HANDBOOK
OF
COMPUTER
NETWORKS

HANDBOOK

— OF —

COMPUTER NETWORKS

Key Concepts, Data Transmission, and Digital and Optical Networks

Volume 1

Hossein Bidgoli

Editor-in-Chief

California State University

Bakersfield, California

BICENTENNIAL

1807

WILEY

2007

BICENTENNIAL

John Wiley & Sons, Inc.

Copyright © 2008 by John Wiley & Sons, Inc. All rights reserved

Published by John Wiley & Sons, Inc., Hoboken, New Jersey
Published simultaneously in Canada

For general information on our other products and services or for technical support, please contact our Customer Care Department within the United States at (800) 762-2974, outside the United States at (317) 572-3993 or fax (317) 572-4002.

Wiley also publishes its books in a variety of electronic formats. Some content that appears in print may not be available in electronic books. For more information about Wiley products, visit our web site at www.wiley.com.

Library of Congress Cataloging-in-Publication Data:

Handbook of computer networks / edited by Hossein Bidgoli.
    3 v. cm.
   ISBN 978-0-471-78458-6 (cloth vol 1 : alk. paper)
   ISBN 978-0-471-78459-3 (cloth vol 2 : alk. paper)
   ISBN 978-0-471-78460-9 (cloth vol 3 : alk. paper)
   ISBN 978-0-471-78461-6 (cloth set : alk. paper)
   1. Computer networks Handbooks, manuals, etc. I. Bidgoli, Hossein.
TK5105.5.H32 2008
004.6–dc22
                                     2007012619

Printed in the United States of America

10 9 8 7 6 5 4 3 2 1

To so many fine memories of my mother Ashraf, my father Mohammad, and my brother Mohsen, for their uncompromising belief in the power of education.

About the Editor-in-Chief

Hossein Bidgoli, Ph.D., is professor of Management Information Systems at California State University. Dr. Bidgoli helped set up the first PC lab in the United States. He is the author of 43 textbooks, 27 manuals, and over five dozen technical articles and papers on various aspects of computer applications, information systems and network security, e-commerce, and decision support systems published and presented throughout the world. Dr. Bidgoli also serves as the editor-in-chief of *The Internet Encyclopedia, The Handbook of Information Security,* and *The Encyclopedia of Information Systems.*

The Encyclopedia of Information Systems was the recipient of one of the Library Journal's Best Reference Sources for 2002 and *The Internet Encyclopedia* was recipient of one of the PSP Awards (Professional and Scholarly Publishing), 2004. Dr. Bidgoli was selected as the California State University, Bakersfield's 2001–2002 Professor of the Year.

Editorial Board

Contents

Volume III: Distributed Networks, Network Planning, Control, Management, and New Trends and Applications

Part 1: Distributed Networks

Contributors

Tarek F. Abdelzhaer
University of Illinois, Urbana-Champaign
Mo Adda
University of Portsmouth, United Kingdom
Kemal Akkaya
Southern Illinois University, Carbondale
Fatih Alagöz
Bogazici University, Turkey
Omar Al-Bayari
Al-Balqa' Applied University, Jordan
Ala Al-Fuqaha
Western Michigan University, Kalamazoo
Jamal N. Al-Karaki
The Hashemite University, Jordan
Nirwan Ansari
New Jersey Institute of Technology
Ismail Ari
Hewlett-Packard Laboratories, Palo Alto, CA
Manuel Arriaga
New York University
Vijay Atluri
Rutgers University
Mark Baker
University of Reading, United Kingdom
Mario Baldi
Politecnico di Torino, Italy
Xiaoyi Bao
University of Ottawa, Canada
Valmir C. Barbosa
Universidade Federal do Rio de Janeiro, Brazil
Elyes Ben Ali Bdira
University of Sharjah, UAE
Keren Bergman
Columbia University
Larry A. Bergman
Jet Propulsion Laboratory (JPL), California Institute
of Technology
Bhagyavati
DeSales University
Qi Bi
Bell Laboratory, Alcatel-Lucent Technologies Inc.
Hossein Bidgoli
California State University, Bakersfield
David Blockus
Independent Consultant
Fernando Boavida
University of Coimbra, Portugal
Benjamin Bock
Secure Business Austria
Noureddine Boudriga
University of the 7th of November, Tunisia
Nicholas David Bowman
Michigan State University
Thomas C. Bressoud
Denison University

Linda Bruenjes
Lasell College
Stephen F. Bush
GE Global Research
Werner Bux
IBM Corporation, Switzerland
Rajkumar Buyya
The University of Melbourne, Australia
John Cameron
University of Ottawa, Canada
Lillian N. Cassel
Villanova University
Tom S. Chan
Southern NH University
Kavitha Chandra
University of Massachusetts, Lowell
Hsiao-Hwa Chen
National Sun Yat-Sen University, Taiwan
Liang Chen
University of Ottawa, Canada
Thomas M.Chen
Southern Methodist University
Zhuojun Joyce Chen
University of Northern Iowa
Jau Ming Chew
University of Portsmouth, United Kingdom
Jaehak Chung
Inha University, Republic of Korea
Song Ci
University of Nebraska, Lincoln
Tim Collins
University of Birmingham, United Kingdom
Marco Conti
Institute of Informatics and Telematics (IIT), Italian
National Research Council (CNR), Italy
David Coquil
University of Passau, Germany
Luís Cordeiro
University of Coimbra, Portugal
Marco Cremonini
University of Milan, Italy
Marilia Curado
University of Coimbra, Portugal
Leslie L. Daigle
Cisco Systems, Herndon, Virginia
Pragati Dalal
Canisius College
Marcos Dias de Assunção
The University of Melbourne, Australia
Serge Demidenko
Massey University, New Zealand, and Monash
University, Malaysia
Hans-Peter Dommel
Santa Clara University

Kais Dridi
Université de Moncton, Canada

Arjan Durresi
Louisiana State University

Akihiro Enomoto
University of California, Irvine

Patrick J. Fahy
Athabasca University, Canada

Guangbin Fan
Intel Corporation

Farid Farahmand
Central Connecticut State University

Clayton Ferner
University of North Carolina at Wilmington

Daniel R. Fesenmaier
Temple University

Frank H.P. Fitzek
Aalborg University, Denmark

Sara Foresti
University of Milan, Italy

Dario Forte
University of Milano, Crema, Italy

Immanuel Freedman
Independent Consultant, Harleysville, Pennsylvania

Keita Fujii
University of California, Irvine

Muneo Fukaishi
NEC Corporation, Japan

Bruce Garrison
University of Miami

Z. Ghassemlooy
Northumbria University, United Kingdom

Filippo Giannetti
University of Pisa, Italy

William R. Gillis
WSU Center to Bridge the Digital Divide

James E. Goldman
Purdue University

Ulrike Gretzel
Texas A&M University

Qijun Gu
Texas State University

Xiaoyuan Gu
Technical University of Braunschweig, Germany

Mohsen Guizani
Western Michigan University

Sghaier Guizani
University of Quebec, Canada

Hong Guo
LLRC, Ontario Public Service, Canada

Mohamed A. Haleem
Stevens Institute of Technology

Habib Hamam
Universite de Moncton, Canada

Mohamed Hamdi
University of 7th of November, Carthage, Tunisia

Jon Hamkins
Jet Propulsion Laboratory, Pasadena, California

Omar M. Hammouri
University of Mississippi

Raymond A. Hansen
Purdue University

Shinsuke Hara
Osaka City University, Japan

David Harley
Small Blue-Green World, United Kingdom

Muhannad Harrim
Western Michigan University, Kalamazoo

Robert W. Heath
The University of Texas, Austin

Hamid Hemmati
Jet Propulsion Laboratory, California Institute of Technology

Murad Hizlan
Cleveland State University

Chengdu Haung
University of Illinois, Urbana-Champaign

Yuheng Huang
Qualcomm Inc.

James M. Hudson
PayPal, an eBay, Inc. Company

Gurdeep Singh Hura
University of Maryland, Eastern Shore

Hassan Ibrahim
The University of Maryland, College Park

François Ingelrest
IRCICA/LIFL University, France

Tariq Jadoon
Lahore University of Management Sciences (LUMS), Pakistan

Raj Jain
Washington University, St. Louis

Sushil Jajodia
George Mason University

Abbas Jamalipour
University of Sydney, Australia

Krishna Jayakar
Penn State University

Bandula Jayatilaka
Binghamton University, SUNY

Tao Jiang
University of Michigan, Dearborn

Stefan Joe-Yen
Northrup Grumman Corporation

Ari Juels
RSA Laboratories

Stella Kafetzoglou
National Technical University of Athens, Greece

Joonhyuk Kang
Information and Communications University (ICU), South Korea

Heather Kanuka
Athabasca University, Canada

Katz Marcos
Aalborg University, Denmark

Rick Kazman
University of Hawaii, Manoa

Azhar M. Khayrattee
Florida Institute of Technology

Yassine Khlifi
Carthage University, Tunisia

Chang-Su Kim
Korea University, Seoul

Nancy J. King
Oregon State University

David Klappholz
Stevens Institute of Technology

Markus Klemen
Vienna University of Technology, Austria

Harald Kosch
University of Passau, Germany

Jim Krause
Indiana University, Bloomington

Prashant Krishnamurthy
University of Pittsburgh

Peter Kroon
LSI, Pennsylvania

C.C. Jay Kuo
University of Southern California

Stan Kurkovsky
Central Connecticut State University

Yu-Kwong Kwok
The University of Hong Kong, Hong Kong

Amor Lazzez
CN&S Research Lab., University of the 7th of
November at Carthage, Tunisia

Allen H. Levesque
Worcester Polytechnic Institute

Matthew Liotine
University of Illinois, Chicago

Natalia M. Litchinitser
University of Michigan, Ann Arbor

Jingxuan Liu
Frostburg State University

Mei-Ling L. Liu
Cal Poly San Luis Obispo

Peng Liu
Penn State University

Qingchong John Liu
Oakland University

Xiang Liu
Bell Laboratories, Lucent Technologies

Zhu Liu
AT&T Laboratories, Middletown, NJ

Asim Loan
University of Management and Technology, Lahore,
Pakistan

David G. Loomis
Illinois State University, Normal

Robert D. Love
LAN Connect Consultants

Albert Lozano-Nieto
Pennsylvania State University

Ying Lu
University of Nebraska, Lincoln

Xuming Lu
University at Buffalo, SUNY

Michele Luglio
University of Rome Tor Vergata, Italy

Marco Luise
University of Pisa, Italy

Yuanqiu Luo
New Jersey Institute of Technology

Aarne Mämmelä
VTT Technical Research Centre of Finland

Konstantinos Markantonakis
Royal Holloway, University of London, United
Kingdom

Manish Marwah
University of Colorado, Boulder

Mustafa M. Matalgah
University of Mississippi

Prabhaker Mateti
Wright State University

Emilio Matricciani
Dipartimento di Elettronica e Informazione
Politecnico di Milano, Italy

Ketan Mayer-Patel
The University of North Carolina at Chapel Hill

Keith Mayes
Royal Holloway, University of London, United
Kingdom

Cavan McCarthy
Louisiana State University

Patrick McDaniel
Pennsylvania State University

Daniel McFarland
Rowan University

Matthew K. McGowan
Bradley University

Amel Meddeb
University of the 7th of November at Carthage, Tunisia

Alfred Mertins
University of Lübeck, Germany

M. Farooque Mesiya
Rensselaer Polytechnic Institute

Marcus Messner
Virginia Commonwealth University

Mark Michael
Research in Motion Limited, Canada

Brent A. Miller
IBM Corporation

Milos Milosevic
Schlumberger Wireline Acquisition and Control
Systems

Mário Minami
University of São Paulo, Brazil

Shivakant Mishra
University of Colorado, Boulder

Jelena Mišić
University of Manitoba, Canada

Vojislav B. Mišić
University of Manitoba, Canada

Shaheed N. Mohammed
Marist College

Edmundo Monteiro
University of Coimbra, Portugal

Michael Moore
University of California, Irvine

Syed H. Murshid
Florida Institute of Technology

Arun Srinivasa Murthy
Villanova University

B. Muthukumaran
Gemini Communication Limited, India

Tadashi Nakano
University of California, Irvine

Keivan Navaie
Tarbiat Modares University, Iran
Amiya Nayak
University of Ottawa, Canada
Thomas Neubauer
Vienna University of Technology, Austria
Darren B. Nicholson
Rowan University
Jennifer Nicholson
Rowan University
Richard Nieporent
Johns Hopkins University
Peng Ning
North Carolina State University
Paul W. Nutter
University of Manchester, United Kingdom
Mohammad S. Obaidat
Monmouth University
S. Obeidat
Arizona State University
Yoram Ofek
University of Trento, Italy
Yutaka Okaie
University of California, Irvine
Hong Ong
Oak Ridge National Laboratory, Tennessee
Priscilla Oppenheimer
Southern Oregon University
Raymond R. Panko
University of Hawaii, Manoa
G.I. Papadimitriou
Aristotle University, Thessaloniki, Greece
Symeon Papavassiliou
National Technical University of Athens, Greece
C. Papazoglou
Aristotle University, Thessaloniki, Greece
Stefano Paraboschi
University of Bergamo, Italy
Amanda Peart
University of Portsmouth, United Kingdom
Kenneth Pedrotti
University of California, Santa Cruz
Stephan Pfletschinger
Centre Tecnològic de Telecomunicacions de
Catalunya (CTTC), Barcelona, Spain
Ronnie J. Phillips
Colorado State University
Thomas L. Pigg
Jackson State Community College
Martin Placek
The University of Melbourne, Australia
A.S. Pomportsis
Aristotle University, Greece
Dan Port
University of Hawaii, Manoa
G.N. Prezerakos
Technological Education Institute of Piraeus, Greece
Eddie Rabinovitch
ECI Technology
Miguel Arjona Ramírez
University of São Paulo, Brazil
Jeremy L. Rasmussen
Sypris Electronics

Indrajit Ray
Colorado State University
Mustapha Razzak
Université de Moncton, Canada
David R. Reavis
Texas A&M University, Texarkana
Slim Rekhis
CNAS Research Lab., University of
Carthage, Tunisia
Jian Ren
Michigan State University, East Lansing
Vladimir V. Riabov
Rivier College
James A. Ritcey
University of Washington
Emilia Rosti
Università degli Studi di Milano, Italy
Liam Rourke
Nanyang Technological University, Singapore
Balqies Sadoun
Al-Balqa' Applied University, Jordan
Antonio Saitto
Telespazio, Italy
Hamidreza Saligheh
Harvard University
Atul A. Salvekar
Intel Corporation
Pierangela Samarati
University of Milan, Italy
Nabil J. Sarhan
Wayne State University
Damien Sauveron
University of Limoges, France
Michel Savoie
Communications Research Center (CRC), Canada
Mark Schaefer
OnStar Corporation
Chadwick Sessions
Northrup Grumman Corporation
Mark Shacklette
The University of Chicago
William A. Shay
University of Wisconsin, Green Bay
John Lucas Sherry
Michigan State University
Carolyn Siccama
University of Massachusetts, Lowell
Douglas C. Sicker
University of Colorado, Boulder
Farhan Siddiqui
Wayne State University
David Simplot-Ryl
Université de Lille, France
Robert Slade
Independent Consultant, Canada
Robert Slagter
Telematica Instituut, The Netherlands
Benjamin A. Small
Columbia University
Anthony H. Smith
Purdue University
Min Song
Old Dominion University

Hideyuki Sotobayashi
National Institute of Information and
Communications Technology, Japan

Lee Sproull
New York University

William Stallings
Independent Consultant

Mark Stamp
San Jose State University

Charles Steinfield
Michigan State University

Ivan Stojmenovic
University of Birmingham, UK and University of
Ottawa, Canada

Norman C. Strole
IBM Corporation

Koduvayur P. Subbalakshmi
Stevens Institute of Technology

Tatsuya Suda
University of California, Irvine

Anthony Sulistio
The University of Melbourne, Australia

Wayne C. Summers
Columbus State University

Vahid Tarokh
Harvard University

Colleen Taugher
WSU Center to Bridge the Digital Divide

Marvi Teixeira
Polytechnic University of Puerto Rico

Vassilis Tsaoussidis
Democritos University of Thrace, Xanthi, Greece

Michael Tunstall
University College Cork, Ireland

Okechukwu C. Ugweje
University of Akron

Zartash Afzal Uzmi
Lahore University of Management Sciences (LUMS),
Pakistan

Shahrokh Valaee
University of Toronto, Canada

I.S. Venieris
National Technical University of Athens, Greece

Srikumar Venugopal
The University of Melbourne, Australia

Sabrina De Capitani di Vimercati
University of Milan, Italy

Linda Volonino
Canisius College

Mohamed El-Wakil
Western Michigan University, Kalamazoo

Youcheng Wang
University of Central Florida

James. L. Wayman
San Jose State University

Troy Weingart
University of Colorado, Boulder

Edgar R. Weippl
Vienna University of Technology, Austria

Stephen A. Weis
Google

Risto Wichman
Helsinki University of Technology, Finland

Barry Wilkinson
University of North Carolina, at Charlotte

Tin Win
Monash University, Malaysia

Raymond F. Wisman
Indiana University Southeast

Paul L. Witt
Texas Christian University

Albert K.S. Wong
Hong Kong University of Science and Technology,
Hong Kong

Michael Workman
Florida Institute of Technology

Jing Wu
Communications Research Centre (CRC), Canada

Geoffrey G. Xie
Naval Postgraduate School

Jiang Xie
University of North Carolina, Charlotte

Xu Yan
Hong Kong University of Science and Technology,
Hong Kong

Wei Ye
University of Southern California

Chee Shin Yeo
The University of Melbourne, Australia

Si Yin
New Jersey Institute of Technology

Jia Yu
The University of Melbourne, Australia

Viktor Zaharov
Polytechnic University of Puerto Rico

Faouzi Zarai
University of the 7th of November, Tunisia

S. Zeadally
University of the District of Columbia

Jingyuan Zhang
University of Alabama

Nan Zhang
Hong Kong University of Science and Technology,
Hong Kong

Qinqing Zhang
Bell Laboratory, Alcatel-Lucent Technologies Inc.

Qiong (Jo) Zhang
Arizona State University, West Campus

Jiying Zhao
University of Ottawa, Canada

Mingshan Zhao
Dalian University of Technology, People's Republic of
China

Wen-De Zhong
Nanyang Technological University, Singapore

Chi Zhou
Illinois Institute of Technology

Jin Zhu
University of Northern Iowa

Junaid Ahmed Zubairi
State University of New York, Fredonia

Preface

The *Handbook of Computer Networks* is the first comprehensive examination of the core topics in the computer network field. *The Handbook of Computer Networks*, a 3-volume reference work, with 202 chapters, 3400+ pages, is a comprehensive coverage of the computer network field with coverage of the core topics.

The primary audience is the libraries of 2-year and 4-year colleges and universities with Computer Science, Computer Engineering, Network Engineering, Telecommunications, Data Communications, MIS, CIS, IT, IS, Data Processing, and Business departments, public and private libraries and corporate libraries throughout the world, and educators and practitioners in the networking and telecommunications fields.

The secondary audience is a variety of professionals and a diverse group of academic and professional courses for the individual volumes.

Among industries expected to become increasingly dependent upon the computer networks and telecommunications and active in understanding the many issues surrounding this important and fast-growing field are: government agencies, military, education, libraries, health, medical, law enforcement, accounting firms, law firms, justice, manufacturing, financial services, insurance, communications, transportation, aerospace, energy, biotechnology, retail, and utilities.

Each volume incorporates state-of-the-art core information and computer networks and telecommunications topics, practical applications, and coverage of the emerging issues in the computer networks field.

This definitive 3-volume *Handbook* offers coverage of both established and cutting-edge theories and developments in the computer networks and telecommunications fields. The *Handbook* contains chapters from global experts in academia and industry. The *Handbook* offers the following unique features:

1. Each chapter follows a unique format including Title and Author, Outline, Introduction, Body, Conclusion, Glossary, Cross-References, and References. This unique format assists the readers to pick and choose various sections of a chapter. It also creates consistency throughout the entire series.

2. The *Handbook* has been written by more than 270 experts and reviewed by more than 1000 academics and practitioners chosen from around the world. These diverse collections of expertise have created the most definitive coverage of established and cutting-edge theories and applications of this fast-growing field.

3. Each chapter has been rigorously peer reviewed. This review process assures the accuracy and completeness of each topic.

4. Each chapter provides extensive online and off-line references for additional reading. This will enable the readers to go further with their understanding of a given topic.

5. More than 1000 illustrations and tables throughout the series highlight complex topics and assist further understanding.

6. Each chapter provides extensive cross-references. This helps the readers to read other chapters related to a particular topic, providing a one-stop knowledge base for a given topic.

7. More than 2500 glossary items define new terms and buzzwords throughout the series, assisting in understanding of concepts and applications.

8. The *Handbook* includes a complete table of contents and index sections for easy access to various parts of the series.

9. The series emphasizes both technical as well as managerial issues. This approach provides researchers, educators, students, and practitioners with a balanced understanding and the necessary background to deal with problems related to understanding computer networks and telecommunications issues and to be able to design a sound computer and telecommunications system.

10. The series has been developed based on the current core course materials in several leading universities around the world and current practices in leading computer, telecommunications, and networking corporations. This format should appeal to a diverse group of educators and researchers in the networking and telecommunications fields.

We chose to concentrate on fields and supporting technologies that have widespread applications in academic and business worlds. To develop this *Handbook*, we carefully reviewed current academic research in the networking field in leading universities and research institutions around the world.

Computer networks and telecommunications, network security, management information systems, network design and management, computer information systems (CIS), and electronic commerce curriculums, recommended by the Association of Information Technology Professionals (AITP) and the Association for Computing Management (ACM) were carefully investigated. We also researched the current practices in the networking field carried out by leading networking and telecommunications corporations. Our work assisted us in defining the boundaries and contents of this project. Its chapters address technical as well as managerial issues in the networking and telecommunications fields.

TOPIC CATEGORIES

Based on our research, we identified nine major topic areas for the Handbook:

- Key Concepts
- Hardware, Media, and Data Transmission
- Digital and Optical Networks
- LANs, MANs, and WANs
- The Internet, Global Networks, and VoIP
- Cellular and Wireless Networks
- Distributed Networks
- Network Planning, Control, and Management
- Computer Network Popular Applications and Future Directions

Although these nine categories are interrelated, each addresses one major dimension of the computer networks and telecommunications fields. The chapters in each category are also interrelated and complementary, enabling readers to compare, contrast, and draw conclusions that might not otherwise be possible.

Though the entries have been arranged logically, the light they shed knows no bounds. The *Handbook* provides unmatched coverage of fundamental topics and issues for successful design and implementation of a computer network and telecommunications systems. Its chapters can serve as material for a wide spectrum of courses such as:

Grid Computing
Distributed Intelligent Networks
Multimedia Networking
Peer-to-Peer Networks
Cluster Computing
Voice over IP
Storage Area Networks
Network Backup and Recovery Systems
Digital Networks
Optical Networks
Cellular Networks
Wireless Networks
Telecommunications Systems
Computer Network Management

Successful design and implementation of a sound computer network and telecommunications systems requires a thorough knowledge of several technologies, theories, and supporting disciplines. Networking researchers and practitioners have had to consult many resources to find answers. Some of these sources concentrate on technologies and infrastructures, some on applications and implementation issues, and some on managerial concerns. This *Handbook* provides all of this relevant information in a comprehensive three-volume set with a lively format.

Each volume incorporates core networking and telecommunications topics, practical applications, and coverage of the emerging issues in the networking and telecommunications fields. Written by scholars and practitioners from around the world, the chapters fall into nine major subject areas:

Key Concepts

Chapters in this group examine a broad range of topics. Fundamental theories, concepts, technologies, and applications related to computer networks, data communications, and telecommunications are discussed. These chapters explain the OSI reference model and then discuss various types of compression techniques including data, image, video, speech, and audio compression. This part concludes with a discussion of multimedia streaming and high definition television (HDTV) as their applications are on the rise. The chapters in this part provide a solid foundation for the rest of the Handbook.

Hardware, Media, and Data Transmission

Chapters in this group concentrate on the important types of hardware used in network and telecommunications environments and then examine popular media used in data communications including wired and wireless media. The chapters in this part explain different types of modulation techniques for both digital and optical networks and conclude with coverage of various types of multiplexing techniques that are being used to improve the efficiency and effectiveness of commutations media.

Digital and Optical Networks

Chapters in this group discuss important digital and optical technologies that are being used in modern communication and computer networks. Different optical switching techniques, optical devices, optical memories, SONET, and SDH networks are explained.

LANs, MANs, and WANs

This group of chapters examines major types of computer reworks including local, metropolitan, and wide area networks. Popular types of operating systems used in a LAN environment are discussed, including Windows and Linux. The chapters also examine various types of switching techniques including packet, circuit, and message switching. The chapters discuss broadband network applications and technologies and conclude with a discussion of multimedia networking.

The Internet, Global Networks, and VoIP

Chapters in this group explore a broad range of topics. They review the Internet fundamentals, history, domain name systems, and Internet2. The architecture and functions of the Internet and important protocols including TCP/IP, SMPT, and IP multicast are discussed. The chapters in this group also explain the network and end-system quality of service and then discuss VoIP and its various components, protocols, and applications.

Cellular and Wireless Networks

Chapters in this group explain cellular and wireless networks. Major standards, protocols, and applications in the cellar environment are discussed. This includes a detailed coverage of GSM, GPRS, UMTS, CDMA, and TDMA. The chapters in this group explore satellite communications principles, technologies, protocols, and applications in detail. The chapters conclude with coverage of wireless wide area networks and wireless broadband access.

Distributed Networks

The chapters in this group investigate distributed networks, their fundamentals, architectures, and applications. Grid computing, cluster computing, and peer-to-peer networks are discussed in detailed. These chapters also explore storage area networks, fiber channels, and fault tolerant systems. This part concludes with a discussion of distributed algorithms and distributed databases.

Network Planning, Control, and Management

The chapters in this group discuss theories, methodologies, and technologies that enhance successful network planning, control, and management. After discussion of network capacity planning and network modeling, the chapters concentrate on the identification of threats and vulnerabilities in a network environment. The chapters then present a number of tools and technologies that if properly utilized could significantly improve the integrity of data resources and computer networks by keeping hackers and crackers at bay. This part concludes with a discussion of business continuity planning, e-mail, and Internet use policies, and computer network management.

Computer Network Popular Applications and Future Directions

Chapters in this group present several popular applications of computer networks and telecommunications systems. These applications could not have been successfully utilized without a sound computer network and telecommunications system. Some of these applications include conferencing, banking, electronic commerce, travel and tourism, and Web-based training and education. This part concludes with a discussion of future trends in computer networking including biologically inspired networking, active networks, and molecular communication.

Specialists have written the *Handbook* for experienced and not so experienced readers. It is to these contributors that I am especially grateful. This remarkable collection of scholars and practitioners have distilled their knowledge into a fascinating and enlightening one-stop knowledge base in computer networks and telecommunications that "talks" to readers. This has been a massive effort, but one of the most rewarding experiences I have ever had. So many people have played a role that it is difficult to know where to begin.

I should like to thank the members of the editorial board for participating in the project and for their expert advice on help with the selection of topics, recommendations for authors, and reviewing the materials. Many thanks to more than 1000 reviewers who devoted their time by providing advice to me and the authors for improving the coverage, accuracy, and comprehensiveness of these materials.

I thank my senior editor Matt Holt, who initiated the idea of the *Handbook*. Through a dozen drafts and many reviews, the project got off the ground and then was managed flawlessly by Matt and his professional team. Matt and his team made many recommendations for keeping the project focused and maintaining its lively coverage.

Jessica Campilango, our editorial coordinator, assisted our authors and me during the many phases of its development. I am grateful for all her support. When it came to the production phase, the superb Wiley production team took over. Particularly I want to thank Deborah Schindlar and Miriam Palmer-Sherman, our production editors. I am grateful for all their hard work. I also want to thank Lynn Lustberg, our project manager from ICC Macmillan Inc. Her thoroughness made it easier to complete the project. I am grateful to all her efforts. I thank Kim Dayman and Christine Kim, our marketing team, for their impressive marketing campaign launched on behalf of the *Handbook*.

Last, but not least, I want to thank my wonderful wife, Nooshin, and my two children, Mohsen and Morvareed, for being so patient during this venture. They provided a pleasant environment that expedited the completion of this project. Mohsen and Morvareed assisted me in sending out thousands of e-mail messages to our authors and reviewers. Nooshin was a great help in designing and maintaining the authors' and reviewers' databases. Their efforts are greatly appreciated. Also, my two sisters, Azam and Akram, provided moral support throughout my life. To this family, any expression of thanks is insufficient.

Hossein Bidgoli
California State University, Bakersfield

Guide to The Handbook of Computer Networks

The Handbook of Computer Networks is a comprehensive coverage of the relatively new and very important field of computer networks and telecommunications systems. This reference work consists of three separate volumes and 202 different chapters on various aspects of this field. Each chapter in the Handbook provides a comprehensive overview of the selected topic, intended to inform a broad spectrum of readers, ranging from computer network professionals and academicians to students to the general business community.

In order that you, the reader, will derive the greatest possible benefit from *The Handbook of Computer Networks*, we have provided this Guide. It explains how the information within it can be located.

Organization

The Handbook of Computer Networks is organized to provide the maximum ease of use for its readers. All of the chapters are arranged logically in these three volumes. Individual volumes could be used independently. However, the greatest benefit is derived if all three volumes are investigated.

Table of Contents

A complete table of contents of the entire Handbook appears at the front of each volume. This list of chapter titles represents topics that have been carefully selected by the editor-in-chief, Dr. Hossein Bidgoli, and his colleagues on the Editorial Board.

Index

A Subject Index for each individual volume is located at the end of each volume. This index is the most convenient way to locate a desired topic within the Handbook. The subjects in the index are listed alphabetically and indicate the page number where information on this topic can be found.

Chapters

The author's name and affiliation are displayed at the beginning of the chapter. All chapters in the Handbook are organized according to a standard format as follow:

Title and Author
Outline
Introduction
Body
Conclusion
Glossary
Cross References
References

Outline

Each chapter begins with an outline indicating the content of the chapter to come. This outline provides a brief overview of the chapter, so that the reader can get a sense of what is contained there without having to leaf through the pages. It also serves to highlight important subtopics that will be discussed within the chapter. For example, the chapter "The Internet Fundamentals" includes sections for Information Superhighway and the World Wide Web, Domain Name Systems, Navigational Tools, Search Engines, and Directories.

The Outline is intended as an overview and thus it lists only the major headings of the chapter. In addition, second-level and third-level headings will be found within the chapter.

Introduction

The text of each chapter begins with an introductory section that defines the topic under discussion and summarizes the content of the chapter. By reading this section the readers get a general idea regarding a specific chapter.

Body

The body of each chapter discusses the items that were listed in the outline section of each chapter.

Conclusion

The conclusion section provides a summary of the materials discussed in a particular chapter. This section leaves the readers with the most important issues and concepts discussed in a particular chapter.

Glossary

The glossary contains terms that are important to an understanding of the chapter and that may be unfamiliar to the reader. Each term is defined in the context of the particular chapter in which it is used. Thus, the same term may be defined in two or more chapters with the detail of the definition varying slightly from one chapter to another. The Handbook includes approximately 2700 glossary terms. For example, the chapter "The Internet Fundamentals" includes the following glossary entries:

Extranet A secure network that uses the Internet and Web technology to connect two or more intranets of trusted business partners, enabling business-to-business, business-to-consumer, consumer-to-consumer, and consumer-to-business communications.

Intranet A network within the organization that uses Web technologies (TCP/IP, HTTP, FTP, SMTP, HTML, XML, and its variations) for collecting, storing, and disseminating useful information throughout the organization.

Cross References

All the chapters in the Handbook have cross references to other chapters. These appear at the end of the chapter, following the chapter text and preceding the References. The cross references indicate related chapters that can be consulted for further information on the same topic. The Handbook contains more than 2000 cross references in all. For example, the chapter "The Internet Fundamentals" has the following cross references:

Electronic Commerce, Electronic Data Interchange (EDI), Electronic Payment Systems, History of the Internet, Internet2, Internet Domain Name System, Information Retrieval on the Internet.

References

The References appears as the last element in a chapter. It lists recent secondary sources to aid the reader in locating more detailed or technical information. Review articles and research papers that are important to an understanding of the topic are also listed. The References in this Handbook are for the benefit of the reader, to provide references for further research on the given topic. Thus, they typically consist of a dozen to two dozen entries. They are not intended to represent a complete listing of all materials consulted by the author in preparing the chapter.

PART 1

Key Concepts

The Telecommunications Industry

David G. Loomis, *Illinois State University, Normal*

INTRODUCTION

What exactly is the telecommunications industry? The industry, in fact, is hard to define because technological advances cause the industry to continually redefine itself. Indeed, the only constant in the telecommunications industry is that it is always changing. So it is a somewhat dubious task to write a chapter on such a dynamic market. Nevertheless, this chapter will attempt to provide an overview that segments the industry into different markets and shows where these markets are converging or overlapping.

This chapter will look at the industry through the eyes of an economist and policy maker rather than through the eyes of a technologist. Many of the other chapters in this book will focus on various technologies used in the industry, but this chapter will concentrate on the supply and demand of telecommunications services to the mass market: the consumer and small business marketplace. Although it may seem easier to write about economics because technologies change rapidly, the economics of supply and demand change rapidly, too, as the technological possibilities expand.

The telecommunications industry has been and will continue to be in the midst of convergence for some time. *Convergence* means that industry segments that were once separate and distinct are now overlapping and merging to provide similar competing services. Because of convergence, it is hard to draw lines of separation within the industry that are clear and meaningful. For the purposes of this chapter, we will define the three industry segments as voice, video, and data. From a purely technological standpoint, one could define voice and video as just different types of data; from the consumer perspective, however, these products are different in use and access, at least currently. Within each industry segment, there are wireline and wireless technologies that deliver these products. For voice communications, we have the choice of traditional landline phones or wireless phones. Cable television (wireline or coaxial cable), broadcast, and satellite (wireless) can deliver video. Data delivery can be done by dialup, broadband technologies such as *direct subscriber line* (DSL) and cable modem (wireline), and *wireless fidelity* (WiFi) as well as by satellite and data services provided by cell phone companies (wireless).

What is causing this convergence? There are several drivers. The first and primary driver is technology, specifically the Internet. Internet protocol was once limited to data traffic such as e-mail and Web pages, but now it is being used to provide voice services such as *voice over IP* (VoIP) and video (e.g., *Internet protocol television*, or IPTV). Voice and video (television), which were once analog, have become digitized and delivered over an IP network. This transition has not always been smooth or easy. Two problems have plagued the transport of voice and video over IP networks: latency and prioritization. Voice and video communications require the information to arrive in the same order in which it was sent and without more than a split-second delay. Without this requirement, a packet of a conversation might arrive out of order and result in a jumbled and garbled mess. Likewise, delays of a second or more are especially noticeable in voice and video communication but are mere inconveniences to traditional data traffic such as e-mail. IP networks initially had problems transporting real-time voice and video, but the problems of latency and prioritization have largely been overcome.

But how and why did this technological change take place? In the United States, much of the freedom to allow this technological change came from the Telecommunications Act of 1996 (TA96) and associated rulings by the Federal Communications Commission (FCC). The FCC chose not to regulate nascent technologies out of existence and allowed them time to develop and mature. The intent of TA96 was "to provide for a pro-competitive, deregulatory national policy framework designed to accelerate rapidly private sector deployment of advanced telecommunications and information technologies and services to all Americans by opening all telecommunications markets to competition" (Duesterberg and Gordon 1997, 2). Thus, the second cause of convergence is the legislative and regulatory restructuring that allowed the technologies to adapt and change.

Underlying both the first two reasons of technology and restructuring is the basic economic incentive to reduce costs, increase revenues, and, ultimately, maximize profits. If VoIP can provide landline voice to customers at a much cheaper price than traditional landline networks, then there is a great economic incentive to develop it. If IPTV can enhance the revenue stream and leverage the investment for "fiber to the premises" (FTTP) and "fiber to the curb" (FTTC) projects, then the economic incentives will drive development and allocate resources to overcome technological challenges. Ultimately, it is consumer demand and willingness to pay coupled with cost-effective technological innovation that is driving convergence.

Customers seem to be driven to purchase four products: (1) landline voice, (2) high-speed Internet access, (3) TV and entertainment, and (4) wireless voice and data. These four products have become known as the "quadruple play" by companies that seek to provide all of these services to customers, sometimes as bundles. Many telecommunications companies have merged in recent years either to increase their market share or market reach within one or more of these product areas or to provide a new product that they had not already offered to customers. For example, SBC merged with AT&T, and Cingular (owned by SBC and BellSouth) bought out AT&T Wireless. Verizon then merged with MCI, and the new AT&T (SBC–AT&T) plans to merge with BellSouth. These mergers and others have resulted in an industry that is dominated by large multimarket oligopolies.

After completing these mergers, the resulting companies have become the market leaders in each of the quadruple play markets except for TV and entertainment. The new AT&T is the second-largest local landline company (it will be the largest after its proposed merger with BellSouth), the largest long-distance company, the largest wireless provider (Cingular–AT&T Wireless), and the largest provider of DSL (and a nationwide IP network from the old AT&T). Verizon is the largest local landline company, the second-largest long-distance company, the second-largest wireless provider (Verizon Wireless with 45 percent owned by Vodafone), and the second-largest provider of DSL (and a nationwide IP network from MCI's uunet). Both companies have plans to aggressively build their fiber networks to provide TV and entertainment services.

The rest of this chapter is organized as follows. First, we will explore the landline voice market with its historical segments of local and long distance. Second, the wireless voice market will be examined along with its interactions with the landline market. Third, the video and data markets will be explained along with the wireline and wireless technologies used to supply these markets. Finally, the U.S. telecommunications market will be compared to telecommunications markets in other developed countries.

LANDLINE VOICE MARKET

Landline voice is the oldest of the telecommunications markets discussed here; historically, it was the entire telecommunications industry. Before 1970, the landline voice market was mostly served by AT&T with its affiliated local Bell operating companies. During the 1970s and 1980s, the FCC allowed increased competition for long-distance and customer-premises equipment that culminated in the divestiture of AT&T in 1984. The divestiture required the creation of a precise definition for local and long-distance calls. This somewhat arbitrary distinction between long-distance and local telecommunications had no real foundation in cost or demand considerations. Because the distinction was a creation of regulation, market forces have caused the two markets to merge. Convergence and corporate mergers are blurring any remaining distinctions between this historical separation. SBC, the largest local company, has recently merged with AT&T, the largest long-distance company; and Verizon, the second-largest local company, has merged with MCI, the second-largest long-distance company.

Long-Distance Voice Market

Historically, long-distance voice service was provided as a monopoly service by AT&T. During the 1960s and 1970s, the FCC allowed other companies—namely, Microwave Communications Inc. (MCI) and others—to provide long-distance services in direct competition with AT&T. This policy eventually led to the divestiture of AT&T from its local telephone subsidiaries and full-fledged competition in the long-distance industry. This movement from a regulated monopoly provision of services to competitive services from many companies would be repeated throughout different industry segments.

Long-distance rates have declined significantly since the divestiture of AT&T in 1984. Figure 1 shows the decline in rates from 1984 to 2003. In 1984, the average price of a long-distance call was almost sixty cents per

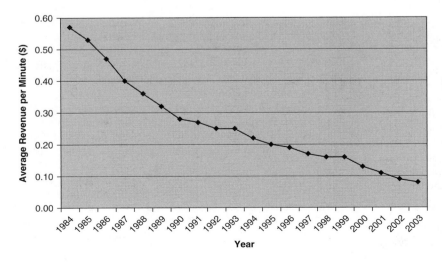

Figure 1: Average revenue per minute for interstate and international calls (in 2003 dollars), 1984–2003

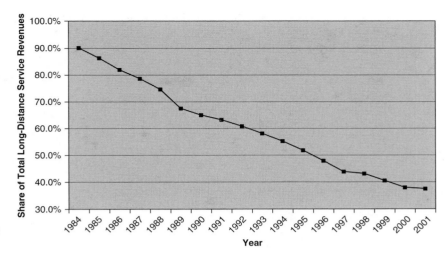

Figure 2: AT&T's share of total long-distance revenues, 1984–2001

minute (in 2003 dollars), but the average price was less than ten cents per minute by 2003. Much of the decline resulted from lower costs to connect calls to local telephone networks (Taylor and Taylor 1993). AT&T's market share declined from more than 90 percent in 1984 to less than 40 percent in 2001 (see Figure 2). MCI and Sprint were the second- and third-largest providers of long distance during this time, and their market shares grew as AT&T's declined. Table 1 shows the annual market share for the long-distance market between 1984 and 2001 (the most recent year the FCC produced these statistics). By 2001, MCI's market share had grown to 23.4 percent, and Sprint's had grown to 9.3 percent.

Overall, the traditional long-distance landline voice market is in serious decline for two reasons. First, the "death of distance" (Cairncross 2001) has been caused by a shift in long-distance traffic away from the public switched telephone network (PSTN) onto private data networks and the public Internet. This shift was first led by international traffic that could avoid voice call termination charges and high regulated prices by carrying the voice traffic over data lines. Even within the United States, regulatory policies caused prices for domestic long-distance calls to be high above their marginal cost. These high margins eroded as competitive alternatives became available. The second reason for the decline of the long-distance landline voice was the high market penetration of wireless phones with significantly different pricing. In 1998, AT&T Wireless's Digital One Rate incorporated long distance into the company's wireless plan at no additional charge above that for airtime. This pricing plan was quickly adopted by other wireless firms. Under this plan, customers had monthly bundles of minutes on their wireless phone contracts that they would lose if they were not used. Thus, the effective marginal price of a long-distance call on a wireless phone was zero as long as users did not exceed their allotted minutes. Not long after this, wireless plans included free calls during nights and weekends (e.g., airtime during night and weekends did not count against customers' monthly allotments of minutes). Thus, customers shifted much of their usage away from landline long distance and onto wireless phones.

Regulation of the long-distance market also changed substantially during this time (Sappington and Weisman

Table 1: Percentage Shares of Total Toll Service Revenues for Long-Distance Carriers, 1984–2001

Year	AT&T	MCU	Sprint	All Other Long Distance Carriers
1984	90.1	4.5	2.7	2.6
1985	86.3	5.5	2.6	5.6
1986	81.9	7.6	4.3	6.3
1987	78.6	8.8	5.8	6.8
1988	74.6	10.3	7.2	8.0
1989	67.5	12.3	8.4	11.8
1990	65.0	14.5	9.7	10.8
1991	63.2	15.6	9.9	11.3
1992	60.8	18.1	9.7	11.5
1993	58.1	19.7	10.0	12.3
1994	55.2	20.7	10.1	14.0
1995	51.8	24.6	9.8	13.8
1996	47.9	25.6	9.7	26.8
1997	43.8	25.6	9.5	21.0
1998	43.1	23.5	8.5	24.9
1999	40.5	23.7	9.8	26.0
2000	37.9	22.4	9.0	30.7
2001	37.4	23.4	9.3	23.8

Source: Federal Communications Commission (2003), Table 7.

1996). Even after divestiture, AT&T was regulated under *rate-of-return regulation* by the FCC; it is one of the heaviest forms of regulation because it limits both profits and prices. Because MCI and Sprint had much lower market shares, they were not regulated but still filed their rates with the FCC. This asymmetric regulation allowed MCI and Sprint to know AT&T's rates with certainty and respond in a competitive manner. The FCC changed from rate-of-return regulation to price-cap regulation in 1989, but not until 1995 was AT&T declared nondominant and effectively deregulated.

Local Voice Market

The path taken by the local voice market has been similar to that of the long-distance market. Each local market was historically served by a monopoly local telephone company that was rate-of-return regulated by the state regulatory board. Most cities and heavily populated areas were served by subsidiaries of AT&T until divestiture in 1984. At divestiture, local telephone subsidiaries were separated from AT&T's long-distance and equipment pieces. The local telephone pieces of AT&T were broken into seven different companies called *regional Bell operating companies* (RBOCs): NYNEX, Bell Atlantic, BellSouth, Ameritech, Southwestern Bell, US West, and Pacific Telesis. These companies corresponded to different geographic regions of the country (see Figure 3). The companies did not serve all customers in their regions but only major population centers. Other local telephone companies known as *independents* (because they were independent of the Bell system), served customers in the other areas.

Local telephone companies did not face competition until much later than their long-distance counterparts. In fact, competition in the local market came about because of competition in long distance. Competition in local markets started in large urban areas where new start-up companies provided direct connections from the customer to the long-distance network and thereby bypassed the local telephone network. This competition arose because of artificially high regulated rates that the local telephone companies charged to long-distance companies to connect their networks to customers. Much of this bypass was uneconomic in the sense that it was caused by regulatory rules rather than underlying differences in costs. The upstart companies became known as *competitive access providers* (CAPs) or *alternative local transport companies* (known as ALTs). These companies continued to expand the local telecommunications services they offered until full-fledged local competition was introduced by TA96. These upstart companies became known as *competitive local exchange carriers* (CLECs) after this legislation. The traditional local telephone companies then became known as *incumbent local exchange carriers* (ILECs). Several rules from TA96 sought to put CLECs on an equal footing with ILECs. One rule was *local number portability*. For many business and individuals, changing phone numbers when changing phone service presented a great barrier to switch carriers. Because the ILECs started with all the customers, this gave them an unfair advantage in a fully competitive marketplace. To combat that advantage, local number portability required that all phone companies allow their customers to take their phone number with them when they changed local companies (Black 2002, 99).

Rates for local telephone service did not decline as they did in the long-distance market. In fact, the recurring monthly charge for basic telephone service has increased from 1986 to 2004 as shown in Figure 4: The average monthly residential charge rose from $17.70 in 1986 to $24.31 in 2004 (in nominal dollars). Part of the increase in local residential rates has been a shift in recovering costs away from per-minute charges (*access charges*) charged to long-distance companies and toward per-line *subscriber line charges* (SLCs) charged to end users.

The total number of switched access lines has decreased from a high of approximately 192.5 million lines in December 2000 to approximately 175.5 million in December 2005 (FCC 2006, 5). Much of the decline has been caused by people disconnecting second lines that were used for Internet connections or teenagers. These individuals have switched to broadband connections for Internet use and substituted wireless phones for teenagers. ILECs have suffered not only from the overall decline in the size of the market but also from competition with

Figure 3: RBOC regions at AT&T's divestiture, 1984

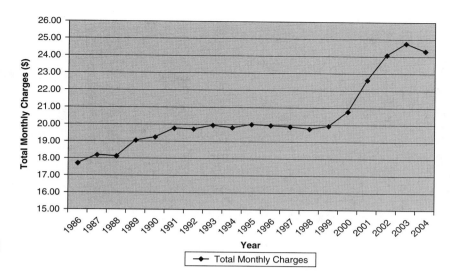

Figure 4: Total monthly charges for local services in urban areas, 1986–2004

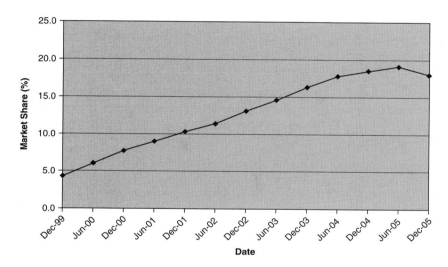

Figure 5: Growth in CLEC market share, 1999–2005

CLECs. CLEC market share has increased steadily from 4.3 percent in December 1999 to 17.8 percent in June 2004 (see Figure 5).

In addition to suffering from the decline in second lines, the local wireline market faces competitive threats from so-called intermodal forms of competition for primary lines to a household. Loomis and Swann (2005) have shown clear links among wireless, wireline, and broadband telecommunications. In the future, more and more households will go "wireless-only" and disconnect their wireline services. Others will shift their voice usage toward *voice over IP* (VoIP), using their broadband connections and disconnecting their traditional landline phones.

The local landline market has changed considerably because of mergers since AT&T's 1984 divestiture. Figure 3 (RBOCs at divestiture) has changed to Figure 6 (RBOCs today). In 1997, Bell Atlantic merged with NYNEX to become the new Bell Atlantic. In 2000, the new Bell Atlantic merged with GTE, the largest independent telephone company, to become Verizon. Verizon merged with MCI in 2006. Southwestern Bell Corporation changed its name to SBC Communications in 1995 and acquired Pacific

Telesis in 1997, SNET in 1998, and Ameritech in 1999. SBC merged with AT&T in late 2005 and took on the AT&T name for the company. On March 5, 2006, the new AT&T announced plans to purchase BellSouth. US West was acquired by Qwest, a long-distance company in 2000. Thus, only AT&T, Verizon, and Qwest will remain from the eight companies formed from the 1984 divestiture of AT&T.

Long-Distance and Local Voice Market

Markets that are in decline often see industry consolidation through mergers as a means to decrease costs in order to survive in a shrinking market. The local and long-distance markets have seen much industry consolidation with the top local provider (SBC) merging with the top long-distance company (AT&T) and the second-largest local company (Verizon) merging with the second-largest long-distance company (MCI). With these mergers, the distinction between local and long distance is difficult to discern except as a regulatory artifact.

In spite of blurring lines between long distance and local services, two important regulatory and public policy decisions concern the interaction between these two

Figure 6: RBOC regions, 2006

industry segments. These decisions include universal service and intercarrier compensation.

Universal service is the public policy of having a telephone network that is available, integrated, and affordable to all Americans (Mueller 1997). Historically, long-distance calls were priced above their marginal costs in order to price local telephone service below its marginal cost. This cross-subsidization was approved by both federal and state regulators to ensure that local telephone service would be affordable to most people. The divestiture of AT&T broke the linkage between long-distance and local rates. As AT&T long distance faced more competition, policy makers feared that local rates would increase and that households would disconnect their local phone service. Local rates did increase following divestiture, but households did not disconnect their phones. Instead, households responded to their total bill in which local rates increased but long-distance rates decreased even more rapidly. As a result, the market penetration rate rose from 91.4 percent in 1984 to 93.3 percent in 1990 (Hausman and Belinfante 1993).

In addition to the cross-subsidy issue from long distance to local, TA96 added the e-rate program under the category of universal service. The e-rate program provides subsidies ranging from 20 percent to 90 percent for Internet access to schools and libraries, depending on how disadvantaged they are. The fund was capped at $2.25 billion, and the amount of requests for funding quickly exceeded the funds available. This program fundamentally changed the understanding of universal service. Previously, only landline voice service was treated as needing support under universal service; the e-rate program now extends this same type of support to Internet access.

Another area of universal service is support for high-cost rural telephone companies. The RBOCs generally serve only densely populated areas of their states. These areas are generally cheaper to serve because of economies of scale and geographical considerations. Each area of a state that is not served by an RBOC is served by an independent telephone company. The independents serve

areas that are less densely populated, more rural, and therefore of higher cost. Because of the policy of geographic rate averaging, the high-cost rural telephone companies have needed subsidies to continue to maintain low rates. These funds have come from high access charges for long-distance calls as well as surcharges on bills of all telecommunications service providers.

Access charges are a large part of the second public policy decision concerning local and long distance services: intercarrier compensation. *Intercarrier compensation* started with access-charge plans around the time of divestiture. Because AT&T was split between its long-distance and local pieces, a mechanism of prices had to be developed to charge long-distance companies for their use of the local telephone network in order to connect a long distance call. Economists had argued that these charges should only include variable traffic-sensitive costs of completing the long-distance calls; the fixed non–traffic-sensitive costs should be paid for by end users in the form of a per-line charge (later called the *subscriber line charge*, or SLC). Because of rate shock and concerns about universal service, the SLC was not set high enough to pay for all of the non–traffic-sensitive costs; the remainder was collected through increases in access charges above the traffic-sensitive cost level. This decision ultimately led to bypassing of local networks and the rise of CAPs and CLECs as discussed earlier.

TA96 recognized that the system of access charges was flawed and needed to be overhauled. The law charged the FCC with developing a solution, and the FCC devoted the third of its trilogy of orders from TA96 to *access-charge reform*. The FCC reform plan, however, has a large failure. Instead of raising the SLC, the FCC created a brand new charge—a *presubscribed interexchange carrier charge* (PICC)—that the local companies charged to the long-distance companies based on the number of customers who had that company as their default long-distance carrier. Revenue raised from this new charge was used to lower access charges. The FCC also distinguished between primary and other lines coming into a residence and allowed the SLC and PICC to be higher for nonprimary lines. The

FCC wanted the long-distance companies to absorb the PICC charges as their per-minute access charges declined. Instead, the companies passed on the new PICC charges to consumers as a new fee and, in some cases, charged more than the PICC charge. The end result was worse than if the FCC had simply raised the SLC directly. After two years, the FCC admitted its mistake and eliminated the PICC charge and began raising the SLC.

Intercarrier compensation includes more than just access charges for long-distance service. Because TA96 formalized rules for full-blown local competition between ILECs and CLECs, intercarrier compensation has also included payments, called *reciprocal compensation*, between ILECs and CLECs for terminating local traffic between subscribers. Reciprocal compensation rates were set at a fraction of the price of access charges even though the physical act of terminating a phone call is the same whether it originates across the country or across the street. Charging different prices for the same service is referred to as *price discrimination* by economists and invites *arbitrage* (buying in the low market and selling in the high market) unless there is an easy way to prevent it. In the case of reciprocal compensation, CLECs could accept long-distance traffic from the long-distance company and pass it on to the ILEC as local traffic. The CLEC would only pay the low per-minute reciprocal compensation rate, and the long-distance company would avoid the much higher access-charge rate. This act would be even easier if the CLEC and the long-distance company were part of the same holding company. Thus, there was pressure to lower access charges and make reciprocal compensation rates higher than their marginal cost.

One byproduct of having reciprocal compensation rates higher than their marginal costs was that CLECs could make a profit from terminating local traffic. One type of customer with the highest amount of terminating traffic is the Internet service provider (ISP). ISPs with dialup access have large modem banks that allow individuals to connect to the Internet by placing local calls. If the ISP is a customer of the CLEC and the individual connecting to the Internet is a customer of the ILEC, then the ILEC must pay the CLEC per-minute reciprocal compensation for the duration of the Internet connection. In this way, some CLECs received 40 percent to 70 percent of their total revenue from reciprocal compensation from the ILECs. The FCC eventually ruled that a call to an ISP was not a local call and therefore should not be subject to reciprocal compensation rules. This ruling placed some CLECs into bankruptcy.

The rules for intercarrier compensation get even more difficult when VoIP providers and wireless carriers are added to the mix. Efforts to reform intercarrier compensation and the universal service fund in order to provide a consistent plan that addresses many of the concerns already raised have been led by coalitions of industry players and regulators. One plan, known as the Missoula Plan (named for the town in which the group met at one point), was filed with the FCC in August 2006 and will be the subject of comments and debate in the coming years. The Missoula Plan task force has worked under the auspices of the National Association of Regulatory Utility Commissioners (NARUC) and is sponsored by AT&T, BellSouth, and Cingular, as well as by approximately one-quarter of the small rural companies. Qwest, Verizon, and most wireless providers have reserved judgment on the plan.

WIRELESS VOICE MARKET

The wireless voice segment of the telecommunications industry has been one of its fastest-growing segments. This segment started in 1985 when two cellular providers were awarded licenses in each geographic territory by the FCC. One license was given to the landline company, and the other was awarded by a combination of merit hearings and lottery. This duopoly structure did not make for a competitive environment, but the industry grew at a rapid clip because of the high demand for mobility in communications. This robust demand led to calls for the FCC to allocate more radio spectrum to wireless telephony. As a result, an additional 120 megahertz (MHz) of radio spectrum was sold by the FCC in its broadband personal communication system (PCS) auctions from December 1994 to January 1997 (compared to 50 MHz for cellular at that time). In all, 2074 licenses were awarded, and more than $20 billion was bid.

To ensure more competition than under the former duopoly structure, the FCC imposed a spectrum cap such that no single company could have a license for more than 45 MHz in any single market. In November 2001, the FCC raised that limit to 55 MHz; in January 2003, the commission eliminated the spectrum cap altogether. The elimination has led to mergers and industry consolidation. In 2004, Cingular bought AT&T Wireless (at that time, a company independent of AT&T Long Distance); in 2005, Alltel bought Western Wireless and Sprint merged with Nextel. These mergers helped solidify the dominance of four nationwide wireless carriers—Cingular, Verizon Wireless, Sprint-Nextel, and T-Mobile—with several smaller regional carriers. The firms' market shares are shown in Table 2.

In August 2006, the FCC began an auction of an additional 90 MHz of wireless spectrum. The bidders with the largest upfront deposit include a consortium of satellite TV providers, including DirecTV and EchoStar; and a group of cable TV companies, including Comcast, Time Warner Cable, and Cox Communications. Wireless providers T-Mobile, Cingular, and Verizon Wireless have also registered at the auction to acquire additional spectrum.

Table 2: Market Share by Subscriber for the Top Four Mobile Telephone Operators

Mobile Telephone Operator	Market Share (%)
Cingular Wireless	27.1
Verizon Wireless	24.2
Sprint PCS	11.9
T-Mobile	9.6

Source: Federal Communications Commission. 2005. Tables 2 and 4.

In 2008, the FCC will auction off additional spectrum that is now occupied by local television stations.

Before the creation of these nationwide carriers, the wireless industry was served by smaller regional carriers. Because customers wanted to use their wireless phones outside of their carriers' regions, each company developed roaming agreements so its customers could utilize another company's network while in its territory. The charges for using this roaming feature were passed along to the customer. Because roaming charges were much higher than the standard home rate for calls, customers complained frequently and loudly to their carriers. The development of nationwide carriers allowed consumers to use their own companies' networks and choose pricing plans that would avoid all roaming charges.

Wireless subscribers and revenues have increased rapidly over time. Figure 7 shows the rapid increase in the number of wireless subscribers, and Figure 8 shows the increase in minutes of use over wireless networks. As of December 2003, nationwide wireless penetration was 54 percent. The average minutes used per month increased from 255 minutes in 2000 to 599 minutes in 2003. Figure 9 shows that the average total bill for wireless has declined greatly with the slight increase in recent years because of increased usage.

The wireless industry has experienced several pricing innovations that have spurred its growth. The first innovation was AT&T's Digital One Rate, which was introduced in May 1998. This plan combined wireless airtime and long-distance charges into a single rate, effectively absorbing the long-distance surcharge for long-distance calls made on wireless phones. This pricing plan was quickly copied by the other wireless companies. As mentioned earlier, this type of pricing plan cut landline long-distance usage significantly. On the flip side, it spurred wireless growth because of the "savings" in long distance that was introduced in this plan. In January 2004, AT&T Wireless also introduced mobile-to-mobile calling whereby calls to another AT&T Wireless subscriber would be free. These free calls did not count against a customer's monthly allotment of minutes; the plan helped spur customers to get their friends and family to switch to the same carrier. Similar "in-network" plans were introduced later by many other wireless companies.

Wireless companies have also provided customers with discounted or sometimes even free phones with a one- or

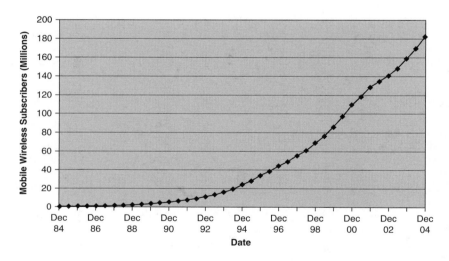

Figure 7: Number of mobile wireless subscribers, 1984–2004

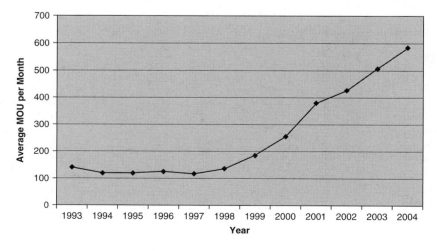

Figure 8: Average minutes of mobile wireless telephone use (MOU) per month, 1993–2003

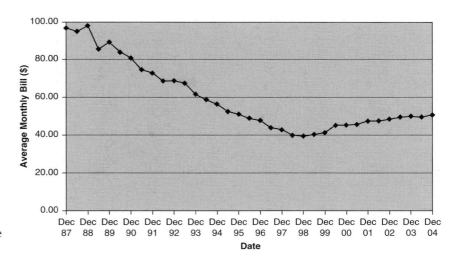

Figure 9: Average monthly bill for mobile wireless telephone service, 1987–2004

two-year contract. Providing a discount for the cost of buying a phone in order to use the wireless service lessened the upfront financial burden of getting service even if the monthly charge was higher as a result. Wireless companies have also signed exclusive deals with phone manufacturers to capture consumer interest in the latest technology. One example is Cingular's exclusive limited-time contract with Motorola to sell its RAZR line of phones.

As wireless phones increasingly became a substitute for landline usage, many customers started to see their wireless phones as substitutes for their landline phones. Surveys have shown that 10 percent to 15 percent of households have "cut the cord" and gone wireless only. This percentage has been highest among younger people and new households. One problem that the wireless industry faced in this substitution was that one landline phone could serve many individuals in the household. If the household consisted of a family of four, this would mean four separate wireless plans to substitute for one landline phone. To effectively lower the price of this substitution and spur growth elsewhere, the wireless companies introduced family plans in which family members could join another family member's plan for as low as $10 per month and share their bundled minutes. These family plans lowered the price for a household to substitute wireless phones for its landline phone.

As discussed earlier, local number portability required local landline companies to allow their customers to keep their local telephone numbers when they switched carriers. This rule applied only to landline companies, so a wireless customer who changed carriers would have to change phone number and notify all of his or her contacts of the new number. This hassle gave customers a great incentive to stay with their current providers and hindered free and equal competition in the market. In November 2003, the FCC required companies in the top one hundred markets to implement local number portability and roll it out nationwide by May 2004.

Unlike landline telecommunications, the FCC and state regulatory commissions do not regulate and never have regulated wireless firms' prices or profits. However, the FCC does hold power over the wireless spectrum licenses that the wireless companies use and can impose rules on how the firms operate; one example is the ruling on local number portability.

As the cellular industry began, the FCC required all U.S. providers to use a single analog standard called *advanced mobile phone service* (AMPS). In the mid-1990s, the wireless providers began building second-generation (2G) networks that used digital technology. These 2G networks were better than the AMPS network because they had better signal quality and used the radio spectrum more efficiently. The FCC did not mandate a 2G standard, and two different types of standards developed. The first set of standards takes samples by time and is similar to time division multiplexing of landline networks. The time-slicing techniques include *time division multiple access* (TDMA), *global system for mobile* (GSM), and *integrated digital enhanced network* (iDEN). GSM was the standard used in Europe, and most U.S. companies that started using TDMA, like Cingular, have since switched to GSM. Nextel uses the iDEN standard. The second set of standards used complex algorithms to compress digital signals. This standard is called *code division multiple access* (CDMA), and it is used by Verizon Wireless and Sprint PCS. TDMA was proven to work on a large scale sooner and enjoyed a "first-mover" advantage. CDMA is more sophisticated and expensive but ultimately was able to use radio spectrum more efficiently than TDMA. However, once a company has chosen a standard, switching technologies becomes expensive. Third-generation wireless services (3G) have been developed in Europe and Asia. Two competing standards are available: universal mobile telephone service (UMTS) (also called WCDMA), which was mandated in Europe; and CDMA2000, which is used in parts of Asia.

Of the five nationwide mobile telephone operators, Cingular and T-Mobile use TDMA or GSM as their 2G digital technology, Sprint PCS and Verizon Wireless use CDMA, and Nextel uses iDEN. Verizon Wireless has deployed $1 \times$ RTT technology throughout its network. Discussion of the wireless carriers upgrade plans to 3G networks will be delayed until the section on data and Internet access.

VIDEO AND CABLE TELEVISION

Before the advent of cable TV, video programming was delivered by over-the-air broadcasts. The FCC licensed television channels to broadcast over *very high frequency* (VHF) from channels 2 to 13 and *ultrahigh frequency* (UHF) for channels above 13. In a typical local market, the FCC would license three to four VHF channels and several more UHF channels. A VHF station is often affiliated with one of the major commercial television net-works: ABC, CBS, NBC, and, later, FOX. Some of these stations are owned by the network, and some are independently owned but have the right to carry the network programming in their particular markets. Although a small percentage of homes receive their video programming from over-the-air broadcasts, the local network affiliated stations are usually carried to homes over cable TV and satellite (Nuechterlein and Weiser 2005, 360).

Cable TV started as noncommercial community antenna TV and was not originally seen as a competitive threat to broadcast TV over the airwaves. However, as more and more cable-only channels became available and more and more homes were passed by cable TV, cable TV became increasingly popular. As of June 2004, 98.8 percent of homes in the United States are passed by cable TV and 61 percent of homes passed subscribed to cable TV (FCC 2005, 14). Cable TV firms use coaxial cable to deliver cable content, and their networks were traditionally one-way networks that delivered video content from the cable headend to end users. To provide cable modem service (discussed in the next section), cable firms had to upgrade their networks to become two-way networks so that users could send as well as received information.

Although local broadcast stations were being seen by fewer and fewer people over the airwaves, they were still seen by many people on their cable systems as cable TV companies retransmitted local over-the-air stations on their cable systems. At first, this seemed to "save" the local broadcast channels from a slow death as the over-the-air market shrank, but station owners soon became jealous as other content channels received payment from the cable firms for their channels while the broadcast channels were essentially free. To change this situation, the Cable Act of 1992 gave broadcasters the right to forbid retransmission without their consent. This property right gave broadcasters the ability to negotiate a fee from a cable company for retransmission of its station. The broadcaster could waive this right and require the cable TV operator to carry its station under "must carry" rules. In most cases, broadcasters did not receive high monetary compensation but were able to negotiate additional channel "slots" on a cable firm's lineup in exchange for the right to use its local network channel.

In addition to broadcast TV, cable operators faced competition from another "wireless" provider. By the mid-1990s, *direct broadcast satellite* (DBS) providers such as DirecTV and Dish Network entered the video-delivery market. The DBS market share of the video market has increased steadily, reaching 25 percent by 2004, as shown in Table 3. Among cable TV firms, Comcast is the largest with more than 21 million customers (see Table 4). Taking the video market as a whole, Comcast has the largest market share with 23 percent, and DirecTV has a

Table 3: Direct Broadcast Satellite Market Share as Percentage of Multichannel Video Programming Distribution

Date	Market Share (%)
June 2000	15.65
June 2001	18.67
June 2002	20.83
June 2003	22.68
June 2004	25.09
June 2005	27.72

Source: Federal Communications Commission. 2006a. Table B-1.

Table 4: Number of Subscribers for Top Cable TV Firms, 2004

Company	Number of Subscribers
Comcast	21,569,521
Time Warner	10,955,507
Cox	6,386,867
Charter	6,211,505
Adelphia	5,426,991
Cablevision	2,944,235
Bright House	2,187,410
Mediacom	1,532,110

Source: Federal Communications Commission. 2005. *Eleventh annual report on the status of competition in the market for delivery of video programming, February 2005*, Tables B-1 and B-3.

Table 5: Top Ten Firms by Market Share in the Video Market as a Whole, 2005

Rank	Company	Market Share (% of Subscribers)
1	Comcast	22.99
2	DirecTV	15.72
3	EchoStar	12.27
4	Time Warner	11.69
5	Cox	6.73
6	Charter	6.37
7	Adelphia	5.50
8	Cablevision	3.22
9	Bright House	2.34
10	Mediacom	1.55

Source: Federal Communications Commission. 2006. *Twelfth annual report on the status of competition in the market for delivery of video programming, February 2006*, Table B-3.

market share of 16 percent. The top ten firms are shown in Table 5.

Within the cable TV industry, firms are organized as *multiple system operators* (MSOs). There has been significant consolidation in the cable TV industry and across the landline telecommunications industry and cable TV. In 1998, AT&T, the largest long-distance company at the time, bought TCI, then the largest cable TV operator. Then, in 1999, AT&T bought Media One, the fifth-largest cable TV operator. TCI and Media One became AT&T Broadband, which was sold in 2001 to Comcast, the second-largest MSO. It seems that the convergence between cable TV and landline voice communications took longer than AT&T anticipated, and the cable TV properties were more valuable to another MSO than they were to a long-distance landline voice company.

Prices for cable TV have risen steadily over the past several years. Figure 10 shows the average price for basic service, while Figure 11 shows the average total cable bill for customers overall. Basic cable service has risen from $11.57 in 1997 to $13.80 in 2004, but the average total monthly bill has almost doubled from $24.34 in 1995 to $45.32 in 2004.

Cable TV has been regulated and deregulated several times. Before 1984, some municipalities regulated cable TV rates in addition to awarding local franchises.

However, the Cable Act of 1984 removed cable systems from municipal rate regulation where it existed. Because of this deregulation and other causes, cable rates rose 43 percent from 1986 to 1989. This sudden rise in rates led to calls for federal rate regulation. Thus, the Cable Act of 1992 required the FCC to regulate cable TV rates. This lasted until the Telecommunications Act of 1996 removed rate regulation for all cable services except basic-tier cable service.

In addition to high prices and both the regulation and deregulation of prices, the industry has also faced controversy surrounding so-called à la carte pricing. À la carte pricing refers to a pricing scheme in which consumers would only pay for channels they wanted and would not be required to buy packages or tiers of programming. Cable TV firms have consistently claimed that such a pricing scheme would raise the costs to all consumers because programming and advertising is based on the number of subscribers and this number would be reduced under such a scheme. The FCC originally agreed with the industry's analysis but has changed its mind recently. To head off a requirement to offer à la carte pricing, several firms have begun to offer "family-friendly" packages to placate the most vocal advocates of à la carte pricing.

Cable TV providers not only face current competition from DBS but also now face future competition from

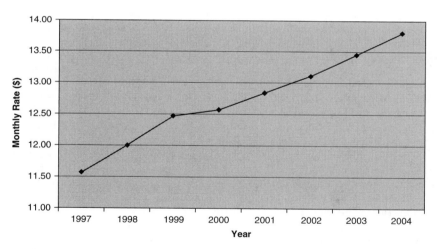

Figure 10: Average monthly rates for basic services, 1997–2004

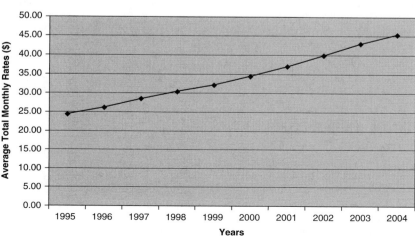

Figure 11: Average monthly rates, 1995–2004

the RBOCs that are rolling out fiber networks to provide IPTV in addition to high-speed Internet access. IPTV is projected to offer several enhancements over traditional cable TV, including greater interactivity, easier guides and channel changing, and even more channels. RBOCs have been hindered in their efforts to roll out video services because of local franchise agreements. Cable TV companies usually have franchise agreements with local municipalities, and the RBOCs argue that it would be too expensive and onerous to negotiate city-by-city franchise agreements in order for them to provide service. They have asked Congress to issue a national franchise license for them to provide video programming nationwide and have already obtained statewide franchise authority in several states.

If one takes a larger definition of the relevant market, cable TV also faces competition from videotape and DVDs and Internet video downloads such as iTunes and video iPod. With convergence comes another emerging distribution channel for video programming: the Internet. Web sites such as YouTube, Google Video, MSN video, and Yahoo Video are increasing the amount of free and paid content for viewers. In addition, TV networks are distributing their content over their own Web sites and partnering with others to sell online versions of their TV content.

The video programming and distribution industry is also somewhat vertically integrated. Several cable TV systems own parts of many of the programming channels that they and others carry on their systems. For example, Cablevision has a 60 percent ownership of American Movie Classics, Cox owns 24.6 percent of Discovery Channel, and Time Warner completely owns HBO. TV networks are owned by larger corporations that also own video content and programming. CBS is owned by Viacom, NBC is owned by General Electric and Vivendi, ABC is owned by Disney, and FOX is owned by News Corporation. Vertical integration could make it difficult for new firms to enter in competition with the cable TV firms. The Cable Act of 1992 required cable firms to make their own programming available on reasonable terms to rivals. This requirement was renewed by the FCC in 2002.

Some cable TV firms are offering voice communications (local and long distance) over their broadband cable modem systems in direct competition with the RBOCs and the long-distance companies. Most of the firms are using VoIP to provide these services over their broadband cable-modem networks. Several cable companies have also partnered with Sprint-Nextel to offer wireless phones. Convergence is taking place as RBOCs enter the video market and cable TV firms offer voice services. Both types of firms are gearing up to provide the quadruple play of voice, video, data, and wireless.

DATA AND INTERNET ACCESS

Although there was talk of alternative "information superhighways" in the 1980s, the Internet has taken over as the data network for the consumer market. The Internet is a network of networks that use the TCP/IP protocols. The Internet evolved from ARPAnet, which was developed in the 1960s by the Department of Defense; and NSFNET, which linked universities and supercomputers in the 1980s.

Despite having these roots in government funding, the Internet was privatized on April 30, 1995. There were then five major backbone providers: uunet, ANS, SprintLink, BBN, and MCI. By 2000, uunet and ANS were brought by MCI WorldCom, BBN was part of Genuity, MCI's old network was owned by Cable and Wireless, and AT&T had created its own IP network using its own fiber and purchasing IBM's Global Network. These backbone providers had peering arrangements to exchange traffic and provide links to regional networks and ISPs.

The exponential growth of the Internet would not have occurred without the development of easy-to-use end-user applications. The first applications were e-mail systems that could exchange messages between systems. End-user e-mail interfaces became easier to use with more and more features. Netscape and its World Wide Web browser popularized the use of the Internet beyond simply e-mail, and customer demand grew rapidly. The explosive growth of Web sites and extensions of basic browser functions drove consumers to demand access to the Internet and, eventually, higher speed access.

Starting in the mid-1990s, the number of residential second lines soared, driven by demand for dialup Internet access (Cassel 1999). It was not long before the attraction of always-on connectivity, faster speeds, and declining prices spurred a switch from second lines to broadband technologies. *Broadband* is defined by the FCC as speeds 200k or faster in one direction, which is low by some standards. The current technologies that offer broadband speeds are cable modems, DSL, satellite, and WiFi. The broadband market shows the greatest evidence of convergence, with cable TV firms offering cable modem service and landline voice companies offering DSL. As shown in Figure 12, cable modems have the highest percentage market share of the broadband market with 59 percent; ADSL follows with 37.2 percent. Cable modems were first to the marketplace, but ADSL has tried to close the gap in recent years with lower pricing that has led to increased market share. Table 6 shows the number of lines served by various companies that provide cable modems, with Comcast being the largest provider. Table 7 shows the

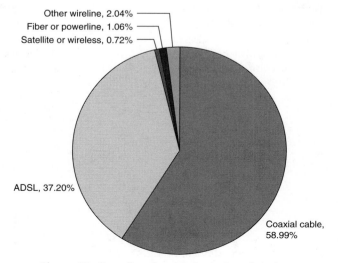

Other wireline, 2.04%
Fiber or powerline, 1.06%
Satellite or wireless, 0.72%
ADSL, 37.20%
Coaxial cable, 58.99%

Figure 12: Broadband technologies' market share

Table 6: Major Cable Modem Providers, Ranked by Subscribership, First Quarter 2005

Company	Number of Subscribers
Comcast	7,410,000
Time Warner	4,120,000
Cox	2,750,000
Charter	1,980,000
Adelphia	1,490,000
Cablevision	1,440,000
Total North America	21,150,000

Source: Leichtman Research Group, cited in *The digital fact book*. 2005. 7th ed.

Table 7: Major DSL Providers by Subscribership, First Quarter 2005

Company	DSL Subscribers
SBC	5,610,000
Verizon	3,940,000
BellSouth	2,350,000
Qwest	1,120,000
Sprint	550,000
Covad	550,000
Total North America	14,700,000

Source: Leichtman Research Group, cited in *The digital fact book*. 2005. 7th ed.

various companies that provide ADSL, with SBC being the largest.

Landline broadband faces increasing competition from wireless technologies. The wireless technology with the most users is WiFi, which is used in home wireless networks and coffee shops. WiFi is also used by *wireless Internet service providers* (WISPs) to provide Internet services in rural communities. WiMAX is an emerging wireless technology that promises wider ranges and faster speeds than WiFi; thus, it may be a better competitor to wireline broadband. Sprint-Nextel recently announced its intention to build a "4G" wireless broadband network using WiMAX technology.

In addition to private companies building wireless broadband networks, cities and local governments have taken the initiative to build new networks. WiFi networks are being deployed across much larger geographies such as the cities of Philadelphia and San Francisco. In these cases, city governments are taking the initiative to have the technology deployed by partnering with private firms to build and manage the networks. These cities already have wireline broadband services available to most city residents. In other cases, smaller rural municipalities are looking to build broadband networks where private companies have not deployed any broadband technologies. Other cities have opted for a landline fiber solution similar to the Utah Telecommunication Open Infrastructure Agency (UTOPIA) project. Municipal broadband has been a politically controversial topic, with private firms looking to bar municipalities from providing broadband services out of fear that subsidies from taxpayers will provide an unequal playing field and potentially delay or stop private investment.

Another politically sensitive issue concerning the Internet has been called "net neutrality." *Net neutrality* does not have a precise definition but usually refers to a policy that broadband providers cannot charge content providers to send information over their broadband lines to end users. This policy debate begin when broadband providers such as Verizon, AT&T, and Comcast proposed charging content providers such as Google and Yahoo to send data over their lines. The providers would create "fast lanes" for high-bandwidth applications such as movie downloads or streaming video. The providers claim that this would ensure these applications have the bandwidth available when they need it and would support enhanced infrastructure. Critics claim that users will end up paying twice for access to content.

Aside from Sprint's announcement concerning WiMAX, wireless companies are already upgrading their networks to provide wireless data that surpass minimum broadband speeds. Until the major carriers upgraded their networks, less than 2 percent of their mobile traffic was data. Their second-generation networks—using GSM, CDMA, and TDMA—yielded data speeds of 9.6 to 19.2 kilobytes per second (kbps). Recently, however, several networks have been upgrading to third-generation network technologies such as *evolution data optimized* (or *only*) (EvDO) in major cities across the United States. These third-generation networks allow broadband speeds for laptops, personal digital assistants (PDAs), and cell phones from anywhere the signal reaches. Verizon Wireless launched its CDMA2000 1 × EVDO network in late 2003 and now offers it in several major U.S. cities. Sprint began to deploy this same technology in July 2005. Cingular Wireless is planning to deploy WCDMA with *high-speed data packet access* (HSDPA) technology in many major U.S. markets. This technology will allow average download speeds of 400 kbps to 700 kbps with burst rates of up to several megabytes per second (Mbps); CDMA2000 1 × EV-DO, on the other hand, delivers average user speeds of 400 kbps to 700 kbps and allows maximum data-throughput speeds of 2.4 Mbps.

INTERNATIONAL TELECOMMUNICATIONS

Although much of this chapter has focused on the U.S. telecommunications market, similar convergence of industry markets has occurred elsewhere in the world. In some cases, the United States has been in the forefront of these changes; in other cases, notably wireless and broadband data, the United States has lagged behind. The movement of landline voice services from monopoly to competition in both local and long distance has followed the U.S. pattern with some delay. In many cases, countries first had to transition from state-owned telecommunications monopolies to private, regulated firms. In Canada, several telephone companies were owned by provincial governments. In the United Kingdom, British Telecom was privatized in 1985. In other parts of Europe, France Telecom and Deutsche Telecom moved from state-owned telephone and telegraph monopolies to private companies. In Japan, Nippon Telephone and Telegraph Corporation started the process in 1985, but in 1996 it was restructured into a holding company with a separate long-distance division and two local telephone companies, NTT East and NTT West.

After privatization, all of these countries opened their landline markets to competition. In 1985, the United Kingdom opened entry into telecom services and Japan allowed long distance and international calling competition. Canada allowed competition in long distance in 1992 and local competition in 1997. The European Union opened all telecommunications markets to competition in 1998 (Crandall 2005).

On the wireless telecommunications front, the move toward competition took a similar but delayed path in mimicking the U.S. experience. Most of the developed countries only had one or two wireless carriers as late as 1991. Even today, many countries only have two to four wireless carriers competing. In spite of being in the forefront in wireline and wireless competition, the United State has lagged behind in its auction of 3G radio spectra and deployment of 3G services. In addition, the United States ranked tenth in broadband penetration at the end of 2003 (Organisation for Economic Co-operation and Development 2005, 129).

CONCLUSION

Having looked at each of the telecommunications industry segments separately, we clearly see that each segment faces competitive inroads by other industry segments. The landline voice market (both local and long-distance) faces competition from wireless voice and cable TV companies. Cable TV firms are facing increasing competition from DBS firms and local telephone companies using IPTV. Local voice companies, cable TV firms, and wireless firms are competing for the broadband data market. Large multimarket firms will continue to increase their market shares or market reach in each of the quadruple play markets of landline voice, high-speed Internet access, TV and entertainment, and wireless voice and data.

GLOSSARY

Advanced mobile phone service (AMPS): Wireless analog standard used in the United States.

Alternative local transport carrier (ALT): Smaller local landline company that provided bypass of the ILEC network. These companies later became known as CLECs.

Code division multiple access (CDMA): A 2G wireless standard that uses complex algorithms to compress the digital signal.

Competitive access provider (CAP): Smaller local landline company that provided bypass of the ILEC network. These companies later became known as CLECs.

Competitive local exchange carrier (CLEC): Smaller, upstart company that competes with ILECs for local landline voice customers.

Digital subscriber line (DSL): A broadband Internet access service provided by LECs.

Direct broadcast satellite (DBS): Wireless video providers such as DirecTV and Dish Network that compete with cable TV companies.

Evolution data optimized (or only) (EvDO): A third-generation wireless standard that enables broadband data speeds on wireless networks.

Federal Communications Commission (FCC): The federal agency created by the Communication Act of 1934, which regulates interstate telecommunications.

Fiber to the curb (FTTC): The use of fiber optic cable to the pedestal or neighborhood and copper or coaxial cable from that point to the home.

Fiber to the premises (FTTP): The use of fiber optic cable directly to the home that replaces copper or co-axial cable.

Global system for mobile (GSM): A 2G wireless network standard that uses time-slicing techniques.

High-speed data packet access (HSDPA): A 3G wireless data standard.

Incumbent local exchange carrier (ILEC): Traditionally regulated monopoly providers of local voice landline services.

Integrated digital enhanced network (iDEN): A 2G wireless network standard that uses time-slicing techniques.

Internet protocol television (IPTV): Delivers video (television) programming to homes using Internet protocols.

Internet service provider (ISP): Company that provides Internet access to end users.

Multiple system operators (MSO): Cable TV companies that provide video programming via many different local systems.

National Association of Regulatory Utility Commissioners (NARUC): Umbrella organization representing state and federal regulatory commissions.

Presubscribed interexchange carrier charge (PICC): New charge as a result of TA96 instituted by the FCC to lower switched access fees. Charged by local companies to long-distance companies.

Public switched telephone network (PSTN): The traditional voice network operated by ILECs and long-distance voice companies.

Regional Bell operating company (RBOC): Any of seven local telephone companies created from the divestiture of AT&T in 1984.

Second generation (2G): Wireless network standards that use digital technology, including TDMA and CDMA.

Subscriber line charge (SLC): Per-line prices charged to end users that started around the time of divestiture.

Telecommunications Act of 1996 (TA96): The most recent, wide-ranging telecommunication law; technically, a rewrite of the Communications Act of 1934.

Third generation (3G): Wireless network standards that provide faster data transmission and include UMTS and WCDMA.

Time division multiple access (TDMA): A 2G wireless network standard that uses time-slicing techniques.

Universal mobile telephone service (UMTS): A 3G wireless standard also known as WCDMA.

Voice over Internet protocol (VoIP): Using Internet protocols to transmit voice conversations over data networks.

Wireless fidelity (WiFi): The popular name given to 802.11 standards for transmitting data wirelessly.

Wireless Internet service provider (WISP): Company that provides Internet access to end users using wireless technology, usually over an unlicensed spectrum.

Worldwide interoperability for microwave access (WiMAX): A newer wireless standard that allows higher speed and longer ranges than WiFi.

CROSS REFERENCES

See *Cable Modems; Data Communications Basics; DSL (Digital Subscriber Line); Voice Communications Systems: KTS, PBX, Centrex, and ACD; Voice over IP (VoIP)*.

REFERENCES

Black, S. K. 2002. *Telecommunications law in the Internet age*. San Diego: Academic Press.

Cairncross, F. C. 2001. *The death of distance: How the communications revolution is changing our lives*. Boston: Harvard Business School Press.

Cassel, C. A. 1999. Demand for and use of additional lines by residential customers. In *The future of the telecommunications industry: Forecasting and demand analysis*, edited by D. G. Loomis and L. D. Taylor, 43–59. Norwell, MA: Kluwer Academic Publishers.

Crandall, R. W. 2005. *Competition and chaos: U.S. telecommunications since the 1996 Telecom Act*. Washington, DC: Brookings Institution, 2005.

Duesterberg, T. J., and K. Gordon. 1997. *Competition and deregulation in telecommunications: The case for a new paradigm*. Indianapolis: Hudson Institute.

Federal Communications Commission (FCC). 2003. *Statistics of the long distance telecommunications industry, May 2003*. Washington, DC: Industry Analysis and Technology Division Wireline Competition Bureau.

———. 2005. *Eleventh annual report on the status of competition in the market for delivery of video programming, February 2005*. Washington, DC: Industry Analysis and Technology Division Wireline Competition Bureau.

———. 2006. *Local telephone competition: Status as of December 31, 2005*. Washington, DC: Industry Analysis and Technology Division Wireline Competition Bureau.

Hausman, T., and A. Belinfante. 1993. Effects of the breakup of AT&T on telephone penetration in the United States. *American Economic Review* (May): 178–84.

Loomis, D. G., and C. M. Swann. 2005. Intermodal competition in local telecommunications markets. *Information Economics and Policy* 17(1): 97–113.

Mueller, M. L., Jr. 1997. *Universal service: Competition, interconnection, and monopoly in the making of the American telephone system*. Cambridge: MIT Press.

Nuechterlein, J. E., and P. J. Weiser. 2005. *Digital crossroads: American telecommunications policy in the Internet age*. Cambridge: MIT Press.

Organisation for Economic Co-operation and Development. 2005. *OECD communications outlook 2005*. Paris: Author.

Sappington, D. E. M., and D. L. Weisman. 1996. *Designing incentive regulation for the telecommunications industry*. Cambridge: MIT Press.

Taylor, W. E., and L. D. Taylor. 1993. Postdivestiture long-distance competition in the United States. *American Economic Review* (May): 185–90.

FURTHER READING

Breznick, A. 2005. Baby Bells trump cable on data front. www.cabledatacomnews.com/dec05/dec05-5.html (retrieved February 10, 2006).

Brock, G. W. 1994. *Telecommunication policy for the information age*. Cambridge: Harvard University Press.

———. 2003. *The second information revolution*. Cambridge: Harvard University Press.

Crandall, R. W., and H. Furchtgott-Roth. 1996. *Cable TV: Regulation or competition*. Washington, DC: Brookings Institution.

Crandall, R. W., and L. Waverman. 1995. Talk is cheap: *The promise of regulatory reform in North American telecommunications*. Washington, DC: Brookings Institution.

Federal Communications Commission (FCC). 2003. *Statistics of the long distance telecommunications industry, May 2003*. Washington, DC: Industry Analysis and Technology Division Wireline Competition Bureau.

———. 2005. *High-speed services for Internet access, 2004*. Washington, DC: Industry Analysis and Technology Division Wireline Competition Bureau.

———. 2005. *Report on cable industry prices, 2004 05-12*. Washington, DC: Industry Analysis and Technology Division Wireline Competition Bureau.

———. 2005. *Tenth annual report and analysis of competitive market conditions with respect to commercial mobile services September, 2005*. Washington, DC: Industry Analysis and Technology Division Wireline Competition Bureau.

———. 2005. *Trends in telephone service, 2004*. Washington, DC: Industry Analysis and Technology Division Wireline Competition Bureau.

———. 2006. *Twelfth annual report on the status of competition in the market for delivery of video programming, February, 2006*. Washington, DC: Industry Analysis and Technology Division Wireline Competition Bureau.

Johnson, L. L. 1994. *Toward competition in cable television*. Cambridge: MIT Press.

Laffont, J.-J., and J. Tirole. 2000. *Competition in telecommunications*. Cambridge: MIT Press.

Lenard, T. M., and M. J. Pickford. 2005. *The digital economy fact book*. 7th ed. Washington, DC: Progress Freedom Foundation.

Maxwell, K. 1999. *Residential broadband*. New York: John Wiley & Sons.

McKnight, L. W., and J. Bailey, eds. 1997. *Internet economics*. Cambridge: MIT Press.

McKnight, L. W., W. Lehr, and D. D. Clark. 2001. *Internet telephony*. Cambridge: MIT Press.

McMillan, J. 1994. Selling spectrum rights. *Journal of Economic Perspectives* 8(3): 145–62.

Schneiderman, R. 1997. *Future talk: The changing wireless game*. New York: IEEE Press.

Shapiro, C., and H. R. Varian. 1999. *Information rules*. Boston: Harvard Business School Press.

Vogelsang, I., and B. M. Mitchell. 1997. *Telecommunications competition*: *The last ten miles*. Cambridge: MIT Press.

Webb, W. 2001. *The future of wireless communications*. Boston: Artech House.

Data Communications Basics

Hossein Bidgoli, *California State University, Bakersfield*

INTRODUCTION

This chapter reviews principles of data communications and looks at data communications components and various types of networking systems. It discusses the role of data communications in delivering timely and relevant multimedia information for decision-making purposes. Important concepts in the data communications environment will be reviewed, including data codes, analog and digital transmission, serial and parallel transmission, transmission modes, elementary data flow, protocols, and the open system interconnection reference model. The chapter also reviews data communications applications, including electronic data interchange and electronic commerce. The chapter concludes with a discussion on the growing convergence of voice, video, and data, and it highlights the importance of data communications field in the business world. The materials presented in this chapter will be further discussed in following chapters and should provide a background for the rest of the *Handbook*.

DEFINING DATA COMMUNICATIONS

The electronic transfer of data from one location to another is called *data communications*. The efficiency and effectiveness of any *computer-based information system* (CBIS) is measured in terms of the timely delivery of relevant and accurate information. Data communications enable a CBIS to deliver information where and when it is needed.

In today's national and international organizations, data may be collected in different cities, states, and even countries. If an effective data communications system is in place, then geographic organizational distribution does not impose any problems in the collection and distribution of relevant information. Data can be collected anywhere, processed, and delivered to any location throughout the world. An effective data communications system can significantly improve the efficiency and effectiveness of a CBIS by improving the flexibility of data collection and transmission. By using a portable computer, a personal digital assistant (PDA), or a palmtop computer and a communications system, an executive can communicate with his or her office at any time and from any location.

Data communications is the fundamental basis of the growing concept of the "virtual organization." This new trend indicates that an organization is not limited to its physical boundary. Various functions can be outsourced, and the results can be delivered to the organization in a timely manner by using a data communications system. A typical virtual organization requires minimal office space. Employees telecommute, and services to customers are provided through communications systems. Data communications systems are the backbone of the growing phenomena of the information superhighway and the Internet.

As Box 1 shows, the applications of data communication systems can be seen anywhere.

Box 1: Applications of data communication systems

- airline reservation systems
- audio conferencing
- automated credit card services
- automated teller machines (ATMs)
- computer conferencing
- data, voice, video, image, and fax transmissions
- distance learning and virtual learning systems
- e-government
- electronic data interchange (EDI)
- electronic commerce (EC)
- electronic file transfer
- electronic funds transfer
- electronic mail (e-mail) and instant messaging
- electronic shopping
- groupware and group support systems
- insurance applications
- Internet and global networks
- law-enforcement applications
- online banking
- online tax returns
- stock market applications
- telecommuting
- time-sharing applications
- video conferencing

BASIC COMPONENTS OF A DATA COMMUNICATIONS SYSTEM

A typical data communications system may include the following components:

- sender and receiver devices,
- modems, and
- communications media (channels).

Sender and Receiver Devices

A sender or receiver device may include one of the following components:

- input/output device;
- smart terminal;
- intelligent terminal, workstation, or microcomputer;
- network computer; or
- other type of computer.

The input/output (I/O) device, also known as a *dumb terminal*, is used only to send or receive information; it has no processing power.

A *smart terminal*, on the other hand, is an input/output device with a limited degree of processing capability. It can perform certain processing tasks, but it is not a full-featured computer. This type of device is used on factory floors and assembly lines for data collection and transmission to a main computer system.

An *intelligent terminal*, *workstation*, or *microcomputer* serves as both an input/output device and stand-alone system. Using this type of device, the remote site is able to perform processing tasks without the support of the main computer system.

A *network computer* (NC) is a diskless computer that runs software from and saves all data to a *server*, which is a computer that provides a particular service to the client computers on the network. NCs may become more popular in the near future and should be used extensively in place of intelligent terminals. These low-priced computers can connect a user to the Internet and other networks.

Other types of computers used as input/output device include minicomputers, mainframe computers, and supercomputers.

Modems

A *modem* (modulator-demodulator) converts digital signals to analog signals that can be transferred over an analog telephone line. *Analog signals* are continuous wave patterns and are produced naturally, such as by the human voice. They are related to a continuously variable physical property, such as voltage, pressure, or rotation. *Digital signals*, on the other hand, are distinct on or off, 0 or 1, binary electrical signals. Digital signals are encoded information in a binary system, such as 0 or 1. All computers process data in digital format. Once analog signals arrive at their destination, a second modem converts them back into digital format before they enter the receiving computer.

To establish a communications link, the two devices must be synchronized. This means that both devices must start and stop at the same point. Synchronization is achieved through protocols. *Protocols* are conventions and rules that govern a data communications system. They cover error detection, message length, speed of transmission, and so forth.

Protocols also help to ensure compatibility among different manufacturers' devices.

Communications Media

Communications media, or *channels*, connect the sender and receiver devices. Communications media can be either conducted (wired or guided), such as coaxial cable, or they can be radiated (that is, transmitted wirelessly) to receiving devices such as satellite. A communications medium can be either a point-to-point or a multipoint medium. In a point-to-point system, only one device uses the medium. In a multipoint system, several devices share the same medium.

IMPORTANT EVENTS IN THE GROWTH OF DATA COMMUNICATIONS IN NORTH AMERICA

Modern communications started in 1837 when Samuel Morse constructed a working telegraph system. Table 1

Table 1: Major Data Communications Event in North America

Event	Year
Telegraph invented	1837
Western Union founded	1856
Telephone invented	1876
Bell Company founded	1877
AT&T created	1885
Telephone system regulation begins in Canada	1892
Telephone system regulation begins in United States	1910
Direct-dial long-distance service begins	1951
IBM introduces remote job entry	1954
First U.S. communications satellite sent into orbit	1958
FCC approves private microwave communication networks	1959
Satellites begin to transmit international telephone calls	1962
Packet-switching network concept proposed by the Rand Corporation	1964
Carterfone court decision permits non-Bell telephone equipment to be used	1968
ARPAnet (the foundation of the Internet) begins operation	1969
Court permits MCI to provide long-distance services	1970
Ethernet LAN specifications formulated	1972
IBM announces its systems network architecture (SNA)	1974
Microcomputer LANs introduced	1982
Breakup of AT&T into seven regional Bell operating companies	1984
Cellular phones begin service	1984
Telecommunications Act of 1996 deregulates U.S. telephone system	1996
More than 50 percent of American households own a personal computer	1998
SBC and AT&T merge	2005
Lucent and Alcatel merge	2006

highlights important events in North America that have led to today's modern communications systems.

DATA-PROCESSING CONFIGURATIONS

Over the past sixty years as the computer field has advanced, three types of data-processing configurations have emerged: centralized, decentralized, and distributed.

Centralized Data Processing

In a *centralized data-processing system*, one central location performs all data-processing tasks. In the early days of computer technology (1950s and 1960s), this type of processing was justified because data-processing personnel were in short supply; economy of scale, both in hardware and software, could be realized; and only large organizations could afford computers.

Decentralized Data Processing

In a *decentralized data-processing system*, each user, office, department, or division has its own computer. All data-processing tasks can be implemented within each separate organizational unit. This system is certainly more responsive to the user than centralized processing. Nevertheless, decentralized systems have certain problems, including lack of coordination among organizational units, the excessive cost of having many systems, and duplication of efforts.

Distributed Data Processing

Distributed data processing (DDP) solves two of the major problems associated with the first two types of data-processing configurations: (1) lack of responsiveness in centralized processing, and (2) lack of coordination in decentralized processing. Distributed data processing has overcome these problems by maintaining centralized control while decentralizing operations.

In DDP, processing power is distributed among several locations. Databases, processing units, or input/output devices may be distributed. A good example is a newspaper publishing business in which reporters and editors are scattered around the world. Reporters gather news stories, enter them into their personal computers (PCs), edit them, and use a communications medium to forward them to the editor in charge. The reporter and the editor can be thousands of miles apart. Since the mid-1970s, with advancements in networking and microcomputers, this type of data-processing configuration has gained popularity. Some of the unique advantages of a DDP system include:

- access to unused processing power by an overused location;
- design modularity (i.e., computer power can be added or removed based on need);
- distance and location independence;
- increased compatibility with organizational growth by the addition of workstations;
- fault tolerance because of the availability of redundant resources as a security measure (i.e., if one component fails, a redundant component will take over);
- resource sharing (e.g., of expensive high quality laser printers);
- system reliability (i.e., system failure can be limited to only one site); and
- user orientation (i.e., the system is more responsive to user needs).

Some of the disadvantages of DDP include dependence on communications technology, incompatibility among equipment, and more challenging network management.

IMPORTANT CONCEPTS IN DATA COMMUNICATIONS

To better understand a data communications system and its operations, several keywords and concepts should be defined. These keywords and concepts will be further explained throughout the *Handbook*.

Data Codes

Computers and communications systems use *data codes* to represent and transfer data among various computers and network systems. Three popular types of data codes are:

- Baudot code,
- ASCII (American standard code for information interchange), and
- EBCDIC (extended binary coded decimal interchange code).

The *Baudot code* was named after French engineer Jean-Maurice-Emile Baudot. It was first used to measure the speed of telegraph transmissions. It uses five-bit patterns to represent the characters A to Z, the numbers 0 to 9, and several special characters. Using Baudot code up to thirty-two characters can be represented mathematically as $2^5 = 32$. This is not enough, however, to represent all the letters of most alphabets (uppercase and lowercase) and special characters.

To overcome this limitation, Baudot code uses *downshift* (11111) and *upshift* (11011) character code. By doing this, as many as sixty-four different characters can be defined, doubling the code's original size. This process is similar to typing using the keyboard. If the caps lock key on the keyboard is pressed, then all of the characters typed after this will be transmitted as uppercase; as soon as it is pressed again, all the characters will be transmitted as lowercase. Therefore, using Baudot, every character except for a space is either an upshift character or a downshift character. For example, 10001 represents both the letter Z and + (the plus sign). The letter Z is a downshift character, and the plus sign is an upshift character. Although Baudot code is no longer used, it illustrates how information is transmitted by a small number of bit combinations.

In the early 1960s, the American National Standards Institute developed the American Standard Code for Information Interchange, or *ASCII* (pronounced *ask-ee*). It is the most common format for text files, is used extensively in PC applications, and is ubiquitous on the Internet. In an ASCII file, each alphabetic, numeric, or special character is represented with a seven-bit binary number (a string of seven 0's or 1's). As many as 128 characters can be represented ($2^7 = 128$). UNIX and DOS-based operating systems and the majority of PC applications use ASCII for text files. Windows NT and 2000 use a newer code called *unicode*. The extended ASCII is an eight-bit code used by IBM mainframe computers that allows 256 ($2^8 = 256$) characters to be represented.

Extended binary coded decimal interchange code, or *EBCDIC* (pronounced "ehb-suh-dik") is a binary code for alphabetic and numeric characters that IBM developed for its mainframe operating systems. It is the code for text files used in IBM's OS/390 operating system that many corporations run on IBM's S/390 servers. In an EBCDIC file, each alphabetic, numeric, and special character is represented with an eight-bit binary number (a string of eight 0's or 1's). As many as 256 characters (letters of the alphabet, numerals, and special characters) can be represented ($2^8 = 256$). Conversion programs allow different operating systems to change a file from one code to another. Table 2 illustrates selected examples of ASCII and EBCDIC.

Serial versus Parallel Transmission

In *serial transmission*, data travels in a single-file bit stream, one bit following after another. In other words, the network cable is like a one-lane road along which computers either send or receive information at any given time. In *parallel transmission*, an entire byte is transmitted at one time. Telephone lines are serial; PC printer cables are usually parallel. A network interface card takes data traveling in parallel as a group and restructures it so that it will flow through the one-bit wide path on the network cable. A network interface card is an expansion card that is required to connect a computer to a *local area network* (LAN).

Transmission Modes

Transmission modes include synchronous, asynchronous, and isochronous. In *synchronous transmission*, several characters are blocked together in parallel for transmission. At the beginning and end of each block there are empty bits, but these make up a small percentage of the total number of messages. Synchronous transmission is used to reduce overall communications costs.

In *asynchronous transmission*, each character is sent serially through a medium as an independent message. Each message is one character long, and the character is preceded by a start bit and ended with a stop bit. This type of transmission is more expensive than synchronous

Table 2: Selected Keyboard Symbols in ASCII and EBCDIC

Symbol	ASCII	EBCDIC
Space	0100000	01000000
A	1000001	11000001
B	1000010	11000010
Z	1011010	11101001
a	1100001	10000001
b	1100010	10000010
z	1111101	10101001
*	0101010	01011100
%	0100101	01101100
(	0101000	01001101
0	0110000	11110000
1	0110001	11110001
9	0111001	11111001

transmission but may be more accurate. The *parity bit* is used for an error-checking procedure in which the number of 1's must always be the same—either odd or even—for each group of bits transmitted without error.

There are two types of parity: even and odd. In *even parity*, the bits are counted before they are transferred; if the total number of 1 bits is even, then the parity bit is set to 0 (the sum of the bits must be even). If the number of 1 bits is odd, then the parity bit is set to 1, making the result even. An *odd parity* bit is set to 1 if the number of 1's in a given set of bits is even (making the total number of 1's odd).

In *isochronous transmission*, the elements of both synchronous and asynchronous forms of transmission are combined. Each character is required to have both a start bit and a stop bit; however, as in synchronous data transmission, the sender and receiver are synchronized.

Data Flow

The three elementary types of data flow are simplex, full duplex, and half-duplex. In a *simplex transmission*, communication can take place in only one direction: A warehouse sends its daily transactions to the main office, for example. Radio and television signal transmissions are examples of simplex transmission.

In a *half-duplex transmission*, communication takes place in both directions, but not at the same time. This is similar to a walkie-talkie radio; only one person can talk at a time. The amount of time required for half-duplex data flow to switch between sending and receiving is called *turnaround time*. The turnaround time for different circuits varies and can be obtained from their technical specification manual.

In a *full-duplex transmission*, communication can take place in both directions at the same time.

OPEN SYSTEM INTERCONNECTION (OSI) REFERENCE MODEL

In 1979, the International Organization for Standardization (ISO) developed the *open system interconnection (OSI) reference model*. The OSI reference model is a seven-layer architecture that defines the method of transmission of data from one computer to another over a network. The model is used to control and describe the flow of data

between the physical connection to the network and the end-user application. The seven layers are as follow:

layer 7, or application layer;
layer 6, or presentation layer;
layer 5, or session layer;
layer 4, or transport layer;
layer 3, or network layer;
layer 2, or data-link layer; and
layer 1, or physical layer.

Each layer in the architecture performs a specific task. It only communicates with the layers directly above and below it; no communications are allowed directly between layers that are not directly adjacent to one another. For example, the session layer (layer 5) can only communicate with the presentation and transport layers (6 and 4, respectively).

The lowest layers—1 and 2—define the network's physical media such as network adapter cards and the cable. They also define how data bits will be transmitted over the medium. The highest layers define how user applications will access communication services. The higher the layer, the more complex its function.

Each layer provides a specific service or action that prepares the data to be transmitted over the network to another computer. The layers are separated from each other by boundaries called *interfaces*. Requests are passed from one layer, through the interface, to the next layer, and each layer builds on the services or actions provided by the layer below it.

Although the OSI model is the best known and most widely used model for describing network communications, it has been criticized for being difficult to understand and for the long time spent to have it finalized. Table 3 provides a description and the purpose of each layer in the open systems interconnection model.

The basic purpose of each layer is to provide services to the next layer. Virtual communication occurs between peer layers of the sending and receiving computers. For example, the transport layer adds information to the packet that only the transport layer on the receiving computer can interpret.

To send a packet from a source computer to a destination computer, information is sent down through each of the seven layers, picking up formatting or addressing information from each layer as it proceeds. The completed

Table 3: The Open Systems Interconnection (OSI) Model

OSI Layer	Layer Name	Focus
7	Application	Program-to-program transfer of information
6	Presentation	Text formatting and display code conversion
5	Session	Establishing, maintaining, and coordinating communication
4	Transport	Accurate delivery, service quality
3	Network	Transport routes, message handling and transfer
2	Data-link	Coding, addressing, and transmitting information
1	Physical	Hardware connections

packet, having passed through all seven layers, is then transmitted out of the network interface card, over the network cable, to the destination computer. At the destination computer, the packet is sent up through each of the seven layers in the reverse order. Each layer reads and strips away the information sent to it by its peer layer on the sending computer, then passes the packet up to the next layer. When the packet finally arrives at the application layer on the destination computer, all of the formatting and addressing information has been stripped away and the information is back in its original form.

On the sending computer, information must be passed through all of the lower layers before being transmitted over the network cable. On the receiving end, the information is passed up from the lowest to the highest layer. This means that only the physical layer is capable of communicating directly with its counterpart layer on another computer. No other layer can pass information directly to its counterpart layer on another computer.

The following sections describe the purpose of each of the seven layers of the OSI model and identify the services they provide to adjacent layers.

Layer 7: The Application Layer

The top (seventh) layer of the OSI model is the application layer. It provides services to and receives services from layer 6, the presentation layer. The application layer serves as the window that application programs use to access network services. This layer provides the services that directly support user applications such as software for file transfer, database access, and e-mail. It is application dependent and performs different tasks in different applications.

Programs, which use services of the network, reside in this layer. These programs are the ultimate consumers of network services of the lower layers. The transmission of messages used by these programs is the primary goal of the lower protocols. This is the end user's access to the network system. The application layer handles general network access, flow control, and error recovery. Its main objective is to provide a set of utilities for application programs. Examples of application layer programs are:

- AppleShare (Apple);
- file transfer protocol (FTP);
- hypertext transfer protocol (HTTP), the protocol used to access World Wide Web documents written in *hypertext markup language* (HTML); and
- X.400.

Layer 6: The Presentation Layer

The presentation layer provides services to and receives services from layers 7 and 5 (application and session, respectively). The layer formats the message and is known as the network's translator. It translates data from a format provided to it by the application layer from the sending computer into a commonly recognized format. At the destination computer, the presentation layer translates the commonly recognized format back into a format that the receiving computer's application layer can

understand. It might perform data compression, protocol conversion, and data translation.

Data encryption and character set translation such as ASCII to $\leftrightarrow$ EBCDIC and vice versa are also performed by protocols at this layer. The redirector utility operates here and literally redirects requests for input/output operations to resources on a network server. Examples of presentation layer protocols are *hypertext transfer protocol* (HTTP) and *AppleShare file protocol* (AFP).

Layer 5: The Session Layer

The session layer provides services to and receives services from layers 6 and 4 (presentation and transport). The layer is responsible for establishing a dialogue between computers and establishes, maintains, and breaks connections or "conversations" between computers over the network. It is responsible for dialogue control by regulating which side transmits, when, and for how long. Session initiation must arrange for all of the desired and required services between session participants such as logging onto the network, transferring files, and checking security.

The session layer also provides synchronization by placing checkpoints at specific intervals in the data stream to help prevent large data losses. With the use of checkpoints, if the network fails, only the data after the last checkpoint has to be retransmitted.

Examples of session layer protocols are *transmission control protocol* (TCP) and *network basic input/output system* (NetBIOS).

Layer 4: The Transport Layer

The transport layer provides services to and receives services from layers 5 (the session layer) and 3 (the network layer). The transport layer (sometimes called the *host-to-host* or *end-to-end layer*) is responsible for providing flow control and error handling. This layer generates the receiver's address and ensures the integrity of the transmitted messages. The transport layer ensures that packets are delivered error-free, in sequence, and with no losses or duplications. This layer also provides various methods of flow control, ordering of received data, and acknowledgment of correctly received data. It is responsible for breaking large blocks of data into smaller packets, if needed, and eliminating duplicate packets.

At the destination computer, the transport layer unpacks messages, reassembles the original messages, and sends an acknowledgment of receipt. Examples of transport layer protocols include TCP and *sequenced packet exchange* (SPX) (Novell).

Layer 3: The Network Layer

The network layer provides services to and receives services from the transport and data-link layers (4 and 2). The layer is responsible for message addressing and routing as well as addressing messages and translating logical addresses and names into physical addresses. It also determines which path a packet should take based on network conditions and priority of service. The network layer also handles tasks such as packet switching, routing, and controlling data congestion. Software at this layer accepts messages from the transport layer and ensures that the packets are directed to their proper destination. Examples of network layer protocols include TCP, the *Internet protocol* (IP), and *internetwork packet exchange* (IPX) (Novell).

Layer 2: The Data-Link Layer

The data-link layer provides services to and receives services from layers 3 and 1 (network and physical, respectively). The layer oversees the establishment and control of the communications link; its primary task is to resolve the problems caused by damaged, lost, or duplicate messages so that succeeding layers are protected against transmission errors and can assume that no errors take place. The layer also is responsible for the detection of physical errors, notification of such errors, and establishing and terminating logical links. It performs error detection, correction, and retransmission of packets if necessary.

Generally, the source computer's data-link layer waits for an acknowledgment from the destination computer's data-link layer. The destination data-link layer detects any problems with the transmission. If an acknowledgment is not received, then the source data-link layer initiates a retransmission.

When the 802 standards committee (an industry standards-setting group) decided that more detail was necessary at the data-link layer, the layer was divided into two sublayers: the *logical link control* (LLC) and the *media access control* (MAC) sublayers. The LLC is the higher of the two sublayers, and it manages data-link communication and defines the use of logical interface points called *service access points* (SAPs). The MAC sublayer provides shared access for the computers' network adapter cards to the physical layer. The MAC sublayer communicates directly with the network adapter card and is responsible for delivering error-free data between two computers on the network. It performs most of the data-link layer functions such as error detection and retransmission.

Examples of data-link layer implementation are Ethernet, token bus, and token ring.

Layer 1: The Physical Layer

The physical layer provides services to and receives services only from layer 2, the data-link layer. The physical layer is the lowest layer of the OSI model. It specifies the electrical connections between the computer and the transmission medium (such as the network cable). This layer defines the physical media through which the host communicates over the network. For example, it defines the number and function of each pin on a connector.

The layer is primarily concerned with transmitting binary data (0's and 1's), or bits, over a communication network and defines the rules by which binary data are transmitted, including the appropriate electrical or optical impulse, electrical voltages, and full duplex or half-duplex data flow and connector cable standards such as RS232, RS449, or radio frequency. This layer is also responsible for data encoding and bit synchronization, ensuring that when a bit is transmitted as a 1, it is received as a 1 (not as a 0) at the destination computer.

The physical media can be coaxial, fiber-optic, or twisted-pair cable. The layer defines the specifics of implementing a particular transmission medium. It defines the type of cable, frequency, terminations, and so forth. The physical layer can be changed to other new technologies as they are developed without affecting the operation of upper layers, assuming that the interlayer interfaces are implemented properly.

Examples of physical layer implementation include:

- token ring;
- ArcNet;
- Ethernet:
  - 10Base-2, for thin Ethernet (coaxial) cable, commonly known as "thinnet";
  - 10Base-5, for thick Ethernet (coaxial) cable, commonly known as "thicknet";
  - 10Base-T, for unshielded twisted-pair cable, commonly known as "twisted pair";
  - 10Base-F, for fiber-optic cable, commonly known as "fiber"; and
  - other higher speed Ethernets now available, including 100BASE-FX, 100BASE-SX, and 100BASE-BX; and
- wireless:
  - broadcast radio;
  - infrared light;
  - microwave radio; and
  - spread-spectrum radio.

NETWORK TYPES

There are three major types of network systems: *local area network* (LAN), *wide area network* (WAN), and *metropolitan area network* (MAN).

A LAN system connects peripheral equipment that is in close proximity. Usually, this kind of system is limited to a certain geographical area such as a building, and one company owns it. The geographical scope of a LAN can be from a single office to a building or an entire campus. The speed of LANs varies from 10 Mbps (million bits per second) to 10 Gbps (trillion bits per second). A LAN is usually a prerequisite for an automated office in which word processing, e-mail, and electronic message distribution are integrated in one system. To establish a LAN system, careful planning and a thorough assessment of a particular organization's information needs are required.

A WAN system does not limit itself to a certain geographical area. It may span several cities, states, or even countries. Usually, several different parties own the system. The geographical scope of a WAN can be from between two or more cities to crossing international borders. The speed of a WAN depends on the speed of its individual interconnections (called *links*), and it can vary from 28,800 bps to 155 Mbps. As an example, consider a company that has its headquarters in Washington, D.C., and an office in each of thirty states. With a WAN system, all of these offices can be in continuous contact with

Table 4: LAN, WAN, and MAN Comparison

	LAN	**WAN**	**MAN**
Ownership Speed Scope	Usually one party 100 Mbps to 10 Gbps A building to a campus	More than one party 28.8 Kbps to 155 Mbps Intercity to international	One to several parties 34 Mbps to 155 Mbps One city to several contiguous cities

the headquarters and send and receive information. An airline reservation system is another good example of a WAN. A customer can reserve an airline ticket in the United States and pick it up in Asia or Africa.

A WAN system may use many different technologies. For example, it may use different communication media (coaxial cables, satellites, and fiber optics) and terminals of different sizes and sophistication (PCs, workstations, and mainframes) and be connected to other networks.

A committee of the Institute of Electrical and Electronic Engineers has developed specifications for a public, independent, high-speed network that connects a variety of data communications systems, including LANs and WANs in metropolitan areas. This new set of standards is called a *metropolitan area network* (MAN). A MAN is designed to deliver data, video, and digital voice to all organizations within a metropolitan area. Its geographical scope usually covers a city and contiguous neighboring cities. The speed of MANs varies from 34 Mbps to 155 bps. Table 4 compares these three types of networks.

APPLICATIONS OF DATA COMMUNICATIONS

Early in this chapter we saw several applications of data communications. Volume 3 of the *Handbook* explores several applications of data communications and networking. For now, we would like to introduce two popular applications of data communications: electronic data interchange and electronic commerce. With the rapidly increasing popularity of the Internet, these applications are gaining more users.

Electronic Data Interchange

Data communications can help companies transmit data electronically over telephone lines and other communications media. These data can be directly entered into a trading partner's business application. However, data communications can only solve a part of the problem. The data are captured first and then electronically transmitted. Some manual intervention must take place here. This is where *electronic data interchange* (EDI) plays such an important role. For the purpose of this chapter, we define EDI as follows:

A computer-to-computer exchange of data in a public or industry standard format using public or private networks among trading partners. Such an exchange may include requests for quotation, purchase orders, student information, invoices, or transaction balances.

As this definition indicates, standard formats play a critical role in an EDI environment. Sending e-mail or faxes or posting through bulletin boards does not require a specific data format and standard.

Electronic data interchange was initially developed to improve response time, reduce paperwork, and eliminate potential transcription errors. EDI represents the application of computer and communications technology, supporting innovative changes in business processes. It uses a comprehensive set of standards and protocols for the exchange of business transactions in a computer-compatible format. This may cover the following applications:

- acknowledgments of business transactions,
- financial reporting,
- inquiries,
- invoices,
- order status,
- payments,
- pricing,
- purchasing,
- receiving,
- scheduling, and
- student information.

EDI is the closest option to implementing a paperless business-transaction processing system. Many businesses use EDI as a substitute for their usual method of communication where paper documents such as purchase orders, invoices, or shipping notices were physically carried from department to department, mailed or faxed from one organization to another, or manually re-entered into the computer of the recipient. Also, organizations use EDI to electronically communicate, having documents and other types of information transmitted immediately and accurately in a computer-compatible format.

EDI is different from sending e-mail or sharing files through a network (LANs, WANs, or MANs) or through an electronic bulletin board. Using these communications systems, the format of the transmitted data must be the same for the sender and receiver or successful communication will not result. When EDI is used, the format of the data does not need to be completely the same. When documents are transmitted, the translation software of EDI converts the document into an agreed-upon standard format. Once the data are received, translation software changes them into the appropriate format.

An EDI message is held within two parts known as *envelopes*. The *outside envelope* contains the interchange control information to address the message being

Table 5: Advantages and Disadvantages of EDI

Advantages	Disadvantages
Improved competitiveness Improved convenience Increased control in payments Increased customer service Increased response and access to vital information Reduced errors in ordering, shipping and receiving Reduced labor costs Reduced order lead time, resulting in reduced inventory	Different standards May incur additional costs Security issues Supplier dependence

transmitted. It can be compared to a common paper envelope that will send a letter. The *inside envelope* (the content) consists of header information, or control information such as source and destination addresses and other protocol information; and signature authentication. This inside envelope can be compared to the content of the letter that is sent in the regular paper envelope.

Table 5 summarizes EDI's advantages and disadvantages.

Electronic Commerce

Electronic commerce (EC) encompasses all the activities that a firm performs when selling and buying services and products when using computers and communications technologies. In broad terms, EC includes a host of related activities such as online shopping, sales-force automation, supply-chain management, electronic payment systems, and order management. In the last section, EDI was discussed; EC is the next step in this evolutionary progression. Technologies and applications used by EC may include (Blinch 1998; Chakravarty 1998):

- direct connectivity using LANs, MANs, and WANs;
- electronic data interchange;
- electronic mail;
- the Internet, intranets, and extranets; and
- value-added networks.

Among the products and services that customers purchase online are:

- airline tickets and travels,
- apparel and footwear,
- books and music,
- computer hardware and software, and
- flowers and gifts.

The advantages of electronic commerce include:

- doing business around the globe seven days a week, twenty-four hours a day;

- gaining additional knowledge about potential customers;
- improved customer service;
- improved relationships with the financial community;
- improved relationships with suppliers;
- increased return of capital because no or minimal inventory is needed;
- increased flexibility and ease of shopping;
- increased return on investment; and
- increased number of potential customers.

Possible capacity and throughput problems, initial investment, and security issues are among the important disadvantages of electronic commerce. However, all indications point to the elimination of these problems thereby paving the way for EC to become a common took among all types of businesses.

CONVERGENCE OF VOICE, DATA, AND VIDEO

In the data communications field, the term *convergence* refers to the integration of voice, video, and data to provide timely and relevant multimedia information for decision-making purposes. Convergence is not just about technology. It is about services and new ways of doing business and interacting with society. In the past, separate networks were used to transmit data, voice, and video. This is changing as the technology supports such integration and as the demand for integrated services is on the rise. The integration of voice and data is almost complete in WANs.

Major carriers offer services that seamlessly integrate voice and data on the same network. The integration of voice and data has been slower in LANs mainly because of the lack of capacity and bandwidth. The integration of video with voice and data requires substantial network upgrades required by the significant bandwidth needed to carry video on the same network. However, this is changing with the increased availability of high-speed technologies such as *asynchronous transfer mode* (ATM) and *Gigabit Ethernet* (GbE) and an increased demand for new applications that require the integrated technology. Gigabit Ethernet is a LAN transmission standard that features a data-transmission rate of one billion bits per second (1 Gbps). ATM is a packet-switching service that operates at speeds of 25 to 622 Mbps.

In packet switching, small units of information known as *packets* are transmitted along the best route available between the sender and receiver. The service handles multimedia data such as text, graphics, audio, and video. The end points of the convergence market are distribution (e.g., bandwidth on demand by any medium) and content (e.g., video, audio, and data).

More and more content providers, network operators, and telecommunications and broadcasting giants, among many others, are being swept into a convergence of technologies. All the old rules about who delivers what and to whom are breaking as once-separate technologies are merging on the information superhighway. Convergence has an impact not only on technology development and products, but also on companies and individuals. Convergence is even affecting national boundaries, with increasing numbers of companies having global access to information and even beginning to undertake worldwide project development using the Internet. Convergence is just starting; as it increases, the boundaries between products and national borders will blur even further. Convergence is possible because of a unique combination of factors that has just only begun to exist, including technological innovation, changes in market structure, and regulatory reform. Common applications of convergence include:

- e-commerce,
- entertainment (the number of television channels available will increase substantially, and movies and video on demand will become a reality),
- increased availability and affordability of video and computer conferencing, and
- consumer applications (virtual classrooms, telecommuting, virtual teams, and so forth).

The Internet is probably the most important driving force behind the growth and popularity of the convergence phenomenon. It is a vehicle for the delivery of both existing services (for example, e-mail, video, sound, and voice telephony) and completely new services. The Internet is displacing traditional computer networks and showing signs of how it may provide a platform that, over time, replaces traditional methods of trading. For example, traditional business-to-business trading on closed corporate networks is giving way to commerce on global open networks.

The Internet is also providing an alternative means of offering core telecommunications business activity (even if differences in quality still distinguish the two services) through the delivery of telephony. The Internet is also a significant platform for broadcasting services. Advances in digital technologies are helping to move the convergence of technologies forward, and when standards become available and accepted, the rate of change may speed up even further.

The lack of bandwidth is probably the most significant obstacle for the widespread applications of the convergence technologies. As new users come online, bandwidth demands increase exponentially. In addition, corporate and consumer securities and privacy are other issues that must be resolved before convergence can really take off. Security measures such as firewalls and sophisticated encryption routines are parts of the solution (Akers 1998; Bidgoli 2002; Caldwell and Foley 1998).

WHY DO MANAGERS NEED TO KNOW ABOUT DATA COMMUNICATIONS?

Data communications have become a vital and integral part of the corporate infrastructure. In fact, they have become so interwoven into the fabric of corporate activity that it has become difficult to separate the core functions of the enterprise from the data communications that enable and support that very activity.

Data communications applications can enhance the efficiency and effectiveness of decision makers by ensuring the timely delivery of relevant information. For example, data communications supports just-in-time delivery of goods, resulting in reduced inventory costs and increased competitive advantage for organizations that effectively use this technology. Large corporations such as Wal-Mart, Home Depot, J.C. Penney, Dow Chemical, UPS, and FedEx are examples of companies that have been successfully using data communications technologies in order to stay ahead of their competitors. Companies such as Ford and Intel are using virtual teams to cut across boundaries of geography, time, and organization to put together powerful teams that develop products quickly and effectively.

Data communication systems have generated opportunities for companies to use e-mail instead of the postal system and to transfer files online rather than by shipping magnetic tapes and disks. An integrated network enhances managerial control, shortens product- and service-development life cycles, and provides better information to those who need it most. Most important, an integrated network is a crucial part of an organization's international information systems infrastructure. Data communications applications directly or indirectly affect all types of organizations. The following are some of the highlights of this growing technology.

- More employees will get their education online through virtual classrooms that use data communications technologies. This will bring the latest in technology and product information right to an employee's workstation.
- Online searches over the Internet and other networks bring the latest information on products, services, and innovation right to the employee.
- The Internet and data communications will facilitate and enable lifelong learning, and knowledge will become an asset of even further importance for individuals in the future.
- Boundaries between work life and personal life will become ever more diffuse as data communications become widely available both in homes and businesses.
- Improved data communications technologies will reduce the cost and complexity of staying in touch with people.
- Customers will be able to use their televisions and PCs to access the Internet, shop, make phone calls, and conduct video and computer conferencing.

There are at least seven critical areas within the data communications field that managers should clearly understand:

1. the basics of data communications and networking;
2. the Internet, intranets, and extranets;
3. proper deployment of wired and wireless networks;
4. network security issues and measures;
5. organizational and social effects of data communications;

6. globalization issues; and
7. applications of data communications.

The *Handbook* will explain these various areas in several chapters in detail.

CONCLUSION

This chapter discussed data communications and networking principles. It introduced basic components of a data communications system, types of networks, and important events in data communications growth in North America. The chapter introduced some of the important keywords and concepts in the data communications field, including data codes, serial and parallel transmission, transmission modes, data flow, and the open system interconnection reference model. The chapter discussed electronic data interchange and electronic commerce as two of the fastest-growing applications of data communications. We concluded with a brief discussion on the convergence of data, voice, and video and a brief discussion on why managers need to know about data communications.

GLOSSARY

Communications media: Channels that connect sender and receiver devices. Communications media can be either conducted (wired or guided), such as coaxial cable; or radiated (wireless) such as satellite.

Data codes: Formats used to represent and transfer data among various computers and network systems. Popular types include Baudot, ASCII, and EBCDIC.

Data communications: The electronic transfer of data from one location to another.

Electronic commerce (EC): All of the activities a firm performs to sell and buy services and products using computers and communications technologies.

Electronic data interchange (EDI): A computer-to-computer exchange of data in a public or industry standard format using public or private networks among trading partners.

Local area network (LAN): A network that connects peripheral equipment that is in close physical proximity. Usually this kind of system is limited to a certain geographical area such as a building, and one company usually owns it.

Metropolitan area network (MAN): A network that is designed to deliver data, video, and digital voice to all organizations within a metropolitan area. The geographical scope of a MAN usually covers a city and contiguous neighboring cities.

Modem: Abbreviation of modulator-demodulator; this device converts digital signals to analog signals and vice versa for transference over analog telephone lines.

Open system interconnection (OSI) reference model: A seven-layer architecture that defines the method of transmission of data from one computer to another over a network.

Wide area network (WAN): A type of network that is not limited to a certain geographical area. It may span several cities, states, or even countries. Usually, several different parties own it. The geographical scope of a WAN can be from intercity to international borders.

CROSS REFERENCES

See *Local Area Networks; Metropolitan Area Networks; Terrestrial Wide Area Networks*.

REFERENCES

Akers, J. 1998. Ten ways to prepare for convergence. *Business Communications Review*, 28(2): S9.

Bidgoli, H. 2002. *Electronic commerce: Principles and practice*. San Diego: Academic Press.

Blinch, R. 1998. Convergence coming: Voice, data and video convergence prompts mergers in the telecommunications industry. *Computer Dealer News*, 13 July, p. 34.

Caldwell, B., and J. Foley. 1998. *IBM means e-business*. http://www.informationweek.com/668/68iuebz.htm (accessed April 30, 2007).

Chakravarty, S. N. 1998. The convergence factor. *Forbes*, July 27, p. 46.

FURTHER READING

Bidgoli, H. 2000. *Handbook of business data communications: A managerial perspective*. San Diego: Academic Press.

Kogan, A., E. F. Sudit, and M. A. Vasarhely. 1997. The era of electronic commerce. *Management Accounting*, September, pp. 26–30.

Margolin, B. 1997. Chip makers keeping pace with changing modem technologies. *Computer Design*, August, pp. 101–102.

Romei, L. K. 1997. Networking connectivity gains momentum. *Managing Office Technology*, May, pp. 16–18.

Data-Link Layer Protocols

Stefan Joe-Yen and Chadwick Sessions, *Northrop Grumman Corporation*

INTRODUCTION

This chapter discusses the data-link layer and the protocols associated with it. The data-link layer provides two major classes of services. First, it provides a mechanism for managing access to shared physical transmission resources. Second, it is the preliminary level of data abstraction that allows for error correction and flow control, including the retransmission of data. This addresses the issue of reliable data transfer over a network medium that is susceptible to error.

As discussed in other chapters, the *open system interconnection* (OSI) network model (ISO 1994) manages the complexity of network communications by separating protocols into a hierarchical arrangement comprising seven layers. As we move from layers 1 through 7, the associated protocols become closer to user-level abstractions and move away from the details of physical data transmission.

The data-link layer is layer 2 in the OSI model and thus exists closest to the hardware level. The OSI model is designed such that nonadjacent layers do not directly communicate with each other. Therefore, the data-link layer only has knowledge of the physical and network layers (1 and 3, respectively). Thus, the data-link layer serves as the first level of abstraction away from transmission media and toward more data-oriented functionality.

Over the history of computer networking, several data-link layer protocols have been implemented. As hardware and software needs have evolved, some of these schemes have fallen out of use. This chapter will take a look at both legacy and current protocols. However, the emphasis will be on the current implementations that the reader is more likely to encounter.

This chapter covers theoretical issues as well as practical details of existing data-link layer protocols as outlined below.

Physical Communication Architectures

The primary task of the data-link layer is to ensure that data transmissions over physical network connections are conducted reliably. Because of the close connection to the physical layer, abstractions implemented in the data-link layer must still make use of specific aspects of the physical layer. Therefore, even at one layer above the physical layer, *network topology* plays an important role. The chapter will examine some of the details of network architecture and topology as they pertain to data-link layer implementations.

Access Control and Signaling

Many data-link implementations divide the functional concerns of shared media access and error correction between two sublayers. The *media access control* (MAC) sublayer is responsible for addressing the shared media access at the physical transmission level, while a *logical link control* (LLC) sublayer abstracts media access and multiplexing and provides for error correction. Although some access protocols do not divide the data-link layer in this fashion, the MAC and LLC sublayers are explicitly defined in Institute for Electrical and Electronics Engineers (IEEE) standards. The chapter will examine these sublayers in detail.

Specific Examples

The chapter concludes with a discussion of specific protocol implementations such as Ethernet, high-level data-link control (HDLC), fiber distributed data interface (FDDI), and token ring as examples of different schemes for addressing the data-link layer's concerns. The specifications and operations of each in their primary network environments are also discussed.

DATA TRANSFER

The physical layer provides the mechanism for transmitting data across the transmission medium. It is not concerned with the higher-level semantics of the data, but solely with the transformation of data into electromagnetic or optical signals to be expressed in a wired or wireless medium. As such, it does not implement mechanisms to detect whether signals have been transmitted or received reliably. This is the responsibility of the next level of the OSI networking protocols: the data-link layer (also shortened in the following to just "link layer").

The link layer provides several high-level services related to data transfer. Whereas the physical layer handles data on a bit-level basis, link layer protocols package data from the network layer into *frames* for transmission. The frames contain the metadata that provide for the transmission of the data to the correct node as well as ensure the reliability of transfer. The link layer can be designed to detect whether the data frames it receives contain errors and attempt to correct these errors. The link layer can also provide mechanisms to inspect the flow of data along the physical medium and to ensure that nodes are transmitting and receiving data at an optimal rate.

Network Topologies and Addressing

The physical layer is home to different technologies with an array of different media. The media may include copper wire, optical fibers, or specific radio frequency channels in wireless and satellite transmissions. Devices that are connected to each other across the media are called *nodes*. The nodes and their connections may be arranged in various shapes known as *network topologies*. To identify these nodes, the link layer uses a MAC addressing scheme to identify the various devices on the network. This is a distinct addressing scheme from the Internet protocol (IP) addressing that is used by the network layer. MAC addresses are unique, and most data-link implementations allow for unicast or broadcast messaging. Unicast messages are sent to a single recipient, whereas broadcast messages are sent to every node on the network. The link layer may also support multicast addressing in which a message is sent to multiple recipients defined in a group.

The topologies, the nodes, and the physical media can be described in either physical or logical terms. The *physical topology* is the arrangement of the actual wiring between or among the nodes, including any signal-extending hardware such as repeaters. The *logical topology* is a description of the network based on node connectivity (regardless of physical medium) and addressing. The data-link layer is more concerned with the logical topology of the network, although during discussion of actual link layer implementations, the choice of physical medium topology can still affect the operation of the data-link layer (e.g., the choice between a point-to-point link versus a shared bus). The following is a list of common logical topologies. There can be confusion in topology discussions, because one type of logical topology can be implemented in a different type of physical topology. Yeh and Siegmund (1980) and Stallings (1984) give good early overviews of different network topologies.

Bus

The oldest and simplest topology is the *bus*. All nodes connected to a bus share the medium, and all data are broadcast to every node regardless of individual destination. Because the data are broadcast, each node has no responsibility (unlike the ring topology reviewed next) to retransmit frames not addressed to it. However, because the medium is shared, link utilization can decrease from frame collisions when the number of nodes increases.

Early physical implementations of the logical bus were physical buses, but today the vast majority of these layouts are implemented as stars (described below).

Ring

An early alternate topology to the bus was the *ring* topology. Nodes in a ring are connected to each other in a loop. Messages are sent from node to node (in a clockwise or counterclockwise fashion), and each node acts as a repeater (i.e., a node does not necessarily drop a message even if it is not the intended recipient). Usually, only one node is allowed to act as a transmitter at a time. This is controlled by token passing. The authorization *token* is a bit sequence that contains control information. The network has one authorization token, which is passed around from node to node. Only the node with the token may transmit.

Although the logical ring can be physically designed as a ring, star topologies with special token-passing hubs are the majority of physical designs.

Star

Although it can be more efficient than a bus, the ring architecture still passes redundant data and involves nodes that may not be the intended target. This issue is addressed by the *star* topology. In the star topology, one node called a *hub* acts as a central point for data transmission. If this hub is simply passive and retransmits all incoming frames onto the other legs of the star, then the logical star topology, while physically a star, is simply a logical bus. However, if the hub is "intelligent" and only passes frames to the correct node, then the logical topology is a true star.

The intelligent type of hub known as a *switching hub* keeps track of the unique MAC addresses of the other nodes in the network and allows for efficient point-to-point communication. It can also handle point-to-multipoint broadcasting by reserving a special address that indicates the message is intended for all nodes and then distributing messages addressed to the broadcast address to all connected nodes. Designs based around either passive or switching hubs have the significant drawback that the hub is a single point of failure. The hub must remain operational or the entire LAN is disabled.

Tree

The *tree* topology is a combination of the star and bus topologies described above. In a tree, the central hubs of multiple star networks are connected to a shared bus.

IEEE

The IEEE 802 group of protocols (IEEE 2001) split the responsibilities of the data-link layer into two sublayers. The low-level access to nodes on the network, including the addressing scheme described above, is handled by the *media access control* (MAC) layer. In addition to providing the mechanism for implementing logical topologies, the MAC sublayer implements protocols for resource sharing in which multiple nodes must use the same physical medium as a link. Above the MAC sublayer is the more abstract logical link control (LLC) sublayer. The LLC delineates data and allows for error checking and flow control. The next two sections describe the facilities of LLC and MAC sublayers.

LOGICAL LINK CONTROL

The *logical link control* sublayer provides some higher-level services for multiplexing and demultiplexing transmissions on the MAC sublayer, as well as other optional services for detecting and retransmitting dropped frames and flow control. The following describes different services provided by the LLC (IEEE 1998).

Framing

The logical link control provides services to the network layer by creating meaningful blocks of information in the data. These data segments are called *frames*. It is the responsibility of the link layer to reliably transfer frames from point to point in the network. The link layer views transmissions in a strictly peer-to-peer fashion. It does not have a representation of the entire network but knows about nodes that can act as transmitters and receivers of frames.

The details of framing schemes vary between the numerous implemented link layer protocols. However, the basic idea is the same. Headers and trailers that contain transmission metadata are appended to the message data passed to the data-link layer from the higher OSI layers to form a frame. Frames are managed and sent to the physical layer for transmission. After frame reception, any link layer metadata are stripped from the frame before they are handed upward to the network layer. This encapsulation scheme is the hallmark of a layered network model, whether it is OSI or TCP/IP.

Error Detection and Data Recovery

Data transfer is an incompletely reliable process. The physical signals are subject to noise that can interfere with the transmission process to the extent that data become corrupted. Error detection and correction schemes attempt to compensate for the physical limitations and increase data reliability. Algorithms that attempt to counter bit errors include checksums, parity checks, longitudinal redundancy checks, and cyclic redundancy checks. Once errors are found, fixes include retransmitting and error-correcting codes. Kurose and Ross (2005) is one of several texts that supply overviews of the different algorithms.

Checksum

A simple form of redundancy checking is to treat the message data as a series of one-byte integers and then appending the sum of the integers modulo 255 as a check value. The receiver recomputes the checksum on the data it receives. If the checksum does not match, then the data are marked as corrupt. Of course, because different byte combinations may add to the same value, checksumming is not perfect and can allow errors to pass. The term *checksum* is also commonly used in a generic fashion to describe the other types of checking algorithms.

Parity Checking

One of the simplest forms of error detection is called *parity checking*. A single check bit is added to the message data before transmission. The value of this bit represents whether the number of bits with a value of 1 in the message data is odd or even. On reception, the receiver checks the data to see if the parity of the received data matches the reported parity.

Parity checking is not a robust method for error detection because the errors introduced by noise often occurs in bursts. Several bits may be changed simultaneously; this would create an error undetectable by the receiver by inspecting the check bit. Any even number of errors would produce a valid checksum and not detect the corrupt data. For example, the original sent pattern 10111011 (with an even parity of 1) corrupted to 10111000 would be received as correct because it would have the same parity value.

Longitudinal Redundancy Checking

The *longitudinal redundancy checking* (LRC) method improves on the parity checking scheme by examining the reliability across multiple bytes of the frame. LRC works by adding an additional block of check bits after several bytes of data. By treating the entire block as a two-dimensional array, parity can be checked for each row and column in the array. It is still subject to burst error, but it requires a greater number of errors and in certain patterns to generate a valid checksum for corrupt data.

Cyclic Redundancy Check

Cyclic redundancy check (CRC) is another kind of checksum algorithm that generates the check values by viewing the data bits as the coefficient of a polynomial. The data polynomial (after multiplying by x^n, where n is the degree of the CRC polynomial) is divided by a generator polynomial, and the remainder (with no carry) is used as the check value. CRC makes use of the mathematical properties of polynomials limited to binary coefficients to form what amounts to a hash code that should identify data reliably. CRC checksums do have a possibility of colliding (different bit values producing the same checksum), but with modern CRCs this is usually not a concern.

Common CRCs (and hence polynomial lengths) include CRC-16 and CRC-32 (16 and 32 represent the checksum's bit length). CRCs, especially with the larger polynomials, are quite robust to bit errors, including burst errors. Because CRCs are widely used, optimization of the implemented algorithms is important (Stone, Greenwald, Partridge, and Hughes 1998).

Forward Error-Correcting Codes

In addition to error detection, check bits can also be used for error correction. Some error correcting codes, such as Reed-Solomon, use the polynomial interpretation of the data (see the section on CRC coding above) to reconstruct corrupted data by sending an oversampled representation of the same polynomial. Thus, even if some data are lost or corrupted, the original can be determined and reconstructed. Unlike Reed-Solomon, which computes on blocks of data, another popular type of error-correcting code—*forward error correcting*—operates on the bit stream. Other correction codes, such as Hamming codes, use multiple check bits, so if data bits are changed, the check pattern will change in a manner that identifies the position of the altered bit.

Retransmission

Error correcting codes' primary drawback is the increase in size of the transmitted frame. If bandwidth is limited, it is often more efficient and convenient to signal the sending node to retransmit the frame if the receiving node determines the data were corrupted in transit. The sender may wait for a specific signal from the receiver that indicates the need for retransmission. Conversely, the sender may resend if it does not receive an acknowledgment from the receiver after a certain amount of time. *Automatic requests for retransmission* (ARQs) are part of flow control discussed in the next section.

Flow Control

Flow controls are various mechanisms to ensure that data are not transmitted faster than the receiver can handle. Two common schemes are *blocking* and *sliding window* (Tanenbaum 1981). However, a data-link implementation may eschew any flow control and assume that a higher layer is taking the responsibility of flow control.

Blocking

Blocking protocols control data flow by implementing a turn-based system. In the simplest form of blocking, the sender sends a packet and waits for an *acknowledgement* (ack) signal sent back from the receiving node. Because only one packet is sent between each ack, a blocking scheme is highly inefficient.

Sliding Window

In the sliding window scheme for flow control, the receiving node maintains a buffer for received packets that may be larger than the packet size. This allows the transmitter to send multiple packets to the receiving node without waiting for an ack signal. The receiver (which sets the initial window size) transmits the window size; as the buffer fills, this transmitted size shrinks. If the size reaches zero, the transmitter will stop sending packets, but as the size increases, the sender may increase the number of packets it sends between ack signals. If the window size is sufficient, then packet transmission is essentially continuous, thus maximizing the throughput.

Automatic Retransmission Requests

Automatic retransmission requests (ARQs) occur when the receiver detects an error indicating that a frame is lost or corrupted. If a frame is lost, then it may not send an ack for a time period that exceeds the sender's predetermined time-out. The sender then retransmits the packet. The receiver may report a corrupted frame by sending a *nack* signal (not acknowledged message) back to the sender. In the sliding window scheme described above, the nack may contain frame sequence information that indicates which of multiple packets need to be resent. In the so-called go-back-*n* schemes for ARQ, the sender retransmits the corrupted frame and all the frames that followed. In another approach to ARQ, known as *selective reject*, only the corrupted frame is retransmitted.

MEDIA ACCESS CONTROL

The media access control (MAC) sublayer is closer to the hardware than the LLC. It is responsible for using the physical layer for controlling access to the physical transmission medium, and it determines who has the right to transmit on a shared medium at any one time.

MAC Addresses

The MAC sublayer is also the assignment point of the link layer addressing. MAC addresses are used to deliver link layer frames to the different hosts on the link.

MAC addresses can be universally or locally administered. Universally administered addresses are assigned to each link layer device by the manufacturer. Part of the MAC address is the *organizationally unique identifier* (OUI) that is unique to each manufacturer. The rest of the address, known as the *extension identifier*, is arbitrarily determined by the manufacturer (as long as each is unique), usually using a one-up numbering with possible groupings across different models. A single manufacturer can register and pay for multiple OUIs, and these assignments are made open to the public.

Locally administered addresses are determined by the local system administrator and override the universally assigned address. To determine whether a given MAC address is local or universal, the second least-significant bit of the most significant byte can be analyzed. If it has the value of 1, then the address is administered locally; otherwise, it is administered universally.

MAC-48 was the first IEEE MAC address and was specified in the Ethernet protocol. It was named so because of its forty-eight–bit address space. The OUI is contained in the first three bytes of MAC-48, leaving twenty-four bits of addressing for the manufacturer to assign. MAC-48 technically designates link layer addresses for network hardware; the term *EUI-48* (trademarked by the IEEE) designates any other hardware and software. MAC-48 and EUI-48 are assigned from the same numbering space. Example protocols originally using MAC-48 include FDDI, ATM, and most of the IEEE 802 networks (Ethernet, Wi-Fi, Bluetooth, and token ring).

Although it will still be a while before the EUI-48 address space is exhausted, for future growth the IEEE defined EUI-64 (IEEE 2006). This sixty-four–bit address has a twenty-four–bit OUI and forty bits reserved for manufacturer assignment. This gives each OUI more than one trillion unique address assignments. The IEEE stated that each manufacturer who requests an OUI will not be able to request a second one until it has exhausted more than 90 percent of the original address space. IEEE 1394 (Firewire) is the best known protocol to use EUI-64 addresses.

An EUI-48 address can be encapsulated in an EUI-64 address for compatibility purposes. To encapsulate, a special label with hex value of FFFE is added between the OUI and extension identifier. The actual extension identifier is not changed.

MULTI-ACCESS LINK CONTROL

In many networking situations, several nodes must share the same physical transmission media. For example, in a wired LAN, several computers may need to transmit along the same wire. In wireless transmissions, some nodes need to use the same transmission channel. The link layer protocol has the responsibility to ensure that all the users of a shared resource successfully complete their transmissions. Various protocols for multi-access channel control have been developed. They can be roughly divided into the classes described next. Each has its advantages and disadvantages.

Fixed Assignment

One means of sharing the transmission resource is to assign each node a fixed slot on the resource for its use. The slots are assigned using various aspects of the signal such as frequency or timing. Most research on resource sharing concerns satellite systems and links (Elbert 1999).

Time Division Multiple Access

In the *time division multiple access* (TDMA) scheme, a single frequency can be shared by multiple users by defining and assigning time slices in which each user has the exclusive right to use the frequency. The users alternate in rapid succession, transmitting only within their allotted segment of time. With many users, this scheme requires precise and complex synchronization: If the timing is incorrect, then a user's data may drift into another's time slot. The pulsed nature of the transmissions can also create radio frequency interference as a side effect.

Frequency Division Multiple Access

The *frequency division multiple access* (FDMA) scheme allows multiple transmitters to share a single carrier frequency by subdividing it into frequency subchannels, each modulating the carrier around a slightly different range of frequencies. Each transmitter is assigned a different subchannel. Because the transmitters are all modulating the same carrier, the multiple messages are carried as a single signal along the medium. However, there is some wasted space because of needed *guard* space between each subchannel. The guard space is a gap to prevent interference between subchannels. The size of the guard space depends on many factors, including signal strength and frequency of transmission.

Spread Spectrum

The schemes above are mechanisms for sending several messages along a single frequency channel. Spread-spectrum mechanisms take the opposite approach and split a message across a frequency spectrum. In *frequency hopping spread spectrum* (FHSS), the data are segmented and each segment is transmitted over a different frequency pattern determined by a pseudorandom process. A matched pseudorandom process is applied at the receiving end to track the varying frequencies necessary to reconstruct the message. Because numerous messages are being spread at random across a broad band, the bandwidth is used efficiently. A single message is not confined to a single frequency, so it is robust against the catastrophic interference effects that occur when different signals are transmitted along two spectrally adjacent frequencies.

Code Division Multiple Access

Code division multiple access (CDMA) splits the message across frequencies and encodes each frequency with orthogonal codes (e.g., Walsh codes).

Random Access

Fixed assignment is stable but can be inefficient (especially when there are few nodes transmitting) or too centralized. Another scheme for shared access tries to maximize the usage of bandwidth by allowing any resource to transmit at any time. Of course, this can lead to collisions, but it also can simplify the network architecture.

ALOHA

The *ALOHA network* (ALOHAnet) was implemented at the University of Hawaii in 1970. It is considered a seminal prototype in computer networking. Concepts developed for ALOHA are still in use today on LANs and other networks that need to efficiently share physical resources. Instead of assigning a fixed slot in time or frequency to a node as discussed in the previous section, ALOHA introduced the concept of *packets* by which messages would be sent in small segments at intervals that allow each node the chance to transmit a packet when an opening occurs. Because the nodes are transmitting asynchronously, two nodes may attempt to transmit at the same time, resulting in a collision in which data from both packets would be lost or corrupted. ALOHA dealt with collisions by retransmitting lost packets after a random time-out period. The random time-out at each node usually prevented a repeat collision when the failed senders tried to retransmit (Abramson 1970).

Carrier Sense Multiple Access

The random access scheme developed on ALOHAnet has evolved into a variety of *carrier sense multiple access* (CSMA) protocols. "Carrier sense" means a node first listens on the network for the presence of a carrier, indicating a message is being sent. If no carrier is detected, then the node begins transmission (Kleinrock and Tobagi 1975). Collisions may still occur, and they are handled differently by assorted CSMA protocol variants. The mechanism used by the Ethernet is known as *CSMA with collision detection* (CSMA/CD). If a node begins to send and the current on the network exceeds an expected threshold, then it registers as a collision. The node immediately stops sending data and instead sends a signal to indicate a collision has occurred. The lost data can be retransmitted when the link is clear (Metcalfe and Boggs 1976).

DATA-LINK PROTOCOL IMPLEMENTATIONS

Many link layer protocol implementations have been specified and employed throughout the years of networking one computer to another. This section delves into more details for some of the more popular protocols: HDLC, token ring, FDDI, and Ethernet. However, before discussing these, a brief discussion will be given for the data-link interfaces to the network layer.

The functionality of a network adapter card's link layer is broken up between the firmware on the card and the software in the operating system. To simplify hardware production, the majority of the link layer's code is in the software drivers. Three primary device driver specifications can be used to interface with a network card: *open data-link interface* (ODI), *network driver interface specification* (NDIS), and *packet driver*. These specifications simplify interface implementation (no need for compiling individual drivers for each machine configuration) and allow multiple protocols to be bound to a single network card.

ODI was created by Novell and Apple for their NetWare and Macintosh operating systems, respectively. One of the first protocol stacks written under ODI was *internetwork packet exchange/sequenced packet exchange* (IPX/SPX) (Novell 2006). NDIS was created by Microsoft and 3Com for use in Microsoft's Windows operating systems, as well as IBM's OS/2 (Microsoft Corporation 2006). The third major interface, packet driver, was written by John Romkey while at FTP Software. The major (and nontechnical) difference is that packet driver specification is open source, along with the implemented drivers (Crynwr Software 2006).

High-Level Data-Link Control

The *high-level data-link control* (HDLC) protocol was developed by the International Organization for Standardization (ISO). Originally comprising four standards (ISO 3309, 4335, 6159, and 6256), it is now currently defined in ISO 13239 (ISO 2002). The protocol roots are in IBM's *synchronous data-link control* (SDLC) protocol.

Frame

A synchronous protocol, HDLC relies on the physical layer for clocking and frame transmission and reception synchronization. HDLC links identify the beginning and ending of a frame with a special set of bits known as the *frame delimiter*. The frame delimiter, which has a hex value of 7E (01111110), is guaranteed not to be inside of the frame. If the frame data do contain this value, then they must be escaped. If there are no data to be sent, then the link may send consecutive frame delimiters to keep the channel synchronized.

On synchronous links, a process called *bit stuffing* is used to escape the frame delimiter. During transmission of the data portion of the frame, the sender simply inserts a zero after any string of five 1's. The receiver examines the next bit after receiving those five 1's. If it is a zero, then the zero is removed and the receiver knows it is still processing data; however, if it is a 1, then the receiver must know the current byte of data is the frame delimiter. For asynchronous links, *byte stuffing* (or *control-octet transparency*) with a control byte of hex value 7D is used. This control byte is sent before any byte with a 7D or 7E value, and then the data byte has its fifth bit inverted. The receiving byte, by recognizing the control byte and reversing the inversion, can detect the difference between control bytes, frame delimiters, and data.

In addition to the frame delimiter, a basic HDLC frame has four fields: address, control, data, and frame check sequence.

The *address* is the destination address of the frame. The length can be arbitrary, but usually is zero (point-to-point links), eight, or sixteen bits. The first bit can be used to designate a unicast (0) or multicast (1) address. The *control* field is an eight- or sixteen-bit value that defines whether the frame represents user data or control (protocol independent) data. *Data* are sets of information bits from the layer above. Their lengths can be variable. The *frame check sequence* (FCS) is used to check for bit errors and is calculated over the address, control, and data fields. Being sixteen bits long, CRC-16 is a common FCS algorithm.

Token Ring

History

The token ring interface for networking was first developed at IBM during the 1970s. Subsequently, the protocol was standardized in IEEE 802.5 (IEEE 2003). It has largely been replaced by Ethernet for LAN implementations, but it is still used where redundant, reliable transmission of data is desired. Token ring networks were originally implemented on shielded twisted-pair copper wires, but newer implementations can use fiber-optic or unshielded twisted-pair cables.

Architecture

This chapter earlier discussed the topology of a token ring network. The computers in a network are connected to each other in a loop and pass a control signal known as the *token*. In IEEE 802.5 token rings, the token is an instance of command frame (described below). If a node on the network receives the token and has data to send, it appends the data to the token and converts the token into a data frame. This message continues to circulate around the ring until it reaches its intended destination. The destination computer copies the message, reports the receipt to a special segment of the frame, and then *continues* to pass it around the ring until it returns to the source. The source can inspect the segment of the frame reserved for the destination computer to determine whether the data were received successfully. If the message was received without errors, the source computer removes the message and passes the token as a control frame once again.

Frame

The token ring protocol provides for two frame types. The unmodified token or control frame consists of three one-byte fields: start delimiter, access control byte, and end delimiter.

The *start delimiter* indicates the arrival of the token at a receiving node. The *access control byte* contains information about the token priority and a means to detect whether the token is spinning endlessly around the ring. It also contains a bit that identifies the frame as a token and not a data/command frame. The *end delimiter* marks the end of the token.

When a node adds data to the token and unsets the token bit in the access control byte, the frame now becomes a data/command frame with the following additional fields that are inserted after the access control byte: frame control byte, destination and source address, data, and frame check sequence.

The *frame control byte* indicates whether the frame is a data frame or a control frame. If a control frame is identified, then it specifies the type of control represented. The *destination address* is the six-byte MAC address of the intended recipient of the message. The *source address* is the six-byte MAC address of the message sender. *Data* contains the message data. The *frame check sequence* (FCS) field is provided for error checking.

Fiber Distributed Data Interface

History
The *fiber distributed data interface* (FDDI) is an optical networking standard for LANs. It was developed in the mid-1980s in support of distributed applications because existing LAN technology based on token ring and Ethernet protocols could not support the networking needs of high-speed workstations used in science and engineering. FDDI also addresses the concerns of mission critical applications. It was designed to provide a robust and reliable network. FDDI is standardized by various ANSI standards.

Architecture
FDDI is primarily based on a token ring network. The FDDI protocol defines a 100 Mbps token-passing, dual ring LAN using fiber-optic cable. The reliability concerns of a single failed link bringing down the entire network are addressed by using a counter-rotating dual ring architecture. Traffic on each ring flows in opposite directions. One ring is designated as the primary ring and the other as the secondary ring.

During normal operation, only the primary ring is used to carry data. If any station on the dual ring fails, a segment of the secondary ring is used in conjunction with the original ring to rearrange the topology, wrapping it into a single ring. This wrapped ring allows for uninterrupted data flow.

Attachment Points
There are several ways to connect FDDI devices to a network. FDDI defines two types of node called *stations* and *concentrators*. Each may be single-attached or dual-attached for a total of four node types.

Single-attached devices are attached to one ring (usually the primary ring) of the counter-rotating architecture. Dual-attached rings are attached to both the primary and secondary rings. Concentrators are different from stations by acting as hubs to allow other devices to attach, either as single or dual stations. Concentrators come as *dual-attachment concentrators* (DACs) or *single-attachment concentrators* (SACs).

Dual Homing
Dual homing can be used for critical devices that need extra security against ring failures. Dual-homed devices connect to two different concentrators. One concentrator is designated as the primary or active concentrator, and the other is designated as the secondary or passive device. If the active concentrator or the link it is on fails, then the passive concentrator becomes active.

Frame
The FDDI frame format is similar to the token ring format described above. It consists of eight fields: *preamble, start delimiter, end delimiter, destination and source address, data, frame check sequence,* and *frame status*. The FDDI frame is essentially a token ring frame (Otto and Thomas 1996).

Ethernet

History and Overview
Arguably the most successful of the link layer protocols, practically every home or office has an Ethernet technology making up its LAN. Created in the 1970s at the Xerox Corporation (Metcalfe and Boggs 1976) and after a successful Ethernet version 1 specification developed by Xerox, Intel, and Digital Equipment Corporation, the IEEE developed the 802.3 Ethernet standards (IEEE 2005). IEEE 802.3 is what most references use as a standard in discussing Ethernet, even though Ethernet version 2 frames are still popular in networks.

Ethernet is not a single protocol but a range of protocols and technologies for layers 1 (physical) and 2 (data link) of the networking stack. Table 1 shows the mapping of the Ethernet layers to the OSI network model. This chapter only briefly mentions the physical specifications of Ethernet and instead focuses on the data-link properties, including describing common frame formats.

Within the data-link layer, the Ethernet protocols are divided into two sublayers: the *MAC* and *MAC client*. If the Ethernet adapter is in a normal end host, or *data terminal equipment* (DTE), the MAC client is a LLC. The LLC provides access between the link and network layers through a well-defined interface given in IEEE 802.2 specifications. If the Ethernet adapter is instead located in *data communication equipment* (DCE), the MAC client is a *bridge entity*. Defined by IEEE 802.1, bridge entities

Table 1: Mapping of the Ethernet Data-Link and Physical Layers to the OSI Model

ISO Reference Model	Ethernet Reference Model

Application layer
Session layer
Presentation layer
Transport layer
Network layer
Link layer
Physical layer
	Ethernet independent
	    protocols
	MAC client
	Media access control
	Specific media physical
	    protocols

Source: Cisco Systems 2004.

provide interfaces for connecting LANs regardless of protocol homogeneity.

The MAC sublayer provides access to the physical layer and defines the Ethernet frame format. Across a variety of Ethernet technologies and speeds (some with extensions to the basic frame format), the MAC sublayer is protocol specific. A primary responsibility of the MAC sublayer is the encapsulation of the data given from the higher layer (i.e., LLC) by wrapping Ethernet fields around the data and producing a valid Ethernet frame. Once a frame is constructed, the MAC must start the transmission process of the frame, as well as handle any errors arising during the transmission process.

Physical Specifications and Data Rates

The different physical specifications and implementations of Ethernet can be grouped by the bandwidth that each technology provided. The first Ethernet standards specified bandwidths of 10 Mbps. Fast Ethernet bumped the bandwidth to 100 Mbps, Gigabit Ethernet increased bandwidth to 1000 Mbps, and the recent 10-Gigabit Ethernet standard specifies a 10,000 Mbps bandwidth. Table 2 lists examples of Ethernet specifications grouped by speed along with columns for types of cabling and possible topologies.

Sharing the Medium

Ethernet shares the medium between all the users on the link by using a scheme mentioned earlier known as *carrier sense multiple access with collision detection* (CSMA/CD). This multiple-access scheme requires no centralization of host transmission, no special token frames, and no time slots. The algorithm does require the Ethernet adapter to determine when the link is free to transmit (carrier sense) and to determine when different hosts have transmitted frames concurrently (collision detection).

The CSMA/CD algorithm can be written in pseudocode as follows.

Step 1: An Ethernet frame is prepared for transmission with data from the network layer.

Step 2: If the link media is busy, then wait.

Step 3: Transmit the frame.

Step 4: Listen for colliding frames. If there is no collision, the frame has been successfully transmitted and the algorithm can restart at step 1.

Step 5: If collision detected, transmit a *jam signal.*

Step 6: Abort the entire process for the frame if the number of transmission attempts has been exceeded.

Step 7: Wait a computed back-off time before re-entering step 2.

Once the Ethernet adapter has detected a busy carrier in step 2 and has to wait, the adapter also has to wait an additional amount of time called the *interframe gap* (or *interframe spacing*) once the medium is clear. The interframe gap is a type of rest period between Ethernet frames to allow network adapters to get ready for the next frame. Gap time minimums are based on the amount of time to transmit ninety-six bits, so the interframe gap time is relative to each Ethernet technology's transmission speeds.

The *jam signal* in step 5 is a thirty-two–bit signal that makes sure all the other hosts on the link detect colliding frames. The jam signal is necessary because it is possible for not enough signal energy to be generated and transmitted back to the first transmitting host for it to detect a collision if the second sending host immediately stopped transmitting when a collision was detected.

In step 7, the back-off time is computed by an *exponential back-off* algorithm: given that the network adapter is attempting to transmit a frame that has experienced n collisions, the adapter waits $512k$ bit-times where k is chosen randomly with $0 \leq k < 2^m$ and m is the minimum of n, and the standard back-off limit of 10. With a wait time based on a power of 2 and a maximum wait time

Table 2: Ethernet Specifications

Ethernet Family	Speed	Technology	Cabling	Topology
Standard Ethernet	10 Mbps	10Base5 10Base2 10Base-T 10Base-F	Coaxial (thicknet) Coaxial (thinnet) Twisted pair Fiber-optic	Bus Bus Star Star
Fast Ethernet	100 Mbps	100Base-TX 100Base-T4 100Base-FX 100Base-SX	Cat5 twisted pair Cat3 twisted pair Fiber-optic (laser) Fiber-optic (LED)	Star Star Star Star
Gigabit Ethernet	1000 Mbps	1000Base-T 1000Base-LX 1000Base-SX	Cat5 twisted pair Fiber-optic (laser) Fiber-optic (LED)	Star Star Star
10-gigabit Ethernet	10000 Mbps	10GBase-T 10GBase-SR 10GBase-LR 10GBase-LX4	Cat5/5e/6 twisted pair Fiber-optic (multimode) Fiber-optic (single mode) Fiber-optic (multiplexed)	Star Star Star Star

Source: Compiled from various sources, including IEEE 802 standards.

bounded by the back-off limit, the back-off algorithm is more formally noted as a *truncated binary exponential back-off*. The exponential back-off algorithm ensures two things: (1) a random wait time to make sure two colliding hosts do not retransmit at the same time and recollide and (2) a longer and longer wait time for duplicate colliding frames to reduce the amount of collisions on a busy Ethernet network.

Efficiency

Much literature has been dedicated to the analysis of the performance and efficiency of the various Ethernet technologies. Deriving a simple closed-form efficiency equation is difficult, given the number of empirical factors in an Ethernet link. Kurose and Ross (2005), citing Lam (1980) and Bertsekas and Gallagher (1991), have given an approximation of Ethernet efficiency:

$$Efficiency = \frac{1}{1 + 5(t_{propagation}/t_{transmission})}$$

The maximum time of energy from a signal propagating between the most distant adapters is $t_{propagation}$, and the time to transmit the largest Ethernet frame is $t_{transmission}$. From the above relationship, two conclusions can be formed: When propagation times rise, efficiency goes down (or becomes perfect when the time nears zero); and when the size of the Ethernet frames becomes smaller, efficiency goes down (or becomes perfect when the frame size approaches infinity).

Frame

There are seven basic Ethernet frame fields: preamble, start-of-frame delimiter, destination address, source address, type or length, data, and frame check sequence. Advanced Ethernet standards, such as Gigabit Ethernet, may extend or modify these.

The *preamble* is a seven-byte bit-synchronization pattern of alternating 0's and 1's. Following the preamble is the one-byte *start-of-frame delimiter* (10101011) that marks the beginning of a valid Ethernet frame.

After these eight bytes of synchronization and signaling, the actual Ethernet data follows, starting with the *destination address* and *source address*. Each address is six bytes and is also known as a MAC address. The destination MAC address can represent a single host address (unicast) or a group of addresses. If the first bit of the destination is a 0, then the address is an individual host, but a 1 represents a group of hosts. Furthermore, if a group of addresses is specified, the grouping can be based on all the hosts on the link (broadcast) or a logical subset of users (multicast). A multicast address is an a priori agreed-to address for the group, whereas the broadcast address bits are all set to 1's.

The next field can either be the *type* field or *length* field. The IEEE 802.3 Ethernet standard defines the two-byte field following the source address as the length field, marking the number of bytes in the data field. Other Ethernet standards' frames, most notably the Ethernet II frame (also known as the DIX frame, named from the joint work by the Digital Equipment Corporation, Intel, and Xerox) treat this field as a type field, noting the type of protocol in the network layer that generated the frame. A majority of implemented Ethernet networks use the DIX frames, and the 802.3 specification now recognizes either use of the type or length field as valid. An Ethernet frame is limited to 1500 bytes by 802.3. If the type or length field's value is less than or equal to 1500, then the field's value represents the value of the data field. Type values are defined by field values greater than or equal to 1536 (0×600).

The *data* field follows the type or length field. The minimum length of the data field is 46 bytes, whereas the maximum length is 1500 bytes. If the data from the network layer are less than 46 bytes, then padding bytes are added to the user data. The maximum length of the data field is also known as the *maximum transmission unit* (MTU). Ethernet is such a ubiquitous protocol that modern operating systems IP stacks default to generating 1500 byte datagrams for the Ethernet frame. However, if the datagram traverses a part of the network with a smaller MTU, then it is the responsibility of the network layer (i.e., the IP layer), to split the datagram.

The final standard Ethernet field is the four-byte *frame check sequence* field. It is an error-detection field containing a thirty-two–bit cyclic redundancy check value. The CRC value is computed using the values of the data, length or type, and both address fields. Because Ethernet is defined as a connectionless and unreliable service, the responsibility for a frame with a bad CRC lies with the higher layers, and the failed CRC frames are dropped by the network card driver. The frame's data would only be retransmitted if a higher layer was using a reliable service such as TCP.

Because of the higher transmission speeds of Gigabit Ethernet, the minimum frame size was increased to 520 bytes for 1000base-T and 416 bytes for 1000Base-X implementations. To retain compatibility with the basic Ethernet frame, the possible extra padding these increased minimums bring are not added in the data field (as described above) but in an extra *extension* field. This extension field is appended to the end of the frame.

Another Gigabit Ethernet update to the original specification was the addition of a *frame burst mode*. In this mode, a host is allowed to send additional frames up to 65,536 bit times without giving up the medium. In between the "bursting" frames, the sending host fills the interframe gaps with extension bits so that the other hosts know not to attempt to transmit (Cisco Systems 2004).

Transmission Modes

The original standard transmission mode for Ethernet is half-duplex. On a single Ethernet link only one host can be transmitting data at a time. For the host to receive data, it must stop transmitting. Every Ethernet standard must work at half-duplex. Usually, performance metrics and Ethernet parameters are given assuming half-duplex transmission.

Transmission in full duplex began as an optional mode for Ethernet, but because almost every adapter supports it, has become the de facto standard. Full duplex mode is actually simpler than half-duplex mode, but it does require two point-to-point links to be established between the target Ethernet nodes. Once the two links are established, Ethernet data flows in one direction on one link and in the opposite direction on the other. This removes media contention, thus removing collisions and retransmitted frames. The original requirement to keep the interframe gap is still needed, although frame extension bits for short frames are not necessary (Cisco Systems 2004).

CONCLUSION

We hope this chapter has provided a foundation for understanding the data-link layer. Located one step above the physical layer, the layer is vital for reliable transmissions between nodes in a computer network. It is important to understand the different link layer specifications and the various implementations that exist and how they both influence and are influenced by the network topologies and physical media. Errors in engineering the data-link layer could range from slight (selecting an incorrect frame size) to severe (providing no collision detection for a busy shared bus). Such mistakes can lead to correspondingly severe and negative consequences in the overall efficiency of network communication.

GLOSSARY

Automatic retransmission request (ARQ): A strategy for error correction in which the sender retransmits a frame if an acknowledgement message is not received within a specified time period.
Data-link layer: Layer 2 of the OSI model.
Frame: Logical grouping of data to be transmitted across the network.
Frame acknowledgement signal (ack): A signal sent from the receiver to the transmitter to indicate a frame was successfully transmitted.
Logical link control (LLC): Higher-level sublayer of the data-link layer.
Logical topology: Abstract arrangement of nodes on the network independent of wiring.
Media access control (MAC): Lower-level sublayer of the data-link layer.
Nack: Frame has not successfully received signal.
Node: A device that acts as a transmitter or a receiver on the network.
Physical topology: Arrangement of the physical wiring between nodes on a network.
Token: Special control sequence that is used especially in networks with ring topologies.

CROSS REFERENCES

See *Data Communications Basics; Network Layer Protocols; Session, Presentation and Application Layer Protocols; Transport Layer Protocols.*

REFERENCES

Abramson, N. 1970. The ALOHA system—Another alternative for computer communications. *Proceedings of Fall Joint Computer Conference*, 37: 281–85.
Bertsekas, D., and R. Gallagher. 1991. *Data networks*. 2nd ed. Englewood Cliffs, NJ: Prentice Hall.
Cisco Systems. 2004. Fiber distributed data interface. Chap. 9 in *Internetworking technologies handbook*, 4th ed., edited by J. Kane. Indianapolis: Cisco Press.
Crynwr Software. 2006. Packet driver specification (retrieved August 14, 2006, from www.crynwr.com/).
Elbert, B. 1999. *Introduction to satellite communication*. 2nd ed. Boston: Artech House Publishers.
IEEE (Institute for Electrical and Electronics Engineers). 1998. *IEEE standard for local and metropolitan area networks: Logical link control: 802.2*. New York: Author.
———. 2001. *IEEE standard for local and metropolitan area networks: Overview and architecture: 802*. New York: Author.
———. 2003. *IEEE standard for local and metropolitan area networks: Token ring access method and physical layer specifications: 802.5*. New York: Author.
———. 2005. *IEEE standard for local and metropolitan area networks: Carrier sense multiple access with collision detection (CSMA/CD) access method and physical layer specifications*. New York: Author.
———. 2006. *Guideline for 64-bit global identifier (EUI 64) registration authority* (retrieved August 20, 2006, from http://standards.ieee.org/regauth/oui/tutorials/EUI64.html).
ISO (International Organization for Standardization). 1994. *Information technology—Open systems interconnection—Basic reference model: The basic model*. Number 7498-1.
———. 2002. *Information technology–Telecommunications and information exchange between systems–High-level data link control (HDLC) procedures*. Number 13239.
Kleinrock, L., and F. A. Tobagi. 1975. Packet switching in radio channels: Part I—Carrier sense multiple-access modes and their throughput-delay characteristics. *IEEE Transactions on Communications*, 23(12): 1400–16.
Kurose, J. F., and K. W. Ross. 2005. *Computer networking: A top-down approach featuring the Internet*. 3rd ed. Boston: Addison Wesley.
Lam, S. 1980. A carrier sense multiple access protocol for local networks. *Computer Networks*, 4: 21–32.
Metcalfe, R. M., and D. R. Boggs. 1976. Ethernet: Distributed packet switching for local computer networks. *Communications of the Association for Computing Machinery*, 19(7): 395–404.
Microsoft Corporation. 2006. *NDIS—Network driver interface specification* (retrieved August 20, 2006, from www.microsoft.com/whdc/device/network/ndis).
Novell. 2006. ODI LAN driver components (retrieved August 20, 2006, from the Novell Developer Network Web site at http://developer.novell.com/wiki/index.php/ODI_LAN_Driver_Components).
Otto, C., and S. Thomas. 1996. *FDDIXPress administrator's guide*. Document no. 007-0813-060. Silicon Graphics (retrieved August 21, 2006, from http://techpubs.sgi.com/library/tpl/cgi-bin/getdoc.cgi/0650/bks/SGI_Admin/books/FDDIX_AG/sgi_html/ch01.html).
Stallings, W. 1984. Local networks. *Computing Surveys*, 16(1): 3–41.
Stone, J., M. Greenwald, C. Partridge, and J. Hughes. 1998. Performance of checksums and CRC's over real data. *IEEE/ACM Transactions on Networking*, 6(5): 529–43.
Tanenbaum, A. S. 1981. Network protocols. *Computing Surveys*, 13(4): 453–89.
Yeh, J. W., and W. Siegmund. 1980. Local network architectures. *Proceedings of the third ACM SIGSMALL symposium and the first SIGPC symposium on small systems*, pp. 10–14.

Network Layer Protocols

Muhannad Harrim, Mohamed El-Wakil, and Ala Al-Fuqaha, *Western Michigan University, Kalamazoo*

INTRODUCTION

A protocol is a collection of standard conventions and rules that govern communication between entities in the same or different environments. The *Internet protocol* (IP) serves to interconnect systems in packet-switched networks. IP is the routed network layer protocol of the Internet that encapsulates upper-layer protocols (e.g., TCP and *user datagram protocol*, or UDP) packets as *datagrams* for transmission over various layer 2 technologies such as Ethernet, wireless fidelity (WiFi), and point-to-point protocol (PPP).

IP offers unreliable connectionless services and depends on transport layer protocols such as TCP and UDP to deliver error-free, duplication-free flow control and sequenced delivery of packets. To fulfill its objective—that is, transmission of datagrams end to end—the IP performs three main tasks: *addressing, fragmentation and reassembly,* and *packet forwarding*.

Each network interfacing card attached to end hosts or routers is identified by a unique address called an *IP address*. When a datagram is received by a system, the IP module residing on that system accesses the *header* of the datagram to obtain the destination IP address and forward the datagram toward the destination accordingly.

When datagrams are transmitted from one network to another that has a smaller *maximum transmission unit* (MTU) size, the IP performs fragmentation to enable the datagrams to fit on the underlying link layer protocols. Specific fields and flags in the IP header of a datagram provide all of the necessary information required to reassemble the fragments to re-create the original datagram. This reassembly process is performed at the ultimate destination of the datagram.

The selection of the next hop through which a datagram is forwarded from the source host to the destination host is called *datagram forwarding*. The IP module determines the next hop by consulting the routing table and makes its forwarding decision accordingly.

IP is a *routed network layer protocol*. This means that routers can forward IP packets through an internetwork toward their intended destination. On the other hand, *routing protocols* maintain the routing tables so that they reflect the actual topology of the network. Routing protocols are categorized into *interior gateway protocols* (IGPs) and *exterior gateway protocols* (EGPs).

EGPs route datagrams between *autonomous systems* (i.e., multi-internetwork environments), while IGPs route datagrams within a single routing domain or an autonomous system (a single administrative entity). Examples of IGPs include: *routing information protocol* (RIP and RIPv2), *interior gateway routing protocol* (IGRP), *enhanced interior gateway routing protocol* (EIGRP), *open shortest path first* (OSPF), and *intermediate system to intermediate system* (IS-IS). An example of an EGP is the *border gateway protocol* (BGP).

An IP datagram consists of a header and data (i.e., *payload*). Figure 1 shows the structure of an IP datagram header. Explanations of some of the important fields follow.

- *Type of service*: This set of abstract unified parameters indicates a certain service request.
- *Precedence, delay, throughput,* and *reliability*: These form the whole set of the abstract parameters and define the handling mechanism of datagram transmissions through the internetwork by mapping them into real service types.
- *Time to live*: A time limit is assigned by the sending host for the datagram to be delivered to its destination. If the time to live for a datagram reaches zero before it reaches the destination, the datagram will be discarded. This mechanism limits the upper-bound lifetime of

datagrams, thus suppressing undesired loops, discarding undelivered datagrams, and sometimes preventing old datagram duplications.

- *Options*: These provide predefined optional routing methods. It is up to the sender to choose one or not. Nevertheless, Internet modules of each node should be able to interpret it and react accordingly. Option definitions include *security, loose secure routing, strict secure routing, record route, stream identifier*, and *Internet timestamp*.

- *Header checksum*: This error-detection mechanism enforces the correctness of a datagram's header, ensuring that the processing of the datagram is done accurately during the whole transmission process. When an error occurs, it will be reflected in the *checksum*.

Working with the IP, the *Internet control message protocol* (ICMP) is a companion protocol that is responsible for detecting and reporting errors to the source entity.

IP ADDRESSING

Each router or host on the Internet is assigned at least one unique global identity called an *IP address*. Names given to entities over the network could not replace IP addresses because the IP protocol uses the IP addresses to perform forwarding, and the *address resolution protocol* (ARP) maps IP addresses to their corresponding link layer addresses. The *domain name system* (DNS) maps IP entity names to IP addresses and vice versa.

Having a fixed length of thirty-two bits, IP addresses are formatted into a decimal notation such as: 128.244.65.18. Each IP address consists of two parts: *network number* and *host number*.

IP addresses are divided into five classes: A, B, C, D, and E (see Figure 2). In class A, the most significant bit of the leftmost byte is zero; that is followed by seven bits that represent the network number and twenty-four bits for the host number. That means that the network numbers 1 through 126 are class A networks. Note that

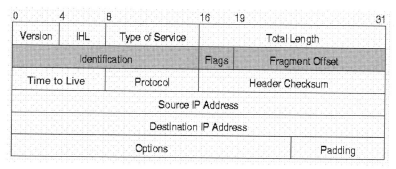

Figure 1: IP datagram header

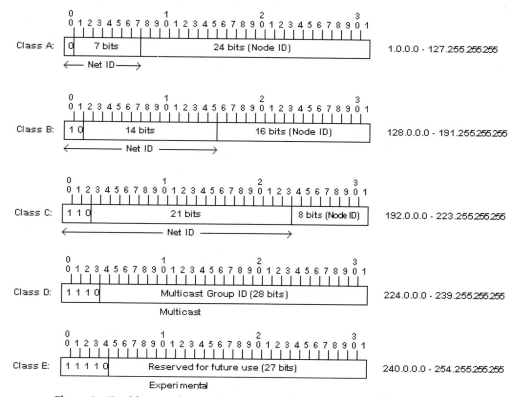

Figure 2: IP addresses classes. Source: www.cisco.com/warp/public/701/3.html

the network number 127 represents a local machine and is used for loopback.

In class B addresses, the two most significant bits of the leftmost byte are 10, followed by fourteen bits that represent the network number and sixteen bits for the host number. Class B network numbers are in range from 128 to 191.

In class C addresses, the three most significant bits of the leftmost byte are 110, followed by twenty-one bits for the network number and eight bits for the host number.

The above implies a maximum of 126 class A networks, each having as many as 16 million hosts. There are 16,000 class B networks with 65,000 hosts per network. Class C addresses provide approximately 2 millions networks, each consisting of 253 hosts. The Internet Corporation for Assigned Names and Numbers (ICANN) is responsible for assigning and mapping the network numbers.

Besides the aforementioned classes, class D is used for *multicasting*. This allows data to be sent to several destinations instead of just a single destination. Finally, class E is reserved for future use.

Network masks provide a method for specifying the network and host numbers in IP addresses. Having the mask and the IP addresses represented in binary notation would make it easier to identify the network number and the host number for each IP address. Classes A, B, and C have their own default masks. The default mask of class A addresses is 255.0.0.0; for class B, the default mask is 255.255.0.0; and for class C, the default mask is 255.255.255.0.

If we have the class A address 8.20.15.1, then:

```
IP address    : 00001000.00010100.00001111.00000001
Mask          : 11111111.00000000.00000000.00000000
Network       : 00001000.00000000.00000000.00000000
number
(binary)
Network       : 8.0.0.0
number
(decimal)
Host number   : 00000000.00010100.00001111.00000001
(binary)
Host number   : 0.20.15.1
(decimal)
```

For class B, if we have the address 145.14.34.4, then:

```
IP address    : 10010001.00001110.00100010.00000100
Mask          : 11111111.11111111.00000000.00000000
```

```
Network       : 10010001.00001110.00000000.00000000
number
(binary)
Network       : 145.14.0.0
number
(decimal)
Host number   : 00000000.00000000.00100010.00000100
(binary)
Host number   : 0.0.34.4
(decimal)
```

For class C, if we have the address 196.10.33.2, then:

```
IP address    : 11000000.00001010.00100001.00000010
Mask          : 11111111.11111111.11111111.00000000
Network       : 11000000.00001010.00100001.00000000
number
(binary)
Network       : 196.10.33.0
number
(decimal)
Host number   : 00000000.00000000.00000000.00000010
(binary)
Host number   : 0.0.0.2
(decimal)
```

SUBNETTING

Subnetting is the process of logically dividing a given network into a group of smaller networks called *subnets*. Subnetting serves to organize large networks as a collection of smaller networks that follow the organizational structure of companies or organizations. Subnetting also improves performance through traffic control.

Internet addresses with subnetting are represented as:

<Network number><Subnet number><Host number>

The host number part is reduced to allow the subnet number to fit in the whole address. The trade-off in assigning bits from the host number to the subnet number is that each bit assigned would cut the maximum number of hosts to the half within the subnet and double the number of subnets in the network. Table 1 illustrates this point for class C addresses.

In the other classes, the table would be bigger because the host part is larger (sixteen bits for class B, twenty-four bits for class A), so potentially more subnetting designs are possible.

Table 1 Number of Subnets versus Number of Hosts in a Class C Network

Number Bits for Subnet	Number of Subnets	Number of Bits for Host	Number of Hosts
1	2	7	126 (128 − 2)
2	4	6	62 (64 − 2)
3	8	5	30 (32 − 2)
4	16	4	14 (16 − 2)
5	32	3	6 (8 − 2)
6	64	2	2 (4 − 2)

Table 2: Possible Designs for Class C Networks

Bits in Subnet Field	Number of Subnets	Bits in Host Field	Number of Hosts	Comments
2	4	6	62	Too few subnets
3	8	5	30	Good balance
4	16	4	14	Too few hosts

Table 3: Possible Designs for Class B Networks

Bits in Subnet Field	Number of Subnets	Bits in the Host Field	Number of Hosts	Comments
3	8	13	8,190	Too few subnets
4	16	12	4,094	Too few subnets
5	32	11	2,046	Good balance
6	64	10	1,022	Good balance
7	128	9	510	Good balance
8	256	8	254	Too few hosts

Table 4: Network Addresses and Host Addresses for a Class C Network with Subnet

Network Address	Valid Host Addresses
192.178.130.0	192.178.130.1 to 192.178.130.62
192.178.130.64	192.178.130.65 to 192.178.130.126
192.178.130.128	192.178.130.129 to 192.178.130.190
192.178.130.192	192.178.130.190 to 192.178.130.254
255.255.255.192	

In class A, the maximum number of subnets is 4,194,304 subnets with just two hosts in each one. In class B, the maximum number of subnets is 16,384 subnets with just two hosts in each. As illustrated in Table 1, class C subnetting design provides a maximum of 64 subnets.

An organization with class C network that requires seven distinct networks with a maximum number of twenty-eight hosts per each subnetwork can assign a three-bit subnet field to obtain a total of eight subsets, each with thirty hosts as illustrated in Table 2 below.

A larger organization with a class B network that requires eighteen subnetworks and a maximum of 445 hosts per subnetwork can design a solution based on the information in Table 3.

If a subnet mask of a class C network is 255.255.255.192, then it means that only two bits are assigned from the host number to the subnet number; the result is four subnets, each with as many as sixty-two hosts.

Let the organization's IP network be 192.178.130.0. If the previous subnet mask is used, then the organization's network will be segmented into four networks as shown in Table 4.

CLASSLESS INTERDOMAIN ROUTING

Because the Internet is running out of IP addresses and organizations do not fully utilize class B addresses, this class is getting more crowded and exhausted. A short-term solution for such problems is *classless interdomain routing* (CIDR) or supernetting.

The two primary functions of CIDR are (1) allocating address space throughout the Internet and (2) providing a method to aggregate routing information.

Address space allocation and the aggregation of routing information within a hierarchical topology is done automatically and smoothly for *single-homed* clients (i.e., those with one bandwidth provider). It is more complicated when clients are *multihomed*: They have multiple addresses with possibly different service providers. The routing information for these clients must be advertised by the supporting service provider, and whenever organizations change their service provider, it is recommended that these organizations migrate their address allocations to the new service provider's address space to save more address space and make routing more efficient and smooth.

The main idea of supernetting is to assign blocks from class C network numbers to a network service provider, where an organization using a specific service provider will be assigned mask subsets pointing to its provider address space. In this way, the hierarchical routing implies that any client using a service provider for network connectivity will be routed via its provider infrastructure even if the client or organization is multihomed.

Organizations that implement supernetting in their networks use IGPs that support classless routing such as OSPF. Older IGPs have the ability to receive supernet information but cannot distribute such information in their current routing domains.

The major benefits of using CIDR include: (1) preventing more occupation and exhaustion of class B address space by allocating flexible and variously sized blocks of class C address space, and (2) controlling the growth rate of routing tables by significantly decreasing the entries in these tables.

Restructuring of IP addresses is required to apply CIDR. Instead of being limited to network prefixes of eight, sixteen, or twenty-four bits, prefixes can be used anywhere from thirteen to twenty-seven bits. Thus, blocks of class C addresses can be allocated to networks as small as thirty-two hosts—or as large as more than 500,000 hosts. This supports more flexibility in assigning addresses to an organization's network in ways that would meet its requirements.

The representation of CIDR address includes the standard thirty-two–bit IP address and the prefix that indicates the number of bits used for the network number. For example, in the CIDR address 211.78.4.39/24, the "/24" indicates that the first twenty-four bits are used to identify the network number; the remaining bits identify the host number (see Table 5).

Consider the block of 2,048 class C network numbers beginning with 192.24.0.0 and ending with 192.31.255.0 allocated to a single network provider whom we will call "RA." A supernetted route to this block of network numbers would be described as 192.24.0.0 with mask of 255.248.0.0.

If this service provider should connect six clients as in Table 6, then the service provider should assign addresses to the clients as follows:

C1: Addresses from 196.12.0.0 to 196.12.7.0. This block of networks is described by the route 196.12.0.0 and mask 255.255.248.0.

C2: Addresses from 196.12.16.0 to 196.12.31.0. This block is described by the route 196.12.16.0, mask 255.255.240.0.

C3: Addresses from 196.12.8.0 to 196.12.11.0. This block is described by the route 196.12.8.0, mask 255.255.252.0.

C4: Addresses from 196.12.12.0 through 196.12.15.0. This block is described by the route 196.12.12.0, mask 255.255.252.0.

C5: Addresses 196.12.32.0 and 196.12.33.0. This block is described by the route 196.12.32.0, mask 255.255.254.0.

C6: Addresses 196.12.34.0 and 196.12.35.0. This block is described by the route 196.12.34.0, mask 255.255.254.0.

To make this example more realistic, assume that C4 and C5 are multihomed through "RB," another service provider. Further assume the existence of a client "C7" who was originally connected to "RB" but has moved to "RA."

C7: Allocate 196.32.0.0 through 196.32.15.0. This block is described by the route 196.32.0.0, mask 255.255.240.0.

For the multihomed clients, we will assume that C4 is advertised as primary via "RA" and secondary via "RB"; C5 is primary via "RB" and secondary via "RA."

Assume that "RA" and "RB" are connected via some common "backbone" provider "BB." Result advertisements from "RA" to "BB" will be:

C4 primary advertisement: 196.12.12.0 to 255.255.252.0.
C7 primary advertisement: 196.32.0.0 to 255.255.240.0.

Table 5: Examples of CIDR Prefixes

CIDR Prefix	Number of Equivalent Class C	Number of Host Addresses
/27	1/8	32
/26	1/4	64
/25	1/2	128
/24	1	256
/23	2	512
/22	4	1,024
/21	8	2,048
/20	16	4,096
/19	32	8,192
/18	64	16,384
/17	128	32,768
/16	256 (= 1 class B)	65,536
/15	512	131,072
/14	1,024	262,144
/13	2,048	524,288

Table 6: Example of Class C Network Allocation

Client	Number of Equivalent Class C Networks	Number of Host Addresses
C1	8	≤ 2,048
C2	16	< = 4,096
C3	4	< = 1,024
C4	4	< = 1,024
C5	2	< = 512
C6	2	< = 512

Remainder of RA primary advertisement: 196.12.0.0 to 255.248.0.0.

For RB, the advertisements must also include C4 and C5 as well as its block of addresses. Result advertisements from "RB" to "BB" will be:

C4 secondary advertisement: 196.12.12.0 to 255.255.252.0.
C5 primary advertisement: 196.12.32.0 to 255.255.254.0.
Remainder of RB primary advertisement: 196.32.0.0 to 255.248.0.0.

NETWORK ADDRESS TRANSLATION

Network address translation (NAT) is another short-term solution along with CIDR and subnetting to the scarce IP addresses limitations and scaling problems. A *stub domain* is a domain that handles network traffic from and to hosts inside the domain. Whenever a communication outside the stub domain is needed, the IP addresses—only the ones communicating outside the domain—should be reformed to be globally unique. The IP addresses inside one's stub domain are not globally unique and are reused in many different domains.

Here comes the role of NAT, which is nothing but a router function or model that is set to a stub border router. At the end points of a stub domain, where it shares borders with other outside domains and networks, NAT must be configured at these end or exit points, having the same translation table in all distinct end points within the same domain.

NAT's tables carry two parts of data: (1) the reusable addresses, also known as *local addresses*, that are used internally in a stub domain; and (2) the global addresses that are unique and used to communicate with global networks. NAT provides external communication ability to the Internet or other networks and domains by translating these reusable addresses and mapping them with unique global IP addresses.

To illustrate how NAT works, let's have two stubs, A and B, that internally use class A address 20.0.0.0. Stub A's NAT is assigned the class C address of 198.76.29.0, and stub B's class C address is 198.76.27.0. When stub A host 10.40.66.5 wants to send datagrams to stub B host 10.88.12.21, it uses the global unique address 198.76.27.4 for the destination's address and sends the datagrams to its corresponding router. The stub router translates the source host address 10.40.66.5 in the IP header to globally unique address 198.76.29.15 and uses a static route for the net 198.76.0.0; as a result, the packets are sent to the next router in a different network. Before the datagram is transmitted to the destination, stub B router maps the destination's address 198.76.27.4 in the IP header to the available host that owns this global address and forwards the datagram to the that host.

The address translations used by NAT are done transparently. Both host and routers require no changes or knowledge about the mappings or translations of local addresses to global ones.

Having NAT installed, end-point stub routers never advertise the local addresses to the global network's backbones; global information from the backbones, however, can be advertised via the stub domains.

Because the hosts in the backbone cannot tell which address or source host has sent the packets, this whole matter increases the privacy of the hosts. As useful as it is, there is a negative effect: Security can be breached easily and the tracking methods could become difficult because locating the IP address would be challenging: It is unknown to the global backbone. Such scenarios are used in sending junk mails, hacking, and otherwise abusing the net. Other NAT drawbacks include (1) potential misaddressing problems, (2) the need to use sparse end-to-end matrices to avoid having huge translation tables that would affect performance, (3) difficulties in running some applications, and (4) problems with *simple network management protocol* (SNMP), DNS, and other protocols.

FRAGMENTATION AND REASSEMBLY

Sometimes a large datagram—that is, one larger than the MTU—reaches a network. In such a case, the router receiving the datagram either drops it and returns an ICMP message saying "Datagram too big," or it fragments the datagram into smaller datagrams that can be handled by the network. The latter option is called *fragmentation*.

When the fragments reach the destination host, they will be recombined in a process known as *reassembly*.

The IP address header consists of three vital parts for the fragmentation and reassembly process: identification, fragmentation flags, and fragmentation offset.

The *identification* is a sixteen-bit unique number assigned by the sending entity. Via the identification bits, the destination host can recognize different arriving fragments and assemble the ones with the same identification, along with the same source, destination, and protocol identification to form the original datagram.

The *fragmentation flags* section is a three-bit number divided into three parts: the *must be zero* (MBZ) bit, which is always set to zero; the *do not fragment* (DF) bit; and the *more fragments* (MF) bit.

If the DF equals zero, then the routers can fragment this datagram if necessary. If the DF is set, then the datagram will not be fragmented under any circumstances; if it cannot be delivered without fragmentation, then it will eventually be dropped.

```
DF          (1 bit)
Value       Description
0           Fragment if necessary
1           Do not fragment
```

When set, the MF flag indicates that more fragments can be expected and this one is not the last. But if the MF is zero, this is the last fragment.

```
MF          (1 bit)
Value       Description
0           No more fragments (last fragment)
1           More fragments follow this fragment
```

The fragmentation offset, which is thirteen bits long, represents the position or order of the fragment in the whole datagram; in other words, it identifies the order or sequence of the fragment relative to the others. The first fragment always has the offset of zero.

These fields provide enough information to reassemble datagrams.

The fragmentation process works as follows: Several new datagrams (i.e., fragments) that comply with the current network MTU are created. The original datagram IP header is copied verbatim to the new datagrams IP headers. The data of the original datagram are divided into eight-byte blocks and distributed among the newly created datagrams. An eight-byte block is called a *number of fragment blocks* (NFB). Every fragment must be assigned an integral number of the eight-byte blocks, except the last fragment. In all fragments, the total length field is set to the size of the data in the fragment. In the first fragment, the fragment offset is set to zero. For the other fragments, the fragment offset is set to the value of the fragment offset in the original datagram plus the summation of the NFB value of the preceding fragments. Finally, the MF flag is set to 1 in all fragments except the last.

It is possible that the source hosts perform the fragmentation instead of the routers, but that would necessitate a *path MTU* discovery so the source host knows the smallest MTU value along the path to the destination. Path MTU discovery is not always guaranteed to succeed because it depends on ICMP messages, which are blocked by some networks as a countermeasure to *denial of service* (DOS) attacks.

When a fragment reaches its destination, it is checked to see if it belongs to a datagram that is being currently assembled or to a new datagram. If the just-arrived fragment belongs to a new datagram, then a new data buffer and a bitmap are allocated. The bitmap is used to keep track of which fragments have arrived.

If all fragments belonging to a datagram arrive within a specified time period, then the assembled datagram is passed to the transport layer; otherwise, the partially assembled datagram is dropped.

To give an example of fragmentation and reassembly, we have a datagram with 624 bytes of data; the MTU is 544 bytes (see Figure 3).

Fragmentation of the datagram into two fragments will solve the problem. The first fragment is shown in Figure 4, and the second (last) fragment is shown in Figure 5.

4 bits	8 bits	16 bits	32 bits	
Ver = 4	IHL = 5	Type of service	Total length = 644	
Identification = 405			MF = 0	Fragment offset = 0
Time to live = 123	Protocol = 6		Header checksum	
Source address				
Destination address				
Option + padding (no options)				
Data = 624 bytes				

Figure 3: Example of an IP datagram with large data payload

4 bits	8 bits	16 bits	32 bits	
Ver = 4	IHL = 5	Type of service	Total length = 540	
Identification = 405			MF = 1	Fragment offset = 0
Time to live = 119	Protocol = 6		Header checksum	
Source address				
Destination address				
Option + padding (no options)				
Data = 540 bytes				

Figure 4: Example of the first fragment of a large IP datagram

4 bits	8 bits	16 bits	32 bits	
Ver = 4	IHL = 5	Type of service	Total length = 124	
Identification = 405			MF = 0	Fragment offset = 86
Time to live = 119	Protocol = 6		Header checksum	
Source address				
Destination address				
Option + padding (no options)				
Data = 84 bytes				

Figure 5: Example of the last fragment of a large IP datagram

ROUTING

Routing is the process of passing a packet from one node to another in a network until this packet reaches its intended destination. The network nodes that are dedicated to routing are called *routers*. Routers perform routing through tables known as *routing tables*. For example, in Figure 6, the routing table in router A would tell whether a packet going from PC 1 to a server will go through router B or C. Building routing tables could be done either manually (i.e., *static routing*) or automatically (i.e., *dynamic routing*).

Static Routing

Static routing is a simple method in which users manage and arrange routes through a relatively small network. To do so, one should either draw routing diagrams (usually done in real-life scenarios) or create routing tables.

Assume that R1, R2, and R3 are three routers for this network. A, B, and C are selected hosts in the network; each exists in a different subnet. Another host, D, in another external network is connected with this network. Assume the network address is 198.10.12.0 of class C (255.255.255.0) and let the subnets' addresses be as shown in Figure 7.

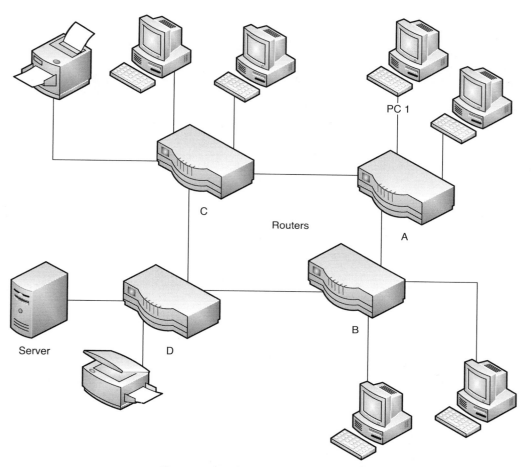

Figure 6: Simple network with four routers

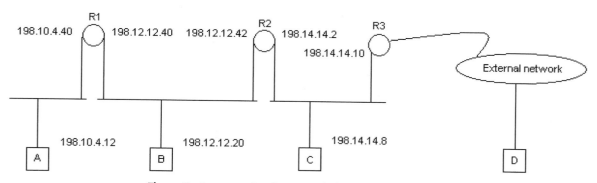

Figure 7: An example of a network that uses static routing

For the network to communicate with the external network, note that NAT is supposed to be installed on router R3 router, the end-point router.

The next step is to pinpoint the *default gateways* (dg) and connect them between the nodes (host and routers) and their default routers or gateways (see Figure 8). After that, specific routes' expressions are computed and supplemented to provide particular complementary routes along the default gateways to control the flow to the opposite side (to the left in this scenario) without the need to pass through default gateways. These expressions simplify the routing paths between nodes in understandable and easy notations such as R(X, Y, →Z), which means there is a route to the network subnet X that has the mask Y through the gateway Z.

Figure 9 represents the complete diagram that simulates a static routing principle for this network.

To configure the routes of a network in real life, we simply use the *route* add* command for each subnet address connected to its designated gateway. To do that in the previous scenario, it would be similar to the following:

To configure host A routes:

```
route  add  198.12.12.0  mask  255.255.255.0
198.10.4.40
```

If host A is connected to another router that connects to a subnet in the opposite direction (to its left), then that route should be added as well.

To configure host B routes:

```
route add 198.10.4.0 mask 255.255.255.0 198.12.
12.40
route  add  198.14.14.0  mask  255.255.255.0
198.12.12.42
```

To configure host C routes:

```
route  add  198.12.12.0   mask  255.255.255.0
198.14.14.2
route add (External Address) mask 255.255.255.0
198.14.14.10
route  add  198.10.4.0  mask  255.255.255.0
198.14.14.2
```

One can monitor the applied routing table in the local network by running *netstat*** command with the *r* and *n* options—*r* to display routing table and *n* to show IP addresses in their numeric notation (see Figure 10).

The result shows destinations (hosts or routers) and their corresponding default gateways along with other features such as the netmasks, interfaces, and metrics.

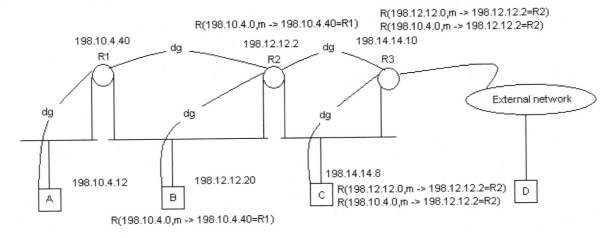

Figure 8: An example of a network that uses static routing with default gateways added

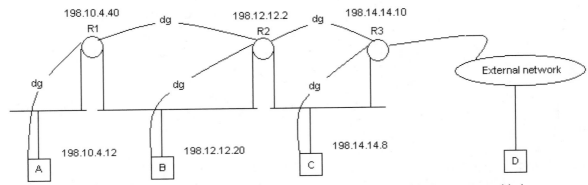

m in the R expressions stands for the mask = 255.255.255.0

Figure 9: An example of a network that uses static routing with routing expressions added

---

* Available for Windows, Linus, and Unix Systems.　　　　　* Available for Windows and Unix Systems.

```
C:\>netstat -rn

Route Table
===========================================================================
Interface List
0x1 ........................... MS TCP Loopback interface
0x2 ...00 14 22 ed 66 33 ...... Broadcom 440x 10/100 Integrated Controller - Pac
ket Scheduler Miniport
0x3 ...00 16 6f 2f 32 27 ...... Intel(R) PRO/Wireless 2200BG Network Connection
 - Packet Scheduler Miniport
===========================================================================
Active Routes:
Network Destination        Netmask          Gateway       Interface  Metric
          0.0.0.0          0.0.0.0        10.23.4.5      10.23.4.6     30
        10.23.4.4  255.255.255.252        10.23.4.6      10.23.4.6     30
        10.23.4.6  255.255.255.255        127.0.0.1      127.0.0.1     30
   10.255.255.255  255.255.255.255        10.23.4.6      10.23.4.6     30
        127.0.0.0        255.0.0.0        127.0.0.1      127.0.0.1      1
        224.0.0.0        240.0.0.0        10.23.4.6      10.23.4.6     30
  255.255.255.255  255.255.255.255        10.23.4.6      10.23.4.6      1
  255.255.255.255  255.255.255.255        10.23.4.6              3      1
Default Gateway:        10.23.4.5
===========================================================================
Persistent Routes:
  None
```

Figure 10: An example of retrieving the local network routing table using netstat

Another method to configure routes in a network is to use ICMP route redirect messages. This method cuts the complexity of declaring routes for the hosts all over the network; it only requires specifying routers' special routes.

Note that there are no routes expressions for the hosts. This will lead to datagrams routing only through default gateways, which will forward them using the default gateway or the assigned routes. This method is certainly easier, yet it would affect the performance and the traffic by depending only on the default gateways.

Dynamic Routing

Dynamic routing is less intuitive but more effective and easily scalable when compared to static routing. It is also more resilient to failed routers than static routing because routers can automatically update their routing tables without administrator intervention. Dynamic routing can be classified into three broad categories: *distance vector routing*, *link state routing*, and *policy-based routing*.

Distance Vector Routing

Distance vector routing is a protocol that particularly applies the *Bellman-Ford algorithm* to find the optimal paths in a network by utilizing vector, direction, and distance concepts to gather the required routing information and tables.

Routing information protocol (RIP) is one of the most common protocols to apply distance vector routing to compute the paths between the routers in a network. RIPv2 is the second version of the original RIP protocol and has nearly replaced RIPv1.

In a RIP network, routers exchange messages with each other that contain their own routing table entries represented as destination IP addresses and their corresponding distances computed in terms of hops. In this way all of the nearby routers acquire the most updated and new routing data and update theirs accordingly. The updated data aim to reduce the path distance by minimizing the number of crossed hops.

Quagga, a free software suite, can be used to configure RIPv2 routing, among other routing protocols, on Linux systems.

Link State Routing

Link state routing is a competitor to distance vector routing; with the latter, the routers exchange information only with the neighboring ones, but in link state routing the routers exchange information with all other routers in the network. A router sends messages containing the information (routing metrics) that are identified as *link state advertisements* (LSAs) to all neighboring routers. These routers exchange the advertisements with their neighbors as well and so on. This method of exchanging messages is also known as *flooding*.

The flooding of advertisements is commenced whenever updates occur. If there are no route updates, then there will not be any messages exchanged—unlike the distance vector, which depends on periodic broadcasting of messages.

This grants the network more efficiency and stability because there will not be that much traffic caused by the multicasting of the advertisements. It is only activated whenever route updates occur and does not necessarily include all the routers in the network, only those relevant to these updates.

Link state routing, then, is more efficient and stable by maintaining a degree of traffic control over the distance vector routing. In addition, distance vector routing has a lot of problems such as the convergence and count-to-infinity dilemma; these distinguish the link state over the distance vector protocols.

One of the most common link state routing approaches is the *open shortest path first* (OSPF). This protocol uses specific algorithms—basically, the *Dijkstra algorithm*—to compute the shortest routes between nodes in the network by forming a tree with routers as nodes. It then tries to figure out the distances and costs between these nodes to conclude the best routes.

OSPF passes around different types of packets that sum up the whole process (see Table 7).

The *hello* packets are distributed usually during the initiation to find out neighboring routers. The *database description* and *link state request* packets are engaged in the creation of adjacency and contiguity connections among routers. The *link state update* and *link state acknowledgment* packets are the core of the routes and metric update as well as the flooding part.

All messages or packets share an ordinary twenty-four–byte header, which is formatted as shown in Figure 11.

OSPF provides logical arrangements of networks such as where nodes can be encapsulated within areas. This reduces the traffic and the congestion of updates flooding beyond network capacity. It also cuts down the unnecessary update messages through other areas where these messages are not really claimed. Although the network topology can be divided into several different areas, all of these areas should be joined to a central one called the *backbone area*.

Policy Routing

Policy routing is a flexible way of routing that allows customizable routing of packets according to the policies and rules with which a specific organization's traffic should comply. Network administrators are able to control routing mechanisms as well as packet flows in their network system by publishing defined policies that policy-based routing protocols must follow.

Policy routing is different from the other dynamic routing protocols (distance vector and link state). It is an exterior gateway protocol (EGP) that is implemented in multi-autonomous systems, not a single one.

Table 7: OSPF Packets Types

Type	Packet Name
1	Hello
2	Database description
3	Link state request
4	Link state update
5	Link state ACK

8	16	32
Version	Type	Packet length
Router ID		
Area ID		
Checksum	Authentication type	
Authentication		

Figure 11: OSPF header fields

Border gateway protocol (BGP) is a policy-based routing protocol that uses a path vector algorithm to discover the optimal path. However, if routing policies are defined, it adopts these policies as its method in resolving the route selections. BGP uses TCP as a transport mechanism in message exchanges. The main functionality of BGP systems is to link with other BGP autonomous systems and exchange routing and reachability data to help in path selection without breaking any policy enforced in the network traffic.

Different messages are exchanged in BGP; each message has its own distinct format and header. BGP messages are divided into four categories according to its type: open, update, notification, and keepalive messages. *Open* messages are transmitted right after connection between hosts is established. A *keepalive* message is sent to the source to confirm the open message reception. *Update* messages transport the routing information to the nodes and are also used as a way to advertise routes. Keepalive messages are exchanged frequently to ensure that connectivity remains alive between hosts and prevent any connection timeout. *Notification* messages are passed around on any error detection.

MULTICAST ROUTING

Multicast routing is a mechanism that allows an IP datagram to be delivered to a host group—that is, multiple hosts represented in a single IP address. In a multicast, the sent datagram is neither promised to be delivered to all members of the destined group host nor delivered in the exact sequence as other datagrams.

There are no restrictions for any host in joining or leaving any host group at any time. Also, there are no limitations on the total number of hosts permitted in host groups or the locations of host groups. A host does not need to belong to a certain group to be able to have datagrams sent to it. A host can join more than one group at the same time.

A class D IP address is the one that handles the multicast technique. The first four bits—which are the high-order bits of (1110)—followed by the host group ID together represent the multicast group address or class D IP address. It ranges from 224.0.0.0 to 239.255.255.255. Some of the group addresses are already assigned by the Internet Assigned Numbers Authority (IANA); these addresses are called *permanent host groups*. For example, 224.0.0.1 is allocated to the permanent host group of all IP hosts and gateways in that subnet.

To perform multicasting, specific kinds of routers that support multicasting, called *multicast routers*, are employed; they could be separate from or work with normal routers. A multicast router in a certain subnet could be linked to another multicast router in a different subnet, and the latter could be linked to another, and so forth, creating what's called a *multicast backbone* (Mbone). Mbone is a collection of autonomously administered multicast regions, each specified by one or more multicast routers.

The *Internet group management protocol* (IGMP) is just a reporting protocol, similar to ICMP, but its purpose is to allow hosts to send reports throughout the network to inform the neighboring multicast routers about their "joins" or memberships to host groups.

From time to time, multicast routers transmit query messages to get the latest information about the memberships to a particular region or network. Whenever those queries are not replied to, the multicast router surmises that there are no members in that group and that it should not be involved with any forwards or multicasts. Any time a host joins that group (or any empty group), it should instantly send a report notifying the multicast routers that the host group has a member and is qualified to receive multicasts.

As mentioned earlier, only multicast routers have the ability to forward multicast datagrams; therefore, one method that allows routers that are missing multicasting support to send multicast datagrams and link with other multicast-enabled routers is called *tunneling*. Tunnels are virtual point-to-point links that allow the multicast datagram to be encapsulated in a normal (unicast) datagram in order to be transferred freely through available gateways.

Different algorithms are involved in multicast routing: *distance vector multicast routing protocol* (DVMRP), *multicast open shortest path first* (MOSPF), and protocol-independent multicast (PIM). Each region could choose any of these algorithms, forcing all multicast routers in that region to use only the same algorithm. All regions, however, can be linked together despite algorithm differences through a common region called *region backbone*, which runs the *distance vector multicast routing protocol* (DVMRP). This way, only border multicast routers in the regions should be able to interconnect with the backbone through the DVMRP.

DVMRP uses several remarkably different algorithms. *Truncated reverse path broadcasting* (TRPB), *reverse path broadcasting* (RPB), and *reverse path multicasting* (RPM) are different algorithmic approaches that handle the forwarding of multicast datagrams and the creation of distribution trees distinctively. Whereas TRPB concentrates on creating a shortest-path distribution tree with the ability to prune all unnecessary interfaces, RPB is less efficient in a way that it does not have the pruning feature, resulting in datagram duplication. However, a much better solution in forwarding datagrams is to use RPM, which holds out the distribution tree of all source and group pairs.

DVMRP multicasts periodically so that it can manage to deliver the datagrams to new members of the destination host groups. Hence, this brings some scaling and performance difficulties to the surface.

MOSPF, on the other hand, optimizes the path between the source and destination by computing the shortest possible distance between them. By using a type of spanning tree called *Steiner tree*, which preserves group members' routes and statistics, a router attempts to forward the datagrams within the optimal path between the source and the potential host group's destinations.

Although, in this manner, path utilization could be maximized between source and group, the overall internetwork utilization is more often disrupted.

In the forwarding process, each router located in the multicast datagram's path must preserve cached details (called *forwarding cache*) that hold information about the router from which the datagram was received (the *upstream node*) and the interfaces the datagram should head out of (the *downstream interfaces*). Each entry in the cache is based on two elements: (1) the local database that indicates the router's directly linked nodes and their corresponding group memberships, and (2) the shortest path tree that connects the source to remotely bound group members.

Unlike the previous protocols, PIM is a flexible multicast pattern that does not rely on any particular unicast protocol. It has the ability to get along with the entire set of currently implemented unicast algorithms. *Sparse mode PIM* (PIM-SM) and *dense mode PIM* (PIM-DM) are two common implementations of this protocol.

In PIM-SM, a router receives join and prune messages from neighboring routers. These messages serve to guide the router to forward datagrams to specific interfaces. The virtual point at which join and prune messages are intersected to accumulate a tree with only active members (sending and receiving nodes) is called the *rendezvous point* (RP). The RP is the most fundamental component to this protocol; when a router wants to forward the datagram, it sends the RP the same matches with the receiving nodes where they notify the RP. Once the data stream begins to flow from sender to RP and then to receiver, the routers positioned along the forwarding path refresh and update the path automatically to avoid any unnecessary gateways or branches until the forwarded datagrams reach the designated group members.

PIM-DM, on the other hand, considers all downstream nodes to be eligible to receive the multicast datagrams, so basically the network is flooded with the multicast datagrams and *reverse path forwarding* (RPF) is used to suppress the multicast datagrams' duplication. After flooding, if any branch in the network does not have group members, then it is pruned for a certain period. Whenever a new member joins a pruned branch, the updated router forwards the datagram to that branch to deliver it to the group member, changing it to an active branch.

In summary, the main distinctions between PIM-DM and PIM-SM are that in the former there are no scheduled joins monitored or any periodic updates (just clear prunes and grafts) and there is no RP.

PIM-DM and PIM-SM can be blended together in the same network, but a PIM-DM router cannot be set to be downstream of a PIM-SM router.

QUALITY OF SERVICE ROUTING

Quality of service (QoS) is the capability to provide guarantees that a requested service will be delivered according to a certain standard of quality. QOS involves assigning different priorities to different users or data flows. This contrasts with typical Internet behavior, which is based on *best effort delivery*. In best effort, users and data flows are treated equally. Best effort is suitable for applications such as e-mails and FTP, but it may not be suitable for newer applications such as streaming multimedia IP telephony. QOS is more importance for limited capacity networks.

In the following subsections, three QOS protocols will be presented: differentiated services (DiffServ), integrated services (IntServ), and multiprotocol label switching (MPLS).

Differentiated Services

Differentiated services (DiffServ) is based on classifying packets and handling them according to this classification. The DiffServ protocol itself does not have standard classifications but recommends four such classes. The establishment of classes is left to the network operators. Packet classification may depend on source address, destination address, or traffic type. Packets can have DiffServ markings that request certain service, but DiffServ routers are not obliged to honor these markings. DiffServ recommends four classes of services: (1) *default*, which is equivalent to best-effort service; (2) *expedited forwarding* for low-loss, low-latency traffic; (3) *assured forwarding*; and (4) *class selector*, which is equivalent to the IP header's precedence field.

Integrated Services

Integrated services (IntServ) was proposed as an approach to provide end-to-end QOS that real-time applications require by explicitly handling available resources to distinguish one packet stream from another. IntServ has four fundamental core components that establish such QOS integrated service: (1) packet scheduler, (2) classifier, (3) admission control, and (4) resource reservation protocol (RSVP).

The *packet scheduler* uses queuing and sometimes timers to handle the forwarding and policing of different packet streams. Packet scheduling is implemented at the data-link layer. To control the traffic and classify the different packet streams, each packet is mapped into a certain class, depending on some header value or additional classification number appended in the packet. Packets of the same class receive the same management from the packet scheduler. All of that is performed by the *classifier*.

Admission control manages the decision making in a router or host to receive a QOS for a new flow without influencing earlier guarantees. It is invoked at each host or router in the network to either accept or reject QOS requests via special route. The admission control algorithm must be consistent with the service model, and it is logically part of traffic control. The major role of the admission control is guaranteeing that QOS requests are satisfied. It also has important roles in imposing some administrative policies such as authentication upon resource reservations, accounting, and administrative reporting.

The final component of IntServ is the *resource reservation protocol*, which is needed to preserve a flow-specific state in the end-point nodes residing in the path of the traffic stream. Its main purpose is to explicitly signal the QOS requests of a specific application's traffic through the interfaces (nodes) located in the boundary regions along the taken route. Whenever a required bandwidth is reserved at the end points along the path, the application can commence the signaling or transmitting of packets. To simplify things, the signaling responsibility for transmitting QOS request is done through the RSVP that notifies routers about the application program's QOS request.

Two parameters are used to generally describe the operation of resource reservation: (1) the *flow spec*, which describes the resource quantity to be reserved; and (2) the *filter spec*, which describes the packet subset obtaining those reserved resources.

Multiprotocol Label Switching

A separate mechanism that is considered a fundamental section of QOS is called *multiprotocol label switching* (MPLS) because it is feasible in any network layer protocol and depends on label-based forwarding in transmitting packets.

MPLS confers QOS aims and advantages. It provides a great deal of flexibility to divert and control traffic streams, avoid network congestion spots and delays, and provide QOS utilities.

In any network, each router is independently capable of choosing the next router or hop and to thereafter forward the packet, relying on both the vital information concealed in the packet's header and the routing algorithm it is implementing.

In details, packets are divided to *forwarding equivalence classes* (FECs). These are, in turn, appended in the routing tables and referred to its designated next hop. This means that all packets belonging to a particular FEC will go along the same route or multipath routes associated with that FEC.

Each FEC is assigned a particular small identifier called a *label*. Once a packet arrives at a MPLS-supported router called a *label-switching router* (LSR), certain algorithms (the type depends on the packet's header) map the packet into its corresponding FEC. After that, the FEC-associated label is tagged to the packet before forwarding. Now the packet is ready to be forwarded to the next router, and instead of analyzing the packet each time it arrives at a router, the label associated with that packet (only representing FEC) is used as an index in the routing table to find out the path to the next hop; this is called a *label-switching path* (LSP).

To achieve a certain degree of QOS, the *precedence* and *class-of-service* fields represented in the header of a packet can be referenced from the label, avoiding analysis and allowing faster access. This means that labels are not only simple representations or indices to FECs but also class-of-service and precedence providers. In case of precedence, FECs prioritized to higher priority will use a higher-priority LSP, and the lower priority FECs will use lower-priority LSP.

Label distribution protocol (LDP) is responsible for the distribution and preservation of the relationship between the labels and FECs in MPLS. Other protocols may replace LDP such as *constraint route label distribution protocol* (CR-LDP), and resource reservation protocol–traffic engineering (RSVP-TE).

MOBILE INTERNET PROTOCOL

In the network, a node must be attached and assigned an IP address so that it can receive datagrams transmitted to it or it will never receive the datagrams. Having the capability to both exchange datagrams and change the point of attachment in the network is achieved through the *mobile IP's* mechanism. This mechanism usually applies to nodes that are connected to the network or Internet via a wireless link.

Although this mechanism allows a node to change its point of attachment to a network; the node preserves its own IP address throughout the changing of networks or subnets.

To preserve exchanging datagrams in both the old network and the newly visited one, special routers called *home agent* and *foreign agent* are needed. The home agent is situated in the mobile's node home (permanent network) and delivers the datagrams destined to the mobile node when it is away or attached to another network (foreign network). The foreign agent is situated in the mobile's node visited (i.e., foreign) network and serves the mobile node as long as it is a registered guest. It also delivers the datagrams destined to the mobile node tunneled by the home agent.

A mobile node is not necessarily a host that can attach to different networks. It could be a router that is mobile along with its network or an entire set of mobile networks.

In a home network, the mobile node functions naively. As it enters a foreign network, the mobile node acquires a new temporary IP address called the *care-of address*. The mobile node then registers the newly acquired care-of address to the home agent through distribution of *registration requests* and *registration replies* messages. This process is inverted (i.e., deregistration) when the mobile node returns back to the home network by also using the registration requests and replies.

This registration allows the home agent to seize the datagrams destined to the mobile node's home IP address and then tunnel and transmit those datagrams to the mobile node's care-of address (which might be transmitted directly to the node or to the foreign agent first). The home agent checks the destination IP address in the header of the datagram to see if it is exactly equivalent to any of its mobile nodes registered in a foreign network and accordingly tunnels or drops the seized datagrams. Tunneling also enables the exchange of ICMP messages redirected to the original senders if some trouble or error is generated during the datagram's transmission; this is called the *tunnel soft state mechanism.*

Mobile nodes have the ability to send datagrams directly to routers or hosts using available routing algorithms. Datagrams sent from mobile nodes are certainly no compelled do not have to go to the home agent.

There are two forms of care-of addresses: (1) the foreign agent care-of address and (2) co-located care-of address. The *foreign agent care-of address* represents the IP address of the foreign agent and is provided by *agent advertisement* messages. This means that the datagrams sent by the home agent to the mobile node of such a care-of address will arrive first at the foreign agent. The foreign agent itself will decapsulate the mobility and additional headers off these tunneled datagrams and send them to the mobile node. The advantage of this form is that it allows multiple mobile nodes to share the same care-of addresses, which will save many IP addresses for other uses.

On the other hand, the *co-located care-of address* is the one obtained by other external mechanisms to represent the IP address of the mobile node as a local IP address. It could be a temporary IP address automatically generated by the node itself via the *dynamic host configuration protocol* (DHCP) or an assigned permanent IP address to be used whenever the mobile node is in a foreign network. In this form, the mobile node itself represents the care-of address and is responsible for the tunneling and decapsulation of the received datagrams. The advantage of co-located care-of address is the absence of any intermediate (foreign agent) intervention.

In a foreign network, the mobile node cannot exchange datagrams with the foreign agent using direct and standard IP-routing protocols because those protocols rely once and for all on the destination IP address (in this case, the home IP address of the mobile node) presented in the header of the datagrams. The solution is that the foreign agent and mobile node have a common network gate or interface with the attaching link between both of them in which the mobile node and the foreign agent seize the use of standard IP-routing protocols and exchange packets via the link layer level.

INTERNET PROTOCOL 6

The Internet has become a basic element in every aspect of life, leading to huge demands and tremendous consumption of IP addresses to host different Web applications and commercial Web sites, and so on. This demand has steadily grown, making IP addresses scarcer each day. A solution to this problem is the new IP protocol called *IPv6.*

The main improvements of IPv6 over the current IPv4 are the new address and header structures. The IPv4 header is shown in Figure 12, and the IPv6 header appears in Figure 13.

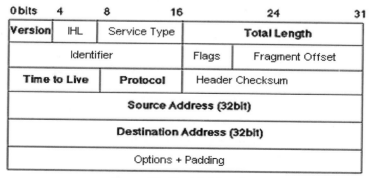

Figure 12: The IPv4 header

IPv6 Header Structure

The *version* represents the protocol used to send this packet. The *class* (traffic class) is used only by the source hosts and forwarding routers to specify certain classes and priorities provided for the IPv6 datagram. The purpose is to provide some QOS capabilities such as integrated and differentiated service models for the new IPv6 packets in a simpler manner than the complicated configuration of classifying streams.

The *flow label* is used to specify the type of QOS handling required for a datagram sent from a specific source address to a specific destination. Datagrams that share the same flow must be sent with the same source address, destination address, and flow label, and datagrams that do not belong to any flow have a flow label value of 0.

Payload length is the size of the rest of the datagram, including the extension headers.

The *next header* describes the header type following this header. The values are similar to that used for IPv4. Table 8 shows some of the possible values.

Table 8: Next Header Field Possible Values

Decimal Value	Header
0	Hop-by-hop options
1	ICMP
2	IGMP
6	TCP
17	UDP
41	Encapsulated IPv6
43	Routing
44	Fragment
46	RSVP
50	Encapsulating security payload
51	Authentication
58	ICMPv6
59	No next header
60	Destination options

The *hop limit* field is the maximum number of hops that this datagram should go through. On each passed hop, the hop limit is decremented by one; if the value reaches zero, then the datagram is dropped.

The *source address* represents the 128-bit address of the source host, and the *destination address* represents the 128-bit address of the destination host.

In addition to the standard header, a set of additional extension headers cooperates with it. The set should have the same sequence of order summed up in the following:

1. Hop-by-hop options header
2. Destination options header (for mediatory destinations)
3. Routing header
4. Fragment header
5. Authentication header
6. Encapsulating security payload header
7. Destination options header (final)
8. Upper-layer header

When the next header field value is equivalent to 59 in the IPv6 header or any extension header, this reveals that no header follows.

The Hop-by-Hop Options Header

The *hop-by-hop options header* is used to set some values and options inspected by each hop (node) along the datagram's delivery route to the destination (see Figure 14).

The *next header* defines the header type to follow this header.

The *header extension length* is the total size of the hop-by-hop options header without the first eight octets, and it is presented in eight-octet units.

Options is a variable field; its length can be any multiple of eight-octet blocks, and it describes some the predefined options such as the *pad 1*, which corresponds to one-octet padding; *pad n*, which corresponds to *n*-octets padding; and other options.

Destination Options Header

The *destination options header* is used to set certain options inspected only by destination nodes along the datagram's delivery route. This header might represent the destination options for both the intermediate destinations and the final destination but in two separate headers

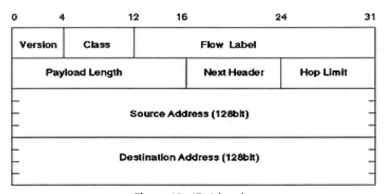

Figure 13: IPv6 header

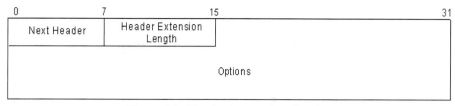

Figure 14: Hop-by-hop options header

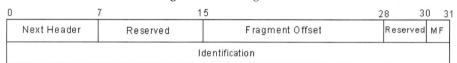

Figure 15: Destination options header

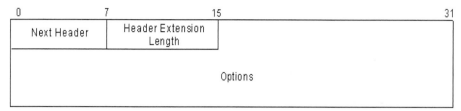

Figure 16: Routing header

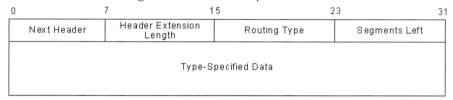

Figure 17: Fragment header

(see Figure 15). The fields included in this header have the same description as the ones included in the hop-by-hop options header.

Routing Header

The *routing header* identifies the nodes (routers) to be visited along the datagram's route to the destination (see Figure 16).

The *routing type* indicates a particular routing header variant. The *segments left* field is the number of remaining route nodes still to be visited preceding the destination; the value is decremented in each visited router. If segments left is equal to 0, then the receiving node ignores this header and advances to process the next one.

The *type-specified data* is a multiple of an eight-octet variable that is dependent on the routing type. If routing type is 0, then the type-specified data is nothing but the addresses of the intermediate destinations to be visited.

Fragment Header

In the *fragment header*, fragmentation takes place in a separate header extension; this is unlike the IPv4 datagram, which is included in the same header. The fragment header is used whenever a source node needs to transmit a datagram that is larger than the MTU allowed across the path leading to the destination.

Unlike IPv4, fragmentation is carried out only by the source node, not by routers along the destination path (see Figure 17).

The *reserved fields*, which are zeros, are ignored in each receiving node and preserved for future needs. The *fragment offset* identifies the order or sequence of the fragment relative to the start of the fragmentable part of the original datagram.

The *more flag* (MF) section is either 1, which means more fragments follow; or 0, which means the header carrying datagram is the last fragment.

The *identification* is a unique number assigned by the source node and specifies a single value to all fragments of the original datagram. In this way, the destination host can recognize different arriving fragments and assemble the ones with the same identification, along with the same combination of source and destination addresses.

To send datagrams that are too large to fit in the MTU of the delivery path, source nodes may apportion the datagram into several fragments, each considered as a separate packet to be reassembled in the end at the destination node as presented in Figure 16 (see Figure 18).

The Authentication Header

The *authentication header* offers data verification, data integrity, and data origin authentication for datagrams. It also offers protection against replays, an optional service chosen by the receiving node whenever a *security association* (SA) is present (see Figure 19).

The *payload length* identifies size of the authentication header represented in eight-octet units. If the authentication is zero, then the value of this field equals 2.

| Unfragmentable part | First fragment | Second fragment | ... | Last fragment |

Original datagram

| Unfragmentable fragment | Fragment header | First fragment |
| Unfragmentable fragment | Fragment header | Second fragment |

.
.
.

| Unfragmentable Fragment | Fragment Header | Last Fragment |

Figure 18: Large datagram and its corresponding fragments

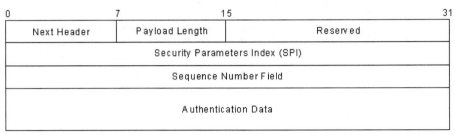

Figure 19: The authentication header

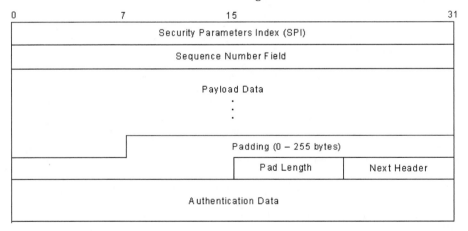

Figure 20: Encapsulating security payload header

Security parameters index (SPI) specifies the SA associated with the datagram. The SPI of value 0 is reserved for local, and values ranging from 1 to 255 are reserved by the IANA for future implementation.

The *sequence number field* is an incrementing counter that sets the antireplay. If the antireplay is activated (default case), then the sequence number is seized and should be reset for the sender and receiver.

Authentication data is a variable field of multiple eight-octet units, which describes the *integrity check value* (ICV) for the datagram through an authentication algorithm. Examples of the implemented authentication algorithms are the *data encryption standard* (DES) and *message digest* (MD5).

Encapsulating Security Payload Header

The *encapsulating security payload header* provides confidentiality, data origin authentication, connectionless data integrity, an optional antireplay feature, and limited traffic-flow confidentiality. The combination of offered services may vary—for example, confidentiality could be presented independently of all other services. This header can be associated with the authentication header to combine confidentiality and authentication features; this would lead to a higher degree of security and privacy (see Figure 20).

SPI, sequence number field, and authentication data are all of the same as in the authentication header. The *payload data* is a variable field of multiple eight-octet units that contains the data encapsulated within the header.

The *padding* field fills the header with nonfunctional data of size range between zero and 255 bytes presented in zeros or as random binary data based on many factors such as the implemented algorithm. The padding can be thought of as a privacy supporter that hides the actual size of the datagram and conceals a network's traffic information.

The *pad length* specifies the total size of the padding field presented in the header. The value of this field ranges from zero to 255.

Upper-Layer Header

Also known as the *pseudo header*, the *upper-layer header* has been modified to include the compulsory checksum computation over 128-bit addresses. Transport layer (upper layer) for IPv4 includes 32-bit source and destination addresses, whereas in IPv6 the structure should incorporate the 128-bit addresses of both source and destination nodes in order to execute their checksum over the TCP or UDP stream.

In IPv4, the checksum incorporated in UDP datagrams is optional. In IPv6, the checksum in the pseudo header is obligatory. IPv6 destination nodes dispose of UDP datagrams that have a zero checksum, and in turn transmit an ICMPv6 error message (see Figure 21).

The same pseudo header structure is also used for the ICMPv6 checksum. The *source address* is the 128-bit address of the sending node. The *destination address* represents the address of the final destination, even if the datagram has a routing header. The *next header* specifies the implemented link layer protocol (6 for TCP, or 17 for UDP). It might yet vary if there are extension headers that come in-between.

The *upper-layer packet length* is the size of the upper-layer header along with the data (TCP header plus TCP data or UDP header plus UDP data).

Addressing

The most obvious distinguishing part of IPv6 is its possession of much larger sizes of addresses. The size of an address in IPv6 is 128 bits, which is four times the larger than an IPv4 address. A 32-bit address space allows for 2^{32} (4,294,967,296) potential addresses, whereas IPv6 allows 2^{128} potential addresses.

The representation of addresses is also quite different from IPV4. Whereas IPv4 notates the addresses in four binary segments separated by dots, IPv6's 128-bit address is divided into 16-bit boundaries, and each 16-bit block is converted to a four-digit hexadecimal number and delimited by colons. The originated format is referred as *colon-hexadecimal*.

An example of the address format is:

```
00DA:04D3:0000:0000:2F 3C:02BA:0000:872D
```

IPv6 representation can be further simplified by removing the leading zeros within each sixteen-bit block. However, each block must have at least a single digit. Because of the suppression of the leading zero, the address becomes more simplified. Furthermore, multiple entire zero-value blocks can be compacted to only a double colon—::—and it is only done once in a single address so the number of zeros can be determined just as in the following:

```
DA:4D3::2F3C:2BA:0:872D
```

Note that the sole zero is still there; if it were compressed, then the number of zeros in the first double colon—::—and in the second would be ambiguous, so the compression should be used only once in each address to be able to identify it.

Subnetting is also supported in IPv6 addresses through subnet prefixes that exactly resemble IPv4's CIDR, where the notation is presented as address- or prefix-length just as in the following:

```
DA:4D3::2F3C:2BA:0:872D/64
```

The utilization of 128 bits for the IPv6 addresses awards superior levels of hierarchy and flexibility that eventually equip the Internet with upgraded hierarchical addressing and routing mechanisms.

Address types supported in IPv4 are also supported in the IPv6: unicast and multicast addresses.

Also, a new address type called *anycast* is supported only in IPv6; it defines an address that is allocated to multiple interfaces of usually different routers, where a datagram sent to one anycast address will be directed to the nearest interface with same address. Anycast addresses are typically assigned out of the unicast addresses. So, considering a case of a unicast address pointing to multiple interfaces, it becomes an anycast address and is no longer a unicast address. Anycast can be useful in determining the routers in a definite domain or in a subnet or determining particular routes through a certain service provider's gateways.

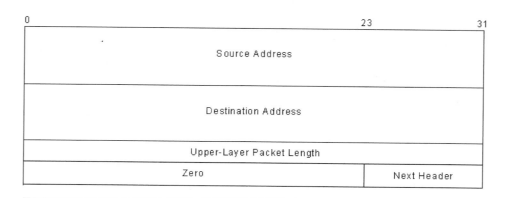

Figure 21: Upper-layer header

Summary of Features

What characterizes the IPv6 is the set of features and extensions that provide entire and enhanced network surroundings.

Larger numbers of addresses are made possible (128 bits instead of 32 bits), address configuration is made easier, and all types of datagrams can be expanded. Header format has become simpler than that specified for the older version to improve the performance and speed of datagrams processing in the network.

More enhanced options have been introduced with no restrictions and space limitations on the options in general, which creates more flexible protocol and easier adaptability to future modifications or additions.

IPv6 can be configured automatically through *plug and play*, reducing the administration and deployment overhead. Configuration can be done through DHCP server or without it by automatically configuring the use of IPv6 addresses in the link.

QOS is effectively supported by introducing the flow label field in the datagram header (labels defined for specific datagram streams), which makes QOS more applicable than in IPv4.

Authentication, confidentiality, and security options that guarantee the datagrams' integrity and privacy through the network are appended to the collection of options extensions.

Finally, efficient interoperability and backward compatibility with IPv4 is supported.

IPV4 AND IPV6 INTEROPERABILITY

Because IPv4 has been widely spread all over the globe's networks and the Internet and its address space is becoming scarce, using IPv6 becomes more attractive. It is impossible to immediately replace all deployed IPv4 addresses by IPv6, so the solution is to have them both interoperable and coexistent. *Tunneling, dual stacking,* and *translation* are all proposed solutions in preserving interoperability between IPv6 and IPv4.

Tunneling

To put up with IPv4 nodes, IPv6 nodes should support the entire IPv4 execution model. These types of nodes—which are supposed to be able to carry out both IPv6 and IPv4 implementation—are called *IPv6/IPv4 nodes*. IPv6/IPv4 nodes have the capability to exchange both sorts of datagrams (IPv4 and IPv6), and they can communicate straightforwardly with both IPv4 and IPv6 nodes.

Tunneling—or *IPv6-over-IPv4 tunneling*—is a way of seeking interoperability between both versions of IP. IPv6 datagrams are wrapped inside IPv4, enabling them to be transmitted through IPv4 networks and gateways.

The *encapsulating source node* (or *entry node*) prepares an IPv4 header and encapsulates the IPv6 datagram with it before transmitting it through a tunnel. When the encapsulated datagram arrives, the *decapsulating node* (or *exit node*) accepts it, eliminates the IPv4 header, and processes the IPv6 datagram. It recognizes that the encapsulated datagram is an IPv6 one by checking the protocol field; if it is equivalent to 41, then the decapsulating node detaches and discards the IPv4 header and forwards the IPv6 datagram to the upper layer (see Figure 22).

Configured tunneling and *automatic tunneling* are two means of applying the tunneling mechanism over an internetwork. By using configured tunneling, the end-point address of the tunnel is concluded from the configuration information in the source node that encapsulates the datagram. The tunnels' end-point addresses should be stored somehow in the encapsulating node. When the node transmits the datagram via a tunnel, the destination of that datagram is determined from the tunnel's end point address itself.

Routing tables contribute to the tunneling decision, specifying whether the datagrams require tunneling or not, based on the destinations stored in these tables.

Automatic tunneling, on the other hand, has the tunnels' end-point addresses specified by the datagram itself. The tunnel extracts the 32-bit IPv4 compatible address of the destination from the datagram's header and considers it as the destination address of the datagram. If a datagram's addresses are not IPv4 compatible, then such datagrams cannot be tunneled automatically. An IPv6 address is 128 bits long; its IPv4 compatibility is determined by comparing a static routing table record of prefix value (0:0:0:0:0:0/96) with the address in the IPv6 header. If the two prefixes are similar, then the address is IPv4 compatible and the automatic tunneling is carried out. This guarantees that only IPv6 addresses that have IPv4 addresses

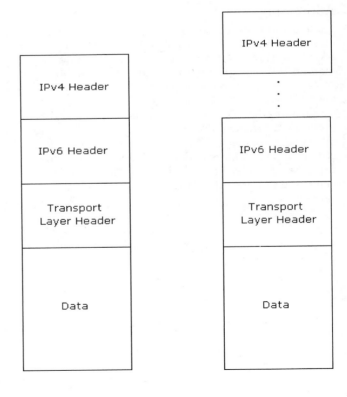

Encapsulation   Decapsulation

Figure 22: Encapsulation and decapsulation of IPv6 datagrams in and out of IPv4 datagrams

format in their last (low-order) 32 bits and that match this prefix criteria qualify for automatic tunneling.

Dual Stacking

The dual stack IPv6-dominant transition mechanism (DSTM) is another proposed technique to handle the interoperability between IPv4 and IPv6. It concentrates on the deployment of the new IPv6 networks and the capability to interchange datagrams with existing IPv4 networks.

DSTM applies existing protocols and does not define its own protocol or algorithm; it uses Ethernet, fiber distributed data interface (FDDI), or point-to-point protocol (PPP) in physical layers and the same protocol in upper layers that can bear both versions of datagrams (see Figure 23).

In DTSM, the address server allocates IPv4 addresses to the network nodes using certain protocols such as DHCPv6. DTSM concentrates on having IPv6 dominant, so IPv6 routing tables and mechanisms are used, which will lessen management overhead for IPv4 interoperability.

When DTSM client nodes acquire the assigned IPv4 addresses, the IPv4 datagram to be transmitted is encapsulated in an IPv6 header and transmitted through *tunnel end points* (TEPs) until it reaches a DTSM border router.

The *dynamic tunnel interface* (DTI) enables the client nodes to send an IPv4 datagram over the IPv6 TEP as well as receive IPv4 datagrams from IPv6 TEP. It is the DTSM server's responsibility to provide the TEPs for all DTSM nodes.

The border router decapsulates the encapsulated IPv4 datagram, discards the IPv6 header, and forwards the datagram to the destination node as if it is in normal IPv4 architecture.

The DSTM address pool module provides IPv4 addresses to allow DSTM clients to obtain unique IPv4 addresses. The lifetime of an address is also preserved in the pool and can be supplied to the client node along with the address.

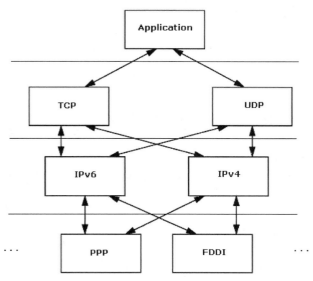

Figure 23: Dual stack

Translating (Network Address Translation)

Network address translation (NAT) can be also used in the transition between IPv4 and IPv6. *Translation* means altering an IPv4 address to another. As for interoperability, however, the core is in either translating IPv4 addresses to IPv6 addresses, IPv6 addresses to IPv4 addresses, or both by applying *NAT protocol translation* (NAT-PT).

NAT-PT assigns IPv4 addresses to IPv6 nodes out of an address pool that contains only global unique IPv4 addresses; it then prepares sessions in which IPv6 network and IPv4 network addresses are bound and communication is thus established between the different networks. Routing throughout this whole process is transparent between both networks' end-point nodes. However, the session between both nodes that enables the sending and receiving of datagrams must maintain the same route as well as the same router.

There are two sorts of NAT-PT: traditional and bidirectional. *Traditional NAT-PT* sessions are unidirectional, only outgoing from the IPv6 network. In *bidirectional NAT-PT*, the sessions allow flow in both directions between IPv4 and IPv6 networks.

Traditional NAT-PT is also divided into two classes: *basic NAT-PT* and NAT-PT. The first translates the source IP address and other fields such as IP, TCP, UDP, and ICMP header checksums of IPV6 outgoing datagrams, or the destination IP address and fields in case of incoming datagrams scenario. The latter translates all those previously mentioned plus transport identifiers such as the TCP and UDP ports and the ICMP query IDs.

In bidirectional NAT-PT, the sessions across the two networks are constructed in either's node, which means that both the IPv4 and IPv6 networks' nodes are capable of initiating such connections or sessions. An IPv4 node should resolve the IPv6 network's node address via DNS in order to access it and vice versa.

INTERNET PROTOCOL SECURITY AND VIRTUAL PRIVATE NETWORKS

Internet Protocol Security

Internet protocol security (IPSec) is a security-based mechanism at the IP layer level that provides IPv4 and IPv6 with a useful set of security services. Access control, connectionless integrity, data-origin authentication, antireplay protection, encryption techniques, and traffic-flow confidentiality are all included in the IPSec services framework.

IPSec is one outcome of many applied methods involving the *authentication header* (AH), the *encapsulating security payload header* (ESP), and cryptographic key algorithms.

The implementation of such services in one's network traffic does not compromise the communication with other networks that use either different security techniques and algorithms or no security services at all for their traffic, which guarantees the interoperability between networks that implement different IPSec mechanisms.

Routers that implement an IPSec are called *security routers* or *security gateways*. Usually, IPSec operates in hosts or security gateway networks based on defined algorithms stored in a database called a *security policy database* (SPD) and managed by the network administrator or a network application. Certain fields in datagram headers are accessed in the SPD and the relevant process for these datagrams is determined: drop them, allow them to pass, or grant them IPSec services.

Security association (SA) is the environment or connection that handles the security services accompanied by the traffic stream. It is the part that completes the whole concept of security services and IPSec, making use of AH or ESP, which are IPSec mechanisms. For a communication between two nodes, two SAs are required (one for every stream direction).

Two distinct modes are supported in SA: transport mode and tunnel mode. In the transport mode, the SA is associated between two hosts (not routers). If ESP is used, then a transport mode SA provides security services only for higher-layer protocols, not reaching the IP header or any header before the ESP header. In the case of AH, the security services reach parts of the IP header, extension headers, and some options within the IPv4 header: the IPv6 hop-by-hop options header or the IPv6 destination extension headers.

In tunnel mode, SA is provided between either two hosts—a host and a security router—or security routers. Security routers do not support the transport mode, so if any security router is on a communication edge then the incorporated SA is tunnel mode.

Two headers are used in tunnel mode SA: the outer and inner IP headers. The outer IP header relates to the IPSec processing destination (*mediatory destination*), whereas the inner IP header defines the final destination.

If AH is applied in this mode, IPSec's SA is supplied to the entire tunneled datagram along with the inner IP header and the upper-layer protocol header, as well as portions of the outer IP header mentioned in the transport mode. But if ESP is applied, then only the tunneled datagram obtains select security services. Nevertheless, ESP-based tunnel mode can be used to provide some kind of confidential traffic stream between two security routers because of the encryption of the inner IP header, which maintains the low profiles of the source and the destination. This applies to the dynamic connectivity of mobile nodes to a network in tunneled ESP SA under the protection of a firewall.

Virtual Private Networks

A *virtual private network* (VPN) is a network that links remote clients or sites with each other within a surrounding backbone via virtual gateways.

Companies and enterprises can allow their remote users, clients, employees, and any other party to access their private networks via secure virtual connections (basically, tunnels) that direct them to the Internet and the specified backbone that surrounds the VPNs, providing more simplicity and scalability instead of connecting them via heavy dedicated connections such as WANs.

To make it simple, remote entities in a network can link in a secure scalable behavior through routing to the Internet to reach their private LAN.

All of the sites in a VPN could belong to a single enterprise; in this way, a VPN is considered an intranet. If the sites belong to distinct parties, then this kind of VPN is called an *extranet*. A VPN site can be in both an intranet and one or more extranets, which means there are no restrictions in belonging to different VPNs.

Edge devices are used to configure VPNs and connectivity between sites and clients. *Provider edge* (PE) routers link to *customer edge* (CE) routers or switch at a definite data link level such as Ethernet, PPP, frame relay, and so forth. In this way, the whole connection is established to enable remote access of authorized clients to VPN sites.

Remote clients can connect to the Internet using whatever attainable connectivity method—as fast as DSL or cable or as slow as a dialup connection—and then reach the VPN server at a certain enterprise or corporate site.

To ensure a massive boundary of security handling, IPSec is applied in the surrounding backbone of a VPN to ensure authentication, privacy, encryption, and other security services offered by its core.

Other security modules and procedures include having *authentication, authorization, and accounting* (AAA) servers, symmetric and public key encryptions, and firewalls that prevent communication with unauthorized users or data. When appended, QOS features give more functionality as well as intensive reliability and throughput.

VPNs are considered valuable alternatives to network structures such as WANs and LANs. Instead of using both of these latter structures, VPN can handle connectivity no matter the geographic distance via secured, encrypted, and scalable links.

Extending geographic connectivity, improving security (through IPSec, AAA servers, etc.), improving throughput and productivity, offering global and remote connectivity and compatibility, simplifying the network topology, and saving cost and time are all advantages of VPNs.

GLOSSARY

Address resolution protocol (ARP): A protocol that maps a host's network layer address (e.g., IP address), to the hardware address (e.g., MAC address).

Anycast: A routing scheme in which the best (i.e., nearest) destination among a set of destinations will receive the packet.

Bellman-Ford algorithm: An algorithm that can figure out the shortest path between two nodes in a weighted graph, even if some of the weights are negative.

Border gateway protocol (BGP): A routing protocol that routes packets between autonomous systems. It is considered to be the core routing protocol of the Internet.

Checksum: A value that accompanies a piece of data (e.g., a packet) that helps determine whether these data have changed (i.e., corrupted) between a source and a destination. For example, a checksum may be the number of set bits in a packet.

Classless interdomain routing (CIDR): An IP addressing technique that replaced the IP address classes (A, B, C, D, and E). It allowed combining networks in supernets, reducing routing overhead.

Datagram: An entity of data that could be transmitted over a network. It carries information (e.g., source address, destination address) that allows it to be transmitted from a source to a node.

Denial of service (DOS) attack: An attack that intends to wastefully consume network resources. A DOS attack overloads a network by sending excessive traffic that the network cannot accommodate.

Differentiated services (DiffServ): A mechanism for assigning classes to network traffic so that certain traffic classes get precedence over other classes. For example, voice traffic—which needs low latency—may get precedence over e-mail and Web traffic. DiffServ is a QOS technique.

Dijkstra algorithm: An algorithm that can figure out the shortest path between two nodes in a weighted graph when the all the weights are non-negatives.

Distance vector multicast routing protocol (DVMRP): A protocol based on RIP for multicasting a packet over an IP network.

Domain name system (DNS): Allows communication with a host without knowing its hard-to-remember IP address (e.g., 141.218.143.20) by associating human-readable names (e.g. www.cs.wmich.edu) to hosts. Translating between such two addresses is done through a domain name server.

Dynamic host configuration protocol (DHCP): Enables a device on an IP network to request and receive an IP address from a server. It simplifies networks administration.

Ethernet: A local area network (LAN) architecture that uses bus or star topology. Ethernet defines standards for both the physical and data-link layers.

Exterior gateway protocol (EGP): A protocol used to exchange routing tables between neighboring autonomous systems.

Forwarding equivalence class (FEC): A group of packets are treated the same with respect to their forwarding path and how they are forwarded. Such packets exhibit similar properties.

Host: A device connected to a network (e.g., a computer). For TCP/IP networks, every host is identified by an IP address.

Integrated services (IntServ): A QOS architecture that depends on allocating required resources to deliver data before sending the actual data.

Interior gateway protocol (IGP): Protocol used to exchange routing information within an autonomous system.

Internet control message protocol (ICMP): An extension to the IP that is used to relay information such as "a datagram cannot reach its destination" and "this host is not reachable."

Internet protocol (IP): A network layer protocol that facilitates exchanging packets among hosts in a network.

Internet protocol security (IPSec): A group of protocols that is intended to secure IP packets through encryption and authentication.

Label-switching path (LSP): A path within an MPLS network.

Label-switching router (LSR): A special router used by MPLS networks to relay labels.

Link state advertisement (LSA): Message sent by a router to communicate needed information for the OSPF routing protocol to work. There are five types of LSAs.

Maximum transmission unit (MTU): The maximum size of a packet that can be handled by a given networking device (e.g., a router).

Multicast open shortest path first (MOSPF): A multicast routing protocol.

Multicast routing or multicasting: Sending the same packet to different destinations.

Multiprotocol label switching (MPLS): A protocol that integrates parts of layers 2 and 3.

Netstat: A utility program for Windows and UNIX-based operating systems that retrieves information about current network connections and routing tables.

Network: Two or more computers connected together via a communications medium.

Network address translation (NAT): The rewriting of an IP address when a packet is going through a router or a firewall. Usually, NAT is used to protect hosts and reduce the number of IP addresses used by a network.

Open shortest path first (OSPF): A link-state routing protocol that depends on sending LSAs to other routers within a network.

Payload: Data carried by a packet.

Point-to-point protocol (PPP): Protocol used to establish a direct connection between two nodes in a network.

Quality of service (QOS): The ability to guarantee a specific level of service in terms of throughput, delay, and so on by prioritizing traffic so that more important traffic receives better service.

Quagga: A free routing software suite that provides implementation of many routing protocols (e.g., OSPF, RIP, and BGP).

Resource reservation protocol–traffic engineering (RSVP/TE): A protocol that allows resources to be reserved throughout a path for traffic.

Routing information protocol (RIP): The most enduring interior gateway protocol routing protocol. RIP works by sending out routing information periodically and whenever the network topology changes. When a router receives new routing information, it updates its own table.

Simple network management protocol (SNMP): A part of the IP protocol (application layer) that is used to manage network devices and solve network problems. It is used mainly by network administrators.

Subnet: Short for *subnetwork*. A network belonging to an organization can be divided into subnetworks. Typically, a subnetwork is served by a router and shares a common IP address prefix.

Supernet: A group of contiguous subnetworks addressed as a single subnet.

Throughput: The amount of data transmitted from one node to another in a given amount of time.

Transmission control protocol (TCP): The most commonly used transport layer protocol. It provides reliable communications over the unreliable IP protocol.

The combination of TCP and IP is referred to as *TCP/IP*.

User datagram protocol (UDP): A transport layer protocol that gives no reliability guarantees. Packets transmitted using UDP may arrive out of order or be dropped without notice.

Virtual private network (VPN): A private network owned by an organization but built from publicly available resources. For example, the Internet could be used as a communication medium for a private network. Typically, a VNP is secured via authentication and encryption.

Wireless fidelity (Wi-Fi): A set of standards and technologies that allows wireless connection to a network through an access point.

CROSS REFERENCES

See *Data Communications Basics; Data Link Layer Protocols; Session, Presentation and Application Layer Protocols; Transport Layer Protocols.*

REFERENCES

Adams, A., J. Nicholas, and W. Siadak. 1994. Protocol independent multicast—dense mode (PIM-DM): Protocol specification (revised). RFC 3973, NextHop Technologies, ITT A/CD, NextHop Technologies, March 1994.

Atkinson, R., and S. Kent. 1998. IP authentication header. RFC 2402, @Home Network, BBN Corp, November 1998.

———. 1998. Security architecture for the Internet protocol. RFC 2401, @Home Network, BBN Corp, November 1998.

Blake, S., Black, D., Carlson, M., Davies, E., Wang, Z., and W. Weiss. 1998. An architecture for differentiated services. RFC 2475, Torrent Networking Technologies, EMC Corporation, Sun Microsystems, Nortel UK, Bell Labs Lucent Technologies, Lucent Technologies, December 1998.

Braden, R., Clark, D., and S. Shenker. 1994. Integrated services in the Internet architecture: An overview. RFC 1633, ISI, MIT, Xerox PARC, June 1994.

Clark, D. 1982. IP datagrams reassembly algorithms. RFC 815, MIT, July 1982.

Deering, S. 1989. Host extensions for IP multicasting. RFC 1112, Stanford University, August 1989.

———, and R. Hinden. 1998. Internet protocol, version 6 (IPv6) specification. RFC 2460, Cisco Systems, Nokia, December 1998.

———, and R. Hinden. 1998. Internet protocol version 6 (IPv6) addressing architecture. RFC 3513, Cisco Systems, Nokia, December 1998.

Egevang, K., and P. Francis. 1994. The IP network address translator. RFC 1631, Cray Communications, NTT, May 1994.

El Zarki, M., and J. Liebeherr. 2003. *Mastering networks: An Internet lab manual.* Boston: Addison-Wesley.

Estrin, D., Farinacci, D., Helmy, A., Thaler, D., Deering, S., Handley, M., Jacobson, V., Liu, C., Sharma, P., and L. Wei. 1998. Protocol independent multicast-sparse mode (PIM-SM): protocol specification. RFC 2362, USC, Cisco Systems, USC, UMICH, XEROX, UCL, LBL, USC, USC, Cisco Systems, June 1998.

Fuller, V., Li, T., Yu, J., and K. Varadhan. 1993. CIDR address strategy. RFC 1519, BARRNet, Cisco Systems, MERIT, OARNet, September 1993.

Gilligan, R., and E. Nordmark. 1996. Transition mechanisms for IPv6 hosts and routers. RFC 1933, Sun Microsystems Inc, April 1996.

Huston, G.. 2000. Next steps for the IP QOS architecture. RFC 2990, Telstra, November 2000.

Miyakawa, A., Shirasaki, Y., Takenouchi, A., and T. Yamazaki. 2005. A model of IPv6/IPv4 dual stack Internet access service. RFC 4241, NTT Communications, December 2005.

Mogul, J. 1984. Internet subnets. RFC 917, Stanford University, October 1984.

Moy, J. 1991. The OSPF specification version 2. RFC 1247, Proteon Inc, January 1991.

———. 1994. Multicast extensions to OSPF. RFC 1584, Proteon Inc, March 1994.

Partridge, C., Waitzman, D., and S. Deering. 1988. Distance vector multicast routing protocol. RFC 1075, BBN STC, Stanford University, November 1988.

Perkins, C. 1996. IP mobility support. RFC 2002, IBM, October 1996.

Postel, J. 1981. Internet protocol. RFC 791, USC/Information Sciences Institute, September 1981.

———. 1983. The TCP maximum segment size. RFC 879, USC/Information Sciences Institute, November 1983.

Rekhter, Y., and E. Rosen. 1999. BGP/MPLS VPNs. RFC 2547, Cisco Systems, March 1999.

Rosen, E., Callon, R., and A. Viswanathan. 2001. Multiprotocol label switching architecture. RFC 3031, Cisco Systems, Inc., Juniper Networks Inc, Force10 Networks Inc, January 2001.

Srisuresh, P., and G. Tsirtsis. 2000. Network address translation–protocol translation (NAT-PT). RFC 2766, Campio Communications, BT, February 2000.

Steenstrup, M. 1993. An architecture for inter-domain policy routing. RFC 1478, BBN Systems and Technologies, June 1993.

Stevens, R.. 1994. *TCP/IP illustrated.* Vol. 1: *The protocols.* Boston: Addison-Wesley, 1994.

Transport Layer Protocols

Vassilis Tsaoussidis, *Democritus University of Thrace, Xanthi, Greece*

INTRODUCTION

Transport protocols are designed to deliver data to the network layer at the sender side and receive data from the same layer at the receiver's end in order to deliver it to the appropriate application protocol. Therefore, the functionality and efficiency of the transport layer determines the ability of applications to operate effectively. However, application service demands vary widely. Some—such as e-mail, HTTP, and FTP—require reliable data delivery along with a fast service; others, such as multimedia applications, may emphasize speedy transmission, even at the cost of reliability. Although the diversity of applications may imply a corresponding diversity of transport protocols, in practice two main protocols handle transmissions for a wide range of applications at the transport layer: the *transmission control protocol* (TCP) (RFC 793)* and the *user datagram protocol* (UDP) (RFC 768). The latter has been introduced as a simple protocol that allows programmers to build required functionality on top of it. The former began as a protocol with enhanced functionality that includes reliability, data sequencing, and flow control; it has evolved as a sophisticated protocol that manages congestion control and stability and also allows for fair resource allocation in dynamic and heterogeneous systems.

In both protocols, functionality is encoded in the protocol header and appears in each data packet. Therefore, each packet needs to have at least a structure appropriate for recording the process where data need to be delivered. Communication at this layer is enabled through the use of port numbers that identify each process. The 16-bit field of the packet header allows for 65,000 distinct ports; the first 1023 are reserved from application protocols such as FTP (port 21), telnet (port 23), and HTTP (port 80). That said, each receiver's application "listens" to some predetermined port; the transport layer delivers the data to that particular port, enabling data demultiplexing at that level.

Transport layer functions, however, need to handle efficient delivery of data as well, not just demultiplex data correctly. Efficiency here involves several aspects such as ordering of packets, flow, and congestion control. Therefore, functionality has been developed for packet sequencing, receiver buffer reporting, and estimation of network dynamics, coupled with corresponding transmission strategies. The latter has been one of the major research problems at that layer because of its complexity: Balancing efficient channel utilization, fair resource allocation, and network stability in a dynamically changing environment with unknown number of flows, unknown bandwidth, and asynchronous service times was definitely not an easy task. The design target has evolved around the concept of network equilibrium, its characteristics, and convergence dynamics. That complexity did not allow for mathematically tractable optimal solutions; optimization also had to be experimentally valid.

Today, TCP is the dominant protocol for most Internet applications, whereas UDP is the protocol of choice for most real-time applications. However, new protocols have emerged today to support specific applications such as IP telephony.

We discuss the core functions of the transport layer, such as the sliding window, flow control, and congestion control along with corresponding performance metrics. We also detail the theoretical basis for the mechanisms incorporated into TCP. We then discuss various versions of TCP and present new protocols along with a prescribed framework for potential improvements. We detail the *stream control transmission protocol* (SCTP) as the designated transport protocol for telephony of IP networks, and we present the recently emerging new classes of transport protocols. We then describe the collaborative nature of the transport and network layer from the perspective of transport protocols.

---

*Requests for Comments can be found at www.rfc-editor.org/rfc.html

CORE FUNCTIONS AT THE TRANSPORT LAYER

The *transmission control protocol* (Postel 1981) is the dominant protocol at the transport layer. It carries more than 95 percent of the Internet traffic and allows for reliable data delivery, packet* reordering, flow, and congestion control. However, TCP functionality is not optional; that is, applications do not have the luxury of selecting only some particular set of TCP functions. Within this context, the protocol may not be appropriate for applications that intend to exploit network trade-offs. For example, multimedia applications may need to favor transmission speed at the cost of reliability or fairness at the cost of efficiency. Traditionally, the alternative choice has been the *user datagram protocol* (UDP), a protocol with almost no functionality. Indeed, UDP has only functionality for demultiplexing of data. In support of this argument, we present the protocol's header in Figure 1.

We note that even basic error detection is optional in UDP. However, the design choice of an almost-no-functionality protocol at this layer was not coincidental. A programmer may use the demultiplexing functions of the protocol (the combination of source-destination port) to deliver data to the appropriate process and incorporate the functionality of choice within the application protocols. In this way one can avoid the obligatory functions of TCP and exploit the performance trade-offs for the benefit of the application protocol. The lack of functionality is also reflected in the protocol header; its simplicity also contributes to render UDP a fast communication protocol.

On the contrary, TCP includes functionality for the following operations:

- connection establishment and termination,
- graduated consumption and detection of available bandwidth,
- reliability of transmission,
- packet ordering,
- flow control, and
- congestion avoidance and control.

We describe next the protocol functionality as it is encoded in the protocol's header. Note that the transport layer may also contribute in path *maximum transmission unit* (MTU) discovery, which traditionally belongs to the IP layer. A relevant working group exists (the PMTUD working group) that aims to specify a robust method for determining the IP maximum transmission unit supported over an end-to-end path. Various weakness in the current methods are documented in RFC 2923 and have proven to be a chronic impediment to the deployment of new technologies that alter the path MTU such as tunnels and new types of link layers.

TCP HEADER

The fields *Source Port* and *Destination Port* determine from and to whom a packet is delivered; together with *SrcIPAddress* and *DestIPAddress* of IP, they form a unique identifier. The field *Sequence Number* is used for packet reordering and also for identification of duplicate packets (see Figure 2).

Note that TCP is byte-oriented and hence the field *Sequence Number* holds the ID of the first byte of each segment. The field *Acknowledgment* allows for reporting at the receiver side; reporting is somewhat strange (for a reason): Each time a packet x is delivered, the receiver acks the $x+1$, meaning it now expects $x+1$. In addition, $x+1$ acknowledges all previously delivered packets as well; in case a previous acknowledgment has been lost, a following ack suffices for the sender to verify previous packet delivery. The aforementioned policy, called *cumulative acknowledgments*, has its cost: The receiver cannot always report precisely the concrete packet received, and it is possible for it to receive new packets out of sequence but report only the next expected packet (in fact, the first byte of the packet). The transmission strategy of TCP is therefore strictly based on the acknowledgment progress; lack of acknowledgments for consistency causes suspension of transmission as well. This policy is known as the *ack-clocking* mechanism of TCP. The field *HdrL* refers to a segment's header length in units of thirty-two bits and is necessary because of the optional nature of some fields, which results in unknown header length. The header also allows for six distinct *flags:*

- *syn, fin,* which are used in connection establishment, and termination;
- *reset,* which is used when unexpected data are received;
- *push,* which signifies urgent data delivery;

0 16 31

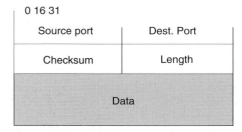

Figure 1: UDP header

---

*TCP's terminology for packet is *segment*. We use both terms throughout this text.

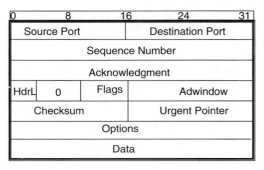

Figure 2: TCP header

- *urgent pointer*, which indicates use of the urgent pointer; and

- *ack*, which reports acknowledgments.

The fields *SYN* and *ACK* are used during connection establishment, which is implemented using a three-way handshake algorithm. The sender initiates a connection request by marking the *syn* flag of the TCP header and assigns a random sequence number x (see Figure 3). The receiver responds by also marking the *syn* flag and assigns a sequence number y. In the same response, the receiver marks the acknowledgment field with the $x+1$ number, which means that the receiver now waits for the segment with a sequence of bytes starting from $x+1$. The sender acknowledges the response of the receiver similarly—that is, it marks the acknowledgment field with $y+1$ and enters the establishment phase. As soon as the acknowledgment arrives at the receiver, the connection is established.

The order of events may differ occasionally. For example, the sender and the receiver may request connection establishment simultaneously or some request or acknowledgment may be lost. In any case, an establishment phase is confirmed when both the sender and the receiver

have issued one *syn* request and received one corresponding *ack* for their request.

The field *Adwindow* (for *advertised window*) is where buffer space is reported and is used for flow control. The field *Checksum* is used for error detection. Finally, options are possible: The field *Options* has been widely used not only for evaluating new versions but also for enhancing the functionality of existing versions through the use of time stamps and so on.

Now consider that the sender starts transmitting segments from this window. If *acks* do not arrive, then transmission is suspended. By default, retransmission is triggered by time-outs (although more sophisticated ways have also been deployed). Therefore, reliability requires:

- acknowledgments;
- buffers at both the sender and the receiver to hold packets in flight and out of order, respectively;
- time-out to trigger retransmission; and
- sequence numbers to allow for distinction of duplicate packets and ordering.

As shown in the sliding window operation of Figure 4, the sender maintains pointers that determine the transmission window, based largely on the pace of *acks*. For example, given the limitation of buffer space, which restricts sending to the amount of

$$\text{Last byte written} - \text{Last byte acked}$$

the lack of new acks does not allow the pointer *last byte acked* to move forward, resulting in suspended transmission. The pointers at the receiving end allow for *flow control:* The receiver reports the amount

$$\text{Adwindow} = \text{MaxRcvBuffer} - (\text{LastByteRcvd} - \text{Last ByteRead}) \qquad (1)$$

to the sender, which incorporates the pace at which the receiving application reads data from the buffer and, in turn, determines the

$$\text{EffectiveWindow} = \text{AdWindow} - \text{Data\_in\_flight} \qquad (2)$$

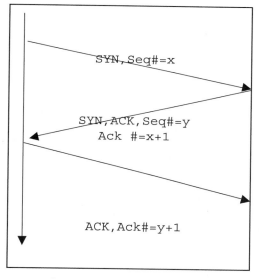

Figure 3: Three-way handshake

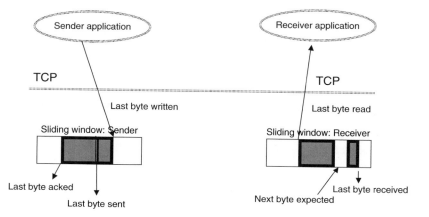

Figure 4: Sliding window operation

where

$$Data\_in\_flight = (LastByteSent - LastByteAcked) \quad (3)$$

Obviously,

$$LastByteWritten - LastByteAcked \leq MaxSendBuffer \quad (4)$$

Retransmission

Retransmission in TCP is triggered by either a time-out event or a *three-duplicate acknowledgment* (3-DACK). In the event of a segment loss, the delivery of consequent segments triggers *duplicate acks* (dacks). Three such dacks indicate the loss of a segment, and retransmission is then initiated. Because the delivery of out-of-order segments is possible, a single dack does not suffice to convince the sender that the segment is lost; three dacks are more convincing. In the event of persistent congestion, more segments may be lost. In that case, dacks may not be generated and the sender will thus time-out. The time-out will trigger retransmission as well. We describe in more detail in the section on congestion control the different retransmission policies of various TCP versions that correspond to time-out or three-dack events, respectively.

Time-Out

The retransmission time-out policy of standard TCP is governed by the rules of RFC 2988. Most existing TCP versions implement that standard. The algorithm is based solely on *round-trip time* (RTT) measurements in an effort to capture dynamic network conditions by measuring the variation of the RTT samples. In particular, the *retransmission time-out* (RTO) is calculated upon each ack arrival after smoothing out the measured samples and weighting the recent history. In this way, the time-out reflects the weighted average delay currently in the network rather than the instantaneous network delay. Furthermore, the time-out takes into account the RTT variation measured during the previous transmission rounds. More precisely, upon each ack arrival, the sender updates the RTT variation:

$$RTTVAR = {}^{3}\!/_{4} \times RTTVAR + 1/4 \\ \times |SRTT - RTT\_sample| \quad (5)$$

This smoothes the expected RTT before calculating the retransmission time-out:

$$SRTT = 7/8 \times SRTT + 1/8 \times RTT\_sample \quad (6)$$

Finally, it calculates the retransmission time-out value,

$$RTO = SRTT + max(G, 4 \times RTTVAR) \quad (7)$$

where RTTVAR holds the RTT variation and SRTT the smoothed RTT. G denotes the timer granularity, which is incorporated in order to assign a lower bound for the retransmission time-out to protect it against spurious time-outs (Sarolahti and Kojo 2003) (i.e., when RTT equals the timer granularity).

Zhang (1986) identifies several drawbacks of the TCP retransmission timer, reports its intrinsic limitations, and concludes that mainly external events should trigger retransmissions; timers should be used only as a last notification of packet loss. The Eifel algorithm (Ludwig and Gurtov 2005; Ludwig and Meyer 2003) focuses on spurious time-outs. A *spurious time-out* happens in case of a sudden delay spike on the link, where the round-trip delay exceeds the expected value calculated for the retransmission time-out. As a result, all data in flight are falsely considered lost and are being retransmitted. The Eifel algorithm uses the TCP time-stamp option to detect spurious timer expirations. Once a spurious time-out is detected, the sender does not back off, but instead restores the transmission rate to the recorded rate before the time-out event. The *forward RTO algorithm* (F-RTO) (Sarolahti and Kojo 2003) targets the detection of spurious time-outs, too. Instead of using time-stamp options, the algorithm checks the ack packets that arrive at the sender after the timer's expiration. F-RTO observes whether the acks advance the sequence number, concludes whether the time-out was spurious, and determines the appropriate recovery policy accordingly.

Both of the above algorithms (Eifel and forward RTO) are currently in the standardization process of the Internet Engineering Task Force. Both algorithms consider outstanding data packets only after the timer expires, although the nature of the problem also calls for design modifications of the time-out itself. Recently, Chandrayana et al. (2006) investigated the problem of TCP flow synchronization, too, and identified anomalies in TCP's transmission policy. More precisely, they report TCP performance problems in terms of fairness (i.e., TCP treats unfairly flows with long RTTs) and window synchronization. They attempt to break flow synchronization by randomizing the sending times in TCP. Psaras, Tsaoussidis, and Mamatas (2005) have shown that time-out adjustments, based solely on RTT estimations, do not correspond to the level of flow contention. The authors investigated the behavior of TCP in high-contention scenarios and confirmed that it is possible for the time-out to decrease while contention increases. The authors conclude that this anomaly is the result of flow synchronization.

CONGESTION CONTROL

A network is considered congested when too many packets try to access the same router's buffer, resulting in packets being dropped. In this state, the load exceeds the combined network and buffer capacity. During congestion, actions need to be taken by both the transmission protocols and the network routers not only to avoid a congestive collapse but also to ensure network stability, high throughput, and fair resource allocation to network users. Indeed, during a collapse, only a fraction of the existing bandwidth is utilized by traffic that finally reaches the receiver.

The sender maintains a *congestion window* (cwnd) to record the amount of data the network can hold, an approach similar to the Adwindow and the receiver. Then the sender needs to calculate the *sending window* as the minimum of the two windows [i.e., min(adwindow, cwnd)] minus the *data in flight*. This way, both the receiver and network overflow can be avoided (Floyd 2000; Jacobson 1988).

The real issue, however, is how to assign values to congestion windows that correspond to current network dynamics. Unlike the receiver's buffer, for which the receiver can report accurate measurements of free space to the sender, the network state cannot be reported for two reasons: (1) Network and transport protocols differ, hence extra mechanisms are required for cross-layer communication; and (2) whatever network buffer capacity may be reported to the sender cannot be trusted because flows may write there anytime. Therefore, it appears reasonable to seek a way to estimate the overall network state or monitor the network dynamics rather than calculate precise capacities. However, monitoring the dynamics is half the story. What remains unknown is the level of flow contention; even if each flow knew the available network buffer capacity, the value of the congestion window cannot be determined because bandwidth sharing requires knowledge of the *fair share* as well. Congestion control therefore requires window adjustments in a manner that the system of flows will converge to some equilibrium where resources are well utilized and sharing is possible. How can we adjust the congestion window to guarantee both efficiency and fairness? We address this issue in the following sections.

PERFORMANCE METRICS

Several metrics have been proposed and used for evaluating various performance aspects at the transport layer. Because of the several performance trade-offs at this layer, it becomes difficult to capture a protocol's behavior by a single metric. Indeed, new performance aspects require new metrics. For example, the contribution of a protocol's transmission policy to energy consumption requires a new metric; energy expenditure cannot capture the particular contribution of this layer alone.

A major task of the protocols at this layer is to regulate traffic in a manner that allows for the efficient utilization of resources (i.e., bandwidth) and fair allocation to participating users. That said, metrics characterize system performance as well as user's application efficiency. For example, although a system may appear as highly efficient in bandwidth utilization, there might be users that do not really experience that performance had the allocation of bandwidth not been fair. From another perspective, utilization itself is not the whole story, because bandwidth may be consumed by headers, retransmissions, and control packets. Therefore, utilization and efficiency have to be occasionally distinguished. Network utilization is usually captured by *throughput*, which is defined as:

$$\text{Throughput} = \text{Data transmitted/Connection time} \quad (8)$$

The metric *goodput* is widely used to capture the application efficiency instead of the network utilization scores. The goodput for each flow is defined as:

$$\text{Goodput} = \text{Original data/Connection time} \quad (9)$$

where original data is the number of bytes delivered to the high-level protocol at the receiver (i.e., excluding retransmitted packets) and connection time is the amount of time required for the corresponding data delivery. Because goodput is an average rate and as such cannot capture the fluctuations in time, the metric can be further extended in accordance with Zhang and Tsaoussidis (2001). The *allotted system goodput* (ASG), for example, can be defined as the system goodput within a short sampling period (usually at a timescale of several RTTs) and could be used to capture the particularity of protocol behavior over time in dynamically changing environments.

The protocol efficiency can also be studied from another perspective. *Overhead* can be used as a metric to realize the protocol transmission effort to complete reliable data delivery:

$$\text{Overhead} = (\text{Bytes sent} - \text{original bytes})/\text{Bytes sent} \quad (10)$$

where *bytes sent* is the total bytes transmitted by TCP senders and *original bytes* is the number of bytes delivered to the higher level protocol by all receivers, excluding retransmitted packets and TCP header bytes. This metric captures the portion of consumed bandwidth, or the percentage of the transmitted data, that is wasted on packet retransmissions and protocol header overhead. Similar metrics may also be derived to capture the protocol effort as the amount of unexploited available resources or even the protocol's energy saving potential (see Mamatas and Tsaoussidis 2006 for more details).

Fairness is a common metric and is measured by the *fairness index*, which is defined in Bakre and Badrinath (1995) as:

$$FairnessIndex = \frac{\left(\sum_{i=1}^{n} throughput_i \right)^2}{n \sum_{i=1}^{n} throughput_i^2} \quad (11)$$

where *throughput*$_i$ is the throughput of the *i*th flow measured at a timescale of connection time. Similarly, *allotted fairness* can be defined as the corresponding fairness within a short sampling period; it is used to capture the system fairness over time under dynamic traffic loads. *Allotted throughput* can also be used to compute the *short-term fairness*, which is derived from the traditional fairness index:

$$ShortTermFairness = E_t \left\{ \frac{\left(\sum_{i=1}^{n} throughput(t)_i \right)^2}{n \sum_{i=1}^{n} throughput(t)_i^2} \right\} \quad (12)$$

where, $E_t\{\}$ denotes the computation of the mean along the time, and *throughput(t)*$_i$ is allotted throughput of the *i*th flow over time *t*.

To investigate the performance smoothness observed by end users (i.e., transmission gaps), the allotted throughput of individual flows $throughput(t)_i$ can be used to observe the performance fluctuations. In this context, *coefficient of variation* (COV) (see Yang and Lam 2000; Zhang and Tsaoussidis 2001) can be used to gauge the throughput smoothness experienced by flow i:

$$CoV_i = \frac{\sqrt{E_t\{thoughput_i^2(t) - E_t\{thoughput_i(t)\}^2}}{E_t\{thoughput_i(t)\}} \quad (13)$$

For a system with multiple flows, the system COV is the average of COVs of all flows.

NETWORK AS A BLACK BOX

If we consider the network as a *black box* that only provides binary feedback to network flows upon congestion, all of the control burden is shifted to end users. Regardless of the network particularity or the current network state, the algorithm will react similarly in all cases because no further information is available to end users. However, the goal of each sender is to operate independently but nevertheless to adjust its rate (or window) in a manner that the total bandwidth of the network will be expended fairly and effectively. From its algorithmic perspective, the above problem is challenging because the distributed entities (sources) neither have any prior or current knowledge of the other entities' states nor know the system's capacity and the number of competitors. Hence, the goal of fairness and efficiency appears initially difficult to attain. However, if the system is entitled to a prescribed behavior and the entities agree on common transmission tactics, then convergence* to fairness becomes feasible (Lahanas and Tsaoussidis 2003 "Exploiting"). *Additive increase, multiplicative decrease* (AIMD) (Chiu and Jain 1989), the traditional congestion control algorithm of the Internet, operates within that scope: It increases additively the rate of the senders (by a value α) until the system reaches congestion. Upon congestion, all senders decrease their rate multiplicatively using a decrease ratio, β.

The goals we set for congestion avoidance and control are to:

- achieve high bandwidth utilization,
- converge to fairness more quickly,
- minimize the length of oscillations, and
- maintain high responsiveness.

Although the sources may discover their fair share early on, the dynamics of real systems in practice prohibit a straightforward adjustment; instead, they call for continuous oscillations as a means of discovering the available bandwidth. *Smoothness* is reflected by the magnitude of the oscillations during multiplicative decrease. *Responsiveness* is measured by the number of steps (or RTTs) to reach an equilibrium (i.e.. to equate the windows in order to be in a fair state).

---

*Convergence to fairness should be perceived as the procedure that enables different flows that consume different amount of resources each to balance their resource usage.

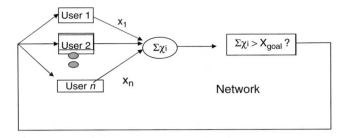

Figure 5: Synchronous control system model of *n* users sharing a network (Chiu and Jain 1989)

A synchronous-feedback control system model is shown in Figure 5. In congestion control, the load change is the response in one occurrence. This event is a binary feedback. The synchronous model is characterized by a synchronous generation of responses in congruity with Chiu and Jain (1989). The system response is 1 when bandwidth is available and 0 when bandwidth is exhausted. The instruction to the system entities (sources) is to increase or decrease their data rate, respectively. Note that, in real networks, the responsive behavior of the system is not administered by any centralized authority with additional knowledge of the network dynamics, it is simply a packet drop because of congestion that naturally happens when bandwidth is exceeded.

The system has *n* users (flows), and the instantaneous throughput for the flow i is X_i. The system's goal is to operate at an optimal point X goal. Note that this point is not necessarily bandwidth B because throughput might decrease before we reach B. We assume that responses are synchronous and consequently the duration of RTTs is common for all flows. Hence, the sources respond uniformly by decreasing their windows in response to a 0 signal; they increase their windows by one in response to a signal of 1 (in the case of classical AIMD). The limitations of the system are derived from these dynamics of packet networks:

- Bandwidth B is limited,
- each flow is not aware of the throughput rates (window sizes) of other flows,
- each flow is not aware of the number of competitors in the channel, and
- no flow is aware of the size of bandwidth B.

Multiplicative decrease guarantees that different window sizes will gradually equate because the gap between the windows is gradually reduced. The decrease ratio determines the length of oscillation, which reflects the convergence speed as well, however, at the cost of smoothness. Figure 6 depicts the graduated adjustments of the windows of two users. After each multiplicative decrease (e.g., halving the window in TCP) the gap between the two user windows is reduced and the total resources used approach the line where user demand is equal. Although both users increase their windows, the gap remains constant but the resource utilization approaches the line Total demand = C.

Although the synchronous model is widely adopted, it is associated with a number of assumptions or

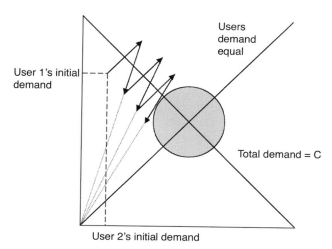

Figure 6: AIMD dynamics described in Chiu and Jain (1989)

simplifications that may not really hold in real networks. We note that some drawbacks of the simplified synchronous model are somewhat canceled experimentally because of the wide use of long FTP flows. In a recent work, Lahanas and Tsaoussidis ("t-AIMD" 2003) described an asynchronous-feedback model that corresponds to the diverse round-trip times (RTTs) of competing flows within the same communication channel. In this system, authors show that congestion epoch, which equals the RTT of a flow times the number of additive increases, is common knowledge among all competing flows. Based on this knowledge, they proposed a new algorithm that increases the consumption rate proportionally to the RTT of the flow using a mechanism that adjusts the sizes of the windows of the competing flows at the end of each congestion epoch. Long RTT flows are relatively favored because their window is increased more quickly than in a traditional AIMD scheme. The system reaches a window-based equilibrium. This mechanism, named τ-AIMD, introduces an extra adaptive component τ to the additive increase formula of AIMD.

In two papers, Yang, Kim, and Lam (2001) and Yang and Lam (2000) compare AIMD and *multiplicative additive increase, multiplicative decrease* (MAIMD) and introduce general AIMD. They show that the convergence speeds of AIMD and MAIMD are similar. Furthermore, MAIMD has some advantages; for example, its speed to use available network bandwidth can be much faster than AIMD. Authors have made their investigations using an asynchronous system model in which users can have different round-trip times.

Incorporating the Additive Increase, Multiplicative Decrease Algorithm into TCP

Standard TCP applies graduated multiplicative and additive adjustments to the sender's congestion window in order to guarantee stability and fairness to other flows that possibly attempt to simultaneously utilize the channel's bandwidth. The additive increase multiplicative decrease (AIMD) algorithm is used to implement TCP window adjustments. Based on the analysis of Chiu and Jain, the algorithm achieves stability and converges to fairness

in situations where the demand (of competing flows) exceeds the channel's bandwidth. Tahoe, Reno, and SACK are the three most common reference implementations of TCP. They rely on lost segments to detect congestion so that a flow can adjust its rate to its available share. We discuss each version in turn.

TCP Tahoe congestion control algorithm includes *slow start*, *congestion avoidance*, and *fast retransmit* mechanisms (Allman, Paxson, and Stevens 1999; Postel 1981). It also implements an RTT-based estimation of the retransmission time-out. In slow start, the sender increases its window size by one segment each time an acknowledgment is received until it reaches the *slow start threshold* (SSTHRESH). From that point onward, it increases the window by one segment each time a *full window* of acknowledgments is received (*congestion avoidance* phase). In the *fast retransmit* mechanism, a number of successive dacks (the threshold is usually set at three) that are carrying the same sequence number triggers a retransmission without waiting for the associated time-out event to occur. Note that the slow start threshold is halved whenever a congestion event is detected; the threshold is then increased in accordance with the congestion window.

TCP Reno introduces *fast recovery* in conjunction with *fast retransmit*. The idea behind fast recovery is that a dack is an indication of available channel bandwidth because a segment has been successfully delivered. This, in turn, implies that the congestion window (cwnd) should actually be incremented upon a dack delivery. In particular, receiving the threshold number of dacks triggers fast recovery: The sender retransmits one segment and sets the congestion threshold to half the current cwnd. Then, instead of entering slow start as in Tahoe, the sender increases its current cwnd by the predetermined threshold number. The fast recovery stage is completed when an acknowledgement for new data is received.

Although Reno significantly improves the behavior of Tahoe TCP when a single packet is dropped from a window of data, it degrades performance when multiple packets are dropped. A modification of Reno, named *New Reno* (Floyd and Handley 1999), changes the sender's behavior during fast recovery and reduces Reno's time-outs in case of multiple packet drops. New Reno remains in fast recovery until all of the data (which it has initiated during fast recovery) have been acknowledged. TCP SACK (Mathis et al. 1996) adds *selective acknowledgments* (sacks) and *selective repeat* to TCP. A comparative evaluation of the aforementioned versions can be found in Fall and Floyd (1996).

AIMD Fast Convergence

A recent improvement to AIMD—*additive increase, multiplicative decrease with fast convergence* (AIMD-FC)—was proposed in Lahanas and Tsaoussidis ("Exploiting" 2003). AIMD-FC positively affects efficiency and fairness. It is not based on a new algorithm but on an optimization of AIMD during the convergence procedure that enables the algorithm to converge more quickly and achieve higher efficiency. AIMD-FC increases the bandwidth utilization of AIMD from 3/4 to 5/6.

AIMD-FC departs from AIMD and the following four observations:

1. During the additive increase phase, an equal amount of system resources is allocated to each flow. This amount (k) is public or common knowledge (i.e., it is known to every flow in the system).

2. AIMD affects both the initial windows and the amount of system resources (k), that has been fairly allocated during the multiplicative decrease phase. Note that the manipulation of the initial (and unknown) windows is the real target for achieving fairness.

3. The average distance of actual utilization from the capacity line (see Figure 6) when the system is in equilibrium depends only on the multiplicative decrease factor (Chiu and Jain 1989).

4. Two algorithms may need the same number of cycles to converge to fairness—for example, two variants of AIMD with different additive increase rate but the same multiplicative decrease ratio. The number of increase steps determines the relative efficiency of the algorithm to converge to fairness.

Practically, fairness is achieved in AIMD-FC by releasing (through multiplicative adjustments of the windows) the initial resources of the flows (which are unknown to other flows) because, during the additive increase phase, the flows increase their resource consumption uniformly. So, it is becoming apparent that the distinctive difference of AIMD and AIMD-FC concerns the portion of the congestion window that is affected by multiplicative decrease (this portion is called *decrease window*).

MEASUREMENT-BASED CONGESTION CONTROL

One can measure network conditions, estimate the available bandwidth or even flow contention, and obtain some knowledge about the network. However, measurements are taken at time instances that may not necessarily represent current network dynamics or may not correspond to the overall conditions. As a consequence, protocols may not manage to accurately estimate the load and predict its duration, resulting in either wrong estimations or wrong recovery strategies. Furthermore, some generic questions cannot really be addressed with certainty: How frequently should we measure the network? How far can we trust our measurements? How responsive should the recovery strategy be? How shall we associate the instantaneous measurements of congestion with the network load over some sufficiently long but also sufficiently recent time period? That said, the network may not be a black box, but it is certainly not better than *gray*, occasionally involving a considerable risk.

TCP Vegas

A well-designed, measurement-based congestion avoidance mechanism is TCP Vegas (Brakmo and Peterson 1995). Vegas defines *base RTT* to be the *minimum of all measured RTTs* and *expected rate* to be the *ratio of the congestion window to base RTT*. The sender measures the *actual rate* based on the sample RTTs. If the difference between the expected rate and actual rate is below a lower bound, then the congestion window increases linearly during the next RTT. If the difference exceeds an upper bound, then TCP Vegas decreases the congestion window linearly during the next RTT. According to Brakmo and Peterson (1995), Vegas achieves better transmission rates than Reno and Tahoe.

TCP Real

TCP Real (Tsaoussidis and Zhang 2002; Zhang and Tsaoussidis 2001) employs a receiver-oriented and measurement-based congestion control mechanism that significantly improves TCP performance over heterogeneous (wired and wireless) networks and over asymmetric paths. TCP Real goes beyond the limitation of ack-based binary feedback. It estimates the level of contention and distinguishes the reason of packet losses. TCP Real relies on the following:

- *receiver-oriented congestion detection*, which abrogates the impact of false assessments at the sender because of lost or delayed acknowledgments on a lossy reverse path (the receiver measures the network condition and attaches the results to the acks sent back to the sender); and

- *measurements*, which are based on wave patterns that distinguish the nature of a packet loss because of congestion or transient wireless errors.

A *wave* (originally introduced in Tsaoussidis, Badr, and Verma 1999) consists of a number of fixed-sized data segments sent back-to-back, matching the inherent characteristic of TCP to send packets back-to-back. The receiver computes the data-receiving rate of a wave, which reflects the level of contention at the bottleneck link. If a packet drop results from a wireless error, then the data-receiving rate will not be affected by the gap of missing packets because the wave size is published to the receiver. The congestion window is multiplicatively reduced only when a drop is associated with congestion.

TCP Westwood

In TCP Westwood (Casetti et al. 2001; Mascolo et al. 2001), the sender continuously measures the rate of the connection by monitoring the rate of returning acks. Upon three duplicate acknowledgments or a time-out, the slow start threshold and the congestion window are set to be consistent with the effective bandwidth used at the time the packet loss is experienced. No specific mechanism exists to support error classification and the corresponding recovery tactics for wired or wireless networks, albeit the proposed mechanism appears to be effective over symmetric wireless links because of its efficient congestion control.

One can go beyond the blind algorithms or the high risk of estimations and actually ask the network for help. Of course, precision comes at some cost. Besides the practical difficulty of layer collaboration and the issue of convincing people to add functionality (and invest money) to their network, the issue of recovery strategies remains. In other words, even when the network is really a *green* box (which practically is extremely difficult), changes may be so rapid and unpredictable that our costly and painful effort to obtain some information may go wasted. An approach to calculate the fair share without any network support was published in Attie, Lahanas, and Tsaoussidis (2003).

Bimodal Mechanism

Bimodal congestion avoidance and control mechanism (Attie, Lahanas, and Tsaoussidis 2003) measures the fair share of the total bandwidth that should be allocated for each flow at any point during the system's execution. If the fair share were known, then the sources could avoid congestion by adjusting immediately after the fair share was discovered to a new state in which the bandwidth allocation of each flow is exactly its fair share. However, bandwidth availability not only is a matter of channel capacity but also is dependent on the number of participating flows and the transmitting behavior of the sources. So, fair share can be measured only in an equilibrium state. The authors proposed a *bimodal mechanism*, which is based on the idea that upward and downward adjustments need to operate in association with the system state. Action is determined based on whether the system is in equilibrium (fair share is known) or not (fair share is unknown).

When the fair share is unknown, the algorithm behaves like AIMD until two congestion cycles have passed, which suffices to recalculate the fair share. The algorithm then sets the bandwidth allocation for flow f to ε (where ε is a small tunable parameter) times the calculated fair share and shifts to *known fair share* mode. So, bimodal congestion control algorithm explicitly calculates the fair share and converges in two congestion cycles to the fair share. In this mode, the algorithm continues to use additive increase and multiplicative decrease, but the multiplicative decrease factor is ε instead of β. This algorithm calculates fair share explicitly, and so fairness is not compromised in this approach. Furthermore, because this algorithm restricts its flows to use only their fair share, it can be used in conjunction with any other transport protocol (e.g., standard AIMD-based protocols) without monopolizing for itself most of the available bandwidth. This is in contrast with the TCP-friendly protocols, which attempt to grab available bandwidth. Of course, this algorithm will not work well in conjunction with other protocols that aggressively (and unfairly) grab a disproportionate share of the bandwidth for their flows.

FRAMEWORK FOR POTENTIAL IMPROVEMENTS

The application requirements and the limitations of congestion control circumscribe a framework for potential improvements. We identify five distinct cases of interest that have been discussed in the recent literature (see Tsaoussidis and Matta 2002).

Additive increase leads naturally to congestion, which, in turn, degrades throughput for two reasons:

1. Routers need time to recover even from a transitory congestive collapse and sources need time to detect and retransmit missing packets (Fall and Floyd 1996).

2. Congestion control is triggered upon congestion; the window is adjusted backward and the time-out is extended, which in turn degrades the protocol's capability to detect and exploit error-free conditions and bandwidth availability, respectively.

Additive increase is not efficient when the network dynamics encompass rapid changes of bandwidth availability. For example, when short flows that cause congestion complete their task, bandwidth becomes available. Similarly, when a hand-off is completed in a cellular network, the entire channel's bandwidth becomes available. A more rapid response is then clearly indicated (Tsaoussidis and Matta 2002).

Multiplicative decrease causes transmission gaps that hurt the performance of real-time applications that experience jitter and degraded goodput. Furthermore, multiplicative decrease with a factor of one-half or a window adjustment to two packets characterizes a rather conservative strategy.

Error detection lacks an appropriate classification module that would permit a responsive strategy oriented by the nature of potential errors. In other words, when errors appear to be transient because of short-lived flows or random wireless interference, congestion control mechanisms (i.e., time-out extension and multiplicative window adjustment) are triggered unduly. The insufficient error detection and classification may also lead to unfair bandwidth allocation in mixed wired and wireless networks. By default, flows that experience wireless errors do not balance their bandwidth loss with a more aggressive recovery, although such behavior could be justified: Flows that experienced no losses have occupied extra bandwidth at the router temporarily when the wireless errors forced some senders to back off.

A source-based decision on the transmission rate, based on the pace of the acknowledgments, necessarily incorporates the potentially asymmetric characteristics (e.g., ack delays or losses) of the reverse path (Balakrishnan, Padmanabhan, and Katz 1997). Hence, the sender's transmission rate does not always reflect the capacity of the forward path. This situation has a direct effect on efficiency because available bandwidth remains unexploited.

Several proposals have been presented to tackle the problems of TCP over wireless and mobile networks. Most of these proposals rely on some form of local retransmission at the wired and wireless border (e.g., Bakre and Badrinath 1995; Balakrishnan et al. 1995; Goff et al. 2000). Some recent protocols restrict the modifications at the transport level (see also Papadimitriou and Tsaoussidis, "Transport Layer" 2006). *Freeze TCP* (Goff et al. 2000) distinguishes hand-offs from congestion through the use of the advertised window. WTCP (Sinha et al. 1999) implements a rate-based congestion control replacing entirely the ack-clocking mechanism. *TCP probing* (Tsaoussidis and Badr 2000) grafts a *probing cycle* and an *immediate recovery* strategy into standard TCP in order to control effectively the throughput and overhead trade-off. Although TCP probing deals effectively with both throughput and energy performance in heterogeneous networks because of its probing mechanism, it may not satisfy the requirements of delay-sensitive applications for reduced transmission gaps. TCP Westwood (Casetti et al. 2001; Mascolo et al.; Wang 2001) relies on bandwidth estimation to set the slow start threshold and the congestion window on three duplicate acknowledgments or a timeout. No specific mechanism exists to support error classification and the corresponding recovery tactics for wired and wireless networks, albeit the proposed mechanism appears to be relatively effective over symmetric wireless links because of its efficient congestion control. Naturally, a sender-based strategy does not cancel the TCP deficiency over asymmetric channels.

TCP-FRIENDLY PROTOCOLS

A new family of protocols has recently emerged, namely the *TCP-friendly protocols* (Floyd, Handley, and Padhye 2000; Floyd Handley, Padhye, and Widmer 2000; Handley et al. 2001; Feng, et al. 1997). Congestion control was designed based on two fundamental requirements: (1) to achieve smooth window adjustments, which is done by reducing the window decrease factor during congestion; and (2) to compete fairly with TCP flows, which is achieved by adjusting the increase rate calculated from a TCP throughput equation. *TCP-friendly rate control* (TFRC) (Handley et al. 2001) is an equation-based TCP-friendly congestion control protocol. The sender explicitly adjusts its sending rate as a function of the measured rate of loss events to compete fairly with TCP. A loss event consists of one or more packet drops within a single round-trip time. The receiver calculates the loss event rate and reports feedback to the sender. The benefit of TFRC is its "gentle" rate regression upon congestion. *General additive increase, multiplicative decrease* (GAIMD) Yang and Lam (2000) generalizes TCP by parameterizing the congestion window increase value α and decrease ratio β. It provides a balancing relationship between α and β to guarantee friendliness:

$$\alpha = 4(1 - \beta^2)/3 \tag{14}$$

Originally departing from the model of Padhye et al. (2000) and based on experiments, Yang and Lam (2000) have chosen $\beta = 7/8$ as the appropriate value* for the reduced window (i.e., less rapidly than TCP does). For $\beta = 7/8$, (1) gives an increasing value $\alpha = 0.31$.

Obviously, the choice of parameters α and β directly affects the "responsiveness" of the protocols to conditions of increasing contention or bandwidth availability. Indeed, the combined dynamics of α and β from equation 1 exploit an interesting trade-off: A choice of α that allows for rapid bandwidth consumption (additive increase) is counterbalanced by a friendliness-driven response with multiplicative decrease, rendering the protocol inappropriate for real-time applications.

The differences between TCP, TFRC,** and GAIMD congestion control lie mainly in the specific values of α and β. Their similarities lie in their AIMD-based congestion

control, a characteristic that enables us to include them both in the family of TCP (α, β) protocols. Standard TCP is therefore viewed here as a specific case of TCP (α, β) with $\alpha = 1$, $\beta = 0.5$. From our perspective, TCP-friendly protocols are designed to satisfy specific application requirements; however, as it was shown in Tsaoussidis and Zhang (2005), they may exhibit further weakness when bandwidth becomes available rapidly. Apparently, the trade-off between responsiveness and smoothness can be controlled to favor some applications, but it will cause other damages. Considering the variability of network conditions and the duration of flows, the equation-based recovery may provide weak guarantees for friendliness.

Rate adaptation protocol (RAP) (Rejaie, Handely, and Estrin 1999) is a rated-based protocol that employs an AIMD algorithm for the transmission of real-time streams. The sending rate is continuously adjusted by RAP in a TCP-friendly fashion by using feedback from the receiver. The protocol uses layered encoding and the associated component—namely, *layer manager*—tries to deliver the maximum number of layers that can fit in the available bandwidth. Rate adaptation is performed on a timescale of round-trip times, but layers are added and dropped on a longer timescale. However, because RAP fully complies to AIMD, it causes short-term rate oscillations, mainly because of multiplicative decrease. Furthermore, RAP occasionally does not result in interprotocol fairness.

Datagram congestion control protocol (DCCP) (Kohler, Handley, and Floyd 2003) is a new transport protocol that provides a congestion-controlled flow of unreliable datagrams. DCCP is intended for time-sensitive applications that have relaxed packet loss requirements. The protocol aims to add to a UDP-like foundation the minimum mechanisms necessary to support congestion control, such as possibly reliable transmission of acknowledgement information.

Several TCP protocol extensions have emerged to overcome the standard TCP limitations, providing more efficient bandwidth utilization and sophisticated mechanisms for congestion control, which preserve the fundamental QOS guarantees for time-sensitive traffic. Sisalem and Schulzrinne (1998) proposed protocols of the family of *TCP-friendly* such as *TCP-friendly rate control* (TFRC) (Goff et al. 2000), where transmission rate is adjusted in response to the level of congestion, as indicated by the loss rate. Multiple packet losses in the same RTT are considered as a single loss event by TFRC, hence the protocol follows a more gentle congestion control strategy. The protocol eventually achieves the smoothing of the transmission gaps and therefore is suitable for applications requiring a smooth sending rate, such as streaming media. However, this smoothness has a negative effect as the protocol becomes less responsive to bandwidth availability (Tsaoussidis and Zhang 2005).

REAL-TIME TRANSPORT PROTOCOL

Real-time transport protocol (RTP) (Schulzrinne et al. 1996) is the standard for transmitting delay-sensitive traffic across packet-based networks. The protocol runs on top of UDP or TCP and provides end-to-end network

---

*Note that although β was so far called the *multiplicative factor*, its value determines the size of the window; that is, 7/8 means that the window was reduced by 1/8th.

**In fact, TFRC has several other mechanisms that differ from TCP.

transport functions, which are suitable for real-time applications over multicast or unicast networks. RTP, in a complementary role, uses the sequence information to determine whether the packets are arriving in order, and it uses the time-stamping information to determine packet interarrival times. The data transport is augmented by *real-time control transport protocol* (RTCP), which allows the monitoring of data delivery. RTP and RTCP are designed to be independent of the underlying transport and network layers.

Papadimitriou and Tsaoussidis ("Evaluating" 2006) study transport protocol performance from the perspective of real-time applications. More precisely, they evaluate TCP and UDP supportive role in terms of real-time QOS, network stability, and fairness. A new metric for the evaluation of real-time application performance is proposed to capture both bandwidth and delay requirements. Using this metric as a primary criterion in their analysis, the authors reach conclusions on the specific effects of wireless links, real-time traffic friendliness, and UDP and TCP protocol efficiency. Furthermore, Papadimitriou and Tsaoussidis ("Evaluating" 2006) quantify the effects of satellite links on TCP efficiency and streaming video delivery.

STREAM CONTROL TRANSMISSION PROTOCOL

Like TCP, *stream control transmission protocol* (SCTP) (RFC 2960) provides a reliable transport service, ensuring that data are transported across the network without error and in sequence. Like TCP, SCTP is a session-oriented mechanism, meaning that a relationship is created between the end points of an SCTP association before data transmission, and this relationship is maintained until all data transmission has been successfully completed.

However, traffic characteristics and requirements of signaling as well as conventional telephony (i.e., SIP traffic) have found TCP too limiting. Easy but still inefficient solutions have incorporated reliable, congestion-aware data transfer in the application layer protocol, which runs on top of the simple, message-oriented UDP. TCP's limitations for such applications can be summarized as follows (RFC 2960 and RFC 3286).

1. The combined reliable data transfer and strict order-of-transmission delivery of data: Some applications need reliable transfer without sequencing of packets, while others would be satisfied with partial ordering of the data. In both of these cases. TCP inevitably causes additional delays.

2. The stream-oriented nature of TCP, which is occasionally insufficient for some applications: Such applications must add their own record marking to delineate messages along with the use of the push field of the TCP header.

3. The limited scope of TCP sockets complicates the task of providing highly available data transfer capability using multihomed hosts.

4. TCP is relatively vulnerable to denial-of-service attacks.

STCP satisfies the aforementioned requirements. It is positioned between the SCTP user application and a connectionless packet network such as IP. SCTP has been approved by the Internet Engineering Task Force as a proposed standard. The basic service offered by SCTP is the reliable transfer of user messages (in contrast to TCP's bytes) between peer SCTP users. It performs this service within the context of an association between two SCTP end points. SCTP provides the means for each SCTP end point to provide the other end point (during association start-up) with a list of transport addresses (i.e., multiple IP addresses in combination with an SCTP port) through which that end point can be reached and from which it will originate SCTP packets. The association spans transfers over all of the possible source and destination combinations that may be generated from each end point's lists. The name *stream control transmission protocol* is derived from the multistreaming function provided by SCTP. This feature allows data to be partitioned into multiple streams that they have the property of independently sequenced delivery so that message loss in any one stream will only initially affect delivery within that stream and not in others. In contrast, TCP assumes a single stream of data and ensures that delivery of that stream takes place with byte-sequence preservation. Although this is desirable for delivery of a file or record, it causes additional delay when message loss or sequence error occurs within the network. When this happens, TCP must delay delivery of data until the correct sequencing is restored either by receipt of an out-of-sequence message or by retransmission of a lost message.

The SCTP transport service can be decomposed into a number of functions, including sequenced delivery, association within streams, user data fragmentation acknowledgment-based reliable service, congestion avoidance, packet validation, and path management.

SYNERGISTIC APPROACHES

The traditional *drop tail* technique for managing router queue lengths is to set a maximum length for each queue, append incoming packets to the tail of the queue until the maximum length is reached, and then reject (drop) subsequent incoming packets until the queue size decreases because a packet from the head of the queue has been transmitted. On the other hand, *random early detection* (RED (Floyd and Jacobson 1993) drops or marks incoming packets with a dynamically computed probability when the average queue size exceeds a minimum threshold. This probability increases with the average queue length and the number of packets accepted since the last time the packet was dropped. The average queue length, $\bar{q}$, is estimated as an exponentially weighted moving average as follows:

$$\bar{q} \leftarrow (1 - w) * \bar{q} + w * q \qquad (15)$$

where w, the weight of the moving average, is a fixed (small) parameter and q is the instantaneous queue length. As $\bar{q}$ varies from *min th* to *max th*, the packet-dropping probability varies linearly from 0 to *max p*.

An initial drop probability, p, is calculated using a drop function, F, given as:

$$F = \begin{cases} 0 & \bar{q} < \min\_th \\ \dfrac{\max\_p(\bar{q} - \min\_th)}{(\max\_th - \min\_th)} & \min\_th < \bar{q} < \max\_th \\ \max\_p + \dfrac{(\bar{q} - \max\_th)}{(1 - \max\_p)/\max\_th} & \max\_th < \bar{q} < 2\max\_th \\ 1 & \bar{q} > 2\max\_th \end{cases}$$

(16)

Therefore, F grows linearly from 0 to $max\ p$ when $\bar{q}$ increases from $min\ th$ to $max\ th$, and F grows linearly from $max\ p$ to 1 if $\bar{q}$ increases further from $max\ th$ to $2\ max\ th$. The actual probability, P, is a function of the initial probability, p, and a *count* of the number of packets enqueued since the last packet was dropped—that is, $P = p/(1 - count * p)$. In the original RED buffer management scheme, $F = 1$ if $\bar{q} > max\ th$. Later, Floyd recommended the use of the "gentle" variant of RED, which uses the dropping function F above.

RED attempts to provide negative feedback to sending hosts by dropping packets from among various flows probabilistically before the gateway's queue overflows. RED's strategic goal is to prevent high delays and burst drops; it achieves this by dropping packets when contention boosts up (i.e., the queue steadily builds up) before queue overflow. Although packet control is necessarily local, the management perspective of RED is not confined by strict locality: Each drop is expected to trigger a congestion-oriented response from the corresponding sender, and the dropping mechanism selects packets at random, causing more drops to flows that transmit at higher rates. RED's design was intended for TCP and adaptive transport protocols that respond to packet-drop events at the routers. RED, for example, collaborates perfectly with Reno because a packet drop triggers multiple dacks and the sender enters a congestion avoidance phase—unlike Tahoe, which falls back to the initial window size. A great advantage of RED is its implicit synergy: No modification is required to protocol headers of both layers.

CONCLUSION

Transport layer protocols incorporate mechanisms for the delivery of data. There is no standardized functionality for such protocols; they can provide a reliable service, ordering of packets, flow control, congestion control, or application-oriented rate control. Their performance cannot be characterized by a single metric, and there are many trade-offs involved. For example, reliability comes at the expense of time, congestion control has its cost on real-time application performance, and efficiency has its cost on fairness.

More sophisticated protocols have been developed recently to handle specific aspects of applications and allow collaboration—implicit or explicit—with other layers. Because the network lacks a centralized mechanism for monitoring the behavior of users or user applications, the functionality of the transport layer has a crucial role on network stability and resource-sharing capability.

GLOSSARY

Additive increase multiplicative decrease (AIMD): The standard transport protocol strategy to bring a system into equilibrium.

Congestion: A situation in which buffers are fully occupied and packets are being dropped.

Congestion control: Usually implemented in collaboration by the transport and the network layer. The transport layer regulates the transmission rate, and the network layer drops packets when the network is congested.

Flow control: A widely used mechanism to avoid overflowing in the receiver's buffer.

Goodput: A performance measure of transmitted data over time, excluding protocol overhead and retransmitted data, associated with the efficiency of protocol strategies.

Random early detection or drop (RED): A mechanism to drop packets before congestion occurs in order to avoid multiple packet drops and implicitly inform senders about forthcoming congestion.

Reliable service: A service that guarantees delivery of packets and is usually implemented using buffers at both the sender and the receiver, sequence numbers, time-outs, and acknowledgments.

Responsiveness: A measure of the ability of a system to converge to equilibrium.

Smoothness: A measure of the oscillations during transmission.

CROSS REFERENCES

See *Data Communications Basics; Data Link Layer Protocols; Network Layer Protocols; Session, Presentation and Application Layer Protocols.*

REFERENCES

Allman, M., V. Paxson, and W. Stevens. 1999. *TCP congestion control.* RFC 2581, April.

Attie, P. C., A. Lahanas, and V. Tsaoussidis. 2003. Beyond AIMD: Explicit fair-share calculation. In *Proceedings of ISCC 2003*, June, pp. 727–34.

Bakre, A., and B. R. Badrinath. 1995. I-TCP: Indirect TCP for mobile hosts. *In Proceedings of the 15th International Conference on Distributed Computing Systems*, May, p. 136.

Balakrishnan, H., V. Padmanabhan, and R. Katz. 1997. The effects of asymmetry in TCP performance. In *Proceedings of ACM Mobicom '97*, September, pp. 219–41.

Balakrishnan, H., S. Seshan, E. Amir, and R. H., Katz. 1995. Improving TCP/IP performance over wireless networks. In *Proceedings of ACM Mobicom '95*, November, pp. 2–11.

Brakmo, L. S., and L. L. Peterson. 1995. TCP Vegas: End to end congestion avoidance on a global Internet. *IEEE Journal on Selected Areas in Communications*, 13(8): 1465–80.

Casetti, C., M. Gerla, S. Mascolo, M. Y. Sanadidi, and R. Wang. 2001. TCP Westwood: Bandwidth estimation for enhanced transport over wireless links. In *Proceedings of ACM Mobicom*, New York, July, pp. 287–97.

Chandrayana, K., S. Ramakrishnan, B. Sikdar, and S. Kalyanaraman. 2006. On randomizing the sending times in TCP and other window based algorithms. *Computer Networks*, 50(3): 422–47.

Chiu, D.-M., and R. Jain. 1989. Analysis of the increase and decrease algorithms for congestion avoidance in computer networks. *Computer Networks and ISDN Systems*, 17(1): 1–14.

Fall, K., and S. Floyd. 1996. Simulation-based comparisons of Tahoe, Reno, and SACK TCP. *Computer Communication Review*, 26(3): 5–21.

Feng, W., D. Kandlur, S. Saha, and K. Shin. 1997. Understanding TCP dynamics in an integrated service Internet. In *Proceeding of ACM NOSSDAV '97*, May 1997.

Floyd, S. 2000. *Congestion control principles*. RFC 2914, September.

Floyd, S., and M. Handley. 1999. *The New Reno modification to TCP's fast recovery algorithm*. RFC 2582, April.

Floyd, S., M. Handley, and J. Padhye. 2000. *A comparison of equation-based and AIMD congestion control* (available from www.aciri.org/tfrc/).

Floyd, S., M. Handley, J. Padhye, and J. Widmer. 2000. Equation-based congestion control for unicast applications. In *Proceedings of ACM SIGCOMM 2000*, August, pp. 43–56.

Floyd, S., and V. Jacobson. 1993. Random early detection gateways for congestion avoidance. *IEEE/ACM Transactions on Networking*, 1(4): 397–413.

Goff, T., J. Moronski, D. Phatak, and V. V., Gupta. 2000. Freeze-TCP: A true end-to-end enhancement mechanism for mobile environments. In *Proceedings of IEEE INFOCOM 2000*, March, pp. 1537–45.

Handley, M., J. Pahdye, S. Floyd, and J. Widmer. 2001. *TCP friendly rate control (TFRC): Protocol specification*. RFC 3448, Proposed Standard, January.

Jacobson, V. 1988. Congestion avoidance and control. In *Proceedings of ACM SIGCOMM 88*, August.

Kohler, E., M. Handley, and S. Floyd. 2003. *Designing DCCP: Congestion control without reliability* (available at www.icir.org/kohler/dccp/).

Lahanas, A., and V. Tsaoussidis. 2003. Exploiting the efficiency and fairness potential of AIMD-based congestion avoidance and control. *Computer Networks*, 43(2): 227–45.

———. 2003. t-AIMD for asynchronous receiver feedback. In *Proceedings of ISCC 2003*, June, pp. 735–40.

Ludwig, R., and A. Gurtov. 2005. *The Eifel response algorithm for TCP*. RFC 4015.

Ludwig, R., and M. Meyer. 2003. *The Eifel detection algorithm for TCP*. RFC 3522.

Mamatas, L., and V. Tsaoussidis. 2006. *Transport protocol behavior and energy-saving potential*. Sixth International Workshop on Wireless Local Networks (WLN 2006) in conjunction with IEEE LCN 2006, Tampa, Florida.

Mascolo, S., C. Casetti, M. Gerla, M. Y., Sanadidi, and R. Wang, 2001. TCP Westwood: Bandwidth estimation for enhanced transport over wireless links. In *Proceedings of ACM Mobicom*, Rome, July 16–21.

Mathis, M., J. Mahdavi, S. Floyd, and A. Romanow. 1996. *TCP selective acknowledgement options*. RFC 2018, April.

Padhye, J., V. Firoiu, D. Towsley, and J. Kurose. 2000. Modeling TCP Reno performance: A simple model and its empirical validation. *IEEE/ACM Transactions on Networking*, 8(2): 133–45.

Papadimitriou, P., and V. Tsaoussidis. 2006. Evaluating TCP mechanisms for real-time streaming over satellite links. In *Proceedings of the Fourth IEEE International Conference on Wired and Wireless Internet Communications*, Bern, Switzerland, May, pp. 62–74.

———. 2006. On transport layer mechanisms for real-time QoS. *Journal of Mobile Multimedia*, 1(4): 342–63.

Postel, J. 1981. *Transmission control protocol*. RFC 793, September.

Psaras, I., V. Tsaoussidis, and L. Mamatas. 2005. CA-RTO: A contention-adaptive retransmission time-out. In *Proceedings of IEEE ICCCN*, San Diego.

Rejaie, R., M. Handely, and D. Estrin. 1999. RAP: An end-to-end rate-based congestion control mechanism for real-time streams in the Internet. In *Proceedings of IEEE INFOCOM '99*, April.

Sarolahti, P., and M. Kojo. 2003. *Forward RTO-recovery (F-RTO): An algorithm for detecting spurious retransmission time-outs with TCP and the stream control transmission protocol (SCTP)*. RFC 4138.

Schulzrinne, H., S. Casner, R. Frederick, and V. Jacobson. 1996. RTP: *A transport protocol for real-time applications*. RFC 1889, IETF, January.

Sinha, P., N. Venkitaraman, R. Sivakumar, and V. Bharghavan. 1999. WTCP: A reliable transport protocol for wireless wide-area networks. In *Proceedings of ACM Mobicom '99*, August, Seattle, pp. 231–41.

Sisalem, D., and H. Schulzrinne. 1998. The loss-delay adjustment algorithm: A TCP-friendly adaptation scheme. In *Proceedings of ACM NOSSDAV '98*, July, pp. 215–26.

Stewart, R., Q. Xie, K. Morneault, C. Sharp, H. Schwarzbauer, T. Taylor, I. Rytina, M. Kalla, L. Zhang, and V. Paxson. 2000. *Stream control transmission protocol*. Proposed Standard. RFC 2960, October.

Tsaoussidis, V., and H. Badr. 2000. TCP-probing: Towards an error control schema with energy and throughput performance gains. In *Proceedings of the 8th International Conference on Network Protocols*, November, pp. 12–21.

Tsaoussidis, V., H. Badr, and R. Verma. 1999. Wave and wait protocol: An energy-saving transport protocol for mobile IP-devices. In *Proceedings of the 7th International Conference on Network Protocols*, October, 301–10.

Tsaoussidis, V., and I. Matta. 2002. Open issues on TCP for mobile computing. *Journal of Wireless Communications and Mobile Computing*, 2(1): 3–20.

Tsaoussidis, V., and C. Zhang. 2002. TCP real: Receiver-oriented congestion control. *Journal of Computer Networks*, 40(4): 477–97.

———. 2005. The dynamics of responsiveness and smoothness in heterogeneous networks. *IEEE Journal on Selected Areas in Communications*, 23(6): 1178–89.

Yang, Y. R., M. S. Kim, and S. S. Lam. 2001. Transient behaviors of TCP-friendly congestion control protocols. In *Proceedings of IEEE INFOCOM 2001*, April.

Yang, Y. R., and S. S., Lam. 2000. General AIMD congestion control. In *Proceedings of the 8th International Conference on Network Protocols*, November, pp. 187–96.

Zhang, C., and V. Tsaoussidis. 2001. TCP-real: Improving real-time capabilities of TCP over heterogeneous networks. In *Proceedings of ACM NOSSDAV 2001*, June, pp. 189–98.

Zhang, L. 1986. Why TCP timers don't work well. In *Proceedings of ACM SIGCOMM*, pp. 397–405.

Session, Presentation, and Application Layer Protocols

Chadwick Sessions, *Northrop Grumman Corporation*

INTRODUCTION

The first four layers of the *open system interconnection* (OSI) *reference model* and the *TCP/IP reference model* are roughly synonymous in function: They move network data from one host to the other. Above the transport layer, however, the models differ. The TCP/IP model has one more layer, the *application layer;* whereas the OSI model uses three more—the application, presentation, and session layers—to represent the same functionality.

The OSI model's bottom four layers (physical, data-link, network, and transport) are the most studied by networking neophytes. In stark contrast, the top three layers (application, presentation, and session), which are not completely realized in the TCP/IP model, are often overlooked. The OSI model, designed by committee, explicitly had a goal of specifying layers that would solve the problem of communicating heterogeneous data and creating complex dialogs between varied autonomous systems (see Figure 1). The Internet model, on the other hand, evolved from a developing network focused on moving bits around, not on standardizing software application functions.

Even if the higher OSI layers are not widely implemented in explicit, separate layers, each serves a definite purpose. The presentation layer forces a designer into abstracting the way data are represented, leading to more maintainable code, better code re-use, and a higher chance of interoperability among communicating processes. Designing for the session layer leads to better management of complicated data streams. Also, fully utilizing the application layer allows for clear modularization of networking services and higher levels of code re-use.

ISO AND ITU REFERENCE LAYER DESCRIPTION
Framework

Work on what would become the OSI reference model began in the late 1970s and culminated in 1984 as the International Organization for Standardization (ISO) international standards document 7498. This standard was actually a joint development with the International Telegraph and Telephone Consultative Committee (CCITT), which has since been reorganized into the Telecommunication Standardization Sector of the International Telecommunication Union (ITU-T).

ISO 7498 is a collection of four documents: 7498-1 (ISO 1994b), *The Basic Model*; 7498-2, *Security Architecture*; 7498-3, *Naming and Addressing*; and 7498-4, *Management Framework*. Over time, supporting ISO and ITU-T standards augmented the basic model, adding in-depth description of the layers' services. Later revisions to the reference documents streamlined or adapted the model to new ideas in the networking world. However, the changes have not shifted the model from its tightly coupled seven-layer framework.

Being a joint effort, each ISO standards document has a mirror recommendation document from the ITU-T. To reduce confusion, the references in the rest of this chapter will refer to the ISO standard document numbers. Table 1 gives a listing of referenced ISO standards, their ITU-T counterparts, and their mappings to the OSI layers. The table is compiled from the 35.100 (open systems interconnection) standards section of the ISO Web site (www.iso.org) and the ITU-T X (data networks and open

Application

Presentation

Session

Transport

Network

Data-link

Physical

Figure 1: Layers in the OSI reference model. Source: ISO 1994b.

Table 1: Selected Application, Presentation, and Session Layer ISO and ITU Documents

Layer	Topic	ISO/ITU Document
All	Basic reference model Security architecture Naming and addressing Management framework	7498-1/X.200 7498-2/X.800 7498-3/X.650 7498-4/X.700
Application	Layer structure ACSE service definition Connection-oriented ACSE protocol Connectionless-oriented ACSE Protocol Application object service Connection-oriented application service object Connectionless-oriented application service object RTSE service definition and protocol ROSE service definition and protocol CCRSE service definition and protocol Distributed transaction processing	9545/X.207 8649 (ISO 1996a)/X.217 8650/X.227 10035/X.237 15953/X.217bis 15954/X.227bis 15955/X.237bis 9066/X.218,X.228 9072 (ISO 1989)/X.219,X.229 9804 (ISO 1998), 9805/X.851-853 10026/X.860-862
Presentation	Service definition Connection-oriented protocol Connectionless-oriented protocol ASN.1 specification ASN.1 encoding rules: BER, CER, and DER ASN.1 encoding rules: PER ASN.1 encoding rules: XER	8822 (ISO, 1994c)/X.216 8823/X.226 9576/X.236 8824/X.680 8825-1 (ISO, 2002)/X.690 8825-2/X.691 8825-4/X.693
Session	Service definition Connection-oriented protocol Connectionless-oriented protocol	8326 (ISO 1996b)/X.215 8327/X.225 9548/X.235

Source: Compiled from ISO and ITU Web sites: www.osi.org and www.itu.org

system communications) section of the ITU Web site (www.itu.org).

Application Layer

Zimmermann (1980) succinctly describes the six other layers in the OSI model as existing "only to support this layer." No common network protocols exist here, only end-user processes (or applications) that initiate and receive communications from other application-layer processes. Any software has an application component, but e-mail readers, Web browsers, instant messengers, and multiplayer games are common programs that make good application examples because each relies heavily on the network stack.

The ultimate goal of the application layer is to communicate information, but the OSI model (ISO 1994b) identifies other possible responsibilities for the layer:

- communicating processes' addresses,
- quality of service acceptable for the communications link,
- process error recovery obligation,
- security requirements,
- process synchronization, and
- requiring abstract syntaxes.

Larmouth (1995) gives a good overview of the history of the application layer and the motivations behind changes since its inception. When the OSI model first defined the application layer, it did so with the idea that applications are large, monolithic pieces of software with a tightly structured access to presentation-layer services. It broke the application entity (the portion of the application that provides OSI model support) into two parts: the user element and the *application service element* (ASE). The user element depended on the ASE for communication functionality as well as for providing an interface to services in the lower layers. The ASE itself was broken in two main modules: the *specific-application service element* (SASE) and the *common-application service element* (CASE). SASEs were network pieces custom to the specific application such as database access or file sharing.

Common-application service elements were networking elements used by many different applications. Different CASEs can be used many times in a single application entity. The OSI model originally defined four CASEs:

- *association control service elements* (ACSE) create an associative link between applications in preparation for network communications (ISO 1996a);
- *remote operations service elements* (ROSE) create a request-reply mechanism to allow for remote operations across the ACSE link (ISO 1989b);

- *reliable transfer service elements* (RTSE) allow reliable messaging while keeping the more complicated lower layers transparent (ISO 1989a); and
- *commitment, recurrence, and recovery service elements* (CRSE) act as coordinators for multiple application communications (ISO 1998).

In the 1980s, the structure of the application layer was changing. The concept of the user element was removed, and the CASE and SASE elements were combined into an application service element. Applications were now thought of as a collection of ASEs. Each ASE used a set of *service primitives* to communicate with the presentation layer and provide a high-level service (from which more ASEs could be built). This *nested service primitives model* provided a problem to an application programmer because of the complexities that could arise from naively combining ASEs. It would be ambiguous from looking at just the ASE primitives as to which lower-level services were mapped to the ASE; this would lead to multiple synchronization points (when the developer wanted only one) or incorrect ordering of messages through the combined ASEs.

Later in that decade, a new application-layer standard (ISO 1994a) created a new *application-layer structure* (ALS). Developed from a concern about coordinating network activity over more than one connection, the ALS defined new building blocks for an application entity. First, it grouped all ASEs for a single application association into a *single association object* (SAO). Within each SAO was a *single association control function* (SACF) that managed the ASEs. An application entity might have multiple SAOs and these were grouped into a *multiple association object* (MAO). Likewise, the MAOs were controlled by a *multiple association control function* (MACF).

Unfortunately, the new ALS did not address problems in the *commitment, concurrency, and recovery* (CCR) and *transaction processing* (TP) standards (ISO 1992, 1998). Briefly, these standards are concerned with the use of consistent operations. An example of keeping consistent would be a banker moving money between two institutions. The complete transaction requires two separate subtransactions (a debit and a credit), but the transaction would only be valid (i.e., consistent) if both subtransactions were successful. In other words, each action should only be committed if successful and, likewise, the other action also successful. One solution is to implement a two-phase commitment system. A related concept in TP is *atomic* transactions that are all-or-nothing operations that guarantee database consistency.

Amendment I of ISO 9545 (1994) addressed the CCR and TP problem by almost completely rewriting the standard to create the *extended application-layer structure* (XALS). The first major change was moving the SAO, MAO, SACF, and MACF concepts from the main text and into an annex because it was decided they were not necessary for combining ASEs. The concept of an *application service object* (ASO) was added, reflecting the shift to objects at the start of the 1990s. Each ASO was a collection of one and only one *control function* (CF) and a collection of ASOs or ASEs. Each ASE was defined to be basic and with no component parts. With this new structure,

an *application entity* was defined as the outermost ASO. In addition, this outermost ASO's CF was the service that specified the presentation services instead of having the ASEs specify them.

Another choice an application must make is the mode of connection. The OSI model defines two types of network communications initiated by an application: *connection-oriented* (connection mode) and *connectionless-oriented* (connectionless mode). Connection-oriented communication requires that cooperating processes follow a standard protocol to establish, maintain, and tear down the communications link. Connectionless-oriented information transfers have no explicit link setup (to be useful, of course, the receiving processes must at least listen for any incoming data).

The choice between a connection- or connectionless-oriented data transfer by the application layer is determined by factors such as overhead allowance, transmit speed, and message complexity. The choice can also affect how lower layers construct and transmit their data. In fact, the OSI model allows certain layers (physical, data-link, network, and transport) to convert between modes. However, the session and presentation layers are never allowed to convert between different modes: They are tied to the application's layer mode.

Presentation Layer

The penultimate layer of the OSI model is the presentation layer (ISO 1994c). Because it is not guaranteed that communicating processes will share the same representation of data, it is the job of the presentation layer to provide services to allow applications to transform their data into representations that other applications can understand. A classic and simple example of different data representations is the case of ASCII systems communicating with terminals using EBCDIC characters. In more complex cases, an application has a highly structured data representation that needs more than a simple one-line conversion routine.

Each application's data are considered to be encoded by a language, or *syntax*, and the presentation layer utilizes a special *transfer syntax* to solve the problem of moving data between the two representations. There can be more than one usable transfer syntax for a given application's abstract syntax. Combined with the fact that each application can have more than one representation for its data, multiple combinations of transfer syntaxes and abstract syntaxes may be possible. The ISO model defines a *presentation context* as a singular abstract and transfer syntax association. Each combination is a unique set to an application entity, and each is usually assigned a unique identifier. Multiple presentation contexts could be pairs of abstract and transfer syntaxes that are disparate in nature or simply syntax pairs that have different parameterizations. It is up to the application to define each presentation context.

When a connection-mode link between applications is established, the two communicating presentation layers must negotiate the transfer syntaxes to be used. The originating side sends possible syntaxes available to it, so the receiving presentation layer can choose the transfer syntax it understands. In connectionless-mode, the sending presentation layer chooses a transfer syntax with no negotiation. However, the receiving application must be able to translate the chosen syntax, so usually there would need to be an a priori selection of a transfer syntax.

Service Primitives

The application layer accesses the presentation layer's service primitives through the *presentation-service access point* (PSAP). The presentation layer has only one unique primitive of interest: the *P-Alter-Connect*. This primitive allows the negotiation of the presentation context discussed previously.

The rest of the presentation primitives are mirrors of the session-layer primitives. These copies give an application entity, which only has direct access to the presentation layer, access to the myriad session services. Replicating functions is the price for keeping a tightly layered model, but there is one difference between the session and presentation primitives: Whereas the session primitives have strings of octets as their data values, the presentation primitives have the same data in the applications abstract syntax. This transformation is the result of the application of the transfer syntax and its encoding rules.

Abstract Syntax Notation 1 and Basic Encoding Rules

The representation of a transfer syntax itself requires a standard notation to allow for wide-scale re-use of data definitions and operability between heterogeneous systems. *Abstract syntax notation 1* (ASN.1) is a joint ISO and ITU standard notation to do just that (ISO 2002a). ASN.1 is a textual language that is powerful enough to represent data structures that have recursive or nonmandatory elements. Before ASN.1, previous attempts at a standard notation included the *Backus-Naur form* (BNF) *notation*. Yet no standardization for BNF materialized, even though it was a powerful enough language (Larmouth 1995).

The ASN.1 is based on a set of primitive (e.g., Boolean, integer, real) and structured (e.g., set, sequence, choice) types to define a data representation. These types can be assigned values and organized into modules. Additional language features incorporate the ability to include subtyping and recursion. ASN.1 included a macro notation before 1994 when the introduction of the *information class object* deprecated it. Information class objects are similar to macros except they are placed within an object framework.

Before an ASN.1-defined transfer syntax can communicate data, the ASN.1 structures must actually be converted, or encoded, into a bit stream of octets. Because of the desired flexibility of ASN.1 and the presentation layer itself, these encoding rules are separate from the ASN.1 language. Encoding rules for ASN.1 include *basic encoding rules* (BER), *canonical encoding rules* (CER), *packed encoding rules* (PER), *lightweight encoding rules* (LWER) and *XML encoding rules* (XER).

Briefly, the use of a *type, length, and value* (TLV) encoding scheme can describe BER (ISO 2002b). ASN.1 encodes primitive types as a TLV triplet. ASN.1 structured types are recursively defined by having a nested TLV within an encapsulating *value* field (which is in its own TLV triplet). Each TLV field translates to a whole number of octets; in most usages, the type (T) and length (L) fields will impose a two-octet overhead for every primitive. Other encoding rules such as PER attempted to decrease this high overhead of BER. Usually, though, reduced overhead means encoding complexity and CPU usage increase. Although other rules attempted to do the opposite, LWER is meant to have a fast processing time, but not necessarily the most compact form. Other encoding rules, such as XER, encode ASN.1 into standard and popular document languages such as *extensible markup language* (XML).

Session Layer

The session layer manages the "dialogue" between two communicating application entities. For a connectionless-oriented link, the only function the session layer performs (besides error handling) is to provide any transport-to-session address mappings. In a connection-oriented link, services include:

- establishment and release of the session,
- selection of normal or expedited data transfer,
- management of tokens,
- management of activities,
- checkpoint synchronization and resynchronization, and
- handling of exceptions.

The rest of the session-layer description focuses on the activities in a connection-oriented session (ISO 1996b).

During the establishment of the session, the higher presentation-layer entities establish a session connection and can cooperatively set any parameter values needed for the dialogue. The session layer also provides an orderly session release for the presentation entities without losing data. In addition, with a risk of data loss, the higher presentation or session layer can abort a session.

Again, Larmouth (1995) gives a description of the motivations behind the creation of the session layers and the problems they attempt to solve. Many of the session layer's services developed in a time of unreliable and slow links. The establishment of checkpoints and their resynchronization between two applications were driven by communication failures that forced a retry of a data send. If these data constituted a large file, then it would be helpful if the network stack could periodically create synchronization points where two applications could reset and start their communications over again without restarting from the beginning.

The session layer provides two types of synchronization: minor and major. *Minor* synchronization is usually used when only one application (simplex) is talking because of the reduced complexities. During a minor checkpoint, the sending application inserts a marker (actually a type of session token) into the data stream. Once the receiving application reads this marker, it knows that the two applications have a common point at which to restart their monologue. *Major* synchronization is used when two applications are both communicating (duplex). The algorithm for the major synchronization is outside the scope of this chapter, but it allows for resynchronizing applications to have common checkpoints in the data stream.

The use of tokens in the session dialog was primarily created to overcome a specific issue in duplex links. Historically, many network protocols (and their applications) become simpler if the communicating applications do not talk simultaneously. One advantage of this is that software does not have to worry about an input and an output queue at the same time. One option is for the applications to take turns sending data, which the session layer implements with a special token. The token is appended to the data stream whenever a sending application is finished with its current communication and acts as a signal for the other application to begin sending.

With modern computers able to multitask and most languages able to support threading, multiple sending and receiving queues are trivial to implement, thus eliminating the requirement for tokens. Fast and reliable links have reduced, but not eliminated, the need for checkpointing.

The concept of a session activity comes from the days of Teletex communications. The document transmissions were independent activities and marked as such. Today, of course, the use of this activity has little benefit for the majority of non-Teletex applications. However, the application entity has full control of the session activity services and can use the activity primitives to divide its dialogue into arbitrary activities.

Service Primitives

Without going into detail about each one, the numerous session primitives fall into fourteen functional units: kernel, negotiated release, half-duplex, duplex, expedited data, typed data, capability data exchange, minor synchronize, symmetric synchronize, major synchronize, resynchronize, data separation, exceptions, and activity management. As said earlier, these primitives repeat at the presentation level.

TCP/IP PROTOCOL SUITE EXAMPLES

The only layer the TCP/IP explicitly defines of the OSI's top three is the application layer in RFC 1123 (Braden, 1989). RFC 1123 is a far different document than the OSI application standard. The RFC does not define service elements or submodules in the layer. Instead, it gives a brief introduction of the goals of application development (such as error logging and robustness) and then describes certain requirements that applications must follow (such as host names and numbers and type of service). However, the bulk of the document is a description of the basic types of applications found on the Internet: telnet, file transfer protocol (FTP), simple mail transfer protocol (SMTP), and domain name service (DNS). This may not seem the best way to set a standard, but it follows the basic philosophy of the Internet: Creation is through usage, not through a priori standards.

It is generally considered that the TCP/IP's application layer subsumes the OSI presentation and session layers, but there is no explicit mention of this subsumption in the TCP/IP *Request for Comments* (RFC) (Socolofsky and Kale 1991, for example). With no explicit layers or protocols to handle presentation or session functions, application designers are free to develop their own representations and

protocols. Over time, many of these developments have become de facto standards and textbook examples to map back to the OSI model. The problem with direct mapping of TCP/IP protocols to OSI layers is that TCP/IP software will encapsulate functionality from many layers into a single protocol that cannot be mapped to a specific OSI layer. The following examples will show off the overlapping layer services.

TCP Session Establishment

The TCP connections created between two applications are commonly called *sessions*. These sessions, which are simply the TCP/IP transport protocol handling connection establishment and control (Iren, Amer, and Conrad 1999), really do not map to the OSI session layer. The session layer provides services to the data streams that flow across the TCP-created link.

World Wide Web

Because of its ubiquity and popularity, the World Wide Web has become almost synonymous with the Internet. The advantage of separating the Web browser from the underlying data representation and services becomes apparent when one considers the numerous combinations of browsers, multimedia, and page languages that exist.

Web pages are served to a browser through the *hypertext transfer protocol* (HTTP) (Fielding et al. 1999), which is a fairly simple protocol and is usually considered at the application level, although its services can be mapped to the session layer. Its ability to create persistent Web connections gives HTTP session-level services. Before HTTP 1.0, a Web browser required separate TCP connections to download each element of a complex Web page. However, newer versions of HTTP keep a TCP connection open and stream in the different Web elements with a series of "get" statements. This "pipelining" raises the efficiency of downloading intricate Web pages, thus decreasing load time.

Even though the different elements of the Web page are primarily encoded in *hypertext markup language* (HTML), a varied number of other formats also can be found on a served page, including pictures, animations, music, and movies. These formats are specified as *multipurpose Internet mail extensions* (MIME) content types in the HTTP messages. This presentation-layer service allows the Web browser to identify content type and determine the compatibility to play it, as well as allow the user to install software for unknown MIME content (Freed and Borenstein 1996).

Hypertext transfer protocol secure (HTTPS) is the secure form of HTTP. It is not a separate protocol per se, but simply HTTP implementing a type of encrypting protocol such as *transport layer security* (TLS) or its predecessor *secure sockets layer* (SSL). Being a type of encryption, TLS (Dierks and Allen 1999) would seem to naturally fall into the presentation layer, even though it does have the word *transport* in its name. Indeed, the actual encryption of the Web page can be seen as existing at the presentation level because the encryption represents just another type of data representation. Also, the exchange of certificates and other encryption parameters could be a type of data representation negotiation. Yet TLS can also be mapped to the session layer, because it forms its own session (connection) between host and client and manages this data stream. It is protocols such as HTTPS—a combination of two protocols that both share services between the presentation and session layers—that make it a nontrivial problem to map real services based on the TCP/IP model directly to the OSI reference model.

Distributed Applications

Whereas serving a Web page is a simple request-and-receive transaction, data communications between many distributed applications become more complicated once processes need to distribute objects or execute remote code. The following common distributed services are mapped to the OSI model as we explain.

Named Pipes

A *named pipe* is a method of interprocess communication in UNIX and other operating systems (although other operating systems may have different operational semantics). A named pipe is a persistent service that allows processes to connect and disconnect with it (unlike an *unnamed pipe*, which is destroyed when the process that created it has finished). A named pipe can manage multiple flows within it by allowing multiple applications to connect to it through access points in the file system. Named pipes also implement session commands such as O_NONBLOCK, which allows for non-blocking read or write commands. The named pipe is one of the classic examples of mapping a real, common service to the session layer.

Remote Procedure Call

A *remote procedure call* (RPC) is a method for executing code remotely. An RPC (Sun Microsystems 1988) is generic in itself, but there are several RPC versions: *open network computing* (ONC), *distributed computing environment* (DCE), and ISO RPC to name a few. Barkley (1993) compares these different versions nicely. Each RPC has an associated representation. ONC RPC has *external data representation* (XDR), DCE RPC has *network data representation* (NDR), and ISO RPC has ASN.1 (of course!). Riding on top of the transport layer, RPC allows a process to transparently call a procedure even if the target machine is local or halfway around the world.

Barkley (1993) admits that there is some argument, however, as to where a remote procedure call fits on the OSI model. Because it requires a presentation-level data representation for communicating between heterogeneous environments, one argument is that an RPC is strictly an application-level service. This does fit the layering of the OSI model.

The counterargument is that RPC provides enough "dialogue" manipulations to make it a session-level service and the presentation-layer representation should be simply relegated to a common data encoding (instead of an entire presentation-layer protocol). Session services include:

- transaction IDs to match request and replies,
- versioning for both the RPC protocol and participating applications,

- authentication fields, and
- error handling.

Voice over Internet Protocol

Internet telephony, otherwise known as *voice over Internet protocol* (VoIP), is becoming a common alternative to traditional POTS (plain old telephone system) phones or even cellular phones. Entire books have been written about this new Internet service, but this section will briefly describe some of the high-level protocols and services of VoIP and how they map to the top three OSI layers.

End-user applications for VoIP include POTS telephones plugged into analog-to-digital routers to telephony software running on a personal computer. Regardless of the interface, the application has the function of presenting and receiving the multimedia of the communications and allowing user-level control of the call. The application also determines the actual services that need to be implemented at the lower levels. For example, a simple analog phone will not need any video *coders-decoders* (codecs). Likewise, a static PC-to-PC connection would have no need for three-way calling services. However, by keeping the application functionality modularly separate from the lower levels, application hardware or software is upgradeable and user privileges changeable, thus minimizing upgrade costs.

H.323

Below the VoIP application layer, H.323 (International Telecommunication Union 2003) is an umbrella standard that includes large set of protocols and services for VoIP call setup, management, and teardown. Several protocols in H.323 are usable as example mappings to OSI's presentation and session layers.

The H.323 presentation-layer services generally comprise codecs that are used to encode and decode the voice communications. Each codec runs a different encoding rate, leading to different levels of voice quality. Some common codecs include G.711 (64 kbps audio), G.729 (8 kbps speech), and G.723.1 (5.3 or 6.3 kbps speech). Video codecs are available as well, including H.261 and H.263. Keeping the codecs at the presentation layer allows VoIP systems to change data-encoding rates to match network congestion or update newly released codecs without modifying the user application.

A bulk of the call management responsibility falls on the transport layer, but some session-level services also affect the media stream or call dialogue. Services at the transport layer and below are grouped in a *call signaling* class. Functionality that controls the communication stream are called *call control* services and include the management of the different media (audio, video, and text) that can be sent across a VoIP connection and the exchange of capabilities so each end-point application knows which media streams and data rates can be used.

The *registration admission status* (RAS) messages facilitate gateway discovery and registration, name resolution (IP address ↔ H.223 address), admission and bandwidth control, and status requests. Along with RAS, protocol H.245 provides services that could map to the session layer. The H.245 protocol allows the setting of a master-and-slave configuration, exchange of capabilities, and management of the multimedia streams. Both of these protocol's messages are encoded in the independent representation ASN.1.

Sun Microsystem's Network File System

Introduced in 1985, Sun Microsystem's *network file system* (Sun-NFS) has functionality that can be mapped to all three upper layers. Sun-NFS was designed to be independent of the operating system, machine, and even transport architecture. This transparency has made it a popular file system, especially in the UNIX world. Sun-NFS is currently at version 4 (Shepler et al. 2000), with this recent version simplifying and unifying the protocol.

The application services of NFS are the procedures and operations that a user or another process can perform. Standard file operations include opening, writing, closing, locking, and attribute modification. End users may directly use the Sun-NFS through the operating system or through a secondary process interacting with the file system.

At the presentation level, NFS uses *external data representation* (XDR) as its data-representation language. Less general than ASN.1, XDR focuses more on actual systems. For example, XDR assumes *real* numbers conform to the IEEE floating point standard representation. ASN.1 also is more expressive, because XDR has no module capability or macro functionality. However, XDR can be significantly faster in encoding and decoding, and it is certainly a simpler representation language than ASN.1.

SUN-NFS has a session service built over the transport layer that is independent of any transport connection. This session allows voluntary or involuntary disconnections without server context loss. These sessions also cache authentication-service settings.

Sun-NFS uses Sun's *open network computing* (ONC) RPC to call its remote file methods on the network. Because of Sun-NFS the ONC RPC has become one of the more prevalent remote procedure call flavors. In addition to the normal RPC commands, Sun-NFS version 4 added a *compound* service functionality to its RPC operations that provides greater session functionality. The COMPOUND command allows multiple file operations using one RPC request, therefore increasing the efficiency of file system operations.

CONCLUSION

The OSI reference model provides for a highly detailed model for distinct application, presentation, and session layers. Clearly, not every application needs or uses the explicit layering described by the model. If they do, then most common applications do not tightly structure their code as much as the OSI model has detailed, especially in the application layer.

However, not taking any design requirements from the OSI model because of its complexity is like throwing the baby out with the bathwater. Separating out session and presentation services is a way of reducing the complexity of programming applications on the Internet. With many distributed applications handling multiple remote clients on different platforms, separating out dialogue (session) and representation (presentation) functions from the main functionality of the software can only be described as good design. With changing network topologies and newer hardware, programmers can focus software changes at particular layers without affecting the end-user functionality. It is the author's opinion that any future construction of a new networking framework will include some features of the OSI's application, presentation, and session layers, albeit in a form that is more friendly to real-world network programming.

GLOSSARY

Application layer: The seventh (top) layer in the OSI model and TCP/IP reference models. In the OSI model, the layer below it is the presentation layer. In the TCP/IP reference model, it is the transport layer.

Extensible markup language (XML): A markup language designed to specify many different types of data using tags. Its standards body is the World Wide Web Consortium (W3C).

Hypertext transfer protocol (HTTP): The protocol used in communicating pages on the World Wide Web. The current version is 1.1.

International Organization for Standardization (ISO): An international body that creates standards ranging from manufacturing processes to data communications.

International Telecommunication Union (ITU): An international body that creates standards (or recommendations) specializing in telecommunications (radio, satellite, and networking, among others).

Open system interconnection (OSI) reference model: An abstract network model defined in numerous ISO standards. The layers are application, presentation, session, transport, network, data link, and physical. The model defines services at each layer and describes how each layer interacts with the layers above and below it to transmit data.

Presentation layer: The fifth layer in the OSI model. The layer provides services to translate data between different syntaxes. The TCP/IP model does not implement this layer.

Remote procedure call (RPC): A protocol for executing programs remotely.

Session layer: The sixth layer in the OSI model. The layer provides services to manage the flows, or dialogues, of applications. The TCP/IP model does not implement this layer.

Syntax: The rules that define a correct language. In data communications, sending and receiving computers may use different syntaxes to encode their data. Before use, a process must translate foreign syntaxes into usable ones.

TCP/IP reference model: A set of protocols and standards that the Internet and most commercial networks implement. The model is chiefly defined in documents known as Requests for Comments (RFCs).

Voice over Internet protocol (VoIP): A protocol used to transmit and receive voice communications over a network.

CROSS REFERENCES

See *Data Communications Basics; Data Link Layer Protocols; Network Layer Protocols; Transport Layer Protocols.*

REFERENCES

Barkley, J. 1993. *National Institute of Standards and Technology interagency report 5277: Comparing remote procedure calls* (retrieved January 29, 2006, from http://hissa.nist.gov/rbac/5277/).

Braden, R., ed. 1989. *Requirements for Internet hosts—Application and support.* RFC 1123.

Dierks, T., and C. Allen. 1999. *The TLS protocol, version 1.0.* RFC 2246.

Fielding, R., J. Gettys, J. Mogul, H. Frystyk, P. Leach, and T. Berners-Lee. 1999. *Hypertext transfer protocol—HTTP/1.1.* RFC 2616.

Freed, N., and N. Borenstein. 1996. *Multipurpose Internet mail extensions (MIME). Part two: Media types.* RFC 2046.

Iren, S., P. D. Amer, and P. T. Conrad. 1999. The transport layer: Tutorial and survey. *ACM Computing Surveys,* 34: 360–404.

International Organization of Standards (ISO). 1989. *Information processing systems—Text communication—Remote operations. Part 1: Model, notation, and service definition.* Number 9072.

———. 1994a. *Information technology—Open systems interconnection—Application layer structure.* Number 9545.

———. 1994b. *Information technology—Open systems interconnection—Basic reference model: The basic model.* Number 7498-1.

———. 1994c. *Information technology—Open systems interconnection—Presentation service definition.* Number 8822.

———. 1996a. *Information technology—Open systems interconnection—Service definition for the association control service element.* Number 8649.

———. 1996b. *Information technology—Open systems interconnection—Session service definition.* Number 8326.

———. 1998. *Information technology—Open systems interconnection—Service definition for the commitment, concurrency and recovery service element.* Number 9804.

———. 2002. *Information technology—ASN. 1 encoding rules: Specification of basic encoding rules (BER), canonical encoding rules (CER) and distinguished encoding rules (DER).* Number 8825-1.

International Telecommunication Union. 2003. *ITU-H Recommendation H.323: Packet-based multimedia communications systems* (available at www.itu.int/rec/T-REC-H.323/e).

Larmouth, J. 1995. *Understanding OSI.* Chapter 9 (retrieved January 29, 2006, from www.isi.salford.ac.uk/books/osi/all.html).

Shepler, S., B. Callaghan, D. Robinson, R. Thurlow, C. Beame, M. Eisler, et al. 2000. *NFS version 4 protocol.* RFC 3010.

Socolofsky, T., and C. Kale. 1991. *A TCP/IP tutorial.* RFC 1180.

Sun Microsystems. 1988. *RPC—Remote procedure call protocol specification.* RFC 1050.

Zimmermann, H. 1980. OSI reference model: The ISO model of architecture for open systems interconnection. *IEEE Transactions on Communications,* 28: 425–32.

FURTHER READING

International Organization for Standards (ISO). 1989. *Information processing systems—Text communication—Reliable transfer. Part 1: Model and service definition.* Number 9066-1.

———. 1992. *Information technology—Open systems interconnection—Distributed transaction processing. Part 1: OSI TCP model.* Number 10026-1.

———. 2002. *Information technology—Abstract syntax notation one (ASN.1): Specification of basic notation.* Number 8824-1.

Digital Transmission

Marvi Teixeira and Viktor Zaharov, *Polytechnic University of Puerto Rico*

INTRODUCTION

Digital information transmission systems can be used to transmit signals that are originally in *digital* form (i.e., at a given time the signals can only take a finite set of allowed values within their input range) or transmit signals that are originally *analog* in nature (i.e., at any given time they can take any values within a given input range). Note that the range in question could be amplitude, phase, or frequency. Analog signals, however, must undergo a procedure called *analog to digital conversion* before they can be digitally transmitted (we discuss this later).

The section starts with comments regarding the idea behind digital information transmission and an empirical description regarding the effect of noise in these systems followed by a comparison between digital information transmission and analog information transmission. Digital data transmission technology is then summarized, starting with analog to digital conversion, channel bandwidth, *baseband transmission* (transmission of information at the same frequency range in which the information originated), *passband transmission* (i.e., transmission of information at a frequency that is upshifted, with respect to the original range, to a much higher frequency range). Next, the different modes of transmission and signaling schemes are reviewed, followed by a formal discussion regarding digital transmission systems affected by noise.

INFORMATION TRANSMISSION: ANALOG VERSUS DIGITAL
Analog versus Digital Signal Transmission: A Comparison

When an analog information waveform, such as that produced by a musical instrument, is transmitted using an analog system, it is desirable that the same waveform (except for a delay and some attenuation) appears at the receiver input. Any change, because of ever-present channel noise, in the decoded signal constitutes a distortion and

cannot be undone. Therefore, the main objective of the analog systems is to reproduce the analog waveform with as much fidelity as possible. As such, the ratio of the signal power to the noise power—that is, *signal-to-noise ratio* (SNR)—appears to be the best measure for rating system performance in meeting the stated objective. The larger the SNR, the better the analog system performance.

For the remainder of the discussion, keep in mind that an analog information waveform can be digitalized by a procedure called *analog-to-digital conversion*, after which the signal can also be handled by a digital transmission system (the idea is discussed in depth later). The idea behind digital transmission is based on transmitting only a finite set of distinctive waveforms (symbols). A number of these symbols can be used to encode each finite allowed signal level within the signal input range. In this case, because each transmitted symbol is known a priori, the receiver task is simply to determine from the received noisy signal which symbol actually arrived. The more dissimilar the symbols (symbol *distance*), the less chance of making the wrong identification. Clearly, the best measure for rating the performance of such a system in the presence of noise is the error rate at the receiver decision stage. This is called *symbol error rate* (SER); as we will see, it is closely related to the *bit error rate* (BER) or *probability bit error* (P_b). The smaller the bit error rate, the better the digital system performance.

Noise in Communication Systems: Digital versus Analog

One advantage of digital transmission is that each time the receiver makes a correct decision, the effect of channel noise on the current symbol is completely removed. This is also useful when information needs to be transmitted over long distances. In such cases, the effect of channel noise can be diminished by breaking the long channel path into several segments, each using regenerative repeaters that detect and *regenerate* the arriving symbol to its original form (thus improving the SNR by eliminating input noise); they can then be retransmitted along the next channel segment. As a consequence, the effect of noise within each individual channel segment is not compounded when the overall channel is considered. Repeaters that boost the signal power can also work as an advantage for analog transmission systems; unfortunately, they also increase the received noise power. Note that these are not *regenerative* repeaters. In practice, the SNR is actually degraded at the output of each repeater of analog information because of the addition of internal repeater noise. For analog systems, to maintain the same SNR as the number of repeaters increases, the transmitted power must be increased linearly (Proakis and Salehi 2005).

As another example of analog versus digital transmission, consider *frequency modulation* (FM) and *pulse code modulation* (PCM), both of which are studied later. These are well known to exchange bandwidth for SNR. Consider that doubling the transmission bandwidth in FM quadruples the SNR, whereas only a small increase of 12.5 percent in bandwidth for PCM systems is required to achieve the same improvement in SNR. On top of this advantage, PCM systems can also use regenerative repeaters along the transmission path as described above (Lathi 1998).

Summary of Advantages: Digital over Analog Information Transmission

Some of the advantages of digital information transmission systems over analog information transmission systems involve their behavior in the presence of noise. One advantage, for example, is the use of regenerative repeaters in digital communication; this allows the signal to be restored at the end of each channel segment, thus preventing the accumulation of errors. This permits the transmission of signals without (or with little) distortion over long distances. Analog systems, on the other hand, can transmit analog messages over maximum distances that are limited by the available transmitting power. Digital systems also have the capacity to do highly sophisticated preprocessing and post-processing of data, digital storage of data and error correction, and error detection. Note that digital transmission lends itself to the use of techniques such as time division multiplexing and code division multiple access systems, particularly in the form of *direct sequence spread spectrum*. The use of microprocessor-based digital hardware allows system upgrades by doing software updates. This is the only way to upgrade, for example, the systems of distant deep space probes. Digital data transmission systems are also amenable to encryption schemes for security and privacy protection. Finally, there is the issue of cost. The cost of digital hardware has been decreasing steadily with time while its performance and capacities have been increasing at an incredibly fast pace.

DIGITAL DATA TRANSMISSION: AN OVERVIEW
Digital Transmission Systems
The following sections describe with detail some of the main aspects of digital information transmission.

The first step in transmitting an analog signal through a digital system will be to sample the signal in order to change it from the continuous time domain to the discrete time domain. The amplitude of each sample will then be encoded using a finite number of bits. This will map the amplitude of each sample to one of a finite set of allowed amplitude values (the *quantization stage*). At this point, the signal changes from analog (sample amplitudes can take any value within a range) to digital (amplitude can have only a finite set of allowed values within a range). Each amplitude level is therefore encoded using n quantization bits that are then transmitted through a baseband channel using the selected line coding. Within this topic, there are several issues such as synchronization, bit error rate, line coding, baseband transmission, passband transmission, and others that will be tackled later.

Analog-to-Digital Conversion: Sampling

The *sampling theorem* is a fundamental tool that supports the conversion of signals from the continuous to the discrete time domain for further processing. Because most real-world signal sources have amplitudes that vary continuously within a range (analog signals), they are usually converted into digital form. The first step in the digitalization process is *time sampling* followed by the second step, *quantization*, which converts the time sample's amplitude into a stream of digital symbols. Each stream encodes one of a finite set of allowed amplitudes values or quantization levels. The second step is where the actual analog-to-digital conversion (A/D) occurs. The time sampling procedure is discussed next, and later some A/D converters are described.

The Sampling Theorem
Let $g(t)$ be a band-limited baseband analog signal with highest frequency component of B Hz, and let $g_s(t)$ be a discrete time signal obtained from $g(t)$ by sampling it at discrete instants in time: $t_n = nT_s, n = 0, \pm 1, \pm 2, ...,$. If the sampling interval is constrained to $T_s \leq 1/(2B)$, then the original continuous time signal, $g(t)$, can be perfectly reconstructed from its samples in $g_s(t)$ (Oppenheim, Schafer, and Buck 1999). Should $g(t)$ be a non–band-limited signal or band limited to a frequency higher than B, then an *anti-aliasing* filter must be used before sampling at $T_s \leq 1/(2B)$ in order to band limit the signal to B Hz. Note that the sampled signal is a discrete time analog signal because the amplitude of each time sample is still analog—that is, it can vary continuously within the signal amplitude range. The sampling operation can be mathematically modeled as a multiplication of the continuous time signal by a train of impulse functions:

$$g_s(t) = g(t) \sum_{n=-\infty}^{\infty} \delta(t - nT_s) \tag{1}$$

If the analog signal $g(t)$ has a Fourier transform $G(f)$; $g(t) \Leftrightarrow G(f)$ then the sampled signal, $g_s(t)$, has a periodic spectrum, $G_s(f)$, with spectral replicas centered at frequencies nf_s (Lathi 1998; Oppenheim, Schafer, and Buck 1999); that is,

$$g_s(t) \Leftrightarrow G_s(f) = \frac{1}{T_s} \sum_{n=-\infty}^{\infty} G(f - nf_s) \tag{2}$$

where $f_s = 1/T_s$ is the sampling frequency and $f_s = 2B$ is called the *Nyquist rate*, or minimum rate at which a band-limited continuous time signal can be sampled without the occurrence of aliasing. In general, when there is aliasing, or overlap of the spectral replicas in the spectrum of the sampled signal $G_s(f)$ (see Figure 1b), the original signal cannot be reconstructed from its samples.

The continuous time signal, $g(t)$, can be reconstructed if we recover its original spectrum from among the spectral replicas corresponding to the spectrum $G_s(f)$ of the sampled signal $g_s(t)$. This can be done by filtering the sampled signal with an ideal *low-pass filter* (LPF) with cutoff frequency B Hz and impulse response $h_{LP} = 2B \, \text{sinc}(2\pi Bt) = 2B \frac{\sin(2\pi Bt)}{2\pi Bt}$. Hence,

$$g(t) = g_s(t) * h_{LP}(t) = \sum_{n=-\infty}^{\infty} g\,(nT_s)2B\,\text{sinc}[2\pi B(t - nT_s)] \tag{3}$$

where * is the convolution sign and the sinc function is as defined above.

The sampling operation in both time and frequency domain is depicted in Figure 1. Sampling in time corresponds to a periodic replication of the original spectrum in frequency. It is clear by looking at Figure 1b that if sampling is done at less than the Nyquist rate—$f_s < 2B$—then there will be an aliasing effect whereby the spectral replicas will overlap and perfect reconstruction by using an ideal LPF will not be possible. Note that this particular figure assumes $f_s = 2B$ and therefore the maximum frequency content in the signal is assumed to be $B = f_s/2$. In practice, f_s is usually selected strictly greater than $2B$.

The sampling theorem gives a clue about the *maximum information rate* that can be transmitted without errors through a noiseless channel of bandwidth B Hz. Assuming no noise, such a channel can transmit error free a signal band limited to B Hz. Because a signal of bandwidth B Hz can be completely reconstructed from samples taken at the rate $f_s = 2B$ Hz (note that these samples are independent because they are taken at the minimum sampling rate that allows signal reconstruction from its samples), this implies that a noiseless channel of bandwidth B Hz is able to transmit error free a maximum of $2B$ *independent* pieces of information per second, which is equivalent to, say, two independent pieces of information per second per Hz of bandwidth (Lathi 1998).

In practice, a periodic train of pulses of finite width is used instead of a train of delta functions. In this case, the spectral replicas that appear in the spectrum of the sampled signal are not identical to each other. The baseband spectral replica, however, is an undistorted version of the original signal spectrum. Therefore, the original signal can still be recovered by passing the sampled signal through a low pass reconstruction filter.

Pulse Modulation

The idea behind *pulse modulation* is to sample the analog information waveform and use the amplitude value of each sample to alter one of the parameters of a pulse placed at the sampling point. Depending on the pulse parameter being changed—namely, pulse amplitude, pulse position, or pulse width—this method leads to pulse amplitude modulation (PAM), pulse position modulation (PPM) or pulse width modulation (PWM). These techniques will be discussed in detail elsewhere in this handbook.

In *instantaneous sampled* or *flattop* PAM, the amplitude of each pulse at time nT_s is equal to the amplitude of the sample value at time $t_n = nT_s$; $g(nT_s)$ (see Figure 2). Note that this PAM signal is still analog because the amplitude of the pulses can vary continuously within a range. Afterward, the PAM signal can be converted into a digital signal by quantizing the amplitude of each pulse, thus

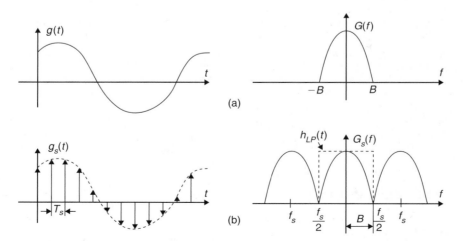

Figure 1: Sampling of analog signals and their reconstruction—(a) analog signal and its Fourier transform, (b) sampled signal and its Fourier transform

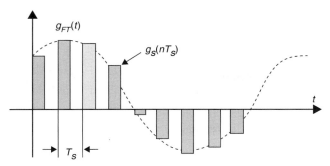

Figure 2: Flat-top or instantaneous sampled pulse amplitude modulation

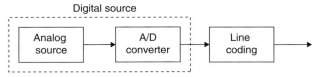

Figure 3: Baseband digital transmission system

permitting only a finite set of values to be the allowable amplitude values. So the conversion of a continuous time analog signal to a PAM signal could be considered a first step in the full digitalization of the signal (Proakis and Salehi 2005; Lathi 1998). A second modality called *natural sampled* PAM discussed elsewhere in this handbook.

Baseband Digital Transmission

A baseband information signal has a low frequency spectrum concentrated around frequency $f = 0$ and it is transmitted within the same frequency range. For a baseband digital transmission system, a digital source and a line encoder are needed. An *analog-to-digital converter* (A/D or ADC) is also needed to transform the analog information waveform into a digital data source (Figure 3). Baseband modulation schemes such as *pulse code modulation* (PCM), *differential pulse code modulation* (DPCM), and *delta modulation* (DM) are considered later in this section.

PCM: Quantization and Companding

PCM can be seen as an application of analog-to-digital conversion technology. In the first stage, an analog signal is transformed into a flattop PAM signal; in the second stage, each amplitude level of the resulting PAM pulses are encoded into finite length digital words (Lathi 1998; Couch 2001; Electrical Engineering Training Series undated). The block diagram of a PCM system is shown in Figure 4. The fact that the analog amplitude of each pulse

is converted into a finite length digital word means that there is only a finite set of "legal" values or levels (quantization levels) that can be adopted to describe the amplitude of each pulse.

An *n*-bit quantizer assigns the closest of the $2^n = M$ quantization levels as the quantized amplitude of each pulse. The difference between the analog amplitude and the quantized amplitude is called the *quantization error*. If we consider that for each sample value there is a corresponding quantization error value, then we can talk about a quantization error signal. It can be shown that such an error signal can be modeled as a white noise signal whose amplitude values, which can be positive or negative, have a uniform probabilistic distribution within the length of a quantization step (constant probability density function). Thus, the side effects of quantizing the signal are basically the same as those of adding noise to the signal. Those effects are therefore called *quantization noise*. When uniform quantization is used, the quantization step is $\Delta = 2g_p/M$, where g_p is the peak value of the flat-top sampling signal, $g_{FT}(t)$, $2g_p$ is the total amplitude range, and M is the number of quantization levels. Assuming that the quantization error is uniformly distributed in the range $(-\Delta/2, +\Delta/2)$, the variance or power of the quantization noise is $\sigma_\Delta^2 = g_p^2/3M^2$, and the *signal power to quantization noise power* (S/N) at the output of the quantizer will be (Lathi 1998):

$$\frac{S}{N} = \frac{\overline{g^2(t)}}{\sigma_\Delta^2} = 3M^2 \frac{\overline{g^2(t)}}{g_p^2} \qquad (4)$$

where $\overline{g^2(t)}$ is a time-averaged mean square value, or average power of the input analog signal.

As follows from equation 4, the output S/N is a linear function of the average power of the input signal. Hence, when the average power is rather small for a weak input signal, the output S/N can decrease dramatically. To achieve some advantage in the output SNR a scheme termed *nonuniform quantization* is used. In nonuniform quantization, the step size of the quantizer is reduced for small amplitude values and progressively increased for larger values. Such types of nonuniform quantization can be achieved by first passing the analog signal through a nonlinear device whose transfer characteristics follow the profile of certain compression curves; after that, a uniform quantizer can be used. These nonlinear curves can also be generated by a piecewise linear approximation. When compression is used at the transmitter, expansion has to be used at the receiver. To correctly restore the original analog signal, the nonlinear functions used for compression and expansion must be inverses of each other. This technique of compressing and expanding is known as *companding* (Lathi 1998).

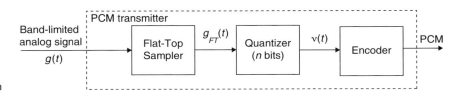

Figure 4: PCM transmission system

Two types of compression laws are accepted as standards: the μ-law and the A-law. In North America, a μ-law type of compression characteristics is used. It is defined by

$$m_o(t) = \frac{\ln\left(1 + \mu\left|m_{in}(t)\right|\right)}{\ln(1+\mu)} \times sign\{m_{in}(t)\} \quad (5)$$

where $m_o(t)$ and $m_{in}(t)$ are the output and input signals to the compressor normalized by their peak values.

In Europe, the A-law compression characteristic is applied, defined as

$$m_0(t) = \begin{cases} \dfrac{A\, m_{in}(t)}{1 + \ln A}, \\ \qquad 0 \le \left|m_{in}(t)\right| \le \dfrac{1}{A}, \\ \dfrac{1 + \ln[A\left|m_{in}(t)\right|]}{1 + \ln A} \times sign\{m_{in}(t)\}, \\ \qquad \dfrac{1}{A} \le \left|m_{in}(t)\right| \le 1. \end{cases} \quad (6)$$

The two standard laws of equations 5 and 6 are depicted in Figure 5 for different values of the parameters μ and A. Typical values for such parameters are μ = 255 and A = 87.6.

The relation of output SNR for companded PCM is given by

$$\frac{S_o}{N_o} = 3a\, 2^{2n} \quad (7)$$

where $L = 2^n$, $a = (1 + \ln A)^{-2}$ for A-law compression and, $a = [\ln(1+\mu)]^{-2}$ for μ-law compression.

Differential Pulse Code Modulation

In practice, adjacent samples of an analog signal (voice, for example) are not completely independent. This effect is more marked, considering that in practice most sampling operations are carried out at rates slightly higher than the Nyquist rate. Therefore, adjacent samples taken from an analog signal contain some redundancy. As a consequence, the transmitted bandwidth is wasted when the redundant samples are transmitted. One way to minimize redundancy is to transmit just the difference

between adjacent samples. The amplitude range of the transmitted information is therefore reduced, thus allowing the use of fewer quantization bits. To reduce even further the amplitude range being transmitted, instead of transmitting the difference between current and previous samples, what can be transmitted is the *difference* between the current sample and its predicted value based on the quantized version of previously transmitted samples. Any good prediction scheme will render a prediction value much closer to the value of the current sample than that of the previous sample value. Such method of digital transmission is called *differential pulse code modulation* (DPCM) (Lathi 1998; Couch 2001).

As shown in Lathi (1998), if the number of transmission bits is the same, then the S/N improvement of DPCM over PCM system is $\alpha = \overline{g^2(t)}/\overline{d^2(t)}$, where $d(t)$ is the difference between the amplitude value of the current sample and its predicted value based on previous samples; $\overline{g^2(t)}$ and $\overline{d^2(t)}$ are the average powers of $g(t)$ and $d(t)$ signals, respectively.

Delta Modulation

The idea of *delta modulation* (DM) is to increase the correlation between adjacent samples by oversampling above the Nyquist rate in order to achieve such a small difference between the current sample value and its predicted value that it can be encoded using only one bit ($L = 2$). Therefore, DM is a version of DPCM in which the difference in signal values, d_n, can be represented by two quantizing levels—namely, $\pm\delta$—that correspond to positive or negative differences. Actually both DM and DPCM use the *quantized* values of the previously transmitted samples to predict the value of the current sample. This is because the receiver has available only quantized values of previously transmitted samples. The DM transmission system is depicted in Figure 6.

The integrator provides staircase approximation to the analog signal by a step $\pm\delta$, where the sign depends on the d_n sign as depicted in Figure 7.

DM is subject to two types of quantization errors. In one case, when the staircase approximation cannot follow the signal because it is rapidly rising, the so-called slope overload effect, slope overload noise arises (Lathi 1998). In the second case, *granular noise* affects slow varying signals, becoming encoded in an almost square wave

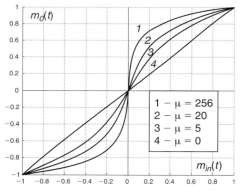
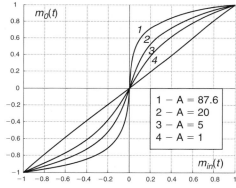

Figure 5: μ - and A-compression laws

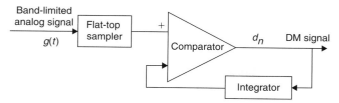

Figure 6: DSM transmission system

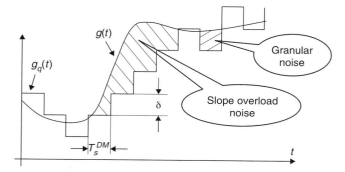

Figure 7: Regions where slope overload and granular noise occur

fashion. As follows from Figure 7, to avoid slope overload, the staircase slope must be equal to or greater than the maximum analog signal slope; that is,

$$\delta/T_s^{DM} \geq \left(\frac{dg(t)}{dt}\right)_{max} \qquad (8)$$

As shown in Couch (2001), for a voice frequency (VF) signal to avoid overload noise the corresponding value δ should be

$$\delta \geq \frac{1600\pi g_p}{f_s^{DM}} \qquad (9)$$

where g_p is a peak value of $g(t)$ and $f_s^{DM} = 1/T_s^{DM}$ is the oversampling rate being used.

The output S/N for a DM system that operates with VF signals can be written in the form

$$\frac{S_o}{N_o} = 2\frac{3(f_s^{DM})^3}{(1600\pi)^2 B} \times \overline{\frac{g^2(t)}{g_p^2}} \qquad (10)$$

The main attractions of DM are simplicity and low cost, although with the decline in price for digital components the low-cost advantage is probably no longer relevant. Note that delta modulation is inferior to PCM for high SNR cases.

Channel Bandwidth for PCM, DPCM, and DM

To find the transmitted bandwidth for PCM, we recall that PCM allows transmitting information at a bit rate given by

$$R_b = 1/T_b = \frac{1}{T_s/n} = nf_s = 2nB \qquad (11)$$

As follows from the sampling theorem, $2B$ samples can be transmitted per second per Hz over a channel of bandwidth B Hz. Because each $2B$ sample is quantized and thus encoded into n bits, we need to send $2nB$ pieces of information per second; therefore, the minimum transmission bandwidth will be half that value, or

$$B_{Tmin} = nB = R_b/2 \qquad (12)$$

Writing n as B_{Tmin}/B in equation 12 and substituting it in equation 7 yields

$$\frac{S_o}{N_o} = \alpha 2^{2(B_{Tmin}/B)} \qquad (13)$$

This means that SNR can be controlled by the transmission bandwidth. It follows from equation 13 that to increase the SNR linearly when using PCM, the transmission bandwidth needs only to be increased logarithmically.

The transmission bandwidth required by DPCM is reduced, compared with PCM, by the coefficient $\beta = n_{PCM}/n_{DPCM}$, where n_{PCM} and n_{DPCM} are the number of bits required for the transmission of the same analog signal at the same output SNR using PCM and DPCM, respectively.

Because the output of a DM transmission system only has one bit, the transmission bit rate of the DM system is $R_b = f_s^{DM}$. Hence, the minimum transmitted bandwidth required for delta modulation is $B_{Tmin} = f_s^{DM}/2$.

Line Coding

Line coding or *transmission coding* is the process of coding our information bits (0's and 1's) into electrical pulses (waveforms) in order to transmit them over a channel. Several signal formats that can be used.

Various types of line coding can be designed, depending on different applications as well as different channel characteristics (LoCicero and Patel 1999). There are two major categories of line codes: return to zero (RZ) and non-return to zero. In RZ coding, the level of the pulse returns to zero during the bit interval. In *non-return to zero* (NRZ) coding, the level of the pulse during the entire bit interval does not change. Line coding formats can also be classified according to the polarity of the voltage levels used to represent the data. For example, in unipolar signaling, the zero level and only one polarity—either positive or negative—is used. In polar signaling, both positive and negative voltage levels are used. In bipolar signaling, positive, negative, and zero voltage levels are used. The most important features that are considered when choosing a line code are the following seven.

1. *Timing.* Line codes should contain enough timing information for synchronization with the transmitter.
2. *Transmission bandwidth.* The bandwidth should be as small as possible.
3. *Probability of error.* The detection error probability should be as small as possible for a given transmission bandwidth and power.
4. *Transparency.* For every possible data sequence, the coded signal can be decoded without problems at the receiver. Note that long strings of 0's or 1's can give synchronization problems in some codes.

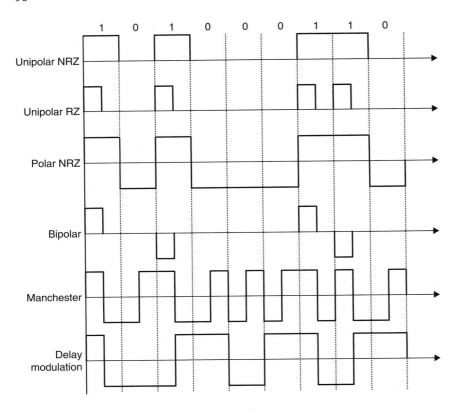

Figure 8: Line coding formats

5. *Memory.* If the current waveform depends on past binary data, then the code is said to have memory; otherwise, the code is memoryless.

6. *Adequate power spectral density profile.* Because AC coupling is used at repeaters, the line code power spectral density should not have a DC component.

7. *Error detection and correction capabilities.* The line code should lend itself to some method of error correction and, if possible, error detection.

The more widely used line coding formats are the following (see Couch 2001; LoCicero and Patel 1999; Haykin 2000): unipolar NRZ (binary on-off keying), unipolar RZ, polar NRZ, polar RZ (alternate mark inversion, or AMI), Manchester coding, delay modulation (Miller code), binary *n* zero substitution (BNZS), and high-density bipolar *n* (HDBN). The above line coding formats are depicted in Figure 8 for the binary input data: 101000110.

Unipolar NRZ (Binary On-Off Keying). In unipolar NRZ line code, a binary 1 is represented by a nonzero voltage level, and a binary 0 is represented by a zero voltage level. This is a memoryless code. The major advantages of unipolar NRZ are ease of generation and a relatively small bandwidth of R_b Hz. There are a few disadvantages with this line code: A loss of synchronization can result with a long sequence of 1's or 0's, the code has no error-detection capability, there is a significant DC component, and the error-rate performance is not as good as that of polar line codes.

Unipolar RZ. In unipolar RZ line code, a binary 1 is represented by a nonzero voltage level during one-half of the bit period. A binary 0 is represented by a zero voltage level during the entire bit duration. This is a memoryless code.

The main advantages of unipolar RZ are ease of generation and the presence of a discrete spectral component at the symbol rate, which allows for straightforward timing recovery. The code's disadvantages are that it has a nonzero DC component, which can lead to DC wander and that a long string of 0's will lead to loss of synchronization; there is no error-detection capability; the bandwidth requirement is $2R_b$ Hz, which is higher than that of NRZ signals; and the bit error-rate performance is worse than that of polar line codes.

Polar NRZ. In polar NRZ line code, a binary 1 is represented by a positive voltage and a binary 0 is represented by a negative voltage over the full bit period. This is a memoryless code. The advantages of polar NRZ include a low-bandwidth requirement of R_b Hz, good error probability, and a zero DC component. Some of the disadvantages include no error-detection capability and long strings of 1's or 0s potentially resulting in loss of synchronization.

Bipolar (Alternate Mark Inversion, or AMI)
In the bipolar or AMI scheme, a binary 1 is represented by alternating the positive and negative voltage levels, which return to zero for one-half of the bit period; a binary 0 is represented by a zero voltage level during the entire bit duration. This is a level code with memory. The AMI code is widely used in telephony. It has no DC component and completely avoids the DC wander problem. This code has error-detection capabilities and a low-bandwidth requirement of R_b Hz. Some of the AMI's codes disadvantages

are a bit error-rate performance that is worse than that of the unipolar and polar waveforms and possible loss of synchronization from long strings of 0's.

Manchester Coding.

In the Manchester code, a binary 1 is represented by two mid-bits with positive voltage of the first mid-bit and negative voltage of the second mid-bit. A binary 0 is represented as the exact opposite of a binary 1. A negative or positive mid-bit transition indicates a binary 1 or binary 0, respectively. It has no memory. This line code is used in Ethernet local area networks (LANs). The advantages of this code include zero DC content, ease of timing information extraction, and a bit error-rate performance identical to polar NRZ. The code's main disadvantages are a larger bandwidth than any of the other regular codes and no error-detection capability.

Delay Modulation (Miller Code).

In the delay modulation or Miller line code, a binary 1 is represented by a transition at the mid-bit pulse, and a binary 0 is represented by transition of the whole bit duration pulse. A 0 followed by another 0 changes signal polarity. Delay modulation is a transition code with memory. Some of the advantages of this code are that despite no distinct spectral null within the $2R_b$ Hz band, most of the energy is contained in less than $0.5R_b$ Hz, it shows low DC content, it provides good timing content, and it has a bit error-rate performance that is comparable to the other polar line code. One important disadvantage is that it has no error-detection capability.

Binary N Zero Substitution (BNZS).

The AMI code has many desirable properties of a line code. Its major limitation, however, is that a long string of zeros can lead to loss of synchronization and timing jitter. The *binary* N *zero substitution* (BNZS) attempts to improve AMI by substituting a special code of length N for all strings of N zeros in order to maintain the synchronization ability. Furthermore, the special code is chosen in such a way that the desirable properties of AMI coding are retained—that is, DC balance and error-detection capability. BNZS codes require memory. Three common BNZS codes are used: B6ZS, B3ZS, and B8ZS.

In a B6ZS code, a stream of six consecutive zeros is replaced by one of the two special codes according to the rule: If the last pulse was positive (+), then the special code is: $0 + - 0 - +$. If the last pulse was negative (−), then the special code is: $0 - + 0 + -$. Here a zero indicates a zero voltage level for the bit period, a plus designates a positive pulse, and a minus indicates a negative pulse.

There are four pulses introduced in order to facilitate timing recovery. The special code causes two AMI pulse violations, one in its second bit position and the other in its fifth bit position. These violations are easily detected at the receiver so it can receive the zeros without loosing synchronization.

In a B3ZS code, a stream of three consecutive zeros is replaced by either B0V or 00V, where B denotes a pulse that obeys the rule of the AMI and V denotes a pulse violating the AMI convention. The violation always occurs in the third bit position of the substitution code, so it can be easily detected so that zero replacement can be made at the receiver. B3ZS is used in the digital signal-3 (DS-3) signal interface in North America.

The Table 1 presents the B3ZS substitution rules.

A B8ZS code is similar to the B6ZS code. Here a stream of eight consecutive zeros is replaced by one of two special codes according to the following rule. If the last pulse was positive (+), the special code is $0\ 0\ 0 + - 0 - +$. If the last pulse was negative (−), the special code is $0\ 0\ 0 - + 0 + -$. There are two bipolar violations in the special codes—at the fourth and seventh bit positions. The B8ZS code is used to provide transparent channels for the integrated services digital network (ISDN) on T1 lines.

High-Density Bipolar N (HDBN) Line Coding.

High-density bipolar N *(HDBN) line coding* is especially similar to the BNZS code. If a stream of N + 1 consecutive zeros appears, they are replaced by a special code of length N + 1 containing certain AMI violations (to facilitate detection). One specific HDBN code is HDB3. In this code, a stream of four consecutive zeros is replaced by either B00V or 000V. Here the violation always occurs in the fourth bit position so that it can be easily detected and replaced by zero at the receiver. The Table 2 presents the HDB3 substitution rules.

Pulse Shaping: Intersymbol Interference

Transmission of baseband rectangular pulses through a band-limited communication channel causes pulse distortion and, as a consequence, *intersymbol interference* (ISI). The problem occurs because the time-limited pulse has an unlimited spectrum, but because the channel is band-limited, the transmitted pulse spectrum becomes limited as well. As the pulse spectrum becomes band-limited, the rectangular pulse itself becomes distorted and is no longer time-limited. The lack of a time limit for the duration of the pulse causes interference, in the time domain, with adjacent pulses (ISI). So the necessary condition to avoid ISI seems to be the requirement that the pulse to be

Table 1: B3ZS Substitution Rules

Number of B Pulses Since Last Violation	Polarity of Last B Pulse	Substitution Code	Substitution Code Form
Odd	Negative (−)	00−	00V
Odd	Positive (+)	00+	00V
Even	Negative (−)	+0+	B0V
Even	Positive (+)	−0−	B0V

Table 2: HDB3 Substitution Rules

Number of B Pulses Since Last Violation	Polarity of Last B Pulse	Substitution Code	Substitution Code Form
Odd	Negative ($-$)	$000-$	000V
Odd	Positive ($+$)	$000+$	000V
Even	Negative ($-$)	$+00+$	B00V
Even	Positive ($+$)	$-00-$	B00V

transmitted must have a spectrum that vanishes for frequencies that are outside the channel bandwidth—or, in other words, the pulses should be also band-limited to avoid spectrum mutilation during transmission. The main problem is that a band-limited pulse cannot be simultaneously time-limited. Therefore, it is clear that intersymbol interference is a problem inherent to all practical band-limited channels. To avoid ISI, a better technique is needed.

There exists what is known the *Nyquist criterion for zero ISI*. The pulse-shaping problem to avoid ISI occurrence can be formulated as follows: The appropriate pulse must be synthesized with a compact localization in both time and frequency domains. Furthermore, to avoid affecting adjacent pulses, the transmitted pulse has to be adjusted so that it has nonzero amplitude at its center and zero amplitude at all other signaling instants (adjacent pulses center) (Lathi 1998):

$$g(t) = \begin{cases} 1, & t = 0 \\ 0, & t = \pm nT_b \end{cases} \quad (14)$$

The pulse $p(t) = \text{sinc}(\pi R_b t)$, where $R_b = 1/T_b$ and T_b is the bit period, is the only one that satisfies the previous requirements. It has a compact bandwidth of $R_b/2$ and satisfies the above criteria to avoid ISI (Figure 9). However, this sinc-type shape has two practical inconveniences. The pulse starts at $-\infty$ and therefore it is impractical; furthermore, if it were to be truncated in time, its bandwidth would increase beyond the stated value of $R_b/2$ Hz. On top of this problem, this pulse decays so slowly, at a rate of $1/t$, that the synchronization of the clock in the receiver sampling circuit must be absolutely perfect to avoid the

ISI that would occur because of any deviation from the exact sampling instant. Unfortunately, it is known that, in practice, sampling instants deviate because of pulse time jitter. As a result of the slow pulse decay, the cumulative effect of the interference from remaining pulses amounts to a large value. There are other reasons for these types of deviations from the exact sampling instants such as little change in the data rate R_b at the transmitter and little change in the sampling rate at the receiver.

Because of these problems, Nyquist considered other pulse shapes that have a slightly wider bandwidth. The idea is to find pulse shapes that go through zero at adjacent sampling points and yet have an envelope that decays much faster than $1/t$. One solution is to generate the pulse as the impulse response of the raised cosine–rolloff Nyquist filter with the frequency transfer function (Couch 2001):

$$G(f) = \begin{cases} 1, & |f| < f_1, \\ 0.5\left\{1 + \cos\left[\dfrac{\pi|f| - f_1}{2\,\Delta f}\right]\right\}, & f_1 < |f| < B_T, \\ 0, & |f| > B_T, \end{cases} \quad (15)$$

where $\Delta f = B_T - R_b/2$, and $f_1 = R_b/2 - \Delta f$.

The ratio $r = 2\Delta f/R_b$ is called the roll-off factor. Figure 10 shows the pulse in question as the impulse response of the raised cosine-rolloff Nyquist filter and the frequency transfer function of this filter for the bit rate $R_b = 20$ Hz and three roll-off factors, $r = 0$, $r = 0.5$, and $r = 1$.

Because $0 < r < 1$, the transmission bandwidth varies from $R_b/2$ to R_b, depending on the choice of r; for any r, it can be calculated as $B_T = (1 + r)R_b/2$. A higher r gives a higher transmission bandwidth. The pulse decays quickly as $1/t^3$ and therefore this type of pulse is less sensitive to small deviations in bit rate, sampling rate, timing jitter, and the like. Hence, the clock timing requirements can now be relaxed.

At this point, the filter is not yet a causal filter. Noncausal filters are not physically realizable. Causal filters have impulse responses that are zero for negative time. Therefore, this filter can be made approximately causal by delaying its impulse response by an appropriate amount of time, t_0. Such delay causes the peak of the impulse response to move to the right along the time axis. The anticausal tail becomes negligible because of the large order of decay ($1/t^3$) of the filter impulse response.

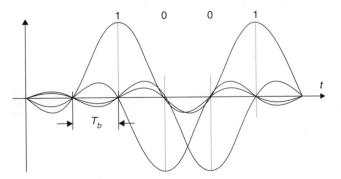

Figure 9: Sinc-type waveforms

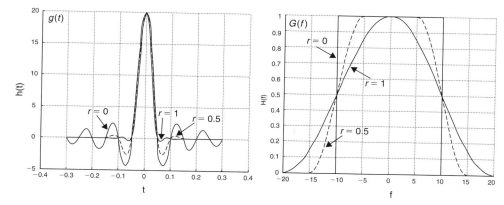

Figure 10: The raised cosine roll-off Nyquist filter characteristics—(a) impulse response (b) spectral characteristics

The introduced time delay leads to a filter with transfer characteristics $G(f)e^{-j\omega t_0}$.

Timing Extraction and Jitter

As mentioned above, to avoid ISI, the clock in the receiver must be synchronized perfectly with the transmitter clock. This requires the transmission of some type of clock signal to maintain timing information. This clock synchronization signal must have a precise frequency and phase relationship with respect to the received input signal. As usual, the synchronization is derived either directly from the input signal (self-synchronization) or from a separate channel that is used only to transmit the synchronization information (pilot clock). A third method would be to have both, with the transmitter and receiver to abide by an independent master timing source. Deriving the synchronization information directly from the incoming signal is more desirable, but the complexity of the bit synchronizer circuit depends on the timing properties of the applied line code. For example, the PSD of BNZS code has a delta function at the frequency that coincides with the bit rate—that is, $f = R_b$. Hence, the bit synchronization clock signal can be extracted by passing the received BNZS waveform through a narrowband bandpass filter with central frequency R_b Hz.

Timing jitter is caused by variations in sampling instants or pulse positions. Interference, noise, and so on can cause the variation of pulse position in the receiver despite the originally transmitted pulses being exactly located. In these cases, the effect of time jitter occurs randomly. Other types of jitter are pattern dependent (because of various causes); as such, their effects are cumulative down the string of regenerative repeaters placed along the channel.

Time Division Multiplexing and Frequency Division Multiplexing

The use of pulse modulation lends itself to the simultaneous transmission of several signals through the same channel. The idea is to use the common channel on a time-sharing basis—that is, different time slots will be adjudicated to different signals in a certain order. Each signal will transmit one (or various) information pulses in its time slot. It will then wait for the other signals to use their time slots until is time to transmit again. Therefore when using *time division multiplexing* (TDM), signals will take turns in time to transmit through the channel. When using this modality, signals are transmitted at the same frequency but use different time slots.

The modality of *frequency division multiplexing* (FDM) also permits the simultaneous transmission of several signals through a common channel of a given bandwidth. Here, however, each signal occupies a different frequency range. The sum of each signal frequency range cannot exceed the available channel bandwidth. When using this modality, signals are transmitted at the same time but using different frequencies.

Digital Passband Transmission

In digital *bandpass transmission*, a carrier waveform $A_c \cos(2\pi f_c t)$ with frequency f_c and amplitude A_c is used to encode the incoming baseband modulating signal, $m(t)$, into a bandpass waveform or modulated signal. This encoding is called *modulation*. The carrier waveform, $A_c \cos(2\pi f_c t)$, is used to shift the spectrum of the original baseband waveform by an amount f_c. Shifting the spectrum to a higher frequency range may allow the binary data to be transmitted over a radio link using an antenna of reasonable dimensions.

The modulation process can involve the variation of the amplitude, frequency, or phase of the sinusoidal carrier in accordance with the incoming data. Thus, there are three basic digital modulation schemes known as *amplitude shift keying* (ASK), *phase shift keying* (PSK), and *frequency shift keying* (FSK) (Haykin 2000). Figure 11 depicts the resulting modulated waveforms when the input binary data are 10110.

If the baseband waveform $m(t)$ is an on-off signal, then multiplication by the carrier produces an ASK signal that can be written as

$$s(t) = \begin{cases} A_c g(t) \cos \omega_c t, & m(t) = 1 \\ 0, & m(t) = 0, \end{cases} \quad 0 \leq t \leq T_b \quad (16)$$

where $g(t)$ is the transmitted pulse shape.

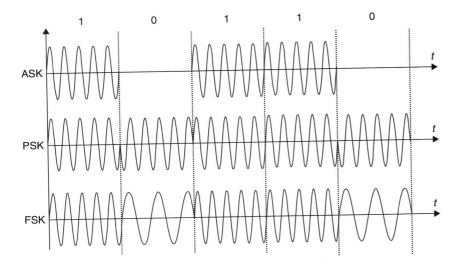

Figure 11: Basic digitlal carrier modulation waveforms

By definition, this is a *double-sideband suppressed carrier* (DSB-SC) AM signal. The spectrum of the ASK waveform is

$$S(f) = \frac{A_c}{2}[G(f - f_c) + G(f + f_c)] \qquad (17)$$

If $m(t)$ is a polar signal, then the corresponding modulated signal is a **PSK** waveform; that is,

$$s(t) = \begin{cases} A_c g(t)\cos\omega_c t, & m(t) = 1 \\ A_c g(t)\cos(\omega_c t - \pi), & m(t) = 0 \end{cases} \qquad (18)$$

Here a binary 1 in the baseband stream corresponds to the phase 0 in the bandpass waveform, and a binary 0 in the baseband stream corresponds to the phase π in the bandpass waveform. The PSK signal has the same double-sideband spectral characteristic as the ASK signal.

When the carrier frequency is changing according to a binary data stream, the modulation is called *frequency shift keying* (FSK). Binary FSK modulated signals are written as

$$s(t) = \begin{cases} A_c g(t)\cos 2\pi f_1 t, \, m(t) = 1, \\ A_c g(t)\cos 2\pi f_2 t, \, m(t) = 0, \end{cases} \quad 0 \le t \le T_b \qquad (19)$$

The spectrum of FSK may be visualized as the linear superposition of two interleaved ASK signals with frequencies f_1 and f_2.

Digital Transmission Systems: Noise and Detection Error

Suppose a stream of baseband binary information is being transmitted though an *additive white Gaussian noise* (AWGN) channel. As a consequence, the received signal will contain the desired signal, $g(t)$, plus additive white

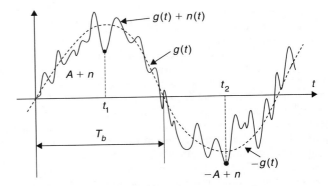

Figure 12: The received signal corrupted by noise

Gaussian noise, $n(t)$, as shown in Figure 12 for polar signaling, where $+g(t)$ corresponds to a transmitted binary 1 and $-g(t)$ corresponds to binary 0.

The decision about what pulse was transmitted is done at discrete values of time, t_k, $k = 1, 2, 3,\ldots$. It is reasonable for polar transmission to assign a detection threshold equal to zero (Lathi 1998). In other words, despite the additive noise, if the pulse amplitude value at the sampling instant t_k is positive, a 1 was received. If the pulse amplitude at the sampling instant is negative, a 0 was received. The AWGN is a random process with Gaussian *probability density function* (PDF) that will influence the detection decision at the output of the receiver. The probability of making the correct decision, or the probability of no error, is the probability of receiving a 1 (or 0) given that a 1 (or 0) was transmitted, which is $P(1|1) = P(A + n > 0)$ and $P(0|0) = P(-A + n < 0)$. The error occurs when a 0 is detected given that a 1 was transmitted (or vice versa). The probability of error can be written as $P(0|1)$, $P(1|0)$ or, in general, as $P(\in|1) = P(A + n < 0), P(\in|0) = P(-A + n > 0)$. Taking into account that $n(t)$ is a white noise with Gaussian PDF: $p(n) = \left(1/\sqrt{2\pi\sigma_n^2}\right)\exp\left(-n^2/2\sigma_n^2\right)$, the probability of error can be calculated as the area under the PDF when $n > A$ or $n < -A$. Because of the symmetry of the Gaussian PDF, the two areas have the same value—that is,

$$P(\in|0) = P(\in|1) = \frac{1}{\sqrt{2\pi\sigma_n^2}} \int_A^\infty e^{\frac{n^2}{2\sigma_n^2}} dn$$

$$= \frac{1}{\sqrt{2\pi}} \int_{A/\sigma_n}^\infty e^{\frac{\alpha^2}{2}} d\alpha = Q\left(\frac{A}{\sigma_n}\right)$$

(20)

where $Q(x) = \frac{1}{\sqrt{2\pi}} \int_x^\infty e^{\frac{\alpha^2}{2}} d\alpha$ is a tabulated integral (Lathi 1998).

The average error probability for the polar signaling is $P(e) = 0.5[P(\in|0) + P(\in|1)] = Q(A/\sigma_n)$, where the relation A/σ_n can be viewed as a root square of the SNR, or $S/N = A^2/\sigma_n^2$. For the on-off signaling, the obvious detection threshold is $A_p/2$ and the error probability is $P(\in|1) = P(n > A_p/2)$ or $P(\in|0) = P(n < -A_p/2)$. The average error probability is $P(e) = Q(A/(2\sigma_n))$. For bipolar signaling and assuming thresholds at $A_p/2$ and $-A_p/2$, the average error probability is $P(e) = 1.5Q(A/2\sigma_n)$ (Lathi 1998; Couch 2001; Haykin 2000).

Optimum Threshold Detection

Optimum threshold detection implies maximization of the A/σ_n ratio, which is the argument of the Q function, in order to minimize the average error probability. This leads to the *matched filter* concept. The following discussion can be expanded by reading this material as presented in Lathi (1998). For a received pulse $p(t)$ or $g(t)$, a matched filter maximizes the output S/N at the decision-making instant, and its value is $(S/N)_{max} = 2E_g/N_0$, where E_g is the energy of the pulse $g(t)$, and N_0 is the *power spectral density* (PSD) of the AWGN. Hence, the minimum probability of error for the detection of this pulse is $P_e = Q\left(\sqrt{2E_g/N_0}\right)$.

In binary digital communications, two distinct pulses are used. Let's say that pulse corresponds to the transmission of a binary 1 and pulse $q(t)$ corresponds to the transmission of a binary 0. In an optimum binary receiver (see Figure 13), the output at the matched filter stage, at the sampling instant T_b, is a Gaussian random

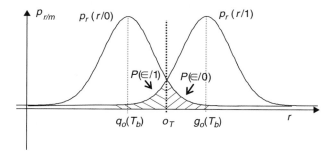

Figure 14: PDF of the random variable r at the output of the matched filter stage

variable (because of the additive Gaussian noise) of value $r(T_b) = g_o(T_b) + n_o(T_b)$ or $r(T_b) = q_o(T_b) + n_o(T_b)$, depending on which pulse, $g(t)$ or $q(t)$, did arrive. Note that $g_o(T_b)$, $q_o(T_b)$, and $n_o(T_b)$ are output values of the matched filter at sampling instant T_b. The PDF of $r(T_b)$ is depicted in Figure 14.

As shown in Lathi (1998), the bit error probability or *bit error rate* (BER) P_b in this case is $P_b = Q\left(\sqrt{(E_g + E_q - 2E_g E_q)/2N_0}\right)$, where E_g and E_q are the energies of $g(t)$ and $q(t)$, respectively (Lathi 1998). When two distinct pulses are used, the optimum threshold can be found as $o_T = 0.5(E_g - E_q)$. The performance of an optimum receiver in terms of the BER when baseband binary signaling (such as polar, on-off, and bipolar) and bandpass signaling (such as ASK, PSK, and FSK) are used leads to the following relations: $P_b = Q\left(\sqrt{2E_b/N_0}\right)$ for the polar and PSK cases; $P_b = Q\left(\sqrt{E_b/N_0}\right)$ for the on-off, FSK coherent detection, and ASK coherent detection cases; and $P_b = 1.5Q\left(\sqrt{E_b/N_0}\right)$ for the bipolar case. The ASK and FSK can be detected in noncoherent mode, based on envelope detection. The performance is $P_b = (1/2) \exp[-E_b/2N_0]$ for both ASK and FSK (Lathi 1998).

Furthermore, PSK signaling can be detected in differential coherent mode (Couch 2001; Haykin 2000). The resulting modulation is called *differential phase shift keying* (DPSK). The performance of DPSK is $P_b = (1/2) \exp[-E_b/2N_0]$. Figure 15 shows P_b versus E_b/N_0 in dB for different baseband and bandpass binary signaling schemes.

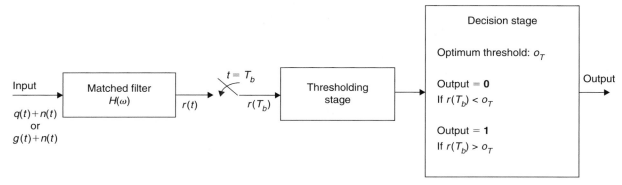

Figure 13: Optimum binary detection system

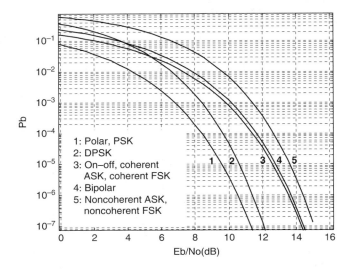

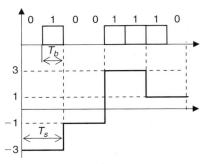

Figure 17: The formation of a four-level signal

Figure 15: Error probability for different binary signaling modes

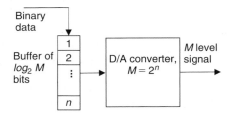

Figure 16: Converting binary data into M-ary symbols

M-ary Communications

M-ary communications implies the transmission of M symbols instead of two symbols such as in binary signaling. It is commonly used in data communication to achieve higher spectrum efficiency, which is defined as an information rate per unit of band, that is, R/B (Xiong 2000). M-ary symbols are obtained by converting a sequence of $\log_2 M$ binary digits into a corresponding M-ary symbol by *digital-to-analog* (D/A) *conversion*, as presented in Figure16. Because a single M-ary symbol carries the information of $\log_2 M$ binary digits, the transmitted power or transmission bandwidth, depending on the case, may have to be increased to keep the same performance level. On the one hand, if several amplitudes are used to distinguish the symbols, then it is clear that signal power will need compensation. On the other hand, if different frequencies are used to differentiate the symbols, then signal bandwidth will have to be increased.

As an example, a four-level signal is presented in Figure 17, where a digital-to-analog converter transforms the binary data into a four different symbols according to the rule $11 \rightarrow +3$, $10 \rightarrow +1$, $00 \rightarrow -1$ and $01 \rightarrow -3$. The resulting symbols form the baseband four-level signal (4-PAM).

When the carrier $A_c \cos 2\pi f_c t$ of frequency f_c and amplitude A_c is used to encode an M-ary baseband signal, any of the following bandpass signaling modes can result: multiphase shift keying, multiamplitude shift keying, and combined multiphase-multiamplitude signaling (Proakis and Salehi 2005; Lathi 1998).

In *m-ary phase shift keying* (M-PSK) modulation, the information is incorporated on the different phase shifts that affect the carrier. The M possible phases $\theta_k = 2\pi k/M$, $k = 0, 1,..., M-1$ are used. The general representation of a set of M carrier phase–modulated signal waveforms is

$$s_k(t) = g(t)\cos(2\pi f_c t + \frac{2\pi k}{M}) = g(t)a_k \cos(2\pi f_c t)$$
$$-g(t)b_k \sin(2\pi f_c t), k = 0, 2,..., M-1, 0 \leq t \leq T \quad (21)$$

where $a_k = \cos\dfrac{2\pi k}{M}$, $b_k = \sin\dfrac{2\pi k}{M}$ are the in-phase and quadrature components, respectively, and $g(t)$ is the transmitting filter pulse shape. Therefore, a phase-modulated signal may be viewed as two carriers in quadrature with amplitudes $g(t)a_k$ and $g(t)b_k$.

M-ary quadrature amplitude modulation (M-QAM) is a combined multiphase-multiamplitude signaling scheme. The transmitted signal has the form

$$s_k(t) = A_k g(t)\cos(2\pi f_c t + \varphi_k) = a_k g(t)\cos(2\pi f_c t)$$
$$-b_k g(t)\sin(2\pi f_c t), k = 0, 2,..., M-1, 0 \leq t \leq T \quad (22)$$

where $a_k = A_k \cos\varphi_k$, $b_k = A_k \sin\varphi_k$, $A_k = \sqrt{a_k^2 + b_k^2}$, $\varphi_k = \tan^{-1}(b_k/a_k)$.

M-QAM multisymbol signaling schemes are generated by letting a_k and b_k take on multiple values. M-QAM may be interpreted as multilevel amplitude modulation that is applied independently on each of the two quadrature carriers.

Sometimes, M-PSK as well as M-QAM signals are represented using two orthonormal basis functions (Proakis and Salehi 2005; Xiong 2000):

$$s_k(t) = s_{kc}\psi_1(t) + s_{ks}\psi_2(t) \quad (23)$$

where $\psi_1(t) = \sqrt{\dfrac{2}{E_g}} g(t)\cos 2\pi f_c t$ and $\psi_2(t) = -\sqrt{\dfrac{2}{E_g}} g(t)\sin 2\pi f_c t$ are the orthonormal basis functions and the elements of the vectors are $s_{kc} = \sqrt{\dfrac{E_g}{2}} a_k$, $s_{ks} = \sqrt{\dfrac{E_g}{2}} b_k$.

Therefore, both M-PSK and M-QAM signals can be geometrically represented as a two-dimensional vector:

$$\mathbf{s}_k = \left(\sqrt{\frac{E_g}{2}} a_k, \sqrt{\frac{E_g}{2}} b_k \right) \quad (24)$$

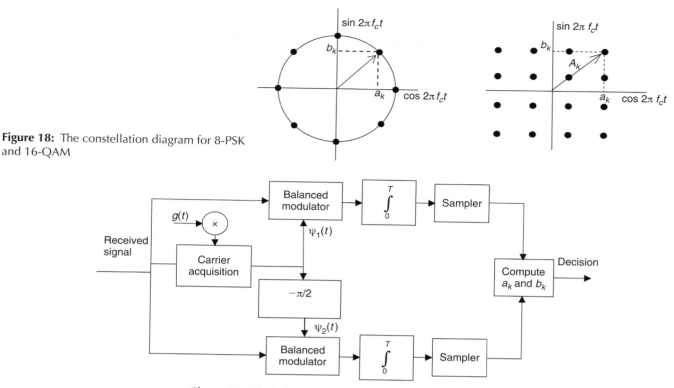

Figure 18: The constellation diagram for 8-PSK and 16-QAM

Figure 19: Block diagram of M-PSK and M-QAM transmitter

It is useful to represent the M-PSK and M-QAM signals in a two-dimensional constellation diagram by locating the set of the points $\{a_k, b_k\}$. Figure 18 depicts the constellation diagram for 8-PSK and 16-QAM. As an example, a block diagram of an M-ary bandpass transmitter is presented in Figure 19. The $\log_2 M$ successive binary input pulses are stored and then converted into the pair of numbers (a_k, b_k) that are used to modulate two quadrature carrier terms, $\cos(2\pi f_c t)$ and $\sin(2\pi f_c t)$, respectively. Depending on the values $\{a_k, b_k\}$, the transmitter can be applied either to M-PSK or M-QAM modulation.

The structure of the optimum receiver in the presence of white Gaussian noise for M-PSK (M-QAM) signals is presented in Figure 20 (Proakis and Salehi 2005; Xiong 2000), where the received signal (23), which eventually includes an additive noisy component, is multiplied by two orthonormal functions $\psi_1(t)$ and $\psi_2(t)$. After the integration and sampling stages, the elements of the received vector are $s_{kc} = \sqrt{\dfrac{E_g}{2}} a_k$, $s_{ks} = \sqrt{\dfrac{E_g}{2}} b_k$ if no noise is included.

Pros and Cons of the Different M-ary Communication Techniques

The main advantage of multiamplitude signaling is the reduction on transmitted bandwidth by a factor of $\log_2 M$ compared with the binary case for the same rate of information transmission. Although the transmission bandwidth is reduced (Lathi 1998; Xiong 2000), the transmission

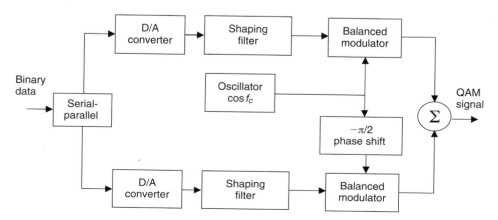

Figure 20: Block diagram of M-PSK and M-QAM optimum receiver

power increases as M^2, which can be viewed as a trade-off or cost to be paid for the reduction in bandwidth. As we said, when using M-PAM, M-QAM, and M-PSK for a fixed bit rate, the channel bandwidth decreases as the number of signals, M, increase. As M increases, the system increases its bandwidth efficiency (Proakis and Salehi 2005). However, an increase in M also means an increase in error probability (lower performance) that can be compensated by an increase in signal power that, in turn, decreases the power efficiency. Therefore, on the one hand, this brings us to the conclusion that M-ary, M-PAM, M-QAM, and PSK are amenable to bandwidth-limited communication channels such as telephone channels as long as there is enough power to support the multiple signaling phases and amplitudes (Proakis and Salehi 2005). Within this framework, it can also be said that M-QAM is better than M-PSK for large signal constellation sizes. On the other hand, multitone signals (use of different frequencies instead of different amplitudes or phases) are suitable for large bandwidth but power-limited channels (Lathi 1998).

Error Correction and Detection

The transmission of information over a communication link always results in some degradation in the quality of the information because of noise and interferers. In analog links, the degradation is measured in the form of a decrease in signal-to-noise ratio. In digital links, the degradation is measured in terms of the bit error rate. An essential difference between analog and digital transmission is that the quality of a digital signal can be improved by the use of error-correction techniques. In a digital system, some extra redundant bits are added to the data stream that not only can indicate when an error occurs but also point to the particular bit or bits that have been corrupted. Afterward, the communication system can correct the errors that were detected.

Systems that only detect errors (error-detection systems) must make a decision about what action to take when an error is detected: ignore the error, flag the error, send a block of information again, or estimate the error and replace the corrupted data.

Systems that detect and correct errors (e.g., a *forward error correction* or FEC system) generate codes that can detect and correct some errors in a given data stream. The number of errors that can be corrected strongly depends on the number of redundant bits. An increase in the number of redundant bits results in a reduction of the data rate. This is because the redundant bits are not data bits. In practice, there is a trade-off between the number of redundant bits added to the information data bits and the rate at which information is sent over the link.

In some FEC systems, the number of redundant bits is equal to the number of data bits, resulting in a halving of the data rate for a given channel transmission rate. This is called *half-rate FEC*. It has some advantages: It is easier to implement than other rates because it simplifies clock synchronization between the input data stream and the output coded stream.

The most widely used codes in FEC systems are linear block codes, cyclic block codes, and convolutional codes.

Linear block codes are codes in which n-bit code words contain k message bits and $(n - k)$ redundant check bits. A codeword with n bits of which k bits are message data is denoted as (n, k). In a systematic linear block code, the first k bits of the code word are the message bits, and the remaining $(n - k)$ bits are the parity bits.

A large number of binary cyclic codes have been found, many of which have been named after the people who first proposed them. The best known binary cyclic codes are the *Bose-Chaudhuri-Hocquenghem codes* (BCH), the Reed-Solomon codes, and the Golay codes. For example, the Golay code is a (23, 12) cyclic code that corrects all patterns of three or fewer bit errors.

The performance of FEC systems compared with other systems that do not apply error correction is considerably better. For instance, adding half-rate FEC to the data streams using convolutional coding leads to a roughly 3-dB improvement in *carrier-to-noise ratio* (CNR) at the baseband output of the receiver (Lathi 1998).

Capacity of a Band-Limited AWGN Channel

Channel capacity can be defined as the maximum rate of information transmission that can be achieved over a channel. As a rule, all communication systems involve the use of noisy channels, a fact that reduces the capacity of the overall transmission channel. For an *additive white Gaussian noise* (AWGN) channel, where the additive Gaussian noise is band-limited and zero mean, the capacity C is given by Shannon's law as

$$C = B \times \log_2\left(1 + \frac{S}{N}\right) \text{ bit/s} \qquad (25)$$

where B is the channel bandwidth in Hz, S/N is the received signal-to-noise ratio, and the channel capacity, C, gives the maximum possible information transmitted per second (Lathi 1998).

When the channel bandwidth goes to infinity, $B \rightarrow \infty$, the channel capacity reaches an upper limit. Assuming that $N = N_0 B$, where N_0 is the single-sided noise power spectral density in watts per hertz, the limit can be found (Lathi 1998) to be

$$\lim_{B \to \infty} C = \lim_{B \to \infty} B \times \log_2\left(1 + \frac{S}{N_0 B}\right) = 1.44 \frac{S}{N_0} \qquad (26)$$

Equation 26 is known as the *Shannon bound*. It shows that for finite power signals and noise, the channel capacity remains finite in spite of infinite channel bandwidth.

Multiple-Access Techniques

Multiple access permits the resources of a communication system to be shared by a large number of users who are seeking to communicate with each other. In particular, the sharing of available bandwidth has to be accomplished without causing severe interference among users. For example, in a satellite link, many earth stations can access a single satellite transponder from widely different locations at the same time. Another example is cellular communications: Many mobile handsets can access a base station at the same time.

Some basic types of multiple access techniques can be identified: *frequency division multiple access* (FDMA), *time division multiple access* (TDMA), *code division multiple access* (CDMA), *space division multiple access* (SDMA), and *random access* (RA).

In FDMA, the available frequency band is broken into *sub-bands* that are assigned to different users. To reduce interference between users, *guard bands* are introduced. These guard bands relax filtering requirements as well.

In TDMA, each user is allocated the full available frequency band but only for a short duration of time called a *time slot*. Guard times are inserted between the assigned time slots to reduce interference between users and relax the synchronization requirements.

CDMA includes *direct-sequence CDMA* (DS-CDMA) and *frequency-hopping CDMA* (FH-CDMA). In DS-CDMA, each user is assigned a unique code that distinguishes this user from other users. The assigned code is in the form of a much higher rate *pseudonoise* (PN) sequence of bits (chips) that are used to encode the data bits. The higher chip rate accounts for the spreading of the spectrum. Only those who possess the right PN code can decode the transmission of a particular user.

Each user is allocated the channel's full spectral and temporal occupancy. An important advantage of CDMA over both FDMA and TDMA is that, because of the encoding, it can provide secure communications. In FH-CDMA, for each successive time slot, the frequency bands assigned to users are reordered in a pseudorandom manner.

In SDMA, the spatial separation of earth mobile units is exploited. In particular, multibeam antennas can be used to separate signals by pointing them along different directions. Different mobile users can access the base station simultaneously, at the same frequency, at the same time or even using the same PN code.

CONCLUSION

A brief overview of some techniques used in the area of digital information transmission has been presented. Digital transmission has taken over the field of information transmission, and its further development is continually being fueled by market demand. The current trend is one of permanent falling prices for most digital communication devices and a steady increase in their capabilities and performance. There is no end in sight to this trend except, maybe, for the continuous increase in the component count in integrated circuits, which at some point may reach the current technology miniaturization limits. New technologies, such as nanotechnology, are already on the horizon to help sustain the future growth of this field.

GLOSSARY

Additive white Gaussian noise (AWGN): A random process with Gaussian probability density function that is added to the information signal and as such influences the detection decision at the output of a receiver.

Alternate mark inversion (AMI) code: Pseudoternary signal where no pulse encodes a 0 and a pulse $p(t)$ or $-p(t)$, with consecutive pulses having alternating polarities, encodes a 1. The fact that consecutive 1's are encoded with pulses of alternate sign facilitates error detection.

Amplitude shift keying (ASK): The amplitude of a carrier waveform varies (shift) among two amplitude values (usually A and 0) in order to encode 1's and 0's. If the amplitude shifts among more than two values it is called M-ASK, where M is the number of possible amplitudes.

Analog to digital converter (A/D or ADC): Transforms an analog information waveform into a digital data source.

Bandpass transmission: A type of transmission in which the spectrum of the original information is shifted to a much higher frequency, specifically around the frequency of the carrier waveform.

Baseband transmission: A type of transmission in which the transmitted signal has a spectrum concentrated around frequency $f = 0$.

Binary N zero substitution (BNZS): When N successive 0's are detected, they are suppressed and substituted by a particular sequence of N bits that includes a deliberate bipolar violation that can be easily detected and corrected. This avoids the loss of synchronization caused by too many consecutive 0's. The value of N depends on the standard.

Delta modulation (DM): A form of DPCM in which the difference between the actual sample value and that of the predicted sample valued inferred from the previously quantized sample values is encoded using only one bit. The use of only two levels for encoding such a difference is made possible by oversampling, which increases adjacent sample correlation and thus reduces the prediction error.

Differential pulse code modulation (DPCM): A technique by which the difference between the actual sample value and that of the predicted sample value inferred from the previously quantized sample values, is encoded using N bits. The smaller range of the difference, compared to the full sample value provides the following choice: Keep the same number of quantizations bits and improve the SNR or keep the same SNR and decrease the transmission bit rate.

Frequency shift keying (FSK): The frequency carrier waveform is varied (shifted) among a set of prescribed discrete frequency values in order to encode the binary bits.

High-density bipolar N line coding (HDBN): Is a code that when N + 1 consecutive zeros appear, the group of zeros is changed by one of certain N + 1 digit sequences. To avoid the loss of synchronization caused by a run of several zeros, the replacement sequences are chosen to include some binary 1's to help keep proper timing and deliberately violate the bipolar rule for easy identification.

Intersymbol interference (ISI): Then spreading of a pulse beyond its interval, which causes it to interfere with adjacent and nearby pulses.

Low-pass filter (LPF): Filter that blocks higher frequencies that are beyond a certain cutoff frequency.

M-ary communications: Communication using M symbols.

Matched filter: A filter that maximizes the output S/N at the decision-making instant when the expected symbol arrives at the receiver.

Multiamplitude shift keying (M-ASK): The amplitude of a carrier waveform varies (shifts) among the elements of a discrete set of M previously accorded values in order to encode the binary bits.

Multiphase-multiamplitude quadrature amplitude modulation (M-QAM): The phase and the amplitude of a carrier waveform varies (shifts) among the elements of a discrete set of M previously accorded values in order to encode the binary bits.

Multiphase shift keying (M-PSK): The phase of a carrier waveform varies (shifts) among the elements of a discrete set of M previously accorded values in order to encode the binary bits.

Non-return to zero (NRZ): Line codes using pulses that maintain a nonzero value during the complete bit period; thus, their amplitudes can never "return to zero."

Phase shift keying (PSK): The phase of a carrier waveform varies (shift) among a discrete set of phase values in order to encode 1's and 0's. In particular, if the phase shifts between two values, it is called BPSK. If the phase shifts among M values, it is called M-PSK

Power spectral density (PSD): For random processes, it is given by the Fourier transform of the autocorrelation function. It gives an idea of how signal power is allocated with relation to the signal frequency content.

Probability density function (Pdf): For a random variable X the Pdf $f_X(x)$, if it exists, is defined as the derivative of the *cumulative distribution function* (Cdf). The Cdf is the probability of the event $\{X \le x\}$—that is, $F_X(x) = P[X \le x]$.

Pulse amplitude modulation (PAM): The amplitude of a pulse is used to encode the value of the sample.

Pulse code modulation (PCM): A system by which an analog signal is sampled at a rate F_s samples per second and then the amplitude of each sample is quantized (adopting one out of L possible values) using N bits. The sampling rate F_s is usually 8000 samples per second, N is 8, and L is 256 for regular telephone communication.

Return to zero (RZ): Line codes using pulses that do not maintain a nonzero value during the complete bit period.

Signal-to-noise ratio (S/N or SNR): Ratio of the power of the information signal to the power of the noise signal that accompanies the information signal.

CROSS REFERENCES

See *Analog Transmission*; *Line Coding*; *Pulse Amplitude Modulation*; *Sources of Errors, Prevention, Detection and Correction*.

REFERENCES

Couch, L. W. II. 2001. *Digital and analog communication systems*. 6th ed. Upper Saddle River, NJ: Prentice Hall.

Electrical Engineering Training Series. Undated. *Pulse-code modulation*. New Port Richey, FL: Integrating Publishing (retrieved from www.tpub.com/neets/book12/49l.htm).

Haykin, S. 2000. *Communication systems*. 4th ed. New York: John Wiley & Sons.

Lathi, B. P. 1998. *Modern digital and analog communication systems*. New York: McGraw Hill.

LoCicero, J. L., and B. P. Patel. 1999. *Mobile communications handbook*. Boca Raton, FL: CRC Press.

Oppenheim, A. V., R. W. Schafer, and J. R. Buck. 1999. *Discrete-time signal processing*. 2nd ed. Upper Saddle River, NJ: Prentice Hall.

Proakis, J., and M. Salehi. 2005. *Fundamentals of communication systems*. Upper Saddle River, NJ: Prentice Hall.

Van Trees, H. L. 2002. *Detection, estimation, and modulation theory. Part I*. 2nd ed. New York: John Wiley & Sons.

Xiong, F. 2000. *Digital modulation techniques*. Boston: Artech House.

FURTHER READING

General Topics

Gibson, J. D. 2002. *The communications handbook*. New York: CRC Press.

Sklar, B. 2001. *Digital communications: Fundamentals and applications*. 2nd ed. Upper Saddle River, NJ: Prentice Hall.

M-ary Modulation

Simon, M. K. 2001. *Bandwidth-efficient digital modulation with application to deep-space communications*. Publication 00-17. Pasadena: Jet Propulsion Laboratory, California Institute of Technology.

Modulation, ISI, and Time Extraction

Benedetto, S., and E. Bigliery. 1999. *Principles of digital transmission: With wireless applications*. New York: Kluwer Academic.

Passband Digital Transmission

Ha, R., M. Borran, and D. Rajan. 2002. *Digital transmission over passband channels* (retrieved from http://cnx.org/content/m10032/2.7/).

Wilson, S. G. 1995. *Digital modulation and coding*. Upper Saddle River, NJ: Prentice Hall.

Pulse Code Modulation

Waggener, W. N. 1998. *Pulse code modulation systems design*. Boston: Artech House.

Sampling

Johnson, C. R. Jr., and W. A. Sethares. 2003. *Telecommunication breakdown*. Upper Saddle River, NJ: Prentice Hall.

Weisstein, E. W. Sampling theorem. From *MathWorld* (retrieved from http://mathworld.wolfram.com/SamplingTheorem.html).

Time Division Multiplexing

Gilbert, H. 1990. *Digital networking and T-carrier multiplexing*. New York: John Wiley & Sons.

McNicol, D. 2004. *A primer of signal detection theory*. Mahwah, NJ: Lawrence Erlbaum Associates.

Ziemer, R. E., and W. H. Tranter. 2001. *Principles of communication: Systems, modulation and noise*. 5th ed. New York: John Wiley & Sons.

Analog Transmission

Hamidreza Saligheh, *Harvard University*
Joonhyuk Kang, *Information and Communications University, Daejeon, South Korea*
Jaehak Chung, *Inha University, Incheon, South Korea*
Vahid Tarokh, *Harvard University*

INTRODUCTION

The main purpose of a communication system is to transmit information through a communication channel between a transmitter and a receiver. In general, the information is converted into a signal that varies in an unpredictable and random manner. These random information-bearing signals are broadly subdivided into two categories: *digital* and *analog*. Digital signals are constructed with a fixed and finite number of possible choices or selections, usually called symbols, and abruptly change from one symbol to another at discrete instants of time. For example, a text is a digital signal constructed from approximately fifty symbols. Analog signals accept any value between given limits and typically vary smoothly and continuously over time. The analog signals are acquired from natural analog sources—for example, the temperature or atmospheric pressure at certain locations (Pierce and Noll 1990).

ANALOG MODULATION

Information-bearing signals can be in the form of *baseband signals*. The term *baseband* refers to the band of frequencies that represents the original signal produced by a source of information. These signals are not always suitable for direct transmission over a given channel. In fact, the appropriate use of the communication channel requires a shift of the range of baseband frequencies into other frequency ranges that are efficient for transmission and a corresponding shift back to the original frequency range after reception. A shift of the range of frequencies in a signal is accomplished using *modulation*, which is defined as the process by which some characteristics of a carrier are varied in accordance with the information-bearing signal. A common form of the carrier

in *analog modulation* is a *sinusoidal wave*. The baseband information-bearing signal is referred to as the *modulating wave*, and the bandpass signal resulting from the modulation process is referred to as the *modulated wave*. Although the modulation process is performed at the transmitter, we usually need the original baseband signal to be restored at the receiver. This is accomplished through a process known as *demodulation*, which is the reverse of the modulation process (Haykin 2001).

The modulation process is performed to achieve one or more of the following objectives (Proakis and Salehi 2002; Ziemer and Tranter 2001):

1. match the baseband signal to the passband characteristics of the channel after translation into a bandpass signal,
2. accommodate for simultaneous transmission of signals from several message sources, and
3. expand the bandwidth of the transmitted signal to increase the noise immunity in a noisy channel.

Frequency multiplexing is an example of the second process. It is commonly used in long-distance telephone transmissions in which many narrowband voice channels are accommodated in a wideband coaxial cable. The bandwidth of such a cable is typically some megahertz, and the bandwidth of each voice channel is approximately 4 kilohertz (khz). The cable bandwidth is divided into intervals of 4 khz, and one voice channel is transmitted in each interval. Therefore, each voice channel must be processed (modulated) in order to shift its spectrum into the appropriate frequency slot. At the receiver, the reverse process of demodulation is necessary.

Basically, the transmitter of an analog communication system consists of a modulator and the receiver consists

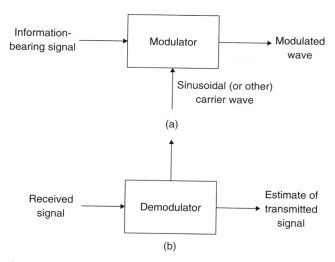

Figure 1: Basic elements of a continuous-wave communication system: (a) transmitter, (b) receiver

of a demodulator, as shown in Figure 1. In addition to the modulated wave, the received signal in the demodulator includes channel noise and distortion. Therefore, the performance of the communication system in the presence of these degradations depends on the type of the modulating wave and the employed modulation scheme. Typically in a communication system, the analog signals are converted into digital signals via sampling and quantization, because digital signals can be made more immune to noise (Ziemer and Tranter 2001; Lathi 1998).

Analog Modulation versus Pulse Modulation

In analog modulation, some parameters of a sinusoidal carrier wave are varied in accordance with the information-bearing signal. These parameters are *amplitude*, *frequency*, or *phase* of the sinusoidal carrier wave. Depending on the type of the modulating wave, these variations will result in a certain kind of modulation as follows (Haykin 2001);

- For an analog signal, these continuous variations may result in *amplitude modulation* (AM), *frequency modulation* (FM), or *phase modulation* (PM), respectively.
- For a digital binary signal, these discrete variations may result in *amplitude shift keying* (ASK), *frequency shift keying* (FSK), or *phase shift keying* (PSK), respectively.

In contrast to analog modulation, in *pulse modulation* some parameters of a pulse train are varied in accordance with the information-bearing signal. Again, depending on the type of transmission signal, there are two families of pulse modulation: *analog pulse modulation* and *digital pulse modulation*, as follows (Haykin 2001; Gagliardi 1988);

- In analog pulse modulation, a periodic pulse train is used as the carrier wave, and some features of each pulse—for example, amplitude, duration, or position—are continuously varied in accordance with the corresponding sample value of the signal. These variations result in *pulse amplitude modulation* (PAM), *pulse duration*

modulation (PDM), or *pulse position modulation* (PPM), respectively.

- In digital pulse modulation, the signal is represented in a form that is discrete in both time and amplitude. Therefore, the transmission takes place in digital form as a sequence of *coded pulses*.

Analog transmission requires high frequency circuitry, but it is known to have the following advantages over digital transmission (Lathi 1998):

- flexible frequency band allocation for different sources,
- suitability for wireless transmission where the signal frequency needs to be sufficiently high for antenna length restriction,
- amenability to band-limited electronic devices.

In general, the choice of modulation depends on several factors (Haykin 2001; Proakis and Salehi 2002):

- the characteristics of the information-bearing signal;
- the channel characteristics, such as the type of the transmission medium and the type of channel disturbances;
- performance requirements; and
- economic factors in practical implementations.

In this chapter, we study analog-modulation systems for both analog and digital signals in a noise-free environment. Real communication is always accompanied by noise; however, the objective of this chapter is to represent basic ideas of analog modulation.

Noise in Analog Transmission

The term *noise* is usually used to refer to unwanted signals that tend to disturb the transmission and processing of signals in communication systems and over which we have incomplete control. In the design of communication systems for transmitting information through physical channels, it is convenient to construct mathematical models that reflect the most important characteristics of the transmission medium (Haykin 2001; Proakis and Salehi 2002).

The simplest mathematical model for a communication channel is the additive noise channel as illustrated in Figure 2. In this model, the transmitted signal, $s(t)$, is corrupted by an additive random noise process, $n(t)$. Physically, the additive noise process arises from electronic components and amplifiers at the receiver of the communication system or from interference caused in transmission. If the noise is introduced primarily by electronic components and amplifiers at the receiver, then it may be characterized as *thermal noise*. This type of noise is statistically characterized as a *Gaussian noise process*.

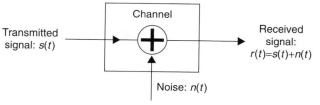

Figure 2: The additive noise channel

Therefore, the resulting mathematical model for the channel is usually called the *additive Gaussian noise channel* or *additive white Gaussian noise* (AWGN) *channel* if the noise is wideband with a constant spectral density (expressed as watts per hertz of bandwidth). This model does not account for the phenomena of fading, frequency selectivity, interference, nonlinearity, or dispersion. However, it produces simple and tractable mathematical models that are useful for gaining insight into the underlying behavior of a system before these other phenomena are considered. The AWGN channel is a good model for many satellite and deep space communication links. It is not a good model for most terrestrial links because of multipath, terrain blocking, interference, and so on. However, for terrestrial path modeling, AWGN is commonly used to simulate background noise of the channel under study in addition to the multipath, terrain blocking, interference, ground clutter, and self-interference that modern radio systems encounter in terrestrial operation (Ziemer and Tranter 2001; Wikipedia 2007; Downing 1964; Schwartz 1980).

ANALOG MODULATION FOR ANALOG SIGNALS

The general expression for a sinusoidal carrier is

$$c(t) = A_c \cos(2\pi f_c t + \varphi_c) \tag{1}$$

where A_c, f_c, and φ_c are amplitude, frequency, and phase of the carrier signal, respectively. These three parameters may be varied for the purpose of transmitting an information-bearing analog signal $m(t)$ to result in amplitude, frequency, and phase modulation, respectively. In effect, the modulation process converts the signal $m(t)$ from baseband to produce a bandpass signal in the neighborhood of the center frequency, f_c. Figure 3 displays the waveforms of amplitude-modulated and frequency-modulated signals for the case of sinusoidal modulation and a single-tone

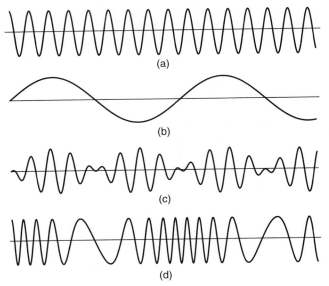

Figure 3: AM and FM signals produced by a single tone; (a) carrier wave $c(t)$; (b) sinusoidal modulating signal $m(t)$; (c) amplitude modulation; (d) angle (frequency) modulation

modulating waveform. This figure clearly explains the major differences between amplitude modulation and frequency or phase modulation. In fact, frequency modulation and phase modulation are both special cases of *angle modulation*. Basically, in this case, the only difference between frequency modulation and phase modulation is a phase shift in the modulated signal.

AMPLITUDE MODULATION

As noted above, in *amplitude modulation* (AM), the message signal $m(t)$ affects the amplitude of the carrier signal, $c(t)$. There are four main implementation methods for AM: double-sideband AM (DSB AM), double-sideband suppressed carrier AM (DSB-SC AM), single-sideband AM (SSB AM), and vestigial sideband AM (VSB AM).

Double-Sideband Amplitude Modulation

In *double-sideband amplitude modulation* (DSB AM), the carrier amplitude is proportional to the instantaneous amplitude of the modulating signal

$$s(t) = [1 + m(t)]c(t) = A_c[1 + m(t)] \cos(2\pi f_c t + \varphi_c) \tag{2}$$

In practice $|m(t)| \leq 1$ so that $A_c[1 + m(t)] \geq 0$ for an undistorted envelope and easy demodulation. If this condition is not satisfied, the AM signal is said to be *overmodulated*, and its demodulator hardware becomes more complex (Haykin 2001).

Although, in practice, the message signal $m(t)$ is unknown, here we consider a deterministic signal. In such a case, the spectrum of the AM signal $s(t)$ is

$$\begin{aligned} S(f) &= \mathcal{F}[m(t)] \otimes \mathcal{F}[A_c \cos(2\pi f_c t + \phi_c)] \\ &\quad + \mathcal{F}[A_c \cos(2\pi f_c t + \phi_c)] \\ &= \frac{A_c}{2}\Big[e^{j\phi_c} M(f - f_c) + e^{j\phi_c}\delta(f - f_c) + e^{-j\phi_c} \\ &\quad M(f + f_c) + e^{-j\phi_c}\delta(f + f_c)\Big] \end{aligned} \tag{3}$$

where $M(f)$ represents the Fourier spectrum of $m(t)$—that is, $m(t) \xleftarrow{\mathcal{F}} M(f)$, and $\mathcal{F}$, $\otimes$, and $\delta(\cdot)$ denote the Fourier transform, the convolution, and the Dirac delta function, respectively. Figure 4 illustrates such an AM signal in both time and frequency domains as well as the basic structure of modulator when the input signal is fed as $1 + m(t)$. We observe that the spectrum of a DSB AM signal occupies a bandwidth that is twice the bandwidth of the message signal W. In fact, the magnitude of the spectrum of the message signal, $m(t)$, is translated or shifted in frequency by an amount of f_c. The phase of the message signal is also translated to the same frequency and offset by the carrier phase, φ_c, which is not shown in this figure. The frequency contents of the modulated signal $S(f)$ in the frequency band $|f| > f_c$ is called the *upper sideband* (USB) of $S(f)$, and the frequency content in the frequency band $|f| < f_c$ is called the *lower sideband* (LSB) of $S(f)$. Note that either one of the sidebands of $S(f)$ contains all the frequencies that exist in $M(f)$, therefore it is called a *double-sideband* (DSB) AM signal (Shanmugan 1979; Couch 2001).

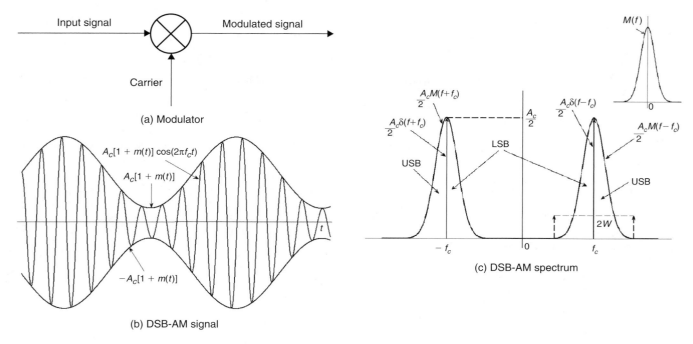

(a) Modulator

(b) DSB-AM signal

(c) DSB-AM spectrum

Figure 4: DSB AM signal and its spectrum

As stated above, $|m(t)| \leq 1$ is a necessary condition to have an easy demodulation for the DSB AM signal (see Figure 4b). In this case, the envelope has the same shape as $m(t)$ (although riding on a *direct current*, DC), and therefore it is possible to detect the desired signal $m(t)$ by using a simple envelope detection. Otherwise, we have to employ other demodulation techniques that require generation of a local carrier for the demodulation. Thus, the condition for envelope detection of an AM signal is $1 + m(t) \geq 0$, for all t (Haykin 2001; Proakis and Salehi 2002).

It is sometimes convenient to express $m(t)$ as $m(t) = \beta m_n(t)$ where $m_n(t)$ is normalized such that its minimum value is -1; the scalar factor β is called the *modulation index*. The modulation index or modulation depth indicates how much the modulated variable varies around its original level. Using this factor, the *modulation efficiency* of a DSB AM signal is defined as the ratio of the power in the modulated signal that contributes to the transmission of the message to the total power in the modulated signal; this is given by

$$\eta \overset{\Delta}{=} \frac{\beta^2 P_{m_n}}{1 + \beta^2 P_{m_n}} \qquad (4)$$

where P_{m_n} is the power in $m_n(t)$ (Proakis and Salehi 2002). As an example for the special case of tone modulation, we have $\eta = \dfrac{\beta^2}{2 + \beta^2}$ with the condition that $0 \leq \beta \leq 1$. In this case, the modulation efficiency η takes its maximum of 33 percent in the best condition when $\beta = 1$. In practical situations and for the case of envelope detection ($|m(t)| \leq 1$), this efficiency is usually lower than 25 percent.

This is the price that must be paid for the advantage of envelope detection in AM (Haykin 2001; Lathi 1998).

Generation of DSB AM signals

DSB AM is produced by multiplying together the carrier and the input signal $1 + m(t)$ as depicted in Figure 4a. The multiplication can be achieved using a network with a nonlinear behavior—for example, a diode modulator (as shown in Figure 5). The input/output characteristics of this circuit are written in terms of a power series:

$$V_{out} = aV_{in} + bV^2_{in} + cV^3_{in} + \cdots \qquad (5)$$

If $V_{in} = A_c \cos 2\pi f_c t + m(t)$, then the output is given by

$$V_{out} = A_c \cos (2\pi f_c t)[a + b_m(t)] + \text{other terms} \qquad (6)$$

As "other terms" are higher frequency components that are easily filtered off, the diode produces the required modulation.

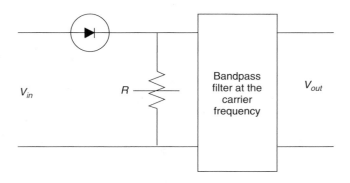

Figure 5: Diode modulator to generate DSB AM

Another method to generate AM signals is to employ a switching modulator; this is explained in Lathi (1998).

Demodulation of DSB AM Signals

The *detection* (i.e., *demodulation*) of DSB AM can be broadly considered under two headings: noncoherent and coherent. Traditionally, broadcast receivers use envelope detection. With the advent of the integrated *phase-locked loop* (PLL), coherent detectors are now attractive. The envelope (noncoherent) detector physically reproduces the envelope of the modulated carrier. The detector is basically a half-wave rectifier that commonly makes use of a silicon diode and a *low-pass filter* (LPF) as shown in Figure 6a.

When $|m(t)| \leq 1$, the rectifier eliminates the negative part of the modulated signal without affecting the message signal. In other words, the rectified signal is equal to $s(t)$ when $s(t) > 0$ and zero when $s(t) < 0$. The message signal is recovered by passing the rectified signal through an LPF whose bandwidth matches that of the message signal. The combination of the rectifier and the LPF is called an *envelope detector*. Ideally, the output of this detector is in the form of $a + bm(t)$, where a represents a DC component and b is a gain factor resulting from the signal modulator. The DC component can be eliminated by passing $d(t)$ through a transformer whose output is then $bm(t)$. The operation of an envelope detector in the presence of a square-wave message signal is shown in Figure 6b (Haykin 2001; Proakis and Salehi 2002).

Double-Sideband Suppressed Carrier Amplitude Modulation

The total power transmitted in a DSB AM signal is the sum of the carrier power and the total power in the sidebands.

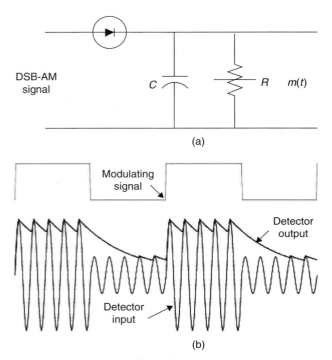

(a)

(b)

Figure 6: Envelope detector for DSB AM

If the modulating signal is a single tone, then the modulation efficiency based on equation 4 is 33 percent in the best situation. If the carrier can be suppressed, or at least reduced in amplitude, then practically all of the transmitted power is used for signal. This is more important when the received signal is distorted by noise because it produces a higher effective *signal-to-noise ratio* (SNR) than when the full carrier is transmitted. This motivates us to propose a new AM scheme called *double-sideband suppressed carrier* (DSB-SC) AM. The price paid for removing the carrier is an increase in the complexity of the detector (Lathi 1998).

The DSB-SC AM signal is obtained by multiplying the message signal $m(t)$ with the carrier signal $c(t)$ as follows

$$s(t) = m(t)\, c(t) = A_c m(t) \cos(2\pi f_c t + \varphi_c) \quad (7)$$

The spectrum of this modulated AM signal $s(t)$ is given by

$$S(f) = \mathcal{F}[m(t)] \otimes \mathcal{F}[A_c \cos(2\pi f_c t + \phi_c)]$$
$$= \frac{A_c}{2}[e^{j\phi_c} M(f - f_c) + e^{-j\phi_c} M(f + f_c)] \quad (8)$$

and is shown in Figure 7, where $M(f)$ represents the Fourier spectrum of $m(t)$ and $M(0) = M(f)|_{f=0}$. This spectrum is similar to what is shown for DSB AM in Figure 4, except for the Dirac delta functions used to illustrate the existence of carrier $A_c \cos(2\pi f_c t)$ in the modulated signal. For this reason, the signal resulting from this modulation is called *suppressed carrier signal*. In addition, the structure of the DSB-SC AM modulator is basically the same as the one proposed in Figure 4; it uses the proper input signal $m(t)$, which is the modulating signal in this case. Similar to the case of DSB AM, it is to be noted that the bandwidth occupancy of DSB-SC AM is $2W$ when the bandwidth of the message signal is assumed to be W.

Generation of DSB-SC AM signals

Modulation of DSB-SC AM is achieved in several ways. Important modulators include multiplier modulators, nonlinear modulators, and switching modulators (Couch 2001). All of these techniques are simply different methods of implementing the multiplication operation shown in Figure 4a by different methods: Multiplier modulators take advantage of analog multipliers, nonlinear modulators use nonlinear devices (e.g., see Figure 5), and switching

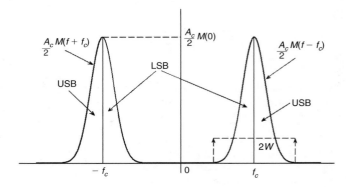

Figure 7: DSB-SC AM spectrum

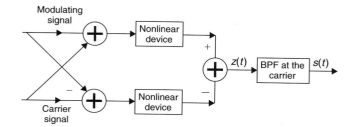

Figure 8: Nonlinear modulator to generate DSB-SC AM

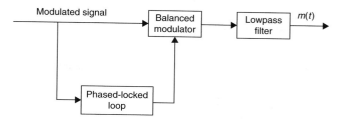

Figure 9: Demodulator for DSB-SC AM signal

modulators employ a simple switching operation. Here we explain nonlinear modulators in more detail.

As previously stated, modulation can be achieved by using nonlinear devices such as semiconductor diodes or transistors. Figure 8 depicts one possible scheme that uses two identical nonlinear elements. If the input/output characteristics of the nonlinear elements are represented by the same relationship as in equation 5, then the signal $z(t)$ is represented by

$$z(t) = 2am(t) + 4bm(t)A_c\cos 2\pi f_c t + \text{other terms} \qquad (9)$$

Whereas the spectrum of $m(t)\cos 2\pi f_c t$ is centered at the carrier frequency, if $m(t)$ and "other terms" are filtered off properly through the *bandpass filter* (BPF), the proposed structure produces the desired modulated signal. This structure is called a *single balanced modulator* (Proakis and Salehi 2002; Lathi 1998).

Demodulation of DSB-SC AM Signals

This type of modulation requires coherent detection. Because no tone component with the frequency f_c is transmitted, the required component must be generated through a local oscillator. Special circuits are required to ensure that the local oscillator is locked in phase to the incoming signal.

Let us assume that the incoming signal (in the absence of noise and through the ideal channel) is represented by $A_c m(t)\cos(2\pi f_c t + \varphi_c)$. Suppose we demodulate the received signal by first multiplying $r(t)$ by a locally generated sinusoid $\cos(2\pi f_c t + \varphi)$, where φ is the phase of the sinusoid, and then passing the product signal through an ideal LPF with bandwidth W. This process yields $\frac{1}{2} A_c m(t)\cos(\varphi_c - \varphi)$. So, depending on the value of φ, the detected signal is deviated or vanished. Therefore, we need a *phase-coherent* or *synchronous demodulator*. This phase-locked sinusoid to the phase of the received carrier at the receiver can be generated in two ways: by adding a carrier component to the transmitted signal (pilot tone) or using the phase-locked loop demodulator noted above and shown in Figure 9. The addition of a pilot tone has the disadvantage of wasting some portion of energy on the pilot. The PLL, on the other hand, generates a phase-coherent carrier signal that is mixed with the received signal in a single balanced modulator. The output of this modulator is then passed through a LPF of bandwidth W to keep the desired signal and eliminate "other terms." See Proakis and Salehi (2002) and Lindsey and Simon (1978) for more information on the PLL's characteristics and operation.

Single-Sideband Amplitude Modulation

The reason to suppress the carrier component in the DSB-SC AM is that it contains no information. It can also be observed that the signal information transmitted in the LSB is the same as is transmitted in the USB. If either one is suppressed, it is possible to send the same information with half of the employed bandwidth $2W$ for two proposed techniques in which W is the bandwidth of the baseband information-bearing signal. This is the main motivation to introduce *single-sideband amplitude modulation* (SSB AM).

The SSB AM signal is represented as follows:

$$s(t) = A_c m(t)\cos 2\pi f_c t \mp A_c \hat{m}(t)\sin 2\pi f_c t \qquad (10)$$

where $\hat{m}(t)$ is the *Hilbert transform* of $m(t)$, and plus or minus tells us which sideband we obtain. The Hilbert transform is basically a linear filter with $h(t)$, $1/\pi t \xleftrightarrow{\mathscr{F}} H(f) = -j\,\text{sgn}(f)$, where $\text{sgn}(\cdot)$ denotes the sign function. In fact, using the Hilbert transform is only one method to generate an SSB AM signal. Another method is to generate a DSB-SC AM signal and then employ a filter that is able to select either the USB or the LSB of the original signal.

As explained above, an *upper single-sideband* (USSB) AM can be obtained by eliminating the lower sidebands of a DSB-SC AM signal by passing $m(t)$ through a high-pass filter (HPF) with transfer function $H_U(f) = U(f - f_c) + U(-f - f_c)$, where $U(\cdot)$ denotes the unit step function. Therefore, the spectrum of the USSB AM signal $s_U(t)$ is given by

$$S_U(f) = A_c M(f - f_c)U(f + f_c) + A_c M(f + f_c)U(-f - f_c) \qquad (11a)$$

where $M(f)$ represents the Fourier spectrum of $m(t)$. Similarly, a *lower single-sideband* (LSSB) AM can be obtained by eliminating the upper sidebands of a DSB-SC AM signal by passing $m(t)$ through a HPF with transfer function $H_L(f) = 1 - U(f - f_c) - U(-f - f_c)$, which is in effect the complement of the $H_U(f)$ in the frequency domain. Therefore, the spectrum of the LSSB AM signal $s_L(t)$ is given by

$$S_L(f) = A_c M(f - f_c)U(f + f_c) + A_c M(f + f_c)U(-f + f_c) \qquad (11b)$$

Figure 10 shows the spectrum of two kinds of SSB AM for the message signal $m(t) \xleftrightarrow{\mathscr{F}} M(f)$ shown in Figure 4c, where $M(f)$ represents the Fourier spectrum of $m(t)$ and $M(0) = M(f)\,|_{f=0}$. In Figure 10, the USSB AM spectrum is shown in white while the LSSB AM spectrum is gray. We observe that the bandwidth occupancy of this signal is W (Haykin 2001; Gagliardi 1988; Couch 2001).

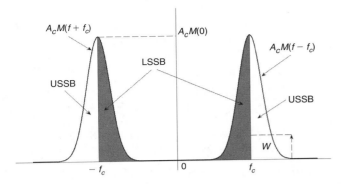

Figure 10: SSB AM spectra

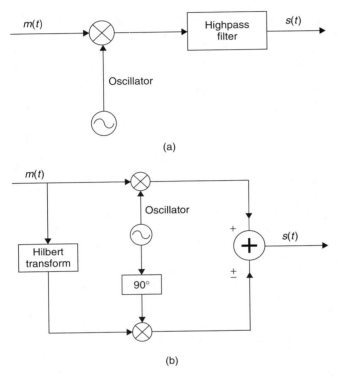

Figure 11: Generation of SSB AM signal: (a) Selective-filtering method, (b) Phase-shift method

Generation of SSB AM signals

Two methods are commonly used to generate SSB AM signals. The first uses sharp cutoff filters to eliminate the undesired sideband; the second method uses phase-shifting networks based on the Hilbert transform. These methods are shown in Figure 11 (Proakis and Salehi 2002; Lathi 1998).

Selective-Filtering Method. We can produce an SSB AM signal from DSB-SC AM by filtering off one of the sidebands as shown in Figure 11a. The filtering process is relatively difficult to accomplish at high frequency when the sideband separation would be a tiny fraction of the filter center frequency. The problem is considerably eased if the initial modulation takes place at a low carrier frequency (in the range of 100 khz). The selected sideband can then be shifted to the required frequency range—from 3 to 30 megahertz (Mhz)—by a second modulation. As the

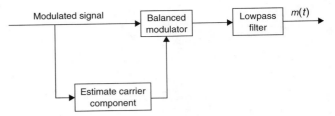

Figure 12: Demodulator for SSB AM signal

side-bands of the second modulation are spaced with a wider distance in frequency, less exact filtering is necessary.

Phase-Shift Method. An interesting alternative method is based on the Hilbert transformation. Using two blocks of DSB-SC AM modulator, this modulator basically implements equation 10 for two different possible SSB AM signals (depicted in Figure 11b). Note that the two kinds of SSB AM signals are shown by ± signs in equation 10 and correspondingly by ± signs in Figure 11b.

Demodulation of SSB AM Signals

Because no carrier is transmitted in SSB AM, the demodulation of a SSB AM signal also requires coherent detection and local oscillators. In the case of signals with almost no DC power (such as speech signals), it is common to add a small carrier component to the transmitted signal. In such a case, a configuration similar to that in Figure 12 may be used to demodulate the SSB AM signal (Proakis and Salehi 2002).

Vestigial Sideband Amplitude Modulation

Vestigial sideband amplitude modulation (VSB AM) is usually used for wideband modulating signals such as television, where the bandwidth of the modulating signal can be extended as much as 5.5 Mhz (with a total bandwidth of 11 Mhz for a DSB AM transmission). With such a wide bandwidth, the cost of an SSB AM transmitter will be high because of frequency response requirements on the sideband filter, while the bandwidth requirement for DSB AM is not easily affordable. Therefore as a compromise, we allow a part of the unwanted sideband, referred to as a *vestige*, and the whole of the other side band to appear at the output of the modulator. This way, we simplify the design of the sideband filter at the cost of a little increase in the transmitted bandwidth. The resulting signal is called *vestigial sideband* (VSB) AM signal.

To generate the VSB AM signal, we generate a DSB-SC AM signal and pass it through a sideband filter with more relaxed characteristics compared to sideband filters used for SSB AM generation. If $h(t)$ and $H(f)$ represent the impulse and frequency responses of the employed sideband filter, respectively—that is, $h(t) \xleftrightarrow{\mathcal{F}} H(f)$—then the modulated signal in both time and frequency domains is given by

$$s(t) = [A_c m(t) \cos 2\pi f_c t] \otimes h(t) \qquad (12a)$$

$$S(f) = \frac{A_c}{2}[M(f - f_c) + M(f + f_c)]H(f) \qquad (12b)$$

Based on the structure of the VSB AM demodulator (shown later in Figure 15), the filter $H(f)$ is chosen in a way that the message signal at the output of the demodulator is undistorted. In fact, the signal spectrum at the output of the ideal low-pass filter is $A_c/4\, M(f)\,[H(f-f_c)+H(f+f_c)]$. Therefore, the VSB filter characteristics must satisfy the condition (Proakis and Salehi 2002; Lathi 1998):

$$H(f-f_c)+H(f+f_c) = \text{constant}, \qquad |f| \leq W \qquad (13)$$

Figure 13 shows the frequency response characteristics of a desired filter, $H(f)$, to generate the VSB AM signal in the case of the upper sideband VSB AM, as well as the frequency response of the upper VSB AM signal for the signal proposed in Figure 4c. As we observe, the bandwidth of $H(f)$ and therefore the bandwidth of VSB AM signal is $W + V$; an extra V is added to implement the VSB AM and relax the stringent condition on the ideal filters used in DSB AM. Similarly, the lower VSB AM signal is explained by considering the fact that the frequency response of lower VSB is the mirror of what is seen in this figure around the lines $\pm f_c$ (Proakis and Salehi 2002; Lathi 1998).

Generation of VSB AM signals

VSB AM is produced by filtering the corresponding DSB AM signal as discussed above. Figure 14 shows the general structure of a VSB AM modulator.

Demodulation of VSB AM signals

Figure 15 shows the general structure of a VSB AM demodulator. To implement this coherent detector, in VSB

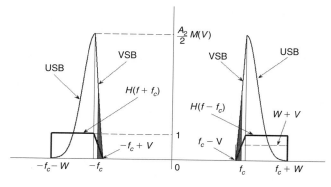

Figure 13: Frequency response of the upper VSB AM signal and its corresponding filter, H(f)

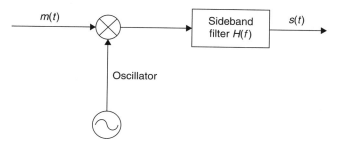

Figure 14: Generation of VSB AM signal

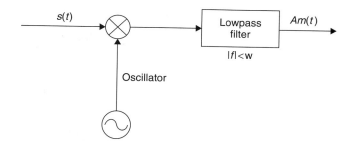

Figure 15: Demodulation of VSB AM signal

a carrier is generally transmitted along with the message sidebands. The existence of the carrier component makes it possible to extract a phase-coherent reference for demodulation in a balanced modulator as shown in Figure 12 (Proakis and Salehi 2002).

ANGLE MODULATION

As an alternative to amplitude modulation, information can be transmitted by varying the phase angle of a sinusoidal signal. This variation can impact either the phase or the frequency of the sinusoid, which results in *phase modulation* (PM) or *frequency modulation* (FM), respectively. These two modulations are often jointly referred to as *angle modulation*. Angle modulation is inherently nonlinear, difficult to implement, and even more difficult to analyze. In addition, angle modulation has a bandwidth expansion property. The effective bandwidth in an angle-modulated signal is generally many times the bandwidth of the message signal. But angle-modulation systems have a high degree of noise immunity when the transmitted signal energy is quite limited (Haykin 2001; Roberts 1977).

Representation of FM and PM Signals

An angle-modulated signal is written as

$$s(t) = A_c \cos(\theta(t)) = A_c \cos(2\pi f_c t + \varphi(t)) \qquad (14)$$

where $\theta(t)$ is the phase angle that is proportional to a function of the modulating signal, and $\varphi(t)$ is the phase drift. If we define its instantaneous frequency as $f_i(t) \triangleq \dfrac{1}{2\pi}\dfrac{d}{dt}\theta(t)$, we get

$$f_i(t) = f_c + \frac{1}{2\pi}\frac{d}{dt}\phi(t) \qquad (15)$$

This equation is the main one to define FM and PM. In fact, if $m(t)$ is the message signal, then FM and PM modulated signals are defined as follows:

$$f_i(t) - f_c = k_f m(t) = \frac{1}{2\pi}\frac{d}{dt}\phi(t) \quad \text{FM} \qquad (16a)$$

$$\phi(t) = k_p m(t) \qquad\qquad\qquad \text{PM} \qquad (16b)$$

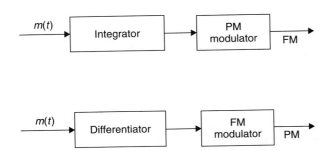

Figure 16: A comparison between FM and PM modulators

where k_f and k_p are frequency and phase *deviation constants*. This implies

$$\phi(t) = \begin{cases} 2\pi k_f \int_{-\infty}^{t} m(\xi)d\xi & \text{FM} \\ k_p m(t) & \text{PM} \end{cases} \qquad (17)$$

This equation shows a close relationship between FM and PM signals: The phase modulation of the integral of a message is equivalent to its frequency modulation—or the frequency modulation of the derivative of a message is equivalent to its phase modulation. This duality characteristic, which is shown in Figure 16, helps us describe and analyze these two modulations in parallel.

Spectral Characteristics of Angle-Modulated Signals

Because of the inherent nonlinearities of angle-modulated signals that are caused by angle time variations, precise spectral analysis of these signals is extremely difficult. In fact, such an analysis usually results in mathematically intractable equations, even for simple message signals. In this part, we study the spectral characteristics of an angle-modulated signal for two simple cases: (1) a narrowband angle-modulation system ($\varphi(t) \ll 1$, for all t) and (2) a simple sinusoidal message signal. See Proakis and Salehi (2002) and Lathi (1998) for further readings on the (spectral) characterization of different message signals.

Narrowband Angle Modulation

If an angle-modulation system is designed such that $\varphi(t) \ll 1$, for all t, then the phase-modulated signal is approximated by (Proakis and Salehi 2002)

$$S(t) \approx A_c \cos 2\pi f_c t - A_c \varphi(t) \sin 2\pi f_c t \qquad (18)$$

Therefore, the narrowband angle modulation is the same as amplitude modulation when the message signal $m(t)$ is modulated on a sine carrier rather than a cosine carrier. The spectrum analysis of this kind of angle modulation is similar to an AM signal; its bandwidth is twice that of the message signal's bandwidth. Of course, this bandwidth is just an approximation to the real bandwidth of the phase-modulated signal. For a precise characterization of the spectral properties of this signal, we should keep more

higher-order terms in the approximation of the modulated signal $s(t)$.

Angle Modulation for a Sinusoidal Signal

Considering a sinusoidal message signal $m(t) = A_m \cos 2\pi f_m t$, an angle-modulated signal (FM and PM signals) is represented by

$$s(t) = A_c \cos (2\pi f_c t + \beta \cos 2\pi f_m t) \qquad (19)$$

where β is the modulation index—that is, $\beta_f \triangleq \dfrac{k_f A_m}{f_m}$ for FM modulation or $\beta_p \triangleq k_p A_m$ for PM modulation. It is also possible to extend the definition of the modulation index for a general nonsinusoidal signal, $m(t)$, as $\beta_f \triangleq \dfrac{k_f \max[|m(t)|]}{W}$ for FM modulation or $\beta_p \triangleq k_p \max [|m(t)|]$ for PM modulation, where W denotes the bandwidth of the message signal $m(t)$ (Proakis and Salehi 2002). Because the modulating signal is a periodic function with period f_m^{-1}, we are able to rewrite it in terms of its Fourier series expansions. This expansion method for $m(t)$ results in another expansion for $s(t)$ based on *Bessel functions of the first kind of order* n—that is, $J_n(\beta)$—as follows Proakis and Salehi (2002):

$$s(t) = \sum_{-\infty}^{+\infty} A_c J_n(\beta) \cos (2\pi(f_c + nf_m)t) \qquad (20)$$

From this equation, we observe that in the case of a sinusoidal modulating signal, the actual bandwidth of the angle-modulated signal depends on $f_c \pm nf_m$—that is, the bandwidth is infinite. However, because the Bessel function is accurately approximated by $J_n(\beta) \approx \dfrac{\beta^n}{2^n n!}$ for small values of β, the amplitude of higher-order Bessels in this expansion rapidly tend to decrease. Therefore, we are able to define an effective bandwidth for this modulated signal. Usually, the effective bandwidth of an angle-modulated signal contains at least 98 percent of the signal power. Such a definition results in the effective bandwidth as

$$B_c \approx 2(\beta + 1)f_m \qquad (21)$$

where β is the modulation index and f_m is the frequency of the sinusoidal message signal (Proakis and Salehi 2002). Substituting the appropriate values for β in FM or PM cases, the effective bandwidth B_c is given by

$$B_c = \begin{cases} 2(k_f A_m + f_m) & \text{FM} \\ 2(k_p A_m + 1)f_m & \text{PM} \end{cases} \qquad (22)$$

We observe that the variations of A_m have almost the same effect on the variations of B_c in both FM and PM cases. However, in most cases of interest with a large value of β, the variations of f_m have a substantial effect on the variations of B_c of a PM signal compared to an FM signal (Shanmugan 1979; Roberts 1977).

Features of Angle Modulation

As a general fact, any modulation process involves the generation of new frequencies that are not present in the input signal. This is true for both amplitude- and angle-modulation schemes. Usually, amplitude-modulation methods are called *linear modulation methods*, although DSB AM is not linear in the strict sense. Specifically, angle-modulation methods are time-varying and nonlinear systems. Based on this nonlinearity, they have the feature of exchanging signal power for transmission bandwidth. This is a unique feature of angle-modulation schemes compared to amplitude-modulation methods. In fact, we can show that for an angle-modulation system, the SNR is roughly proportional to the square of the transmission bandwidth B_c (Lathi 1998; Roberts 1977).

Immunity of Angle Modulation to Nonlinearities (and Noise)

An interesting feature of angle modulation is its constant amplitude, which makes it less sensitive to nonlinearities. The effect of nonlinearities are lumped into the generation of some higher-order harmonics in the output of the nonlinear distortive component. These harmonics are easily filtered out by an LPF detector. Therefore, the nonlinearity does not destroy the information. Preserving the information in the presence of nonlinearity is the advantage of using this kind of modulation in microwave applications.

Generation of Angle-Modulation Signal

Basically, there are two ways to generate FM (angle modulation) signals: *indirect generation* from a narrowband angle-modulated signal or *direct generation* by variations of the frequency of a voltage-controlled oscillator.

Direct Generation

One method to generate an angle-modulated signal is to design an oscillator whose frequency changes with the input signal, biased at f_0—that is, when the input voltage is zero, the oscillator generates a sinusoid with frequency f_0. There are two approaches to design such an oscillator, which is usually called a *voltage-controlled oscillator* (VCO). One approach is to use a *varactor diode*, while the second approach is through a *reactance tube*. See Proakis and Salehi (2002) and Lathi (1998) for more details on these two approaches.

Indirect Generation

Another method to generate an angle-modulated signal is to first generate a narrowband angle-modulated signal and then change it to a wideband signal. These two steps are shown in parts a and b of Figure 17, respectively. As it is explained in the preceding section on the spectral characteristics of angle-modulated signals, the narrowband angle modulator is basically a conventional AM modulator with slight modifications.

The next step is to generate the wideband angle-modulated signal employing the narrowband angle-modulated signal. This is possible by applying the

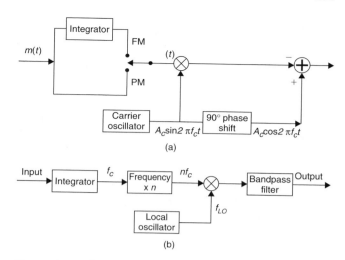

Figure 17: Indirect generation of analog modulated signal; (a) generation of narrowband angle-modulated signal; (b) generation of angle-modulated signal

signal at frequency f_c to a nonlinear element and then passing its output through a BPF at the central frequency, nf_c. If the frequency nf_c is not the desired carrier frequency, then we tune the frequency of the output signal using the local oscillator with frequency f_{LO}. This stage basically consists of a mixer and a BPF, and performs up or down conversion to shift the frequency to the desired center frequency. Therefore, using the narrowband modulated signal $A_c \cos(2\pi f_c t + \varphi(t))$, we have $A_c \cos(2\pi (nf_c - f_{LO})t + n\varphi(t))$ as the wideband angle-modulated signal (Proakis and Salehi 2002; Roberts 1977).

Demodulation of an Angle-Modulation Signal

The primary function of an angle-modulation detector is to produce an output that is proportional to the angle of the modulated wave—that is, the FM demodulator should produce an output proportional to the instantaneous frequency of the modulated signal, while the PM demodulator produces an output proportional to the phase of the modulated signal (see equation 16). On the other hand, as the structure of FM and PM modulators are almost the same (see Figure 17), here we just explain different methods to implement an FM demodulator.

The information in an FM signal is in the instantaneous frequency $f_i = f_c + k_f m(t)$. Therefore, a frequency demodulator should somehow be able to extract this information from the received modulated signal (with noise!). In general, there are two types of FM (angle) demodulators: a demodulator based on an AM demodulator and an *FM demodulator with feedback* (FMFB) (Haykin 2001; Proakis and Salehi 2002; Lindsey and Simon 1978; Roberts 1977).

FM Demodulator Based on AM Demodulator

We can implement an FM demodulator by an AM signal whose amplitude is proportional to the instantaneous frequency of the FM signal and then using an AM demodulator to recover the message signal. Figure 18 shows

Figure 18: A general FM demodulator

the general structure of this kind of FM demodulator in two steps.

To implement the first step in converting the FM signal to an AM signal, it is enough to pass the FM signal through a filter whose frequency response is approximately a straight line in the bandwidth of the FM signal; that is,

$$|H(f)| = a + b(f - f_c) \quad \text{for} \quad |f - f_c| < B_c/2 \quad (23)$$

Many circuits can be used to implement such a filter. One candidate is a simple differentiator with $|H(f)| = 2\pi f$, while the other candidate is a balanced discriminator (Proakis and Salehi 2002). The whole purpose of this filter is to have a linear-shaped response at the output so as to have the instantaneous frequency of the modulated signal appear at the amplitude of the converted (AM) signal.

FM Demodulator with Feedback

Figure 19 shows a totally different approach to demodulate an FM signal by using feedback in the FM demodulator to narrow the bandwidth of the FM detector. In fact, the bandwidth of the discriminator and the subsequent LPF is designed to match the bandwidth of the message signal, $m(t)$.

An alternative to the FMFB demodulator is the use of a *phase-locked loop* (PLL). Figure 20a shows the general structure of a PLL-FM demodulator; its equivalent linearized structure in the presence of small phase error is depicted in Figure 20b. In this structure, the demodulator input is the modulated signal (phase), and the demodulator output is proportional to the message signal, $m(t)$. We assume that the input of the VCO is $v(t)$—that is, the instantaneous output frequency of the VCO is $f_c + k_v v(t)$ where k_v ($kv > 0$) is the VCO constant. Therefore, the output of the VCO is given by

$$y_v(t) = A_v \sin(2\pi f_c t + \phi_v(t)) \quad (24a)$$

$$\phi_v(t) = 2\pi k_v \int_0^t v(\xi)d\xi \quad (24b)$$

The phase comparator output is the phase error $\phi_e(t) \triangleq \phi(t) - \phi_v(t)$. In the case of a small phase error—that is, $|\varphi_e(t)| \ll 1$—we are able to use the linearized PLL structure depicted in Figure 20b. Using this equivalent

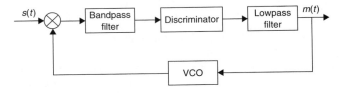

Figure 19: General structure of an FMFB demodulator

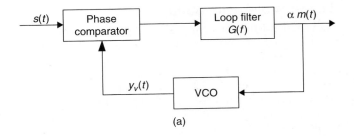

(a)

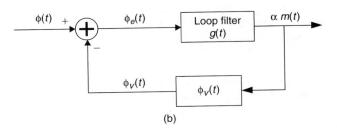

(b)

Figure 20: PLL-FM demodulator; (a) general structure, (b) linearized PLL

linear structure, we analyze the output of the PLL-FM demodulator (or the input of the VCO, $v(t)$). Based on this analysis (see Proakis and Salehi 2002), the output of the demodulator is proportional to the message signal—that is, $v(t) \propto m(t)$, if

$$k_v \left| \frac{G(f)}{f} \right| \gg 1 \quad (25)$$

Employing this condition, we get $v(t) \approx \dfrac{k_f}{k_v} m(t)$. Note that the bandwidth of the filter $G(f)$ should be the same as the bandwidth of the message signal, W. This fact has the advantage of limiting the output noise to the bandwidth W. For some more references, see Haykin (2001), Ziemer and Tranter (2001), Freeman (1998), and Gitlin, Hayes, and Weinstein (1992) and references therein.

ANALOG MODULATION FOR DIGITAL SIGNALS

What we have studied to this point deals with analog transmission of the analog message signal, $m(t)$. In contrast, there are situations when the information-bearing signal is a digital signal that is a sequence of symbols that are selected from a fixed and finite number of possible symbols. In general, the analog modulation of digital signals is known as *passband digital transmission* as the spectrum of the signal is transformed to the passband frequency. Figure 21 shows different techniques used in this form of transmission: amplitude shift keying, frequency shift keying, and phase shift keying. Here we briefly explain these transmission schemes. See Chapter 7 for more details on passband digital transmission (Haykin 2001; Turin 1969; Smith 1985; Sklar 1988).

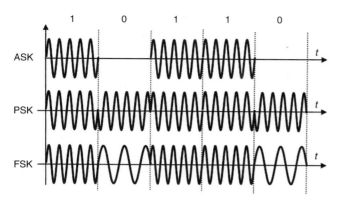

Figure 21: Analog modulation of digital signals or passband digital transmission; amplitude shift keying (ASK), phase shift keying (PSK), and frequency shift keying (FSK)

Amplitude Shift Keying

Amplitude shift keying (ASK) is the name used for AM when we use it to transmit data signals. The ASK signal is generated by multiplication of data signals by a carrier $A_c \cos 2\pi f_c t$. This process effectively shifts the data spectrum to the carrier's center frequency. As seen for DSB AM, the bandwidth of ASK is twice that of the original data signal because it contains the carrier plus upper and lower sidebands. This means that the original 110-baud signaling rate requires a transmission bandwidth of 220 hz using ASK.

Frequency Shift Keying

Frequency shift keying (FSK) is the binary equivalent of FM. In this case, a binary 0 is transmitted as a carrier at frequency f_1, and a binary 1 is transmitted as a tone, f_2. In this way, the binary signal effectively modulates the frequency of the carrier. Although, strictly speaking, FSK is the same as FM, it is usually more convenient to consider FSK as the sum of two ASK waveforms with different carrier frequencies. The spectrum of the FSK is thus the sum of the spectra of the two ASK waves. Therefore, the bandwidth of the FSK signal is given by $B_c \approx 2W$ $(\beta + 1)$, where W is the bandwidth of the data signal and β is the modulation index (Smith 1985; Sklar 1988). This equation is similar to the corresponding rule for continuous FM, as proposed in equation 21. This rule is usually known as *Carson's rule*.

Phase Shift Keying

Phase shift keying (PSK) is the binary equivalent of PM. In PSK, the binary information-bearing signal is transmitted either as zero phase shift or a phase shift of π radians. This is equivalent to multiplying the carrier signal by either $+1$ or -1, respectively. The bandwidth is thus the same for ASK. Because there is no DC component in the modulating signal, the carrier in the PSK spectrum is suppressed. This form of PSK is sometimes referred to as binary PSK (BPSK), which is equivalent to binary DSB-SC AM.

CONCLUSION

In this chapter, we studied the essentials of analog transmission of message data in the form of continuous-wave information-bearing signals. The chapter covers important techniques of generating and demodulating continuous-wave modulated signals. This analog form of modulation is made up of a sinusoidal carrier that encodes the message data in its amplitude or angle (frequency or phase) to form the information-bearing signal. Therefore, we distinguished two categories of analog transmission—amplitude modulation and angle modulation—and discussed different forms of each category.

Amplitude modulation (AM) is classified into four types: (1) double-sideband AM, in which the upper and lower sidebands are transmitted in full, accompanied by the carrier wave; (2) double-sideband suppressed carrier AM, in which only the upper and lower sidebands are transmitted; (3) single-sideband AM, in which only the upper sideband or lower sideband is transmitted; and (4) vestigial sideband AM, in which almost the whole of one sideband and a vestige of the other sideband are transmitted in a complementary manner.

Angle modulation is classified into frequency modulation (FM) and phase modulation (PM). In FM, the instantaneous frequency of a sinusoidal carrier is varied in proportion to the message signal; however, in PM, the phase of the carrier is varied in proportion to the message signal.

GLOSSARY

Additive white Gaussian noise (AWGN): A communication channel in which the only impairment is the linear addition of wideband or white noise with a constant spectral density and a Gaussian distribution of amplitude.

Amplitude modulation (AM): A technique used in electronic communication, most commonly for transmitting information via a radio carrier wave, and works by varying the strength of the transmitted signal in relation to the information being sent.

Amplitude shift keying (ASK): A form of modulation that represents digital data as variations in the amplitude of a carrier wave.

Bandpass filter (BPF): A device that passes frequencies within a certain range and rejects (attenuates) frequencies outside that range.

Double-sideband (DSB): A technique in conventional AM transmission in which the carrier and both sidebands are present.

Double-sideband suppressed carrier (DSB-SC): A form of DSB in which the carrier is removed.

Frequency modulation (FM): A form of modulation that represents information as variations in the instantaneous frequency of a carrier wave.

Frequency shift keying (FSK): A form of frequency modulation in which the modulating signal shifts the output frequency between predetermined values.

Lower sideband (LSB): A band of frequencies lower than the carrier frequency.

Lower single-sideband (LSSB): A technique in AM transmission in which the lower sideband is present.

Low-pass filter (LPF): A filter that passes low frequencies but attenuates (or reduces) frequencies higher than the cutoff frequency.

Phase-locked loop (PLL): A closed-loop feedback control system that generates and outputs a signal in relation to the frequency and phase of an input "reference" signal.

Phase modulation (PM): A form of modulation that represents information as variations in the instantaneous phase of a carrier wave.

Phase shift keying (PSK): A digital modulation scheme that conveys data by modulating the phase of a the carrier wave.

Pulse-amplitude modulation (PAM): A pulse modulation technique for a signal in which the message information is encoded in the amplitude of a series of signal pulses.

Pulse-duration modulation (PDM): A pulse modulation technique for a signal in which the message information is encoded in the duty cycle of a series of signal pulses.

Pulse-position modulation (PPM): A pulse modulation technique for a signal in which the message information is encoded in the position of a series of signal pulses.

Signal-to-noise ratio (SNR): An electrical engineering concept defined as the ratio of a signal power to the noise power corrupting the signal.

Single-sideband (SSB): A technique in AM transmission in which one of the sidebands (either lower or upper) is present.

Upper sideband (USB): A band of frequencies higher than the carrier frequency.

Upper single-sideband (USSB): A technique in AM transmission in which the upper sideband is present.

Vestigial sideband (VSB): A sideband that has been only partly cut off or suppressed.

Voltage-controlled oscillator (VCO): An electronic oscillator specifically designed to be controlled in oscillation frequency by a voltage input. The frequency of oscillation is varied with an applied DC voltage, while modulating signals may be fed into the VCO to generate FM, PM, or PDM.

CROSS REFERENCES

See *Digital Transmission; Frequency and Phase Modulation; Pulse Amplitude Modulation; Sources of Errors, Prevention, Detection and Correction.*

REFERENCES

Couch, L. 2001. *Digital and analog communication systems*. 6th ed. Upper Saddle River, NJ: Prentice Hall.

Downing, J. 1964. *Modulation systems and noise*. Englewood Cliffs, NJ: Prentice Hall.

Freeman, R. 1998. *Telecommunications transmission handbook*. 4th ed. New York: John Wiley & Sons.

Gagliardi, R. 1988. *Introduction to communications engineering*. 2nd ed. New York: John Wiley & Sons.

Gitlin, R., J. Hayes, and S. Weinstein. 1992. *Data communications principles*. New York: Plenum.

Haykin, S. 2001. *Communications systems*. 3rd ed. New York: John Wiley & Sons.

Lathi, B. 1998. *Modern digital and analog communications systems*. 3rd ed. New York: Oxford University Press.

Lindsey, W., and M. Simon. 1978. *Phase-locked loops and their applications*. New York: IEEE Press.

Pierce, J., and A. Noll. 1990. *Signals: The science of telecommunications*. New York: Scientific American Library.

Proakis, J., and M. Salehi. 2002. *Communication systems engineering*. 2nd ed. Upper Saddle River, NJ: Prentice Hall.

Roberts, J. 1977. *Angle modulation: The theory of systems assessment*. IEE Communications Series 5. London: Institution of Electrical Engineers.

Schwartz, M. 1980. *Information transmission, modulation, and noise: A unified approach*. 3rd ed. New York: McGraw-Hill.

Shanmugan, K. 1979. *Digital and analog communications systems*. New York: John Wiley & Sons.

Sklar, B. 1988. *Digital communications: Fundamentals and applications*. Englewood Cliffs, NJ: Prentice Hall.

Smith, D. 1985. *Digital transmission systems*. Princeton, NJ: Van Nostrand Reinhold.

Turin, G. 1969. *Notes on digital communications*. Princeton, NJ: Van Nostrand Reinhold.

Wikipedia. 2007. Additive white Gaussian noise (retrieved from http://en.wikipedia.org/wiki/Additive_white_Gaussian_noise).

Ziemer, R., and W. Tranter. 2001. 5th ed. *Principles of communications: Systems, modulation, and noise*. New York: John Wiley & Sons.

FURTHER READING

For further readings on analog transmission, analog modulation, noise in analog systems, and related topics, the interested reader can look at the preceding references as well as the following:

Haykin, S., and M. Moher. 2006. *An introduction to digital and analog communications*. 2nd ed. New York: McGraw-Hill.

Proakis, J. G., M. Salehi, and G. Bauch. 2003. *Contemporary communication systems using MATLAB*. 2nd ed. New York: Thomson Engineering.

Roden, M. S. 1999. *Analog and digital communication systems*. New York: McGraw-Hill.

Ryerson University. 2007. Course information for ELE 635, Communication systems (retrieved from www.ee.ryerson.ca:8080/~courses/ele635/).

San Francisco State University. No date. *Syllabus for ENGR 449* (retrieved from http://userwww.sfsu.edu/~tcooklev/course449.html).

Stremler, F. G. 1990. *Introduction to communication systems*. 3rd ed. New York: McGraw-Hill.

Sunde, E. 1969. *Communications systems engineering theory*. New York: John Wiley & Sons.

Taub, H. 1986. *Principles of communication systems*. 2nd ed. New York: McGraw-Hill.

Wozencraft, J., and I. Jacobs. 1965. *Principles of communication engineering*. New York: John Wiley & Sons.

Voice Communications Systems: KTS, PBX, Centrex, and ACD

Hassan Ibrahim, *University of Maryland, College Park*

INTRODUCTION

The pervasive use of voice communications systems in society cannot be overemphasized. Today, a *key telephone system* (KTS) enables its users to make telephone calls by simply pushing buttons (hence, the name *key*). Telephone systems have become highly sophisticated with multiline telephones and accessories that allow a user to place a call on a selected line while simultaneously placing another caller on hold and using intercom features to communicate between phones at the same location—or even activating other systems and devices. Understanding how the basics of that technology work and how they can be made to serve individual and corporate users is vital.

The digital communications revolution has resulted in the convergence of voice, data, and video communications. With communications technology advancements, new services and their associated costs must be considered in light of the business or social functions they are supposed to serve. This chapter is intended for those who have an interest in the topic, without assuming they already have extensive knowledge of the subject. It presents the development and applications of voice communications technologies, starting with the basics (such as how the voice is translated into electric signals) to more advanced and contemporary topics (such as VoIP).

A BRIEF HISTORY OF VOICE COMMUNICATIONS

Modern voice communications have been historically dependent on the invention of the telephone and the evolution of its technology. However, when the telephone was first invented, it did not necessarily receive the welcome it deserved. At the time, it was considered by the telegraph industry as having too many shortcomings to be seriously considered as a means of communication and thus inherently of no value. Over the years since, however, voice communication technologies advanced and their use became global.

In 1885, the American Telephone and Telegraph (AT&T) Company was incorporated as a subsidiary of the American Bell Telephone Company. AT&T's corporate charter laid out the firm's mission:

> Connect one or more points in each and every city, town or place in the State of New York with one or more points in every other city, town or place in said State and in each and every other of the United States, Canada and Mexico; and each and every of said cities, towns and places is to be connected with each and every other city, town or place in said states and countries, and also by cable and other appropriate means with the rest of the known world (AT&T 2007).

Such a bold statement was made less than a decade after the telephone's invention. In reality, it took AT&T several decades to accomplish that mission.

Some of the major milestones in its history in the United States are shown in Table 1.

THE TELEPHONE SYSTEM
Transmitter and Receiver Operation

The first task in technology-based voice communications is to translate the voice's acoustic waves into electronic

Table 1: Major Events in U.S. Telecommunications History

Year	Event
1837	Invention of the telegraph by Samuel Morse
1876	Invention of the telephone by Alexander Graham Bell
1934	Creation of the Federal Communications Commission (FCC) to regulate interstate telephone traffic
1958	First U.S. communications satellite sent into orbit
1959	FCC approves private microwave communications networks
1963	First geosynchronous orbiting satellite (SYNCOM II) launched
1984	Divestiture of American Telephone and Telegraph (AT&T)
1985	Cellular radio telephones introduced
1996	Telecommunications Reform Act of 1996 passed

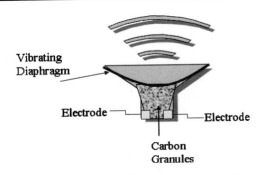

Figure 1: Components of the telephone mouthpiece

signals. These signals are then able to travel over wired and wireless networks. Upon reaching their destination, they are retranslated back into their original sound form for the receptor to understand. These translation and re-translation tasks are handled at the telephone's mouth- and earpieces, respectively.

Voice waves spoken at the mouthpiece push against a sensitive flexible diaphragm that in turns presses together carbon granules that connect two electrodes (see Figure 1). The degree of conductivity of the granules and consequently the strength of the signal passing between the electrodes depends on how well the granules are compressed together. Hence, the variation in the sound waves at the mouthpiece vibrates the diaphragm, which changes the degree of compressions of the granules, resulting in signals with variable strengths passing the two electrodes and emulating the variations in the original sound waves.

At the receiving end, the earpiece contains an electromagnet that faces a moveable diaphragm. Arriving electric signals create variable levels of magnetism in the electromagnet, which in turn causes the diaphragm to move in a corresponding way. This produces sounds that correspond to the original sound waves entered into the mouthpiece.

Dialing Systems

The telephone numbering system was created in order to identify each user in a unique way. Today's telephone number systems include a comprehensive list of country codes for individual nations and city codes, in addition to individual telephone numbers. In any given country, some form of hierarchical system is followed in assigning the telephone numbers.

For example, in the United States, the first three digits signify the area code, which is associated with a particular geographic location. This is followed by a prefix of three digits that signify the local switching office or exchange, and then four digits that identify the individual subscriber. Originally, all area codes in the United States had a 1 or a 0 in the middle digit while no exchange numbers were allowed to have those numerals, which made it easier for telephone switches to differentiate between the two. Once all of the areas codes that followed that system were completely used, new area codes with numerals other than a 1 or a 0 as the center digit were introduced, starting with area code 770, which is used outside of Atlanta, Georgia (Goldman and Rawles 2004, 170).

Rotary Dialing

The earlier form (and one still used in some countries) of dialing phone numbers was done though a rotating disc on the face of the telephone set that carried the numerals 0 through 9. By manually rotating the disk using one of those ten digits, the telephone produces a string of electric pulses that correspond to the dialed digit. Once those electrical pulses reach the phone company's local exchange, the arms of electromechanical switches move to create the needed connection between the caller and the call destination. This system is slow, inaccurate, and no match for the incredible growth in demand for voice communications.

Dual Tone Multifrequency: The Touch Tone System

The clumsiness and frequent inaccuracy of that rotary system led to the development of a more user-friendly and accurate system known as *touch tone dialing* or *dual tone multifrequency* (DTMF). In DTMF, each digit in the phone number is "dialed" by simply pushing down a button to create a signal with a unique frequency that is associated in the telephone network with a particular digit (see Figure 2). As the signals arrive at the switching office, they are processed by electronic microprocessors that control smaller and faster relays that make the connections.

VOICE COMMUNICATIONS NETWORK INFRASTRUCTURE
The Central Office

Earlier generations of telephone networks required massive hardwiring of towns and cities in order to connect different callers directly to each other through dedicated wires. As both the number of telephone users and their

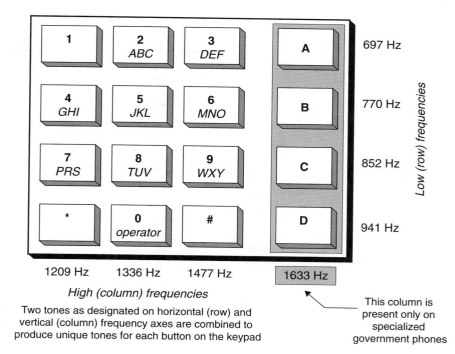

				697 Hz
1	**2** ABC	**3** DEF	**A**	770 Hz
4 GHI	**5** JKL	**6** MNO	**B**	852 Hz
7 PRS	**8** TUV	**9** WXY	**C**	941 Hz
*	**0** operator	#	**D**	

Low (row) frequencies

1209 Hz   1336 Hz   1477 Hz   1633 Hz

High (column) frequencies

Two tones as designated on horizontal (row) and vertical (column) frequency axes are combined to produce unique tones for each button on the keypad

This column is present only on specialized government phones

Figure 2: The touch tone dialing system. Source: Reprinted with permission from J. E. Goldman. 2004. *Applied data communication*. New York: John Wiley & Sons

desire to reach more people increased, hardwiring all of the necessary lines became a nightmare, and cities became blighted with jungles of wires hanging on telephone poles. The solution came with the introduction of the *switching office* (also known as *central office*, or CO). Because each individual user is connected to a particular CO, only one wire is needed per user. By interconnecting the switching offices, callers anywhere can reach each other with minimal wiring requirements because connections are established through the switching offices.

The CO method required having a telephone numbering system (as previously discussed) that was totally dependent on human operators—commonly known as *switchboard operators*—to physically plug cables into corresponding sockets to create the connections. First, young men were hired to do the job, but with many complaints about their lack of professionalism and prank calls, they were replaced with female operators who were better trained and more professional in conducting the tasks. The system worked well for awhile until an automated switchboard was developed. Strangely enough, the automated switchboard was apparently invented by Almon Brown Strowger, an undertaker in Kansas City, Missouri (Sveum 2000, 117). Strowger was convinced that he was losing customers to a competitor, whose wife was a switchboard operator and who intentionally routed business calls intended for Strowger to her husband's office.

Today, all over the world automated systems in switching offices facilitate connections in the voice communications industry. The switching office usually serves a limited geographic region and is connected to end users by a connection known as "the last mile" or the "local loop" (Figure 3). As mentioned before, a switching office is assigned a unique exchange number in the telephone system that end users inherit as the prefix of their telephone numbers.

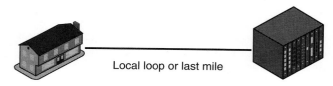

Local loop or last mile

Figure 3: The local loop

Public Switching Telephone Network

The *public switching telephone network* (PSTN) is the oldest interconnected worldwide network that crosses many countries and telephone company boundaries. It is also known as the *plain old telephone service* (or *system*) (POTS). In many countries, the telephone company is government-owned and typically considered part of what is commonly known as a *public* (or *post*), *telephone and telegraph* (PTT); in these cases, it enjoys complete monopoly over a nationwide market, which is similar to what AT&T had before its divestiture in 1984.

A telephone network is typically set up as a hierarchy of switching offices connected by *trunk lines*. The value of a hierarchical structure is in its efficient way of providing adequate switching capacity in the network without unnecessary investment. In the United States, AT&T built a hierarchy of five levels known as *classes*. A class 5 CO, placed at the bottom of the hierarchy, is the local switching office that is directly connected to end users. A call from one user to his or her immediate neighbor is most likely to be routed directly through the same class 5 CO, freeing the rest of network from the burden of having to carry that traffic.

A call placed to a destination that cannot be reached directly through the same exchange is moved up the hierarchy to a class 4 switching office that can then route

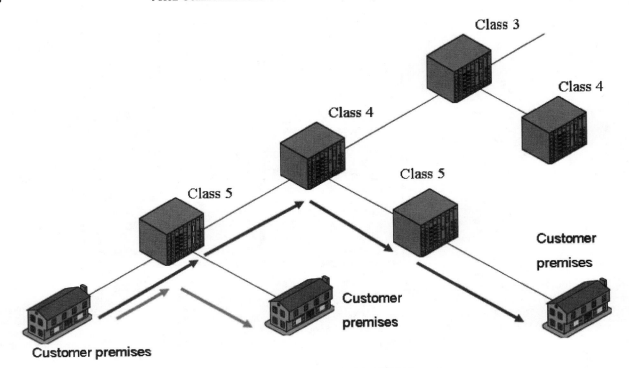

Figure 4: Routing calls through the PSTN hierarchy

the call down to the class 5 CO in the locality of the destination or move it up to a class 3 or higher CO until an open route to the destination is established. The call is then routed down until it reaches a class 5 CO and is then routed to the intended party (Figure 4).

Local Access and Transport Areas

The geographic region served by a telephone company can be divided into different areas known as *local access and transport areas* (LATAs). In the United States, AT&T divided the country into 161 LATAs (Goldman and Rawles 2004, 169). A call bound to a destination within a given LATA is considered a *local call* for the telephone company, and the customer is charged accordingly (Gelber 1997, 130). A call placed to a number outside a designated LATA is considered either an *out-of-area call* or a *long-distance call*, depending on the destination. *Intra*-LATA calls are typically handled by a local phone company, which is usually referred to as a *local exchange carrier* (LEC); *inter*-LATA calls are handed over to an *interexchange carrier* (IXC) for delivery to the LATA of the called

party (see Figure 5). Note that a geographic region covered by an area code is not necessarily considered a LATA. In fact, several LATAs could be covered by a given area code (Goldman and Rawles 2004, 164).

Point of Presence

For an IXC to access an end user, it can set up its own network, in essence duplicating the LEC's network. A more cost-efficient way is to simply rely on the LEC network that already exists to provide access to the "last mile" by connecting its network directly to one of the switching offices of the LEC. The switching office where the IXC connection to the LEC network takes place is known as *point of presence* (POP).

An IXC that can provide service to international calls is known as an *international common carrier* (ICC). Countries negotiate not only which ICCs may provide service in their territories but also settlement call charges on bilateral basis. Such bilateral agreements often bring uneven pricing schemes for calls placed to neighboring countries.

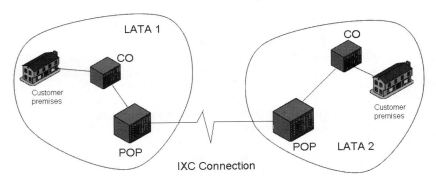

Figure 5: Local area and transport areas and POPs

Trunk Lines

The switching offices placed in different service regions and neighborhoods are interconnected through high-speed lines that use different types of multiplexing technologies that allow carrying multiple conversations simultaneously and thus improve network efficiency. Those lines that interconnect the switching offices are known as *trunk lines*. Earlier generations of trunk lines were built to handle analog signals. Over the years, most have been upgraded to carry digital signals, and many have been upgraded to fiber-optic cabling, even though many of the so-called last mile connections continue to be analog lines.

VOICE DIGITIZATION TECHNOLOGIES

Digital signals provide better quality and capacity utilization compared to analog signals, leading the telecommunications industry to shift to digital technologies in their infrastructures, including in switching offices and trunk lines. Digital signaling technologies translate a message into an equivalent binary sequence of 0's and 1's. This not only allows information to be coded more precisely (see PCM below) but also allows easier error detection and correction during transmission. Attempting to accomplish the same level of quality through analog transmission is more difficult, imprecise, and inefficient.

To allow an analog signal arriving from a local loop to be handled by a digital switching office and then digital trunk lines, a digitization process is employed to convert the analog signal into an equivalent digital signal. To represent analog signals, which have continuous form, into digital signals, which are discrete in nature, *voice digitization* is employed. Voice digitization relies on a sampling theorem that states that if a signal is sampled at regular intervals of time and at a rate higher than twice the significant signal frequency, then the samples will contain all of the original signal's information. Given that most human voice communications are typically between 300 hz and 3400 hz (a bandwidth less than 4000 hz), some 8000 samples per second are considered a sufficient and acceptable standard in voice digitization technologies, which include various forms of pulse modulation (see Figure 6).

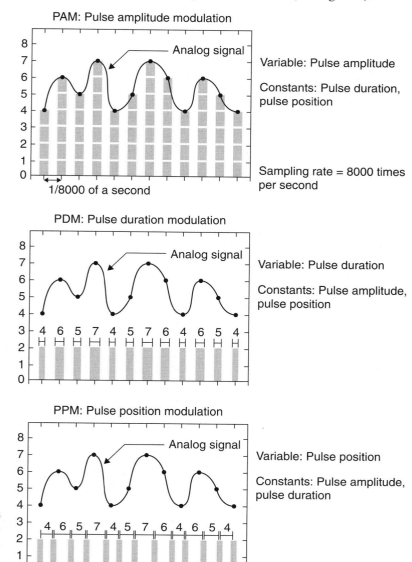

Figure 6: Voice digitization techniques system. Source: Reprinted with permission from J. E. Goldman. 2004. *Applied data communication*. New York: John Wiley & Sons

Pulse Modulations

Four main methods of pulse modulation are used in modern voice digitization: pulse amplitude modulation, pulse duration modulation, pulse position modulation, and pulse code modulation.

Pulse amplitude modulation (PAM) produces electrical pulses with variable *amplitude* (or *signal strength*) in ways that correspond to variations in the analog signal. *Pulse duration modulation* (PDM) produces electrical pulses with variable *durations of time*, also in ways that correspond to variations in analog signals. *Pulse position modulation* (PPM) produces electrical pulses with variable *durations between pulses* (Goldman and Rawles 2004, 174).

Pulse code modulation (PCM) is currently the most widely used form of digitization technology. PCM samples the analog signal (as stated earlier, at the rate of 8000 samples per second) and then produces binary codes that correspond to the variations in the analog signal (see Figure 7). A *coder-decoder* (codec) device or software is used to facilitate that process (Fitzgerald and Dennis 2005, 98).

Voice Compression

Voice compression is a sophisticated form of PCM known as *adaptive differential PCM* (ADPCM) that transmits only the approximate difference between two consecutive pulses, which is a more efficient way to use available bandwidth to send and receive communication signals. Voice compression is widely used in today's telephone systems.

VOICE COMMUNICATIONS SERVICES

Digital signals brought new flexibility to telephone networks and made possible the introduction of more advanced services. Among the voice communications services that are popular with many businesses are *toll-free services*, *900 services*, and *wide area telecommunications services* (WATS) (Beyda 2005, 19).

Toll-Free Service

Toll-free service is not as free as it sounds. It is only free to the caller because the called party (the toll-free service

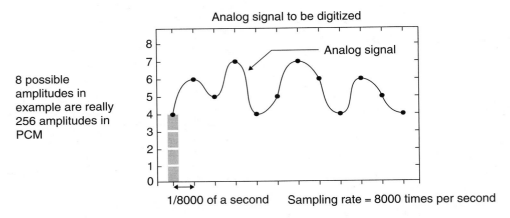

8 possible amplitudes in example are really 256 amplitudes in PCM

Step 1: Sample Amplitude of Analog Signal

Amplitude in example at sample position 1 (the gray shaded box) is 4

Step 2: Represent Measured Amplitude in Binary Notation

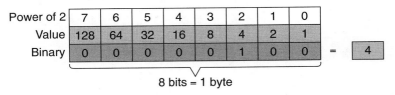

Power of 2	7	6	5	4	3	2	1	0		
Value	128	64	32	16	8	4	2	1		
Binary	0	0	0	0	0	1	0	0	=	4

8 bits = 1 byte

Step 3: Transmit Coded Digital Pulses Representing Measured Amplitude

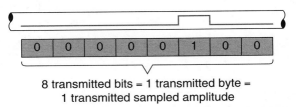

0	0	0	0	0	1	0	0

8 transmitted bits = 1 transmitted byte =
1 transmitted sampled amplitude

Figure 7: Pulse duration modulation system. Source: Reprinted with permission from J. E. Goldman. 2004. *Applied data communication*. New York: John Wiley & Sons

subscriber) pays for the calls. This way customers or other users can reach the toll-free service subscriber in a convenient and economic way, calling from anywhere, anytime, and for any length of time without having to worry about the costs of their calls. The toll-free service provider is typically one of the IXCs, which charges its subscribers a cheaper rate than that for direct dial services.

In the United States, for many years the 800 area code signified that the number was a toll free number. However, over the years, the demand for toll-free numbers grew along with the desire of many businesses to have numbers that could be easily associated with their names, products or services, or even their logos (such as 800-CALL ATT). This required the introduction of new area codes such as 866, 877, and 888. By having these area codes designated in the telephone network for toll-free service, the accounting task for these calls can be easily handled.

Another challenge that toll-free service providers faced was that their numbers were assigned as blocks to particular carriers. That meant that when a subscriber changed its carrier, it could no longer hold onto the same toll-free number that it had used and publicized on its literature or in its commercials. The solution came in the form providing access to the carriers' switching offices through a master toll-free numbers database. In this way, switching offices could automatically determine which carrier was supposed to carry particular toll-free traffic.

900 Services

Like toll-free services, a 900 service is an inbound call to the subscriber but paid for by the caller and usually at a much higher rate than a normal long-distance call. Good examples for subscribers to such services include technical support companies and tax consultation services. More recently, U.S. embassies in some countries provide a similar service for callers who want to check on the status of their visa applications (Forouzan 2003, 185).

Wide Area Telecommunications Services

With a *wide area telecommunications service* (WATS), a subscriber (typically a business) may buy calls in a specified volume at a highly discounted price from the telephone company. In this way the subscriber enjoys substantial savings when compared to paying for individual calls. The main advantages to the carrier are a guaranteed cash flow as well as better capacity planning for its network (Forouzan 2003, 185).

PRIVATE BRANCH EXCHANGE

A *private branch exchange* (PBX) is a privately owned, on-site switching telephone facility operated by an enterprise. It emulates the function of a CO in the PSTN. The PBX and all of its lines that are connected to individual employees are the property of the enterprise, so all internal calls are handled by the PBX without the involvement of the phone company. However, local and long-distance calls are routed from the PBX to the local phone company or an IXC respectively. In addition to providing telephone-switching capabilities, a PBX supports many of the business needs that have come to be part of normal organizational activities such as conference calls, call waiting and call forwarding, voice messaging, and automatic call distribution as well as providing links to databases.

Purpose and Benefits

An enterprise that wishes to provide hundreds or thousands of workers with their own telephone service and unique phone numbers can get similar numbers of lines from a telephone company. This would have a tremendous cost, however. Because it is unlikely that all users will be on the phone at the same time, using a PBX would facilitate phone services by using only few lines from the local company and providing each user with an individual phone number. Internal calls can be made using *reduced dialing*—that is, by using the last four or five digits of the phone number—while external calls can typically be made by first dialing "9" to request an outside line from the PBX. Initially, a PBX would be found at a medium-to large-sized business enterprise, government agency, or educational institution, but PBXs now are available in much smaller sizes and at more affordable prices (Thurwachter 2000, 531).

Architecture

A PBX is made of four major components: the central processing unit, station or line card, trunk card, and a switching matrix (Goldman and Rawles 2004, 198).

The *central processing unit* (CPU) is the brain of the PBX and is responsible for controlling the switching matrix and managing the call traffic of the network as well as facilitating the services requested by a user such as call waiting, call forwarding, voice mail, and so on.

The *station* (or *line*) *card* is the point of contact between the individual user and the network. A PBX is usually built according to a modular design of station cards, providing the flexibility needed to expand the PBX's capacity as the number of users increase.

The *trunk card* connects the PBX to a telephone company for external local and long-distance calls.

The *switching matrix* is responsible for creating, maintaining, and terminating the needed physical connections between the callers. If the call is intended for an internal number, then an electronic connection is established through the matrix by connecting the station cards of the caller to the intended destination's card. For calls placed to outside numbers, the switching matrix routes the call to the trunk card, and from there to the local phone company or directly to the point of presence of an IXC (see Figure 8).

Features and Services

PBX provides four main categories of features:

1. users-related PBX services,
2. switchboard operator–related or receptionist-related services,

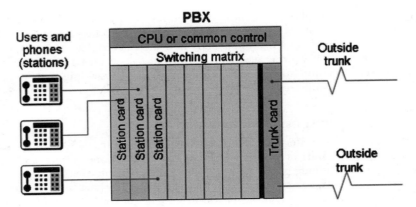

Figure 8: The PBX architecture system. Source: Reprinted with permission from J. E. Goldman. 2004. *Applied data communication.* New York: John Wiley & Sons

3. data and voice integration, and

4 control over the usage of PBX and organization's resources.

First, user services include commonly used features such as display of dialed number, speed dialing, redialing of the last number, call waiting and playing on-hold music or messages, call forwarding, automatic (incoming) number identification, conference calling, intercom, and camp on (Panko 2005, 526).

Most of these features are self-explanatory, but *camp on* may need clarification. This feature frees the user from the frustration of calling a number that is constantly busy. The user dials the desired phone number, pushes the "camp on" button, and hangs up. The system then automatically keeps dialing the number as many times as it has been programmed to do; once the call gets through, the phone on the caller's side rings to signify that the called party has been reached (Beyda 2005, 28).

Second, there are those PBX-supported tasks that were traditionally carried out by human receptionists, such as the following:

- Distributing incoming calls to appropriate destinations. This is handled by a feature called *automatic call distribution* (ACD), which answers incoming calls and then routes them to the intended person or department or the next available help desk.
- Taking messages for individuals who are away from their desks or on other lines. This is handled by an electronic voicemail feature.
- Paging someone who is away from his or her desk such as a plant manager or physician who is making his or her rounds.
- Automatic nighttime transfer of calls to a guard station or an answering service as in the case of an emergency call that arrives after working hours at a physician's office.

Third, PBX data and voice integration allows the system's users to use their phones as input/output devices (instead of a computer terminal) to access data stored in computer files. This feature is different from computer telephony integration, which will be discussed later, in that the telephone is the main input/output device. Among the most popular features of data and voice integration are

interactive voice response and interfacing with wide area networks (Fitzgerald and Dennis 2005, 449).

Interactive voice response (IVR), which is widely used in phone banking, allows callers to use the telephone to interface with a bank's database.

Interfacing with a *wide area network* (WAN) connection such as an *integrated services digital network* (ISDN) or a leased T1 lines allows the PBX to support voice and data traffic simultaneously in an organization.

Finally, a PBX can collect a wealth of data through its extensive call monitoring and control features. That enables an organization's management to monitor the use of resources, improve efficiency, and have better control over assets. Among those features are least cost routing, station message detail reporting, and call restriction.

In *least cost routing*, a PBX can automatically route outgoing calls in the least expensive way, given different options of long-distance carriers or WATS (described earlier).

Station message detail reporting (SMDR) monitors and reports all incoming and outgoing calls with detailed charges. With this feature, management can monitor how users spend their time on the phone (e.g., to see whether they are talking to family and friends or conducting legitimate business), how long it takes to answer customer questions or process orders, and how many sales calls are made by a particular salesperson on any given day. SMDR can provide a *nonrepudiation capability* that allows management to investigate a customer's complaints about important orders (placements, cancellations, and so on) and whether and when a call took place and who answered a particular call.

Call restriction is another important feature that prevents certain extensions from making external calls, long-distance calls, or 900 calls.

Common PBX standards allowed for the interoperability of PBX systems from different manufacturers, which made it possible for an organization to mix and match different components of its telephone system (central or desk units). The major vendors of PBX systems are Avaya, Nortel, Lucent Technologies, NEC, Mitel, and Siemens Rolm. Some newer PBX systems are built in scaled-down versions with limited features that are just enough to support the needs of a small or home office. Others are built with wireless integration capabilities that can support the increasing growth in wireless network infrastructures.

When selecting a PBX system, careful consideration is needed to ensure that the desired features are available or can be supported by the system, because certain features need to be available in the station (desk) unit and be supported by the system (central) unit. In general, station features include automatic redial, call forwarding, speed dialing, call transfer, call waiting, camp on, and conference calling. System features, on the other hand, typically include automatic call distribution, data communication, least cost routing, paging, SMDR, and voice messaging.

Centrex

A Centrex service could simply be defined as a PBX that is physically located at the central office of a local phone company (Stallings 2005, 23). With a centrex, an organization does not need to invest in a PBX with all of its related costs of operation, maintenance, and upgrades; instead, it leases switching capacities from the local phone company at the local CO. Members of an organization can still call each other with reduced dialing, using only the extension of the called party. Although those calls are physically routed through the phone company's CO, they would be considered internal to the organization and not charged by the phone company as local calls (Crane 1999, 680).

A centrex can be an economical alternative for an organization that cannot afford the up-front cost of buying a PBX but wants the flexibility of adding more switching capacity as the organization grows. On the one hand, a centrex frees an organization from the headaches related to capacity management, operation and maintenance costs, and keeping up with constant PBX technological advancements. On the other hand, the phone company enjoys a guaranteed business and cash flow in addition to leveraging its investment in CO switching capabilities that otherwise could have been idle.

Virtual PBX

A *virtual PBX* is created by interconnecting several PBXs at one site or at multiple sites, often by leased lines (see Figure 9). Users within the same organization across cities or even countries can access one another with reduced dialing and substantially cheaper cost than having to pay for hundreds of long and overseas calls.

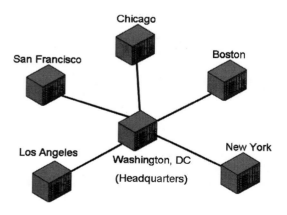

Figure 9: The virtual PBX

An example of a virtual PBX is found at the University of Maryland, College Park, which uses two PBX units. One unit mainly serves student dorms; the other serves faculty, staff, and administration. Faculty and staff calls are mostly placed during normal daytime working hours while students are in their classes. Most of the students' calls are placed in the afternoon and later when most faculty and staff have left for the day. By tying together the two PBX units, the university is able to balance traffic load between the two PBXs by taking advantage of the idle capacity of the PBX that is not heavily in use at the time.

Note that a virtual PBX can be created by tying together a number of centrex facilities that can be configured by the centrex-hosting local phone company. Similarly, a global virtual PBX can be implemented for a multinational corporation through international common carriers (ICCs), which are telephone companies that provide international service (e.g., Sprint, British Telecom, and Deutsch Telecom).

Automatic Call Distribution versus PBX

Automatic call distribution (ACD), which was discussed earlier, can be part of as well as ancillary to a PBX. A business such as an airline's ticketing center may get ACD functionality from a stand-alone ACD system without having to invest in a full-fledged PBX system. Just as with the ACD featured in a PBX, incoming calls are answered, the caller or type of service requested is identified, and then the call is routed to the right extension to handle that call (Carr and Snyder 2003, 58).

Digital PBX

For many years, organizations had to invest in separate voice and data communications infrastructures, which were typically managed by two different departments. The voice network was managed by a facilities department, while the data network was managed by the information technology department. That distinction was meaningful when voice was coded and transmitted as analog signals while data was primarily transmitted in a digital form. However, the digital communications revolution converged different means of communications: voice, data, video, and images. Under pressure to cut the cost of duplicated resources and to minimize departmental conflicts, organizations realized that they had to unify their information (including voice and data) systems into completely digital networks. That need was fulfilled by the introduction of digital PBXs that were able to handle both voice and data networks simultaneously and route outgoing voice and data traffic to different voice and data networks (Carr and Snyder 2003, 59). Organizations now can deal with just one service provider to manage all of their investment in communications technologies. Users can plug their desktop computers into the telephone network and communicate without having to go through a modem. By avoiding having to convert signals back and forth between analog and digital led to major improvements in the network's quality, speed, and throughput.

Standards

The International Organization for Standardization (ISO) has developed standards for interoperability between PBXs that are made by different vendors. This has allowed enterprises the flexibility they need to shop around and mix and match equipment that best fits their needs without being chained to a single vendor. ISO's *Q-signaling* (QSIG) standards have enabled the interoperability among PBXs that are interconnected via ISDN lines. Q.931 is an ISDN standard that enables the interconnection between PBXs and PSTN services. In turn, an organization can create a virtual PBX network that may encompass a collection of its own PBXs as well as centrex services across a wide geographic area (Stamper and Case 2003).

The growing demand for VoIP (discussed next) has manifested itself in a new generation of PBXs that interoperate with the Internet as well as with other data networks (Dooley 2005, 326). A traditional PBX included trunk lines connected to the PSTN (the local phone company or a long-distance carrier or both). Now a modern digital PBX can support IP telephony through an IP call manager that places and receives calls to and from the Internet. Such a PBX can connect the organization's voice and data traffic to the rest of the globe. With the use of intelligent network management systems, the organization's traffic is routed to the best connection, either over the PSTN or over the Internet, based on the nature of the traffic, the reliability of the network, the destination, and the cost of service (Beasley 2004, 411).

VOICE OVER INTERNET PROTOCOL

The convergence of voice and data communications took a major leap forward with the introduction of the Internet and its global access. In the past, modems were used to allow data to travel over the PSTN, a network that was created to carry exclusively for voice communication. Now, however, the Internet, which was created primarily to carry data, can now carry voice through a technology known as *voice over Internet protocol* (VoIP). VoIP enables digitized voice signals (or video for that matter) to be formatted in a manner similar to data packeting; these packets can then travel with data over the same physical network simultaneously (Black 2000, 13).

Many individual and corporate users alike started to use the Internet to place phone calls, bypassing completely local and long-distance phone companies, and hence reducing their phone bills. Those users employed the microphone and speakers on their personal computers (PCs) as voice communication input/output devices. Although these users were able to place and receive calls on their PCs, the voice quality was poor and unpredictable. The main reason for that was that the Internet's infrastructure and protocols allow individual packets to travel over the network through different physical paths, which may lead to delayed and possibly out-of-sequence arrival. With data transmission such as e-mail, that is not a problem because the recipient does not read the e-mail until the entire message has been delivered. On the other hand, voice and video traffic is time sensitive, requiring that packets arrive in short and fixed time intervals in order to maintain proper audible quality.

The interest in VoIP provided a window of business opportunity for companies such as Vonage and Skype to move in and offer a higher-quality VoIP service. The market of VoIP service providers is rapidly growing, and they are gradually grabbing more and more customers away from traditional voice communications market leaders in local and long distance such as Verizon and Sprint.

COMPUTER TELEPHONY INTEGRATION

Computer telephony integration (CTI) combines two of the most widely used technologies in society today: the computer and the telephone. CTI serves numerous business applications such as telemarketing, technical support hotlines, and customer service centers. With CTI, businesses can advertise a nationwide toll-free number to their customers for placing orders, resolving products' technical problems, or questioning credit card charges. CTI uses an ACD unit or a PBX to examine incoming calls and identify the caller's telephone number, caller-entered account number, or type of service requested. It then uses that information to search a computer database for information on the identified caller, the product in question, or the credit card charge that is the subject of inquiry. As it routes the call to the most appropriate desk to handle the call, it also forwards to that desk's computer the relevant information that was obtained from the database.

For example, a CTI system may use a caller's area code to identify the region from which the call originated and then route it to the appropriate regional sales office along with the caller's purchase history and credit limits that appear on the sales representative's computer screen as that call is routed to his or her desk. In other applications, using the caller-entered credit card number, a CTI system can retrieve the transactions history of that credit card, which can help the account representative answer the caller's questions efficiently and accurately. With CTI capability, the public can call a government agency and order specific forms which the system can automatically retrieve from its database and then forward the documents to a provided fax number or e-mail address.

One of the most useful features of CTI is the ability to provide users with a unified message box for all of their voice messages, e-mails, and text and video messages. With this feature, users can check one place—the computer screen—for all of their messages, which are marked by different icons to indicate the type of message received. Users can then read their e-mail or play recorded voice or video messages.

Architecture

CTI can be implemented on different scales using different platforms, depending on the size of the organization and type of application. A small business such as a

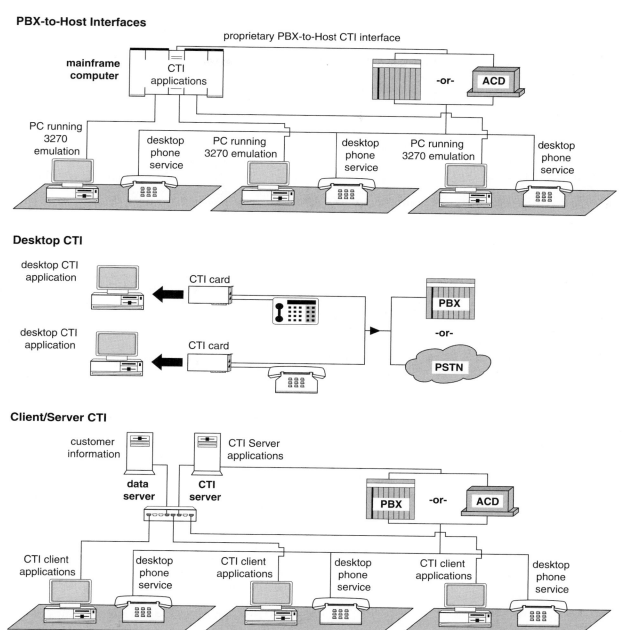

Figure 10: CTI architectures system. Source: Reprinted with permission from J. E. Goldman. 2004. *Applied data communication.* New York: John Wiley & Sons

fast-food outlet can benefit from a desktop-based CTI system. That system involves adding a CTI card to the personal computer, driver software, and a database management system on its hard drive. Although this is a scaled-down CTI system, it enables a store manager to relate a phone order to a customer in the store's database, identify his or her address, directions to the customer's premise, purchase history, and billing information.

A more common implementation of CTI in larger organizations could be based on mainframe or (single or multi-tier) client-server architecture, depending on the size of the organization, volume of transactions, and level of security desired (see Figure 10). The system could be distributed and internetworked to facilitate access by multiple sites.

CONCLUSION

Voice communications have always been an important aspect of human life. The invention of the telephone more than a century ago and all of the subsequent related technologies have made global voice communications a possibility for the first time in human history. Voice communication technology will continue to advance, and so will the dependence of society on it, from the individual chatting with friends to corporations conducting their business using voice communications systems. The advancements of such technologies will also continue to shape and reshape those enterprises whose business is facilitating voice communications infrastructure and all of its related services.

GLOSSARY

Automatic call distribution (ACD): Feature that can be provided by a PBX or stand-alone device that answers incoming calls and routes them to the most appropriate extension.

Central office (CO): A telephone company switching office where calls are routed to their appropriate designations.

Centrex: A *private branch exchange* (PBX) service hosted by a telephone company in one of its central offices.

Computer telephony integration (CTI): A technology that allows organizations to interface incoming calls with related data stored in the organization's database.

Dual tone multifrequency (DTMF): A dialing system that creates a signal with a unique frequency for each dialed digit.

Interexchange carrier (IXC): A telephone company (typically, a long-distance carrier) that carries phone traffic between local access areas.

Local access and transport area (LATA): A geographic region designated by the phone company for local calls.

Local exchange carrier (LEC): A telephone company that carries local phone traffic within a LATA.

Local loop: The connection between the customer premise and the local telephone company's central office.

Point of presence (POP): The central office where the interexchange carrier (IXC) is connected to the local access and transport area (LATA).

Private branch exchange (PBX): An on-site, privately owned switching facility.

Voice digitization: The process of converting voice analog signals into equivalent digital signals that can be transmitted by digital lines.

Voice over Internet protocol (VoIP): Using the Internet to carry digitized voice communications.

Wide area telecommunications services (WATS): A service that a business can subscribe to through a phone company to get a specific volume of calls at a highly reduced rate.

CROSS REFERENCES

See *BISDN (Broadband Integrated Services Digital Network); Messaging Systems: Facsimile and Voice Processing; Public Switched Telephone Network (PSTN); Pulse Amplitude Modulation; Voice over IP (VoIP); Voice over MPLS and VoIP over MPLS.*

REFERENCES

AT&T. 2007. *History of AT&T* (retrieved from www.att.com/history/).

Beasley, J. S. 2004. *Networking*, 408–15. Upper Saddle River, NJ: Prentice Hall.

Beyda, W. J. 2005. *Data communications*. 4th ed., 6–28. Upper Saddle River, NJ: Prentice Hall.

Black, U. D. 2000. *Voice over IP*, 1–30. Upper Saddle River, NJ: Prentice Hall.

Carr, H. H., and C. A. Snyder. 2003. *The management of telecommunications*. 2nd ed., 42–63. New York: McGraw-Hill/Irwin.

Crane, E. B. 1999. *Telecommunications: Primer*. 2nd ed., 675–80. Upper Saddle River, NJ: Prentice Hall.

Dooley, A. 2005. *Business data communication*, 325–26. Upper Saddle River, NJ: Prentice Hall.

Fitzgerald, J., and A. Dennis. 2005. *Business data communications and networking*. 8th ed., 96–9, 449–50. New York: John Wiley & Sons.

Forouzan, B. A. 2003. *Business data communications*, 179–84. New York: McGraw-Hill/Irwin.

Gelber, S. 1997. *Data communications today*, 128–35. Upper Saddle River, NJ: Prentice Hall.

Goldman, J., and P. Rawles. 2004. *Applied data communications*. 4th ed., 164–204. New York: John Wiley & Sons.

Panko, R. R. 2005. *Business data networks and telecommunications*. 5th ed., 252–63, 526–29. Upper Saddle River, NJ: Prentice Hall.

Stallings, W. 2005. *Business data communications*. 5th ed., 22–3. Upper Saddle River, NJ: Prentice Hall.

Stamper, D., and T. Case. 2003. *Business data communications*. 6th ed., 198–202. Upper Saddle River, NJ: Prentice Hall.

Sveum, M. 2000. *Data communications*, 113–20. Upper Saddle River, NJ: Prentice Hall.

Thurwachter, C. 2000. *Data and telecommunications*, 531–34. Upper Saddle River, NJ: Prentice Hall.

Messaging Systems: Facsimile and Voice Processing

Albert K. S. Wong, Nan Zhang, and Xu Yan, *Hong Kong University of Science and Technology, Hong Kong*

INTRODUCTION

The word *facsimile*—from the Latin *fac* and *simile*, meaning "to make similar"—refers to the telecommunication technology used for transmitting graphical information over a distance. Also called *fax* for short, facsimile came into widespread use in the 1970s and 1980s following the standardization effort by the International Telegraph and Telephone Consultative Committee (CCITT, now known as ITU-T). The peak annual sales of fax machines reached twenty million units in the late 1990s. Today, an estimated seventy million fax machines have been installed worldwide, and twelve to fifteen million units are sold each year.

The fax machine is an indispensable part of many business establishments as a simple-to-use document transmission and messaging tool. Fax transmission works for both handwritten and printed documents, and a fax machine can be turned on around the clock to work across time zones. Today, close to half of all calls on the telephony network are estimated to be facsimile calls.

In the first part of this chapter, we describe the history, technology, and future of facsimile. We also discuss the future of facsimile in the increasingly Internet-centric telecommunication world.

HISTORICAL PERSPECTIVE

A less known fact in the history of telecommunications is that Samuel Morse's 1844 patent on the telegraph was preceded by the patent for electrical facsimile in 1843 by Scottish physicist Alexander Bain. Unlike the telegraph, which has transformed communications, facsimile saw limited commercial application in the nineteenth century. From the 1920s to the 1960s, facsimile was primarily a series of commercial failures: picture telegraphy by various post, telegraph, and telephone (PTT) administrations; Telefax by Western Union; fax broadcasting by newspapers and radio stations; and so on. Not until the 1970s did facsimile take root in the business application world in Japan and the 1980s that it found worldwide adoption. In the first part of this chapter, we provide a historical perspective on the development of the facsimile technology from the 1840s to its modern embodiment in the telephony network–based group 3 standard and data network–based group 4 standard.

Ancient Telegraphy

The story of the runner who died from exhaustion after delivering the message of victory from Marathon to the Greeks in Athens in 490 B.C. is frequently used to illustrate the desirability of finding less arduous means for telecommunications. From the ancient world to the present, drums, torch and smoke signals, homing pigeons, and semaphores have been used to convey messages over long distances. A network of water telegraph systems was installed throughout the Roman Empire by 150 B.C. These water telegraph systems used the draining of water from water tanks as timers so that durations of specific drum or torch signals could be timed and specific messages conveyed. The invention of the telescope in the early seventeenth century pushed forward the development of optical telegraphy, also called *semaphore*, which is based on the arrangement of flags, lights, or mechanical arms installed in towers that can be seen from a distance. In the late eighteenth century, a French system by Claude Chappe was adopted and widely deployed in Napoleon's empire. Chappe's system, which was based on mechanical arms that could be rapidly rearranged by ropes and pulleys, achieved rates of communications that were comparable to those achieved by the earliest electrical telegraphs.

Electrical Telegraphy and Early Facsimile

The idea of electrical telegraphy came to Samuel Morse in 1832. His successful demonstration of the telegraph to the U.S. Congress in 1844 heralded the age of electrical communications. Morse's invention is significant not only in the apparatus but also in his concept of a code that uses sequences of dots and dashes to represent the alphabets. Morse introduced the notion of an efficient code by assigning shorter sequences to the more commonly used letters of the alphabet.

Although Morse's telegraph was focused on transmitting alphabets, the facsimile system was pursued around the same time for the transmission of handwritings and drawings. In fact, in 1843, one year before Morse's patent, an English patent was issued to Scottish physicist Alexander Bain for his "recording telegraph," the first known design of a facsimile system. Bain's system used a battery-driven electric pendulum clock. At the transmitter, on each swing of the pendulum, a stylus traced across a metal typeface, making and breaking an electrical circuit. At the receiver, a similar pendulum and stylus traced over a damp electrolytic paper that was blackened whenever there was a current flow, producing a marking that represented a reproduction of the raised typeface.

In 1848, English physicist Frederick Bakewell obtained the patent for an alternative facsimile machine design. Bakewell's design differed from Bain's in two ways. First, instead of the pendulum, Bakewell used a rotating drum with leadscrew to perform the mechanical "scanning." The rotation of the drum was driven through a gear train by a weight that was lowered by gravity. Second, instead of a typeface, an insulating ink on a metal surface was used at the transmitter.

Bain's and Bakewell's designs were both hampered by the difficulty in achieving good synchronization between the transmitter and receiver. Bain's pendulum system used a synchronizing electrical pulse and a latch magnet to start and stop each pendulum swing. This synchronization system was prone to lightning and atmospheric disturbances that might induce current pulses on the line. Bakewell never fully resolved the synchronization problem for his drum-based design.

In 1861, an Italian named Giovanni Caselli patented the *pantelegraph*, a facsimile machine design that was based on both a pendulum and a drum. The pantelegraph made use of the leadscrew to move the stylus by one line for each pendulum swing. As with Bakewell's machine, the image to be transmitted was drawn with an insulating ink on a metal surface. Caselli adopted Bain's electric clock system for synchronization and introduced improvements that would eliminate most errors resulting from extraneous current pulses. The pantelegraph was received with such great enthusiasm in Paris that the Pantelegraph Society was created to prepare for its full exploitation. Customers from as far away as the imperial court of China came to observe the system's demonstration. In 1865, the world's first commercial facsimile service commenced operation between the French cities of Paris and Lyon. Unfortunately, despite an enthusiastic beginning, the pantelegraph did not live up to its full potential. First, the Pantelegraph Society failed to seize the opportunity to vigorously promote the device; instead it waited passively for orders to arrive. Second, the pantelegraph was invented just when the world was investing heavily in the telegraph network. In France, Chappe's semaphore network was being replaced by the telegraph. The French Telegraph Administration, concerned that the pantelegraph might jeopardize its investment in the telegraph network, imposed a heavy tariff on the pantelegraph service for the transmission of written messages, intending that pantelegraph service would be limited to the transmission of drawings and signatures, services that could not be performed by the telegraph. In Italy, the pantelegraph faced similar political obstacles. Eventually, in 1870, the pantelegraph service was discontinued. Caselli died, disappointed, in 1891.

The pantelegraph was an ingenious design in its time. Working units of the pantelegraph still exist in museums today. Units kept at the Musée National des Techniques and the Postal Museum in France were turned on in 1961 and 1982; as reported in an article in the June 1995 issue of *La Revue*, a publication of the Musée, the units "operated faultlessly, six hours a day, for months." The museum units operated at a speed of 120 lines per minute. Figure 1 shows a working pantelegraph and its scanning unit. The device stands more than 2 meters tall.

The facsimile systems introduced by Bain, Bakewell, and Caselli were all based on mechanical contact scanning by a stylus. In 1902, Arthur Korn of Germany introduced the first facsimile device based on optical scanning. In Korn's system, the film negative of a photograph was put on a revolving glass drum inside a cylinder. Light from a transmitter lamp was focused on the film, passing through the film as well as the glass drum, and reflected by a prism onto a selenium cell that produced a current in response. The receiver was also based on photographic recording on film. As relays and spark gap modulators were found too slow to be varying light sources for recording, Korn developed an electromagnetic light shutter that was a piece of aluminum foil hung by a loop of wire in a magnetic field. The flow of current deflected the aluminum foil and blocked or passed the light from the receiver lamp that was focused on the foil. In 1904, Korn sent telephone wire photos from Munich to Nuremberg, a distance of more than 600 miles. In 1907, Korn sent the first wire photos from continent Europe to England. In 1922, a photo of Pope Pius XI was sent from near Rome to Berlin and then radioed to a navy radio station in Maine, United States. The transmission of this picture took forty minutes. Later, Korn developed a radio system

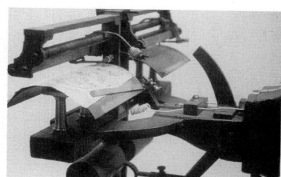

Figure 1: Pantelegraph. Source: Retrieved from http://chem.ch.huji.ac.il/~eugeniik/history/caselli.html.

so that maps, sketches, and aerial photos could be sent from aircraft in what was called a "phototelegraph."

Shortly following Korn, Edouard Belin (1876–1963) of France constructed in 1907 and perfected by 1925 an alternative optical-based system, the Belinograph. Belin's system operated not on the film negative but directly on the image that was placed on a cylinder and scanned with a powerful light beam. The reflected light was converted into electrical current. The Belinograph, widely used in Europe by the news media in the 1930s and 1940s, formed the basic principle of all subsequent facsimile machines (Through the Wires, no date).

Early Applications and Failures

During the years between the first and second world wars, many commercial fax operations were launched. World War I brought great progress to electronics and radio, and along came improved facsimile system designs such as Bartholomew and MacFarlane's Bartlene system (1920), AT&T's telephotography machine (1924), RCA's Photoradio (1924), and various designs by Western Union (1924 and later). According to an AT&T study, eighteen different facsimile systems were operational or in development in 1928.

In the Bartlene system, a screen image was first created according to the same principle used in newspaper printing: gray scale was represented by dots of different sizes. The sizes of the dots were then transmitted as a telegraph message over the standard Western Union telegraph cable. As such, the Bartlene system was a digital system.

AT&T's telephotography machine operated on similar principles as Korn's machine and was one of the first systems that operated over the telephone network using conditioned private lines. To achieve synchronization, the drum and motor was in a servo frequency control loop using an accurate tuning fork, housed in a constant temperature oven, for frequency reference. The telephotography machine (see Figure 2) was used mainly to transmit newspaper wire photos such as photographs of Babe Ruth.

The RCA system was based on radio transmission. Similar to AT&T's system, the RCA system employed a tuning fork in a constant temperature oven. An amplifier took the tuning fork frequency reference and generated the current for driving the motor. Amplitude of the scanned signal was converted into the duration of an on-off RF signal, a process known as *constant frequency variable dot* (CFVD) modulation.

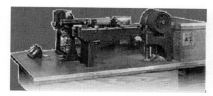

Figure 2: AT&T's telephotography machine. Source: Retrieved from www.att.com/attlabs/reputation/timeline/24fax.html).

Fueled by competition in news reporting, facsimile was widely used for the transmission of pictures worldwide by the late 1920s. Services were provided by European PTTs, AT&T, and news agencies such as the Associated Press, NEA Acme, Reuters, and *The New York Times*. But these services were never profitable in terms of business. They faced competition from the less timely but far cheaper alternative: airmail. Although European PTTs were keeping money-losing businesses alive to maintain the capability, AT&T sold its Wirephoto business to Associated Press in 1934. The start of World War II virtually finished off all public picture facsimile services because of the lack of countries to communicate with (Coopersmith 1993, 1994).

During this time, facsimile was also used to transmit maps, terrain drawings, and weather charts. During World War II, such uses were adopted in a widespread fashion by both sides. In 1955, the U.S. Weather Bureau developed a weather facsimile network using dedicated leased lines for transmitting weather data around the country.

Western Union was a major developer and user of facsimile from the 1930s to 1960s. The company's approach, interestingly, was to make facsimile an extension of the telegraph. Facsimile offered to Western Union the potential of error avoidance and cost saving by eliminating telegraph operators. Facsimile equipment between its own offices and the offices of its large customers also allowed Western Union to deliver telegrams without a courier. Figure 3 shows a DeskFax system that was developed by Western Union in 1935. The DeskFax was the first large-scale deployment of facsimile. Eventually, more than 50,000 units were in customer offices in the 1950s. Fax services accounted for $42 million of Western Union's $255 million revenue in 1958.

In the 1960s, in the face of rapidly changing technology, Western Union's refusal to treat and develop facsimile as an independent service caused DeskFax to eventually disappear from the scene.

Another noteworthy episode in the history of facsimile was fax broadcasting. Before and after World War II, newspapers and radio stations cooperated to introduce radio facsimile receivers into individual homes so that newsprints could be broadcasted into the home anytime during the day. By 1940, forty stations in the United States were experimenting with nighttime fax broadcasting

of newspapers. This effort was interrupted by the war but was renewed afterward. In 1948, the FCC created a new radio facsimile standard based on FM instead of AM. It supported 4-inch- and 8-inch-wide facsimiles, with synchronization provided by 60 hz power lines. Fax broadcasting eventually died because of the high cost and unpleasant smell of the recording paper, as well as the insufficient quality of the received newsprint.

Modern Systems: Timelines for Group 1 to 4 Standards

The trigger that led to the widespread adoption of facsimile in the 1980s was the adoption of a standard protocol for sending faxes at a rate of 9600 bps in 1980. This standard is known as the *group 3 standard*. Later, a group 4 standard emerged that was designed to work over ISDN lines. Because the widespread deployment of ISDN has never materialized as initially envisioned, group 4 facsimile has never taken off and the group 3 standard continues to drive facsimile operation today. Group 3 is a digital standard. Before group 3, the group 1 and group 2 analog standards existed but were not universally adopted by manufacturers. Before group 3, the facsimile world was characterized by incompatible machines and limited deployment. In this section, we provide a brief timeline for the development of modern facsimile standards.

In the United States, the Electronic Industries Association (EIA) established the TR-29 technical committee to work on the facsimile standard in 1962. The effort was not fully embraced by the participants, who were hesitant to disclose their designs and accept proposals that would require them to modify their designs. Nevertheless, in 1966, EIA published Standard RS-328, *Message Facsimile Equipment for Operation on Switched Voice Facilities Using Data Communication Equipment*, a set of standards that allowed a high degree of tolerance together with a recommended "eventual standard." This was the first U.S. standard. Although few manufacturers upgraded to the eventual standard, with RS-328, a large number of machines from different manufacturers could begin to interoperate, even though pages might be stretched or have their edges cut off. The common speed was 6 minutes per 8.5- × 11-inch page.

CCITT (now ITU-T) began the group 1 international standard effort in 1968 based on RS-328 and adopted the final standard in 1974 with minimal participation from U.S. companies. Although RS-328 used *frequency modulation* (FM) with 1500 hz representing "white" and 2400 hz representing "black," the group 1 standard specified 1300 hz as "white" and 2100 hz as black. The scanning speed for group 1 was four minutes per page.

Following what happened at CCITT, U.S. manufacturers began to work together more closely in the TR-29 meetings. Companies such as Xerox and Graphic Sciences were developing faster systems that offered group 1 transmission quality. Xerox's design also was based on FM but Graphic Sciences' design was based on *amplitude modulation* (AM), which allowed the transmission of gray scale. Working through a U.S. Department of State CCITT group, U.S. manufacturers were much better represented at CCITT. With good collaborative support from the

Figure 3: DeskFax. Source: Retrieved from www.westernunion. gr/netemtts/HISTORYPHOTO.HTM.

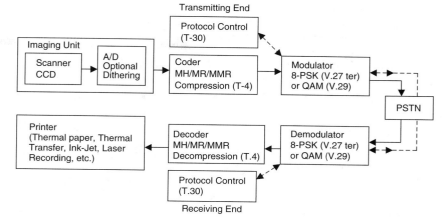

Transmitting End

Figure 4: Block diagram of a group 3 fax machine

British Facsimile International Consultative Committee (BFICC), the group 2 standard adopted in 1976 opened the door to a true global standard. Group 2 was based on *amplitude modulation-phase modulation with vestigial sideband* (AM-PM VSB) at a carrier frequency of 2100 hz; it allowed a transmission speed of three minutes per page.

It was also in the mid-1970s that the sophistication and cost of the three underlying technologies for facsimile improved to a reasonable level. During the 1960s, the center of activities for facsimile had shifted to Japan. Fax machines first had become popular there, where the use of *kanji* (a system of writing using Chinese characters) made typing difficult; it was much faster to handwrite kanji, which gave facsimile transmission an advantage. It was also the Japanese who first mastered the skill for efficient and low-cost manufacturing. Following the group 2 standard, Japanese manufacturers became dominant players in the global market.

Group 3 fax is today's dominant facsimile standard. Its standardization effort began in 1975, around the same time that the group 2 standard was adopted. Group 3 (G3) is a digital standard, and operation of a group 3 facsimile system no longer depends on the synchronization between transmitter and receiver. Adoption of group 3 occurred in 1980 and led to the widespread adoption of facsimile in the office and home in the 1980s. The group 3 standard includes modulation schemes, an end-to-end digital control protocol, variable transmission rates, coding schemes for data compression, and error control. Generally, G3 fax achieves a transmission rate of one minute per page.

The group 4 facsimile standard was adopted in 1984. It was intended for use over the new *public switched data network* (PSDN) based on ISDN. It also adopted the *open system interconnection* (OSI) layered model for computer communications. It defined classes of machines with different levels of capabilities, covered transmission over different networks, and included other services such as Telex. Instead of being a pure image, a document to be transmitted in group 4 may contain a layout structure with text as well as graphics. Many of the features defined for group 4 facsimile were also adopted as options for group 3. Like ISDN, group 4 fax was never widely deployed.

In the 1990s, with the mass adoption of personal computers and peripherals, new facsimile standards for the Internet-centric world came to the scene. These included

the PC fax and T.38. As of today, group 3 fax remains the main staple of facsimile. It is the easiest to use and an indispensable form of communications for many businesses and households.

In the remainder of this chapter, we will discuss the technology involved in groups 3 and 4 facsimiles, as well as emerging Internet-centric standards.

GROUP 3 FACSIMILE
Overall Architecture

The block diagram of a group 3 fax machine is shown in Figure 4. Components include an image scanner with an analog-to-digital converter (ADC), a coder-decoder, and a modem. At the transmitting end, the imaging unit converts a document into a digital image, and then the coder compresses the image to reduce the number of bits that need to be transmitted; the modulator sends the compressed data over a telephone line. At the receiving end, the demodulator recovers the compressed and transmitted data, the decoder expands the compressed data, and the printer produces a duplicate of the original document (ITU-T 1988, 2003).

The resolution specified for group 3 fax is 1728 pel* per standard scan line of 215 millimeter (mm) ± 1 percent horizontally and 3.85 lines per mm ± 1 percent vertically. The standard vertical resolution of G3 is identical to that of G1 and G2 faxes. Horizontally, although G3 is a digital system, G1 and G2 are analog systems and are not represented by pels. Options for 2 × and 4 × vertical resolutions and wider horizontal scan-line width, higher horizontal resolutions, or both are also allowed. Standard G3 focuses on the transmission of halftone images so that each pel is either a black or white—that is, either 0 or 1. A dithering scheme may be used with the ADC so that any gray scale in the original picture can be reflected by the density of black pels. For printing, a variety of recording technologies are available today. The imaging and printing system will be discussed in the next section.

The raw digital image is compressed by a coder using either a one-dimensional *modified Huffman* (MH)

---

*A discrete, metrically measured picture element.

code or a two-dimensional *modified READ*** (MR) code. These codes utilize two facts: (1) Most fax images contain large numbers of continuous white pels, and (2) there are usually few changes between two successive scan lines. At the receiver, the compressed data are decompressed. Because errors may occur in the transmission, error-correction and error-concealment schemes are used to minimize their impact. Modulation methods can be:

- 2.4 or 4.8 Kbps *phase shift keying* (PSK), according to V.27ter, when operating over the general PSTN;
- 7.2 or 9.6 Kbps *quadrature amplitude modulation* (QAM), according to V.29; or
- 9.6 Kbps or 14,400 *trellis modulation*, according to V.17, when the facsimile is operating a high-quality switched circuit or leased line.

The procedures for communications between a transmitting fax machine and a receiving G3 fax terminal over the PSTN are governed by a set of protocols specified in Recommendation T.30 by ITU-T (2005). Procedures involved include:

- call establishment and call release;
- compatibility checking, status, and control command;
- checking and supervision of line conditions; and
- control functions and facsimile operator recall.

A fax terminal may be *automatic* in that it is capable of performing all of the procedures above, or it may be *manual* in that some of the procedures may require actions to be taken by an operator. Procedures are specified for all combinations of automatic and manual transmitting and receiving terminals. Communications of control information between terminals are based on frequency tone signals as well as binary coded signaling. The binary coded signaling is based on *high-level data-link control* (HDLC).

Various annexes were added to the T.4 (ITU-T 2003) standard to provide enhancements to G3 fax, including:

a. optional error-correction mode;
b. optional file-transfer mode to permit the transmission of any data file;
c. optional character mode to permit the transmission of character-coded documents based on the T.30 standard for transmitting character-coded control data;
d. optional *mixed mode* (MM) to permit the transmission of both character-coded and facsimile-coded data;
e. optional continuous-tone color mode;
f. facsimile group 3 64-kbps option F (G3F) for operation over ISDN;
g. transmission of color and gray-scale images using lossless coding scheme;
h. *mixed raster content* (MRC) mode; and
i. optional continuous-tone color mode.

**An acronym for *relative element address designate*.

Imaging and Printing

A standard G3 facsimile terminal supports the following paper sizes: ISO A4, ISO B4, ISO A3, North American letter (215.9 mm × 279.4 mm) and legal (215.9 mm × 355.6 mm). The pel density of G3 facsimile is "unsquare," unlike that of the square G4. The T.4 standard has now focused on the metric-based pel, and specifies:

a. a standard resolution of 3.85 lines/mm ±1 percent in vertical resolution;
b. optional higher resolution of 7.7 lines/mm ±1 percent and 15.4 lines/mm ±1 percent in vertical direction;
c. 1728 black and white picture elements along the standard scan line length of 215 mm ±1 percent;
d. optionally, 2048 black and white picture elements along a scan line length of 255 mm ±1 percent;
e. optionally, 2432 black and white picture elements along a scan line length of 303 mm ±1 percent;
f. optionally, 3456 black and white picture elements along a scan line length of 215 mm ±1 percent;
g. optionally, 4096 black and white picture elements along a scan line length of 255 mm ±1 percent;
h. optionally, 4864 black and white picture elements along a scan line length of 303 mm ±1 percent.

Imaging

Drum scanners were broadly used in the past. In the drum scanner, the scanning spot traces horizontally (or *helically*) across a page as the drum turns. Brightness information on the page is converted by a photosensor into a signal one spot at a time. This spot corresponds to a *pel* in the case of a halftone (black-and-white) image and a *pixel* in the case of gray-scale or color images.

A modern scanner used in G3 typically works on more than one spot at a time. An array of 1728 or more tiny *charge-coupled device* (CCD) photosensors focuses on all spots across a horizontal line on the page simultaneously so that a document can be scanned one line at a time. The number of photosensors is scaled proportionally to the page width and supported resolution. In this way, a document can be scanned far more quickly. The photosensor array can be implemented on a small CCD chip in the case of a camera-style scanner, or it can be implemented along a bar of the same width as the document in the case of a contact image scanner.

The disadvantage of the camera-style scanner is its large size: An optical path distance of approximately 30 centimeters (cm) is needed to focus light from the illuminator reflecting off the scanned page onto the CCD chip through a lens with a 10:1 image reduction. A mirror system can be used to fold the optical path and reduce the size of the scanner. For the contact scanner, an array of integrated *light-emitting diodes* (LEDs), photosensors, and lenses distributed along a bar is placed directly above the scanned document. The LEDs illuminate the picture elements, and the photosensors detect the reflected light. The contact scanner allows for a more compact design and provides uniform image quality without distortion at the edges of the page. The LEDs demand much lower power (Streetman and Banerjee 2006).

The photosensor works by accumulating a voltage in proportion to the amount of light incident on it. During scanning, each photosensor's voltage is read and converted to a single-bit digital value by an ADC. A 0 bit represents a white pel, and a 1 bit represents a black pel. An *automatic background control* circuit is used in most group 3 terminals so that any off-white background of the original will not be converted into black. The original group 3 standard was intended for transmitting bilevel textual images. The printing technology in the 1980s was also bilevel. The technique of dithering was frequently used to enhance the quality of the resulting digital image from the scanning process. We will describe the process of dithering in a later section.

Printing

We now discuss several printing technologies that are most commonly used in fax terminals.

The invention of thermal paper recording brought significant improvements over earlier technologies such as electrolytic paper and contributed to the widespread adoption of fax. It provided better image contrast, did not fade, cost less, and did not emit an unpleasant odor as did electrolytic paper. Thermal paper is coated with a dye and an oxidized material on a base. Upon heating, the dye and the oxidized material fuse and produce a mark. In a thermal paper printer, the printer head is made up of a row of small resistor-based heating elements. The supply of a current pulse provides the heating needed to produce the mark on the paper. One disadvantage of thermal paper recording is that the recorded image deteriorates if the paper is later exposed to heat.

Thermal-transfer recording works according to principles similar to thermal-paper recording, with the difference that the heat is applied to a transfer film over a plain white paper so that the dye is transferred to the white paper. The thermal-transfer printer costs more than the thermal-paper printer, and the recording materials ("ink") used also cost more, but the printer uses standard paper that can be conveniently handled and is not sensitive to heating and light.

The laser printer and the LED printer are both based on similar electrostatic principles. In the laser printer, a rotating mirror scans a laser beam across the recording paper and produces an electrostatic charge on each spot on the paper. The presence of an electrostatic charge causes the recording material (the "toner") to adhere to the spot, and as the paper rolls out of the printer, a "fuser" applies heat to the paper and melts the toner into the paper. In an LED printer, an array of LEDs is used instead of a scanning laser beam. Figure 5 shows the major component in a laser printer.

Ink-jet recording has been most widely adopted in desktop PC printing. Earlier ink-jet printers appeared long before group 1 fax terminals but were not popular because of the effort needed both to clean print heads to prevent clogging and to refill ink reservoirs. Widespread success came with the availability of replaceable cartridges and print jets. Although the ink-jet printer costs less than a laser or LED printer, the per-page cost is much higher.

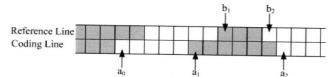

Figure 5: Major component in a laser printer

Coding

Consider a binary image at a resolution of 1728 pels per line and 1068 lines per page (3.85 lines per mm with a page length of 277 mm) created from the scanning process of a G3 terminal. Uncompressed, 1,845,504 bits are needed to represent this image, and it will take 384 seconds (more than 6 minutes) to transmit this image over a phone line at 4800 bps. The scanned image, however, typically contains redundant information and can be compressed significantly.

The modified Huffman code noted earlier is used by all G3 fax terminals. Two variations—the *modified READ* (MR) code and *modified modified READ* (MMR) codes—are supported as options. A newer coding scheme is *trellis coding*. These coding methods reduce the amount of data to be sent over the phone lines and therefore the time needed to send each page. We first describe the modified Huffman and modified READ coding schemes.

Modified Huffman Coding

The MH coding scheme is a so-called one-dimensional coding scheme as one line of data is scanned and coded for transmission at a time. In contrast, in MR coding each line is scanned and compared to the previous line. The coder encodes only the changes. The MR coding achieved greater compression than MH but is less robust against transmission errors. Both schemes make use of the fact that there are typically long strings of 0's and 1's in a scanned line or in the difference between the current line and the previous line.

In MH, a line is decomposed into alternating white runs and black runs (strings of 0's and strings of 1's) that sum to 1728 bits (at standard resolution). Each code word represents a run-length of either all white pels or all black pels, and the code table is designed so that more likely run lengths are assigned shorter code words. To maintain color synchronization, all data lines begin with a white run-length code word. A white run length of zero is sent if the actual scan line starts with a black run. Two types of code words are used: *terminating code words*, which encode values from 0 to 64; and *makeup code words*, which encode values in multiples of 64. Hence, a run length is encoded either by one terminating code word or a makeup code word followed by a terminating code word. The white run lengths and the black run lengths should sum to 1728 for each line. To provide error checking, an *end-of-line* (EOL) code word is also included. The sum of the run lengths between two EOL code words should equal 1728. Any discrepancy is an indication of transmission errors. Table 1 shows extracted portions of tables in ITU-T Recommendation T.4.

Table 1: Extracted Portions of Tables in from ITU-T Recommendation T.4 (2003)

Tab.1 T.4 – Terminating codes

White run length	Code word	Black run lenth	Code word
0	00110101	0	0000110111
1	000111	1	010
2	0111	2	11
3	1000	3	10
4	1011	4	011
5	1100	5	0011
6	1110	6	0010
7	1111	7	00011
8	10011	8	000101
9	10100	9	000100
10	00111	10	0000100
11	01000	11	0000101
12	001000	12	0000111
13	000011	13	00000100
14	110100	14	00000111
15	110101	15	000011000
16	101010	16	0000010111
17	101011	17	0000011000
18	0100111	18	0000001000
19	0001100	19	00001100111
20	0001000	20	00001101000
21	0010111	21	00001101100
22	0000011	22	00000110111
23	0000100	23	00000101000
24	0101000	24	00000010111
25	0101011	25	00000011000
26	0010011	26	000011001010
27	0100100	27	000011001011
28	0011000	28	000011001100
29	00000010	29	000011001101
30	00000011	30	000001101000
31	00011010	31	000001101001
32	00011011	32	000001101010
33	00010010	33	000001101011
34	00010011	34	000011010010
35	00010100	35	000011010011
36	00010101	36	000011010100
37	00010110	37	000011010101
38	00010111	38	000011010110
39	00101000	39	000011010111
40	00101001	40	000001101100

Table 1 (Continued)

Tab.1 T.4 – Terminating codes

White run length	Code word	Black run lenth	Code word
41	00101010	41	000001101101
42	00101011	42	000011011010
43	00101100	43	000011011011
44	00101101	44	000001010100
45	00000100	45	000001010101
46	00000101	46	000001010110
47	00001010	47	000001010111
48	00001011	48	000001100100
49	01010010	49	000001100101
50	01010011	50	000001010010
51	01010100	51	000001010011
52	01010101	52	000000100100
53	00100100	53	000000110111
54	00100101	54	000000111000
55	01011000	55	000000100111
56	01011001	56	000000101000
57	01011010	57	000001011000
58	01011011	58	000001011001
59	01001010	59	000000101011
60	01001011	60	000000101100
61	00110010	61	000001011010
62	00110011	62	000001100110
63	00110100	63	000001100111

Tab.1 T.4 – Make up Codes

White run length	Code word	Black run lenth	Code word
64	11011	64	0000001111
128	10010	128	000011001000
192	010111	192	000011001001
256	0110111	256	000001011011
320	00110110	320	000000110011
384	00110111	384	000000110100
448	01100100	448	000000110101
512	01100101	512	0000001101100
576	01101000	576	0000001101101
640	01100111	640	0000001001010
704	011001100	704	0000001001011
768	011001101	768	0000001001100
832	011010010	832	0000001001101
896	011010011	896	0000001110010

Table 1 (Continued)

Tab.1 T.4 – Make up Codes

White run length	Code word	Black run lenth	Code word
960	011010100	960	0000001110011
1024	011010101	1024	0000001110100
1088	011010110	1088	0000001110101
1152	011010111	1152	0000001110110
1216	011011000	1216	0000001110111
1280	011011001	1280	0000001010010
1344	011011010	1344	0000001010011
1408	011011011	1408	0000001010100
1472	010011000	1472	0000001010101
1536	010011001	1536	0000001011010
1600	010011010	1600	0000001011011
1664	011000	1664	0000001100100
1728	010011011	1728	0000001100101
EOL	000000000001	EOL	000000000001

NOTE: It is recognized that terminals exist which accommodate larger paper widths maintaining the standard horizontal resolution. This option has been provided for by the addition of the make-up code set defined in this table.

Tab.1 T.4 – Make up Codes

Run length (black and white)	Make-up codes
1792	00000001000
1856	00000001100
1920	00000001101
1984	000000010010
2048	000000010011
2112	000000010100
2176	000000010101
2240	000000010111
2304	000000010111
2368	000000011100
2432	000000011101
2496	000000011110
2560	000000011111

NOTE: Run length in the range of lengths longer than or equal to 2624 pels are coded first by the make-up code of 2560. If the remaining part of the run (after the first make-up code of 2560) is 2560 pels or greater, additional make-up code(s) of 2560 are issued until the remaining part of the run becomes less than 2560 pels. Then the remaining part of the run is encoded by terminating code or by make-up code plus terminating code according to the range as mentioned above.

Modified READ Coding

The MR is a lossless two-dimensional coding technique for bilevel images, a superset of the modified Huffman code. It is used by many facsimile terminals.

In MR, we define a *changing element* as an element with a color (i.e., black or white) that is different from that of the previous element on the same line. It was estimated that 75 percent of changing elements occur within one position to the left or right of a corresponding changing element in the previous line. In MR, the position of each changing element in the current line is encoded with respect to the position of a corresponding reference

Table 2: Modified READ Coding

Code	Explanation
a_0	The reference or starting changing element on the coding line. At the start of the coding line, a_0 is set on an imaginary white changing element situated just before the first element on the line. During the coding of the coding line, the position of a_0 is defined by the previous coding mode.
a_1	The next changing element to the right of a_0 on the coding line.
a_2	The next changing element to the right of a_1 on the coding line.
b_1	The first changing element on the reference line to the right of a_0 and of opposite color to a_0.
b_2	The next changing element to the right of b_1 on the reference line.

element either on the previous line or on the same line. Because transmission errors will lead to error propagation to subsequent lines, a K parameter is defined to limit the number of successive lines that can be coded two-dimensionally. A maximum K value is defined under different vertical resolutions:

- Standard vertical resolution: $K = 2$
- Optional higher vertical resolution:
  - 200 lines/25.4 mm, $K = 4$
  - 300 lines/25.4 mm, $K = 6$
  - 400 lines/25.4 mm, $K = 8$
  - 600 lines/25.4 mm, $K = 12$
  - 800 lines/25.4 mm, $K = 16$
  - 1200 lines/25.4 mm, $K = 24$

To explain how MR coding works, we define the following elements with reference to Table 2.

At any instance, the MR encoder chooses one of three coding modes based on the relative positions of the changing elements defined in Table 2. The *pass mode* is identified when b_2 lies to the left of a_1. When this occurs, a_0 is set immediately below b_2 (to a'_0) in preparation for the next coding (see Figure 6).

The *vertical mode* is identified when b_2 does not lie to the left of a_1 and the distance $|a_1b_1|$ is less than or equal to 3 (see Figure 7). In this case, we encode the distance

a_1b_1 by one of seven values: $V(0)$, $V_R(1)$, $V_R(2)$, $V_R(3)$, $V_L(1)$, $V_L(2)$, and $V_L(3)$. The subscripts R and L indicate whether a_1 is to the left or to the right of b_1. After the encoding occurs, the position of a_0 is reset to a_1.

If b_2 does not lie to the left of a_1 but the distance $|a_1b_1|$ is greater than 3, then the horizontal mode is identified (see Figure 8). In this case, we encode both the run lengths a_0a_1 and a_1a_2 using the code words H + $M(a_0a_1)$ + $M(a_1a_2)$, where H is the flag code word 001 taken from the two-dimensional code table, and $M(a_0a_1)$ and $M(a_1a_2)$ are code words that represent the length and "color" of the runs a_0a_1 and a_1a_2, respectively, and are taken from the appropriate white or black one-dimensional uncompressed code tables (see Table 1). Note that an entrance code precedes the uncompressed code. After a horizontal mode encoding, the position of a_0 is set on a_2.

Table 3 shows the two-dimensional code table from ITU Recommendation T.4 (2003). Figure 9 shows the flowchart that specifies the coding procedure. The one-dimensional uncompressed code table, also from T.4, is shown in Table 4.

The modified modified READ (MMR) codes are part of the group 4 facsimile standard and will be described in the enhancement section.

Protocol

As discussed earlier, a fax terminal is automatic if it is capable of performing all of the protocol procedure without operator action. Otherwise it is considered manual. ITU-T Recommendation T.30 (2005) classifies eight operating methods as shown in Table 5.

Note that while the direction of fax transmission is usually from the calling terminal to the called terminal,

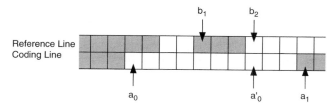

Figure 6: Pass model

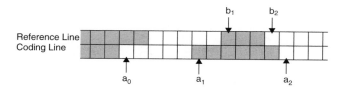

Figure 7: Vertical model

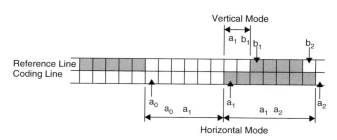

Figure 8: Horizontal mode

Table 3: Two-Dimensional Code Table

Mode	Elements to be coded		Notation	Code word
Pass	b_1, b_2		P	0001
Horizontal	a_0a_1, a_1a_2		H	001 ÷ M(a_0a_1) ÷ M(a_1a_2) (Note 1)
Vertical	a_1 just under b_1	$a_1b_1 = 0$	V(0)	1
	a_1 to the right of b_1	$a_1b_1 = 1$	$V_R(1)$	011
		$a_1b_1 = 2$	$V_R(2)$	000011
		$a_1b_1 = 3$	$V_R(3)$	0000011
	a_1 to the left of b_1	$a_1b_1 = 1$	$V_L(1)$	010
		$a_1b_1 = 2$	$V_L(2)$	000010
		$a_1b_1 = 3$	$V_L(3)$	0000010
Extension	2-D (extensions) 1-D (extensions)			0000001xxx 000000001xxx (Note 2)

Note 1 – Code M() of the horizontal mode represents the code words in Tables 2 and 3.

Note 2 – It is suggested the uncompressed mode is recognized as an optional extension of two-dimensional coding scheme for Group 3 terminals. The bit assignment for the xxx bits is 111 for the uncompressed mode of operation whose code table is given in Table 5.

Note 3 – Further study is needed to define other unspecified xxx bit assignments and their use for any further extensions.

Note 4 – If the suggested uncompressed mode is used on a line designated to be one-dimensionally code, the coder must not switch into uncompressed mode following any code word ending in the sequence 000. This is because any code word ending in 000 followed by a switching code 000000001 will be mistaken for an end-of-line code.

Source: ITU-T Recommendation T.4.

the standard also allows for transmission from the called terminal to the calling terminal.

The time sequence of a facsimile call consists of the following five phases.

Phase A: Call establishment

Phase B: Premessage procedure (with an identification section and a command section)

Phase C: Message transmission (includes phase C1, in-message procedure; and phase C2, message transmission)

Phase D: Postmessage procedure

Phase E: Call release

The time sequence of a facsimile call is shown in Figure 10.

Each of the eight operating methods requires a slightly different procedure sequence. Here we provide a high-level description of the procedure sequence under method 4-T, where an automatic terminal calls an automatic terminal and the direction of facsimile transmission is from calling terminal to called terminal.

Phase A: Call Setup

The sending terminal dials the receiving terminal through the PSTN and sends the *calling tone* (CNG) that indicates that the call is from a fax terminal. CNG is a 1100-hz beep at a 0.5 second on, 3 second off cycle. The called terminal answers by going off-hook and, after a 0.2 second delay, sends back to the calling terminal the *called terminal identification* (CED) answer tone. CED is a continuous

2,100-hz +15hz tone with a duration exactly between 2.6 and 4 seconds.

Phase B: Premessage Procedure

The receiving terminal sends its *digital identification signal* (DIS) at 300 bps to declare its capabilities and options supported such as:

- modem types supported,
- resolution,
- coding scheme for compression,
- maximum paper length,
- minimum time needed to record a scanned line at the receiver, and
- nonstandard features.

The calling terminal then sends a *digital command signal* (DCS) to lock the receiving terminals into the selected capabilities and options followed by an all-zeros 1.5-second training signal (TCF) for the data modem. After its modem is trained, the receiving terminal is ready and sends a *confirmation-to-receive* signal (CFR).

Phase C: Message Transmission

The calling terminal sends a training signal again, followed by the image data for the entire page.

Phase D: Postmessage Procedure

The calling terminal sends a *return-to-control* (RTC) signal and switches the modem back to 300 bps. If no more

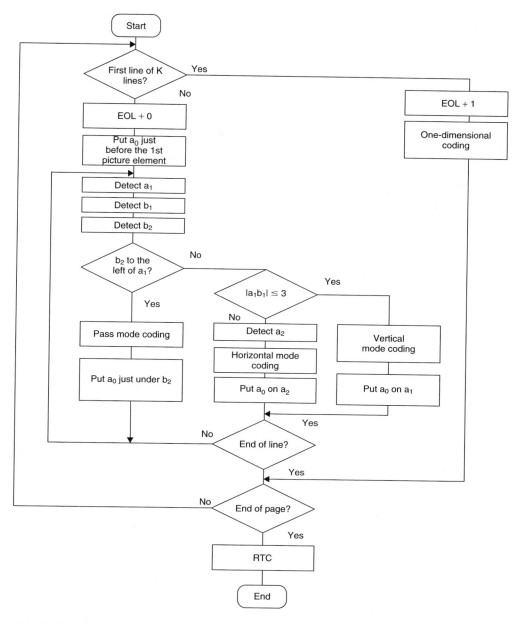

Figure 9: Flowchart of coding procedure

Table 4: Uncompressed Mode Code Words

Entrance code to uncompressed mode	On one-dimensionally coded line: 000000001111 On two-dimensionally coded line: 0000001111	
	Image pattern	Code word
	1	1
	01	01
Uncompressed mode code	001	001
	0001	0001
	00001	00001
	00000	000001
		0000001T
	0	00000001T
Exit from uncompressed mode code	00	000000001T
	000	0000000001T
	0000	00000000001T
T Denotes a tag bit which tells the colour of the next run (blank = 1, white = 0)		

Table 5: Eight Transmission Operating Methods

			Direction of Facsimile Transmission	
Operating Method	Calling Terminal	Called Terminal	Calling Terminal to Called Terminal	Called Terminal to Calling Terminal
1	Manual	Manual	1-T	1-R
2	Manual	Automatic	2-T	2-R
3	Automatic	Manual	3-T	3-R
4	Automatic	Automatic	4-T	4-R

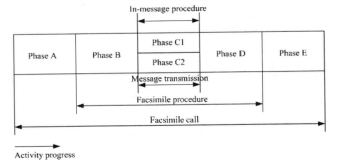

Figure 10: Sequence of a facsimile

pages are forthcoming, an *end-of-procedure* (EOP) signal is sent, and the called terminal replies with the *message-confirmation* (MCF) signal to indicate that the page has been received successfully. The terminals then proceed to phase E. If more pages are to follow, then a *multipage signal* (MPS) is sent instead of an EOP, and the terminals return to the beginning of phase C. Alternatively, the calling terminal may also send an *end-of-message* (EOM); in this case, the terminals return to the beginning of phase B. If operator intervention is requested, then a *procedural interrupt* (PRI) command (such as PRI-EOP, PRI-MPS, or PRI-EOM) is sent and the terminals return to the beginning of phase B. A complete list of postmessage commands and responses can be found in T.30 (ITU-T 2005).

Phase E: Call Release

The calling facsimile sends a *disconnect* (DCN) signal and both terminals release the call.

All binary-encoded procedural data are transmitted at 300 bits per second ±0.01 percent using the V.21 channel number two modulation system and encapsulated in HDLC frames for frame labeling, error checking, and acknowledgment of correct reception. All new binary-encoded transmissions are preceded by a preamble that consists of a sequence of HDLC flags (0111 1110) with a duration of 1 second ±15 percent. This preamble ensures that all elements of the communication channel, such as echo suppressors, are properly conditioned before the transmission of data.

Error Control

The communication channel provided by the telephone network introduces error to digital data transmissions.

The use of an EOL code at the end of each scanned line provides a means for error detection and containment. A number of error conditions may occur:

- EOL occurring before 1728 pels have been decoded,
- more than 1728 pels have been decoded before the occurrence of EOL,
- invalid bit pattern received, and
- in two-dimensional coding, invalid reference to a previous line.

Without EOL, erroneous decoding because of a transmission error may propagate through the entire page. With EOL, transmission errors often lead to annoying streaks in the output page. Before the adoption of the optional error correction mode by ITU-T (Annex A of Recommendation T-4), various error-concealment schemes were used by vendors to minimize the effect of transmission errors. These schemes included:

- all erroneous lines printed white until the first correct MH coded line was received;
- all erroneous lines replaced by the last correctly received line until the next correctly coded line was received; and
- the first erroneous lines replaced by the last correctly received line and all subsequent erroneous lines printed white.

The first erroneous line is decoded and printed normally based on MH or MR up to where the error occurs. After that, the pel from the previous line is printed and also used as reference for the decoding of the next received line in the case of MR.

In the optional error correction mode defined by ITU-T, an HDLC frame structure is used to transmit the coded scan line. A selective *automatic repeat request* (ARQ) scheme is used so that the receiver may request the retransmission of bad frames. The communication channel operates in the half-duplex mode. After four requests for retransmission of the same frame, the transmitter may stop or execute procedures for modem speed fallback.

The error-correction mode provides a basis for other new features such as binary file transfer and operation over ISDN.

Other Enhancements

The *optional file transfer* mode in Annex B of T-4 allows the transfer of any data file with or without additional information. Four file transfer modes are supported:

1. *basic transfer mode* (BTM) for the exchange of files of any kind without any additional information;
2. *document transfer mode* (DTM) for the exchange of files of any kind with a structured file description (file name, file type, file coding, etc.) that may be processed automatically or read by the user at the receiving side;
3. *binary transfer mode* (BFT), which is similar to DTM, with structured file description processed automatically only at the receiving side; and
4. *electronic data interchange for administration commerce and transport* (EDIFACT) transfer, or the exchange of EDIFACT files according to ISO 9735.

The *optional* character mode in Annex C of T-4 supports the reliable transfer of character coded documents by means of the T-30 protocol and the Annex A error-correction mode. The repertoire of graphic characters supported includes those allowed by ISO/IEC 8859-1 and the box-drawing characters repertoire in registered ITU-T set ISO 72. A basic page format of fifty-five lines with seventy-seven characters each is assumed, and control functions are incorporated to act on the formatting of the document and character attributes.

The optional mixed mode in Annex D allows pages with both facsimile-coded and character-coded information to be transferred between terminals. Again, the use of the error-correction mode is mandatory.

Next, we discuss a number of enhancements made to support the transfer of gray-scale and color images. These enhancements include the use of:

- clumped and ordered dithering to create bilevel representation of gray-scale images;

- JPEG as described in Annex E, optional continuous-tone color mode; and
- JBIG as described in Annex G, transmission of color and gray-scale images using lossless coding schemes.

Group 3 was originally designed for bilevel (i.e., black and white) images such as those created by handwriting and line drawings. Gray-scale images are also frequently encountered by a fax machine, so dithering was employed by vendors to achieve better results for such images. Dithering is performed only by the transmitting terminal and is not part of the T-4 standard.

For the case of standard G3 fax, each pel is either a 1 or a 0. If a fixed threshold is used for this single-bit analog-to-digital decision, any gray-scale information in the original will be lost and the resulting digital image may frequently show blocks of black and white areas. With dithering, this threshold is varied either randomly or systematically, so that the gray scale in the original can be reflected by a varying density of black pels in the resulting digital image, a technique used broadly in black-and-white printing (Yasuda et al. 1985; Jarvis, Judice, and Ninke 1976). The mechanism of dithering is illustrated in Figure 11.

In random dithering, the decision threshold is varied randomly. In *clumped dithering* and *ordered dithering*, the decision threshold is varied according to a fixed pattern. Figure 12 shows a clumped dithering scheme in which an

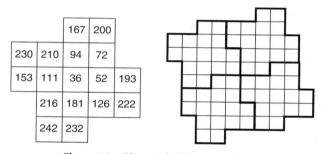

Figure 12: Clumped dithering scheme

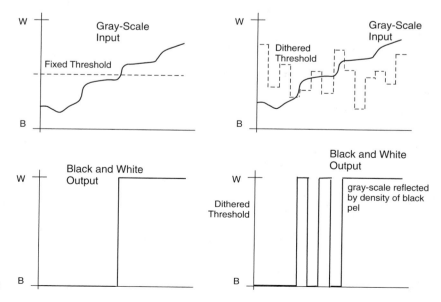

Figure 11: The dithering process

8	136	40	168
200	72	232	104
56	184	24	152
248	120	216	88

Figure 13: Ordered dithering scheme

image is made up of repetitive and interlocked clusters of 17 pels. The decision thresholds, based on 256 brightness levels, are varied in a fixed pattern as we move away from the center of the cluster. This way, regions of different brightness levels in the original image will be represented by clusters of black dots of different density in the bilevel image. This technique is equivalent to the halftone screening process used for printing photos in newspapers.

The idea of ordered dithering is similar to that of clumped dithering. In ordered dithering, the cluster is a square matrix. A 4 × 4 Bayer-type ordered dither threshold matrix is shown in Figure 13.

The problem in applying dithering to group 3 fax images is that the efficiency of the MH and MR codes is greatly reduced because dithering greatly reduces the run lengths of 1's and 0's.

The use of *JPEG*, the Joint Photographic Experts Group standard for encoding continuous-tone color fax images, was added to the group 3 standard in 1994. This option is described in Recommendation T-42 and Annex E of T-4. JPEG specifies two classes of coding processes: *lossy* and *lossless*. The lossy process is based on discrete cosine transform (DCT), and the lossless process is based on predictive coding. Group 3 adopted the $(L^x a^x b^x)$ color space defined by the Commission international de l'Eclairage (CIE) in 1976. The three components are L^x for lightness and a^x and b^x for chrominance. T-42 also defined the following different multilevel image-transfer modes:

- *lossy gray-scale mode* (LGM),
- *lossy color mode* (LCM).
- *lossless gray-scale mode* (LLGM), and
- *lossless color mode* (LLCM).

The selection of these modes is accomplished through the DIS and DCS frames described in T-30.

Although JPEG is a popular color image coding standard, it suffers from low efficiency when bilevel images, particularly textual and handwriting images, are encoded.

Following T.42, Recommendation T.43 defines a lossless encoding option that is intended for images with textual and line drawing content and limited color information. T.43 uses the color encoding scheme specified in T.82 (JBIG), and defines four types of images:

- one bit per color CMYK* or RGB** images,
- palettized color images,
- continuous-tone color, and
- gray scale.

---

* Cyan, magenta, yellow, black.
** Red, green, blue.

Different color representation, bit-plane decomposition, and coding methods are defined for these different image types. This option is described in Table 6 (from Annex G of T.4); Table 6 includes T.4's Annex G tables for image mode classification and color and gray-scale mode classification.

The *error correction mode* (ECM) specified in Annex A must be used for data transfer under the JPEG option and the JBIG option.

Lastly, the *mixed raster content* (MRC) option described in Annex H of T.4 defines a way to efficiently represent raster-oriented pages that contain a mixture of multilevel (e.g., continuous-tone and palletized color) and bilevel (e.g., text and line art) images. Standardized in Recommendation T.44, MRC does not introduce new encodings or resolutions but achieves enhanced efficiency by combining different encoding schemes and different spatial and color resolutions on a single page. It decomposes an image with a three-layer model consisting of the following layers:

- foreground (multilevel, text color),
- mask (bilevel, text shape, and rectangular text and continuous-tone outline)
- background (multilevel, continuous-tone images).

Considering that device memory may be limited in facsimile terminals, MRC provides ways to divide a page into horizontal strips. The maximum strip size is negotiated and may range from 256 lines to the full length of the scanned page. Although the mask layer must span the whole area of a strip, the foreground and background layers may cover only part of the strip. There are also three types of strips, each one depending on the type of data it contains:

- a *three-layer strip* (3LS) contains all three layers (foreground, mask, and background),
- a *two-layer strip* contains either the mask and foreground layers or the mask and background layers, and
- a *one-layer strip* contains only one of the three layers, with the other two set to fixed values.

NEW FACSIMILE SYSTEMS
The Group 4 Standard

The group 4 recommendation is designed for digital networks and makes use of the open system interconnection (OSI) seven-layer model for communications. Groups 3 and 4 facsimiles provide similar performance, and both use a similar set of encoding schemes for images. The main focuses for group 4 facsimile were operation over the then-emerging ISDN and interoperability of facsimile with other messaging systems and services. Under the group 4 standard, a facsimile terminal may bring new capabilities such as:

- interworking with remote computers as an input/output device (e.g., the fax terminal as keyboard, printer, and scanner or the computer as a storage and processing device for optical character recognition) and

Table 6: Image Mode Classification

Image type	Coding sub-mode class	Image specification	Number of bit-planes to be coded
One bit per color image	One bit per color image	One bit per colour image using RGB or CMY(K) primaries	CMY(K) image: 4 bit-planes CMY image: 3 bit-planes RGB image: 3 bit-planes
Palettized color image	Basic palettized color	Palettized image using 12 bits or less entries and 8 bits/comp.precision table	1 to 12 bit-planes (palette-table: up to 4096 entries 2 octets/entry)
	Extended palettized color	Palettized image using 13 to 16 bits entries and 8 bits/comp. precision table or 16 bits or less entries and 12 bits/comp.precision table	13 to 16 bit-planes (palette-table: 4097 to 65536 entries 3 octets/entries) or 1 to 16 bit-planes (palette-table: up to 65636 entries 6 octets/entry)
Continuous-tone image	Colour 8 bits/comp.color 12 bits/comp.color	2–8 bits/comp. 9 to 12 bits/comp.color image	2 x 3–8 x 3 bit-planes 9 x 3–12 x 3 bit-planes
	Gray-scale 8 bits gray-scale 12 bits gray-scale	2–8 bits 9 to 12 bits gray-scale image	2–8 bit-planes 9–12 bit-planes

Source: ITU-T. 2003 Recommendation T.4.

Table 7: Group 4 Recommendations Used in Conjunction with Recommendation T.6

Recommendation	Subject Covered
T.503	A document application profile for the interchange of group 4 facsimile documents
T.521	Communication application profile for document bulk transfer based on the session service (according to the rules defined in T.62 bis)
T.563	Terminal characteristics for group 4 facsimile apparatus
T.73	Document interchanges protocol for telematic services
T.62	Control procedures for Teletex and group 4 facsimile services
T.62 bis	Control procedures for Teletex and group 4 facsimile services based on Recommendations X.215/X.225
T.70	Network-independent basic transport service for Telematic services
F.161	International group 4 facsimile service

- interworking with the public data network for e-mail and other messaging services.

Under group 4, three classes of fax terminals are defined:

class 1, sending and receiving facsimile documents only at 200 pels/inch;

class 2, scanning, sending, receiving, and printing facsimile documents at 300 pels/inch; and

class 3, having class 2 capabilities plus a keyboard.

The initial image-encoding scheme for group 4 fax is MMR, which is specified in Recommendation T.6. MMR is designed for communication channels with no error or low error rates. In MMR, the starting line is assumed to be a white line, and all lines are encoded as differences from the line above. EOL is not used, so if an error occurs, all subsequent lines will become invalid until an "all white" or "all black" line is received. T.6 is used in conjunction with the recommendations for group 4 shown in Table 7.

In addition, the following recommendations are also applicable for classes 2 and 3 terminals:

- terminal equipment for use with Teletex (T.60),
- character repertoire and coded-character sets for international Teletex (T.61), and
- terminal capabilities for mixed modes of operation (T.72).

The MMR coding procedure is described by the flowchart in Figure 14. The code tables used are the same as those in MR.

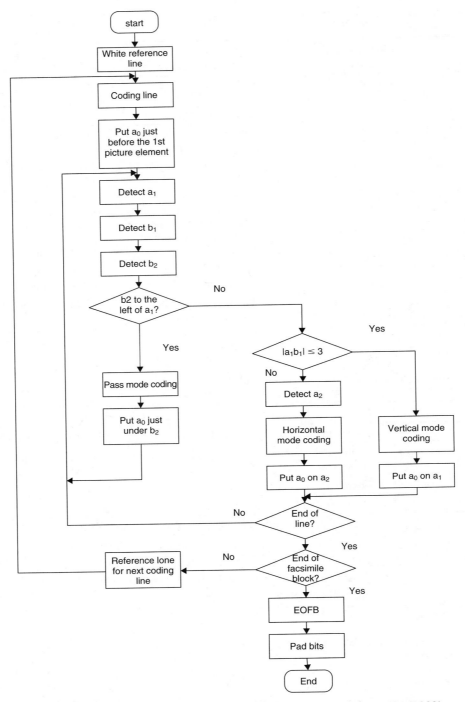

Figure 14: MMR coding procedure. Source: ITU-T Recommendation T.4 (2003).

Internet-Based Systems

The transmission of facsimiles over packet networks was considered before the emergence of the Internet. ITU-T's 1992 recommendations X.5, X.38, and X.39 provided a set of standards for the transmission of facsimiles over the X.25 packet network in a so-called real time mode: where end-to-end negotiations take place between transmitting and receiving terminals so that all standard and

common nonstandard facsimile features and options can be retained to the highest degree possible.

The use of X.25-based fax requires the transmitting terminal to connect to a *facsimile packet assembly and disassembly* (FPAD) device through the PSTN. The originating FPAD determines and makes connection to the terminating FPAD through the X.25 network, and the terminating FPAD makes connection to the receiving fax terminal through the PSTN. The connection to the originating FPAD can be *manual*, resulting in two-stage dialing by the user; or *automatic* so that the use of the FPAD and packet network becomes transparent to the user.

A second type of facsimile transmission over packet networks is the *store-and-forward service*, which is designed to operate over messaging systems such as X.400 and precludes the use of real-time negotiation. Store-and-forward fax is described in ITU-T's F.162 and F.163. Instead of the FPAD in X.25 facsimile, the *store-and-forward unit* (SFU) is used. Access to the SFU follows a two-stage procedure that is similar to the FPAD access procedure. Notification of delivery failure to the sender is required, but notification of success is optional. Delivery information may indicate delivery to the SFU (level 1), or delivery to the receiving terminal (level 2). The lack of real-time negotiation means that the SFU may need to be sent re-encoded high-resolution pages if the receiving fax terminal is capable only of receiving at a lower resolution. The SFU may also be capable of storing address lists such that a single fax message can be delivered to multiple recipients.

With the emergence of the Internet in the 1990s, the focus of facsimile over packet networks shifted. Standardization work began for facsimile service for which, in addition to the PSTN or ISDN, a portion of the transmission path may be an IP network (e.g., the Internet) (see Figure 15). This scenario is known as *fax over packet* or *fax over IP* (FoIP). A set of objectives for FoIP were drafted by ITU-T Study Group 8 in early 1997 that stipulated that FoIP standards should cover two basic scenarios:

1. Fax terminals can be *Internet-aware fax* (IAF) devices directly connected to the Internet or traditional fax terminals connected to gateways through PSTN or ISDN.

2. Service can be in real-time or store-and-forward mode. In real-time mode, the terminals negotiate and receive acknowledgments during the fax transmission (similar to traditional facsimile). In store-and-forward mode, facsimile data can be stored and delayed before delivery (similar to e-mail service).

The first recommendation from the study group was 1988's Draft Recommendation F.185 (ITU-T 1988), which described guidelines applicable to the support of both groups 3 and 4 over the Internet (with much left for further study for group 4) and covered both the real-time and store-and-forward modes. The real-time mode for group 3 fax was further standardized in ITU-T Recommendation T.38, which was approved in September 2005. The store-and-forward mode was further standardized in ITU-T Recommendation T.37, which has yet to be approved. In T.37, two modes of operation—*simple mode* and *full mode*—are defined. The simple mode means that capabilities exchange and receipt confirmation are not required but may be provided using optional e-mail functions outside the scope of the recommendation. The full mode means that capabilities exchange and confirmation are required. Simple mode operation is specified in T.37, whereas full mode operation is for further study. T.37 is based on the use of Internet e-mail.

As described in T.38, in real-time Internet facsimile, the contents and sequence of message exchanges between the transmitting and receiving terminals follow those used in conventional fax over PSTN or ISDN to the highest degree possible. The transmitting terminal receives a confirmation of receipt by the receiving terminal before disconnection, and the call duration is similar to fax over PSTN and ISDN. Consider the standard group 3 terminal in Figure 15. To transmit a fax, the terminal first accesses an emitting gateway through the PSTN following the T.30 standard. The emitting gateway then connects to the receiving gateway using an Internet call establishment and control procedure that can be H.323, *session initiation protocol* (SIP), or H.248. The receiving gateway, in turn, makes a PSTN call to the called group 3 terminal. For real-time FoIP, once the PSTN connection is established on both ends, the two group 3 terminals are linked and all standard T.30 session establishment and capabilities negotiations can be carried out directly between them. The transmitting gateway demodulates the T.30 transmissions from PSTN or ISDN, maps the facsimile data into an octet stream using the *Internet facsimile protocol* (IFP) format, and transmits the data through the IP network to the receiving gateway using either TCP or UDP. A key consideration is that the IP portion of the transmission path should have a reasonably low delay so that the requirements specified in F.185 can be met (ITU-T 1998). Recommendation

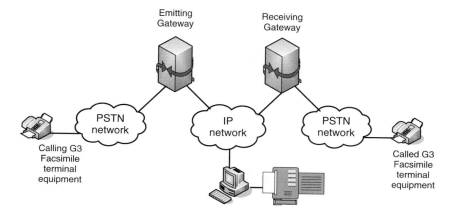

Figure 15: Standard group 3 terminal

T.38 focuses mainly on the operation of devices directly connected to the Internet: the gateways and an IAF device such as a personal computer. T.38 also describes implementation guidelines concerning the preamble packet, intervals between a training packet and an image data packet, and adjustment of T.30 timer values.

The supported call establishment and control protocols—H.323, SIP, and H.248—were originally specified for VoIP. Each of these protocols uses a different architecture and model for call establishment and control. SIP, which was created by the Internet Engineering Task Force (IETF) and is regarded as the most Internet-centric protocol of the three, with be discussed further later in this chapter.

Fax image quality is ensured by error control in the IP network in addition to mechanisms specified in T.30: reliable data transfer via TCP over IP, and higher-layer error control of UDP over IP.

The operation of FoIP may depend on other supporting functions such as directory services for conversion between PSTN and IP addresses, network hunting and selection, user authentication and billing, and network management (SNMP or others), among other functions. These supporting functions are not addressed in T.38 but are covered to various degrees under the H.323, SIP, and H.248 protocols and frameworks. Standardizing these functions will help implement a network based on third-party management devices, including sharing such devices with other Internet gateways such as Internet telephony and video, remote access, and e-mail.

Note that there is also a serious effort from the Internet community to further develop Internet fax. IETF's Internet Fax Working Group has been active since 1996. Documents generated by this group are important references and can be found on the group's Web site (www.imc.org/ietf-fax/). Request for Comment (RFC) 2542, for example, provides the terminology and goals for Internet fax. RFC 2880 describes how to map T.30 group 3 fax into Internet fax. RFC 2301 describes the *tagged image file format* (TIFF) representation of image data for black-and-white and color facsimiles.

As discussed earlier, the simple mode of store-and-forward Internet fax was specified in ITU-T Recommendation T.37. It was based on Internet e-mail, and T.37 draws heavily on relevant IETF protocols for e-mail transport and retrieval—*simple mail transfer protocol* (SMTP), *extended simple mail transfer protocol* (ESMTP), *post office protocol 3* (POP3), and *Internet messaging access protocol 4* (IMAP4)—and on various RFCs for multipurpose Internet mail extensions (MIME). T.37 defines an *offramp gateway* as equipment capable of receiving e-mail and relaying it to one or more group 3 or 4 fax terminals, and a *mailstore* as equipment that is capable of receiving e-mail and storing it for later retrieval by a receiver (see Table 8).

VOICE PROCESSING
Historic Perspectives and Types of Voice Processing Application
Because voice is the most common way for people to communicate, most technologies in the telecommunications industry have been developed for voice processing ever since the telephone was invented by Bell in 1876. Voice processing is currently a significant part of the industry.

Voice processing involves a variety of technologies that can be categorized into two main areas: call directing and message manipulation (Tetschner 1993). This part of the chapter will focus on these two areas. As time goes on, increasing numbers of voice-processing applications will be developed such as *voice recognition* and *voice over IP* (VoIP). Among the essential tools of voice processing are automatic call distribution, auto attendant features, interactive voice response, and voice message systems.

CALL DIRECTING APPLICATIONS
Automatic Call Distribution
Automatic call distribution (ACD) was originally an application that could distribute incoming calls to a free agent under a previously configured rule that was both inflexible and uneven (Nuasis 2006). Recently, with the ACD being implemented in more and more areas, lots of other parameters have been added to the system, which makes it an increasingly effective telecommunication tool that can evenly distribute incoming calls to a group of people.

ACD is usually used in customer service centers where there are high volumes of incoming calls. Generally speaking, ACD is a load-balancing system that can spread incoming calls to different agents evenly. The rules of distribution in various situations are different from one another, but there are some basic rules: *time of day* (TOD) routing, *day of week* (DOW) or *day of year* (DOY) routing, *area code* or *exchange* routing, and *percentage allocation* routing, among others. Under these rules, ACD can set up a smooth and ordered connection between customers and agents. A typical answer flow of ACD is shown in Figure 16.

ACD can be integrated into the company's *private branch exchange* (PBX). In this scenario, incoming calls from customers are delivered directly to the ACD for processing. This PBX architecture is simple and easy to implement, but it has its limitations; it is suitable for companies that have only one customer service center. Another mode—namely, the ACD system—can be used with a telecom center server. An incoming call will be first identified in the telecom center server and then routed to the appropriate ACD through a local exchange network under the rules that each company needs. Multiple ACDs within the company can also set up connections between each other to guarantee that the service is still available even when some ACDs do not work or all agents behind some ACDs are busy. The ACD can automatically route the calls to other ACDs as in the 800 system. But this process is complex and will increase the cost of management.

With the advancement of technologies, the ACD is becoming more and more sophisticated. For example, with the help of number-identifying systems and customer databases, the agent can immediately obtain necessary information when a call comes in. This will help the agent answer customer inquiries more efficiently. Nevertheless, ACD may not be appropriate for all business.

Table 8: T.37 Implementation Requirements for Simple Mode Store-and-Forward Fax

Sender		
Required	Send image data as a single MIME multipage RFC 2301 Profile S file	RFC 2305 §2.2.3
	Provide notice in case of local transmission problems	RFC 2305 §2.3.1
	Provide a return address of an Internet e-mail receiver that is MIME compliant	RFC 2049
Strongly recommended	Include message ID	RFC 2305 §2.2.1
	Use Base 64 encoding for image data	
Optional	Use other TIFF profiles if it has prior knowledge that such profiles are supported by the receiver (e.g., RFC 2301 Profile F for G4)	RFC 2305 §4
	Provide notice on receipt of DSN or other notifications	RFC 1894
Receiver		
Required	Be MIME compliant except that it is not required to offer to place a MIME attachment in a file and it may print a received file rather than display	RFC 2305 §2.2.2
	Be capable of processing multiple MIME RFC 2301 Profile S image files within a single message	RFC 2305 §2.2.4
	Provide notice in case of reception or processing problems	RFC 2305 §2.3.2
Optional	Use other TIFF profiles (e.g., RFC 2301 Profile F for G4)	RFC 2305 §4
Offramp gateway (when implemented)		
Required	Be SMTP compliant	RFC 821
	Provide delivery failure notification	RFC 1894, RFC 2305 §2.3.1
	Be able to process PSTN/FAX e-mail addresses	RFC 2303, RFC 2304
	Comply with relevant ITU recommendations relating to facsimile transmission	T.30
	Attempt to relay authorized e-mail to the corresponding facsimile terminals G3	RFC 2305 §3.2
	Ensure that local legal requirements relating to facsimile transmissions are met	
Strongly recommended	Use DSN for delivery failure notification	RFC 2305 §2.3.1, RFC 1894
	Use an approved mailbox access protocol when serving multiple users	RFC 2305 §2.1.3
Optional	Translate image data into a format acceptable by the receiving G3 facsimile terminal	RFC 2305 §2.1.2
	Use a mailbox access protocol when serving a single mail recipient	RFC 2305 §2.1.3
Mailstore (when implemented)		
Required	Be SMTP compliant	RFC 821
	Provide delivery failure notification in the form of a DSN	RFC 1894

Source: ITU-T Recommendation T.37, Table 1.1.

Auto Attendant

Today's business relies on voice processing, and customers of such businesses expect voice-processing systems to perform around the clock and have the flexibility to provide all of the functionalities they need. Although an ACD system can provide access to hundreds of agents, it is still not a good tool for the modern business because it gives customers no choice except waiting to be accessed. Nobody will feel satisfied by hearing "All agents are busy now. Please hold on for X minutes!" In this case, other tools to manage the networks are needed.

An *auto attendant* (AA) system allows callers to be automatically transferred to an intended extension without a receptionist's intervention. A receptionist, who acts as the telephone operator, can be reached by pressing "0" on most systems. An auto attendant is a feature on most modern PBX and key telephone systems (Tetschner 1993).

Auto attendant (AA) phone systems can be fully configured and customized to meet the company's need to answer all incoming calls. Figure 17 shows an AA system's basic answer flow.

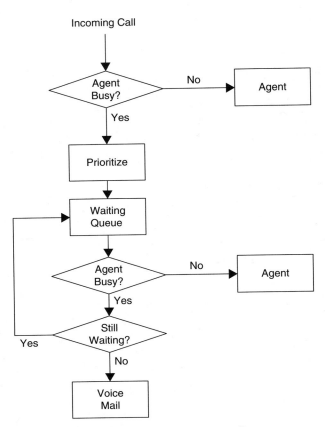

Figure 16: Typical ACD answer flow

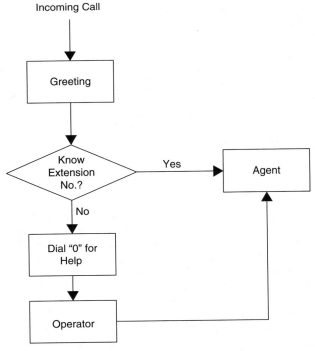

Figure 17: Answer flow of an auto attendant

The AA is designed to take responsibility for answering *frequently asked questions* (FAQs) away from human agents, who can save their time and serve customers who really need assistance. It can also help companies reduce the cost of management.

The AA usually has the following functions: answering the telephone, announcing options to a caller, accepting input from a caller, and forwarding the call to a human agent if no options are chosen.

Interactive Voice Response

Neither ACD nor AA systems can entirely replace the human agent. Although ACD and AA can improve the efficiency of the system, answer FAQs, and balance loads, final answers or information must still come from human agents, so we need a system with more intelligence.

Interactive voice response system (IVRS) is one such system. The IVR is an automated telephony system that interacts with callers, gathers information, and routes calls to appropriate recipients. An IVRS accepts a combination of voice telephone input and touch-tone keypad selection, and provides appropriate responses in the form of voice, fax, callback, e-mail, and other possible media. It allows callers to select an option from a voice menu or from an interface within this system. In recent years, the latest IVRSs accepts not only the keypad but also natural language speech as input (Bates and Gregory 2001).

As discussed above, the auto attendant can also give callers information, but an IVRS is different. Normally, the data retrieved from an IVRS is stored in other systems such as databases. The IVRS provides an interface between a caller and those other systems where the caller's information is stored. For example, a caller can access his or her bank account through an IVRS.

In most cases, the IVRS should incorporate computers. Figure 18 shows the basic architecture an IVRS. An IVRS can reduce the number of human agents but not eliminate the need for them. When a caller needs to speak to a customer service agent, the call still needs to be redirected to an ACD for queuing.

Outbound Dialers

In the modern business market, just waiting for customers' calls may be not enough. Many companies need a technology that will automatically help them reach potential customers.

Predictive dialers, which were developed from auto-dialers, are the technology these companies need. A predictive dialer is a computerized system that automatically dials batches of telephone numbers for connection to agents assigned to sales or other campaigns. A predictive dialer not only automatically dials telephone numbers for call agents who are free but also uses a variety of statistical algorithms to predict both the availability of agents and called parties, and then directs the calling process to the appropriate agents. Predictive dialers are widely used in call centers. They discard unanswered calls, engaged numbers, disconnected lines, answers from fax machines, answering machines, and similar automated services, and only connect agents with calls answered by people.

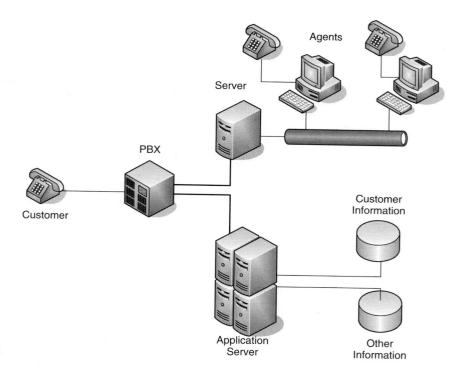

Figure 18: Architecture of an IVRS

There are two types of predictive dialer: the *software dialer* and the *hardware dialer*. The operating principles of both types are the same, but the software dialer is cheaper while the hardware dialer can provide more function.

A *progressive dialer* is another type of outbound dialer. It will automatically dial numbers for a human agent, but the agent must take action on each call to handle the request from customers. Apparently, it is not as efficient as the predictive dialer (see Table 9).

In some cases, outbound system need to be mixed with inbound systems—for example, with *blended dialing*. In blended dialing, whenever a new outbound record is requested, the phone is first put into the ACD queue. If an inbound phone call is received, it will be processed instead of the outbound record.

Voice Messaging

With the help of ACD, AA, and IVR, a company now may need fewer human agents but cannot totally eliminate

the need for them. For those companies with small numbers of people, there might be times when everyone is engaged. For such small companies, they need another technology called a *voice messaging* (VM) system.

The VM system, invented by Gordon Matthews, is a centralized system of managing telephone messages for a large group of people. VM uses a centralized server rather than an answer machine at each individual telephone. Most VM systems also have the ability to forward messages to another voice mailbox, send messages to multiple voice mailboxes, add voice notes to a message, store messages for future delivery, make calls to a telephone or paging service when a message is received, transfer callers to another phone for personal assistance, and play different message greetings to different callers (Bates and Gregory 2001).

Sometimes, VM systems can be integrated with the AA system to give callers more choices.

Table 9: Progressive Dialing versus Predictive Dialing

	Progressive	Predictive	Predictive
		30 agents	70 agents
Abandonment (%)		1	5
Time talking (%)	53	70	7
Talk time per hour (min.)	31:48	41:59	45:27

Source: Jones 2002.

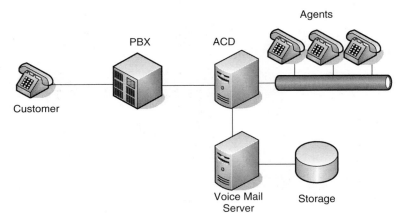

Figure 19: Typical voice messaging system architecture

ARCHITECTURE AND EXAMPLE SYSTEMS

Figure 19 shows a typical voice messaging system architecture. With this architecture, the voicemail system usually allows the following functions:

- message dictation to the system;
- message delivery to the called party;
- indication to called parties that they have new messages;
- stored messages can be listened to, forwarded, or deleted by the called people; and
- the attribute of the voice mailbox can be modified by users.

A typical VM system is the one provided by a mobile phone operator. When the called party does not answer the phone, the calling party will be redirected to the VM system and invited to record a short voice message. The VM system will provide some indication of a missed call voice message to the called party by a *short message service* (SMS). The called party then calls his or her mailbox in the VM system to retrieve the message and can then decide to store, forward, or delete the message.

Implementing a VM system requires careful consideration. For example, the allowed length of a message should be calculated carefully; the length will depend on where and how the voicemail will be stored. In addition, not everyone likes to talk to a machine, so the VM system should be integrated with other technologies such as ACD, AA, and IVR.

Audio Messaging Interchange Specification

In today's business world, voicemail boasts an installed base of more than 10 million mailboxes and 500,000 systems (Daniels and Goh 1998). Most major suppliers of voicemail systems provide their own standards for delivering voice messages between their systems. However, interworking among different systems may become a problem for some customers.

The *audio messaging interchange specification* (AMIS) is a series of standards aimed at addressing the problem of how voice-messaging systems produced by different vendors can be networked and interact with each other (AMIS Group 1992). The AMIS contains two specifications: *AMIS-analog specification* (AMIS-A) and *AMIS-digital specification* (AMIS-D), the latter based on completely digital interaction between two voice-messaging systems. The definitions for the two specifications are given as follows.

The AMIS-A method relies on telephone channels for connection, using *dual-tone, multifrequency* (DTMF) signaling and message transmission in analog form (AMIS Group 1992). AMIS-D, on the other hand, is based on the International Telecommunication Union (ITU)'s X.400 series of messaging recommendations. All of the control information and the voice message itself is conveyed between systems in digital form (AMIS Group, 1993).

AMIS-Analog

AMIS-A provides a mechanism for transferring voice messages among voicemail systems with similar functions but different architectures and technologies. It provides defined formats for identifying message origins and destinations, addressing messages, and sending, receiving, and replying to messages.

AMIS-A provides an open access networking, which means that when two voicemail systems support AMIS-A, the users within these two systems can send messages to each other without any problems. AMIS-A systems are designed to be used on the PSTN, accessing the telephone network via dialup ports that are addressed using *international direct dialing* (IDD) telephone numbers (and direct distance dialing for calls within country) (AMIS Group 1992). An IDD number contains a country code, area code, and local telephone number.

AMIS-A meets the needs of small system users and vendors. Because small systems have low traffic volumes, setting up a new network such as a completely digital one is therefore not necessary. Because of the use of analog DTMF control signaling and analog audio message transmission, AMIS-A can be implemented in the existing network without adding networking equipment.

AMIS-A is designed for simple implementation. It only supports the most common functions of different VM systems such as sending, receiving, and replying to

Table 10: AMIS Digital Stack

Layer Number	Layer Name	AMIS Digital Recommendations
7	Application	MHS X.400
6	Presentation	X.409
5	Session	X.225 BAS
4	Transport	X.224
3	Network	X.25 Packet
2	Data Link	X.25 LAPB
1	Physical	V.32 or V.35

Source: AMIS Group 1993.

messages. It does not require password exchange, and all addressing information required for call setup, message delivery, and message reply can be provided by the voice-messaging subscriber. Furthermore, AMIS-A is designed such that no significant changes are required for user interfaces at terminal devices. Messages transmitted using AMIS-A should be transposable to and from existing system formats.

As discussed above, AMIS-A also specifies a maximum message length and a maximum number of messages that may be delivered per session, a consideration of the storage capacity limits of the typical AMIS-A system. In addition, these limits help avoid situations in which one party occupies the system for overly long periods of time. The AMIS-A protocol enforces these limits by providing a mechanism for the destination system to reject messages that exceed the length limit and to terminate sessions when the message limit is exceeded (AMIS Group 1993).

The disadvantage of AMIS-A is that it does not support extended features such as message receipt notification, importance, or privacy. To achieve parity between different voice-messaging systems, the specification was depressed to a point where the technology no longer provided the robust, full-featured functionality desired by customers (Candell 2004). Fundamentally, customers had to give up some functions in order to gain the ability to communicate with other users in different systems. This compromise did not meet the needs of the market, and vendors scrambled to find an alternative solution that could take advantage of the full features of their messaging system and thus give themselves a competitive advantage in the marketplace (Rabiner 1994). The AMIS-digital protocol described following can provide full function and more complex networking capabilities for customers.

AMIS-Digital

Two alternative protocol stacks are supported in AMIS-digital. One stack—X.25—is in strict accordance with the seven-layer *open systems interconnection* (OSI) model of the International Standards Organization (ISO) (AMIS Group 1993). The other protocol stack matches the X.25 stack in the upper layers but replaces it with TCP/IP in the lower layer. This protocol stack is thus called the

TCP/IP stack. Both alternatives provide an effective base for the X.400 messaging protocol used in AMIS-digital (AMIS Group 1993). The X.25 stack is the baseline for the AMIS-D protocol. The TCP/IP stack on a VM system is optional.

The emphasis of the X.25 stack in AMIS-digital is on circuit-switched transmission facilities. When using the TCP/IP stack, different AMIS-D nodes will be connected by local area network (LAN). All of the LANs can be connected by IP routers to form a whole system. In addition, it is easy to connect VM systems to the Internet by IP routers.

The AMIS-D protocol stack is structured in seven layers (see Table 10). Each layer performs specific functions and provides services to the next higher layer. Implementation at each level can be developed separately (AMIS Group 1993).

A store-and-forward mode is used in an AMIS-D VM system. This concept is realized in the AMIS-digital protocol by separating the message-transfer functions from the user-to-user functions. This allows delivery to an intermediate message relay node without requiring delivery to a user, thereby providing the functionality of a tandem node (AMIS Group 1993). In this way, the topology will be more efficient. It will concentrate traffic through certain nodes to better utilize high-bandwidth digital services for those VM systems with lower volume messages. Sometimes, the store-and-forward topology can also act as a gateway between two protocols—for example, between AMIS-D and AMIS-A. For the X.25 stack only, another mode can be used. It assumes that a direct connection (switched or nonswitched) will exist to transport messages between sending and receiving systems. This model is, in fact, a subset of the store-and-forward model (AMIS Group 1993).

A message transmitted by an AMIS-D VM system can have some attributes that will be visible to both message senders and receivers. These message attributes are maximum length, maximum number of addresses, privacy, sending priority, importance, and sending time stamp.

The maximum length for an AMIS-D messages is eight minutes. The maximum number of addresses for a single AMIS-D message is 128. A message can be marked by its sender to be "private," which means that it is not allowed to be forwarded or redirected by any recipient. But if the receiving system does not support this feature, the message will be rejected. A sending system may allow any of as many as three transmitting priorities for a message: urgent, normal, and low. A sending system can also mark one of three importance levels to a message: high, normal, and low. Finally, the message-sending time stamp means that each message transmitted in AMIS-D VM systems be tagged with the date and time when it is sent by its originator.

Message senders can receive one of several kinds of notification upon message delivery:

- nondelivery notification (NDN),
- delivery notification (DN),
- nonreceipt notification (NRN),
- receipt notification (RN), and
- service notification (SN).

As discussed above, the main advantage of AMIS-D is that it can provide more features than AMIS-A. Table 11 shows the differences between these two VM systems.

Computer Telephony Integration and Unified Messaging

In fact, computers have already appeared in the systems discussed above. For example, with the help of computers, agents can access customers' names, addresses, and telephone numbers before a call is distributed by an ACD system. The voice traffic can also be encoded into a digital format and stored on the hard disk of computer as a database.

Standards

Computer telephony integration (CTI) is the technology that allows coordinated interactions between telephones and computers. As contact channels have expanded from voice to data and now include e-mail, Web, and fax, CTI has expanded to integrate all customer contact channels (voice, e-mail, Web, fax, etc.) with computer systems (Asatani 1998).

CTI can have several basic functions such as calling party information display, on-screen dialing, on-screen phone control, coordinated phone and data transfers between two parties, and call center phone control. Some other advanced functions such as call routing can be provided by a CTI system.

There are two modes of CTI, namely, *first-party control* and *third-party control*. For the first mode, only the computer associated with the phone can control the phone by sending commands directly to it. In the second mode, a dedicated telephony server that connects the telephone network and the computer network is required. The user's computer has no direct connection to the telephones; the action is actually conducted by the dedicated telephony server. Information about a phone call can display on the corresponding computer's screen while commands to control the phone can be sent from the computer to the telephony server.

An effective CTI can significantly reduce the cost and improve the quality of data handling in the telephony system.

Unified Messaging

Unified messaging (UM) is the integration of different streams of messages such as e-mail, fax, voice, and video into a single mailbox that is accessible from a variety of

Table 11: Comparison of AMIS-D and AMIS-A Protocols

Feature	Digital	Analog
Send	Yes	Yes
Receive	Yes	Yes
Reply	Yes	Yes
Notification of nondelivery	Yes	Yes
Delivery notification	Yes	No
Forward	Yes	No
Full duplex message flow	Yes	No
Message importance indicator	Yes	No
Message privacy	Yes	No
Message sending priority	Yes	No
Nonreceipt notification	Yes	No
Originating message time stamp	Yes	No
Receipt notification	Yes	No
Separate originator's voice name	Yes	No
Service notification	Yes	No

devices (Arbanowski and van der Meer 1999). It is a technology that can replace simple voicemail. UM systems were expected to take advantage of the ubiquity of computers, personal digital assistants (PDAs), smartphones, and 3G networks.

As more and more messaging systems are used in daily life, some people need to receive message notifications no matter when and where, while others do not want to be interrupted by uncontrolled messages. As a result, people are unsatisfied when they manage and keep track of their message on multiple devices and systems, for example, voice mail on PBXs, voice mail on PSTN, mobile phones, fax, e-mail, and instant messaging. Consequently, the UM system is viewed as a better choice as a personal agent.

A unified messaging system provides the ability to reach people almost anywhere and anytime and with the flexibility of allowing people to program and decide when the notifications should be delivered. With the help of unified messaging, customers can reduce the number of mailboxes that they must check for incoming voice, fax, and e-mail messages. They can access all their messages from one interface. On the other hand, service providers and network operators can also benefit from UM. They only need to manage a single UM system rather than multiple message system.

Several vendors and service providers can provide UM solutions, including Cisco, Alcatel, Nortel, Microsoft, and Siemens. Figure 20 shows the basic model of a UM system from Cisco.

The main new network element in the design of a unified message system is the *universal message store*, which is under the control of a unified message system server (Sinnreich and Johnston 2001). The unified message and store can be implemented in various ways by existing protocols such as SIP, XML, HTTP, SMTP, and *real-time streaming protocol* (RTSP). Figure 21 illustrates an example of unified messaging by SIP, which will be discussed in the next section.

If the called party does not answer the phone, then the UM server will store the caller's voice message. The notification method depends on a user's settings.

The Session Initiation Protocol (SIP) and the Component Server Architecture for Unified Messaging

Session initiation protocol (SIP) is an Internet application-layer protocol intended for the control of multimedia communication sessions: the establishment, modification, and termination of multimedia calls over the Internet. SIP was developed by the IETF's Multiparty Multimedia Session Control (MMUSIC) Working Group, with work starting in the mid-1990s and reaching maturity in 2002. Modeled after the hypertext transfer and simple mail transfer protocols, SIP is hailed as the third application-layer protocol of the Internet, and the Internet application layer protocol that will herald in the age of multimedia communications over the Internet. In November 2000, SIP was accepted as the signaling protocol for the *IP multimedia subsystem* (IMS), which was defined by the Third-Generation Partnership Project (3GPP) as the core network of the future to support mobile as well as fixed-line voice and multimedia communications. Since then, SIP has been recognized as the leading signaling protocol for VoIP. SIP represents also the apex manifestation of the client-server model prevalent in the Internet until the emergence of the peer-to-peer model in the early 2000s. In this section, we will describe how SIP and the component server architecture provide the vision of a flexible and dynamic model for the support of converged unified communications.

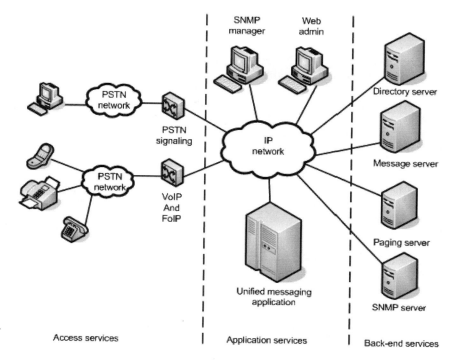

Figure 20: Unified messaging model.
Source: www.cisco.com 2002

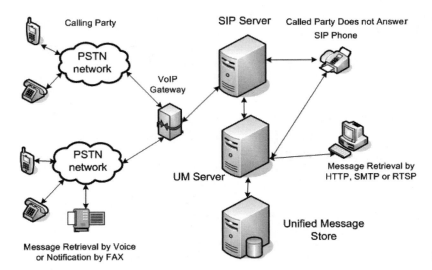

Figure 21: Figure 18 Unified messaging by SIP

In the previous section we described the notion of unified messaging. Unified communications (UC) can be viewed as UM with the addition of call control to integrate real-time sessions with messaging. Converged unified communications means the support of UC over a common network: the Internet.

SIP Characteristics

The following is a description of the characteristics of SIP:

First, SIP is a text-based Internet application-layer protocol that uses a request-response model. There are header lines in the request and a response code in the response. All of these are similar to HTTP and SMTP.

Second, SIP uses the *uniform resource indicator* (URI) for addressing. URI is a generalization of the *uniform resource locator* (URL) used for e-mail and Web addresses. Like e-mail and the Web, SIP uses the *domain name system* (DNS) to convert e-mail-like destination address of "users" to the network address of "servers" that serve the users. SIP may make use of other directory systems such as ENUM, which will enable SIP to handle addresses in the form of E.164 telephone numbers. The analogy with e-mail makes obvious SIP's global scalability and mobility. Although it takes a telephone company expensive equipment and software and significant deployment time to provide telephony services to a new community, it takes no more than a couple of hours to set up an e-mail server and allow everyone in a new company or department to enjoy sending and receiving e-mails to and from anyone around the world. Whereas a fixed line telephone number is tied to a fixed location and a mobile telephone number is tied to a mobile phone (or SIM card), an e-mail address is independent of location and device. A user can be behind any device in any location while retrieving his or her e-mails.

Third, SIP makes use of *session description protocol* (SDP), which was originally designed to support the description of multicast sessions over the Internet, to describe how the end systems would like to communicate with each other (IP address, port number, codec types,

bit rates, and so on). SIP provides the carrier service for the SDP message.

Fourth, SIP follows the "smart client, dumb network" paradigm of the Internet. SIP and the IP network provide the mechanism for the *rendezvous* function—that is, "finding" and connecting to the destination—while the service logics are implemented in the end systems. It is up to the end systems to decide how to process an incoming call request. Many conventional PBX and PSTN call features—such as call hold, transfer, call forward, call screening, and call waiting—can be easily implemented with call logics in the call server or in the end systems. New services can be provided by additional servers (service controller, presence server, databases, IVR, UM store, voicemail, text-to-speech converter, media mixers, event schedulers, and so on) based on what is known as the component server architecture paradigm. Services can also be created dynamically through the use of *call processing language* (CPL) in XML scripts, SIP *common gateway interface* (CGI) similar to the CGI for Web servers, or SIP Java servlets. The mix-and-match of new servers, dynamic service logic, and easy integration of SIP with other Internet protocols make SIP and the component server architecture the key model for service creation and orchestration over the Internet.

Fifth, SIP supports a variety of request types known as *SIP methods*. Five request types are described here to illustrate SIP's capability: INVITE, REGISTER, SUBSCRIBE, NOTIFY, and MESSAGE. A SIP INVITE request contains an SDP that informs the called party the intention of a communication session. A REGISTER request allows a user to register its current network address and current status so that the network can locate the user when needed. A SUBSCRIBE request allows a user to express his or her desire to be informed of specified events. A NOTIFY request informs the recipient of an event. A MESSAGE request transports an instant message body that is delivered to the recipient. REGISTER, SUBSCRIBE, NOTIFY, and MESSAGE bring capabilities that are not found in the conventional telephone network.

The first standard version of SIP is version 2.0, which was defined in RFC 2543 in March 1999. As many

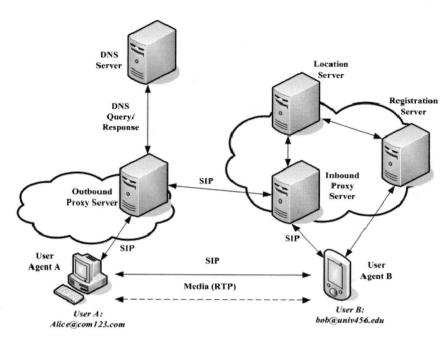

Figure 22: Basic SIP servers and the SIP routing trapezoid

shortcomings were identified, SIP version 2 was revised substantially in RFC 3261, which was accepted in June 2002. The basic SIP architecture, which consists of user agents (UAs), outbound and inbound proxy servers, a location server, and a registration server, together with the SIP routing trapezoid, is illustrated in Figure 22. User A, who currently sits behind user agent A (a notebook computer), wishes to call user B. On behalf of user A, user agent A generates a SIP INVITE message to user B using B's SIP address, which is *bob@univ456.edu*, and sends this INVITE message to its serving outbound proxy sever. The outbound proxy queries the DNS system to find the inbound proxy server serving the *univ456.edu* domain and then forwards the INVITE to the inbound proxy server. The inbound proxy server then queries its location server, a local database, to find the current network address(es) of user agent(s) serving user B, and forward the INVITE message accordingly.

Note that user B may be using multiple user agents at the same time, and the inbound proxy may opt to fork the INVITE message to multiple destinations. The INVITE message contains the network address of user agent A as a return address, so that the responding user agent B may choose to respond to user agent A directly without the trapezoidal routing. Also, the INVITE message and the response contain SDP bodies specifying the network address, port number, and media type for the communication session. Once the SIP INVITE and response exchange is completed, the media session can flow directly between user agent A and user agent B.

In the component server architecture, servers are added to provide messaging and other services, using SIP as the basic call control and messaging protocol. These other servers may include:

- *UM server* and *UM store* to handle and store messages,
- *media server* to play announcements and other media,

- *IVR server* to provide interactive voice response functions such as touch tone detection and voice recognition,
- *presence server* to keep track of availability and the presence of users,
- *notification server* to accept and fulfill requests for notification of events, and
- *authentication* and *security server* to support security functions.

INTERNET-BASED SYSTEMS AND NEW PROTOCOLS

We conclude this section by mentioning that although there are individual Internet-centric protocols for VoIP and messaging, no other protocol integrates voice and messaging in as comprehensive a manner as SIP. MGCP and MEGACO, for instance, are other popular protocols for VoIP. They do not address messaging. *Extensible messaging and presence protocol* (XMPP), for example, is an open, XML-based protocol for conveying near real-time, extensible instant messaging and presence information. Although it does not address the setup of real-time communication sessions, XMPP is the core protocol for the *jabber instant messaging and presence technology*. Deployed by Google Talk, XMPP is used by millions of people worldwide. IETF's XMPP working group has produced several RFCs: RFC 3920, RFC 3921, RFC 3922, and RFC 3923. It remains to be seen if SIP-based instant messaging system will reach a similar level of popularity.

CONCLUSION

In the first part of this chapter, we began with a review of the history of the development of facsimile, followed by a detailed description of the group 3 standard which has since its first adoption in 1980 defined the operation of the modern fax machine – for over a quarter century. Our description of the group 3 standard included the coding, specifically the modified READ (MR) code and the modified modified READ (MMR) code, the protocol, and various proposed enhancements. Then we described new facsimile systems including the group 4 standard which was intended for operation over ISDN has not seen wide-spread application, facsimile over X.25, and most recently, internet-based systems which can be real-time or store-and-forward.

Facsimile is a messaging system for images. The second part of this chapter covered messaging for voice. We began with a description of call directing applications including automatic call distribution (ACD), auto attendant (AA), interactive voice response (IVR), outbound dialer, and voice messaging (VM), followed by an overview of the Audio Messaging Interchange Specification (AMIS). Then the concept of computer telephony integration (CTI) and unified messaging (UM) were introduced. We finished the chapter with a description of the session initiation protocol (SIP), mentioned also in the section on internet-based facsimile, as potentially the protocol to unify different call directing and voice/text/image messaging applications in an internet-centric component server-based architecture.

GLOSSARY

AM: Amplitude Modulation is a technique used in electronic communication. AM works by varying the strength of the transmitted signal in relation to the information being sent.

AM-PM VSB: Mplitude/Phase Modulation with Vestigal Sideband

BFICC: British Facsimile International Consultative Committee

CCD: Charge-Coupled Device is an analog shift register, enabling analog signals to be transported through successive stages controlled by a clock signal.

CFVD: Constant Frequency Variable Dot

CTI: Computer Telephony Integration is technology that allows interactions on a telephone and a computer to be integrated or co-ordinated.

DCS: Digital command signal

DCT: Discrete cosine transform is a Fourier-related transform similar to the discrete Fourier transform (DFT), but using only real numbers.

DIS: Digital identification signal

DSCP: Differentiated Services Code Point is a field in the header of IP packets for packet classification purposes.

DTM: Document Transfer Mode

DYMF: Dual tone multi frequency

ECM: Error Correction Mode is an optional transmission mode built into Class 1 fax machines or fax modems.

EIA: Electronic Industries Association

FoIP: Fax-over-IP

FPAD: Facsimile Packet Assembly/Disassembly

HDLC: High Level Data Link is a bit-oriented synchronous data link layer protocol developed by the International Organization for Standardization (ISO)

IAF: "Internet-aware" fax

IETF: Internet Engineering Task Force develops and promotes Internet standards, cooperating closely with the W3C and ISO/IEC standard bodies; and dealing in particular with standards of the TCP/IP and Internet protocol suite.

IMS: IP Multimedia Subsystem is an architectural framework, originally designed by the wireless standards body 3GPP, for delivering IP multimedia services to end users.

ITU: International Telecommunication Union

IVR: Interactive Voice Response is a phone technology that allows a computer to detect voice and touch tones using a normal phone call.

LDP: Label Distribution Protocol is a protocol in which two Label Switch Routers (LSR) exchange label mapping information.

LSR: Label Switching Router is a type of a router located in the middle of a Multiprotocol Label Switching (MPLS) network.

MH: is used in fax machines to encode black on white images.

MIME: Multipurpose Internet Mail Extensions is an Internet Standard that extends the format of e-mail.

MPLS: Multi Protocol Label Switching is a data-carrying mechanism which emulates some properties of a circuit-switched network over a packet-switched network.

MRC: Mixed Raster Content is a process of using image segmentation methods to improve the contrast resolution of a raster image composed of pixels.

NGN: Next Generation Network is a broad term to describe some key architectural evolutions in telecommunication core and access networks that will be deployed over the next 5–10 years.

QAM: Quadrature Amplitude Modulation is a modulation scheme which conveys data by changing (modulating) the amplitude of two carrier waves.

OSI: Open Systems Interconnection

PSK: Phase Shift Keying is a digital modulation scheme that conveys data by changing, or modulating, the phase of a reference signal.

READ: Relative Element Address Designate

PTT: Post, Telegraph, and Telephone administrations

SIMPLE: Session Initiation Protocol for Instant Messaging and Presence Leveraging Extensions

SIP: Session Initiation Protocol is an application-layer control (signaling) protocol for creating, modifying, and terminating sessions with one or more participants.

SMTP: Simple Mail Transfer Protocol is the de facto standard for e-mail transmissions across the Internet.

SNMP: Signaling Network Management Protocol is used by network management systems to monitor network-attached devices for conditions that warrant administrative attention.

TCP/IP: Transmission Control Protocol/Internet Protocol

XMPP: Extensible Messaging and Presence Protocol is an open, XML-based protocol for near-real-time, extensible instant messaging (IM) and presence information.

CROSS REFERENCES

See *Analog Transmission*; *Voice Communications Systems: KTS, PBX, Centrex, and ACD*; *Voice over IP (VoIP)*; *Voice over MPLS and VoIP over MPLS.*

REFERENCES

AMIS Group. 1992. AMIS-analog protocol.

———. 1993. AMIS-digital protocol.

Arbanowski, S., and S. Van der Meer. 1999. Service personalization for unified messaging systems. *Computers and Communications*, 156–63.

Asatani, K. 1998. Standardization on multimedia communications: Computer-telephony-integration-related issues. *Communications Magazine*, 36: 105–9.

Bates, R. J., and D. W. Gregory. 2001. *Voice and data communications handbook.* New York: McGraw-Hill.

Candell, E. 2004. *High-level requirements for Internet voice mail.* RFC 3773 (retrieved from www.faqs.org/rfcs/rfc3773.html).

Cisco. 2002. Unified messaging (available at www.cisco.com).

Coopersmith, J. Facsimile's false starts. *IEEE Spectrum*, February 1993. 30(2): 46–50.

———. 1994. The failure of fax: When a vision is not enough. *Business and Economic History*, 23(1): 272–282.

Daniels, B. R., and M.-J. Goh. 1998. Voice and fax messaging in an Internet world (retrieved from www.tmcnet.com/articles/itmag/0998/0998toc.htm).

File format for Internet fax. 1998. RFC 2301, March.

ITU-T. 1988. Recommendation F.185. *Internet facsimile: Guidelines for the support of the communication of facsimile documents*, June.

ITU-T. 1988. Recommendation T.1. *Standardization of phototelegraph apparatus.* Blue Book.

———. 2003. Recommendation T.4. *Standardization of group 3 facsimile terminals for document transmission*, July.

———. 2005. Recommendation T.30. *Procedures for document facsimile transmission in the general switched telephone network.* September.

———. 1998. Recommendation T.37. *Procedures for the transfer of facsimile data via store-and-forward on the Internet*, June.

———. 2005. Recommendation T.38. *Procedures for real-time group 3 facsimile communication over IP networks*, September.

Jarvis, J. F., C. N. Judice, and W.H. Ninke. 1976. A survey of techniques for continuous tone pictures on bilevel displays. *Computer Graphics and Image Processing*, 5: 13–40.

Jones, C. T. 2002. White paper on dialing methods.

Handley, M., H. Schulzrinne, E. Schooler, and J. Rosenberg. 1999. *SIP: Session initiation protocol.* RFC 2543.

Internet fax T.30 feature mapping. 2000. RFC 2880, August.

Nuasis Corporation. 2006. Compelling reasons for VoIP in the enterprise contact center (retrieved from http://searchcrm.bitpipe.com/detail/RES/1137778296_114.html?hdl_contprof).

Rabiner, L. R. 1994. The role of voice processing in telecommunications. Second IEEE Workshop, Interactive Voice Technology for Telecommunications Applications, pp. 1–8.

Sinnreich, H., and A B. Johnston. 2001. *Internet communications using SIP*, 151–9. New York: Wiley Computer Publishing.

Streetman, B. G., and S. K. Banerjee. 2006. *Solid state electronic devices.* 6th ed. Upper Saddle River, NJ: Prentice Hall.

Terminology and goals for Internet fax. 1999. RFC 2542, March.

Tetschner, W. 1993. *Voice processing.* Boston: Artech House.

Through the wires. No date. Fax machine (retrieved from http://library.thinkquest.org/27887/gather/history/fax.shtml).

Yasuda, Y., Y. Yamazaki, T. Kamae, and K. Kobayashi. 1985. Advances in FAX. In *Proceedings of the IEEE*, 73(4): 706–30.

Zeadally, S., and F. Siddiqui. 2004. Design and implementation of a SIP-based VoIP architecture. In *Proceedings of the 18th International Conference on Advanced Information Networking and Application* (AINA '04), 187–190.

Zhang, Y. 2002. SIP-based VoIP network and its interworking with PSTN. *Electronics and Communication Engineering*, 273–282.

Public Switched Telephone Network

Jingxuan Liu, *Frostburg State University*
Nirwan Ansari, *New Jersey Institute of Technology*

INTRODUCTION

The *public switched telephone network* (PSTN) is an aggregation of circuit-switched networks that is optimized for continuous real-time voice communications. Originally a network of fixed-line analog telephone systems, the PSTN guarantees the *quality of service* (QoS) for voice communications characterized by short session time, continuous channel holding, and narrowband bandwidth requirement.

This chapter focuses on the important PSTN components and the provisioned network services, PSTN-enabling technologies and equipments, and the network's performance and management.

Basic Concepts

This section describes the PSTN network access, components, and provisioned services.

Network Access

PSTN features a sophisticated network infrastructure with various components, thereby providing a rich variety of services. The PSTN network can be partitioned into three segments as shown in Figure 1: the access networks or local loops, the local exchange networks, and the interexchanges or gateways that interface with long-distance and other networks.

In PSTN, a communication request originates from *customer premise equipment* (CPE) such as a telephone or fax machine that is connected to the access network. A typical connection request may be from residential customers or from business office users. In the latter case, a *private branch exchange* (PBX) may be used to provide private switched services.

The access network, or the *local loop*, is the bridge between the subscribers and the core network. An access network consists of CPEs, PBXs, and access lines lead to

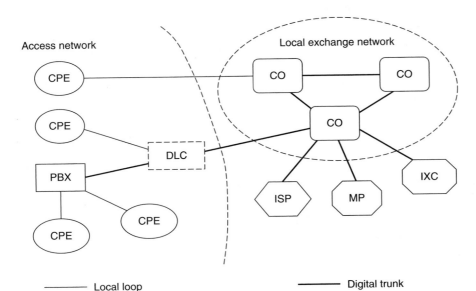

Figure 1: Network access

Local loop ———— Digital trunk

digital loop carriers (DLCs) or the *local exchanges* (LXCs). DLCs are highly efficient digital transmission systems that reduce the analog line length and economically expand the access network. The access network also includes the logic to control the traffic flow over the access lines.

The core of the PSTN is the local exchange network that interconnects *central offices* (COs). A central office is the physical location where local service providers terminate subscriber lines and locate switching equipments. When it is necessary, connection requests are forwarded by or received from other service providers such as an *interexchange carrier* (IXC) to other local exchange networks, a *mobile provider* (MP) to wireless networks, or an *Internet service provider* (ISP) to the Internet.

Access Services

Access services are categorized into residential subscriber lines and trunks. *Residential subscriber lines* provide connections between residential CPEs and central offices or DLCs.

Trunks are used to provide connections to the PBX. There are three types of trunks: two-way local exchange trunks, direct inward dialing trunks, and direct outward dialing trunks.

Two-way local exchange trunks allow both incoming and outgoing calls. *Direct inward dialing trunks*, also known as DID trunks, are designed for incoming calls only. One benefit of DID trunks is that they allow the caller to dial a number directly rather than go through a centralized attendant. Another benefit of a DID trunk is that although it may appear to be a private line, it is able to support one hundred different numbers with a group of twenty-five to thirty-five trunks. *Direct outward dialing trunks*, also known as DOD trunks, are designed for outgoing calls only. They are used when an access code such as the number 9 is dialed to reach an outside line's dial tone before the actual number is dialed.

Transport Services

Transport services comprise network switching, transmission, and related services that support information transfer between the originating and terminating access facilities. The underlying facilities include local exchanges, tandem switches, toll and transit switches, international gateways, and interoffice transmission equipment. Transport services, which demand the coordination among communication equipments, carriers, and service providers, can be classified into switched services, nonswitched services, and virtual private networks.

There are two types of *switched services*: public and private. *Public switched services* include local calling, long-distance calling, international calling, directory assistance, operator assistance, and emergency services. *Private switched services* can be CPE-based or carrier-based. In case of CPE-based private switched services, the customer can add capabilities to the telephone systems in the PBXs by a feature called *electronic tandem networking*, which can be used to gain flexibility in routing around congestion points. With carrier-based private switched services, a customer can use a centrex to partition and implement extensions across multiple local exchanges and to switch

traffic between those locations. The *centrex* is a central office-based telephone service that provides an alternative to PBX. Centrex service includes free calling within the local exchange area, access to long-distance networks, and an abbreviated dialing plan that can be used to dial between any two phones that are in the centrex.

Nonswitched services include leased lines, *foreign exchange* (FX) lines, and *off-premises exchanges* (OPX). When connected by leased lines, two locations or two devices are always on, using the same transmission path. FX lines allow customers to make toll calls that appear to be local calls. The OPX setup provides a nice solution: lease a circuit to each off-premise location and tie it in as if it were part of the PBX.

A *virtual private network* (VPN) is a concept that originated from the circuit-switched network environment. A VPN defines a network in which the customer traffic is isolated over shared service provider facilities. The underlying facilities of a VPN include the carrier public network augmented by network control points and service management systems. Traffic on a VPN is routed through the public network as if it were in a facilities-based private network.

Service Providers

PSTN services are offered by the following major types of providers (Goleniewski 2005).

- An *interexchange carrier* (IXC) is the carrier for long-distance and international communications. AT&T (acquired by SBC), MCI (acquired by Verizon), Sprint, and Qwest are the primary IXCs in the United States.
- *Public telecommunications operators* (PTOs) are the incumbent carriers in countries other than the United States.
- *Incumbent local exchange carriers* (ILECs) are the original common carriers that had or still have monopoly rights in the local loop. In the United States, these would be one of four so-called baby Bells: Qwest, SBC, BellSouth, and Verizon.
- *Competitive local exchange carriers* (CLECs), which are competitors of ILECs and products of the Telecommunications Act of 1996.
- *Data competitive local exchange carriers* (DCLECs) are companies that provide data service to end users such as DSL service providers.
- *Ethernet local exchange carriers* (ELECs) provide Ethernet solutions in local loops and metropolitan areas. Among others, *Ethernet passive optical network* (EPON) technology provides a feasible solution that makes this new service possible.
- *Value-added network* (VAN) providers offer pipe connections from one location to another location as well as additional services—such as error detection and correction, and protocol and language conversion—to enable interoperability across the network.

PSTN Architecture

According to their functionalities, facilities in PSTN systems are classified into four categories: customer premise equipment nodes, switching nodes, transmission nodes, and service nodes.

A *customer premise equipment* (CPE) node interfaces the customer and the access network. Its main function is to transmit and receive customer information as well as exchange control information with the local exchange network. CPE nodes include PBXs, key telephone systems, single-line telephones, and facsimile machines.

Switching nodes interconnect transmission facilities at various locations and route traffic through a network. They set up the circuit connections for a signal path based on the number dialed. Switching nodes include the local exchanges (Freeman 2004), tandem switches that route calls between local exchanges within a city, toll offices that route calls to and from other cities, and international gateways that route calls to and from other countries. Primary network intelligence is contained in the local exchanges and tandem switches. The toll switches provide long-distance switching and network features, and local exchanges provide the local switching and telephony features to which customers subscribe. Figure 2 illustrates the relationship between different telephone exchanges.

Transmission nodes provide communication paths that carry user traffic and network control information between the nodes in a network. They are equipped with *transport media* such as twisted pair wires, coaxial cable, microwave transmitters, satellites, and fiber-optic cabling; and *transport equipment* such as amplifiers, repeaters, multiplexers, *digital cross-connects* (DCCs), and *digital loop carriers* (DLCs).

Service nodes handle *signaling*, or the transmission of information to control the setup, holding, charging, and releasing of connections, as well as the transmission of information to control network operations and billing.

PSTN Numbering Plan

The PSTN numbering plan is an important part of call routing. ITU-T E.164 (2005) lays out a framework for PSTN addressing. Each telephone consists of one or more of the following parts.

- The *subscriber number* identifies a subscriber within a local numbering area. A local numbering area is one

in which two subscribers can reach each other using the same dialing procedure. The area can be further divided into two parts: exchange code and local code. An *exchange code* is used to identify an exchange within a numbering area. A *local code* is used to uniquely identify a subscriber within the exchange.

- An *area code* (or *trunk code*) is a digit or string of digits that identifies an area within a country. It is also known as a *city code* in some countries.
- A *country code* is a one- to three-digit number that identifies a country (defined in ITU-T E.163).
- An *international access code* is a prefix that asks the local exchange to route a call to an international gateway.
- A *toll access code* is a prefix for domestic long-distance (toll) calls.
- An optional *network access code* allows access to the external network from a PBX CPE.

Figure 3 shows the general numbering plan for international and domestic calls.

Generally speaking, each country or region has its own numbering plan under the framework of ITU-T E.164. In North America, for example, the North American Numbering Plan Administration (NANPA) regulates numbering in Canada, the United States and its territories, and nations of the Caribbean. The NANPA works with industry consensus forums through the Alliance for Telecommunications Industry Solutions (ATIS) and its Industry Carriers Compatibility Forum (ICCF). ATIS's Industry Numbering Committee (INC) is responsible for the technical definition and use of the North American numbering plan's (NANP's) resources. The NANP specifies some numbers for special services, such as N11 and N00 (where N = 2 ··· 9). For a complete coverage of NANP, refer to ATIS (2005, 2006) and Web sites listed at the end of this chapter.

Evolution and Standardization

The earliest telephones required no switching because they were installed on a dedicated-line basis (Deese 1984). It quickly became evident that such a one-on-one arrangement was inefficient to meet growing economic

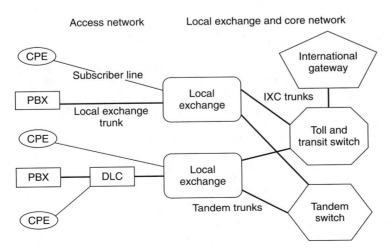

Figure 2: Types of PSTN nodes and their interrelationships

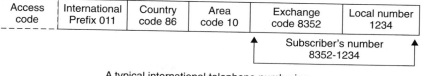

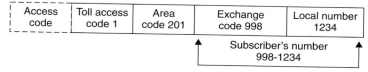

A typical international telephone numbering
(for a call from the United States to China)

A typical domestic long-distance
numbering within the United States

Figure 3: Typical telephone numbering plans (international and domestic) (access code is optional)

and social needs. The newer telephone network began to emerge when telephones were connected to a central location in which an operator could connect and disconnect telephone lines from any pair of subscribers to the service whose lines terminated in that location. In North America, the location was called the *central office*.

To facilitate interconnection, telecommunication equipment must comply with national, regional, or international standards. The most recognized institute of standardization is the International Telecommunication Union (ITU), which has two subsidiary organizations, the Telecommunications Standardization Sector (ITU-T) and the Radiocommunication Sector (ITU-R). Before 1993, ITU-T was called the International Consultative Committee on Telephone and Telegraph (CCITT).

The ITU-T publishes its standardized documents as recommendations. *Synchronous digital hierarchy* (SDH) (ITU-T 2006, G.707) and *signaling system number 7* (SS-7) (ITU-T 1993, Q.700) are two examples of more than 2900 ITU-T recommendations.

In North America, the *American National Standards Institute* (ANSI) is the organization that administers and coordinates the U.S. standardization and conformity assessment system. *Synchronous optical network* (SONET) is one of the thousands of standards approved by ANSI.

PSTN TRANSPORT MECHANISMS

Although the PSTN was created using analog voice connections through manual switchboards, it started to migrate to a digital-based network in the 1980s. Since 1997, North American long-distance networks and local exchange carriers have been nearly 100 percent digital (Freeman 2004).

Digital transmission outperforms analog transmission in three main aspects. First, noise does not accumulate as it does in an analog system. Noise accumulation stops at each regenerative system repeater where digital signals are fully regenerated. Such accumulation is a major concern in analog design. Second, the digital format lends itself ideally to solid-state technology and integrated circuits. Third, such transmission is compatible with digital data, telephone signaling, and computers.

In the following discussions, we will only focus on digital transmission mechanisms and digital networks.

The Digital Transmission System

In this section, we describe the fundamental transmission mechanisms that are essential to digital-based PSTN systems. For a more detailed discussion on digital transmission, readers are referred to "Digital Transmission."

Pulse Code Modulation

To transmit analog voice traffic over the digital network, voice signals must be converted to a digital format. There are two commonly used conversion methods: *pulse code modulation* (PCM) (ITU-T 1988, G.711), which is used almost exclusively in the digital PSTN, and *delta modulation*, which is widely employed by many of the world's armed forces. Here we discuss the PCM method.

To develop a PCM signal from an analog signal, three steps are required: sampling, quantization, and coding. The result is a *serial binary signal* or *bit stream*. Figure 4 shows the bit streams in different coding formats for the same analog signal. The *bipolar* PCM mode, also known as *alternate mark inversion* (AMI), is the format actually used in the PSTN network (ITU-T 1998, G-704). In the bipolar PCM mode, the marks—that is, the 1's—have only 50 percent duty cycle. The advantages of using the bipolar mode are twofold: (1) There is no direct current (DC) in the transmit lines, so transform coupling can be used along the lines; and (2) the power spectrum of the transmitted signal is centered at a frequency equal to one-half the bit rate (Freeman 2004, Sklar 2001).

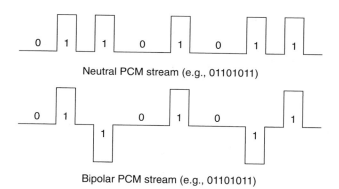

Neutral PCM stream (e.g., 01101011)

Bipolar PCM stream (e.g., 01101011)

Figure 4: Neutral PCM versus bipolar PCM bit streams

According to the *Nyquist sampling theorem* (Sams 1976), the nominal 4-khz voice channel would be sampled at a rate of 8000 samples per second. The time between two samples is therefore 1/8000 second = 125 μsec and is called a *frame*.

After sampling, each sample is quantized and encoded. Modern PCM systems use an 8-bit code to quantize each sample. At the sampling rate of 8000 hz, each voice channel needs to transmit at $8 \times 8000 = 64$ kbps. This signal rate is called the *digital signal zero* (DS-0) rate or E-0, which is the basic rate for all digital transmission systems.

Line Code

As previously discussed, in the PSTN, PCM signals are transmitted to the cable in the bipolar mode, which reduces noise, and eliminates DC return so that transformer coupling can be used on the line. One drawback of the bipolar mode, however, is that when a long string of 0's is transmitted, a timing issue may arise because the repeaters and decoders have no way of extracting timing without transmissions. This issue can be solved by prohibiting long strings of 0's. Two coding systems are available.

One solution is called *BNZS coding* in which the Nth 0 of N constitutive 0's are substituted by 1. For example, a B6ZS code substitutes a signal with a string of six 0's. B6ZS is widely used in the subscriber loop carrier.

Another solution is the *high density binary 3* (HDB3) coding system, where 3 indicates the substitution for binary sequences with more than three consecutive 0's. With HDB3, the second and third 0's are transmitted unchanged. The fourth 0 is transmitted to the line with the same polarity as the previous mark sent, which is a violation of the bipolar coding. The first 0 may or may not be modified to ensure the successive violations are of opposite polarity. HDB3 is used in E series PCM systems and is similar to B3ZS.

Frame Format

The frame is an essential concept underlying all digital transmission systems of PSTN. Two frame formats are widely used in PSTN: *digital signal 1* (DS-1) *frame* or *T-1 frame*, and *common European postal telegraphy 1* (CEPT-1) *frame* or *E-1 frame*.

In the DS-1 frame, twenty-four DS-0 channels are each allotted an 8-bit *time slot* (TS)—that is, 125 μsec/24 = 5.2 μsec. DS-1 time slots are numbered from 1 to 24, or TS1 to TS24. To synchronize the receiver, a frame bit is added to each frame. The DS-1 frame thus consists of $(24 \times 8) + 1 = 193$ bits. At the sampling rate of 8000 hz, the line rate for DS-1 frame is thus $193 \times 8000 = 1,544,000$ bps or 1.544 Mbps. Figure 5 shows the DS-1 frame format.

Higher rates are achievable by multiplexing DS-0 channels and are referred to as *digital signal* n (DS-*n*), where *n* can be 2, 3, and so on.

In the DS-1 system, supervisory signaling is "in-band," with bit 8 of every sixth frame "robbed" for supervisory signaling. Two enhancement schemes are widely used: *superframe* (SF) and *extended superframe* (ESF). A SF is illustrated in Figure 6 (ITU-T 1998, G.704).

An ESF is similar to an SF, with enhancement of signaling and usage of S-bits, as specified in ITU-T G.704 (1998).

In the CEPT-1 or E-1 PCM systems, a frame consists of thirty-two channels (TS0–31), thirty of which are used to carry voice or data; the remaining two channels transmit synchronization alignment (TS0) and signaling information (TS16). Each time slot is 125/32 = 3.906 μsec. An E-1 frame thus contains $32 \times 8 = 256$ bits, resulting in a line rate of $256 \times 8000 = 2,048,000$ bps or 2.048 Mbps. Table 1 shows the E-1 frame format.

In TS0, a synchronizing code word is transmitted every second frame, occupying digits 2 through 8 as below:

E–1 synchronizing code word: 0011011

In those frames without the synchronizing code word, the second bit of TS0 is set to 1.

The frame format and the digital hierarchy (see the section below) define the PSTN carriers into T, E, and J categories, as described in the next section.

Internetworking between Hierarchies

When two different hierarchies (i.e., the T1- and E1-based systems) internetwork at the boundary between two countries, a time-slot interchange procedure occurs, whereas the *digital cross-connect* (DCC) maps the 8-bit time slots from one hierarchy into the corresponding time slots in the other hierarchy. Although a time slot that carries data patterns will be mapped across unchanged, a time slot that carries voice speech requires the PCM *A*-law to μ-law conversion, or vice versa, at the internetworking point. Figure 7 depicts the internetworking between the T1- and E1-based hierarchies.

Differences between the T1 and E1 Network and Broadband Integrated Services Digital Network

We introduce this subsection mainly for completeness. Generally speaking, both T1- and E1-based networks and ISDN networks can transmit data and speech traffic. Specifically, the ISDN can run on top of the T1- and E1-based infrastructure and serve as layer 3 (the network layer) in the OSI model. Although T1- and E1-based networks employ the *channel associated signaling* (CAS) model, which

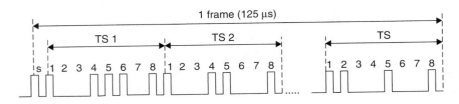

Figure 5: DS-1 frame format (frame length 193 bits in 125 μsec)

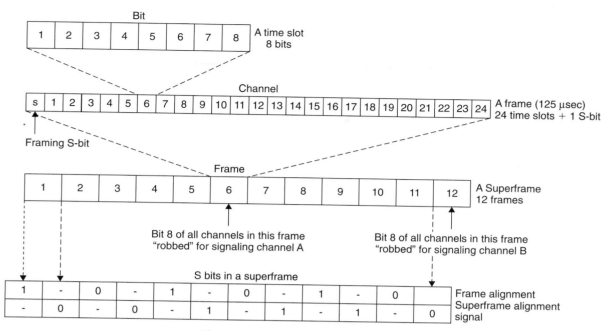

Figure 6: A DS-1 superframe structure

Table 1: Allocation of TIme Slots in an E-1 Frame

TS0	TS1	...	TS15	TS16	TS17	...	TS31
Framing	Voice Channels			Signaling	Voice Channels		

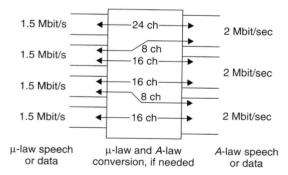

Figure 7: Internetworking between T1- and E1-based hierarchies

requires the signaling be carried on the same physical medium as that of the data or speech traffic, *broadband integrated services digital network* (BISDN) adopts the *common channel signaling* (CCS) model, which allows the separation of signaling traffic and data or speech traffic and utilizes SS-7 as its signaling protocol. (We will discuss CCS and SS-7 shortly.) For more detailed discussion on BISDN, please refer to Chapter 73 of this handbook.

Plesiochronous Digital Hierarchy

Plesiochronous digital hierarchy (PDH) is the first system designed to transmit voice in PSTN using the digital format. PDH is an asynchronous infrastructure in the sense that each component—such as exchange, multiplexer, cross-connect, repeater, and so on—gets its clocking pulse from different sources that are synchronous but have minute fluctuations in timing.

PDH defines an integrated digital network that can carry any kind of digital information such as digitized voice, data, and video. PDH also specifies the different transmission levels, or data rates, and the number of channels that can be contained within each level.

Three different standards of the PDH Infrastructure have been adopted in different regions of the world. *T-carriers* adopt the DS-1 frame format and DS-*n* digital hierarchy and are deployed throughout North America. *E-carriers* adopt the CEPT-1 frame format and are deployed throughout Europe and the majority of other nations around the world, including large parts of Asia, Latin America, and Africa. *J-carriers*, only operating in Japan, adopt the DS-1 frame format but follow the J-*n* digital hierarchy. Table 2 summarizes the signal levels and hierarchy supported by each carrier.

Although T-*n* (*n* = 1, 2, 3, 4, 5) means the infrastructure (Bellcore 1994) carrier type or service type, and DS-*n* (n = 1,2,3,4,5) is used to indicate the signal level and interface type, they have been used interchangeably in most locations, except where confusion might result. It is also true for CEPT-*n* and E-*n*.

Lower-level signals can be multiplexed to higher-level signals by using multiplexers. Figure 8 (Clark 1996) shows how the North American digital hierarchy works.

Table 2: Signal Rate and Hierarchy

Digital Signal Level	T-Carrier		E-Carrier		J-Carrier	
	Line Rate (Mbps)	Number of DS-0/T-1	Line Rate (Mbps)	Number of E0/E-1	Line Rate (Mbps)	Number of DS-0/J-1
Level 0 (DS-0, CEPT0)	0.064	1/0	0.064	1/0	0.064	1/0
Level 1 (T-1/DS-1, J-1, E-1/CEPT-1)	1.544	24/1	2.048	32/1	1.544	24/1
DS-1-C	3.162	48/2				
Level 2 (T2/DS-2, E2/CEPT2, J-2)	6.312	96/4	8.448	128/4	6.312	96/4
Level 3 (T3/DS-3, E/CEPT3, J-3)	44.736	672/28	34.368	512/16	32.064	480/20
Level 4	274.176	4032/168	139.264	2048/64	97.728	1440/60
Level 5	400.352	6048/252	565.148	8192/256	397.200	5760/240

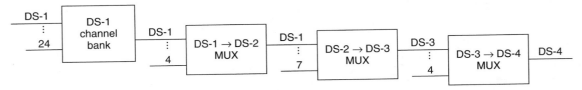

Figure 8: The T-carrier digital hierarchy

PDH Components

The PDH system depends on the following key components to implement the network.

Transmission Media. PDH signals can be transmitted over a variety of transmission media, depending on the signal rate. For example, T-1, E-1, or J-1 services can be provided over copper pairs; and T3, E3, or J-3, or high rates, can be provisioned over coaxial cable, microwave, or optical fiber. PDH operates on four-wire circuits—that is, it always operates in full duplex mode.

Repeaters. Repeaters are devices that are deployed between exchanges to amplify and regenerate signals.

Channel Service Units. *Channel service units* (CSU) are interfaces that terminate each end of a T-, E-, or J-carrier.

Data Service Units. *Data service units* (DSU) are interfaces that extend data services to the user's premise.

Multiplexers. *Multiplexer* (MUX) devices are used to format higher-level signals from lower-level ones within the digital hierarchy.

Digital Loop Carriers. Also known as remote terminals, or concentrators, *digital loop carriers* (DLCs) are deployed to improve efficiency and reduce costs by reducing the analog facility and sharing pairs among many multiplexed conversations.

Digital Cross-Connects. *Digital cross-connects* (DCCs) are devices that are deployed to cross-connect exchange channels from one facility to another, using their key feature, which is known as *add and drop*. DCCs are used to route or reroute traffic around connection or failure and allow customers to dynamically reconfigure their own networks. Generally, DCCs can provide four levels of switching: between DS-3s and DS-3s (or E-3s and E-3s), between DS-1s and DS-1s (or E-1s and E-1s), between DS-0s and E-0s, and potentially within a DS-0 (E-0) channel.

Synchronous Optical Network and Synchronous Digital Hierarchy

The *synchronous optical network* (SONET) provides digital formats extending to 40 Gbps or more. SONET is a North America standard (Bellcore 1994, GR-253-CORE). The equivalent European format recommended by ITU-T is called *synchronous digital hierarchy* (SDH) (ITU-T 2001, G.703; 2006, G.707). They are similar in frame format and can accommodate the standard DS-*n* or E-*n* line rates. In contrast to PDH, SONET or SDH is a synchronous infrastructure, meaning that each network element draws its clocking pulses from one clocking source.

SONET and SDH Architecture

SONET and SDH introduced the notion of a ring operation to address network survivability by handling rapid restoration. As shown in Figure 9, SONET and SDH nodes are linked by a dual counter-rotating ring of fiber

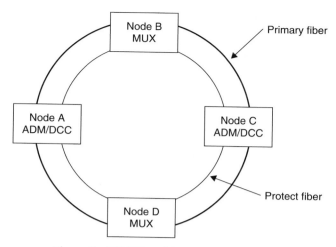

Figure 9: SONET and SDH ring architecture

pairs. One pair of fibers, where information flows in a clockwise manner, is designated as the *primary fiber*. Designed to carry information in a counter-clockwise manner, the other pair of fibers are called the *protect fiber*. In case the primary fiber is cut between nodes A and B, information can still be delivered from node A to B via a path from A to D to C to B. This dual ring architecture enables immediate recovery—within 50 milliseconds (Bellcore 1994, GR-253)—from small-scale outages. A major disaster may break both rings at the same time, and thus the counter-rotating ring would not ensure network survivability.

SONET and SDH Signal Hierarchy

Similar to PDH, SONET and SDH (ITU-T 1988, G.801) define their size of frame as 125 μsec. SONET defines a family of signal levels, called *synchronous transport signal* (STS). The basic signal rate is STS-1: 51.840 Mbps (Bellcore 1994, GR-253). The optical counterpart of STS-1 is *optical carrier level 1* (OC-1).

Higher-level SONET signals are obtained by synchronously multiplexing lower-level modules, resulting in STS-*N* or OC-*N* signals. The rate of STS-*N* is *N* times the rate of STS-1.

SDH refers to its frame as *synchronous transport module* (STM) and defines its lowest line rate as STM-1 at 155.520 Mbps (ITU-T 1988, G.702), which is equivalent to

that of OC-3 or STS-3. Higher-level STM-*N* signals have line rates of *N* times the line rate of STM-1.

The signal hierarchy of SONET and SDH is shown in Table 3.

SONET and SDH Frame Format

An STS-1 frame is a specific sequence of 810 bytes, which is divided into transport overhead and payload and can be used to transport DS-3 signals or a variety of sub DS-3 signals if *virtual tributary* (VT) is used. An STS-1 frame, shown in Figure 10 (Bellcore 1994, GR-253-CORE), is constructed as a ninety-column by nine-row structure. The line rate is

$$810 \times 8 \times 8000 = 51.84 \, \text{Mbps}$$

A frame is transmitted row by row from top to bottom, and each row is transmitted column by column from left to right.

The first three columns (total 27 bytes) of the STS-1 frame are the *transport overhead*, which is used to carry frame control relative information. The remaining $87 \times 9 = 783$ bytes per frame are allocated to the *synchronous payload envelope* (SPE) signal. This provides a channel capacity of 50.11 Mbps in the STS-1 signal structure for carrying tributary payloads intact across the synchronous network.

An STS-*N* frame is formed by *byte interleaving* STS-1 and STS-*M* frames (M < N). An STM-N frame is equivalent

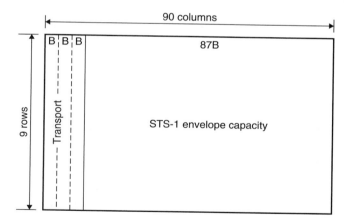

Figure 10: SONET STS-1 frame format (B = 8-bit byte)

Table 3: SONET and SDH Signal Hierarchy

OC-*N* Level	STS-*N* Electrical Level	STM-*N* Electrical Level	Line Rate (Mbps)
OC-1	STS-1	(STM-0)	51.48
OC-3	STS-3	STM-1	155.52
OC-12	STS-12	STM-4	622.08
OC-48	STS-48	STM-16	2488.32 (2.5G)
OC-192	STS-192	STM-64	9953.28 (10G)
OC-768	STS-768	STM-256	39813.12 (40G)

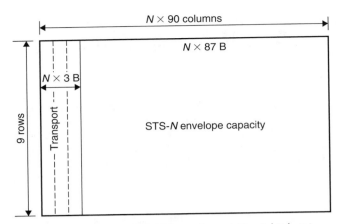

Figure 11: SONET STS-*N* frame format (B = 8-bit byte)

to an STS-3N frame. Figure 11 shows an STS-N frame. Because the frame rate of 8000 frame per second in a STS-*N* signal is the same as that of the PDH frame rate, a byte within the STS-*N* structure represents a channel bandwidth of 64 kbps (8 bits/byte × 8000 bytes/sec). This is the same rate of a PCM voice channel or a DS-0 or E-0 channel.

Virtual Tributary and Virtual Container

The SONET *virtual tributary* (VT) (Bellcore 1994, GR-253) and SDH *virtual container* (VC) (ITU-T 1999, G.708) structures are designed to support sub-STS and sub-STM-1 payloads such as DS-1 and E-1. There are four sizes of VTs—VT1.5, VT2, VT3, and VT6—and four sizes of VCs (VC1–4). Their rates and standards are shown in Table 4.

Key Components

SONET and SDH were built for and largely rely on fiber-optic transmission media. Both systems include a variety of *multiplexers* and digital cross-connects. There are two major categories of SONET and SDH MUXes:

1. *Terminal MUXes* enable signals to move from one optical level to another level.
2. *Add and drop MUXes* (ADMs) facilitate easy dropping and adding of payload and are one of the key building blocks of the SONET and SDH network.

Figure 12 shows the major functionalities of terminal MUX and ADM.

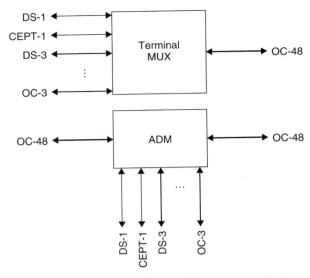

Figure 12: SONET and SDH MUXes versus ADMs

DCCs can also be divided into two categories. *Wideband DCCs* terminate SONET and SDH and DS-3 and E-3 signals and switch at DS-0, DS-1 and E-1, and VT or VC levels. *Broadband DCCs* interface at various SONET and SDH signal levels as well as the legacy DS-3 and E-3 levels, and can make cross-connections at the DS-3 and E-3 and OC-1 level.

SWITCHING AND SYNCHRONIZATION
Digital Switching
Types of Switching
A digital switch's architecture contains two elements: *time-division switching* (T) and *space-division switching* (S). A switch comprises T and S elements in an arbitrary order. For example, the AT&T number 4 ESS is a TSSSST, 5 ESS is TST, and Nortel DMS-100 is TSTS.

Time-division switching involves time-slot interchange, moving data in each time slot from the incoming bit stream to an outgoing bit stream but in a different order of time slots, in accordance with the preset destination for each time slot.

A T switch, or *time-slot interchanger* (TSI), contains at least two elements: a data buffer and a time-slot controller. The data buffer is used to store the incoming bit

Table 4: SONET and SDH VT and VC

VT/VC Level	Line rate (Mbps)	Standard	Columns in a frame
VT-1.5/VC-1	1.728	DS-1	3
VT-2/VC-2	2.304	E-1	4
VT-3	3.456	DS-1C	6
VT-6	6.912	DS-2	12
Async DS-3/VC-3	44.736/34.368	DS-3/E-3	78/60
VC-4	139.264	DS-4/E-4	243

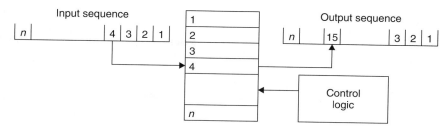

Figure 13: A simplified diagram of a time switch

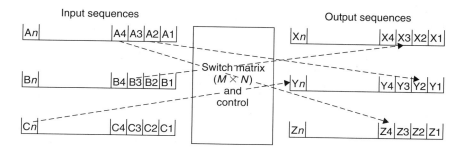

Figure 14: A space switch

stream, and the time-slot controller moves the data in the buffer to the outgoing bit stream in a preset order. This operation is illustrated in Figure 13. The data buffer has the same number of cells as the number of time slots.

Figure 13 shows a single inlet–outlet switch. In case of the DS-1 system, the switch can handle twenty-three stations besides the calling subscriber. To increase the capacity of a switch, a *space switch* (S) is used to move time slots in a trunk to another trunk in the same time-slot position. Figure 14 shows this concept.

The key component of a space switch is a $M \times N$ switch matrix, where M and N represent the number of input trunks and output trunks, respectively. If $M = N$, then the switch is nonblocking (for tandem and transit switches). If $M > N$, then the switch concentrates. If $M < N$, then the switch expands. Local switches usually have $M \neq N$.

Multistage Switches

A digital switch comprises time and space switches in an arbitrary order. Figure 15 illustrates a time-space-time (TST) switch concept. The first stage of the switch is the *time-slot interchangers* (TSI) or time stages that interchange time slots in the time domain between external incoming digital channels and subsequent space stage. The space

stage (a $M \times N$ switch) provides connectivity between time stages at the input and output. When no blocking occurs in the TST switch, the capacity of the TST is min $(M, N) \times C$, where C is the number of TDM time slots per input trunk. However, blocking can happen in the TST even though the space switch is nonblocking. Blocking occurs in TST if there is no internal space-stage time slot available. During blocking, the link from the inlet time stage and the link to the outlet time stage are both idle. A TST switch is nonblocking if

$$L = 2C - 1$$

where L is the number of space stage time slots, and C is the number of external TDM time slots (Freeman 2004).

A space-time-space (STS) switch is a reversal of a TST switch. It consists of a space switch as the input stage, followed by an array of TSIs whose outputs feed another space switch. Figure 16 shows an STS switch, where the sizes of the two space switch matrices are not necessarily the same.

The architecture of a TST switch is more complicated than that of an STS switch. The TST switch is more cost-effective because time-slot expansion can be achieved at less cost than space expansion. Such expansion is required

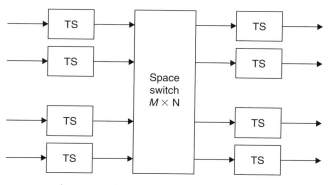

Figure 15: A time-space-time switch (TST)

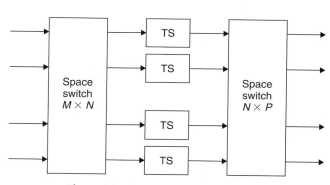

Figure 16: A space-time-space switch

as link utilization increases. Bellamy (2000) states that STS is favored for small switches because of reduced implementation complexities. For large switches with heavy traffic loads, the implementation advantages of TST over STS are dominant. For example, AT&T 5 ESS, a large TST switch, can handle more than 100,000 lines. With a 10:1 concentration rate, 5 ESS can achieve blocking probability of 1.5 percent for an average busy season (AT&T 1994).

Digital Network Synchronization

Needs for Synchronization

When a PCM bit stream is transmitted from one element to another over a link, the transmitter and receiver need to be synchronous to decode the received information. The synchronization has to be done at three levels: bit level, time-slot level, and frame level.

The bit synchronization requires that both the transmitter and the receiver operate at the same rate, and the receiver decodes the bit at the midposition of the incoming bit. Time-slot synchronization is needed but is done when a frame is synchronized.

For the DS-1 frame, there is a frame bit. If the twelve-frame *superframe* (SF) is adopted, it has twelve framing bits. The frame alignment pattern is 101010 and is located in the odd-numbered frames. The superframe-alignment pattern is 001110 and is located in the even-numbered frame. In case of the twenty-four–frame *extended superframe* (ESF), the frame alignment pattern is 001011, and the framing bit occurs only once in four frames.

The E-1 frame has a dedicated framing and synchronization channel in time slot 0 (channel 0). The receiver detects the bit pattern 0011011 in channel 0 from bits 2 to 8 of every other frame. Once this pattern is detected, the receiver knows when the frame starts.

All digital switches have a master clock that is used to clock the outgoing bit stream. The switch also derives the timing from the incoming bit transitions for the incoming bit stream. The standards require that every switch in a digital network generates outgoing bit streams whose bit rate is extremely close to the nominal bit rate. To achieve this goal, all switches in the network have to be synchronized (Bellcore 1994, GR-436). Network synchronization can be accomplished by synchronizing the master clocks in all switch nodes so that each switch node has the same average bit rate. Buffer storage is used at the transmission interface to absorb the differences between the actual line bit rate and the average rate. Without network-wide synchronization, slips will occur.

The other factor to cause slips is *phase wander and jitter* in the digital stream. Phase wander and jitter can be caused by such environmental effects as changing ambient temperature. In case of underflow slips, the last frame just before the clip occurs is repeated. Adequate buffering in the digital line interface can prevent the overflow slips.

Methods of Network Synchronization

There are several methods that can be employed to synchronize the digital networks (ITU-T 1997, G.811; Bellcore 1994, GR-436).

The first method is *plesiochronous operation*. In this case, each switch clock is free running, but each node switch has identical high-stability clocks operating at the nominal rate. The stability of the clock should range from 1E-11 to 5E-13 per month. The disadvantage of this method is that each node has such a high-precision clock, which may incur a high cost burden to a commercial network. This method is popularly deployed in the interfaces between autonomous networks, such as those between LEC and ILCs. ITU-T G.811 (1997) also recommends the plesiochronous operation for international links.

The second method of synchronization is to employ *mutual synchronization* among all network nodes, each of which exchanges frequency references, thereby establishing a common network clock frequency.

The third method to synchronize a digital network is to *synchronize with an external source*, such as geographical positioning system, which disseminates coordinated universal time known as UTC. This method is widely deployed in military systems as well as private networks.

The fourth method used in network synchronization is to *utilize a hierarchical timing distribution system*. This scheme is broadly used in North American networks. Figure 17 shows the synchronization scheme, which is part of a recommendation from Bellcore. In this scenario, different stratum level clocks are deployed at different network nodes. A stratum 1 clock is the *primary reference source* (PRS) of the accuracy of 1E-11 or better. Stratum 2 clocks are typically deployed as part of tandem and transit switches. Stratum 3 clocks are suitable for local exchanges, while stratum 4 clocks are good for channel banks.

The last method for network synchronization is to apply the *master-slave method*. In this scheme, a master clock is synchronized to an external reference, and all other clocks within the network slave to the master clock.

SIGNALING SYSTEMS

The signaling systems are the nerve of the PSTN as network equipment and transmission media are its muscle. A large amount of control information needs to be passed back and forth between network elements to set up and complete a call. Signals can be categorized into four types.

1. *Supervisory signals* handle the on-hook/off-hook condition. When a user picks up a phone handset, an

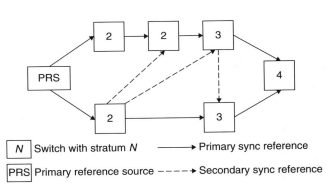

Figure 17: NA hierarchical network synchronization

off-hook signal is sent to the local exchange to indicate that a dial tone is desired. When the call is completed and the user hangs up (on-hook), an on-hook signal is sent to ask to terminate the connection.

2. *Address signals* carry the numbers dialed, including country code, city code, area code, prefix, and subscriber number. The address signal is the routing instruction to the network hierarchy.

3. *Informational signals* provide various enhanced services such as the call waiting service. These signals are optional to set up a call.

4. *Alerting signals* include ringing tones, busy tones, and other alerts.

Signaling takes place in two key parts of the network: (1) in the access network, where it is called *loop signaling*, and can take either analog or digital formats; and (2) in the core, where it is referred to as *interoffice signaling*. There are two mechanisms for interoffice signaling system. One is called *channel associated signaling* (CAS); it sends signals over the same truck as of the data path. The other is called *common channel signaling* (CCS), and it sends signals over a separate trunk or network to set up and release calls on other trunks. Figure 18 illustrates these two mechanisms.

Signaling in Analog Systems

Many signaling systems have been used in the analog PSTN, including E and M signaling (DC-based signaling) and AC signaling. AC signaling can be further divided into in-band and out-of-band signaling. There are three categories of in-band signaling: *single frequency* (2600 hz), *two frequency* (2400 hz and 2600 hz), and *multifrequency* (MF). Out-of-band signaling is a single frequency system, using 3825 hz for the ITU-T region and 3700 hz for North America.

Despite the many systems, the MF signaling is the only one that is still widely used in current access networks. MF signaling is an in-band system that uses five to six frequencies, two for each tone. ITU-T R1 and R2 are two most popularly deployed MF signaling systems in the access network.

R1: North American MF Signaling

R1 Signaling uses two out of five frequencies (700 hz, 900 hz, 1100 hz, 1300 hz, and 1500 hz) to form the signaling code. Additional signals for control functions are provided by combinations using a sixth frequency (1700 hz). Table 5 contains digits and other control functions and their corresponding frequency pairs.

R2: European MF Signaling

R2 is a European regional signaling code listed in ITU-T Recommendation Q.441. R2 uses full combinations of two out of six tone frequencies to form fifteen frequency pairs. The number of pairs is doubled in each direction by having groups I and II in the forward direction, and groups A and B in the backward direction, as shown in Table 6.

Tables 7 and 8 illustrate the signaling frequencies used in North America. The *dual tone multifrequency* (DTMF) signaling, or so called touch tone, uses seven frequencies and covers ten digits (0–9), "*," and "#," as illustrated in Table 7. Also shown in Table 7 is the traditional dial-pulse signaling (i.e., breaks). Table 8 specifies the alerting and call progress signals (Bellcore 1991).

ITU-T Signaling System Number 7

The ITU-T has defined a family of signaling from ITU-T *signaling system number* 1 (SS-1) to *signaling system number* 7 (SS-7). Among these standards, SS-7 is designed for broadband digital systems and is widely used in the current PSTN (ITU-T 1993, Q.700; ITU-T 1993, Q.703). SS-7 is a CCS-based signaling system that enables the

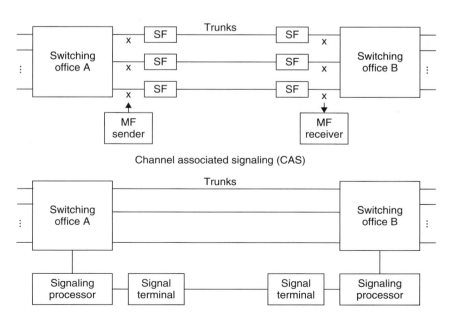

Figure 18: CAS and CCS signaling

Table 5: The R1 signaling code

Digit or special function	Frequency pair (hz)	Description
1	700, 900	
2	700, 1100	
3	900, 1100	
4	700, 1300	
5	900, 1300	
6	1100, 1300	
7	700, 1500	
8	900, 1500	
9	1100, 1500	
0	1300, 1500	
KP	1100, 1700	Preparatory for digits
ST	1500, 1700	End-of-pulsing sequence
STP	900, 1700	Used with traffic service position system
ST2P	1300, 1100	Same as STP
ST3P	700, 1700	Same as STP
Coin collect	700, 1100	Coin control
Coin return	1100, 1700	Coin control
Ring back	700, 1700	Coin control
Code 11	700, 1700	Inward operator
Code 12	900, 1700	Delay operator
KP1	1100, 1700	Terminal call
KP2	1300, 1700	Transit call

Table 6: R2 Signaling

Signaling index number for groups I, II and A, B	Frequencies (hz)						Forward group I, II Backward group A, B
	1380	1500	1620	1740	1860	1980	
	1140	1020	900	780	660	540	
1	x	x					
2	x		x				
3		x	x				
4	x			x			
5		x		x			
6			x	x			
7	x				x		
8		x			x		
9			x		x		
10				x	x		
11	x						x
12		x					x
13			x				x
14				x			x
15						x	x

Table 7: North America DTMF and dial pulse

Digit	Dial pulse (breaks)	Touch tone (DTMF (hz)
0	10	941, 1336
1	1	697, 1209
2	2	697, 1336
3	3	697, 1477
4	4	770, 1209
5	5	770, 1336
6	6	770, 1477
7	7	852, 1209
8	8	852, 1336
9	9	852, 1477
*		941, 1209
#		941, 1477

Table 8: Audible tones used in North American DTMF

Tone dial	Busy (station)	Busy (network)	Ring return	Off-hook	Recording warning	Call waiting
Frequencies HZ	350	480	480	440	MF 1400	440
440	620	620	480	howl		
Cadence continuous	0.5 sec on	0.2 sec on	2 sec on	1 sec on,	0.5 sec on	0.3 sec on
0.5 sec off	0.3 sec off	4 sec off	1 sec off	15 sec off		9.7 sec off

ISDN services. SS-7 is also known to have been deployed in a well-defined data network. Each SS-7 link is a full duplex digital transmission channel with bandwidth of 56 kbps (for T- and J-carrier) or 64 kbps (for E-carrier). Multiple voice channels can share a single SS-7 link.

SS-7 Network Architecture

SS-7 itself is a packet-based data network designed to control the operation of the underlying voice networks. A SS-7 network (ITU-T 1993, Q.705) requires three key components: *service switching points* (SSPs), *service control points* (SCPs), and *signal transfer points* (STPs). SSPs and SCPs are the signaling end points of the SS-7 networks. To guarantee the high reliability and high availability of signal delivering, the SS-7 networks adopt a fully redundant architecture as shown in Figure 19.

The STPs and SCPs are usually deployed in pairs, and a backup pair of STPs can be deployed with the primary pair (as shown in the network of carrier 1), thus providing full redundancy of the signal path. SCPs are the centralized nodes that contain the network configuration and call-completion database. STPs are responsible for

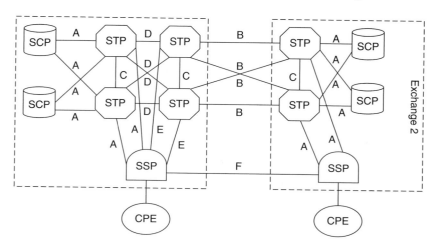

Figure 19: SS-7 network architecture

interpreting the SS-7 messages and routing them between network nodes and databases. SSPs are the originating and terminating points of calls.

Links in the SS-7 network are designated with particular names according to the network components that they connect.

A (access) links interconnect STPs and SSPs or SCPs.
B (bridge) links interconnect primary STP pairs between two carriers or two central offices.
C (cross) links interconnect the paired STPs.
D (diagonal) links connect the backup and primary STP pairs.
E (extended) links connect the SSPs to the backup pair of STPs.
F (fully associated) links connect two SSPs directly.

SS-7 Structure

SS-7 is internally implemented into a layered structure with two major parts: *message transfer part* (MTP) and *user part* (UP). The MTP can be further divided into three sublayers of *signaling data link, signaling link control*, and *signaling network functions*. UPs are classified according to the type of services they support. Currently, three UPs exist: *telephone user part* (TUP), *data user part* (DUP), and *ISDN user part* (ISUP). To facilitate the understanding of the SS-7 layered structure, it can be related to the OSI standard seven-layer networks as shown in Figure 20.

Signaling Data Link.

The signaling data link (layer 1) is a full duplex transmission path for signaling, containing two data channels operating together in opposite directions at the same rate. The digital transmission channels may be derived from a multiplex signal at 1.544, 2.048, or 8.448 Mbps having a frame format as defined in ITU G.704 (1998), or they may be from digital multiplex bit streams having a frame structure specified for data circuits in ITU X.50, X.51, X.50 bis, and X.51 bis. The operational signaling data link is exclusively dedicated to the use of SS-7 signaling between two signaling points. No other information may be carried by the same channels with the signaling information.

Signal Link Control. The signal link control (layer 2) deals with the transfer of signaling messages over one signaling link directly connecting to signaling points. Signaling messages are transferred over the signaling link in variable-length signal units, which include signaling information and transfer control information for proper operation of the signaling link. The signaling link functions include (1) *signaling unit delimitation and alignment*, (2) *error detection and correction*, (3) *initial alignment*, (4) *error monitoring*, and (5) *flow control*.

Signaling Network Functions. The signaling network functions (layer 3) can be broken into two categories: signaling message handling and signaling network management.

Signaling message handling ensures that a signaling message originated by a particular user part is delivered to the same user part at the destination point. Dependent on the environment, the delivery may be through the F links or via one or more STPs.

Signaling network management includes three parts: *signaling traffic management, signaling link management*, and *signaling route management*.

Signaling traffic management controls message routing, signaling traffic transfer, and flow control. Signaling link management controls the locally connected signaling link sets. In the event of changes in the availability of a local link set, it initiates and controls actions with the objective of restoring the normal availability of that link set. Signaling route management transfers information about changes in availability of signaling routes in the signaling network to enable the remote signaling points to take appropriate signaling actions.

Signaling Connection Control Part. The *signaling connection control part* (SCCP) (layer 4) provides additional functions to the *message transfer part* (MTP) for both

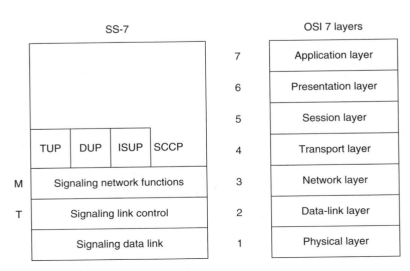

Figure 20: Relationship between SS-7 and OSI model

connectionless and connection-oriented services between switches and specialized centers in telecommunication networks. SCCP mainly provides logical signaling connections within the SS-7 network and a transfer capability for the *network service signaling data units* (NSDUs). Three user parts (UPs) are also supported in the position of SCCP. Each user part corresponds to a specific service, such as the aforementioned TUP, DUP, and ISUP.

NETWORK PERFORMANCE AND MANAGEMENT
Network Performance

Network performance measurements ITU-T G.821 (2002) and G.826 (2002) recommend a set of network performance measurements that should be satisfied by all network elements to guarantee QoS.

Bit error rate or *ratio* (BER) should be less than 1E-6 in all networks.

Loss of signal (LOS) in the connection is detected by the local exchange.

Alarm indication signal (AIS) is sent from a remote exchange to indicate an alarm condition has been detected.

Errored second (ES) is a one-second period in which one or more bits are in error or during which LOS or AIS is detected.

Severely errored second (SES) is a one-second period that has a bit error ratio? 1 E-3 $\geq$ or during which LOS or AIS is detected.

Errored second ratio (ESR) is the ratio of ES to the total seconds in the available time during a fixed measurement interval. The performance objective for ESR is < 0.002.

Severely errored second ratio (SESR) is the ratio of SES to total seconds in available time during a fixed measurement interval. The performance objective for SESR is ESR < 0.08.

Unavailable seconds (UAS) are declared when a unidirectional connection experiences ten consecutive SESs and no SES is detected for a period of 10 consecutive seconds. UAS starts at the beginning of the 10 consecutive SESs and ends at the beginning of 10 consecutive non-SESs. For bidirectional connection, the connection is in the unavailable state when either or both directions are in the unavailable state.

Error Detection and Correction Mechanism
Many mechanisms deployed in the PSTN network are used to detect possible bit errors. Most of them can detect or correct one bit error within a frame.

Parity Check. Parity check is a simple mechanism that takes one bit out of an 8-bit byte to avert the parity of the byte. For example, for an even parity-enforced system, a 1010110 string will be appended "0" to keep its even parity. For an odd parity system, a "1" will be appended to make it hold odd number of "1" bit in the byte. This mechanism can only detect an odd number of errors.

Frame Check Sequence. Frame check sequence (FCS) is an error-detection method that sums the 1's in a vertical column of all characters, including the 1's in the eighth bit position. The sum is then appended to the end of the message block. The FCS method can detect one error per bit column.

Cyclic Redundancy Check. Cyclic redundancy check (CRC) is an advanced method that employs complicated algorithms to calculate the FCS, which can be 16- or 32-bits long. The FCS is determined by generating polynomials. ANSI and ITU-T define different generating polynomials. For CRC-16:

$$CRC\text{-}ITU\text{-}T = X16 + X12 + X5 + 1$$
$$ANSI\ CRC\text{-}16 = X16 + X15 + X2 + 1$$

CRC-16 can detect error bursts of as many as 16 bits.

Forward Error Correction. Forward error correction (FEC) uses codes to detect bit errors. Two typical codes are used: block and convolutional. Block codes take k information bits and c parity bits. A Hamming distance is a measure of a code's error detection and correction capability. For example, to detect N erred digits, a Hamming distance of $N + 1$ is required. To correct the error, $2N + 1$ is required.

A convolutional code is formed by convoluting a string of digits with the response function of the encoder. Modulo-2 is used to form check digits.

FEC is good at detecting random errors only. It does not help with burst errors. Some techniques, such as interleaver and deinterleaver, can be used to preprocess the digit stream before they are transmitted and after they are received (Freeman 2004).

Network Management
Basics of Network Management
Network management for PSTN, also known as *surveillance and control* (or SC) in the Bellcore standards (Bellcore 1994, BOC notes), is mainly aimed at maintaining a high level of network utilization efficiency, minimizing the effects of the network overloads, and supporting the Bell operating company's national security emergency preparedness commitment. To achieve these objectives, three important functions need to be implemented: network traffic management (NTM), network service, and service evaluation.

An NTM center provides real-time surveillance and control of message traffic in *local access and transport area* (LATA) telephone networks. The goal of the NTM center is to increase call completions and optimize the use of available trunks and switching equipment. Using information collected from the traffic flows and control capability of the network elements, the operator of the network can optimize the utilization of the network.

Among other functions, the NTM renders relief on traffic overload conditions, including generic network overload, focused overload, and switching system overload.

The reduction of a generic network overload is achieved by deploying techniques such as code blocking, call gapping, and protective trunk group controls. A focused overload, which may result from media stimulation (such as news programs, call-in contests, etc.) or events that cause mass calling to public service agencies, can be managed using code controls or choke networks. Last but not least, NTM can relieve switching system overload, which is caused when the offering load is much higher than the engineered capacity; this is done by employing congestion time-outs with short holding times on the circuit group.

Typical NTM controls are described as follows:

Cancel control prevents overflow traffic from or to a trunk.

Skip route control directs some traffic to bypass a specific circuit group and advance to the next route.

Code block control blocks some percentage of traffic routed to a specific destination code.

Call gapping control uses an adjustable timer to stop all calls to a specific code for a time interval.

Circuit directionalization control changes two-way circuits to one-way operation.

Circuit turndown control removes one- or two-way circuits from service.

Reroute control redirects traffic from congested or failed routes to other groups.

NTM optimizations are based on four principles:

First, keep all trunks filled with messages. Because the network is normally trunk limited, it is beneficial to optimize the ratio of messages to nonmessages on any trunk group. NTM controls are designed to reduce nonmessage traffic flow and allow more call completions, resulting in higher customer satisfaction and increased revenues.

Second, give priority to single-link connections. In a network with alternate-routing support, some calls are alternate routed and therefore must use more than one link to complete a call. During the overload situation, the use of multilinks to complete a call occurs more frequently, and the possibility of a multilink call blocking other call attempts is greatly increased. This is the reason that some NTM blocks a portion of alternate-routed calls to give preference to first-routed traffic.

Third, use available trunking. The network is typically engineered to accommodate average business day peak-hour calling requirements. Focused overloads and holiday calling can cause network failures and switching system outages. In these cases, NTM can be activated to reroute calls to the available trunks.

Fourth, inhibit switching congestion. A large number of ineffective attempts that exceed the engineered capacity of the switching systems can cause switching congestion. NTM can be activated to remove the ineffective attempts.

Network Management Systems

The goal of the *network management system* (NMS) is to provide automated means to remotely monitor a network for (1) level of performance (e.g., BER, ES, LOS, and LOF), (2) equipment failures and circuit outages, and (3) level of traffic load and network usage.

Currently, there are three categories of NMS with respective protocols:

Bellcore transaction language 1 (TL1), which is mostly deployed in the North American PSTN;

TCP/IP based simple network management protocol (SNMP); and

ISO -supported common management information protocol (CMIP).

TL1 is a protocol defined in Bellcore's GR-199 (2002), GR-811 (1997), and GR-831 (1996) that imposes syntax, semantics, information structure, and other rules for uniform construction of TL1 messages. TL1 is the most widely used management protocol in telecommunications. It is the telecom industry's only cross-vendor, cross-technology human-machine language that manages the majority of SONET and access infrastructure in North America. In TL1, messages are used to manage the network elements (NEs) and observe faults and events emitted by NEs. In other words, in facilities and equipment that have a TL1 management protocol, TL1 messages are used to operate, administer, maintain, and provision equipment. There are two main types of standards-defined TL1 messages (Bellcore, 1996, 1997, 2002): (1) commands and responses and (2) autonomous events.

Commands and Responses. Commands and responses are initiated by a user and consist of two parts: a request to the NE to get or set information, and a response from the NE containing completion or status codes and requested or chained information.

Autonomous Events. Autonomous events, alarmed or otherwise, are emitted by the NE to indicate some change in its status.

Depending on the TL1 interface for the device, as well as the *element management system* that is used to manage the device, the user executes TL1 requests via a *graphic user interface* (GUI) or a *command line interface* (CLI) and receives notifications from the NE (autonomous events) in a designated location such as stdout, a GUI application, a file, and so on. TL1's widespread acceptance is due in large part to its ease of use. A TL1-conformant message is easy to read, and each message component is easily identifiable. Figure 21 shows an example of a SET ATTR message, which sets alarm condition attributes for specific entities.

Figure 22 shows the basic architecture of a TL1-based NMS. For more details on TL1 message definitions, refer to GR-831 (Bellcore 1996).

SNMP NMS SNMP, defined by the Internet Engineering Task Force (ITEF), is the most dominant method for devices on a data network to relay network management to the centralized management consoles. The SNMP protocol contains three components: the SNMP protocol itself, the *management information base* (MIB), and the *structure of management information* (SMI). Figure 23 shows the architecture of an SNMP NMS. For details on the SNMP protocols and defined MIBs, see Case et al. (1996a, 1996b, 1996c).

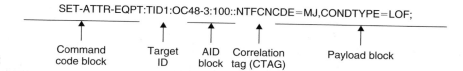

Figure 21: A typical TL1 command format

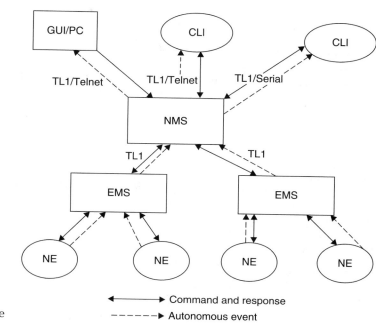

Figure 22: TL1 NMS architecture

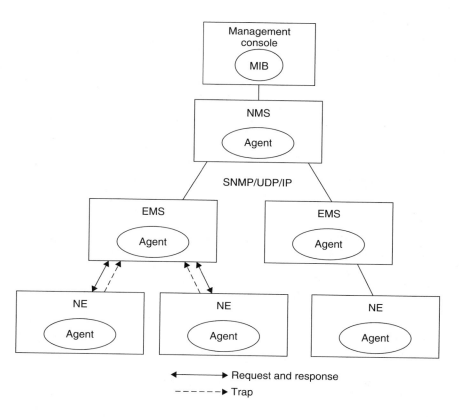

Figure 23: SNMP NMS architecture

Common Management Information Protocol NMS.
Common management information protocol (CMIP) is an ISO development designed to operate in the OSI environment. CMIP uses *managed objects* (MOs) to model platforms and devices (Warrier et al. 1990). Each CMIP agent maintains a *management information tree* (MIT). CMIP is used to create, change, delete, and retrieve MOs in the MIT.

CMIP is a more versatile protocol but requires approximately five times as much memory as SNMP. It is much more complex than SNMP. Although SNMP uses connectionless transport protocols (UDP and TCP) to transport messages, CMIP relies on standard OSI layers for communication and utilizes connection-oriented transport. For more information about CMIP, see Aidarous and Plevyak (1993).

CONCLUSION

This chapter has briefly discussed the basic concepts of the PSTN network, including its service provisioning, network architectures, frame formats, transport mechanisms, synchronization mechanisms, signaling systems, network performance measurement, and network management. PSTN is an evolving network that has adopted new available technology and facilities—such as digital cross-connect, SONET, fiber optics, and so on—to increase its capacities and enhance its services.

A significant trend in PSTN development is the evolution to the *next generation network* (NGN). ITU defines NGN as a packet-based network that provides full services of voice, data, video, multimedia, and mobility. Users of NGN should be offered unrestricted access to different service providers. The next generation gateway switches will provide seamless interoperability between the circuits that connect PSTN and packet-switching networks such as IP backbones, ATM networks, and MLPS networks. They will support a variety of telephony signaling protocols such as H.323, *session initiation protocol* (SIP), and *media gateway control protocol* (MGCP) for communicating with the underlying SS-7 architecture. SS-7 signaling will continue to play a key role in NGN, supporting packet-based telephony networks using class 4 (toll) and class 5 (local exchange) switches.

NGN will support at least these features: (1) a packet-switching network with capacity in the range of terabits per second (TBPS) or more; (2) an optical-based core network to take advantages of the abundant bandwidth in the light spectrum; (3) multiservice access with intelligent networking applied to the public data infrastructure as well as the Internet; and (4) access moving toward the broadband realm on both a wire and wireless basis. To include access, edge, core, and service layers, a complete NGN PSTN transformation can be spread over several years.

GLOSSARY

Central office (CO): A physical location where local service providers terminate subscriber lines and locate the switching equipment that interconnects those lines.

Channel associated signaling (CAS): An electronic means of signaling in which the signal is carried on the same physical path as the data.

Common channel signaling (CCS): An electronic means of signaling between any two switching systems that is independent of the voice path.

Competitive local exchange carrier (CLEC): A telephone company that competes with an ILEC.

Customer premise equipment (CPE): Equipment that is located on the customer's premises and is owned and managed by the customer.

Digital loop carrier (DLC): A type of concentrator; also known as a *remote concentrator*.

Dual tone multifrequency (DTMF): A method of signaling that uses two frequencies to stand for a key on the keypad.

E-*n*: A time-division multiplexed, digital transmission facility that operates at an aggregate rate of multiples of 2.048 Mbps. E-carrier is a PCM system that uses 64 kbps (E-0) for a voice channel. The basic E level is E-0 (64 kbps); higher levels are E-1 (2.048 Mbps), E-2 (8.488 Mbps), and so on.

Incumbent local exchange carrier (ILEC): A telephone company that provides local service in the United States; came into existence after enactment of the Telecommunications Act of 1996.

Interchange carrier (IXC): A long-distance telephone company that offers circuit-switched, leased-line, or packet-switched services.

Plesiochronous digital hierarchy (PDH): The first generation of digital hierarchy that defines transmission rates and frame formats; that is, T-carrier for North America, E-carrier for ITU-T countries, and J-carrier for Japan.

Private branch exchange (PBX): A telephone switch that is located on the customer's premises and establishes voice circuits between users.

Public switched telephone network (PSTN): The complete traditional public telephone system that includes the telephones and local and interchange trunks.

Pulse code modulation (PCM): A scheme that is used to convert a voice signal into a digital bit stream for transmission. A common method to digitize the speech is to use an 8-bit code word and sampling at 8000 times per second to produce the basic rate of 64 kbps.

Signaling system number 7 (SS-7): A telecommunication signaling protocol defined by the ITU-T. The SS-7 architecture is set up in a way so that any node can exchange signaling with any other SS-7 signaling-enabled node, not just signaling between switches that are directly connected.

Synchronous digital hierarchy (SDH): An ITU-T standard for digital broadband communications.

Synchronous optical network (SONET): An ANSI standard that has been incorporated into the SDH standard and that defines a line-rate hierarchy and frame formats for use with high-speed optical fiber.

T-*n*: The North American standard of the PDH, a time-division multiplexed, digital transmission system. The T-carrier is a PCM system that uses 64 kbps (T-0) per channel as the basis of the hierarchy. The higher rates are T-1 (1.544 Mbps), T-2 (6.312 Mbps), and so on.

CROSS REFERENCES

See *Analog Transmission*; *Digital Transmission*; *SONET/SDH Networks*; *Telephone Number Mapping (ENUM)*.

REFERENCES

Aidarous, S., and T. Plevyak. 1995. Telecommunications network management into the 21st century. Piscataway, NJ: IEEE Press.

ATIS. 2005. *U.S. numbering and dialing plan within the United States*. ATIS-0300076. Washington, DC: Author.

———. 2006. *North American numbering plan numbering resource: Utilization/forecast reporting (NRUF) guidelines*. ATIS-0300068. Washington, DC: Author.

AT&T. 1994. *5ESS switch and 5ESS-2000 switch system description*. 235-100-125. Winston-Salem, NC: Author.

Bellamy, J. C. 2000. *Digital telephony*. 3rd ed. New York: John Wiley & Sons.

Bellcore. 1991 *BOC notes on the LEC networks—1990*. SR-TSV-002275, no. 1. Piscataway, NJ: Author.

———. 1994 *BOC notes on the LEC networks*, no. 2. Piscataway, NJ: Author.

———. 1994. *Digital network synchronization plan*. GR-436-CORE. Piscataway, NJ: Author.

———. 1994. *Synchronous optical network (SONET) transfer systems: Common generic criteria*. GR-253-CORE. Piscataway, NJ: Author.

———. 1996. *Operations application messages—Language for operations application messages*, no. 1. GR-831-CORE. Piscataway, NJ: Author.

———. 1997. *Operations application messages—TL1 messages index*, no. 3. GR-811-CORE. Piscataway, NJ: Author.

———. 2002. *Operations application messages—Memory administration messages*, no. 5. GR-199-CORE. Piscataway, NJ: Author.

Case, J., K. McCloghrie, M. Rose, and S. Waldbusser. 1996a. *RFC 1902—Structure of management information for version 2 of the simple network management protocol (SNMPv2)*. San Jose, CA: Cisco.

———. 1996b. *RFC 1905—Protocol operations for version 2 of the simple network management protocol (SNMPv2)*. San Jose, CA: Cisco.

———. 1996c. *RFC 1907—Management information base for version 2 of the simple network management protocol (SNMPv2)*. San Jose, CA: Cisco.

Clark, M. P. 1996. *Networks and telecommunications design and operation*. Chichester, England: John Wiley & Sons.

Deese, R. 1984. A history of switching. *Telecommunications*, no. 23.

Freeman, R. L. 2004. *Telecommunication system engineering*. 3rd ed. New York: John Wiley & Sons.

Goleniewski, L. 2005. *Telecommunications essentials*. Boston: Addison-Wesley.

ITU-T. 1988. G.702. *Digital hierarchy bit rates*.

———. 1988. G.711. *Pulse code modulation (PCM) of voice frequencies*.

———. 1988. G.801. *Digital transmission models*.

———. 1993. Q.441. *Signaling code: Specifications of signalling system R2*.

———. 1993. Q.700. *Introduction to ITU-T signaling system no. 7*.

———. 1993. Q.703. *Signaling link*.

———. 1993. Q.705. *Signaling network structure*.

———. 1997. G.811. *Timing characteristics of primary reference clocks*.

———. 1998. G.704. *Synchronous frame structures used at 1544, 6312, 2048, 8448 and 44 736 kbit/s hierarchical levels*. Geneva.

———. 1999. G.708. *Sub STM-0 network node interface for the synchronous digital hierarchy (SDH)*. Geneva.

———. 2001. G.703. *Physical/electrical characteristics of hierarchical digital interfaces*.

———. 2002. G-821. *Error performance of an international digital connection operating at a bit rate below the primary rate and forming part of an Integrated Services Digital Network*.

———. 2002. G.826. *End-to-end error performance parameters and objectives for international, constant bit-rate digital paths and connections*.

———. 2005. E.164. *The international public telecommunication numbering plan*.

———. 2006. E.163. *Numbering plan for the international telephone service*.

———. 2006. G.707. *Network node interface for the synchronous digital hierarchy (SDH)*. Helsinki.

Sams, H. W. 1976. *Reference data for radio engineers*. 6th ed. Indianapolis: ITT.

Sklar, B. 2001. *Digital communications: Fundamentals and applications*. 2nd ed. Upper Saddle River, NJ: Prentice Hall.

Warrier, U., L. Besaw, L. LaBarre, and B. Handspicker. 1990. RFC 1189. *Common management information services and protocols for the Internet (CMOT and CMIP)*.

WEB SITES

The following Web sites offer more information on the organizations and standards discussed in this chapter:

- ANSI documents are available at www.ansi.org.
- ITU-T recommendations are available at www.itu.int.
- TL1 information is available at www.tl1.com/library/TL1/TL1_Protocol/.
- ATIS documents are available at www.atis.org, and www.atis.org/inc/index.asp.
- Complete coverage of NANP is available at www.nanpa.com.

Information Theory

David Blockus, *Independent Consultant* and Mark Stamp, *San Jose State University*

INTRODUCTION

In his classic paper, Shannon (1948) states, "The fundamental problem of communication is that of reproducing at one point either exactly or approximately a message selected at another point."

Beginning from this premise, Shannon proceeded to develop a beautiful, coherent, and surprisingly complete mathematical theory of communication. In this chapter, we outline some of the key elements of Shannon's theory and then turn our attention to a wide array of related topics. Although some of these related topics might go slightly beyond the usual definition of information theory, all are relevant to topics that appear in this volume.

SHANNON'S THEORY
Background and Basics

The diagram in Figure 1 models a general communication system. As the diagram shows, errors may occur during transmission because of the "noise source."

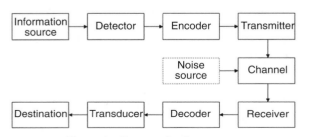

Figure 1: Communication system

Each block in Figure 1 will be discussed to some extent in this chapter. The topic of this section—Shannon's theory—deals with the "transmitter → channel → receiver" path and the effect of noise on this crucial part of a communication system.

Channel Capacity

Suppose that we transmit seven-bit ASCII characters using eight bits for each (there is one parity bit) over a 1 Mb/sec link. Then we are able to transmit $1,000,000(7/8) = 875,000$ bits of information per second; this is the channel capacity, C. Note that the capacity is not the number of bits transmitted, but the number of information bits transmitted.

More generally, the transmitted symbols need not all be of the same length. In this case, we define the capacity as

$$C = \lim_{T \to \infty} \frac{\log N(T)}{T}$$

where $N(T)$ is the number of different symbol strings of length T. When log is taken to be $\log_2$, this formula gives the correct result in the case where the symbols are all of the same length. This is often the case of interest in modern communications systems where bits, bytes, (fixed size) packets, and so on are transmitted.

Entropy

Entropy is the fundamental concept of Shannon's theory. At the time Shannon developed his mathematical theory of communication, the term *entropy* was established and widely used in physics. Why did Shannon choose to use the same term for his new concept? According to Tribus and McIrvine (1971), Shannon said that

> My greatest concern was what to call it. I thought of calling it "information," but the word was overly used, so I decided to call it "uncertainty." John von Neumann had a better idea. [H]e told me, "You should call it entropy, for two reasons. In the first place your uncertainty function goes by that name in statistical mechanics. In the second place, and more important, nobody knows what entropy really is, so in a debate you will always have the advantage."

Why is uncertainty the "right" thing to measure? One of the fundamental problems Shannon was concerned with was compression. To compress data, we compress the redundant information—that is, the parts that are "certain" or knowable from other parts of the data can be removed. At the extreme, if we have a string of bits that will always be all 1's, then it has no uncertainty (equivalently, it is entirely redundant, and we say that its entropy is zero), and this string compresses to nothing. In other words, we do not even need to transmit the string at all because it is entirely known to the sender and receive beforehand. On the other hand, if we have a random string of bits, with all bit strings being equally probable, then, on average, such a string will not compress.

Let X be a random variable. Then we denote the entropy of X as $H(X)$. We define entropy with respect to an underlying probability distribution. This assures us that the entropy will not change because of a trivial change such as a change of label from "bits" to "heads or tails." We also denote the entropy function as $H(p_0, p_1, ..., p_{n-1})$, where the arguments p_i are the underlying probabilities—that is, each p_i is nonnegative and the sum of the probabilities is 1.

What properties should the entropy function $H(X)$ satisfy? We would like the function to satisfy the following conditions.

First, the function $H(p_0, p_1, ..., p_{n-1})$ should be a real-valued continuous function of its arguments. This is desirable because, intuitively, a small change in the arguments should result in a small change in the function value.

Second, if all outcomes are equally likely, then the more outcomes there are, the larger the entropy—that is, $H(1/n, 1/n, ..., 1/n) \leqslant H(1/(n+1), 1/(n+1), ..., 1/(n+1))$. For example, if we flip a fair coin, there are only two possible outcomes whereas when we roll a die there are six possible outcomes, so the outcome of a roll of a die is more uncertain than the outcome when a coin is flipped.

Third, if an outcome is viewed as the result of successive outcomes, then the original entropy H is the weighted sum of the entropies leading to the outcome. For example, suppose that we roll a die and the three outcomes of interest are "even," {1,3}, and {5}. Then the entropy function for this experiment is $H(1/2, 1/3, 1/6)$. On the other hand, we could view this same experiment as having outcomes "even" and "odd," with the "odd" outcome being

further split into {1,3} and {5}. The probabilities in these two cases are illustrated below.

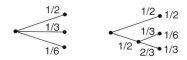

In this case, we require that $H(1/2, 1/3, 1/6) = H(1/2, 1/2) + 1/2 H(1/3, 2/3)$. In general, we require that $H(p_0, ..., qp_j, (1-q)p_j, ..., p_{n-1}) = H(p_0, ..., p_j, ..., p_{n-1}) + p_j H(q, 1-q)$ for $0 < q < 1$. Because these experiments are equivalent, we clearly want the entropies to be the same. The point of this assumption is that we want the entropy to be linear in this specific sense.

Shannon (1948) proved the following result.

Theorem: The only H satisfying the three assumptions above is of the form

$$H(p_0, p_1, ..., p_{n-1}) = -K \sum_{i=0}^{n-1} p_i \log p_i$$

where K is a positive constant.

We choose $K = 1$, and we take *log* to be log_2, which yields the entropy function $H(p_0, p_1, ..., p_{n-1}) = -\Sigma p_i \log_2 p_i$. Note that because of the choice of logarithm, the entropy can be measured in bits as discussed above.

In any experiment with n equally likely outcomes, we have

$$H(p_0, p_1, ..., p_{n-1}) = -\log(1/n) = \log n$$

For example, if we flip a fair coin, there is one bit of uncertainty, and the entropy in this case is indeed 1. On the other hand, rolling a single die has entropy of $\log 6 = 2.58$. In this way, we can quantify the increased uncertainty of a roll of a die as compared to a flip of a coin.

Entropy has many equivalent interpretations. One interesting interpretation is that, roughly speaking, entropy gives the minimum number of yes-no questions that need to be asked to determine an outcome (Trappe and Washington 2002). For example, suppose that we flip two fair coins and count the number of heads. Then the entropy is:

$$-1/4 \log 1/4 - 1/2 \log 1/2 - 1/4 \log 1/4 = 3/2$$

In this case, we can determine the actual number of heads with, on average, 1.5 questions as follows. First, we ask, "Is the number of heads odd?" If the answer is yes (which occurs with probability 1/2), then we are done; if not, it takes one more question to precisely determine the number of heads.

Entropy is also the number of bits of information inherent in a given outcome. When we flip three fair coins, the entropy is three; in any particular flip of three fair coins, we thus learn three bits of information. Similarly, the entropy is the minimum number of bits required to represent an event on a digital computer.

In other words, the uncertain bits are all that need to be stored because any remaining parts are completely predictable. Therefore, entropy is intimately related to data compression.

As an illustrative example, we now briefly consider the entropy of English while simultaneously defining additional concepts related to entropy. Suppose we eliminate all punctuation, special characters, and spaces and use only lowercase letters. With these restrictions, English text is limited to twenty-six characters. If the individual letters were independent, then the entropy per letter would simply be $-\Sigma p_i \log p_i$, where p_i is the probability of the ith letter. If all letters were equally likely, then this would yield an entropy value of $1/26\Sigma\log 26 = 4.7$, which implies that there are approximately 4.7 bits of uncertainty in each letter. But in English text the letters do not each occur with an equal probability. In a large selection of English text, the letter "e" will have a frequency of more than 12 percent, while "q" will appear far less than 1 percent of the time. Taking these relative frequencies into account, the entropy of English is reduced to approximately 4.2—that is, there are only some 4.2 bits of uncertainty per letter.

In reality, there are far less than 4.2 bits of uncertainty per letter of English text. For example, the letter "x" is unlikely to be followed by the letter "z," while the letter "q" is extremely likely to be followed by "u." This information is not accounted for in the entropy calculation based on individual letter frequencies. To account for such information, we need to consider the 26^2 digraphs, aa, ab, ac, ..., zz and compute the entropy of each letter, given the previous letter. But then we can make the same argument regarding trigraphs, quadgraphs, and so on. As a result, the precise entropy of English would need to be calculated as $\lim_{N\to\infty} \dfrac{H(N)}{N}$, where $H(N)$ is the entropy of English N-graphs.

It is only practical to enumerate English N-graphs for small values of N, so it appears that a reasonable estimate of the entropy of English might be difficult to obtain. However, Shannon (1951) proposed the following practical approach to obtain an upper bound on the entropy of English. Suppose we have a deterministic machine that will predict the next letter of an English text based on the previous letters. Given an English text, the predictor machine is used to make guesses until the next letter is guessed correctly. Once the letter is guessed correctly, we record the number of guesses required, the letter is revealed, and the machine is then used to guess the next letter. This process continues until we have obtained a sequence of numbers (the numbers of guesses) corresponding to the sequence of letters. Then the original text can be reconstructed directly from the sequence of numbers using the predictor machine. Therefore, the entropy of English can be no greater than the entropy of the sequence of numbers.

Now suppose that we replace the predictor machine with an English-speaking human. The sequence of number is no longer sufficient to reconstruct the text—because of the nondeterministic nature of humans—but the resulting sequence of numbers should still provide a reasonable approximation because English-speaking humans provide a reasonable approximation to a predictor machine. Using this approach (with humans), we can simply use the relative frequency of each number that occurs and thereby approximate the entropy of English. This experiment yields an estimate of the entropy of English text of slightly more than one bit per letter.

Consider the *relative entropy* of English text—that is, the fraction of uncertainty (or information) in English letters relative to the uncertainty of random text, which, as noted above, has the maximum possible uncertainty. This relative entropy is given by $\dfrac{H}{\log(26)}$, where H is the entropy of English text. Let $R = 1 - \dfrac{H}{\log(26)}$. Then R is the fraction of English that is certain, and therefore R, or the *redundancy*, gives the fraction of English text that does not carry any information. For English, we have $R \approx 0.75$, which, among other things, implies that, optimally, we should be able to compress English text by a ratio of approximately 4 to 1. Huffman coding comes reasonably close to achieving this theoretical bound.

Shannon (1948) discusses several "interesting properties" of his entropy function, H, that we briefly summarize here.

1. We have $H = 0$ only when there is no uncertainty in the outcome. More precisely, $H = 0$ if and only if $p_i = 1$ and $p_j = 0$ for all $j \neq i$.

2. The entropy H is maximized when the uncertainty with respect to the underlying probability distribution is maximized. This follows from the fact that, for a given n, the value of H is maximized at $\log n$ precisely when $p_i = 1/n$ for all i, which is the most uncertain case.

3. The entropy of a joint event is never more than the sum of the entropies of the individual events. Consider, for example, an event X with n possible outcomes and an event Y with m possible outcomes, with joint probability distribution $p(i, j)$. Then

$$H(X, Y) = -\sum_{i,j} p(i, j) \log p(i, j)$$

and it is not difficult to see that

$$H(X) = -\sum_{i,j} p(i, j) \log \sum_{j} p(i, j)$$

and

$$H(Y) = -\sum_{i,j} p(i, j) \log \sum_{i} p(i, j)$$

From these expressions it follows that $H(X, Y) \leq H(X) + H(Y)$.

4. The more uniform the probabilities, the greater the entropy. For example, if p_1 and p_2 are both replaced with $(p_1 + p_2)/2$, then the new entropy will be at least as great as the original entropy.

5. Consider two random variables, X and Y, as in property 3 above, where X and Y need not be independent. The conditional entropy of Y, denoted $H(Y|X)$, should measure the amount of uncertainty in Y, given knowledge of X. The conditional probability of the event that Y is j given that X is i is given by

$$p_i(j) = p(i,j) / \sum_j p(i,j)$$

Then the conditional entropy of Y given X is defined as

$$H(Y|X) = -\sum_{i,j} p(i,j) \log p_i(j)$$

In words, the conditional entropy measures the uncertainty of Y, on average, when X is known. It is easily shown that $H(X,Y) = H(X) + H(Y|X)$. This important result means that the uncertainty in the joint event is given by the uncertainty of X plus the uncertainty of Y when X is known.

6. Combining properties 3 and 5 yields $H(Y|X) \leqslant H(Y)$. This matches with the intuition that knowledge of X cannot increase the uncertainty of Y. In fact, $H(Y|X) < H(Y)$ unless X and Y are independent, in which case equality holds.

Noise and the Fundamental Theorem

Here we present a simple example of a noisy channel and consider the role that entropy has to play in such a situation. Then we give Shannon's fundamental theorem and mention one of its implications.

Shannon (1948) considers the following example of a noisy channel. Suppose we have a source that transmits bits at a rate of 1000 per second with an equal probability for 0 and 1. Suppose that during transmission, errors occur, so that 1 percent of the bits are received in error. Clearly, the rate of transmission of information is less than 1000 bits per second, but how much less? Because we expect 10 errors in each 1000 transmitted bits, the "obvious" answer is 990 bits per second, but this fails to account for the fact that the receiver does not know a priori which bits are correct and which are in error. In the extreme, suppose that the received bits are random with equal probability of 0 and 1. Then approximately 500 bits would be "received" correctly; but we certainly cannot claim that 500 bits of information was transmitted, because the same result would be obtained by simply flipping a coin at the receiving end.

Shannon defines the rate of information transmission as $R = H(X) - H(X|Y)$—that is, the rate at which information is transmitted is the rate at which it was sent, $H(X)$, minus the information that is "missing" at the received end, which can be viewed as the ambiguity in the received signal. The conditional entropy $H(X|Y)$, which goes by the name of *equivocation*, measures the uncertainty in X, given the received signal Y. In the example above, with a 1 percent chance of error, if a 0 is received, then it is 99 percent certain that a 0 was sent and a 1 percent chance that a 1 was sent (and vice versa in the case

where a 1 is received). Consequently, the equivocation in this example is

$$H(X|Y) = -(0.99 \log_2 0.99 + 0.01 \log_2 0.01) \approx 0.081$$

This gives the number of bits of uncertainty per symbol. Because one bit of information is transmitted per symbol and 1000 bits per second are sent, the rate of transmission of information is $1000 - 81 = 919$ bits per second. On the other hand, if the received bits are random, then the equivocation would be

$$H(X|Y) = -(0.5 \log 0.5 + 0.5 \log 0.5) = 1$$

in which case, $1000 - 1000 = 0$ bits of information are transmitted. This agrees with our intuition that no information has been transmitted in such a scenario.

Define the capacity of a discrete channel with noise as $C = \max (H(X) - H(X|Y))$, where the maximum is over possible information sources to the given channel. In the case where there is no noise, $H(X|Y) = 0$, and the capacity is simply the maximum amount of information that can be fed into the channel, which is consistent with the definition of capacity given above. If $H(X|Y) > 0$, then the capacity is reduced by a corresponding amount. Shannon's fundamental theorem states that it is possible to send information through the channel at the rate C "with as small a frequency of errors or equivocation as desired" (Shannon 1948). However, if we try to send information at rate $C + R$ through the channel, then the equivocation must be at least R. Shannon's fundamental theorem can be stated as follows.

> **Theorem:** Let a discrete channel have capacity C and a discrete source have entropy (per second) of H. If $H \leqslant C$, then there exists a coding system such that the output of the source can be transmitted over the channel with an arbitrarily small frequency of errors (or an arbitrarily small equivocation). If $H > C$, it is possible to encode the source so that the equivocation is less than $H - C + \in$, where $\in$ is arbitrarily small. There is no method of encoding that gives an equivocation less than $H - C$.

One consequence of Shannon's fundamental theorem is that "good" error correcting codes exist. However, Shannon's proof of this theorem does not provide a particularly useful road map for constructing such codes. An enormous amount of research has been conducted since the initial publication of this result in an effort to find codes that approach the bound promised by Shannon.

This completes our brief overview of Shannon's theory. For more details on the basic theory, Shannon (1948) remains surprisingly relevant, readable, and concise. Numerous sources discuss the theory and extend it in various directions. The book by Trappe and Washington (2002) has a brief but highly readable introduction to various mathematical aspects of the theory; MacKay (2002) contains a thorough treatment of the basic theory and includes many fascinating advanced topics; and the books by Ash (1990), Cover and Thomas (1991), and Reza (1994) are just a few of the many other excellent sources available.

DIGITAL SAMPLING OF SIGNALS

Most modern communication networks have increasingly migrated to digital, rather than analog, signal formats for several important reasons. The processing speed and data throughput rates of general purpose computers and *digital signal processors* (DSPs) have grown exponentially over recent years. The relatively lower cost of designing, fabricating, assembling, and maintaining digital electronics has won out over that of systemwide custom analog circuitry. Digital systems offer more modularity and scalability, and they permit more efficient communications channel utilization via packetized transport mechanisms, and broadband, spread spectrum, frequency-hopping methods.

Modern electronic circuits sample analog signals at discrete time intervals, usually with uniform temporal spacing. It is no surprise that such a circuit is called an *analog-to-digital converter* (ADC). It can be implemented using many different methods, including successive approximation, flash (totem-pole comparator configurations), sigma-delta feedback, and multistage error correction (Frerking 1994; Brannon 1995). A high-quality ADC can be an extremely expensive electrical circuit component, relatively speaking. Thus, different designs make various trade-offs among conversion rate, precision (bit depth dynamic range), accuracy (faithful representation of the actual input value), and cost. One must analyze carefully the actual requirements dictated by the particular application in order to choose wisely an appropriate ADC component.

There are other, less obvious, issues regarding ADC performance. First, note that the digital amplitude is quantized discretely into 2^n levels, where n is the number of ADC output bits. However, it is easy to show that the statistically averaged resolution of the ADC is roughly one-third of a bit. Consider the probability distribution, whereby an analog signal value x ranges uniformly between a digital output transition amplitude of magnitude ka to $(k \mid 1)a$, with k being a positive integer, as given in Figure 2.

We can calculate the statistical root-mean-square (RMS) error σ_x as follows. First,

$$\int_{ka}^{(k+1)a} P(x)\,dx = \frac{1}{a}[(k+1)a - ka] = 1, \text{ so that } \langle x \rangle$$

$$\equiv \int_{ka}^{(k+1)a} xP(x)\,dx = \frac{1}{a}\left[\frac{x^2}{2}\right]_{ka}^{(k+1)a} = \frac{1}{2}(2k+1)a$$

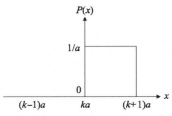

Figure 2: Probability for analog signal x to cause digital transition level a

and

$$\langle x^2 \rangle \equiv \int_{ka}^{(k+1)a} x^2 P(x)\,dx = \frac{1}{a}\left[\frac{x^3}{3}\right]_{ka}^{(k+1)a} = \frac{1}{3}(3k^2 + 3k + 1)a^2$$

Then the variance is given by

$$\sigma_x^2 \equiv \int_{ka}^{(k+1)a} (x - \langle x \rangle)^2 P(x)\,dx = \langle x^2 \rangle - 2\langle x \rangle^2 + \langle x \rangle^2$$

$$= \langle x^2 \rangle - \langle x \rangle^2$$

Its square root, or RMS value, which measures the standard deviation, is

$$\sigma_x^2 \equiv a^2 \left\{ \frac{1}{3}(3k^2 + 3k + 1) - \frac{1}{4}(4k^2 + 4k + 1) \right\} = \frac{1}{12}a^2$$

Finally, we have

$$\sigma_x = \frac{1}{\sqrt{12}}a \approx \frac{1}{3}a \quad \text{(roughly speaking)}$$

Several important issues affect ADC performance. Major influences include sampling time jitter, sample and hold circuitry time jitter, limited slewing rate for tracking rapid changes in signal amplitude, nonlinear response in the circuitry, and spurs in frequency response resulting from clock harmonic noise components (Brannon 1995; Frerking 1994; Masta 1999; Oppenheim, Schafer, and Buck 1999). It is surprising that many of these problems can be minimized by dithering the sampled signal with a small amount of asynchronous noise. In fact, the noise can be as large as a full amplitude quantization level.

The added noise offers two main benefits. First, it tends to smooth out large, abrupt jumps in output level in the time domain. Second, it reduces the harmonic spurs in the frequency domain at the minor expense of raising the overall asynchronous spectral noise floor. Dither noise can be provided by means as simple as using a noisy high-impedance input resistor. A more sophisticated approach involves using a linear feedback shift register (LFSR) to generate a pseudo-random number generator with a long repetition period in the digital output stage. More details may be found in the references cited above.

Time Domain Representation

Many interesting analog signals vary relatively smoothly with time and are often quasi-periodic in nature. This suggests the utility of a truncated Fourier series in order to allow a limited number of terms in approximating the analog signal well. Later we will examine some other important representations for describing analog signals. In general, we can use any complete set of orthonormal functions as a basis for the representation of a signal.

We often use a sinusoidal representation for an analog signal, using real-valued functions $a(t)$ for amplitude and $\phi(t)$ for phase.

The *instantaneous amplitude* is $x(t) = a(t)e^{i\phi(t)}$. The *instantaneous frequency* is given by $f(t) = \dfrac{1}{2\pi}\dfrac{d\phi(t)}{dt}$. We will see that one cannot simultaneously specify both the amplitude and frequency without some fundamental limitations on their relative precision. If the signal is not complex, as is often the case, then one can simply take the real part of $x(t)$. Traditional methods of broadcasting radio signals modulate a carrier wave by changing $a(t)$ in the case of amplitude modulation (AM), and $\sigma(t)$ in the case of frequency modulation (FM). AM signals use a constant carrier wave frequency, $f(t) = f_c$. FM signals use a constant amplitude, $a(t) = a_c$. Nevertheless, in both cases the signal spectrum will occupy a range of frequencies, or bandwidth, centered about the carrier wave frequency. If the carrier wave frequency is zero, then the signal is said to be *basebanded*.

We usually work with signals that have limited time duration or frequency bandwidth. We will see that each of these limited intervals affects the other. When the analog signal is sampled at discrete intervals, the representation changes from a continuous function $x(t)$ to a finite length sequence of n values, $x_0, x_1, x_2, ..., x_{n-1}$.

Major considerations for discrete sampling of analog signals include dynamic range and sampling rate. The particular application will dictate an appropriate cost and performance trade-off with respect to ADC bit depth, speed, and precision. In the case of dynamic range, one must adjust the gain properly to map the full analog amplitude range without clipping to utilize all of the ADC bits. The sampling rate must be at least twice the Nyquist frequency. One must usually employ an analog low-pass filter before the ADC to reject unwanted high-frequency signals and avoid aliasing in the captured spectrum. As an alternative, one can oversample the analog signal, apply a digital low-pass filter after the ADC, and decimate the filtered digital signal, retaining only a smaller bandwidth of interest. In a similar way, signals generated by modulating a very-high-frequency carrier wave can be basebanded via analog input circuits before discrete sampling at lower rates, or else oversampled at higher rates and basebanded via digital postprocessing. We will discuss this in more detail in a later section.

Frequency Domain Representation

All signals that we process will be limited necessarily in both temporal duration and frequency bandwidth. One can view the power density of a sampled signal as being distributed either in the time domain or in the frequency domain. These viewpoints are complementary but distinct representations of the signal. We will see that merely by limiting the time duration of a sampled signal, a *monochromatic* tone will spread in the frequency domain. Similarly, limiting the frequency bandwidth of a signal will be accompanied by a spread, or *uncertainty*, in temporal localization and duration.

Discrete Fourier Transform

Given a continuous time-domain analog signal $x(t)$, one can convert it to its equivalent counterpart, $X(f)$, in the frequency domain, and vice-versa, by means of the continuous Fourier transform pair. The formulas relating these two are

$$X(f) = \int_{-\infty}^{+\infty} x(t)\, e^{+i2\pi ft}\, dt$$

and

$$x(t) = \int_{-\infty}^{+\infty} X(f)\, e^{-i2\pi ft}\, df$$

These transforms are linear in the sense that the transform of a sum of signals is equal to the sum of the transforms of each signal individually. This follows easily from the definitions because

$$\int_{-\infty}^{+\infty} (a(t) + b(t))\, e^{+i2\pi ft}\, dt = \int_{-\infty}^{+\infty} a(t)\, e^{+i2\pi ft}\, dt + \int_{-\infty}^{+\infty} b(t)\, e^{+i2\pi ft}\, dt$$

and

$$\int_{-\infty}^{+\infty} (A(f) + (B(f))\, e^{-i2\pi ft}\, df = \int_{-\infty}^{+\infty} A(f)\, e^{-i2\pi ft}\, df + \int_{-\infty}^{+\infty} B(f)\, e^{-i2\pi ft}\, df$$

Signals that are discretely sampled in the time domain as a sequence of n amplitude values $x_0, x_1, x_2, ..., x_{n-1}$ require some modifications to this Fourier transform pair. Specifically, in the discrete case, we have

$$X_k = \sum_{j=0}^{n-1} x_j\, e^{+i2\pi jk/n}$$

and

$$x_j = \frac{1}{n} \sum_{k=0}^{n-1} X_k\, e^{-i2\pi jk/n}$$

We will see later that an optimal choice for the number of samples is such that n is a power of 2. Note that a finite length sequence of discretely sampled data is necessarily periodic with period n.

The so-called Fourier kernel or twiddle factor—$e^{\pm i2\pi jk/n}$—comprises the nth roots of unity, lying on the unit circle in the complex plane. Nicely detailed analyses of these concepts can be found in Frerking (1994); Krauss, Shure, and Little (1998); Oppenheim, Schafer, and Buck (1999); Press et al. (1992); Reid and Passin (1991).

If we call the uniform time sampling interval $\Delta t = \tau$, with total sampled time duration $n\tau$, then the uniform frequency sampling interval is given by $\Delta f = 1/(n\tau)$. The Nyquist frequency is given by $f_N = n\,\Delta f/2 = 1/(2\,\tau)$. Note that this dimensional information does not appear explicitly in the abstract formulas specified by the *discrete Fourier transform* (DFT) pair. The DFT maps the n values $x_j = x(t_j)$, with $0 \leq j \leq (n-1)$, into n values $y_k = y(f_k)$, with $0 \leq k \leq (n-1)$. The sequence of time values at which the signal is sampled is given by $t_j = 0, \tau, 2\tau, \ldots, (n-1)\tau$. However, the input signal must be band limited to avoid aliasing, such that $|f_k| \leq f_N = n\,\Delta f/2 = 1/(2\,\tau)$, for all k. The factor of 2 in the denominator of this relation reveals that negative, as well as positive, frequencies are needed to completely specify the frequency domain representation of a (complex-valued) signal. Hence, the sequence of frequency values at which the signal is sampled is given by:

$$f_k = \pm 0, +1/(n\,\tau), \ldots, +[(n/2)-1]/(n\,\tau), \pm 1/(2\,\tau)$$
$$= \pm f_N, -[(n/2)-1]/(n\,\tau), \ldots, -1/(n\,\tau)$$

This arrangement of terms is often called *wraparound order*. The frequency terms rise in value from $+0$ to $+f_N$, jump to $-f_N$, then increase back up to -0. There are two redundancies: one at $+0 \Leftrightarrow -0$ and another at $+f_N \Leftrightarrow -f_N$. This is somewhat bizarre, and hence given the special, albeit appropriate, name of *wraparound order*. The name seems to arise from the fact that as the negative frequency abscissas rise toward zero, they actually decrease in modulus. It is important for at least two reasons. First, it explicitly indicates that sampling needs to be done at more than twice the Nyquist frequency because we get equal amounts of positive and negative frequency abscissas. Second, the wraparound speaks to the finite, discrete sampling, giving rise to periodicity, and the danger of aliasing, should we neglect to band limit the signal. The aliased frequencies first add onto and corrupt the edges of the interval near DC. As their frequency increases, they corrupt more of the interval toward the Nyquist frequency in the middle from either or both ends. Just as a finite length sequence of discretely sampled data in the time domain is necessarily periodic with period n, so too is the frequency domain representation.

If the signal time-domain amplitudes are real-valued, then the frequency domain values are complex conjugate pairs, symmetric about $f = 0$, *i.e.*, $y_{(m+n/2)} + y^*_{(-m+n/2)}$, with $0 < m < n/2$. Furthermore, y_0 and $y_{(n/2)}$ are each self-conjugate and hence real-valued. This is perhaps more obvious when one examines the following relations for the continuous Fourier transform pair. We have

$$X(f) = \int_{-\infty}^{+\infty} x(t)e^{+i2\pi ft}dt, X^*(f) = \int_{-\infty}^{+\infty} x^*(t)e^{-i2\pi ft}dt$$

and $x^*(t) = x(t)$, so that

$$X^*(f) = \int_{-\infty}^{+\infty} x^*(t)e^{-i2\pi ft}dt = \int_{-\infty}^{+\infty} x(t)e^{+i2\pi(-f)t}dt = X(-f)$$

Processing Overhead

The formulas for the DFT indicate a sum of n terms, each of which involves a multiply and accumulate (MAC) calculation. Furthermore, there are n such sums. Thus, a brute force computation is of polynomial order of complexity $O(n^2)$. However, there exists a clever, recursive algorithm, called the *fast Fourier transform* (FFT), popularized by Cooley and Tukey (1965). This algorithm reduces the order of complexity to $O(n\log_2 n)$ (Frerking 1994; Krauss, Shure, and Little 1998; Oppenheim, Schafer, and Buck 1999; Press et al. 1992; Reid and Passin 1991). The method entails repeated subdivision of the DFT into interleaved even and odd terms, dividing the complexity by a factor of 2 at each subdivision. This technique effectively reduces the DFT summation to $O(\log_2 n)$. However, there are still n sums to calculate, and hence the overall computation is $O(n\log_2 n)$. For this method to succeed, it is imperative that n be an exact power of 2. If the number of data samples does not satisfy this criterion initially, then it is advantageous to enforce the criterion, by either adding extra data samples with zero value (zero padding) or throwing some data samples away.

When the number of data samples is extremely large, it is often necessary to break the data set into smaller subsets and apply a smaller length DFT to each data subset. This is clearly necessary when sampling a data stream for a long period of time. In that case, it is important not only to reduce processing overhead, but also to track spectral data characteristics that are changing with time. The most commonly used method for breaking the data stream into subsets is to use a *sliding buffer frame*. Usually, it is recommended that there be a 50 percent overlap between successive data frames. In this case, overlapped results are added together. This technique also mitigates issues variously called *ringing transients*, *Gibb's phenomena*, or *diffraction anomalies* associated with sharp cutoffs in the data stream. A better technique for eliminating undesirable effects due to sharp cutoffs in the data stream is to employ *windowing*, discussed in a later section, which effectively smooths the data at the edges of the sliding frame buffer. Finally, one can alternatively use zero padding of each successive frame buffer instead of overlapping adjacent buffers.

The effect of sharp cutoffs is particularly noticeable in some images published by newspapers. Some images are compressed tightly for transmission over a satellite communications channel with limited bandwidth, using the lossy compression afforded by the ubiquitous JPEG algorithm (Pennebaker and Mitchell 1992). JPEG compresses eight-by-eight blocks of pixels successively without overlap or windowing. High-compression ratios yield visual *blocking* anomalies by which image contrast levels change abruptly.

Performance can also be greatly enhanced by using modern processor hardware architectures. Several key developments specifically address the type of calculation required to perform DFTs. Special processor instruction sets include MAC operations and so-called barrel-shifted addressing modes to unwind the interleaved nature of the recursive FFT algorithm. The chain of self-similar MAC operations lends itself well to *single-instruction,* multiple-data (SIMD) architectures. Processors with *reduced instruction set computing* (RISC) architectures easily permit data pipelines, effectively reducing MAC overhead to a single machine clock cycle after initial setup. Often one can simultaneously decode a data sample's memory address, load an earlier data sample into a register, and perform a MAC operation on an earlier data sample—all in a single clock cycle. A common processor architecture feature that improves throughput is inclusion of multiple execution units on the same die. Another improvement stems from utilization of multiple address and data buses. Finally, some architectures use vector, or array, processors on the die. These architectural enhancements were formerly unique to highly specialized *digital signal processors* (DSPs). However, nowadays even general purpose commodity processors, such as Power PCs and Pentiums, include these improvements.

Correlation Operator and Power Spectrum

The correlation operator is often used to compare one signal against another for a match. Common applications include signal detection and analysis used in radar and sonar (Oppenheim, Schafer, and Buck 1999; Oppenheim 1978). One is usually interested in shifts in time or frequency between the two signals. A shift in time, or lag, may provide information such as target range, because of the finite speed of signal propagation. A change in frequency may provide information such as target speed resulting from the Doppler shift. The time domain formulas for the continuous and discrete correlation are given as a function of lag by

$$r(t) = \int_{-\infty}^{+\infty} a(t + \tau) b(\tau)\, d\tau$$

and

$$r_k = \sum_{j=0}^{n-1} a_{k+j} b_j$$

respectively.

Note that each finite-length, discretely sampled signal sequence is necessarily periodic, and thus there are wraparound issues. Thus, if $(k + j) \geq n$, then $a_{(k+j)} = a_{(k+j-n)}$. In addition, the time lags represented by r_k are arranged in wraparound fashion. Thus, positive lags occur for $0 < k < n/2$, negative lags occur for $n/2 < k < n$, $r_{+0} = r_{-0}$, and $r_{+n/2} = r_{-n/2}$. If one wishes to circumvent the periodic nature of the finite sample sequence, one must zero pad the frame buffer to the larger length $(2n - 1)$. However, the end points of the resulting correlation will have large errors of estimation because fewer data points actually enter into the calculation for large values of lag.

FFT methods can play an important role here because of frequency domain properties of the correlation operator. If $A(f)$, $B(f)$ are the Fourier transforms of the time domain signals $a(t)$, $b(t)$, then the Fourier transform of their correlation is given simply as the product $C(f) = A(f)B(-f)$. Recall that if the time domain signal is real-valued, then $B(-f) = B^*(f)$, and thus $C(f) = A(f)B^*(f)$ in that common situation. One can often obtain significant performance gains by transforming into the frequency domain, calculating the product, and then transforming back to the time domain to find the time lag response of the correlation in the now familiar wraparound order.

When one correlates the signal with itself—a process called the *autocorrelation*—one can measure the overall power in the signal. The total power can be obtained by integrating the differential *power spectral density* (PSD) over the full range in either the time or the frequency domain. According to Parseval's theorem, this must remain invariant, whether calculated in the time domain or in the frequency domain. The power density per unit time is given by $|x(t)|^2$ in the continuous case or $|x_j|^2$ in the discrete case. The power density per unit frequency is given by $|X(f)|^2$ in the continuous case or $(1/n)|X_k|^2$ in the discrete case. Recall that if the signal is real, then $X^*(f) = X(-f)$, or $X^*_k = X_{(n-k-1)}$, when $0 < k < (n - 1)$. In the discrete case, $X_0 = X^*_0$ and $X_{n-1} = X^*_{n-1}$ are real-valued. Then the total power is, in the continuous case,

$$\int_{-\infty}^{+\infty} \left| x(t) \right|^2 dt = \int_{-\infty}^{+\infty} \left| X(f) \right|^2 df$$

while in the discrete case it is given by

$$\sum_{j=0}^{n-1} \left| x_j \right|^2 = \frac{1}{n} \sum_{k=0}^{n-1} \left| X_k \right|^2$$

Sensor Characteristics

Ideal sensors would have perfect calibration accuracy and extremely fine-grained precision. Alas, ideal sensors do not exist. Calibration can be a thorny issue if the sensor response varies nonlinearly over the full dynamic range. Improper calibration gives rise to systematic error offsets. Sophisticated detection circuitry, or postprocessing following detection, can ameliorate this problem. A simple example is afforded by the audio cassette. Because of the limitations in high-frequency response and dynamic range of audiotape magnetic storage, the signal is *companded*, or reduced in dynamic range when recorded on tape, and expanded during playback. In addition, different tape technologies require different bias and equalization.

Another problem with nonideal sensors is limited precision or resolution. The response function is necessarily smeared because of statistical error in the signal-detection process. The detector output can be represented mathematically by the convolution of the actual signal and the sensor response function. This operation is described in the next section. In theory, it is possible to deconvolute the sensor response function from the detected signal to obtain a more ideal signal representation. However, this process is fraught with peril. One issue stems from the need for detailed information concerning the sensor response function over a wide range of operating characteristics. Another issue stems from inadvertent introduction of noise and systematic uncertainty via deconvolution where the signal-to-noise ratio is small. One popular technique for such a deconvolution process is called *optimal Wiener filtering* (Krauss, Shure, and Little 1998; Press et al. 1992).

Convolution Operation

The convolution operation is mathematically similar to the correlation operation. In practice, however, these two operations have quite different applications. The correlation operation is used to evaluate the degree of match between a measured signal and a reference signal. Radar signals reflected from a target can reveal its range and speed via correlation with the transmitted signal. The convolution operation is commonly used to model the smeared response function of an imperfect detection process. In the case of convolution, the response function is time-reversed—that is,

$$\nu(t) = \int_{-\infty}^{+\infty} a(t - \tau) b(\tau) \, d\tau$$

and

$$\nu_k = \sum_{j=0}^{n-1} a_{k-j} b_j$$

The time reversal results from the time-ordered manner in which the smeared detector response function samples the signal. However, mathematically the convolution result remains invariant whether one time reverses the response function or the signal.

Usually, the response function has a smaller period than that of the signal and must be zero padded to have the same length as the sequence of signal samples. The periodic nature of the discrete representations yields wraparound properties similar to those that arose in the case of the correlation operator. There is also a corresponding relationship in the frequency domain. If $A(f)$, $B(f)$, $V(f)$ are the Fourier transforms of $a(t)$, $b(t)$, $v(t)$, then $V(f) = A(f)B(f)$. Thus, here again, we may profitably employ the FFT to reduce significantly the overall computation load.

Sampling Issues

There are special requirements for a discretely sampled sequence to accurately represent a continuous analog signal. The sampling rate must exceed twice the Nyquist frequency: $f_s \geqslant 2f_N$. The analog signal must be bandwidth-limited via filtering so that its highest frequency component is less than the Nyquist frequency: $|f_{max}| \leqslant f_N$. Nevertheless, there are issues associated with finite, quantized intervals in both the time domain and the frequency domain. For example, the sampling rate will dictate the width of the frequency bins, thus determining the frequency resolution. The location of the bin edges can influence the interpretation of the power spectral density, $|X(f)|^2$. Therefore, several nearby narrowband frequency spikes in the signal being sampled may become smeared together in the discrete power spectral density periodogram. Oversampling—namely, choosing $f_s \gg 2f_N$—can improve spectral resolution but incurs a processing performance penalty. Oversampling can assist in resolving nearby frequency spikes but may not provide a clear separation if the spikes occur close to bin edges. We will consider these issues in more detail below, illustrating the nature of these problems, and suggest methods to ameliorate their influence (Krauss, Shure, and Little 1998).

Figure 3 shows a "pure tone" at 1 kHz, the peak sensitivity of the human auditory system, with a duration of ten periods. Note that the real part of the frequency domain amplitude spreads or leaks symmetrically around the central maximum at 1 kHz. This effect occurs both in the continuous and (necessarily) the discrete sampled signal domains. Figure 4 illustrates the same 1-khz tone with twice the duration of twenty periods.

Figure 4 illustrates an "intrinsic" increase in absolute frequency resolution in the continuous domain. The mathematical function that describes the form of the power spectral density in the frequency domain is related to the transcendental function called *sinc*. (A popular electronics store in Silicon Valley has adopted this shape as an architectural embellishment.) We have $x(t) = e^{-i2\pi f_0 t}$ and

$$X(f) = \int_0^{mT} x(t) e^{+i2\pi f t} dt \quad \text{and, hence,}$$

$$X(f) = \left[\frac{1}{2\pi(f - f_0)} e^{+i2\pi(f - f_0)t} \right]_0^{mT}$$

$$= \frac{1}{2\pi(f - f_0)} [e^{+i2\pi(f - f_0)mT} - 1]$$

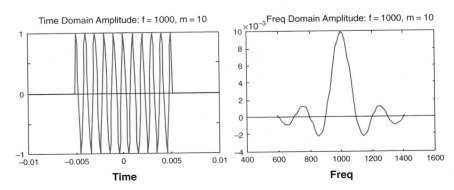

Figure 3: Simple tone, frequency = 1000 hz, duration = 10 periods

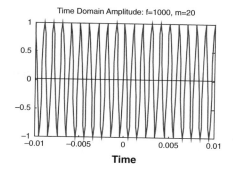

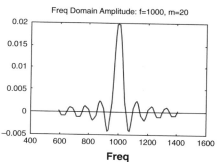

Figure 4: Simple tone, frequency = 1000 hz, duration = 20 periods

It follows that

$$\left|X(f)\right|^2 = X(f)X^*(f) = \frac{1}{2}\left[\frac{1}{\pi(f-f_0)}\right]^2$$

$$\times \left[1 - \cos(2\pi(f-f_0)mT)\right] = \left[\frac{\sin(\pi(f-f_0)mT)}{\pi(f-f_0)}\right]^2$$

The multiplier m in the numerator of $|X(f)|^2$ provides the resolution enhancement in the power spectral density in the frequency domain. There is a reciprocal relationship between the spread in the time domain and the spread in the frequency domain representations of the signal. This relationship is the basic idea behind the Heisenberg uncertainty principle in quantum mechanics. It is possible to quantify this result mathematically (Messiah 2000; Reid and Passin 1991; Reza 1994). We can calculate the standard deviation, or root-mean-square, for the time spread as well as for the frequency spread:

$$\sigma_t^2 \equiv \left\langle t^2\right\rangle - \left\langle t\right\rangle^2 = \int_{-\infty}^{+\infty} (t-\left\langle t\right\rangle)^2 \left|x(t)\right|^2 dt \text{ and}$$

$$\sigma_f^2 \equiv \left\langle f^2\right\rangle - \left\langle f\right\rangle^2 = \int_{-\infty}^{+\infty} (f-\left\langle f\right\rangle)^2 \left|X(f)\right|^2 df$$

The inequality $\sigma_t\sigma_f \geq \dfrac{1}{4\pi}$ follows from a Cauchy-Schwarz relation.

Quantum mechanics associates the energy of a system with a wavelike frequency through the relation $E = hf$. Here h is Planck's constant, the quantum scale parameter, which has the units of angular momentum. This theory also associates physical observables with linear operators in an abstract Hilbert space. The spectra of these operators, or *eigenvalues*, are the possible measured values for the associated physical observable *eigenstates*. Operators that cannot be simultaneously diagonalizable do not commute and give rise to the Heisenberg uncertainty principle—that is,

$$\sigma_t\sigma_E \geq \frac{h}{4\pi} = \frac{\hbar}{2} \text{ and } \sigma_x\sigma_p \geq \frac{h}{4\pi} = \frac{\hbar}{2}$$

where E is energy, p is linear momentum, and $\hbar = h/(2\pi)$.

This principle points out that, because of particle-wave duality, one cannot simultaneously localize, with unlimited precision, physical quantities associated with complementary representations, such as energy (frequency) and time or position and momentum. These conclusions follow directly from the probabilistic nature of measurement in quantum mechanics, as well as from its fundamental postulates. Information theory is concerned mainly with the probabilistic nature of measurement. However, there are additional important considerations regarding causality, because of relativity theory, which states that information cannot be transferred faster than the speed of light. Recent theoretical work and experimental evidence have established the validity of the quantum entanglement of states and confirm a strict interpretation of quantum theory. These developments refute the Einstein-Podolsky-Rosen (1935) conjecture, which favored undiscovered "hidden variables," in opposition to a probabilistic theory. These recent results, as well as relativity theory, also dismiss more fanciful notions such as superluminal communication. More information on theoretical and experimental results can be found in selected references such as Bell (1964); Aspect, Grangier, and Roger (1982); and Tittel (1998). A particularly approachable book for popular audiences is the delightful historical analysis by Aczel (2003). These principles constitute the foundations for quantum information theory and quantum cryptography (more properly termed *quantum key exchange*).

Returning to the classical physics domain, there are important practical considerations that stem from the analogy of the uncertainty principle. Because of spectral leakage into nearby frequency bins, one may be tempted to increase the sampling rate or increase the number of the samples per frame buffer (or both). The first method can mitigate problems with the analog filtering in the input stage by increasing the Nyquist frequency or else provide finer-grained frequency bins if the Nyquist frequency is held constant. Note, however, that increasing the sampling rate, while holding the Nyquist frequency constant, does not reduce the spectral leakage into nearby bins. Instead, the bins simply have smaller intrinsic width (Press et al. 1992). The second method statistically improves intrinsic spectral resolution at the expense of slower tracking of spectral changes in nonstationary signals. There is yet another method to assist interpretation of the power spectral density, called *windowing*, described in the next section.

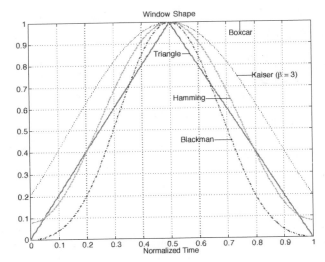

Figure 5: Window shapes in time domain

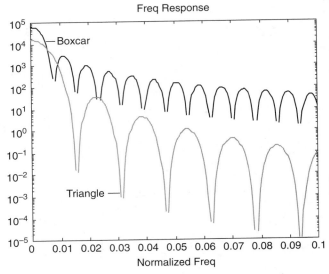

Figure 6: Window frequency response (boxcar, triangle)

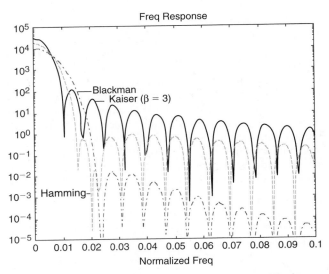

Figure 7: Window frequency response (Hamming, Blackman, Kaiser)

Data Block Windowing

Many windowing or envelope functions are employed to taper off the amplitude range of a signal frame buffer at its initial and final temporal domain values. Figures 3 and 4 used a boxcar window. In general, one can reduce spectral width of the main frequency lobe by choosing a window with a narrow central peak and rapid fall-off on either side. However, the windowed signal displays larger spectral leakage into sideband frequencies. Following from Figure 5, we see that Figures 6 and 7 indicate the main frequency lobe as the leftmost peak. The side lobes caused by leakage extend to the right. These observations follow directly from the "uncertainty principle" inequality outlined above. An "optimal" trade-off between main lobe resolution and side-lobe leakage can be achieved by using a Gaussian or bell-shaped window function that corresponds to exact equality in the "uncertainty principle" formula. In other words, the Fourier transform of a Gaussian curve also has a Gaussian shape. A Gaussian distribution for the random variable x, with mean $\langle x \rangle$, and standard deviation σ_x, is given by

$$g(x) = \frac{1}{\sqrt{2\pi}\sigma_x} e^{-(x-\langle x \rangle)^2/(2\sigma_x^2)}$$

However, the exponential function results in a costly calculation penalty so that similarly shaped approximations are used in practice. A linear triangular window, obtained by integrating (smoothing) a boxcar, still has an awkward cusp. Thus, one usually resorts to smoother, nonlinear window functions. Common functional shapes include truncated polynomial series for trigonometric functions (Hamming, Blackman) or Bessel functions (Kaiser). The Kaiser window can be adjusted to have a large central width (small b parameter) or a small central width (large b parameter). Figures 5, 6, and 7 illustrate the window shapes in the time domain and their corresponding frequency response (Krauss, Shure, and Little 1998). In all cases, one must trade off narrowness of a spectral peak against sideband ripple by adjusting the window shapes accordingly. Note also the potential for problematic spurs in the frequency domain in Figures 5, 6, and 7.

SIGNAL CODING

Some excellent sources for more detailed information on coding theory are MacKay (2002), Press et al. (1992), Reza (1994), Trappe and Washington (2002). Of course, there are many other good sources in books, articles, and on the Internet.

Most familiar data types contain a lot of redundant information. A simple example is written language. One can omit most vowels (but not consonants) of longer words in written language and still permit meaningful information transfer. For example, given the vowel-less text

Th qck brwn fx jmpd vr th lz dg

it is not difficult to determine that the original text was

The quick brown fox jumped over the lazy dog.

In musical chords, an analogous phenomenon occurs when a note or two are excised yet the human auditory perceptual process fills in the missing tones, especially a pleasant-sounding phantom fifth interval.

Depending on the structure of the data messages and contextual usage, one can apply a variety of coding techniques to reduce information entropy and necessary transmission bandwidth. It is clear that this goal is desirable to improve channel efficiency. In addition, it opens up headroom for additional "out of band" information that can be used for error detection or correction in noisy channels and control signals to be transmitted along with the message data information.

Error-detection techniques are usually varied according to the nature of the encoded signal. These methods are closely tied to various forms of error correction used in practice. One rather simple technique for mitigating errors is repetition of message packets, followed by majority logic processing. This is often called *message redundancy*. Another popular technique is retransmission via a handshake between sender and receiver. In this scenario, a second smaller code is encapsulated within the message packet to verify integrity. Common verification codes include parity bits, checksums, cyclic redundancy codes, and hash functions. All of these techniques have different trade-offs in efficiency and robustness. Extremely noisy channels obviously reduce effective transmission bandwidth dramatically, necessitating hardware upgrades or simultaneous transmission over multiple redundant pathways.

Real-Valued Scalar Signals

Most sensor data consist of real-valued quantities. However, this is not always the case, particularly in the case of digital radio frequency transmissions. Earlier we described a commonly used circular function representation for an analog signal using real-valued functions $a(t)$ for amplitude and $\phi(t)$ for phase, where $x(t) = a(t)e^{i\phi(t)}$ and $f(t) = \frac{1}{2\pi}\frac{d\phi(t)}{dt}$.

We can represent a noncomplex sinusoid simply by taking the real part, $\text{Re}(x(t))$. Conversely, one can convert a real-valued signal to an analytic complex-valued signal by using a Hilbert transform. The term *analytic* is used in the strict mathematical sense, as defined in the theory of complex-valued functions of complex variables. It is often more convenient to manipulate complex-valued functions (required to be analytic). This technique is introduced early in courses of study in analog electronics, optics, and so on. More information can be found in Frerking (1994); Krauss, Shure, and Little (1998); and Oppenheim, Schafer, and Buck (1999).

Modern digital hardware has become extremely computationally fast and inexpensive. Thus, nowadays specialized sensors bridge the domains between an analog signal source and a digital input to digital processors, both general and specialized in nature. Only a few decades ago, it was customary to perform computationally complex operations such as the FFT by utilizing specially fabricated piezoelectric quartz crystals, with nonlinear time delay, called *surface acoustic wave* (SAW) processors.

Most people nowadays, of course, focus attention on the digital data stream. Digital signal processing has become the dominant method because of many factors, including low cost, modularity, scalability, and reduced calibration and maintenance costs.

Real-valued signals possess a unique symmetry in their frequency domain representation. Recall that, given a continuous time-domain analog signal $x(t)$, one can convert it to its equivalent counterpart $X(f)$ in the frequency domain, and vice-versa, by means of a continuous Fourier transform pair. In the case of real-valued signals, $x^*(t) = x(t)$. Then, from the definition of the Fourier transform,

$$X(f) = \int\limits_{-\infty}^{+\infty} x(t)e^{+i2\pi ft}dt$$

we have

$$X^*(f) = \int\limits_{-\infty}^{+\infty} x^*(t)e^{-i2\pi ft}dt = \int\limits_{-\infty}^{+\infty} x(t)e^{+i2\pi(-f)t}dt = X(-f)$$

from which it easily follows that $X^*(+f) = X(-f)$. Of course, the same type of symmetry occurs for discretely sampled real-valued signals.

Complex-Valued Signals

As discussed above, mathematical operations on complex-valued signals tend to be more tractable. There are important cases where the complex-valued representation of signals are necessary. One example is a 120-V AC, 60-hz current in a power line that possesses both amplitude and phase. Another example is an optical signal, comprising coupled varying electric and magnetic fields. An optical signal possesses yet another important property—polarization—because a light quantum, or photon, has nonzero spin angular momentum ($s = 1\hbar$). A technical point is that a photon, being massless, travels at the speed of light. Thus, it possesses only two, rather than three, polarization states. Different representations for these two orthogonal polarization states commonly use either {vertical planar, horizontal planar} or {left circular, right circular}. We use the term *optical* broadly to cover the full range of the electromagnetic (EM) spectrum. EM signals commonly in use range from khz to Mhz to Ghz and beyond (e.g., high-energy gamma rays). Technically, the power line signal is merely an extremely low-frequency optical signal.

I/Q Representation of Signals

In many important situations it is necessary to use complex-valued signals whose real and imaginary parts do not obey the symmetries discussed earlier. In other words, $x^*(t) \neq x(t)$ and $X^*(+f) \neq X(-f)$. However, we usually want to enforce an analyticity condition on signals of interest. The analyticity condition imposes a causal behavior on such signals as well as enforcing more "well-behaved" mathematical properties. The analyticity condition can be enforced either by Hilbert transformer circuitry in the case of continuous domain signals or a digital Hilbert transform in the case of discretely sampled signals. For such signals in the time domain, the real part is commonly called "I," while the imaginary part is called "Q." These symbols were defined for historical reasons to specify the in-phase and quadrature components (the latter meaning 90 degrees out of phase). Much more information may be found in Frerking (1994).

There is a different kind of "symmetry" (perhaps better called "broken symmetry") for analytic complex-valued signals. For this kind of signal, one can choose between two different and distinct possible situations for the frequency domain representation: All negative frequency components are zero $X(-f) = 0$ or (exclusive *or*) all positive frequency components are zero $X(+f) = 0$. This condition is critically important for shifting signals up in frequency from baseband or shifting them down toward baseband. In other words, modulating or demodulating a carrier wave with the signal of interest does not incur a penalty of spectral reflections. One can also multiplex many band-limited signals onto a single higher-bandwidth communication channel.

To illustrate the importance of this type of signal (besides the case of cable TV), consider *magnetic resonance imaging* (MRI) diagnostic medical equipment. Magnetic Resonance Imaging is a less popularly frightening term than the underlying physics of *nuclear magnetic resonance* (NMR). Human bodies are mostly water, whose molecules consist of two hydrogen atoms and one oxygen atom. The nucleus of a hydrogen atom is a single proton, which possesses a nonzero spin angular momentum. Such objects in most cases rotate in the presence of an external magnetic field like a compass needle in the Earth's magnetic field. Furthermore, it is possible to alter the proton's precession by resonant absorption of an RF signal (Mhz range). One can detect the weak excitation and subsequent relaxation of the proton's precession to diagnose tumors and even monitor metabolic processes dynamically in real time on TV.

Digital Modulation Schemes

Several signal-modulation schemes are (perhaps) more complicated than either AM or FM. Here we consider two specific examples of digital modulation, namely, pulse code modulation and quadrature amplitude modulation.

Earlier we discussed (implicitly) *pulse code modulation* (PCM). This is simply the digital sampling and quantization of analog signal streams at regular intervals. When people "rip" audio tracks from CDs, they extract the digitized audio. However, the PCM stream is usually repackaged with wrappers into a segmented data structure. The resulting file has a different internal structure, depending on certain standards. The standards are provided mainly by the operating system vendor rather than by the actual software-ripping application. In the case of audio CDs, the PCM-modulated data consist of two interleaved

(stereo) streams. Each PCM stream is discretely sampled at a rate of 44.100 khz and a range of 16 bits. Thus, theoretically, the Nyquist frequency is 22.050 khz, and the dynamic range is 96 dB. Of course, the actual, as opposed to theoretical, bandwidth and dynamic range are somewhat smaller, depending on the instrumentation and recording equipment.

The theoretical bandwidth far exceeds the hearing range of most people, except perhaps for gifted children. An interesting consequence of the theoretical 96 dB dynamic range is that one often needs to keep turning the audio playback amplifier gain up (to hear the quieter sections) or down (to avoid ear damage). There is so much headroom, that many people reduce it by subsequently compressing it with perceptual filters. Of course, the other reason for compression is to reduce the file size by roughly a factor of ten.

Quadrature amplitude modulation (QAM) performs a mixture of two different signals 90 degrees out of phase. The term *quadrature* arises from the fact that the two signals are orthogonal. It is desirable, because it affords a minimal bandwidth over wires. By using a multisymbol constellation in the I/Q domain, the bandwidth requirement is reduced. Depending on the noise in the channel, one may need to employ a smaller number of symbols. This affords a smaller chance of intersymbol errors. QAM is used for encoding the two TV chroma signals. It was also used for transmitting data over 9600 bits per second (bps) telephone lines. More information can be found in Frerking (1994) and Krauss, Shure, and Little (1998). An example of a QAM constellation appears in Figure 8. In this case, each symbol is represented by four different values for both I and Q. This popular modulation scheme is called 16-QAM because it encodes sixteen distinct four-bit symbols.

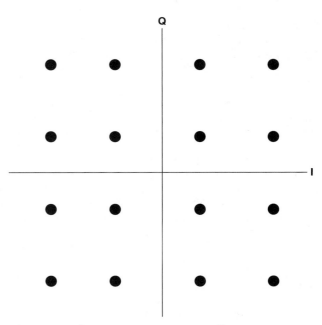

Figure 8: QAM (I/Q) constellation

Parity Bits

Parity bits constitute an extremely simple coding method. One merely adds all individual binary bits in a digital message packet using mod 2 arithmetic. This is equivalent to applying right or left shifts, masking off either the *least significant bit* (lsb) or the *most significant bit* (msb), and XOR ing the bit in an accumulator. This is a highly efficient calculation for digital processors. For example, a digital byte 10110011 yields a parity bit 1, while a byte with an even number of one bits yields a parity bit of 0. Sending a single parity bit per byte can detect a transmission error. However, it cannot perform correction because it is unclear which bit, including the parity bit, flipped during transmission. Sending more parity bits by breaking up the byte into overlapping fragments can offer more robust error correction but the overhead becomes quite large.

Checksums

A common checksum involves adding each *n*-word sequence into a one-word accumulator. This is attractive from both the standpoint of computational efficiency and small packet-size augmentation. It can determine fairly reliable occurrences of message packet corruption but offers little chance of error correction. Retransmission via handshake can recover a corrected message packet.

Hash Functions

Cryptographically secure hash functions are a type of checksum. Most hashes, like checksums, produce a result that has smaller measure than the message used as input to the hash function. This is a mapping from a larger space to a smaller space—that is, a many-to-one function. It is clear that many different messages can produce the same hash code, called a *collision*, as illustrated in Figure 9. However, good hash functions are designed so that it is computationally infeasible to find any two messages with the same hash value. Thus, it is common practice to transmit both a message and its hash to ensure that no transmission error or tampering has occurred in transit. Many software distributions employ this method, often using the hash function *message digest algorithm* 5 (MD5).

A collision was recently discovered for MD5, so it is now considered "broken." Another popular standard, the *secure hash algorithm* 1 (SHA-1), has also been broken recently. Although no SHA-1 collision has yet appeared (as of the time this chapter was written), it is clear that an actual collision will soon be found. More information can be found in Wang and Yu (2005).

A useful feature of hash functions is randomization as well as message-size reduction. In other words, the same message may be mapped to different hashes in a pseudo-random fashion by including a short random value known as a "salt."

All checksum techniques are able to detect certain types of random errors. In addition to the detection of random errors, cryptographic hash functions provide the ability to detect malicious tampering. In other words, for most checksum methods, an intelligent adversary can change a message in a way that a checksum remains valid. But if a cryptographically secure hash function is used, any change to the data will result in a different checksum.

Cyclic Redundancy Codes

Cyclic redundancy codes (CRCs) are designed to offer a degree of simple error correction as well as detection. However, because they are based on linear operations, the error-detection feature is vulnerable to spoofing by an adversary. A highly useful feature of CRCs is that their mathematical calculations can be implemented efficiently in digital hardware.

Cyclic codes (CC) are aptly named in the sense that any cyclic permutation of a member's elements yields another member of that code. Let element X_0 be a member of cyclic code C, $X_0 \in C$, $X_0 = (x_0, x_1, x_2, ..., x_n) \in C$, then also $X_2 \in C$, where $X_2 = (x_2, x_3, x_3, ..., x_n, x_0, x_1)$, and so forth for all cyclic permutations.

CRCs are a specific type of CCs. The most commonly used representation to implement a CRC employs fixed-length linear combinations of polynomial terms. Each term in the linear combination corresponds to an increasing power (by one integral unit). Given an element X of a code C, $X \in C$, we can realize its implementation by

$$X = \sum_{k=0}^{n-1} a_k z^k = a_0 z^0 + a_1 z^1 + \cdots + a_{n-1} z^{n-1}$$

The polynomials are defined over a finite field. Specifically, calculations employ modular arithmetic based on polynomial division. Usually, the coefficient for each polynomial term uses mod 2 arithmetic, being either 0 or 1. For more information, see Press et al. (1992), Stamp (2005), and Trappe and Washington (2002).

Gray Codes

Gray codes, named after Frank Gray, were designed at Bell Labs in the mid-twentieth century (Gray 1953). They helped mitigate the occasional large data errors caused by a single bit flip in a noisy channel. For instance, in ones-complement representation, a decimal 8 is represented as binary 1000, while flipping the msb yields binary 0000, which is equivalent to decimal 0. This is a shift of eight decimal units. The ones-complement representation

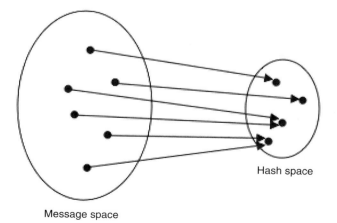

Figure 9: Hash collisions

increments the least significant bit by one bit, with a carry to the next most significant bit, as the decimal count increases by one. This is a natural coding technique because it maps our usual radix-10 integer counting system directly into the corresponding radix-2 integer counting system. In contrast, the Gray code sequence for decimal 0,1, …, 8, increases as 0000, 0001, 0011, 0010, 0110, 0111, 0101, 0100, 1100. Note that each successive term in the sequence differs by only a single bit with respect to its neighbors both left and right.

The pattern may seem peculiar at first, but there is an interesting underlying structure. In ones-complement representation, bit 0 has a cycle of one, bit 1 has a cycle of two, bit 2 has a cycle of four, and so forth. In the Gray code, bit 0 has a cycle of two, bit 1 has a cycle of four, bit 2 has a cycle of eight, and so forth. The Gray code can be implemented efficiently in digital hardware by using a recursive, reflection-about-the-midpoint algorithm. More details can be found in Frerking (1994), Press et al. (1992), and Trappe and Washington (2002).

Hamming Codes

Hamming Codes (Hamming 1980) were also designed at Bell Labs in the mid-twentieth century. There is some confusion, concerning prior art versus official publication, for a large number of clever coding techniques around this time. The major players, in alphabetic order, are Golay, Golomb, Gray, Hamming, Shannon, and unnamed others.

Hamming codes—more precisely, the Hamming [7,4] code—maps four input bits into a seven-bit output code word. The structure of this mapping is a linear transformation (nonsquare matrix), from a four-dimensional space to a seven-dimensional space. It is clear that the overhead involved nearly doubles the transmission bandwidth. However, the significant benefit is that this method can correct a single-bit error and detect a double-bit error. The method used to find the flipped bit is to apply a linear operator (nonsquare matrix), derived from the encoding matrix, to the received code word. If the three-bit result is (0,0,0), then no error occurred. If any result bit is nonzero, then one uses a lookup table (dictionary) to determine the flipped bit.

A four-bit message vector can be converted into a seven-bit Hamming codeword by multiplying (mod 2) on the right by the following matrix:

$$\begin{vmatrix} 1000110 \\ 0100101 \\ 0010011 \\ 0001111 \end{vmatrix}$$

Error detection and correction can be performed by multiplying (mod 2) the transmitted seven-bit code word on the right by another matrix:

$$\begin{vmatrix} 1 & 1 & 0 \\ 1 & 0 & 1 \\ 0 & 1 & 1 \\ 1 & 1 & 1 \\ 1 & 0 & 0 \\ 0 & 1 & 0 \\ 0 & 0 & 1 \end{vmatrix}$$

If the result is nonzero, then the flipped bit is given by the number of the correction matrix row that matches the 3-bit result. More details can be found in Trappe and Washington (2002).

DATA COMPRESSION
Signal Compression

It is usually desirable to remove redundant information from a signal by reducing its entropy. Furthermore, this is somewhat surprisingly most often realizable—within limits. It is useful to remove entropy from each specific signal according to its particular nature. The entropy of a particular kind of signal determines the degree of compressibility. If it is then needed to compensate for noisy channels, one can apply common, standardized, signal-independent methods to include required data-integrity checks transmitted along with the compressed signal packets. Compression algorithms may be either lossless or lossy. Lossy compression algorithms reduce entropy by removing information, which cannot later be restored. This feature is tolerated in many cases of interest when it is deemed that the excised information content is less important for the specific method of using the signal.

Arguably one of the earliest "modern" digital, lossless, compression algorithms is Morse code, a type of pulse-width modulation (see Figure 10). To spare human operators from digital carpal tunnel syndrome and improve the efficiency of transmitting coded messages over telegraph wires, a symbol table or dictionary was devised. This technology predated the invention of analog telephones. Of course, now we have come full circle and use digital telephony. In general terms, a *dictionary data structure* is a mapping between an input key and an output value. Morse code maps a letter of the printable alphabetical characters (ASCII codes 0×20 through 0×76) to a pulse-width pattern. It improves efficiency, at least to a first-order approximation, by using the smallest code for the most commonly used letter in the English language and, conversely, using a longer code for least probably used letters or other characters. This can be seen for the letters given in Figure 10.

Note that there must be a pause (greater than one long pulse width) between symbols transmitted to avoid confusion during decoding. Below we will examine ways of

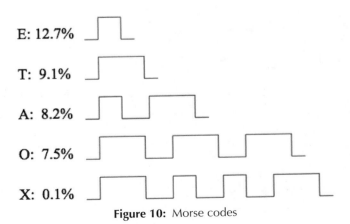

Figure 10: Morse codes

removing the long pause while retaining the unique decoding of the transmitted message.

Early in the twentieth century, telephone transmissions relied on analog basebanded AC signals with a bandwidth from a few decahertz to kilohertz. This has been dubbed plain old telephone system (POTS). An important feature of this system was the need for switching a dedicated channel to allow one or more ("party line") customers to tie up a circuit. This system morphed into the public telephone switched network (PTSN). During this time, the nature of the signals were analog on the transmitting and receiving end but converted into digital packets between switching centers. The first "crossbar switches" were literally bars of copper that were moved by electromagnetic relays with a deafening racket. Later, of course, solid state digital circuitry replaced the relay arrays. The digital channel supported a signal with a bandwidth of 64 kbits/sec.

An interesting type of signal compression used was named *compansion*. This is a nonlinear compression algorithm. In North America, the particular algorithm used is called μ-law. A similar algorithm called *A*-law is used in Europe. Because human auditory perception is inherently nonlinear, it was realized that digital channel bandwidth could be effectively reduced, with little noticeable degradation in perceived quality, by nonlinear compression at the transmitter, followed by the inverse nonlinear expansion at the receiver. Although this compression algorithm is invertible, it is (somewhat) lossy when applied to signals in the digital domain. One can discretely sample human speech using a twelve-bit nonlinear ADC, producing an eight-bit output word. Then one can compress and expand using the μ-law relations

$$y = f(x) = \text{sgn}(x)\frac{\ln(1 + \mu|x|)}{\ln(1 + \mu)}$$

and

$$x = f^{-1}(y) = \text{sgn}(y)\frac{1}{\mu}\left\{(1 + \mu)^{|y|} - 1\right\}$$

where $\mu = 255$, and the normalized signal lies within the range $-1 \le x, y \le +1$.

Huffman Codes

A Huffman code is a type of more complicated offspring, resulting from marriage between run-length encoding and the concept of Morse code. It is a lossless compression algorithm that uses a dictionary. Run-length encoding relies on multiple sequential occurrences of symbols. Instead of transmitting each symbol n times, it transmits a pair {symbol code, count}. Obviously, if multiple occurrences of each symbol are rare, then there may be expansion rather than compression. Run-length coding might be useful for sparse occurrences of symbols above a more prevalent and constant background field. Furthermore, run-length coding has no overhead resulting from output symbol delays. Morse code uses a single fixed-length symbol as input to its dictionary but achieves compression

efficiency by adjusting the dictionary according to the probability of occurrence of each key. Yet it suffers from output symbol delays.

A Huffman code employs a dictionary but constructs the keys as symbol groups. It also adjusts the dictionary structure so that more commonly occurring input symbol groups yield smaller output symbol sizes. There is no extra delay between transmission of output symbols. Usually, a Huffman algorithm first scans (possibly several times) a test signal stream segment so that it can build the weighted dictionary. Then the dictionary is subsequently used without further modification. Of course, if the input signal is quasi-stationary and has lower bandwidth than that of the digital processor implementing the Huffman coder, one could periodically rebuild the dictionary. In any case, the dictionary structure must be transmitted along with the output data stream to allow successful decoding at the receiver.

A Huffman dictionary is constructed by building a binary tree data structure, after scanning the test input data chunk, and storing probabilities of occurrence for successively more complicated symbol groups and stopping at some predetermined upper limit to the multisymbol group size. Next, it builds the dictionary binary tree by starting with the most complex (largest) multisymbol group, then keeps bifurcating as it successively prunes the size of multisymbol groups. As it bifurcates from the root of the tree, the least probable daughter symbol group, called a *terminal leaf node*, is assigned a 0 bit. The more probable daughter is awarded a 1 bit and allowed to continue to bifurcate.

Consider the following example, which is similar to the example discussed in Trappe and Washington (2002). Suppose we have four symbols—denoted A, B, C, and D—that occur with probabilities 0.5, 0.1, 0.3, and 0.1, respectively. We can construct the Huffman code as follows. First, the symbols are listed in descending probability. Because B and D are equally probable, these two symbols can be listed in either order. The procedure that follows is illustrated in Figure 11.

The actual codes are read from right to left in Figure 10 so that the code for A is 1, the code for C is 01, the code for B is 001, and the code for D is 000. More

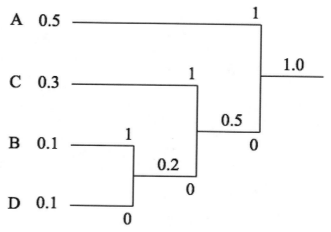

Figure 11: Huffman coding

information can be found in Press et al. (1992) and Trappe and Washington (2002).

JPEG Compression

JPEG is an acronym for Joint Photographic Experts Group. This committee produced a document that outlined specifications for lossy compression of single image frames. Specific implementation details were left open to designers as long as they complied with the standards. Nevertheless, a single, specific implementation structure quickly gelled and is in common usage.

The human visual system has some peculiarities, in that it perceives certain features of the visual field much better than other features. For instance, the human retina has far more sensors (rods), which perceive gray-scale levels, than it has color sensors (cones). Furthermore, the rods are more sensitive than the cones and are positioned more favorably in order to sample the incoming light. The JPEG algorithm allocates only half as many sampled bits to the red- and blue-like natures of the signal than it does to the gray-scale nature. This provides an immediate compression factor of 75 percent, at least for color images. This technique was discovered in the early part of the twentieth century and implemented in the unequal allocation of television bandwidth to color versus gray scale.

The eye is also more sensitive to low-scale frequencies than to high-scale frequencies. For instance, the eye better perceives the large rectangles of solid color of a Mondrian painting than it does the finely divided, alternating lines and spaces of a mesh screen. The space of scale frequency has two dimensions because it corresponds to the two-dimensional FFT (actually, discrete cosine transform, or DCT) of the two-dimensional light-intensity input. Fourier transforms of two-dimensional data frames are extremely costly in computational overhead. One must first transform each row and then again each column in turn. Without the speedup that the FFT provides, this would computationally cost $O(M^2N^2)$ for a frame with M rows by

N columns. Using FFT techniques, this can be reduced to $O(MN\log_2(M + N))$, a vast improvement.

In addition, a great deal of study has been undertaken to determine the most optimal type of transform to employ, specifically well tailored to human visual perception. Nominally, the best choice was a DCT. The cosine function is even under reflection about the abscissa origin. This property assists in smoothly matching interframe boundaries. The entire visual frame is subdivided into eight-by-eight pixel blocks. The DCT is applied independently to each block. Thus, because this is a boxcar window, there are noticeable "ringing artifacts" at block boundaries, especially at high compression ratios.

After the DCT has been applied, the resulting transform amplitudes are weighted such that low-scale frequencies receive higher weights, while high-scale frequencies receive lower weights. This is the how the main signal compression is done.

Finally, the compressed signal is Huffman coded, affording additional modest compression. More information can be found in Beauchamp (1984), Pennebaker and Mitchell (1992), and Pratt (2001).

Figure 12 illustrates typical compression (8×) and extremely tight compression (32×). Notice that the tightly compressed image has "blocky artifacts" near regions of sharply changing luminance.

MPEG

MPEG is an acronym for Motion Picture Experts Group. It is a committee for outlining specifications for streams of synchronization time codes, image frame components, and audio frames. The image frames, and audio frames, are separately compressed in a lossy fashion. The algorithms for video compression are quite different from the algorithms used to compress audio. However, both classes of algorithms exploit nuances of the human perceptual system. Specific implementation details are left open to designers, as long as they comply with the standards. Refer to the preceding section on JPEG compression for

Figure 12: JPEG compression; 8× (left), 32× (right)

more details concerning lossy compression of still image frames.

The MPEG standards are an extremely complicated and evolving hierarchy of modes. Major milestones in this hierarchy have been designated MPEG-1, MPEG-2, and MPEG-4. Note carefully that the numerical suffix does not in fact indicate improvements achieved during a historical timeline. Instead, each of these three standards regimes specifies general restrictions on bandwidth and classification of the compression algorithms. More information can be found in Mitchell et al. (1996) and Pratt (2001).

Text documents can usually be compressed, in a lossless fashion, by at least a factor of two, using variants of the commonly exploited ZIP/GZIP archival software. This class of software uses lossless compression algorithms, pioneered by Abraham Lempel, Jacob Ziv, and Terry Welch (LZW) in the early 1980s. Audio and video streams do not compress well using the LZW algorithms. Instead, newer classes of perceptual-based compression algorithms were developed.

In this chapter, we do not outline the rich history in the development of audio or video compression techniques. Before MPEG, midrange hardware modules and software applications assembled sequences of still frames. Each frame was processed using a variant of DCT/JPEG compression. This method was often labeled "motion JPEG." Each manufacturer developed proprietary, and mostly noninteroperable, methods and storage formats.

Unlike motion JPEG, MPEG video compression performs interframe tracking. This mechanism incorporates three types of image frames: I, P, and B. The intracoded frames are anchors, encoded by JPEG, without reference to other image frames. The *predictive* frames track changes between earlier I and P frames. The *bidirectionally predictive* frames track changes between earlier and upcoming I or P frames. The block-based *motion tracking* determines a group of most probable block motion vectors. In image regions where block tracking fails, the JPEG algorithm is used by default. The compression ratio is usually enhanced over that of motion JPEG at the cost of additional complexity in the algorithm.

OTHER TOPICS

Here we briefly mention two interesting alternative coding transforms. The first, the *Walsh transform*, is specially designed for processing digital pulse trains rather than sinusoids. The second, the *wavelet transform*, is a recursive, self-similar transform. It is specially designed for processing a signal type that lies between a pure time-domain representation, and a pure frequency-domain representation. Each transform type in turn is extremely powerful for manipulating its specialized signal representations. These representations may seem rare compared to the better-known sinusoids but have risen in importance in the past several decades.

Walsh Transforms

Most signals in the analog domain can be described efficiently by a truncated Fourier series with a finite number

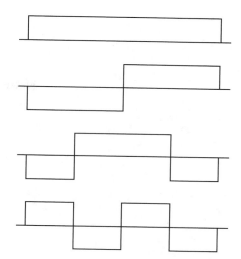

Figure 13: Walsh transform basis functions

of terms. For sequences of pulses (pulse trains) such as Morse-coded streams, the sharp discontinuities are not well represented by smoothly varying sinusoids. Thus, the Fourier transform of rectangular wave signals yields poor results. For somewhat similar reasons, a boxcar-windowed Fourier transform of a sinusoidal signal has certain issues because of the rectangular boxcar window. The Walsh transform domain is analogous to the frequency domain, except that its representation uses only two values for both input and output: -1, $+1$. The first four Walsh functions, ordered by increasing number of zero crossings, are illustrated in Figure 13.

Both Fourier transforms and Walsh transforms use particular complete sets of orthonormal basis functions. In the case of Fourier transforms, the basis functions are sinusoids. In the case of Walsh functions, the basis functions are rectangular waves of varying width and delay or phase. Both transforms are specific implementations of general abstract number-theoretic transforms. Another implementation, the Hadamard transform, has a domain similar to that of the Walsh domain but uses three values for both input and output: -1, 0, $+1$. In some abstract sense, one can think of the Walsh basis as measuring the position and direction of the zero crossings of the Hadamard basis. (This analogy cannot be stretched too far.) Walsh functions are also important in studying *sequency theory* for streams of two-valued numbers.

There are (at least) two main problems with generalized abstract number-theoretic transforms. First, the time and phase (sequency) ordering, and the corresponding transform indexing or duration and rate, are usually not as conceptually straightforward as in the case of the Fourier sinusoid bases. Second, the FFT calculation speedup from $O(N^2)$ to $O(N \log N)$ cannot usually be extended to the case of generalized abstract number-theoretic functions. In specific cases, it can be done, but the performance enhancement is not as significant as in the FFT case. There is, in fact, a fast Walsh transform (FWT), which is not as "fast" as the FFT, but is a significant step in that direction. More information concerning Walsh transforms and sequency theory can be found in Beauchamp (1984).

Figure 14: Wavelet compression; 8× (left), 32× (right)

Wavelet Transforms

In the case of Fourier transforms, the basis functions consist of orthonormal, complex-valued circular functions (sinusoids). These basis functions work well for smoothly varying signals but rather poorly for signals with sharp transitions such as pulse trains. One metric for "working well" often means that the signal can be approximated by truncating the linear series of weighted basis states, using fewer terms. A second important issue is the discrete sampling of continuously changing signals. This reduces the region of periodicity to a finite frequency interval with repeated, or aliased, copies. If the signal was not properly band-limited via filtering before sampling, then one suffers aliasing contamination. This is effectively a "feed-through" between successive band edges.

One can view the finite number of successive terms in the FFT, or DCT, as successive powers of a basis frequency, with different phase shifts. In an abstract sense, it is analogous to starting with one period of a sinusoid, followed by various stretchings (frequency changes), and translations (phase shifts). In the cases of the FFT or DCT, the complementary representations are the time domain versus the frequency domain. However, sometimes we would like to use some representation in between. In other words, we would sacrifice some time localization for better simultaneous frequency localization and conversely. The wavelet transforms provide just such a mixed worldview.

The wavelet transforms, pioneered by Ingrid Daubechies, start with an abstract base wavelet and then perform stretches and shifts on this base wavelet, summing all the (weighted) pieces. However, the input data stream must first be buffered into a large frame (such as an entire image frame) as opposed to smaller chunks (such as an eight-by-eight pixel subframe). Then that full frame buffer must be rescanned several times during the operation of the wavelet transform. More information can be found in Daubechies (1992), Meyer (1993), and Strang and Nguyen (1996).

Here we consider a specific application of wavelets, namely, still image frame compression, as in the JPEG-2000 specification. Even though it is now 2007, and wavelet compression methods have been in (limited) use since the early 1990s, JPEG-2000 remains largely unused. As one increases the usual JPEG compression factor to large values, one clearly notices the visually unpleasant artifacts near edges of rapid contrast change. An example is a light-colored garment in front of a dark background field. This is commonly observed in newspaper photos broadcast by satellite channels with limited bandwidth. In the case of wavelets, as the compression factor increases, instead of diffraction anomalies at edges, one notices instead a soft blurring of the resultant still image frame. More information can be found in Strang and Nguyen (1996).

Wavelet compression of still image frames uses other important features in addition to the wavelet bases. A popular implementation employs a pair of matched quadrature mirror filters using seven-tap and nine-tap FIR linear phase filters. Figure 14 illustrates modest compression (8×) and tight compression (32×). Notice that the tightly compressed image has blurred softly in contrast to the case of standard JPEG compression illustrated in Figure 12. The "blocky artifacts" have been smoothed out.

CONCLUSION

In this chapter, we first presented details regarding Shannon's theory. which formulates a concise methodology for describing the information content of data transferred between different locations. In particular, the theory considers characteristics of the communications channel, including data content, signal transducers, channel capacity, noise and error rate, and ultimately the integrity of data at the receiver. An important measure of the data is information redundancy. Shannon developed a metric for data redundancy, which he named *entropy*, and which is analogous to the concept in thermodynamics and statistical mechanics. The data transfer rate depends critically on channel capacity and integrity. Low channel capacity can be mitigated by careful removal of information redundancy—that is, by data compression. Conversely, noisy channels can be mitigated by increasing the size of the data by adding redundancy codes.

The rest of the chapter presented a brief introduction to digital signal processing, integrity of transferred data, and data compression. Digital coding and data transfer permit significant improvements over older analog technology. These improvements include enhanced data transfer reliability, lower overall cost, superiority in modular design and implementation, and more efficient use of available channel bandwidth.

The signal processing introduction comprised general and specific topics. We discussed digital sampling of signals and important methods to overcome some fundamental issues. The sampling rate is a crucial factor, which must be carefully matched to the bandwidth of the data. The data must first be prefiltered or oversampled to avoid corruption in the frequency domain. These considerations lead to techniques for expressing data content in the time and frequency domains. Mathematical methods for relating these two domains mainly use integral transforms in the analog regime, and their discrete expression in the digital regime. An important method uses the Fourier transform, which permits significant speed advantages because of work by Cooley, Tukey, and earlier researchers.

The rest of the article presents a brief introduction to several specialized topics, illustrating current techniques to enhance data transfer reliability and eliminate data redundancy.

GLOSSARY

Coding theory: The science of transmitting data over a channel in such a way that errors can be detected and, in some cases, automatically corrected at the receiving end. This is distinct from source coding, where the goal is to compress the data (see Huffman coding below).

Cyclic redundancy code (CRC): An error-detecting code that is computed by long division, with the remainder being the CRC value. These codes are particularly good at detecting burst errors.

Discrete cosine transform (DCT): A mathematical operator that transforms an image from the pixel amplitude space into the scale frequency space (and vice-versa), using a basis consisting of orthogonal cosine functions.

Entropy: In information theory, a measure of the amount of randomness or uncertainty. In communication systems, entropy is a fundamental concept related to error-correcting codes, data compression, and so on.

Fast Fourier transform (FFT): A recursive mathematical method that significantly speeds up a Fourier transform.

Fourier transform: A method for writing a function in terms of sinusoidal functions of various frequencies. The Fourier transform is used to convert between the *time domain* and *frequency domain* representations of a function.

Gray code: A method of listing binary *n*-tuples so that successive terms differ in exactly one bit position.

Hamming code: An error-correcting code that can detect all one- and two-bit errors and can correct all one-bit errors per block. A *block* consists of seven bits, where four bits are data.

Hash function: A function in which the output *summarizes* the input data. Typically, such functions compress an arbitrary size input to a fixed size output, with the output acting as a fingerprint of the data. One use for such functions is to detect errors in the input data by comparing the hash value to a previously computed hash value. Cryptographic hash functions are a special class of such functions that are resistant to intelligent attacks, as opposed to simply detecting random errors.

Huffman coding: A lossless form of data compression that uses probabilistic information about the data so that the more common symbols are represented with fewer bits than the less common symbols.

Information theory: The mathematical theory of communication founded by Claude Shannon in 1948.

JPEG: A lossy form of compressing images.

MPEG: A lossy compression method for video.

Nyquist rate: The minimum sampling rate that can be used so that the signal can be reconstructed from the samples. The Nyquist rate is twice the highest frequency that the signal contains.

Run length encoding (RLE): A simple *compression* method whereby a string of repeated symbols is replaced by one copy of the symbol and its run length. For example, AAAAAAAAAA could be replaced by 10 A. In many cases, this approach will greatly compress the data, but in some cases it can actually expand the data.

Walsh transform: A generalized Fourier transform that, like the Fourier transform, can be implemented efficiently.

Wavelet transform: A transform technique that is an alternative to the Fourier transform.

Windowing: A function that is zero outside of some "window" or range. When data are multiplied by such a function, they are then also zero outside of the window. Such a window can be used, for example, to restrict the Fourier transform to a particular time interval.

CROSS REFERENCES

See *Data Compression*; *Digital Transmission*; *Frequency and Phase Modulation*; *Sources of Errors, Prevention, Detection and Correction*.

REFERENCES

Aczel, A. D. 2003. *Entanglement: The unlikely story of how scientists, mathematicians, and philosophers proved Einstein's spookiest theory*. New York: Plume (Penguin Group USA).

Ash, R. B. 1990. *Information theory*. New York: Dover.

Aspect, P., Grangier, and G. Roger. 1982. Experimental Realization of Einstein-Podolsky-Rosen-Bohm Gedankenexperiment: A New Violation of Bell's Inequalities. *Physical Review Letters* 49, 91 (1982).

Beauchamp, K. 1984. *Applications of Walsh and related functions: With an introduction to sequency theory.* New York: Academic Press.

Bell, J. S. 1964. On the Einstein-Podolsky-Rosen paradox. *Physics*, 1: 195.

Brannon, B. 1995. *Overcoming converter nonlinearities with dither.* Analog Devices Application Note AN-410.

Cooley, J. W., and J. W. Tukey. 1965. An algorithm for the machine computation of complex Fourier series. *Mathematics of Computation*, 19: 297–301.

Cover, T. M., and J. A. Thomas. 1991. *Elements of information theory*: New York: John Wiley & Sons.

Daubechies, I. 1992. *Ten lectures on wavelets.* Philadelphia: Society for Industrial and Applied Mathematics.

Einstein, A., B. Podolsky, and N. Rosen. 1935. Can quantum-mechanical description of physical reality be considered complete? *Physical Review* 47: 777.

Frerking, M. 1994. *Digital signal processing in communications systems.* New York: Springer.

Gray, F. 1953. Pulse code modulation. U.S. patent no. 2,632,058.

Hamming, R. 1980. *Coding and information theory.* Upper Saddle River, NJ: Prentice-Hall.

Krauss, T. P., L. Shure, and J. N. Little. 1998. *Signal processing toolbox for use with MATLAB.* Natick, MA: The Math Works.

MacKay, D. J. C. 2002. *Information theory, inference & learning algorithms.* New York: Cambridge University Press.

Masta, B. 1999. Dither: Making a lemon into lemonade. Interstellar Research (available at www.daqarta.com/TM05.HTM).

Messiah, A. 2000. *Quantum mechanics.* Mineola, NY: Dover Publications.

Meyer, Y. 1993. Wavelets: *Algorithms and applications.* Translated by R. D. Ryan. Philadelphia: Society for Industrial and Applied Mathematics.

Mitchell, J. L., W. B. Pennebaker, C. E. Fogg, and D. J. LeGall. 1996. *MPEG video compression standard.* New York: Springer.

Oppenheim, A. V. 1978. *Applications of digital signal processing.* Upper Saddle River, NJ: Prentice Hall.

———, R. W. Schafer, and J. R. Buck. 1999. *Discrete-time signal processing.* Upper Saddle River, NJ: Prentice Hall.

Pennebaker, W. B., and J. L. Mitchell. 1992. *JPEG: Still image data compression standard.* New York: Springer.

Pratt, W. K. 2001. *Digital image processing.* New York: Wiley-Interscience.

Press, W. H., B. P. Flannery, S. A. Teukolsky, and W. T. Vetterling. 1992. *Numerical recipes in C: The art of scientific computing.* New York: Cambridge University Press.

Reid, C. E. and T. B. Passin. 1991. *Signal processing in C.* New York: John Wiley & Sons.

Reza, F. M. 1994. *An introduction to information theory.* Mineola, NY: Dover Publications.

Shannon, C. E. 1948. A mathematical theory of communication. *Bell System Technical Journal*, 27 (July and October): 379–423, 623–56 (available at http://cm.bell-labs.com/cm/ms/what/shannonday/shannon1948.pdf).

———. 1951. Prediction and entropy of printed English. *Bell System Technical Journal*, 30: 50–64.

Stamp, M. 2005. *Information security: Principles and practice.* New York: Wiley-Interscience.

Strang, G., and T. Nguyen. 1996. *Wavelets and filter banks.* Wellesley, MA: Wellesley College.

Tittel, W., et al. 1998. Violation of Bell inequalities by photons more than 10 km apart. *Physical Review Letters*, 81: 3563.

Trappe, W., and L. C. Washington. 2002. *Introduction to cryptography with coding theory.* Upper Saddle River, NJ: Prentice Hall.

Tribus, M., and E. C. McIrvine. 1971. Energy and information. *Scientific American*, 224 (September): 178–84. See also M. Tribus, *Some observations on systems, probability, entropy and management* (available at http://deming.ces.clemson.edu/den/sys_entropy.pdf).

Wang, W., and H. Yu. 2005. How to break MD5 and other hash functions. In *Advances in cryptology*, edited by Ronald Cramer, 19–35. From EUROCRYPT 2005, 24th Annual International Conference on the Theory and Applications of Cryptographic Techniques, Aarhus, Denmark, May 22–26.

Data Compression

Chang-Su Kim, *Korea University, Seoul,* and C.-C. Jay Kuo, *University of Southern California*

INTRODUCTION

Rapid advances in computing and communication technologies support lifestyles in the information age, which features an increasing demand for a wide range of multimedia services, including voice, audio, and video services. Multimedia data, however, require a huge amount of storage space or high transmission bandwidth. There are two approaches to support multimedia services. One increases the capacity of storage devices and transmission channels, and the other compresses data compactly, thereby exploiting existing system capacity. System capacity has increased continuously, but the need for more storage space and higher bandwidth is increasing at an even faster pace. Moreover, new types of multimedia data are emerging. Therefore, extensive efforts have been made to develop data compression techniques to use limited storage space and bandwidth effectively.

Data compression is ubiquitous in our daily lives, and its application list is extensive. For example, it would take a much longer time to browse Web sites on the Internet that contain audiovisual information if there were no data compression techniques. Data compression enables us to send photographs or music files efficiently via e-mail. Also, digital TV broadcasting, real-time video streaming, and the storage of high-quality video on digital versatile disc (DVD) are possible because of video compression technology, which compresses a huge amount of video data efficiently. Recently, mobile communications have become popular, and there is an explosive demand for mobile multimedia services such as wireless Internet, mobile commerce (m-commerce), and game services. Data compression is one of the key technologies that enable the transmission of multimedia data as well as voice over bandwidth-limited wireless channels.

Data compression can be classified into two categories (Witten, Moffat, and Bell 1999): lossless and lossy techniques. In *lossless compression,* an encoder compresses the source data in such a way that the decoder can reconstruct the original data exactly from the compressed data. The lossless property is essential in some applications, such as the compression of texts, medical imaging, and satellite imaging for remote sensing, where even small changes in data may lead to undesirable results. Also, lossless compression techniques are used to archive numerous types of data without loss of information.

In contrast, *lossy compression* attempts to achieve better compression by allowing loss of information during the compression procedure. There is a trade-off between the accuracy of reconstructed data and the compression performance. Audio and video data are usually compressed in a lossy way because the human perceptual system can tolerate a modest loss of audiovisual information. Moreover, audio and video data require much larger storage spaces than text. For example, consider a video clip with a frame rate of 15 frames/sec. If each frame consists of 176×144 pixels and the color information of each pixel is represented with 24 bits, then the video clip requires the transmission bandwidth of about 9 Mbps. Suppose we want to transmit the clip over a 56-Kbps modem. The compression performance is often measured by the compression ratio, defined by

$$\text{Orignal data size/Compressed data size}$$

In this case, we need a very high compression ratio, approximately 160 (= 9 Mbps/56 Kbps), and thus it is reasonable to select lossy compression techniques.

In 1948, Shannon established the field of information theory (Shannon 1948), which measures the amount of information in data quantitatively. Since the late 1960s, the subject of data compression has undergone extensive study, and numerous concepts and algorithms have been developed. In this chapter, we survey lossless and lossy compression techniques and exemplify their application areas.

LOSSLESS COMPRESSION

In lossless compression, an exact duplicate of the original data can be reproduced after the compression and decompression procedures. We introduce several concepts and tools for lossless compression in this section.

Table 1: Examples of Codes

Symbol	Probability	Code 1	Code 2	Code 3	Code 4
A	0.5	0	0	0	11
B	0.25	1	10	01	0
C	0.25	10	11	11	10
Average length		1.25	1.5	1.5	1.75

Examples of Codes

In most digital computers, data are represented by binary numbers. Also, data are converted into binary numbers before transmission over digital communication channels. Data *compression* or *coding* refers to the mechanism of assigning binary strings to samples of a data source in a compact way. The set of binary strings is called a *code*, and each string is called a *code word*.

Suppose that a communication system transmits a sequence of symbols (or samples) selected from an alphabet {*A,B,C*} and that the probabilities of the symbols are given by

$$p(A) = 0.5, p(B) = 0.25, p(C) = 0.25 \qquad (1)$$

Table 1 shows four codes for this alphabet. The average length of a code is defined by

$$L = p(A)l(A) + p(B)l(B) + p(C)l(C)$$

where $l(A)$, $l(B)$, and $l(C)$ are the numbers of bits assigned to symbols A, B, and C, respectively. Code 1 seems to be most efficient because it requires the least number of bits to transmit each sample on the average, but it cannot be used in communication systems because more than two sequences of samples can yield the same binary sequence. Let us assume that the decoder receives the binary sequence 10. Both C and BA are encoded into the same sequence 10. Therefore, the decoder cannot determine whether it is generated by C or BA. To avoid this ambiguity, a code should be uniquely decodable—that is, every distinct sequence of samples should be mapped into a different binary sequence.

Code 2 is a uniquely decodable code. A code is called a *prefix code* if no code word is a prefix of any other code word. Therefore, code 2 is also a prefix code. Figure 1(a) is the tree representation of code 2. Each code word is a

leaf node, because code 2 is a prefix code. Therefore, every binary sequence can be deciphered without ambiguity by traversing the tree. Let us decode 01110. Starting from the *root node*, the decoder traverses to the left child if the input bit is 0 and to the right child otherwise. When the decoder meets a leaf node, it outputs the corresponding symbol and starts again from the root node. Thus, 01110 can be deciphered into 0 11 10 = ACB. Note that every prefix code is a uniquely decodable code, and each code word in a prefix code can be decoded instantaneously without reference to future code words.

However, not every uniquely decodable code is a prefix code. Code 3 is a uniquely decodable code but not a prefix code. Figure 1(b) shows its tree representation. The code word for A lies on the path from the root node to the code word for B, because 0 is a prefix of 01. Therefore, when the decoder meets 0, it needs to check future bits to properly decode symbols. When 0 is followed by an even number of 1's, it is decoded into A. Otherwise, it is decoded into B. For example, 011110111 is decoded into 0 11 11 01 11 = $ACCBC$. In the worst case that a binary sequence is a concatenation of a single 0 and an infinite number of 1's, the code 3 decoder need check infinitely many future bits to decode the first sample. The decoding of a nonprefix code hence may incur an unbounded delay and is more complex than that of a prefix code.

The goal of code design is to find an optimal uniquely decodable code that provides the minimum average length. It can be shown (Cover and Thomas 1991) that the minimum average length can be achieved also by a prefix code. Therefore, we can restrict our attention only to the set of prefix codes, which are instantaneously decodable. Code 2 actually achieves the minimum average length. Code 4 is also a prefix code, but less efficient than code 2. It assigns a longer code word to the symbol A than the symbol B, although A is more probable than B. It is readily seen that an efficient code should assign longer code words to less probable symbols.

Entropy

In 1948, Shannon published "A Mathematical Theory of Communication," which founded the field of information theory. He developed a set of concepts that are necessary to understand the process of communication quantitatively. One concept is *entropy*, which measures the amount of information or uncertainty in a data source. More specifically, the entropy of a data source is the number of bits required on the average to describe a sample of the data source. The entropy depends only on the probability

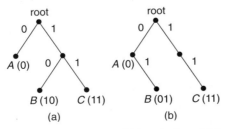

Figure 1: Tree representations of (a) code 2 and (b) code 3 in Table

distribution of symbols and has nothing to do with what the data represent.

As mentioned previously, an efficient code should assign longer code words to less probable symbols. Thus, the information or uncertainty of a symbol should be defined to be inversely proportional to its probability p. To find an adequate inversely proportional function, let us consider an alphabet that consists of sixteen equiprobable symbols. Because the symbols have the same probability (1/16), they should be assigned code words of the same length. Obviously, the optimal code consists of the four-bit binary representations of decimal numbers 0–15:

$$0000\ 0001\ 0010\ 0011\ 0100\ 0101\ 0110\ 0111$$
$$1000\ 1001\ 1010\ 1011\ 1100\ 1101\ 1110\ 1111$$

Hence, a symbol of probability 1/16 has four-bit uncertainty. Similarly, considering an alphabet that consists of 2^n equiprobable symbols, it can be seen that a symbol of probability $1/2^n$ has n-bit uncertainty. In general, a symbol of probability p has $\log_2 (1/p)$-bit uncertainty. Note that $\log_2(1/(1/2_n)) = \log_2 2^n = n$.

Consider a random data source X consisting of n symbols, which have probabilities $p_1, p_2, ..., p_n$. The entropy $H(X)$ of the data source is the average uncertainty of the symbols and thus given by

$$H(X) = \sum_{i=1}^{n} p_i \log_2 \frac{1}{p_i} \qquad (2)$$

This derivation of entropy is oversimplified. The entropy can be derived rigorously from three axioms (Shannon 1948). Moreover, the entropy has the profound meaning that at least $H(X)$ bits/sample are required to encode a data source X losslessly, no matter what compression scheme is employed. In other words, $H(X)$ is the fundamental lower bound for the average length that a code can achieve. For example, the entropy of the alphabet in Table 1 is

$$0.5 \log_2 \frac{1}{0.5} + 0.25 \log_2 \frac{1}{0.25} + 0.25 \log_2 \frac{1}{0.25} = 1.5$$

Therefore, no code can achieve less than 1.5 bits/sample on the average, which is the average length of code 2 in Table 1.

Huffman Coding

Huffman coding constructs an optimal prefix code that provides the minimum average length (Huffman 1952). It is based on the observation that the optimal code should allocate longer code words to less probable symbols. Let us consider a random data source with n symbols. Without loss of generality, we assume that

$$p_1 \leq p_2 \leq ... \leq p_{n-1} \leq p_n$$

where p_i denotes the probability of the ith symbol. Then the code word lengths should satisfy

$$l_1 \geq l_2 \geq ... \geq l_{n-1} \geq l_n$$

Probability	Huffman Tree	Codeword
0.45		0
0.25		10
0.1		1100
0.1		1101
0.08		1110
0.02		1111

Figure 2: Construction of a Huffman code

where l_i is the code word length of the ith symbol. Note that if $l_1 > l_2$, then the last $(l_1 - l_2)$ bits of the longest code word can be trimmed without violating the prefix condition. In other words, the code is not optimal. Hence, l_1 should be equal to l_2. Moreover, the optimal code can be designed such that the two longest code words should differ only in the last bit.

As shown in Figure 1(a), a prefix code can be represented by a binary tree. The above observations mean that the two least probable symbols should correspond to the two deepest nodes in the tree, and the two nodes should be siblings. Therefore, we can construct the optimal tree using a bottom-up method. Figure 2 illustrates how to construct a Huffman code. First, we merge two least probable symbols, while assigning 0 and 1 to the last bits of the corresponding code words. The merged node is treated as a new symbol with the probability 0.1, which is the sum of the two child node probabilities. Second, we find again two least probable symbols. There are three symbols with the probability 0.1 at this stage. We arbitrarily merge two symbols among the three symbols into a new symbol and assign the probability 0.2 to the merged symbol. Proceeding in this way, we can merge all nodes into the root node. Then the original symbols are assigned the code words, which are the top-down concatenations of branch bits.

It can be shown (Cover and Thomas 1991, Chapter 5) that the average length $L(X)$ of the Huffman code for a random data source X satisfies

$$H(X) = L(X) < H(X) + 1 \qquad (3)$$

For example, the entropy of the probability distribution in Figure 2 is 2.0872, whereas the Huffman code achieves the average length 2.15. $L(X) = H(X)$ if and only if the probability of each symbol is dyadic—that is, equal to 2^{-k} for some non-negative integer k.

The upper bound in equation 3 indicates that the Huffman coding scheme introduces at most one bit of over-head as compared to the entropy. This overhead may cause a problem in some situations. Suppose that a communication system transmits samples selected from an alphabet [A,B], and $p(A) = 0.99$ and $p(B) = 0.01$. The entropy of the alphabet is 0.0808. But, as shown in $p(A)$ in the left column of Table 2, the Huffman code requires 1 bit/sample on the average, which is approximately twelve times higher than the entropy. We can reduce the overhead by encoding n consecutive samples simultaneously. In the middle column of Table 2, two consecutive samples are grouped into a block, and the Huffman code is constructed for the set of possible blocks. The Huffman code introduces at most 1 bit overhead per block, hence

Table 2: Huffman Coding of Grouped Samples

No grouping			Grouping of 2 samples			Grouping of 3 samples		
Symbol	Probability	Code	Block	Probability	Code	Block	Probability	Code
A	0.99	0	AA	0.9801	0	AAA	0.970299	0
B	0.01	1	AB	0.0099	10	AAB	0.009801	100
			BA	0.0099	110	ABA	0.009801	101
			BB	0.0001	111	ABB	0.000099	11100
						BAA	0.009801	110
						BAB	0.000099	11101
						BBA	0.000099	11110
						BBB	0.000001	11111
Average bits/sample = 1			Average bits/block = 1.0299			Average bits/block = 1.06		
			Average bits/sample = 0.515			Average bits/sample = 0.3533		

at most 1/2 bit overhead per sample. In general, if we design the Huffman code for n-sample blocks, it incurs only $1/n$ bit overhead per sample. Therefore, by increasing n, we can achieve an average bits/sample arbitrarily close to the entropy, which is the theoretical lower bound.

Arithmetic Coding

Huffman coding may require the grouping of more and more samples to achieve an average bits/sample that is arbitrarily close to the entropy. However, the grouping of samples introduces transmission delay and requires a higher computational load and a larger storage space for the code word table. Arithmetic coding is an alternative coding scheme that provides a near-optimal compression performance without requiring the grouping of samples. It treats a whole sequence of samples, called a *message*, as a single unit, but can be implemented to generate output code words incrementally as samples arrive (Bell, Cleary, and Witten 1990).

In arithmetic coding, a message is mapped to an interval of real numbers between 0 and 1. The interval length is proportional to the probability of the message, and any number in the interval can be used to represent the message. Less probable messages yield longer sequences of bits, while more probable messages yield shorter sequences.

For example, suppose that the alphabet is [A, B, C], and the symbol probabilities are $p(A) = 0.6$, $p(A) = 0.3$, and $p(C) = 0.1$. In Figure 3, the messages starting with A, B, and C are respectively mapped to the half-open intervals [0, 0.6), [0.6, 0.9), and [0.9, 1), according to their probabilities. Let us encode a message BCA. Because it starts with B, it is first mapped to the interval [0.6, 0.9). Then the interval is divided into three subintervals—[0.6, 0.78), [0.78, 0.87), and [0.87, 0.9)—that correspond to the messages starting with BA, BB, and BC, respectively. Note that the length ratio of the subintervals is set to

$$0.18 : 0.09 : 0.03 = 6 : 3 : 1 = p(A) : p(B) : p(C)$$

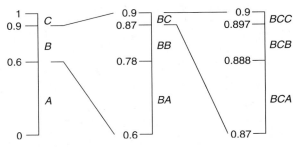

Figure 3: Illustration of arithmetic coding

and 0.18, 0.09, and 0.03 are the probabilities of the messages starting with BA, BB, and BC, respectively. Similarly, [0.87, 0.9) is further divided into three subintervals, and the messages starting with BCA are mapped to [0.87, 0.888).

The two end points can be written in binary numbers as

$$0.87 = \frac{1}{2} + \frac{1}{2^2} + \frac{1}{2^4} + \frac{1}{2^5} + \cdots = 0.11011\cdots$$

$$0.888 = \frac{1}{2} + \frac{1}{2^2} + \frac{1}{2^3} + \frac{1}{2^7} + \cdots = 0.11100\cdots$$

The prefix "0." can be omitted because every number within the unit interval [0, 1) is less than 1. Therefore, the interval [0.87, 0.888) can be represented in the binary form [11011..., 11100...). The encoder can transmit an arbitrary number within this interval to specify that the message starts with BCA. For example, it can transmit the sequence of three bits, 111, which corresponds to 0.875 in decimal. Then the decoder can follow the same division procedure in Figure 3 and know that 0.875 lies within the interval [0.87, 0.888), hence the message starts with BCA.

However, the decoder cannot determine when the message ends. Because 0.875 lies also within the interval [0.87, 0.8808) that corresponds to the set of messages starting with *BCAA*, it can also represent the message *BCAA*. To make the arithmetic code uniquely decodable, we can add a special symbol to the alphabet that indicates the termination of a message. If the special symbol is assigned a small probability and a message is long, then the addition of the special symbol leads to only a minor degradation in the compression performance.

Arithmetic coding is superior to Huffman coding in many respects. It can achieve a near-optimal performance without grouping samples. Also, it can be easily used in an adaptive way. In some applications, the probability distribution of alphabets cannot be predetermined and should be trained and updated based on the statistics of the data stream itself. To be adaptive to the change in the probability distribution, Huffman coding should regenerate the code word table (Gallager 1978), which is computationally inefficient. In contrast, arithmetic coding can adjust itself to the updated probability distribution simply by changing the lengths of intervals in the division procedure.

Dictionary Coding

Both Huffman coding and arithmetic coding assume that a data source generates a sequence of independent samples and do not consider the dependence between samples. However, samples are dependent on one another in many data sources. For example, consider the following words from a text source:

Inte*net, com*ter, n*two*ks, d*ta, compre*sion

where * denotes a missing letter. We can reasonably recover the words as

Internet, computer, networks, data, compression

based on our knowledge of frequently used words. In other words, the missing letters can be retrieved by exploiting the dependence between letters—that is, by the context.

Dictionary coding achieves data compression by replacing blocks of consecutive samples with indices into a dictionary (Bell, Cleary, and Witten 1990, Chapter 8). The dictionary should be designed to contain symbol blocks that are frequently used. If sufficient prior knowledge of a particular data source is unavailable, then the dictionary can be built adaptively from the source itself. Many adaptive dictionary coding schemes are modifications of one of two approaches, *Lempel-Ziv coding 1977* (LZ77) and *Lempel-Ziv coding 1978* (LZ78) (Ziv and Lempel 1977, 1998). Popular file compression tools such as ZIP and ARJ are variations of LZ77. LZW is one of the most popular modifications of LZ78 and is used in the UNIX command "compress," the V.42 bis standard for data compression over modem, and the *graphics interchange format* (GIF) for compressing graphical images.

Let us describe the encoding and decoding procedures of LZW. The encoder parses an input sequence into nonoverlapping symbol blocks in a dictionary and represents each block with its index to the dictionary. The blocks in the dictionary are also referred to as the *words*. The

Table 3: Dictionary Construction in LZW Coding with Input Sequence *ABABABBBBA*

Index	Dictionary	Comment
1	*A*	initial
2	*B*	dictionary
3	*AB*	(A) + B
4	*BA*	(B) + A
5	*ABA*	(AB) + A
6	*ABB*	(AB) + B
7	*BB*	(B) + B
8	*BBA*	(BB) + B

dictionary is initialized with the single symbols in the alphabet and grows during the encoding. Suppose that the alphabet is {*A,B*}, and an input sequence is given by

ABABABBBBA

The encoder first parses the longest word in the dictionary from the input sequence. As shown in Table 3, the initial dictionary contains two words, *A* and *B*. Thus, the longest word is *A* and is represented by the index 1. Then it is concatenated with the next sample *B* to form a new word *AB* in the dictionary. Similarly, the next longest word *B* is represented by the index 2, and is concatenated to the next sample *A* to form a new word *BA*. In this way, the input sequence can be parsed into

$$(A)_{AB}(B)_{BA}(AB)_{ABA}(AB)_{ABB}(B)_{BB}(BB)_{BBA}(A) \qquad (4)$$

where the parsed words are enclosed in parentheses, and the newly formed words in the dictionary are written as subscripts. Consequently, the input is represented by the index sequence of strings in parentheses in equation 4:

$$1\ 2\ 3\ 3\ 2\ 7\ 1$$

The decoder can reconstruct the input sequence from the index sequence by emulating the behavior of the encoder. It also starts with the initial dictionary, consisting of two words, *A* and *B*. Thus, the first index 1 is decoded into *A*, which should be concatenated to the next sample to form a new word in the dictionary. Thus, the decoder looks ahead at the next index 2 that corresponds to a word *B*, and inserts the new word *AB* into the dictionary. Similarly, the decoder reconstructs a word *B* from the second index 2, looks ahead at the next index 3 to find out that the next sample is *A* and inserts a new word *BA* into the dictionary.

Proceeding in this way, the third and fourth indices 3 are decoded into *AB*, respectively, and two new words, *ABA* and *ABB*, are inserted into the dictionary. Then the decoder reconstructs the word *B* from the fifth index 2. The next step is to look ahead at the next index 7 to find out the next sample, denoted by *, and concatenate B and * to construct a new word *B** in the dictionary. This requires caution. Note that the index 7 cannot be directly parsed into a word because the dictionary contains only six words and the seventh word is being constructed at this stage. However, we know that the seventh word starts with *B*, thus the next sample * is *B*. Therefore, the seventh word in the dictionary is *BB*, and the decoder can continue.

Adaptive dictionary coding can be used to compress all types of data, thus being classified as a universal coding scheme. However, care should be taken with its use. It can compress a data source effectively, provided that the source generates frequently recurring patterns or groups of samples. Text data provide a good example. In contrast, dictionary coding is not the most efficient way to compress natural image data, speech, and so on that contain relatively few repetitive patterns. These data can be more effectively compressed by employing other approaches that are described later.

Run-Length Coding

Run-length coding (Jayant and Noll 1984, Chapter 10) is suitable for compressing data that contain large segments of constant sample values. It replaces a sequence of samples by a sequence of pairs, $\{(s_k, r_k)\}$, representing sample values s_k's and run lengths r_k's. For example, suppose that an input sequence is given by

$$AAAABBCCCBBBBBB$$

It starts with a run of *A*'s with length 4, followed by a run of *B*'s with length 2. Thus, the first pair is (*A*,4) and the second pair is (*B*,2). Thus, the input sequence is converted into

$$(A,4),(B,2),(C,3),(B,6)$$

The sequence of pairs $\{(s_k, r_k)\}$ is usually encoded using the Huffman coding technique.

Run-length coding can effectively compress binary and facsimile images that contain long runs of black (0) and white (1) pixels. Because white and black runs alternate, the colors (or sample values) of runs need not be encoded. To avoid the ambiguity, the color of the first run is assumed to be white, and the white run of length 0 is encoded if the sequence starts with a black pixel. For example, a sequence of pixels

$$000111110111001$$

is converted into a sequence of run lengths

$$0, 3, 5, 1, 3, 2, 1$$

The decoder can know from the first run length 0 that the sequence starts with a black pixel and interpret the following numbers as the lengths of black and white runs alternately.

LOSSY COMPRESSION

Lossless compression schemes can encode data sources with discrete alphabets only. However, many data sources are analog; that is, their symbols may have arbitrary values from a continuous range of amplitudes.

The lossless description of a continuous sample requires an infinite number of bits. Thus, a finite representation of a continuous sample inevitably incurs some loss of precision; this is called the *quantization error*. Moreover, even if a data source has a discrete alphabet, lossy compression techniques can describe a discrete sample more compactly by allowing some distortion.

In rate-distortion theory (Cover and Thomas 1991, Chapter 13), it was shown theoretically that there is a trade-off relation between the bit rate (in bits/sample) and the distortion. As more distortion is allowed, data can be compressed more compactly. The goal of lossy compression techniques is to minimize the distortion subject to a given bit-rate requirement or, equivalently, to achieve the lowest bit rate subject to a given distortion requirement.

A measure of distortion should be defined in lossy compression techniques. The most common measure is the squared error, defined by

$$d(x, \tilde{x}) = (x - \tilde{x})^2$$

where x is the original sample and $\tilde{x}$ is the reconstructed sample. Also, the mean squared error between two vectors $\mathbf{x} = (x_1, x_2, ..., x_n)$ and $\tilde{\mathbf{x}} = (\tilde{x}_1, \tilde{x}_2, ..., \tilde{x}_n)$ is defined by

$$d(\mathbf{x}, \tilde{\mathbf{x}}) = \frac{1}{n} \sum_{i=1}^{n} (x_i - \tilde{x}_i)^2$$

The squared error distortion is simple to use and has the intuitive meaning that it measures the power of the error signal. Thus, it is used in this section to evaluate the performances of lossy compression techniques.

Scalar Quantization

Quantization is the process of representing a large or infinite set of values with a smaller set (Gersho and Gray 1991, Part II). In scalar quantization, the input and output sets are composed of scalar values. An N-point scalar quantizer partitions the real line into N cells $R_i = \{r : x_{i-1} < r \le x_i\}$ for $i = 1, 2, ..., N$, and maps input values within a cell R_i to an output point y_i. Suppose that we have a data source modeled by a random variable X with *probability density function* (Pdf) $f_X(x)$. Then, the quantizer yields the average distortion or the mean squared error given by

$$D = \int_{-\infty}^{\infty} (x - Q(x))^2 f_X(x)dx$$
$$= \sum_{i=1}^{N} \int_{R_i} (x - y_i)^2 f_X(x)dx$$

where Q denotes the quantizer mapping. Because the quantizer has N output points, each output point can be represented with $\lceil \log_2 N \rceil$ bits, where $\lceil a \rceil$ denotes the smallest integer greater than or equal to a. In other words, the bit rate of the quantizer is given by

$$R = \lceil \log_2 N \rceil \text{ (bits/sample)}$$

when fixed-length code words are used to encode the output indices.

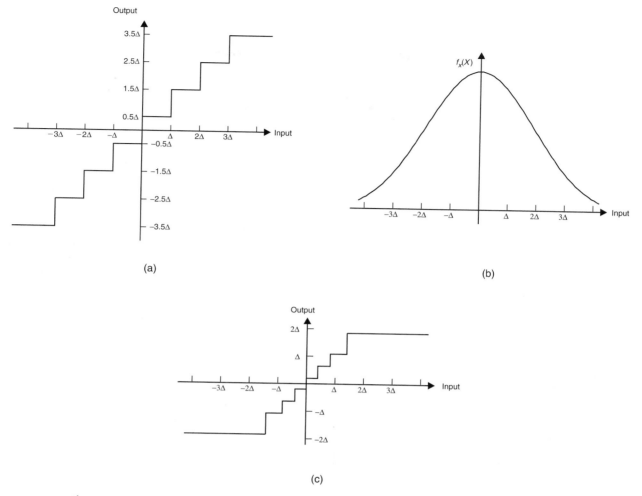

Figure 4: (a) uniform quantizer, (b) Pdf of a random variable, and (c) Lloyd quantizer for Pdf in (b)

For example, Figure 4(a) shows the input-output graph of an eight-point quantizer whose mapping, Q, is given by

$$y = Q(x) = \begin{cases} 3.5\Delta & \text{if } x > 3\Delta, \\ 0.5(2n-1)\Delta & \text{if } (n-1)\Delta < x \leq n\Delta \\ & (n = -2, -1, \ldots, 3) \\ -3.5\Delta & \text{if } x \leq -3\Delta. \end{cases}$$

Except for the two outermost cells, every cell has the same length Δ. Thus, it is called a *uniform quantizer*. The bit rate is 3 bits/sample when fixed-length code words are employed, because the quantizer has eight output points. However, output points can be described more compactly because they do not have the same probability. Suppose that a random variable X has a Pdf $f_X(x)$ shown in Figure 4(b). The probability P_i of the ith output point is given by

$$P_i = \int_{R_i} f_X(x)dx \quad (1 \leq i \leq 8)$$

Note that the fourth and fifth output points have higher probabilities than other points. Therefore, entropy coding

schemes such as Huffman coding and arithmetic coding can achieve a higher compression ratio than fixed-length coding by exploiting the nonuniform probability distribution of the output indices.

In practice, for a random variable with a Pdf such as the one shown in Figure 4(b), the uniform quantizer is not the optimal eight-point quantizer that yields the lowest average distortion. Notice that a quantizer can reduce the average distortion by approximating the input more precisely in regions of higher probability. The optimal quantizer should make cell sizes smaller in regions of higher probability.

The Lloyd algorithm (Lloyd 1982) is an iterative method that finds a locally optimal quantizer for a given Pdf, which is based on two sufficient conditions for the optimal quantizer. First, an output point y_i should be the centroid of the corresponding cell R_i,

$$y_i = \frac{\int_{R_i} xf_X(x)dx}{\int_{R_i} f_X(x)dx} \quad (5)$$

Second, a cell boundary point x_i should be the midpoint between two adjacent output points,

$$x_i = \frac{y_i + y_{i+1}}{2} \qquad (6)$$

The Lloyd algorithm first determines output points by equation 5 after fixing boundary points. These output points are then used to select boundary points by equation 6. These two steps are repeatedly applied until the change between the obtained average distortions becomes negligible. Because each step reduces the average distortion, the Lloyd algorithm always converges to a locally optimal quantizer. Figure 4(c) shows the Lloyd quantizer for the Pdf in Figure 4(b). Note that the Lloyd algorithm assigns smaller cell sizes around the origin to approximate regions of a higher probability more accurately.

Vector Quantization

As shown in Table 2, the overhead of Huffman coding can be reduced by grouping samples together and encoding them as a single block. Moreover, as in dictionary coding, the grouping makes it easy for the encoder to exploit possible dependencies between samples. Vector quantization is the generalization of scalar quantization that quantizes a block of scalar samples jointly.

Figure 5 illustrates a two-dimensional vector quantizer that partitions a unit square $[0,1] \times [0,1]$ into seven cells. The black dot in a cell depicts the output point of the cell. In this quantizer, the configuration of these cells is completely determined by the locations of the output points. More specifically, the ith cell C_i is given by

$$C_i = \{x \in [0,1] \times [0,1] : d(x, y_i) \leq d(x, y_j) \text{ for } 1 \leq j \leq 7\}$$

where y_i denotes the ith output point. A vector x belongs to the ith cell if y_i is the nearest output point to x among all output points. This configuration of cells is called the *Voronoi diagram of output points*, and the quantizer is called the *nearest neighbor quantizer*. With the nearest neighbor quantizer, the encoder needs to store only the codebook consisting of output points without requiring any information on the geometrical configuration of cells. For an input vector, the encoder compares its distances to the output points and records the index of the nearest output point.

If a set of output points is fixed, the Voronoi diagram is the best configuration of cells that minimizes the average distortion. Also, as in equation 4, the output points should be centroids of the corresponding cells to minimize the average distortion. Therefore, in the same way as the Lloyd algorithm, we can design a locally optimal vector quantizer for a Pdf by refining the configuration of cells and the locations of output points iteratively. This is called the *generalized Lloyd algorithm* (GLA) (Gersho and Gray 1991, Chapter 11).

Vector quantization has several advantages over scalar quantization. First, it can effectively exploit possible correlations between samples. Consider a two-dimensional random variable $X = (X_1, X_2)$ that is uniformly distributed over the two shaded quadrants in Figure 6(a). Because the marginal Pdf of X_1 or X_2 is uniform over the interval $[0,1]$, its optimal scalar quantizer is a uniform quantizer. If we encode each component independently by a four-point uniform scalar quantizer, the unit square is partitioned into sixteen rectangular cells as shown in Figure 6(b). This scheme requires 2 bits per component. However, note that components X_1 and X_2 are correlated with each other and the probability density over the upper-right and lower-left quadrants in Figure 6(a) is zero. Therefore, we can encode variable X with an eight-point vector quantizer in Figure 6(c), which requires only 1.5 bits per component while achieving the same distortion as given in Figure 6(b).

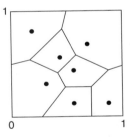

Figure 5: An example of a 2D vector quantizer

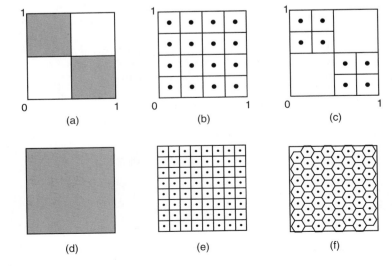

(a)   (b)   (c)

(d)   (e)   (f)

Figure 6: Advantages of vector quantization over scalar quantization (Gersho and Gray 1991, Chapter 11)-(a) probability density function; (b) scalar quantization for (a); (c) vector quantization for (a); (d) probability density function; (e) square cell partitioning for (d); (f) hexagonal cell partitioning for (d)

As shown in Figure 6(b), scalar quantization of each component leads only to a rectangular cell partitioning in the two-dimensional space. Similarly, it leads only to a cubic cell partitioning in the three-dimensional space and so on. In contrast, vector quantization has a freedom in choosing multidimensional cell shapes. Therefore, even if the components of a multidimensional variable are statistically independent, vector quantization can provide better performance than scalar quantization. For example, suppose that the components of a variable $X = (X_1, X_2)$ are independent of each other and uniformly distributed as shown in Figure 6(d). Figures 6(e) and 6(f) are a square partitioning and a hexagonal cell partitioning for this Pdf, respectively. The square cells and the hexagonal cells are of the same size. Thus, if we assume that the number of output points is large and the boundary effects are negligible, then the hexagonal partitioning requires the same rate as the square partitioning. However, the hexagonal partitioning provides lower average distortion than the square partitioning because the maximum distance between two points within the hexagon is smaller than that within the square.

Vector quantization is used to compress various kinds of data, including speech and image data. However, the main drawback of vector quantization is that it often requires a large storage space and high computational complexity. Consider a vector quantizer for image data that encodes each eight-by-eight pixel region as a block at the rate of 0.5 bits per pixel. Each block is encoded with $32 = 8 \times 8 \times 0.5$ bits and the codebook is, hence, composed of $2^{32} \cong 4 \times 10^9$ vectors. If each pixel value is represented with a single byte, then both the encoder and the decoder require about $8 \cdot 8 \cdot 4 \times 10^9$ bytes ($\cong 256$ Gbytes) to store the codebook. Also, if the nearest neighbor rule is used to find the code word, then a brute-force encoder would compute 4×10^9 vector distances to encode each block, which is not acceptable in practice. Hence, to reduce the storage space and the computational burden, several techniques have been developed such as *lattice vector quantization*, *tree-structured vector quantization*, and *shape-gain vector quantization* (Gersho and Gray 1991, Chapter 12).

Predictive Coding

Many data sources generate a sequence of samples that are highly correlated to one another. Hence, in many cases we can predict the future sample based on the past and current samples, although perfect prediction is not necessarily possible. Prediction plays an important role in data compression systems because it enables the removal of redundancy in data to achieve a high compression ratio. In predictive coding, the encoder predicts each sample from previous ones and transmits the prediction error instead of the original sample. Then the decoder makes the same prediction as the encoder and uses the prediction error to compute the original sample. The entropy of the prediction error is generally lower than that of the original sample; thus, the prediction error can be more compactly compressed with lossless or lossy compression tools.

Let us consider an image compression system. Figure 7(a) shows the Lena image and its enlarged face region. The image consists of 512×512 pixels. Each pixel

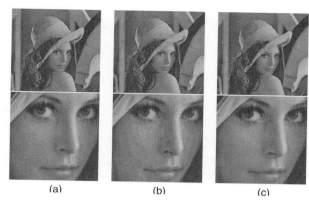

(a) (b) (c)

Figure 7: Lena images-(a) original image, (b) quantized image, and (c) image obtained by predictive quantization

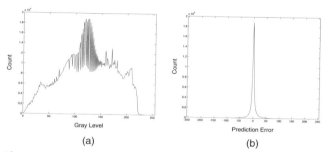

(a) (b)

Figure 8: Histograms of (a) original gray levels and (b) prediction errors

has a gray level within [0,255], and is represented by a single byte. Figure 8(a) is the histogram of gray levels obtained from other test images. For each gray level, the histogram shows the number of pixels in the test images that have that gray level. Thus, after normalization, the histogram can be employed as an approximation of the Pdf of gray levels. Based on the approximation of the Pdf, we can design a sixteen-point scalar quantizer using the Lloyd algorithm. The sixteen output points are

$$\{16, 30, 42, 58, 70, 84, 98, 114, 129, 143, \\ 159, 173, 187, 200, 209, 217\}$$

Figure 7(b) is the image quantized by this quantizer. It can be observed that the quantization error degrades the image quality. The rate is 4 bits per pixel, and the mean squared error is 18.974. We use the mean squared error to evaluate image quality because it is easy to compute. However, other quantitative measures are designed to provide more accurate estimation of subjective image quality (Agaian, Panetta, and Grigoryan 2001).

We can achieve better performance using predictive coding techniques because adjacent pixels in typical images have similar gray levels. Suppose that the encoder compresses pixels in a raster scan order (Wang, Osterman, and Zhang 2002). Figure 8(b) is the histogram of prediction errors where each pixel is predicted from the average of the past three neighboring pixels: left, upper, and upper-right pixels. Note that the prediction errors are concentrated around 0 and much more compactly

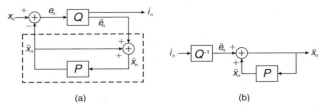

Figure 9: (a) DPCM encoder; (b) DPCM decoder

distributed than the original pixel values in Figure 8(a). For this distribution, the codebook of the sixteen-point Lloyd quantizer is given by

$\{-56, -35, -25, -19, -15, -11, -7, -3,$
$\qquad 0, 4, 8, 12, 17, 21, 32, 53\}$

Figure 7(c) is the image obtained by predictive quantization. During the prediction, the encoder uses the reconstructed values of past three pixels, instead of the original values, to avoid the mismatch between the encoder and the decoder. Then the encoder quantizes the prediction error and transmits the output index to the decoder. In the decoder, the same prediction is performed, and then the quantized error is added to the prediction value to reconstruct a pixel. Note that Figure 7(c) provides better image quality than Figure 7(b). The mean squared error is 5.956.

The general structure of a predictive quantization system (Gersho and Gray 1991, Chapter 7) is shown in Figure 9. This system is also called *differential pulse code modulation* (DPCM). The predictor, P, generates the prediction $\hat{x}_n$ of the nth sample x_n based on the past reconstructed samples $\tilde{x}_{n-i}$ ($i = 1,2,\cdots$). The most common predictor is the linear predictor, given by

$$\hat{x}_n = \sum_{i=1}^{m} a_i \tilde{x}_{n-i}, \qquad (7)$$

where a_i's are weighting coefficients. The quantizer Q quantizes the prediction error $en = x_n - \hat{x}_n$ into an output point $\tilde{e}_n$, and transmits the output index i_n. In the decoder, the dequantizer Q^{-1} converts the index i_n into the output point $\tilde{e}_n$, and adds it to the prediction $\hat{x}_n$ to reconstruct $\tilde{x}_n$.

Transform Coding

In *transform coding*, a sequence of source samples is represented by another sequence of transform coefficients, whose energy is concentrated in relatively few coefficients. Because the coefficients have different statistics, they can be quantized more effectively than the original samples. In the decoder, the quantized coefficients are inverse transformed to reconstruct the samples.

The *discrete cosine transform* (DCT) (Jayant and Noll 1984, 558–60) provides excellent energy compaction for highly correlated data. The DCT of a sequence a is related to the *discrete Fourier transform* (DFT) and can be computed by fast algorithms based on the *fast Fourier transform* (FFT). Thus, it is employed in various image

and video compression standards. The DCT of an N-point sequence $a = (a_0, a_1, \ldots, a_{N=1})$ is defined as

$$x_j = c_j \sum_{i=0}^{N-1} a_i \cos\left[\frac{\pi(2_i + 1)j}{2N}\right] \quad \text{for } j = 0, 1, \ldots N - 1,$$

where $c_0 = \sqrt{1/N}$ and $c_j = \sqrt{2/N}$ for $j = 1, 2, \ldots N - 1$.

The sequence of transform coefficients $x = (x_0, x_1, \ldots, x_{N-1})$ can be inverse transformed into the original samples by

$$a_i = \sum_{j=0}^{N-1} c_j x_j \cos\left[\frac{\pi(2i + 1)j}{2N}\right] \quad \text{for } i = 0,1,\ldots N - 1,$$

This can be rewritten as

$$a = \sum_{j=0}^{N-1} x_j b_j$$

where b_j is a basis vector, whose ith element is equal to $c_j \cos[(\pi (2i + 1) j) /(2N)]$.

Figure 10 shows the eight basis vectors for the eight-point DCT. When j is low, the samples in b_j are slowly varying, and the coefficient x_j represents a low-frequency component in the signal. On the other hand, for high j, x_j represents a high-frequency component corresponding to rapid variations between samples. As mentioned previously, many data sources generate a sequence of highly correlated samples. In such a case, high-frequency coefficients usually have smaller magnitudes than low-frequency coefficients. For example, consider the sequence of samples

(97, 102, 117, 135, 139, 140, 137, 130).

The eight-point DCT of these samples yields the coefficients

(352.5, −37.5, −25.2, 2.1, 1.8, 4.1, −0.7, −1.1)

Note that most energy is concentrated in the first three coefficients. Let us assume that the encoder transmits only the first three coefficients after quantizing them into the nearest integers. Then the decoder fills in the other

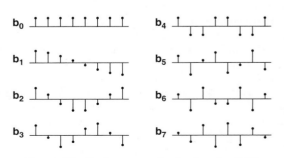

Figure 10: Basis vectors for the 8-point DCT

coefficients with zeros and performs the inverse transform on

$$(353, -37, -25, 0, 0, 0, 0, 0)$$

to obtain approximate samples

$$(95.1, 104.6, 119.3, 132.7, 140.0, 139.9, 135.4, 131.4)$$

The reconstruction errors are relatively small, although only the first three quantized coefficients are employed in the reconstruction. In image compression systems, 2D-DCT is employed, and the transform coefficients are encoded by more sophisticated coding schemes such as *zonal* or *threshold coding* (Jain 1989, 508–10).

In most applications, the length of a signal is unbounded or too large to be transformed as a whole. Consequently, a source signal is partitioned into blocks of samples, and the DCT is applied independently to the blocks. In this case, the DCT is called a *block transform*. The DFT, the *discrete sine transform* (DST), the *Hadamard transform* are other examples of block transforms (Jain 1989, Chapter 5). The main disadvantage of block transforms is that they cannot exploit possible correlations between blocks.

Sub-Band and Wavelet Coding

Being different from block transforms, the *sub-band transform* involves no partitioning of samples, and thus possible correlations between blocks can be exploited. Figure 11 shows a two-channel sub-band coding system that transforms an input sequence into two frequency sub-bands. First, the encoder applies two analysis filters, H_0 and H_1, to an input sequence a, respectively. Then the outputs are downsampled by a factor of 2 to generate two sequences, x_0 and x_1. In general, H_0 is a low-pass filter and H_1 is a high-pass filter. Thus, x_0 represents low-frequency components in the original sequence, while x_1 represents high-frequency components. Both x_0 and x_1 can be quantized and coded differently according to their characteristics. In the decoder, the quantized sequences $\tilde{x}_0$ and $\tilde{x}_1$ are upsampled by inserting a zero between every two consecutive samples and then processed by synthesis filters G_0 and G_1 to reconstruct the input sequence approximately.

The analysis and synthesis filters can be designed so that the decoder reconstructs the original sequence losslessly when there is no quantization error (i.e., $\tilde{x}_0 = x_0$ and $\tilde{x}_1 = x_1$). If this condition is satisfied, then the set of the analysis and synthesis filters is called the *perfect reconstruction filter bank*. Several methods have been proposed for the design of perfect reconstruction filter banks,

driven by applications of sub-band coding of speech and image signals (Vetterli and Kovačević 1995, Chapter 3).

In the wavelet representation, a signal is hierarchically decomposed using a family of basis functions that is built by scaling and translating a single prototype function (Mallat 1989). The *wavelet transform* facilitates the multi-resolution analysis of a signal by reorganizing the signal as a set of details appearing at different resolutions. The wavelet transform has a close relationship with the sub-band transform, and the *discrete wavelet transform* (DWT) can be obtained by applying the two-channel sub-band transform to the low-pass sub-band recursively.

Figure 12 shows the sub-band decomposition of the Barbara image. First, we filter each row using two analysis filters and then downsample the filtered sequences to obtain low (L) and high (H) frequency sub-bands. In this Figure, the 9-7 filter bank (Antonini et al. 1992) is employed. Then, in the same way as the row decomposition, we decompose each column to obtain LL, LH, HL, and HH sub-bands.

This 2-D sub-band decomposition is recursively applied to the LL sub-band to obtain the DWT. Figure 13 shows the three-level wavelet decomposition of the Barbara image. The LL_3 sub-band approximates the original image at the coarsest resolution. The HL_i sub-bands contain vertical edge components at different resolutions ($i = 1, 2, 3$). Similarly, the LH_i and HH_i sub-bands contain horizontal and diagonal details, respectively. It can be seen that the signal energy is concentrated in the coefficients in the LL_3 sub-band. Therefore, the wavelet

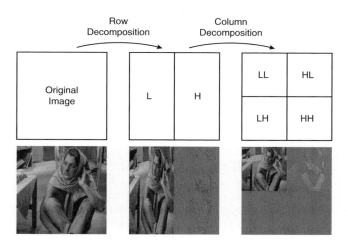

Figure 12: Sub-band decomposition

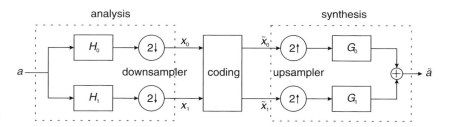

Figure 11: A sub-band coding system

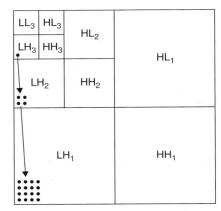

Figure 13: Three-level wavelet decomposition

coefficients can be compressed effectively based on the adaptive quantization by allocating a higher bit rate to the LL_3 sub-band than to other sub-bands (Vetterli and Kovačević 1995, Chapter 7).

Shapiro (1993) proposed an image compression algorithm, called *embedded zerotree wavelet* (EZW). His algorithm exploits interband correlations of DWT coefficients using zerotrees. Figure 13 illustrates a zerotree. The twenty-one coefficients, depicted by dots, represent the horizontal edge components of the same region in the original image. Thus, if the one coefficient in the LH_3 sub-band is less than a threshold, it is probable that the other twenty coefficients in the finer sub-bands also are less than the threshold. In such a case, the twenty-one coefficients are said to form a zerotree. Shapiro combined the concept of zerotrees with bit-plane coding and adaptive arithmetic coding to compress the DWT coefficients efficiently. The DWT is also used in the recent image compression standard JPEG2000 (Taubman and Marcellin 2002).

APPLICATIONS

A data compression system can be conceptually divided into a data modeler and a parameter coder. To compress a certain type of data, its characteristics should be first analyzed and modeled. Then, according to the data model, parameters are extracted from input data and compressed using one or more techniques in the previous two sections. The compression performance depends on how accurately the source data are modeled as well as how efficient the parameter coder is.

For example, letters in a text can be modeled as independent variables and each letter can be Huffman encoded, irrespectively of its position in the text, according to the probability distribution of letters. Alternatively, we can adopt the model that the probability of a letter depends on the preceding letter and design several Huffman code word tables, one for each preceding letter. Similarly, the preceding n letters can be employed as a conditioning class, and a Huffman code word table can be designed for each conditioning class. As n increases, the characteristics of text data can be more accurately approximated,

and text data can be more compactly encoded at the cost of higher complexities of the encoder and the decoder (Bell, Cleary, and Witten 1990, Chapter 2).

Therefore, when designing the data modeler and the parameter coder, we need consider several requirements of an individual application, including the desired compression ratio, tolerable distortion, and complexities of the encoder and the decoder.

Several applications of text compression are considered below. The approaches and application areas of speech and audio compression, image compression, and video compression are described in *Image Compression*, *Video Compression*, and *Speech and Audio Compression*. By reducing the sizes of text files, we can use the limited storage space in a computer more effectively and save communication time for sharing files between computers. In the UNIX environment, "compress" and "gzip" are often used as file compression tools. Also, in PC environments, ARJ and ZIP are popular compression tools. All of these tools are variations of Lempel-Ziv dictionary coding techniques. They can losslessly compress typical text data to 30 percent to 40 percent of its original size because text data contain many redundancies and frequently recurring patterns.

Recently, context-based adaptive arithmetic coding has been studied to compress text data more efficiently (Witten, Neal, and Cleary 1987). Moffat, Neal, and Witten (1998) reported that their arithmetic coder requires 2.20 bits/letter for a text file excerpted from the *Wall Street Journal*, while the "gzip" utility requires approximately 2.91 bits/letter. The text file has the zero-order letter entropy of 4.88 bits/letter, which is the minimum required bit rate when letters are modeled as independent variables.

CONCLUSION

Data compression is one of the key technologies that enable Internet and mobile communications. It has been extensively studied since the late 1960s, and various compression algorithms have been developed to store and transmit multimedia data efficiently. In this chapter, we classified data compression into lossless and lossy techniques and described key algorithms for each class.

GLOSSARY

Code: A set of binary strings assigned to symbols of a data source.

Code word: A binary string in a code.

Compression ratio: The ratio of original data size to compressed data size.

Data coding: A synonym for data compression.

Data compression: A mechanism of representing data in a compact way.

Decoder: A device that reproduces original data from compressed data.

Decompression: A mechanism of reproducing original data from compressed data.

Encoder: A device that compresses data.

Entropy: The amount of information or uncertainty in a data source, or the minimum number of bits required on average to describe a sample of the data source.

Lossless compression: Compressing data such that an exact duplicate of the original data can be reproduced at the decoder.

Lossy compression: Data compression that allows loss of information.

CROSS REFERENCES

See *Image Compression*; *Information Theory*; *Speech and Audio Compression*; *Video Compression*.

REFERENCES

Agaian, S. S., K. Panetta, and A. M. Grigoryan. (2001). Transform-based image enhancement algorithms with performance measure. *IEEE Transactions on Image Processing*, 10: 367–82.

Antonini, M., M. Barlaud, P. Mathieu, and I. Daubechies. 1992. Image coding using wavelet transform. *IEEE Transactions on Image Processing*, 1: 205–20.

Bell, T. C., J. G. Cleary, and I. H. Witten. 1990. *Text compression*. Upper Saddle River, NJ: Prentice Hall.

Cover, T. M., and J. A. Thomas. 1991. *Elements of information theory*. New York: John Wiley & Sons.

Gallager, R. G. 1978. Variations on a theme by Huffman. *IEEE Transactions on Information Theory*, 24: 668–74.

Gersho, A., and R. M. Gray. 1991. *Vector quantization and signal compression*. Norwell, MA: Kluwer Academic Publishers.

Huffman, D. A. 1952. A method for the construction of minimum-redundancy codes. *Proceedings of IRE*, 40: 1098–1101.

Jain, A. K. 1989. *Fundamentals of digital image processing*. Upper Saddle River, NJ: Prentice Hall.

Jayant, N. S., and P. Noll. 1984. *Digital coding of waveforms: Principles and applications to speech and video*. Upper Saddle River, NJ: Prentice Hall.

Lloyd, S. P. 1982. Least squares quantization in PCM. *IEEE Transactions on Information Theory*, 28: 129–37.

Mallat, S. G. 1989. A theory for multiresolution signal decomposition: The wavelet transform. *IEEE Transactions on Pattern Analysis and Machine Intelligence*, 11: 674–93.

Moffat, A., R. M. Neal, and I. H. Witten. 1998. Arithmetic coding revisited. *ACM Transactions on Information Systems*, 16: 256–94.

Shannon, C. E. 1948. A mathematical theory of communication. *Bell System Technical Journal*, 27: 379–423, 623–56.

Shapiro, J. M. 1993. Embedded image coding using zerotrees of wavelet coefficients. *IEEE Transactions on Signal Processing*, 41: 3445–62.

Taubman, D. S., and M. W. Marcellin. 2002. *JPEG2000: Image compression fundamentals, standards and practice*. Norwell, MA: Kluwer Academic Publishers.

Vetterli, M., and J. Kovačević. 1995. *Wavelets and subband coding*. Upper Saddle River, NJ: Prentice Hall.

Wang, Y., J. Ostermann, and Y. Q. Zhang. 2002. *Video processing and communications*. Upper Saddle River, NJ: Prentice Hall.

Witten, I. H., A. Moffat, and T. C. Bell. 1999. *Managing gigabytes: Compressing and indexing documents and images*. San Francisco: Morgan Kaufmann.

Witten, I. H., R. M. Neal, and J. G. Cleary. 1987. Arithmetic coding for data compression. *Communications of the ACM*, 30: 520–40.

Ziv, J., and A. Lempel. 1977. A universal algorithm for sequential data compression. *IEEE Transactions on Information Theory*, 23: 337–43.

———. 1978. Compression of individual sequences via variable-rate coding. *IEEE Transactions on Information Theory*, 24: 530–36.

Image Compression

Alfred Mertins, *University of Lübeck, Germany*

INTRODUCTION

Image compression can generally be categorized into lossless and lossy compression. Obviously, lossless compression is most desirable because the reconstructed image is an exact copy of the original. The compression ratios that can be obtained with lossless compression, however, are fairly low and typically range from three to five, depending on the image. Such low compression ratios are justified in applications where no loss of quality can be tolerated, which is often the case in the compression and storage of medical images. For most other applications such as Internet browsing and storage for printing, some loss is usually acceptable. Allowing for loss then allows for much higher compression ratios.

Early image compression algorithms have mainly focused on achieving low distortion for a given, fixed bit rate, or, conversely, on achieving the lowest rate for a given maximum distortion. Although these goals are still valid, modern multimedia applications have led to a series of further requirements such as spatial and *signal-to-noise ratio* (SNR) scalability and random access to parts of the image data. For example, in a typical Internet application, the same image is to be accessed from various users with a wide range of devices (from a low-resolution palm top computer to a multimedia workstation) and via channels ranging from slow cable modems or wireless connections to high-speed wired local area networks. To optimally utilize available bandwidth and device capabilities, it is desirable to transcode image data within the network to the various resolutions that best serve the respective users. On-the-fly transcoding, however, requires that compressed image data be organized in such a way that different content variations can be easily extracted from a given high-resolution code stream. The new JPEG 2000 standard takes a step in this direction and combines abundant functionalities with a high compression ratio and random code stream access.

It is also worth mentioning that image coders are usually asymmetrical in the sense that the encoding process takes much more computational power than the decoding.

This is because the encoder often needs to select the best compression strategy and parameters for a given image or image region before it can start encoding the intensity values, whereas the decoder just receives the encoder's selection and code stream and decodes it in a straightforward manner. The compression standards often only specify the decoder, leaving room for developers to optimize their encoders.

This chapter gives an overview of some of the most important image compression tools and techniques. We first look at an introductory example that already shows some of the key ideas behind image compression. Then we discuss the theoretical background of data compression and review the discrete cosine and wavelet transforms, which are the two most important transforms in image compression. Subsequently, we look at state-of-the-art embedded wavelet compression methods and give an overview of standards for the compression of images. Finally, a number of conclusions and an outlook are given.

AN INTRODUCTORY EXAMPLE OF IMAGE COMPRESSION

Consider the gray-scale image in Figure 1a. There are 256 possible levels of gray that are commonly expressed by integer numbers ranging from zero (black) to 255 (white). The encoding requires 8 *bits per pixel* (bpp) when a fixed-length code is used. To achieve a compression ratio of 8, we can quantize the pixels to 1 bit, expressing whether a pixel value is larger than 127. The resulting decoded image can be seen in Figure 1b, where only two different levels of gray are visible.

Figure 1c shows the magnitude of the *two-dimensional discrete Fourier transform* (2D-DFT) of the image. We see that most of the signal energy is concentrated in the low-frequency range (the center of Figure 1c), which results from the fact that the image has flat regions with approximately the same level of gray. In a subsequent step, the frequency-domain representation has been quantized with equal step size for all coefficients and then encoded

Figure 1: Example of image compression. (a) The original image with a size of 256 × 320 pixels and 256 levels of gray. (b) Image directly quantized and encoded at 1 bpp. (c) Fourier transform of the image, with frequency axes ranging from −π to π in both horizontal and vertical directions. (d) Image reconstructed from quantized Fourier coefficients at a rate of 1 bpp. (e) Fourier transform carried out on blocks of 32 × 32 pixels. (f) Image reconstructed from quantized block-wise Fourier coefficients at a rate of 1 bpp.

with a Huffman code (see below). In this case, most of the bits are spent for transmitting the large low-frequency coefficients, and only few bits are used for the high-frequency content. The result of encoding the image at a rate of 1 bpp is depicted in Figure 1d. We see that the quality is already much better than for the direct image quantization.

Actual coding standards do not transform the entire image but usually divide it into smaller blocks in order to have a better chance of capturing flat regions in the blocks and limit the spreading of individual quantization errors over the entire reconstructed image. The magnitude of a blockwise 2D-DFT with block size 32 × 32 is depicted in Figure 1e. The reconstructed image after quantization and Huffman encoding at 1 bpp is shown in Figure 1f. Now the quality within each block is better than in Figure 1d, but the block boundaries become clearly visible. Further reducing the block size reduces the visibility

of block boundaries, but overdoing this reduces the coding efficiency, with 1-pixel blocks being the limit. Most block-based coding standards adopt a block size of 8 × 8 pixels. Instead of the DFT, one often uses the discrete cosine transform (see below). A way to achieve high coding efficiency without blocking artifacts it to use overlapping blocks, which is the case for the wavelet transform discussed later in this chapter.

ELEMENTS OF SOURCE CODING THEORY
The Rate-Distortion Trade-Off

The mathematical background that describes the trade-off between compression ratio and fidelity was established by Shannon (1959) in his work on rate-distortion (RD) theory. To study the implications of the theoretical

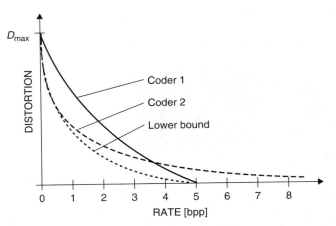

Figure 2: Distortion-rate curves for different coders

results obtained by Shannon on the performance of any practical coder, we consider the graphs in Figure 2 that show the distortion obtained with different coders versus the rate required to store the information. Such graphs obtained for a specific image and encoding algorithm are known as *operational distortion-rate curves*. The distortion is typically measured as the *mean squared error* (MSE) between the original and the reconstructed image, and the rate is measured as the required average number of bits per pixel.

As one might expect, all coders show the same maximum distortion at rate zero (no transmission). With increasing rate, the distortion decreases and different coders reach the point of zero distortion at different rates. Coder 1 is an example of a coder that combines lossy and lossless compression in one bit stream and that is optimized for lossless compression. Coder 2, on the other hand, is a lossy coder that shows good performance for low rates but reaches the lossless stage only at extremely high rates. The lowest curve shows the minimum rate required to code the information at a given distortion, assuming optimal compression for any rate. This is the desired curve, combining lossy and lossless compression in an optimal way.

Coding Gain through Decorrelation

The simplest way to compress an image in a lossy manner would be to quantize all pixels separately and provide a bit stream that represents the quantized values. This strategy is known as *pulse code modulation* (PCM). For example, an 8-bit gray-scale image whose pixels $x_{m,n}$ are integers in the range from 0 to 255 could be compressed by a factor of four through neglecting the six least-significant bits of the binary representations of $x_{m,n}$, resulting in an image with only four different levels of gray. Entropy coding (see below) of the PCM values would generally allow for increased compression, but such a strategy would still yield a poor trade-off between the amount of distortion introduced and the compression ratio achieved. The reason for this poor behavior of PCM is that the spatial relationships between pixels are not utilized.

Images usually contain a large amount of spatial correlation that can be exploited to obtain compression schemes with a better RD trade-off than that obtained with PCM. For this, the data first need to be decorrelated, and then quantization and entropy coding can take place. Figure 3 shows the basic structure of an image coder that follows such a strategy. The quantization step is to be seen as the assignment of a discrete symbol to a range of input values. In the simplest case, this could be the assignment of symbol a through the operation $a = \text{round}(x/q)$ where q is the quantization step size. The inverse quantization then corresponds to the recovery of the actual numerical values that belong to the symbols (e.g., the operation $\hat{x} = q \cdot a$). The entropy coding stage subsequently endeavors to represent the generated discrete symbols with the minimum possible number of bits. This step is lossless. Errors occur only because of quantization.

One of the simplest decorrelating transforms is a prediction error filter that uses the knowledge of neighboring pixels to predict the value of the pixel to be encoded and then outputs the prediction error made. In this case, the coding paradigm changes from PCM to *differential PCM* (DPCM). To give an example, Figure 4 shows a neighborhood relationship where the previously decoded pixel values $x_{m-1,\,n-1}$, $x_{m-1,\,n}$, $x_{m-1,\,n+1}$ and $x_{m,\,n-1}$ can be used to predict the actual value $x_{m,\,n}$. A coding gain of DPCM over PCM arises from the fact that the prediction error usually has much less power than the signal itself and can therefore be compressed more efficiently.

Modern state-of-the-art image compression algorithms use transforms such as the *discrete cosine transform* (DCT) or the *discrete wavelet transform* (DWT) to

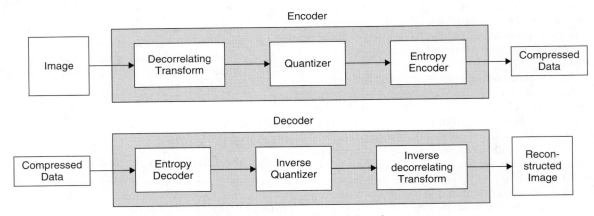

Figure 3: Typical image encoder and decoder structures

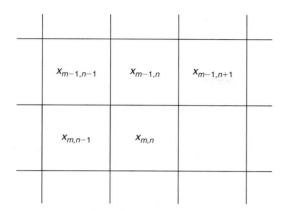

Figure 4: Context modeling

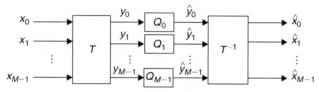

Figure 5: Transform coding

carry out decorrelation. These transforms are extremely efficient in decorrelating the pixels of an image and are employed in several compression standards such as JPEG (Wallace 1992) and JPEG 2000 (Joint Photographic Experts Group 2000).

To see how and why *transform coding* works, we consider the system in Figure 5. The input is a zero-mean random vector $x = [x_0, x_1,..., x_{M-1}]^T$ with correlation matrix $R_{xx} = E[xx^T]$, where $E[\cdot]$ denotes the expectation operation. The output $y = Tx$ of the transform is then a zero-mean random process with correlation matrix $R_{yy} = TR_{xx}T^T$. Because the random variables $y_0, y_1,..., y_{M-1}$ stored in y may have different variances, they are subsequently quantized with different quantizers $Q_0, Q_1,..., Q_{M-1}$. In the synthesis stage, the inverse transform is applied to reconstruct an approximation $\hat{x}$ of the original vector x based on the quantized coefficients $\hat{y}_0, \hat{y}_1,..., \hat{y}_{M-1}$. The aim is to design the system in such a way that the MSE $E[||x-\hat{x}||^2] = \sum_{k=0}^{M-1} E\{(x_k - \hat{x}_k)^2\}$ becomes minimal for a given total bit budget. Three questions arise: (1) What is the optimal transform T given the properties of the source? (2) How should an available bit budget B be distributed to the different quantizers? (3) What are the optimal quantization levels? Answers to these questions have been derived for both unitary and biorthogonal transforms. We will briefly discuss the results for the unitary case.

The optimal scalar quantizers Q_k that minimize the individual error variances $\sigma_{q_k}^2 = E_{q_k^2}$ with $q_k = y_k - \hat{y}_k$ for a given number of quantization steps are known as Lloyd-Max quantizers (Lloyd 1957; Max 1960). Important properties of these optimal quantizers are $E\{q_k\} = 0$ (zero-mean error) and $E\{q_k\hat{y}_k\} = 0$ (orthogonality between the quantized value and the error). When assuming such optimal quantizers in a transform-coding framework and restricting the overall average bit rate to a budget B, one obtains the bit-allocation rule $2^{B_k} \sim \sigma_{y_k}^2$, where B_k is the number of

bits spent to encode y_k and σ_{yk}^2 is the variance of y_k (Jayant and Noll 1984). This rule intuitively makes sense as more bits are assigned to random variables with a larger variance. Moreover, another important result is that in an optimal setting, each quantizer contributes equally to the total output distortion.

To answer the question which transform is optimal for a given coding task, we consider the coding gain defined as $G_{TC} = \sigma_{PCM}^2/\sigma_{TC}^2$ where σ_{PCM}^2 is the error variance of simple PCM and σ_{TC}^2 is the error variance produced by transform coding, both at the same average bit rate B. With the optimal quantizers discussed above, one obtains (Jayant and Noll 1984)

$$G_{TC} = \frac{\frac{1}{M}\sum_{k=0}^{M-1}\sigma_{y_k}^2}{\left(\prod_{k=0}^{M-1}\sigma_{y_k}^2\right)^{1/M}}$$

which is the ratio of the arithmetic and geometric mean of the coefficient variances. Among all unitary transforms T, this quotient is maximized when R_{yy} is diagonal and thus when the transform coefficients are uncorrelated. This decorrelation is accomplished by the *Karhunen-Loève transform* (KLT).

The expression for the coding gain can be interpreted as follows:

1. A maximum coding gain is obtained if the coefficients y_k are mutually uncorrelated.
2. The more unequal the variances $\sigma_{y_k}^2$ are, the higher the coding gain is because a high dissimilarity leads to a high ratio of arithmetic and geometric mean. Consequently, if the input values x_k are already mutually uncorrelated a transform cannot provide any further coding gain.
3. With increasing M, one may expect an increasing coding gain that moves toward an upper limit as M goes to infinity. In fact, one can show that this is the same limit as the one obtained for DPCM with ideal prediction (Jayant and Noll 1984).

It is interesting to note that the above-mentioned expression for the coding gain also holds for *sub-band coding* based on uniform, energy-preserving filter banks. A more general expression for the coding gain has been derived by Katto and Yasuda (1991). Their formula also holds for biorthogonal transform and sub-band coding as well as other schemes such as DPCM.

Vector Quantization

Vector quantization (VQ) is a multidimensional extension of *scalar quantization* in that an entire vector of values is encoded as a unit. Let x be such an N-dimensional vector of values, and let x_i, $i = 1, 2,..., I$ be a set of N-dimensional code vectors stored in a codebook. Given x, a vector quantizer finds the code vector x_i from the codebook that best matches x and transmits the corresponding index i. Knowing i, the receiver reconstructs x as x_i. In the simplest case, one could think of x as being a block of an image, and then the code vectors x_i would be images as well.

An often-used quality criterion to determine which vector from the codebook gives the best match for x is the Euclidean distance $d(x, x_i) = \|x - x_i\|^2$. Theoretically, if the vector length N tends to infinity, then VQ becomes optimal and approaches the performance indicated by rate-distortion theory. In practice, however, the cost associated with searching a large codebook is the major obstacle. See Gersho and Gray (1991) for discussions of computationally efficient forms of the VQ technique and details on codebook design.

Fractal Coding

The idea of fractal coding is to exploit the self-similarity of the content of an image in different resolutions and at different locations. Given an image x, the encoder determines a contractive affine transformation T with a fixed point being close to x and transmits the parameters of T. The decoder iterates the transform T, starting from an arbitrary image and converging to the fixed point of T. The method yields good results on certain classes of images, but it is not widely used and lacks the efficiency and flexibility of transform- and wavelet-based coders.

Block-Truncation Coding

Block-truncation coding (BTC) (Delp and Mitchell 1979) is a lossy, block-adaptive encoding scheme that operates on small image regions. It quantizes a local region of an image in such a way that a number of moments are preserved in the quantized output. If, for example, the mean and variance are to be preserved, the encoder transmits two reconstruction values a and b together with a bitmap indicating whether a pixel is above or below a threshold. If a pixel value is below the threshold, it is reconstructed as a, otherwise as b. The values a and b are chosen to preserve the mean and variance within the block. Extensions to higher-order moments are possible.

Entropy Coding

Assigning the same code length to all symbols generated by a source is not optimal when the different symbols occur with different probabilities. In such a case, it is better to assign short code words to symbols that occur often and longer code words to symbols that occur only occasionally. The latter strategy results in variable-length codes and is the basic principle of entropy coding. Variable-length codes are employed in lossless image compression as well as for the compression of quantizer indices in lossy schemes.

A simple source model is the *discrete memoryless source* (DMS), which produces random variables X_i taken from an alphabet A $=\{a_1, a_2, \ldots, a_L\}$. The symbols a_i may, for example, identify the various steps of a quantizer and are assumed to occur with probabilities $p(a_i)$. The first-order entropy of the source is defined as

$$H = -\sum_{i=1}^{L} p(a_i) \log_2 p(a_i)$$

and describes the average information per symbol (in bits). According to this expression, the more skewed the probability distribution, the lower the entropy. For any given number of symbols L the maximum entropy is obtained if all symbols are equally likely. The entropy provides a lower bound for the average number of bits per symbol required to encode the symbols emitted by a DMS.

The best-known entropy-coding methods are *Huffman coding, arithmetic coding*, and *Lempel-Ziv coding*. Huffman coding produces a uniquely decipherable prefix code. As an example, consider the symbols a_1, a_2, a_3, a_4 that occur with probabilities 0.5, 0.25, 0.125, 0.125, respectively. A fixed-length code would use 2 bits per symbol. A possible Huffman code is given by $a_1 : 0$, $a_2 : 10$, $a_3 : 110$, $a_4 : 111$. This code only requires 1.75 bits per symbol on average, which is the same as the entropy of the source. In fact, one can show that Huffman codes are optimal and reach the lower bound stated by the entropy when the symbol probabilities are powers of 1/2. To decode a Huffman code, the decoder must know the code table that has been used by the encoder. In practice, this means that either a specified standard code table must be employed or the code table must be transmitted to the decoder as side information.

In arithmetic coding, there is no one-to-one correspondence between symbols and code words; the coding assigns variable-length code words to variable-length blocks of symbols. The code word representing a sequence of symbols is a binary number that points to a subinterval of the interval [0,1) that is associated with the given sequence. The length of the subinterval is equal to the probability of the sequence, and each possible sequence creates a different subinterval. The advantage of arithmetic over Huffman coding is that it usually results in a shorter average code length, and arithmetic coders can be made adaptive to learn the symbol probabilities on the fly so that no side information in form of a code table is required.

In 1977 and 1978, Lempel and Ziv published two universal coding methods that are commonly referred to as LZ77 and LZ78, respectively. Universal coding aims at asymptotically achieving the lowest possible bit rate without having prior knowledge of the distribution of symbols. It does this by encoding entire phrases of symbols at once. In 1984, Welch published the LZW algorithm (Welch 1984), which is a modified version of LZ78. The LZW algorithm became quite popular in image compression because of its use in the GIF format (see below), but it incurred licensing royalties, so several software developers looked for alternatives such as modifications to the older LZ77 algorithm.

TRANSFORMS FOR IMAGE COMPRESSION
The Discrete Cosine Transform

The *discrete cosine transform* (DCT) is used in most current standards for image and video compression. Examples are JPEG, MPEG-1, MPEG-2, MPEG-4, H.261, H.263, and H.264. To be precise, there are four different DCTs defined in the literature; according to the categorization introduced by Rao and Yip (1990), it is the DCT-II that is used for image compression. Because there is no ambiguity throughout this text, we will simply call it the DCT.

The DCT of a two-dimensional signal $x_{m,n}$ with m, $n = 0, 1,..., M - 1$ is defined as

$$y_{k,l} = \frac{2\gamma_k\gamma_\ell}{M} \sum_{m=0}^{M-1}\sum_{m=0}^{M-1} x_{m,n} \cos\frac{k(m+\frac{1}{2})\pi}{M}$$
$$\times \cos\frac{\ell(n+\frac{1}{2})\pi}{M}, \quad k,\ell = 0,1,...,M-1$$

with

$$\gamma_k = \begin{cases} 1/\sqrt{2} & \text{for } k = 0 \\ 1 & \text{otherwise.} \end{cases}$$

The DCT is a unitary transform, so the inverse transform (2D-IDCT) uses the same basis sequences. It is given by

$$x_{m,n} = \sum_{k=0}^{M-1}\sum_{\ell=0}^{M-1} \frac{2\gamma_k\gamma_\ell}{M} y_{k,\ell} \cos\frac{k(m+\frac{1}{2})\pi}{M}$$
$$\times \cos\frac{\ell(n+\frac{1}{2})\pi}{M}, \quad m,n = 0,1,...,M-1$$

The popularity of the DCT comes from the fact that it almost reaches the coding gain obtained by the KLT for typical image data while having implementation advantages. Fast implementations can be obtained through the use of FFT algorithms or through direct factorization of the DCT formula (Rao and Yip 1990). The latter approach is especially interesting for the two-dimensional case where two-dimensional factorizations led to the most efficient implementations (Duhamel and Guillemot 1990; Fang, Hu, and Shih 1999).

In image compression, the DCT is usually used on non-overlapping 8×8 blocks of the image rather than on the entire image in one step. The following aspects have led to this choice. First, from the theory outlined above and the good decorrelation properties of the DCT for smooth signals, it is clear that, to maximize the coding gain for typical images, the blocks should be as big as possible. On the other hand, with increasing block size, the likelihood of capturing a nonstationary behavior within a block increases. This, however, decreases the usefulness of the DCT for decorrelation. Finally, quantization errors made for DCT coefficients will spread out over the entire block after reconstruction via the IDCT. At low rates, this can lead to annoying artifacts when blocks comprise a combination of flat and highly textured regions or if there are significant edges within a block. These effects are less visible if the block size is small. Altogether, the choice of 8×8 blocks has been found to be a good compromise between exploiting neighborhood relations in smooth regions and avoiding annoying artifacts because of inhomogeneous block content.

Figure 6 shows an example of the blockwise 2D-DCT of an image. The original image of Figure 6a has a size of 144×176 pixels, and the block size for the DCT is 8×8. Figure 6b shows the blockwise-transformed image, and Figure 6c shows the transformed image after rearranging the coefficients in such a way that all coefficients

(a)

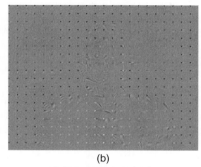

(b)

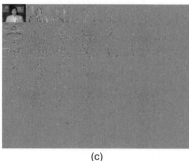

(c)

Figure 6: Example of a blockwise 2-D DCT of an image. (a) Original image (144×176 pixels); (b) transformed image (block size 8×8, 18×26 blocks); (c) transformed image after reordering of coefficients (8×8 subimages of size 18×26)

with the same physical meaning (i.e., coefficients $y_{k,l}$ from the different blocks) are gathered in a subimage. For example, the subimage in the upper-left corner of Figure 6c contains the coefficients $y_{0,0}$ of all the blocks in Figure 6b. These coefficients are often called *DC coefficients* because they represent a constant signal equal to the average pixel value within a block. Correspondingly, the remaining sixty-three coefficients of a block are called *AC coefficients*. From Figure 6c, one can see that the DC coefficients carry the most important information on the entire image. Toward the lower-right corner of Figure 6c, the amount of signal energy decreases significantly.

The Discrete Wavelet Transform

The discrete wavelet transform (DWT) is a tool to hierarchically decompose a signal into a multiresolution pyramid. It offers a series of advantages over the DCT. For example, contrary to the blockwise DCT, the DWT has overlapping basis functions, resulting in less-visible artifacts when coding at low bit rates. Moreover, the

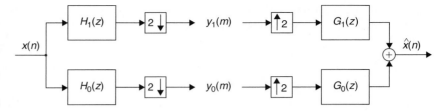

Figure 7: Two-channel filter bank

multiresolution signal representation offers function-alities such as spatial scalability in a simple and generic way. Although most of the image compression standards are based on the DCT, the new still image compression standard JPEG 2000 and parts of the MPEG-4 multi-media standard rely on the DWT (Joint Photographic Experts Group 2000; Moving Picture Experts Group 1999). Also, the FBI standard for the compression of fingerprints uses the wavelet transform (Brislawn 1995).

For discrete-time signals, the DWT is essentially an octave-band signal decomposition that is carried out through successive filtering operations and sampling-rate changes. The basic building block of such an octave-band filter bank is the two-channel structure depicted in Figure 7. The terms $H_k(z)$ and $G_k(z)$ in Figure 7 denote the z-transforms of the respective filter impulse responses $h_k(n)$ and $g_k(n)$, $k = 0, 1$, where the z-transform of a sequence $a(n)$ is computed as $A(z) = \sum_{n=-\infty}^{\infty} a(n)z^{-n}$. $H_0(z)$ and $G_0(z)$ are low-pass filters, whereas $H_1(z)$ and $G_1(z)$ are high-pass filters. The blocks with arrows pointing downward indicate downsampling by factor two (i.e., taking only every second sample), and the blocks with arrows pointing upward indicate upsampling by two (insertion of zeros between the samples). Downsampling serves to eliminate redundancies in the sub-band signals, while upsampling is used to recover the original sampling rate. Because of the filter characteristics (low pass and high pass), most of the energy of a signal $x(n)$ with low-pass characteristic will be stored in the sub-band samples $y_0(m)$. Because $y_0(m)$ occurs at half the sampling rate of $x(n)$, it appears that the filter bank structure concentrates the information in fewer samples as it is required for efficient compression. More efficiency can be obtained by cascading two-channel filter banks to obtain octave-band decompositions or other frequency resolutions. For the structure in Figure 7 to allow *perfect reconstruction* (PR) of the input with a delay of n_0 samples [i.e., $\hat{x}(n)=x(n - n_0)$], the filters must satisfy

$$H_0(-z)G_0(z) + H_1(-z)G_1(z)=0$$

and

$$H_0(z)G_0(z) + H_1(z)G_1(z) = 2z^{-n0}$$

The first equation guarantees that the aliasing components that are present because of the subsampling operation will be compensated at the output; the second equation ensures that no amplitude distortions occur. In addition to the above-mentioned PR conditions, the filters should satisfy $H_0(1) = G_0(1) = \sqrt{2}$ and $H_1(1) = G_1(1) = 0$, which are essential requirements to make them valid wavelet filters. Moreover, they should satisfy some regularity constraints as described in (Daubechies 1992). It should be noted that the above two PR constraints hold for biorthogonal

two-channel filter banks. Paraunitary (energy-preserving) filter banks and the corresponding orthonormal wavelets additionally require the stronger condition

$$\left|H_0\left(e^{j\omega}\right)\right|^2 + \left|H_0\left(e^{j(\omega+\pi)}\right)\right|^2 = 2$$

to hold. Apart from the special case where the filter length is two, this condition can only be satisfied by filters with nonsymmetric impulse responses (Vaidyanathan 1985). Because symmetric filters are highly desirable because they allow for simple boundary processing (see below), paraunitary two-channel filter banks and the corresponding orthonormal wavelets are seldom used in image compression.

For the decomposition of images, the filtering and downsampling operations are usually carried out separately in the horizontal and vertical directions. Figure 8 illustrates the principle. To ensure that the analysis process results in the same number of sub-band samples as there are input pixels, special boundary processing steps are required. These will be explained below. An example of the decomposition of an image is depicted in Figure 9. One can see that the DWT concentrates the essential information on the image in a few samples, resulting in a high coding gain.

When decomposing a finite-length signal (a row or column of an image) with a filter bank using linear convolution, the total number of sub-band samples is generally higher than the number of input samples. Methods to resolve this problem are *circular convolution* (Woods and O'Neil 1986), *symmetric extension* (Smith and Eddins 1990; Bradley, Brislawn, and Faber 1992) and *boundary filtering* (de Queiroz 1992; Herley 1995; Mertins 2001). In the following, we will describe the method of symmetric extension, which is the one most often used in practice. It requires the filters in the filter bank to have linear phase, which means that biorthogonal filters or wavelets must be used. We will address the procedure for filters with odd and even length separately.

If the filter impulse responses have odd lengths, then linear phase means that they obey the *whole sample symmetry* (wss) shown in Figure 10a or they have whole sample asymmetry. For filters with wss, which are common in image compression, the symmetric extension of the signal has to be carried out with wss as well, as depicted in Figure 10b. A signal of length N is thus extended to a periodic signal $x_{wss}(n)$ with period $2N - 2$ and symmetry within each period. When decomposing such an extended signal with the corresponding analysis filter bank, the obtained sub-band signals will also be periodic and show symmetry within each period. The type of sub-band symmetry depends on the filter and signal lengths. For the case where

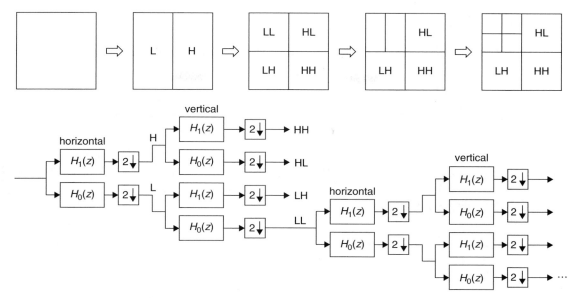

Figure 8: Separable two-dimensional octave-band filter bank

Figure 9: Example of a two-dimensional octave-band decomposition

N is even, the obtained sub-band symmetries are depicted in Figures 10c and 10d. One can easily see that only a total number of N distinct sub-band samples need to be stored or transmitted, because from these N samples the periodic sub-band signals can be completely recovered. Feeding the periodic sub-band signals into the synthesis filter bank and taking one period of the output finally yields perfect reconstruction.

Linear-phase filters with even length have the *half-sample symmetry* (hss) in Figure 11a for the low-pass and the *half-sample antisymmetry* (hsas) in Figure 11b for the high-pass. In this case, the hss extension in Figure 11c is required, resulting in an extended signal with period $2N$ and symmetry within each period. Again, the sub-band signals show symmetries that can be exploited to capture the entire information on a length-N input signal in a total number of N sub-band samples. The sub-band symmetries obtained for even N are depicted in Figures 11d and 11e.

Note that the extension schemes described above can also be used for cases where N is odd, resulting in different sub-band symmetries. Moreover, with the introduction of two different subsampling phases, they can be used to define nonexpansive DWTs for arbitrarily shaped objects (see, e.g., Danyali and Mertins 2004 and the references therein).

EMBEDDED WAVELET CODING

Early wavelet image coders used to employ run-length and entropy coding for further compression of the quantized wavelet coefficients. Run-length coding was found particularly useful for coding long stretches of zeros that frequently occur within the higher bands. Although such coders can perform reasonably well for a fixed bit rate, they do not offer much flexibility, and especially do not allow for progressive transmission of the wavelet coefficients in terms of accuracy. A new era of wavelet coders

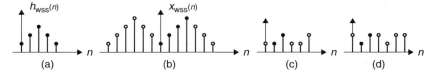

Figure 10: Symmetric extension for odd-length filters. (a) Impulse response with whole sample symmetry (wss); (b) periodic extension with wss of a signal with length $N = 4$ (the original signal is marked with black dots); (c) sub-band periodicity obtained for filter lengths $L = 3 + 4k$ with k being an integer; (d) sub-band periodicity for filter lengths $L = 5 + 4k$

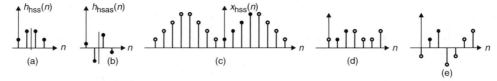

Figure 11: Symmetric extension for even-length filters. (a) Impulse response with half-sample symmetry (hss); (b) half-sample antisymmetry (hsas); (c) periodic signal extension with half-sample symmetry; (d) hss-hss, obtained with hss filter; (e) hsas-hsas, obtained with hsas filter

started with Shapiro's *embedded zerotree wavelet* (EZW) coder (Shapiro 1993), which was the first coder that looked at simultaneous relationships between wavelet coefficients at different scales and produced an entirely embedded code stream that could be truncated at any point to achieve the best reconstruction for the number of symbols transmitted or received. The key idea of the EZW coder was the introduction of *zerotrees*, which are sets of coefficients gathered across scales that are all quantized to zero with regard to a given quantization step size and can be coded with a single symbol. All coefficients within a zerotree belong to the same image region. The formation of zerotrees and the parent-child relationships within a zerotree are shown in Figure 12a. From looking at the wavelet transform in Figure 9, it is clear that it is quite likely that all coefficients in such a tree may be quantized to zero in a smooth image region. The concept of EZW coding was refined by Said and Pearlman (1996), who proposed a coding method known as *set partitioning in hierarchical trees* (SPIHT), a state-of-the-art coding method that offers high compression and fine granular SNR scalability. Both the EZW and SPIHT coders follow the idea of transmitting the wavelet coefficients in a semi-ordered manner, bit plane by bit plane, together with the sorting information required to identify the positions of the transmitted coefficients.

In the following, we will have a closer look at the SPIHT coder, which is more efficient in transmitting the sorting information. In fact, the SPIHT algorithm is so efficient that additional arithmetic coding will only result in marginal improvements (Said and Pearlman 1996).

The SPIHT coder uses three lists to organize the sorting of coefficients and the creation of the bit stream. These are a *list of insignificant pixels* (LIP), a *list of insignificant sets* (LIS), and a *list of significant pixels* (LSP). During initialization, the coordinates of the coefficients in the lowest band are stored in the LIP, and three-quarters of them are also stored in the LIS where they are seen as roots of insignificant sets. Figure 12b illustrates the structure of a set where each coefficient has four offspring. The LSP is left empty at this stage. A start threshold T is defined as $T = 2^n$ with $n = [\log_2(y_{max})]$ and y_{max} being the magnitude of the largest sub-band coefficient.

After initialization, the algorithm goes through sorting and refinement stages with respect to T. During the sorting phase, each coefficient in the LIP is compared with the threshold T, and the result of the comparison (a symbol being 0 or 1) is sent to the channel. If a coefficient exceeds T, then its sign is transmitted and its coordinate moved to the LSP. In a second phase of the sorting pass, each set having its root in the LIS is compared with T, and

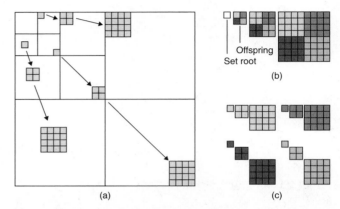

Figure 12: Formation of sets. (a) Sets and zerotrees within the wavelet tree; (b) set; (c) set of (b) partitioned into four subsets

if no coefficient exceeds T, then a zero is sent to the channel. If at least one coefficient within a set is larger than T, then a 1 is sent and the set gets subdivided into the four offspring and four smaller sets. The offspring are tested for significance, and their coordinates are moved to the appropriate list (LIP or LSP). The offspring coordinates are also used as roots for the four smaller sets. See Figures 12b and 12c for an illustration of set partitioning. The significance test and subdivision of sets are carried out until all significant coefficients with respect to T have been isolated. At the end of the procedure with threshold T, all coordinates of significant coefficients are stored in the LSP and their signs have been transmitted along with the sorting information required to identify the positions of the transmitted coefficients. In the next stage, the threshold is halved, and the accuracy of the coefficients in the LSP is refined by sending the information of whether a coefficient lies in the upper or lower half of the uncertainty interval. Then the next sorting pass with the new threshold is carried out and so on. The procedure is repeated until a bit budget is exhausted or the threshold falls below a given limit.

The SPIHT decoder looks at the same significance tests as the encoder and receives the answers to the tests from the bit stream. This allows the decoder to reconstruct the sub-band coefficients bit plane by bit plane. The reconstruction levels are always in the middle of the uncertainty interval. This means that if the decoder knows, for example, that a coefficient is larger than or equal to 2^k (with some k) and smaller than 2^{k+1}, it reconstructs the coefficient as 1.5×2^k. The bit stream can be truncated at any point to meet a bit budget, and the decoder can reconstruct the best possible image for the number of bits received.

An interesting modification of the SPIHT algorithm called *virtual SPIHT* has been proposed by Khan and Ghanbari (2001). This coder virtually extends the octave decomposition until only three set roots are required in the LIS at initialization. This formation of larger initial sets results in more efficient sorting during the first rounds where most coefficients are insignificant with respect to the threshold. Further modifications include, for example, three-dimensional extensions for coding of video (Kim, Xiong, and Pearlman 2000).

Although EZW and SPIHT coding cater well to SNR embeddedness, they do not allow for spatial scalability in the sense that a given bit stream for an $M \times N$ image can be easily parsed into a bit stream for an image of size $(2^{-k}M) \times (2^{-k}N)$ with k being a positive integer. In addition, object-based access is not originally included. These limitations have been overcome by the highly scalable set partitioning algorithm of Danyali and Mertins (2004). This method uses separate lists for the different spatial resolution levels and creates a bit stream that is both SNR and resolution embedded. Higher resolution levels that are not required for a certain target resolution can be easily removed on the fly by a simple parser. Moreover, the method allows for the encoding of arbitrarily shaped objects.

Another efficient and progressive encoding scheme that does not exploit spatial significance trees is the so-called *embedded block coding with optimized truncation* (EBCOT) proposed by Taubmann (2000). This method first encodes blocks of wavelet-transform coefficients in a bit plane by bit plane manner, using a context-dependent arithmetic coding technique. This step results in independent embedded bit streams for each code block. During the individual encoding processes, points of the *rate-distortion* (RD) curves for each code block are determined and stored. In a second step, given an actual bit budget and the stored samples of the RD curves, the optimal bit allocations and thus the code-stream truncation points for the individual blocks are found through a postcompression rate-distortion optimization. By using this principle for several stepwise increasing budgets, a progressively layered code stream is generated. This is illustrated in Figure 13, which shows the formation of layers from the individual embedded code streams.

IMAGE COMPRESSION STANDARDS

A large number of image formats exists. The simplest one is the *bitmap* (BMP) format, which encodes the color components of an image in uncompressed form. The *tagged*

image file format (TIFF) is a container format that allows for the inclusion of various image formats. It is best known for its lossless mode (either uncompressed or losslessly compressed); a TIFF file may, however, also include a lossy-encoded JPEG image (see following). In the following, we will describe the most important formats that achieve significant compression or are widely used throughout the Internet.

GIF

The *graphics interchange format* (GIF) is a lossless image coding format based on the LZW algorithm. It became quite popular for encoding computer-generated images such as buttons on Web sites. GIF allows for interlacing the lines of an image in the order 0, 8, 16,..., 4, 12, 20,..., 2, 6, 10,..., 1, 3, 5, 7,..., which helps to see a reasonable approximation of the image earlier during transmission. GIF is limited to 256 different colors, so it is not well suited for natural images. Because of the licensing problems for the LZW algorithm mentioned earlier, GIF has been abandoned by some software developers who did not want to pay royalties; it has been replaced with the PNG format, which has been intentionally developed as a license-free coding method.

PNG

PNG stands for *portable network graphics* and is a losslessly compressed image format. It was designed as a license-free format that would also overcome some of GIF's limitations such as the low color depth. PNG uses a lossless compression method called *deflation* in combination with the prediction of actual pixel colors from previously seen colors. The deflation algorithm consists of LZ77, followed by a variable-length code. PNG allows for up to 48-bit color depth and offers a more sophisticated interlacing scheme than GIF. The interlacing in PNG is truly two-dimensional and yields a clearer low-resolution image earlier during transmission.

JPEG

JPEG is an industry standard for digital image compression of continuous-tone images developed by the Joint Photographic Experts Group, which is a group of experts nominated by leading companies, academia, and national standards bodies. JPEG was approved by the principal members of ISO and IEC JTC1 as an international standard (IS 10918-1) in 1992 and by the CCITT as recommendation T.81, also in 1992. It includes the following modes of operation (Wallace 1992): a sequential mode, a progressive mode, a hierarchical mode, and a lossless mode. In the following, we will discuss the so-called baseline coder, which is a simple form of the sequential mode that encodes images block by block in scan order from left to right and top to bottom. Image data are allowed to have 8-bit or 12-bit precision. The baseline algorithm is designed for lossy compression with target bit rates in the range of 0.25 to 2 bits per pixel (bpp). The coder uses blockwise DCT, followed by scalar quantization and entropy coding based on run-length and Huffman coding. The general

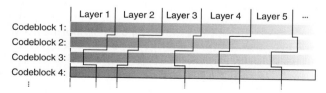

Figure 13: Formation of layered code stream from embedded code streams of individual code blocks

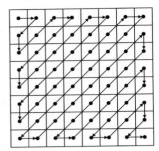

Figure 14: Zigzag scanning order in JPEG

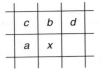

Figure 15: Context modeling in JPEG-LS

structure is the same as in Figure 3. The color space is not specified in the standard, but mostly the YUV space is used with each component treated separately.

After the blockwise DCT (block size 8×8), scalar quantization is carried out with uniform quantizers. This is done by dividing the transform coefficients $y_{k,\ell}, k, \ell = 0, 1, \ldots, 7$ in a block by the corresponding entries $q_{k,\ell}$ in an 8×8 quantization matrix and rounding to the nearest integer: $a_{k,\ell} = \mathrm{round}(y_{k,\ell}/q_{k,\ell})$. Later in the reconstruction stage, an inverse quantization is carried out as $\hat{y}_{k,\ell} = q_{k,\ell} \cdot a_{k,\ell}$. Particular, perceptually optimized quantization matrices have been included in the standard as a recommendation, but they are not a requirement and other quantizers may be used. To obtain more flexibility, all quantization matrices are often scaled such that step sizes $q'_{k,\ell} = D \cdot q_{k,\ell}$ are used instead of $q_{k,\ell}$ The factor D then gives control over the bit rate.

The quantized coefficients in each block are scanned in a zigzag manner, as shown in Figure 14, and are then further entropy encoded. First, the DC coefficient of a block is differentially encoded with respect to the DC coefficient of the previous block (DPCM), using a Huffman code. Then the remaining sixty-three quantized AC coefficients of a block are encoded. The actual coefficient values are Huffman encoded together with the run of zeros from the last nonzero coefficient along the zigzag scanning pass using a two-stage Huffman coding technique with predefined codebooks. The special treatment of zero runs is used, because the occurrence of long stretches of zeros during the zigzag scan is quite likely and coding of individual zeros would be inefficient. If all remaining coefficients along the zigzag scan are zero, then a special end of block symbol is used.

JPEG-LS

JPEG-LS is a standard for lossless and near lossless compression of continuous-tone images (Joint Photographic Experts Group 1997). In the near lossless mode, the user can specify the maximum error ε that may occur during compression. Lossless coding means $\varepsilon = 0$. The performance of JPEG-LS for lossless coding is significantly better than the lossless mode in JPEG.

To achieve compression, context modeling, prediction, and entropy, coding based on Golomb-Rice codes are used. Golomb-Rice codes are a special class of Huffman codes for geometric distributions. The context of a pixel x is determined from four reconstructed pixels a, b, c, d in the neighborhood of x, as shown in Figure 15. Context

is used to decide whether x will be encoded in the run or regular mode.

The run mode (run-length coding) is chosen when the context determines that x is likely to be within the specified tolerance ε of the last encoded pixel. This may be the case in smooth image regions. The run mode is ended either at the end of the current line or when the reconstruction error for a pixel exceeds ε. To encode the run length, a modified Golomb-Rice code is applied.

The regular mode is used when, based on the context, it is unlikely that x lies within the tolerance ε of the previously encoded pixel. In this mode, a prediction for x is computed based on the three neighboring values a, b, and c according to

$$\hat{x} = \begin{cases} \min(a,b) & \text{if } c \geq \max(a,b) \\ \max(a,b) & \text{if } c \leq \min(a,b) \\ a + b - c & \text{otherwise.} \end{cases}$$

This predictor adapts to local edges and is known as a *median edge detection predictor*. In a second step, the prediction is corrected by a context-dependent term to remove systematic prediction biases. The difference between the bias-corrected prediction and the actual value is then encoded using a Golomb-Rice code.

JBIG

The acronym JBIG stands for Joint Bilevel Image experts Group, which is a group of nominees from industry, academia, and government bodies that is working on both ISO and ITU-T standards. JBIG targets the compression of bilevel images, or images that contain only two possible colors (e.g., black and white). When JBIG was created, the aim was to replace older bilevel facsimile standards such as the ITU-T Recommendations T.4 (MH, MR) and T.6 (MMR) with more efficient and flexible techniques.

JBIG has first developed the ISO/IEC 11544 (ITU-T T.82) standard (also known as JBIG1) for the compression of bilevel images. JBIG1 has been designed for lossless and progressive (i.e., lossy-to-lossless) coding, but its capabilities for lossy coding are quite limited.

To see how JBIG1 works, let us consider the encoding of a pixel in a page of digitized text. For such a bilevel image, given the knowledge of some neighboring pixels, one can often infer with high probability what the color of the actual pixel will be. For example, if all neighboring pixels are white, then the probability for the pixel being white will be high. This principle is used in JBIG1 to select one of several arithmetic coders that are optimized for different neighboring pixel configurations. In doing so, a better overall efficiency can be achieved than with a single arithmetic coder.

Figure 16: Neighborhood systems for the low-resolution layer in JBIG1

The neighborhood system used in JBIG1 for the low-resolution part is depicted in Figure 16. The pixels marked o and A are previously encoded ones, and the pixel marked X is the one to be encoded. The position of the pixel marked A is variable and can be chosen to capture some structure (such as vertical lines) in the image. With 10 neighboring pixels, there are $2^{10} = 1024$ different possible neighborhood pixel configurations, and each one yields a different probability for the pixel X to be black or white. Therefore, JBIG would select the best arithmetic coder from 1024 possible ones, depending on the neighborhood pattern.

In the progressive mode, the low-resolution pixels are included in the context for the high-resolution layer together with previously encoded high-resolution pixels. There are four different neighborhood templates with 10 pixels each, so 4096 different neighborhood patterns exist. Consequently, the algorithm selects one of 4096 possible arithmetic coders to encode the pixel.

More recently, a new recommendation known as JBIG2 (lossy and lossless coding of bilevel images) has been published as ISO/IEC 14492 and ITU T.88. It directly targets lossless, lossy, and lossy-to-lossless bilevel image compression. In addition to quality-progressive coding, JBIG2 also includes content-progressive coding, which means that different types of image data are successively added (for example, first text, then halftones). Different compression methods and context models may be applied for text, halftones, and other binary image content. There are a number of fixed templates like in JBIG1, but there exist also adaptive templates for better capturing document structures. Moreover, JBIG2 handles multipage documents in an explicit way.

JPEG 2000

The JPEG 2000 standard is a new standard for still image compression that provides a series of functionalities that were not addressed by the original JPEG standard (Christopoulos, Skodras, and Ebrahimi 2000; Joint Photographic Experts Group 2000). The main features of JPEG 2000 are as follows:

- It can code any type of image (bilevel, continuous tone, multicomponent) with virtually no restriction on image size.

- It handles a wide range of compression factors from 200:1 to lossless.

- It offers progressive transmission by accuracy (signal-to-noise ratio) and spatial resolution.

- It handles lossless and lossy compression within one bit stream.

- It uses random code stream access.

- It demonstrates robustness to bit errors.

- It uses region of interest with improved quality.

To be backwardly compatible with JPEG, the new JPEG 2000 standard includes a DCT mode similar to JPEG, but the core of JPEG 2000 is based on the wavelet transform. JPEG 2000 is being developed in several stages, and in the following we refer to the baseline JPEG 2000 coder as specified in part 1 of the standard. The structure of the baseline JPEG 2000 coder is essentially the one in Figure 3, with the wavelet transform of Figure 8 as the decorrelating transform. To allow for processing of extremely large images on hardware with limited memory resources, it is possible to divide images into tiles and carry out the wavelet transform and compression for each tile independently. The wavelet filters specified are the Daubechies 9-7 filters (Antonini et al. 1992) for maximum performance in the lossy mode and the 5-3 integer-coefficient filters (LeGall and Tabatabai 1988) for an integrated lossy-to-lossless mode. Boundary processing is carried out using the extension scheme for odd-length filters with whole-sample symmetry discussed above.

The quantization stage uses simple scalar quantizers with a dead zone around zero. The quantizer index a that results from quantizing a variable x with step size q is given by

$$
a = \begin{cases} \text{sign}(x) \left\lfloor \frac{|x|}{q} + \xi \right\rfloor, & \frac{|x|}{q} + \xi > 0 \\ 0, & \text{otherwise} \end{cases}
$$

The value of ξ is set to $\xi = 0$ in part 1 of the JPEG 2000 standard, and it is variable with $\xi \in [-1, 1)$ in part 2. Given the quantizer index a, the reconstructed value $\hat{x}$ is computed as

$$
\hat{x} = \begin{cases} \text{sign}(a) \left(|a| - \xi + \delta \right) q, & a \neq 0 \\ 0, & a = 0 \end{cases}
$$

The value for δ satisfies $0 \le \delta < 1$ and is typically chosen as $\delta = 0.5$ so that the reconstructed value lies in the middle of the uncertainty interval. The step sizes for the quantizers are determined from the dynamic ranges of the coefficients in the different sub-bands. In the lossless mode where all sub-band coefficients are integers, the step size is one. The quantized coefficients within each sub-band are then grouped into code blocks that are encoded separately. Independent compression of sub-bands in code blocks is the key to random code-stream access and simple spatial resolution scalability. Only the code blocks referring to a certain region of interest at a desired spatial resolution level of the wavelet tree need to be transmitted or decoded. SNR scalability is achieved through the layer technique described earlier for the EBCOT method.

To demonstrate the performance of JPEG 2000 and provide a comparison with the older JPEG standard, Figure 17 shows some coding examples. One can see that JPEG produces severe blocking artifacts at low rates (in this example, 0.5 bpp) whereas JPEG 2000 tends to produce slightly blurry images. At the higher rate of 2 bpp, both

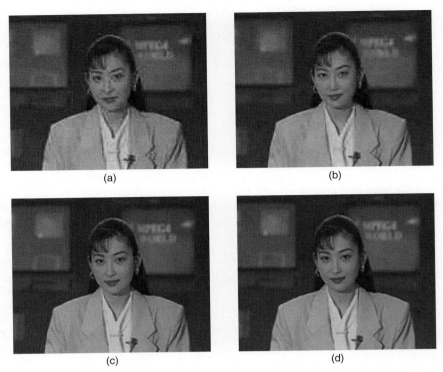

Figure 17: Coding examples (144 × 176 pixels). (a) JPEG at 0.5 bpp; (b) JPEG 2000 at 0.5 bpp; (c) JPEG at 2 bpp; (d) JPEG 2000 at 2 bpp

standards yield good quality images that can hardly be distinguished by the human eye, but JPEG 2000 still has the better signal-to-noise ratio.

Part 2 of the standard includes optional techniques such as trellis-coded quantization (Kasner, Marcellin, and Hunt 1999), which are not required for all implementations. Part 3 addresses Motion JPEG 2000 and defines a file format for storing sequences of images and gives support for associated audio. However, unlike in video coding, each frame is coded independently using JPEG 2000. Applications of this technique are, for example, the storage of video clips using digital still cameras, high-quality frame-based video recording and editing, digital cinema, and medical and satellite imagery. Part 4 addresses conformance and testing, and part 5 contains a reference software. Part 6 describes a file format for document imaging that can be used for storing multipage documents with many objects per page. Part 7 has been abandoned. Part 8 addresses security aspects and ownership protection. Part 9 defines interactive protocols and tools for supporting image and metadata delivery in the context of a networked environment. The main component of part 9 is a client/server protocol (JPIP) that may be implemented on top of HTTP and is designed to handle several different formats for the image data such as complete JPEG or JPEG 2000 files and incremental streams that take full advantage of JPEG 2000's scalability features. Part 10 addresses genuine volumetric image compression rather than frame-wise coding as in Motion JPEG 2000. Part 11 targets wireless multimedia applications, and part 12 is a joint initiative of JPEG and MPEG that aims to create a common file format for future applications using timed sequences of media data.

CONCLUSION

This chapter has reviewed general concepts and standards for still-image compression. We started by looking at theoretical foundations of data compression and then discussed some of the most popular image compression techniques and standards. We saw that different algorithms are used for different types of images. For example, computer-generated images have other properties than natural images and allow for different compression techniques. Moreover, bilevel images require other algorithms than gray-scale and color images. This makes clear that there is and will be a large variety of tools and techniques for still-image compression. Regarding natural images, from today's point of view the diverse functionalities required by many multimedia applications are best provided by coders based on the wavelet transform. As demonstrated in the JPEG 2000 standard, wavelet-based coders even allow the integration of lossy and lossless coding, which is a feature that is highly desirable for applications such as medical imaging where the highest quality is needed. The compression ratios obtained with lossless JPEG 2000 are in the same order as the ones obtained with dedicated lossless methods. However, because lossless coding based on the wavelet transform is still in an early stage, we may expect even better integrated lossy and lossless wavelet-based coders to be developed in the future. In addition to improving on lossless coding, the current research challenges include achieving better error resilience, more flexible object-based access and manipulation, and the incorporation of more up-to-date knowledge of human perception in lossy compression.

GLOSSARY

Differential pulse code modulation (DPCM): A coding technique in which prediction errors are quantized and coded.

Discrete cosine transform (DCT): A transform that is used to decorrelate image blocks.

Discrete wavelet transform (DWT): A multiresolution analysis method that is used in image compression to decorrelate image data.

Embedded block coding with optimized truncation (EBCOT): A technique to generate layered codestreams.

Embedded zerotree wavelet coding (EZW): A wavelet-based coding technique that exploits relationships between wavelet coefficients at different scales.

Karhunen-Loève transform (KLT): A decorrelating transform, also known as principal component analysis.

Lempel-Ziv-Welch algorithm (LZW): A universal coding method.

Pulse code modulation (PCM): A coding technique where signal samples are quantized and encoded separately and independently.

Quantization: The assignment of a discrete symbol to a range of input values.

Set partitioning in hierarchical trees (SPIHT): A wavelet-based coding technique that exploits relationships between wavelet coefficients at different scales.

Vector quantization (VQ): A coding technique where signal samples are quantized and encoded jointly.

CROSS REFERENCES

See *Data Compression*; *Information Theory*; *Speech and Audio Compression*; *Video Compression*.

REFERENCES

Antonini, M., M. Barlaud, P. Mathieu, and I. Daubechies. 1992. Image coding using wavelet transform. *IEEE Transactions on Image Processing*, 1(2): 205–20.

Bradley, J. N., C. M. Brislawn, and V. Faber. 1992. Reflected boundary conditions for multirate filter banks. In *Proceedings of the International Symposium on Time-Frequency and Time-Scale Analysis*, 307–10, Victoria, BC, Canada.

Brislawn, C. M. 1995. Fingerprints go digital. *Notices of the AMS*, 42(11): 1278-83.

Christopoulos, C., A. Skodras, and T. Ebrahimi. 2000. The JPEG 2000 still image coding system: An overview. *IEEE Transactions on Consumer Electronics*, 46(4): 1103–27.

Danyali, H., and A. Mertins. 2004. Flexible, highly scalable, object-based wavelet image compression algorithm for network applications. *IEE Proceedings: Vision, Image, and Signal Processing*, 151(6): 498–510.

Daubechies, I. 1992. *Ten lectures on wavelets*. Philadelphia: Society for Industrial and Applied Mathematics.

Delp, E. J., and O. R. Mitchell. 1979. Image compression using block truncation coding. *IEEE Transactions on Communications*, 27(9): 1335–42.

de Queiroz, R. L. 1992. Sub-band processing of finite length signals without border distortions. In *Proceedings of the IEEE International Conference on Acoustics, Speech, and Signal Processing*, 5: 613–6, San Francisco.

Duhamel, P., and C. Guillemot. 1990. Polynomial transform computation of the 2-D DCT. In *Proceedings of the IEEE International Conference on Acoustics, Speech, and Signal Processing*, 1515–8, Albuquerque, New Mexico.

Fang, W., N. Hu, and S. Shih. 1999. Recursive fast computation of the two-dimensional discrete cosine transform. *IEE Proceedings: Visual Image Signal Processing*, 146(1): 25–33.

Gersho, A., and R. M. Gray. 1991. *Vector quantization and signal compression*. Norwell, MA: Kluwer Academic Publishers.

Herley, C. 1995. Boundary filters for finite-length signals and time-varying filter banks. *IEEE Transactions on Circuits and Systems II*, 42(2): 102–14.

Jayant, N. S., and P. Noll. 1984. *Digital coding of waveforms*. Englewood Cliffs, NJ: Prentice Hall.

Joint Photographic Experts Group. 1997. *JPEG-LS final committee draft*. ISO/IEC JTC1/SC29/WG1 FCD14495-1.

———. 2000. *JPEG 2000 final draft international standard, part I*. ISO/IEC JTC1/SC29/WG1 FDIS15444-1.

Kasner, J. H., M. W. Marcellin, and B. R. Hunt. 1999. Universal trellis coded quantization. *IEEE Transactions on Image Processing*, 8(12): 1677–87.

Katto, J., and Y. Yasuda. 1991. Performance evaluation of sub-band coding and optimization of its filter coefficients. In *Proceedings of SPIE Visual Communication and Image Processing*, 95–106.

Khan, E., and Ghanbari, M. 2001. Very low bit rate video coding using virtual SPIHT. *Electronic Letters*, 37(1): 40–2.

Kim, B.-J., Z. Xiong, and W. A. Pearlman. 2000. Low bit-rate scalable video coding with 3-d set partitioning in hierarchical trees (3-D SPIHT). *IEEE Transactions on Circuits and Systems for Video Technology*, 10(8): 1374–87.

Le Gall, D., and A. Tabatabai. 1988. Sub-band coding of digital images using short kernel filters and arithmetic coding techniques. In *Proceedings of the IEEE International Conference on Acoustics, Speech, and Signal Processing*, 761–4, New York.

Lloyd, S. P. 1957. Least squares quantization in PCM. In *Institute of Mathematical Statistics Society Meeting*, 189–92, Atlantic City, New Jersey.

Max, J. 1960. Quantizing for minimum distortion. *IRE Transactions on Information Theory*, 7–12.

Mertins, A. 2001. Boundary filters for size-limited paraunitary filter banks with maximum coding gain and ideal DC behavior. *IEEE Transactions on Circuits and Systems II*, 48(2): 183–8.

Moving Picture Experts Group. 1999. MPEG-4 video verification model, version 14. Generic coding of moving pictures and associated audio. ISO/IEC JTC1/SC 29/WG 11.

Rao, K. R., and P. Yip. 1990. *Discrete cosine transform*. New York: Academic Press.

Said, A., and W. A. Pearlman. 1996. A new fast and efficient image codec based on set partitioning in hierarchical trees. *IEEE Transactions on Circuits and Systems for Video Technology*, 6(3): 243–50.

Shannon, C. E. 1959. Coding theorems for a discrete source with a fidelity criterion. *IRE Nat. Conv. Rec.*, 4: 142–63.

Shapiro, J. M. 1993. Embedded image coding using zerotrees of wavelet coefficients. *IEEE Transactions on Signal Processing*, 41(12): 3445–62.

Smith, M. J. T., and S. L. Eddins. 1990. Analysis/synthesis techniques for sub-band coding. *IEEE Transactions on Acoustics, Speech, and Signal Processing*, 38(8): 1446–56.

Taubmann, D. 2000. High performance scalable image compression with EBCOT. *IEEE Transactions on Image Processing*, 9(7): 1158–70.

Vaidyanathan, P. P. 1985. On power-complementary FIR filters. *IEEE Transactions on Circuits and Systems*, 32(12): 1308–10.

Wallace, G. K. 1992. The JPEG still picture compression standard. *IEEE Transactions on Consumer Electronics*, 38(1): 18–34.

Welch, T. A. 1984. A technique for high-performance data compression. *IEEE Computer*, 17(6): 8–19.

Woods, J., and S. O'Neil. 1986. Sub-band coding of images. *IEEE Transactions on Acoustics, Speech, and Signal Processing*, 34(5): 1278–88.

Video Compression

Immanuel Freedman, *Independent Consultant, Harleysville, Pennsylvania*

INTRODUCTION

What Is Video Compression?

Video compression is a method of reducing the amount of digital data used to represent a sequence of images that normally vary in time and are intended to portray motion.

This chapter focuses on principles of video compression in a cumulative presentation that follows from chapters in this volume on information theory, data compression, image compression, high-definition television (HDTV), and error correction. The presentation intersperses practical examples with just-in-time theoretical analysis.

In this chapter, the first section introduces and demonstrates the need for video compression. The second, third, and fourth sections describe and discuss standards developed by the Joint Photographic Experts Group (JPEG), the International Telecommunication Union (ITU), and the Moving Picture Experts Group (MPEG). The fifth section refers to proprietary codecs developed by Microsoft, Real Networks, On2 Technologies, and Euclid Discoveries, including a proprietary codec standardized by the Society of Motion Picture and Television Engineers (SMPTE). The last section before the conclusion provides a simple evaluation of commercially available codecs for real-time communications.

Why Do We Need Video Compression?

Many people would like to hold conversations over video telephone systems, such as the *freedom of mobile multimedia access* (FOMA) system developed by NTT DoCoMo (Tachikawa 2003). Other people would like to watch digital movies on their cable television systems, store and retrieve video on demand from high-density optical disks, or videoconference with business partners. The required data rate (frame rate × frame size × color depth) usually exceeds the available communications bandwidth, a problem for which video compression provides a technical solution.

Visual Inspection

As a practical example, Figure 1 shows images of frames numbered 1231 to 1233 from *The Emotion of Space* movie (National Aeronautics and Space Administration 2001), indicating a scene change at frame 1232 and motion sequence from frames 1232 to 1233.

The 3219 frames of this movie, which is 215 seconds in length, include monochrome still images, historic monochrome video, color video with rapidly moving objects, animation sequences, human faces, and crowd scenes. The movie has frame size 320 × 240 pixels, 24-bit color depth (8 bits each for the red, green, and blue channels), and an average frame rate of 15 frames per second (fps). Real-time transmission without compression requires 27.7 megabytes per second (Mbps), not considering the audio tracks. This bit rate is far above the capacity of a typical 384-kbps FOMA video telephone connection or 1.5-Mbps digital television channel under optimal conditions.

Visual inspection of Figure 1 reveals considerable overlap between frames 1232 and 1233 but discontinuous change of scene between frames 1231 and 1232 (a likely

Figure 1: Images of frames 1231 to 1233 from the NASA movie *The Emotion of Space* showing scene change at frame 1232 and motion sequence from frames 1232 to 1233

result of editing). The space suit color (not shown in these gray-scale images) contrasts well with the background, which indicates *spectral redundancy*. Each frame depicts a small number of recognizable visual objects, which indicates local *spatial redundancy*. The motion of the astronauts indicates *temporal redundancy*. The viewer focuses attention on the motion of the astronauts and the expressions on their faces, which indicates *psychovisual redundancy* (i.e., redundancy related to human perception of vision).

Accordingly, this chapter shows how video compression methods solve the problems of communicating *The Emotion of Space* over bidirectional videophones by reducing spectral, spatial, temporal, and psychovisual redundancies while also addressing rate control, scalability, error resilience, and applications. In addition, the chapter shows how video compression methods solve problems in distributing digital cinema movies, transmitting and receiving NASA's Mars Exploration Rover image sequences, storing and retrieving high-definition television sequences, and videoconferencing with business partners.

Video Compression

Video compression trades communications bandwidth and media storage space for picture quality and processor cycles.

Video compression methods are described as *lossless*, *lossy*, *progressive*, or *hybrid*. Unlike lossless methods, which are exact and reversible, lossy methods are approximate and irreversible. The term *lossy* arose by analogy with a concept familiar to electrical engineers: the dissipation of electrical energy as heat in the transmission of power. Quoting Shannon (1948), "The fundamental problem of communication is that of reproducing at one point either exactly or approximately a message selected at another point." In multidisciplinary environments, the terms *exact* and *approximate* are often more acceptable than the terms *lossless* and *lossy*. *Progressive* methods provide a sequence of approximations that may become exact. *Hybrid* methods preserve picture quality by exactly coding residuals from compressed approximations. This chapter points out lossless, lossy, progressive, and hybrid methods when appropriate.

Remotely sensed images (such as radar and satellite images) are often noisy. The image noise carries information about sensor characteristics, background, and unresolved images. Although researchers frequently state that image noise is incompressible, identifying noise process parameters or reporting noise summary statistics conveys information that can be used to reconstruct the noise.

Rate-Distortion Bound

For a small reduction in picture quality (distortion), lossy methods often yield far greater reduction in data rate than quality-preserving lossless methods. The *Shannon rate-distortion bound* refers to the minimum average bit rate required to encode a data source for a given average distortion; it is useful for exploring the limits of compressibility for a *memoryless image source*, which selects each pixel's luminance value independently of all of the others (see "Information Theory" and "Image Compression"). With perfect reconstruction of data, the bit rate at zero distortion is equal to the source entropy, a measure of the information contained in the source. In practice, many researchers compare the effectiveness of video compression algorithms by plotting empirically determined quality measures as a function of observed bit rate for a specified set of video sequences. Almost invariably, the observed video quality improves with increased bit rate.

Equation 1 defines Shannon's entropy H for an image in units of *bits per pixel* (bpp), where $p(I)$ is the probability of pixel value I.

$$H = -\sum_{I=0}^{2^m-1} p(I)log_2 p(I) \tag{1}$$

The observed histogram of pixel values over all video sequence frames determines the observed Shannon's entropy.

Video Quality Metrics

Let each frame have N*M pixels with bit depth m. Let the pixel value at location (i, j) in frame k be $I(i, j, k)$ for the original frame and $\hat{I}(i, j, k)$ for the reconstructed frame. To measure video quality, Equation 2 exhibits the *mean square error* and *peak signal-to-noise ratio* (PSNR) for a video sequence of K frames.

$$MSE = \frac{1}{NMK}\sum_{k=1}^{K}\sum_{j=1}^{N}\sum_{i=1}^{M}\left[I(i,j,k) - \hat{I}(i,j,k)\right]^2$$

$$PSNR = 20\log_{10}\left(\frac{2^m - 1}{\sqrt{MSE}}\right) \tag{2}$$

Although many researchers use PSNR as a measure of video quality, measuring the quality of a video sequence reconstructed from compressed imagery is an application-dependent task.

Subjective evaluation requires a group of human observers—preferably not experts in image quality assessment—to view and rate video quality in terms of a scale of impairments that range from "imperceptible" to "very annoying." The BT.500-11 standard developed by the radiocommunication sector of the International Telecommunications Union titled "Methodology for the Subjective Assessment of the Quality of Television Pictures" (ITU-R 2002), recommends a specific system and prescribes viewing conditions, range of luminance presented to the viewer panel, number and experience of viewers, monitor contrast, selection of test materials, and suggested processes for evaluating test results. The *double stimulus impairment scale* (DSIS) and the *double stimulus continuous quality scale* (DSCQS) are particularly noteworthy. Subjective tests are costly and not highly reproducible. Two standards set by the American National Standards Institute (ANSI) are of value here: T1.801.01-1995 (ANSI 1995) provides a set of test scenes in digital format while T1.801.02-1996 (ANSI 1996) provides a dictionary of commonly used video quality impairment terms.

Objective evaluation techniques include the ANSI T1.803.03-2003 (Annex A) standard, which lists a set of objective test criteria used to measure video quality in one-way video systems, applying objective tests closely related to known features of the *human visual system* (HVS). A video quality metric software implementation of the Annex A standard is currently available from the Institute for Telecommunication Sciences, which is the research and engineering branch of the U.S. government's National Telecommunications and Information Administration.

Lossless Entropy Coder

Consider independently compressing each frame of the 3219 RGB video frames of *The Emotion of Space* depicted in Figure 1. Recall from "Data Compression" that a lossless entropy coder converts a sequence of input symbols into a sequence of bits such that the average number of bits approaches the entropy of the symbols. Figure 2a depicts a lossless entropy encoder, and Figure 2b depicts a lossless entropy decoder corresponding to Figure 2a. An encoder and corresponding decoder together form a *codec*.

The lossless entropy coder selected for this example is a *Witten-Neal-Cleary adaptive arithmetic coder* according to the implementation developed by Witten et al. (1987). This arithmetic coder represents a message as an interval of real numbers between zero and one. Successive symbols of the message reduce the interval, increasing the number of bits required to represent the interval according to symbol probabilities generated from a model updated as the symbols are encoded.

Lossless Entropy Coder Performance

Figure 3 shows the result of compressing all 3219 frames of *The Emotion of Space* with the Witten-Neal-Cleary coder together with the Shannon's entropy according to Equation 1. The Figure also indicates the arithmetically encoded bit rate and Shannon's entropy according to Equation 3 for each frame, expressed in bpp:

$$\text{bit rate} = 24 \bullet \left(\frac{\begin{array}{c}\text{compressed frame}\\\text{size in bits}\end{array}}{\begin{array}{c}\text{original frame}\\\text{size in bits}\end{array}} \right) \text{bits-per-pixel} \quad (3)$$

Horizontal lines indicate the movie average bit rate and Shannon's entropy. The arithmetically encoded bit rate and Shannon's entropy are highly variable, which is appropriate for the highly variable information content including scene changes and fades. The average arithmetically encoded bit rate is 18.68 bpp, which is approximately 4.918 bpp above the average Shannon's entropy of 13.76 bpp. Encoding *The Emotion of Space* at approximately 384 kbps requires 24 bpp × (384 kbps/27.7 Mbps) = 0.333 bpp.

Motion DCT Codec

To further illustrate the above concepts, consider independently compressing each of the 3219 RGB video frames of *The Emotion of Space* with a simplified block transform coder based on the *discrete cosine transform* (DCT) and a lossless entropy coder. Figure 4 shows a block diagram for an initial version of this simple coder, reminiscent of the well-known baseline image coder standardized by the JPEG.

Each frame has $N*M$ pixels for each color component. If $N = 0 \pmod{B}$ and $M = 0 \pmod{B}$, then each frame can be covered without padding by contiguous nonoverlapping blocks of $B \times B$ pixels.

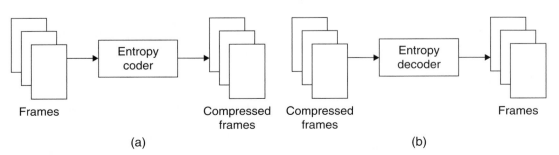

Figure 2: Lossless entropy (a) encoder and (b) decoder

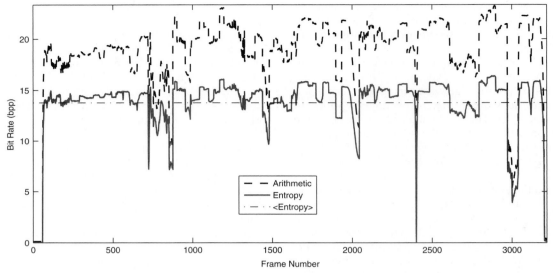

Figure 3: Arithmetic coding (bpp) and Shannon's entropy versus frame number for *The Emotion of Space* (NASA, 2001)

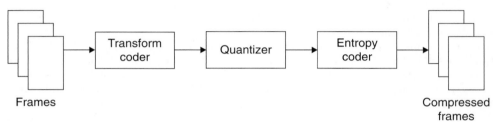

Frames

Compressed
frames   **Figure 4:** Motion DCT encoder

The DCT is widely used for video coding because the transform coefficients are independent of frame content and effectively reduce spatial redundancy by decorrelating the pixel values. For highly correlated adjacent pixels, the DCT performs nearly as well as the optimal Karhunen-Loève transform, which has coefficients laboriously calculated from the pixel values of each frame.

Equation 4 gives the two-dimensional separable DCT of the pixel values $I(x, y)$ for pixels at block coordinates (x, y) where $x \in [0, ..., B - 1]$, $y \in [0, ..., B - 1]$:

$$DCT(m,n) = \frac{1}{\sqrt{2B}} C(m)C(n) \sum_{x=0}^{B-1} \sum_{y=0}^{B-1} I(x,y)$$
$$\cos\left[\frac{(2x+1)m\pi}{2B}\right] \cos\left[\frac{(2y+1)n\pi}{2B}\right]$$
$$C(i) = \frac{1}{\sqrt{2}}, i = 0$$
$$1, i > 0 \tag{4}$$

Approximating the coefficients $DCT(m, n)$ by uniform scalar quantization, Equation 5 shows how to obtain the quantized coefficients $QDCT(m, n)$ by rounding and division with positive integer quantization parameter Q:

$$QDCT(m,n) = \text{round}\left(\frac{DCT(m,n)}{Q}\right) \tag{5}$$

The decoder reconstructs coefficients DCT' according to Equation 6:

$$DCT'(m,n) = Q \bullet QDCT(m,n) \tag{6}$$

Equation 7 shows how to reconstruct image blocks $\bar{B}(x,y)$ from the quantized coefficients $QDCT(m, n)$. Note that rounding ensures lossy compression even when the quantization parameter Q is set to unity.

$$\bar{B}(x,y) = \frac{1}{\sqrt{2N}} \sum_{m=0}^{N-1} \sum_{n=0}^{N-1} C(m)C(n)QDCT(m,n)$$
$$\cos\left[\frac{(2x+1)m\pi}{2N}\right] \cos\left[\frac{(2y+1)n\pi}{2N}\right]$$
$$C(i) = \frac{1}{\sqrt{2}}, i = 0$$
$$1, i > 0 \tag{7}$$

The *minimum coded unit* (MCU) is the minimum amount of image data that a coder can code. For noninterleaved image data, Equations 4 and 7 indicate that the motion DCT coder can compress or decompress as little as one $B \times B$-pixel block. Hence, the motion DCT coder can provide easy access to compressed image blocks for nonlinear editing together with a low level of latency (delay) for encoding and decoding.

A lossless entropy coder encodes the quantized coefficients $QDCT(m, n)$. The lossless entropy coder selected

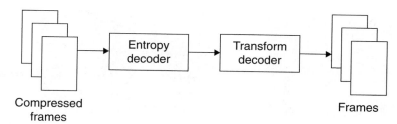

Figure 5: Motion DCT decoder

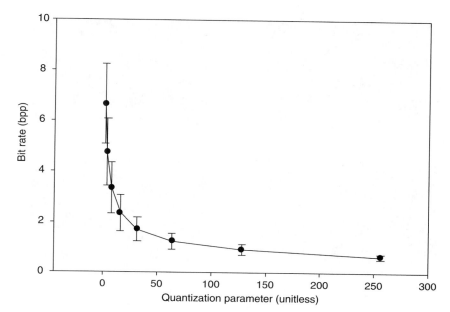

Figure 6: Motion DCT average and standard deviation bit rate (bpp) versus quantization parameter for *The Emotion of Space* (3219 frames)

for this example is the Witten-Neal-Cleary arithmetic coder described above.

Figure 5 shows a block diagram for an initial version of a simple decoder that decodes the compressed frames into quantized coefficients QDCT (*m, n*) with an entropy decoder according to Witten et al. (1987). A transform decoder restores image blocks from the quantized coefficients according to Equation 5.

Motion DCT Performance

Figure 6 shows the observed average and standard deviation in bpp versus quantization parameter for 3219 frames of *The Emotion of Space* encoded by the motion DCT encoder implemented in MATLAB and the C programming language. Quantization parameter values ranging from 2 to 256 result in bit rates ranging from 6.64 to 0.651 bpp.

Figure 7 shows a panel of gray-scale images representing color frame 1232 of *The Emotion of Space* compressed by the motion DCT coder to bit rates (a) 6.63, (b) 4.74, (c) 3.35, (d) 2.36, (e) 1.70, (f) 1.26, (g) 0.927, and (i) 0.651 bpp. These images illustrate lossy, progressive compression with quantization parameters Q = 2, 4, 8, 16, 32, 64, 128, and 256 corresponding to the above bit rates.

Figure 8 shows the objective video quality versus bit rate (bpp) measured by the PSNR metric according to Equation 2 and the *video quality metric* (VQM) software implementation of the T1.803.03-2003 Annex A standard (ANSI 2003). The VQM is measured on the aforementioned DSIS (5 = imperceptible, 4 = perceptible but

not annoying, 3 = slightly annoying, 2 = annoying, and 1 = very annoying).

The VQM objective video quality assessment agrees substantially with the subjective video quality assessment described above. Within the visually acceptable range of observed VQM values (approximately 3 to 5 on the DSIS), the observed PSNR metric values range from approximately 30 to 60 dB.

In summary, the motion DCT codec illustrates the principles of spatial redundancy reduction but does not achieve the goal of communicating *The Emotion of Space* over bidirectional videophones at a near constant bit rate of 384 kbps with acceptable video quality. Several standardized video codecs perform better than the motion DCT codec.

Standards

Standards are requirement documents that indicate detail only in areas of agreement between standards participants (who are often competitors). Practicing the standards requires proprietary technology, for which some patent holders have agreed to provide licenses on reasonable and nondiscriminatory terms.

Note that the standards typically specify reference decoders, not encoders. Although this chapter presents encoding techniques, encoders typically comply with the standard if the standard reference decoder can decode the bit stream they produce. This approach to standardization maximizes flexibility and innovation while ensuring a modicum of interoperability between implementations.

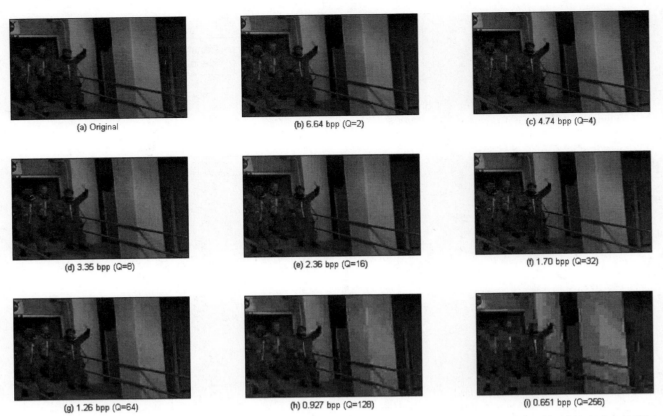

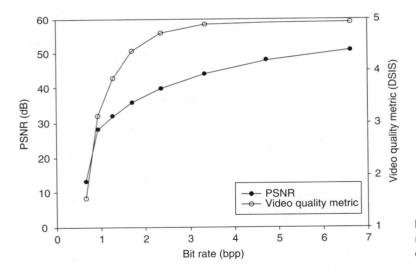

Figure 7: Panel of gray-scale images representing color frame 1232 of *The Emotion of Space* compressed by the Motion DCT coder to bit rates (b) 6.64, (c) 4.74, (d) 3.35, (e) 2.36, (f) 1.70, (g) 1.26, (h) 0.927, and (i) 0.651 bpp

Figure 8: PSNR and video quality metric versus bit rate (bpp) for a 30-second duration of *The Emotion of Space*, frames 1230 to 1679

JPEG CODECS

Motion JPEG—although never standardized—derives from the baseline JPEG standard for compression and coding of continuous-tone still images, 10918-1:1994 (ISO/IEC 1994).

The baseline JPEG standard encodes images with an arbitrary number of color components, comprising data samples having precision ranging from two to sixteen bits. This standard supports four encoding modes: sequential DCT-based, progressive DCT-based, lossless, and hierarchical.

Motion JPEG-LS (also never standardized) derives from the JPEG standard for lossless and near-lossless compression of continuous tone still images, ISO/IEC 14495-1:1999(E). This standard improves and extends methods for baseline JPEG lossless encoding.

Part 3 of the JPEG 2000 standard for the JPEG 2000 image-coding system, 15444-3 (ISO/IEC 2002), standardizes Motion JPEG 2000. Motion JPEG 2000 is the most efficient, compressive, and flexible JPEG codec to date and so forms the primary topic of this section.

Spectral Domain

Motion JPEG and Motion JPEG-LS support an arbitrary number of color components without recommending or mandating any color space for spectral compression, although the JPEG standard cites an example based on a color space with luminance and chrominance color components.

Motion JPEG 2000 derives spectral compression from Parts 1 and 2 of the current JPEG 2000 standard, 15444-1 and 15444-2 (ISO/IEC, 2004a, 2004b). JPEG 2000 transforms image colors to reduce spectral redundancy. The *human visual system* (HVS) is typically more sensitive to changes in brightness than color, with peak color sensitivity to green. Accordingly, JPEG 2000 supports color transformation of images in the RGB color space to the YC_rC_b color space given by Equation 8, where Y denotes image brightness signal (luma) while C_r and C_b denote red and blue color difference signals (chroma), respectively. A downsampling filter typically reduces the resolution of both C_r and C_b components by a factor of two in both horizontal and vertical directions:

$$
\begin{bmatrix} Y \\ C_r \\ C_b \end{bmatrix} = \begin{bmatrix} 0.299 & 0.587 & 0.114 \\ -0.1688 & -0.3313 & 0.5 \\ 0.5 & -0.4187 & -0.08131 \end{bmatrix} \begin{bmatrix} R \\ G \\ B \end{bmatrix} \quad (8)
$$

In addition to the YC_rC_b color space above, JPEG 2000 supports an integer *reversible color transform* (RCT) given by Equation 9, where V_1 denotes the luma signal, while V_2 and V_3 denote chroma signals, respectively:

$$
\begin{aligned}
V_1 &= \left\lfloor \frac{1}{4}(R + 2G + B) \right\rfloor \\
V_2 &= B - G \\
V_3 &= R - G
\end{aligned} \quad (9)
$$

To preserve reversibility, if any image component is unsigned, JPEG 2000 Part 1 Annex G specifies shifting the level of the unsigned component with depth *bits* by subtracting 2^{bits-1} and storing the transformed values at one-bit greater precision than the original component.

JPEG 2000 Part 2 supports additional color spaces, such as Commission Internationale de l'Éclairage (CIE) XYZ tri-stimulus color values, together with color transforms for spectral decorrelation of multiple component images, which are often required by scientific and medical applications.

Reversible Color Transform

Figure 9 shows (a) red, (b) green, and (c) blue components of frame numbered 1232 from *The Emotion of Space* together with luma V_1 (d) and chroma V_2(e), V_3(f) components, following a reversible color transform from RGB to RCT color space.

To measure the effectiveness of color decorrelation, Equations 10 and 11 compare the covariance of samples between frame 1232 color components $\tilde{\mathbf{R}}_{RGB}$ (before) and $\tilde{\mathbf{R}}_{RCT}$ (after) transformation from RGB to RCT color space.

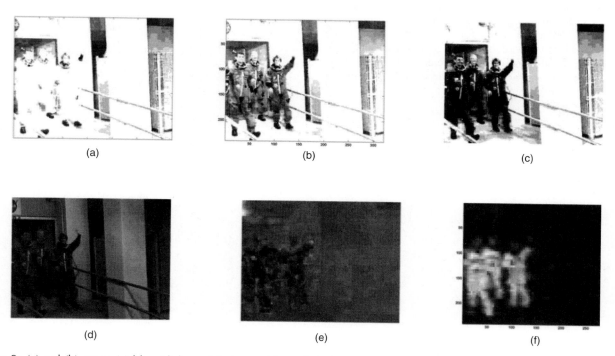

(a)   (b)   (c)

(d)   (e)   (f)

Figure 9: (a) red (b) green (c) blue (d) luma (e) chroma V_2, and (f) chroma V_3 components of frame numbered 1232 from *The Emotion of Space*

$$\tilde{\mathbf{R}}_{RGB} = 1000^* \begin{bmatrix} 1.573 & 1.334 & 1.303 \\ 1.334 & 1.886 & 2.041 \\ 1.303 & 2.041 & 2.279 \end{bmatrix}$$

$$\tilde{\mathbf{R}}_{RCT} = 1000^* \begin{bmatrix} 1.719 & 0.1293 & -0.4010 \\ 0.1293 & 0.0842 & -0.1866 \\ -0.4010 & -0.1866 & 0.7900 \end{bmatrix} \quad (10)$$

$$G_{color} = \frac{\sum_{n=1}^{3} \tilde{\mathbf{R}}_{RGB}^2(n,n)}{\sum_{n=1}^{3} \tilde{\mathbf{R}}_{RCT}^2(n,n)} = 10 \log_{10}\left(\frac{5.738}{2.213}\right) = 3.449 \text{ dB}$$

$$(11)$$

The transformation from RGB to RCT color space provides 3.449 dB variance gain by substantially reducing correlation between color components.

Spatial Domain

Motion JPEG

The frequency distribution of DCT AC coefficients, as determined by Equation 4 for $m > 0$ and $n > 0$, is often described by a Laplacian (symmetric exponential) distribution. The DC coefficients ($m = 0$, $n = 0$) are typically distributed differently from the AC coefficients with relatively high block-to-block correlation. The fraction of nonzero-quantized AC coefficients often varies as a mild power law with average bit rate.

The JPEG committee recommended different treatments for DC and AC coefficients because of the high block-to-block correlation for DC coefficients and that quantization clears many AC coefficients. A Huffmann or arithmetic lossless entropy coder encodes the transform coder output. The transform coder emits the difference between the DC coefficients for the current and previous blocks in row major order. As shown in Figure 10, the transform coder scans AC coefficients in zigzag order from the coefficient labeled 1 to the coefficient labeled

63 to increase the run length of zeros, which it identifies and codes efficiently.

The JPEG committee selected the 8 × 8-pixel block size for transform coding, a decision practical at that time. A full frame block size would have reduced blocking impairments at the expense of increased computational resource. Operating in a hierarchical mode, a 4 × 4-pixel block size would more likely than not have reduced impairments at the edges of visual objects.

Distribution of DCT Coefficients

Recalling the Motion DCT coder described above, Figure 11 shows the frequency distribution of discrete transform AC coefficients for Motion DCT *The Emotion of Space* as determined by Equation 4 for $m > 0$ and $n > 0$. Let y denote the frequency and x denote the value of the DCT AC coefficient. A Laplacian (symmetric exponential) distribution $y = a \exp - |x/b|$ where $a = 1.27 \bullet 10^8$, $b = 6.84$ fits this distribution with coefficient of determination $r^2 = 0.854$ for all RGB color components. For DC coefficients, the observed block-to-block correlation is (74 ± 18%, 75 ± 18%, 58 ± 36%) for the red, green, and blue color components, respectively.

Figure 12 shows the fraction of nonzero-quantized AC DCT coefficients versus average bit rate (bpp) for the

0	2	5	9	14	20	27	35
1	4	9	13	19	26	34	42
3	7	12	18	25	33	41	48
6	11	17	24	32	40	47	53
10	16	23	31	39	46	52	57
15	22	30	38	45	52	56	60
21	29	37	44	50	55	59	62
28	36	43	49	54	58	61	63

Figure 10: Zigzag sequence for 8 × 8-pixel DCT coefficients

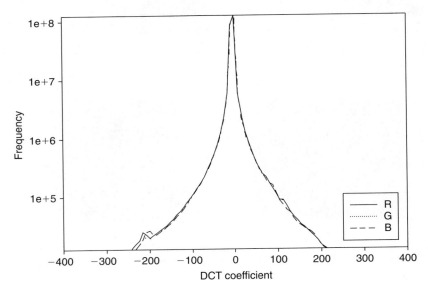

Figure 11: Frequency distribution of AC DCT coefficients for *The Emotion of Space* in color space

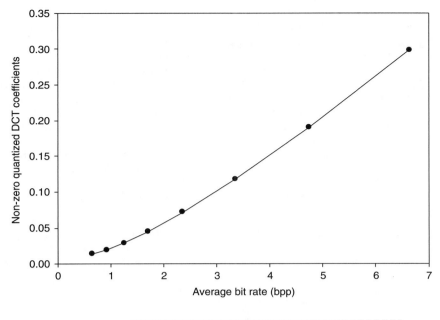

Figure 12: Fraction of nonzero quantized DCT coefficients versus average bit rate (bpp) for *The Emotion of Space*

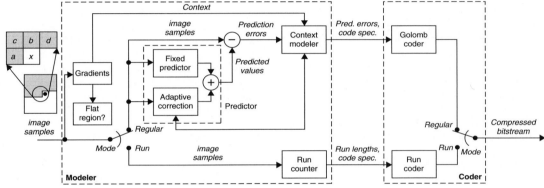

Figure 13: JPEG-LS block diagram after Weinberger et al. 1999

NASA movie and Motion DCT coder. Let y denote the fraction of nonzero-quantized DCT coefficients and x denote the average bit rate (bpp). A power curve $y = a^{bx}$ fits the data for all RGB color components, where $a = 0.0224 \pm 0.00037$ and $b = 1.37 = 0.0095$ with coefficient of determination $r^2 = 0.999$.

Whereas Figures 11 and 12 illustrate distributions observed for the motion DCT encoder, the corresponding distributions for generic transform coders often take these forms.

Quantization Matrices

The JPEG standard generalizes Equations 5 and 6 to Equations 12 and 13 by quantizing each AC coefficient separately in terms of a quantization matrix $Q(m, n)$ where $m, n \in [1,...,7]$. The matrix allows an encoder to allocate bits between sub-bands:

$$QDCT(m,n) = \text{round}\left(\frac{DCT(m,n)}{Q(m,n)}\right) \quad (12)$$

$$DCT'(m,n) = Q(m,n) \bullet QDCT(m,n) \quad (13)$$

Note that the JPEG standard does not mandate specific tables for quantization, Huffmann encoding, or arithmetic encoding, and it provides a default table only for arithmetic encoding. To decode a JPEG-compliant bit stream, the encoder tables must be available in the bit stream or from a separate source.

Motion JPEG-LS. Motion JPEG-LS provides hybrid lossless and near-lossless coding without using transforms. The current (1999) version is based on a low-complexity encoder termed LOCO-I (Weinberger et al. 1999).

Figure 13 shows the JPEG-LS block diagram and an image data sample (marked by x) in the context of its reconstructed nearest neighbors (a, b, c, d), whose pixel values the encoder combines to form a set of selectable linear predictors of x. Equation 14 gives the fixed predictor denoted by $\hat{x}_{MED}$, in terms of the pixel values a, b and c:

$$\hat{x}_{MED} = \begin{cases} \min(a,b) \text{ if } c \geq \max(a,b) \\ \max(a,b) \text{ if } c \leq \max(a,b) \\ a - b + c \text{ otherwise} \end{cases} \quad (14)$$

The fixed predictor $\hat{x}_{MED}$ is the median of three fixed predictors, a, b, and $a + b - c$, and it tends to pick b when there is a vertical visual edge to the left of the current location, a, when there is a horizontal visual edge above the current location, and $a + b - c$, when no edge is detected. The JPEG-LS standard assumes that the integer context-dependent prediction residuals $\varepsilon = x - \hat{x}_{MED}$ follow the normalized biased Laplacian distribution with decay rate θ and bias $\mu = R - s$, $R = \lfloor \mu \rfloor$, $0 \leqslant s < 1$, given by Equation 15 with normalization factor denoted by $C(\theta, s)$:

$$P(\theta, \mu) = C(\theta, s)\theta^{|\varepsilon - R + s|}, \varepsilon = 0, \pm 1, \pm 2, \ldots,$$
$$C(\theta, s) = (1 - \theta)/(\theta^{1-s} + \theta^{s}) \qquad (15)$$

The adaptive correction shown in Figure 13 subtracts a low-complexity estimate of R, the integer part of the bias, from the prediction residuals. Equation 16 gives the distribution of residuals after adaptive correction:

$$P(\theta, s) = C(\theta, s)\theta^{|\varepsilon + s|}, \varepsilon = 0, \pm 1, \pm 2, \ldots, \qquad (16)$$

The context modeler in Figure 13 partitions the triplet of pixel value differences $\mathbf{g} = \{d - b, b - c, c - a\}$ into a fixed number of equiprobable regions. The run coder then codes the partitioned prediction residuals with a run-length code that the Golomb coder codes with a near-optimal entropy code.

In the near-lossless mode, the JPEG-LS encoder controls the maximum absolute error between a reconstructed image component and the corresponding value in the original image by quantizing prediction residuals.

Motion JPEG 2000. Figure 14 shows a block diagram for a Motion JPEG 2000 encoder, while Figure 15 shows a block diagram for the corresponding decoder.

"Image Compression" addresses wavelet transforms together with JPEG 2000 tier-1 and tier-2 codecs (see Taubman and Marcellin 2001).

Motion JPEG 2000 derives scalability of image size, bit rate, and quality from Part 1 of the JPEG 2000 standard. Spatial transforms recommended by JPEG 2000 include reversible 5/3 tap and irreversible 9/7 tap wavelets. Quantization of wavelet coefficients is a mechanism for lossy compression methods based on the irreversible 9/7 tap filter. The section discussing rate control and JPEG codecs addresses bit allocation and packetization for rate control by *post compression rate distortion* (PCRD), which provides mechanisms for lossy compression methods based on the reversible 5/3 tap filter.

Distribution of Wavelet Coefficients

As an example, consider a video frame filtered by an analysis filter with low-pass coefficients $\{-1/8, 2/8, 6/8, 2/8, -1/8\}$ and high-pass coefficients $\{1/2, 1, 1/2\}$. This is a 5/3 tap filter because it has five low-pass and three high-pass filter coefficients. The low-pass coefficients provide a low-resolution version of the image, while the high-pass coefficients provide a low-resolution version of the residuals needed for perfect reconstruction of the image. Applying this filter (implemented in MATLAB) three times to a square window sized 240×240 pixels of *The Emotion of Space* in the RCT color space provides three levels of detail in both horizontal and vertical directions that yield the frequency distribution of wavelet coefficients shown in Figure 16.

The Laplacian distribution $y = \exp\left(-\left|\dfrac{x}{b}\right|\right)$ describes the frequency distribution shown in Figure 16 for color components (V_1, V_2, V_3) where $a = (1.03, 1.19, 1.19) \bullet 10^8$, $(b = 6.96, 6.09, 6.02)$ with coefficient of determination

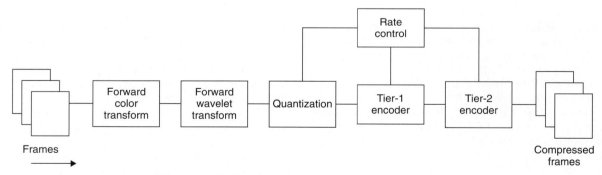

Figure 14: Block diagram for a Motion JPEG 2000 encoder

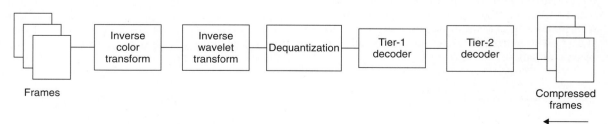

Figure 15: Block diagram for a Motion JPEG 2000 decoder

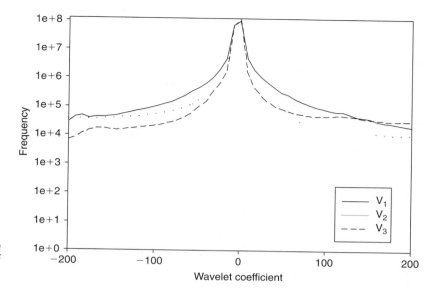

Figure 16: Frequency distribution of 5/3 tap wavelet coefficients after three-level analysis of *The Emotion of Space* in RCT color space

$r^2 = (0.849, 0.866, 0.867)$, respectively. The empirical distribution of wavelet transform coefficients is often Laplacian; the section on rate control and JPEG codecs will use this property to explain the derivation of a functional form for the rate-distortion function at low bit rates.

Temporal Domain

An alternative approach to video compression considers a sequence of images as multiple components of a single image, an approach supported by multiple component transforms defined in Part 2 of the JPEG 2000 standard. A two-dimensional spatial and one-dimensional temporal transform applied in any order provide a three-dimensional wavelet transform (e.g., Levy and Wilson 1999; Gokturk and Aaron 2006). If each single image comprises a group of frames, then the number of frames in the group is a key decision, based on considerations of error resilience and latency together with ease of editing, detecting scene changes, and detecting transitions.

In particular, U.S. Patent 6,823,129 to Goertzen discloses a motion image recording and storage system based on a three-dimensional transform, which Quvis developed into a practical digital cinema solution.

Three-Dimensional Compression

As a practical example, consider the compression of frames 1230 to 1679 of *The Emotion of Space* with the Kakadu implementation of the JPEG 2000 standard, choosing a 15-frame group of RGB frames for the multiple component transform. For this example, the encoder applies a YC_bC_r color transform to the color components of each frame to reduce spectral redundancy, a reversible 5/3-tap wavelet transform to both spatial components of each frame to reduce spatial redundancy, and a two-level Haar wavelet transform between adjacent frames to the luminance components Y to reduce temporal redundancy. The 5/3-tap wavelet transform has low-pass coefficients $(1, 0, 1.402, 1, -0.3441, -0.7141)$ and high-pass filter coefficients $(1, 1.772, 0)$. The two-level Haar wavelet

Figure 17: Frame 1232 of *The Emotion of Space* after three-dimensional wavelet compression to 0.33 bpp per frame by the Kakadu implementation of a JPEG 2000 multiple component transform

transform yields the normalized sum and difference of luminance for corresponding pixels in adjacent frames and has matrix coefficients $\frac{1}{\sqrt{2}}\begin{bmatrix} 1 & 1 \\ 1 & -1 \end{bmatrix}$. Figure 17 shows frame 1232 of *The Emotion of Space* compressed to 0.33 bpp target bit rate by this method. By visual inspection, the video quality is good with slight blurring and flickering. Strong visual edges appear to have occasional coronas. The measured average video quality metrics are PSNR = 35.72 and VQM = 4.14.

Psychovisual Domain

Video compression systems use perceptual methods for at least the following tasks: choosing color spaces, optimizing quantization matrices, assessing subjective quality, assessing practical significance of codec enhancements, suppressing flicker artifacts, and enhancing regions of interest.

Choosing Color Spaces

The earlier section on spectral domain indicated color spaces that reduce spectral redundancy based on the HVS being more sensitive to changes in brightness than color, with peak color sensitivity to green.

Optimization of JPEG Quantization Matrices

Regarding optimization of JPEG quantization matrices, U.S. Patent 5,629,780 to Watson discloses a method for image data compression having minimal perceptual error.

A series of psychovisual experiments measured the threshold luminance and chrominance at which observers could just notice individual DCT basis functions presented as images. The experiment varied viewing conditions, including the mean absolute luminance of the display device, the (veiling) luminance cast on the display device by background illumination, and the pixel size in terms of pixels per degree of visual angle (horizontal and vertical).

Consider the DCT coefficient of order (m, n) in image block with index k, denoted by DCT (m, n, k), quantized to QDCT (m, n, k) by a quantization matrix $Q(m, n, k)$, according to Equation 17:

$$QDCT(m,n,k) = \text{round}\left(\frac{DCT(m,n,k)}{Q(m,n,k)}\right) \quad (17)$$

Equation 17 indicates that the maximum possible quantization error is $Q(m, n, k)/2$.

Denote by $t(m, n, k)$ the observed threshold at which a typical viewer can just notice the DCT basis function of order (m, n) in image block with index k. Choosing $Q(m, n, k) < 2 \bullet t(m, n, k)$ ensures that typical viewers will not notice quantization errors.

Visual thresholds $t(m, n, k)$ increase with mean luminance of image block ("light adaptation") and decrease with the presence of patterns of similar spatial frequency and orientation ("contrast masking"). Furthermore, the perceived image quality depends on the perceptual quantization error from all image blocks, not only the block indexed by k.

Equation 18 gives an approximate power law formula for the effect of light adaptation on visual thresholds $t(m, n, k)$ for $m, n \neq 0$, valid for mean absolute luminance above $10\,\text{cd}\,\text{m}^{-2}$. Let $T(m, n)$ denote the visual thresholds determined in the above psychovisual experiments, with average DC coefficient set to $C(0, 0)$ when the display device has mean absolute luminance denoted by L_0 and (veiling) background absolute luminance denoted by $L_V = VL_0$:

$$t(m,n,k) = T(m,n,L_0) \bullet \left(\frac{V + DCT(0,0,k)/C(0,0)}{V + 1}\right)^a \quad (18)$$

Typical values for the parameters in Equation 18 are $L_0 = 40\,\text{cd}\,\text{m}_{-2}$, a = 0.65, and $V = 0.05$. The average DC coefficient $C(0, 0)$ can usually be set to the nominal value 1024 for an 8-bit color component. Applying contrast masking to $t(m, n, k)$ threshold in accordance with the widely used model developed by Legge and Foley (1980) results in the masked threshold $M(m, n, k)$ given by Equation 19 in terms of power law exponent $W(m, n)$ in the range [0, 1]:

$$M(m,n,k) = \max[t(m,n,k), DCT(m,n,k)^{W(m,n)} \\ \bullet\, t(m,n,k)^{1-W(m,n)})] \quad (19)$$

For $W(m, n) = 1$, the threshold is proportional to the luminance, a behavior known as *Weber's law*. A typical empirical value for the exponent $W(m, n)$ is 0.7.

Expressing the quantization errors observed by a typical viewer as $d(m, n, k) \bullet M(m, n, k)$, the $d(m, n, k)$ values are measured in units of *just noticeable difference* (jnd). Equation 20 gives the perceptual error $P(m, n)$ for the DCT coefficients of order (m, n) obtained by pooling the quantization errors from all blocks using a widely used metric (the L_β norm). A typical value for $\beta(m, n)$ is 4:

$$P(m,n) = \left(\sum_k |d(m,n,k)|^{\beta(m,n)}\right)^{\frac{1}{\beta(m,n)}} \quad (20)$$

Finally, Equation 21 yields the overall perceptual error, P, obtained by pooling the $P(m, n)$ values with a possibly different exponent β_f:

$$P = \left(\sum_{m,n} P(m,n)^{\beta_f}\right)^{\beta_f} \quad (21)$$

If we choose the conservative value $\beta_f \rightarrow \infty$, then only the largest absolute error matters, and the perceptual error metric reduces to Equation 22:

$$P = \max(P(m,n)) \quad (22)$$

Minimizing the perceptual error, P, at specified bit rate R yields a quantization matrix optimized for each block k at bit rate R. The DCTune software tool currently available from the National Aeronautics and Space Administration (NASA) embodies these concepts.

Optimization of JPEG Quantization Matrices

As an example, consider using the DCTune software tool to compress frames 1230 to 1679 of *The Emotion of Space*, viewed from the default 7.125 picture heights, display device mean absolute luminance $40\,\text{cd}\,\text{m}^{-2}$, and default bit rate tolerance 5 percent.

With the goal of communicating *The Emotion of Space* over bidirectional videophones with acceptable video quality, Figure 18 shows a panel of gray-scale images representing color frame 1232 compressed by the DCTune software tool to target bit rates (a) 0.927, (b) 0.651, and (c) 0.33 bpp (corresponding to 384 kbps data rate).

The observed bit rates and corresponding PSNR and VQM video quality metrics for frames 1230 to 1679 are as follows:

- bit rate = (0.9091 ± 0.1139, 0.6405 ± 0.0715, 0.3252 ± 0.0217) bpp,

Figure 18: Panel of gray-scale images representing color frame 1232 of *The Emotion of Space* compressed by the DCTune coder to bit rates (a) 0.927, (b) 0.651, and (c) 0.33 bpp

(a)   (b)   (c)

8	8	8	10	16	40	255	255
6	10	8	10	14	24	255	255
8	8	14	28	255	255	255	255
10	10	18	40	112	255	255	255
16	124	28	255	255	255	255	255
28	24	100	255	255	255	255	255
126	255	255	255	255	255	255	255
255	255	255	255	255	255	255	255

Figure 19: Exemplary quantization matrix for luminance *Y* color component of frame 1232 of *The Emotion of Space* at 0.33 bpp target bit rate, compressed by the DCTune coder

Figure 20: Perceptual error map of frame 1232 of *The Emotion of Space* at 0.33 bpp target bit rate, pooled over 16 × 16-pixel regions, compressed by the DCTune coder

- PSNR = (40.53 ± 3.32, 37.84 ± 3.38, 10.7 ± 0.39) dB, and
- VQM = (4.828, 4.632, 3.732), respectively.

At target bit rate 0.33 bpp, the video quality metric value VQM = 3.732 implies that, consistent with the results of visual inspection, DCTune compression provides video of acceptable quality because the impairments are perceptible but not annoying.

Figure 19 shows an exemplary quantization matrix for the luminance *Y* color component of frame 1232 at 0.33 bpp target bit rate.

Figure 20 is a gray-scale image that indicates the result of applying Equation 22 to pool overall perceptual errors over 16 × 16-pixel regions for the same frame and bit rate, where lighter values indicate larger perceptual errors.

Practical Significance of Codec Enhancements

Although it is often useful to apply statistical tests to test the null hypothesis that the PSNR values resulting from codec comparisons have the same statistical distribution (statistical significance), it is even more useful to test whether the effect is large enough to be practically useful (practical significance). Many researchers consider a codec enhancement to be practically significant if it improves PSNR by 0.5 dB or VQM by approximately one unit on the DSIS scale.

Compare the video quality metric values VQM = (4.828, 4.632) at target bit rates (0.927, 0.651) bpp that result from DCTune compression of frames 1230 to 1679 of *The Emotion of Space* with the values that result from Motion DCT compression of the same frames VQM = (3.191, 2.044) at the same bit rates (0.927, 0.651) reported in Figure 18. Because the VQM values improved by more than one unit on the DSIS scale, optimizing the quantization matrices has practical significance.

Suppressing Flicker Artifacts

To take account of the HVS's varying sensitivity to spatial frequencies, JPEG 2000 Part 1 Annex J.8 recommends weights for visual weighting schemes. These schemes include visual progressive coding, with layers separately weighted for the viewing conditions appropriate to each layer, by modifying the distortion weights for each component provided to the rate-distortion optimizer. JPEG 2000 Part 3 Annex B recommends weights for a five-level wavelet decomposition of YC_bC_r video, based on the observed typical visual CSF measured at the midpoint of each sub-band. Part 3, Annex B observes that visual weighting can reduce the incidence of some flickering artifacts that appear when displaying a visual sequence, even though individual images do not show an annoying artifact. Leontaris et al. (2006) suggest that many flickering artifacts are due to (1) small temporal variations in input luminance that give rise to large variations in dequantized wavelet coefficients and (2) uneven rate allocation between code blocks across subsequent frames. An intuitive approach is to truncate all code blocks to the same truncation length throughout each image or for as many images as possible.

Enhancing Regions of Interest

Part 1, Annex H of the JPEG 2000 standard supports region-of-interest signaling in which the encoder creates a mask selecting quantized transform coefficients for better quality encoding. A compliant encoder scales down the background (nonmasked) quantized transform coefficients with a scaling factor s chosen for each component so that the smallest nonzero foreground (masked) quantized transform coefficient is larger than the largest background coefficient. The encoder writes the scaling factor into the code stream. All coefficients less than 2^s belong to the background. A compliant decoder retrieves the scaling factor, s, for the current component from the code stream and scales up any coefficient less than $2^s \times 2^s$.

Foveated Regions of Interest

Faces and facial expressions often attract human attention. Rapid motion of peripheral objects across the field of view is often distracting (Colmenarez et al. 1999). Bounding regions of attention and distraction allow Motion JPEG 2000 to use the JPEG 2000 region-of-interest capability in Annex H to encode the regions at a relatively higher bit rate. Wang and Bovik (2001) incorporate HVS models into a scalable encoder. The HVS spatial resolution peaks in the direction the eye is currently looking (foveation point) and decreases dramatically away from this direction. Geisler and Perry (1998) report a CSF model that fits experimental data, given by Equation 23, where CT denotes the visible contrast threshold, CT_0 minimal visible contrast threshold, f spatial frequency (cycles/degree), e angular displacement of foveation point from observer's retina, α spatial frequency decay constant, and e_2 half-resolution angular displacement decay constant:

$$CT(f,e) = CT_o \exp\left(af\, \frac{e + e_2}{e_2} \right) \tag{23}$$

Equation 24 gives their best-fit measurements:

$$\begin{aligned} a &= 0.106 \\ e_2 &= 2.3 \\ CT_0 &= \frac{1}{64} \end{aligned} \tag{24}$$

Equation 25 defines contrast sensitivity, CS, as the inverse of the contrast threshold:

$$CS(f,e) = \frac{1}{CT(f,e)} \tag{25}$$

Observing a point in an image of width N pixels, at distance d from the retina with perpendicular viewing distance v between the retina and the image plane measured in image widths, yields Equation 26 for the retinal angular displacement of a point in the image:

$$e = \tan^{-1}\left(\frac{d}{Nv} \right) \tag{26}$$

Equation 27 gives the highest perceptible frequency, f_m, which is the smaller of the Nyquist frequency, $f_{Nyquist}$, and the cutoff frequency at maximum contrast $CT_c = 1$:

$$\begin{aligned} f_{Nyquist}(v) &= \frac{1}{2}\,\frac{\pi N v}{180} \left(\frac{\text{cycles}}{\text{degree}} \right) \\[6pt] f_c(e) &= \frac{e_2 \ln\left(\dfrac{1}{CT_0} \right)}{\alpha(e + e_2)} \left(\frac{\text{cycles}}{\text{degree}} \right) \\[6pt] f_m(v,e) &= \min\left(f_{Nyquist}(v), f_c(e) \right) \end{aligned} \tag{27}$$

Hence, Equation 28 gives the foveation-based contrast sensitivity for viewing a point with spatial frequency f, at distance d from the retina, with perpendicular viewing distance v between the retina and the image plane:

$$S_f(v,f,d) = \begin{cases} \dfrac{CS(v,f,d)}{CS_0} & \text{if } f \le f_m(v,d) \\ 0 & \text{otherwise} \end{cases} \tag{28}$$

The authors select human faces as foveation points in the wavelet transform domain, detected by a binary template-matching algorithm similar to that proposed by Wang and Chang (1996). The template includes bounds in chroma and bounding rectangle aspect ratio. Chroma bounds for skin tone are narrow for each race, regardless of ethnicity. Human faces are contiguous regions with typical aspect ratios in the range 1.4–1.6 and tilt $\pm 30°$, so the typical aspect ratios of their bounding rectangles are in the range 1–1.7. The video frame size bounds the rectangles, together with a lower limit based on the threshold for face detection, typically 32×32 pixels. Noting that human faces have discontinuities at eyes, nose, and mouth, the algorithm accepts only candidate faces with sufficiently high pixel variance.

As a practical example, consider viewing an image from a typical distance of six image widths. Figure 21 shows the contrast sensitivity according to Equation 28 normalized to peak value 1.0. The *full width at half maximum*

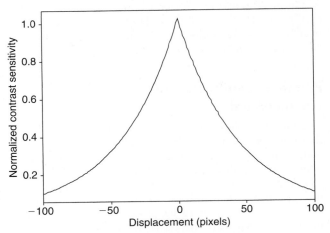

Figure 21: Normalized contrast sensitivity versus displacement for viewing images 240 pixels wide from a perpendicular distance of six image widths

Figure 22: Foveated uncompressed image of *The Emotion of Space*, frame 1232, with fixation point within the rightmost astronaut's face

(FWHM) contrast sensitivity is approximately 60 pixels displacement centered on zero displacement.

Figure 22 displays a foveated image of *The Emotion of Space*, frame 1232, with fixation point within the rightmost astronaut's face.

The Kakadu implementation of the JPEG 2000 standard (Taubman and Marcellin 2001) supports regions of interest. Defining a mask with foreground regions of interest centered on each astronaut's face of width and height 60 pixels, covering approximately 14 percent of the pixels, allows encoding frame 1232 with twenty image layers at bit rates from lossless to 0.33 bpp rate, with distortion minimized at higher priority in the foreground than the background.

Rate Control

In general, the information content of digital video sources varies in complexity from scene to scene. *Constant bit rate* (CBR) encoding has the goal of maintaining a (near) constant bit rate for the transmission channel coder by varying the reconstructed video quality. *Variable bit rate* (VBR) has the goal of maintaining (near) constant quality by varying the bit rate allocated to scenes of varying complexity.

To achieve goals of CBR or VBR encoding, consider rate-control algorithms that control a generic block transform encoding process by encoding each image separately at a desired bit rate or image quality. In particular, they control the encoding process by adjusting the quantizer step size in accordance with the slope of the rate-distortion curve.

In particular, the Motion JPEG 2000 standard supports the *postdistortion rate control* algorithms recommended by Part 1, Annex J.10 of standard 15444-1 (ISO/IEC 2004a). These algorithms optimize the bit allocation by adjusting the quantizer step size according to the slope of the rate-distortion curve evaluated for each code block in each sub-band independently (see "Image Compression").

Generic Lagrangian Rate Control

To see how this works, consider an image decomposed into N sub-bands corresponding to the transform coefficients arranged into a linear sequence ($N = 64$ for the 8×8-pixel DCT). In general, the transform coefficients have unequal variances, and the algorithm allocates bits to each sub-band to minimize the overall distortion. Normalizing the transform coefficient variance in sub-band i to unity by transform normalization factor T_i, a quantizer designed for transform coefficients with zero mean and unit variance can quantize the sub-band to bit rate R_i. Each sub-band contributes an amount $D_i(R_i)$ to distortion in the reconstructed image. If the distortion measure (such as mean square error) is additive across sub-bands, then the observed fraction of transform coefficients in sub-band i is n_i and the observed transform coefficient variance is σ_i, so the normalization factor is $T_i = \sigma_i^{-1}$. The resulting image distortion D is given by Equation 29, ith image bit rate R given by Equation 30:

$$D = \sum_{i=1}^{N} n_i T_i D_i(R_i) \qquad (29)$$

$$R = \sum_{i=1}^{N} n_i R_i \qquad (30)$$

In general, larger quantizer step sizes clear more coefficients (e.g., Equation 12). Adjusting the quantizer step size selects R_i by adjusting n_i and σ_i.

Minimizing the distortion, D, at a desired bit rate, $R < R_{\max}$, by the well-known method of Lagrange multipliers is equivalent to minimizing the functional L given by Equation 31:

$$L = \sum_{i=1}^{N} n_i T_i D_i(R_i) - \lambda \sum_{i=1}^{N} n_i R_i \qquad (31)$$

Differentiating the functional L with respect to R_i yields Equation 32:

$$L' = \sum_{i=1}^{N} n_i \{T_i D_i'(R_i) - \lambda\} \qquad (32)$$

Setting $L' = 0$ yields λ, given by Equation 33:

$$\lambda = T_i D_i'(R_i) \; \forall i \, \varepsilon [1, N] \qquad (33)$$

Hence, λ is proportional to the slope of the rate-distortion curve for sub-band i evaluated at bit rate R_i. The value of λ is the same for all sub-bands. In practice, the rate-control algorithm adjusts the quantizer step size for each sub-band i by a search method that solves the bit allocation Equation 33 using a theoretical or empirical form of rate-distortion function $D_i(R_i)$ and adjusting the value of λ until the algorithm achieves the desired overall bit rate R.

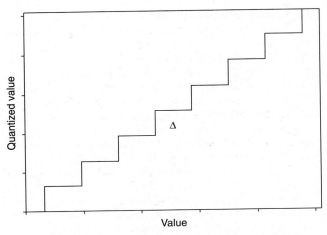

Figure 23: Uniform scalar quantizer with step size Δ

Rate-Distortion Function

To develop a theoretical rate-distortion function $D_i(R_i)$ for relatively high bit rates, consider the fixed-rate uniform scalar quantizer given by Equation 5 with step size $Q = \Delta$ depicted in Figure 23. This is termed a *midtread* quantizer because zero is a possible output value.

Assuming a uniform distribution of m-bit source data, Equation 34 gives the uniform scalar quantizer bit rate, R, and mean square error distortion, D (e.g., Sayood 2006):

$$R = m - \left\lfloor \log_2 \Delta \right\rfloor,$$
$$D = \frac{1}{12}\Delta^2 \Rightarrow D = \frac{1}{12}2^{-2(R/m)} = \varepsilon^2 \bullet 2^{-2R} \quad (34)$$

Consider an image sampled from a source distribution with variance σ_X^2. Equation 35 gives the mean square error distortion for image samples $D_X(R)$ quantized at rate R by a uniform scalar quantizer (or nonuniform scalar quantizer with sufficiently high resolution):

$$D_X(R) \cong \varepsilon^2 \sigma^2 x 2^{-2R} \quad (35)$$

Here ε^2 is a form factor depending on the source *probability distribution function* (pdf). The form factor for a uniform pdf is $\varepsilon^2 = \frac{1}{12}$.

Consider an orthonormal transform T with coefficients Y_n, $n = 0, ..., N - 1$ drawn from a distribution with variance $\sigma_{Y_n}^2$, each contributing R_n to the rate when quantized by a uniform scalar quantizer (or nonuniform scalar quantizer with sufficiently high resolution). Equation 36 gives the mean square error distortion for image samples at rate R resulting from quantization of transform coefficients to rates R_n, which is the rate-distortion function required by Equation 33:

$$R = \sum_{n=0}^{N-1} R_n$$
$$D_T(R) \cong \frac{1}{N}\sum_{n=0}^{N-1}\varepsilon^2 \sigma_{Y_n}^2 2^{-2R} \quad (36)$$

To obtain an empirical form for the overall rate-distortion function $D(R)$ useful for generic transforms and scalable video coders at low bit rates, Dai et al. (2004) combine the Laplacian empirical distribution of generic transform coefficients (e.g., the distribution of DCT and wavelet coefficients discussed above) with the almost linear empirical relation between the number of nonzero quantized generic transform coefficients and the observed bit rate (He and Mitra 2001). If the source variance is σ_x^2, then Equation 37 expresses the resulting form of the overall rate-distortion function, $D(R)$, in terms of empirical coefficients a, b, c:

$$D = \sigma_x^2 - (a \log_2^2 R + b \log_2 R + c)R \quad (37)$$

Differentiating Equation 37 yields the slope of the rate-distortion curve $D'(R)$ required by Equation 33 for Lagrangian generic rate control.

Iterative Generic Rate-Control Algorithm

The Lagrangian generic rate-control algorithm explained above is accurate but computationally intensive, encoding every sub-band completely by entropy coding before adjusting the quantizer step size.

Tzannes (2002) describes a reasonably accurate but less computationally intensive iterative rate-control algorithm. Although initially intended for wavelet transforms, the algorithm is applicable to arbitrary sub-band transforms and proceeds by:

1. compressing the first image of the sequence to a bit rate $R_{achieved}$ based on an empirical value of λ determined by rate-distortion analysis;

2. repeating steps 3 to 5 until the algorithm has compressed the last image of the sequence;

3. calculating the rate-control error between the achieved bit rate $R_{achieved}$ and target bit rate R_{target} as

$$RC_{error} = \frac{R_{achieved} - R_{target}}{R_{target}} \quad (38);$$

4. correcting the value of λ using first-order control,

$$\lambda_{new} = \lambda_{previous} * (1 - RC_{error}) \quad (39); \text{ and}$$

5. compressing the next image in the sequence based on λ_{new}.

Iterative Rate Control

Consider applying the iterative rate-control algorithm expressed by steps 1 to 5 above to frames 1230 to 1679 of *The Emotion of Space* with Motion JPEG 2000 compression and target bit rate 0.33 bpp. Figure 24 shows the result of compressing frame 1230 to a range of bit rates from 0.1 to 1.0 bpp by the Kakadu implementation of JPEG 2000 with a single-layer reversible transform (Taubman and Marcellin 2001).

Denoting by D the mean square error distortion and by R the bit rate, the Equation $\log_{10}(D) = D_0 + a\log_{10}(R)$

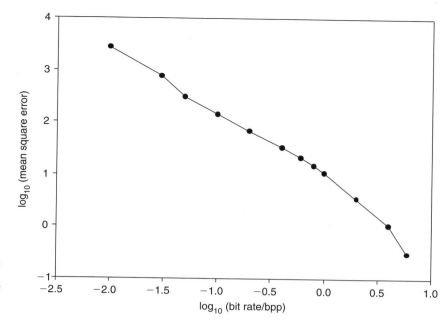

Figure 24: Mean square error versus bit rate (bpp) for *The Emotion of Space*, frame 1230, encoded by the Kakadu implementation of the JPEG 2000 reversible transform

fits the curve shown in Figure 24 with $D_0 = 0.8826$, $a = -1.322$, and coefficient of determination $r^2 = 0.9909$. The interpolated rate-distortion slope $\lambda = -43.66$ at target bit rate 0.33 bpp. Applying the iterative rate-control algorithm, defined by steps 1 to 5 above, to frames 1230 to 1679 of *The Emotion of Space* yields bit rates with coefficient of variation 0.98 percent, compared to the more accurate but computationally intensive Lagrangian rate-control algorithm, which yields bit rates with coefficient of variation 0.75 percent.

Error Resilience

Transmission channels are often prone to error (see "Sources of Errors, Prevention, Detection, and Correction"). Because the JPEG standards encode frames independently, the damaging effect of channel errors does not propagate across frames. In particular, Motion JPEG 2000 further relies on resynchronization markers and data partitions for limiting error propagation such as code blocks (spatial domain) and precincts (wavelet domain). The resynchronization markers are special codes inserted by encoders that enable decoders to resynchronize in the presence of errors. The current JPEG 2000 standard does not recommend any specific error correction or concealment method. (For a review of video error concealment methods, see Wang and Zhu 1998.)

Dufaux and Ebrahimi (2003) simulation experiments indicate that Motion JPEG 2000 is highly resilient to channel errors that are typical of low bit rate wireless channels.

Scalability

In streaming video applications, the servers often serve a large number of users with differing screen resolutions and network bandwidth. In particular, the available Internet network bandwidth fluctuates over a wide range because of factors such as traffic variability and network congestion. Spatially scalable coding provides different resolutions, while temporally scalable coding provides

different temporal resolutions (or frame rates) to accommodate different users by widening the range of bit rates. *Signal-to-noise ratio* (SNR) scalable coding ensures a minimum video quality at the receiver end by sacrificing the least important information when transmission errors and packet losses occur. Encoders may truncate embedded bit streams provided by fine granularity scalable coding to arbitrary quality, spatial, or temporal resolution.

In the progressive DCT-based mode, a Motion JPEG encoder codes 8×8-pixel blocks in zigzag order in multiple scans through each image. At each scan, the encoder either partially codes the DCT coefficients for each block by selecting bands of coefficients for coding each block (spectral selection), selecting ranges of bits for coding each coefficient with the most significant bits encoded first (successive approximation), or both. In the hierarchical mode, a Motion JPEG encoder may encode each image as a succession of frames. The first frame for each component provides a reconstructed reference frame for prediction in subsequent frames that encodes the differences between source components and reference reconstructed components. A Motion JPEG encoder in hierarchical mode may build a pyramid of spatial resolutions by up- or downsampling the source components. A Motion JPEG encoder may offer the capability of progressive coding to a final lossless stage if the encoder codes the differences by lossless methods at the final stage.

In the near-lossless mode, a Motion JPEG-LS encoder may adjust the quantization of prediction residuals to control the maximum absolute error between a reconstructed image component and the corresponding value in the original image.

The JPEG 2000 standard recommends SNR and fine granularity scalable coding for each image via multiple layers of *embedded block coding with optimized truncation* (EBCOT) (see "Data Compression"). Motion JPEG 2000 encoders may provide SNR and fine granularity spatially scalable coding of image sequences by derivation from the JPEG 2000 standard.

Applications

This section explores practical applications of the concepts discussed previously.

Digital Cinema System

As an example of Motion JPEG 2000 compression, the Digital Cinema Initiatives (DCI) consortium's Digital Cinema System Specification v. 1.0 specifies that digital cinema decoders must support Motion JPEG 2000 compression for each video frame (Digital Cinema Initiatives 2005). Two formats are specified: (1) a 4K format comprising 4096×2160 pixel frame size, 36-bpp color depth, and 24 fps frame rate; and (2) a 2K format specified at a 2048×1028 pixel frame size, 36-bpp color depth, and a choice of either 24 or 48 fps frame rate.

To reduce spectral redundancy, the DCI consortium specified a color space defined in terms of CIE primary colors $X'Y'Z'$, displayed as output values XYZ by a display device with nonlinear response. Equation 40 specifies the overall color space with luminance and chrominance measured in absolute values (cd/m²):

$$X = P \times \left(\frac{X'}{4095} \right)^{2.6}, \ Y = P \times \left(\frac{Y'}{4095} \right)^{2.6}, \ Z = P \times \left(\frac{X'}{4095} \right)^{2.6}$$
$$X'\varepsilon[0\ldots4095], Y'[0\ldots4095], Z'\varepsilon[0\ldots4095]$$
$$P = 53.27 \ \text{cd/m}^2$$

$$(40)$$

Notable digital cinema releases include *Chicken Little* (Disney) and *Moonmathora!* (Mayalolam).

Mars Exploration Rover Camera System

NASA's Mars Exploration Rover (MER) mission currently carries nine cameras for navigation and reconnaissance. According to Kiely and Klimesh (2003), the MER onboard system uses ICER, an algorithm closely related to JPEG 2000, to compress each 1024×1024-pixel image independently at 12-bit depth to bit rate from approximately 1 bit/pixel to nearly lossless. The MER transmission channel has fixed length packets. To fill the transmission packets efficiently, ICER implements a rigorous byte quota, together with a quality goal, whichever comes first. To contain transmission channel errors, ICER partitions the wavelet coefficients into precincts corresponding to rectangular regions in each image. The MER onboard system transmits each precinct separately.

ITU CODECS

The International Telecommunication Union (ITU) recommends a series of standards for the moving picture component of audiovisual services.

ITU-T Standards H.261, H.262, H.263, and H.264

H.261

ITU standard H.261 recommends a video codec for audiovisual services over telephone lines at $p \times 64$ kbit/sec where p is in the range of 1 to 30. Intended for use at video bit rates between 40 kbit/sec and 200 kbit/sec, the codec was standardized initially in 1990 and revised in 1993. The source coder operates on noninterlaced pictures occurring at 30,000/1001 fps (approximately 29.97 fps) in either *common intermediate format* (CIF) or quarter CIF (QCIF) with frame sizes 352×288 and 176×144 pixels, respectively. Videoconferencing over telephone lines is an appropriate application for the H.261 standard, which is a superseded standard maintained for backward capability.

H.262

The ITU and the Motion Picture Experts Group (MPEG) jointly standardized H.262, also known as MPEG-2. This chapter discusses the popular MPEG-2 codec below under "MPEG Codecs."

H.263

ITU standard H.263 addresses video coding for low bit rate video communications for arbitrary video bit rate, standardized initially in 1997 and revised in 2005. The source coder can operate on five standardized video source formats that are submultiples or multiples of CIF: sub-QCIF, QCIF, CIF, 4CIF, and 16CIF. The coder can operate using a broad range of custom video formats. Profiles are subsets of the standard that are intended for a specific range of applications. Videoconferencing is an appropriate application for the H.263 standard.

H.263 is a superseded standard, also maintained for backward capability.

H.264

The ITU and MPEG jointly standardized H.264, also known as MPEG-4 Part 10 or *advanced video codec* (AVC). This standard recommends coding methods for the moving picture component of audiovisual services with the intention of providing twice as much compression as previously standardized codecs without using a substantially increased computational resource. The source coder can operate on noninterlaced and interlaced video components. Applications cover, among other things, digital storage media, television broadcasting, and real-time communications including videoconferencing. Profiles are subsets of the standard that are intended for a specific range of applications. In many applications, it is currently neither practical nor economic to implement a decoder that is capable of dealing with all of the hypothetical uses of a particular profile, so the standard further specifies levels within each profile. This chapter discusses the H.264 profiles below. H.264 is the most efficient, compressive, and flexible ITU codec to date, so it forms the primary topic of this section.

Generic Encoder and Decoder

Each ITU standard includes the specification of a *hypothetical reference decoder* (HRD). An encoder complies with a standard if it encodes a bit stream decodable by the HRD.

Figure 25 illustrates a block diagram for a generic ITU decoder, which is considerably simpler than that for the generic encoder.

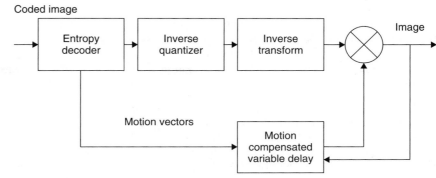

Figure 25: Block diagram for a generic ITU decoder

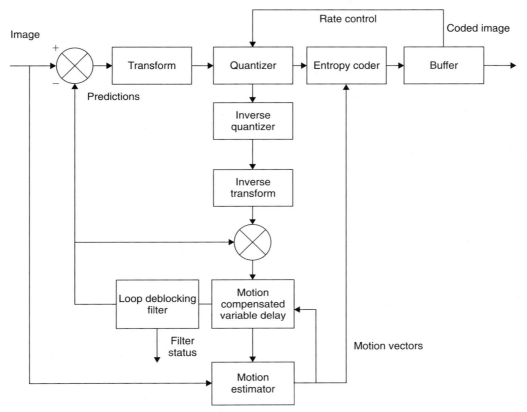

Figure 26: Block diagram for a generic ITU source encoder

Figure 26 shows a block diagram for a generic ITU source encoder. The source encoder reduces spatial, spectral, temporal. and psychovisual redundancy by prediction, block transformation, and quantization.

Spatial Domain

H.261

The H.261 standard specifies encoding and decoding of picture sequences. Each of the CIF and QCIF noninterlaced picture formats comprises luminance and color difference samples, with the color difference samples at half the resolution of the luminance samples. In accordance with ITU Recommendation BT.601 (the current version in force is BT.601-7), H.261 encodes luminance samples in the range 16 (black) to 235 (white) and color difference

samples in the range from 16 to 240, with the zero level of color difference encoded as 128. H.261 partitions each picture into *groups of blocks* (GOBs), macroblocks, and blocks. A GOB is a region defined by 176×48 pixels of luminance samples and the spatially corresponding 88×24 pixels of color difference samples for each color component. A macroblock is 16×16 pixels of luminance samples and the spatially corresponding 8×8 pixels of color difference samples for each color component. A block is 8×8 pixels of luminance samples and the spatially corresponding 4×4 pixels of color difference samples for each color component. In the decoder, H.261 recommends a deblocking filter to reduce the incidence of visible blocking artifacts. An H.261-compliant encoder codes pictures independently (*intra* mode) or by reference to past pictures decoded and stored in a buffer (*inter* mode).

The H.261 standard recommends transforming picture samples by an 8×8 DCT. The standard further recommends quantizing AC coefficients with the scalar quantizer defined in Equations 12 and 13 above, using the same quantization parameter $Q \in [2,4,6 \ldots 60,62]$ for all coefficients in a macroblock. H.261 recommends quantizing DC coefficients with fixed step size $Q = 8$ and further recommends arranging the coefficients in zigzag order, encoding zero-quantized transform coefficients by run-length encoding, with separate encoding for blocks in which all quantized transform coefficients are zero. H.261 also recommends encoding the resulting bit stream with an entropy coder in the form of a specific variable length code. In the decoder, H.263 recommends a deblocking filter to reduce the incidence of visible blocking artifacts.

H.263

The H.263 standard specifies decoding of picture sequences. The H.263 specification partitions each picture into GOBs or slices. A GOB comprises $k * 16$ lines, where k is an integer in the range 1 to 4, depending on picture format and encoder resolution mode. H.261 further partitions each GOB into macroblocks. Each macroblock is 16×16 pixels of luminance samples and the spatially corresponding 8×8 pixels of color difference samples for each color component, except in *reduced resolution update* (RRU) mode. In the RRU mode, each macroblock is 32×32 pixels of luminance samples and the spatially corresponding 16×16 pixels of color difference samples for each color component. A block is 8×8 pixels of luminance samples and the spatially corresponding 4×4 pixels of color difference samples for each color component. The criteria for choice of mode and transmitting a block are not subject to recommendation. Slices are rectangular picture regions comprising a whole number of macroblocks, and the H.263 standard allows transmission of the corresponding transform coefficients in arbitrary macroblock order. H.263 recommends transforming transmitted blocks using an 8×8 DCT, quantizing and entropy coding the resulting coefficients with a variable length code. The standard defines a quantization process similar to that defined for the H.261 standard, except that H.263 does not define the quantizer decision levels. An H.263-compliant encoder codes pictures independently (intra mode) or by reference to immediate past or future pictures decoded and stored in a buffer (inter mode).

H.264

The H.264 standard enables encoding and decoding of image sequences. An encoder can choose whether to scan any of the images in a progressive or field-interlaced manner (see "High Definition Television (HDTV)"). The H.264 standard also supports high-definition television standards through scalable aspect ratio, resolution, and frame rate.

Images intended for interpretation by an H.264 decoding process are termed *primary pictures*. Each primary picture can be associated with at least one *auxiliary picture* comprising information (such as opacity samples) intended for interpretation by a display process. A cropping rectangle specifies the width and height of primary pictures.

An H.264 compliant encoder codes images independently (intra mode) or by reference to arbitrary past or future images decoded and stored in a buffer (inter mode).

H.264 supports *intra* (I), *predicted* (P), and *bidirectionally* (B) predicted pictures, with exemplary temporal structure of I, P, and B pictures shown in Figure 27.

Each image comprises one or more sample arrays, representing monochrome (luma) or color (chroma) samples with or without auxiliary arrays. The terms *luma* and *chroma* avoid implying a linear transfer function that is often associated with absolute luminance and chrominance.

Each image comprises an integer number of *macroblocks*, each comprising 16×16 luma samples and any chroma samples associated with the luma samples. *Slices* partition images into arrays of macroblocks. Figure 28 illustrates a picture divided into two slices. The H.264 standard further characterizes slices as *intra* (I), *predicted* (P),

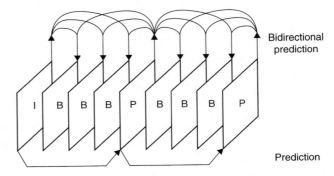

Figure 27: Example of temporal picture structure. Reproduced by permission of ISO

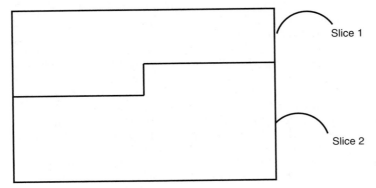

Figure 28: A picture divided into two macroblock slices after H.264. Reproduced with the kind permission of ITU

bidirectionally (B) predicted, *switching intra* (SI), and *switching predictive* (SP). The SP slice type facilitates efficient switching between precoded pictures, especially between pictures from bit streams coded at different rates, while the SI slice type facilitates random access and error recovery. *Macroblock to slice group maps* further group slices into sets of macroblocks, which is useful for defining foreground, background, and special patterns such as checkerboards and regions of interest. *Submacroblocks* partition each macroblock in regions as small as 4×4 luma samples. Figures 29, 30a, and 30b illustrate the Morton scanning order for macroblocks and submacroblock partitions, starting from the upper-left sample.

When coding in intra mode, an encoder begins by predicting the current macroblock or submacroblock luma and chroma from a context formed from its available decoded neighbors. The H.264 standard specifies three categories of intra mode spatial prediction: *intra 16 × 6*, *intra 8 × 8*, and *intra 4 × 4*. In the intra 16×16 mode, an encoder predicts the luma component of all 16×16 pixels of a macroblock from samples of its available decoded and reconstructed (but not filtered) macroblock neighbors. An encoder can choose between predictions made in four modes: vertical, horizontal, DC, and plane.

H.264 Prediction of Intra-Coded Luma Samples

Figure 31 shows a luma (Y) macroblock that contains an astronaut's face from frame 1232 of *The Emotion of Space* and has been transformed from RGB to YC_bC_r color space. This macroblock is bounded by frame coordinates (112, 80) to (127, 95) in the 240×320-pixel frame. In Figure 31, this macroblock is bounded by image coordinates (2, 2) to (17, 17) as measured from the top lefthand corner. Figure 31 additionally depicts an image row from the macroblock above the current macroblock and an image column from the macroblock to the left of the current macroblock.

Figure 32 shows the intra 16×16 luma predictions for the macroblock in Figure 31, together with a quality metric, the median absolute error (MAE). The vertical

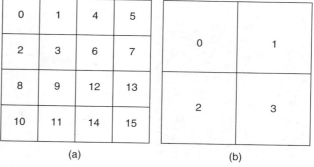

Figure 30: Morton scanning order for (a) 4 × 4 luma samples and (b) 8 × 8 luma samples after H.264. Reproduced by permission of ITU

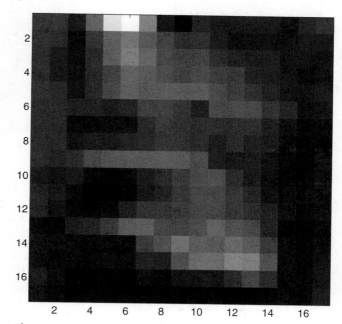

Figure 31: Luma macroblock bounded by frame coordinates (112, 80) to (127, 95) from frame 1232 of *The Emotion of Space*

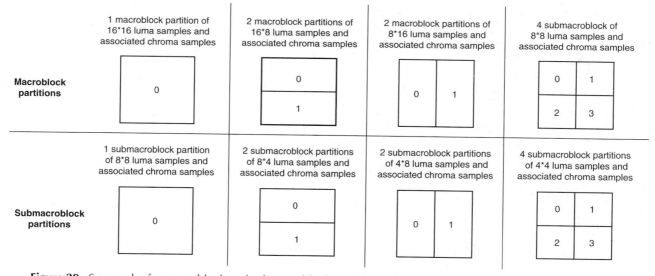

Figure 29: Scan order for macroblock and submacroblock partitions after H.264. Reproduced by permission of ITU

Vertical (MAE=13.96)

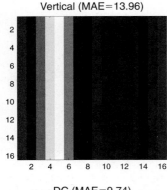

Horizontal (MAE=8.85)

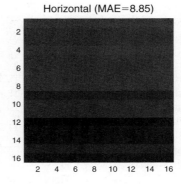

DC (MAE=9.74)

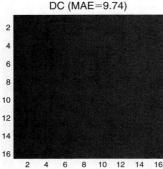

Plane (MAE=10.14)

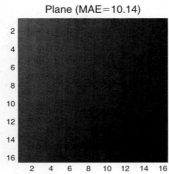

Figure 32: Intra 16×16 luma predictions for the macroblock shown in Figure 31, together with their MAE. The horizontal prediction has the least MAE

mode copies the top row of available previously decoded pixels (H) into all rows of the predicted macroblock. The horizontal mode copies the left column of available previously decoded pixels (V) into all columns of the predicted macroblock. The DC prediction averages the H and V pixels uniformly across the predicted macroblock, adding 0.5 to the predicted luma value before rounding. The plane prediction applies bilinear interpolation to the H and V pixels of the predicted macroblock, adding 0.5 to the luma value before rounding and clipping m-bit luma values to the range $[0, 2^m - 1]$. In this example, the horizontal prediction has the least MAE of these four prediction modes. Although an H.264-compliant encoder may reasonably select the intra 16×16 horizontal luma prediction mode, the standard does not oblige it to do so.

The H.264 standard specifies nine directional prediction modes for 8×8 luma and 4×4 luma submacroblocks. These prediction modes result from bilinear interpolation of the available previously decoded samples above and to the left of the current submacroblock, with coefficients specified for each direction. If the macroblock luma samples are predicted by intra coding, then so are the associated chroma samples with 8×8 prediction modes similar to those described above for 16×16 luma samples. "Temporal Domain" below addresses methods for reducing temporal redundancy together with inter-coding modes.

The decoder needs to know the prediction modes for each 4×4 submacroblock. Because prediction modes between adjacent submacroblocks within the same slice are typically highly correlated, the decoder calculates and applies the most probable mode unless it receives side information in the form of an eight-valued mode selector.

The encoder transforms each macroblock or submacroblock partition of residuals after the prediction modes are decided and the predictions have been subtracted from the corresponding pixel values. A hierarchical encoder can dynamically select any of the partition sizes indicated in Figure 29 for its tree structure. Selecting small partition sizes near edges and larger partition sizes in smooth regions tends to reduce blocking artifacts.

One approach to H.264 mode selection is to perform a full search of prediction mode space to select the prediction mode that minimizes a measure of distortion according to a Lagrangian functional. Jagmohan and Ratakonda (2004) report a relatively time-efficient learning algorithm for H.264 mode selection that uses a simple distortion measure and fast search for motion vectors.

Spatial Transform

The H.264 standard transform for 4×4 submacroblocks is a low-complexity *integer cosine transform* (ICT), an integer approximation to the DCT defined by Equation 41:

$$\text{Define } a = \frac{1}{2}, \ b = \sqrt{\frac{1}{2}} \cos\left(\frac{\pi}{8}\right), \ c = \sqrt{\frac{1}{2}} \cos\left(\frac{3\pi}{8}\right).$$

$$DCT_{4 \times 4} = \begin{bmatrix} a & a & a & a \\ b & c & -c & -b \\ a & -a & -a & a \\ c & -b & b & -c \end{bmatrix}$$

$$ICT_{4 \times 4} = \begin{bmatrix} 1 & 1 & 1 & 1 \\ 2 & 1 & -1 & -2 \\ 1 & -1 & -1 & 1 \\ 1 & -2 & 2 & -1 \end{bmatrix} \tag{41}$$

ICT calculations are reversible in integer arithmetic and require only additions and shifts. The ICT is real and orthogonal but not orthonormal. The ICT has the same matrix structure as the 4×4 DCT.

Similarly, the H.264 standard defines an 8×8 ICT for 8×8 submacroblocks. When the encoder selects the 16×16 intra prediction mode with the 4×4 transform, the 16 DC coefficients of the 4×4 luma submacroblocks are selected and further transformed by a 4×4 Hadamard transform for increased compression in visually smooth regions as are the DC coefficients of all 4×4 chroma submacroblocks. Equation 42 gives the 4×4 Hadamard transform:

$$H_{4 \times 4} = \begin{bmatrix} 1 & 1 & 1 & 1 \\ 1 & 1 & -1 & -1 \\ 1 & -1 & -1 & 1 \\ 1 & -1 & 1 & -1 \end{bmatrix} \tag{42}$$

The Hadamard transform is real, symmetric and orthogonal, and reversible in integer arithmetic, and it requires only additions and subtractions.

Quantizer

A uniform scalar dead zone quantizer quantizes the transformed picture components. Referring to Figure 23, which depicts a one-sided uniform scalar quantizer, a uniform scalar dead zone quantizer additionally quantizes to zero all coefficients having absolute value less then a predetermined threshold. This ensures that a zero reconstruction level is available (see Yu 2004). The H.264 standard specifies a scalar quantizer according to a choice of fifty-two step sizes indexed by a *quantization parameter* (QP). An increase of approximately six in QP doubles the quantizer step size. An encoder can choose different values of QP for luma and chroma components. Note that the quantizer incorporates scaling factors for the ICT, an orthogonal but not orthonormal transform.

Reminiscent of the JPEG standards, a *zigzag scan* (frame mode) or *alternate scan* (field mode) orders the quantized transform coefficients corresponding to each 4×4 submacroblock so that higher-variance coefficients are traversed earlier and the run lengths of zero are increased.

Entropy Coder

H.264 standardizes a choice of entropy coders to encode the scan, including *context adaptive variable length code* (CAVLC) and *context adaptive binary arithmetic coding* (CABAC). For CAVLC, the H.264 standard provides a syntax element to report the total number of nonzero-quantized transform coefficients in a scan, together with the number of trailing ones, defined as consecutive transform coefficient levels equal to 1 at the end of a scan. Note that He and Mitra (2001) found an almost linear relationship between the number of nonzero coefficients and rate for several algorithms closely related to H.264, including H.263 and MPEG-4. The term *context adaptive* means that an encoder implementing CAVLC can choose between several VLC tables according to the local statistics of the bit stream. CABAC maintains separate arithmetically encoded streams for different H.264 syntax elements and

typically provides increased coding efficiency relative to CAVLC, with considerably increased demands on computational resources. Transform coefficients account for the vast majority of syntax elements coded by CABAC. Osorio and Bruguera (2006) point out that even though CABAC provides a 10 percent to 15 percent improvement over baseline CAVLC entropy coding, the real-time H.264 encoding of standard and high-definition television video sequences requires at least millions of symbols per second when the encoder uses CABAC rather than CAVLC. The processor workload increases by approximately two orders of magnitude if the encoder also uses *rate-distortion optimization* (RDO), which is a method of trying several different encoding modes to find one that optimizes the balance between bit rate and distortion.

Marpe et al. (2003) provide a rationale for CABAC from the viewpoint of an encoder. The encoding process includes the steps of *binarization, context modeling,* and *binary arithmetic coding*. Binarization maps a binary sequence, termed a *bin string*, to a specified syntax element. Each binary element of a bin string is termed a *bin*. If the syntax element is binary-valued, then binarization is equivalent to a step of identity mapping. In the regular coding mode, context modeling includes selecting a probability model that may depend on previously coded syntax elements or bins, followed by selecting a regular arithmetic coding engine. In the bypass coding mode, context modeling includes selecting a simplified arithmetic coding engine without selecting an explicit context model. Arithmetic coding includes encoding the bin with a binary arithmetic coder.

Loop Deblocking Filter

The H.264 standard recommends an optional in-loop deblocking filter to reduce the visual annoyance from blocking artifacts resulting from ringing at 4×4-pixel or 8×8-pixel block boundaries. The filter provides a modest improvement of approximately 0.3 dB PSNR (Wei et al. 2005) at considerable implementation cost. Zhong et al. (2005) demonstrate that human viewers do not always prefer this adaptive filter and that subjective tests indicate a bimodal distribution of preferred filter strengths.

Spectral Domain

H.261 and H.263

The H.261 and H.263 standards support monochrome and YC_bC_r color spaces with 4:2:0 color-sampling schemes (see "High Definition Television (HDTV)"), with color-difference samples located between the corresponding luminance samples.

H.264

Standard H.264 supports 4:2:0, 4:2:2, and 4:4:4 color-sampling schemes and directly supports monochrome, RGB, and YC_bC_r color spaces, together with unspecified monochrome or CIE color tri-stimulus values, usually denoted by *XYZ*, with or without an auxiliary array for quantities such as opacity. Recently, Malvar and Sullivan (2003) proposed a reversible color transform of residuals from RGB (4:4:4) to a YC_oC_g color space with color differences relative to orange and green, respectively. Equations

43 and 44 respectively define the direct and inverse RCT color transforms:

$$
\begin{bmatrix} Y \\ C_o \\ C_g \end{bmatrix} = \begin{bmatrix} \dfrac{1}{4} & \dfrac{1}{2} & \dfrac{1}{4} \\ \dfrac{1}{2} & 0 & \dfrac{-1}{2} \\ \dfrac{-1}{4} & \dfrac{1}{2} & \dfrac{-1}{4} \end{bmatrix} \begin{bmatrix} R \\ G \\ B \end{bmatrix} \tag{43}
$$

$$
\begin{bmatrix} R \\ G \\ B \end{bmatrix} = \begin{bmatrix} 1 & 1 & -1 \\ 1 & 0 & 1 \\ 1 & -1 & -1 \end{bmatrix} \begin{bmatrix} Y \\ C_o \\ C_g \end{bmatrix} \tag{44}
$$

A reversible integer color transform results from applying an S transform (Adams et al. 2002) to the direct color transform defined by Equations 43 and 44. By definition, a forward S transform maps the integer vector $\begin{bmatrix} x_0 \\ x_1 \end{bmatrix}$ to the integer vector $\begin{bmatrix} y_0 \\ y_1 \end{bmatrix}$ by the transformation Equation 45, with corresponding inverse S transform defined by Equation 46:

$$
\begin{bmatrix} y_0 \\ y_1 \end{bmatrix} = \begin{bmatrix} \left\lfloor \dfrac{1}{2}(x_0 + x_1) \right\rfloor \\ x_0 - x_1 \end{bmatrix} \tag{45}
$$

$$
\begin{bmatrix} x_0 \\ x_1 \end{bmatrix} = \begin{bmatrix} t \\ t - y_1 \end{bmatrix}, \; t \gg y_0 + \left\lfloor \dfrac{1}{2}y_0 + 1 \right\rfloor \tag{46}
$$

Applying Equation 45 to Equation 43, Equation 47 yields the forward integer RCT, where $>>$ denotes the arithmetic shift operator. Equation 48 yields the inverse integer RCT corresponding to Equation 44:

$$
\begin{aligned}
C_o &= R - B \\
temp &= B + (C_o 1) \\
C_g &= G - temp \\
Y &= temp + (C_g 1)
\end{aligned} \tag{47}
$$

$$
\begin{aligned}
temp &= Y - (C_g 1) \\
G &= C_g + temp \\
B &= temp - (C_o 1) \\
R &= B + C_o
\end{aligned} \tag{48}
$$

Malvar and Sullivan (2003) report that this reversible color transform yields a coding gain of 4.54 dB on the widely used 24-image RGB Kodak color still image set available from the Rensselaer Polytechnic Institute Center for Image Processing Research.

Temporal Domain

H.261
Recall that Motion JPEG 2000 compresses each picture independently. The H.261 standard allows an encoder to choose whether to encode each picture independently (intra coding) or relative to predictions based on previously reconstructed pictures (inter coding). The H.261 standard recommends forcing the encoder to intra mode with an update pattern that the encoder is free to choose. The suggested pattern is to update at least once every 132 transmitted pictures to control the accumulation of irreversible DCT mismatch errors. Although the encoder is free to choose the method of interpicture prediction, the H.261 standard specifies optional motion compensation (see Jain 1989 or Sayood 2006), followed by an optional spatial loop deblocking filter to reduce the incidence of blocking artifacts.

The H.261 standard specifies motion compensation between pictures in terms of motion vectors encoding differences between pictures. The decoder will accept one motion vector per macroblock for the luminance component to pixel accuracy. The standard specifies halving this motion vector and rounding the values toward zero to obtain a motion vector for both color components. Moving cameras (pan and zoom), moving objects, shadowing, changing lighting, and editing video all contribute to differences between pictures.

Accordingly, the H.261 standard specifies that horizontal and vertical motion vector components must be in the range $[-15...15]$ pixels and that valid motion vectors must be within the coded picture area. A positive value for the horizontal or vertical motion vector component indicates that the corresponding macroblock is spatially to the right or below the predicted macroblock. The encoder is free to choose the method for determining motion vectors.

H.263
The H.263 standard allows an encoder to choose whether to encode each picture by intra coding or relative to predictions based on a previous intrapicture (P pictures) or one previous and one future intrapicture that have the same picture size (B pictures). There are four optional additional types of predicted picture: PB, improved PB, EI, and EP.

The decoder accepts one motion vector per macroblock to half-pixel accuracy unless the decoder selects the optional *advanced prediction mode*, when the decoder accepts four motion vectors per macroblock to half-pixel accuracy. In the optional *unconstrained motion vectors* mode, motion vectors may point outside picture boundaries.

H.264
The H.264 standard allows an encoder to choose whether to encode each picture or each slice by intra coding or relative to predictions based on arbitrary previous and future pictures, including predicted pictures (inter coding). The H.264 standard supports variable block sizes for motion compensation, from the 16×16 macroblock to the 4×4 submacroblock, and accepts as many as 16 motion vectors per macroblock stored at quarter-pixel precision. The motion vectors may point outside the picture boundaries. Choi and Jeon (2006) describe a hierarchical motion search for H.264 variable-block-size motion compensation that provides quality (PSNR) similar to full search

but approximately 10 times faster by adjusting the search center and search pattern according to the distribution of sub-block motion vectors.

H.264 Interframe Motion Compensation

Interframe coding is a method of reducing redundancies between successive images. It is especially useful when there is little change in content from one image to the next.

Motion compensation seeks to encode differences between frames, considering moderate motion. Moving visual objects, moving cameras, changing lighting conditions, and editing scenes all contribute to differences between successive images in a video sequence.

To see how this works, consider a buffer storing a number N of available decoded frames (typically five). The frames can be past, present, or future. To simplify this discussion, choose $N = 2$ and focus on a specific block B_1 in image I_1. If an encoder can find a closely matching block B_2 in image I_2, then the vector location of block B_2 in image I_2 relative to the location of block B_1 in image I_1 is termed the *motion vector*. The H.264 standard recommends differential encoding of motion vectors for transmission.

Consider again frames 1231 to 1233 of *The Emotion of Space* and, in particular, the astronaut's face macroblock in frame 1232, bounded by frame coordinates (112, 80) to (127, 95). Frame 1232 is a scene change from frame 1231; as the astronaut walks forward from frame 1232 (time code 01:22.133) to frame 1233 (time code 01:22.200), audience flash photography enhances luma and blue chroma. By visual inspection, the astronaut's face is not present in frame 1231.

To obtain motion vectors to half-pixel and quarter-pixel accuracy, a compliant encoder first interpolates luma samples to half-pixel precision by filtering horizontally, vertically, or both with the six-tap *finite impulse response* filter $\frac{1}{32}[1 \quad -5 \quad 20 \quad 20 \quad -5 \quad 1]$. Averaging neighboring values horizontally, vertically, or diagonally yields quarter-pixel interpolation. Likewise, a compliant encoder interpolates chroma samples by bilinear interpolation to quarter-pixel or eighth-pixel accuracy as required.

An encoder is free to choose the method for matching blocks. Typically, an encoder selects a matching block by minimizing an error metric such as the MSE or MAE. If the error metric exceeds a specific threshold or a spatial prediction is a closer match, then an encoder may decide to intra code the block. One possible method for matching blocks is a full search, which is resource intensive but easy to parallelize. Alternatives to full search include *logarithmic search, hierarchical search, conjugate direction,* and *gradient search* techniques (Jain 1989).

As an example, Figure 33 illustrates the popular three-step search (TSS) introduced by Koga et al. (1981). Starting with a predicted search center, the encoder searches a 6×6-pixel region around the search center with 3-pixel step size, evaluating an error metric at the search center's eight nearest neighbors. The position yielding the minimum error becomes the new search center (shaded in

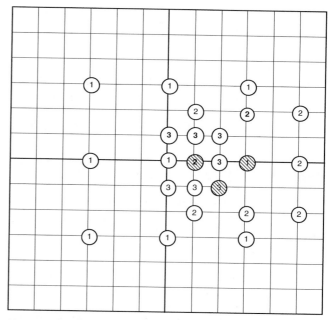

Figure 33: Three-step search converging on a position of minimum error at (2, −1)

Figure 34). The encoder repeats the search from this new center, decrementing the step size by one, until it finds the best match or decides to intra code the block.

Let us apply TSS on a pixel grid to match the luma macroblock bounded by frame coordinates (112, 80) to (127, 95) in frame 1232 with a luma macroblock in frame 1233, based on initial search center (120, 88) in frame 1233 coordinates. If we use the MAE, the result is motion vector (+2, +3) with MAE = 4. Let us further refine the search of nearest neighbors on a half-pixel grid starting from the match found on the pixel grid, followed by a refinement search of nearest neighbors on a quarter-pixel grid starting from the match found on the half-pixel grid. The result is the motion vector (+2.0, +3.0) to quarter-pixel accuracy. Because the best match intra prediction results in a value of MAE = 8.85, an encoder may choose inter prediction based on the frame 1233 interpolated macroblock values found in the search. If an encoder decides to use more than one reference frame (which itself may be the result of a temporal prediction), the temporal predictions from the reference frames are weighted and combined.

Psychovisual Domain

The H.263 and H.264 standards support perceptual quantization through custom quantization tables. As an example of how to derive such custom quantization tables for the H.264 standard, Hu and Gibson (2005) explore the threshold at which human observers notice the test patterns that result from quantizing to zero ICT coefficients, one coefficient at a time. Based on small-sample subjective tests with five subjects, the authors show that using the nonuniform quantization matrices (derived by measuring thresholds to quantize the transform coefficients) results in improved perceptual quality for several well-known video sequences.

Error Resilience

H.261. The H.261 standard recommends forced updating of pictures in intra mode at least once every 132 transmitted pictures, together with a *Bose-Chaudhuri-Hocquenghem* (BCH) forward error-correcting code in the encoder.

H.263. The H.263 standard supports an *enhanced reference picture selection* mode in which a decoder may reconstruct predicted pictures from alternate reference pictures stored in picture memories. The standard further recommends a BCH error-correcting code in the encoder.

H.264. The H.264 standard incorporates several error-resilience tools, including independent compression of slices. An encoder can specify that spatial prediction of macroblocks within temporally predicted slices use only macroblocks that were themselves spatially predicted in intra mode. Multiple reference picture support ensures that if transmission errors adversely affect a reference picture, other reference frames are available for reconstruction. *Flexible macroblock ordering* allows transmission of macroblocks in arbitrary order, spreading the impact of transmission errors over many frames instead of one. Data partitioning allows separation of syntax elements into different packets of data that may receive unequal protection. Transmission of redundant slices ensures replacement of primary slices that are corrupted or lost. Finally, a picture count separates the timing information from the picture number in case the timing information is corrupted or lost.

Rate Control

H.261

The H.261 standard Annex B recommends that a compliant encoder buffer its output and apply a *leaky-bucket* rate-control algorithm.

To understand how a leaky-bucket rate-control algorithm smoothes traffic bursts, consider a decoder buffer of capacity B bits. The initial buffer fullness parameter is $F \leq B$ bits. Let R be the peak rate (bps) at which bits enter the decoder buffer, which is initially empty. As bits arrive, the buffer fills up; when the buffer contains F bits, the decoder instantaneously removes all the bits in the buffer for processing. A compliant encoder sends no more bits until there is room in the buffer. The initial delay for the buffer to fill up is $D = F/R$, measured in seconds. Hence, the decoder receives a bit stream at a fixed rate, even though the buffer input receives a bit stream at variable rate.

The H.261 standard specifically recommends operating the encoder and decoder synchronously at the same clock frequency and CIF rate. Denoting the peak bit rate by R_{max} kbps, the standard specifies the decoder buffer

size to be $\left\lceil \dfrac{4R_{max}}{29.97} \right\rceil + 256$ kb. The decoder buffer is initially empty. The decoder examines the buffer at CIF intervals (approximately 33 msec) and if at least one complete coded picture is stored in the buffer, the decoder removes all the data corresponding to the earliest picture for processing. Immediately after removing the data, the buffer must contain less than $\left\lceil \dfrac{4R_{max}}{29.97} \right\rceil$ kb.

H.263

The H.263 standard generalizes this leaky-bucket rate-control algorithm with decoder buffer size set to $\left\lceil \dfrac{4R_{max}}{PCF} \right\rceil + P_{max}$ where *PCF* denotes the *picture clock frequency* (input picture rate) and P_{max} denotes the maximum number of bits per picture that have been negotiated for use in the bit stream. The buffer is initially empty. The decoder examines the buffer at *PCF* intervals and, if at least one complete coded picture is stored in the buffer, the decoder removes all the data corresponding to the earliest picture for processing. Immediately after removing the data, the buffer must contain less than $\left\lceil \dfrac{4R_{max}}{PCF} \right\rceil$ kb.

For the purpose of rate control, the H.263 standard defines a complete coded picture as an *I picture, P picture, PB picture,* or *improved PB picture.*

H.264

The H.264 standard Annex C specifies a *hypothetical reference decoder* (HRD) with a leaky-bucket rate-control algorithm, including a coded picture buffer, an instantaneous decoding process, a decoded picture buffer, and an output cropping process.

Milani et al. (2003) describe an iterative rate-control algorithm based on analysis by He and Mitra (2001), similar to that described by Tzannes (2002), and discussed in the section on rate control. In particular, the method of rate control modifies the quantization step size while coding different macroblocks according to a target fraction of transform coefficients quantized to zero to achieve the desired bit rate for the currently available bandwidth. To see how this works, let Δ denote the uniform quantizer step size and $p_x(a)$ denote the probability of observing a transform coefficient $x < a$ then Equation 49 yields $\rho(\Delta)$, the fraction of transform coefficients quantized to zero:

$$\rho(\Delta) = \sum_{|a|<\Delta} p_x(a) \qquad (49)$$

An H.264 encoder may use fixed values of Δ, referred to as *integer quantization parameters*, denoted by $QP \in [0, 1, 2, ..., 51]$. Note further that an H.264 encoder will not code any bits for a picture if all the transform coefficients are null for that picture, so Equation 50 describes an empirical linear relation with slope $-\lambda$ between the observed bit rate denoted by R and the fraction of transform coefficients quantized to zero, denoted by ρ:

$$R(\rho) = \lambda(1 - \rho) \qquad (50)$$

Equation 51 gives an empirical Laplacian form for the observed distribution $p_x(a)$ as reported by Milani et al. (2003) for I and P frames, where $\delta(a)$ is the Dirac delta function and α, β, γ are empirical constants:

$$p_x(a) = \gamma \exp(-\beta|a|^\alpha) \qquad (51)$$

Similarly, Equation 52 gives an empirical Laplacian plus impulsive form for the observed distribution $p_x(a)$ as reported by Milani et al. (2003) for B frames, where α', β', γ' are empirical constants:

$$p_x(a) = \alpha'\delta(a) + \beta'\exp\left(-\frac{2|a|}{\gamma'}\right) \qquad (52)$$

In Equation 51, normalization may determine the variable γ, while the mean and variance of the observed distribution $p_x(a)$ may determine the variables α, β. Similarly, in Equation 52, normalization may determine the variable β', while the mean and variance of the observed distribution $p_x(a)$ may determine the variables α', γ'.

Let $I_m(x, y)$ and $\hat{I}_m(x, y)$ be respectively the original and predicted pixel value at position (x, y) in the 16×16-pixel macroblock indexed by m in a frame having N_{MB} macroblocks. Equation 53 defines the current macroblock activity $act(m)$ and the current frame average activity $\langle act \rangle$:

$$act(m) = \sum_{y=0}^{16} \sum_{x=0}^{16} \left| I_m(x, y) - \hat{I}_m(x, y) \right|$$
$$\langle act \rangle = \frac{1}{N_{MB}} \sum_{m=0}^{N_{MB}} act(m) \qquad (53)$$

Equation 54 gives a quadratic approximation to the relations $\alpha(\langle act \rangle), \beta(\langle act \rangle), \gamma(\langle act \rangle)$:

$$\alpha\left(\langle act \rangle\right) = \alpha_0(\rho) + \alpha_1(\rho) \bullet \langle act \rangle + \alpha_2(\rho) \bullet \langle act \rangle^2$$
$$\beta\left(\langle act \rangle\right) = \beta_0(\rho) + \beta_1(\rho) \bullet \langle act \rangle + \beta_2(\rho) \bullet \langle act \rangle^2 \qquad (54)$$
$$\gamma\left(\langle act \rangle\right) = \gamma_0(\rho) + \gamma_1(\rho) \bullet \langle act \rangle + \gamma_2(\rho) \bullet \langle act \rangle^2$$

Equation 55 gives an approximation to the relation $\alpha'(\langle act \rangle)$:

$$\alpha'\left\langle act \right\rangle = \alpha'_0(\rho) + \alpha'_1(\rho) \bullet \log\left(\langle act \rangle\right) + \alpha'_2(\rho) \bullet \log$$
$$\log\left(\langle act \rangle\right) \qquad (55)$$

Milani et al. (2003) report that they tabulated the observed coefficients $\alpha_i(\rho), \beta_i(\rho), \alpha'_i(\rho), \gamma'_i(\rho)$ as a function of ρ to yield a parametric approximation to the observed distribution $p_x(a)$.

Following Milani et al. (2003), a method for controlling the bit rate of a bit stream encoded by an H.264

encoder allocates $G_{k,0}$ bits to encode the GOP indexed by k. The method starts by allocating $\bar{G}$ bits to encode the whole group of N at frame rate denoted by F_r and target bit rate denoted by R_b, as given by Equation 56:

$$\bar{G} = \frac{R_b \bullet N}{F_r} \qquad (56)$$

Equation 57 shows how the method corrects for the difference between the target and actual number of bits used after coding the GOP indexed by $(k - 1)$, denoted by δG_{k-1}:

$$G_{k,0} = \delta G_{k-1} + \bar{G} \qquad (57)$$

Equation 58 shows how the method selects a target bit rate T_n for the frame indexed by n in the current GOP, where n_i denotes the number of remaining frames of type $i \in \{I, P, B\}$ in the GOP, $K_{i,j}$ denotes the target bit ratio between frames of type i and frames of type j, where $i, j \in \{I, P, B\}$:

$$T_n = K'_i \frac{G_{k,n}}{1 + K_{I,P} \bullet n_P + K_{I,P} \bullet K_{P,B} \bullet n_B}, \, i \in \{I, P, B\} \qquad (58)$$
$$K'_I = K_{I,P} \bullet K_{P,B}, \, K'_P = K_{P,B}, \, K'_B = 1$$

Equation 59 updates the available number of bits for the frame indexed by $n + 1$ in the current GOP, denoted by $G_{k,n+1}$ after the current frame has been encoded by a number of bits, denoted by S_n:

$$G_{k,n+1} = G_{k,n} - S_n \qquad (59)$$

The quantization parameter $QP \in [0,1,2,\ldots,51]$ drives the target bit rate T_n for H.264 encoders. Recalling Equation 50, the average fraction of transform coefficients quantized to zero for the frame indexed by n, denoted by ρ_n, is given by Equation 60, where the constant λ may be estimated from previously coded pictures (e.g., the frame indexed by $(n - 1)$ in the current GOP):

$$\rho_n = 1 = \frac{T_n}{\lambda} \qquad (60)$$

Equation 49 determines the average quantization step size for the current picture indexed by the integer quantization parameter, denoted by $\langle QP_n \rangle$ from the average fraction of transform coefficients quantized to zero for the frame indexed by n, denoted by ρ_n, and the distribution $p_x(a)$, parameterized as shown in Equation 53 through Equation 55. Milani et al. (2003) recommend clipping the value of $\langle QP_n \rangle$ to the range $[\langle QP_{n-1} \rangle - 3, [\langle QP_{n-1} \rangle - 3]]$ to avoid producing objectionable quality differences between different picture zones. To smooth the coding distortion over different macroblocks, Milani et al. (2003) further correct the quantization parameter for each macroblock. Let

ρ_m^p denote the observed fraction of transform coefficients quantized to zero and B_m^p denote the number of bits used to code the current picture after coding the macroblock indexed by m of the frame indexed by n in the current GOP. For the target number of bits used to code the current picture, denoted by T_n, the remaining number of bits is $B_m^R = T_n - B_m^p$. Recalling Equation 60, Equation 61 gives the target remaining fraction of transform coefficients quantized to zero, denoted by ρ_m^R, to achieve the target number of bits, denoted by B_m^R, in a frame where total number of macroblocks is denoted by N_{MB}:

$$\rho_m^R = 1 - \frac{B_m^R}{\lambda} \bullet \frac{N_{MB}}{N_{MB} - m} \tag{61}$$

The H.264 standard relates the quantization step size, denoted by Δ, to the integer quantization parameter $QP \in [0,1,2,...,51]$, according to Equation 62:

$$\Delta \approx 0.67 \bullet 2^{\frac{QP}{6}} \tag{62}$$

Defining $\delta k = \frac{0.67}{C} \bullet 2^{\frac{\langle QP_n \rangle}{6}}$, with the empirical constant C set at $C = 3000$ to avoid creating strong variation in bit rate and visual quality across different macroblocks, Equation 63 gives the quantization parameter QP_{m+1} for the macroblock indexed by $(m + 1)$:

$$QP_{m+1} = \begin{cases} \langle QP_n \rangle + 3 \text{ if } 1 + 3 \bullet \delta k \leq k < +\infty \\ \langle QP_n \rangle + 2 \text{ if } 1 + 2 \bullet \delta k \leq k < 1 + 3 \bullet \delta k \\ \langle QP_n \rangle + 1 \text{ if } 1 + \delta k \leq k < 1 + 2 \bullet \delta k \\ \langle QP_n \rangle \text{ if } 1 - \delta k \leq k < 1 + \delta k \\ \langle QP_n \rangle - 1 \text{ if } 1 - 2 \bullet \delta k \leq k < 1 - \delta k \\ \langle QP_n \rangle - 2 \text{ if } 1 - 3 \bullet \delta k \leq k < 1 - 2 \bullet \delta k \\ \langle QP_n \rangle - 3 \text{ if } -\infty < k < 1 - 3 \bullet \delta k \end{cases} \tag{63}$$

To ensure that there are enough transform coefficients quantized to zero for ρ_m^p to be estimated, Milani et al. (2003) additionally set $QP_m = \langle QP_n \rangle$ until $B_m^p \geq 0.1 \bullet T_n$.

Miyaji et al. (2005) point out that assigning the same number of bits to each GOP, as recommended by Equation 56, requires a HRD buffer size equal to the largest number of bits generated by a frame in the GOP. An inappropriate choice of buffer size may lead to unacceptable delay, frozen video, or jerky motion. Furthermore, assigning the number of bits to each GOP using Equation 56 may lead to quality fluctuations because the picture information content is not considered.

Following Miyaji et al. (2005), Equation 64 gives an approximate quadratic relation between the *sum of absolute deviation* (SAD) of the prediction error in each macroblock, denoted by S, and the number of bits generated for the macroblock by an H.264 encoder using fixed values of quantization parameter without rate-distortion optimization:

$$bits = a \bullet S^2 + b \bullet S + c \tag{64}$$

Miyaji et al. (2005) determine the coefficients a, b, c by a method of least squares.

The H.264 standard supports *instantaneous decoding refresh* (IDR) pictures in which all slices are I or SI slices that cause the decoding process to mark all reference pictures as "unused for reference" immediately after decoding the IDR picture. An H.264 decoder can decode all following pictures without interframe prediction from any picture decoded before the IDR picture.

To avoid HRD buffer underflow, the number of bits of the current frame must be less than the HRD buffer level just before encoding the current frame and also larger than the number of bits that may be consumed by the following IDR frame. To avoid HRD buffer overflow, the HRD buffer level just before encoding the next frame must be lower than the maximum level at the next GOP boundary.

Miyaji et al. (2005) propose a method of allocating the number of bits to each frame according to the number of bits predicted by the observed value of SAD and a parameter related to the slope of the HRD buffer transition in a GOP, denoted by GW.

Let N denotes the number of frames in the GOP, B denote the maximum HRD buffer level, be denote the number of bits that are available for allocation to the first frame of the next GOP, Bh_i denote the HRD buffer level just before encoding the frame indexed by $i \in [1,2,...,N]$, and b_i denote the number of bits used in encoding the frame indexed by i. Equation 65 gives the *underflow limit*, denoted by B_U, and the *overflow limit*, denoted by B_O:

$$B_U(i) = \frac{be - (Bh_0 - b_0)}{N} i + (Bh_0 - b_0)$$
$$B_O(i) = \frac{B - Bh_1}{N - 1}(i - 1) + Bh_1 \tag{65}$$

Let $B_I(i)$ denote the line that equally divides the "safe area" between the underflow and overflow limits of the HRD buffer level. The HRD buffer level will progress around the line $B_I(i)$ if b_i is allocated to the frame indexed by i according to Equation 66, where BR denotes the maximum bit rate and FR denotes the maximum frame rate:

$$Bh_i - b_i + \frac{BR}{2FR} = B_I(i) \tag{66}$$

Define the parameter GW as the ratio of b_i to the average bit number for each frame. In accordance with Equation 66, Equation 67 gives the value of the parameter GW_i for the frame indexed by i:

$$GW_i = \frac{Bh_i - B_I(i)}{\dfrac{BR}{FR}} + \frac{1}{2} \tag{67}$$

Miyaji et al. (2005) determine the value of GW at the start of the GOP by using Equation 67 when $i = 2$.

To allocate the number of bits to each frame, Miyaji et al. (2005) use the frame SAD in accordance with the quadratic relation given by Equation 64, estimated for each fixed value of the quantization parameter, denoted by QP, so that Equation 68 gives the target number of bits for each frame, denoted by TB_i:

$$TB_i = f(SAD, QP) \qquad (68)$$

Applying the weighting parameter $GW = GW_2$ to ensure that the HRD buffer level will progress around the line that equally divides the "safe area" between the underflow and overflow limits of the HRD buffer level, Equation 69 gives the target bit rate for each frame, denoted by T_i:

$$T_i = TB_i \bullet GW \qquad (69)$$

Miyaji et al. (2005) further recommend allocating the number of bits for each macroblock in accordance with Equation 70, where TM_j and SAD_j are a target bit rate and observed SAD for the macroblock indexed by j:

$$TM_j = \frac{SAD_j}{\sum_j SAD_j} \bullet T_i \qquad (70)$$

Equation 71 controls the cumulative number of bits generated from the first macroblock of the current frame to the macroblock indexed by j, denoted by BM_j, in terms of the average value of the quantization parameter QP for the preceding macroblocks, denoted by $\langle QP \rangle$ and a target value of QP for the current macroblock, denoted by QP_j:

$$2^{\frac{QP_j - \langle QP \rangle}{6}} = \frac{BM_{j-1}}{\sum\limits_{k=1}^{j-1} BM_k} \qquad (71)$$

Scalability

Many networks are subject to congestion. A method for reducing the impact of channel bandwidth fluctuations on video bit streams is to encode a base layer of video at a bit rate substantially below the channel capacity together with at least one enhancement layer; the combined base and enhancement layer bit streams result in video at a predetermined bit rate when sufficient bandwidth is available. Figure 34 shows a block diagram for a two-layer scalable video codec (after Ghanbari 1989).

Ghanbari (1992) reports an adapted H.261 two-layer video codec for transmitting *variable bit rate* (VBR) video over *asynchronous transmission mode* (ATM) networks. Ghanbari and Seferidis (1995) report a two-layer video codec where both the base layer and enhancement layer codecs are H.261 codecs with interframe coding in each layer. Ng et al. (1996) report a two-layer spatially scalable codec having an H.261 encoder in the base layer to provide a *constant bit rate* (CBR) QCIF-resolution bit stream, together with an enhancement layer having a pyramidal DCT encoder with perceptual quantization of residuals. The combination of base layer and enhancement layer bit streams provides a VBR CIF-resolution bit stream.

Qi et al. (2001) and Blaszak et al. (2002) report fine granularity spatially scalable encoding with multiple enhancement layers for VBR video transmitted over ATM

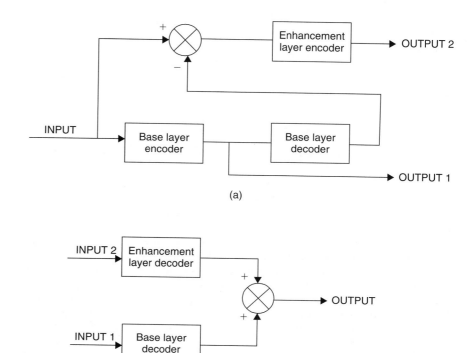

Figure 34: Block diagram of two-layer video codec (after Ghanbari, 1989)

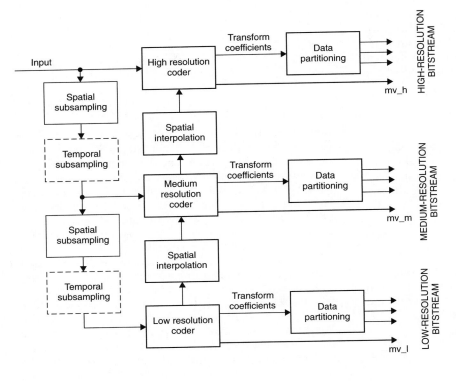

Figure 35: Block diagram of three-layer scalable coder (after Blaszak et al. 2002)

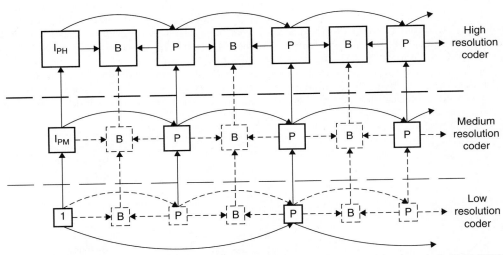

Figure 36: Exemplary image sequence for three-layer encoder (after Blaszak © 2002 IEEE)

and wireless networks. In particular, wireless networks are subject to fading and transmission error. Figure 35 shows a block diagram for the three-layer hybrid motion-compensated encoder with spatial and temporal scalability after Blaszak et al. (2002), who indicate that the medium- and high-resolution bit streams are appropriate for narrowband, middleband, and wideband networks, respectively.

Advantageously, all three coders may comply with video compression standards such as H.263. The proposed structure covers spatial resolutions QCIF for the low-resolution layer, CIF for the middle-resolution layer, and 4CIF for the high-resolution layer. The encoder estimates motion vectors mv_l for the low-resolution layer independent

of the motion vectors mv_m and mv_h estimated for the higher-resolution layers. Each layer may use fine granularity scaling to adapt to channel bandwidth fluctuations.

Figure 36 shows how the three-level encoder applies spatial and temporal subsampling by skipping frames.

Ugur and Nasiopoulos (2003) report a method for combining bit stream switching and fine granularity scalability for H.264 scalable video transmission that is compatible with standard H.264 encoders and decoders. In that paper, the H.264 fine granularity scalability mechanism has a base layer encoded at bit rate R_{base} and an enhancement layer encoded using bit-plane encoding up to a maximum bit rate R_{max}. The stream-switching mechanism switches between a limited number of streams encoded at different bit rates at *switching predictive* (SP) frames rather than I frames, which allow identical reconstruction of frames even if they are predicted from different reference frames. In the combined system, fine granularity scalability accommodates low-bandwidth variations with respect to the base layer, while stream switching accommodates high-bandwidth variations that exceed a predetermined threshold.

The method determines the rates for each stream by optimizing the total distortion measure D given by Equation 33 for a given bandwidth R_{avail}, where R_i denotes the bit rate allocated to the base stream labeled by $i \in [1,2,...,n]$, $R_1 = R_{min}$, $R_{n+1} = R_{max}$, $R_1 \leq R_2 ... \leq R_{n-1} \leq R_n$ and $D_i^{bp\_j}$ denotes the distortion of the base stream labeled by i sending bp_j bit planes to the enhancement layer:

$$D = \sum_{i=1}^{n} \left(\sum_{R_{avail}=R_i}^{R_{avail}=R_{i+1}} D_i^{bp} \right) \tag{72}$$

Profiles

Annex A of the H.264 standard, which is currently the most advanced, flexible, and compressive ITU video codec, specifies seven capability profiles—*baseline, main, extended, high, high 10, high 4:2:2, and high 4:4:4*—and levels for these capability profiles. Each profile is a subset of H.264 capabilities, intended for a specific kind of application, as follows:

- *baseline profile* (BP), which is intended for video-conferencing and mobile applications that require the lowest cost and least computational resource;
- *main profile* (MP), which has been widely replaced by the high profile;
- *extended profile* (XP), which is intended for streaming video applications;
- *high profile* (HiP), which is intended for broadcast and disc storage applications, specially for high-definition television applications;
- *high 10 profile* (Hi10P), which is intended for broadcast and storage applications (and extends the high profile by supporting as many as 10 bits per sample of decoded picture precision);
- *high 4:2:2 profile* (Hi422P), which is intended for broadcast and storage applications (and extends the high 10 profile for professional applications that use interlaced video with support for the 4:2:2 chroma sampling format); and
- *high 4:4:4 profile* (Hi444P), which is currently a deprecated profile.

Table 1 shows a capability matrix for the above profiles.

Applications

High-Definition Video Storage

High-capacity optical disks developed by the Blu-Ray Disc Association and the DVD Forum can store 50 GB or 30 GB, respectively, on dual-sided 12-centimeter discs. By comparison, a dual-sided 12-centimeter *digital video disc* (DVD) can store only 17 GB. These high-capacity optical disk readers and writers use blue-violet lasers that operate at a 405-nanometer wavelength to read and write pits that are smaller and closer together than pits read and written by DVD readers and writers using red lasers that operate at a 650-nanometer wavelength.

As an example, the Blu-Ray Disc Association and DVD Forum have adopted the high profile of H.264 (together with the MPEG-2 and SMPTE 421M WMV 9 codecs discussed later in this chapter) for high-definition television content stored on high-capacity optical disks.

H.264 typically allows a Blu-Ray or high-definition DVD (HD-DVD) disk to store up to four hours of high-definition video encoded at 23 Mbps to 25 Mbps, compared to two hours for MPEG-2.

MPEG CODECS

The Motion Picture Experts Group (MPEG) started in 1988 as International Standards Organization (ISO) Working Group JTC1/SC29. The goal of MPEG is to develop standards for the digital compression of audiovisual signals. MPEG membership currently exceeds 300 experts.

MPEG-1

The MPEG team published the MPEG-1 standard in 1993 as 11172-2 (ISO/IEC 1993), with four updates issued between 1996 and 2006. The standard specifies a decoding process for moving pictures and associated audio. MPEG-1 is primarily applicable to noninterlaced digital video formats preferably having a *standard intermediate format* (SIF) of 288 lines of 352 pixels with picture rates approximately 24 hz to 30 hz at bit rates up to approximately 1.5 Mbps and visual quality similar to the well-known *video home system* (VHS).

The MPEG-1 standard assumes a video input in YC_bC_r color space with 4:2:0 sampling for spectral redundancy reduction. Reminiscent of JPEG, the recommended method for spatial redundancy reduction is 8×8-pixel block-based DCT coding with visually weighted scalar quantization, zigzag coefficient ordering, differential encoding of DC coefficients between blocks, and run-length coding of AC coefficients quantized to zero followed by *variable length code* (VLC) entropy coding. MPEG-1 defines blocks as 8×8-pixel regions and macroblocks as 16×16-pixel regions.

The MPEG-1 standard recommends motion-compensated transform coding of pixel value differences between observed and predicted pictures. It is the responsibility of the encoder to determine appropriate motion vectors, and the standard does not recommend any method for doing so.

MPEG-1 supports *intra* (I), *predicted* (P), *bidirectionally predicted* (B), and *DC-coded* (D) pictures. MPEG-1 encoders never use B frames as references for prediction. D pictures are intra coded with DC transform coefficients but no AC transform coefficients to facilitate fast-forward and reverse playback operations. The standard recommends a

Table 1: H.264 Profile Capability Matrix

	Baseline	Extended	Main	High	High 10	High 4:2:2	High 4:4:4
I and P slices	X	X	X	X	X	X	X
B slices		X	X	X	X	X	X
SI and SP slices		X					
Multiple reference frames	X	X	X	X	X	X	X
Loop deblocking filter	X	X	X	X	X	X	X
CAVLC entropy coder	X	X	X	X	X	X	X
CABAC entropy coder			X	X	X	X	X
Flexible macroblock order	X	X					
Arbitrary slice order	X	X					
Redundant slices	X	X					
Data partitions		X					
Interlaced pictures			X	X	X	X	X
4:2:0 chroma format	X	X	X	X	X	X	X
4:0:0 monochrome format				X	X	X	X
4:2:2 chroma format						X	X
4:4:4 chroma format							X
8-bit sample depth	X	X	X	X	X	X	X
9-and 10-bit sample depth					X	X	X
11-and 12-bit sample depth							X
8 × 8 and 4 × 4 adaptive transforms				X	X	X	X
Quantization scaling matrices				X	X	X	X
Quantization parameters for C_b and C_r separately				X	X	X	X
Residual color transform							X
Predictive lossless codes							X

subset of the coding parameters known as the *constrained parameters*, which are defined as follows:

- horizontal picture size ≤ 768 pixels,
- vertical picture size ≤ 576 lines,
- picture area ≤ 396 macroblocks,
- picture rate ≤ 30 Hz,
- pixel rate ≤ 396 × 25 macroblock/second,
- motion vector range ≤ [−64, ... ,63.5] pixels at half-pixel accuracy,
- input buffer size ≤ 327,680 bits, and
- bit rate ≤ 856 kbps at near constant bit rate.

An encoder may skip macroblocks in P and B pictures that have no associated motion vectors or for which the motion vector is zero. MPEG-1 recommends that the encoder force the use of an intra-coded macroblock at least once every 132 times that it is encoded in a P picture without an intervening I picture, as recommended by the H.261 standard to control the accumulation of floating-point inverse DCT mismatch error. Because the output bit rate is variable, MPEG-1 recommends that a compliant encoder implement a leaky-bucket rate-control buffer, which is specified as the MPEG-1 standard *video buffer verifier* (VBV).

The two-layer scalable video codecs developed by Ghanbari (1992), Ghanbari and Seferidis (1995), and Ng et al. (1996), discussed in the section on scalability, can be adapted for MPEG-1 scalable video coding.

Applications of the MPEG-1 standard include *video compact disc* (VCD) compression and decompression.

MPEG-2

Developed from 1990 to 1995, the MPEG-2 standard is widely deployed and currently jointly standardized by ITU and MPEG with multiple updates as H.262 and ISO/IEC

Table 2: Display and Transmission of an Exemplary Group of 12 MPEG-2 Intra (I), Predicted (P), and Bidirectional (B) Pictures

Display	B	B	I	B	B	P	B	B	P	B	B	B
Frame	1	2	3	4	5	6	7	8	9	10	11	12
Transmit	I	B	B	P	B	B	P	B	B	P	B	B
Frame	3	1	2	6	4	5	9	7	8	12	10	11

13818-2:2000. The MPEG-2 standard, based on the DCT, shares many features with the H.264 standard, operating on noninterlaced and interlaced video; it delivers approximately half as much compression as H.264 using considerably less computational resources. MPEG-2 supports scalable compression in which a compliant decoder can extract useful video from portions of a compressed bit stream. MPEG-2 operates on pictures in YC_bC_r color space with 4:2:0, 4:2:2, and 4:4:4 sampling formats using the 8×8-pixel DCT, and it accepts one motion vector per 16×16-pixel macroblock at half-pixel accuracy. MPEG-2 is capable of encoding standard definition television at bit rates from approximately 3 Mbps to 15 Mbps and high-definition television at approximately 15 Mbps to 30 Mbps.

Table 2 shows the relationship between an exemplary group of I, P, and B pictures. The different picture types typically occur in a repeating GOP sequence. I pictures are coded using information only from that picture. P pictures are coded using forward prediction from previous I or P pictures. A compliant encoder codes B pictures from previous and succeeding frames using I or P pictures (but not other B pictures, which H.264 allows). This, in turn, implies that the encoding order may be markedly different from the display order. Because decoding B pictures requires both past and future pictures to be available, the presence of B pictures adds considerably to the encoder delay.

The MPEG-2 standard specifies five capability profiles: *simple, main, SNR scalable, spatially scalable,* and *high*. Levels for each capability profile are also specified. Each profile is a subset of MPEG-2 capabilities as follows:

- *Simple profile* supports noninterlaced video in 4:2:0 sampling format without B pictures.
- *Main profile* supports noninterlaced and interlaced video in 4:2:0 sampling format with I, P, and B pictures.
- *SNR scalable profile* provides two layers with the same spatial resolution but different picture quality.
- *Spatially scalable profile* provides two layers with arbitrary spatial resolution and picture quality, each coded without regard for the other.
- *High profile* supports interlaced and noninterlaced video in the 4:2:2 sampling format.

The two-layer scalable video codecs developed by Ghanbari (1992), Ghanbari and Seferidis (1995), and Ng et al. (1996) can be adapted for MPEG-2 scalable video coding. The multiple enhancement layer scalable video codec reported by Blaszak et al. (2002) can also be adapted for MPEG-2 scalable video coding.

The MPEG-2 simple profile at main level requires only I and P frames, thus reducing encoding delay. Video-conferencing is an appropriate application for the MPEG-2 simple profile (Tudor 1995), although the H.261, H.263, and H.264 standardized codecs are more widely used for that purpose.

MPEG-4

The MPEG Web site provides detailed information about MPEG standards and includes an overview. In particular, H.264 is the ITU name for the ISO/ITU joint standard MPEG-4 Part 10.

MPEG-4 is an extensible toolbox of algorithms that addresses the coding of audiovisual objects throughout an extended bit range from approximately 5 bps to more than 1 Gbps. The standard addresses video compression together with audio and systems elements.

MPEG-4 standardizes only bit stream syntax and decoder algorithms. Standardization of H.264 has now overtaken the MPEG-4 visual codec IEEE:14496-2 based on the DCT (ISO/IEC 2004). However, the Koenen (2002) overview of the MPEG-4 standard illustrates concepts such as encoding scenes containing visual objects and sprites, which the H.264 standard does not directly incorporate. In particular, MPEG-4 allows a *shape-adaptive discrete cosine transform* (SA-DCT) to encode visual objects of arbitrary shape (not just rectangles) together with texture. SA-DCT calculations use predefined orthonormal sets of *one-dimensional discrete cosine transform* (1D-DCT) functions within an 8×8-pixel block (Sikora 1995). A set of 1D-DCT functions of the same length as each column encodes a visual object of arbitrary shape in the vertical direction. Next the algorithm shifts the visual object's rows to the left border of the 8×8-pixel block and a set of 1D-DCT functions of the same length as each row encodes the object. This technique results in a block with as many DCT coefficients as the visual object has pixels. A compliant decoder requires contour information to decode the coefficients. This technique is appropriate for applications such as nonlinear editing of video objects when an editor selects a visual object's contours by manual intervention or downstream keying.

The MPEG-4 standard additionally supports coding audiovisual objects, including static and dynamically generated *sprites*, which are still images representing backgrounds visible throughout a scene of a video sequence. Figure 37 depicts an audiovisual scene containing scrolling text, audio, background sprite, arbitrarily shaped video, and graphics.

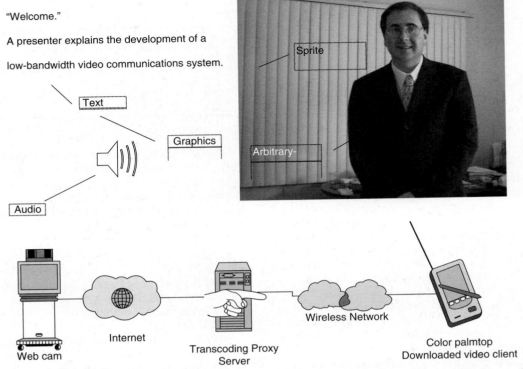

Figure 37: Audiovisual scene containing scrolling text, audio, background sprite, arbitrarily shaped video, and graphics

The MPEG-4 standard currently supports scalability of visual objects through the profiles illustrated in Table 3.

The multiple enhancement layer scalable video codec reported by Blaszak et al. (2002), as discussed earlier in the section on scalability and JPEG codecs, can also be adapted for MPEG-4 scalable video coding. The MPEG-4 standard additionally supports *visual object plane* (VOP) spatial and temporal scalability via methods for generalized scalable coding together with methods for fine granularity scalable coding. In particular, the MPEG-4 standard supports spatial temporal scalability of rectangular VOPs and temporal scalability of arbitrarily shaped VOPs. The MPEG-4 standard supports fine granularity scalable coding via truncation of bit streams coding DCT coefficient bit planes.

MPEG-7

The MPEG-7 standard 159383 (ISO/IEC 2002) defines a multimedia content description interface to provide fast

Table 3: MPEG-4 Standard Scalable Profiles

Profile	Objects	Use
Simple visual	Rectangular video objects	Mobile networks
Simple scalable visual	Temporal and spatial scalable objects	Internet
Core visual	Arbitrarily shaped and temporally scalable	Internet multimedia
N-bit visual	Core visual, but 4–12 bits pixel depth	Surveillance
Scalable texture visual	Spatial scalable coding of still (texture) objects	Games, still cameras
Core scalable	Temporal and spatially scalable arbitrarily shaped objects	Internet, mobile, broadcast
Advanced scalable texture	Arbitrarily shaped texture and still images	Image browsing
Advanced core	Arbitrarily shaped video objects and still image objects	Interactive multimedia streaming over Internet
Fine granularity scalability	Truncation of bit stream at any bit position to adapt delivery quality as required	Any

and efficient methods for searching, filtering, and identifying multimedia content. In particular, Part 3 of the MPEG-7 Standard focuses on metadata for visual content such as still images, video. and three-dimensional models.

Part 3 of the MPEG-7 Standard specifies the following elements:

- *Description schemes* describe entities or relationships that pertain to multimedia content. They specify the structure and semantics of their components, which may be description schemes, descriptors, or data types.
- *Descriptors* describe features, attributes, or groups of attributes of multimedia content.
- *Data types* are the basic reusable data types employed by description schemes and descriptors.
- *Description definition language* defines description schemes, descriptors, and data types by specifying their syntax and allows their extension (currently based on extensible markup language, or XML).
- System tools that support delivery of descriptions and multiplexing of descriptions with multimedia content, synchronization, and file format.

Part 3 of the MPEG-7 standard provides the following visual description tools:

- *basic structures*, such as descriptor containers (grid layout, time series, and multiple view), together with basic supporting tools (temporal interpolation and a spatial two-dimensional coordinate system);
- *visual features*, such as
  - *color*, such as color feature descriptors (dominant color, scalable color, color layout, color structure, and group of frames, group of pictures color descriptor, together with color supporting tools (color space and color quantization);
  - *texture*, such as homogeneous texture, texture browsing, and edge histogram;
  - *shape*, such as region shape, contour shape, and 3D shape;
  - *motion*, such as camera motion, motion trajectory, parametric motion, and motion activity;
  - *localization*, such as region locator and spatio-temporal locator; and
- other structures, such as face recognition.

Schafer et al. (2000) suggest using metadata currently defined in the MPEG-7 standard to improve coding efficiency. In particular, if the production process generates information about cut and fade transitions, an encoding strategy can switch off predictive coding when no motion compensation model would be useful. If the production process provides visual object metadata from an editing or chroma color process (such as blue screen), an encoding strategy can provide for separate coding of moving objects, background, and transparent layers—which is especially useful when a motion compensation model is unable to predict the appearance or disappearance of moving objects. If the production process provides camera motion metadata, this will facilitate global motion compensation coding of MPEG-4 sprites. Finally, an encoding strategy may use information about color and texture histograms or distribution to adjust bit allocation or quantizer values.

OTHER CODECS

This section of the chapter discusses proprietary and other codecs.

SMPTE 421M (WMV 9)

Microsoft proposed Windows Media Video 9 (WMV9) codec, renamed VC-1. In 2006, the Society of Motion Picture and Television Engineers (SMPTE)* standardized this codec as SMPTE 421M (SMPTE 2006).

SMPTE 421M competes with the H.264 standard based on the 8×8-pixel DCT, with particular strength in compressing interlaced content widely available to the broadcast and video industries. Although the SMPTE 421M and H.264 are broadly similar standards, specific differences between SMPTE 421M and H.264 include overlapped transforms, intensity compensation, display metadata with so-called pan-and-scan windows, and leaky-bucket rate control.

Overlapped transforms reduce blocking artifacts by using coefficients from neighboring blocks in the block reconstruction. SMPTE 421M emulates an overlap transform by smoothing 8×8-pixel block boundaries before applying an in-loop deblocking filter. Consider the three image blocks depicted in Figure 38.

The overlap transform algorithm filters all of the reconstructed pixels in the four-pixel wide boundary (shown crosshatched in Figure 38), applying a filter to pixels at vertical edges (such as a_0, a_1, b_1, and b_0) followed by pixels at horizontal edges (such as p_0, p_1, q_1, and q_0). In particular, the algorithm filters the 2×2 corner pixels (shown as a rectangle in Figure 39) in both vertical and horizontal directions. Equations 73 and 74 define the overlap smoothing filter, which filters input pixel values $[x_0 \ x_1 \ x_2 \ x_3]$ to output pixel values $[y_0 \ y_1 \ y_2 \ y_3]$:

$$\begin{bmatrix} y_0 \\ y_1 \\ y_2 \\ y_3 \end{bmatrix} = \frac{1}{8} \left\{ \begin{pmatrix} 7 & 0 & 0 & 1 \\ -1 & 7 & 1 & 1 \\ 1 & 1 & 7 & -1 \\ 1 & 0 & 0 & 7 \end{pmatrix} \begin{bmatrix} x_0 \\ x_1 \\ x_2 \\ x_3 \end{bmatrix} + \begin{bmatrix} r_0 \\ r_1 \\ r_0 \\ r_1 \end{bmatrix} \right\} \tag{73}$$

$$r_0 = 4, \ r_1 = 3 \text{ (odd-numbered rows and columns)}$$
$$r_0 = 3, \ r_1 = 4 \text{ (even-numbered rows and columns)} \tag{74}$$

---

* The SMPTE is a multidisciplinary organization focused on developing standards for the motion imaging industry. Started in 1916 as the Society for Motion Picture Engineers, the society embraced television engineering in 1950.

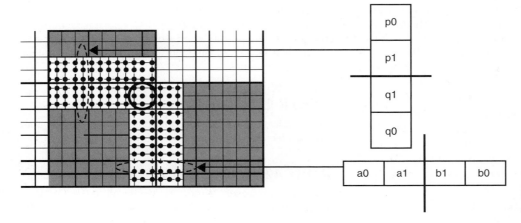

Figure 38: Overlap smoothing of 8 × 8-pixel blocks

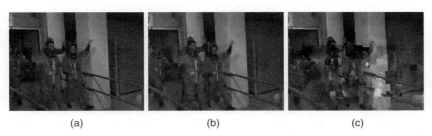

(a)   (b)   (c)

Figure 39: Images of frame numbered 1251 from *The Emotion of Space* encoded by (a) the MPEG-4 codec after flipping bits, (b) the VP70 codec software before flipping bits, and (c) the VP70 codec software after flipping bits

The SMPTE 421M standard recommends methods for detecting fade sequences and compensating luminance in fade sequences for efficient coding. Optional display metadata provide a compliant decoder with information such as the geometry of decoded pictures, together with pan-and-scan windows, which are subpictures that provide alternate display formats such as a 4:3 aspect ratio picture-in-picture display within an anamorphic 16:9 aspect ratio picture.

Many proprietary codecs have not yet received formal standardization. Of current interest are RealVideo (Real Networks), TrueMotion VP7 (On2 Technologies), and EuclidVision (Euclid Discoveries).

RealVideo-10

Real Networks released RealVideo-1 in 1997, based on a proprietary implementation of the H.263 standard. The technical summary for the current version (RealVideo-10) describes a scalable block-based transform coder with spatial prediction, temporal prediction, motion compensation, and psychovisual filtering (Real Networks 2003). RealVideo-10 relates to U.S. patents 5,854,858 and 5,917,954 granted to Girod et al. These patents disclose a multiresolution coder in which the encoder can decide to provide low-resolution pictures for coding by a 4 × 4-pixel DCT after averaging 2 × 2-pixel regions in the input pictures. Coding blocks by a 4 × 4-pixel DCT requires considerably less computational resource than coding blocks by an 8 × 8-pixel DCT. The encoder inserts the 4 × 4-pixel DCT coefficients into the lowest 4 × 4 coefficients of the corresponding 8 × 8-pixel blocks in the input pictures, with the remaining 48 coefficients set to zero for each 8 × 8-pixel block.

TrueMotion VP7

U.S. Patent 7,027,654 granted to Ameres et al. and assigned to On2 Technologies discloses a video compression system for vector architectures such as Intel's multimedia extensions. The disclosed encoder includes a motion estimator, a block-based 8 × 8 DCT, a quantizer, a variable length encoder, and a loop filter for smoothing block edges. The encoder includes a deblocking filter and an edge-enhancing deringing filter, both designed for implementation on vector processors. The deblocking filter uses simple linear calculations and one-dimensional filters to remove blocking artifacts and gather information for use by the edge-enhancing deringing filter (similar to a symmetric neighborhood filter).

The TrueMotion VP7 white paper (On2 Technologies 2005) suggests that the proprietary codec implements 4 × 4-pixel transforms, improved motion compensation allowing the representation of complex patterns of motion, and second-order coding of transform DC coefficients. The VP7 codec also implements a motion vector filter, deblocking and deringing filters, a scene change detector for automatic key frames, and a method for adapting to changes in light level.

EuclidVision

Euclid Discoveries claims to have developed an object-based coding technology that leverages the MPEG-4 standard. Note that the MPEG-4 standard supports object-based video coding, which is especially useful when the video sequence is a composite formed by an editor from known video objects stored separately in a video database.

In principle, if the video objects identified in a scene have substantially different statistical characteristics, such as "talking head" video on a smooth featureless background, object-based coding methods provide substantial improvements in compression ratio and video quality in comparison with picture-based coding methods.

Euclid Discoveries has published five provisional patent applications related to object-based video coding. The most recently published application, U.S. 20060233448 to Pace et al., apparently discloses an apparatus and method for processing video data. By segmenting video pictures into video objects, the method allows prioritization of these objects for separate compression. The method detects and tracks objects through successive pictures, together with specific features of these objects—such as the eyes or nose in a face—via multiresolution analysis of the spatial gradient of optical flow. The method also performs motion compensation by analyzing the translation, rotation, and scaling of a mesh of vertices that connect discrete regions for each picture (similar to a wireframe model). In the preferred embodiment, the method determines the motion displacement for each vertex relative to an interpolated polygon neighborhood by block-based matching in a rectangular tile neighborhood. The method additionally removes outliers by a robust process such as the RANSAC algorithm (Fischler and Bolles 1981).

EVALUATION

Consider selecting a commercially available video codec for deployment in a hypothetical wireless videophone system operating over a 384 kbps link. To be acceptable, a solution must be cost-effective, the visual quality acceptable to viewers, the encoding and decoding latency each less than approximately 0.25 second, and the battery life maximized. For this example, cost-effectiveness, latency, and battery life are more important factors than visual quality. If the wireless channel degrades through network congestion, rain fading, or multipath propagation, then the reconstructed visual quality must degrade gracefully. The solution must be capable of yielding an average bit rate within 5 percent of the target bit rate and robustly decode video transmitted over a channel that has a relative error rate up to approximately 10^{-5} per second after error correction.

The requirement for graceful degradation of visual quality suggests a solution based on a spatially and temporally scalable codec, effective at bit rates up to approximately 384 kbps (typically 360 kbps when audio tracks are considered). Of the codecs discussed in this chapter, these requirements imply that the only candidates are H.264, H.263, MPEG-4, Motion JPEG 2000, VC-1, RealVideo-10, and TrueMotion VP7 (EuclidVision is not currently widely available). The MPEG-2 standard scalable profiles are appropriate only for target bit rates from approximately 3 Mbps to 15 Mbps, whereas MPEG-1, Motion JPEG, and Motion JPEG-LS do not recommend scalable solutions.

In particular, consider real-time encoding of *The Emotion of Space*, frames 1230 to 1679, at 15 fps in 24-bit color on a hypothetical 624-MHz processor with 32 MB memory. Although the architectures are not directly comparable, consider benchmarking commercially available codecs on a Windows XP Professional workstation with a dual 1.7-GHz processor and 1 GB memory.

Selecting a Commercially Available Video Codec for Deployment

For this example, the candidates are the H.264, H.263, MPEG-4 Visual and Motion JPEG 2000 implemented by Lead Tools, SMPTE 421M implemented by Microsoft as WMV9 in Windows Media Encoder Series 9, RealVideo-10 implemented by Real Networks in Real Producer, and True Motion software version 0 (VP70) implementing the VP7 codec developed by On2 Technologies. Each implementation has a small number of user-adjustable configuration parameters. Table 4 tabulates the experimental results.

To maximize encoding speed and battery life, the H.264 codec configuration was constant bit rate with target set to 360 kbps, output frame rate set to 15 fps, entropy coding type set to CAVLC (rather than CABAC), and motion estimation set to the "very fast" option. Because rate control appears not to be effective unless the group of pictures comprises at least two pictures, the GOP structure is one P picture between successive I pictures and no B pictures to minimize latency. The observed visual quality and latency are acceptable. The bit rate is more than 5 percent above the target bit rate, and the compression speed is about half real-time using 2.6 times the platform CPU and 1.7 times the platform memory.

To maximize encoding speed and battery life, the H.263 codec configuration was constant bit rate with target set to 360 kbps and output frame rate set to 15 fps. Every frame is a key frame, to minimize latency, with quality improved by selecting the deblocking filter and advanced intra coding options. The visual quality is slightly blocky with corona around strong visual edges and slight flickering with soft contrast. Although latency is acceptable, visual quality is unacceptable. The average bit rate is quite far from the target bit rate, perhaps requiring improved rate control. The compression speed is some five times faster than real time using approximately 2.2 times the platform CPU and one times the platform memory.

To maximize encoding speed and battery life, the MPEG-4 codec configuration was fast motion vector search, without four motion vectors per macroblock or half-pixel motion vector accuracy. The configuration selects one P picture between every two I pictures to minimize latency. By experiment, quality factor $Q = 10$ yields average bit rate 492 kbps bit rate, whereas $Q = 12$ and $Q = 11$ yield 307.8 kbps and 325 kbps average bit rate, respectively. Adopting $Q = 11$, the visual quality is slightly blocky with slight flickering. The visual quality and latency are acceptable. The average bit rate would benefit from improved rate control. The compression speed is approximately 3.75 times faster than real time using 2.99 times the platform CPU and less than the platform memory.

The Motion JPEG 2000 codec configuration was 77:1 compression for 360-kbps target bit rate. The average bit rate is 389 kbps. The visual quality is slightly blurry with slight flickering. The visual quality and latency are acceptable. The average bit rate is within 8 percent of the target bit rate, and the codec could benefit from slightly improved rate control. The compression speed is

Table 4: Video Compression Experimental Results

Codec	Configuration	Average bit rate (kbps)	Elapsed time (sec)	Peak processor utilization (%)	Peak memory (Mb)	Average PSNR (dB)	VQM general model (DSIS)	Latency (sec)
H.264	CBR CALVC Very fast GOP = 2 (IPIP)	418	63	48	54	20.69	3.64	0.13
H.263	Deblocking filter Advanced intra coding GOP = 1	209	6	40	31	18.45	2.7	0.2
MPEG-4 visual	Q = 11 Fast search GOP = 21 motion vector per macroblock Full pixel accuracy	325	8	55	28	20.62	3.89	0.13
Motion JPEG 2000	77:1	389	23	48	24	20.71	3.86	0
WMV9	384 kbps	403.9	31	91	120			
RV40	384 kbps Normal video One-pass	362	25	81	39			
VP70	Live encoding Target = 678 kbps Speed 8 Sharpness 4 Noise reduction off Undershoot 95% Overshoot 105% Quantizer [4, 56] Prebuffer = 0 Optimal buffer = 0 Max buffer = 0	362	9	48	43	22.98	4.16	0.13

approximately 30 percent faster than real time using 2.5 times the platform CPU and approximately 75 percent of the platform memory.

The WMV9 codec configuration was 384-kbps target bit rate. The average bit rate is 403.9 kbps. The visual quality is very good. The average bit rate (measure by file size) is more than 5 percent above the target bit rate. The compression speed is approximately real time using 5.2 times the platform CPU and 3.75 times the platform memory. Multiple compression layers support graceful degradation but were not configured for this experiment.

The RealVideo-10 codec configuration selects a 384-kbps audience (350 kbps video) for single-layer video without audio and "normal video" with one-pass video encoding. The visual quality is very good. The average bit rate is within 5 percent of the target bit rate. The compression speed is 17 percent faster than real time using approximately 5.4 times the platform CPU and 1.2 times the platform memory. Multiple compression layers support graceful degradation but were not configured for this experiment.

The VP70 codec configuration is 384 kbps CBR for live encoding, with speed 8, sharpness 4, noise reduction off, undershoot 95 percent, overshoot 105 percent, quantizer [4, 56], prebuffer 0, and buffer 0. By experimentation,

setting the target bit rate to 678 kbps yields a 362-kbps file. The visual quality is very good with acceptable latency. The compression speed is 3.3 times faster than real time using 2.6 times the platform CPU and 1.34 times the platform memory. An optimized implementation with better rate control or a 34 percent increase in platform memory could make VP70 a stronger candidate. Hence, MPEG-4 and VP70 were selected for subsequent bit-error resilience tests.

Bit-Error Resilience Tests

A simplified bit-error resilience test flipped bits with uniform random distribution for 10^{-5} of the bytes in each output file. The MPEG-4 bit-flipped output file played to completion in Windows Media Player 9 without noticeable bit error-induced artifact. The VP70 bit-flipped output file played to completion in Windows Media Player 9 with some frames having rectangular regions with changed colors, such as frame 1251. Figure 39 shows gray-scale images of frame 1251 (a) encoded by the MPEG-4 codec but not visibly damaged by flipping bits, (b) frame 1251 encoded by the VP70 codec before flipping bits, and (c) the VP70 codec after flipping bits.

Table 5 tabulates the measured visual quality metrics before and after flipping bits.

Table 5: Visual Quality Metric for *The Emotion of Space,* Frames 1230 to 1679*

Codec	Average PSNR (dB)	VQM General Model (DSIS)
MPEG-4	20.62	3.89
MPEG-4 (after)	20.58	3.85
VP70 (before)	22.98	4.16
VP70 (after)	20.57	3.52

* Encoded by MPEG-4 and VP70 codec software before and after flipping bits.

In this educational example, the MPEG-4 codec would be more likely than not selected for deployment on technical grounds.

CONCLUSION

This chapter has discussed principles by which digital video signals are compressed, and we have reviewed applicable standards developed by JPEG, MPEG, ITU, and SMPTE, together with proprietary codecs developed by Microsoft, Real Networks, On2 Technologies, and Euclid Discoveries. The chapter provided a simple example of codec evaluation based on commercially available codecs for-real time communications.

GLOSSARY

Foveation point: The point at which the eye is looking.
Frame: An image from a video sequence.
Lossless: A reversible and exact process.
Lossy: An irreversible and approximate process.
Minimum coded unit (MCU): The minimum amount of image data that a coder can code.
Picture clock rate: The input picture rate.
Scene: A sequence of frames.

CROSS REFERENCES

See *Data Compression*; *Image Compression*; *Information Theory*; *Speech and Audio Compression*.

REFERENCES

Adams, M. D., F. Kossentini, and R. K. Ward. 2002. Generalized S transform. *IEEE Transactions on Signal Processing*, 50: 2831–42.

ANSI. 1995. Standard T1.801.01-1995. *Digital transport of video teleconferencing/video telephony signals: Video test scenes for subjective and objective performance assessment* (revised 2001).

———. 1996. Standard T1.801.02-1996. *Digital transport of video teleconferencing/video telephony signals: Performance terms, definitions and examples* (revised 2001).

———. 2003. Standard T1.803.03-2003. *Digital transport of one-way video signals: Parameters for objective performance assessment* (revision of T1.801.03-1996).

Blaszak, L., M. Domanski, and S. Mackowiak. 2002. Scalable video compression for wireless systems. In *Tenth National Symposium of Radio Science*, pp. 336–40.

Choi, I. W., and B. Jeon. 2006. Hierarchical motion search for variable-block-size motion compensation. *Optical Engineering*, 45(1): 17002–10.

Colmenarez, A., B. Frey, and T. S. Huang. 1999. Detection and tracking of faces and facial features. In *1999 Proceedings of 1999 International Conference on Image Processing*, Kobe, Japan, Oct. 25–8, vol. 1, pp. 657–61.

Dai, M., D. Loquinov, and H. Radha. 2004. Rate distortion modeling of scalable video coders. In *Proceedings of 2004 International Conference on Image Processing*, Singapore, Oct. 24–7, vol. 2, pp. 1093–6 (retrieved from http://irl.cs.tamu.edu/people/min/papers/icip2004-RD.pdf).

Digital Cinema Initiatives. 2005. Digital cinema system specification v1.0 (retrieved from www.dcimovies.com).

Dufaux, F., and T. Ebrahimi. 2003. Motion JPEG 2000 for wireless applications. In *Proceedings of the First International Workshop on JPEG 2000*, Lugano, Switzerland, July 8, pp. 2036–9 (retrieved from www.emitall.com).

Fischler, M. A., and R. C. Bolles. 1981. Random sample consensus: A paradigm for model fitting with applications to image analysis and automated cartography. *Committee of the ACM*, 24: 381–95.

Geisler, W. S., and J. S. Perry. 1998. A real-time foveated multiresolution system for low-bandwidth video communication. In *Proceedings of Human Vision and Electronic Imaging III*, San Jose, CA, Jan. 24–30, vol. 3299, pp. 294–305.

Ghanbari, M. 1989. Two-layer coding of video signals for VBR networks. *IEEE Journal on Selected Areas in Communications*, 7(5): 771–81.

———.1992. An adapted H.261 two-layer video codec for ATM networks. *IEEE Transactions on Communications*, 40(9): 1481–90.

———, and V. Seferidis. 1995. Efficient H.261-based two-layer video codecs for ATM networks. *IEEE Transactions on Circuits and Systems for Video Technology*, 5(2): 171–5.

Gokturk, S. B., and A. M. F. Aaron. 2006. Applying 3D methods to video for compression (retrieved from http://ai.stanford.edu/~gokturkb/3DCompression/3DForCompression.pdf).

He, Z., and S. Mitra. 2001. A unified rate-distortion analysis framework for transform coding. *IEEE Transactions on Circuits and Systems for Video Technology*, 11: 1221–36.

Hu, J., and J. D. Gibson. 2005. Intra-mode indexed nonuniform quantization parameter matrices in AVC/H.264. In *Proceedings of the Asilomar Conference on Signals, Systems, and Computers*, Pacific Grove, California, Oct. 30–Nov. 2, pp. 746–50.

ISO/IEC. 1993. Standard 11172-2. *Information technology—Coding of moving pictures and associated audio for digital storage media at up to about 1,5 Mbit/s—Part 2: Video.*

————. 1994. Standard 10918-1. *Information technology—Digital compression and coding of continuous-tone still images: Requirements and guidelines*.

————. 2002. Standard 15444-3. *Information technology—JPEG 2000 image coding system—Part 3: Motion JPEG 2000*.

————. 2002. Standard 15938-3. *Information technology—Multimedia content description interface—Part 3: Visual*.

————. 2004a. Standard 15444-1. *Information technology—JPEG 2000 image coding system: Core coding system*.

————. 2004b. Standard 15444-2. *Information technology—JPEG 2000 image coding system: Extensions*.

————. 2004. Standard 14496-2. *Information technology—Coding of audio-visual objects*.

ITU-R. 2002. Recommendation BT.500-11. *Methodology for the subjective assessment of the quality of television pictures*, June.

————. 2007. Recommendation BT.601-6. *Studio encoding parameters of digital television for standard 4:3 and wide-screen 16:9 aspect ratios*, January.

ITU-T. 2005. Recommendation H.264. *Advanced video coding for generic audiovisual services*.

Jagmohan, A., and K. Ratakonda. 2004. Time-efficient learning theoretic algorithms for H.264 mode selection. In *Proceedings of International Conference on Image Processing*, Singapore, Oct. 24–7, pp. 749–52.

Jain, A.K. 1989. *Fundamentals of digital image processing*. Upper Saddle River, NJ: Prentice-Hall.

Koga. T., K. Linuma, A. Hirano, Y. Iijima, and T. Ishiguro. 1981. Motion-compensated interframe coding for video conferencing. In *Proceedings of National Telecommunication Conference '81*, New Orleans, LA, December, pp. G5.3.1–.5.

Kiely, A., and M. Klimesh. 2003. The ICER progressive wavelet image compressor. In *Interplanetary Network Progress Report*, 42(155) (retrieved from http://ipnpr.jpl.nasa.gov/progress_report/42-155/155J.pdf).

Koenen, R. 2002. MPEG-4 overview (v.21 Jeju version). ISO/IEC JTC1/SC29/WG11 N4668 (retrieved from www.m4if.org/resources/Overview.pdf).

Legge, G. E., and J. M. Foley. 1980. Contrast masking in human vision. *Journal of the Optical Society of America*, 70(12): 1458–71.

Leontaris, A., Y. Tonomura, and T. Nakachi. 2006. Rate control for flicker artifact suppression in Motion JPEG2000. In *Proceedings of the IEEE International Conference on Acoustics, Speech, and Signal Processing*, Toulouse, France, May 14–9, pp. 11–41.

Levy, I. K., and R. Wilson. 1999. Three dimensional wavelet transform video compression. In *1999 IEEE International Conference on Multimedia Computing and Systems*, Florence, Italy, July 7–11, vol. 2, pp. 924–28.

Malvar, H., and G. Sullivan. 2003. YCoCg-R: A color space with RGB reversibility and low dynamic range. JTC1/SC29/WG11 and ITU-T Q6/SG16, Document JVT-H031r2, May (retrieved from http://research.microsoft.com/~malvar/papers/JVT-I014r3.pdf).

Marpe, D., et al. 2003. Context-based adaptive binary arithmetic coding in the H.264/AVC video compression standard. *IEEE Transactions on Circuits and Systems for Video Technology*, 13(7): 620–36.

Milani, S., et al. 2003. A rate control algorithm for H.264 encoder. In *Sixth Baiona Workshop on Signal Processing in Communications*, Baiona, Spain, Sept. 8–10, pp. 390–6.

Miyaji, S., Y. Takishima, and Y. Hatori, 2005. A novel rate control method for H.264 video coding. In *IEEE International Conference on Image Processing*, 2005, Genoa, Italy, Sept. 11–4, vol. 2., pp. II 309–12.

National Aeronautics and Space Administration. 2001. *The Emotion of Space* (retrieved from ftp://ftp.hq.nasa.gov/pub/pao/images).

Ng, K. T., S.C. Chan, and T.S. Ng, 1996. A multiresolution two-layer video codec for networking applications. In *IEEE Third International Conference on Signal Processing*, Beijing, China, Oct. 14–18, pp. 1071–4.

On2 Technologies. 2005. TrueMotion VP7 video codec (retrieved from www.on2.com).

Osorio, R. R., and J. D. Bruguera. 2006. High-throughput architecture for H.264/AVC CABAC compression system. *IEEE Transactions on Circuits and Systems for Video Technology*, 16(11): 1376–84.

Qi, W., W. Feng, L. Shipeng, Z. Yuzhuo, and Z. Ya-Qin. 2001. Fine-granularity spatially scalable video coding. In *Proceedings of the IEEE International Conference on Speech, Acoustics, and Signal Processing*, 3: 1801–4.

Real Networks. 2003. RealVideo 10 technical overview version 1.0 (retrieved from www.realnetworks.com).

Sayood, K. 2006. Introduction to data compression. 3rd ed. San Francisco: Elsevier.

Schafer, R. G., et al. 2000. Improving image compression: Is it worth the effort? In *Tenth European Signal Processing Conference*, Tampa, Florida, Sept. 5–8 (retrieved from http://iphome.hhi.de/smolic/docs/).

Shannon, C. E. 1948. A mathematical theory of communication. *Bell System Technical Journal*, 27: 379–423, 623–56.

Sikora, T. 1995. Low complexity shape-adaptive DCT for coding of arbitrarily shaped image segments. *Signal Processing and Image Communications*, 7: 381–95.

SMPTE. 2006. Standard SMPTE-421M . *VC-1 compressed video bitstream format and decoding process*.

Tachikawa, K. 2003. A perspective on the evolution of mobile communications. *IEEE Communications Magazine*, 41: 66–73.

Taubman, D. S., and M. W. Marcellin. 2001. *JPEG 2000: Image compression fundamentals, standards and practice*. Norwell, MA: Kluwer Academic.

Tudor, P. N. 1995. MPEG-2 video compression. *Electronics and Communication Engineering Journal*, 7(6): 257–64.

Ugur, K., and P. Nasiopoulos. 2003. Combining bitstream switching and FGS for H.264 scalable video transmission over varying bandwidth networks. In *2003 IEEE Pacific Rim Conference on Communications, Computers, and Signal Processing*, Victoria, BC, Canada, Aug. 28–30, 2: 972–5.

Tzannes, A. P. 2002. An iterative rate control technique for motion JPEG2000. In *Applications of Digital Image Processing XXV, SPIE*, 4790: 220–7.

Wang, H., and S. F. Chang. 1996. Automatic face region detection in MPEG video sequences. In *Electronic Imaging and Multimedia Systems*, SPIE Photonics China, Beijing, China, Nov. 4, 1996 (retrieved from www.ee.columbia.edu/ln/dvmm/publications/96/wang96b.pdf).

Wang, Y, and Q.-F. Zhu. 1998. Error control and conceal-ment for video communication: A review. In *Proceed-ings of the IEEE*, 86(5): 974–97.

Wang, Z., and A. C. Bovik. 2001. Embedded foveation im-age coding. *IEEE Transactions on Image Processing*, 10(10): 1397–1410.

Wei, J., et al. 2005. Tile boundary artifact reduction using odd tile length and the low-pass first convention. *IEEE Transactions on Image Processing*, 14(8): 1033–42.

Weinberger, M., et al. 1999. The LOCO-I lossless image compression algorithm: Principles and standardiza-tion into JPEG-LS. Hewlett-Packard Laboratories Technical Report No. HPL-98-193R1 (Nov. 1998; re-vised Oct. 1999). Reprinted in *IEEE Transactions on Image Processing*, 9 (Aug. 2000): 1309–24.

Witten, I. H., et al. 1987. Arithmetic coding for data com-pression. *Communications of the ACM*, 30(6): 520–40.

Yu, J. 2004. Advantages of uniform scalar dead-zone quantization in image coding system. In *International Conference on Communications, Circuits and Systems*, Chengdu, China, June 27–29, vol. 2, pp. 805–8.

Zhong, Y., et al. 2005. Perceptual quality of H.264/AVC deblocking filter. In *IEE International Conference on*

Visual Information Engineering, Glasgow, UK, Apr. 4–6, pp. 379 –84.

FURTHER READING

For further information on the topics in this chapter, see the following Web sites:

Blu-Ray Disc Association: www.blu-raydisc.org

Center for Image Processing Research: www.cipr.rpi.edu

Digital Cinema Initiatives: www.dcimovies.com

DVD Forum: www.dvdforum.com

Euclid Discoveries: www.euclid.com

HP Labs (LOCO-I/JPEG-LS): www.hpl.hp.com/loco/

MathWorks (MATLAB): www.mathworks.com

MPEG: www.chiariglione.org/mpeg

MPEG-4 Industry Forum: www.m4if.com

National Telecommunications and Information Agency: www.its.bldrdoc.gov

NASA: http://vision.arc.nasa.gov

NTT DoCoMo: www.nttdocomo.com

Real Networks: www.real.com

On2 Technologies: www.on2.com

Speech and Audio Compression

Peter Kroon, *LSI, Allentown, Pennsylvania*

INTRODUCTION

Audible signals such as speech and music are acoustic sound waves. They are analog waveforms characterized by pressure changes that propagate through a medium such as air or water. The waveforms are created by a vibrating source such as a loudspeaker or musical instrument and received by a receptor such as a microphone diaphragm or eardrum. An example of a simple waveform is a pure tone. It consists of a periodic signal that repeats its waveform shape many times per second. The number of repetitions per second is its *frequency* and is measured in hertz (Hz). Audible tones are typically in a range of 20 to 20,000 Hz, which is referred to as the *bandwidth* of audible signals. The tone will create a sound pressure displacement that is related to its amplitude. Signals with high amplitude will sound louder than signals with low amplitude, and the range from soft to loud is called *dynamic range*. Complex sounds (e.g., the sound of a piano or speech) consist of a combination of many tones of different frequencies and amplitudes that vary over time.

Using a microphone, one can capture the acoustic waveform and convert this into an electric signal. This electric signal or waveform can be converted back to an acoustic signal by using a loudspeaker. To represent this analog waveform as a digital signal, it is necessary to find a numerical representation that preserves its characteristics. The process of converting an analog signal to a digital signal is usually referred to as *digitization*. A digital representation of audio and speech signals has many advantages. It is easier to combine with other media such as video and text, and it is easier to make the information secure by encrypting it. Digital representations also enable procedures to protect against impairments when transmitting the signals over error-prone communication links. The main disadvantage is that straightforward digitization of analog signals results in data rates that require much more capacity of the physical channel than the original analog signal. Before we provide examples of this dilemma, let us first take a look at the principles of digitization.

To digitize an analog audio signal, it is necessary to sample the signal at discrete instances of time at a rate equivalent to or more than twice the highest bandwidth that exists in the signal (this is the *sampling* or *Nyquist theorem*). The frequency that the signal is sampled with is referred to as the *sampling frequency*. Typical sampling frequencies for speech signals are between 8 and 16 kHz, while for music signals ranges between 16 and 48 kHz are more common. To get a digital representation, the sample values need to be represented with a discrete set of numbers represented by a binary code. This process is referred to as *quantization*. In contrast to sampling, which allows the perfect reconstruction of the original analog waveform, quantization will introduce errors that will remain after reconstructing the analog signal. The *quantization error* (defined as the difference between the analog sample value and its discrete value) can be made smaller by using more bits per sample. For example, an 8-bit number allows $2^8 = 256$ different values, while a 16-bit number allows 65,536 different values. For speech, signals between 8 and 16 bits per sample are adequate, while for high quality music signals 16 to 24 bits per sample are commonly used.

The digitization process of sampling and quantization as described above is referred to as *pulse coded modulation* (PCM). The total bit rate for a PCM signal is given by:

$$\text{sampling rate} \times \text{number of bits per sample} \times \text{number of audio channels}$$

For a stereo signal on a compact disc (CD), this means $44{,}100 \times 16 \times 2 \times 1{,}411{,}200$ bits per second (1411 Mb/s). As illustrated in Figure 1, the typical bit rate needed for

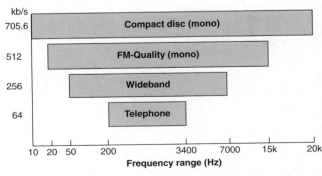

Figure 1: Relationship between audio band-width and bit rate for mono signals

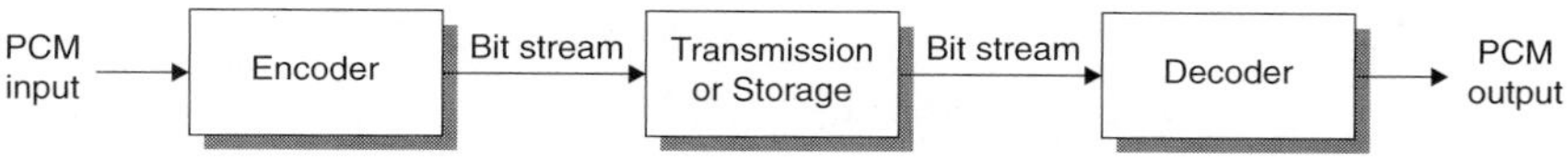

Figure 2: Block diagram of a generic coding or compression operation

PCM input → Encoder → Bit stream → Transmission or Storage → Bit stream → Decoder → PCM output

various signals can be quite high. For storage and transmission purposes, these rates quickly become prohibitive. Although disk-based storage has become cheaper and high-speed Internet connections are more commonplace, it is still difficult to stream compact disc data directly at 1.4 Mb/sec or store hundreds of uncompressed CD's on a hard disk.

The main goal of *audio* and *speech compression* is to find a more efficient digital representation of these signals. Because most signals start as simple sampled PCM signals, it is useful to use the resulting relative reduction in bit rate as a measure of efficiency. It should be pointed out that a reduction in bit rate is not always the main objective. For example, one could increase the bit rate to make the signal more robust against transmission errors. In that case, the generic term *coding* is more appropriate. In this chapter, we will use both terms interchangeably. Figure 2 shows the generic compression operation. The *encoder* takes the PCM input signal and generates the compressed *bit stream*. The bit stream is either transmitted to the *decoder* or stored for later retrieval. The decoder takes the bit stream and generates the corresponding decoded PCM signal, which is a rendering of the original input PCM signal.

In the remainder of this chapter, we will focus on reducing the bit rate of speech and audio signals while providing the best possible signal quality. At this point, it is good to point out that quality is a difficult attribute to quantify because it has many dimensions. Most of these dimensions are associated with its application, and it is important to set proper objectives when designing or choosing a particular compression algorithm. For example, for speech communications, it could be important to have a consistent performance for various input conditions such as clean speech, noisy speech, input-level variations, and so on. For compression of music signals, it could be important to have a consistent performance for various types of music or to preserve as much as possible audio bandwidth and stereo image. As will be clear later, this quality objective will be constrained by other factors such as the *delay* (the time needed to encode and decode a signal) and *complexity* (the number of arithmetic operations or memory use) of the methods used.

Speech and audio compression applications can be divided in two classes: *broadcasting* (e.g., streaming) and *communications* (e.g., Internet telephony). Each class has different requirements, as can be seen from Table 1.

There are two principal approaches to compression of digital signals: *lossless* and *lossy* compression. Lossless compression techniques take advantage of the redundancies in the numerical representation. For example, instead of using uniformly 16 bits per sample, one could use a new mapping that assigns symbols of shorter length to the most frequent values. Or if the signal values change slowly between sample values, then one could use fewer bits by encoding the differences instead. Lossless compression is a reversible operation, and both input and output signal samples of Figure 2 will be identical. Lossy compression

Table 1: Difference in Requirements for Broadcasting and Communications

Feature	Broadcasting	Communications
Characteristic	One-way transmission	Two-way transmission
Delay	Not important	Important
Encoder complexity	Not important	Important
Decoder complexity	Important	Important
Technology	Audio coding	Speech coding

techniques, on the other hand, assume that the signal has a human destination, which means that signal distortions can be introduced as long as the listener is not able to either hear them or has no serious objections. Lossy compression is not reversible, and the input and output signal samples of Figure 2 will be different. For many signals, this difference would be unacceptable; but for audio signals, one only worries about audible differences. If the differences are inaudible, then the lossy coding techniques used are often referred to as *perceptually lossless* coding techniques. But even if the differences were clearly audible, it still will be acceptable for many applications. A good example is the difference between telephone speech and natural speech, where the telephone signal is significantly limited in bandwidth (typically less than 4 kHz).

In practice, the use of lossless coding for audio and speech signals results in a limited compression efficiency, and its use is restricted to high quality applications such as the DVD audio. The compression efficiency for lossy coding can be significantly higher; consequently, perceptually lossless and lossy coding are the main approaches used in most audio and speech compression applications. Speech compression takes this approach one step further by also assuming that humans generate the source signal, which gives it certain properties that can be taken advantage of by the compression algorithms. As a result, speech compression can achieve especially high compression efficiency. Figure 3 gives a summary of the typical bit rates and applications.

Compression for Packet Networks

The compression algorithms described in this chapter are used for communication and broadcasting over wired and wireless networks. Errors that get introduced in the bit stream during transmission can introduce serious degradations in the decoded signal. In contrast to analog signals, where transmission impairments mainly introduce additional noise in the audio signal, digital signals subjected to bit stream errors result in pops, clicks, and other annoying artifacts. Especially in wireless applications, one is likely to encounter transmissions errors, and it is

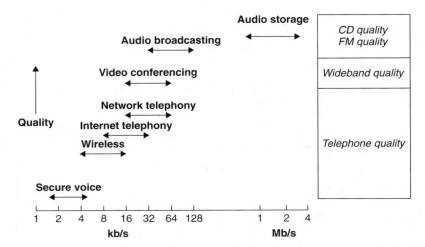

Figure 3: Typical bit rates and applications for speech and audio compression

common to add additional information for *error correction and detection*. However, even with the use of error-correction techniques, it is still possible that bit errors remain in the bit stream. The sensitivity of a decoder to random bit errors (in other words, its relative effect on the decoded signal quality) should be taken into account in such an application. For wired networks, the transmissions channels are usually good and transmission errors are unlikely. However, in packet networks (e.g., the Internet), it is possible that packets do not arrive on time. Because the decoder cannot request retransmission, this information is considered to be lost. To avoid gaps in the signal, it is necessary to fill in the missing information. This technique is referred to as *error mitigation*. Sophisticated error mitigation techniques work quite well for segments up to 40 msec to 50 msec but are of limited effect for longer erroneous bursts, in which case the best option is to mute the signal. It is important to realize that for applications where transmission errors can occur, the overall quality of a coder (including the use of error correction and mitigation) could be dominated by its robustness to channel impairments.

Traditional compression applications are optimized for the underlying application (e.g., a cellular system). These systems are homogeneous in the sense that all terminals and links meet certain minimum requirements in throughput and capabilities. The Internet is a much more heterogeneous network where end points can be quite different in capabilities (e.g., low-end versus high-end, PC versus laptop, wired versus wireless), and connection throughput (dialup versus broadband). One solution would be to use *scalable* coders in which the same coding structure can be used for operation at different bit rates by simply changing some of its parameter settings. This requires a handshaking process between transmitter and receiver side to agree on the bit rate to be used. Moreover, if a throughput issue comes up somewhere in the middle of a link, it would require decoding the higher rate first and then subsequent encoding at the lower rate. The resulting *transcoding* operation introduces additional delay and a significant degradation in quality because coding distortions are compounded. A better approach is the use of *embedded* coders. In embedded coders, there is a core bit stream from which each decoder needs to decode the signal with a certain basic quality. One or more enhancement layers enhance this core layer. Each enhancement layer will increase the average bit rate and the quality of the decoded signal. The encoder generates the core layer and enhancement layers, but the decoder can decode any version of the signal as long as it contains the core layer.

This is illustrated in Figure 4. Apart from adjusting for various throughput rates, embedded coders can also be

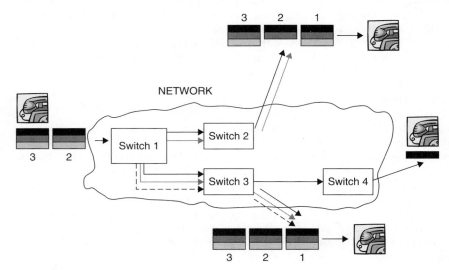

Figure 4: Use of embedded coders in a heterogeneous network

used for temporarily alleviating congestion. If too many packets arrive at a given switch (e.g., switch 2 in Figure 4), the switch can decide to temporarily drop some enhancement packets to avoid congestion. As long as this is not done for extended periods of time and the enhancement layers have a fine granularity, this process will only introduce limited audio degradation. The embedded coding approach will alleviate packet loss problems but will not avoid them. Packet losses of the core information will still be a source of quality degradation. *Multidescriptive* coders can be seen as a superset of embedded coders. In this technique, the encoder creates two or more descriptions of the signal, each of which can be decoded independently and each with a similar quality. When more descriptions are received, they are combined to produce an output of higher quality than is possible with fewer descriptions. As long as the packet losses for each description are independent of the other descriptions, by adding more descriptions it is possible to significantly reduce the probability that all descriptions suffer from a packet loss at the same time. The increased robustness is a trade-off with the need to transmit more information. In practice, it is difficult to design efficient scalable coders and multidescriptive coders, and this topic is still an active area of research.

Speech and Audio Quality Assessment

The quality assessment of lossy speech and audio compression algorithms is a complicated issue. Quite often we want to assess not only the quality of the compression algorithms, but also the quality delivered by these algorithms in a typical operating scenario, which means including other aspects of the delivery chain as well, such as the quality of the network or the quality and type of playback equipment. Because the coders use perceptual techniques, it is important to use human listeners. Even in this case, care has to be taken to get reliable and reproducible results. Choice of test material, number of listeners, training of listeners, test format (e.g., ordering of playback, inclusion of original), and playback scenario (e.g., headphones versus loudspeakers) all affect the outcome of the test, and it is necessary to design the test to minimize the effect of these factors. Testing perceptually lossless coders (no audible differences when compared to original) will be different from assessing the performance of lossy coders. The latter will be complicated because trade-offs have been made in many dimensions that will produce different listener responses. Examples are the trade-off between audio bandwidth and signal quantization distortions or the stability of the reproduced stereo image. A well-designed test will try to eliminate all these biases and should produce a reproducible result.

Assessment of speech is even more involved, because it involves two-way communications and most material is context sensitive. *Mean opinion scores* (MOS), a type of testing in which panels of listeners rate the quality of short sentences on a five-point scale, are the most common.Refinements of these tests provide the original reference and the corresponding processed and compressed signal. In that case, the scores reflect a comparison that can be single-sided (degradation MOS) or two-sided (comparison MOS). Besides speech quality, one can also test speech intelligibility, although this is usually not an issue for bit rates of 4 kbs and higher.

It should be appreciated that none of the testing methods described above can fully predict how people experience the quality in a real-world scenario, which involves talking to people whose voices they know or listening to music they like.

Tests with human subjects are expensive and time-consuming, and one would like to use objective measures that could predict subjective quality based on a comparison between original and processed version. For lossy compression, simple objective measures such as segmental *signal-to-noise ratio* (SNR) measurements are meaningless. A more effective approach is to include models that mimic our auditory system and use the resulting model output to predict subjective quality. Two standards based on such an approach have been recently recommended: (1) ITU-R BS.1387 (perceptual estimate of audio quality, or PEAQ) for the assessment of audio compression techniques and (2) ITU-T P.862 family of standards (perceptual estimate of speech quality, or PESQ) for the assessment of telephony quality speech compression techniques. Both methods rely on comparing the reference input and (decompressed) output signal. Such an approach reflects reasonably well subjective tests of high audio quality in which listeners rate the degradation relative to the reference. However, typical subjective tests for speech quality do not include direct comparisons with the reference. This means that the PESQ is unable to reflect the quality of the original signal. To address this shortcoming, ITU-T has introduced P.563, which is a single-ended measure for speech quality that does not need a reference. Although these methods have shown to be quite accurate for some scenarios, they should always be used with caution and with a clear understanding of their shortcomings.

SPEECH-CODING TECHNIQUES

Efficient digital presentation of speech signals has been a topic of research since the 1940s, but only since the early 1990s have many applications become technically and economically feasible. Digital cellular telephony has been one of the main applications for speech coding, and many digitization choices were chosen to be compatible with wired digital networks. For example, the speech signals are sampled at 8 kHz (thereby limiting the signal bandwidth to 4 kHz), single channel (mono), and 8 to 16 bits per sample. The communication application puts a constraint on the *delay* introduced by the compression operation. Not only is it difficult to have a natural two-way conversation with one-way delays exceeding 200 msec, but also it is more noticeable to hear echoes introduced, for example, by the acoustic coupling between loudspeaker and microphone (e.g., speakerphone) at either end of the communication link. For conferencing applications that involve more than two parties, each party will hear the combination signal of all other participants. Because this combining of the signals needs to be done in the PCM domain, it is necessary to decompress the signals, digitally combine them, and compress them again. The delay introduced by compression will now be compounded, thereby reinforcing the problems mentioned above. Most compression algorithms introduce delay because they analyze the signal in blocks or frames with durations of 10 msec to 30 msec to better characterize the signal behavior and its variations.

For communication applications, it is also important to put constraints on the *complexity* of the compression operation because each end point needs both an encoder and a decoder. This is even more relevant for wireless applications where the end point is battery-powered because high complexity will reduce battery life. Complexity is defined in terms of computational load (MIPS) and memory usage (RAM and ROM). For most speech and audio-coding algorithms, there is an asymmetry in complexity, and the encoder can be several more times complex than the decoder.

Most speech coders are based on the lossy compression paradigm and take advantage of the properties of both the auditory system and the speech production mechanism. The latter can be taken advantage of by using so-called parametric coders. With these coders, the speech signal is modeled by a limited number of parameters, which are usually related to the physical speech production mechanism. The parameters are obtained from analyzing the speech signal and then quantized before transmission. The decoder will use these parameters to reconstruct a rendering of the original signal. When comparing the input and output waveforms, the resemblance can be weak, but the signals can sound quite similar. Using parametric approaches, it is feasible to achieve low bit rates (2 kbs to 4 kbs) with a reasonable quality. The quality is limited by the accuracy of its model. This is illustrated in Figure 5. To avoid this limit in quality, a more common approach is to use waveform-approximating coders. These coders maintain the waveform of the original signal as much as possible while taking advantage of the properties of both the speech production and auditory mechanisms. The resulting quality is better at the expense of higher bit rates; at lower bit rates, the quality of a waveform coder will be less than a parametric coder operating at the same low rate.

Speech produced by humans has certain properties that can be taken advantage of for compression. It has limited energy above 8 kHz, and it has a limited dynamic range. This allows sampling with frequencies between 8 kHz and 16 kHz, and PCM quantization with 1216 bits/

sample. Using nonuniform quantization (i.e., the quantizer step sizes are small for small input values and large for large input values), it is possible to quantize telephony speech with 8 bits per sample. Figure 6 shows a waveform and its corresponding spectrogram. Looking at this figure, we see that the envelope of the amplitudes change slowly as a function of time. The spectrogram shows that certain frequencies are stronger than others. These emphasized frequencies, called *formants*, are caused by resonant frequencies in the human vocal tract in response to the glottal excitation signal. The resonant frequencies are moved by changing the shape of the mouth cavity over time. The relative position of these formants defines the sounds and vowels that we perceive. We can also see a more harmonic component, which results from the periodic excitation by the vocal cords. The estimate of the fundamental frequency of this harmonic excitation is referred to as the *pitch* and varies between 100 and 250 Hz for males and 200 to 400 Hz for females.

All of these features are produced by the human articulatory system, which changes slowly in time because it is a biological system driven by slowly moving muscles. As a result, the formants can be effectively represented by a slowly varying adaptive digital filter, the *linear* or *short-term prediction* filter. With only ten predictor coefficients updated once every 20 msec, it is possible to accurately reproduce the evolution of speech formants.

Figure 7 shows a short segment of a speech signal and the corresponding signal after filtering it with this adaptive linear prediction filter. This figure shows another generic characteristic of speech signals: Some segments are more noiselike or *unvoiced* and others are more periodic or *voiced*. Voiced segments have distinct pitch, whereas the pitch of unvoiced segments is undefined. The filtered signal is called the *residual* signal. Because this signal has a reduced dynamic range and less variance, it can be quantized with fewer bits per sample. Although it is possible to derive the prediction coefficients without explicitly

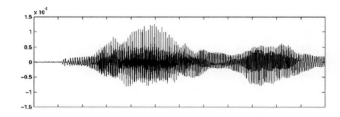

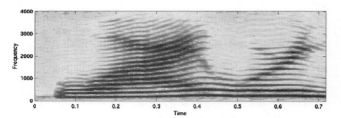

Figure 6: Time waveform of the utterance "Why were you away a year, Roy?" spoken by a female speaker (top) and corresponding spectrogram (bottom). The spectrogram shows the power spectrum as a function of time, where the gray level indicates the power levels from low (white) to high (black)

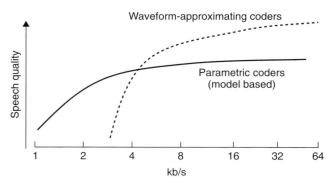

Figure 5: Quality versus bit rate curves for waveform and parametric coders

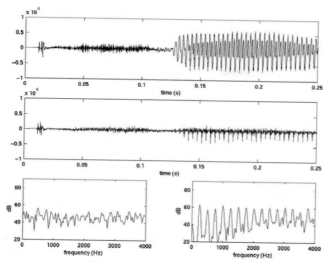

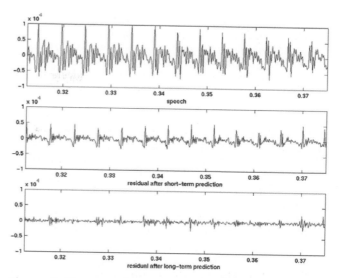

Figure 7: Time waveform (top), corresponding residual signal (middle), and spectra of the residual signal (bottom) for the first part of the sentence (left) and second part of the sentence (right)

Figure 8: Time waveform (top), short-term residual signal (middle), and long-term residual signal (bottom)

transmitting them (*backward adaptation*), it is more common (especially for lower-rate coders) to quantize and transmit the predictor coefficients explicitly (*forward adaptation*). Numerous methods are available, and the most effective methods require only 1500 to 2000 bits/sec for transmitting ten coefficients every 10 to 20 msec. Predictor efficiency can be further improved by recognizing that speech signals contain significant periodic components for voiced sounds (e.g., vowels). A *long-term* or *pitch predictor* is able to predict the periodic component, resulting in an even more noiselike residual signal. The long-term predictor consists of variable delay line with a few filter coefficients. The delay and coefficients are updated once every 5 msec to 10 msec. The most typical configuration is *forward adaptive*, which means that approximately 1500 to 2000 bits per second are needed for transmitting the long-term predictor parameters. Figure 8 shows the signals after short- and long-term prediction, respectively.

The signal shown at the bottom of Figure 8 resembles a noiselike signal with a reduced correlation and reduced dynamic range. As a result, it can be quantized more efficiently. At this point, we have all of the components needed for a linear predictive-based coder. A block diagram is

shown in Figure 9. The signal is filtered with the *short-term filter*, A(z), and *long-term filter*, P(z), and the remaining residual signal is quantized. The predictor parameters and quantized residual signal are transmitted or stored. After decoding the quantized residual signal, the decoder filters this signal through the inverse long-term and short-term prediction filters. Note that, without quantization of the residual signal, the decoder can exactly reproduce the original signal. For quantization of the residual signal, many techniques exist. The simplest quantizers are scalar uniform or nonuniform PCM quantizers. For acceptable results, at least 4 to 5 bits per sample are needed. Even refinements such as adaptive quantization, in which the step sizes are adjusted over time, will not reduce the number of bits per sample significantly.

More efficient quantization can be obtained through the use of *vector quantization* (VQ), in which multiple samples are quantized simultaneously. This is achieved by having a number of possible representative sample sets or *codebook*. The quantization is achieved by selecting the codebook entry (each entry containing multiple samples) that is the best representation of the signal to be quantized. The codebook index corresponding to this

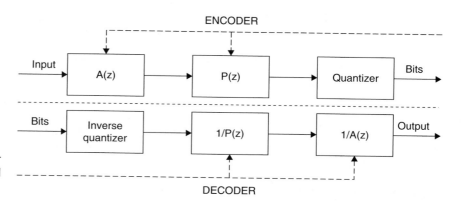

Figure 9: Block diagram of a linear predictive-based coder with short-term and long-term prediction

entry is transmitted, and the decoder, which has a similar codebook, uses this index to look up the corresponding values. Although the lowest quantization rate for scalar quantization is one bit per sample, VQ allows fractional bit rates. For example, quantizing two samples simultaneously using a one-bit codebook will result in 0.5 bits per sample. More typical values are a ten-bit codebook with codebook vectors of dimension forty, resulting in 0.25 bits/sample. The objective of both scalar and vector quantization is to find the quantized value that is the closest to the original nonquantized input. In the block diagram of Figure 9, one can argue that the overall goal is not to find the best quantized residual values but the best quantized speech signal. Especially for coarse quantization (few bits per sample), this becomes an important distinction. A powerful technique used in speech coding is *analysis by synthesis* in which the effect of quantization is determined by examining the effect on the decoded output. This is accomplished by operating the diagram of Figure 9 in the configuration shown in Figure 10.

In this figure, the encoder of Figure 9 is enhanced with a local decoder. In most practical coders, the predictors are still computed as usual. The quantization of the residual signal is done in an analysis-by-synthesis fashion. If we assume that we use a codebook, then the essence of this approach requires that for each codebook vector we perform local decoding and compare the resulting prototype output with the original input signal. The codebook vector that gives the best approximation is selected. Note that with this paradigm we are indirectly creating a quantized residual signal, and this signal is often referred to as *excitation* signal. Instead of directly comparing the original input signal, and the quantized and decoded rendering of this signal, an error-weighting filter is introduced that better reflects the way our auditory system perceives distortions. Note that this weighting is much simpler than the complex auditory models used in audio coding. The block diagram of Figure 10 forms the basis for a family of coders generically referred to as *code-excited linear predictive* (CELP) coders. Most modern standards are based on this principle. A large amount of research has been done on efficient codebook structures that not only give the best performance but also are manageable in terms of search and memory requirements. A commonly used structure is the so-called algebraic codebook, which consists of a few nonzero pulses with deterministic positions.

For any speech coder, several techniques can be used to further improve its performance. Some of these techniques can be done independently of the coder, although in practice it makes sense to take advantage of the parameters already computed by the coder. Preprocessing techniques that are useful are *gain control* and *noise suppression*. The latter can be quite sophisticated but highly effective, especially for the lower-rate speech coders, which typically do not handle background noise well. A widely used form of postprocessing is *postfiltering*. In this process, the decoded speech signal is slightly distorted in a way that suppresses the coding noise and enhances the signal. If done with care, it can clean up the signal, resulting in a perceived quality improvement.

Another technique that has found some popularity is taking advantage of the fact that conversational speech comes in bursts because talkers speak at alternating times. Sometimes, there can be large pauses between words. This can be exploited by only transmitting when active speech is present. When speech is not active, no signal is transmitted. Because, on average, people speak one-half of the time, this technique has the potential to reduce the bit rate by half. To make this *discontinuous transmission* approach work, a *voice activity detector* (VAD) is needed. For speech without background noise, this approach can work quite well. When background noise is present (e.g., car sounds), it is more difficult to get reliable decisions from the VAD. Moreover, when no talker is active and no signal is transmitted, the receiver side needs to substitute a replacement signal. This is referred to as *comfort noise*. For high levels of background noise, it is difficult to have this comfort noise match its characteristics. Hence, more sophisticated systems transmit low-rate information about the background noise, such as energy and spectral characteristics, at average rates of 1 kbs to 2 kbs. The resulting system is a *variable bit rate* (VBR) system. This concept could be further extended to coding the speech on a frame-by-frame basis with a different bit rate depending on the characteristics of the signal, or it could be controlled by the overall communication system. Variable bit rate systems are able to produce similar quality as fixed bit rate systems but at a lower average bit rate. However, the system issues become more complicated because of the need to track all these rate changes throughout the whole communication chain.

Speech-Coding Standards

For communications purposes, it is important to establish standards to guarantee interoperability between equipment from different vendors or between telecommunication services between different geographic areas. Telecommunication standards are set by different standard bodies, which typically govern different fields of use. The International Telecommunications Union (ITU-T) establishes worldwide telephony and communications standards, while regional standards bodies such as the European Telecommunications Standards Institute (ETSI), and Telecommunications Industry Association define standards that are more regional in character (e.g., wireless standards), although this distinction is disappearing because of globalization. It is also common to have the same coding standard adopted by more than one standard body. For example, the ITU-T G722.2 wideband coder and the ETSI/3GPP AMR-WB coder are referring to the same standard. Table 2 summarizes the most relevant ITU-T and ETSI speech-coding standards.

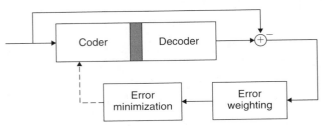

Figure 10: Analysis-by-synthesis encoder with error weighting

Table 2: Summary of Relevant ITU-T and ETSI Narrowband (8 kHz Sampling Rate) Speech-Coding Standards

Coder	Algorithm	Rate (kbs)	Frame size	Complexity	Quality
G.711	μ-law/A-law	64	1	*	*****
G.726	ADPCM	16, 24, 32, 40	1	**	**_*****
G.727	ADPCM	16, 24, 32, 40	1	**	**_*****
G.728	LD-CELP	16	5	*****	*****
G.729	CS-ACELP	8	80	****	****
G.723.1	MP-MLQ	6.3	240	****	***
	ACELP	5.3	240	****	**
AMR-NB	ACELP	4.75–12.2	160	****	**_****

*Quality and complexity are indicated by asterisks; with * meaning low and ***** meaning high.*

Table 3: ITU-T and ETSI Wideband and Superwideband Speech Coders

Coder	Algorithm	Sample rate (kHz)	Rate (kbs)	Frame size	Complexity	Quality
G.722	ADPCM	16	48, 56, 64	1	*	***_****
G.722.1	Transform	16	24, 32	320	***	***_****
G.722.1 Annex C	Transform	32	24, 32, 48	320	***	****
G.722.2/AMR-WB	CELP	16	6.6–23.85	320	****	**_****

*Quality and complexity are indicated by asterisks; with * meaning low and ***** meaning high.*

Note that several other speech-coding standards exist, specifically for military and government applications. Typically, the bit rates are significantly lower (less than 4 kbs), and the resulting quality is lower than typical civilian cellular communications standards.

Besides the main standard there are many extensions or, in ITU-T terms, annexes. G.729 Annex A, for example, is a low-complexity version of G.729 that generates bit-compatible output. It requires only half the complexity at the expense of a minor degradation in speech quality. Other annexes of G.729 define a low-rate and high bit rate versions and integration with VAD.

Most of the discussion has focused on coders for 8-kHz sampling rate, which limits the audio bandwidth to 4 kHz. With the availability of new end points, it is now more feasible to provide higher quality output, specifically increased audio bandwidths. A commonly used sampling rate is 16 kHz, which supports audio bandwidths up to 8 kHz. More recently, some standards have been established for superwide band coders that support audio bandwidths of 14 kHz using a 32-kHz sampling rate. Table 3 summarizes several ITU-T and ETSI standards that have been defined for encoding these so-called wideband signals.

Most of these ITU-T standards not only have a detailed technical description of their underlying algorithms but also are accompanied by reference source code and test vectors. The source code is provided as floating-point C code, fixed-point C code, or both. Fixed-point code reflects implementation on signal processor and VLSI chips, which are typically used in most portable devices.

It is worthwhile mentioning that although standards make the technology readily available, they are not license free. In most cases, proper royalty agreements have been obtained before one can use the coder in a commercial application. Although G.729 is one of the more commonly used coders used in *voice over Internet protocol* (VoIP) applications, the need to pay royalties has affected its deployment. This has created the opportunity for open-source royalty-free coders such as the iLBC coder, which has been adopted by IETF as a standard. This coder has as an additional advantage that it does not require information from past frames, which reduces its coding efficiency but makes it extremely robust against packet losses.

In general, all the above speech-coding algorithms are highly effective for the compression of speech and speechlike signals (noisy speech), but in general not the best for music signals. This is to a large extent because of the speech-modeling components incorporated in these coders. As will be discussed in the next chapter, audio coders do not make assumptions about the underlying production model and hence work in general much better for music and other signals. However, at the lower rates and for speech signals specifically, these coders tend to produce coding artifacts. As a result, there is a transition area where neither coder paradigm is optimal. Recent advances in the field have produced coders that try to fill that void by offering hybrid architectures that use both speech- and audio-coding paradigms and adaptively combine these elements as a function of signal content. The AMR-WB+ coder standardized by ETSI is one example, and other proposals can be found in the literature. However, to declare these coders as truly universal coders might be a far stretch, and it is unlikely that there ever will be a single truly universal coder that covers all possible application scenarios and constraints.

AUDIO-CODING TECHNIQUES

The most common high-quality audio distribution format is based on the compact disc format introduced in the early 1980s. The signal is encoded using PCM with 16 bits/ sample at a 44.1 kHz sampling rate. For stereo signals, this means a data rate of $44,100 \times 16 \times 2 = 1.41$ Mbs. More recent formats such as the DVD audio support as many as 24-bit samples in multichannel format (e.g., 5.1) and sampling rates as much as 192 kHz, resulting in even higher data rates. For most practical purposes, these signals will be used as the digitized source signals. For Internet streaming and computer storage applications, it is necessary to reduce these rates significantly and bring them in the 32 kbs to 128 kbs range. As discussed earlier, this can be accomplished by the use of perceptual lossless coders, which take advantage of the limitations of our auditory system. For CD quality, it is possible to make signals sound perceptually indistinguishable from the original at 64 kbs per channel (128 kbs for stereo). At lower rates, we lose some of the information, but if done by proper combinations of bandwidth reduction, reduced dynamic range, and mono instead of stereo, the resulting signal will still be acceptable for many applications.

Perceptually lossy and lossless compression use two main techniques. First, we have the *irrelevancy* removal, which removes parts of the signal that we cannot hear. The second technique, *redundancy* removal, finds the most compact signal representation. Irrelevancy removal exploits the properties of the human auditory system.

The human auditory system is a highly sophisticated system with tremendous capabilities. It acts as a converter of acoustic waves to auditory nerve firings while performing a spectral analysis as part of this process. The auditory system has been shown to have masking properties. *Masking* describes the process in which one signal becomes inaudible in the presence of another signal. In other words, under certain circumstances it is possible to make quantization noise inaudible while the decoded audio signal is present.

Masking can happen both in time and in frequency. Understanding the principles of masking has taken many decades of research using both physiological and physical measurements. Masking data are obtained through psycho-acoustical studies in which subjects are exposed to test signals and asked about their ability to detect changes (e.g., increases in frequency, audibility, etc). Most of the understanding of masking is based on simple tones and noise. Because complex signals can be viewed as a composite of time-varying tones, a common approach has been to derive the masked threshold by analyzing the signal tone by tone in specific frequency bands that are common to the human auditory system. These bands are called *critical bands* and are spaced nonuniformly with increasing bandwidth for higher frequencies. In each critical band, the signal and its corresponding masking function are calculated, and the masked threshold is derived as a superposition over the complete frequency band. Note that the actual procedure is much more complicated, taking into account several interactions and signal characteristics (e.g., if the signal is noiselike or tone-like). Figure 11 gives an example of the power spectrum of a signal and its corresponding masked threshold. In this figure, as long as the quantization noise remains below the solid stepped line, it will be inaudible.

In general, the model that is used to derive the masked thresholds is referred to as the *psychoacoustic* or *perceptual* model. Building a good perceptual model and matching it properly to a given coder structure is a complex task. Note also that for a given coder structure (or coder standard such as MPEG-1 layer 3), it is possible to

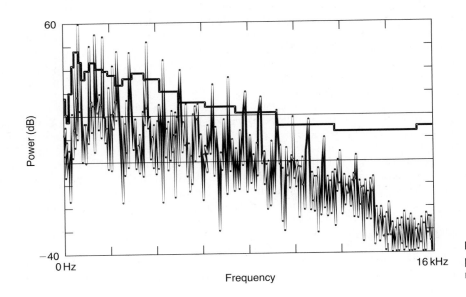

Figure 11: Example of signal frequency power spectrum and its corresponding masked threshold (solid stepped line)

improve the perceptual model while still being compliant to the standard. This also explains the differences in various encoders that all support the same standard. To achieve redundancy removal, and at the same time take advantage of the frequency domain masking properties, it is beneficial to perform a spectral decomposition of the signal by means of a filter bank or transform. Most modern audio coders are based on some form of lapped transform that not only provides computational efficiency but also allows perfect reconstruction. In other words, the process of transform and its inverse will produce the original (although delayed) version of the original time signal. The transform sizes and overlaps will be chosen in such a way that the signal is critically sampled (i.e., the number of frequency components is the same as the number of time samples). The size of the transform will determine the spectral resolution. A larger transform will provide a better spectral resolution at the expense of a decreased time resolution. A common solution is to make the transform size adapt to the signal. For stationary signals, a large transform size is chosen; for nonstationary signals or onsets, a smaller transform size is chosen. Typically, sizes vary from 256 to 2048 samples for sampling rates in the 20 kHz to 40 kHz range. This process is called *window switching*, and care is taken to make sure that the whole process is invertible. A commonly used transform is the *modified discrete cosine transform* (MDCT). It uses a transform of length $2M$ samples, which advances M samples between adjacent transforms. It is critically sampled, and only M coefficients are generated for each $2M$ set of input samples. Computationally efficient implementations have contributed to the widespread use of the MDCT in many audio-coding standards.

Figure 12 shows a generic block diagram of an audio encoder that incorporates the filter bank and the perceptual model. The resulting spectral components (MDCT coefficients) are quantized in such a way that the resulting quantization noise is inaudible. This is accomplished by using the masking level obtained from the *perceptual model*. The amount of noise is controlled by the resolution of the quantizer. By choosing a different quantizer step size, the amount of noise can be quantized. Typically, the same quantizer is used for a set of coefficients, and the corresponding step size for that set is transmitted to the decoder. Note that because of quantization, the decoded signal will be different from the original (i.e., lossy coding). To accomplish perceptually lossless coding, we need to make sure that the quantization noise remains below the masked threshold. The redundancy removal is accomplished by encoding the quantizer indices with lossless coding techniques (e.g., Huffman coding). To avoid confusion, it should be clear that this is a lossless coding technique on quantizer indices, hence the overall operation is still a lossy coding operation. The resulting bit rate will be variable and signal-dependent. In many implementations, an iterative procedure is used to find the optimum quantizer step sizes that result in coding noise below the masked threshold; this will result in the lowest possible bit rate.

The decoder operation performs the operation in reverse without the need for a perceptual model. A generic block diagram of an audio decoder is shown in Figure 13. After reconstructing the coefficients, the signal is transformed back to the time domain ready for playback.

The block diagrams of Figures 12 and 13 are the principle for coding a single audio channel. For encoding multiple channels (N channels), we could in principle use N of these encoder-decoder pairs. However, in practice we would like to take advantage of the possible correlations that exist between the various channels. Also, for transparent coding, we should take into account that masking levels will differ for signals that are spatial in nature. Some distortions that are inaudible in each individual channel will become audible when listening to its multichannel version (e.g., in stereo).

Most state-of-the-art audio coders will produce a variable bit rate. In most communication scenarios, a fixed bit rate is more desirable. This is accomplished by a buffering scheme that interacts with the coder quantization decisions. Designing buffering schemes that minimize

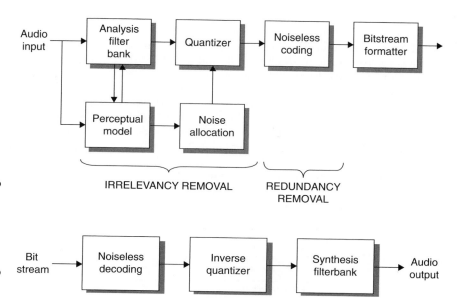

Figure 12: Block diagram of generic audio encoder

Figure 13: Block diagram of generic audio decoder

buffer size (and its corresponding delay) and minimize impact on audio quality turns out to be a challenge, and various solutions exist, each with its own advantages and disadvantages.

Enhanced Audio-Coding Techniques

The audio-coding techniques discussed in the previous section achieve significant compression efficiency and can produce stereo CD quality audio at bit rates as low as 80 kbs to 128 kbs. At the same time, there is a need for acceptable quality stereo coding of audio at bit rates as low as 24 kbs. Two signal dimensions that have recently been successfully explored and resulted in additional standardization activities are efficient coding of high-frequency information and the encoding of spatial information as typically captured in multichannel signals (e.g., stereo and surround). It should be noted that these dimensions are now explored in a similar context as lossy compression where certain a priori decisions are made that will result in certain nonreversible signal degradation. However, these trade-offs when done properly will produce quite acceptable audio quality at lower bit rates and will enable additional applications. Because this approach can be viewed as an extension to existing lossy and lossless audio coders, it is useful to incorporate them as shown in Figure 14.

The input audio signal is analyzed and possibly modified by the extension analysis module. The extension parameters are typically transmitted as part of the core bit stream. The original or modified audio signal is encoded using the core audio encoder with appropriate settings. At the decoder side, the core audio bit stream is decoded as usual, and the extension synthesis module uses this decoded audio signal together with the transmitted extension bits to reconstruct the final audio output. One advantage of this approach is that these extensions can be added in a backward-compatible manner, which is critically important for coders that are widely used. The compatibility is such that legacy decoders can decode the core bit stream but obviously cannot process the transmitted extension information. In that case, the resulting signal could be severely limited in audio bandwidth and be mono instead of stereo.

As mentioned, one dimension to explore is audio bandwidth. To encode a signal with its full audio bandwidth requires a significant number of bits. At the same time, most listeners will have difficulty hearing frequencies beyond 11 kHz to 15 kHz, somewhat as a function of age. Some encoders will limit the audio bandwidth a priori; but, depending on the listener, this trade-off could be unacceptable. A better approach is to recognize that it is good to have high frequency content, but that an approximation of this part of the signal is adequate to most

people and for most signals. Such approach is enabled by a technique referred to as *bandwidth extension*. The basic principle is to encode the original audio signal up to a certain predetermined bandwidth. The higher frequency content is not explicitly transmitted but approximated from the transmitted low-frequency audio signal. Such an approach is possible because most signals show some correlation between low- and high-frequency contents. Moreover, this approximation is enhanced by analyzing the original high-frequency content and deriving guidance parameters that can help with reconstruction of the missing high frequencies at the decoder side. These guidance parameters are transmitted as a separate (low-rate) bit stream or added to the core bit stream. A widely used bandwidth extension technique is *spectral band replication* (SBR) first introduced as a commercial enhancement as part of mp3PRO and aacPlus, and later standardized in MPEG-4. SBR approximates the higher-frequency information by a transposed version of the lower-frequency band, and the guidance parameters provide information about the details of this transposition as well as the energy envelope of the nontransmitted higher frequencies. If the transmitted lower-band cutoff frequency is chosen to be not too low (e.g., above 9 kHz), the resulting audio quality will be quite good at bit rates as low as 48 kbs for stereo. It is possible to lower this cutoff frequency; but, depending on signal contents, distortions will be audible, although in most cases they will be not objectionable. The bit rate for the guidance information is typically a few kbs.

As mentioned, the other dimension to explore is spatial information existing in stereo and multichannel audio. To encode a multichannel signal requires a significant number of bits, especially for surround signals (e.g., 5.1). Although modern coders take advantage of the correlation between the various channels, at lower bit rates it is necessary to reduce the number of channels and transmit multichannel as stereo or stereo as mono. Similar to bandwidth extension, it was recognized that it is important to have spatial information but that it is possible to approximate this signal feature. The spatial content is not explicitly transmitted, but spatial features are extracted from the original signal and transmitted as a separate (low-rate) bit stream or added to the core bit stream. This technique is referred to as *spatial audio coding*. The signal to be encoded with the core audio coder is a modified version of the original signal. In its extreme case, this modified signal is a mono version of the input signal obtained by downmixing the input signal using a linear combination of the various signals. The mono signal is using conventional audio-coding techniques, or it could be encoded using the bandwidth extension techniques described above. The spatial features of the input signal are analyzed and encoded separately. The decoder first reconstructs the core audio signal, and the extension

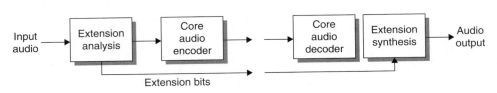

Figure 14: Generic block diagram for adding extensions

synthesis reinserts the spatial features to create the multichannel output signal. The spatial features contain frequency-dependent level and delay information between the various channels and can be encoded with a 5 kbs to 20 kbs. For a stereo signal, the savings are substantial, but the best savings are obtained when encoding surround sound signals (e.g., the 5.1 format). Although the results using a downmixed mono signal are quite impressive, for backward-compatibility reasons it is beneficial to use a downmixed stereo signal. In that case, legacy receivers will continue to receive the same stereo content, while enhanced receivers will be able to render the surround sound signal. The methods used are quite robust and work with both automatic and manual downmixes. One version of this technology has been incorporated as a proprietary enhancement to mp3 as MPEG-3 surround. A more advanced and flexible version has been standardized as an amendment to MPEG-4 audio.

Audio-Coding Standards

Two types of standards exist. The first type is based on a sanctioning by a standard organization (e.g., ISO and its MPEG standards). The second type is based on a proliferated proprietary de facto standard (e.g., Windows Media Player, RealPlayer, Dolby AC-3, etc.). In both cases, proper licensing is needed to use these standards in commercial applications. The MPEG coding standards are widely used for audio and video. The well-known mp3 standard is actually MPEG-1, layer 3. Table 4 summarizes the MPEG audio standards.

The MPEG standards are defined in a different way than most ITU-T speech-coding standards. They consist of a normative part that defines the bit stream syntax and the decoder description (sometimes accompanied by reference C code). As a result, anyone should be able to implement proper decoders. The encoder is described in the informative part and just describes the algorithmic concepts and operating modes. However, to build good encoders, it is necessary to understand the algorithms, and the standard document will not provide details on how to build a good encoder. As a result, standard compliant encoders can be quite different in performance. However, sometimes adoption of certain standards such as MPEG audio by other standard organizations (e.g., 3GPP) that require more normative definitions of the encoders has helped proliferate good reference encoders.

Besides the coders based on the traditional coding paradigm described above, other paradigms exist as well. These alternative paradigms play a role in very low rate coding. Two paradigms that have become part of the MPEG-4 standards are structured audio and parametric audio coding. *Structured audio* consists of a set of tools that can be used to generate music in a way similar to a music synthesizer. It also contains a structured way of describing musical scores and its subsequent conversion to sound using synthesizers. A structured audio bit stream describes how to build the synthesizers and provides the musical score and information on how to play this on the synthesizer. The resulting description can be quite compact and low bit rate (only several kbs). The resulting audio signal can be especially high quality, and because

Table 4: Overview of Various MPEG Audio Standards

Standard	Year	Rates for transparency (stereo, 44-kHz sampling)	Channels	Comments
MPEG-1 audio, layer 1	1992	384 kbs	Mono, stereo	48-, 44.1-, 32-kHz sampling rates
MPEG-1, layer 2	1992	192–256 kbs	Mono, stereo	48-, 44.1-, 32-kHz sampling rates
MPEG-1, layer 3	1992	128–160 kbs	Mono, stereo	48-, 44.1-, 32-kHz sampling rates
MPEG-2, layers 1–3	1994	See MPEG-1 rates	Mono, stereo, and I backward- compatible 5.1 multichannel	MPEG-1 + enhancements; supports lower sampling rates
MPEG-2, AAC	1997	96–128 kbs	Mono, stereo, multichannel up to 48 channels	Not compatible with MPEG-1, -2; supports 96-kHz sampling
MPEG-4 version 1	1998	96–128 kbs	Mono, stereo, multichannel	Supports various coding tools
MPEG-4 version 2	1999	96–128 kbs	Mono, stereo, multichannel	Supports error robustness tools
MPEG-4 audio 1 amendment	2003	48–96 kbs	Mono, stereo, multichannel	Bandwidth extension
MPEG-4 spatial audio coding	2006	64–128 kbs	Stereo and multichannel	

many modern music productions use synthesizers extensively, it can be especially close to some originals. *Parametric audio coding* uses similar ideas as those used in speech compression by modeling some of the production mechanisms of the music sounds. Although it will work well for some sounds, it is difficult to make this technique work consistently for a large variety of input signals.

APPLICATIONS

Two popular Internet applications of speech and audio compression are telephony (e.g., Vo IP) and music downloading and streaming. The IP data network is used to transport digitized (and compressed) audio signals. However, several layers of protocol need to be added to match the application: for example, information about the order of the information, indication of which packets have been received, and so on. To provide a complete phone service, it is necessary to support numbering schemes, billing and call setup protocols, and servers that can act as intermediaries between end points.

Another challenge in transmitting real-time sensitive data over a packet data network is the fact that the Internet is a best effort network. This means that one cannot guarantee the on-time arrival of the audio data; this may result in interruptions in the audio or it may introduce unacceptable delays. In other words, *quality of service* (QoS) cannot be guaranteed for real-time communications. Many recent efforts have focused on improving this situation. For example, new protocols support differentiation of the packets in terms of being real-time critical or not, and improved routing schemes reducing the overhead needed for traffic-flow management. To give real-time sensitive data a better guarantee of arrival, it is necessary to prioritize these packets. Keep in mind that prioritization can only work if other packets can get a lower priority and if routers can handle these priority requests. To reduce the impact of variations in arrival times, it is common to apply buffering of the packets. For one-way communications such as streaming, that is a manageable solution; for real-time applications such as VoIP, this buffering can only be done with a limited buffer size before conversational speech becomes impaired.

There are two popular ways of distributing music over the Internet. *Downloading* is a copy operation from a server that contains the original or compressed version of the material. The downloading will typically use the TCP/IP protocol, and one has to wait until all of the material has been downloaded before being able to play the music. Once downloaded, the same material can be played repeatedly. The other common way of music distribution is *streaming,* which is similar to radio broadcasting. The material is transmitted to the end user, but the signal is played out almost instantaneously without local storage. Similar to the VoIP scenario, it is necessary to buffer the packets to compensate for late arrival. Because this is a broadcast or one-way communication scenario, the amount of buffering can be large (a few to 30 seconds). Although, in principle, the buffers could be made even larger, it will create large delays before a player produces an audible signal. From a user interface perspective, this is undesirable. Hence, sophisticated

buffer control has been developed to make sure that a continuous throughput is maintained while a relatively small buffer is maintained. Some streaming services accomplish this by reducing the coder rate temporarily if the average available connection rate cannot support the initial streaming rate.

The compression techniques used are typically based on audio-coding algorithms because most material that is being streamed will be music. For lower rates, it is possible that speech-coding algorithms are used instead. A commonly used format is the mp3 (MPEG-1 layer 3) format that runs at bit rates varying from 64 kbs to 128 kbs. For streaming applications, it is possible to use proprietary coders, as long as the decoders are available as downloads. However, most content providers will only support one or two formats; as a result, a couple of proprietary standards have become de facto standards. Examples are Microsoft's Windows Media Player and Real Networks' RealPlayer. These proprietary coders have a reasonable quality versus bit-rate performance while trading off other parameters such as delay, complexity, and audio bandwidth. As should be clear from the previous sections, the best quality is obtained at higher bit rates (e.g., 96 kbs to 128 kbs); at lower rates (e.g., 24 kbs to 64 kbs), trade-offs will be made in reducing the audio bandwidth, or even switching to mono. However, use of advanced audio techniques such as bandwidth extension and spatial audio coding help to reduce the bit rates without compromising the audio quality too much. Note also that even at the same bit rate and using the same format, differences in quality could exist because of the quality of the source material and the encoder used. For most streaming applications, it is important that a variety of rates can be accommodated to support the various connection speeds. It is also important that the decoder has a relative low complexity to allow it to run on the host processor. With the advances in computing speed, this has become less of an issue. However, if these formats are used for downloading in portable players, complexity becomes an issue because it is related to battery life and cost.

CONCLUSION

This chapter has explained the basics of speech and audio coding and their applications to Internet telephony and Internet streaming. It should be clear that, especially for the lower bit rates, there is no single coder that is good for all applications and that careful tailoring toward the application is important. Speech and audio coding is a mature field with many available solutions. Based on our current knowledge, and the various constraints that exist, it is expected that future developments in this field will focus less on compression efficiency and more on application-specific issues such as scalability, error robustness, delay, and complexity. Specifically, solutions that use the same algorithmic architecture to support a large range of applications, bit rates, signals, and quality levels are of interest. Another area of interest is coders that can be used to provide both lossless and lossy solutions using a similar algorithmic framework.

GLOSSARY

Audio compression: The process of reducing the amount of digital information to describe audio and speech signals while maintaining the audio quality as much as possible.

Code excited linear prediction (CELP): A technique based on analysis by synthesis and widely used in speech compression standards.

Digitization: The process of creating a digital version of an analog signal by sampling and quantization.

Error mitigation: The process of reducing the perceivable impact of transmission errors of a compressed audio signal.

International Telecommunications Union (ITU): The organization that sets standards for global communications.

Linear prediction: A commonly used technique in speech compression to remove redundancies in a speech signal.

Lossless compression: An audio compression technique that uses redundancies of the signal to achieve compression. The (decompressed) output signal will be identical to the input signal.

Lossy compression: An audio compression technique that uses redundancies and irrelevancies of the signal as well as acceptable quality compromises to achieve compression. The (decompressed) output signal will be different and sound different compared to the input signal.

Motion Picture Experts Group (MPEG): An organizational part of the International Organization for Standardization that sets worldwide standards for media compression.

Perceptually lossless compression: A particular subset of lossy compression techniques in which the differences between input and (decompressed) output signals are measurable but not audible.

Quality of service (QoS): A term commonly used in the context of Internet communications and broadcasting to describe consistency in delivering a particular signal quality.

Quantization: The process of converting an analog value into a discrete digital value.

Sampling frequency: The rate at which analog signal samples are digitized. The value of the sampling frequency will be twice the highest possible frequency that can be contained in the signal.

Streaming: The process of delivering audio signals over a packet network for continued broadcasting.

Transcoding: The process of converting from one compressed format to another by decoding and encoding.

If the coders used are lossy coders, the transcoding process typically introduces additional degradation.

CROSS REFERENCES

See *Data Compression*; *Image Compression*; *Information Theory*; *Video Compression*.

REFERENCES

Bosi, M., et al. 1997. ISO/IEC MPEG-2 advanced audio coding. *Journal of Audio Engineering Society*, 45(10): 789–814.

Faller, C., et al. 2002. Technical advances in digital audio radio broadcasting. *Proceedings of the IEEE*, 90(8):1303–35.

Kleijn, W. B., and K. K. Paliwal, Eds. 1995. S*peech coding and synthesis*. New York: Elsevier.

Kondoz, A. M. 1994. *Digital speech: Coding for low bit rate communication systems*. New York: John Wiley & Sons.

Madisetti, V. K., and D. B. Williams, Eds. 1998. *The digital signal processing handbook*. New York: CRC Press.

Painter, T., and A. Spanias. 2000. Perceptual coding of digital audio. *Proceedings of the IEEE* (April), pp. 451–513.

Pohlman, K. C. 2000. *Principles of digital audio*. 4th ed. New York: McGraw-Hill.

Quatieri, T. F. 2001. *Principles of discrete-time speech processing*. Upper Saddle River, NJ: Prentice Hall, October 2001.

WEB REFERENCES

www.itu.int: International Telecommunications Union (ITU). Contains descriptions, code, and test vectors of various speech coder standards (e.g., G.72X series and quality measurement techniques P series).

www.iso.org: International Organization for Standardization (ISO). Contains descriptions, reference code, and test vectors of various MPEG audio standards.

www.3gpp.org: Contains descriptions, reference code, and test vectors of various global system for mobile communications standards as well as adopted MPEG standards (26 series).

www.ilbc.org: Home pages for royalty free coders standardized by IETF for Internet telephony.

www.chiariglione.org/mpeg: Home page for MPEG standardization activities.

www.mp3surround.com: Home page for MP3Surround. Contains software and demos.

Multimedia Streaming

Nabil J. Sarhan, *Wayne State University*

INTRODUCTION

Multimedia streaming enables users to access multimedia data in real time by pipelining data delivery and playback. This pipelining allows the playback of a video or an audio file to start promptly, as opposed to requiring the user to wait for the whole file to download. Streaming offers other important advantages as well. In particular, it has the capability of conveying live events, such as news and sports games. Moreover, it can alleviate copyright concerns because the streamed files are not written to the user's hard disk. The data arrive piece by piece, and each piece is decoded, played back, and then discarded.

Streaming is employed by various multimedia networking applications: *video on demand* (VOD), *live streaming*, and *interactive real time*. VOD delivers stored multimedia content to users and allows them to apply VCR-like operations such as pause, resume, fast forward, and fast rewind. By contrast, live streaming offers live multimedia content. Naturally, users cannot fast forward through multimedia data with this application. Other interactive operations, however, such as pause and rewind, may be applied with local storage of appropriate portions of the data. On the other hand, interactive real-time applications such as Internet telephony and videoconferencing, allow users to communicate with each other in real time.

Multimedia streaming has grown dramatically in popularity over the Internet. Currently, streaming is widely used by television and radio stations, news companies, e-tailers, entertainment companies, and many others. "State of the Consumer Streaming Market," a December 2005 report by comScore Networks, demonstrates the broad reach of streaming, showing that more than 100 million U.S. users—approximately 60 percent of the U.S. online population—access online digital media by streaming and downloading in a month. Moreover, in August that year, nearly two-thirds of U.S. Internet users had streamed audio or video through a portal, and almost 50 percent had done so from an entertainment Web site. In addition, more than 17 percent of these users streamed content from music Web sites, and 15 percent had streamed from retail Web sites. (The report does not provide statistics for streaming usage in other countries.)

This chapter discusses the basics of multimedia streaming over the Internet. First, it illustrates how streaming works then discusses the standardized network protocols used for streaming and their coordination in a streaming session. The chapter proceeds by discussing the main challenges in streaming multimedia over the Internet. It also surveys the main approaches and techniques that can be used to address these challenges. Finally, the design of streaming servers is discussed, covering the main aspects of admission control, resource sharing, request scheduling, and storage subsystem management.

HOW STREAMING WORKS: AN OVERVIEW

An Internet user can request the streaming of a stored multimedia file by clicking on its hyperlink, which points to a description file rather than the actual multimedia file. The description file contains the URL of the multimedia file and its type of encoding. For example, the description file may have the following line:

```
rtsp://www.univserv.edu/~user/AlienSong.mov
```

The URL descriptor "rtsp://" identifies the requested media stream. When the user clicks on the hyperlink, the Web browser retrieves and opens the description file and then launches the appropriate *media player* such as Real Player, Windows Media Player, or QuickTime. Subsequently, the media player establishes a connection with the corresponding *streaming server*, which decomposes the file into packets and sends them as a stream to the client's media player. The media player decompresses the multimedia content and begins the playback after some buffering time in order to remove the variation in the source-to-destination packet delay. This variation is usually called *delay jitter*. Removing the delay jitter is essential because multimedia data must be presented to the user with the same timing as the original recording. The media player also performs error correction in order to handle packet losses caused by network congestion. Figure 1 further explains the streaming process. Note that the Web and streaming servers can be

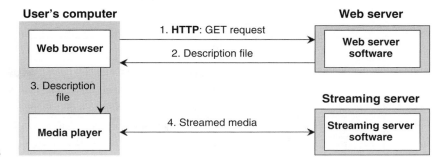

Figure 1: Multimedia streaming process

implemented on the same machine. The connection between the streaming server and the client is bidirectional because of user interactions.

Let us now discuss in more detail the communication between the streaming client and the streaming server. This communication usually involves coordination among three application-layer protocols: *real-time streaming protocol* (RTSP), *real-time protocol* (RTP), and *real-time control protocol* (RTCP). The functions of these protocols can be explained as follows:

- RTSP manages the streaming session. In particular, it is used to initiate and control the delivery of multimedia streams. Basically, it supports such user interactions as play, pause, resume, fast forward, fast rewind, and stop (teardown).
- RTP provides end-to-end delivery services for multimedia streams such as payload type identification, sequence numbering, and time stamping. It can be viewed as a sublayer of the transport protocol. It runs on top of the *user datagram protocol* (UDP) or the *transport control protocol* (TCP). UDP, however, is preferable for multimedia streaming as will be explained later.
- RTCP supports monitoring of data delivery and provides intermedia synchronization and participant identification services.

Figure 2 illustrates the coordination among these protocols through a simple example. After retrieving the description file, the client issues the RTSP setup command, and the server responds by establishing an RTSP session and informing the client. The client then issues the play command, and the server replies by granting the request.

Now the delivery of the stream begins, using the transport protocol specified by the setup command (RTP/UDP in this example). RTCP is used as well to provide important control information. Finally, the client issues the RTSP teardown command to stop the streaming service. Although not shown in this figure, the client can apply other interactive operations, such as pause and resume, during the RTSP session. The example shows only one multimedia stream, but there can actually be more than one stream. For instance, a movie may be delivered in separate audio and video streams. In such a case, RTCP can help synchronize these streams.

STREAMING PROTOCOLS

We now discuss in more detail the network protocols used for streaming.

Real-Time Streaming Protocol

RTSP is a control protocol defined by IETF RFC 2326. Its function resembles a VCR remote control. RTSP manages the streaming session but does not deliver the data by itself (although its connection may be used in certain cases to tunnel RTP traffic). It uses text-based messages, which can be transported using TCP or UDP. RTSP is generally similar to HTTP, but with significant differences. For example, RTSP supports both client-to-server and server-to-client requests. Moreover, RTSP maintains a session state (whereas HTTP is stateless). Furthermore, the data with RTSP are carried out-of-band using another protocol, typically RTP.

Table 1 lists and describes various types of RTSP requests. The setup request creates an RTSP session for the

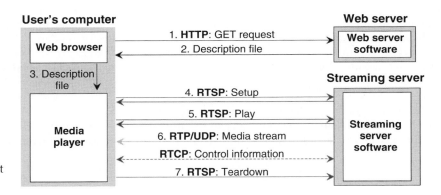

Figure 2: Coordination among different protocols in multimedia streaming

Table 1: Types of RTSP Requests

Method	Direction	Desired Action
DESCRIBE	C → S	Server returns a description of the presentation or object
ANNOUNCE	C → S	Client posts description to server
	S → C	Server updates session description
OPTIONS	C ↔ S	Requester determines options supported by the other part
SETUP	C → S	Server allocates resources and creates a session
PLAY	C → S	Server starts sending data
RECORD	C → S	Clients starts recording a data stream
PAUSE	C → S	Server halts the delivery temporarily
REDIRECT	S → C	Client connects to a another server
GET_PARAMETER	C ↔ S	Server or client retrieves a parameter value
SET_PARAMETER	C ↔ S	Server or client changes a parameter value
TEARDOWN	C → S	Server stops stream delivery and frees resources

specified presentation or multimedia object. All later requests by the client must include the generated session number. The play request supports absolute positioning by specifying the range within the stream to be played out. Fast forward and fast rewind can be requested by specifying the speed value.

Real-Time Protocol

Streaming applications typically employ RTP, which is defined by IETF RFC 3550. Basically, it provides end-to-end delivery services for real-time data, including payload type identification, time stamping, sequence numbering, and source identification. These services can be described as follows:

- Payload identification: The payload type field in the RTP header identifies the format of the RTP payload and determines how it can be interpreted by the application. Examples of payload types are PCM, MPEG audio, motion JPEG, H.262, MPEG-1 video, and MPEG-2 video.
- Time stamping: The time stamp field in the header reflects the sampling instant of the first byte in the RTP data packet. The receiver uses the time stamps to remove the packet delay jitter introduced by the network and thus reconstruct the original timing of the multimedia content.
- Sequence numbering: The sequence number field in the header is incremented by one for each RTP data packet sent. It can be used by the recipient to detect any packet loss and thus perform the necessary correction action.
- Source identification: The *synchronization source identifier* (SSRC) field in the header identifies the source of the RTP stream. Each source generates a random number when its stream starts and uses the number as an identifier. (The RTP implementation should make sure that each source will have a unique identifier.) In some situations, a participant may generate multiple streams in

an RTP session. For example, one stream can be from a microphone and another from a camera. In such situations, each source must have a different SSRC.

RTP also supports delivery to multiple recipients using multicasting when this service is provided by the network.

Real-Time Control Protocol

RTCP is a control protocol that works along with RTP. It is also specified by IETF RFC 2326. RTCP packets do not encapsulate RTP packets or any parts of multimedia data. They are separate packets that are sent periodically to give feedback on the quality of data distribution and to provide membership information.

Let us now discuss the different types of RTCP packets.

- Receiver report (RR): This packet contains the reception statistics from participants who are not active senders for each stream they receive. These statistics include the last sequence number received, the fraction of packets lost, the largest packet number received, and the interarrival jitter for each RTP stream.
- Sender report (SR): This packet includes both reception and transmission statistics for participants who are active senders. The reception statistics are the same as those in RR, but the transmission statistics contain the number of packets sent and the number of bytes sent. In addition, SR contains important information for intermedia synchronization: RTP time stamps and their corresponding *network time protocol* (NTP) time stamps. (NTP time stamps indicate the wall clock time.)
- Source description items (SDES): This packet contains textual information that describes a source, such as the participant's name, telephone number, and e-mail address.

- BYE: This packet is used to indicate the end of participation.
- Application-specific functions (APP): This packet is intended for experimental use as new applications and features are developed.

These RTCP packets can be used to provide the following services.

- *Quality of service* (QoS) monitoring and congestion control: The primary function of RTCP is to provide feedback on the quality of data distribution. This function is related to TCP's congestion and flow control functions. The shared reception and transmission statistics help senders, receivers, and network managers. In particular, senders can adjust their transmission rates (by changing the encoding for instance), while receivers can know whether the congestion is local, regional, or global. On the other hand, network managers can use the feedback information to evaluate the performance of multicast distribution.
- Intermedia synchronization: RTP multimedia streams may advance at different rates. They also typically have different time offsets to prevent some possible security attacks. Hence, the SR of an active sender contains the current RTP time stamp of the stream and its corresponding wall clock time. This information can be used by receivers to synchronize different incoming streams. For instance, a receiver can use the information to perform lip synchronization for a video.
- Source identification: This function is performed by sending SDES packets so that participants in a session will know each other.
- Control information scaling: The frequency of sending RTCP packets should be controlled in order to prevent the control traffic from overwhelming the network. RTCP limits the control traffic to at most 5 percent of the overall session traffic.

STREAMING OVER THE INTERNET: CHALLENGES AND APPROACHES

Streaming multimedia over the Internet faces significant challenges. The Internet provides only a best effort service, thus there are no guarantees whatsoever on bandwidth, delay jitter, or packet-loss rate. The best effort service works well for many applications, such as Web browsing, FTP, and e-mail but, unfortunately, it is not well suited for multimedia streaming. The time-varying bandwidth, packet delay, and packet loss make accessing multimedia data in real time challenging.

We now discuss the main approaches and techniques used to address these challenges.

Rate Control and Rate Shaping

The available bandwidth between any two nodes on the Internet is unknown and varies with time. Sending data at a higher rate than the available bandwidth leads to network congestion and subsequently packet loss, while sending data at a lower rate underutilizes the bandwidth

and possibly reduces audio and video quality. Thus, congestion control is required. For multimedia streaming, congestion control requires two mechanisms: *rate control* and *rate shaping*. Rate control estimates the available bandwidth and determines the data's transfer rate based on the available bandwidth. Rate shaping, on the other hand, forces the source (streaming server) to send the stream at the rate determined by rate control.

Rate Control

Multimedia data can be streamed by using TCP, which employs an *additive increase, multiplicative decrease* (AIMD) rule. The transmission rate is increased at a constant rate when no congestion is inferred (based on packet loss, delay, or delay jitter); otherwise, the transmission rate is halved. Using TCP for streaming multimedia causes serious problems. First, TCP retransmits lost packets to live up to its guarantees of reliable communication. Such retransmissions amplify the already high delay in the delivery of packets. These retransmissions, however, may not be necessary because multimedia data is loss tolerant. In particular, packet losses cause glitches, which can be concealed partially or fully (as will be discussed later). Second, the AIMD rule leads to wide variations in the instantaneous throughput (in the form of a sawtooth pattern). These variations are problematic for multimedia streaming. Third, TCP has a slow-start phase. Hence, the UDP is usually preferable to TCP. UDP's transmission rate can be controlled in a TCP-friendly manner by matching TCP throughput on a macroscopic scale while avoiding the wide variations in instantaneous throughput (Mathis, Semke, and Mahdavi 1997; Padhye et al. 2000; Tan and Zakhor 1999; Floyd et al. 2000).

Rate control can be performed by the source or the receiver. Source-based rate control is inefficient when a multimedia stream is sent to multiple recipients using multicasting (i.e., one-to-many communication). For such an environment, a receiver-based technique called *layered multicast* (McCanne, Jacobson, and Vetterli 1996) can be used. This technique uses *layered compression* schemes, which encode the multimedia file into a *base* layer and one or more *enhancement* layers. The base layer provides low but acceptable and usable quality, whereas each enhancement layer refines the quality further. With the layered multicast technique, the source transmits each layer on a separate multicast channel, while the receiver determines the number of channels to listen to based on the current network condition. The receiver changes the number of channels dynamically by adding channels when no congestion is detected and dropping channels when congestion occurs.

Although TCP is less suitable than UDP for streaming multimedia, TCP accounts for the majority of streaming traffic over the Internet (Merwe, Sen, and Kalmanek 2002). A primary reason for UDP's limited usage is that many network administrators close their firewalls to UDP traffic. The study (Wang et al. 2004) shows that TCP generally provides satisfactory streaming performance when the achievable TCP throughput is roughly twice the multimedia bit rate. The performance was considered satisfactory when the fraction of late packets was less than 10^{-4} for a startup delay of approximately 10 seconds.

Rate Shaping

The question arises now as to how the compressed multimedia object can be "shaped" or transformed to fit the available bandwidth. This is the function of rate shaping. Several techniques can be used for rate shaping, including *transcoding*, *multirate switching*, and *layered compression*. These can be described as follows.

- With transcoding, the video or audio is decoded and then re-encoded to the desired bit rate. Unfortunately, transcoding requires extensive computations and produces video and audio quality that is worse than if the streamed content were to be encoded directly at the target bit rate.

- With multirate switching, multiple copies of the multimedia object are made available at different bit rates, each of which targets a common network connection speed (such as dialup modem, DSL, cable, T1 line, etc.). The client can switch dynamically during the streaming session from one bit rate to another that best suits the current available bandwidth. This technique removes effectively both shortcomings of transcoding. It increases, however, the required storage capacity and has limited ability to adapt to the current bandwidth because only a small number of copies, and thus a small number of target bit rates, can practically be made available in actual servers.

- Layered video compression encodes the video into multiple layers and lets the client determine the number of received layers. Unfortunately, data overlap among the different compression layers reduces the compression efficiency compared with nonlayered schemes. The overall storage requirement, however, is much smaller than multirate switching.

Client-Side Buffering

The streamed multimedia content should be played back at a constant rate. For instance, a video recorded at 30 frames/sec should be played back at that same rate. Streaming that file through the Internet leads to variations in the end-to-end packet delays (delay jitter). The delay jitter causes perceptual problems in the reconstructed video. Hence, a playout buffer can be used at the receiver (the client side) to smooth out the variations in the packet delay. Buffering can also absorb, to a certain degree, the variability in the available bandwidth. Unfortunately, these advantages come at the expense of increasing the initial delay.

Error Control

As discussed earlier, UDP is more suitable than TCP for transporting multimedia data. Because UDP does not ensure reliable delivery, the purpose of error control is to address the problem of packet loss that would otherwise severely degrade the playback quality. Error control techniques can be classified into four main classes: *forward error correction*, *delay-constrained retransmission*, *error-resilient coding*, and *error concealment*.

Let us now briefly discuss the different error control approaches. Additional information can be found in Wang and Zhu (1998); Wang, Ostermann, and Zhang (2002); and Apostolopoulos, Tan, and Wee (2002).

Forward Error Correction

Forward error correction (FEC) adds redundant information that can be used in the case of packet loss to reconstruct the original information. For example, a video stream can be divided into segments, each of which is packetized into k packets of actual data and l packets of error control information. A segment can be reconstructed fully if any k packets are received correctly. Otherwise, the perceptual quality might be affected if no further error control is provided.

Delay-Constrained Retransmission

As mentioned earlier, UDP does not retransmit lost packets so as to avoid any additional delays. In certain situations, however, it may be desirable to retransmit a lost packet, particularly if the expected delay will be within a certain range. For example, delay-constrained retransmission can be implemented by the receiver as follows. When the receiver detects the loss of a packet, it sends a request to the server to retransmit that packet if

$$\mathrm{T}_{curr} + RTT < T_{disp} + T_s \qquad (1)$$

where T_{curr} is the current time, RTT is the network round trip time, T_{disp} is the time the packet is scheduled for display, and T_s is a safety threshold. Otherwise, the receiver relies on error concealment to deal with the packet loss.

Error-Resilient Coding

The error-resilient coding approach addresses the packet-loss problem from the compression perspective by changing the compression algorithm so that it can be resilient to some types of error caused by packet loss. Current video compression standards use motion-compensated prediction between frames and block-based spatial transforms (such as DCT) for each frame, followed by entropy encoding (such as Huffman coding). These standards are highly susceptible to packet loss, which may cause significant error propagation and loss of bit stream synchronization. Thus, the purpose of error-resilient coding is to limit error propagation and reduce the scope of error in the reconstructed video or audio.

Error Concealment

Error concealment tries to minimize the negative impact of packet loss on the perceptual quality of the multimedia content. Basically, the lost information can be predicted based on other received information. For example, videos exhibit significant degrees of spatial locality (within frames) and temporal locality (between frames) that can be used to interpolate the missing information. Generally, there are three main approaches for error concealment: *spatial interpolation*, *temporal interpolation*, and *motion-compensated temporal interpolation*.

- With spatial interpolation, missing pixels in a frame can be interpolated based on neighboring pixels in the same frame.

- Temporal interpolation uses the corresponding pixels in a correctly received previous frame. This approach does not consider any possible motion between the two frames and thus is effective only for low-motion videos.
- Motion-compensated temporal interpolation is more effective for high-motion videos. Basically, it considers possible movements (which can be detected by examining motion vectors) in predicting the missing information.

Other Approaches

The shortcomings of the Internet's best-effort service can be mitigated in many other ways, including the following:

- *Internet service providers* (ISPs) can reduce packet delay and packet loss by adding more bandwidth and switching capacity.
- Multicasting can be employed to use server bandwidth and network resources efficiently. It can be implemented at the IP level (Giuliano undated; SprintLink undated), which is most effective but challenging and currently not widely deployed. It can also be implemented at the application level by using *multicast overlay networks* (Jannotti et al. 2000; Chu, Rao, and Zhang 2000; Castro et al. 2002). The overlay consists of multiple servers scattered across the network.
- ISPs can use *Web caching* (also called *proxy caching*) to bring the content closer to the clients and to reduce the traffic on the access links of these ISPs to the Internet.
- *Content delivery networks* (CDNs) can be used to replicate multimedia files and place them at the edges of the Internet closer to the clients.

The need for the Internet, however, to provide services beyond the best-effort service has grown spectacularly. Therefore, many frameworks have been developed for providing QoS. These frameworks include the *integrated services* (IntServ) model (Clark, Shenker, and Zhang 1992; Braden, Clark, and Shenker 1994; Braden et al. 1997; White 1997) and the *differentiated services* (DiffServ) model (Blake et al.1998; Bernet et al. 1998). The IntServ model requires fundamental changes to the Internet so that applications can reserve bandwidth in each link between the sender and the receiver. This model uses the *resource reservation protocol* (RSVP) (Braden et al. 1997; Guerin, Blake, and Herzog 1997; Li and Rekhter 1998) to set up paths and reserve resources along them. In contrast, the DiffServ model requires only minor changes to the Internet by introducing only few classes and giving packets differentiated services based on their assigned classes. The reader is recommended to refer to Xiao and Ni (1999) and Kurose and Ross (2004) for additional information on Internet QoS.

STREAMING SERVER DESIGN

Streaming servers face significant challenges to support large numbers of concurrent customers because of the requirements of real-time playback and high transfer rates. This section focuses on servers that stream stored multimedia content, *video on demand* (VOD) servers in particular. The design of these servers is more challenging than live-streaming servers because multiple clients of the same video can be at different playback points and unrestricted support for interactive operations is desirable.

We now discuss the main design aspects for streaming servers: admission control, resource sharing, request scheduling, and storage subsystem management.

Admission Control

The basic function of the admission control unit is to ensure that the real-time performance requirements of all admitted requests are met. There are three main approaches for admission control: *deterministic* (Ferrari 1990; Gemmell and Christodoulakis 1992; Cheng, Chen, and Chen 2000), *predictive* (Vin et al. "Admission control," 1994; Bao and Sethi 1999), and *statistical* (Vin, Goyal, and Goyal 1994; Zimmermann and Fu 2003). The deterministic approach provides hard QoS guarantees by admitting new requests only if the real-time requirements of all existing requests are guaranteed to be met. Thus, this approach must assume the worst case for system parameters (including the disk seek time, rotational latency, and transfer rate). The predictive and statistical approaches increase the utilization of resources by providing soft QoS guarantees. Hence, they admit new requests if the real-time requirements of existing requests are *likely* to be met. Both of these approaches reach their decisions by using statistical analysis. The predictive approach uses actual measurements of server utilization, whereas the statistical approach is entirely parameter-based.

Resource Sharing

Streaming servers—VOD servers, in particular—can support limited numbers of concurrent customers because of the required real-time and high-rate transfers. Resource-sharing techniques face this challenge by using the multicast facility and exploiting the high locality of reference in multimedia access patterns. The main classes of resource-sharing techniques include *batching, stream merging*, and *periodic broadcasting*. These classes are briefly discussed below, but only some of the more popular techniques are covered.

Batching

With batching, the requests to the same videos are accumulated and serviced together by utilizing the multicast facility. Batching, therefore, offloads the underlying storage subsystem and efficiently uses server bandwidth and network resources.

Stream Merging

Stream-merging techniques combine streams when possible to reduce the delivery costs. These techniques include *stream tapping and patching* (Carter and Long 1997; Hua, Cai, and Sheu 1998), *transition patching* (Cai and Hua 1999), and *hierarchal stream merging* (Eager, Vernon, and Zahorjan 1999, 2001).

Patching expands the multicast tree dynamically to include new requests. A new request joins immediately

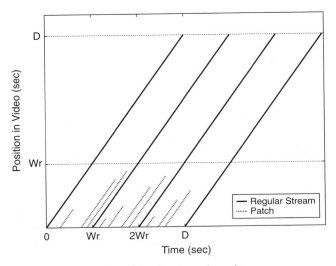

Figure 3: Clarification of patching

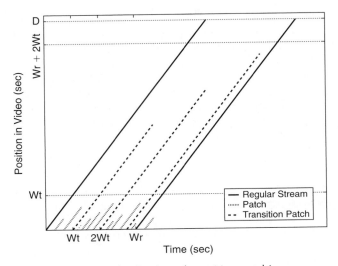

Figure 4: Clarification of transition patching

the latest multicast stream for the object and receives the missing portion as a patch using a unicast stream. When the playback of the patch is completed, the client continues the playback of the remaining portion using the data received from the multicast stream and already buffered locally. The cost of servicing a new request is determined by its temporal skew to the latest multicast stream. To avoid the continuously increasing cost of patch streams, regular streams (i.e., multicast streams of the whole video) are typically retransmitted every prespecified period of time, which is called *regular window* (Wr). Figure 3 further explains the concept. In the figure, D is the video length in seconds. Typically, Wr is much smaller than D, but the figure is meant only for a simple clarification.

Transition patching allows some patches to be sharable by extending their lengths. It introduces another multicast stream called *transition patch*. The threshold to start a regular stream is Wr as in patching, and the threshold to start a transition patch is called the *transition window* (Wt). The transition patch length is equal to the difference between the starting times of the transition patch and the last regular stream plus $2 \times Wt$, whereas the length of the patch is equal to the difference between the starting times of the patch and the latest transition stream or regular stream. Hence, the maximum possible patch length is Wt, and the maximum possible transition patch length is $Wr + 2 \times Wt$. Figure 4 further illustrates the concept. A possible scenario for a client is to start listening to its own patch and the transition patch; when its patch is completed, it starts listening to the regular stream.

Both patching and transition patching are extended with *hierarchal stream merging*, whereby streams can merge multiple times during their lifetimes to form dynamic merge trees. Eager, Vernon, and Zahorjan (1999) analyzed different policies for creating merge trees. The best performer among these policies is *earliest reachable merge target* (ERMT). With ERMT, which was shown to perform near optimally, a new client or a newly merged group of clients snoops on the closest stream that it can merge with if no later arrivals preemptively catch them.

Periodic Broadcasting

Periodic broadcasting protocols divide each supported multimedia object (usually video) into multiple segments and broadcast them periodically on dedicated server channels. Thus, they can service unlimited numbers of customers but can be used only for the most popular objects, and they require customers to wait until the next broadcast times of the first segments. Note that as the number of segments increases, the maximum waiting time shortens (because the length of the first segment is reduced). A large number of broadcasting techniques has been proposed. These techniques differ in terms of the maximum waiting time achieved by the same server bandwidth, the required client download bandwidth, and buffering space.

Basically, broadcasting protocols can be classified into the following three main classes (Hu 2001):

- Class A partitions the objects into increasing size of segments and transmits them periodically on dedicated logical channels. This class is based on the idea of *pyramid broadcasting* (Viswanathan and Imielinski 1995) and includes *skyscraper broadcasting* (SB) (Hua and Sheu 1997) and *fast broadcasting* (FB) (Juhn and Tseng 1998). Both SB and FB allocate each channel a fixed bandwidth, b, that is equal to the object consumption (playback) rate. SB partitions the segment according to the series {1, 2, 2, 5, 5, 12, 12, 25, 25, 52, 52, ...}. The partitioning series determines the relative segment size. (Note that the first segment is the smallest in order to reduce the maximum waiting time.) SB requires the client to download from only two channels at any one time. FB, however, employs the partitioning series {1, 2, 4, ..., 2^{K-1}, 2^K }, where K is the number of channels. FB is more efficient in server bandwidth, but it requires the client to download from all channels. Other protocols in this class include *Fibonacci broadcasting* (Hu 2001) and *reliable periodic broadcast* (Mahanti et al. 2003).

- Class B partitions objects into equal-sized segments and transmits them in logical channels of decreasing bandwidth. Thus, it requires much less server bandwidth than class A. Using segments of increasing size is less efficient because each entire segment must be broadcast at the same bandwidth and periodicity while the data at the end of a segment could have been broadcast at lower bandwidth (Pâris, Carter, and Long 1999). This class is based on *harmonic broadcasting* (HB) (Juhn and Tseng 1997), which allocates channel i bandwidth b/i. The client here is required to download from all channels simultaneously. HB may not be able to meet the real-time playback requirements in certain cases. This problem was resolved by later HB-based techniques, including *cautious harmonic* (Pâris, Carter, and Long "Efficient broadcasting," 1998), *quasi harmonic* (Pâris, Carter, and Long "Efficient broadcasting," 1998), and *polyharmonic* (Pâris, Carter, and Long "Low bandwidth," 1998).

- Class C is a hybrid of classes A and B. It is based on *pagoda broadcasting* (Pâris, Carter, and Long 1999) and uses fixed-length segments like class B and equal bandwidth logical channels like class A. The main objective is to reduce the number of logical channels that should be managed by the server compared with HB while achieving close reductions in server bandwidth. Thus, Pagoda broadcasting divides each object into fixed-size segments and maps segments to a small number of logical channels of equal bandwidth and uses time-division multiplexing to ensure that successive segments are broadcast at the proper decreasing frequencies.

Qudah and Sarhan (2006) provide additional information and a detailed analysis of resource-sharing techniques.

Request Scheduling

VOD servers maintain a waiting queue for each video. The purpose of the scheduling unit is to select for service an appropriate queue whenever the server has sufficient resources. Many scheduling policies exist, including *first-come, first-served* (FCFS) (Dan, Sitaram, and Shahabuddin 1994), *maximum queue length* (MQL) (Dan, Sitaram, and Shahabuddin 1994), and *maximum factored queue length* (MFQL) (Aggarwal, Wolf, and Yu 2001). They can be described as follows:

- FCFS acts fairly by selecting the queue with the oldest request.
- MQL maximizes the number of requests serviced at any time by selecting the longest queue. It is, however, extremely biased against unpopular objects because they have shorter queue lengths.
- MFQL attempts to minimize the mean request waiting time by selecting the queue with the *largest factored queue length*. The factored length of a queue is defined as its length divided by the square root of the relative access frequency of its corresponding video. MFQL is more fair toward unpopular objects than MQL but less fair than FCFS.

A detailed analysis of scheduling policies can be found in Sarhan and Das ("Simulation," 2003). In Sarhan and Das ("New class," 2004), a new class of scheduling policies for providing time-of-service guarantees was proposed. Providing time-of-service guarantees can enhance customer-perceived QoS and influence customers to wait, thereby increasing server throughput.

Storage Subsystem Management

Storage subsystems play a significant role in the performance, scalability, and reliability of multimedia servers. The main design aspects of multimedia storage subsystems include *disk striping*, *fault tolerance*, and *cache management*.

Disk striping (Shenoy and Harric 1999) is used to increase the disk I/O bandwidth.

To address the reliability problem of hard disk drives, multimedia servers employ fault-tolerance techniques that can be classified as either *parity-based* (Berson, Golubchik, and Muntz 1995; Tewari et al. 1996) or *mirror-based* (Mourad 1996; Haskin 1998).

The objective of cache management is to reduce the load on the storage subsystem by caching portions of the multimedia data (videos in particular) in the main memory of the server. *Interval caching* (Dan et al. 1995) is a cache-management technique that exploits the locality of reference by caching intervals between successive streams. Basically, it attempts to pair each playback request with an immediately preceding request for the same video that is currently being serviced. When the server accepts a request for service from the cache, it starts to cache the data of the preceding stream while retrieving and transferring them to the client. and the compression method used. Interval caching uses the available cache (memory) space efficiently by ensuring that only the shortest intervals are cached at any time. *Generalized interval caching* (Dan and Sitaram 1996) extends interval caching to handle workloads of short and long videos. It does not require paired streams to be concurrent because short videos are unlikely to have concurrent accesses. Hence, when two paired streams are not concurrent, the technique caches the entire corresponding video. Interval caching has also been adapted to cache multimedia data in network-attached disk environments (Sarhan and Das "Integrated resource," 2003; "Caching," 2004).

Cache management is essential, regardless of the resource-sharing techniques used. Interval caching works well with batching, but it is not well suited for other resource-sharing techniques such as patching, transition patching, and ERMT. In Qudah and Sarhan (2006), a statistical approach for cache management was proposed for multimedia servers using various resource-sharing techniques. With this approach, the server periodically computes video access frequencies and determines the data to be cached. Besides being performance effective, this approach is easy to implement and incurs small overhead because updates are triggered only when the workload varies considerably. The results show that this approach for cache management is highly effective in reducing the disk I/O bandwidth requirements. For example, with a cache size of only 2 percent of the total size of videos, these requirements can be reduced by as much as 16 percent for systems with moderate request rates. Moreover, these reductions increase with the request arrival rate.

CONCLUSION

Streaming multimedia data over the Internet is typically performed by coordination among three application-layer protocols: *real-time streaming protocol* (RTSP), *real-time protocol* (RTP), and *real-time control protocol* (RTCP). RTSP manages the streaming session and supports user interactions, while RTP provides end-to-end delivery services for multimedia streams, including payload type identification, sequence numbering, and time stamping. RTCP is used to support monitoring of the data delivery and provide intermedia synchronization and participant identification services.

Multimedia streaming presents serious challenges to both the network and the server. The Internet provides only a best-effort service and thus makes no guarantees on bandwidth, delay jitter, or packet-loss rate. The best-effort service works well for many applications but is not well suited for multimedia streaming. The main ways to mitigate the shortcomings of the best-effort service can be summarized as follows:

- UDP can be used instead of TCP not only to avoid the additional delays caused by retransmitting lost packets but also to avoid the wide variations in the instantaneous available bandwidth.
- Rate-control and rate-shaping techniques can be used to address the time-varying available bandwidth. Rate control estimates the available bandwidth and determines the data-transfer rate based on the available bandwidth; rate shaping forces the source (streaming server) to send the stream at the rate determined by rate control using transcoding, multirate switching, or layered compression. When a multimedia stream is sent to multiple recipients using multicasting, receiver-based rate control is more suitable than source-based. With receiver-based rate control, the multimedia object is encoded into multiple layers that are transmitted separately, and the recipient determines the number of layers to listen to, dynamically based on its available bandwidth to the source.
- The client can use a playout buffer to smooth out the delay jitter and absorb (to some degree) the variability in the network bandwidth.
- Error-control techniques can be employed to handle packet loss when UDP is used. These techniques can be classified into four main categories: *forward error correction* (FEC), *delay-constrained retransmission, error-resilient coding,* and *error concealment*. FEC adds redundant information that can be used to reconstruct the missing data. With delay-constrained retransmission, lost packets are retransmitted if they are expected to arrive before their scheduled playback time. Error-resilient coding changes the compression algorithm to be resilient to some errors caused by packet loss. Error concealment exploits the spatial and temporal locality of multimedia data by interpolating the missing information.

The design of streaming servers—*video on demand* (VOD) servers, in particular—faces a significant challenge to support large numbers of concurrent requests. Without smart management of server resources, the network bandwidth and disk I/O bandwidth will be consumed quickly after servicing only a small number of customers. Resource-sharing techniques such as stream merging and periodic broadcasting face this challenge by utilizing the multicast facility. Stream-merging techniques combine streams when possible to reduce the delivery costs, whereas periodic protocols divide each supported multimedia object into multiple segments and broadcast them periodically on dedicated server channels. Request scheduling, admission control, and storage management are other important design aspects that can significantly affect the server's overall performance. To meet the high disk I/O bandwidth requirement, multimedia objects are typically striped across multiple disks that can be accessed concurrently.

ACKNOWLEDGMENT

I would like to thank the anonymous reviewers for their insightful and helpful comments and suggestions.

GLOSSARY

Batching: A resource-sharing technique that accumulates requests for the same multimedia streams and services them together using multicasting.

Error control: A variety of techniques used to deal with packet loss and data corruption. The main classes of error-control techniques for multimedia streaming are *forward error correction, delay-constrained retransmission, error-resilient coding,* and *error concealment*.

Multimedia streaming: Pipelining the delivery and playback of multimedia data.

Periodic broadcasting: A group of resource-sharing techniques that divide multimedia objects into segments and broadcast them periodically on dedicated server channels. They include *skyscraper broadcasting, harmonic broadcasting,* and *pagoda broadcasting*.

Rate control: A congestion control mechanism that estimates the available bandwidth and determines the data-transfer rate based on the available bandwidth.

Rate shaping: A congestion control mechanism that forces the data source (streaming server) to send the stream at the rate determined by rate control.

Real-time control protocol (RTCP):   A network protocol used in conjunction with *real-time protocol* (RTP) to support the monitoring of data delivery and provide intermedia synchronization and participant identification services.

Real-time protocol (RTP):   A network protocol that provides end-to-end delivery services for multimedia streams. These services include *payload type identification, sequence numbering,* and *time stamping*.

Real-time streaming protocol (RTSP):   A network protocol that manages streaming sessions of multimedia data. It supports such user interactions as play, pause, resume, fast forward, fast rewind, and stop (teardown).

Resource sharing: Techniques that reduce the delivery costs of multimedia streams by using multicasting. The main classes of resource sharing techniques are *batching, stream merging,* and *periodic broadcasting*.

Stream merging: A group of resources sharing techniques that combine some multimedia streams (when possible) to reduce the delivery costs. These techniques include patching, transition patching, and earliest reachable merge target (ERMT).

CROSS REFERENCES

See *Computer Conferencing: Protocols and Applications.*; *High Definition Television (HDTV)*; *Sources of Errors, Prevention, Detection and Correction*; *TCP/IP Suite*.

REFERENCES

Aggarwal, C. C., J. L. Wolf, and P. S. Yu. 2001. The maximum factor queue length batching scheme for video-on-demand systems. *IEEE Transactions on Computers*, 50(2): 97–110.

Apostolopoulos, J. G., W. Tan, and S. J. Wee. 2002. *Video streaming: Concepts, algorithms, and systems*. Technical Report HPL-2002-260. Palo Alto, CA: Mobile and Media Systems Laboratory, HP Laboratories.

Bao, Y., and S. Sethi. 1999. Performance-driven adaptive admission control for multimedia applications. In *Proceedings of IEEE International Conference on Communications*, September, Tokyo, pp. 199–203.

Bernet, Y., J. Binder, S. Blake, M. Carlson, S. Keshav, E. Davies, et al. 1998. A framework for differentiated services. IETF Internet draft (May).

Berson, S., L. Golubchik, and R. R. Muntz. 1995. Fault tolerant design of multimedia servers. In *ACM SIGMOD International Symposium on Management of Data*, May, Cambridge, MA, USA, pp. 364–75.

Blake, S., D. Black, M. Carlson, E. Davies, Z. Wang, and W. Weiss. 1998. *An architecture for differentiated services*. IETF RFC 2475, December.

Braden, R., D. Clark, and S. Shenker. 1994. *Integrated services in the Internet architecture: An overview*. IETF RFC 1633, June.

Braden, R., L. Zhang, S. Berson, S. Herzog, and S. Jamin. 1997. *Resource reservation protocol (RSVP–version 1 functional specification)*. IETF RFC 2205, September.

Cai, Y., and K. A. Hua. 1999. An efficient bandwidth-sharing technique for true video on demand systems. In *Proceedings of ACM Multimedia*, October, Orlando, FL, USA, pp. 211–4.

Carter, S. W., and D. D. E. Long. 1997. Video-on-demand server efficiency through stream tapping. In *Proceedings of Sixth International Conference on Computer Communications and Networks*, September, Las Vegas, NV, USA, pp. 200–7.

Castro, M., P. Druschel, A. Kermarrec, and A. Rowstron. 2002. SCRIBE: A large-scale and decentralized application-level multicast infrastructure. *IEEE Journal on Selected Areas in Communications*, 20(8): 1489–99.

Cheng, S.-T., C.-M. Chen, and I.-R. Chen. 2000. Dynamic quota-based admission control with sub-rating in multimedia servers. *Multimedia Systems*, 8(2): 83–91.

Chu, Y.-H., S. G. Rao, and H. Zhang. 2000. A case for end system multicast. In *Proceedings of the ACM SIGMETRICS Conference on Measurements and Modeling of Computer Systems*, June, Santa Clara, CA, USA, pp. 1–12.

Clark, D. D., S. Shenker, and L. Zhang. 1992. Supporting real-time applications in an integrated services packet network: Architecture and mechanism. In *Proceedings of the ACM SIGCOMM*, August, Baltimore, Maryland, USA, pp. 14–26.

Dan, A., D. M. Dias, R. Mukherjee, D. Sitaram, and R. Tewari. 1995. Buffering and caching in large-scale video servers. In *Digest of Papers, IEEE International Computer Conference, March*, San Francisco, CA, USA, pp. 217–25.

Dan, A., and D. Sitaram. 1996. A generalized interval caching policy for mixed interactive and long video workloads. In *Proceedings of Multimedia Computing and Networking Conference*, January, San Jose, CA, US, pp. 344–51.

Dan, A., D. Sitaram, and P. Shahabuddin. 1994. Scheduling policies for an on-demand video server with batching. In *Proceedings of ACM Multimedia*, October, San Francisco, CA, US, pp. 391–8.

Eager, D. L., M. K. Vernon, and J. Zahorjan. 1999. Optimal and efficient merging schedules for video-on-demand servers. In *Proceedings of ACM Multimedia*, October, Orlando, Florida, USA, pp. 199–202.

———. 2001. Minimizing bandwidth requirements for on-demand data delivery. *IEEE Transactions on Knowledge and Data Engineering*, 13(5): 742–57.

Ferrari, D. 1990. *Client requirements for real-time communication services*. IETF RFC 1193, November.

Floyd, S., M. Handley, J. Padhye, and J. Widmer. 2000. Equation-based congestion control for unicast applications. In *Proceedings of the ACM SIGCOMM*, August, Stockholm, pp. 43–56.

Gemmell, J., and S. Christodoulakis. 1992. Principles of delay-sensitive multimedia data storage retrieval. *ACM Transactions on Information Systems*, 10(1): 51–90.

Giuliano, L. Undated. *Deploying native multicast across the Internet*. White paper (available at www.sprintlink.net/multicast/whitepaper.html).

Guerin, R., S. Blake, and S. Herzog. 1997. Aggregating RSVP-based QoS requests. IETF Internet Draft, November.

Haskin, R. L. 1998. Tiger shark: A scalable file system for multimedia. *IBM Journal of Research and Development*, 42(2): 185–97.

Hu, A. 2001. Video-on-demand broadcasting protocols: A comprehensive study. In *Proceedings of IEEE INFOCOM*, April, Anchorage, AK, USA, pp. 508–17.

Hua, K. A., Y. Cai, and S. Sheu. 1998. Patching: A multicast technique for true video-on demand services. In *Proceedings of ACM Multimedia*, September, Bristol, England, pp. 191–200.

Hua, K. A., and S. Sheu. 1997. Skyscraper broadcasting: A new broadcasting scheme for metropolitan video-on-demand system. In *Proceedings of ACM SIGCOMM*, September, Cannes, France, pp. 89–100.

Jannotti, J., D. K. Gifford, K. L. Johnson, M. F. Kaashoek, and J. W. O'Toole. 2000. Overcast: Reliable multicasting with an overlay network. In *Proceedings of the Fourth Symposium on Operating System Design and Implementation*, October, San Diego, pp. 197–212.

Juhn, L., and L. Tseng. 1997. Harmonic broadcasting for video-on-demand service. *IEEE Transactions on Broadcasting*, 43(3): 268–71.

———. 1998. Fast data broadcasting and receiving scheme for popular video service. *IEEE Transactions on Broadcasting*, 44(1): 100–5.

Kurose, J. F., and R. W. Ross. 2004. *Computer networking: A top-down approach featuring the Internet*. 3rd ed. Boston: Addison Wesley.

Li, T., and Y. Rekhter. 1998. *Provider architecture for differentiated services and traffic engineering (PASTE)*. IETF RFC 2430, October.

Mahanti, A., D. L. Eager, M. K. Vernon, and D. J. Sundaram-Stukel. 2003. Scalable on-demand media streaming with packet loss recovery. *IEEE/ACM Transactions on Networking*, 11(2): 195–209.

Mathis, M., J. Semke, and J. Mahdavi. 1997. The macroscopic behavior of the TCP congestion avoidance algorithm. *Computer Communications Review*, 27(3): 67–82.

McCanne, S., V. Jacobson, and M. Vetterli. 1996. Receiver-driven layered multicast. In *Proceedings of the ACM SIGCOMM*, August, Stanford, CA, USA, pp. 117–30.

Merwe, J. V. der, S. Sen, and C. Kalmanek. 2002. Streaming video traffic: Characterization and network impact. In *Proceedings of the Seventh International Workshop on Web Content Caching and Distribution*, August, Boulder, CO, USA.

Mourad, A. 1996. Doubly-striped disk mirroring: Reliable storage for video servers. *Multimedia Tools and Applications*, 2: 273–9.

Padhye, J., V. Firoiu, D. F. Towsley, and J. F. Kurose. 2000. Modeling TCP Reno performance: A simple model and its empirical validation. *IEEE/ACM Transactions on Networking*, 8(2): 133–45.

Pâris, J.-F., S. W. Carter, and D. D. E. Long. 1998. Efficient broadcasting protocols for video on demand. In *Proceedings of the International Symposium on Modeling, Analysis and Simulation of Computer and Telecommunication Systems*, July, Los Alamitos, CA, USA, pp. 127–32.

———. 1998. A low bandwidth broadcasting protocol for video on demand. In *Proceedings of the Seventh International Conference on Computer Communications and Networks*, October, Lafayette, LA, USA, pp. 690–9.

———. 1999. A hybrid broadcasting protocol for video on demand. In *Proceedings of the Multimedia Computing and Networking Conference*, January, San Jose, CA, USA, pp. 317–26.

Qudah, B., and N. J. Sarhan. 2006. Analysis of resource sharing and cache management in scalable video-on-demand. In *Proceedings of the Fourteenth International Symposium on Modeling, Analysis, and Simulation of Computer and Telecommunication Systems*, September, Monterey, CA, USA, pp. 327–34.

Sarhan, N. J., and C. R. Das. 2003. An integrated resource sharing policy for multimedia storage servers based on network-attached disks. In *Proceedings of the International Conference on Distributed Computing Systems*, May, Providence, RI, USA, pp. 136–43.

———. 2003. A simulation-based analysis of scheduling policies for multimedia servers. In *Proceedings of the Annual Simulation Symposium*, March, Orlando, FL, USA, pp. 183–90.

———. 2004. Caching and scheduling in NAD-based multimedia servers. *IEEE Transactions on Parallel and Distributed Systems*, 15(10): 921–33.

———. 2004. A new class of scheduling policies for providing time of service guarantees in video-on-demand servers. In *Proceedings of the Seventh IFIP/IEEE International Conference on Management of Multimedia Networks and Services*, October, San Diego, pp. 127–39.

Shenoy, P., and V. Harric. 1999. Efficient striping techniques for variable bit rate continuous media file servers. *Performance Evaluation Journal*, 38(2): 175–99.

SprintLink. Undated. Sprintlink multicast (online article available at www.sprintlink.net/multicast).

Tan, W., and A. Zakhor. 1999. Real-time internet video using error resilient scalable compression and TCP-friendly transport protocol. *IEEE Transactions on Multimedia*, 1(2): 172–86.

Tewari, R., R. Mukherjee, D. M. Dias, and H. M. Vin. (1996, May). Design and performance tradeoffs in clustered video servers. In *International Conference on Multimedia Computing and Systems*, May, San Jose, CA, USA, pp. 144–50.

Vin, H., P. Goyal, and A. Goyal. 1994. A statistical admission control algorithm for multimedia servers. In *Proceedings of the Second ACM International Conference on Multimedia*, San Francisco, pp. 33–40.

Vin, H. M., A. Goyal, A. Goyal, and P. Goyal. 1994. An observation-based admission control algorithm for multimedia servers. In *Proceedings of Conference on Multimedia Computing and Systems*, Boston, pp. 234–43.

Viswanathan, S., and T. Imielinski. 1995. Pyramid broadcasting for video on demand service. In *Proceedings of Multimedia Computing and Networking Conference*, February, San Jose, CA, USA, pp. 66–77.

Wang, B., J. Kurose, P. Shenoy, and D. Towsley. 2004. Multimedia streaming via TCP: An analytic performance study. In *Proceedings of the Twelfth Annual ACM International Conference on Multimedia*, October, New York, pp. 908–15.

Wang, Y., J. Ostermann, and Y.-Q. Zhang. 2002. *Video processing and communications*. Upper Saddle River, NJ: Prentice Hall.

Wang, Y., and Q.-F. Zhu. 1998. Error control and concealment for video communication: A review. *Proceedings of the IEEE*, 86(5): 974–97.

White, P. P. 1997. RSVP and integrated services in the Internet: A tutorial. *IEEE Communications Magazine*, 35(5): 100–6.

Xiao, X., and L. M. Ni. 1999. Internet QoS: A big picture. *IEEE Network Magazine*, 13(2): 8–18.

Zimmermann, R., and K. Fu. 2003. Comprehensive statistical admission control for streaming media servers. In *Proceedings of the Eleventh ACM International Conference on Multimedia*, November, Berkeley, CA, USA, pp. 75–85.

High-Definition Television

Jim Krause, *Indiana University, Bloomington*

INTRODUCTION

Ever since the first black-and-white television image was displayed, both developers and viewers have sought ways to make it better: to add more resolution, to increase the contrast ratio, and to be able to faithfully replicate the color spectrum. An obvious yardstick to measure the progress and quality of television has been cinematic film, which for years has been capable of providing high-resolution moving images. Imagine TV developers in 1939 who watched the cinematic premiere of *The Wizard of Oz* or *Gone with the Wind*. What would they think after returning to their homes to face the comparatively small and grainy images on black-and-white television sets?

With *high-definition television* (HDTV), the gap has narrowed. George Lucas shot the last additions to his popular *Star Wars* collection using high-definition video cameras. More and more HDTV sets have made their way into a growing number of residential households. Despite the fact that we are closer than ever to having a high-definition cinema experience in all of our homes, obstacles remain. Broadcasters need cost-effective production tools. Consumers want to be able to purchase, record, and play back their favorite programs easily and at relatively low cost. The Federal Communications Commission (FCC) planned to end all analog television broadcasts by 2006, but recent legislation pushed this cutoff date back to February 17, 2009.

As we consider HDTV, it is useful to trace its evolution and maintain some perspective. *High definition* is a relative term. It is higher resolution—but higher than what?

This chapter will examine the environment in which HDTV has developed and identify some of its more important technical characteristics.

HISTORY OF TELEVISION

The exact beginning of what most of us refer to as television is debatable. In 1842, Alexander Bain managed to transmit a still image over wire, inventing what can readily be called the first fax machine. In 1884, Paul Gottlieb Nipkow went a step further and discovered (and patented) a way to scan a moving image and transmit it sequentially. Nipkow's process used two synchronized spinning disks, each with a spiral pattern of holes in it. On the transmitting side, a disk was placed between the subject and a light-sensitive element. The receiving side had a similar disk placed between a light source and the viewer. The resolution of Nipkow's disk system depended on the number of holes in the disk. His system was thought to have been able to achieve between eighteen and thirty lines of resolution and marked the beginning of the era of electro-mechanical television.

However, John Logie Baird, a Scottish inventor, publicly demonstrated what some consider the first recognizable video image of a human face on January 26, 1926. Baird's gray-scale image, presented to members of the Royal Institution in London, had only some thirty lines of resolution. Baird used a spinning disk similar to Nipkow's that was embedded with lenses and provided an image just clear enough to display a human face. Baird's television proved to be popular. His company, Baird Television Development Company, continued working to improve and refine the image. The maximum resolution ever achieved by his electromechanical system was approximately 240 lines (British Broadcasting Corporation undated).

But electromechanical television was cumbersome, and interest diminished as developers realized that an electronic process was necessary in order to provide higher levels of resolution. In 1934, Philo Farnsworth gave a public demonstration of an all-electronic system. The system used a camera on one end and a *cathode ray tube* (CRT) to serve as a display on the receiving end. Both camera and CRT used an electron beam controlled by modulating a magnetic field. Compared to electromechanical TV, the all-electronic system was more convenient and interest in TV broadcasting soared. Other developers soon began developing improved versions of television and began successfully marketing them to the public.

The Search for Standards: The FCC and the NTSC

The FCC oversees radio, wire, cable, satellite, and television broadcast in the United States. Established by the Communications Act of 1934, the FCC initially set out to regulate the ever-increasing use of the broadcast spectrum. One of the FCC's early challenges was setting technical standards for television. In 1936, the Radio Manufacturers Association (RMA) recommended a standard for television using 441 horizontal scan lines and 30 frames per second (fps) with a 4:3 aspect ratio. The public was accepting of the 4:3 aspect ratio because it was close to existing 16- and 35-millimeter (mm) film formats, which used the *Academy aperture* (an 11:8 aspect ratio). A major manufacturer, the Radio Corporation of America, embraced this standard and had already begun broadcasting and manufacturing TV receivers capable of displaying 441 scan lines.

Many opponents, however, argued that more picture detail was necessary. After a series of formal hearings, the FCC urged the RMA to form the *National Television System Committee* (NTSC) in 1940. Its goal was to set technical standards for the broadcast of black-and-white television. The next year, the NTSC established its first set of standards; they kept the 4:3 aspect ratio but called for a higher resolution image with 525 scan lines refreshing at a rate of 30 interlaced frames (or 60 fields) per second. Each interlaced frame consisted of two fields. First, the odd lines were scanned for field 1, then the even lines were scanned for field 2. Television stations were allotted 6 MHz of bandwidth per channel, which ultimately covered a frequency range spanning from 54 MHz to 890 MHz on the broadcast spectrum.

Color Television

In order for signals to broadcast color, the original NTSC standard for black-and-white television had to be revised. NTSC presented an update in 1953. Creating the new standard was no easy task because engineers had to make color broadcasts backward-compatible with the large base of existing black-and-white televisions (ten million sets had been sold by 1949). To do so, engineers split the

signal into two components: (1) *luminance*, referred to as *luma*, which contained the brightness information; and (2) *chrominance*, which contained the color. The color information was encoded onto a 3.58-MHz subcarrier added onto the video signal. Black-and-white sets could ignore the color subcarrier using only the luma portion while color sets could take advantage of both. Unfortunately, the color subcarrier interacted with the sound carrier, creating minor visible artifacts. To reduce interference, the field refresh rate of 60 Hz was slowed down by a factor of 1000/1001 to 59.94 Hz. Instead of running at 30 fps, broadcast television downshifted to 29.97 fps.

PAL and SECAM

Although the United States, Canada, and Mexico adopted NTSC standards based on a 60-Hz frequency, most other countries developed color television systems based on 50 Hz. (The refresh frequencies varied because they were dependent on the operating frequency of a region's electrical systems.) Most versions of *phase alternating line* (PAL) and *séquential colour avec mémoire* (SECAM), while still employing a 4:3 aspect ratio, had 625 horizontal scan lines. The 100 extra scan lines provided more picture detail but some people felt the slower 25-Hz scan rate created a noticeable flicker.

High-Definition Advances

During the next thirty years, many improvements were made in cameras, production and broadcast gear, and television receivers. Despite these advances, the quality of analog broadcast was still limited to the NTSC standard of 60 fields and 525 horizontal scan lines. To take television to the next level, the entire analog broadcasting system had to be replaced. Several manufacturers had developed and were already using *high-definition* (HD) digital television systems. The exact format had yet to be determined, but it was clear that the replacement for analog would use digital television technology. What was needed was a set of standards to ensure compatibility.

Advanced Television Systems Committee

In 1982, industry associations, corporations, and educational institutions formed the Advanced Television Systems Committee (ATSC). This not-for-profit organization develops voluntary standards for advanced television systems, including enhanced analog TV, *digital TV* (DTV), *standard definition TV* (SDTV), *high-definition TV* (HDTV), and data services. The ATSC's published broadcast standards are voluntary unless adopted and mandated by the FCC.

In 1987, The FCC formed an advisory committee on advanced television service. The goal was to explore the issues of advanced television technologies and to advise the FCC in both technical and public policy matters accordingly. By 1989, there were as many as twenty-one proposed systems submitted by various proponents. After a peer review process, the field was narrowed down to four systems. Proponents of these systems formed what would become known as the *Grand Alliance:* AT&T, General Instrument Corporation, Massachusetts Institute of Technology, Phillips Consumer Electronics, David Sarnoff

Table 1: ATSC Digital Standard A/53E Supported Formats

HDTV/SDTV	Horizontal lines	Vertical lines	Aspect ratio	Frame rate
SDTV	640	480	4:3	23.976p, 24p, 29.97p, 30p, 59.94p, 60p, 59.94i, 60i
SDTV	704	480	4:3 and 16:9	23.976p, 24p, 29.97p, 30p, 59.94p, 60p, 59.94i, 60i
HDTV	1280	720	16:9	23.976p, 24p, 29.97p, 30p, 59.94p, 60p
HDTV	1920	1080	16:9	23.976p, 24p, 29.97p, 30p, 59.94i, 60i, 60p

i = *interlaced*, p = *progressive*

Research Center, Thomson Consumer Electronics, and Zenith Electronics Corporation. The Grand Alliance built a working prototype of an HDTV terrestrial broadcasting system that used MPEG-2 compression. After a series of testing, the ATSC proposed DTV Standard A/53 that specified the protocol for high-definition broadcasting through a standard 6-MHz channel. DTV Standard A/52 outlined the use of digital audio through Dolby Digital, or AC-3, compression.

In December 1996, the FCC adopted most of the standards proposed by the ATSC, mandating that broadcasters begin broadcasting digitally. According to the ATSC, within one year of the November 1, 1998 rollout, more than 50 percent of the U.S. population was in a position to receive digital broadcasts. During a transitional period, television would be broadcast both digitally under the FCC's digital terrestrial television guidelines and through traditional analog means. Congress has voted to terminate analog broadcasting by February 2009, although the deadline could be extended.

DIGITAL TELEVISION, STANDARD DEFINITION TELEVISION, AND HIGH-DEFINITION TELEVISION

Although the NTSC standards defined one analog format, ATSC created a framework supporting several digital formats. The ATSC's DTV broadcasting standards provide for SDTV and HDTV programming using several possible frame rates. Because the technology is relatively new, there is a considerable amount of confusion among consumers regarding HDTV. DTV broadcasts can be either high definition or standard definition. SDTV can use either the 4:3 or 16:9 aspect ratios, but HDTV always uses the 16:9 aspect ratio (see Table 1).

Comparison to Standard Definition Television

Assuming an NTSC standard definition display of approximately 640 × 480 pixels, a 1080 × 1920 HDTV image has nearly seven times more pixels (see Figure 1). But in addition to the greater visual detail that the increased pixels provide, there are many other notable improvements that contribute to a heightened viewing experience. The delivery method of ATSC programming is considered to be an improvement over that of the NTSC. Analog television is susceptible to interference such as ghosting and

snow. DTV is digitally compressed; although not immune to all interference, such compression does eliminate a great deal of broadcast-related distortion. Because the signal is digital, the data either arrive perfectly intact or are noticeably absent.

Another improved element is audio. The ATSC standards call for AC-3, or Dolby Digital, sound; this can provide 5.1 surround sound as well as provide support for multiple audio bit streams. This allows broadcasters to deliver programming in multiple languages.

TECHNICAL ASPECTS
Codecs

Codec is short for both *compressor-decompressor* and *coder-decoder* and refers to a manner in which data are compressed and uncompressed. Compression can be achieved with software, hardware, or a combination of the two. In uncompressed form, a 1920 × 1080 HDTV signal requires nearly 1 Gigabyte per second (Gbps) of bandwidth. A *high-definition serial digital interface* (HD-SDI), specified by SMPTE 292M,* can carry high-definition video, as many as sixteen channels of embedded audio, and ancillary data at a nominal data rate of 1.485 Gbps. To squeeze the data into a form that can be reliably broadcast within a 6-MHz section of bandwidth, the signal must be compressed approximately at a 50:1 ratio. The ATSC DTV standard conforms to the main profile syntax of MPEG-2 compression standard.

As used in the current distribution of digital television, MPEG-2 uses *interframe* compression, which compresses both spatially and temporally. *Intraframe* codecs such as those for digital video (DV) treat each frame individually and thus only compress spatially. Because MPEG-2 can compress over time as well as space, it is capable of delivering a high-quality image in a smaller amount of bandwidth than an intraframe codec can deliver. A great deal of MPEG-2's efficiency is because it compresses the video into *groups of pictures* (GOPs) and not simply individual frames. In MPEG-2 compression, images are divided into *macroblocks*, which are typically areas of 16 × 16 pixels. The GOPs are created with three types of pictures: I, P, and B frames. *I frames* are intracoded frames, which are sometimes referred to as *index frames*. *P frames* are

---

*A standard developed by the Society of Motion Picture and Television Engineers.

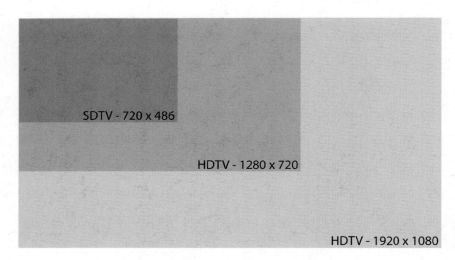

SDTV - 720 x 486

HDTV - 1280 x 720

HDTV - 1920 x 1080

Figure 1: Comparison of standard and high definition video formats (illustration courtesy of Tabletop Productions)

predicted frames, and *B frames* are bidirectional frames. A GOP starts with an I frame. In MPEG-2 compression, P frames are compared to the previous I or P frame. If there is a difference, a proper vector is determined to move the macroblock. If there is no change (if there is no movement within the shot), the bit rate can be reduced significantly. B frames work similarly but reference previous and future frames.

Some compression methods use intraframe compression, which treats every frame individually, compressing one after the next. These types of compressors such as M-JPEG or DV, facilitate editing because each frame is independent of the others and can be accessed at any point in the stream. Because MPEG-2 breaks the video stream into chunks known as GOPs, ease of editing is reduced in favor of maximizing compression. Although MPEG-2 is perhaps ideal for transmission, its multiframe GOP structure is not optimized for editing. It is possible to edit MPEG-2 without recompression as long as an edit point resides on a GOP boundary.

Metadata

DTV broadcasts with MPEG-2 also provide for *metadata* to be included along with the signal. Metadata are auxiliary information related to the program or its content and can include information such as audio dialog level data, closed captioning content, format descriptor tags, and *digital rights management* (DRM) data. Metadata can be processed at many stages along the delivery path.

Interlaced versus Progressive Scanning

An NTSC video signal is made up of 525 scan lines. On a CRT display, the image is created by an electron beam that excites phosphors on the face of the screen. The electron beam scans each row from left to right and then jumps back to draw the next line. The excited phosphors on CRT displays decay quickly after the electron beam makes its sweep. Because of the decay, images displayed at about 30 fps present a noticeable flicker. To reduce the flicker, the display frequency had to be increased. To achieve this, the frame was broken down into two fields. The first field displays only the odd lines, while the second displays only the even lines. So, instead of drawing approximately 30 fps, interlacing uses two fields, one after the next, at the rate of nearly 60 times a second.

Interlacing creates some unfortunate visible artifacts. Visual elements with fine horizontal lines will tend to flicker when displayed. In addition, capturing still frames or creating slow-motion effects shows temporal artifacts because the two fields have not been captured simultaneously, but 1/60th of 1 second apart. Other problems can occur when converting footage shot at 24 fps into 60-Hz interlaced fields.

By contrast, in progressively scanned video, the entire frame is captured all at once without two separate fields (see Figure 2).

Frame Rates

The ATSC standards bring new possible frame rates and also provide the ability to comply with existing,

Field 1 is sampled first and contains only the odd lines.

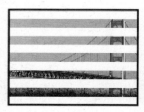

Field 2 sampled 1/60th of a second later contains the even-lines.

A complete frame consists of field 1 and field 2.

Figure 2: Interlaced scanning. For illustrative purposes, the number of scan lines has been greatly reduced (illustration courtesy of Tabletop Productions)

traditional standards. Broadcast video under the NTSC standards employs an interlaced frame composed of two separate fields. As stated earlier, for technical reasons the refresh rate was reduced from 60 Hz to 59.94 Hz. In common terminology and documentation, sometimes the true 29.97 or 59.94 frame rates are used but often this figure is rounded up for the sake of convenience: 29.97 becomes 30 and 59.94 becomes 60. Because of this and the fact that the frame-numbering protocol used in time code is based on the rate of 30 fps, many people mistakenly think that the NTSC frame rate is a whole number. ATSC standards support both the NTSC 0.1-percent reduced frame rates as well as whole-integer frame rates of 24, 30, and 60.

Frame rate has a direct impact on the bandwidth required to carry a signal. A 60p signal would require approximately twice the bandwidth needed by a 60i signal.

One frame rate that is appealing to digital video cinematographers is 24p because it has been the standard film frame rate used by the motion picture industry for decades. This lessens the steps and expense required to transfer a copy to film for theatrical release and also helps the video look more like film.

Color Space

Computer-based digital imaging systems typically operate in an RGB color space or a variant of it. Broadcast video transmission, however, adopted a color difference model not only because the signal had to be compatible with existing black-and-white televisions but also because it had to take up as little bandwidth as possible. Most professional video cameras (both SDTV and HDTV) capture images into an RGB color space via three *charge-coupled devices* (CCDs). However, a growing number of cameras are using *complementary metal oxide semiconductor* (CMOS) sensors. Initially captured in uncompressed form, the RGB values are processed and converted into a color difference mode.

In the color difference system, the color signal can be numerically represented with three values: Y, B-Y, and R-Y. Mathematically, Y represents the value of the luma portion; B-Y and R-Y represent the two color difference values. The formulas used to derive the color difference values vary depending on the application. YIQ was the color-encoding system originally developed for NTSC while YUV was used for PAL. YPbPr uses a slightly different formula that is optimized for component analog video, while YCbCr uses a different scaling factor that is optimized for digital video.

Humans are more sensitive to spatial detail in brightness than in color information. Because of this, most of the important detail needed to comprehend an image is provided through the luma portion of the video signal. Engineers found they could throw out more than half of the color information and still get pleasing results. Compared to RGB, the Y, B-Y, R-Y scheme can store color data in a smaller amount of space and thus use less bandwidth when broadcast.

Color Sampling

Unless working in an uncompressed RGB mode, the color signal is converted into a color difference system. After converting the RGB, the signal is sampled, quantized, compressed (usually), and then recorded to tape, hard drive, optical disk, or, in some cases, a memory card.

Color-sampling figures convey the manner in which the luma and color components are sampled for digitizing and are typically presented as a ratio with three figures: x:x:x. The first figure is usually "4" and refers to the number of luma samples. The second two figures correspond to the number of samples for the two color difference signals. For instance, DV's 4:1:1 states that for every four luma samples, only one sample is taken for each of the color difference samples. A 4:2:2 format (such as DVC Pro50 or digital Betacam) means that for every four luma samples taken, two samples will be taken of each of the color difference signals. A 4:1:1 format would record half of the color information that a 4:2:2 format would. When a codec is represented by a 4:4:4, it is typically referring to an RGB signal.

The 4:2:0 color sampling format comes in a few different variants. As usually employed in MPEG-2, the color difference signals are sampled at half the rate of the luma samples but also reduced in half vertically.

Although formats using lower color-sampling ratios require less bandwidth, those with higher sampling ratios are preferred for professional editing, keying, and compositing.

Quantization

After sampling, the signal must be quantized—that is, assigned a numerical value. The number of quanta corresponds to bit depth. Video signals are usually captured into 8-bit or 10-bit per color channel formats. An 8-bit sample has 256 possible values, while a 10-bit sample has 1024 possible values. Generally speaking, a 10-bit sample will take more storage space but offer more contrast information.

Format Conversion

Because of the numerous types of media and formats in use, it is often necessary to convert from one type of format to another. *Transcoders* provide a means for doing so. Some can convert analog signals into digital (referred to as *A to D*) or digital into analog (*D to A*). Others provide a means to provide pulldown, de-interlacing, upconverting, and downconverting. *Upconverting* occurs when content is transferred to a superior format. *Downconverting* is copying to a format of lesser quality—for example, downconverting HD footage into SD footage. Sometimes it is necessary to manipulate the visual or pixel aspect ratio or change the image size (scaling). Other common transcoding tasks include changing the format temporally (vary the frame rate) and interlacing or de-interlacing the image. Bidirectional interfaces allow transfers from one format to another, such as from HD-SDI to analog component or SDI to HDMI.

Aspect Ratio Conversion

One benefit of HDTV is that its aspect ratio more closely matches that of widescreen film formats. Its 16:9 or 1.78:1 aspect ratio is close, but not quite as wide as the

Table 2 Common Aspect Ratios

Common Aspect Ratios	
Aspect Ratio	Application
4:3 or 1.33:1	Traditional television and 16 mm and 35 mm film
1.37:1	Academy aperture
16:9 or 1.78:1	Widescreen television
1.85:1	Standard theatrical widescreen
2.20:1	70 mm
2.40:1	CinemaScope

popular 35-mm anamorphic widescreen (see Table 2 and Figure 3). Some may argue that the widescreen format is at a disadvantage for playing old movies such as *The Wizard of Oz* or *Gone with the Wind,* but in general widescreen formats have become more favored for film since the 1950s.

Although HDTV content is designed to fill a 16:9 frame, the display of programming from other sources with varying aspect ratios is also possible. Programs shot in the 4:3 aspect ratio or in wider cinematic formats can easily be displayed inside a 16:9 frame without distortion by shrinking the image. Unfortunately, it is quite common to see broadcasters delivering images with the improper aspect ratio (example A of Figure 4). Traditional 4:3 content is ideally viewed on widescreen displays by presenting the image as large as possible and centered within the frame (example B). This is sometimes referred to as *pillar boxing.* This allows the original image to be seen as it was intended. Some broadcasters magnify the 4:3 image so that it fills the entire 16:9 frame (example C). This can often be identified by the lack of headroom. Content from cinematic formats with wider aspect ratios can be accurately displayed within the 16:9 frame with *letterboxing* (example D). It is also frequently necessary

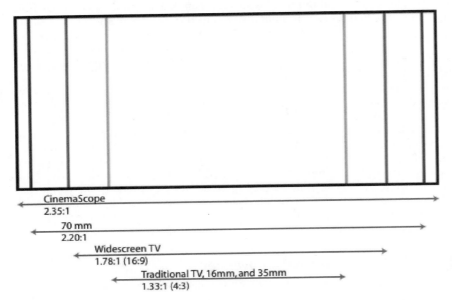

CinemaScope
2.35:1

70 mm
2.20:1

Widescreen TV
1.78:1 (16:9)

Traditional TV, 16mm, and 35mm
1.33:1 (4:3)

Figure 3: Common aspect ratios (illustration courtesy of Tabletop Productions)

Example A 4:3 content improperly displayed within a 16:9 frame. The image has been stretched to fill the entire frame.

Example B 4:3 content properly displayed in the center of the 16:9 frame.

Example C 4:3 content scaled up in order to fill the entire 16:9 frame.

Example D Content from a 70mm film with a 2.20:1 aspect ratio letterboxed within the 16:9 frame.

Figure 4: Content with varying aspect ratios displayed within a 16:9 frame (images courtesy of Table top Productions)

to present widescreen programming inside of traditional 4:3 displays with letterboxing.

The ATSC standard supports an *active format descriptor* (AFD) data tag that can be embedded into the encoded video. The AFD data tag describes the aspect ratio of the signal when it does not extend to the edges of the frame. If utilized, the receiver or set top box can decode the AFD data tag and display the signal with the proper aspect ratio.

The 3-2 Pulldown

A common frame conversion task is required by the frequent need to change 24p content into 60i. Such is the case when converting film (which runs at 24 fps) into 60i. This 3-2 *pulldown*, sometimes called the *telecine process*, is also required when changing 24p video into 60i. Some systems employ a 2-3 pulldown; although reversing the order, this achieves the same end result.

The basic idea between the 3-2 pulldown is that four frames of 24p footage are converted into five interlaced video frames. It is called 3-2 (or 2-3) because each consecutive 24p frame is transferred into two fields followed by three fields, then two fields, and so on. One step is to slow the film down by 0.1 percent to the rate of 23.976 frames per second. In Figure 5, we have four frames of 24p material, labeled A, B, C, and D. The first video frame contains two fields of frame A. The second video frame contains one field of A and the second field of B. The third video frame contains one field of B and one of C. The fourth video frame contains two frames of C. The fifth video frame contains two fields of D.

IMPLEMENTATION

The HDTV production chain typically begins with a high-definition camera or a project shot on film that is then converted to a digital format. However, other means are possible. Much of director Tim Burton's recent stop-motion feature film *The Corpse Bride* was shot with a Canon digital still camera and then transferred to digital video for editing. Many commercials, cartoons, and full-length features have been created solely with two-dimensional or three-dimensional animation software.

Cameras

HDTV cameras were used long before the ATSC standards were in place. Because of the move to DTV and the growing acceptance of HDTV by consumers, many broadcasters are choosing to replace retired or existing standard definition equipment with high-definition camera gear. Although higher-end production cameras suitable for studio or digital cinematography can cost more than $200,000 apiece, many professional HD camcorders used for daily production tasks can be found between $20,000 and $60,000. Recently, a few companies have released HDTV camcorders priced less than $1500 targeted to consumers. Generally speaking, camcorders with high-quality lenses that are capable of writing higher data rates and recording images up to 1920 × 1080 pixels in varying frame rates occupy the higher end of the price range. Camcorders with lower-quality optics that use lower data rates, GOP-based compression, and have fewer frame rate options can be found at the lower end of the price range.

Recording and Playback Formats

Recording, storage, and playback of HDTV content can be done in several ways. As in standard definition digital video, the data can be written to tape, hard drive, optical disk, or random access memory (RAM). The following are some of the more popular formats currently used for high-definition video production. (Refer to Table 3 for side-by-side comparisons.)

D-VHS

The D-VHS consumer format from JVC records onto VHS tapes using an MPEG-2 stream at as high as a 28.2-Mbps data rate. It is backward-compatible with VHS appealing

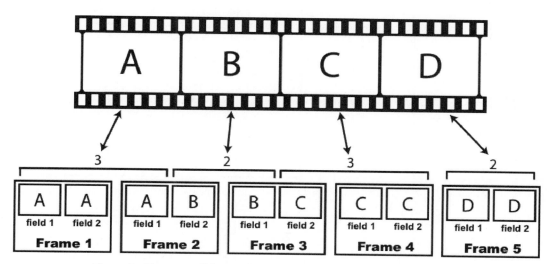

Figure 5: The 3-2 pulldown (illustration courtesy Tabletop Productions)

Table 3: Comparison of HD Field and Production Formats

Name	Format	Pixel dimensions (recorded)	Color sampling	Bit depth	Compression	Data rate	Audio channels
HDV	1080 60i 1080 50i 720 60p 720 50p 720 30p 720 24p	1440 × 1080 1280 × 720	4:2:0 4:2:0	8 8	MPEG-2 MPEG-2	25 Mbps 19.7 Mbps	2 2
XDCAM HD	1080 60i 1080 50i 1080 30p 1080 25p 1080 24p	1440 × 1080	4:2:0	8	MPEG-2	Adjustable: 18 Mbps 25 Mbps 35 Mbps	4
D9-HD	1080 60i 720 24p	1280 × 1080 960 × 720	4:2:2	8	DCT	100 Mbps	8
DVCPRO HD (D12)	1080 60i 1080 50i 720 60p 720 50p	1280 × 1080 1440 × 1080 960 × 720	4:2:2	8	DCT	100 Mbps	8
D5 HD	1080 60i 1080 30p 1080 24p 720 60p	1920 × 1080 1280 × 720	4:2:2	8 10	DCT	235 Mbps	8
HDCAM (D11)	1080 60i 1080 50i 1080 25p 1080 24p	1440 × 1080	3:1:1	8	DCT	140 Mbps	4
HDCAM SR	1080i 60 1080i 50 1080PsF 30 1080PsF 29.97 1080PsF 25 1080PsF 24 1080PsF 23.98 720p	1920 × 1080	4:2:2 at 440 Mbps 4:4:4 at 880 Mbps	10	MPEG-4	440 Mbps	12

to consumers with sizable VHS tape collections. It is not considered a viable commercial production format.

HDV

Canon, Sony, and JVC offer lower cost HDV cameras that record at a maximum resolution of 1440 × 1080. HDV uses a form of MPEG-2 compression that can be recorded onto mini-DV cassettes. In 1080i mode, HDV can record a 25-Mbps signal. In 720p mode, it records at 19 Mbps. Because MPEG-2 employs GOPs instead of discrete frames, HDV data is often upconverted into a different format for editing. Because the data rate is relatively low, HDV content can easily be transferred over a FireWire (IEEE-1394) connection.

DVCPRO HD

Also known as D12, DVCPRO HD was developed by Panasonic and has versions that record on magnetic tape as well as to memory cards. The 100-Mbps data rate is still low enough to be transferred over a FireWire connection from a videotape recorder into an editing system. DVCPRO HD is restricted to a maximum resolution of 1280 × 1080 pixels.

XDCAM HD

Sony's tapeless XDCAM HD format records onto Blu-Ray optical disks using several possible frame rates and codecs. It can record HD content using MPEG-2 encoding at 35 Mbps or DVCAM at 25 Mbps. Its HD resolution is restricted to 1440 × 1080 pixels.

D-5 HD

Developed by Panasonic in 1991, the D-5 format has been updated to HD. It records at a 235-Mbps data rate and can handle 720 and 1080 content at most possible frame rates.

HDCAM

Sony's HDCAM format records onto 1/2-inch videocassettes at several possible frame rates. It uses a 140-Mbps data rate and supports as many as four channels of audio. It, too, is restricted to a maximum resolution of 1440 × 1080 pixels.

HDCAM SR

Sony's higher end version of HDCAM shares some of the same features but can write data rates as high as 880 Mbps with as many as twelve audio channels.

Editing

Although linear, tape-to-tape editing is still viable (and sometimes best suited for the job), most editors work with computer-based, nonlinear editing systems. With dozens of vendors making HD-capable editing systems, many codecs are available. Some require proprietary hardware to use, while others are hardware-independent. In addition to the standard 8- and 10-bit depths, there are also higher-end, 16-bit codecs available from companies such as Pinnacle and Digital Anarchy.

Although HDTV is routinely compressed using MPEG-2 for transmission and delivery, uncompressed or mildly compressed data are preferred for editing. Because it is often necessary for editors to composite many layers of content together in order to create special effects, the signal must be kept as pristine as possible. This is why editors will often upconvert footage to a codec with better bit depth and higher resolution.

Video Capture

HDTV data may be brought into a computer through FireWire, HD-SDI, or digital or analog component capture. Footage can be transferred into an editing system bit for bit, or it can be encoded into a codec that is more suitable for editing. A detailed discussion of HD editing codecs is outside the scope of this chapter, but color space, bit depth, and compression are three factors that should be considered along with the overall format and frame rate. In addition, certain broadcast channels or clients have precise technical requirements that may affect the choice of codecs. As mentioned previously, 10-bit files contain more information than 8-bit files but also require more storage. Projects with demanding chroma-keying or color-compositing needs will be better served by codes with higher color sampling ratios (4:2:2 over 4:1:1, etc.). Similarly, compressed footage requires less bandwidth at the trade-off of some quality loss. Lastly, choosing a lossless codec that operates in a 4:4:4 resolution will offer the highest quality but at the expense of requiring the greatest amount of storage.

Video Storage, Servers, and Networks

In uncompressed form, HDTV content requires more disk space than standard definition video and a larger bandwidth to access or deliver media. Consider this comparison. An hour of standard definition DV footage with a stereo pair of 16-bit audio tracks captured at 25 Mbps takes approximately 14 Gb of disk space. An hour of 10-bit 1920 × 1080 HD footage with a pair of 24-bit audio channels requires nearly 600 Gb of space. The same footage captured in RGB uncompressed would fill almost 900 Gb.

Video editing, production, and broadcast delivery systems often require several streams of video to be accessed simultaneously. As well as providing access to multiple users, HDTV data must be safeguarded in some way. A common approach to this utilizes network-based storage architecture. Typical systems incorporate a video server that allows for multiple connections and interfaces with a *redundant array of independent disks* (RAID) storage device. Although HD content can be stored and retrieved over standard or Fast Ethernet connections, the high bandwidth and constant throughput required to deliver HD in professional applications requires the use of fibre channel or 10-Gigabit Ethernet. Architecture for storage systems will likely be based on a *storage area network* (SAN) or *network attached storage* (NAS). Either way, they will likely rely on RAID storage. RAIDs use multiple hard drives in a single enclosure that are written to and read simultaneously. Common RAIDs used for HD storage are the following:

- RAID 0 stripes the data across two or more disks. No parity information for redundancy is recorded, so there is no protection offered against data loss. If one drive goes out, all of the data are lost.

- RAID 3 uses at least three or more drives. Parity information is recorded on one of the disks while the data are striped evenly across the other drives. RAID 3 arrays can be backed up with relative ease if one of the drives goes bad.
- RAID 5 contains three or more drives per set. Parity information is stored on all of the drives equally. RAID 5 sets can generally handle data transfers more quickly than can RAID 3.
- RAID 50 (5 + 0) uses two or more RAID 5 sets striped together into a single RAID 0. Each RAID 5 element typically is on an individual controller. RAID 50 provides an excellent mix of fast read and write speeds and redundancy.

Display Technologies

HDTV content can be viewed using several different technologies including the aforementioned CRT, *liquid crystal display* (LCD), plasma, *digital light processing* (DLP), and *liquid crystal on silicon* (LCoS). Displays can be "direct view" with the image generated on the screen's surface or projected from the front or rear. Each technology has its strengths and weaknesses. Although some experts argue that traditional CRT displays are the best means to accurately monitor color, their vacuum tube construction ultimately renders them unsuitable for large, widescreen displays. Because of their limitations, other microdisplay technologies such as LCD, plasma, DLP, and LCoS have gained favor in both consumer and professional markets. In addition to these, there are other viable HDTV display technologies including *organic light-emitting diode, grating light valve, nano-emissive*, and *surface-conductive electron emitter* displays.

Besides pixel resolution, important factors to consider when comparing different displays include contrast, brightness, and color. In addition, how well the displays scale and de-interlace images is significant. These factors ultimately determine why some displays look better than others or are more suitable for a particular installation or location.

CRT

CRT monitors draw the lines one after the next, from top to bottom, to make an entire frame. Generally speaking, they have pleasing color balance performance and wide viewing angles. Because of their use of vacuum tubes, the displays cannot be constructed much larger than 40 inches or so. They weigh more than the other types of displays, use a significant amount of power, and generate heat. Rear-projection monitors typically use three CRTs (red, green, and blue) that converge onto a projection screen. Rear-projection CRT displays have good colors and black levels, but they are heavy, take up sizable amounts of room, and suffer from low output and limited viewing angles. Front-projection systems offer excellent resolution and are still favored by many people but are large and require periodic maintenance to ensure proper convergence and focus.

LCD

LCD HDTV monitors work by casting light through an array of cells sandwiched between two polarized planes. LCD monitors come in both flat-panel and rear-projection varieties. Flat-panel, direct-view monitors have become popular as computer and DTV monitors because of their brightness, high contrast, and relatively long life span. Traditionally, LCDs have had a slower response time and lessened viewing angles than their CRT counterparts, but their speed and angle of view have been improved in recent years. Unlike plasma monitors, LCDs do not suffer from *burn-in* damage that results when a static or constantly illuminated image area begins to dim over time.

Plasma

Like LCD monitors, plasma HDTV sets are thin and are made of cells that correspond to pixels sandwiched between glass plates. Plasma cells contain three separate gas-filled subcells, one for each color. When a current is applied to a subcell, it ionizes the gas-emitting ultraviolet light. The ultraviolet light in turn excites fluorescent substances in the subcells that emit red, blue, or green light. Compared to LCD, plasma sets can cost more but have larger viewing angles. Although they also can suffer from low-level noise in dark material, in general they have deeper blacks. Some older plasma sets suffered from burn-in and limited life spans, but these have been improved in recent years.

DLP

Digital light processing is a technology used in projection displays. In DLP monitors, light is reflected off an array of microscopic hinged mirrors. Each tiny mirror corresponds to a visible pixel. The light is channeled through a lens onto the surface of the screen. Single-chip DLP projectors can display 16.7 million colors. Although some manufacturers claim their three-chip DLP projectors can display 35 trillion colors, critics have observed that humans are only capable of discerning some 10 million.

LCoS

LCoS projection systems use liquid crystals arranged in a grid in front of a highly reflective silicon layer. The liquid crystals open and close, either allowing light to be either reflected or blocked.

Cables and Connectors

With the large and growing number of cameras, displays, recorders, and playback devices for both professional and consumer markets, numerous connection options are available. HDTV production equipment typically features digital inputs and outputs, along with legacy analog formats for both monitoring and additional I/O flexibility. Because HDTV content is digital data that are routinely stored, delivered, and processed over networked systems, standard computer connectivity such as Ethernet, WiFi, and USB can be used. Note, however, that the limited bandwidth of these connections might not support real-time delivery. In addition to the aforementioned computer connections, the following connectors are commonly used in HDTV equipment.

HD-SDI

A SMPTE 292-Mb serial digital interface (HD-SDI) connection provides for transfers up to 1.485 Gbps over a 75-ohm coaxial cable. This is a standard method of transferring an HDTV signal from one device to another, such as from a digital recorder to an editing system. As many as sixteen channels of digital audio can be delivered along with the video.

IEEE-1394: FireWire or i.Link

Created as a versatile multimedia serial bus, IEEE-1394, commonly referred to by Apple as FireWire and by Sony as i.Link, allows bidirectional connectivity between a growing number of computers and multimedia devices. Two variations of FireWire support either 400 Mbps or 800 Mbps.

Component

Both analog and digital color difference connectors can be found on HDTV equipment. In the case of digital connections, YCbCr is used. Analog uses YPbPr, with audio being handled through a separate connection.

HDMI

A *high-definition multimedia interface* (HDMI) connection can carry both multichannel audio and video through one cable. It is found on some satellite and cable boxes along with a growing number of consumer and semi-professional gear.

DVI

Digital video interface (DVI) connections are commonly found connecting computers and flat-panel displays. DVIs can be connected to HDMI with an adaptor. There are three types of DVI interfaces: (1) DVI-A contains only analog connections, (2) DVI-D only digital, and (3) DVI-I supports both analog and digital.

DisplayPort

This new display interface is physically smaller than a DVI connector and supports resolutions up to 2048 × 1536 pixels at 30 bits per pixel. It is designed to replace DVI and LVDS connectors and can be used for both external and internal display connections.

UDI

The *unified display interface* (UD) is another new interface for PCs and consumer electronic devices designed to replace the VGA standard. It is designed to be compatible with HDMI and DVI interfaces, delivering high-definition video and metadata through a single connector.

Broadcast Transmission and Reception

Overall, the traditional model of broadcast transmission over the radiofrequency spectrum is unchanged. However, DTV requires broadcasters to replace analog with digital transmission gear and consumers to upgrade to digital receivers. The new technologies and digital infrastructure are providing broadcasters with new options such as multicasting. Within a single 6-MHz section of bandwidth, a broadcaster can deliver a 1080i HDTV broadcast, offer multiple audio and video streams along with a variety of data, or both.

Reception

HDTV programming can be received via traditional terrestrial broadcast, cable, satellite, or even Internet protocol television (IPTV). To receive HDTV programming (via DTV broadcast), end users need a receiver with an ATSC-compliant tuner. Cable and satellite companies currently provide set-top tuners and demodulators. Some contain *personal video recorders* (PVRs) that are capable of recording and playing back both standard and high-definition content. Many new HDTV sets referred to as "plug and play" or "digital cable ready" can interface with the digital service providers by means of a security card (known as a *cableCARD*), which is a small card with integrated circuits that plugs into the back of the console. Interfacing with the broadcast service providers through some form of return channel is necessary in order to use services such as *pay-per-view* (PPV), *video on demand* (VOD), or, in some cases, interactive programming.

Terrestrial

This traditional over-the-air system of transmission uses radio frequencies allocated by the FCC. TV stations broadcast from a single point, or through ancillary translators or repeaters that rebroadcast the originating signal, to end users who are physically located within the station's receiving area. Reception of terrestrially broadcast DTV requires an antenna and limits the reception to those located within a TV station's service area. Although new sets are being manufactured with DTV-compatible tuners, stand-alone set-top devices will be available so that existing analog televisions can still be used. It should be noted that existing antennas would work fine for DTV broadcasts.

Cable

Cable service providers retransmit programming to end users over coaxial or optical cable. One main benefit of digital cable is the ability to offer a wide variety of programming as well as provide a broadband Internet connection. Two-way digital cable is uniquely structured, providing a built-in return channel facilitating the use of PPV, VOD, and interactive programming.

Satellite

Direct broadcast satellite (DBS) service transmits digitally compressed programming to users via small, K_u band antennas. Like cable, satellite service providers retransmit existing content and offer a variety of programming packages.

Internet Protocol Television

Interest and development is growing rapidly in IPTV, which provides DTV service over a broadband connection. Wire-service broadband providers, such as telephone companies, who have not traditionally been vested in television, seem to have the most interest in developing the technology. There is also growing interest in providing IPTV use over standard 802.11g wireless networks.

Usage and Saturation

A recent survey carried out by Panasonic in December 2005 (Broadcast Newsroom 2005) reported that 26 percent of U.S. households would own or would have purchased a high-definition set by the end of 2006. Given the imminent demise of analog broadcasting and the growth of HDTV content, it is safe to assume that figure will continue to grow.

The National Association of Broadcasters (NAB) maintains a growing list of stations that have made the move to digital broadcast. In December 2005, 1550 stations were broadcasting digitally. As of January 2006, the major commercial broadcasting networks (ABC, CBS, FOX, and NBC) had begun to offer most of their prime time programming in HD form. The Discovery Channel runs 24-hour HDTV programming, and PBS HD was expanding its schedule as well. Major satellite and cable service providers DirecTV, Dish Network, Comcast, and Insight all offer an increasing lineup of HDTV programming along with time-shifting PVRs.

IMPACT OF HIGH-DEFINITION TELEVISION

Users

According to studies, HDTV results in a heightened sense of "presence" (Bracken 2005) in viewers—that is, the viewer has a sense of being *in* the televised environment. Another aspect of presence is the degree to which the technological medium is ignored as attention becomes focused on the content. Because HDTV delivers an increased viewing experience, it is also suggested that levels of media effects will rise as well. The primary factors leading to the increased feeling of presence include screen size and image quality. Bracken's research found that subjects viewing HDTV content felt an increased feeling of immersion or involvement in the material. Participants also reported feeling a greater spatial presence of objects as well as an increased sense of the televised characters' expressions and body language.

Television Production

HDTV's wider aspect ratio and more detailed image are two elements that affect production. Sets, graphics, and other production elements that may have served well for the 4:3 aspect ratio needed to be redesigned to fill the wider space. The increased visual clarity has forced designers to spend considerably more money on sets, set dressings, and props. With the old analog system, fake, painted-on books might have served well for a bookshelf backdrop, but now viewers can see more detail so real books, or at least better paint jobs, are needed. There has been some press about the need for TV actors to invest in cosmetic surgery, or at least spend more time in makeup, because of the greater detail HDTV provides. This is mostly a myth. The likenesses of film talent have been displayed at a much greater size and with far more

clarity on large movie screens for years. By using soft lights and decreasing the angle of key lights, lighting designers can greatly reduce the appearance of wrinkles and imperfections. Contrast reduction filters also can help minimize blemishes and small shadows.

Digital Video Discs

High-definition DVD manufacturers are currently engaged in a format war, with the major contenders being Blu-Ray and HD-DVD. Both formats have considerable industry backing. The formats are similar in using the familiar 120-mm diameter CD-sized discs, but they use higher-frequency 405-nm wavelength lasers that are capable of writing and reading data more tightly together. Players of both formats are being made that are capable of reading existing analog DVDs.

Blu-Ray Discs

Single-layer Blu-Ray discs can hold approximately 25 Gb, and dual-layer discs can hold some 50 Gb writing MPEG video at data rates as high as 36 Mbps. Although the Blu-Ray lasers are not directly compatible with existing DVDs and CDs, an additional optical pickup device achieves playback.

High-Definition DVDs

The DVD Forum, an industry group whose purpose is to establish technical standards for DVD technology has sided with the HD-DVD format. Although HD-DVD players write with the same 36 Mbps rate as the Blu-Ray format, a single-sided disc can only hold 15 Gb and a dual layer disc approximately 30 Gb.

Feature Films

The era of digital cinema began when George Lucas released *The Phantom Menace* digitally to select theatres on June 18, 1999. Digital cinema replaces traditional film distribution and projection with digital delivery and projection. Digital cinema may use high-definition technology, but it is not directly tied to ATSC's DTV standards. The formats currently used in digital cinema provide even higher resolution than HDTV, including 2K (2048 × 1080) and 4K (4096 × 2160). Much of the equipment and interconnections used for HDTV production also work with digital cinema formats.

Using digital cameras to shoot a motion picture project is referred to as *digital cinematography*. Some filmmakers have resources to shoot with larger, ultrahigh definition cameras such as Panavision's Genesis, but most are opting to shoot in HDTV or with even smaller, standard-definition formats because of the mobility, ease of editing, and low cost. Digital cinematography provides filmmakers with a means to shoot, edit, and master a project in the digital realm. With digital cinema, they now have a direct path into theatrical distribution. Although some film production companies view HDTV and digital cinema as a threat, many studios are major proponents who see it as a way to reduce the costly expense of duplication and distribution. A single 35-mm film print can cost more than $1500 to produce. Other benefits include the fact that there is no loss of quality after multiple viewings and that more advertising can be run and edited more quickly and efficiently.

The 1999 *Phantom Menace* screenings used media and projectors that were only capable of producing 1280 × 1080 sized images, but current installations are using more advanced technology. The latest digital projectors are capable of displaying images with pixel dimensions of 4096 × 2160. Christie, a leading manufacturer of high-definition projectors for the digital cinema market, has agreements to install 2300 projection systems by November 2007.

CONCLUSION

As analog broadcast retires, and as broadcasters and viewers transition to DTV, HDTV programming, products, and services will continue to grow exponentially. Although both broadcasters and consumers may have experienced a few bumps as they have transitioned to DTV, the move will come more cheaply, more quickly, and more easily as products and services become more widespread and people grow accustomed to the new technology.

Savvy shoppers have already become familiar with HDTV along with the nuances of different displays and formats. According to the Consumer Electronics Association, in 2003, total dollar sales figures of HDTV sets surpassed those of analog sets. The purchasing process for uninformed consumers has been made easier by the FCC, which has required that manufacturers include ATSC-compatible digital tuners in their TVs. The FCC also has established a standard for *digital cable ready* (DCR) televisions, known as "plug and play." This allows cable subscribers to receive digital and high-definition programming without the need for a set-top box.

One interesting phenomenon is that despite advances and increased availability in HDTV gear and service, the demand for low-definition video has also increased. Although some consumers might watch the latest episode of *Lost* or *Desperate Housewives* on large HDTV sets, a growing number are downloading 320 × 240 sized versions onto their iPods and portable digital media players.

HDTV has brought a more cinematic experience into viewers' homes and, with digital cinema, delivered the film industry a few of the benefits of television. However, HDTV has much lower resolution than 70-mm film. It is only a matter of time before some will begin pressuring for another increase in quality.

GLOSSARY

Aspect ratio: A ratio of screen width compared to height.

Bandwidth: The amount of data that can be sent through a signal path.

Digital TV (DTV): A standardized system of transmission and reception of digital television over radio frequencies.

Downconvert: Converting a higher-resolution format into a lesser-resolution format.

High-definition TV (HDTV): A high level of DTV that is capable of displaying 720p or 1080i television content using a 16 × 9 aspect ratio.

Interlace scan: A technique used in NTSC broadcasts in which a television image is created with two separate fields.

Letterboxing: The effect of an image presented in a display with a narrower aspect ratio. When this occurs, horizontal black bars are visible at the top and bottom of the screen.

Metadata: In the digital television context, refers to data about the programming such as start and stop times, titles, and information on the following show.

MPEG-2: A version of the MPEG video file format used to deliver digital video (from *Moving Picture Experts Group*).

Multicast: When a broadcaster splits its bandwidth into separate channels or program streams.

Personal video recorder (PVR): A digital recorder that allows a user to record, store, and playback video such as television broadcasts from a hard drive.

Progressive scanning: Method of scanning all of the scan lines from top to bottom sequentially without two interlaced fields.

Standard definition TV (SDTV): The lowest quality level of DTV that is capable of displaying 480i television content.

Upconvert: Converting a lower-resolution format into a higher-resolution format.

Widescreen: Term that describes displays with an aspect ratio greater than 4:3.

CROSS REFERENCES

See *Digital Transmission*; *Multimedia Streaming*; *Video Compression*; *Video Conferencing*.

REFERENCES

Bracken, C. C. 2005. Presence and image quality: The case of high-definition television. *Media Psychology*, 7(2): 191–205.

British Broadcasting Corporation. Undated. Online article available at www.bbc.co.uk/history/historic_figures/baird_logie.shtml.

Broadcast Newsroom. 2005. Online article available at www.broadcastnewsroom.com/articles/viewarticle.jsp?id=36377.

ADDITIONAL RESOURCES

Advanced Television Systems Committee: www.atsc.org/
Consumer Electronics Association (CEA): www.ce.org/
DTV Digital Television (an informational site run by the FCC): www.dtv.gov
Federal Communications Commission: www.fcc.gov/
HDV Organization: www.hdv-info.org/
HDTV Magazine: www.hdtvmagazine.com/
Museum of Television (Toronto, Ontario): www.mztv.com
TV Technology: www.tvtechnology.com/

PART 2

Hardware, Media, and Data Transmission

Modems

Darren B. Nicholson and Jennifer A. Nicholson, *Rowan University*

INTRODUCTION

Few would disagree that the emergence of tele- and data-communication technologies—specifically, the ability to both transmit and receive voice, video, and data—has had profound impacts on both our personal and professional lives. Although many have contributed to the progression of modern-day communication networks, the works of Samuel Morse and Alexander Graham Bell (i.e., Morse code and the telephone network, respectively) provide the foundation for much of the last mile, or local loop, communication infrastructure in use today. In other words, the same basic physical circuitry between residential homes and a telephone company's central or end office remains unchanged. Thus, even in today's technology-driven economy, consumer-based, network-capable technologies (e.g., computers, video games), although digital in nature, continue to utilize, at least in the last mile, both guided and wireless analog-based circuitry (e.g., dialup, cable, wireless). As such, translational protocols and devices are necessary.

In this chapter, we discuss one such device: the modem. Modems first emerged as a communication solution to the binary-analog dichotomy that existed between computer data and existing voice-grade circuits. Specifically, computers produce binary or discrete data (e.g., 1's and 0's), whereas the existing telephone circuitry and hardware are designed to transmit analog data—that is, data that are continuous in nature and constantly varying. Essentially, to transmit discrete data over voice-grade circuits, digital data must be *modulated* or converted to analog signals. Similarly, the receiving computer requires that all incoming analog signals be *demodulated*—that is, converted back to binary data. As such, the term *modem* emerged as a contraction of these two primary functions—modulation and demodulation—and traditionally has been defined as any physical, networking device that allows computers, or other binary-based

technologies, to transmit data over standard telephone or plain old telephone service (POTS) lines.

With the proliferation of the Internet and World Wide Web, the definition of modems, like many other networking technologies, has evolved. For example, Horak (2002, p.182) writes, "Modems modulate and demodulate signals. In other words, they change the characteristics of the signal in some way." From this definition, the term *modem* subsumes any device that meaningfully modifies data for the purposes of transmission. In this chapter, the traditional definition is used to refer to dialup modems, while Horak's definition is used to accommodate broadband modems (e.g., cable, DSL, and wireless).

The chapter begins by providing a brief historical perspective. This is followed by a high-level discussion of how dialup modems work. We then classify modems on several salient dimensions: their architecture, locality, mode of transmission, and synchronization. Following this, modem protocols, or standards, are discussed and presented (e.g., data flow, data rate, compression, and error checking). Subsequently, we present and summarize what we term here as *next-generation modems* (e.g., wireless, cable, optical). Finally, last mile connectivity technologies and trends are discussed.

HISTORICAL PERSPECTIVE

In this section, we present a succinct history of modems. For a comprehensive historical review, see AT&T (undated "Milestones," undated "History"), Green (2000), and Horak (2002).

Modems were first introduced and used in the government sector in the 1950s, specifically as a data transmission solution for the North American Air Defense Command (NORAD). Mainstream commercial usage of modems began with AT&T's introduction of the Bell 103 in 1962. Initially, modems were primarily used for connecting remote terminals to servers and mainframes.

Until the mid-1980s, modem speeds (signals per second or baud) and data rates (bits per second or bps) made little progress (300 to1200 bps). This slow advancement was principally because of the dominant host-based application architecture and lack of standards. In other words, other than the presentation logic, the server or mainframe performed all primary application functions (e.g., data storage, data access, application logic). However, as application architectures evolved (e.g., client-based and client server–based), and as standardization became a central theme, data rates advanced more quickly.

By the mid-1980s, many of the signaling, fallback, error-detection and -correction, and standardization hurdles were overcome (these, and many of the other terms used herein, are defined in the glossary or discussed in greater detail in the sections that follow). During this same time period, new modulation (e.g., amplitude, frequency, and phase) and echo cancellation techniques were also being successfully employed. As a result, data transmission speeds of 9600 bps became commonplace.

The 1990s were a time of great advancement. As the Internet and World Wide Web continued to proliferate, engineers began experimenting with ways to increase modem speeds beyond the limits of purely analog-based modems (e.g., V.34+). By this time, with the exception of the local loop, virtually all of the telephone circuitry in the *public switched telephone network* (PSTN) was digital. It was thus reasoned that if the transmission remained digital between central or end offices, the data throughput rates could be dramatically increased. In other words, it would meaningfully reduce the number of digital-to-analog conversions and, as a result, reduce the amount of data that would be compromised or lost during each conversion (a bit of data is compromised or lost during each digital-to-analog conversion). From this logic, the V.90 and V.92 standards were born, and data rates went from 14,400 bps in early 1990 to 56,000 bps by the end of the decade.

These advancements, like earlier modem technologies, were immediately embraced by the International Telecommunications Union (ITU), and became the recognized international standard (V.90 and later V.92) by the turn of the century. It is believed that the V.92 standard, or 56K(Kbps), is the maximum—or, at the very least, the penultimate—data rate possible for dialup modems given the dedicated bandwidth (4000 Hz) and Federal Communications Commission (FCC) power limitations of voice-grade circuits on the local loop, which limit the maximum download transmission rate to 53 Kbps.

In the next section, we discuss dialup modem components and their functionality.

MODEM FUNCTIONALITY

In the most general sense, modems are used to modify binary or digital data in some way that affords transmission over guided (e.g., twisted-pair, coax) or wireless (e.g., radio, infrared, microwave) media. Although transparent to the network user, traditional dialup modems automatically dial and redial, monitor call progress, negotiate and agree on protocols and features (known as the "handshake"), and terminate calls. Figure 1 illustrates the process of modulating and transmitting digital data with a dialup modem via the analog local loop and digital PSTN. What follows is a discussion of the V.92 dialup modem standard, as well as its key features and components.

The V.90/92 standards became the first *hybrid*, or analog-digital, modems. Essentially, V.90/92 series modems increased data rates beyond purely analog modems (e.g., V.34+) through the use of *pulse code modulation* (PCM), specifically by inverting the codec process. The term *codec* derives from a contraction of the device's two primary functions: to code and to decode (that is, a codec at each central or end office is employed to digitize analog voice signals as well as decode digitized voice signals back into their analog counterparts for the purpose of transmitting voice data over the PSTN). Instead of sampling analog voice signals 8000 times per second via one of 256 quantizing levels (the number of levels deemed necessary to digitize the human voice without degradation), V.90/92 modems are engineered to recognize 8-bit digital symbols (any of the 256 possible amplitudes, or sample heights, used in PCM) 8000 times per second.

As such, current V.92 modems are designed to provide downstream speeds as high as 56 Kbps—that is, (8 bits − 1 control bit) × (8000 samples per second) = 56 Kbps—and upstream speeds as high as 48 Kbps. Note, however, that actual transmission speeds are limited by both regulatory

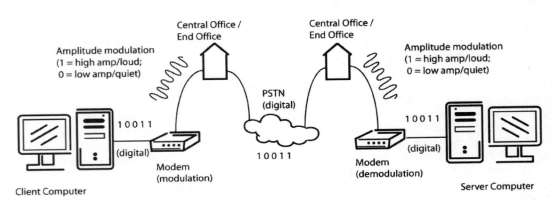

Figure 1: Modem example

conditions (e.g., the FCC in North America) and circuit conditions (the latter is discussed to a greater extent in the section titled "Modem Standards"). As such, transmission speeds rarely if ever reach these theoretical transmission rates. In addition to reversing the codec process, the V.92 standard also supports many new features such as quick connect, modem on hold, PCM upstream, and V.44 data compression. The *quick connect* feature reduces the initial handshake time from 30 seconds to 10 to 20 seconds. The *modem-on-hold* feature allows users to accept incoming voice calls without compromising or releasing their data connection. *PCM upstream* affords both the transmitter and receiver the option to receive PCM schemes so that data transmission speeds can, in theory, reach data rates as high as 56 Kbps. We now turn to a discussion on the inner components of a traditional dialup modem.

In general, dialup modems have three primary components: a *microcontroller unit* (MCU), a *data pump unit* (DPU), and a *data access arrangement* (DAA).

Microcontroller Unit

The MCU has four primary functions: (1) to check for errors in the data (V.42), (2) to compress the data (V.44), (3) to provide fax capabilities, and (4) to convert parallel transmissions into serial transmissions when needed. If the modem is Hayes-compatible (see Wikipedia 2006 "Hayes"), then the MCU utilizes the Hayes AT command set to control the modem—that is, to send and receive data. When the MCU finishes processing, it transfers data to the DPU.

Data Pump Unit

The *data pump unit* (DPU) has three key parts: *random access memory* (RAM); *read-only memory* (ROM), or *electrically erasable programmable ROM* (EEPROM); and a *digital signal processor* (DSP). The DPU receives initial instructions from ROM, and it uses RAM for temporary storage during calculations. The DPU is responsible for modulation and echo cancellation—that is, it is responsible

for converting the binary data to analog data. When the DPU finishes processing, the data are sent to the DAA.

Data Access Arrangement

The *data access arrangement* (DAA) is the modem's physical interface to POTS lines. Essentially, it is a female, voice-grade, RJ-11 telephone jack.

The process described above is based on a transmission sequence. Note that the receiving sequence or process, in general, would be in reverse order, and that some of the component functionalities (e.g., MCU) also would be reversed—that is, decompressed, as opposed to compressed. Figure 2 illustrates the movement, as well as the transformation, of data through the modem's MCU, DPU, and DAA.

In the next section, we discuss various traditional dialup modem classification schemes.

CLASSIFICATION SCHEMES

Dialup modems can be classified on several salient dimensions. At a functional level, they can be distinguished from one another based on their architectural configuration. Modems also can be further classified based on *locality* (internal versus external), *transmission mode* (simplex versus half-duplex versus full duplex), and *synchronicity* (asynchronous versus synchronous). Each classification scheme is discussed next.

Architecture

An architectural classification is based on whether the MCU, DPU, and DAA functionalities are part of the physical modem or part of the computer. For example, if the MCU, DPU, and DAA functions are performed solely by the modem, then it is referred to as a *controller modem*. Conversely, if the MCU, DPU, and DAA functions reside on the PC, the modem is referred to as a *software modem*. Finally, if the MCU is on the PC but the DPU and DAA reside on the modem, then it is referred to as a *controllerless modem*.

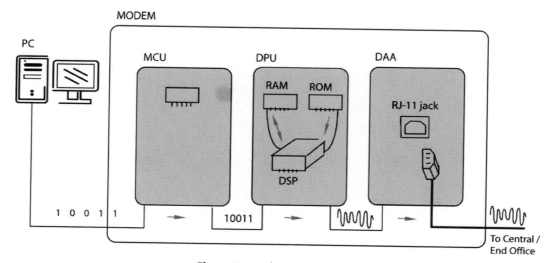

Figure 2: Modem functionality

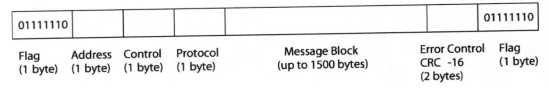

01111110						01111110
Flag (1 byte)	Address (1 byte)	Control (1 byte)	Protocol (1 byte)	Message Block (up to 1500 bytes)	Error Control CRC -16 (2 bytes)	Flag (1 byte)

Figure 3: Point-to-point packet

Locality

Modems can be broadly classified as either *internal* or *external*. The former refers to a modem attached to a PC's expansion slot, whereas the latter refers to a stand-alone modem that lies between a PC and the POTS connection—for example, one that connects via external serial, parallel, USB, or PCMCIA jacks or slots. It is important to note that most current PCs ship with internal modems, although expansion slot–based broadband connectivity cards are still frequently used (e.g., 802.11 g PC-MCIA and USB wireless cards).

Transmission Mode

Modems can also be classified based on their mode of transmission: as *simplex*, *half-duplex*, or *full duplex*. The distinction is based on how data may flow between two or more networked devices. In other words, simplex is data flow in one direction only; half-duplex is data flow in both directions, but not at the same time; and full duplex is data flow in both directions at the same time.

Synchronicity

Lastly, *synchronicity* refers to the way in which modems transmit characters or data. Asynchronous modems rely on start-and-stop bits to demarcate characters or packets and frames, whereas synchronous modems use clocking to separate characters or packets and frames, the latter being much faster. An example of a synchronous *point-to-point protocol* (PPP) packet, typically used for Internet access over dialup modems (Wikipedia 2006 "Internet"), is presented in Figure 3.

In the next section, modem standards are discussed.

MODEM STANDARDS

Standards are paramount for achieving interoperability. Essentially, standards ensure that hardware and software from different vendors can work together—that is, they define a set of rules known as *protocols* (Dennis 2002). Two of the more well-known standards are the *open systems interconnectivity* (OSI) and Internet (TCP/IP) protocol stacks. Although the former was developed by the International Organization for Standards (ISO) in 1984 and the latter emerged from the Internet paradigm (Wikipedia 2006 "OSI"), they remain important conceptual foundations (especially the latter) on which most commercial data networks are built and managed today. As an example, the Internet protocol stack defines five interdependent layers, each of which performs a specific set of operations in the transmission of data between computing devices (Fitzgerald and Dennis 2005; Wikipedia 2006 "Internet"). See Table 1 for an overview.

Table 1: Protocol Stacks

OSI Model	Internet Model	General Tasks	Common Standards
7. Application layer	5. Application layer	Provide utilities for end user applications	HTTP; HTML IMAP, POP, SMTP MPEG; H.323
6. Presentation layer		Formats data for the presentation to end user	Middleware-RPC; MOM; CORBA/IIOP; CICS; DTP
5. Session layer		Initiating, maintaining, and terminating user sessions	
4. Transport layer	4. Transport layer	Breaks up messages into manageable blocks	TCP; SPX
3. Network layer	3. Network layer	Addresses and determines the route of messages	IP; IPX
2. Data link layer	2. Data link layer	Creates start and end blocks; determines when to transmit; error checking	Ethernet; ATM; FDDI ISDN; PPP
1. Physical layer	1. Physical layer	Physically connets the user to the network	Cat 5; Cat 3; twisted pair; coax; fiber; wireless

Table 2: ITU-T Modem Standards

Standard	Properties
Bell 103	300 bps, frequency modulation (FSK)
V.22	1200 bps, phase modulation (PSK)
V.22bis	2400 bps, quadrature amplitude modulation (QAM)
V.32	9600 bps; 4800 bps and 9600 bps fallback; quadrature amplitude modulation (QAM)
V.32bis	14400 bps; 12000 bps and 7200 bps fallback; trellis-coded modulation (TCM)
V.34	28800 bps; 24000 bps and 19200 fallback; trellis-coded modulation (TCM)
V.34+	Increased data rate of V.34 to 33600 bps
V.42	Error correction
V.42bis	Lempel-Ziv data compression
V.44	Improved V.42bis data compression; compression used in V.92 standard
V.90	33600 bps upstream; 56000 bps downstream; single analog digital conversion
V.92	48000 bps upstream; 56000 bps downstream; single analog digital conversion modem on hold; quick connect increases upstream

Although the ISO is credited with standardizing the networking layers, it is the work of other standards-making or enforcing bodies such as the Institute of Electrical and Electronics Engineers (IEEE), International Telecommunications Union–Telecommunications Group (ITU-T), the American National Standards Institute (ANSI), and the Internet Engineering Task Force (IETF) that ensures interoperability at and between each layer. Two of these organizations—IEEE and ITU-T—are salient to the current context. The IEEE is the standards-making body for wireless modems (we will discuss these devices later), whereas ITU-T, a technical standards body of the United Nations, governs the standards for dialup modems. A summary of the most salient ITU-T modem standards (all starting with a "V") is presented in Table 2.

In reviewing the ITU-T and IEEE modem standards, the three key concepts on which modem standards rest emerge: modulation, error checking, and compression. Before visiting each concept in greater detail, we first broach the topic of baud rate and data rate.

Data Rate

Data rate can be defined as the number of symbols or symbol spaces transmitted per second multiplied by the number of bits per symbol or symbol space. *Baud rate* can be defined as the number of times per second that the transmission signal can or does change. As such, the term *symbol rate* is synonymous with baud rate. For example, if the circuit's baud rate is 1200, then 1200 symbols can be transmitted in one second. In other words, if one bit of data was transmitted for each symbol or symbol space, then the data rate would also be 1200 bps. However, if two bits were sent per symbol and the baud rate was 1200 bps, then the effective data rate would be 2400 bps (2 bits per symbol = 1200 symbols per second = 2400 bps). Note that

baud and data rate are different concepts: The first is a change in symbols per unit of time, whereas the latter is the number of bits of data sent per unit of time. However, they are equivalent whenever a single bit is transmitted per symbol or symbol space.

In addition to baud or symbol rate and bits per symbol, several factors influence effective data rates. First, noise may be a problem in the analog local loop, or last mile, depending on the type and quality of the transmission medium. For instance, twisted-pair copper wire tends to be antenna-like, absorbing electromagnetic and radio frequency signals that effectively corrupt the original signal and reduce data rates. Second, the type of modulation scheme invoked impacts the number of bits transmitted per symbol or data rate. Third, error checking, although necessary, reduces the effective data rate because of the additional data that are appended to each message for the purposes of detecting and correcting errors. Lastly, data compression algorithms, unlike the other three factors, may be used to increase the effective data rate by reducing the total number of bits that need to be transmitted (in some instances, a ratio of 1:6).

The first factor—noise—is external to the modem itself—that is, it is an issue with the circuit or connection media (e.g., twisted-pair, fiber) and, in the context of this discussion, needs no further elaboration. The last three factors—modulation, error checking, and data compression—are fundamental to modem standards. As such, they are elaborated on in greater detail next.

Modulation

Modulation refers to the way in which the shape of a carrier wave can be meaningfully modified so as to increase the number of bits per symbol or data rate. Carrier waves, or voice-grade analog waves, have three important

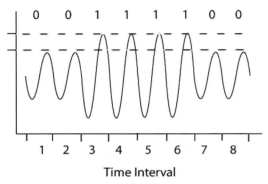

Figure 4: Amplitude modulation

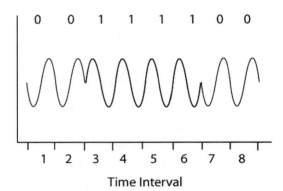

Figure 6: Phase modulation

properties: amplitude, frequency, and phase. *Amplitude* refers to the height of the wave (the human ear recognizes this property as loudness), *frequency* refers to the length of the wave (the human ear recognizes this property as pitch), and *phase* refers to the wave's initial direction. Based on these wave characteristics, three basic modulation techniques emerge: amplitude, frequency, and phase modulation.

In *amplitude modulation* (also called *amplitude shift keying*), the height of the wave is systematically varied. One height can be used to represent a 0, and the other height can be used to represent a 1 (see Figure 4).

In *frequency modulation* (also called *frequency shift keying*), the number of waves per symbol space is systematically varied. One frequency can be used to represent a 0, and another can be used to represent a 1. For example, 2400 Hz can be used to represent a 0 during one given symbol space (if the baud rate is 300, then the symbol space would be 1/300 of a second), and 1200 Hz can be used in another symbol space to represent a 1 (see Figure 5).

In *phase modulation*, the direction (e.g., up to the right or down to the right) that the wave starts out at the beginning of a symbol space is systematically varied. One phase can be used to represent a 0, and another can be used to represent a 1. For example, in one symbol space, the carrier wave can be forced up and to the right, representing a 1; and, in another symbol space, the carrier wave can be forced down and to the right, representing a 0 (see Figure 6).

Based on the properties of binary data (1 or 0 only), increasing the bits per symbol beyond 1 would require creating a number of amplitudes or modulations equal to the maximum number of possible combinations for a given number of bits. For example, if one wanted to transmit two bits per symbol, then four different wave heights, frequencies, or phase shifts would be needed (e.g., 11, 10, 01, and 00). Similarly, if three bits per symbol were desired, then eight different modulation levels would have to be defined (e.g., 111, 110, 101, 100, 011, 010, 001, and 000). In general, if n is defined as the number of bits per symbol or symbol space, then the formula for determining the appropriate number of modulations, regardless of modulation technique, is 2^n (2 raised to the number of bits per symbol).

Many of the more sophisticated modulation standards combine modulation techniques to maximize the number of bits per symbol (e.g., QAM and TCM). For example, in *quadrature amplitude modulation* (QAM), eight different phases and two different amplitudes are combined. The net result is a modulation technique that can transmit four bits per symbol—that is, it affords the creation of sixteen unique symbols, each defining one of sixteen different four-bit combinations ($2^4 = 16$). Building on QAM, *trellis-coded modulation* (TCM) can transmit 6, 7, 8 and 9.8 bits per symbol (Fitzgerald and Dennis 2005).

Error Checking

Error checking refers to the way in which modems append outgoing data and evaluate incoming data for errors. Like other modem protocols, error checking also has experienced considerable evolution (see Table 3). In general, if a data block is found to be error free, then the receiver transmits an *acknowledgment* block (ack). If it is not error free, then the receiver transmits a *negative acknowledgment* block (nack). The nack then notifies the sender that a specific data block, or frame, had errors and needs to be resent.

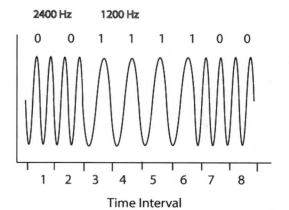

Figure 5: Frequency modulation

Table 3: Error-Detection Protocols

Error Protocol	Block Size	Checking Algorithm
X Modem	128 bytes	Checksum
Y Modem	1024 bytes	Cyclical Redundancy Check
Z Modem	512 bytes	Cyclical Redundancy Check
Kermit	Dynamic	Checksum
V.42 (LAPM)	128 bytes	Cyclical Redundancy Check

Data Compression

Data compression refers to the process of finding commonality in data and transmitting a shortened version of the message for the purpose of increasing data throughput. Current compression protocols (V.44) like Lempel-Ziv (LZ) compress data at ratios as high as 6:1 (Fitzgerald and Dennis 2005). Essentially, LZ compression creates a dictionary of two-, three-, and four-character combinations in any previously uncompressed set of data and represents repeat occurrences as dictionary indexes, as opposed to the actual character combination. For example, a V.34+ modem utilizing LZ compression (V.42bis) can, depending on the file type (e.g., text, graphics, executable), produce effective data rates in excess of 200 Kbps (Fitzgerald and Dennis 2005). Moreover, V.92 modems (utilizing V.44 compression), depending on the file type, are purported to improve throughput by as much as 120 percent relative to V.42bis. Note, however, that the relative effects of V.42bis and V.44 compression standards on actual throughput vary widely in the extant networking literature. Table 4 illustrates the compression effects of V.24bis and V.44 on text and graphics files (Digit-Life 2004).

Thus far, the primary focus of the chapter has been on dialup modems. In the next section, several broadband technologies—cable, DSL, and wireless modems—are reviewed. Note, however, that many of the concepts discussed to this point (e.g., standardization, modulation, compression, and error checking) are foundational for broadband modems as well. In other words, binary or digital data must still be modulated and demodulated, compressed and decompressed, and checked for errors.

BROADBAND MODEMS

Despite advancements in modem technology (e.g., V.92), the unrelenting integration of voice, video, and data on the Internet and World Wide Web continues to outpace traditional voice-grade circuits in ways that greatly diminish quality of service. Furthermore, traditional dialup modems may even be prohibitive for many of today's data-intensive applications and services (e.g., videoconferencing and online video games). A new generation of modems called *broadband modems* has thus been developed to overcome the limitations associated with traditional dialup modems. In this section, several broadband modems are reviewed: cable, DSL, and wireless.

Cable Modems

Several industries offer broadband alternatives to traditional dialup modems. One such industry is cable television. Many of today's cable entertainment providers, in addition to cable television, provide shared multipoint access to the Internet. Cable modems, in theory, can provide download speeds as high as 55 Mbps and upstream speeds of 10 Mbps. Today, however, speeds for both downstream and upstream are typically no greater than 2 Mbps (Fitzgerald and Dennis 2005). Currently, cable infrastructures (i.e., private *hybrid fiber-coax*, or HFC, networks) remain proprietary and therefore lack standardization. Although several protocols are in use, the de facto protocol is *data over cable service interface specification* (DOCSIS). Figure 7 shows a typical cable modem configuration.

In general, cable modems work by transmitting data to a line splitter within or near the customer's premise. The line splitter combines (upstream) or splits (downstream) the television and Internet data streams. From the splitter, the signals are carried to the cable company's fiber node. The fiber node contains an *electrical-to-optical* converter that converts cable signals to fiber-optic signals. The fiber node then connects directly to the cable company's distribution hub via a separate downstream and upstream fiber-optic cable. The upstream data is then processed by the cable company's *cable modem termination service* (CMTS), which handles various Internet protocols necessary for routing data traffic.

Table 4: Relative Compression Efficiency of V.42bis and V.44

Compression	Text File		Graphics File	
	Units	Effective Data	Units	Effective Data
None	1.00	1017	1.00	1018
V.42bis	5.53	5617	2.39	2427
V.44	7.16	7282	3.29	3344

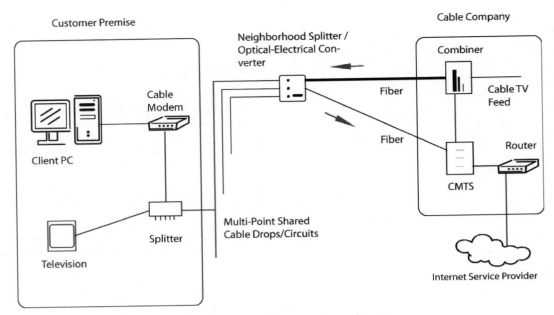

Figure 7: Cable modem example configuration

Downstream traffic, which may include both Internet data and television video, is merged via the cable company's combiner. The combiner then transmits the data by way of fiber optic to the cable company's fiber node. The optical-to-electrical converter on the fiber node then converts the fiber signal to a cable signal and sends it down the cable drop. The line splitter on the customer's premise then separates the data streams into Internet and television data and sends the Internet data to the modem, which either converts it for computer use or retransmits it. It is important to note that all cable users on a given cable drop share the multipoint cable circuit, and, as such, the cable modem at each premise may actually process much of the other users' downstream and upstream data, making security an issue.

Digital Subscriber Lines

Digital subscriber lines (DSL) are another broadband alternative. Unlike cable modem technology, DSL technology is a point-to-point technology. As such, compared to cable modems, privacy becomes less of a concern, and the overall bandwidth is dedicated, as opposed to being shared by 300 to 1000 cable users. Because DSL is a telecommunications technology, the ITU-T acts as the standards body. Digital subscriber lines overcome traditional voice-grade circuit limitations in the last mile or local loop by circumventing the traditional voice-grade switching equipment at the central or end office. Dialup limitations do not so much lie in the twisted-pair copper but more so on the voice-grade switching equipment, which is limited to 4000 Hz. The copper wires in the local loop have a physical capacity of as much as 1 MHz (1 million cycles per second). Telephone companies leverage the available bandwidth by simply placing different terminating

equipment at the customer's premise and at the central office. Figure 8 illustrates a common DSL configuration.

Similar to cable modems, the *customer's premise equipment* (CPE) may include a splitter to separate traditional voice-grade data from other data. The DSL modem, sometimes referred to as a *DSL router*, combines the functions of a modem and the functions of a *frequency division multiplexer* (FDM). Essentially, FDM creates several logical circuits from one physical circuit. This is done by transmitting voice-grade data at 4 kHz and, in many instances, creating two additional and distinct frequencies for upstream and downstream data, the latter being considerably larger in bandwidth.

Digital subscriber line modems transmit data to a telecommunication company's central office, specifically the telephone company's *main distribution facility* (MDF). Similar to the CPE splitter, the MDF has a splitter that directs voice-grade data to the telephone network and all other data to the phone company's *digital subscriber line access multiplexer* (DSLAM). Next, the DSLAM converts the data and either transmits it as *asynchronous transfer mode* (ATM) data for further retransmission (e.g., to an ISP) or directly routes it through the phone company's point-of-presence (its own ISP). The reverse process (downstream) is relatively the same.

Many types of DSL are currently available throughout the world. The most common is *asymmetric DSL* (ADSL). Asymmetric DSL uses FDM to create three logical circuits: one 4-kHz voice-grade circuit, one 384-Kbps circuit for upstream, and one 1.5-Mbps high-speed circuit for downstream. A second common type of DSL is *very-high-data-rate DSL* (VDSL). VDSL, or *short-loop ADSL*, is used for distances of less than 4500 feet. It also uses FDM to create three logical circuits from a single physical circuit, with theoretical data rates of 51.84 Mbps downstream and

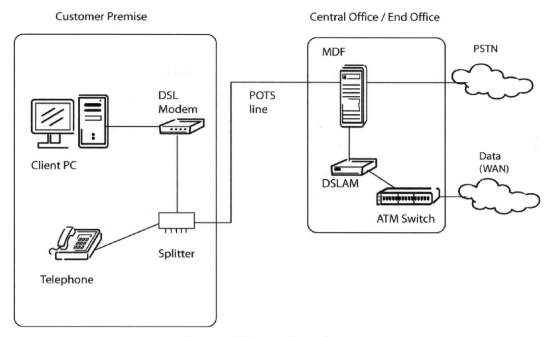

Figure 8: DSL example configuration

2.3 Mbps upstream on drops less than 1000 feet. A third type of DSL in use is *wireless DSL* (WDSL). This remains a good solution for instances in which transmitters have unobstructed line of sight. Both point-to-point and multipoint WDSL architectures are available. Both versions typically can provide data rates as high as 11 Mbps.

Wireless Modems

Wireless modems convert digital data into radio or cellular signals. These are transmitted to the nearest receiver (wireless access point or cell tower) and routed appropriately. Several standards are in existence and vary depending on the mobile device, transmitter, or application layer in use. For WLAN (WiFi and Bluetooth) and WiMAX standards, IEEE is the standards body (see IEEE 2006a, 2006b). Several standards for smaller handheld, mobile devices also exist, including *wireless application protocol* (WAP) and *wireless application environment* (WAE).

In general, cellular phone connections are markedly slower than V.92, cable, and DSL. They do, however, provide ubiquitous connectivity. Data rates, as well as signal footprints, vary considerably for WLAN and WiMAX technologies. Two 2.4-GHz WLAN standards remain popular today: 802.11b and 802.11 g. The 802.11b standard provides data rates as high as 11 Mbps, and 802.11 g provides data rates as high as 54 Mbps. For both, however, these are theoretical data rates, and data rates diminish quickly the farther one is from the wireless access point. In theory, WiMAX (IEEE 802.16) has the capability to deliver wireless services as far as thirty miles away. A single WiMAX tower is purported to have the capacity to deliver the equivalent bandwidth of sixty T1 lines (1.544 Mbps each) and one hundred DSL or cable lines. Although the data rate and coverage (or footprint) for WiMAX are still in question, it is reasonable to expect even more impressive bandwidth and coverage as WiMAX and other emergent wireless technologies advance.

CONCLUSION

In this chapter, modems were defined and a brief history of dialup technologies was provided. The process of transmitting binary data via dialup modems was also presented. The salient functional components of a dialup modem—MCU, DPU, and DAA—as well as salient modem classifications, were also discussed. The important role of standards, as well as the primary bodies for standards making and enforcing for networking in general and modem-based technologies specifically were presented as well. Three primary concepts underlying modem standards—modulation, error checking, and data compression—as well as their impact on data rates were also discussed. Lastly, three broadband modem categories—cable, DSL, and wireless—were identified and presented as alternatives to the waning dialup standards.

With the introduction and proliferation of broadband technologies, as well as the relentless integration of voice, video, and data, the probability of seeing traditional or analog-digital hybrid modem data rates or adoption rates increase in any meaningful way is extremely suspect. Essentially, the dialup modem is to networking as the horse and buggy is to global transportation: It remains viable but is limited at best. The overwhelming trend in network access and connectivity—at least in the local loop or last mile—has shifted and continues to shift toward both broadband wired (e.g., DSL, cable, Ethernet to the home, fiber to the home, and broadband over power lines) and wireless (e.g., 3G cellular data services and WiMAX) technologies.

GLOSSARY

American National Standards Institute (ANSI): The principal standards-setting body in the United States. ANSI is a nonprofit, nongovernmental organization that supports in excess of 1000 trade organizations, professional societies, and companies. ANSI is also a member of ITU-T and ISO.

Amplitude modulation: The form of modulation in which the amplitude of the carrier is varied in accordance with the instantaneous value of the modulating signal.

Asymmetric digital subscriber line (ADSL): A data-link layer technology that provides high-speed communication over traditional telephone lines.

Asynchronous transfer mode (ATM): A communication switch that affords transmission rates as high as 622 Mbps. ATM is especially well suited for multimedia transmission, including the integration of voice, video, and data.

Broadband: A type of data transmission in which a single medium can carry several channels at once.

Cable modem: A modem designed to operate over co-axial cable lines used by cable TV.

Controller-less modem: A modem in which the microcontroller is actually part of the computer device instead of the modem.

Controller modem: A modem that contains a microcontroller unit, a data pump unit, and a data access arrangement.

Data access arrangement (DAA): Provides the analog circuits that electrically isolate the modem from the phone line, separating the modem from the telephone line's higher voltage and allowing the modem to interface with the telephone network.

Data compression: A technique that allows devices to transmit or store the same amount of data in fewer bits.

Data pump unit (DPU): That part of the modem responsible for converting binary data to analog data.

Digital subscriber line (DSL): A data-link layer technology that provides high-speed communication over traditional telephone lines.

Digital subscriber line access multiplexer (DSLAM): The multiplexer used by telephone companies for connecting to, and handling, data transmitted on multiplexed DSL circuitry.

Echo cancellation: Used in higher-speed modems to isolate and filter out echoes when half-duplex transmissions use stop-and-wait automatic repeat request protocols.

Frequency division multiplexing (FDM): The technique of dividing a voice-grade circuit into subcircuits, each covering a different frequency range so that each circuit can be employed as though it were an individual circuit.

Frequency modulation: A form of modulation in which the frequency of the carrier is varied in accordance with the instantaneous value of the modulating signal.

Institute of Electrical and Electronics Engineers (IEEE): An organization composed of scientists and students and best known for developing standards for the computer and electronics industry.

Internet Engineering Task Force (IETF): A large, open international community of network designers, operators, vendors, and researchers concerned with the evolution of the Internet architecture and its smooth operation.

International Organization for Standards (ISO): An international standards-making body best known in data communications for developing the internationally recognized seven-layer network model called the open systems interconnection (OSI) reference model.

International Telecommunications Union (ITU): An intergovernmental organization through which public and private organizations develop telecommunications. The ITU was founded in 1865 and became a United Nations agency in 1947. It is responsible for adopting international treaties, regulations, and standards that govern telecommunications.

Microcontroller unit (MCU): A modem's internal processor or controlling unit.

Phase modulation: A form of modulation in which the phase of the carrier is varied in accordance with the instantaneous value of the modulating signal.

Quadrature amplitude modulation (QAM): A sophisticated modulation technique that combines eight phases and two amplitudes to generate a unique four-bit code for each one of sixteen unique modulations or symbols.

Very high data rate digital subscriber line (VDSL): A DSL technology designed to provide very high data rates over very short distances of less than 4500 feet.

Wireless fidelity (WiFi): Generically used when referring to any 802.11 network.

Wireless local area network (WLAN): A type of local-area network that uses high-frequency radio waves rather than wires to communicate between nodes.

WiMAX: The name commonly given to the IEEE 802.16 standard.

Wireless modem: A modem that accesses a private wireless data network or a wireless telephone system.

CROSS REFERENCES

See *Cable Modems*; *Frequency and Phase Modulation*; *Pulse Amplitude Modulation*; *Sources of Errors, Prevention, Detection and Correction*.

REFERENCES

AT&T. Undated. History of the AT&T network (retrieved January 5, 2006 from www.att.com/history/nethistory).
———. Undated. Milestones in AT&T History (retrieved January 5, 2006 from www.att.com/history/milestones. html).

Dennis, A. 2002. *Networking in the Internet age*. New York: John Wiley & Sons.

Digit-Life. 2004. Modem comparison: V.44 against V.42bis (retrieved June 12, 2006 from www.digit-life.com/articles/compressv44vsv42bis).

Fitzgerald, J., and A. Dennis. 2005. *Business data communications and networking*. New York: John Wiley & Sons.

Green, J. H. 2000. *The Irwin handbook of telecommunications*. New York: McGraw-Hill.

Horak, R. 2002. *Communications systems and networks*. Indianapolis: Wiley Publishing.

IEEE. 2006a. Standards (retrieved May 25, 2006 from www.ieee.org/web/standards/home/index.html).

———. 2006b. Wireless standards zone (retrieved May 25, 2006 from http://standards.ieee.org/wireless).

Wikipedia. 2006. Hayes command set (retrieved May 21, 2006 from http://en.wikipedia.org/wiki/Hayes_command_set).

———. 2006. Internet protocol suite (retrieved May 23, 2006 from http://en.wikipedia.org/wiki/Internet_protocol_suite).

———. 2006. OSI model (retrieved May 23, 2006 from http://en.wikipedia.org/wiki/OSI_Mod).

Conducted Communications Media

Thomas L. Pigg, *Jackson State Community College*

INTRODUCTION

The Internet consists of millions of digital passages that carry signals all over the world. These conduits that connect us to the World Wide Web come in many shapes, sizes, and modes. The bewildering assortment and seemingly endless conduits—more commonly referred to as *communication media*—that are used to connect computers together can be boiled down to two types: conductive cable and wireless. Conductive media is simply a hardwired connection that requires someone to physically join network devices with some type of cable. The three major types of cable are coaxial, twisted-pair, and fiber-optic. The focus of this chapter is on conducted communications media. Wireless communication is the alternative to conducted communications media and is accomplished using a variety of broadcast transmission technologies, including radio, terrestrial microwave, and satellite communications.

To aid in understanding conductive communications media, a short explanation of network transmission basics is discussed, followed by a detailed exploration of the three major types of media mentioned earlier. In addition, we present the similarities and contrasts between these media. Finally, the suitability and application of each type of conducted media along with security concerns is discussed.

OVERVIEW OF NETWORK TRANSMISSION BASICS

Network Transmission Basics

When computers communicate over the Internet or on private networks, they must follow certain communication protocols. In short, each computer that connects to a network must follow rules that govern the type of hardware and software that is used for access to the network. These protocols consist of signal types and speeds, cable layouts, and communications access schemes.

Baseband and Broadband

Bandwidth is the range of frequencies that a particular network transmission media can carry. It also reveals the maximum amount of data that can be carried on the medium. A baseband transmission is a single fixed signal that uses the entire available bandwidth. Baseband signals use a single channel to communicate with devices on a network; this allows computers to transmit and receive data on one cable (Tittel and Johnson 2001). Baseband communications are typically used for *local area networks* (LANs). When LANs expand into a *metropolitan area network* (MAN) or a *wide area network* (WAN), baseband systems do not provide the bandwidths that are adequate for these larger networks.

Network connections that attach several LANs together, such as MANs or WANs, or that allow remote access from external users or networks to local servers often require multichannel bandwidths because of increased traffic flow. Broadband transmissions help to meet these needs. In contrast to the discrete digital signals produced in baseband communications, broadband transmission generates an analog carrier frequency that carries multiple digital signals or multiple channels. This concept is much like cable television systems that carry many channels on one cable.

The decision to use baseband or broadband is determined by the application. If the network consists of a single LAN, then baseband would be the best choice. If an organization has computer networks that spread over several geographic areas, then multiple channels of communications between locations may be needed; this can be achieved only through broadband applications. Note that it is the network type and the particular network device that determines whether a signal is baseband or broadband, not the transmission media.

Cable Access Methods

A *cable access method* is how data is placed on the transmission media. Data are formatted into small pieces called *packets*. A packet contains header and trailer information about the contents, source, destination, error checking, and the actual data. A packet typically contains a specific amount of information, normally 1 to 2 kilobytes, that is defined by the particular network protocol being used. It is a lot like an envelope used to hold a letter to be mailed. The outside of the envelope contains a destination address along with sender information. This information is used by the postal service to deliver the mail to its destination. When a wrong destination address is used, the postal service can notify the sender by means of the return address. Network packets are handled in a similar way (Tittel and Johnson 2001).

Packets are placed on the communications line in several ways. Typically, the communication media used in a LAN will be shared by all network devices. In most cases, only one device can transmit information on the communication media at a time. This will often be in the form of a broadcast. A broadcast by a computer will be received by all of the devices connected to the particular network segment. For example, Ethernet, a widely used LAN protocol, uses a cable access method called *carrier sense multiple access with collision detection* (CSMA/CD). This method is a lot like a two-way radio broadcast, which allows only one person to talk at one time. CSMA/CD requires each participating network workstation to first listen to the communication line to determine whether it is clear before attempting to broadcast a packet of information, because it is possible that two or more workstations will begin broadcasting their packets at almost the same time. If this occurs, then the *collision detection* (CD) feature of CSMA/CD will instruct the conflicting workstations to cease transmissions and assign a random delay before they are allowed to attempt to send another packet of data. Without a random delay, the colliding workstations would continue to rebroadcast at the same time, causing more collisions. It should be noted that a small number of collisions are normal but should not exceed 5 percent of all network traffic. Occasionally, a defective *network interface card* (NIC) may cause excessive collisions by constantly broadcasting packets. This is called a *broadcast storm* (Tittel and Johnson 2001).

A similar access method used by AppleTalk networks is called *carrier sense multiple access with collision avoidance* (CSMA/CA). This scheme is similar to CSMA/CD except that it attempts to avoid collisions altogether. Network devices accomplish this by sending a short broadcast requesting control of the network segment before sending a packet. This helps prevent collisions of complete packets, thus reducing network traffic because of rebroadcasting packets (Tittel and Johnson 2001).

Another type of access method is called *token passing*, and it is used by token-ring protocol. Token passing eliminates network collisions altogether by passing a token from node to node on the network in one direction. A *token* is similar to a packet. When a network device receives a token, it examines it to determine whether its contents are for that particular node. If not, then the network node rebroadcasts the token to the next device on the network. When the token finds its destination, it unloads the data and rebroadcasts an empty token to the next device. The empty token will ask each passing node whether it has any data to send. The empty token is passed on down the line until a device generates information to place in the empty token (Tittel and Johnson 2001).

Network Topologies

A *network topology* is the physical cable layout or configuration. There are three basic types: star, bus, and ring. Each network protocol (i.e., Ethernet, token ring) will specify the cable type and topology supported. The *star* topology, as illustrated in Figure 1, requires a central wiring point for all network devices on a particular network segment. A device called a *hub* or *concentrator* is used to serve this purpose. A hub is a multiport repeater that regenerates signals received. In some applications, a device called a *switch* is used. A switch is more intelligent than a hub because it can learn which devices are connected to its ports and send packets directly to the destination port only, thus reducing network traffic.

The *bus* topology (see Figure 2) requires no special external device for computers to connect with it. It consists of network nodes connected to the communications media via a special T-connector that connects the computer's NIC to the bus (see Figure 3). Notice in Figure 2 that a small box is shown at both ends of the bus. This represents a terminator that is required for this cable layout (see Figure 4). Its purpose is to prevent *signal bounce*, which occurs when a cable is not terminated. Signal bounce is the result of a broadcast signal that continues to oscillate. The terminator is used to absorb the signal once it has reached the end of the cable, thus eliminating signal bounce.

The *ring* topology (see Figure 5) is similar to bus topology in that each computer is connected directly to its neighbor without the need for a hub or other special device. The big difference between the two is that ring

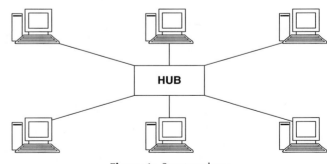

Figure 1: Star topology

Figure 2: Bus topology

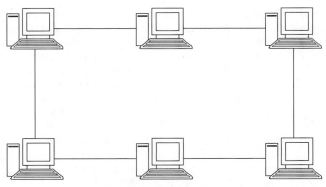

Figure 5: Ring topology

Figure 3: T-connector

Figure 4: Terminator

topology provides a closed-loop design that does not require termination.

In some applications, more than one topology may be used. This is typically called a *mesh* or *hybrid* topology. This is often the case when different types of communications media are used for the same network. Later in this chapter, we discuss the characteristics of different network cables and see that each cable type is best suited for a particular topology. In some situations, a network might need to utilize different cable types in order to accomplish the best overall network performance, which might require the use of multiple topologies.

A mesh or hybrid topology does not necessarily require the use of different communications media. For example, the token ring protocol uses a topology called a *star-wired ring* that may utilize only one type of cable, as shown in Figure 6. In this example, *multistation access units* (MAUs) or concentrators are used to connect the network devices. The MAUs are then connected to each other in a physical ring configuration. The physical connection to the MAU represents the star portion of the topology; however, a logical continuous ring is actually created when using MAUs and the token-ring cabling system. Figure 6 only shows the physical connections even though a token is passed into and back out of each MAU

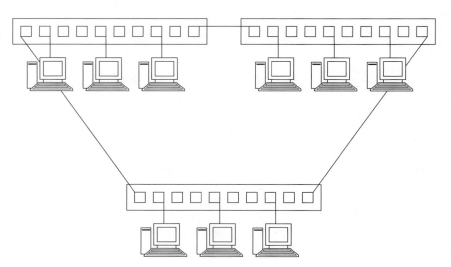

Figure 6: Star-wired ring

port that has a device connected to it in a continuous loop that forms the logical ring.

Each topology has its advantages and disadvantages. For example, the bus topology has the advantage of low cost because it does not require any special devices to connect computers. A disadvantage, however, is that if there is a break in any of the cables, the entire network segment will go down because of a loss of termination. The task of finding the broken cable could be somewhat difficult without the help of a fairly expensive cable analyzer. On the other hand, computers connected to a star topology would most likely remain operating on the network if one of the cables malfunctioned between a device and a hub. Star topology requires more wire than a bus topology, and it also requires hubs or switches, which adds more cost. Ring topology has an advantage over bus and star topologies because it typically provides an alternate path for data transmission in case of a cable break. For instance, a star-wired ring topology provides a logical continuous ring that provides a redundant path if a cable were to be cut.

The purpose of this section on network transmission basics is to establish the concepts and characteristics related to conducted transmission cable. Each media type differs in physical and electrical-optical characteristics as well as in application. The following section discusses the three major types of conducted transmission cable: coaxial, twisted-pair, and fiber-optic.

COAXIAL CABLE

Coaxial (or simply *coax*) *cable* is used in a wide range of applications, including television, radio, and computer network communications. This section looks at the physical makeup of coaxial cable and the specific characteristics that distinguish different types.

Components

Coaxial cable consists of an inner and outer conductor that share the same axis, which is how it got its name, coaxial (Carr 1999). The inner conductor, sometimes called the *conducting core*, is typically made of a copper alloy. Most applications use a solid core, except where flexibility is required, and then a stranded core may be used. The outer conductor is either braided metal or foil; this acts as a conductor and a shield to reduce interference. An *insulator*, or, more accurately, a *dielectric*, is between the two conductors. Depending on the type of coax, this material is made out of Teflon or an inert gas. Finally, for protection, there is an *outer sheath* that surrounds the inner components. This is made from polyvinyl chloride (PVC) or special fire-retardant material for installations where wire must be run in the plenum areas above the false ceilings in a building (Carr 1999; Tittel and Johnson 2001).

Coaxial cables come in a variety of forms: flexible, helical line, and hard line. Flexible coax is made of flexible material in the outer conductor, typically braid or foil. This cable is mostly found in LANs and home television-to-antenna connections. Helical line coax is a semiflexible cable that consists of a slightly more rigid, spiral-wound outer conductor. Normally, this type of cable is used for network backbones or interconnections between networks that require long cable runs. This type of cable is able to carry a signal over longer distances at higher frequencies than can flexible cable types. Hard-line coaxial cable is used to connect equipment that transmits in the microwave frequency range. This form of coax uses a thin-walled pipe as an outer conductor that is rigid and difficult to work with. As the frequency of a transmitted signal increases, there is a greater chance of the signal radiating beyond the outer conductor, which also acts as a shield, thus resulting in signal loss. In the case of external electromagnetic interference, the type of outer conductor will determine which frequencies will be rejected from the transmitted signal (Carr 1999).

Another characteristic of coaxial cable is its *impedance*. Impedance, measured in ohms, is the resistance of a cable to the transmitted signal (Tittel and Johnson 2001). Carr (1999) stated that the lowest loss of signal occurs at higher impedances; however, more power can be achieved when the impedance is low. Cable television uses coaxial cable rated at 75-ohm impedance because of its lower signal attenuation with long cable runs. Most network and radio applications use 50-ohm impedance as a middle ground between low signal loss and more power.

Cable manufacturers use a *radio government* (RG) specification for the coaxial cables they produce. Cable television uses RG-6, RG-11, or RG-59 spec cable. All of these are rated at 75 ohms. RG-6 and RG-11 are larger diameter cables used for major trunk lines. RG-59 is employed between the trunk lines and the customer's television.

RG-58 and RG-8 are 50-ohm cables used for computer network communications. As does cable television, computer networks use trunk lines to connect network segments together. RG-8 is the cable used for trunk lines or network backbones and is often referred to as *thickwire Ethernet*, or *thicknet* for short. RG-58 is used with *thinwire Ethernet*, or *thinnet*, to interconnect smaller segments of the network (Tittel and Johnson 2001).

Coaxial Cable Network Applications

Thickwire Ethernet

Thicknet (RG-8) is typically used as an Ethernet backbone to connect various network segments together. Thicknet can be used to directly interconnect devices on the network, but usually thinnet is used for this purpose. Thicknet uses the bus topology with the CSMA/CD cable access method. Normally it is used as a network backbone, which consists of a length of RG-8 cable with network devices, such as hubs, connected to it. Each device connected to the backbone requires a special device called a *transceiver*. The transceiver is connected to the coax by use of a *vampire tap* (see Figure 7). A special cable then attaches the transceiver to the device through its *attachment unit interface* (AUI) port (see Figure 8).

Each conducted transmission cable exhibits certain standardized characteristics that describe its advantages and disadvantages within network applications. Table 1 describes thickwire Ethernet characteristics. Each cable type reviewed contains similar specifications. The reason there is a maximum length is because of *attenuation*, which is the reduction in signal strength that occurs

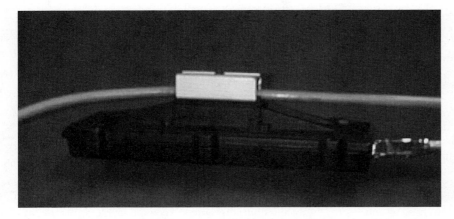

Figure 7: Thickwire coax attached to transceiver via vampire tap

Figure 8: AUI cable connected to a transceiver

Table 1: Thickwire Ethernet Specifications

Characteristic	Specification
Maximum cable segment length	500 m
Maximum total network length	2500 m
AUI (drop cable length)	50 m
Maximum number of devices per segment	100
Maximum number of segments	Five connected by four repeaters, with not more than three populated segments
Bandwidth	10 Mbps*
Termination	50 ohms
Cable access method	CSMA/CD

* Megabits per second

as cable lengths increase. At some point, the signal loss becomes excessive and causes the network to stop functioning. As with this and other wire specifications, cable manufacturers rely on Institute of Electrical and Electronics Engineers (IEEE) standards when producing their products. The Ethernet standards for thicknet and thinnet are covered in the IEEE 802.3 specification (Tittel and Johnson 2001).

Table 1 shows a total network cable length of 2500 meters (m), which is based on the *5-4-3 rule*. This rule states that each network cannot exceed a total of five cable segments connected by four repeaters, with not more than three of the segments populated by nodes (see Figure 9).

Figure 9 shows five complete cable segments. Each segment is connected to a device called a *repeater*. A repeater is used to compensate for the attenuation caused by cable lengths that exceed 500 m for thicknet. Its function is to amplify and repeat what it receives so that its signal will be strong enough to reach another repeater or the end of the next cable segment. Note that two segments do not have any network devices connected to them. This implies that only three of the five segments may have network devices attached. Tittel and Johnson (2001) stated that in reality this means that any two network devices cannot be separated by more than four repeaters (five segments) with three populated segments. So the 5-4-3 rule does not say a network is limited to only five segments. It states only that network devices cannot communicate with each other if they are separated by more than five segments. In addition, the 5-4-3 rule helps with signal timing and reduces the collision activity.

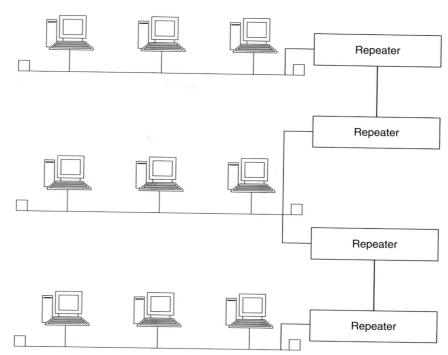

Figure 9: 5-4-3 rule diagram

The AUI or drop cable length refers to the cable that attaches to the transceiver unit connected via the vampire tap to the thickwire Ethernet backbone. This type of connection is used to connect such devices as repeaters or hubs to the Ethernet backbone. The AUI cable must be less than 50 m long.

Table 1 shows a maximum of one hundred devices per segment for thickwire Ethernet. Every time a device is attached to an Ethernet backbone, there will be some signal loss. Any device attached beyond the limit is not guaranteed to function properly. When designing a network, these limits should not be pushed. If a segment is fully populated, then there is no room for expanding a network without adding another segment, assuming that the network does not already have the maximum allowable five segments.

Some IEEE specifications, such as bandwidth, are preset and cannot be altered. If the network bandwidth will not support the needs of the network, then a different protocol or standard will need to be used. The bandwidth specification of 10 Mbps for thickwire Ethernet describes how much data can be transmitted, which ultimately determines the speed of communications. As with all bus topologies using coax, a terminator is required at both ends of the bus to eliminate signal bounce. Because thicknet coaxial cable is designed for 50-ohm impedance, a 50-ohm *terminator* is required. A terminator is simply a connector that has been retrofitted with a 50-ohm resistor between the inner and outer conductors.

Thinwire Ethernet

Networks can be quickly set up using little more than RG-58 cable and a few connectors. Thinwire cable is commonly used to interconnect computers or other network devices on a network segment using the bus topology.

Figure 10: British naval connector or bayonet nut connector (BNC)

In the past, thinnet was one of the most popular transmission cables for Ethernet networks because of its low cost and ease of setup.

Thinnet cable uses a special connector called a *British naval connector* or *bayonet nut connector* (BNC) (see Figure 10). Computers and other network devices are connected to the bus topology by way of a BNC T-connector (see Figure 3), which connects to the NIC. The NIC is a transceiver that provides the physical connection between the network device and the transmission media. In addition, the NIC is responsible for packaging the data coming from the network device into a form acceptable to the network cable.

As with thicknet, thinnet follows the IEEE 802.3 standard with regard to the use of RG-58 coaxial cable. Table 2

Table 2: Thinwire Ethernet Specifications

Characteristic	Specification
Maximum cable segment length	185 m
Maximum total network length	925 m
Maximum number of devices per segment	30
Maximum number of segments	Five connected by four repeaters, with three populated segments
Bandwidth	10 Mbps
Termination	50 ohms
Cable access method	CSMA/CD

summarizes these cable specifications. Notice that thinnet characteristics are similar to thicknet except in cable lengths and number of devices per segment. Also, there is no specification for a drop cable for thinwire Ethernet because the NIC serves the same function as the external transceiver used by thicknet (Tittel and Johnson 2001).

The physical characteristics of thinwire coax attenuate signals over shorter distances than does thickwire. This is typically not an issue because thinnet is normally used to interconnect computers within a relatively small area. In situations where computers need to be separated by more than 185 m, a repeater can be used to accommodate these devices. The low cost of this wire often outweighs the distance limitations.

The number of devices that can be attached to a thinnet bus topology is thirty. This is fewer than can be attached to thicknet because of the reasons noted in the previous paragraph for cable length. Be aware that a network can have more than one segment. With repeaters, thinwire Ethernet can support multiple populated segments. The 802.3 standard specifies a maximum of 1024 devices per network as long as the 5-4-3 rule is followed; however, with that many devices network performance would be dismal at best and thus not practical (Tittel and Johnson 2001).

In addition to network protocol standards for Ethernet and token ring, IEEE references cable-type standards such as 10Base5 and 10Base2 for thickwire and thinwire, respectively. The number 10 represents the bandwidth of the cable specification. *Base* refers to a baseband (single-channel) signal type, and the last number represents the maximum length of a network segment in meters rounded to the nearest hundred. For example, 10Base5 refers to a coaxial cable that carries a baseband signal transmitted at 10 Mbps with a maximum segment length of 500 m (thicknet). Thinnet is referenced by 10Base2, meaning a baseband signal with a 10-Mbps bandwidth at 200 m, approximately. In reality, thinwire Ethernet can only support 185 m segments. Twisted-pair and fiber-optic cables carry 10BaseT and 10BaseF IEEE cable standards. These are discussed in more detail later.

There are several advantages to using coaxial cables for computer networks. For LANs, RG-58 uses the bus topology, which offers lower cost options and ease of installation. Also, the outer shielding of coax provides moderate protection from interference. 10Base2 applications allow for fairly long cable runs compared with other cables such as twisted pair. The major drawback of coax is its narrow bandwidth compared with contemporary applications using twisted-pair and fiber-optic cable. Plus, thicknet installations can be somewhat difficult and expensive because of the rigidity of the cable, the rather difficult task of installing network connections, and the overall cost of the interface devices. Generally speaking, the days of coaxial cable infrastructures are waning. The majority of installations use twisted-pair and fiber optic cabling.

TWISTED-PAIR CABLE

Twisted-pair cable consists of one or more pairs of twisted wire. Twisted pair has a longer history than coaxial cable, but its usage was restricted to voice until the 1980s. Omninet or 10Net began to use twisted pair in the early 1980s for PC-based LANs. One of the first PC applications using twisted-pair cable was in 1984, when IBM introduced the token-ring network protocol. By the end of the 1980s, Ethernet technology began using twisted pair. Some advantages of twisted-pair over coaxial cable include its light weight and flexibility; in some cases, existing twisted-pair cables within buildings can be used without having to install new wiring (Network Magazine 1999).

Components

Twisted-pair media comes in two forms: *shielded twisted pair* (STP) and *unshielded twisted pair* (UTP). STP consists of several pairs of twisted wires that are surrounded by a foil shielding and an outer jacket or sheath. The number of wire pairs can vary from either two or four for basic telephone and network applications to hundreds of pairs for major communication trunk lines. Each wire within the pair consists of a solid or stranded copper center core surrounded by an insulating cover. Stranded wire is typically used where greater flexibility is required.

The twist in each pair of wire reduces *cross talk*. When a signal travels down the wire, it produces a magnetic field. If not controlled in some way, this can produce unwanted interference with other pairs of wire within the same cable (cross talk). The twist in the pairs works to reduce the effects of cross talk. It also helps to reduce the magnetic field's effect on other pairs. Cables with more twists per foot offer the best performance and are normally more expensive. The foil shielding that surrounds the twisted pairs blocks sources of interference from electronic noise outside of the cable in addition to keeping stray noise from escaping to the outside world. STP is often the choice of transmission media when heavy electrical or electronic equipment exists near cable runs. It may also be used to increase network security by reducing the amount of outside signal radiation that could be intercepted by inductive signal equipment used by someone trying to intercept sensitive network communications.

Figure 11: Unshielded twisted-pair (UTP) cable

The outer sheath exists to protect the inner components of the cable. Like many cables, twisted-pair jackets are made of some form of PVC or special plenum sheaths that are used in applications that require nontoxic and fire-resistant cable.

UTP is basically the same as STP except that it does not have a foil shield (see Figure 11). Without the shield, it is more prone to cross talk and other forms of interference, although some cross talk is reduced because of the twists in the pairs of wire.

UTP is probably the most popular cable type for networks today. The Electronic Industries Alliance (EIA) and the Telecommunications Industries Association (TIA), with the endorsement of the American National Standards Institute (ANSI), have defined several categories of UTP cable for different applications (Network Magazine 1999; Fogle 1995; Tittel and Johnson 2001). Category 1 is traditionally used for telephone and voice transmissions. Category 2 is capable of data transmissions as high as 4 Mbps. Category 3 is certified for up to 10 Mbps for 10BaseT Ethernet and suitable for 4-Mbps token ring. New technology applications, including 100BaseT4 and 100Base-VG AnyLAN, can utilize this lower rated cable for 100-Mbps bandwidth. Category 4 can handle up to 16 Mbps, which includes token ring 16 Mbps and 10-Mbps Ethernet applications. Category 5 cable type supports bandwidths of as much as 100 Mbps.

At the turn of the century, a new enhanced category 5 (CAT5E) cable was introduced that boosted the performance limits of the original category 5 cables. These improvements include further reduction in signal attenuation and cross talk, and they also provide problem-free full duplex transmissions.

Up to this point, we have used the term *bandwidth* to describe the speed at which data travels on the transmission media. In reality, two factors are involved in the speed of data transmissions: bandwidth and data rates. A more precise definition for bandwidth would be the carrying capacity of a signal, which is typically measured in megahertz (Mhz). A good illustration of this would be like a highway. Some highways consist of only two lanes, where others may consist of ten or more lanes. The more lanes a highway has, the better the traffic flow. Thus, the higher the bandwidth rating of a cable, the more data traffic it can handle (Kish 1998).

The data-rate measure is simply the amount of data that passes through the transmission media in a given period of time, which is measured in bits per second (bps). The data rate is directly influenced by the amount of data being transmitted and the bandwidth of the media, just as the traffic flow on a highway will be influenced by the number of lanes and the number cars that need to use that highway to get to their destinations (Kish 1998).

The bandwidth capacity of a cable has been specified in cables prior to CAT5, but it did not seem to be as much of a factor until now when bandwidth is everything with today's electronic superhighways. Both category 5 and 5E cables specify 100-Mhz bandwidth signals. Without getting into the specific details of calculating the data rates of CAT5 and CAT5E, it suffices to say that these cables are being pushed to their limits when trying to achieve 1 Gb/sec transmission rates, which is becoming the data-rate standard today for LAN interconnect speeds.

In 2002, a category 6 cable was introduced that offers higher performance specs along with a greater bandwidth of 250 Mhz. CAT6 cabling systems are better able to meet the bandwidth demands associated with 1 and 10 Gb/sec requirements that are typical with today's LANs. To take advantage of the more stringent specifications of the CAT6 cable, installations must incorporate jacks, patch cables, and panels that meet the CAT6 requirements. Mixing older CAT5 components with CAT6 cabling would bring the overall cable infrastructure down to CAT5 standards.

On the horizon, the proposed category 7 cable will support bandwidths up to 600 Mhz and further reduce cross talk and signal loss. CAT7 cable will also incorporate newly designed cable connection components including jacks and patch panels that will function better at the higher frequencies. The overall trend in twisted-pair cabling standards focus on increasing performance and stability at higher frequencies (bandwidths) (Black Box Explains 2005; Global Technologies 2002; Kish 1998).

Twisted-Pair Cable Network Applications

Twisted-pair cable uses a special modular connector for categories up to and including CAT6. Standard telephone wire uses a four-connection plug called an RJ-11. For network applications, an eight-connector RJ-45 is used (see Figure 12). UTP wire pairs often consist of a solid core with a thin layer of insulation. The installation of RJ-45 connectors, called *insulation displacement connectors* (IDCs), requires a special crimping tool that pushes the connector into the insulated wire. When each connector is pushed into the wire, the insulation is pierced just enough to make contact with the center core of the wire (Spurgeon 2000).

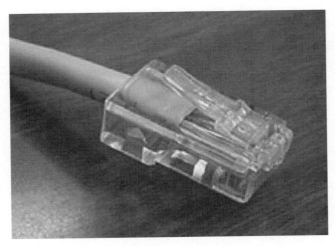

Figure 12: RJ-45 connector

Figure 13: RJ-45 connection to a network interface card

Table 3: Ethernet Twisted-Pair Cable Specifications

Characteristic	Specification
Maximum cable segment length	100 m
Maximum number of devices per segment	1
Bandwidth 10BaseT 100BaseT4, 100BaseTX 1000BaseT	10 Mbps 100 Mbps 1,000 Mbps
Topology	Star
Cable access method	CSMA/CD

Twisted-pair cable is typically used for point-to-point wiring, such as with star topology configurations. UTP is connected to a network device via a NIC's RJ-45 jack (see Figure 13), with the other end connected to a hub, switch, or router. In some cases, a patch panel or punch-down block may be used to better organize cabling before it is attached to the devices.

There are several IEEE Ethernet standards for twisted-pair media. The most documented are the 10BaseT, 100BaseT, and 1000BaseT standards (see Table 3). All twisted-pair Ethernet standards require a maximum cable length of 100 m and use star topology, which allows only one network connection for each cable segment. Note that this is considerably less than the coaxial cable specifications. It is much more difficult to control high-frequency signals over twisted-pair; thus, shorter cable runs are used to cut down on the effects of a harsher electrical environment (Spurgeon 2000). The major differences between 10BaseT, 100BaseT, and 1000BaseT are their data rates: 10, 100, and 1000 Mbps, respectively.

Each IEEE specification describes which wire type is most suitable for a particular application. Category 3 cable is adequate for 10BaseT applications. In fact, only two of the four pairs of wire are actually used. The 100BaseT standard is a bit more complicated. There are three cable

configurations for the 100BaseT standard: 100BaseT4, 100BaseTX, and 100BaseFX. 100BaseT4 can produce 100-Mbps bandwidth using all four pairs of category 3, 4, 5, 5E, and 6 cables. With 100BaseTX, only two pairs of category 5, 5E, or 6 cables are used to transmit and receive at 100 Mbps. 100BaseFX is the fiber-optic extension for 100BaseT. 100BaseT is often referred to as Fast Ethernet.

One of the newest technologies, Gigabit Ethernet, transmits 250 Mbps over each of the four pairs of category 5E or 6 wires simultaneously for a total bandwidth of 1 Gbps. Gigabit Ethernet is ideal for network backbones that connect network switches and hubs together. Many are now talking about 10-Gigabit Ethernet, which is in its early stages of development and implementation. Currently, the IEEE specification for 10-Gigabit Ethernet is for the use of fiber-optic cable, but development for a copper-based standard is underway and predicted to be completed within the next few years. Once a twisted-pair specification comes to fruition, the cost for this super high-speed Ethernet standard will be greatly reduced (10 Gigabit Ethernet Alliance 1999, 2002; Tittel and Johnson 2001; Violino 2003).

Ethernet standards for UTP follow TIA/EIA 568 standards. Wire pairs within a particular category of cable are color coded. The preferred 568 standard dictates that wire pairs will consist of a green wire paired with a white wire with a green stripe, an orange wire paired with a white wire with an orange stripe, a blue wire paired with a white wire with a blue stripe, and a brown wire paired with a white wire with a brown stripe. Each pair will be attached to a specific connection on the RJ-45 connector (see Figure 14). *Tip* and *ring* are used to identify the connections made by each pair. These terms come from the old telephone systems, which required a patch cable to connect one telephone line to another. The connector on the patch cable consisted of a tip at the end and a ring separated by an insulator that separated the two conductors. These two conductors provided the path for transmitting or receiving communications. Traditional analog telephone lines require only one pair for operation. Network transmissions typically require two or four pairs. Note the earlier discussion regarding the required pairs for each of the Ethernet standards 10BaseT, 100BaseT, and 1000BaseT (Spurgeon 2000).

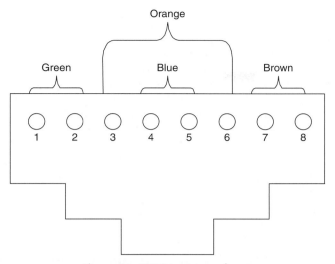

Figure 14: T568A wiring scheme

Table 4: Token-Ring Cable Specifications

Characteristic	Specification
Maximum cable segment length	101 m (type 1) 45 m (type 3) 100 m (cat 3) 225 m (cat 5) 400 m (STP)
IEEE specification	802.5
Bandwidth	4, 16, or 100 Mbps
Topology	Star-wired ring
Cable access method	Token passing

The majority of network device connections using UTP use *straight-through wiring*, which means that both ends of the RJ-45 connector are wired exactly the same way. Each pair of cables either transmits or receives data. Likewise, each NIC transmits data through certain connections and receives through others via its RJ-45 port. If a straight cable was connected to two NIC ports, then the result would be that the transmit connections of both ports would be connected to each other, as would the receive links. It should be apparent that when one NIC transmitted, the other would not receive it because of the direct connections between the ports. Therefore, there must be some kind of crossover that makes a connection between the transmit and the receive pairs. In reality, most network connections between devices are made via hubs or switches. These devices provide the crossover for the transmit and receive pairs.

For some applications, a special *crossover cable* is required. A crossover cable is made by crossing pairs two and three on the opposite end of the connecting cable. This allows two network devices to be connected independently without using a hub or other central wiring point. For example, if a small office with two computers wanted to network, it could build or buy a crossover cable and connect the NICs from both computers together to form a small network without the expense of a hub. Crossover cables are also used to connect hubs or switches together if they are not supplied with an *uplink port*. Uplink ports are optional ports that take care of uncrossing the links between these centralized wiring points.

In comparison, there are several advantages and disadvantages to twisted-pair and coaxial cabling. Coax appears to have the distance contest won but is losing the bandwidth race. During the mid- to late 1980s, coax was the wire of choice, but now twisted-pair seems to be the predominate cable used for most LAN interconnections. Twisted-pair cable offers great flexibility within network design and layout in addition to its lower cost for material and installation. Even though maximum cable runs are shorter than coax, 100 m is still a significant distance

for most network connections. With applications being developed to use the newest categories of UTP—CAT6 and CAT7—the potential advances for twisted-pair cable are encouraging with regard to increased bandwidth and expanded connection options.

Token-Ring Cabling

In the mid-1980s, IBM developed the token-ring architecture that used a special type of twisted-pair wiring. IBM engineered a cabling system that included nine cable types, numbered from one to nine. These cable types included STP, UTP, and fiber-optic media. For token-ring networks, types 1 (STP) and 3 (UTP) were the most prevalent. Type 1 cable allowed for lengths of up to 101 m, with a maximum data rate of 16 Mbps. Because of its lack of shielding, type 3 cable runs were limited to 45 m and a data rate of 4 Mbps (Tittel and Johnson 2001). Today, most token-ring applications use UTP category 3 or 5 cable with RJ-45 connectors. As noted in Table 4, there have been some improvements in cable lengths with the use of these media (Feit 2000).

The IEEE specification for token ring is 802.5, which describes the data rate of 4 or 16 Mbps using the token-passing cable access method. In 1999, *high-speed token ring* (HSTR) introduced an improved bandwidth that resulted in a data rate of 100 Mbps with twisted-pair or fiber-optic cable. Token ring uses a star-wired ring topology (see Figure 6). Fault tolerance is probably the biggest advantage the token-ring architecture has to offer because of the logical continuous ring that is created when using the IBM cabling system along with the star-wired ring topology that provides a dual path for data transmission. Theoretically, if a cable is cut, the token-ring network can continue to operate because of the redundant path. Another plus is the use of the token-passing access method, which eliminates collisions (Dean 2003; Feit 2000; Tittel and Johnson 2001).

FIBER-OPTIC CABLE

The bandwidth capacities of coax and twisted pair are dwarfed by that of fiber-optic cable. Consider that the capacity of a simple telephone line to carry data is equivalent to the flow of liquid through a drinking straw. It would take a tunnel large enough to drive a bus through to equal the bandwidth of a single fiber-optic strand using today's technologies. Furthermore, if technology existed to fully utilize fiber-optic capabilities, then it would take a tunnel the diameter of the moon to handle the flow of liquid equal to its potential bandwidth (Jamison 2001).

Fiber-optic cable carries optical pulses rather than electrical signals, which eliminates any possible electrical interference. All types of conducted communication media are vulnerable to electronic eavesdropping to some degree, but fiber-optic cable is less prone to eavesdropping because its signal does not radiate outside of the media as does copper-based wire. Therefore, the only way to intercept data from fiber-optic cable would be to tap into it, which would require a great deal of effort and skill.

Fiber-optic cable lengths are measured in kilometers rather than meters, which greatly reduces the number of signal-repeating devices required for long-distance cable runs. One of the most impressive characteristics is the high volumes of data that can be pumped through optical fibers. All this makes fiber-optic cable the medium of choice for many WAN applications, where network traffic can cause major bottlenecks (Tittel and Johnson 2001). In addition, many people believe that fiber-optic cables may become the norm rather than the exception for interconnecting network devices on a LAN (Kostal 2001; Sinks and Balch 2001; Vickers 2001).

Components

Fiber-optic cable consists of three components: a fiber core, cladding, and a protective outer sheath. The *inner core* is either glass or plastic fiber. Plastic is used when a flexible cable is needed; however, plastic cable is more susceptible to attenuation than glass, which limits the length of the cable. *Cladding* provides a coating that keeps the light waves within the fiber. The outer *protective jacket* is used to protect the fiber inside (Tittel and Johnson 2001).

Fiber Modes

Fiber-optic cable comes in two forms: single and multiple mode. Single-mode fiber is best for applications that require great distances. This fiber is narrow and requires an extremely focused source of data transmission that can keep the light waves on a straight, continuous path. The narrow internal core makes room for one-way traffic only. This reduces obstacles (stray light) that might interfere with the delivery of packets, resulting in more reliable transmissions over longer distances. A laser is normally used as the generating source for single-mode transmissions because it can produce the narrow band of light needed (Jamison 2001).

Multimode fiber (MMF) is less expensive than single-mode because its transmission devices consist of light-emitting diodes (LEDs), which are not as costly as laser sources. MMF fibers also have a larger core than single mode. A wider core helps to compensate for information loss because of light dispersion when using less precise light-emitting sources. A larger core allows the light wave to bounce around, which results in shorter transmission distances. The connections to the fiber are easier to make to the larger core, however. MMF is ideal for shorter cable runs within single buildings for LAN backbones (Jamison 2001).

Fiber-Optic Cable Network Applications

There are four major types of fiber connectors: *straight* (ST), *straight connection* (SC), *medium interface connector* (MIC), and *subminiature type A* (SMA) (see Figure 15). ST is often used for interconnections between individual fibers and optical devices. When joining optical fibers, an SC connector may be used. This connector consists of connections for two fibers: one for receiving and the other for sending. MIC connectors are one-piece connectors similar to the SC used to connect both the transmit and the receive fibers. It is primarily used with the *fiber distributed data interface* (FDDI) protocol. As with the ST connector, SMA uses individual connectors for each fiber. The major difference is that SMA uses either a straight or a stepped ferrule to ensure a precise fit, whereas the ST connector uses a bayonet twist-lock connection (Tittel and Johnson 2001).

The major differences between fiber-optic and other cable types are fiber optics' long-distance cable runs and high bandwidth. For example, the maximum fiber length for the 100BaseFX Ethernet standard is 2000 m, and the data rate for 1000BaseSX tops out at 2000 Mbps. More recently, the 10GBaseSR, 10GBaseLR, and 10GBaseER standard reach 10,000 Mbps. These specifications easily exceed other cable specifications. The potential of fiber-optic cable is limited by the technology that exists today. As the cost of fiber declines and the advances in transmission devices continue to improve, the use and performance of fiber will continue to grow.

In some applications, fiber optic is not needed for its high bandwidth but to facilitate long cable lengths or to block unwanted electrical interference. For example, the

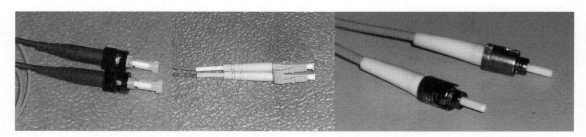

Figure 15: Fiber-optic cable with connectors

Table 5: Fiber-Optic Cable Specifications

Characteristic	Specification
Maximum cable segment length	2000–40,000 m
IEEE specification	802.3
Bandwidth	100–10,000 Mbps
Topology	Star
Cable access method	CSMA/CD

100BaseFX specification supports the use of fiber-optic cable. With the exception of distance, the other specifications for 100BaseFX are essentially the same as that described for UTP cabling (see Table 5). Token ring also has a cable specification for the use of fiber optic for connecting its MAUs. Again, this does not fully utilize fiber optic's full bandwidth potential, but it allows for longer cable runs.

Fiber-optic applications do not stop at 100 Mbps. Gigabit Ethernet, 1000BaseLX and 1000BaseSX each sport data rates of 1000 Mbps. The major difference in these two standards is the type of laser used. 1000BaseLX uses a long-wavelength laser that can transmit a signal over 5000 m of fiber in full duplex mode. A short-wavelength laser is used in 1000BaseSX applications that support a maximum cable length of 550 m and 2000 Mbps data rates in full duplex mode. Still in its early stages, 10-Gigabit Ethernet is sure to accelerate the use of fiber-optic cable into the future (10 Gigabit Ethernet Alliance 2002; Tittel and Johnson 2001).

The only thing holding fiber-optic transmission rates at bay is the devices used to drive the signals through the fibers. As noted at the beginning of this section, the potential of fiber-optic media is truly enormous. Currently, the primary application for fiber-optic cabling is for long connections and network backbones. There are some limited applications of direct connections between individual computers and hubs, but many people feel that this will increase over time as equipment and installation costs continue to decrease.

COMPARISONS AND CONTRASTS

When comparing and contrasting the advantages and disadvantages of the various types of cables, the particular application must be considered. It may be true that fiber-optic cable has the potential to transmit data at much faster rates than UTP, but if bandwidth is not an issue, then the added complexity involved in installing fiber optic where it is not needed would make it a bad choice. Table 6 compares and contrasts each cable type discussed in this chapter, showing more clearly how a particular cable may be applied (Tittel and Johnson 2001).

No hard and fast rules govern cable selection. Each business or industry must evaluate and determine its specific cabling needs. From the discussion in this chapter, it should be fairly obvious that the use of coaxial cable is fading, which means that plans for new network installation would best avoid using coax. This will help narrow down cable selection to twisted-pair, fiber-optic cable, or both. The physical size, number of devices, and distances between devices will also inform planning decisions.

MEDIA SECURITY

When designing a network infrastructure, the security of conductive communications media should be a strong consideration in the overall network design. Most common security breaches are the result of someone hacking into an organization's network through security holes in user-authentication policies or vulnerabilities in network operating systems from far distances. Security flaws of this order seem to upstage the potential risks associated with the physical security of network devices and cabling, but these risks do exist. For example, a network's infrastructure could be at risk if the physical cable routes are not carefully thought out. The physical path of a cable must be secure to prevent someone from tapping into the network, which would result in an unauthorized connection. Also, connecting devices such as hubs or switches placed on the floor or up in a crawl space in a common area of a building may pose a security risk.

As noted earlier, the physical location of the network cabling has the potential to create a security risk if not protected. Copper cabling, such as coax and twisted-pair, are probably the most vulnerable because of the simplicity of splicing into an exposed cable. Areas of special concern would be the cable routes that run through or above common areas of a building, along with cables that are run outside of the building or underground. In many ways, tapping into a computer network by an unauthorized cable tap may make a network more vulnerable to attacks than from external security threats. If access is gained via

Table 6: Comparison of Cable Types

Cable	Bandwidth	Length	Interference	Installation	Cost
Thinwire coax	10 Mbps	185 m	Moderate	Easy	Low
Thickwire coax	10 Mbps	500 m	Low	Hard	High
UTP	100 Mbps	100 m	High	Easy	Low
STP	1000 Mbps	100 m	Moderate	Moderate	Moderate
Fiber-optic	10 Gbps	100 km	None	hard	Very high

a wire tap to the internal network infrastructure, external security measures such as firewalls would provide no protection. Also with direct access to the LAN, a person might be able to use eavesdropping or sniffing utilities to access security devices and reconfigure them to allow external access. Once a security device has been reconfigured, sensitive company data (such as product design secrets, customer information, and financial data) might be lost or stolen (Campbell, Calvert, and Boswell 2003).

Another risk involving communications media security is electronic eavesdropping. Cable that uses a copper-type conductor can be vulnerable because of the electromagnetic emissions it produces. With the right type of equipment, sensitive network traffic could be intercepted. Twisted-pair cables used in Ethernet applications are most likely targets for electronic eavesdropping because most of these cables are not shielded. This type of threat is often hard to combat if a network is constructed using nonshielded wire.

Once the potential physical security threats have been identified, it is fairly simple to eliminate many of these concerns. With regard to wiretaps, network designs should make sure that all cable runs are not exposed to unsecured areas. In cases in which cables must be routed in public areas or outside of buildings, copper-based media should be replaced with fiber-optic cable, which is difficult to tap. Several options of protection are available for electronic eavesdropping. One is to reduce electromagnetic emissions by using a shielded twisted-pair cable. Another, although expensive, option would be to replace copper-type transmission media with fiber-optic cables, which would eliminate any possible electronic emissions. Of course it would be expensive to use fiber throughout an entire network. A final alternative, which is orthogonal to transmission media decisions, would be to encrypt any sensitive company information before it is transmitted over the communication lines (Campbell, Calvert, and Boswell 2003).

Threats to a network's physical transmission media are real and need to be considered in all infrastructure designs. In most cases, it is not expensive for an organization to protect its network from wiretaps and eavesdropping. Business and industry need to consider the possible holes in physical security and plan cable runs and use cable types that will reduce or eliminate the possible risks to the internal network. In addition, using encryption for sensitive data transmissions should protect against any breach of security with regard to electronic eavesdropping.

CONCLUSION

Conductive transmission cables provide the highway for data communications. This chapter has discussed the most popular types of cable in use today. As times change, the applications and uses for these various cable types will change. Some limiting factors for conductive transmission media are cable attenuation and the devices that drive the information through them such as NICs, hubs, and switches. We saw that data rates for twisted-pair cable have increased from approximately 1 to 1,000 Mbps over the past twenty years. Transmissions speeds over fiber-optic cable are only now being realized. What are the limits? What does the future hold for conductive transmission cables? How do wireless technologies fit into network communications? No one knows the answers to these questions, but at least the questions are being asked, so researchers can continue to experiment and produce new applications for all transmission options.

GLOSSARY

Bandwidth: The maximum range of frequencies a communications medium can carry.
Baseband: A digital transmission signal that uses a single channel to communicate with devices on a network.
Broadband: An analog transmission that carries multiple digital signals over multiple channels.
Cross talk: An electromagnetic field surrounding certain types of cable that may interfere with adjacent wires.
Hub: A central wiring point for network devices configured in a star topology. Its purpose is to repeat the broadcast packets to all connected nodes.
Impedance: The resistance of conducted communications media to a transmitted signal.
Insertion loss: The loss or attenuation of a signal that occurs each time a device is inserted into a network using conductive communications media.
Local area network (LAN): A collection of computers connected to a network within a single floor or building.
Network interface card (NIC): An electronic device that is installed in a network node that provides a link to the network media.
Node: Any device connected directly to a network.
Packet: An entity that contains data plus other information (such as destination, origination, and error-checking bits) and is transmitted over a network.
Protocol: A set of rules that specify how communicating entities will format data and process events.
Signal attenuation: The loss of signal strength as data travels the length of the cable that is caused by the cable, connectors, or other devices on the conducted communication medium.
Terminator: A device attached to a cable configured with a bus topology that eliminates signal bounce.
Topology: The physical cabling configuration of a network.

CROSS REFERENCES

See *Ethernet LANs*; *Local Area Networks*; *Optical Fiber Communications*; *Token Ring LANs*; *Wireless Channels*.

REFERENCES

Black Box Explains. 2005. Retrieved from www.blackbox.com/Tech_Support/Black_Box_Explains.aspx?cid=45&bid=2033.
Campbell, P., B. Calvert, and S. Boswell. 2003. *Security + guide to network security fundamentals*. Toronto: Course Technology.
Carr, J. J. 1999. Coax 'n' stuff. *Popular Electronics*, 16(9): 77–9.

Dean, T. 2003. *Enhanced networking + guide to networks*. Toronto: Course Technology.

Feit, S. 2000. *Local area high speed networks*. Upper Saddle River, NJ: New Riders.

Fogle, D. 1995. Lay of the LAN: Cabling basics. *Network Magazine*, April 1, www.networkmagazine. com/showArticle.jhtml?articleID=8702649 (retrieved March 21, 2005).

Global Technologies. 2002. Cat 5E, cat 6, cat 7 cable (retrieved from www.globaltec.com/catext100.html).

Jamison, E. 2001. Finding out about fiber. *Poptronics*, 2(11): 21–3.

Kish, P. 1998. *Enhanced cabling solutions for gigabit networks*. Fort Mill, SC: NORDX/CDT.

Kostal, H. 2001. Switching to all-optical networks. *Lightwave*, 18(13): 106–8.

Network Magazine. 1999. Cabling (retrieved from www. networkmagazine.com/article/NMG20000724s0010).

Sinks, C., and J. Balch. 2001. Fiber snakes its way closer to the desk. *Lightwave*, 18(11): 86–8.

Spurgeon, C. E. 2000. *Ethernet: The definitive guide*. Cambridge, MA: O'Reilly.

10 Gigabit Ethernet Alliance. 1999. Gigabit Ethernet: Accelerating the standard for speed (retrieved from www.10gea.org/Tech-whitepapers.htm).

———. 2002. 10 Gigabit Ethernet technology overview white paper (retrieved from www.techonline.com/ community/member_company/non_member/tech_ paper/5308/content_21170).

Tittel, E., and D. Johnson. 2001. *Guide to networking essentials*. Toronto: Course Technology.

Vickers, L. 2001. Emerging technology: Is fiber optic destined for the desktop. *Network Magazine* (retrieved from www.networkmagazine.com/article/ NMG20010103S0004).

Violino, B. 2003. Cutting 10G costs with copper. *Network World Fusion* (retrieved from www.nwfusion.com/ research/2003/092210gcopper.html).

Wireless Channels

Okechukwu C. Ugweje, *University of Akron*

INTRODUCTION

The current popularity of wireless communication system is driven mainly by the commercial success of the second-generation digital mobile wireless standards, as well as the technological advances in device implementations and sophisticated signal-processing algorithms. With the continued growth of mobile radio communications, the study of radio wave propagation is even more important in determining system parameters and facilitating design and development. Future generation wireless systems are no longer used to transmit voice only but instead transmit large multimedia data. Currently, the demand for very high data rate Internet access for mobile users and the desire for multimedia services through the Internet with seamless connectivity is driving the need to design high-speed reliable wireless communication systems. Characteristics such as bandwidth on demand capability, global roaming, and interoperability are desirable. However, to achieve these improvements, accurate characterization and modeling of the channel is essential. Hence, the importance of developing effective propagation models for wireless communication systems cannot be overemphasized.

The goal of this chapter is to present a tutorial on wireless channels in general by examining the fundamental terminology, definitions, concepts, and modeling techniques. First, we introduce the concept of radio wave propagation, which is fundamental in any wireless communication system. Then the losses associated with large-scale propagation and their mechanisms are characterized. This is followed by examining the channel-modeling techniques for small-scale fading effects, and the characterization of the fading environment in a wireless channel.

RADIO WAVE PROPAGATION

Propagation is the process of wave motion from the *transmitter* (Tx) to the *receiver* (Rx). During propagation, the signal amplitude may be attenuated. The signal may also be subjected to *time variability* (signal strength and quality varies with time), *space variability* (signal strength and quality varies with location and distance), and *frequency variability* (signal strength and quality differs on different frequencies). This implies that the transmitted signal in the channel is attenuated, delayed, and phase-distorted, with noise and possibly interference added, thereby presenting fundamental limitation on the system *quality of service* (QoS). Because of the limitation of the channels, sophisticated signal design, transmission, and reception schemes are required to maintain reliable communication.

Before we can design better wireless communication systems, we must thoroughly understand the characteristics of the channel because it imposes limitations on the quality of the transmission. Because of this, wireless systems engineers are now more interested in understanding and predicting radio wave propagation characteristics in various environments (urban, suburban, indoor, etc.). For example, the study of propagation is used to determine where base stations should be placed, what transmission powers should be used, what radio channel is to be assigned to a cell, and what types of handoff decision strategies or algorithms are to be used. To design an efficient wireless communication system, it is important to understand how a radio frequency (RF) signal is transformed from the time it leaves a Tx to the time it reaches the Rx. The various mechanisms of radio wave propagation are summarized in this section.

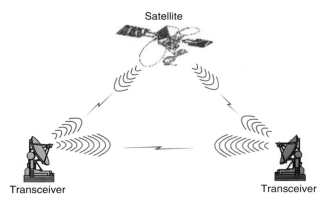

Figure 1: Illustration of free space LOS propagation

Free Space Propagation

By definition, *free space* (FS) is a region of space in which there are no obstacles to get in the way, no gases to absorb energy, and nothing to scatter radio waves. Free space is essentially a vacuum by definition. When a radio wave propagates in free space, it is the approximation to "ideal" propagation in which other mechanisms of propagation (discussed below) are not present or significant. It is simply a mode of propagation that requires a direct *line of sight* (LOS) for the radio waves to propagate between the Tx and Rx, unobstructed via a single path. In FS propagation, a radiated radio wave from a Tx in a given direction will ideally propagate outward from the Tx towards the Rx in a straight line traveling at the speed of light. Free space propagation involving direct LOS is illustrated in Figure 1. This mode of propagation is present in many terrestrial microwave and satellite communication systems.

Radio LOS is a necessary but not sufficient requirement to obtain FS propagation. The first *Fresnel zone* clearance is also needed (SoftWright 1999). The first Fresnel zone illustrated in Figure 2, for directional antennae, describes that portion of the radio wave path in which there are no obstacles. It is an ellipsoidal region surrounding the direct beam between the Tx and the Rx antennae. Additional Fresnel zones (second, third, etc.) may contain some level of obstacles that exist beyond the boundaries of the first Fresnel zone. Microwave systems using waveguides and parabolic antennae have approximately one-half the total transmitted energy in the first Fresnel zone, which accounts for some 25 percent of the total received energy. Microwaves passing an obstacle such as a hilltop, a building, or a tree may have part of their strength obstructed, thereby decreasing the signal level at the receiving antenna. Thus, full path clearance is desired for LOS and free space propagation. If at all possible, an LOS microwave path should be laid out with first Fresnel zone clearance.

Suppose that the source of the radio wave is from an isotropic antenna (i.e., a source radiating equally in all directions). The total energy is uniformly spread out over a spherical area around the source. In practice, it is of interest to know the received power, P_r, relative to an isotropic radiator at a distance d or simply how much energy gets from the transmit antenna to the receive antenna. This power is simply the incident power flux density, S_{inc}, multiplied by the effective capture area (or aperture) of the antenna, A_{eff}, such that

$$
\begin{aligned}
P_r &= S_{inc} \times A_{eff} \\
&= \left(\frac{P_t G_t}{4\pi d^2}\right) \times \left(\frac{G_r \lambda^2}{4\pi}\right) = P_t G_t G_r \left(\frac{\lambda}{4\pi d}\right)^2 \quad (1) \\
&= EIRP \times G_r \left(\frac{\lambda}{4\pi d}\right)^2 \ watts,
\end{aligned}
$$

where P_t is the transmit power output, G_t is the transmit antenna gain, G_r is the receive antenna gain, λ is the wavelength, and $EIRP = G_t P_t$ is the *effective isotropic radiated power* (EIRP).

Equation 1 is the well known Friis equation, which represents the ideal received signal assuming no loss in the channel. It is evident from Equation 1 that as the propagation distance increases, the radiated energy is spread out over a larger distance d such that the received power decreases in proportion to d^2 or at the rate of 20 dB per decade.

Mechanism of Radio Wave Propagation

Beside the idealistic FS propagation, there are other propagation mechanisms such as reflection, refraction, diffraction, scattering, and absorption. A brief overview of these mechanisms is presented below.

Reflection

Reflection occurs when a radio wave strikes an object with larger dimensions compared to its wavelength. The part

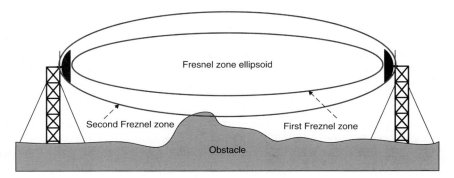

Figure 2: Fresnel zone clearance between transmitter and receiver

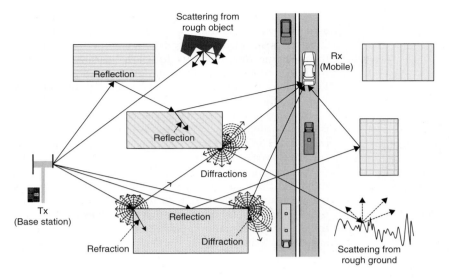

Figure 3: Illustration of the wireless propagation mechanisms *reflection, diffraction, refraction,* and *scattering*

of the wave that is not reflected back loses some of its energy by being absorbed into the material; the remaining wave passes through the reflecting object. All radio waves will undergo some level of reflection if the propagation wave encounters abrupt changes in the physical medium (see Figure 3). The more abrupt the discontinuity, the more pronounced the reflection; depending on the type of material, the RF energy can be partially reflected, fully reflected, or absorbed. From the properties of the two media, one could compute the amount of reflection. If the incident object is a good conductor, then the wave is totally reflected with angle of incidence the same as angle of reflection. Reflecting rays from different surfaces may interfere constructively or destructively at the receiver. In microwave systems, the waves usually reflect from ground and surrounding objects, producing multiple-ray paths between the Tx and the Rx, a phenomenon known as the *multipath propagation*.

Refraction

Refraction is the bending of radio waves. A radio wave can be refracted or bent if it is transmitted into ionized layers (e.g., the atmosphere) or at the boundary between two dielectrics. When the incident wave propagates into another medium at an angle, refraction occurs. When radio waves propagate from a medium of one density to a medium of another density, the speed of the wave changes, causing the waves to bend at the boundary of the two media and toward the denser medium or where the radio wave's velocity is the least. For example, in the atmosphere, as the wave enters the denser layer of charged ions, its upper portion moves faster than its lower portion, causing the abrupt speed increase at the upper layer and thereby causing the wave to bend back toward the Earth. The amount of refraction a radio wave undergoes depends on the ionization density of the layers, the frequency of the radio wave, the angle at which the radio wave enters the layer, and the physical characteristics or refractive index of the medium.

Diffraction

The mechanism of *diffraction* occurs when a radio wave encounters some obstruction along its path and tends to propagate around the edges and corners and behind the obstruction. Each time a radio wave passes an edge such as a corner of a building, it bends around the edge and continues to propagate into the area shadowed by the object. This is illustrated in Figure 3, where the arrows are used to indicate the direction of propagation and how the signal reaches the areas around the corner because of sources of secondary waves situated at the corner of the obstacle. The more the waves have to bend around a corner, the more they lose their energy. The areas to which the rays have to bend more gain relatively less additional field strength than the areas to which the rays can proceed almost linearly. The field strength of the secondary waves is much smaller than that of the primary wave. In practice, the diffracted waves can be neglected if there is a LOS between the Tx and the Rx. The height or dimension of the obstruction affects the amount of diffraction at the wavelength of the transmission. The same obstruction height may produce lower diffraction loss at higher λ than at lower λ. Radio waves with long wavelengths compared to the diameter of an obstruction are easily propagated around the obstruction. As the wavelength decreases, the obstruction causes more and more attenuation until, at extremely high frequencies, a definite shadow zone develops.

Scattering

Waves are attenuated through molecular absorption in a way similar to sound waves being absorbed in the wall between two adjacent rooms. It is the result of small objects and irregularities in the channel, rough incident surfaces, or particles in the atmosphere. It occurs when the radio wave encounters objects with dimensions that are on the order of or smaller than the propagating wavelength; this causes the signal to spread in all directions. *Scattering*, as in diffraction, causes energy to be radiated in many different directions, and the amount of scattering depends on the surface roughness of the scattering object. Scattering has been proven to be one of the most difficult mechanisms to model, and its theoretical prediction is also more complicated to analyze. Scattering can be neglected in many practical cases compared to other mechanisms such as diffraction, reflection, and combinations of reflections and diffractions.

Absorption

Absorption describes the process of radio energy penetrating a material or substance and being converted to heat. When radio waves propagate in the atmosphere and in higher degree materials such as glass, concrete, and wood, RF energy can be absorbed. Two cases of absorption of radio waves are prevalent. One occurs when radio waves are incident on a lossy medium, and the other results from atmospheric effects. When a radio wave strikes an object, the incident wave propagates into the lossy medium and the radio energy experiences exponential decay with distance as it travels into the material. The wave is either totally dissipated or will reemerge from the material with smaller amplitude and continue to propagate. Particles in the atmosphere also absorb RF energy. Absorption through the atmosphere depends on weather conditions such as humidity, drizzle, heavy rain, fog, snow, and hail. Absorption of RF energy through the atmosphere is not significant and may be ignored at frequencies below 10 GHz.

Multipath Propagation

The term *multipath* is simply used to describe the multiple propagation paths of a radio wave as it travels from the Tx to the Rx. *Multipath propagation* (MP) is the result of the collective effect of the different propagation mechanisms discussed above. In other words, when all of the different propagation mechanisms are significant, it is more likely that the radio wave may take multiple paths as it propagates from the Tx to the Rx.

An illustration of multipath propagation is shown in Figures 3 and 4. In Figure 3, the mobile unit receives multiple radio waves from the fixed base station (BS). As the mobile unit moves, the wireless channel's characteristics change and may impact adversely on the quality of the received signal. In Figure 4, a radio wave transmitted from the transmitter denoted as Tx can get to the receivers through many paths. Observe that four waves are received by receiver 1 (denoted as Rx_1). One path is the direct wave from Tx to Rx_1. Another path is the basic ground reflected wave (Tx–A–Rx_1). The third wave is reflected, diffracted, or both from a surrounding object B. Waves can also refract and diffract from the atmospheric layers to a receiver (e.g., Tx–C–Rx_1). So at Rx_1, the received signal is a combination of the direct, ground, reflected, and refracted radio waves that constitute the multipath components. These waves, having traveled different paths, arrive at the receiver Rx_1 at different times, with different amplitudes, and possibly with different phases. A similar situation can occur at receivers Rx_2, Rx_3, Rx_4, and Rx_5, depending on the distance and location. Receivers at Rx_3 and Rx_4 may experience waves with greater angle of incidence, delay, and multiple refractions from the atmospheric layers.

Radio waves that are received in phase reinforce each other and produce a stronger signal at the receiver, while those that are received out of phase produce weak or faded signal. Small alterations in the transmission path may change the phase relationship of the waves, causing periodic fading. In other words, multipath propagation leads to the phenomenon of *multipath fading* discussed later in this chapter. Because the multipath radio waves are attenuated differently and arrive with different path gains, time delays, and phases, they can interfere with the direct rays or with one another, causing significant fluctuations and hence degradation in the system performance. The resultant signal may vary widely in amplitude and phase, depending on the distribution of intensity and relative propagation time and bandwidth of the transmitted signal. If the Rx is a mobile unit, then the number of

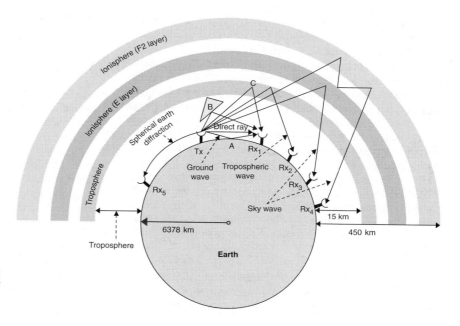

Figure 4: Multipath propagation consisting of several modes and mechanisms of propagation

paths may change drastically when the mobile changes its position or when the number of intervening obstacles increase or decrease.

Indoor Propagation

The use of wireless systems indoors introduces one of the biggest design challenges in communication systems. Since the advent of the IEEE 802.11 standard in 1997, the number and the use of *wireless local area networks* (WLANs) has continued to grow in popularity. WLAN-capable devices can now be found in laptops, desktops, personal digital assistants, gaming systems, and even *voice over Internet protocol* (VoIP) phones. These networks are primarily targeted for indoor use and are most often based on either the IEEE 802.11–type protocols using the unlicensed bands at 2.4–2.5 GHz or 5.15–5.85 GHz. Because of the popularity of these devices, lately more interest has been paid to the properties of indoor wireless channels.

Indoor propagation is somewhat different from the outdoor propagation environment, although it is characterized by the same propagation mechanisms. However, the influence and variability of the environment is much stronger indoors because the propagation distances covered are much smaller. Indoor propagation is affected by building layout (e.g., number of walls), construction materials, building type, the locations of transceivers or access points, as well as the propagating wavelength. Walls and obstacles made of different materials obstruct RF energy differently. The position and type of antenna mounting strongly influence the propagation (e.g. antennae mounted at the desk level, on the ceiling, or on the wall). In general, indoor channels may be classified as either LOS or obstructed with varying degrees of clutter. Detail presentation on the indoor propagation can be found in Hashemi (1993).

CHANNEL MODELING

Modeling the radio channel has always been one of the most difficult parts of wireless system design. Before wireless communication systems can be designed and deployed, accurate propagation characteristics of the environment are required. A variety of propagation models are available for approximating the channel characteristics. These models provide some insight into the effects of different channel characteristics on wireless communication systems. Some of the characteristics are determined analytically, and some are modeled statistically using measured propagation data. Measurements have been performed to obtain propagation loss information and signal-power variations for conventional radio communication systems (Anderson, Rappaport, and Yoshia 1995; Fleury and Leuthold 1996; Molkdar 1991). These measurements and studies have shown that, in general, radio wave propagation in the wireless channel can be decomposed into three components (Rappaport 2002; Prasad 1998):

1. Large-scale propagation path loss models that indicate the dependency of the mean power of the received signal to the distance d between the Tx and the Rx. These

models assume that the propagation is fairly constant over a large area and the signal is slowly time-varying. These models are used to (a) predict the mean signal strength between the Tx and the Rx for arbitrary d, (b) characterize the signal strength over large distances, (c) predict local average signal strength, (d) characterize statistical median path loss, and (e) predict coverage areas and service availability.

2. Medium-scale, slow-varying path loss models having log-normal distributions include medium-scale components that capture variations in the signal power over distances much larger than a few wavelengths. The idea is that the signal power measured at two different locations may be different from each other for the same Tx to Rx separation. It is commonly represented in terms of the mean signal strength and its variation around the mean resulting from shadowing.

3. Small-scale propagation models characterize the fast-varying signal with randomly distributed amplitude with or without LOS connection. These models describe the fading effects from rapid fluctuations of the radio wave amplitude over a short period of time (a few milliseconds up to seconds) or over a short travel distance (a few wavelengths) (Rappaport 2002). The small-scale models consider the fading associated with the superposition of the multipath radio waves at the receiver. The fading effects in the channel could be severe when the transceivers or the surrounding environments are in motion. With mobility, the received signal power may fluctuate by as much as 40 dB by moving a fraction of the wavelength.

In this section, we present a summary of the large- and medium-scale propagation modeling of the channel. The main objective is to present several methods of predicting path loss of a radio link between the Tx and the Rx. In practice, the aim is to deliver sufficient signal power to the Rx so that the required performance objective is achieved.

Path Loss Modeling

Path loss (PL) is a term used to characterize the relationship between the transmitted power, P_t, and received power, P_r, in a radio link. There are several PL models depending on the environment and the assumptions made. For example, *simple analytical models* are used for understanding and predicting individual paths and specific obstruction cases. We also have *general area models* used mainly for early system dimensioning, primarily driven by statistics and measurements. Finally, there are *point-to-point models* that are essentially analytical models used for detailed area coverage and system planning. These models are summarized in Figure 5, and the general concepts of the most commonly used models are highlighted in this section.

Free Space Propagation Path Loss

Although a transmitted radio wave in free space encounters no obstructions, the energy of the wave spreads out as it propagates. This spreading out of energy results in

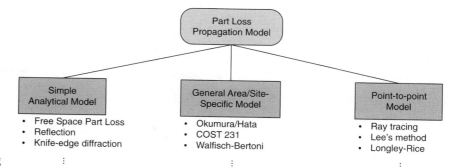

Figure 5: Propagation path loss modeling

the lowering of the intensity of the wave at some distance d from the source. This reduction in intensity is commonly referred to as *loss*. This is the loss that would be expected in an FS propagation environment or in a region free of any obstacles—the ideal case.

Calculating FS transmission loss is quite simple. Consider a Tx with power P_t coupled to an antenna that radiates energy equally in all directions (isotropic antenna). At a distance d from the Tx, the radiated power is distributed uniformly over a spherical area of $4\pi d^2$ (i.e., the surface area of a sphere of radius d). The channel attenuation, α, is defined as the ratio of the received power P_r and transmitted power P_t, which is given as

$$\alpha = \frac{P_r}{P_t} = G_t G_r \left(\frac{\lambda}{4\pi d}\right)^2 = G_t G_r \frac{1}{PL_{fs}}, \qquad (2)$$

where PL_{fs} (in dB) is the FS path loss. This implies that the signal-loss factor after accounting for transmit and receive antenna gains is given by

$$PL_{fs}(d) = \left(\frac{4\pi d}{\lambda}\right)^2 = \left(\frac{4\pi d f}{c}\right)^2, \qquad (3)$$

where f is the carrier frequency and c is the speed of light in FS. Notice that PL_{fs} is proportional to f^2 and d^2, the classic square-law dependence of signal power level and distance. Any doubling of the range or frequency increases PL_{fs} by a factor of 4 and reduces the received power in Equation 1 by a factor of 4 Note that PL_{fs} is valid only in the far-field range of $d_f > 2D^2/\lambda$ (or, equivalently, $d_f \gg D$ and $d_f \gg \lambda$), where D is the maximum dimension of the antenna.

We can express PL_{fs} in dB as follows:

$$PL_{fs}(d)_{dB} = 10\log_{10}\left(\frac{4\pi d}{\lambda}\right)^2 = 20\log_{10}\left(\frac{4\pi d}{\lambda}\right)$$

$$= \begin{cases} 32.45 + 20\log_{10} d + 20\log_{10} f, \\ \quad (d \text{ in km}, f \text{ in MHz}) \\ 36.6 + 20\log_{10} d + 20\log_{10} f, \\ \quad (d \text{ in miles}, f \text{ in MHz}) \end{cases} \qquad (4)$$

Hence, for a given frequency and distance, it is easy to compute precisely the PL_{fs}. The relationship between path loss and distance as well as frequency is clearly shown in

Equation 4. Each time the distance doubles, another 6 dB of signal is lost under FS conditions.

One may wonder as to why FS path loss is proportional to d^2 because, after all, the propagation is taking place in a vacuum (i.e., free space). But recall that the so-called loss is not a loss in the real sense because the wave is not dissipating energy, but simply spreading out. Because P_r is the product of incident power flux density and effective area (see Equation 1), it is also inversely proportional to d^2, which results in a decrease in intensity as the wave propagates. This is the reason why PL_{fs} is often referred to as *spreading loss*.

Another point that troubles some people when they see equations 3 or 4 is that path loss also increases as the square of the frequency. Does this mean that the transmission medium is inherently lossier at higher frequencies? Because antennae are more directive at high frequency, the losses instead should be decreasing as the frequency increases.

To explain this, notice that, although absorption of RF energy by various materials (buildings, trees, water vapor, etc.) tends to increase with frequency, it does not apply to free space propagation. The frequency dependence in this case results solely from the decrease in the effective gain of the receiving antenna as the frequency increases. This is reasonable because the electrical physical size of a given antenna type is inversely proportional to wavelength. If we double the frequency, the linear electrical dimensions of the antenna increase by a factor of 2 and the capture area by a factor of 4. The antenna therefore captures four times the power flux density at the higher frequency versus the lower one, and it delivers 6 dB more signal to the receiver. However, in most cases, we lose part of this 6 dB back by a decrease in the antenna's efficiency and hence the gain of the receiving antenna.

Path Loss over Smooth Plane

FS propagation is seldom the only mechanism of propagation in wireless channels. Under normal propagation conditions, LOS path may have adequate Fresnel zone clearance and still have path loss significantly different from PL_{fs}. If this is the case, the cause is probably multipath propagation resulting from reflections. This mode of propagation is used to account for multiple reflections of radio waves over a smooth plane, which depends not only on the Tx–Rx distance and wavelength but also on the heights of the Tx and Rx antennae.

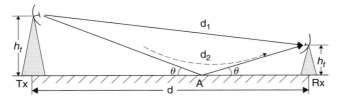

Figure 6: Two-ray propagation model

One common source of reflections is the ground, which is considered as a smooth surface. Ground reflection can be a major determinant of path loss and tends to be more of a factor on paths in rural areas compared to urban areas, because the ground reflection path in urban areas will often be blocked by the clutter of buildings and other infrastructure.

To illustrate this concept, a two-ray model is often used to demonstrate the effect of multipath propagation on the average received power. It assumes that the transmitted radio wave reaches the stationary Rx through a direct LOS path and indirectly by perfect reflection from the ground. This scenario is illustrated in Figure 6. The radio wave at the Rx is the sum of the FS propagation and a single reflected wave from the ground. The two rays arriving at the Rx can have different phases and, in the worst case, they can cancel each other out.

Assume for simplicity that the transmit and receive antennae are both isotropic radiators separated by distance d. The direct ray travels a distance d_1, and the reflected ray travels a total distance of d_2 to reach the receiving antenna after reflecting from point A. The angle of incidence θ and angle of reflection are the same. The path loss in this case depends on the relative amplitude and phase relationship of the two signals. In cases where the ground-reflected path has Fresnel clearance and suffers little loss, the reflected amplitude may approach that of the direct path. Thus, depending on the relative phase shift of the two paths, we may have an enhancement of as much as 6 dB over the direct path alone or cancellation resulting in additional path loss of 20 dB or more. The amplitude and phase of the reflected wave depend on several variables—including conductivity and permittivity of the reflecting surface (reflection coefficient), frequency of the wave, angle of incidence, and polarization—that are beyond the scope of this chapter. More detailed analysis can be found in Rappaport (2002) and Mark and Zhuang (2003).

Taking into account the phase difference, the received signal power is given by Mark and Zhuang (2003):

$$P_r(d) = P_t G_t G_r \left(\frac{\lambda}{4\pi d}\right)^2 \left[1 + \alpha_f e^{-j\beta_f} e^{j(\theta_2 - \theta_1)}\right]^2, \quad (5)$$

where α_f and β_f are the amplitude attenuation and carrier phase shift of the reflection wave, respectively. If $\alpha \cong 1$ (i.e., reflection loss is negligible), and $\beta_f = \pi$, for $\theta \ll 1$, then Equation 5 can be simplified to

$$P_r(d) = 4P_t G_t G_r \left(\frac{\lambda}{4\pi d}\right)^2 \left[\sin^2\left(\frac{2\pi h_r h_t}{\lambda d}\right)\right] \quad (6)$$

Hence, the corresponding path loss is (Mark and Zhuang 2003)

$$PL_{2-ray}(d) = -10\log_{10}\left\{4\left(\frac{\lambda}{4\pi d}\right)^2\left[\sin^2\left(\frac{2\pi h_r h_t}{\lambda d}\right)\right]\right\} dB, \quad (7)$$

after accounting for the transmitting and receiving antennae gains.

The result in Equation 7 is consistent with previous results that, in general, the path loss increases with the distance d. Also, a plot of Equation 7 (see Mark and Zhuang 2003, Figure 2.17) will show that the path loss has alternate minima and maxima as the distance between the Tx and the Rx increases.

Log-Distance Path Loss with Shadowing

Free space and the two-ray path loss models predict the received power as a deterministic function of distance, frequency, and antenna heights. Both models represent the mean received power at distance d In practice, however, the received power at some distance d is a random variable resulting from variation of the environment. The average received power varies from location to location in a random manner (Bertoni 2000). More precisely, the logarithmic value of the received signal power at distance d is normally distributed with standard deviation σ_{dB} around the logarithm of the local mean power. The magnitude of the standard deviation indicates the severity of signal fluctuations caused by irregularities in the receiving and transmitting antennae surroundings. The log-distance model generalizes path loss to account for environmental factors. The log-normal model allows for random power variations around the area mean power.

This model consists of two parts. The first part, given by

$$\overline{P}_r(d) = P_r(d_0)\left(\frac{d}{d_0}\right)^n, \ d \ge d_0, \quad (8)$$

predicts the path loss as the average received power, $\overline{P}_r(d)$, at distance d, where d_0 is a close-in reference distance, $P_r(d_0)$ is the reference received signal at distance d_0, and n is known as the path loss exponent, which is dependent on the environment. In this case, the path loss measured in dB is given by

$$\overline{PL}(d)_{dB} = \overline{PL}(d_0) + 10n\log_{10}\left(\frac{d}{d_0}\right). \quad (9)$$

The fact that the environment in the same Tx–Rx separation may be vastly different at two different locations is not considered by Equation 9. But path loss at a particular location is random and log-normally distributed about the mean.

The second part, denoted as X_σ, accounts for the shadowing effect, which reflects the variation of the received power at certain distances. X_σ is a zero-mean Gaussian-distributed random variable (in dB) with standard

Table 1: Typical Values of Path Loss Exponent n and Shadowing Deviation σ_{dB}

	Environment	Path loss exponent n	σ_{dB}(dB)
Outdoor	Free space	2.0	4.0–12
	Urban cellular/PCS	2.7–3.5	4.0–12
	Shadowed urban cellular/PCS	3.0–5.0	4.0–12
Indoor	Propagation LOS	1.6–1.8	3.0–6.0
	Office, soft partition	4.0–6.0	9.6
	Office, hard partition	4.0–6.0	7.0
	Factory, LOS	1.6–2.0	3.0–5.8
	Factory, obstructed	2.0–3.0	6.8

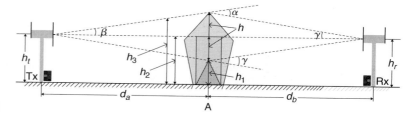

Figure 7: Diffraction loss calculations

deviation σ (also in dB). The standard deviation is larger than zero; in case of severe signal fluctuation, measurements indicate that it can be as high as 12 dB (Rappaport 2002).

Hence, the overall model of log-distance *path loss with shadowing* (PLWS) is represented by

$$\overline{PL}_{plws}(d)_{dB} = \overline{PL}(d_0) + 10n\log_{10}\left(\frac{d}{d_0}\right) + X_\sigma. \quad (10)$$

When the standard deviation, σ_{dB}, is zero, the log-normal model reduces to the conventional log-normal path loss model without shadowing, which could be seen as a specific case of the more general log-normal model. Some typical values of n and σ_{dB} are shown in Table 1. Larger values of n or σ_{dB} correspond to more obstructions or deviation from the mean value, respectively, and hence faster reduction in the average received power or variations.

Diffraction Path Loss

Diffraction loss is the loss of radio energy from obstructions (or shadowing) along the path of propagation that arise when the direct LOS is obstructed by objects larger than the λ. To calculate the loss introduced by these obstacles, obstructions that diffract signals are treated like sharply defined objects known as *knife edges* (Rappaport 2002). Loss is dependent on the number and geometry (especially the height) of the obstructions. Depending on the number of obstacles, the loss could be calculated assuming a single knife edge or multiple knife edges. It also measures the height of obstruction in relation to the height of antennae.

Figure 7 summarizes the geometry for the computation of path loss assuming single knife-edge obstruction.

A single obstruction with different heights represented by a triangle, a rectangle, and a pentagon are located at point A. Several cases are possible. The transmitter height (h_t) and receiver height (h_r) could be the same ($h_t = h_r$) or, more naturally, $h_t > h_r$. The obstruction heights denoted as h_1, h_2, and h_3 are compared with h_t and h_r as well as with λ. The same obstruction height may produce lower diffraction loss at higher λ than at lower λ. Radio waves grazing the top of the obstructions are shown as dotted lines. The angles of incidents and reflections are shown as α, β, and γ.

As in the two-ray propagation model, the path and the phase difference of the direct path and the diffracted wave can be estimated from the geometry of the environment with the obstruction taken into consideration. It can be shown that the phase difference can be approximated as

$$\Delta\theta = \frac{2\pi\Delta d}{\lambda} \simeq \frac{2\pi}{\lambda} \times \frac{(d_a + d_b)h^2}{2d_a d_b}, \quad (11)$$

with the parameters of Equation 11 shown in Figure 7, where h is the height from the LOS ray to the height of the obstruction.

To quantify diffraction losses, $\Delta\theta$ is normalized by the Freshnel-Kirchoff diffraction parameter v, such that $\Delta\theta = \pi v^2/2$, where v is a dimensionless parameter given by

$$v = h\sqrt{\frac{2}{\lambda}\left(\frac{1}{d_a} + \frac{1}{d_b}\right)} = h\sqrt{\frac{2(d_a + d_b)}{\lambda d_a d_b}} \quad (12)$$

By convention, v is positive when the direct path is blocked (i.e., the obstacle has positive height, $h > 0$) and negative when the direct path has some clearance (i.e., the obstacle has negative height, $h < 0$). When the direct path just grazes the object, then $h = v = 0$. Therefore, the knife-edge diffraction gain or loss in dB is then given as a function v according to the following equation (Rappaport 2002):

$$G_d(dB) = \begin{cases} 0 & v \leq -1 \\ 20\log(0.5 - 0.62v), & -1 \leq v \leq 0 \\ 20\log(0.5\exp(-0.95v)), & 0 \leq v \leq 1 \\ 20\log\left(0.4 - \sqrt{0.1184 - (0.38 - 0.1v)^2}\right), & 1 \leq v \geq 2.4 \\ 20\log(0.225/v), & v > 2.4 \end{cases}$$

(13)

For multiple obstructions between the Tx and the Rx, approximate techniques for computing diffraction loss have been proposed in Bullington (1977), Epstein and Peterson (1953), and Deygout (1966, 1991). In Bullington (1977), multiple obstructions are replaced by a single equivalent obstruction at the point where the LOS from the Tx and Rx intersect. This results in oversimplification of the model. In Epstein and Peterson (1953), loss of individual obstructions is calculated by drawing LOS between each obstacle. Then the diffraction loss of each obstacle is added to obtain the overall loss. This gives poor results when the obstructions are especially close to each other. In Deygout (1966, 1991), a search for the "main" obstacle location—that is, the point where the highest value of v occurs along the path—is first determined and used to compute the loss. Then diffraction losses over "secondary" obstacles are added to the diffraction loss over the main obstacle. The approach can achieve reasonably good agreement with more rigorous approaches, but in general it overestimates the diffraction loss in increasingly greater amounts as the path length increases.

EMPIRICAL PATH LOSS MODELS

Most mobile communication systems operate in complex propagation environments that cannot be accurately modeled by the large-scale path loss models described above. Several models based on measurements have been used to predict path loss in typical operating environments. These models are mainly based on measurements in a given frequency range and geographical area and then developed into analytical approximations of propagation losses. However, application of the models is not restricted to the frequencies or geographical areas on which they were developed. In practice, many cellular system designs use these models as a basis for performance analysis, to estimate link budgets, cell sizes and shapes, capacity, and handoff criteria. In this section, the most common types of empirical models are summarized.

Okumura Model

One of the most common models for signal prediction in urban areas is the *Okumura model* (Okumura, Ohmori, and Fukuda 1968). The model is based on detailed analysis of measurements made in Tokyo and its suburbs in late 1960s and early 1970s. The collected data included measurements on terrestrial wireless microwave channel,

which takes into account some of the propagation parameters and terrain information. With the measured data, Okumura produced analytical expression and a set of curves giving the median attenuation relative to free space in an urban area as a function of effective Tx and Rx antenna height. Different curves were produced for different coverage areas such as open, quasi open, suburban, and urban areas. The measurement were conducted with effective Tx antenna height $h_t = 200\,m$ and effective Rx antenna height $h_r = 3\,m$, $1 \leq d \leq 100\,km$, and $150 \leq f \leq 1920\,MHz$.

The analytical structure of the Okumura model is given by

$$L_p(d) = PL_{fs} + A_{mu}(f,d) - G(h_t) - G(h_r) - G_{area}, \quad (14)$$

where $L_p(d)$ is the median value of the propagation path loss, $A_{mu}(.)$ is the median attenuation relative to FS, $G(h_t)$ is the base station height gain factor, $G(h_r)$ is the mobile station height gain factor, and G_{area} is the gain resulting from the environment. The antenna height gains are strictly a function of height, and the model is valid for Rx antenna heights ranging from $30\,m$ to $1000\,m$.

To determine path loss using Okumura's model, PL_{fs} is first determined, and then the correction values $A_{mu}(.)$, $G(.)$, and G_{area} are obtained from either the plots or equation and then added to the PL_{fs} according to Equation 14.

Okumura's model typically results in $10\,dB$ to $14\,dB$ standard deviations between path loss predicated by the model and actual measurements in urban and suburban cellular systems. This model has served as the basis for high-level design of many existing wireless systems and has spawned several newer models adapted from its basic concepts and numerical parameters.

Hata Model

The *Hata model* is another commonly used empirical PL model (Hata 1980). This model is the empirical formula derived from Okumura's path loss measurements. The objective is to facilitate automatic calculation without the need for plots. The Hata PL equations are given as follows:

$$L_p\,(urban) = 69.55 + 26.16\log f - 13.82\log h_t$$
$$+ (44.9 - 6.55\log h_t)\log d - a(h_r)$$
$$L_p\,(suburban) = L_p(urban) - 2(\log(f/28))^2 - 5.4$$
$$L_p\,(rural) = L_p(urban) - 4.78(\log f)^2 - 18.33\log f - 40.98,$$

(15)

where the parameters in this model are the same as the Okumura model. The Rx antenna gain correction factors are given by

$$a(h_r) = \begin{cases} (1.1\log f - 0.7)h_r - (1.56\log f - 0.8), \\ \quad\text{suburban, rural} \\ 8.29(\log 1.54h_r)^2 - 1.1, \\ \quad\text{urban} \quad f \leq 300\,MHz \\ 3.2(\log 11.75h_r)^2 - 4.97, \\ \quad\text{urban} \quad f > 300\,MHz. \end{cases}$$

(16)

This model is most suitable for use when $150 \leq f \leq 1500\,\text{MHz}$, $30 \leq h_t \leq 200\,\text{m}$, $1 \leq h_r \leq 10\,\text{m}$, and $1 \leq d \leq 20\,\text{km}$. Although the Hata model does not imply path-specific corrections, which are available in Okumura model, it has significant practical value and provides predictions comparable to the Okumura model, especially when $d > 1\,\text{km}$. At distances less than 30 km, Hata values compare favorably within ± 1 dB of the Okumura values. At distances beyond 30 km, the Okumura curves drop below the Hata values. At 100 km, the difference varies from 7 dB to 15 dB.

This model is well suited for outdoor macrocell but not for personal communication systems, which have cells on the order of 1 km radius or less. Thus, it is a good model for first-generation cellular systems but does not model propagation well in current cellular systems with smaller cell sizes.

The COST-231 Model

The COST-231 model developed by the European Cooperative for Scientific and Technical (COST) research committee is one extension of the Hata model (COST 1991). It extends the model to the 1.8–2.0 GHz band in anticipation for use in the 1900 MHz PCS band. The COST path loss model is given by:

$$L_p(\text{urban}) = 46.3 + 33.9\log f - 13.82\log h_t - a(h_r) \\ + (44.9 - 6.55\log h_t)\log d + C_M, \qquad (17)$$

where the city size correction factor $C_M = 0$ for medium city and suburban area and $C_M = 3\,\text{dB}$ for metropolitan centers. The COST-231 model parameters have the following ranges: $1500 \leq f \leq 2000\,\text{MHz}$; $30 \leq h_t \leq 200\,\text{m}$; $1 \leq h_r \leq 10\,\text{m}$; and $1 \leq d \leq 20\,\text{km}$.

Walfisch-Bertoni Model

One of the drawbacks of the Okumura-type models discussed previously is that they do not consider the impact of diffraction from surrounding buildings. As cellular mobile radio systems migrated from 800 MHz (or 900 MHz) to 1800 MHz (or 1900 MHz), the effect of propagation became more pronounced at 1800 (or 1900 MHz) compared to 800 (or 900 MHz). Reflections are more effective, shadowings from obstructions are deeper, foliage absorption is more attenuative, and penetration into buildings through openings became more effective, but material absorption within buildings and their walls is more severe. Consequently, the net result is the greater signal loss for systems in the 1800 MHz (or 1900 MHz) range compared to the 800 MHz (or 900 MHz) range. Overall, coverage radius of a 1800 MHz (or 1900 MHz) base station compared to 800 MHz (or 900 MHz) is approximately two-thirds the distance, which would be obtained with the same effective radiation power and same antenna height. In this type of environment, the Okumura-type models will not work well.

For these reasons, Walfisch and Bertoni (1988) developed a model aimed at improving the accuracy by exploiting the actual propagation mechanisms involved. This model considers the effect of rooftop diffraction and ray "channeling," which is significant in big metropolitan area. The Walfisch-Bertoni (WB) part loss model is given by

$$PL_{WB} = PL_{fs} + PL_{FT} + PL_{MS}, \qquad (18)$$

where PL_{fs} is given in Equation 3, PL_{FT} is the rooftop-to-street diffraction and scatter loss, and PL_{MS} is the multiscreen diffraction loss. This model has been considered for use by the Radiocommunication sector of the International Telecommunication Union (ITU-R) in the International Mobile Telecommunications 2000 (IMT 2000) standards activities (Sarkar et al. 2003).

Wideband PCS Microcell Model

Another model of interest is the *wideband PCS model* (Feuerstein et al. 1994). It is essentially a two-ray ground reflection model for a LOS microcell environment. The measurement was conducted for a cellular system in California's San Francisco Bay Area using 20 MHz pulsed Tx at 1900 MHz with $h_t = 3.7\,\text{m}$, 8.5 m, and 13.3 m; and h_r of 1.7 m. If d_f represents the distance at which the first Fresnel zone just becomes obstructed by the ground, and assuming flat ground reflection, the average path loss given by this model is

$$\overline{PL}(d) = \begin{cases} 10n_1\log(d) + \overline{PL}(d_0) & \text{for } 1 < d < d_f \\ 10n_2\log(d/d_f) + 10n_1\log(d_f) + \overline{PL}(d_0) & \text{for } d > d_f, \end{cases} \qquad (19)$$

where n_1 and n_2 are the path loss exponents, which are functions of the environment, and

$$d_f = (1/\lambda)\sqrt{16h_{te}^2 h_{re}^2 - \lambda^2(h_{te}^2 + h_{re}^2) + (\lambda^4/16)}. \qquad (20)$$

This model is a double regression model, assuming regression breakpoint at the first Fresnel zone clearance. The model fits measured data well and agrees with the log-distance path loss model for dense urban microcell environments.

Longley-Rice Model

The Longely-Rice model (Longley and Rice 1968) is used for point-point communication systems under different types of terrain and over the frequency ranges from 40 MHz to 100 GHz. It is usually referred to as the *irregular terrain model* in which the median transmission loss is predicted using the path geometry of the terrain profile and the refractivity of the troposphere. Urban factors account for additional attenuation because of urban clutter near the receiving antenna. The signal strength of the radio wave in different environments is predicted using different techniques such as two-ray ground reflection and knife-edge techniques. This model is essentially a computer program with general input to the program including frequency, distance, antenna heights, polarization, surface

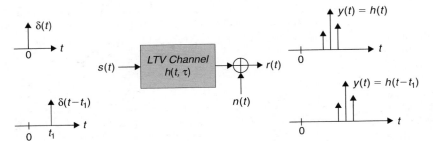

Figure 8: A wireless channel model as a linear system with impulse response h(t, τ) and noise n(t)

refractivity, Earth radius, climate conditions, and ground conductivity. Other specific parameters include antennae horizon and elevation angle, transhorizon distance, and terrain irregularity. This model does not consider the effects of buildings, foliage, and multipath propagation.

Durkins Model

The Durkin model (Durkin 1977) is similar to the Longly-Rice model. It is a computer simulator for predicting field strength contours over irregular terrain. It consists of two parts: the ground profile and the expected path loss. The *ground profile* is reconstructed from the topographic data of the proposed surface along the radial distance joining transmitter and receiver. It is used to model LOS and diffraction derived from obstacles and local scatters and assumes that all the signals are received along the radial (no multipath). The second part calculates the expected path loss along the radial by moving the receiver location in order to deduce signal strength contour. This model seems to have a pessimistic prediction in narrow valleys and tries to identify weak reception areas. The major disadvantage of this model is that it cannot adequately predict propagation effects because of foliage and buildings and cannot account for multipath propagation.

STATISTICAL WIRELESS CHANNEL MODEL

In the previous section, we examined the characteristics of the signal strength through the wireless channel based on large-scale signal propagation or fading. The average strength of the received signal is determined as a function of the Tx–Rx distance and frequency. However, because of multipath propagation and the complex interactions of the radio wave with the environment, the received signal consists of many radio waves with randomly distributed amplitudes, phases, and angles. Although the large-scale characteristics of the channel are necessary for proper link budget design, the small-scale statistical characteristics are vital in proper Rx design.

In this section, we examine the small-scale propagation effects of the wireless channel commonly known as *multipath fading*. This involves the rapid and often dramatic fluctuation of signal amplitude and phase resulting from the multipath phenomena. Unlike large- and medium-scale propagation, multipath fading is a result of the rapid fluctuation in the multipath signal amplitude over a short period of time or over short distances. Our discussion of

small-scale multipath fading will be a summary because of space limitations.

Channel Impulse Response

Multipath fading of the wireless channel is commonly described by the impulse response, which introduces a filtering action on the signal. Figure 8 represents a *linear time variant* (LTV) channel, where $h(t, \tau)$ is the time-variant impulse response. An impulse at the transmitter will result to multiple impulses at the receiver. The main goal is to statistically characterize the rapid fluctuations of the amplitudes, delays, and phases of the multipath signal. If the channel is bandlimited, then $h(t, \tau)$ can be described by the complex baseband equivalent representation. However, a more realistic representation is to model the multipath channel by taking different snapshots of complex baseband equivalent impulse responses at discrete time intervals. This implies that at time t, the channel can be modeled as a linear filter with time-varying impulse response given by

$$h(t,\tau) = \sum_{k=0}^{N(t)-1} \alpha_k(t,\tau) e^{-j2\pi f_c \tau_k(t) + \phi_k(t,\tau)} \delta(\tau - \tau_k(t)) \quad (21)$$

where $\alpha_k(t, \tau)$ and $\tau_k(t)$ are the amplitudes and excess delay of the kth multipath component, respectively; $\delta(.)$ is the unit impulse function; and $2\pi f_c \tau_k(t) + \phi_k(t, \tau)$ represents all mechanisms of phase shifts of the kth multipath component; while $N(t)$ represents the number of multipath components, which generally can be a function of time. Most often, the phase shifts are represented as one variable—that is, $2\pi f_c \tau_k(t) + \phi_k(t, \tau). = \theta_k(t, \tau).$

In a wireless channel, all of the parameters—$\alpha_k(t, \tau)$, $\tau_k(t)$, $\theta_k(t, \tau)$ and $N(t)$—are unknown and, because they change over time, are often characterized as random processes. The amplitude attenuation $\alpha_k(t, \tau)$ may be obtained from the path loss and shadowing models described above, while $\theta_k(t, \tau)$ depends on delay and Doppler shift. It is commonly assumed that these two random processes are independent. If the multipath components have variable propagation delays that depend only on the receiver location and not on time, then the system can be modeled as a linear time-invariant filter.

Note that the phase $\theta_k(t, \tau)$ is most often assumed to be uniformly distributed over $[0, 2\pi]$, whereas the path gain model and distribution function depend on the nature of the channel and the propagation environment. The path gain distribution is commonly assumed to be a Rayleigh-, Racean-, or Nakagami-distributed random variable, but details of these distributions are beyond the scope of this chapter.

Using Equation 21, the received signal given by

$$r(t) = s(t) * h(t,\tau) + n(t)$$
$$= \text{Re}\left\{\left(\sum_{k=0}^{N-1} \alpha_k(t)\, e^{-j\theta_k(t)} x(\tau - \tau_k(t)) e^{j2\pi f_c t + \phi_0}\right)\right\} + n(t),$$

(22)

is a superposition of all signal arriving at the Rx with various amplitudes, phases, and time delays, where * is the convolution operator; $x(t)$ is a complex baseband equivalent signal (with bandwidth B, power P_t, carrier frequency f_c, and an arbitrary initial phase ϕ_0), and $s(t) = \text{Re}\{x(t)e^{j(2\pi f c t + \phi 0)}\}$ is the transmitted signal. From Equation 22, one can conclude that the received signal is a series of time-delayed, phase-shifted, attenuated versions of the transmitted signal. At times, the complex-valued vectors $r(t)$ add destructively to reduce the power level of the receiver or add constructively to produce a large signal value.

One way to model a time-variant multipath channel is by using the *tapped delay line* model illustrated in Figure 9. The channel model consists of a tapped delay line with uniformly spaced taps. The tap spacing between adjacent taps is $T_c = 1/B$, the time resolution that can be achieved by transmitting a signal of bandwidth B. The tap coefficients denoted as $c_n(t)$, $n = 1, 2, ..., N$, are usually modeled as complex-valued, uncorrelated Gaussian random processes. The length of the delay line corresponds to the amount of time dispersion in the multipath channel, which is usually called the *multipath spread* denoted as $T_m = N/B$, where N represents the maximum number of possible multipath signal components.

Channel Transfer Functions

Because time and frequency are inversely related, $h(\tau, t)$ can also be examined in the frequency domain via Fourier transformation. In addition to impulse response $h(\tau, t)$, the channel can be characterized by the time-variant transfer function $H(f, t)$, the channel output Doppler-spread function $D(f, v)$, and the delay Doppler-spread function $S(\tau, v)$.

Time-variant transfer function is the Fourier transform of the impulse response with respect to the delay variable τ and is given by

$$H(f, t) = F_\tau[h(\tau,t)] = \int_{-\infty}^{\infty} h(\tau,t)e^{-j2\pi f\tau}\, d\tau \quad (23)$$

At any instant, $H(f, t)$ characterizes the channel in the frequency domain. If the channel changes with t, then $H(f, t)$ also changes with t. However, for a time-invariant channel, the impulse response is independent of the time variable t, and the transfer function varies only with the frequency variable f and is independent of t. Conversely, the inverse Fourier transform of the transfer function will give the impulse response. As a wireless channel can be characterized equivalently in frequency domain, a channel being time varying in the time domain means a channel is introducing Doppler shifts in the frequency domain. In fact, a wireless channel usually introduces continuous Doppler shifts, which results in the spectral broadening of the transmitted signal in the frequency domain.

The output Doppler-spread function $D(f, v)$, which is the channel gain associated with the Doppler shift v at frequency f, is the Fourier transform of the time-variant transfer function $H(f, t)$ with respect to the time variable, t, and is defined as

$$D(f, v) = F_t[H(f,t)] = \int_{-\infty}^{\infty} H(f,t)e^{-j2\pi vt}\, dt \quad (24)$$

Hence, time variation of the impulse response is equivalent to the Doppler shift in the frequency domain.

Another function of interest is the delay Doppler-spread function $S(\tau, v)$, which is the Fourier-transform

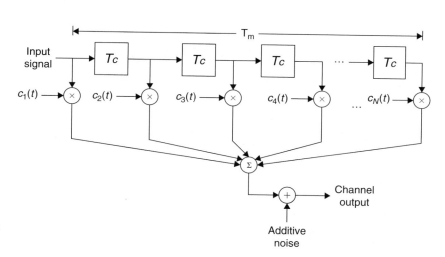

Figure 9: Equivalent model for a time-variant multipath channel

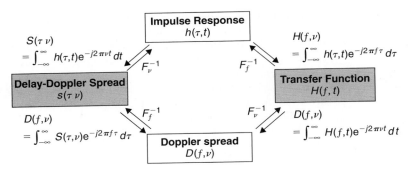

Figure 10: Relationship between the system functions

of the time-variant impulse response with respect to the time variable t, which is defined as

$$S(\tau,v) = F_t[h(\tau,t)] = \int_{-\infty}^{\infty} h(\tau,t)\,e^{-j2\pi vt}dt \qquad (25)$$

Because the transmitted signal and the received signal can be represented in time or frequency domain, we can characterize the channel in time or frequency domain using the above four functions: $h(t, \tau)$, $H(f, t)$, $D(f, v)$, and $S(\tau, v)$. The relationship between these channel functions is shown in Figure 10. These functions enable us to characterize the channel in time and frequency domains, as well as in distance and velocity relationship.

Channel Scattering Functions

In practice, the channel may change with time in a random manner. This means that $h(t, \tau)$, $H(f, t)$, $D(f, v)$, and $S(\tau,v)$ are random processes and will require additional characterization. These functions are random processes with zero mean. In particular, $h(t, \tau)$ is a *wide sense stationary* (WSS) process and uncorrelated at τ_1 and τ_2, for any t. Such a channel is said to be a *wide sense stationary uncorrelated scattering* (WSSUS) channel.

This channel model is an important class of practical channels in which it is assumed that the signal variations on the paths arriving at different delays are uncorrelated, such that the statistical properties of the channel do not change with time. Hence, the channel can be examined in terms of the correlation functions.

The correlation functions of a WSSUS channel are related to the above system functions and can be represented by four correlation functions denoted as

$$P_h(\tau, \Delta t),\ P_H(\Delta f, \Delta t), P_D(\Delta f, v),\ \text{and}\ P_S(\tau, v) \qquad (26)$$

where $P_h(\tau, \Delta t)$ is called the *space-time correlation function*, $P_H(\Delta f, \Delta t)$ is the *spaced-time, spaced-frequency correlation function*, $P_D(\Delta f, v)$ is the *spaced-frequency Doppler spread function*, and $P_S(\tau, v)$ is the *delay Doppler spread function*. Details of these functions can be found in Proakis (2000).

By allowing one of the variables in Equation 26 to be zero, the following one-dimensional functions can be obtained:

1. *power delay profile* (also known as the *multipath intensity profile*), $P_h(\tau)$;
2. *frequency correlation function*, $P_H(\Delta f)$;
3. the *time correlation function*, $P_H(\Delta t)$; and
4. the *Doppler power spectrum*, $P_S(v)$.

$P_h(\tau)$ portrays the time-domain behavior of the channel whereas $P_H(\Delta f)$ portrays the frequency-domain behavior of the channel. The relationship of these correlation functions and the associated fading parameters is illustrated in Figure 11. Through these correlation functions, important statistical characteristics of the channel can be determined.

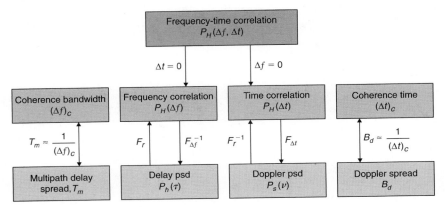

Figure 11: Relationship between system correlation functions

STATISTICAL PARAMETERS OF THE WIRELESS CHANNEL

From the impulse response, transfer functions, and correlation functions discussed above, several channel statistical parameters can be obtained. These parameters can provide insight into the effect of the channel on the transmitted signal. These statistical parameters include the power delay profile, time dispersion or delay spread, frequency domain correlation, Doppler spectrum (shift and spread), coherence bandwidth, and coherence time. As indicated above, these parameters and functions are random in nature and are characterized statistically. They directly affect receiver design and are useful for the proper descriptions of the channel in order to estimate the performance and methods of mitigating the effects of fading.

Power Delay Profile

The *power delay profile* $P_h(\tau)$, or *multipath intensity profile*, is the expected power (spatial average over a local area) per unit of time received with a certain excess delay. It is obtained by averaging a large set of impulse responses. It indicates the level of dispersion or distribution of transmitted power over various multipaths. From $P_h(\tau)$, we can compute the correlation of fading at different carrier frequencies and determine the multipath delay spread T_m, defined as the range of nonzero values of $P_h(\tau)$. T_m is an important parameter in characterizing wireless channels. The signal bandwidth B_S when compared to T_m will indicate the frequency selectivity and distortion level of the signal in the channel. Hence, from the power delay profile, we can compute the statistics describing the time-dispersion characteristics of the channel.

Time Dispersion

Recall that one of the most important differences between wireless and wired channels is that the wireless channel varies with time. Because of the mechanisms of propagation, time dispersion of the wireless channel varies widely from one location to another, and the resulting multipath channel response appears random as well. In multipath channel, each path has a different path length and different time of arrival at the receiver. This leads to the cumulative signal being smeared or spread in time, a phenomenon commonly known as *delay spread*. Because *time dispersion* depends on the geometrical relationships among the Tx, the Rx, and the surrounding physical objects, some parameters that can quantify the multipath channel are needed. Time dispersion can be characterized with channel parameters such as *excess delay, mean excess delay, root mean square* (RMS) *delay spread*, and *maximum excess delay*. These delays are determined in comparison to the first arrival path signal at the receiver with delay τ_0. *Mean excess delay*, $\bar{\tau}$, or the *mean delay spread*, is the average delay measured in relation to the first arrival delay τ_0. The *RMS delay spread* of the channel denoted as τ_{rms} is the square root of the second centralized moment of the power delay profile—that is, τ_{rms} is the standard deviation about the mean excess delay of the reflections weighted

proportional to their energies. The value of τ_{rms} describes the time delay spread in a multipath channel beyond what would be expected for free space LOS transmission. It characterizes the time dispersive nature or the multipath spread of the channel, which can be used to estimate the potential effect of conditions such as data rate of the signal and *intersymbol interference* (ISI). For reliable communication over a fading channel, it is required that the symbol period be greater than τ_{rms} (i.e., $T_s \gg \tau_{rms}$) in order to minimize the distortion in the channel. Because T_s is inversely proportional to the data rate, the inverse of τ_{rms} can be taken as a measure of the data-rate limitations of a fading multipath channel. Finally, the *maximum excess delay* is the maximum delay spread τ_m, which measures the time delay during which multipath power falls below a threshold, say, $X\ dB$. Numerical computation of these delays can be found in Proakis (2000).

Doppler Effect

In general, the output signal of a linear system does not have frequency components different from those of the input signal. However, both nonlinear and time-varying systems introduce new frequency components other than those existing in the input signal. In a wireless propagation environment, because of the mobility of users, surrounding scatterers, or both, the channel is linear but time variant. As a result, a wireless channel introduces frequency shifts to the transmitted signal, a Doppler-effect phenomenon. Because of the relative motion of Tx and Rx in mobile wireless channels, a Doppler frequency shift is impressed on the frequency of the transmitted signal. The Doppler shift, f_d, is given by $f_d = (v/\lambda)\cos(\theta)$, where v is the relative velocity between the Tx and Rx, λ is the wavelength of the transmitted signal, and θ is the angle of incident of received signal relative to direction of motion. This means that the received signal will be the frequency-shifted version of the transmitted signal. When the relative transceiver velocity varies with time, f_d will also vary with time.

Doppler spread, B_D (also known as the *maximum delay spread*), is the range of frequency over which Doppler power spectrum is nonzero. It represents the strength of the Doppler shift at different frequencies caused by movements of the terminals or objects close by. It is an indication of how the channel characteristics are changing with time, and it measures the spectral broadening caused by time rate of change of the channel.

Coherence Time and Bandwidth

From the multipath delay profile and the Doppler effect of the channel, the wireless channel is further characterized in time and frequency. The coherence time and coherence bandwidth are two additional parameters that are useful in characterizing fading and multipath effects in wireless channels. The coherence time, T_c, of the channel is used to characterize the time-varying nature of the frequency dispersiveness of the channel in time domain. It is a statistical measure of the time duration over which the channel impulse is invariant—that is, the time that impulse response is stationary. This implies that two signals arriving with time separation greater than T_c are affected differently. Different symbols that are transmitted over the channel within the coherence time are affected by the same amount of fading. Different symbols that are transmitted over the channel outside the coherence time are most likely faded by different amounts. T_c is obtained by taking the reciprocal of the Doppler spread—that is, $T_c = 1/B_D$.

On the other hand, the coherence bandwidth, B_c, is a statistical measure of the bandwidth over which the channel characteristics of the signal (magnitude and phase) are highly correlated. Within this bandwidth, all frequency components of a signal will be affected similarly by the channel, and the channel is said to be "flat." B_c is obtained as the reciprocal of the multipath spread and is defined as $B_c = 1/T_m$. Two signals separated in frequency greater than B_c will fade independently—that is, the statistical properties of the two signals are independent.

FADING IN WIRELESS CHANNELS

There are different types of fading. The type of fading experienced by a signal propagating through a wireless channel depends on the characteristics of the channel and nature of the transmitted signal. Depending on the parameters of the signal (e.g., wavelength, bandwidth, symbol period) and the channel parameters (e.g., RMS delay spread, Doppler spread), different transmitted signals will undergo different types of fading in the channel. Small-scale fading can be categorized based on two aspects: multipath delay spread (T_m) and Doppler spread (B_d). T_m leads to time dispersion and frequency selectivity of the channel. In this case, the channel may be classified as *flat fading* or *frequency selective fading*. T_m is a channel parameter in time domain, whereas the phenomenon in which the channel is flat or frequency selective corresponds to the frequency domain. Thus, the time-domain parameter, T_m, influences the channel characteristic in frequency domain.

On the other hand, Doppler spread (B_d) leads to frequency dispersion and time-selective fading. In this case, the channel may be classified as *fast-fading* or *slow-fading*. B_d is a channel parameter in frequency domain, whereas the phenomenon that the channel changes fast or slow is a time-domain effect. Therefore, the frequency domain parameter, B_d, influences the channel characteristic in time domain.

Knowing these relationships will help us design the system and determine the exact behavior of the signal in the channel. A summary of the fading effects in the wireless channel is illustrated in Figure 12.

If the coherence bandwidth, B_c, of the channel is much larger than the bandwidth of the transmitted signal, B_s, then the received signal undergoes flat fading. In that case, the symbol period is much longer than the multipath delay spread of the channel. In contrast, if B_c is smaller than B_s, the received signal suffers from frequency-selective fading. In this case, the symbol period T_s is smaller than T_m. When this happens, the received signal is distorted and ISI is induced. This means that it is much more difficult to model frequency-selective fading channels compared to flat fading channels, because each multipath has to be treated differently. Therefore, it is preferable to deal with a flat fading channel for signal transmission. Because we cannot change the multipath delay spread and coherence bandwidth of the channel, we can only try to design the symbol period T_s and signal bandwidth B_s such that flat fading of the channel results for the transmitted signal. Hence, to improve the performance of the transmission, given the delay spread, we choose a value for T_s that will result in a flat fading channel instead of a frequency-selective channel.

Based on the Doppler spread, the channel can be classified as *fast-fading* or *slow-fading*. If the channel impulse response (in time domain) changes quickly within T_s—that is, if the coherence time, T_c, of the channel is smaller than T_s—the received signal experiences fast fading. This will result in signal distortion. On the other hand, if the channel impulse response changes at a much

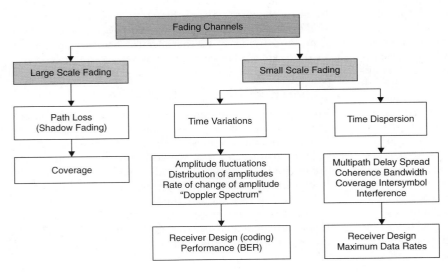

Figure 12: Summary of fading effects in wireless channel

Table 2: Classifications of Small-Scale Fading

Categorization basis	Fading types	Condition
Multipath delay spread	Flat	$B_s < B_c; T_s \geq 10\tau_{rms}$
	Frequency-selective	$B_s > B_c; T_s < 10\tau_{rms}$
Doppler spread	Fast	$T_s > T_c; B_s < B_d$
	Slow	$T_s < T_c; B_s > B_d$

slower rate than the transmitted baseband signal, then the received signal experiences slow fading. This means that the channel is stationary over certain symbol periods. It is easy to see that a slow-fading channel is preferable because it results in a more stable transmission quality.

Unfortunately, the Doppler spread is not determined by a system's design, although we can try to design T_s and B_s to achieve slow fading on the transmitted signal. In this case, given the Doppler spread, we choose B_s that will result in a slow-fading condition instead of a fast-fading one, resulting in better performance. The different types of fading and the conditions that give rise to them are summarized in Table 2.

CONCLUSION

The recent development in wireless communications has led to the emergence of new systems and services and yet the limitations of the wireless channel remain the same. These new systems and services strive to increase capacity and improve the QoS. For future generations of wireless systems that will require higher frequencies, smaller cell sizes, and more complex channel environments, there is a need for more accurate channel models and better site-specific propagation prediction models. New techniques such as smart antennae and multiple input and multiple output systems need new propagation prediction models to characterize the joint spatio-temporal channel. In this chapter, we have presented a review of the wireless channel characteristics in terms of large- and small-scale fading characteristics, as well as a review of the propagation prediction models that range from simple empirical formulas to modern site-specific models based on ray tracing. The channel characteristics in space domain are related to large-scale path loss. Small-scale fading presents the random fluctuations because of multipath propagation. This is a vast topic, and we have only scratched the surface in this chapter.

GLOSSARY

Attenuation: Weakening of radio frequency signals because they are partially blocked or absorbed. A process heavily dependent on the frequency of the radio wave and on the physical environment and material.

Autocorrelation: A measure of the similarity between a signal and a time-shifted replica of itself; a special case of cross-correlation.

Coherence bandwidth: One effect of multipath propagation is delay spread, which causes frequency-selective fading. The coherence bandwidth is a measure of the delay spread whereby the larger the delay spread, the smaller the coherence bandwidth.

Coherence time: The time interval over which the received signal may be regarded as approximately constant.

Constructive interference: Interference that occurs when waves arriving at the receiver combine to form a single stronger wave. The strength of the composite wave depends on how closely in phase the two component waves are.

COST 231: The European Cooperation in Science and Technology program committee that deals with future mobile systems.

Delay spread: An effect of multipath for a digital interface in which multiple reflections of the same signal arrive at the receiver at different times, creating a noticeable degradation in signal quality.

Destructive interference: Interference that occurs when waves arriving at the receiver combine to form a single weaker wave. Usually occurs when waves that are out of phase combine to form a composite wave that is weaker than any of the component waves.

Doppler shift: The difference between the frequencies of the transmitted wave and of the echo received from a moving target.

Doppler spectrum: The power spectrum of the complex signal, expressed as a function of Doppler frequency or Doppler velocity.

Doppler spread: The width of the Doppler spectrum, measured in units of either frequency or velocity, which is usually defined as the standard deviation of the Doppler velocity about its mean value.

Fading: The random variation of the signal amplitude, phase, or both as a result of radio wave interactions with the transmission environment.

Free space loss: The power loss of a signal as a result of its spreading out as it travels through space. As a wave travels, it spreads out its power over space—that is, as the wave front spreads, so does its power.

IEEE 802.11: A WLAN standard (or set of standards) operating at 2.4 GHz and with data rates as high as 1 Mbps.

Industrial, scientific, and medical (ISM) band: A license-free band that is set aside for industrial, scientific, and medical equipment.

Isotropic radiator: A completely nondirectional antenna (one that radiates equally well in all directions). This antenna exists only as a mathematical concept and is used as a known reference to measure antenna gain.

Line of sight (LOS): Transmission in which the transmitting and receiving stations (antennae) can see each other—that is, a clear path between transmitting and receiving stations.

Multipath: A phenomenon whereby a radio signal reaching a receiving antenna arrives by multiple paths because of the various mechanisms of propagation. By traveling different distances to the receiver, the reflections arrive with different time delays and signal strengths. Signals that are in phase will add to one another. Signals that are out of phase will cancel one another.

Multipath fading: Fading that occurs when the direct path wave destructively interferes with its reflections at the receiver. The destructive interference is a result of the reflected waves arriving at the receiving end out of phase with the direct path transmitted wave.

Path loss: The average attenuation undergone by a radio wave as it propagates between the transmitter and a receiver. The loss may be the result of many effects, including free space loss, refraction, reflection, and absorption.

Personal communications service (PCS): Within the United States, an allocated 1.9-GHz band; the allocated spectrum is 120 MHz wide and is licensed as two 30-MHz segments for 51 major trading areas and three 10-MHz segments for 493 basic trading areas.

Radio frequency (RF): Also used generally to refer to the radio signal generated by the system transmitter or to the energy present from other sources that may be picked up by a wireless receiver.

Reflections: RF waves can reflect off of basically almost anything in the transmission environment. The reflections may vary in phase and strength from the original wave.

Root mean square (RMS): The square root of the average value of the square of the instantaneous signal amplitude; a measure of signal amplitude.

Scattering function: The average power density at the output of a fading channel as a function of the delay and Doppler shift.

Shadowing: Random fading resulting from blockage by objects in the signal path.

Voice over Internet protocol (VoIP): A technology that integrates voice and data transmission over the Internet.

Wide-sense stationary (WSS) process: A process whose mean and autocorrelation function are time-invariant.

Wide-sense stationary uncorrelated scattering (WSSUS): The statistical characterization of mobile radio channels with parameters of the channels (i.e., the appropriate system functions) assumed to be wide-sense stationary both *in time* and *in frequency*.

Wireless: Description of radio-based systems that allow transmission of telephone or data signals through the air without a physical connection such as a metal wire or fiber-optic cable.

Wireless local area network (WLAN): A flexible data communication system implemented as an extension to or as an alternative for a wired LAN. With WLANs, users can access shared information without looking for a place to plug in.

CROSS REFERENCES

See *Cellular Communications Channels*; *Conducted Communications Media*; *Mobile Radio Communications*.

REFERENCES

Anderson, J. B., T. S. Rappaport, and S, Yoshia. 1995. Propagation measurements and models for wireless communication channels. *IEEE Communications Magazine*, 33: 42–9.

Bertoni, H. 2000. *Radio propagation for modern wireless systems*. Upper Saddle River, NJ: Prentice Hall.

Bullington, K. 1977. Radio propagation for vehicular communications. *IEEE Transactions on Vehicular Technology*, November, 295–308.

COST. 1991. *Urban transmission loss models for mobile radio in the 900 and 1800 MHz bands*. Technical report (European cooperation in the field of scientific and technical research EURO-COST 231). The Hague: Author.

Deygout, J. 1966. Multiple knife-edge diffraction of microwaves. *IEEE Transactions on Antennas and Propagation*, 14(4): 480–9.

———. 1991. Correction factor for multiple knife-edge diffraction. *IEEE Transactions on Antennas and Propagation*, 39(8): 1256–8.

Durkin, J. 1977. Computer prediction of service areas for VHF and UHF land mobile radio services. *IEEE Transactions on Vehicular Technology*, November, pp. 323–7.

Edwards, R., and J. Durkin. 1969. Computer prediction of service area for VHF mobile radio networks. *Proceedings of the IEE*, 116(9): 1493–1500.

Epstein, J., and D. W. Peterson. 1953. An experimental study of wave propagation at 840 M/C. *Proceedings of the IRE*, 41(5): 595–611.

Feuerstein, M. J., K. L. Blackard, T. S. Rappaport, S. Y. Seidel, and H. H. Xia. 1994. Path loss, delay spread, and outage models as functions of antenna height for microcellular system design. *IEEE Transactions on Vehicular Technology*, 43(3): 487–98.

Fleury, B. H., and P. E. Leuthold. 1996. Radiowave propagation in mobile communications: An overview of European research. *IEEE Communications Magazine*, 34: 70–81.

Hashemi, H. 1993. Impulse response modeling of indoor radio propagation channels. *IEEE Journal on Selected Areas in Communications*, 11(7): 967–78.

Hata, M. 1980. Empirical formula for propagation loss in land mobile radio services. *IEEE Transactions on Vehicular Technology*, 29(3): 317–25.

Longley, A. G., and P. L. Rice. 1968. Prediction of tropospheric radio transmission over irregular terrain, a computer method. ESSA Technical Report ERL 79-ITS 67. Washington, DC: U.S. Government Printing Office.

Mark, J., and W. Zhuang. 2003. *Wireless communications and networking*. Upper Saddle River, NJ: Prentice Hall.

Molkdar, D. 1991. Review on radio propagation into and within buildings: Microwaves, antennas and propagation. *IEE Proceedings H*, 138(1): 61–73.

Okumura, Y., E. Ohmori, and K. Fukuda. 1968. Field strength and its variability in VHF and UHF land mobile service. *Review Electrical Communications Laboratory*, 16(9,10): 2935–71.

Prasad, R. 1998. *Universal wireless personal communications*. Boston: Artech House Publishers.

Proakis, J. G. 2000. *Digital communications*. 4th ed. Boston: McGraw-Hill.

Rappaport, T. S. 2002. *Wireless communications: Principles and practice*. Upper Saddle River, NJ: Prentice-Hall.

Sarkar, T. K., Z. Ji, K. Kim, A. Medouri, and M. Salazar-Palma. 2003. A survey of various propagation models for mobile communication. *IEEE Antennas and Propagation Magazine*, 45(3): 51–82.

SoftWright. 1999. Fresnel zone clearance (retrieved Oct. 16, 2006 from www.softwright.com/faq/engineering/Fresnel%20Zone%20Clearance.html).

Walfisch, J., and H. L. Bertoni. 1988. A theoretical model of UHF propagation in urban environments. *IEEE Transaction on Antennas and Propagation*, AP-36: 1788–96.

Sources of Errors, Prevention, Detection, and Correction

Syed H. Murshid and Azhar M. Khayrattee, *Florida Institute of Technology*

INTRODUCTION

Imperfections in the transmission media and disturbances in the surrounding environment are the main causes of errors. A significant portion of bandwidth can be lost because of errors. If data transmission was error free, then data communication would be a lot faster and cheaper. No transmission media is error free. Even fiber-optic cables, known for their reliability and used for extremely high-speed data communication links between continents, experience data corruption to some degree. Errors are caused by many factors, including type of transmission media, environmental effects, type of signal, and modulation scheme used. Error sources can be attributed to three major categories—namely, attenuation, distortion, and noise. However, there are techniques such as error detection and error correction that can be used to ensure data integrity. This is usually done by including redundant bits along with the data unit. Popular error-detection methods include parity check, cyclic redundancy checks, and so on. Hamming code is discussed as one example of an error-correction technique.

SOURCES OF ERRORS AND PREVENTION
Attenuation

Data are generally transmitted across communication networks in the form of electromagnetic waves (electrons or photons according to the wave-particle duality principle). Similar to a car losing energy to friction as it moves, electromagnetic waves also tend to lose energy as they propagate through a medium. This loss of energy is referred to as *attenuation* (see Figure 1). The causes of attenuation include absorption and scattering of electrons or photons in the medium. Because work is done to overcome absorption and scattering, energy is released, usually as heat.

The attenuation level can be calculated by

$$P_{out} = P_{in}e^{-\alpha z}$$

where α is attenuation level and z is distance traveled by a wave in some medium.

For practical purposes, attenuation is generally expressed as the ratio of the output power to the input power, and generally expressed in decibels (dBs):

$$Attenuation(dB) = 10\log_{10} \frac{P_{out}}{P_{in}} dB$$

Attenuation is a physical property of the transmission media and cannot be eliminated. However, it is possible to mitigate its effects through the process of amplification. The components used to amplify signals are called *amplifiers* or *repeaters*. Amplification applied to a signal is often referred to as *signal regeneration*. It should be noted that attenuation and amplification are opposing processes.

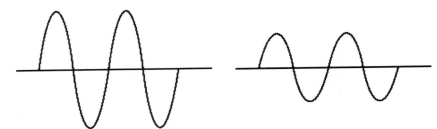

Figure 1: Effect of attenuation on amplitude of signal

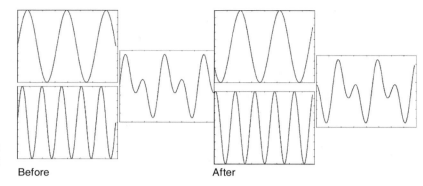

Figure 2: Distortion resulting from the different propagation constants and phases of the different Fourier components

Before   After

In general, if

$$10\log_{10}\frac{P_{out}}{P_{in}}\,dB = \begin{cases} -ve & \Rightarrow & attenuation \\ 0, & \Rightarrow & unity\ gain \\ +ve & \Rightarrow & amplification \end{cases}$$

Distortion

The propagation speed of an electromagnetic wave in a medium depends on its refractive index. In addition, data transmission is not limited to perfect sinusoids. Complex signals are often used. Jean Baptiste Joseph Fourier proved that any signal is composed of multiple harmonically related sinusoids, each of which has a different frequency and each of which can be considered as a different propagation mode with a different propagation constant. So each mode travels at a somewhat different speed; their net effect at the destination can be determined by using the superposition principle. The differential delay between the different sinusoids causes changes in the phase relationships, which leads to distortion of the signal. This is graphically illustrated by the amplitude versus time plots in Figure 2.

Distortion is sometimes referred to as *delay distortion* or *dispersion* (in fibers). Modal distortion can be reduced by compensating for the different propagation constants.

Noise

As mentioned earlier, another source of error in data transmission is noise. Unlike attenuation and distortion, it is often difficult to accurately quantize noise because of its random occurrence. Probabilistic methods are generally used to predict and counteract these effects. The common types of noise include white noise, impulse noise,

induced noise, cross talk, echo, and jitter. The effect of noise is quantized by the *signal-to-noise ratio* (SNR):

$$SNR = \frac{P_{signal}}{P_{noise}} \qquad or \qquad SNR(dB) = 10\log_{10}\left(\frac{P_{signal}}{P_{noise}}\right)$$

White Noise

White noise is also referred to as *thermal* or *Johnson noise* or *Nyquist noise*. White noise is caused by the random motion of electrons in the medium that generates a relatively constant random signal. The root mean square (rms) white noise voltage V_n can be expressed as:

$$V_n = \sqrt{4k_B T\Delta fR}\,,$$

where k_B is Boltzmann's constant, T is temperature in degrees kelvin, Δf is bandwidth, and R is resistance of the circuit element. (See Figure 3.)

White noise can be eliminated by the use of filters. Removing white noise from a digital signal is often termed *signal regeneration*.

Impulse Noise

Impulse noise, also known as *burst noise*, is mostly caused by sudden changes in power. It is common because of many environmental factors that affect transmission media such as lightning and power surges. Analog signals affected by impulse noise are difficult to restore. As for digital signals, the higher the bit rate, the more consequent the impact of impulse noise. Impulse noise can be reduced in analog signals by the use of specialized filters. Digital signal processing on digital signals can reduce the effect of impulse noise (see Figure 4).

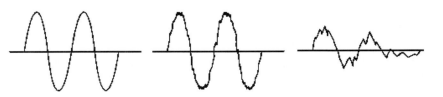

Figure 3: Effects of white noise; extreme noise can degrade the signal beyond recognition (amplitude versus time plots)

Figure 4: Digital signal affected by impulse noise

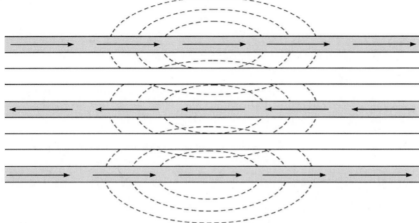

Figure 5: Cross talk between different transmission wires

Induced Noise

Any electromagnetic disturbance coming from the surrounding environment is classified as *induced noise*. Components such as motors and other electrical appliances are responsible for induced noise because they emit radio frequency waves and hence act as antennas. Transmission media often act as receivers, capturing these waves that lead to interference and subsequently corrupt the signal. This type of interference is commonly termed *radio frequency interference* (RFI). Induced noise is not always constant but can be prevented by shielding.

Cross Talk

Cross talk is another type of induced noise caused by coupling between different wires. As mentioned in the previous section, some wires can act as antennas while others act as receivers. Cross talk is many times experienced with analog communication links—for example, when someone hears another phone conversation on top of the desired conversation on the same line. Cross talk is usually constant. As it is induced noise, it can be prevented with proper shielding. (See Figure 5.)

Echo

Echo is generated by the reflection of the original signal. This generally occurs wherever there is a discontinuity in the medium. Coaxial and fiber-optic cables are prone to noise because of echo. Severe echo can corrupt the original signal. Echo is usually constant and can be prevented through proper termination of the cables.

Collision

Collision occurs when two or more hosts attempt to send data packets simultaneously over the same transmission line. (Details of collision will be discussed in a later chapter.) Data packets travel along the transmission line as electromagnetic waves. When two or more waves occupy the same medium simultaneously, they interfere and thus corrupt the original information. Collision is prevented by the medium access control sublayer (also discussed in detail in a later chapter).

Jitter

Small timing irregularities during digital signal transmission cause *jitter*. Jitter is accentuated by high transmission rate for digital signals, especially when the same signal is transmitted multiple times. The effects of jitter can be minimized by several techniques, including slower transmission rates, the use of fewer repeaters, and better-quality electronic components.

ERROR DETECTION

As previously discussed, data transmission is susceptible to corruption. The extent of corruption primarily depends on the transmission medium. For example, an optical fiber is more reliable than a twisted-pair. The types of data corruption (or errors) can be classified into two categories: single-bit error and burst error. A *single-bit error*, as the name implies, refers to errors where only one bit has altered—that is, a 1 has changed to a 0 or vice the versa. Any other error, where more than one bit is altered, is called a *burst error*.

To detect errors, we need to know the original data. We could send each data unit more than once until the receiving party acknowledges it. However, this method would not be efficient. A bandwidth-efficient way to detect errors within a data unit is to append extra bits.

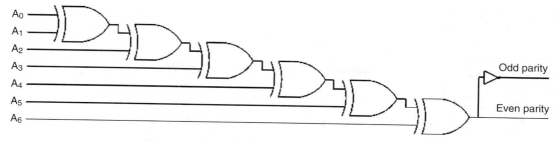

Figure 6: Circuit for calculating and checking parity

Parity Check

The receiving system can then check for consistency using the extra bits. Once the consistency is verified, the extra bits are discarded. These extra bits are termed as *redundant* or *check bits*. The data unit together with the redundant bits is usually called a *code word*. In the following sections, we will discuss how to generate the redundancy bits and how to detect errors using them.

Parity Check

Parity check is the most common, least expensive, and simplest error-detection algorithm. It is sometimes referred to as *vertical redundancy check*. This technique uses one bit as the redundant bit. There are two implementations of parity check—namely, even parity and odd parity. For *even parity*, the goal is to make the number of 1's in the code word even. Conversely, odd parity makes the number of 1's odd. For example, 101000 becomes 1010001 with odd parity and 101000 0 with even parity. The parity bit computation and check is implemented using an exclusive-*or* gate arrangement similar to that shown in Figure 6.

Parity check can detect all single-bit errors. It can also detect burst errors provided the total number of altered bits is odd. For example: 11001100 and 11001101 differ by one bit, which is detected by even parity check. The data units 10101010 and 01001010 differ by three bits, which is also detected by even parity check. However, if the number of bits altered is even, then parity check will fail. For example, 10010011 and 11110011 differ by two bits and yet have the same even parity. On the whole, despite being fast and cheap to implement, parity check is not especially reliable in detecting burst errors.

Longitudinal Redundancy Check

The *longitudinal redundancy check* (LRC) is an extension of parity checking. LRC uses parity checking to detect burst errors. The idea is to use multiple parity bits for one data unit. To implement LRC, the data unit is segmented into multiple portions; then the parity check for each of these portions is calculated and appended to the original data unit.

The data unit to be transmitted is segmented and arranged in rows and columns. The parity for each corresponding column is then calculated and appended to the original data unit. For example if we have a block of twenty-four bits, we can rearrange the data into four rows, each with six bits, and calculate the parity bit for each column and append it to the original data unit, which then becomes 24 + 6 = 30 bits long.

For example, we want to transmit 101010 011100 001101 110011. If we choose to break the message into four segments, we calculate the LRC with even parity as follows:

Segment 1	1	0	1	0	1	0
Segment 2	0	1	1	1	0	0
Segment 3	0	0	1	1	0	1
Segment 4	1	1	0	0	1	1
LRC	0	0	1	0	0	0

Therefore, the code word becomes 101010 011100 001101 110011 001000

Now suppose the data block 110001 101010 111011 101010 is corrupted to 110001 101001 001011 101010. The LRC bits will change from 001010 to 111001. Hence, this four-bit error is detected. Note how the total number of bits changed per column is odd. From this example, it is clear that LRC can detect multiple-bit errors or burst errors. However, if the total number of bits altered per column is even, then LRC will fail. For example, suppose the same data block gets corrupted to 110000 101011 111011 101010. Because the LRC bits remain unchanged, 001010, the LRC algorithm fails. We should expect this because we know that parity check fails when the total number of bits altered is even.

Block Sum Check

Block sum check is yet another implementation of parity check to detect burst errors. It is quite similar to LRC, but instead of only appending the parity for the columns, we also append the parity for the rows. The data unit is rearranged into a block, and the parity for both the rows and the columns is calculated. The resulting set of bits is referred to as the *block sum*. Figure 7 illustrates how block sum works.

As we observe, if the total number of errors in any column is even, then the error can be detected (LRC fails in such scenarios). Similarly, if the total number of errors in any row is even, then the error is detected. Block sum checking increases the probability of detecting burst errors as compared to LRC. However, if two bits are altered

	P$_0$	A$_6$	A$_5$	A$_4$	A$_3$	A$_2$	A$_1$	A$_0$
	1	0	0	0	0	0	0	0
	1	0	1	0	1	0	0	0
	0	1	0*	0	0	1*	1	0
	0	0	1	0	0	0	0	0
	1	0	1	0	1	1	0	1
	0	1	0*	0	0	0*	0	0
	1	1	1	0	0	0	1	1
	1	0	0	0	0	0	1	1
P$_1$	1	1	0	0	0	0	1	1

Figure 7: Block sum example

in any two columns and rows simultaneously, then block sum fails. An example of such a failure is denoted by (*) in Figure 7.

Cyclic Redundancy Check

In the previous sections, we covered various implementations of parity check. We used longitudinal redundancy check and block sum check to compensate for the single-bit error-detection limitation of parity-checking algorithms. Despite these limitations, both methods were successful in detecting burst errors. However, the receiver end has to wait for the complete code word to arrive before performing any checks. Note also that the receiver end has no means of detecting which part of the data has corrupted; therefore, in case of any errors, the entire code word has to be sent again, which wastes bandwidth.

Cyclic redundancy check (CRC) is another error-detection scheme that compensates for all of the limitations of the various parity check methods. It is based on polynomial codes and binary division. Calculations are performed in modulo 2 arithmetic. In essence, the CRC method divides the data unit by a divisor (called the *generator polynomial*) and uses the remainder bits as redundant bits. The receiver then divides the code word by the same divisor, and a remainder of zero verifies the integrity of the data. The number of redundant bits used must be one less than the number of bits in the divisor for the CRC to be valid.

The conversion of CRC binary data to polynomial codes proceeds as follows. Each bit is represented by a polynomial term with coefficient 0 or 1 (the value of that particular bit). Consider an *n*-bits long data unit, where each bit is represented by a term x^{n-1}, with coefficient either 0 or 1, depending on the value of that particular bit. The least significant bit has position 0, and the most significant bit has position *n*. For example, consider 11010: the polynomial equivalent is $1.x^{5-1} + 1.x^{4-1} + 0 x^{3-1} + 1.x^{2-1} + 0.x^{1-1} = x^4 + x^3 + x$.

Let the generator polynomial be $G(x)$ of degree g and the transmitted data unit $D(x)$ of degree d and length m. The following steps describe the process of generating the CRC bits.

1. Append g zero bits to the low order of the data unit, which now becomes $m + g$ bits long. Let $D_{m+g}(x)$ represent the new polynomial.
2. Divide $D_{m+g}(x)$ by $G(x)$ using modulo 2 division.
3. Replace the g-appended zero bits by the remainder of the previous operation in the polynomial $D_{m+g}(x)$. The new polynomial, $T(x)$, represents the code word to be transmitted.

To detect errors using CRC, divide $T(x)$ by $G(x)$. If the remainder is not zero, then there is an error.

The following example illustrates CRC bit generation. Let $D(x) = x^9 + x^7 + x^6 + x^4 + x^2 + 1$ and $G(x) = x^4 + x + 1$. Find the CRC bits and the frame to be transmitted.

The message is 1010010101; $G(x)$ is 10011. Because $G(x)$ is five bits long, we should append four zeros to the message before performing modulo 2 division. Therefore, the message becomes 1010010101 0000:

					1	0	1	0	1	0	1	0	1	0				
1	0	0	1	1	1	0	1	1	0	1	0	1	0	1	0	0	0	0
					1	0	0	1	1									
						1	0	1	1	0								
						1	0	0	1	1								
							1	0	1	1	0							
							1	0	0	1	1							
								1	0	1	1	0						
								1	0	0	1	1						
									1	0	1	0	0					
									1	0	0	1	1					
										1	1	1	0					

The remainder is 1110. Now we append this remainder to the original message to get the code word 1010010101 1110.

To check for errors on the receiver end, we perform modulo 2 division again:

					1	0	1	0	1	0	1	0	1	0				
1	0	0	1	1	1	0	1	1	0	1	0	1	0	1	1	1	1	0
					1	0	0	1	1									
							1	0	1	1	0							
							1	0	0	1	1							
									1	0	1	1	0					
									1	0	0	1	1					
											1	0	1	1	1			
											1	0	0	1	1			
													1	0	0	1	1	
													1	0	0	1	1	
																		0

As we can see, the remainder is, in fact, confirming the integrity of the data. Now suppose our code word suffered from a burst error such as this: 1<u>1001</u>101011110. We perform the CRC check:

					1	1	0	1	1	0	1	1	1	0				
1	0	0	1	1	1	1	0	0	1	1	0	1	0	1	1	1	1	0
					1	0	0	1	1									
						1	0	1	0	1								
						1	0	0	1	1								
								1	1	0	0	1						
								1	0	0	1	1						
									1	0	1	0	0					
									1	0	0	1	1					
											1	1	1	1	1			
											1	0	0	1	1			
												1	1	0	0	1		
												1	0	0	1	1		
													1	0	1	0	1	
													1	0	0	1	1	
															1	1	0	0

We can confirm that the remainder is not zero, so there is an error. A brief description of CRC operation is provided next for interested readers.

CRC Operation

Suppose we transmitted $T(x) = 10001010101$ and it was corrupted by $E(x) = 0001000100$, where the 1's represent positions where errors occurred. Then the received bit string would be $T(x) + E(x)$ (the + sign stands for exclusive-*or* or modulo 2 addition). The receiving party would perform $\frac{T(x) + E(x)}{G(x)}$ or $\frac{T(x)}{G(x)} + \frac{E(x)}{G(x)}$. But because $\frac{T(x)}{G(x)} = 0$, the error depends on the result of $\frac{E(x)}{G(x)}$.

Case 1: Single-Bit Errors

$E(x) = xi$, where i is the error bit position. If $G(x)$ has more than one term, then $E(x)$ will never be divisible by $G(x)$, and hence the error will be detected.

Case 2: Double-Bit Errors

$E(x) = x^i + x^j$, where $i > j$ and both represent bit error positions. We rewrite $E(x)$ as $E(x) = x^j(x^{i-j} + 1)$. To be able to detect this type of error, first, $G(x)$ must not be divisible by x; second, $G(x)$ must not divide $x^k + 1$, for any k up to $i - j$.

Case 3: Total Number of Erroneous Bits Is Odd

For an odd number of bit errors, the polynomial $E(x)$ will have an odd number of terms. To catch this type of error, $x + 1$ must be a factor of $G(x)$. It turns out that no polynomial with an odd number of terms has $x + 1$ as a factor in the modulo 2 system.

Case 4: Burst Errors

If the burst error is of length k, then $E(x) = x^i(x^{k-1} + \cdots + 1)$. $G(x)$ will not have x^i as a factor if it has a term in x^0. So, if the degree of $(x^{k-1} + \cdots + 1)$ is less that that of $G(x)$, then the remainder will never be zero. If the degree of $(x^{k-1} + \cdots + 1)$ is greater than or equal to the degree of $G(x)$, then the remainder will not necessarily be zero.

Summary of CRC Operation

In short, we should choose the generator polynomial such that it is not divisible by x but is divisible by $x + 1$. Such a generator polynomial with degree r will detect:

1. all single-bit errors,
2. all double-bit errors,
3. all odd-numbered bit errors (burst errors),
4. all burst error $\leq r$ in length, and
5. most burst errors $> r$ in length (if length $= r + 1$, probability of detection is $(2^{r-1} - 1)/2^{r-1}$ and if length $> r + 1$, probability of detection is $(2^r - 1)/2^r$).

An example of a CRC polynomial used in the IEEE 802 standard is $x^{32} + x^{26} + x^{23} + x^{22} + x^{16} + x^{12} + x^{11} + x^{10} + x^8 + x^7 + x^5 + x^4 + x^2 + x^1 + 1$. Based on the previous discussions, we can verify that this polynomial detects all bursts errors of length thirty-two or less and all burst errors with odd numbers of bits.

The hardware implementation of CRC is based on a shift register and exclusive-*or* gates as illustrated in Figure 8. Assume that $G(x) = x^4 + x + 1$. The bit string enters the circuit from the right.

Checksum

All of the error-checking methods discussed so far are mostly used by the lower-layer protocols. The upper-level protocols use the *checksum* method, which is based on the redundancy principle (like parity check, LRC, block sum check, and CRC). To calculate the redundancy bits, the sender party divides the data unit equally into two or more segments. These segments are then added together using one's complement. Any generated carry is added to the sum to ensure that the sum has the same length as the segments. The complement of the sum is then appended to the original data unit as redundant bits. To detect errors, the receiver system determines the sum of the segments (the same length used by the sender) in the code word. If the complement of the sum is zero, then the data are error free.

Examples

Suppose we want to determine the code word for 1010111011100011 using checksum. First, we break the bit string into equal segments (let us divide it into two for simplicity). Then we calculate the checksum as follows:

Carry	1	1		1	1	1		
Segment 1	1	0	1	0	1	1	1	0
Segment 2	1	1	1	0	0	0	1	1
Sum	1	0	0	1	0	0	0	1
Add carry								1
New sum	1	0	0	1	0	0	1	0
Checksum	0	1	1	0	1	1	0	1

Therefore, the code word is 1010111011100011 01101101.

To verify the checksum, assume we use the above code word:

Carry	1	1		1	1	1	1	
Segment 1	1	0	1	0	1	1	1	0
Segment 2	1	1	1	0	0	0	1	1
Checksum	0	1	1	0	1	1	0	1
Sum	1	1	1	1	1	1	1	0
Carry								1
New sum	1	1	1	1	1	1	1	1
Complement	0	0	0	0	0	0	0	0

Because the result is zero, this is error free.

Assume the code word suffered a burst error and the new transformation is now 1010000111100011 01101101:

Carry	1	1		1	1	1	1	
Segment 1	1	0	1	0	0	0	0	1
Segment 2	1	1	1	0	0	0	1	1
Checksum	0	1	1	0	1	1	0	1
Sum	1	1	1	1	0	0	0	1
Carry								1
New sum	1	1	1	1	0	0	1	0
Complement	0	0	0	0	1	1	0	1

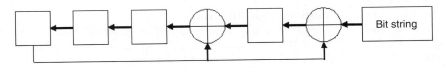

Figure 8: CRC circuit

Because the new complement is not zero, it indicates a burst error.

Checksum detects all errors with odd numbers of bits, and most errors with even numbers of bits. However, there may be instances when an error with an even number of bits may go undetected. The following example illustrates such an instance:

Carry	1	1		1	1	1	1	
Segment 1	1	0	1	0	1	0	1	1
Segment 2	1	1	1	0	0	1	1	0
Checksum	0	1	1	0	1	1	0	1
Sum	1	1	1	1	1	1	1	0
Carry								1
New sum	1	1	1	1	1	1	1	1
Complement	0	0	0	0	0	0	0	0

Note how the complement is still zero despite the burst error. Such an error will go undetected. Table 1 synthesizes several references (Forouzan 2001; Halsall 1996; Tanenbaum 2002; Shay 1999) that summarize the different error-detection techniques and their advantages and limitations.

ERROR CORRECTION

Having seen how the detection of single-bit errors and burst errors works, we now need to devise methods to correct them. In the event of an error, there are only two possible alternatives: either correct it or request that the original data be retransmitted. When dealing with single-bit errors, data retransmission wastes significant amount of bandwidth. It is not worth retransmitting the whole data unit for just one erroneous bit, so if at all possible avoid retransmission. The receiver, then, needs some type of automatic error-correcting mechanism. For binary data, error correction is fairly easily accomplished. If a bit should not be 1, then it must be 0—and vice versa. Therefore, the error-correcting mechanism only needs to locate the error and complement its value. In practice, it is more efficient to only correct errors when the error is limited to one, two, or three bits because of the fact that the bigger the burst error, the more redundant bits are needed to accurately correct the errors. Therefore, in these scenarios, retransmission is more efficient.

Single-Bit Error Correction

As discussed earlier, the simplest way to detect single bit errors is parity check. The key to error correction is to locate the error; correcting it involves complementing the bit. So if we want to detect and correct the error, we must

Table 1: Summary of Error-Detecting Methods

Detection Method	Advantages	Limitations
Parity check (vertical redundancy check)	• Simple and fast to implement • Always detects single-bit errors • Always detects odd-numbered bit errors	• Cannot detect errors when even number of bits are corrupted
Longitudinal redundancy check	• Always detects single-bit errors • Can detect most burst errors	• Fails when the number of bits altered per column is even within the block arrangement
Block sum check	• Always detects single-bit errors • Better than LRC in detecting burst errors	• Fails where an even number of bits are altered in any two columns and rows simultaneously within the block arrangement
Cyclic redundancy check	• Most efficient and reliable • Detects all single-bit errors • Detects all double-bit errors • Detects all odd-numbered errors • Detects all burst errors $\leq r$ in length • Detects most burst errors $> r$ in length (if length $= r + 1$, probability of detection is $(2^{r-1}-1)/2^{r-1}$ or if length $> r + 1$, probability of detection is $(2^{r-1}-1)/2^r$)	• Somewhat more complex to implement when compared to other parity check techniques
Checksum	• Simpler to implement than CRC • Always detects single-bit errors • Always detects odd-numbered bit errors • Detects most even-numbered bit errors	• Occasionally fails when an even number of bits are corrupted

Table 2: Hamming Code for a Seven-Bit-Long Data Unit

10	9	8	7	6	5	4	3	2	1	0
d_6	d_5	d_4	r_3	d_3	d_2	d_1	r_2	d_0	r_1	r_0

Table 3: Erroneous Bit Detection Using Hamming Code

$r_3r_2r_1r_0$	Invalid parity checks	Erroneous bit position
0000	None	None
0001	d_0	0
0010	d_1	1
0011	d_0 and d_1	2
0100	d_2	3
0101	d_0 and d_2	4
0110	d_1 and d_2	5
0111	d_0, d_1, and d_2	6
1000	d_3	7
1001	d_0 and d_3	8
1010	d_1 and d_3	9
1011	d_0, d_1, and d_3	10

locate it. Hence, we need to include enough redundant bits so that we can locate the exact position of the error in the data unit. For a data unit m bits long, the redundant bits should be able to designate at least $m + 1$ states, pointing to no error, error in position 1 through error in position m. However, we also need to accommodate for errors in the redundancy bits themselves. Therefore, if we have r redundant bits, then the total number of states that need to be designated is $m + r + 1$. Because r bits can represent 2^r states, and we want to represent at least $m + r + 1$ states, we can solve for the ceil value of r from $2^r = m + r + 1$. Finally, using a code developed by R. W. Hamming—the *Hamming code*—we can detect the erroneous bits. The *Hamming distance* is defined as the number of different bits between the actual and received code word.

The Hamming Code

The Hamming code segments the data unit and calculates the even parity bits for each segment. The parity bits are then inserted at strategic positions in the transmitted data unit, as determined by $2^i + 1$, where i is the redundant bit number, assuming we start from position 0. To illustrate this concept, consider a data unit seven bits long: $d_6\,d_5\,d_4\,d_3\,d_2\,d_1\,d_0$. Using $2^r = m + r + 1$ with $m = 7$, the least integer value of the required redundancy bits (r) is 4. These redundant bits are called r_3, r_2, r_1, and r_0, and they are placed at strategic positions. The resulting Hamming code is shown in Table 2.

The even parity bits are calculated for the following data bits:

r_0 is calculated for positions 0, 2, 4, 6, 8, and 10.
r_1 is calculated for positions 1, 2, 5, 6, 9, and 10.

r_2 is calculated for positions 3, 4, 5, and 6.
r_3 is calculated for positions 7, 8, 9, and 10.

The Hamming code is tabulated in such a fashion that the combination of correct and erroneous parity reveals the location of the erroneous bit. It should be noted that r_0 is calculated using bits whose binary representations have a 1 in the zero position. Similarly, r_1 is calculated using bits with 1 in the first position and so forth. Table 3 illustrates this concept.

As an example, consider the message 1001011. The code word is

10	9	8	7	6	5	4	3	2	1	0
1	0	0	1	1	0	1	0	1	0	0

Assume that the code word transforms to 10011110100 because of a single bit error.

Checking each parity bit, we see that:

$$r_0 \text{ is } 0, r_1 \text{ is } 0, r_2 \text{ is } 1, r_3 \text{ is } 0$$

Therefore, the error is in location 0100. From Table 3, the location 0100 corresponds to d_2; and referring to Table 2, d_2 corresponds to location 5.

Burst-Error Correction

As previously discussed, the Hamming code is highly efficient at correcting single-bit errors. But we still have burst errors to deal with. To handle them, we can modify the Hamming code algorithm.

Table 4: Hamming Code Word Arrangement

d_6	d_5	d_4	r_3	d_3	d_2	d_1	R_2	d_0	r_1	r_0
d_6	d_5	d_4	r_3	d_3	d_2	d_1	R_2	d_0	r_1	r_0
d_6	d_5	d_4	r_3	d_3	d_2	d_1	R_2	d_0	r_1	r_0
d_6	d_5	d_4	r_3	d_3	d_2	d_1	R_2	d_0	r_1	r_0
d_6	d_5	d_4	r_3	d_3	d_2	d_1	R_2	d_0	r_1	r_0

The principle stays the same. The Hamming code words are arranged in a matrix before they are transmitted. The following two steps outline the process of encoding and transmitting the data.

1. Arrange the Hamming code words in a fashion so that they form a block or matrix (similar to the LRC arrangement).
2. Transmit the matrix one column at a time (instead of the conventional row method).

The receiver then reconstructs the original matrix one column at a time. Once the original matrix has been reconstructed, error correction is applied to each row. This technique ensures error correction even if the entire column is corrupted by a burst error. However, if multiple columns are corrupted in a fashion that leads to multiple erroneous bits in single row, then this technique will fail.

Suppose we want to transmit a data unit that is thirty-five bits long. First, we segment the data unit into segments: five in this case. Then we compute the Hamming code word for each segment: $d_6\,d_5\,d_4\,r_3\,d_3\,d_2\,d_1\,r_2\,d_0\,r_1\,r_0$. Finally the code words are arranged as shown in Table 4 and transmitted column-wise.

Table 5 summarizes the Hamming code and some other popular satellite and RF communication error-correction techniques. The details of most of these techniques are beyond the scope of this text. However, expected growth in wireless networking will make these techniques important, so the important features of the Hamming code and some other relevant techniques are tabulated in terms of their properties and applications by summarizing Hamming (1980), Peterson (1981), 4i2i Communications (2004a, 2004b, 2004c), Morelos-Zaragoza (1996), Wicker (1995), and Blelloch and Maggs (undated), for the interested reader in Table 5.

Table 5: Comparison of Various Error-Correcting Methods

Error-Correcting Method	Properties	Applications
Hamming code	• Corrects all single-bit errors • Can be modified to correct 2- or 3-bit errors • May fail to detect some error combinations	• Reliable network links • Computer memory
Golay code	• Perfect Golay code encodes 12 bits into 23 bits, denoted by (23, 12) • Corrects all errors with 3 bits or less • Extended Golay code (with 1 additional parity bit) can correct errors as long as 4 bits	• Because of low latency and short code word length, usually used in real-time applications and radio communications • Packet data communications • Mobile and personal communications • Radio communications • NASA deep space missions (Voyager 1 and 2) Communications
BCH code	• BCH code of length $n = 2^m - 1$ with generator polynomial with roots $a^1, a^2, \ldots a^{2t}$ can correct t-bit errors	• Used in digital communications and mass storage
Reed-Solomon code	• Code word has n data bits and k check bits • Errors up to $(n - k)/2$ can be corrected • Ensures high-quality throughput in real time	• Storage devices such as CDs and DVDs • Mobile communications • Digital communications over noisy channels

(continued)

Table 5: *(Continued)*

Convolution code	• Used on data stream rather than data blocks • Previous bits are used to encode following bits in data stream • Encoded using finite state machines; decoded using Viterbi algorithm • Computation-intensive, hence more difficult to implement but extremely powerful error-correcting capabilities	• Usually used where bit-error rate is relatively high and retransmission is not feasible such as satellite and deep space communications
Turbo codes	• High-performance error-correcting code based on convolution code • Encoded data stream consists of: 3 subunits: payload data, parity for data, and parity bits for known permutation of data. • Both parities are calculated using convolution code	• Usually used to achieve maximum data transfer over noisy bandwidth-limited channels • Deep space and satellite communications • 3G wireless networks

CONCLUSION

Data communication is straightforward, but there are many factors that can corrupt information as it travels along a transmission media. To ensure data integrity, many preventive measures can be taken. For instance, shielding counteracts the effects of cross talk, impulse noise, and induced noise. Other specialized filters remove other types of noise such as white noise. Amplifiers reduce the effect of attenuation and so forth. Despite all of these preventive measures, errors can still creep into data. As a result, the integrity of data cannot always be ensured. To achieve reliable data transmission, error-detection and error-correction schemes are needed.

As the term implies, *error detection* is used to detect errors in transmission. Techniques include parity check, LRC, block sum check, CRC, and checksum. Once an error has been detected, there are two options: correct it or request retransmission. Retransmission protocols used by the data-link layer include *positive acknowledgment with retransmission* (PAR) or *automatic repeat request* (ARQ), and *sliding window* protocols (*go back n* and *selective repeat*). There are many techniques that can be employed to correct errors, including the popularly used Hamming code.

GLOSSARY

Attenuation: The loss of energy when a signal travels through a medium.
Block sum check: Modification of LRC to allow detection of some burst errors.
Checksum: Error checking based on 1's complement addition.
Code word: Used to define a data unit together with its redundancy bits.
Cyclic redundancy check (CRC): Error checking based on polynomials. Most reliable error-detecting method.

Distortion: Often caused by the different speeds associated with each component of a complex signal.
Hamming code: Code that makes use of multiple even parity check bits inserted at strategic positions in the transmitted data unit to correct single bit errors.
Impulse noise: Noise caused by spikes.
Induced noise: Noise caused by electromagnetic interference.
Longitudinal redundancy check (LRC): Modification of parity check to allow detection of double bit errors.
Parity: Even and odd parity; simplest way to check for single bit errors or errors where the total number of bits is odd.
Redundancy bits: Bits added to check for or correct errors. They do not form part of the original data.
White noise: Usually random; also referred to as background noise.

CROSS REFERENCES

See *Cellular Communications Channels*; *Conducted Communications Media*; *Data Compression*; *Mobile Radio Communications*; *Wireless Channels*.

REFERENCES

4i2i Communications. 2004a. *Convolutional encoder/ Viterbi decoder IP core* (retrieved from www.4i2i.com/ viterbi.htm).
———. 2004b. *Golay encoder/Decoder IP core* (retrieved from www.4i2i.com/golay.htm).
———. 2004c. *Reed-Solomon codes* (retrieved from www.4i2i.com/reed_solomon_codes.htm).
Blelloch, G., and B. Maggs. Undated. *Error correcting codes* (retrieved from www.cs.cmu.edu/afs/cs.cmu.edu/ project/pscico-guyb/realworld/www/errorcorrecting. html).
Forouzan, B. A. 2001. *Data communications and networking*. New York: McGraw-Hill Higher Education.

Halsall, F. 1996. *Data communications, computer networks and open systems*. Boston: Addison Wesley.

Hamming, R. W. 1980. *Coding and information theory*. Englewood Cliffs, NJ: Prentice Hall.

Morelos-Zaragoza, R. 1996. *The error correcting codes (ECC) page* (retrieved from www.eccpage.com).

Peterson, W. W. 1981. *Error correcting codes*. Cambridge: MIT Press.

Shay, W. A. 1999. *Understanding data communications and networks*. Boston: PWS-Kent.

Tanenbaum, A. S. 2002. *Computer networks*. Upper Saddle River, NJ: Prentice Hall.

Wicker, S. B. 1995. *Error control systems*. Upper Saddle River, NJ: Prentice Hall.

Routers

Min Song, *Old Dominion University*

INTRODUCTION

Routers are networking devices that operate at the network layer (layer 3) of the OSI reference model. They are used to connect two or more computer networks. In the simplest case, a router consists of a computer with at least two network interfaces that support routing protocols. The main function of routers is to route packets across the networks from a source to a destination. Two processes inside the routers accomplish this function. The first process is *route processing*, or determining the best route to move packets from source to destination and filling this routing information into a routing table. The routing process is independent of the packet arrivals; it is performed by running the routing protocols periodically or in an event-triggered manner. By exchanging routing information with other routers in the network, each router is capable of constructing a complete picture of the entire network topology and thus finding the optimal routes to a destination.

The second process is *packet forwarding*, or looking up in the routing table to find the particular outgoing interface to use for each incoming packet, and moving the packet from the incoming interface to the outgoing interface. The forwarding process happens every time a packet arrives. When a router receives a packet, it uses the information contained in the packet header and the information contained in the routing table to decide whether to forward the packet to an appropriate outgoing interface or to respond to the packet for local processing. When the router responds to the incoming packet, it will behave as an end system rather than as an intermediate system. When the router decides to forward the packet, the packet is forwarded from the arriving interface to the outgoing interface through the switching backplane. The packet then is sent to the next host, which may or may not be the ultimate destination. If not, the next hop is typically another router or switch. As the packet moves across the network, its physical address changes from hop to hop, but its protocol address remains the same, which is the protocol address of the ultimate destination host.

A general purpose processor usually controls the operation of routers. Although both route processing and packet forwarding can also be implemented in the general purpose processor, advanced routers separate these processes by employing a number of distributed processors that are capable of performing specific tasks. Furthermore, modern high-performance routers use special high-performance network interfaces that include an onboard forwarding engine to speed up operation.

Routers are deployed at every level in the Internet. Routers in small office and home offices connect a small number of users to an *Internet service provider* (ISP). Routers in enterprise networks connect multiple *local area networks* (LANs) within the enterprise and ultimately connect them to the Internet backbone. Routers in the Internet backbone link together ISPs and enterprise networks with long-distance trunks. Because computer networks come in a variety of sizes and architectures, routers need to be designed specifically to meet these needs and be flexible enough to allow for changes in order to provide diverse services. The design of routers has an enormous impact on every aspect of the router's performance and consequently the network's performance.

ROUTER HARDWARE COMPONENTS

We start this section by introducing the main hardware components in traditional or first-generation routers. As shown in Figure 1, a traditional router is a rather simple piece of equipment with the following hardware components: network interfaces, shared bus, and routing processor.

Network Interfaces

Network interfaces are the hardware components that connect a router to the network and perform in- and outbound packet transmission to and from their immediate neighbors, which could be routers, switches, or normal hosts. Typically, two different modules—namely, input port card and output port card—perform the functions of

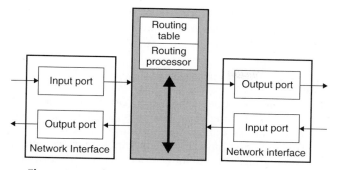

Figure 1: Hardware components in a traditional router

network interfaces. In Figure 1, each interface has one input port and one output port. In practice, multiple input and output ports are often gathered together on the same network interface. The protocols running on each interface are determined by the network that connects each interface. Figure 2 illustrates the main hardware modules on each port.

Next, we introduce the main functions performed on each input and output port with a focus on the layer 3 processing.

Input Port

The primary functions performed on the input port are verifying the integrity of the packet, modifying the packet header, and looking up the routing table to obtain the next hop information so that the packet can be forwarded to the appropriate output port. In particular, the following series of actions are performed on a packet's arrival.

IP Packet Verification. After passing the checking at layers 1 and 2, the packet is verified at layer 3 by checking the fields of version number, header length, and header checksum in the packet header. Only well-formed packets are placed in a shared memory pool for further processing; otherwise, the packet is discarded and an ICMP error message is returned to the original source.

An Interrupt Called on the Routing Processor. The routing processor is notified of the arrival of the packet. The routing processor then records the packet's location in memory and schedules a process to find out to which output port the packet should be sent.

Destination IP Address Parsing and Table Lookup. The destination address of the packet is extracted. If the packet is for this router (i.e., the destination address matches a router interface address), it is forwarded to the appropriate higher-layer protocol such as TCP. If it is for a remote host, then the routing table is examined to find the outgoing interface. The selected interface corresponds to the entry where the largest number of leading address bits match the destination address. In the case when the router does not know how to forward the packet, the packet is typically dropped. If the packet has multiple destinations (i.e., it is a *multicast* packet), then a set of output interfaces is chosen.

Packet Lifetime Control. The packet is discarded if the value of the *time to live* (TTL) field has decreased and is zero or negative. In this case, an ICMP error message is sent to the original source. The packet lifetime control is one effective approach to preventing packets from wandering around forever.

Handling Standard IP Options. Some packets require IP options handling such as *source routing* (the originating host chooses the route to the destination), *security* (the originating host specifies how secret the packet is), and *time stamp* (which makes each router append its own address and time stamp).

Handing Other Options. In reality, routers also need to handle *tunnels* (packets carrying other packets inside them), *network address translation* (i.e., map local private IP addresses to public global IP addresses and vice versa), *quality of service* (QoS) features (such as priority for some packets), and *packet filtering* (filtering packets according to security rules by looking at the packet's contents).

Packet Forwarding. At this point, the packet is ready to be forwarded to the output port. When all packets ahead of this packet in the transmit interface queue have been sent, the interface controller transmits the packet. If the packet has multiple destinations (multicasting), one copy is transmitted to each of the destined output ports. The arriving interface then interrupts the routing processor to tell it that the packet has been sent. The memory buffer is now freed by returning it to the set of buffers available for new arriving packets.

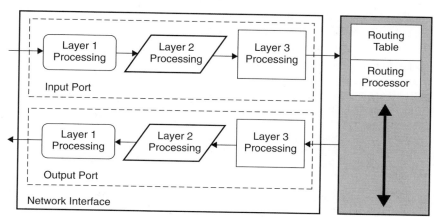

Figure 2: Network interfaces

The processing described above is known as *basic forwarding*; all packets are processed following the same procedures. In reality, however, many packets are sent by the same source to the same destination. In this case, once the first packet has been processed and forwarded, the router understands the way to forward all successive packets to the same destination. Therefore, the router stores the forwarding decision after it has been made. Using the *cached* information (destination address, port number, and any necessary details), the forwarding process can be faster. This is known as *fast forwarding*. With fast forwarding, a packet is handled immediately using an entry in the fast-forwarding cache without scheduling an interrupt to the routing processor. Just like any other caching system, it is unwise to keep the cached routing information for too long. Changes in network conditions require invalidating the entries in the routing table and, accordingly, the fast-forwarding cache. Thus, fast forwarding is highly effective at the edge of networks or within private networks (where there are comparatively few destination addresses and routes). It provides little advantage at the center of networks.

Output Port

The primary functions performed at the output port are to construct the outgoing packets and transmit them to the outgoing links. In particular, the following series of actions are performed on the output port.

Fragmentation. The output port checks the *maximum transfer unit* (MTU) of the output network interface. Packets larger than the interface's MTU must be fragmented into a suitable size for transmission. If a packet is received that has the *do not fragment* (DF) bit set, then the packet should not be fragmented but instead discarded if it is larger than the MTU of the output network interface.

Checksum Recalculation. Because at least the TTL field always changes from hop to hop, the header checksum needs to be recalculated.

Destination Physical Address. By looking in the *address resolution protocol* (ARP) cache, the medium access control address of the next hop router is found. If there is no such entry, an ARP request can be sent. The physical address is then added, and the packet is linked into the list of packets to be sent in the appropriate output interface.

Packet Scheduling. A packet is typically placed in a queue waiting for transmission. If there is a single *first in, first out* (FIFO) queue, then a simple first-come-first-service policy is used. More complicated packet-scheduling algorithms are needed to allocate the link bandwidth and service order among users if there are multiple queues on the output port. More information about packet scheduling can be found in "Packet Switching".

Packet Transmission. The packet is finally sent to the outgoing link with the physical address set to the next hop

router. When complete, the buffer (memory) allocated to the packet is released, and it may be used to store a new received packet.

Shared Bus

The shared bus connects the router's other components. It serves as a switching backplane to forward packets from the input interface to the output interface. A new arriving packet is first moved from the input interface buffer, across the shared bus, to the *central processing unit* (CPU), where the routing decision is made. The packet then is transferred across the bus again to the output interface buffer, where it waits to be transmitted to the link. Apparently, only one packet at a time can be transferred over the bus. Moreover, as the number of interfaces increases, the arrival rate of packets increases, or both, the demand on the bus grows.

In addition to the shared bus architecture, traditional routers also employ another similar architecture named *shared memory-based backplane* as shown in Figure 3 (Kurose and Ross 2003).

In this system, incoming packets are written into the shared-memory pool. The routing processor then reads the header information from the memory and makes the routing decisions. The switching operation therefore consists of removing a pointer from the receiving queue and copying the value of the pointer to the appropriate transmit queue. The memory would have to be a two-port design that allows simultaneous reads and writes at different memory addresses at the same time. Reading only the header saves a great deal of activity on the bus, but the system must be designed so that the network interfaces know which headers have been updated so they can remove the packets from memory and forward then to the next hop. As the link speed and router size increase, the shared memory and CPU may become the performance bottleneck and make the switching capability limited.

Both the shared-bus and shared-memory architectures make multicasting much simpler than other architectures. As packets move on the bus, it is simply a matter of informing multiple network interfaces to take packets off the bus and send them out to their respective links.

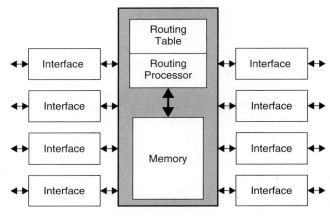

Figure 3: Shared memory-based backplane

Routing Processor

The routing processor executes routing protocols, constructs and maintains the routing table, and performs the forwarding function. In addition, the routing processor also performs management functionalities such as link up and down management and system control. For example, it responds to any *Internet control message protocol* (ICMP) messages it receives, and it may generate ICMP error messages when error events are detected (such as a packet received that cannot be routed because the address is not known). These functions do not apply to every packet; therefore, they are performed relatively infrequently.

The routing protocols define the information from the packet that a router uses to find a particular entry in the routing table, as well as the exact procedures that the router uses for finding the entry. The forwarding function consists of a set of algorithms that a router uses to make a forwarding decision on a packet.

The routing table contains lists of IP destination addresses and the appropriate network interfaces to be used to reach the destination. A default entry may be specified for all addresses not explicitly defined in the table. Figure 4 shows the routing table for the given network. The structure of the routing table varies, depending on the routing protocol used. The minimum information included in the routing table is a triple of <Destination, Next hop, Metric>. Here the metric specifies the cost of reaching the next host. It could be as simple as a single measure (such as hops, physical distance, bandwidth, or measured delay) or as complex as a function of hops, physical distance, bandwidth, communication cost, average traffic load, and measured delay. Figure 4 illustrates the structure of a routing table using the *distance vector routing* algorithm. For clarity, a single measure (hops) is used as the metric.

The routing table is constructed by using information supplied when the router is configured (installed). Although the routing table may be configured manually, it is usually configured automatically using a routing protocol. The routing protocol allows a router to periodically exchange information to all of its neighboring routers about the contents of its own routing tables. After a period of time, the router becomes aware of all the possible routes to reach each end system connected at any point in the network. It therefore adds the information to its own routing table about the other routers to which it is connected, building a picture of how to reach other parts of the network. Routers near the center of a network generally have enormous routing tables, whereas those nearer the edges have smaller tables.

There are two basic approaches to construct a routing table (Comer 2004 "Computer networks"): static routing and dynamic routing.

Static Routing

In static routing, a program or network administrator computes and installs routes to be followed when a router boots; the routes do not change. Although this approach is simple, it is not flexible enough to allow change in routes based on dynamic network conditions.

Dynamic Routing

In dynamic routing, a program builds an initial routing table when a router boots; the program then updates the table as conditions in the network change. This approach provides the capability for a network to handle problems automatically. The two well-known routing algorithms for distributed route computation are the *distance vector algorithm* and the *link state routing algorithm* (Tanenbaum 2003).

Static routing is applicable when network topologies do not change significantly and route calculations can be performed offline. Typically, however, the dynamics of networks necessitate more sophisticated algorithms to allow routers to adapt to rapidly changing network conditions. For interior routing within each network that is controlled by a common network administrator (such a network is often referred to as an *autonomous system*), *open shortest path first* (OSPF) is the predominant protocol. OSPF operates by abstracting the autonomous system into a directed graph. In the graph, nodes represent routers or LANs, and arcs represent the lines connecting routers and LANs. Each node measures the cost (distance, delay, bandwidth, etc.) to each of its neighbors and send its updates either to all other nodes in the system by

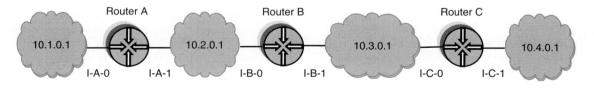

Routing table for router A			Routing table for router B			Routing table for router C		
10.1.0.1	I-A-0	0	10.1.0.1	I-B-0	1	10.1.0.1	I-C-0	2
10.2.0.1	I-A-1	0	10.2.0.1	I-B-0	0	10.2.0.1	I-C-0	1
10.3.0.1	I-A-1	1	10.3.0.1	I-B-1	0	10.3.0.1	I-C-0	0
10.4.0.1	I-A-1	2	10.4.0.1	I-B-1	1	10.4.0.1	I-C-1	0

Figure 4: Routing table

broadcasting or to certain nodes in the system by multicasting. Eventually, every node in the system knows the complete picture of the entire system and thus is able to compute the shortest path to every other node.

Although OSPF is the recommended routing protocol within an autonomous system, a different protocol—*border gateway protocol* (BGP)—is frequently used between autonomous systems. BGP is fundamentally a distance vector protocol. It operates by maintaining the cost to each destination and keeping the track of the path used. Instead of just telling each neighbor its estimated cost to every other destination, each BGP router tells its neighbors the exact path it is using to reach the destination. BGP routers communicate with each other by establishing TCP connections and send updated router table information only when one host has detected a change.

Another important feature of BGP is that it is a policy-based routing protocol. Typical policies involve political, security, and economic considerations (Metz 2001; Tanenbaum 2003). For example, a corporate autonomous system might want the ability to send and receive packets from any other network. However, it might not want to deliver packets originating in one foreign autonomous system and ending in another foreign autonomous system, even though it is on the shortest path between the two autonomous systems. It should be noted that many other routing protocols, such as *routing information protocol* (RIP) and *enhanced interior gateway routing protocol* (EIGRP), are also widely used in practice. More information about routing protocols can be found in Chapter 4.

ROUTER DESIGN ISSUES

The first generation of routers (Figure 1) was based on software implementation on a single general-purpose CPU. They benefited from the ability to be easily upgraded and modified. However, this simple architecture inevitably yielded low performance because of the following reasons. First, the overall processing speed is definitely limited by the single CPU. Second, the software implementation of routing is inefficient because most of the operations could be conveniently implemented in hardware. Third, for the shared-bus architecture, packets need to travel twice through the shared bus. This brings significant overhead and delay.

Next we introduce the design goals and techniques for modern high-performance routers.

Design Goals

High-performance routers are designed in an attempt to achieve the following goals:

High Throughput
Throughput is the number of packets the router can forward each second. This defines the aggregate packet-forwarding capacity of the router. Factors that affect throughput include the traffic model, buffer management, and packet scheduling.

Low Latency
Latency is the amount of time from the moment a packet leaves the outgoing interface to the moment a packet arrives at the incoming interface. This time is determined by several factors, including the packet-processing time, routing table lookup time, calculations of routes, queuing time, and transmission time.

High Scalability
Scalability is the number of input and output ports the router can support with a good performance. It can be measured in terms of both the rate of increase in cost and the maximum possible router size.

High Reliability
Reliability is the total number of failures regardless of whether the failures result in router downtime.

High Availability
Availability is the percentage of time that the router is operating—that is, the total time the router is operational divided by the total time elapsed since the last failure.

Low Cost
The overall cost of a router is proportional to the number of ports, which in turn depends on the amount and kind of memory it uses, the processing power, and the complexity of the communication protocols used between the components.

Design Techniques

The techniques to achieve the above goals are summarized as follows.

Hardware Implementation
More and more of the packet-forwarding functions are performed in hardware. The improvement in the integration of CMOS technology has made it possible to implement a large number of functions in *application-specific integrated circuit* (ASIC) components.

Parallelism
Separate banks of forwarding engines and port cards are interconnected by *switching fabrics* (SFs) to either achieve higher performance or allow the use of lower-cost components.

Distributed Forwarding Decision Making
The forwarding decision can be made locally on the interfaces. This leaves the routing processor to focus on the overall system management rather than on packet processing.

Flexibility
Although switch-based fabric (hardware) has been widely employed, network processor-based routers have also attracted attention for their flexibility and active routing capabilities.

Quality of Service
Advance queuing and scheduling algorithms make it possible to provide differentiated quality of services.

EVOLUTION OF ROUTER ARCHITECTURES

Although some first-generation routers cache the routing decisions on each interface, the overall performance is still significantly limited by the central CPU and shared medium. Over the last decades, the evolution of router architecture has experienced several generations as follows.

Shared Processor-Based Architecture

As shown in Figure 5, in addition to the traditional routing processor, there are multiple distributed processing units (CPU and memory), and they are connected to network interfaces through the shared bus (Puzmanova 2002).

Each processing unit is associated with a group of interfaces and handles all packets received by the group of interfaces. In this design, an arriving packet could be sent to the available distributed CPU instead of the central routing processor. This dramatically reduces the load that would burden the routing processor. In addition, packets from the same flow (a stream of packets that have the same source and destination) could be always sent to the same CPU to speed up the process.

Dedicated Processor-Based Architecture

As shown in Figure 6, in dedicated processor-based architecture, each interface is equipped with a dedicated forwarding processor.

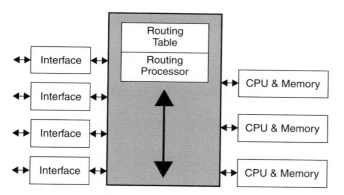

Figure 5: Router with shared processor

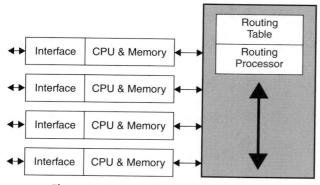

Figure 6: Router with dedicated processor

The forwarding processors do not take part in route processing; instead, they periodically receive all routing information from the router's routing processor. In doing so, a shadow copy of the routing table is stored on each of the forwarding processors. With local copies of the routing table, the forwarding decision can be made locally without invoking the routing processor. This approach allows the forwarding processor on each interface to handle large numbers of destination IP addresses, even when there are large numbers of route changes. It therefore scales well to core routers and is used in high-speed routers.

Switch-Based Architecture

The performance of the dedicated processor-based architecture is limited by the speed of the general purpose CPU and the shared bus. In the switch-based architecture (Figure 7), there are two major innovations.

First, the general purpose CPU is replaced by a specially designed forwarding engine. An appropriate ASIC is designed for each protocol processing task and then replicated on each network interface (Aweya 1999). The second innovation is that the shared bus is replaced by a crossbar switch fabric (McKeown 1997; Partridge et al. 1998). Hence all input and output ports are fully interconnected. A transmission path is dynamically configured between an input and an output. Therefore, multiple packets can be transmitted across the fabric simultaneously.

The performance of the switch architecture shown in Figure 7 can be further improved by deploying parallel technique in the implementation of forward engine and switch fabric. Figure 8 depicts the architecture of the forwarding engine where parallelism is achieved by partitioning forwarding functions among five different processors or ASICs (Kumar, Lakshman, and Stiliadis 1998). Because it performs only one type of function, each processor or ASIC needs only access the data associated with a particular function. Thus, the memory required is much smaller and can be more quickly acquired.

The performance of the switch-based router can also be boosted by using multiple crossbar switches in parallel

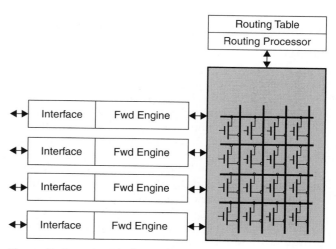

Figure 7: Router with forwarding engine and switch-based fabric

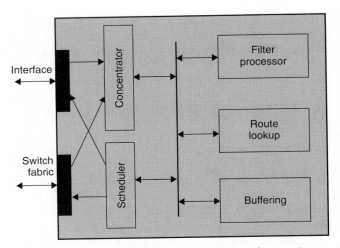

Figure 8: Parallel implementation of forwarding engine

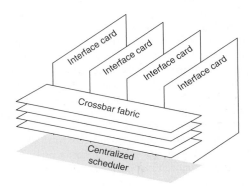

Figure 9: A four-way parallel crossbar switch

(McKeown 1997). Figure 9 demonstrates a switching backplane that has four parallel crossbars.

In Figure 9, during each time slot, all of the crossbar "slices" are set to the same configuration, presenting a four-bit wide bus from each interface card to the switch core. A centralized scheduler connects to each interface card and determines the configuration of the crossbar switch at each time slot.

NEW DEVELOPMENTS IN ROUTER DESIGN

With the transformation of the Internet into a ubiquitous commercial infrastructure for conducting business, research, education, and entertainment, the ability to guarantee QoS and provide diverse services has become as important as providing massive bandwidth. Unfortunately, the bottleneck of the Internet has moved from links to routers with the rapid provisioning of higher performance links and the introduction of wavelength division multiplexing (Chao and Degermark 1999). As an effort to alleviate the bottleneck, new developments in router design have emerged dramatically. The differentiated service architecture (Blake et al. 1998) has been designed to provide a simple, easy-to-implement, low-overhead tool to support applications with diverse QoS requirements. In this architecture, the administration defines a set of service classes, each corresponding to a certain level of QoS requirements. When a user signs up for the differentiated service, its packets are classified as one type of class by using the current *type of service* field (IPv4) or *traffic class* field (IPv6). Routers within the differentiated service domain then use this field to provide differentiated quality of services. At the routing protocol side, *IP switching* (Newman et al. 1997) and *multiprotocol label switching* (Rosen, Viswanathan, and Callon 2001) have been proposed to speed up the switching and routing process. In the rest of this section, we present the new hardware developments.

Buffer Management

Buffers are critically important hardware components in modern routers. Given the fact that only one packet can be transmitted to the external link at any cycle, routers need buffers at the output side to temporarily store the backlogged packets in the following scenarios: (1) the network is congested and thus the packet transmission speed must slow down, and (2) multiple packets are forwarded to the same output port at the same cycle. Similarly, routers need buffers at the input side for the following reasons. Because of the stochastic nature of the packet arrival process and the heterogeneous nature of connected links, it is likely that multiple input ports have packets destined to the same output port at the same cycle, a phenomenon called *output contention*. Given the current technology, the switch fabric is not able to forward all of the contending packets, so the remaining packets must be stored at the input port. As more and more packets are backlogged at the input port, packets with different destinations start to contend for the resource within the switch fabric, a phenomenon called *input contention*. Moreover, contention may also occur within the switch fabric, a phenomenon called *internal contention*. All of these contentions need to be solved by placing buffers at the appropriate location.

Next we briefly introduce the three basic queuing schemes: output queuing, input queuing, and virtual output queuing.

Output Queuing

In output queuing, buffers are allocated at the output ports. Typically, they are organized as multiple queues to support multiple classes of services. Incoming packets are immediately forwarded to the appropriate output port and stored in one of the queues. Because packets are queued directly at the output links to which they must be transmitted, the output links will never suffer from the starvation. By employing one of the weighted fair queuing policies (Zhang 1995), the best delay throughput performance can be easily obtained. To implement the output queuing scheme, however, the switch fabric must operate N times faster than the external links in a router of N ports. This is impossible for routers with more ports or higher link rates. As an example, consider a router with 16 ports operating at 2.5 Gbps. One path in the switch fabric must be able to transfer at $2.5 \times 16 = 40$ Gbps to accommodate the worst case. This requirement is too high for the implementation of both fabric and memories.

Input Queuing

In input queuing, buffers are allocated on the input ports. Traditionally, the entire buffer was organized as one queue. If more than one packet is destined for the same output, only one packet can be transmitted. The other packets are temporarily buffered at the input ports. For routers with Gigabit links, the switch fabric needs to operate only slightly faster than the links. Although the speed constraint of fabric is removed, the router performance is significantly degraded due to the *head of line* (HOL) blocking (Karol, Hluchyj, and Morgan 1987). Moreover, it is difficult to control the packet delay bounds resulting from the input contention.

Virtual Output Queuing

The widely employed queuing policy for modern routers is *virtual output queuing* (VOQ). In a VOQ-based router, each input port organizes the buffer into N logical queues, each associated with an output port. It has been shown that VOQ is able to provide a maximum throughput of 100 percent (McKeown et al. 1999). To better improve the link utilization, buffers are allocated on both input and output sides. This is called *combined input and output queuing* (CIOQ) as shown in Figure 10.

In Figure 10, the VOQ scheme is employed on the input port, and a single FIFO queue is employed on the output port. It has been proved that a router with CIOQ behaves identically to a router with output queuing if the fabric of CIOQ router operates $2 - 1/N$ faster than the external links (Chuang et al. 1999).

Multicast Queuing

To efficiently support multicast traffic (i.e., traffic with multiple destinations), special attention is needed in the queuing design. Simply considering multicast as a special case of unicast does not allow queuing to be scalable. For example, VOQ is commonly believed to be the best queuing scheme for unicast traffic but is not suitable for multicast traffic. For multicast traffic, in order to implement the VOQ-based architecture, in total $2^N - 1$

queues are needed at each input port. This is impractical for large routers. One simple queuing policy for multicast traffic is to allocate one queue at each input port (Hui and Renner 1994). Given independent and identically distributed traffic and a random packet-scheduling algorithm, the throughput λ versus fanout f (the number of destinations) is given as follows:

f	1	2	4	8	16
λ	0.59	0.69	0.78	0.85	0.90

An advanced multicast queuing policy allocates multiple queues at each input port (Bianco et al. 2003; Song et al. 2005). Because more queues provide more scheduling spaces, the throughput can be increased significantly. Under the same traffic and scheduling policy as in Hui and Renner (1994), the throughput λ versus fanout f is given as follows when three queues are allocated at each input port:

f	1	2	4	8	10	16
λ	0.78	0.84	0.88	0.92	0.93	0.95

Before we conclude the topic of buffer management, it is important to note that other aspects of buffer management deserve equal attention in router design. These include the buffer's speed and size, both of which grow linearly with the external link rate. To handle the speed problem, one solution (Iyer, Kompella, and McKeown 2002) is to take advantage of the density of DRAM and the speed of SRAM. Specifically, a small fast SRAM holds (caches) the heads and tails of queues, allowing arriving packets to be written quickly to the tail and departing packets to be read quickly from the head. The large DRAMs are used for bulk storage, holding the majority of packets in each queue that are at neither the head nor the tail. A memory manager shuttles packets between the SRAM and the DRAM. To handle the

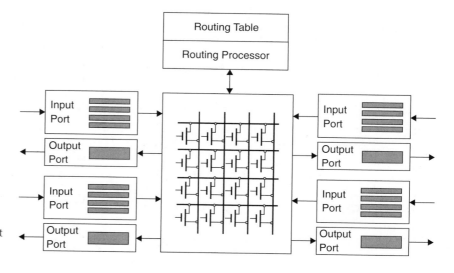

Figure 10: Combined input and output queuing scheme

size problem, one suggestion (Villamizar and Song 1994) is that the capacity of a port should have enough buffers to hold as many packets as could pass through the buffer in end-to-end round-trip time.

Active Networking

Active networking is a new communications paradigm for data networks. With active networking, the network is no longer viewed as a passive move of bits but as a more general computation engine: Packets injected into the network may be modified, stored, or redirected as they are being transported. To do this, routers are expected to perform more customized computing functionalities that could be customized on a per-user or per-application basis. For example, a user of an active network could send a customized compression program to a router within the network and request that the router execute that program when processing the user's packets.

There are two primary approaches to implement the active networking (Tennenhouse et al. 1997). In the first approach, users send a trace program to each router and arrange for the program to be executed when their packets are processed. The second approach is that packets themselves contain the program that can be recognized and executed by routers. The fundamental difference between these two approaches is the *out-of-band* (first approach) or *in-band* (second approach) transmission of the executable code.

With the wide deployment of active networking, more and more active services are becoming standard services shared by many users and applications. As a result, advanced router architectures include the use of *plug-ins* to dynamically reconfigure the router (Decasper et al. 2000). Plug-ins are basically specialized blocks that perform certain tasks. Because a router must be able to handle many different types of traffic, plug-ins provide a way to dynamically scale the amount of processing that has to be done on a packet to provide the most efficient packet handling possible given a set of plug-ins. When a special packet is detected and it is determined that a plug-in is needed, the plug-in management system loads the plug-in and reroutes the packet to the plug-in. Plug-ins may also work with other plug-ins to fully process packets. The strength of a plug-in is its ability to be removed from the processing chain and dynamically work together with other plug-ins. After these plug-ins are installed, subsequent packets that require similar processing can make use of the plug-in more quickly than when they were first invoked.

As a note to active networking, care must be taken when deploying the active services. Computing functions should be placed in the network only if they can be cost-effectively implemented there (Bhattacharjee, Calvert, and Zegura 1997). The semantics of any active features must be carefully constrained so that interactions among different users can be predicted by a user who is using the active service and functions (Reed, Saltzer, and Clark 1998). Moreover, large-scale deployment of active services involves significant challenges in interoperability, security, and scalability.

Network Processor

Modern routers require the flexibility to support new protocols and network services without changes in the underlying hardware components. However, the traditional general purpose processor-based routers are not applicable for modern high-speed networks because of their low performance. The continuing advances in integrated circuit technology are making it possible to implement network processor-based router architecture. A network processor is a special purpose, programmable hardware device that combines the low cost and flexibility of a *reduced instruction set computer* (RISC) with the speed and scalability of ASIC chips (Comer 2004 "Network systems"). Network processors are designed to be implemented on a single chip that integrates many small, fast processor cores, each tailored to perform a specific networking task.

The first step in developing an architectural design of the network processor requires an identification of important functions. These functions are then partitioned into two groups. The first group—called *ingress*—focuses on arriving packets; the second group—*egress*—focuses on departing packets. To implement both ingress and egress, specific software architecture needs to be implemented. Figure 11 depicts the software architecture of the network processor. A classifier (C) first reads the packets from an input port. The forwarder (F) is selected based on certain fields in the packet header. Each forwarder then procures packets from the input queue and executes some predefined function to the packet; the modified packet is then transmitted to its output queue. The transformation of packets occurs in the forwarders. The output scheduler (S) selects one of the nonempty output queues and transmits the associated packet to the output port.

Network processors are flexible to maintain low overall cost. They are not limited to a particular protocol or particular layer of the stack. This results in the usage of network processor in any layer of the stack in applications

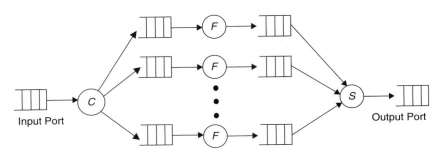

Figure 11: Software architecture of network processor

such as a layer 2 bridge, a layer 3 router, a layer 4 splicer, or a layer 5 load balancer. Because a network processor offers the ability to program and change its behavior, the system that uses network processors can be designed and implemented more quickly because no changes are required in hardware.

Secure Routing

Many of the protocols that are in widespread use were designed with the assumption that no users on the network are malicious. Gateway routers do not typically verify the source address of an incoming packet, making it easy to "spoof" packets. Routers rely on both temporal and spatial locality for doing fast routing table lookup, but an incoming stream of packets with randomly generated destination addresses can cause worst case table lookup latencies and grind routers to a halt. For this reason, there is another table called the *filter table* along with the routing table. The filter table is usually manually configured and contains a list of addresses and other packet header details that, if they match a received packet, will cause the packet to be either discarded by the network interface immediately or forwarded directly to the routing processor for further processing. This may be used to deny access to particular protocols or to prevent unauthorized packets being forwarded. More information about network security can be found in the *Handbook of Information Security* (Bidgoli 2006).

CONCLUSION

In this chapter, we studied routers from the hardware perspective. We introduced the main hardware components and their functions, and we reviewed the evolution of router architectures. For each type of architecture, we analyzed the strengths and weaknesses as well as the design issues. To support the ever-growing services supported by the Internet, specialized network processors are being developed to address the specific needs of network activities and perform active networking by using plug-ins. As Internet traffic continues to grow, we anticipate that the newest development in router design will be to create special purpose routing control platforms to facilitate routing traffic. In addition, because the computer networks come in a variety of sizes and architectures, routers need to be designed specifically to meet these needs and be flexible enough to allow for changes in order to provide diverse services.

GLOSSARY

Address resolution protocol (ARP): A protocol that maps an Internet protocol address to a physical machine address that is recognized in the local network.

Application-specific integrated circuit (ASIC): A microchip designed for a special application such as a transmission protocol.

Enhanced interior gateway routing protocol (EIGRP): A network protocol that lets routers efficiently exchange information. EIGRP evolved from interior gateway routing protocol (IGRP); routers using

either EIGRP and IGRP can interoperate because the metric used with one protocol can be translated into the metrics of the other protocol.

Head of line (HOL) blocking: A phenomenon that a blocked HOL packet prevents the packets behind it from receiving service. This happens because only the HOL packets can be transmitted.

Internet control message protocol (ICMP): A message-control and error-reporting protocol between a host and a router. It is also used to test the Internet.

Internet protocol (IP): A networking layer protocol by which packets are delivered from one computer to another on the Internet.

Open systems interconnection (OSI): A standard description or reference model for how messages should be transmitted between any two points in a communication network.

Router: A networking device that determines the next network point to which a packet should be forwarded toward its destination.

Routing information protocol (RIP): A widely used protocol for managing router information within a self-contained network such as a corporate LAN or an interconnected group of such LANs. It is one of several internal gateway protocols.

Switching fabric (SF): Combination of hardware and software that moves packets from the input ports to the output ports.

Virtual output queuing (VOQ): A queuing mechanism in which each input port organizes the buffer to N logical queues, each associated with an output port.

CROSS REFERENCES

See *Bridges*; *Circuit Switching*; *Message Switching*; *Packet Switching*; *Switches*.

REFERENCES

Aweya, J. 1999. *IP router architectures: An overview*. Nortel Networks (retrieved March 9, 2006 from www.owlnet. rice.edu/~elec696/papers/aweya99.pdf).

Bhattacharjee, S., K. L. Calvert, and E. W. Zegura. 1997. Active networking and the end-to-end argument. *Proceeding of the International Conference on Network Protocols*, pp. 220–8.

Bianco, A., P. Giaccone, E. Leonardi, F. Neri, and C. Piglione. 2003. On the number of input queues to efficiently support multicast traffic in input queued switches. *Proceeding of High-Performance Switching and Routing*, pp. 111–6.

Bidgoli, H. 2006. *The handbook of information security*. Vol. 1. New York: John Wiley & Sons.

Blake, S., D. Black, M. Carlson, E. Davies, Z. Wang, and W. Weiss. 1998. An architecture for differentiated services. RFC 2475 (retrieved March 9, 2006 from http://rfc.net/rfc2475.html).

Chao, H. J., and M. Degermark. 1999. Next-generation IP switches and routers. *IEEE Journal on Selected Areas in Communications*, 17(6): 1009–11.

Chuang, S. T., A. Goel, N. McKeown, and B. Prabhakar. 1999. Matching output queueing with a combined input/output switch. *IEEE Journal on Selected Areas in Communications*, 17(6): 1030–9.

Comer, D. E. 2004. *Computer networks and Internets with Internet applications*. (4th ed. Upper Saddle River, NJ: Prentice Hall.

———. 2004. *Network systems design using network processors*. Upper Saddle River, NJ: Prentice Hall.

Decasper, D., Z. Dittia, G. Parulkar, and B. Plattner. 2000. Router plugins: A software architecture for next-generation routers. *IEEE/ACM Transactions on Networking*, 8(1): 2–15.

Hui, J. Y, and T. Renner. 1994. Queuing analysis for multicast packet switching. *IEEE Transactions on Communications*, 42(2–4): 723–31.

Iyer, S., R. R. Kompella, and R. McKeown. 2002. *Designing buffers for router line cards*. Stanford University HPNG Technical Report TR02-HPNG-031001 (retrieved March 9, 2006 from http://kailash.ucsd.edu/~ramana/).

Karol, M., M. Hluchyj, and S. Morgan. 1987. Input versus output queueing on a space division switch. *IEEE Transaction on Communication*, 35(12): 1347–56.

Kumar, V. P., T. V. Lakshman, and D. Stiliadis. 1998. Beyond best effort: Router architectures for the differentiated services of tomorrow's Internet. *IEEE Communications Magazine*, 36(5): 52–164.

Kurose, J. F., and K. Ross. 2003. *Computer networking, A top-down approach featuring the Internet*. 2nd ed. Boston: Addison Wesley.

McKeown, N. 1997. A fast switched backplane for a gigabit switched router. *Business Communications Review*, December.

———, A. Mekkittikul, V. Anantharam, and J. Walrand. 1999. Achieving 100% throughput in an input-queued switch. *IEEE Transactions on Communications*, 47(8): 1260–67.

Metz, C. 2001. Interconnecting ISP networks. *IEEE Internet Computing*, 5(2): 74–80.

Newman, P., G. Minshall, T. Lyon, and L. Huston. 1997. IP switching and gigabit routers. *IEEE Communication Magazine*, 35(1): 64–9.

Partridge, C., P. P. Carvey, E. Burgess, et al. 1998. A 50-Gb/s IP router. *IEEE/ACM Transactions on Networking*, 6(3): 237–48.

Puzmanova, R. 2002. *Routing and switching: Time of convergence?* Boston: Addison Wesley.

Reed, D. P., J. H. Saltzer, and D. D. Clark. 1998. Active networking and end-to-end arguments. *IEEE Network*, 12(3): 69–71.

Rosen E., Viswanathan, A., and Callon, R. (2001). *Multiprotocol label switching architecture*. RFC 3031 (retrieved March 9, 2006 from www.rfc-archive.org/getrfc.php?rfc=3031).

Song, M., W. Zhu, A. Francini, and M. Alam. 2005. Performance analysis of large multicast switches with multicast virtual output queues. *Journal of Computer Communications*, 28(2): 189–98.

Spalink, T., S. Karlin, L. Peterson, and Y. Gottlieb. 2001. Building a robust software-based router using network Processors. *Proceedings of the Eighteenth ACM Symposium on Operating Systems Principles*, pp. 216–29 (retrieved March 9, 2006 from www.cs.cornell.edu/People/egs/syslunch-fall01/sosp/spalink.pdf).

Tanenbaum, A. S. 2003. *Computer networks*. 4th ed. Upper Saddle River, NJ: Prentice Hall.

Tennenhouse, D. L., J. M. Smith, W. D. Sincoskie, D. J. Wetherall, and G. J. Minden. 1997. A survey of active network research. *IEEE Communications Magazine*, 35(1): 80–6.

Villamizar C., and C. Song. 1994. High performance TCP in ANSNET. *Computer Communication Review*, 24(5): 45–60.

Zhang, H. 1995. Service disciplines for guaranteed performance service in packet-switching networks. *Proceeding of IEEE*, 83: 1374–96.

Switches

Min Song, *Old Dominion University*

INTRODUCTION

Switches are frequently referred to as layer 2 devices because they principally operate at the data link layer of the *open systems interconnection* (OSI) reference model (Day and Zimmermann 1983). As one of the most important interconnecting devices in today's networks, switches are often used to connect multiple segments of a large *local area network* (LAN) in order to extend the length of the LAN and increase its effective bandwidth. The interconnection of switches provides a large-scale network without reducing individual end host performance. In addition, switches can be used to directly connect individual hosts to form a LAN. The main task of switches is to forward frames from the inbound link to the outbound link based on the information contained in the frames. In addition, switches also play an important role in network security and traffic management.

In a generic switch, the main hardware components include several line cards or interfaces, a high-speed switching fabric, and a control unit. The line cards connect the switch to other networking devices, which could be LANs, other switches, routers, or individual hosts. On each line card, there are several port cards with links running the appropriate layer 2 protocols to communicate with the port cards at the other end of the link. The switching fabric forwards these frames to the appropriate output ports. The forwarding process is guided by the forwarding table, which is constructed and maintained by the control unit. The control unit also performs management functions such as link up or down management, and system control. Advanced line cards may also have embedded memories and control units to perform local processing.

The architectures of the contemporary switches vary widely and evolve rapidly. As a result, many switches with diverse features appear on the market. Unlike the traditional switches that operate at layer 2, these switches operate at both layers 2 and 3. Some even have the capability of supporting multiple network paradigms such as *Internet protocol* (IP) networks and *asynchronous transfer mode* (ATM) networks. Therefore, the definition of the *switch* has changed over time. Nevertheless, the fundamental functionalities of switches—interconnecting networking devices and forwarding frames—have never been changed. Based on this thought, we classify switches by two dimensions: communication spectrums and network paradigms.

In the remainder of this chapter, we first introduce the switch hardware components, some representative switch architectures, and switch performance metrics. We then present two types of switches: The first type is the LAN switch, which includes Ethernet switches and token ring switches. For both Ethernet and token ring switches, the *virtual LAN* (VLAN) switching capability is also discussed. The second type is the *wide area network* (WAN) switch, which includes packet switches and ATM switches. For both packet and ATM switches, the multicast switching capability is briefly studied. Finally, new switch architectures that require no speedup and support both unicast and multicast traffic are discussed.

SWITCH ARCHITECTURES
Hardware Components

As we mentioned earlier, all switches have conceptually the same hardware components: input port cards, output port cards, a switching fabric, and a control unit. As a matter of fact, a switch and a classic computer share many similar hardware components. A general purpose computer equipped with several network line cards and suitable software can provide the same function as a switch. The biggest difference, however, is that the general purpose computer performs switching more slowly than a switch because of the fact that all frames from different links must pass through a common I/O bus. Every frame crosses the I/O bus twice and is written to and read from main memory once. Therefore, the aggregate throughput is limited to either half of the main memory bandwidth or half of the I/O bus bandwidth. The aggregate throughput of switches can be significantly improved by employing a high-performance switching fabric and

375

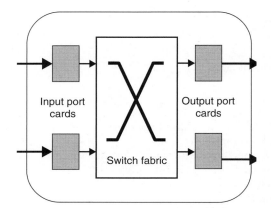

Figure 1: The main hardware components of a generic switch

distributed processing facility. Next we introduce some representative switch fabric architectures. For simplicity, an $N \times N$ switch is assumed, which means there are an equal number of input and output ports.

Figure 1 shows the main hardware components of a generic switch. Depending on which type of device they are connected to, the input port cards perform totally different tasks. For example, if an input port card connects to an Ethernet LAN, then the main tasks of the port card are to build and maintain the *forwarding table* that maps between the *medium access control* (MAC) addresses and the output ports and to determine which output port a frame should be sent to. On the other hard, if an input port card connects to an ATM link, then the main tasks of the port card would be to set up and manage the *virtual path identifier* (VPI) and *virtual circuit identifier* (VCI) table and determine which output port a cell should be sent to. Nevertheless, many input port cards perform the same fundamental tasks as follows:

- provide a link enable and disable function;
- reformat a frame from the external format to the internal format;
- determine which output port or ports a frame should be sent to;
- buffer the frames that cannot be sent to the switch fabric at the current cycle (if there are multiple buffers on the input port card, then a scheduling algorithm is needed to determine which frame can be transmitted to the output port at the current cycle); and
- maintain configuration values, error flags, and statistics counters.

Similarly, the fundamental tasks of the output port cards are as follows:

- reformat a frame from the internal format to the external format;
- buffer the frames that cannot be transmitted to the link at the current cycle;
- determine by a scheduling algorithm which frame can be transmitted to the link at the current cycle if there are multiple buffers on the output port card; and

- maintain configuration values, error flags, and statistics counters.

The primary task of the switch fabric is to quickly forward frames from the input ports to the output ports. When a switch fabric receives a frame passed from the input port, it forwards the frame to the output port based on the information either contained in the frame or sent from a control unit. A simple switch fabric has only one stage, whereas a complex switch fabric may have multiple stages with each one having different functions.

Representative Switch Architectures

In this section, we introduce representative switch architectures that are used to build large-scale switches.

Shared-Memory Switches

In shared-memory switches, all input ports and output ports share the same memory (as shown in Figure 2). Shared-memory switches are also called shared-buffer switches, in which memories are organized as linked-list buffers. (There are four linked lists in Figure 2.) The switch operates as follows. Incoming frames are sequentially written to the appropriate locations of the shared memory. The memory addresses for writing incoming frames and for reading stored frames are provided by a central control unit (not shown in the figure). There are two approaches in determining how the entire memory is shared among the output ports. The first approach is *complete partitioning* in which the entire memory is divided into N equal parts and each part is assigned to a particular output port. The second approach is *full sharing* in which the entire memory is shared by all output ports without any reservation. In this design, mechanisms such as an upper and lower bound on the memory space are needed to prevent monopolization of the memory by any output ports.

The main advantage of shared-memory switches over other switch designs is that a much smaller memory is enough to achieve the same blocking probability (Walrand and Varaiya 2000). Because its memory space is shared among its switch ports, a shared-memory switch achieves a high buffer utilization efficiency (Tatipamula and Khasnabish 1998). Another advantage is that more complex memory-sharing schemes can be readily implemented to provide different levels of service and thus guarantee

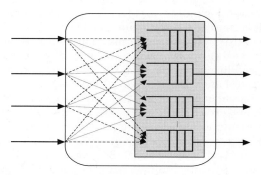

Figure 2: The architecture of a 4×4 shared-memory switch

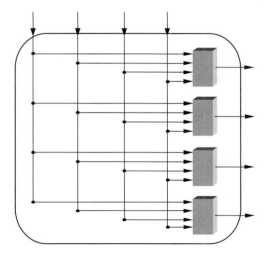

Figure 3: The architecture of a 4×4 crossbar switch

Crossbar Switches

In a crossbar switch, every input port has a connection to every output port. As shown in Figure 3, a crossbar switch consists of N^2 crosspoints. When appropriately configured, these crosspoints connect every input port to every output port, allowing N frames to be transmitted each cycle. To deal with the output contention that occurs when multiple frames are destined to the same output port, two approaches can be employed. In the first approach, a crossbar switch provides buffers on the output port cards. In the second approach, a high-performance central scheduler is used to configure the crosspoints (McKeown et al. 1997). Both approaches can greatly increase the aggregate bandwidth of the switch when implemented appropriately. Crossbar switches can be used as a basic switching element to construct a multistage switch such as a Benes switch (discussed later).

Crossbar switches hold the most promise because of their architectural simplicity, modularity, nonblocking structure, and good support of multicast traffic. However, the implementation complexity of crossbar switches increases as fast as N^2, making crossbar switches impractical for switches with a many ports.

frame delay and frame loss ratio. In addition, shared-memory switches intrinsically provide good support for multicast traffic (Francini and Chiussi 2002). When a multicast frame arrives, only a single copy is stored in the shared buffer. The frame will then be read multiple times to different output ports (Saito et al. 1994).

The main limitation of the shared-memory switch is that the memory and the central control unit must run at least N times faster than the link speed. As the link speed and size increase, the shared memory and central control unit may become the performance bottleneck and limit the switching capability. A more promising design is to provide multiple paths between the input ports and the output ports. These paths operate concurrently so that multiple frames can be transmitted across the switch simultaneously. The total capacity of the switch is thus the product of the bandwidth of each path and the number of paths that can transmit frames concurrently. Switches based on this design, such as crossbar switches, are called *space-division switches*.

Knockout Switches

Knockout switches are one type of switch that has been designed to reduce the complexity of crossbar switches (Yeh, Hluchyj, and Acampora 1987). The complete connectivity between the input ports and output ports is accomplished by N separate broadcast buses as shown in Figure 4. The address filters identify the frames that have the right output port numbers. Given that the likelihood that all input ports send frames to the same output port is small, the concentrator at each output port fairly chooses l out of N frames destined for the same output port in a single cycle.

The fairness in choosing l out of N frames is achieved by having all of the frames against each other in a form of knockout tournament to select l winners from N contestants. It works as follows. The tournament has l sections,

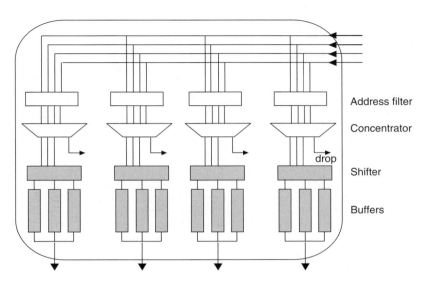

Figure 4: The architecture of a 4 × 4 knockout switch

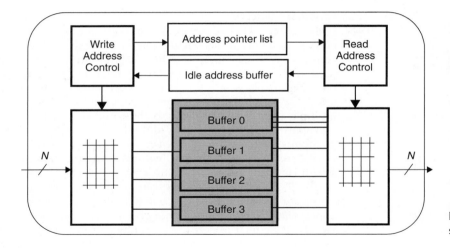

Figure 5: The architecture of a space-time, space-division switch

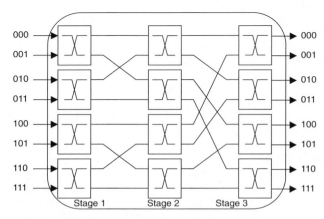

Figure 6: The architecture of an 8×8 Banyan network

each of which determines a winner. In the first section, a winner is randomly chosen. All the losers then go to compete in the second section. A winner is randomly chosen again. All of the losers then go to compete in the third section, and so on. Because only one winner is selected in each section, l frames are selected and all of the rest are dropped. The selected l frames go into the shifter, which distributes the frames uniformly over the multiple output buffers. Although knockout switches reduce the complexity of crossbar switches, they do increase the possibility of frames being dropped. In Figure 4, for example, if more than three frames are destined to the same output port in a cycle, then one of them will be dropped.

Another technique to reduce the complexity of crossbar switches is to combine the space-division and time-division techniques (Tatipamula and Khasnabish 1998). As shown in Figure 5, switches using this technique have a crossbar switch at both input and output ports. The two crossbars are connected by the shared memory. The *write address control* (WAC) extracts the header information from incoming frames and configures the input-side crossbar switch. The WAC also returns the frame location pointer to the *address pointer list* and receives the next available location from the *idle address buffer*. Similarly, the *read*

address control configures the output-side crossbar switch, returns the location pointers of transmitted frames to the *idle address buffer*, and receives the new memory location from the *address pointer list*. The memory operation speed is only required to be $k + 1$ faster than the link speed, where k is the speedup factor ($k = 3$ in Figure 5) of reading speed to writing speed in each cycle.

Self-Routing Switches

Self-routing switches use many small, interconnected switching elements (typically a 2×2 switch) in which frames find their own way through the switch fabric based on a sequence of local switching decisions made at each switching element (Peterson and Davie 2000). Figure 6 shows the architecture of an 8×8 Banyan network, where the port numbers are presented in binary format. The switch elements in stage 1 look at the most significant bit of the output port number and route the frame to the top output port if that bit is a 0 or to the bottom if it is a 1. Switch elements in stage 2 look at the second bit, and those in stage 3 look at the least significant bit. There will be no collision if the destinations of the frames are in an ascending order.

The main advantages for this type of switch are as follows:

- a linear complexity of $n\log_2 n$,
- a self-routing property (i.e., no control mechanism is needed for routing frames),
- a parallel structure (i.e., several frames can be processed simultaneously), and
- modular and recursive structures (i.e., large-scale switches can be built).

The main flaw of this type of switch is its internal blocking structure. This inevitably causes both internal and output contention and degrades the switch performance. Possible approaches to solve this problem are as follows.

- Allocate buffers within the switching elements to release contention. The buffer size could be just one.

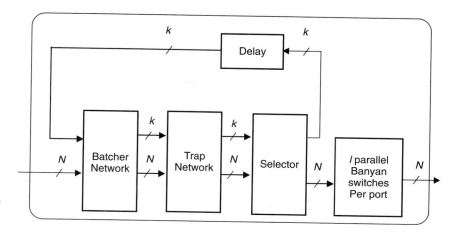

Figure 7: The architecture of the sunshine switch

- Add more stages to accommodate the output contention. Frames are examined at every augmented stage to determine whether they have arrived at their output ports. If so, they will be sent to the output link. Otherwise, they are routed to the next stage and will be examined again. This type of switch is called a *Benes switch*.
- Put a Batcher network in front of the Banyan network to permute frames into an ascending order. With a combination of Batcher and Banyan networks, the switch can deliver all frames to the destined output ports, as long as there are no frames heading to the same output port.

Sunshine Switch

To remove the restriction of no frames heading to the same output port required in Batcher-Banyan networks, the sunshine switch adds three components (Giacopelli et al. 1991) as shown in Figure 7.

The first component is a *trap network*. It identifies up to *l* frames that will be delivered to the same output port and marks up to *k* frames that need to be recirculated back to the Batcher network. The second is a *selector* that distributes those *l* frames to *l* parallel Banyan switches and sends back those *k* frames. The third component is a set of *delay* units that align the timing of the recirculated frames with the new frames. In addition, the sunshine switch uses *l* multiple parallel Banyan switches to allow up to *l* frames with the same output port destination at the same cycle. Using multiple, usually identical switching planes can significantly increase the switch throughput and reliability. This technique has been employed by several designs (Iyer and McKeown 2001 "Speedup"; Turner and Yamanaka 1998).

Performance Metrics

The switch performance can be measured by four metrics. The first is switch *throughput*, which reflects how many frames the switch can forward per second. It is usually measured in bits per second (bps). For comparison and theoretical analysis purposes, however, a normalized throughput is often used. In this case, a 100 percent throughput means that the switch has achieved the maximum switching capability. For a switch with N inputs (outputs) and a link speed of s, the maximum throughput is Ns. The achieving throughput, however, is typically less than Ns because of output contention. Many queuing schemes and scheduling algorithms are designed to alleviate the impact of contention.

The second matrix is *latency*, which reflects how long it takes on average to forward a frame from the input port to the output port. It is usually measured in milliseconds or microseconds depending on the bandwidth of the internal switch fabric and the external links. Several factors contribute to the overall latency, including processing delay, queuing delay, and forwarding delay. The third metric is *frame loss ratio*, which is measured as the percentage of the number of frames dropped to the total number of frames received. Buffer overflow is the primary reason for frame loss. The fourth metric is *complexity*, which may be quantified by the number of crosspoints, the buffer size, the speed of bit streams inside the switch, or the time running the scheduling algorithm. The main goal of a switch design is to achieve a high performance with desirable features such as good scalability (a function of N) and low cost.

LAN SWITCHES

LAN switches are the devices that connect multiple LAN segments. They improve the effective bandwidth by separating collision domains and selectively forwarding frames to the right segments. LAN switches offer plug-and-play operation and support dynamic switching. Most of them also have such network management capabilities as monitoring or remote monitoring. LAN switches are similar to bridges in that both operate in layer 2 of the OSI reference model. The primary differences between them are as follow.

- Switches provide much higher port density at a lower cost than do bridges (Kurose and Ross 2003). The higher port density results in several desirable features, such as a high aggregate forwarding rate, full duplex operation, and fewer users per segment. By operating in a full duplex mode, switches can send and receive frames at the same time over the same interface. By having fewer users per segment, each host receives a dedicated bandwidth and does not need to contend with other hosts.

- Switches can be configured to make more intelligent decisions with respect to forwarding frames. For instance, switches typically provide a better quality of service than bridges by employing advanced queuing schemes and intelligent dropping policies. Most commercial switches can be configured to only accept frames from specific MAC addresses on specific ports.

- Switches have two switching modes: *store-and-forward* switching and *cut-through* switching; bridges only perform store-and-forward switching. Usually, cut-through is implemented entirely in hardware, and store-and-forward is implemented in software.

LAN switches make the forwarding decision by looking up the forwarding table maintained on each input port card. When a LAN switch is first plugged in, the forwarding table is empty. When a frame arrives at input port *i*, the switch uses a technique called *flooding* to send the frame to all output ports except port *i*. Meanwhile, the switch inspects the MAC address of the frame and learns that port *i* can be used in the future to forward frames with that particular MAC address. This process is called *backward learning*. The forwarding table is fully completed when all of the devices connected to the switch have either sent or received frames. After that, the switch determines which port to forward an incoming frame to by looking up the forwarding table.

The forwarding table is dynamically updated through the backward learning process. Unfortunately, a simple denial-of-service attack can quickly fill the forwarding table by generating tens of thousands of MAC addresses. When the table is full, the switch cannot learn any additional addresses, so the frames from new addresses are flooded throughout the entire LAN. This results in poor network performance. To prevent this from happening, security policies need to be imposed during the learning process. One approach is to provide the specification of the number of MAC addresses that can be learned by a particular switch port (Dubrawsky 2002). If the limit is exceeded, the switch will disable the port to protect the network.

LAN switches employ two switching modes: *store-and-forward* switching and *cut-through* switching. In store-and-forward switching, the switch first stores the entire frame in the input buffer and then processes the frame by doing error checking and looking up the forwarding table. The frame is discarded if its contents are compromised. If the outbound link of the frame is free, the switch sends the frame to that particular link via the switch fabric; otherwise, the switch temporarily stores the frame in the input buffer. In cut-though switching, the entire frame need not be stored in the input buffer. As long as the header information (e.g., the destination MAC address) of the frame is available, the frame is immediately forwarded to the output buffer. If the output link is free, then the frame can be immediately transmitted. There is no error checking. Thus, cut-through switching usually causes less latency than store-and-forward switching but raises the risk of transmitting compromised frames.

The most widely employed LAN switches in today's networks are Ethernet switches and token ring switches. Based on the topology of switches, each can be further classified as follows (Puzmanova 2002):

- *backbone switches* that connect a LAN into high-speed protocols such as Gigabit Ethernet or ATM.
- *workgroup switches* that connect multiple segments that form a large LAN, and
- *desktop switches* that connect individual hosts for dedicated bandwidth.

Note that the difference between these three types of switches mainly lies in the interfaces. The interfaces in a backbone switch operate at especially high speeds, and the interfaces in a desktop switch operate at lower speeds. In fact, an advanced switch may have several different types of interfaces. This will become clear in the following discussion. A switch with different types of interfaces is called an *asymmetric switch* (Kane 2004).

Ethernet Switches

Ethernet switches are used to interconnect Ethernet LANs. Figure 8 illustrates the configuration of a switched Ethernet LAN with two Ethernet switches and seven hosts. The link speeds vary from, for example, 10 Megabits per second (Mbps) to 10 Gigabits per second.

The forwarding table in an Ethernet switch contains the following fields: MAC address, outgoing port number, and timer.

The MAC address refers to the destination address of the frame. The outgoing port number refers to which port should be used to transmit the frame to that particular MAC address. The timer indicates the age of the entry—that is, the association of the MAC address to the outgoing port number is only valid before the timer expires. The significance of the timer is used to accommodate the dynamic property of LANs in which links or hosts might go down or move. Thus, the association of a MAC address to a port number is valid only within a given period of time.

Token Ring Switches

Token ring switches are used to interconnect token ring LANs. Each port in a token ring switch supports either 4 Mbps or 16 Mbps ring speeds, which are configurable through the system software. Ports can be configured to one or multiple logical ring groups. Figure 9 illustrates the configuration of one token ring switch and one Ethernet switch connecting two LANs.

A token ring switch can perform switching in one of three modes. In the first mode, *transparent switching*, the switch uses the backward learning technique to learn which ring can be accessed through which port. This learned information is used to determine how to forward frames. If an arriving frame is destined for a MAC address that has not yet been learned by the switch, then the frame is flooded to all ports belonging to the same group on the switch, excluding the port that received the frame.

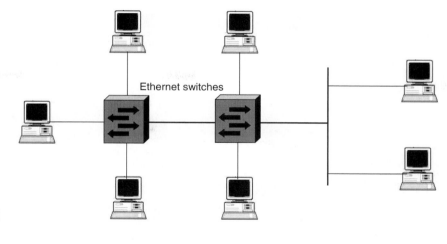

Figure 8: A switched Ethernet LAN

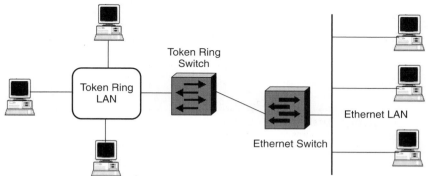

Figure 9: The configuration of a token ring switch and an Ethernet switch

The second mode is *source-route transparent switching*, which combines source-route bridging and transparent bridging. Under this mode, a switch makes forwarding decisions based on the data in the *routing information field* (RIF), if present. The RIF details each interface and path through which the traffic is flowing. If a frame does not contain a RIF, then the switch will perform transparent switching.

The third mode is source-route switching. Under this mode, the source host needs to determine the path to reach the destination host. The path is represented by route descriptors carried in frames. Intermediate switches forward the frames based on these descriptors. Source-route switching has become popular for switches that offer *microsegmentation*, a feature that allows multiple switch ports to be given the same logical ring number so that frames are switched either by destination MAC address on the logical ring segment or by the route descriptors carried in source-routed frames (Puzmanova 2002).

VLAN Switching Capability

A LAN built and designed only with traditional LAN switches, such as Ethernet switches and token ring switches, appears as a flat network topology consisting of a single broadcast domain. A *virtual LAN* (VLAN) is a logical grouping of hosts that appear to one another as if they are on the same physical LAN segment even though they spread across multiple LAN segments. Only the hosts that are in the same VLAN belong to the same broadcast domain. This allows a network administrator to logically segment a LAN into different broadcast domains. VLANs provide several advantages, including increasing the flexibility, reducing the network load, and ensuring security. Figure 10 shows two VLAN switches connecting seven hosts into three VLANs.

In Figure 10, the hosts that are equipped with VLAN-capable Ethernet interfaces can generate or receive 802.1Q frames directly to or from the switch. In case a host belongs to multiple VLANs, it creates virtual interfaces (cloned interfaces) for each VLAN to which the host belongs. The two LAN switches are configured to understand VLAN memberships and 802.1Q frames. The VLAN memberships specify which hosts belong to which VLAN. Therefore, a VLAN switch maintains two tables: a membership table and a forwarding table. The forwarding table can be built using the backward learning technique discussed earlier. The membership table must be configured by the system administrator. The following methods are used (Tanenbaum 2003):

- Every port is assigned a VLAN identifier.
- Every MAC address is assigned a VLAN identifier.
- Every layer 3 protocol or IP address is assigned a VLAN identifier.

Figure 11 shows the frame formats of 802.3 and 802.1Q. It can be seen that the only change in 802.1Q is the addition of a pair of two-byte fields. The first one is the VLAN protocol ID, which has the value of 0×8100. The second

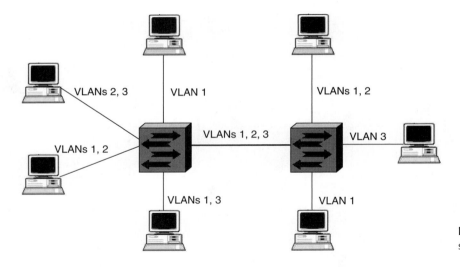

Figure 10: Two VLAN switches connect seven hosts into three VLANs

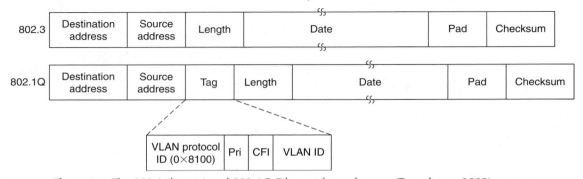

Figure 11: The 802.3 (legacy) and 802.1Q Ethernet frame formats (Tanenbaum 2003)

field contains three subfields: a twelve-bit VLAN identifier, a one-bit flag denoting whether MAC addresses in the frame are in canonical format, and a three-bit field indicating the priority of the frame. When a VLAN frame arrives at a VLAN-aware switch, the switch uses the VLAN identifier as an index in a forwarding table to find out which ports to send it on.

Spanning Tree Algorithm

To increase reliability, two or more switches are used in parallel between pairs of LANs. This deployment, however, also creates loops in the network topology. When loops occur, some switches see stations appear on both sides of the switch. This condition confuses the forwarding algorithm and allows duplicate frames to be forwarded. To provide both path redundancy and loop-free topology, the *spanning tree algorithm* (Perlman 1999) defines a tree in which some switches, ports on switches, or both are active and others are blocked. The blocked switches or ports constitute the disconnected portions of the original topology, thus creating the tree topology. Note that a blocked switch does not participate in frame forwarding, but it does listen to all transmissions, monitoring all activity and ensuring the health of other nonblocked switches. If one network segment becomes unreachable, the spanning

tree algorithm reconfigures the tree topology and reestablishes the link by activating the blocked path.

The basic idea behind the spanning tree algorithm is that switches transmit special messages called *bridge protocol data units* (BPDUs) to calculate a spanning tree. Each BPDU contains the following minimal information:

- the identifier of the current root switch,
- the cost of the path to the root from the transmitting port,
- the identifier of the switch that sends the BPDU, and
- the identifier of the transmitting port.

The switch's identifier, called the *switch ID*, is eight bytes long and contains a switch priority (two bytes) and the lowest MAC address (six bytes) among the switch's MAC addresses. Each port ID is sixteen bits long with two parts: a six-bit priority setting and a ten-bit port number. If all switches are enabled with default settings, then the switch with the lowest ID in the network is elected the root of the spanning tree and is henceforth referred to as the *root switch*. However, because of traffic patterns, the number of forwarding ports, or line types, this switch might not be the ideal root switch. The ideal switch can become the root switch by increasing its priority (lowering the numerical priority number).

The exchange of BPDUs results in the following:

- One switch is elected as the root switch.
- The minimum-cost path to the root switch is calculated for each switch.
- A designated switch for each LAN segment is selected. This is the switch closest to the root switch through which frames will be forwarded to the root switch.
- A root port for each switch is selected. This is the port that provides the best path from the switch to the root switch.
- Ports included in the spanning tree algorithm are selected.

To monitor the *health* of the spanning tree, the root switch periodically broadcasts a *hello BPDU* on its branches. The reception of this broadcast hello BPDU by switches at the next level on the tree in turn triggers a transmission of a HELLO BPDU along their branches. This continues down the tree until it reaches the leaf switch, which transmits a hello BPDU on its local LAN segments primarily for the benefit of any blocked switches that might be attached at that level to signal its continued health. If at any point a switch in the tree does not send a hello BPDU within a specified interval of time, the neighboring switches (including blocked ones) will sound the alarm by initiating a new round for creating a spanning tree. In the event that the root switch begins to fail or have network problems, the spanning tree algorithm allows the other switches to immediately reconfigure the network with another switch acting as the root switch.

WAN SWITCHES

WAN communications occur between geographically separated sites connected by one or more subnets. In most WANs, the subnet consists of two distinct components: WAN links and WAN switches. The *WAN links* are the transmission media to move packets between hosts. The *WAN switches* are the devices that connect WAN links. They are designed to efficiently share both public and private WAN facilities among multiple users. WAN switches differ in many aspects such as switching technology and switching capability. However, all of them offer two fundamental functionalities: packet queuing and packet switching. This chapter concentrates on packet queuing. Information about packet switching can be found in Chapter 68.

Packet queuing means that when multiple packets want to access the same resource, only one of them can get access. The others must be temporarily stored in the buffers that are most often organized in logical queues. According to the location of the buffers, there are five different queuing schemes: input queuing, output queuing, shared-memory queuing, virtual output queuing, and combined input-and-output queuing. In *input queuing* switches, packets are first stored in the buffers located on the input port before they are scheduled to access the switch fabric. If more than one packet is destined for the same output port, then only one packet is switched. Others are temporarily stored at the input buffer. An input queuing switch has the advantage that the operation speed of the switch fabric needs to be only slightly higher than the external link speed, which makes the implementation easier. However, the switch throughput is limited to 58.6 percent because of the well-known *head of line* (HOL) blocking phenomenon (Karol, Hluchyj, and Morgan 1987). Moreover, it is hard to provide delay guarantees in input queuing switches.

In *output queuing* switches, incoming packets are immediately switched from the input port to the output port and stored in the buffers located on the output port. Output queuing switches have the best possible performance for all traffic distributions, especially for those applications in which traffic behavior is difficult to predict. To implement the output queuing, however, the switch fabric needs to operate N times faster than the external links. This is because all N arriving packets may be destined for the same output port in the same cycle, so the fabric may become a bottleneck. The shared memory queuing technique has been illustrated in Figure 2. As we already learned, the main problem for this type of switch is that the memory and the central control unit must run at least N times faster than the link speed. This makes shared-memory queuing less attractive for large high-speed switches.

In *virtual output queuing* switches, buffers are allocated on the input port card. To completely overcome the HOL blocking, each input port organizes the buffer to N logical queues, each associated with an output port. A packet scheduler chooses up to N packets from the total N^2 logical queues to transmit to N output ports and thus achieves a 100 percent throughput. The nice feature of the virtual output queuing technique is that the operation speed of the switch fabric needs to be only slightly higher than the external link speed. To further improve the switching capability and accommodate diverse link speeds, buffers are also allocated at the output ports. This queuing technique, depicted in Figure 12, is called *combined input-and-output queuing* (McKeown, Prabhakar, and Zhu 1999).

Three primary WAN switches are widely used in today's networks: packet switches, ATM switches, and circuit switches. This chapter concentrates on the first two types. Next we introduce the specific designs and features of two types of WAN switches. For clarity, we will use the term *packet* to represent the protocol data unit when introducing packet switches and use the term *cell* when introducing ATM switches.

Packet Switches

Packet switches are one of the primary devices that form the backbone of the WAN. Unlike the traditional LAN switches that operate at layer 2, packet switches make switching decisions based on layer 3 information—that is, on IP addresses. Because of this, packet switches are similar to the well-known network layer device, the *router*. They both use IP addresses to make the forwarding decision and both offer layer 3 features such as security management, flow control, and IP fragmentation. The primary difference between them is that WAN switches do not perform the *routing process*, which is actually the

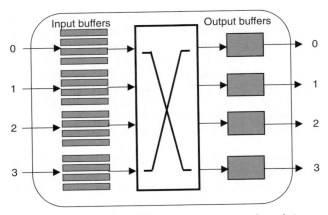

Figure 12: The architecture of a 4×4 combined input-and-output queuing switch

main task of routers. Figure 13 illustrates three packet switches within a packet-switched WAN.

Other important services and features supported by most packet switches are (Puzmanova, 2002):

- automatic line quality monitoring,
- end-to-end error control,
- network monitoring,
- restricted and multiple addressing options,
- hunt group facilities,
- priority and preemption facilities, and
- fast select to minimize call-processing overhead.

ATM Switches

ATM switches are the primary devices in ATM networks. They are frequently used to construct a high-speed backbone for WANs. The design of ATM switches is based on the *cell-switching* technique in which every packet is broken into equal-sized cells at the input port. More information about cell switching can be found in Chapter 72. Figure 14 illustrates ATM switches within a cell-switched WAN.

Most ATM switches support the following important services and special features:

- set up and maintain the end-to-end connections;
- perform the *virtual path identifier* (VPI) and *virtual circuit identifier* (VCI) table lookup to decide the outgoing cell's VPI and VCI;
- provide feedback information from the output port to the input port;
- resequence cells to the order in which they came into the input port in case cells are out of order;
- perform congestion control; and
- decide which cells should be discarded if needed (for bursty data connections, it is better to discard the entire frame rather than a few cells from each of many frames).

ATM switches can also be used to construct a LAN. In doing so, a LAN emulation technique is needed so that the traditional applications do not need to make any changes.

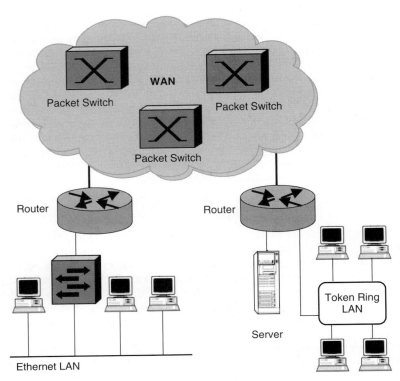

Figure 13: Packet switches within a packet-switched WAN

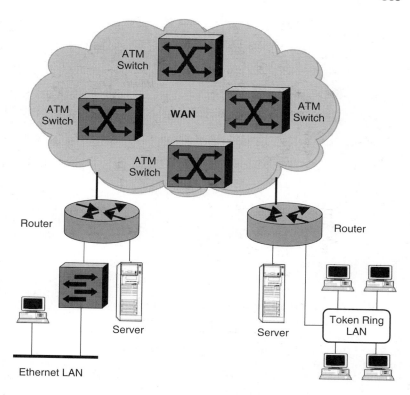

Figure 14: ATM switches with a cell-switched WAN

Multicast Switching Capability

Traditionally, the design of packet switches is optimized for supporting unicast traffic. As the fraction of multicast traffic on the Internet is continuously growing, the ability to efficiently support both unicast and multicast traffic becomes increasingly important. The design challenge of multicast switches stems from the nature of multicast packets—that is, a multicast packet has multiple destinations. The number of destinations for a multicast packet is termed *fanout*. In unicast switches, once a packet is transmitted to the destined output port, the packet can be removed from the buffer. However, in multicast switches, a packet can only be removed from the buffer if all of its destinations have received a copy of the packet. Simply considering multicast as a special case of unicast does not allow the architecture to be scalable. In this section, we introduce the architecture of multicast switches by addressing two specific issues: packet replication and multicast queuing.

Packet Replication

The *packet-replication* procedure in a multicast switch can be performed either with or without a copy network. With a dedicated copy network, multicast packets are first replicated in the copy network and then forwarded to distribution networks and routing networks (Chao et al. 1997). Without a dedicated copy network, the packet replication can be performed in three ways.

First, to perform the replication at the input side, a multicast packet with a fanout of f is copied to f queues based on its destinations. Then each copy is handled exactly the same as a unicast packet. This works only if the

multicast traffic is a small fraction of the total traffic and the switch fabric operates faster than the external links.

Second, to perform the replication inside the switch fabric, one approach is to take advantage of the nice feature of shared-memory switches—that is, good support of multicast traffic (Francini and Chiussi 2002). Another approach is to use parallel crossbar-based fabrics as shown in Figure 15 (Iyer and McKeown 2001 "Making").

Third, the packet-replication process can also be performed at the output side of the switch as shown in Figure 16 (Chao and Choe 1995).

Among these approaches, it appears that the parallel crossbar-based fabrics approach is the most attractive

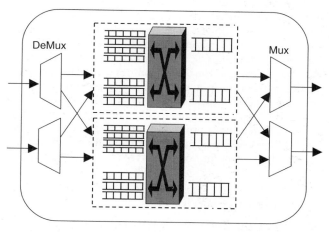

Figure 15: A 2 ×2 multicast switch based on parallel crossbar-based fabrics

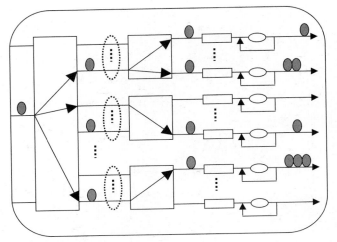

Figure 16: A switch performing multicasting at the output side

because of the following reasons. First, it is possible that multiple copies of the same multicast packet can be forwarded to different output ports during the same cycle. Provided that only one packet is transferred to each output at each cycle, the cost of transferring one multicast packet equals the cost of transferring one unicast packet. Second, multiple bus transactions can occur simultaneously, which means that the fabric will not be a potential bottleneck.

Multicast Queuing

Multicast queuing is entirely different from unicast queuing. For unicast, it is commonly believed that *virtual output queuing* (VOQ) is the best queuing scheme in terms of achieving a high switch throughput. To achieve the same performance for multicast switches, $2^N - 1$ queues are needed at each input port, which makes it impractical for large-scale switches. One simple multicast queuing scheme is to allocate a single *first-in, first-out queue* at each input port for multicast traffic (Hui and Renner 1994). Although this scheme can be easily implemented because of its simplicity, the HOL blocking significantly limits the switch throughput and the link utilization.

To overcome the HOL blocking, window-based queuing was introduced such that packets other than the HOL packet are allowed to be transmitted before the HOL packet during the current cycle (Chen et al. 2000). The increased scheduling space results in a better throughput. The price paid for this is that a reordering circuit is needed at each output port and the input queues must have the random access capability. Another design to alleviate the HOL blocking is to allocate multiple multicast queues at each input port (Bianco et al. 2003; Song et al. 2005). Because more queues provide more scheduling spaces, the throughput can be increased significantly.

NEW DEVELOPMENT
No Speedup Requirement Architectures

As we pointed out earlier, although output queuing switches have the best possible performance for all traffic

distributions, the switch fabric needs to operate N times faster than the external links. Thus, the switch fabric may become a bottleneck. The combined input-and-output queued switch architecture shown in Figure 12 can potentially achieve the performance comparable to that of an output-queued switch if the switch fabric operates two times faster than the external links (Krishna et al. 1998). However, the speedup requirement of switch fabric needs memories with shortened access time and requires a scheduler to make scheduling decisions within reduced time, which is quite difficult even for a speedup of two. Two new switch architectures that require no speedup have been recently proposed: *parallel switching architecture* (Iyer and McKeown 2001 "Making") and *multiple input/output-queued* (MIOQ) switch architecture (Lee and Seo 2006).

The parallel switching architecture is composed of input demultiplexers, output multiplexers, and parallel switches. An incoming stream of packets is spread packet by packet by a demultiplexer across the parallel switches and then recombined by a multiplexer at each output port. For an $N \times N$ MIOQ switch, the architecture is composed of N input buffers at each input port, M output buffers at each output port, k parallel crossbar switches, and a scheduler. As shown in Figure 17, each parallel switch is connected with each input via an ingress line and connected with each output via an egress line. Therefore, with k parallel crossbars, each input sends up to k packets to k ingress lines and each output receives up to k packets from k egress lines. However, because no speedup of any component is assumed, only one packet from each input buffer can be selected and transmitted via one k parallel switch.

Mixed Traffic Switching Capability

Traditionally, the design of packet switches is optimized for supporting unicast traffic. As the fraction of multicast traffic on the Internet continuously grows, the ability to efficiently support mixed unicast and multicast traffic becomes increasingly important. Two central challenges are how to avoid HOL blocking and how to buffer unicast and multicast packets. One design is to maintain N virtual output queues for unicast traffic and one multicast queue for multicast traffic (McKeown et al. 1997; Andrews, Khanna, and Kumaran 1999). Although this queuing policy can be easily implemented because of its simplicity, multicast HOL blocking significantly limits the switch throughput. Another design to alleviate multicast HOL blocking is to assign a multicast packet into one of the virtual output queues that correspond to one of the packet's destinations (Francini and Chiussi 2002; Minkenberg 2000). But because multicast traffic is mixed together with unicast traffic, the overall packet delay is compromised considerably. To efficiently support both unicast and multicast traffic, new switch architecture was recently proposed as shown in Figure 18 (Zhu and Song 2006).

In this architecture, each input port maintains N unicast queues based on virtual output queuing technique and M ($M < N$) multicast queues based on a load-balancing policy. Both theoretical analysis and simulation studies suggest that this architecture exhibits a promising

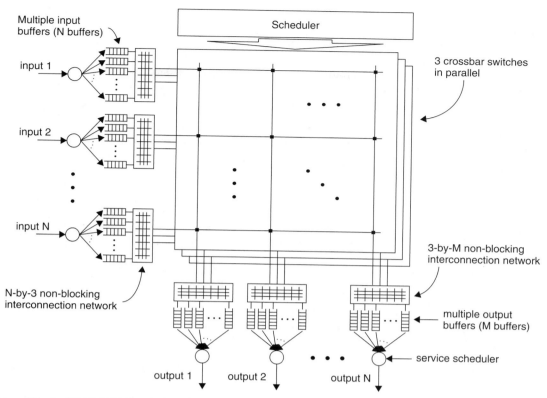

Figure 17: An $N \times N$ MIOQ switch architecture with three crossbar switches in parallel (Lee & Seo, 2006)

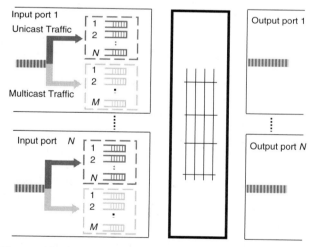

Figure 18: An $N \times N$ switch supporting both unicast and multicast traffic (Zhu & Song, 2006)

performance in terms of throughput, delay, and packet loss ratio.

CONCLUSION

We have introduced the architecture of LAN switches and WAN switches. For each type of switch, we presented the main hardware components and their functionalities, the switching modes, the main design issues, and the main services and features. For LAN switches, we have studied the VLAN switching capability and the spanning tree algorithm. For WAN switches, we have addressed the design challenges of multicast switches. Specifically, we presented the techniques of multicast packet replication and multicast queuing. New development in packet switches design was also discussed. We concluded that the fundamental functionalities of switches are interconnecting networking devices and forwarding frames. Four metrics have been defined to measure switch performance. Factors that affect switch performance and the technologies that improve switch performance were also discussed.

The architectures of contemporary switches are continuously evolving. We anticipate that future switches will provide better end-to-end quality of service guarantees for each application, ensure reliable and secure services, and continuously reduce design complexity and cost.

GLOSSARY

Asynchronous transfer mode (ATM): A high-speed multiplexing and switching method utilizing fixed-length cells of fifty-three octets to support multiple types of traffic.

Header error control (HEC): A field in a packet or cell header that contains information to detect and correct errors in the cell header.

Head of line (HOL) blocking: A phenomenon in which a blocked HOL packet prevents the packets behind it from receiving service. This happens because only the HOL packets can be transmitted.

Local area network (LAN): A data communications system that lies within a limited spatial area, has a specific user group, has a specific topology, and is not a public switched telecommunications network but may be connected to one.

Medium access control (MAC): A sublayer of the data-link layer that controls how the shared medium—for example, an Ethernet cable—is accessed by the machines attached to the medium.

Switch: A networking device that operates at data-link layer, forwards frames, and interconnects LANs.

Switching fabric (SF): Combination of hardware and software that moves data from input ports to output ports.

Virtual channel identifier (VCI): A sixteen-bit field in an ATM cell's header that identifies the cell's next destination as it travels through an ATM network.

Virtual LAN (VLAN): A network of computers that behaves as if the computers are connected to the same wire even though they may be physically located on different segments of a LAN.

Virtual output queuing (VOQ): A queuing mechanism in which each input port organizes the buffer to N logical queues, each associated with an output port.

Virtual path identifier (VPI): An eight-bit field in an ATM cell's header that identifies the virtual path (a bundle of virtual channels that have the same end point) to which the cell belongs as it travels through an ATM network.

Wide area network (WAN): A physical network that provides data communications to a larger number of independent users than are usually served by a LAN and is spread over a larger geographic area than that of a LAN.

CROSS REFERENCES

See *Bridges*; *Circuit Switching*; *Local Area Networks*; *Message Switching*; *Packet Switching*; *Routers*; *Terrestrial Wide Area Networks*.

REFERENCES

Andrews, M., S. Khanna, and K. Kumaran. 1999. Integrated scheduling of unicast and multicast traffic in an input-queued switch. *Proceedings of IEEE INFOCOM*, 3: 1144–51.

Bianco, A., P. Giaccone, E. Leonardi, F. Neri, and C. Piglione. 2003. On the number of input queues to efficiently support multicast traffic in input queued switches. *Proceedings of High-Performance Switching and Routing*, Torino, Italy, pp. 111–6.

Chao, H. J., and B. S. Choe. 1995. Design and analysis of a large-scale multicast output buffered ATM switch. *IEEE/ACM Transaction on Networking*, 3(2): 126–38.

Chao, H. J., B. S. Choe, J. S. Park, and N. Uzun. 1997. Design and implementation of abacus switch: A scalable

multicast ATM switch. *IEEE Journal on Selected Areas in Communications*, 15(5): 830–43.

Chen, W. T., C. F. Huang, Y. L. Chang, and W. Y. Hwang. 2000. An efficient packet-scheduling algorithm for multicast ATM switching systems. *IEEE/ACM Transactions on Networking*, 8(4): 517–25.

Day, J. D., and H. Zimmermann. 1983. The OSI reference model. *Proceedings of the IEEE*, 71(1): 1334–40.

Dubrawsky, I. 2002. *Safe layer 2 security in-depth* (retrieved from www.cisco.com/warp/public/cc/so/cuso/epso/sqfr/sfblu_wp.pdf).

Francini, A., and F. M. Chiussi. 2002. Providing QoS guarantees to unicast and multicast flows in multistage packet switches. *IEEE Journal on Selected Areas in Communication*, 20(8): 1589–1601.

Giacopelli, J., J. Hickey, W. Marcus, W. Sincoskie, and M. Littlewood. 1991. Sunshine: A high-performance self-routing broadband packet switch architecture. *IEEE Journal on Selected Areas in Communications*, 9(8): 1289–98.

Hui, J. Y., and T. Renner. 1994. Queuing analysis for multicast packet switching. IEEE Transactions on Communications, 42(2–4): 723–31.

Iyer, S., and N. McKeown. 2001. Making parallel packet switches practical. Proceedings of *IEEE INFOCOM*, 3: 1680–7.

———. 2001. On the speedup required for a multicast parallel packet switch. *IEEE Communication Letters*, 5(6): 269–71.

Kane, J., ed. 2004. *Internetworking technologies handbook*. 4th ed. Indianapolis: Cisco Systems.

Karol, M., M. Hluchyj, and S. Morgan. 1987. Input versus output queueing on a space division switch. *IEEE Transaction on Communication*, 35(12): 1347–56.

Krishna, P., N. S. Patel, A. Charny, and R. Simcoe. 1998. On the speedup required for work-conserving crossbar switches. *Proceedings of the Sixth International Workshop Quality of Service*, Napa, CA, pp. 225–34.

Kurose, J. F., and K. Ross. 2003. *Computer networking: A top-down approach featuring the Internet*. 2nd ed. Boston: Addison Wesley.

Lee, H.-I., and S.-W. Seo. 2006. Matching output queueing with a multiple input/output-queued switch. *IEEE/ACM Transactions on Networking*, 14(1): 121–32.

McKeown, N., M. Izzard, A. Mekkittikul, W. Ellersick, and M. Horowitz. 1997. Tiny Tera: A packet switch core. *IEEE Micro*, 17(1): 26–33.

McKeown, N., B. Prabhakar, and M. Zhu. 1999. Matching output queueing with combined input and output queuing. *IEEE Journal on Selected Areas in Communications*, 17(6): 1030–38.

Minkenberg, C. 2000. Integrating unicast and multicast traffic scheduling in a combined input- and output-queued packet-switching system. *Proceedings of International Conference on Computer Communications and Networks*, Las Vegas, NV, pp. 127–34.

Perlman, R. 1999. *Interconnections: Bridges, routers, switches, and internetworking protocols*. 2nd ed. Boston: Addison-Wesley.

Peterson, L. L., and B. S. Davie. 2000. *Computer networks: A systems approach*. 2nd ed. San Francisco: Morgan Kaufmann.

Puzmanova, R. 2002. *Routing and switching: Time of convergence?* Boston: Addison Wesley.

Saito, H., H. Yamanaka, H. Yamada, M. Tuzuki, H. Koudoh, Y. Matsuda, and K. Oshima. 1994. Multicasting function and its LSI implementation in a shared multibuffer ATM switch. *Proceedings of IEEE INFOCOM*, pp. 315–22.

Song, M., W. Zhu, A. Francini, and M. Alam. 2005. Performance analysis of large multicast switches with multicast virtual output queues. *Journal of Computer Communications*, 28(2): 189–98.

Tanenbaum, A. S. 2003. *Computer networks*. 4th ed. Upper Saddle River, NJ: Prentice Hall.

Tatipamula, M., and B. Khasnabish. 1998. *Multimedia communications networks: Technologies and services.* *Boston*: Artech House.

Turner, J., and N. Yamanaka. 1998. Architectural choices in large scale ATM switches. *IEICE Transactions on Communication*, E81-B(2): 120–37.

Walrand, J., and P. Varaiya. 2000. *High-performance communication networks*. 2nd ed. San Francisco: Morgan Kaufman Publishers.

Yeh, Y., M. Hluchyj, and A. Acampora. 1987. The knockout switch: A simple, modular architecture for high-performance packet switching. *IEEE Journal on Selected Areas in Communication*, SAC-5: 1274–83.

Zhu, W., and M. Song. 2006. Integration of unicast and multicast scheduling in input-queued packet switches. *Journal of Computer Networks*, 50(5–6): 667–87.

Bridges

Zartsh Afzal Uzmi and Tariq Mahmood Jadoon, *Lahore University of Management Sciences, Pakistan*

INTRODUCTION

A LAN segment is usually restricted to span a small geographical area and may only support a small number of hosts (Forouzan 2002). Adding more hosts can cause the performance of the LAN segment to degrade. Furthermore, if the geographical span of the LAN segment is increased, end stations may no longer be able to communicate. However, LAN segments can be joined together, without an appreciable performance degradation, by means of a bridge (Wikipedia 2007). Using many bridges, a conglomerate of LAN segments—an *extended LAN*—can be created that may cover a reasonably large geographical area, typically a campus, supporting a larger number of end stations. The term *LAN* is used in the literature to refer to either a LAN segment or an extended LAN.

The end stations (or *hosts*, as they are sometimes called) are connected to a *local area network* (LAN) using one of many LAN technologies, several of which have been standardized by the 802 committee of the Institute of Electrical and Electronic Engineers (IEEE). The most commonly used LAN technology is based on the *carrier sense multiple access with collision detection* (CSMA/CD) protocol and was standardized by the IEEE 802.3 subcommittee. Another LAN standard based on CSMA/CD is Ethernet (also referred to as Ethernet II or DIX Ethernet as standardized by Digital Equipment Corporation, Intel, and Xerox), and it is quite similar to the one standardized by the IEEE 802.3 subcommittee (Firewall 2007). In fact, the CSMA/CD-based LANs in use today are those that have been standardized by IEEE 802.3 and are backward-compatible with Ethernet; both are usually referred to as *Ethernet*. Therefore, we will also use the terms 802.3 LAN and Ethernet LAN interchangeably, unless we need to highlight the differences between the two. Because CSMA/CD-based LANs are the most prevalent these days (Tanenbaum 2002), these will be our primary focus in this chapter and any reference to a LAN will implicitly mean an 802.3 or an Ethernet LAN.

The Ethernet standardization included two layers of the networking stack: the physical layer and the data link layer. Because bridges are meant to connect various LAN segments, they also implement the physical and data link layers of the networking stack. The data link layer of the networking stack is subdivided into the *media access control* (MAC) sublayer, which depends on the actual physical technology (e.g., Ethernet or token ring); and the *logical link control* (LLC) sublayer, which is independent of the physical technology used to implement the LAN and allows sharing of the data link resources by providing a unified interface that supports a common set of services (Forouzan 2003). A brief description of tasks accomplished by some relevant subcommittees of the IEEE 802 committee is given in Table 1, and Figure 1 shows a picture of the networking stack standardized by this committee.

A LAN segment uses a physical medium that is shared by all of the end stations connected to that segment. In other words, the physical medium is of a broadcast type, and the end stations or hosts contend with one another to transmit a chunk of data, referred to as a *frame*, on the LAN segment. All such stations are said to be in the same collision domain. If two stations transmit at the same time, then a collision happens and a back-off mechanism is used by the hosts to retry the transmission of the frame (Keiser 2001).

Sometimes, either a hub or a repeater is used to connect many LAN segments together. Many such devices use store-and-forward technology; others may forward

Table 1: Tasks of Various IEEE 802 Subcommittees

Subcommittee	Assigned/Accomplished Tasks
802.1	Common issues
802.2	Logical link control (LLC)
802.3	CSMA/CD-based LANs
802.4	Token bus LAN
802.5	Token ring LAN

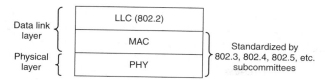

Figure 1: Networking stack showing the layers standardized by the IEEE 802 committee

the frame as it is being received. In the former case, each LAN segment has its own independent collision domain; whereas in the latter case, LAN segments connected through the device are part of the same collision domain. In either case, both LAN segments belong to the same broadcast domain; although the use of a hub or repeater has extended the range and increased the capacity, an *extended* LAN has not been formed. Unfortunately, distinguishing a hub from a repeater has become quite difficult these days with the proliferation of devices that enjoin LAN segments. We will not attempt to differentiate between these devices, especially because most devices available these days use store-and-forward technology. A bridge also enjoins LAN segments and uses store-and-forward technology and may well be confused with a hub or a repeater, but we will clearly differentiate a bridge from other LAN devices as a LAN device that can run the spanning tree algorithm. Most bridges also learn end station addresses and perform selective forwarding based on such learning.

The terms *MAC bridge, Ethernet bridge, LAN switch*, and *Ethernet switch* all refer to a bridge. Note, however, that a *switch* is a generic term and may sometimes refer to devices other than bridges (Perlman 2000). The term *LAN segment* may refer to a single LAN segment or different segments connected through a hub or repeater within the same collision or broadcast domain. An extended LAN is a topology of many LAN segments that are connected using one or more bridges.

Every broadcast medium must use a mechanism to identify the sender and the receiver. On CSMA/CD-based LANs, a *LAN address* (also known as *MAC address, Ethernet address, hardware address,* or *physical address*) is used to identify the sender and the intended receiver (Stallings 2006). Every Ethernet frame contains a source LAN address and a destination LAN address. IEEE has standardized 48-bit addresses for use with IEEE 802.3 LANs. LAN addresses are globally unique and are *burned* into a LAN card by the manufacturer. The first three octets of each 48-bit LAN address represent the *vendor code*, also referred to as the *organizationally unique identifier* (OUI), and indicate a block of 2^{24} LAN addresses. A vendor, who may purchase one or more blocks of LAN addresses, assigns the last three octets of a block to uniquely identify the complete 48-bit address. Note that a single vendor may buy address blocks, each of which has different OUIs. An example Ethernet address using a well-accepted representation is 00:0F:1F:B2:0E:CC, where 000F1F represents the manufacturer (Dell), and the remaining portion is selected by the manufacturer uniquely for each card.

The sending host includes the source and destination LAN addresses within each frame. The last bit of the first octet of the destination LAN address is the first bit

that is sent on the physical medium. A 0 value of this bit means that the desired destination is a single host, while a 1 in this bit position designates a multicast destination address, indicating that this frame is intended for multiple hosts. Because of the broadcast nature of the LAN, every connected station receives every frame transmitted in the same broadcast domain and immediately examines the destination address. If the destination address is a unicast LAN address different from the receiving station's address, then the frame is discarded (otherwise, it is processed further). Bridges, on the other hand, must process all of the frames received at all of their ports, a *port* being a physical point connecting a bridge to a LAN. We refer to this mode of listening, where a bridge listens to (and processes) every frame, as *promiscuous listening*. For efficiency reasons, end hosts do not usually listen promiscuously, but bridges must listen promiscuously because they are meant to forward frames from one segment to other segments.

TRANSPARENT BRIDGES

Bridges can be broadly classified as either *transparent* or *source-routing*. Bridges are transparent in the sense that two stations on two different segments of an extended LAN, formed by using transparent bridges, communicate as if they are on the same LAN segment. In other words, end stations and other bridges are unaware of the presence of a transparent bridge in the network. On the other hand, source-routing bridges explicitly forward frames to other source-routing bridges in the network by specifying a path included within the frames. In this chapter, we will only consider transparent bridges because those are the ones commonly used in practice. Figure 2 shows several end stations connected to a LAN segment, whereas Figure 3 indicates the same end stations divided onto two LAN segments connected through a bridge. If the bridge is transparent, the end stations will not notice any difference in topology in the two cases.

The two obvious benefits of bridges are an increased number of supported end stations and an extension in the geographical range over which a LAN can be used. A third, not so obvious, benefit is the potential for increased transmission rate per LAN segment. This benefit stems from

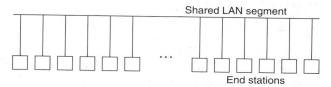

Figure 2: Stations connected to a LAN segment

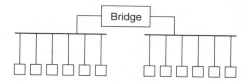

Figure 3: A bridge connecting two LAN segments

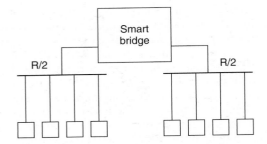

Figure 4: A transparent bridge with smart forwarding

the fact that bridges may forward frames *smartly* such that a frame is not blindly forwarded to every LAN segment as is done by other store-and-forward LAN devices (such as repeaters and hubs). Instead, a bridge forwards the traffic only to those LAN segments where necessary. This limits the traffic on a given LAN segment, resulting in the possibility of accommodating more traffic per segment. To illustrate this benefit, consider a LAN segment with an average traffic of R packets per second. If we divide the stations on this LAN segment into two groups, one on each LAN segment, on either side of a smart bridge as shown in Figure 4, then the average traffic on each segment will be $R/2$ packets per second. On average, half of the traffic generated on each segment is directed for the same segment while the other half is destined for the other segment. Thus, the average traffic on each segment is $3R/4$, and it must not exceed the throughput capacity, C, of the segment—that is, $3R/4 < C$, which means that the effective transmission rate may exceed C up to a value $4C/3$ and is in contrast with the case when a single segment was used and the effective transmission rate was limited to the value C.

The increase in effective transmission rate depends not only on the number of segments and bridges used to make an extended LAN topology but also on the configuration in which the segments and bridges are connected. Note that the increase in transmission rate is possible because we assume that the bridges do not unnecessarily forward frames to all segments; such is not the case with other LAN devices that do not perform any learning, whether or not they use a store-and-forward mechanism.

BRIDGE OPERATION

From earlier discussion, we learned that the end stations or hosts are connected to LAN segments, and LAN segments are connected to one another by means of bridges to form an extended LAN or simply a LAN. We may use a router to connect two LAN segments, but this results in the two segments belonging to two different broadcast domains. In such a case, end hosts on different segments will need to communicate using a different mechanism compared to what would be used if they were on the same segment (Matthews 2005; Olifer and Olifer 2006).

Transparent bridges listen to every frame promiscuously on each physical interface (port) and either filter (i.e., do not forward) or store and forward the frame to some of the other ports based on a local database called *filtering database* or *forwarding database* (FDB). The

entries in an FDB indicate the port (or ports) where a frame for a given destination should be forwarded. To populate the forwarding database, for every received frame, the source LAN address is stored together with the port on which the frame is received. This is indicative of the fact that the transmitting end station is approachable through that particular port. The forwarding database is created in a memory area called the *station cache*. Sometimes, the terms *forwarding database* and *station cache* are used interchangeably. It is likely that a station might move from one place to another, necessitating that the FDB entries be refreshed periodically.

For each received frame, the bridge examines the destination LAN address; if it is found to be a unicast address, then the forwarding database is searched for the destination LAN address in the frame. If the destination LAN address is not found in the FDB, then the frame is forwarded to all of the ports except for the one on which it is received. However, if an entry for the destination LAN address is found in the FDB, the frame is forwarded to the corresponding port in that FDB entry. The frame is not forwarded at all if the port number in the FDB is the same as the one on which the frame is received, a situation that arises when the source and destination stations reside on the same LAN segment.

Learning and Forwarding Operation

To illustrate the learning and forwarding mechanism, consider the topology shown in Figure 5, adapted from Perlman (2000).

Suppose that the first frame transmitted in this topology is directed from P to L. To begin with, we assume that the station cache is empty. The bridge forwards the frame to ports 2 and 3 and makes an entry in the FDB that station P is approachable through port 1. Next assume that M transmits a frame destined for P. Because the station cache now includes the station P, the frame is only forwarded to port 1. If the next frame is transmitted from station Q with P as the destination, the frame is not forwarded at all on any of the ports because the bridge determines that the source and the destination both reside on the same LAN segment. Note that the broadcast nature

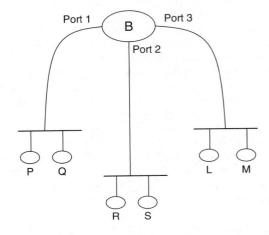

Figure 5: Learning and forwarding in a transparent bridge

of the LAN segment ensures that station P would have received this frame directly. Finally, if station R transmits a frame with S as the destination, the frame is forwarded to ports 1 and 3 because there is no entry for station S in the FDB at that time.

The same learning and forwarding mechanism as described above is independently used at each bridge in the extended LAN. In fact, just as the end stations do not notice the presence of transparent bridges in an extended LAN, other bridges also remain unaware of the presence of transparent bridges in an extended LAN topology. Each bridge builds its own FDB based on the frames received at each port (or through manual intervention by the network administrator) and forwards or filters frames according to the FDB entries, irrespective of the FDB entries of other bridges.

Loop-Free Operation

It is clear from the bridge operation described in the previous section that a bridge may make copies of a frame received at one of its ports for further transmission to some of its other ports. This means that an extended LAN topology with loops is prone to the proliferation of frames, and frames may run in loops forever. Furthermore, the presence of loops may also cause the learning process to become unstable. Thus, it appears that loops in extended LANs should be avoided at all cost. However, loops may provide path redundancy when a portion of the extended LAN fails and, therefore, enforcing a loop-free topology by careful deployment of network resources (bridges and LAN segments) is not necessarily desirable. Instead, bridges in the topology may be designed to run a distributed protocol that logically prunes part of the topology in order to avoid loops. This pruning is obtained by blocking some ports of bridges and is temporary in the sense that the blocked ports may be unblocked if some portion of the network fails.

In the normal operation of bridges, some ports remain part of the extended LAN such that data frames are received from and transmitted to these ports while some ports are blocked for data frames. Here we differentiate between *data frames*, which are generated by the end stations; and *control frames*, which are generated by bridges and communicated to other bridges to ensure proper working through a distributed protocol. This protocol reduces the original topology into a spanning tree which, by definition, connects all nodes (i.e., bridges) in a loop-free manner. Although data frames are not allowed across blocked ports, bridges may receive control frames on such ports.

The distributed protocol must use an algorithm to automatically reconfigure an arbitrary topology into a loop-free topology in a short bounded time without significant overhead (i.e., without transmitting too many control frames). The reduced topology is loop-free and is obtained by eliminating the blocked ports from the complete original topology. We call this reduced topology an *active topology*, which necessarily is a spanning tree. A popular algorithm for finding the active topology, originally designed by Radia Perlman, is called the *spanning tree algorithm* (STA), and it implicitly includes the protocol

for exchanging control frames between the bridges. Sometimes, the STA is also referred to as the *spanning tree protocol* (STP); we will use both STA and STP interchangeably. Newer versions of STA have also been proposed and are used in practice. The STA is the key ingredient of bridge operation and is given in detail in the following section. Subsequent sections will cover applications and variations of this algorithm.

SPANNING TREE ALGORITHM

In an extended LAN (also known as a *switched Ethernet*), each bridge (or Ethernet switch or layer 2 switch) runs a distributed protocol, the *spanning tree protocol* (STP) (which is sometimes referred to as the *spanning tree algorithm*, or STA) to facilitate the formation of a spanning tree of the extended LAN (IEEE Standards Committee 2004). The resulting spanning tree is used by the bridges to forward (or filter) the frames from one LAN segment to another.

The spanning tree is formed when bridges exchange control information among themselves. This step does not require that any end station be attached to any of the LAN segments; the (address) learning process, on the other hand, requires that end stations are attached to LAN segments. Furthermore, learning is solely based on the information originated by the end stations and is not dependent on the information originated by bridges.

Description

The terms *spanning tree algorithm* and *spanning tree protocol* are usually used interchangeably (and we will also use them as such here), but there is a clear difference between the two. An implementation of the STA runs on each bridge in the extended LAN, while the STP is used to exchange information among bridges to create a spanning tree in order to eliminate loops that may exist in the topology. Thus, STA and STP both support each other during the formation of a spanning tree. As already mentioned, a spanning tree is needed in a topology of LAN segments connected by bridges because loops in the network topology create instability in learning besides the endless circulation of multicast and broadcast traffic.

The spanning tree is created by an exchange of special messages between bridges called *configuration bridge protocol data units*, or *configuration BPDUs*. We will use the term *BPDU* to refer to *configuration BPDUs* throughout this chapter. In the spanning tree protocol, bridges exchange and process the BPDUs. Toward this end, one bridge is selected to be the root of the spanning tree. The spanning tree thus created consists of shortest paths from each bridge to the root.

To explain the spanning tree algorithm and protocol, we assume that the BPDU message has the following form:

<Root ID>.<Cost>.<Transmitting Bridge ID>.
<Transmitting Port ID>

Thus, a BPDU contains all of the information given in Table 2.

Table 2: Information Contained in BPDUs

Data	Explanation of Data
Root ID	ID of the bridge currently believed to be or known to be the root
Transmitting bridge ID	ID of the bridge transmitting this BPDU
Cost	Cost of the least cost path from the transmitting bridge to the currently known root
Transmitting port ID	ID of the port that transmits the BPDU

Protocol Operation

As described above, the protocol serves to build a tree in which one bridge is determined to be the root, while the other bridges make up a spanning tree. Bridges can only forward data frames toward or away from the root bridge.

Each bridge is assigned a unique bridge ID, typically by an administrator based on the Ethernet addresses of its ports, and the root bridge is determined to be the one with the lowest bridge ID (LinuxNet 2007). When a bridge first boots up, it has no information about other bridges on the LAN, so it believes that it is the root bridge itself. Therefore, it builds a BPDU of the form `<its bridge ID>.<0>.<its bridge ID>.<Port ID>` and transmits this BPDU on each of its ports. A BPDU transmitted by a bridge on a given port is multicast to all of the bridges on the LAN segment to which it is connected via that port. Likewise, a bridge receives BPDUs sent by all of the other bridges on that segment. The bridge must process the received information and reevaluate which bridge it now believes to be the root bridge and the distance to the new root bridge. Depending on the BPDUs received, the bridge may *block* some of its ports and *designate* others. Finally, the bridge sends out this newly determined information on all designated ports. The process of sending, receiving,

and processing BPDUs continues until a stable spanning tree is formed. After the algorithm converges, one bridge has been elected as the root bridge, while all other bridges have calculated their shortest path cost to the root bridge. An example of a spanning tree in a given topology is shown in Figure 6.

The bridge with bridge ID 20 (or simply bridge 20) is determined to be the root bridge because it has the lowest bridge ID. Thus, all of its ports are designated. Every other bridge has found its root port and either designated or blocked all other ports. A root port is the port that leads to the root bridge along the shortest path, and a designated port is an unblocked port connected to a segment. A blocked port is not part of the spanning tree, and no data traffic flows through it.

In Figure 6, bridge 50 has two ports that lead to the root with the same cost. In this case, the transmitting port ID of bridge 20 is used to determine that port 1 of bridge 50 should be the root port (details shortly).

There can only be one designated bridge per LAN segment, and it is the bridge with the lowest cost to the root. Thus, the root bridge is designated on all of the LAN segments to which it is connected, and all ports of the root bridge are designated. In case of a tie in determining the designated bridge for a LAN segment, the bridge with the lowest bridge ID is chosen. Thus, for segment 3, bridge 57 (rather than bridge 78) is chosen as the designated bridge.

Protocol Algorithm

The protocol algorithm is described below (Cisco 1997).

1. Initially, each bridge assumes itself to be the root bridge and transmits the following BPDU on each of its ports:

   <Transmitting Bridge ID>.<0>.<Transmitting Bridge ID>.<Transmitting Port ID>

2. During a period of time (called a *cycle*, which can be arbitrarily short), each bridge receives BPDUs on each of its ports. For each port, the bridge saves the "best" among all of the BPDUs received and determines the

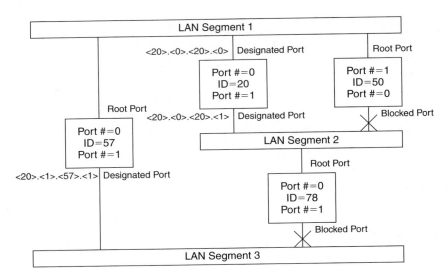

Figure 6: Spanning tree example

BPDU that it would transmit on that port. When comparing the BPDUs, we use the following rules:

- A BPDU with a lower root bridge ID is "better" than any other BPDU with a higher root bridge ID.
- If the above rule results in a tie (i.e., the root bridge ID is the same), then a BPDU with lower cost is "better" than any other BPDU with higher cost.
- If both the above rules result in a tie (i.e., the root bridge ID and cost are the same), then a BPDU with a (numerically) lower transmitting bridge ID is "better" than any other BPDU with a higher transmitting bridge ID.
- If all three rules above result in a tie (i.e., the root bridge ID, cost, and transmitting bridge ID are the same), then a BPDU with a lower transmitting port ID is "better" than any other BPDU with a higher transmitting port ID.

Examples:

<29>.<15>.<35>.<0>is better than
<31>.<12>.<32>.<1>

<35>.<15>.<80>.<2>is better than
<35>.<18>.<38>.<1>

<35>.<80>.<39>.<1>is better than
<35>.<80>.<40>.<0>

<35>.<15>.<80>.<0>is better than
<35>.<15>.<80>.<1>

3. If a bridge receives a BPDU on a port that is better than the one that it would have transmitted on that port, it no longer transmits BPDUs on that port (that port will be named as either root port or blocked port). Therefore, when the algorithm stabilizes, only one bridge on each segment (the designated bridge for that segment) transmits BPDUs on that segment.

Based on the received BPDUs from all interfaces, each bridge independently determines the identity of the root bridge (which will eventually converge to a single identity). After receiving BPDUs, the bridge ID of the "newly determined" root bridge is therefore the minimum of a bridge's own bridge ID and the root ID contained in all other received BPDUs. Each bridge is able to determine its lowest cost to the root, its root port, and its designated ports, if any.

As an example, assume that bridge B has a bridge ID of 18. Suppose that the "best" BPDU received by bridge B on each of its ports is as given in Table 3.

From the best BDPUs received by bridge B on its ports, it is clear that both port 1 and port 2 received BPDUs containing the lowest root ID. Bridge B has bridge ID 18, which is greater than 12. Therefore, bridge B is not the root bridge, and after B receives the BPDUs listed in Table 3, bridge B now believes that bridge 12 is the root bridge. Bridge B must also determine the cost to the root bridge; this cost is calculated by adding 1 to the lowest cost reported to bridge 12 by any of the best BPDUs given in Table 3. Likewise, bridge B must also select its root port—the port through which the root bridge can be

Table 3: Examples of the Best BPDUs Received on Each Port

Port Number	Best BPDU Received on the Port
Port 1	<12>.<85>.<51>.<0>
Port 2	<12>.<85>.<32>.<2>
Port 3	<81>.<0>.<81>.<1>
Port 4	<15>.<31>.<27>.<1>

reached via the smallest cost. Because the BPDUs received at ports 1 and 2 report the same cost to root (i.e., 85), the cost to root for bridge B is 1 + 85 = 86, and because the transmitting bridge ID is lower in the BPDU received at port 2, bridge B selects port 2 as its root port. Bridge B no longer transmits BPDUs on port 2.

Bridge B now constructs a BPDU <12>.<86>.<18>. <possible port number on bridge B>. This BPDU is better than the ones received at ports 3 and 4, so bridge B becomes a designated bridge for the two LAN segments, one connected to port 3 and the other to port 4. Ports 3 and 4 are the designated ports, and bridge B continues to transmit BPDUs on these ports.

Finally, the BPDU that bridge B would send out is not better than the BPDU received at port 1. Port 1 is, therefore, blocked; bridge B no longer transmits BPDUs out of this port.

Thus, bridge B has determined the following:

- the root bridge and bridge B's root port (bridge 12 and port 2),
- its own distance (cost) to the root (86),
- ports for which it is designated (3, 4), and
- blocked ports (1).

4. At each step, a bridge must decide which ports to include in the spanning tree and which ports to exclude. The root port and all designated ports are included, whereas all blocked ports are excluded. Thus, in the above example, ports 2, 3, and 4 are included in the spanning tree while port 1 is excluded.

Bridges place all ports included in the spanning tree in the "forwarding" state. A bridge receives and transmits frames on ports in the forwarding state. Bridges, however, neither accept nor transmit data on blocked ports (this does not apply to BPDUs).

By having all bridges run the same algorithm, a spanning tree will be formed that connects every LAN segment into a loop-free tree. Data frames can therefore be transported along the branches of the tree.

Address Learning and Frame Forwarding

When a data frame arrives at a port on a bridge, the bridge must determine on which outgoing port the frame should be transmitted. The decision is made using the aforementioned forwarding database, which is simply a table

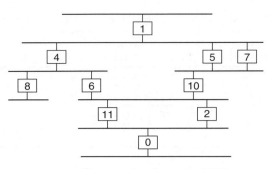

Figure 7: Application of STP

containing the destination MAC addresses and the appropriate output port that should be used to reach those destinations.

To maintain the FDB and forward frames correctly to the destinations, a bridge will use the following procedure.

1. When a bridge receives a frame, the bridge stores the frame's source address in the forwarding database along with the port on which the frame was received.
2. The bridge then looks up the frame's destination address in the forwarding database:
   - If the destination address is found, the bridge forwards the frame on the outgoing port specified in the forwarding database (except when the frame is received from the same port).
   - If the destination address is not found, the bridge forwards the frame on all of the outgoing ports except for the one on which the frame was received.

STP Example

We notice that the spanning tree algorithm is simply a distributed version of the shortest-path algorithm: Once a root bridge is determined, the shortest paths from every other bridge to the root bridge are included in the active topology. To illustrate the application of the STP, consider the topology shown in Figure 7.

For this topology, we demonstrate the step-by-step procedure used by the spanning tree protocol and algorithm in a sequence of diagrams. In each diagram, we show one full cycle of the exchange of BPDUs. Progressing through these cycles, the topology converges to a final loop-free topology (the last in the sequence of diagrams). In each cycle, we also indicate BPDUs exchanged between bridges (without being particular about the port numbers for selecting the best BPDU). The sequence is shown in Figures 8 and 9.

Reconfigurations and STP

One goal of the spanning tree protocol is to allow for the formation of a new spanning tree in case the extended LAN topology changes. Topology changes are part of regular LAN operation, with segments and bridges added, removed, or moved around in the topology. These changes may also result by upgrading a segment to run at a higher speed (e.g., from 100 Mb/s to

1 Gb/s). Sometimes, a topology change also occurs when a segment or a bridge (or another LAN device) malfunctions. The STP should deal with topology changes efficiently and quickly find a new spanning tree.

For spanning tree maintenance, the STP acts as a *soft state protocol*, which means that bridges must be periodically assured of the health of the LAN topology. For this purpose, in addition to the best configuration message received at each blocked or root port, bridges store an *age field*. The bridge continues to increment the age field until a configuration BPDU is received, at which time the age field is reset. Otherwise, the age field reaches the *MaxAge*, at which point the bridge assumes that the topology has changed and consequently runs the STA from the start.

Under normal operation, the root bridge generates and then transmits the configuration BPDUs at every *hello time* with the age field set to zero within the message. When any downstream bridge receives a message coming from the root (received at the root port), it transmits a BPDU on designated ports with the age field set to zero within the message. Thus, if the root bridge fails or the path to the root bridge becomes unavailable, a bridge stops receiving fresh messages and eventually times out (the age field becomes equal to MaxAge) at which point the root bridge, cost to the root bridge, and the root port are all calculated from scratch. Although timing out on root ports will always cause everything—root, cost to root, and root port—to be recalculated, timing out on a blocked port may or may not indicate a significant change in topology and thus may not warrant a fresh running of the spanning tree protocol.

Reconfigurations and Loops

When an extended LAN undergoes a topology change and reconfiguration, different ports of the bridges change their state. The blocked ports (across which data frames were not allowed in an active topology) may now be required to change their state to forwarding (by becoming root or designated ports). Similarly, ports that were previously in the forwarding state may now be required to move to a blocking state. Because the STP converges after some iterations, it is possible that temporary loops and temporary disconnections will appear, even though the new final topology is guaranteed to be loop-free. Even if they are temporary, loops cause frame proliferation, and therefore it is desirable to avoid temporary loops in a changing topology. The STP used in bridges ensures that loops are avoided by forcing ports in the blocking state to wait for some time before switching to the forwarding state. This wait period is set to be large enough to allow the topology change information to propagate through the network. Obviously, a port that needs to move to the blocking state in the new topology from the forwarding state in the old topology is allowed to switch state immediately. This may cause temporary disconnections, resulting in frame drops, which is an acceptable LAN behavior as reliable delivery of data is left to the higher layer protocols.

When a port is being moved from the blocking state to the forwarding state, the IEEE 802.1D standard defines two intermediate states during the wait period (see IEEE Standards Committee 2004). In the *listening*

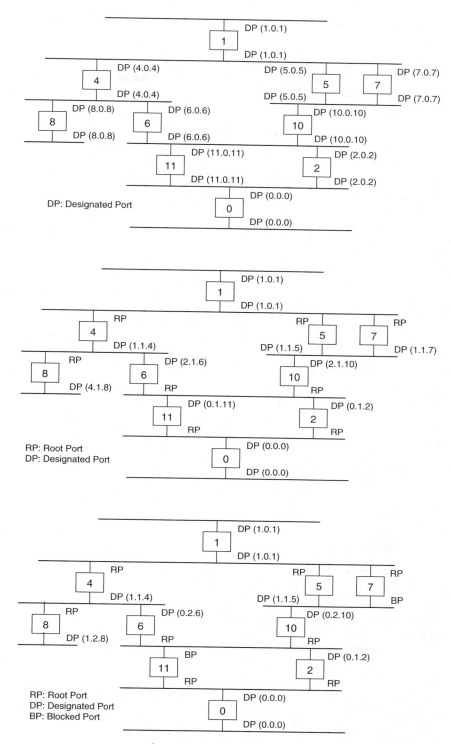

Figure 8: Applying STP, part 1

intermediate state, the bridge listens but does not learn station addresses through that particular port; in the *learning* intermediate state, address learning is enabled. In both intermediate states, bridges do not forward any data frames. A state diagram reproduced from the IEEE 802.1D standard depicting state transitions from blocking state to forwarding state is shown in Figure 10.

BPDU Format

The configuration BPDUs exchanged between bridges for the operation of the STP have a generic format as given in Figure 11. The TC flag in the bridge message format indicates a *topology change*. When a bridge notices that a port has moved into or out of the blocked state, it transmits

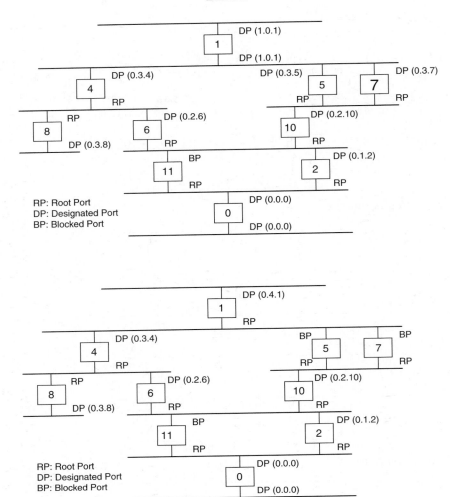

Figure 9: Applying STP, part 2

a topology change notification on the segment connected to its root port (by setting the TC flag). The bridge designated on that segment (which receives the topology change notification on the designated port) sets the *topology change acknowledgement* (TCA) flag in the next BPDU transmitted onto that segment; this is done to inform the bridge that has launched the topology change notification that action is being taken about the reported topology change. In addition to sending an acknowledgement (by means of TCA flag) to the bridge indicating the topology change, this bridge also relays the topology change notification on its own root port toward the root bridge. In this manner, the topology change notification reaches the root bridge, which sets the TC flag in its BPDUs for a time period equal to the sum of MaxAge and *forward delay*. The forward delay time is a network-wide parameter that indicates the longest distance between any two bridges in the extended LAN, and it may be set by the network manager to ensure that the topology change notification

is propagated to all of the bridges in the extended LAN before a port is actually moved from the blocking state to the forwarding state.

BRIDGES AND LAN MULTICAST

When a source intends to send a frame to multiple receivers, a naive solution is to broadcast the frame throughout the extended LAN so that it is transmitted on every segment and received by all of the hosts. Hosts that are interested in this frame pass it to their higher layers, while hosts that are uninterested in this frame drop it at the link layer. This solution has some inherent problems. First, broadcasting multicast traffic over slower links might cause those links to saturate. Second, transmitting a message to a large number of stations in an extended LAN when it is only intended for a few stations does not seem to be a reasonable option, even if all the links in the LAN have high capacity.

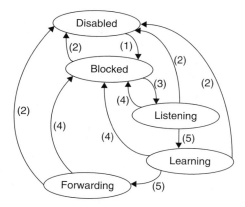

1) Port Enabled → Management
2) Port Disabled → Management
   or failure
3) Selected as RP or DP
4) Ceases to be RP or DP
5) One forward delay elapses

Figure 10: The transition from blocking to forwarding state

Number of octets

2	Protocol Identifier			
1	Version			
1	Message Type			
1	TCA	Reserved	TC	Flags
8	Root ID			
4	Cost of Path to Root			
8	Bridge ID			
2	Port ID			
2	Message Age			
2	Max Age			
2	Hello Time			
2	Forward Delay			

Figure 11: Format of message exchanged between bridges

A solution to disseminate multicast traffic only through those portions of the LAN where it is actually required is to allow the end stations or hosts to explicitly indicate their interest in receiving traffic on given multicast addresses. Entries for multicast addresses are entered into the same filtering database that is used to forward or filter unicast addresses. Such multicast entries may either be added statically by a network manager or entered dynamically by using a protocol derived from *group attribute registration protocol* (GARP) (see the following section) called *GARP multicast registration protocol* (GMRP). If a bridge only allows static multicast entries (that may be manually entered), the bridge is said to be providing *basic filtering services*. In contrast, the provision of *extended filtering services* requires that the bridge also allows

that dynamic multicast forwarding entries be entered into the FDB. In either case, a bridge must allow static unicast entries (entered manually) as well as dynamic unicast entries (through the address learning process). A bridge conforming to the IEEE 802.1D standard must provide basic filtering services and may optionally provide extended filtering services.

As with unicast FDB entries, multicast forwarding entries in a bridge's FDB enlist the set of ports on which a frame should be forwarded, indicating the presence of at least one end station, approachable through a listed port, that is interested in receiving that particular multicast frame. Thus, each port of a bridge keeps track of the interest of end stations that may be accessible through that port. Note that if multiple end stations, accessible through a port of a bridge, are interested in receiving a multicast frame, it is only necessary for the bridge to transmit just one copy of the frame on that port.

End stations indicate their interest in receiving a frame destined for a specific multicast address using GMRP. Although the details encompassed by GMRP are too many to describe here (see the IEEE 802.1D standard in IEEE Standards Committee 2004)), GMRP includes mechanisms that allow end stations to register (i.e., indicate interest in a multicast group address) or deregister membership information with the bridges attached to the same LAN segment. GMRP also allows bridges to disseminate multicast group registration information throughout the extended LAN. For each bridge in the extended LAN, a port is marked to forward a multicast frame on a port if at least one member of that multicast group is accessible through that port. Similarly, forwarding of multicast traffic on a port is retracted when all members of the multicast group that are accessible through that port have deregistered.

As a result of GMRP operation, frames sent to a particular multicast group address can be received on all LAN segments to which at least one end station that is interested in receiving frames sent to that multicast group address is attached. A multicast frame is also transmitted on those LAN segments that are on the way (i.e., along the active topology) from the source of the multicast frame to any intended recipient of that frame. Note that the source of a multicast frame may reside anywhere in the topology and may not need to explicitly register for that multicast address unless it also wishes to receive frames sent to that multicast address. Thus, any station that wishes to send frames to a particular group can do so from any point of attachment in the extended LAN. This property is sometimes referred to as the *open host group concept*.

GENERIC ATTRIBUTE REGISTRATION PROTOCOL

As described in the preceding section, dissemination and distribution of interest in a particular multicast group is a function of GMRP for which it uses GARP. In fact, GARP may be used to register for and disseminate information about any generic attribute in a bridged LAN. A multicast group address is just one example of a generic attribute. Thus, GMRP may be considered as an application that uses GARP service. Another application that uses the services of GARP, in much the same way that GMRP does, is *GARP VLAN registration protocol* (GVRP). GVRP uses the services of GARP to disseminate information about *virtual LAN IDs* (VLAN IDs), which is another generic attribute. The attributes registered, deregistered, or propagated through GARP are opaque to GARP itself in the sense that it is up to the application (such as GMRP or GVRP) to interpret a generic attribute.

GARP Operation

The two principal control messages used in GARP to register (or deregister) an attribute are *join message* and *leave message*. Join message is initiated by an end station (and relayed by the bridges) to register an attribute. Leave message is initiated by an end station (and relayed by the bridges) to deregister an attribute.

There are other messages that are derived from these two principal messages, details of which can be found in the IEEE 802.1D standard. The join and leave messages are initiated by end stations to register or deregister for a particular attribute (a VLAN ID or a multicast group address).

As previously mentioned, if multiple end stations, all accessible through a port of a bridge, are interested in receiving a multicast frame, then it is only necessary for the bridge to transmit just one copy of the frame on that port. Thus, if there are multiple end stations on a single segment, all interested in a given attribute, only one of them needs to register for the said attribute. This indicates to the bridges connected to that segment that there is at least one end station on this segment that is interested in receiving frames corresponding to the given attribute, and thus the bridges will forward the frame on their ports attached to this segment. In contrast, a bridge will not forward a frame with given attributes on a given port if no one has indicated an interest in that attribute from that port, indicating that none of the interested recipients is accessible through this port.

For each bridge that implements an application that uses GARP, a GARP *participant* exists at each port for each application (such as GMRP or GVRP). Each GARP participant further consists of a GARP *application* component and a *GARP information declaration* (GID) component. Although the application component has more to do with the application (attribute type and values, how to send frames to the application, etc.), the GID component is more relevant with the actual declaration (register and deregister) and dissemination of an attribute. The GID component further consists of two state machines: (1) an *applicant* state machine that keeps track of the interest level of end stations in a given attribute and (2) a *registrar* state machine that allows the bridge to selectively forward (or filter) a frame for a given attribute. When someone registers for an attribute, the associated registrar at the port, after listening to the registration message, should be moved to a state (IN) for that attribute. While in the IN state for an attribute at a given port, the bridge should forward the frames on that port for that attribute. A leave message (or a time-out) for a given attribute on a given

port should cause the registrar move to a state labeled MT, indicating that there is no need for the bridge to forward a frame with that attribute on that port.

Virtual LANs and GVRP

An extended LAN may span a large campus covering a large subnetwork with many end stations. It is likely that people in one department are not interested in receiving frames that really belong to another department. This calls for the formation of *virtual LANs* (VLANs) on the active topology such that the unicast, multicast, or broadcast traffic remains limited to a portion of the active topology (the VLAN). Thus, a VLAN is a collection of LAN segments and end stations connected to them within an extended LAN that has exactly the same properties of an independent LAN (Seifert 2000). In an extended LAN comprising several VLANs, traffic belonging to a VLAN is restricted from reaching users in other VLANs.

End stations indicate their interest in one or more VLANs by sending register message for those VLANs on the segments to which they are attached. The register message includes the generic attribute, which, in this case, is the VLAN ID. Differentiation among traffic belonging to different VLANs is accomplished by the addition of VLAN tags (VLAN ID or VID) to frames; bridges use VIDs to appropriately filter the frames.

The VID is attached with a frame as an additional data called a *tag*. A tag consists of sixteen bits, twelve of which are used for the VID. It is expected that VLAN deployment in a bridged LAN is incremental so that some station will still be VLAN-unaware. Such legacy stations are not able to handle the VLAN tags. Thus, VLAN-aware bridges must ensure that tagged frames (frames that include VLAN tags) are untagged before they are forwarded to a legacy station. Thus, each bridge maintains a set of ports called *untagged set* that consists of ports through which frames that are transmitted shall be sent untagged. In other words, a bridge removes the tags (if already present) from the frames before forwarding them to any port that is included in the untagged set.

The actual realization of a VLAN is made possible by means of another set called the *member set*, which consists of those ports that are included in a given VLAN. Each bridge maintains a member set corresponding to each VLAN. Because a VLAN is a subset of the spanning tree, none of the blocked ports may be included in any member set of any bridge. In an extended LAN where all bridges are VLAN-aware, traffic belonging to a VLAN is restricted to that VLAN and is not allowed to leave the VLAN.

A VLAN is also represented by a tree (a VLAN is a subset of spanning tree, and different VLANs may overlap) that is confined to some (or all) of the nodes (bridges) in the extended LAN. Forwarding and filtering of frames on a VLAN is quite similar to how it is done if VLANs are not implemented. However, learning is done on each VLAN independently. In other words, for each VLAN, the port through which particular end stations can be reached is determined and entered into the FDB for that VLAN. Sometimes, shared learning on multiple VLANs is also desirable and can be configured using another parameter (FID) of bridges. Many commercial bridges available these days are VLAN-aware, and their VLAN capabilities are frequently used.

CONCLUSION

Bridges are an essential part of today's local area networks. They allow a LAN to scale from a small building to a large campus, as well as from a few stations to a large number of stations. Bridges perform learning to avoid unnecessarily forwarding data traffic onto LAN segments. This selective forwarding can also be used to register specific attributes with the bridges such that traffic corresponding to a multicast group or a virtual LAN is forwarded to the appropriate interfaces.

A *spanning tree protocol* (STP) is used by the bridges to determine the active topology over which data frames will flow in an extended LAN. Recent versions of STP include *rapid spanning tree protocol* (RSTP) (Cisco 2006), which results in faster convergence to a final spanning tree after a topology change. This is possible by allowing ports to move from blocked state to forwarding state a bit sooner. Another variation of STP is *multiple spanning tree protocol* (MSTP) (Cisco 2007), which uses overlapping multiple spanning trees, each with its own root bridge, to efficiently utilize the LAN segments in an extended LAN.

Traditionally, bridges are considered as the devices that just extend the scope of a local area network in a given campus, while different campuses are connected to each other using routers (Kurose and Ross 2004). However, advances and cost-effectiveness of Ethernet technology has led to the use of Ethernet standards over a larger metropolitan area (Metro Ethernet Forum 2007). In this case, subscribers or branch offices of a larger business may be connected using bridges, thus forming a LAN that covers an entire metropolitan area.

GLOSSARY

Active topology: A topology comprising portions of a bridged LAN over which transmission of data is allowed. Control traffic is usually used to obtain an active topology and may be transmitted over portions of the local area network that are not part of the active topology.

Bridge: A layer 2 packet switch that receives a frame from any of its interfaces and appropriately forwards that frame to some of its other interfaces.

Bridge protocol data unit (BPDU): A frame that is used to exchange control traffic between bridges that run the spanning tree protocol.

Broadcast domain: The extent of an extended LAN. All devices in the same broadcast domain can be reached by sending a frame to the data link layer broadcast address.

Carrier sense multiple access with collision detection (CSMA/CD): A multi-access protocol in which each transmitter senses the carrier before transmission and also uses a mechanism to detect a collision.

Collision domain: The extent of a physical medium in which two or more frames cannot coexist without interfering.

Designated bridge: The bridge responsible for relaying data frames on a given LAN segment. A given bridge may be designated for multiple LAN segments.

Extended LAN: A conglomerate of LAN segments joined by bridges.

Forwarding database (FDB): In a bridge, a table that lists the forwarding information and maps a destination MAC address to a set of outgoing ports.

Frame: A formatted block of data sent from one node to an adjacent node in a computer network. A frame is an entity that is dependent upon the link layer technology.

GARP multicast registration protocol (GMRP): Protocol used to register and deregister multicast group addresses in a bridged LAN for which an end station or a bridge is interested in receiving data traffic.

Generic attribute registration protocol (GARP): Protocol used to register and deregister attributes whose corresponding data traffic is of interest to a bridge or an end station.

GVRP GARP VLAN: Registration protocol used to register and deregister *virtual local area networks* (VLANs) in a bridged LAN.

Hub: A LAN device that connects two or more LAN segments, usually on separate collision domains. It does not run the spanning tree algorithm or perform any learning on these segments. A hub broadcasts a frame received on a port to all of the other ports.

Local area network (LAN): Used to signify either a LAN segment or an extended LAN.

Logical link control (LLC): The upper sublayer of the data link layer. It is independent of the underlying physical layer and acts as an interface between the MAC layer and the network layer.

Media access control (MAC): The layer in a layered network architecture that provides an addressing and channel access control mechanism to many nodes connected to the same physical media.

Packet: A formatted block of data carried by a computer network from one node to another.

Packet switch: A network device that receives packets from any of its incoming interfaces and appropriately forwards it to some of its outgoing interfaces based on the information contained in the packet header.

Repeater: A LAN device that connects two or more LAN segments, usually on the same collision domain. It does not run the spanning tree algorithm or perform any learning on these segments. A repeater broadcasts a frame received on a port to all of the other ports.

Root bridge: The bridge with the lowest identification number.

Router: A layer 3 packet switch that forwards layer 3 packets based on the information in the packet header.

Spanning tree: A loop-free active topology that traverses all the bridges in a bridged LAN comprising a set of LAN segments connected by the bridges. A spanning tree is obtained by using the spanning tree protocol.

Spanning tree algorithm (STA): The algorithm used by the spanning tree protocol to find a spanning tree that can be used as active topology in a bridge's local area network.

Spanning tree protocol (STP): The protocol used to find a spanning tree in a bridged local area network.

Transparent bridge: Bridges are transparent in the sense that two stations on two different segments of an extended LAN, formed by using transparent bridges, communicate as if they are on the same LAN segment.

Virtual local area network (VLAN): A subset of a bigger local area network. Data traffic in a VLAN is confined within the subset that represents the VLAN.

CROSS REFERENCES

See *Circuit Switching*; *Local Area Networks*; *Message Switching*; *Packet Switching*; *Routers*; *Switches*; *Terrestrial Wide Area Networks*.

REFERENCES

Cisco. 1997. Understanding spanning-tree protocol (retrieved from www.cisco.com/univercd/cc/td/doc/product/rtrmgmt/sw_ntman/cwsimain/cwsi2/cwsiug2/vlan2/stpapp.htm)

———. 2006. Understanding rapid spanning tree protocol (802.1w) (retrieved from www.cisco.com/warp/public/473/146.html).

———. 2007. Understanding multiple spanning tree protocol (802.1s) (retrieved from www.cisco.com/warp/public/473/147.html).

Firewall.cx. 2007. *The site for networking professionals* (retrieved from www.firewall.cx).

Forouzan, B. A. 2002. *Local area networks*. New York: McGraw-Hill.

———. 2003. *Data communications and networking*. 3rd ed. New York: McGraw-Hill.

IEEE Standards Committee. 2004. *802.1D-2004 (802.1D MAC Bridges)*.

Keiser, G. 2001. *Local area networks*. New York: McGraw-Hill.

Kurose, J. F., and K. W. Ross. 2004. *Computer networking: A top-down approach featuring the Internet*. 3rd ed. New York: Addison Wesley.

LinuxNet. 2007. Bridge (retrieved from http://linux-net.osdl.org/index.php/Bridge).

Matthews, J. 2005. *Computer networks: Internet protocols in action*. New York: John Wiley & Sons.

Metro Ethernet Forum. 2007. What is carrier Ethernet? (retrieved from www.metroethernetforum.org).

Olifer, N., and V. Olifer. 2006. *Computer networks: Principles, technologies and protocols for network design*. New York: John Wiley & Sons.

Perlman, R. 2000. *Interconnections: Bridges and routers*. Redwood City, CA: Addison Wesley.

Seifert, R. 2000. *The switch book: The complete guide to LAN switching technology*. New York: John Wiley & Sons.

Stallings, W. 2006. *Data and computer communications*. 8th ed. Upper Saddle River, NJ: Prentice Hall.

Tanenbaum, A. S. 2002. *Computer networks*. 4th ed. Upper Saddle River, NJ: Prentice Hall.

Wikipedia. 2007. Network bridge (retrieved from http://en.wikipedia.org/wiki/Networkbridge).

Pulse Amplitude Modulation

Muneo Fukaishi, *NEC Corporation, Japan*

INTRODUCTION

Increases in the performance of *large-scale integrated* (LSI) circuits have enabled the amount of data that can be input or output from an LSI chip to be dramatically increased. Concurrent with these technological innovations has been increasing demand for high-speed data link systems that use high-speed interface LSIs capable of speeds in the gigabit-per-second (Gbps) range. These improvements in interface performance lead to better system performance for computers and networks. Although LSI performance increases with device miniaturization, design innovations are also needed to get the most out of device performance. A multivalue transmission technique using *pulse amplitude modulation* (PAM) is one candidate for overcoming these limitations and increasing the effective data bandwidth.

This chapter reviews several approaches for improving communication performance. First, the building blocks of communication LSIs and the trends underlying the development of high-speed communication LSIs are shown. PAM is then introduced, and its advantages and disadvantages are discussed by comparing it with nonmodulated data transmission or normal binary *non-return to zero* (NRZ) signal transmission. Finally, the likely appreciations of data transmission using the multivalue transmission technique are presented.

COMPONENTS FOR HIGH-SPEED INTERFACE

Figure 1 shows the system components of a serial communication system: transmitter (TX), channel, and receiver (RX). The TX converts several bitwide digital information streams into a single bitwide signal, or *serial signal*, in the transmission medium or communication channel. For electrical communication, the most commonly used channels are a board trace, coaxial cable, and twisted-pair cable.

An optical fiber is used for optical communication. The RX at the other end of the channel receives the transmitted signal and restores the original digital information.

Examples of block diagrams of the TX and RX are shown in Figures 2 and 3, respectively. The TX is composed of a data-generation block (*encoder*), serializer (*multiplexer*, or MUX), and driver (*output buffer*). The encoder receives multi-bitwide data and regenerates encoded data to increase not only the transmission accuracy but also the operating margin of the receiver; for example, an 8B10B encoder is widely used in high-speed interface specifications because it guarantees DC balancing and a maximum run length of five for the serial data in the channel. The encoded data are then serialized into high-speed serial data by the MUX and output by the output buffer. A differential output buffer is often used for the output buffer because of its high tolerance to noise. A frequency synthesis *phase-locked loop* (PLL) generates a high-speed clock signal from a low-speed reference signal.

The RX is composed of a data receiver (*input buffer*), data recovery block (*clock and data recovery*, or CDR,

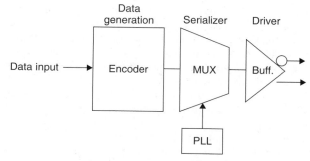

Figure 2: Transmitter block diagram

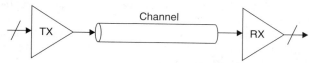

Figure 1: System components

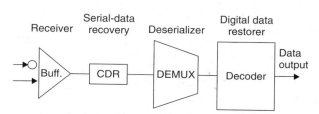

Figure 3: Receiver block diagram

circuit), deserializer (*demultiplexer*, or DEMUX), and digital data restorer (*decoder*). The input buffer converts the small swing signals on the channel to a full-swing signal to be handled in the RX circuit. The high-speed serial data must be sampled at the optimal phase clock signal, so the CDR adjusts the clock signal phase. The recovered data are then deserialized by the DEMUX and restored to the original digital data by the decoder; for example, the 10B8B decoder is used for the 8B10B encoder.

There are two important issues related to achieving high-speed data transmission: (1) high-speed signaling to transmit high-speed data and (2) high-speed chip operation, especially clock generation and timing recovery. The high-speed signaling is mentioned in detail in the following sections. The clock and timing issue, which is very important for accurate signal transmission and reception, is introduced next. Briefly here, the jitter of the clock generator in the TX, like that of the PLL, is directly transferred to the output signal, where it degrades the transmitted waveform. The timing recovery circuit (the CDR in Figure 3), which is often embedded in the RX, adjusts the phase of the clock in the RX to sample the transmitted signal at the optimal position.

REQUIREMENTS FOR WIRED COMMUNICATION

There are three approaches to address the demand for greater transmitted data volumes: (1) increase the number of channels, (2) increase the data-transmission speed, and (3) increase the transmission efficiency. Increasing the number of channels leads to the cost being multiplied by the number of channels. Therefore, it is more cost effective to increase the speed because this does not need an increase in the number of channels. The available increasing in data-transmission speed, however, is limited by the performance of devices and channel medium.

Although semiconductor device performance has increased with miniaturization, the circuit operating speed cannot be increased as the data rate is increased. To overcome this limitation, a parallel architecture has been proposed (Figure 4). Compared with the conventional single architecture (Figure 4a), which requires a clock signal of the same frequency as the transmitted data rate (e.g., a 10-GHz clock signal is necessary for 10-Gbs transmission), the parallel architecture shown in Figure 4b overcomes device limitations by using multiple clocks with different phases. In this parallel architecture, the clock frequency decreases as the number of different-phase clocks increases. As the number of multiphase clocks increases, the clock frequency can be decreased. This approach, however, requires highly precise clock-phase control because any distortion of the phase differences directly increases the jitter of the output data.

The trends underlying the development of high-speed serial data communication LSIs that incorporate *complementary metal oxide semiconductor* (CMOS) technology are shown in Figure 5. The transmission data rate has been increased in proportion to reductions in the gate length: operating speeds of 1 and 3 Gbps have been achieved with 0.8-μm to 0.5-μm and 0.15-μm CMOS devices by using

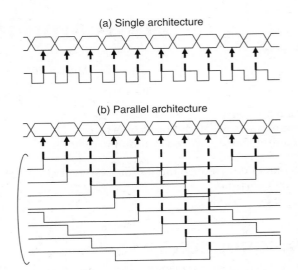

Figure 4: Serializer and deserializer architectures

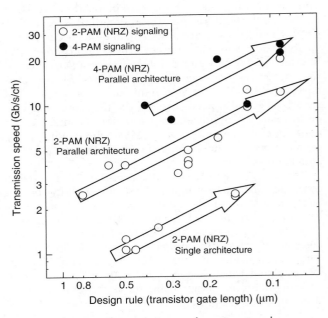

Figure 5: Transmission performance trends

the single architecture and normal *two-level pulse amplitude modulation* (2-PAM) or NRZ signaling. The maximum transmitted data rate is determined by the device performance and will be only about 4 to 5 Gbps for a 0.1-μm CMOS. In contrast, the parallel architecture overcomes device performance limitations by using multiple different-phase clocks. For example, a 4-Gbps data rate is achieved with a 0.25-μm CMOS, and a 6-Gbps data rate with a 0.18-μm CMOS. The maximum transmitted data rate reaches more than 10 Gbps with a 90-nm CMOS.

The channel performance limitation depends on the size and construction of the channel material such as the conductor and dielectric materials. For example, Figure 6 shows the transmission medium performance of a *printed circuit board* (PCB) with a 1-m long trace; it shows received data amplitude versus transmission

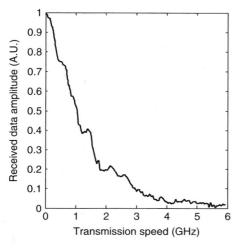

Figure 6: Transmission medium performance

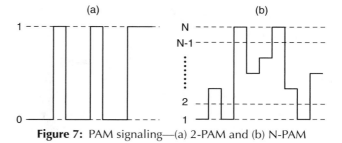

Figure 7: PAM signaling—(a) 2-PAM and (b) N-PAM

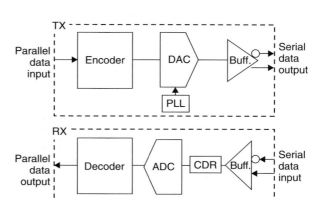

Figure 8: Block diagrams for PAM transmitter and receiver

speed. Signal attenuation increases with frequency. The attenuation derives from the medium's series resistance, which is caused mainly by the skin effect and dielectric loss. Figure 6 indicates that high-speed data are received as a small-amplitude signal. For example, when 10-Gbps NRZ data is transmitted with a 1-V swing at the transmitter, the received data amplitude is attenuated to less than 50-mV. The channel performance, moreover, depends on channel length. If we want to increase system performance while continuing to utilize existing system equipments, the transmission data speed will need to be increased while the same channel medium or channel performance and length is kept. However, the received data's amplitude decreases and they cannot be received at the RX because of channel performance degradation. This means that the improvements in data volume that can be achieved by increasing the data speed are limited.

Therefore, the third approach—increasing transmission efficiency—is expected to be effective at improving the transmitted data volume. As mentioned with Figure 5, a higher speed can be achieved by using four-level PAM (4-PAM) signaling, which is more efficient than 2-PAM (NRZ) signaling. A data rate of 10 Gbps has been achieved with 0.4-μm technology, and more than 20 Gbps has been reached with 90-nm technology. The figure indicates that the maximum data rate is dependent on the circuit design (e.g., a parallel architecture) and data signaling (e.g., PAM) rather than on the design rule or gate length. PAM, especially, has been found to be more effective at increasing the data rate in low-speed devices.

To summarize the requirements for high-speed serial data transmission, the transmitted data volume is limited by the transmission medium performance more than by device performance. This means that improving transmission efficiency, or decreasing the effective data speed on the transmission medium, is important for increasing the data volume or improving system performance.

DATA SIGNALING

This section introduces data signaling to decrease the effective data speed on the transmission medium.

Transmitting multiple bits in each transmit time decreases the required data rate for the channel. The simplest multilevel transmission scheme is pulse amplitude modulation. The waveform of the N-level pulse amplitude modulation (N-PAM) is compared with 2-PAM or NRZ signaling in Figure 7. In N-PAM, each symbol time comprises $\log(N)/\log(2)$ bits of information. This means that the same datarate can be achieved with a low effective transmission speed on the channel or a higher data rate can be achieved with the same effective speed. For example, the data rate per channel reaches 10 Gbps with 4-PAM when 0.4-μm CMOS is used, although it is approximately 4 Gbps with an eight-phase parallel architecture using the same technology. And it reaches more than 20 Gbps with 90-nm technology. As the amplitude modulation level is increased, the total volume of the transmitted information can be increased.

The PAM scheme requires a *digital-to-analog converter* (DAC) for the TX and an *analog-to-digital converter* (ADC) for the RX, as shown in Figure 8. The serializer in the serial interface TX is replaced with a modulator, or DAC. In the RX, the deserializer is replaced with a demodulator, or ADC. Any effort to increase the volume of the transmitted information confronts with two challenges: increase the transmission data rate and increase the amplitude modulation level. Increasing the amplitude modulation level requires a high *signal-to-noise ratio* (SNR) for the DAC and ADC. On the other hand, if we increase the data rate, then high-speed operation is mandatory for the DAC and ADC because they are located in the last stage of the TX and the first stage of the RX, respectively, and both operate at the highest speeds in the system. Moreover, both the DAC and ADC have a trade-off between higher data

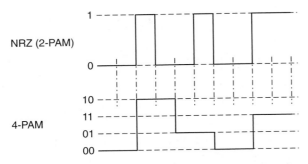

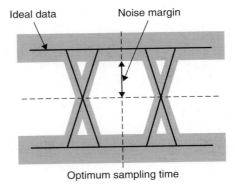

Figure 9: Comparison between NRZ and 4-PAM signaling

Figure 11: Generalized NRZ eye pattern

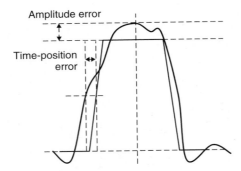

Figure 10: Waveform with noise

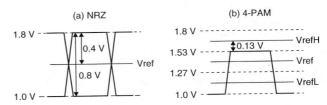

Figure 12: Transmitted voltage levels and reference voltage (Vref) levels—(a) binary modulation and (b) 4-PAM

throughput and higher SNR. Taking this trade-off into account, 4- to 5-PAM transmission is reasonable at the Gigahertz bandwidth.

The logic level of a 4-PAM transmitted waveform is compared with NRZ in Figure 9. In 4-PAM, each symbol time comprises two bits of information. Therefore 4-PAM reduces the data rate to half that of an NRZ transmission; in other words, twice the data rate can be achieved with the same bandwidth. The voltage swing of 4-PAM is one-third that of an NRZ transmission.

We now consider the problem of a signal contaminated by additive noise, as represented by the receiver diagrammed in Figure 10. To receive transmitted data, we should sample it at a position close to the center timing of the transmitted data. The signal amplitude is variable because of noise: The difference between ideal data and actual data that contain noise represents the amplitude error. The signal transit timing is also variable because of noise: The difference between ideal data and noised data at the center of the signal amplitude is the time-position error. Figure 11 shows a generalized NRZ signaling eye pattern with noise. Here, only *additive white Gaussian noise* (AWGN) is considered; another large noise source, *intersymbol interference* (ISI), is discussed later. The optimum sampling time corresponds to the maximum eye opening. Noise partially closes the eye and thereby reduces the noise margin. When synchronization between the received data and the sampling timing is derived from the zero crossings of the received data, zero-crossing distortion because of noise produces jitter in the receiver clock, which determines the sampling timing, and results in nonoptimum sampling times. The slope of the eye pattern in the vicinity of the zero crossings indicates the sensitivity to timing error.

When the amplitude error for an ideal data pattern is assumed to be almost the same independent of signaling, such as NRZ or multilevel PAM, the large received data amplitude leads to the large noise margin. The received data amplitude is considered here. Examples of signal voltage levels obtained for NRZ and 4-PAM transmissions are shown in Figure 12. The reference voltages (Vref, VrefH, and VrefL) are necessary to determine the correct data for 4-PAM transmission, while NRZ transmission does not always need the reference voltage because the difference in signals can be used to determine data. The voltage difference input to the voltage detector is equal to the full voltage swing under ideal conditions in NRZ transmission. The difference in 4-PAM transmission is equal to the difference between the input and reference voltages: it is one-sixth that of NRZ transmission when the reference voltages are set at the midpoint of the PAM levels. The voltage margin of PAM transmission is therefore less than one-sixth that of NRZ transmission. When a differential input buffer is used to receive 4-PAM, the voltage margin of PAM is one-third that of NRZ.

Figure 13 shows an eye diagram for data received through a channel with loss where ISI is not considered. The transmission data rate is the same for NRZ and 4-PAM signaling in this comparison. Therefore, the attenuation was set at –20 dB for NRZ signaling and –10 dB for 4-PAM signaling because channel loss is usually proportional to the transmission speed. In this case, the received eye diagram was reduced to 80 mV for NRZ signaling with 0.8 V transmitted at the transmitter and to 80 mV for 4-PAM as well. However, considering the reference voltage to determine correct data at the receiver, the difference between the reference voltage and the received data voltage level was 40 mV for 4-PAM. Therefore, the voltage margin for

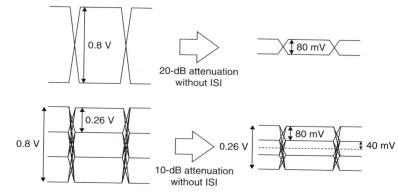

Figure 13: Signal for NRZ and 4-PAM received through channel with attenuation

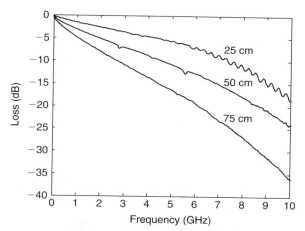

Figure 14: Transmission medium performances

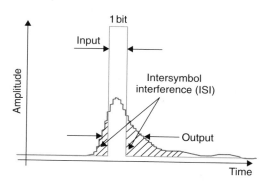

Figure 15: Intersymbol interference (ISI)

4-PAM was approximately one-half that for NRZ. This comparison indicates that a higher SNR is required for a 4-PAM receiver than for an NRZ receiver.

CHANNEL PERFORMANCE LIMITATIONS AND SIGNALING COMPARISONS

Examples of channel characteristics of a PCB using a material with a low dielectric constant (low k) are shown in Figure 14. Signal attenuation increases with medium length and frequency. In general, signal attenuation is proportional to medium length and data speed. For example, at a frequency of 5 GHz and for a channel length of 25 cm, the channel loss is approximately −6 dB. It increases to −12 dB for a channel length of 50 cm and to −18 dB for one of 75 cm. The channel loss reaches −18 dB at 10 GHz for a channel length of 25 cm and exceeds −35 dB for one of 75 cm. When the transmission channel has loss, the transmitted data swing either decreases or is attenuated, and the voltage margin required to detect correct data at the receiver is reduced. When the loss becomes larger, the output no longer swings fully. The time-domain effect of the frequency-dependent attenuation is shown in Figure 15. A single square pulse is fed into the 25-cm PCB. The attenuation of the input pulse reduces the signal amplitude

by more than 50 percent. The lower frequency attenuation produces the signal's long settling tail. As a result, the values of the previously transmitted bits affect the current bit's waveform. This interference, called *intersymbol interference* (ISI), reduces the transmitted signal's timing and voltage margins. The total effect on transmitted random data is a significant closure of the resulting data eye. The effect of ISI is greater for high-speed and long-distance transmission. Therefore, this ISI hinders efforts to improve the data speed and transmission length.

The way to achieve higher data speed, even with a large loss channel, is to compensate for the frequency dependence of the channel transfer function. An equalizer is widely used to do this. The pre-emphasis technique as one type of equalizer as shown in Figure 16. The pre-emphasis

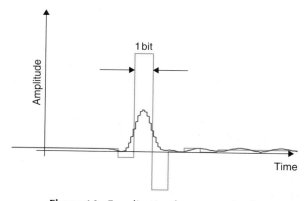

Figure 16: Equalization by pre-emphasis

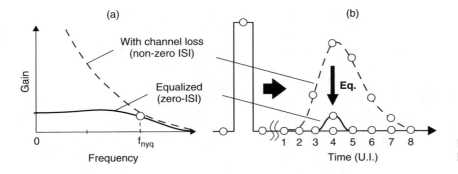

Figure 17: (a) Transfer function and (b) single-bit response for 2-PAM (NRZ) signaling

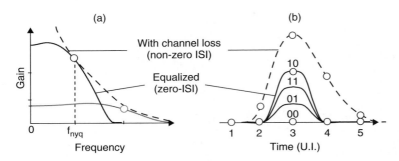

Figure 18: Transfer function (a) and single bit response (b) for 4-PAM signaling

transfer function is set to the inverse of the channel transfer function. As a result, the total transfer function with the channel and the pre-emphasis becomes flat up to the transmitted data frequency, and ISI is compensated.

Figure 17a shows an example of a transfer function, and Figure 17b shows the single bit response for 2-PAM (NRZ) signaling. Without channel equalization, frequency-dependent channel loss causes ISI, which results in the data received at each sampling timing having not only values of 0 or 1 but also intermediate values (nonzero ISI). As a result, binary input data cannot be successfully restored. Channel equalization assures Nyquist-rate bandwidth in the frequency domain—that is, zero ISI in the time domain. This zero ISI means that binary input data can be successfully obtained as binary output data.

Figure 18a shows the transfer function and Figure 18b the single-bit response for 4-PAM signaling. The 4-PAM coding makes it is possible to halve the symbol rate. Therefore, channel equalization only has to ensure one-half the Nyquist-frequency bandwidth of 2-PAM to achieve zero ISI. Moreover, the signal amplitude is still kept larger than that of 2-PAM because the effect of channel loss is smaller than in 2-PAM.

However, 4-PAM results in increased sensitivity to cross talk and reflection because the 4-PAM signal includes a maximum transition, which causes proportional cross-talk, whereas the data eye amplitude is one-third of the maximum transition.

In response to this situation, *duobinary signaling* has been developed. This type of partial response signaling can be helpful in reducing the required maximum frequency on the channel because it allows for a controlled amount of ISI to be removed afterward. In duobinary signaling, channel loss and equalization combine to produce ISI. An eye diagram of duobinary signaling is shown in Figure 19.

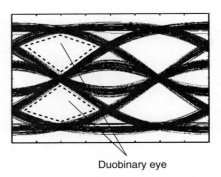

Duobinary eye

Figure 19: Eye diagram for duobinary signaling

The transfer function and single bit response for duobinary signaling are shown in Figure 20. The transfer function of duobinary is expressed as the z-function $1+z^{-1}$. Received data are produced by adding current input data and previous input data. Therefore, the transfer function results in binary input data being output as a duobinary three-level signal: $1 + (1) = 2, 1 + (0)/0 + (1) = 1, 0 + (0) = 0$, where the value inside each set of parentheses denotes a preceding data bit. Because transmitted data are binary, the data output at the transmitter has to operate at the same speed as that of 2-PAM, and the data received timing is also the same as 2-PAM. However, the Nyquist frequency of duobinary signaling through the channel is smaller than that of 2-PAM. Therefore, the data speed on the transmission channel is eased. Recent LSIs can operate at high speed because of improvements in device performance. However, the transmission channel performance cannot be improved in a similar manner to the device performance improvements. Therefore, reducing the Nyquist frequency

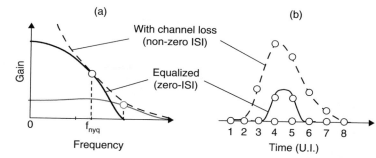

Figure 20: (a) Transfer function and (b) single-bit response for duobinary signaling

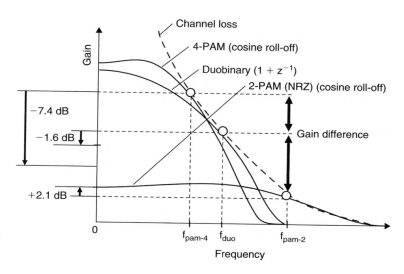

Figure 21: Comparison of transfer functions for 2-PAM, 4-PAM, and duobinary signaling schemes

of data through the channel is an effective way to achieve high-speed data transmission.

The data eye amplitudes of 2-PAM, 4-PAM, and duobinary signals can be compared by using the channel loss value at a corresponding Nyquist frequency: f_{nyq} (2-PAM), $f_{nyq}/2$ (4-PAM), and $2f_{nyq}/3$ (duobinary), where f_{nyq} is one-half the symbol rate of 2-PAM. Although duobinary is not a type of Nyquist signaling but a partial response signaling, here the Nyquist frequency of duobinary signaling is defined to compare its characteristics with those of the other signaling types. The Nyquist frequency value was determined from the sampling frequency at which the original waveform can be recovered by the optimum duobinary single bit response with a 1.5-Tsymbol transition time, where Tsymbol is the symbol interval for 2-PAM/duobinary.

Each relationship between Nyquist frequency and received data eye amplitude is calculated from theoretical transfer curves for 2/4-PAM (cosine roll-off) and duobinary $(1 + z^{-1})$. Those for these three types of signaling are compared in Figure 21. The eye amplitude of the 2-PAM signal is 2.1 dB above the gain at f_{nyq}. The eye amplitude of the 4-PAM signal is 7.4 dB below the gain at $f_{nyq}/2$ because of four-level signaling. In contrast, the eye amplitude of the duobinary signal with three levels is only 1.6 dB below the gain at $2f_{nyq}/3$. This is because although the 4-PAM signal includes the maximum transition between the lowest and highest levels, the duobinary signal only includes transitions between adjacent levels. That is why duobinary

signaling has better immunity to cross talk and reflection than does 4-PAM, which is proportional to the maximum transition.

At each Nyquist frequency, when the difference in channel loss between duobinary and 2-PAM is larger than 3.7 dB, the duobinary eye amplitude will be larger than that of 2-PAM. In the same way, when the difference between duobinary and 4-PAM is less than 5.8 dB, the duobinary eye amplitude will be larger than that of 4-PAM. When the difference is larger than 5.8dB, on the other hand, the duobinary eye amplitude will be smaller than that of 4-PAM. Regarding the comparison between 2-PAM and 4-PAM, when the difference in channel loss between 2-PAM and 4-PAM is larger than 9.5 dB, the 4-PAM eye amplitude will be larger than that of 2-PAM. To summarize the relationship between channel loss and received data eye amplitude of these three signaling types, the 4-PAM data eye is larger for a large channel loss and the 2-PAM eye is larger for a small channel loss.

One example of the comparison is given in Figure 22, which shows the eye amplitudes of 2-PAM, 4-PAM, and duobinary calculated using previous analyses and actual channel loss values at each Nyquist frequency. The effective data rate was set at 12-Gbps for all types of signaling. This figure indicates that 2-PAM has a larger eye amplitude than 4-PAM for a short channel length. This is because the channel loss is small for a the short channel length, so the loss difference between the Nyquist frequencies of 2-PAM and 4-PAM is less than 9.5 dB. In contrast, for a long

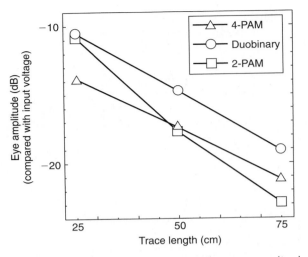

Figure 22: Comparison of transmitted data eye amplitudes for 2-PAM, 4-PAM, and duobinary signaling schemes with 12-Gbps data rate and low-*k* PCB

channel length, 4-PAM has a larger amplitude than 2-PAM because the loss is large enough, having a loss difference larger than 9.5 dB. Although duobinary always has a larger eye amplitude than 2-PAM and 4-PAM for channel lengths up to 75 cm according to this estimation, 4-PAM will be more effective than duobinary for longer length or with larger channel loss.

Figure 23 shows the results of measurements made through low-k PCB traces with lengths of (a) 75 cm, (b) 50 cm, and (c) 25 cm. The one on the left of Figure 23

is for 2-PAM signaling, whose eye opening indicates horizontal ISI caused by a steep roll-off. The one on the right of Figure 23a is for duobinary signaling and shows a 3.5-dB larger eye amplitude and 1.5 times larger eye width. Figures 23b and 23c are eye diagrams more than 50- and 25-cm traces of the same material. The eye openings of the 2-PAM and duobinary are comparable to that of the 50-cm trace. When the high-frequency loss of the trace is relatively small, as in a 25-cm trace, 2-PAM signaling has a larger eye opening than duobinary signaling.

To summarize the signaling comparison, the dependence of the maximum transmission length on data rate is shown in Figure 24. This was estimated using an FR4 PCB trace. Equalization techniques, such as pre-emphasis and receiver equalization, improve the transmission length about two times. Several signaling techniques (for example, PAM or duobinary signaling) improve the transmission length even more, and it reaches 50 cm at 10 Gbps. When a longer length is required, better channel performance will be necessary, and noise immunity techniques are also essential to achieve high-speed and long-distance transmission. Moreover, optical transmission is one candidate for achieving a length longer than 1 m and a transmission speed higher than 10 Gbps.

APPLICATIONS

This section discusses applications that have been determined to be suitable for PAM transmission, including duobinary transmission. Serial communication applications and their required bandwidths are shown in Figure 25. Serial communication is widely used, regardless of the

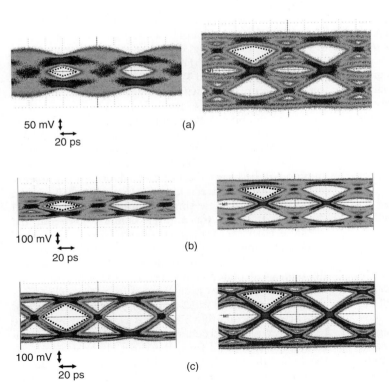

Figure 23: Comparison of measurement data eyes of 2-PAM and duobinary with 12-Gbps data rate

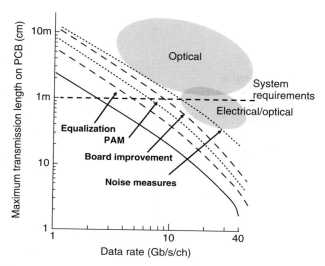

Figure 24: Techniques for high-speed and long-distance transmission

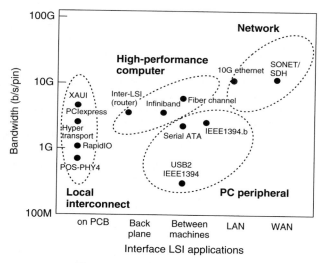

Figure 25: Interface applications

over a long transmission length or large frequency-dependent loss in channels. For example, the 100BASE-T2 and 1000BASE-T standards for Ethernet adopt 5-PAM signaling, and several proposals for 10GBASE-T have been considered, including twelve-, ten-, and eight-level PAM (12-PAM, 10-PAM, and 8-PAM).

To achieve high-speed circuit operation, let us consider the relationship between the maximum operating frequency of circuits and the gate length. The maximum frequency is inversely proportional to the gate length or design rule, as shown in Figure 5. By simply extrapolating the fitting line, we can see that we should be able to reach 5-Gbps operation with 0.1-μm CMOS technology if we use a single architecture, which operates with the same frequency clock signal as the transmitted data rate. A more radical design is obviously needed to overcome the conventional circuit limitations and further improve the circuit performance. The parallel architecture and circuit technique have achieved twice the performance of the conventional design, as shown in Figure 5. This circuit technique is independent of the design rule, so it is always effective at doubling the processing speed. The maximum transmitted data rate, for example, has exceeded 10 Gbps with 90-nm CMOS. Moreover, it has reached more than 20 Gbps with 4-PAM transmission techniques using 90-nm technology. Oversampling, in which sophisticated decision control logic can operate at a lower frequency, with multiphase clocks is also an effective approach for getting the most out of CMOS characteristics. For example, 4-Gbps operation can be achieved with 500-MHz, eight-phase clock signals by using 0.5-μm CMOS technology, and 12-Gbps operation using 3-GHz and four phases. These architectures for high-speed operation with lower-speed devices are supported by the high level of integration of CMOS technology compared with non-CMOS technology.

Another important point for achieving high-data bandwidth transmission is sophisticated equalization techniques, such as the pre-emphasis, liner equalizer, and the decision feedback equalizer. These approaches make it possible to increase the transmission length with high-speed data on large-loss media. They are also supported by the high level of integration of CMOS.

On the other hand, we have to solve several design issues on the road to high operating speed LSIs. As supply voltage and design rules are reduced in accordance with device scaling, *signal integrity* problems become serious. One major drawback of CMOS push-pull operation is the large switching noise induced by sudden current flows on the power and ground lines. Switching noise on the power and ground lines, for example, can reach approximately 100 mV. The digital switching noise could cause delay time variations or errors in logical operation. The silicon substrate itself is another source of digital switching noise. Substrate noise, for example, reaches some 50 mV. Analog circuits, such as the PLL and preamplifier, are highly sensitive to this noise. These types of switching noise degrade transmission data because the noise degrades the accuracy of the clock signal, which determines the transmission data timing and directly affects the data waveforms.

To increase the data bandwidth or channel length by using the PAM, we need to apply noise immunity techniques because the received data are degraded or

channel length or application. The transmission rate of serial communication has been increased to beyond the Gigahertz range. From the perspective of the transfer function, PAM is effective for increasing the total bandwidth of transmitted data while keeping the data rate low when the frequency dependence of channel loss is high. Applications using PAM therefore fall into two types: (1) transmission with a large loss and (2) transmission with a fixed operating speed because of some limitation imposed on device performance.

Large-loss transmission means long-distance communication, such as in the backplane, between machines, or in a LAN, as shown in Figure 25. Regarding device limitation, it is effective to achieve a higher data bandwidth with a low-speed device in the early stage after a product has been launched on the market. Its effect, however, declines as process technology is improved. Therefore, applications using the PAM technique are focused on those communications

attenuated when the receiver circuit noise becomes larger as the operating speed increases. Moreover, PAM signaling has multiple data eyes at the same received timing. Therefore, the SNR of PAM signaling is smaller than that of 2-PAM or NRZ signaling.

Using an optical fiber as the channel is an effective way to increase the channel length. In a case such as this, the output buffer is replaced with a laser driver, and the input buffer is a photo detector. The application of PAM technique to optical communications presents a new problem: The linearity of the laser driver and the photo detector emerges as a new obstacle to surmount.

CONCLUSION

This chapter presented a brief review of recent research on high-speed communication technology. Pulse amplitude modulation was presented as one solution for increasing the amount of data transmitted while simultaneously maintaining a low data rate. PAM effectively increases the data-transmission bandwidth through large-loss transmission channels or in long-distance communication. The development of a PAM transceiver involved surmounting several significant obstacles. One was the challenge of eliminating the trade-off between higher data throughput and improved signal-to-noise ratio for received data. Another was achieving a sufficient voltage margin for the attenuated transmitted signal.

GLOSSARY

Duobinary: A type of partial response signaling. The transmitted pulse is based on the sum of last two bits.
Eye diagram: Diagram used to visualize the waveforms that are used to send multiple bits.
Intersymbol interference (ISI): Distortion of received signal; the previously transmitted bits affect the current bit's waveform.
Non-return to zero (NRZ): Binary code with two levels.
Nyquist frequency: The highest frequency that can be coded at a given sampling rate in order to be able to fully reconstruct the signal. It is equal to one-half the signal's sampling frequency.
Pre-emphasis: Based on FIR. filters, to be performed to boost high frequency signal content on the transmitter side.
Reference voltage: The voltage to determine received data.

CROSS REFERENCES

See *Optical Transmitters, Receivers, and Noise*; *Signaling Approaches*.

REFERENCES

Chen, D.-L., and M. O. Baker. 1997. A 1.25Gb/s, 460mW CMOS transceiver for serial data communication. *IEEE International Solid-State Circuits Conference Digest of Technical Papers*, February, pp. 242–3.

Ewen, J. F., A. X. Widmer, M. Soyuer, K. R. Wrenner, B. Parker, and H. A. Ainspan. 1995. Single-chip 1062Mbaund CMOS transceiver for serial data communication. *IEEE International Solid-State Circuits Conference Digest of Technical Papers*, February, pp. 32–3.

Fiedler, A., R. Mactaggart, J. Welch, and S. Krishnan. 1997. A 1.0625Gbps transceiver with 2x-oversampling and transmit signal pre-emphasis. *IEEE International Solid-State Circuits Conference Digest of Technical Papers*, February, pp. 238–9.

Frajad-Rad, R., C.-K. K. Yang, M. A. Horowitz, and T. H. Lee. 1999. A 0.4-μm CMOS 10-Gb/s 4-PAM pre-emphasis serial link transmitter. *IEEE Journal of Solid-State Circuits*, 34(5): 580–5.

———. 2000. A 0.3-μm CMOS 8-Gb/s 4-PAM serial link transceiver. *IEEE Journal of Solid-State Circuits*, 35(5): 757–64.

Fukaishi, M., K. Nakamura, H. Heiuchi, Y. Hirota, Y. Nakazawa, H. Ikeno, H. Hayama, and M. Yotsuyanagi. 2000. A 20-Gb/s CMOS multichannel transmitter and receiver chip set for ultra-high-resolution digital displays. *IEEE Journal of Solid-State Circuits*, 35(11): 1611–18.

Fukaishi, M., K. Nakamura, M. Sato, Y. Tsutsui, S. Kishi, and M. Yotsuyanagi. 1998. A 4.25-Gb/s CMOS fiber channel transceiver with asynchronous tree-type demultiplexer and frequency conversion architecture. *IEEE Journal of Solid-State Circuits*, 33(12): 2139–47.

Gu, R., J. M. Tran, H.-C. Lin, A.-L. Yee, and M. Izzard. 1999. A 0.5-3.5Gb/s low-power low-jitter serial data CMOS transceiver. *IEEE International Solid-State Circuits Conference Digest of Technical Papers*, February, pp. 352–3.

Hur, Y., M. Maeng, C. Chun, F. Bien, H. Kim, S. Chandramouli, E. Gebara, and J. Laskar. 2005. Equalization and near-end crosstalk (NEXT) noise cancellation for 20-Gb/s 4-PAM backplane serial I/O interconnections. *IEEE Transactions on Microwave and Techniques*, 53(1): 246–55.

Krishna, K., D. A. Yokoyama-Martin, A. Caffee, C. Jones, M. Loikkanen, J. Parker, R. Segelken, J. L. Sonntag, J. Stonick, S. Titus, D. Weinlader, and S. Wolfer. 2005. A multigigabit backplane transceiver core in 0.13-um CMOS with a power-efficient equalization architecture. *IEEE Journal of Solid-State Circuits*, 40(12): 2658–66.

Kudoh, Y., M. Fukaishi, and M. Mizuno. 2003. A 0.13-μm CMOS 5-Gb/s 10-m 28AWG cable transceiver with no-feedback-loop continuous-time post-equalizer. *IEEE Journal of Solid-State Circuits*, 38(5): 741–6.

Landman, P., K. Brouse, V. Gupta, S. Wu, R. Payne, U. Erdogan, R. Gu, A.-L. Yee, B. Parthasarathy, S. Ramaswamy, B. Bhakta, W. Mohammed, J. Powers, Y. Xie, L. Wu, L. Dyson, K. Heragu, and W. Lee. 2005. A transmit architecture with 4-tap feedforward equalization for 6.25/12.5Gb/s serial backplane communication. *IEEE International Solid-State Circuits Conference Digest of Technical Papers*, February, 66–7.

Lee, K., S. Kim, Y. Shin, D.-K. Jeong, G. Kim, V. DaCosta, and D. Lee. 1998. A jitter-tolerant 4.5Gb/s CMOS interconnect for digital display. *IEEE International Solid-State Circuits Conference Digest of Technical Papers*, February, pp. 310–1.

Lee, M.-J. E., W. J. Dally, and P. Chiang. 2000. Low-power area-efficient high-speed I/O circuit techniques. *IEEE Journal of Solid-State Circuits*, 35(11): 1591–9.

Menolfi, C., T. Toifl, R. Reutemann, M. Ruegg, P. Buchmann, M. Kossel, T. Morf, and M. Schmatz. 2005. A 25Gb/s PAM4 transmitter in 90nm CMOS SOI. *IEEE International Solid-State Circuits Conference Digest of Technical Papers*, February, pp. 72–3.

Nakamura, K., M. Fukaishi, H. Abiko, A. Matsumoto, and M. Yotsuyanagi. 1998. A 6 Gbps CMOS phase detecting DEMUX module using half-frequency clock. *1998 Symposium on VLSI Circuits Digest of Technical Papers*, June, pp. 196–7.

Sinsky, J. H., M. Duelk, and A. Adamiecki. 2005. High-speed electrical backplane transmission using duobinary signaling. *IEEE Transactions on Microwave Theory and Techniques*, 53(1): 152–60.

Soda, M., H. Tezuka, S. Shioiri, A. Tanabe, A. Furukawa, M. Togo, T. Tamura, and K. Yoshida. 1997. A 2.4-Gb/s CMOS clock recovering 1:8 demultiplexer. *1997 Symposium on VLSI Circuits Digest*, June, pp. 69–70.

Sonntag, J., J. Stonick, J. Gorecki, B. Beale, B. Check, X.-M. Gong, J. Guiliano, K. Lee, B. Lefferts, D. Martin, U.-K. Moon, A. Sengir, S. Titus, G.-Y. Wei, D. Weihlader, and Y. Yang. 2002. An adaptive PAM-4 5 Gb/s backplane transceiver in 0.25-µm CMOS. *IEEE 2002 Custom Integrated Circuits Conference Digest*, pp. 363–6.

Stojanovic, V., A. Ho, B. W. Garlepp, F. Chen, J. Wei, G. Tsang, E. Alon, R. T. Kollipara, C. W. Werner, J. L. Zarbe, and M. A. Horowitz. Autonomous dual-mode (PAM2/4) serial link transceiver with adaptive equalization and data recovery. *IEEE Journal of Solid-State Circuits*, 40(4): 1012–26.

Stonic, J. T., G.-Y. Wei, J. L. Sonntag, and D. K. Wenlader. 2003. An adaptive PAM-4 5-Gb/s backplane transceiver in 0.25-µm CMOS. *IEEE Journal of Solid-State Circuits*, 38(3): 436–43.

Tanabe, A., M. Soda, Y. Nakahara, T. Tamura, K. Yoshida, and A. Furukawa. 1998. A single-chip 2.4-Gb/s CMOS optical receiver IC with low substrate cross-talk pre-amplifier. *IEEE Journal of Solid-State Circuits*, 33(12): 2148–53.

Tanahashi, T., M. Kurisu, H. Yamaguchi, T. Nedachi, M. Arai, S. Tomari, T. Matsuzaki, K. Nakamura, M. Fukaishi, S. Naramoto, and T. Sato. 2001. A 2Gb/s 21CH low-latency transceiver circuit for inter-processor communication. *IEEE International Solid-State Circuits Conference Digest of Technical Papers*, February, pp. 60–1.

Toifl, T., C. Menolfi, M. Ruegg, R. Reutemann, P. Buchmann, M. Kossel, T. Morf, and M. Schmatz. 2005. A 22 Gbit/s PAM-4 receiver in 90nm CMOS-SOI technology. *2005 Symposium on VLSI Circuits Digest of Technical Papers*, June, pp. 380–3.

Verghese, N. K., T. J. Schmerbeck, and D. J. Allstot. 1995. *Simulation techniques and solutions for mixed-signal coupling in integrated circuits*. Norwell, MA: Kluwer Academic Publishers.

Widmer, A. X., and P. A. Franaszek. 1983. A DC-balanced, partitioned-block, 8B/10B transmission code. *IBM Journal of Research Development*, 27: 440–51.

Yamaguchi, K., K. Sunaga, S. Kaeriyama, T. Nedachi, M. Takamiya, K. Nose, Y. Nakagawa, M. Sugawara, M. Fukaishi. 2005. 12Gb/s duobinary signaling with ×2 oversampled edge equalization. *IEEE International Solid-State Circuits Conference Digest of Technical Papers*, February, pp. 70–1.

Yang, C.-K. K., R. Farjad-Rad, and M. A. Horowitz. 1998. A 0.5-µm CMOS 4.0-Gbit/s serial link transceiver with data recovery using oversampling. *IEEE Journal of Solid-State Circuits*, 33(5): 713–22.

Yang, C.-K. K., and M. A. Horowitz. 1996. A 0.8-µm CMOS 2.5 Gb/s oversampling receiver and transmitter for serial links. *IEEE Journal of Solid-State Circuits*, 31(12): 2015–23.

Yang, C.-K. K., and K.-L. J. Wong. 2003. Analysis of timing recovery for multi-Gbps PAM transceivers. *IEEE 2003 Custom Integrated Circuits Conference Digest*, pp. 67–72.

Zerbe, J. L., P. S. Chau, C. W. Werner, T. P. Thrush, H. J. Liaw, B. W. Garlepp, and K. S. Donnelly. 2001. 1.6 Gb/s/pin 4-PAM signaling and circuits for a multi-drop bus. *IEEE Journal of Solid-State Circuits*, 36(5): 752–60.

Zerbe, J. L., C. W. Werner, V. Stojanovic, F. Chen, J. Wei, G. Tsang, D. Kim, W. F. Stonecypher, A. Ho, T. P. Thrush, R. T. Kollipara, M. A. Horowitz, and K. S. Donnelly. 2003. Equalization and clock recovery for 2.5 – 10-Gb/s 2-PAM/4-PAM backplane transceiver cell. *IEEE Journal of Solid-State Circuits*, 38(12): 2121–30.

Frequency and Phase Modulation

Albert Lozano-Nieto, *Pennsylvania State University*

INTRODUCTION

Angle modulation denotes the types of modulations in which the angle of a carrier is varied according to the amplitude of the modulating baseband signal. In this type of modulation, the amplitude of the carrier is kept at a constant value. There are several ways in which the phase of the carrier— $\theta(t)$—can be changed in accordance with the modulating signal. The two classes of angle modulation are frequency modulation and phase modulation.

PRINCIPLES OF FREQUENCY MODULATION

Frequency modulation (FM) is based on changing the instantaneous frequency of a carrier according to the amplitude of the baseband modulating signal. Conceptually, FM can be implemented by a modulating signal that changes with time placed at the input of a *voltage-controlled oscillator* (VCO). The frequency at the output of the VCO can be written as:

$$f_i(t) = f_c + k_0 v_m(t) \tag{1}$$

in which $f_i(t)$ is the instantaneous output frequency of the VCO, f_c is the output frequency of the VCO in the absence of a modulating signal, $v_m(t)$ is the modulating signal, and k_0 is the VCO constant expressed in Hz/V.

Assuming that when $v_m = 0$ then $f_i(t) = f_c$, Equation 1 can be rewritten as:

$$f_i(t) = f_c + \Delta f_c \tag{2}$$

with $\Delta f_c = k_0 v_m(t)$.

Therefore, the variations in f_c follow exactly the variations in the amplitude of the modulating signal.

An angle-modulated signal can be expressed as:

$$s(t) = A \cos \theta(t) \tag{3}$$

With $\theta(t)$ being the time-varying angle displacement of the signal. Equation 3 can be rewritten as:

$$s(t) = A \cos(\omega t + \Phi) \tag{4}$$

In Equation 4, the angle variations can be the result of ωt or Φ. When Φ is changed depending on the modulating signal, the resulting complex signal is called *phase modulation* and will be studied in detail later in this chapter. When the ωt angle is changed depending on the modulating signal while keeping Φ constant, the resulting signal is called *frequency modulation*.

Modulation Index

The *modulation index* is a parameter that measures the relative amounts of information-to-carrier amplitude in the resulting modulated signal and is specifically used to determine spectral power distribution. Assuming for simplicity a sinusoid as the modulating signal, the modulation index is defined as the peak phase-angle deviation of the carrier.

To find the instantaneous frequency of a FM signal, we need to consider the fundamental relationship between frequency and phase. The *angular frequency* (ω) of a signal can be written as:

$$\omega = \frac{d\theta}{dt} \tag{5}$$

Therefore, using the relationship between linear and angular frequency in equation 1, we can write:

$$\frac{d\theta}{dt} = 2\pi f_c + 2\pi k_0 v_m(t) \tag{6}$$

Integrating this yields:

$$\theta(t) = \int_{-\infty}^{t} 2\pi f_c \, dt + \int_{-\infty}^{t} 2\pi k_0 \, v_m(t) dt \qquad (7)$$

The first integral can be evaluated immediately, therefore:

$$\theta(t) = 2\pi f_c t + \theta_0 + \int_{-\infty}^{t} 2\pi k_0 \, v_m(t) \, dt \qquad (8)$$

with θ_0 being the arbitrary phase at $t = 0$.

This then leads to the general form of the FM equation:

$$S_{FM}(t) = A \cos \left[2\pi f_c t + 2\pi k_0 \int_{-\infty}^{t} 2\pi k_0 \, v_m(\lambda) d\lambda \right] \qquad (9)$$

Equation 8 shows that, in general, the instantaneous phase of a FM signal is dependent on the type of modulating signal. Again assuming for simplicity a sinusoidal modulating signal such as $v_m(t) = V_{pk} \cos(2\pi f_m t)$ for use in Equation 8, and assuming that the initial phases are zero, it is then possible to write:

$$\theta(t) = 2\pi f_c t + \left(\frac{k_0 V_{pk}}{f_m} \right) \sin 2\pi f_m t \qquad (10)$$

Therefore,

$$\theta(t) = 2\pi f_c t + \left(\frac{\Delta f_c(pk)}{f_m} \right) \sin 2\pi f_m t \qquad (11)$$

Substitution of Equation 11 in Equation 3 gives the equation that mathematically describes the FM signal:

$$S_{FM}(t) = A \cos(2\pi f_c t + m_f \sin 2\pi f_m t) \qquad (12)$$

$$\text{with } m_f = \left(\frac{\Delta f_c(pk)}{f_m} \right) \qquad (13)$$

The parameter described in Equation 13, m_f is the *modulation index* for a sinusoidal modulating signal expressed in radians. Equation 12 shows that m_f is the peak of the phase-angle signal, which also changes with time following a sine form.

Narrowband Frequency Modulation

The frequency spectrum of a FM signal depends on both the modulating signal and the modulation index. Because the modulated FM signal is a nonlinear function of the modulating signal, its spectrum must be evaluated on a case-by-case basis. It has been shown that for a sinusoidal modulating signal like those considered here, the amplitudes of the spectral components are giving by Bessel functions of the modulation index, m_f. However, in special cases—for example, in those cases in which the modulating index is small, or *narrowband FM* (NBFM)—it is possible to simplify the resulting function. Assuming a sine-modulating signal and after some trigonometric manipulation, Equation 11 can be rewritten as:

$$\begin{aligned} s_{FM}(t) = {} & A(\cos(m_f \sin \omega_m t) \cos \omega_c t) \\ & - A(\sin(m_f \sin \omega_m t) \sin \omega_c t) \end{aligned} \qquad (14)$$

In those cases with small modulation indexes, we can do the following approximations:

$$\cos(m_f \sin \omega_m t) \approx 1 \text{ and } \sin(m_f \sin \omega_m t) \approx m_f \sin \omega_m$$

Therefore, the FM signal described in Equation 13, assuming small modulations indexes, can be approximated as:

$$s_{FM}(t) \approx A(\cos \omega_c t) - A(m_f \sin \omega_m t) \sin \omega_c t \qquad (15)$$

The first term in Equation 15 is a carrier signal, while the second term is the sidebands. Focusing now on the sidebands term, we can rewrite it as:

$$\begin{aligned} A(m_f \sin \omega_m t) \sin \omega_c t = {} & \left(\frac{A m_f}{2} \right) \cos(\omega_c - \omega_m)t \\ & - \left(\frac{A m_f}{2} \right) \cos(\omega_c + \omega_m)t \end{aligned} \qquad (16)$$

Equations 15 and 16 show that the spectrum of a NBFM consists of a carrier with constant amplitude and two sidebands with a form similar to double sideband with suppressed carrier. Its peak amplitude depends on the amplitude of the modulating signal as well as the modulating index. Therefore, the bandwidth required to transmit the NBFM signal includes the carrier and a single set of sidebands separated in $\pm\omega_m$ from the carrier frequency. The validity of this conclusion—and therefore the assumption of working with a NBFM signal—is better as the value of m_f is lower, but in any case it cannot exceed approximately 0.25 for the approximation to remain valid.

Wideband Frequency Modulation

When the previous approximation cannot be used because of the higher value of the modulation index, Equation 13 describes the time dependence of the FM signal. From this equation, it is possible to observe how the amplitude variations of the carrier components become quite complicated. In fact, the amplitudes of the carrier at the different frequencies cannot be evaluated in a closed form. The peak amplitude of the carrier for a FM signal with modulation index m_f is given by the Bessel function of first kind of order zero as $V_c pk = A J_0(m_f)$. In general, the amplitude of any sideband is given as

$$V_n pk = A J_n(m_f) \qquad (17)$$

where A is the amplitude of the modulating signal and $J_n(m_f)$ is the Bessel function of first kind of order n that can be easily found in the tables elsewhere.

An important implication from these equations is that the spectrum of the FM signal has theoretically infinite components. In a practical manner, $J_n(m_f)$ tends to zero for values of n large enough for any given modulation index, so for practical purposes we can consider the FM signal as being limited in bandwidth. One criterion is to limit the value of sidebands with amplitude higher than 1 percent of the amplitude of the unmodulated carrier (Proakis and Salehi 1994). Bessel functions decay more slowly with increasing values of the modulation index m_f. Therefore, FM signals with larger modulation indexes have a much wider power spectral as it could be qualitatively suggested by the definition of modulation index.

We can also use this approach to evaluate the bandwidth of the NBFM signal. By considering the Bessel functions for a modulation index of 0.25, it is possible to see that only the first-order sidebands have amplitudes that exceed 1 percent of the unmodulated carrier. This in turn results in a power spectrum that contains the carrier and a single sideband at each side as it was discovered in the previous section using a different approximation.

A somewhat alternative and empirical criteria to establish the bandwidth of the FM signal for practical purposes without resorting to evaluating the Bessel functions is known as *Carson's rule*. Carson's rule states that for small values of the modulation index the spectrum of the FM signal contains the carrier frequency and one pair of sideband frequencies separated in f_m Hz from the carrier at frequency f_c. Carson's rule also states that, for larger values of the modulation index, the bandwidth of the FM signal can be found as:

$$B = 2(m_f + 1)f_m \qquad (18)$$

Equation 18 clearly shows how increasing values of the modulation index will results in higher values of spectral bandwidth.

MODULATION METHODS FOR FREQUENCY MODULATION

There are two basic methodologies for generating a FM signal: direct method and indirect method. In the *direct method*, the frequency of a carrier is directly varied according to the amplitude of the modulating signal. In the *indirect method*, a balanced modulator generates a NBFM signal; by further multiplying in frequency, it is possible to achieve the desired frequency carrier and frequency deviation. These two methods are further developed in the upcoming sections.

Modulation Techniques for FM

The most basic approach to generating a FM signal by the direct method is by using a voltage controlled oscillator. The VCO is followed by a buffer amplifier and finally amplified to its final output power by the appropriate power amplifiers. Because of the nonlinearity of the FM signal, it is possible to use nonlinear amplifiers operating near their saturation point and therefore increase the efficiency of the whole system.

However, because VCOs are notorious for exhibiting poor frequency stability, it is necessary to introduce additional circuitry to solve this problem. One of the most common approaches is to use a feedback circuit that stabilizes the frequency of the carrier. Another method is to generate the FM signal from a phase-modulation signal as we will discuss later in this chapter.

For practical applications, however, the best approach is to use one of the several commercial integrated circuits designed and optimized for these applications. For example, the family of integrated circuits MAX2605 to MAX2609 from Maxim are a series of highly stable VCOs with central frequencies that range from 45 MHz to 650 MHz. Application note 1869 from the same manufacturer shows how to use these circuits to generate low-power FM signals in the commercial broadcasting band (Maxim Semiconductor 2003). National Semiconductor has also several solutions to generate FM signals with the traditional LM566 and LM565 pair of chips (National Semiconductor 1975). In the higher frequency ranges, the TRF6900 from Texas Instruments provides in a single chip a solution to NBFM and FSK transmission in the 900-MHz ISM band (Texas Instruments 2005). Given the recent development of digital circuits and, in particular, *digital signal processing* (DSP), it is also possible to generate high-quality FM signals using all-digital circuitry. The advantages of not requiring periodic recalibration or it drifts with temperature or power supply variations make it advantageous even with its initial increased complexity (Analog Devices undated). Although this list of options is not exhaustive, it indicates the practical directions to follow at the time of implementing a system to generate FM signals.

Demodulation Techniques for FM

The demodulation circuits for FM signals are based on the *superheterodyne principle*, similar to those for *amplitude-modulated* (AM) signals. However, because in FM signals there is no information in the amplitude of the carrier, it is not necessary to use automatic gain control circuits.

In general, a FM demodulator produces an output voltage that is proportional to the instantaneous frequency of the signal at its input. Using an approach similar to the one used to develop equation 1, we can develop the equation for the FM demodulator:

$$v_0(t) = k_d f(t) \qquad (19)$$

in which $f(t)$ is the instantaneous input frequency for the FM demodulator, $v_0(t)$ is the output demodulated signal, and k_d is the gain of the demodulator, expressed in V/Hz.

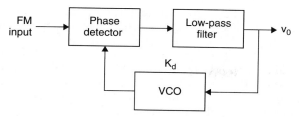

Figure 1: Basic structure of a PLL

There are three possible ways of implementing Equation 19: (1) a demodulator based on *phase-locked loops* (PLL), (2) demodulators based on slope detection (also known as *FM discriminators*), and (3) quadrature detectors.

Figure 1 shows the basic structure of a FM demodulator based on a PLL. If we call $f_c(t)$ the FM signal at the input of the demodulator, we can write:

$$f_c(t) = k_0\, v_m(t) \qquad (20)$$

where k_o is the constant of the VCO for the modulator and $v_m(t)$ is the modulating signal.

In the circuit of Figure 1, the output of the VCO (k_d) is compared with the input signal using a phase comparator, producing an output voltage that is proportional to the phase difference. The phase difference signal is in turn fed back into the VCO to control the output frequency. Therefore, changes between the frequency of the FM signal and the signal generated by the VCO are converted into changes in the amplitude of the output signal, V_o.

The slope detection demodulation method is based on taking the time derivative (slope) of the FM signal and following it with envelope detection. We can write the expression for the FM signal at the input of the demodulator as:

$$v_{FM}(t) = A\cos[2\pi f_c t + \theta(t)]$$

with $\theta(t)$ given by Equation 8 as $\theta(t) = 2\pi f_c t + \theta_0 + \int 2\pi k_0\, v_m(t)dt$.

After the FM signal $v_{FM}(t)$ is passed through a differentiator—a filter with transfer function has a gain that increases linearly with frequency—the signal at the output of the differentiator is:

$$v_{fil} = -A\left[2\pi f_c t + \frac{d\theta(t)}{dt}\right]\sin(2\pi f_c t + \theta(t)) \qquad (21)$$

After the signal v_{fil} is passed through an envelope detector, its output is:

$$\begin{aligned} v_o(t) &= -A\left[[2\pi f_c t] + \frac{d}{dt}\theta(t)\right] \\ &= A[2\pi f_c t + 2\pi k_0\, v_m(t)] \end{aligned} \qquad (22)$$

The DC value contained in Equation 22 can be easily eliminated by filtering, resulting in an output voltage that is proportional to the original modulating signal.

Quadrature detection is another method for demodulating the FM signal. It is based on a network that shifts the phase of the incoming FM signal by an amount proportional to its instantaneous frequency, followed by a phase detector between the original FM signal and the signal at the output of the network. With this approach, the output voltage is proportional to the instantaneous frequency of the incoming FM signal. This type of FM demodulation is therefore based on a frequency-to-amplitude conversion.

Similarly to FM modulator circuits, it is possible to find high-quality FM demodulators based on different integrated circuits. For example, the CD4046B from Texas Instruments is an extremely versatile PLL that has been widely used for demodulation purposes. Other integrated circuits, such as the TRF6900 from Texas Instruments, are transceivers that can be used to implement the transmitter and receiver for a digital FM system (Texas Instruments 2003). The AD8348 integrated circuit from Analog Devices is a demodulator based on quadrature detection that can work in the frequency range from 50 MHz to 1000 MHz, thus making it extremely flexible for a large number of applications. Another chip from Analog Devices is the AD650 chip that is a voltage-to-frequency and frequency-to-voltage converter, making it suitable to FM generation and detection, although in this case the frequency range is limited to 1 MHz.

PERFORMANCE OF THE FREQUENCY-MODULATED SIGNAL

Because FM is a nonlinear modulation, the analysis of noisy FM systems can be quite complicated, so some approximations and generalizations need to be made. At the same time, this nonlinearity proves to be critical to make FM signals more robust than linearly modulated signals. We need to remember that a FM signal carries the information in its frequency—that is, in the sequence of its zero-crossings. Because noise is normally additive, it affects the amplitude of the FM signal but has a much lower effect in changing its zero crossings. It is then usual for receivers to clip or limit the amplitude of the FM signal before frequency detection in order to provide a constant amplitude signal at its input.

Noise in the Frequency Modulated Signal

Assuming the previous FM signal $v_{FM}(t) = A\cos[2\pi f_c t + \theta(t)]$ with $\theta(t)$ given by Equation 8, its phasor has a constant amplitude of A volts and an angle of $2\pi\theta(t)$, circling around in the complex plane. The noise is a random process that can be decomposed into its quadrature components:

$$n(t) = x(t)\cos 2\pi f_c t - y(t)\sin 2\pi f_c t \qquad (23)$$

where $x(t)$ and $y(t)$ are random processes (Proakis 2001). Figure 2 represents these phasors in the complex plane.

Adding the noise phasor to the FM signal, the resulting signal has a different amplitude and phase. The change in amplitude is irrelevant because no information is

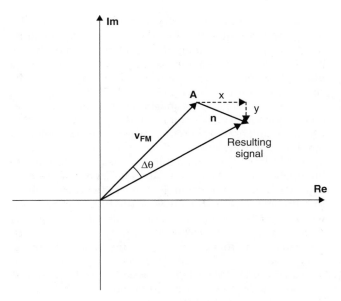

Figure 2: Phasor diagram for noise in the FM signal

contained in the amplitude, so the only important change is in the phase ($\Delta\theta$). As long as the amplitude of the noise does not exceed the value A, the change in phase $\Delta\theta$ will be less than 45 degrees. This situation is not unusual because the amplitude of the noise will normally be lower than the amplitude of the FM signal.

The expression for the resulting signal $r(t)$ can be written as:

$$r(t) = \sqrt{[A + x(t)]^2 + y(t)^2} \cos\left[2\pi f_c t - \tan^{-1}\left(\frac{y(t)}{A + x(t)}\right)\right]$$

(24)

When the resulting signal is demodulated, the limiter will keep its amplitude constant, therefore its output will only respond to the cosine term. After the limiter, the signal is then passed through the discriminator-envelope detector, resulting in the following signal (Roden 2001):

$$\frac{d\theta}{dt} = \frac{[x(t) + A]\dfrac{dy}{dt} - y(t)\dfrac{dx}{dt}}{y(t)^2 + [x(t) + A]^2}$$

(25)

With the assumption of a high carrier-to-noise ratio [$A \gg x(t)$ and $ZA \gg y(t)$], Equation 25 can be rewritten as:

$$\frac{d\theta}{dt} \approx \frac{\dfrac{dy}{dt}}{A}$$

(26)

Equation 26 gives the change in the phase angle originated as a result of additive noise.

Noise Capture in the Frequency-Modulated Signal

The previous equations show the improvement in noise performance of the FM detector when the amplitude of

the signal is larger than the amplitude of the noise. If the amplitude of the noise is larger than the amplitude of the signal, the detector locks onto the noise and suppresses the signal. This phenomenon is known as *noise capture* and is commonly seen while listening to a distant FM station in a car as we drive away from the station, noting that it gets to a point in which the station drops out totally and is replaced by static. At this point, the FM receiver has locked onto the noise instead of the signal. This is one of the main drawbacks of FM systems in which the noise performance drops to zero after a certain threshold *signal-to-noise ratio* (SNR). A similar effect occurs when two signals are broadcasted simultaneously: The FM receiver will lock onto the stronger signal and ignore the weaker signal.

Trade-Off between Signal-to-Noise Ratio and Bandwidth for the FM Signal

In the FM signal, the SNR before the detection depends on the bandwidth of the filters in the receiver, the power of the received carrier, and the power of the noise signal. However, the signal-to-noise ratio after the detection process is a function of the maximum frequency of the message (f_m), the modulation index (m_f), and the SNR at the input (Rappaport 1996).

The signal-to-noise ratio at the output of a properly designed FM detector can be written as (Couch 1993):

$$(SNR)_o = 6(m_f + 1)m_f^2 \overline{\left(\frac{m(t)}{V_p}\right)^2} (SNR)_i$$

(27)

with V_p being the peak voltage of the modulating signal $m(t)$ and m_f, the modulation index. We must take into consideration that Equation 27 is only valid for high carrier-to-noise ratios. The expression of the SNR and the input is given by:

$$(SNR)_i = \frac{A_c^2 / 2}{2N_o(m_f + 1)Bw}$$

(28)

where A_c is the amplitude of the carrier, N_o is the noise density (assumed to be white noise), and Bw is the bandwidth of the filter used.

In the simplified case of a modulating sinusoidal signal, $m(t) = A_m \sin \omega_m t$, Equation 27 results in:

$$(SNR)_o = 3(m_f + 1)m_f^2 (SNR)_i$$

(29)

Equation 29 clearly shows that by increasing the modulating index m_f for the FM signal, it is possible to increase the signal-to-noise ratio at the output of the demodulator. However, as it was described earlier in the chapter, an increase in m_f results in an increase of the transmission bandwidth. Thus, the increase in $(SNR)_o$ is at the expense of using higher amounts of bandwidth, and therefore the designer of a FM system must carefully analyze signal-to-noise and bandwidth requirements in order to reach a compromise. From Equation 18, we can see that for large values of m_f the transmission bandwidth is proportional to the modulation index m_f. Therefore, Equation 29 shows that the SNR at the output of the demodulator increases with the cube of the transmission bandwidth, thus making it an excellent technique for the transmission of fading signals. It can also be shown (Rappaport 1996) that given the same conditions for the carrier and noise values, the detection of FM signals result in much higher values of $(SNR)_o$ than for AM signals. Frequency modulations improve performance through the adjustment of the modulation index at the transmitter and not the transmitted power. This is not the case of AM signals because, being a linear modulation technique, it does not trade bandwidth for SNR.

All of the previous considerations are valid only if the SNR at the input of the detector exceeds the threshold for which the detector locks onto the signal and not onto the noise. For the majority of detectors in practical applications, this threshold for $(SNR)_i$ has an approximate value of 10 dB, although with some additional circuitry it can be improved down to 6 dB.

FREQUENCY MODULATION FOR DIGITAL SIGNALS: FREQUENCY SHIFT KEYING

When the modulating signal is a digital signal instead of an analog signal, the resulting frequency-modulating signal receives its own specific name: *frequency shift keying* (FSK). Contrary to analog FM in which the instantaneous frequency of the carrier can have any value within its maximum deviation frequency, in FSK the number of possible carrier instantaneous frequencies is limited to a given subset. The most basic case, in which only two instantaneous frequencies can be transmitted, is called *binary FSK* (BFSK). For more complex systems, and to increase the bit transmission rate, the number of possible instantaneous carrier frequencies is higher, normally a power of 2. This situation is called *M-ary FSK*, where M represents the total number of different possible instantaneous frequencies. These two approaches are explained in further detail in the following subsections.

Binary Frequency Shift Keying

Binary frequency shift keying transmits two different frequencies (f_0 and f_1) to represent a logic 0 or a logic 1 following an established protocol. The transmission of BFSK can be easily accomplished by having two oscillators operating at frequencies f_0 and f_1, followed by a switch that will select one or the other based on the digital input. Although this is a simple procedure, it results in discontinuities of the carrier frequency at the time of switching. This in turn results in additional high-frequency components, thus needing a much wider bandwidth transmission.

BFSK can also be generated using the VCO approach in a manner similar to analog signals. Because the digital modulating signal will never have a zero rise or settling time, this digital modulation is in fact an analog modulation with a very short transition time. In this case, the

carrier has a continuous and smooth transition, therefore guaranteeing phase continuity and requiring a narrower spectrum for transmission. This method is known as *continuous phase frequency shift keying* (CPFSK). Although it has been introduced here for BFSK, it can also be readily applied for multilevel modulation systems.

Similar to analog FM, the spectrum for BFSK signals is complex and strongly dependent on factors such as the separation between the transmitted frequencies f_0 and f_1 and the symbol rate. Two special cases deserve deeper study: When the spacing between the two frequencies is made exactly equal to the symbol rate, the resulting FSK modulation is called *Sunde's FSK*. The power spectral density in this case can be written as (Bateman 1999):

$$G(f)_{Sunde's\ FSK} = \frac{1}{4}\left[\delta\left(f - 0.5\frac{1}{T_b}\right) + \delta\left(f + 0.5\frac{1}{T_b}\right)\right] + \frac{4T_b}{\pi^2}\left[\frac{\cos(\pi f T_b)}{4f^2 T_b^2 - 1}\right]^2 \quad (30)$$

with T_b being the symbol rate.

Equation 30 shows that the spectrum for Sunde's FSK contains two discrete spectral lines at the two symbol frequencies—given by the first component of the equation—plus a broader spectral band given by the last component of the equation.

Minimum shift keying (MSK) is a type of *continuous phase modulation* (CPM). Its power spectral density is (Bateman 1999):

$$G_{MSK}(f) = \frac{16T_b}{\pi^2}\left[\frac{\cos(2\pi f T_b)}{16f^2 T_b^2 - 1}\right] \quad (31)$$

Comparing Equations 29 and 30, we can easily see that the power spectral density for MSK is similar to the one for Sunde's FSK without the energy at the two discrete frequencies. Moreover, the main lobe for MSK is much narrower because it can be expected from the narrower frequency separation between symbols. However, it is also important to note the advantage of the pronounced spectral lines that appear on Sunde's FSK to lock on and demodulate the FSK signal.

In general, the detection of BFSK signals can be achieved by means of either noncoherent or coherent detection. *Noncoherent detection* is based on simultaneously injecting the BFSK into two bandpass filters, each one tuned to the transmitted frequencies, f_0 or f_1, as shown in Figure 3. The output of each filter is connected to an envelope detector, and their outputs are combined to reconstruct the baseband modulating signal.

Alternatively, noncoherent FSK detection can be achieved by applying the FSK signal to the input of a PLL. The output of the internal VCO will switch between frequencies following the signal at the output of the PLL, thus locking onto the incoming FSK signal so that the output changes between the logic levels of 0 and 1, depending on the frequency of the incoming signal.

The coherent detection of BFSK signals can be achieved with the approach outlined in Figure 4.

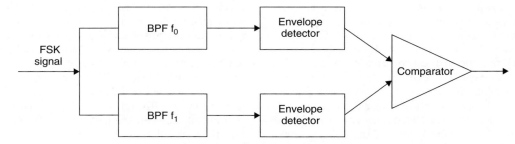

Figure 3: Noncoherent FSK detection

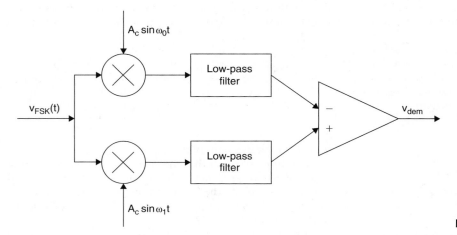

Figure 4: Coherent FSK detection

This approach requires the generation of two carriers with the same exact frequencies and phases as those used at the transmitter. Let us assume in the following analysis that the instantaneous frequency of the carrier at this moment is ω_1—that is, $v_{FSK} = A \sin \omega_1 t$. The output of the first mixer, the generator with a carrier at ω_0 is:

$$
\begin{aligned}
v_1(t) &= A\,A_c \sin(\omega_1 t)\sin(\omega_0 t) \\
&= \frac{A\,A_c}{2}\cos(\omega_1 - \omega_0)t - \frac{A\,A_c}{2}\cos(\omega_1 + \omega_0)t
\end{aligned}
\tag{32}
$$

The output of the lower mixer, the generator with a carrier at ω_1 is:

$$
v_2(t) = A\,A_c \sin^2(\omega_1 t) = \frac{A\,A_c}{2}(1 - \cos(2\omega_1 t))
\tag{33}
$$

The last term in Equation 32 and the second term in Equation 31 can be easily removed by the low-pass filter. If the first term in Equation 31 falls within the pass band of the low-pass filter, it must be eliminated by a notch filter for the DC value that appears in Equation 33 to be the only input into the comparator. However, the use of the notch filter has limitations because of its long transition process. The resulting DC signal is connected at the input of a comparator that will result in a logic 1 at its output.

A similar sequence of events happens when the instantaneous frequency of the FSK signal is ω_0. In this case, the DC value will be applied at the other input of the comparator. Therefore, the output of the comparator is a logic 0.

The *bit error rate* (BER) performance for BFSK modulations depends on the type of detection (coherent versus noncoherent) used in the demodulation process. In general, for a given BER, coherent detection requires approximately 3 dB less SNR (specified as energy per bit divided by noise spectral density) than noncoherent demodulation, thus resulting in a more robust type of detection. This advantage is at the cost of increased complexity. In the case of noncoherent detection, the BER can be expressed as (Bateman 1999):

$$
BER_{BFSK,Non-Coh} = 0.5\,e^{\frac{-0.5 E_b}{N_o}}
\tag{34}
$$

while for coherent detection, the BER is:

$$
BER_{BFSK,Coh} = 0.5\,erfc\left(\sqrt{\frac{E_b}{2 N_o}}\right)
\tag{35}
$$

where $erfc(x)$ is the complementary error function of the variable x (the values of which can be easily found in the appropriate mathematical tables) and E_b, the average energy per bit.

There are integrated circuits in the market that perform FSK transmission, reception, or both. The integrated circuit MAX7032 from Maxim is a FSK transceiver with a carrier frequency from 300 MHz to 450 MHz selectable by the user. The MAX7031 is similar, although it can only operate in three fixed frequencies in that range. From the same manufacturer, the MAX1479 is an ASK/FSK transmitter and the MAX1471 is an ASK/FSK receiver in that specific frequency range. In some cases, it may be necessary to implement the FSK system with a VCO using the approaches outlined in this section. The integrated circuit MAX2754 is a 1.2 GHz VCO with linear modulation input to build the FSK system.

The TRF4903 chip from Texas Instruments is a radio frequency transmitter based on VCO that has been designed to implement FSK systems, while the TRF6900 is a FSK transceiver in the 800-MHz to 900-MHz band (Texas Instruments 2001). The majority of commercial FSK transmitters, receivers, or transceivers are designed for frequency operation in the ISM band. The ADF7901, ADF7011, and ADF7010 from Analog Devices are all FSK transmitters in the ISM band frequency range. In general, when it is necessary to operate in another frequency range, it is possible to do so by using a VCO with the appropriate frequency band.

M-ary Frequency Shift Keying

The demands for higher transmission speed have spurred the development of techniques for transmission of more than just two states. As long as the number of states transmitted is finite, the resulting form of communication is still digital in nature but no longer binary. M-ary transmission designates this type of multisymbol transmission, where M indicates the number of levels used.

M-ary FSK is based on utilizing M-frequencies in a manner similar to BFSK. The key aspect for this type of modulation is the appropriate separation of the frequencies used. If we desire to maintain the same frequency separation for BFSK, we can easily see that M-ary FSK will require a higher transmission bandwidth. On the opposite side, we can squeeze a number of frequencies into the same space utilized by BFSK and improve the transmission bandwidth. However, in this last case, the noise immunity of the M-ary FSK system decreases when compared to the BFSK. By utilizing a specific set of frequencies, it is possible to find the best trade-off between noise immunity and transmission bandwidth. These are known as *orthogonal frequencies* and represent the best choice to increase the noise immunity of the whole system. The set of orthogonal frequencies is given by:

$$f_m = f_c + \frac{m}{2T_s} \tag{36}$$

where f_m represents each one of the orthogonal set of frequencies $m = 1, 2, \ldots M f_c$ is the carrier frequency, and T_s is the period for the symbol rate.

For example, the orthogonal frequencies for an 8-ary FSK system with a symbol rate of 1400 symbols per second and a carrier frequency of 1000 Hz can use the following set: 1000 Hz, 1700 Hz, 2400 Hz, 3100 Hz, 3800 Hz, 4500 Hz, and 5200 Hz with the same starting phase.

A good approach for M-ary FSK detection is to use coherent demodulators similar to the one shown in Figure 4. In this case, we will need M multipliers, each one with an oscillator at one of the frequencies from the orthogonal set, thus increasing the complexity of the system.

As easily expected, as the number of symbol states (M) increase, the BER rate improves, albeit at the expense of bandwidth. The BER rate for a given set of M-ary FSK using orthogonal frequencies is difficult to derive for the general case and must be normally calculated numerically (Proakis 2001).

PRINCIPLES OF PHASE MODULATION

Phase modulation (PM) is another form of angle modulation. Although it is not much used for analog signals, it is the modulation of choice for satellites, deep-space missions, and those occasions that require a strong noise immunity. When a phase is modulated with a particular modulating signal, the derivative of the phase (frequency) is also modulated with the same signal.

Phase modulation is expressed mathematically by varying the phase of a higher-frequency carrier with a constant frequency in Equation 4 [$s(t) = A\cos t(\omega t + \Phi)$]. In the case of PM, the phase Φ is proportional to the modulating signal, $v_m(t)$:

$$\Phi(t) = k_p v_m(t) \tag{37}$$

in which the constant k_p is expressed in rad/V and is called *phase modulator sensitivity*.

Therefore, the general expression for the PM signal is:

$$s_{PM}(t) = A\cos(2\pi f_c t + k_p v_m(t)) \tag{38}$$

If we assume again a sinusoidal modulation signal $v_m(t) = V_{pk}\cos(2\pi f_m t)$, then the PM signal can be written as:

$$s_{PM}(t) = A\cos(2\pi f_c t + k_p V_{pk}\cos 2\pi f_m t) \tag{39}$$

Using $\Delta\Phi(t) = k_p V_{pk}$, Equation 39 becomes:

$$s_{PM}(t) = A\cos(2\pi f_c t + \Delta\Phi(pk)\cos 2\pi f_m t) \tag{40}$$

The value $\Delta\Phi(pk)$ represents the peak deviation of the sinusoidally varying carrier phase angle, so it can be seen as the modulation index for the PM signal. Therefore, Equation 40 can be rewritten as:

$$s_{PM}(t) = A\cos(2\pi f_c t + m_p \cos 2\pi f_m t) \tag{41}$$

It is interesting to compare this last equation with Equation 11, which describes the FM signal. We can see that both of them are similar with the difference being in the modulation term; for the FM signal, it is the derivative of the modulating signal. Figure 5 shows a block diagram for *narrowband phase modulation* (NBPM) generation in the more general case for the modulating signal.

Similar to the approach used to develop the narrowband FM signal and using the appropriate trigonometric identities and assuming a low modulation index ($\Delta\Phi < 0.25$), the equation for the NBPM signal can be written as:

$$s_{NBPM}(t) \approx A(\cos \omega_c t) - A(m_p \cos \omega_m t)\sin \omega_c t \tag{42}$$

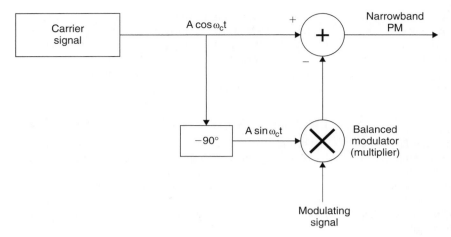

Figure 5: Block diagram for NBPM generation

Once again, it is possible to see the similarities between the equations that describe NBFM and NBPM signals with the difference in the sidebands being the different derivative.

Techniques for Phase Modulation Generation

When using a VCO, wideband phase modulators are the same as frequency modulators except that they first differentiate the modulating signal before entering the VCO. This and similar techniques can be used with the approaches regarding commercial integrated circuits that have been presented earlier for FM generation. For a given modulation index, the sidebands, spectrum, and power of the sinusoidal FM and PM are identical. The only way to see the difference between these two types of modulation in practice is by using a spectrum analyzer modifying the modulation frequency. The modulation index for the PM signal will remain constant, while for the FM signal it will change as the value m_f is dependent on f_m, but m_p and f_m are independent.

A difference in their practical use is that although a large number of practical systems use FM with analog and digital modulating signals, phase modulation is used almost exclusively with digital signals.

PHASE MODULATION FOR DIGITAL SIGNALS: PHASE SHIFT KEYING

A digital signal can also modulate a carrier by changing its phase. The resulting signal is called *phase shift keying* (PSK). The following sections will explore binary and multilevel phase shift keying systems.

Binary Phase Shift Keying

In PSK, the information is contained in the instantaneous phase of the modulated carrier. Usually, this phase is imposed and measured with respect to a known and selected phase of the carrier. For binary phase shift keying in which the modulating signal has two levels, the phase states are 0 and 180 degrees.

The basic method to generate BPSK is depicted in Figure 6. In this approach, the modulating signal has a

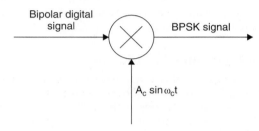

Figure 6: Basic approach for BSPK generation

bipolar form—that is, $v_m(t)$ can take these two values: $+A$ or $-A$ volts. The output of the BPSK generator can be written as:

$$v_{BPSK}(t) = v_m(t) A_c \sin \omega_c t \qquad (43)$$

Using trigonometric identities, Equation 43 can be rewritten as:

$$v_{BPSK}(t) = A_c \sin(\omega_c t + \theta) \qquad (44)$$

where the values of θ can be 0 or 180 degrees.

For coherent detection, the ideal PSK detector needs to know perfectly the phase of the unmodulated carrier. This requirement can be problematic because any phase error (Φ) of the locally generated carrier reduces the effective voltage at the output of the detector in $\cos(\Phi)$, thus degrading the signal-to-noise ratio. To avoid this problem, one particular process for detecting BPSK actually derives a phase-coherent reference, as shown in Figure 7.

Let us assume the signal at the input of the demodulator as:

$$v_{BPSK}(t) = B v_m(t) \sin \omega_c t \qquad (45)$$

with B being the combined amplitude of the BPSK signal. The signal at the output of the squaring circuit is:

$$v_1(t) = B^2 v_m^2(t) \sin^2 \omega_c t = \frac{B^2}{2} v_m^2(t)(1 - \cos 2\omega_c t) \qquad (46)$$

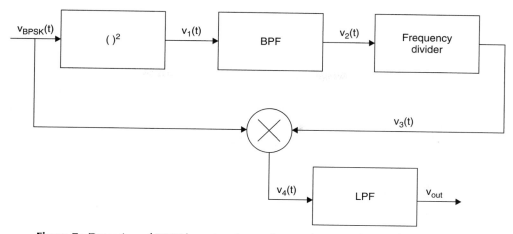

Figure 7: Detection of BPSK by extracting a phase-coherent reference from the signal

The original $v_m(t)$ had two possible values (A and $-A$). After the squaring circuit, $v_1(t)$ becomes:

$$v_1(t) = \frac{C^2}{2}(1 - \cos 2\omega_c t) \qquad (47)$$

with the value $C = AB$ incorporating all of the amplitude values.

The bandpass filter eliminates the DC component, therefore, $v_2(t)$ is:

$$v_2(t) = \frac{C_1^2}{2}\cos 2\omega_c t \qquad (48)$$

The signal $v_2(t)$ is then fed into a frequency divider. This divides the frequency by two and shifts the phase. The signal at its output, $v_3(t)$, is:

$$v_3(t) = \frac{C_2^2}{2}\sin \omega_c t \qquad (49)$$

Finally, $v_3(t)$ is multiplied by the original BPSK signal given by Equation 44. The value of the resulting signal, $v_4(t)$ is:

$$v_4(t) = \frac{C_1^2}{2}Bv_m(t)(\sin \omega_c t)(\sin \omega_c t) \\ = Dv_m(t)\sin^2 \omega_c t = Dv_m(t)(1 - \cos 2\omega_c t) \qquad (50)$$

The low-pass filter eliminates the last term in Equation 40, so the final output voltage is:

$$v_{out}(t) = Dv_m(t) \qquad (51)$$

The signal represented by Equation 51 is a reproduction of the original digital modulating signal that has been recovered from the BPSK signal. In practice, there are problems with this method, requiring the use of more sophisticated approaches such as differential data encoding and differential PSK modulation.

The BER for BPSK is given by Equation 52 (Bateman 1999):

$$BER_{PSK} = 0.5\,erfc\left(\sqrt{\frac{E_b}{N_o}}\right) \qquad (52)$$

where $erfc(x)$ is the complementary error function of the variable x, E_b is the detected energy per bit, and N_o is the noise spectral density.

M-ary Phase Shift Keying

We can apply the same concepts described for M-ary FSK to PSK signals, resulting in a M-ary PSK signal. The four-level PSK signal (quarternary encoding) remains in use, receiving the name of *quadriphase shift keying* (QPSK). The QPSK signal has four different states that are determined by four different phase shifts for the transmitted signal. Therefore, the difference between phases is 90 degrees. Figure 8 shows a basic block diagram for the generation of the QPSK signal.

The digital modulating signal $v_m(t)$ is applied into a two-bit serial-to-parallel converter, so the resulting signals $v_1(t)$ and $v_2(t)$ change at one-half the rate of $v_m(t)$. This has the advantage of reducing the required transmission bandwidth as in the case of M-ary modulations. The output QPSK signal will be:

$$v_{QPSK} = v_1(t)\cos \omega_c t - v_2(t)\sin \omega_c t \qquad (53)$$

Although the two terms that make up the voltage in Equation 45 are centered at the same carrier frequency and their magnitude spectra overlap each other, they do not interfere because they are in phase quadrature. In other words, all of the spectral components of the first term are 90 degrees out of phase with those of the second term, making them independent from each other.

The detection of the QPSK signal follows the inverse process as shown in Figure 9.

The QPSK signal is applied at the input of the demodulator and has the same form as Equation 45, although

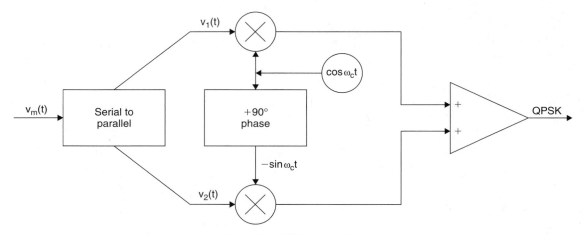

Figure 8: QSPK generation

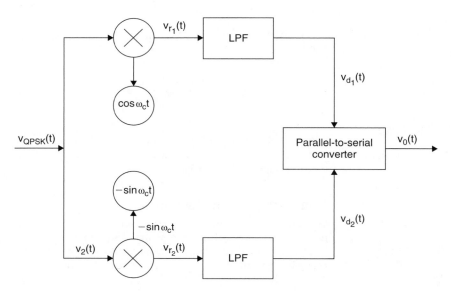

Figure 9: QPSK detection

with a different amplitude to indicate the changes in level during the transmission process:

$$\nu_{d,QPSK} = A\nu_1(t)\cos\omega_c t - A\nu_2(t)\sin\omega_c t \qquad (54)$$

The expression for the signals at the output of the two multipliers, $\nu_{r1}(t)$ and $\nu_{r2}(t)$ after using the appropriate trigonometric identities are:

$$\nu_{r1}(t) = \frac{A}{2}\nu_1(t) + \frac{A}{2}\nu_1(t)\cos 2\omega_c t - \frac{A}{2}\nu_2(t)\sin 2\omega_c t$$
$$\qquad (55)$$
$$\nu_{r2}(t) = \frac{A}{2}\nu_2(t) - \frac{A}{2}\nu_2(t)\cos 2\omega_c t - \frac{A}{2}\nu_1(t)\sin 2\omega_c t$$

The terms at $2\omega_c$ are eliminated by the low-pass filter, thus resulting in the following signals $\nu_{d1}(t)$ and $\nu_{d2}(t)$ at their output:

$$\nu_{d1}(t) = \frac{A}{2}\nu_1(t)$$
$$\qquad (56)$$
$$\nu_{d2}(t) = \frac{A}{2}\nu_2(t)$$

Equation 56 shows the existence of two separate streams of digital data that are then combined into a single stream by the parallel-to-serial converter, thus recovering the original digital modulating signal.

QPSK modulation allows for sending information at twice the speed of BPSK using the same bandwidth without compromising the BER performance over BPSK at the expense of using multilevel signals. A recent variation of QPSK now widely used in the majority of digital radio modems is the format called π/4 QPSK. The difference between these two formats is that in π/4 QPSK the set of four symbols is rotated by 45 degrees at every new symbol transmission. This ensures that the modulation envelope of the filtered QPSK signal never crosses zero, so the peak to mean ratio of the modulation is minimized. This type of modulation can be easily implemented by a digital signal processor (Texas Instruments 1996).

More complex modulation schemes combine digital amplitude modulation with digital phase modulation, resulting in the *quadrature amplitude modulation* (QAM) approach. The analysis of these modulations goes beyond the scope of this article and can be easily found elsewhere in this volume.

The MAX2720 and MAX2721 integrated circuits from Maxim are direct QPSK modulators that are suitable for work in the 1.7 GHz to 2.5 GHz band and also incorporate a power amplifier to minimize the need for external parts in a design. Similarly, members of the MAX2361 family are complete quadrature QPSK transceivers optimized to work in cellular phones. Similar products can also be found from Texas Instruments—for example, the GC41164/6 quad digital transmitter chips. The AD7011 chip from Analog Devices is a $\pi/4$ DQPSK transmit port that employs a differential QPSK modulator with the $\pi/4$ rotation explained above, and the AD9853 from the same manufacturer is a programmable digital QPSK modulator that can also be employed for QAM transmissions (Maxim Semiconductor 2000).

CONCLUSION

Phase and frequency modulation are two types of angle modulation, which is based on changing the angle of a carrier signal in accordance with the amplitude of the modulation signal that contains the information to be transmitted. When the modulating signal is a digital signal, the resulting frequency-modulated signal and process receive the name of *frequency shift keying*, while for phase modulation it is named *phase shift keying*. This chapter has studied both analog and digital modulations, providing examples of commercial devices suitable for their hardware implementations. Although analog angle modulations have been prevalent in the past, digital angle modulations are now more widely used, leaving analog modulation mostly to broadcasting applications.

GLOSSARY

Analog: Pertaining to or consisting of a signal or parameter that is continuously and infinitely variable.

Bandwidth: The data-transmission capacity of a communications system, channel, network, or medium.

Binary: Based on or consisting of two parts, components, or possibilities.

Demodulation: The process of reversing the effects of modulation, thereby restoring the original modulating signal.

Digital: Pertaining to information, such as data, that is represented in the form of discrete units called *digits*, especially that expressed in binary digits.

Frequency: For a periodic phenomenon, the number of complete cycles per unit of time. When the unit of time is one second, the unit of frequency is the hertz.

Modulation: The process of modifying a characteristic of a wave or signal proportionally to a characteristic present in another wave or signal.

Noise: Usually, an unwanted electrical disturbance, often random or persistent in nature, that affects the quality or usefulness of a signal or adversely affects the operation of a device.

Phase: For a given periodic phenomenon, the portion of the complete cycle that has been completed as measured from a given reference point.

Spectrum: A range of energies arranged in order of increasing or decreasing wavelengths or frequencies.

CROSS REFERENCES

See *Digital Phase Modulation and Demodulation; Frequency Division Multiplexing (FDM); Sources of Errors, Prevention, Detection and Correction.*

REFERENCES

Analog Devices. Undated. *Application Note 543: High quality, all-digital RF frequency modulation generation with the ADSP-2181 DSP and the AD9850 direct digital synthesizer* (retrieved from www.analog.com/UploadedFiles/Application_Notes/545038480AN-543.pdf).

Bateman, A. 1999. *Digital communications*. Menlo Park, CA: Addison-Wesley.

Couch, L. W. 1993. *Digital and analog communication systems*. New York: Macmillan

Maxim Semiconductor. 2000. *Application Note 686: QPSK demodulation demystified* (retrieved from www.maxim-ic.com/appnotes.cfm/appnote_number/686).

———. 2003. *Application Note 1869: Single-chip FM transmitter extends home-entertainment system* (retrieved from www.maxim-ic.com/appnotes.cfm/appnote_number/1869).

National Semiconductor. 1975. *Application Note 46: FM remote speaker system* (retrieved from www.national.com/an/AN/AN-146.pdf).

Proakis, J. G. 2001. *Digital communications*. 4th ed. New York: McGraw-Hill.

———, and M. Salehi. 1994. *Communication systems engineering*. Upper Saddle River, NJ: Prentice Hall.

Rappaport, T. S. 1996. *Wireless communications*. Upper Saddle River, NJ: Prentice Hall.

Roden, M. S. 2001. *Analog and digital communication systems*. Los Angeles: Discovery Press.

Stanley, W., and J. Jeffords. 2006. *Electronic communications: Principles and systems*. Clifton Park, NY: Thomson Delmar Learning.

Texas Instruments. 1996. Implementing a $\pi/4$ shift D-QPSK baseband modem using the TMS320C50. *Proceedings of the First European DSP Education and Research Conference*. SPRA341 (retrieved from http://focus.ti.com/lit/an/spra341/spra341.pdf).

———. 2001. Application Report SLAA121. *Implementing a bidirectional, half-duplex FSK RF link with TRF6900 and MSP430* (retrieved from http://focus.ti.com/lit/an/slaa121/slaa121.pdf).

———. 2003. Application Report SCHA002A. *CD4046B Phase-lock loop: A versatile building block for micropower digital and analog applications* (retrieved from http://focus.ti.com/lit/an/scha002a/scha002a.pdf).

———. 2005. Application Report SWRA033E. *Designing with the TRF6900 single-chip RF transceiver* (retrieved from http://focus.ti.com/lit/an/swra033d/swra033d.pdf).

Carrierless Amplitude Phase Modulation

Tim Collins, *University of Birmingham, UK*

INTRODUCTION

Carrierless amplitude phase (CAP) *modulation* is a standard used in computer networks in order to communicate at high data rates, often over relatively low-quality cable. A widely used application is in the provision of *asymmetrical digital subscriber lines* (ADSL); these lines provide broadband network access to residential customers using the same unshielded copper twisted pairs already used for voice telephony and ISDN services (Paradyne Corporation 2000). In many such cases, this use has been superseded by more elaborate *discrete multitone* (DMT) systems that are favored for their ability to counter narrowband interference. CAP, however, is still widely used in many countries. It has also found applications in *asynchronous transfer mode* (ATM) *local area networks* (LANs) using low-quality unshielded cabling for high data-rate communication (Im et al. 1995). In both of these applications, CAP modulation has been adopted primarily because of its high bandwidth efficiency and low implementation costs.

FUNDAMENTALS OF AMPLITUDE PHASE MODULATION

Many of the underlying principles behind CAP are identical to those of *quadrature amplitude modulation* (QAM). The only fundamental difference between them is in their implementation. Figure 1 illustrates block diagrams of a QAM transmitter and receiver as well as those of an equivalent CAP transmitter and receiver.

In either case, the first part of the transmission process is *encoding*. This stage splits the incoming data stream into blocks of binary data, usually between two and eight bits, depending on the modulation scheme. Each block of data is encoded into a single pair of amplitude-weighted impulses. The amplitude weights, denoted a_n and b_n (n being the symbol index), are chosen from a look-up table and are often referred to as a single complex value, $A_n = a_n + jb_n$. A plot of all possible values of A_n on the complex plane is known as the *signal constellation*. Figure 2 shows

an example of how four bits can be encoded in this way. CAP line codes are usually referred to in the form CAP-*M* (or sometimes *M*-CAP), where *M* is the number of points in the signal constellation. The example in Figure 2 is for a sixteen-point constellation, hence CAP-16. Sixteen permutations of a_n and b_n allow the transmitter to encode four bits per symbol. In general, $\log_2(M)$ bits per symbol are encoded.

After encoding, the subsequent modulation is then performed in such a way that two orthogonal signals are produced. These are then summed together before transmission. Upon reception, the orthogonality of the two summed modulated signals allows them to be separated, after which the a_n and b_n values can be estimated and the original encoded data symbol recovered. The last stage is to decode the symbol, A_n, in order to recover the block of binary digits that was transmitted.

The difference between a QAM and CAP system is how the two streams of amplitude-modulated impulses generated by the encoder are transformed into a pair of bandlimited, orthogonal, modulated signals in the transmitter and how the amplitudes of the original impulses are recovered in the receiver.

In the QAM transmitter, modulation is a two-stage process. The encoder output symbols are first low-pass filtered. This restricts the bandwidth of the signal to that of the transmission channel and, consequently, spreads the data impulses in the time domain (see Figure 3). The envelope of an individual symbol is the same as the impulse response of the filters. Therefore, they are often referred to as *pulse-shaping filters*. The baseband signal produced by the pulse-shaping filters is then multiplied by either the in-phase or quadrature phase carrier (i.e. a sine or a cosine wave). This produces a pair of orthogonal modulated signals, which are simply summed before transmission.

Carrierless Amplitude Phase Modulation

In a CAP modulator, the low-pass filtering and modulation are effectively combined into a single pair of filters,

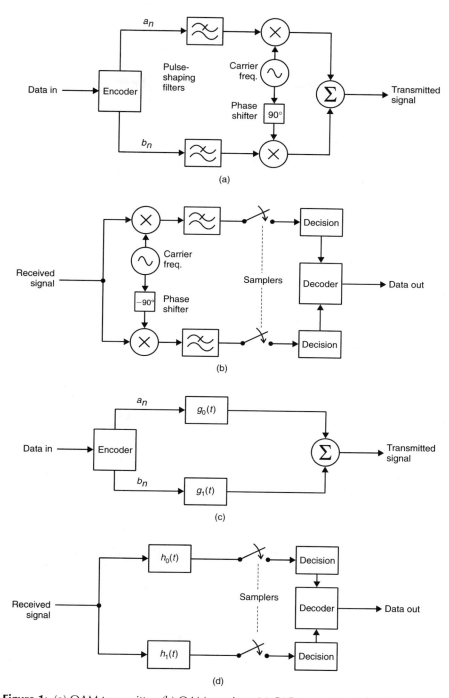

Figure 1: (a) QAM transmitter, (b) QAM receiver, (c) CAP transmitter, (d) CAP receiver

one for each channel. The filters are designed to be orthogonal and to have a bandpass response according to the requirements of the transmission channel. Usually, this is achieved by designing the two impulse responses to have the same amplitude envelope multiplied by either a cosine or a sine wave. Figure 4 shows the impulse responses of a pair of filters suitable for this purpose.

The bandpass responses of the filters means that the signals produced will already be centered at the required carrier frequency and will also be orthogonal. As no separate carrier frequency multiplication is required, this scheme is known as *carrierless amplitude phase modulation*.

It is clear that the design of the pair of filters determines the bandwidth that the modulated signal will occupy. This, in turn, is specified by the intended application. For example, a typical upstream ADSL channel may occupy the band of frequencies between 30 kHz and 160 kHz. In this case, the filters must be designed to have a center frequency of 95 kHz and a bandwidth of 130 kHz. This implies a maximum symbol rate of 130 kbaud,

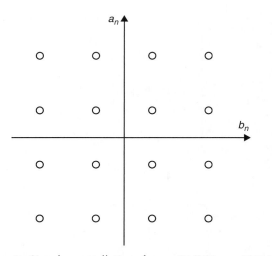

Figure 2: Signal constellation for a CAP-16 or QAM-16 encoder

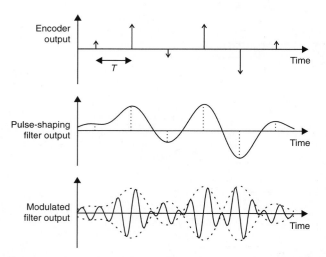

Figure 3: Example waveforms from one channel of a QAM modulator

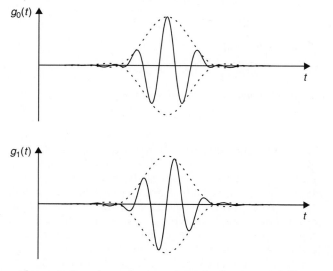

Figure 4: Impulse responses of a pair of orthogonal filters

although in practice an excess bandwidth of up to 100 percent is employed, giving typical symbol rates of between 65 kbaud and 100 kbaud. If CAP-16 is used, then each symbol would represent four bits, giving a data rate of between 260 kbits and 400 kbits per second.

In the 51.84 Mbps ATM LAN application described by Im et al. (1995), on the other hand, the band used is between 0 and 25.92 MHz, giving a center frequency of 12.96 MHz and a bandwidth of 25.92 MHz. In this system, the excess bandwidth is 100 percent, so the symbol rate is exactly half the bandwidth at 12.96 Mbaud. This particular system uses CAP-16 giving four bits per symbol and, therefore, the final data rate of 51.84 Mbps.

Carrierless Amplitude Phase Modulation versus Quadrature Amplitude Modulation

A reasonable question at this stage would be "Which is better—CAP or QAM?" The answer would be, "It depends on the implementation." A glance at Figure 1 would suggest that the CAP implementation is much simpler. It does, however, require precisely designed filters to ensure orthogonality. In practice, this is trivial in a software implementation using a pair of *finite impulse response* (FIR) filters but much more difficult in a hardware-only system. By contrast, the QAM architecture consists only of elements that are relatively straightforward to implement in hardware.

In terms of the fundamental limitations in performance, a CAP system can be considered identical to an equivalent QAM one. There are, however, practical differences that arise because of the differences in the receiver implementation. In particular, the effects of carrier frequency tracking and symbol timing synchronization are different in their nature.

IMPLEMENTATION
Transmitter Implementation

Referring to the block diagram in Figure 1, the transmitted signal can be written as:

$$s(t) = \sum_{n=-\infty}^{\infty} [a_n g_0(t - nT) + b_n g_1(t - nT)] \qquad (1)$$

where a_n and b_n are the real and imaginary parts of A_n, the nth encoded data symbol; T is the symbol period; and $g_0(t)$ and $g_1(t)$ are the impulse responses of the in-phase and quadrature phase filters, respectively. The design of these filters must fit the following specification:

- The bandwidths of the filters do not exceed the bandwidth of the transmission channel, and
- the impulse responses of the two filters are orthogonal with respect to one another—that is, $\int g_0(t)g_1(t)\, dt = 0$.

The reason for the first criterion is obvious; one job of the pulse-shaping filters is to restrict the bandwidth of the signal. The second criterion is required to ensure that the two components of each data symbol—a_n and b_n—can be separated in the receiver. In practice, satisfying these criteria is achieved by using filters that form a Hilbert pair (i.e., the Fourier transform of one is identical to that of the other, only rotated through a phase shift of 90 degrees). Usually, the form of the two filters will be

$$g_0(t) = w(t)\cos(2\pi f_c t) \text{ and } g_1(t) = w(t)\sin(2\pi f_c t) \quad (2)$$

where $w(t)$ is the amplitude window function common to both filters and f_c is the center frequency of the transmission channel. Provided that the center frequency is higher than the largest frequency component of the amplitude window, the cosine and sine functions ensure that the orthogonality condition is satisfied. They also allow the signal to be modulated to a specified center frequency, f_c. The window function, $w(t)$, is designed to shape the spectrum of the transmitted signal and restrict it to the specified bandwidth.

A commonly used family of amplitude windows is the *raised cosine form*, so named after the shape of their Fourier transform (Chen, Im, and Werner 1992). Such windows are favored because the spectrum is well confined to a predictable bandwidth without the requirement for filters with excessively long impulse responses. Figure 5 shows an example of a raised cosine window (a *von Hann window*) in the time and frequency domains. It can be seen that the spectral energy is well contained within the bandwidth, $2/T$ (i.e., 100 percent excess bandwidth in this case). In the time domain, $w(t)$ theoretically extends infinitely. In practice, however, the temporal side lobe levels decay quickly, and the response can be truncated without adversely affecting the frequency spectrum.

Square-root raised cosine filters are another popular choice. These have the advantage that the energy is spread a little more evenly in the frequency domain although higher side lobes in the time domain necessitate longer filter responses.

Receiver Implementation

When a CAP signal is received, it is processed by separate in-phase and quadrature phase filters with impulse responses of $h_0(t)$ and $h_1(t)$. To optimize the performance of the system against additive white Gaussian noise, one would expect these to be matched filters—that is, their impulse responses would be time-reversed versions of $g_0(t)$ and $g_1(t)$. In many cases, however, this is not used because it would result in an undesirable amount of *intersymbol interference* (ISI). As an example, Figure 6 shows the effect of using a matched filter for a raised cosine

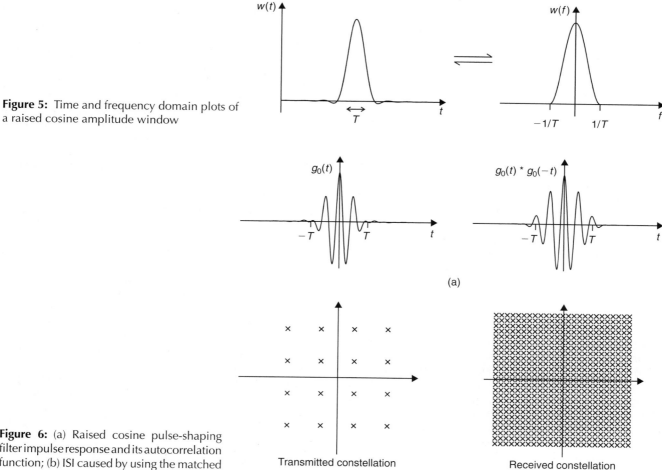

Figure 5: Time and frequency domain plots of a raised cosine amplitude window

Figure 6: (a) Raised cosine pulse-shaping filter impulse response and its autocorrelation function; (b) ISI caused by using the matched filter alone for a CAP-16 system

Transmitted constellation

Received constellation

(a)

(b)

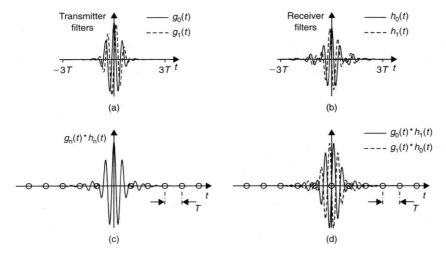

Figure 7: (a) Pair of raised cosine transmitter filter impulse responses, (b) their corresponding receiver filter responses, and (c and d) the convolution of the two. Circles indicate values that should be zero to ensure perfect reconstruction.

pulse-shaping filter with 100 percent excess bandwidth. Note that at delays of $\pm T$, the autocorrelation function of the filter response is a significant nonzero value. This translates into the ISI apparent in Figure 6a.

Ideally, the filters used in the receiver should be designed such that the following conditions are satisfied:

- $g_n(t)*h_n(t)$ is unity for zero time delay,
- $g_n(t)*h_n(t)$ is zero for time delays that are nonzero integer multiples of T, and
- $g_n(t)*h_{1-n}(t)$ is zero for all time delays that are integer multiples of T, including zero,

where $n = 0$ or 1 and * represents convolution.
An example of an appropriate pair of transmitter and receiver filter responses is shown in Figure 7.

Adaptive Filtering

Although it is possible to design appropriate receiver filter responses in advance that meet the criteria above, this is seldom done in practice mainly because the ISI caused by the transmitter filter is often insignificant when compared with the ISI caused by the response of the channel itself.

The channel response obviously will vary from application to application. In most cases, however, propagation through a communications channel can be modeled as

$$y(t) = \sum_m c_m s(t - \tau_m) + n(t) \qquad (3)$$

where $y(t)$ is the received signal, $s(t)$ is the transmitted signal, $n(t)$ is the additive noise or interference, and the coefficients c_m and τ_m correspond to the attenuation and the propagation loss of the mth discrete propagation path from source to receiver. The physical mechanism that causes multiple propagation paths depends on the application. For example, in a wireless system it will be the result of multiple reflections from scatterers near the propagation path. In a cabled system, however, it will result from reflections along the cable caused by scattering at impedance-mismatched junctions.

An alternative and more compact form of Equation 3 is:

$$y(t) = c(t) * s(t) + n(t) \qquad (4)$$

where $c(t)$ is the impulse response of the channel. Note that $c(t)$ can rarely be considered to be completely time-invariant. For example, when communicating via a cable the channel response will appear to be relatively constant but will, in fact, change slowly over time as environmental conditions evolve. In a mobile wireless communications scenario, by comparison, $c(t)$ will be continually varying over time as the relative positions of the transmitter, receiver, and scatterers change.

A nonideal channel impulse response causes ISI in just the same way as the transmission filter and its effects therefore can be cancelled (or at least suppressed) in the same way by designing an appropriate receiver filter. There are, however, two significant differences. First, the ISI caused by the channel can often have a much greater extent, affecting several symbols rather than just the immediate neighbors. Also, the channel response is not necessarily known in advance and may, in fact, vary with time. For the latter reason, adaptive filters (also known as *adaptive equalizers*) are generally employed for the two receiver filters. Figure 8 shows an example of a simulated channel response and the measures that an adaptive filter takes in order to correct (or equalize) it.

In fact, there are various adaptive filter designs that can be used to suppress ISI (Qureshi 1985). The simplest form is a linear feed-forward equalizer (as used in Figure 8), usually a finite impulse response filter whose tap weights are determined adaptively in order to minimize the difference between the input and output of the decision-making block. In applications with high signal-to-noise ratios, the response of the adaptive filter will iteratively converge toward the convolution of the ideal receiver, $h_n(t)$, and the band-limited inverse filter to the channel response. There are, however, problems with this approach. First, to perfectly equalize the channel response with a linear equalizer, long adaptive filter responses may be needed. The ideal inverse filter response will often be several times longer than the spread of the channel. Not only are long filters more

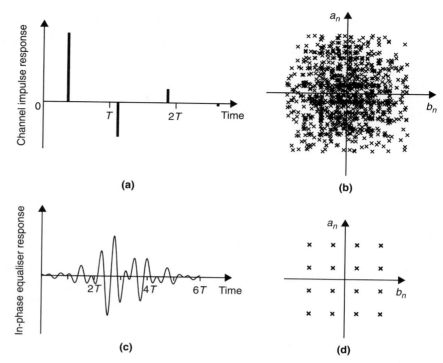

(a)

(b)

Figure 8: (a) Simple simulated channel response, (b) resulting received constellation, (c) required equalizing receiver filter response, and (d) effect on the equalized constellation (the transmission filter used is the same as in Figure 7)

(c)

(d)

computationally costly to implement but also they adapt more slowly. Second, if the channel response exhibits deep nulls in the frequency domain, then a linear equalizer will attempt to correct for this by introducing high gains at those frequencies. This can result in the ambient noise being amplified undesirably, giving no net improvement in the final error rate and perhaps even increasing it.

A more effective approach is often the use of a nonlinear equalizer, typically employing a decision feedback equalizer (Proakis 1995). A block diagram of a CAP receiver with decision feedback equalization is shown in Figure 9 (Zlatanovici et al. 1999).

The equalizer consists of two types of filters: feedforward and feedback. Effectively, the feedback filters take the decisions made for previous symbols, convolve them with an estimate of the channel response, and then subtract this from the input to the decision block. Both the in-phase and quadrature phase decisions must be fed back for each equalizer, resulting in four adaptive feedback filters in total. If the combined channel response and transmitter filter is minimum phase (i.e., there are no precursors to the main arrival), then the feedback filters alone can perfectly cancel out the ISI. This assumes that the filter length is at least as long as the spread of the channel

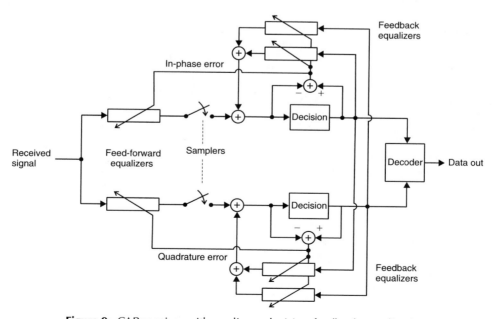

Figure 9: CAP receiver with nonlinear decision-feedback equalization

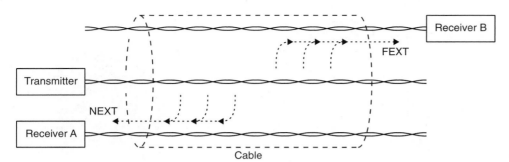

Figure 10: NEXT and FEXT interference sources

and that all the decisions are correct. Typically, the transmitter filter response is not minimum phase, so the feedforward filters are also needed to gather together the energy spread within one or two symbols from the current sample point. By incorporating feedback filters, the feedforward filters can usually be quite short, often no more than a few taps in length.

The tap weights of the filters are derived adaptively in an attempt to constantly minimize the error signal. Several adaptive algorithms exist for this purpose. The choice of algorithm typically is a compromise among rate of adaptation, steady-state error, and computational complexity. For applications with cable as the transmission medium, the propagation path is relatively stable. In such cases, a simple *least mean squares* (LMS) algorithm is sufficient. For more variable channels such as wireless, optical, or acoustic ones, however, a more rapidly adapting algorithm such as the *recursive least square* (RLS) can be more appropriate.

Cross Talk

Like any form of cabled transmission, CAP systems are vulnerable to interference sources sharing the same bandwidth. Cross talk is a particular type of interference caused by signals being coupled from other pairs of wire sharing the same cable. It is distinct from other forms of interference in that it is possible to suppress it using techniques other than simply improving the shielding of the cables. Figure 10 shows the sources of cross talk in a cable sharing several pairs of wires.

Two types of cross talk are illustrated in Figure 10: *near-end cross talk* (NEXT) and *far-end cross talk* (FEXT). NEXT is caused by a transmitter interfering with the reception of neighboring equipment at the same end of the cable. Receiver A is subject to NEXT from the transmitter in Figure 10. FEXT, on the other hand, is caused when a transmitted signal interferes with reception at the opposite

end of the cable as with receiver B in Figure 10. In general, as a consequence of the propagation loss along the length of the cable, NEXT is a much stronger source of interference than FEXT and is often the only one that is processed against. NEXT suppression can be achieved most easily when the source of the cross talk is employing the same modulation scheme as the desired signal to be received. This situation is sometimes known as *self-NEXT*. The two most common approaches to suppress NEXT are *NEXT cancellation* and *NEXT equalization*.

NEXT cancellation works by introducing an extra adaptive filter into the system as illustrated in Figure 11. The new filter attempts to simulate the NEXT propagation path from the transmitter, causing the interference to the receiver suffering from it. Adaptive filtering, driven by the receiver error signal, is used in a similar way as in a decision feedback equalizer. When the adaptive filter response converges toward the same transfer function as the NEXT path, the interference will be completely subtracted from the incoming signal. Note that the diagram in Figure 11 assumes that there is only one source of NEXT. This implies that the cable contains just two pairs of wires and that there is only one transmitter and one receiver at each end of the cable. If there are more NEXT sources, then extra cancellation filters are required.

NEXT equalization works using exactly the same adaptive equalization architecture already discussed. The only difference is that the receiver filters now have an extra constraint to satisfy, as explained below. If the impulse response of the transmission channel is denoted by $p_{TX}(t)$ and the impulse response of the NEXT interference path is denoted by $p_{NEXT}(t)$, then the receiver filters must satisfy the following criteria:

1. $g_n(t)*p_{TX}(t)*h_n(t)$ is unity for zero time delay,
2. $g_n(t)*p_{TX}(t)*h_n(t)$ is zero for time delays that are nonzero integer multiples of T,

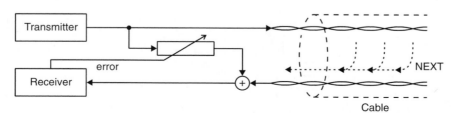

Figure 11: Simple NEXT canceller

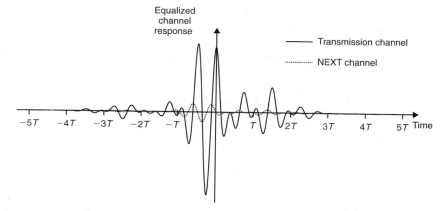

Figure 12: Convolution of the transmission filter and simulated channel impulse responses after NEXT equalization

3. $g_n(t)*p_{TX}(t)*h_{1-n}(t)$ is zero for all time delays that are integer multiples of T, and

4. $g_n(t)*p_{NEXT}(t)*h_n(t)$ and $g_n(t)*p_{NEXT}(t)*h_{1-n}(t)$ are zero for all time delays that are integer multiples of T where $n = 0$ or 1 in each case.

Note that the first three criteria are the requirements for successful operation with no cross talk. The forth criterion is the extra constraint. Figure 12 shows an example of the convolved impulse responses of the in-phase transmitter and receiver filters and simulated transmission and NEXT propagation channels. Note that the equalized responses are zero for all integer multiples of the symbol period, T, except for the transmission channel response, which is unity at zero time delay.

The extra constraint that the presence of NEXT imposes on the adaptive equalizer cannot be satisfied without cost. To successfully equalize both a transmission channel and a NEXT source, an extra degree of freedom is required in the shape of considerable excess bandwidth and a fractionally spaced linear equalizer (Petersen and Falconer 1991). In theory, an additional 100 percent excess bandwidth is required for each NEXT source to be equalized. In practice, systems rarely use more than 100 percent excess bandwidth in order to maintain bandwidth efficiency, in which case the receiver will automatically equalize the most dominant NEXT source. This situation can compare favorably against the additional requirements of several NEXT cancellers under the same circumstances. It has been observed (Im et al. 1995) that NEXT cancellation receivers, in general, do not operate reliably in a multiple interferer scenario.

TIMING AND SYNCHRONIZATION
Synchronization Requirements

As with any coherent communications system there is an exacting requirement for the receiver and transmitter clocks to be locked in terms of both their frequency and phase. In QAM systems, two oscillators must be synchronized: the carrier frequency for downconversion and the symbol-timing clock for sampling the data symbols (Franks 1980). In a CAP receiver, by comparison, there is no carrier frequency and only the symbol-timing clock must be synchronized. This does not necessarily make the

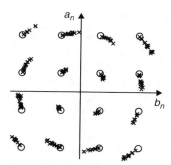

Figure 13: Effect of uncompensated 0.01 percent timing drift on 200 symbols in a CAP-16 system

task any simpler because the tolerance requirements are much more stringent in a CAP system than the symbol-clock tolerance limits in an equivalent QAM receiver. Figure 13 shows the effects of a 0.01 percent error in the receiver clock frequency of a CAP system of more than 200 symbols. In an equivalent QAM receiver, such an error in the symbol timing would be imperceptible. The effect observed in Figure 13 is broadly equivalent to an error in the downconvertor oscillator rather than the symbol timing. With CAP demodulation, a single clock effectively performs both tasks.

Note that the simulation used for Figure 13 did not incorporate any kind of timing compensation. In practice, the adaptive equalizer would constantly attempt to minimize the error and would partly compensate for the timing drift. This would lead to tap rotation whereby the coefficients of the feed-forward equalizers shift toward the left or the right in an attempt to counter the drifting clock. Eventually, the equalizers would fail as they would run out of taps, so it is essential that some form of external symbol-timing recovery processing is also used.

Synchronization Implementation

There are two main categories of algorithm and circuit used to recover the symbol timing from a coherently modulated received signal: *decision-directed* and *non-decision-directed*. These are also known as *data-aided* and *nondata-aided* systems in some texts. In a decision-directed system, the data outputs from the receiver are fed back and compared with the input to the decision block.

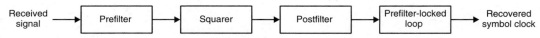

Figure 14: Simple symbol-timing recovery circuit

The phase difference between the two is measured and averaged over time by suitable filtering. Any nonzero average phase error can be interpreted as the receiver clock being slightly ahead or behind the transmitter clock and can be compensated appropriately. The detail of how this basic idea is achieved varies between systems but most are based on this fundamental idea.

A simpler method that has found favor in many CAP applications is a nondecision-directed approach. Nondecision-directed symbol-timing estimators generally try to extract the timing information completely independently from the rest of the receiver. They do this by attempting in some way to extract the cyclostationary statistics of the received signal and recover the cyclic frequency that will correspond to the symbol rate of the modulated data. A simple example of a nondecision-directed symbol timing recovery circuit is shown in Figure 14.

CAP signals exhibit *cyclostationarity* in that their variance is not constant over time but varies periodically with the symbol rate. The circuit in Figure 14 recovers this cyclic frequency by a relatively simple process. First, the signal is prefiltered, often by a matched filter, to optimize the noise performance of the estimator. Then a squarer is used to generate a stable tone at the symbol rate. After squaring, the signal will still contain unwanted artifacts caused by the data symbols. A postfilter in the form of a narrowband filter centered at the expected symbol rate extracts the exact symbol rate and suppresses the jitter caused by the variations of the data themselves.

Figure 15 shows the spectra of typical CAP signals as they are being processed by such an estimator. Note the spikes at frequencies of $\pm 1/T$ in the squarer output spectrum; this is the desired symbol timing frequency. Although it is clear to see these spikes on the spectrum, there is obviously also a large amount of "noise" at other frequencies that must be suppressed by the bandpass filtering provided by the postfilter. Finally, the phase-locked loop locks onto the symbol rate frequency and generates the sample clock to be used by the CAP demodulator.

There are numerous variations on this basic theme. In some cases, the squaring operation is replaced by a different nonlinear function (Proakis 1995); in others, the prefiltering is made slightly more elaborate in an attempt to reduce timing jitter. In particular, the use of two separate prefilters, both narrowband but centered at different frequencies $1/T$ apart, is a promising approach (Kim et al. 1998). Instead of a squarer, the outputs of the two filters are multiplied together before postfiltering. This has the advantage of reducing timing jitter and also reducing the oversampling requirements of the receiver signal processor.

Acquisition

The discussion of adaptive equalization, NEXT equalization, and synchronization all make the assumption that

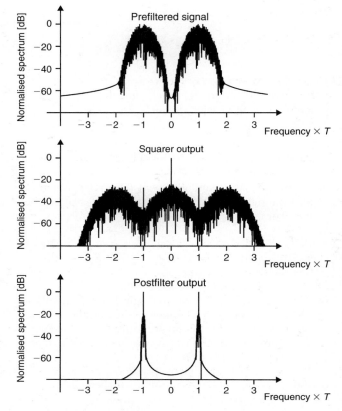

Figure 15: Prefiltered CAP signal, squarer output, and postfilter output

the receiver is already running and that the equalizer has already converged. In other words, the equalization and timing recovery sections of the receiver are operating in a tracking mode rather than an acquisition one. When the receiver is first switched on and connected, the adaptive filter coefficients will not equalize the channel because they have not had a chance to adapt to it. As a result, any initial amplitude and phase estimates made by the receiver will be erroneous because of the uncompensated ISI. This, in turn, will hinder the convergence of the equalizers and make the phase of the timing recovery circuit unreliable.

To allow the receiver to initialize successfully, preset training or synchronization sequences of data are usually inserted periodically into the transmission. On start-up, the receiver waits for a synchronization sequence that can be identified using correlation (or similar) processing. During the first and subsequent synchronization sequences, the equalizers can adapt based on the difference between the filter output and the known data symbols rather than the decoded estimates. This means that equalizer convergence is not hindered by the effects of noise

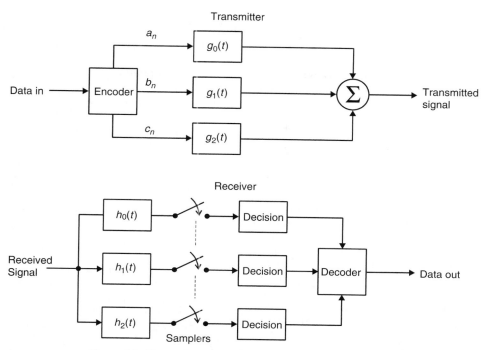

Figure 16: Three-dimensional CAP transmitter and receiver

caused by incorrect decisions. Furthermore, as the ISI and any NEXT interference are suppressed, the phase of the clock recovery circuit will become much more closely aligned with the correct transmitted phase. Depending on the nature of the channel response, adequate equalizer convergence can often be achieved after just a few tens of symbols so the overhead incurred by their occasional insertion into the transmission is not necessarily significant.

MULTIDIMENSIONAL CARRIERLESS AMPLITUDE PHASE MODULATION
Three-Dimensional Carrierless Amplitude Phase Modulation

For a CAP system to work, it is vital that the transmitter-receiver filter combinations satisfy the orthogonality (or "perfect reconstruction") criteria outlined earlier. It has been proposed that it is possible to synthesize sets of more than two filter pairs that satisfy this condition while retaining appropriate spectral constraints. Given that this is possible, one has the potential to build a multidimensional CAP system (Shalash and Parhi 1999). Figure 16 shows a block diagram of such a system.

Having three transmission filters means that there are now three streams of encoded data that can be transmitted simultaneously instead of two. In Figure 2, the constellation of a two-dimensional CAP system with four possible signal levels per channel (a or b) was shown. Four levels per channel equates to $4^2 = 16$ possible symbols. Using four levels per channel again in a three-dimensional CAP system gives us $4^3 = 64$ possible symbols (i.e., an increase from four to six bits per symbol). The signal constellation for this system is shown in Figure 17.

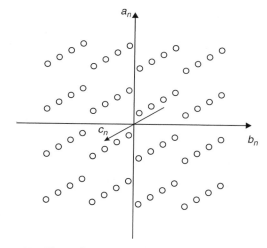

Figure 17: Three-dimensional CAP-64 signal constellation

For this system to work, the perfect reconstruction criteria must be satisfied. These were outlined earlier for conventional two-dimensional CAP. In a system of arbitrary dimension, D, the criteria may be rewritten as

$$r_{nm}(kT) = \begin{cases} \delta(k) & \text{if } n = m \\ 0 & \text{if } n \neq m \end{cases} \quad (5)$$

where $r_{nm}(\tau) = g_n(t)*h_m(t)$, $n = 0, 1, ..., (D-1)$, $m = 0, 1, ..., (D-1)$, k is any integer, and $\delta(k)$ is the Kronecker delta function.

There are several ways to satisfy the conditions of Equation 5. One is to specify the desired transmission filter amplitude response and then search for a set of responses that satisfy Equation 5 while approximating the desired spectral shape as closely as possible. The search is performed using a minimax optimization algorithm (Shalash and Parhi 1999).

Several flaws have been observed with this approach (Tang, Thng, and Li 2003). In particular, neglecting to constrain the spectral shape of the receiver filters can make this system highly noise-sensitive in a practical application. An alternative optimization method has been proposed by these authors whereby the constraint in Equation 5 is appended by the additional constraint

$$h_n(t) = g_n(-t) \qquad (6)$$

In other words, the receiver filters are matched filters for the corresponding transmission filter. The minimization condition is changed in this approach to merely state that the out-of-band spectral content of the filters should be zero; no constraints are placed on the in-band amplitude. Although one might think that the constraint in Equation 6 gives optimal noise performance, in practice the relaxation of the transmitter spectral shape specification means that highly nonuniform spectra can arise from this approach. As such, the use of matched filters only optimizes the noise performance given a particular waveform spectrum but does not necessarily give the best possible performance given the power and bandwidth available.

Although neither approach is entirely ideal, they both succeed in satisfying the condition of Equation 5 and therefore producing a set of filters that are suitable in theory for three-dimensional CAP. In fact, both approaches are also easily extensible to higher dimensions. Figure 18

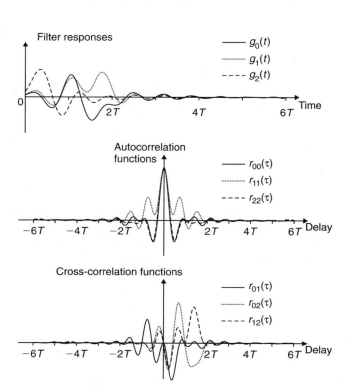

Figure 18: Set of filter responses for three-dimensional CAP (Tang, Thng, and Li 2003), their autocorrelation functions, and their cross-correlation functions

shows an example set of responses for a three-dimensional CAP transmitter (Tang, Thng, and Li 2003). Because the receiver filters are the same as the matched filters, their compliance with Equation 5 can be observed through their autocorrelation functions ($n = m$) and their cross-correlation functions ($n \neq m$). These are also shown in Figure 18. Note that they meet the constraints of Equation 5 by all being zero for time delays that are integer multiples of T except for the autocorrelation functions at zero delay, which are all unity.

Multidimensional CAP Advantages and Disadvantages

At first glance, one might conclude that adding extra dimensions gives the system extra throughput without the need for additional bandwidth or without compromising the noise performance. This is, however, not true; the increase in throughput does not come without cost. It has been observed by Tang, Thng, and Li (2003) that the most significant potential advantage of multidimensional CAP is the relative simplicity in terms of receiver implementation as compared with an equivalent two-dimensional CAP. It can be easier to implement several lower-rate equalizers in parallel rather than two higher-rate ones.

Published work on the subject (up to 2007) focuses on simulations rather than realistic practical experiments. Possible limitations of multidimensional CAP systems in practice have not been reported so far. It is felt that the constraints that the additional dimensions place on the adaptive equalizers will probably compromise their ability to equalize NEXT interference and may affect their performance in multipath environments. It is also likely that the synchronization tolerances required for reliable operation may become tighter for higher dimensions. The received energy from dimensions other than the one to which an equalizer is "tuned" appears between the symbol sampling instants. If the number of dimensions is increased, then the magnitude of this energy also increases and the potential interference that would leak through because of small timing or equalization errors becomes greater.

CONCLUSION

Carrierless amplitude phase modulation has found many uses in high data-rate digital communications and computer-networking systems. The transmitter and receiver architectures are particularly suited to modern digital signal processor-based systems. Although CAP has been largely superseded by discrete multitone systems in many ADSL systems, it is still used in many countries. It also finds use in ATM local area networks.

In many applications, CAP finds favor because of its high bandwidth efficiency and low implementation costs. Where it has been replaced by alternative technologies, this has often been the result of relatively poor performance of CAP against narrowband interference sources.

Recent advances in multidimensional CAP show theoretical promise in terms of further simplifying receiver operation in future systems. It is apparent, however, that researchers must address several technical issues before this becomes a realistic proposition.

GLOSSARY

Adaptive equalizer: An equalizer whose coefficients adapt in order to continually counter the effects of a time-varying channel response.

Asymmetrical digital subscriber line (ADSL): A popular method for providing broadband data services alongside voice communications using existing copper telephone cables.

Asynchronous transfer mode (ATM): A network and data-link layer protocol most commonly used in WAN applications.

Carrierless Amplitude Phase (CAP) modulation: A communications method used in computer networks.

Cross talk: Undesirable coupling of signals from one communications circuit to another.

Cyclostationarity: A characteristic of a signal whose statistical properties vary periodically with time.

Discrete multitone (DMT) modulation: Also known as *orthogonal frequency division multiplexing* (OFDM), a communications method used in some ADSL systems as an alternative to CAP.

Equalizer: A filter used to modify the frequency spectrum of a signal in order to remove or suppress the effects of the channel response.

Far-end cross talk (FEXT): Cross talk caused by signals coupling from a source located at the opposite end of a cable to the receiver.

Finite impulse response (FIR) filter: A digital filter realized by performing a weighted summation of the contents of a shift register. It is equivalent to the mathematical procedure of convolution with a sampled set of coefficients.

Integrated services digital network (ISDN): An early communications standard used to transmit both voice and data signals over standard copper telephone cables.

Intersymbol interference (IS): An undesirable source of interference whereby one symbol in a modulated data stream overlaps in time with neighboring symbols. It is generally caused by temporal smearing because of the effects of pulse-shaping filters or a nonideal propagation channel.

Least mean squares (LMS): An iterative optimization technique that attempts to minimize the mean square error of a system using a gradient descent algorithm.

Local area network (LAN): A geographically small computer network consisting of several interconnected machines usually located in the same building.

Near-end cross talk (NEXT): Cross talk caused by signals coupling from a source located at the same end of a cable as the receiver.

Quadrature amplitude modulation (QAM): A digital communications technique similar in principle to CAP but differing in the way it is implemented.

Recursive least squares (RLS): An iterative optimization technique used as an alternative to LMS. It generally exhibits faster convergence but higher steady state error than LMS.

Wide area network (WAN): A geographically large computer network consisting of several interconnected machines that may be located in different parts of the world.

CROSS REFERENCES

See *Frequency and Phase Modulation*; *Pulse Amplitude Modulation*; *Sources of Errors, Prevention, Detection, and Correction*.

REFERENCES

Chen, W. Y., G. H. Im, and J. J. Werner. 1992. Design of digital carrierless AM/PM transceivers. *AT&T/Bellcore Contribution* TlEl.4/92-149.

Franks, L. E. 1980. Carrier and bit synchronization in data communication: A tutorial review. *IEEE Transactions on Communications*, 28(8): 1107–20.

Im, G.-H., D. B. Harman, G. Huang, A. V. Mandzik, M.-H. Nguyen, and J.-J. Werner. 1995. 51.84 Mb/s 16-CAP ATM LAN Standard. *IEEE Journal on Selected Areas in Communications*, 13(4): 620–32.

Kim, K., Y. Song, B. Kim, and B. Kim. 1998. Symbol timing recovery using digital spectral line method for 16-CAP VDSL system. *Proceedings of IEEE Global Telecommunications Conference* (GLOBECOM), 6: 3467–72.

Paradyne Corporation. 2000. *The DSL sourcebook*. Largo, FL: Paradyne Corporation.

Petersen, B. R., and D. D. Falconer. 1991. Minimum mean square equalization in cyclostationary and stationary interference-analysis and subscriber line calculations. *IEEE Journal on Selected Areas in Communications*, 9(6): 931–40.

Proakis, J. G. 1995. *Digital communications*. New York: McGraw-Hill.

Qureshi, S. U. H. 1985. Adaptive equalization. *Proceedings of the IEEE*, 73(9): 1349–87.

Shalash, A. F., and K. K. Parhi. 1999. Multidimensional carrierless AM/PM Systems for digital subscriber loops. *IEEE Transactions on Communications*, 47(11): 1655–67.

Tang, X., I. L. J. Thng, and X. Li. 2003. A new digital approach to design 3-d CAP waveforms. *IEEE Transactions on Communications*, 51(1): 12–16.

Zlatanovici, R., A. Manolescu, L. Kabulepa, and M. Glesner. 1999. Decision feedback equalizers for carrierless amplitude/phase modulation receivers. *Semiconductor Conference, CAS '99 Proceedings*, 1, 127–30.

Minimum Shift Keying

Tao Jiang, *University of Michigan*

INTRODUCTION

In digital communication systems, a key technique is the *modulation scheme*, which maps the digital information into analog waveforms that match the characteristics of the channel. One of the important digital modulation schemes is *minimum shift keying* (MSK), which combines many attractive characteristics, including constant envelope, compact power spectrum, good error rate performance, simple demodulation, and easy synchronization. These features make MSK an excellent digital modulation technique that is suitable for digital links, in which the bandwidth must be conserved and that can utilize efficient transmitter design with nonlinear devices.

MSK was first developed in the late 1960s (Doelz, Heald, and Collins Radio Co. 1961; Buda 1972). Since then, it has been successfully used in many communication fields (Pasupathy 1979). Table 1 highlights notable dates in MSK history.

We begin with a description of MSK, including its mathematical representation and performance. Then we discuss how to realize the MSK modulator, in particular the transmitter and receiver design, as well as synchronization. Similar to MSK, we also discuss the basics and implementation issues for GMSK modulation. Finally, we review the latest development of MSK and GMSK, followed by a short conclusion.

MINIMUM SHIFT KEYING

In this section, we briefly review related modulation techniques such as frequency shift keying and continuous phase frequency shift keying. Then we introduce the mathematical model of MSK and compare its performance with other modulation schemes. Finally, we discuss how to implement the MSK modulation system.

Fundamentals

Mathematical Model

To introduce MSK, we first consider a simpler digital modulation scheme: *frequency shift keying* (FSK). Typically,

Table 1: Brief History of MSK Development

Date	Development
1972	MSK first used by Data Transmission Company (Sullivan 1972)
1972	MSK applied to domestic satellite system by AT&T (Brady 1972)
1977	Canadian communications technology satellite (Taylor et al. 1977)
1981	GMSK technique proposed (Murota and Hirade 1981)
1991	MSK applied to digital European cordless telecommunications (Feher 1991)
Since 1998	GMSK applied to global system for mobile (GSM) communications successfully. MSK and GMSK are attractive digital modulation concepts for B3G.

in one symbol duration, the FSK signal can be expressed as:

$$s_i(t) = \sqrt{\frac{2E_b}{T_b}} \cos(2\pi f_i t), \; i = 1, 2, \dots, M, \; 0 \le t \le T_b \quad (1)$$

where E_b is the energy per bit, T_b is the bit duration, f_i is the ith carrier frequency, and M is the total number of difference frequencies. Clearly, the waveforms of different carriers have the same energy, and the cross-correlation coefficient of two waveforms is

$$\rho_{km} = \frac{1}{T_b} \int_0^{T_b} \cos[2\pi(f_m - f_k)t] dt \quad (2)$$

If we define Δf as the frequency separation between successive carriers, we can get $f_m - f_k = (m - k)\Delta f$. Therefore

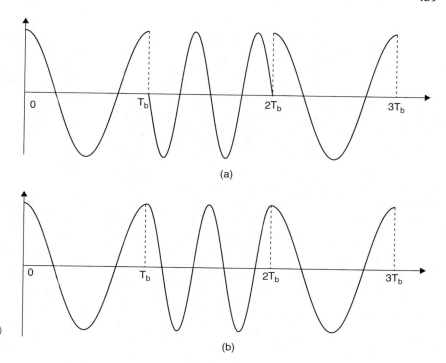

Figure 1: Comparison of (a) FSK with (b) CPFSK signal waveforms

$$\rho_{km} = \frac{1}{T_b} \int_0^{T_b} \cos[2\pi(m-k)\Delta ft]dt$$
$$= \frac{\sin[2\pi T_b(m-k)\Delta f]}{2\pi T_b(m-k)\Delta f} \tag{3}$$

We can see that $\rho_{km} = 0$ when $m \neq k$ and $\Delta f = 1/(2T_b)$. Because $|m - k|$ corresponds to adjacent frequency slots, $\Delta f = 1/(2T_b)$ represents the minimum frequency separation between adjacent frequencies that can guarantee the orthogonality of M possible waveforms (Proakis 1995). To transmit M possible waveforms, a simple solution is to utilize $M = 2^k$ separated oscillators tuned to the desired frequencies and to select one of the M frequencies according to the particular k bit symbol that is to be transmitted in a signal interval of duration kT_b. The output of such a simple system can be seen in Figure 1a, in which we can clearly observe that the phase of FSK signals is discontinuous. Because an FSK system switches abruptly from one oscillator output to another in successive signaling intervals, FSK signal has the relatively large spectral side lobes outside of the main spectral band of the signal, and consequently FSK modulation scheme requires a large frequency band. To resolve this problem, *continuous phase frequency shift keying* (CPFSK) modulation has been proposed, and the corresponding carrier-modulated signal over one bit duration can be expressed as

$$s_i(t) = \sqrt{\frac{2E_b}{T_b}} \cos(2\pi f_i t + \Theta_k) \tag{4}$$
$$i = 1, 2, \ldots, M, \quad kT_b \leq t \leq (k+1)T_b$$

where Θ_k is a continuous function of time and k is zero or a positive integer.

We consider the simplest form of CPFSK—the binary CPFSK—in which $M = 2$. According to Equation 4, the binary CPFSK can be written as

$$s_i(t) = \sqrt{\frac{2E_b}{T_b}} \cos[2\pi(f_c + s_k f_d)t + \Theta_k] \tag{5}$$
$$i = 1, 2, \quad kT_b \leq t \leq (k+1)T_b$$

with $f_c = (f_1 + f_2)/2$, $f_d = (f_1 - f_2)/2$, where $f_1 > f_2 > 0$ and $s_k = \pm 1$, depending on the input data. To keep continuous phase at time kT_b, $2\pi(f_c + s_{k-1}f_d)kT_b + \Theta_{k-1} = 2\pi(f_c + s_k f_d)kT_b + \Theta_k$ modulo 2π, which results in a recursive expression defining $\Theta_k = \Theta_{k-1} = 2\pi(s_{k-1} - s_k)f_d kT_b$ modulo 2π. Therefore, the variation of the phase over one bit duration can be written as

$$\Theta(t) = 2\pi s_k f_d t + \Theta_k \quad kT_b \leq t \leq (k+1)T_b \tag{6}$$

If we replace the f_d with $h/(2T_b)$, where h is known as the modulation index or deviation ratio, we have

$$\Theta(t) = \pi h s_k \frac{t}{T_b} + \Theta_k \quad kT_b \leq t \leq (k+1)T_b \tag{7}$$

Because $\Theta((k+1)T_b) - \Theta(kT_b) = \pi h s_k$, the phase is increased by πh when $s_k = +1$, and it is decreased by $-\pi h$ when $s_k = -1$. A CPFSK signal has been shown in Figure 1b; clearly, its phase is always continuous at the bit transition instants.

MSK is a special binary CPFSK with $h = \frac{1}{2}$ in Equation 7, and thus MSK signal can be written as

$$s(t) = \sqrt{\frac{2E_b}{T_b}} \cos\left[2\pi\left(f_c + \frac{s_k}{4T_b}\right)t + \Theta_k\right] \quad (8)$$

$$kT_b \le t \le (k+1)T_b$$

Obviously, the frequency separation of MSK is $\Delta f = f_2 - f_1 = 2f_d = 1/(2T_b)$, which is the minimum frequency separation that is necessary to ensure the orthogonality of the signal $s_1(t)$ and $s_2(t)$ over a signaling interval of length T_b. This explains why binary CPFSK with $h = \frac{1}{2}$ is called *minimum shift keying*.

Using trigonometric functions to expand Equation 8, we have

$$s(t) = \sqrt{\frac{2E_b}{T_b}} \begin{array}{l} \cos(2\pi f_c t)\cos\left(s_k \dfrac{\pi t}{2T_b} + \Theta_k\right) \\[2mm] -\sin(2\pi f_c t)\sin\left(s_k \dfrac{\pi t}{2T_b} + \Theta_k\right) \end{array} \quad (9)$$

Without loss of generality, we choose $\Theta_0 = 0$, which results in $\Theta_k = 0$ or π modulo 2π, because $\Theta_k = \Theta_{k-1} + k(s_{k-1} - s_k)\pi/2$. Therefore, the MSK signal can been rewritten as

$$s(t) = \sqrt{\frac{2E_b}{T_b}} \begin{array}{l} a_I(t)\cos\left(\dfrac{\pi t}{2T_b}\right)\cos(2\pi f_c t) \\[2mm] + a_Q(t)\sin\left(\dfrac{\pi t}{2T_b}\right)\sin(2\pi f_c t) \end{array} \quad (10)$$

where $a_I(t) = \cos(\Theta_k)$ and $a_Q(t) = -s_k \cdot \cos(\Theta_k)$.

Figure 2 shows various components of the MSK signal defined by Equation 10. Figure 2a shows the binary bit stream $\{a_k(t)\}$ to be sent, which has been broken into staggering of the I-component $\{a_I(t)\}$ and Q-component $\{a_Q(t)\}$ data streams, respectively. Figure 2b shows the sinusoidal shaped in-phase bit stream waveform of the $\{a_I(t)\}$ stream. Figure 2c shows the in-phase signal yielded by multiplying the waveform shown in Figure 2b with the in-phase carrier $\cos 2\pi f_c t$. Similarly, the sinusoidal shaped odd-bits stream and the quadrature signal are shown in Figure 2d and 2e, respectively. Finally, the MSK signal $s(t)$ is shown in Figure 2f, which is the sum of signals shown in Figure 2c and 2e. From Figure 2b and 2d, we can observe that at time kT_b ($k = 0, 1, \dots$), only one of the components (I component or Q component) is 1 while the other is zero. The orthogonality between I component and Q component simplifies detection algorithm, hence it can reduce power consumption in a mobile communication receiver.

If we define $m(t)$ as the sinusoidal pulse, namely,

$$m(t) = \begin{cases} \sin\left(\dfrac{\pi}{2T_b}t\right) & 0 \le t \le 2T_b \\[2mm] 0 & otherwise \end{cases} \quad (11)$$

We can rewrite Equation 10 as

$$s(t) = \sqrt{\frac{2E_b}{T_b}} \begin{array}{l} \displaystyle\sum_{n=-\infty}^{\infty} a_I(t) \cdot m(t - 2nT_b) \cdot \cos(2\pi f_c t) \\[2mm] + \displaystyle\sum_{n=-\infty}^{\infty} a_Q(t) \cdot m(t - 2nT_b - T_b) \cdot \sin(2\pi f_c t) \end{array} \quad (12)$$

where n is an integer. From Equations 10 or 12, it is clear that MSK can be interpreted as being composed of two quadrature data—$a_I(t)$ and $a_Q(t)$—in an *offset quadrature phase-shift keying* (OQPSK) modulation (Pasupathy 1979) or *staggered quadrature phase shift keying* (SQPSK) (John 1998) signaling system. The *in-phase stream* $a_I(t)$ and the *quadrature stream* $a_Q(t)$ are weighted by sinusoidal functions before modulating the carrier. Consequently, MSK is also a constant amplitude and frequency modulated signal. However, in contrast to pure OQPSK, $a_I(t)$ and $a_Q(t)$ of MSK signal are dependent on each other.

Figure 3 shows the difference between OQPSK and MSK waveforms when an input bit stream is [1 1 0 0 0 1 1 1]. Clearly, MSK signal has continuous phase, and its phase transition is a type of continuous linear phase shift. Figure 3b shows the OQPSK waveform undergoing a phase shift of $\pm\pi/2$ and its offset of T_b between I component and Q component helps to avoid π phase shift.

It is instructive to sketch the set of phase trajectories $\{\Theta_k\}$ generated by all possible values of the input bit stream $\{a_k\}$. For example, in the case of MSK with binary bits $a_k = 0, 1$, the set of phase trajectories beginning at time $t = 0$ is shown in Figure 4. All of these possible phase diagrams are called a *phase tree*. When the phase tree is reduced modulo 2π, it is called a *phase trellis* (Gulak and Shwedyk 1986). Figure 5 shows an example of a phase trellis for MSK signal, where a phase shift of $+90$ degrees represents a data bit 1 being transmitted and a phase shift of -90 degrees represents a bit 0 being transmitted. From these figures, clearly we can find that the phase at nT_b (n is positive integer) takes a set of discrete values, and over the interval of each bit the phase of the MSK waveform is advanced or retarded by exactly 90 degrees. Therefore, the peak-to-peak frequency shift of the MSK signal equals to its one-half of the bit rate.

Performance

Power spectral density (PSD) is a common characteristic used to compare the bandwidth of communication signals. The unfiltered PSD of a MSK signal can be been accurately expressed as (Pasupathy 1979; Morais and Feher 1979)

$$G_{MSK}(f) = \frac{16P_c T_b}{\pi^2}\left(\frac{\cos 2\pi f T_b}{1 - 16f^2 T_b^2}\right)^2 \quad (13)$$

where P_c is the power of the modulated waveform, T_b is the bit duration, and f is the frequency offset of the carrier. For comparison, here we also write out the PSD of OQPSK signal:

$$G_{OQPSK}(f) = 2P_c T_b\left[\frac{\sin 2\pi f T_b}{2\pi f T_b}\right]^2 \quad (14)$$

Obviously, $G_{MSK}(f)$ and $G_{OQPSK}(f)$ are different as shown in Figure 6. It is clear to note that the width of the main lobe of the MSK spectrum is 1.5 times larger than that of the OQPSK spectrum. However, side lobes in MSK fall off faster, which makes MSK more bandwidth efficient.

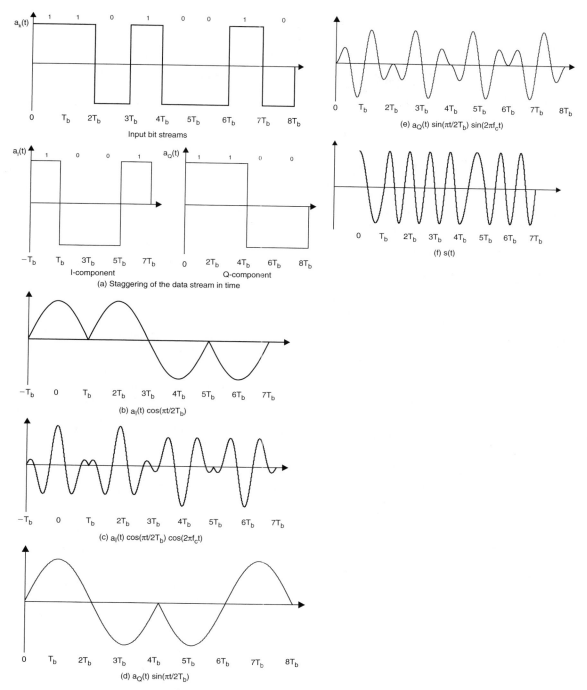

Figure 2: Processing of the composite MSK signal

Another measure of the compactness of a modulation spectrum is bandwidth B, which contains 99 percent of the total power. For MSK, $B \cong 1.2/T_b$; and for OQPSK, $B \cong 8/T_b$ (Gronemeyer and McBride 1976). This indicates that MSK may be spectrally more efficient than OQPSK in wideband links. However, as shown in Figure 6, the MSK spectrum has a wider main lobe than that of OQPSK, which suggests that in narrowband links MSK may not be the preferred modulation scheme. However, with the right filtering in narrowband links, bandwidth efficiency

of MSK can be the same as that of OQPSK (Morais and Feher 1979).

Furthermore, the performance of MSK modem can be generally quantified by measurement of the bit error rate. Simon and Wang have compared the error probability of differential demodulation of MSK to that of limiter discriminator demodulation in *additive white Gaussian noise* (AWGN) and in partial-band noise jamming (Simon and Wang 1983). Masamura and Mason have analyzed the theoretical and experimental validation for differential

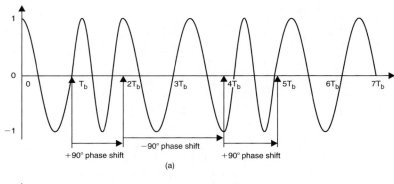

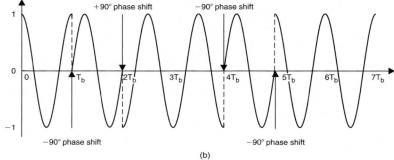

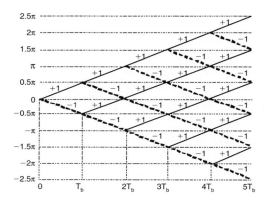

Figure 4: The phase tree of MSK

Figure 3: Comparison of (a) MSK and (b) OQPSK signal waveforms

demodulation of MSK with nonredundant error correction (Masamura et al. 1979; Mason 1987).

In an AWGN channel, the optimum receiver for coherent MSK, which uses correlation demodulation or matched filter demodulation, yields the same BER as that of coherent FSK:

$$P_e \cong Q\left(\sqrt{\frac{2E_b}{N_0}}\right) \tag{15}$$

where P_e is the probability of bit error, $N_0/2$ is the PSD of the AWGN channel, and $Q(t) = \frac{1}{\sqrt{2\pi}} \int_t^\infty e^{\frac{r^2}{2}} d\tau$. For non-coherent MSK, the optimum receiver for MSK yields the

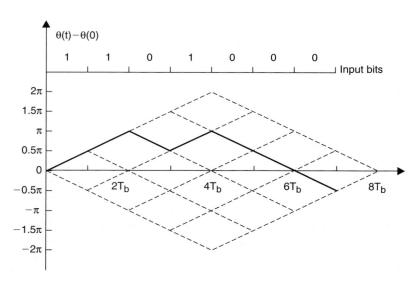

Figure 5: An example of the MSK phase trellis (the solid line is the phase trajectory path)

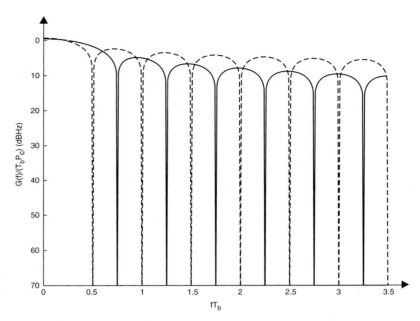

Figure 6: Power spectral density of MSK and OQPSK (the solid curve corresponds to MSK, and the dashed curve corresponds to OQPSK)

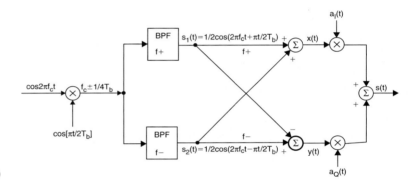

Figure 7: Basic MSK modulator (Pasupathy 1979)

same P_e as that of the noncoherent FSK over the AWGN channel:

$$P_e \cong \frac{1}{2} e^{\left(\frac{1}{2}\frac{E_b}{N_0}\right)} \qquad (16)$$

Implementation

Transmitter

Ziemer and Ryan examined some methods of implementation of MSK for high data-rate applications (Ziemer and Ryan 1983). A typical MSK modulator is shown in Figure 7 (Taylor et al. 1977; Fielding, Berger, and Lochhead 1977; Pasupathy 1979). The multiplier produces two-phase coherent signals at the frequencies $f_+ = f_c + 1/(4T_b)$ ($s_k = +1$) and $f_- = f_c - 1/(4T_b)$ ($s_k = -1$). The biggest advantage of forming *binary frequency shift keying* (BFSK) signals by this method is that the signal coherence and the deviation ratio are largely unaffected by variations in the data rate (Taylor et al. 1977; Pasupathy 1979). The BFSK signals, after being separated by means of *narrow-band pass filters* (NBPF), are combined to form the corresponding I component and Q component. These carriers are then multiplied with the odd and even bit streams

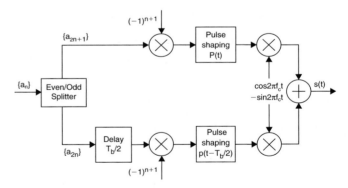

Figure 8: Precoded MSK transmitter

$a_I(t)$ and $a_Q(t)$ with T_b offset to produce the MSK-modulated signal $s(t)$ as defined in Equation 10.

As a special modulator, the precoded MSK transmitter is a combined differential decoder with MSK modulator as shown in Figure 8 (Simon, Hinedi, and Lindsey 1995). A compensating differential decoder should be needed following I-component and Q-component demodulation and detection at the receiver when a differential encoder is used in a conventional MSK modulator. Such a

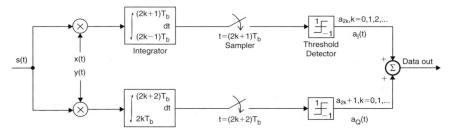

Figure 9: Basic MSK receiver (Pasupathy 1979)

combination of differential encoding at the transmitter and differential decoding at the receiver results in a loss in power perf ormance relative to that obtained by conventional MSK. However, the precoded MSK does not need a differential decoder at the receiver. Therefore, precoded MSK has an improvement in power performance with the same identical spectral as the conventional MSK.

Receiver

A typical MSK receiver is shown in Figure 9. The received signal $s(t)$ is multiplied by the in-phase carrier $x(t)$ and quadrature carrier $y(t)$; they are then followed by the integrate and dump circuits, respectively. The multiplier integrator constitutes the correlation detection, which is an optimum coherent detection operation for a signal in white Gaussian noise without any *intersymbol interference* (ISI). Note that the integration interval is $2T_b$. When $s(t)$ is multiplied by $x(t) = \cos(\pi t/2T_b)\cos(2\pi f_c t)$, the low-frequency component equals $a_I(t)(1 + \cos \pi t/T_b)/4$. Hence, the polarity of the sampler output determines the value of $a_I(t)$. Similarly, the operation on the quadrature channel determines the value of $a_Q(t)$.

Synchronization

Imperfect phase and timing nonsynchronization degrade the MSK signal performance. *Synchronization* is the coordination of occurrences to operate in unison with respect to time and carriers. Figure 10 shows the basic MSK synchronization recovery circuit. The clock signal at one-half of the bit rate is recovered from $s(t)$ and the reference waveforms $x(t)$ and $y(t)$. Although the MSK signal $s(t)$ has no discrete components that can be used for synchronization, it produces strong discrete spectral components at $2f_c + 1(2T_b)$ and $2f_c - 1(2T_b)$ after passing

through a *squarer*. This squarer can be defined as squaring both sides of Equation 8—namely,

$$
\begin{aligned}
s^2(t) &= \cos^2\left[2\pi f_c t + \frac{s_k \pi}{2T_b} + \Theta_k\right] \\
&= \frac{1}{2} + \frac{1}{2}\cos\left[4\pi f_c t + \frac{s_k \pi}{T_b}t + 2\Theta_k\right]
\end{aligned}
\tag{17}
$$

Note that $2\Theta_k$ becomes either 0 or 2π and therefore drops out. In effect, this squarer doubles the modulation index and produces an FSK signal with $\Delta f = 1/T_b$, which is known as *Sunde's FSK* (Bennett and Rice 1963), and its phase of each tone is a constant. This means that we can lock to each of these tones with a *phase-locked loop* (PLL) and divide each output frequency by two, then produce a pair of reference signals $s_1(t) = \frac{1}{2}\cos[2\pi f_c t + \pi t/(2T_b)]$ and $s_2(t) = \frac{1}{2}\cos[2\pi f_c t - \pi t/(2T_b)]$. Consequently, we can get the sum and difference of the reference signals $s_1(t)$ and $s_2(t)$, respectively:

$$
\begin{aligned}
s_1 + s_2 &= \frac{1}{2}\cos\left(2\pi f_c t + \frac{\pi t}{2T_b}\right) + \frac{1}{2}\cos\left(2\pi f_c t - \frac{\pi t}{2T_b}\right) \\
&= \cos\left(\frac{\pi t}{2T_b}\right)\cos(2\pi f_c t) = x(t)
\end{aligned}
\tag{18}
$$

$$
\begin{aligned}
s_1 - s_2 &= \frac{1}{2}\cos\left(2\pi f_c t + \frac{\pi t}{2T_b}\right) - \frac{1}{2}\cos\left(2\pi f_c t - \frac{\pi t}{2T_b}\right) \\
&= \sin\left(\frac{\pi t}{2T_b}\right)\sin(2\pi f_c t) = y(t)
\end{aligned}
\tag{19}
$$

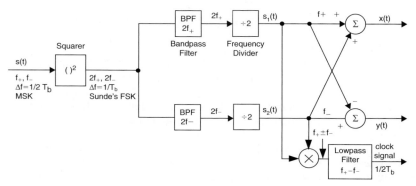

Figure 10: Basic MSK synchronization recovery (Pasupathy 1979)

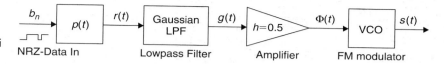

Figure 11: GSK modulator structure (Borowski and Feher 1995)

Equations 18 and 19 show that the reference carriers of $x(t)$ and $y(t)$ can be obtained from $s_1 + s_2$ and $s_1 - s_2$, respectively. To obtain a clock reference signal, the signal $s_1(t)s_2(t) = \frac{1}{4}\cos\left(2\pi f_c t + \frac{\pi}{2T_b}t\right)\cos\left(2\pi f_c t - \frac{\pi}{2T_b}t\right) = \frac{1}{8}$

$\left[\cos(4\pi f_c t) + \cos\left(\frac{\pi}{T_b}t\right)\right]$ goes through a PLL designed to

run a frequency of $1/(2T_b)$. Therefore, the resultant signal is proportional to $\sin(\pi t/T_b)$, which is the desired timing waveform. This is the reason why the MSK modulation format lends itself to easy self-synchronization.

Summary for MSK

MSK has some excellent properties that make it an attractive alternative when high bandwidth efficiency is required. These characteristics are summarized as follows:

1. MSK is a special type of CPFSK with a frequency deviation equal to one-half of the bit rate, and its modulus envelope is a constant. The continuous phase nature of MSK makes it highly desirable for high-power transmitters driving highly reactive loads.
2. MSK can also be viewed as a form of OQPSK signaling with the Q component delayed by one bit period in which the symbol pulse is a half-cycle sinusoid rather than the usual rectangular form.
3. The phase of the radio frequency carrier at the bit transition instants is continuous. Therefore, MSK can be demodulated with simple synchronization circuits.
4. In wideband communication links, MSK is spectrally more efficient than OQPSK. In narrowband links, it is preferred because of its wider main lobe.

GAUSSIAN MINIMUM SHIFT KEYING

Gaussian minimum shift keying (GMSK) is a frequency modulation scheme that has been widely applied in some of the most prominent communication standards around the world. GMSK improves the spectral efficiency of MSK by using a Gaussian-shaped impulse response filter.

Fundamentals

Mathematical Model

As mentioned in the previous section, MSK modulation has some good properties such as a constant envelope. However, the spectrum of MSK is too loose, and MSK does not satisfy some requirements with respect to out-of-band radiation for some mobile radio (Murota and Hirade 1981). To make the MSK output power spectrum more compact, we can select a *low-pass filter* (LPF) to meet the following conditions: (1) narrow bandwidth and sharp cutoff to suppress high-frequency components, (2) small

overshoot impulse response to prevent excess deviation of the instantaneous frequency, and (3) preservation of an integrated filter output pulse capable of accommodating a 90-degree phase shift to ensure coherent demodulation. A premodulation Gaussian LPF, which satisfies the above requirements, is adopted for GMSK modulation in which the data sequence is passed through a Gaussian LPF filter, and the output of the filter is MSK-modulated (Murota and Hirade 1981).

Figure 11 shows the block diagram of the structure of a GMSK *voltage-controlled oscillator* (VCO) modulator. If the Gaussian filter is left out, one obtains the modulator structure of MSK. First, an antipodal *non-return-to-zero* (NRZ) sequence $b_n \in (-1, 1)$ is converted to a stream of rectangular pulses $r(t) = \sum_n b_n \cdot p(t - nT_b)$, where T_b is the symbol interval. $p(t) = 1$ when $t \in (0, T_b)$, otherwise $p(t) = 1$.

The next operation is to generate the filtered pulse stream

$$g(t) = r(t) * h(t) \tag{20}$$

where $h(t)$ is the impulse response of the Gaussian filter.

Then the phase $\Phi(t)$ of the carrier wave frequency can be obtained by $\Phi(t) = 2\pi f_c \cdot t + 2\pi f_m \cdot \int_0^t g(\tau)d\tau$ around a carrier frequency f_c, where f_m is the peak frequency deviation and the phase is normalized to 0 at $t = 0$. Therefore, the instantaneous frequency of the modulated signal will be $f(t) = \frac{1}{2\pi}\frac{d\Phi}{dt} = f_c + f_m \cdot g(t)$. It is clear that the modulated GMSK carrier is determined by f_m, and f_m is determined by the bit rate, just like the MSK signal $f_m = 1/(4T_b)$ (Linz and Hendrickson 1996; Pasupathy 1979).

Finally, a VCO or equivalent digital synthesis method can produce the GMSK signal $s(t) = \cos[\Phi(t)]$. Consequently, the GMSK signal can be written as

$$s(t) = \sqrt{\frac{2E_b}{T_b}}\cos(2\pi f_c t)\cos\left\{2\pi f_m \cdot \left[\int_0^t g(\tau)d\tau\right]\right\}$$
$$- \sqrt{\frac{2E_b}{T_b}}\sin(2\pi f_c t)\sin\left\{2\pi f_m \cdot \left[\int_0^t g(\tau)d\tau\right]\right\} \tag{21}$$

For GMSK, $h(t)$ is a key parameter, and its Fourier transform pair (Adachi and Ohno 1988) is

$$H(f) = e^{-\alpha^2 f^2} \tag{22}$$

$$h(t) = \frac{\sqrt{\pi}}{\alpha}e^{\frac{\pi^2}{\alpha^3}t^2} \tag{23}$$

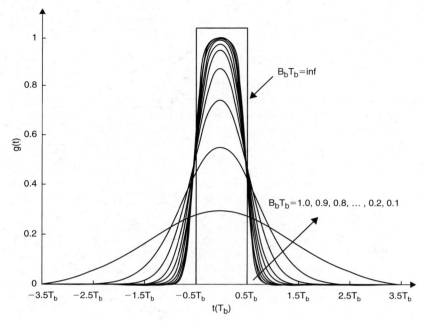

Figure 12: Shapes of $g(t)$ with different B_bT_b

The term α is defined as (Linz and Hendrickson 1996)

$$\alpha = \frac{\ln(2)}{2(B_bT_b \cdot 2\pi f_b)^2} \tag{24}$$

where $B_b = B_{3dB}$ and B_{3dB} is 3-dB bandwidth, $f_b = 1/T_b$. Consequently, the typical pulse response $g(t)$ can be written as

$$g(t) = \left\{ Q\left[2\pi B_b \frac{t - T_b}{\sqrt{\ln 2}} \right] - Q\left[2\pi B_b \frac{t + T_b}{\sqrt{\ln 2}} \right] \right\} \tag{25}$$

where $Q(t) = \frac{1}{\sqrt{2\pi}} \int_t^\infty e^{-\frac{\tau^2}{2}} d\tau$.

B_bT_b is a common design parameter of the GMSK modulator. Figure 12 shows different shapes of $g(t)$ with different B_bT_b. When $B_bT_b = \inf$, the GMSK is the same as the MSK.

Figure 13 shows a GMSK signal with $B_bT_b = 0.2$. It is clear that Gaussian filtered pulses overlap each other, giving rise to ISI (Diana and Tien 2001). Therefore, GMSK has a more compact spectrum than MSK. However, the GMSK has the more available frequency spectrum as a cost of increased ISI (Grellier and Comon 1998; Huang, Fan, and Huang 2000). Large ISI allows the spectrum to be more compact, but it also makes the demodulation more difficult.

An *eye diagram* is a simple and convenient tool for studying the effects of ISI for GMSK modulation as shown in Figure 14. The effect of ISI is a reduction of the eye opening and an increase in the number of paths in the eye diagram. The eye of the instantaneous frequency is relatively poorer in comparison to the I component and the Q component. This indicates that extracting modulation information from the instantaneous frequency would

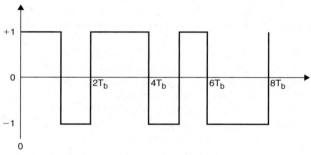

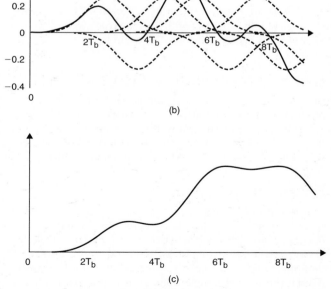

Figure 13: Processing of the composite GMSK signal with $B_bT_b = 0.2$—(a) input bit stream, (b) output filtered pulse (solid curve; the dashed curve corresponds to the filtered pulse for every bit), and (c) continuous phase

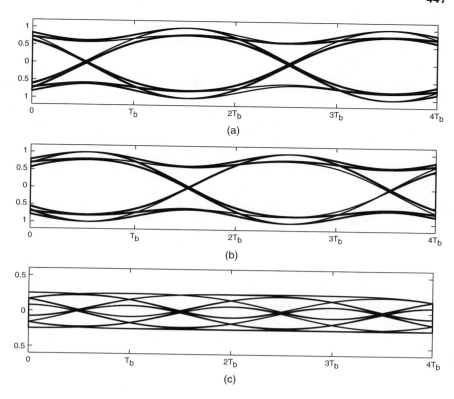

(a)

(b)

(c)

Figure 14: Eye diagrams of GMSK with $B_bT_b = 0.25$—(a) and eye diagram of the I component; (b) eye diagram of the Q component; (c) eye diagram of instantaneous frequency

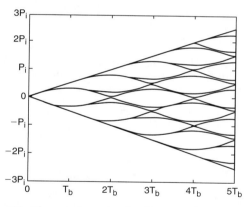

Figure 15: Phase trajectories for GMSK with $B_bT_b = 0.25$

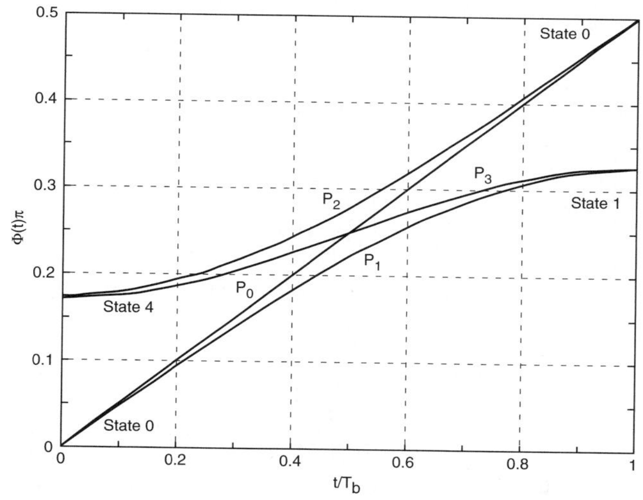

Figure 16: Four possible basic paths in the GMSK phase trajectories

yield rather poor performance, and high B_bT_b trades the spectral efficiency with the lower the level of ISI.

It is known that the phase transition of MSK is linearity in every bit duration. However, the phase transition of GMSK is nonlinearity. We call curves of phase transition *phase trajectories* as shown in Figure 15. A Gaussian premodulation filter smoothes the phase trajectory of the MSK signal to limit instantaneous frequency variations, which results in a GMSK signal with a much narrower bandwidth. Further, one fundamental concept in Laurent's work states that any phase modulator can be approximated using a set of amplitude modulators, where the phase-shaping filter of the phase modulator is replaced by an equivalent set of filters for the amplitude modulators. For GMSK, the first filter is the most significant pulse, and more than 99 percent of the energy is contained in it. Hence, GMSK can be well approximated

by only using the first term of the Laurent expansion (Laurent 1986).

In fact, for GMSK signals, all state transition paths in the phase trajectories can be generated from four basic paths; these are labeled P_0 to P_3 in Figure 16 (Hellosoft 2002).

Performance

Figure 17 displays the output-normalized spectra of GMSK signals versus the normalized frequency difference from the carrier center frequency with different B_bT_b. As B_bT_b decreases, the side-lobe levels fall off rapidly, causing an increase in bandwidth efficiency, which

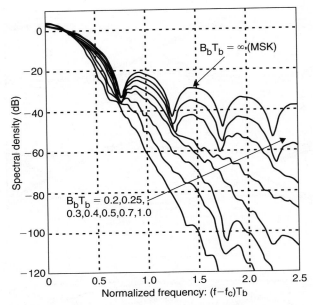

Figure 17: Power spectral density of GMSK (Murota and Hirade 1981)

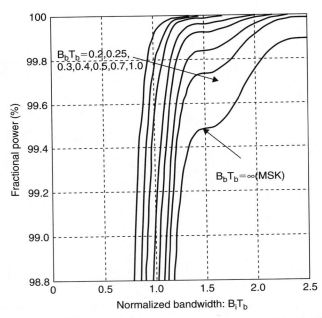

Figure 18: Fractional power ratio of GMSK (Murota and Hirade 1981)

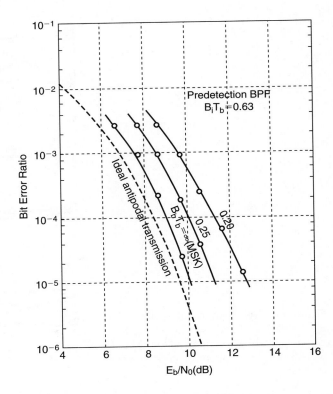

Figure 19: Static BER performance (Murota and Hirade 1981)

means that small $B_b T_b$ are desirable to achieve good spectral efficiency.

Figure 18 shows the fractional power ratio of GMSK versus the normalized bandwidth. For GMS, when $B_b T_b = 0.25$ and 0.5, 99.0 percent of the signal powers are contained in a bandwidth of $0.86/T_b$ and $1.04/T_b$, respectively. When $B_b T_b = 1.0$, the graph yields a wider spectrum, indicating a loss in power efficiency (Mandayam 2005).

Similar to MSK, the performance of GMSK modem can be generally quantified by measurement of BER. The static BER performance in the nonfading environment can be approximated as (Murota and Hirade 1981)

$$P_e \cong Q\left(\sqrt{\frac{2\alpha E_b}{N_0}}\right) \qquad (26)$$

where $Q(t) = \dfrac{1}{\sqrt{2\pi}} \int\limits_{t}^{\infty} e^{-\frac{\tau^2}{2}} d\tau$ and α has been defined in Equation 24. Compared to MSK, it is clear that $p_e^{GMSK} > P_e^{MSK}$. This arises from the trade-off between power and bandwidth efficiency: GMSK can achieve better bandwidth efficiency than MSK at the cost of power efficiency.

Figure 19 shows experimental results for static BER performance in the nonfading channel, where the normalized 3-dB down bandwidth $B_i T_b$ of the predetection Gaussian NBPF is a nearly optimal 0.63. When $B_b T_b$ is greater than 0.63, the degradation caused by premodulation filtering remains mild (Ishizuka and Yasuda 1984).

For high SNR, the BER of a GMSK signal transmitted in an AWGN channel is approximated as (Asano and Pasupathy 2002)

$$P_e = \frac{1}{2} erfc\left(\sqrt{\frac{d_{min}^2 E_b}{2N_0}}\right) \qquad (27)$$

where $erfc(x) = \dfrac{2}{\sqrt{\pi}} \int\limits_{x}^{\infty} e^{-t^2} dt$ and d_{min} is the normalized minimum Euclidean distance. For GMSK modulation, the approximate maximum of d_{min} is $\sqrt{2}$, which corresponds to the performance of optimal antipodal signaling (Murota and Hirade 1981).

However, when the modulated GMSK signals transmitted in a quasi stationary slow Rayleigh fading channel, the dynamic BER can be approximated as (Murota and Hirade 1981)

$$P_e(\Gamma) \cong \frac{1}{2}\left(1 - \sqrt{\frac{\alpha\Gamma}{\alpha\Gamma+1}}\right) \cong \frac{1}{4\alpha\Gamma} \qquad (28)$$

where Γ is the average SNR.

Implementation

Transmitter
Some existing methods can implement GMSK modulation for high data rate applications as follows:

1. The first method is to select the frequency deviation of CPFSK and make it the minimum possible and then filter the baseband modulating signal with a Gaussian filter (Linz and Hendrickson 1996). Therefore, it requires that the modulation index of the VCO exactly equal 0.5. However, the modulation index of the conventional VCO-based transmitter drifts over time and temperature, so it is hard to keep the center frequency within the allowable value under the restriction of maintaining the linearity and the sensitivity for the required frequency modulation (Murota and Hirade 1981).

2. Another attractive method is a *polar modulator*, and its principal design issue is the need for precise matching of the amplitude and phase delays through the feedback loops (McCune and Sander 2003). A polar modulator architecture has been proposed to avoid the external radio frequency filters that would likely be necessary with other transmitter topologies and for compatibility with existing *global system for mobile* (GSM) communications transmitters for an efficient dual-mode solution (Sander, Schell, and Sander 2003). Meanwhile, a system-level analysis of a polar modulator for GMSK reveals that inadequate bandwidths in the phase modulation and amplitude modulation paths result in spectral regrowth, which can violate the transmit mask requirement as imposed by the standard (Elliott et al. 2004).

3. The third method is to employ a quadrature baseband process followed by a quadrature modulator (Ishizuka and Hirande 1980). With this implementation, the modulation index must be maintained at exactly 0.5.

A typical PLL GMSK modulator is shown in Figure 20; a $\pi/2$-shift BPSK modulator is followed by a suitable PLL phase smoother. The transfer characteristics of this modulator can ensure that the output power spectrum satisfies the required condition (Murota and Hirade 1981).

Receiver
Similar to MSK, a GMSK signal also can be demodulated either differentially or coherently depending on the performance and complexity requirements. For an orthogonal coherent detector, it is difficult to recover the reference carrier and the timing clock. The most typical method is *de Buda's modulator* (De Buda 1972) as shown in Figure 21. In this demodulator, the reference carrier is recovered by dividing by four the sum of the two discrete frequencies contained in the frequency doubler output; the timing clock is directly recovered by their difference.

Coherent demodulation is common in GMSK systems (e.g., the GSM). It requires knowledge of the reference phase or exact phase recovery, local oscillators, and the PLL and carrier recovery circuits. Thus, the complexity and cost of the demodulator will be increased. Coherent demodulation is also required to facilitate linear equalization, which is necessary to compensate ISI caused by the multipath effect and the premodulation and predetection filtering (Laster 1997). The performance of coherent demodulation may degrade in fading channels because of imperfect tracking of the received signal phase.

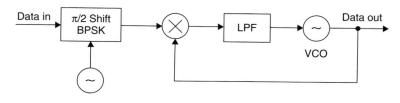

Figure 20: PLL-type GMSK modulator

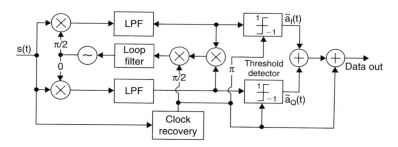

Figure 21: Coherent detector for GMSK

However, noncoherent demodulation is generally less expensive and easier to build than coherent demodulation because it does not need to generate the coherent signal. Therefore, noncoherent demodulation is often preferable, although it can degrade performance under certain channel conditions. Several types of noncoherent demodulation exist, including the differential demodulator and the limiter discriminator (Simon and Wang 1983).

Summary for GMSK

Although GMSK can be generated from MSK, it still has its own characteristics as follows:

1. GMSK modulation focuses on phase as the modulation variable; it turns out that the GMSK is superior in terms of its spectral efficiency.
2. The phase of the GMSK signal is continuous and smoothed by a Gaussian filter. Therefore, GMSK has a more compact spectrum than MSK. However, it suffers more ISI.
3. The degree of Gaussian filtering is expressed by $B_b T_b$. Low values of $B_b T_b$ create significant ISI. When $B_b T_b$ is less than 0.3, an ISI combating mechanism is required.
4. GMSK has a main lobe 1.5 times that of MSK.

EXTENSIONS OF MSK AND GMSK

When MSK is combined with partial response signaling, such as a Gaussian filter, the communication system can achieve more spectral efficiency. However, when phase transitions are spread over several symbol periods, the complexity of the demodulator will increase. Especially when the channel has fixed bandwidth, the increased spectral efficiency is required only for high symbol-rate transmission. When a low-rate data stream is submitted, a receiver with less complexity can complete the transmission. Therefore, it is critically important how to select a reasonable trade-off among bandwidth and system complexity and performance of the modulation through the judicious choice of the modulation parameters. To obtain high performance with low complexity, MSK and GMSK have recently been extended to *multi-amplitude MSK* (MAMSK) (Simon 1976; Weber, Stanton, and Sumida 1978), *optical MSK* (OMSK) (Sakamoto, Kawanishi, and Izutsu 2005), *pulse-driven GMSK* (PDGMSK) (Hetling

and Rhodes 1998), and N-GMSK (Javornik, Kandus, and Burr 2001).

Multi-Amplitude MSK

Just as the name multi-amplitude MSK implies, MAMSK signals can be considered as the superposition of some MSK signals. For example, a two-level MAMSK signal can be expressed as

$$s(t) = 2A\cos[2\pi f_c t + \phi_1(t:I)] \\ + A\cos[2\pi f_c t + \phi_2(t:J)] \tag{29}$$

where $\quad \phi_2(t:I) = \dfrac{\pi}{2}\displaystyle\sum_{k=-\infty}^{n-1} I_k + \dfrac{\pi}{2T_b} I_n(t-nT_b), nT_b \leq t \leq$

$(n+1)T_b, \phi_2(t:J) = \dfrac{\pi}{2}\displaystyle\sum_{k=-\infty}^{n-1} J_k + \dfrac{\pi}{2T_b} J_n(t-nT_b), nT_b \leq t \leq$

$(n+1)T_b$, I_k and J_k are the function of the information sequence (Simon 1976; Proakis 1995). Therefore, MAMSK still keeps the phase continuity property, and it can provide high spectral efficiency. However, its amplitudes of the constituent signals are not equal (as shown in Figure 22), and this prevents the phase trajectory from passing through the origin.

When two orthogonal MSK signals are superposed, we call this special type of MAMSK an *orthogonal MSK* (Ahmed 2002). Consequently, the orthogonal MSK signal can be demodulated using a receiver architecture similar to the parallel receiver architecture for MSK. The only difference is that two correlators for MSK receiver are replaced with four correlators for orthogonal MSK receiver. Also, the performance of orthogonal MSK is worse than MSK or BPSK, although they are orthogonal.

Optical MSK

In optical communication systems, it is important to transmit data with a more compact spectrum to increase spectral efficiency and improve dispersion tolerance in the optical links. It is found that the synchronous control technique cannot offer the condition required for the MSK format, where frequency deviation is $1/(4T_b)$ (Sakamoto, Kawanishi, and Izutsu 2005). To solve this problem and realize external modulation in MSK format, OMSK has been proposed to achieve continuous-phase modulation with a narrower frequency deviation, $1/(4T_b)$.

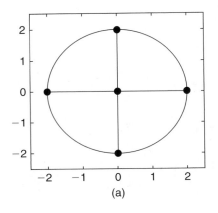

(a)

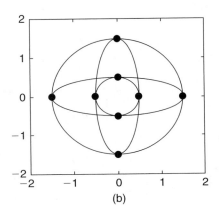

(b)

Figure 22: Constellation diagrams of the MAMSK signal—(a) constituent signals have equal amplitude; (b) constituent signals have unequal amplitude

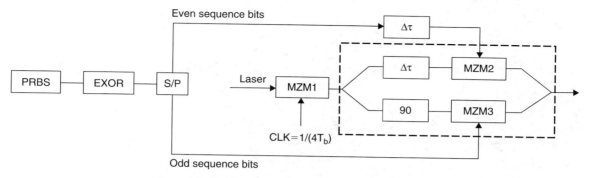

Figure 23: The basic structure of the OMSK modulator

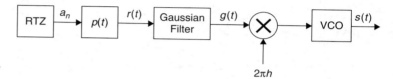

Figure 24: PDGMSK signal modulator

Figure 23 shows the basic structure of the OMSK modulator (Jinyu et al. 2005). First, a *pseudo-random binary sequence* (PRBS) is precoded using an *exclusive OR* (EXOR) gate and then separated by a *serial-to-parallel* (S/P) converter to form the odd-numbered-bit and even-numbered-bit sequences for driving two *Mach-Zender modulators* (MZM)—namely, MZM3 and MZM2, respectively.

The first MZM (MZM1) is used for *carrier suppressed return-to-zero* (CSRZ) pulse generation, which is driven by a clock signal with a frequency of $1/(4T_b)$ and is biased at the null point. Then the CSRZ pulses are fed into the second modulator for MSK modulation, which consists of two arms. The upper arm has a one-bit delay, $\Delta\tau = 1T_b$, and MZM2. The lower arm has a 90-degree phase shifter and MZM3. MZM2 and MZM3 are biased at the null point and driven by two data streams of even bits and odd bits, respectively. This driving condition provides either π or 0 phase shift in each arm according to the values of the bit streams.

Therefore, in the OMSK-modulated signal, the phase of all of the even-numbered bits are either 0 or π, while the phase of all of the odd-numbered bits are either $\pi/2$ or $3\pi/2$. The 1 bit is modulated with $\Phi_n = \Phi_{n-1} = \pi/2$, but $\Phi_n = \Phi_{n-1} = \pi/2$ for bit 0.

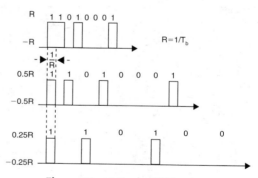

Figure 25: Bipolar RTZ pulses

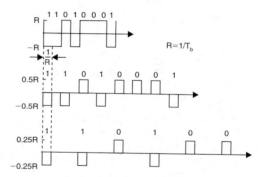

Figure 26: Unipolar RTZ pulses

Pulse-Driven GMSK

To simplify the architecture of GMSK demodulator, the PDGMSK was proposed. Figure 24 shows the data processing in a PDGMSK modulator and the *return-to-zero* (RTZ) data stream input to generate a PDGMSK signal (Hetling and Rhodes 1998). For PDGMSK, B_bT_b is the same as that of the GMSK. The corresponding stream ofectangular pulses $r(t) = \sum_n a_n \cdot p(t - nT_b)$ where $p(t) = 1/T_b$ when $|t| < T_b/2$, otherwise $p(t) = 0$. For the bipolar waveform, a_n belongs to the set $\{-1, +1\}$, but for the unipolar waveform, it is from the set $\{0, 2\}$. As the symbol rate decreases, the input sequence will change to a bipolar

RTZ sequence (Figure 25). However, it will become a series of pulses with a unipolar RTZ sequence (Figure 26).

Consequently, the output signal of the PDGMSK modulator can be expressed as

$$s(t) = \sqrt{\frac{2E_b}{T_b}} \cos\left[2\pi f_c t + \pi \cdot \sum a_n q(t - nT_b)\right] \quad (30)$$

Normally, phase transition function is defined as $q(t) = \int_{-\infty}^{t} g(\tau) d\tau$. The instantaneous frequency response of the Gaussian $g(t)$ is the same as Equation 25.

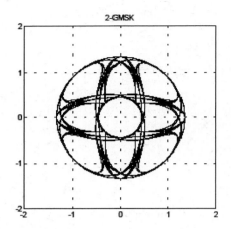
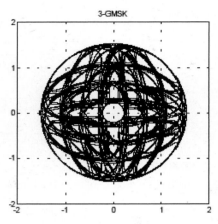

Figure 27: N-GMSK signal constellation diagrams (Javornik, Kandus, and Burr 2001)

N-GMSK

Just as its name implies, the N-GMSK signal is the superposition of N GMSK signals with different amplitudes. When $N = 1$, N-GMSK is the same as the conventional GMSK. Therefore, the N-GMSK signal can be written as

$$s(t, \alpha_1, \alpha_2, \ldots \alpha_n) = \frac{\sum_{i=1}^{N} s(t, \alpha_t)}{\sqrt{\sum_{i=1}^{N} 2^{2(i-1)}}} \qquad (31)$$

where $s(t, \alpha_i) = 2^{i-1} \sqrt{2E_b/T_b} \cos(2\pi f_c t + \Phi(t, \alpha_i) + \Phi_i)$ is the ith GMSK component and $\{\alpha_i\}$ is an infinitely sequence of independent data symbols with $\alpha_i \in \{-1, +1\}$, $i \in N \cdot \Phi(t, \alpha_i) = \pi \sum_{k=-\infty}^{n} \alpha_k q(t - kT), nT_b \leq t \leq (n+1)T_b$. The phase response $q(t)$ is defined as

$$q(t) = \begin{cases} \dfrac{1}{2T_b} \displaystyle\int_0^t Q\left(2\pi B_b \dfrac{\tau - T_b/2}{\sqrt{\ln 2}}\right) \\ \qquad - Q\left(2\pi B_b \dfrac{\tau + T_b/2}{\sqrt{\ln 2}}\right) d\tau & t \geq 0 \\ 0 & t < 0 \end{cases} \qquad (32)$$

where $Q(t) = \dfrac{1}{\sqrt{2\pi}} \displaystyle\int_t^\infty e^{\frac{\tau^2}{2}} d\tau$ and B_b is the bandwidth of a LPF having a Gaussian shaped spectrum.

Figure 27 shows the scattering diagrams for 2-GMSK and 3-GMSK with $B_b T_b = 0.3$. It is clear that the N-GMSK signals never reach the zero signal energy, which can improve the signal performance in nonlinear channels. The power spectra of the N-GMSK signals depend on modulation level and bandwidth of the Gaussian prefilter.

CONCLUSION

The fundamentals, implementations, and system impacts of MSK and GMSK have been reviewed. The overall performances of MSK and GMSK—including the coherent and noncoherent demodulations, implementation penalty, and tolerance to transmission impairments—have been comprehensively evaluated. Some forward-looking extensions of MSK and GMSK have been briefly discussed, and they are expected to be a promising modulation format for modern wireless communication systems.

GLOSSARY

Additive white Gaussian noise (AWGN): AWGN is one channel model in which only impairment is the linear addition of wideband or white noise with a constant spectral density and a Gaussian distribution of amplitude.

Binary frequency shift keying (BFSK): A form of frequency modulation that modulates input signals by 0- and 180-degree phase shifts.

Continuous phase frequency shift keying (CPFSK): A variation of frequency shift keying; its phase is continuous.

Continuous phase modulation (CPM): A method for modulation of data commonly used in wireless modems with continuous phase.

Frequency modulation (FM): A form of modulation that represents information as variations in the instantaneous frequency of a carrier wave.

Frequency shift keying (FSK): A form of frequency modulation; its modulating signal shifts the output frequency between predetermined values.

Gaussian minimum shift keying (GMSK): A special kind of MSK; it can improve the spectral efficiency by using a Gaussian-shaped impulse response filter

I component: In-phase component

Minimum shift keying (MSK): A type of continuous phase frequency shift keying; it is encoded with bits that alternate between quarternary components, with the Q component delayed by one-half the symbol period.

Multi-amplitude minimum shift keying (MAMSK): Superposition of some MSK signals.

Non-return-to-zero (NRZ): A data transmission method in which the 0's and 1's are represented by different polarities, typically positive for 0 and negative for 1.

Offset quadrature phase shift keying (OQPSK): A variant of phase shift keying modulation; it usually uses four different values of the phase to transmit information.

Optical minimum shift keying (OMSK): A type of continuous phase modulation used in optical communication systems in which narrower frequency deviation equals one-quarter of symbol period.

Phase-locked loop (PLL): An electronic control system that generates a signal that is locked to the phase of an input signal.

Phase shift keying (PSK): A digital modulation scheme that conveys data by changing or modulating the phase of a input signal.

Pulse-driven Gaussian minimum shift keying (PDGMSK): A special GMSK demodulator; its signal is generated by a return-to-zero (RTZ) data stream.

Q component: Quadrature component

Quadrature phase shift keying (QPSK): A form of phase modulation; it can be viewed as a quaternary modulation that uses four points on the constellation diagram that are equally spaced around a circle.

Staggered quadrature phase shift keying (SQPSK): Namely, QPSK; it is a variant of phase shift keying modulation using four different values of the phase to transmit.

Voltage controlled oscillator (VCO): An electronic oscillator specifically designed to be controlled in oscillation frequency by a voltage input.

CROSS REFERENCES

See *Optical Transmitters, Receivers, and Noise*; *Digital Communications Basics*.

REFERENCES

Adachi, F., and K. Ohno. 1988. Performance analysis of GMSK frequency detection with decision feedback equalization in digital land mobile radio. *Proceedings of the IEE, Part F: Radar and Signal Processing*, 135(3): 199–207.

Ahmed, Y. 2002. A model-based approach to demodulation of co-channel MSK signals (master's thesis, Virginia Polytechnic Institute and State University Graduate School).

Asano, D. K., and S. Pasupathy. 2002. Optimization of coded GMSK systems. *IEEE Transactions on Information Theory*, 48: 2768–73.

Bennett, W. R., and S. O. Rice. 1963. Spectral density and autocorrelation functions associated with binary frequency shift keying. *Bell Systems Technical Journal*, 42: 2355–85.

Borowski, J., and K. Feher. 1995. Nonobvious correlation properties of quadrature GMSK, a modulation technique adopted worldwide. *IEEE Transactions on Broadcasting*, 41: 69–75.

Brady, D. M. 1972. FM-CPSK: Narrowband digital FM with coherent phase detection. In *Proceedings of IEEE International Conference Communications*, Washington, DC, October, pp. 4412–6.

De Buda, R. 1972. Coherent demodulation of frequency shift keying with low deviation ratio. *IEEE Transaction on Communications*, 20: 429–35.

Diana, M. J., and M. N. Tien. 2001. Bandwidth-efficient modulation through Gaussian minimum shift keying. *Crosslink* (retrieved from www.aero.org/publications/crosslink/winter2002/03.html).

Doelz, M. L., E. H. Heald, and Collins Radio Co. 1961. Minimum-shift data communication system. U.S. Patent 2,977,417, filed March 28, 1961.

Feher, K. 1991. Modems for emerging digital cellular mobile radio systems. *IEEE Transactions on Vehicular Technology*, 40: 355–65.

Fielding, R. M., H. L. Berger, and D. L. Lochhead. 1977. Performance characterization of a high data rate MSK and QPSK channel. In *Proceeding of IEEE International Conference on Communications*, Chicago, June pp. 3242–6.

Grellier, O., and P. Comon. 1998. Blind equalization and source separation with MSK inputs. In *Proceeding of International Symposium on Optical Science Conference*, pp. 26–34.

Gronemeyer, S. A., and A. L. McBride. 1976. MSK and offset QPSK modulation. IEEE Transactions on Communications, 24: 809–20.

Gulak, G. P., and E. Shwedyk. 1986. VLSI structures for Viterbi receivers: Part II—encoded MSK modulation. *IEEE Journal on Selected Areas in Communications*, 4: 155–9.

Hellosoft A. P. 2002. Efficient GMSK modulator targets GSM designs. *CommsDesign* (retrieved from www.commsdesign.com/design_corner/showArticle.jhtml?articleID=16505388).

Hetling, K., and R. R. Rhodes. 1998. Pulse driven Gaussian minimum shift keying. *Proceedings of MILCOM 98*, Bedford, MA, pp. 511–4.

Huang Y. L., K. D. Fan, and C. C. Huang. 2000. A fully digital non-coherent and coherent GMSK receiver architecture with joint symbol timing error and frequency offset estimation. *IEEE Transactions on Vehicular Technology*, 49: 863–73.

Ishizuka, M., and K. Hirande. 1980. Optimum Gaussian filter and deviated-frequency-locking scheme for coherent detection of MSK. *IEEE Transactions on Communications*, 28: 850–7.

Ishizuka, M., and Y. Yasuda. 1984. Improved coherent detection of GMSK. *IEEE Transactions on Communications*, 32: 308–11.

Javornik, T., G. Kandus, and A. Burr A. 2001. The performance of N-GMSK signals in non-linear channels. *Fourth International Symposium on Wireless Personal Multimedia Communications*, Aalborg, Denmark, pp. 391–4.

Jinyu, M., D. Yi, W. Yangjing, et al. 2005. Optical minimum-shift keying modulator for high spectral efficiency WDM systems. *ECOC Proceedings*, 14, 781–2.

Proakis, J. G. 1995. *Digital communications*. 3rd ed. New York: McGraw-Hill.

Laster, J. D. 1997. Robust GMSK Demodulation using demodulator diversity and BER estimation (doctoral dissertation, Virginia Polytechnic Institute and State University).

Laurent, P. A. 1986. Exact and approximate construction of digital phase modulations by superposition of amplitude modulated pulses. *IEEE Transactions on Communications*, 34: 150–60.

Linz, A., and A. Hendrickson. 1996. Efficient implementation of an I-Q GMSK modulator. *IEEE Transactions on Circuits and Systems—II: Analogy and Digital Signal Processing*, 43: 14–23.

Mandayam, N. 2005. QPSK, OQPSK, CPM probability of error for AWGN and flat fading channels (retrieved from www.winlab.rutgers.edu/~narayan/Course/Wless?lectures05/lect9.pdf).

Masamura, T., S. Samejima, Y. Morihiro, and H. Fuketa. 1979. Differential detection of MSK with nonredundant error correction. *IEEE Transactions on Communications*, 27, 912–8.

Mason, L. J. 1987. Error probability evaluation for systems employing differential detection in a Rician fast fading environment and Gaussian noise. *IEEE Transactions on Communications*, 35: 39–46.

McCune, E., and W. Sander. 2003. EDGE transmitter alternative using nonlinear polar modulation. *Proceedings of the International Symposium on Circuits and Systems*, 3: 594–7.

Elliott, M. R., T. Montalvo, B. P. Jeffries, F. Murden, J. Strange, A. Hill, S. Nandipaku, and J. Harrebek. (2004). A polar modulator transmitter for GSM/EDGE. *IEEE Journal of Solid-State Circuits*, 39: 2190–9.

Morais, D. H., and K. Feher. 1979. Bandwidth efficiency and probability of error performance of MSK and offset QPSK systems. *IEEE Transactions on Communications*, 27: 1794–1801.

Murota, K., and K. Hirade. 1981. GMSK modulation for digital mobile radio telephony. *IEEE Transactions on Communications*, 29: 1044–50.

Pasupathy, S. 1979. Minimum shift keying: a spectrally efficient modulation. *IEEE Communications Magazine*, 17: 14–22.

Sakamoto T., Kawanishi T., and Izutsu M. (2005). Optical minimum-shift keying with external modulation scheme. Optics Express, 13, 7741–7747.

Sander, W. B., S. V. Schell, and B. L. Sander. 2003. Polar modulator for multimode cell phones. *Proceedings of the IEEE International Custom Integrated Circuits Conference*, 439–45.

Simon, M. K. 1976. An MSK approach to offset QASK. *IEEE Transactions on Communications*, 24: 921–3.

———, S. M. Hinedi, and W. C. Lindsey. 1995. *Digital communication techniques: Signal design and detection*. Upper Saddle River, NJ: Prentice Hall.

———, and C. C. Wang. 1983. Differential versus limiter-discriminator detection of narrow-band FM. *IEEE Transactions on Communications*, 31: 1227–34.

Sullivan, W. A. 1972. High capacity microwave system for digital data transmission. *IEEE Transactions on Communications*, 20: 466–70.

Taylor, D. P., S. T. Ogletree, H. C. Chan, and S. S. Haykin. 1977. A high speed digital modem for experimental work on the communications technology satellite. *Canadian Electrical Engineering Journal*, 2: 21–30.

Weber, W. J. III, P. H. Stanton, and J. T. Sumida. 1978. A bandwidth compressive modulation system using multi-amplitude minimum shift keying. *IEEE Transactions on Communications*, 26: 543–51.

Ziemer, R. E., and C. R. Ryan. 1983. Minimum-shift keyed modem implementations for high data rates. *IEEE Communications Magazine*, 21: 28–37.

Optical Differential Phase Shift Keying

Xiang Liu, *Bell Laboratories, Lucent Technologies*

INTRODUCTION

Evolution of Optical Transport Networks

Optical transport networks are evolving quickly to adapt to the ever-increasing demands of telecommunication needs, as most noticeably seen in the explosive growth in transmission capacity demands. The channel data rate in modern optical transport networks is migrating from 2.5 Gb/s to 10 Gb/s. A data rate of 40 Gb/s per channel is also on the horizon for commercial deployment. In addition to increases in data rate per channel, the number of channels per fiber is also increased through *wavelength-division multiplexing* (WDM) or *dense wavelength-division multiplexing* (DWDM) to further improve overall transmission capacity. Besides the demand for high capacity, optical transport networks desire long unregenerated optical transmission distance to effectively support metropolitan, regional, and national network applications. Moreover, flexible wavelength management, enabled by elements such as *reconfigurable optical add-drop multiplexers* (ROADM), is often utilized to make optical networks transparent and scalable. Optical transport networks are expected to continue to evolve to offer higher capacity, longer reach, and more flexible wavelength management and to do so with minimized operational expenditure and capital expenditure.

The evolution of optical transport networks is empowered by technological innovations in several key elements of an optical communication system, one of which is the *optical transponder*. An optical transponder consists of a transmitter that encodes information on a light wave through optical modulation and a receiver that recovers the information. An essential part of an optical transponder is its modulation format, which defines how the information is encoded at the transmitter and how it is recovered at the receiver. Furthermore, modulation format has strong system-level implications because the transmission performance of an optical signal in an optical network is related to how the signal is modulated. Different

modulation formats have different receiver sensitivities that relate to the required *optical signal-to-noise ratio* (OSNR), different spectral efficiencies, and different tolerances to transmission impairments such as *chromatic dispersion* (CD), *polarization mode dispersion* (PMD), optical filtering, and fiber nonlinearity (Forghieri, Tkach, and Chraplyvy 1997). This chapter is devoted to a specific type of optical modulation format—namely, *optical differential phase shift keying* (ODPSK).

Overview of Optical Modulation Formats

Generally, there are four basic physical attributes of a light wave that can be used through optical modulation to carry information: amplitude, phase, frequency, and polarization. The most common optical modulation format is *intensity modulation with direct detection* (IM-DD) (often called *on-off keying*, or OOK), in which the light intensity is turned on and off to represent the 1 and 0 states of a digital signal. Even though OOK has poor receiver sensitivity as compared to most other modulation formats, it is widely used in optical communications because of its simple transmitter and receiver configurations. Another common type of optical modulation is *phase modulation*. *Optical phase shift keying* (OPSK) utilizes the phase of a light wave to carry information. To recover the information, an OPSK receiver uses *homodyne detection* or *heterodyne detection* with the help of an *optical local oscillator* (OLO). The use of an OLO increases the receiver complexity and cost as compared to direct-detection receivers that do not need OLOs. Homodyne detection, however, offers superior receiver sensitivity and other benefits.

In ODPSK, information is encoded onto a light wave by the phase difference between adjacent bits and recovered by an optical demodulator followed by a direct-detection circuitry. A digital precoder is needed to ensure that the recovered data are the original data. *Optical frequency shift keying* (OFSK) and polarization shift keying are less commonly used, mainly because appropriate transmitters and

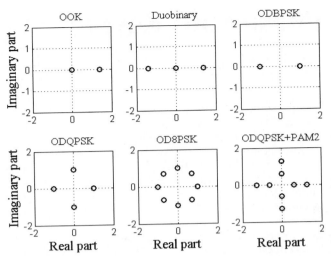

Figure 1: Constellation diagrams of OOK, duobinary, ODBPSK, ODQPSK, OD8PSK, and ODQPSK + PAM2. The average signal power is normalized to unity

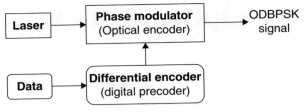

Figure 2: Schematic of an ODBPSK transmitter

receivers are less readily available and often exhibit poorer transmission performance. More than one of the four physical attributes may be simultaneously modulated to either carry more information bits per symbol or mitigate a certain transmission penalty. Ho (2005 "Phase") provides more details on various optical modulation formats.

Constellation diagrams are often used to illustrate different modulation formats. In a constellation diagram, the real and imaginary parts of the complex fields of a modulated optical signal at the centers of bit periods are plotted. Figure 1 shows the constellation diagrams of OOK, duobinary (Price and Le Mercier 1995), *optical differential binary phase shift keying* (ODBPSK) (Giles and Reichmann 1987; Tamura et al. 1990), *optical differential quadrature phase shift keying* (ODQPSK), *optical differential eight-level phase shift keying* (OD8PSK), and a combined *ODQPSK and two-level pulse amplitude modulation* (ODQPSK+PAM2). Note that the ODPSK constellation diagrams are identical to their OPSK counterparts. By creating more states in the symbol constellation, it is possible to increase spectral efficiency or the amount of information carried in each time slot, but this approach also tends to increase the required OSNR for a given *bit error rate* (BER) because of a reduced separation between symbols. Note that the constellation diagrams, although informative, are of limited use. Details about the modulation format, such as the intensity and phase profiles over each bit period and how the symbols are distinguished from each other, are not conveyed. The following sections of this chapter present detailed descriptions on different variants of ODPSK.

OPTICAL DIFFERENTIAL BINARY PHASE SHIFT KEYING
Implementation

This section describes the implementation of ODBPSK, including various transmitter and receiver configurations.

The ODBPSK transmitter generally consists of three components: a laser, a digital precoder, and an optical phase modulator (Gnauck and Winzer 2005) as shown in Figure 2. The laser output serves as an optical carrier, with a requirement on the maximal allowable laser linewidth. Finite laser linewidth causes phase noise that in turn causes an OSNR penalty. The penalty resulting from a given laser linewidth will be discussed in a later section. A digital precoder, which performs the differential precoding, is needed so that the recovered data are the original data. The key component of an ODBPSK transmitter is the optical phase modulator needed for optical encoding. For ODBPSK, digital data 1 or 0 is encoded as an optical phase difference of 0 or π between adjacent bits. Optical phase modulation can be realized through an electro-optical material such as lithium niobate (LiNbO$_3$) or gallium arsenide (GaAs), whose indexes of refraction change with an applied voltage (Heismann, Korotky, and Veselka 1997).

Two common types of modulators effectively realize phase modulation. The first is based on a single waveguide made of an electro-optical material, which is referred to as a *single-waveguide phase modulator*. The second is based on a zero-biased Mach-Zehnder interferometer with one such waveguide in each of its two arms, which is often referred to as a *Mach-Zehnder phase modulator*. Figure 3 shows the schematic diagrams of the two types. Assuming an unlimited modulator bandwidth, the output optical field from a Mach-Zehnder modulator that is biased at null can be expressed as

$$E_{output}(t) = E_{input}(t) \cdot \left[e^{j\frac{V_1(t)}{V_\pi}\pi} - e^{j\frac{V_2(t)}{V_\pi}\pi} \right] / 2 \cdot e^{-j\frac{\pi}{2}}$$

$$= E_{input}(t) \cdot \sin\left[\frac{V_1(t)}{V_\pi}\pi \right] \qquad (1)$$

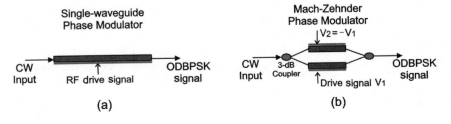

Figure 3: Schematic of optical phase modulators based on single-waveguide (a) and Mach-Zehnder (b) configurations

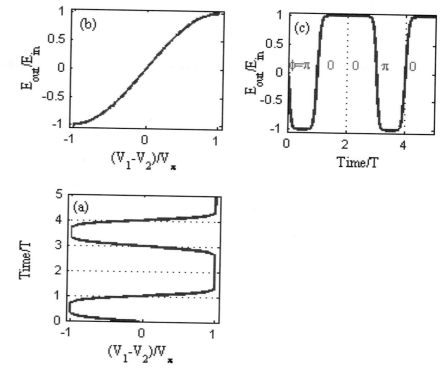

Figure 4: Operation principle of the Mach-Zehnder phase modulator for ODBPSK

where $V_1(t)$ and $V_2(t) = -V_1(t)$ are the time-varying drive voltages applied to the first and second arms of the Mach-Zehnder interferometer and V_π is the voltage needed to introduce an optical phase change of π on the optical wave passing through each of the two arms. Here an extra phase delay of $-\pi/2$ between the output and the input fields is used for convenience. Evidently, an optical phase change of exactly π is obtained when the drive voltages change signs. In addition, with a voltage swing of V_π applied to each arm, the output signal intensity is maximized. Figure 4 shows the operation principle of the Mach-Zehnder phase modulator. The dual-drive configuration can be replaced by a single-drive configuration with an internal push-pull design, in which case a voltage swing of $2\ V_\pi$ is desired and the modulator driver power consumption increases. The single-drive configuration removes the requirement of the precise timing alignment between V_1 and V_2. For LiNbO$_3$-based modulators, the dual-drive configuration is implemented with z-cut LiNbO$_3$ waveguides and the single-drive configuration with x-cut LiNbO$_3$ waveguides.

The single-waveguide phase modulator has the advantages of low loss, no need for bias control, and an absence of modulator bandwidth limitation–induced signal amplitude fluctuations. However, it has the drawbacks of the presence of modulator bandwidth limitation–induced phase fluctuations and a stringent drive voltage requirement for realizing the exact π phase shift. On the other hand, the Mach-Zehnder phase modulator has the advantages that the exact π phase shift can be obtained even with nonexact drive voltages, and there is no modulator bandwidth limitation–induced signal phase fluctuations. However, the use of the Mach-Zehnder phase modulator requires an accurate bias control (at extinction or null) and causes some signal amplitude fluctuations because of

limited modulator bandwidth that can be suppressed by operating the modulator in the saturation ranges of its intensity transfer function. Typically, the bias needs to be controlled within $\pm 0.1 V_\pi$ around the null point to avoid noticeable penalty. Overall, the Mach-Zehnder phase modulator, because of its capability of generating exact phase modulations, is preferred over the single-waveguide phase modulator in high-speed ODBPSK transmissions.

Return-to-zero (RZ) pulse formatting is usually used in association with ODBPSK to improve its transmission performance (Xu, Liu, and Wei 2004; Gnauck and Winzer 2005). Unlike *non-return-to-zero* (NRZ) pulse formatting, RZ pulse formatting minimizes the optical intensity between any adjacent bits and offers higher receiver sensitivity and a higher degree of immunity to *intersymbol interference* (ISI), which may result from linear and nonlinear transmission effects. RZ-ODBPSK has become the modulation format of choice for many record-setting high-capacity, long-haul transmissions (Gnauck and Winzer 2005). The generation of an RZ-ODBPSK signal usually requires one modulator for pulse generation and another modulator for phase modulation as shown in Figure 5a. RZ pulse formats also have several variants such as *chirp-free RZ*, *chirped RZ* (CRZ), *carrier-suppressed RZ* (CSRZ), and $\pi/2$ *alternate-phase RZ* $\pi/2$-AP RZ) (Gnauck et al. 2004 "Comparison"). Different RZ formats have different spectral profiles that lead to different tolerances to chromatic dispersion, optical filtering, and so on. Chirped RZ format may also offer higher tolerance to nonlinear effects (Mu et al. 2002). Fully phase-correlated RZ-ODBPSK signals at 80 Gb/s and 160 Gb/s have also been demonstrated (Möller et al. 2003; Möller et al. 2004). For RZ-ODPSK, the centers of the bits need to be aligned with the peaks of the RZ pulse train. Typically, the alignment accuracy needs to be

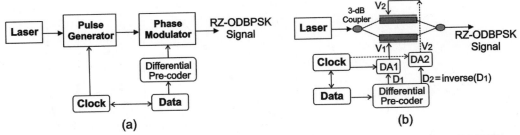

Figure 5: (a) Schematic of a RZ-ODBPSK transmitter based on two modulators; (b) schematic of a CRZ-ODBPSK transmitter based on a single dual-driver Mach-Zehnder modulator

within 20 percent of the pulse duration to avoid noticeable penalty.

To reduce the complexity of an RZ-ODPSK transmitter, a single Mach-Zehnder modulator has been used to simultaneously perform the RZ pulse formatting and phase modulation functions based on different methods (Liu and Kao 2005). Both chirp-free and chirped RZ-ODBPSK signals have been generated. Figure 5b shows the schematic of a single modulator-based chirped RZ-ODBPSK transmitter. The original data are first differentially encoded to form two complementary NRZ signal streams, D1 and D2, which are later converted to RZ format by two differential amplifiers, DA1 and DA2, with two clock signals whose frequency equals the *bit rate* (BR) (Liu and Kao 2005). The two RZ drive signals provide voltages V_1 and V_2, which are synchronously applied to the two arms of the MZM, which is biased at null, to modulate the light from the CW laser to generate the CRZ-ODPSK signal. In this driving scheme, neither V_1 nor V_2 can be nonzero or zero simultaneously. This is because when $V_2 \neq 0$, the inverted data bit is 1 or the data bit is 0, and thus V_1 (which is the logical AND operation result for the data bit and the clock whose peak is aligned with the bit center) should be 0 and vice versa. The optical intensity transfer function can be expressed as

$$\left| \frac{E_{output}(t)}{E_{input}(t)} \right|^2 = \begin{cases} \sin^2\left[\pi \dfrac{V_2(t)}{2 \cdot V_\pi} \right] & \text{when } V_1(t) = 0; \\[4mm] \sin^2\left[\pi \dfrac{V_1(t)}{2 \cdot V_\pi} \right] & \text{when } V_2(t) = 0. \end{cases} \quad (2)$$

The signal optical phase can be written as

$$\text{phase}(t) = \begin{cases} \tan^{-1}\left\{ \dfrac{\sin[\pi \cdot V_2(t) / V\pi]}{\cos[\pi \cdot V_s(t) / V_\pi] - 1} \right\} \\ \qquad \text{when } V_1(t) = 0; \\[4mm] \pi + \tan^{-1}\left\{ \dfrac{\sin[\pi \cdot V_1(t) / V\pi]}{\cos[\pi \cdot V_1(t) / V_\pi] - 1} \right\} \\ \qquad \text{when } V_2(t) = 0. \end{cases} \quad (3)$$

Apparently, there is an identical phase variation or chirp across each bit when V_1 and V_2 have the same nonzero temporal profile. Upon differential detection, what matters

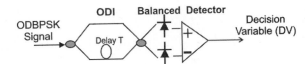

Figure 6: Schematic of an ODBPSK receiver

is only the phase difference between adjacent bits, which is either 0 or π, as needed for ODBPSK encoding. The sign and magnitude of the chirp can be changed by varying V_1 and V_2.

An interesting variant of DBPSK is $\pi/2$-ODBPSK (Wei et al. 2003). The $\pi/2$-ODBPSK format differs from ODBPSK in that the phase between successive bits always changes by plus or minus 90 degrees. A $\pi/2$-RZ-ODBPSK format has been realized by ODBPSK combined with $\pi/2$-AP RZ pulse formatting. This format has been shown to yield slightly better receiver sensitivity when tight optical filtering is used, as well as better tolerance to polarization mode dispersion when filtering is present (Wei et al. 2003).

The ODBPSK receiver generally consists of three components: a one-bit *optical delay interferometer* (ODI), a balanced detector, and *clock and data recovery* (CDR) circuitry, as shown in Figure 6. The one-bit ODI is needed for demodulating the ODBPSK signal into two complementary OOK signals that can be directly detected by intensity detectors. The signal is first split into two paths that have a certain path difference so that the signal at the end of one path is delayed by approximately one bit period, denoted as T, with respect to that of the other path. This effectively causes two adjacent bits to interfere with each other; depending on their phase difference of 0 or π, they interfere constructively or destructively. The constructively and destructively interfered signal components exit the ODI through its constructive and destructive output ports, respectively, and are detected by a balanced detector that consists of two matched photodiodes. The photocurrents generated by the two matched photodiodes are subtracted, and the current difference is then converted to a voltage difference before it is used for CDR with a nominal decision threshold at approximately zero. The CDR circuitry can be similar to those conventionally used for OOK detection. Mathematically, the *decision variable* (DV) can be expressed as

$$\text{DV}_{\text{ODBPSK}}(t) = \text{Re}[E_{RX}(t) \cdot E_{RX}^*(t - T)] \quad (4)$$

where E_{RX} is the normalized optical field of the ODBPSK signal entering the receiver, Re[x] is the real part of a complex variable x and * denotes to complex conjugate.

The ODIs are commonly made based on an all-fiber design, a planar light wave circuit design, a free-space optics design (Liu et al. 2005 "Athermal"), or a LiNbO$_3$ platform (Cho et al. 2004). Note that a precise phase control of the phase difference between the two optical paths of the ODI is required. The penalty associated with a nonexact phase difference will be discussed in a later section. Because the phase difference may be changed by environmental temperature, accurate temperature control and stabilization of the ODI are usually required. Athermal ODIs have been demonstrated by using a free-space optics design. They are capable of demodulating 40-Gb/s ODBPSK signals that are on the ITU 50-GHz grid over the entire C+L band in the temperature range of 0 to ~70°C (Liu et al. 2005 "Athermal"). In addition to temperature changes, laser frequency drifts also affect the phase difference, so the ODI is desired to be able to track the laser frequency drifts and adjust the phase difference accordingly.

Balanced detectors are usually used for ODBPSK in order to take advantage of the higher receiver sensitivity offered by ODBPSK over OOK. Without taking the receiver sensitivity advantage, an ODBPSK signal can be received by a single detector that detects the signal component from either the constructive port or the destructive port of the ODI. Effectively, the signal components from

the constructive and destructive ports are of the optical duobinary format and the alternating mark-inversion format (Gnauck et al. 2004 "Comparison"), which exhibit unique spectrum characteristics. Figure 7 shows typical simulated optical spectra of an ODBPSK signal, and its filtered components from the constructive and destructive ports of a one-bit ODI. Figure 8 shows the simulated ODBPSK eye diagrams measured by a balanced detector and a single detector. The optical and electronic bandwidths of the receiver are assumed to be 2× and 1× the signal data rate, respectively. The eye diagrams measured at the constructive and destructive ports of the ODI are different because of the NRZ formatting of the ODBPSK signal and the optical filtering induced destructive interference between any adjacent bits that are out of phase by π. The special optical duobinary signal format is also referred to as *DI-duobinary*, which, like conventional optical duobinary, offers high tolerance to chromatic dispersion tolerance and optical filtering.

Back-to-Back Performance

In this section, we evaluate the performance of ODBPSK in the back-to-back configuration without considering optical fiber transmission penalties. Because optical *amplified spontaneous emission* (ASE) noise is the predominate noise source in optical transport systems where optical amplifiers are extensively used, we evaluate receiver

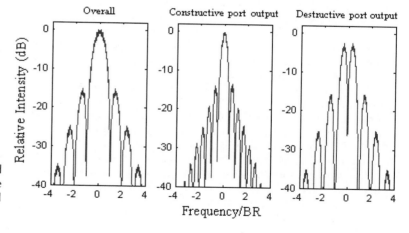

Figure 7: Typical spectra of an ODBPSK signal and its filtered components from the constructive and destructive ports of a one-bit ODI. The spectral resolution is 5 percent of the BR

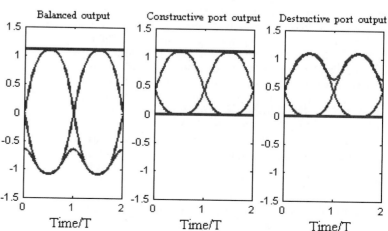

Figure 8: Typical ODBPSK eye diagrams detected by a balanced detector, and a single detector at the constructive and destructive ports of the ODI

sensitivity in terms of the required optical signal-to-noise ratio for a given bit error rate and assess the performance degradation caused by a given impairment in terms of the increase in the required OSNR (or the OSNR penalty) it causes. We first briefly introduce the common numerical methods for performance evaluation of ODPSK and then describe the ideal receiver sensitivity of ODBPSK, followed by implementation penalties caused by various imperfections in the transmitter and receiver designs.

Numerical methods for performance evaluation of a given optical modulation format are important because they provide a theoretical guidance on the upper bond of the performance of the format, as well as the individual and combined impacts of various degradation sources. Numerical performance evaluation often provides insights that are not readily available from experimental investigations. There are three main categories of numerical methods based on analytical modeling, semi-analytical modeling, and Monte Carlo simulation. Among the three categories, methods based on Monte Carlo simulation are most versatile because they are capable of taking into consideration virtually all of the system aspects, including various nonlinear effects. They are, however, most time-consuming. They are thus often used for evaluating system performance at high BER values (e.g., higher than 1E-5). This may be sufficient for optical transport systems that adopt *forward error correction* (FEC), and the raw BER values of interest are in the range between 1E-2 and 1E-5. A new type of Monte Carlo simulation method called the *multicanonical Monte Carlo* (MMC) method (Yadin, Shtaif, and Orenstein 2005) has been shown to provide a relatively more efficient way of estimating system performances at low BER values. The MMC method is based on an iterative technique that is designed to more quickly obtain the probabilities of rare events by applying proper biasing to randomly generated noise vectors in Monte Carlo simulations.

Analytical methods, on the other end of the spectrum, provide especially fast performance evaluations and often offer clear physical intuitions on the impacts of individual impairments. The trade-off is that assumptions, sometimes oversimplified, have to be made to derive analytical descriptions of an optical transmission system. For example, matched optical filtering is usually assumed in the receiver in order to obtain analytical description of the *probability density function* (PDF) of the decision variable. Simplified fiber transmission-link configurations are often used to analytically describe nonlinear effects. A simple yet useful performance indicator of an ODPSK signal is the differential phase Q-factor introduced by Wei, Liu, and Xu (2003 "Q factor"). When the phase noise can be approximated as Gaussian-distributed, it offers quick assessment of the signal quality in both linear (Wei et al. 2003 "Q factor") and some nonlinear regimes (Wei, Liu, and Xu 2003 "Numerical").

Semi-analytical methods are between the analytical and Monte Carlo methods in terms of needed computational efforts. Most linear and nonlinear impairments result in bit pattern–dependent ISI. Semi-analytical methods can take into consideration the bit pattern–dependent ISI by averaging the BERs over all possible bit patterns while each BER may be analytically calculated with a known PDF of the decision variable. When only linear effects are considered and the noise is Gaussian-distributed, there is a useful technique called the *Karhunen–Loève series expansion* (KLSE). In the KLSE, the signal and noise are expanded into Karhunen–Loève series (Proakis 2000) so that the *moment generation function* (MGF) of the decision variable, which is related to the PDF through Laplace transformation, can be expressed in a closed form. The BER values can then be obtained through numerical integrations. The KLSE method is applicable for assessing the impact of various linear effects such as optical and electrical filtering in the receiver (Winzer, Chandrasekhar, and Kim 2003; Bosco and Poggiolini 2005), chromatic dispersion, and PMD (Wang and Kahn 2004).

For simplicity and clarity, most performance assessments presented in this chapter will be based on analytical methods, particularly when discussing linear effects. Semi-analytical and Monte Carlo methods will be used primarily for studying nonlinear effects.

Receiver sensitivity indicators are useful for representing the performance of a receiver for a signal with a certain modulation format. In an optically pre-amplified receiver, its receiver sensitivity is usually indicated by the required *signal-to-noise ratio per bit*, SNR_b, for achieving a given BER. The SNR_b is defined as

$$\mathrm{SNR}_b = \frac{\varepsilon_b}{N_0} = \frac{P_s}{N_0 \cdot BR} \qquad (5)$$

where ε_b is the signal energy per bit, P_s is the signal power, N_0 is the ASE noise spectrum density per polarization, and BR is the bit rate of the signal. The physical meaning of the SNR_b is the ratio between the signal power and the power of the single polarized optical noise within a bandwidth of the signal bit rate.

A conventionally used term to represent the SNR in optical fiber communications is OSNR, defined as the ratio between the signal power and the power of optical noise of two polarization states within a fixed bandwidth of 0.1 nm (or 12.5 GHz at a signal wavelength of approximately 1550 nm). OSNR relates to SNR_b as

$$\mathrm{OSNR} = \frac{\mathrm{SNR}_b \cdot BR}{2 \cdot 12.5\,\mathrm{GHz}} \qquad (6)$$

As an example, at bit rates of 10 Gb/s and 40 Gb/s, the OSNR values are approximately −4 dB and 2 dB higher than the SNR_b values, respectively.

Another commonly used indicator for the receiver sensitivity of an optically pre-amplified receiver is the required number of *photons per bit* (PPB) to achieve a given BER. The PPB of the input signal is related to the SNR_b of the amplified signal as

$$\mathrm{PPB} = n_{sp} \times \mathrm{SNR}_b \qquad (7)$$

where n_{sp} is related to the *noise figure* (NF) of the optical pre-amplifier. For an ideal optical pre-amplifier which has a NF of 3 dB or $n_{sp} = 1$ (Ho 2005 "Phase"), SNR_b and PPB happen to be equal.

Optimal receiver sensitivity is obtained when the receiver uses a matched optical filter and no postdetection electrical filter (Proakis 2000; Ho 2005 "Phase"). For homodyne or heterodyne OBPSK, we have the following dependence of BER on SNR_b:

$$\text{BER}_{\text{OBPSK}} = \frac{1}{2} erfc\left(\sqrt{SNR_b}\right) \qquad (8)$$

For direct-detection ODBPSK with polarization filtering at the receiver so that only the noise component whose polarization is aligned with that of the signal is detected with the signal, we have

$$\text{BER}_{\text{ODBPSK}\_1p} = \frac{\exp(-SNR_b)}{2} \qquad (9)$$

For direct-detection ODBPSK without polarization filtering at the receiver, we have

$$\text{BER}_{\text{ODBPSK}\_2p} = \frac{\exp(-SNR_b)}{2}\left(1 + \frac{SNR_b}{4}\right) \qquad (10)$$

For direct-detection OOK with polarization filtering at the receiver, we have

$$\text{BER}_{\text{OOK}\_1p} = \frac{1}{2}\left[1 - Q\left(2\sqrt{SNR_b}, 2\sqrt{SNR_b \cdot V_{th}}\right)\right] \\ + \frac{1}{2}\exp(-2SNR_b \cdot V_{th}) \qquad (11)$$

where V_{th} is the decision threshold normalized to the signal peak power, and $Q(a,b)$ is the first-order Marcum Q function (Weisstein 2005):

$$Q(a,b) = e^{-(a^2+b^2)/2} \cdot \sum_{m=0}^{\infty}\left(\frac{a}{b}\right)^m I_m(ab), \quad a \le b$$
$$= 1 + e^{-(a^2+b^2)/2}I_0(ab) \qquad (12)$$
$$- e^{-(a^2+b^2)/2} \cdot \sum_{m=0}^{\infty}\left(\frac{b}{a}\right)^m I_m(ab), \quad a > b$$

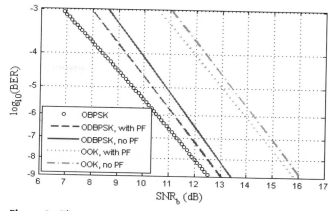

Figure 9: The optimal BER performances of OBPSK, ODBPSK, and OOK with and without polarization filtering (PF)

where and $I_m(x)$ is the mth-order modified Bessel function of the first kind. The optimal decision threshold satisfies

$$I_0\left(4SNR_b \cdot \sqrt{V_{th}}\right)\exp(-2SNR_b) = 1 \qquad (13)$$

The optimal BER for direct-detection OOK can thus be numerically calculated by solving Equations 11 through 13.

For direct-detection OOK without polarization filtering at the receiver, we have (Ho 2005 "Phase")

$$\text{BER}_{\text{OOK}\_2p} = \frac{1}{2}\left[1 - Q_2\left(2\sqrt{SNR_b}, 2\sqrt{SNR_b \cdot V_{th}}\right)\right] \\ + \frac{1}{2}\exp(-2SNR_b \cdot V_{th}) \cdot (1 + 2SNR_b \cdot V_{th}) \quad (14)$$

where

$Q_2(a,b) = Q(a,b) + \frac{b}{a}e^{-(a^2+b^2)/2} \cdot I_1(ab)$ and the optimal decision threshold can be numerically calculated.

Figure 9 shows the BER performances of OBPSK, ODBPSK, and OOK with and without *polarization filtering* (PF). Table 1 summarizes the receivers' sensitivities at BER = 1E-3 and 1E-9 for the above signal formats.

Table 1: Receiver Sensitivity Comparison among Different Binary Signal Formats

		OBPSK	ODBPSK		OOK	
			with PF	no PF	with PF	no PF
BER = 10^{-9}	PPB	18	20	22	38.3	40.7
	SNR_b	12.5 dB	13 dB	13.4 dB	15.8 dB	16.1 dB
	$OSNR_{10G}$	8.5 dB	9 dB	9.4 dB	11.8 dB	12.1 dB
BER = 10^{-3}	PPB	4.8	6.2	7.2	11.2	12.7
	SNR_b	6.8 dB	8 dB	8.6 dB	10.5 dB	11 dB
	$OSNR_{10G}$	2.8 dB	4 dB	4.6 dB	6.5 dB	7 dB

Ideal optical pre-amplifier with NF = 3 dB assumed. $OSNR_{10G}$ is the required OSNR values for a 10-Gb/s signal.

With polarization filtering at the receiver, the receiver sensitivity of ODBPSK is slightly worse than that of the OBPSK: approximately 0.45 dB at BER = 10^{-9}. This penalty is often referred to as *the differential detection penalty*. The differential detection penalty increases for ODPSK formats that have more than two symbols per bit, as will be discussed in later sections. Without polarization filtering, the receiver sensitivity of ODBPSK is further worsened by approximately 0.4 dB at BER = 10^{-9}. Two commonly used modulation and detection configurations are direct-detection ODBPSK and OOK that does not have the polarization filtering. The ODBPSK outperforms the OOK by approximately 2.7 dB at BER = 10^{-9}: This is commonly referred to as the *3-dB advantage of ODBPSK over OOK* in optical transmissions.

Implementation impairments result in degradations in receiver sensitivity. The most significant impairment in a back-to-back ODBPSK transmitter-receiver configuration is the phase error resulting from nonexact phase matching between the two arms of the ODI. The phase error usually comes from temperature-induced phase mismatch or laser frequency offset from the passband center of the ODI. With the consideration of the phase error, we have for direct-detection ODBPSK with polarization filtering at the receiver (Ho 2005 "Phase")

$$
\begin{aligned}
\text{BER}_{\text{ODBPSK\_1}p} &= Q(a,b) - \frac{1}{2}e^{-(a^2+b^2)/2} \cdot I_0(ab), \\
a &= \sqrt{2\text{SNR}_b}\left|\sin(\phi_e/2)\right|, \\
b &= \sqrt{2\text{SNR}_b}\left|\cos(\phi_e/2)\right|,
\end{aligned}
\tag{15}
$$

where ϕ_e is the phase error, and $I_0(x)$ is the zero-order modified Bessel function of the first kind, and $Q(a,b)$ is the first-order Marcum Q function.

For direct-detection ODBPSK without polarization filtering at the receiver, we have

$$
\begin{aligned}
\text{BER}_{\text{ODBPSK\_2}p} &= Q(a,b) - \frac{1}{2}e^{-(a^2+b^2)/2} \cdot I_0(ab) \\
&+ \frac{1}{8}e^{-(a^2+b^2)/2}\left(\frac{b}{a} - \frac{a}{b}\right) \cdot I_0(ab),
\end{aligned}
\tag{16}
$$

where the last term on the right-hand side of the equation represents the error contribution from the noise component whose polarization is orthogonal to that of the signal. When the phase error becomes zero, Equations 15 and 16 reduce to Equations 9 and 10, respectively. Figure 10 shows the OSNR penalty as a function of the phase error for direct-detection ODBPSK.

The phase error that results from laser frequency offset, f_e, can be expressed as

$$
\phi_e = 2\pi \frac{f_e}{\text{FSR}} \approx 2\pi \frac{f_e}{\text{BR}}
\tag{17}
$$

where FSR is the free spectral range of the ODI. Usually, the FSR of the ODI equals the bit rate of the ODBPSK signal, and thus the phase error resulting from a same laser frequency offset or uncertainty decreases as the bit

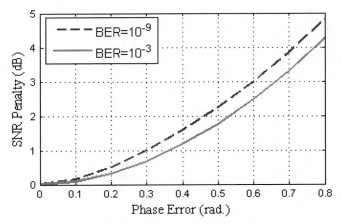

Figure 10: The OSNR penalty as a function of the phase error for direct-detection ODBPSK without polarization filtering at BER = 10^{-9} and BER = 10^{-3}

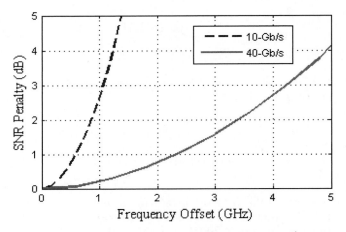

Figure 11: The OSNR penalty (at BER = 10^{-3}) as a function of the laser frequency offset in 10-Gb/s and 40-Gb/s ODBPSK system using one-bit ODIs. No polarization filtering is used

rate of the ODBPSK signal increases. Note that any laser has a finite linewidth or frequency jitter that causes random phase errors with a given distribution (e.g., the Lorentzian distribution) and degrades the performance of ODPSK. The linewidth of commonly used DFB lasers is on the order of a few megahertz, which causes negligible penalty for ODPSK signals with bit rates of multigigabits per second. However, laser frequency drift resulting from temperature and aging may cause sufficiently large frequency offset (e.g., > 1 GHz) and severe degradation of the ODPSK performance. Figure 11 shows the OSNR penalty as a function of the laser frequency offset in 10-Gb/s and 40-Gb/s ODBPSK systems. In addition, the phase error because of a certain temperature change of the ODI is proportional to the length difference between the two arms of the ODI, which is inversely proportional to the signal bit rate. So the higher the signal rate, the higher the tolerance of the direct-detection ODBPSK to laser frequency uncertainties and temperature changes at the receiver. This makes ODBPSK particularly suitable for high-speed optical transmissions.

Another receiver imperfection is the nonexact one-bit delay of the ODI. ODBPSK is more tolerant to the delay mismatch than RZ-ODBPSK. Negligible OSNR penalty was observed when an ODI with a FSR of 50 GHz was used for demodulating a 42.7-Gb/s ODBPSK signal (Liu et al. 2005 "Athermal"). The use of 50-GHz ODI, when its passband is also locked on the ITU grid, has the advantage of being able to demodulate any or multiple ITU-specified WDM ODBPSK channels.

Other receiver imperfections such as the arrival time mismatch and amplitude mismatch between the two electrical signals detected by the balanced detector and receiver also contribute to the degradation of the ODBPSK receiver sensitivity. Generally, the associated penalties become negligible when the time and amplitude mismatches are less than 5 percent of the bit period and nominal amplitude, respectively (Gnauck and Winzer 2005). Because the amplitude mismatch is related to the finite common-mode rejection of the balanced detector, so the required common-mode rejection is desired to be higher than approximately 13 dB.

Transmission Performance

Generally, optical signals experience loss, chromatic dispersion, polarization mode dispersion, and fiber nonlinearity during propagation in fiber. The propagation equations governing the evolution of the slow varying amplitudes of the two polarization components of an optical field, A_x and A_y, satisfy (Agrawal 2001)

$$
\begin{aligned}
&\frac{\partial A_x}{\partial z} + \beta_{1x}\frac{\partial A_x}{\partial t} + \frac{j}{2}\beta_2\frac{\partial^2 A_x}{\partial t^2} + \frac{\alpha}{2}A_x \\
&= j\gamma\left(\left|A_x\right|^2 + \frac{2}{3}\left|A_y\right|^2\right)A_x + \frac{j\gamma}{3}A_x^*A_y^2\exp(-2j\Delta\beta z) \\
&\frac{\partial A_y}{\partial z} + \beta_{1y}\frac{\partial A_y}{\partial t} + \frac{j}{2}\beta_2\frac{\partial^2 A_y}{\partial t^2} + \frac{\alpha}{2}A_y \\
&= j\gamma\left(\left|A_y\right|^2 + \frac{2}{3}\left|A_x\right|^2\right)A_y + \frac{j\gamma}{3}A_y^*A_x^2\exp(2j\Delta\beta z)
\end{aligned}
\tag{18}
$$

where $\Delta\beta = \beta_x - \beta_y$ is the wave-vector mismatch between the two polarization components, α is the fiber loss coefficient, β_2 is related to fiber chromatic dispersion coefficient as

$$
D(z) = -\frac{2\pi c}{\lambda^2}\beta_2(z)
\tag{19}
$$

β_{1x} and β_{1y} and is related to *differential group delay* (DGD) between the two polarization components as

$$
\text{DGD}(z \to z + dz) = \left|\beta_{1x} - \beta_{2x}\right|dz
\tag{20}
$$

and γ is the fiber nonlinear coefficient. The conventional units for the fiber CD coefficient, DGD (or first-order PMD), and fiber nonlinearity are ps/km/nm, ps, and W/km, respectively.

Tolerance of ODBPSK to Chromatic Dispersion

Chromatic dispersion causes pulse broadening in the time domain that leads to ISI and consequently degrades the receiver sensitivity of an optical signal. The tolerance to CD is usually defined as the allowed CD range, [CD_{min}, CD_{max}] (in units of ps/nm), within which the receiver sensitivity penalty is less than a given value—for example, 2 dB. For signals with chirp-free modulation formats, $CD_{max} = -CD_{min}$, and

$$
CD_{max} = \frac{P}{SR^2}
\tag{21}
$$

where SR is the symbol rate of the signal and p is a factor that depends on the signal pulse format and modulation format. The SR of a signal is its bit rate divided by $\log_2(N_s)$, where N_s is the number of the symbols in the constellation diagram of the signal format. The CD tolerance decreases quadratically with the increase of the signal bit rate for a same format. NRZ pulse-formatted signals, because of their relatively narrow optical spectra, usually have higher CD tolerance than RZ pulse-formatted signals. Optically filtered signals usually also offer higher CD tolerance than unfiltered or less filtered signals. The CD tolerance of ODBPSK is found to be higher than that of OOK (Wang and Kahn 2004). This can be partially attributed to the fact that in ODBPSK, a moderate CD causes primarily phase distortions instead of amplitude distortions, and the phase distortions on adjacent bits are correlated (Liu, Mollenauer, and Wei 2004).

Tolerance of ODBPSK to Polarization Mode Dispersion

Polarization mode dispersion is one of the major obstacles in high-speed (e.g., 40-Gb/s) long-haul transmissions. ODBPSK is found to have a slightly higher PMD tolerance than OOK (Xie et al. 2003). Because of the stochastic nature of PMD and its wavelength dependence, PMD mitigation is normally done on a per-channel basis through *PMD compensation* (PMDC). From a system perspective, cost-effective PMD mitigation is essential. Although forward error correction is effective in correcting random errors, it is ineffective in the presence of PMD-induced burst errors. It is found that substantial improvement in PMD tolerance can be achieved over a broad bandwidth by using *distributed fast polarization scramblers* (D-FPSs) and FEC (Liu et al. 2005 "Demonstration"). The D-FPSs physically change the instantaneous PMD of an optical link in a time interval shorter than the FEC code's *burst error correction period* (BECP) so that PMD-induced burst errors can be effectively corrected. It is also shown that this PMD mitigation scheme is even more effective for ODBPSK with balanced detection than for OOK. Substantial improvement in PMD tolerance was achieved in an ODBPSK system that uses a standard *Reed-Solomon FEC code* (RS-FEC) and an *enhanced FEC* (eFEC) code with a 7 percent overhead (Liu et al. 2005 "Improved"). It was also found that the PMD mitigation scheme remains effective in the presence of moderate polarization-dependent loss (Liu et al. 2005 "Demonstration"). Figure 12 shows the simulated relative required OSNR as a function of the

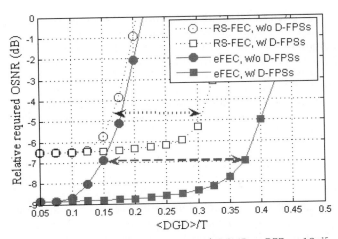

Figure 12: Simulated relative required OSNR at BER = 10^{-15} versus <DGD> in NRZ-DPSK systems that use the RS-FEC or the eFEC

Table 2: PMD Tolerance of NRZ-DPSK (at 2-dB Penalty)

	Without FEC	With RS-FEC	With eFEC
Without D-FPSs	0.185 T	0.170 T	0.155 T
With D-FPSs	0.185 T	0.310 T	0.375 T

mean DGD divided by the bit period T, denoted as DGD /T. Table 2 summarizes the PMD tolerance in ODBPSK systems that employ the RS-FEC or eFEC code without and with the use of D-FPSs. The targeted output BER is 10^{-15}. Evidently, the improvements in PMD tolerance are further increased by D-FPSs in systems that use eFEC than in systems that use RS-FEC. Note also that without the use of D-FPSs, the PMD tolerance of systems with the eFEC is actually lower than that with the RS-FEC.

Tolerance of ODBPSK to Optical Filtering

Optical filters are widely used in optical transport systems. Optical filters are often used in wavelength routing elements for optical add drop functions. High tolerance to optical filtering is desired for modern networks because signals tend to pass multiple *optical add drop multiplexers* (OADMs) with many filters. Generally, the signal quality is affected by the passband characteristics of a filter in terms of its bandwidth, loss ripple, and phase ripple or *group-delay ripple* (GDR). ODBPSK with balanced detection is found to be more tolerant of tight optical filter bandwidth than conventional OOK with the same data rate (Gnauck and Winzer 2005). This is related to the high tolerance of ODBPSK to ISI (Gnauck and Winzer 2005). Loss ripple and phase ripple are common imperfections of optical filters. The signal degradation resulting from these ripples depends on the ripple period, ripple magnitude, and how the signal center frequency is located with respect to the ripple peaks. The degradation can become most severe when the ripple period coincides with the signal bit rate. It is also found that the degradation

resulting from the ripple is dependent on the phase relationship among the signal bits (Liu, Mollenauer, and Wei 2004). Therefore, the loss and phase ripples influence ODBPSK signals differently as compared to OOK signals. For example, ODBPSK, unlike OOK, is highly tolerant to phase ripple when a peak or valley is aligned with the signal center frequency. As another example, optical duobinary signal has a compact optical spectrum and high tolerance to narrow optical filter bandwidth, but it is especially sensitive to phase ripple. In an optical transmission system with multiple optical filters, judicious control of the loss and phase ripples in filters is necessary to minimize the overall penalty of a given signal because of the concatenated filtering. Finally, optical filters generally exhibit finite extinction ratios that may cause coherent cross talk that is detrimental to signal quality. ODPSK is found to have higher tolerance to coherent cross talk than OOK (Liu et al. 2004 "Tolerance"), which makes it a good candidate in transparent optical networks with multiple filters.

Tolerance of ODBPSK to Fiber Nonlinearity

Nonlinear effects in WDM optical transmissions can be categorized into intrachannel nonlinear effects and interchannel effects (Essiambre, Raybon, and Mikkelsen 2002). Interchannel effects include *cross-phase modulation* (XPM) and *four-wave mixing* (FWM) among different wavelength channels, and intrachannel effects include *self-phase modulation* (SPM), *intrachannel XPM* (IXPM), and *intrachannel FWM* (IFWM). For ODPSK, there is a unique type of nonlinear effect, commonly referred to as the *Gordon-Mollenauer effect*, which was first reported by Gordon and Mollenauer (1990). The Gordon-Mollenauer effect causes nonlinear phase noise by converting the ASE noise–induced signal amplitude fluctuations to phase fluctuations through SPM. The Gordon-Mollenauer effect can be extended to the generation of nonlinear phase noise resulting from the interaction of ASE noise and the XPM. Generally, these nonlinear effects degrade signal quality by introducing distortions and noises in signal amplitude and phase. Phase distortions and noises are minor concerns in OOK, but they are important and sometimes major concerns for ODBPSK. The importance of each nonlinear effect in a particular optical transmission system depends on the system parameters. The FWM among different wavelength channels is usually managed to have minimal impact in modern dispersion-managed WDM transmission systems. For WDM systems with tighter channel spacing, the XPM among wavelength channels becomes more important. For single-channel effects, SPM and Gordon-Mollenauer effect are of primary concerns in systems where adjacent optical pulses are not severely overlapping during transmission, as in most 10 Gb/s systems, while the IFWM and IXPM become primary concerns in systems where adjacent optical pulses are severely overlapping during transmission, as in most 40 Gb/s systems. A simple assessment of the signal quality after nonlinear transmission is given by the differential phase Q factor (Wei, Liu, and Xu 2003 "Q factor") described next. The impact of the Gordon-Mollenauer phase noise and the IFWM-induced phase and amplitude distortions on ODBPSK will be briefly discussed.

The differential-phase Q factor is defined as

$$Q_{\Delta\phi} = \frac{\pi}{\sigma_{\Delta\phi,0} + \sigma_{\Delta\phi,\pi}} \qquad (22)$$

where $\sigma_{\Delta\phi,0}$ and $\sigma_{\Delta\phi,\pi}$ are, respectively, the standard deviations of the differential phase between two adjacent bits on the 0 and π rails, where the phase noise is caused by the ASE noise and the Gordon-Mollenauer effect. The bit error rate of the signal can be obtained by

$$\text{BER} = \text{erfc}\left(\frac{Q_{\Delta\phi}}{\sqrt{2}}\right) \qquad (23)$$

The simple method assumes that the nonlinear phase noise is Gaussian-distributed, which is an approximation that is valid in some nonlinear transmission systems. In Gordon-Mollenauer noise-limited systems, this method is found to qualitatively reproduce the result obtained from the direct error counting method except for a relatively small offset. This method captures the essence of the SPM penalty in ODPSK systems and predicts the optimum launch power quite accurately. The optimum signal power in a DPSK system is found to correspond to a mean SPM-induced nonlinear phase shift of approximately 1 radian (Gordon and Mollenauer 1990; Wei, Liu, and Xu 2003 "Numerical"). The nonlinear phase noise from single-channel Gordon-Mollenauer effect can be effectively reduced by a lumped *nonlinear phase shift compensation* (NPSC) scheme (Liu et al. 2002; Hansryd, van Howe, and Xu 2005). Signal Q-factor improvement of as much as 6 dB can be realized by NPSC. The effectiveness of NPSC is reduced in DWDM transmission, particularly when the channel spacing is small, because interchannel XPM-induced phase noise cannot be compensated by NPSC.

In dispersion-managed 40-Gb/s transmissions, the Gordon-Mollenauer effect is usually much reduced because of strong pulse breathing. A major nonlinear penalty in 40-Gb/s ODBPSK is IFWM-induced phase and amplitude distortions. Remarkably, it is found that ODBPSK suffers less IFWM penalty than OOK with the same average power. This is attributed to the fact that signal peak power is lower in ODBPSK than OOK with the same average power,

and there exists a correlation between the IFWM-induced nonlinear phase shifts of any two adjacent bits (Wei and Liu 2003). Figure 13 shows the simulated phasor diagrams of a 40-Gb/s RZ-OOK signal and a 40-Gb/s RZ-ODBPSK signal that have the same average power after transmission over a symmetrically dispersion-managed link. The simulated signal pattern is a PRBS of length $2^9 - 1$, which is sufficient for capture most of the intrachannel nonlinear interactions in the dispersion-managed transmission. Evidently, there is a severe eye-closure penalty in the OOK signal because of the generation of ghost pulses while ODBPSK suffers relatively smaller eye closure in the phase domain (see the center subplot). It is interesting that the variance of differential phase, as shown in the right subplot, is almost the same as (instead of twice as large as) that of the absolute phase, showing a strong correlation between the IFWM-induced phase noises of two adjacent bits. Experimentally, ODBPSK is also found to offer higher tolerance to nonlinear effects than OOK in most pulse-overlapped 40-Gb/s transmissions (Gnauck and Winzer 2005).

A semi-analytical method has been developed to estimate the BER of an optical channel by taking into consideration the deterministic phase and amplitude distortions resulting from the IFWM (Ho 2005 "Error"; Wei et al. 2006). The overall BER can be obtained by

$$\text{BER} = \sum_{i=1}^{N} \text{BER}_i \qquad (24)$$

where BER_i is the expected BER for the ith bit out of a simulated N-bit sequence, which can be analytically calculated by

$$\text{BER}_i = Q(a_i, b_i) - \frac{1}{2}e^{-(a_i^2 + b_i^2)/2}I_0(a_i b_i) \qquad (25)$$

where $Q(a,b)$ is the first-order Marcum Q function described in Equation 12 and

$$a_i = \sqrt{\frac{\text{SNR}_b}{2}}\left|\Delta u_i - \Delta u_{i-1}\right|, \quad b_i = \sqrt{\frac{\text{SNR}_b}{2}}\left|2 + \Delta u_i + \Delta u_{i-1}\right| \qquad (26)$$

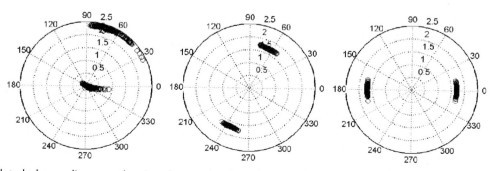

Figure 13: Simulated phasor diagrams showing the amplitude and phase at the centers of signal bits in RZ-OOK (left) and RZ-ODBPSK (center), and the mean amplitude of adjacent bits and differential phase between them in RZ-ODBPSK (right) after pulse-overlapped nonlinear transmission

where Δu_i is the normalized complex amplitude of the IFWM-induced ghost pulse in the ith bit, which can be obtained by numerically solving the governing signal propagation equation (e.g., Equation 18) with the ASE noise excluded. It is found that the IFWM penalty depends on a dispersion map, and a symmetric dispersion map gives smaller IFWM penalty than a nonsymmetric dispersion map (Wei et al. 2006). This is attributed to the absence of the IFWM-induced amplitude fluctuations when a symmetric map is used.

OPTICAL DIFFERENTIAL MULTILEVEL PHASE SHIFT KEYING

Optical differential quadrature phase shift keying (ODQPSK) is a promising modulation format (Griffin 2005) that offers doubled spectral efficiency as compared to ODBPSK and suffers only slightly in terms of receiver sensitivity.

Implementation of ODQPSK

The transmitter for ODQPSK is similar to that for ODBPSK except that the phase modulator should be able to generate four differential-phase levels (0, $\pi/2$, π, and 1.5π) rather than two levels (0 and π) as in ODBPSK; a different precoder is also needed. These four phase levels can be generated by using a nested Mach-Zehnder modulator or using a Mach-Zehnder modulator together with a single-waveguide phase modulator that encodes a 0 or $\pi/2$ phase modulation. A nested Mach-Zehnder modulator is usually preferred because exact phase levels are more readily achievable as discussed earlier. Figure 14 shows the schematic of an ODQPSK transmitter consisting of a nested Mach-Zehnder modulator for phase encoding. Figure 14 also shows the schematic of an ODQPSK receiver, which consists of two ODIs to demodulate the *in-phase* (I) and *quadrature* (Q) tributaries of the signal and two balanced detectors. Mathematically, the two decision variables can be expressed as

$$DV_I(t) = \mathrm{Re}[e^{j\frac{\pi}{4}}E_{RX}(t) \cdot E_{RX}^*(t-T)]$$
$$DV_Q(t) = \mathrm{Im}[e^{j\frac{\pi}{4}}E_{RX}(t) \cdot E_{RX}^*(t-T)] \quad (27)$$

where E_{RX} is the normalized optical field of the ODQPSK signal entering the receiver, and Re[x] and Im[x] are,

respectively, the real and imaginary parts of a complex variable. Note that the ODQPSK demodulator can be simplified by using an optical hybrid with a single optical delay (Cho et al. 2004; Doerr et al. 2005)

For the optical encoding and detection configurations shown in Figure 14, the relations among the precoder outputs and the original data are shown in Table 3 (Ho 2005 "Phase"). The precoder outputs at the kth bit, p_k and q_k, can be obtained by performing the following logic operations on the original data at the kth bit, a_k and b_k, and the previous outputs of the precoder, p_{k-1} and q_{k-1}, according to the following equation

$$p_k = \bar{a}_k\bar{b}_k\bar{p}_{k-1} + \bar{a}_kb_kq_{k-1} + a_k\bar{b}_k\bar{q}_{k-1} + a_kb_kp_{k-1}$$
$$q_k = \bar{a}_k\bar{b}_k\bar{q}_{k-1} + \bar{a}_kb_k\bar{p}_{k-1} + a_k\bar{b}_kp_{k-1} + a_kb_kq_{k-1} \quad (28)$$

Back-to-Back Performance of ODQPSK

For reference, we first describe the optimal receiver sensitivities. For homodyne or heterodyne OQPSK, we have (Proakis 2000).

$$\mathrm{BER}_{\mathrm{OQPSK}} = \frac{1}{2}\,erfc\left(\sqrt{\mathrm{SNR}_b}\right) \quad (29)$$

For direct-detection ODQPSK with polarization filtering at the receiver, we have

$$\mathrm{BER}_{\mathrm{ODQPSK\_1}p} = Q(a,b) - \frac{1}{2}e^{-(a^2+b^2)/2}I_0(ab),$$
$$\text{with } a = \sqrt{2\mathrm{SNR}_b(1-1/\sqrt{2}}, \text{ and}$$
$$b = \sqrt{2\mathrm{SNR}_b\left(1+1/\sqrt{2}\right)}. \quad (30)$$

Similar to Equation 16, for direct-detection ODQPSK without polarization filtering at the receiver, we have

$$\mathrm{BER}_{\mathrm{ODQPSK\_2}p} = Q(a,b) - \frac{1}{2}e^{-(a^2+b^2)/2} \cdot I_0(ab)$$
$$+ \frac{1}{8}e^{-(a^2+b^2)/2}\left(\frac{b}{a} - \frac{a}{b}\right) \cdot I_1(ab), \quad (31)$$

where a and b are the same as those given in Equation 30. Figure 15 shows the BER performances of OQPSK and

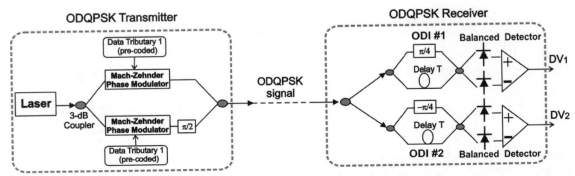

Figure 14: Schematic of an ODQPSK transmitter based on a nested Mach-Zehnder phase modulator and an ODQPSK receiver

Table 3: Relations among Precoder Outputs and Original Data for ODQPSK Transmitter and Receiver Configuration in Figure 14 (Ho 2005 "Phase")

Original data ($a_k b_k$)	Optical phase difference	First precoder output, p_k	Second precoder output, q_k
(00)	π	$\bar{p}_{k-1}$	$\bar{q}_{k-1}$
(01)	$\pi/2$	q_{k-1}	$\bar{p}_{k-1}$
(10)	1.5π	$\bar{q}_{k-1}$	p_{k-1}
(11)	0	p_{k-1}	q_{k-1}

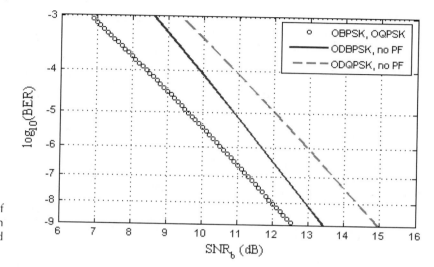

Figure 15: The optimal BER performances of OQPSK and ODQPSK without polarization filtering, as compared to those of OBPSK and ODBPSK

ODQPSK without polarization filtering, as compared to those of OBPSK and ODBPSK. The OQPSK performs the same as the OBPSK, while the ODQPSK (without polarization filtering) exhibits a differential detection penalty of ~2.4 dB. Comparing the ODQPSK with the ODBPSK, the relative sensitivity penalty of the ODQPSK is ~1.5 dB at BER = 10^{-9} and ~0.8 dB at BER = 10^{-3}. These performance differences were experimentally verified (Gnauck et al. 2006). In optical transmission systems with modern FEC codes, the raw BER of interest is high, and the receiver sensitivity disadvantage of the direct-detection ODQPSK as compared to the ODBPSK becomes small.

Similar to ODBPSK, ODQPSK also suffers from implementation imperfections. Particularly, ODQPSK is highly sensitive to the phase errors. The BER of an ODQPSK signal in the presence of a phase error, ϕ_e, is

$$
\begin{aligned}
\text{BER}_{\text{ODQPSK}\_\phi_e} = \frac{1}{2} \big[&\text{BER}_{\text{ODQPSK}}(a_+, b_+) \\
&+ \text{BER}_{\text{ODQPSK}}(a_-, b_-) \big],
\end{aligned}
$$

$$
\text{with } a_{\pm} = \sqrt{2\text{SNR}_b \left[1 - \cos\left(\frac{\pi}{4} \pm \phi_e \right) \right]}, \quad \text{and} \quad (32)
$$

$$
b_{\pm} = \sqrt{2\text{SNR}_b \left[1 + \cos\left(\frac{\pi}{4} \pm \phi_e \right) \right]},
$$

where $\text{BER}_{\text{ODQSPK}}()$ is obtained from Equation 30 or 31, depending on whether there is polarization filtering at the receiver. Figure 16 shows the OSNR penalty (at BER = 10^{-9}) of a 40-Gb/s ODQPSK as a function of the laser frequency offset, as compared to that of a 40-Gb/s ODBPSK signal. ODQPSK requires approximately 5.5 times tighter laser frequency accuracy (Kim and Winzer 2003).

Transmission Performance of ODQPSK

For the same symbol rate, multilevel formats usually have lower CD tolerance than binary formats. However, for the same bit rate, multilevel formats are more tolerant to CD. ODQPSK, by encoding two bits per symbol, offers higher tolerance to CD and PMD than ODBPSK. At 42.7 Gb/s, the CD-induced penalty reaches 2 dB at approximately ±130 ps/nm (Gnauck et al. 2006). The PMD tolerance of ODQPSK is approximately twice as large as that of ODBPSK (Gnauck et al. 2006). RZ-ODQPSK is also found to have good tolerance to fiber nonlinearity and optical filtering (Cho et al. 2003; Gnauck et al. 2004 "Spectrally"). The disadvantages of ODQPSK as compared to ODBPSK include slightly lower receiver sensitivity and higher sensitivity to the phase error. ODQPSK is attractive for systems where high spectral efficiency and high tolerance to CD and PMD are desired.

Generalized ODMPSK

Higher spectral efficiency can be obtained by using ODMPSK formats with more phase levels. *Optical differential 8-ary PSK* (OD8PSK) has been proposed and demonstrated by (Kim and Li 2004). Generally, for an ODMDPSK transmitter, $\log_2(M)$ binary phase modulators are usually needed to encode the M phase levels, or $\log_2(M)$ binary data tributaries. For an ODMPSK receiver, a series of

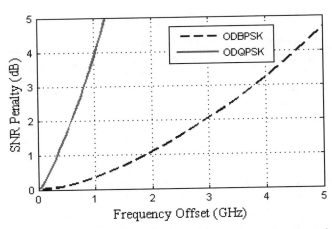

Figure 16: The OSNR penalty (at BER = 10^{-9}) as a function of the laser frequency offset in 40-Gb/s ODQPSK and ODBPSK systems using one-bit ODIs. No polarization filtering is used

decision variables are needed to decode the $\log_2(M)$ binary data tributaries. A straightforward demodulation scheme is to use $M/2$ ODIs with the following different phase offsets (between the two arms of each ODI):

$$\Delta\phi_{\mathrm{ODI}}(m) = \frac{[1 - 2(m-1)]\pi}{M}, \text{ with } m = 1, 2, \dots, \frac{M}{2} \quad (33)$$

For the demodulation of OD8PSK, four ODIs are needed, and the phase offsets in the ODIs are $\pi/8$, $-\pi/8$, $-3\pi/8$, and $-5\pi/8$, respectively. Because there are correlations among the decision variables obtained by the $M/2$ ODIs, the number of the needed ODIs may be reduced with the help of analog radio frequency components (Han, Kim, and Li 2004).

The receiver sensitivity of an OMPSK signal can be straightforwardly estimated from the minimum Euclidean distance between the two closest symbols in its constellation diagram. The receiver sensitivity penalty (in dB) of OMPSK as compared to OBPSK can be approximated as (Ho 2005 "Phase")

$$\Delta\mathrm{SNR}_b(\mathrm{OMPSK} \Leftrightarrow \mathrm{OBPSK}) \approx$$
$$- 20\log_{10}\left[\sin\left(\frac{\pi}{M}\right) \cdot \sqrt{\log_2(M)}\right] \quad (34)$$

For ODMPSK signals, the errors are dominated by differential phase noise. We define an effective "differential-phase distance" between the two closest symbols of ODMPSK signal in its constellation diagram as

$$d_{\Delta\phi}(\mathrm{ODMPSK}) = \frac{2\pi}{M} \cdot \frac{1}{\sqrt{2}} = \frac{\sqrt{2}\pi}{M} \quad (35)$$

where the factor of 2 comes from the fact that the differential-phase deviation is 2 times as large as the absolute phase deviation, assuming that the optical noise–induced phase fluctuations in adjacent signal bits are independent Gaussian random variables. At low BERs, we can express the receiver sensitivity penalty (in dB) of ODMPSK as compared to the OBPSK as

$$\Delta\mathrm{SNR}_b(\mathrm{ODMPSK} \Leftrightarrow \mathrm{OBPSK}) \approx -20\log_{10}$$
$$\left[\frac{d_{\Delta\phi}}{2} \cdot \sqrt{\log_2(M)}\right]$$
$$= -20\log_{10}\left[\frac{\pi}{\sqrt{2}M} \cdot \sqrt{\log_2(M)}\right] \quad (36)$$

Figure 17 shows the receiver sensitivity penalties of OMPSK and ODMPSK as compared to OBPSK versus the number of phase levels. The sensitivity penalties are large (>3 dB) for formats with $M > 4$. In addition, the differential detection penalty approaches 3 dB as M increases. This suggests that ODMPSK formats with $M > 4$ are only viable in systems with sufficiently high OSNR.

Combined ODMPSK and Pulse Amplitude Modulation

Another way to achieve high spectral efficiency is by combining ODMPSK with PAM. The simplest such format is

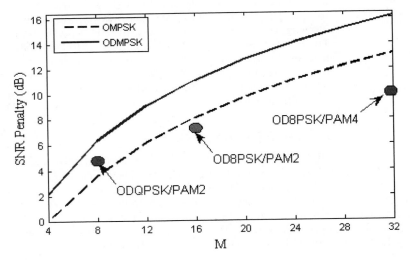

Figure 17: The receiver sensitivity penalties of OMPSK and ODMPSK as compared to OBPSK as a function of the number of phase levels. The symbols are for ODMPSK/PAM-N formats

the combination of ODBPSK and a two-level PAM (Liu et al. 2003). For an ODMPSK/PAM-N signal, its ideal receiver sensitivity is optimized when the Euclidean distances between two adjacent PAM levels in its constellation diagram not only are equal but also equal to the effective "differential-phase distance" between the two closest symbols. The optimal locations of the $M \times N$ symbols of an ODMPSK/PAM-N signal are thus

$$s(m,n) = c \cdot \exp\left(j\frac{2\pi m}{M}\right) \cdot \left(1 + \frac{\sqrt{2}\pi n}{M}\right), \text{ with}$$
$$m = 0,1,\ldots,M-1, \text{ and } n = 0,1,\ldots,N-1 \quad (37)$$

where c is a normalization factor. It can be estimated that the receiver sensitivity penalty of the ODMPSK/PAM-N as compared to the OBPSK is

$$\Delta\text{SNR}_b(\text{ODPMSK/PAM-N} \Leftrightarrow \text{OBPSK}) \approx$$
$$-10\log_{10}\left\{\left(\frac{d_{\Delta\phi}}{2}\right)^2 \cdot \left[\begin{matrix}1+(N-1)d_{\Delta\phi}\\+\frac{1}{6}(N-1)(2N-1)d_{\Delta\phi}^2\end{matrix}\right]^{-1} \cdot \log_2(M \cdot N)\right\}$$
$$= -10\log_{10}\left\{\frac{\pi^2}{2M^2} \cdot \left[\begin{matrix}1+(N-1)\frac{\sqrt{2}\pi}{M}\\+(N-1)(2N-1)\frac{\pi^2}{3M^2}\end{matrix}\right]^{-1} \cdot \log_2(M \cdot N)\right\} \quad (38)$$

ODQPSK/PAM-2 is a three-bit/symbol format that has been demonstrated (Hayase et al. 2004). The theoretical receiver sensitivity penalty as compared to OBPSK (having the same bit rate) is 4.7 dB, approximately 1.7 dB smaller than OD8PSK, which is also a three-bit/symbol format. At four and five bits per symbol, the ODMPSK/PAM-N offer higher optimal receiver sensitivities than ODMPSK, as shown in Figure 17. However, ODMPSK/PAM-N generally suffers more implementation penalty and nonlinear penalty (because of SPM-induced phase offsets between symbols with different intensities) than ODMPSK.

Polarization Multiplexed ODPSK

A commonly used means to double spectral efficiency is via *polarization multiplexing*, with the trade-off of increased complexity at both the transmitter and receiver. Because the polarization of a signal after fiber transmission is uncertain and time-varying, polarization monitoring and tracking are required for polarization demultiplexing. Furthermore, in WDM transmissions, interchannel XPM may lead to nonlinear polarization scattering, which causes the polarization to vary on a bit-by-bit basis and may make polarization demultiplexing impossible. ODPSK, by having nearly identical intensity profiles in all of the bit slots, exhibits smaller XPM effects and smaller nonlinear polarization scattering than OOK (Liu, Xu, and Wei 2004). High spectral-efficiency transmissions have been demonstrated using polarization multiplexing and ODQPSK (Wree et al.

2003; Cho et al. 2004). A special case of polarization multiplexing is *polarization bit interleaving*, which is used to mitigate intrachannel nonlinear penalties rather than doubling spectral efficiency. Note that large PMD can severely degrade the performance of polarization-multiplexed signals.

FORWARD-LOOKING TOPICS

As ODPSK is evolving to be a potential candidate for many applications in optical communications, there are many forward-looking topics that deserve further study. A few are briefly mentioned in the following.

Improved Detection of ODPSK

As shown in a previous section, there exists a differential detection penalty for the receiver sensitivity of direct-detection ODPSK as compared to homodyne or heterodyne OPSK. The differential detection penalty can be reduced by expanding techniques used in wireless communications such as multichip ODPSK (Nazarathy and Simony 2005) and data-aided multisymbol phase estimation (Liu 2006) to ODPSK. With multichip detection or multisymbol phase estimation, a more accurate phase reference can be obtained so that the performance of ODPSK can approach that of homodyne-detection OPSK. By extracting a more accurate phase reference, the tolerance of ODPSK to nonlinear phase noise (e.g., resulting from the Gordon-Mollenauer effect) can also be increased (Nazarathy and Simony 2005; Liu 2006). With the advances of high-speed electronics, future efforts are expected to improve the detection of ODPSK through high-speed analog-to-digital conversion and *digital signal processing* (DSP), even in the presence of transmission impairments. Note that DSP techniques can also be applied to improve the homodyne detection of OPSK. Soft detection can also be used in combination with FEC to further improve the performance of ODQPSK (Kramer et al. 2003; Mizuochi et al. 2004).

Wavelength Conversion and Optical Regeneration of ODPSK

Wavelength conversion and optical regeneration are emerging techniques in modern optical transport networks. Unlike OOK, ODPSK encodes data in optical phase, so wavelength conversion of ODPSK has to be phase preserving. Similarly, the regeneration of an ODPSK signal has to include restoration in optical phase in addition to *reamplification* in signal intensity, *reshaping* of signal waveform, and *retiming* (3R) that are sufficient in the regeneration of an OOK signal. A regenerative all-optical wavelength conversion scheme, based on a Mach-Zehnder interferometer with differentially driven semiconductor optical amplifiers, was demonstrated for a 40-Gb/s ODBPSK signal (Kang et al. 2005). A regenerative amplification scheme for ODBPSK that is capable of suppressing both phase and amplitude noises has also been demonstrated (Shin et al. 2006). More efforts may be seen in cost-effective implementations of the wavelength conversion and regeneration of ODSPK in future optical networks.

Optical Packet Switching Based on ODPSK

Optical packet switching (OPS) and *optical burst switching* (OBS) are regarded as promising transport technologies. In OPS and OBS systems, a challenging issue is the need of burst-mode receivers that are capable of fast resynchronization to different data packets or bursts with different amplitudes and timings. Direct-detection ODPSK with balanced detection has a fixed optimal decision threshold at approximately zero and may allow burst-mode detection to be more easily implemented than in the OOK case. Optical label switching is an interesting switching method. Orthogonal ODPSK modulation and intensity modulation have been used for encoding payload and label signals on a same wavelength channel (Liu et al. 2004 "Transmission"). ODPSK is expected to play an important role in future high-speed OPS and OBS networks.

CONCLUSION

The fundamentals, principles, implementations, and system impacts of ODPSK have been reviewed. The overall performance of ODPSK, including optimal receiver sensitivity, implementation penalty, and tolerance to transmission impairments, are comprehensively evaluated. Some forward-looking topics have been briefly discussed. ODPSK, by exhibiting several advantages over OOK, is expected to be a promising modulation format for modern optical transport networks.

ACKNOWLEDGMENT

The progress on ODPSK summarized in this chapter implicitly represents the works of many researchers and developers around the world, and in this limited space the author was unable to include all of the contributions. The author is especially grateful to his colleagues working in this field in the Bell Laboratories for fruitful collaborations and valuable discussions. Among them are S. Chandrasekhar, C. R. Doerr, D. A. Fishman, D. M. Gill, A. H. Gnauck, I. Kang, Y.-H. Kao, G. Kramer, J. Leuthold, C. J. McKinstrie, L. F. Mollenauer, L. Möller, Y. Su, A. J. van Wijngaarden, X. Wei, P. J. Winzer, C. Xie, and C. Xu. The author is also indebted to C. R. Giles and A. R. Chraplyvy for their support.

GLOSSARY

Bit error rate (BER): The ratio between the number of bits that are incorrectly received and the number of the total bits that are transmitted over a given period of time in a communication system.

Chromatic dispersion (CD): An effect that causes different optical wavelength components to travel at different speeds.

Cross-phase modulation (XPM): A nonlinear optical effect that imposes a change in optical phase on an optical signal by another optical signal via the optical Kerr effect.

Forward error correction (FEC): A digital communication technique for error control whereby the sender adds redundant data to its messages, which allows the receiver to detect and correct errors.

Intrachannel four-wave mixing (IFWM): The four-wave mixing interaction among different symbols in a same wavelength channel.

Non-return to zero (NRZ): A pulse format used in telecommunication signals in which the signal power does not drop to zero after each symbol that has a nonzero power.

On-off keying (OOK): A modulation format that represents digital data as the presence (on) or absence (off) of a carrier wave.

Optical delay interferometer (ODI): An optical interferometer having two interference paths whose optical lengths are different.

Optical differential binary phase shift keying (ODBPSK): An optical modulation format that represents digital data by two possible differences between the optical phases of two adjacent symbols, 0 and π.

Optical differential multilevel phase shift keying (ODMPSK): An optical modulation format that represents digital data by M possible differences between the optical phases of two adjacent symbols, 0, $2\pi/M$, $4\pi/M$, ... , and $2\pi(M-1)/M$.

Optical differential phase shift keying (ODPSK): An optical modulation format that represents digital data by the difference between the optical phases of two adjacent symbols.

Optical differential quadrature phase shift keying (ODQPSK): An optical modulation format that represents digital data by four possible differences between the optical phases of two adjacent symbols: 0, $\pi/2$, π, and $3\pi/2$.

Optical phase shift keying (OPSK): An optical modulation format that represents digital data by the optical phase of a carrier wave.

Optical signal-to-noise ratio (OSNR): The ratio between the signal power and the power of optical noise of two polarization states within a fixed bandwidth of 0.1 nm (or 12.5 GHz at a signal wavelength of approximately 1550 nm).

Photons per bit (PPB): The number of optical photons used to carry each information bit.

Polarization mode dispersion (PMD): A form of modal dispersion in which two different polarizations of light in a waveguide, which normally travel at the same speed, travel at different speeds because of random imperfections and asymmetries, causing random spreading of optical pulses.

Pulse amplitude modulation (PAM): A form of signal modulation in which the message information is encoded in the amplitude of a series of signal pulses.

Return to zero (RZ): A pulse format used in telecommunication signals in which the signal power drops (returns) to zero after each symbol that has a nonzero power.

Self-phase modulation (SPM): A nonlinear optical effect that imposes a change in optical phase on an optical signal by the signal itself via the optical Kerr effect.

Wavelength-division multiplexing (WDM): An optical communication technology that multiplexes multiple optical carrier signals on a single optical fiber by using different wavelengths (colors) of laser light to carry different signals.

CROSS REFERENCES

See *Minimum Shift Keying (MSK)*; *Optical Fiber Communications*.

REFERENCES

Agrawal, G. P. 2001. *Nonlinear fiber optics*. 3rd ed. San Diego: Academic Press.

Bosco, G., and P. Poggiolini. 2005. The impact of receiver imperfections on the performance of optical direct-detection DPSK. *Journal of Lightwave Technology*, 23: 842–8.

Cho, P. S., V. S. Grigoryan, Y. A. Godin, A. Salamon, and Y. Achiam. 2003. Transmission of 25-Gb/s RZ-DQPSK signals with 25-GHz channel spacing over 1000 km of SMF-28 fiber. *IEEE Photonics Technology Letters*, 15: 473–5.

Cho, P. S., G. Harston, C. Kerr, A. Greenblatt, A. Kaplan, Y. Achiam, G. Yurista, M. Margalit, Y. Gross, and J. Khurgin. 2004. Investigation of 2-bit/s/Hz 40-Gb/s DWDM transmission over 4 × 100-km SMF-28 fiber using RZ-DQPSK and polarization multiplexing. *IEEE Photonics Technology Letters*, 16: 656–8.

Doerr, C. R., D. M. Gill, A. H. Gnauck, L. L. Buhl, P. J. Winzer, M. A. Cappuzzo, A. Wong-Foy, E. Y. Chen, and L. T. Gomez. 2005. Simultaneous reception of both quadratures of 40-Gb/s DQPSK using a simple monolithic demodulator. In *Proceedings of Optical Fiber Communication Conference* (OFC '05), Anaheim, CA, USA, vol. 5, postdeadline paper PDP12.

Essiambre, R.-J., G. Raybon, and B. Mikkelsen. 2002. Chap. 6 in *Pseudo-linear transmission of high-speed TDM signals, 40 and 160 Gb/s*, edited by I. P. Kaminov and T. Li. San Diego: Academic Press.

Forghieri, F., R. W. Tkach, and A. R. Chraplyvy. 1997. Chap. 8 in *Fiber nonlinearities and their impact on transmission systems*, edited by I. P. Kaminov and T. L. Koch. San Diego: Academic Press.

Giles, R. C., and K. C. Reichmann. 1987. Optical self-homodyne DPSK transmission at 1-Gbit/s and 2-Gbit/s over 86 km of fiber. *Electronics Letters*, 23: 1180–1.

Gnauck, A. H., X. Liu, X. Wei, D. M. Gill, and E. C. Burrows. 2004. Comparison of modulation formats for 42.7-Gb/s single-channel transmission through 1980 km of SSMF. *IEEE Photonics Technology Letters*, 16: 852–4.

Gnauck, A. H., and P. J. Winzer. 2005. Optical phase-shift-keyed transmission. *Journal of Lightwave Technology*, 23: 115–30.

Gnauck, A. H., P. J. Winzer, S. Chandrasekhar, and C. Dorrer. 2004. Spectrally efficient (0.8 b/s/Hz) 1-Tb/s (25 × 42.7 Gb/s) RZ-DQPSK transmission over 28 100-km SSMF spans with 7 optical add/drops. In *Proceedings in European Conference on Optical Communications* (ECOC), postdeadline paper Th. 4.4.1.

Gnauck, A. H., P. J. Winzer, C. Dorrer, and S. Chandrasekhar. 2006. Linear and nonlinear performance of 42.7-Gb/s single-polarization RZ-DQPSK format. *IEEE Photonics Technology Letters*, 18: 883–885.

Gordon, J. P., and L. F. Mollenauer. 1990. Phase noise in photonic communications systems using linear amplifiers. *Optics Letters*, 15: 1351–3.

Griffin, R. A. 2005. Integrated DQPSK transmitters. *Proceedings of OFC 2005*, paper OWE3.

Han, Y., C. Kim, and G. Li. 2004. Simplified receiver implementation for optical differential 8-level phase-shift keying. *Electronics Letters*, 40: 1372–3.

Hansryd, J., J. van Howe, and C. Xu. 2005. Experimental demonstration of nonlinear phase jitter compensation in DPSK modulated fiber links. *IEEE Photonics Technology Letters*, 17: 232–4.

Hayase, S., N. Kikuchi, K. Sekine, and S. Sasaki. 2004. Chromatic dispersion and SPM tolerance of 8-state/symbol (binary ASK and QPSK) modulated signal. *Proceedings of OFC*, paper Th. M3.

Heismann F., Korotky S. K., and Veselka J. J. (1997). Chap. 9 in *Lithium niobate integrated optics: Selected contemporary devices and system applications*, edited by I. P. Kaminov and T. L. Koch. San Diego: Academic Press.

Ho, K.-P. 2005. Error probability of DPSK signals with intrachannel four-wave mixing in highly dispersive transmission systems. *IEEE Photonics Technology Letters*, 17: 789–91.

———. 2005. *Phase-modulated optical communication systems*. New York: Springer

Kang, I., C. Dorrer, L. Zhang, M. Rasras, L. Buhl, A. Bhardwaj, S. Cabot, M. Dinu, X. Liu, M. Cappuzzo, L. Gomez, A. Wong-Foy, Y. F. Chen, S. Patel, D. T. Neilson, J. Jaques, and C. R. Giles. 2005. Regenerative all optical wavelength conversion of 40-Gb/s DPSK signals using a semiconductor optical amplifier Mach-Zehnder interferometer. *Proceedings of ECOC*, postdeadline paper Th. 4.3.3.

Kim, C., and G. Li. 2004. Direct-detection optical differential 8-level phase-shift keying (OD8PSK) for spectrally efficient transmission. *Optics Express*, 12: 3415–21.

Kim, H., and P. J. Winzer. 2003. Robustness to laser frequency offset in direct-detection DPSK and DQPSK systems. *Journal of Lightwave Technology*, 21: 1887–91.

Kramer, G., A. Ashikhmin, A. J. van Wijngaarden, and X. Wei. 2003. Spectral efficiency of coded phase-shift keying for fiber-optic communication. *Journal of Lightwave Technology*, 21: 2438–45.

Liu, X. 2006. Data-aided multi-symbol phase estimation for receiver sensitivity enhancement in optical DQPSK. In *Proceedings of Coherent Optical Technologies and Applications* (COTA), Topical Meeting, Whistler, British Columbia, Canada, paper CThB4.

———, C. R. Giles, X. Wei, A.-J. van Wijngaarden, Y.-H. Kao, C. Xie, and L. Möller. 2005. Improved PMD tolerance in systems using enhanced forward error correction through distributed fast polarization scrambling. In *Proceedings of ECOC*, paper We1.3.6.

———, C. R. Giles, X. Wei, A.-J. van Wijngaarden, Y.-H. Kao, C. Xie, L. Möller, and I. Kang. 2005. Demonstration of broad-band PMD mitigation in the presence of PDL through distributed fast polarization scrambling and forward-error correction. *IEEE Photonics Technology Letters*, 17: 1109–11.

———, A. H. Gnauck, X. Wei, Y. C. Hsieh, C. Ai, and V. Chien. 2005. Athermal optical demodulator for OC-768 DPSK and RZ-DPSK signals. *IEEE Photonics Technology Letters*, 17: 2610–12.

————, and Y.-H. Kao. 2005. Chirped RZ-DPSK based on single Mach-Zehnder modulator and its nonlinear transmission performance. *IEEE Photonics Technology Letters*, 17: 1531–3.

————, Y.-H. Kao, M. Movassaghi, and R. C. Giles. 2004. Tolerance to in-band coherent crosstalk of differential phase-shift-keyed signal with balanced detection and FEC. *IEEE Photonics Technology Letters*, 16: 1209–11.

————, L. F. Mollenauer, and X. Wei. 2004. Impact of group-delay ripple in transmission systems including phase-modulated formats. *IEEE Photonics Technology Letters*, 16: 305–7.

————, X. Wei, Y.-H. Kao, J. Leuthold, C. R. Doerr, and L. F. Mollenauer. 2003. Quaternary differential-phase amplitude-shift-keying for DWDM transmission. *Proceedings of ECOC*, paper Th. 2.6.5.

————, X. Wei, R. E. Slusher, and C. J. McKinstrie. 2002. Improving transmission performance in differential phase-shift-keyed systems by use of lumped nonlinear phase-shift compensation. *Optics Letters*, 27: 1616–18.

————, X. Wei, Y. Su, J. Leuthold, Y.-H. Kao, I. Kang, and R. C. Giles. 2004. Transmission of an ASK-labeled RZ-DPSK signal and label erasure using a saturated SOA. *IEEE Photonics Technology Letters*, 16: 1594–6.

————, C. Xu, and X. Wei. 2004. Performance analysis of time/polarization multiplexed 40-Gb/s RZ-DPSK DWDM transmission. *IEEE Photonics Technology Letters*, 16: 302–4.

Mizuochi, T., Y. Miyata, T. Kobayashi, K. Ouchi, K. Kuno, K. Kubo, K. Shimizu, H. Tagami, H. Yoshida, H. Fujita, M. Akita, and K. Motoshima. 2004. Forward error correction based on block turbo code with 3-bit soft decision for 10-Gb/s optical communication systems. *IEEE Journal of Selected Topics in Quantum Electronics*, 10: 376–86.

Möller, L., Y. Su, C. Xie, X. Liu, J. Leuthold, D. M. Gill, and X. Wei. 2003. Generation and detection of 80-Gbit/s return-to-zero differential phase-shift keying signals. *Optics Letters*, 24: 2461–3.

Möller, L., Y. Su, C. Xie, R. Ryf, C. R. Doerr, X. Liu, and L. L. Buhl. 2004. Generation of a 160-Gb/s RZ-DPSK Signal and its detection with a one-bit Mach-Zehnder interferometer. *Proceedings of ECOC*, paper PDP Th.4.4.6.

Mu, R.-M., T. Yu, V. S. Grigoryan, and C. R. Menyuk. 2002. Dynamics of the chirped return-to-zero modulation format. *Journal of Lightwave Technology*, 20: 47–57.

Nazarathy, M., and E. Simony. 2005. Multichip differential phase encoded optical transmission. *IEEE Photonics Technology Letters*, 17: 1133–5.

Price, A. J., and N. Le Mercier. 1995. Reduced bandwidth optical digital intensity modulation with improved chromatic dispersion tolerance. *Electronics Letters*, 31: 58–9.

Proakis, J. G. 2000. *Digital communications*. 4th ed. New York: McGraw-Hill.

Shin, M., P. S. Devgan, V.S. Grigoryan, and P. Kumar. 2006. SNR improvement of DPSK signals in a semiconductor optical regenerative amplifier. *IEEE Photonics Technology Letters*, 18: 49–51.

Tamura, K., S. B. Alexander, V. W. S. Chan, and D. M. Boroson. 1990. Phase-noise-canceled differential phase-shift-keying (PNC-DPSK) for coherent optical communication systems. *Journal of Lightwave Technology*, 8: 190–201.

Wang, J., and J. M. Kahn. 2004. Impact of chromatic and polarization-mode dispersions on DPSK systems using interferometric demodulation and direct detection. *Journal of Lightwave Technology*, 22: 362–71.

Wei X., A. H. Gnauck, D. M. Gill, X. Liu, U.-V. Koc, S. Chandrasekhar, G. Raybon, and J. Leuthold. 2003. Optical π/2-DPSK and its tolerance to filtering and polarization-mode dispersion. *IEEE Photonics Technology Letters*, 15: 1639–41.

Wei, X., and X. Liu. 2003. Analysis of intrachannel four-wave mixing in differential phase-shift keying transmission with large dispersion. *Optics Letters*, 28: 2300–2.

————, S. H. Simon, and C. J. McKinstrie. 2006. Intrachannel four-wave mixing in highly dispersed return-to-zero differential-phase-shift-keyed transmission with a nonsymmetric dispersion map. *Optics Letters*, 31: 29–31.

————, and C. Xu. 2003. Numerical simulation of the SPM penalty in a 10-Gb/s RZ-DPSK system. *IEEE Photonics Technology Letters*, 15: 1636–8.

————, and C. Xu. 2003. Q factor in numerical simulation of DPSK with optical delay demodulation (retrieved from http://arXiv.org/physics/0304002).

Weisstein, E. W. 2005. Marcum Q-function (retrieved from http://mathworld.wolfram.com/MarcumQ-Function.html).

Winzer, P. J., S. Chandrasekhar, and H. Kim. 2003. Impact of filtering on RZ-DPSK reception. *IEEE Photonics Technology Letters*, 15: 840–2.

Wree, C., N. Hecker-Denschlag, E. Gottwald, P. Krummrich, J. Leibrich, E.-D. Schmidt, B. Lankl, and W. Rosenkranz. 2003. High spectral efficiency 1.6-b/s/Hz transmission (8 × 40 Gb/s with a 25-GHz grid) over 200-km SSMF using RZ-DQPSK and polarization multiplexing. *IEEE Photonics Technology Letters*, 15: 1303–5.

Xie, C., L. Möller, H. Haunstein, and S. Hunsche. 2003. Comparison of system tolerance to polarization mode dispersion between different modulation format systems. *IEEE Photonics Technology Letters*, 15: 1168–70.

Xu, C., X. Liu, and X. Wei. 2004. Differential phase-shift keying for high spectral efficiency optical transmissions. *IEEE Journal of Selected Topics in Quantum Electronics*, 10: 281–93.

Yadin, Y., M. Shtaif, and M. Orenstein. 2005. Bit-error rate of optical DPSK in fiber systems by multicanonical Monte Carlo Simulations. *IEEE Photonics Technology Letters*, 17: 1355–7.

DMT Modulation

Stephan Pfletschinger, *Centre Tecnològic de Telecomunicacions de Catalunya, Barcelona, Spain*

INTRODUCTION

Discrete multitone (DMT) is a digital transmission scheme that belongs to the class of *multicarrier modulation* (MCM) schemes, the key function of which is to partition a high-rate data stream into a large number of low-rate streams and to transmit them in parallel over equidistantly spaced subchannels. As the occupied bandwidth of a signal is reciprocal to its symbol rate, the sum of all low-rate bit streams occupies the same bandwidth as the high-rate signal. The main feature of MCM is that the low-rate (and hence narrowband) signals are much less susceptible to channel impairments; thus, reconstruction of the subchannel signals at the receiver side is simplified to a great extent. However, all subchannels have to be received in parallel and must be processed simultaneously, a requirement that can only be met in an economic way with digital signal processing. Because of the usually large number of carriers, the subchannel signals can be well adapted to the channel characteristics. As a consequence, multicarrier systems such as DMT offer the ability to maximize the data throughput over frequency-selective channels such as telephone subscriber lines. Thus, it does not come as a surprise that the main application of DMT is the transmission of broadband data over such lines, which are known as *asymmetric digital subscriber lines* (ADSLs) and *very high data rate digital subscriber lines* (VDSLs) (Bingham 2000).

The earliest ideas for MCM date back to the late 1950s when the first multicarrier systems were developed for military high-frequency transmission. The idea of synchronously modulating several narrowband signals onto equidistant carriers with overlapping spectra was realized as early as 1957 in the Collins Kineplex system (Doelz, Heald, and Martin 1957), which used *phase shift keying* (PSK) modulation to transmit 3000 bits/sec over twenty

subcarriers with overlapping spectra. This early system already made use of a guard time to prevent *intersymbol interference* (ISI). In the 1960s, this was followed by other high-frequency military systems.

The groundbreaking idea of using the *discrete Fourier transform* (DFT) instead of oscillator banks for modulation became widely known with the classical paper of Weinstein and Ebert (1971). Cimini (1985) investigated and suggested the use of MCM over mobile channels. Multicarrier systems had still not found their way into applications, but with the ascent of digital signal processing and the substantial progress in semiconductor technology in the early 1990s, Bingham (1990) concluded that the time had come for MCM. Kalet (1989) and Kasturia, Aslanis, and Cioffi (1990) provided in-depth investigations of the potential of MCM, and the race was on. Nowadays, MCM is being applied in many digital transmission systems, and it is still the preferred option for new developments such as fourth-generation cellular systems.

Apart from DMT, another well-known multicarrier scheme is *orthogonal frequency division multiplex* (OFDM), with which DMT has many basic principles in common. OFDM is a passband modulation scheme that is applied for wireless communication, while DMT is a baseband system and is normally used in wireline applications. Moreover, DMT offers the possibility of adjusting the modulation and transmit power in each subchannel (bit loading) and can thus be well adapted to frequency-selective channels.

Because MCM can be interpreted as a further development of *frequency division multiplexing* (FDM), in the next section we explain classical FDM principles and then derive the basics of multicarrier modulation such as the orthogonality criterion and show the need for the guard interval. In the third section, we turn our attention to the digital system model and develop the probably most important characteristic of DMT, which is the decomposition of a frequency-selective broadband channel into parallel nonselective narrowband channels. The fourth section then goes into some implementation details such as equalization strategies, considering also an insufficient guard interval, and outlines the problem of the peak-to-average power ratio. Implementation alternatives with filter banks and variants of the guard interval are given. In the fifth section, we describe how adaptive bit loading can be used to maximize the transmission rate by making use of fundamental principles from information theory. Finally, the last section portrays the main applications of DMT and looks at recent advances with multi-user DMT.

BASICS OF MULTICARRIER MODULATION
Frequency Division Multiplexing

With FDM, the available bandwidth of the transmission medium is partitioned into a number of nonoverlapping frequency bands in order to transmit various signals simultaneously on the same medium. The basic block diagram is depicted in Figure 1. Each band-limited baseband signal $x_\nu(t)$ is modulated onto a complex carrier $\exp(j\omega_\nu t)$ with carrier frequencies ω_0, ..., ω_{N-1}. The received FDM signal is demodulated with the complex conjugate carrier $\exp(-j\omega_\nu t)$ and then *low-pass* (LP) filtered to obtain the baseband signal $y_\nu(t)$. The FDM signal at the transmitter output is given by

$$s(t) = \sum_{\nu=0}^{N-1} x_\nu(t)e^{j\omega_\nu t} \qquad (1)$$

Here and in the following we use the equivalent baseband notation for the output signal—that is, $s(t)$ is the complex envelope of the transmit signal, and the channel in Figure 1 is the equivalent baseband channel (for details, see, e.g., Haykin 2001).

Considering the spectra of the signals $x_\nu(t)$ on the νth branch, denoted by $x_\nu(t) \leftrightarrow X_\nu(\omega)$, we have

$$x_\nu(t)e^{j\omega_\nu t} \leftrightarrow X_\nu(\omega - \omega_\nu) \qquad (2)$$

and hence the spectrum of the transmitter output signal

$$s(t) \leftrightarrow S(\omega) = \sum_{\nu=0}^{N-1} X_\nu(\omega - \omega_\nu) \qquad (3)$$

The spectrum $S(\omega)$ is shown for an exemplary case in Figure 2. In classical FDM systems, the frequencies ω_ν have to be chosen in such a way that the spectra of the modulated signals do not overlap. If all baseband signals $x_\nu(t)$ have the same bandwidth, then the carrier frequencies are chosen to be equidistant. However, the described FDM system wastes valuable bandwidth because some space is needed in the form of a guard band to accommodate the transition between the pass- and the stopband of each branch's signal.

This drawback of wasted spectrum can be overcome by multicarrier modulation such as DMT, which allows for a certain overlap between the spectra of the subchannel signals. Because spectral overlap in general could lead to signal distortions and cross talk, conditions to ensure the possibility of signal reconstruction have to be elaborated. This is addressed in the next section.

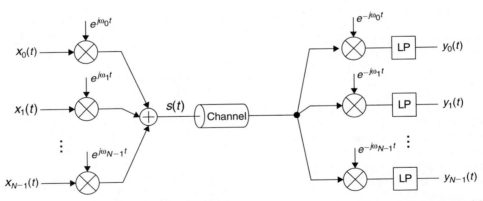

Figure 1: Analog frequency division multiplexing. The baseband signals $x_0(t)$, ..., $x_{N-1}(t)$ are modulated on different carriers and are transmitted over a common channel

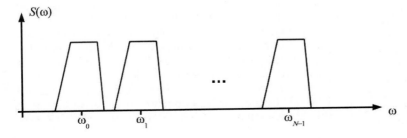

Figure 2: Exemplary spectrum $S(\omega)$ of the FDM signal $s(t)$

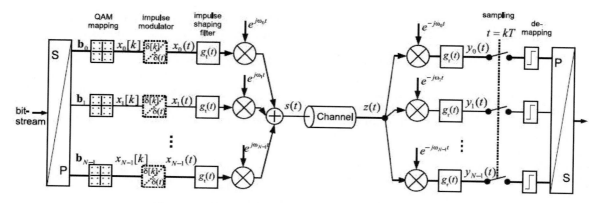

Figure 3: Block diagram of a general multicarrier system

Orthogonality Criterion

In a multicarrier system as depicted in Figure 3, the incoming bit stream is divided into N bit streams of lower rate and then mapped to *quadrature amplitude modulation* (QAM) symbols $X_\nu[k]$, $\nu = 0, 1, ..., N - 1$. The QAM symbols are taken out of a discrete alphabet—that is, $X_\nu[k] \in A_X$. In a multiple-access system, these sequences stem from different sources, which does not affect the following treatment as long as the sequences are synchronized. The QAM symbols $X_\nu[k]$ with $k \in Z$ constitute a discrete time sequence $\{..., X_\nu[0], X_\nu[1], ...\}$, which is translated by the impulse modulator into a continuous time function

$$x_\nu(t) = T \sum_{k=-\infty}^{\infty} X_\nu[k] \cdot \delta(t - kT) \qquad (4)$$

Here $\delta(t)$ is the Dirac delta function, which is defined by $\delta(t) = 0$ for $t \neq 0$ and $\int_{-\infty}^{\infty} \delta(t) dt = 1$. Note that the impulse modulator is a theoretical concept that provides a mathematically rigorous transition from discrete time to continuous time signals but does not correspond to any identifiable circuit in a practical implementation. In the following, we write continuous time signals with parentheses, such as $s(t)$, and discrete time signals with brackets such as $s[n]$.

The signal after the impulse-shaping filter is $T\sum_k X_\nu[k] \cdot g_t(t - kT)$, where $g_t(t)$ denotes the impulse response of the impulse-shaping filter. These signals are modulated onto the subcarrier frequencies ω_ν, and together they form the output signal

$$s(t) = T \sum_{\nu=0}^{N-1} e^{j\omega_\nu t} \sum_{k=-\infty}^{\infty} X_\nu[k] \cdot g_t(t - kT) \qquad (5)$$

The carrier frequencies ω_ν are equidistant and thus integer multiples of the subcarrier spacing $\Delta\omega$:

$$\omega_\nu = \nu \cdot \Delta\omega, \quad \nu = 0, 1, ..., N - 1 \qquad (6)$$

Although all practical multicarrier systems are realized with digital signal processing, we will use the analog model of Figure 3 in this section because the analysis can be done more conveniently and the basic principles of MCM can be visualized more clearly with this model. In the following sections, we will continue with a digital system model.

The output signal $s(t)$ can be either real or complex-valued. If complex-valued, $s(t)$ is considered as the complex envelope, and the channel is the equivalent baseband channel.

The receiver input signal $z(t)$ is demodulated and filtered by the receiver filters with impulse response $g_r(t)$, resulting in the signal

$$y_\mu(t) = \left(z(t)e^{-j\omega_\mu t}\right) * g_r(t) = \int_{-\infty}^{+\infty} z(\tau)e^{-j\omega_\mu \tau} g_r(t - \tau) d\tau,$$
$$\mu = 0, 1, ..., N - 1 \qquad (7)$$

where $*$ denotes convolution. For the moment, we assume an ideal channel—that is, $z(t) = s(t)$—and obtain from Equation 7 with Equations 5 and 6

$$y_\mu(t) = T \int_{-\infty}^{\infty} \sum_{\nu=0}^{N-1} e^{j(\nu-\mu)\Delta\omega\tau} \sum_k X_\nu[k] g_t(\tau - kT) g_r(t - \tau) d\tau \qquad (8)$$

To obtain a discrete time sequence again, this signal is sampled at $t = kT$:

$$Y_\mu[k] = y_\mu(kT)$$
$$= T \int_{-\infty}^{\infty} \sum_{\nu=0}^{N-1} e^{j(\nu-\mu)\Delta\omega\tau} \sum_\ell X_\nu[\ell] g_t(\tau - \ell T) g_r(kT - \tau) d\tau \qquad (9)$$

From this expression for the received signal after sampling, we can observe two types of interference.

1. *Intersymbol interference* (ISI), a transmit symbol $X_\nu[k]$ which is sent at time k on subcarrier ν influences previous and subsequent received samples $Y_\nu[\ell]$, $\ell \neq k$ on the same subcarrier.

2. *Intercarrier interference* (ICI), a transmit symbol $X_v[k]$ on subcarrier v has an impact on received symbols $Y_\mu[\ell]$, $\mu \neq v$ on other subcarriers—that is, cross talking occurs between adjacent subcarriers.

Now the objective is to recover the transmit sequences at the receiver without distortion. Because our system is linear and time-invariant, we can restrict the analysis to the evaluation of the response to a single transmit symbol on one subcarrier. We can then make use of the superposition theorem for the general case of arbitrary input sequences, which can be written as a linear combination of time-shifted unit impulses.

Without loss of generality, we assume that the system model in Figure 3 has zero delay—that is, the filters $g_t(t)$ and $g_r(t)$ are noncausal. We assume that one unit impulse $\delta[k]$ is transmitted at time $k = 0$ on subcarrier v:

$$X_i[k] = \delta[v - i] \cdot \delta[k], \quad i = 0, \ldots, N - 1. \tag{10}$$

Here

$$\delta[k] = \begin{cases} 1 & \text{for } k = 0 \\ 0 & \text{for } k \neq 0 \end{cases} \tag{11}$$

is the discrete time equivalent of the Dirac delta function. The desired received signal is

$$Y_\mu[k] = \delta[v - \mu] \cdot \delta[k] \tag{12}$$

In this case, the received signal is free of interference at the sampling instants. This does not put any condition on the signal $y_\mu(t)$ between the sampling instants. However, to gain further insight into the nature of ISI and ICI, we take a step back and consider the signals before they are sampled at the receiver. The transmitter output signal for the sequence in Equation 10 is

$$s(t) = T\, g_t(t)e^{jv\Delta\omega t} \tag{13}$$

which is also the receiver input signal $z(t)$ because we assume an ideal channel. The *elementary impulse* $r_{v-\mu}(t)$ is defined as the response $y_\mu(t)$ to the transmitter input in Equation 10:

$$r_d(t) = T \int_{-\infty}^{\infty} e^{jd\Delta\omega t} g_t(\tau)g_r(t - \tau)d\tau \tag{14}$$

Here we set $d = v - \mu$ because the elementary impulse depends only on the difference of the subcarrier indices. The condition for no interference can now be formulated as

$$r_d(kT) = \delta[d] \cdot \delta[k] \tag{15}$$

This can interpreted as the multicarrier version of the Nyquist criterion because it forces not only the absence of

ISI but also zero ICI. If we set $d = 0$, then Equation 15 simplifies to the Nyquist criterion for single-carrier systems. In the context of general multicarrier systems and filter banks, Equation 15 is often called the *orthogonality criterion* or the criterion for *perfect reconstruction*.

For standard multicarrier systems without guard interval, $g_t(t)$ and $g_r(t)$ are both rectangular with duration T. With the subcarrier spacing $\Delta\omega = 2\pi/T$, we obtain the elementary impulses

$$r_0(t) = \begin{cases} 1 - |t|/T & \text{for } |t| \leq T \\ 0 & \text{elsewhere} \end{cases}$$

$$r_d(t) = \begin{cases} \dfrac{\text{sgn}(t)(-1)^d}{j2\pi d}\left(1 - \exp\left(jd\dfrac{2\pi}{T}t\right)\right) & \text{for } |t| \leq T, \ d \neq 0 \\ 0 & \text{elsewhere} \end{cases} \tag{16}$$

These functions are shown in the top left section of Figure 4 and help us understand the characteristics of ISI and ICI. We clearly see that at the sampling instants $t = kT$ no interference is present. This is not the case between the sampling instants where significant cross talk comes from the adjacent subchannels. The oscillation frequency of the cross talk increases with the distance d between transmitter and receiver subchannel index, whereas the amplitude decreases proportionally to $1/d$. Because of this slow decline, many adjacent subchannels contribute to the cross talk between the sampling instants. As long as this cross talk is zero at the sampling instants, no interference occurs there. However, it cannot be ignored for other time instants, as becomes clear from the eye diagram at the top right of Figure 4, which corresponds to the real part of $y_\mu(t)$ when the transmit symbols are 16-QAM modulated. Although the orthogonality condition of Equation 15 is fulfilled, the horizontal eye opening tends to zero, producing decision errors even for tiny sampling jitter or channel influences.

Introduction of the Guard Interval

An effective solution to increase the horizontal eye opening is the introduction of a *guard interval*. It is introduced by choosing different impulse responses $g_t(t) \neq g_r(t)$ at transmitter and receiver. The duration of the guard interval is

$$T_G = T - T_u \tag{17}$$

where T and T_u denote the length of the impulse response of the transmitter and receiver filter $g_t(t)$ and $g_r(t)$, respectively. Both impulse responses are rectangular and symmetric to $t = 0$. The subcarrier spacing is now given by

$$\Delta\omega = \frac{2\pi}{T_u} \tag{18}$$

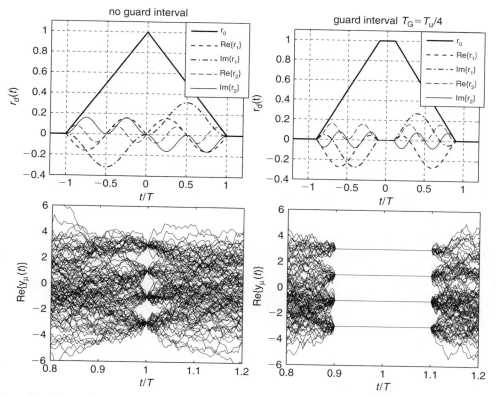

Figure 4: Elementary impulses (above) and eye diagrams (below) of a multicarrier system with rectangular impulse shapes, 16-QAM modulation, and $N = 256$ subcarriers. Left: Without guard interval. Right: Guard interval $T_G = T_u/4$

For the elementary impulses follows

$$r_0(t) = \begin{cases} \dfrac{-|t| + T - T_G/2}{T - T_G} & \text{for } \dfrac{T_G}{2} \le |t| \le T - \dfrac{T_G}{2} \\[2ex] 1 & \text{for } |t| < \dfrac{T_G}{2} \\[2ex] 0 & \text{for } |t| > T - \dfrac{T_G}{2} \end{cases} \tag{19}$$

$$r_d(t) = \begin{cases} \dfrac{\operatorname{sgn}(t)(-1)^d}{j2\pi d} \\[1ex] \left(\exp\left(j\pi \operatorname{sgn}(t) d \dfrac{T_G}{T_u} \right) - \exp\left(jd \dfrac{2\pi}{T_u} t \right) \right) \\[1ex] \qquad \text{for } \dfrac{T_G}{2} \le |t| \le T - \dfrac{T_G}{2}, \quad d \ne 0 \\[1ex] 0 \qquad \text{elsewhere} \end{cases} \tag{20}$$

As can be observed from the bottom of Figure 4, there are now flat regions around the sampling instants $t = kT$ that prevent any interference. This holds also for a channel

with an impulse response shorter than T_G. The horizontal eye opening is now as long as the guard interval. During this period, no information is transmitted and thus the spectral efficiency is reduced by the factor T_G/T.

PRINCIPLES OF DMT
Implementation with Digital Signal Processing

Although the continuous time model we treated in the previous section is valuable for the theoretical system analysis, the implementation of MCM systems has been exclusively realized with digital signal processing ever since the technique became available. We obtain the discrete time system model depicted in Figure 5 by sampling the continuous time model in Figure 3 with the sampling period T_A. The impulse modulators are replaced by upsamplers that insert $N_s - 1$ zero samples after each incoming symbol $X_v[k]$. The basic time intervals are hence given by

$$\begin{aligned} T &= N_s \cdot T_A & \text{duration of DMT symbol,} \\ T_u &= N \cdot T_A & \text{``useful'' time interval,} \\ T_G &= G \cdot T_A & \text{duration of guard interval.} \end{aligned} \tag{21}$$

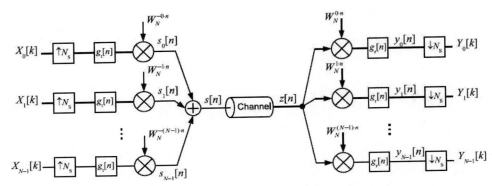

Figure 5: Transmitter and receiver for digital multicarrier transmission

In the following, we will use the discrete time index k for the "slow" sampling time T or T_u and the index n for the "fast" time T_A. In accordance with Equation 17, one DMT symbol contains $N_S = N + G$ samples.

For the complex carriers in Figure 3, we obtain with Equations 6 and 18 and $t = n\,T_A$

$$\exp(j\omega_\nu n T_A) = \exp\left(j\frac{2\pi}{N}\nu n\right) = W_N^{-\nu\cdot n} \quad (22)$$

where we define the *twiddle factor*, W_N, which is also the Nth root of unity:

$$W_N = \exp\left(-j\frac{2\pi}{N}\right) \quad (23)$$

Because we have made no assumptions about the filters $g_t(t)$ and $g_r(t)$, the sampling theorem is in general not fulfilled and thus the discrete time system model does *not exactly* represent the analog model. This explains the difficulties that arise when trying to derive the discrete time model from its continuous time counterpart. Nevertheless, it is a reasonable approximation, and the presented concepts such as the elementary impulses and the orthogonality criterion can be applied in the same way.

We now adopt *causal* discrete time filters:

$$g_t[n] = \begin{cases} 1/\sqrt{N} & \text{for } n = 0,1,\ldots,N_S - 1 \\ 0 & \text{elsewhere} \end{cases} \quad (24)$$

With this transmit filter, we can write for the output signal of the transmitter in Figure 5:

$$s[n] = \sum_{\nu=0}^{N-1} W_N^{-\nu n} \sum_{k=-\infty}^{\infty} X_\nu[k] g_t[n - kN_S]$$
$$= \frac{1}{\sqrt{N}} \sum_{\nu=0}^{N-1} X_\nu\left\lfloor n/N_S \right\rfloor W_N^{-\nu n} \quad (25)$$

The rectangular pulse shape lets the sum over k disappear and allows us to write the output signal as a single sum using the integer division $\lfloor n/N_S \rfloor = n$ div N_S. Note that

the periodicity of the twiddle factor, W_N, is not identical to the filter length N_S. This is due to the guard interval and creates some subtle effects, as we will observe in the following.

In Equation 25, we recognize one expression of the discrete Fourier transform pair:

$$\text{DFT:} X_\mu = \frac{1}{\sqrt{N}} \sum_{\nu=0}^{N-1} x_\nu W_N^{\nu\mu}, \quad \text{IDFT:} x_\nu = \frac{1}{\sqrt{N}} \sum_{\mu=0}^{N-1} X_\mu W_N^{-\nu\mu}$$
$$(26)$$

We can thus identify the input signals $\{X_0[k], \ldots, X_{N-1}[k]\}$ as a block with index k and consider the blockwise *inverse discrete Fourier transform* (IDFT):

$$x_i[k] = \frac{1}{\sqrt{N}} \sum_{\nu=0}^{N-1} X_\nu[k] W_N^{-\nu i}, i = 0,1,\ldots,N-1 \quad (27)$$

The double-indexed sequence $x_i[k]$ contains the inverse discrete Fourier transformed input signals $X_\nu[k]$, which allows us to express the transmitter output signal of Equation 25 as

$$s[n] = x_{\mathrm{mod}_N(n)}\left\lfloor n / N_S \right\rfloor \quad (28)$$

where we introduced the modulus operator to keep the index in the specified range. Note that because of the periodicity of W_N, this is not strictly necessary here but will prove useful later.

For each block of N input samples, $N_S = N + G$ output samples are produced. The first block with $k = 0$ yields the output sequence

$$\{s[0],\ldots,s[N_S - 1]\} = \{x_0[0],\ldots,x_{N-1}[0], x_0[0],\ldots,x_{G-1}[0]\}$$

while the second block $(k = 1)$ gives the output

$$\{s[N_S],\ldots,s[2N_S - 1]\} = \{x_G[1],\ldots,x_{N-1}[1], x_0[1],\ldots,x_{2G-1}[1]\}$$

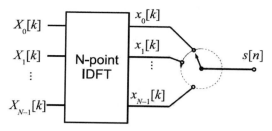

Figure 6: Inverse discrete Fourier transform with parallel-serial conversion

We observe that each output block contains the symbols $x_0[k]$, ..., $x_{N-1}[k]$ plus G additional samples taken out of the same set. The calculation of $s[n]$ applying a block-wise IDFT is illustrated in Figure 6: A block of N input symbols is first IDFT-transformed and then parallel-serial converted. The conmutator puts out N_S symbols for each block by turning more than one revolution, resting after each block in a different position. Thus, although each block contains all transformed symbols, the ordering and the subset of doubled samples vary. To overcome this inconvenience and to facilitate the block processing at the receiver side, practically all DMT systems compute a block of N samples by inverse DFT processing and insert the additional samples at the beginning of the block. Therefore, this common form of the guard interval is also called *cyclic prefix* (CP). Hence, a DMT block with index k will be ordered as follows:

$$\underbrace{x_{N-G}[k], x_{N-G+1}[k]\dots, x_{N-1}[k]}_{G \text{ guard samples}}, \underbrace{x_0[k], x_1[k]\dots, x_{N-1}[k]}_{N \text{ data samples}}$$

For this ordering, we can define the double-indexed output signal

$$s_\nu[k] = x_{\mathrm{mod}_N(\nu-G)}[k] = \frac{1}{\sqrt{N}} \sum_{i=0}^{N-1} X_i[k] W_N^{-(\nu-G)i} \quad (29)$$

From this, the output signal $s[n]$ is given as

$$s[n] = s_{\mathrm{mod}_{N_S}(n)}\left[\lfloor n / N_S \rfloor\right] \quad (30)$$

This operation ensures that each transmitted block is independent of the previous one, which simplifies the signal processing significantly. We will later see that—by an appropriately chosen guard time—this will hold also at the receiver side.

Baseband Transmission with Multicarrier Modulation

Because the DMT signal is transmitted over baseband channels, it has to be ensured that the output signal $s[n]$ is real-valued. In the following, we will derive the conditions that allow us to use the usual complex-valued QAM modulation on the subcarriers but nevertheless obtain a real-valued output signal.

To obtain a real-valued output, the samples $x_i[k]$ according to Equation 27 also have to be real. By decomposing $x_i[k]$ into real and imaginary parts and after some simple calculations, we obtain the conditions for the input sequences:

$$\begin{aligned} X_0[k], X_{N/2}[k] &\in \mathbb{R} \\ X_\nu &= X_{N-\nu}^* \quad \text{for } \nu = 1, 2, \dots, \frac{N}{2} - 1 \end{aligned} \quad (31)$$

To simplify the transmitter scheme, we can choose X_0 and $X_{N/2}$ as the real and imaginary part of one QAM symbol as indicated in Figure 7. For practical implementations, this is of minor importance because X_0 and $X_{N/2}$ are usually set to zero anyway. The reason for this will become clear when we look at the spectral properties of the DMT signal.

System Description with Matrix Notation

We have seen that the transmitter processes the data blockwise, resulting in a simple implementation without the need to store data from previous blocks. We now describe how this block independence can be extended to the receiver when including the influence of the channel. Figure 8 shows a block diagram for the complete DMT transmission system. For the moment, we focus on the signal only and consider the influence of the noise later. The receiver input signal is then given by

$$z[n] = s[n] * h[n] = \sum_m s[m]h[n-m] \quad (32)$$

where the discrete time *channel impulse response* (CIR), $h[n]$, includes the influence of the digital-analog and analog-digital conversion as well as any analog filters in the transmission chain. We assume that the CIR has finite length—that is, $h[n]$ has nonzero values only for $n = 0, 1, \dots, G$:

$$h[n] = 0 \quad \text{for } n < 0 \text{ or } n > G \quad (33)$$

As depicted in Figure 8, we define the vectors

$$\begin{aligned} \mathbf{x} &= (x_0, x_1, \dots, x_{N-1})^T, \quad \mathbf{s} = (s_0, s_1, \dots, s_{N+G-1})^T \\ &= (x_{N-G}, \dots, x_{N-1}, x_0, \dots, x_{N-1})^T \\ \mathbf{z} &= (z_0, z_1, \dots, z_{N+G-1})^T, \quad \mathbf{y} = (y_0, y_1, \dots, y_{N-1})^T \\ &= (z_G, z_{G+1}, \dots, z_{N+G+1})^T \end{aligned} \quad (34)$$

After the removal of the guard interval, we obtain for the components of the receive vector $\mathbf{y}$

$$y[n] = z[n+G] \text{ for } n = 0, 1, \dots, N-1 \quad (35)$$

Using Equations 32 through 34, we can write

$$\begin{aligned} y[n] = &\sum_{m=0}^{G-1} x[m-G+N]h[n+G-m] \\ &+ \sum_{m=G}^{N+G-1} x[m-G]h[n+G-m] \end{aligned} \quad (36)$$

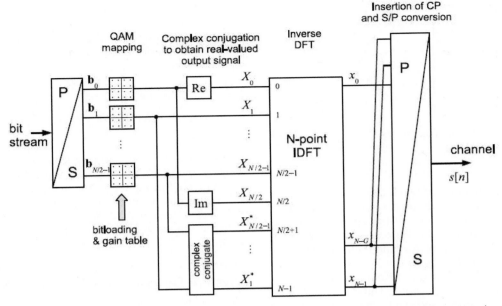

Figure 7: DMT transmitter. The bit sequence is first mapped to QAM symbols, which together with their complex conjugates form the input of the inverse DFT processor. Finally, the cyclic prefix is inserted and the symbols are converted to a serial data stream

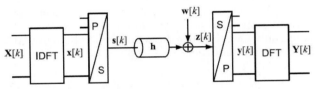

Figure 8: DMT receiver. After serial-parallel conversion, the input symbols are DFT processed. The receiver discards the symbols corresponding to the cyclic prefix

which can be expressed in matrix notation as follows

$$
\mathbf{y} = \begin{pmatrix} y_0 \\ y_1 \\ \vdots \\ y_{G-1} \\ y_G \\ y_{G+1} \\ \vdots \\ y_{N-1} \end{pmatrix} = \underbrace{\begin{pmatrix} h_0 & 0 & \cdots & 0 & h_G & \cdots & h_2 & h_1 \\ h_1 & h_0 & 0 & \cdots & 0 & h_G & \cdots & h_2 \\ \vdots & \vdots & \ddots & \ddots & & & \ddots & \vdots \\ h_{G-1} & h_{G-2} & \cdots & h_0 & 0 & \cdots & 0 & h_G \\ h_G & h_{G-1} & h_{G-2} & \cdots & h_0 & 0 & \cdots & 0 \\ 0 & h_G & h_{G-1} & \cdots & h_1 & h_0 & 0 & \cdots \\ \vdots & & \ddots & \ddots & & \ddots & \ddots & \vdots \\ 0 & \cdots & 0 & h_G & h_{G-1} & \cdots & h_1 & h_0 \end{pmatrix}}_{\mathbf{H}} \begin{pmatrix} x_0 \\ x_1 \\ \vdots \\ x_{G-1} \\ x_G \\ x_{G+1} \\ \vdots \\ x_{N-1} \end{pmatrix} = \mathbf{Hx}
$$

(37)

This Equation with the *circular* matrix

$$(\mathbf{H})_{nm} = h[\mathrm{mod}_N(n-m)] \text{ with } n,m = 0,1,\ldots,N-1 \quad (38)$$

expresses the *circular convolution* (Oppenheim and Schafer 1989), which corresponds to a multiplication in the frequency domain, and which can also be written as

$$y[n] = x[n] \otimes h[n] = \sum_{m=0}^{N-1} x[m]h[\mathrm{mod}_N(n-m)] \quad (39)$$

From this point of view, the cyclic prefix transforms the linear convolution of Equation 32 into a circular convolution. Because the matrix $\mathbf{H}$ is circular, its eigenvalues λ_μ and eigenvectors ϑ_μ are given by

$$\lambda_\mu = \sum_{i=0}^{N-1} h[n]W_N^{\mu i}, \ \vartheta_\mu = \frac{1}{\sqrt{N}} \begin{pmatrix} W_N^{-0} \\ W_N^{-\mu} \\ \vdots \\ W_N^{-(N-1)\mu} \end{pmatrix}, \mu = 0,1,\ldots,N-1$$

(40)

This can be easily verified by checking the characteristic Equation $\mathbf{H}\vartheta_\mu = \lambda_\mu\vartheta_\mu$. We recognize the eigenvectors ϑ_μ as the columns of the inverse DFT matrix:

$$\mathbf{F}^{-1} = (\vartheta_0, \vartheta_1, \cdots, \vartheta_{N-1}) \quad (41)$$

The DFT matrix is unitary—that is, its inverse is identical to its conjugate transpose: $\mathbf{F}^{-1} = \mathbf{F}^{\mathrm{H}}$. As a consequence of these special eigenvectors and eigenvalues, we can diagonalize the channel matrix with the DFT matrix:

$$\mathbf{FHF}^{\mathrm{H}} = \mathbf{D} = \mathrm{diag}(\lambda_0,\ldots,\lambda_{N-1}) \quad (42)$$

with $\mathbf{X} = (X_0[k],\ldots, X_{N-1}[k])^T$ and $Y = (Y_0[k], \ldots, Y_{N-1}[k])^T$, so we can write

$$\mathbf{Y} = \mathbf{Fy} = \mathbf{FHx} = \mathbf{FHF}^{\mathcal{H}}\mathbf{X} = \mathbf{DX} \quad (43)$$

or

$$Y_\mu[k] = \lambda_\mu \cdot X_\mu[k] \quad (44)$$

We can now describe the input-output relationship of the whole transmission system in Figure 8 with a single diagonal matrix. The result shows that because of the cyclic prefix, the parallel subchannels are independent and perfect reconstruction can be realized by a simple one-tap equalizer per subchannel at the output of the receiver DFT. As equalization is done after the DFT, this equalizer is often referred to as *frequency domain equalizer* (FEQ).

Following from Equation 40, we can interpret the eigenvalues λ_μ of the channel matrix as the DFT of the CIR. If we define the discrete time Fourier transform of the CIR as

$$H(\omega) = \sum_{n=0}^{N-1} h[n]e^{-j\omega nT_A} \qquad (45)$$

we see that the eigenvalues in Equation 40 are nothing else than the values of the channel transfer function at the frequencies $\omega_\mu = \mu \cdot \Delta\omega$:

$$\lambda_\mu = H(\omega_\mu) \qquad (46)$$

Because DMT is a baseband transmission scheme, the impulse response $h[n]$ is real-valued and therefore its spectrum shows hermitian symmetry:

$$\lambda_0, \lambda_{N/2} \in \mathbb{R}; \quad \lambda_\mu = \lambda_{N-\mu}^* \quad \mu = 1,\dots,N/2-1 \qquad (47)$$

Let us now summarize the results, which highlight some of the main features of DMT. We have seen that the insertion of the cyclic prefix translates the linear convolution of Equation 32 into the circular convolution of Equation 39, which corresponds to a simple multiplication in the frequency domain as long as the impulse response of the channel is not longer than the guard interval. In this case, no interblock and intercarrier interference occur, and each subchannel signal is only weighted by the channel transfer function at the subcarrier frequency. It is this remarkable property that made multicarrier schemes such as DMT and OFDM so popular.

If the CIR exceeds the guard interval, then the described features are not valid anymore. To overcome this problem, which might appear in ADSL for especially long lines, an additional equalizer has to be introduced as outlined later (in the section titled "Equalization for Insufficient Guard Interval Length").

Spectral Properties of DMT Signals

For the calculation of the spectrum of the output signal, we consider the system model in Figure 5, which leads to a straightforward and comprehensible calculation. First we consider one modulated subchannel with the input signal given in Equation 10. This leads to the output signal and the corresponding spectrum:

$$s[n] = g_t[n] \cdot W_N^{-vn} \leftrightarrow S(\omega)$$
$$= \sum_{n=-\infty}^{\infty} g_t[n]W_N^{-vn}e^{-j\omega nT_A} = \sum_n g_t[n]W_N^{\left(\frac{\omega}{\Delta\omega}-v\right)n} \qquad (48)$$

where for the last expression we made use of Equations 18 and 21. For the rectangular pulse-shaping filter of Equation 24, we obtain for the output spectrum:

$$S(\omega) = \frac{1}{\sqrt{N}}\begin{cases} \dfrac{1-W_N^{\left(\frac{\omega}{\Delta\omega}-v\right)N_S}}{1-W_N^{\left(\frac{\omega}{\Delta\omega}-v\right)}} & \text{for } \omega \neq v \cdot \Delta\omega \\ N_S & \text{for } \omega = v \cdot \Delta\omega \end{cases} \qquad (49)$$

In Figure 9a, the magnitude of the spectrum is depicted for the case that subcarrier $v \in \{10,11,12\}$ is modulated. The spectrum is quite similar to a $\sin(\omega)/\omega$ function but not identical because the system model in Figure 5 is discrete time. Another consequence is that $S(\omega)$ is periodic with $\omega_A = 2\pi/T_A = N\cdot\Delta\omega$. Note that the spectrum of a single subcarrier with carrier frequency $v\Delta\omega$ does *not* have zero crossings at the adjacent subcarrier frequencies $(v \pm m)\Delta\omega$ unless the guard interval is zero. Although in the literature it is often suggested that spectral nulls at adjacent subcarrier frequencies is tantamount to orthogonality, it is clear from Figure 9 that this condition is not necessary. Note also that to obtain a real-valued output signal, according to Equation 31, we also must send a unit impulse on subchannel $N - v$.

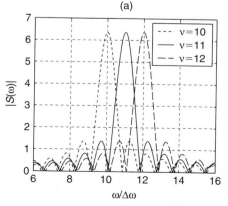
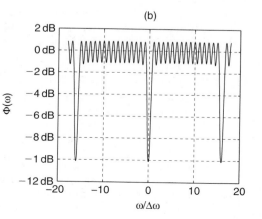

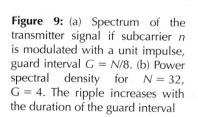

Figure 9: (a) Spectrum of the transmitter signal if subcarrier n is modulated with a unit impulse, guard interval $G = N/8$. (b) Power spectral density for $N = 32$, $G = 4$. The ripple increases with the duration of the guard interval

To calculate the *power spectral density* (PSD) of a DMT signal, we now consider stochastic input sequences $X_\nu[k]$, which are uncorrelated with zero mean and unit variance. Then the PSD of the output signal $s_\nu[n]$ corresponding to one subcarrier is given by

$$\Phi_\nu(\omega) = \frac{1}{N_S} |G(\omega)|^2 \qquad (50)$$

where

$$G(\omega) = \sum_n g_t[n] e^{-j\omega m T_A} = \frac{1}{\sqrt{N}} \begin{cases} \dfrac{1 - W_N^{\omega N_S/\Delta\omega}}{1 - W_N^{\omega/\Delta\omega}} & \text{for } \omega \neq 0 \\ N_S & \text{for } \omega = 0 \end{cases} \qquad (51)$$

From this we obtain the PSD of the output signal $s[n]$ as

$$\Phi_s(\omega) = \frac{1}{N_S} \sum_{\substack{\nu=-(N/2-1) \\ \nu \neq 0}}^{N/2-1} |G(\omega - \nu \cdot \Delta\omega)|^2 \qquad (52)$$

which is depicted in Figure 9b for a system with $N = 32$. All subcarriers are modulated with unit power, except for carriers $\nu = 0$ and $\nu = N/2$. As the anti-aliasing low pass in the digital-analog converter has a cutoff frequency of $\omega_A/2 = N \cdot \Delta\omega/2$, the carriers in this frequency region cannot be modulated. Therefore, at least the carrier at $\nu = N/2$ remains unused. Because the anti-aliasing filter is not arbitrarily selective, usually many more subcarriers are left unmodulated. The carrier at $\nu = 0$ is normally not used either because most channels do not support a DC component.

IMPLEMENTATION ASPECTS

Having established the basic principles of DMT, in this section we specify further details that are important for implementation, starting with the one-tap equalizer made possible by the cyclic prefix. Because for especially long channels this simple and elegant method is not sufficient, we give a sketch of equalization strategies for the case of an insufficient guard interval. One major drawback of MCM is the problem of high peak power, which we outline and briefly sketch possible solutions. Finally, we describe implementation alternatives such as MCM with filter banks and some variants of the guard interval.

Frequency Domain Equalization

The signal after DFT processing at the receiver is given by

$$Y_\mu[k] = \lambda_\mu \cdot X_\mu[k] + w_\mu[k] \qquad (53)$$

where $w_\mu[k]$ represents the noise on subchannel μ. In many practical cases, the noise on the channel can be modeled as *additive white Gaussian noise* (AWGN). After DFT processing, the noise is still white and Gaussian. In the

following, we assume that the post-DFT noise is Gaussian but not necessarily white—that is, the variance $\sigma_\mu^2 = E[|w\mu[k]|^2]$ may vary from subchannel to subchannel.

Because the parallel subchannels are only affected by the constant eigenvalues of the channel matrix according to Equation 53, a simple one-tap equalizer with coefficient ψ_μ per subchannel is sufficient to recover the transmit signal:

$$\hat{X}_\mu[k] = \psi_\mu \cdot Y_\mu[k] = \psi_\mu \lambda_\mu X_\mu[k] + \psi_\mu w_\mu[k] \qquad (54)$$

The simplest equalization strategy disregards the noise and simply recovers the transmit symbol by dividing through the channel transfer coefficient:

$$\psi_\mu = \frac{1}{\lambda_\mu} \Rightarrow \quad \hat{X}_\mu[k] = X_\mu[k] + \frac{1}{\lambda_\mu} w_\mu[k] \qquad (55)$$

Although this strategy is easy to implement, it has the drawback of noise amplification, which is especially severe for strongly attenuated subchannels. If we denote by $p_\mu = E[|X_\mu[k]|^2]$ the signal power on subchannel μ, then we can write for the SNR after equalization:

$$\gamma_\mu = |\lambda_\mu|^2 \cdot \frac{p_\mu}{\sigma_\mu^2} \qquad (56)$$

From this expression, it is obvious that the SNR can be severely degraded if the channel is strongly attenuated.

This equalization strategy can be significantly improved by taking into account the noise power: the *minimum mean square error* (MMSE) equalizer minimizes the quadratic error $E[|\hat{X}_\mu - X\mu|^2]$. This is achieved by the MMSE equalizer coefficients

$$\psi_\mu = \frac{\lambda_\mu^*}{|\lambda_\mu|^2 + \dfrac{\sigma_\mu^2}{p_\mu}} \qquad (57)$$

and leads to the postequalization SNR

$$\gamma_\mu = |\lambda_\mu|^2 \frac{p_\mu}{\sigma_\mu^2} + 1 \qquad (58)$$

which gives a significantly better performance than in the first case, especially for strongly attenuated subchannels with $\lambda_\mu \ll 1$.

Although the objective of the above equalizers is to recover the symbol $X_\mu[k]$, this is only an intermediate step in the reception. Each transmit symbol $X_\mu[k]$ corresponds to a number of bits, and the objective is to recover as much information as possible about the transmitted bits. In nearly all modern communication systems, channel coding is applied and the decoder at the receiver will work most efficiently if provided with *reliability information* about each bit. Each transmit symbol is taken out of a finite symbol alphabet—that is, $X_\mu[k] \in A_X$—and corresponds to a bit vector $\mathbf{b}_\mu = (b_{\mu,1}, \ldots, b_{\mu,Q})^T$, where $b_{\mu,q} \in \{0,1\}$.

Because, according to Equation 53, the subchannels are parallel and independent, in the following we focus solely on subcarrier μ.

On each subcarrier, a bit vector is mapped to a QAM symbol—that is,

$$X_\mu[k] = \text{map}(\mathbf{b}_\mu) \qquad (59)$$

Whereas a hard demapper first equalizes the symbols and then calculates the corresponding bit sequence, a *soft demapper* computes for each detected bit a soft value that contains information about the reliability of this bit. A common measure is the *a posteriori probability* (APP) *log-likelihood value* (L value) of $b_{\mu,q}$, which is defined as

$$L_D(b_{\mu,q}|Y_\mu) = L_A(b_{\mu,q}) + L_E(b_{\mu,q}|Y_\mu) = \ln \frac{P[b_{\mu,q} = 1|Y_\mu]}{P[b_{\mu,q} = 0|Y_\mu]} \qquad (60)$$

where

$$L_A(b_{\mu,q}) = \frac{P[b_{\mu,q} = 1]}{P[b_{\mu,q} = 0]} \qquad (61)$$

is the *a priori L value* of $b_{\mu,q}$ and $L_E(b_{\mu,q}|Y)$ is the *extrinsic information*. The a priori knowledge may stem from a channel decoder if iterative decoding is applied. If no such knowledge is available, then the L-value $L_A(b_{\mu,q})$ is simply set to zero. The extrinsic information is given by

$$L_E(b_{\mu,q}|Y_\mu) = \ln \frac{\displaystyle\sum_{\mathbf{b}\in B_{q,1}} p(Y_\mu|\mathbf{b})\exp(\mathbf{b}_{\bar{q}}^T \mathbf{A}_{\bar{q}})}{\displaystyle\sum_{\mathbf{b}\in B_{q,0}} p(Y_\mu|\mathbf{b})\exp(\mathbf{b}_{\bar{q}}^T \mathbf{A}_{\bar{q}})} \qquad (62)$$

where

$$p(Y_\mu|\mathbf{b}_\mu) = p(Y_\mu|X_\mu) = \frac{1}{\pi\sigma_\mu^2}\exp\left(-\frac{\left|Y_\mu - \lambda_\mu X_\mu\right|^2}{\sigma_\mu^2}\right) \qquad (63)$$

is the conditional probability distribution function of the received noisy signal, $\mathbf{A} = (A_{\mu,1},\ldots,A_{\mu,Q})^T$ is the vector of a priori values corresponding to the bit vector $\mathbf{b}_\mu$, and $\mathbf{A}_{\bar{q}}$ denotes this vector without its qth component. The sums are taken over all bit vectors that have a 1 or 0 in the qth position—that is, $B_{q,j} = \{\mathbf{b} : b_q = j\}$.

The extrinsic L value is finally given as

$$L_E(b_{\mu,q}|Y_\mu) = \ln \frac{\displaystyle\sum_{\mathbf{b}\in B_{q,1}} \exp\left(-\frac{\left|Y_\mu - \lambda_\mu X_\mu\right|^2}{\sigma_\mu^2} + \mathbf{b}_{\bar{q}}^T \mathbf{A}_{\bar{q}}\right)}{\displaystyle\sum_{\mathbf{b}\in B_{q,0}} \exp\left(-\frac{\left|Y_\mu - \lambda_\mu X_\mu\right|^2}{\sigma_\mu^2} + \mathbf{b}_{\bar{q}}^T \mathbf{A}_{\bar{q}}\right)} \qquad (64)$$

This value is passed to the channel decoder, which performs the inverse operation to the encoder in the transmitter. This calculation of soft bits as input to a channel decoder corresponds to a fundamental principle in digital communications that says no information should be discarded until a final decision is taken.

Equalization for Insufficient Guard Interval Length

As we have seen in the previous sections, one main feature of DMT is the low complexity of the single-tap equalization that is achieved by the insertion of the guard interval. However, if the CIR length occupies a significant fraction of the symbol time T, and if the number of subcarriers cannot be increased, then the necessary guard interval length would lead to a significant reduction in useful transmission time T_u and therefore decrease the spectral efficiency. This situation might occur in applications such as ADSL over long telephone lines, but alternative solutions have been investigated in order to cope with impulse responses that exceed the guard interval length. Basically, two methods as illustrated in Figure 10 can be distinguished:

1. In *time domain equalization* (TEQ), the received signal is equalized before being transformed by the DFT. Loosely speaking, the objective of this equalizer is to "shorten" the CIR.
2. In *frequency domain equalization* (FEQ), the equalizer is placed after the DFT which—in contrast to the simple one-tap equalizer described in the previous section—and generally considers several subcarriers and DMT symbols jointly.

Good overviews about equalization strategies for DMT can be found in Pollet et al. (2000) and Arslan, Evans, and Kiaei (2001). The final objective of the equalizer is usually to maximize the transmission rate, which has to be translated into a criterion for the equalizer coefficients.

Time Domain Equalization

It has been shown by al-Dhahir and Cioffi (1996) that the computation of the TEQ coefficients for rate maximization leads to a highly nonlinear optimization problem with several local minima. Because the equalizer coefficients must be initialized during the training phase in real time, modem designers resort to simpler criteria that depend more directly on the equalizer coefficients. A natural choice for the TEQ objective function is to "shorten" the CIR. The equalizer produces an "effective" CIR— $h_{\text{eff}}[n] = h[n] * a[n]$—that is shorter than the guard interval. Several criteria for this "channel shortening," such

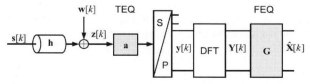

Figure 10: Receiver with time- and frequency-domain equalizers

as the *mean square error* (MSE) with respect to a target impulse response or the signal energy within a window of length G, can be applied (Schur, Speidel, and Angerbauer 2000).

Frequency Domain Equalization

A rather natural choice to combat the effects of an insufficient guard interval is to use an equalizer after the receiver DFT that spans several subcarriers and DMT symbols. This can be seen as an extension of the simple one-tap equalizer described in the previous section. Karp, Trautmann, and Fliege (2004) showed that ISI and ICI can be completely removed by a block equalizer based on the zero-forcing criterion, as long as there are some unused subcarriers, which is the normal case in practical DMT systems. The resulting equalizer matrix is sparse, which means that the implementation cost of this block equalizer is rather low.

The Peak-to-Average Power Ratio Problem

One of the major difficulties of multicarrier systems when it comes to practical implementation is related to its high *peak-to-average power ratio* (PAPR). In multicarrier systems, the peak power of the output signal is significantly higher than its average power, leading to high linearity requirements for the power amplifier and requiring a huge range and high resolution for the digital-to-analog and analog-to-digital converter.

Based on the system model in Figure 3, we can define the PAPR as

$$\eta = \frac{\max\left\{|s(t)|^2\right\}}{E\left[|s(t)|^2\right]} \qquad (65)$$

We assume that all subchannels use the same QAM constellation and that the sequences $X_\mu[k]$ are uncorrelated. Then for 2^Q-QAM with square constellations—that is, Q is even—the average signal power of $X_\mu[k]$ is given by

$$E_S = \frac{2^Q - 1}{6} d^2 \qquad (66)$$

where d is the distance between two adjacent signal points. The signal power of the output signal $s(t)$ is

$$E\left[|s(t)|^2\right] = N \cdot E\left[|s_0(t)|^2\right] = N T E_S \int_{-\infty}^{+\infty} |g_t(t)|^2\, dt \qquad (67)$$

The output signal $s(t) = T\sum_k \sum_{v=0}^{N-1} e^{j\omega_v t} X_v[k] g(t - kT)$ takes on its maximum when all terms $e^{j\omega_v t} X_v[k]$ have the same phase. Denoting by $A = \max\{|X_v[k]|\}$ the maximum value of the signal constellation, the maximum output signal power is

$$\max\left\{|s(t)|^2\right\} = \left(ANT\sum_k |g(kT)|^2\right)^2 \qquad (68)$$

For square constellations, it holds that $A = \frac{\sqrt{2}}{2}(2^{Q/2} - 1)d$. We further assume normalized transmitter filters—that is, $\int |g(t)|^2\, dt = 1$—which finally yields the PAPR:

$$\eta = N \cdot \frac{3(2^{Q/2} - 1)^2}{2^Q - 1} \cdot T \cdot \left(\sum_k |g(kT)|^2\right)^2 \qquad (69)$$

From this expression, we see that the transmit filter has a minor influence on the PAPR, which is dominated by the number of subcarriers N. This is intuitive, because amplitude peaks occur when all subcarriers are in phase and the amplitudes simply add up.

Another explanation for the high PAPR when the number of subcarriers is large comes from the central limit theorem. When N becomes large, the amplitude distribution of the output signal, which is the sum of N independent subcarrier signals, tends to a Gaussian distribution, which has infinite PAPR. From an information theory perspective, this is an advantage of multicarrier systems: To achieve the Shannon capacity of a Gaussian channel, the transmitter signal has to be Gaussian distributed, too.

The PAPR problem has been recognized by the scientific community and a great number of partial solutions exist. Van Nee and Prasad (2000) classify the PAPR reduction techniques into the following three groups.

1. *Distortion of the transmit signal before the power amplifier.* This includes clipping and nonlinear companding, which indeed reduces the PAPR but on the other hand originates additional out-of-band emissions and in-band distortions (see e.g. O'Neill and Lopes 1995).
2. *Coding techniques to exclude sequences with a high peak power.* Because there are few sequences with a high power, not much overhead is required. However, the computational complexity of this approach can be significant (Van Nee 1996; Tarokh and Jafarkhani 2000).
3. *Probabilistic methods* that, for example, modify the phases of the QAM constellations by pseudorandom sequences or methods that make use of spreading (Müller-Weinfurtner 2000).

These methods allow us to reduce the PAPR, but they come at the price of increased complexity and signaling overhead. There seems to be no unique and optimal solution to this problem, hence research is still active in this field. A comprehensive description of state-of-the-art methods to achieve a low PAPR can be found in the book by J. Tellado (2000).

Implementation as Filter Bank

So far, we only considered implementations with rectangular pulse shape. In fact, this is by far the most common option for practical systems, and from Figure 7 it is not obvious how to realize nonrectangular pulse shapes. For this purpose, the more general scheme in Figure 5 is much better suited. As long as the condition for perfect reconstruction is satisfied, the transmit and receive filters may be chosen to fulfill any optimization criterion. A common objective for the design of the pulse-shaping filter is to reduce the spectral side lobes of the transmit signal (see e.g. Cherubini, Eleftheriou, and Ölçer 2002).

Although the filter bank implementation in Figure 5 is well suited for system analysis and for getting a good understanding of the system, it is not efficient for implementation. Similar to rectangular pulse shaping, which can be realized with a simple IDFT, MCM systems with pulse shaping can be implemented more efficiently with DFT processing. In addition to the IDFT processor, a polyphase filter bank is required as depicted in Figure 11.

We assume that the impulse response $g[n]$ has length $KN_S + 1$ and is symmetrical to $KN_S/2$, where K is the filter lengths in multiples of DMT symbols:

$$g[n] = 0, \quad \text{for } n < 0, n > KN_S$$
$$g[n] = g[KN_s - n] \tag{70}$$

Note that this allows us to define filters of nearly arbitrary length that can be used to impose stringent conditions on the spectral properties of the output signal. The polyphase filter bank in Figure 11 consists of N_S filters with impulse responses:

$$g_i[k] = g[kN_S + i], \ i = 0, 1, \ldots, N_S - 1, k \in \mathbb{Z} \tag{71}$$

This decomposition of $g[n]$ into N_S filters of lower sampling rate is called *polyphase decomposition of type* 1 (Vaidyanathan 1990 and 1993; Fliege 2000) and reads in the other direction:

$$g[n] = g_{\text{mod}_{N_S}(n)}\left[\lfloor n/N_S \rfloor\right] \tag{72}$$

It can be shown easily that the implementation in Figure 11 is equivalent to the MCM system in Figure 5. Because the polyphase filter bank operates at a fraction of the sampling rate of the direct implementation in Figure 5, the first variant is preferred for practical implementation.

Variants of the Guard Interval

Besides the most commonly applied cyclic prefix, there are other alternatives for the implementation of the guard interval. In this section, we briefly outline these alternatives, starting with a compact matrix notation of the cyclic prefix.

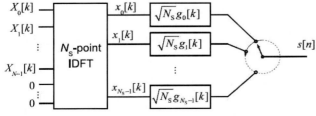

Figure 11: Transmitter with IDFT and polyphase filter bank

Cyclic Prefix

As we saw earlier, after the inverse Fourier transform, the last G samples of each DMT block are copied and inserted at the beginning of the block. We can thus write the output of the transmitter as

$$\mathbf{s}[k] = [\mathbf{F}_{\text{cp}} \ \mathbf{F}]^H \mathbf{X}[k] \tag{73}$$

where $\mathbf{F}$ is the DFT matrix and $\mathbf{F}_{\text{cp}}$ is the $N \times G$ matrix that is formed by the last G columns of $\mathbf{F}$. The received signal after the DFT is given by

$$\mathbf{Y}[k] = \mathbf{D} \mathbf{X}[k] + [\mathbf{0}_{N \times G} \ \mathbf{F}] \mathbf{w}[k] \tag{74}$$

where $\mathbf{D}$ is a diagonal matrix as we saw in the previous section.

Zero Padding

Multicarrier modulation with zero padding has been proposed relatively recently by Scaglione, Giannakis, and Barbarossa (1999) and has been considered for wireless transmission by Muquet et al. (2002). It has been shown that in the noiseless case, zero padding allows us to recover the transmit symbol regardless of the channel zero locations—that is, the transmit symbol can even be recomputed at the receiver if the matrix $\mathbf{H}$ according to Equation 37 has zero eigenvalues. This is not possible with a cyclic prefix where a channel zero at a subcarrier frequency will inevitably destroy that subchannel's symbol. However, it has to be noted that this argumentation is rather academic because it only holds for noiseless channels that, in reality, never occur.

With zero padding, the transmitter output is given by

$$\mathbf{s}[k] = [\mathbf{F} \ \mathbf{0}_{N \times G}]^H \mathbf{X}[k] \tag{75}$$

The receiver input signal is now

$$\begin{aligned}
\mathbf{z}[k] &= \tilde{\mathbf{H}} \mathbf{F}_{\text{zp}} \mathbf{X}[k] + \mathbf{w}[k] \\
&= [\tilde{\mathbf{H}}_0 \ \tilde{\mathbf{H}}_{\text{zp}}][\mathbf{F} \ \mathbf{0}_{N \times G}]^H \mathbf{X}[k] + \mathbf{w}[k] \\
&= \tilde{\mathbf{H}}_0 \mathbf{F}^H \mathbf{X}[k] + \mathbf{w}[k],
\end{aligned} \tag{76}$$

where $\widetilde{\mathbf{H}}$ is the $N_S \times N_S$ lower triangular Toeplitz matrix whose first column is $(h0 \ldots h_G \ 0 \ldots 0)^T$, and $\widetilde{\mathbf{H}} = [\tilde{\mathbf{H}}_0 \ \tilde{\mathbf{H}}_{\text{zp}}]$ is its partition into the first N and the last G columns. $\tilde{\mathbf{H}}_0$ is also Toeplitz and nonsingular—that is, it is always invertible. For zero padding, a slightly more complex receiver is in order because the Toeplitz matrix $\widetilde{\mathbf{H}}$ *cannot* be diagonalized by the Fourier matrix as was the case with the circular matrix $\mathbf{H}$ in Equation 37. If we adopt the MMSE criterion for the equalization of the input signal in Equation 76, then we obtain the equalization matrix

$$\mathbf{G} = \mathbf{F} \tilde{\mathbf{H}}_0^H \left(\frac{N_0}{E_S} \mathbf{I}_{N_S} + \tilde{\mathbf{H}}_0 \tilde{\mathbf{H}}_0^H \right)^{-1} \tag{77}$$

Thus, the signal after equalization is given by

$$\mathbf{Y}[k] = \mathbf{G}\,\mathbf{z}[k] = \mathbf{G}\,\mathbf{H}_0\,\mathbf{F}^H\,\mathbf{X}[k] + \mathbf{G}\,\mathbf{w}[k] \quad (78)$$

The matrix $\mathbf{GH}_0\,\mathbf{F}^H$ is approximately diagonal; based on this observation, further receiver processing can be implemented based on soft demapping as outlined in the section on frequency domain equalization. For further details, see also Pfletschinger and Sanzi (2004).

Pseudorandom Postfix

The idea of the pseudorandom postfix is partially inspired by the zero-padding guard interval and shares some of its advantages (Muck et al. 2003). However, instead of appending G zero samples to each DMT symbol, a pseudorandom sequence is inserted. Because this sequence is known beforehand, the receiver can use this knowledge for channel estimation.

Similar to zero padding, the transmitted signal is given by

$$\mathbf{s}[k] = [\mathbf{F}\,\mathbf{0}_{G\times N}]^H\,\mathbf{X}[k] + [\mathbf{0}_{1\times N}\ \mathbf{c}]^T \quad (79)$$

where $\mathbf{c} = (c_0, c_1,..., c_{G-1})^T$ is the pseudorandom postfix. Muck et al. (2003) propose several equalization schemes with different performance and complexity trade-offs for this multicarrier scheme. The basic advantage of this scheme is its ability to facilitate channel estimation in the receiver, especially if the Doppler spread is large.

CAPACITY AND ADAPTIVE BIT LOADING
Capacity of Frequency-Selective Channels

Shannon (1948) showed in his seminal work that the maximum bit rate for reliable communication over a noisy channel is given by the *channel capacity*. For an AWGN channel with complex-valued transmit signals, transmit power E_S, and noise power N_0, this capacity is given by

$$R = \log_2\left(1 + \frac{E_S}{N_0}\right) \quad (80)$$

The maximum achievable rate R is measured in bits per channel use, which is equivalent to bps/Hz when applied to a discrete time channel model. Because DMT decomposes the broadband channel into parallel independent subchannels, according to Equation 53 we can use this expression to compute the capacity per subchannel. The transmit and noise power on subchannel μ are given by $p_\mu = E[|X_\mu[k]|^2]$ and $\sigma_\mu^2 = E[|w_\mu[k]|^2]$, respectively. This gives the subchannel capacity

$$R_\mu = \log_2\left(1 + \frac{|\lambda_\mu|^2\,p_\mu}{\sigma_\mu^2}\right) = \log_2(1 + T_\mu p_\mu) \quad (81)$$

where we defined the *channel gain-to-noise ratio* (CNR):

$$T_\mu = \frac{|\lambda_\mu|^2}{\Gamma\cdot\sigma_\mu^2} \quad (82)$$

For the following considerations on channel capacity and transmit power, it is sufficient to describe the channel by its CNR. The factor Γ denotes the SNR gap, which for the moment is set to unity. If the channel is frequency-selective, which is the usual case for DMT, then the simple AWGN formula of Equation 80 cannot be applied. However, because DMT decomposes the broadband channel into parallel, frequency nonselective subchannels, we can compute the capacity of the subchannel and obtain the capacity of the broadband channel as the sum of all subchannel capacities.

This sum capacity depends on the distribution of the total transmit power on the subchannels; thus, a natural question to ask is: How should the transmit power $\bar{P}$ be allocated in order to maximize the channel capacity $R = \Sigma_\mu R_\mu$? This can be formulated rigorously as the following optimization problem:

$$\begin{aligned} \max. \quad & \sum_{\mu=1}^{M} R_\mu \\ \text{s.t.} \quad & \sum_{\mu=1}^{M} p_\mu \leq \bar{P},\ p_\mu \geq 0 \end{aligned} \quad (83)$$

where $\mu = 1, 2, ..., M$ denotes the available subcarriers, and $\bar{P}$ is the available transmit power. The solution to this problem is the famous *water-filling* solution (Gallager 1968):

$$p_\mu = \max\left\{0, P_0 - \frac{1}{T_\mu}\right\},\ \text{with } P_0 \text{ such that } \sum_\mu p_\mu = \bar{P} \quad (84)$$

The name of this solution comes from the nice graphical representation of the formula, which is depicted in Figure 12. We can interpret the inverse CNR $1/T_\mu$ as the bottom of a bowl, into which we fill an amount of water that corresponds to $\bar{P}$. The water will distribute itself such that the depth corresponds to the wanted function p_μ.

The water-filling solution finds the optimum power allocation to maximize the channel capacity. In a practical system, we need to consider implementable *modulation and coding schemes* (MCS) that operate at a rate below capacity. Moreover, only a small number of eligible MCS, each corresponding to a given code rate, is usually available.

To make use of the water-filling solution for practically implementable MCS, we can introduce the SNR gap, which provides a link between the information-theoretic channel capacity and the bit rate for (coded) QAM. The SNR gap Γ is the additionally required SNR in QAM modulation with a given target *bit error ratio* (BER) to achieve the bit rate R. In other words, if for the SNR γ the channel

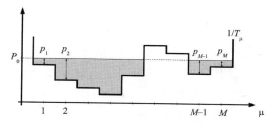

Figure 12: Water-filling diagram. The inverse CNR $1/T_\mu$ can be interpreted as the bottom of a bowl. If this bowl is filled with an amount of water that corresponds to the available transmit power, then the depth corresponds to the optimum power allocation per subchannel

capacity is R, then with QAM we need an SNR of $\Gamma\gamma$ to achieve the same rate R.

Algorithms for Bit and Power Loading

For practical QAM modulation, the optimization problem of Equation 83 must be formulated in a slightly different way. Instead of the channel capacities, we have to consider bit rates b_μ, which are taken out of a discrete set $B = \{r_1, r_2, \ldots, r_Q\}$. An associated set, $\gamma = \{\gamma_1, \gamma_2, \ldots, \gamma_Q\}$, denotes the required SNRs to achieve these rates at a given BER. The modulation and coding scheme is sufficiently described by these two sets for a given target BER.

Apart from maximizing the bit rate, another common criterion is the minimization of the transmit power for a given target bit rate.

Maximum bit rate:

$$
\begin{array}{ll}
\max & \sum_\mu b_\mu \\
\text{s.t.} & \sum_\mu p_\mu \le \bar{P}, \ p_\mu \ge 0, \ b_\mu \in B
\end{array}
\tag{85}
$$

Minimum transmit power:

$$
\begin{array}{ll}
\min & \sum_\mu p_\mu \\
\text{s.t.} & \sum_\mu b_\mu \ge b_{\min}, \ p_\mu \ge 0, \ b_\mu \in B
\end{array}
\tag{86}
$$

An algorithm that can be applied to both criteria is the *Hughes-Hartogs algorithm* (Hughes-Hartogs 1987). This is the optimal algorithm for the discrete optimization problems of Equations 85 and 86 and can be considered as the discrete version of the water-filling solution.

The Hughes-Hartogs algorithm is relatively simple and can be described in a few lines:

$p_{\text{tot}} = 0, \ b_m = i_m = 0 \ \forall m = 1, \ldots, M$

$\Delta p_m = \gamma_1/T_m \ \forall m = 1, \ldots, M$

while $\sum_m b_m < b_{\min}$ and $p_{\text{tot}} < \bar{P}$

$\hat{m} = \arg\min_m \{\Delta p_m\}$ // find subcarrier with smallest power increment

$p_{\text{tot}} = p_{\text{tot}} + \Delta p_{\hat{m}}$ // increment total transmit power

if $p_{\text{tot}} < \bar{P}$

    $i_{\hat{m}} = i_{\hat{m}} + 1, \ b_{\hat{m}} = r_{i_{\hat{m}}}$ // increment rate on chosen subcarrier

    if $i_{\hat{m}} < Q$ // rate increment still possible on chosen subcarrier?

$$\Delta p_{\hat{m}} = \left(\gamma_{i_{\hat{m}+1}} - \gamma_{i_{\hat{m}}}\right)\Big/T_m$$

    else

$$\Delta p_{\hat{m}} = \infty$$ // subcarrier fully loaded

    end if

end if

end while

The basic idea of this algorithm is to increase the rate of the subchannel that requires the least power for this rate increment. The algorithm first calculates the power increment for transmitting the next higher rate on each subcarrier. Then the subchannel with the lowest power increment is selected and—if neither the power nor the bit rate constraint is exceeded—the next higher bit rate is allocated to this subchannel. This process is repeated until the power or rate constraint is about to be exceeded. The algorithm can be used for both rate maximization or power minimization by simply setting the other constraint to infinity. It was originally formulated for uncoded QAM, but by defining the set B with noninteger rates, it can also be applied to coded QAM. The mapping between transmit power and rate, which substitutes Equation 81, is implicitly given by the set of minimum SNRs γ.

Although the Hughes-Hartogs algorithm provides the best solution, it is not the most efficient one from an implementation point of view. This issue has been addressed by various authors who have presented suboptimal but computationally more efficient solutions. These are too numerous to be listed, so we mention as an example the solution of Sonalkar (2002) and the references therein.

Significant contributions in this area have been provided first by Chow (1993) and later by Yu and Cioffi (2001), who formalized the observation that the capacity is reduced only to a small extent by constant power allocation. They describe a solution that allocates constant transmit power to a subset of the available subcarriers and illustrate a low-complexity algorithm that finds this subset. Moreover, they provide a bound on the rate loss with respect to the optimum water-filling solution.

The Hughes-Hartogs and the constant power algorithm are illustrated in the water-filling diagram in Figure 13.

APPLICATIONS AND EXTENSIONS OF DMT
The First Main Application: ADSL

The DMT modulation scheme has been selected as standard for asymmetric digital subscriber lines, a technique

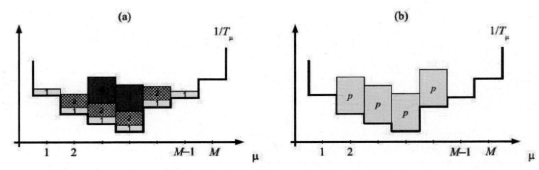

Figure 13: (a) Bit allocation with the Hughes-Hartogs algorithm. Bits are allocated to the subchannel with the smallest power increment. (b) Constant power water filling. Constant power is allocated to a properly chosen subset of all subchannels

for providing high-speed data services over the existing copper-based telephone subscriber line infrastructure. Typically, these phone lines are unshielded twisted pairs that share the same cable with multiple other pairs. Hence, the performance of ADSL depends on the noise environment and cable loss. When lines are bound together in a cable, they produce cross talk from one pair to another at levels that increase with frequency and the number of cross-talking pairs or disturbers. For this reason, cross talk is one major noise source. Additional disturbances stem from impulse noise and possibly from radio frequency interferers. Beside that, line attenuation increases with frequency and distance. DMT is well suited for the wide variations in the ADSL channel characteristics. In particular, rate adaptation on a subchannel basis is quite straightforward for DMT in order to optimize the ADSL transmission system. In the sequel, certain aspects of an ADSL system are regarded.

The parameters of the DMT modulation scheme for downstream transmission are determined by the ADSL standard (ITU-T 1999) as follows:

- FFT size of $N = 512$. Excluding the two subcarriers at $\nu = 0$ and $\nu = N/2$, at most 255 usable parallel subchannels result.
- sampling rate $f_A = 1/T_A = 2.208 \cdot 10^6$ samples/s
- guard interval length $G = N/16 = 32$ samples
- adaptive bit loading with a maximum number of 15 bits per subcarrier (this corresponds to QAM with $2^{15} = 32768$ constellation points)
- a flat transmit power spectral density of approximately -40 dBm/Hz. As the spectrum ranges up to $f_A/2 = 1.104$ MHz, the transmit power is approximately 20 dBm.

Because ADSL services share the same line with the plain old telephone service (POTS), a set of service filters (POTS-splitter) at the customer premises and the network node separate the two frequency bands. Usually, POTS signals occupy a bandwidth up to 4 kHz. To allow a smooth and inexpensive analog filter for signal separation, ADSL services can use a frequency range from 25 kHz to as high as 1.1 MHz.

For a comprehensive overview of xDSL technology, see the books of Bingham (2000) and Starr, Cioffi, and Silverman (1999), as well as the June 2002 issue of the *IEEE Journal of Selected Areas in Communications* (vol. 20, no. 5).

DMT for Power Line Communications

Power line communication (PLC) systems aim at using the ubiquitous power line grid as a medium for last-mile access networks. As with ADSL, the key idea for economic feasibility is to use an advanced transmission scheme over an existing medium. One of the principal differences between the telephone subscriber line and the power line grid is that in the first system each user has a dedicated line while the latter is a shared medium; hence for PLC a multiple-access scheme is required. DMT can be extended straightforwardly to a multi-user scheme by allocating to each user a subset of the available subcarriers.

Another variant of PLC uses the power line for in-home communication, making use of the existing infrastructure of wires and wall outlets to provide a broadband LAN and thus constitute an alternative to WLAN for in-home use.

The major impairments of the power line channel are the frequency-dependent attenuation and considerable noise, which is typically far from the typical AWGN model. It is strongly colored and has multiple impulse components. In addition, narrowband interference from external radio sources is coupled into the network. DMT with adaptive bit loading can cope well with frequency-selective channels, colored noise, and narrowband interference by allocating more bits to subchannels with high SNR and apply lower rates on noisier subchannels.

A good high-level overview of PLC can be found in Majumder and Caffery (2004), while details on coding and modulation for PLC are given by Biglieri (2003). Up-to-date information can also be found in the July 2006 special issue of the *IEEE Journal on Selected Areas in Communications* (vol. 24, no. 7).

Advanced DMT Techniques

The prime application of DMT is ADSL, which connects individual users over the existing telephone subscriber line to a central office, which is connected to a backbone network such as the Internet. These subscriber lines consist usually of twisted pairs that form part of a bigger cable bundle. Because the individual pairs are not shielded, electromagnetic coupling results in significant cross talk between the twisted pairs of different users. This creates a multi-user environment, which gives the opportunity for significant performance gains by treating the individual DMT systems jointly—that is, as a multi-user system. The main degrees of freedom for multi-user optimization come from the possibility for frequency-selective power allocation and from the possibility of coordinating transmission or reception of different users' signals. These techniques are known as *dynamic spectrum management* (see Cioffi 2005; Song and Chung 2002) and the following two main methods can be identified.

Multi-User Power Allocation with Iterative Water Filling

In this approach, all users optimize their own transmit PSD by considering the cross talk of all other users. This method is computationally inexpensive but nevertheless powerful and can be applied in a distributed or centralized version. If applied to an *interference channel*, the distributed algorithm converges to a Nash equilibrium (Yu, Ginis, and Cioffi 2002), while the centralized version converges to the maximum sum rate for a *multiple-access channel* (Yu et al. 2004).

Vectored DMT

In the downstream, the signals for all users in the same cable binder can be transmitted *cooperatively* by applying predistortion techniques. Ideally, these predistortions are designed such that, after passing through the channel, the received signals at the customers' modems are free of interference.

Both techniques have the potential to significantly increase the throughput on digital subscriber lines at a more than reasonable implementation cost.

CONCLUSION

The features and the underlying principles of DMT modulation have been explained. The criterion for orthogonality has been described, and the relationship between analog and digital system models have been illustrated. It has been shown how a broadband channel is divided into parallel frequency nonselective subchannels. This partitioning paves the way for DMT to adapt easily to frequency-selective channels and to approach the limits set by the channel capacity. For the main application of DMT—the transmission over digital subscriber lines—substantial performance gains can be achieved by considering the multi-user nature of the transmission environment.

GLOSSARY

Channel capacity: This fundamental figure of merit for a given channel model determines the maximum rate at which information can be reliably transmitted. This concept was developed by Shannon in his groundbreaking work and is therefore also called *Shannon capacity*. The channel capacity can be seen as the upper bound of the bit rate for any realizable modulation and coding scheme.

Convolution: Describes a mathematical operation to compute the output signal of a linear system. The output signal is given as the convolution of the input signal with the impulse response. In frequency domain, the corresponding operation is the multiplication with the frequency response.

Digital subscriber line (DSL): Comprises all techniques for digital transmission over existing telephone subscriber lines. The most famous variant is *asymmetric digital subscriber line* (ADSL).

Discrete Fourier transform (DFT): Discrete variant of the Fourier transform that can be implemented very efficiently with digital signal processing if the number of input and output elements is a power of 2. In this case, it is also called *fast Fourier transform* (FFT).

Eye diagram: A plot of the signals after the receiver filter during the interval of the sampling period. This diagram gives a visualization of the expected intersymbol interference and the vulnerability of the system to phase jitter.

Log-likelihood value (L-value): Gives information about the reliability of a detected bit. A large positive L-value signifies that the bit is surely a 1, while a large negative value corresponds to a probable 0. If no information about the bit is available, then the L-value is zero.

Nyquist criterion: This criterion defines the condition on the transmit and receive filters to ensure that at the sampling instants the received signal is not influenced by preceding or successive samples—that is, that the received signal is free of intersymbol interference.

Phase shift keying (PSK): Digital modulation format that modulates only the phase of the carrier frequency while the amplitude is kept constant.

Quadrature amplitude modulation (QAM): Digital modulation format that modulates the phase and the amplitude of the carrier frequency. This can be considered as the concurrent modulation of two sinusoidal carriers that are shifted in phase by 90 degrees.

Water filling: The term used to describe the method for optimal power allocation in a frequency-selective channel. The name comes from the visualization of a water basin into which a certain amount of water is poured. The wanted function corresponds to the water depth.

CROSS REFERENCES

See *Digital Communications Basics*; *DSL (Digital Subscriber Line)*; *Frequency Division Multiplexing (FDM)*; *Orthogonal Frequency Division Multiplexing (OFDM)*.

REFERENCES

Akansu, A. N., P. Duhamel, X. Lin, and M. de Courville. 1998. Orthogonal transmultiplexers in communication: A review. *IEEE Transactions on Signal Processing*, 46(4): 979–95.

Al-Dhahir, N., and J. M. Cioffi. 1996. Optimum finite-length equalization for multicarrier transceivers. *IEEE Transactions on Communications*, 44(1): 56–64.

Arslan, G., B. L. Evans, and S. Kiaei. 2001. Equalization for discrete multitone transceivers to maximize bit rate. *IEEE Transactions on Signal Processing*, 49(12): 3123–35.

Biglieri, E. 2003. Coding and modulation for a horrible channel. *IEEE Communications Magazine*, 41(5): 92–8.

Bingham, J. A. C. 1990. Multicarrier modulation for data transmission: An idea whose time has come. *IEEE Communications Magazine*, May, pp. 5–14.

———. 2000. *ADSL, VDSL, and multicarrier modulation*. New York: John Wiley & Sons.

Cherubini, G., E. Eleftheriou, and S. Ölçer. 2002. Filtered multitone modulation for very high-speed digital subscriber lines. *IEEE Journal on Selected Areas in Communications*, 20(5): 1016–28.

Chow, P. S. 1993. Bandwidth optimized digital transmission techniques for spectrally shaped channels with impulse noise (doctoral dissertation, Stanford University).

Cimini, L. J. 1985. Analysis and simulation of a digital mobile channel using orthogonal frequency division multiplexing. *IEEE Transactions on Communications*, 33(7): 665–75.

Cioffi, J. M. 1990. *A multicarrier primer*. ANSI T1E1.4 Committee Contribution, Nov.

———.2005. Dynamic spectrum management project (retrieved from www.stanford.edu/group/cioffi/dsm/).

Doelz, M. L., E. T. Heald, and D. L. Martin. 1957. Binary data transmission techniques for linear systems. *Proceedings of the IRE*, 45: 656–61.

Fliege, N. J. 2000. *Multirate digital signal processing: Multirate systems, filter banks, wavelets*. New York: John Wiley & Sons.

Gallager, R. G. 1968. *Information theory and reliable communication*. New York: John Wiley & Sons.

Haykin, S. 2001. *Communications systems*. New York: John Wiley & Sons.

Hughes-Hartogs, D. 1987. Ensemble modem structure for imperfect transmission media. U.S. patent 4,679,227, issued July 7, 1987.

ITU-T. 1999. Recommendation G.992.1. Asymmetric digital subscriber lines (ADSL) transceivers, June.

Kalet, I. 1989. The multitone channel. *IEEE Transactions on Communications*, 37(2): 119–24.

Karp, T., S. Trautmann, and N. J. Fliege. 2004. Zero-forcing frequency-domain equalization for generalized DMT transceivers with insufficient guard interval. *EURASIP Journal on Applied Signal Processing*, 10: 1446–59.

Kasturia, S., J. T. Aslanis, and J. M. Cioffi. 1990. Vector coding for partial response channels. *IEEE Transactions on Information Theory*, 36(4): 741–62.

Majumder, A., and J. Caffery. 2004. Power line communications: An overview. *IEEE Potentials*, 23(4): 4–8.

Muck, M., M. de Courville, M. Debbah, and P. Duhamel. 2003. A pseudo random postfix OFDM modulator

and inherent channel estimation techniques. In *IEEE Globecom*, San Francisco, December, pp. 2380–4.

Müller-Weinfurtner, S. 2000. *OFDM for wireless communications: Nyquist windowing, peak-power reduction, and synchronization*. Aachen, Germany: Shaker.

Muquet, B., Z. Wang, G. B Giannakis, M. de Courville, and P. Duhamel. 2002. Cyclic prefixing or zero-padding for wireless multicarrier transmissions? *IEEE Transactions on Communications*, 50(12): 2136–48.

O'Neill, R., and L. B. Lopes. 1995. Envelope variations and spectral splatter in clipped multicarrier signals. *IEEE PIMRC*, Toronto, September, 1: 71–5.

Oppenheim, A. V., and R. W. Schafer. 1989. *Discrete-time signal processing*. Englewood Cliffs, NJ: Prentice Hall.

Pfletschinger, S., and F. Sanzi. 2004. Iterative demapping for OFDM with zero-padding or cyclic prefix. In *IEEE International Conference on Communications* (ICC), Paris, June, pp. 842–6.

Pollet, T., M. Peeters, M. Moonen, and L. Vandendorpe. 2000. Equalization for DMT-based broadband modems. *IEEE Communications Magazine*, 38(5): 106–13.

Scaglione, A., G. B. Giannakis, and S. Barbarossa. 1999. Redundant filterbank precoders and equalizers. Part I: Unification and optimal designs. Part II: Blind equalization, synchronization and direct equalization. *IEEE Transactions on Signal Processing*, 47(7): 1988–2022.

Schur, R., J. Speidel, and R. Angerbauer. 2000. Reduction of guard interval by impulse compression for DMT modulation on twisted pair cables. In *IEEE Globecom*, San Antonio, November, pp. 1632–6.

Shannon, C. E. 1948. A mathematical theory of communication. *Bell System Technical Journal*, 27: 379–423, 623–56.

Sonalkar, R. V. 2002. Bit- and power-allocation algorithm for symmetric operation of DMT-based DSL modems. *IEEE Transactions on Communications*, 50(6): 902–6.

Song, K. B., and S. T. Chung. 2002. Dynamic spectrum management for next-generation DSL systems. *IEEE Communications Magazine*, October, pp. 101–109.

Starr, T., J. M. Cioffi, and P. J. Silverman. 1999. *Understanding digital subscriber line technology*. Englewood Cliffs, NJ: Prentice Hall.

Tarokh, V., and H. Jafarkhani. 2000. On the computation and reduction of the peak-to-average power ratio in multicarrier communications. *IEEE Transactions on Communications*, 48(1): 37–44.

Tellado, J. 2000. *Multicarrier modulation with low PAR: Applications to DSL and wireless*. Norwell, MA: Kluwer Academic Publishers.

Vaidyanathan, P. P. 1990. Multirate digital filters, filter banks, polyphase networks, and applications: A tutorial. *Proceedings of the IEEE*, 78(1): 56–93.

———. 1993. *Multirate systems and filter banks*. Englewood Cliffs, NJ: Prentice Hall.

Van Nee, R. D. J. 1996. OFDM codes for peak-to-average power reduction and error correction. In *IEEE Globecom, London*, November, pp. 740–4.

Van Nee, R., and R. Prasad. 2000. *OFDM for wireless multimedia communications*. Boston: Artech House.

Weinstein, S. B., and P.M. Ebert. 1971. Data transmission by frequency-division multiplexing using the discrete Fourier transform. *IEEE Transactions on Communication Technology*, 19(5): 628–34.

Yu, W., and J. M. Cioffi. 2001. On constant power water-filling. *IEEE International Conference on Communications* (ICC), Helsinki, June, 6: 1665–9.

Yu, W., G. Ginis, and J. M. Cioffi. 2002. Distributed multiuser power control for digital subscriber lines. *IEEE Journal on Selected Areas in Communications*, 20(5): 1105–15.

Yu, W., W. Rhee, S. Boyd, and J. M. Cioffi. 2004. Iterative water-filling for Gaussian vector multiple access channels. *IEEE Transactions on Information Theory*, 50(1): 145–52.

Pulse Position Modulation

Jon Hamkins, *Jet Propulsion Laboratory, California Institute of Technology, Pasadena, California*

INTRODUCTION

Pulse position modulation (PPM) is a signaling format in which the temporal positions of pulses are modulated by a message. In this chapter, we explore the history, fundamentals, and modern design principles of PPM. As we shall see, the PPM signal format has a long history and a bright future.

History

Early references to PPM in the electrical engineering literature use the term *pulse position modulation* unevenly to refer to any one of a multitude of transmission schemes in which pulse positions are modulated by a message. In several early descriptions of PPM (Lacy 1947; McAulay 1968; Riter, Boatright, and Shay 1971), the frequency of the pulses was held fixed and information was contained in the continuous variation of a pulse from its nominal position. This has been referred to as *PPM with a fixed reference* (Ross 1949); in today's terminology, it would be referred to as *analog PPM*. When the pulse positions can take on only discrete values, as is the case in modern designs, the early literature referred to the modulation as *quantized PPM* (QPPM) (Pettit 1965).

In another early scheme, the frequency of pulses was held fixed, with the center of each pulse not varying at all from the nominal frequency. The information was contained in the variation in the position of the rising (and symmetrically falling) edge of the pulse. To maintain a constant energy per pulse, the amplitude was varied inversely to the pulse width. In today's terminology, this is more properly termed *return-to-zero pulse width modulation* and *pulse amplitude modulation*.

These and other types of pulsed transmissions have been in use since at least World War II ("Pulse position" 1945) and expressed in early *private branch exchange* (PBX) implementations by AT&T (Meiseand and DeStefano 1966). Indeed, the concept of pulsed transmission is much older than that: Native Americans used it in their smoke signals, with one puff meaning "Attention," two in rapid succession meaning "All is well," and three in rapid succession meaning "Danger" or "Help" (Tomkins 2002). Several decades ago, the optical communications literature came on what is now the standard definition of PPM (Gagliardi and Karp 1976), which is a specific form of QPPM. In this chapter, to avoid confusion, we shall define and analyze PPM in only this standard way.

Applications

PPM has a rich history of applications in optical, radio frequency, and acoustical communications.

Optical Communications Links

In recent years, the dominant application of PPM has been optical communications. PPM has long been suggested for use in optical systems because its potential for a high peak-to-average power ratio naturally fits the physical properties of lasers, which may emit a pulse of light with a high peak power but which output a much lower average power. Such a property has been shown to be an efficient means of transmitting at high data rates, even when background light interferes.

Using PPM, a laser sends a pulse of light delayed in proportion to the value of the message being transmitted. The light pulses can be either transmitted through free space, including to and from outer space (Wilson and

Lesh 1993; Wilson et al. 1997; Townes et al. 2004), or coupled to an optical fiber (Palais 2004; Ohtsuki and Kahn 2000). The receiver detects the delay of the light pulse to decipher the intended message. [In the case of earlier demonstrations (Wilson and Lesh 1993; Wilson et al. 1997) pulse lasers were used, but not PPM specifically.]

In one impressive PPM application, NASA developed technology for high-speed optical transmission from a Mars orbiter, originally set to launch in 2009, to Earth (Townes et al. 2004). The system supports data rates as high as 50 Mbps over a distance of 150 million kilometers using a laser with an average output power of 5 W, which is one hundred times faster than Mars–Earth data rates achieved as of this writing. The link design uses 32-ary and 64-ary PPM (Moision and Hamkins 2003), depending on link conditions, highly accurate pointing algorithms (Lee, Ortiz, and Alexander 2005), reception with either the 5-meter Hale telescope on Palomar Mountain or an array of smaller telescopes (Candell 2005), efficient photodetectors (Biswas and Farr 2004), and a specially developed *error-correction code* (ECC) that operates within 1 decibel (dB) of the Shannon limit (Moision and Hamkins 2005, "Coded"). Laboratory demonstrations showed the proper operation of a multi-Mbps end-to-end system under expected link conditions, but a new emphasis on human flight missions within NASA has forced the cancellation of this robotic mission.

Another free space optical application that uses PPM is the infrared links for the consumer mobile electronics devices that are becoming ubiquitous. The Infrared Data Association has developed the IrDa standard (Knutson and Brown 2004) which includes, among other modes, a "fast infrared" mode that operates at 4 Mbps using 4-ary PPM. Laptop computers, cell phones, personal information managers, cameras, printers, and many other consumer devices now have IrDa-compliant transceivers. Infrared television remote controls do not typically use the IrDa standard, but they often operate with a type of PPM as well (Casier, De Man, and Matthijs 1976). For example, JVC, Mitsubishi, NEC, Philips, Sanyo, Sharp, and Toshiba manufacture televisions that use PPM as the format for infrared remote control. An NEC data sheet (NEC Corporation 1994) contains a description of a representative signaling format.

Remotely Controlled Vehicles

Remotely controlled aircraft, watercraft, vehicles, and robots routinely use PPM as a method of accurately obtaining controlling information from the operator. Signals transmitted with radio frequency pulses have time delays that are proportional to several controls (e.g., the angles of ailerons, elevators, and rudder and steering and throttles) that the operator desires to set.* PPM is chosen for this application because the vehicles and vessels require low-complexity receivers (especially aircraft), and the

---

*In 1898, Nikola Tesla was issued the first patent (U.S. patent 613, 809) for remote-controlled vessels. The patent, however, primarily concerns the mechanical positions of brushes and contact plates and does not propose PPM. The controlling actions are made by directly rendering a given circuit either active or inactive, according to the signal transmitted from a remote operator.

electronics needed to convert a pulse to a motor position are simple.

Medical Sensors

A sensor may be implanted in or attached externally to medical patients who require close monitoring of blood pressure, blood flow, temperature, the presence of certain chemicals, and the vital signs of a baby during birth. The sensor can transmit radio waves to a remote receiver that displays or records the data. PPM is an efficient transmission for this application, particularly for analog data such as these, thereby providing the longest possible battery life before inconvenient sensor replacement (Bornhoft et al. 2001).

Oil and Coal Drilling

Drilling is necessary in both the oil and coal industries for both exploration and methane drainage. Automatic monitoring of the borehole trajectory, bit thrust, and torque during drilling assists greatly in drilling the longest, straightest, and most accurately aimed holes. To do this, so-called measure-while-drilling or logging-while-drilling techniques are used, by which pressure pulses in the drilling fluid are modulated with PPM at the end of the drill bit down the hole and detected at the surface (Marsh et al. 2002).

Underwater Acoustic Communications Links

PPM can also be used for acoustic underwater signaling. A short acoustical tone is transmitted with a delay that is a linear function of the value being sent (Riter, Boatright, and Shay 1971). In addition to ocean communication on Earth, this technique has been considered for the exploration of Europa, a moon of Jupiter with a thin layer of ice and liquid water beneath. In this mission scenario, a probe would penetrate the surface and communicate with acoustic PPM back to a surface spacecraft.

FUNDAMENTALS OF PPM
Definition of PPM

PPM is a modulation format that maps message bits to pulse positions. In the modern use of the term, a PPM *symbol* comprises M slots, exactly one of which contains a pulse. Input message bits determine which of the M positions is used. For the simplest mapping, M is typically taken to be a power of 2, in which case $\log_2 M$ message bits specify one of the M possible positions of the pulse, as shown in Figure 1. If the slots are numbered $0, 1, ..., M - 1$, then in the mapping shown in Figure 1, the decimal representation of the bits is the number of the slot containing the pulse. As a shorthand, M-ary PPM is often referred to as M-PPM (not to be confused with *multipulse* PPM, or MPPM, discussed later in this chapter).

Mathematically, M-ary PPM may be described as the encoding of a k-bit source $\mathbf{U} = (U_1, ..., U_k) \in [0,1]^k$ to yield a signal $\mathbf{X} = (0, ..., 0, 1, 0, ..., 0) \in [0,1]^M$, $M = 2^k$, which contains a single one in the position indicated by the decimal representation of $\mathbf{U}$.

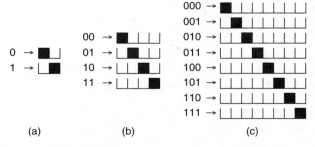

Figure 1: M-ary PPM maps $\log_2 M$ bits to a pulse in one of M positions—(a) binary PPM, (b) 4-ary PPM, (c) 8-ary PPM

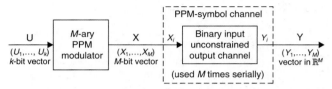

Figure 2: Block diagram of PPM modulator and memoryless channel

PPM Channel Model

To facilitate the analysis in this chapter, we now formalize a description of the channel model. The transmission channel for each slot, the *slot channel*, is a binary-input unconstrained-output channel, with input $X \in \{0,1\}$ and output $Y \in \mathbb{R}$. When no pulse is transmitted in a slot, $X = 0$; and when a pulse is transmitted in a slot, $X = 1$. We define $f_{Y|X}(y|x)$ as the *conditional probability density* (or mass) of receiving $Y = y$ in a slot, given $X = x$.

The PPM symbol $\mathbf{X} = (X_1, \ldots, X_M)$ is transmitted via M uses of the slot channel and results in the received vector $\mathbf{Y} = (Y_1, \ldots, Y_M) \in \mathbb{R}^M$. This is illustrated in Figure 2. We let $S = \{\mathbf{x}_1, \ldots, \mathbf{x}_M\}$ be the set of M-PPM symbols. Each $\mathbf{x}_k = (x_{k,1}, \ldots, x_{k,M})$ is a binary M-vector with one 1 in position k, and $M - 1$ zeros in all other positions. We define $f_{\mathbf{Y}|\mathbf{X}}(\mathbf{y}|\mathbf{x})$ as the conditional probability density of receiving $\mathbf{Y} = \mathbf{y}$ in the M slots, given $\mathbf{X} = \mathbf{x}$.

If the slot channel is memoryless, then every slot of the transmission is conditionally independent of every other slot, given the transmitted sequence. In other words, if PPM symbols $\underline{\mathbf{x}} = (\mathbf{x}^{(1)}, \ldots, \mathbf{x}^{(N)})$ are transmitted, where each symbol $\mathbf{x}^{(i)} \in S$ is a binary M-vector as described above, then the conditional probability or probability density of receiving the real M-vector $\underline{\mathbf{y}} = (\mathbf{y}^{(1)}, \ldots, \mathbf{y}^{(N)})$ factors over the symbols and slots as

$$f_{\underline{Y}|\underline{X}}(\underline{y}|\underline{x}) = \prod_{i=1}^{N}\prod_{j=1}^{M} f_{Y_j^{(i)}|X_j^{(i)}}(y_j^{(i)}|x_j^{(i)}) \qquad (1)$$

For this type of channel, there is no intersymbol interference and no interslot interference. If the slot channel is also stationary, then each factor in Equation 1 simplifies to $f_{Y|X}(y_j^{(i)}|x_j^{(i)})$.

The likelihood ratio of receiving value y in a slot is denoted by $L(y) \triangleq \dfrac{f_{Y|X}(y|1)}{f_{Y|X}(y|0)}$, which for algebraic convenience we assume to be finite for all y. We also assume that

$L(y)$ is monotonic in y, as is the case for many channels of practical interest (e.g., Poisson, Gaussian, and Webb-McIntyre-Conradi) (Vilnrotter, Simon, and Srinivasan 1999). The log-likelihood ratio is denoted $\Lambda(y) = \log L(y)$. $F_{Y|X}(y|1)$ $(F_{Y|X}(y|0))$ denotes the cumulative distribution—that is, the probability that a received signal (nonsignal) slot has value less than or equal to y.

Several common probability densities arise in PPM applications. Perhaps the most common is the Poisson distribution, which arises for optical communications:

$$f_{Y|X}(k|0) = \frac{K_b^k e^{-K_b}}{k!}, k \in \{0\} \cup \mathbb{N} \qquad (2)$$

$$f_{Y|X}(k|1) = \frac{(K_s + K_b)^k e^{-(K_s + K_b)}}{k!}, k \in \{0\} \cup \mathbb{N} \qquad (3)$$

where K_b is the average number of background photons detected when $X = 0$ and $K_s + K_b$ is the average number of signal and background photons detected when $X = 1$. Several other models for optical communications may arise, depending on whether the system is limited by shot noise or thermal noise; whether the photodetector is a PIN diode, a *photomultiplier tube* (PMT), or an *avalanche photodiode detector* (APD); and which of various approximations are used. The equations governing these models are discussed in depth in Dolinar et al. (2006) and Gagliardi and Karp (1995) and summarized here in Table 1. In each case, m_0 and σ_0^2 denote the mean and variance conditioned on $X = 0$, and m_1 and σ_1^2 denote the corresponding quantities conditioned on $X = 1$. We define the slot *signal-to-noise ratio* (SNR) as $\beta = (m_1 - m_0)^2/\sigma_0^2$, the "excess SNR" as $\gamma = (m_1 - m_0)^2/(\sigma_1^2 - \sigma_0^2)$, and the "bit SNR" as $\beta_b = \beta/(2R_c \log_2 M)$, where R_c is the ECC code rate ($R_c = 1$ if uncoded).

Bit-to-PPM Symbol Mappings

Figure 1 shows one mapping of user bits to pulse positions. We refer to this as a *bit-to-symbol* mapping. Each $\log_2 M$ bit corresponds to one PPM symbol. There are many choices—indeed, $M!$ choices—for the bit-to-symbol mapping. One question naturally arises: What is the best choice of the bit-to-symbol mapping?

If we suppose, as is consistent with typical applications, that the slot channel is either slowly varying or stationary, then we arrive at a convenient result: The performance of the system is equivalent under every bit-to-symbol mapping. To see this, we note that one bit-to-symbol mapping can be obtained from any other bit-to-symbol mapping by a suitable reordering of the coordinates of the transmitted slots. For example, if bits 11 are mapped to PPM symbol $(0,0,0,1)$ in one bit-to-symbol mapping and to $(0,1,0,0)$ in another, then we may transform the first mapping to the second, in part, by moving the fourth slot to the second position. Because the channel is stationary and the slots are conditionally independent, the reordering does not affect the statistics of the channel, and the performance will be the same.

In this situation, the choice of bit-to-symbol mapping is made for the convenience of the implementation.

Table 1: Probability mass functions probability density functions of several optical channel models*

Channel model	pmf or pdf
Poisson	$f_{Y|X}(k|x) = \dfrac{m_x^k e^{-m_x}}{k!}$, where $m_0 = K_b, m_1 = K_s + K_b, k \in \{0\} \cup \mathbb{N}$,
AWGN	$f_{Y|X}(y|x) = \dfrac{1}{\sigma_x} \phi\left(\dfrac{y - m_x}{\sigma_x}\right), y \in \mathbb{R}$, where $\phi(x) = \frac{1}{\sqrt{2\pi}} e^{-x^2/2}$
McIntyre–Conradi**	$f_{Y|X}(k|x) = \sum_{n=1}^{k} \dfrac{n \Gamma\left(\frac{k}{1-k_{eff}} + 1\right)\left[\frac{1+k_{eff}(G-1)}{G}\right]^{n+k_{eff}k/(1-k_{eff})}\left[\frac{(1-k_{eff})(G-1)}{G}\right]^{k-n} K_x^n e^{-K_x}}{k(k-n)! \Gamma\left(\frac{k_{eff}k}{1-k_{eff}} + n + 1\right) n!}$
WMC**	$f_{Y|X}(y|x) = \dfrac{1}{\sqrt{2\pi\sigma_x^2}}\left(1 + \frac{y-m_x}{\sigma_x \delta_x}\right)^{-3/2} \exp\left[-\dfrac{(y-m_x)^2}{2\sigma_x^2\left[1+\frac{y-m_x}{\sigma_x \delta_x}\right]}\right], y \in \mathbb{R}$
WMC +Gaussian	$f_{Y|X}(y|x) = \int_{m_x - \delta_x \sigma_x}^{\infty} \frac{1}{\sqrt{2\pi\sigma_n^2}} \exp\left[-\frac{(y-t)^2}{2\sigma_n^2}\right] \cdot \frac{1}{\sqrt{2\pi\sigma_x^2}}\left(1 + \frac{t-m_x}{\sigma_x \delta_x}\right)^{-3/2} \exp\left[-\dfrac{(y-m_x)^2}{2\sigma_x^2\left(1+\frac{t-m_x}{\sigma_x \delta_x}\right)}\right] dt$

*In each case, for $x \in \{0,1\}$, m_x and σ_x^2 are the mean and variance when $X = x$, respectively
**Webb, McIntyre, and Conradi 1974

Table 2: Common Bit-to-Symbol Mappings for 8-ary PPM

Natural	Gray	Anti-Gray	PPM pulse position
000	000	000	0
001	001	111	1
010	011	001	2
011	010	110	3
100	110	011	4
101	111	100	5
110	101	010	6
111	100	101	7

The typical mapping is the *natural* mapping, in which the decimal representation of the bits is equal to the slot position of the pulse in the PPM symbol. The natural mapping is shown in Figure 1 and in Table 2.

Many applications, especially high-speed applications, risk interslot interference. This occurs, for example, when a laser pulse width is wider than a slot epoch, or when the detector bandwidth is not sufficiently high to prevent the detected pulse from spreading across slot boundaries. This introduces memory into the channel, and equation 1 no longer holds. In addition, the choice of the symbol mapping affects performance.

For uncoded PPM on a channel with interslot interference, a PPM symbol with a pulse in the ith position is generally more likely to be incorrectly detected as having a pulse in the $(i-1)$th or $(i+1)$th position than in any other position. Thus, a *Gray code* mapping (Gray 1953) helps reduce the bit error rate. A Gray code has the property that adjacent PPM symbols correspond to input bits that

differ in at most one position, as seen in Table 2. For example 00,01,11,10 is a Gray code. PPM symbol errors that are off by only one slot result in only one bit error when a Gray code is used, instead of an average of $M(\log_2 M)/(2(M-1))$ bit errors that would result from a symbol error in a system employing a random bit-to-symbol mapping.

There are many distinct Gray code labelings (Agrell et al. 2004), but, to good approximation, all Gray codes have the same performance. One common and easily constructed Gray code is the *binary-reflected Gray code*. This code of size n bits is built from the code of size $n-1$ bits by appending a copy of the code in reverse order and prepending a 0 to the original code and a 1 to the new copy. For example, the Gray code 00,01,11,10 is copied in reverse order (10,11,01,00) and prepended with a 1, becoming the Gray code 000,001,011,010,110,111,101,100, as shown in Table 2.

Coded PPM refers to a system in which the input to the bit-to-symbol mapper has been previously encoded by an ECC. When coded PPM is used on a channel with interslot interference, often the opposite bit-to-symbol effect is needed, namely, the property that adjacent PPM symbols correspond to input bits that differ in as *many* positions as possible. Loosely speaking, the reason for this is that the ECC and PPM detectors work best when they complement each other, with the PPM detector determining roughly where the pulse is within a few slot positions and the structure of the ECC determining the specific slot position. If adjacent ECC code words correspond to slots that are in near proximity, neither the ECC nor the PPM detector can determine the correct slot exactly.

Therefore, a good bit-to-symbol mapping for coded PPM is often an *anti-Gray mapping*, in which adjacent M-ary PPM symbols correspond to input bits that differ in either $\log_2 M$ or $\log_2(M-1)$ bit positions. An anti-Gray code may be constructed from the binary-reflected

Gray code using the following method. Beginning with the first half of the Gray code (the words beginning with a 0), insert after each word its 1's complement negation (bitwise exclusive OR with the all 1's). In the original Gray code, words are all distinct, and all have a zero in the first position; therefore, the words in the anti-Gray code are also distinct. This mapping is shown in Table 2.

System Design Considerations

The bandwidth, power, efficiency, and throughput of a PPM system are interrelated parameters. Proper design of a near-optimal PPM system requires a careful examination of these parameters (Moision and Hamkins 2003; Hamkins and Moision, 2005) and a well-defined system optimization metric.

A *bandwidth constraint* is a limitation on the minimum slot width, T, in order to eliminate, or allow only a given level of, *intersymbol interference* (ISI). A *peak power constraint* is a limitation on the power within slots containing a signal. For example, for the optical Poisson channel, the peak power is $K_s hc/(\lambda T)$ W, because there are an average of K_s photons in the signal slot of duration T seconds and each photon has energy hc/λ J, where λ m is the wavelength of the photon, $h = 6.626 = 10^{-34}$ J $\cdot$ s is Planck's constant, and $c = 3 \times 10^8$ m/s is the speed of light. An average power constraint is a limitation on the average power over all slots, or, in this same example, $K_s hc/(\lambda MT)$. The photon efficiency of the system is the number of bits per photon that the system achieves, or $R_c \log_2 M/K_s$ bits/photon, where R_c is the code rate of the ECC ($R_c = 1$, if uncoded). The throughput of the system is $R_c \log_2 M/(MT)$ bits/s.

An example helps illustrate a potential pitfall of the PPM system design. Suppose photon efficiency were paramount in an optical PPM system. Then the design naturally leads one to using a very large PPM order M, because photon efficiency $R_c \log_2 M/K_s$ is increasing in M. Intuitively, this makes sense, because a pulse is rarely sent (only 1 out of M slots), but it represents many ($\log_2 M$) bits. However, if there is a limited bandwidth, then increasing M necessarily reduces the data rate. Furthermore, if the peak power is limited, then increasing M reduces the average power as well (because $\log_2 M/M$ is decreasing), which can increase the error rate of the system.

The example above shows one reason why a penchant for maximizing photon efficiency, or any other single system parameter, can be a mistake. A better question to ask is, Within the power and bandwidth constraints of a system, what is the highest throughput that can be reliably achieved with a coded PPM system of acceptable implementation complexity? The answer to this can be found by following a series of steps:

1. Determine the average power, peak power, bandwidth, and implementation complexity limitations of the system.
2. Set the slot width equal to the minimum allowed by the bandwidth and complexity constraints.
3. Compute the capacity of the PPM channel under these constraints, for various PPM orders M, and identify the PPM order M^* having the highest capacity, and the

corresponding data rate in bits per second or bits per slot.
4. Design an ECC, and associated encoder and decoder, with performance near the capacity of M^*-ary PPM.

In some applications, such as deep space communications where the received signal is especially weak, the use of ECC is essential, and the procedure above is necessary to arrive at a successful design. On the other hand, for other applications, such as remote-controlled aircraft, signaling on fiber-optic cabling, and the mining and medical applications, signal power may not be an issue, and instead simplicity considerations may dominate the link design.

DETECTION OF PPM SIGNALS
Maximum Likelihood Detection of Uncoded PPM

After observing $\mathbf{Y} = (Y_1, ..., Y_M)$, the receiver must decide which PPM symbol $\mathbf{X} \in S$ was sent. The decision rule that minimizes the probability of error is the *maximum a posteriori* (MAP) rule, given by $\text{argmax}_\mathbf{x} f_{\mathbf{X}|\mathbf{Y}}(\mathbf{x}|\mathbf{y})$. When the symbols are sent with equal likelihood, an application of Bayes's rule implies that the MAP decision is equivalent to the *maximum likelihood* (ML) decision, given by

$$\hat{\mathbf{X}} = \underset{\mathbf{x}}{\text{argmax}}\, f_{\mathbf{Y}|\mathbf{X}}(\mathbf{y}|\mathbf{x}) \qquad (4)$$

On a memoryless stationary channel, the conditional probability (or probability density) of receiving $\mathbf{Y} = \mathbf{y}$, given $\mathbf{X} = \mathbf{x}_k$, is

$$\begin{aligned} f_{\mathbf{Y}|\mathbf{X}}(\mathbf{y}|\mathbf{x}_k) &= f_{Y|X}(y_k|1)\left(\prod_{i \neq k} f_{Y|X}(y_i|0)\right) \\ &= \frac{f_{Y|X}(y_k|1)}{f_{Y|X}(y_k|0)}\left(\prod_{i=1}^{M} f_{Y|X}(y_i|0)\right) \end{aligned}$$

The ML symbol decision rule is $\hat{\mathbf{X}} = \mathbf{X}_{\hat{k}}$, where

$$\hat{k} = \underset{k}{\text{argmax}}\, f_{\mathbf{Y}|\mathbf{X}}(\mathbf{y}|\mathbf{x}_k) = \underset{k}{\text{argmax}}\, L(y_k) = \underset{k}{\text{argmax}}\, y_k \quad (5)$$

and where we made use of the monotonicity of the likelihood ratio. Equation 5 is maximized by the index k corresponding to the largest slot value—that is, the ML detection rule is to choose the symbol corresponding to the largest observed slot value. The rule has also been generalized to hold for multipulse PPM on a Poisson channel (Georghiades 1994) and arbitrary discrete memoryless channels (Hamkins and Moision 2005), as well as for even more general modulations (Hamkins et al. 2004).

Maximum Likelihood Detection of Coded PPM

A block of N PPM symbols (each a binary vector of length M) is an element of the Cartesian product $S^N = S \times \cdots \times S$. A block code is a subset $C \subset S^N$. When codeword from

C are transmitted on the channel, the ML codeword decision is the codeword $\mathbf{x} \in C$. that maximizes Equation 1. Following the same method as in the uncoded case above, the ML decision is $\underline{\hat{\mathbf{X}}} = (\mathbf{x}_{\hat{k}_1}, ..., \mathbf{x}_{\hat{k}_N})$ where $\underline{\hat{k}}$ is given by

$$\hat{k} = \operatorname*{argmax}_{\underline{k}:(x_{k_1}, ..., x_{k_N}) \in C} \prod_{i=1}^{N} f_{\mathbf{Y}|\mathbf{X}}\left(\mathbf{y}^{(i)} | \mathbf{x}_{k_i}\right) \qquad (6)$$

$$= \operatorname*{argmax}_{\underline{k}:(x_{k_1}, ..., x_{k_N}) \in C} \prod_{i=1}^{N} L\left(y_{k_i}^{(i)}\right) \qquad (7)$$

$$= \operatorname*{argmax}_{\underline{k}:(x_{k_1}, ..., x_{k_N}) \in C} \log \prod_{i=1}^{N} L\left(y_{k_i}^{(i)}\right) \qquad (8)$$

$$= \operatorname*{argmax}_{\underline{k}:(x_{k_1}, ..., x_{k_N}) \in C} \sum_{i=1}^{N} \Lambda\left(y_{k_i}^{(i)}\right) \qquad (9)$$

In other words, the ML rule chooses the PPM code word that maximizes the sum of the log-likelihood ratios of its pulsed slots. As can be seen from Equation 9, the ML decision requires storing all of the slot values from all of the symbols in the block. This is called a *soft decision decoder*. Maximum likelihood decoding of modern codes is usually too complex to be practical, and instead the codes are decoded using suboptimal methods. On the other hand, Equation 9 demonstrates that the set of slot likelihood ratios is a sufficient statistic for ML decoding. Turbo codes, turbo-like codes, and low-density parity check codes are each decoded using slot likelihood ratios (Benedetto et al. 1996) and an iterative algorithm that attempts to approximate the ML decoder, typically with good results.

A lower complexity decoder results when symbol decisions are made first and then fed into the decoder. In this *hard decision decoder*, an initial vector of k's are made according to Equation 5—that is, using symbol-by-symbol decisions—and these are fed to the decoder, which attempts to correct the errors. This is the method used in a conventional decoder for a Reed-Solomon code, for example. An additional penalty, generally of approximately 2 dB, results from using a hard decision decoder compared to a soft decision decoder.

PERFORMANCE OF PPM

We now derive general formulas for the PPM *symbol error rate* (SER) and *bit error rate* (BER), as a function of the channel statistics $f_{Y|X}(y|x)$. The derivation assumes that the channel is memoryless and stationary, and that slot and symbol timing are perfectly known.

Symbol Error Rate and Bit Error Rate of Uncoded PPM

On a continuous-output memoryless channel, the PPM symbol error probability, P_s, is the well-known performance (Gallager 1968) of an ML detector for M-ary orthogonal signaling:

$$P_s = 1 - \Pr(Y_1 = \max[Y_1, ..., Y_M] | X_1 = 1)$$
$$= 1 - \int_{-\infty}^{\infty} f_{Y|X}(y|1) \left[\int_{-\infty}^{y} f_{Y|X}(y'|0) \, dy'\right]^{M-1} dy \qquad (10)$$

Equation 10 may be evaluated numerically by first producing a table lookup for the bracketed term and then computing the outer integral numerically in the usual way (Press et al. 1992).

When the channel outputs take on discrete values, there is a possibility of a tie for the maximum count. Suppose a value of k is detected in the slot containing the pulse, l nonsignal slots also have count k, and the remaining nonsignal slots have count strictly less than k. Then the correct decision is made with probability $1/(l + 1)$. Otherwise, an error is made. By summing over all possible values of k and l, it follows that

$$P_s = 1 - \sum_{k=0}^{\infty} \sum_{l=0}^{M-1} \Pr\begin{bmatrix} \text{correct decision when } l \\ \text{nonsignal slots tie the sig-} \\ \text{nal slot for the maximum} \\ \text{count} \end{bmatrix}$$
$$\times \Pr\begin{bmatrix} \text{exactly } l \text{ of } M-1 \\ \text{nonsignal slots have} \\ \text{value } k, \text{ all others} \\ \text{smaller} \end{bmatrix} \times \Pr\begin{bmatrix} \text{signal slot} \\ \text{has value } k \end{bmatrix} \qquad (11)$$

$$= 1 - \sum_{k=0}^{\infty} \sum_{l=0}^{M-1} \frac{1}{l+1} \binom{M-1}{l} f_{Y|X}(k|0)^l F_{Y|X}$$
$$\times (k-1|0)^{M-l-1} f_{Y|X}(k|1) \qquad (12)$$

An extension of Equation 12 to n-pulse PPM, $n \geq 2$, is straightforward and involves a triple summation in place of the double summation (Hamkins and Moision 2005). After some algebraic manipulation, Equation 12 can be rewritten in a single summation as (Hamkins 2004)

$$P_s = 1 - \frac{1}{M} \sum_{k=0}^{\infty} L(k) \left(F_{Y|X}(k|0)^M - F_{Y|X}(k-1|0)^M\right) \qquad (13)$$

where $L(k)$ is the likelihood ratio. On a noiseless channel, $f_{Y|X}(0|0) = 1$, and the erasure probability is $f_{Y|X}(0|1)$; thus, Equation 13 can be simplified to

$$P_s = \frac{(M-1)f_{Y|X}(0|1)}{M} \qquad (14)$$

This is consistent with the fact that the symbol decision (guess) is wrong $M - 1$ out of M times when no signal is received.

Once the PPM symbol is detected, it is mapped to a string of $\log_2(M)$ bits via the inverse of the encoding mapping (see Table 2). There are $M/2$ symbol errors that will produce an error in a given bit in the string, and there are $M - 1$ unique symbol errors. Thus, assuming all symbol errors are equally likely, the resulting BER is

$$P_b = \frac{M}{2(M-1)} P_s \qquad (15)$$

where P_s is given by Equation 10 or Equation 13.

We now proceed to evaluate the error-rate expressions above for a couple of specific channel models: the

Poisson channel and the *additive white Gaussian noise* (AWGN) channel. The reader is reminded that the error rates derived here assume perfect slot and symbol timing and a memoryless, stationary channel. If timing jitter or intersymbol interference were present, for example, then performance would degrade.

Poisson Channel

For $K_b > 0$, the SER in Equation 13 becomes

$$P_s = 1 - \sum_{k=0}^{\infty} \left(1 + \frac{K_s}{K_b}\right)^k \frac{e^{-K_s}}{M} \left(F_{Y|X}(k|0)^M - F_{Y|X}(k-1|0)^M\right) \tag{16}$$

where $F_{Y|X}(k|0) = \sum_{m=0}^{k} \frac{K_b^k e^{-K_b}}{k!}$. When $K_b = 0$, from Equation 14 we have

$$P_s = \frac{(M-1)e^{-K_s}}{M} \tag{17}$$

and from Equation 15 we see that $P_b = \frac{1}{2}e^{-K_s}$, which is independent of M and equal to that of on-off keying. This is shown in Figure 3a. As K_b increases, the dependence on M grows and the performance for each M degrades, as seen in Figure 3b and 3c. It is not appropriate to interpret performance versus K_s as a measure of power efficiency, however. K_s is proportional to the *peak* power. The average transmitter power is proportional to K_s/M photons per slot. Whereas low values of M in Figure 3a, 3b, and 3c produce a lower BER compared to high values of M, the situation is reversed in Figure 3d, 3e, and 3f, which plot versus K_s/M. The performance is also shown relative to the photon efficiency, $\log_2 M/K_s$ bits/photon, in Figure 3g, 3h, and 3i, where it is also seen that high values of M are more photon efficient. Note that there is an average

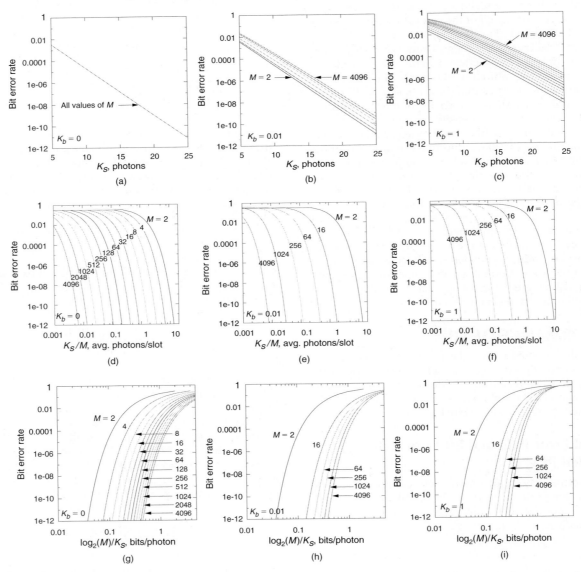

Figure 3: BER of uncoded M-PPM signaling on a Poisson channel versus quantities proportional to peak power (a, b, and c), average power (d, e, and f), and photon efficiency (g, h, and i) for $M = 2$ to 4096 and $K_b = 0, 0.01, 1$

power difference of approximately 30 dB between $M = 2$ and $M = 4096$ (Figure 3d, 3e, and 3f) and a photon-efficiency difference of approximately 10 dB (Figure 3g, 3h, and 3i). The performance is also shown in terms of the slot SNR $\beta = K^2_s/K_b$ in Figure 4a through 4d, where we see little dependence on M; when plotted in terms of the bit SNR $\beta_b = K^2_s/(2K_b \log_2 M)$, the 30 dB gap manifests itself again.

AWGN Channel

The probability of symbol error is given by Equation 10, which becomes

$$P_s = 1 - \int_{-\infty}^{\infty} \frac{1}{\sigma_1} \phi\left(\frac{x - m_1}{\sigma_1}\right) \Phi\left(\frac{x - m_0}{\sigma_0}\right)^{M-1} dx \quad (18)$$

$$= 1 - \int_{-\infty}^{\infty} \sqrt{\frac{\gamma}{\beta + \gamma}} \phi\left(\sqrt{\frac{\gamma}{\beta + \gamma}}\left(v - \sqrt{\beta}\right)\right) \Phi(v)^{M-1} dv \quad (19)$$

where $\phi(x) = \frac{1}{\sqrt{2\pi}} e^{-x^2/2}$ is the standard normalized Gaussian probability density function, $\Phi(x)$ is its cumulative distribution function, and, as defined earlier, $\beta = (m_1 - m_0)^2/\sigma^2$ and $\gamma = \frac{(m_1 - m_0)^2}{\sigma_1^2 - \sigma_0^2}$. If $\sigma_1 = \sigma_0$, then $\gamma = \infty$ and Equation 19 simplifies to

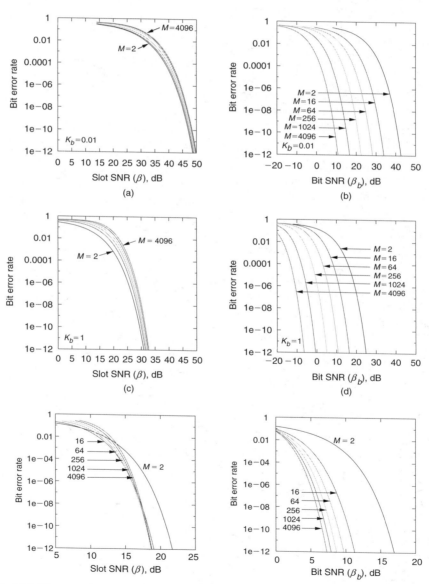

Figure 4: BER of uncoded M-PPM signaling—(a) Poisson channel versus slot SNR, (b) Poisson channel versus bit SNR, (c) Poisson channel versus slot SNR, (d) Poisson channel versus bit SNR, (e) AWGN channel versus slot SNR, and (f) AWGN channel versus bit SNR

$$P_s = 1 - \int_{-\infty}^{\infty} \phi\left(x - \sqrt{\beta}\right)\Phi(x)^{M-1}dx \qquad (20)$$

The BER P_b is then given by Equation 15 and can be expressed in terms of the bit SNR $\beta_b = \beta/(2R_c \log_2 M)$. This is shown in Figure 4e and 4f.

Performance of Coded PPM

A full treatment of the subject of code design and performance is beyond the scope of this chapter. In lieu of the expanded discussion, we summarize the conventional approaches and recent advancements in the area and direct the reader to references where the complete details are contained.

Conventional Coded PPM Approaches

As mentioned earlier in this chapter, the initial PPM applications were analog in nature and, of course, did not use any coding. Shortly after quantized, now conventional, PPM became common in the literature, it was realized that an ECC could substantially improve performance.

Reed-Solomon (RS) *codes* (Lin and Costello 1983) were among the first codes proposed for use with PPM (McEliece 1981). An RS(n, k) code is a linear block code that encodes every block of k data symbols into n code symbols, where each symbol is an element of the Galois field with $q = n + 1$ elements, denoted GF(q) (Lin and Costello 1983). Most commonly, q is a power of 2, $q = 2^s$, in which case each symbol is conveniently represented by s bits. Thus, the code can also be viewed as a (sn, sk) binary code.

The beauty of RS-coded PPM is that the RS code symbols in GS(q) are a natural fit with the nonbinary nature of PPM signaling. One can use RS(n, k) with M-PPM, $M = n + 1$, by assigning each RS code symbol to one PPM symbol. On the other hand, if system constraints push one toward small M, this leads to small block-length codes that have limited coding gain. This problem can be overcome, in part, by using a longer RS code and splitting RS code symbols across multiple PPM symbols (Hamkins and Moision 2005).

Recent Advancements in Coded PPM: Serially Concatenated PPM

An ECC maps information bits to coded bits, whereas PPM maps these coded bits to PPM symbols. We may consider the combination of the code and modulation as a single large code that maps information bits directly to symbols transmitted on the channel. If the ECC is conducive to iterative decoding (Benedetto et al. 1996), then one effective technique for decoding the large code is to iteratively decode the modulation and the ECC.

Following this approach, codes have been developed for the deep space optical PPM channel that operate within 1 dB of the capacity limit (Moision, Hamkins, and Cheng 2006), several dB better than RS-coded PPM, and more than 1 dB better than turbo-coded PPM which does not iteratively demodulate the signal (Hamkins and Srinivasan 1998). A representative example of the *serially concatenated PPM* (SCPPM) code is shown in Figure 5. The code is the serial concatenation of a convolutional code, a bit interleaver, an accumulator (differential encoder), and PPM. The specific design involves optimizing the PPM order, code rate, and convolutional code, given the design constraints (Moision and Hamkins 2003). The code is decoded iteratively (Moision and Hamkins 2005, "Coded"), using standard turbo-decoding principles. The complexity may be reduced by discarding most of the slot likelihood ratios without noticeably affecting performance (Moision and Hamkins 2005, "Reduced"), and other complexity-reducing implementation techniques (Cheng, Moision, and Hamkins 2006) make it possible to produce a 50 Mbps decoder on standard FPGA hardware that became available in 2006.

The performance of various rate 1/2 codes on a Poisson channel is illustrated in Figure 6, along with channel capacity. The channel was set to $K_b = 0.2$ background photons per slot, which is typical for the existing MLCD-class design for reception from Mars. The SCPPM code performs within approximately 0.75 dB of soft decision capacity and well beyond the performance of hard decision capacity. There is a gap of 1.5 dB between hard decision and soft decision capacity for this channel. Recall from earlier that an approximate 2 dB gap exists between hard and soft decision decoding. The 2-dB gap is a rule of thumb that applies to a wide range of coded communications systems, but it is not a theorem. For the optical application, the gap between hard and soft decision decoding for the optical channel is not actually fixed; instead, it varies with the channel model and operating conditions. In fact, the hard and soft capacity gap for the Poisson channel is zero when $K_b = 0$, because hard and soft decisions are equivalent in that case; the gap increases to several dB with increasing K_b.

Figure 6 also shows the performance of two RS codes. The RS (63,31) code has symbols that are matched to the PPM order; it operates at approximately 4.25 dB from soft decision capacity when the BER is 10^{-6}. The longer block length RS (4095,2047) code reduces this gap to 3.7 dB. The gap remains several dB away from soft decision

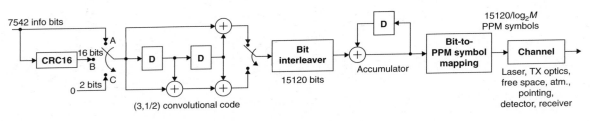

Figure 5: The SCPPM encoder

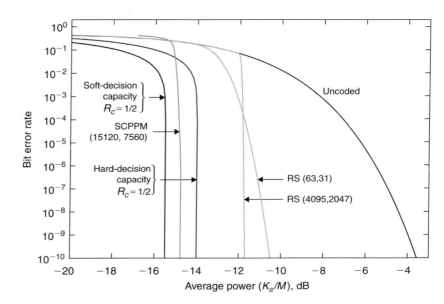

Figure 6: Performance of uncoded, RS-coded, and SCPPM-coded 64-PPM versus average power on a Poisson channel with $K_b = 0.2$

capacity, in part because of its use of hard decision decoding.

SYNCHRONIZATION

To detect symbols properly, a PPM receiver must acquire the PPM symbol timing—that is, identify the boundaries of the PPM symbols. The total timing may either be determined directly, or the problem may be partitioned into one of determining the slot timing and symbol timing sequentially. Figure 7 illustrates this for the case of 4-PPM. The transmitted PPM symbols in the upper part of the figure are misaligned by a slot offset and symbol offset at the receiver, shown in the lower part of the figure. The total timing error is the difference of the symbol offset and the slot offset.

Blind Synchronization

A *blind synchronizer* is one that operates without any knowledge of the PPM symbols being transmitted—that is, when no pilot or repetition signal is available. This is the case for any system in which transmitted PPM symbols consist solely of those that result from a modulation of coded or uncoded user data.

The PPM slot synchronization problem is closely related to the well-studied problem of symbol timing recovery of radio frequency *binary phase shift keying* (BPSK) signals. They both can be solved by arithmetically combining the energy detected in certain intervals of time in such a way that an error signal is generated that is proportional to the timing error. Two differences are that in PPM the signal energy is confined to a single slot among M slots instead of appearing in every slot, and the signal is on-off instead of antipodal.

For BPSK, timing recovery can be accomplished with a *digital transition tracking loop* (DTTL). For PPM, the analogue of the DTTL is a decision-directed slot recovery loop (Srinivasan, Vilnrotter, and Lee 2005), which is illustrated in Figure 8. As described in Srinivasan, Vilnrotter, and Lee (2005):

> A PPM signal delayed by the timing error $\Delta > 0$ is passed to the top branch that outputs the integrated slot values and selects the slot corresponding to the maximum value over an arbitrarily defined "pseudo-symbol." In the lower branch, the signal is further delayed by one symbol duration and passed to the error detector, which multiplies it by a "chopping function"—a square

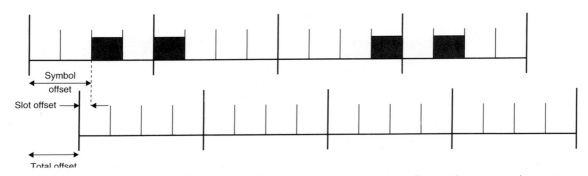

Figure 7: The transmitted symbols (top) result in a slot offset and symbol off set at the receiver (bottom)

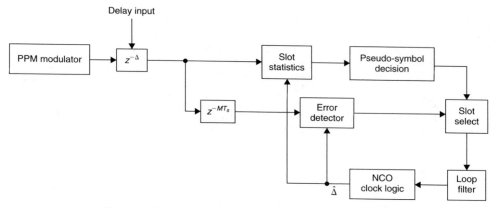

Figure 8: Decision-directed slot synchronization of PPM

wave at the slot frequency—and integrates over the duration of a slot, each slot. The signal is then gated by the slot selector from the upper branch in order to create the timing error signal, which is filtered and then passed to the numerically controlled oscillator ..., which outputs the slot clock. Note that symbol synchronization need not be assumed for this algorithm to work. If the initial pseudo-symbol interval contains two signal pulses, there will simply be two main contenders for the maximum slot to be picked by the slot selector, only one of which can be picked to contribute to the error detector. On the other hand, if the pseudo-symbol interval contains no signal pulse, a noise slot will be picked as the maximum, effectively increasing the symbol-error rate ... in the PPM decision process.

Following slot synchronization, symbol synchronization is performed. If aligned, each PPM symbol will contain exactly one pulse. The number of signal pulses per (potentially misaligned) PPM symbol may be estimated by comparing slot values to a threshold. PPM symbol synchronization can be accomplished by, for example, comparing the slot offset that maximizes the number of PPM symbols having exactly one pulse exceeding the threshold.

In some designs, *dead time* is inserted between every PPM symbol. This can aid in symbol synchronization, because a correlation against the channel output will reveal no signal energy during the dead time. Dead time is sometimes needed in Q-switched laser communications, for example, to allow sufficient time for the laser to recharge before the next pulse is transmitted. Dead time does not cost the transmitter any power, but because it lowers the data rate it is usually avoided when possible.

Synchronization Using Pilot Tones

In some PPM applications (Lacy 1947), a *pilot tone* was transmitted along with the modulated pulses to simplify the synchronization process. A pilot tone is a series of reference pulses, perhaps even full PPM symbols, inserted throughout the PPM symbol stream.

For example, a single known PPM symbol (e.g., $\mathbf{x}_1$) may be inserted after every nth PPM symbol. If there are s samples per slot, then M-PPM symbol synchronization is achieved by forming a length-sM vector sum of channel outputs over many blocks of sM samples. If the user data are random—that is, independent and equally likely a priori to take on any PPM value—then the samples in the slot corresponding to the pilot tone slot will have a disproportionately large correlation compared to the other slots. This accomplishes both slot and symbol synchronization in a low-complexity fashion.

Because a pilot tone is an unmodulated signal not representing any user information, its use reduces the efficiency of the transmission in terms of both bits per joule and bits per second. Therefore, the pilot tone is generally used as infrequently as the successful operation of the synchronization system allows. Also, care must be taken for uncoded PPM systems because the pilot signal might not be discernible in the presence of a string of all zeros in the user data—for example, as might occur in a raster scan of a dark area of an image.

CAPACITY OF PPM ON AN OPTICAL CHANNEL

Shannon (1948) demonstrated that for any communications channel, as long as the rate of transmitting information is less than some constant, C, it is possible to make the average error probability arbitrarily small by coding messages into a large enough class of signals. The constant C is called the *capacity* of the channel. Characterizing the capacity of the optical channel provides a useful bound on the data rates achievable with any coding scheme, serving as a benchmark for assessing the performance of a particular design.

The capacity will be a function of the received optical signal and noise powers, the modulation, and the detection method. The loss in capacity by restricting the modulation to PPM is small in the low average power regime where the deep space optical channel currently operates (Hamkins and Moision 2005; Wyner 1988; Boroson 2006).

We divide the capacity into two categories depending on the type of information provided to the decoder by the receiver. In one case, the receiver passes hard PPM decisions on to the decoder. The hard decision capacity may be expressed as a function of the probability of uncoded PPM symbol error, P_s, derived for several channel models presented earlier. In the second case, the receiver passes soft log-likelihood ratios to the decoder. In this case, the soft decision capacity may be expressed as a function of the channel statistic $f_{Y|X}$. The soft decision capacity is at least as large as the hard decision capacity, as the slot counts provide additional information to the decoder.

General Capacity Formulas

The hard decision PPM channel is an M-ary input, M-ary output, symmetric channel with capacity given by (Gallager 1968):

$$C = \log_2 M + (1 - P_s)\log_2(1 - P_s)$$
$$+ P_s \log_2 \left(\frac{P_s}{M - 1} \right) \text{ bits per PPM symbol} \quad (21)$$

where P_s is the probability of incorrect PPM symbol detection, given by Equation 10 or Equation 13.

The soft decision capacity is given by (Moision and Hamkins 2003):

$$C = E_{\mathbf{Y}} \log_2 \left[\frac{ML(Y_1)}{\sum_{j=1}^{M} L(Y_j)} \right] \text{ bits per PPM symbol} \quad (22)$$

an expectation over $\mathbf{Y}$, where $L(y) = f_{Y|X}(y|1)/f_{Y|X}(y|0)$ is the channel likelihood ratio, the Y_j have density $f_{Y|X}(y|1)$ for $j = 1$ and density $f_{Y|X}(y|0)$ otherwise.

The M-fold integration in Equation 22 is often intractable. However, it is straightforward to approximate the expectation by a sample mean. A quick approximation follows from the lower bound

$$C \geq E \log_2 \left[\frac{M}{1 + \frac{M - 1}{L(Y_1)}} \right] \text{ bits per PPM symbol} \quad (23)$$

which is a good approximation for large M, reducing the M-fold integration (or set of M-dimensional vector samples) needed to evaluate Equation 22 to a one-dimensional integral (or set of scalar samples).

Capacity of PPM on Specific Channels

Poisson Channel

We consider first the Poisson channel. The behavior of the case $K_b = 0$ has a particularly simple form. When $K_b = 0$, we have

$$L(k) = \begin{cases} e^{-K_s} & k = 0 \\ \infty & k > 0 \end{cases}$$

and Equation 22 reduces to

$$C = (\log_2 M)(1 - e^{-K_s}) \text{ bits/PPM symbol}$$

When $K_b = 0$, only signal photons are detected. If any signal photons are detected, then the signal is known exactly. If no photons are detected, then all M candidate symbols are equally likely. Because the received statistic takes binary values, the soft and hard decision capacities are equal.

When $K_b > 0$, we have $e^{-K_s} \left(1 + \frac{K_s}{K_b} \right)^k$, and Equation 22 becomes

$$C = (\log_2 M)\left(1 - \frac{1}{\log_2 M} E_{Y_1,\dots,Y_M} \log_2 \left[\sum_{i=1}^{M} \left(1 + \frac{K_s}{K_b} \right)^{(Y_j - Y_1)} \right] \right)$$

The case $K_b = 1$ is illustrated in Figure 9 as a function of average power (to within a constant factor) K_s/M for a range of M. In the plot, an average power constraint would be represented by a vertical line. A peak constraint can be shown (Moision and Hamkins 2003) to result in an upper limit on the PPM order. Hence, the maximum data rate subject to both peak and average power constraints can be identified using Figure 9.

AWGN Channel

For the AWGN channel, the likelihood ratio reduces to

$$L(y) = \sqrt{\frac{\gamma}{\beta + \gamma}} \exp \left[\frac{\beta v^2 + 2\gamma\sqrt{\beta}v - \gamma\beta}{2(\beta + \gamma)} \right]$$

where $v = (y - m_0)/\sigma_0$ (recall that β and γ were defined earlier). The capacity reduces to

$$C = \log_2 M - E \log_2 \sum_{j=1}^{M} \exp \left[\frac{(V_j - V_1)\beta(V_j + V_1) + 2\gamma\sqrt{\beta}}{2(\beta + \gamma)} \right]$$

bits per PPM symbol, where $V_j = (V_j - m_0)/\sigma_0$ for $j = 1, \dots, M$, or, when $\sigma_1 = \sigma_0$,

$$C = \log_2 M - E \log_2 \left[\sum_{j=1}^{M} e^{\sqrt{\beta}(V_j - V_1)} \right] \text{ bits per PPM symbol}$$

$$(24)$$

RELATED MODULATIONS
On-Off Keying

On-off keying (OOK) is another slotted modulation in which each slot contains either a pulse (1) or no pulse (0). In general, OOK allows any pattern of zeros and ones, and thus it is a generalization of several other modulation types. As such, the capacity of a channel using OOK is an upper bound on the capacity of a channel using one of its special case modulations. PPM is a special case of OOK, with the constraint that there is exactly one pulse

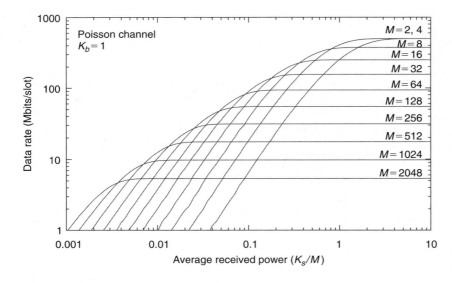

Figure 9: Capacity of M-PPM on a Poisson channel when $K_b = 1$

per M slots. Duty-cycle constrained OOK is another special case of OOK in which the fraction of slots with pulses is constrained to a specific number (Boroson 2006; Barron 2004). Duty-cycle constrained OOK is closely related to PPM, because each can have a duty cycle of $1/M$; it is also a generalization of PPM, because it does not require a frame of M slots to contain exactly one pulse.

Multipulse PPM

Multipulse PPM (MPPM), first proposed in Herro and Hu (1988), is a generalization of PPM that allows more than one pulse per symbol. In n-pulse M-slot MPPM there are n unique symbols that correspond to the possible ways to populate M slots with n pulses. This is illustrated in Figure 10 when $n = 2$ and $M = 8$. When $n > 1$, the mapping from message bits to MPPM symbols becomes more

complicated, as $\binom{M}{n}$ is not a power of 2—that is, each multipulse symbol corresponds to a noninteger number of bits. This complication can be avoided by using a MPPM subset of size $2^{\left\lfloor \log_2 \binom{M}{n} \right\rfloor}$ (Sato, Ohtsuki, and Sasase 1994), which reduces throughput.

A recent result (Hamkins and Moision 2005) shows that in many cases of practical interest, the capacity of MPPM is not substantially greater than that of conventional PPM. The added complexity of implementing MPPM would not be justified in those cases. When the average power is sufficiently high, corresponding to an optimum PPM size of approximately 16 or less, then MPPM or more general modulations (e.g., Barron 2004) can begin to show power-saving gains of 1 dB or more over conventional PPM.

Overlapping PPM

Overlapping PPM (OPPM) is a generalization of PPM proposed in Lee and Schroeder (1977). In OPPM, each symbol interval of length T is divided into NM chips of duration $T_c = T/(NM)$. A pulse occupies N chips and is constrained to be entirely contained within the symbol epoch. This is shown in Figure 11 with $N = 3$ and $M = 4$. When $N = 1$, we have ordinary PPM as discussed above in which $\log_2 M$ bits are transmitted per T seconds. When $N > 1$, the pulse can be in one of $NM - N + 1$ positions (the last $N - 1$ positions are disallowed because the pulse must be completed contained within the symbol boundary), and we have $\log_2[NM - N + 1]$ bits per T seconds—that is, nearly an additional $\log_2 N$ bits per T seconds for large M. OPPM imposes more stringent synchronization requirements, and special synchronizable codes may be used to aid in this (Calderbank and Georghiades 1994).

Note that OPPM may result from a PPM modulation in which the slot width is accidentally or intentionally set too small. This can happen when the slot widths are defined too narrowly for the pulse width being transmitted or when the bandwidth of the detectors does not support the full resolution of the slot. Whatever the cause, the result is intersymbol interference. Even with perfect synchronization, the modulation set is not orthogonal, and

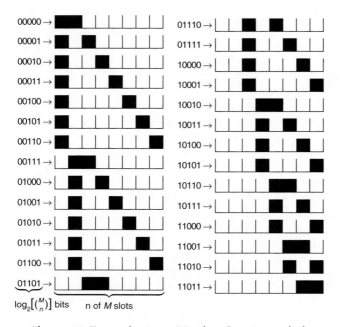

Figure 10: Two-pulse 8-ary PPM has $\binom{8}{2}$ = 28 symbols

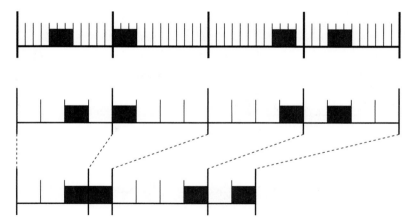

Figure 11: Each OPPM symbol with $N = 3$ and $M = 4$ has twelve chips. The pulse may begin in any of ten positions

Figure 12: A 4-ary PPM meassage (top) and the corresponding 4-ary DPPM message (bottom)

thus the raw SER performance will be degraded compared to PPM.

The intersymbol interference degradation may be mitigated with an ECC. This was recognized by Georghiades (1989), who proposed a trellis-coded modulation in conjunction with PPM and OPPM. The optimal receiver structure for this coded modulation involves a Viterbi decoder, and performance of this receiver for the AWGN and Webb channel models has been determined (Srinivasan 1998; Kiasaleh and Yan 1998).

Analog PPM

Analog PPM (Lacy 1947; McAulay 1968; Riter, Boatright, and Shay 1971; Ross 1949) may be viewed as the asymptotic limit of OPPM, in which the discrete chips that mark the permissible times at which a pulse may become infinitesimally narrow. In this way, the concepts of a slot and chip disappear entirely, and the pulse delay from the beginning of the symbol is simply an analog value. The position of a pulse is linearly related to the value of the analog message intended to be transmitted. For this modulation format, unless another synchronization method is provided, it may be necessary to transmit an auxiliary pulse to identify the beginning of each symbol.

The performance of such systems, in terms of the power efficiency or the effective information throughput achieved, is generally not comparable to conventional PPM with discrete slots, especially because an ECC is conceptually difficult to apply to an analog modulation format. However, this is compensated by the remarkable simplicity of the analog circuit that can measure the delay of the pulse. For the remote-controlled aircraft application mentioned early in the chapter, these lightweight receiver electronics are critical to a successful design, and analog PPM is often used. Several parameters—such as the position of the rudder, aileron, and elevators—can be independently controlled, and each parameter may take on infinitely many values.

Differential PPM

In *differential PPM* (DPPM) (Zwillinger 1988), also called *truncated PPM* (TPPM) and *digital pulse interval modulation* (DPIM), throughput is increased by beginning a new PPM symbol immediately following the slot containing the pulse. In other words, nonpulsed slots of a PPM symbol that follow a pulsed slot are flushed. This is shown in Figure 12. Information is conveyed in DPPM by the amount of separation between pulses. In one sense, this means that symbol synchronization is easier than in PPM: In PPM, the detection of a pulse does not assist much in determining the boundary of the PPM symbol, whereas in DPPM the symbol always sends with a pulse. On the other hand, the variable length of the symbols imposes a significantly more challenging synchronization problem than PPM because a missed pulse detection would lead to a *deletion* of a symbol from the symbol stream. Symbol deletions are generally fatal in both uncoded transmission (which is typically validated by a cyclic redundancy check) and to decoding algorithms. There may be methods of averting the synchronization problems with DPPM by buffering data and performing an appropriate sequence-detection algorithm. DPPM increases the throughput per unit time by almost a factor of two because symbols are on average only half as long as they would be with ordinary PPM.

Wavelength Shift Keying

From the viewpoint of communication theory, *wavelength shift keying* (WSK) (Dolinar et al. 2006), is similar to PPM of the same dimension. Instead of placing a single pulse of laser light of a given wavelength into one of M time-disjoint time slots, WSK places a single laser pulse of one of M disjoint wavelengths. This is shown in Figure 13. At the receiver, a filter bank completely separates the wavelengths before detection. Like PPM, this modulation is orthogonal. Therefore, if the channel is statistically

Figure 13: 4-ary WSK uses four frequencies in one time slot for each two bits

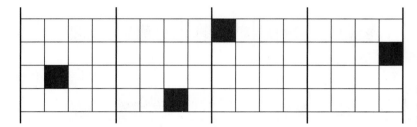

Figure 14: 4-ary WSK with 4-PPM uses four frequencies (in rows) and four times slots (in columns) for each four bits per symbol

identical at the various wavelengths, the maximum likelihood rules presented in the earlier section "Detection of PPM Signals" and the performance presented in the section "Performance of PPM" carry over to WSK as well.

Combined PPM and Wave Shift Keying

WSK transmits a pulse during every time slot. One way to reduce the required average laser power is to use a combination of PPM and WSK (Dolinar et al. 2006): By restricting the laser pulse to one of M time-slots, but allowing the laser pulse to take on any of N wavelengths, the low average laser power of conventional PPM can be maintained with the added advantage of increased data rate. This can be demonstrated by observing that the dimensionality of the signal space has been increased from M dimensions (PPM) to NM dimensions.

Combined PPM and WSK is an orthogonal signaling scheme. Therefore, if the channel is statistically identical at the various wavelengths, then the maximum likelihood rules presented in "Detection of PPM Signals" and the performance presented in "Performance of PPM" carry over to combined PPM and WSK as well (see Figure 14). The performance is the same as PPM, but with NM dimensions instead of M. The probability of correct detection is given by Equations 10 and 13, but with M replaced by NM.

The information throughput of this combined modulation scheme is $\log_2 NM = \log_2 N + \log_2 M$ bits per symbol period, or $\log_2 N$ more than M-PPM alone. For a given bandwidth, the throughput of combined PPM and WSK is higher than PPM alone. However, this modulation scheme requires N detectors, one for each wavelength, instead of just one. In addition, a method (e.g., high-dispersion grating) is needed to direct each distinct wavelength to a different detector.

CONCLUSION

Pulse position modulation is a modulation format with a rich set of applications in optical, radio frequency, and acoustical communications. The modern usage of PPM refers to a modulation format in which a binary input of $\log_2 M$ bits determines which of M slots is to have a pulse in it. This modulation has a high peak-to-average power ratio. The precise mapping of bits to PPM symbols may or may not affect performance, depending on the system; under typical circumstances, the maximum likelihood detection of a PPM symbol corresponds to the slot with the largest received value. A general formula for the capacity of PPM is known; thus, given bandwidth and power

constraints, an appropriate near-capacity error-correcting code can be designed for many typical applications.

GLOSSARY

Channel capacity: The maximum mutual information between the input and output of a channel among all possible inputs to the channel. This determines the maximum data rate that is supportable by a given stochastic channel.

Gray code: An ordered set of binary vectors in which adjacent vectors differ in exactly one bit. An *anti-Gray code* is an ordered set of binary vectors in which adjacent vectors differ in either all positions or all but one position.

Maximum likelihood (ML) detection: The ML detection of a signal received from a channel is the value of the channel input that, among all possible channel inputs, maximizes the conditional probability density function of the observed channel output given the channel input.

Pulse position modulation (PPM): A signaling format in which the temporal positions of pulses are modulated by a message.

Reed-Solomon code: An error-correcting code popularly used with PPM signaling.

Serially concatenated PPM: An error-correcting code comprising the serial concatenation of a convolutional code, interleaver, and PPM.

Slot: An interval of time during which a 1 or a 0 is transmitted. In an optical communications application, a laser pulse would either be present or absent during this time interval.

Symbol error rate (SER): The probability that a symbol is detected in error, typically under the assumption of ML detection.

Symbol synchronization: The temporal alignment of a received stream of slots with the true symbol boundaries of the transmitted signal.

CROSS REFERENCES

See *Optical Fiber Communications*; *Wavelength Division Multiplexing (WDM)*.

REFERENCES

Agrell, E., J. Lassing, E. Strom, and T. Ottosson. 2004. On the optimality of the binary reflected Gray code. *IEEE Transactions on Information Theory*, 50(12): 3170–82.

Barron, R. J. 2004. Binary shaping for low-duty-cycle communications. *International Symposium on Information Theory* (ISIT), Chicago, June 22–July 2, p. 514.

Benedetto, S., D. Divsalar, G. Montorsi, and F. Pollara. 1996. A soft-input soft-output maximum a posteriori (MAP) module to decode parallel and serial concatenated codes. *TDA Progress Report*, 42(127): 1–20 (available at http://ipnpr.jpl.nasa.gov/progress_report/42-127/127H.pdf).

Biswas, A., and W. Farr. 2004. Detectors for ground-based reception of laser communications from Mars. In *Lasers and Electro-Optics Society* (LEOS), 1: 74–5.

Bornhoft, R., B. P. Brockway, M. Kunz, G. Lichtscheidl, B. Lindstedt, and P. A. Mills. 2001. Frame length modulation and pulse position modulation for telemetry of analog and digital data. U.S. Patent 6,947,795, issued October 2001.

Boroson, D. M. 2006. Private communication.

Calderbank, A. R., and C. N. Georghiades. 1994. Synchronizable codes for the optical OPPM channel. *IEEE Transactions on Information Theory*, 40: 1097–1107.

Candell, L. 2005. LDES: A prototype array optical receiver for the mars laser communications demonstration program. In *2005 Digest of the LEOS Summer Topical Meetings*, San Diego, July 25–27, 2005, pp. 13–14.

Casier, H., H. De Man, and C. Matthijs. 1976. A pulse position modulation transmission system for remote control of a TV set. *IEEE Journal of Solid-State Circuits*, 11(6): 801–9.

Cheng, M., B. Moision, and J. Hamkins. 2006. Implementation of a coded modulation for deep space optical communications. Information Theory and Applications Workshop, University of California at San Diego, February 6–10.

Dolinar, S., J. Hamkins, B. Moision, and V. Vilnrotter. 2006. Optical modulation and coding. Chap. 4 in *Deep space optical communications*, edited by H. Hemmati. New York: John Wiley & Sons.

Gagliardi, R., and S. Karp. 1976. *Optical communications*. New York: John Wiley & Sons.

———. 1995. *Optical communication*. New York: John Wiley & Sons.

Gallager, R. 1968. *Information theory and reliable communication*. New York: John Wiley & Sons.

Georghiades, C. N. 1989. Some implications of TCM for optical direct-detection channels. *IEEE Transactions on Communications*, 37: 481–7.

———. 1994. Modulation and coding for throughput-efficient optical systems. *IEEE Transactions on Information Theory*, 40: 1313–26.

Gray, F. 1953. Pulse code communication. U.S. Patent 2,632,058, issued March 1953.

Hamkins, J. 2004. Accurate computation of the performance of *M*-ary orthogonal signaling on a discrete memoryless channel. *IEEE Transactions on Communications*, 51(11): 1844–5.

———, M. Klimesh, R. McEliece, and B. Moision. 2004. Capacity of the generalized PPM channel. In *International Symposium on Information Theory* (ISIT), Chicago, June, p. 337.

———, and B. Moision. 2005. Multipulse pulse-position modulation on discrete memoryless channels, *IPN Progress Report*, pp. 42–161. http://ipnpr.jpl.nasa.gov/progress_report/42-161/161L.pdf.

———, and M. Srinivasan. 1998. Turbo codes for APD-detected PPM. In *Proceedings of the Thirty-Sixth Annual Allerton Conference on Communication, Control and Computing*, Urbana, Illinois, USA, September, pp. 29–38.

Herro, M. A., and L. Hu. 1988. A new look at coding for APD-based direct-detection optical channels. *IEEE Transactions on Information Theory*, 34: 858–66.

Kiasaleh, K., and T.-Y. Yan. 1998. T-PPM: A novel modulation scheme for optical communication systems impaired by pulse-width inaccuracies. *TMO Progress Report*, 42(135): 1–16 (available at http://ipnpr.jpl.nasa.gov/progress_report/42-135/135G.pdf).

Knutson, C. D., and J. M. Brown. 2004. *IrDA principles and protocols: The IrDA library*. Vol. 1. Salem, UT: MCL Press.

Lacy, R. E. 1947. Two mutichannel microwave relay equipments for the United States Army Communication Network. *Proceedings of the I.R.E. and Waves and Electrons*, 33: 65–9.

Lee, G. M., and G. W. Schroeder. 1977. Optical PPM with multiple positions per pulse width. *IEEE Transactions on Communications*, 25: 360–4.

Lee, S., G. G. Ortiz, and J. W. Alexander. 2005. Star tracker-based acquisition, tracking, and pointing technology for deep-space optical communications. *IPN Progress Report*, 42(161): 1–18. http://ipnpr.jpl.nasa.gov/progress_report/42-161/161L.pdf.

Lin, S., and D. J. Costello, Jr. 1983. *Error control coding: Fundamentals and applications*. Englewood Cliffs, NJ: Prentice Hall.

Marsh, L. M., C. Sun, B. K. Pillai, and L. Viana. 2002. Data recovery for pulse telemetry using pulse position modulation. U.S. Patent 6963290, issued November 2002.

McAulay, R. J. 1968. Numerical optimization techniques applied to PPM signal design. *IEEE Transactions on Information Theory*, 14: 708–16.

McEliece, R. J. 1981. Practical codes for photon communication. *IEEE Transactions on Information Theory*, 27: 393–8.

Meiseand, H. A., and V. R. DeStefano. 1966. A new self-contained private branch exchange utilizing electronic control and metallic crosspoints. *IEEE Transactions on Communications Technology*, 14: 763–7.

Moision, B., and J. Hamkins. 2003. Deep-space optical communications downlink budget: Modulation and coding. *IPN Progress Report*, 42(154): 1–28 (available at http://ipnpr.jpl.nasa.gov/progress_report/42-154/154K.pdf).

———. 2005. Coded modulation for the deep-space optical channel: Serially concatenated pulse-position modulation. *IPN Progress Report*, 42(161): 1–26 (available at http://ipnpr.jpl.nasa.gov/progress_report/42-161/161T.pdf).

———. 2005. Reduced complexity decoding of coded PPM using partial statistics. *IPN Progress Report*,

42(161): 1–20 (available at http://ipnpr.jpl.nasa.gov/progress_report/42-161/161O.pdf).

———, and M. Cheng. 2006. Design of a coded modulation for deep space optical communications. Information Theory and Applications Workshop, University of California at San Diego, February 6–10.

NEC Corporation. 1994. MOS integrated circuit μPD6121, 6122, NEC datasheet (retrieved from www.datasheetarchive.com/semiconductors/download.php?Datasheet=2205902).

Ohtsuki, T., and J. M. Kahn. 2000. BER performance of turbo-coded PPM CDMA systems on optical fiber. *Journal of Lightwave Technology*, 18: 1776–84.

Palais, J. C. 2004. *Fiber optic communications*. 5th ed. Englewood Cliffs, NJ: Prentice Hall.

Pettit, R. 1965. Use of the null zone in voice communications. *IEEE Transactions on Communications*, 13(2): 175–82.

Press, W. H., S. A. Teukolsky, W. T. Vetterling, and B. P. Flannery. 1992. *Numerical recipes in C.* New York: Cambridge University Press.

Pulse position modulation technic. 1945. *Electronic Industries*, December, pp. 82–7, 180–90.

Riter, S., P. A. Boatright, and M. T. Shay. 1971. Pulse position modulation acoustic communications. *IEEE Transactions on Audio and Electroacoustics*, 19: 166–73.

Ross, A. E. 1949. Theoretical study of pulse-frequency modulation. *Proceedings of the I.R.E.*, 37: 1277–86.

Sato, K., T. Ohtsuki, and I. Sasase. 1994. Performance of coded multi-pulse PPM with imperfect slot synchronization in optical direct-detection channel. In *International Conference on Communications, Conference Record*, New Orleans, May 1–5, pp. 121–5.

Shannon, C. E. 1948. A mathematical theory of communication. *Bell Systems Technical Journal*, 27: 379–423, 623–56.

Srinivasan, M. 1998. Receiver structure and performance for trellis-coded pulse position modulation in optical communication systems. *TMO Progress Report*,

42(135): 1–11. http://ipnpr.jpl.nasa.gov/progress_report/42-135/135H.pdf

———, V. Vilnrotter, and C. Lee. 2005. Decision-directed slot synchronization for pulse-position-modulated optical signals. *IPN Progress Report*, 42(161): 1–12. http://ipnpr.jpl.nasa.gov/progress_report/42-161/161R.pdf

Tomkins, W. 2002. Smoke signals (retrieved from www.inquiry.net/outdoor/native/sign/smoke-signal.htm).

Townes, S., B. Edwards, A. Biswas, D. Bold, R. Bondurant, D. Boroson, J. Burnside, D. Caplan, A. DeCew, R. DePaula, R. Fitzgerald, F. Khatri, A. McIntosh, D. Murphy, B. Parvin, A. Pillsbury, W. Roberts, J. Scozzafava, J.Sharma, and M. Wright. 2004. The Mars laser communication demonstration. In *Proceedings of the IEEE Aerospace Conference*, 2: 1180–95.

Vilnrotter, V., M. Simon, and M. Srinivasan. 1999. Maximum likelihood detection of PPM signals governed by arbitrary point-process plus additive Gaussian noise. *IEEE Electronics Letters*, 34: 1132–3.

Webb, P. P., R. J. McIntyre, and J. Conradi. 1974. Properties of avalanche photodiodes. *RCA Review*, 35: 234–78.

Wilson, K., M. Jeganathan, J. R. Lesh, J. James, and G. Xu. 1997. Results from phase-1 and phase-2 GOLD experiments. *TDA Progress Report*, 42(128): 1–11 (available at http://ipnpr.jpl.nasa.gov/progress_report/42-128/128K.pdf).

Wilson, K. E., and J. R. Lesh. 1993. An overview of the Galileo Optical Experiment (GOPEX). *TDA Progress Report*, 42(114): 192–204 (available at http://ipnpr.jpl.nasa.gov/progress_report/42-114/114Q.pdf).

Wyner, A. D. 1988. Capacity and error exponent for the direct detection photon channel–Part II. *IEEE Transactions on Information Theory*, 34: 1462–71.

Zwillinger, D. 1988. Differential PPM has a higher throughput than PPM for the band-limited and average-power-limited optical channel. *IEEE Transactions on Information Theory*, 34: 1269–73.

Digital Phase Modulation and Demodulation

Zartash Afzal Uzmi, *Lahore University of Management Sciences, Pakistan*

INTRODUCTION

In computer and communication networks, where different layers communicate at the peer level, a study of physical layer is necessary to understand the concept of information communication at the most fundamental level and how information is physically communicated from one point to another. Communication at the physical layer is the most fundamental way of providing connectivity to numerous hosts in a computer network such as the Internet. The physical layer provides connectivity between two directly connected nodes whether they are connected through a wire as in the IEEE 802.3 standard or through a wireless link as in the IEEE 802.11 standards.

In a computer network such as the Internet, end systems communicate with each other through a network that is largely a collection of communication links connected through packet switches. In almost all cases, the communication between end systems will be in the form of packets. At times, a circuit switch is used to provide an interface to end users, as in the case of users communicating through dialup connections. In a layered architecture, the network layer and the layers above it provide end-to-end connectivity between the end systems. The data-link layer, however, provides connectivity between two directly connected nodes, where a node can be an end system or an intermediate switch. The data-link layer is responsible for transporting physical frames between two directly connected or adjacent nodes. A frame is nothing more than a sequence of bits; for transporting a frame between two adjacent nodes, the data-link layer uses the services of a physical layer that is responsible for physically transporting individual bits.

In this chapter, we will consider communication of digital data only at the physical layer. This can be accomplished by various methods, one of which is *digital phase modulation* (DPM). Sometimes, digital phase modulation is used synonymously with *phase shift keying* (PSK), which is only a special case of DPM. Our focus will be on the generation and detection of digital phase modulated signals and their various properties. In the next section, we provide background for understanding communications at the physical layer, eventually leading to a definition of digital phase modulation.

BACKGROUND

At the physical layer, the communication of digital data between two directly connected nodes is carried out in one of the two fundamental ways. The first way is by using baseband communication whereby the digital data are transmitted without altering the frequency spectrum of the digital message signal or the digital baseband signal. The baseband digital communication (also known as *baseband pulse transmission*) is, therefore, a direct transportation of a digital baseband signal that is generated by directly representing digital symbols in one of the various electrical pulse shapes. Baseband digital transmission is carried over baseband channels, which are usually low-pass in nature. The second way of transporting digital data is by means of passband communication whereby the digital data to be transported are used to generate a passband digital signal that is then transmitted to the receiver.

A passband digital signal is generated by using the digital data symbols to alter some characteristics of a carrier, which is usually sinusoidal. The characteristics of a sinusoidal carrier that may be modified by the digital data include the amplitude, phase, and frequency, resulting in digital amplitude, digital phase, and digital frequency modulation, respectively. Thus, we define *modulation* as the process in which a message signal alters the properties of a carrier signal (Wikipedia 2007, "Modulation"). As a result of modulation, the frequency spectrum of the modulated signal is usually quite different from that of the baseband signal or message signal. The spectrum of the modulated signal may be obtained from the spectrum of the baseband signal in a way that depends on the type of modulation and the carrier frequency.

The message signal or the modulating signal can either be analog or digital. However, in computer networks, the message signal is almost always digital: Symbols are selected from a discrete set and sent one after the other every symbol period (or signaling period). The modulation in which the modulating signal is digital is called *digital modulation*. Because a digital signal is obtained by choosing one symbol from a discrete set, a simple way of performing digital modulation is to switch the amplitude, frequency, or phase of the carrier based on the symbol selected from that discrete set. In this form, digital modulation is also termed as *keying*. In *amplitude shift keying*, for example, the amplitude of the carrier wave is switched every symbol period from one value to another based on a symbol selected from the discrete set, which includes all possible digital symbol values.

We may now define a special form of digital phase modulation called *phase shift keying* (PSK). In PSK, the phase of a carrier—usually sinusoidal—is shifted at the start of each symbol interval directly in accordance with the digital data that need to be communicated from transmitter to the receiver in that interval (Wikipedia 2007, "Phase-shift keying"). If the digital data are binary, there are only two possible symbol values (typically, 0 and 1), and the simplest way to achieve PSK is to transmit one of the two possible sinusoidal waves phase shifted by 180 degrees with respect to each other when one of the two possible symbols is to be sent. In PSK, the information to be communicated is exclusively encoded in the phase of the carrier at the beginning of every symbol interval. The envelope remains constant in a PSK signal, while the frequency also remains constant throughout a given symbol. However, an abrupt phase transition happens at symbol boundaries, causing frequency impulses.

Other modulation methods exist, in addition to PSK, in which the information can be exclusively sent in the phase of the carrier. All such digital modulation methods in which the phase of the carrier contains the information to be transferred are classified as *digital phase modulation*. By this definition, the amplitude of a DPM signal should remain constant. Because phase and frequency are related to each other, a generic digital phase modulation may also be viewed as a digital frequency modulation scheme. In particular, *continuous phase modulation* (CPM) is a nonlinear modulation scheme that falls under phase as well as frequency modulation.

Digital phase modulation can either be linear or nonlinear. Linear DPM can further be *without* memory (also known as *coherent PSK* with *binary phase shift keying*, *quadriphase shift keying*, and *offset quadriphase shift keying* as examples) or *with* memory (such as differential PSK). In nonlinear digital phase modulation with memory, the modulated signal is constrained to maintain a constant envelope and continuous phase, avoiding abrupt changes in phase. CPM is an example of nonlinear digital phase modulation with memory. A special case of CPM is *continuous phase frequency shift keying* (CPFSK). A famous modulation scheme called *minimum shift keying* is a further special case of CPFSK.

Coherent PSK is the simplest form of digital phase modulation and is used whenever the receiver is able to locally generate the carrier with correct frequency and phase; otherwise, the differential form is preferred. If the coherent form is used, then the demodulator must track the carrier by using a carrier recovery circuit. Any errors

in tracking lead to performance degradation of the overall communication, resulting in higher bit error rates. Demodulation of CPM signals is usually accomplished by using coherent demodulators followed by sequence detectors.

A description of DPM requires understanding the terminology used in a digital communication system. We therefore first consider a baseband communication system to introduce the terminology before we set out to describe the DPM techniques in more detail.

DIGITAL COMMUNICATION SYSTEMS

In a digital communication system, the information to be sent from transmitter to receiver is always encoded in the form of digital data. If the information to be sent is already in the digital format, then the sender is not required to take any extra effort when using the digital communication system. If, however, the information to be sent is analog, such as the voice in a *voice over Internet protocol* (or VoIP) call between two end users, it is the responsibility of the sender to convert the analog information (voice) into digital format by employing analog-to-digital conversion. Obviously, the receiver will need to reverse the process by constructing an analog signal from the received digital signal.

Baseband Signal Representation

To become familiar with the terminology of digital communication systems, we start by defining a baseband digital signal as follows:

$$x(t) = \sum_{n=-\infty}^{\infty} a_n p(t - nD)$$

Usually, this signal will be available at the output of an analog-to-digital converter. This signal is also known as a digital *pulse amplitude modulation* (PAM) signal and is transmitted as is in a baseband digital system. However, in passband digital systems such as PSK, the signal $x(t)$ is fed to a modulator before subsequent transmission. In the above expression, $x(t)$ is the baseband digital signal, $p(t)$ is the pulse shape, and a_n is the nth digital symbol that needs to be sent from the transmitter to the receiver. For a binary digital system, the symbol a_n represents one single bit and will take one of the two possible values—that is, a_n will belong to a set whose cardinality is 2. In many cases, a_n will be a symbol representing more than a single bit; in such cases, a_n will belong to a set with higher cardinality. Note that D is the duration of one symbol in the above expression, and its inverse is called the *symbol rate*. For binary digital systems, each symbol will represent a single bit, and the symbol rate will be equal to the *bit rate*. However, if a_n belongs to a set with cardinality 4, then each symbol a_n will represent two binary digits (bits), and the bit rate will be twice the symbol rate. In general, if a_n belongs to a set with cardinality M, then the bit rate is $\log_2 M$ times the symbol rate. We usually use T_b for bit duration, where T_b is related to D for an M-ary digital signal as $D = T_b \log_2 M$. Obviously, for binary signals, $M = 2$ and $D = T_b$.

Line Codes

It is important to understand the baseband digital formats (also referred to as *line codes*) because the passband digital signals (including digital phase modulation or PSK) are generated by modulating a carrier according to the baseband digital signal. Line codes or baseband digital formats are defined by selecting the parameters a_n and $p(t)$ in the expression for a baseband digital signal. Spectral properties of line codes depend on the pulse shape $p(t)$, the symbol values a_n, and the symbol rate $1/D$, and they play an important role in signal transmission. In this chapter, we only describe line codes that are of relevance to the material presented here. For a complete reference of line codes, see Barry, Lee, and Messerschmitt (2003).

The *non-return-to-zero* (NRZ) or *unipolar NRZ* or *nonpolar NRZ* format is characterized by $a_n \in \{0, 1\}$ and $p(t) = A \Pi (t/D)$ or any time-shifted version, where $\Pi (t)$ is defined as:

$$\Pi(t) = \begin{cases} 1 & |t| \le \frac{1}{2} \\ 0 & \text{otherwise} \end{cases}$$

The NRZ format corresponding to the binary sequence 101101 is shown in Figure 1, along with other baseband digital formats.

The *return-to-zero* (RZ) format is characterized by an $a_n \in \{0, 1\}$ and $p(t) = A \Pi (\frac{t+D/4}{D/2})$ or any shifted version. Because the signal level returns to zero in the middle of the bit value, we should expect relatively higher frequency components in RZ compared with NRZ format, an undesirable effect. However, the RZ format aids the

receiver in synchronization by guaranteeing a return to zero in the middle of the bit.

The polar NRZ format has the same pulse shape as the unipolar NRZ counterpart, but it uses an alphabet $a_n \in \{-1, +1\}$. Similarly, polar RZ is similar to unipolar RZ except that $a_n \in \{-1, +1\}$ for the polar case. These formats are shown in Figure 1 for the binary sequence 101101. Note that for the RZ and NRZ formats, for either polar or unipolar case, the signal has a nonzero DC value that is usually an undesirable characteristic. A popular digital baseband signal format is *Manchester encoding*, which guarantees zero DC value irrespective of the proportions of 1's and 0's in the digital signal. Manchester encoding format is also shown in Figure 1 along with other binary formats. All of these baseband digital signal formats are for the binary case where $D = T_b$—that is, the symbol period is the same as the bit period. In general, the symbol period will be greater than or equal to the bit period.

Passband Signal Representation

The passband digital signal is obtained by modulating a carrier with a baseband digital signal. This process is referred to as *passband modulation*, and the carrier wave used is usually a sinusoidal wave. For communication over wireless channels and for longer distances, passband communication is used whereby passband signals are transmitted over the communication channel. Passband modulation is also employed whenever the communication medium is to be shared for multiple simultaneous communications over different frequency bands, as in standard commercial AM and FM radio. A large number of digital modulation schemes are used in practice (see section 1.5 of Xiong 2000). One of the most basic schemes for passband digital transmission is digital phase modulation in which the phase of the carrier is modified according to the digital baseband signal. In the rest of the chapter, we describe and analyze various DPM schemes with a particular focus on PSK. The reader is referred to Proakis (2000) and Anderson and Sundberg (1991) for details of more advanced DPM techniques. Phase shift keying is a special case of DPM in which the phase of the carrier is selected, in accordance with the digital symbol, at the beginning of the symbol interval. Thus, in PSK, phase discontinuities are observed at the start of *symbol intervals* (or *symbol boundaries*). In another type of DPM, continuous phase modulation, there are no phase discontinuities but the phase is allowed to vary throughout the symbol interval in a continuous manner.

Let us first introduce the mathematical representation of a passband digital signal. Any passband digital signal $x_c(t)$ is completely described by its in-phase and quadrature components and a carrier frequency. Mathematically, we write

$$x_c(t) = x_I(t) \cos 2\pi f_c t - x_Q(t) \sin 2\pi f_c t$$

where $x_c(t)$ is the modulated signal or passband signal, $x_I(t)$ is the in-phase component of the passband signal, $x_Q(t)$ is the quadrature component of the passband signal, and f_c is the frequency of the sinusoidal carrier.

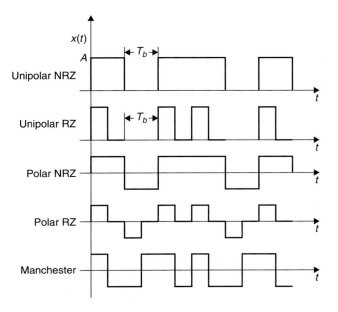

Figure 1: Digital PAM formats for unipolar NRZ, unipolar RZ, bipolar NRZ, bipolar RZ, and split-phase Manchester encoding for binary data 101101

Using the famous Euler's equation $e^{j\theta} = \cos\theta + j\sin\theta$, we can write the above expression as

$$x_c(t) = \Re[x_B(t)e^{j2\pi f_c t}]$$

where $x_B(t)$ is called the baseband equivalent signal or the complex envelope of the passband signal and is given by

$$x_B(t) = x_I(t) + jx_Q(t)$$

The in-phase and quadrature components and the complex envelope are all low-pass signals. The passband signal can be completely described by knowing the carrier frequency and the complex envelope. We may further note that the power spectral density of the passband signal is completely obtained from the power spectral density of the complex envelope by knowing the carrier frequency (Carlson, Crilly, and Rutledge 2002).

Constellation Diagrams

In passband digital systems, such as those that use digital phase modulation or PSK, a symbol is sent as a digital signal from the transmitter to the receiver during every symbol interval. The signal sent in each interval is chosen from a set whose cardinality depends on the level of modulation. For binary modulation, for example, the signal sent in each interval is chosen from one of the two possible signals and represents a single bit of information. For quaternary modulation, the signal sent in each symbol interval represents two binary bits and is chosen from a set of four signals.

For passband digital modulation, the signal sent in each symbol is represented by the expression for $x_c(t)$ given in the preceding section on passband signal representation and can be considered as a weighted combination of two orthogonal basis functions $\phi_1(t)$ and $\phi_2(t)$. For phase shift keying, a possible set of such basis functions is:

$$\phi_1(t) = \sqrt{\frac{2}{T}}\cos 2\pi f_c t$$

$$\phi_2(t) = -\sqrt{\frac{2}{T}}\sin 2\pi f_c t$$

where f_c is the frequency of each of the basis functions, and T is its reciprocal.

The digital passband signal transmitted in each interval is obtained by taking the weighted sum of $\phi_1(t)$ and $\phi_2(t)$, where the weights are obtained by selecting some appropriate values for $x_I(t)$ and $x_Q(t)$. Note that the basis functions $\phi_1(t)$ and $\phi_2(t)$ chosen above are not only orthogonal to each other—that is, $\int_T \phi_1(t)\,\phi_2(t)\,dt = 0$—but also have unit energy—that is, $\int_T \phi_1{}^2(t)\,dt = \int_T \phi_2{}^2(t)\,dt = 1$. To find the projection of a signal point along the basis function $\phi_1(t)$, we may simply use

$$x_{c1,\phi_1} = \int_T x_{c1}(t)\phi_1(t)\,dt$$

where $x_{c_i}(t)$ is one of the two possible signals that can be transmitted within a symbol interval, and x_{c_1,ϕ_1} is the projection of $x_{c_1}(t)$ along the basis function $\phi_1(t)$.

We usually show the projections along the basis functions as a point in a plane where the axes represent the basis functions. Each point in such a two-dimensional plane refers to a signal in one symbol interval. The figure obtained by displaying all possible points is called a *constellation diagram*. Thus, a binary digital system has a constellation diagram with only two points, while the constellation diagram of a quaternary signal contains four points in the plane of basis functions (Wikipedia 2007, "Constellation diagram"). Example constellation diagram for commonly used PSK schemes are given in subsequent sections.

GENERATION OF COHERENT PSK SIGNALS

In this section, we introduce the process of generating a coherent PSK signal. To this end, we first provide a mathematical representation of the PSK signals. To develop an understanding of PSK signals, we start with the simplest of the PSK signals: the *binary phase shift keying* (BPSK) signal, which is also known as a *binary antipodal signal*. Any reference to PSK would implicitly mean coherent PSK, unless stated otherwise.

Representation of BPSK

The BPSK signal is represented by two points on the constellation diagram. Corresponding to each constellation point, the two possible digital passband signals, one of which is selected for transmission in each symbol interval, are given by:

$$x_{c1}(t) = A\cos 2\pi f_c t$$
$$x_{c2}(t) = -A\cos 2\pi f_c t$$

In terms of the basis functions given in the preceding section on constellation diagrams, these two passband signals are

$$x_{c1}(t) = A\sqrt{\frac{T}{2}}\phi_1(t)$$

$$x_{c2}(t) = -A\sqrt{\frac{T}{2}}\phi_1(t)$$

The projection of $x_{c_1}(t)$ along the two axes in the constellation diagram is

$$x_{c1,\phi_1} = \int_T x_{c1}(t)\phi_1(t)\,dt = A\sqrt{\frac{T}{2}}$$

$$x_{c1,\phi_2} = \int_T x_{c1}(t)\phi_2(t)\,dt = 0$$

Similarly, the projection of $x_{c_2}(t)$ along the two axes in the constellation diagram is

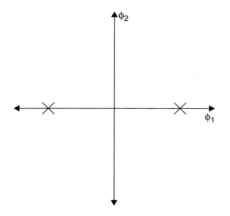

Figure 2: Constellation diagram for BPSK

$$x_{c2,\phi_1} = \int_T x_{c2}(t)\phi_1(t)dt = -A\sqrt{\frac{T}{2}}$$

$$x_{c2,\phi_2} = \int_T x_{c2}(t)\phi_2(t)dt = 0$$

The constellation diagram in Figure 2 shows $x_{c_1}(t)$ and $x_{c_2}(t)$ as points on the plane of basis functions. Both constellation points lie along the $\phi_1(t)$ axis with no component along $\phi_2(t)$. Furthermore, the two constellation points are 180 degrees from each other. The total number of constellation points (i.e., two in this case) indicate that the constellation diagram belongs to a binary digital system. For a quaternary system, the constellation diagram would contain four constellation points, as will be explained in later sections.

Every signal has an associated energy; therefore, each point in a signal constellation diagram has an associated transmitted energy. The average energy of all of the signal points in a constellation diagram is referred to as *transmitted energy per symbol*. For a binary constellation (i.e., with two constellation points), the transmitted energy per symbol is equal to the *transmitted energy per bit*, usually denoted by E_b. Thus, for BPSK signals, the energy of signal $x_{c_1}(t)$ within one symbol interval is

$$\begin{aligned}
E_{x_{c_1}} &= \left\langle x_{c1}(t)x_{c1}(t)\right\rangle \\
&= \int_T x_{c1}(t)c_{c1}(t)dt \\
&= \int_T \frac{A^2T}{2}\phi_1(t)\phi_1(t)dt \\
&= \frac{A^2T}{2}
\end{aligned}$$

By symmetry, the energy of the signal $x_{c_2}(t)$ within one symbol interval is $E_{x_{c_2}} = \frac{A^2T}{2}$. In general, the energy of a signal point is given by the sum of squares of projections along each basis function. Thus, for BPSK, the energy for the first constellation point is given by

$$\begin{aligned}
E_{x_{c1}} &= \sqrt{x^2_{c1,\phi_1} + x^2_{c1,\phi_2}} \\
&= \frac{A^2T}{2}
\end{aligned}$$

Finally, the transmitted energy per bit for BPSK is given by averaging the energy per bit corresponding to each signal point in the constellation:

$$\begin{aligned}
E_b &= \frac{\left\langle x_{c1}(t)x_{c2}(t)\right\rangle + \left\langle x_{c2}(t)x_{c2}(t)\right\rangle}{2} \\
&= \frac{A^2T}{2}
\end{aligned}$$

Generation of BPSK

In practice, a binary digital signal consists of bits, a sequence of 1's and 0's, and one of the two signals in BPSK constellation is assigned to each bit. For example, for the BPSK signals given in the preceding section, a 1 can be represented by $x_{c_1}(t)$ while a 0 can be represented by $x_{c_2}(t)$. Thus, the transmitted signals that correspond to each bit value will be as shown in Figure 3. The assignment of bit values to one of the constellation points is completely arbitrary, and the transmitter and receiver must use the same assignment. For example, for BPSK representation in the previous section, one could assign $x_{c_1}(t)$ to bit value 0 and $x_{c_2}(t)$ to bit value.

A simple method to generate the BPSK signal is to take the polar NRZ baseband signal and multiply it with the sinusoidal carrier at frequency f_c, as shown in Figure 4. The resulting product will be a BPSK signal and is shown in Figure 5 for an example binary sequence 101101. The carrier frequency is deliberately chosen to be an integer multiple of the inverse of symbol period. It will be shown in the section on demodulation that this is not a strict requirement on the carrier frequency as long as it is much larger than the inverse of the symbol period.

Representation and Generation of QPSK

The *quadriphase shift keying* (QPSK) signal is represented by four points on the constellation diagram. As usual, for every symbol period, we select one from the four symbols for transmission during the same symbol period. However, in this case, each symbol represents two information bits and therefore the symbol period is twice the bit period. The four signals, each corresponding to one constellation point, are given by the generic expression for passband signals:

$$x_c(t) = x_I(t)\cos 2\pi f_c t - x_Q(t)\sin 2\pi f_c t$$

To generate the QPSK signal, we need to find the in-phase and quadrature components, $x_I(t)$ and $x_Q(t)$, for each of the four signal points. These components are listed in Table 1.

Thus, for example, the expression for the signal $x_{c_1}(t)$ that corresponds to the first constellation point is

$$\begin{aligned}
x_{c1}(t) &= \frac{A}{\sqrt{2}}\cos 2\pi f_c t - \frac{A}{\sqrt{2}}\sin 2\pi f_c t \\
&= \frac{A}{2}\sqrt{T}\phi_1(t) + \frac{A}{2}\sqrt{T}\phi_2(t)
\end{aligned}$$

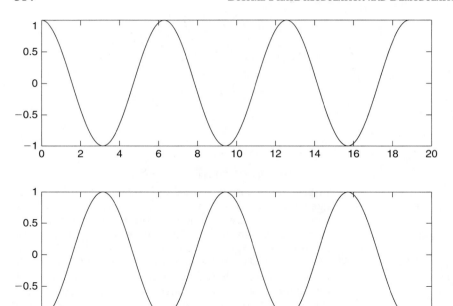

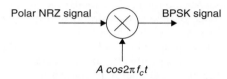

Figure 3: Signal set for BPSK with $A = 1$

Figure 4: Generation of BPSK signal from polar NRZ signals

Then the projections of $x_{c_1}(t)$ on the axes representing the two basis functions are

$$x_{c1,\phi_1} = \int_T x_{c1}(t)\phi_1(t)dt = \frac{A}{2}\sqrt{T}$$

$$x_{c1,\phi_2} = \int_T x_{c1}(t)\phi_2(t)dt = \frac{A}{2}\sqrt{T}$$

The projections of other signal points on the basis functions can be similarly determined. The complete constellation diagram for the QPSK signal is shown in Figure 6.

For QPSK, one symbol represents two signal bits, which means that the energy per bit is one-half the energy per symbol. The energy per symbol can be determined by taking the average energy for each signal point in the constellation. For the first constellation point, the corresponding energy, if that symbol is transmitted in one symbol period, is given by

$$\begin{aligned} E_{x_{c1}} &= \left\langle x_{c1}(t)x_{c1}(t)\right\rangle \\ &= \int_T x_{c1}(t)x_{c1}(t)dt \\ &= \frac{A^2T}{2} \quad \text{(using orthonormality of basis functions)} \end{aligned}$$

This energy can also be determined by taking the sum of squares of projections along each basis function, as given below:

$$\begin{aligned} E_{x_{c1}} &= \sqrt{x_{c1,\phi_1}^2 + x_{c1,\phi_2}^2} \\ &= \frac{A^2T}{2} \end{aligned}$$

By symmetry, the energy of other signal points within one symbol interval is $\frac{A^2T}{2}$, and thus the transmitted energy per symbol is $\frac{A^2T}{2}$. Finally, the energy per bit for QPSK is

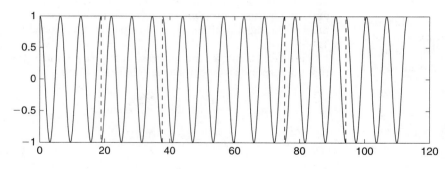

Figure 5: BPSK-transmitted signal for bit sequence 101101

Table 1: In-Phase and Quadrature Components of a QPSK Signal

Constellation point signal	In-phase component, $x_I(t)$	Quadrature component, $x_Q(t)$
$x_{c1}(t)$	$\dfrac{A}{\sqrt{2}}$	$\dfrac{A}{\sqrt{2}}$
$x_{c2}(t)$	$-\dfrac{A}{\sqrt{2}}$	$\dfrac{A}{\sqrt{2}}$
$x_{c3}(t)$	$-\dfrac{A}{\sqrt{2}}$	$-\dfrac{A}{\sqrt{2}}$
$x_{c4}(t)$	$\dfrac{A}{\sqrt{2}}$	$-\dfrac{A}{\sqrt{2}}$

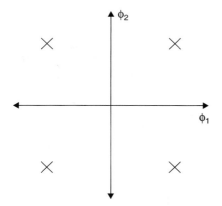

Figure 6: Constellation diagram for QPSK

$$E_b = \frac{1}{2}\frac{A^2 T}{2}$$
$$= \frac{A^2 T}{4}$$

Now that we have expressions for each signal point in the QPSK constellation, the generation of the QPSK signal becomes straightforward. First, we emphasize that each constellation point represents two signal bits and, as in the case of BPSK, every possible pair of bits needs to be mapped onto one of the constellation points. Because there are four possible combinations a bit pair may take—00, 01, 10, and 11—we have just enough constellation points to map these bit pairs. Once again, the mapping is arbitrary as long as a single bit pair maps onto a single constellation point. Next, we note from Table 1 that in-phase and quadrature component pairs can be generated by mixing two polar NRZ BPSK signals. Thus, the QPSK signal can be generated by adding two BPSK signals that are generated using *quadrature carriers*. To generate the two BPSK signals, we split the polar NRZ encoded information bits into even and odd numbered bits using a demultiplexer and perform individual BPSK modulation as shown in Figure 7.

M-ary PSK

The constellation points in BPSK and QPSK signals may be considered as lying along a circle, where one constellation point can be obtained by adding some phase shift to another constellation point. The two constellation points in BPSK are 180 degrees apart, at 0 degrees and 180 degrees, whereas the constellation points in QPSK lie at 45, 135, 225, and 315 degrees along a circle whose radius can be computed from the projections of any point along the two basis functions. In both cases, the circle along which the constellation points lie has a radius equal to the square root of the transmitted energy per symbol.

The idea of placing the constellation points along a circle in the basis functions plane can be extended to higher modulation levels. For example, in 8-PSK (or 8-ary PSK) eight points are spaced at 45 degrees from adjacent points along a circle in the plane formed by the two basis functions, as shown in Figure 8. This also means that the signal energy of each constellation point is the same and is equal to the transmitted energy per symbol. For M-ary PSK, there are M constellation points along a circle in the basis function plane and each constellation point represents $\log_2 M$ bits transmitted in each symbol.

M-ary PSK signals can be generated by generalizing the idea of generating the QPSK signal from two BPSK signals. Theoretically, one signal point on the M-ary constellation can be obtained from another by adding appropriate phase shift to the modulated signal. Practically, every possible $\log_2 M$-bit sequence is mapped onto a constellation point. When a given bit sequence of length $\log_2 M$ bits occurs in the message stream, the signal corresponding to the mapped constellation point is transmitted

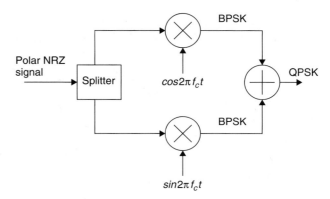

Figure 7: Generation of QPSK signal from polar NRZ signals

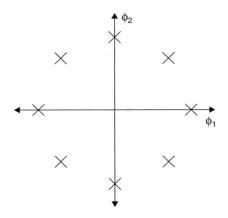

Figure 8: Constellation diagram for M-ary PSK

in the symbol interval. To generate the signal corresponding to a constellation point, the in-phase and quadrature components of the signal are summed after modulating with $\cos 2\pi f_c t$ and $\sin 2\pi f_c t$, respectively.

DEMODULATION OF COHERENT PSK SIGNALS

As mentioned in the early background section, coherent PSK is used when the receiver or the demodulator is able to locally generate the carrier with correct phase and frequency. To this end, the coherent receiver tracks the carrier by using a carrier recovery circuit. We will briefly describe the carrier recovery circuit in the later section on synchronization and carrier recovery while discussing synchronization and its effects on the performance of PSK signals. For this section, we assume that the demodulator has some mechanism to track the carrier and will somehow be able to generate the carrier with the correct frequency and phase. We will also assume that the transmitted signal does not encounter any imperfection or noise in the channel. In real communications, however, the received signal will not be an exact replica of the transmitted signal, only a noisy version of it. This will lead to occasional errors in making a decision at the demodulator about what was sent from the transmitter. For an understanding of the demodulation process, we may ignore the channel imperfections and later evaluate the effects of noise once the demodulation process is completely understood.

A simple construction of a coherent BPSK receiver is shown in Figure 9, where $r(t)$ is the received signal. Ignoring the noise, the received signal in each symbol interval

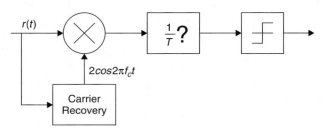

Figure 9: Demodulation of BPSK signals

is equal to the signal corresponding to one of the two constellation points in the BPSK constellation. Recall from the earlier section on BPSK that the two possible symbols in each symbol interval are:

$$x_{c1}(t) = A\cos 2\pi f_c t$$
$$x_{c2}(t) = -A\cos 2\pi f_c t$$

For a single symbol period, the received signal will thus be equal to either $xc_1(t)$ or $xc_2(t)$. In general, for $-\infty < t < \infty$, the received signal $r(t)$ can be written in terms of a polar NRZ signal using the previously discussed mechanism for generating a BPSK. In other words,

$$r(t) = \sum_{n=-\infty}^{\infty} a_n p(t - nT)\cos 2\pi f_c t$$

where $a_n \in \{-1, +1\}$ and $p(t) = A\Pi(\frac{t}{T})$. Thus, the signal $\hat{r}(t)$ at the output of the integrator is given by

$$
\begin{aligned}
\hat{r}(t) &= \frac{1}{T}\int_T r(t)^2 \cos 2\pi f_c t \, dt \\
&= \frac{1}{T}\int_{(k-\frac{1}{2})T}^{(k+\frac{1}{2})T} \left(\sum_{n=-\infty}^{\infty} a_n A\Pi\left(\frac{t-nT}{T}\right)\cos 2\pi f_c t \right) 2\cos 2\pi f_c t \, dt \\
&= \frac{1}{T}\int_{(k-\frac{1}{2})T}^{(k+\frac{1}{2})T} Aa_k 2\cos^2 2\pi f_c t \, dt \\
&= \frac{Aa_k}{T}\int_{(k-\frac{1}{2})T}^{(k+\frac{1}{2})T} (1 + \cos 4\pi f_c t)\, dt \\
&= Aa_k + \frac{Aa_k}{4\pi T f_c}[\sin 4\pi f_c (k+\tfrac{1}{2})T - \sin 4\pi f_c(k-\tfrac{1}{2})T] \\
&= Aa_k + \frac{Aa_k}{4\pi T f_c} 2\cos 4\pi f_c kT \sin 2\pi f_c T
\end{aligned}
$$

In the above expression, the second term is approximately equal to zero if $f_c T \gg 1$, and is exactly zero if f_c is an integer multiple of $1/T$. Thus, the input to the decision device, shown as the last box in Figure 9, is approximately (or exactly if f_c is an integer multiple of $1/T$ equal to Aa_k). The decision device infers that $a + 1$ was sent from the transmitter if the input to the decision device is greater than 0 and decides that $a - 1$ was sent otherwise. Thus, in the absence of noise, one can completely and perfectly recover the transmitted signal using the above demodulation scheme. The presence of noise in the signal would cause the input to the decision device to be different from Aa_k, depending on the magnitude of the noise, and may lead to occasional errors in inferring what was sent from the transmitter.

The demodulator for QPSK and M-ary PSK can be constructed on a similar principle, whereby the in-phase and quadrature components are demodulated separately and then combined to generate the transmitted signal (Xiong 2000).

SPECTRAL CHARACTERISTICS OF PSK SIGNALS

The *power spectral density* (PSD) of a modulated signal is a direct indication of the bandwidth efficiency of the modulation scheme. A modulated signal with *wider* PSD consumes more transmission bandwidth compared to a signal that has narrower PSD. We will provide expression for the power spectral density of M-ary PSK signals, which can be specialized for $M = 2$ (BPSK) and $M = 4$ (QPSK). To simplify things, we use the fact that for pass-band signals with certain properties, the PSD can be obtained by dividing by the symbol duration the power spectral density of the corresponding baseband signal. A BPSK signal generated from the polar NRZ signal in the previous section on BPSK possesses these properties and, therefore the PSD of the BPSK signal is simply 1/T times the PSD of the underlying polar NRZ signal shifted to baseband. Recall that the BPSK signal is given by

$$x_c(t) = \sum_{n=-\infty}^{\infty} a_n p(t - nT) \cos 2\pi f_c t$$

whose underlying baseband signal is the following polar NRZ signal:

$$x(t) = \sum_{n=-\infty}^{\infty} a_n p(t - nT)$$
$$= \sum_{n=-\infty}^{\infty} a_n A \Pi \left(\frac{t - nT}{T} \right)$$

The energy spectral density of $x(t)$ in a single symbol period is given by the squared Fourier transform of $x(t)$ by considering just one symbol period. Thus, if $\tilde{x}(t)$ represents the single symbol of $x(t)$, then a possible value of $\tilde{x}(t)$ is $a_n A \Pi(\frac{t}{T})$. The Fourier transform $\tilde{X}(f)$ of $\tilde{x}(t)$ is, therefore, $a_n AT$ sinc fT. Thus, the *energy spectral density* (ESD) of the signal $x(t)$ is $a_n^2 A^2 T^2$ (sinc $fT)^2$; and because $a_n \in \{-1 + 1\}$, the ESD of $x(t)$ is $A^2 T^2$ (sinc $fT)^2$. Then the PSD of the polar NRZ signal $x(t)$ is given by its ESD divided by the symbol period—that is,

$$\text{PSD of } x(t) = S_x(f) = 1/T \; A^2 T^2 (\text{sinc } fT)^2$$
$$= A^2 T (\text{sinc } fT)^2$$

Finally, the baseband-shifted PSD of BPSK signal is given by the PSD of the baseband polar NRZ signal divided by the symbol period T. Thus,

$$\text{Shifted PSD of BPSK} = S_{x_c}(f) = 1/T \; A^2 T (\text{sinc } fT)^2$$
$$= A^2 (\text{sinc } fT)^2$$

It can be seen that the PSD of a polar NRZ signal falls off with squared frequency and crosses the first null at $fT = 1$ or $f = 1/T$. Thus, the PSD of a BPSK signal will also fall off with squared frequency, will be centered at f_c, and will hit the first null at $f_c \pm 1/T$. The PSD of a BPSK signal for the positive frequencies is shown in Figure 10.

The PSD of a QPSK signal can be easily determined by considering the structure that was used earlier (in the section on the representation and generation of QPSK) for the generation of BPSK by taking the sum of two independently generated BPSK signals. In other words, in one symbol period, we generate two independent BPSK signals, each of which has a corresponding baseband polar NRZ signal given by $a_n \frac{A}{\sqrt{2}} \Pi \left(\frac{t}{T} \right)$. Because this signal is $1/\sqrt{2}$ times the polar NRZ signal $\tilde{x}(t)$ considered above, its PSD is one-half of the PSD of the BPSK signal considered above. However, the QPSK is generated by summing up

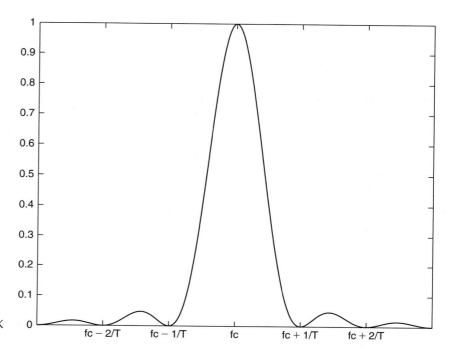

Figure 10: Power spectral density of BPSK signals

two such independent BPSK signals; thus, the PSDs are also added, and the PSD of the QPSK signal has the same expression as in the case of BPSK and is given below:

$$\text{Shifted PSD of QPSK} = 2 \times (A/\sqrt{2})^2 (\text{sinc } fT)^2$$
$$= A^2 (\text{sinc } fT)^2$$

This expression for power spectral density is also correct for an M-ary PSK modulation with parameter $A = \sqrt{2E/T}$, where E and T are energy per symbol and symbol period, respectively.

ERROR PERFORMANCE OF PSK SIGNALS

An important performance parameter of any digital modulation scheme is the average number of bits that are inferred incorrectly at the receiver. In an ideal communication channel, no errors are observed, but practical channels are noisy, which means that the signals transmitted through the channel are contaminated by noise. We usually model the noise as additive white Gaussian noise (Wikipedia 2007, "Additive white Gaussian noise") —that is, the probability density function of noise, which is assumed to be added to the transmitted signal, follows a Gaussian distribution, and individual noise samples are uncorrelated with each other, leading to flat power spectral density.

The effect of additive noise is to add an undesirable random parameter (voltage, phase, or frequency) to the actual signal. This results in a received signal that has moved away from the original constellation point used for that signal in that symbol period. For distinguishing the received signals corresponding to two neighboring constellation points, the receiver usually places the decision boundary midway between the two points. Thus, for the BPSK signal, where the two constellation points are at $\pm A\sqrt{T/2}$, the decision boundary is the vertical line midway between the two constellation points. Thus, received signals in the first and fourth quadrant are mapped to $\pm A\sqrt{T/2}$, while the signals in the second and third quadrant are mapped to $-A\sqrt{T/2}$. Similarly, for QPSK, the lines along the horizontal and vertical axes form the decision boundaries. An error results when the noise added to the signal is such that the contaminated signal crosses a decision boundary such that it is mistakenly regarded as belonging to a neighboring constellation point.

Although the effect of additive noise is simply to move the received signal away from its corresponding constellation point with the addition of an undesirable random parameter, the signals also undergo fading in wireless communication channels. Fading may increase the bit error rates by many times compared to those obtained in additive noise channels only (Rappaport 2001). In this chapter, we only include the bit error rates (or probability of bit errors) in *additive white Gaussian noise* while omitting the error rates for fading channels that can be found in more advanced texts (e.g., Proakis 2000; Barry, Lee, and Messerschmitt 2003).

To find the bit error rate (or error probability) of BPSK, we recall from the earlier section on the representation of BPSK that the BPSK transmitter sends one of the two possible symbols, $xc_1(t)$ or $xc_2(t)$, in each symbol interval. There are two possible ways a receiver can make an error: (1) $xc_1(t)$ was transmitted, but the additive noise pushed the received signal into the region that corresponds to $xc_2(t)$; or (2) $xc_2(t)$ was transmitted, but the additive noise pushed the received signal into the region that corresponds to $xc_1(t)$. For obtaining a quantitative expression, we consider additive noise with a constant two-sided power spectral density of $N_0/2$ and Gaussian distribution after demodulation, which is given by:

$$f_N(n) = \frac{1}{\sqrt{\pi N_0}} e^{-\frac{n^2}{N_0}}$$

The probability of error in a single bit interval is given by the sum of probabilities of two mutually exclusive events (Couch 1995):

1. The transmitter sent $xc_1(t)$ and the receiver detected $xc_2(t)$, which happens when additive noise after demodulation is less than xc_{1,ϕ_1}.
2. xc_1The transmitter sent $xc_2(t)$ and the receiver detected $xc_1(t)$, which happens when additive noise after demodulation is greater than $-xc_{2,\phi_1}$.

If the probability of sending $xc_1(t)$ is the same as the probability of sending $xc_2(t)$, which is usually the case, then by symmetry the error probability is given by the probability that the demodulated noise is greater than $x_{c1,\phi_1} = A\sqrt{\frac{T}{2}} = \sqrt{E_b}$. Thus, the bit error probability $P_{b,\text{BPSK}}$ is given by

$$P_{b,\text{BPSK}} = P\{\text{Additive Noise} > \sqrt{E_b}\}$$
$$= \int_{\sqrt{E_b}}^{\infty} \frac{1}{\sqrt{\pi N_0}} e^{-\frac{n^2}{N_0}} dn$$
$$= Q\left(\sqrt{\frac{2E_b}{N_0}}\right)$$

where $Q(\cdot)$ is the tail of the standard Gaussian distribution (a Gaussian distribution with zero mean and unit variance).

A similar method of error probability analysis for QPSK can be carried out and is given in Haykin (2000). In summary, for QPSK, the symbol error probability is given by

$$P_{S,\text{QPSK}} = 2Q\left(\sqrt{\frac{E}{N_0}}\right)$$

where E is the symbol energy, and for QPSK the symbol energy is twice the bit energy as explained in the earlier section on BPSK representation—that is, $E = 2E_b$. With using a special encoding technique called *Gray encoding*, the probability of bit error in QPSK can be kept at one-half of the probability of symbol error. Thus, the bit error rate for QPSK is given by

$$P_{b,\text{QPSK}} = \frac{1}{2} \times 2Q\left(\sqrt{\frac{E}{N_0}}\right)$$

$$= Q\left(\sqrt{\frac{E}{N_0}}\right)$$

$$= Q\left(\sqrt{\frac{2E_b}{N_0}}\right)$$

which is the same as the bit error rate for BPSK. Thus, coherent QPSK delivers the same bit error rates as coherent BPSK but has the capability of transmitting data twice as fast, keeping other parameters constant. Thus, in practice, coherent QPSK is a preferred modulation scheme when compared with coherent BPSK (Simon, Hinedi, and Lindsey 1994).

SYNCHRONIZATION AND CARRIER RECOVERY

As we observed in the section "Demodulation of Coherent PSK Signals," coherent demodulation of coherent PSK requires the availability of a correct carrier frequency and phase at the receiver. This can be accomplished by using a carrier recovery circuit that usually employs a *phase-locked loop* (Xiong 2000). In fact, if the transmitter chooses to include an extra *pilot* signal at the carrier frequency (at which the PSK signals have no spectral components), the receiver may use this pilot signal to acquire the synchronization. If the pilot signal is not included in the transmitted signal, then carrier recovery is accomplished by using a nonlinear circuit. A newer approach to carrier synchronization is by setting up a DSP algorithm that maximizes the likelihood estimate of the carrier phase in an iterative manner (Haykin 2000).

Differential PSK does not require carrier synchronization because it can use noncoherent detector. However, both coherent and differential modulation require another type of synchronization called *symbol synchronization*. Note from the BPSK demodulation discussed earlier that the integral operation in the demodulator is carried out over precisely one symbol time. Therefore, the receiver must somehow determine the start and end of each symbol. Symbol synchronization, also referred to as *clock recovery*, is extremely important for correct detection of symbols and is usually implemented in DSP before performing carrier synchronization.

From the demodulation process, we note that the accuracy of clock recovery (or symbol synchronization) and phase synchronization determines the accuracy of the decisions taken at the receiver. It is shown in Xiong (2000) that a phase synchronization error of ϕ will result in a reduction in the amplitude of the signal that is fed to the decision device by a factor $\cos \phi$. Thus, the bit error probability of the BPSK signal in the presence of a phase error ϕ will be given by

$$P_b = Q\left(\sqrt{\frac{2E}{N_0}} \cos \phi\right)$$

From this equation, we note that the argument of the Q function is directly affected by the phase error, and thus even small local carrier phase errors may significantly affect the bit error rates of coherent BPSK systems.

SPECTRUM CONTROL IN DIGITAL PHASE MODULATION

Coherent PSK signals undergo abrupt phase transitions at the beginning of symbol intervals, causing high-powered spectral side lobes that may interfere with adjacent channels. To illustrate the abrupt phase transitions, let us consider the example of QPSK signal described earlier in "Representation and Generation of QPSK." The QPSK constellation shown in Figure 6 consists of four points, exactly one of which is transmitted in one symbol period, corresponding to a two-bit sequence that appears in the bit stream of message signal during that symbol period. The signal transmitted in one symbol interval does not depend on the signal transmitted in a previous or future symbol interval. Thus, the constellation point in each symbol interval is chosen independently. Because the constellation points represent signals with differing phases (at 45, 135, 225, and 315 degrees), phase change at each symbol boundary could be 0 degrees, ±90 degrees, and ±180 degrees.

Another issue related to abrupt phase transitions turns up when we consider the demodulator that invariably uses a bandpass filter before detection in order to limit the amount of additive white Gaussian noise. Some PSK transmitters will also include the bandpass filter to limit the side lobe power and consequent interference with adjacent frequency bands. Passing a PSK signal through a bandpass filter causes amplitude variation through a phenomena called FM-to-AM conversion (Carlson, Crilly, and Rutledge 2002). This amplitude variation can deteriorate the error rate performance of the overall system.

To combat abrupt phase transitions at the beginning of symbol intervals, variations of PSK have been devised. One such variation for QPSK is called *staggered QPSK* or *offset-keyed* (or *offset*) *QPSK*, abbreviated OQPSK. Using OQPSK, constellation points chosen in any two consecutive symbol periods are not allowed to be diagonally opposite to each other, thus avoiding the ±180-degree phase transition at the beginning of the symbol period. Thus, the allowable phase transitions at the beginning of a symbol period are limited to 0 degrees and ±90 degrees. OQPSK is generated by delaying the bit stream responsible for generating the quadrature component by half a symbol period. Although OQPSK exhibits the same bit error performance as exhibited by QPSK, it results in reduced amplitude fluctuations after bandpass filtering when compared with QPSK.

The use of OQPSK limits the phase transitions to at most ±90 degrees at the beginning of a symbol interval. These phase transitions can be eliminated altogether by using CPM. In CPM, the phase transitions, which happen at the beginning of a symbol interval in case of QPSK and OQPSK, are spread over the whole symbol interval in such a way that a phase continuity is maintained throughout the symbol period, including the symbol boundaries. A generic continuous phase modulated signal is given by

$$x_c(t) = \sqrt{\frac{2E}{T}} \cos(2\pi f_c t + \phi_0 + \phi(t))$$

where the variable portion of phase $\phi(t)$ is given by

$$\phi(t) = 2\pi h \sum_{j=0}^{n} a_j q(t - jT)$$

and where $q(t)$ is called the phase-shaping pulse and h is the modulation index. The phase-shaping pulse $q(t)$ is related to the frequency-shaping pulse $g(t)$ as:

$$q(t) = \int_{-\infty}^{t} g(y)dy$$

Note that the expression of CPM signal $x_c(t)$ indicates that the CPM is a variation of frequency modulation; however, because of a direct relationship between frequency and phase (instantaneous frequency is the derivation of instantaneous phase), a CPM signal can either be viewed as a frequency-modulated or a phase-modulated signal. When $g(t)$ is a rectangular pulse of duration LT, we get a special family of CPM called L-REC CPM. For $L = 1$, we get 1-REC CPM, which is also known as *continuous phase frequency shift keying*. A further specialization of CPFSK with $h = 1/2$ yields the well-known *minimum shift keying* (MSK). For demodulation purposes, a usual way to interpret a CPM signal is to consider it as a concatenation of a trellis code followed by memoryless modulation (Wilson 1995). Thus, the demodulation of CPM signals may be carried out by a linear demodulator followed by a sequence detector.

CONCLUSION

Digital phase modulation is a widely used modulation technique in computer and communication networks. This type of modulation has an attractive property—it maintains a constant envelope—and is therefore suitable for communication in nonlinear channels. Many existing communication networks use phase shift keying or other digital phase modulation schemes for communication at the physical layer. Specifically, current wireless LAN standards such as IEEE 802.11b, IEEE 802.11g and others such as Bluetooth and GSM make use of digital phase modulation in various transmission modes.

We studied the methods for generating and demodulating the PSK signals and also learned PSK signal representation in the signal space. We evaluated the PSK schemes with respect to the error probabilities they offer and briefly described the two types of synchronization required in coherent systems. Expressions for bit error rates for BPSK and QPSK are provided in this chapter, and we learned that, keeping other parameters the same, QPSK delivers data at twice the rate of BPSK and therefore is a preferred modulation technique.

Phase shift keying is the simplest form of digital phase modulation. Constant envelope is the most notable and useful property of PSK signals. In general, all DPM schemes maintain a constant envelope. Furthermore, PSK undergoes abrupt phase changes at symbol boundaries, resulting in relatively high energy at higher frequency side lobes. This abrupt phase change can be subsided by using techniques such as offset QPSK, which limits the phase jump at symbol boundaries. Furthermore, CPM allows a complete elimination of abrupt phase changes at symbol boundaries by allowing a continuous change of phase throughout the symbol. CPM signals may be viewed as coding followed by modulation and therefore may be demodulated by using a coherent demodulator followed by a sequence detector. By avoiding abrupt phase changes, CPM avoids high power in side lobes, resulting in spectrally efficient modulation.

GLOSSARY

Bit error rate: The average number of bits received in error when a digital signal is sent from one point to another.
Carrier signal: A signal or wave that is a relatively high-frequency signal, usually a sinusoidal. One property of a carrier signal—phase, frequency, or amplitude—is varied according to a message signal that needs to be transmitted from one point to another.
Constellation: The representation of signal points of a digital modulation scheme on a plane whose axes are represented by orthonormal basis functions.
Continuous phase frequency shift keying (CPFSK): A special case of CPM in which the frequency-shaping pulse is rectangular with a duration equal to the symbol interval.
Continuous phase modulation (CPM): A digital modulation in which the modulated signal is constrained to maintain a constant envelope and continuous phase, avoiding abrupt changes in phase.
Demodulation: The process of extracting the message signal from the modulated signal received at the receiving end of a communication system.
Message signal: An electrical signal, typically a representative of a physical quantity, that is usually transmitted from the source to the destination in a communication system.
Minimum Shift Keying (MSK): A special case of CPFSK. In particular, MSK is CPFSK with a minimum modulation index that results in orthogonal signaling.
Modulation: The process of varying some property (amplitude, phase, or frequency) of a carrier signal according to a message signal that needs to conveyed to the receiver.
Phase shift keying (PSK): A modulation method in which the phase of a carrier signal is varied directly in accordance with a digital message signal.
Synchronization: The process in which two quantities are made to vary in unison. In PSK, two types of synchronization are needed: phase synchronization and symbol synchronization.

CROSS REFERENCES

See *Minimum Shift Keying (MSK)*; *Optical Fiber Communications*.

REFERENCES

Anderson, J. B., and C.-E. W. Sundberg. 1991. Advances in constant envelope coded modulation. *IEEE Communications Magazine*, 29: 36–45.

Barry, J. R., E. A. Lee, and D. G. Messerschmitt. 2003. *Digital communication*. 3rd ed. New York: Springer.

Carlson, A. B., P. B. Crilly, and J. C. Rutledge. 2002. *Communication systems*. 4th ed. New York: McGraw-Hill

Couch, L. W. II. 1995. *Modern communication systems: Principles and applications*. Upper Saddle River, NJ: Prentice-Hall.

Haykin, S. 2000. *Communications systems*. 4th ed. New York: John Wiley & Sons.

Proakis, J. G. 2000. *Digital communications*. 4th ed. New York: McGraw-Hill.

Rappaport, T. S. 2001. *Wireless communications: Principles and practice*. 2nd ed. Upper Saddle River, NJ: Prentice-Hall.

Simon, M. K., S. M. Hinedi, and W. C. Lindsey. 1994. Digital communication techniques: Signal design and detection. Upper Saddle River, NJ: Prentice-Hall.

Wikipedia. 2007. Additive white Gaussian noise (retrieved from http://en.wikipedia.org/wiki/Additive_white_Gaussian_noise)

———. 2007. Constellation (retrieved from http://en.wikipedia.org/wiki/Constellation_diagram).

———. 2007. Modulation (retrieved from http://en.wikipedia.org/wiki/Modulation).

———. 2007. Phase shift keying (retrieved from http://en.wikipedia.org/wiki/Phase-shift_keying).

Wilson, S. G. 1995. *Digital modulation and coding*. Upper Saddle River, NJ: Prentice-Hall.

Xiong, X. 2000. *Digital modulation techniques*. Boston: Artech House Publishers.

Line Coding

Asim Loan, *University of Engineering and Technology, Lahore, Pakistan*

INTRODUCTION

Information is sent from one point in the network to another and can be converted to either a digital signal or an analog signal. This chapter deals with the shaping of digital data so that it is suitable for transmission over a channel. The digital messages can be stored in the memory of the computer and include data, text, numbers, graphical images, audio, and video. Passband systems have a relatively constant attenuation over the bandwidth because the carrier frequency is much larger compared to the signal bandwidth and the cross-talk coupling loss is also relatively frequency-independent. In baseband modulation, however, data are transmitted directly without resorting to frequency translation. A variety of waveforms have been studied, and the ones that have good power, spectral efficiency, and adequate timing information are used for converting the data, a sequence of bits, to a digital signal. These baseband modulation waveforms are called *line codes*, *baseband waveforms*, or *pulse-coded modulation* (PCM) codes. Line coding is an issue in baseband systems (compared to the passband systems) that operate over

cable because the channel exhibits a large variation in attenuation over the bandwidth of interest and also has a large variation in cross-talk coupling loss. However, improvement in performance of these systems is possible by controlling the power spectrum of the transmitted signal.

In the next section, we give an overview of the fundamentals of optimum detection of binary (and multiple-level) signals in *additive white Gaussian noise* (AWGN) and briefly describe how to calculate the *power spectral density* (PSD) of random digital signals. For more details, the interested reader is referred to Simon, Hinedi, and Lindsey (1995).

The rest of the chapter is broadly divided into two categories of line codes: those that are suitable for transmission over (1) wireline links and (2) optical fiber. Line codes that are appropriate over wireline systems are discussed in the third section and can be broadly divided into four subclasses: *non-return to zero* (NRZ), *return-to-zero* (RZ), *pseudoternary* (PT) and *biphase* (see Figure 1). These line codes will be compared based on their spectral characteristics, bandwidth, error performance, error-detection

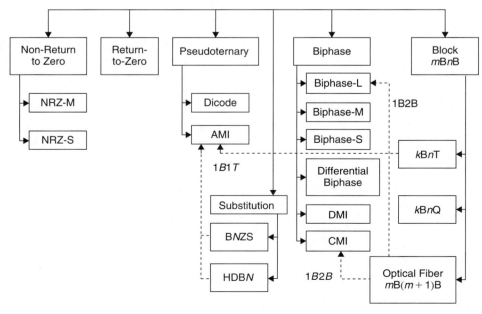

Figure 1: Line code tree

capability, self-synchronization ability, and bit sequence independence or transparency. Substitution codes overcome the shortcomings of the pseudoternary line codes—the most popular wireline line codes—by exchanging the consecutive zeros with various control signals that improve the timing information of the original codes. Block codes are not limited to binary and introduce redundancy through which the characteristics of the line code can be controlled. The nonbinary block codes (ternary and quaternary) are used in wireline systems where bandwidth is a premium. However, because the optical sources and detectors operate in the nonlinear mode, binary block codes are preferred in optical fiber transmission systems where abundant bandwidth is available. The block codes used for optical fiber are discussed in the last major section.

PROBABILITY OF BIT ERROR AND POWER SPECTRAL DENSITY

This section gives an overview of fundamentals of optimum detection of binary (and multilevel) signals in channels disturbed by AWGN and the basics of PSD calculations for digital random signals.

Probability of Bit Error

The probability of making a bit error after transmission through an AWGN channel is discussed in this section. The AWGN channel model implies that channel frequency response is flat and has infinite bandwidth. The only distortion introduced is by the additive white Gaussian noise. This is not an accurate model for practical channels except probably the satellite channel, but it is reasonably accurate as long as signal bandwidth is much narrower than that of the channel.

From the signal-detection viewpoint, binary line code (i.e., code that uses two signals to transmit information) presents one of two hypotheses:

$$
\begin{array}{llll}
H_1 : s_1(t) & 0 \le t \le T_b & \textit{apriori probability } p_1 & (1) \\
H_2 : s_2(t) & 0 \le t \le T_b & \textit{apriori probability } p_2 &
\end{array}
$$

Signal energies are $E_1 = \int_0^{T_b} s_1^2(t)dt$, $E_2 = \int_0^{T_b} s_2^2(t)dt$, and the correlation coefficient between the two signals is $\rho_{12} = \dfrac{1}{\sqrt{E_1 E_2}} \int_0^{T_b} s_1(t)s_2(t)dt$ where $|\rho_{12}| \le 1$. When a matched filter receiver is used, the bit error probability, P_b, of equally likely binary signals, in AWGN with zero mean and variance $N_0/2$, is given by Simon, Hinedi, and Lindsey (1995):

$$
P_b = Q\left(\sqrt{\frac{E_1 + E_2 - 2\rho_{12}\sqrt{E_1 E_2}}{2N_0}}\right) \tag{2}
$$

where $Q(x)$ represents the area under the tail of a unit normal variate—that is, the normal random variable has a zero mean and unit variance. The bit error probability

is minimum for antipodal signals—in other words, when $\rho_{12} = -1$ and 3 dB worse for equal energy binary orthogonal signals, or when $\rho_{12} = 0$.

For M-ary signals, the minimum error probability receiver computes (Simon, Hinedi, and Lindsey 1995)

$$
l_j = \ln(p_j) - \frac{1}{N_0}\sum_{i=1}^{N}(r_i - s_{ij})^2 \quad j = 1,2,\cdots\cdots,M \tag{3}
$$

and chooses the largest l_j. For equally likely signals, the decision rule reduces to calculating the distance between the signals and selects the signal that is at a minimum distance. The received signal is given by

$$
r(t) = s_j(t) + n(t) \quad j = 1,2,\cdots\cdots,M \tag{4}
$$

where $n(t)$ is AWGN with zero mean and variance $N_0/2$. Note also that r_i are statistically independent Gaussian random variables with variance $N_0/2$:

$$
r_i = \int_0^{T_b} r(t)\,\Phi_i(t)dt \quad i = 1,2,\cdots\cdots,N \tag{5}
$$

$\Phi_i(t)$ are N orthonormal basis functions. The projection of $s_j(t)$ onto $\Phi_i(t)$ is s_{ij}:

$$
s_{ij} = \int_0^{T_b} s_j(t)\,\Phi_i(t)dt \quad \begin{array}{l} i = 1,2,\cdots,N \\ j = 1,2,\cdots,M \end{array} \tag{6}
$$

Power Spectral Density

A general formula for calculating the power spectrum of digitally modulated baseband waveforms is presented below. It can be used for most of the binary line codes. However, for other codes, different methods to calculate PSD will have to be employed.

A digital random signal $s(t)$ can be represented by

$$
s(t) = \sum_k a_k g(t - kT_S) \tag{7}
$$

where $\{a_k\}$ represents the binary or multilevel random data sequence and $g(t)$ is a filter that shapes the spectrum. For binary signaling, $T_s = T_b$ where T_b is the time it takes to send one bit and T_s is the symbol duration. The power spectral density of $s(t)$ is (Simon, Hinedi, and Lindsey 1995)

$$
S(f) = \frac{|G(f)|^2}{T_S}\sum_n R[n]\exp(-j\omega nT_S) \tag{8}
$$

where $R[n] = E(a_k a_{k+n})$ is the autocorrelation function of the data sequence and, in general, $E(XY) \overset{\Delta}{=} \int_{-\infty}^{\infty}\int_{-\infty}^{\infty} xy\, f_{XY}(x,y)dxdy$. Thus, the PSD of a line code is determined by its (1) pulse shape and (2) the statistical properties of the data sequence.

For uncorrelated $\{a_k\}$:

$$R[n] = \begin{cases} \sigma_a^2 + \eta_a^2 & n = 0 \\ \eta_a^2 & n \neq 0 \end{cases} \quad (9)$$

where σ_a^2 is the variance of $\{a_k\}$ and η_a^2 is the square of the mean of $\{a_k\}$. Using the Poisson sum formula for binary signals, we have (Simon, Hinedi, and Lindsey 1995):

$$S(f) = \frac{|G(f)|^2}{T_b}\sigma_a^2 + \frac{\eta_a^2}{T_b^2}\sum_n |G(nT_b^{-1})|^2 \delta(f - nT_b^{-1}) \quad (10)$$

The first term in Equation 10 represents the continuous part of the power spectral density and depends only on the pulse shape used. Pulse shape should be selected such that the desired properties of line codes (see the following section) are met. The second term in the above equation represents discrete components, weighted by the pulse shape, $1/T_b$ a part in frequency that aids in timing recovery. This term can be reduced to zero by (1) a zero mean sequence—that is, one that consists of equally likely and symmetrically placed symbols in the complex plane; or (2) a pulse shape whose spectrum is zero at all multiples of $1/T_b$. Later we will show that unipolar RZ codes, with rectangular pulses, have this discrete component at zero frequency. However, note that polar versions can be made unipolar by rectification, from which the timing can be easily recovered.

In the following, we will assume that 1's and 0's are equally likely in the data sequence. Moreover, $\{a_k\}$ may represent the original data sequence or its differentially encoded form. Later in the chapter, we will see that the NRZ (NRZ-L, NRZ-M, and NRZ-S), RZ (polar or unipolar) family, and pseudoternary (AMI-RZ, AMI-NRZ, dicode RZ, and dicode NRZ) families as well as biphase-L can be written as Equation 7. Thus, the above expression, for PSD—Equation 10—represents their spectral densities. However, biphase-M, biphase-S, and substitution line codes cannot be represented as Equation 7, so other means must by used to calculate their spectral densities (Xiong 2000).

To find the spectral density of a *wide sense stationary* (WSS) signal, we need to find the autocorrelation function $R(\tau)$ first and then, according to the Wiener-Khintchine theorem, the Fourier transform of the function will give the spectral density (Simon, Hinedi, and Lindsey 1995).

BASIC LINE CODES FOR WIRELINE SYSTEMS

This section compares various basic wireline line codes. The comparison is based on their spectral characteristics, bandwidth, error performance, error-detection capability, self-synchronization ability, redundancy, and transparency. The basic line codes considered are:

- the non-return-to-zero family, including *NRZ-level* (NRZ-L), *NRZ-mark* (NRZ-M), and *NRZ-space* (NRZ-S) (including unipolar and polar subclasses);
- the return-to-zero family, including unipolar and polar subclasses;

- the pseudoternary family, including alternate mark inversion, dicode NRZ, and dicode RZ;
- the substitution codes that include binary N zero substitution and high-density bipolar N;
- the biphase family, which includes biphase-level (or Manchester), biphase-mark, and biphase-space; and
- the multilevel block code family, which includes $kBnT$ and $kBnQ$ codes.

There are other codes that do not belong to any of the classes while some may belong to more than one family.

The reason for a large selection of line codes is because of differences in performance that lead to different applications. The features to look for in choosing a line code are described below (Xiong 2000; Bellamy 2000; Barry, Lee, and Messerschmitt 2003).

Self-synchronization: A digital signal is preferred that includes timing information (self-synchronizing as opposed to sending a pilot signal that wastes bandwidth or synchronizes to a master clock) in the data being transmitted. This can be achieved if there are a suitable number of transitions in the signal that alert the receiver to the beginning, middle, or end of the pulse. Thus, formats with higher transition density are desired.

Spectrum suitable for channel: For lossless transmission, the spectra of the line codes should match the channels over which information is being transmitted. For example, for alternating current (AC) coupled channels, a line code whose spectrum has negligible energy near DC (zero frequency) should be used. Furthermore, line code should have a bandwidth that is small compared to the channel bandwidth so that channel-induced *intersymbol interference* (ISI) is not a problem.

Transmission bandwidth: The bandwidth should be as narrow as possible and may be reduced by using multilevel transmission techniques.

Low error probability: Receivers should be able to recover the information from the corrupted signal with a low probability of bit error.

Error detection capability: Line codes should preferably have a built-in error-detection capability.

Bit sequence independence (transparency): The bit pattern in a line code should not affect the ability to accurately recover the timing information.

Differential coding: If 1's and 0's are encoded such that they are negative of each other and then are transmitted over a medium on which it is impossible to determine an absolute phase reference, then 1's will be decoded as 0's and vice versa. To overcome this polarity inversion problem, either the source is differentially encoded or line codes that are inherently differential are used. In the latter case, a 1 or a 0 causes a transition in the code. Thus, decoding reduces to detecting whether the current state is the same or different from the previous.

Redundancy: By allowing redundancy (i.e., having an information bit rate less than the information-carrying capacity), we can make the transmitted data symbols statistically dependent, regardless of the statistics of the

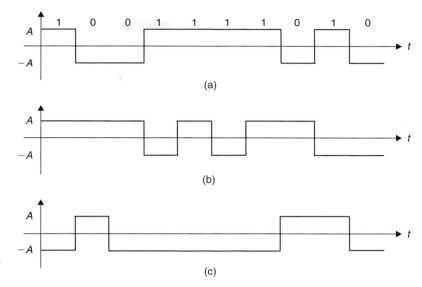

Figure 2: Polar NRZ waveforms—(a) NRZ–L, (b) NRZ—M, (c) NRZ–S

information, and hence exercise control over the power spectrum of the transmitted signal.

Non-Return-to-Zero Codes

Digital transmission systems send pulses along a link, usually a wire or fiber line within a cable. Two levels of pulse amplitude are used to distinguish between a 1 and a 0 in polar NRZ-L format (see Figure 2a). For an equally likely binary data sequence, the waveform has no DC component. The line code is relatively easy to generate, but when the data contain a long string of 0's or 1's, the received signal may not carry enough timing-recovery information and therefore the receiver may lose synchronization.

In NRZ-M [or *NRZ-invert* (NRZ-I)] format, the level changes whenever a *mark* (or 1) occurs in the sequence and no change takes place for a space (or 0) (see Figure 2b). The NRZ-S waveform is similar but encoded in the opposite sense (see Figure 2c). Thus, NRZ-M and NRZ-S are differentially encoded versions of NRZ-L. The main advantage of NRZ-M and NRZ-S over NRZ-L is their immunity to polarity reversals.

The NRZ family can be made unipolar (i.e., only one polarity—positive or negative—is used) by changing the lower level (–A volts) to zero. This line code is referred to as *on-off signaling* and is widely used in optical fiber systems where the sources and detectors operate in the nonlinear region (Bellamy 2000). For equally likely 1's and 0's, unipolar waveforms have a nonzero DC level of $A/2$ volts, whereas their polar counterparts do not. The disadvantage of on-off signaling is waste of power because of the transmitted DC level; thus, the power spectrum is nonzero at DC (see Equation 19).

A constant level in the NRZ-encoded waveforms contains no transitions and hence a lack of timing content. This shortcoming can be overcome by (1) scrambling (or randomizing), which is a process that makes data look more random by eliminating long strings of 1's and 0's; or (2) transmitting a separate synchronization sequence.

NRZ-L is used in digital logic. NRZ-M is used in magnetic tape recording. In telecommunication applications,

the NRZ format is limited to short-haul links because of its timing characteristic.

Bit Error Rate of NRZ Codes NRZ-L is polar with

$$s_1(t) = +A \qquad 0 \le t \le T_b$$
$$s_2(t) = -A \qquad 0 \le t \le T_b \tag{11}$$

$\rho_{12} = -1$, $E_1 = E_2 = A^2T_b$, therefore polar NRZ-L is antipodal with the best error performance—that is, $P_b = Q\left(\sqrt{2A^2T_b/N_0}\right) = Q\left(\sqrt{2E_b/N_0}\right)$, where the average bit energy

$$E_b = (E_1 + E_2)/2 = A^2T_b$$

For unipolar NRZ-L:

$$s_1(t) = +A \qquad 0 \le t \le T_b$$
$$s_2(t) = 0 \qquad 0 \le t \le T_b \tag{12}$$

$\rho_{12} = 0$, $E_1 = A^2T_b$, $E_2 = 0$, or $P_b = Q\left(\sqrt{A^2T_b/2N_0}\right)$ $= Q\left(\sqrt{E_b/N_0}\right)$: 3 dB worse than polar NRZ-L where $E_b = A^2T_b/2$ (see Figure 3).

NRZ-M and NRZ-S are modulated by a differentially encoded data sequence. The coded sequence is then differentially decoded back to the original data sequence. The current and previous bits of coded sequence are used to produce the current bit of the original sequence. Thus, the error probability, P_b', is (Xiong 2000)

$$P_b' = (1 - P_b)P_b + P_b(1 - P_b) = 2(1 - P_b)P_b$$
$$\approx 2P_b = 2Q\left(\sqrt{2E_b/N_0}\right) \quad \text{for small } P_b \tag{13}$$

Note that if the current bit is in error, then it and the next bit (because the current bit is used as a reference) will be erroneously decoded. Thus, in differential decoding, one

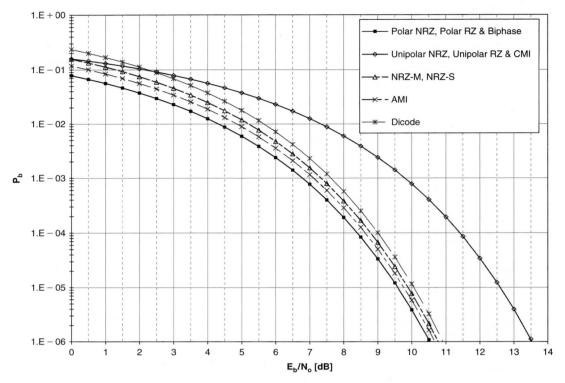

Figure 3: Probability of bit error

bit error affects two decoded bits (see Figure 3). However, the ambiguity in the reference bit will only affect the first decoded bit and, if desired, can be removed by agreeing on the reference bit in advance or by calculating the phase of the reference bit from a known transmitted sequence.

Power Spectral Density of NRZ Codes. NRZ-M and NRZ-S are generated by modulating the differentially encoded data sequences using the NRZ-L format. If the original binary data are equally likely, then the differentially encoded data are also equally likely—that is, statistical properties of the sequences used for modulation are the same for NRZ-L, NRZ-M, and NRZ-S. From the section on the probability of bit error and power spectral density, we know that if their pulse-shaping function is also the same, then the spectral densities are also the same because the power spectrum depends on the pulse shape used and the statistical properties of the data sequence.

NRZ formats' pulse-shaping function is a square pulse in $[0,T_b]$ seconds—that is,

$$g(t) = rect\left(\frac{1}{T_b}\right) = \begin{cases} 1 & 0 \le t \le T_b \\ 0 & else \end{cases} \tag{14}$$

$$\begin{aligned} G(f) &= T_b\left[\frac{\sin(\pi f T_b)}{\pi f T_b}\right]\exp(-j\pi f T_b) \\ &= T_b\text{sinc}(\pi f T_b)\exp(-j\pi f T_b) \end{aligned} \tag{15}$$

Because the data sequence is equally likely, the correlation function in Equation 9 becomes

$$R[n] = \begin{cases} (A)^2\dfrac{1}{2} + (-A)^2\dfrac{1}{2} = A^2 & n = 0 \\ (A)(A)\dfrac{1}{2}\dfrac{1}{2} + (-A)(-A)\dfrac{1}{2}\dfrac{1}{2} + 2(-A)(A)\dfrac{1}{2}\dfrac{1}{2} = 0 & n \ne 0 \end{cases} \tag{16}$$

Thus, the power spectral density is

$$S(f) = A^2 T_b\left[\frac{\sin(\pi f T_b)}{\pi f T_b}\right]^2 \tag{17}$$

From Equation 17, we can see that the spectral density is a squared sinc function with first null at $f T_b = 1$. The signal energy is concentrated around zero frequency, and null bandwidth, B_{null}, is R_b. Note that the power spectral density is a non-bandlimited function. There are various definitions of bandwidth, and the interested reader is referred to Benedetto and Biglieri (1999). In this chapter, the bandwidth referred to is always null to null.

In Figure 4, A is selected such that the normalized average power of the polar NRZ-L signal is one. To calculate A, assume that the transmitted sequence is periodic—that is, [1 0 1 0 1 0 ⋯]. It can then be easily shown that $A = 1$ satisfies the unity normalized average power constraint.

A DC component of $A/2$ volts is present in unipolar NRZ and appears as an impulse function, with a strength

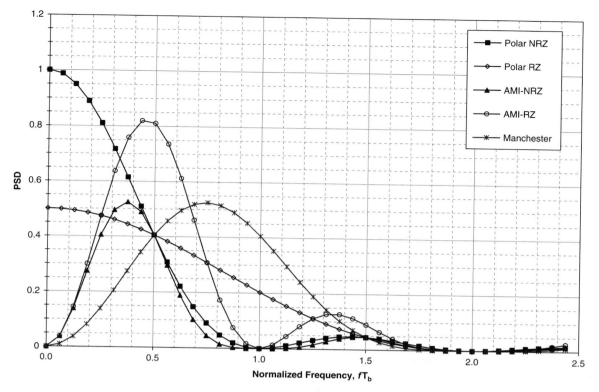

Figure 4: Power spectral density

$A^2/4$ watts at DC in the power spectrum. For equally likely data sequence the values of mean and variance are

$$\eta_a = E(a_k) = (A)\frac{1}{2} + (0)\frac{1}{2} = \frac{A}{2}$$

$$\sigma_a^2 = E[(a_k - \eta_a)^2] = (A - A/2)^2\frac{1}{2} + (0 - A/2)^2\frac{1}{2} = \frac{A^2}{4}$$

(18)

Thus, the power spectral density, from Equation 10, is

$$S(f) = \frac{A^2 T_b}{4}\left[\frac{\sin(\pi f T_b)}{\pi f T_b}\right]^2 + \frac{A^2}{4}\delta(f)$$

(19)

because the sinc function is zero at multiples of nR_b and exists only for $n = 0$. For $A = \sqrt{2}$, the normalized average power of the unipolar NRZ signal equals 1. Thus, the power spectra of polar NRZ and unipolar NRZ are the same with the only difference that the unipolar NRZ contains an impulse at DC corresponding to the nonzero mean of the signal.

Multiline Transmission, Three-Level Codes. The scheme of *multiline transmission, three-level* (MLT-3) codes is similar to NRZ-I, but it cycles through the three levels (+1, 0, and −1) to transmit a 1—that is, signal transitions from one level (say positive or zero or negative) to the next (say, zero, negative, or positive) at the beginning of 1 and stays at the same level for 0 (see Figure 5). This line coding technique is used in 100BaseT Ethernet ("Line code" undated).

Return-to-Zero Codes

The shortcoming of the NRZ family—lack of timing information—can be overcome by introducing more transitions in the waveform or trading self-synchronization capability for increased bandwidth. The receiver can use these transitions to update and synchronize its clock. To change with every bit, we need more than just two values. One solution is return-to-zero encoding, which uses three values: positive, negative, and zero. However, its disadvantage is that it uses a wider bandwidth than the NRZ waveform.

In polar RZ format, 1's and 0's are represented by positive and negative half-period pulses, respectively

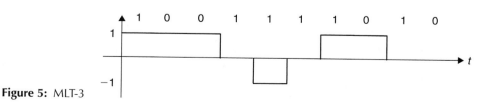

Figure 5: MLT-3

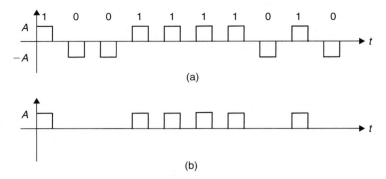

Figure 6: RZ waveforms—(a) polar, (b) unipolar

(see Figure 6a). This waveform ensures two transitions per bit and consequently has no DC component.

In the unipolar RZ format, a 1 is represented by a positive pulse for a half-bit period, which then returns to zero level for the next half period, resulting in a transition in the middle of the bit. A 0 is represented by the zero level for the entire bit period (see Figure 6b). A delta function (i.e., nonzero DC level) exists at $f = 0$, $\pm R_b$ in the power spectrum of the transmitted signal, which can be used for bit timing recovery at the receiver. However, the disadvantage of this code is that it requires 3 dB more power than polar RZ signaling for the same probability of symbol error. By making the sequence look more random (via scrambling), the long stream of 0's can be eliminated in the unipolar RZ scheme.

Bit Error Rate of RZ Codes. Polar RZ signals are:

$$s_1(t) = \begin{cases} +A & 0 \le t \le T_b/2 \\ 0 & else \end{cases} \tag{20}$$

$$s_2(t) = -s_1(t)$$

$\rho_{12} = -1$, $E_1 = E_2 = A^2T_b/2$, therefore polar RZ is antipodal and has the best performance with $P_b = Q\left(\sqrt{2E_b/N_0}\right)$. The average bit energy is

$$E_b = (E_1 + E_2)/2 = A^2T_b/2$$

For unipolar RZ:

$$s_1(t) = \begin{cases} +A & 0 \le t \le T_b/2 \\ 0 & else \end{cases} \tag{21}$$

$$s_2(t) = 0$$

$\rho_{12} = 0$, $E_1 = A^2T_b/2$, $E_2 = 0$ or $P_b = Q\left(\sqrt{A^2T_b/4N_0}\right)$ $= Q\left(\sqrt{E_b/N_0}\right)$: 3 dB worse performance than polar RZ with $E_b = A^2T_b$ (see Figure 3).

When the bit energy of unipolar RZ is the same as that of unipolar NRZ, the amplitude of the former must be $\sqrt{2}$ times that of the latter. However, if amplitudes are fixed, then unipolar NRZ will have twice the energy of unipolar; thus, its error probability is lower.

Power Spectral Density of RZ Codes. For RZ formats, the pulse-shaping function is a square pulse with half-bit duration—that is,

$$g(t) = rect\left(\frac{t}{T_b/2}\right) = \begin{cases} 1 & 0 \le t \le T_b/2 \\ 0 & else \end{cases} \tag{22}$$

$$G(f) = \frac{T_b}{2}\left[\frac{\sin(\pi f T_b/2)}{(\pi f T_b/2)}\right]\exp(-j\,\pi f T_b/2) \tag{23}$$

For an equally likely data sequence, the correlation function of the polar RZ signaling is the same as that for polar NRZ—that is,

$$R[n] = \begin{cases} A^2 & n = 0 \\ 0 & n \ne 0 \end{cases} \tag{24}$$

The power spectral density is

$$S(f) = \frac{A^2T_b}{4}\left[\frac{\sin(\pi f T_b/2)}{(\pi f T_b/2)}\right]^2 \tag{25}$$

As can be seen from Equation 25, the spectral density is a stretched version with frequency axis scaled up twice—that is, all bandwidths are double that of NRZ (i.e., the null bandwidth, B_{null}, is $2R_b$). The value of $A = \sqrt{2}$ makes the normalized average power of the polar RZ signal equal to 1 and has been used to plot the PSD in Figure 4.

For the unipolar RZ format, the pulse shape is the same as above in Equation 22. The data sequence, its mean, and its variance are same as those for unipolar NRZ (Equation 18). Thus, the power spectral density, after substituting Equation 23 into Equation 10, is

$$S(f) = \frac{A^2T_b}{16}\left[\frac{\sin(\pi f T_b/2)}{(\pi f T_b/2)}\right]^2 \times \left[1 + R_b \sum_{n=-\infty}^{\infty}\delta(f - nR_b)\right] \tag{26}$$

The value of $A = 2$ satisfies the constraint of unit normalized average power of the unipolar RZ signal. It can be easily seen from Equation 26 that the bandwidths are double those of the corresponding NRZ signal.

Pseudoternary Codes

The baseline or DC wander is caused by a slow decay in amplitude of a long string of 1's or 0's or whenever there is an imbalance in the number of 1's and 0's (Bellamy 2000). The impairment makes the receiver lose its reference to distinguish between the two levels and is a problem that can be solved through coding of transmitted data symbols—that is, a zero at DC is introduced in the spectrum by forcing the data symbols to be correlated. Moreover, the only way redundancy can be introduced without increasing the baud rate is by increasing the number of levels (Barry, Lee, and Messerschmitt 2003). In a pseudoternary line code, we use three-level data symbols to transmit one bit of information, which also helps reduce baseline wander. However, with these codes we also suffer a reduction in noise immunity because for the same peak power level, a smaller noise level causes an error (compared to biphase codes).

Three levels ($\pm A$, 0 volts) are used. The most popular, *alternate mark inversion* (AMI) codes, belong to this group. They are often called *bipolar codes* (Bellamy 2000).

In AMI-RZ format, a 1 is represented by an RZ pulse and consecutive 1's are represented with alternating polarities. A 0 is represented by the zero-level, hence an average voltage level of zero is maintained (see Figure 7a). In AMI-NRZ, coding rule is the same as AMI-RZ except that the symbol pulse has a full length of T_b — 100 percent duty cycle (see Figure 7b). The average level is still zero, but like unipolar RZ, the lack of transitions in a string of 0's causes synchronization problems.

Dicode NRZ and dicode RZ also belong to this group. These formats are also called *twinned binary* and encode the changes in a data sequence—that is, in dicode NRZ, a 1 to 0 transition or a 0 to 1 transition changes signal polarity. If the data remain constant, then a zero-voltage level is output (see Figure 7c). In dicode RZ, the same coding rule applies except that the pulse is only half-bit wide (see Figure 7d). Dicodes and AMI codes are related through differential coding (Xiong 2000).

These formats are used in baseband data transmission and magnetic recording. AMI-RZ formats are used in telemetry systems and are also being used by AT&T for T1 carrier systems.

Bit Error Rate of Pseudoternary Codes. The AMI-NRZ code consists of three types of signals:

$$
\begin{aligned}
H_1 &: s_1(t) = A & 0 \le t \le T_b & \quad p_1 = 1/4 & \textit{Transmit 1} \\
H_2 &: s_2(t) = -A & 0 \le t \le T_b & \quad p_2 = 1/4 & \textit{Transmit 1} \\
H_3 &: s_3(t) = 0 & 0 \le t \le T_b & \quad p_3 = 1/2 & \textit{Transmit 0}
\end{aligned}
\tag{27}
$$

The probability of bit error in AWGN is given by the following expression:

$$
\begin{aligned}
P_b &= p_1 \Pr(error|s_1) + p_2 \Pr(error|s_2) + p_3 \Pr(error|s_3) \\
&= p_1 \int_{-\infty}^{-A/2} f_N(n|s_1)dn + p_2 \int_{A/2}^{\infty} f_N(n|s_2)dn + 2p_3 \int_{A/2}^{\infty} f_N(n|s_3)dn \\
&= 2p_1 \int_{-\infty}^{-A/2} f(n|s_1)dn + 2p_3 \int_{A/2}^{\infty} f(n|s_3)dn \\
&= \frac{1}{2}Q\left[\frac{A}{2\sigma_n}\right] + Q\left[\frac{A}{2\sigma_n}\right] = \frac{3}{2}Q\left[\frac{A}{2\sigma_n}\right]
\end{aligned}
\tag{28}
$$

For the matched filter receiver, the above probability of error becomes (Couch 2001)

$$
P_b = \frac{3}{2}Q\left[\sqrt{\frac{2E_b}{N_0}}\right]
\tag{29}
$$

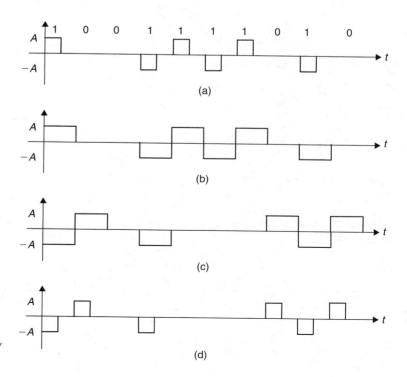

Figure 7: Pseudoternary waveforms—(a) AMI-RZ, (b) AMI-NRZ, (c) dicode NRZ, (d) dicode RZ

For AMI-RZ, the same error performance, as in Equation 29, is obtained (Couch 2001) (see Figure 3). Dicodes and AMI are related via differential encoding. Thus, similar to NRZ-M and NRZ-S, the probability of bit error for the dicode is twice the bit error probability of its AMI counterparts (Xiong 2000).

Power Spectral Density of Pseudoternary Codes.
For AMI codes, the data sequence takes on three values:

$$a_k = \begin{cases} +A & binary\,1 & p_A = 1/4 \\ -A & binary\,1 & p_{-A} = 1/4 \\ 0 & binary\,0 & p_0 = 1/2 \end{cases} \tag{30}$$

$$R[0] = E(a_k^2) = \frac{1}{4}(A)^2 + \frac{1}{4}(-A)^2 + \frac{1}{4}(0)^2 = \frac{A^2}{2} \tag{31}$$

Adjacent bits are correlated because of alternate mark inversion. An adjacent bit pattern in the original binary sequence must be one of these: (1,1), (1,0), (0,1), and (0,0). The possible values of product $a_k a_{k+1}$ are: $-A^2$, 0, 0, and 0, and each has a probability of 0.25. Thus,

$$R[1] = E(a_k a_{k+1}) = \frac{1}{4}(A)(-A) + \frac{1}{4}(0) + \frac{1}{4}(0) + \frac{1}{4}(0) = -\frac{A^2}{4} \tag{32}$$

When $n > 1$, $a_k a_{k+n}$ are uncorrelated. Possible values of product $a_k a_{k+n}$ are $\pm A^2$, 0, 0, and 0, and each occurs with a probability of 0.25 (Couch 2001). Thus,

$$R[n > 1] = E(a_k a_{k+n}) = \frac{1}{8}(+A)(+A) + \frac{1}{8}(+A)(-A) = 0$$

$$R[n] = \begin{cases} A^2/2 & n = 0 \\ -A^2/4 & |n| = 1 \\ 0 & |n| > 1 \end{cases} \tag{33}$$

Thus, the power spectral density for AMI-RZ is

$$\begin{aligned} S(f) &= \frac{1}{T_b}|G(f)|^2 \left[\frac{1}{2} - \frac{1}{4}\exp(j\omega T_b) - \frac{1}{4}\exp(-j\omega T_b) \right] \\ &= \frac{1}{T_b}|G(f)|^2 \left[\frac{1}{2} - \frac{1}{2}\cos(\omega T_b) \right] \\ &= \frac{A^2 T_b}{4} \left[\frac{\sin(\pi f T_b/2)}{(\pi f T_b/2)} \right]^2 \sin^2(\pi f T_b) \end{aligned} \tag{34}$$

For $A = 2$, the normalized average power of the AMI-RZ signal is 1. The null bandwidth, B_{null}, is R_b (see Figure 4).

The power spectral density of AMI-NRZ can be obtained by replacing $T_b/2$ with T_b in $G(f)$ of AMI-RZ because both of them have the same coding rules; the only difference is in the pulse width. Thus,

$$S(f) = \frac{A^2 T_b}{2} \left[\frac{\sin(\pi f T_b)}{\pi f T_b} \right]^2 \sin^2(\pi f T_b) \tag{35}$$

a value of $A = \sqrt{2}$ satisfies the normalized average power constraint of unity. The null bandwidth, B_{null}, is R_b. Note that the bandwidths of AMI-RZ and AMI-NRZ are the same.

Dicodes can be constructed using AMI rules and a differentially encoded sequence—that is,

$$s(t) = \sum_{k=-\infty}^{\infty} d_k g(t - kT) \tag{36}$$

where $\{d_k\}$ is the pseudoternary sequence derived from the original data sequence $\{a_k\}$ and is

$$d_k = a_{k-1} - a_k = \begin{cases} +1 & binary\,1 & p_1 = 1/4 \\ -1 & binary\,1 & p_{-1} = 1/4 \\ 0 & binary\,0 & p_0 = 1/2 \end{cases} \tag{37}$$

Thus, the power spectral density of dicodes is the same as those of AMI; therefore, the bandwidth is also the same (Xiong 2000).

Substitution Codes
The AMI code is a preferred choice because of its (1) narrow bandwidth, (2) lack of DC component, (3) error-detection capability (resulting from alternate mark inversion), (4) ease in synchronization (because of transitions in each binary 1 bit), and (5) absence of DC wander (because of inefficient use of the ternary code space). However, a string of 0's will result in a long period of zero level that will cause loss of synchronization. This problem results from the linearity of the AMI code because linearity implies that an all-zero bit sequence is translated into a zero signal. The solution to this problem is therefore to modify the line code and make it nonlinear. One way to alleviate this problem is to substitute the long string of zeros with a special sequence with intentional bipolar violations that can be readily detected and consequently replaced at the receiver. Two popular zero substitution families are considered in this section: (1) binary N-zero substitution (BNZS) and (2) high-density bipolar N (HDBN). These codes have been used in T1 carrier systems.

Binary N-Zero Substitution Codes.
The BNZS code modifies AMI by performing a substitution for a block of N consecutive zeros. The substituted block, which contains one or more positive or negative pulses to ensure timing recovery, takes advantage of the fact that only 2^{N+1} patterns of N transmitted symbols are allowed by AMI and therefore substitutes one of the nonallowed blocks for the all-zeros block. At the receiver, this nonallowed block is readily detected and replaced with the all-zero bit block (Barry, Lee, and Messerschmitt 2003).

All BNZS formats have no DC component and retain the balanced feature of AMI. There are two kinds of BNZS codes: (1) nonmodal and (2) modal.

In nonmodal code, two substitution sequences are allowed, and the choice among them is based solely on the polarity of the pulse immediately preceding the zeros to be replaced. Substitution sequences must contain an equal number of positive and negative pulses to maintain

DC balance. The substitution sequences may also contain zeros. For nonmodal codes, N must be at least 4 (Xiong 2000). Some practical balanced nonmodal codes are B6ZS and B8ZS. For example, in the B6ZS case, if the polarity of the pulse preceding the six zeros is negative ($-$), then the sequence to be substituted is $0 - + 0 + -$ whereas if the polarity of the pulse preceding the six zeros is positive ($+$), then the suggested substitution sequence is $0 + - 0 - +$ (Bellamy 2000). Thus, the polarity of the pulse immediately preceding the six zeros and the polarity of the last pulse in the sequence to be substituted is the same. For B8ZS, the two substitution sequences corresponding to a negative and positive pulse, preceding the eight zeros, are $0\,0\,0 - + 0 + -$ and $0\,0\,0 + - 0 - +$, respectively (Bellamy 2000).

In the modal case, more than two substitution sequences are provided, and the choice of the sequences is based on the polarity of pulse immediately preceding the zeros to be replaced as well as the previous substitution sequence used. For modal codes, N is 2 or 3 (Xiong 2000). Modal code substitution sequences need not be balanced, and balance is achieved by properly alternating the sequences. A block of $0\,0\,0$ is replaced by $B\,0\,V$ or $0\,0\,V$, where B represents a normal bipolar alternation that conforms to AMI rule, V represents bipolar violation, and 0 represents no pulse. If the polarity of the pulse preceding the three zeros, is negative (positive) and the number of bipolar pulses since last substitution is odd, then replace $0\,0\,0$ with $0\,0\,V$. However, if the preceding pulse is negative (positive) and if the number of 1's since last substitution is even, then replace $0\,0\,0$ by $B\,0\,V$ (see Figure 8). In a long-time average, the polarity of these extra pulses will cancel each other so that there will be no DC component.

B3ZS and B6ZS are specified for DS-3 and DS-2, respectively, and B8ZS is specified as an alternative to AMI for DS-1.

No results of bit error probability of BNZS codes are available in the literature. They are conditioned AMI codes, therefore their bit error probabilities must be quite close to those of AMI codes (Xiong 2000).

The power spectrum calculation for BNZS codes is based on a flow graph of the pulse states and is quite involved. Moreover, the spectrum depends on the substitution sequence used and the statistical property of the data sequence. The interested reader is referred to (Xiong 2000) and (Bellamy 2000).

High-Density Bipolar N Codes.

High-density bipolar N codes limit the number of consecutive 0's to N by replacing the $(N+1)$th zero by a bipolar violation. Moreover, to avoid a DC component, the code is made modal. Substitution sequences are (Xiong 2000)

$$HDB: B\,0\,0 \cdots 0\ V \text{ or } 0\,0\,0 \cdots 0\ V \qquad (38)$$

In HDB3 line coding, strings of greater than three zeros are excluded. The coding algorithm is similar to the B3ZS algorithm described in the previous section. If the polarity of the pulse preceding the three zeros is negative (positive) and the number of bipolar pulses since last substitution is odd, then replace $0\,0\,0\,0$ by $0\,0\,0\,V$. However, if the preceding pulse is negative (positive) and if the number of 1's since last substitution is even, then replace $0\,0\,0\,0$ with $B\,0\,0\,V$ (see Figure 9).

Two commonly used HDBN codes are HDB2 and HDB3. HDB2 is identical to B3ZS. HDB3 is used for coding of 2.048, 8.448, and 34.368 Mbps streams within the European digital hierarchy.

Biphase Codes

With the help of substitution codes, the pseudoternary family of codes gains self-synchronizing capability. However, this comes at a price: not the bandwidth (NRZ-L has the same bandwidth) but the increased code space (from binary to ternary). The pseudoternary family does not use the code space efficiently. It will be seen in the section on multilevel block line codes that the code efficiency of AMI is only 63 percent; to achieve higher code efficiencies, the input block size will have to be increased. The desirable characteristics (error detection, self-synchronizing, and lack of DC wander capabilities) of pseudoternary codes can be achieved with binary codes but at the expense of bandwidth. The biphase family of codes uses one cycle of square wave to represent 1's and its opposite phase to represent 0's. The most famous code belonging to this family is the biphase level, which is better known as *Manchester* (or *diphase* or *split-phase*). The Manchester encoding signal is shown in Figure 10a. Note that the pulse shapes for 0 and 1 are arbitrary and can be exchanged. For Manchester encoding, the signal contains strong timing components because a transition is present in the center of each bit interval. Moreover, the positive and negative polarities of 0 and 1 are equal, therefore there is no DC wander. The only drawback—besides twice the bandwidth, which makes it vulnerable to near-end cross-talk and ISI (Barry, Lee, and Messerschmitt 2003)—is that it has no error-detection capability.

In the *biphase-mark code*, a transition is always present at the beginning of each bit. For a 1, there is a second transition in the middle of the bit, while there is no second transition for a 0—that is, it is encoded as a level

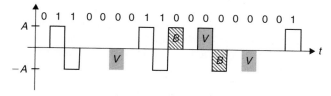

Figure 8: B3ZS-coded waveform

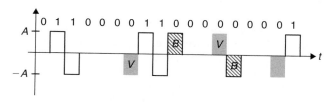

Figure 9: HDB3-coded waveform

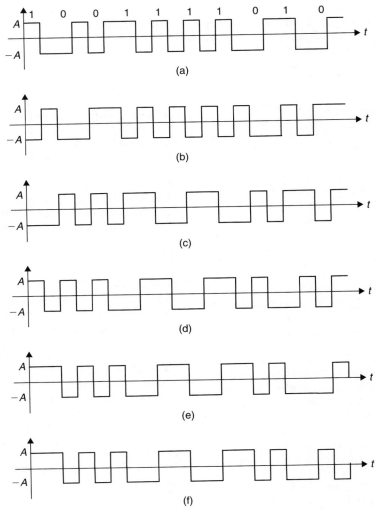

Figure 10: Biphase waveforms—(a) biphase-L, (b) biphase-M, (c) biphase-S, (d) differential biphase, (e) CMI, (f) DMI

(see Figure 10b). In the *biphase-space code*, the opposite coding rule applies (see Figure 10c). Because there is at least a transition in each bit interval, the codes contain adequate timing information.

Conditioned biphase level is differentially encoded biphase-L and is also referred to as *differential Manchester*. Like all differentially encoded signals, the information resides in signal transitions—that is, a change in level—at the beginning of the bit interval, from the preceding one, which indicates that a 0 was transmitted; whereas absence of a transition means a 1 was sent (see Figure 10d). Because data are differentially encoded, this format is also immune from polarity reversals. The biphase-S is identical to Differential Manchester if the zero reference of the former is changed by half a bit.

The *code mark inversion* (CMI) code is a combination of the AMI-NRZ and Manchester. It is similar to AMI-NRZ because 1's are alternately encoded as A or $-A$ volts. It is related to Manchester because a 0 is represented by a half-cycle square wave of a particular phase, such as level A volts for first half bit and $-A$ volts for second half bit, or vice versa (see Figure 10e). The signal has no energy at

DC, and the transition density over AMI-NRZ is improved significantly. Error detection is possible by monitoring occurrence of alternating 1's. There is no ambiguity between 1's and 0's. The technique is insensitive to polarity reversals because decoding is possible by simply comparing the second half of the bit with the first half.

The *differential mode inversion* (DMI) code is again a combination of AMI-NRZ and Manchester. Its coding rule for 1's is the same as that of CMI. However, its coding rule for 0's is different: $0 \rightarrow -A, A$ or $0 \rightarrow A, -A$ so that no pulses in a sequence have pulse widths wider than the bit duration (see Figure 10f).

To be used for digital subscriber loops, the power spectrum of the transmitted signal should (1) be zero at zero frequency because no DC transmission passes through a hybrid transformer and (2) be low at high frequencies because transmission attenuation in a twisted pair is most severe at high frequencies and between adjacent twisted pairs increases dramatically at high frequencies because of increased capacitive coupling (Haykin 2004).

The biphase code is a good choice where implementation simplicity is desirable and the distance between transmitter and receiver is modest, as in a *local area network* (LAN). The biphase family has been used in magnetic recording, optical communications, and in some satellite telemetry links. The Ethernet or IEEE 802.3 standard for LAN uses Manchester coding. Differential Manchester has been used for IEEE 802.5 standard for token ring, using either baseband coaxial cable or twisted-pair. Because it uses differential coding and is immune to polarity inversions, differential Manchester is preferred for a twisted-pair channel. CMI has been chosen for coding of 139.246 Mbps multiplex within the European digital hierarchy.

Bit Error Rate of Biphase Codes. Biphase-L signals are antipodal with

$$
s_1(t) = \begin{cases} +A & 0 \le t \le T_b/2 \\ -A & T_b/2 \le t \le T_b \end{cases}
$$

$$
s_2(t) = -s_1(t)
$$

(39)

$\rho_{12} = -1$, $E_1 = E_2 = A^2 T_b = E_b$, and therefore the probability of error is $P_b = Q\left(\sqrt{2A^2 T_b/N_0}\right) = Q\left(\sqrt{2E_b/N_0}\right)$, which is the same as NRZ-L because both have the same average bit energy and are antipodal (see Figure 3).

Conditioned biphase-L has a bit error probability approximately two times that of biphase-L because it is just differentially encoded biphase-L.

The error performance of CMI is 3 dB worse than Manchester signaling when bit-by-bit detection is used (Bellamy 2000):

$$
P_b \approx Q\left(\sqrt{\frac{E_b}{N_0}}\right)
$$

(40)

This error performance is the same as that of unipolar codes (see Figure 3). For details, see Xiong (2000). Improved performance can be obtained by using maximum likelihood Viterbi decoding (Bellamy 2000).

Power Spectral Density of Biphase Codes. For biphase-L, the pulse shape is half-positive and half-negative—that is,

$$
g(t) = \begin{cases} 1 & 0 \le t \le T_b/2 \\ -1 & T_b/2 \le t \le T_b \\ 0 & else \end{cases}
$$

(41)

$$
G(f) = T_b\left[\frac{\sin(\pi f T_b/2)}{(\pi f T_b/2)}\right]\sin(\pi f T_b/2)\exp(-j\pi f T_b)
$$

(42)

The correlation of the data sequence is

$$
R[n] = \begin{cases} (A)^2\dfrac{1}{2} + (-A)^2\dfrac{1}{2} = A^2 & n = 0 \\ (A)(A)\dfrac{1}{2}\dfrac{1}{2} + (-A)(-A)\dfrac{1}{2}\dfrac{1}{2} + 2(A)(-A)\dfrac{1}{2}\dfrac{1}{2} = 0 & n \ne 0 \end{cases}
$$

(43)

Thus, the power spectral density is

$$
S(f) = A^2 T_b\left[\frac{\sin(\pi f T_b/2)}{\pi f T_b/2}\right]^2 \sin^2(\pi f T_b/2)
$$

(44)

For $A = 1$, the normalized average power constraint of unity is satisfied (see Figure 4). The power spectrum of conditioned biphase-L is the same as that of the biphase-L because it is merely a differentially encoded biphase-L, and differential encoding does not change the probability density function of equally likely data.

Although biphase-M and biphase-S use different waveforms to encode data, they have the same power spectrum if marks and spaces are equally likely in a data sequence. Note that their waveforms are close to that of biphase-L in terms of pulse shapes and number of transitions (biphase-S is differentially encoded biphase-L if the zero reference is shifted by half a bit for the former), therefore their power spectrum is the same as that of biphase-L.

Multilevel Block Line Codes

In a block code, k bits are mapped into n data symbols drawn from an alphabet of size L with the constraint

$$
2^k \le L^n
$$

(45)

When equality is not met, there is available redundancy that can be used to accomplish desirable goals such as minimizing baseline wander or providing energy for timing.

Two basic techniques used in block coding are (1) translation of a block of input bits to a block of output symbols that uses more than two levels per symbol or (2) insertion of additional binary pulses to create a block of n binary symbols that is longer than the number of information bits m. The first technique applies to cases in which bandwidth is limited but multilevel transmission is possible, such as metallic wires used for digital subscriber loops. The second technique is mainly used in optical transmission where modulation is limited to two levels (on-off, optical sources and detectors operate in a nonlinear mode) but can withstand a small increase in transmission rate because a wide bandwidth is available. All basic line codes can be viewed as special cases of block codes.

Ternary *kB*n*T* Codes

This is a class of codes that maps k binary bits into n ternary symbols, where $n < k$. AMI can be considered as 1B1T code.

The efficiency of a block code is the ratio of the actual information rate to theoretical maximum information rate. NRZ encodes one bit into a 1-binary encoded symbol, therefore its efficiency is $\log_2(2)/\log_2(2) = 1$. AMI encodes one bit into a 1-ternary symbol, therefore its efficiency is $\log_2(2)/\log_2(3) = 0.63$. Manchester encodes one bit into two binary symbols, therefore its efficiency is $\log_2(2)/[2 \times \log_2(2)] = 0.5$.

AMI and its derivative pseudoternary codes (dicode RZ and dicode NRZ) transmit only one bit per symbol whereas the capacity of a ternary symbol is $\log_2(3) = 1.58$ bits.

Table 1: Efficiency of $kBnT$ Codes

k	1	3	4	6	7
n	1	2	3	4	5
$\eta = \dfrac{k \log_2(2)}{n \log_2(3)}$	0.63	0.95	0.84	0.95	0.89
	1B1T	3B2T	4B3T	6B4T	7B5T

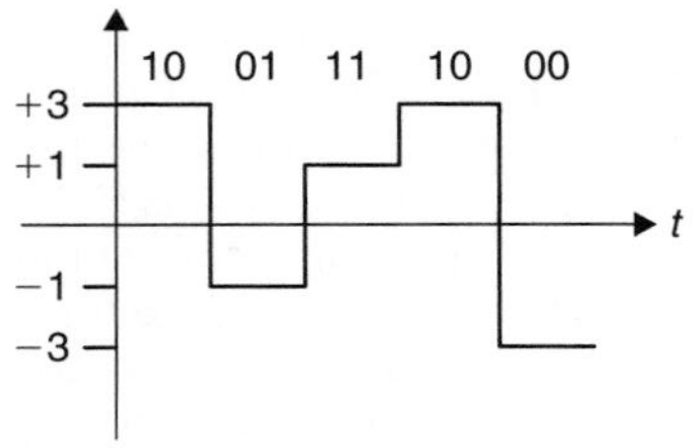

Figure 11: The 2B1Q waveform

Moreover, little control over the power spectrum is provided. A much broader class of pseudoternary codes—the $kBnT$ codes, where k is the number of information bits and n is the number of ternary symbols per block—addresses these shortcomings. If we choose the largest k possible for each n, we get a table of possible codes (up to $k = 7$) (see Table 1).

As the block size increases, we generally achieve greater efficiency. Greater efficiency implies better noise immunity on many channels, because it translates into a lower symbol (baud) rate for a given bit rate and hence a reduced noise bandwidth. However, greater efficiency also implies reduced redundancy, and hence less control over the statistics of transmitted signal (power spectrum, timing recovery, density of 1's, etc.). The 4B3T code seems to be a reasonable compromise between these competing goals and hence has been used widely in digital subscriber loop applications.

The 4B3T Code. This code maps a combination of four bits to twenty-seven possible combinations of three ternary digits. The ternary sequence 000 is not used, but all other combinations are used. The code uses three codebooks; a codebook defines a mapping between bit patterns of input and output for an encoder. The three codebooks contain words that are biased toward positive polarity, negatively biased, or neutral. The algebraic sum of recently transmitted symbols, also known as the *digital sum* or *disparity*, determines which codebook is to be used. If disparity is positive, then code words from the negatively biased codebook are selected and vice versa. If disparity is neutral, then code words from the neutral codebook are selected. This ensures that the transmitted code has zero DC content.

For the 4B3T line code, the power spectral density depends on the selection of a particular codebook. Multiple choices of codebooks exist because sixteen information bits can be mapped to twenty-seven different ternary codes in a variety of ways.

The 4B3T coding is used on T148 span lines developed by ITT Telecommunications (Bellamy 2000).

The 8B6TCode. The 8B6T code substitutes an eight-bit group with a six-symbol ternary code. Eight bits can represent 256 possibilities; a six-symbol ternary signal can represent 729 possibilities—that is, some codes are not used. Thus, a code can be designed that can maintain synchronization and also has error checking capability. This code is used in 100 Mbps Ethernet (Moloney 2005).

Quaternary Code: 2B1Q. In this code, binary data are mapped into one of four levels. The disadvantage with multilevel signaling is that it requires greater SNR for a given error rate. Thus, the 2B1Q code represents a four-level pulse amplitude modulated signal (see Figure 11). Assuming 1 and 0 are equiprobable, the 2B1Q code has zero DC on the average. The signaling baud rate is half of the bit rate. It offers the greatest baud reduction and the best performance with respect to near-end cross talk and ISI. It is because of this desirable property that the 2B1Q code has been adopted as the North American standard for digital subscriber loops ("Line code" undated).

The power spectrum of the 2B1Q code is given by Chen (1998):

$$S(f) = \frac{5}{9} T_{2B1Q,baud\ rate} \left[\frac{\sin(\pi f T_b)}{\pi f T_b} \right]^2 \qquad (46)$$

CODES FOR OPTICAL FIBER SYSTEMS

Line codes used in optical fiber systems should also satisfy the requirements that are desired for basic line codes (see the previous "Basic Line Codes for Wireline Systems"). Because the optical sources and detectors operate in nonlinear mode, the best suited line code is the one that has two levels: unipolar scrambled (or randomized) NRZ-L or on-off keying. Because there is plenty of bandwidth available (no advantage is gained by using multilevel signaling) in optical fiber systems, the inherent disadvantage of a lack of timing information in the line code can be overcome by including extra timing transitions for a small bandwidth penalty. Moreover, there is no polarity ambiguity in direct detection optical receivers, therefore resorting to differential encoding is unnecessary. The DC level of the line code affects the gain of some photodiodes. However, it is easy to control variations in the DC level in an optical system than in a wireline system, so for optical fiber the line codes should be DC-constrained instead of DC-balanced.

In intensity modulated practical optical fiber communication systems, a symbol is represented by the optical source's light intensity, therefore AMI cannot be used in such systems because it uses three levels (-1 for off, 0 for half intensity, and $+1$ for full intensity) and thus suffers from nonlinearity of the source. However, in phase modulated optical fiber communication systems, optical AMI has been implemented by coding the phase of light with π phase difference to achieve the coding of $+1$ and -1. When high data speed is not a requirement, then Manchester or CMI codes are used in optical fibers. When CMI is used for optical transmission, two levels of $\pm A$ are replaced by A and 0—that is, the code waveform is unipolar. This unipolar CMI has the same spectral shape as polar CMI with the only difference that the spectrum has a DC component. Unipolar DMI is also used in optical transmission systems (Xiong 2000).

Just as with wireline systems, block coding can also be used in optical fiber transmission systems. The m information bits are mapped to a block of n binary symbols where $n > m$. The additional pulses can be selected such that timing content is increased in the block line code. The modulation of choice is binary because the optical sources and devices operate in the nonlinear mode.

The mBnB Block Codes

Transitions in a data stream can be ensured by scrambling (or randomizing) the long string of zeros. The same goal can be achieved by introducing *redundancy*. Redundancy not only gives flexibility over controlling timing and DC wander but also aids in detecting errors. Block coding to some extent achieves these two goals.

A special case of block codes occurs when $L = 2$, which means we transmit a binary signal. For this case, we have the simpler constraint $k \le n$—in other words, we must transmit a block of n bits that is larger than the number of bits k at the input to the line coder. These codes are useful for media such as optical fiber that prefer to operate in one of the two states (on or off) and for which the additional bandwidth required is easier to achieve.

One primary motivation in the design of line codes has been the elimination of the DC content of the coded signal because of AC coupling of the medium. It might appear that this problem goes away for media such as optical fiber and magnetic recording because there are no transformers required. However, this is not really the case because it is especially difficult to build DC-coupled high-speed electronics for preamplification and so forth (Barry, Lee, and Messerschmitt 2003).

When $n > m + 1$, because of decoding logic or a small look-up table, it is difficult to implement these codes in high-speed transmission systems. For $n = m + 1$, the mB $(m + 1)$B codes are known as *bit-insertion codes* and are popular in high-speed fiber optical transmission because of its simple codec design. However, to increase code efficiency, a large m (greater than 1) must be chosen.

The 2B3B DC-Constrained Code.

This code constrains rather than suppresses the DC component and thus makes it possible to use redundancy for error detection. Data bits 1 and 0 are converted to $+$ and $-$, respectively. Then a third symbol $+$ or $-$ is added to make combinations of one $+$ and two $-$'s. The code produces a constant DC component of $-1/3$ (Xiong 2000).

The 4B5B Code.

With a four-bit input block, we can have sixteen different groups. With a five-bit code, we can have thirty-two possible codes. This means we can map some of the five-bit groups to four-bit groups. Some of the five-bit codes are not used. We can employ a strategy to choose only the five-bit codes that help us in synchronization and error detection. To achieve synchronization, we can use the five-bit codes in such a way that we do not have more than three consecutive 0's or 1's—that is, select five-bit codes that contain no more than one leading 0 and no more than two trailing 0's. Because only a subset of five-bit codes are used, if one or more of the bits in the block is changed in such a way that one of the unused codes is received, the receiver can easily detect the error. After substitution, we can use one of the basic wireline line coding techniques discussed above to create a signal. This code is used for Ethernet 100 Mbps and *fiber distributed data interface* over optical fiber (Moloney 2005). The 4B5B code increases the line rate by 25 percent. CMI and biphase (1B2B codes) increase the line rate by 100 percent.

The 7B8B code is being used in a 565-Mbps terrestrial system being developed by British Telecom and in a 280-Mbps NL1 submarine system being developed by STC of Great Britain.

The Carter Code (8B9B).

This code was proposed for PCM systems. The eight-digit character is transmitted either unchanged or with the digits inverted (i.e., marks for spaces and spaces for marks), depending on which condition will reduce total disparity (the numerical sum of symbols in the sequence) since the start of transmission. Thus, the DC component will be zero over a long period. The efficiency of the Carter code is 0.9464.

The m B1P Code.

This code inserts an odd parity bit after every m bits. Odd parity ensures that there is a 1 in every $m + 1$ bits. A Manchester signal is a 1B1P signal. The 24B1P line code is being used in the trans-Pacific submarine cable (TPC-3) system.

The m B1C Code.

In the coding process, a complementary bit (i.e., complement to the last bit of the block) is inserted at the end of every block of m information bits. The maximum number of consecutive identical symbols is $m + 1$, which occurs when the inserted bit and m succeeding bits are the same. The Manchester code is a degenerate case of the 1B1C code (Bellamy 2000). The code has been adopted by Nippon Telegraph and Telephone (NTT) in its F-1.6G optical system in the form of 10B1C.

CONCLUSION

Based on the coding rules, the simplest of all line codes is the NRZ family. The NRZ signal occupies a narrow bandwidth, but it lacks other desired characteristics such as adequate timing content, error-detection capability, and lower signal energy near low frequencies. Timing content is increased in the RZ-coded signal by allowing more transitions at the expense of the signal bandwidth. The RZ-coded signals, however, still have substantial energy near DC, which also make them unsuitable for AC-coupled circuits. The three-level pseudoternary codes provide the same timing information as RZ-coded signals but in a narrower bandwidth. Their spectra have no DC components, and near-DC components are small, also making the codes suitable for transmission on AC-coupled circuits. Their performance, however, is worse than polar NRZ

Table 2: Line Codes and Digital Systems

Code	Digital system
Non-return to zero	Digital logic and short-haul telecommunication links
Differential NRZ	Magnetic tape recording
Multiline transmission-3	100baseT Ethernet
Alternate mark inversion	Telemetry systems, especially AT&T T1 carrier systems
Binary N zero substitution	DS1 ($N = 8$), DS2 ($N = 6$), and DS3 ($N = 3$)
High-density bipolar 3	European digital hierarchy: E2, E3, and E4
Biphase (1B1C or 1B2B)	Local area network
Differential biphase	IEEE 802.5 token ring
Code mark inversion (1B2B)	139.246-Mbps European digital hierarchy
4B3T	T148 span line
8B6T	100-Mbps Ethernet
2B1Q	Digital subscriber loops
Optical Fiber Systems	
4B5B	100-Mbps Ethernet and FDDI over optical fiber
7B8B	565-Mbps system of British Telecom
8B9B	Pulse coded modulation
24B1P	Trans-Pacific submarine cable (TPC-3)
10B1C	F-1.6 G optical by NTT

signals. Substitution codes can be used in conjunction with pseudoternary codes to alleviate the latter's timing recovery problem if a long string of zeros occurs. The biphase codes occupy the same bandwidth as the RZ-coded signals, but their spectra contain no DC or very small near-DC components. Their error performance is no better than the NRZ-coded signals. The diphase code contains ample timing recovery information because it contains at least one transition per symbol; this property makes it widely used. However, the AMI family of codes is more suitable for band-limited channels and is therefore preferred over diphase. The block line codes add redundancy, which aids in error detection and benefits timing recovery. However, the disadvantage is that the transmission rate is increased and should only be used on channels where bandwidth availability is not an issue. Block codes are not limited to only binary: Multilevel block codes increase the efficiency of the line codes, reduce bandwidth requirements, and can be designed to have a zero or constant DC component. Finally, the binary block codes that are easier to encode and decode—for example, bit-insertion block codes—are more suitable for optical transmission systems because the devices operate in the nonlinear mode.

Table 2 lists digital systems where the aforementioned line codes are being used.

GLOSSARY

Alternate mark inversion (AMI): A bipolar line coding technique that uses three levels—positive, negative,

and zero—and is the most widely used technique because it has good spectral characteristics, better error-detection capability, and superior timing recovery ability compared to other line codes.

Binary N zero substitution (BNZS): A line coding technique that replaces a string of N zeros by another sequence that is readily detected and replaced at the receiver by an all-zeros sequence.

Biphase codes: A line coding technique that uses half-period pulses with different phases. Manchester or diphase or split phase codes belong to this family.

Bipolar: A line coding technique that uses three levels: positive, negative, and zero.

Codebook: A codebook defines mapping between input and output bit patterns of an encoder.

Code mark inversion (CMI): A line coding technique that replaces the zero level in the AMI waveform by two levels: $+A$ for first half bit duration and $-A$ for the second half bit duration or vice versa.

High-density bipolar N (HDB N): A line coding technique that limits the number of consecutive zeros to N by replacing the $(N + 1)$th zero by a bipolar violation.

kBnT codes: A family of line code that maps k binary digits into n ternary symbols, where $n < k$. AMI is a 1B1T code.

Line coding: The process of converting the binary digits to waveforms that are suitable for transmission over the baseband channel.

mBnB codes: This family of line codes converts a block of m binary digits into a block of n binary digits, where $m < n$. CMI and DMI are 1B2B codes.

Non-return to zero (NRZ): A line coding technique in which the signal does not return to zero during the duration of the bit.

Pseudoternary (PT): A line coding technique that uses three-level data symbols to transmit one bit of information. AMI codes also belong to this group and these are also called *bipolar codes*.

Return to zero (RZ): A line coding technique in which the signal returns to zero during the duration of the bit.

Unipolar: A line coding technique that uses only one signal level for bit representation in addition to zero.

CROSS REFERENCES

See *Digital Communications Basics*; *Digital Phase Modulation and Demodulation*; *Optical Fiber Communications*.

REFERENCES

Barry, J. R., E. A. Lee, and D. G. Messerschmitt. 2003. *Digital communication*. New York: Springer.

Bellamy, J. C. 2000. *Digital telephony*. New York: John Wiley & Sons.

Benedetto, S., and E. Biglieri. 1999. *Principles of digital transmission with wireless applications*. Norwell, MA: Kluwer Academic.

Chen, W. Y. 1998. *Simulation techniques and standards development for digital subscriber line systems*. New York: Macmillan Technical Publishing.

Couch, L. W. 2001. *Digital and analog communication systems*. Upper Saddle River, NJ: Prentice Hall.

Haykin, S. 2004. *Communication systems*. New York: John Wiley & Sons.

Line code. Undated. (Retrieved from www.answers.com/topic/line-coding.)

Moloney, A. 2005. Line coding (retrieved from www.electronics.dit.ie/staff/amoloney/dt021_4/lecture-9.pdf).

Simon, M. K., S, M. Hinedi, and W. C. Lindsey. 1995. *Digital modulation techniques: Signal design and detection*. Upper Saddle River, NJ: Prentice Hall.

Xiong, F. 2000. *Digital modulation techniques*. Boston: Artech House Publishers.

FURTHER READING

The following reading list includes the original sources for those who are interested in learning more about the history of line codes.

4B3T Code

Waters, D. B. 1983. Line codes for metallic systems. *International Journal on Electronics*, 55: 159–69.

Binary N Zero Substitution

Johannes, V. I., A. G. Kaim, and T. Walzman. 1969. Bipolar pulse transmission with zero extraction. *IEEE Transactions on Communications*, 17: 303–10.

Carter Code

Carter, R. O. 1965. Low disparity binary coding system. *Electronic Letters*, 1(3): 67.

CMI and 2B3B DC-Constrained Code

Takasaki, Y., M. Tanaka, N. Maeda, K. Yamashita, and K. Nagano. 1976. Optical pulse formats for fiber optic digital communications. *IEEE Transactions on Communications*, 24: 404–13.

Dicode

Aaron, M. R. 1962. PCM transmission in the exchange plant. *Bell System Technical Journal*, 14(99): 99–141.

Dicode and High-Density Bipolar N Codes

Croisier, A. 1970. Introduction to pseudoternary transmission codes. *IBM Journal of Research Development*, July, pp. 354–67.

mB1C Code

Yoshikai, N. K., K. Katagiri, and T. Ito. 1984. mB1C code and its performance in an optical communication system. *IEEE Transactions on Communications*, 32(2): 163–8.

Spread Spectrum

Murad Hizlan, *Cleveland State University*

INTRODUCTION

Information about spread spectrum was particularly hard to come by until the late 1970s because of its military origins and classified status. Starting in the 1980s, however, there was a huge growth in spread-spectrum research, followed in the 1990s by an explosive growth in civilian applications. Rather than attempting a likely futile summary of the technical literature on spread spectrum within the confines of this chapter, we will introduce a more intuitive glimpse of spread spectrum, concentrating on its general properties, touching on its well-known applications, and presenting simple results about its robustness.

OVERVIEW OF SPREAD SPECTRUM

A discussion of spread spectrum would be exceptionally dull, if not entirely impossible, without reference to its intriguing origins and captivating applications. Although volumes can be written on either of these subject matters, we introduce a brief summary here.

Historical Origins

Much of the early history of spread spectrum can be tied to military applications, mainly starting with World War II. Although *spark gap* transmitters of the early wireless era and wideband FM transmitters of the 1920s and 1930s transmitted spread spectrum-like signals, the first traceable patent on true spread spectrum, "Secret Communications Technique," was granted in 1942 to the most unlikely of co-inventors: an actress and a composer (Markey and Antheil 1942).

Hedy Lamarr (Markey), a Hollywood movie actress, and George Antheil, an avant-garde composer, turned over their invention to the U.S. government for use in the war effort, and the details of their patent were kept as a military secret for several decades (Scholtz 1982). By the time military secrecy was lifted and commercial use of spread spectrum began, the patent had long expired, having awarded no monetary gain to the inventors.

Intentional use of spread spectrum can be considered to have started with World War II (Simon et al. 1984, 39–42). The early research and development were mainly for applications in communications, navigation beacons, and radar jamming countermeasures. Although it is known that both the Allies and the Axis powers developed and implemented spread-spectrum systems, much of that work remains classified. In fact, most of the research and development in spread spectrum from the 1950s until the early 1970s were supported by the military and kept classified. An example, however, of a well-known application of spread spectrum in the military is its use in satellites by the U.S. military through modems such as the USC-28 (Satellite Communications 2004).

The dawn of spread spectrum use in civilian applications came about in 1980, after the declassification of the technology by the military, when the Federal Communications Commission specified the regulations for civilian spread-spectrum transmissions through Title 47, Section 15.247 of *Code of Federal Regulations* (Federal Communications Commission 2004).

Modern Applications

Although civilian applications of spread spectrum started to appear in the 1980s, they have exponentially increased throughout the 1990s and early 2000s. Ironically, the world's largest single spread-spectrum system today has its roots in the military and is used for navigation rather than communication. The *global positioning system* (GPS) was initially developed, funded, and operated by the U.S. Department of Defense primarily for the military (Parkinson and Spilker 1996), but it is now available for unrestricted civilian use around the world with full existing accuracy (Clinton 2000). The system incorporates a space segment consisting of satellites transmitting the GPS signal, a control segment monitoring and uploading the orbital and time reference data, and a user segment consisting of inexpensive GPS receivers for position fixing.

Another widespread application of spread-spectrum technology is in wireless multiple-access networking. The IEEE 802.11b standard (IEEE 802.11 Working Group 1999) for *wireless local area networks* (WLANs), for example, allows wireless networking at data rates up to 11 Mb/s using *direct sequence spread spectrum* (DSSS) over the 2.4-GHz band. Although there exist several different flavors of the 802.11 standard—collectively known by the popular name *Wi-Fi* (Wi-Fi Alliance 2005) but with some forms using techniques other than spread spectrum—802.11b has revolutionized wireless computing. Another example of wireless networking using spread spectrum is the Bluetooth technology (Bakker, McMichael Gilster, and Gilster 2002), which employs *adaptive frequency-hopping* spread spectrum for *personal area networks* (PANs). The use of Bluetooth has particularly exploded over the last few years.

Another modern application of spread spectrum that has enjoyed widespread acceptance is in digital cellular telephony. Simply known as CDMA (for *code division multiple access*), this application is based on DSSS and follows the IS-95 standard (Garg and Rappaport 2000) that was originally spearheaded by Qualcomm. CDMA technology is currently employed by several wireless service providers in the United States, including Sprint and Verizon. Also based on CDMA technology, *wideband CDMA* (W-CDMA) (Holma and Toskala 2002) and *CDMA2000* (Garg and Rappaport 2000) are candidate standards for third-generation (or 3G) wireless services.

Although there are many other applications of spread spectrum, one that has been explicitly obvious to the average consumer over the years—cordless telephones—has seen terms such as *direct sequence* and *spread spectrum* liberally used (Good, Cheng, and Hae-Seok 2000). Today, spread-spectrum technology is used to suppress interference and allow uncoordinated multiple access in several models of cordless phones.

BASIC CONCEPTS

Several basic concepts will help us understand the beneficial attributes of spread-spectrum modulation. Although these attributes can be well established through a rigorous theoretical development, here we seek a more intuitive treatment of the basic concepts leading to these attributes.

Robust Communications

A communication system is said to be *robust* if it is designed to work reasonably well, staying *strong* and *healthy*,

in the presence of varying and usually severe interference. One can argue that the main feature of spread spectrum in communication is its robustness. This robustness allows spread-spectrum communication systems to reliably operate under various types of interference, ranging from hostile jamming in the case of military applications to multiuser interference for mainstream civilian applications.

The robustness of spread-spectrum modulation can be explained in terms of several properties of the spread-spectrum signal such as bandwidth expansion, randomness, and redundancy. A spread-spectrum signal possesses a considerable amount of redundancy by its nature. Although this redundancy is attained through different means, depending on the type of spread spectrum being used, it can intuitively be tied to the fact that spread spectrum occupies a bandwidth that is much greater than would otherwise be required by the underlying modulation scheme. This redundancy, of course, can easily be interpreted as leading to robustness.

Another property of spread-spectrum modulation that leads to its robustness is the randomness property. As will be explained later, spread-spectrum modulation can be viewed as a random modulation scheme transmitting a signal that appears to be random to third observers. Of course, this signal is not random to the intended receiver, and any apparent randomness is *removed* by the receiver, which at the same time makes any interference—hostile or not—behave like random noise. This allows a spread-spectrum communication system to operate in a robust manner in the presence of arbitrary interference.

Spectrum Spreading

The main characteristic of spread spectrum is that it occupies a bandwidth that is much larger than what would ordinarily be needed for modulating the data to be transmitted. Such bandwidth expansion is not a unique characteristic of spread spectrum in itself, but it is exclusive in the sense that it is used in spread spectrum for combating interference other than *additive white Gaussian noise* (AWGN) (Pursley 2005, 560).

What makes bandwidth expansion work for spread spectrum in combating interference is the process of *despreading*, or contracting the bandwidth to its original size at the receiver. The same process that performs the despreading for the spread-spectrum signal works to spread the bandwidth of any interfering signal that would be added during transmission. As a result, the despread signal is in effect hit by an interfering signal with a *power spectral density* (PSD) that is much smaller than the PSD of the interference in the channel.

The PSD illustrations of Figure 1 show the effect of spectrum spreading. Figure 1a illustrates the PSD of a modulated arbitrary data signal before spectrum spreading. In Figure 1b, the PSD of this signal is shown as it is transmitted through the channel after the spreading process; the PSDs of narrowband and wideband interference are also shown. Here the signal bandwidth is expanded approximately four times, accompanied by a fourfold decrease in its PSD, while the PSDs of narrowband and wideband interference are as they would be in the channel.

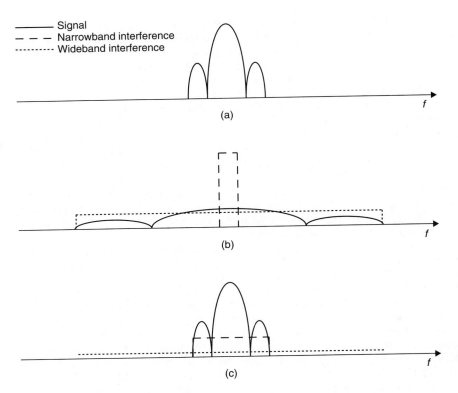

——— Signal
— — — Narrowband interference
·········· Wideband interference

(a)

(b)

(c)

Figure 1: Power spectral density (a and b) before and after the spreading process and (c) after the despreading process

Finally, Figure 1c shows the PSDs of the spread-spectrum signal, the narrowband interference, and the wideband interference after the despreading process. Although the despreading process at the receiver re-creates the original PSD of the modulated signal, it also spreads the PSDs of the interference terms picked up during transmission. The net result is smaller PSDs for the interference terms and thus less harm inflicted on the signal.

The underlying assumption for all of this to work is that the interference should have a bounded average power, or *bounded energy*. This is true, of course, for the types of interference that spread spectrum is good at combating. In the case of AWGN, for which this condition is not satisfied, spectrum spreading has no effect on performance (Pursley 2005, 560).

Processing Gain

In cases where spread-spectrum modulation is effective in combating interference, we might be interested in determining how much gain in performance can be attained by using spread spectrum instead of some classical narrowband modulation technique. *Processing gain* is the parameter that expresses this performance advantage. In fact, processing gain expresses this advantage not only for interference rejection but also for *any* application of spread spectrum.

There are various ways to define and evaluate processing gain depending on the particular application of spread spectrum. For arbitrary interference rejection, for instance, we may define it as the improvement in signal-to-interference ratio in going from a narrowband modulation scheme to spread-spectrum modulation. In most cases, however, processing gain turns out to be equal to

the bandwidth expansion factor (Sklar 2001, 735–8). For this reason, *processing gain* and *bandwidth expansion factor* are interchangeably used in many sources, even though this usage is technically incorrect.

Jamming Game Viewpoint

Most treatments of spread-spectrum modulation, especially when dealing with performance analysis, make reference to a *jammer* or a *jamming* signal (for example, Nazari and Ziemer 1988; Su and Milstein 1990; Teh, Kot, and Li 1999). Although this reference partially results from historical reasons and the military origins of spread spectrum, a jamming type of interference presents a perfect setting for illustrating the robustness and interference-rejection capability of this modulation scheme. A hostile jammer that is intentionally trying to impede communication can be considered to be the worst type of interference among those with the same average power, and a spread-spectrum system that does well under such interference is a robust communication system that is expected to do at least better under other types of interference. As such, performance analyses of spread-spectrum systems in the presence of jamming signals are equally valuable for nonmilitary applications.

Communication in the presence of a jammer can be considered in terms of game theory (Osborne 2004), where one player (the communicator) is trying to incur the least damage while the opponent (the jammer) is trying to inflict the most damage on the first player. An analysis of this game would lead to a minimax solution in which the best communication and jamming strategies under a given set of constraints can be determined (Hughes and Hizlan 1990). Nevertheless, in the absence of such an approach, spread-spectrum modulation has been shown over several decades to be a good strategy for the communicator regardless of the strategy followed by the jammer.

Random Modulation

Spread-spectrum modulation can be viewed as a random modulation scheme in which the data to be transmitted are modulated in a way that appears to be random to a third observer other than the transmitter and the receiver. The pseudorandom sequences and their various derivatives used in the creation of spread-spectrum modulation introduce this apparent randomness into the transmitted signal.

From an intuitive standpoint, the randomness of the transmitted signal allows spread spectrum to combat interference, whether it is hostile jamming or more benign forms of disturbance, by randomly and thus unpredictably occupying a small portion of the available signal space at any given time. This way, a hostile jammer does not know what portion of the signal space to jam *effectively*, and other types of interference do not cause any significant harm *most* of the time.

From a more rigorous standpoint, a form of random modulation in which the transmitted signal vector is uniformly distributed on the surface of an *N*-dimensional sphere has been shown to be asymptotically optimal for combating unknown and arbitrary interference (Hughes and Hizlan 1990), and spread spectrum is known to be a particularly effective special case of the general class of random modulation schemes. As such, spread-spectrum modulation is especially suited for combating unknown and arbitrary interference.

ADVANTAGES OF SPREAD SPECTRUM

Spread-spectrum modulation has several advantages or beneficial attributes that make it useful for various applications. Some of these make spread spectrum useful for military applications, while others make it effective for multiuser civilian applications.

Low PSD, Low Probability of Detection, and Low Probability of Intercept

One main attribute of a spread-spectrum signal is its low PSD. This is the result of spreading the bandwidth of a finite power signal over a much larger bandwidth, as illustrated in Figure 1a and 1b. In practice, the bandwidth expansion, and the resulting PSD reduction, can be by a factor of tens to hundreds for commercial applications to more than a thousand for military applications (Roberts 1995).

For civilian applications, the low PSD of the spread-spectrum signal allows it to coexist with narrowband signals of much higher PSD over the same band without causing undue interference on them. The spread-spectrum signal simply appears as low levels of background noise as far as the narrowband users are concerned. Of course, the spread-spectrum signal itself effectively combats interference from the narrowband signals.

Low power spectral density has other advantages for military applications. For one, the spread-spectrum signal with an extremely low PSD can be effectively buried under background noise, making it practically undetectable to anyone other than the intended receiver, resulting in what is known as *low probability of detection* (LPD) or *low probability of intercept* (LPI). Any adversary would try to detect the presence of a communicator's signal using a device called a *radiometer* (Dillard 1979). Spread-spectrum signals have been shown to exhibit good LPD and LPI properties (Sklar 2001, 722).

Even when detected, spread spectrum affords a level of security to the message that it carries. This is because of the pseudorandom nature of the spreading of the signal. By no means can this type of security be compared to cryptography, but it would be relatively secure from casual eavesdroppers. An adversary with sufficient computing power and sufficient time to observe the transmitted spread-spectrum signal can, however, determine the pseudorandom spreading sequence used and therefore decipher the message (Ziemer and Peterson 2001, 604–5).

Arbitrary Interference Rejection

Interference rejection is an attribute of spread spectrum that is advantageous for both military and civilian applications. For military applications, the interference takes the form of a hostile jammer that intentionally tries to hinder communication, arguably the most damaging kind of interference. For civilian applications, the interference might be from various sources such as narrowband users of the same frequency band, signals from other spread-spectrum users in a multiple-access setting, or reflections of the user's own transmission in a multipath situation, among others. Regardless of the kind of application, or the type of interference, spreading of the bandwidth before transmission and despreading after reception are what help with arbitrary interference rejection.

As illustrated in Figure 1b and 1c, the interfering signal itself gets spread during the process of despreading at the receiver, thus resulting in a much smaller PSD for the interference than before. Although only two examples of interference are illustrated in Figure 1, it should be obvious that any type of interference, whether from a hostile jammer or a more benign source, will undergo the same type of reduction in PSD.

Another way to explain interference rejection is to consider the spread-spectrum signal as randomly occupying only a small fraction of a huge number of available signal dimensions at any given time. Any interference with bounded average power has to occupy the whole available signal space with a small amount of power or only a small number of available signal dimensions (which most of the time will not coincide with the signal itself) with a large amount of power. In either case, the interference is rendered ineffective.

High Resolution Time-of-Arrival Measurements

Range measurement or position determination can be accomplished by measuring the time a given pulse takes to propagate through a channel, assuming that the pulse propagates at the speed of light. Such a measurement suffers primarily from the uncertainty in determining the exact time of arrival of the pulse being detected. Because the rise time (or the fall time) of a pulse is inversely proportional to its bandwidth, high-bandwidth pulses afford much better resolution in time-of-arrival determination (Sklar 2001, 723–4).

A spread-spectrum signal is especially suited for time-of-arrival and therefore range measurements because of its markedly large bandwidth. In fact, some types of spread spectrum transmit long sequences of pulses of especially short duration, further aiding the time of arrival measurement through, in effect, an averaging of numerous highly precise measurements. The result is exceptionally precise range determination. The global positioning system is based on this very concept, accurately determining the user's location through precise measurements of the range between the user and satellites with known locations.

Code Division Multiple Access

Code division multiple access happens to be the most widespread civilian use of spread-spectrum technology, with the most common example being the CDMA wireless phone infrastructure. The idea is based on the fact that spread spectrum rejects interference, including those from other spread-spectrum users within the same frequency band. Unlike frequency division multiple access or time division multiple access, in CDMA all users occupy the same frequency band at the same time, separated by the spreading codes assigned to each user. This allows for better utilization of the available spectrum among multiple users and graceful degradation of the performance as more users are added.

In essence, each user in a CDMA setting transmits with quite low PSD, thereby inflicting little damage on any other user. Of course, as more users are added, the cumulative interference incurred by any one user gets larger, limiting the total number of users in the channel. In CDMA applications, the spreading codes assigned to each user are specifically designed to have as small a cross-correlation as possible so that the interference from one user on another is almost negligible. This, of course, requires a measure of collaboration among the users, which the nature of multi-access applications readily provides.

TYPES OF SPREAD SPECTRUM

Spread-spectrum modulation can be implemented in many different ways. Although two of these methods, *direct sequence spread spectrum* and *frequency-hopping spread spectrum*, overwhelmingly dominate, other methods such as *time-hopping spread spectrum* and various hybrids of these techniques have been defined and implemented.

Direct Sequence Spread Spectrum

Direct sequence spread spectrum arguably represents the most common implementation of spread-spectrum modulation. It involves the multiplication of a phase-modulated data signal by a pseudorandom *chipping*

sequence of ± 1's running at a rate that is much higher that the data rate. This process can be equivalently perceived as multiplying the ± 1 data sequence by the higher-rate chipping sequence and then phase modulating the product sequence. The bandwidth of the resulting spread-spectrum signal is determined by the rate of the chipping sequence rather than the rate of the data sequence. The term *direct sequence* refers to the generation of spread spectrum through a direct multiplication of the data sequence with the chipping sequence.

To visualize this process, consider Figure 2. Figure 2a represents a bipolar data sequence of four bits taking on the values $+1$, -1, $+1$, and $+1$, while Figure 2b represents a bipolar pseudorandom chipping sequence running at a rate that is eight times faster than the data rate. The product of the two sequences, which would phase modulate a carrier to generate the direct sequence spread-spectrum signal, is shown in Figure 2c. Clearly, in this example, the bandwidth of the spread-spectrum signal would be eight times larger than the signal bandwidth with only the data sequence performing the phase modulation.

The underlying modulation in direct sequence spread spectrum is either *binary phase shift keying* (BPSK) or *quaternary phase shift keying* (QPSK). Although QPSK has twice the bandwidth efficiency of BPSK for the same error performance, this is not the reason for choosing QPSK, even though it is slightly more complicated, for some direct sequence implementations. Rather, QPSK resists some types of jamming better and is more difficult to detect than BPSK (Ziemer and Peterson 2001, 577–83). The demodulation of DSSS is accomplished by multiplication of the received signal by a synchronously generated chipping sequence to remove spreading, followed by demodulation of the underlying signal.

Frequency-Hopping Spread Spectrum

Frequency-hopping spread spectrum is a commonly used type of spread-spectrum scheme that is based on frequency modulation. In this implementation, the carrier frequency is chosen from a large set of carrier frequencies that together constitute the spread-spectrum bandwidth. A pseudorandom sequence is used to select the carrier frequency to use at any given time. The name *frequency hopping* refers to the modulated carrier that appears to be hopping from one frequency to another.

There are two main types of frequency-hopping spread spectrum: *slow* frequency hopping and *fast* frequency hopping. In slow frequency hopping, one or more data symbols are transmitted per hop, whereas in fast-frequency hopping, one or more hops are made per data symbol. The underlying modulation in frequency-hopping spread spectrum can be *binary frequency shift keying* (BFSK) or M-*ary frequency shift keying* (MFSK). In either case, the demodulation is performed noncoherently because of the difficulty of phase synchronization among rapidly changing carrier frequencies.

To visualize the frequency-hopping spread spectrum, consider Figures 3 and 4. A slow frequency-hopping spread-spectrum system using 4-ary FSK with two data symbols per hop is illustrated in Figure 3. Every two symbols, a new set of four carrier frequencies (a *hop block*)

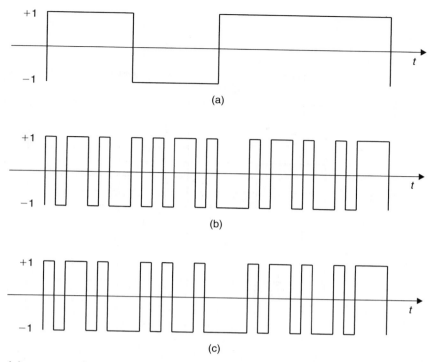

Figure 2: Illustration of direct sequence spread spectrum—(a) data sequence, (b) chipping sequence, and (c) product sequence

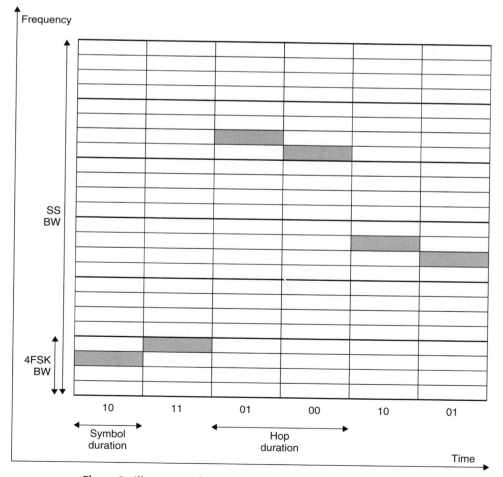

Figure 3: Illustration of slow frequency-hopping spread spectrum

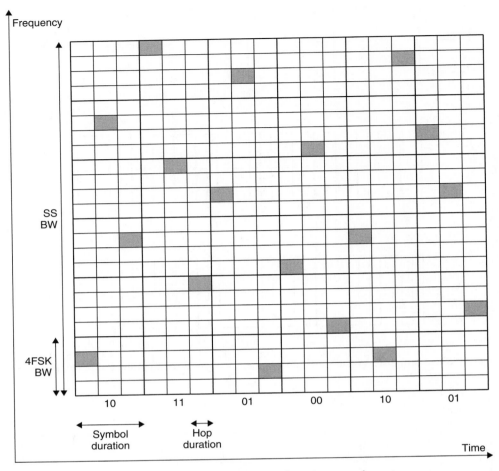

Figure 4: Illustration of fast frequency-hopping spread spectrum

is pseudorandomly selected among the six possible sets. Within each hop, the carrier frequency is assigned in increasing order of the decimal representation of the two-bit symbol. In this example, the spread-spectrum bandwidth, denoted by *SS BW*, is six times the underlying 4-ary FSK bandwidth, denoted by *4FSK BW*. Using similar values and notation, a fast frequency-hopping spread-spectrum system using 4-ary FSK with three hops per data symbol is illustrated in Figure 4. Again, in this example, the spread-spectrum bandwidth is six times the 4-ary FSK bandwidth.

Although fast frequency-hopping spread spectrum would be more difficult to implement than a slow one because of the higher hopping rate, it is more advantageous because it introduces frequency diversity for each symbol, resulting in better resistance to partial band jamming. The demodulation in either case is accomplished by a noncoherent receiver synchronously hopping to the same set of frequencies as selected by the pseudorandom sequence at the transmitter.

Time-Hopping Spread Spectrum

In time-hopping spread spectrum, each data bit is transmitted as a short-duration pulse whose position within the bit time is determined by a pseudorandom sequence.

Although time hopping suppresses interference as well as direct sequence or frequency hopping does and can be employed for multi-access purposes, it does not provide nearly the level of security against eavesdropping afforded by either of the two other methods, and it is easier to jam as well.

To visualize the time-hopping spread spectrum, consider Figure 5. A four-bit data sequence is illustrated in Figure 5a, while the pseudorandom position modulation of a short-duration pulse is shown in Figure 5b. The product of the two signals, which is shown in Figure 5c, represents time-hopped data, which would then modulate a carrier. The bandwidth of the resulting time-hopping spread-spectrum signal, as determined by the duration of the pulse, would be much higher than the bandwidth of the underlying data in actual implementation.

Demodulation of the time-hopping spread spectrum involves detection during time intervals as determined by a hopping sequence synchronized to the one at the transmitter.

Hybrids and Other Methods

Combinations of the aforementioned methods can also be used to implement spread-spectrum modulation as hybrid systems. Although clearly more difficult to implement

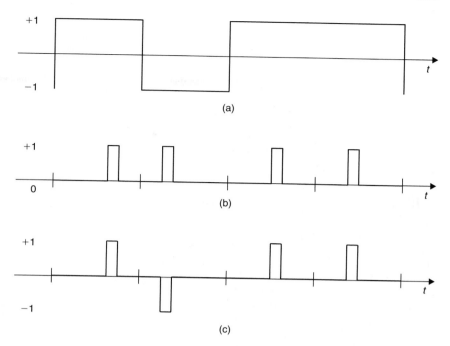

Figure 5: Illustration of time-hopping spread spectrum—(a) data sequence, (b) pseudorandom pulse position modulation, and (c) time-hopped data pulses

than pure spread-spectrum methods, hybrid systems are sometimes employed in an effort to reap the unique benefits of different spread-spectrum techniques. Common hybrid techniques include *direct sequence and frequency hopping* hybrids and *direct sequence and time hopping* hybrids.

Another possible method for spread-spectrum modulation is to use *pulsed FM* or *chirp* modulation (Maes and Steffey 1996). In pulsed FM spread-spectrum systems, the carrier frequency is frequency modulated by a pseudorandom sequence at the beginning of each symbol. This method can also be viewed in a sense as a frequency-hopping spread-spectrum scheme in which hops are continuous in frequency rather than discrete.

DIRECT SEQUENCE SPREAD SPECTRUM

As a simple example of DSSS, consider an uncoded BPSK direct sequence spread-spectrum system with a correlation receiver operating in the presence of arbitrary interference.

System Definition

As illustrated in Figure 6, the transmitter transmits a binary message every T seconds through the BPSK direct sequence spread-spectrum signal

$$x(t) = b(t) \cdot c(t) \cdot \sqrt{2P} \, \cos(\omega_c t), \qquad (1)$$

where $b(t) = \sum_i b_i u_T(t - iT)$ is the data waveform, $c(t) = \sum_j a_j u_{T_c}(t - jT_c)$ is the chipping waveform, $u_\tau(t) = \begin{cases} 1, & 0 \le t < \tau \\ 0, & \text{otherwise} \end{cases}$ is the unit pulse waveform of duration τ seconds, $b_i \in \{\pm 1\}$ is the data sequence, $a_j \in \{\pm 1\}$ is the chipping sequence modeled as an independent and identically distributed sequence of equally likely random variables, $T_c = T/N$ is the chip duration for N chips per bit, P is the signal power, and ω_c is the carrier frequency.

The channel adds interference $s(t)$ to the transmitted signal. As shown in Figure 6, the receiver is a simple

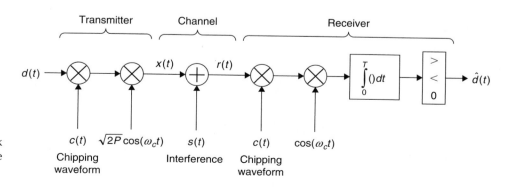

Figure 6: Conceptual block diagram of BPSK direct sequence spread spectrum

correlation receiver that performs an estimate of the transmitted bit by evaluating

$$\hat{b} = \text{sgn}\left(\int_0^T r(t) \cdot c(t) \cos(\omega_c t) dt\right) \qquad (2)$$

It should be clear that multiplication of the received signal $r(t)$ with a replica of the chipping waveform despreads the spread-spectrum signal (because $a_j^2 = 1$) while spreading the interference at the same time.

Arbitrary Interference Performance

There is a significant body of knowledge regarding the performance of DSSS in the presence of various types of interference, ranging from numerous kinds of jamming signals to different multi-access settings. Rather than attempting to summarize all of these results, we consider DSSS from a robust communications point of view and present its worst-case performance in the presence of an unknown and arbitrary interference of bounded energy, the so-called arbitrarily varying channel (Hughes and Narayan 1987). This type of an analysis allows us to take into account any form of interference, as long as it is uncorrelated with the transmitted signal, without having to refer to specific statistical descriptions.

Assume that the transmitted signal $x(t)$ is corrupted by an unknown and arbitrary interfering signal, as shown in Figure 6, so that

$$r(t) = x(t) + s(t) \qquad (3)$$

is received. The only restrictions on $s(t)$ are that it is independent of the transmitted signal $x(t)$ and it satisfies a constraint on its energy:

$$\int_0^T s^2(t) dt \le E_I \qquad (4)$$

Note that although $s(t)$ covers a substantial range of interference situations, it cannot model multipath interference (Sklar 2001, 771–2, 947–78) or repeat-back type jammers (Simon et al. 1994, 142) where the interference is correlated with the signal. The performance measure is defined as the worst-case error probability of the system under all $s(t)$ satisfying the energy constraint

$$\epsilon_{DS} = \sup_{s(t)} \text{Pr}\left\{\hat{b} \ne b\right\} \qquad \text{subject to (4)} \qquad (5)$$

In Figure 7, an upper and a lower bound to the worst-case error probability, ε_{DS}, of this system operating with $N = 20$ chips per bit are plotted as a function of signal-to-noise ratio, E_b/E_I (where E_b is the energy per bit), in the absence of AWGN (Hizlan and Hughes 1991). Also plotted in Figure 7 is a fundamental lower bound to the worst-case error probability of *any* random binary modulation scheme: No uncoded binary system of any kind can have a better worst-case error probability than this bound (Hizlan and Hughes 1991). We see from Figure 7 that at 10^{-6}, the worst-case error probability of uncoded direct sequence spread spectrum is no more than 1.8 dB

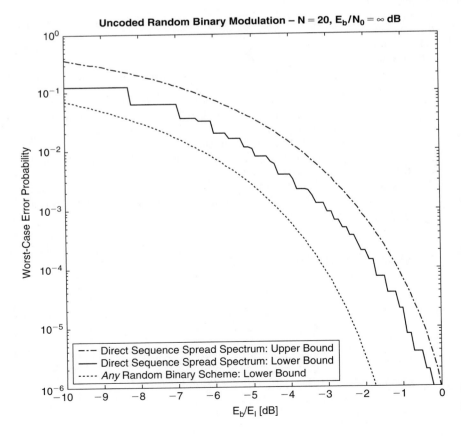

Figure 7: Arbitrary interference rejection performance of DSSS

away from what is theoretically possible. We can therefore claim that uncoded DSSS is remarkably good at arbitrary interference rejection.

Although not presented here, similarly remarkable worst-case performance results have been shown for uncoded DSSS in multipath channels (Hizlan and Liu 1999) and for coded DSSS in the arbitrarily varying channel (Hizlan and Hughes 1998).

FREQUENCY-HOPPING SPREAD SPECTRUM

A frequency hopping spread-spectrum system can be implemented as a *block hopper* or an *independent hopper*, regardless of whether it is a slow or fast frequency-hopping system. In a block hopper, each hop is made into a contiguous block of *M* frequencies, within which MFSK modulation takes places. In this type of a system, MFSK modulation and frequency hopping are separately performed. In the independent hopper, MFSK modulation and frequency hopping are combined into a single frequency synthesis process, resulting in hops to individual carrier frequencies rather than frequency blocks. Here a simple example of a block hopping system is presented.

System Definition

As shown in Figure 8a, the transmitter sends an *M*-ary message $1 \leq m \leq M$ every *T* seconds by transmitting the signal

$$x(t) = \sqrt{2P}\, \cos\!\left((\omega_c^{(m)} + \omega_h^{(j)})t\right), 1 \leq m \leq M, 1 \leq j \leq N \quad (6)$$

where $\omega_c^{(m)}$ is the carrier frequency corresponding to message *m* and $\omega_h^{(j)}$ is one of the *N* available hop block frequencies pseudorandomly selected by the *pseudonoise* (PN) sequence. Although $\omega_c^{(m)}$ stays fixed for the entire message duration of *T* seconds, the timing of $\omega_h^{(j)}$ depends on whether slow or fast frequency hopping is utilized, and it is not explicitly specified in this model. The high-pass filter in Figure 8a is in place to select the upconverted frequencies from the mixer.

The receiver illustrated in Figure 8b "de-hops" the received signal $r(t)$ to the original MFSK frequencies by downconverting through a synchronously running replica of the transmitter PN generator. The image-reject filter removes the image frequencies before the downconversion process. The rest of the receiver operates as a conventional noncoherent MFSK receiver to produce an estimate of the transmitted message, $\hat{m}$.

CODE DIVISION MULTIPLE ACCESS

Although *code division multiple access* refers to the multiple-access technique by which spreading codes are used to discriminate among users, the use of *CDMA* has become synonymous with the well-known implementation of this technology in wireless telephony. Rather than addressing this particular implementation, we consider a DSSS multiple-access system as a simple example of CDMA.

System Definition

Consider a communication scenario in which *K* asynchronous users share a multiple-access channel through

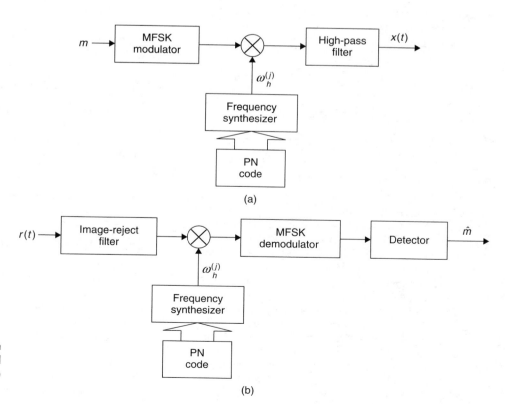

Figure 8: Conceptual block diagram of MFSK frequency-hopping spread spectrum for (a) transmitter and (b) receiver

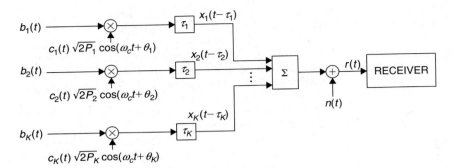

Figure 9: DSSS CDMA model

the use of BPSK direct sequence spread spectrum, as shown in Figure 9. Each user transmits a signal

$$x_k(t) = \sqrt{2P_k}\, b_k(t) c_k(t) \cos(\omega_c t + \theta_k), \quad 1 \le k \le K \quad (7)$$

where $b_k(t)$ is the data waveform and $c_k(t)$ is the chipping waveform as defined in the direct sequence example, P_k is the received power, and θ_k is the phase angle for user k. The receiver receives time-delayed signals from all of the transmitters corrupted by AWGN:

$$r(t) = \sum_{k=1}^{K} x_k(t - \tau_k) + n(t) \quad (8)$$

where τ_k is the propagation delay associated with transmitter k and $n(t)$ is AWGN. Without loss of generality, assume that the receiver is locked on to the phase and time delay of transmitter 1. As in the direct sequence example, the correlation receiver obtains an estimate of a transmitted bit b by computing

$$\hat{b} = \text{sgn}\left(\int_0^T r(t) \cdot c_1(t - \tau_1) \cos(\omega_c(t - \tau_1) + \theta_1) dt \right) \quad (9)$$

where the integral is over the T-second bit interval.

Multiple-Access Performance

It should be noted that multiple-access performance of spread spectrum can be expressed in terms of the interference rejection capability of spread spectrum. Multiple-access interference is wideband interference, which would be spread out by the despreading mechanism in the receiver, thereby reducing its effect by a factor that is essentially equal to the processing gain of the system. Rather than attempting to summarize the substantial amount of existing results on CDMA performance, we consider CDMA from a robust communications point of view and present its worst-case performance. The performance measure is therefore the worst-case error probability of the above-defined system where the worst case is taken over all transmitter powers $P_k \ge 0$, $2 \le k \le K$, phase angles $\theta_k \in [0, 2\pi)$, $2 \le k \le K$, and time delays

$\tau_k \in [0, T)$, $2 \le k \le K$ subject to a constraint on the detected interference power:

$$\varepsilon_{CDMA} = \max_{\substack{P_k, \theta_k, \tau_k \\ 2 \le k \le K}} \Pr\left\{ \hat{b} \ne b \right\} \quad \text{subject to}$$
$$\text{detected interference power} \le P_I. \quad (10)$$

In Figure 10 (Hizlan and Hughes 1988), an upper and a lower bound to ε_{CDMA} for this multiple-access system operating with $K = 15$ transmitters and $N = 31$ chips per bit are plotted as a function of postdetection signal-to-interference ratio, P_s/P_I (where P_s is the detected signal power), in the presence of AWGN with signal-to-noise ratio $E_b/N_0 = 15$dB. Also plotted in Figure 10 is the average error probability of this system for the case of multiple-access interference being modeled as AWGN. We observe from Figure 10 that, at 10^{-5}, the worst-case error probability of the example system is no more than 2 dB away from its average error probability in the presence of AWGN with equivalent interference power. Even under worst-case assumptions, therefore, DSSS does a very good job of rendering multi-access interference harmless, making it behave much like low-level AWGN.

PSEUDONOISE SEQUENCES

Pseudonoise or *pseudorandom* sequences constitute a fundamental building block of spread-spectrum systems whether they are used directly as in DSSS or indirectly as in frequency-hopping or time-hopping spread spectrum. They are deterministic in nature so that they can be synchronously generated both at the transmitter and the receiver, but they exhibit several properties that make them appear like random sequences.

Methods of Generation

Because a pseudorandom sequence is essentially a sequence of numbers approximating the samples of a random variable, any random number generation algorithm can be used to generate it. On the other hand, because pseudorandom numbers used in spread spectrum are plain binary numbers, simple generation methods exist and are preferred for use.

One such method that is commonly used is the *linear feedback shift register* method, as illustrated in Figure 11. The tap coefficients c_i are 1 or 0, meaning there is either

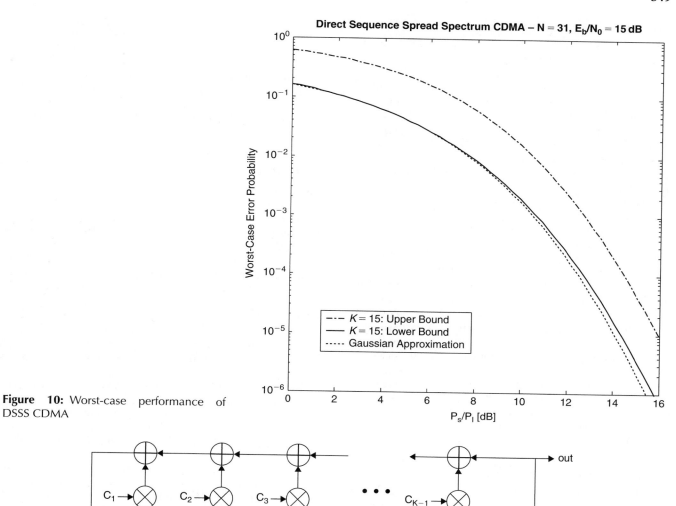

Figure 10: Worst-case performance of DSSS CDMA

Figure 11: Linear feedback shift register PN sequence generators

a feedback connection or not; the addition is modulo-2 addition; and the shift register is initialized to a nonzero state before sequence generation begins. Because the maximum number of distinct states, excluding the all-zero state, is $2^K - 1$ for a K-stage shift register, the period of the longest sequence that can be obtained is also $2^K - 1$. The all-zero state is excluded because, if it occurs, the rest of the sequence will all be zeros.

If the tap coefficients are chosen just right, the longest period can be attained, resulting in what is called an *m-sequence*, or maximal length sequence. This method can clearly generate extremely long sequences with modest-size shift register implementations. These PN sequences exhibit good randomness properties as will be described later.

In multiple-access applications, PN sequences with low cross-correlation values are desired in order to minimize interference among multiple users. There are several common ways of generating such sequences. One well-known set constitute *Gold* codes (Gold 1967), which

are simply generated through a modulo-2 sum of two *m*-sequences. Each user in the multiuser environment has to use a different code from the set obtained by using different initial states for one of the two shift registers. The two *m*-sequences are specifically chosen to form what is called a *preferred pair*, resulting in the desired cross-correlation properties.

Another set of PN sequences with minimal cross-correlation values constitutes the *Kasami* sequences (Kasami 1966). Kasami sequences have better cross-correlation properties than Gold codes (smaller maximum autocorrelation), but they provide a smaller number of codes and therefore support a smaller number of users for a given code length.

The *Walsh* codes are still another well-known set of PN sequences for multiuser applications (Ziemer and Peterson 2001, 610–1). One way to generate them is through the use of a *Hadamard* matrix, in which each row is orthogonal to any other. As such, Walsh codes have zero cross-correlations, but only if they are perfectly synchronized.

Properties of PN Sequences

Although Gold codes, Kasami codes. and Walsh codes exhibit good cross-correlation properties, pure m-sequences display especially good randomness properties. Randomness properties of m-sequences can be stated in terms of the balance, run length, and autocorrelation properties (Haykin 2001, 482–3).

M-sequences are balanced in terms of the number of 1's and 0's generated in one period. In fact, because m-sequences have odd periods, it can be shown that the number of 1's generated in one period is always one more than the number of 0's generated. This distribution approximates the expected value for a purely random binary sequence of equally likely numbers.

Defining a run of length l as a subsequence of l identical symbols within the m-sequence, run lengths also exhibit a balanced distribution. More specifically, half of all the runs (of 1's and 0's) in an m-sequence have run length 1, one-fourth of all the runs have run length 2, one-eighth of all the runs have run length 3, and so on. Also, the number of runs of 1's and runs of 0's for each run length are equal. The only exception, resulting from the odd period of the m-sequence, is for the single 1 run and the single 0 run, where the length of the 1 run is one more than the length of the 0 run.

The normalized periodic autocorrelation function of an m-sequence with period N is 1 for a cyclic shift of the sequence by an integer multiple of the period, and $-1/N$ for any other cyclic shift. This, of course, is a tiny number for large N, approximating an uncorrelated sequence.

Choosing a PN Sequence

For arbitrary interference rejection, LPI or LPD applications, anti-jam applications, or ranging applications, m-sequences are usually adequate because they have good randomness properties. Note, however, that because m-sequences are based on linear generation methods, they are relatively easy to decode and therefore provide only minimal security against eavesdropping. If security is a concern, then nonlinear generation methods should be utilized (Key 1976).

For multiuser applications, minimal cross-correlation among PN sequences is more important then their individual randomness properties. For such applications, Gold codes, Kasami codes, or Walsh codes can be used. As stated before, Walsh codes have perfect (zero) cross-correlation but only if synchronized. Therefore, their application is limited to synchronous multiple-access systems. For asynchronous systems, Gold codes or Kasami codes can be considered. Although Gold codes support more users for a given code length, they exhibit larger cross-correlations than Kasami codes. However, with the larger number of users, the cumulative interference will also be larger. The trade-off between the two should therefore be considered.

CONCLUSION

Although spread spectrum led a quiet and secretive life of several decades under military safeguard, it is now enjoying a vibrant new lease on life in the civilian world. This should come as no surprise, however, given the many desirable features of spread spectrum such as robustness, interference rejection, low power spectral density, and multiple-access capability. Even the sole fact that it can coexist in the same band with other narrowband applications is enough to make spread spectrum highly sought after in today's exceedingly crowded frequency spectrum. It is therefore safe to predict that spread spectrum will enjoy an ever-increasing number of applications in the future.

GLOSSARY

Anti-jam: A characteristic of a communication system designed to resist jamming or intentional blocking. *See also* Jammer.

Bluetooth: An industrial specification for wireless *personal area networks* (PANs), Bluetooth provides a relatively secure and low-cost way to connect and exchange information between devices such as wireless phones, PDAs, laptops, and computer peripherals through short-range wireless connections.

CDMA2000: A family of *third-generation* (3G) mobile telecommunications standards that utilize *code division multiple access* based on the older CDMA digital cellular telephony standard and remaining compatible with it.

Code division multiple access (CDMA): A method of multiple access that allows many users to share the same communication channel through the use of individual spreading codes. CDMA also refers to a particular digital cellular telephony system that utilizes this scheme.

Direct sequence spread spectrum (DSSS): A method of spread spectrum in which spreading the bandwidth is accomplished by directly multiplying the data signal with a much higher-rate pseudorandom sequence.

Frequency hopping spread spectrum (FHSS): A method of spread spectrum in which spreading the bandwidth is accomplished by pseudorandomly switching (or hopping) the carrier frequency over a wide range of frequencies.

IEEE 802.11: A set of *wireless local area network* (WLAN) standards developed by Working Group 11 of the IEEE LAN/MAN Standards Committee (IEEE 802).

Interim Standard 95 (IS-95): Developed under Telecommunications Industry Association and Electronic Industries Alliance standards to define the second-generation digital cellular telephony standard better known as CDMA.

Jammer: A transmitting device used in electronic warfare to obstruct or foil transmission of the adversary's signals; also, the entity that performs such action.

Low probability of detection (LPD): A characteristic of transmissions, such as spread-spectrum signals, that are difficult to detect because of attributes such as low-power spectral density or high directivity.

Low probability of intercept (LPI): *See* Low probability of detection.

Multiple access: Type of communications in which more than one user accesses and communicates over a common channel.

Pseudonoise (PN) or pseudorandom sequence: An algorithmically generated sequence of numbers that appear to be random.

Robust communications: Type of communications designed to provide a minimum specified level of performance regardless of the kind of interference in the channel in which it operates.

Spread spectrum: A class of modulation schemes in which the transmission bandwidth is made much larger than the information bandwidth through a process that is independent of the transmitted data.

Time hopping: A method of spread spectrum in which bandwidth spreading is accomplished by transmitting extremely narrow pulses that are pseudorandomly pulse position modulated.

Wideband code division multiple access (W-CDMA): A third-generation (3G) wideband digital cellular telephony standard utilizing spread-spectrum multiple access; it is slated to be a successor to the worldwide second-generation standard of the *global system for mobile communications* (GSM).

Wi-Fi: A shortened form of *wireless fidelity* and a trademark of the Wi-Fi Alliance. Wi-Fi defines product compatibility standards for *wireless local area networks* (WLANs) based on the IEEE 802.11 standards.

CROSS REFERENCES

See *Code Division Multiple Access (CDMA)*; *Spread Spectrum Signals for Digital Communications*.

REFERENCES

Bakker, D. M., D. McMichael Gilster, and R. Gilster, eds. 2002. *Bluetooth end to end*. New York: Hungry Minds.

Clinton, W. J. 2000. Selective availability (retrieved from www.navcen.uscg.gov/gps/selective_availability.htm).

Dillard, R. A. 1979. Detectability of spread-spectrum signals. *IEEE Transactions on Aerospace and Electronic Systems*, 15, 526–37.

Federal Communications Commission. 2004. Operation within the bands 902–928 MHz, 2400–2483.5 MHz, and 5725–5850 MHz (47CFR15.247) (retrieved from www.access.gpo.gov/nara/cfr/waisidx_04/47cfr15_04.html).

Garg, V. K., and T. S. Rappaport, eds. 2002. *IS-95, CDMA and CDMA2000: Cellular/PCS systems implementation*. Upper Saddle River, NJ: Prentice Hall.

Gold, R. 1967. Optimal binary sequences for spread spectrum multiplexing. *IEEE Transactions on Information Theory*, 13: 619–21.

Good, P., J. Cheng, and C. Hae-Seok. 2000. A highly integrated radio for high performance, low-cost 2.4 GHz ISM cordless applications. *Microwave Symposium Digest of 2000 IEEE MTT-S International Microwave Symposium*, Boston, June 11–16, pp. 269–72.

Haykin, S. 2001. *Communication systems*. 4th ed. New York: John Wiley & Sons.

Hizlan, M., and B. L. Hughes. 1988. Bounds on the worst-case bit-error probability for asynchronous spread-spectrum multiple-access. In *Proceedings of the IEEE International Conference on Communications 1988*, Philadelphia, June 12–15, pp. 1410–4.

———. 1991. On the optimality of direct-sequence for arbitrary interference rejection. *IEEE Transactions on Communications*, 39: 1193–6.

———. 1998. Worst-case error probability of a spread-spectrum system in energy-limited interference. *IEEE Transactions on Communications*, 46: 286–96.

Hizlan, M., and X. Liu. 1999. A worst-case analysis of direct-sequence spread-spectrum in multipath channels. *Journal of the Franklin Institute*, 336: 611–25.

Holma, H., and A. Toskala, eds. 2002. *WCDMA for UMTS: Radio access for third generation mobile communications*. 2nd ed. New York: John Wiley & Sons.

Hughes, B. L., and M. Hizlan. 1990. An asymptotically optimal random modem and detector for robust communication. *IEEE Transactions on Information Theory*, 36: 810–21.

Hughes, B. L., and P. Narayan. 1987. Gaussian arbitrarily varying channels. *IEEE Transactions on Information Theory*, 33: 267–84.

IEEE 802.11 Working Group. 1999. *IEEE Std 802.11b-1999 (R2003)* (retrieved from http://standards.ieee.org/getieee802/download/802.11b-1999.pdf).

Kasami, T. (1966). *Weight distribution formula for some class of cyclic codes*. Tech. Rep. R-285, AD632574. University of Illinois, Urbana: Coordinated Science Laboratory.

Key, E. 1976. An analysis of the structure and complexity of nonlinear binary sequence generators. *IEEE Transactions on Information Theory*, 22: 732–6.

Maes, M. E., and J. R. Steffey. 1996. License free spread spectrum and FSK wire industrial data communications. In *Proceedings of the IEEE Northcon 1996*, Seattle, November 4–6, pp. 107–13.

Markey, H. K., and G. Antheil. 1942. Secret communication system. U.S. Patent 2,292,387, filed June 10, 1941.

Nazari, N., and R. E. Ziemer. 1988. Computationally efficient bounds for the performance of direct-sequence spread-spectrum multiple-access communications systems in jamming environments. *IEEE Transactions on Communications*, 36: 577–87.

Osborne, M. J. 2004. *An introduction to game theory*. New York: Oxford University Press.

Parkinson, B. W., and J. J. Spilker Jr., eds. 1996. *Global positioning system: Theory and applications, vols. I–III*. Washington, DC: American Institute of Aeronautics and Astronautics.

Pursley, M. B. 2005. *Introduction to digital communications*. Upper Saddle River, NJ: Prentice Hall.

Roberts, R. 1995. The ABCs of spread spectrum: A tutorial (retrieved from www.sss-mag.com/ss.html).

Satellite Communications. 2004. *Army* (October) (retrieved from www.ausa.org/webpub/DeptArmyMagazine.nsf/byid/DeptArmyMagazine.nsfmainhome).

Scholtz, R. A. 1982. The origins of spread-spectrum communications. *IEEE Transactions on Communications*, 30: 822–52.

Simon, M. K., J. K. Omura, R. A. Scholtz, and B. K. Levitt. 1994. *Spread spectrum communications handbook*. New York: McGraw-Hill.

Sklar, B. 2001. *Introduction to digital communication.* 2nd ed. Upper Saddle River, NJ: Prentice Hall.

Su, C.-M., and L. B. Milstein. 1990. Analysis of a coherent frequency-hopped spread-spectrum receiver in the presence of jamming. *IEEE Transactions on Communications*, 38: 715–26.

Teh, K. C., A. C. Kot, and K. H. Li. 1999. Partial-band jammer suppression in FFH spread-spectrum system using FFT. *IEEE Transactions on Vehicular Technology*, 48: 478–86.

Wi-Fi Alliance. 2006. Learn about Wi-Fi (retrieved from www.wi-fi.org/OpenSection/index.asp).

Ziemer, R. E., and R. L. Peterson. 2001. *Digital communications: Fundamentals and applications.* 2nd ed. Upper Saddle River, NJ: Prentice Hall.

Frequency Division Multiplexing

Zhu Liu, *AT&T Laboratories, Middletown, New Jersey*

INTRODUCTION

Frequency division multiplexing (FDM) is a technique in which the available bandwidth of a transmission channel is divided by frequency into narrower bands such that each band is used for a separate voice, video, or data transmission. When *amplitude modulation* (AM) radio broadcasting started at the beginning of the twentieth century, the pioneering electrical engineers modulated different radio programs to different frequencies so that they could be broadcast simultaneously. FDM was first employed in the 1930s in the analog carrier system to transmit several voice channels on a single physical circuit. Based on FDM, *multicarrier modulation* (MCM) was invented in the late 1950s, and *orthogonal frequency division multiplexing* (OFDM), a special form of MCM with densely spaced subcarriers (typically dozens to thousands), was introduced in 1970. Unlike FDM, in which each signal is carried by one carrier on a particular frequency band, MCM transmits a signal by splitting it into several components and sending each component over separate subcarrier. The details of OFDM are discussed in Chapter 39 of this handbook.

Nowadays, the FDM technique has application in many modern communication systems: for example, telephone, mobile phone, wireless *local area networks* (LANs), TV broadcast systems, radio broadcast systems, broadband Internet connections, and microwave and satellite communication systems (Freeman 1998; Minoli 2003; Rappaport 2001; Roddy 2006). Although different modulation techniques are adopted in these systems, the theme of transmitting multiple signals by sharing the frequency resource is the same.

In this chapter, we introduce the basic theories underlying FDM and discuss a few of its applications. The concept corresponding to frequency division multiplexing in the optical domain is known as *wavelength division multiplexing* (WDM), and it is discussed in detail in "Wavelength Division Multiplexing."

This chapter is organized as follows. The next section introduces the fundamentals of signal and Fourier transform, which are useful for the discussion in the rest of the chapter. The following two sections explain the theories of amplitude modulation and frequency modulation and

illustrate several typical AM and *frequency modulation* (FM) schemes. We then describe the general mechanism of FDM and present a few of its exemplary applications. Finally, we draw conclusions in the final section.

SIGNAL AND FOURIER TRANSFORM

Fourier analysis can transform the representation of a signal in the time domain into a representation of the signal in the frequency domain. The Fourier transform can isolate individual components of a complex signal for easier detection and manipulation. Analyzing and processing a signal in the frequency domain is a powerful tool in signal processing, communications, and many other areas. In this section, we briefly introduce the continuous Fourier transform and some properties of Fourier transforms. For more details, please refer to the textbook by Oppenheim, Wilsky, and Nawab (1996).

Let $x(t)$ be a signal in the time domain, where t is the time. The Fourier transform of $x(t)$, denoted by $F\{x(t)\} = X(f)$, where f is the frequency, is defined by the following formula:

$$X(f) = \int_{-\infty}^{\infty} x(t)\exp[-j2\pi ft]dt, \ where \ j = \sqrt{-1}$$

With equal validity, $X(f)$ gives a representation of the original signal $x(t)$ in the frequency domain. Generally, $X(f)$ is a complex function, and it is often convenient to express $X(f)$ in exponential form: $X(f) = |X(f)|e^{j\Phi(f)}$. The magnitude function $|X(f)|$ is called the Fourier spectrum of $x(t)$, $\Phi(f)$ is its phase angle. The square of the spectrum $|X(f)|$ is commonly referred to as the *power spectrum of $x(t)$*.

Given $X(f)$, we can obtain $x(t)$ by applying the inverse Fourier transform:

$$x(t) = \int_{-\infty}^{\infty} X(f)\exp[j2\pi ft]df$$

The above two equations are called the *Fourier transform pair*. Table 1 lists the Fourier transform pairs of a few

Table 1: Fourier Transform Pairs of Typical Signals

$x(t)$	$X(f)$
1	$\delta(f)$
$\delta(t)$	1
$e^{j2\pi f_0 t}$	$\delta(f - f_0)$
$\cos(2\pi f_0 t)$	$\frac{1}{2}[\delta(f - f_0) + \delta(f + f_0)]$
$\sin(2\pi f_0 t)$	$1/2j[\delta(f - f_0) + \delta(f + f_0)]$
$\begin{cases} 1 & \|t\| < t_0 \\ 0 & otherwise \end{cases}$	$2t_0\mathrm{sinc}(2t_0 u),\ where\ \mathrm{sinc}(t) = \dfrac{\sin(\pi t)}{\pi t}$

Table 2: Property of Fourier Transform

Property	Formulae
Duality	$F\{X_1(t)\} = x_1(-f)$
Scaling	$F\{ax_1(t)\} = ax_1(-f)$
Linearity	$F\{ax_1(t)\} + bx_2(t)\} = aX_1(f)\} + bX_2(f)$
Translation	$F\{x_1(t - t_0)\} = X_1(f)e^{-j2\pi t_0 f}$
	$F\{x_1(t)\, e^{-j2\pi f_0 t}\} = X_1(f = f_0)$
Convolution	$F\{x_1(t) \otimes x_2(t)\} = X_1(f)X_2(f),$
	$where\ \ x_1(t) \otimes x_2(t) = \displaystyle\int_{-\infty}^{\infty} x_1(\tau)x_2(t - \tau)\, d\tau$
	$F\{x_1(t)x_2(t)\} = \displaystyle\int_{-\infty}^{\infty} X_1(u)X_2(f - u)\, du$

typical signals. Note that in the table, $\delta(*)$ is the Dirac delta function.

The Fourier transform of a cosine signal, $\cos(2\pi f_0 t)$, contains two delta functions in the frequency domain, one at f_0, and the other at $-f_0$, which is negative. The convention of negative frequency serves as a powerful mathematical tool in signal analysis. In fact, the use of negative frequency is mandatory for representing real signals—for example, the cosine signal in the frequency domain.

From the definition, it is straightforward to show that the Fourier transform satisfies a few nice properties, including linearity and duality. Assuming that a and b are two constants, $x_1(t)$ and $x_2(t)$ are two signals, and $X_1(f)$ and $X_2(f)$, are their Fourier transforms, we list several important properties of Fourier transform in Table 2. These properties will be referred to in the rest of this chapter.

When $x(t)$ is a real signal, $|X(f)|$ is symmetric with respect to the origin. Figure 1 shows the waveform and the power spectrum of a typical speech signal. To reveal the details of high frequency components of the signal, we plot $20\log|X(f)|$ in Figure 1b. The symmetry of the spectrum is clearly shown in that figure. The symmetry means that, for a real signal, no information is lost if we only consider the positive frequency components. The frequency component at $f = 0$ is called the *direct current* (DC) component, and the frequency components of nonzero frequencies are called the *alternating current* (AC) component. Although the human voice covers a wider frequency range (from 100 Hz to 8000 Hz), research has shown that the intelligent part of human speech is carried in the range of 300 Hz to 3400 Hz (Rabiner 1993). Figure 1b shows that the energy of the voice power spectrum actually concentrates in this band.

AMPLITUDE MODULATION

Modulation is the process of varying a carrier signal in order to convey information. The purpose of modulation is to create a signal with frequencies in a desired part of the spectrum that are more compatible with the system. A carrier signal is normally a cosine wave at a certain frequency. It can be represented by the following function:

$$v_c(t) = A_c\cos(2\pi f_c t + \Phi(t))$$

where A_c is the amplitude, and $2\pi f_c t + \Phi(t)$ is the angle.

Generally, there are two types of modulations: amplitude modulation and angle modulation. *Amplitude modulation* utilizes the carrier's amplitude to convey information, and *angle modulation* embeds the information in the angle of the carrier signal. Angle modulation can be further

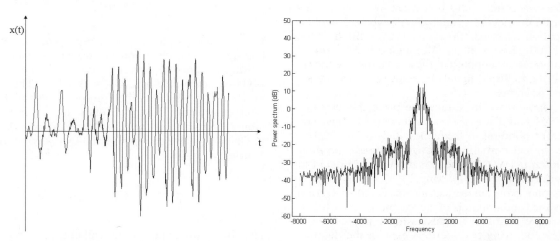

Figure 1: Waveform and power spectrum of a voice signal—(a) waveform and (b) power spectrum

categorized into *frequency modulation* and *phase modulation*. In frequency modulation, the instantaneous frequency varies relative to the information signal; in phase modulation, the instantaneous phase varies with the information signal. Because phase modulation is similar to frequency modulation, we do not cover it in this chapter. Interested readers may refer to Schweber (2002).

In this section, we briefly introduce three common amplitude modulation techniques: the basic AM modulation, the suppressed carrier and single sideband AM, and vestigial sideband AM. The frequency modulation will be addressed in the next section.

The Basic AM Modulation

Assume $f(t)$ is the information signal and $v_c(t) = A_c \cos(2\pi f_c t)$ is the carrier signal; the basic AM modulation scheme modifies amplitude of the carrier, A_c, with $f(t)$ by the following formula:

$$s_{AM}(t) = [A_c + f(t)]\cos(2\pi f_c t)$$

To simplify the analysis, we assume that the information signal is a sinusoid, $f(t) = A_i \cos(2\pi f_i t)$. Then the above formula becomes

$$s_{AM}(t) = [A_c + A_i \cos(2\pi f_i t)]\cos(2\pi f_c t)$$
$$= A_c[1 + \beta_{AM}\cos(2\pi f_i t)]\cos(2\pi f_c t),$$
$$\text{where } \beta_{AM} = A_i/A_c$$

β_{AM} is called the AM index, and $|\beta_{AM}| \leq 1$. Figure 2(a) shows the waveforms of the carrier signal and the information signal, where $f_c = 10$, $A_c = 2$, $A_i = 1$, and $f_i = 1$. In the time domain, the envelope of the carrier follows the information signal.

Let $F(f)$ and $V_c(f)$ represent the Fourier transforms of $f(t)$ and $v_c(t)$. Table 1 tells us that $F(f) = A_i[\delta(f - f_i) + \delta(f + f_i)]/2$, and $V_c(f) = A_c[\delta(f - f_c) + \delta(f + f_c)]/2$. The two spectrums are shown in Figure 2b, each containing two Dirac delta functions at $\pm f_i$, and $\pm f_c$, respectively. Figure 3a shows the waveform of the modulated signal, $s_{AM}(t)$. Let $S_{AM}(f)$ denote its Fourier transform. From the convolution property listed in Table 2, we know that the Fourier transform of the product of two signals is the convolution of the Fourier transforms of the two signals. $S_{AM}(f)$ can be computed as follows:

$$S_{AM}(f) = \frac{A_c}{2}[\delta(f - f_c) + \delta(f + f_c)]$$
$$+ \left[\frac{A_i}{2}(\delta(f - f_i) + (\delta(f + f_i))\right]$$
$$\otimes \left[\frac{1}{2}(\delta(f - f_c) + (\delta(f + f_c))\right]$$
$$= \frac{A_c}{2}[\delta(f - f_c) + \delta(f + f_c)]$$
$$+ \frac{A_i}{4}[\delta(f - f_c - f_i) + \delta(f - f_c + f_i)$$
$$+ \delta(f + f_c - f_i) + \delta(f + f_c + f_i)]$$

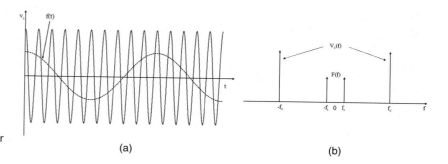

Figure 2: Information signal and carrier signal—(a) waveform and (b) spectrum

(a)

(b)

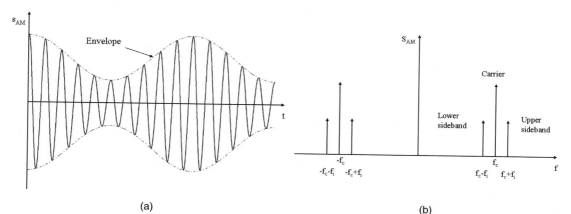

(a)

(b)

Figure 3: Modulated signal of the basic AM modulation—(a) waveform and (b) spectrum

Figure 3b plots the spectrum of the modulated signal. It is composed of the spectrum of the original carrier at $\pm f_c$ and two copies of the spectrum of the information signal whose origins are shifted to $\pm f_c$. Let us take a closer look at the copy centered at f_c. The two delta functions at $f_c - f_i$ and $f_c + f_i$ are called the *lower sideband* (LSB) and the *upper sideband* (USB), respectively. Two observations from Figure 3b are that (1) more energy is spent on the carrier signal than on the information signal and (2) the modulated signal takes twice the bandwidth of the baseband information signal.

There are several methods to demodulate the basic AM modulation, and the simplest one is the envelope detector. It detects the envelope of the incoming signal by first rectifying the signal by a diode and then removing high frequency components that are outside of the spectrum of information signal by a resistor-capacitor low-pass filter. The main disadvantage of the envelope detector is that it is not particularly linear and the distortion level may be high. Coherent demodulation technique provides superior quality, and we will discuss it in the next section.

Suppressed Carrier and Single Sideband AM

Basic AM spends more energy on the carrier signal than on the information signal. Besides, the two sidebands carry the identical spectrum information, and they require twice the bandwidth of the modulating signal. To solve these two issues, the carrier and the one of the sidebands (LSB or USB) in Figure 3b could be removed. When only the carrier is removed, it is called *double-sideband suppressed carrier* (DSB-SC) AM. When both carrier and one sideband are removed, it is called *single-sideband suppressed carrier* (SSB-SC) AM.

The carrier can be suppressed by removing the DC component of the envelope in Figure 3a. The modulated signal becomes $s_{DSB-SC}(t) = f(t)\cos(2\pi f_c t)$, and its Fourier transform is $S_{DSB-SC}(f) = [F(f - f_c) + F(f + f_c)]/2$. Let $f(t) = \cos(2\pi f_i t)$, then we have $s_{DSB-SC}(t) = \cos(2\pi f_i t)\cos(2\pi f_c t)$, and the spectrum of the DSB-SC signal is shown in Figure 4a.

If we want to remove the LSB, an ideal high-pass filter with a cutoff frequency at f_c has to be applied. On the other hand, an ideal low-pass filter with a cutoff frequency at f_c can get rid of the USB. In reality, because either low-pass or high-pass filters have a certain transition

band, we cannot cleanly remove one sideband without affecting the other. If the information signal takes limited bandwidth, for example, a voice signal takes the frequency band from 300 Hz to 3400 Hz, a certain amount of transition band (in this case, 600 Hz) is tolerated.

Following the example shown in Figure 4a, if we just keep the upper sideband, then the spectrum of the SSB-SC signal is $S_{SSB-SC}(f) = [\delta(f - f_c - f_i) + \delta(f + f_c + f_i)]/4$, and its time domain expression is $s_{SSB-SC}(t) = 0.5\cos(2\pi (f_i + f_c) t)$. The spectrum of $s_{SSB-SC}(t)$ is shown in Figure 4b. In this special case, the modulated signal actually has a constant amplitude, which is quite different from the basic AM and DSB-SC AM cases. It is obvious that the envelope detector cannot demodulate the SSB-SC modulated signal.

Both DSB-SC and SSB-SC can be demodulated by coherent demodulation, which is accomplished by remodulating the modulated signal with a local carrier signal with the same frequency and in phase with the original carrier signal—for example, $\cos(2\pi f_c t)$. In the frequency domain, the remodulation basically shifts the spectrum of the modulated signal by f_c and $-f_c$, which recovers the baseband spectrum of the original signal with a few high-frequency components (images). After filtering out the high-frequency components, the information signal is recovered.

Vestigial Sideband AM

Vestigial sideband (VSB) AM is a scheme between the basic AM and the suppressed sideband AM. When the information signal contains low frequency or even the DC component, it is impossible to implement the suppressed sideband AM. In VSB AM, while one sideband of the modulated signal is kept, part of the other sideband is kept also. The modulation procedure is shown in Figure 5a. $H_{VSB}(f)$ is the vestigial sideband filter. The Fourier transform of $s_{VSB}(t)$ is

$$S_{VSB}(f) = \tfrac{1}{2} H_{VSB}(f)[F(f - f_c) + F(f + f_c)]$$

Figure 5b gives an example of the vestigial sideband filter with part of the lower sideband and the entire upper sideband retained.

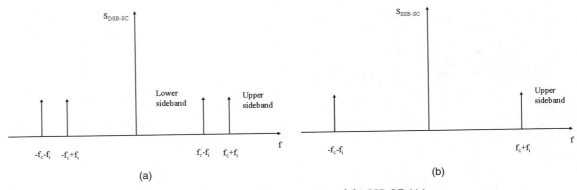

Figure 4: Spectra of (a) DSB-SC and (b) SSB-SC AM

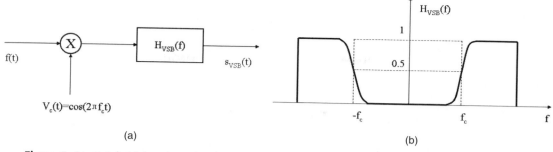

Figure 5: Vestigial sideband amplitude modulation—(a) generation of VSB signal and (b) VSB filter

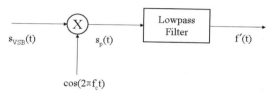

Figure 6: Demodulation of the VSB signal

The demodulation of the VSB signal can be achieved by coherent demodulation with the right low-pass filter. Figure 6 shows the diagram of a VSB demodulator.

From Figure 6, we have $s_p(t) = s_{VSB}(t)\cos(2\pi f_c t)$. By the convolution property listed in Table 2, we can compute the Fourier transform of $s_p(t)$ as follows:

$$
\begin{aligned}
S_p(f) &= \tfrac{1}{2}[S_{VSB}(f - f_c) + S_{VSB}(f + f_c)] \\
&= \tfrac{1}{4}[H_{VSB}(f - f_c)[F(f - 2f_c) + F(f)] \\
&\quad + H_{VSB}(f + f_c)[F(f) + F(f + 2f_c)]] \\
&= \tfrac{1}{4}[F_f[H_{VSB}(f - f_c) + H_{VSB}(f + f_c)] \\
&\quad + \tfrac{1}{4}[H_{VSB}(f - f_c)F(f - 2f_c) \\
&\quad + H_{VSB}(f + f_c)[F(f + 2f_c)]
\end{aligned}
$$

The second item of $S_p(f)$ in the last equation contains high-frequency components, and it can be removed by a suitable low-pass filter. For the first item, to ideally recover the information signal $f(t)$, $H_{VSB}(f)$ has to satisfy the following condition:

$$
H_{VSB}(f - f_c) + H_{VSB}(f + f_c) = \text{constant}
$$

This means that $H_{VSB}(f)$ is complementary-symmetric about the carrier frequency f_o, as shown in Figure 5b. The most popular VSB filters are root-raised cosine filters and linear roll-off filters. They are widely used in data communication systems and TV broadcasting systems, respectively.

FREQUENCY MODULATION

In frequency modulation, the information signal is represented by the instantaneous frequency of a carrier signal.

In contrast to AM, it offers many advantages in noise reduction, signal fidelity, and power efficiency, but it also requires more complex circuits for the transmitter and receiver. In this section, we present the basic theory of frequency modulation.

Assume the information signal is $f(t)$ and the carrier signal is $v_c(t) = A_c\cos(2\pi f_c t)$. Then the time domain representation of the FM signal $s_{FM}(t)$ is given by the following formula:

$$
s_{FM}(t) = A_c\cos\left(2\pi\int_0^t [f_c + K_{FM}f(\tau)]d\tau\right)
$$

where K_{FM} is the constant that controls the frequency deviation. Based on the above formula, we can easily compute the instantaneous frequency of $s_{FM}(t)$ as $f_{FM}(t) = f_c + K_{FM}f(t)$.

Figure 7 shows an example of frequency modulation. The information signal $f(t)$ and the original carrier $v_c(t)$ are the same as those shown in Figure 2a. In this example, we set $K_{FM} = 1$.

Comparing Figure 7 to Figure 3a, we can see the difference between AM and FM: AM modulates the amplitude of the carrier without changing the carrier's frequency, and FM keeps the amplitude of the carrier constant but modulates the instantaneous frequency of the carrier.

To study the FM spectrum, we use a sinusoidal modulating signal $f(t) = A_i\cos(2\pi f_i t)$. In this case, $s_{FM}(t)$ can be written as

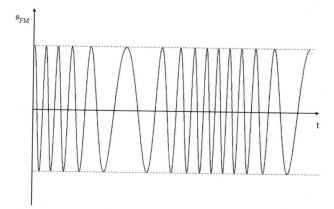

Figure 7: Waveform of a frequency-modulated signal

$$s_{FM}(t) = A_c \cos\left(2\pi \int_0^t [f_c + K_{FM}A_i \cos(2\pi f_i \tau)]d\tau\right)$$

$$= A_c \cos\left(2\pi f_c t + \frac{K_{FM}A_i}{2\pi f_i}\sin(2\pi f_i t)\right)$$

$$= A_c \cos(2\pi f_c t + \beta_{FM}\sin(2\pi f_i t)),$$

$$where\ \beta_{FM} = \frac{K_{FM}A_i}{2\pi f_i}$$

$$= A_c \cos(2\pi f_c t)\cos(\beta_{FM}\sin(2\pi f_i t))$$
$$- A_c \sin(2\pi f_c t)\sin(\beta_{FM}\sin(2\pi f_i t))$$

β_{FM} in the above equation is called the *modulation index* of the FM signal, which is the ratio of the peak frequency deviation to the carrier's frequency. Depending on the value of β_{FM}, FM can be classified into narrowband FM when $\beta_{FM} < 0.2$ and broadband FM otherwise.

For narrowband FM, we have the following approximation:

$$\cos(\beta_{FM}\sin(2\pi f_i t)) \approx 1,\ \sin(\beta_{FM}\sin(2\pi f_i t)) \approx \beta_{FM}\sin(2\pi f_i t)$$

Then $s_{FM}(t)$ becomes

$$s_{FM}(t) = A_c \cos(2\pi f_c t) - A_c\beta_{FM}\sin(2\pi f_i t)\sin(2\pi f_c t)$$
$$= A_c \cos(2\pi f_c t) + \frac{A_c\beta_{FM}}{2}[\cos(2\pi(f_c + f_i)t)$$
$$- \cos(2\pi(f_c - f_t)t)]$$

Comparing this equation to the time representation of AM signal $s_{AM}(t)$, we know that they are similar. Both modulated signals have a carrier component and two sidebands. The bandwidth of narrowband FM is also twice the bandwidth of the information signal. The Fourier transform of $s_{FM}(t)$ is

$$S_{FM}(f) = \frac{1}{2}[\delta(f - f_c) + \delta(f + f_c)]$$
$$+ \frac{A_c\beta_{FM}}{4}[\delta(f - f_c - f_i) + \delta(f + f_c + f_i)]$$
$$- \frac{A_c\beta_{FM}}{4}[\delta(f - f_c + f_t) + \delta(f + f_c + f_i)]$$

Figure 8 plots $S_{FM}(f)$. Compared to Figure 3b, the spectrum of a narrowband FM signal is similar to the spectrum of an AM signal. One dissimilarity is that the signs of the two sidebands of $S_{FM}(f)$ are different.

For broadband FM, we can express $\cos(\beta_{FM}\sin(2\pi f_i t))$ and $\sin(\beta_{FM}\sin(2\pi f_i t))$ in series of the *Bessel functions* of the first kind $J_n(\beta_{FM})$ (Cantrell 2000):

$$\cos(\beta_{FM}\sin(2\pi f_i t)) = J_0(\beta_{FM}) + 2\sum_{n=1}^{\infty}J_{2n}(\beta_{FM})\cos(2n2\pi f_i t)$$

$$\sin(\beta_{FM}\sin(2\pi f_i t)) = 2\sum_{n=1}^{\infty}J_{2n-1}(\beta_{FM})\sin(2n-1)2\pi f_i t)$$

Interested readers can find more details about Bessel functions of the first kind in the appendix. Plugging these

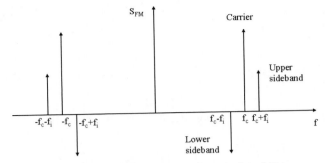

Figure 8: Fourier transform of narrowband FM

two equations into the original $s_{FM}(t)$ and applying a few properties of Bessel functions, we get

$$S_{FM}(t) = A_c \sum_{n=-\infty}^{\infty} J_n(\beta_{FM})\cos(2\pi(f_c + nf_i)t)$$

and its Fourier transform $S_{FM}(f)$ is

$$S_{FM}(f) = \frac{A_c}{2}\sum_{n=-\infty}^{\infty} J_n(\beta_{FM})[\delta(f - f_c - nf_i) + \delta(f + f_c + nf_i)]$$

From the above equation, we know that the spectrum of an FM signal contains infinite components, where the component at the carrier's frequency is determined by $J_0(\beta_{FM})$ and the components of the nth sideband are determined by $J_n(\beta_{FM})$. Figure 9 illustrates the spectrum of a broadband FM signal. Theoretically, the bandwidth of an FM signal is infinite, but normally we can safely ignore the high-order sidebands when $|J_n(\beta_{FM})|$ is small enough. The bandwidth can also be estimated by *Carson's rule*, which is $W = 2f_i(1 + \beta_{FM})$.

The simplest way to demodulate the FM signal is through the use of an FM discriminator such as that shown in Figure 10. The output of the differentiator $s_d(t)$ is

$$s_d(t) = A_c 2\pi[f_c + K_{FM}f(t)]\sin\left(2\pi \int_0^t [f_c + K_{FM}f(\tau)]d\tau\right)$$

$S_d(t)$ is basically a sinusoidal function with envelope $f_c + K_{FM}f(t)$. This form is similar to the modulated signal of the basic amplitude modulation, and an envelope detector can extract the signal $f_c + K_{FM}f(t)$.

FREQUENCY DIVISION MULTIPLEXING

Multiplexing refers to a process by which multiple information signals are combined for transmission in one physical channel. Basically, there are two types of multiplexing: *frequency division multiplexing* (FDM) and *time division multiplexing* (TDM). Figure 11 illustrates the concepts of FDM and TDM. In FDM, each signal takes a certain band within the bandwidth of the channel, and all signals are transmitted simultaneously. In TDM, all signals take the entire available bandwidth, and each signal is transmitted for a certain period of time.

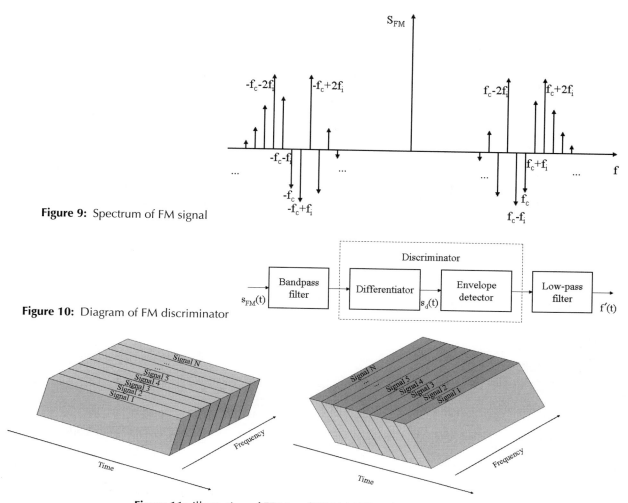

Figure 9: Spectrum of FM signal

Figure 10: Diagram of FM discriminator

Figure 11: Illustration of FDM and TDM (a) FDM (b) TDM

Figure 12 shows the diagram of an FDM system. Normally, the system consists of three main parts: the transmitter, the channel, and the receiver. The entire bandwidth of the channel is split into a set of nonoverlapping bands, and each band is used for transmitting one information signal. On the transmitter side, because the input signals may not be strictly band-limited signals, low-pass filters must be applied to remove any unwanted high-frequency component of the input signals. Then the spectrum of each information signal is moved to the desired band of frequency by the modulator. Before summing all modulated signals together and sending them through the shared channel, each modulated signal goes through a bandpass filter to prevent any spectral overlap among the modulated signals.

On the receiver side, the received signal is passed to a set of bandpass filters to extract the modulated signals. Then each modulated signal passes the demodulator and a low-pass filter to recover the corresponding baseband signal.

One key challenge in an FDM system is to eliminate the interference among different frequency bands, mainly because of the harmonics of the modulated signals caused by the nonlinearity of the modulators. This type of interference is called *cross talk*. To effectively reduce the cross talk, the carriers' frequencies have to be designed carefully, and certain guard bands need to be inserted between the adjacent frequency bands.

FDM has been widely used in many communication systems. Although some communication systems rely on proprietary wires or cables, many other systems actually share the same radio frequency spectrum, which is a finite nature resource. Table 3 lists the radio frequency spectrum that is suitable for radio communications. Note that in the table, ITU refers to the International telecommunication Union, which is responsible for many global communication standards and recommendations.

To meet the increasing demand of this limited resource because of rapid development of new radio-based services and to optimize the usage of the resource, it has to be regulated by governments and international standards organizations (U.S. Department of Commerce 2003; Roke Manor Research 2004). The way to manage the spectrum is to divide the radio frequency spectra into blocks of various sizes that meet the requirements of different services and to allocate them to services on an exclusive or shared basis, either for free use or licensed usage. Table 4 lists the spectrum range of a few common broadcast services in the United States.

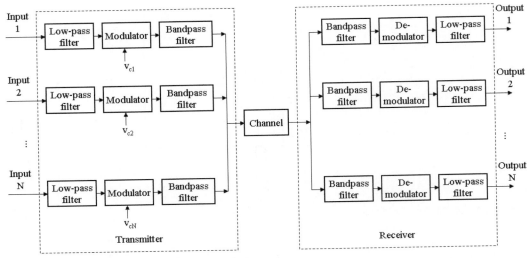

Figure 12: Diagram of the FDM system

Table 3: Radio Frequency Spectrum

ITU band / Designation	Frequency	Wavelength	Sample application
1 ELF (extreme low frequency)	3–30 Hz	100–10 mm	Communication with submarines
2 SLF (super low frequency)	30–300 Hz	10–1 mm	
3 VF (voice frequency)	300–3000 Hz	1–0.1 mm	Communication within mines
4 VLF (very low frequency)	3–30 kHz	100–10 km	Avalanche beacons
5 LF (low frequency)	30–300 kHz	10–1 km	AM (long-wave) broadcasts
6 MF (medium frequency)	300–3000 kHz	1–0.1 km	AM (medium-wave) broadcasts
7 HF (high frequency)	3–30 MHz	100–10 m	Shortwave broadcasts and amateur radio
8 VHF (very high frequency)	30–300 MHz	10–1 m	FM and television broadcasts
9 UHF (ultrahigh frequency)	300–3000 MHz	100–10 cm	Television broadcasts, mobile phones, wireless LANs
10 SHF (super high frequency)	3–30 GHz	10–1 cm	Microwave devices, wireless LANs, radars
11 EHF (extreme high frequency)	30–300 GHz	1–0.1 cm	Radio astronomy
Decimeter	300–3000 GHz	1–0.1 mm	Night vision

Table 4: Broadcast Frequencies

Broadcast service	Broadcast frequencies
AM radio	535 kHz–1605 kHz
TV band I (channels 2–6)	54 MHz–88 MHz
FM radio	88 MHz–108 MHz
TV band II (channels 7–13)	174 MHz–216 MHz
TV band III (channels 14–69)	470 MHz–806 MHz

APPLICATIONS OF FREQUENCY DIVISION MULTIPLEXING

As mentioned previously, FDM has been widely used in various areas, including the analog carrier system, FM radio, terrestrial TV broadcast systems, and space remote sensing. In this section, we discuss a few representative FDM applications: specifically, the analog carrier system, the NTSC TV broadcast system, and the FM radio broadcast system.

Analog Carrier System

In an analog carrier system, *single sideband* (SSB) is adopted to combine multiple voice channels in one medium such as analog microwave and coaxial cable. The frequency of speech can range from approximately 100 Hz to 8 kHz. However, the primary components necessary for speech are contained in the range of 300 to 3400 Hz. Considering the guard band, each voice channel is assigned 4 kHz as its bandwidth. In this section, we represent the spectrum as a triangle, as shown in Figure 13. The voice spectrum is marked by the gray area in the figure. Representing the spectrum by a triangle makes it easy to locate the low- and high-frequency components simply by their spectral

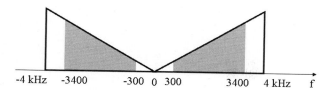

Figure 13: Spectrum of one voice channel

Table 5: FDM Multiplex Levels

Level	Capacity (Channels)
Group	12
Basic supergroup	60
Basic mastergroup	300
Basic supermastergroup	900

densities. In Figure 13, the low-frequency component has small spectral density, and the high-frequency component has large density. This is normally not true in reality, but the representation is convenient in illustrating the multiplexing scheme in the analog carrier system. For example, we can easily identify the two sidebands of a modulated signal based on the shapes of their spectra.

The U.S. carrier system was initiated by the American Telephone and Telegraph (AT&T) and the ITU-T (originally the CCITT, Consultative Committee on International Telegraph and Telegraph). They are responsible for the

international standard for the FDM hierarchy. In this section, we will focus on the hierarchy specified by the ITU-T. Table 5 lists a few hierarchies in the ITU-T recommendations (ITU-T 1993). The FDM hierarchy ranges from a single voice channel up to a basic super master group as illustrated in Figure 14.

The basic group is composed of twelve voice channels, as shown in Figure 15. The basic group occupies 48 kHz of bandwidth between 60 kHz and 108 kHz. Single sideband suppressed carrier modulation is utilized. In an ITU-T recommendation (ITU-T 1993), the lower sidebands are universally selected.

Five basic groups are translated up to a higher frequency range, and they become the basic supergroup. As shown in Figure 16, the carrier frequencies are 420 kHz for group 1, 468 kHz for group 2, 516 kHz for group 3, 564 kHz for group 4, and 612 kHz for group 5. The basic supergroup occupies 240 kHz of bandwidth between 312 kHz and 552 kHz.

Similarly, one basic mastergroup contains five supergroups. Figure 17 shows the formation of a mastergroup. There is a guard band of 8 kHz between adjacent supergroups. For example, the upper band of the first modulated supergroup is 1052 kHz, and the lower band of the second modulated supergroup is 1060 kHz, leaving 8 kHz in between. Consequently, each basic mastergroup takes a total of 1232 kHz bandwidth between 812 kHz and 2044 kHz.

The multiplexing procedure for the supermastergroup is shown in Figure 18. It is composed of three mastergroups and occupies the band between 8516 kHz and 12,388 kHz. Each mastergroup takes 1232 kHz, and there

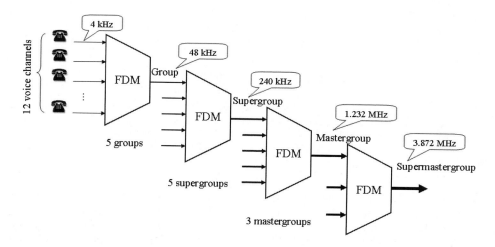

Figure 14: DFM hierarchy

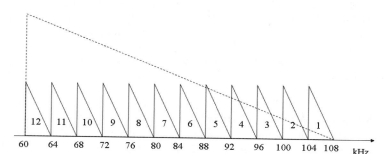

Figure 15: The ITU-T basic group

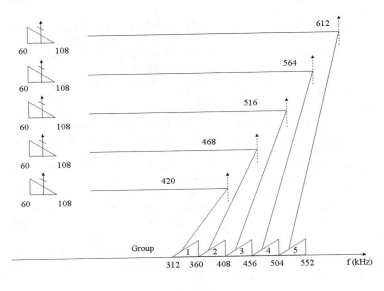

Figure 16: Formation of supergroup (ITU-T G.233)

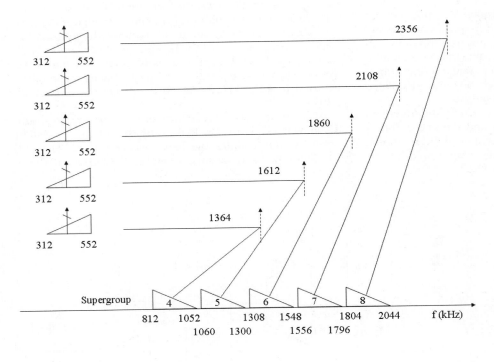

Figure 17: Formation of mastergroup (ITU-T G.233)

is a guard band of 88 kHz between adjacent mastergroups. The carrier frequencies are 10,560 kHz, 11,880 kHz, and 13,200 kHz, respectively.

In the U.S. telephone network, there are more multiplex levels (Minoli 2003). For example, AR6A level has the capacity of 6000 voice channels, L5 level has 10,800, and L5E has 13,200 voice channels. Although the analog carrier system had dominated the global telephone network for many decades, it has given way to the recent digital technology.

NTSC TV Broadcast System

There are three major analog television systems: *National Television System Committee* (NTSC), *phase alternating line* (PAL), and *sequential color with memory* (séquential colour avec mémoire, or SECAM). Figure 19 shows the geographical distribution of the three systems around the world (Wikipedia undated). NTSC is the committee that developed the television standards for the United States, which are also used in Canada, Japan, South Korea, and several Central and South American countries. Both the committee and the standard are called NTSC. In this section, we focus on the spectrum structure of the NTSC channel and the FDM scheme in the NTSC system.

In a television set, color pictures are displayed by producing the three primary colors, red (R), green (G), and blue (B). For the purpose of efficient transmission and backward compatibility to the black-and-white television system, the RGB components in the NTSC system are

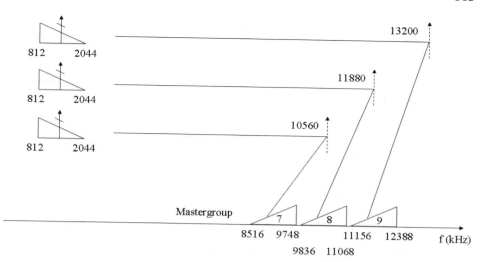

Figure 18: Formation of super-mastergroup (ITU-T G.233)

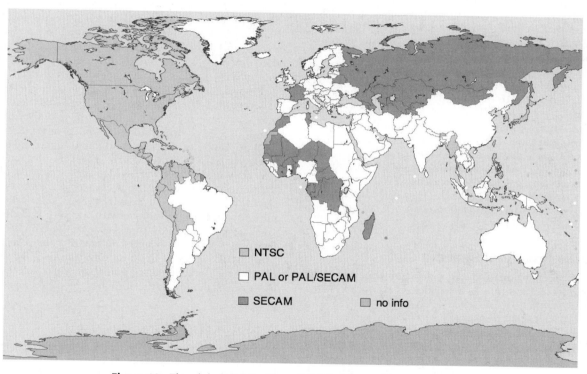

Figure 19: The global distribution of NTSC, PAL, and SECAM systems

transformed into one luminance component, Y, and two chrominance components I (orange-cyan balance) and Q (green-magenta balance). I and Q components have the virtue of requiring much less bandwidth for subjectively acceptable picture quality than the Y component. Y component takes 4.2 MHz bandwidth, but very good picture rendition can be achieved in most cases with I and Q band-limited to 1.4 MHz and 0.5 MHz, respectively (Netravali and Haskell 1995).

Figure 20 shows how the video signal and audio signals are multiplexed into a 6 MHz bandwidth. The Y component is modulated using vestigial sideband AM. Each sideband of the Y component is 4.2 MHz wide, and the entire upper sideband and only 750 kHz of the lower

sideband are transmitted. The video carrier is 1.25 MHz above the lower bound of the channel. The I and Q components are *quadrature amplitude modulated* (QAM) with suppressed carrier. QAM is a modulation scheme that modulates two carrier waves by the information signals. These two waves, usually a sine and a cosine signal with the same frequency, are called *quadrature carriers*. The color subcarrier is 4.79545 MHz above the lower bound. The modulated I signal covers from −1.5 MHz to +0.5 MHz from the color subcarrier, sent as double sideband; and the modulated Q signal covers from –0.5 MHz to +0.5 MHz from the subcarrier, also sent as double sideband. The audio signal is frequency modulated at the highest 250 kHz of each channel. The main audio carrier is

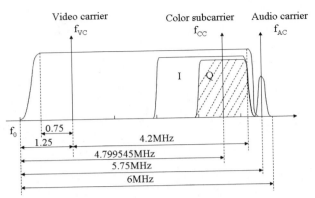

Figure 20: Spectrum of one NTSC channel

4.5 MHz above the video carrier. The audio signal modulation is compatible with the FM radio broadcast system.

In the NTSC system, a guard band occupies the lowest 250 kHz of the channel to avoid interference between the video signal of the current channel and the audio signals of the next channel down.

In North America, terrestrial TV broadcasting operates on channels 2 to 6 (VHF low band, from 54 MHz to 88 MHz), 7 to 13 (VHF high band, from 174 MHz to 216 MHz), and 14 to 69 (UHF TV band, from 470 MHz to 806 MHz). Table 6 lists the frequency band, the video carrier frequency, and the color and audio subcarrier frequencies for each channel in the VHF band.

For cable TV (CATV), channels 2 through 13 operate on the same frequencies as broadcast TV as shown in Table 6. Channels 14 to 22 take the frequency band from 120 MHz to 174 MHz, and channels 23 to 94 take the band from 216 MHz to 648 MHz.

FM Radio Broadcast System

Both AM modulation and demodulation can be easy, which led to the boom in AM broadcasts from the 1920s

through the late 1950s. FM radio, and later stereo FM radio, were both developed in the United Sates. The first experimental FM radio station, W1XOJ, was granted a construction permit by the Federal Communications Commission (FCC) in 1937. FM became the mainstream in 1978 when the number of FM stations surpassed that of AM stations. According to the FCC, more than 12,000 FM stations now operate in the North America alone (Federal Communications Commission undated).

FM radio was originally assigned a frequency band of 42 MHz to 50 MHz with 200 kHz channel spacing by the FCC in 1940; the FCC moved the band to 88 MHz and 106 MHz in 1945. Throughout the world, the FM broadcast band is 87.5 to 108.5 MHz. In the United States, FM broadcast stations operate between 87.9 MHz and 107.9 MHz; in China, it is between 92 MHz and 108 MHz. Japan is the only exception, running FM broadcasts in the band of 76 MHz to 90 MHz with 100 kHz channel spacing.

A *pilot tone multiplex system* was added to FM radio in the early 1960s to allow FM stereo transmissions. To be backward-compatible with monaural FM receivers, the left (L) and right (R) audio channels are transformed into the sum (L + R) and the difference (L − R) signals for modulation, instead of being modulated directly.

Figure 21 shows the stereo multiplexing scheme in FM broadcasting. The sum signal (L + R) takes the baseband part that covers 15 kHz bandwidth, and the difference signal (L − R) is amplitude-modulated onto 38 kHz by a DSB-SC modulation. The modulated signal takes a frequency band of 23 kHz to 53 kHz. A 19-kHz pilot tone, which is exactly one-half of the 38-kHz subcarrier frequency, is then added to indicate the presence of a stereo-encoded signal. A guard band of ±4 kHz (15–23 kHz) protects the pilot tone from interference with the sum and difference signals. When the pilot tone is absent, the FM receiver just recovers the baseband signal. Otherwise, the receiver doubles the frequency of the pilot tone and uses it to demodulate the difference signal and then generates the stereo sounds based on both the sum and the difference signals.

Table 6: Standard NTSC Television Frequencies in VHF Band (MHz)

Channel	Band	Video carrier frequency	Color subcarrier frequency	Audio subcarrier frequency
2	54–60	55.25	58.8295	59.75
3	60–66	61.25	64.8295	65.75
4	66–72	67.25	70.8295	71.75
5	76–82	77.25	80.8295	81.75
6	82–88	83.25	86.8295	87.75
7	174–180	175.25	178.8295	179.75
8	180–186	181.25	184.8295	185.75
9	186–192	187.25	190.8295	191.75
10	192–198	193.25	196.8295	197.75
11	198–204	199.25	202.8295	203.75
12	204–210	205.25	208.8295	209.75
13	210–216	211.25	214.8295	215.75

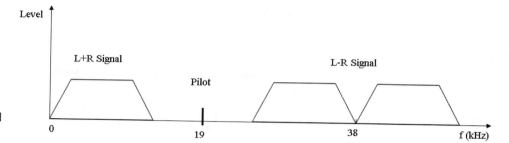

Figure 21: Stereo multiplexed signal in FM radio broadcasting

The stereo multiplexing system has been further extended to add an extra, even higher frequency 57 kHz subcarrier (the third harmonic of the pilot), which is used to carry low-bandwidth digital radio data system information, allowing digitally controlled radios to provide extra features.

Normally, the content of FM broadcasting is speech and music, and their spectrum energy concentrates at the low frequencies within the baseband. The noise power spectral density at the output of the FM demodulator is proportional to the square of the frequency (Stremler 1990) with the effect that noise dominates at the high frequencies within the baseband. This deteriorates the signal-to-noise ratio for the high-frequency band. One technique to solve this problem is pre-emphasizing the high-frequency components of the audio or music signals before transmission and de-emphasizing the high-frequency components after receiving, such that the high-frequency noise is effectively reduced without affecting the fidelity of the original audio signal.

CONCLUSION

In this chapter, we presented the frequency division multiplexing technology. To give a reasonably complete and in-depth coverage of this topic, we introduced the underlying theories, including the basic Fourier transform, amplitude modulation, and frequency modulation; described the principles of FDM; and discussed three exemplary applications of FDM—the analog carrier telephone network, the TV broadcast system, and the FM radio broadcast system.

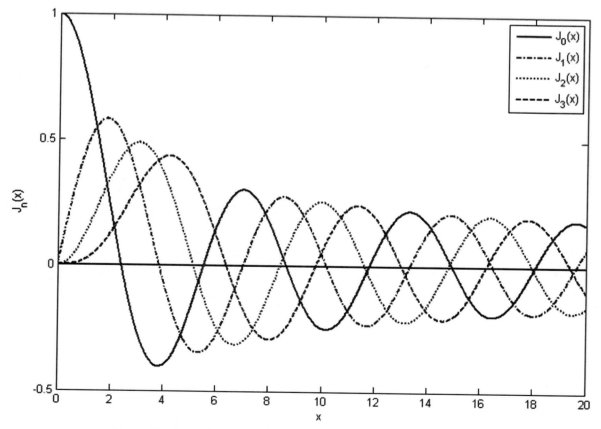

Figure 22: Bessel functions of the first kind, $J_n(x)$, with $n = 0, 1, 2,$ and 3

FDM technologies have enabled a wide range of historical and modern telecommunication systems, and hence significantly affected our daily lives and contributed to the civilization of the human being. Surely, FDM will continue to serve as the basis for many new communication technologies and services in the future.

APPENDIX: BESSEL FUNCTION OF THE FIRST KIND

Bessel functions of the first kind, denoted by $J_n(x)$, are defined as the solutions to the Bessel differential equation

$$x^2 \frac{d^2 y}{dx^2} + x \frac{dy}{dx} + (x^2 - n^2) y = 0$$

which are nonsingular at the origin. They can also be represented by their Taylor series expansions around $x = 0$,

$$J_n(x) = \sum_{m=0}^{\infty} \frac{(-1)^m \left(\frac{x}{2}\right)^{n+2m}}{m!(m+n)!}$$

Figure 22 illustrates $J_n(x)$ with $n = 0, 1, 2$, and 3.

The following are a few useful properties of Bessel functions of the first kind when n is an integer.

1. Relationship of $J_n(x)$ and $J_{-n}(x)$:

$$J_{-n}(x) = (-1)^n J_n(x)$$

2. Sum identity:

$$\sum_{n=-\infty}^{\infty} J_n(x) = 1, \quad \text{for } \forall x$$

3. Approximation when x is small ($x \to 0$):

$$J_0(x) \approx 1$$
$$J_1(x) \approx x/2$$
$$J_n(x) \approx 0, n > 1$$

4. Derivative identity:

$$\frac{d}{d_x}[x^n J_n(x)] = x^n J_{n-1}(x)$$

For an in-depth discussion about the Bessel functions, please refer to Cantrell (2000).

GLOSSARY

Amplitude modulation: A process of varying a carrier signal in which the amplitude of the carrier varies relative to the information signal.

Analog carrier system: A system that transmits more than one voice channel over a wideband path by modulating each channel on a different carrier frequency.

Carrier signal: Normally, a single frequency signal that can be modulated to carry analog or digital signal information.

Frequency division multiple access (FDMA): A technology that enables multiple users to share a physical communication channel by frequency division multiplexing.

Frequency division multiplexing (FDM): A technique in which the available bandwidth of a transmission channel is divided by frequency into narrower bands such that each band is used for a separate voice, video, or data transmission.

Frequency modulation (FM): A process of varying a carrier signal in which the instantaneous frequency of the carrier varies relative to the information signal.

Modulation: A process of varying a carrier signal in order to convey information.

Multiplexing: A process in which multiple information signals are combined for transmission in one physical channel.

National Television System Committee (NTSC): The committee that developed the television standards for the United States and which are also used in Canada, Japan, South Korea, and several Central and South American countries. Both the committee and the standard are referred to by *NTSC*.

CROSS REFERENCES

See *Frequency and Phase Modulation*; *Orthogonal Frequency Division Multiplexing (OFDM)*; *Statistical Time Division Multiplexing (STDM)*; *Time Division Multiplexing (TDM)*; *Wavelength Division Multiplexing (WDM)*.

REFERENCES

Cantrell, C. D. 2000. *Modern mathematical methods for physicists and engineers*. New York: Cambridge University Press.

Freeman, R. L. 1998. *Telecommunications transmission handbook*. 4th ed. New York: John Wiley & Sons.

Federal Communications Commission. Undated. FM radio database (retrieved from www.fcc.gov/mb/audio/fmq.html).

ITU-T. 1993. Recommendation G.233. *Concerning translating equipments*, November.

Minoli, D. 2003. *Telecommunications technology handbook*. 2nd ed. Boston: Artech House.

Netravali, A.N., and B. G. Haskell. 1995. *Digital pictures representation, compression, and standards*. 2nd ed. New York: Plenum Press.

Oppenheim, A.V., A. S. Wilsky, and S. H. Nawab. 1996. *Signals and systems*. 2nd ed. Upper Saddle River, NJ: Prentice Hall.

Rabiner, L., and B. H. Juang. 1993. *Fundamentals of speech recognition*. Englewood Cliffs, NJ: Prentice Hall.

Rappaport, T. 2001. *Wireless communications*. 2nd ed. Upper Saddle River, NJ: Prentice Hall.

Roddy, D. 2006. *Satellite communications*. 4th ed. New York: McGraw-Hill.

Roke Manor Research. 2004. The UK Frequency allocations (retrieved from www.roke.co.uk/download/ datasheets/UK_Radio_Frequency_Allocations.pdf.

Schweber, W. L. 2002. *Electronic communication systems*. 4th ed. New York: Pearson Education.

Stremler, F. G. 1990. *Introduction to communication system*. 3rd ed. New York: Addison Wesley.

U.S. Department of Commerce. 2003. United States frequency allocations: The radio spectrum (retrieved from www.ntia.doc.gov/osmhome/allochrt.pdf).

Wikipedia. Undated. NTSC-PAL-SECAM distribution map (retrieved from http://en.wikipedia.org/wiki/ Image:NTSC-PAL-SECAM.png).

Time Division Multiplexing

William A. Shay, *University of Wisconsin, Green Bay*

INTRODUCTION
Shared Communication Lines

When it comes to data transmissions, most would agree that higher bit rates are better. If you have ever upgraded to a faster computer or disk drive or switched from a dialup Internet connection to broadband or DSL service, then you no doubt discovered that the faster response times helped you work (or play) more efficiently. Some of us old-timers remember when the first 3.5-inch drives became available. The ability to get a file in just a couple of seconds was a wonderful improvement over the 5.25-inch drives. Now with the hard disk drives and flash memory sticks available today, those 3.5 inch disks are all but obsolete.

The same is true of communication networks: Faster is generally better. Speed does have its drawbacks, however. First, it is more expensive; second, there is a point of diminishing returns. In other words, after a certain point, many users cannot use the increased speed and there is little to gain by further increasing the bit rate capacities. For example, communications links in some networks are now capable of bit rates of more than 1 Gigabit per second (Gbps). However, devices such as telephones and workstations simply do not generate the volume of data necessary to make use of that speed. One might infer from this that developing high-speed networks is therefore not important because most users cannot utilize their full potential. This is not true, however. Suppose the communication network shown in Figure 1 supports a bit rate of 10 Megabits per second (Mbps). If the only activity involves two PCs communicating at that rate, then the network likely serves its purpose. However, if several hundred PCs need to communicate with one another, then the total amount of data that must be transmitted per second will in all likelihood exceed the 10-Mbps rate. Thus, in

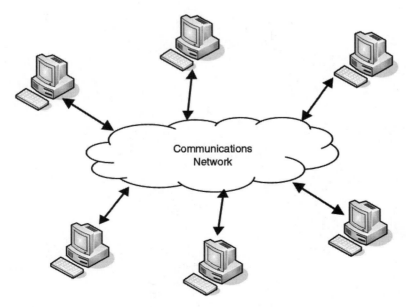

Figure 1: Many users communicating over a network

this case, the 10-Mbps limit creates a serious bottleneck. Increasing the bit rate will reduce that bottleneck.

A good analogy is a road through a large city. If there were only a few cars using it, then a single lane road would be sufficient. If, however, during rush hour the road is shared by many more vehicles, then there is a need to move them quickly. Consequently, the vehicle-carrying capacity of a single lane becomes insufficient and multiple lanes are required to increase the capacity. Similarly, communication links in a network are shared by many, and there is a need to move far more data than can be generated by a single workstation.

Multiplexer

Now that we have established the need for high-speed capabilities to transmit data from many devices, we must connect those devices to the network. One could provide a high-speed connection between a communications network and every device that uses it. It would be a little like building multilane highways directly to everyone's house. However, the cost of doing this is not justified. One approach is to develop high-speed communication networks but somehow reduce the cost of connecting devices to them by using links with lower bit rates. Because many devices do not require high bit rates, those links should service the devices just fine. However, defining connections to the network for each possible device becomes an issue. In Figure 1, each device has a separate connection to the network. Figure 2 shows an alternative using a *multiplexer* (sometimes called *MUX*), a device that combines transmissions from multiple sources onto a single communications link. These devices could be telephones, workstations, cable TV stations broadcasting TV signals, or any of a variety of devices capable of sending and receiving information. The multiplexer may also route transmissions in the reverse direction—that is, from the network to any of the devices.

In general, a multiplexer's output line to the network has a much higher bit rate than any of the input lines from the sources. This way it can utilize the network's high bit rate and, by providing a single connection for multiple users, provide a more efficient way for multiple users to connect to the network.

There are several forms of multiplexing. One is *frequency division multiplexing;* it deals with analog signals

such as those in an analog cable television network. It works by modulating different analog signals onto different frequency ranges and producing a single but more complex analog signal consisting of frequencies from all the different ranges. This technique is discussed in "Frequency Division Multiplexing (FDM)." Another form is *wavelength division multiplexing* and works by combining multiple optical signals, each with a different wavelength of light, into a different optical signal consisting of the combined wavelengths. It is typically used for transmission over an optical fiber. "Wavelength Division Multiplexing (WDM)" discusses this approach. There is also *optical multiplexing;* as the name suggests, it deals with the combining of optical signals (see "Synchronous Optical Code Division Multiplexing Systems"). The focus of this chapter is on time division multiplexing, which works primarily by combining digital data from different sources into a common bit stream.

TIME DIVISION MULTIPLEXERS
Basic Operations

A *time division multiplexer* (TDM) will interpret its inputs as a collection of *bit streams*. These bits are then combined and transmitted together. Figure 3a illustrates the basic process. Suppose A, B, C, and D represent bit streams from distinct sources headed into the multiplexer. The multiplexer scans each input line, grabs some bits from each line, combines them into a single bit stream, and then sends the stream over the output line. As the bits are being sent, the TDM repeats the process by grabbing more bits from each of the input lines and then combines and transmits them as soon as the previous bits have been sent. If the timing is right, the multiplexer will grab more bits just in time to transmit them immediately following the previous ones. This process keeps the output line active and makes full use of its capacity. Each group of bits is allocated a small amount of time for transmission over the output line, hence the term *time division multiplexing.*

Because the bit groups came from different sources, it is logical to assume they each have different destinations and that the multiplexer has a companion device on the other end of the transmission line. Figure 3b shows the device called a *demultiplexer* accepting a single bit stream from its input, extracting substreams of bits as they arrive, and routing the substreams out along different output lines. As with the multiplexer, timing is an issue. If the timing is right, a substream of bits destined for the first output line arrives just as the demultiplexer routes the previous substream over the last output line.

Bit-Interleaved Multiplexers

Although the previous discussion outlines the general approach to multiplexers, there are different types of multiplexers. For example, a *bit-interleaved multiplexer* will take one bit at a time from each input line and combine them before transmitting them over the output line. Figure 4 shows an example. One bit from each stream is taken from each input line and transmitted one after another. The spaces between each set of four bits are

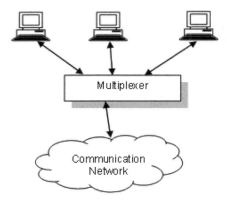

Figure 2: Multiplexing low-speed devices onto a high-speed network

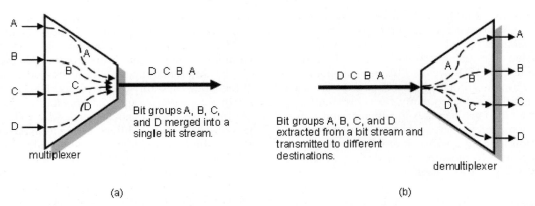

Figure 3: Merging bit groups from multiple sources into a single frame for transmission

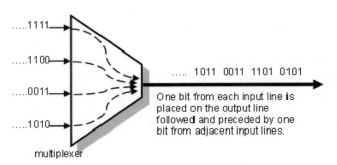

Figure 4: Bit-interleaved multiplexing—one bit from each input line is combined into a common stream

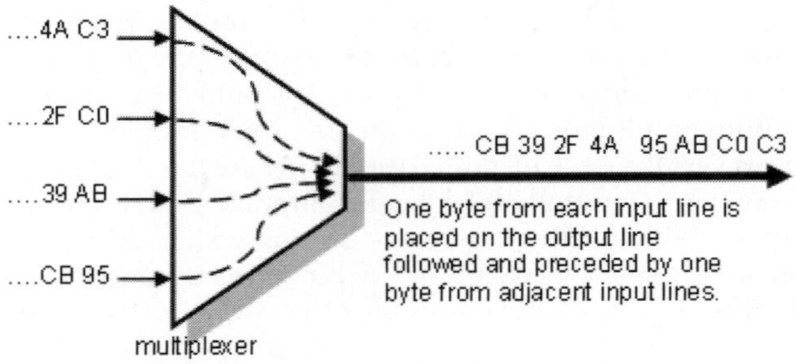

Figure 5: Byte-interleaved multiplexing

inserted there for clarity. The main idea is that the right-most group, 0101, consists of the rightmost bits from each input stream. The adjacent group to the left consists of the second rightmost bits from each input stream. This pattern continues for each group.

Bit-interleaved multiplexing tends to be efficient and requires little buffering capabilities, in contrast to other forms described shortly. However, bit-interleaved multiplexing is not usually the best match for many microprocessor-based devices, whose data are organized by bytes. However, a few applications use the technology. For example, Tsukada et al. (1996) describe an application for bit-interleaved multiplexing in the design of photonic ATM switches. Bit-interleaved multiplexing is also used in the T-carrier system. We discuss T-carrier system later, and Goralski (2002) also provides a more detailed discussion of the technology.

Byte-Interleaved Multiplexers

Byte-interleaved multiplexing works in a similar fashion except that a full byte is transferred from an input line to the output line between bytes from adjacent lines. For example, suppose the inputs in Figure 5 are expressed in hexadecimal format. Then every two hexadecimal digits represent one byte. The multiplexer routes one byte from an input line to the output line before getting the byte from the next input line. Byte-interleaved multiplexing is also used in the previously mentioned T-carrier system. However, we need to present additional topics before we describe its use.

Framing

A common approach in multiplexing involves framing the output. In other words, data that are transmitted over the output line are placed into a *frame*, a unit of transmission that is consistent with the protocol governing the output line. Figure 6 illustrates how this works. The bit streams A_1, B_1, C_1, and D_1 enter the multiplexer through different input lines. The multiplexer creates a frame with those bits as input and then transmits the frame over the outgoing line. It then gathers A_2, B_2, C_2, and D_2, creates another frame, and sends it. The process continues as long as the sources are providing bit streams for the outgoing frames.

Transmission Rates

An important part of the multiplexer's design depends in part on the input and output transmission rates. How quickly should the multiplexer transmit bits over the outgoing line? For example, suppose data from a source arrive at a rate of 10 Mbps. If the multiplexer transmits them at the same rate, there is a problem because bits from other inputs are also arriving, thus making the combined input bit rate much larger than 10 Mbps. If there were ten such inputs, then the combined bits arrive at the multiplexer at a rate of 100 Mbps and the multiplexer should be able to send them at that same rate.

In general, if source bits from the combined inputs arrive faster than the previous frame can be sent, then frames are generated more quickly than they can be forwarded. If the multiplexer has no capacity to store the extra frames, then there will be problems. Input lines must

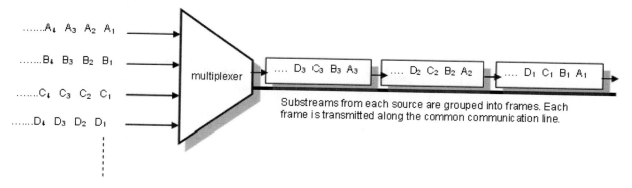

Figure 6: Framing TDM output

not provide the multiplexer with information faster than it can release the information without some type of buffering capacity. On the other hand, if the source bits arrive too slowly, then the previous frame will have been sent and the multiplexer either waits for enough bits to arrive or sends a frame that is only partially full. Either way, the output line is not used to its fullest capacity.

An ideal situation occurs when the combined input rate (the sum of bit rates from each source) equals the output bit rate. For example, suppose that there are n sources, r_i is the input rate from the ith source, and r_{output} is the bit rate of the output line. Mathematically, we express this as

$$\sum_{i=1}^{n} r_i = r_{output}$$

This is consistent with our previous example of ten ($n = 10$) inputs, each with a 10-Mbps rate, and one output line with a rate of 100 Mbps. However, we will discuss an alternative shortly.

Synchronous TDM

There are two different types of TDMs, and we introduce one here: *synchronous TDM*. However, we must first define the concept of a time slice. A *time slice* is a portion of the outgoing frame that is reserved specifically for data from one of the input lines. A synchronous TDM is a multiplexer that reserves a time slice for each input line, thus guaranteeing that every outgoing frame will carry some data from each input line, assuming that such data are available. In Figure 6, each frame consists of four time slices, each containing bits from one of the four input lines. Furthermore, those slices are guaranteed. For example, as long as there are bits arriving from the first input line, some of them are guaranteed to go out with each departing frame. Similar comments can be made for each of the other input lines.

Synchronous TDMs have an important advantage in applications where a certain amount of bandwidth between two points must be guaranteed to meet the needs of the application. Perhaps the most visible example is the infrastructure that we know as the telephone system. Making a telephone call involves establishing a real-time connection between two telephones. The underlying

hardware ensures that digitized voice data will travel between numerous pairs of telephones simultaneously with almost no noticeable delays. It does this, in part, by using synchronous TDMs that guarantee that each link in the path between two phones is able to carry part of the telephone conversation with every frame it transmits. This provides for a smooth and consistent flow of voice data without the delays that buffering data at intermediate sites might cause. Note the contrast with performance you may have observed while downloading large files where the rate of arriving data increases and decreases over time. We will describe additional details of this process later in this chapter.

Variable Input Rates

Not all multiplexers operate in as simple an environment as we have described. Sometimes there is an issue that deals with the relative rates of input lines with respect to each other. The previous scenario has assumed that bits arrive from all sources at the same rate. Under this assumption, each source is assigned to one time slice inside of each frame. However, what if the rates among the input lines differ? For example, what if the bits from the first source, A, arrive at a rate twice that of all the other sources? In such a case, the process shown in Figure 6 does not work well. When all the bits in A_1 arrive, only one-half of the bits from each of groups B_1, C_1, and D_1 have arrived; the multiplexer cannot fill the time slices associated with those groups. One approach is to simply transmit the frame with the times slots reserved for groups B, C, and D only half full. This, of course, underutilizes the outgoing bandwidth capacity.

Figure 7 shows another way to deal with this situation. Because the bit rate of the first input line is twice that of each of the other lines, the multiplexer receives bit groups A_1 and A_2 in the same amount of time that it receives B_1, C_1, and D_1. Because the multiplexer has these five bit groups, it can allocate five time slices of the outgoing frame, one for each group. Thus, A_1 and A_2 occupy two consecutive time slices but otherwise occupy the same frame as B_1, C_1, and D_1. Similarly, bit groups A_3 and A_4 occupy the same frame as B_2, C_2, and D_2, and so on.

However, even this example does not cover all cases. The assumption that the first input had a rate twice that of the others was convenient. However, what if the rate

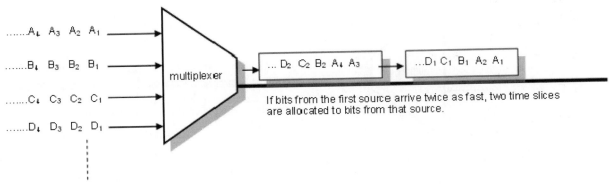

Figure 7: Framing data assuming different input rates

from source A was 1.4 times that of the others? As before, when the first bit group from A arrives, there is still an insufficient number of bits from the other groups to fill the respective time slices. If the TDM waits for the other bit groups to arrive, then there are too many bits from source A to fill one time slice but not enough to fill two time slices. One approach to this problem is for the TDM to perform *bit stuffing*, sometimes called *bit padding*. This means the TDM will fill as many time slices in a frame as is possible for the fastest input line. If the last time slice is not full, then the TDM will insert extra bits so that the time slice has the same number of bits as the other slices. These bits are not part of the data flow and are there solely to maintain a constant size for all the time slices in the frame. At the opposite end, the demultiplexer removes the padded bits and discards them. For example, assuming that A provided bits at 1.4 times the rate of other sources, then bits from A would fill the first time slice but only 40 percent of the second. The remaining 60 percent of that slice would consist of padded bits.

Inactive Input Lines

There are still other scenarios we have not mentioned. The discussion so far has assumed the input lines are always transmitting bits. As long as bits are arriving on an input line, the time slices in the outgoing frame are occupied, even if only partially. However, a logical question to ask is, What if there are no bits arriving on a particular input? One approach is to simply do bit stuffing in an entire time slice (or more if several lines are quiet). In such cases, the number of meaningful bits transmitted per unit of time may fall well below the bit rate of the outgoing line and the line becomes underutilized. In an extreme case, the number of stuffed bits could actually be larger than the number of data bits.

In response, another alternative is to increase n, the number of input lines, so that

$$\sum_{i=1}^{n} r_i > r_{output}$$

Although the bits would then potentially be arriving faster than they can be sent, such designs are used in cases where it is expected that some of the inputs will generally be inactive and that active lines would produce bits at a rate comparable to r_{output}. Of course, these multiplexers must also be designed to account for periodic bursts where, for short periods of time, they can handle the extra bits. This may involve buffering the input streams and creating variable-sized frames. Such a device is called a *statistical multiplexer*. Some variations are called *concentrators* or *asynchronous TDMs*.

In general, a statistical multiplexer will allocate a time slice of an outgoing frame to whatever input line needs it. Data from different inputs may occupy different time slices in the outgoing frame. Furthermore, there is no guarantee that arriving input will be sent out with the next outgoing frame. If there is a surge of activity, then the input may have to be buffered until another outgoing frame can accommodate it, thus causing a delay in the transmission of the data. Note the contrast with synchronous TDMs that guarantee that a part of every outgoing frame is reserved for data from each of its inputs. The potential delay in the transmission is a disadvantage in systems where data must be transmitted in timely fashion without delay. On the other hand, it is useful in cases where data transfer is bursty such as with the Internet. For example, there may be periods of high transfer rates if a PC is downloading a large file and periods of extremely low rates if the PCs user is casually following Web links. In such cases, the TDM can handle a larger number of input lines than a synchronous TDM could. Other examples include *point-of-sales* terminal (cash registers) in stores, remote meters, and even lottery or gaming machines.

An analysis of statistical multiplexers can be difficult because of the random way in which the sources send data. Many questions must be answered. How frequently will the combined input rates exceed the output rate? How often will all sources be busy? How large must the internal buffers be to handle temporary surges? Because data from different input lines may occupy different times slices, how does the demultiplexer know how to handle them? How long are the delays when surges occur? One approach to the analysis uses *queuing theory*, a field of mathematics that defines models for studying events such as waiting in lines (queues) for events to occur. It can be applied to many areas, including communications systems in which input streams may arrive in random patterns. In such cases, the events are the transmissions over the output lines. Stallings (2004), Walrand (2000), and Martin (1972) contain introductory discussions of queuing theory. Also, because statistical time division multiplexing is the topic of the chapter "Statistical Time Division Multiplexing (STDM)," we will not discuss it further here.

T-CARRIER SYSTEM

Our next step is to describe a common environment in which TDMs are used. Much of what we think of as the telephone system was designed to transmit digitized voice signals over high-speed media such as optical fiber or microwaves. In fact, years ago AT&T developed a complex hierarchy of communications systems used to multiplex voice and data signals and transmit them all over the United States. The *T-carrier system* is used primarily in North America and Japan. European countries and most of the rest of the world use a similar but different system known as the *E-carrier system*.

History

The history of the T-Carrier System dates back to the 1960s when AT&T developed the technology to deal with the growing number of telephone users. As new homes were built, telephone wires had to be installed between them and the existing central offices of the local phone company. As neighborhoods grew, there was a need for additional central offices to accommodate them, and communication links had to be established between central offices. Rather than provide wires for all of the new users, AT&T needed a better way to route all of the customers' phone calls between central offices. This was the beginning of what is known as the *T1 line*.

T1

The T-carrier system consists in part of a synchronous byte-interleaved multiplexer that combines digital signals from twenty-four different sources into a common frame called a *digital signal* 1 (DS-1) *frame* (Figure 8). This frame is then transmitted over a T1 line. The T1 multiplexer takes eight bits at a time from each source and places each eight-bit group into a time slice of the outgoing DS-1 frame. This time slice defines a channel between a specific source and destination. If the source and destinations are telephones, then each time slice in effect transmits part of a telephone conversation between those phones. In such cases, the T1 multiplexer is sometimes called a *T1 channel bank*.

In addition to the twenty-four channels, the frame contains an extra bit, called a *framing bit*, at the beginning of each frame. Thus, each frame contains $24 \times 8 + 1 = 193$ bits. The framing bit allows the demultiplexer to determine the beginning of the frame and, consequently, identify the exact location of each channel inside the frame so that it may extract those bits and route them appropriately. The framing bit also has other functions that we describe shortly.

Figure 9 provides one possible context for using a T1 carrier system. At each source is a telephone. The telephone generates an analog signal that represents the sound of the person's voice. However, because most of the telephone system is digital, the analog signals must be converted to a digital representation. A device called a *codec* does this. It will sample the analog signal at a rate of 8000 samples per second using a method called *pulse code modulation* to take the samples. Depending on the signal's characteristics at the time of the sample, the codec generates eight bits that are then transmitted to the multiplexer.

The reason for the sampling rate of 8000 samples per second results from the well-known Nyquist theorem (Forouzan 2007), which states that an analog signal can be reconstructed from its digital representation if samples are taken at a rate at least twice that of the signal's highest frequency. Because 4000 Hz is at the upper end of the telephone's bandwidth range, a sampling rate of 8000 times per second is used.

Each eight-bit sample then occupies one time slice in the DS-1 frame, and consecutive samples from the same source are stored in successive DS-1 frames. The voice messages are thus transmitted using many DS-1 frames to a demultiplexer. This demultiplexer extracts the bits from each time slice and routes them toward their appropriate destination, where they eventually are converted back to analog signals that represent the sound of a person's voice. The net effect is that up to twenty-four phone conversations are transmitted over the same T1 line using the channels in a DS-1 frame.

We stated previously that the bit rate of a synchronous multiplexer's output must be able to accommodate the combined rates of the input lines. Each eight-bit sample is generated at a rate of 8000 samples per second, yielding a bit rate of 64 kbps. To support this speed, T1 must transmit a DS-1 frame every 1/8000 of a second, or 8000 frames per second. In other words, it must transmit 8000×193 bits each second for a bit rate of 1.544 Mbps. However, because one bit for each frame is overhead, the

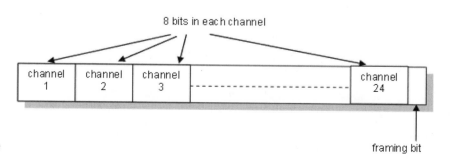

Figure 8: A 193-bit DS-1 frame

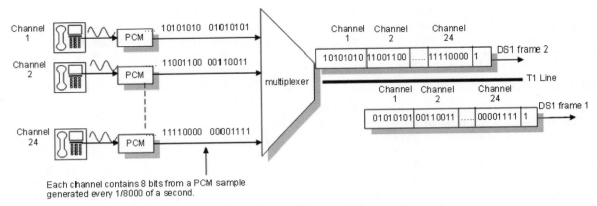

Figure 9: T1 carrier system

bit rate to move real data (also called *payload data*) is actually reduced by 8 kbps to 1.536 Mbps.

Superframe and Extended Superframe Format

Typical implementations of T1 actually combine multiple DS-1 frames into a larger frame structure to facilitate administration and synchronization. In fact, there are two different framing techniques in which multiple DS-1 frames are combined into either a *superframe* (SF) or *extended superframe* (ESF) format. A superframe consists of twelve DS-1 frames as shown in Figure 10; the process of creating it is called *D-4 framing*. However, not all DS-1 frames are the same. For example, the framing bits from the twelve frames occur in the pattern 1-0-0-0-1-1-0-1-1-1-0-0. Although this bit pattern may seem arbitrary, there is a reason for it. Inside a superframe, the framing bits are divided into two categories. The framing bits from each of the odd-numbered frames are *terminal framing* bits and occur in the pattern 1-0-1-0-1-0. The receiving demultiplexer knows the pattern and uses the alternating sequence to keep the frames and, of course, the channels synchronized.

The framing bits in even-numbered frames are *signal framing* bits and occur in the pattern 0-0-1-1-1-0. In this case, the transition of a signal framing bit from a 0 to a 1 (or vice versa) is significant. For example, the signal framing bit changes from 0 to 1 in the sixth frame and from a 1 to a 0 in the twelfth frame and identifies those frames as ones that carry additional control information. Superframes store that information in the least significant bits

of each of the twenty-four channels in both the sixth and twelfth frames. This means that two bits can be used to describe the status of each channel for each superframe. For example, if the channel corresponds to a telephone connection, then the bits can specify whether either phone is "on-hook" or "off-hook." The use of these bits for control removes a small part of the voice data. This process is called *bit robbing* but has little effect in cases where the data are a voice signal.

The ESF is similar to the SF and was designed to provide more functionality and control information such as error detection and maintenance communication. It also makes use of more advanced technology so that fewer synchronization bits are needed. One difference from the SF format is that the ESF consists of twenty-four DS-1 frames instead of twelve. Another difference is in how the 193rd bit in each of the twenty-four DS-1 frames is used. Of those twenty-four bits, only six are used for synchronization; they appear in frames 4, 8, 12, 16, 20, and 24. Six more bits (from frames 2, 6, 10, 14, 18, and 22) are used for *cyclic redundancy check* (CRC). These bits are calculated from existing data and are used to detect transmission errors. More information about CRC can be found in Shay (2004). The remaining twelve bits from the odd-numbered frames define an administrative channel that is used to communicate performance information and alarms (problems on the T1 line).

Like the SF format, the ESF also uses bit robbing from DS-1 frames 6, 12, 18, and 24. Using more bits than in the SF format allows more options in describing the status of each channel. To be sure, the details of T1 are complex and impossible to cover in this chapter. Additional

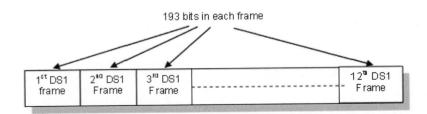

Terminal Frame alignment bit pattern (first bit in each odd numbered frames): 1-0-1-0-1-0
Signaling Frame alignment bit pattern (first bit in each even numbered frames): 0-0-1-1-1-0
Combined pattern: 1-0-0-0-1-1-0-1-1-1-0-0

Figure 10: T1 superframe format

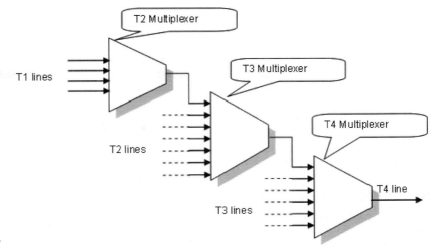

Figure 11: Digital services hierarchy

information may be found in Hajbandeh (2000) and is also available from Wikipedia (undated, "Digital signal 1") and NComm (2001).

Plesiochronous Digital Hierarchy

The T1 rate of 1.544 Mbps is slow when compared with the capabilities of optical fibers and the needs for high-speed traffic along the backbone of a communications network. However, T1 is only one part of a digital hierarchy of services known as the *plesiochronous digital hierarchy* (PDH). As defined by the ITU-T standard G.702, PDH is designed to transmit large amounts of information over a digital transport infrastructure. The standard specifies additional carrier and signal designations with more channels and faster bit rates. Figure 11 shows how the carriers and channels relate, and Table 1 lists the designations, number of channels, and bit rates for each.

According to Figure 11, four T1 lines enter a T2 multiplexer, which multiplexes them to generate a DS-2 frame, and then transmits the frame on the outgoing T2 line. There are important differences between multiplexing at this level and the previous one. First, the DS-2 frame is formed by bit multiplexing the incoming data from T1 lines. Second, the multiplexer also adds control bits to the T2 line at the rate of 136 kbps. These control bits perform similar functions as previously mentioned, distinguishing between successive DS-2 frames, but also include stuffed bits to account for any differences in the timing of incoming DS-1 signals. Four DS-1 frames collectively provide input at a rate of $4 \times 1.544 = 6.176$ Mbps. Add

the overhead of 136 kbps, and the required bit rate of a T2 line is 6.312 Mbps.

Proceeding in similar fashion, seven T2 lines are input to another bit-interleaved multiplexer, which generates a DS-3 frame on an outgoing T3 line. This multiplexer adds another 552 kbps of overhead, pushing the required bit rate of a T3 line to 7×6.312 Mbps + 552 kbps = 44.736 Mbps. Finally, the last multiplexer combines the data from six T3 lines into a DS-4 frame, adds yet more overhead bits, and sends them over a T4 line at a rate of 274.176 Mbps.

The exact format of the various frames and the specifics of all the overhead and control bits are beyond what this chapter can cover. For those who are interested, more information is available in Goralski (2002), Cisco Systems (2004), Juniper Networks (1998), and Digital Link (1996).

As mentioned previously, this system is used in North America and Japan. However, most of the rest of the world uses the E-carrier system ("E" for European) that, although similar in concept, is incompatible to the T-carrier system. For example, where T1 defines twenty-four 8-bit channels and a bit rate of 1.544 Mbps, E1 defines thirty-two 8-bit channels and a bit rate of 2.048 Mbps. It also provides methods similar to T1 for synchronization and conveying channel status. This standard also groups multiple E1 frames together into a multiframe format, but we will not elaborate on specifics. Also, as with the T-carrier system, there is a hierarchy defined by different levels of multiplexing. Table 2 shows the designations and rates at each of the levels.

Table 1: ITU G.702 PDH Specifications

Carrier	Frame designator	Number of channels	Transmission rate (Mbps)
T1	DS-1	24	1.544
T2	DS-2	96	6.312
T3	DS-3	672	44.736
T4	DS-4	4032	274.176

Table 2: E-Carrier Service

Carrier	Number of channels	Transmission rate (Mbps)
E1	30	2.048
E2	120	8.448
E3	480	34.368
E4	1920	139.264

SONET AND SDH

PDH and the E-carrier system are by no means the only digital carrier systems. In fact, before the breakup of AT&T in 1984, each telephone company had its own TDM technology. After 1984, local companies had to interface with multiple long-distance providers, which generated a need to develop standards. One standard that grew from this need is the *synchronous optical network* (SONET) developed by Bellcore (Bell Communications Research). It is described by ANSI standards T1.105, T1.106, and T1.117. Yet another system is the *synchronous digital hierarchy* (SDH) defined by ITU-T standard G.707, G.708, and G.709. Although there are differences, the two systems share much; at this level, we will make no distinction and simply refer to the technology as SONET-SDH. "SONET/SDH Networks" discusses these technologies, as does Shay (2004), Kularatna (2004), Ramaswami and Sivarajan (2002), Leon-Garcia and Widjaja (2000), Goralski (2002), and Wikipedia (undated, "Synchronous"). However, two components relate to our discussion on time division multiplexing and we describe them here.

Add-Drop Multiplexer

Figure 12 shows a simplified view of the components that make up a SONET-SDH network. One important component in SONET is the *add-drop multiplexer* (ADM). SONET ADMs may form a ring, often connecting points in large metropolitan areas, in a state, or even across a multistate region. The ADM is a synchronous byte-interleaving multiplexer that extracts traffic from outside the ring and merges it with existing traffic already on the ring. An ADM also works in reverse by providing an exit for ring traffic.

Although the term *multiplexer* is used, it is a little different from the time division multiplexer we described previously. The ADM need not multiplex all external signals into a common frame. In fact, a frame may already contain multiplexed data from a previous ADM and may be traveling the ring when it arrives at another ADM. That ADM, in turn, may add data from an external source to that frame. In other words, the entire frame is not multiplexed, just part of it. Demultiplexing works analogously. Some, but not necessarily all, of the data may be extracted from a frame at an ADM and routed elsewhere; it is not

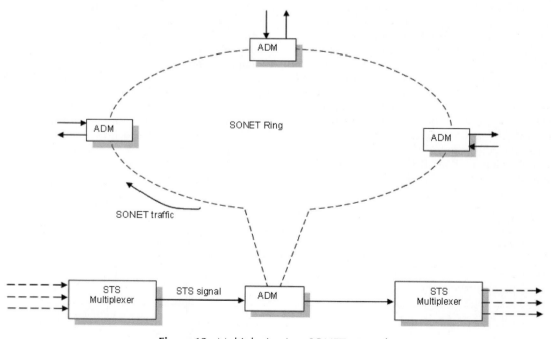

Figure 12: Multiplexing in a SONET network

Table 3: SONET-SDH multiplexing hierarchy

STS level	Optical carrier designation	Bit rate (Mbps)
STS-1	OC-1	51.840
STS-3	OC-3	155.520
STS-12	OC-12	622.080
STS-24	OC-24	1244.160
STS-48	OC-48	2488.320
STS-192	OC-192	9953.280
STS-768	OC-768	39813.120

necessary to demultiplex the entire frame's contents. This is perhaps analogous to a rapid transit system. At the beginning of the run, all passengers board a bus and find a seat (complete multiplexing); at the end, everyone leaves (complete demultiplexing). However, along the route, passengers can board or depart at designated stops (add-drop multiplexing).

SONET-SDH Hierarchy

Just as there is a hierarchy for the T-carrier system, there is one for SONET-SDH also. The basic unit of transmission is the *synchronous transport signal* 1 (STS-1) frame, which contains 810 bytes. Each frame is transmitted once every 125 microseconds along an optical fiber line. Lines that carry STS-1 frames have the designation *optical carrier 1* (OC-1). Sometimes, the signal is called an *OC-1 signal*. Previously cited references describe the contents of this frame, and we restrict our attention here to the hierarchy defined by multiplexing slower lines into faster ones.

Bytes from multiple STS-1 frames can be byte-multiplexed into higher level STS-*n* frames, and each is transmitted over another fiber with a designation of OC-*n*. The value of *n* represents the number of STS-1 frames contained by the STS-*n* frame. Furthermore, because of the synchronous nature of the technology, no additional overhead bits are added as was the case in the T-carrier system. As a result, the bit rate of OC-*n* signals is obtained by multiplying the bit rate of the OC-1 signal by the value of *n*. So, for example, the bit rate of an OC-3 signal is three times the bit rate for an OC-1 signal or 3×51.84 Mbps = 155.52 Mbps. The bit rate for an OC-48 signal is $48 \times 51.84 = 2488.32$ Mbps = 2.48832 Gbps. Table 3 summarizes the SONET-SDH rates and designations.

CONCLUSION

In summary, time division multiplexing combines bits from multiple sources into a single bit stream. Bit-interleaved TDMs combine individual bits from multiple sources, and byte-interleaved TDMs combine bytes from multiple sources. Frequently, the multiplexed data are stored in a single transmission unit called a *frame* (the process is called *framing*). Synchronous TDMs guarantee that some data from each input will occupy a time slice of

an outgoing frame. In such cases, the bit rate of the outgoing line must match the combined bit rates of the input lines. In contrast, statistical TDMs do not dedicate a particular time slice in a frame to a given input. Data may be buffered, waiting to be transmitted in a subsequent outgoing frame. Carrier systems that rely on multiplexing are the T-carrier system, E-carrier system, and SONET-SDH. All define a hierarchy of frame types and bit rates and use multiplexing to combine lower bit-rate lines into a single higher bit-rate line. However, the manner in which they perform the multiplexing varies.

GLOSSARY

Add-drop multiplexer: Device used to extract traffic from outside a SONET-SDH ring and merge it with existing traffic already on the ring.

Bit-interleaved multiplexer: The process of routing one bit at a time from each of several inputs and transmitting the bits in sequence over a shared communication line

Bit rate: Number of bits that can be transmitted per second.

Bit stream: Term used to describe the bit interpretation of an incoming or outgoing electrical or optical signal.

Bit stuffing: Process of inserting extra bits into a frame to fill out a time slice that can only be partially filled.

Byte-interleaved multiplexer: The process of routing one byte at a time from each of several inputs and transmitting the bytes in sequence over a shared communication line.

DS-1 line: A digital signal designator for the transmission of data over a T1 line.

Framing: The process of grouping a bit stream into a physical unit of transmission called a *frame*.

Framing bit: An overhead bit added to a data stream to mark the beginning of a frame and to synchronize the receiver with the frame's time slices.

Plesiochronous digital hierarchy: Standard for a digital service system, defined in part by a hierarchy of multiplexers, each generating signals that are input to the next multiplexer in the hierarchy.

Pulse code modulation: A process that samples analog signals and generates a bit stream dependent on the signal's characteristics.

Synchronization: Making sure that two or more devices use timing that is consistent with each other.

Synchronous time division multiplexer: A multiplexer that reserves a fixed portion of the outgoing frame to data from each of the input lines.

T1 carrier: A digital carrier service with twenty-four channels and a bit rate of 1.544 Mbps.

Time division multiplexing: Process of accepting digital signals from several sources, storing them into a single bit stream, and sending the stream over a communications link.

Time slice: A small amount of time during which bits from a specified source are placed into a frame before transmission.

CROSS REFERENCES

See *Frequency and Phase Modulation*; *Frequency Division Multiplexing (FDM)*; *Orthogonal Frequency Division Multiplexing (OFDM)*; *Statistical Time Division Multiplexing (STDM)*; *Wavelength Division Multiplexing (WDM)*.

REFERENCES

Cisco Systems. 2004. Plesiochronous TDM (retrieved from www.harmontraining.com/GK/08_Plesiochronous%20TDM_R1.ppt).

Digital Link. 1996. T3 fundamentals (retrieved from www.quickeagle.com/PDF/Services/t3fund.pdf).

Forouzan, B. A. 2007. *Data communications and networking*. 4th ed. New York: McGraw-Hill.

Goralski, W. 2002. *SONET/SDH*. 3rd ed. New York: McGraw-Hill.

Hajbandeh, R. 2000. T1, T3, and SONET networks. In *Network design: Principles and applications*, edited by G. Held, 175–94. Boca Raton, FL: Auerbach Publications.

Juniper Networks. 1998. T3 and E3 interfaces overview (retrieved from www.juniper.net/techpubs/software/jseries/junos74/jseries74-config-guide/jN144F1.html).

Kularatna, N., and D. Dias. 2004. *Essentials of modern telecommunications systems*. Boston: Artech House.

Leon-Garcia, A., and I. Widjaja. 2000. *Communication networks: Fundamentals concepts and key architectures*. New York: McGraw-Hill.

Martin, J. 1972. *Systems analysis for data transmission*. Englewood Cliffs, NJ: Prentice-Hall.

NComm. 2001. Communication developers handbook (retrieved from www.ncomm.com/new_site/pdf/NComm-Handbook2006EarlyEdition.pdf).

Ramaswami, R., and K.N. Sivarajan. 2002. *Optical networks: A practical perspective*. 2nd edition. San Francisco: Morgan Kaufmann.

Shay, W. A. 2004. *Understanding data communications and networks*. 3rd ed. Boston: Course Technology.

Stallings, W. 2004. *Data and computer communications*. 7th ed. Upper Saddle River, NJ: Prentice-Hall.

Tsukada, M., W. De Zhong, T. Matsunaga, M. Asobe, and T. Oorhara. 1996. An ultrafast photonic ATM switch based on bit-interleaved multiplexing. *Journal of Lightwave Technology*, 14: 1979–85.

Walrand, J., and P. Varaiya. 2000. *High-performance communication networks*. 2nd ed. San Francisco: Morgan Kaufmann.

Wikipedia. Undated. Digital signal 1 (retrieved from http://en.wikipedia.org/wiki/Digital_Signal_1).

Wikipedia. Undated. Synchronous optical networking (retrieved from http://en.wikipedia.org/wiki/Synchronous_optical_networking).

Statistical Time Division Multiplexing

Kavitha Chandra, *University of Massachusetts, Lowell*

INTRODUCTION

A communications network is defined by its access components and its local and backbone transport infrastructures. Transmission lines such as copper wire, coaxial cable, optical fiber, microwave, and radio frequency links serve to interconnect these components enabling information transfer to take place over long distances. With the exception of the copper wire pair transmitting analog signals between the telephone and the central office switch, almost all other levels in a network implement digital transmission. In digital networks, access devices convert an analog information signal such as voice or video to digital format through the process of sampling, quantization, and coding. Using digital modulation principles, blocks of digital data are mapped to time waveforms and are propagated over the transmission medium. The transport infrastructure is often hierarchical in design. The transmission capacities of the links progressively increase as one moves from the point of access to the core of the network. Access networks aggregate the traffic generated by individual subscribers for transport over higher-capacity links. Traffic from multiple access networks may be further concentrated at successive stages along the transmission path. The process of traffic concentration, also referred to as *multiplexing*, is integral to network design, allowing network providers achieve economies of scale.

Multiplexing refers to the process of combining multiple information-bearing signals onto a single output line. A multiplexer is composed of a set of input and output channels with associated control circuitry, buffers, and a switching mechanism. This concept emerged in the early 1900s with the evolution of the *public switched telephone network* (PSTN). Major George O. Squier (Schwartz 2004) is credited with inventing the carrier multiplexing of telephone signals, having filed a prominent patent in 1911 titled "Multiplex Telephony and Telegraphy." Subsequently, AT&T developed commercial carrier multiplexing systems that modulated several analog voice signals onto high-frequency carrier signals. Each voice grade channel was allocated a 3-kilohertz signal bandwidth with 500-hertz guard bands on each side and shifted to a unique carrier frequency. Frequency division multiplexing was the basis for the successful increase in the capacity of the AT&T L series carrier coaxial systems. The series that began in 1944 with the L1 system carrying 600 telephone conversations, was followed by the improved 1800-call capacity of the L3 system and ended in the 1970s with the L5 system carrying more than 100,000 circuits that multiplexed both telephone and television signals. The coaxial cable–based L systems in the telephone network were supported by microwave radio transmission links and relay stations that were built in the 1950s for transcontinental and interstate calls.

Digital transmission began in the early 1960s, and Time Division Multiplexing (TDM) became a networking standard. AT&T introduced a *digital signaling* (DS-N) hierarchy with supporting carrier systems to transport digitized voice signals, where N represents the level. The T1 carrier for example, operating at 1.544 Mbps and referred to as the DS-1 rate, offered an order-of-magnitude capacity improvement over analog carrier systems. The transmission took place using two twisted-pair copper lines for full duplex communication. Digital carriers were originally used by AT&T to ease congestion in heavily populated areas and in the core switching network. Subsequently, these systems became available to the public and were used for carrying voice and data traffic from private networks to the local exchange switch or to an Internet access router. The long-haul microwave transmission systems and L-carrier coaxial systems were eventually replaced in the 1980s by fiber-optic transmission lines. After AT&T's divestiture, optical transmission systems were standardized under the *synchronous optical network* (SONET) hierarchy in North America and a corresponding *synchronous digital hierarchy* (SDH) in the rest of the world. SONET also implements TDM but uses a synchronous time format—byte interleaving—in contrast to the multiple clock rates or plesiochronous timing used in the DS hierarchy.

Multiplexing principles are fundamental also to the operation of packet-switched data networks. Packets are variable-sized, information-carrying units generated from audio, video, and data applications. Multiplexing on data networks takes place asynchronously on the time scale of the packet. Until recently, the delay and loss performance of Internet traffic was controlled by provisioning high-capacity links and operating at low to moderate levels of link utilization. The need to provide service guarantees for real-time voice and video applications led to the *asynchronous transfer mode* (ATM) network, which was proposed in the 1990s as a platform for a broadband integrated services

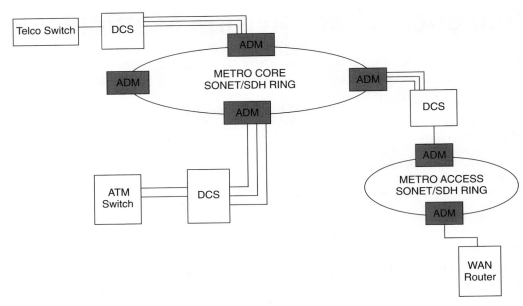

Figure 1: Current architecture of metro core and access networks

digital network. ATM networks implement virtual circuits with varying quality classes for controlling the performance of traffic flows. During this time, network traffic measurement, modeling, and methods for evaluating the capacity gains achieved by statistical multiplexing became important research fields in the data network community. These studies identified the difficulties in the exact characterization of the complex traffic patterns and prediction of the resulting multiplexing efficiency. With respect to the *open systems implementation* (OSI) model for data networking, ATM networks typically appear as a layer 2 (data link) technology and access the SONET-SDH backbone for long-haul transport. SONET backbones also admit a variety of other access interfaces that generate both TDM voice and packet multiplexed data.

The general architecture of a metropolitan area network serving both voice and data transport is depicted in Figure 1. In this figure, the core network is accessed by telephone company switches, ATM switches, and SONET access rings through *digital cross connect* (DCS) systems and *add-drop multiplexers* (ADMs). ADMs can add or drop lower-rate signals to or from higher-rate optical signals, respectively. The synchronous nature of SONET allows addition or dropping without the need for demultiplexing the original signal. DCS systems serve to interface links of varying capacity and provide functions of switching, multiplexing, and demultiplexing. Typically, interface-specific equipment is needed and provided by different vendors. In this architecture, data traffic is time division multiplexed onto a reserved circuit on the SONET backbone. Because these circuits are provisioned with minimum capacities in units of DS-1 rates and data traffic is inherently a variable rate process, it can result in an inefficient utilization of network resources. Packet data traffic continues to be the dominant consumer of network bandwidth, thus creating a critical need for various levels of multiplexing control for transport over optical backbones.

The next section provides an overview of the design and functionality of time division multiplexers. The section titled "Statistical Packet Division Multiplexing" discusses packet division multiplexing and presents packet traffic features that affect multiplexing performance. New protocols proposed for improving statistical multiplexing performance on the SONET-SDH transport infrastructure are discussed in the section preceding the conclusion.

TIME DIVISION MULTIPLEXING

A functional diagram of a time division multiplexer (Held 1999) is shown in Figure 2. The n source streams at the input are aggregated into TDM frames composed of a fixed number of time slots. The position of the data and the number of time slots allocated per source in each frame are fixed parameters. The frames are transmitted over an output link with a transmission rate that is typically greater than the sum of the average bit rates of the input streams. To compensate for the lower arrival rates, each stream is individually buffered by input and output adapters. The central controller polls each input buffer in a predetermined sequence, blocks a sequence of bits from each buffer, and packs the information into the format of a TDM frame along with necessary synchronization information. These frames are buffered again at the output, compensating for any difference in the switching speed of the controller relative to the available frame transmission rate.

The block size associated with each source can range from one bit per source to one character per source or a combination of these levels, based on the application. In the case of a telephone network, the input streams to the multiplexer are digitized speech signals arriving at a rate of 64 kbits/sec. The multiplexer admits $n = 24$ source streams and allocates eight bits per source in each TDM frame and one bit for synchronizing the transmitter and

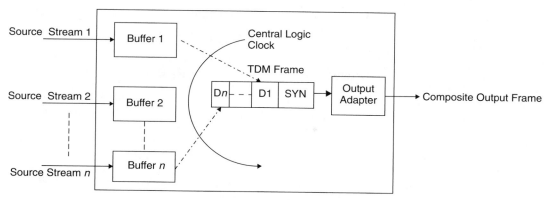

Figure 2: Time division multiplexer

receiver. The resulting TDM frame consist of 193 data bits and is 125 microseconds in duration for transmission over a link with a capacity of 1.544 Mbps. The digital signal transmission hierarchy specified by the American National Standards Institute (ANSI) refers to the 64-kbps signaling rate of each voice channel as a base rate, denoting it DS-0. The next level, DS-1, corresponds to 1.544 Mbps, the transmission rate of the T1 carrier, and onto which twenty-four DS-0 channels can be multiplexed.

The T1 carrier was implemented in telephone networks with the objective of improving the utilization of trunk lines between central office switches (Fultz and Penick 1965; Travis and Yaeger 1965). Current T1 carriers use twisted-pair copper, coaxial cable, optical fiber, or microwave transmission technology. Note that the T1 standard is prevalent in North America and Japan. The European counterpart to T1 is the E1 carrier, standardized by the International Telecommunications Union (ITU) and operating at 2.048 Mbps with capacity for thirty-two voice channels. Higher levels of signaling hierarchy include DS-2 (96 voice channels at 6.312 Mbps on T2 carriers), DS-3 (672 channels at 44.736 Mbps on T3 carriers), and DS-4 (4032 channels at 274.176 Mbps on T4

carriers). Figure 3 shows the progressive time division multiplexing hierarchy from the DS-0 rate of the voice channel up to the DS-4 level that terminates with a backbone of the long-distance network. The digital channel bank provides the encoding and formatting required for multiplexing the received signals onto a higher-capacity carrier. It can also demultiplex the aggregate stream into individual source signals. The multiplexer denoted M12 can aggregate four DS-1 streams and generate a DS-2 signal with a rate of 6.312 Mbps carrying ninety-six voice channels. The intermediate M1C multiplexer combines two DS-1 signals for transmission over a T1C carrier at 3.152 Mbps. Similarly, an M13 multiplexer combines three DS-1 streams into a signal with a bit rate of 44.7 Mbps for transport over a T3 carrier system. The M23 aggregates seven DS-2 signals onto the T3 carrier, and the M34 multiplexes six DS-3 signals for transmission over a higher-order T4 carrier at 274.176 Mbps.

To understand how this signaling hierarchy maps in the transport architecture, consider the PSTN. At the lowest level, the transport network consists of the copper wire local loops from subscriber telephones connecting to line concentrators that may be located in a neighborhood or

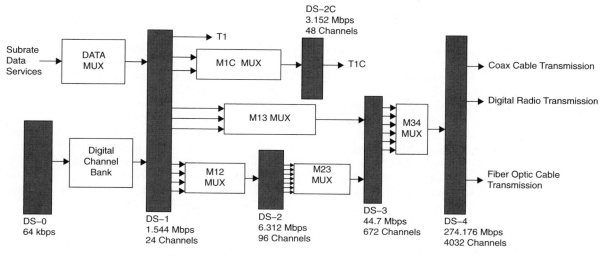

Figure 3: North American digital signal hierarchy

directly to switches in central offices belonging to a *local exchange carrier* (LEC). The line concentrators, also referred to as *digital loop carriers*, extend service to remote areas by performing functions of routing, analog-to-digital conversion, multiplexing, and demultiplexing of outgoing and incoming calls respectively. These systems connect to a circuit switch located within the LEC through fiber-optic or microwave links. AT&T's SLC-96 introduced in 1979, for example, supports ninety-six lines on five T1 line pairs, the additional pair being required for reliability. The LECs connect to the interexchange carrier network operated by long-distance providers through their points of presence. The long-distance network consists of fiber-optical cable and ground- and satellite-based microwave systems. After the divestiture of AT&T in 1984, ANSI proposed the SONET standard for fiber-optic transmission to overcome existing proprietary systems. To enable interoperability between systems satisfying North American standards and those in the rest of the world, the ITU subsequently created the synchronous digital hierarchy such that SONET may be considered a subset of the global standard SDH.

The SONET digital hierarchy is defined using *synchronous transport signals* (STS) and *optical carriers* (OC) starting with the base rate of 51.84 Mbps (STS-1) and optical connect OC-1. It is followed by STS-3 at 155.5 Mbps and the OC-3 carrier onto which three DS-3 signals can be multiplexed. Higher-bandwidth carriers include the OC-12 (622 Mbps), OC-48 (2.488 Gbps), OC-192 (9.953 Gbps), and OC-768 (39.813 Gbps). From the multiplexing viewpoint, SONET admits input streams of different capacities and performs a byte-interleaved multiplexing starting from the base signal STS-1. In the synchronous hierarchy, all systems in SONET have the same average clock rate. This feature allows many STS-1 signals to be concatenated for multiplexing without the need for bit stuffing that is required in the plesiochronous hierarchy. The STS-1 frame length is maintained at 125 microseconds, repeating at a rate of 8000 frames per second. It contains 810 bytes organized in 9-byte rows and 80-byte columns. SONET-SDH is therefore optimized to carry voice traffic that is predictively encoded and generating fixed source rates. SONET also supports the multiplexing of asynchronous streams from T1 and T3 systems as well as streams arriving from other synchronous or plesiochronous systems. Sub-STS-1 levels can also be defined using low-rate *virtual tributaries* (VTs) such as VT 1.5 (1.728 Mbps), VT 2 (2.3 Mbps), VT 3 (3.456 Mbps), and VT 6 (6.912 Mbps). When the required service rate is below DS-3, it is allocated using VTs that are synchronously multiplexed and visible as individual streams at the higher rates. Therefore each tributary can be extracted from the multiplexed stream without need for demultiplexing the higher-rate signal. Although this hierarchy is optimized to carry digital voice from the PSTN, the transport of data traffic using the available levels of granularity in link capacity can be inefficient. It is often the case that the TDM circuit will be underutilized. This feature results from the variable data rate and burst type of transmission patterns that characterize most data applications. To examine the integration of data services on TDM systems, packet division multiplexing is discussed next.

STATISTICAL PACKET DIVISION MULTIPLEXING

Introduced in the 1970s for data transfer on ARPANET (Kleinrock 1972; Kleinrock and Naylor 1974), the first computer network, packet multiplexing continues to be the basic transmission mode on the Internet. It is enabled by the *transmission control protocol and Internet protocol* (TCP/IP) suite (Cerf and Kahn 1974) that ensures reliable end-to end data delivery between hosts and across networks. In the 1980s, the Internet consisted of a single backbone utilizing T1 and T3 lines to interconnect *local area networks* (LANs) at universities and national laboratories. The Internet is now composed of many backbones under the control of commercial network providers who establish peering arrangements to ensure connectivity across the different networks. The backbone networks are typically SONET-based and served by various types of access and data-link layer technologies.

On packet networks, routers and switches perform multiplexing on a packet-by-packet basis. The features of the multiplexed output stream will be governed by the statistical characteristics of all of the traffic flows that are aggregated. Statistical multiplexers can be modeled as queueing systems with finite waiting room and served by transmission links of fixed capacity. The output link capacity is higher than the aggregate average rate of the input streams but typically lower than their aggregate peak rate. Packets arriving at the input ports and destined to an output link are admitted and served, typically on a first-in, first-out (FIFO) basis. The buffers smooth out large variations in the input rate but also produce variable queueing delays and packet losses. Priority-based service may also be implemented by allocating *virtual paths* (VPs) as in ATM networks. The VPs are occupied by traffic flows multiplexed under a specified packet loss or delay tolerance constraint. By allocating output link capacities that are between the average and peak rates of the input traffic, statistical multiplexers attempt to balance the performance requirements of the source traffic flows while efficiently using the available output link capacity. The *statistical multiplexing gain* (SMG) represents the ratio of the number of sources admitted under statistical multiplexing and the number admitted under peak rate allocation. An efficient system operates with SMG values that are greater than 1. Admission control rules for grouping traffic into an ATM virtual circuit or for general packet multiplexing relate input traffic parameters to the performance metrics and determine the type and number of flows that can be aggregated.

To characterize the multiplexing efficiency of packet switched networks, many studies have examined the traffic patterns generated by packet data, voice, and video applications. It is well known that data traffic sources originating from applications such as file transfer or Web browsing alternate between bursts of high-rate transmission activity and periods of low or no activity. Streaming video and audio applications, based on the coding mechanism used, generate either a constant or a continuously varying packet rate. One measure of traffic variability is the ratio of peak to average packet rate exhibited by the traffic source. The objective of multiplexing traffic at successively higher levels of the network hierarchy is to reduce this ratio, thus creating a more uniform traffic rate that can efficiently use network resources. Queueing delays and blocking can also be controlled in these cases because capacity overflow will be a low-probability event. Such a feature requires that the traffic flows being multiplexed satisfy certain statistical properties, such as having a low degree of determinism or correlation in their temporal arrival patterns and independence from the traffic variations of other flows being multiplexed. A brief review of packet traffic measurement and modeling studies conducted over the last three decades is presented next.

Packet Traffic Features

Packet traffic arriving at a multiplexer is characterized by considering the dynamics of the packet interarrival times and the packet sizes. These features determine the workload generated on the link and the network. Analyses of workload measurements on LANs (Jain and Routhier 1986; Schoch and Hupp 1980; Murray and Enslow 1984) and wide area networks (Tobagi 1978) have identified random periods of activity during which packet clusters occur with small interarrival times and are followed by random durations of relatively slow to moderate packet rate. Jain and Routhier (1986), in their measurement and modeling study of traffic on a token ring network, determined that the system hardware and network protocols had significant impact in shaping the traffic patterns. They proposed a packet train model and attributed the time between packet clusters to be a function of user access at the application level, whereas the intracluster statistics were a function of the network hardware and software. The influence of protocol-dependent features in Internet traffic has been presented also by Paxson and Floyd (1996) and Caceres et al. (1991)

Traffic features generated by flows consisting of a mix of voice, data, video, and control information have been found to exhibit some of the most complex behavior. In particular, this intermix shows evidence of deterministic trends as well as statistical variations. The interarrival times of *integrated services digital network* (ISDN) traffic generated from a user's terminal was shown (Meier-Hellstern et al. 1991) to be modeled by superposing gamma and power-law type of probability density functions. Nonstationary features such as a time-varying mean rate and a slow decay rate in the tail of the interarrival time distributions were found in Ethernet traffic generated by workstations (Gusella 1991). To describe Ethernet traffic invariance when observed on multiple time scales, Leland et al. (1994) proposed that traffic be modeled as a *self-similar* process. This model implies that traffic features such as its variance remain statistically invariant even when aggregated over increasing time scales. In comparison, teletraffic models that capture the arrival patterns of telephone calls to a switch and the call holding times are simpler and more tractable for predicting the multiplexing performance. As shown by Erlang (1909), teletraffic processes can be adequately represented by Poisson distributions for the number of call arrivals in a time interval and by a negative exponential probability density function for characterizing the call holding times.

Although no single model has been able to capture all of the complexity observed in packet traffic measurements, approximate models that capture some of the features that affect queueing performance have been proposed. *Fractional Brownian motion* (FBM) is considered by Norros (1995) as the fundamental model for generating self-similar features. Although this model can represent the trend in the long-range correlation of the traffic, it fails to capture short-range variations that affect the performance of finite buffer queues (Ryu and Elwalid 1996). To account for the limitations of the FBM model, a multifractal representation has been proposed in later studies (Vehel and Riedi 1997; Feldmann, Gilbert, and Willinger 1998). This model allows characterization of the high-frequency end of the traffic spectrum, allowing short-term effects to be modeled.

Zhang et al. (2003) investigated traffic carried on OC-3, OC-12, and OC-48 backbone links using multiple time scales ranging from 1 to 10^4 milliseconds. The small time-scale variations were found to be essentially uncorrelated, unlike the fractal and multifractal features observed in previous studies of LAN traffic. This feature may be attributed to the large-scale aggregation that takes place on high-capacity links, generating marginal distributions of the workload that approach Gaussian statistics. In an analysis of Web traffic collected on a 100-Mbps Ethernet link, Cao et al. (2001 "Nonstationarity") modeled the traffic distributions as a function of the connection rate. With increase in the connection rate, the traffic features tended toward Poisson characteristics and independence. At lower rates, a Weibull distribution with a rate-dependent shape parameter was shown to characterize the packet interarrival times. The features of traffic generated on an OC-48 backbone link of an Internet service provider were investigated by Karagiannis et al. (2004). They showed that in the subsecond time scale, traffic approaches Poisson behavior, whereas at the multisecond time scales it exhibits nonstationarity oscillating around a global mean value. This study also points to nonstationary features in the Bellcore Ethernet data previously studied in Leland et al. (1994). The origin of nonstationarity is hypothesized to result from aggregation of arrival processes with a high degree of variability among the individual streams.

The effect of statistical multiplexing of Internet traffic on long-range dependence (LRD) features is examined in (Cao et al. 2001). The statistical multiplexing effect was quantified with respect to the *number of active connections* (NAC), considering traffic from 100-Mbps Ethernet, 156-Mbps ATM interfaces, and 622-Mbps packet over SONET interfaces. It was shown that both traffic workload and interarrival times exhibited LRD at all levels of NAC but generally tended to decrease with the NAC. The emphasis on examining LRD in traffic is primarily to describe the expected value and variance of the queueing delay and the blocking probabilities in network multiplexers. Livny, Melamed, and Tsiolis (1993) showed that when the arrival process is characterized by LRD, the expected queueing delays and blocking probabilities are higher than those generated by Poisson processes at the same level of utilization. Under these traffic assumptions and to preserve *quality of service* (QoS), network service providers have been operating at less than

50 percent network utilization levels. The study in Cao et al. (2001 "Effect"), however, points out that when multiplexing level is taken into account by considering the number of active connections, networks that are subject to high NAC can afford to operate at higher levels of utilization.

The exact analysis of queueing delays and blocking generated by correlated arrival processes is generally intractable. Stochastic models of traffic that can capture some if not all of the correlation features inherent in traffic measurements have been proposed for analyzing the multiplexer performance. A review of some of these approaches is presented next.

Performance Models for Packet Multiplexers

Various approaches for estimating the queueing and multiplexing performance have been proposed considering descriptors that capture the level of correlation in the traffic. In this context, the *index of dispersion of counts* (IDC) and the *index of dispersion of intervals* (IDI) have been useful traffic descriptors for a qualitative prediction of the effect of correlated traffic bursts in queues (Sriram and Whitt 1986; Heffes and Lucantoni 1986). Using the random variable $N(t)$ to represent the number of packets arriving in a time interval t, the IDC is derived as the ratio of the variance and expected value of $N(t)$. The IDI is obtained similarly using the packet interarrival times instead of the counts given by $N(t)$. The limiting value of $N(t)$ as $t \rightarrow \infty$ for a stationary arrival process can be shown to be directly related to the normalized autocorrelation coefficients of the arrivals (Gusella 1991). Sriram and Whitt (1986) consider a highly variable renewal process (Sevast'yanov 2001 "Renewal") to model a single voice source and apply the IDI to characterize the superposition of these processes. The limiting value of IDI as the number of sources tend to infinity can characterize the effect of the arrival process on the congestion characteristics of a FIFO queue in heavy traffic. This work also shows that the positive dependence in the packet arrival process is a major cause of congestion in the multiplexer queue at heavy loads. Buffer sizes larger than a critical value as determined by the characteristic correlation time scale will allow a sequence of dependent interarrival times to build up the queue, causing congestion. Limiting the size of the buffer, at the cost of increased packet loss, is proposed as an approach for controlling congestion. To control packet loss that occurs from dependence in the arrival process, Sriram and Lucantoni (1989) propose dropping the least significant bits in the queue when the queue length reaches a given threshold. They show that under this approach the *queue performance* is comparable to that of a Poisson traffic source.

Another performance parameter that encompasses the features of both the traffic and the queue parameters is the *peakedness* value (Eckberg 1983, 1985). The peakedness captures the ratio of the variance and expectation of the number of busy servers in a queue that can theoretically be approximated to have an infinite number of servers. The calculation requires a functional description of both the probability distribution function and autocorrelation function of the workloads arriving at the queue.

In addition, the arrival process may be characterized by a time-varying random arrival rate and its covariance density function. The application of peakedness to estimate the blocking probability of finite server systems is presented in Fredericks (1980), and its application for analysis of delay systems is given by Eckberg (1985).

To characterize the probability distribution of the buffer occupancy in a statistical multiplexer, at least two characteristic time scales must be taken into consideration. The small time-scale correlations that are a result of packets arriving back to back generate what is known as *packet level congestion* and a characteristic decay rate in the queue distribution for small queue sizes. At the other end of the time scale, referred to as *burst-scale congestion*, large queue sizes are formed by the occurrence of multiple traffic sources transmitting at their peak rate (Norros et al. 1991; Roberts and Virtamo 1991; Roberts 1992). If the multiplexer buffer sizes are large enough, both of these effects are manifest in the queue and affect the transmission performance. Finite state Markov chain models designed to capture the correlation features of traffic (Sevast'yanov 2001 "Markov") can be applied to model the temporal features at small to moderate time scales. Considered jointly with a workload distribution that specifies the state dependent arrival rate, the steady-state distributions of buffer occupancy can be derived.

Methods for efficiently multiplexing digital video sources are of particular importance. Packet video exhibits significant variations in the packet rate during scene changes and when the encoder is refreshed to adapt to new information. By aggregating frames from independent video sources, a moderate to high link utilization may be achieved with statistical multiplexing. To evaluate this hypothesis, finite state Markov chains have been applied to model packet video frame rate variations. Markov chains have a limited ability to capture some of the short- and long-range correlations evident in the intra- and interscene variations of the video frame rates. Applying a two-state, on-off Markov process to model a low-activity videophone signal, Maglaris et al. (1988) derived the multistate Markov chain representation for the multiplexed process. The superposition of moderate activity videoconference data was modeled by Heyman, Tabatbai, and Lakshman (1992). Considering a multistate Markov chain model for the source, they assumed the transitions from a given state to other states followed a negative binomial probability distribution. The state dimension ranged from 400 to 500. This structure, however, could not address the short-term correlations in the traffic of a single source (Heyman and Lakshman 1996). Video sources with moderate activity (Sen 1989) and full-motion video (Yegenoglu, Jabbari, and Zhang 1993; Skelly, Schwartz, and Dixit 1993) have also been represented by discrete time Markov chains and state-dependent autoregressive processes. The problem of selecting an adequate number of states and spectral content in the Markov chain model of a single source so as to capture the scaling effects under multiplexing is discussed in Chandra and Reibman (1999).

There are several advantages in representing a traffic source using a discrete or continuous time Markov chain. Two or more sources represented using Markov chains can be combined to yield another Markov chain that represents the statistically multiplexed process. The queueing performance of the multiplexed stream and the multiplexing efficiency can be computed using fluid buffer models (Anick, Mitra, and Sondhi 1982). Fluid flow analysis assumes that the source rate varies continuously in time as captured by a finite state continuous time Markov process. This approach is suitable when the packet sizes are small relative to the link capacity and a large number of sources are multiplexed. The computational model allows the estimation of the delay and loss distributions in multiplexers fed by Markov-modulated fluid sources and served at a constant rate.

Markov chains described using K states are completely characterized by a K-dimensional square matrix Q whose off-diagonal elements specify the rates of transition between states and an associated diagonal rate matrix R that specifies the rate-generation process in each state. The result of multiplexing N statistically identical sources, each represented by (Q, R), is a new Markov process represented by square matrices (Q_N, R_N) of dimension $M = K^N$. The matrices Q_N and R_N can be computed using the N-fold Kronecker sums $Q \oplus Q \oplus .... \oplus Q$ and $R \oplus R \oplus .... \oplus R$, respectively. The cumulative probability distribution $F(x) = Prob[X \leq x]$ of the buffer occupancy X can be obtained by solving the first-order differential equation $\frac{dF(x)}{dx} = \underline{F}(x)[Q_N D_N^{-1}]$, where the vector $\underline{F}(x):[F_1(x)F_2(x) .... F_M(x)]$ and elements $F_i(x)$, $i = 1, 2 ... M$ represent the cumulative probability when the source is in state i. The matrix $D_N = [R_N - CI]$ represents the drift between the input rates and the link capacity or service rate denoted by C. Here I is the identity matrix. The solution to the differential equation can be represented using the eigenvalues and eigenvectors of $Q_N D_N^{-1}$. The cumulative probability is given as $F(x) = \sum_{i=1}^{M} F_i(x) = 1 + \sum_{i:z_i < 0} a_i e^{-z_i x}$, where the summation is over those eigenvalues z_i that are less than zero. The coefficients a_i are functions of the eigenvalues and eigenvectors (Walrand and Varaiya 1996; Schwartz 1996) of $Q_N D^{-1}$, solved using the appropriate boundary conditions of X. The asymptotic decay rate of the complementary distribution function $G(x) = Pr[X > x] = 1 - F(x) = \sum_{i:z_i < 0} a_i e^{-z_i x}$ for large x is an important performance metric that determines the multiplexing efficiency. The dominant eigenvalue will govern this feature.

The fluid buffer analysis described above becomes computationally intensive as N increases for sources with a large dimension K. In such situations, asymptotic approximations to the model may be obtained for large buffer sizes and small delay or loss probabilities (Abate, Choudhury, and Whitt 1994). In this approximation, $G(x) \sim \alpha e^{-\beta x}$, $x -> \infty$, where α is referred to as the asymptotic constant and β is the largest negative eigenvalue of the matrix $Q_N D^{-1}$. The asymptotic decay rate $-\beta$ is a function of the service rate C and may be determined with relative ease. The asymptotic constant, however, requires knowledge of all of the system's eigenvectors and eigenvalues. Approximate methods for estimating for Markovian systems are derived in Addie and Zukerman (1994) and Elwalid et al. (1995). Although most of the asymptotic representations have considered Markovian sources, there have been some results for traffic modeled as stationary Gaussian processes

(Choe and Shroff 1998) and fractional Brownian motion (Norros 1995).

Often, $G(0)$ is assumed to be unity in the heavy traffic regime. From this assumption, an effective bandwidth representation of a source, which serves as a descriptor of multiplexer performance, can be derived. The limiting form of the tail probabilities as $x \to \infty$ can be represented as $G(x) \approx e^{-\beta x}$. To achieve a specified value of β that satisfies given performance constraints, the required capacity may be shown (Elwalid and Mitra 1993) to be obtained as the maximal eigenvalue of the matrix $\left[R_N + \frac{Q_N}{\beta} \right]$. This capacity is referred to as the *effective bandwidth* (EB) of the multiplexed source. In the limit, as β approaches zero and ∞, the EB approaches the source average and peak rate, respectively. However, as noted by Choudhury, Lucantoni, and Whitt (1996), the effective bandwidth approximation can lead to conservative estimates for highly variable traffic sources that undergo significant smoothing under multiplexing. It was shown that the asymptotic constant was itself asymptotically exponential in the number of multiplexed sources N. For traffic sources with indices of dispersion greater than those of Poisson sources, this parameter decreased exponentially in N, reflecting the multiplexing gain of the system.

The EB characterization of a multiplexed system is particularly useful for admission control in multiservice networks (Elwalid and Mitra 1993; Kesidis, Walrand, and Chang 1993; Chang and Thomas 1995). Its utility has been compared with other types of admission control in Knightly and Schroff (1999): scheduling based on average and peak rate information (Ferrari and Verma 1990), refinements of EB from large deviation principles (Kelly 1996), and maximum variance approaches based on estimating the upper tails of Gaussian process models of traffic (Choe and Shroff 1998). To examine how EB can be utilized, assume that K classes of traffic are to be admitted into a node served by a link capacity C packets per second. If N_i sources of type i exist, each characterized by an effective bandwidth E_i, the simplest admission policy is given by the linear control law, $\sum_{i=1}^{K} N_i E_i \leq C$. The effective bandwidths are derived taking into consideration the traffic characteristics and performance requirements of each class and available capacity C. Defining the traffic generated by type i source on a time scale t by a random variable $A_i[0,t]$, the effective bandwidth derived from large-deviations principles (Kelly 1996) is given by $E_i(s,t) = \frac{1}{st} \log E\left[e^{sA_i[0,t]} \right]$, where the parameter s is related to the decay rate of $G(x)$ and captures the multiplexing efficiency of the system. It is calculated from the specified probability of loss or delay bounds (Schwartz 1996). The term on the right is the log moment generating function of the arrival process (Weisstein 1999 "Moment"). The workload can be described over a time t that represents the typical time taken for the buffer to overflow starting from an empty state. For a fixed value of t, the EB is an increasing function of s and lies between the mean and peak values of $A_i[0,t]$. This may be shown by a Taylor series approximation of E_i as $s \to 0$ and $s \to \infty$. respectively (Weisstein 1999 "Taylor"). Methods for deriving E_i for different traffic classes are discussed in Chang (1994). The aforementioned model assumes that all of the multiplexed sources have the same QoS requirements. If they do not, all sources achieve the performance of the most stringent source. Kulkarni, Gun, and Chimento (1995) consider an extension of this approach for addressing traffic of multiple classes. For the superposition, because the total workload is given by $A[0,t] = \sum_{i=1}^{K} A_i[0,t]$, the effective capacity C_e of the multiplexed system is $C_e = \sum_{i=1}^{K} E_i$. The admission control algorithm compares C_e with available capacity C and if $C_e < C$ allows the new source to be admitted into the system.

The problem of statistical multiplexing has been discussed in this section with reference to traffic characteristics and approaches for evaluating the performance of multiplexers modeled as queues. To support these algorithmic approaches, the network infrastructure must include appropriate protocols and technology. A brief review of proposals in this area is presented in the next section.

PROTOCOLS FOR STATISTICAL TIME DIVISION MULTIPLEXING SUPPORT

Transport architectures in next generation networks must be designed to better support the demand for packet data, voice, and video services. This will require more flexible approaches for integrating packet-switched services into the optical transport plane and protocols that can improve the control of end-to-end quality of packet traffic. To better utilize the existing SONET-SDH circuit capacity, a statistical time division multiplexing framework will be required at both access interfaces and network elements within the optical backbone. A packet-aware optical transport paradigm will allow customization of packet delivery services while leveraging the stability and security of the well-tested optical transport systems. At the access level, legacy Ethernet services will probably continue to expand through Fast and Gigabit Ethernet technologies.

A hybrid integrated service, *Ethernet over SONET* (EoS), is envisioned by most network providers as the emerging model for which controlled service and improved bandwidth utilization are to be designed. In support of this, several technologies and protocols are under various stages of investigation and evaluation. These include *virtual concatenation* (VCAT), *link capacity adjustment scheme* (LCAS), *generic framing procedure* (GFP) (Hernandez-Valencia, Cholten, and Zhu 2002; Henrique-Valencia 2002 02; Cavendish et al. 2002) and *resilient packet ring* (RPR) (Davik et al. 2004) for integrating Ethernet and SONET. In addition, *multiprotocol label switching* (MPLS) (Awduche 1999; Rosen, Viswanathan, and Callon 2001) and *generalized MPLS* (GMPLS) protocols (Mannie 2004) provide approaches for controlling quality through label-switched paths on Internet protocol (IP) and optical networks respectively.

In the current transmission architecture, IP packets are carried over SONET-SDH using packet-over-SONET standards. Here the packets are transported using link layer point-to-point protocol after being encapsulated into byte-stuffed high-level data link control frames. They are then byte mapped into the contiguously concatenated SONET-SDH payload envelopes. Contiguous concatenation allows the transport of payloads that exceed the basic STS-1 *synchronous payload envelope* (SPE) by concatenating multiple SPEs contiguously and transporting them as one unit. The concatenated containers are referred to as STS-*nc*, where *n* takes values of 3,12,48,192 generating rates of 155,622,2448 and 9792 Mbps, respectively. The limitation in the granularity of output link capacities can yield underutilized bandwidth. For example, a 100-Mbps Fast Ethernet connection will be allocated a 155 Mbps STS – 3c container, and a Gigabit Ethernet link will be assigned the 2.5-Gb STS-48c capacity resulting in significant underutilization. Using VCAT, the Fast Ethernet connection can be assigned two STS-1 channels, and Gigabit Ethernet can be carried on seven STS-3s or twenty-one STS-1s, all of which can be combined in a single *virtual concatenation group* (VCG). An important feature is that each path in the VCG can be transported independently of others in the group, and VCG members can occupy noncontiguous time slots. Only the initiating and terminating equipment need to be aware of the VCAT functionality. VCAT will also allow provisioning for fractional or subrate Ethernet services if full Ethernet capacity is not currently being utilized by the source. The link concatentation using increments of 1.5 Mbps is referred to as *low-order VCAT*, whereas concatenation using increments of 50 Mbps is the high-order VCAT. The application of VCAT to implement low-overhead protection of EoS transport is discussed in Acharya et al. (2004).

To improve the flexibility afforded by VCAT, LCAS has been proposed (ITU-T 2001 "Link"). LCAS is a signaling protocol that allows dynamic bandwidth adjustment on SONET without disrupting existing service and often takes place in real time. It can be applied to remove and add connections in a VCG and to recover failed paths while retaining end-to-end connectivity for the entire group. For the time it takes to recover the failed path, the source will experience a reduced throughput rather than a full outage. For example, on recognizing a failed member in a VCG, LCAS enables the sink network element to communicate to the source element implementing the VCG to modify its concatenation rules. The combined VCAT and LCAS functions can be utilized as an intelligent bandwidth management system for SONET-SDH. It can afford continuity in service that is set up at the access network and can integrate with IP QoS policies such as the *differentiated services* (DiffServ) architecture and the MPLS framework proposed by the Internet Engineering Task Force (IETF 1998). The GFP proposed by ITU standardization sector and ANSI (ITU-T 2001 "Generic") is an international standard in support of VCAT, providing the framing process for mapping a wide range of data streams into SONET-SDH frames. Data streams can be generated from multiple higher-layer protocols and network technologies such as IP, Ethernet, or fibre channel. In the frame-mapped GFP adaptation, the data signal frame is mapped entirely into one GFP frame. This allows transparency with data-link layer functions and parameters and can be optimized for packet switching. An Ethernet frame, for example, with size varying from 46 kbytes to 65 kbytes is encapsulated into a GFP frame consisting of an eight-byte header. In the block-code oriented or transparent GFP adaptation, GFP operates on the coded character stream rather than the protocol data units. Fixed-size GFP frames are encapsulated on the decoded data character stream, creating efficient block codes that can be transported with minimum latency. It therefore supports delay-sensitive circuit-emulation applications and is targeted for Gigabit Ethernet and storage network protocols. The basic requirement for GFP is that upper-layer data signals must be octet-aligned, and lower layers such as SONET-SDH must also provide an octet-synchronous path.

As packet traffic continues to consume network bandwidth, retaining packet awareness at all levels of network hierarchy becomes an important design feature. The concept of a packet-aware metro transport network is discussed in Afferton et al. (2004). They propose deployment of Ethernet switching and transport at the metro level and consider the RPR protocol for carrying packet traffic over the access rings. RPR is configured above GFP and provides a medium access-level protection scheme. SONET rings typically consist of a fully configured backup ring that is utilized if the primary ring experiences a failure. RPR can eliminate the need for such redundancy at the physical layer while offering network availability that is comparable with the sub–50-millisecond resiliency of SONET-SDH ring architecture. By removing the need for a second physical circuit, bandwidth utilization can be effectively doubled. RPR also supports three QoS classes—A, B, and C—where class A is highest priority with bandwidth and jitter guarantees; class B is intermediate level, requiring bandwidth guarantee; and class C refers to best effort traffic. RPR applies admission control schemes to enforce the quality requirements.

The aforementioned protocol enhancements are designed to improve the multiplexing flexibility of conventional time division multiplexing systems. The objective of making optical transport networks packet aware is also important when viewed from the perspective of improved traffic-engineering methodologies that have been implemented in traditional packet-switching networks. In this context, *multiprotocol label switching* (MPLS) (Adwuche 1999; Rosen, Viswanathan, and Callon 2001) and its extension GMPLS are among the protocols proposed by the IETF for controlling QoS on Internet paths. MPLS is designed to emulate the circuit-switched flow transfer of telephone networks. Edge routers implementing MPLS attach labels to packets identifying them as belonging to a particular *label-switched path* (LSP). At each label-switching router in the transmission path, an outgoing label is placed on the packet, based on which packets are routed. Forward equivalent classes are generated based on packets with the same labels, and they may represent flows with common service class, source-destination endpoints or other service criteria. MPLS allows the integration of link layer parameters such as the link capacity and latency into labels that are accessible at the higher IP layer. These labels serve to generate a constraint-based routing paradigm. MPLS is used in conjunction with the *resource reservation protocol* to implement traffic engineering and QoS service on the network. To implement MPLS, routers must map the QoS parameters in the labels through an appropriate admission control and queueing process that preserves the service constraints. The method for implementing these features at required Gigabit rates is not specified under any standards but rather implemented as proprietary algorithms in switches and routers currently installed. However, they follow the general recommendations of the DiffServ architecture (IETF 1998) in which traffic is aggregated and provided differentiated service quality on a hop-by-hop basis.

GMPLS allows the extension of MPLS into the optical physical layer, supporting optical label-switched paths using *wavelength division* or *time division multiplexing* (WDM and TDM). At the physical transport layer, GMPLS-enabled routers and network elements set up optical label-switched paths between the nodes of the core transport network. The IP network affords many levels of granularity in capacity for creating label-switched paths, whereas a limited set of capacities is available on SONET or WDM physical layers. Therefore, multiple label-switched paths generated on IP paths must be appropriately multiplexed to maximize the utilization of WDM or TDM paths on the optical channel (Zhang and Qiao 2000).

CONCLUSION

The need for statistical multiplexing will continue increasing in proportion with the increasing traffic generated by variable and intermittent rates of packet-switched voice, video, and data sources. In support of this, network architects are expanding the role of traditional local access network multiplexing technologies such as Ethernet to the level of metro and core transport networks. To better utilize the significant widespread optical transport infrastructure that exists worldwide, SONET-SDH transport systems are being provided with the capability to implement more flexible forms of traffic aggregation and bandwidth management. As optical networks become more data-centric, network elements that support multiple services and new protocols to enforce service level agreements are under development. Multiservice networks will require interfaces that can function both as packet switches and optical cross connects and support hybrid packet and wavelength multiplexing for high-capacity demands. The design objective of such systems is to seamlessly integrate into the optical plane the multiple capacity demands of traffic flows routed using MPLS label-switched paths on the IP segment of the transmission path. The traditional manual management of path connectivity is being updated through the development of a distributed optical control plane that will facilitate adaptive traffic management, signaling, routing and recovery from faults. Protocols such as generalized MPLS are configured to distribute information on bandwidth availability, topology, and network status that will help network nodes configure constraint-based traffic aggregation and route selection.

The problems of packet traffic characterization and prediction of performance of statistical multiplexers continue to be challenging issues in network design. The current understanding of traffic patterns suggests that traffic descriptors must be considered at multiple time scales and that traffic features are significantly influenced by transport and control protocols and the queueing experienced during transmission. In general, traffic models applied for analyzing multiplexers can change from hop to hop and must be derived after taking into consideration system issues such as buffer size, link capacity, and system utilization. At the access to the optical network, traffic models for aggregation must address the issues of how best to maximize the utilization of the optical capacity. A suite of protocols for virtual concatenation, link capacity adjustment, and generic framing are being applied to increase the flexibility of the optical plane while retaining the robustness and security of SONET-SDH networks.

GLOSSARY

Add-drop multiplexer (ADM): Technique for demultiplexing a high-rate signal into its lower-rate components so as to multiplex another low-rate signal.

Asynchronous transfer mode (ATM): A switching and multiplexing technique that operates on fixed-length 53-byte cells and provides a virtual connection-oriented delivery while controlling packet delay, jitter, and loss. Applies traffic parameters such as peak and average rates for controlling performance.

Broadband integrated services digital network: Standards for switching, multiplexing, and transporting integrated voice, video, and data sources using ATM. Transmission rates are higher than 1.544 Mbps.

Digital cross connect (DCS): System for switching and multiplexing low-speed voice and data signals onto high-speed lines and for demultiplexing high-speed signals into their lower-rate components.

Digital loop carrier: System that multiplexes low-rate signals from end users onto high-speed digital lines such as T1 and performs the reverse operation for transmission to end users' telephone or computers.

Digital signal (DS-N) hierarchy: Standard signal rates for time division multiplexed systems, where $N = 0, 1, 2, 3, 4$ represent 64 kbps and 1.544, 6.312, 44.736, and 274.176 Mbps, respectively.

Fast Ethernet: An enhanced version of standard Ethernet that can transfer data at a rate of 100 Mbps.

Fibre channel: Storage and networking interface technology capable of transmitting data between computers at rates as high as 10 Gbits per second.

High-level data link control: Format for delimiting frames in a packet multiplexing scheme.

Integrated services digital network (ISDN): A flexible telephone service that allows digital voice and data communications using multiple bidirectional bearer channels, each with capacity as high as 64 kbps.

Kronecker sum: Sum of two matrices A and B of dimension N and M, respectively, is given by $A \oplus B = A \otimes I_{M \times M} + I_{N \times N} \otimes B$, where the symbol $\otimes$ represents the Kronecker or tensor product. The Kronecker product of two matrices $C_{N \times N} \otimes D_{M \times M}$ replaces each element of C by the product of the element and the matrix D, resulting in a matrix of dimension $N \times M$.

Long-range dependence (LRD): The process autocorrelation function decays hyberbolically rather than exponentially.

Open systems interconnect (OSI): Standard for data communications over a network. Consists of seven layers of protocols starting from the lowest physical or data transport layer and moving up in sequence to the data-link layer, network or Internet protocol layer, transport layer, session, presentation, and application layers.

Optical carrier: Standardized transmission speeds in SONET-SDH fiber-optic networks.

Plesiochronous digital hierarchy: Signals are not exactly synchronized to a standard rate but operate with some variation around the nominal value.

Point-to-point protocol: Standard for serial communications over the Internet; defining protocol for the modem to transfer and receive data packets with other systems.

Self-similar: Property exhibited by fractals and chaotic systems in which certain statistical or deterministic properties remain invariant with scale.

Synchronous digital hierarchy (SDH): International networking standard with a base transmission rate of 155 Mbps.

Synchronous optical network (SONET): ANSI standard for synchronous data transmission on optical media.

Tributary: The lower-rate signal forming an input to a multiplexer.

Virtual circuit (VC): A communications channel that provides sequential transport of ATM cells between two ATM end stations.

Virtual path (VP): A logical association or a bundle of virtual circuits.

Wavelength division multiplexing (WDM): Multiplexing data sources using multiple wavelengths and transmission over a single optical fiber.

CROSS REFERENCES

See *Frequency and Phase Modulation*; *Frequency Division Multiplexing (FDM)*; *Orthogonal Frequency Division Multiplexing (OFDM)*; *Time Division Multiplexing (TDM)*; *Wavelength Division Multiplexing (WDM)*.

REFERENCES

Abate, J., G. L. Choudhury, and W. Whitt. 1994. Asymptotics for steady-state tail probabilities in structured Markov queueing models. *Stochastic Models*, 10: 99–143.

Acharya, S., B. Gupta, P. Risbood, and A. Srivastava. 2004. PESO: Lowe overhead protection for Ethernet over SONET transport. In *Proceedings of INFOCOM 2004*, pp. 165–175.

Addie, R. G., and M. Zukerman. 1994. An approximation for performance evaluation of stationary single server queues. *IEEE Transactions on Communication*, 42: 3150–60.

Afferton, T. S., R. D. Doverspike, C. R. Kalamanek, and K. K. Ramakrishnan. 2004. Packet-aware transport for metro networks. *IEEE Communications Magazine*, 42(3): 121–36.

Anick, D., D. Mitra, and M. M. Sondhi. 1982. Stochastic theory of a data-handling system with multiple sources. *Bell Systems Technical Journal*, 8: 1871–94.

Awduche, D. O. 1999. MPLS and traffic engineering in IP networks. *IEEE Communications Magazine*, 37: 42–7.

Caceres, R., P. Danzig, S. Jamin, and D. Mitzel. 1991. Characteristics of wide-area TCP/IP conversations.

Proceedings of ACM/SIGCOMM, September, Zurich, pp. 101–12.

Cao, J., W. S. Cleveland, D. Lin, and D. X. Sun. 2001. The effect of statistical multiplexing on the long-range dependence of Internet packet traffic. *Bell Labs Technical Report* (retrieved from http://cm.bell-labs.com/cm/ms/departments/sia/InternetTraffic/webpapers.html).

———. 2001. On the nonstationarity of Internet traffic. In *Proceedings of ACM Sigmetrics* (ACM SIGMETRICS 2001), Cambridge, MA, pp. 102–1 June, Montreal, Paper 4.4B-3.

Eckberg, A. E. Jr. 1985. Approximations for bursty (and smoothed) arrival queueing delays based on generalized peakedness. In *Eleventh International Teletraffic Congress*, 1985, Kyoto, June, Paper 3.1A-4.

Elwalid, A., D. Heyman, T. V. Lakshman, D. Mitra, and A. Weiss. 1995. Fundamental bounds and approximations for ATM multiplexers with applications to video teleconferencing. *IEEE Journal of Selected Areas in Communication*, 13: 1004–16.

Elwalid, A. I., and D. Mitra. 1993. Effective bandwidth of general Markovian traffic sources and admission control of high speed networks. IEEE/ACM Transactions on Networking, 1(3): 329–43.

Erlang, A. K. 1909. The theory of probabilities and telephone conversations. *Nyt Tidsskrift for Matematik B*, 20: 33.

Feldmann, A., A. Gilbert, and W. Willinger. 1998. Data networks as cascades: Investigating the multifractal nature of Internet WAN traffic. In *Proceedings of the 1998 ACM SIGCOMM Conference*, September, Vancouver, pp. 42–55.

Ferrari, D., and D. Verma. 1990. A scheme for realtime channel establishment in wide-area networks. *IEEE Journal of Selected Areas in Communication*, 8: 368–79.

Fredericks, A. A. 1980. Congestion in blocking systems: A simple approximation technique. *Bell System Technical Journal*, 59: 805–27.

Fultz, K. E., and D. B. Penick. 1965. The T1 carrier system. *Bell Systems Technical Journal*, 44(7): 1405–51.

Gusella, R. 1991. Characterizing the variability of arrival processes with indexes of dispersion. *IEEE Journal of Selected Areas of Communications*, 9(2): 203–11.

Heffes, H., and D. M. Lucantoni. 1986. A Markov-modulated characterization of packetized voice and data traffic and related statistical multiplexer performance. *IEEE Journal of Selected Areas on Communications*, 4: 856–68.

Held, G. 1999. *High speed digital transmission networking*. New York: John Wiley & Sons.

Henrique-Valencia, E. 2002. Hybrid transport solutions for TDM/Data networking services. *IEEE Communications Magazine*, 40(5): 104–12.

Hernandez-Valencia, E., M. S. Cholten, and Z. Zhu. 2002. The generic framing procedure (GFP): An overview. *IEEE Communications Magazine*, 40(5): 63–71.

Heyman, D., A. Tabatbai, and T. V. Lakshman. 1992. Statistical analysis and simulation study of video teletraffic in ATM networks. *IEEE Transactions on Circuits and Systems for Video Technology*, 2: 49–59.

Heyman, D. P., and T. V. Lakshman. 1996. Source models for VBR broadcast-video traffic. *IEEE/ACM Transactions on Networking*, 4: 40–8.

IETF. 1998. An architecture for differentiated services. RFC 2475, December.

ITU-T. 2001. Generic framing procedure (GFP). Draft Recommendation G.7041.

———. 2001. Link capacity adjustment scheme (LCAS). Draft Recommendation G.7042/Y.1305.

Jain, R., and S. A. Routhier. 1986. Packet trains-measurements and a new model for computer network traffic. *IEEE Journal on Selected Areas in Communications*, 4(6): 986–95.

Karagiannis, T., M. Molle, M. Faloutsos, and A. Broido. 2004. A nonstationary Poisson view of Internet traffic. In *Proceedings of IEEE INFOCOM 2004*, March, Hong Kong, pp. 1558–69.

Kelly, F. 1996. *Stochastic networks: Theory and applications*. New York: Oxford University Press.

Kesidis, G., J. Walrand, and C. Chang. 1993. Effective bandwidths for multiclass Markov fluids and other ATM sources. *IEEE/ACM Transactions on Networking*, 1(4): 424–8.

Kleinrock, L. 1972. Performance models and measurement of the ARPA computer network. In *Online 72 Conference Proceedings*, September, Uxbridge, Middlesex, England, 2: 61–85.

———, and W. Naylor. 1974. On measured behavior of the ARPA network. In *AFIPS Conference Proceedings*, May, Chicago, 43: 767–80.

Knightly, E. W., and N. B. Schroff. 1999. Admission control for statistical QOS: Theory and Practice. *IEEE Network*, 13(2): 20–9.

Kulkarni, V. G., L. Gun, and P. F. Chimento. 1995. Effective bandwidth vectors for multiclass traffic multiplexed in a partitioned buffer. *IEEE Journal on Selected Areas in Communication*, 6(13): 1039–47.

Leland, W. E., M. S. Taqqu, W. Willinger, and D.V. Wilson. 1994. On the self-similar nature of Ethernet traffic (extended version). *IEEE/ACM Transactions on Networking*, 2(1): 1–15.

Livny, M., B. Melamed, and A. K. Tsiolis. 1993. The impact of autocorrelation on queueing systems. *Management Science*, 39(3): 322–39.

Maglaris, B., D. Anastassiou, P. Sen, G. Karlsson, and J. D. Robbins. 1988. Performance models of statistical multiplexing in packet video communications. *IEEE Transactions on Communications*, 36(7): 834–44.

Mannie, E. 2004. Generalized multiprotocol label switching (GMPLS). RFC 3945. IETF, October.

Meier-Hellstern, K. S., P. E. Wirth, Y. Yan, and D.A. Hoeflin. 1991. Traffic models for ISDN data users: Office automation application. In *Teletraffic and data traffic: A period of change*, edited by A. Jensen and V. B. Iversen, 167–72. New York: Elsevier Science.

Murray, D. N., and P. H. Enslow Jr. 1984. An experimental study of the performance of a local area network. *IEEE Communications Magazine*, 22: 48–53.

Norros, I. 1995. On the use of Fractional Brownian Motion in the theory of connectionless networks. *IEEE Journal of Selected Areas of Communication*, 13(6): 953–62.

————, J. W. Roberts, A. Simonian, and J. T. Virtamo. 1991. The superposition of variable bit rate sources in an ATM multiplexer. *IEEE Journal of Selected Areas in Communication*, 9(3): 378–87.

Paxson, V., and S. Floyd. 1996. Wide-area traffic: The failure of Poisson modeling. *IEEE/ACM Transactions on Networking*, 3(3): 226–44.

Roberts, J. W., and J. T. Virtamo. 1991. The superposition of periodic cell arrival streams in an ATM multiplexer. *IEEE Transactions on Communications*, 39: 298–303.

Roberts, W. ed. 1992. *Performance evaluation and design of multiservice networks* (COST 224 final report). Brussels: Commission of the European Communities.

Rosen, E., A. Viswanathan, and R. Callon. 2001. Multiprotocol label switching architecture. Number RFC-3031. IETF.

Ryu, B. K., and A. Elwalid. 1996. The importance of long-range dependence of VBR video traffic in ATM traffic engineering: Myths and realities. In *Proceedings of ACM SIGCOMM '96*, October, California, 26(4): 3–14.

Schoch, J. F., and J. A. Hupp. 1980. Performance of the Ethernet local network. *Communications of the ACM*, 23(12): 711–21.

Schwartz, M. 1996. *Broadband integrated networks*. Upper Saddle River, NJ: :Prentice Hall.

————. 2004. Origins of carrier multiplexing: Major George Owen Squier and AT&T (retrieved from www.ieee.org/portal/cms_docs_iportals/iportals/aboutus/history_center/conferences/che2004/Schwartz.pdf).

Sen, P., B. Maglaris, N. Rikli, and D. Anastassiou. 1989. Models for packet switching of variable bit-rate video sources. IEEE Journal on Selected Areas in Communication, 7(5): 865–69.

Sevast'yanov, B. A. 2001. Markov chain (retrieved from http://eom.springer.de/M/m062350.htm.

————. 2001. Renewal theory (retrieved from http://eom.springer.de/R/r081250.htm).

Skelly, P., M. Schwartz, and S. Dixit. 1993. A histogram based model for video traffic behavior in an ATM multiplexer. *IEEE/ACM Transactions on Networking*, 1(4): 447–59.

Sriram, K., and D. M. Lucantoni. 1989. Traffic smoothing effects of bit dropping in a packet voice multiplexer. *IEEE Transactions on Communications*, 37(7): 703–12.

Sriram, K., and W. Whitt. 1986. Characterizing superposition arrival processes in packet multiplexers for voice and data. *IEEE Journal on Selected Areas in Communication*, 4(6): 833–46.

Tobagi, F. A. 1978. Modeling and measurement techniques in packet communication networks. In *Proceedings of the IEEE, November*, 66(11): 1423–47.

Travis, L. F., and R. E. Yaeger. 1965. Wideband data on T1 carrier. *Bell Systems Technical Journal*, 44(8): 1567.

Vehel, J. L., and R. Riedi. 1997. Fractional Brownian motion and data traffic modeling: The other end of the spectrum. In *Fractals in Engineering*, edited by J. L. Vehel, E. Lutton, and C. Tricot, 185–202. New York: Springer.

Walrand, J., and P. Varaiya. 1996. *High-performance communication networks*. San Francisco: Morgan Kaufmann.

Weisstein, E. W. 1999. Moment generating function (retrieved from http://mathworld.wolfram.com/MomentGeneratingFunction.html).

————. 1999. Taylor series (retrieved from http://mathworld.wolfram.com/TaylorSeries.html).

Yegenoglu, F., B. Jabbari, and Y. Zhang. 1993. Motion classified autoregressive modeling of variable bit rate video. *IEEE Transactions on Circuits and Systems for Video Technology*, 3: 42–53.

Zhang, X., and C. Qiao. 2000. "An effective and comprehensive approach for traffic grooming and wavelength assignment in SONET/WDM rings," IEEE/ACM Trans. Networking, vol. 8, no. 5, pp. 608–617, 2000.

Zhang, Z., V. J. Ribeiro, S. Moon, and C. Diot. 2003. Small-time scaling behaviors of Internet backbone traffic: An empirical study. *Computer Networks*, 48(3): 315–34.

Orthogonal Frequency Division Multiplexing

Shinsuke Hara, *Osaka City University, Japan*

INTRODUCTION

Orthogonal frequency division multiplexing (OFDM) is a special form of *multicarrier modulation* (MCM), the purpose of which is to split a high-rate data stream into a number of lower rate data streams that are transmitted simultaneously over a number of subcarriers. The first systems using MCM were military high-frequency (HF) radio links in the late 1950s (Mosier and Clabaugh 1958) and early 1960s (Zimmerman and Kirsch 1967). OFDM, which was patented in the United States in 1970 (Chang 1970), then abandoned the use of analog steep bandpass filters that completely separated the spectrum of individual subcarrier and instead chose time domain waveforms such that mutual orthogonality was ensured even though the spectra overlapped. Such a waveform can be easily generated and detected using the *inverse discrete Fourier transform* (IDFT) and *discrete Fourier transform* (DFT) at the transmitter and receiver, respectively (Weinstein and Ebert 1971). However, for a relatively long time, implementational aspects of OFDM such as the computational complexity of the DFT appeared prohibitive, not to speak of other problems such as the stability of oscillators at transmitter and receiver, the linearity required in radio-frequency power amplifiers, and the power backoff associated with it. After many years of intensive research and development for mobile communications, digital audio broadcasting, and data transmission over telephone lines in the 1980s; for *asymmetric digital subscriber line* (ADSL), *power line communications* (PLC), digital broadcasting, and wireless *local area networks* (LANs) in the 1990s; and for wireless broadband access in the early 2000s, many of the major implementational problems have been solvable and OFDM has become part of several worldwide standards (Cimini 1985; Alard and Lassalle s1989; Bingham 1990; ANSI 1998; Lin et al. 2002; Dambacher 1996; European Telecommunications Institute 1996; Association of Radio Industries and Businesses 2000; IEEE 1999, 2003, 2006).

This chapter is organized as follows. The next section provides an overview of OFDM, including its origin, the use of DFT, the insertion of cyclic prefix, and the use of channel coding to combat frequency-selective fading. The third and fourth sections present drawbacks related to OFDM transmitters and receivers, respectively. The fifth section addresses resource allocation in OFDM. The last section before the conclusion introduces applications of OFDM in several standards of digital broadcasting, wireless LANs, and broadband wireless access, among others.

PRINCIPLES OF ORTHOGONAL FREQUENCY DIVISION MULTIPLEXING

This section will revisit the principle of OFDM and its history from its origin to current coded OFDM.

Origins

Figure 1 compares a conventional *single-carrier modulation* (SCM) and a MCM, where f_c denotes the carrier frequency (Hara and Prasad 2002). At the transmission side, $S_{SCM}(f; t)$, $S_{MCM}(f; t)$, B_{SCM}, and B_{MCM} denote the frequency spectra and bandwidths of the SCM and MCM signals, respectively. Furthermore, for MCM, f_k, $F_k(f; t)$, N_{SC}, and Δf denote the frequency of the kth subcarrier, the frequency spectrum of pulse waveform of the kth subcarrier, the total number of subcarriers, and the subcarrier separation, respectively. The frequency spectrum of the MCM signal is written as

$$S_{MCM}(f;t) = \sum_{k=1}^{N_{SC}} F_k(f;t)$$

(See Figure 1a.)

If the impulse response of a channel has a delay spread because of multipath propagation, then the channel

591

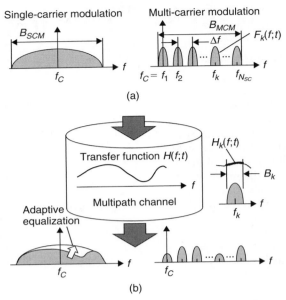

Figure 1: Comparison of SCM and MCM—(a) frequency spectra of transmitted signals and (b) frequency spectra of received signals

response in the frequency domain, which is called the *transfer function*, has a large variation, as shown in Figure 1. Such a channel is called a *multipath channel*, and the channel model is true for wired channels such as metallic cables and power lines and wireless channels in urban, rural, and indoor environments. In general, a multipath channel has a bandwidth where channel variations are highly correlated; it is called the *coherence bandwidth*. When a signal is transmitted through a multipath channel, if the coherence bandwidth is small compared with the bandwidth of the transmitted signal (i.e., the delay spread is not negligibly small as compared with the information symbol period), the channel is said to be *frequency-selective* because different spectral components of the transmitted signal experience different attenuations through the channel.

On the other hand, in general, the channel state in telephone systems does not change often, whereas the channel state in wireless systems, especially in mobile systems, always changes because of Doppler frequency spread. Such a channel with a time-varying nature is called a *multipath fading channel*; it is more hostile to information transmission, because the receiver needs to track the variation of the channel to successfully recover the transmitted data.

Through a frequency-selective multipath channel characterized by the transfer function $H(f; t)$, the frequency spectra of the SCM and MCM signals at the receiver side are written as

$$R_{SCM}(f;t) = H(f;t)S_{SCM}(f;t)$$

and

$$R_{MCM}(f;t) = H(f;t)S_{MCM}(f;t) = \sum_{k=1}^{N_{SC}} H_k(f;t)F_k(f;t)$$

respectively (see Figure 1b), where $H_k(f; t)$ denotes the channel transfer function corresponding to B_k, which is the frequency band occupied by the kth subcarrier. For SCM, because of the multipath propagation, the received signal is rich in *intersymbol interference* (ISI), so adaptive equalization in the time or frequency domain is required to reject or effectively combine intersymbol interferers. On the other hand, for MCM, when the number of subcarriers is large, the amplitude and phase response of $H_k(f; t)$ can be assumed to be constant over B_k, so $R_{MCM}(f; t)$ can be approximated as

$$R_{MCM}(f;t) \cong \sum_{k=1}^{N_{SC}} H_k(t)F_k(f;t)$$

where $H_k(t)$ denotes the complex-valued pass loss for the kth subcarrier. Therefore, the receiver requires no equalization or, at most, one-tap equalization for each subcarrier (see "Insertion of Cyclic Prefix" below for details).

The first systems employing MCM were military HF radio links in the late 1950s and early 1960s, such as Kineplex (Mosier and Clabaugh 1958) and KATHRYN (Zimmerman and Kirsch 1967), where nonoverlapped, band-limited orthogonal signals were used because of difficulty in precisely controlling the frequencies of subcarrier local oscillators and detecting subcarrier signals with analog filters.

The concept of MCM employing time-limited orthogonal signals, which is almost the same as the current OFDM, dates back to 1960 (Marmuth 1960). Defining the symbol period at subcarrier level as T_s, the mathematical expression of the transmitted signal $s(t)$ is written as

$$s(t) = \sum_{i=-\infty}^{+\infty} \sum_{k=1}^{N_{SC}} c_{ki} e^{j2\pi f_k(t-iT_s)} f(t - iT_s) \qquad (1)$$

where c_{ki} denotes the ith information symbol at the kth subcarrier, and $f(t)$ denotes the pulse waveform of the symbol. When the rectangular pulse waveform is used, $f(t)$ is given by

$$f(t) = \begin{cases} 1, & (0 < t \le T_s) \\ 0, & (t \le 0, t > T_s) \end{cases} \qquad (2)$$

so f_k and Δf are respectively written as

$$f_k = f_c + \frac{(k-1)}{T_s} \qquad (3)$$

$$\Delta f = \frac{1}{T_s} \qquad (4)$$

Figure 2 compares baseband data transmissions ($f_c = 0$) with a serial rectangular pulse waveform (Figure 2a) and with parallel sinusoidal waveforms resulting in an OFDM waveform (Figure 2b). Here the subscript i is dropped in Equation 1 for the sake of simplicity. Note

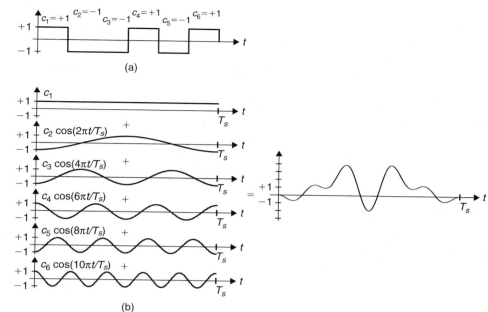

Figure 2: Comparison of transmitted waveforms—(a) rectangular pulse waveform for baseband serial data transmission and (b) baseband parallel data transmission with sinusoidal waveforms and resulting OFDM waveform

that the name *OFDM* appeared in the U.S. patent issued in 1970 (Chang 1970).

Use of the Discrete Fourier Transform

Sampling $s(t)$ $(iT_s < t \le (i + 1)T_s)$ with sampling period of t_{spl} $(=T_s/N_{SC})$, the transmitted signal in a discrete form is written with a column vector $(N_{SC} \times 1)$ as

$$
\begin{aligned}
\mathbf{s}_i &= [s(iT_s + t_{spl}), \ldots, s(iT_s + qt_{spl}), \ldots, s(iT_s + N_{SC}t_{spl})]^T \\
&= \mathbf{W}^{-1}(N_{SC})\mathbf{c}_i
\end{aligned}
\tag{5}
$$

where $(*)^T$ denotes the transpose of $(*)$, and $\mathbf{W}^{-1}(N_{SC})$ and $\mathbf{c}_i$ denote the N_{SC}-point IDFT matrix $(N_{SC} \times N_{SC})$ and the ith symbol (column) vector $(N_{SC} \times 1)$, respectively:

$$
\begin{aligned}
\mathbf{W}^{-1}(N_{SC}) &= \left\{ w_{qk}^{-1} \right\} \\
w_{qk}^{-1} &= \frac{1}{\sqrt{N_{SC}}} e^{j2\pi \frac{(q-1)(k-1)}{N_{SC}}}
\end{aligned}
\tag{6}
$$

$$
\mathbf{c}_i = [c_{1i}, c_{2i}, \ldots, c_{N_{SC}i}]^T
\tag{7}
$$

Equation 5 shows that the transmitted symbol vector is recovered at the receiver by means of the DFT:

$$
\hat{\mathbf{c}}_i = \mathbf{W}(N_{SC})\mathbf{s}_i
\tag{8}
$$

where $(\hat{*})$ is used to distinguish the recovered symbol vector from the transmitted symbol vector and $\mathbf{W}(N_{SC})$ denotes the N_{SC}-point DFT matrix given by

$$
\begin{aligned}
\mathbf{W}(N_{SC}) &= \left\{ w_{qk} \right\} \\
w_{qk} &= \frac{1}{\sqrt{N_{SC}}} e^{-j2\pi \frac{(q-1)(k-1)}{N_{SC}}}.
\end{aligned}
\tag{9}
$$

Figure 3 shows the discrete representation of a baseband OFDM system. As we can see, the use of IDFT and DFT totally eliminates the bank of subcarrier oscillators at the transmitter and receiver (Weinstein and Ebert 1971). The N_{SC}-point IDFT and DFT requires the number of complex multiplications of N_{SC}^2, but if the number of DFT points is selected as the power of 2, it can be replaced by the N_{SC}-FFT (fast Fourier transform), which requires a number of complex multiplications of $(N_{SC}/2)\log_2 N_{SC}$ (Mitra and Kaiser 1993). This results in reduced computational complexity and thus power consumption at the transmitter and receiver, so in OFDM systems the number of DFT points is usually chosen as the power of 2. Note that the number of subcarriers is not always chosen as the power of 2. For example, both the edge subcarriers are often not used for data transmission to reduce adjacent channel interference.

Besides its military application, OFDM's use in mobile communications was first suggested by Cimini (1985), and a telephone modem based on OFDM was developed

Figure 3: Discrete representation of a baseband OFDM system—(a) transmitter and (b) receiver

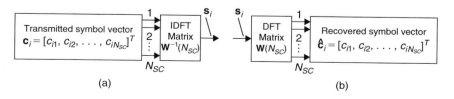

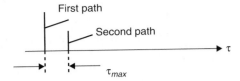

Figure 4: An instantaneous impulse response of a multipath channel

as the first commercial product in the late 1980s (Bingham 1990).

Insertion of Cyclic Prefix

As mentioned earlier in the discussion of OFDM's origins, a multipath channel can be characterized by an impulse response with delay spread in the time domain. Figure 4 shows an instantaneous impulse response of a multipath channel only with two paths, where τ_{max} denotes the time delay between the first and second paths (Hara and Prasad 2002).

After an OFDM signal goes through the channel, the receiver receives two signals. In the following, we deal with the first arrival signal as the desired one in the sense that the receiver is synchronized to it, whereas the second arrival signal is a delayed one. Figure 5 shows three

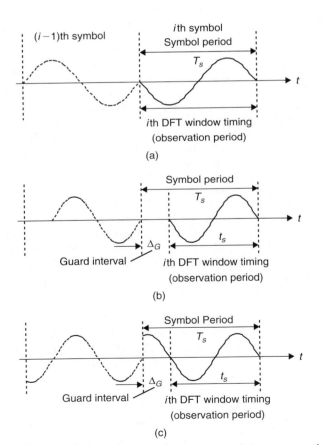

Figure 5: Transmitted signals—(a) no guard time interval insertion, (b) guard time interval insertion, and (c) cyclic prefix insertion

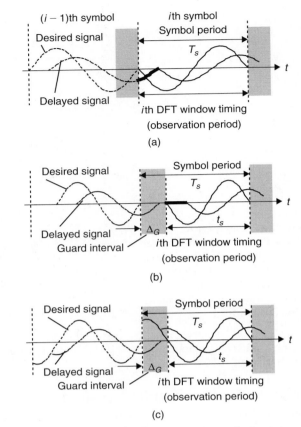

Figure 6: Received signals—(a) no guard time interval insertion, (b) guard time interval insertion, and (c) cyclic prefix insertion

transmitted signals, whereas Figure 6 shows the corresponding three received signals. Note that here we pay attention only to waveforms at a certain subcarrier ($f_c = 0$, $k = 2$).

Without a guard time interval between successive OFDM symbols, ISI from the $(i-1)$th symbol gives a distortion to the ith symbol (compare Figures 5a and 6a and see the thick line in Figure 6a). If we employ a guard time interval (no signal transmission) with length of $\Delta_G > \tau_{max}$, we can perfectly eliminate ISI. This scheme is called *zero-padded OFDM*, and it was first suggested in Weinstein and Ebert (1971). However, in this scheme, the sudden change of waveform contains higher spectral components, so they result in *inter(sub)carrier interference* (ICI) (compare Figures 5b and 6b and see the thick line in Figure 7b).

Figure 5c shows the cyclic prefix insertion technique to perfectly eliminate ICI, where the OFDM symbol is cyclically extended in the guard time interval (Alard and Lassalle 1989; Peled and Ruiz 1980). Paying attention to the ith DFT window with width of t_s in Figure 6c, we can see two sinusoidal signals with full width, so it results in no ICI.

For more general multipath channels, the effect of cyclic prefix can be mathematically explained as follows. Assume that a multipath channel has an impulse response with a length of L paths (samples) $h_1, \ldots, h_L$. To eliminate the ISI resulting from the multipath propagation, the length of the inserted cyclic prefix M should be

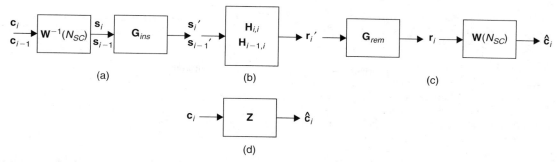

Figure 7: Matrix and vector representation of OFDM system—(a) transmitter, (b) channel, (c) receiver, and (d) input/output relationship

greater than or equal to $L - 1$, namely, $M \geq L - 1$. The ith cyclically prefixed signal is written in a vector form as

$$\mathbf{s}_i' = \mathbf{G}_{ins}\mathbf{s}_i \tag{10}$$

where $\mathbf{s}_i'$ and $\mathbf{G}_{ins}$ denote the ith cyclically prefixed signal vector $((N_{SC} + M) \times 1)$ and the cyclic prefix insertion matrix $((N_{SC} + M) \times N_{SC})$, respectively:

$$\mathbf{s}_i' = [s_{1i}, s_{2i}, \dots, s_{(N_{SC}+M)_i}]^T \tag{11}$$

$$\mathbf{G}_{ins} = \begin{bmatrix} \mathbf{0}_{M \times (N_{SC}-M)} \mathbf{I}_{M \times M} \\ \mathbf{I}_{N_{SC} \times N_{SC}} \end{bmatrix} \tag{12}$$

where $\mathbf{0}_{\alpha \times \beta}$ and $\mathbf{I}_{\alpha \times \alpha}$ denote the zero matrix with size of $\alpha \times \beta$ and the identity matrix with size of $\alpha \times \alpha$, respectively.

Through the channel, the ith received signal contains contributions from not only the ith transmitted signal but also the $(i - 1)$th transmitted signal. Assume that the receiver has been synchronized to the received signal—that is, it has accurately known the boundary between the ith and $(i - 1)$th signals. In this case, neglecting the channel noise, the received signal vector $r_i' = [r_{1i}', r_{2i}', \dots, r_{(N_{SC}+M)i}']^T$ $((N_{SC} + M) \times 1)$ is written as

$$\mathbf{r}_i' = \mathbf{H}_{i,i}\mathbf{s}_i' + \mathbf{H}_{i-1,i}\mathbf{s}_{i-1}' \tag{13}$$

where $\mathbf{H}_{i,i}$ and $\mathbf{H}_{i-1,i}$ denote the ith impulse response matrices $((N_{SC} + M) \times (N_{SC} + M))$ contributed from the ith and the $(i-1)$th transmitted signal, respectively:

$$\mathbf{H}_{i,i} = \begin{pmatrix} h_1 & 0 & \cdots & \cdots & \cdots & 0 \\ \vdots & h_1 & \ddots & \ddots & \ddots & \vdots \\ h_L & \vdots & \ddots & \ddots & \ddots & \vdots \\ 0 & h_L & \ddots & h_1 & \ddots & \vdots \\ \vdots & \ddots & \ddots & \vdots & \ddots & \vdots \\ 0 & \cdots & 0 & h_L & \cdots & h_1 \end{pmatrix} \tag{14}$$

$$\mathbf{H}_{i-1,i} = \begin{pmatrix} 0 & \cdots & 0 & h_L & \cdots & h_2 \\ \vdots & \ddots & \ddots & \ddots & \ddots & \vdots \\ \vdots & \ddots & \ddots & \ddots & \ddots & h_L \\ \vdots & \ddots & \ddots & \ddots & \ddots & 0 \\ \vdots & \ddots & \ddots & \ddots & \ddots & \vdots \\ 0 & \cdots & \cdots & \cdots & \cdots & 0 \end{pmatrix} \tag{15}$$

The receiver removes the cyclic prefix from the received signal before demodulation. The received signal vector after the cyclic prefix removal $\mathbf{r}_i = [r_{1i}, r_{2i}, \dots, r_{N_{SC}i}]^T (N_{SC} \times 1)$ is written as

$$\mathbf{r}_i = \mathbf{G}_{rem}\mathbf{r}_i' \tag{16}$$

where $\mathbf{G}_{rem}$ denotes the cyclic prefix removal matrix $(N_{SC} \times (N_{SC} + M))$:

$$\mathbf{G}_{rem} = [\mathbf{0}_{N_{SC} \times M} \mathbf{I}_{N_{SC} \times N_{SC}}] \tag{17}$$

Taking into consideration for $M \geq L - 1$

$$\mathbf{G}_{rem}\mathbf{H}_{i-1,i} = \mathbf{0}_{N_{SC} \times (N_{SC}+M)} \tag{18}$$

Substituting Equations 13 and 17 into Equation 16 leads to

$$\begin{aligned} \mathbf{r}_i &= \mathbf{G}_{rem}(\mathbf{H}_{i,i}\mathbf{s}_i' + \mathbf{H}_{i-1,i}\mathbf{s}_{i-1}') \\ &= \mathbf{G}_{rem}\mathbf{H}_{i,i}\mathbf{s}_i' \\ &= \mathbf{G}_{rem}\mathbf{H}_{i,i}\mathbf{G}_{ins}\mathbf{s}_i \\ &= \mathbf{D}\mathbf{s}_i \end{aligned} \tag{19}$$

where

$$\mathbf{D} = \mathbf{G}_{rem}\mathbf{H}_{i,i}\mathbf{G}_{ins} \tag{20}$$

Equation 19 clearly shows that the cyclic prefix perfectly eliminates the ISI resulting from the $(i - 1)$th transmitted signal. Furthermore, direct calculation of Equation 20 reveals that with the impulse response vector $\mathbf{h} = [h_1,...,$ $h_L, 0,..., 0]^T$ ($N_{SC} \times 1$), $\mathbf{D}$ can be written as

$$\mathbf{D} = [\mathbf{h}^0, \mathbf{h}^1, ..., \mathbf{h}^v, ..., \mathbf{h}^{N_{SC}-1}] \quad (21)$$

where $\mathbf{h}^v$ denotes the v-cyclic shifted channel impulse response vector. $\mathbf{D}$ is called a *circulant matrix* ($N_{SC} \times N_{SC}$), and with the DFT and IDFT matrices, it can be diagonalized (Davis 1979) as

$$\mathbf{D} = \mathbf{W}^{-1}(N_{SC})\mathbf{Z}\mathbf{W}(N_{SC}) \quad (22)$$

where $\mathbf{Z}$ is defined as

$$\mathbf{Z} = diag\{\mathbf{W}(N_{SC})\mathbf{h}^0\} = diag\{\mathbf{z}\} \quad (23)$$

where $\mathbf{z} = [z_1,...,z_{N_{SC}}]^T$ denotes the frequency response vector of the channel ($N_{SC} \times 1$) and $diag\{\mathbf{z}\}$ denotes the diagonal matrix ($N_{SC} \times N_{SC}$) with main diagonal elements of $z_1,..., z_{N_{SC}}$. Consequently, inserting a cyclic prefix replaces the convolution of the channel impulse response by its circular convolution, which is equivalently expressed in the discrete frequency domain as multiplication of the channel frequency response. Defining the DFT output vector $\mathbf{W}(N_{SC})\mathbf{r}_i$ as $\hat{\mathbf{c}}_i = [\hat{c}_{i1},..., \hat{c}_{iN_{SC}}]^T$ ($N_{SC} \times 1$) with Equations 5, 19, and 22, it can be written as

$$\begin{aligned} \hat{\mathbf{c}}_i &= \mathbf{W}(N_{SC})\mathbf{r}_i \\ &= \mathbf{W}(N_{SC})(\mathbf{W}^{-1}(N_{SC})\mathbf{Z}\mathbf{W}(N_{SC}))\left(\mathbf{W}^{-1}(N_{SC})\mathbf{c}_i\right) \\ &= \mathbf{Z}\mathbf{c}_i \end{aligned} \quad (24)$$

Taking into consideration that $\mathbf{Z}$ is the diagonal matrix with elements of $z_1,..., z_{N_{SC}}$, finally we have

$$\hat{c}_{ik} = z_k c_{ik} \ (k = 1,..., N_{SC}) \quad (25)$$

Equation 25 clearly shows that, through the channel, the symbol transmitted over the kth subcarrier is multiplied by its frequency response. In other words, if the receiver estimates the frequency response of the channel, then it can easily recover the transmitted data. Figure 7 shows the matrix and vector representation of a baseband OFDM system.

Before finishing this discussion on the effect of cyclic prefix, note that the cyclic prefix insertion technique is applicable not only to OFDM but also to SCM. Indeed, an SCM system, with DFT processing and the use of cyclic prefix for frequency domain equalization, has essentially the same performance and complexity as an OFDM system (Sari, Karam, and Jeanclaude 1994).

Now let us come back to the analog representation of OFDM signal. Modifying Equations 1 through 4, the transmitted signal with the cyclic prefix is written as

$$s(t) = \sum_{i=-\infty}^{+\infty} \sum_{k=1}^{N_{SC}} c_{ki} e^{j2\pi f_k (t - iT_s)} f(t - iT_s) \quad (26)$$

$$f(t) = \begin{cases} 1, (-\Delta_G < t \leq t_s) \\ 0, (t \leq -\Delta_G, t > t_s) \end{cases} \quad (27)$$

$$f_k = f_c + \frac{(k-1)}{t_s} \quad (28)$$

$$\Delta f = \frac{1}{t_s} \quad (29)$$

where T_s, Δ_G and t_s denote the OFDM symbol period, cyclic prefix length, and observation period (often called the *useful symbol length*), respectively, and they satisfy the following equation:

$$T_s = \Delta_G + t_s \quad (30)$$

The OFDM waveform is expressed by Equations 26 through 30 in the sense that it is transmitted and received with the IDFT and DFT and that it has a cyclic prefix. Now we have reached the "current form" of OFDM. Figure 8 shows the cyclic prefix insertion technique, the frequency spectrum of the pulse waveform, and the frequency spectrum of the transmitted signal in the current form of OFDM.

Before moving on to the next section, note that the cyclic prefix also gives OFDM signal a drawback. Remember that the subcarrier separation of the OFDM signal

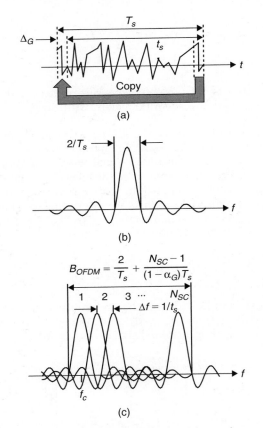

Figure 8: Current form of OFDM—(a) cyclic prefix extension technique, (b) frequency spectrum of the pulse waveform, and (c) frequency spectrum of the ODM signal

without the cyclic prefix is $1/T_s$ (see Equation 4), whereas that with the cyclic prefix is $1/t_s$ (see Equation 29). T_s is larger than t_s, so $1/T_s$ is smaller than $1/t_s$. This means that inserting the cyclic prefix makes the subcarrier separation a bit larger. For example, the bandwidth in terms of the main lobe is calculated as $B_{OFDM} = 2/T_s + (N_{SC} - 1)/[(1 - \alpha_G) T_s]$, where α_G is the cyclic prefix factor defined as $\alpha_G = \Delta_G/T_s$. If the number of subcarriers is large, then the bandwidth of the OFDM signal normalized by total symbol transmission rate $R = N_{SC}/T_s$ is written as $B_{OFDM}/R = 1/(1 - \alpha_G) \approx 1 + \alpha_G$. This means that the cyclic prefix insertion widens the bandwidth of the OFDM signal by Δ_G.

Coded OFDM

To show that channel coding gives OFDM more robustness against frequency-selective fading, this subsection will demonstrate the *bit error rate* (BER) performance of a coded OFDM system by computer simulation (Hara and Prasad 2002). As shown later in the third and fourth sections of this chapter, OFDM has some drawbacks, such as sensitivity to nonlinear amplification at the transmitter and sensitivity to carrier frequency offset and difficulty in DFT window synchronization at the receiver. However, here we assume that such drawbacks have been overcome—that is, we assume linear amplification, no carrier frequency offset, and perfect DFT window synchronization.

When an OFDM signal is transmitted through a frequency-selective fading channel, some subcarriers experience high attenuation whereas others experience low attenuation. We can imagine that if we employ a channel coding scheme over subcarriers, we can improve the BER by means of a frequency diversity effect.

Error-correcting codes such as convolutional codes are often designed for channels where the errors are random. However, in a frequency-selective fading channel, signal fade causes bursty errors, because the time-varying nature of the channel makes the level of the received signal fall below the noise level and the fade duration contains several transmitted data. To make such codes work well even in a frequency-selective fading channel, an interleaving technique is commonly used to transform the bursty channel into a channel with random errors by reordering the encoder outputs at the transmitter.

Figure 9 shows the block diagram of a bit-interleaved coded OFDM system to investigate the BER performance, where *quadrature phase shift keying* (QPSK) and coherent detection and a half-rate convolutional code are assumed with constraint length of 7 and bit interleaving

depth of 8 within one OFDM symbol. Note that the subcarrier arrangement of the physical layer standard (IEEE 802.11a PHY) is used (IEEE 1999). In addition, two kinds of Rayleigh fading channels are assumed. One is a frequency-nonselective Rayleigh fading channel in which a single Rayleigh-distributed path is in the multipath delay profile. The other is a frequency-selective Rayleigh fading channel in which there are three independent and identical Rayleigh-distributed paths with the identical average power in the multipath delay profile (Proakis 2001). For both channels, a quasi-static fading is assumed in which the temporal variation is negligibly small over one OFDM symbol whereas it is independent symbol by symbol.

Figure 10 shows the BER performance against the average E_b/N_0 (the ratio of signal energy per bit to spectral density of noise) in the frequency-nonselective and quasi-static Rayleigh fading channel (see Figure 11a) and in the frequency-selective and quasi-static Rayleigh fading channel (see Figure 11b), respectively. Each figure contains a theoretical result as well as a computer simulation result, and the theoretical derivation on the BER is given in Proakis (2001). In Figure 11a, there is no diversity effect even if the channel coding is employed because all of the subcarriers are subject to the same attenuation at one time. On the other hand, in Figure 11b, the third-order diversity effect is obtained. It is well known that the degree of freedom in the time domain is the same as that in the frequency domain, because they are related to each other through a linear transform of DFT (Monsen 1973). Therefore, in this case, through the channel coding, the third-order gain is obtained as a frequency diversity effect instead of as a path diversity effect.

TRANSMISSION OF OFDM SIGNALS

Figure 12 shows the block diagram of an OFDM transmitter, where the blocks for interleaving and channel coding are omitted. This section will discuss the issues related to two blocks in the figure: the *digital-to-analog* (D/A) converter and a power amplifier.

Resolution of Digital-to-Analog Converter

Equation 26 shows that the OFDM signal is composed of a number of sinusoidal signals, each one independently modulated by information data to transmit. Therefore, by the central limiting theorem, the signal becomes like a Gaussian noise; more precisely, its amplitude becomes complex-valued and Gaussian-distributed, thus its

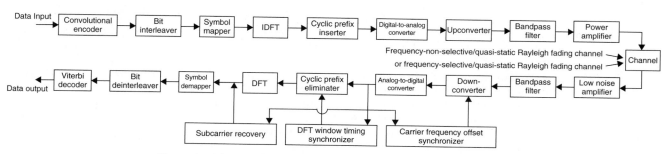

Figure 9: A bit-interleaved, convolutionally encoded OFDM system

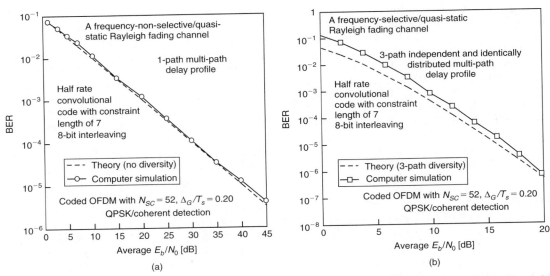

Figure 10: BERs of the OFDM system in (a) frequency-nonselective and quasi-static Rayleigh fading channel and (b) frequency-selective and quasi-static Rayleigh fading channel

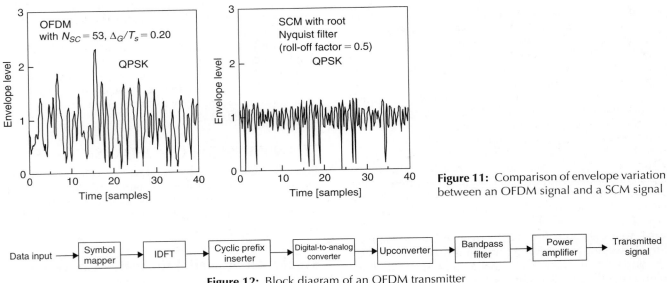

Figure 11: Comparison of envelope variation between an OFDM signal and a SCM signal

Figure 12: Block diagram of an OFDM transmitter

envelope becomes Rayleigh-distributed. Figure 12 compares the envelope variation between an OFDM signal and an SCM signal, where the QPSK with $N_{SC} = 53$ and $\Delta_G/T_s = 0.2$ is assumed for the OFDM signal whereas the QPSK with root Nyquist filter (roll-off factor = 0.5) is assumed for the SCM signal. It can be seen from the figure that the OFDM signal has a large envelope variation, whereas the values of the SCM envelope concentrate on a certain level. Figure 13 compares the probability density functions of the envelope level between the two signals, which more clearly highlights the difference. A large variation in the envelope level also means a large difference between peak and average powers, so it is said that OFDM has a high *peak-to-average-power ratio* (PAPR).

In the transmitter, the signal generated in a digital domain is D/A-converted before upconversion. The dynamic

range of the input amplitude determines the resolution of the D/A converter, so a high resolution is required for the D/A converter in the OFDM transmitter.

Power Amplification of OFDM Signals

In general, a highly efficient power amplifier is preferable at the transmitter, especially in a mobile terminal that is driven by a battery. However, such a highly efficient power amplifier has a nonlinear characteristic that clips the amplitude of input signal. The sudden clips of the input amplitude generate higher spectral components in the power spectrum of the signal, so it results in a spectrum spreading.

As mentioned above, the OFDM signal is like a Gaussian noise with a large envelope variation, so even if we

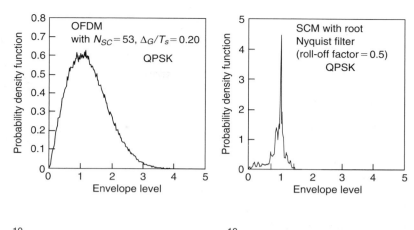

Figure 13: Probability density functions of the envelope for the OFDM and SCM signals

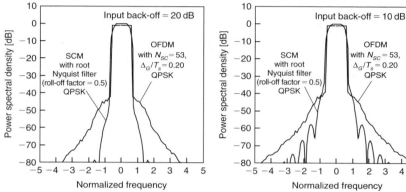

Figure 14: Power spectral densities of the OFDM and SCM signals after a nonlinear amplification

try to reduce the spectrum spreading with a large input backoff to a nonlinear amplifier, we cannot perfectly eliminate sudden inputs of the larger amplitudes beyond the saturation point of the nonlinear amplifier. Furthermore, the outband radiation generated by a subcarrier also becomes ICI for its neighboring subcarriers. Therefore, the severe ICI drastically deteriorates the transmission performance.

Figure 14 compares the power spectral densities of the OFDM and SCM signals after a nonlinear amplification. Here the horizontal axis denotes the frequency normalized by the data transmission rate, and a European Telecommunications Standards Institute (ETSI) BRAN high-power amplifier model (Johansson and Potsher undated) is assumed with input backoffs of 20 dB and 10 dB. As compared with the SCM signal, the OFDM signal has a large outband radiation even for the large input backoff of 20 dB. The sensitivity to nonlinear amplification is often pointed out as one of major drawbacks of OFDM.

There are mainly two methods to increase the power efficiency when amplifying OFDM signals. One method is to reduce the PAPR of the OFDM signal. For example, *selected mapping* (SLM) (Bauml, Fischer, and Huber 1996) multiplies an input symbol sequence by each of the phase sequences to generate alternate input symbol sequences. After applying the IDFT to all of the alternative symbol sequences, SLM selects the one with the lowest PAPR. On the other hand, *partial transmit sequence* (PTS) (Muller and Huber 1997) partitions an input symbol sequences into a number of disjoint symbol subsequences. Applying the IDFT to each symbol subsequence and then summing

the resulting signal subsequences multiplied by a set of distinct rotating vectors, PTS selects the one with the lowest PAPR. Another method is to improve the power efficiency of the amplifier even for varying-envelope input signals. For example, a dynamic biasing method (Saleh and Cox 1983) dynamically controls the direct current voltage with the envelope value of the input signal. On the other hand, *linear amplification with nonlinear components* (LINC) (Cox 1974) is based on the fact that any bandpass signal can be represented by two constant-envelope phase-modulated signals. In addition to these, it is known that some block codes can limit the PAPR within a certain level (Jones, Wilkinson, and Barton 1994).

All of the techniques shown in the above are old. Now, in the early 2000s, to improve the power efficiency of amplifier for the OFDM signal, several variants related to those techniques are now being widely discussed in the research communities on signal processing, wireless communications, and microwave technology.

RECEPTION OF OFDM SIGNALS

Figure 15 shows the block diagram of an OFDM receiver, where the blocks for deinterleaving and channel decoding are also omitted. Here we can easily imagine that, similar to the D/A converter in an OFDM transmitter, a high resolution is required for the analog-to-digital converter in the OFDM receiver.

This section will discuss the issues related to the lower blocks in the figure, such as DFT window timing and

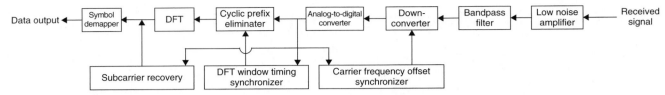

Figure 15: Block diagram of an OFDM receiver

carrier frequency offset synchronization and subcarrier recovery.

DFT Window Timing and Carrier Frequency Offset Synchronization

Equation 25 shows that if it correctly estimates the channel responses for the subcarriers, the receiver can recover the transmitted data. This is true when the receiver has been synchronized to the received signal. Here synchronization at the receiver has two tasks. One is *DFT timing synchronization*—that is, finding a correct timing of the DFT windowing for the received signal. This is extremely difficult, because the OFDM signal is like a Gaussian noise with no distinct boundary between successive OFDM symbols. The second task is *carrier frequency offset synchronization*. There is always a mismatch between the carrier frequencies of local oscillators between a transmitter and receiver. The spectra of subcarriers are densely overlapped in an OFDM signal, so if there exists a carrier frequency offset between a transmitter and receiver, the DFT outputs at the receiver are rich in ICI, resulting in worse transmission performance. Therefore, the receiver needs to accurately estimate and compensate for the carrier frequency offset.

For burst mode transmission in wireless LAN applications, Schmidl's method can jointly accomplish DFT window timing and carrier frequency offset synchronization (Schmidl and Cox 1997). In this method, a pilot OFDM symbol that has two identical halves in the time domain is added at the head of a data burst. Then with the correlation and angle between the first and second halves of the received pilot OFDM symbol, a correct DFT timing and a carrier frequency offset are estimated, respectively.

On the other hand, for continuous mode transmission in digital broadcasting—for example, in *terrestrial integrated services digital broadcasting* (ISDB-T) (Association of Radio Industries and Businesses 2000), two kinds of pilot symbol patterns are used for DFT window timing and carrier frequency offset synchronization: (1) a continuous pilot pattern on the subcarrier with the highest frequency and (2) the scattered pilot pattern in which pilot symbols are inserted at certain subcarriers and certain OFDM symbols.

SUBCARRIER RECOVERY

For OFDM, carrier recovery—namely, generation of a reference signal point—is needed for each subcarrier, so it gives an impression that the complexity of coherent detection is magnified by the number of subcarriers. However, in wired systems, the channel state does not

change often, so coherent detection is not so difficult. For example, coherent detection was employed even by the telephone modem developed in the late 1980s (Bingham 1990) and then by the *discrete multitone* (DMT) receiver for ADSL (Chow, Tu, and Cioffi 1991).

On the other hand, in wireless systems, the channel state always changes, so until the late 1980s, coherent detection was considered to be difficult for OFDM especially in frequency-selective fading channels. Indeed, the *digital audio broadcasting* (DAB) system specified in the late 1980s was based on differential encoding and differential detection that required no subcarrier recovery (Dambacher 1996).

In the early 1990s, discussion of coherent detection of the OFDM signal in the broadcasting system began (Helard and Le Floch 1991) because, to support a higher data transmission rate in a limited frequency bandwidth, higher multilevel modulation techniques such as 16-QAM (quadrature amplitude modulation) and 64-QAM were required with coherent detection. For example, to support coherent detection, the use of scattered pilot symbols was discussed in a frequency-selective fading channel, where a two-dimensional interpolating filter was employed in the frequency domain to estimate the channel response over the subcarrier where the pilot symbol was not available and in the time domain to track the temporal variation of the channel.

Compared with the SCM signal, because of its long symbol period, the OFDM signal is not robust to the temporal variation of channel, the rate of which is determined by a Doppler frequency spread in mobile systems. Therefore, accurately tracking the temporal variation of the channel for subcarrier recovery is one of the most important receiver's tasks in mobile systems. Now in the early 2000s, subcarrier recovery as well as DFT timing and carrier frequency offset synchronization in frequency-selective fading channels is a hot OFDM topic in the research communities of signal processing and wireless communications (Hara and Prasad 2002; Fazel and Kaiser 2003; Hanzo and Keller 2006).

RESOURCE ALLOCATION

In terms of the number of connections in a channel, a system can be categorized as one of two types: single-user or multi-user. A single-user system is one in which there is only a point-to-point connection in a channel, whereas a multi-user system is one in which there are point-to-multipoint connections in a channel.

In wired telephone systems, the channel state does not change often, so the transmitter can easily know the channel state from the receiver through feedback. Indeed, to

Table 1: DAB Parameters

Parameter mode	Mode 1	Mode 2	Mode 3
Bandwidth	1.536 MHz	1.536 MHz	1.536 MHz
Number of subcarriers	1,546	768	384
Modulation and demodulation		DEQPSK/Differential	
Useful symbol length (t_s)	1 ms	250 μs	125 μs
Subcarrier separation (Δf)	3.968 kHz	1.984 kHz	0.992 kHz
Cyclic prefix length (Δ_G)	$t_s/4$ (250 μs)	$t_s/4$ (62.5 μs)	$t_s/4$ (31.25 μs)
FEC		Convolutional code	
Information transmission rate		2.4 Mbps	

maximize the data transmission rate satisfying a certain BER, the telephone modem developed in the late 1980s (Bingham 1990), which is a typical example of a single-user system, adaptively allocated an adequate power and modulation level to each subcarrier. This is called *adaptive power and bit loading*, and, in wired systems, ADSL and PLC transceivers have used the adaptive power and bit loading (Chow, Tu, and Cioffi 1991; Lin et al. 2002).

On the other hand, in mobile wireless communication systems, the channel state changes often, so introducing an adaptive mechanism into a system requires a high rate of adaptation. For example, a frame-by-frame adaptive bit loading was proposed in a multi-user OFDM *time division multiple access* (TDMA) system in which subcarriers with large gains are assigned to higher modulation levels to convey more information per OFDM symbol; subcarriers in deep fade, on the other hand, are assigned to lower modulation levels or are not used for information transmission (Rohling and Grunheid 1996).

Resource allocation is now one of the hot research topics in multi-user OFDM systems. It can offer a multi-user diversity effect by dynamically allocating subcarrier, bit, and power to different users according to their instantaneous channel conditions (Wong et al. 1999). The optimal allocation algorithm is given by the solution of a nonlinear optimization problem, but it is impractical because of its high computational complexity. To reduce the complexity, several algorithms with modification and approximation have been proposed.

APPLICATIONS OF OFDM

The previous sections have given all of the materials required for understanding current OFDM-based systems along with advantages and drawbacks still to be overcome. This section will show several applications of OFDM in already-existing systems.

Digital Broadcasting

Digital audio broadcasting was specified between 1988 and 1992, with its introduction in Europe scheduled in the late 1990s (Dambacher 1996). Table 1 shows the three modes defined in EUREKA 147 DAB, where *differentially*

encoded quadrature phase shift keying (DEQPSK) and differential detection was employed with a convolutional code as a *forward error correction* (FEC).

Based on the successful results from the OFDM-based DAB field trials and measurements in Europe, *terrestrial digital video broadcasting* (DVB-T), with the use of OFDM, was standardized by ETSI in 1996 (European Telecommunications Institute 1996). The United Kingdom first put it into commercial service with multifrequency network use in 1998.

On the other hand, in Japan, the Association of Radio Industries and Businesses (ARIB) standardized ISDB-T in June 2000 (Association of Radio Industries and Businesses 2000). Table 2 shows the three modes defined in the ISDB-T for television. Commercial service successfully began in 2003. The ISDB-T employs QPSK to 64-QAM with coherent detection and DEQPSK with differential detection for mobile reception.

The difference between the DVB-T and the ISDB-T is that the former supports only stationary reception, whereas the latter supports not only stationary but also mobile receptions. In 2004, *handheld digital video broadcasting* (DVB-H), also with the use of OFDM, was standardized for battery-powered handheld receivers by ETSI (2004).

Wireless Local Area Networks

In 1998, the Institute of Electrical and Electronic Engineers (IEEE) 802.11 standardization group decided to select OFDM as a basis for its new 5-GHz wireless LAN standard, which supports data transmission rate from 6 Mbps to 56 Mbps with *binary PSK* (BPSK) to 64-QAM (IEEE undated "Working group"). In the DVB-T and ISDB-T (mentioned in the previous section), OFDM is used in continuous transmission mode for the purpose of broadcasting. On the other hand, this standard— IEEE 802.11a— is the first to use OFDM in packet transmission mode (IEEE 1999). Now there is also the IEEE 802.11g standard based on OFDM, which is available in the 2.4-GHz frequency band (IEEE 2003), and the frequency arrangement of which is the same as that of the IEEE 802.11a standard. Table 3 summarizes the IEEE 802.11a parameters (Van Nee and Prasad 2000).

Table 2: ISDB-T Parameters

Parameter mode	Mode 1	Mode 2	Mode 3
Bandwidth	5.575 MHz	5.575 MHz	5.575 MHz
Number of subcarriers	1405	2809	5617
Modulation	QPSK, 16-QAM, 64-QAM, coherent and DEQPSK, differential		
Useful symbol length (t_s)	252 μs	504 μs	1008 μs
Subcarrier separation (Δf)	3.968 kHz	1.984 kHz	0.992 kHz
Cyclic Prefix Length (Δ_G)	$t_s/4$ (63 μs)	$t_s/4$ (126 μs)	$t_s/4$ (252 μs)
	$t_s/8$ (31.5 μs)	$t_s/8$ (63 μs)	$t_s/8$ (126 μs)
	$t_s/16$ (15.75 μs)	$t_s/16$ (31.5 μs)	$t_s/16$ (63 μs)
	$t_s/32$ (7.875 μs)	$t_s/32$ (15.75 μs)	$t_s/32$ (31.5 μs)
FEC (inner code)	Convolutional code (coding rate = 1/2, 2/3, 3/4, 5/6, 7/8)		
FEC (outer code)	Reed-Solomon code (204, 188)		
Interleaving	Time-frequency domain bit interleaving		
Information transmission rate	3.65–23.2 Mbps		

Table 3: IEEE 802.11a Parameters

Channel spacing	20 MHz
Bandwidth	16.56 MHz (−3 dB bandwidth)
Number of subcarriers	52
Number of pilot subcarriers	4
Useful symbol length (t_s)	3.2 μs
Subcarrier separation (Δf)	312.5 kHz
Cyclic prefix length (Δ_G)	800 ns
FEC	Convolutional code
Interleaving	Frequency domain bit interleaving (within 1 OFDM symbol)
Information transmission rate	6 Mbps (BSPK, coding rate = 1/2)
(modulation, coding rate)	9 Mbps (BSPK, coding rate = 3/4)
	12 Mbps (QSPK, coding rate = 1/2)
	18 Mbps (QSPK, coding rate = 3/4)
	24 Mbps (16-QAM, coding rate = 1/2)
	36 Mbps (16-QAM, coding rate = 3/4)
	48 Mbps (64-QAM, coding rate = 2/3)
	54 Mbps (64-QAM, coding rate = 3/4)
Multiple access method	CSMA/CA (carrier sense multiple access with collision avoidance)

Broadband Wireless Access

The IEEE 802.16 standard defines the WirelessMAN air interface specification for *metropolitan area networks* (MANs); it attempts to replace the "last mile" of wired access with cable modem and digital subscriber line by broadband wireless access (IEEE undated "802.16"). The IEEE 802.16a standard especially defines the air interface as the 2 GHz to 11 GHz band, including both licensed and license-exempt spectra. In the standard, WirelessMAN-OFDM employs an OFDM format with 256 subcarriers with TDMA, whereas WirelessMAN-OFDMA employs an OFDMA (OFDM access) with 2048 subcarriers, where the system performs multiple access by allocating a subset of the multiple subcarriers to an individual receiver. This system also uses frequency hopping spread spectrum for interference suppression.

The IEEE family has been extended to mobile access through the 802.16e standard of December 2005 (IEEE 2006). The IEEE 802.16e has drawn much attention now

Table 4: IEEE 802.16e Parameters

Bandwidth	1.25, 5, 10, and 20 MHz
Number of FFT points	128 (1.25 MHz), 512 (5 MHz), 1024 (10 MHz), and 2048 (20 MHz)
Cyclic prefix length (Δ_G/t_s)	1/4, 1/8, 1/16, and 1/32
FEC	Reed Solomon code
	Convolutional code (coding rate = 1/2, 2/3, and 3/4)
	Convolutional turbo code (optional)
	Block turbo code (optional)
	Low-density parity check
	Code (optional)
Modulation	BPSK (pilot), QPSK, 16-QAM, 64-QAM
Information transmission rate (modulation, coding rate)	1.04 Mbps (1.25 MHz, QPSK, coding rate = 1/2) to 74.81 Mbps (20 MHz, 64-QAM, coding rate = 3/4)
Multiplexing and multiple access	OFDM and OFDMA

because it has been adopted as the physical and medium access control layers protocol in the WiMAX system (WiMAX Forum undated), providing better data handling capability in all-IP services such as video, music streaming, and so on before fourth–generation (4G) cellular systems arrive. Table 4 summarizes the IEEE 802.16e parameters.

MIMO Transmission

In wireless communications, *multiple-input, multiple output* (MIMO) transmission uses multiple antennae at both the transmission and receiver sides (Foschini and Gans 1998). It can increase the data transmission rate or achieve better error-rate performance without increasing the required frequency bandwidth of the transmitted signal, so it is considered to be a promising technique in future wireless communication systems. In MIMO transmission, frequency-nonselective fading needs to be guaranteed in a channel between any pair of transmission and reception antennae. Therefore, to adopt MIMO transmission in a frequency-selective fading channel, its combination with OFDM is suitable. For example, now in the early 2000s, the IEEE 802.11n standard is being finalized (IEEE undated "802.11"). It employs OFDM with four more subcarriers, a short cyclic prefix length, and 2 × 2 MIMO transmission to support much higher data-transmission rates compared with the IEEE 802.11a standard. In addition, MIMO transmission is optionally adopted in IEEE 802.16e (IEEE 2006).

Fourth-Generation Mobile Communication Systems

The introduction of service of 4G mobile communication systems is scheduled around 2010 to 2020, and it will support more than 100 Mbits/sec data rates even for high-speed cruising mobile users. Intensive research on 4G mobile communication systems and related topics are now of great interest to researchers in universities and laboratories all over the world, with OFDM promising to

play a key role in the systems with MIMO transmission (Hara and Prasad 2002; Fazel and Kaiser 2003; Hanzo and Keller 2006).

CONCLUSION

Now in the early 2000s, we are using several standards based on OFDM—for example, DMT for ADSL; European DAB, DVB-T, and DVB-H and Japanese ISDB-T for broadcasting; IEEE 802.11a and IEEE 802.11g for wireless LANs; and IEEE 802.16e for mobile broadband wireless access. OFDM fundamentally has never changed its form since the use of cyclic prefix was proposed in the late 1980s. In this sense, we can doubtlessly say that the technique of OFDM has been matured, although there are still drawbacks to overcome in implementation of OFDM transceivers, such as efficient power amplification in conjunction with reducing the PAPR and the DFT window timing and carrier frequency offset synchronization and subcarrier recovery. Looking at current discussions on OFDM, we can say that OFDM probably will continue to be a promising transmission technique. Because we desire to enjoy more broadband services in wireless systems, OFDM is suitable to combat frequency-selective fading with MIMO transmission.

GLOSSARY

Cyclic prefix: A signal extended in the guard time interval to cyclically and continuously extrapolate signals over subcarriers.

Guard time interval: A time interval inserted between successive symbols to avoid intersymbol interference because of time dispersion of channel.

Inter(sub)carrier interference (ICI): Interference among subcarriers.

Multicarrier modulation: A parallel data transmission method to split a high-rate data stream into a number of lower-rate data streams that are transmitted simultaneously over a number of subcarriers.

Multiple-input, multiple-output (MIMO) transmission: A technique to use multiple antennae at both the transmission and receiver sides to improve data transmission rate or quality without increasing the required bandwidth.

Multi-user diversity: In a large network, at any time there is a user whose channel condition is good with high probability. Multi-user diversity is a technique to improve the overall network capacity by allowing such a user to transmit data at that time. A technique to improve the overall multi-user capacity in a large network where there is a user at any time with high probability whose channel condition is good is to allow such a user to transmit data at that time.

Orthogonal frequency division multiplexing (OFDM): A kind of multicarrier modulation that allows subcarrier overlapping.

Useful symbol: A part of the OFDM symbol that corresponds to the DFT window.

CROSS REFERENCES

See *Frequency and Phase Modulation*; *Frequency Division Multiplexing (FDM)*; *Orthogonal Frequency Division Multiplexing (OFDM)*; *Statistical Time Division Multiplexing (STDM)*; *Time Division Multiplexing (TDM)*; *Wavelength Division Multiplexing (WDM)*.

REFERENCES

Alard, M., and R. Lassalle. 1989. Principles of modulation and channel coding for digital broadcasting for mobile receivers. *EBU Technical Review*, no. 224, pp. 168–90.

ANSI. 1998. Standard T1.413. Network to customer installation interfaces: Asymmetric digital subscriber line (ADSL) metallic interface.

Association of Radio Industries and Businesses. 2000. Standard ARIB STD-B24. Data coding and transmission specification for digital broadcasting, June.

Bauml, R., R. Fischer, and J. B. Huber. 1996. Reducing the peak-to-average power ratio of multicarrier modulation by selected mapping. *Electronic Letters*, 32(22): 2056–7.

Bingham, J. A. C. 1990. Multicarrier modulation for data transmission: An idea whose time has come. *IEEE Communications Magazine*, 28(5): 5–14.

Chang, R. W. 1970. Orthogonal frequency division multiplexing. U.S. Patent 3,488,445, filed Nov. 14, 1966, and issued Jan. 6, 1970.

Chow, J. S., J. C. Tu, and J. M. Cioffi. 1991. A discrete multitone transceiver system for HDSL applications. *IEEE Journal of Selected Areas in Communication*, 9(6): 895–908.

Cimini, L. J. Jr. 1985. Analysis and simulation of a digital mobile channel using orthogonal frequency division multiplexing. *IEEE Transactions in Communications*, 33(7): 665–75.

Cox, D. C. 1974. Linear amplification with nonlinear components. *IEEE Transactions on Communications*, 23(12): 1942–5.

Dambacher, P. 1996. *Digital broadcasting*. London: IEE.

Davis, P. J. 1979. *Circulant matrix*. New York: John Wiley & Sons.

ETSI. 2004. EN 302 304. Transmission system for hand-held terminals (DVB-H).

European Telecommunications Institute. 1996. Specification EN 300 744. Digital broadcasting systems for television, sound and data services; framing structure, channel coding and modulation for digital terrestrial television.

Fazel, K., and S. Kaiser. 2003. *Multi-carrier and spread spectrum systems*. New York: John Wiley & Sons.

Foschini, G. J., and M. J. Gans. 1998. On limits of wireless communications in a fading environment when using multiple antennas. *Wireless Personal Communications*, 6(3): 311–35.

Hanzo, L., and T. Keller. 2006. *OFDM and MC-CDMA: A primer*. New York: Wiley-IEEE.

Hara, S., and R. Prasad. 2002. *Multicarrier techniques for 4G mobile communications*. Boston: Artech House.

Helard, J. F., and B. Le Floch. 1991. Trellis coded orthogonal frequency division multiplexing for digital video transmission. In *Proceedings of GLOBECOM '91*, pp. 785–91.

IEEE. 1999. Standard 802.11a. Wireless medium access control (MAC) and physical layer (PHY) specifications: High-speed physical layer extension in the 5 GHz band.

———. 2003. Standard 802.11g. Wireless LAN medium access control (MAC) and physical layer (PHY) specifications.

———. 2006. Standard 802.16e. Air interface for fixed and mobile broadband wireless access systems amendment for physical and medium access control layers for combined fixed and mobile operation in licensed bands.

———. Undated. 802.11 Working group Web site (www.ieee802.org/11/).

———. Undated. 802.16 Working group on broadband wireless access standards (retrieved from www.ieee802.org/16/).

Johansson, M., and T. Potsher. Undated. Input on power amplifier models. ETSI BRAN document 3ER1073B.

Jones, A. E., T. A. Wilkinson, and S. K. Barton. 1994. Block coding scheme for reduction of peak to mean envelope power ratio of multicarrier transmission schemes. *Electronic Letters*, 30(25): 2098–9.

Lin, Y. J., H. A. Latchman, M. Y. Lee, and S. Katar. 2002. A power line communication network infrastructure for the smart home. *IEEE Wireless Communications*, 9(6): 104–11.

Marmuth, H. F. 1960. On the transmission of information by orthogonal time functions. *AIEE Transactions in Communications and Electronics*, 79: 248–55.

Mitra, S. K., and J. F. Kaiser. 1993. *Handbook for digital signal processing*. New York: John Wiley & Sons.

Monsen, P. 1973. Digital transmission performance on fading dispersive diversity channels. *IEEE Transactions on Communication*, 21: 33–9.

Mosier, R. R., and R. G. Clabaugh. 1958. Kineplex: A bandwidth-efficient binary transmission system. *AIEE Transactions*, 76: 723–8.

Muller, S. H., and J. B. Huber. 1997. OFDM with reduced peak-to-average power ratio by optimum combination of partial transmit sequences. *Electronic Letters*, 33(5): 368–9.

Peled, A., and A. Ruiz. 1980. Frequency domain data transmission using reduced computational complexity algorithm. In *IEEE International Conference on Acoustics, Speech, and Signal Processing*, April, pp. 964–7.

Proakis, J. G. 2001. *Digital communications*. 4th ed. New York: McGraw-Hill.

Rohling, H., and R. Grunheid. 1996. Performance of an OFDM-TDMA mobile communication system. In *Proceedings of IEEE VTC 1996*, May, pp. 1589–93.

Saleh, A. A. M., and D. C. Cox. 1983. Improving the power-added efficiency of FET amplifiers operating with varying-envelope signals. *IEEE Transactions in Microwave Theory and Technology*, 31(1): 51–6.

Sari, H., G. Karam, and I. Jeanclaude. 1994. Frequency-domain equalization of mobile radio and terrestrial broadcasting channels. In Proceedings of GLOBE-COM '94, Nov.-Dec., pp. 1–5.

Schmidl, T. M., and D. C. Cox. 1997. Robust frequency and timing synchronization for OFDM. *IEEE Transactions in Communications*, 45(12): 1613–21.

Van Nee, R., and R. Prasad. 2000. *OFDM for wireless multimedia communications*. Boston: Artech House.

Weinstein, S. B., and P. M. Ebert. 1971. Data transmission by frequency-division multiplexing using the discrete Fourier transform. *IEEE Transactions in Communications Technology*, 19: 628–34.

WiMAX Forum. Undated. Web site at www.wimaxforum. org/home/.

Wong, C. Y., R. S. Cheng, K. B. Letaief, and R. D. Murch. 1999. Multiuser OFDM with adaptive subcarrier, bit, and power allocation. *IEEE Journal of Selected Areas in Communication*, 17(10): 1747–58.

Zimmerman, M. S., and A. L. Kirsch. 1967. The AN/GSC-10 (KATHRYN) variable rate data modem for HF radio. *IEEE Transactions in Communication Technology*, 15: 197–205.

Wavelength Division Multiplexing

Yassine Khlifi and Noureddine Boudriga, *University of the 7th of November at Carthage, Tunisia*
Mohammad S. Obaidat, *Monmouth University*

INTRODUCTION

In recent years, the increasing popularity of the Internet has resulted in a rapidly growing demand for network bandwidth. It is expected that traditional networks will not be able to support the massive traffic resulting from emerging high-bandwidth applications. The demand of multimedia applications is creating an incredible pressure on existing telephony infrastructures that are designed to handle predictable connection-oriented voice traffic. Users are already seeing reduced performance of the Internet, including high delays and network failures. Hence, new technologies were needed to support the bandwidth requirements of subscribers and provide support for new services. Optical fiber technology is becoming the dominant factor for meeting these demands because of its potential capabilities: huge bandwidth, low signal attenuation, low power requirement, low material usage, small space requirement, and low cost. With optical technology, these networks are becoming the appropriate infrastructure for Internet transport. Given the large difference between optical transmission capacity (in tens of Tbps) and electronic data rate (several Gbps), it is expected that optical fibers can scale the increasing volume of information (Papadimitriou et al. 2003).

Currently, links in long-life networks consist almost entirely of optic fibers, with hundreds of thousands of miles of new fiber being deployed every year. Optic fiber offers increased capacity by allowing higher transmission rates over longer distances as compared to copper wires. However, the bandwidth is still limited by the electronic processing and switching speeds at the communication nodes. Three technologies are available in an optical network: *time division multiplexing* (TDM), *synchronous optical network* (SONET), and *synchronous digital hierarchy* (SDH). Currently, the SONET-SDH layer has been used with many traditional networks to offer mechanisms for efficient bandwidth utilization and to provide protection. The SONET-SDH framing structure is widely used in voice transmission in optical networks but is considered to be cumbersome for high-speed links. A new flexible framing scheme is required for next generation optical network to support multiprotocol encapsulation, virtual links, *quality of service* (QoS) differentiation, and link management (Papadimitriou et al. 2003; SONET overview, undated).

The fiber bandwidth can be further exploited by dividing the bandwidth into a number of channels of different wavelengths and by operating each channel at peak electronic rate. This technique is known as *wavelength division multiplexing* (WDM). A WDM network not only provides a huge amount of bandwidth but also may offer data transparency in which the network may carry signals of arbitrary format. Data transparency may be achieved through all-optical transmission and switching of signals without electronic conversions at the intermediate nodes. The major challenge in deploying WDM is to develop architectures and protocols that take full advantage of the benefits offered by WDM. At the same time, the proposed architectures must consider the limitations imposed by current optical device technology. Also, these architectures must support critical services such as bursty traffic while efficiently utilizing the network resources. There are several optical technologies, namely, *wavelength routing* (WR), *optical packet switching* (OPS), *optical label switching* (OLS), and *optical burst switching* (OBS). In WR, end users communicate with one another via all-optical WDM channels, which are referred to as *lightpaths*. An OPS is capable of dynamically allocating network resources with fine packet-level granularity while offering high scalability. An OLS network is proposed to provide a fast switching process based on a set of labels built during the signaling step. An OBS is designed to achieve a balance between the coarse-grained WR and the fine-grained OPS.

In this chapter, we investigate the optical components, optical multiplexing techniques, network architectures, and protocols for WDM networks with the goal of addressing the different issues related to the existing approaches and developed architectures that provide improved performance as well as support for QoS.

This chapter is organized into eight sections. The next section discusses optical multiplexing techniques and major trends in optical components. The third section presents the basic concepts of the WDM technology, as well as its advantages and limitations. The fourth section addresses the different techniques used by optical switching in the WDM networks. The fifth section presents several signaling schemes used by WDM. The sixth section provides a survey of the basic WDM architectures such as broadcast and select and WR networks. The seventh section discusses the QoS models adopted in WDM networks. Finally, the last section before the conclusion gives several critical issues related to the provision of the Internet protocol over WDM.

OPTICAL MULTIPLEXING TECHNIQUES

Bandwidth requirements are expected to increase with time. Therefore, research in optical fiber networks is directed toward achieving high-capacity optical networks. High capacities in optical networks can be achieved by using various optical components and multiplexing techniques. In all-optical networks, concurrency can be provided through time slots (TDM or optical TDM), SONET-SDH, and WDM. In this section, we present an overview of the major optical multiplexing techniques.

Major Optical Components

To transmit data across an optical fiber, the information must first be encoded, or modulated, onto the laser signal (the optical carrier). Analog techniques include amplitude modulation, frequency modulation, and phase modulation. Digital techniques include amplitude shift keying, frequency shift keying, and phase shift keying (Brackett 1990). To enable the operation of the new, vast, and versatile wavelength dimension, new technologies have to be developed. New components that can exercise selection, switching, and routing based on wavelengths were also needed, including optical transmitters, optical receivers, optical amplifiers, *optical cross-connects* (OXC) and *optical add-drop multiplexers* (OADMs).

Optical Fiber

Before describing the optical components, it is essential to understand the characteristics of the optical fiber itself. An optical fiber consists of a central core that is surrounded by a cladding layer whose refractive index is lower than the index of the core. An optical fiber acts as

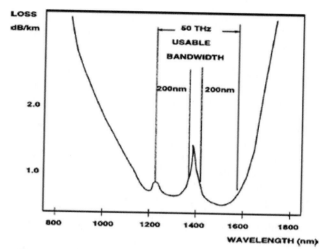

Figure 1: The low-attenuation regions of an optical fiber

a dielectric waveguide to confine light within its surfaces and to guide it in a direction parallel to its axis. The confinement of light is achieved using the so-called total internal reflection, which is done when the angle of incidence of light is greater than the critical angle. Fiber possesses many characteristics that make it an excellent medium for high-speed networking. Figure 1 shows the two low-attenuation regions of optical fiber. The figure also shows the loss attenuation for an optical network in two regions centered at approximately 1300 nanometers (nm) and 1550 nm, respectively, where the attenuation is less than 0.5 dB per kilometer. The total bandwidth for each region is approximately 25 THz.

By using these attenuation areas for data transmission, the signal loss can be made extremely small, thus reducing the number of needed amplifiers and repeaters. Besides its enormous bandwidth and low attenuation, fiber also offers low error rates. Fiber-optic systems typically operate at *bit error rates* (BERs) of less than 10 to 11. Also, fiber transmission is immune to electron magnetic interference and does not cause interference. Naturally, the fiber also has some weaknesses, such as dispersion, nonlinear refraction, and attenuation (when signal attenuation is higher than 0.2 dB/km).

The major forms of dispersion are modal, polarization-mode, and chromatic. *Modal dispersion* occurs only in multimode fibers in which a signal propagates at different speeds. A single mode fiber carries two polarization modes that are indistinguishable in an ideal fiber because of the cylindrical symmetry of the core. However, real fiber deviates from cylindrical symmetry to a more elliptical shape because of the manufacturing process, mechanical stress applied to the fiber, or both. This accidental loss of symmetry results in two distinct polarization modes with different propagation modes. *Polarization mode dispersion* occurs because two polarization modes arrive at different times at the receiver. *Chromatic dispersion* is the consequence of two contributing factors: material dispersion and waveguide dispersion. The first results from the refractive index of silica, which is a function of the spectral components of the signal. The second factor occurs because part of the signal's power propagates on the core and part in the cladding, and they have different refractive indexes.

Optical Transmitter

Optical transmitters can be either tunable or fixed. Tunable lasers can be characterized by the tuning range, tuning time, and information about whether the laser is continuously tunable or discretely tunable. The tuning range is the range of wavelengths over which the laser may be operated. The tuning time is the time required for the laser to tune from one wavelength to another. The most popular tunable lasers are mechanically tuned lasers: acousto-optically and electro-optically tuned lasers or injection current–tuned lasers. Mechanically tuned lasers use a Fabry-Perot cavity that is adjacent to the lasing medium to filter out unwanted wavelengths. They can be tuned by physically adjusting the distance between two mirrors on either end of the cavity so that only the desired wavelength interferes with its multiple reflections in the cavity. A major drawback of mechanically tuned lasers is the tuning time. Because of the mechanical nature of tuning and the length of the cavity, the tuning time is on the order of milliseconds.

In acousto-optically and electro-optically tuned lasers, the index of refraction in the external cavity is changed by using sound waves and electrical current, respectively. The change in the index of refraction results in the transmission of light at different frequencies. In tuned lasers, the tuning time is limited by the time required for light to get back in the cavity at the new frequency (Brackett 1990). Injection current–tuned lasers allow wavelength selection via diffraction grating. Normally, the grating consists of a waveguide in which the index of refraction alternates periodically between two values. The wavelengths that match the period and indexes of the grating are constructively reinforced and propagated through the waveguide, whereas the other wavelengths are not propagated. Depending on the placement of the grating, a laser can be either *distributed feedback* (DFB) or *distributed Bragg reflector* (DBR) laser. In DFB, the grating is placed in the lasing medium, whereas in DBR it is placed outside of the lasing medium. The tuning time for the DBR laser is less than 10 ns.

Optical Receiver

An optical receiver can be either tunable or fixed. The most popular tunable filters are Etalon, acousto-optic, electro-optic, and liquid crystal (LC) Fabry-Perot ("Intellilight dedicated SONET ring," undated). The Etalon comprises a single cavity formed by two parallel mirrors. A signal from an input fiber enters the cavity and reflects a number of times between the two mirrors. A single wavelength can be chosen for propagation through the cavity by adjusting the distance between the mirrors, which can be done mechanically or by changing the index of the material within the cavity. An example of a mechanically tuned Etalon is the Fabry-Perot Etalon receiver (Brackett 1990). In acousto-optic filters, radio frequency waves are passed through a transducer, which is a piezoelectric crystal that converts sound waves to mechanical movement. The sound waves change the crystal's index of refraction

and enable the crystal to act as a grating. By changing the radio waves, a single optical wavelength can be chosen to pass through the filter. The tuning range for acousto-optic receivers covers the spectrum from 1300 nm to 1560 nm and allows approximately one hundred channels. The tuning time of the filters is approximately 10 ms (Yao et al. 2003; Papadimitriou et al. 2003). Electrodes located in the crystal are used to supply current to the crystal. The current changes the crystal's index of refraction, which in turn allows some wavelengths to pass. The tuning time and tuning range of these filters are 10 ns and 16 nm, respectively.

In LC Fabry-Perot filters, the cavity consists of a liquid crystal. Electrical current is used to change the refractive index of the liquid crystal to allow some wavelengths to pass, just as in electro-optic filters. The tuning time of these filters is on the order of a few microseconds while tuning ranges in the order of 30 nm to 40 nm. Fixed receivers use fixed filters or grating devices to filter out wavelengths from a set of wavelengths in a single fiber. The most popular filters or grating devices are diffraction grating, fiber Bragg grating, and thin-film interference filters.

The *diffraction grating* is typically a flat layer of transparent material such as glass or plastic with a row of parallel grooves cut into it. The grating separates light into its component wavelengths by reflecting it with the grooves at all angles. At certain angles, only one wavelength adds constructively while all other wavelengths interfere destructively. Thus, a desired wavelength can be selected by tuning the filter to that wavelength.

In *fiber Bragg grating*, a periodically variable index of refraction is directly photoinduced into the core of an optical fiber. The Bragg grating reflects a given wavelength of light back to the source and passes the other wavelengths. There are two major drawbacks of this method: (1) It induces a grating directly into the core of a fiber, which leads to low insertion loss; and (2) the refractive index in the grating varies with temperature (e.g., an increase in temperature reflects longer wavelengths) (Simmons, Goldstein, and Saleh 1999; Yao et al. 2003; Papadimitriou et al. 2003).

Thin-film interference filters are similar to fiber-grating devices, but they are made by placing alternate layers of low-index and high-index materials onto a substrate layer. Major disadvantages of these filters are their poor thermal stability, high-insertion loss, and poor spectral profile.

Optical Amplifier

Optical amplifiers are important components in the fiber links. They are used to compensate for the attenuation in fibers and for insertion loss in passive optical components such as OXC and OADM. The amplification is usually achieved using *erbium-doped fiber amplifiers* (EDFAs). An EDFA basically consists of small-length optical fibers doped with erbium; they range in length from a few meters to 10 meters. The erbium atoms in the fiber are pumped from their ground state to an excited state at a higher-energy level using a pump source. An incoming signal photon triggers these atoms to come down to their ground state. Thus, incoming signal photons trigger the additional photons, resulting in optical amplification (Brackett 1990).

An optical amplifier is used to amplify a weak or distorted signal with the aim of generating a better optical signal quality. It operates in the optical domain without converting the signal into electrical pulses. It is usually used in long-haul networks where the cumulative loss is large. Current amplifier systems provide extremely low noise and flatter gain, which is advantageous to the optical system. The amplifier output power has steadily increased to nearly +20 dB, which is many times more powerful than the primitive models. A major advantage of EDFAs is that they are capable of amplifying signals with many wavelengths simultaneously. This has provided another way of increasing the capacity: Rather than increasing the bit rate, the bit rate is kept the same and more than one wavelength is used (Yao et al. 2003).

Optical Cross-Connect

A fiber-optical cross-connect element switches optical signals from input ports to output ports. The basic OXC element is the 2×2 cross-point element. It routes optical signals from two input ports to two output ports and has two states: cross state and bar state. In the cross state, the signal from the upper input port is routed to the lower output port, and the signal from the lower input port is routed to the upper output port. In the bar state, the signal from the upper input port is routed to the upper output port, and the signal from the lower input port is routed to the lower output port. Optical cross-point elements have been used in two technologies: (1) the generic directive switch, in which light is physically directed to one of two different outputs; and (2) the gate switch, in which optical amplifier gates are used to select and filter input signals to specific output ports (National Communications System 2002).

Directive switches can be viewed as directional couplers with no gap between the waveguides in the interaction region. When properly fabricated, both cross and bar states can be electro-optically achieved with good cross-talk performance. Cross talk is caused by interference of signals between different wavelengths (interband cross talk) or by interference on the same wavelength on another fiber (intraband cross talk). Interband cross talk must be considered when determining channel spacing where intraband cross talk occurs in switching nodes in which multiple signals on the same wavelength are being switched from different inputs to different output ports. Other types of switches include the mechanical-optical fiber switch and the thermo-optic switch. These devices offer slow switching (in milliseconds) and may be employed in circuit-switched networks. Thermo-optic waveguide switches are operated by the use of the thermo-optic effect. Gate switches operate around 1300 nm and have an optical bandwidth of 40 nm, low polarization dependence (1 dB), and fairly low cross talk (below 40 dB).

Optical Add-Drop Multiplexers

Optical add-drop multiplexers (OADM) are devices that are used to add or remove single wavelengths from a fiber without disturbing the transmission of other signals (see Figure 2). OADM is required for WDM ring and bus networks in order to link the network with local transmitters and receivers. OADMs provide interconnection between network structures. They are generally evaluated in terms

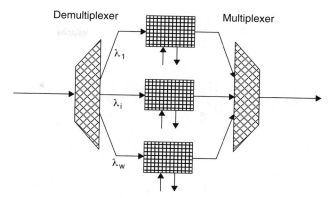

Figure 2: Optical add-drop multiplexer

of performance through cross-talk measurements. Optical cross talk at the same wavelength as the transmitted signal is generally referred to as *homodyne* or *in-band cross talk*. It is particularly serious because it cannot be removed by filtering and has been shown to severely limit network performance (Simmons, Goldstein, and Saleh 1999).

Within homodyne cross talk, incoherent cross talk causes rapid power fluctuations, while coherent cross talk changes the optical power of the signal. Incoherent cross talk occurs in ring and bus networks when the signal and interferer are from different optical sources. It causes power variations at the receiver, resulting in BER degradation. Coherent cross talk in these networks results from multiple paths between ports within OADM. It causes variable attenuation levels between OADM ports. There is no accompanying power penalty because the BER is measured against the optical power at the receiver. Incoherent and coherent cross talk together give a range of possible power penalties, because coherent cross talk can cause variation in both signal and incoherent cross-talk powers at the receiver. The combination of coherent and incoherent cross talk leads to a range of possible BER and power penalties for OADM deployed in a network link.

Optical Multiplexers and Demultiplexers

Optical multiplexers and demultiplexers are used to combine multiple wavelengths onto a single fiber and allow all of the signals to be transferred using the same fiber. These optical components can increase the offered fiber capacity without adding more fibers. They also can receive an optical composite signal that consists of multiple optical frequencies from a fiber and separate it into its frequency components, which are directed to separate fibers. In addition, they can serve as an access point to the optical layer in many more aspects, including other optical devices such OADM and OXC.

Optical Multiplexing

The need for multiplexing is driven by the fact that it is much more economical to transmit data at higher rates over a single fiber than it is to transmit at lower rates over multiple fibers. Multiplexing and demultiplexing aim to transmit multiple signals over a single communication channel. The two common multiplexing techniques are FDM, which separates signals by modulating the data onto different carrier frequencies, and TDM, which separates signals by interleaving bits, one after another. There are three possible multiplexing techniques: (1) time division multiplexing, (2) SONET-SDH and (3) wavelength division multiplexing. TDM is a scheme that combines numerous signals for transmission on a single communications line or channel. Each communication channel is divided into many time segments, each having extremely short duration. A multiplexer at the source of a communication link accepts the input from each individual end user, divides each signal into segments, and assigns the segments to time slots in a rotating sequence.

Optical TDM (OTDM) is a promising multiplexing technique. It is similar to the electronic TDM. The only difference is that OTDM is faster and the devices used have an optical nature ("IP-over-SONET configuration" 2002). The operational principle of OTDM is to interleave several signals in time and then direct them to the same fiber. The main advantages of multiplexing are the facts that only one source is required and that the node equipment is simpler in the single channel architecture. In OTDM, many lower-speed data channels each transmit in the form of ultrashort-duration optical pulses that are time-interleaved to form a single high-speed stream. The resulting data stream is then transmitted over an optical fiber. Special considerations are required to generate ultrashort-duration optical pulses. In particular, gain-switched semiconductor lasers and mode-locked lasers are currently used to generate such optical pulses. However, a gain-switched semiconductor laser has limitations such as the spectral spread, which results from high chirp rates and non-negligible levels of timing jitter. These limitations can be overcome by using optical fibers with appropriate dispersion compensation and optical filtering.

Synchronous Optical Network Technique

SONET is a standard for optical telecommunications transport as defined by the American National Standards Institute. The standard has also been integrated into the synchronous digital hierarchy recommendations of the International Telecommunications Union (ITU) (formerly Consultative Committee on International Telegraph and Telephone, or CCITT) ("IP-over-SONET configuration" 2002). In SONET, the basic signal rate is 51.84 Mbps. This rate is known as the synchronous transport *signal level 1* (STS-1) rate. Similar to other physical-layer transport, SONET describes transmission speed, line encoding, and signal multiplexing. SONET defines this as *optical carrier* (OC) signals, frame format, and *operations, administration, maintenance, and provisioning* (OAM&P) protocol. The fiber-optic transmission rates from OC-1 through OC-192. They are shown in Table 1.

SONET divides a fiber path into multiple logical channels called *tributaries*. A tributary's basic unit of transmission is an STS-1 or OC-1 (optical carrier level 1) signal. Both operate at 51.84 Mbps; STS describes electrical signals, and OC refers to the same traffic when it is converted into optical signals. SONET also allows channels to be multiplexed. Therefore, an OC-12 circuit, for instance, carries traffic from four OC-3 links. A circuit also can carry a single channel. To further understand the elements of SONET, key concepts need to be discussed. Frame format structure is based on the STS-1 equivalent to 51.84 Mbps. Higher levels of signals are integer multiples of the base rate, 51.84 Mbps (Papadimitriou et al. 2003; "IP-over-SONET configuration" 2002; "SONET graphical overview," undated). The STS-1 signal is divided into two main areas: transport overhead and *synchronous payload overhead* (SPE). The SPE is further divided into two overheads: the STS *path overhead* (POH) and the payload. The payload is the data being transported and switched through the SONET network without being demultiplexed at the terminating locations.

STS-1 has a sequence of 810 bytes (6480 bits), which includes overhead bytes and the envelope capacity for transporting payload. The frame consists of a 90 column by 9 row structure with a frame length of 125 ms. This means that 8000 frames are sent per second, because 9×90 bytes/frame $\times 8$ bits/byte $\times 8000$ frames/s = 51.84 Mbps. The order of transmission of bytes is row-by-row from top to bottom and from left to right.

Table 1: Fiber Optical Transmission Rates

OC level	Bit rate (Mbps)	S0 Number	DS-1 Number	DS-3 Number
1	51.84	672	28	1
3	155.52	2016	84	3
6	311.04	4032	168	6
9	466.56	6048	252	9
12	622.08	8064	336	12
18	933.12	12096	504	18
24	1244.16	16128	672	24
36	1866.24	24192	1008	36
48	2488.32	32256	1344	48
96	4976.00	64512	2688	96
192	9952	129024	5376	192

The STS payload pointer provider contained in the transport overhead designates the location of the byte where the STS-1 SPE begins. The STS POH is used to communicate various data such as the pickup and dropoff points. The higher STS-*N* signals are accomplished through byte interleaving of STS-1 modules. SONET provides overhead information that allows simpler multiplexing and greatly expanded operations, administration, maintenance. and provisioning capabilities.

Synchronous Digital Hierarchy

The deployment of synchronous transmission systems is characterized by their ability to interwork with existing plesiochronous systems. Advances in these systems have lead to *plesiochronous digital hierarchy* (PDH), which is a multiplexing technique that allows for combining slightly nonsynchronous rates. PDH has evolved in response to the demand for basic voice telephony and, as such, is not suited for the efficient delivery and management of high-bandwidth connections. For this reason, synchronous transmission has been introduced to overcome these limits ("Synchronous optical network," undated). Synchronous digital hierarchy defines a structure that enables plesiochronous signals to be combined together and encapsulated within a standard SDH signal. The CCITT recommendations defined a number of basic transmission rates within SDH. The first of these is 155 Mbps, normally referred to as STM-1 (where STM stands for synchronous transport module). Higher transmission rates of STM-4, STM-16 and STM-64 (622 Mbps, 2.4 Gbps, and 10 Gbps, respectively) are also defined. The recommendations also define a multiplexing structure whereby an STM-1 signal can carry a number of lower rate signals as payload, thus allowing existing PDH signals to be carried over a synchronous network ("SONET graphical overview," undated).

SDH defines a number of *containers*, each corresponding to an existing plesiochronous rate. Information from a plesiochronous signal is mapped into the relevant container. Each container then has some control information known as the *path overhead* added to it. The path overhead bytes allow the network operator to achieve end-path monitoring such as error rates. Together, the container and the path overhead form a *virtual container* (VC), which has its own frame structure made of nine rows and 261 columns. The first column is called *path overhead*. The payload container, which can itself carry other containers, follows it. Virtual containers can have any alignment within the administrative unit; the pointer in row 4 indicates this alignment. Within the section overhead, the first three rows are used for the regenerator section overhead, and the last five rows are used for the multiplex section overhead. Earlier SDH supports a concept called *virtual containers* ("SONET graphical overview," undated; "Synchronous optical network," undated). Through the use of pointers, VCs can be carried in the SDH payload as independent data packages.

In a synchronous network, all equipment is synchronized to an overall network clock. Notice, however, that the delay associated with a transmission link may vary slightly with time. As a result, the location of virtual containers within an STM-1 frame may not be fixed.

Associating a pointer with each VC accommodates these variations. The pointer indicates the position of the beginning of the VC in relation to the STM-1 frame. It can be incremented or decremented if needed to accommodate the position of the VC. There are different combinations of virtual containers that can be used to fill up the payload area of an STM-1 frame. The process of loading containers and attaching overhead is repeated at several levels in the SDH, resulting in the aggregation of smaller VCs within larger ones. This process is repeated until the largest size of VC is filled. When filled, the large VC is loaded into the payload of an STM-1 frame. When the payload area of the STM-1 frame is full, control information bytes are added to the frame to form the *section overhead*. The section overhead bytes remain with the payload for the fiber section between two synchronous multiplexers. Their purpose is to provide communication channels with alignment and a number of other functions. A higher transmission rate, when required, is achieved by using a relatively straightforward byte-interleaved multiplexing scheme.

Finally, let us notice that under OTDM, each end user should be able to synchronize with one time slot. The optical TDM bit rate is the aggregate rate over all TDM channels in the system, while the optical SONET-SDH rate may be higher than each user's data rate. As a result, the TDM bit rate and the SONET-SDH rate may be much higher than electronic processing speed, Thus, TDM and SONET-SDH are relatively less attractive than WDM, because WDM, unlike TDM or SONET-SDH, has no such requirement. Specifically, WDM is the current favorite multiplexing technology for long-haul communications in optical communication networks because all of the end-user equipment needs to operate only at the bit rate of a WDM channel, which can be chosen arbitrarily.

WAVELENGTH DIVISION MULTIPLEXING TECHNOLOGY

Wavelength division multiplexing divides the large bandwidth of a fiber into many nonoverlapping wavelength bands that can operate simultaneously with the fundamental requirement that each channel operate at a different wavelength. In this section, we introduce basic definitions of WDM and describe its technological evolution. We also highlight its advantages and limitations. We then present different protection schemes used in WDM networks.

Basic Concepts

WDM has been defined as "a technique used in optical fiber communications, by which two or more optical signals having different wavelengths may be combined and simultaneously transmitted in the same direction over one fiber. These signals are then separated, by wavelength, at the distant end." In other words, WDM is a technology that levels optical-fiber cable in ways that allow us to have multiple available bandwidths rather than a single wavelength fiber. As illustrated in Figure 3, optical signals with wavelengths $\lambda 1$, $\lambda 2$, $\lambda 3$, and $\lambda 4$ are multiplexed and simultaneously transmitted in the same direction over a single optical fiber cable. The basic idea is based on

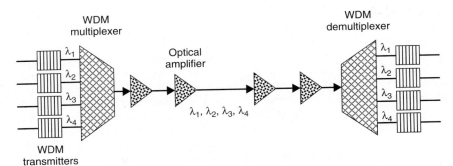

Figure 3: WDM transmission system

simultaneously transmitting several signals using different wavelengths per fiber. This way, WDM provides many virtual fibers on a single physical fiber. Today, WDM can exploit the huge optoelectronic bandwidth difference by requiring that each end user's equipment operate only at electronic rate, although multiple WDM channels from different end users may be multiplexed on the same fiber. Under WDM, the optical transmission spectrum is structured into a number of nonoverlapping wavelength bands, each supporting a single communication channel.

WDM Evolution, Advantages, and Limits

Recently, it has become apparent that the major part of future network traffic will be IP-based. The evolution will go toward IP-over-WDM networks, where several approaches have already been proposed (Chlamtac, Ganz, and Karmi 1992). Each additional layer naturally brings extra overhead to the transmission. Hence, the standard IP over ATM over SONET-SDH over WDM mapping can be considered as an inefficient solution. The other extreme is a direct IP or MPLS over WDM solution: so called λ-labeling or optical label (lambda) switching. It is anticipated that the next generation of the Internet will employ WDM-based optical backbones. Current development activities indicate that WDM networks will be deployed mainly as backbone networks for smaller and larger regions, as well as for metropolitan areas. End users to whom the backbone will be transparent (except for significantly improved response times) will be attached to the network through a wavelength-sensitive switching and routing node.

The evolution of WDM technology has far outpaced the development of applicable standards. This has created a global concern regarding interoperability. Recently, the ITU-T has recommended that vendors use wavelengths in the spectrum range of 1520 nm to 1565 nm, although such a wide range allows for hundreds of system and product variations. Even when vendors agree to use the same wavelengths, there are still the problems of switching channels between networks. There are no immediate standards that take into account such factors as fault management, or power levels, for WDM networks (National Communications System 2002). WDM's main advantages include signal transparency, scalability, flexibility, and ability to upgrade fiber bandwidth. The transparency property makes it possible to support various data formats and services simultaneously. In addition to this great flexibility, transparency protects the investments with respect to future

developments. WDM can support a variety of future protocols without making any changes to the network infrastructure.

As networks migrate from simple point-to-point WDM to optical rings with optical add-drop multiplexers covering applications that span from metropolitan area to ultralong haul, it becomes increasingly more important to also migrate core metroregional transport infrastructures into reconfigurable, manageable, and cost-effective architectures. WDM network components such as reconfigurable OADM and OXC can be used to create WDM networks that can be operated in provisioned mode (wavelength routing) or in switched mode (packet switching, label switching, and burst switching).

Because of their obvious advantages, WDM networks are rapidly deployed in long-distance carriers, local carriers, and enterprise networks. However, there are still a few limitations to be considered for WDM networks. One limitation is the nonlinearity characteristics of fiber optics. Optical fiber nonlinearities will significantly affect the performance of WDM networks. Unless corrected, these nonlinearities will lead to attenuation, distortion, and cross-channel interference. They also place constraints on the spacing between adjacent wavelength channels, reduce the maximum power of the channel, and limit the maximum bit rate. Another limiting factor is the use of wavelength converters. Wavelength conversion has been proposed for use in multihop WDM networks to improve efficiency. Wavelength converters are expensive and may not be economically justifiable because the cost is directly proportional to the number of nodes in the network. Also, several switch architectures have been proposed to allow sharing of converters among various signals at a single switch. However, experiments have shown that the performance of such a network saturates when the number of converters at a switch increases beyond a certain threshold. In addition, a certain type of converter is known to generate significant signal degradation when the output signal is converted to a higher (upconverted) signal. This produces devastating effects when a signal of a transmitted packet passes through multiple converters. However, this type appears to produce desirable results when the output signal is downconverted.

WDM Survivability

A fiber failure in a WDM optical network causes the failure of all of the connections that traverse the failed fiber, resulting in a significant loss of bandwidth and revenue. Thus, the network designer must provide a fault-management technique and also protect against fiber-amplifier malfunction.

Protection Schemes

There are essentially two types of fault-management techniques to combat fiber failures in WDM networks: protection and restoration. In protection, additional capacity is reserved during connection setup, and it is used when the primary connection fails. In restoration, no extra capacity is made available during connection setup; instead, the disrupted connections are rerouted using whatever capacity is available after the fault has occurred. In this subsection, we will discuss these two fault-management strategies in WDM networks.

Protection can be classified into two groups: path protection and link protection. In *path protection*, the traffic is rerouted through a link-disjoint backup route when a link failure occurs on its active path. In *link protection*, the traffic is rerouted only around the failed link. Path protection usually has fewer resource requirements and lower end-to-end propagation delays for the recovered route. In path protection, for each lightpath that is set up, there are two disjoint paths: a primary path and a backup path. The lightpath is set up on the primary path. In case of a link failure, the lightpath is switched to the prereserved backup path. The primary and the backup paths are link-disjoint, whereas the backup paths of different connections may share wavelengths on common links (Chiu and Modiano 2000). The switches on backup paths can be configured at the beginning—that is, when the lightpath is set up on the primary path. No switch configuration is then necessary when the failure occurs. This type of recovery can be extremely fast, but the resources are not utilized efficiently.

Because a protection route for each active route is pre-planned, rerouting is faster and simpler than a restoration, which is usually performed in a distributed manner. Based on the availability of a dedicated protection versus a shared-protection scheme, three types of protection techniques are used in WDM: 1+1 protection, 1:1 protection, and 1:N protection.

In *1+1 protection*, traffic is transmitted on both paths from the source to the destination. The destination receives data from the primary path first. If there is a failure on the primary path, the destination switches over to the backup path and continues receiving. In *1:1 protection*, data are normally not transmitted on the backup path. Thus, we can use the backup path to carry low-priority pre-emptable traffic. If there is a failure on the primary path, the source node is notified (by some protocol) and switches over to retransmit on the backup path. Hence, some data may be lost and the source must be able to retransmit those data. If sharing among backup paths is allowed, the switches on the backup paths cannot be configured until the failure occurs. The recovery time in this scheme is longer, but the overall resource utilization is better than the previous protection. This scheme is called *1:N protection*.

Restoration Schemes

Restoration can be used to provide more efficient routes after the protection has been completed or additional resilience against further faults before the first fault is fixed. Usually, the restoration mechanism is slow (seconds to minutes) and can be computed on the fly by a centralized management system. There are two kind of restoration: link restoration and path restoration. With *link restoration*, all of the connections that traverse the failed link are rerouted around that link. The source and destination nodes of the connections traversing the failed link are unaware of the link failure. The end nodes of the failed link dynamically discover a route around the link for each wavelength in the link. On the occurrence of a failure, the end nodes of the failed link may participate in a distributed procedure to build new paths for each active wavelength on the failed link. When a new route is discovered, the end nodes of the failed link reconfigure their cross-connects to reroute that channel onto the new route. If no new routes are discovered, the relevant connection is blocked.

With *path restoration*, when a link fails, the source node and the destination node of each connection that traverses the failed link are informed about the failure (possibly via messages from the nodes adjacent to the link failure). The source and the destination nodes of each connection independently discover a backup route on an end-to-end basis (possibly using a different wavelength channel). When a new route and wavelength channel are discovered for a connection, network elements such as wavelength cross-connects are reconfigured appropriately, and the connection switches to the new path. If no new routes (and associated wavelength) are discovered for a broken connection, that connection is blocked.

Dense WDM

The WDM network provides the backbone to support existing and emerging technologies with almost limitless amounts of bandwidth capacity. With today's expansion of online services (e.g., the Internet), mobile telephony, and the anticipated emergence of multimedia services, traffic demand will grow quickly, requiring a huge increase in the transport capacity of public networks. WDM and its improvement—*dense wave division multiplexing* (DWDM)—have since proven to be the most promising technology to satisfy the capacity demand in the core network by multiplexing hundreds of Gigabit channels in one fiber. The multiplexing is performed by different lasers emitting light at different wavelengths to form signals that are multiplexed onto a single fiber. A single optical fiber is capable of carrying 10 Terabits per second when DWDM technology is used (Papadimitriou et al. 2003; Brackett 1990).

DWDM has been proposed and deployed in many telecommunication backbones to support growing needs. DWDM systems can upgrade the channel number in optical fibers by using more power or additional signal to noise margin. Technically, WDM and DWDM are similar, but as the name implies, DWDM supports many more wavelengths. The number of wavelengths that a DWDM system can support depends on the ability of the system to accurately filter and separate them. Initial implementations of DWDM systems support either eight or sixteen wavelengths. However, current DWDM systems are capable of supporting thirty-two or sixty-four wavelengths. An end terminal with an ITU-T–compliant wavelength transmitter is directly connected to the DWDM system. An optical amplifier with a gain flatness of ± 1 dB and a maximum total output power of $+21.5$ dBm is a key component in the DWDM system, in which the optical power of each wavelepath is kept at the same level by using EDFA at the input ports of the DWDM system. The next generation of DWDM will have 128 wavelengths, a total capacity of 1.28 Tbps and even more, and networking functions such as OXC and OADM (Zang et al. 2001).

WDM SWITCHING TECHNIQUES

Four major switching techniques have been proposed in the literature for transporting IP traffic over WDM-based optical networks. Accordingly, IP over WDM networks can be classified as WR networks, OPS networks, OLS networks, and OBS networks.

Wavelength Routing

WR networks carry data between access stations in the optical domain without any intermediate optical to and from electronic conversion. This is realized by assigning a path in the network between the two nodes and allocating a free wavelength on all links on the path. Such an all-optical path is commonly referred to as a *lightpath* and may span multiple fiber links without any intermediate electronic processing.

Lightpath Establishment

A lightpath is used to support a connection in a WR network and may span multiple fiber links. In the absence of wavelength conversion, it is required that the lightpath use the same wavelength on all fiber links of the path it uses. This requirement is referred to as the *wavelength continuity constraint*. Continuity may result in an inefficient utilization of WDM channels. Alternatively, when the routing nodes have limited or full conversion capability, it is possible to allocate different wavelengths on the links of the assigned path. Given a set of connections, the problem of setting up lightpaths by routing and assigning a wavelength to each connection is called the *routing and wavelength assignment* (RWA) problem. To establish a lightpath from source to destination, one has to determine a route along which the lightpath can be established and then assign a wavelength to the selected route. Typically, connection requests may be of two types: static and dynamic.

In a *static lightpath establishment* (SLE) problem, the entire set of connections is known in advance and the problem is then to set up lightpaths for these connections while minimizing the usage of network resources (such as the number of wavelengths or the number of fibers). In SLE algorithms, the routing procedure does not vary with time, and the routes for given source-destination pairs are predetermined based on the topology and policies criteria but independent of the current traffic condition in the network.

In *dynamic lightpath establishment* (DLE), a lightpath is set up for each connection request as it arrives, and the lightpath is released after a small period of time. In DLE, a routing algorithm can vary with time and be adaptive

in the sense that it can select a route based on the current network conditions. DLE considers alternate routing, where each source-destination pair is associated with a set of routes. If resources along one route are not available, then another route in the set is examined. When there are multiple routes to choose, the routing algorithm first tries to establish the primary path among the shortest possible routes and then tries to establish its corresponding backup paths also on the shortest possible route.

The objective in dynamic traffic cases is to set up lightpaths and assign wavelengths in a manner that minimizes the amount of connection blocking or maximizes the number of connections that are established in the network. There have been extensive studies to solve both the static and the dynamic RWA problems ("Intellilight dedicated SONET ring," undated). Wavelength-routed connections are fairly static, and they may not be able to accommodate the highly variable and bursty nature of Internet traffic in an efficient manner.

Traffic Grooming

The important advances of high-speed transmission technology creates a large gap between the capacity of an optical channel and the bandwidth requirements of a typical connection request, which can vary in range from tens or hundreds of Mbps up to the full-wavelength capacity. Furthermore, the amount of wavelength channels available for most of the networks of practical size is lower than the number of source-destination connections that need to be made. Traffic grooming poses the problem of how to multiplex (and demultiplex) a set of low-speed traffic streams onto high-capacity channels and switch them at intermediate cross-connects (Chiu and Modiano 2000).

The performance of WR networks depends on the efficient merging of the fractional wavelength link of the nodes into a full or almost full wavelength requirement. This merging of traffic from different source-destination pairs is called *traffic grooming*. Nodes that can groom traffic are capable of multiplexing and demultiplexing lower-rate traffic onto a wavelength and switching it from one lightpath to another. The grooming of traffic can be either static or dynamic. In *static* traffic grooming, the source-destination pairs, whose requirements are combined, are predetermined. In *dynamic* traffic grooming, connection requests from different source-destination pairs are combined, depending on the existing lightpath at the time of request arrival (Zhu and Mukherjee 2001). Even though WR networks have already been deployed, they may not be the most appropriate for the Internet because, for example, it takes at least a round-trip delay to establish a lightpath. This leads to poor wavelength utilization if the connection holding time is especially short. The bursty nature of the data traffic also leads to poor wavelength utilization. Therefore, to fully utilize the wavelength, a sophisticated traffic-grooming mechanism is needed to support statistical multiplexing of data from different users. The objective of traffic grooming is either to maximize the network throughput or to minimize the connection-blocking probability and improve the wavelength utilization, whereas a strategic network design problem is to minimize the total cost (Papadimitriou et al. 2003; Chlamtac, Ganz, and Karmi 1992; Chiu and Modiano 2000).

The following are the four basic grooming options.

1. Single-hop grooming on existing lightpath: The connection is assigned to one existing direct lightpath.
2. Multihop grooming on existing lightpath: Routing takes place on the electrical layer by using more than one existing lightpath and switching the connection in the electrical cross-connect of intermediate nodes.
3. Single-hop grooming on new lightpath: A new lightpath is set up between the source and the destination node. The connection request is routed on the optical layer via this new lightpath.
4. Combined multihop grooming on new and existing lightpath: This is a combination of options 1 and 3. The connection request can be routed on both the electrical and optical layer by using a series of existing and new lightpaths.

Although nonintegrated routing schemes are only capable of grooming on either existing or new lightpaths, integrated routing is able to perform the combined grooming described in option 4.

Optical Packet-Switching Technique

In OPS, a data flow is broken into packets of small size before being transmitted. Routing information is added to the overhead of each packet so that intermediate switches between the source and destination are able to forward the arriving packet. An OPS is capable of dynamically allocating network resources with fine packet-level granularity while offering excellent scalability (O'Mahony 2001). In OPS networks, bit-level synchronization and fast clock recovery are required for packet header recognition and packet delineation. In general, all-optical packet-switched networks can be divided into two categories: *slotted* (or synchronous) and *unslotted* (or asynchronous).

OPS Synchronization

The need for a synchronizer in an optical switch results from delay variations between nodes. These variations are caused by the distance the packet travels in the fiber, chromatic dispersion, and temperature variations. Figure 4 shows a block diagram of the synchronization procedure in a node. An optical splitter directs a small amount of power from the incoming packets into a header-reading circuit. The reading circuit recognizes a special bit stream pattern and prepares to read the header information. Also, the timing information is read and passed to the control unit to configure the synchronization stages and switch fabric. The input synchronization stage aligns the packets into fixed time slots before they enter the switch fabric. The output synchronization stage is used to compensate for any timing drift that occurs during the switching. The required accuracy of synchronization in a system depends on the size and position of the header, payload, and guard time (Yao et al. 2003).

OPS Slotted Network

In slotted networks, packets have fixed size. Slot size is larger than the packet size to allow guard time before and after each packet. Because a node has input fibers from different upstream nodes, the slot boundaries on these fibers are not synchronized. There will be time variation of these boundaries because of different propagation distances and temperature changes. Some synchronization mechanisms need to be implemented to align the slots before the packets enter the space switch. Such mechanism can be realized by using switched *fiber delay lines* (FDLs) of different lengths to create the desired delays with limited resolution. Slotted networks have fewer contentions than unslotted networks because the packets are of the same size and are planed in a joint manner.

OPS Unslotted Network

In an unslotted network, packets may not have the same size and can arrive and enter the switch without being aligned. Therefore, the packet-by-packet switch action could take place at any point in time (Qiao and Yoo 1999). This can lead to contention of different incoming packets for the same outgoing resource. The chance for contention is high because the behavior of the packets is more unpredictable and less regulated. The unslotted networks are easier and cheaper to build, more robust, and more flexible compared to slotted networks. IP traffic is processed and switched at every IP router on a packet-by-packet basis when each contains a payload and header. The header carries the information required for packet routing, whereas the payload carries the actual data. The future and ultimate goal of OPS networks is to process the packet header entirely in the optical domain. With the current technology, it is not possible to do such a task optically. Instead, the header is processed in the electronic domain, and the payload is kept in the optical domain.

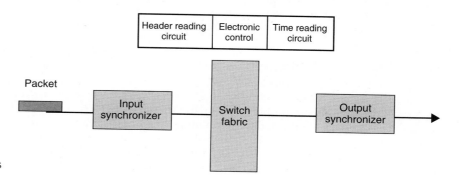

Figure 4: Synchronization of packets

Many technical challenges need to be addressed for this solution to be efficient.

OPS Switching Issues

Optical packet switching is a promising technology as it offers high capacity and data transparency. It is currently in an experimental stage and is not implemented commercially because of the lack of optical buffering. The network control and routing is performed electronically, and the routing information from the packet header has to be converted to electrical form. This problem was solved by transferring the payload and the header with different transmission rates. The header can be transmitted at a relatively slow rate so that it possible to read the header in an electronic form, whereas the data can be transmitted fast in order to benefit from the transmission media. The data rate can be increased by compressing more data into the same time slot. The header and the data can be sent consecutively, separated by a guard time. In OPS networks and photonic slot-routing networks, headers are sent in their own channels. The main idea in these approaches is based on the fact that the headers are sent slowly enough to allow the control information to be read. Higher throughput is accomplished by compressing the payload and increasing the data rate (O'Mahony 2001).

A second issue in OPS networks is synchronization. Most of the optical switches proposed are synchronous and use constant-length packets, meaning that the networks are slotted. This makes controlling and managing the switch easier and facilitates routing and buffering. On the other hand, careful synchronization is required. This synchronization is usually managed using FDL, whereas the issue in OPS networks is the regeneration of optical signal. Optical regenerators are divided into three classes: 1R regenerators are capable of amplification, 2R regenerators can both amplify and reshape signal, and 3R regenerators can amplify, reshape, and retime signals. In recent research efforts, a 3R regenerator was implemented, but using such a regenerator in a network is expensive.

Today's OPS networks are not entirely optical. The signals are converted to electrical form before switching and processing. This means that the major advantages of optical packet switching, (e.g., speed and efficiency) are lost because of the increased delays. All-OPS networks are not coming to commercial use in the few coming years. The biggest problem currently is the lack of optical buffering needed for buffering the packets. In addition, the extremely high switching rates needed in packet networks cause problems. In the near future, the development seems to lead to the integration of optical and electronic networks and the use of optical burst switching.

Optical Burst-Switching Technique

Optical burst switching has received a great attention in recent years as one of the most promising technologies to carry the next-generation optical Internet. OBS combines the advantages of optical circuit switching and optical packet switching while reducing their shortcomings. In OBS networks, the control plane and the data plane are separated, and the signaling is performed out of band (Qiao and Yoo 1999). Although the control plane is done electronically, the data plane is all-optical.

Burst Assembly

One solution, used by OBS, is to aggregate or assemble packets into bursts at ingress nodes in order to keep switching time and associated guard band inefficiencies negligible with respect to the burst sizes. The two main burst assembly algorithms are threshold-based and timer-based.

The Threshold-Based Burst Assembly. This technique requires a single and configurable parameter that corresponds to the burst length (set of packets) stored in the input queue. If the arriving packet reaches this size, the active burst is scheduled to be sent, and its packets are immediately removed from queue. The method offers no delay guarantees under low-input offered load. It may need to wait for a long period of time until this length is reached. However, under high-input offered load, the threshold will be quickly reached, minimizing delay.

Timer-Based Burst Assembly. This method requires a single and configurable parameter that is a time period corresponding roughly to the interdeparture times of the bursts. A time period for each queue is started at the initialization of the system after a burst for that queue is scheduled to be sent immediately when the first packet arrives after the appropriate queue has been emptied. At the expiration of the timer, the burst assembler generates a burst containing all the packets in the buffer at that point. Under low-input load conditions, it guarantees a fixed minimum delay. However, under high-input offered load, it may generate bursts that are extremely large.

Hybrid Burst Assembly. The threshold-based and timer-based algorithms can be used simultaneously to benefit from the advantages of both schemes. In this hybrid system, the burst is sent when one of the constraints is reached (Vokkarane and Jue 2003). For periods of low input load, the timer would expire first, resulting in deterministic burst spacing but randomly sized bursts. For periods of high-input load the threshold would be reached first, resulting in randomly spaced but constant-sized bursts.

OBS Network Architecture

An OBS network consists of optical switches interconnected with WDM links. An optical burst switch transfers a burst coming from an input port to its destination output port. A control message is transmitted ahead of the burst in order to configure the switches along the burst's path. The burst follows the header without waiting for an acknowledgment that resources have been reserved and switches have been configured along the lightpath. The control packet associated with a burst may be transmitted in-band over the same channel as data or on a separate control channel. The source edge nodes are referred to as *ingress nodes* and the destination edge nodes are referred to as *egress nodes*. The ingress edge node assembles incoming packets from client terminals into bursts. The assembled bursts are transmitted completely optically over OBS core nodes without any intermediate storage.

The egress edge node, upon receiving the burst, disassembles the bursts into packets and forwards the packets to destination terminals (Vokkarane and Jue 2003; Qiao and Yoo 1999).

Edge nodes perform the functions of presorting packets, buffering packets, aggregating packets into burst and de-aggregating bursts into their constituent packets. Different burst assembly policies can be used to aggregate data packets into optical bursts. Core routers primarily contain an OXC and a *switch control unit* (SCU). The SCU creates and maintains a forwarding table and is responsible for configuring the OXC (Qiao and Yoo 1999). When the SCU receives a BHP, it identifies the intended destination and consults the router signaling processor to find the intended output port. If the output port is available when the data burst arrives, the SCU configures the OXC to let the data burst pass through. If the port is not available, then the OXC is configured depending on the contention-resolution policy implemented in the network.

Optical Label-Switching Technique

OLS offers seamless integration of data and optical networking while supporting circuit, burst, and packet switching using the optical labels. It provides diverse QoS, class of service (CoS), and type of service. OLS networks separate the control plane and the data plane to facilitate protocol and format independence for data payloads. Interoperability with IP, *multiprotocol label switching* (MPLS), *multiprotocol lambda switching* (MPλS), and other client networks can be achieved with a *generalized MPLS* (GMPLS) extension. In this subsection, we discuss the architecture of OLS networks in light of interoperability and seamless network upgrades in the context of MPLS, MPλS, and GMPLS.

Optical Label-Switching Concept

In OLS networks, the key concept is an efficient and transparent packet-forwarding method using an OLS mechanism that can coexist with legacy WDM technology on the same fiber. New signaling information is added in the form of an optical label that is carried in-band within each wavelength in a multiwavelength transport environment. The optical label, containing routing and control information such as the source, destination, priority, and packet length, will propagate through the network along with the data payload. Each OLS router will read the optical label, look up to the forwarding table, and take the necessary steps to forward the packet. During the optical label-processing stage, the corresponding packet is delayed by an FDL at the input interface before entering the OLS switch fabric. The goal is to reduce the need to manage the delay separating the optical label and its payload. If a packet is to be routed to a wavelength and path where there is already another packet being forwarded, the OLS router will attempt an alternate path.

Label-Switching Structure

The OLS label-encoding method for packet-based networks attaches a label header. This label is four octets long and is segmented into four parts. Figure 5 depicts the label structure in which the first twenty bits contain

Label	Class of service	Label stack	Time to live
20 bits	3 bits	1 bit	8 bits

Figure 5: Label structure

an unsigned integer value that distinguishes the specific traffic route. The next three bits are deemed experimental and are used primarily to provide a means to determine a CoS to relay information to the network routers about how to handle the traffic. The next bit provides a hierarchical label stack function. Finally, the last eight bits represent a conventional time to live that provides network elements with the ability to disregard a packet after a certain length of time to prevent endless recirculation loops through the network (Papadimitriou et al. 2003; Gallaher 2002).

Label-Switching Procedure

The following is a list of commonly used terms and their acronyms that represent the components of an OLS network.

Forwarding equivalence class (FEC): A class or group of traffic based on common parameters such as class of service. It defines a common set of packet-handling parameters.

Label-switched path (LSP): A determined traffic path through the OLS network, from ingress to egress, with the same FEC and intended destination.

Label edge routers (LERs): Routers that are OLS-aware. They are located at the ingress and egress of the OLS network and perform the following functions: (1) computing the LSP through the OLS network, (2) determining an appropriate FEC, (3) appending the OLS label at the ingress of the OLS network, and (d) removing the OLS label at the egress of the OLS network.

Label-switched router (LSR): This is an intermediate router located along the LSP. It inspects the optical label and forwards traffic accordingly. When the LER receives a standard packet containing information destined to traverse the OLS network, it attaches the OLS label. OLS-aware LSR provides high-speed traffic routing by only inspecting the OLS label. The OLS label directs traffic to specific predetermined LSPs, which are FEC-based, aggregate, multipoint-to-point traffic paths through the OLS network. Further packet inspection is not performed until the packet exits the OLS network through the egress LER. Once the egress LER receives the packet, the OLS label is removed and the traffic is routed through the non-OLS destination network without the OLS label (Gallaher 2002). Figure 6 depicts IP traffic traversing an OLS network.

Label stack: The desire to maintain SLA between two networks that are disjoint across a third network results in the implementation of *label stacking*. Label stacking is a hierarchy-based implementation of OLS that helps to provide QoS across multiple third-party networks such as those of an ISP backbone. Additional OLS labels are pushed onto the protocol stack as the packet enters the

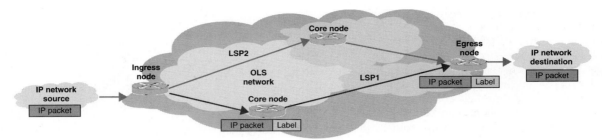

Figure 6: OLS network

intermediate network and are popped off at the egress of the intermediate network. The traffic across the intermediate network is classified as *tunneled traffic*. Label stacking provides a means for best-effort traffic to be marked, classified, and policed to achieve end-to-end QoS (Gallaher 2002).

WDM SIGNALING PROTOCOLS

The signaling technique aims first at constructing routes and scheduling traffic on particular wavelengths. Several signaling techniques have been proposed for WDM networks. Several signaling protocols have been proposed for WDM. In addition to just-in-time, just-enough-time, tell-and-wait, and tell-and-go protocols, an ATM-like protocol has been considered to provide some sort of efficiency in terms of network resources utilization and QoS support (Khlifi et al. 2005). It requires that the transmission of packets is preceded by the setup of a virtual optical communication circuit. It also defines a route between the source and destination composed by an association of fiber links and wavelengths along the chosen route and passing through the FDL (Khlifi et al. 2005). In this section, we present signaling schemes adopted in OBS and OLS techniques.

OBS Signaling Schemes

Signaling and reservation represent fundamental criteria by which OBS can be differentiated from other optical transport technologies. OBS adopts an out-of-band signaling technique in which the header is sent ahead of the burst by a time offset. When a burst is transported over the optical core, a signaling scheme must be implemented in order to allocate resources and configure intermediate switches. Signaling may be implemented in-band, in which a header is transmitted on the wavelength used to transmit the burst, or out-of-band, in which the burst header is transmitted on a separate wavelength. Typically, the connection setup phase of an OBS signaling technique can be one-way or two-way based. In the *one-way scheme*, the source sends out a control packet requesting the intermediate nodes on the path to allocate the necessary resources for the data burst. The primary objective of the one-way based signaling is to minimize the end-to-end delay. Unfortunately, this objective leads to high data loss because of contention of data bursts. In the *two-way scheme*, the request for a resource is sent, and an acknowledgment message confirming a successful assignment of the requested resources is sent back by the destination to the

source. The burst is transmitted only after a connection is established successfully. If any intermediate node in the path is busy, then the request is blocked and the intermediate node takes suitable actions to release any and all of the previously reserved links. The source can choose to retry or drop the request. Therefore, the primary objective of the two-way based techniques is to minimize packet loss, but such an objective leads to high delays.

Just-Enough-Time Scheme

In the *just-enough-time* (JET) technique, a source node first sends a *burst header packet* (BHP) on a control channel toward the destination node. The BHP is processed at each subsequent node in order to establish an all-optical data path for the corresponding data burst. If the reservation is successful, the switch will be configured before the burst arrival. Meanwhile, the burst waits at the source in the electronic domain. After a predetermined offset time, the burst is sent optically on the chosen wavelength (Qiao and Yoo 1999). The offset is computed based on the number of hops from source to destination and the switching time of a core node.

Just-in-Time Scheme

The *just-in-time* (JIT) signaling technique uses immediate reservation, whereas JET signaling adopts delayed reservation. In general, *immediate reservation* is simple and practical to implement but incurs higher blocking because of inefficient bandwidth allocation. On the other hand, implementation of *delayed reservation* is more involved but leads to a higher bandwidth utilization. Delayed reservation and immediate reservation can be incorporated into any signaling technique if the underlying node maintains the relevant information. JIT is similar to JET except that JIT employs immediate reservation and explicit release instead of delayed reservation and implicit release.

Tell-and-Wait Scheme

In the *tell-and-wait* (TAW) technique, a "SETUP" BHP is sent along the burst route to collect channel availability information at every node along the path. At the destination, a channel-assignment algorithm is executed, and the reservation period on each link is determined based on the earliest available channel times of all of the intermediate nodes. A "CONFIRM" BHP is sent in the reverse direction to reserve the channel for the requested duration at each intermediate node. At any node along the path, if the required channel is already occupied, a "RELEASE" BHP is sent to the destination to release the previously reserved resources. If the CONFIRM packet reaches the source successfully, then the burst is sent into the core network (Qiao and Yoo 1999). In the TAW scheme, resources are reserved at any node only for the duration of the burst. Also, if the duration of the burst is known during reservation, then an implicit release scheme can be followed to maximize bandwidth utilization.

Tell-and-Go Scheme

In the *tell-and-go* (TAG) technique, a source first sends a control packet on a separate control channel to reserve bandwidth (and set switches) along a path for the following data that, unlike in circuit switching, can be sent on a data channel without having to receive an acknowledgment first. This implies that the offset time T can be (much) less than the circuit setup time or even zero as in packet switching. After the burst is sent, another control signal (similar to a circuit teardown signal) is sent to release the bandwidth. In this scheme, the burst is transmitted immediately after the control packet (Qiao and Yoo 1999). When arriving to an intermediate node, the control packet attempts to reserve the necessary resources to schedule the burst. Meanwhile, the burst is typically delayed in the optical domain using input FDL.

OLS Signaling Schemes

To reserve resources and manage LSP over the OLS network, it is necessary for the network to have a signaling plane. Two methods have been investigated to provide this plane: *resource reservation protocol with traffic engineering extensions* (RSVP-TE) and *label distribution protocol with constraint-based routing* (CR-LDP). Both methods provide label distribution and LSP creation. The two signaling protocols perform similar functions in OLS networks (Chen, Thomas, and Wu 2000). The main difference between the two is the direction in which the resources are allocated during the signaling process and the transport protocol used. The following subsections summarize these OLS signaling protocols.

RSVP-TE

Resource reservation protocol with traffic engineering extensions operates by providing resources in the reverse direction along the LSP and uses raw IP as an exchange protocol of information. Figure 7 depicts the major steps of RSVP-TE.

The source sends an RSVP-TE *path message* to the receiver to establish the connection. When the ingress LER receives the path message, it injects a *label request* into the path message to request a label binding. The modified path message is then forwarded to the adjacent LSR. The forwarding continues until the path message is received by the egress LER.

When the egress LER receives the path message, it generates an *resv message* that includes a *label object*. The egress LER then propagates the resv message back to adjacent LSRs. When the adjacent LSRs receive the resv message, they will reserve the necessary resources, enter the new LSP label into their forwarding tables, and forward the resv message onto the next adjacent LSR and back toward the source. If, however, a LSR does not accept the resv message for reasons such as unavailability of resources, the LSR will respond to the egress LER with a request to terminate signaling.

Once the ingress LER receives the resv message, it will append the label to the data packets and forward the traffic through the network along the predetermined LSP. Each intermediate LSR along the LSP will inspect only the label, compare it to its forwarding table, and deliver the packet to the next LSR in the LSP.

When the egress LER receives the OLS packets, it will remove the label and deliver the packets to the destination (Awduche, Hannan, and Xiao 2001).

CR-LDP

Label distribution protocol with constraint-based routing operates by allowing resources in the forward direction and uses TCP as its transport protocol. Resources are allocated along each segment of the network in turn. Several methods of label distribution can be implemented with CR-LDP. Downstream-unsolicited and hop-by-hop, explicit-route, downstream-on-demand label distribution can be implemented. Figure 8 depicts downstream-unsolicited label distribution utilizing CR-LDP signaling. The distribution is accomplished when the egress LER advertises without a label request:

1. The egress LER sends out a label-mapping message advertisement to its adjacent LSR.
2. The adjacent LSR then reserves the resources for that egress LER and forwards the message onto its adjacent LSR.

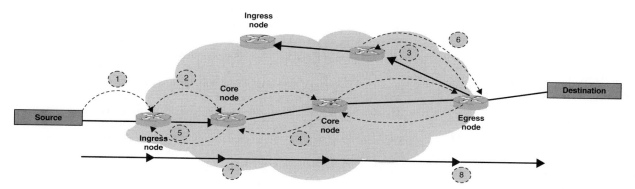

Figure 7: RSVP-TE OLS signaling

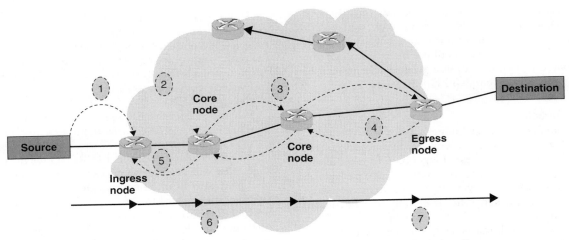

Figure 8: CR-LDP downstream-on demand label distribution OLS signaling

3. Once the ingress LER receives this message, the LSP is established.

Downstream-on-demand label distribution can occur by explicit routing or hop by hop. Whereas the former involves the pre-establishment of an intended LSP path before signaling, the latter operates by reserving the resources in the forward direction, one segment at a time, toward the destination. The latter operates as follows (Chen, Thomas, and Wu 2000):

1. The source attempts to send traffic to the destination through the ingress LER.

2. The ingress LER generates a label request and distributes it to the adjacent LSR.

3. If an adjacent LSR accepts the label request and can allocate the requested resources, then it forwards the label request to its adjacent LSR in the direction of destination.

4. Once the label request is accepted by the egress LER, the latter generates a label mapping and sends it back. When an LSR receives the label mapping, it checks the label ID with the one occurring in the label request message. If it matches, the LSR adds the label to its forwarding table and forwards the label mapping to the next adjacent LSR in the direction of the source.

5. When the ingress LER receives the label mapping, it checks the label ID and adds it to the forwarding table.

6. The label is attached to the packets and the traffic is forwarded through the OLS network along the pre-defined LSP without deep packet inspection.

7. Finally, when the traffic reaches the egress LER, the label is removed.

WDM NETWORK ARCHITECTURES

The commonly used architectural forms for WDM networks are *broadcast and select networks* (BSNs), and *wavelength routing networks* (WRNs). In a BSN (Zang et al. 2001), each transmitter broadcasts its signal on a different channel, and receivers can tune to receive the desired signal. Generally, these networks are based on a passive star coupler. This device is connected to the nodes by fibers in a star topology. It consistently distributes the signals received to the output ports. The main networking problem for these networks is the coordination of pairs of stations in order to agree and tune their systems to transmit and receive on the same channel. Therefore, BSNs are suitable for local area networks and are not scalable. WRNs are composed of one or more wavelength-selective nodes called *wavelength routers* and fibers interconnecting these nodes. Each wavelength router has a number of input and output ports. Signals routed to the same output port should be on different wavelengths. As long as any two channels do not share the same fiber link anywhere on the network, they can use the same wavelength. The wavelength reuse feature results in an interesting reduction in the number of wavelengths required for building a wide network.

Broadcast and Select Networks

Broadcast and select networks are based on the simplest all-optical organization that enables WDM. In this organization, the network infrastructure is entirely composed of glass material that acts as a propagation medium that broadcasts individual transmissions. The network model is illustrated in Figure 9, where the transmitters transmit signals on distinct wavelengths, and the network combines these signals and distributes the aggregate signal to the receivers. The figure shows only the transmitters and receivers. For proper network operation, each end node is able to make connections with any other end node. For this reason, each end node should have access to multiple WDM channels. This can be accomplished by making the transmitters or receivers or both tunable over multiple channels, or having a multiple fixed tuned transmitters or receivers; each is assigned to a different channel on an end node. To avoid interchannel interference, the transmitters are assigned narrow line widths and receivers can filter each channel individually (i.e., narrow bandwidth filters are required). In addition, to improve efficiency, tunable components should cover all of the channels.

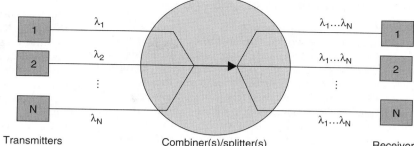

Figure 9: Broadcast and select network   Transmitters   Combiner(s)/splitter(s)   Receivers

Let us assume that there are W channels, each running at a rate of C bits/sec. The broadcast and select organization supports at most W concurrent connections and has a total capacity that is equal to $W \times C$ bits/sec. It is possible to increase the channel bit rate C up to peak electronics rate. It is also possible to have a large aggregate capacity without forcing the limits of electronics on end nodes. Therefore, the capacity of the network is directly proportional to the number of channels available in the network. On the other hand, the number of channels is directly related to the tunability range and bandwidth of lasers and transmitters. In addition, broadcasting and multicasting is possible in BSNs because the receivers have access to entire channels. In other words, it is possible to establish one-to-many and one-to-all connections. In the near future, many applications that require broadcasting or multicasting will be widespread, such as distributed computing, distributed database applications, and interactive video.

Wavelength Routing Networks

The splitting loss and lack of wavelength reuse restrict BSNs from spanning long distances and having large numbers of end nodes with large throughputs. Wavelength routing networks get around these problems by channeling the transmitted power to an appropriate lightpath between the source and destination and reusing the wavelengths in spatially disjointed areas of the network. WRNs are composed of one or more wavelength-selective elements and the fibers connecting them (Karasan and Glu 1998). The wavelength-selective elements are composed entirely of glass material (i.e., no electro-optical conversions) and are called *wavelength routers*. They are capable of routing signals individually. The output port of each signal in a wavelength router is determined by the input port it arrives through and its wavelength. Signals routed to the same output port should be on different wavelengths to avoid mixing different signals.

In WRNs, each wavelength router is connected to one or more wavelength routers or end nodes or both to define a topology in which end-to-end connections between end nodes are established using wavelength channels through one or more wavelength routers. If wavelength routers are ideal, then the connections between the end nodes do not experience any splitting loss and electro-optical conversion. Therefore, an end-to-end connection behaves like a high-speed transparent pipe between end nodes.

If two lightpaths do not share a fiber on their routes, they can be assigned to the same wavelength. Therefore, the spatial reuse of wavelengths can be achieved in WRNs.

Usually, wavelength routers are connected to each other or to end nodes with a pair of fibers. Therefore, bidirectional lightpaths can be established between the end nodes such that each connection follows the same route in the network and is assigned to the same wavelength in counterdirection fibers. To establish a lightpath between two end nodes, one of the transmitters of the source and one of the destination receivers should be tuned to the same wavelength. Therefore, the number of transmitter-receiver pairs in an end node determines the maximum number of lightpaths that can be supported by that particular end node simultaneously. Therefore, end nodes should be equipped with a multitude of tunable and fixed transmitter-receiver pairs to utilize network resources efficiently.

QOS REQUIREMENTS IN WDM NETWORKS
Basic Concepts

The huge bandwidth offered by WDM is promising to reduce the cost of core network equipment and simplify bandwidth management. However, the problem of providing quality-of-service guarantees for several advanced services, such as the transport of real-time packet voice and video, remains largely unsolved for optical backbones. The QoS problem in WDM networks has several fundamental differences compared with the QoS solutions provided in electronic switches. Currently, there is no optical memory, and the use of electronic memory in an optical switch requires *optical-to-electrical* (O-E) and *electrical-to-optical* (E-O) conversions within the switch, which tends to limit the speed of the optical switch. In addition, the use of converters loses the advantage of being bit rate transparent. Furthermore, converters increase the cost of switching significantly. Currently, the only means to provide a limited buffering capability in optical switches is the use of fiber delay lines. Unfortunately, FDLs cannot provide full buffering capabilities. In addition, the wavelength domain provides a further opportunity for contention resolution based on the use of FDL. In this section, we describe the critical issues affecting QoS in WDM based on the optical switching techniques.

Contention Resolution in OPS and OLS Networks

In OPS and OLS networks, contention occurs at a node whenever two or more packets are trying to leave the switch from the same output port on the same wavelength. The way the contention is resolved has a significant effect on the network performance in terms of packet loss ratio, average packet delay, average hop distance, and network utilization. In electrical packet-switched networks, contention is resolved using store-and-forward techniques that require the packets in contention to be stored in a memory and sent out at a later time when the related output port is free. This is possible because of the availability of electronic *random access memory* (RAM). For this, several contention-resolution schemes are explored in OPS networks such as wavelength, time, and space-based schemes (Yao et al. 2003). Three techniques can cooperate to resolve contention: wavelength conversion, optical buffering, and deflection routing.

Wavelength Conversion

Wavelength conversion offers the most effective contention resolution without incurring additional latency while it maintains the shortest path or minimum hop distance. Multiple packets can be sent simultaneously to the same output port (Papadimitriou et al. 2003; Yao et al. 2003).

Optical Buffering

In optical buffering, FDLs are typically used to delay the packets in contention and send them out at a later time. Because FDLs are simply first-in, first-out queues with fixed delays, they are less efficient than the electronic RAM. To be able to resolve contention effectively, a large number of FDLs are usually required. Handling many fibers in a node cannot be an easy task.

Deflection Routing

Packets in contention are deflected to output ports other than to the desired port. This causes part of the network to be used as buffers to store these packets. The disadvantage of deflection is that it introduces extra link propagation delays and causes packets to arrive out of order (Yao et al. 2003; Yao et al. 2000).

Contention Resolution in OBS Networks

Because OBS networks provide connectionless transport, bursts may contend with one another at intermediate nodes. Several techniques are designed to address the contention, including optical buffering, wavelength conversion, deflection routing, and burst segmentation.

OBS Buffering

In OBS networks, FDLs can be utilized to delay burst for a fixed or a variable amount of time. A FDL can be further classified into feed-forward, feedback, and hybrid architectures (Chia et al. 2001). In a *feed-forward* architecture, each FDL connects an output port of a switching element at a given stage to an input port of another switching element in the next stage. In *feedback* architecture, each FDL connects an output port of a switching element at a given stage to an input port of a switching element in the

same stage or at a previous stage. In a *hybrid* architecture, feed-forward and feedback buffers are combined. According to the position of the buffers, burst switches are essentially categorized into three major configurations: input buffering, output buffering, and shared buffering. In *input buffering*, a set of buffers is dedicated for each input port. In *output buffering*, a set of buffers is dedicated for each output port. In *shared buffering*, a set of buffers can be shared by all switch ports. Input buffering has poor performance because of head-of-line blocking. Conversely, output buffering and shared buffering can achieve good performance. However, output buffering requires a significant number of FDLs and larger switches. With shared buffering, all output ports can access the same buffers. Therefore, it can be used to reduce the total number of buffers in a switch while achieving a desired level of packet loss. In the optical domain, shared buffering can be implemented with one-stage feedback recirculation buffering (Zhang, Lu, and Jue 2004) or multistage feed-forward shared buffering (Hunter, Chia, and Andonovic 1998).

Wavelength Conversion

In OBS with wavelength conversion, a contending burst may be switched to any of the available wavelengths on the outgoing link. Although optical wavelength conversion has been demonstrated in laboratory environments, the technology is not yet mature, and the range of possible conversions are somewhat limited (Ramamurthy and Mukherjee 1998). The following are different categories of conversion.

Full Conversion

Any incoming wavelength can be shifted to any outgoing wavelength; thus, there is no wavelength continuity constraint on the end-to-end connection requests.

Limited Conversion

Wavelength shifting is restricted so that not all incoming channels can be connected to all outgoing channels. The restricting on the wavelength shifting will reduce the cost of the switch at the expense of increased blocking.

Fixed Conversion

Fixed conversion is a restricted form of limited conversion, wherein each incoming channel may be connected to one or more predetermined outgoing channels.

Sparse Wavelength Conversion

The networks may comprise a collection of nodes having full, limited, fixed, and no wavelength conversion. For this to work, many wavelength conversion algorithms are used to minimize the number wavelength converters (Xiao and Leung 1999).

Deflection Routing

In deflection routing, a deflected burst typically takes a longer route to its destination, leading to increased delay and degradation in the signal's quality. Furthermore, the burst may loop indefinitely within the network, adding to congestion. Mechanisms must be implemented to prevent excessive path lengths. These may include a maximum-hop counter or a constrained set of deflection alternatives (Jue 2002). In JET-based OBS networks, another concern with deflection is the offset time. It is possible that, if the burst traverses a large number of hops, the burst may overtake the header. Approaches for ensuring sufficient separation include setting a higher initial offset value at the source node and using an FDL at each intermediate node to delay the burst.

Burst Segmentation

Burst segmentation is another approach proposed to reduce packet loss resulting from contention. It is the process of dropping only those parts of a burst that overlap with another burst. Then, when two bursts contend in the OBS network, only those segments of one burst that overlap with the other burst will be dropped. In burst segmentation, the important issue is the decision of which burst segments to drop when a contention occurs between the two bursts. There are two possible approaches for determining which segments to drop: tail dropping and head dropping. In *tail dropping*, the overlapping tail segments of the original burst are dropped. In *head dropping*, the head overlapping segments of the contending burst are dropped. An advantage of dropping the overlapping tail segments of bursts rather than the overlapping head segments is that there is a better chance of in-sequence delivery of packets at the destination, assuming that dropped packets are retransmitted at a later time. A head-dropping policy results in a greater likelihood that packets arrive at their destination out of order; however, the advantage of head dropping is that it ensures that, once a burst arrives at a node without encountering contention, the burst is guaranteed to complete its traversal of the node without preemption by later bursts.

QoS Parameters

Quality of service in WDM networks is characterized by a number of parameters. The following are the most important.

Control Latency

Latency is the time between sending a message from one node and receiving it by another node. This means delay in a transmission path. In a router, latency is the amount of time between receiving a data packet and retransmitting it. This is also referred to as the *propagation delay*.

Jitter

Jitter is a distortion that occurs when data are transmitted over a network and packets do not arrive at their destination in consecutive order or on a timely basis—that is, they vary in latency. In packet-switched networks, jitter is an aberration of the interpacket arrival times compared to the interpacket times of the original transmission. This distortion is particularly damaging to multimedia traffic. For example, the playback of audio or video data may have a jitter.

Bandwidth

Bandwidth is a measure of data-transmission capacity, usually expressed in kbps or megabits per second (Mbps).

Bandwidth indicates the theoretical maximum capacity of a connection, but as the theoretical bandwidth is approached, negative factors such as transmission delay can cause deterioration in quality. If bandwidth is increased, more data can be transferred. Network bandwidth can be visualized as a pipe that transfers data. The larger the pipe, the more data can be sent through it.

Packet Loss

Packet loss means the percentage value of lost packets during a time period. For example, packet loss can be expressed as a percentage.

Availability

Availability is a measure of the percentage of time that a node is in service. Equipment vendors typically claim high availability for their boxes when they attain availability levels in the region of 99.999 percent.

QoS Models

QoS support is another important issue in WDM networks. Applications with diverse requirements urge transport technologies that are carrying the next-generation optical Internet technologies (such as OLS, OPS, and OBS) to provide QoS guarantees. There are two models for QoS: relative QoS and absolute QoS. In the *relative QoS* model, the performance of each class is not defined quantitatively in absolute terms. Instead, the QoS of one class is defined relatively in comparison with other classes. For example, an entity (packet or burst) of high priority is guaranteed to experience lower loss probability than an entity of lower priority. However, the loss probability of a high-priority traffic still depends on the traffic load of lower-priority traffic, and no upper bound on the loss probability is guaranteed for the high-priority traffic.

The *absolute QoS* model provides a worst-case QoS guarantee to applications. This kind of hard guarantee is essential to support applications with delay and bandwidth constraints such as multimedia and mission critical applications. Moreover, the absolute QoS model is preferred in order to ensure that each user receives an expected level of performance. Efficient admission-control and resource-provisioning mechanisms are needed to support the absolute QoS model. QoS models can also be classified based on the degree of isolation between the different traffic classes. In an isolated model, the performance of the high-priority traffic is independent of the low-priority traffic. In a nonisolated model, the performance of the high-priority traffic depends on the low-priority traffic. The degree of isolation can be fixed ahead of time and satisfied using different techniques.

Most QoS differentiation schemes in IP networks focus on providing loss differentiation, delay differentiation, or bandwidth guarantees because IP routers have the capability to buffer packets electronically. However, optical core nodes do not have any electronic buffers, and the data follow an all-optical path from source to destination. Thus, the delay incurred from source to destination results primarily from propagation delay, and bandwidth guarantee is implicitly provided by supporting loss guarantee. Hence, the focus of QoS support in OBS networks is to primarily provide loss differentiation, although a few papers have addressed the problem of providing delay differentiation.

QoS in OBS Networks

In OBS networks, several schemes have been proposed to support the relative QoS model. A differentiated signaling scheme may be used to provide QoS in optical burst switched networks. An additional offset-based JET scheme was proposed for isolating classes of bursts so that high-priority bursts experience less contention and loss than low-priority bursts (Yao et al. 2000). In this additional offset-based reservation scheme, higher-priority class bursts are given a larger offset time than the lower-priority class bursts. By providing a larger offset time, the probability of reserving the resources without conflict for the higher-priority class burst is increased; therefore, the loss experienced by higher-priority class traffic is decreased. The limitation of this approach is that high-priority bursts will experience higher delays; thus, the approach may be capable of satisfying loss requirements but is not capable of meeting delay requirements. Furthermore, it has been shown that this scheme can lead to unfairness, with larger low-priority bursts experiencing higher loss than smaller low-priority bursts (Yao et al. 2000).

Another approach intentionally drops low-priority bursts under certain conditions in order to reduce loss for high-priority bursts. The scheme provides a proportional reduction rather than a complete elimination of high-priority burst losses resulting from contention with low-priority bursts. This proportional QoS scheme based on per-hop information was proposed to support burst loss probability and delay differentiation. The proportional QoS model quantitatively adjusts the QoS metric to be proportional to the differentiation factor of each class. If p_i is the loss metric and s_i is the differentiation factor for class i, then, using the proportional differentiation model, the following will hold for every class: $(p_i/s_i = p_j/s_j)$. To implement this model, each core node needs to maintain traffic statistics, such as the number of burst arrivals and the number of bursts dropped for each class. Hence, the online loss probability of class i, p_i, is the ratio of the number of class i bursts dropped to the number of class i burst arrivals during a fixed time interval. To maintain the differentiation factor between the classes, an intentional burst dropping scheme is employed. A limitation of the scheme is that it can result in the unnecessary dropping of low-priority bursts. Proportional QoS differentiation is also provided by maintaining the number of wavelengths occupied by each class of burst. Every arriving burst is scheduled based on a usage profile maintained at every node. Arriving bursts that satisfy their usage profiles preempt scheduled bursts that do not satisfy their usage profiles so as to maintain the preset differentiation ratio.

QoS Mechanisms

The Quality of Service Forum has defined the different mechanisms that must be carried out to ensure QoS in a network, including the following.

Admission Control

Admission control determines whether a requested connection is allowed to be carried by the network. The main considerations behind this decision are current traffic load, current QoS, requested traffic profile, requested QoS, pricing, and other policy considerations. For QoS-enabled IP networks, admission control, for example, could be performed in setting up RSVP flows or OLS paths.

Traffic Shaping and Conditioning

In QoS-enabled IP networks, it is necessary to specify the traffic profile for a connection to decide how to allocate various network resources. *Traffic shaping and conditioning* ensures that traffic entering at an edge or a core node adheres to the profile specified. Typically, this mechanism is used to reduce the burstiness of a traffic stream. This involves a key trade-off between the benefits of shaping (e.g., loss in downstream network) and the shaping delay. Leaky bucket–based traffic shaping is an example of this mechanism.

Classification and Marking

To provide the requested QoS, it is critical to classify packets so as to enable different QoS treatment. This can be done based on various fields in IP headers and higher-layer protocol headers (e.g., source and destination port numbers for TCP or UDP). Efficient and consistent packet classification is a key problem under active research. Either as a result of a traffic-monitoring mechanism or voluntary discrimination, a packet can be annotated for a particular QoS treatment in the network (e.g. high or low, loss or delay priority). IP packet marking is proposed to be done using the IP header's type of service.

Priority and Scheduling Mechanisms

To satisfy the QoS needs of different connections, nodes need to have priority and scheduling mechanisms. The *priority* feature typically refers to the capability of providing different delay treatment—for example, higher-priority packets are always served before lower-priority packets, both in the context of packet processing and transmission on outbound links. Nodes also implement different loss-priority treatment—that is, higher-loss priority packets are lost less often than the lower-loss priority ones. Nodes also need to have closely related *scheduling* mechanisms to ensure that different connections obtain their promised share of the resources (i.e., processing and link bandwidth). This mechanism also ensures that any spare capacity is distributed in a fair manner. Examples of this mechanism include *generalized processor sharing, weighted round robin, weighted fair queuing,* and *class-based queuing.* Efficient implementation of these mechanisms, their extension to include both delay and bandwidth needs simultaneously, and hierarchical scheduling are active research areas.

Signaling Protocols

To obtain the required QoS from a network, end systems need to signal the network the desired QoS as well as the anticipated offered traffic profile. This has been a fundamental part of various connection-oriented networks (e.g. ATM). However, for connectionless networks (e.g. IP), this is relatively new. Corresponding examples are the signaling associated with the resource reservation and label distribution protocols. Implementation, scalability and the corresponding capabilities to signal different QoS needs are issues under current examination.

ADVANCED ISSUES

As the Internet continues to evolve, it will be expected to support a growing number of applications, including Internet telephony, video conferencing, and video distribution. To support these applications, the network must be capable not only of providing the required bandwidth but also guaranteeing QoS, security, and survivability. A WDM network can provide the necessary bandwidth to support a wide range of multimedia Internet services. WDM networks, however, require the development of suitable devices and network architectures, along with appropriate protocols, to enable service guarantees.

A WDM network not only can provide a huge amount of bandwidth but also may offer the benefit of data transparency in which the network may carry signals of arbitrary format. Data transparency may be achieved through the all-optical transmission and switching of signals without electronic conversions at intermediate nodes. As optical devices mature and become cost-effective and competitive, it is conceivable that, by the end of this decade, optical systems will play a much more significant role in switching technology than today, with many switching and routing functions incorporated into the optical domain.

Several technologies have been proposed to allow for the best utilization of WDM network resources such as OLS, OPS, OBS, and WR. In WR, end users communicate with one another via all-optical WDM lightpaths. WR eliminates the need for buffering in the forwarding path but is poorly suited for rapid provisioning of wide bandwidth data services. OLS provides many desirable features not readily available in conventional networks. Its capability to achieve packet switching as well as burst or circuit switching implies seamless network upgrades and network interoperability. By designing a new signaling protocol that extends GMPLS, OLS can interoperate with MPLS and MPλS networks.

Currently, OPS and OBS techniques are in the experimental stage. The lack of commercially viable optical buffering technology constrains the commercial development of optical packet switches. Also, it is not clear how such switches can be deployed to carry IP traffic. Burst switching seems to be a more commercially viable technology than optical packet switching in the near future—if it can be designed so that it will not require optical buffering. The performance of the various burst switching schemes as well as the size of burst need to be studied in the light of IP traffic. With today's networks experiencing enormous exponential growth, it is important that we develop and take advantage of recent related technologies to keep pace with these increasing demands. WDM is an extremely promising technology for supporting these needs, and by developing architectures and protocols that fully utilize the benefits of WDM, we can ensure that this tremendous growth will continue to grow in the future.

CONCLUSION

In this chapter, we discussed and justified the need for the optical technology to provide bandwidth to carry next-generation Internet. We also provided a survey of the different optical multiplexing techniques, including TDM, SONT-SDH, and WDM. We then presented WDM technology as a solution to support the increasing bandwidth demands of new applications and services. We described with sufficient details the basic concept of this technology, its evolutions, its advantages, and its limits. We also described the most optical switching technologies—OCS, OPS, OBS, and OLS—and we discussed the major signaling schemes proposed in the literature and adopted by these switching technologies. Moreover, we presented in detail the contention resolution methods and stated how to provide service differentiation in optical switched networks and discussed the parameters and models that can be implemented to provide QoS.

GLOSSARY

Dense wavelength division multiplexing (WDM): A way of increasing the capacity of the optical fiber. It carries multiple wavelengths in single strands of the fiber.

Optical burst switching (OBS): A switching technology that can aggregate or assemble packets into bursts at ingress nodes such that the switching times and associated guard band inefficiencies are negligible with respect to the burst sizes.

Optical cross-connect (OXC): An element that switches optical signals from input ports to output ports. A basic cross-connect element is the 2×2 cross-point element. It routes optical signals from two input ports to two output ports and has two states: cross state and bar state.

Optical label switching (OLS): Offers seamless integration of data and optical networking while supporting circuit, burst, and packet switching using the optical labels. The dynamic and agile characteristics of optical label switching indicate its support of diverse QoS and CoS services.

Optical packet switching (OPS): A switching technique in which a data stream is broken into packets of small size before being transmitted. Routing information is added to the overhead of each packet in order to aid intermediate switches between the source and destination nodes.

Optical time division multiplexing (OTDM): An optical multiplexing technique used to enable multiple streams of information to share the same transmission media.

Synchronous optical network-synchronous digital hierarchy (SONET-SDH): A digital transmission standard. Higher layers use optical packet switching; the optical layer is point to point.

Wavelength division multiplexing (WDM): A multiplexing technique in which two or more optical signals with different wavelengths are combined and simultaneously transmitted in the same direction over an optical fiber.

Wavelength routing (WR): Enables optical networks to carry data between access stations in the optical domain without any intermediate optical to and from electronic conversion.

CROSS REFERENCES

See *Frequency and Phase Modulation; Frequency Division Multiplexing (FDM); Orthogonal Frequency Division Multiplexing (OFDM); Statistical Time Division Multiplexing (STDM); Time Division Multiplexing (TDM).*

REFERENCES

Awduche, D. O., A. Hannan, and X. P. Xiao. 2001. *Applicability statement for extensions to RSVP for LSP-tunnels.* Network Working Group (retrieved from www.ietf.org/rfc/rfc3210.txt?number=3210).

Brackett, C. A. 1990. Dense wavelength division multiplexing networks: Principle and applications. *IEEE Journal of Selected Areas in Communications*, 8: 948–64.

Chen, Y., M. Thomas, and W. Wu. 2000. Multi-protocol lambda switching for IP over optical networks. In *Proceedings of SPIE: The International Society for Optical Engineering*, Nov. 6–7, 4211: 165–72.

Chia, M. C., D. K. Hunter, I. Andonovic, P. Ball, I. Wright, S. P. Ferguson, K. M. Guild, and M. J. O'Mahony. 2001. Packet loss and delay performance of feedback and feed-forward arrayed-waveguide gratings-based optical packet switches with WDM inputs out puts. *IEEE/OSA Journal of Lightwave Technology*, 19(9): 1241–54.

Chiu, A., and E. Modiano. 2000. Traffic grooming algorithms for reducing electronic multiplexing costs in WDM ring networks. *Journal of Lightwave Technology*, 18(1): 2–12.

Chlamtac, I., A. Ganz, and G. Karmi. 1992. Lightpath communications: An approach to high bandwidth optical WANs. *IEEE Transactions on Communications*, 40(7): 1171–82.

Gallaher, R. 2002. *An introduction to MPLS* (retrieved from www.convergedigest.com/Bandwidth/archive/010910TUTORIAL-rgallaher1.htm).

Hunter, D. K., M. C. Chia, and I. Andonovic. 1998. Buffering in optical packet switches. *IEEE/OSA Journal of Lightwave Technology*, 16(12): 2081–94.

Intellilight dedicated SONET ring. Undated (retrieved from www.bell-atl.com/network/SONET/).

IP-over-SONET configuration. 2002 (retrieved from http://techweb.com/encyclopedia/defineterm.cgi).

Jue, J. P. 2002. An algorithm for loopless deflection in photonic packet-switched networks. In *Proceedings of the IEEE International Conference on Communications* (ICC), April, pp. 2776–2780.

Karasan, E., and E. A. Glu. 1998. Performance of WDM transport networks. *IEEE Journal on Selected Areas in Communications*, 16(7): 1081–96.

Khlifi, Y., A. Lazzez, S. Guemara El Fatmi, and N. Boudriga. 2005. Optical packet and burst switching node Architecture: Modeling and performance analysis. In *Proceedings of the Eighth International Conference on Telecommunications* (ConTel2005), June 15–17, Zagreb, Croatia, Vol. 2, pp. 507–14.

National Communications System. 2002. *Wavelength division multiplexing (WDM) networks.* Technical information bulletin, TIB 00-3 (retrieved from www.ncs.gov/library/tech_bulletins/2000/tib_00-3.pdf).

O'Mahony, M. J., D. Simeonidou, D. K. Hunter, and A. Tzanakaki. 2001. The application of optical packet switching in future communication networks. *IEEE Communications Magazine*, 39: 128–35.

Papadimitriou, G. I., P. A. Tsimoulas, M. S. Obaidat, and A. S. Pomportsis. 2003. *Multiwavelength optical LANs.* New York: John Wiley & Sons.

Qiao, C., and M. Yoo. 1999. Optical burst switching (OBS): A new paradigm for an optical Internet. *Journal of High Speed Networks*, 8(1): 69–84.

Ramamurthy, B., and B. Mukherjee. 1998. Wavelength conversion in WDM networking. *IEEE Journal on Selected Areas in Communications*, 16(7): 1061–73.

Simmons, J. M., E. L. Goldstein, and A. A. M. Saleh. 1999. Quantifying the benefit of wavelength add-drop in WDM rings with distance-independent and dependent traffic. *Journal of Lightwave Technology*, 17(1): 48–57.

SONET graphical overview. Undated (retrieved from www.cisco.com/warp/public/127/sonet_28081.pdf).

Synchronous optical network. Undated (retrieved from www.iec.org/online/tutorials/acrobat/sonet.pdf).

Vokkarane, V. M., and J. P. Jue. 2003. Prioritized burst segmentation and composite burst assembly techniques for QoS support in optical burst switched networks. *IEEE Journal on Selected Areas in Communications*, 21(7): 1198–1209.

Xiao, G., and Y. Leung. 1999. Algorithms for allocating wavelength converters in all-optical networks. *IEEE/ACM Transactions on Networking*, 7(4): 545–57.

Yao, S., B. Mukherjee, S. J. B. Yoo, and S. Dixit. 2000. All-optical packet-switched networks: A study of contention resolution schemes in an irregular mesh network with variable sized packets. In *Proceedings, SPIE OptiComm*, October, pp. 235–46.

———. 2003. A unified study of contention resolution schemes in optical packet-switched networks. *IEEE/OSA Journal of Lightwave Technology*, March, 21(3), pp. 672–683.

Yoo, M., C. Qiao, and S. Dixit. 2000. QoS performance of optical burst switching in IP over WDM networks. *IEEE Journal on Selected Areas in Communications*, 18(10): 2062–71.

Zang, H., J. P. Jue, L. Sahasrabuddhe, R. Ramamurthy, and B. Mukherjee. 2001. Dynamic lightpath establishment in wavelength routed networks. *IEEE Communications Magazine*, 39(9): 100–8.

Zhang, T., K. Lu, and J. P. Jue. 2004. Differentiated contention resolution for QoS in photonic packet-switched networks. *Journal of Lightwave Technology*, 22(11): 2523–35.

Zhu, K., and B. Mukherjee. 2001. Traffic grooming in an optical WDM mesh network. In *Proceedings of the IEEE International Conference on Communications*, June, Helsinki, Finland, pp. 721–5.

Part 3

Digital and Optical Networks

Digital Communication Basics

Robert W. Heath, *The University of Texas, Austin*
Atul A. Salvekar, *Intel Corporation*

INTRODUCTION

Digital communication is the process of conveying information from a transmitter to a receiver across a physical channel. Typically, information is transformed into digital bits that are processed for transmission. The origin of the binary data is known as a *source*; the destination of the binary data is known as a *sink*.

It is hard to conceive of analog communication or analog physical layer technologies that are comparable to our commonly used digital communication technology. Examples include the analog telephone and AM transmitter-receivers. In these cases, the actual signal of interest is transmitted without digitization. Because of the redundancy of the signal and the difficulty in using advanced techniques for higher data rates, these forms of transmission are not particularly efficient. This is why digital communication is used to carry the majority of information transmission.

Early forms of digital communication using electrical signals date back to the invention of the telegraph by Samuel Morse in the 1830s. The telegraph used Morse code, essentially a mapping from letters to quaternary sequences (long pulses, short pulses, letter spaces, and word spaces) to convey digital information over long distances via cable. Guglielmo Marconi patented a wireless telegraph in 1896: This is the origin of wireless digital communication. The *facsimile* (fax) machine is a sometimes surprising example of early digital communication. First patented in 1843 by Alexander Bain, the fax machine both then and now scans documents line by line and digitally encodes and conveys the presence or absence of ink.

Digital communication systems offer higher quality compared with analog systems, increased security, better robustness to noise, reductions in power, and easy integration of different types of sources such as voice, text, and video. Because the majority of a digital communication system's components are implemented using semiconductor technology, devices can take advantage of the reductions in cost and size in CMOS and other semiconductor technologies.

Digital communication technology is a mix of analog and digital components. The backbone of the Internet uses digital communication over optical fibers. So-called last-mile access technologies including voice-band modems, cable modems, and digital subscriber lines (DSLs) are all digital. Local area networks use different digital communication technologies such as IEEE 802.3 (Ethernet) for wired access or IEEE 802.11 for wireless access. Digital communication allows remote access to the Internet via cellular systems through CDPD in first-generation systems and GPRS, HDR, or EDGE in second-generation systems. Third-generation cellular systems harmonize voice and data access. Examples of upcoming wireless networks include the IEEE 802.16 standard (or WiMAX) and the evolutionary path of the *groupe spéciale mobile* developed by the 3rd Generation Partnership Project called *long-term evolution*.

This chapter presents the fundamentals of digital communication. Many topics of relevance to digital communication are treated elsewhere in this handbook. A broad description of cellular and wireless networks is contained in Volume 2, Part 3. Other modulation schemes are described more in Part 2 of this volume. Readers who are interested in only a cursory overview can read the second section of this chapter. Those who want a more thorough treatment beyond this should read the entire chapter as well as consult select references described in "Further Reading."

FUNDAMENTALS OF DIGITAL COMMUNICATION
Digital Communication System Overview

The physical layer typical of a digital communication system is illustrated in Figure 1. In some systems, various functional blocks may be combined or omitted, depending on the needs of system designers. Some critical control functions such as synchronization are not explicitly highlighted but are discussed in this chapter.

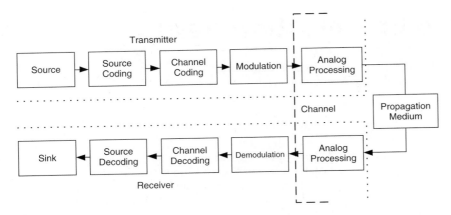

Figure 1: The components of a typical digital communication system

The physical layer is one of several layers of abstraction of a communication network, and it deals with the transmission and reception of raw data. There are several steps in the transmission and reception process, some of which involve *digital signal processing* (DSP) and some of which involve analog processing. Thus, it is important to distinguish that whereas digital communication involves the transmission of digital information, the transmission and reception process involves both digital and analog processing. In this chapter, we focus on the DSP aspects of digital communication, in particular the aspects at the physical layer where the analog waveforms are generated and processed.

The block diagram for a typical digital communication system in Figure 1 is divided into three parts: the transmitter, the channel, and the receiver. The transmitter processes a bit stream of data for transmission over a physical medium. The channel is the physical medium that adds noise and distorts the transmitted signal. It accounts for the propagation medium as well as any analog effects in the transmitter and receiver. The receiver attempts to extract the transmitted bit stream from the received signal.

The first basic transmitter block is devoted to *source encoding*. The purpose of source encoding is to compress the data by removing inherent redundancies. The input to the source encoder will be called $s[n]$, the *source sequence*. The output of the source encoder will be called $i[n]$, the *information sequence*. Source encoding includes both lossy and lossless compression. In lossy compression, some degradation is allowed to reduce the amount of data that need to be transmitted. In lossless compression, redundancy is removed, but upon inverting the encoding algorithm the signal is exactly the same. In other words, if f and g are the source encoding and decoding processes, then $\hat{s}[n] = g[i(n)] = g[f[s(n)]]$; for lossy compression, $s[n] \cong \hat{s}[n]$, and for lossless compression, $s[n] = \hat{s}[n]$. So, data from the source encoder $s[n]$ are transformed into $i[n]$, both of which are in bits. The bit rate R_b is the rate at which information bits are transmitted through the channel.

Following source encoding is *encryption*. The purpose of encryption is to make it difficult for an unintended receiver to interpret the transmitted data. Generally, encryption involves applying a lossless transformation to the information sequence $i[n]$ to produce an encrypted

sequence $e[n] = p(i[n])$. *Decryption* reverses this process by applying an inverse transform $p^{-1}(\cdot)$ to produce $i[n] = p^{-1}(p(i[n]))$. Unlike source coding, encryption does not compress the data; instead, it makes the data unintelligible to an uninformed receiver.

The next block is the *channel coder*. Channel coding adds redundancy to the encrypted sequence $e[n]$ in a controlled way to provide resilience to channel distortions and to improve overall throughput. Using common coding notation, for every k input bits, or information bits, there is an additional redundancy of r bits. The total number of bits is $n = k + r$; the coding rate is defined as k/n. Two types of channel codes are prevalent: forward error-correction codes and error-detection codes. Forward error-correction codes are used to provide redundancy that enables errors to be corrected at the receiver. They come in varieties such as *trellis codes, convolutional codes*, and *block codes* (Bossert 1999). Error-detection codes—*cyclic redundancy check* (CRC) codes being the most common—provide redundancy that allows the receiver to determine if an error occurred during transmission. The receiver can use this information to either discard the data in error or request a retransmission. Channel coding is discussed in more detail in other parts of this handbook.

Following channel coding, the bits are mapped to *waveforms* by the modulator. This is the demarcation point where basic transmitter-side digital signal processing for communications ends. Typically, the bits are mapped in groups to *symbols*. Following the symbol mapping, the modulator converts the digital symbols into corresponding analog waveforms for transmission over the physical link. This can be accomplished by sending the digital signal through a *digital-to-analog* (D/A) converter into a shaping filter and, if needed, mixed onto a higher-frequency carrier. Symbols are sent at a rate of R_s symbols per second (known as the *baud rate*); the symbol period $T_s = 1/R_s$ is the time difference between successive symbols.

The signal generated by the transmitter travels through a propagation medium to the receiver. The medium could be a radio wave through a wireless environment, a current through a telephone wire, or an optical signal through a fiber.

The first block at the receiver is the *analog front end* (AFE), which consists at least of filters to remove unwanted noise, oscillators for timing, and *analog-to-digital*

(A/D) converters to convert the data into the digital regime. There may be additional analog components such as low-noise amplifiers and mixers. This is the demarcation point for the beginning of the receiver-side digital signal processing for digital communication.

As illustrated in Figure 1, the channel is the component of the communication system that accounts for all of the noise and intersymbol interference introduced by the analog processing blocks, the propagation medium, and interfering signals. Noise is a random disturbance that degrades the received signal. Sources of noise include the thermal noise that results from the material properties of the receiver, the quantization noise caused by the D/A and the A/D converters, and the external interference from other communication channels. *Intersymbol interference* is a form of signal distortion that causes the transmitted signal to interfere with itself. Sources of intersymbol interference include the distortion introduced by the analog filters as well as the propagation medium.

The first digital communication block at the receiver is the *demodulator*. The demodulator uses a sampled version of the received waveform, and perhaps knowledge of the channel, to infer the transmitted symbol. The process of demodulation may include equalization, sequence detection, or other advanced algorithms to help combat channel distortions.

Following the demodulator is the *channel decoder*. Essentially, the decoder uses the redundancy introduced by the channel coder to remove errors generated by the demodulation block. The decoder may work jointly with the demodulator to improve performance or may simply operate on the output of the demodulator. Overall, the effect of the demodulator and the decoder is to produce the closest possible $\hat{e}[n]$ given the observations at the receiver.

After demodulation, *decryption* is applied to the output of the demodulator. The objective is to make the information intelligible to the receiver. Generally, decryption applies the inverse transformation $p^{-1}(\cdot)$ corresponding to the encryption process to produce an estimate of the transmitted information $\hat{i}[n] = p^{-1}(\hat{e}[n])$.

The final block in Figure 1 is the source decoder that essentially reinflates the data back to the form it was sent: $\hat{s}[n] = g(\hat{i}[n])$. This is basically the inverse operation of the source encoder. After source decoding, the digital data are delivered to higher-level communication protocols that are beyond the scope of the chapter.

For Internet traffic, common transmitter-receiver pairs include DSL modems, fiber-optic transceivers, local area networks, and even storage devices such as disk drives.

Although their physical media are diverse and the speeds at which they transmit may be significantly different, the fundamental model for each of these digital communication systems is the same.

Processing in the Digital Domain

There are three basic classes of signals in digital communication: continuous time, discrete time, and digital. *Continuous time* signals are those whose value at time t is $x(t)$, where t and $x(t)$ can take values on a continuum—for instance, the real number line or the complex plane. *Discrete time* signals take values only at integer times n, but the signal $x[n]$ takes values on a continuum. Finally, *digital* signals are those that have value at integer times and take on values on some finite (perhaps countably infinite) set.

The link between the analog and the digital domains is through the D/A and A/D converters as illustrated in Figure 2. At the transmitter, the D/A converts a digital signal $x[n]$ to an analog signal $x(t)$ essentially by letting $x(nT_s) = x[n]$ and interpolating the remaining values. At the receiver, the A/D samples the received signal $y(t)$ at some period T (typically a fraction of T_s) to produce $y[n] \cong y(nT)$, where this is approximate equality because $y[n]$ is quantized to some set of values. This new signal is called $y_d[n]$, and is the digital waveform derived from the continuous time waveform $y(t)$.

The Nyquist sampling theorem gives flexibility in the choice of whether to process $y(t)$ or $y[n]$. Ignoring quantization noise, the Nyquist sampling theorem states that if the inverse of the sample rate is greater than twice the maximum frequency in $y(t)$ (or equivalently the bandwidth), then there is no loss in the sampling process. This implies that any processing done on the continuous time waveform can be done equally well on the sampled waveform given that the conditions stated in the Nyquist sampling theorem are satisfied. Several practical considerations, however, make digital the domain of choice.

The biggest advantage of doing as much processing as possible in the digital domain is that it allows full exploitation of the benefits of digital technology. Many digital platforms exist that are highly customizable and easy to alter—for instance, field programmable gate arrays and digital signal processors. This hardware has been designed to have very good tolerances and reproducibility. As the DSP components are relatively easy to change, they are also well suited to adaptation. Analog circuitry is typically not as easy to adjust, and custom design can be expensive.

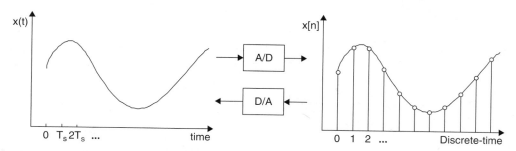

Figure 2: The relationship between a continuous time signal and a discrete time signal

Moreover, even small changes in design or specification tolerances may require wholesale redesign, which may be more costly than adjusting some parameters in a digital platform. Another advantage of processing in the digital domain is a by-product of the shrinking transistor size: It offers both dramatic increases in processing power as well as significant reductions in overall cost. Thus, doing the majority of the processing in the digital domain improves cost, performance, and flexibility. For these reasons, doing processing in the digital domain has become highly relevant to digital communication.

Key Resources: Power and Bandwidth

The two primary resources in any communication system, both digital and analog, are power and bandwidth. Systems whose performance is limited by the available power are *power-limited*, whereas those that are limited by bandwidth are *bandwidth-limited*. Most practical systems are both power- and bandwidth-limited.

The power of a signal is roughly defined as the average energy over time. Mathematically, this is often written as $P = \lim_{T \to \infty} (1/T) \int_{-T/2}^{T/2} |x(t)|^2 \, dt$. Power may be measured in watts but is more often measured in decibels relative to one watt (dB) or one milliwatt (dBm). The decibel is a relative measure that is defined as $(P/Q)_{dB} = 10\log_{10}(P/Q)$. When used to measure the power of P in dB, Q is assumed to be 1 watt, whereas to measure the power of P in dBm, Q is assumed to be 1 milliwatt. Sometimes the notation *dBW* and *dBmW* are used when measuring dB in terms of watts.

There are two different but related notions of power in a communication system: transmit power and the received power. Naturally, the *transmit power* is the average energy over time of the transmitted signal whereas the *received power* is the average energy over time of the received signal.

The transmitted power in a communication system is limited by the maximum power available to transmit a signal. Generally, system performance will be better if there is high transmitted power (and thus received power). Practical constraints on cost, properties of the transmission medium, battery life (in mobile systems), or regulatory constraints generally motivate having a low transmitted power.

Because propagation media are lossy and dispersive, the received power is a function of the transmit power and the channel. In all media, the loss resulting from the

channel increases as some function of the distance between the transmitter and receiver. Thus, the larger the distance, the smaller the received power.

The minimum received power required at the receiver, known as the *receiver sensitivity*, is determined by the parameters of the system, the quality of the hardware, as well as the desired operating characteristics. The range of the system can be inferred from the ratio of the maximum transmit power to the minimum received power. Generally, increased data rate in a given bandwidth or lower *bit error rates* (BERs) increase the required minimum received power.

Besides power, *bandwidth* is the other design constraint in a communication system. Unfortunately, there are many definitions of bandwidth and different notions are used in different systems. The most generic definition of the bandwidth of a signal $x(t)$ is the portion of the frequency spectrum $X(f) = \int_{-\infty}^{\infty} x(t)e^{-j2\pi ft} dt$ dt for which $X(f)$ is nonzero. Because the true bandwidth of a finite duration signal is infinite, systems often use the "3-dB bandwidth," which is the contiguous range of frequencies over which the power spectrum is at least 50 percent of the maximum value. Other definitions of bandwidth are also possible (see Couch 2001 for details.

Note that the definition of bandwidth differs depending on whether the communication system is *baseband* or *bandpass*. Baseband communication systems operate at DC, whereas bandpass communication systems convey information at some carrier frequency f_c. Figure 3 illustrates the different bandwidth notions of absolute and 3-dB bandwidth in each of these types of systems.

The bandwidth available in a communication system depends on the transmission medium. In wireless systems, bandwidth is a precious and expensive commodity that is regulated by the government. Thus, although the theoretical bandwidth of the wireless medium is significant, only a fraction is available to a given communication system. In wireline systems, the bandwidth is determined by the type and quality of the cable and the interconnects. Generally, the larger the bandwidth, the larger the potential data rate that can be supported. Exploiting larger bandwidths, however, typically requires more sophisticated receiver processing algorithms and more expensive analog components.

Bandwidth and power are related through the concept of the *power spectral density* (PSD). The PSD is a measure of the power in a signal as a function of frequency. The integral of the PSD is hence the power of the signal.

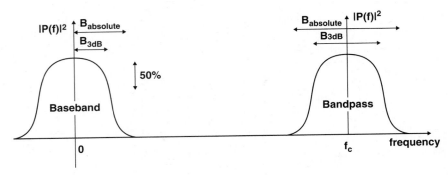

Figure 3: Illustration of two different notions of bandwidth in baseband and bandpass signals

Measures of Performance

There are many potential measures that are used to evaluate the performance of a digital communication system. The choice of a performance measure depends significantly on the application of the system. Broad classes of performance measures include the probability of error, the outage probability, and the capacity. In this chapter, we will discuss the probability of error and the capacity. The *probability of error* is a measure of the rate at which errors occur, whereas the *capacity* is a measure of the maximum data rate that can be supported by a channel with a given *signal-to-noise ratio* (SNR) and an arbitrarily small probability of error.

Of the two measures, the probability of error is the more pragmatic indicator of system performance. There are various flavors of the probability of error, including the probability of bit error, the probability of symbol error, and the probability of frame error. Equivalently, these measures are known as the *bit error rate*, the *symbol error rate* (SER), and the *frame error rate* (FER). In simple transmission mediums, SER and the FER can be determined from the BER; therefore, the BER is a generically studied performance metric.

Essentially, the BER provides the average number of bit errors. For example, a BER of 10^{-2} means that on average approximately one bit out of every one hundred will be in error. The BER can be measured at various places in the receiver but is typically most meaningful after demodulation (the uncoded BER) and after error correction (the coded BER).

The performance needs of the application determine the required BER. For example, voice communication in cellular systems might require a coded BER of 10^{-2}, whereas data communication in the same system might require a coded BER of 10^{-5}. In most communication systems, the uncoded BER is a function of the data rate and the modulation scheme and can be readily related to the signal-to-noise ratio. The SNR is essentially the ratio of the received signal power to the noise power in the signal bandwidth. Thus, the BER is a function of both the received power and the bandwidth of the signal, although more generally the channel model will also play a role.

The fundamental limit to data communications can be most simply described by the so-called capacity of a channel, C, which is the maximum average number of bits that can be supported by a channel with a given SNR at an arbitrarily small probability of error. The capacity is measured in units of bits per second and is essentially a bound on the achievable data rate. Often the capacity is normalized by the bandwidth. The normalized capacity C/B measures the bits per channel use in units of bits per second per hertz. Unlike the BER, the capacity provides an upper bound (instead of the actual performance) of a communication system because it is optimized over all possible modulation and coding schemes. Like the BER, the capacity is typically a function of the SNR, the bandwidth, and the channel.

The capacity is a measure for determining the fundamental limit on the data rate imposed by the given communication channel. The BER is more useful for evaluating the performance of an actual coding and modulation scheme. Typically, a target BER will be defined

and a coding and modulation scheme will be proposed to achieve the largest data rate possible, R. Naturally, it should be the case that $R < C$. Spectrally efficient digital communication systems have a rate R that closely approaches the capacity C for the desired operating point.

IMPORTANT CONCEPTS IN DIGITAL COMMUNICATION
Modulation

The modulator in a digital communication system maps binary data onto waveforms for transmission over the physical channel. The modulator maps a group of bits (or symbols) onto a finite number of waveforms each symbol period. Binary modulations map each bit to one of two possible waveforms, whereas M-ary modulations map each group of $\log_2 M$ bits to one of M possible waveforms. The analog waveforms are designed with the constraints of the channel such as the bandwidth or the carrier frequency in mind.

There are two basic forms of modulation: linear modulation and nonlinear modulation. *Linear modulation* schemes are typically more spectrally efficient—that is, they are able to come closer to the capacity. *Nonlinear modulations* typically have other properties, such as constant envelope, that make them easier to implement and less susceptible to various impairments in the channel. The choice of a modulation scheme depends on the desired throughput, the target BER, the spectral efficiency of the modulation scheme, the power efficiency of the modulation scheme, robustness to impairments, and the implementation cost and complexity.

Modulations may also have memory or they may be memoryless. When a symbol is only a function of the bits from the current symbol period, then it is said to be *memoryless*. When a symbol is a function of the bits from previous symbols periods, the modulation is said to have *memory*. Having memory in the modulation scheme may have practical advantages such as reducing the peak-to-average ratio of the transmitted signal or simplifying noncoherent detection at the receiver. Modulations with memory can also provide additional resilience to errors; thus, they are sometimes called *coded* modulation schemes.

To illustrate the concept of modulation—in particular, linear modulation—let us first define the concept of signal space and then relate that to common modulation formats found in practice. A *vector space* is defined to be a set of vectors (in this case, continuous signals), $\{\phi_i(t)\}$, with two operations: (1) addition of those vectors (i.e., $\phi_i(t) + \phi_j(t)$ is defined and is an element of the vector space) and (2) multiplications of those vectors by a scalar (i.e., $k\phi_i(t)$ is defined and an element of the vector space). Other technical rules for being a vector space can be found in Anton and Rorres (1991). In communications, typically these vectors are orthogonal—that is,

$$\int_{-\infty}^{\infty} \phi_i(t)\phi_j(t)dt = \delta_{ij} \qquad (1)$$

where δ_{ij} is 1 for $i = j$ and 0 otherwise. Because these waveform vectors are orthogonal, they are also a basis for the vector space and are sometimes referred to as *basis functions*.

A digital communication system may be baseband or bandpass, depending on whether the symbols are conveyed at baseband (DC) or at some carrier frequency (see Figure 3). An asymmetric digital subscriber line is an example of a baseband communication system (see also "DSL (Digital Subscriber Line)"). Most digital communication systems are bandpass, including all narrowband wireless systems, optical systems, and cable modems. Although bandpass systems convey information at a carrier frequency, the modulator and demodulator do not need to generate signals at that carrier frequency. Instead, the modulator and demodulator work with the *baseband equivalent* waveform. At the transmitter, the *upconverter* in the analog processing block converts the baseband equivalent signal to the bandpass signal by shifting it to the desired carrier frequency. At the receiver, the *downconverter* in the analog processing block shifts the bandpass signal down to zero frequency. The advantage of the baseband equivalent notion is that it makes the digital operations of the communication system independent of the actual carrier frequency.

Let us first consider baseband *pulse amplitude modulation* (PAM) (see also "Pulse Amplitude Modulation"). PAM transmission is used in *high bit rate digital subscriber lines* (DSL), HDSL-II and G.SHDSL. It is a linear and memoryless modulation. An M-PAM system is a form of M-ary modulation in which $m = \log_2 M$ bits at a time are mapped to an element of the set of M possible amplitudes C_{PAM}, which is the constellation. For 4-PAM, a set of possible amplitudes is $C_{PAM} = \{-3, -1, 1, 3\}$, which are equally spaced apart. A pulse-shaping filter $\phi(t)$ with a bandwidth B is modulated to produce the transmitted waveform $x(t) = \Sigma_n x[n] \phi(t - nT_s)$, where $x[n] \in C_{PAM}$. So the set C_{PAM} is the constellation, $x[n]$ is the symbol transmitted starting at time nT_s, and $\phi(t)$ is the basis waveform. The spectrum of the PAM waveforms is determined by the pulse-shaping filter $\phi(t)$. The choice of pulse-shaping filter is a complicated one involving several competing requirements including resistance to timing jitter, simple implementation, and minimized spectral bandwidth.

A nice generalization of PAM that is preferable for bandpass systems is known as *quadrature amplitude modulation* (QAM). As with PAM, QAM is a linear and memoryless modulation. For simplicity, the M-QAM modulation is defined for M that is a power of four. Let $m = 1/2 \log_2 M$ and consider the same set of 2^m possible amplitudes C_{PAM} and pulse-shaping waveform $\phi(t)$. For M-QAM, at some carrier frequency f_c the transmitted waveform is

$$
\begin{aligned}
x(t) = \left(\sum_n i[n]\phi(t - nT_s)\right)\cos(2\pi f_c t) \\
- \left(\sum_n q[n]\phi(t - nT_s)\right)\sin(2\pi f_c t)
\end{aligned}
\tag{2}
$$

where $i[n] \in C_{PAM}$ corresponds to the symbol transmitted on the in-phase component $\cos(2\pi f_c t)$ and $q[n] \in C_{PAM}$ corresponds to the symbol transmitted on the quadrature component $\sin(2\pi f_c t)$. Assuming that f_c is much greater than $1/B$, the modulated in-phase and quadrature components are orthogonal; thus, QAM has double the data

rate of a PAM system that would use only the in-phase or quadrature component. Of course, recalling the discussion about Figure 3, note that a bandpass QAM system also uses twice the bandwidth of a baseband PAM system and thus the spectral efficiency of QAM at bandpass and PAM at baseband is the same. The ordered pair $(i[n], q[n])$ is the symbol transmitted starting at time nT_s, and $\phi(t) \cos(2\pi f_c t)$ and $\phi(t) \sin(2\pi f_c t)$ are the basis waveforms. For M-QAM, the constellation C_{PAM} is composed of all possible ordered pairs that can be generated from choosing the 2^m – PAM points for the in-phase and quadrature components. Thus, the M-QAM constellation has two dimensions. The baseband equivalent of the QAM signal in Equation 2 is a complex function and is given by

$$
\sum_n (i[n] + jq[n])\, \phi(t - nT_s)
$$

where $j = \sqrt{-1}$. Quadrature modulation schemes have complex baseband equivalents to account for both the in-phase and quadrature components. The spectrum of the QAM waveform is determined by the pulse-shaping filter $\phi(t)$ and is shifted in frequency by f_c. PAM and QAM modulation are illustrated in Figure 4.

Not all bandpass systems are capable of using QAM modulation. For example, in optical transmission phase information is not available, so the constellations are defined for positive amplitudes only. If the constellations values are 0 and A, this is known as *on-off keying*.

Another common form of modulation is *multicarrier modulation* in which several carriers are modulated by QAM modulation simultaneously (see also "DMT Modulation"). These carriers can be thought of as a basis waveform modulated by sinusoids of differing frequencies. This is not easy to accomplish, so an *inverse fast Fourier transform* (IFFT) is used to approximate this operation. The IFFT of a set of constellation points is, in fact, the sum

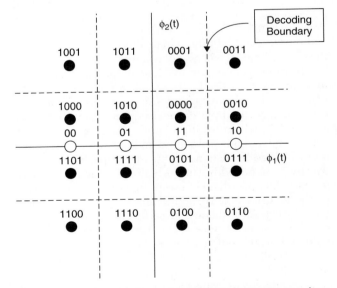

Figure 4: Signal space illustration of PAM and QAM signaling. The solid black circles are QAM, and the white circles are PAM. The numbers above the circles represent the mapping of bits to the constellation points

of a set of sampled sinusoids multiplied by the constellation points. In the digital domain, each of these waveforms can be independently demodulated. These samples are sent through a single pulse-shaping filter (basis waveform) and transmitted through the channel. The receiver samples the waveform and performs the inverse operations, a *fast Fourier transform*. Multicarrier modulation has become important because of its robustness to impulsive noise, ease of equalization, and its ability to do spectral shaping by independently controlling the carriers. *Discrete multitone* is the most common baseband version of multicarrier modulation, whereas *orthogonal frequency division multiplexing* (OFDM) is the most common bandpass version.

Intersymbol Interference Channels

After modulation, the analog waveform $x(t)$ corresponding to an input sequence of bits is transmitted over the communication medium. Communication media—whether fiber-optic cable, coaxial cable, telephone cable, or free space—generally have a dispersive effect on the transmitted signal. The effect of the medium on $x(t)$ is often modeled using a concept from signal processing known as a *linear and time-invariant* (LTI) system. The linearity implies that if $y_k(t)$ is the response to $x_k(t)$, then $\alpha y_1(t) + \beta y_2(t)$ is the response to the input signal $\alpha x_1(t) + \beta x_2(t)$. The time invariance means that the response to $x(t + \tau)$ is $y(t + \tau)$—that is, the behavior of the channel is not a function of time. Practically all physical channels are time-varying (because of changes in environmental factors), especially wireless channels. However, over short periods of time they can be modeled as time-invariant. Optical channels can also exhibit nonlinear behavior and thus other models may sometimes be appropriate.

The LTI assumption about the communication medium allows the distortion to the input signal to be modeled using the convolution operation

$$y(t) = \int_{-\infty}^{\infty} h(\tau)x(t - \tau)d\tau$$

The function $h(\tau)$ is known as the *impulse response* of the channel and includes all of the analog effects in the normal operating regime such as filtering at the transmitter and receiver in addition to the distortion in the medium. From basic Fourier transform theory, LTI systems have the nice property that, in the frequency domain, $Y(f) = H(f)X(f)$, where $Y(f)$ is the Fourier transform of $y(t)$, $H(f)$ is the Fourier transform of $h(t)$, and $X(f)$ is the Fourier transform of $x(t)$. Essentially, the channel acts as a frequency-selective filter that operates on the input signal. LTI systems induce distortion that is multiplicative in the frequency domain.

In an ideal channel, $|H(f)| = 1$ and there is no distortion (only a delay) of the input signal. Equivalently, in the time domain, an ideal channel produces $y(t) = x(t - \tau)$, where τ is an arbitrary delay. When the channel is not ideal, a more serious problem—intersymbol interference—is encountered. To illustrate this concept, suppose that $x(t)$ is generated at baseband using PAM as described in the previous section. In the absence of a channel, ideal

sampling of $x(t)$ at the receiver at time mT_s (more details on this in the next section), results in $\Sigma_n x[n] \phi(mT_s - nT_s)$. The pulse-shaping filter $\phi(t)$, however, is often a Nyquist pulse shape, which means that $\phi(0) = 1$ and $\phi(nT_s) = 0$ for $n \neq 0$. Thus, sampling at time mT_s yields symbol $x[m]$. Now consider a nonideal channel. Let $\phi\sim(t)$ be the convolution of $\phi(t)$ and $h(t)$. For a nontrivial channel, it will generally be the case that $\phi\sim(t)$ is no longer a Nyquist pulse shape and thus $y[m] = \Sigma_n x[n] \phi\sim((m - n)T_s)$. In this case there are multiple superpositions of symbols at each sampling instant—thus the notion of intersymbol interference. Compensating for intersymbol interference is known as *equalization* and is an important part of the receiver processing when intersymbol interference is present.

Noise and Interference

Noise and interference are the most ubiquitous forms of degradation in any communication system. Essentially, both can be modeled as random disturbances that are unrelated to the desired signal. Intersymbol interference also results in degradation, although the effect is different because it causes the signal to interfere with itself. *Noise* usually refers to the disturbances generated in the receiver as a result of the analog components, analog-to-digital conversion, and material properties of the receiver. Generally, noise can be reduced by using higher-quality materials but never eliminated. *Interference* generally refers to disturbances generated by external signals. Typically, interference has more signal structure than noise and thus it can be mitigated by more complex processing at the expense of higher cost.

There are various sources of noise in communication systems. Common examples include thermal noise, shot noise, and quantization noise. *Thermal noise* is a result of the Brownian random motion of thermally excited electrons. It is generated by resistors and the resistive parts of other devices such as transistors. *Shot noise* is more impulsive and may be more related to the signal—for example, the random arrival rates of photons in optical systems. *Quantization noise* is a result of digitizing the amplitude of the discrete time signal. Because thermal noise limits the performance in most systems (with the exception of optical system), we will focus our explanation on thermal noise.

Because noise is fundamentally not deterministic, it is often modeled as a random process. For thermal noise, the Gaussian random process has been found to be adequate for the job. When applied to model thermal noise, the process is assumed to be zero mean, uncorrelated from sample to sample, and have a variance σ^2 that is generally proportional to kBT_e, where k is Boltzmann's constant ($1.23e - 23 \, J/K$), B is the signal bandwidth, and T_e is the effective noise temperature of the device. The latter, T_e, is a parameter determined by the analog portion of the receiver. Essentially, for thermal noise the variance increases linearly as a function of the bandwidth. Thus, for the same transmit power, signals with larger bandwidths incur an additional noise penalty while simultaneously enjoying a higher signaling rate.

The effect of thermal noise is additive, therefore the received signal can be written $z(t) = y(t) + v(t)$, where $v(t)$

is a realization of the noise process. Because $v(t)$ is unknown to the receiver, its presence degrades the performance of subsequent processing blocks. The severity of thermal noise is quantified by the SNR.

The origin of interference is usually an undesired communication signal. Examples include adjacent channel interference, cross talk, and co-channel interference. *Adjacent channel interference* refers to the interference caused by signals operating in adjacent frequency bands. Because practical signals cannot have a finite absolute bandwidth, when the carrier frequencies of two different signals are close together, there is often leakage from one signal to the other. *Cross talk* is a form of interference in wireline systems and results from the electromagnetic coupling among the multiple twisted pairs making up a phone cable. *Co-channel interference* is the wireless equivalent of cross talk. Because of the limited availability of frequencies, wireless cellular systems reuse each carrier frequency. Essentially, co-channel interference is the interference among users sharing the same communication frequency.

Like thermal noise, interference is also additive. Thus, a signal with interference may be written $z(t) = y(t) + \sum_k y_k(t)$, where $y_k(t)$ refers to the distorted interfering signals. Performance degrades because $y_k(t)$ is both random and unknown at the receiver. More generally, noise is also present; thus,

$$z(t) = y(t) + \sum_k y_k(t) + v(t)$$

In some cases, the interference is modeled as another Gaussian noise source. Then performance is characterized by the *signal-to-interference plus noise* (SINR) ratio, which is essentially $P_y/(P_i + P_v)$, where P_y is the power in the desired signal, P_i is the power in the sum of the interfering signals, and P_v is the power in the noise. Systems for which $P_i << P_v$ are called *noise-limited*, whereas those for which $P_v << P_i$ are called *interference-limited*. If the source of the interference is cross talk or co-channel interference, then the interfering signals $\{y_k(t)\}$ all have a structure (modulation, coding, etc.) similar to the desired signal. In this case, advanced signal processing algorithms can be used to mitigate the impact of the interference. Examples of algorithms include *joint demodulation*, in which all of the signals are demodulated simultaneously; *interference cancellation*, in which the interference is partially cancelled; and *optimum filtering*, in which filters are constructed that partially eliminate the interference. Removing or mitigating interference improves performance by reducing the required transmit power to achieve a given BER for a given data rate, by allowing the data rate at a given BER to be increased for a given transmit power, and by mitigating the effect of error floors.

Timing and Synchronization

Before demodulation and symbol recovery at the receiver, several timing and synchronization tasks need to be performed, including phase synchronization, frequency synchronization, symbol timing, and frame synchronization. Synchronization is performed to ensure that the transmitter and receiver operate in a synchronous manner.

The process of synchronization typically consists of first estimating the synchronization error and then correcting this error. Typically, the processing required for synchronization is done in a mixture of the analog and digital domains.

In bandpass systems, information is modulated onto sinusoids as illustrated in the QAM example in Equation 2. To demodulate this signal at the receiver, these sinusoids must be exactly reproduced. The problem of ensuring that the phases are accurate is known as *phase synchronization*. The problem of estimating the transmitted carrier frequency is known as *frequency synchronization*. Estimating and tracking the phase of the sinusoid is typically more difficult than the frequency, although phase differences can sometimes be included as part of the channel and removed during equalization.

At the receiver, the A/D converter samples the analog waveform for subsequent digital processing. Optimal processing requires two aspects of symbol synchronization: symbol timing and sampling clock recovery. *Symbol timing* is the problem of knowing exactly where to sample the received signal. Even in systems with ideal channels, symbol timing errors can lead to intersymbol interference because of timing errors. Often the symbol timing problem is solved by oversampling the received signal and choosing the best subsample. *Sampling clock recovery* refers to the problem of ensuring that the sampling period T_s at the receiver is identical to that at the transmitter. Sampling clock recovery is typically more important in baseband systems than in bandpass systems because in bandpass systems the sampling clock can be derived from the carrier.

In systems in which the fundamental unit of information is a frame and not a symbol, an additional synchronization step is required. This process, known as *frame synchronization*, is required to determine where the beginning of the frame is located. Frame synchronization is often assisted by the presence of synchronization sequences that mark the beginning of the frame.

Demodulation

The goal of the demodulator is to convert the sampled received waveform back into a sequence of bits. Of course, demodulation is highly dependent on the modulation and the channel; therefore, this section provides only a cursory overview.

For an ideal channel, with only an additive noise source, the first step in the demodulation process is to sample the waveform. Typically, this is done via a front-end filter that filters out unwanted noise, followed by a sampler. The sampled data come from an A/D converter, so the data are in the digital domain. The sampled signal includes residual noise left after filtering, the noise from the sampling device, and the signal of interest. For example, assuming perfect timing, synchronization, and no interference, in the presence of an ideal channel the sampled PAM signal at the receiver $y(nT_s)$ is

$$y[n] = x[n] + v[n]$$

where $x[n]$ is the transmitted PAM symbol, $v[n]$ represents the sampled thermal noise and the quantization noise. The samples $y[n]$ are sent through a decision device that processes the data to make a decision. Typically, the decision device determines the most likely symbol from the given constellation that was transmitted. An inverse symbol mapping operation then converts the symbols to bit form.

Because the noise is unknown to the receiver, the role of the decision device is to produce its best "guess" about the transmitted data. One common criterion is to find the symbol that is the most likely input given the observations. If X and Y are vectors representing the input $x[k]$ and the output $y[k]$, respectively, then

$$\hat{X} = \arg\max_X P(X|Y)$$

where $P(X \mid Y)$ is the probability that $x[k] = X$ given that observation of $Y = y[k]$. The maximization is taken over all possible points in the constellation to find the point with the maximum conditional probability and is called the *maximum a posteriori decision*. When the source data are equally likely, it turns out that this is equivalent to the *maximum likelihood detection rule*, which is given by:

$$\hat{X} = \arg\max_X P(Y|X)$$

In this case, the decision rule determines the symbol that was most likely to have produced the observation. For the *additive white Gaussian noise* (AWGN) channel, the above conditional probabilities have a known form.* For instance, when the input symbols are equally likely, it turns out that the detection principle is simply to minimize the Euclidean distance between the observation and the set of possible inputs

$$\hat{X}[k] = \arg\min_{x[k]\in C} \|y[k] - x[k]\|^2 \tag{3}$$

In this case, the detector is known as a *slicer*. The operation of the slicer can be described by Figure 4. For a QAM or PAM waveform, if a received sample is within a decoding boundary of a point, it is mapped to that point. Because of the simple decoding boundaries, the test is essentially a series of threshold tests and hence the name *slicer*.

Slicing is an example of what is known as *hard decoding*. In essence, this term means performing the detection operation in Figure 1 before the channel decoding. In many systems, the detection and channel decoding blocks work together to obtain a better estimate of the transmitted bit sequence. An example of this cooperative behavior is when the detector performs *soft decoding*. In this case, the output of the decoder, is bit likelihoods. Essentially, instead of outputting a 0 or 1 as performed in the slicing operation, a soft detector would output a number between $-\infty$ and $+\infty$, depending on how confident the detector is about the resulting decision. For example, a result of 0.0 might mean that the reliability of the decision is low. Advanced error-control codes such as turbo codes and low-density parity-check codes exploit soft detection as part of their decoding processes (Wicker and Kim 2002).

In the absence of an ideal channel, even with perfect timing and synchronization, there will be intersymbol interference; thus, the sampled PAM signal may have the form

$$y[n] = \sum_{l=0}^{L} h[l]x[n-l] + v[n] \tag{4}$$

where $h[l]$ is the sampled equivalent channel impulse response. Optimum decoding requires considering the channel response in the decision device. Because of the memory in the channel, it is no longer possible to make a decision on a symbol-by-symbol basis. Instead, sequences must be decoded. Thus, given a sequence of observations $\{y[p]\}_{p=0}^{P-1}$, we must determine the sequence $\{x[n]\}_{n=0}^{N-1}$, that was most likely to have been transmitted. We allow for $P \geq N$ at the receiver to account for multiple observations of the received signal via oversampling or multiple antennae, for example. Clearly, the complexity of the search grows with both N and P. Using the fact that memory of the channel is finite, however, allows lower complexity approaches such as the *Bahl, Cocke, Jelenick, and Raviv* (BCJR) *algorithm* to help in maximum a posteriori decoding and the *Viterbi algorithm* for maximum likelihood decoding (see, e.g., Wicker and Kim 2002 for details).

Alternatively, to correct for intersymbol interference, many transmission systems use equalizers that attempt to remove the effect of the channel before the slicing operation. Some common equalizers are *zero-forcing equalizers* (ZFEs) that invert the channel, *minimum mean square error* (MMSE) equalizers that include the effects of noise, and *decision feedback equalizers* (DFEs) that use the detected symbols to remove some portion of the trailing intersymbol interference. Equalization generally gives inferior performance relative to sequence decoding but offers much lower complexity.

One way to simplify linear equalizers is to use orthogonal frequency division multiplexing modulation. As described earlier, OFDM is a form of digital modulation in which information is sent on different subcarriers. OFDM is the modulation scheme of choice in wireless standards such as IEEE 802.11g and IEEE 802.16e. The key concept in OFDM is to create a circular convolution using a cyclic prefix. This allows equalization to be easily performed in the frequency domain courtesy of the fast Fourier transform operations. Using OFDM modulation, it is possible (after several mathematical manipulations) to create the effective input-output relationship

$$Y[n] = H[n]X[n] + V[n] \tag{5}$$

where $H[n] = \sum_{l=0}^{L} h[l] \exp(-j2\pi nl/N)$ and $\{X[n]\}_{n=0}^{N-1}$ are the N symbols transmitted in the OFDM symbol. It is clear that the equalization of Equation 5 is simple, only requiring $Y[n]/H[n]$ instead of the deconvolution operation in Equation 4. An interesting aspect of OFDM is that it can be combined with adaptive modulation, by which the constellation size is varied on each n in

---

*In the AWGN channel, there is no intersymbol interference and the only source of degradation is uncorrelated Gaussian noise.

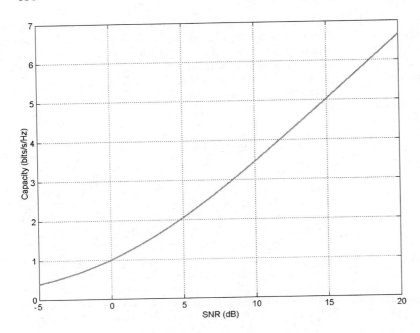

Figure 5: The normalized capacity of an AWGN channel as a function of the SNR

response to $H[n]$ to achieve especially high practical data rates.

A PERFORMANCE EXAMPLE

The AWGN channel provides an analytically tractable baseline case by which performance in other channels can be compared. First, consider the capacity of the AWGN channel. It can be shown in this case that the capacity expression is remarkably simple:

$$C = B \log_2(1 + SNR) \tag{6}$$

where B is the channel bandwidth. The theoretical spectral efficiency that can be achieved in this channel is thus C/B bits per second per hertz. The normalized capacity as a function of SNR is illustrated in Figure 5.

The capacity expression in Equation 6 provides an interesting means for evaluating system performance. For instance, if a coded system provides 3 dB of increased immunity to noise, then the SNR will increase by a multiple of $2 (10 \log_{10} 2 \cong 3\text{dB})$. Hence, the amount of information that can be transmitted will increase by approximately one bit per transmission for high SNR because $\log_2(1 + 2 \cdot SNR) \cong \log_2(2 \cdot SNR) \cong \log_2(SNR) + 1$.

Unlike the capacity, the symbol error rate in an AWGN channel is a function of the modulation scheme that is employed. For uncoded M-PAM or M-QAM transmission, the probability of symbol error is given by

$$P_e = 2 \left(1 - \frac{1}{M}\right) Q \left(\sqrt{\frac{3\, SNR}{M^2 - 1}}\right) \text{ for PAM} \tag{7}$$

$$= 4 \left(1 - \frac{1}{\sqrt{M}}\right) Q \left(\sqrt{\frac{3\, SNR}{M - 1}}\right) - 4 \left(1 - \frac{1}{\sqrt{M}}\right)^2 \left(Q \left(\sqrt{\frac{3\, SNR}{M - 1}}\right)\right)^2$$

for QAM
$$\tag{8}$$

where $Q(x) = 1/\sqrt{2\pi} \int_x^\infty e^{-t^2/2} dt$ for $x = 0$ is the area under the tail of the Gaussian probability distribution function. The probability of symbol error for QAM transmission is illustrated in Figure 6 as a function of SNR. Notice how the error rate exponentially decreases as the SNR increases. Observe that for a given probability of error (at high SNR), there is approximately a 6-dB difference between the SNR required for 4-QAM and 16-QAM or between 16-QAM and 64-QAM.

By inverting the formulas in Equation 7 and Equation 8 for a target probability of error, a useful expression for the maximum spectral efficiency obtained is

$$R = \log_2 \left(1 + \frac{SNR}{\Gamma}\right) \tag{9}$$

where the gap, Γ, can be calculated as a function of M and the target probability of error. Conveniently, Equation 9 allows direct comparison with the capacity in Equation 6. The gap, Γ, effectively determines the loss in capacity—that is, the gap between the actual spectral efficiency and the maximum spectral efficiency. Coded modulation schemes generally reduce the gap (toward the ultimate limit of $\Gamma = 1$). The effect of coding is most often expressed in dB as the coding gain, ΓdB making the effective gap smaller, so that $\Gamma_{db}^{new} = \Gamma_{db} - \Gamma_{db}$.

PRACTICAL DISCUSSION OF WIMAX: A DIGITAL COMMUNICATION STANDARD

WiMAX is a mobile standard that supports speeds beyond 120 km/hr, based on the IEEE 802.162005 standard (Ghosh et al. 2005). IEEE 802.16-2005 is a broad standard for broadband cellular communication and includes

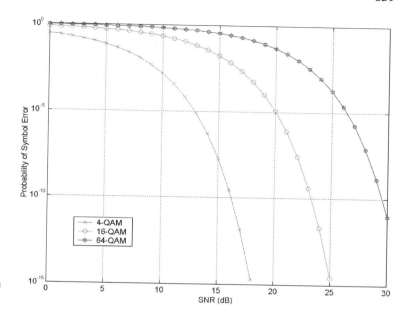

Figure 6: The symbol error rate for QAM transmission in an AWGN channel as a function of SNR

several different deployment options (fixed and mobile), different physical layer solutions, and several advanced communication techniques such as multiple antennae. WiMAX refers to a subset of IEEE 802.16-2005 functionality, agreed upon by an industry consortium known as the WiMAX Forum. WiMAX is perhaps the most cutting edge application of digital communication, at least wireless digital communication, so it is briefly summarized in this section. The purpose is to provide the reader with an appreciation of some of the advanced communication techniques that are on the verge of deployment in commercial wireless systems.

The WiMAX standard is based on the OFDM modulation and is used for reasons of ease of equalization as described earlier. The WiMAX waveform is special: It does not simply use OFDM, it uses multiple access over the OFDM waveform. This is known as *OFDM multiple access* (OFDMA). In OFDM, the band is converted into multiple frequency bins. In OFDMA, these frequency bins are mapped to users. The fundamental frequency unit is called a *subchannel*. For WiMAX, OFDMA has many modes of operation in which the subchannels may or may not be contiguous. For the mandatory mode of operation, the subcarriers are not contiguous. This is intended to give the transmitted data packet frequency diversity. Effectively, in a frequency-selective channel, it is unlikely that many of the subcarriers will be in a notch of the channel. Frequency diversity comes from the fact that the propagation channel is frequency-selective—that is, it varies as a function of location as illustrated in Figure 7.

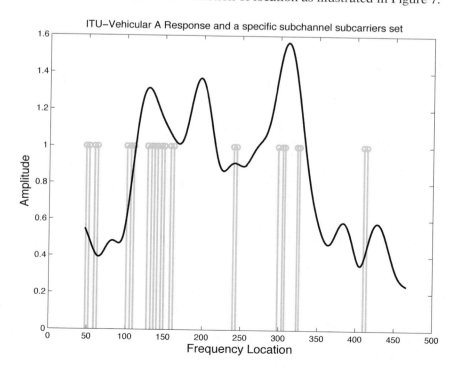

Figure 7: Frequency response of one realization of the ITU vehicular A channel. The stem plot illustrates OFDM subcarriers that are occupied by a given user

The standard WiMAX profile will also include many advanced features such as two-stream spatial multiplexing, beam forming, and convolutional turbo codes. *Spatial multiplexing* is a type of digital modulation used in *multiple-input, multiple-output* communication links. These are communication links with multiple transmit and multiple receive antennae. Spatial multiplexing sends independent information on different transmit antennae, effectively multiplexing the data pipes in space (Bolcskei 2006). *Two-stream spatial multiplexing* increases throughput by doubling the effective size of the constellation to a maximum of two 64-QAM symbols in one symbol period. *Beam forming* also uses multiple transmit antennae but uses them to send one data stream very reliably. Effectively, transmit beams are used to focus the energy at a desired user as a function of frequency. Beam forming can increase throughput by active interference cancellation and increasing the power at the subscriber. Finally, *convolutional turbo codes* are special error-correction codes that are extremely efficient. They use a combination of interleaving and iterative decoding to achieve extremely good error-rate performance. Convolutional coding is used to increase the overall coding gain over traditional convolutional codes.

CONCLUSION

Digital Communication plays an important role in delivering information in computer networks. The fundamentals of digital communication are easy to understand by viewing a digital communication system as a sequence of functions: encryption, source coding, channel coding, and modulation, and their inverse operations. Each forms an area of research and design in and of itself, and all are dealt with in more detail throughout this handbook. Digital communications continues to increase in relevance as our world continues to demand more computation and more information.

GLOSSARY

Analog Front End (AFE): The processing unit before the analog-to-digital converter.

Analog-to-Digital (A/D) Converter: A hardware block which converts analog signals to digital format.

Asymmetric Key Encryption: An encryption process that employs one key for the encryption process and a separate key for the decryption process.

Bandpass: A type of communication signal that has information modulated onto a carrier.

Baseband: A type of communication signal that does not have information modulated onto a carrier.

Bit Error Rate (BER): The average probability of bit error.

Capacity: The maximum data rate for which nearly errorless transmission can occur.

Carrier: Name for the high frequency sinusoid that shifts the spectrum of a baseband signal to higher frequencies, making it bandpass.

Channel Coding: The process of adding redundancy to the transmitted data stream for the purpose of improving resilience to errors caused by the channel.

Ciphertext: The information produced by the process of encryption.

Decryption: The process of transforming encrypted data to its original unencrypted form.

Demodulation: The process of extracting the transmitted digital data from the continuous waveform observed at the receiver.

Digital Signal Processing (DSP): A general name that includes all forms of operations on digital data.

Digital Signature: An encryption-based authentication method employing secret information used to affirm the origin of electronic documents.

Digital-to-Analog (D/A) Converter: This hardware block converts digital data into the analog domain.

Downconversion: Process of converting a bandpass signal to a baseband signal by removing the carrier frequency.

Encryption: The process of encoding data to prevent unauthorized access during transmission.

Field Programmable Gate Array (FPGA): A general purpose array of gates that can be configured by the end user for various applications.

IP Security: An Internet network layer security protocol providing authentication, confidentiality, and message integrity services.

Message Digest Function: An assumed one-way function whose domain is all positive integers and whose range is a set of fixed-length integers.

Modulation: The process of converting digital data to continuous waveforms for transmission on a communication medium.

Orthogonal Frequency Division Multiplexing (OFDM): A type of digital modulation scheme used to help simplify equalization in fading channels.

Plaintext: Information before the process of encryption.

Private Key: A key employed in asymmetric cryptography that is available only to its owner in the protocol.

Public Key: A key employed in asymmetric cryptography that is shared with all participants in the protocol.

Pulse Amplitude Modulation (PAM): A form of modulation in which data are encoded in the amplitude of one basis function.

Quadrature Amplitude Modulation (QAM): A form of modulation in which data is encoded in the amplitude of two basis functions.

Receiver Sensitivity: The minimum required signal level for a receiver to be able to demodulate the received signal.

Secure Socket Layer: An Internet application layer security protocol providing authentication, confidentiality, and message integrity services.

Signal-to-noise ratio (SNR): Essentially the ratio of the received signal power to the noise power.

Source: Generic name for the component that generates the information stream that is the input to the transmitter.

Source encoding: The process of removing redundancy from the information stream provided by the source.

Symbol: A representation of a set of bits in the digital or analog domain.

Symmetric key encryption: An encryption process that employs the same key for both encryption and decryption.

Synchronization: The process of ensuring that the transmitter and receiver operate in a synchronous manner.

Upconversion: Process of converting a baseband signal to a bandpass signal by increasing the carrier frequency.

CROSS REFERENCES

See *Digital Transmission; Frequency and Phase Modulation.*

REFERENCES

Anton, H., and C. Rorres. 1991. *Elementary linear algebra: Applications version.* 6th ed. New York: John Wiley & Sons.

Bolcskei, H. 2006. MIMO-OFDM wireless systems: Basics, perspectives, and challenges. *IEEE Wireless Communications,* 13(4): 31–7.

Bossert, M. 1999. *Channel coding for telecommunications.* New York: John Wiley & Sons.

Cioffi, J. M. Undated. EE 379A—Digital communication: Signal processing (retrieved from www.stanford.edu/class/ee379a/).

———. Undated. EE379B—Digital communication II: Coding (retrieved from www.stanford.edu/class/ee379b/).

———. Undated. EE 379C—Advanced digital communication (retrieved from www.stanford.edu/class/ee379c/).

Couch, L. W. II. 2001. *Digital and analog communication systems.* 6th ed. Upper Saddle River, NJ: Prentice Hall.

Cover, T. M., and J. A. Thomas. 1991. *Elements of information theory.* New York: Wiley-Interscience.

Ghosh, A., D. R. Wolter, J. G. Andrews, and R. Chen. 2005. Broadband wireless access with Wimax/802.16: Current performance benchmarks and future potential. *IEEE Communications Magazine,* 43(2): 129–36.

Hankerson, D., ed. 2000. *Coding theory and cryptography: The essentials.* 2nd ed. New York: Marcel Dekker.

Lee, E., and D. Messerschmitt. 1994. *Digital communication.* Norwell, MA: Kluwer Academic Publishers.

Lin, S., and D. J. Costello. 1982. *Error control coding: Fundamentals and applications.* Englewood Cliffs, NJ: Prentice Hall.

Mengali, U., and A. N. D'Andrea. 1997. *Synchronization techniques for digital receivers.* New York: Plenum.

Oppenheim, A. V., R. W. Schafer, and J. R. Buck. 1999. *Discrete-time signal processing.* 2nd ed. Upper Saddle River, NJ: Prentice Hall.

Proakis, J. G. 2000. *Digital communications.* 4th ed. New York: McGraw-Hill.

Sklar, B. 2000. *Digital communications.* 2nd ed. Upper Saddle River, NJ: Prentice Hall.

Stuber, G. L. 2001. *Principles of mobile communication.* 2nd ed. Norwell, MA: Kluwer Academic Publishers.

Wicker, S. B., and S. Kim. 2002. *Fundamentals of codes, graphs, and iterative decoding.* Norwell, MA: Kluwer Academic Publishers.

FURTHER READING

Digital communications is a broad area that draws on many different but related aspects of electrical engineering. Perhaps the standard academic references for digital communication are *Digital Communications* by John G. Proakis (2001) and *Digital Communication* by Edward Lee and David Messerschmitt (1994). The text *Digital Communications* by Bernard Sklar (2000) provides an intuitive presentation of the concepts of digital communications. Good online information by John Cioffi (undated) is also available. A good technical discussion of digital communication in wireless systems is found in *Principles of Mobile Communication* by Gordon L. Stuber (2001). *Coding Theory and Cryptography: The Essentials* (2000), a reference edited by Darrel Hankerson, provides a good introduction to cryptography, which is perhaps the most relevant aspect of security for digital communications. The standard reference for digital signal processing is *Discrete-Time Signal Processing* (1999) by Alan V. Oppenheim, Ronald W. Schafer, and J. R. Buck. For a basic reference on vector spaces, *Elementary Linear Algebra: Applications Version* (1991) by Howard Anton and Chris Rorres is a good text.

There are many advanced concepts in digital communication that were just barely covered. *Elements of Information Theory* (1991) by Thomas M. Cover and Joy A. Thomas, provides a more thorough introduction to information theory. *Synchronization Techniques for Digital Receivers* (1997) by Umberto Mengali and Aldo N. D'Andrea provides a current treatment of synchronization in digital communication systems. More detail is also available in other chapters of this handbook. Forward error correction is a topic that was only briefly mentioned yet is of significant importance. A classic reference is *Error Control Coding: Fundamentals and Applications* (1982) by Shu Lin and Dan J. Costello. A text that treats some current topics is *Fundamentals of Codes, Graphs, and Iterative Decoding* (2002) by Stephen B. Wicker and Saejoon Kim.

Current research in digital communication appears in a variety of journals, including the *IEEE Transactions on Communications* (www.comsoc.org/pubs/jrnal/transcom. html), the *IEEE Transactions on Signal Processing* (www. ieee.org/organizations/society/sp/), the *IEEE Transactions on Information Theory* (http://www.itsoc.org/publications/journals.htm), among others. Research in the areas of security and digital communication appears in these journals as well as the *ACM Transactions on Information and System Security* (www.acm.org/pubs/tissec/).

Digital Radio Broadcasting

Zhuojun Joyce Chen, *University of Northern Iowa*

INTRODUCTION

Radio broadcasting in the twentieth century was one of the public's main sources of information and entertainment. However, since the widespread acceptance of the compact disc, which was developed for music storage and easy replay, people have become aware of audio quality problems with traditional analog radio broadcasting. With the technological progression of television and computer audio systems, *digital radio broadcasting* (DRB) technologies have been developed for the broadcasting industry to transmit digital audio signals.

DRB services transmit digital radio programs and data services for fixed, portable, and mobile receivers by utilizing DRB technologies to encode audio signals and modulate radio frequencies digitally. DRB has the potential to provide digital radio signals with near-CD fidelity to radio listeners. It eliminates or greatly diminishes reception problems that exist in analog *frequency modulation* (FM) transmission, such as fades and interferences caused by multipath echoes, as well as signal-to-noise ratio problems in analog *amplitude modulation* (AM) transmission. It also supports multicasting and auxiliary data services, such as texts, graphics, and images. In the 1990s, two major DRB technologies have been developed and adopted for terrestrial radio broadcasting: Eureka 147 *digital audiobroadcasting* (DAB), which has been implemented in Europe, Canada, and Australia; and *in-band on-channel* (IBOC), which has been approved by the Federal Communication Commission (FCC) and licensed by radio stations in the United States. In addition, *satellite digital audio radio services* (SDARS) and audio Webcasting became part of digital radio broadcasting.

The Need for Digital Radio Broadcasting

Radio Broadcasting in Contemporary Society

Radio Listeners. Among all types of mass media, radio is still popular in serving the needs of people for entertainment, sports, and information. According to the FCC [Federal Communications Commission (FCC) 2007a], there were 18,739 broadcast radio station totals in the United States as of the end of 2006; they break down as follows:

AM stations	4754
FM commercial	6266
FM educational	2817
FM translators and boosters	4131
Low-power FM	771
Total	18,739

The total number of stations had increased by 409 in just one year, including ninety-six new stations in a low-power FM format that was a new radio service starting in 2005.

Radio reaches 93.7 percent of people each week, and 73.4 percent of people each day, among those aged 12 and older, according to the Radio Advertising Bureau (RAB) (2005). They listen an average of 19.5 hours each week, 2 hours 54 minutes each weekday, and 5 hours each weekend. Listening to radio has become an essential activity while driving automobiles, especially because of its portability and audible nature. According to the RAB report, people aged 12 and older spend 35.7 percent of their total listening time on their home radios, 45.7 percent on their car radios, and 18.6 percent on radios at work or other places during weekdays. Advertisers often use radio to convey information to potential consumers.

According to pretesting surveys, the key messages of major product categories—such as autos, beer, direct-to-consumer medicine, fast food, health and beauty aids, Internet services, and long-distance service—delivered by radio are more communicative to consumers than those from television. The synergy of combined radio and TV advertising is more effective than dual TV commercials for autos, beer, direct-to-consumer drugs, e-business, and travel. Even during prime-time TV hours, radio still reaches 54.6 percent of the population (Radio Advertising Bureau 2005).

Technological Challenges to Analog Radio Systems. AM and FM are the most used audio systems. However, because of the limitations of amplitude modulation technology, AM radio is vulnerable to both internal and external interferences that cause amplitude changes in the AM waveform. In addition, it has particular problems with atmospheric interference, which is heard as static, hiss, and other kinds of noises. The restricted bandwidth of AM systems, approximately ± 5 kHz, further limits the quality of sound. Moreover, because AM radio signals propagate through ground waves during daytime hours, the grounded conductive structures can change the amplitude and phase of an AM waveform, degrading the AM radio signal at the reception end. The daytime coverage area for many AM stations is less than 50 miles; a few powerful AM stations may reach 200 miles. At night, because ionosphere reflectivity increases, the AM signal is transmitted primarily through the reflection of sky waves from the ionosphere. The AM radio signal can reach distant areas thousands of miles away from an AM station, thus causing co-channel interference with stations in those areas that broadcast on the same carrier frequency as the distant AM station. The FCC requires AM stations to either cease operations after sunset or reduce power to avoid such interferences (FCC 2004). To reduce existing AM-band interference, in 1996 the FCC announced an expanded AM band (between 1605 MHz and 1705 MHz) and an eighty-seven station allotment plan for new assignments in the expanded band (FCC 1996).

By comparison with AM radio, FM radio provides higher audio fidelity and is not affected by amplitude interferences. However, there are weaknesses in the FM system. The FM signal is primarily vulnerable to multipath interferences: An original signal may be interfered with by its reflected signals, which cause nulling effects when the direct and reflected signals are received with nearly equal strength in a 180-degree phase shift. Or an original signal may be interfered with by its reflected signals arriving with short delays, resulting in audible interference (FCC 2004; Pohlmann 2000).

Although radio still is a popular medium, various digital audio products such as compact discs, mp3 players, and iPods have rapidly developed and widely occupied the market since the late 1990s. Although people are accustomed to analog radio services, these digital audio devices provide high-fidelity music and have stimulated listeners' desires for high-quality radio broadcasting. Therefore, digital radio broadcasting has become an inevitable demand of radio innovation. The research project aiming to develop DRB formats for the transition from traditional radio broadcasting to DRB began in the late 1980s and early 1990s (Pohlmann 2000).

Digital Audio Technology

Because human hearing is an analog process, analog audio signals need to be digitized for transmission in DRB, with a receiver converting the digital signals back to analog for listening. Sampling and digitizing are the principle processes involved in the conversion of a signal from analog to digital. *Pulse code modulation* (PCM) is the most widely used conversion technique (for details, see Chapter 26). PCM is a digital representation of an analog signal; only the presence or absence of a pulse is necessary to read a digital signal. By and large, a PCM signal can be regenerated without loss because any amplitude changes added on the pulse can be eliminated without affecting the presence or absence of the pulse. In addition, "depending on the sampling frequency and capacity of the channel, several PCM signals can be combined and simultaneously conveyed with time-division multiplexing" (Pohlmann 2000, 51). Along with the digital audio signal, the data for synchronization, error correction, and auxiliary data services can be multiplexed into a PCM stream for reproducing the analog audio signal in the receiver. Depending on the quality of application, the sampling rates used for digital audio are usually in a range from 8 kHz to 192 kHz.

The Development of Digital Radio Broadcasting

Digital radio technological research started in the late 1980s and early 1990s. The Eureka Project 147 was funded in 1987 by the European Commission to design a multiservice digital broadcasting system for fixed, portable, or mobile receivers using a nondirectional antenna. According to the European Telecommunications Standards Institute (ETSI), the Eureka DAB system can operate "at any frequency up to 3 GHz for mobile reception (higher for fixed reception) and may be used on terrestrial, satellite, hybrid (satellite with complementary terrestrial), and cable broadcast networks" [European Telecommunications Standards Institute (ETSI) 2000, 9]. The British Broadcasting Corporation (BBC) has adopted the Eureka 147 DAB technology to operate a *single frequency network* (SFN) digital radio broadcasting system in the United Kingdom. A 12.5-MHz band range of VHF band III spectrum from 217.5 MHz to 230 MHz has been allotted to the BBC for its DAB operations (Bower 1998; FCC 1999). Canada and other European countries are using the L band (1452 MHz to 1492 MHz) to operate Eureka digital broadcasting.

Although in the early 1990s the FCC was concerned about providing a terrestrial and satellite digital audio system in the United States, the commission did not think it was time to discuss DAB standard, testing, licensing, and policy. In 1991, USA Digital Radio Partners, L.P., was established by CBS Radio and the Gannett Co. to develop a digital radio broadcasting system. Westinghouse Electronic Corporation joined the partnership the same year. This partnership developed the IBOC DRB concept (FCC 1998). During the mid-1990s, the National Radio Systems

Committee (NRSC) in collaboration with the Consumer Electronics Manufacturers Association (CEMA, now the Consumer Electronics Association), tested several IBOC systems. However, no viable IBOC system was found not only to provide good quality audio performance but also to eliminate interferences caused by impaired signal conditions. CEMA also conducted the field test of a Eureka 147 system operating in the L band and concluded that the Eureka 147 technology was an ideal DAB system in comparison with other proposed DAB technologies. CEMA's report to the Commission states that of "all the systems tested, only the Eureka system offers the audio quality and signal robustness performance that listeners would expect from a new [DAB] service in all reception environments" (FCC 1999, 7).

However, the FCC did not have the available L-band and VHF band III spectra for implementing Eureka 147 system because L-band was "allocated for the purpose of flight test telemetry, and the spectrum around 221 MHz (in VHF band III) is allocated for the primary purposes of land mobile and amateur use" (FCC 1999, 7). In addition, the U.S. radio broadcasting industry was against adoption of a DRB system that required new spectra and preferred an "in-band" approach that would allow for a smoother transition from analog to digital services. In 1998, USA Digital Radio Partners changed its name to USA Digital Radio (USADR) and filed a petition for rule making that urged the commission to take regulatory steps toward implementing digital radio broadcasting (FCC 1998).

In November 1999, the FCC proposed criteria for evaluating and testing certain DAB systems and considering standard issues (FCC 1999). Subsequently, the DAB subcommittee of the NRSC conducted extensive laboratory tests on several IBOC DRB systems, including comprehensive field and laboratory tests of FM-band and AM-band IBOC systems.

In 2000, USADR merged with Lucent Digital Radio to form iBiquity Digital Corporation. In December 2001, the NRSC proposed that the FCC authorize iBiquity's FM IBOC system as an enhancement to FM broadcasting in the United States (National Radio Systems Committee 2006). The report suggested that the IBOC system bring "an efficient transition to digital broadcasting with minimal impact on existing analog FM reception and no new spectrum requirements" (FCC 1999, 4). In April 2002, the NRSC filed an AM IBOC report that recommended that iBiquity's AM IBOC "should be authorized as a daytime-only enhancement to AM broadcasting, pending further study of AM IBOC performance under nighttime propagation conditions" (FCC 1999, 4).

In October 2002, the FCC announced in its *Digital Audio Broadcasting Report and Order* (DAB R&O) that iBiquity's in-band on-channel technology would be adopted as the standard for DRB and authorized interim requirements for radio stations to initiate DRB voluntarily (FCC 2002b). However, the FCC restricted AM stations from nighttime IBOC operation. iBiquity launched its IBOC consumer brand, HD Radio™, and its commercial rollout to broadcasters began. In 2003, AM and FM stations licensed for HD Radio began DRB in the United States (FCC 2004). Based on iBiquity's AM nighttime IBOC tests, in 2004 the National Association of

Broadcasters (NAB) submitted a recommendation to the commission to permit nighttime AM broadcasts. In May 2007, the FCC extended the IBOC AM station operation hours to "include all hours during which a given station is currently authorized for analog operation, subject to the notification procedures established in the DAB R&O" (FCC 2007b).

The Advantages and Disadvantages of Digital Radio Broadcasting

Both digital and analog radio broadcasting methods have advantages and disadvantages.

Advantages of Digital Radio Broadcasting
- Service: DRB provides both audio and data services.
- Quality: DRB offers the potential to provide near-CD quality audio with higher interference protection.
- Economy: DRB audio and general data services can be offered for free or by subscription.
- Spectrum: DRB offers spectrum efficiency-for example, Eureka 147 allows single-frequency networks and IBOC uses existing frequency channels with the same bandwidth to provide multiple audio services per channel.
- Transmission power: DRB has improved power efficiency, requiring approximately 10 percent of the power of analog radio broadcasting.
- Compatibility: The IBOC system provides both backward and forward compatibility with existing analog broadcasting.

Disadvantages of Digital Radio Broadcasting
- Technical complications: DRB's processes for digital audio coding, modulation, radio frequency (RF) transmission coding, and decoding at the receiver require more expensive equipment for transmitting and receiving.
- Cost: Broadcasters need to invest in new equipment, and listeners need to purchase new radio sets.
- Spectrum: Eureka 147 requires new frequency allocations.
- Compatibility: Eureka 147 radio is an all-digital service. Its receivers are not compatible with analog services.

The following are reasons why listeners in the United States will adopt HD Radio while analog radio remains available.

- There is a replacement cycle. According to iBiquity studies, consumers replace radio sets every ten to fifteen years because they are either out of fashion or dysfunctional.
- Consumers desire better-quality radio programs. HD Radio AM provides near-FM quality, and HD Radio FM can provides near-CD quality. In addition, FM IBOC supports *multicasting*—that is, it allows two or more audio services per channel.
- HD Radio provides free services to listeners. Although satellite radio delivers multichannel CD-quality programs, it charges monthly fees.

- HD Radio broadcasts programs via airwaves. It is more convenient, especially in a mobile situation, than CD or DVD players or mp3 or iPod players. Listeners must carry CDs and DVDs, and mp3 and iPod players require that consumers have the skills to install files.
- HD Radio helps consumers and broadcasters transition smoothly from analog to hybrid (i.e., simulcast digital and analog) radio and finally to all-digital broadcasting.
- Professional organizations such as the HD Digital Radio Alliance provide incentive for adoption, including technical training and strong marketing support to radio stations in the transition process.

The details will be described in the relevant sections.

DIGITAL RADIO BROADCASTING

The technical processes of digital radio broadcasting include audio compression, transmission coding, modulation, and multiplexing. In this chapter, the focus is on how those technical processes are utilized to achieve the various goals of digital radio broadcasting; the detailed technical concepts are described in other chapters of this handbook. However, a few key terms such as *perceptual audio coding, interleaving, phase shift keying, quadrature amplitude modulation,* and *orthogonal frequency division multiplexing* are briefly reviewed before the discussion on the digital radio broadcasting systems.

Technical Foundation of Digital Radio Broadcasting

Perceptual Audio Coding

Perceptual coding of digital audio, or *psychoacoustical coding,* is used to compress the digital audio signal. This technique is based on the spectral and temporal characteristics of the human auditory system. There exists a theoretical threshold curve of human audibility responding to the audio spectrum from 20 Hz to 20 kHz and a theoretical amplitude masking effect (*psychoacoustic masking*). The amplitude masking effect occurs when a louder tone shifts the threshold upward in a frequency region surrounding this tone (see Figure 1). The louder tones

can completely block the softer tones within the range of the frequencies nearby (Bower 1998; Pohlmann 2000).

Based on perceptual coding techniques, a digital audio compression system only codes the audio signal components that the human ear is able to perceive and disregards the components that the ear does not sense, such as a frequency below the intensity threshold level or a frequency blocked by a nearby louder tone. Perceptual coding can also be tailored to the audio quality required by a specific type of audio service. Different bit rates can be used to code speech, sports, stereo music, and other kinds of music. For example, the bit rate of 6 kbps can be used for a monophonic channel and 1024 kbps for a 5.1-channel format (Pohlmann 2000). The BBC is using 192 kbps for its national network stereo radio service and 9 kbps or lower rates for BBC Radio Five Live sports commentaries and Parliament coverage (Bower 1998).

Interleaving

Interleaving is used in a predetermined manner on error corrections for transmission. The output of interleaving is structured in a matrix format. Each matrix is the combination of the audio or data service's signal and the information associated with a specific portion of the transmitted spectrum (Johnson 2000; Peyla 2000). The matrix signal is reassembled in the receiver to reproduce the digital audio. Interleaving techniques involve either dispersing data randomly or adding redundant data in both time and frequency domains. A convolutional interleaver has memory; that is, its operation depends not only on current symbols but also on previous symbols (diversity delayed symbols) (Johnson 2000; Peyla 2000; Pohlmann 2000).

Phase Shift Keying

Phase shift keying (PSK) techniques are commonly used in digital signal modulation. There are orders of PSK such as *binary phase shift keying* (BPSK), *quadrature phase shift keying* (QPSK), and higher-order PSK (8-PSK and 16-PSK), depending on the number of bits transmitted per modulation symbol. A one-bit digital signal applies a binary PSK. In BPSK, two modulation phase shifts represent two states of the PCM binary signal; a binary 0 places

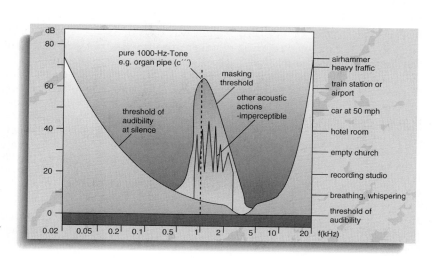

Figure 1: Psychoacoustic masking (Eureka 147 Project 1997)

the carrier in phase 0 degrees, and a binary 1 places the carrier in phase 180 degrees (Pohlmann 2000). The digital symbol rate equals the transmission carrier rate. In QPSK, four phase shifts are used to represent two bits per symbol—that is, 00 places the carrier at 0 degrees, 10 at 90 degrees, 11 at 180 degrees, and 01 at 270 degrees. The digital symbol rate is one-half of the carrier rate. In many circumstances (e.g., Gaussian white noise RF environment) PSK signals generate the lowest *bit error rate* (BER) for a given signal strength (Pohlmann 2000).

QSPK is the most widely used PSK digital modulation method. A QPSK-modulated signal transmitting at 400 kpbs would require a bandwidth between 200 kHz and 400 kHz. The bandwidth for a M-PSK signal is given between $D/\log_2 M$ and $2D/\log_2 M$, where D is the data rate and M is the order of PSK such as in binary ($M = 2$) and in quadrature ($M = 4$) (Pohlmann 2000).

Quadrature Amplitude Modulation

Quadrature amplitude modulation (QAM) is a modulation scheme that uses two orthogonal carriers of the same frequency for amplitude modulation. The phase shift between these two carriers is exactly 90 degrees. Each carrier is amplitude-modulated independently, and the two carriers are combined and transmitted before being separated by demodulation at the receiver. Similarly to PSK, there are 4-QAM (2 bits), 16-QAM (4 bits), 64-QAM (6 bits), and 256-QAM (8 bits). The most used QAMs are 16-QAM (for data) and 64-QAM (for audio signals) (ETSI 2001c; Johnson 2000).

Orthogonal Frequency Division Multiplexing

Orthogonal frequency division multiplexing (OFDM) is an aggregation of a large number of orthogonal subcarriers. The OFDM processing divides the transmitted digital signal into many low bit-rate data streams. It provides a parallel modulation scheme in which the low bit-rate data streams modulate those orthogonal subcarriers, and the modulated subcarriers are transmitted simultaneously (Johnson 2000). The individual subcarriers are typically modulated using the already mentioned PSK or QAM techniques.

Technological Approaches to Digital Radio Broadcasting

In Europe, the Eureka 147 DAB system was developed under the Eureka 147 Project and standardized by the European Telecommunications Standards Institute in 1995. The BBC is operating a single-frequency network Eureka 147 DAB to cover the entire United Kingdom. SFNs using Eureka 147 DAB can be implemented in terrestrial, satellite, or hybrid systems. The Eureka 147 DAB system has also been widely adopted by radio stations in other European countries, Canada, Australia, and several regions in Asia and Africa. The Eureka 147 DAB system is able to simultaneously broadcast five or more high-quality audio channels and various audio-based multimedia services such as text, graphics, and still pictures. It provides opportunities for listeners to receive multimedia radio with pictures and Web pages. Based on the characteristics of the European community, the Eureka 147 technology is well designed to cover a region or area

where a hybrid satellite and terrestrial system can be used for broadcast. For example, a single satellite system's footprint covers the main area, and terrestrial transmitters or repeaters operating on the same frequency are used to fill in the gaps.

Another system is a terrestrial DRB system, the IBOC system, developed in the United States. In October 2002, the FCC (FCC 2002b) approved the IBOC as the technology for U.S. digital radio broadcasting. In 2004, the FCC summarized the IBOC technology as follows:

> iBiquity's IBOC DAB technology provides for enhanced sound fidelity, improved reception, and new data services. IBOC is a method of transmitting near-CD quality audio signals to radio receivers along with new data services such as station, song and artist identification, stock and news information, as well as local traffic and weather bulletins. This technology allows broadcasters to use their current radio spectrum to transmit AM and FM analog signals simultaneously with new higher quality digital signals. These digital signals eliminate the static, hiss, pops, and fades associated with the current analog radio system. IBOC was designed to bring the benefits of digital audio broadcasting to analog radio while preventing interference to the host analog station and stations on the same channel and adjacent channels. IBOC technology makes use of the existing AM and FM bands (In-Band) by adding digital carriers to a radio station's analog signal, allowing broadcasters to transmit digitally on their existing channel assignments (On-Channel). iBiquity IBOC technology will also allow for radios to be "backward and forward" compatible, allowing them to receive traditional analog broadcasts from stations that have yet to convert and digital broadcasts from stations that have converted. Current analog radios will continue to receive the analog portions of the broadcast. (FCC 2004, 2–3)

The HD Radio system (the trademark of iBiquity Digital Corporation's IBOC implementation) is suitable for independent radio stations to broadcast digital radio programs plus data services on their original licensed frequencies. Listeners receive free radio service as well. According to the FCC, as of October 1, 2003, more than 280 radio stations were licensed to iBiquity's technology, which have either begun digital audio broadcasting or were in the process of conversion (FCC 2004). As of late September 2005, 909 radio stations were licensed and 505 had implemented HD Radio on the air, with 28 stations having multiple broadcast channels. Three months later, in December 2005, the licensed stations were up to 1044, on air stations had increased to 703, and multicast stations were 202, which was almost 8 times of the number in September (refer to Table 6).

Other systems also deliver digital audio through direct broadcast satellites such as XM and Sirius in North America, WorldSpace for international satellite radio services, and over the Internet through Webcasting, mp3 and iPod players, and mobile phones.

Eureka 147 DAB System

The Eureka 147 DAB system is designed to provide all-digital audiobroadcasting for mobile, portable, and fixed receivers without the need for a directional antenna. Upon the test results, the Consumer Electronic Manufacturers Association in the United States and the European Telecommunication Standard Institute report that the Eureka 147 system offers reliable and high-fidelity audio with multiple data services. Technically, it can be operated at any spectrum allocation up to 3 GHz for mobile reception, and it can be used for broadcasting on terrestrial, satellite, hybrid, and cable broadcast networks. It can be operated as a single-frequency network in terrestrial or hybrid broadcasting. The recommended spectrums for the Eureka 147 DAB system are: 47.9 MHz to 67.0 MHz for VHF band I, 174.9 MHz to 239.2 MHz for VHF band III, and UHF L band (1452 MHz to 1492 MHz). The BBC's national digital radio services are broadcast as an SFN. This means all the DAB transmitters transmit the BBC multiplexed signals on the same frequency at 225.648 MHz (block 12B of VHF band III) with a bandwidth of 1.54 MHz [British Broadcasting Corporation (BBC) 2006a]. The Eureka DAB system is a highly spectrum- and power-efficient sound and data broadcasting system.

The BBC adopted the Eureka 147 system and began its DAB broadcasts in London in September 1995, operating from five transmitters on a single-frequency network to provide simulcasting of national services on Radio 1, Radio 2, Radio 3, Radio 4, Radio Five Live, and BBC World Service channels (BBC 2006b). In spring 1998, the BBC's national

SNF comprised twenty-seven transmitters that provided BBC's national digital radio services to more than 60 percent of the UK population and served major motorway and road routes (BBC 2006b). In February 2002, the BBC launched its first national digital only radio station, BBC Five Live Sports Extra in the United Kingdom, and subsequently added four new DAB services (1Xtra, 6 Music, BBC 7, and Asian Network) in the same year (BBC 2006d).

A Technical Diagram of Eureka 147 DAB System

A conceptual block diagram of the Eureka 147 DAB system is shown in Figure 2. The top part demonstrates the conceptual process of DAB signals. Each service signal of audio or data is encoded individually at the source level—that is, by an audio encoder or a data encoder. In the channel encoder and time interleaver, each encoded source ensemble is processed with error-correction and interference-protection techniques; the output signal of the interleaving process is a channel of either digital audio or data service. Then all of the channels are multiplexed together with associated service information in the *multiplexer* (MUX). The multiplexer output consists of frequency-interleaved audio and data signals with multiplex control and service information into the *main service channel* (MSC), which is of a predetermined but changeable service configuration. The service information of the multiplexer controller is called the *multiplex configuration information* (MCI). It travels through a *fast information channel* (FIC) that does not pass through the time interleaver in order to avoid the delay generated

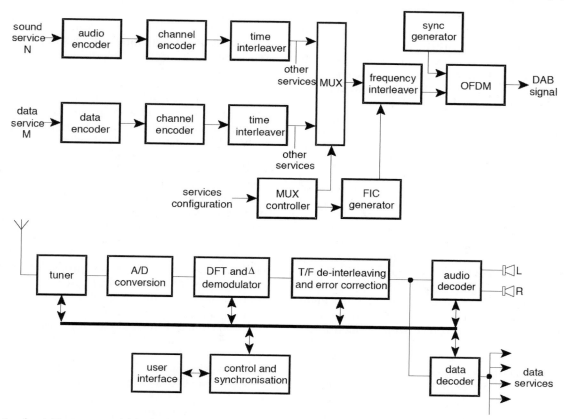

Figure 2: Eureka 147 conceptual block diagram © European Telecommunications Standards 2000. © European Broadcasting Union 2000. Further use, modification, redistribution is strictly prohibited. ETSI standards are available from http://pda.etsi.org/pda/ and http://www.etsi.org/services_products/freestandard/home.htm

by time interleaving. The signals from the MSC and FIC channels are combined with rugged synchronization symbols to form transmission frames. Finally, the digital signals in the transmission frames are modulated with the differential QPSK scheme onto a number of orthogonal frequency division multiplexed subcarriers to generate the DAB transmission signal.

The bottom part of Figure 2 shows a conceptual receiver where the transmitted DAB signal is selected and filtered through a tuner and then downconverted to a multiplexed digital stream, including the wanted DAB ensemble, synchronization data, service information, and other data. The digital stream is then filtered and demodulated. The subsequent stages are the time and frequency de-interleaving processes and error correction used to recover the coded audio programs and service data. The system controller is connected to a user interface that processes the user's commands to retrieve the information in the FIC, which is associated with the program the user is searching. Then the data of the requested program are further processed in an audio decoder, producing the left and right audio signals of the program. The associated program data, such as lyrics and song titles, are recovered in a data decoder.

Multiple Audio and Data Services

The system supports multicasting. The transmitted DAB signal carries a multiplex of various digital services simultaneously, including multichannel radio programs and associated data and other data service. For example, the BBC's national DAB radio uses an SFN for its nationwide broadcasting. It includes eleven channels of radio programs: Radio 1, 2, 3, and 4; 1Xtra, Radio Five Live, Five Live Sports Extra, 6 Music, BBC 7, Asian Network, and World Service. The data services are provided on a small screen and include information about the current program on the radio, such as a plot summary of a play, the name of a track currently being played, e-mail addresses, up-to-the-minute sports results, and competition details. Some of the latest DAB products can pick up a broadcast electronic program guide that provides free, useful program information for as many as seven days before a broadcast, allowing users to program the receiver to record a particular program—or even an entire series of a program—automatically (BBC 2006b).

Audio Encoder. The audio coding techniques used in Eureka 147 is based on a perceptual coding principle. They use advanced digital techniques to remove redundancy and perceptually irrelevant information from the audio source signal. The low bit-rate sub-band coding system used to deliver high-quality audio signals is standardized by the International Organization for Standardization (ISO) and International Electrotechnical Commission (IEC) under the heading ISO/IEC 11172-3 (MPEG-1 audio), and ISO/IEC 13818-3 (MPEG-2 audio) layer 2. Different encoded bit-rate options (e.g., 8, 16, 24, 32, 40, 48, 56, 64, 80, 96, 112, 128, 144, 160 or 192 kbit/s per monophonic channel) are available in the system, and it is possible to provide multichannel sound. Broadcasters can take advantages of these options, depending on the intrinsic quality required

and the number of sound programs to be broadcast (ETSI 2000).

Types of Data. The MSC includes multiple audio service channels, *program-associated data* (PAD), and possible additional data. The PAD are included in each audio service channel, having a variable capacity (minimum 0.333 kbit/s for MPEG-2 audio half-sampling frequency coding or 0.667 kbit/s for full sampling frequency coding), and can be used to convey information linked to the radio program, such as program titles or lyrics, and speech or music indication, as well as text with graphics features. The PAD are incorporated at the end of a DAB audio frame and should not be subject to a different transmission delay (ETSI 2000).

The *multiplex configuration information* is the information that defines the configuration of the main service multiplex. The MCI contains current and forthcoming (in the case of an imminent reconfiguration) details about the services, service components, and subchannels and the linking between these objects. It also includes the identification of the DAB ensemble and a mark of date and time.

Service information (SI) includes data for categorizing (such as basic program service label, time and date, language, and program-type label) and data for monitoring or controlling (such as cross-reference and transmitter identification).

Data for other services, such as the traffic message channel, can be in the form of a continuous stream that can be time-interleaved with audio service data or arranged as packet data services.

Channel Coding and Time Interleaving. The data that represent each of the audio services are processed through energy dispersal scrambling, convolutional coding, and time interleaving. The convolutional encoding process involves adding redundancy to the service data. There are two kinds of error protection: *equal error protection* (EEP) and *unequal error protection* (UEP), which is done by following a preselected pattern. In DAB, for the bit rates of 8, 16, 24, 40 and 144 kbit/s that can be used by MPEG-2 audio half-sampling frequency coding, only EEP can be applied. For audio source-encoded bits that need greater protection than other signals, the UEP profiles are applied. The average code rate, defined as the ratio between the number of audio source-encoded bits and the total number of encoded bits after convolutional encoding, can take a value from 0.35 (the highest protection level) to 0.75 (the lowest protection level). Different average code rates can be applied to different audio sources, subject to the protection level required and the bit rate of the audio source-encoded data. For example, the protection level of audio services carried by cable networks can be lower than that of services transmitted in RF channels. General data services are convolutionally encoded using one of the selected uniform rates. The data carried in the FIC are encoded at a constant 1/3 rate. Time interleaving improves the ruggedness of data transmission in a changing environment (e.g., reception condition in a moving vehicle) but results in a 384 ms transmission delay (ETSI 2000).

Main Service Multiplexer. These encoded and interleaved DAB ensembles (audio programs and data services) are fed to the MUX. In each 24 ms, the data are gathered sequentially into a multiplex frame. The combined bit-stream output from the multiplexer—the MSC—has a gross capacity of 2.3 Mbit/s. Depending on the chosen convolutional code rate, the added protection redundancy can be different from one application to another. Therefore, the net bit rate ranges from approximately 1.7 to 0.6 Mbit/s, accommodated in a DAB signal with a 1.536 MHz bandwidth. At the MUX, all of the program services going through the multiplexing process are brought together and synchronized before the transmission modulation (ETSI 2000).

Fast Information Channel. The FIC is designed to carry the multiplex configuration information, which is accurate and timely information about the current and future content of the MUX. Essential SI items that are associated with the content of the MSC (i.e., for programming selection) must also be carried in the FIC.

The data carried by the FIC are not time-interleaved. It is frequency-interleaved with the MSC ensemble before combining with synchronization for the OFDM modulation. The data carried by FIC are highly protected and frequently repeated to ensure their ruggedness so that a receiver can gain access to any or all of the individual services with a minimum overall delay. When the multiplex configuration is about to change, the new information, together with the timing of the change, is sent in advance within the MCI (ETSI 2000).

Transmission

Transmission Modes. The system provides four transmission modes that allow the use of a wide range of transmitting frequencies, as high as 3 GHz, for mobile reception. These transmission modes are designed to cope with Doppler spread and delay spread for mobile reception in the presence of multipath echoes. Table 1 compares the four transmission mode options for mobile reception in terms of the temporal guard interval duration, nominal maximum transmitter separation, and transmission frequency range (ETSI 2000).

As shown in Table 1, the use of higher frequencies allows smaller guard interval duration and shorter distance between transmitters. Mode I is most suitable for a terrestrial SFN in VHF bands because it allows the greatest distance between transmitters. Mode II can be used for medium-scale SFN in L band and is preferable for local radio applications that require one terrestrial transmitter. Mode III is appropriate for cable, satellite, and complementary terrestrial transmission at all frequencies and for mobile reception at all frequencies up to 3 GHz. This mode has the greatest protection from phase noise. Mode IV is also used in L band and allows greater transmitter spacing in SFNs. However, it is not good for mobile reception because it is less resistant to degradation at higher vehicle speeds (ETSI 2000).

Transmission Frames. To facilitate receiver synchronization, the transmitted signal is built with a frame structure having a fixed sequence of symbols. Each transmission frame encompasses at least three information channels: synchronization channel, fast information channel, and main service channel (see Figure 2). The total frame duration, T_F, varies—including 96 ms, 48 ms, or 24 ms—depending on the selected transmission mode as shown in Table 2 and Figure 3.

The synchronization channel begins with a null symbol with no carrier that is transmitted as an initial synchronization of the frame, followed by a phase reference symbol for differential PSK demodulation.

The FIC includes the MCI and some essential SI associated with the MSC.

The major space of the frame provides the main service channel for the audio programming. The MSC can be a multichannel casting along with other data services. Each audio service within the MSC is allotted with a fixed time slot in the frame. At the beginning of each radio channel, there is a guard interval duration inserted to prevent the reception from multipath fading and interferences. The length of guard interval duration varies, depending on the transmission mode used for the DAB (see Table 2). As an example, the frequency domain of mode III transmission is shown in Figure 3 (ETSI 2000).

The diagrams in Figure 4 show the transmission frames for different transmission modes (ETSI 2001b).

PSK Modulation with OFDM. Phase shift keying is a modulation scheme, and OFDM governs the internal relationship between carriers. The basic process is to divide the digital audio signal into a large number of bit streams that individually have low bit rates (see Figure 5). These digital bit streams are then modulated individually in a PSK scheme (e.g., BPSK or QPSK) onto the carriers that are orthogonal frequency divided. The large number, N, of orthogonal carriers, referring to Table 2 and Figure 4,

Table 1: Parameter Values of Transmission Frame for Each Mode (Eureka 147)

System parameter	Transmission Mode			
	I	II	III	IV
Guard interval duration (µs)	~246	~62	~31	~123
Nominal maximum transmitter separation for SFN (km)	96	24	12	48
Nominal frequency range (for mobile reception)	≤ 375 MHz	≤ 1.5 GHZ	≤ 3 GHz	≤ 1.5 GHz

Source: © ETSI 2000

Table 2: Transmission Parameters for Each Mode (Eureka 147)

System parameter	Transmission Mode			
	I	II	III	IV
Frame duration, T_F (ms)	96	24	24	48
Null symbol duration, T_{null} (µs)	~1297	~324	~168	~648
Guard interval duration, t_Δ (µs)	~246	~62	~31	~123
Useful symbol duration, t_s	1 ms	250 µs	125 µs	500 µs
Total symbol duration, T_s (µs)	~1246	~312	~156	~623
Number of radiated carriers, N	1536	384	192	768

Source: © ETSI 2000

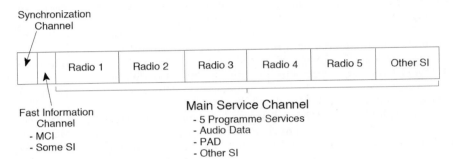

Figure 3: Transmission frame diagram (© ETSI 2000)

can be conveniently generated by a fast Fourier transform process.

The spectrum of the RF output signal is approximately rectangular and Gaussian noiselike, and it occupies a bandwidth of approximately 1.54 MHz (refer to Figure 5). Figure 6 shows an example of the transmitter output spectrum after amplification and filtering. In practice, the peak-to-mean ratio is limited to approximately 8 dB by digital processing. This can be further reduced by additional signal conditioning when coupled with nonlinear amplification in the transmitter (ETSI 2000).

Unique Features of Eureka 147
Prevention from Multipath Interferences. Three main techniques are used in Eureka 147 to alleviate degenerations caused by multipath fading and interferences. In the first, in the presence of multipath propagation, some of the carriers are enhanced by constructive signals, while others suffer destructive interference (frequency selective fading). Therefore, the system provides frequency interleaving by a rearrangement of the digital bit stream among the carriers so that successive source samples are not affected by a selective fade. When the receiver is stationary, the diversity in the frequency domain is the prime means of ensuring successful reception; the time diversity provided by time interleaving provides further assistance to a mobile receiver (ETSI 2000). The second technique uses convolutional coding by adding closely controlled redundancy as the UEP to the signal to be transmitted, providing strong error protection. In the third technique,

a guard interval duration is inserted before each audio data stream, which is longer than the delay to prevent the multipath interferences (ETSI 2000).

Spectrum Efficiency. Efficient spectrum utilization is achieved by (1) frequency interleaving, which supports the use of multiple subcarries for sound coding; (2) time interleaving, which supports the ensemble of low bit rates for sound encoding; and (3) a special feature of frequency reuse, which permits transmitters carrying the same MSC within a broadcasting network to be operated on the same radiated frequency; it is known as the single frequency network. In this case, a gap filler transmitter receives and retransmits the signal on the same frequency without the processes of demodulation and remodulation.

Power Efficiency. Because digital audio transmission using PSK modulation (such as QPSK) and coded OFDM is more immune to amplitude noises and multipath interferences, it is much more power-efficient than analog audio transmission. In the Eureka 147 system, the SFNs tend to have relatively low-powered transmitters (e.g., typically below 10 kW) (ETSI 2001a).

Hybrid Terrestrial Digital Radio Broadcasting: In-Band On-Channel

In-band on-channel was developed by the iBiquity Digital Corporation and approved as the digital radio broadcasting technology by the FCC (FCC 2002b). HD Radio

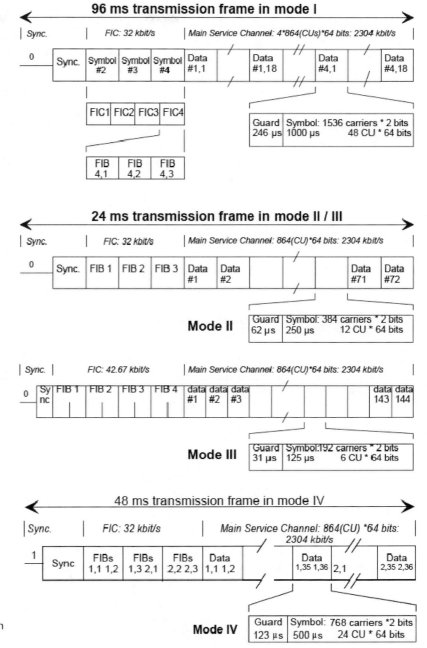

Figure 4: Structure of transmission frame in Eureka 147 (ETSI 2001b, 27)

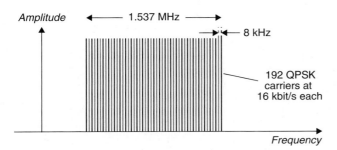

Figure 5: The Eureka 147 signal in the frequency domain (mode III) (Evens 1998, 3)

provides enhanced sound fidelity (near-CD quality), improved reception, and new data services, such as station call letters, song titles, artist identification, stock and news information, and local traffic and weather bulletins.

IBOC is designed to permit a smooth evolution from current analog radio broadcasting to fully digital radio broadcasting. It allows broadcasters to use their current radio spectrum to transmit AM or FM analog signals simultaneously with new digital radio services to mobile, portable, and fixed receivers from terrestrial transmitters on existing AM or FM radio broadcasting channels. The IBOC technology is developed to eliminate the static, hiss, pops, and fades associated with current analog radio

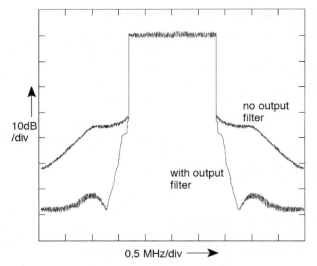

Figure 6: Eureka 147 transmitter output spectrum (ETSI 2000, 15)

that have converted. On the other hand, analog radio receivers continue to receive the analog portions carried by IBOC transmission signals. Moreover, the hybrid IBOC system ensures a "seamless switching from digital to analog reception when the received signal quality is not sufficient for digital audio reception or when digital packets in the DAB signal are corrupted" (National Radio Systems Committee 2005, 8). It is also used for fast channel changes, allowing the receiver to demodulate and play out the analog programming first and then "blend" to its digital version of the same program.

IBOC System Overview

Figure 7 shows the technical flowchart of the IBOC digital radio broadcast system, including three major subsystems specified by NRSC-5-A standard (National Radio Systems Committee 2005): (1) audio and data coding, (2) transport and multiplexing, and (3) RF and transmission.

The basic coding techniques used in the IBOC system for audio coding, error correction, multiplexing, and digital modulation are similar to those used in the Eureka 147 system. The audio coding scheme used in the HD Radio implementation is called "HDC," is proprietary to iBiquity Digital Corporation, and is not specified in the NRSC-5-A standard. However, because IBOC uses the existing analog channel and bandwidth to transmit digital radio signals, the bandwidth limitation and the enclosed analog signals make the transmission process in the IBOC system much more complicated than that in the

systems and to prevent interference to the host analog station and co-channel interference for stations operating on the same frequency channel as well as interference with adjacent channels. It also allows HD Radio receivers to be both backward- and forward-compatible, receiving traditional analog radio broadcasting from stations that have yet to convert and digital broadcasting from stations

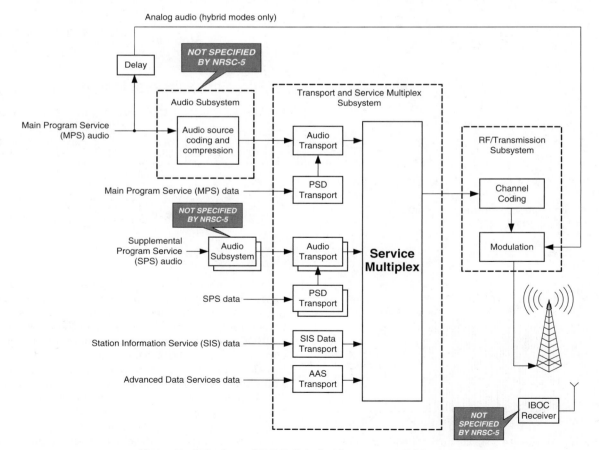

Figure 7: Overview of IBOC digital radio system (NRSC, 2005)

Eureka 147 DAB system. In the following, the discussion is focused on the RF and transmission subsystem.

Audio and Data Input Subsystems

Audio Services. For *main program service* (MPS) audio coding, there is no specific audio coding scheme standardized for the IBOC system. However, the iBiquity HDC technique is the only system to date used in any implementation of the NRSC-5-A standard.

MPS data (MPSD) are program service data associated with the MPS audio and will be integrated into the MPS packet for transmission. *Supplemental program service audio* (SPSA) is the additional program for option.

Supplemental program service (SPS) data are program service data associated with the SPSA and will be integrated into the SPSA packet for transmission.

Each audio service (either the main program service or each individual supplemental program service) has its own source coding, compression, and transport subsystem.

Data Services.

Station information service (SIS) data includes necessary radio station control and identification information such as station call letter and sign identification.

Advanced data services (ADS) include (1) visual effects associated with MPS, SPS, or SIS services; (2) multimedia presentations with audio, text, and image for stock, news, weather, and other entertainment programming; (3) local storage of content for time shifting; (4) targeted advertising; and (5) traffic updates.

Advanced application services is the transport mechanism used to support transmission of ADS and was developed by iBiquity Digital Corporation.

Transport and Service Multiplex Subsystem

The signal processes in the transport and service multiplex subsystems are described as follows.

1. They receive signals and organize audio and data signals into packets, including the packet integrating the main audio program data with the main program service data, the packet of the station information service data, and other packets for advanced data service.

2. They multiplex the main audio program packets into a single data stream together with supplemental program service data and station information data, as well as error detection and addressing (Johnson 2000).

3. In hybrid modes, the RF carrier is directly modulated by the analog audio signal for conventional analog receivers. The analog audio does not pass through the audio compression coding, transport, and multiplexing subsystems, so it needs to be delayed so that the analog audio signal is arriving at the receiver about the same time as the digital signal. This feature ensures that a user can listen to the same program by switching the receiver between analog mode and digital mode. When the signal received in one mode is not good, the receiver can switch to the other mode.

RF Transmission Subsystem

The RF transmission subsystem is called layer 1 in the IBOC technical documents. The output from this subsystem is the complete IBOC radio frequency waveform for transmission. The waveform is spectrally mapped and frequency partitioned across the set of OFDM subcarries (National Radio Systems Committee 2005).

According to the FCC, to prevent reception from interchannel interferences, radio stations in the same local area are not licensed to adjacent channels. The frequencies of those stations are usually two or three channels apart. Therefore, the AM analog radio stations are allotted in 10-kHz (±5 kHz) spacing but can operate within a 20-kHz (±10 kHz) bandwidth. The FM radio stations are licensed in 200 kHz (±100 kHz) spacing but can operate within a 400-kHz (±200 kHz) bandwidth. In IBOC, the hybrid AM broadcasting is operated within ±15 kHz bandwidth, and the all-digital AM can operate within ±10 kHz. Both hybrid and all-digital FM IBOC systems utilize ±200 kHz sidebands.

The RF transmission subsystem includes scrambling, channel coding, interleaving, OFDM subcarrier mapping, OFDM signal generation, hybrid transmission, and upconversion for over-the-air transmission (see Figure 8).

Scrambling. The scrambling process randomizes the bits in each encoded digital audio signal or service data to reduce periodicities of these bits in the time domain. To recover the bit sequence of the digital audio signal on

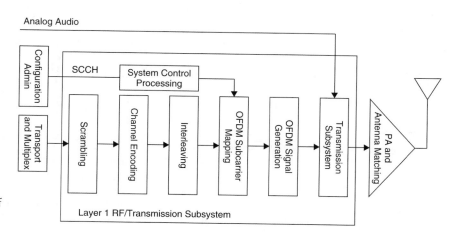

Figure 8: RF transmission subsystem of IBOC (NRSC, 2005)

receivers, the synchronization and coding information data are delivered together with the scrambled digital audio.

Channel Encoding. The channel encoding process generates forward error correction. It is characterized by punctured convolutional encoding (National Radio Systems Committee 2005). A convolutional interleaver has memory; that is, its operation depends not only on current symbols but also on previous symbols (Pohlmann 2000). The convolutional coding ratio between the number of codes for an audio channel and the total codes after the convolutional coding, varies, depending on the characteristics of the audio source and the quality requirement.

Interleaving. The interleaving process is used for error correction. It provides both time and frequency diversity. Frequency interleaving means using multiple subcarriers. Time interleaving creates a diversity delay (time) path that results in main and backup steams. Bit mapping assigns the encoded bits to specific locations in the interleaver output. The interleaver outputs are matrices, including *primary lower* (PL), *primary upper* (PU), *secondary* (S), and *tertiary* (T) sidebands and primary IBOC data service (PIDS) channel (National Radio Systems Committee 2005).

The processes of modulation differ between AM and FM in IBOC.

AM IBOC. The OFDM subcarrier mapping in AM IBOC assigns interleaver partitions to frequency partitions. The input to the OFDM subcarrier mapping is the interleaver matrices (including PL, PU, S, T, and PIDS), and R vector, or the system control data sequence that did not go through the interleaver. According to the standard of NRSC-5-A, one row of each active interleaver matrix and one bit of the system control vector R are processed every T_s seconds ($T_s = 5.805$ ms, i.e., the duration of the OFDM symbol). And all rows in all of the active interleaver matrices are processed sequentially, starting with the first row of the first matrix, to produce a frequency domain representation of the signal (iBiquity Digital 2005a). The interleaver matrices carrying the audio bit streams are transformed into scaled 64-QAM constellation values and mapped to specific subcarriers located in primary and secondary sidebands. And the system control data are transformed into BPSK constellation values and mapped to the reference subcarriers.

Characteristics of the Subcarriers. The OFDM subcarriers are located in the sidebands and defined as *primary* (±10.36 kHz to ±14.72 kHz), *secondary* (±5.09 kHz to ±9.45 kHz), and *tertiary* (±0.36 kHz to ±4.72 kHz) sidebands that are underneath the baseband of the analog AM carrier (see Figure 9). There are also subcarriers assigned to reference data for indicating status and control purpose.

There are eighty-one subcarriers on each side of the unmodulated analog AM carrier, and the frequency span of each subcarrier is 181.7 Hz (iBiquity Digital 2005a; Johnson 2000).

The total power of all OFDM subcarriers for digital audio is significantly lower than the power of the unmodulated analog AM carrier. The primary sideband is −30 dBc/subcarrier and the secondary sideband is −43 dBc/subercarrier or −37 dBc/subercarrier (see Figure 9) (NRSC 2005).

OFDM Signal Generation. OFDM signal generation receives complex frequency-domain vectors of OFDM symbols from the OFDM subcarrier mapping and generates a sequence of complex, baseband, time-domain pulses that represent the digital portion of the AM IBOC signal.

Transmission of Hybrid AM IBOC. The transmission for the hybrid AM IBOC includes analog AM modulator, digital OFDM symbol concatenation, a combination of analog and digital baseband waveforms, and frequency upconversion to the radio frequency—that is, the existing AM channel (shown in Figure 10).

In the analog signal path, the baseband analog signal needs to be delayed to match the timing with its Zcorresponding digital signal and to go through a low-pass filter, either 5 kHz or 8 kHz, to meet the bandwidth

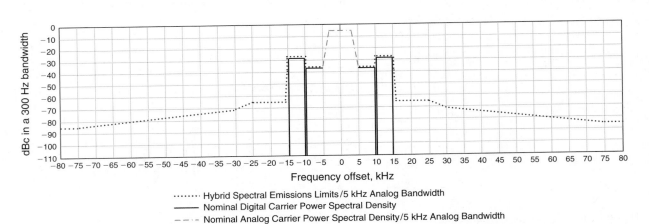

Figure 9: NRSC-5 AM hybrid waveform spectral emission limits for 5-kHz analog bandwidth (NRSC, 2005)

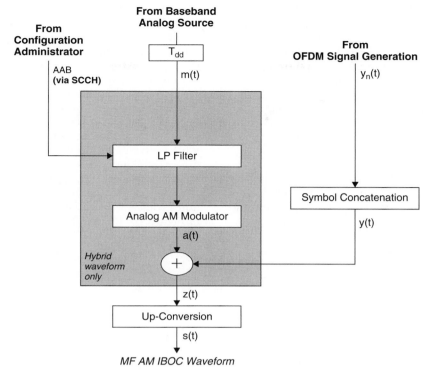

Figure 10: Hybrid AM IBOC transmission (NRSC, 2005)

requirement, when it is then modulated (refer to the respective figures).

In the digital signal path, the individual time-domain OFDM symbols are summed to form a continuum of pulses—that is, the symbol concatenation. The baseband waveforms of the analog and digital signals are combined to produce the complex baseband AM IBOC hybrid waveform. The hybrid is finally upconverted to the RF carrier frequency allocated for its existing AM radio channel.

The AM IBOC hybrid system does not support the stereo analog AM service authorized by the FCC (1998a). Thus, the analog audio signal must be monophonic. During the modulation and transmission, the overall digital

signal must maintain a 90-degree phase relationship to the unmodulated analog AM carrier in order to minimize the interference to the analog signal. Therefore, every other subcarrier in the OFDM subcarriers, which is in a 0-degree relationship with the unmodulated analog carrier, is not used to deliver information. The trade-off for interference protection is that the information content on the subcarriers in the AM IBOC hybrid mode is only half of its capacity (Johnson 2000).

For hybrid AM IBOC transmission, an 8-kHz analog bandwidth (referring to Figure 11) also can be utilized with the same allocation of the sidebands as in the 5-kHz hybrid AM IBOC mode (referring to Figure 9).

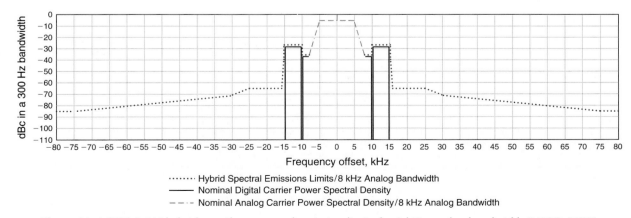

Figure 11: NRSC-5 AM hybrid waveform spectral emission limits for 8-kHz analog bandwidth (NRSC, 2005)

All-Digital AM IBOC. In the all-digital AM IBOC, the analog signal is not transmitted. Therefore, the primary sidebands are located at the baseband area around the unmodulated AM carrier (± .36 kHz to ±4.72 kHz), and the secondary sidebands are ranged from 5.09 kHz to 9.45 kHz, with tertiary from –5.09 kHz to –9.45 kHz (see Figure 12) (NRSC 2005; Johnson 2000). The total bandwidth is reduced. Without the limitation of analog audio QAM, all of the subcarriers can be used for the information content. The power of both sidebands is increased (see Figure 12).

FM IBOC. The principle of OFDM subcarrier mapping in the FM IBOC is similar to that in the AM IBOC. However, in the FM IBOC, the interleaver matrices carrying the audio and data are transformed into scaled QPSK constellation points and mapped to OFDM subcarriers (iBiquity Digital 2005b).

Characteristics of Subcarriers. Although FM radio stations are licensed in 200-kHz spacing, FM analog radio broadcasting usually operates with a bandwidth of ±200 kHz. In the bandwidth of 400 kHz, there are 1092 subcarriers; the span of each subcarrier is 363.373 Hz (iBiquity Digital 2005b); 546 subcarriers spread on each side of the unmodulated FM carrier frequency. The OFDM scheme divides those subcarriers into sixty frequency partitions (see Figure 13). There are eighteen data subcarries and one reference subcarrier in each partition (see Figure 14). The position of the reference subcarrier in a partition varies, either at the beginning or the end as shown in Figure 14. In addition to the reference subcarriers in

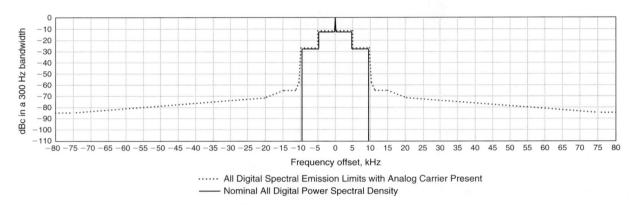

Figure 12: NRSC-5 AM all-digital waveform spectral emission limits (NRSC, 2005)

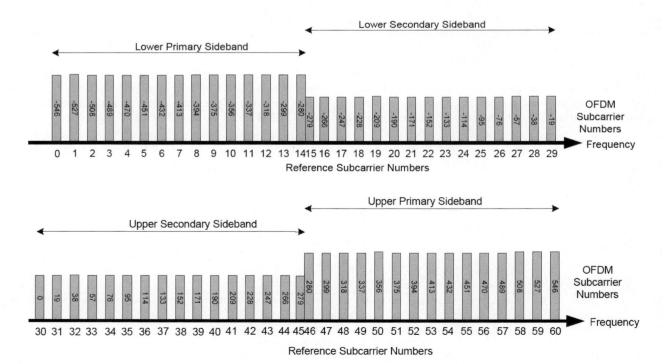

Figure 13: Sideband reference subcarrier spectral mapping (iBiquity Digital Corporation 2005a, 54)

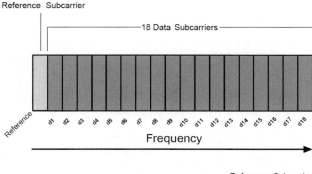

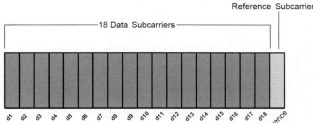

Figure 14: Frequency partitions (iBiquity Digital Corporation 2005b, 12)

the partitions, there are five extra reference subcarriers inserted into the spectrum at subcarrier positions –546, –279, 0, 279, and 546.

OFDM Signal Generation. OFDM signal generation receives complex frequency-domain OFDM symbols from the output of OFDM subcarrier mapping and generates a sequence of complex, baseband, time-domain pulses that represent the digital portion of the FM IBOC signals.

Transmission of the Hybrid FM IBOC. The transmission for the hybrid FM IBOC includes analog FM modulator, digital OFDM symbol concatenation and frequency upconversion to the VHF frequency of the existing FM channel, combination of analog FM RF signal, and digitally modulated RF signals for the hybrid FM IBOC broadcasting (see Figure 15).

The analog audio signal is delayed and sent to the analog FM modulator. The individual time-domain OFDM symbols from the OFDM signal generation are summed to form a continuum of pulses—that is, the processes of symbol concatenation—and then upconverted to the RF carrier frequency allocated to the existing FM channel.

In the hybrid FM IBOC, the analog FM audio signal occupies the baseband between ±129.36 kHz in either monophonic or stereo. The primary digital audio sidebands are ranged from ±129.36kHz to ±198.40 kHz (ten frequency partitions on each side) with the power reduction at –45.8 dBc per subcarrier (see Figures 16 and 17).

It may add one, two, or four extended sidebands to the primary digital sidebands with the power reduction at –45.6 dBc per subcarrier. However, the baseband of the analog FM signal is reduced to ±101.74 kHz (see Figure 18).

All-Digital FM IBOC. In the all-digital FM IBOC spectrum waveform shown in Figures 19 and 20, the analog FM audio signal is removed. The primary sidebands are

fully used to operate the digital audio programming in fourteen partitions on each side (±129.36 kHz to ±198.40 kHz as the main bandwidth; ±101.74 k Hz to ±129.36 kHz as extended bandwidth), and the secondary sidebands with lower power (5, 10, 15, or 20 dB below the power of the primary subcarriers) replace the baseband in a total of twenty-eight partitions (0 Hz to ±69.40 as the main bandwidth, ±69.40 to ±97.02 as extended bandwidth) (see Figures 19 and 20).

Moreover, in the secondary sidebands, twelve subcarriers serve as the secondary protected region, "the area of spectrum least likely to be affected by analog or digital interference" (iBiquity Digital 2005b, 17). As mentioned above, five additional reference subcarriers are inserted at ±198.40 kHz, ±101.74 kHz, and the center (0 Hz from the unmodulated FM carrier).

The transmission system must address several issues of time alignment. For transmission facilities that are equipped to operate IBOC digital radio broadcasting, every data packet transmitted must be properly aligned with GPS (global positioning system) time. Also, the various data packets must be properly aligned with each other. In some service modes, certain packets are purposely delayed by a fixed amount of time to accommodate diversity, combining at the receiver for either interference protection or smoothly switching between the analog signal and the digital signal of the same programming (National Radio Systems Committee 2005).

Digital Radio Mondiale

Because Eureka 147 was developed primarily for the replacement of analog FM services, a small group of broadcasters and manufacturers formed the *Digital Radio Mondiale* (DRM) consortium in March 1998 to develop a digital radio broadcasting system for the radio stations using spectra below 30 MHz such as AM radio, medium frequency (526.5 kHz to 1,606.5 kHz in ITU regions 1 and 3), and high frequency for shortwave radio services (2.3 MHz to 27 MHz) and low frequency (148.5 kHz to 283.5 kHz in ITU region 1) (ETSI 2005). The DRM consortium is a nonprofit organization, including broadcasters, network providers, receiver and transmitter manufacturers, research institutes, and regulatory bodies [Digital Radio Mondiale (DRM) 2006]. As of June 2005, its membership had reached ninety-three organizations from thirty countries (DRM 2005b).

The DRM technology has been supported by the International Telecommunication Union (ITU), the International Electrotechnical Commission (IEC), and the European Telecommunication Standard Institute. In September 2001, ETSI published the DRM system specification (ETSI 2001c) and subsequently updated the specification. The current document was published in October 2005 (ETSI 2005). In March 2005, the DRM consortium voted to extend the system to 120 MHz to ensure digital radio availability worldwide. The design and testing of the extended DRM system are expected to be completed by 2008–10 (DRM 2005a).

The DRM system is designed similarly to the IBOC DAB system. However, it was originally considered to operate the DRM in an all-digital transmission format on a separate

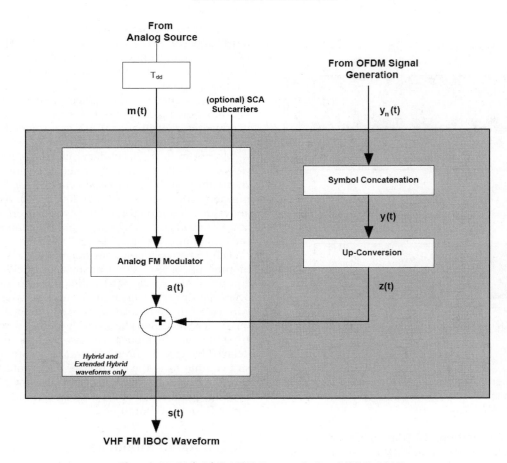

Figure 15: Hybrid FM IBOC transmission (NRSC, 2005)

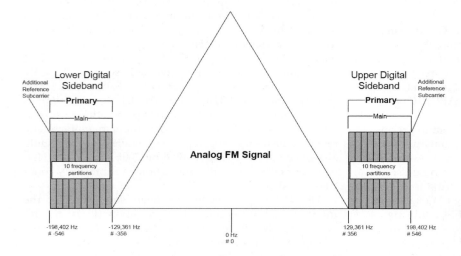

Figure 16: Spectrum of the hybrid FM IBOC transmission signal (iBiquity Digital Corporation 2005b, 15)

channel from its corresponding analog AM service. Moreover, the bandwidth that can be used to carry DRM signals for the AM stations in many countries is narrower than that of the AM IBOC radio broadcasting in the United States. The difference is subject to the frequency planning for AM radio stations. For example, in Europe the AM stations are spaced at 9 kHz rather than 10 kHz as in the United States. In addition, an AM station in European and other countries can be allocated at an adjacent frequency next to another AM station in the same geographic area; in the United States, the planners only allow stations in an adjacent area to be a minimum of two channels (20 kHz) away (Hallett 2003, "History"). Therefore, to avoid the adjacent channel interference, the DRM signal is required to fit in the existing AM broadcast bandwidth, as narrowly as 4.5 kHz or 5 kHz. The DRM signal occupies 4.5 kHz or

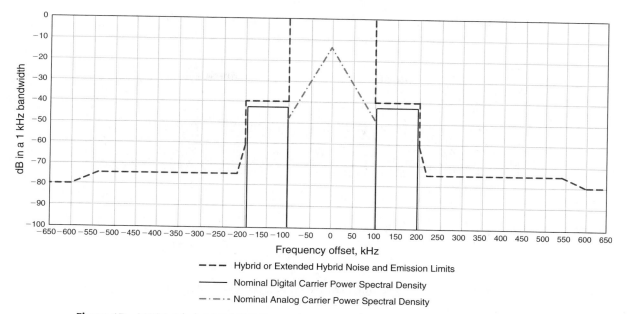

Figure 17: NRSC-5 hybrid FM IBOC waveform noise and emission limits (NRSC, 2005, 25)

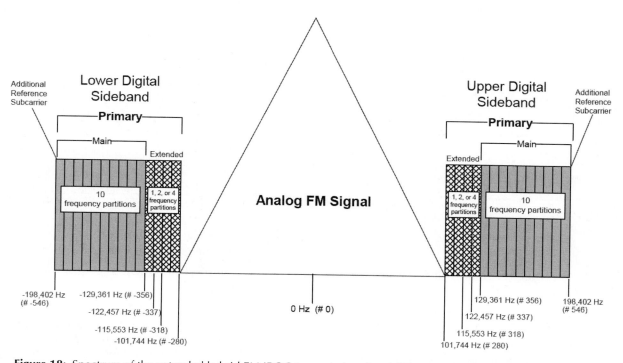

Figure 18: Spectrum of the extended hybrid FM IBOC transmission signal (iBiquity Digital Corporation 2005b, 15)

5 kHz, whereas the other half bandwidth is used to transmit the one sideband of its analog AM signal (ETSI 2001c).

The DRM technology has been developed rapidly. According to H. Donald Messer (2006), DRM technical committee chairman, the DRM can be used with a variety of bandwidth allocations. In all-digital DRM, there are applications for 9/10 kHz RF channel (LF, MF, and HF), 18/20 kHz RF channel (MF and HF), and 50–100 kHz RF channel (VHF bands < 108 MHz). The simulcast DRM (digital plus AM or FM channel) applications include 18/20 kHz (1/2 for DRM), 27/30 kHz (2/3 for DRM), 250–300 kHz (50–100 kHz for DRM), and 15 kHz (10 kHz for DRM and 5 kHz for the one sideband of AM analog signal). DRM technology also can be applied to a single frequency network, automatic frequency switching, a multiple frequency network, an AM signaling system, and displays of program data and other low bit-rate data such as traffic information (Messer 2006).

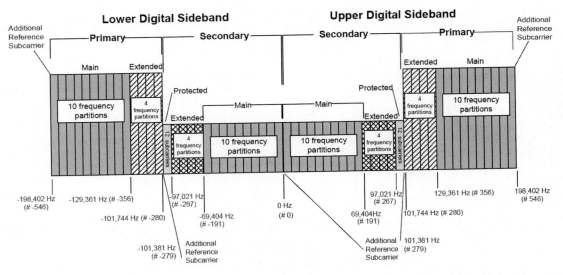

Figure 19: Spectrum of the all-digital FM IBOC transmission signal (iBiquity Digital Corporation 2005b, 17)

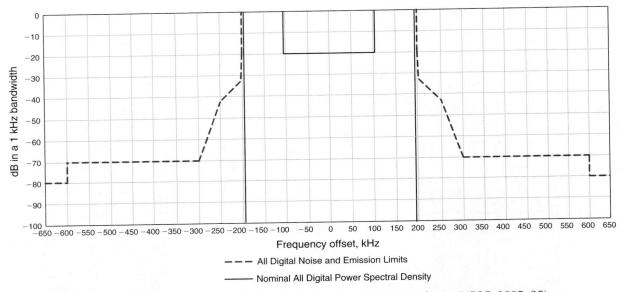

- - - All Digital Noise and Emission Limits

—— Nominal All Digital Power Spectral Density

Figure 20: NRSC-5 all-digital FM IBOC waveform noise and emission limits (NRSC, 2005, 25)

A DRM signal consists of three kinds of data: the *main service channel* (data for all program services), *fast access channels* (service selection information, details of audio encoding information, etc.), and the *service description channels* (details of alternative frequencies, frequency schedules, audio metadata information, etc.). The technical processes of DRM include (1) audio coding, (2) multiplexing, (3) channel coding, and (4) transmission (OFDM cell mapping, OFDM signal generator, and quadrature amplitude modulation) (Hallett 2003, "Development").

Audio Encoding

In the audio coding process, the near-FM quality is achieved by using MPEG-4 *advanced audio coding* (AAC) with *spectral band replication* (SBR), which is called *MPEG-4*

aacPlus. For speech, the audio coding uses *code-excited linear prediction* (CELP) and harmonic vector excitation coding (HVXC) together with SBR to reduce the bit rates.

Kunz (2006) describes the technical concept of SBR in Figure 21. From a technical point of view, SBR is a new method for highly efficient coding of high frequencies in audio compression algorithms. When used in conjunction with SBR, the underlying coder is only responsible for transmitting the lower part of the spectrum. The higher frequencies are generated by the SBR decoder, which is mainly a postprocess following the conventional waveform decoder. Instead of transmitting the spectrum, SBR reconstructs the higher frequencies in the decoder based on an analysis of the lower frequencies transmitted in the underlying coder. To ensure an accurate reconstruction,

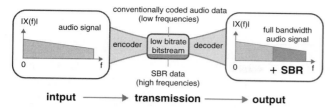

Figure 21: Technical concept of spectral band replication (SBR) (Kunz 2006, 2)

some guidance information is transmitted in the encoded bit stream at a very low data rate.

The reconstruction is efficient for harmonic as well as for noiselike components and allows for proper shaping in the time domain as well as in the frequency domain. As a result, SBR allows full bandwidth audio coding at especially low data rates, thus offering a significantly increased compression efficiency compared to the core coder (Kunz 2006).

Multiplexing

The process in the multiplexing is similar to that in the AM HD Radio system. The multiplexer combines the protection levels of all data and audio services. The data coded with MPEG AAC and CELP in the main service channel use unequal error protection in which higher protection is assigned to more sensitive information. Yet the data coded with HVXC only use equal error protection (ETSI 2005). Because the information carried in the *fast access channel* (FAC) and the *service description channel* (SDC) are used to decode the MSC programming signals, they should be arriving in the receiver before the MSC signals. The FAC and SDC signals pass through neither the multiplexing nor interleaving processes. They are integrated with the MSC signals at the transmission section (ETSI 2005).

Error Protection: Energy Dispersal, Channel Encoder, and Interleaving

The energy dispersal process predetermines selective complementing bits in order to reduce the possibility of a systematic pattern in the transmitted signal. The systematic pattern is vulnerable to the interference caused by the environment. The channel encoder adds redundant

information for error protection and defines the mapping of the digital information onto QAM cells (a cell means one cycle in a waveform). The interleaving spreads consecutive QAM cells onto a sequence of cells separated in time and frequency in order to provide robust transmission of digital radio signals. The pilot generator provides information to demodulate the signal in the receiver (ETSI 2005).

Transmission

In the transmission block, the data from MSC, FAC, and SDC are merging with the information from the pilot generator. The process including OFDM mapping, OFDM signal generation, and modulation.

OFDM Cell Mapping. The OFDM cell mapper collects the different classes of cells and places them on the time-frequency grid that assigns the QAM cells onto specific subcarriers. The mapping constellations are 4-QAM, 16-QAM, or 64-QAM. The output is a frequency representation with time index—that is, the time when the frequency exists.

The time-related OFDM symbol parameters are expressed in multiples of the elementary time period, T, which is equal to 83 ⅓ µs. These parameters are:

- T_g, the duration of the guard interval;
- T_s, the duration of an OFDM symbol; and
- T_u, the duration of the useful (orthogonal) part of an OFDM symbol (i.e. excluding the guard interval).

The OFDM symbols are grouped to form transmission frames of duration T_f (ETSI 2005) (see Table 3).

OFDM Signal Generator. The OFDM signal generator transforms each ensemble of cells with same time index to a time domain representation of the signal. The OFDM symbol is obtained by inserting a guard interval before the time domain representation of the useful ensemble. All OFDM symbols contain data (MSC) cells and reference information cells, including pilot cells and system control information cells. The pilot cells can be used for frame, frequency and time synchronization, channel estimation, and robustness mode identification. The system

Table 3: OFDM Symbol Parameters in Each Transmission Mode in DRM

Parameters list	Robustness mode			
	A	**B**	**C**	**D**
T (µs)	83⅓	83⅓	83⅓	83⅓
T_u (ms)	24 (288 × T)	21⅓(256 × T)	141⅓(176 × T)	9⅓(112 × T)
T_g (ms)	2⅔ (32 × T)	5⅓ (64 × T)	5⅓ (64 × T)	7⅓ (88 × T)
T_g / T_g	1/9	1/4	4/11	11/14
$T_s = T_u + T_g$ (ms)	26⅓	26⅔	20	16⅔
T_f (ms)	400	400	400	400

Table 4: OFDM Frame Parameters in Each Transmission Mode in DRM

Robustness mode	Duration (T_u) (ms)	Carrier spacing $(1/T_u)$ (Hz)	Duration of guard interval (T_g) (ms)	Duration of symbol $(T_s = T_u + T_g)$ (ms)	T_g/T_u	Number of symbols per frame (N_s)
A	24	$41^2/_3$	2.66	26.66	1/9	15
B	21.33	$46^7/_8$	5.33	26.66	1/4	15
C	14.66	682/11	5.33	20	4/11	20
D	9.33	1071/7	7.33	16.66	11/14	24

Source: ETSI 2005, 121

Table 5: Robustness Modes in DRM

Robustness mode	Typical propagation conditions
A	Gaussian channels with minor fading
B	Time and frequency selective channels with longer delay spread
C	As robustness mode B but with higher Doppler spread
D	As robustness mode B but with severe delay and Doppler spread

Source: ETSI 2005, 16

control information includes a FAC and a SDC. Because the OFDM signal consists of many separately modulated carriers, each OFDM symbol can be considered as an ensemble of individual cells, each cell corresponding to either data or reference information modulated on one carrier within this OFDM symbol (ETSI 2005).

Transmission Frame and Superframe. The transmitted signals are organized into transmission frames. Three transmission frames are combined to a transmission superframe. Each transmission frame is in a duration of 400 ms (ETSI 2005), and consists of fifteen to twenty-four OFDM symbols, depending on the robustness modes of transmission (see Tables 4 and 5).

Modulation and Transmission. The modulator converts the digital representation of the OFDM signals into the analog RF signal. This operation includes digital-to-analog conversion to the RF carrier frequency for transmission, as well as bandwidth filtering to comply with the RF protection ratio requirement (ETSI 2005).

SATELLITE DIGITAL AUDIO RADIO SERVICES

There are alternative approaches to the practical implementation of digital radio broadcasting such as Webcasting, cable, and satellite transmission. Among those, *satellite digital audio radio services* (SDARS) have been widely accepted in the United States, especially by the automobile and aircraft industries. Two American companies, XM and Sirius, provide the service in North America, for which subscribers pay a monthly fee.

Regarding SDARS, the FCC allocated a portion of the S band from 2320 MHz to 2345 MHz for national satellite radio broadcasting downlink frequency with a bandwidth of 12.5 MHz for each service. Only two licenses were available. An auction was held with four applicants: CD Radio, American Mobile Radio Corporation (AMRC), Digital Satellite Broadcasting Corporation, and Primosphere Limited Partnership. The two winners were CD Radio ($83.3 million) and AMRC ($89.9 million) (FCC 1997). The term of the renewable SDARS license is eight years. AMRC debuted its service as XM (2332.5 MHz to 2345 MHz) in 2001, and CD Radio launched its service as Sirius (2320 MHz to 2332.5 MHz) in 2002. The SDARS providers offer 120 to 160 digital channels of choice, including music, sports, talk, news, comedy, children's programming, and advanced traffic and weather information. The radio programs reach the receivers directly by satellite or terrestrial repeaters.

As of the end of 2005, XM had 5.9 million subscribers, an increase of 84 percent over 2004 (XM Satellite Radio 2006). Sirius had more than 3.3 million subscribers, an increase of 190 percent over 2004 (Sirius Satellite Radio 2006, "Reports"). Most major brands and affiliates of automakers have made alliances with the SDARS companies to use their radio services. Electronic manufactures are actively participating in the process of developing SDARS radio receivers. The XM and Sirius radio sets are also available in retail stores. The price ranges from $50 to $250. Early in 1997, the FCC ordered XM and Sirius to jointly develop a unified standard for satellite radios so that radio sets can receive both satellite radio channels; the two SDARS providers also planned to make their receivers compatible with existing AM and FM stations (Sirius Satellite Radio 2005). However, this work has progressed slowly.

Another service, WorldSpace Satellite Radio, launched AfriStar and AsiaStar in 1990 to provide sixty-two channels of international satellite radio programming, including news, music, talk, sports, education, spiritual, and special brand content in seventeen languages to

130 countries, including India and China, all of Africa and the Middle East, and most of Western Europe. The company claims that it does not conduct business with people, business, or companies or people doing business with several countries: Burma, Iran, Libya, North Korea, Sudan, Syria, Angola, Serbia, and Montenegro (WorldSpace Satellite Radio, 2007). The content of thirty-two channels are provided by international, national, and regional third parties; thirty channels are produced by WorldSpace-branded stations. WorldSpace owns production studios in Washington, D.C., Bangalore, India and Nairobi, Kenya, where original music and lifestyle channels are created. It also has a programming partnership with the XM Satellite Radio network.

The Development of SDARS in the United States

Satellite digital radio technologies have been developed along with direct satellite television services since the late 1980s. They use similar digital audio coding techniques such as those used to compress audio signals in terrestrial digital video, and they apply frequency or phase modulation to transmit encoded audio signals for the reception of fixed, portable, and cable television receivers. However, as an independent industry, the SDARS only began in the 1990s (FCC 2006a). In 1990, Satellite CD Radio (the predecessor of CD Radio and Sirius) filed a petition with the FCC to allocate spectrum for SDARS and to grant permission for providing CD-quality audio programs to American consumers (FCC 1997a). Initiated by Satellite CD Radio's 1990 petition, the FCC called for investigation into the effects of satellite digital radio services on existing AM and FM stations. The timeline of the SDARS implementation is as follows:

1. November 1992: The FCC established a proceeding to allocate SDARS spectrum domestically and announced a cutoff date of December 15, 1992, for SDARS license applications. Four companies applied for the licenses, including AMRC, Digital Satellite Broadcasting Corporation, Primosphere Limited Partnership, and Satellite CD Radio (FCC 1997a).

2. January 1995: The commission allocated the 2310 MHz to 2360 MHz band for SDARS on a primary basis.

3. June 1995: the FCC requested detailed information on the potential economic impact of SDARS on terrestrial broadcasters. The public notice proposed three possible licensing options and rules to allow expeditious licensing after an option was chosen. The U.S. Congress directed the commission to (a) allocate spectra at 2305 MHz to 2320 MHz and 2345 MHz to 2360 MHz for SDARS to be consistent with international allocations and (b) award licenses in those portions by auction.

4. March 1997: The FCC approved SDARS and announced the date of its auction as April 1, 1997. Despite a petition by the National Association of Broadcasters, the commission did not think the effect of SDARS would be significant on existing free radio service in terms of advertising revenue (FCC 1997a).

5. April 2, 1997: The FCC announced that Satellite CD Radio and AMRC had won the SDARS auction (FCC 1997b).

6. October 1997: The FCC granted two licenses of the S-band frequency. Satellite CD Radio was given the 2320 MHz to 2332.5 MHz spectrum (FCC 1997c), and AMRC was given the 2332.5 MHz to 2345 spectrum (FCC 1997d). The FCC proposed that these satellite licensees begin construction of their space station within one year of the auction, launch and begin their first satellite within four years, and begin to operate their entire system within six years. The FCC determined that satellite DARS license terms should be for eight years. Each license term commences when each service is put into operation and is subject to renewal or termination after the initial eight-year period (FCC 1997a).

XM Satellite Radio

XM Satellite Radio began as AMRC in 1992 and was granted a SDAR license for 12.5 MHz of the S band (2332.5 MHz to 2345.0 MHz) in October 1997 (FCC 1997d). XM is a wholly owned subsidiary of XM Satellite Radio Holdings, Inc. XM Radio is transmitted by satellite, now taking its place alongside AM and FM on the radio dial, as well as by the newly debuted HD Radio in the United States. XM has its corporate headquarters and eighty end-to-end fiber-optic programming and broadcast studios in Washington, D.C., and broadcast facilities in New York; Nashville; Boca Raton, Florida; Southfield, Michigan; and Yokohama, Japan. XM has been publicly traded on the NASDAQ exchange (XMSR) since October 5, 1999.

XM launched two satellites in March and May 2001—Rock and Roll, respectively—in cooperation with Hughes Space and Communications International (now Boeing Space Systems). Both are HS702 geostationary satellites with payloads provided by Alcatel. In September 2001, XM formally launched services in two major markets: Dallas–Fort Worth and San Diego. XM charges a basic monthly subscription fee of $12.95. Under the XM Family plan, subscribers get a discounted rate of $6.99 per month for additional radios. Premium channels are available at an additional monthly cost. Currently, XM uses three Boeing geostationary satellites and approximately 800 terrestrial repeaters located throughout the continental United States. The repeaters receive the XM signal directly from the satellites and then retransmit it to XM radios where the reception directly from the satellite is not acceptable. The repeater network ensures signal coverage, particularly in urban areas where tall buildings and other obstructions may otherwise interfere with signal reception.

XM's programming includes more than 170 digital channels of option from coast to coast, including commercial-free music channels; channels of premier sports coverage, talk, news, comedy, and children's and entertainment programming; and advanced traffic and weather information channels. XM's programming partners include Sesame Workshop, NASCAR, Associated Press, ABC News, CNBC, BBC World Service and BBC Concerts, Radio One, The Sporting News, CNN,

Bloomberg, Fox News, C-SPAN Radio, Disney, and ESPN. XM provides entertainment and data services for the automobile market through partnerships with General Motors, Honda, Toyota, Hyundai, Nissan, and Volkswagen and Audi. As of 2005, XM Radio was being installed in more than 120 different vehicle models.

At the end of December 2001, XM had 28,000 subscribers; 347,000 subscribers at the end of 2002; and 1.36 million subscribers at the end of 2003. XM claimed that it ended 2004 with 3.2 million subscribers and 5.9 million by the end of 2005, reflecting an 84 percent increase in total subscribers over 2004 (XM Satellite Radio 2006, "Reports"). In April 2007, XM announced its first quarter results, indicating that its subscribers reached 7.9 million (XM Satellite Radio 2007, "Investor Information").

XM collaborates with electronics industries such as Delphi, Pioneer, Audiovox, and Yamaha to manufacture radio receivers. The XM Radio receivers are also available at retailers nationwide including Wal-Mart, Best Buy, Circuit City, Sears, and independent dealers. XM Radio receivers are designed for different users: handheld, car plug-in radios, and home tuners. Robust features are embedded in the radio sets, such as more than one hundred channels of programming, LCD display, remote controller, thirty-minute relay, stock ticker, sports score ticker, built-in antenna or FM wireless modulator that translates XM signals to nearby radio sets, and so on. The home tuner can be connected to a television.

Sirius Satellite Radio

Sirius Satellite Radio was originally incorporated as Satellite CD Radio in Delaware in May 1990. Its name was changed to CD Radio in December 1992 and changed again to Sirius Satellite Radio in November 1999. Its headquarters are in New York City's Rockefeller Center. In 1990, Satellite CD Radio filed a petition with the FCC to allocate spectrum for satellite digital audio radio service, and it filed a license application in 1992. In April 1997, Satellite CD Radio successfully won the bid of FCC's auction and was licensed in October 1997 a 12.5-MHz bandwidth of the S band, 2320 MHz to 2332.5 MHz, to provide SDARS radio programming (FCC 1997c). Its uplink transmission spectrum ranges from 7060 MHz to 7072.5 MHz (Sirius Satellite Radio 2003).

Space Systems/Loral launched three operating satellites in the Loral FS-1300 model series in July, September, and December 2000 for Sirius radio services. A fourth satellite, as a spare one, was delivered to ground storage in April 2002. The satellites are designed to have life spans of approximately fifteen years in orbit. Sirius uses the three satellites and almost one hundred terrestrial repeaters to serve subscribers throughout the United States. According to Sirius,

> Each operating satellite travels in a "figure eight" pattern extending above and below the equator, and spends approximately 16 hours per day north of the equator. At any time, two of our three satellites operate north of the equator while the third satellite does not broadcast as it traverses the portion of the orbit south of the equator. This

orbital configuration yields high signal elevation angles, reducing service interruptions that can result from signal blockage. In some areas with high concentrations of tall buildings, such as urban centers, and in tunnels, signals from our satellites may be blocked and reception of our satellite signal can be adversely affected. In many of these areas, we have deployed terrestrial repeaters to supplement our satellite coverage. To date, we have deployed 98 terrestrial repeaters in 61 urban areas. We may deploy additional terrestrial repeaters if we discover that our existing terrestrial repeaters fail to cover a significant number of subscribers or potential subscribers (Sirius Satellite Radio 2003, 6).

In February 2002, Sirius began its service in selected markets, and in July 2002 extended its service nationwide. By charging a monthly subscription fee of $12.95, Sirius provides more than 125 channels of CD-quality audio programs, including sixty-eight channels of commercial-free music and almost sixty channels of news, sports, weather, talk, comedy, public radio, and children's programming (Sirius Satellite Radio 2005). Both Sirius FM-modulated radios and three-band radios (AM/FM/SDARS) have been designed so that the receivers can be plugged into or installed in cars, trucks, recreational vehicles, homes, offices, stores, and even outdoors. Boaters around the country, and as far as 200 miles offshore, can also hear Sirius programming. As of the end of 2002, Sirius had 29,947 subscribers; by the end of 2003, 261,061 subscribers; and by the end of 2004, 1,143,258 subscribers. The company reported that it "ended 2005 with 3,316,560 subscribers, reflecting a 190 percent increase in total subscribers for the year 2004" (Sirius Satellite Radio 2006, "Reports"). In May 2007, Sirius announced its first quarter results, indicating approximately 6.6 million subscribers (Sirius Satellite Radio 2007, "Investor Relations").

Sirius's primary source of revenue is its monthly subscription fee, activation fees, and revenue from limited advertising on its nonmusic channels (Sirius Satellite Radio 2003, 2005). Hertz currently offers Sirius radio at major locations around the country and has signed an agreement with Sirius for charging car renters' activation fees.

Sirius currently has partnership with automobile companies including Audi, BMW, Chrysler, Dodge, Ford, Infiniti, Jaguar, Jeep, Land Rover, Lexus, Lincoln-Mercury, Mazda, Mercedes-Benz, MINI, Nissan, Scion, Toyota, Porsche, Volkswagen, and Volvo to manufacture and sell the vehicles equipped with Sirius radios. The radios are produced by Alpine, Audiovox, Blaupunkt, Clarion, Eclipse, Jensen, JVC, Kenwood, Panasonic, and U.S. Electronics, and they can be purchased at major retailers including Advance Auto Parts, Best Buy, Car Toys, Circuit City, Crutchfield, Good Guys, Wal-Mart, Sears, Tweeter, and Ultimate Electronics along with RadioShack and DISH Network outlets (Sirius Satellite 2006, "Corporate"). In addition, Sirius is also available at heavy truck dealers and truck stops nationwide.

Sirius's state-of-the art studios are located in New York City. It also broadcasts from Los Angeles, Memphis,

Nashville, New Orleans, Houston, and Daytona. Sirius offers sports radio programming, including broadcasting play-by-play action, for more than 350 professional and college teams. Its corporate overview states,

> Sirius programming features news, talk and play-by-play action from the NFL, NBA, NHL, Barclays English Premier League soccer, the Wimbledon Championships and more than 125 colleges, plus live coverage of several of the year's top thoroughbred horse races. SIRIUS is the only radio outlet to provide listeners with every NFL game and airs over 1000 NBA games per season, plus up to 40 NHL games per week. SIRIUS also features programming from ESPN Radio and ESPNews (Sirius Satellite Radio 2006, "Corporate").

AUDIO WEBCASTING

Audio Webcasting is one of the applications developed by streaming media technologies. Streaming media is a technology that converts conventional audio and video signals to compressed digital packets and delivers the packets sequentially in real time through computer networks to players installed on users' computers. The compressed digital packets are reassembled and decompressed into audio and video signals that can be played on users' computers (Mack and Rayburn 2006; Austerberry 2002). Streaming media can be employed to deliver live audio and video programming and provide playlists for simulated live broadcasts of prerecorded audio and video materials or for media on-demand requests. The details of streaming technology are described in Chapter 17. Mp3 and so-called podcasting are other digital audio formats made available on the Internet for downloading to personal players such as mp3 players (audio only) and iPods (audio and video).

Brief History of Audio Webcasting

Audio Webcasting was started by RealNetworks in 1995 through its RealPlayer and RealAudio software. Apple QuickTime, originally used for progressive downloading, became available for Webcasting. Microsoft joined the Webcasting business in 1999. RealNetworks has acquired companies specializing in online software development, music, business management, and distribution and publishing such as Zylom Media Group BV, the Helsinki-based Mr.Goodliving, Seattle-based GameHouse, Listen.com, Netzip, Xing Technology, and Vivo Software. Currently, RealNetworks, Apple QuickTime, and Microsoft Windows Media are three leading proprietary architectures of streaming media compression. Shoutcast is a streaming audio-only system.

To promote Webcasting technology, RealNetworks, QuickTime, and Windows Media provide free downloads of their players that are accepted by Internet browsers for plug-in display of Webcasting materials. Windows Media also offers free encoding software under an agreement with users. Radio networks such as Westwood One, BBC, and ABC Radio, and many independent radio stations provide free audio Webcasting as a supplementary outlet to reach listeners. Satellite radio services XM and Sirius have online radio as well. In addition to supporting Webcasts, those players are commercialized by connecting to advertising, online audiovisual stores, and music industries. Although such free programming as news, sports, and music clips are offered, listeners need to pay subscription fees for high-quality programming or to download music items.

Audio Webcasting System

There are four basic components necessary for operating an audio Webcasting system: streaming audio encoder, streaming audio server, distribution, and streaming audio player. A conceptual diagram of audio Webcasting system is shown in Figure 22.

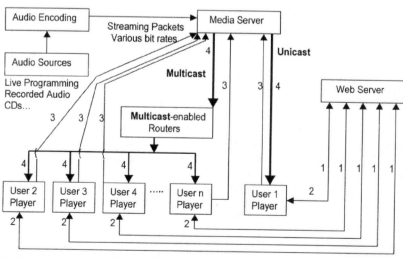

Figure 22: Conceptual diagram of audio Webcasting system

1. User sends a request for an audio Webcasting to a Web server.
2. Web server returns a metafile indicating the URL of the audio Webcast.
3. The user opens the player and sends a request to the relevant media server.
4. The media server sends the audio programming to the player.

Streaming Audio Codec: Encoding and Player

Similarly, the streaming audio codec compression is based on psychoacoustics technology. The encoding compression rate varies depending on the audio source, such as voice or speech and various music formats. Because the delivery is over the Internet, the encoding also takes into account Internet bandwidth and connection speed—for example, dialup modems (56 kbit/s), dual ISDN (128 kbit/ s), cable modems and DSL (300 kbit/s–2 Mbit/s), T1 lines (1.5 Mbit/ s), and 10baseT LAN (3 Mbit/s). For high-quality audio, such as music, variable bit rate coding is used; for limited connection speeds, consistent bit rate coding is used. There are one-pass and two-pass coding processes. During two-pass coding, the first pass is for the codec to gather information about the audio source so that the second pass is able to result in the optimized encoding.

Both RealAudio 10 for bit rates less than 128 Kbps and QuickTime audio apply the MPEG 4 ACC algorism to their stream encoding. Windows Media 10 Professional offers a wide range of steaming applications, from low bit-rate coding at 24 Kbps for audio broadcasting (voice with music), to high bit-rate coding at 320 Kbps to 1.5 Mbps for 7.1 sound systems. The streaming media clip can be encoded for multiple bit rates. It will automatically switch to a lower bit rate for transportation over a lower bandwidth network. Shoutcast uses mp3 encoding.

The players reassemble and decompress the received streaming packets. For missing packets, a player will contact the source to acquire the missing packet in order to recover the audio signal. For this reason, playback starts a few minutes after live programming begins. It will be stopped if there are too many missing packets. All of the basic players are free for downloading, but players with extra features can be purchased. The player can display the Webcasting content in an independent window, embedded in a file, or plugged into a browser. Players are upgraded constantly, and the information about new version and features is sent to the users automatically via e-mail lists. The latest versions of codecs are all backward-compatible with their previous decoders.

Streaming Audio Server: Delivery and Distribution

As shown in Figure 22, the delivery of streaming audio needs media servers. RealNetworks employs Helix Universal Server to stream the RealMedia clips, and it also supports streaming content for QuickTime and Windows Media players. Apple QuickTime uses QuickTime Streaming Server 5.5 that supports QuickTime and international standards such as H.264, MPEG 4, and 3GPP. Apple employs Darwin Streaming Server for Real and Windows Media players, but Darwin Server does not get technical support from the company. Instead, user groups have been organized to discuss and support technical problems. Windows Media streaming is delivered through MMS servers. To ensure live Webcasting, there should be redundant encoders and servers. Each encoder feeds an intake server and then feeds public servers. There is a load balancer or metafile to control the connection between intake servers and public servers (Mack and Rayburn 2006).

Two Internet protocols support the transportation of audio messages: real-time transport protocol, a one-way streaming model; and real-time streaming protocol, an interactive streaming model that allows user control over content such as rewind and fast forward for on-demand users (Austerberry 2002).

Unlike on-the-air broadcasting, the content delivery between a media server and listeners for Webcasting is one-on-one transportation, so-called unicast. Therefore, on unicast the bandwidth needed for content delivery via the Internet is incremental by the number of listeners. According to QuickTime, a server with 4 GB of available disk space supports 10,000 simultaneous streams of 20 kbps ACC audio for live Webcasting and 8000 streams of 20-Kbps ACC audio for on-demand streams. To save the bandwidth, multicast is a content delivery method that transports a single stream to multiple listeners by means of routers and switchers. Listeners do not have direct contact to the server. Instead, they receive Webcasting through their Internet service providers (ISPs), which must install multicast-enabled routers to distribute the content to subscribers and end users. However, unicast is still the major content delivery method because multicast routers have not yet been offered by ISPs.

Advantages and Disadvantages of Webcasting

The Internet has become a new form of mass media. It integrates interpersonal, organizational, mass, and public communication through one medium. Therefore, audio Webcasting possesses many characteristics of the Internet. In this chapter, audio Webcasting is featured as one mass communication that transmits audio programming from one station to many listeners. The advantages and disadvantages of Webcasting follow.

Advantages

1. Interactive process between stations and listeners: It facilitates such services as audio on-demand and downloading music for purchase, and it provides supplementary information about programs, artists, songwriters, and so on.
2. Lower cost of entry: Webcasting does not need transmitters and towers. Media servers and Web servers cost much less than the construction of traditional radio broadcasting infrastructure, and there are few or no regulatory hurdles.
3. Not limited by geography: The Internet is a global medium.
4. Not limited by time: The programming of a popular station can be enjoyed by listeners located in different time zones.
5. Cost-effective for small numbers of listeners: The cost of Webcasting is incremental per listener. Small numbers of receivers would cost less for the delivery fees through the Internet.
6. Quality optimized for different content (such as speech and music) and Internet connection speeds (such as dialup, DSL, and broadband).

Disadvantages

1. Small size of listeners: (a) The penetration of the Internet is smaller than that of traditional radio broadcasting; (b) the Internet's limited bandwidth cannot support large numbers of listeners through unicast; and (c) the incremental cost per listener.

2. Quality: (a) Limited by the bandwidth available on the Internet, the compression ratio is high; and (b) the audio quality of complementary Webcasting from NPR stations and traditional radio stations is fair but worse for listening to free programming from commercial audio Webcasting.

3. Cost: It is not free. The cost is much higher than purchasing a radio set. Webcasting listeners need to have updated computers and subscriptions to their Internet services and the streaming audio and radio materials (paying either for downloading single items or yearly radio passes).

4. Complexity: Because of nonstandardized streaming architectures, listeners need to install three or more players.

5. Technical knowledge and skills are needed for downloading and installing players on personal computers.

Overall, Webcasting is still in its developmental stage in which companies are practicing and public users are trying different new technologies. The FCC and international telecommunication organizations have not yet taken rule-making or licensing actions.

THE IMPLEMENTATION OF DIGITAL RADIO BROADCASTING
Domestic Digital Radio Broadcasting System
United States of America: IBOC HD Radio

Because no spectrum was available in VHF band III or L band for digital audio broadcasting in the United States and U.S. broadcasters were highly supportive of an in-band digital radio broadcast strategy, in October 2002 the FCC approved IBOC as the technology to broadcast digital radio programming (FCC 2002b). In fact, iBiquity has also been actively pursuing adoption of its IBOC technology by the international community. In October 2002, the ITU adopted Recommendation ITU-R BS.1514-1, which endorses iBiquity's AM IBOC technology as a standard for digital broadcasting in the broadcasting bands below 30 MHz (International Telecommunication Union 2002, "System for digital sound"). In January 2007, the ITU approved the recommendation ITU-R BS.1114-6 "Systems for terrestrial digital sound broadcasting to vehicular, portable and fixed receivers in the frequency range 30–3,000 MHz" (ITU 2007). iBiquity's FM IBOC system is listed as its Digital System C (refer to ITU-R BS.1114-6 "Annex 4: Digital System C" at http://www.itu .int/rec/R-REC-BS.1114-6-200701-I/en).

The IBOC technology that uses each station's current frequency and bandwidth to broadcast a hybrid of analog and digital programming has been accepted by the radio industry. HD Radio is the trademark of IBOC technology developed by iBiquity Digital. According to the FCC, as of October 1, 2003, more than 280 radio stations had licenses for iBiquity's technology and had begun HD radio broadcasting or were in the process of conversion (FCC 2004).

iBiquity Digital is the leading company of IBOC technology. It has partnership with companies of receivers, semiconductors, radio broadcasters, automakers, and data service providers, and is supported by financial industries. Among the partners, consumer electronics manufacturers include Alpine, Clarion, Delphi, Denon, Fujitsu Ten, Harman Kardon, iLAB America, JVC, Hyundai AutoNet, Kenwood, Marantz, Mitsubishi, Onkyo, Oritron (Orient Power), Panasonic, Sanyo, Visteon, and Yamaha. Radio broadcasters include ABC, CBS, Clear Channel, Cox Radio, Beasley Broadcast Group, Bonneville International, Citadel Communications, Cumulus Media, Emmis Communications, Entercom Communications, Hispanic Broadcasting, Radio One, Regent Communications, Saga Communications, and Susquehanna Communications. Manufacturing owners include Ford Motor Company, Harris Corporation, Texas Instruments, and Visteon Corporation. Leading financial institutions such as J.P. Morgan Partners, Pequot Capital, and New Venture Partners are also owners of iBiquity Digital.

The National Association of Broadcasters, the National Radio Systems Committee, and the Consumer Electronics Association have been fully participating in evaluation, standard setting, promotion, and training activities to help the transition process from analog radio to digital radio. In October 2004, the NAB conducted an HD Radio workshop in San Diego, California. The certification workshop was "designed to familiarize broadcast engineers and managers with iBiquity Digital Corporation's HD Radio digital audio broadcast system for the AM and FM bands." Experts from iBiquity Digital, equipment manufacturers, consultants, and broadcasters gave presentations on a variety of topics, including "Signal Performance and Antenna Systems For HD Radio," "Transmitters, Tests and Measurements for HD Radio," and "Studios, Audio and Data for HD Radio" (National Association of Broadcasters 2004, "Certification"). Since then, this workshop has been continuously offered online via Webcasting (National Association of Broadcasters 2004, "Workshop Webcast").

There have been a few "firsts" in the history of HD Radio.

In Los Angeles, KROQ 106.7 became the first FM radio broadcaster to convert to HD Radio digital broadcasting on the West Coast, using a Harris Z series exciter to amplify both analog and digital signals. According to the iBiquity report, KROQ's digital broadcasting is generated by a lower power (43-watt) transmitter and delivered through a relatively lower height antenna, but it covers as much of the Los Angeles market as that covered by the station's 4.3 KW analog signal. It not only provides near-CD sound without static, hiss, pops, or fades but also supports on-demand interactive audio that gives listeners more control over what program they want to choose and when they want to listen to it (iBiquity Digital 2006, "KROZ-FM").

In New York City, WOR 710 became the first AM station in the United States to widely test the HD Radio system. WOR first went on the air to test and demonstrate the HD Radio technology for iBiquity Digital on October 11, 2002. iBiquity was able to assess the quality and reliability of the HD Radio system's signal and equipment. WOR became fully licensed in December 2002. The station is impressed by the near-FM quality of the AM digital audio and the elimination of noises and other interferences (iBiquity Digital 2006, "WOR-AM").

On January 7, 2004, the Ultimate Electronics store in Cedar Rapids, Iowa, sold the first HD Radio tuner, a model Kenwood KTC-HR100, to Nathan Franzen. Franzen became the first consumer nationwide to purchase an HD Radio receiver and listen to HD Radio programming. He appreciated the HD Radio sound quality while tuning to the music program from KZIA-FM 102.9 (Z102.9), a radio station in Cedar Rapids. This sale marked the introduction of HD Radio to the consumer market. This event was part of the activities sponsored by the 2004 International Consumer Electronics show in Las Vegas. According to an iBiquity press release, "Cedar Rapids, Iowa, was selected partly because of its heritage as the hometown of Arthur Collins and the Collins Radio Company. In 1925, Collins, as a fifteen-year-old, received radio transmissions for the first time from Greenland. He eventually founded Collins Radio, which provided voice communication technology for every American traveling in space" (iBiquity Digital 2006, "Iowa").

Although the FCC did not announce a cutoff date, the progress in adopting and converting to HD Radio has been quite impressive (see Table 6). As of July 2007, there were 1,344 HD Radio stations on the air. Among those, 627 stations provide multichannel programs to the listeners.

United Kingdom and Other Countries: Eureka 147 and DRM

Eureka 147. In 1994, Eureka 147 was adopted as a world standard (Digital Radio Development Bureau 2006), and in September 1995 the BBC debuted its national digital radio broadcasting in the United Kingdom (BBC 2006c). In accordance with the technological development, trade bodies such as the World DAB (an international nongovernmental organization) and Digital Radio Development Bureau (sponsored by the BBC and UK commercial radio multiplex operators) were established to promote and coordinate the implementation of digital radio services based on the Eureka 147 system. Those nonprofit trade organizations developed membership from more than one hundred companies and organizations in thirty countries. The membership consists of public and private broadcasters, digital radio receiver and other electronic equipment manufacturers, transmission providers, regulators, and governmental bodies. Therefore, technological achievement has been converted to a worldwide commercial marketing success. According to the World DAB, "Over 475 million people around the world can now receive more than 1,000 different DAB services. Commercial DAB receivers have now been on the market since summer 1998. There are now more than 200 different DAB and over 150 DMB receivers commercially available. A receiver archive is available on this site, which exhibits DAB/DMB car radios, hi-fi's, portable receivers, PC cards, USBs, mobile phones, computers and other DAB/DMB equipment that have been developed." (World DAB 2007).

Currently, European countries such as Denmark, Norway, Belgium, the Netherlands, Switzerland, Germany, Spain, Portugal, and Italy have digital radio services. Sweden has been continuously on a national trial of digital radio broadcasting. France began digital radio services in five major cities in October 2005. Finland's national public service broadcasting, YLE Communications, introduced DAB in 1997 but announced in February 2005 that it would shut down DAB to consider other alternatives to implement digital radio broadcasting. Canada, Singapore, Korea, and Australia have launched operational or pilot services. Hong Kong (L band from 1998 to 2001; VHF band III from August 2004 to February 2006), Taiwan, China, and India have begun experimental service, and Mexico and Paraguay have expressed their advanced interest in digital radio broadcasting. Table 7 shows recent status of implementation among European, Asian, and African countries.

A receiver archive is available on World DAB's Web site, which exhibits DAB car radios, stereo systems, portable

Table 6: Stations on-the-Air or Have Licenses for HD Radio™ Technology

	State	Stations On-Air				Stations Multicast			
Date*		I	II	III	IV	I	II	III	IV
1	AK	2	2	7	7	0	0	1	1
2	AL	13	15	20	24	0	4	7	7
3	AR	0	5	6	9	0	0	0	5
4	AZ	2	6	14	27	0	1	5	11
5	CA	57	70	103	134	1	26	42	65
6	CO	16	30	39	47	0	1	11	16
7	CT	11	15	15	18	0	6	15	10
8	DC	0	0	18	21	0	0	10	13
9	DE	0	2	2	3	0	0	1	1
10	FL	36	49	63	88	2	8	16	56

(continued)

Table 6: *(continued)*

Date*	State	Stations On-Air				Stations Multicast			
		I	II	III	IV	I	II	III	IV
11	GA	19	25	26	28	0	8	15	17
12	HI	0	0	0	2	0	0	0	2
13	IA	5	10	10	10	0	1	1	3
14	ID	1	3	3	4	0	0	0	0
15	IL	25	30	35	43	4	15	20	23
16	IN	18	18	25	29	1	10	10	13
17	KS	6	5	10	16	0	3	4	8
18	KY	7	10	10	14	0	0	0	0
19	LA	3	3	4	8	0	0	0	1
20	MA	19	29	32	35	0	15	15	17
21	MD	6	7	9	11	0	5	6	7
22	ME	2	11	11	12	0	0	0	0
23	MI	27	31	41	50	6	13	15	19
24	MN	6	9	17	24	1	2	7	12
25	MO	10	18	24	37	0	0	3	22
26	MS	1	0	0	1	0	0	0	0
27	MT	3	8	8	15	0	0	0	1
28	NC	9	12	22	38	2	1	8	20
29	ND	0	0	0	0	0	0	0	0
30	NE	4	4	6	10	0	0	4	4
31	NH	1	2	4	7	0	0	0	0
32	NJ	7	4	6	7	0	0	1	1
33	NM	5	6	7	7	0	6	6	6
34	NV	4	7	6	8	0	3	3	6
35	NY	28	41	64	88	0	10	24	49
36	OH	29	35	50	72	4	15	20	33
37	OK	5	11	20	21	0	4	5	11
38	OR	11	13	13	16	0	8	3	9
39	PA	20	31	46	61	3	12	19	35
40	RI	2	3	6	9	0	0	0	3
41	SC	5	6	11	18	0	0	0	8
42	SD	0	0	0	4	0	0	0	0
43	TN	9	13	15	28	0	7	7	12
44	TX	33	46	68	93	0	25	29	45
45	UT	4	9	12	17	0	0	3	9
46	VA	9	8	24	30	2	0	6	12
47	VT	0	0	2	4	0	0	1	2
48	WA	14	17	21	28	2	13	15	17
49	WI	9	17	22	34	0	0	4	11
50	WV	2	2	2	11	0	0	0	0
51	WY	0	5	8	16	0	0	0	4
Total		505	703	987	1,344	28	222	362	627

Date: Sept. 25, 2005; II = Dec. 30, 2005; III = Sept. 17, 2006; IV = July 5, 2007
Source: www.ibiquity.com/hd_radio/hdradio_find_a_station

Table 7: Countries on the Air with Eureka 147 Technology

*Country	DAB coverage (%)	DAB services	Initial on-air date
Austria	19		Jan. 1999
Belgium	98	10 stations	1997
Denmark	100	18 channels	Sept. 1995
Finland	40	13 channels	1997 to Aug. 2005
France	25	5 major cities	Oct. 2005
Germany	85	150+ services	Sept. 1993
Italy	65	5 channels	Oct. 2004
Netherlands	70	8 NOS	Feb. 2004
Norway	70	15 channels	Feb. 1999
Spain	50	6 channels	Oct. 2002
Portugal	70	6 channels	1999
Sweden	35	National Trail	1995
Switzerland	58	9 DAB services	Fall 1999
United Kingdom	85	BBC (SFN): 11 national stations, 32 local stations	Sept. 1995
Singapore	100	18 channels	2002
South Korea	N/A	16 channels	Sept. 2004
China	Guangdong, Beijing	DMB (digital mobile)	2005 (pilot in 1999)
Taiwan	N/A	3 national, 3 local	2002 (BBC, CBS)
Hong Kong	N/A (trial)		Aug. 2004 to Feb. 2006
Canada	35	23 channels	Fall 1996 (CBC pilot)
Australia	N/A (trial)	Sydney, Melbourne	Dec. 2003
South Africa	N/A	8 channels	Dec. 1997

Other countries such as Andorra, Brunei, Croatia, Estonia, Hungary, Ireland, Israel, and Slovenia have also started recently.
Source: (1) DAB Ensembles Worldwide (www.wohnort.demon.co.uk/DAB), July 6, 2007; (2) Nyberg 2005; (3) BBC Digital Radio (www.bbc.co.uk/reception/digitalradio/dab.shtml); (4) Huerta 2002; (5) Finland's YLE press release (www.yle.fi/fbc/press_abandondab.shtml> 2/24/05)

receivers, PC cards, and other DAB equipment. According to a sales report by the World DAB Forum (World DAB 2006, "International"), in December 2005 a cumulative total of 2.716 million DAB sets were used in UK homes. Approximately 5.4 million people listened to digital radio on DAB sets (GfK Marketing Services 2005). Approximately 11.1 percent of UK residents lived in DAB households, and there were more listeners to digital radio via DAB sets than via the Internet and DTV combined (RAJAR 2006).

Digital Radio Mondiale. The DRM system has been tested and adopted by counties around the world. DRM broadcasts are now available in Europe, North America, and North Africa. Testing is underway in Latin America and Asia. The DRM services are also delivered online via the DRM Consortium Web site (www.drm.org) and in Germany (www.deutsches-drm-forum.de), France (www.drmfrance.com), and Russia (www.radiostation.ru/drm/index.php), as well as by U.S. DRM group (www.usdrm.com). In September 2005, the

BBC used DRM technology to launch its World Service programming in English to the Benelux countries and neighboring parts of France and Germany (BBC 2005).

During the International Broadcasting Convention (IBC) held in Amsterdam in September 2002, different DRM receivers were demonstrated. According to Jackson (2003, 1),

All the receivers were demonstrated receiving, at different times of the day, live SW transmissions from Sines in Portugal (Deutsche Welle: 1,922 km.), Sackville in Canada (Radio Canada International: 4,892 km), Bonaire in the Netherlands Antilles (Radio Netherlands: 7,796 km.), Juelich in Germany (T-Systems Media-Broadcast: 188 km.) and Rampisham in the UK (VT Merlin Communications carrying BBC WS programmes: 546 km.) and a continuous local 26 MHz SW service of audio with multimedia from Hilversum (RNW: 22 km).

During the ITU's World Radiocommunication Conference in June 2003, leading international, national, and local broadcasters simultaneously sent the world's first live, daily Digital Radio Mondiale broadcasts to Geneva. Broadcasters in Europe (International Broadcasters, BBC World Service, Christian Vision, Deutsche Welle, Radio France Internationale, Radio Netherlands, Radio Vaticana, Swedish Radio International, Voice of Russia, and Wales Radio International), the Middle East (Kuwait Radio and Ministry of Information of Kuwait), and North America (Radio Canada International and Voice of America) participated in the DRM debut broadcasting (DRM 2003).

In September 2005, the world's first, affordable DRM-capable consumer receivers, as well as car radios, were unveiled at the consumer electronics show IFA in Berlin. These products were also showcased in Amsterdam at the IBC that month. Texas Instruments and RadioScape introduced three multistandard, tabletop consumer radios with DRM, DAB, long-wave, medium-wave, and short-wave capabilities. Those radio sets used RadioScape's RS500 module and TI's DRM350 multistandard digital radio baseband. The receivers also possessed a variety of features such as storage, pause, built-in stereo speakers, recording, and playback (DRM 2005b).

International Digital Radio Broadcasting: DRM

The DRM system was originally developed for the band below 30 MHz, including low frequency, medium frequency radio services for AM spectrum stations, and high frequency shortwave stations. The shortwave radio is usually used for international radio broadcasting. The DRM Consortium Web site lists DRM live international broadcast schedules (DRM 2006). Approximately 110 stations worldwide broadcast DRM service daily. Among them, the majority are shortwave radio stations targeting international listeners.

Webcasting

Theoretically, audio Webcasting should be an ideal digital radio format to meet the needs of both domestic and international information, sports, and entertainment. It also provides interactive functions to let listeners control what they want to listen to and when to listen to it with no limitation of time or geography. However, the delivery and distribution of Webcasting is problematic. The quality is not good enough, and the signals are often delayed or interrupted during peak Internet hours. It needs more research and development. Therefore, audio Webcasting currently seems more technological promise than realistic radio industry. It serves for online music purchasing and as a supplementary archiving and promotional tool for traditional audio broadcasting.

CONCLUSION

The three kinds of terrestrial digital radio systems—Eureka 147, in-band on-channel, and Digital Radio Mondiale—have been tested and adopted for domestic and international radio broadcasting. Originally developed to be a supplementary system of Eureka 147, DRM has been used by countries worldwide to replace analog AM and FM radio services allotted in the LF, MF, HF, and VHF spectra. Although Eureka 147 provides excellent-quality radio and data services, DRM seems more attractive to those countries that do not have the resources for extra spectra in VHF band III or L band. The DRM Consortium plays a leading role in developing DRM technology and membership and in coordinating technical and marketing activities internationally. DRM has shown great potential in digital radio broadcasting.

IBOC is the standard of digital audio broadcasting in the United States as approved by the FCC. HD Radio has become an industry standard promoted by the National Association of Broadcasters. Still, the DRM system, as an international standard, is also promoted in the United States by the USA DRM Group. The group is examining "the possibility of using 26 MHz frequencies in the United States in DRM mode for local broadcasting (and maybe even sky wave broadcasting) with low power (10 watts to 1 kilowatt) to cover small areas such as universities and towns" (USA DRM Group 2005).

As a matter of fact, HD Radio provides multicasting capabilities to terrestrial radio stations that maintain analog programs along with digital programs and lets listeners receive programs for free. The 2006 NAB radio show in Dallas and the 2007 NAB convention in Las Vegas paid special attention to promoting and converting to HD Radio. In May 2007, the FCC released rules for HD Radio, such as operating hours and AM nighttime operation (FCC 2007b). The adoption of HD radio grows daily. Up to July 2007, there were 1,344 HD radio stations on air, of which 627 were multicasting (see Table 6). It is important to notice that the current 1,344 HD radio stations constitute approximately 10 percent of the total number of radio stations (13,837, which is the total number of the traditional AM and FM stations, excluding FM translators and boosters, and low-power FM stations) in the United States. Therefore, the conversion from analog to digital radio broadcasting seems an inevitable trend.

The two satellite digital radio services provided by XM and Sirius are still in their growing stages in the United States. The total number of SDARS subscribers reached 14.5 million in the first quarter of 2007 (Sirius Satellite Radio 2007; XM Satellite Radio 2007). The advantage of the SDARS is situated in the potential of program content, which enjoys more freedom of expression than traditional radio broadcasting, and its capability of providing international radio services such as WorldSpace. However, the FCC is closely monitoring the SDARS performance and does not allow interference of the SDARS with conventional free radio.

The competition among satellite radio, HD Radio, and Webcasting in the United States is critical to XM and Sirius satellite radio providers. The satellite radio companies, XM and Sirius, need more collaboration than competition in order to stay strong in the radio market. In February 2007, Sirius and XM reached an agreement to merge and retain the XM name; the consolidated applications were submitted to the FCC for approval in March 2007. According to the merging plan, a new board of directors selected by both Sirius and XM will control the surviving entity and "its equity will be represented equally by former shareholders of XM and Sirius prior to the merger" (FCC 2007c, "Public Notice"). This action initiated a great deal of discussion in the radio industry regarding monopoly and antitrust matters. In June 2007, the FCC issued a notice of proposed rule making to seek comments on this merger application "because the proposed transfer conflicts with language prohibiting such a combination in the Commission's 1997 Order establishing the Satellite Digital Audio Radio Service (FCC 1997a, "SDARS Report & Order"; FCC 2007d). The rule-making focus is on "whether the language in question constitutes a binding Commission rule and, if so, whether the Commission should waive, modify, or repeal the prohibition in the event that the Commission determines that the proposed merger, on balance, would serve the public interest" (FCC 2007d).

Although the satellite radio merge has not been decided, terrestrial HD Radio, SDARS, and audio Webcasting will co-exist. More collaboration among these three outlets will be seen as enhancing program production and distribution in order to better serve the public interest, a mission set up early in the Communication Act of 1934.

GLOSSARY

Audio Webcasting: Audio programs such as news, music, sports, and talk shows are delivered through the Internet and can be accessed through the Web pages of content providers.

Digital Audio Broadcasting (DAB): Trademark of the Eureka 147 project's digital radio broadcasting system.

Digital Radio Broadcasting (DRB): The generic term used to describe digital radio/digital audio broadcasting systems.

Digital Radio Mondiale (DRM): Digital radio broadcasting licensed for the band under 30 MHz. Currently, the DRM technologies are adopted mostly for international radio broadcasting.

Eureka 147: DAB system developed under the Eureka 147 Project and standardized by the European Telecommunications Standards Institute in 1995.

HD Radio: Trademarked IBOC technology implementation that provides enhanced sound fidelity (near-CD quality), improved reception, and new data services.

In-Band On-Channel (IBOC): Developed by the iBiquity Digital Corporation and approved as the digital radio broadcasting technology by the FCC in October 2002.

CROSS REFERENCES

See *Mobile Radio Communications*; *Satellite Communications Basics*; *Speech and Audio Compression*.

REFERENCES

Austerberry, D. 2002. *The technology of video and audio streaming.* New York: Focal Press.

Bower, A. J. 1998. Digital radio: The Eureka 147 DBA system. *BBC Electronic Engineering,* April, pp. 55–56 (retrieved from www/bbc.co.uk/rd/pubs/papers/paper_21/paper_21.shml).

British Broadcasting Corporation (BBC). 2005. BBC launches DRM service In Europe. *BBC World Service,* September 17 (retrieved from www.bbc.co.uk/worldservice/faq/news/story/2005/09/050907_drm_launch_release.shtml).

———. 2006a. Help receiving the BBC (retrieved from www.bbc.co.uk/reception/transmitters/radio_trans/digital_radio.shtml).

———. 2006b. BBC digital radio: The benefits of digital radio (retrieved from www.bbc.co.uk/digitalradio/about/benefits.shtml).

———. 2006c. So how does the BBC fit in? *Research & Development* (retrieved from www.bbc.co.uk/rd/projects/dab/dabbbc.shtml).

———. 2006d. BBC digital radio: The advantages of DAB radio (retrieved from www.bbc.co.uk/digitalradio/about/).

DAB ensembles worldwide. 2007 (retrieved from www.wohnort.demon.co.uk/DAB/).

Digital Radio Development Bureau. 2006. Eureka 147. Technical Information (retrieved from www.drdb.org/index.php?internalPage=tech.php&internalHeaderPage=tech_hd.html).

Digital Radio Mondiale (DRM). 2003. Leading broadcasters to air the world's first, live, daily, Digital Radio Mondiale (DRM) broadcasts during WRC 03, June 16th (news release retrieved from www.drm.org/pdfs/DRMDebutatWRC03.pdf).

———. 2005a. DRM votes to extend its system to 120 MHz: DRM and DAB digital radio systems join forces to ensure digital radio solutions worldwide (press release), March 10 (retrieved from www.drm.org/pdfs/press_release_1.pdf).

———. 2005b. DRM-capable consumer products unveiled at IFA: Sangean, Roberts, Morphy Richards, Bosch, Panasonic, Visteon and CT/AFG/Himalaya (new release), September 4 (retrieved from www.drm.org/pdfs/press_release_118.pdf).

———. 2006. Live broadcasts schedule (retrieved from www.drm.org/livebroadcast/livebroadcast.php).

Eureka 147 Project. 1997. *Eureka 147 digital audio broadcasting.* Köln, Germany: Author (retrieved from www.worlddab.org/images/eureka_brochure.pdf).

European Telecommunication Standard Institute (ETSI). 2000. *Digital audio broadcasting (DAB); Guidelines and rules for implementation and operation; Part 1: System outline.* ETSI TR 101 496-1 v1.1.1 (2000-11). Sophia Antipolis Cedex, France: Author (retrieved from www.etsi.org).

———. 2001a. *Digital audio broadcasting (DAB); Guidelines and rules for implementation and operation; Part3: System features,* ETSI TR 101 496-2 v1.1.2 (2001-05). Sophia Antipolis Cedex, France: Author (retrieved from www.etsi.org).

———. 2001b. *Digital audio broadcasting (DAB); Guidelines and rules for implementation and operation; Part 2: Broadcast network,* ETSI TR 101 496-3 v1.1.2 (2001-05). Sophia Antipolis Cedex, France: Author (retrieved from www.etsi.org).

———. 2001c. *Digital radio mondiale (DRM): System specification, ETSI TS 101 980 v1.1.1, 2001–09* (retrieved from etsi.org/SERVICES_PRODUCTS/FREESTANDARD/home.htm).

———. 2005. *Digital radio mondiale (DRM): System specification, ETSI TS 201 980 v2.2.1, 2005–10* (retrieved from www.etsi.org/SERVICES_PRODUCTS/FREE-STANDARD/home.htm).

Evens, R. H. 1998. An uplinking technique for Eureka 147 satellite DAB. *EBU Technical Review*, Winter. Geneva: EBU.

Federal Communications Commission. 1996. *Comments in response to reconsideration of implementation of the AM expanded band allotment plan.* MO&O, MM docket 87-267, FCC 96-113, 11 FCC Rcd 12444 (retrieved from www.fcc.gov/mb/audio/decdoc/engrser.html#AMEXBAND1).

———. 1997a. Establishment of rules and policies for the digital audio radio satellite service in the 2310-2360 MHz frequency band (SDARS Report & Order). RM No. 8610. Washington, DC: FCC (retrieved from wireless.fcc.gov/auctions/15/releases/fc970070.pdf).

———. 1997b. FCC announces auction winners for digital audio radio service. Public notice DA97-656, April 2. Washington, DC: Author (retrieved from http://wireless.fcc.gov/auctions/15/releases/da970656.pdf).

———. 1997c. International bureau grants satellite digital audio radio authorization to Satellite CD Radio, Inc. Report No. IN 97-31. O&A, DA 97-2191. Washington, DC: FCC (retrieved from www.fcc.gov/Bureaus/International/News_Releases/1997/nrin7036.html).

———. 1997d. International bureau grants satellite digital audio radio subject of document authorization to American Mobile Radio Corporation. Report No. IN 97-33. O&A, DA 97-2210. Washington, DC: FCC (retrieved from www.fcc.gov/Bureaus/International/News_Releases/1997/nrin7038.html).

———. 1998a. 47 Code of Federal Regulation, Sec. 73.128: AM stereophonic broadcasting (cite: 47CFR73.128). 58 FR 66301, Dec. 20, 1993, Revised as of October 1, 2004. Washington, DC: FCC (retrieved from http://frwebgate.access.gpo.gov/cgi-bin/get-cfr.cgi?TITLE=47&PART=73&SECTION=128&YEAR=2004&TYPE=TEXT).

———. 1998b. Amendment of part 73 of the Commission's rules to permit the introduction of digital audio broadcasting in the AM and FM broadcasting services [USADR Petition] petition for rulemaking (FCC RM-9395). Washington, DC: Author (retrieved from www.fcc.gov/Bureaus/Mass_Media/Filings/rm9395.pdf).

———. 1999. *In the matter of digital audio broadcasting systems and their impact on the terrestrial radio broadcast service.* Notice of proposed rule making. MM docket no. 99-325, FCC 99-327. Washington, DC: Author.

———. 2002a. Freeze announced on the filing of AM expanded band major change. Applications public notice, DA 02-239, 17 FCC Rcd 1806 (retrieved from http://hraunfoss.fcc.gov/edocs_public/attachmatch/DA-02-239A1.pdf).

———. 2002b. *Digital audio broadcasting systems and their impact on the terrestrial radio broadcast service.* First Report and Order, MM Docket No. 99-325, FCC 02-286, 17 FCC Rcd 19990. Washington, DC: Author.

———. 2004. *Digital audio broadcasting systems and their impact on the terrestrial radio broadcast service.* Further Notice of Proposed Rulemaking and Notice of Inquiry. MM Docket No. 99-325, FCC 04-99. Washington, DC: FCC.

———. 2006. *Satellite digital audio radio service (SDARS).* Washington, DC: FCC (retrieved from http://www.fcc.gov/ib/sd/ssr/sdars.html).

———. 2007a. Broadcast station totals as of December 31, 2006. *FCC News* (retrieved from http://news.radio-online.com/fcc/totals.pdf).

2007b. Digital audio broadcasting systems and their impact on the terrestrial radio broadcast service. Second Report and Order: First Order on Reconsideration and Second Further Notice of Proposed Rulemaking. MM Docket No. 99-325, FCC 07-33. Washington, DC: FCC (retrieved from http://hraunfoss.fcc.gov/edocs_public/attachmatch/FCC-07-33A1.pdf).

2007c. Sirius Satellite Radio Inc. and XM Satellite Radio Holdings Inc. seek approval to transfer control of FCC authorizations and licenses (Public Notice). MB Docket No. 07-57, DA 07-2417. Washington, DC: FCC.

2007d. Applications for consent to the transfer of control of licenses, XM Satellite Radio Holdings Inc., transferor, to Sirius Satellite Radio Inc., transferee. MB Docket No. 07-57, FCC 07-119. Washington, DC: FCC.

GfK Marketing Services. 2005. Online at www.gfkms.com.

Hallett, L. 2003. The development of the digital radio mondiale technology. *Radio World Online Special Report* (DRM: What's it about?), November 5. Falls Church, VA: IMAS Publishing (retrieved from www.rwonline.com/reference-room/iboc/05_rw_hd_drm_part_II.shtml).

———. 2003. The history of digital radio mondiale and how it compares to HD Radio and Eureka-147. *Radio World Online Special Report* (DRM: What's it about?), October 22. Falls Church, VA: IMAS Publishing (retrieved from http://www.rwonline.com/reference-room/special-report/03_rw_drm_5.shtml).

Huerta, J. M. 2002. DAB: El sistema DAB (Radio Nacional de España) (retrieved from www.rtve.es/dab/queesdab.html).

iBiquity Digital. 2005a. HD Radio air interface design description: Layer 1 AM (Rev. E), March 22. Doc. No. SY_IDD_1012s. Columbia, MD: Author (retrieved from www.nrscstandards.org/Standards/NRSC-5-A/1012sEc.pdf).

———. 2005b. HD Radio air interface design description: Layer 1 FM (Rev. E), March 22. Doc. No. SY_IDD_1011s. Columbia, MD: Author (retrieved from www.nrscstandards.org/Standards/NRSC-5-A/1011sEc pdf).

———.2006. Iowa: First in the nation for HD Radio (press release) (retrieved from www.ibiquity.com/press/pr/010204.htm).

———. 2006. KROQ-FM 106.7—Los Angeles, California (extensive coverage) (retrieved from www.ibiquity.com/hdradio/documents/successstorymediaKROQ-6203Final1.pdf).

———. 2006. WOR-AM 710, New York (retrieved from www.ibiquity.com/hdradio/documents/successstorymediaWOR6203Final1.pdf).

International Telecommunication Union. 2002. System for digital sound broadcasting in the broadcasting bands below 30 MHz (BS.1514 1), November 7 (retrieved from www.itu.int/rec/R-REC-BS.1514-1-200210-I/en).

———. 2007. Systems for terrestrial digital sound broadcasting to vehicular, portable and fixed receivers in the frequency range 30-3 000 MHz. Recommendation ITU-R BS.1114- 6, January (retrieved from www.itu.int/rec/R-REC-BS.1114-6-200701-I/en).

Jackson, P. 2003. *DRM – Progress on the receiver front.* EBU Technical Review, January from www.ebu.ch/en/technical/trev/trev_frameset-index.html).

Johnson, S. A. 2000. *The structure and generation of robust waveforms for AM in-band on-channel digital broadcasting.* Redwood City, CA: iBiquity Digital Corp. (retrieved from www.ibiquity.com/technology/papers.htm).

Kunz, O. 2006. SBR *explained* (white paper). Nuremberg, Germany: Coding Technologies (retrieved from www.codingtechnologies.com/products/sbr.htm).

Mack, S., and D. Rayburn. 2006. *Hands-on guide to Webcasting: Internet event and AV production.* New York: Focal Press.

Messer, H. D. 2006. Summary table of DRM usage possibilities (retrieved from www.drm.org/broadcastmanual/summarytable2.php).

National Association of Broadcasters. 2004. HD Radio certification workshop (retrieved from www.nab.org/conventions/radioshow/2004/hdradio.asp).

———. 2004b. HD Radio workshop Webcast (retrieved from www.nab.org/scitech/HDWebCast/HD2.htm).

National Radio Systems Committee. 2005. *NRSC-5-A: In-band/on-channel digital radio broadcasting standard* (retrieved from www.nrscstandards.org/standards.asp).

———. 2006. *Setting standards for future of radio* (retrieved from www.nrscstandards.org).

Nyberg, A. 2005. DAB roll-out around the world. Presentation at the World DAB Forum, IBC September 9–13, Amsterdam (retrieved from www.worlddab.org/gendocs.aspx).

Peyla, P. J. 2000. The structure and generation of robust waveforms for FM in-band on-channel digital broadcasting. Redwood City, CA: iBiquity Digital Corp. (retrieved from www.ibiquity.com/technology/papers.htm).

Pohlmann, K. C. 2000. *Principles of digital audio.* 4th ed. New York: McGraw-Hill.

Radio Advertising Bureau. 2005. *Radio marketing guide and fact book for advertisers.* 2004–05 ed. New York: Author (retrieved from www.rab.com/public/media/2004rmg&fblow.pdf).

RAJAR (Radio Joint Audience Research). 2006. Platform study Q4, 05 (retrieved from www.rajar.co.uk).

Sirius Satellite Radio. 2003. *2002 Form 10-K annual report.* New York: Author (retrieved from www.sirius.com).

———. 2005. *2004 annual report and proxy statement.* New York: Author (retrieved from www.sirius.com).

———. 2006. *Corporate overview* (retrieved from www.sirius.com/servlet/ContentServer?pagename=Sirius/CachedPage&c=Page&cid=1029348274177).

———. 2006. Reports record subscriber growth and revenue for fourth quarter and full-year 2005 (press release), February 17 (retrieved from www.shareholder.com/sirius/kit.cfm).

———. 2007. SIRIUS Satellite Radio reports strong first quarter 2007 results (investor relations), May 1 (retrieved from investor.sirius.com).

USA DRM Group. 2005. Report on 2005 USA DRM Group meeting. Washington, DC: Radio Free Asia (retrieved from www.usdrm.com/page.php?s=groupMeeting).

World DAB. 2007. Undated. The WorldDMB forum–Working towards the future of digital broadcasting (WorldDMB). (retrieved from www.worlddab.org/worlddab.php).

WorldSpace Satellite Radio. 2007 (retrieved from www.worldspace.com/coveragemaps/interactiveMap.html).

XM Satellite Radio. 2006. XM Satellite Radio Holdings Inc. announces fourth quarter and full year 2005 results (press release), February 16. Washington, DC: Author (retrieved from www.xmradio.com/newsroom/news_room.js).

———. 2007. XM Satellite Radio Holdings Inc. announces first quarter 2007 results (investor information), April 26 (retrieved from http://phx.corporate-ir.net/phoenix.zhtml?c=115922&p=irol-IRHome).

Spread Spectrum Signals for Digital Communications

Filippo Giannetti and Marco Luise, *University of Pisa, Italy*

INTRODUCTION

In the developed countries, the number of wireless access connections between the user terminals of a telecommunication network (phones, laptops, palmtops, etc.) and the fixed, high-capacity transport network has already exceeded the number of wired connections. Untethered communications and computing has become sort of a lifestyle, and the trend will undoubtedly continue in the near future with the development of Wi-Fi hot spots, wireless voice-over-IP (VoIP) terminals, and so on. The picture we have just depicted is what we may call the *wireless revolution* (Rappaport 1991). Beginning in Europe in the early 1990s, it is still ramping up with its adoption by Asian countries (Sasaki, Yabusaki, and Inada 1998). The driving elements of this revolution are the reduction of size and cost, together with the performance increase, of electronic components for *digital signal processing* (DSP), which allows a highly efficient implementation of source and channel coding, modulation, signal synchronization and equalization, and multiple access functionalities. In particular, modern mobile cellular systems have benefited from the adoption of *spread-spectrum* (SS) signaling techniques that will be treated in detail in the following sections.

Second- and Third-Generation Cellular Systems

The real start of the revolution was the advent of *second-generation* (2G) communications, which was inaugurated in 1991 by the well-known *global system for mobile* (GSM)

communications (Padgett, Günther, and Hattori 1995), a digital pan-European *time division multiple access* (TDMA) cellular communication system. Actually, the growth of cellular communications had already started with earlier *first-generation* (1G) analog systems, but the real breakthrough was marked by the initially slow, then exponential, diffusion of GSM terminals, fostered by continent-wide compatibility through international roaming. In the United States, the advent of 2G digital cellular telephony was somewhat slowed down by the coexistence of incompatible systems and the consequent lack of a nationwide accepted unique standard (Padgett, Günther, and Hattori 1995). The two competing 2G American standards were the so-called digital *advanced mobile phone system* (AMPS) IS-54/136, whose technology was developed with the specific aim of being backward-compatible (as far as the assigned radio channels are concerned) with the preexisting 1G analog AMPS system, and the highly innovative *code division multiple access* (CDMA) system *interim standard 95* (IS-95) (Kohno, Meidan, and Milstein 1995; Gilhousen et al. 1991). Although slower to gain momentum, 2G systems in the Americas had the merit of being the first to commercially introduce the SS technology and CDMA that in a few years would have been adopted worldwide for *third-generation* (3G) systems. A similar story about 2G digital cellular telephony could be told about Japan and its personal digital cellular system, which is actually quite similar from a technical standpoint to the American IS-54/136. China did not align itself with any of the digital 2G standards, while India adopted GSM but with a relatively

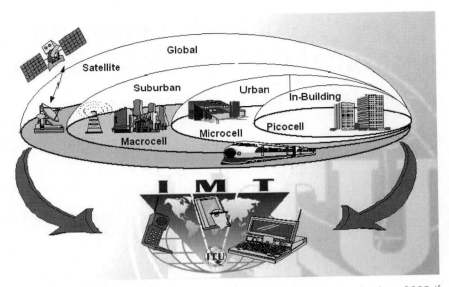

Figure 1: Architecture of a system compliant with International Mobile Telecommunications-2000 (from www.itu.org)

low level of penetration into the market. The number of GSM subscribers in India reached 65 million (i.e., approximately 6.5 percent of the population) by February 2006 (Cellular Operators Association of India 2007).

At the dawn of the third millennium, the International Telecommunications Union based in Geneva, Switzerland, took the initiative of promoting the development of a universal 3G mobile and personal wireless communication system with high capacity and a high degree of interoperability among the different network components (see Figure 1). Under the initiative International Mobile Telecommunications for the Year 2000 (Chia 192), a call for proposals was issued in 1997 to eventually set up the specifications and technical recommendations for a universal system. At the end of the selection procedure, and in response to the different needs of the national industries and telecom operators, three major but incompatible standards survived: *Universal Mobile Telecommunication System* (UMTS) for Europe and Japan (Dahlman et al. 1998; Adachi, Sawahashi, and Suda 1998), *CDMA2000* for the Americas (Knisely et al. 1998) and *time division synchronous code division multiple access* (TD-SCDMA) for China (Li et al. 2005). All are based on a different mixture of TDMA and CDMA technologies, but the real common innovative factor is the universal adoption of SS signals for a maximum of flexibility and multimedia support. A more detailed description of 2G and 3G CDMA-based wireless systems will be presented later.

In the following, we briefly outline the different SS techniques that are currently adopted to establish a multimedia (i.e., voice, video, and data) full duplex link between a *mobile terminal* (MT) and the *base station* (BS) of a cellular radio communication access network.

FUNDAMENTALS OF DIGITAL SPREAD-SPECTRUM SIGNALING
Narrowband

By the term *narrowband*, we indicate a data-modulated signal whose bandwidth around its carrier frequency is comparable to the information bit rate. Most popular narrowband modulated signals are *phase shift keying* (PSK), quadrature amplitude modulation (QAM), and a few nonlinear modulations such as *Gaussian minimum shift keying* (GMSK) which belongs to the broader class of continuous phase modulation (Proakis 1995). More details about these formats can be found in other chapters of this handbook. For the convenience of the reader, before describing SS signals we will review the basics of linearly modulated PSK and QAM signals.

The expression of a bandpass modulated signal $s_{BP}(t)$ is

$$s_{BP}(t) = s_I(t) \cdot \cos(2\pi f_0 t) - s_Q(t) \cdot \sin(2\pi f_0 t) \qquad (1)$$

where f_0 is the carrier frequency and $s_I(t)$ and $s_Q(t)$ are two baseband signals that represent the *in-phase* (I) and *quadrature* (Q) components, respectively, of the *phase-quadrature* (I/Q) modulated signal. A more compact representation of the modulated signal in Equation 1 is its complex envelope (or baseband equivalent), defined as $s(t) \triangleq s_I(t) + js_Q(t)$, where $j \triangleq \sqrt{-1}$. The relationship between the bandpass modulated signal and its own complex envelope is straightforward: $s_{BP}(t) = \Re\{s(t) \cdot \exp(j2\pi f_0 t)\}$, where $\Re\{\cdot\}$ stands for the "real part" of the complex-valued argument. In the case of a linear modulation, the complex envelope of $s_{BP}(t)$ is made of uniformly spaced data pulses as follows:

$$s(t) \triangleq A \cdot \sum_{i=-\infty}^{\infty} d[i] \cdot g_T(t - iT_s) \qquad (2)$$

where $d[i] \triangleq d_I[i] + jd_Q[i]$ is the ith transmitted symbol taken from a constellation of W points lying in the complex plane. The usual assumption is that the ith data symbol $d[i]$ is a random variable with uniform probability distribution over the W-point constellation alphabet and that $d[i]$ is statistically independent of $d[k]$, $i \neq k$. In addition, T_s is the signaling interval (i.e., the inverse of the symbol rate R_s), and $g_T(t)$ is a T_s-energy pulse.

If we denote with P_s the average power of the modulated signal in Equation 1, the average energy per data symbol is $E_s = P_s \cdot T_s$, and the amplitude coefficient in Equation 2 is equal to $A \triangleq \sqrt{2P_s/\mathrm{E}\{|d[i]|^2\}}$, where $\mathrm{E}\{\cdot\}$ stands for statistical expectation. Each symbol $d[i]$ in the constellation is addressed (labeled) by a word of $\log_2(W)$ binary symbols (bits) from a binary information source running at rate $R_b = R_s\log_2(W)$.

The *power spectral density* (PSD) of the signal in Equation 2 is proportional to $|G_T(f)|^2$, where $G_T(f)$ is the Fourier transform of the pulse shape $g_T(t)$. As a result, the (one-sided) spectral occupancy B of a narrowband modulated signal is strictly related to the bandwidth of the pulse shape $g_T(t)$. For instance, in the case of a transmission with *non-return-to-zero* (NRZ) rectangular pulses, the baseband occupancy, evaluated at the first spectral null, is $B = R_s$, whereas in the case of Nyquist's *square root raised cosine* (SRRC) band-limited pulse, the baseband occupancy is $B = (1 + \alpha)R_s/2$, where $0 \leq \alpha \leq 1$ is the pulse roll-off factor. Notice that the bandwidth occupancy B_{RF} of the modulated signal is twice that of the baseband signal—that is, $B_{RF} = 2B$.

Spread Spectrum

With the term *spread spectrum*, we address any modulated signal that has a bandwidth around the carrier frequency that is much larger than its information bit rate. In SS signaling, the bandwidth occupancy of the transmitted signal is intentionally increased well beyond the value required for conventional narrowband transmission, leaving unchanged the transmitted power. This is done to enhance signal robustness against interference, be it intentional (i.e., hostile jamming) or unintentional (e.g., human-made noise or narrow- and wideband transmitters operating on the same carrier frequency), and against the distortion caused by a frequency-selective radio channel. Spectral spreading also reduces the level of radiated power density (i.e., watts per hertz) and thus allows the simultaneous utilization of the same (wide) bandwidth by multiple users (this is called *multiple access*). Spectrum spreading can be essentially accomplished in two ways—namely, by frequency hopping and direct sequence.

Frequency-Hopping Spread Spectrum

Frequency-hopping spread spectrum (FHSS) was conceived in 1941 to provide secure military communications during World War II (Scholtz 1982), and it is based on a simple idea: Just (rapidly) change the transmit carrier frequency every T_{hop} seconds. The radio signal spectrum then "hops" from frequency to frequency following a periodic, pseudo-random (i.e., apparently random) sequence of carrier values to escape hostile jamming or eavesdropping by unauthorized listeners. The long-term spectrum of such signal "spans" a large *radio frequency* (RF) bandwidth and implements a spread-spectrum modulation (Simon et al. 1994; Dixon 1994). The (periodic) frequency hop pattern is also made known to the authorized receiver which is then capable of tracking the transmitted carrier and demodulate the transmitted data. The majority of commercial applications rely on *direct sequence spread spectrum* (DSSS),

while military communications often adopt FHSS because of the larger spreading factors (see "Spectral Spreading Performance Figures" below).

The current most popular technology that uses some form of FHSS is Bluetooth (Haartsen et al. 2000), which is an open standard for short-range, low-power, low-cost, and low-speed wireless data communications. Bluetooth radio interfaces are currently available in PCs and peripherals (allowing cable-free connections), in cell phones and headsets (allowing hands-free telephony), and in many other home appliances and consumer electronic equipments. Bluetooth operates in the unlicensed 2.4-GHz *industrial, scientific, and medical* (ISM) band, which is also used by 802.11 b/g devices, HomeRF devices, portable phones, and microwave ovens. To minimize the amount of interference caused against these devices operating in the same band, Bluetooth radio access is based on an FHSS technology that uses seventy-nine channels, each with a nominal bandwidth of 1 MHz at a "hop" rate of 1600 changes of frequency per second. Tight restrictions about the maximum allowed peak power output in the ISM band limit the range of Bluetooth devices to approximately a few tens of meters.

In the following, we will restrict our attention to the most popular cellular communication standards that account for the vast majority of commercial applications. Therefore, proprietary or local solutions having limited diffusion; military communications, for which scarce up-to-date information is available, will not be dealt with any further. However, the general knowledge of spread-spectrum signals should be enough also to understand the basic operation of such systems.

Direct Sequence Spread Spectrum

Spectral spreading is accomplished by direct multiplication in the time domain of the information-bearing symbols, running at rate $R_s = 1/T_s$, with a sequence of pseudorandom binary symbols (the so-called chips) $c[k]$ running at the much higher rate $R_c \triangleq 1/T_c \gg R_s$, with T_c the chip interval (Dixon 1994; Pickholtz, Schilling, and Milstein 1982; Simon et al. 1994). The result of this product (which is carried out before transmit pulse shaping takes place) is a stream of "chipped" high-rate symbols running at the chip rate R_c. The signal to be transmitted turns out to have a bandwidth occupancy that is much wider than that of conventional modulation schemes—in particular, comparable to the chip rate. The binary sequence $[c[k]]$, addressed as spreading sequence or spreading code, is periodic with period L chips, and has *pseudonoise* (PN) characteristics—that is, zero mean and an autocorrelation sequence as close as possible to an impulse function (Dinan and Jabbari 1998).

DSSS Signal Model

Assuming that one symbol interval T_s spans an integer number M of chip intervals T_c of the spreading sequence (i.e., $M \triangleq T_s/T_c = R_c/R_s$ is an integer), a DSSS signal can be represented as

$$s^{(ss)}(t) \triangleq A \cdot \sum_{k=-\infty}^{\infty} d[k /\!/ M] \cdot c[|k|_L] \cdot g_T(t - kT_c) \qquad (3)$$

where we defined the operators $k//M \triangleq \text{int}(k/M)$, and $|k|_L \triangleq k \bmod L$. The spreading sequence $c[k]$, either real- or complex-valued, runs at rate $R_c = 1/T_c$, and therefore a new T_c-energy chip shaping pulse $g_T(t)$ is generated every T_c seconds. The chip index k "ticks" at the rate R_c, and the spreading code index $|k|_L$ cycles over the interval $0, 1, \ldots, L-1$ every L chip intervals scanning the whole code length. The data index $k // M$ runs at the symbol rate $R_s = R_c/M$—that is, it is updated every M ticks of the index k. The normalization constant is again $A \triangleq \sqrt{2P_s/\text{E}[|d[i]|^2]}$, and the average energy per chip is now $E_c = P_s \cdot T_c$.

Real Spreading

In *real spreading* DSSS (RS DSSS), the spreading sequence $c[k]$ is real-valued, and the chips usually belong to the alphabet $\{-1, +1\}$. In the particular case of complex-valued data $d[i]$, such a DSSS format is named *quadrature real spreading* (Q-RS).

Complex Spreading

In complex spreading DSSS (CS DSSS), the spreading sequence $c[k]$ is complex-valued—that is, $c[k] \triangleq c_I[k] + jc_Q[k]$, where both the real and the imaginary part of the sequence are as in RS above. Two spreading codes are thus needed for the transmission of a CS DSSS signal. This popular spreading technique is employed by several commercial systems (see "A Review of 2G and 3G Standards for CDMA" for more details): IS-95 uses CS with real-valued data symbols $d[i]$, whereas UMTS or CDMA2000 also feature CS with complex data.

DSSS Bandwidth Occupancy

The bandwidth occupancy of the DSSS signal is dictated by the chip rate R_c (as is apparent from Equation 3) and by the shape of the basic pulse $g_T(t)$. For instance, in the case of a DSSS transmission with NRZ rectangular chip shaping, the baseband occupancy of the SS signal in Equation 3, when evaluated at the first spectral null, is $B^{(ss)} = R_c$ and thus $B^{(SS)} \gg B$. However, apart from particular applications, mainly military communications and the global positioning system radiolocation system, the spectrum of the DSSS signal is strictly band-limited because of regulatory issues. This leads to the definition of a band-limited spread spectrum signal (which may sound as a sort of paradox). As in the case of conventional narrowband modulations, spectrum limitation can be achieved by resorting to Nyquist SRRC shaping of the chip pulses so that the bandwidth occupancy becomes $B^{(SS)} = (1 + \alpha)R_c/2$ for the baseband signal and $B_{RF}^{(SS)} = (1 + \alpha)R_c$ for the modulated signal.

Spectral Spreading Performance Figures

The bandwidth spreading of a DSSS system is quantified by two parameters, namely, the spreading factor and the processing gain.

The spreading factor is defined as $M \triangleq T_s/T_c = R_c/R_s$ and represents the ratio between the bandwidth occupancy of the SS signal $B^{(SS)}$ and the bandwidth B of the corresponding narrowband modulated signal with the same symbol rate. Typical values of the spreading factor commonly adopted in commercial wireless communication systems range from 4 to 512. If channel coding is used, and the chip and bit rates are kept constant, the spreading factor is reduced by a factor r, where $r < 1$ is the coding rate. This is easily understood because channel coding has the effect of increasing the symbol rate by a factor $1/r$, thus expanding the signal bandwidth by the same factor before spectrum spreading takes place. Keeping the chip rate constant means keeping the same RF bandwidth, and so the net result is a decrease of the spreading factor.

The processing gain is defined as $G_p \triangleq T_b/T_c = R_c/R_b$ and, in the absence of channel coding, is related to the spreading factor as $G_p = M/\log_2(W)$. As is apparent, the two are coincident only in the case of binary modulation with no channel coding. The processing gain is the standard figure of merit of the antijamming capability of the DSSS signal (Simon et al. 1994).

Short Code

A spreading sequence is called *short code* when one data symbol interval exactly spans a (small) integer number n of the spreading sequence repetition periods—that is, $T_s = nLT_c$. In this case, the spreading factor is $M = nL$. The simplest and most adopted short code spreading arrangement is the case with $n = 1$, whereby the code repetition period is equal to one symbol interval, and $M = L$. An example of signal spreading by a short code, with $M = L = 8$ and NRZ chip shaping is shown in Figure 2. Short code spreading is specified as an option for the *uplink* (UL)—that is, from MT to BS—of UMTS (see "A Review of 2G and 3G Standards for CDMA Mobile Communications" below) to enable multi-user detection.

Long Code

A spreading sequence is called *long code* when its repetition period is much longer than the data symbol duration—that is, $LT_c = T_s$. In this case, the spreading factor is $M \ll L$. An example of signal spreading by a long code, with $M = 8$ and $L = 24$, is shown in Figure 3. Long code spreading is specified for the *downlink* (DL)—that is, from BS to MT—of UMTS and for both the DL and UL of IS-95 and CDMA2000 (see ""A Review of 2G and 3G Standards" for more details).

Pseudorandom Sequence Generators

A real-valued binary spreading sequence $c[k]$ with pseudonoise properties is also called *pseudorandom binary sequence* and can be generated by an m-stage *linear feedback shift register* (LFSR) whose taps are properly set according to polynomial theory (Peterson and Weldon 1972). In particular, it is possible to design sequence generators based on one or more LFSR structures (Dixon 1994; Pickholtz, Schilling, and Milstein 1982; Simon et al. 1994; Dinan and Jabbari 1998) so as to obtain spreading codes with random-like appearance and special features as far as the repetition period and the correlation properties are concerned (Sarwate and Pursley 1980). The reader is referred to Dixon (1994) for further details on the main sets of

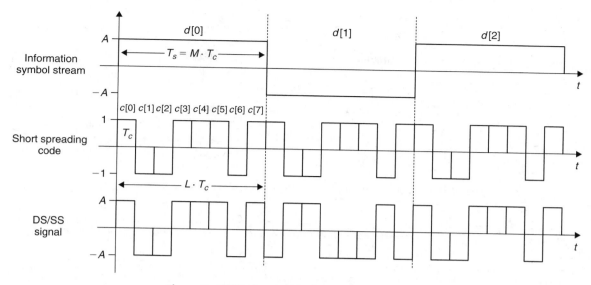

Figure 2: DSSS signal with short code, $M = L = 8$

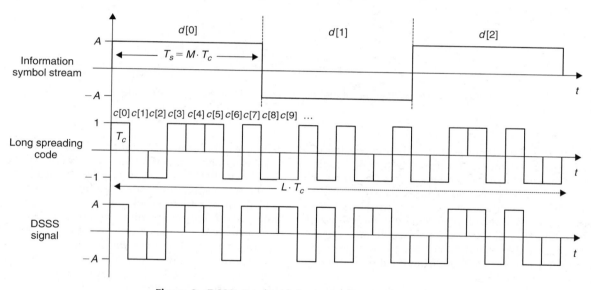

Figure 3: DSSS signal with long code, $M = 8$, $L = 24$

pseudorandom codes used in the practice (maximal length codes, Gold codes, and Kasami codes).

Basic Architecture of a DSSS Modem

Figure 4 shows the general outline of the modulator section of a digital DSSS modem, where, as customary, thick lines denote complex-valued signals (such a graphical notation will be used also in the subsequent diagrams). The information-bearing binary data undergo channel encoding and are mapped onto a complex constellation, thus yielding the data symbol stream $d[i]$ running at symbol rate R_s.

The symbol stream $d[i]$ is then oversampled (repeated) by a factor M, and spectrum spreading is eventually accomplished by direct multiplication with the spreading code $c[k]$ running at chip rate $R_c = MR_s$. Next, chip pulse shaping is performed in the digital domain by a finite

impulse response filter featuring SRRC response $g_T[m]$ and operating at sample rate $R_{sa} \triangleq 1/T_{sa}$ (for instance, $R_{sa} = 4R_c$). The resulting baseband DSSS signal at the filter output is a digital version of the signal in Equation 3 with a sampling frequency R_{sa}. Such a DSSS signal is up-converted to a digital *intermediate frequency* (IF) f_D, then digital-to-analog conversion takes place, followed by conventional analog processing (final upconversion to RF, power amplification, and band limiting) before the signal is sent on the air.

The basic outline of the twin demodulator section is sketched in Figure 5. The analog received signal undergoes RF amplification and filtering, followed by downconversion to IF. In many state-of-the-art implementations, analog-to-digital conversion takes directly place at IF with bandpass sampling techniques as shown. The conversion rate R_{ADC} is invariably faster than the chip rate R_c to perform subsequent baseband filtering with no aliasing issues

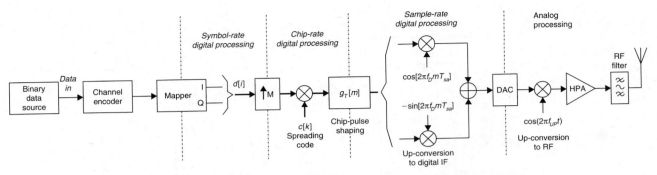

Figure 4: Block diagram of the transmit section of a digital DSSS modem

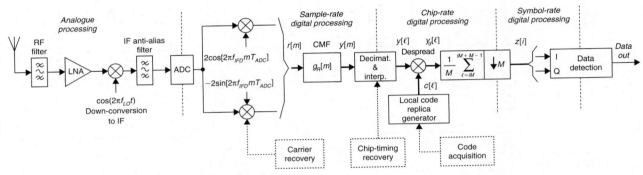

Figure 5: Block diagram of the receive section of a digital DSSS modem

(e.g., $R_{ADC} = 4R_c$). The digital signal is then converted to baseband by an I/Q demodulator driven by a digital oscillator under the control of the carrier synchronization unit (see "Architecture of Spread-Spectrum Receivers"). Each component of the resulting complex signal $r[m]$ is fed to a filter $g_R[m]$ matched to the chip pulse (*chip-matched filter*, CMF). On both I/Q rails, a decimator-interpolator changes the clock rate of the digital signal $y[m]$ and takes the optimum samples $y[\ell]$ at chip rate from the digital stream available at the filter output.

Assuming SRRC chip pulse shaping in the transmitter, propagation channel affected by *additive white Gaussian noise* (AWGN), ideal CMF in the receiver, and perfect chip timing and carrier synchronization, the chip-rate signal $y[\ell]$ at the decimator-interpolator output is

$$y[\ell] = A \cdot d[\ell // M] \cdot c[|\ell|_L] + n[\ell] \tag{4}$$

where $n[\ell]$ is a random process (which represents the contribution of the filtered channel noise) whose I/Q components are independent, identically distributed zero-mean Gaussian random variables with variance $\sigma_n^2 = N_0/T_c$ (N_0 is the one-sided power spectral density of the receiver noise). Subsequently, the spreading code is removed from the received signal by performing the so-called despreading operation:

$$y_d[\ell] = y[\ell] \cdot c[|\ell|_L] = A \cdot d[\ell // M] \cdot c^2[|\ell|_L] \\ + n[\ell]c[|\ell|_L] = A \cdot d[\ell // M] + n'[\ell] \tag{5}$$

where we took into account that $c^2[|\ell|_L] = 1$, and where $n'[\ell]$ is a noise component statistically equivalent to $n[\ell]$. It is seen that despreading requires a local replica $c[\ell]$ of the same spreading code used by the transmitter, and also requires perfect synchronicity of the remote and local codes. After despreading, we are left with a (digital) narrowband rectangular pulse signal plus AWGN. The optimum processing for data detection is thus (digital) integration over a one-symbol period to yield the following complex-valued quantity that is optimum for data detection (also called *sufficient statistics*)

$$z[i] \triangleq \frac{1}{M} \cdot \sum_{\ell=iM}^{iM+M-1} y_d[\ell] = \frac{1}{M} \cdot \sum_{\ell=iM}^{iM+M-1} y[\ell] \cdot c[|\ell|_L] \tag{6}$$

Recalling Equations 4 and 5, we obtain

$$z[i] = \frac{1}{M} \cdot \sum_{\ell=iM}^{iM+M-1} A \cdot d[\ell // M] + \frac{1}{M} \cdot \sum_{\ell=iM}^{iM+M-1} n'[\ell] = A \cdot d[i] + v[i] \tag{7}$$

where $v[i]$ is a noise term whose I/Q components are independent, identically distributed zero-mean Gaussian random variables with variance $\sigma_v^2 = \sigma_n^2/M = N_0/(MT_c) = N_0/T_s$. From Equation 6, we see that despreading accumulation is equivalent to the operation of cross-correlation between the received signal $y[\ell]$ and the local code replica $c[\ell]$, computed on the ith symbol period to yield the ith sufficient statistics $z[i]$. This is why we also speak of *correlation receiver* (CR).

The decision strobe of Equation 7 is eventually passed to the final detector, which may be a slicer to regenerate the transmitted digital data stream or, if channel coding is adopted, a soft-input channel decoder such as a Viterbi algorithm (Viterbi 1967; Viterbi and Omura 1979). Looking at Equation 7, we also see that the sufficient statistics is exactly the same we would obtain in the case of conventional narrowband transmission of the symbol stream $d[i]$ over an AWGN channel with matched filter detection. The conclusion is that spreading-despreading is completely transparent to the end user as far as the bit error rate (BER) performance of the link over an AWGN channel with matched filter detection is concerned.

As already mentioned, Figure 5 also shows ancillary functions—namely, carrier frequency and phase and chip timing recovery, together with spreading code time alignment—that will be dealt with later. Also, other receiver architectures different from the one in Figure 5 (for instance, the so-called zero-IF receiver) are used in the practice.

CODE DIVISION MULTIPLE ACCESS
Frequency, Time, and Code Division Multiplexing

In the DSSS signaling schemes discussed above, the data stream generated by an information source is spread over a wide frequency band using one or two spreading codes. Starting from this consideration, we can devise an access system that allows multiple users to share a common radio channel. This can be achieved by assigning each user a different spreading code and letting all of the signals concurrently access the same frequency spectrum. All of the user signals are therefore transmitted at the same time and over the same frequency band, but they can nevertheless be identified thanks to the particular properties of the spreading codes. The users are kept separated in the code domain, instead of the time or the frequency domain, as in conventional *time* or *frequency division multiple access*, respectively (TDMA and FDMA). Such a multiplexing or multiple-access technique, based on DSSS transmission, is called *code division multiple access*, and the particular spreading sequence identifying each user is also addressed to as signature.

In the DL of a cellular network, the N user signals in DSSS format are obtained from a set of N traffic-bearing channels that are physically co-located into a single site—for instance, the radio base station. The BS keeps all N tributary streams $d_n[k//M]$, $n = 1,2,...,N$ synchronous and performs spectrum spreading on each channel using a set of N different signature codes $c_n[k]$, $n = 1, 2, ...,N$, all having the same start epoch (i.e., the start instant of the repetition period). The resulting *synchronous code division multiplexing* (SCDM) signal is

$$s^{(CDM)}(t) \triangleq A \cdot \sum_{k=-\infty}^{\infty} \left(\sum_{n=1}^{N} d_n[k//M] \cdot c_n[|k|_L] \right) g_T(t - kT_c) \quad (8)$$

The most popular class of binary spreading codes commonly used for SCDM in DL of cellular networks is the *Walsh-Hadamard* (WH) set (Ahmed and Rao 1975; Dinan and Jabbari 1998), which is made of $L = 2^\zeta$ sequences (with ζ an integer) with repetition period L each (in practical systems $L = 32, 64, 128,$ or 256). The WH sequences are orthogonal—that is,

$$\frac{1}{L} \sum_{k=0}^{L-1} c_n[k] \cdot c_m[k] = \begin{cases} 0 & n \neq m \\ 1 & n = m \end{cases} \quad (9)$$

When SCDM is used with WH codes, it is also addressed to as synchronous orthogonal CDM (SOCDM). Demultiplexing of channel i out of the multiplex signal in Equation 8 is easily accomplished by the simple correlation receiver described earlier, provided of course that it uses the signature code $c_i[k]$. Thanks to the orthogonality property of the WH codes, no interference from the other channels is experienced (see also "Multiple Access Interference" below). The set of WH codes of length 2, 4, and 8 is reported in the second, third, and fourth columns of Figure 6, respectively.

In the UL of a cellular network, the DSSS signals are originated by N spatially separated MTs that access the same physical medium (the same RF bandwidth), and their superposition is collected at the receiver antenna. Synchronization of the different sparse MTs is extremely difficult to achieve, and so the access is asynchronous and therefore termed *asynchronous CDMA* (ACDMA). The resulting received signal at the BS receiver is

$$r(t) = \sum_{n=1}^{N} e^{j(2\pi\Delta f_n t + \theta_n)} s_n^{(SS)}(t - \tau_n) + w(t) \quad (10)$$

where τ_n, Δf_n, and θ_n are the propagation delay, carrier frequency, and phase offsets, respectively, of the generic nth signal, and $w(t)$ is an AWGN contribution. We neglect here multipath propagation, which will be dealt with later under "Rake Receiver." Recalling the DSSS signal description presented earlier, the generic nth traffic channel in DSSS format can be expressed as

$$s_n^{(SS)}(t) \triangleq A_n \cdot \sum_{k=-\infty}^{\infty} d_n[k//M \cdot c_n[|k|_L] \cdot g_T(t - kT_c) \quad (11)$$

where A_n, $d_n[i]$, and $c_n[k]$ are the nth channel signal amplitude, data symbols, and signature sequence, respectively. The signal received by a MT in the DL can actually be seen as a special case of Equation 10, with $\tau_n = \tau$, $\Delta f_n = \Delta f$, and $\theta_n = \theta$, for every n—that is, all signal are synchronous and experience the same carrier frequency or phase shift. Orthogonality among asynchronous signals cannot be enforced.

Multirate Code Division Multiplexing

Advanced communication systems (2G and 3G cellular) support different kind of services (e.g., voice, video, data), and so the required bit rate per user can be variable from a few kbit/s up to a few Mbit/s. The spreading scheme has to be flexible enough to allocate signals with different bit rates on the same bandwidth. This can be achieved

Layer 0	Layer 1	Layer 2	Layer 3
$c_0(0)$ $+1$	$c_1(1)$ $+1-1$	$c_2(3)$ $+1-1-1+1$	$c_3(7)$ $+1-1-1+1-1+1+1-1$
			$c_3(6)$ $+1-1-1+1+1-1-1+1$
		$c_2(2)$ $+1-1+1-1$	$c_3(5)$ $+1-1+1-1+1-1+1$
			$c_3(4)$ $+1-1+1-1+1-1+1-1$
	$c_1(0)$ $+1+1$	$c_2(1)$ $+1+1-1-1$	$c_3(3)$ $+1+1-1-1-1-1+1+1$
			$c_3(2)$ $+1-1-1+1+1-1-1+1$
		$c_2(0)$ $+1+1+1+1$	$c_3(1)$ $+1+1-1-1-1-1+1$
			$c_3(0)$ $+1+1+1+1+1+1+1+1$

Figure 6: OVSF codes tree; each layer is the complete set of WH codes of a particular length

basically by three different techniques—multicode, symbol repetition, or variable spreading factor— or a mixture of the three. In the multicode option, if users require a higher bit rate than the one of the basic channel, then they are simply allocated more than one signature code, and the high-rate bit stream is split into a number of parallel lower-rate streams each occupying a single (basic rate) channel. This is done in UMTS and CDMA2000 (see "A Review of 2G and 3G Standards for CDMA"). With symbol repetition, the basic rate is by definition the highest in the network. If a lower rate is needed, then it is obtained by generating a "fake" high-rate stream obtained by repetition a number of times of the same low-rate datum. This is the technique used in IS-95 (see "A Review" later in the chapter). Using a variable spreading factor, the chip rate R_c (and therefore SS bandwidth $B^{(ss)}$) is kept constant, but the spreading factor M is varied according to the bit rate of the signal to be transmitted. This has also to be done without altering the property of mutual code orthogonality outlined above. The solution to this issue, applied in UMTS, CDMA2000, and TD-SCDMA (see "A Review" below) is the special class of codes named *orthogonal variable spreading factor* (OVSF) (Adachi, Sawahashi, and Okawa 1997; Dinan and Jabbari 1998). The OVSF code set is a reorganization of the WH codes into layers, as shown in Figure 6, wherein the codes on each layer have twice the length of the codes in the previous layer. Each code is labeled using an array notation $c_n(k)$, wherein the subscript n denotes the layer, and the index k denotes the code within each layer.

Also, the codes are organized in a tree, wherein any two "children" codes on the layer to the right of a "parent" code are generated by repetition and repetition with sign change, respectively, of the parent. The peculiarity of the tree is that any two codes are not only orthogonal within each layer (each layer is just the complete set of the WH codes of the corresponding length) but also orthogonal across layers, provided that the shorter is not an "ancestor" of the longer one. The shorter code is used for

a higher-rate transmission with a smaller spreading factor, and the longer code is used for a lower-rate transmission with a higher spreading factor (recall that the chip rate is always the same). OVSF are used as channelization code in the DL of both CDMA2000 and UMTS to keep the user channels separated. Unfortunately, the radio signal undergoes distortion during propagation because of the multipath phenomenon, which will be discussed in detail later under "Rake Receiver." Multipath causes the loss of signal orthogonality in spite of the use of OVSF codes. This effect can be mitigated by orthogonality-restoring techniques (channel estimation and equalization) whose efficacy is measured by an orthogonality loss factor that quantifies the receiver performance degradation with respect to the case of perfect code orthogonality (no multipath propagation).

Multiple Access Interference

In the DL of a cellular network each BS sends out an N-channel SOCDM signal so that any MT located within a cell experiences no interference from the other channels in the multiplex thanks to the orthogonality of the channelization WH codes. To see this, assume that the generic mobile receiver intends to detect the useful traffic channel h. The output of the relevant correlation receiver is (see Equation 6)

$$z_h[i] = A_h \cdot d_h[i] + \mu[i] + \nu[i] \tag{12}$$

where $\nu[i]$ is channel noise, and

$$\mu[i] \triangleq \sum_{\substack{n=1 \\ n \neq h}}^{N} \left\{ \frac{1}{M} \cdot \sum_{\ell=iM}^{iM+M-1} A_n \cdot d_n[\ell /\!/ M] \cdot c_n[\ell|\ell|_L] \cdot c_h[\ell|\ell|L] \right\}$$
$$= \sum_{\substack{n=1 \\ n \neq h}}^{N} \left\{ \frac{A_n \cdot d_n[i]}{M} \cdot \sum_{\ell=0}^{M-1} c_n[\ell] \cdot c_h[\ell] \right\} \tag{13}$$

represents a cross-talk term caused by the presence of the other user signals and is addressed as *multiple-access interference* (MAI). Recalling Equation 9, if WH codes are used, then the MAI term $\mu[i]$ vanishes and Equation 12 collapses to Equation 7.

Without entering into further detail, we can easily argue that MAI is, on the contrary, intrinsic to detection of an UL channel. In this case, in fact, the N aggregate DSSS signals of Equation 10 are received by the BS in ACDMA mode. The output of the correlation receiver for channel h can still be put in a form similar to Equations 12 and 13, with a different, slightly more involved expression of the MAI term $\mu[i]$. But now the asynchronous access that is peculiar of the UL prevents the use of orthogonal codes to cancel MAI and $\mu[i] \neq 0$. The usual choice of the channelization codes is thus a set of (long) PN sequences that, thanks to their "randomness," makes $\mu[i]$ similar to additional Gaussian noise, uncorrelated with respect to the useful traffic signal. This approach is pursued in the UL of all of the 2G and 3G commercial systems currently in use.

An MAI-dominated ACDMA system heavily suffers from the so-called near-far effect, where strong-powered users (usually, those located in the vicinity of the receiver in the radio base station) interfere with the weaker ones (usually, those located far from the receiver, i.e., at the edge of a cell). This is why all CDMA cellular systems adopt power control systems that, by continually adjusting the power sent by the user terminals, let the signals from different users arrive at the receiver with well-balanced power (Gilhousen et al. 1991).

Capacity of a CDMA System

In the DL of a cellular network, SOCDM is commonly adopted. Therefore, any BS can radiate a CDM signal containing up to L traffic channels (i.e., the size of the orthogonal code set) without introducing any *quality-of-service* (QoS) degradation because of the presence of multiple users. With WH codes, the spreading factor M is equal to the code length L (short codes), and this represents the key to understanding the interplay between spectrum spreading and multiplexing. Using DSSS transmission, the signal bandwidth is expanded by a factor M, and this is a potential bandwidth waste. But using SOCDM, as many as M signals can be allocated in the same bandwidth with no mutual interference, thus regaining the original bandwidth efficiency. This is exactly what happens with FDMA (whereby the total bandwidth is increased by the number of channels M that are put onto adjacent carriers) and with TDMA (where the channel signaling rate is increased by a factor M to accommodate the M tributary signals). The spreading factor represents thus the ultimate capacity of the DL in a CDMA network, and in this respect CDMA is no better or no worse than FDMA and TDMA.

In the UL, on the contrary, synchronization of the MTs is no longer feasible and ACDMA with long spreading codes (e.g., PN sequences) is adopted. The receiver may experience a significant amount of MAI (as is apparent from Equations 12 and 13) that may cause a significant degradation of the QoS in the terms of BER. The nice feature of ACDMA, also referred to as *graceful degradation property*, is that the QoS degradation can be traded off with a capacity

increase (Gilhousen et al. 1990, 1991). To see this, observe that MAI can be seen as an additional, independent noise term summing up the usual receiver noise contributions. If N traffic channels are active (i.e., the useful one plus $N - 1$ interferers) and all of the interfering channels are received with the same power level P_s, then the MAI can be modeled as a white Gaussian noise process, whose equivalent PSD is found to be

$$I_0 \triangleq \frac{(N-1) \cdot P_s}{B^{(SS)}} = \frac{(N-1) \cdot P_s}{1/T_c} = (N-1) \cdot E_c \qquad (14)$$

All 2G and 3G CDMA systems implement specific power control strategies to ensure that the condition of power balancing is attained within a small error margin. As a consequence, the BS correlation receiver experiences an equivalent total noise PSD given by $N_0 + I_0$. Assuming *quadrature PSK* (QPSK) modulation, the BER of the link is

$$P(e) = Q\left(\sqrt{\frac{2E_b}{N_0 + I_0}}\right) = Q\left(\sqrt{\frac{2E_b}{N_0 + (N-1) \cdot E_c}}\right)$$
$$= Q\left(\sqrt{\frac{2E_b}{N_0} \cdot \frac{1}{1 + (N-1)/G_p \cdot E_b/N_0}}\right) \qquad (15)$$

where $Q(x) \triangleq \sqrt{1/2\pi} \int_x^\infty \exp(-y^2/2)\, dy$ represents the Gauss integral function, and $G_p = E_c/E_b$ is the so-called processing gain. It is apparent that the number N of concurrently active users depends on the specification about the QoS of the link, expressed in terms of a target BER: The lower the required QoS (i.e., the larger is the target BER), the higher the capacity in terms of number of active users. From this standpoint, it is easily seen that the UL capacity of CDMA can be further boosted up by the appropriate use of channel coding (Viterbi 1979).

A more advanced solution to the issue of the MAI is *multi-user data detection* (MUD) wherein demodulation of all of the UL data streams is performed in a single, centralized signal processing unit (Verdù 1998). With such a centralized detection approach, the presence of a certain amount of MAI coming from interfering channels can be accounted for when demodulating the useful, intended channel. This standpoint applies reciprocally to all of the channels, leading to the above-mentioned notion of "multi-user" demodulation. By concurrently observing all of the correlators' outputs, the MAI can be taken into account when detecting each channel, and it can be mitigated or "cancelled" by suitable signal processing. This leap forward in the performance of the CDMA receiver, not surprisingly, comes at the expense of a substantial increase in the complexity (signal processing power) of the demodulator.

Cellular Networks and the Universal Frequency Reuse

As outlined above, multiple access can be granted to DSSS signals by assigning different spreading codes to all of the different active users served by a single BS. In this case, the capacity is limited by the number of orthogonal codes in the DL. With reasonable spreading factors (up to 256), the number of concurrently active channels is too low to serve a large user population such as in a large metropolitan area or a vast suburban area. This also applies to conventional FDMA or TDMA radio networks, where the number of channels is equal to the number of carriers in the allocated bandwidth or the number of time slots in a frame, respectively. In the context of narrow-band signals (FDMA and TDMA networks), the solution to this issue lies in the well-known notion of cellular network with frequency reuse. In a nutshell, the area to be served by the wireless system is divided into smaller cells, and the channels within the RF allocated bandwidth are distributed over the different cells. In so doing, the same channels can be allocated more than once to different cells (they can be reused), provided that the relevant cells are sufficiently far apart so that the mutual interference caused by the use of the same channels on the same frequency is sufficiently low. The distribution of cells on the coverage area (territory) is characterized by the so-called frequency reuse factor Q. Of course, frequency reuse has an impact on the overall network efficiency in terms of users per cell (or users/km²) because the number of channels allocated to each cell is a fraction $1/Q$ of the overall channels allocated to the communications service provider. For instance, in the GSM network Q is equal to 7 or 9. In such a cellular environment, it happens that a mobile user traverses the boundary between two adjacent cells, leaving its own coverage cell to enter another coverage area. To keep possible communications active without service interruption, a network management procedure called *handoff* (or *handover*) is started just before the mobile leaves the "setting" cell to assign new frequency resources to the mobile in the "rising" cell and to disengage the older ones and thus ensure a seamless connection (Rappaport 1991).

In CDMA-based networks, efficiency is maximized by universal frequency reuse whereby the same carrier frequency is used in each cell, and the same OVSF orthogonal codes set (i.e., the same DL channels) are used within each cell on the same carrier. Of course, something has to be done to prevent neighbors at the edge of two adjacent cells from using the same WH code to heavily interfere with each other. The solution is to use a different scrambling code on different cells to cover the channelization (traffic) OVSF codes (Fong, Bhargava, and Wang 1996; Dinan and Jabbari 1998). This arrangement represents a sort of universal code reuse technique, where *code* refers to the (orthogonal) channelization codes in each cell. Denoting with $c_m[k]$, $m = 1, 2, ..., M$, the set of M WH codes to be used by the generic cell u and with $p_u[k]$ the overlaying sequence, the resulting composite spreading signature code is $c'_{u,m}[k] \triangleq p_u[k] \cdot c_m[k]$. The orthogonality between any pair of composite sequences in the same cell is preserved. In a cellular network with universal frequency reuse, the hand-off procedure merely consists of a reassignment of the spreading code at every cell change with no carrier frequency change.

ARCHITECTURE OF SPREAD-SPECTRUM RECEIVERS
Correlation Receiver

This is the conventional receiver for DSSS transmissions and was described in detail earlier. The correlation receiver is optimum in each of the following conditions:

- single-user transmission over the AWGN channel;
- multi-user transmission over the AWGN channel in SOCDM mode (no MAI is experienced by the receiver); and
- multi-user transmission over the AWGN channel in ACDMA mode with long PN codes with a large number of equi-powered active users (allowing the modeling of MAI as an additional white Gaussian noise contribution).

Synchronization Functions

The word *synchronization* refers to those signal-processing functions that in digital communication receivers are carried out to achieve correct time alignment of the incoming waveform with certain locally generated references.

Figure 7 shows the general outline of (the baseband equivalent of) a conventional coherent correlation receiver for DSSS user h in a CDMA system, where we have highlighted the relevant synchronization functions. For the sake of simplicity, the synchronization functions are described for the AWGN case only. After carrier frequency and phase offset correction, the received waveform $r(t)$ is fed to the CMF and then sampled at chip rate. Spectral despreading is performed by multiplying the samples $y_h[\ell]$ by a locally generated replica of the user's code $c_h[\ell]$ and, finally, the resulting sequence is accumulated over

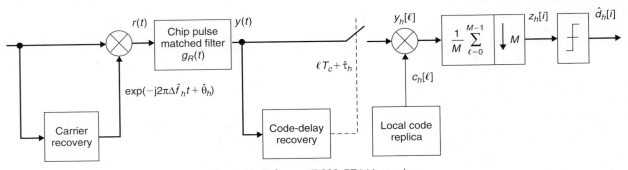

Figure 7: Coherent DSSS CDMA receiver

a symbol period $T_s = MT_c$ (see also the earlier "Fundamentals" section). Correct receiver operation requires accurate recovery of the signal time offset τ_h to ensure that the local code replica is properly aligned with the signature sequence in the received signal. This goal is usually achieved in two steps: (1) coarse alignment is obtained first, and (2) it is used as a starting point for fine code tracking.

From the discussion above it appears that the synchronization problem in CDMA systems is similar to that encountered with narrowband signals, as far as carrier frequency and phase are concerned (Mengali and D'Andrea 1997; De Gaudenzi, Giannetti, and Luise 1998). On the contrary, SS signals are peculiar in the function of delay estimation. As mentioned earlier, data detection relies on the availability at the receiver of a time-aligned version of the spreading code. The delay τ_h must be therefore estimated to ensure such an alignment. The main difference with respect to narrowband modulations is estimation accuracy. In narrowband systems, timing errors must be small compared to the symbol time, whereas in spread-spectrum systems they must be small compared with the chip time, which is M times smaller. This is why, as mentioned above, code delay estimation is broken into two phases: First, a coarse estimate of the delay is obtained (initial acquisition), then the coarse estimate is used to start a continuous process of refinement (fine tracking) (De Gaudenzi, Giannetti, and Luise 1998).

Rake Receiver

The radio signal in a wireless mobile communication system, especially when operating in an urban or indoor environment experiences the phenomenon of *multipath propagation* (Turin 1980). In such scenarios, both the transmit and receive antennae have usually moderate to weak directivity so that the signal can propagate from the transmitter to the receiver through a number of different *propagation paths*. The different paths (or *rays*, as they are called in electromagnetism) result from reflection and scattering on walls, buildings, trees, furniture, and other surfaces or obstacles. A simple model for the received signal at the receiving end is thus

$$r(t) \triangleq \sum_{k=1}^{K} a_k \cdot s^{(SS)}(t - \tau_k) + w(t) \qquad (21)$$

where $s^{(ss)}(t)$ is the (baseband equivalent of) the transmitted DSSS signal, $w(t)$ is the usual channel noise, K is the number of propagation paths, $a_k \triangleq |a_k| \cdot \exp(j\angle a_k)$ is a complex random variable representing the amplitude and phase shift experienced by the signal traveling on the generic kth path, and finally τ_k is the relevant propagation delay. In Equation 21, we neglected for simplicity the time variation resulting from terminal mobility of the channel parameters (amplitudes, phase shifts, and delays). In an urban environment, the amplitude coefficient $|a_k|$ is usually modeled as a Rayleigh random variable, whereas the phase shift $\angle a_k$ is assumed to be uniformly distributed over $[0, 2\pi)$. From Equation 21, the frequency response of the multipath channel turns out to be

$$H(f) = \sum_{k=1}^{K} a_k \cdot e^{-j2\pi f \tau_k} \qquad (22)$$

Typical values of the delays τ_k are 1–10 μs for rural environments, 0.1–1 μs for urban scenarios, and 1–100 ns for indoor propagation. In general, the channel amplitude and phase response from Equation 22 reveal considerable variability over the signal bandwidth, thus causing non-negligible distortion on the received signal: We have a *frequency-selective channel*.

On the multipath channel, the CR is no longer optimal because the additional rays may cause intersymbol interference. A popular way to deal with DSSS signal detection consists of resorting to the *rake receiver*; its architecture is depicted in Figure 8. The rake is a kind of time diversity receiver made of a bank of N_R ($N_R = 3$ in Figure 8) identical conventional DSSS detectors, operating in parallel, and called *fingers* (just like the fingers of a gardener's rake). In the code acquisition phase, DSSS demodulator 1 tries to locate the strongest path within the multipath signal of Equation 21 by finding the strongest correlation peak of the local code replica with the received signal and "tunes" onto it. After this, the other detectors will try to find the second and third strongest paths and lock onto them. To achieve this, they carry out a continuous search around the previously found locations, in particular looking for secondary correlation peaks generated by weaker signal "echoes." The search range is limited to a few chip intervals, depending on the maximum channel delay the receiver has to cope with. Eventually, as shown in Figure 8, each finger of the rake locks onto a different time-delayed replica of the incoming signal (see the time delays τ_i, $i = 1,2,3$), correlates it with a properly shifted version of the local code replica (see the code delays δ_i, $i = 1,2,3$), and yields a decision strobe $z_n[i]$ at symbol rate. This operation mode presumes that the different signal replicas (echoes) can be resolved—that is, they can be singled out by a correlation procedure. This is true only when the difference between the various signal delays is at least approximately one chip time. In this case, in fact, the different signal echoes on the different propagation paths turn out to be uncorrelated (because of the properties of the spreading code) and can be resolved via correlation processing. By resorting to advanced signal-processing techniques, paths separated by less than one chip time can also be resolved.

Assume now for simplicity that finger 1 locks onto path 1, finger 2 onto path 2, and so forth. The different partial decision variables $z_n[i]$ are phase-corrected by $\exp(-j\angle a_n)$ to perform coherent detection. Then, a *combination logic unit* (CLU) controls a combination unit that is in charge of selecting or combining the fingers outputs to provide a final decision strobe $z[i]$ for data detection. The selection and combining criterion may be one of the following:

- *selection combining* in which the CLU just selects the maximum amplitude strobe:

$$z[i]\Big|_{SC} \triangleq z_{\bar{n}}[i] \Leftrightarrow \bar{n} : \left|z_{\bar{n}}[i]\right| = \max_n \left\{\left|z_n[i]\right|\right\} \qquad (23)$$

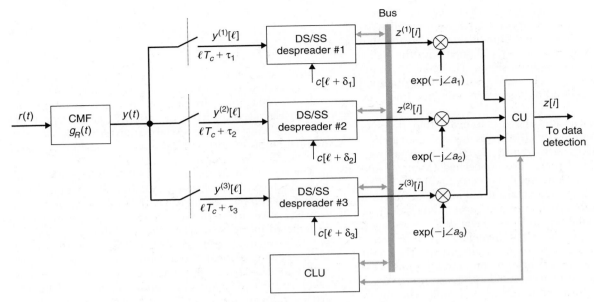

Figure 8: Outline of a rake receiver

- *equal gain combining* in which the CLU sums up all strobes at the fingers outputs (upon carrier phase counter-rotation):

$$z[i]\Big|_{EGC} \triangleq \sum_{n=1}^{N_R} z_n[i] \cdot e^{-j\angle a_n} \qquad (24)$$

- *maximal ratio combining* (MRC) in which the CLU performs a weighted sum of all the strobes at the fingers' outputs:

$$z[i]\Big|_{MRC} \triangleq \sum_{n=1}^{N_R} |a_n| \cdot z_n[i] \cdot e^{-j\angle a_n} = \sum_{n=1}^{N_R} a_n^* \cdot z_n[i] \qquad (25)$$

It can be shown that MRC maximizes the signal-to-noise ratio at the rake output because Equation 25 implements a channel-matched filter. The rake represents the optimum receiver for DSSS single-user reception over multipath channel, provided that all the following conditions are met:

1. the number of the rake fingers is exactly equal to that of the propagation paths;
2. the rake can resolve all the paths—that is, each finger locks onto a different path;
3. interchip interference is negligible—that is, perfect fine time recovery is carried out; and
4. the spreading code is delta-correlated—that is, it has null off-zero autocorrelation.

According to 1 and 2 above, the number of fingers in the rake should be equal to the number of resolvable paths in the channel. In practice, a reasonable trade-off between complexity and multipath robustness is represented in many cases by the choice $N_R = 3$ (De Gaudenzi and Giannetti, 1994, 1998).

A REVIEW OF 2G AND 3G STANDARDS FOR CDMA MOBILE COMMUNICATIONS
Interim Standard 95

The "mother of all" commercial CDMA systems is the American standard IS-95 (Kohno, Meidan, and Milstein 1995) that was issued in 1993 and later evolved into a well-established family of different systems—namely, cdmaOne—whose main representatives are summarized in Table 1. The chip rate is the same in both the UL and the DL and is equal to 1.2288 Mchip/s for a nominal bandwidth occupancy of 1.25 MHz (with roll-off factor 0.2). In the DL, SCDM with length-64 WH codes is used for as many as sixty-four multiplexed channels. The maximum net bit rate on each channel is 9600 bit/s. In addition, some channels are reserved for control. In particular, the channel corresponding to the WH function that is constant throughout the code period bears no data modulation (the so-called pilot channel) and is used as a reference for synchronization and channel estimation (see the preceding section). The traffic channels are all protected against transmission errors by a convolutional forward error-correcting code whose coding rate is $r = 1/2$ so that the actual maximum signaling rate is 19,200 symbol/s. Considering the spreading factor 64 of the WH codes, we end up with the chip rate $19.2 \times 64 = 1228.8$ kchip/s as above. The modulation and spreading format is "real data, complex code" because two different codes are used on the I and Q rails on the same "copy" of the digital datum. The I and Q codes are "long" (although in the standard they are termed *short codes*), and they also serve as scrambling code to perform BS identification. If a lower data rate than 9600 bit/s has to be used, the channel encoder just reclocks the slower output data so as to make them enter the DSSS modulator at the same invariable rate of 19.2 ksymbol/s. This is called *symbol repetition* and allows supported bit rates that are integer submultiples of

Table 1: The cdmaOne Family

System name	System kind	UL frequency band (MHz)	DL frequency band (MHz)
TIE/EIA IS-95	Cellular	824–849	869–894
ANSI J-STD-008	Personal communication system (PCS)	1850–1910	1930–1990
Globalstar	Satellite	1610–1626.5	2483.5–2500

Table 2: UMTS' UTRA-FDD and UTRA-TDD Main System Parameters

Parameter	UTRA-FDD	UTRA-TDD
Frequency Band	UL: 1920–1980 DL: 2110–2170	1900–1920 and 2010–2025
Maximum data rate	2.048 Mbit/s	
Framing	10 msec	
Chip rate	3.840 Mchip/s	3.840 Mchip/s or 1.280 Mchip/s
Pulse shaping	SRRC roll-off factor 0.22	
Carrier spacing	5 MHz	
Spreading factor	4 to 256	Either 1 (no spreading, pure TDMA) or 16
DL multiplexing	SOCDM Optional short codes	SOCDM Short codes
UL multiple access	ACDMA Long codes	
UL pilot channel	Dedicated physical control channel running in parallel with the data channel	"Midamble": short series of pilot symbol at the center of the data burst
DL pilot channel	Common pilot channel plus dedicated pilot symbol in the traffic channels	

the maximum basic rate (in this case, 4800, 2400, and 1200 bit/s).

The arrangement for the UL of IS-95 is a little bit more complicated. We have here ACDMA with extremely long codes, whose periodicity is $2^{42} - 1$ chips. The chip rate is the same as in the DL (1.2288 Mchip/s), as is the basic maximum data rate (9600 bit/s). But the coding rate is now 1/3, and so the symbol rate at the modulator input is $3 \times 9.6 = 28.8$ ksymbol/s. At the other end of the modulator we also have a conventional "real data, complex code" section with scrambling codes. In between, we have multilevel 64-ary modulation with a set of sixty-four orthogonal WH functions (Proakis 1995). Here the WH functions are not used as orthogonal codes to perform multiplexing as they are in the DL. Rather, they are used as symbols in a signal constellation to implement the robust process of orthogonal functions modulation that is suited to efficient noncoherent demodulation. As a consequence, the signaling rate of the orthogonal-modulated stream raises to $28.8/\log_2(64) = 307.2$ ksymbol/s. After ×4 symbol repetition, spreading with the extremely long channelization code and I/Q modulation and scrambling take place. In the UL, the two I/Q components of the modulated signal are staggered in time (i.e., delayed one with respect to the other) by half a chip period. This reduces the envelope fluctuations of the modulated signal, thus preventing distortion by the subsequent stages of nonlinear amplification in the MT radio frequency transmitter.

UMTS and UTRA

In 1998, several telecommunications standards bodies established a collaboration agreement called the 3rd-Generation Partnership Project (3GPP) (3GPP undated), whose scope was to bring forth globally applicable technical specifications and technical reports for a third-generation mobile system. In 2001, the 3GPP produced the 3G Euro-Japanese standard UMTS (release 4) that, despite many substantial differences, incorporated many of the good ideas that were introduced in IS-95 (Ojanpera and Prasad 1998). Table 2 summarizes the main parameters of the two versions of UMTS—namely, *UMTS terrestrial radio access–frequency division duplexing* (UTRA-FDD) and *UMTS terrestrial radio access–time division duplexing* (UTRA-TDD). In UTRA-FDD, the chip rate is 3.840 Mchip/s with a roll-off factor 0.22 for a nominal bandwidth occupancy of 5 MHz, both the UL and the DL. This explains the qualification of "wideband" CDMA of UTRA-FDD. The two links are symmetrical with supported bit rates ranging from 16 (the basic, slowest rate) to 2,048 kbit/s, with variable spreading factor (OVSF codes; see the earlier "Multirate Code Division Multiplexing" section).

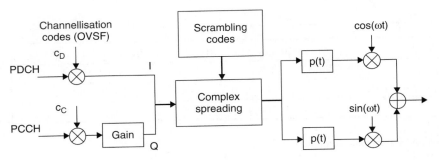

Figure 9: UTRA-FDD UL spreading and modulation

As is seen in Figure 9, each user has a UL *physical dedicated control channel* (PCCH) in addition to the customary traffic channel (*physical dedicated data channel*, PDCH). The two channels, which may have different bit rates, are locally multiplexed and spread with channelization OVSF codes, and the two of them are further scrambled via complex spreading—that is, computing the product between the complex-valued, I/Q spread PDCH/PCCH signal and the complex-valued I/Q scrambling code.

The arrangement for modulation and spreading in the DL (traffic and control channels) is similar but a little bit more complicated (see Figure 10). The presence of the serial-to-parallel converters on the data fluxes indicates that modulation is QPSK (complex binary data), but spreading with the channelization codes (synchronous OVSFs) is real (single code per channel). After I and Q multiplexing, a base-station-unique real scrambling code is applied.

UTRA-TDD is different from UTRA-FDD for the duplexing mode: Instead of placing the UL and the DL on two different carrier frequencies as in FDD, the UL and DL share the same carrier and simply alternate in time (see Table 2). This gives total symmetry of signal format between UL and DL, but on the contrary allows asymmetry of capacity by simply "moving" the boundary between the UL slots and the DL slots in every 10-msec frame as sketched in Figure 11. The signal format is actually somewhat simpler than its FDD counterpart (fixed spreading factor, option for a factor-of-three slower chip rate, etc.), and so UTRA-TDD is left for less demanding applications than FDD.

CDMA2000

As far as the general architecture is concerned (at least from a physical layer perspective), the differences between CDMA2000 and UTRA-FDD are not much relevant. The main differentiation lies in a sort of "multicarrier" mode of CDMA2000 that allows best backward compatibility with IS-95 (Knisely et al. 1998). The chip rates of CDMA2000 are integer multiples of the IS-95 chip rate (for instance, $1.2288 \times 3 = 3.6864$ Mchip/s) so that one wideband CDMA2000 carrier exactly fits into the bandwidth of an integer number of cdmaOne channels. Many features such as OVSF codes, dedicated control channels in the UL, common pilot channel in the DL, coherent demodulation in both the UL and the DL, packet access, and fast power control are shared with UTRA-FDD, and the relevant end-user performance and services are similar. For real worldwide roaming, the design of dual-mode CDMA2000/UMTS terminals is being pursued by most equipment manufacturers.

China's TD-SCDMA

In 1999, the China Wireless Telecommunication Standards group was founded by the People's Republic of China Ministry of Information and Industry and joined the 3GPP. In October 2002, the Chinese ministry assigned a total of 155-MHz asymmetrical bandwidth for the TD-SCDMA standard (Li et al. 2005; TD-SCDMA Forum 2003)

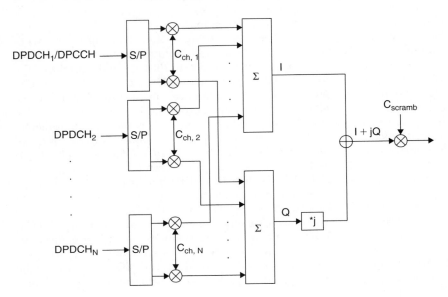

Figure 10: UTRA-FDD DL modulation, spreading, multiplexing, and scrambling

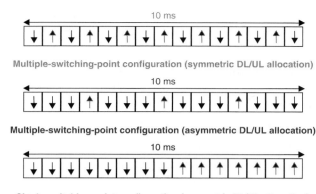

Multiple-switching-point configuration (symmetric DL/UL allocation)

Multiple-switching-point configuration (asymmetric DL/UL allocation)

Single-switching-point configuration (symmetric DL/UL allocation)

Single-switching-point configuration (asymmetric DL/UL allocation)

Figure 11: Asymmetric UL and DL capacity in UTRA-TDD

(1880–1920 MHz, 2010–2025 MHz) plus a supplementary spectrum (2300–2400 MHz). In January 2006, the ministry formally approved TD-SCDMA as the country's standard of 3G mobile telecommunications. Some may say that TD-SCDMA is a variant of UTRA-TDD. Admittedly, the two share several features, starting from the basic arrangement of time division duplexing on a single carrier with dynamic UL and DL allocation. TD-SCDMA also uses TDMA in addition to CDMA to reduce the number of concurrently active codes in a cell. As already stated, the "S" in the acronym of this standard stands for *synchronous*, meaning that the different CDMA channels are always synchronous in both the UL and the DL. The two also share the same framing and spreading and modulation format, just like UTRA-TDD. Designed for 1.6-MHz channels, TD-SCDMA is compatible with 5-MHz unpaired 3G bands in any region of the world. The universal chip rate is 1.28 Mchip/s (much like cdmaOne), and the frame length is 10 ms (see also Figure 12). Each frame

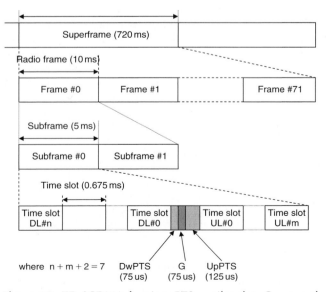

where n + m + 2 = 7   DwPTS   G   UpPTS
(75 us) (75 us) (125 us)

Figure 12: TD-SCDMA framing; PTS = pilot slot; G = guard slot

has seven slots with dynamic but single UL-DL switching point. The information rate of the channel varies with the symbol rate and the spreading factor. The spreading factor ranges from 16 to 1 for both the UL and the DL. Thus, the respective modulation symbol rates vary from 80.0 ksymbols/s to 1.28 Msymbols/s. Modulation is QPSK (8-PSK for higher-rate services with reduced mobility) and channel coding has rates 1/2 and 1/3. Thus, the supported bit rates are 9.6 (packet only), 12.2 (circuit only), 64, 144, 384, and 2,048 kbits/s. Considering all of the features above, we could say that TD-SCDMA is a mix of both the 2G and 3G CDMA systems.

CONCLUSION

Currently, more and more packet-based applications are being developed and put into service (video streaming, voice over IP, etc.), so wireless networks have to face the need for better support of differentiated quality of service, higher spectral efficiency, and higher data rates with full mobility. This need drives a continuously ongoing evolution of 3G systems' technologies (Dahlman and Jou 2006).

Although the end user may not be aware of it, at the same time 3G systems are being commercially developed (and ameliorated), research-and-development laboratories worldwide are also working to devise prototypes and proposals for standards of 4G wireless networks. At the moment, a great many so-called 4G architectures exist, according to the different visions of producers and research labs (Berezdivin, Breinig, and Raytheon 2002; Hui and Yeung 2003). The main ambition of 4G is to combine traditional cellular communications, WLANs, *broadband wireless access* (BWA) systems, and possibly broadcasting into a ubiquitous, universal, broadband, flexible wireless access network that can accommodate business as well residential users, multimedia communications, as well as Internet access. In a word, 4G will go where 3G cannot go.

In this ambitious picture, a variety of signal-processing techniques will be integrated, and SS probably will no longer be the fundamental one as in the previous generation. Many proposals for 4G systems or even 3.5G systems (that is, an intermediate generation between current 3G and long-term future 4G, just like Samsung's Wi-Bro (Cherry 2005), are based on MIMO (multiple-input multiple-output) signal transmission technologies as the factor to boost system capacity (Telatar 1999). With 3G, we can say that SS has attained its full maturity and will be either integrated or replaced by different and at times more advanced techniques. One of them is certainly multicarrier CDMA, which tries to capitalize on the advantages of both SS and MC modulations. Some envisage also the comeback of pure FDMA for multiple access in its modern variant, orthogonal FDMA (OFDMA) (IEEE 802.16 Working Group, undated). In a sense, OFDMA, that has been standardized for BWA applications by the IEEE 802.16 committee (IEEE 802.16 Working Group, undated), is a by-product of the OFDM multicarrier technology mentioned above. Also, the lesson of intentionally broadening the signal spectrum well beyond the Nyquist bandwidth has been completely taken up by those who support *ultra-wide band* (UWB) signaling for short-range communications

("Ultra wide band radio" 2002). In UWB systems, the information conveyed by a single bit is coded into a sequence of ultrashort pulses (less than 1 ns each) whose spectrum is thus spread over a ultrawide bandwidth. Admittedly, this is not conventional DSSS or FHSS but is indeed a form of "wide-spectrum" signaling. The debate among different laboratories and standardization bodies about the pros and cons of such technologies is really hot, so insisting on one instead of on another would be, in the writers' opinion, currently unfair or unmotivated.

GLOSSARY

Chip: One binary symbol of the spreading sequence.

Code: Sequence of pseudorandom binary symbols used in DSSS schemes to spread the bandwidth occupancy of the information-bearing signal. Also termed *spreading sequence*.

Code division multiple access (CDMA): Multiplexing or multiple-access technique based on DSSS transmission wherein all of the user signals are transmitted at the same time and over the same frequency band and are kept separated in the code domain.

Complex spreading (CS): DSSS spreading scheme employing a complex-valued code.

Correlation receiver: Receiver for DSSS transmissions wherein the transmitted data are detected by correlating the incoming received signal with a locally generated replica of the spreading code sequence used by the transmitter.

Despreading: Removal of the spreading code from the received DSSS signal; performed by a correlation receiver.

Direct sequence spread spectrum (DSSS): SS transmission technique wherein the information-bearing symbols are multiplied in the time domain with a sequence of pseudorandom binary symbols running at much higher rate.

Frequency-hopping spread spectrum (FHSS): SS transmission technique wherein the spectrum of the modulated signal "hops" from frequency to frequency following a periodic pseudorandom sequence of carrier values.

Long code: Spreading sequence whose repetition period is much longer than the data symbol duration.

Processing gain: The ratio between the chip rate of the SS signal and the transported bit rate.

Rake receiver: Time diversity receiver made of a bank of identical conventional DSSS detectors, operating in parallel, and suitable for data detection over time-dispersive channels.

Real spreading (RS): DSSS spreading scheme employing a real-valued code.

Short code: Spreading sequence such that a small integer number of the spreading sequence repetition period exactly spans one data symbol interval.

Spreading factor: The ratio between the bandwidth of the SS signal and the bandwidth of the corresponding narrowband modulated signal having the same symbol rate.

Spreading sequence: Sequence of pseudorandom binary symbols used in DSSS schemes to spread the bandwidth occupancy of the information-bearing signal. Also termed *code*.

Spread spectrum (SS): Transmission technique wherein the modulated signal has a bandwidth occupancy around the carrier frequency that is much larger than the information bit rate.

CROSS REFERENCES

See *Code Division Multiple Access (CDMA)*; *Digital Communications Basics*; *Mobile Radio Communications*; *Spread Spectrum*; *Wireless LANs (WLANs)*.

REFERENCES

3GPP. Undated. Online at www.3gpp.org.

Adachi, F., M. Sawahashi, and K. Okawa. 1997. Tree-structured generation of orthogonal spreading codes with different lengths for forward link of DS CDMA mobile radio. *IEE Electronics Letters*, 33(1): 27–8.

Adachi, F., M. Sawahashi, and H. Suda. 1998. Wideband DS-CDMA for next-generation mobile communications systems. *IEEE Communications Magazine*, September, pp. 56–69.

Ahmed, N., and K. R. Rao. 1975. *Orthogonal transforms for digital signal processing*. New York: Springer-Verlag.

Berezdivin, R., R. Breinig, and R. T. Raytheon. 2002. Next-generation wireless communications concepts and technologies. *IEEE Communications Magazine*, March, pp. 108–16.

Cellular Operators Association of India. 2007. Online at http://coai.in/.

Cherry, S. 2005. South Korea pushes mobile broadband. *IEEE Spectrum*, 42(9): 14–16.

Chia, S. 1992. The universal mobile telecommunication system. *IEEE Communications Magazine*, December, pp. 54–62.

Dahlman, E., B. Gudmundson, M. Nilsson, and J. Sköld. 1998. UMTS/IMT-2000 based on wideband CDMA. *IEEE Communications Magazine*, September, pp. 70–80.

Dahlman, E., and Y.-C. Jou. 2006. Evolving technologies for 3G cellular wireless communications systems. *IEEE Communications Magazine*, February, pp. 62–4.

De Gaudenzi, R., and F. Giannetti. 1994. Analysis of an advanced satellite digital audio broadcasting system and complementary terrestrial gap-filler single frequency network. *IEEE Transactions on Vehicular Technology*, 43(2): 194–210.

———. 1998. DS-CDMA satellite diversity reception for personal satellite communication: Satellite-to-mobile link performance analysis. *IEEE Transactions on Vehicular Technology*, 47(2): 658–72.

———, and M. Luise. 1998. Signal synchronization for direct-sequence code-division multiple access radio modems. *European Transactions on Telecommunications*, 9(1): 73–89.

Dinan, E. H., and B. Jabbari. 1998. Spreading codes for direct sequence CDMA and wideband CDMA cellular networks. *IEEE Communications Magazine*, September, pp. 48–54.

Dixon, R. C. 1994. *Spread spectrum systems with commercial applications*. New York: Wiley Interscience.

Fong, M.-H., V. K. Bhargava, and Q. Wang. 1996. Concatenated orthogonal/PN spreading sequences and their application to cellular DS-CDMA systems with integrated traffic. *IEEE Journal on Selected Areas in Communications*, 14(3): 547–58.

Gilhousen, K. S., et al. 1990. Increased capacity using CDMA for mobile satellite communication. *IEEE Journal on Selected Areas in Communications*, 8(4): 503–14.

———. 1991. On the capacity of a cellular CDMA system. *IEEE Transactions on Vehicular Technology*, 40(5): 303–12.

Haartsen, J. C., et al. 2000. The Bluetooth radio system. *IEEE Personal Communications*, February, pp. 28–36.

Hui, S. Y., and K. H. Yeung. 2003. Challenges in the migration to 4G mobile systems. *IEEE Communications Magazine*, December, pp. 54–9.

IEEE 802.16 Working Group. Undated. Broadband wireless access standards (available online at www.ieee802.org/16/).

Knisely, D., et al. 1998. Evolution of wireless data services: IS-95 to CDMA2000. *IEEE Communications Magazine*, October, pp. 140–9.

Kohno, R., R. Meidan, and L. B. Milstein. 1995. Spread spectrum access methods for wireless communications. *IEEE Communications Magazine*, January, pp. 58–67.

Li, B., D. Xie, S. Cheng, J. Chen, P. Zhang, W. Zhu, and B. Li. 2005. Recent advances on TD-SCDMA in China. *IEEE Communications Magazine*, January, pp. 30–7.

Mengali, U., and A.N. D'Andrea. 1997. *Synchronization techniques for digital receivers*. New York: Plenum Press.

Ojanpera, T., and R. Prasad. 1998. An overview of third-generation wireless personal communications: A European perspective. *IEEE Personal Communications*, 5(6): 59–65.

Padgett, J. E., C. G. Günther, and T. Hattori. 1995. Overview of wireless personal communications. *IEEE Personal Communications Magazine*, January, pp. 28–41.

Peterson, W. W., and E. J. Weldon Jr. 1972. *Error-correcting codes*. 2nd ed. Cambridge: MIT Press.

Pickholtz, R. L., D. L. Schilling, and L. B. Milstein. 1982. Theory of spread-spectrum communications: A tutorial. *IEEE Transactions on Communications*, 30: 855–84.

Proakis, J. G. 1995. *Digital communications*. 3rd ed. New York: McGraw-Hill.

Rappaport, T. S. 1991. The wireless revolution. *IEEE Communications Magazine*, November, pp. 52–71.

Sarwate, D. P., and M. B. Pursley. 1980. Cross-correlation properties of pseudorandom and related sequences. *Proceedings of the IEEE*, 68(5): 593–619.

Sasaki, A., M. Yabusaki, and S. Inada. 1998. The current situation of IMT-2000 standardization activities in Japan. *IEEE Communications Magazine*, September, pp. 145–53.

Scholtz, R. A. 1982. The origins of spread-spectrum communications. *IEEE Transactions on Communications*, 30: 822–54.

Simon, M. K., J. K. Omura, R. A. Scholtz, and B. K. Levitt. 1994. *Spread-spectrum communications handbook*. New York: McGraw-Hill.

Telatar, I. E. 1999. Capacity of multi-antenna Gaussian channels. *European Transactions on Telecommunications*, 10: 585–95.

TD-SCDMA Forum. 2003. Available online at www.tdscdma-forum.org.

Turin, G. L. 1980. Introduction to spread-spectrum anti-multipath techniques and their application to urban digital radio. *Proceedings of the IEEE*, 68(3): 328–53.

Ultra wide band radio in multi-access wireless communications. 2002. *IEEE Journal on Selected Areas in Communications* (special issue), 20(9).

Verdù, S. 1998. *Multiuser detection*. Cambridge, UK: Cambridge University Press.

Viterbi, A. J. 1967. Error bounds for convolutional codes and an asymptotically optimum decoding algorithm. *IEEE Transactions on Information Theory*, 13: 260–9.

———. 1979. Spread spectrum communications: Myths and realities. *IEEE Communications Magazine*, May, pp. 11–18.

———, and J. K. Omura. 1979. *Principles of digital communication and coding*. New York: McGraw-Hill.

Optical Fiber Communications

Habib Hamam, *University of Moncton, Canada*
Sghaier Guizani, *University of Quebec, Canada*

INTRODUCTION

The goal of an *optical fiber communication* (OFC) system is to transmit the maximum number of bits per second over the maximum possible distance with the fewest errors. A typical digital fiber-optic link is depicted in Figure 1.

Data encoded as electrical pulses are recoded as optical pulses. Electrical data signals are converted to optical signals via a transducer. The numeral 1 is transmitted as a pulse of light, whereas a 0 has no light output. This modulation is referred to as *on-off keying*.

The use of light as communication methods can be dated back to antiquity if we define optical communications in a broader way. Humans have used mirrors, fire beacons, and smoke signals to convey single pieces of information.

The main idea of using glass fiber to carry an optical communications signal was conceived in the last half of the nineteenth century. However, this idea had to wait for almost a century. In 1966, Charles Kao and George Hockham at Standard Telecommunications Laboratories in England published their famous landmark theoretical

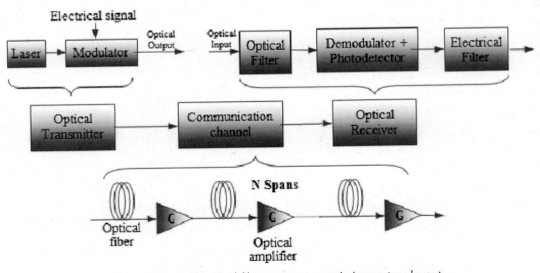

Figure 1: General optical fiber system transmission system layout

paper that described how better forms of glass and low-cost electronics made the idea useful in practical situations (Kao and Hockham 1966). The modern fiber-optic communications started in the 1970s when a gallium arsenide semiconductor laser was invented and the optical fiber loss could be reduced to 20 dB/km in the wavelength region near 1 μm (Dutton 1998).

Over the last four decades, optical communications in public networks evolved from a curiosity to become the dominant technology. Among the thousands of developments and inventions that have contributed to this progress, five major inventions stand out as milestones (Dutton 1998):

1. the invention of the laser in the early 1960s;
2. the development of low-loss optical fiber in the 1970s;
3. the invention of the FBG in the late 1970s;
4. the invention of the optical fiber amplifier in the late 1980s; and
5. the development of the *wavelength-division multiplexing* (WDM) technique in the 1990s.

OPTICAL FIBER TRANSMISSION SYSTEMS
Overview

In general, an optical communications system consists of an optical source, a transmitter, a medium, and a receiver. The digital optical transmission system in which the data bit rate per channel is assumed to be in the range of multi-Gb/s (as many as 40 Gb/s per channel are currently feasible). In the transmitter, a time division multiplexer combines several parallel data channels into a single data stream with a high bit rate. Then a driver stage generates the current required for driving the laser diode directly or the voltage required to drive an external modulator indirectly. *Non-return to zero* and *return to zero* are the most commonly applied modulation formats because of their simple implementation at extremely high speeds.

Similar to frequency-division multiplexing in radio systems, WDM can be used to increase the transmission capacity beyond that limited by the speed of electronics. The idea of WDM is to simultaneously transmit data at multiple carrier wavelengths over a fiber. Interaction among these different channels is minimized by placing these wavelengths sufficiently apart from each other. WDM can expand the capacity of the link into the Terabit/s region, well beyond the capabilities of electrical transceivers (Dutton 1998; Keiser 2000; Agrawal 2002; Zhu et al. 2001; Frignac et al. 2002; Winters and Gitlin 1990).

Traditionally, the optical link span was limited by fiber attenuation, and repeaters had to be placed wherever the optical power dropped below a certain level. To regenerate an optical signal with a conventional repeater, an optical-to-electrical conversion, electrical amplification, retiming, reshaping, and then electrical-to-optical conversion are necessary. This is expensive for a high-speed, multiwavelength system. Instead, optical amplifiers such as erbium-doped fiber amplifiers (EDFAs) are used. Transparent to bit rates and modulation formats, optical amplifiers provide the advantage of easy system upgrading by changing the equipment at the ends of the link. Another advantage is that the optical amplifiers can amplify signals at many wavelengths simultaneously. However, the link now becomes limited by other fiber impairments such as *chromatic dispersion* (CD), *polarization mode dispersion* (PMD), and nonlinear effects in the fiber. For long-haul applications, *dispersion-compensating modules* such as *dispersion-compensation fiber* are placed periodically along the link to compensate for CD.

At the end, an optical demultiplexer routes each wavelength to its designated electrical receiver. In the latter, a photodetector (which can be either a PIN diode or an avalanche photodiode) converts the optical pulses into small current pulses. This low-level signal is amplified by a low-noise preamplifier, followed by a main amplifier, which is either an automatic gain control amplifier or a limiting amplifier. A clock extraction and data regeneration circuit recovers the timing information from the random data and samples the data stream at the appropriate instant. Finally, a serial-to-parallel converter demultiplexes the retimed serial data to a lower rate, where the data are processed by other circuitry.

System Concepts

Fiber-optic communications systems have been deployed worldwide and have certainly revolutionized current telecommunication infrastructures and will continue to do so in the future. Currently, virtually all telephone conversations, cellular phone calls, and Internet packets must pass through some pieces of optical fibers from source to destination. Although initial deployments of optical fiber are intended mainly for long-haul or submarine transmissions, light-wave systems are currently used in virtually all metro and access networks and are considered as a backbone in local area networks.

As shown in Figure 2, a fiber-optic system can generally be seen as a system with three main components: a transmitter (dashed box), a transmission medium (the rest), and a receiver (dashed box). A regenerator might be used if the distance between the transmitter and the receiver is long enough that the signal would be drastically deformed and attenuated before reaching the receiver. As a model, the fiber-optic system is similar to the copper wire system it is replacing. The difference is that fiber optics uses light pulses to transmit information down a fiber instead of using electronic pulses to transmit information down copper lines. In the following sections, we study the three main components in the fiber-optic chain to give a better understanding of how the system works in conjunction with wire-based systems.

A serial bit stream in electrical form is presented to a modulator, which encodes the data appropriately for fiber transmission. A light source—either a *light-emitting diode* (LED) or a laser—is modulated by the modulator and the light is focused into the fiber. The light travels down the fiber (and suffers loss, reducing its intensity). At the receiver end, the light is incident onto a detector and converted to electrical form. The signal is then amplified and fed to another detector, which isolates the individual state changes and their timing. It then decodes the sequence

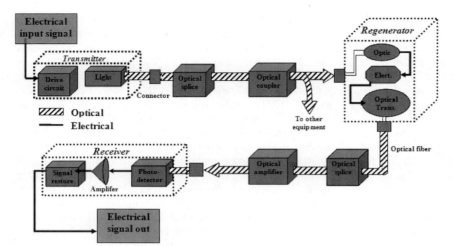

Figure 2: A general view of an optical fiber link

of state changes and reconstructs the original bit stream (Dutton 1998).

Optical Transmitters

A fiber-optic transmitter modulates the intensity of an optical carrier generated by a light source. This can be done in either of two ways: by directly modulating the input power to the light source or by using a separate optical component that changes the intensity of the light leaving the light source. Each approach has its own advantages and disadvantages.

Direct modulation is simple and inexpensive. It is suitable for LEDs and semiconductor lasers because their light output increases with the drive current passing through the semiconductor device once a certain threshold bias current has been exceeded (in the case of the laser). The input signal modulates the drive current, so the output optical signal is proportional to the input electrical signal. However, LEDs take time to respond to changes in the drive current. Semiconductor lasers are much faster, but their optical properties change slightly with the drive current, causing a slight "chirp" in the wavelength as the signal switches on and off. External modulation is needed for high-speed systems (>2.5 Gb/s) to minimize such undesirable nonlinear effects. A variety of external modulators are available either as separate devices or as integral parts of the laser transmitter packages.

Light-Emitting Diode

A LED in essence is a P-N junction solid-state semiconductor diode that emits light when a current is applied through the device. The essential portion of the LED is the semiconductor chip, which is divided into two parts or regions that are separated by a boundary called a *junction*. The P region is dominated by positive electric charges (holes), and the N region is dominated by negative electric charges (electrons). The junction serves as a barrier to the flow of the electrons between the P and N regions. This is somewhat similar to the role of the band gap because it determines how much voltage needs to be applied to the semiconductor chip before the current can flow and the electrons pass the junction into the P region. Band gaps

determine how much energy is needed for the electron to jump from the valence band to the conduction band. As an electron in the conduction band recombines with a hole in the valence band, the electron makes a transition to a lower-lying energy state and releases energy in an amount equal to the band-gap energy. This energy is released in photons. Because the recombinations do not always generate emitted photons, the nonradiative recombinations heat the material. In an LED, the emitted photons may give infrared or visible light.

Lasers

Semiconductor lasers are similar to LEDs in structure. A laser diode is a P-N junction semiconductor that converts the electrical energy applied across the junction into optical radiation. In both laser diodes and LEDs, the wavelength of the output radiation depends on the energy gap across the P-N junction. However, the output from a laser diode is highly coherent and can be collimated, whereas the output from an LED has many phases and is radiated in different directions.

Mach-Zehnder Interferometer Modulators

The *Mach-Zehnder interferometer* (MZI) (named after physicists Ernst Mach and Ludwig Zehnder) is used to split an optical signal into two components and directs them down two separate paths before recombining them. A phase delay between the two optical signals causes them to interfere when recombined, giving an output modulated intensity. Such a device can modulate the optical power from 100 percent (constructive interference) to 0 percent (destructive interference).

MZIs as illustrated in Figure 3 are used in a wide variety of applications within optics and optical communications. The basic principle is that there is a balanced configuration of a splitter and a combiner connected by a pair of matched waveguides. When a phase difference is created between the signals in the two matched waveguides, interference in the recombination process causes differences in the amplitude of the output signal. Thus, an intensity modulator based on an MZI converts changes in phase to changes in signal amplitude. The principle is simple:

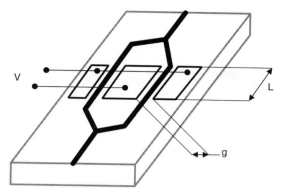

Figure 3: Modulator using Match-Zehender interferometer (L = length, g = width, and V = voltage)

The signal entering the device is split through a Y splitter into two directions. In a properly constructed device, one-half of the signal goes in each direction and polarization is not affected. When there is no phase delay (both arms of the interferometer are equal in length), the signal is recombined at the Y junction (coupler) immediately before the light exits the device. Because the signals in each arm are coherent, they reinforce during recombination. When there is a phase delay of 180 degrees, the output will be zero (Dutton 1998).

Optical Transmission Medium

The optical fiber is the transmission medium. An ideal transmission medium would have no effect on the signal it carries, but any medium inevitably has some effects. In a fiber, the two principal limiting effects on the signal are attenuation of the signal strength and pulse spreading (dispersion). Both depend on how far light travels through the fiber. Attenuation reduces the intensity of the optical signal. Pulse spreading limits the data rate, increases the *bit error rate* (BER) of the digital signal, or reduces the signal-to-noise ratio of an analog signal. Both attenuation and dispersion in the glasses used to make the fiber have low values in the wavelength ranges between 1250 and 1650 nanometers (Dutton 1998).

Optical Amplifiers

An optical amplifier can boost the strength of optical signals so they can travel farther through optical fibers. They amplify light directly in optical form, without converting the signal to electrical form. More details will be given later in "Optical Devices."

Repeaters and Regenerators

Repeater and regenerator first convert the optical signal to electrical form and then amplify it and deliver the electrical signal they generate to another transmitter. That transmitter then generates a fresh optical version of the signal. Regenerators can clean up the effects of dispersion and distortion on optical signals.

Optical Splices

Normally, optical fibers are connected to each other by either connectors or splicing—that is, joining two fibers together to form a continuous optical waveguide.

The generally accepted splicing method is arc fusion splicing, which melts the fiber ends together with an electric arc. For quicker fastening jobs, a "mechanical splice" could be used, too.

Optical Splitters and Couplers

In an optical network there are many situations when it is necessary to combine signals, split them multiple ways, or both. Splitters are designed to split an optical signal into two or more components. Fiber-optic couplers are optical devices that connect three or more fiber ends, dividing one input between two or more outputs or combining two or more inputs into one output. The cable type accepted by fiber-optic couplers could be single-mode or multimode. *Single mode* describes an optical fiber that will allow only one mode to propagate. *Single-mode fiber* (SMF) has an exceptionally small core diameter of approximately 8 μm. It permits signal transmission at extremely high bandwidth and allows long transmission distances.

Optical Receivers

Receivers are the final elements in any communication systems. They convert a signal transmitted in one form into another form. For example, a radio receiver detects weak radio waves in the air and processes them electronically to generate sound. Fiber-optic receivers detect the optical signal emerging from the fiber and transfer the data in the form of an electrical signal. A photodetector generates an electrical current from the light it receives. Electronics in the receiver then amplify that signal and process it to decode the signal. After long distances and for better and improved reception, a preamplifier precedes the photodetector.

Optical Filters

An optical filter is a device that selectively transmits light having certain properties (often, a particular range of wavelengths—that is, a range of colors of light) while blocking the remainder (see "Optical Devices" below).

Photodetectors

The fundamental mechanism behind the photodetection process is optical absorption. The main objective of the photodetector is to receive the optical signal, remove the data from the optical carrier, and output it as a modulated electrical photocurrent through the photoelectric effect. The requirements for a photodetector are fast response, high sensitivity, low noise, low cost, and high reliability. Its size should be compatible with the size of the fiber core.

PROPAGATION OF LIGHT IN OPTICAL FIBERS

The fiber itself is one of the most significant components in any optical fiber system. Because its transmission characteristics play a major role in determining the performance of the entire system, several questions arise concerning optical fibers: What is the structure of the fiber? How does light propagate through the fiber? What is the nature of light traveling through the fiber?

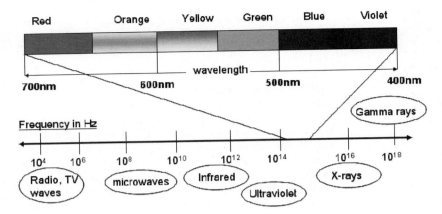

Figure 4: Electromagnetic wave spectrum

The Nature of Light and Its Propagation Characteristics

Through the history of physics, the view of the nature of light has varied. Light is the basis of our most important sensory function. It was generally believed that light consisted of a stream of tiny particles that were emitted by luminous sources. These particles were pictured as traveling in straight lines. However, the answer to the question about what light "really is" varies depending on the situation. Light is usually described in one of three ways: rays, electromagnetic waves, and photons.

The accurate explanation of the electromagnetic nature of light was given by Augustin-Jean Fresnel in 1815. He showed that the approximately rectilinear propagation character of light could be interpreted on the assumption that light was a wave motion, and that the diffraction fringes could thus be accounted for in detail. Later, James Clerk Maxwell in 1864 theorized that light waves must be electromagnetic in nature. Furthermore, observation of polarization effects indicated that light waves are transverse (i.e., the wave motion is perpendicular to the direction in which the wave travels) (Dutton 1998; Keiser 2000; Agrawal 2002; Zhu et al. 2001). Figure 4 illustrates the electromagnetic wave spectrum of light.

Light as an Electromagnetic Wave

An electromagnetic wave consists of two fields: an electric field and a magnetic field, both of which have a direction and a strength (or amplitude). Within the electromagnetic wave, the two fields are oriented at precisely 90 degrees to one another as illustrated in Figure 5. The fields move (by definition, at the speed of light) in a direction 90 degrees to both of them. In three dimensions, we could consider the electric field to be oriented on the x-axis and the magnetic field on the y-axis. Direction of travel would then be along the z-direction.

As the electromagnetic wave travels, the field at any point in space oscillates in direction and strength. Figure 5 shows the electric and magnetic fields separately, but they occupy the same space. They should be overlaid on one another and are only drawn this way in the figure for clarity. We could consider the z-direction in Figure 5 to represent

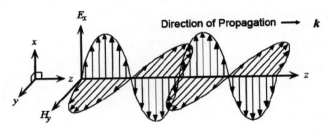

Figure 5: Electric and magentic fields are orthogonal to each other and to the direction of propagation

passing time, or it could represent a wave traveling in space at a single instant in time.

If the electromagnetic wave is watched from a stationary viewpoint, we see that at the start the field is oriented from bottom to top (increasing values of x). Some time later, the field direction reverses. At a still later time, the field direction reverses again back to its original direction (Dutton 1998).

Light Propagation in Multimode Fibers

Fiber types, including *multimode fibers* (MMFs), will be handled below in "Optical Fibers." The key feature of light propagation in a fiber is that the fiber may bend around corners. Provided the bend radius is not too tight—1.4 cm is more or less the minimum for most MMFs and waveguides (Papakonstantinou et al. 2007)—the light will follow the fiber and propagate without loss because of the bends as shown in Figure 6. This observable fact is called *total internal reflection*. A ray of light entering the fiber is guided along the fiber because it reflects from the interface between the core and the cladding, which has a lower *refractive index* (RI). Light is said to be "bound" within the fiber.

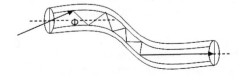

Figure 6: Light propagation in a multimode fiber

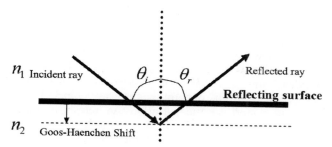

Figure 7: Incident and reflected rays

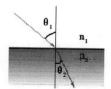

Figure 8: Refraction

If we consider the propagation of a "ray" in a multi-mode step index fiber, the angle of incidence is equal to the angle of reflection. This is illustrated in Figure 7. This means that $\theta_i = \theta_r$.

The important thing to realize about propagation along a fiber is that not all light can propagate this way. The angle of incidence of the ray at the core-cladding interface must be quite small or the ray will pass into the cladding and (after awhile) will leave the fiber. The geometric interpretation of light can be handled more rigorously by electromagnetic theory. In this case, Maxwell equations combined with boundary conditions should be considered.

Geometrical Optics Laws and Parameters

Snell's Law

To understand ray propagation in a fiber, we need one more physics law. This is referred to as *Snell's law*. Referring to Figure 8:

$$n_1 \sin(\theta_1) = n_2 \sin(\theta_2)$$

where n denotes the refractive index of the material. One can notice here that:

1. The angle θ_i is the angle between the incident ray and an imaginary line normal to the plane of the core-cladding boundary;
2. when light passes from a material of a higher refractive index to a material of a lower index, the (refracted) angle θ_2 becomes larger; and
3. when light passes from a material of a lower refractive index to a material of a higher index, the (refracted) angle θ_2 becomes smaller (Dutton 1998).

Critical Angle

If we consider Figure 9, we notice that as the angle θ_1 becomes increasingly larger, so does the angle θ_2. At some point, θ_2 will reach 90 degrees while θ_1 is still well less than that. This is called the *critical angle*. When θ_1 is increased

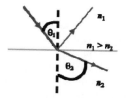

Figure 9: Critical angle

more, refraction ceases and the light is all reflected rather than refracted. Thus, light is perfectly reflected at an interface between two materials of different refractive index if and only if (1) the light is incident on the interface from the side of higher refractive index and (2) the angle θ is greater than a specific critical angle.

If we know the refractive indexes of both materials, then the critical angle can be derived quite easily from Snell's law. At the critical angle, we know that θ_2 equals 90 degrees and $\sin(90) = 1$, so

$$n_1 \sin(\theta_1) = n_2 \quad n_2 < n_1$$

Therefore, $\sin(\theta_1) = \dfrac{n_2}{n_1}$.

Another aspect here is that when light meets an abrupt change in refractive index (such as at the end of a fiber), not all of it is refracted. Usually, approximately 4 percent of the light is reflected back along the path from which it came, depending on the end surface finish (Dutton 1998).

When we consider rays entering the fiber from the outside (into the end face of the fiber), we see that there is a further complication. The refractive index difference between the fiber core and the air will cause any arriving ray to be refracted. This means that there is a maximum angle for a ray arriving at the fiber end face at which the ray will be bound in a propagating mode (Agrawal 2002).

Numerical Aperture

One of the most often quoted characteristics of an optical fiber is its *numerical aperture* (NA), which is intended as a measure of the light-capturing ability of the fiber. However, it is used for many other purposes. For example, it may affect the amount of loss that we might expect in a bend of a particular radius.

Figure 10 shows a ray entering the fiber at an angle close to its axis. This ray will be refracted and later encounter the core-cladding interface at an angle such that

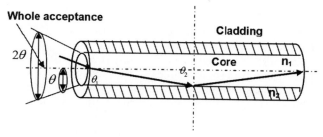

Figure 10: Calculating the numerical aperture

it will be reflected because the angle θ_2 will be greater than the critical angle θ_2. The angle is greater because we are measuring angles from a normal to the core-cladding boundary, not a glancing angle to it. It is clear that there is a "cone" of acceptance (illustrated in Figure 10). If a ray enters the fiber at an angle within the cone, then it will be captured and propagate as a bound mode. If a ray enters the fiber at an angle outside the cone, then it will leave the core and eventually leave the fiber itself.

The NA is the sine of the largest angle contained within the cone of acceptance. Looking at Figure 10, the NA = $\sin(\theta)$. The NA is also found to be given by the following:

$$NA = \sqrt{n_1{}^2 - n_2{}^2}$$

where n_1 = refractive index of the core and n_2 refractive index of the cladding.

Another useful expression is $NA = n_1 \sin(\theta_1)$. This relates the NA to the RI of the core and the maximum angle at which a bound ray may propagate (angle measured from the fiber axis rather than its normal). The typical NA for SMF is 0.1. For MMF, NA is between 0.2 and 0.3 (usually closer to 0.2). NA is related to several important fiber characteristics. It is a measure of the fiber's ability to gather light at the input end (as discussed above). It is also a measure of the contrast in RI between the core and the cladding, so it is a good measure of the fiber's light-guiding properties. The higher the NA, the tighter (i.e., the smaller the radius) the bends in the fiber can be before loss of light becomes a problem.

The higher the NA, the more modes we have. Rays can reflect at greater angles and therefore there are more of them. This means that the higher the NA, the greater will be the dispersion of this fiber (in the case of MMF).

In SMF, a high RI contrast usually implies a high level of dopant in the cladding. Because a significant proportion of optical power in SMF travels in the cladding, we get a significantly increased amount of attenuation because of the higher level of dopant. Thus, as a rule of thumb, the higher the NA of SMF, the higher will be the attenuation of the fiber (Dutton 1998).

Refractive Index

Refractive index is the ratio of the velocity of light in vacuum to the velocity of light in a medium. It is referred to as the *medium's refractive index*, denoted by n and given by

$$n(RI) = \frac{C}{V}$$

where C is the speed of light in a vacuum and V is the velocity of light in the material.

The velocity of light in a vacuum is 3.0×10^8 m/s or approximately 186,000 miles/s. Refractive index of a transparent substance or material is defined as the relative speed at which light moves through the material with respect to its speed in a vacuum. By definition, the refractive index of a vacuum is defined as having a value of 1.0, which serves as a universally accepted reference point.

OPTICAL FIBERS
Conventional Fibers

Like other waveguides, an optical fiber guides waves in distinct patterns called *transverse modes*, which describes the distributions of light energy across the waveguide. The precise patterns depend on the wavelength of light transmitted and on the variations in refractive index across the fiber core. There are three basic types of fiber: *multimode step-index, multimode graded-index,* and *single-mode* or *step-index*.

The difference between the fiber modes is in the way light travels along the fiber. There is a core of 50 microns (μm) diameter for multimode fiber and a cladding of 125 μm diameter (these are the dimensions of standard glass fibers used in telecommunications). (Fiber size is normally quoted as the core diameter followed by the cladding diameter. Thus, the fiber is identified as 50/125.) The cladding surrounds the core. The cladding glass has a different (lower) refractive index than that of the core, and the boundary forms a partially reflecting interface.

Light is transmitted (with low loss) down the fiber by reflection from the boundary between the core and the cladding. This phenomenon is called *total internal reflection*. Perhaps the most important characteristic is that the fiber will bend around corners to a radius of only a few centimeters without any loss of light. The lowest loss occurs at 1.55 microns, and there is also a loss minimum at 1.31-micron wavelengths (Dutton 1998).

Multimode Step-Index Fiber

Fiber that has a core diameter large enough for the light used to find multiple paths is called *multimode fiber* (see Figure 11). For a fiber with a core diameter of 62.5 microns using light of wavelength 1300 nm, the number of modes is approximately 400, depending on the difference in refractive index between the core and the cladding. The problem with multimode operation is that some of the paths taken by particular modes are longer than other paths. This means that light will arrive at different times according to the path taken. Therefore, the pulse tends to disperse (spread out) as it travels through the fiber. This effect is one cause of *intersymbol interference* (ISI). This restricts the distance that a pulse can be usefully sent over multimode fiber.

One way around the problem of (modal) dispersion in MMF is to do something to the glass such that the refractive index of the core changes gradually from the center to the edge. Light traveling down the center of the fiber experiences a higher refractive index than light that travels farther out toward the cladding. Thus, light on the physically shorter paths (modes) travels more slowly than light on

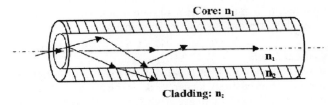

Figure 11: Multimode step-index fiber

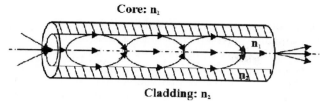

Figure 12: Multimode graded-index fiber

the physically longer paths. The light follows a curved trajectory within the fiber as illustrated in Figure 12. The aim of this is to keep the speed of propagation of light on each path the same with respect to the axis of the fiber. Thus, a pulse of light composed of many modes stays together as it travels through the fiber. This allows transmission for longer distances than in regular multimode transmission. This type of fiber is called *graded-index fiber*. Within this fiber, light typically travels in approximately 400 modes (at a wavelength of 1300 nm) or 800 modes (in the 800 nm band) (Agrawal 2002). A multimode fiber is characterized by its distance multiplied by bandwidth product.

Single-Mode Fiber

Single-mode fibers (also called *monomode fibers*) are optical fibers that are designed to support only a single mode per polarization direction for a given wavelength. As shown in Figure 13, the core diameter is typically between 8 and 9 microns, whereas the diameter of the cladding is 125 microns.

The number of modes allowed in a given fiber is determined by a relationship between the wavelength of the light passing through the fiber, the core diameter of the fiber, and the material of the fiber. This relationship is known as the *normalized frequency parameter*, or *V number*. The mathematical description of the *V* number is given by

$$V = \frac{2 * \pi * NA * r}{\lambda}$$

where NA = numerical aperture, r = core fiber radius (microns), and λ = wavelength (microns).

The electromagnetic wave is tightly held to travel down the axis of the fiber. The longer the wavelength of light in use, the larger the diameter of fiber we can use and still have light travel in a single mode. The core diameter used in a typical single-mode fiber is 9 microns. In practice, it is not quite so simple. A significant proportion (as much as 20 percent) of the light in a SMF actually travels in the cladding. For this reason, the *apparent diameter* of the

core (the region in which most of the light travels) is somewhat wider than the core itself. The region in which light travels in an SMF is often called the *mode field*, and its diameter is quoted instead of the core diameter. We cannot make the core too narrow because of losses at bends in the fiber. When the core is especially narrow, the mode spreads more into the cladding. As the core diameter decreases compared to the wavelength (the core gets narrower or the wavelength gets longer), the minimum radius that we can bend the fiber without loss increases. If a bend is too sharp, the light just comes out of the core into the outer parts of the cladding and is lost.

Single-mode optical fiber is an optical fiber in which only the lowest-order bound mode can propagate at the wavelength of interest. SMFs are best at retaining the fidelity of each light pulse over longer distances and exhibit no dispersion caused by multiple spatial modes; thus, more information can be transmitted per unit time, giving SMFs a higher bandwidth in comparison with MMFs. A typical single-mode optical fiber has a core radius of 5 μm to 10 μm and a cladding radius of 120 μm. Currently, data rates as high as 10 Gigabits per second are possible at distances of more than 60 km with commercially available transceivers.

Unconventional Fibers

Photonic Crystal Fiber

Photonic crystal fiber (PCF) or "holey" fiber is the optical fiber having a periodic structure of cylindrical holes running along the length of the optical fiber as shown in Figure 14. The structures of the PCF have been modified since the introduction of such fibers, including the air-silica fiber, photonic band-gap fiber, and hollow-core photonic crystal fiber. The *air-silica fiber* is the most basic structure. It has a silica background and periodic air holes that surround the silica core, so the core has a high refractive index like a traditional optical fiber. As a consequence, *total internal reflection* (TIR) dominates the guiding mechanism. In *photonic band-gap fiber*, on the other hand, air holes are filled with materials that have higher refractive indexes than the core material (Bise et al. 2002). Obviously, it violates the condition for TIR. However, light is still guided via a different mechanism, the so-called Bragg scattering of constructive or destructive scattering. Finally, the *hollow-core photonic crystal fiber* is air-silica fiber with larger air holes in the core region (Cregan et al. 1999). As a result, the

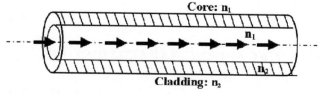

Figure 13: Single-mode fiber. The core diameter is typically between 8 and 9 microns, whereas the diameter of the cladding is 125 microns

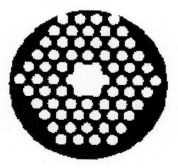

Figure 14: Crosscut view of a photonic crystal fiber

core has a lower refractive index than the cladding, so the guiding mechanism is similar to that of the photonic band-gap fiber.

Holey fibers operating under the TIR principle show significant advantages over their conventional counterparts. For instance, they can be exclusively fabricated out of a single dielectric, thus avoiding interfaces between different materials that might undermine the fiber's performance. The dependence of the cladding's effective index on wavelength permits the manifestation of only a finite number of modes at relatively high frequencies because of the reduction of the difference between the refractive indices of the core and the cladding for increasing frequencies (Birks, Knight, and Russell 1997). Furthermore, it has been theoretically shown and experimentally verified that holey fiber with a triangular lattice of airholes can exhibit endless single-mode operation provided the diameter of the cladding's airholes and the center-to-center spacing of two adjacent holes (lattice constant) are properly chosen (Cregan et al. 1999).

The variation of the cladding's effective index can be optimally turned to advantage, as far as the fiber's dispersion properties are concerned. The wide tailoring of the fiber's design in terms of airhole sizes, shapes, and arrangements provides several degrees of freedom whose proper combination can tune the fiber's dispersion curve. The influence of the design parameters on the dispersion properties of holey fiber has been extensively studied such as both the classical triangular airhole-silica core lattice and other configurations that include additional features—for example, airhole rings of variable diameter and airholes with elliptical cross-sections or doped-silica cylindrical cores (Birks, Knight, and Russell 1997; Saitoh et al. 2003; Ferrando, Silvestre, and Andrés 2001; Hansen 2003). Several types of holey fiber were designed that exhibit favorable dispersion properties, such as zero dispersion at the 1.55-μm operation wavelength and ultraflattened *group-velocity dispersion* (GVD) curves of zero, positive, or negative dispersion over a significant wavelength regime (Crawford, Allender, and Doane 1992; Burylov 1997).

Liquid Crystal Fiber

Nematic liquid crystals are anisotropic materials consisting of rodlike molecules whose axis coincides with the anisotropy's optical axis. The liquid crystal director indicates the local alignment direction and usually varies through the volume of the liquid crystal. When confined in closed cylindrical cavities in the absence of external stimuli, the liquid crystal's director distribution is determined by the physics of elastic theory and the anchoring conditions at the cavity's surface (Saitoh et al. 2003; Ferrando, Silvestre, and Andrés 2001). Under the application of a static electric field, the director's orientation can be controlled because the liquid crystal directors tend to align their axis according to the applied field. In an alternative approach, the properties of nematic liquid crystals can be tuned thermally owing to the dependence of the refractive index values on temperature. The above features have favored their utilization in a number of proposed *opto-electronic* (OE) devices based on photonic crystals (Du, Lu, and Wu 2004; Larsen et al. 2003; Kosmidou, Kriezis, and Tsiboukis 2005; Alkeskjold 2004).

Plastic Optical Fiber

Plastic optical fiber is an optical fiber made from plastic. Traditionally, polymethyl methacrylate is the core material, and fluorinated polymers are the cladding material. The cores of plastic fibers are relatively larger than that of glass fibers (2 mm). The material is a type of plastic and thus quickly absorbs the light traveling through the material. Its lowest loss occurs in the red part of the spectrum rather than in the infrared. Applications for plastic fibers are limited to short-range data transmission. Compared to glass fibers, plastic fibers are less expensive in the overall optical link because of the lower cost of the connector and the splicing used.

Fiber Fabrication

The fiber fabrication process consists of two major stages. The first stage produces a preform, a cylinder of silica of 10 cm to 20 cm in diameter and approximately 50 cm to 100 cm in length. This preform consists of a core surrounded by a cladding with a desired refractive-index profile, a given attenuation, and other characteristics; in other words, this is a desired optical fiber, but on a much larger scale.

In the second stage, the preform is drawn into an optical fiber of the desired size. The preform is made by vapor-phase oxidation, in which two gases—silicon tetrachloride ($SiCl_4$) and oxygen (O_2)—are mixed at high temperature to produce silicon dioxide (SiO_2):

$$SiCl_4 + O_2 \rightarrow SiO_2 + 2Cl_2$$

Silicon dioxide, or pure silica, is usually obtained in the form of small particles (~0.1 μm) called *soot*. This soot is deposited on the target rod or tube layer upon layer to form a homogeneous, transparent cladding material. To change the value of a cladding's refractive index, some dopants are used. For example, fluorine is used to decrease the cladding's refractive index in a depressed-cladding configuration.

The soot for the core material is made by mixing three gases—$SiCl_4$, germanium tetrachloride ($GeCl_4$), and O_2—which results in a mixture of SiO_2 and germanium dioxide (GeO_2). The degree of doping is controlled by simply changing the amount of $GeCl_4$ gas added to the mixture. The same principle is used for doping other materials.

Because deposition is made by the application of silica layers on top of one another, the manufacturer can control the exact amount of dopant added to each layer, thus controlling the refractive-index profile. The vapor-phase oxidation process produces extremely pure material whose characteristics are under the absolute control of the manufacturer.

OPTICAL FIBER CHARACTERISTICS

The need for high-speed data transmission has meant that optical communication systems have experienced a rapid evolution during the last decade. However, one major impairment restricts the achievement of higher bit rates with standard SMF: chromatic dispersion. This is particularly problematic for systems operating in the 1550-nm band. CD and PMD can cause intersymbol interference, which is a major obstacle to reliable high-speed data transmission over optical fiber. As both CD and PMD originate in the optical domain, the most effective compensation schemes use optical equalization. Nonetheless, electrical equalization schemes are also being widely considered because they offer several potential advantages, including compactness, flexibility, and low cost (Winters and Gitlin 1990).

CD is the variation in the speed of propagation of a light-wave signal with wavelength. This phenomenon is also known as *group velocity dispersion* because the dispersion is the result of the group velocity being a function of the wavelength.

Attenuation

Attenuation in fiber occurs as a result of absorption, scattering, and radiative losses of the optical energy. Absorption losses are caused by atomic defects in the glass composition, intrinsic absorption by the atomic resonance of fiber material, and extrinsic absorption by the atomic resonance of external particles (such as the $^-$OH ion) in the fiber. Scattering losses in fiber arise from microscopic variations in the material density and from structural inhomogeneities. There are four kinds of scattering losses in optical fiber: Rayleigh, Mie, Brillouin, and Raman scattering. Radiative losses occur in an optical fiber at bends and curves because of the evanescent modes generated. Figure 15 illustrates the attenuation for SMF with respect to wavelength.

Group Velocity Dispersion and Polarization Mode Dispersion

In SMF there are two types of dispersion: chromatic and PMD. The former is the phenomenon by which different frequencies travel through a fiber with different group velocities, whereas the latter represents a velocity difference between the two orthogonal electric field components of the fundamental mode inside the fiber.

For a single-mode fiber of length L, a specific spectral component at a frequency ω arrives at the other end of the fiber after a propagation delay of $T = L/v_g$, where v_g is the group velocity given by:

$$v_g = \left(\frac{d\beta}{d\omega}\right)^{-1}$$

where β is the mode propagation constant. As a result of the dependence of group velocity on frequency, the different spectral components of the data pulses travel with different velocities along the fiber, arriving at the fiber output dispersed in time. The amount of pulse broadening, as a result of CD, can be quantified as

$$\Delta T \cong \frac{dT}{d\omega}\Delta\omega = \frac{d}{d\omega}\left(\frac{L}{v_g}\right)\Delta\omega = L\frac{d^2\beta}{d\omega^2}\Delta\omega = L\beta_2\Delta\omega$$

The factor $\beta_2 = d^2\beta/d\omega^2$ is the GVD parameter, which provides a measure of how much a pulse broadens in time as the pulse travels along an optical fiber. Depending on the sign of β_2, CD is called *positive* ($\beta_2 > 0$) or *negative* ($\beta_2 < 0$).

CD or GVD increases linearly with the fiber length; its effect on the transmitted and received signal is shown in Figure 16. The GVD is governed by material properties (the dependence of the fiber material's refractive index on the light frequency) and waveguide dispersion (wherein Maxwell's equations yield different β's for different frequencies, depending on the fiber's dimensions). GVD is quantified by a *dispersion parameter*, $D(\lambda)$, that measures the time delay introduced between light at different wavelengths while propagating through a commonly used SMF-28 fiber with a length L:

$$(\tau_{delay} = D(\lambda)\Delta\lambda L) \text{ and } \beta_1 = \frac{\delta\beta}{\delta\omega} = \frac{1}{v_g} \quad \beta_2 = \frac{\lambda^2 D}{4c\pi}$$

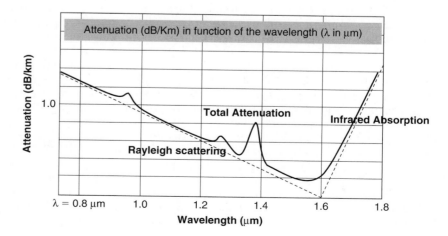

Figure 15: Attenuation for SMF

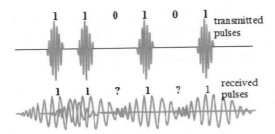

Figure 16: The overall effect of both GVD and PMD (Guizani et al. 2005)

where β_1, β_2 are the first- and second-order dispersions, v_g is the group velocity, C is the speed of light, $D \approx 17$ ps/nm/km in the 1550-nm communication window, and $D(\lambda)\Delta\lambda$ is the wavelength spread. PMD, on the other hand, is caused by the removal of circular symmetry in a fiber resulting from external factors such as temperature or mechanical stress as well as the lack of perfect symmetry in manufacturing. The fraction of the total power contained in one of the polarizations (γ) governs the severity of the PMD. The overall effect of both GVD and PMD is the broadening of pulses propagating through the fiber; this results in intersymbol interference (Winters and Gitlin 1990). In reality, it affects the envelope of the transmitted pulses. ISI leads to closing of the eye diagram (the eye diagram is created by taking the time domain signal and overlapping the traces for a certain number of symbols) at the output, which in turn causes higher BER and increases input power requirements.

Nonlinear Optical Effects

The refractive index of silica has a weak dependence on the optical intensity, I (optical power per effective area in the fiber), and is given by

$$n = n_0 + n_2 I = n_0 + n_2 \frac{P}{A_{eff}}$$

where n_0 is the normal refractive index of the fiber material, n_2 is the nonlinear index coefficient, P is the optical power, and A_{eff} is the effective cross-sectional area of the fiber. In silica, the value of n_2 ranges from 2.2 to 3.4 $\times$ 10^{-8} μm^2/W. This nonlinearity in the refractive index is known as *Kerr nonlinearity* and results in a carrier-induced *phase modulation* (PM) of the propagating signal called the *Kerr effect*. It can cause self-phase modulation, cross-phase modulation, and four-wave mixing (Guizani et al. 2005).

Self-Phase Modulation

The local refractive index is a function of the optical intensity of the propagating signal, so the mode propagation constant also depends on the optical intensity. The power-dependent propagation constant, β, can be written as $\beta = \beta + \gamma P$, where β is the mode propagation constant, which is derived by assuming a constant refractive constant. The nonlinear coefficient γ is defined by $\frac{2\pi n_2}{\lambda A_{eff}}$.

Because this nonlinear PM is self-induced, the nonlinear phenomenon responsible for it is called *self-phase modulation* (SPM). As phase fluctuations translate into frequency fluctuations, SPM and dispersion cause frequency chirping of the optical pulses, which presents a source of error (Guizani et al. 2005).

Cross-Phase Modulation

In WDM systems, where several optical channels are transmitted simultaneously inside an optical fiber, the nonlinear phase shift for a specific channel depends not only on the power of that channel but also on the power of the other channels. Moreover, the phase shift varies from bit to bit, depending on the bit pattern of the neighboring channels. This nonlinear phenomenon is known as *cross-phase modulation* (XPM). Like SPM, XPM may lead to erroneous reception of the transmitted bit sequence (Guizani et al. 2005).

Four-Wave Mixing

Four-wave mixing (WM) is a third-order nonlinearity in silica fiber caused by the Kerr effect. FWM resembles intermodulation distortion in electrical systems. If three optical fields with carrier frequencies f_1, f_2, and f_3 propagating simultaneously in a fiber, the fiber nonlinearity causes them to mix, producing a fourth intermodulation term that is related to the other frequencies by the relation $f_4 = f_1 \pm f_2 \pm f_3$. FWM is an additional source of ISI (Guizani et al. 2005), but more importantly it causes interchannel interference in WDM systems.

OPTICAL DEVICES

In addition to lasers and LEDs, many other optical devices perform useful and necessary functions in an optical communication system. This section describes some of them. We briefly mentioned some optical devices at the beginning of this chapter. Here we discuss those devices in more detail and also describe other optical devices that find uses in optical fiber communications. Many components already in use in radio and radar systems such as circulators, chirped grating reflectors, and compressive receivers were realized in optical form so that the same system designs could now be used in the optical domain.

Circulators

Circulators are passive micro-optic devices of three or more ports in which the ports can be accessed in such an order that when power is fed into any port it is transferred to the next port, the first port being counted as following the last in order. They are unidirectional devices that direct an optical signal (light) from one port to the next in only one direction at a time. Although the direction of the light may be redirected as needed, it must pass to and from ports sequentially (from port 1 to port 2 before traveling to port 3) as illustrated in Figure 17.

Modulators and Switches

An *optical modulator* is a device that allows manipulating a property of light, often of an optical beam such as a laser beam. Depending on which property of light is controlled, we talk about intensity modulators, phase modulators, polarization modulators, and so on.

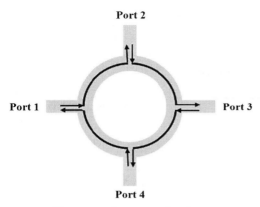

Figure 17: Four-port circulator

Most modulators consist of a material that changes its optical properties under the influence of an electric or magnetic field. The following are some modulators types and their possible applications:

- *fiber-optic* modulators, which are often fiber pig-tailed bulk components;
- *acousto-optic* modulators, which are used for switching or continuously adjusting the amplitude of a laser beam to shift its optical frequency or its spatial direction;
- *electro-optic* modulators, which are used for modifying the polarization, phase, or power of a beam or for pulse picking in the context of ultrashort pulse amplifiers;
- *electro-absorption* modulators, which are used for transmitters in OFC;
- *interferometric* modulators (e.g., Mach-Zehnder modulators), which are often realized in integrated optical circuits and used in optical data transmission; and
- *liquid crystal* modulators, which are used, for example, in optical displays and in pulse shapers and often as spatial light modulators (i.e., with a spatially varying modulation).

Optical modulators are used in widely different application areas such as OFC, displays, active Q switching or mode locking of lasers, and optical metrology.

An optical switch may operate by mechanical means, such as physically shifting an optical fiber to drive one or more alternative fibers, or by electro-optic effects, magneto-optic effects, or other methods. Slow optical switches, such as those using moving fibers, may be used for the alternate routing of an optical transmission path such as around a fault. Fast optical switches, such as those using electro-optic or magneto-optic effects, may be used to perform logic operations.

Optical Amplifiers

The transmission distance of any OFC system is eventually limited by fiber losses. Traditionally, OE repeaters were used to overcome this loss by first converting the optical signal into an electric current and then regenerating it using a transmitter. Such regenerators become quite complex and expensive for WDM light-wave systems.

The alternative approach is to use optical amplifiers that amplify the optical signal directly without requiring its conversion to the electric domain. There are several kinds of optical amplifier. These optical amplifiers have become an integral part of almost all OFC systems installed after 1995 because of their excellent amplification characteristics such as low insertion loss, high gain, large bandwidth, low noise, and low cross talk. The most popular are EDFAs, semiconductor optical amplifiers, and Raman amplifiers.

Fiber Bragg Gratings

An FBG is a periodic perturbation of the refractive index along the fiber length. It is formed by exposure of the core to an ultraviolet optical interference pattern (see Figure 18). The principle of the Bragg grating is illustrated in Figure 19. A part of the incident wave is transmitted at each grating period, and the other part is reflected. For a certain wavelength depending on the period Λ (shown in Figure 18), the reflected waves are in phase. Multiple reflections are not considered in the figure, although they are crucial in fully explaining the device's operation.

The formation of permanent gratings in an optical fiber was first demonstrated by Hill et al. (1978) at the Canadian Communications Research Centre (Maune et al. 2004). They launched intense argon-ion laser radiation into a germania-doped fiber and observed that after several minutes an increase in the reflected light intensity occurred that grew until almost all of the light was reflected from the fiber. Spectral measurements, done indirectly by strain and temperature tuning of the fiber grating, confirmed that a very narrowband Bragg grating filter had been formed over the entire 1-m length of the fiber. This achievement, subsequently called the *Hill gratings*, was an outgrowth of research on the nonlinear properties of germania-doped silica fiber. It established the photosensitivity of germania fiber, which prompted other inquires several years later into the cause of the fiber photo-induced refractivity and its dependence on the wavelength of the light that was used to the form the gratings.

As light moves along the fiber and encounters the changes in refractive index, a small amount of light is reflected at each boundary. When the period of the grating and half of the wavelength of the light are the same, there is constructive interference and power is coupled from the forward direction to the backward direction. Light of other wavelengths destructively interferes with out-of-phase reflections and therefore cannot be reflected and is transmitted instead. The spacing between the grating reflectors determines the wavelength that is reflected. The incoming light is gradually reflected, and the backward-traveling light gradually grows in strength as they are waves coupled by the grating. This is a resonance phenomenon and has some similarities to that in an electromagnetic resonant circuit in electronics. Power from the forward direction is coupled into the resonant circuit and then reflected back. Nonresonant wavelengths are not affected much.

FBGs have proven attractive in a wide variety of optical fiber applications such as:

- narrowband and broadband tunable filters;
- optical fiber mode converters;

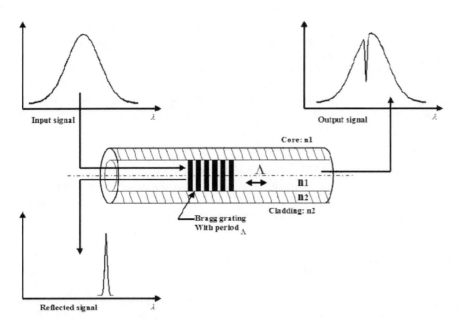

Figure 18: Fiber Bragg granting overview

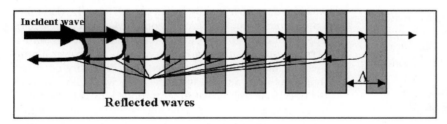

Figure 19: Principle of the Bragg grating (Λ is the grating period)

- wavelength-selective filters, multiplexers, and add-drop Mach-Zehnders;
- dispersion compensation in long-distance telecommunication networks;
- gain equalization and improved pump efficiency in EDFA;
- spectrum analyzers;
- specialized narrowband lasers; and
- optical strain gauges in bridges, building structures, elevators, reactors, composites, mines, and smart structures.

Chirped FBG

The chirped FBG is considered one of the most interesting optical elements to have immediate applications in telecommunications systems. A chirped FBG is used when the spacing of the lines on the grating vary constantly over a miniature range (Figure 20). Shorter-wavelength light

entering the grating travels along it almost to the end before being reflected. Longer-wavelength light is reflected close to the start of the grating (Agrawal 2002). Thus, shorter wavelengths are delayed in relation to longer ones. Because the pulse has been dispersed such that short wavelengths arrive before the long ones, the grating can restore the original pulse shape. It undoes the effects of dispersion (Figure 21). In this sense, it has a similar structure and operates in a similar way to surface acoustic wave chirped reflective gratings developed earlier (Huang, Paige, and Selviah 1986) for use in radar pulse-compression receivers that remove the dispersion on the received pulse.

To show the importance of all of the optical devices discussed herein—the laser, the modulator, the chirped grating, the optical amplifier, the circulator, and the photodetector—an application of an optical link is shown in Figure 21. The electrical signal is transformed into an optical signal by external modulation using a laser source and external modulation, most commonly by means of an

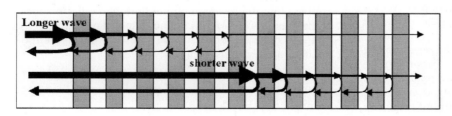

Figure 20: Principle of the chirped grating

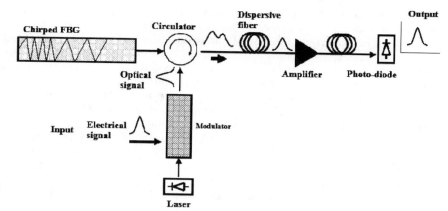

Figure 21: Precompensation of chromatic dispersion by using a chirped grating

MZI. The obtained distortion-free optical signal enters a circulator and goes first through a chirped FBG, where it is intentionally deformed to spread the pulses. Then the optical deformed signal recovers its initial shape after propagation through the dispersive fiber, which compensates the chirped FBG effect (Figure 21). Because a standard single-mode fiber operating at 1550 nm causes negative CD ($D = 17$ ps/nm/km), the chirped FBG should first introduce positive dispersion to enable precompensation. Because attenuation is unavoidable over long distances, optical amplifiers should be used.

Filters

In the world of optics, *filter* often is a broad term that is applied to components that filter out part of the incident light and transmit the rest. In current optical systems, frequency filters are used in front of an LED to narrow the line width before transmission in a form of spectral slicing. In WDM networks, filters are extremely important for many uses, such as (1) placing a filter in front of an incoherent receiver to select a particular signal from many arriving signals and (2) controlling which path a signal will take through a proposed WDM network.

Many filtering principles have been proposed, and many different types of devices have been built. The result is that many kinds of active, tunable filters are available that are essential in WDM networks (Dutton 1998).

In dense wavelength-division multiplexing systems, the wavelengths that are not transmitted through the filter normally are reflected, so they go elsewhere in the system. FBGs are probably the most important optical filter in the communications world. One of the simplest filters in principle is based on the Fabry-Perot interferometer. It consists of a cavity bounded on each end by a dielectric stack mirror. If the mirrors are fixed in relation to each other (such as with spacers), it is called an *Etalon*. If the mirrors can be moved in relation to each other, the device is called an

interferometer and is a narrowband tunable filter. However, this mechanical motion is undesirable, so Fabry–Perot filter cavities have been filled with nematic liquid crystal to give a change in optical path length across the cavity when a low voltage is applied; this changes the effective refractive index of the liquid crystal (Day et al. 1995; Kataoka et al. 2004). These tunable narrowband filters, however, only operate for one incident linear polarization of light, so additional birefringent layers were added inside the cavity to make the device polarization-insensitive (Day et al. 1995; Kataoka et al. 2004).

Repeaters

In an optical fiber communications system, repeaters are used to regenerate an optical signal by converting it to an electrical signal, processing that electrical signal, and then retransmitting an optical signal. Such repeaters are used to extend the reach of optical communications links by overcoming losses resulting from attenuation of the optical fiber and distortion of the optical signal. Such repeaters are known as *optical-electrical-optical* (OEO) because of the conversion of the signal (see Figure 22).

Repeaters have largely been replaced in long-haul systems by optical amplifiers (such as EDFA) because one amplifier can be used for many wavelengths in a WDM system, thereby saving money. Note that a device of this class is sometimes called an *optical amplifier repeater*.

Repeaters have been the method of choice for amplifying an optical signal. A regenerative repeater is a full receiver that reconstructs the bit stream and its timing. This bit stream and its timing are used to drive a transmitter. This means that the repeated signal has all dispersion and noise removed. It is said that repeaters perform the "three R's": *reamplification, reshaping,* and *reclocking.*

So-called 2R repeaters exist but only perform reamplification and reshaping but not reclocking. Repeaters are more complex and more costly than simple amplifiers.

Figure 22: Repeater's components—OE = opto-electrical, EO = electro-optical

They are also highly inflexible because they must be constructed for exactly the wavelength, protocol, and speed of the signal being carried. Because of the high data rates that can be achieved with optical systems, OEO repeaters are expensive to implement; the electronics needed to handle those high data rates are expensive and difficult to construct. Also, because one repeater is required for each wavelength, and many tens of wavelengths may be transmitted down a single fiber, a lot of equipment is required for each fiber. In contrast, an optical amplifier can amplify all of the wavelengths in a single device. An amplifier does not provide the regeneration ability of a repeater, but loss, rather than distortion, is generally the limiting factor in the design of communications systems (Dutton 1998).

CONCLUSION

Since their invention in the early 1970s, the use and demand for optical fiber systems has grown tremendously. OFC now permeate many markets. The most common are telecommunications, medicine, military, automotive, and industrial.

Optical communication applications are widespread, ranging from global networks to local telephone exchanges to subscribers' homes to desktop computers. These involve the transmission of voice, data, and video over progressively shorter distances from thousands of kilometers down to less than a meter within printed circuit boards (Papakonstantinou et al. 2007) in the most recent research.

GLOSSARY

Bit Error Rate (BER): BER is the ratio of bits with errors to the total number of bits that have been transmitted, received, or processed over a given time period. The rate is typically expressed as 10 to the negative power.

Chromatic Dispersion (CD): Different wavelengths travel along an optical medium at different speeds. Wavelengths reach the end of the medium at different times, causing the light pulse to spread. This chromatic dispersion is expressed in picoseconds (of dispersion) per kilometer (of length) per nanometer (of source bandwidth).

Cross-Phase Modulation (XPM): Cross-phase modulation is the change of the optical phase of a light beam caused by the interaction with another beam in a nonlinear medium, specifically a Kerr medium.

Erbium-Doped Fiber Amplifier (EDFA): A purely optical (as opposed to electronic) device used to boost an optical signal. It contains several meters of glass fiber doped with erbium ions.

Fiber Bragg Grating (FBG): A fiber Bragg grating is generally a periodic perturbation of the effective refractive index in the core of an optical fiber.

Group Velocity Dispersion (GVD): Dispersion is a phenomenon that causes the separation of a wave into spectral components with different frequencies due to a dependence of the wave's speed on its frequency. It is most often described in light waves, although it may happen to any kind of wave that interacts with a

medium or can be confined to a waveguide. It is the derivative of the inverse group velocity with respect to either the angular frequency or the wavelength.

Light-Emitting Diode (LED): A light-emitting diode (LED) is a semiconductor device used to transmit incoherent narrow-spectrum light when electrically biased in the forward direction.

Mach-Zhender Interferometer (MZI): MZI splits an optical signal into two components, directs them down into two separate paths, and then recombines them. By inducing a phase delay between the two optical signals, the resulting interference can cause intensity changes.

Optical Fiber Communication (OFC): Fiber-optic communication system is a fiber-optic link providing a point-to-point connection with a single data channel. The data transmitter can be a semiconductor laser, which can be directly modulated via its drive current.

Opto-Electronic (OE): Optoelectronic devices are electrical-to-optical or optical-to-electrical transducers.

Phase Modulation (PM): Phase modulation is one of the three ways of modulating or altering a signal so that it is able to carry information. The other two are amplitude and frequency modulation. Phase modulation is used in high speed modems.

Polarization mode dispersion (PMD): Light transmitted down a single mode fiber can be decomposed into two perpendicular polarization components. Distortion results due to each polarization propagating at a different velocity.

Single-Mode Fiber (SMF): A single-mode optical fiber is an optical fiber in which only the lowest order bound mode can propagate at the wavelength of interest. Unlike multimode fiber, the conventional SMF has a small core diameter ($< 10\ \mu m$).

Wavelength Division Multiplexing (WDM): A way of increasing the information-carrying capacity of an optical fiber by simultaneously operating at more than one wavelength. WDM modulates each of several data streams onto a different color or wavelength called lambda. Each lambda carries an individual optical signal providing the same bandwidth per channel.

CROSS REFERENCES

See *Fiberoptic Filters and Multiplexers*; *Free-Space Optics*; *Optical Transmitters, Receivers, and Noise*.

REFERENCES

Agrawal, G. P. 2002. *Fiber-optic communication systems*. New York: John Wiley & Sons.

Alkeskjold, T. T., J. Lægsgaard, A. Bjarklev, D. S. Hermann, J. Broeng, J. Li, and S.-T. Wu. 2004. All-optical modulation in dye-doped nematic liquid crystal photonic bandgap fibers. *Optics Express*, 12: 5857–871.

Birks, T. A., J. C. Knight, and P. S. Russell. 1997. Endlessly single-mode photonic crystal fiber. *Optics Letters*, 22: 961–3.

Bise, R. T., R. S. Windeler, K. S. Kranz, C. Kerbage, B. J. Eggleton, and D. J. Trevor. 2002. Tunable photonic band gap fiber. In *Optical Fiber Communication*

Conference, vol. 70 of *OSA Trends in Optics and Photonics*, pp. 466–8. Washington, DC: Optical Society of America.

Burylov, S. V. 1997. Equilibrium configuration of a nematic liquid crystal confined to a cylindrical cavity. *Journal of Experimental and Theoretical Physics*, 85: 873–86.

Crawford, G. P., D. W. Allender, and J. W. Doane. 1992. Surface elastic and molecular-anchoring properties of nematic liquid crystals confined to cylindrical cavities. *Physical Review*, A 45: 8693–710.

Cregan, R. F., B. J. Mangan, J. C. Knight, T. A. Birks, P. S. J. Russell, P. J. Roberts, and D. C. Allan. 1999. Single-mode photonic band gap guidance of light in air. *Science*, 285(3): 1537–9.

Day, S. E., D. R. Selviah, H. Manthopoulos, and M. Wiltshire. 1995. Polarization insensitive operation of a liquid crystal Fabry Perot filter for WDM. British Liquid Crystals Society Conference, Exeter, March 29–31.

Du, F., Y.-Q. Lu, and S.-T. Wu. 2004. Electrically tunable liquid-crystal photonic crystal fiber. *Applied Physics Letters*, 85: 2181–3.

Dutton, H. J. R. 1998. *Understanding optical communications*. Upper Saddle River, NJ: Prentice Hall.

Ferrando, A., E. Silvestre, and P. Andrés. 2001. Designing the properties of dispersion-flattened photonic crystal fibers. *Optics Express*, 9: 687–97.

Frignac, Y., G. Charlet, W. Idler, R. Dischler, P. Tran, S. Lanne, S. Borne, C. Martinel, G. Veith, A. Jourdan, J. Hamaide, and S. Bigo. 2002. Transmission of 256 wavelength-division and polarization-division-multiplexed channels at 42.7 Gb/s (10.2 Tb/s capacity) over 3 × 100km of teralight fiber. In *Proceedings of the Optical Fiber Communication Conference and Exhibit* (OFC'02), pp. 1–3.

Guizani, S., H. Hamam, Y. Bouslimani, and A. Chériti. 2005. High bit rate optical communications: Limitations and perspectives. *IEEE Canadian Review* 50: 11–15.

Hansen, K. P. 2003. Dispersion flattened hybrid-core nonlinear photonic crystal fiber. *Optics Express*, 11: 1503–9.

Hill, K. O., Y. Fujii, D. C. Johnson, and B. S. Kawasaki. 1978. Photosensitivity in optical fiber waveguides: Application to reflection filter fabrication. *Applied Physics Letters*, 32: 647–9.

Huang, F., E. G. S. Paige, and D. R. Selviah. 1986. High-performance SAW dispersive delay line using reflective thin metal dot arrays. *Electronics Letters*, 22(12): 653–4.

Kao, K. C., and G. A. Hockham. 1966. Dielectric-fibre surface waveguides for optical frequencies. *Proceedings of the IEE*, 133: 1151–8.

Kataoka, T., S. E. Day, D. R. Selviah, and A. Fernandez. 2004. Polarization-insensitive liquid-crystal Fabry-Perot tunable optical filter. *Digest of Technical Papers* (SID 2004 International Symposium), 35: 1530–3.

Keiser, G. 2000. *Optical fiber communication*. 3rd ed. New York: McGraw-Hill.

Kosmidou, E. P., E. E. Kriezis, and T. D. Tsiboukis. 2005. Analysis of tunable photonic crystal devices comprising liquid crystal materials as defects. *IEEE Journal of Quantum Electronics*, 41: 657–65.

Larsen, T. T., A. Bjarklev, D. S. Hermann, and J. Broeng. 2003. Optical devices based on liquid crystal photonic bandgap fibers. *Optics Express*, 11: 2589–96.

Maune, B., M. Lončar, J. Witzens, M. Hochberg, T. Baehr-Jones, D. Psaltis, A. Scherer, and Y. Qiu. 2004. Liquid crystal electric tuning of a photonic crystal laser. *Applied Physics Letters*, 85: 360–2.

Papakonstantinou, I., K. Wang, D. R. Selviah, and F. A. Fernández. 2007. Transition, radiation and propagation loss in polymer multimode waveguide bends. *Optics Express*, 15(2): 669–679.

Saitoh, K., M. Koshiba, T. Hasegawa, and E. Sasaoka. 2003. Chromatic dispersion control in photonic crystal fibers: Application to ultra-flattened dispersion. *Optics Express*, 11: 843–52.

Winters, J. H., and R. D. Gitlin. 1990. Electrical signal processing techniques in long-haul fiber-optic Systems. *IEEE Transactions on Communications*, 38(9): 1439–53.

Zhu, B., L. Leng, L. Nelson, S. Knudsen, J. Bromage, D. Peckham, S. Stulz, K. Brar, C. Horn, K. Feder, H. Thiele, and T. Veng. 2001. 1.6 Tb/s (40 × 42.7 Gb/s) transmission over 2000 km of fiber with 100-km dispersion-managed spans. In *Proceedings of the Twenty-Seventh European Conference on Optical Communication* (ECOC'01), Sept. 30–Oct. 4, Amsterdam, 6: 16–17.

Optical Transmitters, Receivers, and Noise

Kenneth Pedrotti, *University of California, Santa Cruz*

INTRODUCTION

In a point-to-point optical fiber link, the signal, a train of optical pulses, is launched into the fiber by a transmitter module consisting of a laser or *light-emitting diode* (LED) and its associated control and drive electronics (see Figure 1). After attenuation and distortion by its journey through the fiber, the pulse is detected by a receiver module consisting of a sensitive photodiode to convert the optical signal back into an electrical signal, a low-noise preamplifier, and either a variable gain amplifier or a limiting amplifier. The ratio of the received signal to the noise added by the laser and the receiver determines the accuracy with which the determination of the original signal stream can be determined by a subsequent decision circuit. In this chapter, we describe the basic components, design, and functionality of both transmitters and receivers. Although digital transmission dominates the field of optical fiber transmission, analog transmission is important in remote antenna locations, satellite communications, phased array radar, and cable TV. These and topics related to analog transmission such as linearity are outside the scope of this work, so the interested reader is referred to Cox (2004).

Most data and telecommunication links use a *non-return-to-zero* (NRZ) format, but a *return-to-zero* (RZ) format is sometimes used despite requiring more bandwidth for a given data rate. Our discussion here focuses on systems utilizing these variations of *on-off keyed* (OOK) modulation. Many of the issues involved in the design and characterization of optical transmitters and receivers such as synchronization, line coding, error-correction coding, fiber and transmission impairments, and specific standards are covered elsewhere in this handbook.

In the following, we first will discuss the light sources, modulator, and driver circuits that make up the transmitter.

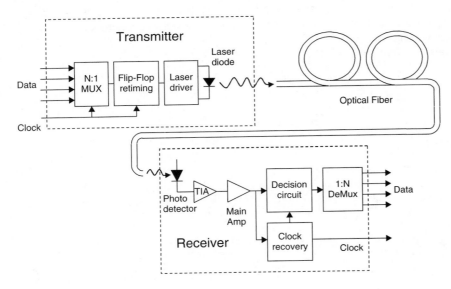

Figure 1: The main elements of a typical point-to-point optical link

Next, fundamental sources of noise encountered in the various stages of an optical link are presented with the intent of allowing the calculation of the *signal-to-noise ratio* (SNR) that determines the achievable error rate in an optical link. Finally, the reception of these signals is treated, starting with the main photodetectors and progressing through representative receiver circuits and system characterization. Both the optical and electronic aspects of these subsystems will be discussed.

OPTICAL TRANSMITTERS

The transmitter subsystem in an optical communication link is responsible for the conversion of the electrical signal into an optical signal. Among the devices used to accomplish this electronic to optical conversion are light-emitting diodes and directly or externally modulated semiconductor lasers. The device choice and approach is driven by cost and performance considerations, chiefly the creation of a faithful replica of the electrical data that is robust to degradation by imperfections in the fiber media and receiver. This becomes translated into a requirement for an emission source whose wavelength lies within a low-attenuation, low-dispersion region of the optical fiber and has a high extinction ratio and low intensity noise. Although the modulated light source is the most important part of a transmitter, state-of-the-art designs must carefully consider the design of the driver circuit and the connection between the driver and the laser. Packaging is also an important issue, requiring an enclosure that is a combination of microwave and optical design approaches. In this section, we survey the various available light emitters, modulators, specifications, and drive electronics used in optical transmitters.

Light Sources

Light-Emitting Diodes

The simplest and cheapest light emitters are LEDs. These are formed from a P-N junction of a direct gap semiconductor such as gallium arsenide (GaAs) or indium gallium arsenide (InGaAs). When a forward voltage bias is applied to the junction, a current flows, resulting in the injection of holes and electrons into the junction region. These carriers then recombine, resulting in the emission of light whose wavelength is characteristic of the band gap of the semiconductor used: 850 nm for GaAs and 1300 nm or 1550 nm for InGaAsP alloys lattice-matched to indium phosphide (InP). For the purpose of achieving good carrier confinement or light emission into a smaller solid angle, the P-N junction is often clad with wider band-gap semiconductor material such as aluminum gallium arsenide (AlGaAs) or InP.

LEDs suffer from three main disadvantages. First, the light that emerges is uncollimated, occupying a large solid angle relative to the acceptance angle of typical optical fibers. LEDs used with large-core fiber can benefit from the use of a lens to capture all of the light, but the inherent low brightness of the sources makes this difficult with small-core fibers. Second, the turnoff time of an LED is limited by the natural recombination time of

carriers in the semiconductor material, typically 5–10 ns for commonly used materials. With the introduction of specific impurities, modulation bandwidths as high as 800 Mbps can be achieved but with reduced light output. These properties make LEDs more attractive for short distance—for example, < 1 km low-capacity < 500 Mbps links. Third, LEDs have a wide spectral bandwidth on the order of 50 nm. This leads to rapid pulse dispersion as well as limits the number of wavelengths that may be used simultaneously on a single fiber.

In resonant cavity LEDs, partially reflective regions above and below the P-N junction form a resonant cavity at the emitted wavelength; they are now becoming available commercially. These have increased brightness because of a reflector behind the active layer. This also results in a narrower linewidth relative to traditional LED structures. The increased light emission allows for longer transmission distances in the face of fiber attenuation. The narrower linewidth allows for higher transmission speeds over longer distances because the pulses are more resistant to spreading in time caused by the chromatic dispersion of the fibers.

New LEDs are also becoming available specifically for use in the shorter wavelength transparency windows of some emerging *plastic optical fibers* (POFs). POF-based link standards are currently targeted at data communications, audiovisual, and automotive applications mostly using 650 nm or 670 nm LEDs, but some are now available that also are optimized for communications use at the 570 and 520 nm POF transmission windows. POF-LED links are typically 10–1000 m long with data rates between 10 Mbps and 250 Mbps.

Laser Diodes

Directly modulated semiconductor lasers greatly surpass LEDs in terms of coupled optical power, narrow optical bandwidth, and switching speed. This enables transmission over much longer distances at higher rates. With the advent of efficient optical amplifiers, it is now possible to reduce or eliminate the impairments resulting from optical attenuation, leaving pulse distortion often as the limiting factor in the attainment of high bit-rate length product fiber links. Optical phase and frequency shifts, referred to as *chirp*, accompany the modulation of semiconductor lasers. These cause spreading and deterioration of the optical pulse as it propagates through dispersive optical fibers. This now becomes the limiting factor in determining the maximum link distance for systems based on these sources. These effects can be reduced by the use of external modulation schemes.

Three basic designs are commonly used in today's systems: *Fabry-Perot* (FP) lasers, *distributed feedback* (DFB) lasers, and *vertical-cavity surface-emitting lasers* (VCSELs). Common to all is a *light versus current* (L/I) characteristic (see Figure 2). Here a relatively small amount of light is emitted below some threshold current; above this value, the light output becomes more intense and rises faster with increasing current. For digitally modulated signals, the current through the diodes is shifted between a current well above threshold and one close to threshold to represent 1's and 0's, respectively. The challenges

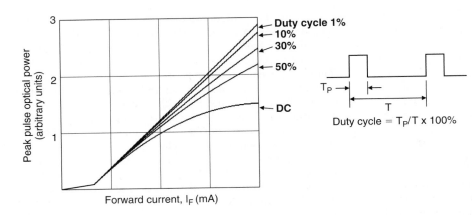

Figure 2: Low T_0 laser diode light versus current characteristic showing the effects of self-heating and modulation duty cycle

encountered in transmitter design arise from nonidealities in this characteristic—chiefly, nonlinearities in this relationship at high currents and changes in the threshold current and slope with temperature and aging. In addition, these devices are highly susceptible to variations in the L/I curve caused by back reflections in the optical path (Twu et al. 1992). The relative intensity noise—the optical noise power normalized to the average noise power—can also be adversely affected by optical reflections. Because of this, *optical isolators* often need to be included in high bit-rate systems, further increasing complexity and cost. The problems caused by temperature and aging can in large part be ameliorated by the use of feedback in the driver circuitry and will be discussed later.

The dynamic response of lasers can also be problematic. When switching, they exhibit time delays and ringing. The time delays are a function of the proximity of the bias in the off state to the threshold level: The further below threshold, the greater the delay. The delay τ_d is given in terms of the delay at threshold τ_{th} (typically ~ 2 ns), the peak drive current I_p, the bias current I_b, and the laser threshold current I_{th} as

$$\tau_d = \tau_{th} \ln\left(\frac{I_p}{I_p + I_b - I_{th}}\right) \quad (1)$$

This delay also has a random component because of variations in the build up of the light to its steady state value that results in signal jitter. To reduce this delay,

the laser is often biased at or slightly above its threshold value trading extinction ratio for turn-on time. Alternatively, the laser can be left on continuously, and its light modulated externally.

When a laser is turned on from its fully off state, it will typically exhibit a high frequency oscillation around its steady state value. This ringing results from a natural relaxation resonance within the laser itself. As current builds, optical gain increases, causing an increase in the number of photons in the laser cavity. As the optical power grows, the consequent rapid recombination by stimulated emission strongly reduces the inverted carrier density and optical gain. This then lowers the optical power density in the cavity, leading to an oscillation as this sequence is repeated. This can result in oscillations at transitions in the large signal response and a second-order small-signal modulation response as shown in Figure 3.

The index of refraction in semiconductors has a dependence on the free carrier density. The large variations in carrier density during these oscillations results in a rapid frequency modulation of the light pulse. Quantitative understanding of this phenomenon is gained through the *laser rate equations* (Price and Pedrotti 2002). Pulse distortion results as the different parts of the pulse, which have slightly different frequencies, travel at different speeds through the dispersive fiber medium. Again, as with turn-on delay, relaxation oscillations can be reduced by bias at or slightly above threshold. The turnoff transient is typically a smooth exponential decay that is somewhat slower than the turn-on time. This asymmetry in the rise and fall times gives rise to pulse width distortion in

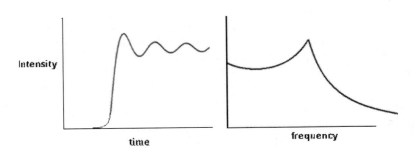

Figure 3: Laser large signal step response versus time (left) and small signal modulation response versus frequency (right)

which the duration of a logic 1 and logic 0 that are equal in the data are not in the optical signal. This is generally compensated for in the drive electronics.

Fabry-Perot Lasers

Fabry-Perot lasers are constructed as shown in Figure 4 using the reflections from the cleaved facets of the laser chip to form the optical cavity. Such cavities combined with repeated traversals by the optical signal result in narrow emission spectra and much smaller angular emission cones relative to LEDs. The high optical intensities in the cavity also result in short stimulated emission lifetimes and rapid turnoff times, leading to higher modulation bandwidths. The active region of FP lasers is typically much thinner than it is wide. This results in an astigmatic beam with a different divergence angle parallel and perpendicular to the plane of the laser substrate. This can pose challenges for the efficient coupling of their radiation into small core fibers.

Distributed Feedback Lasers

Distributed feedback lasers and the closely related *distributed Bragg reflector* (DBR) lasers incorporate grating structures into the gain regions or end regions respectively as shown in Figure 5. This results in a further narrowing of the emission spectra relative to FP laser diodes. The variation of optical propagation velocity with wavelength in optical fibers—chromatic dispersion—leads to pulse broadening with distance. The restriction of the optical emission bandwidth in DFB lasers results in optical pulses that spread less with distance. This means that for a given pulse length or data rate, the bit stream encoded by a DFB laser can propagate further before impairments because of pulse spreading become important. Links using DFB lasers thus achieve higher bit-rate distance products as compared to FP lasers, albeit with a considerable increase in processing complexity and consequent decrease in yield relative to FP lasers. For a more complete treatment of DFB lasers, see Coldren and Corzine (1995).

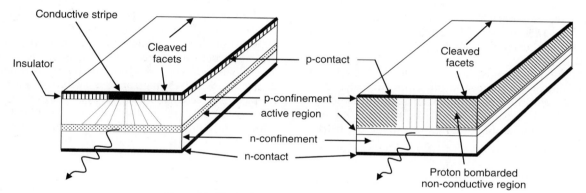

Figure 4: Typical structures of simple Fabry-Perot lasers

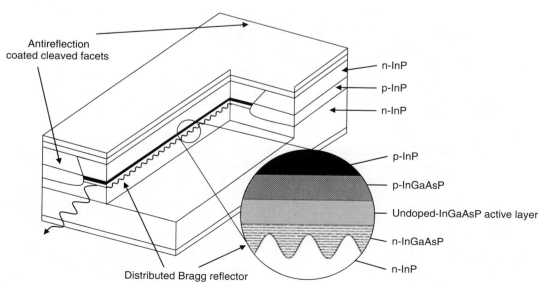

Figure 5: Distributed feedback laser structure

Vertical-Cavity Surface-Emitting Lasers

In VCSELs, the resonant optical cavity is formed perpendicular to the wafer surface. One type of laser structure is shown in Figure 6. A very high reflectivity mirror is first grown composed of many alternating layers of material with different indexes of refraction, with optical thicknesses of one-quarter the desired emission wavelength, to form a Bragg reflector. The active P-N junction region is grown on top, surrounded by spacer layers, and then capped with another Bragg reflector mirror. Although thick and time consuming to grow by the usual epitaxial techniques, a mirror with exceptionally high reflectivity can be produced. A great number of laser structures exist using a variety of materials systems aimed at different performance goals; see, for example, Wilmsen et al. (2001) for a thorough treatment. Some use semiconductor materials for the reflectors; some use dielectrics, mostly for long wavelength emitters; and some use combinations of the two. Many different approaches have also been taken to provide both optical and carrier confinement to the active region and to reduce the sometimes high series resistance and operating voltage. The earliest VCSELs were made from AlGaAs and its alloys and operated in the 850-nm region. Work is continuing, and VCSELs have now been demonstrated at the important 1300-nm and 1550-nm silica fiber transmission windows as well as the shorter 670-nm and 650-nm wavelengths for use with POF.

VCSELS typically have an especially low threshold current, relatively low power outputs, and circular beams that couple well into optical fiber. These desirable characteristics and the advantages in manufacturing and testing afforded by the ability to batch test the lasers before dicing, as is typical with integrated circuits, make them attractive and economical devices. Today, they are used mostly in the 850-nm range using multimode optical fiber for local area networks and other short-distance, high-bandwidth applications for which LEDs are not suitable: most notably, in the optical versions of multi-Gigabit Ethernet implementations. This evolving technology is now spreading into single-mode fiber applications in metropolitan area and wide area networks. This technology is not yet mature or widely used in the longer 1550-nm telecommunication bands.

Tunable Lasers

Tunable lasers are of increasing interest with the advent and wide deployment of *wavelength-division multiplexing* (WDM) systems. The hundreds of wavelengths that can be used in such links creates an inventory and maintenance problem for operators that is solvable by the use of a single or a few distinct tunable lasers. Interest in tunable lasers is also being spurred by their usefulness for wavelength provisioning and wavelength-based routing.

DFB and DBR lasers are thermally tunable. With a typical 0.1 nm/°C tuning coefficient, a 50°C temperature change allows ~5 nm of tuning. Wider tuning can be achieved by the variation of the index of refraction in the grating region of a DBR, usually by free carrier injection. Even wider tuning can be achieved by using a similarly tuned grating structure to selectively couple the desired wavelength between two waveguides with similar propagation constants. Wider tuning range is accompanied by lower frequency selectivity, which can be restored by the use of sampled gratings for the reflectors. Sampled gratings with slightly different grating periods allow wide tuning

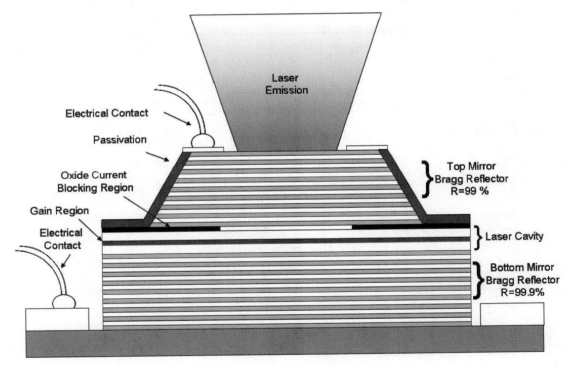

Figure 6: VCSEL structure

in a relatively simple structure. Tunable VCSELs are also available; to date, most have been realized by the micro-mechanical movement of one of the reflective tuning mirrors. Devices with tuning ranges of more than 100 nm are available in some technologies. The need to simultaneously control several currents, voltages, or both—often adaptively—increases the complexity and challenge of transmitter designs based on these devices. Coldren et al. (2004) provide an overview and tutorial introduction to the state-of-the-art in tunable laser technology.

Modulators

External optical modulation is used when the highest data rates and longest transmission distances are of interest. They can switch faster than a directly modulated laser and have less chirping, which reduces the optical pulse spreading. Two types are most often used in optical communications. Semiconductor-based electro-absorption modulators are popular because of their ease of monolithic integration with the *continuous wave* (CW) laser source, high modulation speeds, and reduced chirp relative to lasers. The most common interferometric modulators, however, are the Mach-Zehnder type; these are typically made of lithium niobate, a nonlinear optical material with a high *electro-optic coefficient*. These provide the most precise control over amplitude and phase of the optical signal and are used in the highest performance applications. A current and more detailed treatment of the operation of and comparison between optical modulators is presented by Li and Yu (2003).

Electro-Absorption Modulators

Electro-absorption (EA) modulators are monolithic semiconductor devices that are most often fabricated on InP substrates and use either the Franz-Keldysh or *quantum-confined Stark effect* (QCSE) to vary the effective band edge of a semiconductor region incorporated into an optical waveguide (Wakita 1997). Both of these effects rely on the change in the electric field in the semiconductor in a reversed biased PIN structure (an example is shown in Figure 7). With care and compromise, these modulators can be designed to be compatible with

regard to growth and fabrication, which can allow for monolithic integration of the CW laser and EA modulator as a single device. The main advantage relative to a directly modulated laser is reduced chirp because the frequency modulation associated with the laser relaxation oscillations is avoided (Koyama and Iga 1988). Some residual and unavoidable chirp will remain as implied on fundamental grounds by the Kramers-Kronig relation for the connection between the index of refraction and absorption. Other advantages can accrue because of superior extinction ratio at the desired data rate, lower drive voltages, small size, higher drive impedance, better temperature stability, and improved linearity.

Mach-Zehnder Modulators

Mach-Zehnder modulators (MZMs) operate by splitting a light beam and directing two beams down two different paths before recombining them. This is illustrated in Figure 8. If the phase of the light traveling down one path can be varied relative to the other by the use, for instance, of an electro-optic material such as lithium niobate, then the beams can be caused to arrive either in or out of phase at the beam-combining junction coupled to the exit waveguide. When in phase, the beams recombine to form a propagating mode in the exit waveguide. When out of phase, their amplitudes cancel, no radiation appears in the exit guide, and the optical power is radiated into the crystal substrate. The phase change is controlled by the application of electrical fields across the insulated waveguides, yielding a capacitive drive impedance. Along with the output impedance of the drive electronics, this capacitance determines the maximum modulation rate. The intrinsic electro-optic response is especially fast. These modulators are characterized according to their V_{II}, the voltage necessary for a relative phase shift of Π radians between the waves traveling in the two guides. This is the minimum voltage necessary to change the transmitted signal from fully on to fully off. A typical value is 10 V for a 10-GHz modulator. The V_{II} can be lowered by extending the electrodes along the optical transmission line, but then the drive capacitance of the modulator increases, reducing the bandwidth. The typical ratio of the on-to-off power, the *extinction ratio*, that is practically achieved is better than 20 dB. Better overlap of the optical and applied electrical fields along with differential drive and new materials has been used to reduce V_{II}, and commercial devices are available in the 4–6 V range. This is particularly important for high speed (> 10 Gb/s) operation where the maximum voltage swing provided by transistors is limited by the reduced device geometries necessary for their high-speed operation.

Other materials are also used to realize these types of modulators, including III–V semiconductors, organic nonlinear optical polymers, and silicon. GaAs-based MZMs (which are also based on a bulk electro-optic effect) are demonstrating performance that is close to that achievable with lithium niobate: drive voltages in the range of 5 V but at a smaller size of ~3 cm rather than 5-10 cm lengths typical of Lithium Niobate. Using the QCSE in III–V semiconductor quantum wells, index variations arise that can be used to make MZMs. Relative to lithium niobate, much smaller chip sizes can be realized with lower drive voltage

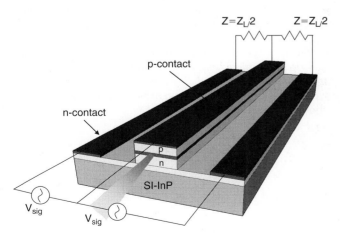

Figure 7: Electro-absorption modulator grown on semi-insulating indium phosphide

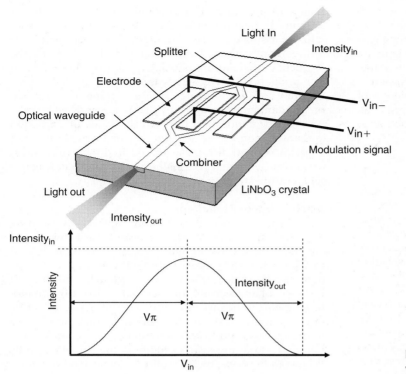

Figure 8: Single Mach-Zehnder modulator (top) with intensity versus voltage characteristic (bottom)

requirements, which allows possible monolithic integration with laser and amplifier components. Disadvantages include higher optical loss, lower extinction ratio, more difficult chirp control, and a narrower wavelength range of operation. Polymer-based MZMs have lower dielectric constants, higher theoretical effective bandwidth, compact size, easier and lower-cost processing, and potential for heterogeneous integration. Stability concerns (both thermal and photochemical), relatively higher optical losses, and limited power-handling capability are the main impediments to more widespread commercial application.

Traveling Wave Modulators

For the highest speed operation the modulating signal is launched down a transmission line in which the propagation velocity of the electrical modulating signal matches that of the optical mode in the adjacent waveguide. This allows a significant increase in bandwidth that is limited only by the time over which the velocity and phase matching can be maintained. This approach is referred to as a *traveling wave modulator;* it also allows for a lower V_{Π} relative to a bulk electrode approach.

Finally for both types of interferometric modulators, if the electrode geometry is such that the induced phase shifts are equal and opposite along the two optical paths, as is obtained with a differential drive, the resulting amplitude modulated signal emerging from the exit waveguide is free of phase modulation (chirp). If independent control of the electrodes on each path is provided, then adjustable amounts of phase, amplitude modulation and chirp can be provided (Gnauck et al. 1991). This is sometimes useful; for example, for optimum transmission over

certain distances and fibers, a small amount of the proper chirp can actually enhance the transmission distance.

Driver Circuits

The electronic driver circuits are designed to transfer the data signal with high fidelity to the optical emitter or modulator, provide a good impedance match to the optical device and compensate for device nonidealities, temperature variation, and aging. Here we describe circuits that are appropriate to driving LEDs, directly modulated lasers, and modulators.

LED Drivers

Given their relatively low maximum modulation rates and stable output characteristics, LEDs are often driven simply and directly in a single-ended configuration by a current source as shown in Figure 9.

The L/I characteristics for an LED are fairly linear and do not typically suffer from the same drift and degradation as laser diodes. For this reason, and particularly where cost is an issue, simple driver approaches like that shown in Figure 9 are often used.

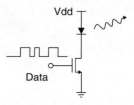

Figure 9: Simple driver for an LED (bias circuitry not shown)

Laser Drivers

Directly modulated lasers are most naturally driven by current sources because the optical signal above threshold is approximately linearly related to the drive current. The laser is biased with a DC bias current (I_{bias}) that sets the off or zero drive value in the vicinity of the laser threshold current. An AC modulation current then varies between zero and a peak value (I_{mod}). This results in the laser biased at I_{bias} in the zero state and $I_{bias} + I_{mod}$ in the on state representing a logical 1. Typically, a current steering circuit using a differential pair is employed (see Figure 10). These circuits can be effectively implemented using either *bipolar junction transistors* (BJTs) or *field effect transistors* (FETs) and possess the following advantages that justify their popularity:

- The roughly constant current draw of the device minimizes the generation of power supply or ground noise because of inductive or resistive parasitics in the supply lines.
- Such a circuit is insensitive to common mode noise such as power supply noise or ground bounce.
- The modulation current can be easily adjusted by variation of the tail current via V_{mod} as indicated in Figure 10.

Also shown in Figure 10 is a monitor photodiode and feedback circuit implementing automatic power control. The monitor diode is mounted so as to intercept the unused light exiting through the back facet of the laser. The diode and circuitry typically has a rather long response time and so measures the average power produced by the laser. In this particular circuit, the laser bias current is adjusted via this feedback loop. This circuit can thus be used to partially compensate for variations in the laser threshold current that result from temperature and aging. This technique would not work if the average number of 1's and 0's (mark density) varied appreciably within the response time of the bias control circuit. Numerous techniques have been used to compensate for threshold variation with temperature and aging, laser L/I characteristic slope, laser L/I characteristic curvature variation and mark-density changes. Most are implemented by use of feedback control based on some combination of the measurement of the electrical data mark density, the peak and average light output that are used to control the laser DC bias current, and the modulation current. For details and a more exhaustive treatment, see Price and Pedrotti (2002). These monitoring circuits can also be used to indicate approaching end of life for the laser

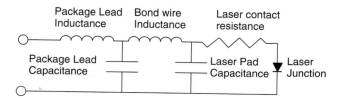

Figure 11: Equivalent circuit of a typical packaged laser diode

diode, allowing preemptive maintenance or switchover to a backup system before an actual failure occurs.

Figure 11 shows an equivalent electrical model for a packaged laser diode. The various parasitic reactances can seriously limit the response speed of the laser. Models such as this can be used in analog circuit simulation programs to simulate the combined performance of the laser, driver circuit, and bias network. The internal carrier dynamics and relaxation oscillations can also be modeled with circuit simulation programs (Wedding 1987). Typically, the sum of the 20 percent to 80 percent rise and fall times should be no more than 0.70 of the bit time to achieve adequate temporal response. Excessively short rise times should also be avoided because, as with relaxation oscillations, they too can lead to undesirable frequency chirp.

The output drive stage is usually preceded by a predriver that consists of several gain stages designed to provide sufficient gain and provide matching between the data source and the low-impedance, high-current load. The signal offset is also controlled by this stage to ensure that the time duration of 1's and 0's is equal. This pulse-width control is used to compensate for pulse-width distortion caused by asymmetric optical turn-on or turnoff delays in the laser. Frequently a flip-flop is provided at the input to allow retiming of the signal with a clean clock. This helps to reduce pulse-width distortion in the incoming data and reduce jitter in the transmitted signal.

Driver-Laser Interface

Most simply, the laser is directly connected to the drive circuit as shown in Figure 12. This approach is well suited to data rates below 1 Gbps, where the laser's parasitic bond wire inductance and capacitance do not pose a serious limitation. Direct drive can be extended to higher frequency by the reduction of packaging parasitics via direct flip-chip mounting of the laser on the driver chip (Pedrotti 1992) or by monolithic integration of the laser with the drive circuitry. This latter approach poses practical fabrication challenges that have so far precluded it from widespread use.

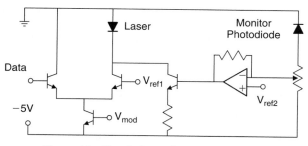

Figure 10: Simple laser driver output stage

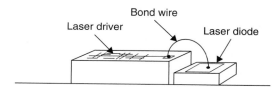

Figure 12: Laser directly connected to the driver chip by a short bond wire

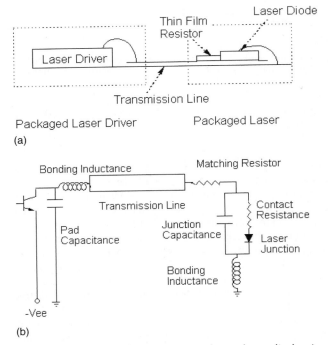

Packaged Laser Driver

(a)

(b)

Figure 13: (a) Laser driver connected to a laser diode via a transmission line and matching resistor; (b) schematic diagram of the equivalent electrical circuit

At higher speeds, for separately packaged lasers, the package and bond wire inductance can induce undesirable ringing in the current pulse. One method to alleviate this is to use a transmission line (12–50 Ω) and a matching network between the drive circuit and the low dynamic impedance (3–8 Ω) of the laser diode. The matching is usually provided by a resistor closely mounted in series with the laser diode (see figure 13) with a value chosen to bring the series resistance of the resistor and laser to that of the driving transmission line. This resistance also aids in suppressing inductive ringing. A back termination is often also used to further suppress ringing because of power reflected back to the driver circuit. Both of these measures significantly increase the power dissipation of the transmitter, with the majority of the power consumed in the matching resistors. When this approach is employed, care must be exercised because of the extra heating of the laser by the nearby matching resistor. Often the bias current needed to bring the laser close to its threshold can be supplied through an inductor whose high impedance at the modulation rate ensures that the bias network does not load the transmission line yet has a low DC impedance, reducing the power dissipation in the laser package.

Modulator Drivers

Both Mach-Zehnder and electro-absorption modulators require a voltage drive. Typically, a precisely controlled DC-voltage bias is supplied to adjust the off state attenuation, and then the modulation is supplied as an AC signal summed with this bias.

EA modulators (EAMs) are typically driven single-ended as with laser drivers. The substrate is usually the cathode and is maintained at a constant voltage. The voltage drive is supplied by driving a current through a parallel resistor mounted close to the device so as to modify the diode reverse bias voltage between the off and on states. The current is supplied by circuits similar to those used with laser drivers. Pulse-width control is often included to compensate for the nonlinear drive characteristic of EAMs that can lead to pulse width distortion.

Mach-Zehnder modulators can be driven either single-ended or differentially. Differential drive is often used because it allows for a reduced absolute voltage swing at the driver output and allows for chirp control. Differential drive can be realized by using both outputs of the current steering stage shown in Figure 10. Automatic bias control can be provided by the injection of a low-frequency pilot tone and optical monitoring of the modulated signal to generate the appropriate feedback signal (Heismann, Korotky, and Veselka 1997).

Packaging

The packaging of optoelectronic components is a challenging interdisciplinary exercise involving materials choices, mechanical design, thermal design, adhesives, electrical bonding, microwave techniques, and optics. Much of the discussion presented here is also relevant to the packaging of receivers and transceivers.

As an example, a rather traditional laser package suitable for high-bandwidth, long-distance data transmission that illustrates many of the packaging concerns and complexity is shown in Figure 14. Here a laser attached to a diamond heat spreader is mounted on a *thermoelectric* (TE) cooler used to stabilize the laser temperature. Behind the rear facet are the monitor photodiode, matching resistor, and transmission line. The laser driver *integrated circuit* (IC) is mounted off the TE cooler to minimize the heat load that it must handle, thus reducing overall power consumption. A ribbon bond connects the laser driver to the transmission line. The electrical signal enters through the high-speed electrical connector, feed through, and transmission line with a controlled 50-Ω impedance throughout. The optical output exits through an optical isolator and is then focused through a *graded index* (GRIN) lens into the optical fiber pigtail. Spherical or more complicated aspheric lenses are sometimes used. Rather than a fiber pigtail, often the optical path is arranged so that a fiber can be inserted directly into a bulkhead fiber connector on the package to ease handling of the packaged part. All of this must be designed to allow hermeticity, precise temperature control, and micron or even submicron optical alignment tolerances over a broad range of environmental conditions. More detailed discussions of techniques, trade-offs, and approaches can be found in Mickelson, Basavanhally, and Lee (1997).

Butterfly packages with controlled impedance lines including laser monitoring and temperature control have often been used at high speeds and where precise wavelength control is desired. Dual in-line packages provide lower cost and lower speed alternatives. The lowest-cost packaging includes an uncooled laser in a TO can that is then mounted using traditional techniques to FR-4 circuit board. Packaging solutions are emerging

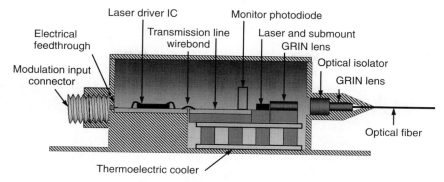

Figure 14: Laser package

that combine an inexpensive uncooled package with an impedance-controlled flex circuit for ease of interface to circuit boards at high data rates.

Uncooled Applications

For many data communication applications, the thermoelectric cooler is dispensed with and a greater range of currents are provided by the laser driver to compensate for the changes in the device with temperature. Device design for such uncooled applications seeks to minimize the laser threshold shift (high T_0) and wavelength shift with temperature. Data communication standards in particular such as those for Gigabit Ethernet, 10Gigabit Ethernet and coarse WDM applications have been developed to tolerate the shift in laser properties with temperature. This ability to dispense with the TE cooler results in significant reduction in power consumption, size, and cost relative to, for example, the cooled lasers used in long-haul dense WDM applications.

Hot-Swappable Transceivers

Many modern transceivers are also packaged to allow hot swapping—that is, insertion or removal from the system without powering down. To accomplish this, the pins that make the various electrical connections are staggered. Typically, as a transmitter or receiver submodule is inserted, the shield connections are made first to help avoid *electrostatic discharge* problems. Next, the ground pins come into contact, followed by power, and lastly the signal connections. Current limiting on the power supply lines is provided to ensure that the local module bypass capacitors do not cause power bus voltage sag. Power on reset routines, now realized in dedicated integrated circuits, orchestrate the series of events that occur during insertion or removal to ensure that sensitive components are not damaged and are powered on into well-defined states.

Multisource Agreements

Active work is proceeding in package development with new connector designs, package miniaturization, cost reduction, standardized of footprint interfaces and functionality being the primary concerns. Although standards bodies can only define the minimum set of requirements on system components to ensure interoperability between components supplied by different vendors, this often leaves many details of the component realizations such as form factor, thermal behavior, electromagnetic compatibility, optical connectors, electrical connectors, electrical interface protocols, and pinouts undefined. To facilitate system acceptance and further ease interoperability *multisource agreements* (MSAs) have evolved to provide plug-compatible and interchangeable parts among a variety of manufacturers. For instance, the XENPAK MSA (www.xenpak.org) defines a 10-Gb Ethernet (IEEE 802.3ae) standard compliant transceiver design that additionally defines the hot-pluggable electrical interface (four wide XAUI), pinout, form factor, optical interface, and connector with additional power supply, thermal, electromagnetic interference, and EMC specifications. Other MSAs include the XFP MSA (www.xfpmsa.org) for a hot-swappable OC-192 SONET/STM-64/10-Gigabit Ethernet, protocol agnostic, parallel electrical, small form factor specification, and its related XFI MSA with a serial electrical interface. The X2 MSA (www.x2msa.org), the small form factor, and the related small form factor pluggable MSA, Gigabit interface converter (relevant documents are available through www.sffcommittee.com), the dense WDM MSA (www.hotplugdwdm.org), and the 300PIN MSA (www.300pinmsa.org) are also examples of the many evolving packaging standards that are continually in development.

Performance Evaluation

As various data-transmission standards have emerged, the testing and evaluation of components has become standardized as well. The intention is to ensure interoperability between devices and subsystems made by different manufacturers. Usually, the transmitter is tested using a long run-length pseudo-random data sequence. The resulting optical signal from the transmitter is detected by a wideband photodetector followed by a low-pass filter with prescribed characteristics. The signal is then displayed on an oscilloscope by overlapping successive bits, all synchronized to the underlying clock, to form what is called an *eye pattern* as shown in Figure 15. A mask is overlaid on the eye diagram. To ensure proper signal shape, the signal trace should not enter the masked areas. Software measures the limits on signal characteristics defined in the standard and also such quantities as extinction ratio and jitter.

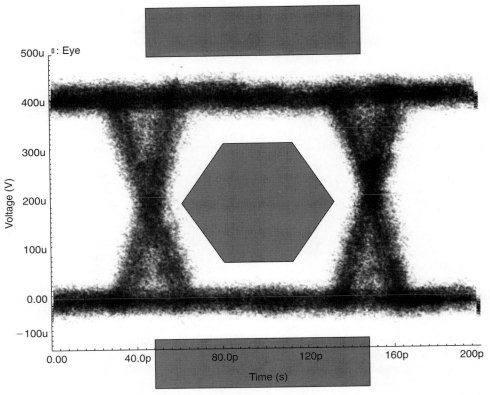

Figure 15: Eye pattern and mask for testing

For long-distance transmission or when using high-dispersion fiber, the effect of the optical bandwidth must be included. Often the best way to do this is to measure the actual error rate after passage through a test fiber. The signal is first launched through an attenuator and a short length of fiber. The signal is attenuated until a specified error rate is observed (typically, $10^{-9} - 10^{-10}$ sec^{-1}) and the received power is measured. Next, a long fiber is inserted in the link and the received power measured to attain the same error rate as obtained previously. After the pulse distortion caused by propagation through the fiber, more receive power is needed to attain the same error rate. The ratio of these two values is known as the *dispersion power penalty* and is commonly expressed in dB. Many other system impairments are also characterized in terms of their power penalties using similar techniques, making this a useful method to quantify trade-offs between and among different implementations, subsystem devices, and techniques.

NOISE

Any unwanted signal in an electronic system is commonly referred to as *noise*. Here, however, we would like to distinguish between noise and interference. *Interference* arises from such sources as undesirable coupling between circuit nodes, the power supply, or sources of other electrical or optical signals external to the communication system. Such sources can usually be reduced to negligible levels by suitably grounding and shielding a system; details of these techniques are provided in

Ott (1988). Here we will refer to *noise* as those inherent fundamental signal variations that arise spontaneously within the system itself. Noise can arise in a general communication system in the transmitter, the communication channel, and the receiver. In typical, well-designed optical communications systems, the most significant noise in terms of its impact on signal fidelity arises in the electronic devices that make up the receiver unless optical preamplification is used. The fundamentals of noise as they pertain to optical links, particularly receivers, is presented here (readers who are familiar with the topic can easily skip to the next section).

Noise in electrical circuits fundamentally arises from the discrete nature of electric charge and the random thermal motions of these carriers in resistive materials, the capture and release of carriers at traps, or the random thermal emission of carriers over potential barriers. Here we briefly describe each of these noise sources—known as thermal noise, flicker ($1/f$) noise, and shot noise, respectively—and their typical role in optical data transmission.

Thermal Noise

The random motions of a large number of charge carriers in an isolated resistor lead to a net long-term average current of zero amps through the device and, one would suppose, zero volts across it. However, given the discrete nature of electric charge and its random thermal motion, more carriers may be traveling in one direction or the other at any instant of time; this leads to a non-zero *root-mean-square* (RMS) current through the device. This fluctuating current leads to a fluctuating voltage across any resistance. The thermal noise power (S) in any resistive element (R) measured in a bandwidth B was shown by Nyquist to be given by:

$$S = 4kTB \qquad (2)$$

where k is Boltzmann's constant. This expression, interestingly, is independent of the resistor value and depends only on the temperature and the bandwidth. The spectrum of the noise has a constant power as a function of frequency and is consequently referred to as *white* noise. In some ways, this takes much of the mystery out of low noise design as there are really only two strategies to pursue in reducing the available thermal noise power: (1) reduction of temperature or (2) reduction of bandwidth. Usually and practically, there is only one: bandwidth reduction.

The RMS noise voltage (V_{rms}) across a resistor is given by

$$V_{rms} = \sqrt{4kTRB} \qquad (3)$$

and the RMS current (I_{rms}) through it by

$$V_{rms} = \sqrt{\frac{4kTB}{R}} \qquad (4)$$

It is easily verified that the product of the two yields the total noise power given above. Note that if the signal is represented by a voltage, then the voltage noise that will corrupt it is reduced by using low resistances. Thus, for those circuit elements with bandwidths that cannot be limited, the available noise voltage can be reduced by using low resistances.

Thermal noise is also present in the resistive channel of *metal-oxide semiconductor field effect transistors* (MOSFETs). The variation of the channel resistance along the length of the channel changes the appearance of the resulting expression, which can be thought of as the sum (integration) of the noise power contributions of a continuously varying set of resistors of different values that make up the channel region. If the necessary integrals are performed, one obtains the expression for the RMS noise current (I_n) in the channel as

$$I_n = \sqrt{4kT\gamma g_m} \qquad (5)$$

where γ, the excess noise factor, is equal to 2/3 and g_m is the small signal transconductance of the FET as determined by its bias state. This result is valid for long-channel devices. For short devices encountered in modern CMOS technology, the overall dependence is similar, but γ typically has a higher value. Figure 16 shows the equivalent circuit model of a noisy MOSFET.

Shot Noise

The discrete nature of electric charge results in an additional source of noise when carriers flow through a potential barrier such as exists in a P-N junction diode, the base-emitter or base-collector junctions of a bipolar junction transistor or through poorly made contacts between dissimilar materials in any electronic device. In these

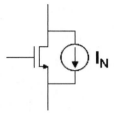

Figure 16: Circuit model of a noisy MOSFET. The noiseless ideal MOSFET is considered to be in parallel with an effective noise generator

devices, the current flows because of the random emission of sufficiently hot carriers over a potential barrier. As a P-N junction is forward biased, the potential barrier is lowered and more carriers have sufficient energy to be emitted across the junction. The current thus consists of a large number of random charge impulses. The Fourier transform or spectral decomposition of such a current exhibits a white spectrum that is constant across frequency. Although the current through the junction has a constant average value (I_{AV}), it exhibits variations around its average value, whose RMS value (I_{shot}) is given by

$$I_{shot} = \sqrt{2q_e I_{AV} B} \qquad (6)$$

where q_e is the charge on the electron. Note that in the absence of an average current, there is no shot noise. This is different from the case of thermal noise, which will be present independently of the current.

Flicker Noise

Flicker noise also known as "one over f" ($1/f$) noise is so called because of the roughly inverse dependence of its power spectral density on frequency. The size of the fluctuations increases as the frequency decreases with a roughly constant power contribution per frequency decade. In electronic devices, it is most often caused by capture and emission processes at carrier traps with widely varying effective trap lifetimes present in the conductive path.

One example of the effect of the contribution from $1/f$ and the other noise sources described above is seen in the differing amounts of noise exhibited by different resistors, with metal film being quieter and carbon composition nosier. Comparing the noise in a metal film and carbon composition resistor, each with the same resistance, the thermal noise in each would be identical but their material dependent $1/f$ contributions could be different. Poor contacts to the resistive elements can also give rise to additional shot noise in resistors.

Typically, $1/f$ noise in MOS devices is attributed to the silicon–silicon dioxide (Si-SiO_2) interface traps over the channel region. Trapped carriers at this interface can be thought of as modifying the effective device threshold voltage at a slow rate as carriers are randomly trapped and released. This causes a variation in the device current that can be modeled as a noise voltage source modulating the gate voltage.

In fact, $1/f$ noise is highly dependent on materials choices and process details between broad classes of devices. As one example of this, because of the way that P-channel MOS transistors have typically been constructed, the carrier flow in their channels is typically farther away from the traps located at the Si-SiO$_2$ interface, leading to lower 1/f noise relative to N-channel MOS devices.

The amount of 1/f noise exhibited by a MOS device can be highly variable within and between process lots as well, and so is often poorly controlled and characterized by manufacturers.

One simple model for the spectral dependence of the flicker noise in MOSFETs is given by a voltage noise source ($V_{1/f}$) in series with the gate that has a RMS value given by the following formula:

$$V_{1/f} = \sqrt{\frac{K}{C_{OX}WLf}} \qquad (7)$$

where K is an empirical factor that is dependent on the device design, materials, and processing; C_{ox} is the gate oxide capacitance per unit area; W and L are the width and length of the gate, respectively; and f is the frequency. The noise power can be seen to decrease linearly with the frequency and with the device area WL. Large area devices are often used to reduce flicker noise in MOS designs.

Often, 1/f noise is characterized by its *corner frequency*, or the frequency at which the lines representing the 1/f noise and the thermal noise intersect on a log-log plot as shown in Figure 17. Bipolar transistors typically exhibit 1/f noise that is roughly 10 dB lower than MOS devices.

Combining Noise Sources

In an operating transmitter or receiver all of these noise sources will be acting simultaneously. However, because each source is usually uncorrelated with any other, their effects at any circuit node do not add linearly as one would expect for a linear time invariant circuit using superposition. Rather, statistical analysis shows that they must be added by the sum of the squares—that is, the noise powers add linearly, not their RMS values. The voltage noise at any given circuit node is thus calculated by finding the noise resulting from each source acting independently at that node and then taking the sum as shown in Equation (8):

$$V_{rmstotal} = \sqrt{V_{rms1}^2 + V_{rms2}^2 + \cdots + V_{rmsn}^2} \qquad (8)$$

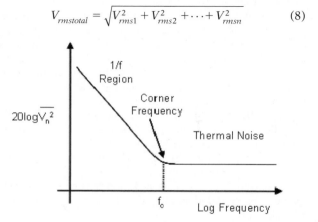

Figure 17: Power spectral density of 1/f and thermal noise showing the corner frequency

Current noise sources are combined in a similar manner. In our treatment of optical transmission links the quantity of greatest concern is the SNR at the decision circuit. This determines the error rate of the system. Conventionally, this is most often and conveniently calculated at the receiver input. This easily allows understanding of the link performance in terms of the optical power and leads to the ability to express impairments in terms of the incurred optical power penalty.

The noise quantity of interest is called the *input referred current noise*. This can be calculated by considering the effect of each noise source independently on the RMS output noise. The various noise voltages are then summed as above, and then the entire RMS output noise is divided by the gain between the input and output. The system can in this manner be assumed noiseless with a single effective noise current source applied at the receiver's input. Often this will be expressed as the noise per root Hz by dividing by the square root of the noise bandwidth of the receiver amplifier. For more in-depth coverage of noise in electrical systems, the interested reader is referred to Motchenbacher and Connelly (1993).

OPTICAL RECEIVERS
Photodetectors

The function of the photodetector is to convert the optical signal into an electrical one. This needs to be done with low noise and high sensitivity. Although many type of photodetectors exist, two are most used in optical fiber communication systems: *PIN diodes* and *avalanche photodiodes* (APDs). These can rapidly and efficiently convert photons into hole-electron pairs and thus create a photocurrent with low noise. Figure 18 shows the dependence of the optical absorption verses wavelength over the range commonly used in optical communications for a number of semiconductors.

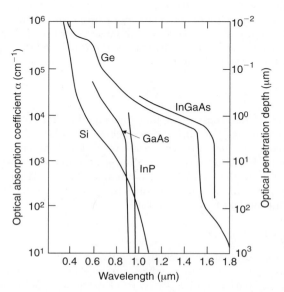

Figure 18: Optical absorption and the 1/e penetration depth versus wavelength for a number of semiconductors commonly used for photodetectors

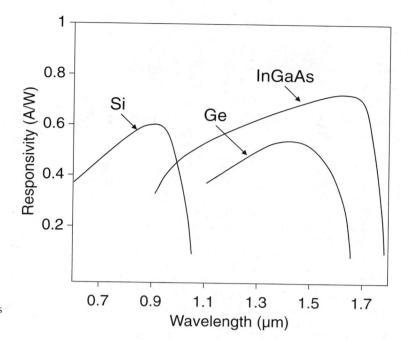

Figure 19: Typical responsivity of PIN photodetectors versus wavelength

Photodetectors are commonly characterized by the following quantities.

The internal quantum efficiency (η_i):

$$\eta_i = \frac{\text{Number of Collected Electrons}}{\text{Number of Photons *Entering* Detector}}$$
$$= \left[1 - e^{-\alpha W} \right] \qquad (9)$$

The external quantum efficiency (η_e):

$$\eta_e = \frac{\text{Number of Collected Electrons}}{\text{Number of Photons *Incident* on Detector}}$$
$$= \frac{i_{ph}/q}{P_o/h\nu} = \left(1 - R_p \right)\left[1 - e^{-\alpha W} \right] \qquad (10)$$

And the responsivity:

$$R = \frac{\text{Photo Current (Amps)}}{\text{Incident Optical Power (Watts)}} = \frac{i_{ph}}{P_o}$$
$$= \frac{q}{h\nu}\left(1 - R_p \right)\left[1 - e^{-\alpha W} \right] \qquad (11)$$

This allows the calculation of the overall device photocurrent for a given illumination as

$$i_{ph} = q\left[\frac{P_o}{h\nu} \right]\left(1 - R_p \right)\left[1 - e^{-\alpha W} \right] = RP_o \qquad (12)$$

In the above expressions, α is the $1/e$ absorption length of the light in the detector active region, W is the width of the absorption region, i_{ph} is the photo current, q is the charge on the electron, P_o is the incident optical power, h is Plank's constant, ν is the frequency of the incident light, and R_p is the reflectivity of the entry surface of the detector. The responsivity vs. wavelength for PIN diodes

realized in a number of different semiconducting materials in shown in Figure 19.

Below we will explore the construction, operation, and noise inherent in these devices.

PIN Diodes

The PIN diode's name reflects its structure: P and N doped semiconductor materials separated by a region of undoped or lightly doped semiconductor referred to as the *intrinsic* (I) layer. In a reverse-biased P-N junction operating below its breakdown voltage, only a small current flows. This consists of thermally generated carriers that, once generated, are rapidly swept by the reverse electric field to the device terminals. If light in which the individual photon energies exceed the band-gap energy of the semiconductor is present, then the photons can be absorbed with the promotion of an electron from the valence band to the conduction band of the semiconductor. The missing electron in the valance band behaves for all intents and purposes like a positively charge particle (called a *hole*), which is analogous to a bubble in a sealed tube of water. The electron promoted into the relatively empty conduction band, now able to easily make transitions to other allowed quantum states, also now becomes mobile. The newly liberated electrons and holes are now free to move in opposite directions under the influence of the electric field imposed by the bias voltage applied to the device. This process is shown in Figure 20.

Two sources of noise are inherent in a PIN diode. One is a shot noise associated with the detection of individual photons. This is sometimes referred to as *quantum noise* because it is associated with the quantized nature of the electromagnetic field. In general, the fluctuations in the number of photoelectrons generated (N_{ph}) is proportional to the square root of N_{ph}. Thus, as the signal increases, so does the noise. The noise, however, increases less rapidly

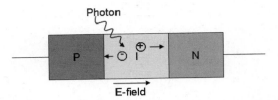

Figure 20: Photon absorption and carrier transport in a PIN junction diode

than the signal, resulting in a steadily improving SNR with increased illumination. In most systems this quantum shot noise is overwhelmed by other noise mechanisms that end up dominating the signal-to-noise ratio and lead to a more intuitively satisfying linear dependence of the SNR on the received signal. The photon shot noise is calculated using Equation (6) with the average photo current during the 1 or 0 used for I_{AV}.

Even when a PIN diode is not illuminated, some small current can be measured when it is under reverse bias. This current is know as *dark current* and is frequently quoted as a measure of quality for a given photodiode. Although it is indicative of material quality, the shot noise associated with this dark current is seldom the limiting source of noise in an optical data link.

Avalanche Photodiodes

In an APD, the photo-generated carriers can acquire enough energy in the intrinsic region so that they can in turn create more hole-electron pairs by collisions with unexcited carriers. This leads to an increased current relative to a simple PIN diode (see Figure 21).

The APD thus has an inherent gain mechanism. This multiplication process also leads to additional noise beyond the photon shot noise. Known as the *excess noise* or *multiplication noise*, this noise is frequently lower than the thermal and $1/f$ electronic noise in the subsequent receiver circuit. In a chain of amplifying elements, the SNR of the chain is dominated by that of the initial amplifier stage. Even though an APD adds more total noise to the system, its gain results in usually a 6–10 dB improvement in SNR. Despite this advantage, the use of APDs is more limited than one might suppose. This is because of the need to carefully control the bias voltage over process, temperature, and aging in order to keep the diode out of avalanche breakdown. This is a sensitive adjustment that usually involves a feedback system. The construction and yield of APDs is similarly problematic because rather complex doping and material profiles are needed for optimum performance, and defects can easily limit yield. The additional time required for the multiplication process and the often larger device dimensions also result in

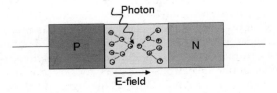

Figure 21: Avalanche photodiode

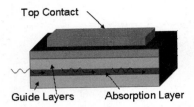

Figure 22: In a waveguide photodetector, light is confined in a small waveguide region to reduce the carrier transit time, allow a small contact with low parasitic capacitance, and thus enable high bandwidth simultaneously with high quantum efficiency

bandwidths somewhat less than can be obtained with a PIN diode. Erbium-doped optical amplifiers also provide an even lower noise source of gain with inherently very high bandwidth, thus supplanting APDs for the more performance-sensitive applications.

Waveguide Photodetectors

The diameter needed for a vertically illuminated photodetector is dependent on the spot size to which the optical mode can be focused. This sets a minimum capacitance, thus setting the maximum speed that the detector can be used with a given preamplifier input impedance. If the detector material has a small absorption coefficient, then the absorption layer must be fairly thick to efficiently detect all of the light. Although this tends to lower the diode capacitance, at high speeds the carrier-transit time can limit the detector-response time. To eliminate the resulting trade-off between responsivity and speed, waveguide detectors can be used (see Figure 22). Here the absorption region is embedded in a semiconductor optical waveguide. The well-confined mode allows the contact area to be small, decreasing the parasitic capacitance; and because the optical power is propagated transversely to the direction of carrier collection, the transit time problem is much reduced. Relatively long absorption lengths can be used without incurring a severe capacitive penalty, thus enabling high bandwidth (~100 GHz) with high efficiency (~50 percent).

Even higher speed operation is possible if the detector electrodes are configured as an electrical waveguide whose mode propagation velocity matches that of the optical signal in what are termed *distributed* photodetectors. In this case, as with waveguide modulators discussed above, the parasitic capacitance is absorbed into the waveguide impedance and the upper bandwidth limit (hundreds of GHz) is then set by the velocity mismatch between the optical and electrical modes.

Transimpedance Amplifiers

Photodetectors are naturally high output-impedance devices, often approximated as a current source for modeling purposes. Signals are usually represented, amplified, and processed as voltages, requiring that the photocurrent be converted into a voltage. This is most often accomplished in the first amplification stage of the receiver by use of a *transimpedance amplifier*. Sometimes called *transresistance amplifiers*, these amplifiers are designed

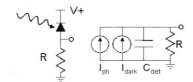

Figure 23: Schematic diagram of a resistor used as the transimpedance. On the right is shown the equivalent model for the sensitivity calculation including the photo current resulting from illumination (I_{ph}), the diode dark current (I_{dark}), the detector's parasitic capacitance, and the resistor (R).

to accept a current as input and provide a proportional voltage at their output. The gain of a transimpedance stage is thus the ratio of the output voltage to the input current and is expressed in the units of resistance, ohms. Below we explore some of the typical receiver stage specifications, followed by some common amplifier circuit topologies and finally the technologies available for their implementation.

Specifications

The two most important specifications for an optical receiver are its bandwidth and its sensitivity.

The bandwidth must be high enough that excessive pulse broadening does not occur. This can lead to *inter-symbol interference* (ISI) and errors in the reconstructed data. Excessive bandwidth, although enhancing the fidelity of the received pulse, also increases the amount of noise that can corrupt the signal and can lead to data errors. The choice of the correct high-frequency limit is thus a compromise. For many NRZ systems, a good rule of thumb is to use a bandwidth of roughly 70 percent of the desired symbol rate. As an example: If a receiver is being designed for use in a 10 Gigabit-per-second system, the optical receiver should have a bandwidth of roughly 7 GHz.

The lower frequency cutoff is also important for proper system operation, particularly for NRZ signals, which can have a considerable amount of signal power in the low-frequency portion of their spectrum. If the amplifier is AC coupled with a low-frequency cutoff that is insufficiently low, then the DC level of the system will appear to wander in a data-dependent manner. This can cause problems at the decision circuit further down the signal-processing chain, leading to errors as well. For many NRZ systems, a low-end frequency response that is 10^{-4} of the symbol rate is desired. For a 10-Gbps NRZ type system, a low-frequency response below 1 MHz is needed, and often 100 kHz or better is used. AC coupling over such a broad bandwidth can be a challenge and is usually accomplished via a combination of several different types of capacitors in parallel. The required high- and low-frequency cutoffs are ultimately determined by the spectral power distribution of the transmitted signal; this, in turn, is determined by the data, the modulation scheme used, and the type of digital coding used.

Receivers must often tolerate a large range of input light intensity because of the uncertainty of the link length and attenuation over which they will be receiving the signal. Hand tuning is undesirable. In addition, for testing purposes it is often desirable to be able to do *loopback* testing in which the local transmitter output is directly connected to the receiver input. This requires that the receiver have a high saturation or overload power, often characterized by the received power at which the receiver input stage response has declined by 1 dB below that expected from a linear extrapolation from lower power inputs. The difference between the saturation power and the power at which the desired *bit error rate* (BER) is just achieved (sensitivity) is defined to be the *dynamic range*.

Resistor as a Transimpedance

Applying the photocurrent from the detector directly to a resistor is the easiest way to convert the current from

the photodetector into voltage as shown in Figure 23. The transimpedance gain is then just the value of the resistor. The problem with this approach is that to achieve a high transimpedance gain using a large value resistor usually results in an unacceptably low bandwidth because of the large R-C time constant created by the photodetector's parasitic capacitance and the resistor. Some receivers are actually built this way with the bandwidth restored by the use of a high-pass filter as an equalizer.

This simple case illustrates the calculation of the signal-to-noise ratio and the error rate in a received signal. The total signal at the input is just I_{ph} the diode photocurrent. The detector is assumed to have a parasitic capacitance C_{det} and a dark current of I_{dark}. The noise is the sum of the noise powers from the photon shot noise, the shot noise associated with the dark current, and the thermal noise of the resistor and is given in Equation (13):

$$\langle i_{noise}^2 \rangle = 2qI_{ph}B + 2qI_{dark}B + \frac{4kTB}{R} \tag{13}$$

The associated Q parameter from which the error rate can be calculated is given by

$$Q \equiv \frac{I_{signal\,p\text{-}p}}{I_{noise\,rms}(1) + I_{noise\,rms}(0)}$$

if the noise is the same for a 0 or a 1 then $\qquad$ (14)

$$Q = \frac{I_{signal\,p\text{-}p}}{2I_{noise\,rms}}$$

This quantity can be thought of as a sort of signal-to-noise ratio. For RZ or NRZ signals, however, the noise can be different, depending on whether the intended symbol is a 1 or a 0 because of the associated photon shot noise. If the photon shot noise is negligible, then Q becomes the signal to noise ratio divided by 2. Once Q has been obtained, the error rate and sensitivity of the link can be calculated.

To a good approximation assuming Gaussian-distributed noise, the probability of error is given by

$$P(E) = \frac{1}{\sqrt{2\pi}} \frac{e^{-[Q^2/2]}}{Q} \tag{15}$$

if the decision level has been optimally chosen. So, for example, if Q is 6, the probability of error is ~10^{-9}. This means that, on average, one bit in a billion would be in error. This is alternately termed the *bit error rate* or *bit error ratio*.

Allied with this is the concept of *receiver sensitivity*. The sensitivity is given as the power required to reach a given BER with a given receiver. The sensitivity is commonly quoted for the 10^{-9} BER but often lower error rates ($\sim 10^{-12}$) are required in practice.

Suppose for the moment that in our simple example receiver that both the thermal and the dark current can be neglected. This leaves the unavoidable photon shot noise as the only noise source. Q is then given by

$$Q = \frac{2I_{ph}}{\sqrt{2qI_{ph}B}} = \sqrt{\frac{2I_{ph}}{qB}} = \sqrt{\frac{2\Phi_{ph}}{B}} = \sqrt{2N_{ph}} \qquad (16)$$

where I_{ph} is the average photo current (hence the factor of 2 to get the peak-to-peak value), Φ_{ph} is the average photon flux in number per second, and N_{ph} is the average number of photons received per bit. The bit time has been taken rather crudely as $1/B$, which rigorously should be the noise bandwidth. If, however, a single pole receiver roll-off is assumed to be set to the recommended 70 percent of the bit rate, then this is not far off. Here we can see that with these assumptions a minimum of eighteen photons per bit on average would be needed for a 10^{-9} BER.

More rigorous analysis using the correct Poisson statistics for the photodetection process gives a true quantum noise limited sensitivity for an OOK signal of

$$N_{ph} = \frac{-\ln(2\,BER)}{2} \qquad (17)$$

which for a BER of 10^{-9} gives a required minimum of ten photons per bit. Given this fundamental limit, we can see why as the bit rate increases the required power per bit does as well. The same number of photons are still required, but they must now be supplied in a shorter amount of time.

One case in which both high bandwidth and ease of use sometimes reward this approach is the use of a 50-ohm resistor and a 50-ohm input-impedance, high-speed amplifier as shown in Figure 24. Although seldom used in practical systems, this is easily built and is sometimes useful for testing and laboratory use.

Fortunately, the bandwidth limitation can be overcome by the use of feedback topologies to realize a broadband transimpedance amplifier. An ideal transimpedance amplifier would have zero input and output impedances. The low input impedance ensures that all of the photocurrent flows into the amplifier input, and the low output impedance would be characteristic of a perfect output voltage drive. To realize such an amplifier, we need to sense the output voltage in parallel and feedback a current in shunt with the photodiode input current. With negative feedback, this will have the effect of lowering the output and

input impedances by the amplifier loop gain. This can be understood from the more formal analysis of feedback circuits or intuitively by realizing that the action of the voltage sensing at the amplifier output combined with negative feedback will tend to hold the output voltage constant over a wider variation of output load, leading to a lower output impedance when the loop is closed. At the input, the return of the feedback signal as a current in shunt will tend to hold the amplifier input voltage constant over a wide variation of input currents as would be characteristic of a low impedance input. As we will see in the more detailed analysis to follow, the chief advantage of the feedback topology is the ability not only to use a high-value resistor to realize a high transimpedance gain but also to escape the bandwidth limitation via the decrease of the input impedance by the loop gain.

Common Transimpedance Amplifier Topology

Although many topologies have been investigated, the one shown in Figure 25 is one of those most often used.

This amplifier consists of a common source stage followed by a source follower. The output voltage is detected by the resistor R_F and is fed back to the input as a current. The equivalent open loop circuit in which the loading effects of the feedback network are taken into account is shown in Figure 26.

From the figure, we can see that the open loop transimpedance gain is approximately

$$R_{TOL} = -R_F g_{m1} R_D \qquad (18)$$

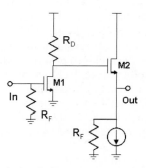

Figure 25: Common transimpedance feedback amplifier topology consisting of a common source stage followed by a source follower stage

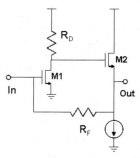

Figure 26: Correctly loaded open loop amplifier corresponding to the closed-loop amplifier shown in Figure 25.

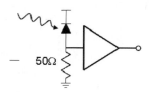

Figure 24: Photodiode using a resistor as the transimpedance followed by a voltage amplifier

The open loop input and output impedances are approximately

$$R_{INOL} = R_F \quad \text{and} \quad R_{OUTOL} = \frac{1}{g_{m2}} \quad (19)$$

The loop gain T of the amplifier is approximately just $-g_{m1}R_D$. Using the usual feedback formalism, this leads to the closed loop values of

$$R_{TCL} = \frac{R_{TOL}}{1+T} = \frac{R_F g_{m1} R_D}{1+g_{m1}R_D} \approx R_F$$

$$R_{INCL} = \frac{R_{INOL}}{1+T} = \frac{R_F}{g_{m1}R_D}$$

$$R_{OUTCL} = \frac{R_{OUTOL}}{1+T} = \frac{1}{g_{m2}g_{m1}R_D} \quad (20)$$

for the transimpedance gain R_{TCL}, the input R_{INCL} and output R_{OUTCL} closed loop resistances. Here we can see explicitly that, whereas the transimpedance gain is maintained at R_F, the input impedance is reduced by the loop gain of the open loop amplifier, reducing the bandwidth limitation seen with the use of a single resistor.

Correct treatment of the calculation of such a receiver's sensitivity is complicated and beyond the scope of this chapter. The difficulties arise from the proper inclusion of the noise bandwidths that must be used for the various noise sources obtained by their integration over the receiver's frequency response. The interested reader is referred to a summary treatment by Smith and Kasper (2002) or the rigorous and detailed treatment found in Personick (1973).

Receiver Blocks

The initial transimpedance amplifier is usually followed by a main amplifier as shown in Figure 1, which is implemented as either an automatic gain control amplifier or sometimes as a more simply implemented limiting amplifier. The purpose in each case is to amplify the signal to a predetermined level for further processing. The signal from the main amplifier is split and applied to the clock recovery and decision circuits. The underlying clock that was used to synchronize the data is recovered, usually by use of a phase-locked loop, and applied to the decision circuit, which in its simplest form can be thought of as a flip-flop. When clocked, it generates a digital output that depends on the analog value at the moment it is clocked. For best signal-to-noise performance, the threshold voltage level and clock timing must be set to the middle of the open data eye.

Transmission impairments—such as chromatic dispersion, chirp in the optical pulse, fiber nonlinearity, polarization mode dispersion, and insufficient component electrical bandwidth—can result in significant pulse distortion leading to ISI and limit the usable link length or maximum data transmission rate. Improvements in component performance or fiber over time tend to reduce these problems for new installations, but it is often desirable to use legacy fiber or lower-cost components at ever greater bit-rate distance products. This limitation is addressed in some systems by either pre- or postelectronic

equalization that offers a low-cost, compact, and relatively simple method to increase link span or bandwidth. When combined with forward error-correction codes, these techniques, which were largely developed for lower-speed wireline and wireless applications, yield significant improvements in link performance. Several approaches are outlined here, but for a more thorough and tutorial discussion the interested reader is referred to Azadet et al. (2002).

Electronic Equalization

Four main techniques are being employed in optical links, *maximum likelihood sequence estimators* (MLSEs), *decision feedback equalizers* (DFEs), *feed-forward equalization* (FFE), and *adaptive threshold control.*

Figure 27 shows a block diagram of a receiver using adaptive threshold control. Here the error monitor block senses the errors as a function of the threshold setting. The threshold is then adjusted to the setting that minimizes the errors induced by noise or pulse distortion.

One way that an FFE can be implemented is shown below in Figure 28. The input signal is delayed a number of times by τ, typically on order of the bit time. The delayed signal samples are then multiplied by analog weighting factors and then recombined in the summation block. This process can be thought of as providing an approximation to a matched filter for the channel. Again, an error monitor circuit is used to adaptively compute the tap weights, often with the aid of initial or periodically recurring training sequences.

FFE implementations are often combined with DFEs; an example is shown in Figure 29. For simplicity, the figure shows a single bit realization, although multiple delays and taps are often used. The DFE operates by adjusting the reference input to the differential amplifier, depending on the value of the previous bit. So, for example, if a 1 was previously detected, the amount of ISI that it contributes to the present bit can be subtracted before the decision circuit. Again, the system can be made adaptive by the use of training sequences or by channel estimation followed by continuous error monitoring and adjustment.

MLSE is a technique that was developed in lower-speed applications, principally for disk drives. This technique

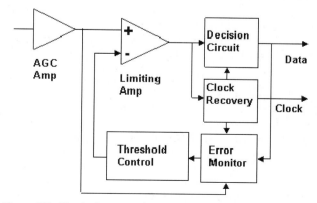

Figure 27: Block diagram of a receiver with adaptive threshold control

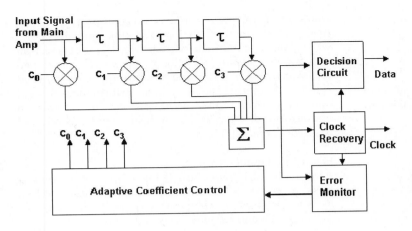

Figure 28: Block diagram of an adaptive feed-forward equalizer using an FIR traversal filter with adjustable tap weights

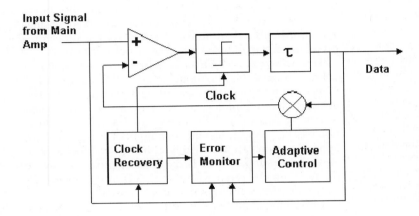

Figure 29: Decision feedback equalizer

makes decisions on the value of not just individual bits but also on sequences. The algorithms used to implement it are often realized digitally, so this approach requires a high-speed analog-to-digital converter with modest resolution. Many standard texts on digital communication treat adaptive equalization and MLSE detection; among them is Proakis (2000).

Electronic Technologies

A variety of circuit technologies are employed to realize transmitter and receiver circuitry. At lower bit rates, CMOS is generally suitable and employed where possible because of its economic advantage in volume production. Higher performance is generally realized by the use of approaches based on silicon BJTs or silicon-germanium (SiGe) *heterojunction bipolar transistors* (HBTs). At the highest bit rates, more exotic processes can be employed using III-V–based semiconductor transistors. The best broadband receiver performance is achieved using InP-based *heterostructure FETs* (HFETs) or *high electron mobility transistors* (HEMTs) that have the virtue of being capable simultaneously of both high F_t and low noise. For laser and modulator drivers for high-bandwidth applications SiGe-based BJTs are often needed. Even this technology becomes inadequate at extremely high bit rates where it is difficult to simultaneously achieve both the necessary F_t and the voltage drive for some modulators. In these cases, GaAs- or InP-based BJTs are often needed.

Good reference works on III-V compound semiconductor-based devices can be found in Liu (1999) and Yuan (1999). Cressler and Niu (2003), Ashburn (2003), and Singh, Oprysko, and Harame (2003) cover the use and development of SiGe HBTs.

Optoelectronic and Photonic Integrated Circuits

The monolithic or hybrid integration of optoelectronic devices such as photodetectors, lasers, and modulators with electronic transistor technologies creates *optoelectronic integrated circuits* (OEICs). This is in contrast to the integration of optical components with optoelectronic devices that leads to *photonic integrated circuits* (PICs). Although demonstrated, monolithic OEIC laser transmitters have not elicited great amounts of interest because of their increased processing complexity with little gain in performance. Hybrid integration via flip-chip bonding of either individual lasers or arrays is used to reduce bonding parasitics and module size. Monolithic OEIC receivers have been more successful, with some reaching commercial production, the most widespread being the integration of GaAs-based MSM detectors with GaAs *depletion mode metal-semiconductor field effect transistors* (D-MESFETs) or HEMTs in an almost completely process-compatible manner. Another natural combination is the combination of PIN detectors with III-V based HBTs. The collector-base junction of the HBT can serve as a passable photodetector with only minimal process alteration. The most successful PICs to date involve the combination of CW-DFB lasers with EAMs for the generation of low-chirp modulated data streams in the multi-Gigabit per second applications and of spot size converters with DFB lasers to ease optical coupling. Rather large PICs that combine arrayed waveguide multiplexers, optical photodiode monitors, tunable DFB lasers, EAMs, and variable optical attenuators integrating more than fifty devices have produced ten 10-Gb/s optical WDM channels on a single chip (Nagarajan et al. 2005). Such high levels of integration with the attendant reduction in expensive alignment steps could provide the impetus needed to further move PICs and OEICs from the research lab to the marketplace. The device performance compromises that inevitably seem to arise for the sake of monolithic integration indicate that OEICs and PICs will likely have the most success in standards-based markets where performance that is "good enough" can be achieved at lower cost.

SILICON PHOTONICS

Although the dominant semiconductor for electronic applications, silicon is a poor light emitter because of its indirect band gap. This also leads to large photon absorption lengths that translate into large and relatively slow photodetectors. The relatively large band gap also makes it transparent at the important glass fiber telecommunications wavelengths of 1.3 and 1.55 nm, although good performance can be achieved at 850 nm, which is the preferred emission wavelength for low-cost and high-speed VCSELs as well as a region of tolerably low loss in both glass multimode fibers and perfluorinated polymer optical fiber, both important for emerging data communication standards. Despite the apparent disadvantages, significant progress has been reported in Si-based OEICs and silicon photonics with much laboratory work focused on methods to create efficient light-emitting devices. Notable has been the report of almost completely process-compatible integration of WDM multiplexers, demultiplexers, waveguides, couplers, modulators, and detectors in a CMOS semiconductor-on-insulator process (Huang et al. 2006). Progress in light emission and integration of optical components with silicon is also reported by Panicia and Koehl (2005) and discussed in some detail in Pavesi and Lockwood (2004) and Reed and Knights (2004). Zimmermann (2004) provides a detailed look at progress in silicon-based OEICs.

CONCLUSION

In this chapter we have provided a detailed summary of the physical layer components and related issues surrounding the optoelectronic components used in optical data links. The two main components are transmitters (consisting of light-emitting devices, optical modulators, and their associated driver circuitry) and receivers (consisting of photodetectors and electronic amplifiers). The influence of optical fiber transmission properties and fundamental processes such as noise are considered as they pertain to the design of transmitters and receivers

for optical links. Specifications, emerging device trends, electronic equalization, optoelectronic integration, packaging issues, and underlying electronic technologies are also discussed.

GLOSSARY

Bragg Reflector: A reflective structure formed by alternating layers of material with different indexes of refraction. The layer spacing is chosen so that the phases of the reflections from the successive layers all add coherently.

Chirp: A frequency shift associated with the on or off switching of a laser diode or modulator.

Dispersion Power Penalty: The power penalty in decibels associated with the increase in receiver optical power level required to achieve a specified error rate when the signal is subjected to a specified amount of chromatic dispersion.

Electro-Absorption (EA) Modulator: Semiconductor modulators using the Franz-Keldysh effect or the quantum-confined Stark effect (QCSE) to vary the effective absorption edge of the material with an applied electric field.

Electro-Optic Coefficient: A measure of the ratio between an applied electric field and the amount of change in the material's index of refraction. This property depends on the material's field orientation, crystal structure, and propagation direction.

Extinction Ratio: The ratio of maximum to minimum attenuation for an amplitude modulator. The term also applies to the ratio (in decibels) of the average optical energy in a logic 1 level to the average optical energy in a logic 0 level of a digitally modulated optical signal.

Eye Pattern: A signal built up by overlapping traces that correspond to all possible sequences of a digital waveform.

Jitter: Random or systematic variations in the arrival times of pulses or transitions in digitally transmitted data. Seen as a horizontal spreading of an eye pattern at the crossover point.

Laser Rate Equations: Set of equations describing the dynamic behavior of electron and photon population densities in a laser under modulation.

Light versus Current (L/I) Characteristic: Plot of light output versus current in a laser.

Mach-Zehnder Modulator (MZM): A two-path optical interferometer that uses phase shifts to provide amplitude modulation.

Non-Return to Zero (NRZ): Digital format in which the logic 1 or 0 pulses occupy the whole bit period (*see also* Return to zero).

Optical Isolator: A device that utilizes the Faraday effect to allow transmission through the device in one direction only; used to isolate lasers from the effects of reflections from external index discontinuities.

Plastic Optical Fiber (POF): Fiber typically based on polymethyl methacrylate but increasingly composed of perfluorinated polymers.

Relaxation Resonance: Internal resonance in a laser diode between electrons and photons.

Return to Zero (RZ): Digital format in which the logic 1 pulses occupy half (or a fraction) of the bit period.

Thermoelectric (TE) Cooler: Device that utilizes the Peltier effect to remove heat from one surface to the other. The direction of current flow determines the direction of heat flow so that the same device can be used to heat or cool as necessary.

Vπ: For phase modulators, the voltage change required to give a phase shift of π radians (180 degrees). In a Mach-Zehnder modulator, this is the minimum voltage needed to change from maximum to minimum extinction.

CROSS REFERENCES

See *Optical Fiber Communications; Fiberoptic Filters and Multiplexers*.

REFERENCES

Ashburn, P. 2003. *SiGe heterojunction bipolar transistors.* New York: John Wiley & Sons.

Azadet, K., E. F, Haratsch, H. Kim, F. Saibi, J. H. Saunders, M. Shaffer, L. Song, and M. L. Yu. 2002. Equalization and FEC techniques for optical transceivers. *IEEE Journal of Solid State Circuits*, 37: 317–27.

Cox, C. H. 2004. *Analog optical links: Theory and practice* (Cambridge studies in modern optics). Cambridge, England: Cambridge University Press

Coldren, L. A., and S. W. Corzine. 1995. *Diode lasers and photonic integrated circuits.* New York: Wiley-Interscience.

Coldren, L. A., G. A. Fish, Y. Akulova, J. S. Barton, L. Johansson, and C. W. Coldren. 2004. Tunable semiconductor lasers: A tutorial. *Journal of Lightwave Technology*, 22: 193–202.

Cressler, J. D., and G. Niu. 2003. *Silicon-germanium heterojunction bipolar transistors.* Boston: Artech House Publishers.

Gnauck, A. H., S. K. Korotky, J. J. Veselka, J. Nagel, C. T. Kemmerer, W. J. Minford, and D. T. Moser. 1991. Dispersion penalty reduction using an optical modulator with adjustable chirp. *Electronics Letters*, 28: 954–55.

Heismann, F., S. K. Korotky, and J. J. Veselka. 1997. Lithium niobate integrated optics: Selected contemporary devices and system applications. *Optical fiber telecommunications*, edited by I. Kaminow and T. L. Koch, IIIB, 377–462. San Diego: Academic Press.

Huang, A., et al. 2006. A 10 Gb/s photonic modulator and WDM MUX/DEMUX integrated with electronics in 0.13μm SOI CMOS. In *Proceedings of the International Solid State Circuits Conference* (ISSCC), February 5–9, San Francisco. Paper 13.7, pp. 244–5.

Koyama, F., and K. Iga. 1988. Frequency chirping in external modulators. *Journal of Lightwave Technology*, 6: 87–93.

Li, G. L., and P. K. L Yu. 2003. Optical intensity modulators for digital and analog applications. *Journal of Lightwave Technology*, 21: 2010–30.

Liu, W. 1999. *Fundamentals of III-V devices: HBTs, MESFETs and HFETs/HEMTs.* New York: Wiley-Interscience.

Mickelson, A. R., N. R. Basavanhally, and Y. Lee. 1997. *Optoelectronic packaging.* New York: Wiley-Interscience.

Motchenbacher, C. D., and J. A. Connelly. 1993. *Low-noise electronic system design.* New York: Wiley-Interscience.

Nagarajan, R., et al. 2005. Large scale photonic integrated circuits. *IEEE Journal of Selected Topics in Quantum Electronics*, 11: 50–65.

Ott, H. 1988. *Noise reduction techniques in electronic systems.* 2nd ed. New York: Wiley-Interscience.

Panicia, M., and S. Koehl. 2005. The silicon solution. *IEEE Spectrum*, 42: 38–43.

Pavesi, L., and D. J. Lockwood, eds. 2004. *Silicon photonics.* New York: Springer.

Pedrotti, K. D., C. W. Seabury, N. H. Sheng, C. P. Lee, R. Agarwal, A. D. M. Chen, and D. Renner. 1992. 6-GHz operation of a flip-chip mounted 1.3-μm laser diode on an AlGaAs/GaAs HBT laser driver circuit ThJ7. In *Proceedings of the Optical Fiber Communication Conference*, February, San Jose, CA, USA.

Personick, S. D. 1973. Receiver design for digital fiber optic communications systems I. *Bell Systems Technical Journal*, 52: 843–74.

Price, A., and K. Pedrotti. 2002. Optical transmitters. Chap. 47 in *The communications handbook*, 2nd ed., edited by J. Gibson. Boca Raton, FL: CRC Press.

Proakis, J. G. 2000. *Digital communications.* 4th ed. New York: McGraw-Hill.

Reed, G. T., and A. P. Knights. 2004. *Silicon photonics: An introduction.* New York: John Wiley & Sons.

Singh, R., M. M. Oprysko, and D. Harame. 2003. *Silicon germanium: Technology, modeling and design.* New York: Wiley-IEEE Press.

Smith, R. G., and B. L. Kasper. 2002. Optical receivers. Chap. 48 in *The communications handbook*, 2nd ed., edited by J. Gibson. Boca Raton, FL: CRC Press.

Twu, Y., P. Parayanthal, B. A. Dean, and R. L. Hartman. 1992. Studies of reflection effects on device characteristics and system performances of 1.5 μm semiconductor DFB lasers. *Journal of Lightwave Technology*, 10(9): 1267–71.

Wakita, K. 1997. *Semiconductor optical modulators.* New York: Springer.

Wedding, B. 1987. SPICE simulation of laser diode modules. *Electronics Letters*, 23(8): 383–4.

Wilmsen, C. W., H. Temkin, L. A. Coldren, P. L. Knight, and A. Miller. 2001. *Vertical cavity surface emitting lasers.* New York: Cambridge University Press.

Yuan, J. S. 1999. *SiGe, GaAs and InP heterojunction bipolar transistors.* New York: Wiley-Interscience.

Zimmermann, H. 2004. *Silicon optoelectronic integrated circuits.* New York: Springer.

FURTHER READING

Kaminow, I., and T. Li. 2002. *Optical fiber telecommunications IVA-components.* San Diego, Academic Press.

Razavi, B. 2003. *Design of integrated circuits for optical communications.* New York: McGraw Hill.

Sackinger, E. 2005. *Broadband circuits for optical fiber communication.* New York: Wiley-Interscience.

Saleh, B. E. A., and M. C. Teich. 1991. *Fundamentals of photonics.* New York: Wiley-Interscience.

Optical Signal Regeneration

Mingshan Zhao, *Dalian University of Technology, People's Republic of China*

INTRODUCTION

It is well known that signals propagating over optical fiber networks are significantly distorted because of a combined effect of amplifier noise accumulation, fiber dispersion, fiber nonlinearity, and inter- or intrachannel interactions. This results in serious limits in both capacity and range of the system transmission. This is especially the case in advanced optical networks based on *wavelength division multiplexing* (WDM), where many channels at different wavelengths and each carrying signals of as much as 40 Gbit/s are sent through long stretches of fiber and are traversing many optical amplifiers and switches. Regardless of the transmission formats [return to zero (RZ), NRZ, or chirped RZ], the induced distortion is reflected in four main types of signal degradation: intensity noise, timing jitter, pulse-envelope distortion (Leclerc, Lavigne, and Chiaroni 2002), and phase noise (Boscolo, Bhamber, and Turitsyn 2006). *Intensity noise* might be more accurately referred to as the uncertainty in the energy content of a given bit slot. Fiber chromatic dispersion coherently mixes the contents of adjacent bits, optical amplification causes beat noise with spontaneous emission, and fiber nonlinearities introduce information-dependent power transfer between WDM channels, all resulting in irreversible bit energy fluctuations.

Timing jitter is the uncertainty in the pulse-mark arrival time, or a synchronization default with respect to the bit stream. The main causes for timing jitter are nonlinearities of *self-phase modulation* (SPM), *cross-phase modulation* (XPM), *polarization-mode dispersion* (PMD), and, for RZ formats, the Gordon-Haus and electrostriction effects (McKinstrie, Santhanam, and Agrawal 2002).

Pulse envelope distortion can be viewed as an irreversible change in the pulse envelope that increases the probability of symbol detection error. A most obvious pulse distortion effect is the fill-up of 0 symbol spaces by *amplified spontaneous emission* (ASE), thus reducing the on-off extinction ratio. Fiber nonlinearities (SPM, XPM), *four-wave mixing* (FWM), stimulated Raman scattering, and PMD are the essential causes of pulse-envelope distortion.

Phase noise is referred to as *bit-to-bit phase fluctuation*. In fiber-optic transmission systems, phase noise is added by ASE from optical amplifiers. Moreover, intra- and interchannel nonlinearities resulting from the Kerr effect in the fiber, such as SPM and XPM, convert amplitude noise (variation of the signal amplitude) to phase noise. As a result, amplitude noise from ASE, dispersion-induced pattern effects, and nonlinearities such as four-wave mixing all introduce nonlinear phase noise. For high-performance fiber-optic transmission, phase-sensitive modulation formats such as *differential phase shift keying* (DPSK) have recently emerged as a promising alternative to conventional *on-off keying* (OOK). The DPSK format carries the information in optical phase shifts of either zero or π between adjacent bits. Unlike the OOK signals, the DPSK signals are sensitive to phase noise. In DPSK transmission systems, phase noise limits the system performance (Boscolo, Bhamber, and Turitsyn 2006).

To limit the above impairments, an efficient and powerful solution regenerates signals at intermediate nodes. This can be realized in two ways for given system impairments from amplifier noise and fiber nonlinearities after some transmission distance. The first, the electronic regeneration, consists of segmenting the system into independent

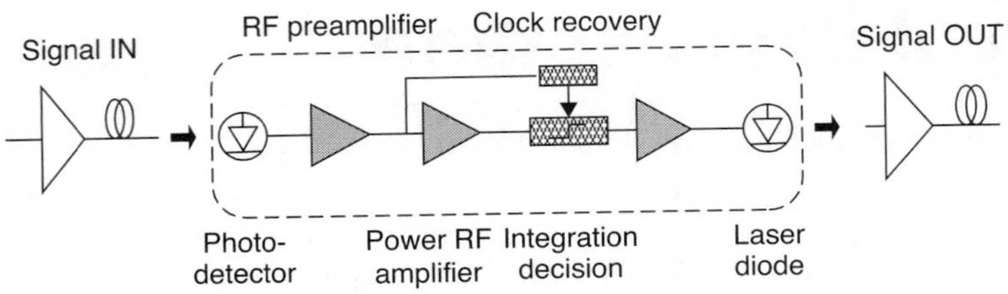

Figure 1: Basic setup of electro-optical regenerator

trunks with full electronic repeaters or transceivers at interfaces. The second is inline optical signal regeneration, which performs the same signal-restoring functions as the electronic approach but with reduced complexity and enhanced capabilities. Several other methods have also been adopted so far: improving the transmission format (e.g., chirped RZ versus NRZ in submarine systems) or reducing power levels (Mu et al. 2002). At the terminal side, the introduction of error-correcting codes has made possible high levels of received signal quality (*bit error rate*, or BER, $< 10^{-7}$), while allowing relatively substantial signal degradation through the transmission line.

Electronic regeneration has been widely used in the networks being deployed today. In electronic regenerators (as seen in Figure 1), the incoming optical signal is converted to the electrical domain by means of a high-speed photodiode. Signal regeneration or processing is then achieved using broadband radio frequency circuitry, after which the regenerated electrical signal is converted back in the optical domain using an electro-optical modulator coupled with a laser diode. As seen in Figure 1, complete integration of such an architecture is rather complex. As the bit rate increases, electronic regenerators become highly expensive and physically more difficult to realize because of the electronic bandwidth bottleneck.

Optical signal regeneration is a promising technique in the evolution of high bit-rate systems, thanks to its strong potential for compact integration and especially high bandwidth. Optical signal regeneration has been one of the most attractive fields of optical fiber communications research. It is now generally accepted that optical signal

regeneration will be the key technique in future photonic networks that require both high-speed optical signals to be transmitted at high qualities over long distances and flexible interconnect of optical network nodes.

In optical signal regeneration, there are three basic signal-processing functions: *reamplifying, reshaping,* and *retiming,* hence the generic acronym *3R* (see Figure 2). Thus, optical amplification (such as with erbium-doped fiber amplifiers, EDFAs) provides a mere *1R* signal-processing function. When retiming is absent, we usually refer to the regenerator as a *2R* device, with only reamplifying and reshaping capabilities. A device with the full 3R capabilities is called a *3R regenerator* and requires clock extraction. There are various ways to define optical signal regeneration. It can refer to pure optical-to-optical signal processing. The *all-optical* label usually refers to the case where the regenerator subcomponents are optically controlled.

This chapter reviews current technology alternatives for optical signal regeneration, considering both theoretical and experimental performance. The second section briefly gives the general principle and the qualification of optical signal regeneration. The third section focuses on regeneration techniques based on the nonlinearities of *semiconductor optical amplifiers* (SOAs). The fourth to seventh sections concern regeneration techniques using multisection lasers, *saturable absorbers* (SAs) or electro-absorption modulators, synchronous modulation, and *nonlinear optical loop mirrors* (NOLMs), respectively. The eighth section discusses other potential implementations of optical signal regeneration.

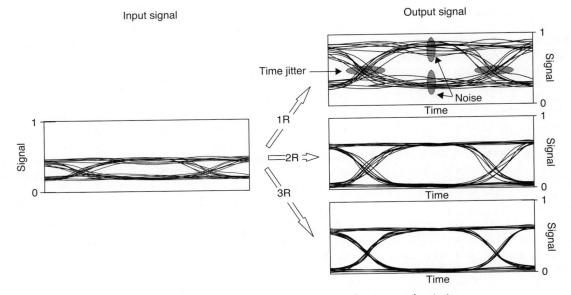

Figure 2: 3R regeneration—reamplification, reshaping, and retiming

THE GENERIC PRINCIPLE AND QUALIFICATION OF OPTICAL SIGNAL REGENERATION
The Generic Principle of Optical Signal Regeneration

Optical signal regeneration has been realized based on different principles: for example, on nonlinear optical gates, synchronous modulation, self-phase modulation, and so on. Optical signal regeneration using nonlinear optical gates has attracted the most interest in the last decade. The generic principle of an optical signal 3R regeneration based on the nonlinear optical gates is illustrated in Figure 3a. A nonlinear gate can be defined as a three-port device in which the second input port is used as a "decision" control such as in SOA gates. It can also be a two-port device, where the input signal acts as its own control, such as in SA gates. The noisy signals to be regenerated are first launched into the reamplification block. Part of the output signal is extracted to recover a synchronized clock signal, while the remnant is fed to the decision block for simultaneous reshaping and retiming. The end block, the decision gate, performs reshaping and retiming and is the regenerator's core element. Ideally, it should also act as a transmitter capable of renewing or restoring optical pulse shapes. In fact, the nonlinear optical gates exhibiting a nonlinear transfer function, as shown in Figure 3b, can also be used as an optical 2R regenerator. At low input powers, the output of the device remains at a low and steady level. Once the input power exceeds a certain power level—that is, the decision threshold—the output rises rapidly up to a steady high level. When the noisy signals to be regenerated are launched into the device, the intensity noise at both 0 and 1 symbols is thus suppressed (i.e., the noise is redistributed) and the *extinction ratio* (ER) is simultaneously improved. The input noisy signals are regenerated.

Figure 4 further illustrates the principle of operation of the optical 3R regenerator based on a nonlinear optical gate. The incoming and distorted signals trigger the nonlinear gate, thus generating a switching window, which is applied to a newly generated optical clock signal so as to reproduce the initial data stream on the new optical carrier.

Clearly, the nonlinear transfer function of the device is the key parameter that governs regenerative properties. It has been shown theoretically that the highest regeneration efficiency (as obtained when considering the less-penalizing concatenation of regenerators) is achieved with an ideal step function (Öhlén and Berglind 1997). Figure 5 shows the theoretical evolution of BER with the number of concatenated regenerators for regenerators having different nonlinear transfer functions. The calculation,

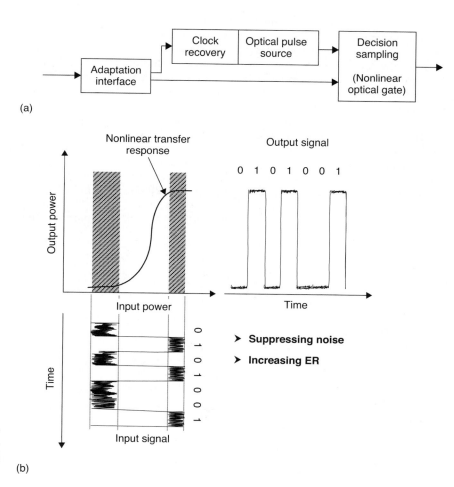

Figure 3: (a) Generic principle of an optical 3R regenerator based on nonlinear optical gates; (b) operating principle of an optical gate with a nonlinear transfer function

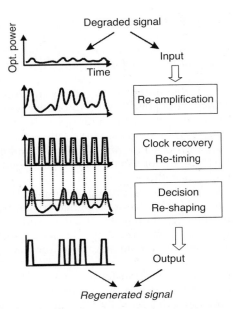

Figure 4: Operation principle of the optical 3R regenerator based on a nonlinear optical gate

however, does not account for dynamic effects or jitter impact in the regenerator cascade. The degree of nonlinear function is characterized through the factor γ, which changes the shape of the nonlinearity from a step function ($\gamma = 0$) to a linear function ($\gamma = 1$). The noise level is adjusted so that the output bit error rate is fixed to 10^{-12} after a single regenerator. As seen in the figure, the smaller the factor γ, the lower the BER and the larger the cascade can be. The optical regenerator with quasi-ideal nonlinear function is therefore of great importance. Different nonlinear optical transfer functions approaching more or less the ideal can be realized in various media such as fiber, SOA, *electro-absorption modulator* (EAM), and laser.

Optical signal regeneration can also be achieved through in-line *synchronous modulation* (SM) associated with *narrowband filtering* (NF) (Leclerc et al. 2003). Modulation can be made on signal intensity (*intensity modulation*, IM) or phase (*phase modulation*, PM), or a combination of both. The SM regenerator includes a *clock recovery* (CR) block, a modulator, and an optical filter. Regeneration through SM-NF intrinsically requires non-linear (soliton) propagation in the trunk fiber following the SM block. More solutions of optical signal regeneration have been proposed recently. A simple optical regeneration system based on self-phase modulation, which was firstly suggested by Mamyshev (1998), is highly attractive. Optical signal regeneration using a nonlinear optical loop mirror is also an attractive approach. More detailed descriptions of these kinds of optical signal regeneration will be given in following sections.

Qualification of Optical 2R Regeneration

The qualification of the regenerative capabilities of an optical signal regeneration device basically consists of the evaluation of a limited number of key parameters such as extinction ratio, power fluctuations, power penalty, and polarization sensitivity. This is practically accomplished by measuring the eye diagrams and BERs. The ER is here defined as $P_s(1)/P_s(0)$, the ratio of the powers (electrical) for 1 symbols and 0 symbols. As mentioned in the previous section, the fill-up of 0 symbol spaces by the ASE degrades the ER. ER improvement achieved with a 2R device proves its regenerative capability. (Note that a mere optical amplification cannot result in any ER improvement.) The BER is defined as the probability of incorrect identification of a bit by the decision circuit of the receiver—that is, the sum of the probabilities of a 1bit being read as 0 and vice versa. The BER is the ultimate test for a digital transmission link. A transmission link is typically characterized by BER as a function of received power. The minimum average power required at the receiver to get a given BER (typically, 10^{-9} or 10^{-10}) is referred to as *receiver sensitivity*. For a given BER and because of transmission impairments, any additional power required at the receiver is called a *power penalty*. Improvement of receiver sensitivity (negative power penalty) for degraded input signals or lower power penalty for "perfect" input signals, because of the insertion of the device, also proves the regenerative capability of the regenerator.

Certainly, validation of the structure and operation margins, the high bit-rate potential, and cascadability

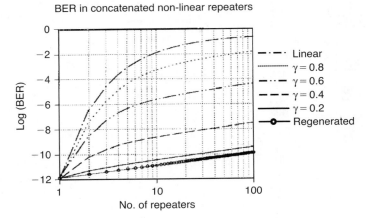

Figure 5: Evolution of the BER with concatenated regenerators for different nonlinear transfer function (i.e., γ parameter)

issues are also important aspects of the qualification of the 2R regenerators. Note that optical regenerators cannot "correct" errors but can only avoid accumulating noise and other impairments. Ideally, the optical regenerator should be tested also in a recirculating loop (Lavigne et al. 2002), especially for 3R regenerators. In that measurement, one might qualify regeneration performance through the evolution of the receiver sensitivity penalty at fixed BERs with respect to key relevant parameters such as *optical signal-to-noise ratio* (OSNR). Evaluation and comparison of regenerative properties then amounts to measuring the minimum OSNR, corresponding for example to a 1-dB penalty on the receiver sensitivity with respect to the first lap, which is tolerated by the regenerative apparatus throughout the cascade. This measurement then reflects the accumulated effects of all degrading factors occurring in the transmission, such as chromatic dispersion, timing jitter accumulation, and amplifier noise, and hence enables the extraction of the actual regenerative performance of the tested device.

In the following sections, we describe current solutions to realize the optical signal regeneration mentioned above. The issue of characterization and performance evaluation is also addressed. As mentioned in the previous section, a key element of optical regenerators is the nonlinear gate, which performs the decision in the optical domain. Such gates have been extensively investigated. This type of decision element uses either monolithic SOA-based (or laser-based) or fiber-based devices. So, in the following sections, we mainly focus on the realization of decision elements (or 2R regenerators) using SOA-based devices, saturable absorbers, electro-absorption modulators, multisection lasers, and fiber-based devices such as nonlinear optical loop mirrors. Some optical 3R regenerators will be given as examples.

OPTICAL SIGNAL REGENERATION BASED ON NONLINEARITIES OF SEMICONDUCTOR OPTICAL AMPLIFIERS

The semiconductor optical amplifier is a prominent key device that acts as the nonlinear element in optical signal regeneration. Because of the maturity of this device technology, market costs are decreasing and integration with other active and passive devices is possible. SOA-based subsystems are being developed to give feasible alternatives for optical signal regeneration. To implement optical signal regeneration, the phenomenon most often used is the SOA's nonlinear gain behavior: the cross-gain modulation and the cross-phase modulation. Another important nonlinear phenomenon, the *nonlinear polarization rotation* (NPR), has also become more attractive and has recently been used for optical signal processing. The four-wave mixing is also an important nonlinear phenomenon of SOAs, but it is less used because of its complex hardware setup and operation, although it presents a high-speed response. All of them—XGM, XPM, NPR, and FWM—are reached under saturated optical gain conditions during SOA amplification, obtained by injecting

either high-input optical powers or electronic bias current into the SOA active cavity or by doing both simultaneously. The first nonlinear process, XGM, is the easiest to implement but the one with the slowest response, so it has the worst converted eye-opening performance. It can be used to cover bit rates not higher than 5 Gbit/s and with a clear input pulse's shape format, because XGM depends on extremely deep carrier density modulation. So, the implementations of optical signal regeneration given in this section will focus on those based on the SOA's XPM and NPR.

Optical Signal Regeneration Using SOA-Based Interferometers

The optical regeneration using SOA-based interferometers is based on a XPM-induced phase shift. Two basic structures have been explored to realize optical regeneration with monolithic SOA-based interferometers, namely, the *Mach-Zehnder interferometer* (MZI) and the *Michelson interferometer* (MI) as shown in Figure 6 and Figure 7, respectively (Leclerc, Lavigne, and Chiaroni 2002). In these structures, both an input signal carried by wavelength λ_1 acting as a pump signal and a local *continuous wave* (CW) signal carried by wavelength λ_2 acting as a probe signal are used. In the Mach-Zehnder interferometer, injection of the signal at λ_1 induces a phase shift through XPM in SOA2, the amount of which depends on the power level $P_{in}(\lambda_1)$. The probe signal at λ_2 is injected into the interferometer, where it splits equally in the two interferometer arms and then recombines at the output, either constructively or destructively depending on the phase difference between the interferometer arms. The phase difference is determined by both a XPM-induced phase shift in SOA2 and a static phase shift in SOA1 and SOA2, as well as changes with $P_{in}(\lambda_1)$. Therefore, the output of the interferometer changes nonlinearly with increasing input signal power as seen in Figure 3b. As explained previously, the nonlinearity of the transfer function induces noise redistribution, resulting in a narrower distribution for marks and spaces and an improvement of the data ER. The interferometer operates as an all-optical 2R regenerator. In the MI, the probe signal is coupled to the interferometer via a circulator and is back-reflected in two SOAs. As in the previous case, only SOA2 induces XPM. The MI type has higher speed potential compared to the MZI type, mainly because of the fact that back reflection doubles the interaction length. The optical bandpass filters in these structures are used for removing the pump signal (wavelength λ_1).

An alternative implementation of the 2R regenerator using an SOA-based interferometer is similar to the previous one but no local CW signal is needed (Wolfson et al. 2000). In this 2R regenerator, a nonlinear phase difference between the two interferometer arms is the result of an SPM (i.e., the phase shift induced by the input signal itself) in both SOAs, which are now asymmetrically biased.

All of the 2R regenerators using SOA-based interferometers have a high integration potential and open the possibility to integrate complex optical functions for optical signal processing. The implementations using SPM

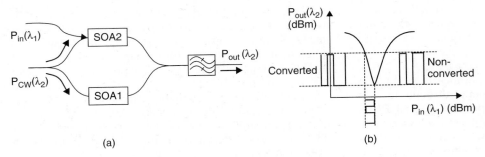

(a)

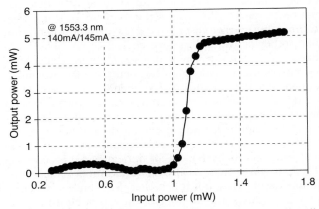

(b)

Figure 6: Principle structure of the 2R regenerator based on a Mach-Zehnder interferometer with SOAs in both arms

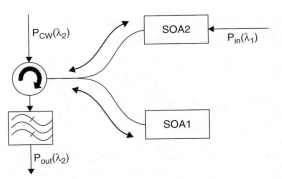

Figure 7: SOA-based Michelson interferometer for 2R regeneration

are simple and cost-effective. The 2R regenerators based on wavelength conversion are more complex because of the probe laser, but they can be easily upgraded to full 3R regeneration if the CW signal at λ_2 is substituted by an optical clock signal. Reshaping and retiming can then be simultaneously obtained using sampling (Chiaroni et al. 1997). Optical regeneration (2R or 3R) based on MIs or MZIs has been demonstrated at 10 Gbit/s (MZI) (Lavigne et al. 1998) and at 20 Gbit/s (MI) (Jepsen et al. 1998). With a differential mode of the SOA-based MZI, the bit rate can be improved to 40 Gbit/s or beyond (Ueno, Nakamura, and Tajima 2001). An asymmetric MZI with a *multimode interference semiconductor optical amplifier* (MMI-SOA) has been proposed (De Merlier et al. 2002) in which the SOA in one arm is replaced by a one-by-one MMI-SOA. This device has the advantage of being small and easy to fabricate, and it also gives a better regeneration characteristic than the above mentioned interferometers. Regeneration at 2.5 Gbit/s has been experimentally demonstrated. In addition, the SOA-based ultrafast nonlinear interferometer is an attractive approach for exceptionally high-speed optical regeneration (Thiele, Ellis, and Phillips 1999).

Optical Signal Regeneration Using Gain-Clamped SOAs

As seen in the previous section, the SOA-based MZI is one of the most attractive implementations of all-optical 2R regeneration because of its high integration potential. This device, however, suffers from a rather slow nonlinear transfer function, which results in limited regeneration efficiency. An all-optical 2R regenerator that has a steep nonlinear transfer function and gives the same benefits

as SOA-based devices would be a highly promising component for the all-optical networks. An all-optical 2R regenerator using an MZI with *gain-clamped SOAs* (GCSOAs) in both arms that does possess all of these features has been proposed and experimentally demonstrated (Zhao, Morthier, and Baets 2002). The operation of this regenerator is based on the specific property of a GCSOA (its amplification in the linear regime is independent of the injected current), whereas the saturation power increases linearly with the injected current. The regenerator has a Mach-Zehnder interferometric structure with gain-clamped SOAs in both arms. The operation of this regenerator is based on the specific property of a GCSOA that its amplification in the linear regime is independent of the injected current, whereas the saturation power increases linearly with the injected current. The two GCSOAs in the Mach-Zehnder interferometer are, in principle, identical and have different biases applied to them. In the linear regime, both arms of the MZI give the same signal gain and a phase delay that differs by a constant. As a result, a completely destructive interference below the input saturation powers of both GCSOAs is obtained at the output of the MZI. Beyond the saturation power of both GCSOAs, the phase difference between both arms is also constant but now different, and the output powers from both GCSOAs are saturated such that a constant output power is also obtained at the output of the MZI and hence a digital-like decision characteristic is achieved with the MZI regenerator. Figure 8 shows the measured static transfer characteristic of the regenerator. The bias currents applied to the two GCSOAs are 140 mA and 145 mA, respectively, and

Figure 8: Measured static transfer characteristic of the all-optical 2R regenerator; injected current to the two GCSOAs is 140 mA/145 mA, and signal wavelength is 1553.3 nm

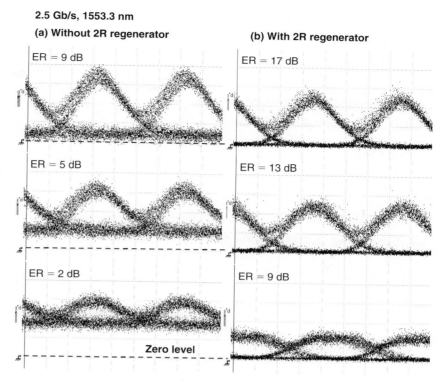

Figure 9: Eye diagrams with and without the 2R regenerator for signals with different extinction ratios at 2.5 Gbit/s [*pseudorandom binary sequence* (PRBS) = $2^{23} - 1$, RZ format]; signal wavelength is 1553.3 nm

the signal wavelength is 1553.3 nm. As we can see, the optical transfer characteristic has a true digital-like shape. For both a logical 1 (high power level) and a logical 0 (low power level) quasi-perfect regeneration is achieved, which is consistent with the simulation result described in the previous section. The output power shifts from the low to the high level over an input power range of approximately 0.2 mW at a threshold power of 1.0 mW. This means that under static conditions an output extinction ratio of 15 dB can be obtained for an input extinction ratio of less than 1 dB.

The eye diagrams with and without the 2R regenerator for the input ERs of 2 dB, 5 dB, and 9 dB are demonstrated in Figure 9, showing the regenerative capabilities of the 2R regenerator under dynamic operation. Clearly, the input signal is regenerated. Both the power level and the noise at the logic 0 are tremendously suppressed, and a strong improvement of the ER is demonstrated. For the input signals with ERs of 5 dB and 9 dB, improvement of 8 dB in ER is obtained. Even for a seriously deteriorated input signal with almost closed eyes (input ER = 2 dB), clearly opening eyes can be obtained with the 2R regenerator, and an ER improvement of 7 dB is still achieved. As the noise at the logical 0 is strongly suppressed after the 2R regenerator, there is no doubt that an improvement in the *signal-to-noise ratio* (SNR) and thus an improvement in receiver sensitivity can be achieved, although no significant intensity noise suppression at the logical 1 is observed.

Optical Regeneration Using Nonlinear Polarization Rotation in SOA

Nonlinear polarization rotation, which is induced by nonlinear effective birefringence, is one of the important nonlinearities in SOAs. For a linearly polarized injected light beam, the state of polarization of the output from the SOA will be different from that at the input but will not change with varying input power level in the linear regime. Although the polarization state of the output in the linear regime is independent of the input power level, it changes rapidly when the SOA becomes saturated because of birefringence effects and transverse electric and transverse magnetic conversion effects (Zhao et al. 2002).

The optical regenerator based on NPR consists of an SOA followed by a polarization controller and a polarizer, as shown in Figure 10 (Zhao et al. 2003). For a linearly polarized injected light beam, the state of polarization

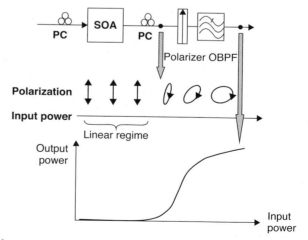

Figure 10: Structure of the 2R regenerator based on polarization rotation in a single SOA

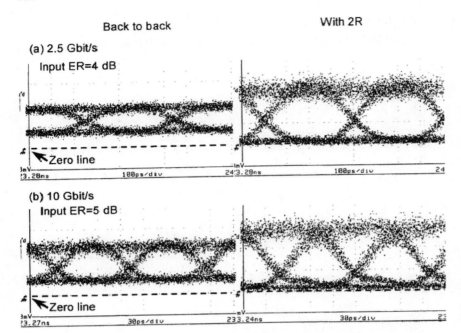

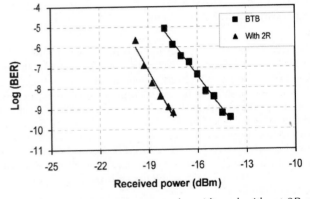

Figure 11: Eye diagrams with and without 2R regenerator for different input signal ER

at the output of the SOA will not change with varying input power level in the linear regime. Hence, by setting the polarizer to block the output beam, a minimal output power (or a logical 0) is obtained below the saturation power of the SOA. Beyond the saturation power of the SOA, the state of polarization of the output from the SOA is changed because of the nonlinear birefringence effects. Both the orientation (i.e., azimuth) and the ellipticity of the polarization vary rapidly with the input power. The polarizer can no longer block the output from the SOA. Hence, a high power level (or a logical 1) is obtained at the output of the polarizer. At the same time, the SOA is saturated and its gain quickly drops with increasing input power, and thus the high power level of the output becomes saturated. As a result, an optical regeneration is realized.

Figure 11 shows the eye diagrams with and without the 2R regenerator for 10 Gbit/s [*non-return to zero* (NRZ), $2^{31}-1$ *pseudorandom bit sequence* (PRBS)] and 2.5 Gbit/s (NRZ, 2^9-1 PRBS), respectively. Clearly, the input signal is regenerated. The eyes become much more open after the 2R regenerator. Figure 12 contains the results from the bit error rate measurement for 2.5 Gbit/s. A receiver sensitivity improvement of more than 3 dB has been obtained at a BER of 10 for a degraded signal. For 10 Gbit/s, a power penalty of 0 dB was found at a BER of 10, and no receiver sensitivity improvement has been obtained. This is because of a polarization relaxation and the induced pattern effect at the falling edge of the signal, as seen in Figure 11, as the SOA used here is not specifically designed for the application proposed above. SOAs with high speed and weak polarization relaxation effect could be fabricated that are better adapted to the optical regeneration based on the nonlinear polarization rotation.

The advantages of this new scheme of all-optical 2R regeneration are its immunity against small signal distortion in the 0 level and a potentially large ER improvement. This results from the flat gain response for small signal

Figure 12: BER measurement results with and without 2R at 2.5 Gbit/s—input ER, 3 dB; input power, 3 dBm

powers and the sudden drop in gain as soon as the linear power range is exceeded. The features of simple configuration, stable operation, and high regenerative capabilities make this new scheme a promising technique for all-optical regeneration in future optical networks.

Optical Signal Regeneration Based on Gain Saturation of Quantum Dot SOA

SOAs can suppress noise and fluctuation when optical signals are on (on level) by utilizing a characteristic known as *gain saturation*, in which the optical gain (amplification rate) falls when a signal is too intense. However, conventional SOAs typically had slow gain saturation response speeds requiring several nanoseconds, thereby impacting the subsequent signal and making such SOAs unusable in all-optical regenerators. Technology developed recently for a new SOA significantly accelerates the response speed of gain saturation (Fujitsu Corporation 2005). It was achieved by observing and focusing on the

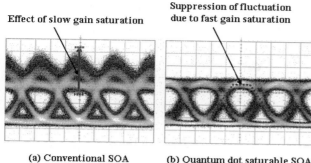

(a) Conventional SOA   (b) Quantum dot saturable SOA

Figure 13: Comparison of output waveform between a conventional SOA and the newly developed quantum dot SOA (signal wavelength = 1550 nm, signal transfer speed = 40 Gbit/s)

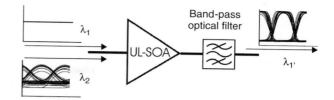

Figure 14: Optical signal regeneration based on channel blue-shift chirp filtering (induced by XPM in UL-SOA amplification)

extremely fast speeds of gain saturation when *quantum dots* were used. By employing quantum dots, gain saturation response time was accelerated to a few picoseconds, one-thousandth the time that was required with conventional SOAs. In addition, through improvements in crystal growth technology of quantum dots and by designing a new device structure, a quantum dot SOA was realized that easily enables gain saturation while achieving high optical gain and high optical output.

By using the new SOA, successful waveform reshaping and suppression of fluctuations of high-speed optical signals at 40Gbit/s were achieved (see Figure 13). Unlike conventional SOAs in which waveform degradation occurred because of slow response time, such waveform degradation is not observed with the quantum dot SOA. By intentionally adding noise to the input signal, significant suppressing of output signal noise was demonstrated. When the input signal was amplified by thirty times (15 decibels), the noise-to-signal ratio was reduced by 40 percent.

The quantum dot SOA will be further optimized. Development of a function to suppress fluctuations when signals are off (off-level fluctuations) and a retiming function are ongoing. The realization of an all-optical 3R regenerator using practical technology is expected in the next four or five years.

Optical Signal Regeneration Based on XPM-Induced Chirp Filtering

The basic scheme for optical signal regeneration based on the XPM-induced blue-shift chirp filtering is composed of an *ultralong SOA* (UL-SOA, length of the SOA $Lz = 10$ mm) and a common WDM short-band filter [*free spectral range* (FSR) of 25, 50, or 100 GHz, with a super-Gaussian-like or a sin-square-like frequency response], as illustrated in Figure 14 (Gallep and Conforti 2004).

As a modulated channel λ_2 propagates inside the extremely long SOA cavity, under high optical gain (just below initial lasing oscillations) it induces gain saturation and phase modulation because of charged carrier's modulation. Simultaneously, the amplification induces XGM and XPM in a co-propagating CW channel λ_1 (Figure 14). Because of the long cavity, the induced chirp correspondent to the XPM can be as high as 10 GHz to 20 GHz (positive),

showing also residual Fabry-Perot oscillations and bit-pattern dependence. By passing the composite output optical signal (the amplified channels λ_1 and λ_2) with the amplified spontaneous emission noise through an abrupt optical filter, the converted signal is obtained when the λ_1 wavelength is rightly positioned at the filter's low-frequency edge, and the modulated channel (λ_2) is positioned out of the bypass window. With this scheme, the second channel and the ASE are totally rejected, and the first channel is also highly attenuated but in such time periods that it presents a huge positive optical chirp induced by the modulation code in λ_2. So the SOA XPM induced chirp (frequency modulation) in the CW channel is transformed in amplitude modulation (FM-AM conversion). In this way, a λ_1' ($\lambda_1 + {\sim}$FSR/2) output channel is obtained with pulses varying from Gaussian-like format (input pulse's shape, low SOA gain) to super-Gaussian-like format (filter response's shape, high SOA gain). Because of the abrupt *S*-like profile in the edge of the filter band, the scheme enables optical 2R regeneration.

It has been shown both theoretically and experimentally that the gain recovery in a long SOA is much faster than in the short one because of the strong ASE in the longer SOA (Girardin, Guekos, and Houbavlis 1998). The UL-SOA has a high-speed potential in optical signal regeneration (Zhao et al. 2005; Bramann et al. 2005).

OPTICAL SIGNAL REGENERATION BASED ON NONLINEAR ABSORPTION DEVICES
Optical Signal Regeneration Using a Saturable Absorber

A saturable absorber has a highly nonlinear transfer function, as shown in Figure 15 (note that the *y*-axis does not refer to the output power there). When illuminated with an optical signal with instantaneous peak power below some threshold P_{sat}, the photon absorption of the SA is high and the device is opaque to the signal. Above P_{sat}, the SA transmission rapidly increases and saturates to an asymptotic value near unity (passive loss neglected). Obviously, such a nonlinear transfer function of the SA makes it possible to use it for 2R optical regeneration (when used together with an optical amplifier).

The SA-based 2R regenerator can reduce the ASE noise level in the 0 symbols, resulting in a higher signal ER and hence improving the system performance. However, because SAs do not provide effective control of amplitude fluctuations, they must be associated with a means of control for marks (1 symbols). This can be accomplished

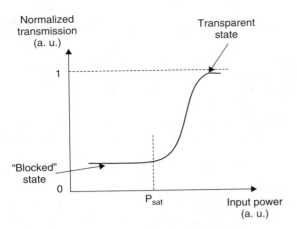

Figure 15: Transfer function of a saturable absorber

by using a cascaded SOA or a narrowband optical filter with nonlinear (soliton) propagation. The SA-based device is simple and has the capability of operating at high bit rate. A 2R regenerator operating together with both an optical filter and nonlinear propagation has been demonstrated at 20 Gbit/s with a specially designed fast SA device (the multiquantum-well microcavity SA) (Leclerc et al. 2000, "Demonstration"). Quite recently, SA-based optical signal regenerators operating at 40 Gbit/s and beyond have been reported. The disadvantages of the SA-based devices are the high-input power requirements and high insertion loss. Further research on SA-based regenerators should address the reduction of saturation energy, the recovery time, the insertion loss, and an increase in the dynamic extinction ratio.

Optical Signal Regeneration Using an Electro-Absorption Modulator

Similar to saturable absorbers, electro-absorption modulators exhibit nonlinear optical transmission characteristics and thus are potential candidates for optical signal regeneration (Cho, Mahgerefteh, and Goldhar 1999). Nonlinear optical transmission in a reverse-biased EAM is achieved by using an intense input optical pulse to produce a large number of photo-generated charged carriers in the highly absorptive waveguide. Drift and diffusion of these photo-generated charged carriers distort and screen the electric field and substantially decreases the absorption coefficient. Reduction of the electric field by the intense pulse significantly decreases the absorption and creates a transmission window for the pulse. Optical

noise such as ASE noise from optical amplifiers, which is not as intense as the data, does not substantially affect the electric field and therefore is absorbed. The recovery time of the absorption after the intense pulse is significantly less than the bit period (50 ps) under high reverse biases. Obviously, the EAM can be used for noise reduction as well as enhancement of extinction ratio. The EAM-based optical signal regenerative devices are especially attractive for high data-rate operation. Optical 2R regeneration at the receiver of 10-Gbit/s RZ data transmitted over 30,000 km using the EAM has been demonstrated (Cho et al. 2000). Recently, optical 3R regeneration using a traveling-wave EAM was proposed and demonstrated (Chou et al. 2005). All of the required functionalities such as clock recovery, pulse generation, and nonlinear decision are implemented with the same device, leading to a highly compact configuration. With a degraded 10 Gbit/s RZ input, 1.0 dB of negative power penalty and 50 percent timing jitter reduction are obtained after regeneration.

OPTICAL 2R REGENERATION USING MULTISECTION LASERS

Recently, two approaches using multisection lasers— namely, the Q-switched, laser-based 2R regenerator and the *distributed feedback* (DFB) laser-based 2R regenerator— have been investigated. The Q-switched, laser-based device consists of three sections: a lasing DFB section, a passive phase tuning, and a second lasing section pumped at transparency and used as a reflector section as seen in Figure 16 (Brox et al. 2001; Möhrle et al. 2002). The combination of passive phase tuning and reflector sections allows the control of the back-reflected signal in amplitude and phase.

The DFB laser integrated with an SOA is shown in Figure 17. In this device, lasing is turned off because of the

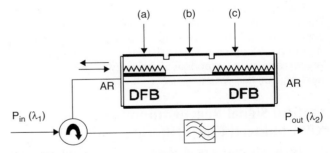

Figure 16: Q-switched, laser-based optical regenerator— (a) laser section, (b) phase tuning section, (c) reflector section

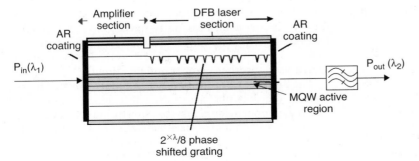

Figure 17: Optical regenerator using a DFB laser integrated with a SOA

gain saturation induced by the injection of a high-power signal (Owen et al. 2000). Both of the two structures deliver optical 2R regeneration through wavelength conversion. The output laser power exhibits a sharply nonlinear response, which results in an efficient optical regeneration.

OPTICAL SIGNAL REGENERATION BASED ON SYNCHRONOUS MODULATION

The use of synchronous modulation for signal reshaping and retiming was first proposed in 1991 (Nakazawa et al. 1991). In that approach, inline synchronous modulation is used to extend the soliton data-transmission distance. Recently, optical signal regeneration based on the inline synchronous modulation technique has been intensively investigated. As mentioned in previous section, SM-based optical signal regenerator includes a CR block, a modulator, and an optical filter (see Figure 18). Regeneration through SM intrinsically requires nonlinear (soliton) propagation in the trunk fiber following the SM block. Therefore, the approach can be referred to as *distributed* optical regeneration, whereas the regeneration described in previous sections can be termed *lumped* regeneration, where 3R is completed within the regenerator and is independent of line transmission characteristics.

In the SM-based optical regeneration, the control effects of modulation over optical pulses are the key points. Both intensity modulation and phase modulation reduce timing jitter regardless of its physical origin (Gordon-Haus, XPM, pulse-to-pulse interactions, or polarization-mode dispersion-induced jitter). However, jitter reduction through PM relies on a time-position-dependent frequency shift of the RZ pulses, resulting in velocity changes because of chromatic dispersion, whereas jitter suppression through IM uses self-forming properties of soliton pulses, which induces detrimental energy fluctuations. These can be efficiently controlled by narrowband filtering. The principle is as follows. In the absence of chirp, the soliton temporal width scales like the reciprocal of its spectral width (Fourier transform limit) times its intensity (fundamental soliton relation). Thus, an increase in pulse intensity corresponds to both time narrowing and spectral broadening. Conversely, a decrease in pulse intensity corresponds to time broadening and spectral narrowing. Thus, the filter causes higher loss when intensity increases, and lower loss when intensity decreases. The filter thus acts as an automatic power control in feed-forward mode, which causes power stabilization. A 1 million km soliton transmission at 10 Gbit/s by synchronous modulation has been experimentally demonstrated.

The optical signal regeneration based on SM associated with NF requires soliton-like pulses; without them, time and intensity noise cannot be controlled. As a result, regeneration and transmission cannot be designed independently from each other. To solve this problem, an improved approach, known as *black-box optical regeneration* (BBOR), was proposed (Dany et al. 1999). The BBOR technique includes an adaptation stage for incoming RZ pulses in the SM-based regenerator, which ensures high regeneration efficiency regardless of RZ signal format (linear RZ, DM-soliton, C-RZ, etc.). This is achieved using a local and periodic soliton conversion of RZ pulses by means of launching an adequate power into some length of fiber with anomalous dispersion. The BBOR approach has been experimentally demonstrated in a 4×40-Gbit/s DM loop transmission (Leclerc et al. 2000, "Simultaneously"). The experimentally results show that at 10,000 km the asymptotic factors of the four channels were measured to be greater than 14.5 dB (5×10^{-8} BER) for $2^{31} - 1$ coding length. The associated system penalty at 10,000 km is only 2 dB compared to a single-channel 40 Gbit/s measurement with SM-NF-based regeneration. Quite recently, 10-Gbit/s RZ transmission over a record distance of 1.25 million kilometers (10,000 loops) using in-line, all-optical 3R regeneration was reported (Zhu et al. 2006).

OPTICAL SIGNAL REGENERATION WITH NONLINEAR OPTICAL LOOP MIRROR

The NOLM is a fiber Sagnac interferometer that has a nonlinear transfer function (a nonlinear input-output power characteristic with slopes larger and smaller than 1). It consists of a fiber coupler and a fiber loop connected to the two output ports of the coupler (see Figure 19a). The phase shift in the interferometer is induced through Kerr effect in the optical fiber. An incoming laser pulse is split into two counterpropagating pulses with different peak powers. Because of the Kerr nonlinearity, these two pulses experience different nonlinear phase shifts that correspond to their peak power. After one round trip, the two pulses interfere at the coupler. This interference is power-dependent and leads to a nonlinear transfer characteristic (see Figure 19b). The flattened region has a slope significantly smaller than 1 and is suitable for signal regeneration in terms of noise reduction. Thus, the SNR is enhanced and bit errors can be reduced.

The NOLM-based optical signal regeneration has been intensively investigated in recent years. Different NOLM configurations have been proposed: for example, dispersion imbalanced NOLM, including dispersive fiber and *highly nonlinear fiber* (HNLF); and imbalanced NOLM,

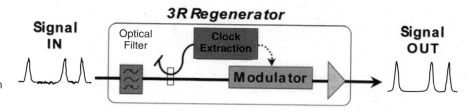

Figure 18: Optical signal regeneration based on synchronous modulation

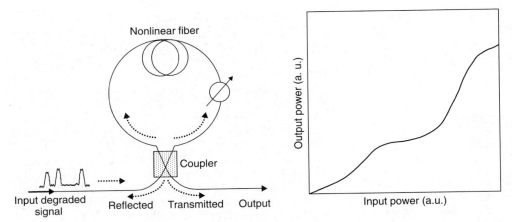

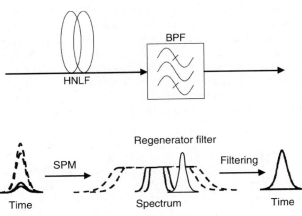

Figure 19: Nonlinear optical loop mirror used for optical signal regeneration

including a HNLF and an attenuator. The common NOLM approach is to use a rather symmetric splitting ratio of the coupler (e.g., 60:40) to compress the noise on the 0 bit while a highly asymmetric NOLM (e.g., 95:5) reduces the noise on the 1 bit. The lower noise suppression on the 0 bit is still good enough for pedestal suppression. The optimum splitting ratio for noise reduction with an asymmetric NOLM needs to be analyzed in the design of a NOLM-based optical signal regenerator. A large number of experimental demonstrations of optical signal regeneration using NOLM technique have been reported in the past years. For example, all-optical, all-passive signal regeneration by reducing the noise imposed on the signal by optical amplification by 12dB with an asymmetric NOLM was experimentally demonstrated (Meissner et al. 2003). An all-optical pulse regenerator suitable for 160-Gbit/s transmission systems, including three stages based on NOLM, was proposed recently (Bogoni et al. 2004). The regeneration was realized based on the idea of splitting the regeneration process in three different steps using easy and well-known ultrafast subsystems. In the first stage, the noise on the spaces is reduced. The second stage transfers the information carried by the input data signal to a clock signal, introducing a logic inversion that transforms the noisy marks into noisy spaces. Finally, the third stage suppresses the residual noise on the spaces. That approach offers advantages in terms of maximum bit rate of the signals that can be regenerated. Experimental results show the suitability of the proposed scheme for the regeneration with a bit rate of 160 Gbit/s. A factor increase from 3.2 to 6.3 was measured for the eye diagram.

The optical signal regeneration mentioned above shows excellent regenerative properties using on-off keying. In fact, the NOLM approach can be upgraded to regeneration of optical signal using phase-encoding modulation formats. A NOLM-based 2R-regenerator, which is capable of regenerating signals modulated in phase-sensitive modulation formats, was recently reported (Striegler et al. 2005). In the advanced system, the key element was a directional attenuator inserted into the NOLM. Numerical simulations show promising performance of the system and capability for the regeneration of RZ-DPSK-modulated signals. The results indicated that regeneration of signals modulated in other phase-sensitive modulation formats

such as duobinary coding, carrier-suppressed RZ, or RZ-DQPSK was also possible.

The key advantage of NOLM-based optical regeneration lies in the near-instantaneous (fs) response of the Kerr nonlinearity, making it highly attractive for ultrahigh bit-rate operation (160 Gbit/s). On the negative side, major limitations come from environmental instability, strong polarization dependence, and difficult integration, mainly because of the requirement of relatively long (kilometer scale) fiber lengths. Polarization-insensitive NOLMs have been realized, although with the same drawbacks concerning integration. The NOLM has promising potentialities for all-optical signal regeneration. With recent developments in HNLFs, however, the required NOLM fiber length could be significantly reduced, dramatically reducing environmental instability.

OTHER POTENTIAL IMPLEMENTATIONS OF OPTICAL SIGNAL REGENERATION
Optical Signal Regeneration Based on Self-Phase Modulation

The operating principle of SPM-based optical signal regeneration is illustrated in Figure 20 (Raybon 2003). An optical pulse launched into the HNLF produces a

Figure 20: Generic principle of optical signal regeneration based on self-phase modulation with bandpass filter

broadened optical spectrum because of the SPM in the fiber. Different intensity pulses give rise to different spectral broadening. An optical filter shifted in wavelength away from the input wavelength acts as an optical decision gate. Shifting the center wavelength of the filter sufficiently far from the input wavelength results in a suppression of noise in the 0's. Similarly, high-intensity pulses give rise to larger spectral broadening, and these components are shifted outside the decision window, resulting in a clamping of fluctuations in the 1's. The regenerated signal is converted to a new wavelength, and the output pulse width is determined by the spectral width of the optical filter. The 2R regenerator provides signal reshaping on one wavelength at a time. Because of the single wavelength nature of the regenerator, its usefulness has been demonstrated both in the transmitter and receivers before and after wavelength multiplexing. The main advantages of the system is the high speed, because of the all-optical nature, the ability to counteract signal distortion regardless of the origin, and the relative simplicity of the experimental configuration. Experiments operating at 160 Gbit/s have utilized this type of regenerator successfully (Mikkelsen et al. 2001). Also, previous experiments at 40 Gbit/s have shown improvements in receiver performance using the regenerator after wavelength have been demultiplexed.

Optical Signal Regeneration Based on Pump-Modulated Four-Wave Mixing

Pump-modulated FWM is a promising technique for optical signal regeneration because of its high-speed performance and the capability to maintain the same logical polarity. Recently, the possibility of 2R regeneration based on pump-modulated FWM using *dispersion-shifted fiber* (DSF) has been demonstrated both theoretically and experimentally (Bogris and Syvridis 2003). The regenerative characteristics of pump-modulated FWM in DSF result from the fact that the OOK modulation for the information encoding is applied on the pump wave and the optical power of the FWM product (the regenerated signal) depends on the square of the pump input optical power, as showing in the following equation (Argyris et al. 2003):

$$P_c(L) = \eta \gamma^2 P_p^2 P_s \cdot \exp(-\alpha L) \cdot \left(\frac{\left[1 - \exp(-\alpha L) \right]^2}{\alpha^2} \right)$$

where P_c, P_p, and P_s are the optical powers of the product, pump, and signal wave, respectively; L is the fiber length; η is the FWM conversion efficiency; γ is the nonlinear fiber coefficient; and η is the fiber attenuation coefficient. Obviously, the dependence of the product wave optical power on the square of the pump wave optical power is translated in a logarithmic scale in a multiplication factor of 2. Thus, in a pump-modulated scheme, the ER of the product wave in dB is twice as much as the pump wave ER.

The regenerative properties of the FWM in the DSF can be also confirmed by the transfer function of the system, giving the dependence of the product wave power on the pump wave power. It has been also shown that the conversion efficiency and the consequent mixing product optical power versus input optical power, under certain operating conditions, saturate when the input optical power is higher or lower than certain value ranges (Bogris and Syvridis 2003). This behavior can be depicted in the corresponding transfer function of the so-called S-shaped function. Two variations of a fiber FWM-based regenerator have been proposed: a single- and a double-stage scheme. In the single-stage approach, the operating conditions of the mixing process are properly adjusted to achieve a compromise between extinction ratio improvement and noise suppression. On the contrary, in the double-stage regenerator, the first stage is adjusted for maximum extinction ratio improvement while the second is used mainly for noise suppression. This dual-stage regenerator transfer function exhibits much broader horizontal regimes for noise suppression and a much steeper intermediate part for extinction ratio enhancement. Note that a bandpass filter is required to extract the regenerated signal and suppress the unwanted output waves at the output of the DSF in the pump-modulated FWM scheme of optical signal regeneration.

The optical signal regeneration scheme utilizing the pump-modulated FWM in DSF generally need a long segment of fiber, and the pump wavelength should be placed near the zero dispersion point of the DSF to maintain the phase-matching condition of FWM. The adoption of high nonlinear DSF can effectively shorten the required fiber length to approximately 1 km, but the dispersion of the fiber still limits the flexibility of operating wavelength. Recently, widely wavelength-tunable FWM using a dispersion-flattened nonlinear photonic crystal fiber has been demonstrated (Chow et al. 2005). With the use of pump-modulated FWM, an improvement of 6 dB in extinction ratio has been shown for a degraded 10-Gbit/s signal, and a power penalty improvement of 3 dB was measured at the 10^{-9} BER level.

Optical Signal Regeneration of Differential Phase Shift Keying Transmission

Most of the regenerators studied so far have been designed to regenerate OOK signals without particular attention to preservation of the signal phase. All-optical regeneration of DPSK transmission by low-complexity and cost-efficient devices that can handle binary phase information would be an attractive technique to improve the performance of DPSK systems. A phase-preserving, all-optical 2R regeneration scheme for phase-encoded signals that exploits a new design of NOLM based on distributed *Raman amplification* in a loop (RA-NOLM) has been proposed (Boscolo, Bhamber, and Turitsyn 2006). It was demonstrated numerically that the combination of the RA-NOLM with narrow spectral filtering provides an additional phase-limiting function in DPSK signal transmission by suppressing the accumulated ASE-induced phase noise. Phase-preserving DPSK signal regeneration using a novel design of a NOLM based on Raman amplification in a loop has been presented at the 40-Gbit/s data transmission rate.

CONCLUSION

The current status of some of the most often investigated technologies and solutions for optical signal regeneration have been reviewed. A variety of solutions were described, including SOA-based nonlinear interferometers and gates, multisection lasers, saturable absorbers, electro-absorption modulators, synchronous modulators, nonlinear optical loop mirrors, HNLF-based self-phase modulation, and fiber-based, pump-modulated, four-wave mixing. Among the solutions, those based on SOAs offer the highest integration potential and have been the focus of much research on optical signal regeneration. They also open possibilities for more complex optical signal processing.

GLOSSARY

Bit error rate (BER): The fraction of bits transmitted that are received incorrectly.

Cross-gain modulation (XGM): A nonlinear optical effect in which the intensity modulation of one wavelength modulates the gain of an active optical device such as a semiconductor optical amplifier (SOA), where another wavelength is propagating and is amplified with modulated gain.

Cross-phase modulation (XPM): A nonlinear optical effect in which the intensity modulation of one wavelength modulates the index of refraction in a material where another wavelength is propagating and therefore modulates its phase.

Electro-absorption modulator (EAM): A chip-level modulation device that modulates light from a laser that is separate from it but may be fabricated on the same wafer. Turning the current on causes absorption of the light.

Extinction ratio (ER): The ratio of the low or off optical power level to the high or on optical power level.

Eye diagram: Shows the proper function of a digital system; the "openness" of the eye relates to the BER that can be achieved.

Four-wave mixing (FWM): A nonlinearity common in optical devices and systems where multiple wavelengths mix together to form new wavelengths called *interfering products*. Interfering products that fall on the original signal wavelength become mixed with and muddy the signal, causing attenuation. Interfering products on either side of the original wavelength can be used for optical functionality such as optical wavelength conversion or optical signal regeneration.

Jitter: Small and rapid variations in the timing of a signal or waveform resulting from noise, changes in component characteristics, voltages, circuit synchronization, and so on.

Mach-Zehnder interferometer (MZI): An interferometer that splits an optical signal into two components and directs them down two separate paths before recombining them. By inducing a phase delay between the two optical signals, the resulting interference can cause intensity changes. Such a device can modulate the optical power from 100 percent (constructive interference) to 0 percent (destructive interference).

Noise figure: The ratio of the output signal-to-noise ratio to the input signal-to-noise ratio for a given element in a transmission system. Used for optical and electrical components.

Non-return to zero (NRZ): A common means of encoding data that have two states termed *zero* and *one* and no neutral or rest position.

Optical signal regeneration: A technology whereby a degraded signal is restored to its original quality. A technology that consists of *reamplification, retiming,* and *reshaping* is called *optical 3R regeneration*. When retiming is absent, the optical regeneration is referred to as *2R regeneration* with only reamplifying and reshaping capabilities. *Reshaping* refers to the suppression of noise and fluctuation of optical signals to reshape signal waveforms. *Retiming* reduces timing fluctuations know as timing jitter, and *reamplification* amplifies optical signals. When these processes do not involve conversion to electronic signals, they are referred to as *all-optical* 3R regeneration.

Phase noise: Rapid, short-term, and random fluctuations in the phase of a wave. It is also referred to as *bit-to-bit phase fluctuation* caused by time domain instabilities in an oscillator, *amplified spontaneous emission* (ASE) from optical amplifiers, and intra- and interchannel nonlinearities resulting from the Kerr effect in the fiber.

Polarization: The direction of the electric field in the light wave. If the electric field is in the y-axis, the light is said to be vertically polarized. If the electric field of the light wave is in the x-axis, the light is said to be horizontally polarized.

Receiver sensitivity: The minimum acceptable value of received power needed to achieve an acceptable BER or performance. It takes into account power penalties caused by the use of a transmitter with worst-case values of extinction ratio, jitter, pulse rise times and fall times, optical return loss, receiver connector degradations, and measurement tolerances. The receiver sensitivity does not include power penalties associated with dispersion or back reflections from the optical path; these effects are specified separately in the allocation of maximum optical path penalty.

Return to zero (RZ): A common means of encoding data that has two information states called *zero* and *one* in which the signal returns to a rest state during a portion of the bit period.

Semiconductor optical amplifier (SOA): A semiconductor device that amplifies an optical signal through the stimulated emission of stored carriers in a semiconductor. The carriers are usually supplied by electrical current.

Signal-to-noise ratio (SNR): A measure of signal quality as the ratio of total signal to total noise. This effectively shows how much higher the signal level is than the noise level.

CROSS REFERENCES

See *Frequency and Phase Modulation; Optical Fiber Communications*.

REFERENCES

Argyris, A., H. Simos, A. Ikiades, E. Roditi, and D. Syvridis. 2003. Extinction ratio improvement by four-wave mixing in dispersion-shifted fibre. *Electronics Letters*, 39: 230–32.

Bogoni, A., P. Ghelfi, M. Scaffardi, and L. Potì. 2004. All-optical regeneration and demultiplexing for 160-Gbit/s transmission systems using a NOLM-based three-stage scheme. *IEEE Journal of Selected Topics in Quantum Electronics*, 10: 192–6.

Bogris, A., and D. Syvridis. 2003. Regenerative properties of a pump-modulated four-wave mixing scheme in dispersion-shifted fibers. *Journal of Lightwave Technology*, 21, 1892–1902.

Boscolo, S., R. Bhamber, and S. Turitsyn. 2006. Design of Raman-based nonlinear loop mirror for all-optical 2R regeneration of differential phase-shift-keying transmission. *IEEE Journal of Quantum Electronics*, 42: 619–24.

Bramann, G., et al. 2005. Two-wave competition in ultralong semiconductor optical amplifiers. *IEEE Journal of Quantum Electronics*, 41, 1260–7.

Brox, O., S. Bauer, C. Bornholdt, D. Hoffmann, M. Möhrle, G. Sahin, and B. Sartorius. 2001. Optical 3R regenerator based on Q-switched laser. In *Technical Digest of the Conference on Optical Fiber Communication* (OFC 2001), March 17–22, Anaheim, CA, USA. Paper MG6, pp. 1–3.

Chiaroni, D., B. Lavigne, A. Jourdan, L. Hamon, C. Janz, and M. Renaud. 1997. 10 Gbit/s 3R NRZ optical regenerative interface based on semiconductor optical amplifiers for all-optical networks. In *Proceedings of European Conference on Optical Communications* (ECOC'97), Sept. 22–25, Edinburgh, UK. Postdeadline paper PD 41, pp. 41–4.

Cho, P. S., D. Mahgerefteh, and J. Goldhar. 1999. All-optical 2R regeneration and wavelength conversion at 20 Gb/s using an electroabsorption modulator. *IEEE Photonics Technology Letters*, 11: 1662–4.

Cho, P. S., P. Sinha, D. Mahgerefteh, and G. M. Carter. 2000. All-optical regeneration at the receiver of 10-Gb/s RZ data transmitted over 30000 km using an electro-absorption modulator. *IEEE Photonics Technology Letters*, 12: 205–7.

Chou, H., Z. Hu, J. Bowers, and D. Blumenthal. 2005. Compact optical 3R regeneration using a traveling-wave electroabsorption modulator. *IEEE Photonics Technology Letters*, 17: 486–8.

Chow, K. K., C. Shu, C. Lin, and A. Bjarklev. 2005. Polarization-insensitive widely tunable wavelength converter based on four-wave mixing in a dispersion-flattened nonlinear photonic crystal fiber. *IEEE Photonics Technology Letters*, 17: 624–6.

Dany, B., P. Brindel, O. Leclerc, and E. Desurvire. 1999. Transoceanic 4×40 Gbit/s system combining dispersion-managed soliton transmission and new "black-box" inline optical regeneration. *Electronics Letters*, 35: 418–20.

De Merlier, J., G. Morthier, P. Van Daele, I. Moerman, and R. Baets. 2002. All-optical 2R regeneration based on integrated asymmetric Mach-Zehnder interferometer incorporating MMI-SOA. *Electronics Letters*, 38: 238–9.

Fujitsu Corporation. 2005. Fujitsu develops world's first semiconductor optical amplifier with signal waveform re-shaping function at 40 Gbps (retrieved from www.fujitsu.com/global/news/pr/archives/month/2005/20050304-01.html).

Gallep, C. M., and E. Conforti. 2004. Wavelength conversion with 2R-regeneration by UL-SOA induced chirp filtering. In *Proceedings of the Eleventh International Conference on Telecommunications* (Telecommunications and Networking, ICT 2004), August 1–6, Fortaleza, Brazil. *Lecture Notes in Computer Science*, edited by J. N. de Souza, P. Dini, and P. Lorenz, 3124: 304–11. New York: Springer.

Girardin, F., G. Guekos, and A. Houbavlis. 1998. Gain recovery of bulk semiconductor optical amplifiers. *IEEE Photonics Technology Letters*, 10: 784–6.

Jepsen, K. S., A. Buxens, A. T. Clausen, H. N. Poulsen, B. Mikkelsen, and K. E. Stubkjaer. 1998. 20 Gbit/s optical 3R regeneration using polarization-independent monolithically integrated Michelson interferometer. *Electronics Letters*, 34: 472–4.

Lavigne, B., D. Chiaroni, L. Hamon, C. Janz, and A. Jourdan. 1998. Performance and system margins at 10 Gbit/s of an optical repeater for long-haul NRZ transmission. In *Proceedings of the European Conference on Optical Communications* (ECOC'98), Sept. 20–24, Madrid. Vol. 1, 559–60.

Lavigne, B., P. Guerber, C. Janz, A. Jourdan, and M. Renaud. 2002. Full validation of an optical 3R regenerator at 20 Gbit/s. In *Technical Digest of Optical Fiber Communication Conference* (OFC2002), March 17–22, Anaheim, CA, USA. Vol. 3: 93–5.

Leclerc, O., G. Aubin, P. Brindel, J. Mangeney, H. Choumans, S. Barre, and J. L. Oudar. 2000. Demonstration of high robustness to SNR impairment in 20 Gbit/s long-haul transmission using 1.5 μm saturable absorber. *Electronics Letters*, 36: 1944–5.

Leclerc, O., B. Dany, D. Rouvillain, P. Brindel, E. Desurvire, C. Duchet, A. Shen, F. Devaux, A. Coquelin, M. Goix, S. Bouchoule, L. Fleury, and P. Nouchi. 2000. Simultaneously regenerated 4×40 Gbit/s dense WDM transmission over 10000 km using single 40 GHz InP Mach-Zehnder modulator. *Electronics Letters*, 36: 1574–5.

Leclerc, O., B. Lavigne, E. Balmefrezol, P. Brindel, L. Pierre, D. Rouvillain, and F. Seguineau. 2003. Optical regeneration at 40 Gbit/s and beyond. *Journal of Lightwave Technology*, 21: 2779–90.

Leclerc, O., B. Lavigne, and D. Chiaroni. 2002. All-optical regeneration: Principles and WDM implementation. In *Optical fiber telecommunications IVA (components)*, edited by I. P. Kaminow and T. Li, 732–83. San Diego: Academic Press.

Mamyshev, P. V. 1998. All-optical data regeneration based on self-phase modulation effect. In *Proceedings of the European Conference on Optical Communications* (ECOC'98), Sept. 20–24, Madrid. Vol. 1: 475–6.

McKinstrie, C. J., J. Santhanam, and G. P. Agrawal. 2002. Gordon-Haus timing jitter in dispersion-managed systems with lumped amplification: Analytical approach. *Journal of the Optical Society of America B*, 19: 640–9.

Meissner, M., M. Rösch, B. Schmauss, and G. Leuchs. 2003. 12 dB of noise reduction by a NOLM-based 2-R regenerator. *IEEE Photonics Technology Letters*, 15: 1297–9.

Mikkelsen, B., G. Raybon, B. Zhu, R. J. Essiambre, P. G. Bernasconi, K. Dreyer, L. W. Stulz, and S. N. Knudsen. 2001. High spectral efficiency (0.53 bits/s/Hz) WDM transmission of 160 Gbit/s per wavelength over 400 km of fiber. In *Technical Digest of the Conference on Optical Fiber Communication* (OFC 2001), Anaheim, CA, USA. Paper THF2, pp. 1–3.

Möhrle, M., C. Bornholdt, O. Brox, S. Bauer, and B. Sartorius. 2002. Multi-section DFB lasers for high speed signal processing/regeneration. In *Technical Digest of the Conference on Optical Fiber Communication* (OFC 2002), March 17–22, Anaheim, CA, USA. Vol. 2: 136–8.

Mu, R. M., T. Yu, V. S. Grigoryan, and C. R. Menyuk. 2002. Dynamics of the chirped return-to-zero modulation format. *Journal of Lightwave Technology*, 20, 47–57.

Nakazawa, M. E., Yamada, H. Kubota, and K. Suzuki. 1991. 10 Gbit/s soliton data transmission over one million kilometers. *Electronics Letters*, 27: 1270–2.

Owen, M., M. F. C. Stephens, R. V. Penty, and I. H. White. 2000. All-optical 3R regeneration and format conversion in an integrated SOA/DFB laser. In *Technical Digest of the Conference on Optical Fiber Communication* (OFC 2000), March 5–10, Baltimore, MD, USA. Paper ThF1, vol. 4: 76–8.

Öhlén, P., and E. Berglind. 1997. Noise accumulation and BER estimates in concatenated nonlinear optoelectronic repeaters. *IEEE Photonics Technology Letters*, 9: 1011–3.

Raybon, G. 2003. Optical 3R regeneration in 40 Gbit/s pseudolinear transmission systems. In *Technical Digest of the Conference on Optical Fiber Communication* (OFC 2003), March 23–28, Atlanta, GA, USA. Paper TuH1, vol. 1: 191.

Striegler, A. G., M. Meissner, K. Cveček, K. Sponsel, G. Leuchs, and Bernhard Schmauss. 2005. NOLM-based RZ-DPSK signal regeneration. *IEEE Photonics Technology Letters*, 17: 639–41.

Thiele, H. J., A. D. Ellis, and I. D. Phillips. 1999. Recirculatingloop demonstration all-optical 3R data regeneration using a semiconductor nonlinear interferometer. *Electronics Letters*, 35: 230–1.

Ueno, Y., S. Nakamura, and K. Tajima. 2001. Penalty-free error-free all-optical data pulse regeneration at 84 Gbit/s by using a symmetric-Mach-Zehnder-type semiconductor regenerator. *IEEE Photonics Technology Letters*, 13: 469–71.

Wolfson, D., T. Fjelde, A. Kloch, C. Janz, A. Coquelin, I. Guillemot, F. Gaborit, F. Poingt, and M. Renaud. 2000. Experimental investigation at 10 Gbit/s of the noise suppression capabilities in a pass-through configuration in SOA-based interferometric structures. *IEEE Photonics Technology Letters*, 12: 837–9.

Zhao, M., J. De Merlier, G. Morthier, R. Baets. 2002. Dynamic birefringence of the linear optical amplifier (LOA) and application in optical regeneration. *IEEE Journal of Selected Topics in Quantum Electronics* (integrated optics and optoelectronics issue), 8: 1399–1404.

Zhao, M., J. De Merlier, G. Morthier, and R. Baets. 2003. All-optical 2R regeneration based on polarization rotation in a linear optical amplifier. *IEEE Photonics Technology Letters*, 15: 305–7.

Zhao, M., G. Morthier, and R. Baets. 2002. Demonstration of extinction ratio improvement from 2 to 9 dB and intensity noise reduction with the MZI-GCSOA all-optical 2R regenerator. *IEEE Photonics Technology Letters*, 14: 992–4.

Zhao, W., Z. Hu, V. Lal, L. Rau, and D. Blumenthal. 2005. Optimization of ultra-long MQW semiconductor optical amplifiers for all-optical 40-Gb/s wavelength conversion. In *Proceedings of the Conference on Lasers and Electro-Optics* (CLEO), May 22–27, Baltimore, MD, USA. Paper CWK5, pp. 1426–8.

Zhu, Z., M. Funabashi, Z. Pan, L. Paraschis, and S. J. B. Yoo. 2006. 10000-hop cascaded in-line all-optical 3R regeneration to achieve 1 250 000-km 10-Gbit/s transmission. *IEEE Photonics Technology Letters*, 18: 718–20.

Optical Sources

Tin Win, *Monash University, Malaysia*

Serge Demidenko, *Massey University, New Zealand, and Monash University, Malaysia*

INTRODUCTION

The fundamentals of light as a propagating electromagnetic wave are presented in the initial part of this chapter. Semiconductor materials and their band-gap energy are introduced, leading to a discussion on the choice of materials for different emission wavelengths. The properties and the principles of laser emission are reviewed along with basic operation of laser diodes. Understanding the structure of *light-emitting diodes* (LEDs) and *laser diodes* (LDs) is important in selecting optical sources for specific applications in optical networks and communications, especially when considering the cost and effectiveness of the source. The resolution in data writing and reading for optical disks depends on the wavelength and the numerical aperture of the source. The optical resolution is discussed and the use of short wavelength laser diodes aimed to increase the data storage capacity of optical disks is introduced. Finally, the discussion on criterion of bit-rate distance products in choosing a proper source for a fiber link is presented.

OPTICAL SIGNALS

Optical signals are modulated electromagnetic waves known as *light*. The frequency range of light used in optical communications and networks is approximately from 200 THz (1.5 μm wavelength) to 1000 THz (300 nm wavelength).

The speed of light v is related to the *magnetic permeability* μ and the *electric permittivity* ε of the medium in which it is propagating as

$$v = \frac{1}{\sqrt{\mu\varepsilon}} \tag{1}$$

In a vacuum, the speed of light is $c = \dfrac{1}{\sqrt{\mu_0\varepsilon_0}} \approx 3 \times 10^8$ ms^{-1}, where $\mu_0 = 4\pi \times 10^{-7}$ H/m and $\varepsilon_0 = 8.85 \times 10^{-12}$ F/m are the permeability and the permittivity of a vacuum, respectively.

The *refractive index n* of a medium is defined as the ratio of the speed of light in vacuum c to the speed v in the medium.

$$n = \frac{c}{v} \tag{2}$$

In optical materials, $\mu \approx \mu_0$ and hence $n = \sqrt{\varepsilon_r}$, where $\varepsilon_r = \varepsilon/\varepsilon_0$ is the relative permittivity of the optical material.

Light is a *transverse electromagnetic wave*, and it is characterized by electric and magnetic fields that are orthogonal to each other as well as perpendicular to the direction of propagation. For a signal propagating in the z-direction, the electric field $\vec{E}(z,t)$ can be expressed as the vector sum of x- and y-components of the *electric field* (E-field) propagating in the z-direction:

$$\vec{E}(z,t) = \vec{E}_x(z,t) + \vec{E}_y(z,t) \tag{3}$$

The x- and y- components of $\vec{E}(z,t)$ propagating in the z-direction can be presented as

$$\vec{E}_x(z,t) = \hat{x}E_{0x}\cos(\omega t - kz + \theta_x) \tag{4}$$

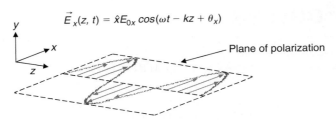

Figure 1: Electric field linearly polarized in the x-direction and propagating in the z-direction

$$\vec{E}_y(z,t) = \hat{y}E_{0y} \cos(\omega t - kz + \theta_y) \tag{5}$$

where $\omega = 2\pi f$ is the angular frequency of the electric field; $k = \dfrac{2\pi}{\lambda}$ is the propagation constant; f and λ are, respectively, the frequency and wavelength of the propagating electric field; θ_x and θ_y are initial phase angles; whereas E_{0x} and E_{0y} are the amplitudes of x- and y-components of $\vec{E}(z,t)$, respectively. Hence,

$$\vec{E}(z,t) = \hat{x}E_{0x} \cos(\omega t - kz + \theta_x) + \hat{y}E_{0y} \cos(\omega t - kz + \theta_y) \tag{6}$$

Polarization is defined as the orientation of the electric field $\vec{E}(z,t)$ in three-dimensional space. *Linearly polarized* light has the E-field in one direction only. The E-field in Equation (4) is linearly polarized in the x-direction while propagating in the z-direction as shown in Figure 1. Likewise, the wave expressed in Equation (5) is linearly polarized in the y-direction while propagating in the z-direction.

The E-field in Equation (6) is *randomly polarized* because the resultant direction of $\vec{E}(z,t)$ depends on the *phase difference* $\theta = \theta_x - \theta_y$ as well as on the amplitudes E_{0x} and E_{0y} of x- and y-components of $\vec{E}(z,t)$. It can be shown that $\vec{E}(z,t)$ is *elliptically polarized* if $E_{0x} \neq E_{0y}$ and $\theta = \theta_x - \theta_y \neq 0, \pi$. If $E_x = E_y$ and $\theta = \theta_x - \theta_y = \dfrac{\pi}{2}$, then the light wave is *circularly polarized*. The polarization as a function of the phase difference $\theta = \theta_x - \theta_y$ with $E_{0x} < E_{0y}$ is summarized in Figure 2. The arrowheads show the directions of rotation of the E-field as the optical wave propagates (out of the page in Figure 2). The E-field makes one complete rotation as the wave propagates one wavelength forward. The optical wave is linearly polarized at $\theta = 0, \pi, 2\pi$. It is elliptically polarized at $\theta = \pi/4, \pi/2,$ and $3\pi/4$, and the E-field makes one complete rotation anticlockwise (looking back into the source) as the wave advances one wavelength. The wave is elliptically polarized at $\theta = 5\pi/4, 3\pi/2,$ and $7\pi/4$ with clockwise rotation.

If $E_{0x} = E_{0y}$ and at $\theta = \pi/2$, then the resultant E-field rotates anticlockwise in a circular path (looking back into the source) and is said to be *left-circularly* polarized. At

$\theta = 3\pi/2$, the resultant E-field rotates clockwise and is referred to as *right-circularly* polarized.

The *polarization mode dispersion* (PMD) in fibers denotes the effect of widening of optical signal pulses when the optical signal propagates along the fiber because of different propagation speeds in each polarization direction. It is difficult to mitigate the PMD effect in optical fiber communication systems as the PMD is not a constant, but is a randomly varying parameter and depends on temperature variation and stress on the fiber.

SEMICONDUCTOR MATERIALS

Semiconductors are materials where all of the energy states in the valence band are filled with electrons while the conduction band is empty at 0 Kelvin. At room temperatures, some of the electrons in the valence band get thermal energy and thus can jump across the energy band gap into the conduction band. The unfilled energy states left behind in the valence band are called *holes*.

Direct and Indirect Band Gaps

The plots of energy band against the momentum vector k are shown in Figure 3 for direct band-gap and indirect band-gap semiconductor materials (Verdeyen 1995).

When an electron in the conduction band recombines with a hole in the valence band, a *photon* of energy $h\nu \geq E_g$ is emitted, where h is the Plank's constant, and E_g is the energy band-gap (atomic energy levels and light emission will be discussed below in the "Fundamentals of Laser" section). The probability of this transition is high in *direct band-gap semiconductor materials* (Verdeyen 1995), where the momentum of the electron is equal to the momentum of the hole and the total energy is conserved. The conduction band minimum energy E_c and the valence band maximum energy E_v occur at the same momentum values.

In an *indirect band-gap* semiconductor material, the conduction and the valence band levels E_c and E_v occur at different k values, and the probability of emission of photons by recombination is especially low because it needs a third particle with appropriate energy for the conservation of momentum.

Therefore, only direct band-gap materials are used for the high emission of photons. The direct band-gap materials are the *group III-V* materials, some of which are gallium arsenide (GaAs), indium phosphide (InP), indium arsenide (InAs), and gallium nitride (GaN).

The probability of occupation of electrons at energy level E_2 (E_1) in the conduction (valence) band is given by the *Fermi-Dirac distribution* (Agrawal 2002):

$$f_c(E_2) = \frac{1}{1 + \exp[(E_2 - E_{fc})/kT]} \tag{7}$$

$$f_c(E_1) = \frac{1}{1 + \exp[(E_1 - E_{fv})/kT]} \tag{8}$$

where E_{fc} and E_{fv} are the Fermi energy levels in the conduction band and the valence band, respectively, k_B is the Boltzmann constant (1.380×10^{-23} J/K) and T is the

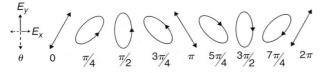

Figure 2: Polarization as a function of phase difference $\theta = \theta_x - \theta_y$ with $E_{0x} < E_{0y}$ (Hecht 2002).

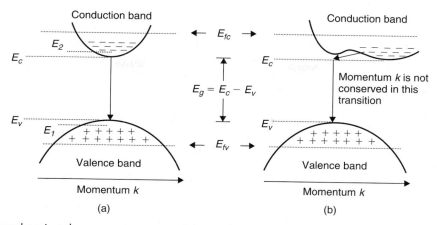

Figure 3: Energy band against the momentum vector k for (a) direct and (b) indirect band-gap semiconductor materials

absolute temperature in Kelvin. The energy level where the probability of being occupied by charge carriers at any temperature is ½ is referred to as the *Fermi energy level*.

To get a population inversion (see "Population Inversion and Pumping" below)—that is, when the number of electrons in the conduction band exceeds the number of electrons in the valence band—the electron occupation probability $f_c(E_2)$ at energy level E_2 in the conduction band must be larger than the electron occupation probability $f_v(E_1)$ at energy level E_1 in the valence band—that is, $f_c(E_2) > f_v(E_1)$.

This can be satisfied from Equation (7) and Equation (8) when

$$E_{fc} - E_{fv} > E_2 - E_1 > E_g \qquad (9)$$

where $E_g = E_c - E_v$, while E_c is the minimum conduction band energy level and E_v is the maximum valence band energy.

In semiconductor lasers (lasers will be discussed in detail in "Fundamentals of Lasers" section below), the population inversion is achieved by injecting charge carriers by means of forward biasing the P-N junction.

Material, Band-Gap, and Wavelength

High-performance *hetero-junction* semiconductor crystals are made of epitaxial layers grown on a substrate. This requires the same crystal structure and the same lattice constant with band-gap energy as large as possible. The same lattice constant is required for different materials in epitaxial crystal growth to reduce the formation of defects and stress in the crystal.

Figure 4 presents the binary compounds with energy band gap plotted against the lattice constant. It shows that aluminum arsenide (AlAs) and GaAs have the same lattice constant and that replacing Ga with Al does not change the lattice constant. GaAs-based optical sources operate in the wavelength range of 0.81 μm to 0.87 μm.

A ternary compound $Al_xGa_{1-x}As$ can be grown on GaAs substrate because replacing Ga with Al does not change the lattice constant. Index x is called the *mole fraction*, and $0 < x < 0.45$. The band-gap energy can be approximated from the empirical formula (Agrawal 2002):

$$E_g(eV) = 1.424 + 1.247x \qquad (10)$$

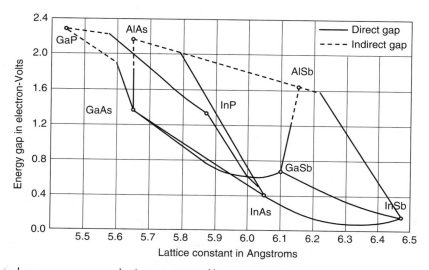

Figure 4: Band-gap energy versus lattice constant of binary compounds at room temperature (Singh 2003)

Table 1: Semiconductor Materials and Emission Wavelengths

Materials			
Active Layer	**Confining Layer**	**Substrate**	**Emission Wavelength (μm)**
InGaN	AlGaN	Al$_2$O$_3$	0.2–0.6
AlGaAs	AlGaAs	GaAs	0.5–0.9
InGaAsP	InGaP	GaAs	0.5–0.9
InGaAsP	AlGaInP	GaAs	0.3–0.5
InGaAsP	AlGaAs	GaAs	0.4–0.8
InGaAsP	InP	InP	0.7–1.6

Source: Nakamura, Pearton, and Fasol (2000)

The quaternary compound InGaAsP can be grown on InP substrate. The In$_{1-x}$Ga$_x$As$_y$P$_{1-y}$ lattice matched to InP if the gallium and arsenic mole fractions x and y are chosen (Buus, Amann, and Blumenthal 2005) such that

$$x = \frac{0.452y}{1 - 0.031y} \qquad (11)$$

The band-gap energy of In$_{1-x}$Ga$_x$As$_y$P$_{1-y}$ can be calculated (Nahory et al. 1978) from the approximate empirical equation

$$E_g(\text{eV}) = 1.35 + 0.668x - 1.17y + 0.758x^2 + 0.18y^2 \\ - 0.069xy - 0.332x^2y + 0.03xy^2 \qquad (12)$$

The emission wavelength range of In$_{1-x}$Ga$_x$As$_y$P$_{1-y}$ hetero-structure diodes is 920 nm to 1670 nm. Optical wavelength of a semiconductor LED or a laser diode can be calculated from the band-gap energy:

$$h\nu = E_g \qquad (13)$$

Because $c = \nu\lambda$, $\lambda_g = \dfrac{hc}{E_g}$, and substituting the value of $c = 3 \times 10^8$ m/s and E_g in the eV unit, λ_g, in nanometer can be calculated as

$$\lambda_g(\text{nm}) \approx \frac{1240}{E_g(\text{eV})} \qquad (14)$$

Semiconductor materials used for fabricating LEDs and laser diodes and their emission wavelength ranges are summarized in Table 1.

For more information on semiconductor materials and structures, readers can refer to Kapon (1999).

LIGHT-EMITTING DIODES

In a forward-biased P-N junction of a group III-V material such as GaAs, the recombination of electrons (in the conduction band) and holes (in the valence band) releases energy in the optical range as a stream of photons. A single-photon LED was first invented in 2002 using a InAs quantum dot layer between the P and N GaAs layers (Yuan et al. 2002; Smalley 2002). Single-photon sources have potential applications in quantum communication and quantum computation (Smalley 2002).

In *homo-junction* LEDs, the recombination takes place in the depletion region and the emitted light is incoherent—that is, photons are emitted in random phases and in all directions. The spectral width is relatively wide (30–60 nm) (Fukuda 1999). For these reasons, homo-junction LEDs are often used for data display purposes, whereas hetero-junction LEDs are more favorable for use in optical and data communications.

Light-emitting diodes are used for transmission with low bit rates (less than 200Mb/s) and for short distances of a few kilometers (Agrawal 2002). LEDs are cheaper than laser diodes and do not need temperature stabilization and optical frequency stabilization circuitry. The driving circuit for direct modulation is simple. However, LEDs have lower cutoff frequencies in the range of less than 100 MHz (Iizuka 2002).

LEDs are made of doped semiconductor materials based on group III-V semiconductors such as GaAs and InP. According to the structure, there are two types of LEDs: *edge-emitting* and *surface-emitting* (see Figures 5 and 6).

Fundamentally, the structures of edge- and surface-emitting LEDs are the same. However, in the surface-emitting type (known also as the *Burrus type*) LEDs, the light output is taken by etching a well through the substrate as shown in Figure 6. The light output is taken in the direction perpendicular to the junction planes.

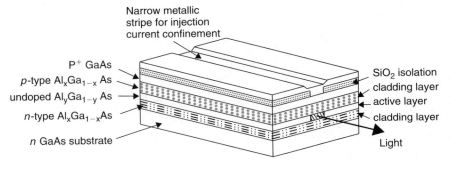

Figure 5: Edge-emitting LED with stripe contact. Typical dimensions: length is 200–400 μm, width is 100–200 μm, height is approximately 50 μm. The active layer thickness is 0.1–0.2 μm, and the light-confining width is less than 10 μm

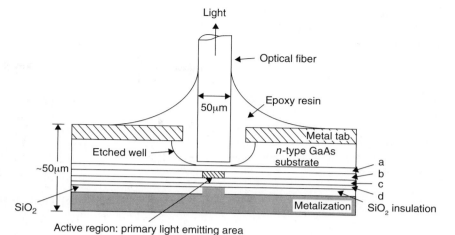

Figure 6: Schematic of double hetero-structure, high-radiance, surface-emitting LED. Optical fiber is bonded with resin to couple the light. Layer (a) N-type Al$_x$Ga$_{1-x}$As = cladding layer; (b) P-type Al$_y$Ga$_{1-y}$As = active layer; (c) P-type Al$_x$Ga$_{1-x}$As = cladding layer; (d) P-type GaAs = capping layer for contact (Burrus and Miller 1971)

Both of the above types use a *double hetero-junction* (DH) to confine the injected carriers when the junctions are forward-biased. A double hetero-junction is made by growing an active region of narrow band-gap material in between the two wide band-gap materials.

LED Spectral Width

The *spectral linewidth* Δλ of an optical source is defined as the *full width at half-maximum* (FWHM) intensity of the emission spectrum as shown in Figure 7. The linewidth is usually measured experimentally.

The typical spectral widths of LEDs are summarized in Table 2. The edge-emitting type of LED has a narrower spectral linewidth than that of the surface-emitting type. This is because shorter wavelength emissions are reabsorbed as the light travels relatively longer distances along the length of the active layer (Fukuda 1999).

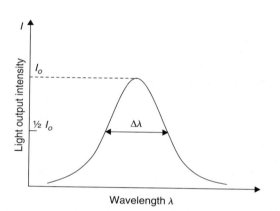

Figure 7: Emission spectrum and FWHM spectral linewidth Δλ

Table 2: Spectral Linewidth of Typical LEDs

LED Material			
Active Layer	**Substrate**	**Emission Wavelength Band (nm)**	**Spectral Linewidth (FWHM) (nm)**
InGaN		465–520 (blue-green)	70
GaP		555 (yellowish green)	60
GaP:N		565 (yellow green)	60
InGaAlP		570–625 (greenish yellow–red)	30
GaAlAs		655 (red)	30
AlGaAs	GaAs	850	40
InGaAsP	InP	1300	110 (surface emitting)
InGaAsP	InP	1300	80 (edge emitting)
InGaASP	InP	1550	130

Source: Blue to red visible wavelength data are from Nakamura, Pearton, and Fasol (2000); infrared wavelength data are from Fukuda (1999).

The spectral linewidth of a LED diode also depends on temperature and can be approximated from the spontaneous emission rate (Agarawal 2002) as

$$\Delta\nu = \frac{1.8 k_B T}{h} \qquad (15)$$

where $k_B = 1.38 \times 10^{-23}$ J/K is the Boltzmann constant, $h = 6.63 \times 10^{-34}$ J-s is the Planck constant, and T is the temperature in Kelvin. The spectral linewidth is often expressed in wavelength width $\Delta\lambda$ in nanometers and can be converted as

$$\Delta\lambda = \frac{\lambda^2}{c}\Delta\nu \quad \text{and hence } \Delta\lambda = \frac{1.8 k_B T \lambda^2}{hc} \qquad (16)$$

For example, the spectral linewidth of a LED at room temperature ($T = 300$ K) and for an emission wavelength of 1300 nm can be estimated as

$$\Delta\lambda = \frac{1.8 \times 1.38 \times 10^{-23} \times 300 \times (1300 \times 10^{-9})^2}{6.63 \times 10^{-34} \times 3 \times 10^8} = 63 \text{ nm}$$

Modulation Response of LEDs

The output intensity of an LED can be modulated by a signal. It can be done by superimposing the signal current on the bias injection current. This type of modulation is known as *direct modulation*. The modulation response of a typical LED is shown in Figure 8. The output signal decreases as the modulation signal frequency increases because of the junction capacitance and the injected carrier lifetime τ_c.

The ratio of optical output power $P_0(\omega)$ at a modulation frequency ω to the power $P_0(0)$ at DC or without modulation can be written as (Fukuda 1999)

$$\frac{P_o(\omega)}{P_o(0)} = \frac{1}{\sqrt{1 + \omega^2 \tau_c^2}} \qquad (17)$$

The optical modulation bandwidth or -3dB frequency f_{3dB} (optical) of an LED is the frequency at which the

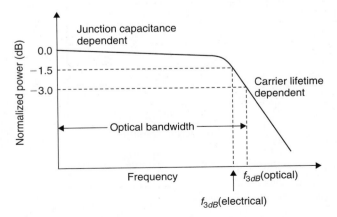

Figure 8: Modulation response of a LED

output intensity decreases to one-half of the intensity at the DC bias point and depends on the carrier lifetime as

$$f_{3dB}(\text{optical}) = \frac{\sqrt{3}}{2\pi\tau_c} \qquad (18)$$

Assuming that the diode threshold current is negligible, the optical output power is directly proportional to the injection current. Then the ratio of the optical output powers $\frac{P_o(\omega)}{P_o(0)}$ in Equation (17) is equal to the ratio of injection current [$I(\omega)$] with signal modulation to the bias current [$I(0)$] without signal modulation (i.e., $\frac{P_o(\omega)}{P_o(0)} = \frac{I(\omega)}{I(0)}$).

Electrical input power P_e is proportional to the square of the injection current ($P_e \propto I^2$) and the electrical -3dB frequency where the input power ratio $P_e(\omega)/P_e(0) = \frac{1}{2}$ occurs at $\frac{I(\omega)}{I(0)} = \frac{1}{\sqrt{2}}$ or at output optical power ratio $\frac{P_o(\omega)}{P_o(0)} = \frac{1}{\sqrt{2}}$. Therefore, from Equation (17), electrical -3dB frequency can be written as

$$f_{3dB}(\text{electrical}) = \frac{1}{2\pi\tau_c} \qquad (19)$$

Therefore, at f_{3dB} (electrical), the output optical power is 70.7 percent of optical output power without modulation. For example, the typical value of a LED carrier lifetime is approximately 5 ns (Fukuda 1999), the value of f_{3dB} (optical) is approximately 55 MHz, and f_{3dB} (electrical) is approximately 32MHz.

Conversion Efficiency of LEDs

The *internal efficiency* η_{int} is defined as the ratio of the number of generated photons to the number of electrons injected by the bias current I:

$$\eta_{int} = \frac{P_{int}/h\nu}{I/q} \qquad (20)$$

where P_{int} is the optical power generated internally and $q = 1.6 \times 10^{-19}$ C is the electron charge.

The ratio of emitted optical output power P_{out} to the internally generated optical power P_{int} is known as the *external efficiency*:

$$\eta_{ext} = \frac{P_{out}}{P_{int}} \qquad (21)$$

The *total power conversion efficiency* η_{tot} of a LED is defined as the ratio of the optical output power P_{out} to the electrical input power P_{in}:

$$\eta_{tot} = \frac{P_{out}}{P_{in}} = \frac{\eta_{ext}\eta_{int}}{V_0 I} = \frac{\eta_{ext}\eta_{int}(h\nu)(I/q)}{V_0 I} = \frac{\eta_{ext}\eta_{int}h\nu}{V_0 q} \qquad (22)$$

where V_0 is the voltage drop across the diode.

If $qV_0 \approx h\nu$, then $\eta_{tot} \approx \eta_{ext}\eta_{int}$, where η_{tot} indicates the overall electrical-to-optical power conversion efficiency, which is also known as *wall-plug efficiency*.

FUNDAMENTALS OF LASERS

In optical networks and optical communications, laser diodes are used for their small size, relatively low price, and narrow spectral linewidth. The word *laser* is an acronym of *light amplification by stimulated emission of radiation*.

Laser Properties

Important laser properties that are different from those of ordinary optical sources such as incandescent lamp, fluorescent lamp, among others, are *monochromaticity*, *coherence*, *brightness*, *directivity*, and *beam divergence*, as described below.

Monochromaticity

Ideally, the laser light is characterized by a single wavelength and is referred to as *monochromatic* light. However, in reality the laser light contains a narrow spread $\Delta\nu$ of frequencies or wavelengths $\Delta\lambda$ called *spectral linewidth*. The spectral linewidth of the laser light depends on the type of laser diode (an element that converts an electrical current into light). A linewidth of a typical Fabry-Perot laser diode lasing at 1550 nm is approximately 1–5 nm (Fabry-Perot lasers will be discussed in detail in the section "Fabry-Perot Laser Resonator" below).

Coherence

In a laser light beam, the photons have the same phase or a constant phase relationship; that relationship of photons in a light beam is known as *coherence*. Because there is a frequency spread of $\Delta\nu$ in a laser light, photons with a small difference in frequencies with each other will get out of phase after a certain time called *coherence time*, which is a measure of temporal coherence. During this coherence time, photons in the laser light will travel coherently in space. The spatial coherence is determined by the distance traveled by the photons in the coherence time and is called *coherence length*. If the spectral linewidth is $\Delta\nu$, then coherence time τ_{coh} is conventionally defined (Milonni and Eberly 1988) as

$$\tau_{coh} = \frac{1}{2\pi\Delta\nu} \quad (23)$$

Coherent length l_c is defined as the distance traveled by laser light in the coherence time τ_{coh}:

$$l_c = \nu\tau_{coh} = \frac{c}{2\pi n \Delta\nu} \quad (24)$$

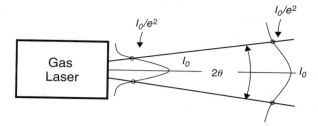

Laser beam spreads out as it is propagating

Figure 9: Gaussian intensity profile with peak intensity at the center of the beam. Beam divergence is defined as the full angle at I_0/e^2 points of the beam profile

where n is the refractive index of the medium. Because $\left|\frac{\Delta\nu}{\Delta\lambda}\right| = \left|\frac{c}{\lambda^2}\right|$, the coherent length l_c can be expressed as

$$l_c = \frac{\lambda^2}{2\pi n \Delta\lambda} \quad (25)$$

As an example, consider an 850-nm edge-emitting laser diode with a spectral width of 1 nm, a coherence length in space of 0.11 mm; in optical silica fiber ($n = 1.45$), it is 0.079 mm. For a 850-nm *distributed feedback* (DFB) laser diode with a spectral linewidth of 0.0001 nm, it has a coherent length of 790 mm in silica optical fiber.

Directivity and Beam Divergence

Multiple reflections of laser light inside a laser cavity results in the highly directional output beam of a laser. Directivity or beam divergence of a laser beam from an atomic (gas) laser source is described by full angle beam divergence 2θ at I_0/e^2, where I_0 is the maximum intensity of the Gaussian intensity distribution as shown in Figure 9.

For a Gaussian beam, the half-divergence angle θ can be derived as (Milonni and Eberly 1988):

$$\theta = \frac{\lambda}{\pi\omega_0} \quad (26)$$

where λ is the *emission wavelength* and ω_0 is the *beam waist* (the smallest beam radius of I_0/e^2 point) at the center of the resonator.

Edge-emitting semiconductor hetero-junction lasers have elliptically shaped spots, and the beam divergence is usually defined by two angles measured in two perpendicular directions: $\theta_\perp$ perpendicular to the junction plane and $\theta_{//}$ parallel to the junction plane as shown in Figure 10. Values of $\theta_\perp$ and are $\theta_{//}$ measured as full angles at

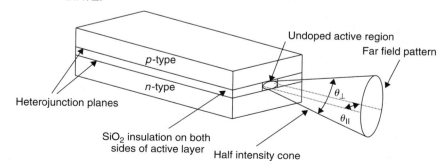

Figure 10: Edge-emitting laser diode illustrating a beam spot at one-half the maximum intensity. The maximum intensity is at the center of the elliptical spot

half-maximum intensity. The value of $\theta_\perp$ is always larger than that of $\theta_\parallel$ because of stronger diffraction from narrower slit-like active layer thickness in the direction perpendicular to the junction plane.

Brightness

Because of their highly directional nature and small beam spots, the brightness or *intensity* (watt per unit area) of lasers is higher than that of incoherent light sources.

Atomic Energy Levels and Emission of Light

Light exhibits both wave nature and particle nature. This is known as the *wave-particle duality*. Quantum mechanics shows that a beam of light consists of light-wave packets (particles) called *photons*. A photon possesses a quantized energy ΔE given by Planck's equation

$$\Delta E = h v \tag{27}$$

where $h = 6.63 \times 10^{-34}$ J-s is the Planck constant and v is the frequency of the light.

An atom has electrons orbiting in different *shells*. The shells are designated with principal quantum number n ($n = 1, 2, 3, \ldots$). The innermost shell has the principal quantum number $n = 1$. Electrons in this shell are in the lowest energy level, which is called the *ground state*. The next shell with the principal quantum number $n = 2$ has higher energy level and so on. Each and every shell is characterized by its own respective energy level.

When an electron from a higher energy level E_2 goes down to a lower energy level E_1, it emits a photon of energy

$$\Delta E = E_2 - E_1 = h v \tag{28}$$

where v is the frequency of the emitted photon and ΔE is the difference of energies between a higher energy level E_2 and a lower energy level E_1 involved in the transition of the electron.

Absorption, Spontaneous Emission, and Stimulated Emission

When a photon of energy hv is incident on an atom, the photon is absorbed and the atom is excited to a higher energy state. The photon is absorbed only when its energy hv is exactly the same as the energy difference $E_2 - E_1$ of the higher and lower energy levels as shown in Figure 11. This process is called *stimulated absorption*.

The natural transition of an atom from the higher energy level E_2 to the lower energy level E_1 can occur at any time, and the emission of a photon occurs in a random direction with a random phase (Figure 11). This type of emission is known as a *spontaneous emission*.

If a photon with the same energy $hv = E_2 - E_1$ is passing nearby, it can trigger the atom to jump down from a higher energy level E_2 to a lower energy level E_1, in which case the emitted photon is in the same direction and in the same phase with the passing photon as shown in Figure 11. This type of emission is known as a *stimulated emission*.

If the transition of the atom from a higher energy level E_2 to a lower energy level E_1 takes place without the emission of a photon, then the energy is transformed into the translational energy of the atom (or vibrational and rotational energy in the case of a molecule). This type of transition is called a *nonradiative de-excitation*.

Population Inversion and Pumping

For a medium at thermal equilibrium with its surroundings, the relative number of atoms at a high energy level E_2 and at a lower energy E_1 is given by the *Boltzmann distribution* as

$$\frac{N_2}{N_1} = e^{\frac{-(E_2 - E_1)}{k_B T}} \tag{29}$$

where N_2 and N_1 are the numbers of atoms at a higher energy level E_2 and at a lower energy level E_1, respectively; $k_B = 1.380 \times 10^{-23}$ J/K is the Boltzmann constant; and T is the temperature in Kelvin (K). The Boltzmann distribution indicates that, at thermal equilibrium, the number of atoms at a higher energy level is lower than that at a lower energy level.

Through the collision of moving particles such as electrons or by absorbing radiations, the atoms of a medium can be excited to higher energy levels. In this situation, if the decay time τ_{21} from E_2 to E_1 is longer than the decay time τ_{10} from E_1 to ground state E_0, then the number of atoms N_2 at an energy state E_2 will be higher than that N_1 of a lower energy state E_1. This is known as *population inversion*.

As mentioned earlier, the atoms or molecules can be excited by colliding with other particles such as high-velocity electrons or molecules as well as by high-energy radiation of an appropriate frequency. In the case of semiconductor laser diodes, by forward biasing the P-N double hetero-junction, the charge carriers are injected to the higher energy band. The electrons in the valence band receive energy to go up into the conduction band. To get laser action, it is necessary to create a population inversion of electrons in the conduction band by continuously injecting the charge carriers into the active layer. This process of creating a larger population at the higher energy level (conduction band for electrons) than that of the lower energy level (valence band) is called *pumping*.

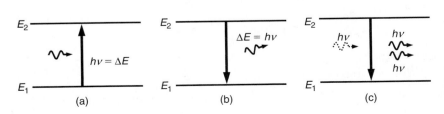

Figure 11: (a) Stimulated absorption, (b) spontaneous emission, and (c) stimulated emission

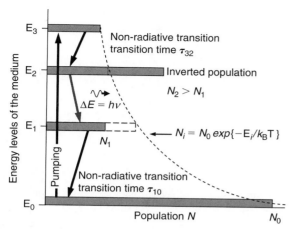

Figure 12: Boltzmann distribution and population inversion

For clarity and completeness, a four-level model of laser pumping in an atomic (gas) medium will be used for explanation. In Figure 12, atoms or molecules at the ground-state energy level E_0 are pumped to a higher energy level E_3. The atoms or molecules decay rapidly to energy level E_2 as nonradiative transition. The transition from E_2 to E_1 is a radiative transition that emits photons. Then, again, the atoms or molecules at energy level E_1 jump down to the grouznd-state energy level E_0 without radiation. The transition time τ_{21} from E_2 to E_1 is much longer than the transition time τ_{32} from E_3 to E_2 and τ_{10} from E_1 to E_0 for the population inversion to achieve. $E_3 \rightarrow E_2$ and $E_1 \rightarrow E_0$ do not have to be nonradiative transitions, although because nonradiative processes are faster, it is better if they are nonradiative.

Figure 13 shows the energy band diagram of a semiconductor. In a semiconductor laser, forward biasing the P-N junction injects or pumps electrons into the energy level E_3 in the conduction band. Then the electron energy decays to the energy level E_2 with a decay time τ_{32} (~10^{-12} sec) (Pearsall 2003). This creates a population inversion of electrons between energy level E_2 and E_1

because at thermal equilibrium there are more electrons in the valence band. An electron transition to E_1 is the recombination with a hole in the valence band, which emits the radiation with the transition time τ_{21} (~10^{-9} sec) (Pearsall 2003). Finally, the electron at the energy level E_1 relaxes to a lower energy level E_0 with a transition time $\tau_{10} < \tau_{21}$.

Fabry-Perot Laser Resonator

Normally, most of the atoms in the population inverted state undergo spontaneous emission and do not contribute to coherent stimulated emission. A resonator with positive feedback is necessary so that the majority of the atoms in the upper laser level will contribute in the coherent stimulated radiation. The resonator has two mirrors with high reflectivity facing each other at a distance L as shown in Figure 14. This arrangement is known as a *Fabry-Perot* (FP) *resonator* (Milonni and Eberly 1988). The photons traveling off-axis are absorbed by the wall of the resonator and eliminated. The photons traveling parallel to the axis of the resonator are reflected back and forth into the resonator by the end mirrors and interact with the atoms, and stimulated emission strongly takes place in the resonator. One of the mirrors has a reflective coating with partial transmission so that a small fraction of the laser light in the resonator is coupled out as a usable laser beam.

The resonance occurs when the resonator optical length nL is equal to an integer multiple of one-half of the free space wavelengths (Iizuka 2002), where n is the refractive index of the gain medium in the resonator:

$$nL = q\frac{\lambda}{2} \quad (30)$$

where q is the number of half-wavelengths in the standing wave in the cavity at resonant frequency as shown in Figure 14. Such a pattern is called the *qth longitudinal mode* of the resonator.

The resonant frequency ν is then

$$\nu = \frac{c}{\lambda} = q\frac{c}{2nL} \quad (31)$$

The frequency spacing between two adjacent resonance modes is

$$\Delta\nu = (q+1)\frac{c}{2nL} - q\frac{c}{2nL} = \frac{c}{2nL} \quad (32)$$

The spacing $\Delta\nu$ is larger for the shorter effective resonator length L.

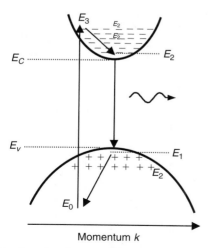

Figure 13: Four-level pumping in semiconductor lasers

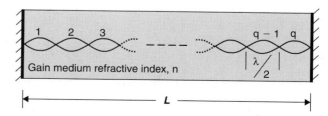

Figure 14: Fabry-Perot laser resonator with gain medium of refractive index n

The number of modes leading to oscillation is determined by the gain linewidth divided by the mode spacing Δv.

Even if the cavity is very short, the number of possible longitudinal modes is still quite large. These modes are called *longitudinal modes* because they can be tuned by changing the cavity length longitudinally.

Laser Gain Curve and Lasing Modes

If the irradiance (sometimes called *intensity*) of the light at one mirror is equal to some value I_0, then after one pass through the laser gain medium in the resonator the intensity grows to a value I as

$$I = I_0 e^{[g(v)-\alpha(v)]L} \qquad (33)$$

where $g(v)$ is the (small signal) gain of the laser medium in the cavity and is a function of frequency v; $\alpha(v)$ is the distributed loss per unit length in the cavity resulting from losses such as scattering and absorption, which are frequency-dependent processes by nonactive molecules or atoms in the medium. If R_1 and R_2 are the reflectivity of the mirrors at each end of the cavity, then after one round trip the intensity becomes

$$I = I_0 R_1 R_2 e^{[g(v)-\alpha(v)]2L} \qquad (34)$$

and the relative gain in intensity in one round trip is

$$G = \frac{I}{I_0} = R_1 R_2 e^{[g(v)-\alpha(v)]2L} \qquad (35)$$

The round trip gain must be greater than unity for initial buildup of lasing and must be equal to 1 at steady state; that is,

$$g(v) \geq \alpha(v) + \frac{1}{2L} \ln\left(\frac{1}{R_1 R_2}\right) = g_{th} \qquad (36)$$

where g_{th} is the threshold gain at steady state.

The conceptual small signal gain curve $g(v)$ of InGaAs (band-gap energy $E_g = 0.75$ eV) is shown in Figure 15 (Asada and Suematsu 1985). The gain is higher for higher carrier density N, which in turn depends on the injection (forward bias) current of a laser diode. This is indicated in Figure 15 by the arrow connecting the gain peaks and showing the trend of growth of the injection current with increasing injection carrier density Ni and the gain.

Normally, the gain curve is wider than the longitudinal mode spacing of the cavity. In long FP resonator-type lasers such as edge-emitting lasers, there would be a few longitudinal cavity modes lasing under the small signal laser gain curve as shown in Figure 16.

The longitudinal mode that coincides with the small signal gain peak will lase more strongly than the adjacent modes as shown in Figure 16. The adjacent modes on either side of the strongest one could have considerable intensity because the difference in gain $g(v)$ between these modes is exceptionally small ($\sim$0.1cm^{-1}) (Agrawal 2002).

Lasers that are lasing with one or two adjacent longitudinal modes together with the main mode are

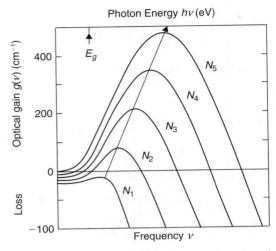

Figure 15: Conceptual gain spectra of a typical semiconductor laser

called *multilongitudinal mode* (MLM) *lasers*. Each mode propagates with different speed when traveling in fibers and contributes to a *group velocity dispersion*. In optical communications, dispersion limits the bit-rate distance product below 10 Gbps-km for systems operating near 1550nm (Agrawal 2002). By appropriately designing the structure and the cavity length, single-mode lasers oscillating at a *single longitudinal mode* (SLM) are

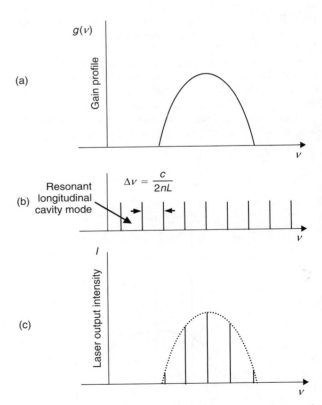

Figure 16: (a) Laser gain curve g(v) at steady state lasing, (b) cavity resonant modes with frequency spacing $\Delta v = c/(2nL)$, and (c) lasing modes under the laser gain profile

fabricated. They are used in high bit-rate, long-haul optical communications.

The *side mode suppression ratio* (SMSR) is defined as the ratio of power of the main mode to the power of the adjacent dominant side mode and is expressed in dB (Agrawal 2002):

$$SMSR = 10\log\left(\frac{P_{mm}}{P_{sm}}\right) \tag{37}$$

where P_{mm} is the main mode power and P_{sm} is the adjacent dominant side mode power. For a good SLM laser, the SMSR exceeds 30 dB (Agrawal 2002).

Spectral Lineshape and Linewidth

The spectrum of the atomic radiation has a *Lorentzian lineshape* because of transition lifetime broadening. The Lorentzian lineshape factor $g(\nu)$ (Iizuka 2002) is expressed as

$$g(\nu) = \frac{\dfrac{\gamma}{2}}{\left(\dfrac{\gamma}{2}\right)^2 + [2\pi(\nu - \nu_0]^2} \tag{38}$$

where $\gamma = (\tau_{21})^{-1}$, τ_{21} is the transition or decay time of the transition from energy level E_2 to energy E_1, and ν_0 is the lasing frequency at which the maximum intensity peak occurs ($\Delta E = E_2 - E_1 = h\nu_0$).

The *spectral linewidth* is defined as the full width at half-maximum of the intensity distribution curve. The spectral line has a width that results from the natural decay lifetime of photons in the cavity. This type of spectral line broadening is called *homogenous line broadening* because each and every atom contributes equally and in the same way in broadening a spectral line.

In semiconductor laser diodes, crystal imperfections, material inhomogeneity, and losses also contribute to spectral line broadening, which is known as *inhomogeneous line broadening*. The actual lineshape depends on the contributions of both homogeneous and inhomogeneous broadening. The spectral linewidth in semiconductor

lasers is also broadened by random spontaneously emitted photons adding into the lasing light. The linewidth $\Delta\nu$ of a semiconductor laser diode is derived (Buus, Amann, and Blumenthal 2005; Henry 1983) as

$$\Delta\nu = \frac{h\nu\nu_g^2(\alpha_L + \alpha_m)\alpha_m n_{sp}}{8\pi P}(1 + \alpha_H^2) \tag{39}$$

where ν_g is the group velocity, α_L is the cavity loss, α_m is the end loss including output as loss, n_{sp} is the spontaneous emission coefficient, P is the optical power per end, and α_H is the linewidth enhancement factor. Equation (39) is known as the *Schawlow-Townes-Henry linewidth equation*.

Lasers of distributed feedback type and *distributed Bragg reflector* (DBR) type laze in single-longitudinal mode and have extremely narrow laser linewidth (the above laser types will be discussed in detail in the section "Distributed Feedback and Distributed Bragg Reflector Lasers" below). Single-longitudinal mode narrow linewidth lasers are used for long-haul optical fiber systems. (Refer to Henry 1982, 1983 for detailed theory on laser linewidths and the noise of semiconductor lasers.)

LASER DIODES

The structures of laser diodes are similar to the structures of LEDs. The only difference is that laser diodes use the Fabry-Perot cavity for light amplification (Figure 17). Typical dimensions of a laser diode crystal are longitudinal direction length of 200–400 µm, lateral direction width of 100–200 µm, and transverse direction height of 50–60 µm. The active layer thickness is 0.1–0.2 µm, and the light-confining width in the active layer is less than 10 µm (the shaded area in the active layer with the slashed line in Figure 17). The active layer is surrounded by lower refractive index cladding and guiding layers on all sides; hence, this type of laser with index guiding is known as a *buried hetero-junction laser*.

In laser diodes, the active layer is grown between two wider band-gap materials, thus forming two hetero-junctions between the active layer and the wider band-gap materials. The injected currents, the injected

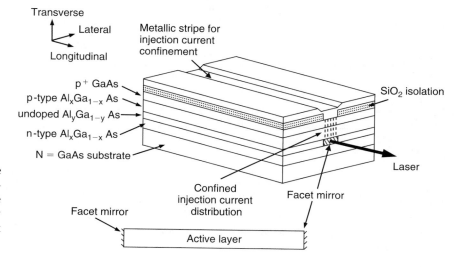

Figure 17: Edge-emitting laser with stripe contact for current confinement. The light-emitting ends are cleaved at a suitable crystal plane to form high-reflectivity facet mirrors required for the Fabry-Perot resonator

carriers, and the emitted light are confined in the thin active layer on the order of a few nanometers up to 0.2 μm thickness and less than 10 μm width so that the lasing threshold current is low and the electrical to light conversion efficiency is high.

Current and Carrier Confinement

The injected current is confined to the small active region by a narrow stripe contact to channel the injected current into the desired area along at the middle of the crystal. There are several other methods used in injection current confinement such as raised resistivity by proton bombardment, barricade by back-biased P-N junction layer, dopant diffused channel, and modulation of layer thickness (Iizuka 2002).

The carrier confinement is achieved by the double hetero-junction structure. The energy-band diagram for a DH structure is shown in Figure 18.

When the junctions are forward-biased, electrons in the cladding N-type material are injected into the undoped active layer. The injected electrons in the active layer cannot penetrate into the P-type cladding because the potential barrier at the P junction push them back into the active layer. Thus, the electrons are confined in the active layer. The injected holes are also confined in the active layer by the potential barrier at the N-junction cladding. The confined electrons and holes recombine in the active layer only, and the energy released from the recombination is emitted as the optical radiation in the active layer.

Light Confinement

The active layer also acts like a dielectric waveguide to guide the emitted light along its length (the longitudinal direction of the FP resonator) toward the end facets. The thickness of the active layer is 0.1–0.2 μm for most laser diodes emitting in the band of 850–1550 nm for use in optical communications. The refractive index of the

active layer is slightly higher than the adjacent P- and N-type cladding layers. The remaining two sides of the active layer are roughened to prevent reflections in the lateral direction. As a result, the emitted light in the active layer is confined by total internal reflections at the boundaries between the active layer and cladding layers. This type of confining and guiding the light along the longitudinal direction of the active layer is called *index guiding*.

The *V* parameter or *normalized frequency* (Kogelnik and Ramaswamy 1974) of a slab waveguide of thickness 2a is given by

$$V = kaNA \qquad (40)$$

where $k = \dfrac{2\pi}{\lambda}$ and $NA = \sqrt{n_1^2 - n_2^2}$ is the numerical aperture of the slab waveguide, n_1 is the refractive index of the active layer, and n_2 is the refractive index of the P- and N-type cladding layers.

In general, if the value of V is $(m-1)\dfrac{\pi}{2} < V < m\dfrac{\pi}{2}$, then there are m number of modes propagating in the slab waveguide. The condition for single-mode propagation is $0 < V < \dfrac{\pi}{2}$. Thus, the number of modes in the active layer can be varied by changing the thickness 2a of the active layer.

The thickness of the active layer is so chosen that only the fundamental mode is propagating in the cavity. Thus, the thickness 2a of the active layer must fulfill the condition

$$2a \leq \frac{\lambda}{2\sqrt{n_1^2 - n_2^2}} \qquad (41)$$

The propagating beam's intensity distribution is shown in Figure 19.

The diffraction from the thinner slit-like active layer at the facets will contribute to a larger output beam divergence. Consequently, in determining the thickness of the active layer, consideration must be taken to balance between the beam width divergence and optical confinement efficiency where the optical confinement factor Γ is defined (Buus, Amann, and Blumenthal 2005) as

$$\Gamma = \frac{\text{Mode power in the active layer}}{\text{Total mode power}} = \frac{\int_{-a}^{a} \left|E_y\right|^2 dy}{\int_{-\infty}^{\infty} \left|E_y\right|^2 dy} \qquad (42)$$

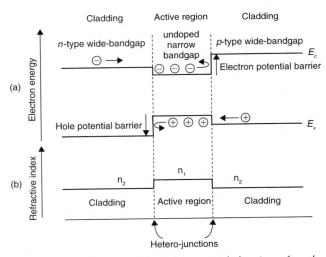

Figure 18: Energy bands and potential barriers for the injection carrier confinement in (a) forward bias condition and (b) refractive indexes of active and cladding layers for index waveguiding

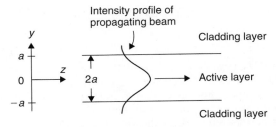

Figure 19: Propagating beam intensity profile

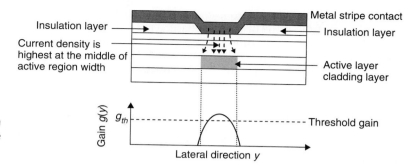

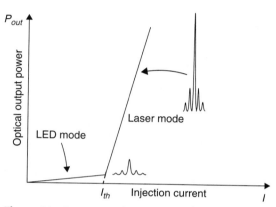

Figure 20: Light is confined around the maximum gain at the center of the active layer width where the gain exceeds the lasing threshold gain g_{th}

where E_y is the electric field propagating along the longitudinal direction (z-direction) and is a function of transverse coordinate y.

Gain guiding occurs in the active layer because of injection current confinement. The injection current density is the highest at the center of the active layer in the lateral direction, and it approaches zero at both the sides of the active layers. Consequently, the injection charge carrier density N and hence the gain g is the highest in the center of the lateral width of the active layer. As a result, stimulated emission of photon is the highest at the center of the active layer. These phenomena are combined and lead to confining the lasing at the center of the active layer where the gain is the highest. Light confinement along the center of the active layers where the gain is the highest is known as *gain guiding* (Figure 20).

The tiny end surfaces of the active layer (facets) are constructed to have high reflectivity by cleaving the crystal at a crystal plane perpendicular to the junction planes, thus forming a Fabry-Perot type cavity along the length of the active layer. The power reflectivity or reflectance R of the cleaved surface is given by *Fresnel's equation* (Hecht 2002; Agrawal 2002):

$$R = \left(\frac{n-1}{n+1} \right)^2 \qquad (43)$$

where n is the refractive index of the active region. For GaAs, $n = 3.5$ and hence the power reflectivity of the facet is 0.3.

Laser Diode Operating Characteristics and Conversion Efficiency

The typical operating characteristic of a laser diode is shown in Figure 21. When the forward bias current (known also as the *injection current*) is less than the threshold current I_{th}, the diode is operating in LED mode. The spontaneous emission is dominant because of insufficient carrier density in the conduction band to get a large enough population inversion and enough gain to overcome losses.

When the bias injection current is increased to the threshold current I_{th}, the population inversion starts to take place and stimulated emission occurs. Above the threshold current I_{th}, the optical output power P_{out} of the laser diode is directly proportional to $(I - I_{th})$. As the biasing current is increased, the peak power increases as well and

Figure 21: Operating characteristic of a laser diode

the spectral linewidth gets narrower [see Equation (39)]. The resonant wavelength of the cavity also increases because of the expansion of the cavity length and an increase in the refractive index by the rising temperature with increasing current (Iizuka 2002). The emission wavelength increases also because the band-gap energy of the gain medium is reduced when the temperature rises as (Iizuka 2002)

$$E_g(T) = E_0 - \frac{\alpha T^2}{\beta + T} \qquad (44)$$

where E_0 is the band-gap energy at 0 K, T is the temperature in Kelvin, α is 4.5×10^{-4} eV/K, and β is 204 K for GaAs and 327 K for $Ga_xIn_{1-x}As_yP_{1-y}$.

Change of cavity length can lead to sudden change in the emission frequency to a lower cavity resonant frequency mode (longer wavelength mode) that coincides with the gain peak. This is known as *mode hopping* (Iizuka 2002). Temperature stabilization circuits using *Peltier thermoelectric devices* (Kasap 2002; Godfrey 1996) are employed to prevent mode hopping and to avoid frequency shifting even inside the same mode.

The slope efficiency or responsivity η_s is defined as (Fukuda 1999):

$$\eta_s = \frac{dP_{out}}{dI} = \eta_d \frac{h\nu}{2q} \qquad (45)$$

where η_d is the external differential quantum efficiency and dP_{out}/dI is the slope of the P-I characteristic at the operating point above the threshold current I_{th}. The factor ½ arises because there are two facets in Fabry-Perot lasers that emit laser light. For Fabry-Perot lasers with coated rear facets or for DFB lasers, ½ should be replaced by unity.

The spontaneously emitted power at threshold current I_{th} is often small compared to the laser power in operation so that dP_{out}/dI can be approximated as $P_{out}/(I - I_{th})$. The lasing output power (from one facet) can be calculated as

$$P_{out} = \frac{1}{2}\eta_d \frac{hv}{q}(I - I_{th}) \qquad (46)$$

The *external quantum efficiency* η_{ext} is defined as the ratio of total photon emission rate to the electron injection rate (Agrawal 2002) and hence can be written as

$$\eta_{ext} = \frac{2P_{out}/hv}{I/q} = \eta_d\left(1 - \frac{I_{th}}{I}\right) \qquad (47)$$

where $\eta_{ext} \approx \eta_d$ for $I >> I_{th}$.

The *total quantum efficiency* (also known as *wall-plug efficiency*) is defined as the ratio of total optical output power to the electrical input power:

$$\eta_{tot} = \frac{2P_{out}}{V_0 I} = \frac{hv}{qV_0}\eta_{ext} \approx \eta_{ext} \qquad (48)$$

because $hv \approx qV_0$. The external quantum efficiency η_{ext} is approximately 40 percent to 60 percent in a typical laser diode (Fukuda 1999).

Modulation Response of Laser Diodes

The signal can be modulated on the laser light by superimposing the signal current to the bias current of the optical source. This type of modulation is known as *direct modulation*. In a direct-modulated laser, the signal output power decreases with increasing modulation frequency. Figure 22 shows the small signal modulation response of a typical laser diode. There is a resonant frequency f_r where the small signal gain increases to a maximum. The value of f_r can be expressed as (Iizuka 2003)

$$f_r = \frac{1}{2\pi\tau_s\tau_n}(I - I_{th})^{\frac{1}{2}} \qquad (49)$$

where τ_s is the photon lifetime in the cavity and τ_n is the electron (carrier) lifetime.

When the modulation frequency increases beyond f_r the output power drops rapidly. The bandwidth is larger for a higher ratio of signal current to threshold current, but the output is lowered as seen in Figure 22. For a wider bandwidth or faster modulation, it is important that the threshold current of the laser diode would be as low as possible.

One undesirable effect in the direct modulation method is *frequency chirping*, or changing of laser light

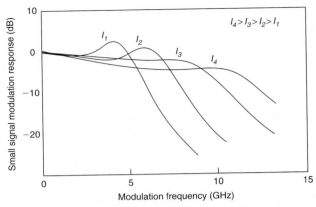

Figure 22: Small signal modulation response of a laser diode

frequency (carrier frequency) by the modulating signal. The frequency of the laser light changes at the rising and falling edges of the signal pulses when direct modulation is used. For the positive chirping parameter, the frequency of the laser decreases at the rising edge of the signal and increases at its falling edge (Li and Yu 2003). The laser frequency changes are opposite for negative chirping parameter. The signal pulse spectrum is broader than that without chirping. Chirping limits the bit rates and hence the performance of the optical communication system. (Refer to Agrawal 2002 for further reading on frequency chirping.)

To avoid frequency chirping, turn-on delay time, and transient effects encountered in direct modulation, *external modulation* schemes are used in bit rates higher than 2.5 Gbps. In the external modulation method, the laser source operates in the *continuous wave mode*—that is, the intensity of the source laser is kept constant by biasing at a constant current. The laser light is passed through an electro-absorption modulator or a LiNbO₃ electro-optic modulator (known as the *Mach-Zehnder modulator*) (Li and Yu 2003) placed next to the laser. When the electrical signal pulses are applied to the modulator, the applied electric field changes the refractive index of the modulator; hence, the intensity of the laser varies in accordance with the signal.

Distributed Feedback and Distributed Bragg Reflector Lasers

To get a single longitudinal mode laser diode, the distributed feedback method (Figure 23) is used for positive feedback instead of the FP resonator. As discussed earlier, the mode spacing Δv is small for a long cavity length L. Fabry-Perot laser diodes usually have longer than 100-μm cavity length, which leads to MLM lasing as the small signal gain curve is wider than the intermode spacing.

In a distributed feedback laser diode, a sinusoidal periodically varying refractive index grating known as a *Bragg grating* (Agrawal 2002) is grown in the guiding layer between the active layer and one of the cladding layers (Figure 24). The refractive index of the guiding layer

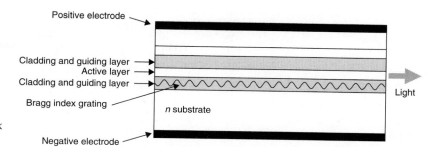

Figure 23: Cross-section of distributed feedback laser diode

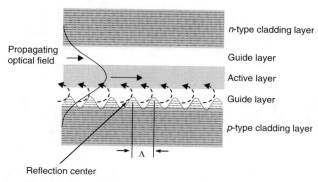

Figure 24: Active, cladding, and guiding layers and the index grating structure of a distributed feedback laser. A single-mode field propagating along the longitudinal direction and the reflected field are shown (Fukuda 1999)

is slightly lower than that of the active layer and higher than that of the cladding layer so that optical confinement is achieved by the slab waveguide structure. The grating next to the active layer reflects light back into the active layer. Each grating tooth acts as a reflection center. The intensity of the reflected light depends on the grating height and shape as well as on the distance between the grating and the active layer (Fukuda 1999).

The spatial periodicity (or *pitch*) Λ of the grating and the equivalent refractive index n_{eq} are the important parameters that are adjusted when fabricating the multilayer crystal to set the lasing wavelength λ of a DFB

laser. The Bragg mode wavelength λ_{Bm} is given as (Fukuda 1999)

$$2\bar{n}\Lambda = m\lambda_{Bm} \tag{50}$$

where $m = 0, 1, 2, \ldots$ is the order of reflection from the grating and $\bar{n}$ is the average equivalent refractive index of the multilayer medium in which the optical wave is propagating (Kogelink and Shank 1972).

The coupled wave theory of distributed feedback lasers indicates that their lasing frequency v of cavity length L is detuned from the Bragg frequency $v_{Bm} = c/\lambda_{Bm}$ and is derived as (Kogelnik and Shank 1972):

$$v = v_{Bm} \pm \Delta v \tag{51}$$

$$\Delta v = \frac{c}{2\bar{n}L}\left[\frac{1}{2} + \frac{1}{\pi}(Phase(\kappa))\right] \tag{52}$$

where κ is the coupling constant, which is a measure of the amount of feedback per unit length imparted by the Bragg grating. The phase of κ is zero for index coupling and $\pi/2$ for gain coupling (Kogelink and Shank 1972). Therefore, there are two lasing frequencies detuned on each side of v_{Bm} as shown in Figure 25. The range between lasing detuned frequencies is known as the *stop band*. For gain coupling $\Delta v = c/2\bar{n}L$, which is the same as cavity frequency mode spacing. Hence, there is a cavity resonance frequency at the Bragg frequency v_{Bm}, and there is no stop band.

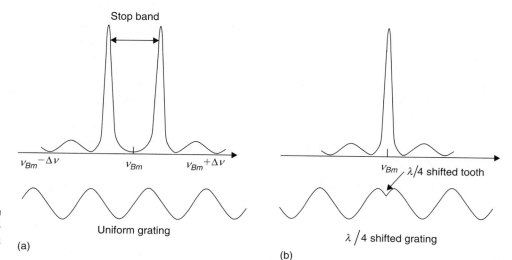

Figure 25: Spectra of (a) uniform grating DFB laser and (b) $\lambda/4$ shifted grating DFB laser (Fukuda 1999)

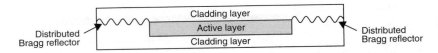

For a uniform grating, there are always two detuned cavity resonance frequencies, one on each side of the Bragg frequency as shown in Figure 25. This is undesirable, and to get a single frequency or a SLM laser, the reflected wave needs an additional phase shift of $\pi/2$ (equivalent to a $\lambda/4$ phase shift in wavelength).

There are several methods to obtain a $\lambda/4$ phase shift to tune the emission at Bragg frequency νBm. One method is to remove one-half of the pitch ($\Lambda/2$) of the grating tooth at the center of the grating as shown in Figure 25b. This is equivalent to $\lambda/4$ shift in wavelength. Such $\lambda/4$ phase-shifted DFB lasers operate in single longitudinal mode at Bragg frequency. Some of the methods employed for $\lambda/4$ shift include etching and adjusting height of the grating tooth at the center of the cavity, using $\lambda/4$ coating at one end of the cavity, and using multi-electrode phase control to select only one of the detuned frequency modes mentioned above (Iizuka 2002).

Gratings can also be grown in one or both the ends of the active layer, replacing the facet mirrors in forming the Fabry-Perot resonator as shown in Figure 26. In this configuration, the gratings are called *distributed reflectors* and the lasers with this configuration are called *distributed Bragg reflector* lasers.

Vertical-Cavity Surface-Emitting Laser

A *vertical-cavity surface-emitting laser* (VCSEL) is one solution for obtaining a single-mode laser with narrow linewidth. Surface-emitting lasers have several advanced properties compared to the edge-emitting type:

1. ease of fabrication with a large-scale integration method;
2. ability to be tested at the wafer level, thus reducing the manufacturing cost;
3. narrow far-field beam divergence with circular beam spot;
4. ability to be used at high bit-rate modulation (>10 Gbps);
5. high coupling efficiency to low numerical aperture fibers;
6. narrower spectral linewidth compared with edge-emitting laser diodes; and
7. low threshold current.

There are several types of surface-emitting lasers, some of which are vertical-cavity surface-emitting types, grating surface-emitting types, deflecting-mirror surface-emitting types, and two-dimension stack-array types. (Refer to Yang and Liang 2003 for further details on these types.)

The schematic diagram of an early type GaAlAs and GaAs VCSEL (Iga et al. 1984) is shown in Figure 27. The laser light is coupled out in the direction perpendicular to the junction plane instead of coupling out from one of

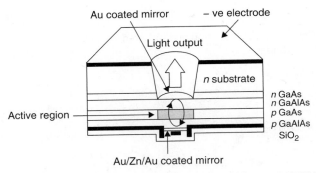

Figure 27: Vertical-cavity surface-emitting laser (VCSEL) (Iga et al. 1984)

the end facets. A mesa well is etched perpendicular to the active layer to couple out the laser light. The length of the vertical cavity is short (~7 µm), hence the mode spacing between two adjacent modes is larger than the gain bandwidth of the laser. Consequently, there exists only a single longitudinal mode in this type of vertical-cavity laser. The output beam has a circular distribution of light, and FWHM beam divergence angle is small (~10°). The lasing wavelength depends on the temperature of the laser diode, and the mode hopping occurs when the change in temperature is extremely high ($\Delta T \approx 800$ K) (Iga et al. 1984).

Later versions of VCSELs use two stacks of multilayer DBRs having from twenty to forty layers per stack, depending on required reflectivity and electrical resistance. Multilayer DBRs are grown on both sides of a thin active layer as shown in Figure 28. Each layer has an optical thickness nd (product of refractive index n and physical thickness d) equal to $\lambda/4$ and has alternating high and low refractive indexes. The reflectivity of this type of DBR is normally higher than 99.5 percent.

There are three types of DBRs used in VCSELs: dielectric, semiconductor, and hybrid. Dielectric DBRs are made of a stack of multilayer dielectrics such as SiO_2 and TiO_2. Semiconductor DBRs are built with a stack of multilayer semiconductors such as GaAs and AlAs. Hybrid type DBRs are constructed with a metal reflector as the outermost layer combined with semiconductor DBR or dielectric DBR. Hybrid type DBRs are not suitable for coupling out the laser because the metal layer has a zero transmission coefficient (Yang and Liang 2003). The two main functions of stacked DBRs are to form a vertical FP optical resonator and to provide a conduction path for the injection current to the active layer.

As noted earlier, electrons have a wave-particle dual nature in quantum mechanics. A moving electron (a particle) has a momentum p and associated wavelength of $\lambda = h/p$ that is known as the *de Broglie wavelength* (Milonni and Eberly 1988). The thickness of the active

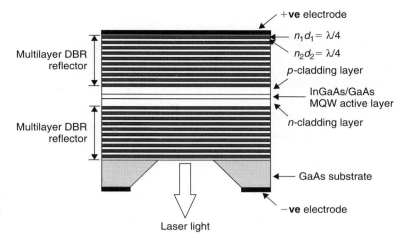

Figure 28: Bottom-emitting VCSEL with etched well in the GaAs substrate for coupling out the light from the bottom

layer in a VCSEL is less than the de Broglie wavelength of the electron. In VCSEL DBR lasers, the thin active layer becomes a *multiquantum well* (MQW) active layer, and the electrons are confined in quantum wells that are each less than the de Broglie wavelength of electrons. The optical gain of a MQW active layer is extremely high and the loss is extremely low (Yang and Liang 2003). Consequently, the threshold current is especially low and the spectral linewidth is especially narrow for a VSCEL. This low threshold current contributes to higher modulation bandwidth. Narrow linewidth, single longitudinal mode lasers are widely used in dispersion-limited, long-haul fiber links.

VCSELs are available for different wavelengths from 650 nm to 1550 nm. The 850 nm VCSELs are the most widely used sources in local area networks and data transfers because of their low cost.

Readers can refer to Suhara (2004) for more information on quantum well structures and stimulated emission in them.

TUNABLE LASER DIODES

In dense wavelength-division multiplexed optical communication systems, sixteen or thirty-two multiplexed channels are normally used. In such applications, tunable lasers are a good alternative to reduce cost. Furthermore, tunable lasers are useful in optical sensing and optical measurements such as reflectometry and optical spectrometry where the tunability of laser wavelengths is an important factor for the applications.

Referring to the Bragg grating equation

$$2\bar{n}\Lambda = \lambda$$

the laser wavelength depends on the average refractive index of the semiconductor material. The basic principle applied for wavelength tuning in laser diodes is to change the refractive index of the active layer and the Bragg grating by varying the carrier injection current.

There are two ways to change the refractive index of the laser diode: (1) change the injection current to vary the refractive index of the DBR or DFB laser diodes and (2) control the temperature of the laser diodes to change the temperature-dependent band-gap energy and the refractive index.

The temperature-control method for tuning can be done by a simple external thermoelectric controller, and it is suitable for sensing and measurements. Injection current tuning is more suitable for applications in communication systems in the wavelength band of 1300–1550 nm.

There are three tuning modes, depending on the structure of the laser diode: (1) discontinuous tuning, (2) continuous tuning, and (3) quasi-continuous tuning. Spectral linewidth and single longitudinal mode lasing need to be sustained throughout the tuning process.

Discontinuous Tuning

In discontinuous tuning, after a narrow tuning range, the wavelength hops suddenly from one longitudinal mode to an adjacent shorter wavelength mode as the tuning current is increased (see Figure 29). At the same time, the overall tuning range achievable is approximately 100 nm.

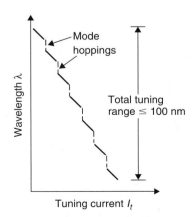

Figure 29: Discontinuous tuning characteristic in a two-section DBR or DFB laser

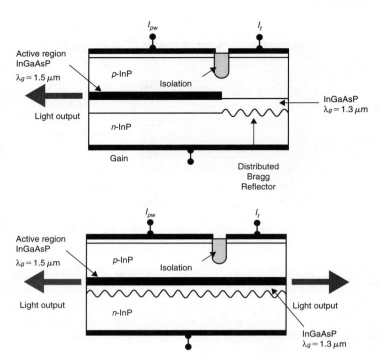

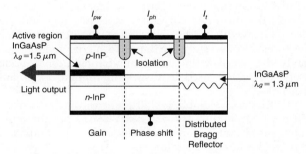

Figure 30: Longitudinally integrated two-section tunable (a) DBR laser and (b) DFB laser

Longitudinally integrated two-section DBR or DFB lasers, shown schematically in Figure 30, are the simplest structures used for discontinuous tuning.

Here I_{pw} is the power control injection current, and I_t is the wavelength tuning control current. Wavelength tuning is carried out by applying different tuning bias current I_t that changes the refractive index of the DBR or DFB section so that it tunes from one mode to another. The wavelength also depends on the output power control current I_{pw} because the varying output power can induce temperature deviations and hence changes of cavity length. Consequently, there is no single independent control for tuning wavelength in laser diodes.

Continuous Wavelength Tuning

In continuous tuning, the wavelength is adjusted in extremely small steps within the spectral width of the lasing main longitudinal mode under the gain curve $g(\nu)$ without

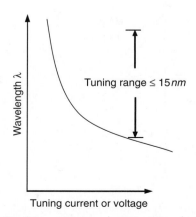

Figure 31: Continuous tuning characteristic of a laser diode

Figure 32: Longitudinally integrated three-section tunable DBR laser (Buus et al. 2005)

changing the mode (see Figure 31). All of the parameters apart from the tuning control current or voltage must be kept constant to ensure the stability of the single longitudinal mode as well as to ensure that the side-mode suppression ratio is above an acceptable value (>30 dB). The tuning range is narrowest (≤ 15 nm) among the three tuning modes (Buus, Amann, and Blumental 2005).

One of the methods for achieving continuous tuning is to use longitudinally integrated three-section DBR as shown in Figure 32. A phase shifter electrode I_{ph} that controls the phase shift of the propagating wave in the active layer is added. Simultaneous adjustment of I_{ph} and I_t enables the user to tune the wavelength continuously within a longitudinal mode. However, the wavelength also depends on the power. Changing the injection current I_{pw} for power adjustment would also change the wavelength. Thus, I_{pw} is usually kept constant when adjusting the phase control current I_{ph} and tuning control current I_t for the desired wavelength in one of the lasing modes as shown in Figure 33.

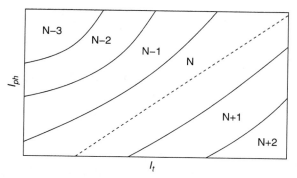

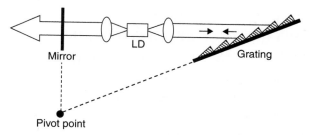

Figure 35: Two-sided external cavity tunable diode laser. Both facets of the laser diode are AR-coated

Figure 33: I_{ph} versus I_t plot for operation of selected longitudinal modes. Continuous tuning is achieved by adjusting I_{ph} and I_t so that these currents stay inside a pair of mode boundaries (solid lines) at which the mode hopping occurs. Dashed line indicates one possible trace of I_{ph} and I_t that fall in single mode N (Yang and Liang 2003)

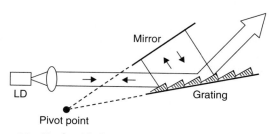

Figure 36: Single-sided external cavity tunable laser. Only one facet facing the external cavity is AR-coated

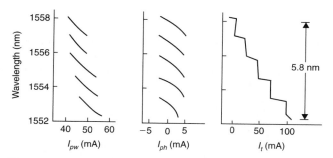

Figure 34: Quasi-continuous tuning characteristics by each of I_{pw}, I_{ph}, and I_t of three-section tunable DBR lasers (Yang and Liang 2003)

Quasi-Continuous Wavelength Tuning

The longitudinal, integrated three-section lasers shown in Figure 32 can also be used in a quasi-continuous tuning mode. The laser output power control current I_{pw} induces temperature change in the laser diode, which leads to the change of emission wavelength. As a result, all three control currents I_{pw}, I_{ph}, and I_t affect the emission wavelength of the laser diode as shown in Figure 34.

Highly precise and sophisticated devices are used to control the tuning so that mode jumping and instabilities are prevented. (Refer to Buus, Amann, and Blumenthal 2005 for details on tunable laser diodes.)

External Cavity Tunable Laser Diodes

Tunable external cavity laser diodes can be employed as an alternative to tunable monolithic laser diodes. However, their tuning speed is slow because of the mechanical movements of gratings and mirrors that are involved in the tuning arrangement.

In an external cavity laser diode, the resonant cavity consists of the diode, which is the gain medium as well as a part of the cavity, and an external cavity for tuning. An extended external cavity is incorporated using a movable grating and a mirror. Gratings and mirrors of extremely small dimensions, the *micro-electromechanical system*, are also used in external cavity tuning. Two examples of the arrangement of tunable external cavity laser diodes are shown in Figures 35 and 36.

In the two-sided external cavity design as shown in Figure 35, the extended cavity, on each side of the *antireflection* (AR) coated laser diode, provides positive feedback. Wavelength selection is achieved by rotating the grating.

Figure 36 shows the single-sided external cavity design that is most commonly used because it has the following advantages: (1) It needs only one AR-coated facet; (2) the arrangement is simple, and it is easy to align the system; and (3) it has excellent performance (Ye 2004).

A continuous, single-mode wavelength tuning without mode hopping over a wide frequency range was obtained by rotating the grating at the pivot point at the intersection of the mirror and grating planes (Levin 2002; Schremer and Tang 1990). The linewidth of external cavity tunable laser sources are narrow (~15 kHz) (Ip et al. 2005).

In addition to the laser diodes discussed above, there are other types of lasers implemented in quite different ways such as quantum cascaded lasers and photonic band-gap lasers. Readers can refer to Lucent Technologies (2000) for more information on quantum cascaded lasers and Nikbin (2006) for photonic band-gap lasers.

OPTICAL DISPERSION AND OPTICAL RESOLUTION IN DATA COMMUNICATION AND STORAGE SYSTEMS

Bit-Rate Distance Product in Optical Communications

In optical communication terms, *dispersion* is the spreading of pulses as they propagate through the optical fiber. A rectangular pulse train consists of a fundamental frequency and higher harmonic frequencies. Different frequency groups propagate with different speeds as well as with different paths in the fiber. A pulse with an initial width of T will have a broadened width of $T + \Delta T$ after propagating through a length of L in the fiber. The dispersion or the spreading of pulse ΔT is proportional to the propagating length L and the modulated source linewidth (in root mean squared value) $\Delta \lambda_s$, and it is given as (Agrawal 2002)

$$\Delta T = |D| L \, \Delta \lambda_s \qquad (53)$$

where D is the chromatic dispersion constant, which is the sum of waveguide and material dispersion constants. D is expressed in practical unit of ps/(km-nm), L in km, and $\Delta \lambda_s$ in nm.

The often-used criterion (Agrawal 2002) is that the dispersion ΔT should be less than or equal to one-quarter of the bit period $T_B = \dfrac{1}{B}$, that is

$$|D| L \, \Delta \lambda_s \le \frac{1}{4B} \qquad (54)$$

where B is the bit rate.

In designing a fiber link while taking into account the dispersion and bit rate, this criterion is often stated as the bit-rate distance product:

$$BL \le \frac{1}{4|D|\Delta \lambda_s} \qquad (55)$$

The bit-rate limitation depends especially on source linewidth. For optical sources with extremely narrow laser linewidths, the bit-rate distance product is derived as (Agrawal 2002)

$$B\sqrt{L} = \frac{1}{4\sqrt{\beta_2}} \qquad (56)$$

where $\beta_2 = \dfrac{\partial^2 \beta}{\partial \omega^2}$ is called the *group velocity dispersion* parameter, and β is the *propagation factor*, which depends on the angular frequency ω of the laser light propagating in the fiber.

Usually, Equation (55) is applied to estimate the probable distance if the bit rate is known. Other factors such as power budget, rise time budget, and so on must be taken into account in determining a fiber link distance at a specified bit rate. For a long-haul fiber link

at high bit rates, laser sources with smaller linewidth $\Delta \lambda_s$ (single-mode lasers) such as DFB and DBR lasers have better performance and have been widely used.

Optical Resolution and Blue Laser Diodes for Data Storage Systems

Beside their use in data communication systems, laser diodes have found wide application in data storage devices such as various optical disks and relevant systems.

The image of a focused uniform beam consists of concentric circular rings known as *Airy's disk* (Hecht 2002) as shown in Figure 37.

The circular spot at the center is brightest, and the intensity of the rings increasingly fades while progressing outward.

The images of two closely spaced spots can be resolved only when the centers of the spots are separated by at least the radius of the central spot. This is known as the *Rayleigh criterion*. The radius of the center spot is given as (Hecht 2002):

$$r = \frac{0.61\lambda}{NA} \qquad (57)$$

Here $NA = n \sin\theta$ is the numerical aperture of the lens used for focusing the spot as shown in Figure 38.

The spacing between two adjacent tracks on an optical data storage disk should be lager than or at least equal to r so that the *pickup head* reads the data without an error. The total data storage capacity on the disk depends on the resolution distance r, which in turn is a function of source wavelength λ and NA. The NA used in a compact disk lens is 0.45 (Pohlmann 1992; Rilum 2000). Currently, laser diodes in infrared region of wavelength 700–780 nm are used in an optical compact disk ROM.

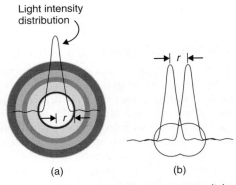

Figure 37: Focused spot of light forming Airy's disks because of the diffraction of light from (a) a circular aperture and (b) two closely placed spots at resolution limit r

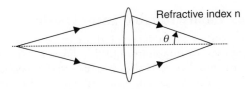

Figure 38: Numerical aperture (at the focusing side) = $n \sin\theta$

As an example, consider a laser diode with a 780-nm emission wavelength used in CD players for recording. The *NA* of the lens is 0.45 and hence, using the Rayleigh criterion, the resolvable distance of writing with a 780-nm laser is 1.06 µm; and for an 830-nm laser, the resolvable distance is 1.13 µm. The standard distance between the adjacent tracks on a CD is 1.6 µm, which is larger than the minimum resolvable distance of 780 nm and 830 nm between the tracks.

To increase data storage capacity, shorter wavelength laser diodes emitting wavelengths in the blue region around 400 nm or shorter are required. Blue laser diodes are made of GaN-based materials such as InGaN, which emits in the wavelength range of 200 nm to 600nm (Table 1). The blue laser diodes have great potential application for increasing the capacity of optical data storage. By using 405-nm blue laser diodes, the storage capacity can be increased by a factor of 2.6 times that of a *digital video discs* (Rilum 2000). Currently, 405-nm VCSEL diodes are available, but their price is still high for use in optical data reading and writing.

CONCLUSION

This chapter presents optical sources that are widely used in various devices and systems related to the field of computer communications, networking, and data storage. The main attention is given to the "workhorses" in the field: light-emitting diodes and laser diodes (fixed wavelength and tunable types). The chapter provides substantial overview of the theoretical foundations of the optical sources technology as well as discusses the technical implementations, benefits, disadvantages, and applications of the sources.

The current fast pace of the technological development in computer engineering and communications implies that new and more efficient optical sources will appear on the stage in the near future. This will lead to significant improvements in characteristics and functionality of existing devices and the systems employed in computer networking as well as to the development, practical implementation, and applications of devices and systems belonging to new generations of computer and data communications technology. For example, the notion of optical computing for many years has been deeply rooted in the scientific and engineering community. There are signs that practical optical computer systems may finally be realized in the near future. Optical computers would use sources with high direct-modulation rates to eliminate the requirement of external modulators, thus leading to the reduction of the optical source components.

Another good example where the progress in optical sources leads to serious advancement in a wide range of areas is the emergence of the commercial GaN blue laser diodes. As a result, the development and implementation of a new generation of high-density digital data storage systems, high-resolution laser printers, medical equipment, and so on is becoming a reality.

Intensive theoretical and applied research in the field of optical sources is currently under way in different countries carried out by a large number of scientists and engineers. For example, substantial efforts by a number of research teams are currently focused on improving such characteristics of tunable laser diodes as output power, repeatability of the tuning range and wavelength, temperature stability, and easiness of tuning, among others.

GLOSSARY

Active layer: The area between two hetero-junctions where the electron-hole recombination and radiation (light) emission takes place inside a laser diode or a light-emitting diode.

Bragg grating: The perturbation of the effective refractive index inside a fiber or inside a laser diode where the reflection of optical wave takes place. The Bragg condition for the reflection grating is $d(\sin\theta_m - \sin\theta_i) = m\lambda$, where d is the spatial period or pitch of the grating, θ_m is the mth order ($m = 0, 1, 2, \ldots$) reflection angle, θ_i is the incident angle, and λ is the wavelength. θ_m and θ_i are measured from the normal to the plane of the grating. In most cases for waves propagating inside *distributed Bragg reflector* (DBR) or *distributed feedback* (DFB) laser diodes, $\theta_i \approx 90°$ and the Bragg condition becomes $d\sin\theta_m = m\lambda$.

Carrier lifetime: The time taken for the electrons in the conduction band to reduce to $\frac{1}{e}$ of the initial electron number because of the recombination process.

Digital video disc (DVD): Optical data storage disk on which high-density data such as movies with high-quality video and sound data can be recorded.

Fresnel equation: The mathematical expression describing the power reflectivity or reflectance R of an interface between two optical media with refractive indices n_1 and n_2, respectively, for a perpendicular incident ray as $R = \left[\dfrac{n_1 - n_2}{n_1 + n_2}\right]^2$.

Group velocity dispersion: Pulse scattering while propagating in the fiber. The group velocity (i.e., velocity with which the intensity maximum propagates in a medium) of a pulse in a fiber depends on frequency. Thus, different spectral components of the pulse travel at different velocities and the pulse is dispersed as it is propagating in the fiber.

Hetero-junction: Junction between two different types of semiconductor materials—for example, the junction between InGaAsP and InP.

Homo-junction: Junction between two semiconductor materials of the same type but differently doped, such as the junction between P-type silicon and N-type silicon.

Junction capacitance: Resultant capacitance from the accumulation of minority carriers (electrons) in the P-type and (holes) in the N-type in the depletion region of a P-N junction.

Peltier effect: The phenomenon of heat transfer between two different metal junctions or two dissimilar semiconductor junctions when a current passes through them. The heat in one junction is carried away by the current and transferred to the other junction. This results in cooling of one junction and heating of the other.

Photon lifetime: The period of time (τ_p) during which the number of photons in a laser cavity decays to $\frac{1}{e}$ or 36.8 percent of the initial photon number after the pumping is stopped. If the initial number of photons in a laser cavity is $N_p(0)$, then the number of photons at time t after the pumping is stopped can be expressed as $N_p(t) = N_p(0)\exp(-\frac{t}{\tau_p})$, where τ_p is the photon lifetime in the cavity.

CROSS REFERENCES

See *Fiberoptic Filters and Multiplexers; Optical Fiber Communications; Optical Transmitters, Receivers, and Noise.*

REFERENCES

Agrawal, G. V. 2002. *Fiber-optic communication systems.* 3rd ed. New York: John Wiley & Sons.

Botez, D., and M. Ettenberg. 1979. Comparison of surface and edge-emitting LED's for use in fiber-optical communications. *IEEE Transactions on Electron Devices*, 26(8): 1230–8.

Burrus, C. A., and B. I. Miller. 1971. Small-area, double-heterostructure aluminum-gallium arsenide electroluminescent diode sources for optical-fiber transmission lines. *Optics Communications*, 4: 307–9.

Buus, J., M.-C. Amann, and D. J. Blumenthal. 2005. *Tunable laser diodes and related optical sources.* 2nd ed. New York: John Wiley & Sons.

Fritz, M. 1996. Digital video discs: Compact discs on steroids. *Wired Magazine* (retrieved from http://www.wired.com/wired/archive/4.07/geek.html).

Fukuda, M. 1999. *Optical semiconductor devices.* New York: John Wiley & Sons.

Godfrey, S. 1996. *An introduction to thermoelectric coolers.* Melcor Corporation (retrieved from http://electronics-cooling.com/Resources/EC_Articles/SEP96/sep96_04.htm).

Hecht, E. 2002. *Optics.* 4th ed. New York: Addison Wesley.

Henry, C. H. 1982. Theory of the linewidth of semiconductor lasers. *IEEE Journal of Quantum Electronics*, 8(2): 259–26.

———. 1983. Theory of the phase noise and power spectrum of a single mode injection laser. *IEEE Journal of Quantum Electronics*, 19(9): 1391–7.

Iga, K., S. Ishikawa, S. Ohkouchi, and T. Nishimura. 1984. Room temperature pulsed oscillation of GAAlAs/GaAs surface emitting injection laser. *Applied Physics Letters*, 45(4): 348–50.

Iizuka, K. 2002. Transmitters. Chap. 14 in *Elements of photonics*, Vol. 2, 893–1016. New York: John Wiley & Sons.

Ip, E., J. M. Kahn, D. Anthon, and J. Hutchins. 2005. Linewidth measurements of MEMS-based tunable lasers for phase-locking applications. *IEEE Photonics Technology Letters*, 17(10): 2029–31.

Kapon, E. 1999. *Semiconductor lasers II: Materials and structures.* San Diego: Academic Press.

Kasap, S. O. 2002. *Principles of electronic materials and devices.* 2nd ed. New York: McGraw-Hill.

Kogelnik, H., and V. Ramaswamy. 1974. Scaling rules for thin film optical waveguides. *Applied Optics*, 13(8): 1857–62.

Kogelnik, H., and C. V. Shank. 1972. Couple-wave theory of distributed feedback lasers. *Journal of Applied Physics*, 43(5): 2327–35.

Levin, L. 2002. Mode-hop-free electro-optically tuned diode laser. *Optics Letters*, 27(4): 237–9.

Li, G. L., and P. K. L. Yu. 2003. Wide-bandwidth optical intensity modulators. In *Handbook of optical components and engineering*, edited by K. Chang, 1009–78. New York: John Wiley & Sons.

Lucent Technologies. 2000. Quantum cascade laser. Bell Labs Innovations, Physical Sciences Research (retrieved from www.bell-labs.com/org/physicalsciences/projects/qcl/qcl.html).

Milonni, P. W., and J. H. Eberly. 1988. *Lasers.* New York: John Wiley & Sons.

Nahory, R. E., M. A. Pollack, W. D. Johnston Jr., and R. L. Barns. 1978. Bandgap versus composition and demonstration of Vegards's law for In1-xGaxAsyP1-y lattice matched to InP. *Applied Physics Letters*, 33: 659–61.

Nakamura, S., S. Pearton, and G. Fasol. 2000. *The blue laser diode: The complete story.* Berlin: Springer-Verlag.

Nikbin, D. 2006. Fiber laser emits light radially (retrieved from http://optics.org/optics/Articles/ViewArticle.do;jsessionid=DBF1A07A639CBE19F44A0570B40E4265?channel=technology&articleId=25048&page=1).

Pearsall, T. P. 2003. *Photonics essentials: An introduction with experiments.* New York: McGraw-Hill.

Pohlmann, K. C. 1992. *The compact disc handbook.* Madison, WI: A-R Editions.

Rilum, J. H. 2000. *Mastering beyond DVD densities 2000.* Optical Disc Corporation Nimbus: Mastering the Next Generation (retrieved from www.optical-disc.com/techpapers/MasteringBeyondDVDDensities.pdf).

Schremer, A. T., and C. L. Tang. 1990. External-cavity semiconductor laser with 1000 GHz continuous piezoelectric tuning range. *IEEE Photonic Technology Letters*, 2(1): 3–5.

Singh, J. 2003. *Electronic and optoelectronic properties of semiconductor structures.* Cambridge, England: Cambridge University Press.

Smalley, E. 2002. LED fires one photon at a time. *Technology Research News* (retrieved from www.trnmag.com/Stories/2001/121901/LED_fires_one_photon_at_a_time_121901.html).

Suhara, T. 2004. *Semiconductor laser fundamentals.* Boca Raton, FL: CRC Press.

Verdeyen, J. T. 1995. *Laser electronics.* 3rd ed. Upper Saddle River, NJ: Prentice Hall.

Yang, J. J., and B. W. Liang. 2003. Semiconductor lasers. In *Handbook of optical components and engineering*, edited by K. Chang, 239–368. New York: John Wiley & Sons.

Ye, C. 2004. *Tunable external cavity diode lasers.* Singapore: World Scientific Publishing.

Yuan, Z., B. E. Kardynal, R. M. Stevenson, A. J. Shields, C. J. Lobo, K. Cooper, N. S. Beattie, D. A. Ritchie, and M. Pepper. 2002. Single-photon source. *Science*, 295: 102–5.

Lambda and Sub-Lambda Switching

Mario Baldi, *Politecnico di Torino, Italy*
Yoram Ofek, *University of Trento, Italy*

INTRODUCTION

Optical switching in the form of whole optical channel or *lambda* (λ) *switching*—that is, a network node switching to one specific output all of the data units of coming in on an optical channel—is well understood. However, the problem of switching fractions of the optical channel (also known as *sub-lambda switching*)—that is, a network node selectively switching to different outputs all of the subsets of the data units of an incoming optical channel—is more challenging and much less understood. Having the capability for sub-lambda switching would result in two basic advantages: (1) efficient use of switching and transmission capacities and (2) extension of the optical network all the way to the edges. Consequently, the two advantages have the potential to provide a major reduction in the overall optical network cost. However, technological challenges remain in realizing sub-lambda switching. This chapter presents and analyzes some of the possible solutions while assessing complexity, scalability, and cost.

To set the context and scope of this chapter, the following assumptions are made regarding sub-lambda switching.

1. No segmentation: Data packets of variable size are switched as a whole.
2. No "stopping" of the serial bit stream: Signals carrying data packets are switched at least once without being digitized—that is, without explicitly decoding and buffering the data packet in the electronic domain. In other words, bits flow continuously in either the optical or electrical domains.

The discussion on sub-lambda switching involves two basic topologies.

1. Linear topology networks: rings or buses in which data packets are possibly removed by their destinations—that is, spatial bandwidth reuse is deployed.
2. Mesh (arbitrary) topology networks.

It is assumed that both topologies form an undirected graph, which implies that data packet transmission is possible in both directions. Because data networks are interconnected to one another, the linear topology network has diminishing importance; therefore, the main emphasis of this chapter is on mesh topology networks.

The main benefit and therefore the motivation for sub-lambda switching are to save on the "expensive" operation of converting: (1) from electronic-to-optical and (2) from optical-to-electronic. However, several challenges must be considered and analyzed in depth to fully appreciate sub-λ switching. The main focus of this chapter is to examine various solutions to those challenges. The following are some of the challenges for sub-lambda switching in the optical domain:

1. Header decoding and processing.
2. Buffering or memory for storing data packets.
3. Speedup of memory access and switch fabric. Assuming that the speed of light is constant, in the optical domain (sub-lambda switching) speedup is always 1—that is, no speedup is possible.
4. Switch control and arbitration—that is, deciding which of multiple packets to forward through the switch to the same output port (also termed a many-to-one problem: from many input ports to one output port).

The main motivation for optical technology has been to solve bottleneck problems: transmission and switching.

Although transmission bottleneck was solved with *wavelength-division multiplexing* (WDM), solutions to the switching bottleneck are still undergoing research and development. Note that relying on overprovisioning to solve other networking problems such as delay and loss will inevitably worsen the switching bottleneck problem.

> Definition 1: Sub-lambda switching. Each data unit is transmitted through optical fibers and switches—without any "stopping" of the serial bit stream–such that each data unit on a given optical channel may be treated differently by network switches.

Regarding *synchronous optical network* (SONET) in the optical domain, the following should be noted. SONET uses only frequency (or clock) synchronization with known bounds on clock and frequency drifts. To overcome possible data loss resulting from clock drifts, SONET uses complex overhead information to accommodate: (1) the accumulation of various delay uncertainties or jitter and (2) the continuous clock drifts from a nominal value. The SONET solution is a sophisticated forwarding of one-byte data units that are transported in time slots (TS). The TS duration in 10 Gb/s is less than one nanosecond. Consequently, it is not possible to realize the sophisticated SONET operation in the optical domain. Therefore, SONET is outside the scope of this chapter.

In the past decade, there has been significant progress in optical switching but further major improvements are still required as discussed in the next major section. As discussed later in "Whole Lambda Switching," mapping the current model of asynchronous packet switching to sub-lambda switching is significantly more complicated than whole lambda switching. Asynchronous packet switching is based on four components: (1) transmission, (2) memory, (3) processing, and (4) switching. To achieve optical networking, all four components should be implemented in the optical domain. As summarized in Table 1, optical transmission is widely deployed, optical switching is commercially viable, optical processing is still difficult, and optical memory using optical fibers is feasible and well understood. However, as discussed later, optical memory is a major implementation obstacle that hinders the realization of optical asynchronous packet switching.

Given the scalability limitations of whole lambda switching soon to be discussed and the technical challenges of asynchronous sub-lambda switching as discussed in later sections, a novel synchronous sub-lambda switching is presented in "Synchronous Sub-Lambda Switching." Finally, the conclusion summarizes this chapter and indicates future directions.

OPTICAL SWITCHING TECHNOLOGIES

The problem of switching, whatever the switched data unit is, can be broadly split into two parts: (1) the actions performed on data units in order to actually move them, which take place in the data plane; and (2) the logic behind it—that is, when and where data units should be moved through the switch, which is the responsibility of the control plane. Although the latter will be the focus of the next sections, below we survey existing solutions for the former in the optical domain—that is, where optical signals are moved from inputs to outputs.

Various technologies are currently available for switching optical signals, and they differ significantly according to various criteria. The main optical switching performance indexes are listed below in order to set a comparison framework before we survey the most popular switching technologies and evaluate them on the basis of the features that are most significant in the context set for this chapter. A more general but high-level and schematic comparison of switching technologies can be found in Ma and Kuo (2003), which also includes summary comparison tables.

Optical Switching Performance Indexes

The following indexes are used to assess optical switching performance.

- *Switching speed*: The time required to change input-output interconnections through a switch. This performance index is particularly critical when implementing sub-lambda switching because, as Definition 1 shows, the switch configuration needs to be changed between data units traveling on the same input optical channel and being switched onto different output optical channels. The lower the switching speed (i.e., the longer the time required to change the switch configuration), the longer the time distance between two subsequent data units and the lower the network throughput.

- *Bit-rate transparency*: Solutions that are transparent to the encoding of information transmitted on an optical channel provide more flexibility and breadth of use.

- *Insertion loss*: The power lost by an optical signal traversing a switch. Low insertion loss is key when signal regeneration should be avoided, which is important, for example, in limiting costs and safeguarding bit-rate transparency.

- *Power equalization*: Deals with the insertion loss changing along different routes (paths) inside the optical switch. This difference should be minimized when the switching pattern (i.e., input ports to output ports interconnection) is changing dynamically.

Table 1: Comparison of Whole λ versus Sub-λ Switching

	Optical Transmission	Optical Memory	Optical Switching	Optical Processing
Whole λ switching	WDM	Not needed	Solutions exist	Not needed
Sub-λ switching	WDM	Solutions exist (sophisticated)	Solutions exist (fewer)	Practical solution needed

- *Cross talk*: The signal interference between channels measured as the ratio of the power leaked to wrong outputs and the power conveyed to the correct output.
- *Polarization sensitivity*: A measure of polarization dependence.
- *Wavelength dependency*: Provides a measurement of how switch properties depend on the wavelength of optical channels being switched. Low wavelength dependency enlarges the deployment potential of a switch.
- *Multicast*: The capability of replicating an input optical signal to various outputs is desirable when multicasting services are to be implemented in the network.
- *Equipment dimensions*: As telecom equipment is usually installed in controlled environments of limited dimensions where space is a valuable resource and real estate is rented out on the basis of the footprint of equipment, their physical dimensions is a major concern as larger equipment imply higher operation cost.
- *Scalability*: As stated above, the main motivation for optical switching is the realization of large-scale, broadband communication infrastructures. The availability of switching elements with a large number of ports to be used as building blocks reduces the complexity of realizing large scale switches featuring (tens of) thousands of inputs and outputs.
- *Nonblocking operation*: Deals with the flexibility to interconnect any input to any idle output. Given that, as discussed later, optical memory is a delicate issue, optical switches need to be strictly nonblocking.
- *Power consumption*: Extremely important because it is connected to several types of costs, including
  - a proper power supply system,
  - the complex design of heat dissipation in the switching system,
  - the large amount of electrical power needed by the switching system,
  - the complex design of heat dissipation in the environment in which many units may be operating, and
  - the large amount of electrical power used by the air conditioning system for the environment in which possibly multiple units are operating.

Optical Switching Technology Overview

Among the various existing optical switching technologies, the ones based on the deployment of *micro electromechanical systems* (MEMS) (De Dobbelaere et al. 2002) are probably among the most mature, best understood, and most sensible from the economical and industrial viewpoints. In general, this solution is based on miniature devices with optical properties (e.g., mirrors, membranes, and waveguides) that perform mechanical actions in response to an electrical stimulus. A popular example is given by switches consisting of two- or three-dimensional arrays of micro mirrors that can be tilted by an electrical field to insert them or exclude them from the path of a light signal. The selection of the specific mirror within an array to reflect the signal determines the output port for the signal.

Common properties of MEMS switches are low cost, sensitivity to vibrations (because of the presence of moving parts), high driving voltages, and high power consumption. Other performance indexes depend significantly on the specific technological solution. For example, switches based on mirrors or other electrostatic actuators have especially low insertion loss and cross talk, but the switching speed is on the order of milliseconds, thus making them unsuitable for sub-lambda switching. On the other hand, planar waveguide switches based on *silicon on insulator* (SOI) (Ollier 2002) are characterized by switching speeds on the order of tens of nanoseconds. However, only small SOI switching elements (1×2, 2×2, or $1 \times N$) are currently manufactured and can be used for realizing small scale switches, such as optical add-drop multiplexers. Instead, large size mirror-based switching elements are available (e.g., 512×512) whose scalability is limited by their own structure: the number of tilting mirrors required to build two- and three-dimensional arrays grows with the square and cube, respectively, of the number of inlets.

Thermo-optic switches are based on thermal phenomena of materials that can be exploited in various ways. Planar light-wave circuit technology leverages on the waveguide thermo-optic effect (Kasahara et al. 2002) and is being used in both digital optical switches and interferometric switches. Other kinds of thermo-optic switches are based on thermocapillarity (Sakata et al. 2001), thermally generated bubbles, and coated microsphere resonators (Tapalian, Laine, and Lane 2002). The size of commercially available switching elements varies significantly, depending on the specific technology. For example, 1×2 switches are built using coated microsphere resonators, whereas switching elements based on thermocapillarity can have a large number of inlets and outlets. In general, thermo-optic switches are characterized by low switching speed as the switch reconfiguration time ranges from a millisecond to tens of milliseconds.

Faster switching speeds, ranging from fractions of nanoseconds to tens of nanoseconds, are offered by *electro-optical switches*. The oldest optical switching solutions belong to this category and are based on the electro-optic properties of lithium niobate ($LiNbO_3$) and on *semiconductor optical amplifiers* (SOA). The former can lead to the implementation of either optical couplers based on interference or digital optical switches whose steplike response depends on the applied voltage (Krähenbühl et al. 2002). A more recent version of digital optical switch is based on lead lanthanum zirconium titanate, which leads to devices with especially good overall performance because of a higher electro-optic coefficient than $LiNbO_3$ (Nashimoto et al. 2001).

Although the first realizations of SOA-based switches (Gallep and Conforti 2002) used optical amplifiers as gates controlled by their bias current, more recent ones are based on Mach-Zehnder interferometers or multimode interference couplers (Earnshaw and Allsopp 2002).

Liquid crystal switches deploy an electro-optic effect to control the polarization of light (Riza and Yuan 1998). Having an electro-optic coefficient much higher than $LiNbO_3$, liquid crystal is one of the most efficient electro-optic materials. However, this kind of switch is characterized by switching speeds on the order of milliseconds. Electroholographic optical switches (Pesach et al. 2000), which are based on controlling the reconstruction of holograms by applying an electric field, feature nanosecond level switching speeds, but require extremely high voltages, which are impractical and expensive. Finally, electronically switchable waveguide Bragg gratings switches (Domash et al. 1997) are a combination of liquid crystal and electroholographic switches.

Acousto-optic switches exploit the properties of crystals such as tellurium dioxide (TeO$_2$) to enable ultrasonic waves to deflect light that traverses them (Enguang, Deming, and Ansh 2000). This technology is currently deployed to manufacture small size switches (e.g., 1×2) with submicrosecond switching speed.

Opto-optical switches exploit nonlinear optic effects in optical waveguides such as two-photon absorption, lightwave self-action, and the Kerr effect to obtain switching functions. Opto-optical switching technologies are still fairly immature and consequently not especially attractive for the near future.

WHOLE LAMBDA SWITCHING

Before we delve into sub-lambda switching, we discuss the advantages and shortcomings of *whole lambda switching* (WλS), another type of optical switching. This can be used as a baseline in the evaluation of benefits and limitations of the various flavors of sub-lambda switching presented in the reminder of this chapter

> Definition 2: Whole lambda switching. All data packets are transmitted through optical fibers and switches such that all data units on a given optical channel are treated the same way by network switches that may not digitize the optical signal carrying them.

Clearly, whole lambda switching represents a more significant paradigm change from current packet and circuit switching than sub-lambda switching does. However, because of its coarse switching granularity, no major technological challenge hampers the implementation and large-scale deployment of whole lambda switching; this is not the case for sub-lambda switching, as summarized by Table 1.

Whole lambda switching aims to create an optical channel between ingress point and egress point to the network such that data units transmitted at the ingress point reach the egress point through a number of optical switches. As switch input-output interconnections are modified only as a result of a provisioning or fault recovery action, a switch controller deployed in whole lambda switching is basically static. Consequently, switch reconfiguration occurs on a long time scale, and any of the various optical switch technologies and architectures presented in the previous section is suitable to whole lambda switching.

Similarly, a data source or a data destination changes optical channel only for provisioning or for fault recovery purposes. Consequently, optical transmitters and receivers with tuning time on the order of milliseconds can be deployed.

The main shortcoming of whole lambda switching stems from its coarse switching granularity. In particular, whole lambda switching suffers a major *scalability* problem because it requires a dedicated optical channel between each pair of access points and egress points. Consequently, when a whole lambda switching backbone has n bidirectional access points, $n^2 - n$ optical channels (lambdas) are potentially required globally through the network. Whenever a new optical channel is set up, a wavelength is chosen for data transmission. A *wavelength routing and assignment* (WRA) problem must be solved in order to choose a wavelength and a path through the network such that the given wavelength is not being used on any of the links constituting the path (see, for example, the discussion in Ramaswami and Sivarajan 1995, 2002). In order for the optical channel to be feasible in the worst case (i.e., all the optical channels traverse the same link), $n^2 - n$ wavelengths are potentially required on each link between network nodes. A large body of literature is available on solving the WRA problem and minimizing the overall number of wavelengths required on each network link.

Given the number of wavelengths that commercially available WDM equipment accommodates on a single fiber, WλS potentially requires parallel fibers to be deployed between nodes. This results in both an increase in the number of physical interfaces of optical switches and the deployment of large quantity of fiber, thus limiting the scalability of the solution and, in turn, undermining the very motivations (discussed at the beginning of this chapter) for resorting to optical switching. For the sake of a numerical example, let's consider an optical backbone with $n = 10,000$ access points, an average optical channel length of 1000 km, and WDM equipment that supports 100 wavelengths per fiber. To get an idea of the extent of WλS scalability issues, consider the worst case requirement of wavelengths per link, which is on the order of n^2 or 10^8 wavelengths. The total amount of fiber required on such a backbone is 10^9 km (i.e., [10^8/100] $\times$ 1000 km), which is equal to circling the Earth 25,000 times. Assuming that 10 km of fiber is 1 kg, the total amount of fiber required is approximately 100,000 tons!

Although the example just given obviously aims only to provide a general appreciation about the extent of the problem, with a smaller number of wavelengths per link there is a non-null probability that the network will be unable to accommodate an optical channel between an ingress point and egress point, although wavelengths are still available on a possible path. This so-called blocking probability depends on the capability of finding an optimal solution to the WRA problem.

Wavelength conversion reduces both the blocking probability and the complexity of the WRA problem— that is, the required number of wavelengths per link that ensures an optical channel between any ingress-egress pair. However, wavelength conversion performed in the optical domain is still an immature technology, and opto-electro-optical transformation is expensive (both in terms of space and power consumption), which works against the main motivations for deploying optical switching.

On the other hand, the WRA problem is made harder by constraints on the set of wavelengths available to ingress and egress points that stem from the tunability characteristics of transmitters and receivers. In fact, transmitters and receivers that are capable of working on a wide range of wavelengths might be impractical from the point of view of cost.

In summary, WλS scalability and efficiency issues lead to various trade-offs in the design and deployment of the technology and are a compelling reason for resorting to sub-lambda switching.

PHYSICAL DIMENSIONS OF OPTICAL MEMORY AND BUFFER

This section analyzes the implications in the optical domain of buffer dimensions traditionally associated with asynchronous packet switching. Although many important challenges exist in the optical domain with other issues such as processing, switching technologies, and switching devices, the discussion of optical memory is particularly significant because it clearly illustrates the need for departing from the current asynchronous packet-switching paradigm when considering the implementation of sub-lambda switching. Various techniques for reducing the memory/buffer requirements are discussed later in "Memory Reduction Techniques for Sub-Lambda Switching."

The following assumptions are derived from what is known about optical devices today.

Assumption 1: Optical memory is implemented with optical fiber, made from silicon, with a diameter of 125 μm.

Thus, optical memory is a delay line or a pipeline with continuously "streaming" photons representing bits of information.

Assumption 2: The speed of light in optical fiber is 200,000 kilometers per second.

In the context of this work, the following two definitions are applied.

Definition 3: *Bulk optical memory* (BOM). An optical fiber that is capable of storing a predefined amount of bits encoded within an optical signal. The access to such bulk optical memory is strictly sequential—that is, first in, first out.

For example, a 1-km fiber is a bulk optical memory that can store 50,000 bits at 10 Gb/s.

Definition 4: *Optical random access memory* (O-RAM). An optical memory wherein each of the stored data units can be accessed at any predefined time (in general, RAM can be accessed at any time), independently of the order in which they entered the O-RAM.

For example, 1 km of fiber at 10 Gb/s tapped (e.g., with 1×2 optical switches) at regular 10-m intervals is an O-RAM that is capable of storing as many as 50,000 bits encoded in data units of 500 bits each. The data units can be accessed in any order through the taps. However,

because the data units are traveling at the speed of light, the access to a data unit at a different time will be done through a different tap. In other words, a common knowledge of time is required in order to use O-RAM.

Device-Level Analysis of Bulk Optical Memory

The physical dimension of optical memory is compared with that of electronic memory—that is, a *dynamic RAM* (DRAM) with equivalent capacity.

Raw Material

A synchronous DRAM chip that is capable of storing 256 Mbits is manufactured with state-of-the-art technology on a $10 \times 10^{-3} \times 10 \times 10^{-3} \times 0.5 \times 10^{-3} = 50 \times 10^{-9}\,m^3$ (or 50×10^{-6} liter) silicon chip.

A 256-Mbit optical memory for an optical signal encoded at 10 Gb/s (thus, each bit is stored in 2×10^{-2} meters of fiber) is realized with a $256 \times 10^6 \times 2 \times 10^{-2} =$ 5,120,000 meter fiber. Because the fiber diameter, core, and cladding is 125×10^{-6} meter, the total volume is $\pi(125 \times 10^{-6}/2)^2 \times 5,120,000 = 62.8 \times 10^{-3}\,m^3$ or 62.8 liters.

Hence, the step from DRAM to optical memory corresponds to a more than 1 million fold decrease in information density. Consequently, if we assume shrinking of the silicon circuitry by a factor of two every eighteen months (as stated by Moore's law), the transition to optical memory translates into a step back of thirty years (as far as device size is concerned)!

Packaging

The above-mentioned 256-Mbit synchronous DRAM chip is contained in a 66-pin package with a volume of $10 \times 10^{-3} \times 23 \times 10^{-3} \times 1 \times 10^{-3} = 230 \times 10^{-9}\,m^3$ or 230×10^{-6} liter.

The fiber needed to realize an equivalent optical memory can, for example, be rolled on a number of spools. For the sake of comparison, the packaging of Corning fiber is considered here. The longest spools that Corning sells are 25.2 km. Hence, building a 256-Mbit optical memory requires 5,120/25.2 × 204 spools occupying a volume of 767 liters (vs. 230×10^{-6} liter of DRAM) and weighing 461 kg. Hence, the step from packaging DRAM to packaging optical memory corresponds to a more than 3 million fold decrease in information density.

Subsystem Analysis of Bulk Optical Memory

Table 2 shows the physical dimensions of BOM required to implement buffers of typical sizes on state-of-the-art IP packet switches for one 10-Gb/s dense WDM channel. The volume and weight of the optical fiber rolled on 25.2-km spools are provided in the last two columns of Table 2. For example, the memory for an all-optical switch with 256 MB of optical memory per channel will weigh 3686 kg.

Obviously, weight is not the only realization constraint. Fiber length is another. *Amplification* is required to compensate the attenuation introduced by transmission over long fibers. Moreover, the signal degenerates because of the distortion introduced along the fibers and by the amplifiers; hence, after traveling a given distance, the

Table 2: Physical Dimensions of BOM for a Single 10-Gb/s Optical Channel

Buffer Size (MBytes)	Fiber Length (km)	Fiber Volume (lt)	Spool Volume (lt)	Spool Weight (kg)
128	20,480	251	3068	1843
256	40,960	503	6136	3686
1000	160,000	1963	23,969	14,400

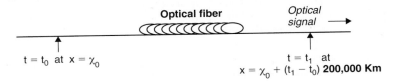

(a)

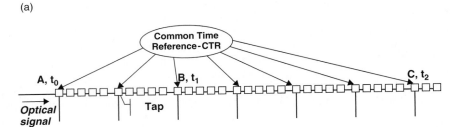

Realistic realization:
        periodic (equally spaced) taps = pipeline forwarding

(b)

Figure 1: The O-RAM (b) is time-dependent (a).

signal must be regenerated. *Regeneration* is an electrical, not an optical, process and encompasses the reamplification, retiming, and reshaping performed by repeaters. As shown in Table 2, the fiber length for a 256-MB buffer is 40,960 km (the same as the Earth's circumference).

Subsystem Analysis of Optical Random Access Memory

Random access implies that at any given time any part of the memory can be accessed. Because the stored optical bits travel along the optical fiber at the speed of light (see Figure 1a), at any given time the bits are in another position along the optical fiber. Consequently, to access such optical memory, there are two requirements (see Figure 1b).

1. *Infinite number of taps*: A tap realized by a 1×2 switch enables the light that is stored in the fiber to either continue along the fiber or be switched out of the fiber.
2. *Common time reference* (CTR): A precise knowledge of time is required in order to access a given sequence of bits at a given spot along the optical fiber. This knowledge of time should be based on the same time reference along the optical fiber (including the ingress edge), which is why it is called a *common* time reference.

Because an infinite number of taps is not feasible, access is possible at predefined times as stated in Definition 4. Two types of O-RAM, which are also referred to as (optical) *programmable delay lines* (PDLs), can be found in the literature: (1) linear delay line or *linear O-RAM* and

(2) parallel delay line or *parallel O-RAM*, shown in Figures 2a and 2b, respectively.

Discussion

The current high-speed, asynchronous packet-switching paradigm is well established with realistic implementation criteria based on optical transmission and electronic switching. The all-optical realization of this paradigm presents multiple challenges. This section has analyzed the optical memory challenge and shown that even though optical memory is well understood and feasible in principle, it hinders the implementation of the current high-speed, asynchronous packet-switching paradigm because of the huge physical size.

We further showed that O-RAM is time dependent and requires a common time reference. As we will show later in "Synchronous Sub-Lambda Switching," CTR is not only required for realizing O-RAM but also essential for minimizing the amount of memory required per optical channel. Furthermore, by using CTR, it is possible to eliminate the need for optical header processing, which, as shown in Table 1, is one of the main challenges in realizing asynchronous sub-lambda switching (e.g., optical burst and packet switching), as discussed in the next sections.

ASYNCHRONOUS SUB-LAMBDA SWITCHING

The discussion on asynchronous sub-lambda switching is divided into mesh (arbitrary) topology and linear topology.

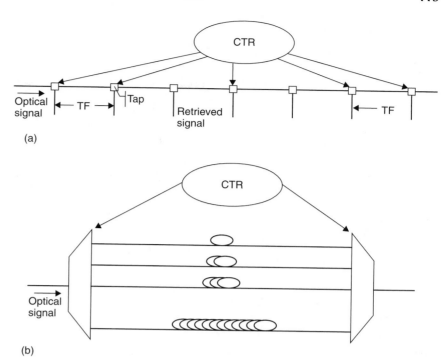

Figure 2: CTR with (a) linear O-RAM and (b) parallel O-RAM

Mesh Topology Networks

In the context of mesh topology, the main implication of asynchronous transmission of packets is that the traffic over the network is not coordinated. Therefore, data packets are subject to congestion and loss just as they are over any other asynchronous packet-switching network. Asynchronous packet switching is an obvious solution for sub-lambda switching because it provides a flexible division of the optical channel into fractions with two major advantages: (1) fine granularity and (2) statistical multiplexing. However, this approach suffers from high complexity because of the following:

- Packet headers are to be optically processed in real time.
- Packet level optical switching—that is, extremely short switching fabric reconfiguration time, is required.
- Without speedup and with limited processing, it is difficult to implement sophisticated scheduling algorithms such as weighted fair queuing, so the service can be unpredictable.
- The relative and well understood optical memory has prohibitive scalability limitation in the optical domain as discussed earlier.

In essence, even if there will be effective solutions for packet header processing and packet-level optical switching, the optical memory and buffer physical dimensions constitute an obstacle that may not be overcome in the foreseeable future.

Current activities on (asynchronous) optical burst switching (see, for example, the discussions in Turner 1999, Rosberg et al. 2003, and Vu et al. 2005) are focusing primarily on optical implementation issues, which are complex and challenging (e.g., header processing). Although burst-level (rather than packet-level) operation somewhat

simplifies some of the optical implementation issues (e.g., header processing and switching speed requirements), it does not affect the unresolved O-RAM issue. Because the relationship between *random access memory* (RAM) requirements and utilization in optical bust switching is not expected to be different from current IP switching, low utilization with reservation can be exploited to reduce RAM requirements. See "Optical Switching Techniques in WDM Optical Networks" for a complete discussion of optical burst and packet switching.

Sub-Lambda Switching over Linear Topology Networks

Linear topology networks have three primary variants: bus, ring, and star. Since the 1980s (see, for example, Ofek 1987) there has been a lot of research work on packet over optical bus and ring networks (see Kazovsky et al. 2000 and Marsan et al. 1997), effectively realizing sub-lambda switching. The main reason for the attractiveness of linear topologies for optical implementations is derived directly from their linearity: There is no congestion (because traffic inside the network has priority over external traffic) and buffering requirements are thus minimal. Conversely, as discussed later in "Memory Reduction Techniques for Sub-Lambda Switching," in asynchronous sub-lambda switching over mesh networks there is congestion, and therefore buffering requirements can be prohibitively large.

The main types of linear topology applicable to sub-lambda switching are: (1) optical buffer insertion ring or bus (see Figure 3), (2) optical slotted ring or bus (see Figure 4), and (3) *passive optical* (star) *network* (PON) (see Figure 5). In the next subsections, these architectures are discussed. Note that there are many ways to describe and realize these ring, bus, and star architectures, and what is described in the following is only one possibility.

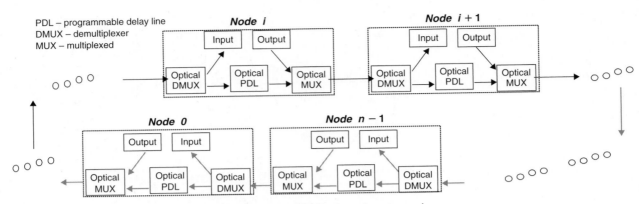

Figure 3: Optical buffer insertion ring or bus

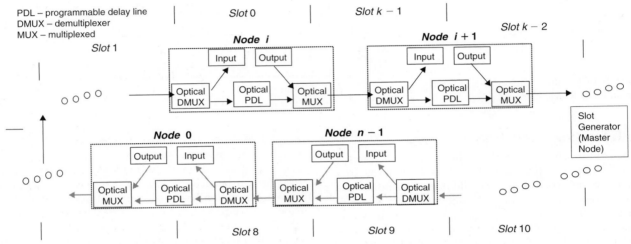

Figure 4: Optical slotted ring or bus

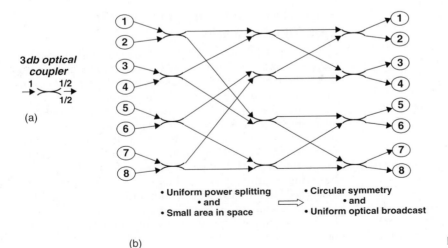

Figure 5: Passive optical network

Optical Buffer Insertion Ring or Bus

An optical buffer insertion ring or bus can be constructed in a way similar to how it is realized in the electronic domain (see, for example, Cidon and Ofek 1993). Figure 3 shows a ring with n nodes (0 to $n - 1$) that is designed to transport variably sized data packets. Each node schematically consists of three parts:

1. An optical *demultiplexer* (DMUX) is a simple 1×2 optical switch that determines whether an incoming

packet should be switched to the node's input or to the optical PDL. This determination is based on decoding the packet header before switching. The header decoding can be done in the electronic domain by converting some of the incoming optical signal to electronics and then using the decoding results for controlling the optical DMUX.

2. An optical *multiplexer* (MUX) is a simple 2×1 optical switch that determines when data packets can be transmitted from the output of the node into the ring. This determination depends on the state of the optical PDL. If the optical PDL is empty, then the node can transmit a packet from its output. The optical MUX control can be done electronically after optically sensing the state of the PDL.

3. An optical programmable delay line can be implemented as shown in Figure 2. Multiple taps are needed to control how long a data packet is delayed by the optical PDL as explained below.

The principle of operation of an optical buffer insertion ring or bus is simple. An incoming packet has priority to be forwarded to the next node over an outgoing packet from the output of the current node. However, an incoming packet will be delayed by the optical PDL if, before its arrival, the node already started to transmit a packet. The maximum delay of an incoming data packet in the optical PDL is one maximum sized packet. This can happen when the node has started to transmit a packet just before the arrival of an incoming packet.

Optical Slotted Ring or Bus

An optical slotted ring or bus can be constructed in a way that is similar to how it is realized in the electronic domain (see, for example, Cidon and Ofek 1993). Figure 4 shows a ring with n nodes (0 to $n - 1$) that is designed to transport data packets with variable sizes. The main difference is that time is divided into time slots of fixed duration. The slots are numbered from 0 to $k - 1$ and are generated by a "slot generator" master node, as shown in Figure 4. Note that an optical slotted ring or bus is sometimes also called a *synchronous* ring or bus. As is apparent from Figure 4, the architecture of optical slotted ring nodes is similar to that of buffer insertion ring nodes.

The principle of operation of an optical slotted ring or bus is simple. Each slot can be either empty or full. Without loss of generality, it is possible to assume that a full slot contains exactly one fixed-size packet. An incoming packet—that is, full slot—has priority to be forwarded to the next node over an outgoing packet from the output of the current node. An incoming packet will be delayed by the optical PDL if, before its arrival, the node already started to transmit a packet. However, the maximum delay in an optical slotted ring can be (much) shorter than an optical buffer insertion ring. In principle, if a node decides to transmit or not transmit at the beginning of each time slot and if the transmission clocks on all links are identical and there is no accumulation of jitter, then the optical PDL can be eliminated. In reality, a small optical PDL is needed.

The node that generates the slots ("Slot Generator" in Figure 4) requires an optical PDL with maximum programmable delay of one time slot. This is necessary to ensure that there is an integer number of time slots (from 0 to $k - 1$) around the ring. Now, for fault tolerance and robustness, it may be reasonable to incorporate the slot generator functionality to all n nodes; consequently, the delay of the optical PDL on all nodes will be capable of introducing a one-time-slot maximum delay.

Passive Optical Network Sub-Lambda Switching

Passive optical networks are an attractive last-mile solution. The basic component typically used in implementing this architecture is the *optical coupler* or *star coupler*. The optical coupler (typically) splits the signal coming in to one of its two inputs evenly to the two outputs as shown in Figure 5a. A large shared (broadcast) medium can be constructed with an array of optical couplers as shown in Figure 5b.

Over the past twenty years, there have been many proposals on how to use optical couplers and PONs. Some of the proposals are synchronous (similar to slotted rings) (see, for example, Ofek 1987), and recent proposals are asynchronous with a medium access control protocol that is a derivation of Ethernet's and hence is called an *Ethernet PON* (EPON) (see, for example, Kramer, Mukherjee, and Pesavento 2001, and Kramer and Pesavento 2002).

The array of optical couplers as shown in Figure 5b can be constructed in a small area in space, so it is possible and simple to synchronize and coordinate the access of all nodes; see, for example, the method presented in Ofek (1988). Transmission in multiple lambdas can also be used on PONs (e.g., arrays of optical couplers); see, for example, the hybrid access protocol proposed in Ofek and Sidi (1993).

MEMORY REDUCTION TECHNIQUES FOR SUB-LAMBDA SWITCHING

Previously, we demonstrated that optical memory might be a major obstacle to realizing sub-lambda switching while assuming the current asynchronous packet-switching paradigm. Specifically, one of the previous sections calculated the physical dimension of optical memory based on optical delay line (i.e., optical fiber), showing that there is at least a factor of 1 million between fiber-based optical memory and solid-state memory. Then in the next section, we showed that sub-lambda switching based on linear topologies and asynchronous packet switching (optical packet or burst switching) on mesh topology provides only a partial solution. Specifically, linear topologies provide limited throughput, whereas optical packet or burst switching largely ignore the actual optical buffering requirement as it arises in equivalent asynchronous packet switching when implemented in electronics. Note that, in electronics, it is simple to implement highly flexible RAM, and therefore the buffering requirement should be lower than in an equivalent optical packet switching that is based on using programmable optical delay lines.

Low utilization is another assumption that is often associated with optical packet switching and optical burst switching over a mesh network. Although optical transmission has high potential capacity, it is not free of charge (as more or less explicitly assumed by many proposed solutions). Furthermore, low utilization already characterizes electronic packet-switching deployment. Nevertheless, today's packet switches are using extremely large buffers that are known to significantly increase the cost of those switches. This dichotomy is extremely interesting, and only time will tell how best to realize asynchronous packet switching in the optical domain. However, it is important to evaluate in depth the relationship between network architecture and the corresponding memory and buffer requirements.

Although there are still unknowns regarding optical processing, amplification, regeneration, and so on, it is clear that the optical memory size should be reduced significantly. In this section, various memory reduction alternatives for mesh networks are analyzed. The analysis is based on the following engineering assumption.

> Assumption 3: Optical fibers, optical channels, transmission bandwidth, network interfaces, memory size, memory access bandwidth, switching fabric capacity, protocol processing, and so on are not free of charge.

High-Level Analysis for Mesh Networks with Arbitrary Topology

First, some switching trade-offs are presented with two main parameters: *time* and *space*. The semantic of *time* in this context refers to whether there is a schedule for sending data units over the network or if there is no schedule. The semantic of *space* in this context refers to whether there is a predefined route for sending data units across the network or a nondeterministic route (i.e., the route was not defined before the data-packet transmission). Four cases shown in Table 3 can be defined by the time and space parameters.

Case 2 in the table is defined by having scheduled times for forwarding data units over nondeterministic routes, which results in a scheme that is not sensible. In other words, it is not practical to schedule the transmission of a data unit over a link when the data unit was actually routed elsewhere.

Case 3 corresponds to the current asynchronous packet-switching paradigm with large random access memory requirements. As discussed before, the current implementation of asynchronous packet switching is not practical for sub-lambda switching. Furthermore, in case 3, large RAM ensures low loss at the expense of long delays (i.e., possibly longer than the propagation delay between source and destination), and the throughput of streaming media applications can be defined only statistically. Note that case 3 also includes various load-balancing methods such as sending data units of the same flow over multiple routes and sending data units to intermediate destinations and to their final destinations.

However, although the relationship between utilization and RAM has been the subject of extensive research in the past three decades, there is still no definitive answer other than to keep utilization (extremely) low or to use (extremely) large RAM. Cases 1 and 4 have small buffer requirements (with no need for optical RAM), and therefore can be used for sub-lambda switching. As it will be shown later using (1) reservation, (2) scheduling, and (3) common time reference (e.g., coordinated universal time), it is possible to maintain full utilization without using any optical RAM (only programmable optical delay lines are required).

In case 4, various well-studied schemes can be used such as hot-potato routing (Baran 1964; Acampora and Shah 1992) or deflection routing (Maxemchuk 1987) as well as convergence routing (Ofek and Yung 1995). In these schemes, data units are stored for only a short period of time (thus requiring only small buffers that can be realized with programmable optical delay lines) and then are forwarded to the next switch even if it is not on the

Table 3: Time and Space Trade-Offs

Space Time	Predefined Routes	Nondeterministic Routes
Schedule	Case 1: Small buffers (RAM not needed)	Case 2:
Loss	None	
Delay	Short	Not sensible
Jitter	Constant	
Throughput	Deterministic	
No schedule	Case 3: Large RAM	Case 4: Small buffers (RAM not needed)
Loss	Low	None
Delay	Long	Long
Jitter	Large	Large
Throughput	Statistical	Unpredictable

best route to their destinations. Consequently, the number of switches traversed can be large, which implies long delays (i.e., much longer than the propagation delay on the shortest path between source and destination). Because data units can be forwarded over a large number of links and a source can transmit only when an outgoing link is idle, the transmission throughput between source and destination is unpredictable. Consequently, their unpredictable delay and throughput make the schemes of case 4 unsuitable for streaming media applications. However, these schemes can perform distributed-computing and parallel-processing applications exceptionally well.

Case 1 has no loss, short delay (i.e., close to the propagation delay between source and destination), and deterministic throughput. Therefore, case 1 is suitable for streaming media applications. Case 1 is traditionally associated with *circuit switching* (CS)—for example, SONET. CS is based on byte-by-byte multiplexing, which is not possible in sub-lambda optical networking. A special case of case 1 is static or whole lambda switching, as discussed earlier. Whole lambda switching is simple to implement; however, as mentioned, its scalability is limited by the *n square* problem (i.e., the potential need of n^2 optical channels) and low utilization (i.e., provisioning of a full wavelength when only a fraction is needed).

The problems that arise with whole lambda switching are fully solved by sub-lambda switching under the conditions of case 1 by a solution called *fractional lambda switching*, which dynamically allocates fractions of an optical channel (i.e., lambda) over predefined routes in the network. This solves the n square problem while ensuring full utilization. Each lambda fraction or *fractional lambda pipe* (FλP) is equivalent to a leased line in CS.

SYNCHRONOUS SUB-LAMBDA SWITCHING

This section describes *fractional lambda switching* (FλS), the novel synchronous sub-lambda switching solution (see, for example, Baldi and Ofek 2003, 2004; Grieco, Pattavina, and Ofek 2005; Nguyen et al. 2005; Ofek 2005), and gives the rationale for its importance and suitability. FλS is based on using a CTR in which time is divided into time frames of duration T_f. Time frames can be viewed as "virtual containers" of IP packets. The time duration of a time frame is a parameter that may change according to the optical link rate. For example, for 10 Gb/s with $T_f = 20$ μs, the virtual container may store as many as 200 Kbits or 25 Kbytes of variably sized IP packets. For this and various other reasons, time frames are quite different from SONET frames and slots. As an example, time frames begin with an explicit delimiter symbol (like the framing flag in PPP), and the contents of two neighboring time frames are separated by a safety margin, which simplifies the implementation of this synchronous sub-lambda switching method.

Another difference between SONET and FλS is that the latter eliminates clock drifts by using a CTR as discussed in the next section. One common time reference established today is the time-of-day international standard called *coordinated universal time* (UTC; also known as

Greenwich mean time, or GMT). Specifically, time is measured by counting the oscillations of the cesium atom in multiple locations. In fact, 9,192,631,770 oscillations of the cesium atom define one UTC second. UTC is available everywhere around the globe from several distribution systems, including U.S. global positioning system (GPS) satellites, the Russian Federation satellite system (GLONASS), and, in the near future, Galileo (the European Union and Japanese satellite system). There are other means for distribution of UTC such as the CDMA cellular telephone system and the two-way satellite time and frequency transfer (TWTFT) technique based on communications satellites. UTC receivers from GPS are available from many vendors with an accuracy of 10–20 nanoseconds. By combining UTC from GPS with local rubidium or cesium clocks, it is possible to have a correct UTC (± 1 μsecond) without an external time reference from GPS for days (with a rubidium clock) and months (with a cesium clock).

FλS Principles of Operation

The operation of FλS is based on the following principles, which are necessary to realize UTC-based *pipeline forwarding* (PF) of time frames—T_f—as shown in Figure 6.

1. Switching of time frames: (a) Each time frame has a predefined duration and contains a payload (plurality of IP packets) with a maximum predefined size (i.e., number of bytes); (b) between two successive payloads there is a safety margin or idle time of a predefined duration; and (c) the payload of a time frame (plurality of IP packets) is switched as a whole from input to output.

2. The idle time or safety margin between two successive payloads is used to change the switching matrix (or permutation) of the optical switch so that the payload of each time frame of a given optical channel can be switched to a different output. This idle pattern can also be used as an explicit delimiter between time frames.

3. Common time reference is UTC and coupled to all switches. The UTC second is divided into a predefined number of equal duration time frames as shown in Figure 7. Time frames are grouped into *time cycles,* and time cycles are grouped into *super cycles,* with the super cycle equal to one UTC second as shown in Figure 7.

4. All received time frames are aligned to UTC such that the delay between inputs of adjacent optical switching fabrics and, consequently, between the inputs of any two optical switching fabrics after alignment is an integer number of time frames. The alignment operation is performed before the optical switching so that time frames coming in to all of the inputs begin at the same time (i.e., are aligned) as shown in Figure 8.

5. A periodic switching pattern through the optical switching fabric repeats every time cycle or super cycle. In other words, during every time frame within a time cycle (or super cycle) the optical switching fabric has a predefined input-output configuration, and the sequence of the input-output configurations repeats every time cycle (or super cycle). This implies that for

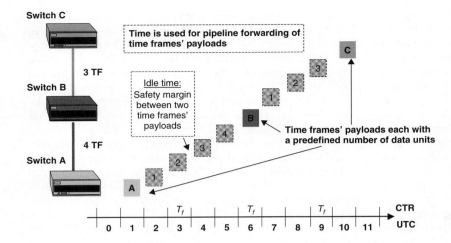

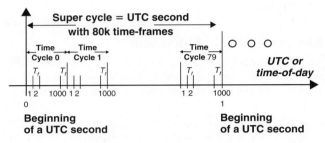

Figure 6: UTC-based pipeline forwarding of time frames

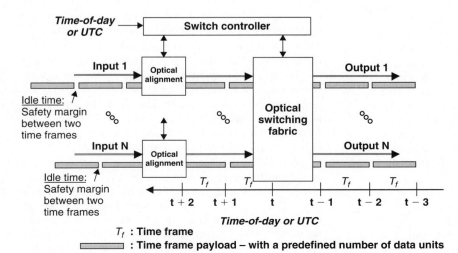

Figure 7: UTC with $T_f = 12.5$ μs

every time frame within a time cycle (or super cycle), (a) the time frame payload is switched to a predefined output and (b) the switching fabric configuration during one time frame is known before its beginning—that is, switch control has low complexity.

UTC-Based Pipeline Forwarding over a Fractional λ Pipe

A fractional lambda pipe, p, is defined along a path of successive FλS switches: $S_p(1)$, $S_p(2)$, ... , $S_p(k)$ such that

the forwarding of a time frame along p has a predefined schedule. More specifically, let:

1. the delay in time frames between inputs of successive optical switching fabrics along p be $d_{1,2}, d_{2,3}, \ldots, d_{k-1,k}$;
2. the time cycle and super cycle duration be c and s time frames, respectively; and
3. the scheduling per FλP repeat itself every $c(s)$ time frames.

Then a time frame forwarded along path p from $S_p(1)$ at t_0 will be forwarded by $S_p(2)$ at $(t_0 + d_{1,2})$ mod c by $S_p(3)$ at $t_0 + d_{1,2} + d_{2,3}$ [mod $c(s)$], and so on; and it will reach the last switch of p, $S_p(k)$, at $t_0 + d_{1,2} + d_{2,3} + \cdots + d_{k-1,k}$ [mod $c(s)$].

The capacity allocated to an FλP is determined by the number of allocated time frames in every time cycle (or super cycle). For example, if $c = 100$ and one time frame per time cycle is allocated for an FλP, then the capacity of the FλP is 1/100 of the optical channel capacity.

Thanks to PF, if all FλPs are unchanged, the switching and forwarding operations along all FλPs at all time frames are known in advance in a reoccurring order every time cycle or super cycle. Consequently, all switches

Figure 8: Incoming time frames are aligned with UTC before reaching the optical switching fabric

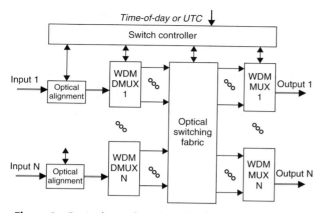

Figure 9: Optical switch with per-optical-fiber alignment

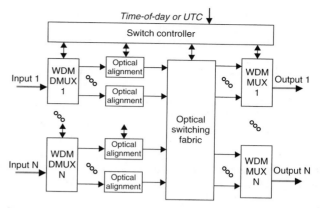

Figure 10: Optical switch with per-optical-channel alignment

know in advance the switching and forwarding operations that are to be performed during every time frame, which greatly simplifies the implementation of the switch controller. The deterministic operation of PF makes FλS suitable for interactive and noninteractive multimedia applications (Baldi and Ofek 2000) and group communications (Baldi, Ofek, and Yener 2000) on a global scale.

CTR and UTC Accuracy

The required CTR accuracy, and hence UTC accuracy, directly affects stability, implementation complexity, and (consequently) cost. With a time frame delimiter, either explicitly transmitted or realized by the idle time between the payloads of two successive time frames, the required UTC accuracy is $\frac{1}{2} \times T_f$ [i.e., UTC $\pm \frac{1}{2}$ (20 μs to 100 μs)]. The reason for such a relaxed requirement is that the UTC is not used to detect the time frame boundaries (because they are detected by the idle times or the explicitly transmitted delimiters) but only to enable the correct mapping of the incoming time frames to the CTR time frames. It is easy to show that as much as $\frac{1}{2} \times T_f$ timing error can be tolerated while maintaining the correct mapping of time frames and without requiring extra buffering.*

FλS Switch Architecture

Two FλS switch architectures are shown in Figures 9 and 10. The main difference between them is where the alignment operation is performed: before the WDM DMUX as in Figure 9 or after the WDM DMUX as in Figure 10. Placing the alignment function before the WDM DMUX is more efficient because it can be done simultaneously on multiple optical channels. However, in some cases, because time frames of different optical channels may be skewed in time over a long fiber, the alignment should be performed on each optical channel separately.

Alignment implies that the beginning of all time frames are aligned with respect to UTC before switching. Implementation of the alignment subsystem in the electronic domain has low complexity because it requires only three queues without memory access speedup with

respect to the input link bandwidth. An optical implementation of the alignment subsystem can be based on a simple optical, programmable delay line. The advantage of optical alignment is it can be performed on multiple optical channels at the same time, provided that the different speed of light did not shift the optical channels too much from one another.

A *switch controller* changes the configuration of the switching fabric before the beginning of each time frame. For each time frame, a switching matrix contains the input-output connections the switching should realize during that time frame. The switch controller can take as much as a whole time frame to download the next switching matrix. Because the switch reconfiguration is so simple and slow (comparable with the control of a T1 add-drop multiplexer), the switch controller can be implemented by means of a microprocessor or a field programmable gate array without requiring the development of complex and costly application-specific integrated circuits.

Each time an FλP is set up or torn down, the switch controller updates the switching matrices corresponding to the time frames allocated to the FλP. Switch controllers of adjacent switches exchange signaling messages to handle FλP creation and release. For example, the resource reservation protocol deployed in the generalized multiprotocol label-switching framework can be adopted as signaling protocols in FλS networks. Notice that, for scalability purposes, the switch controller can include two processors that can easily coordinate the parallel execution of their tasks: one handling switching fabric reconfiguration, the other dealing with signaling and updates of switching matrices.

The properties of FλS can be leveraged also in the design of the switching fabric. Nonblocking switching fabrics and speedup (i.e., transfer rate through the switching fabric higher than the transmission rate on input and output interfaces) are commonly used to maximize the throughput while simplifying the scheduling of the data unit transfer. Deployment of blocking switching fabrics is not practical solution in either circuit switches or packet switches, but it is appealing because of the minimum complexity and hence high scalability and low cost. For example, an $N \times N$ crossbar switch (which is, in the strict sense, nonblocking) contains N^2 crosspoints. However,

---

*An arbitrary timing error can be tolerated on UTC by adding a corresponding buffering capability in the alignment system.

an $N \times N$ Banyan switching fabric implemented, for example, by interconnecting $\log_2 N$ stages of $N/2$ 2×2 crossbar switches (four crosspoints each) contains $2N \times \log_2 N$ crosspoints. For example, a tenfold increase in the required input-output capacity results in a thousand-fold increase in the complexity and cost for a crossbar but only a thirty-fold increase for a Banyan switching fabric.

In FλS, the scope of contention on internal switching resources is limited to a single time frame, and scheduling can be performed—and optimized—off-line (i.e., at FλP setup time). Consequently, blocking can be avoided during switching pattern computation by avoiding conflicting input-output connections during the same TF. Results in Baldi and Ofek (2004) show that (especially if multiple WMD channels are deployed on optical links between fractional λ switches) high link utilization can be achieved with negligible blocking, even when the switching fabric is a Banyan network without speedup.

CONCLUSION

Sub-lambda switching is quite challenging. It has the potential to save on the costly conversions from electronic to optical and from optical to electronic while achieving efficient resource utilization. However, unlike optical transmission and whole lambda switching, sub-lambda switching presents a multitude of challenges that result from the need to perform certain operations in the optical domain. Such operations include (1) buffering, (2) submicrosecond switching time, (3) decoding control information, and (4) changing transmission bit rate. Although such operations are well understood and easily performed in the electronic domain, there is a clear need for further major advancements in high-speed optical switching and processing.

Fractional lambda switching was proposed as a novel optical switching paradigm with the following properties (Baldi and Ofek 2004; Grieco, Pattavina, and Ofek 2005; Nguyen et al. 2005; Ofek 2005): (1) eliminating the need for random access memory, (2) minimizing the need for optical buffers (only used for alignment with UTC), (3) reducing the switching complexity from both the control and switching (optical fabric with speedup of 1 and Banyan topology) point of view, and (4) eliminating the need for header processing, which remains a major challenge in the optical domain.

FλS uses a global common time reference that is realized with UTC to implement pipeline forwarding of time frames, which are virtual containers of 5–20 Kbytes each. Pipeline forwarding over a meshed FλS network requires that the delay between any two switching fabric inputs be an integer number of time frames, which is realized with an alignment to UTC operation before each switching fabric input. Because the time frame boundaries are explicitly identified, a relaxed UTC accuracy of less than one-half of a time frame suffices.

The efficient and deterministic bandwidth provisioning of FλS enables the optical core to be extended toward the edges of the network in the metro and enterprise, thus confining costly header processing to the low-capacity periphery. The fractional lambda pipes realized in FλS networks have the same deterministic characteristics as leased lines in SONET and circuit emulation in ATM. Consequently, FλS eliminates the need for SONET or other service protocols, thus enabling a network "nirvana" in which IP and MPLS packets travel from source to destination without format conversion.

Although FλS is suitable for all-optical implementation, given the state of the art of commercial technology, the most sensible, cost-effective, and scalable solution for sub-lambda switching today is a best-of-breed switch featuring optically interconnected, integrated electronic switching elements.

GLOSSARY

Alignment: The delay between inputs of adjacent switching fabrics and, consequently, between the inputs of any two switching fabrics after alignment, is an integer number of time frames.

Bulk Optical Memory (BOM): An optical fiber capable of storing a predefined amount of bits encoded within an optical signal. The access to such bulk optical memory is strictly sequential or first in, first out.

Common Time Reference (CTR): A common reference established today is the time-of-day international standard called *coordinated universal time* (UTC) or *Greenwich mean time* (GMT). In the context of FλS, the CTR is realized by dividing the UTC second into a predefined number of equal duration (T_f) time frames that are grouped into *time cycles;* time cycles are grouped into *super cycles*, wherein the super cycle is equal to one UTC second.

Fractional Lambda Pipe (FλP): Defined along a path of successive FλS switches: $S_p(1)$, $S_p(2)$, ... , $S_p(k)$ such that the forwarding of a time frame along the FλP has a predefined schedule. Consequently, the switching and forwarding operations along all FλPs at all time frames are known in advance in a reoccurring order every time cycle or super cycle.

Fractional Lambda Switching (FλS): A novel synchronous sub-lambda switching solution based on using a common time reference.

Optical Random Access Memory (O-RAM): An optical memory wherein each of the stored data units can be accessed at any predefined time (in general, RAM can be accessed at any time), independently of the order in which they had entered the O-RAM.

Optical Switching: The actions performed on data units in the optical domain in order to actually move them from the inputs to the outputs of network nodes.

Pipeline Forwarding (PF): A periodic switching pattern through switching fabrics and forwarding pattern through links that repeats every time cycle or super cycle, ensuring that for every time frame within a time cycle (or super cycle) the time frame payload is switched to a predefined output and forwarded to the next hop on its path to the destination.

Sub-Lambda Switching: Network nodes selectively switch to different outputs subsets of the data units incoming on an optical channel—that is, data units are transmitted through optical fibers and switches such that each data unit on a given optical channel may be treated differently by network switches.

Time Frame: Virtual container of 5–20 Kbytes.

Whole Lambda Switching (WλS): Network nodes switch to a specific output all of the data units coming in on an optical channel—that is, data packets are transmitted through optical fibers and switches such that all of the data units on a given optical channel are treated the same way by network switches.

CROSS REFERENCES

See *Optical Fiber Communications; Optical Switching Techniques in WDM Optical Networks*.

REFERENCES

Acampora, A. S., and S. I. A. Shah. 1992. Multihop lightwave networks: A comparison of store-and-forward and hot-potato routing. *IEEE Transactions on Communications*, 40(6): 1082–90.

Baldi, M., and Y. Ofek. 2000. End-to-end delay analysis of videoconferencing over packet switched networks. *IEEE/ACM Transactions on Networking*, 8(4): 479–92.

———. 2003. Comparison of ring and tree embedding for real-time group multicast. *IEEE/ACM Transactions on Networking*, 11(3): 451–64.

———. 2004. Fractional lambda switching: Principles of operation and performance issues. *SIMULATION: Transactions of the Society for Modeling and Simulation International*, 80(10): 527–44.

———, and B. Yener. 2000. Adaptive group multicast with time-driven priority. *IEEE/ACM Transactions on Networking*, 8(1): 31–43.

Baran, P. 1964. On distributed communication networks. *IEEE Transactions on Communications Systems*, 12(1–2): 1–9.

Cidon, I., and Y. Ofek. 1993. MetaRing: A full-duplex ring with fairness and spatial reuse. *IEEE Transactions on Communications*, 41(1): 110–20.

De Dobbelaere, P., K. Falta, L. Fan, S. Gloeckner, and S. Patra. 2002. Digital MEMS for optical switching. *IEEE Communications Magazine*, 40(3): 88–95.

Domash, L. H., Y. M. Chen, P. Haugsjaa and M. Oren. 1997. Electronically switchable waveguide Bragg gratings for WDM routing. In *Digest of the IEEE/LEOS Summer Topical Meetings*, August, Montreal, Quebec, Canada, pp. 34–5.

Earnshaw, M. P., and D. W .E. Allsopp. 2002. Semiconductor space switches based on multi-mode interference couplers. *Journal of Lightwave Technology*, 20(4): 643–50.

Enguang, D., W. Deming, and X. Ansh. 2000. High speed integrated acousto-optic switch with high extinction ratio. In *Proceedings of the Optical Fiber Communication Conference*, March, Baltimore, 2: 139–41.

Gallep, C. M., and E. Conforti. 2002. Reduction of semiconductor optical amplifier switching times by preimpulse step-injected current technique. *IEEE Photonics Technology Letters*, 14(7): 902–4.

Grieco, D., A. Pattavina, and Y. Ofek. 2005. Fractional lambda switching for flexible bandwidth provisioning in WDM networks: Principles and performance. *Photonic Network Communications*, 9(3): 281–96.

Kasahara, R., M. Yanagisawa, T. Goh, A. Sugita, A. Himeno, M. Yasu, and S. Matsui. 2002. New structure of silica-based planar lightwave circuits for low-power thermooptic switch and its application to 8 × 8 optical matrix switch. *Journal of Lightwave Technology*, 20(6): 993–1000.

Kazovsky, L. G., K. V. Shrikhande, I. M. White, D. Wonglumsom, S. M. Gemelos, M. S. Rogge, Y. Fukashiro, and M. Avenarius. 2000. HORNET: A packet-over-WDM multiple access metropolitan area ring network. *IEEE Journal on Selected Areas in Communications*, 18(10): 2004–16.

Krähenbühl, R., M. M. Howerton, J. Dubinger, and A. S. Greenblatt. 2002. Performance and modeling of advanced Ti: LiNbO3 digital optical switches. *Journal of Lightwave Technology*, 20(1): pp. 92–9.

Kramer, G., B. Mukherjee, and G. Pesavento. 2001. Ethernet PON (EPON): Design and analysis of an optical access network. *Photonic Network Communications*, 3(3): 307–19.

Kramer, G., and G. Pesavento. 2002. Ethernet passive optical network (EPON): Building a next-generation optical access network. *IEEE Communications Magazine*, 40(2): 66–73.

Ma, X., and G. S. Kuo. 2003. Optical switching technology comparison: Optical MEMS vs. other technologies. *IEEE Communications Magazine*, 41(11): 16–23.

Marsan, M., A. Marsan, A. Bianco, E. Leonardi, F. Neri, and S. Toniolo. 1997. MetaRing fairness control schemes in all-optical WDM rings. In *Proceedings of the Sixteenth Annual Joint Conference on Computer Communications* (INFOCOM 1997), April, Kobe, Japan. Pp. 752–60.

Maxemchuk, N. F. 1987. Routing in the Manhattan street network. *IEEE Transactions on Communications*, 35(5): 503–12.

Nashimoto, K., H. Moriyama, S. Nakamura, M. Watanabe, T. Morikawa, E. Osakabe, and K. Haga. 2001. PLZT electro-optic waveguides and switches. In *Optical Fiber Communication Conference*, March, Anaheim, CA, USA, 4: PD10–1 to PD10–3.

Nguyen, V. T., M. Baldi, R. Lo Cigno, and Y. Ofek. 2005. Wavelength swapping using tunable lasers for fractional 1 switching. In *Local and Metropolitan Area Networks* (Fourteenth IEEE Workshop on LAN/MAN), Sept. 18–21, Chania, Crete (Greece). Pp. 1–6.

Ofek, Y. 1987. Passive optical star as a building block of a distributed system. *IBM Research Report* (RC 13247), November.

———. 1988. Integration of voice communication on a synchronous optical hypergraph. In *Proceedings of the Seventh Annual Joint Conference on Computer Communications* (INFOCOM'88), New Orleans, Louisiana.

———. 2005. Ultra scalable optoelectronic switching fabric for streaming media over IP. In *IEEE International Symposium on Signal Processing and Information Technology* (ISSPIT 2005), December, Athens. Pp. 245–52.

———, and M. Sidi. 1993. Design and analysis of a hybrid access control to an optical star using WDM. *Journal of Parallel and Distributed Computing*, 17: 259–65.

————, and M. Yung. 1995. MetaNet: Principles of an arbitrary topology LAN. *IEEE/ACM Transactions on Networking*, 3(2): 169–80.

Ollier, E. 2002. Optical MEMS devices based on moving waveguides. *IEEE Journal of Selected Topics in Quantum Electronics*, 8(1): 155–62.

Pesach, B., G. Bartal, E. Refaeli, and A. J. Agranat. 2000. Free space optical cross-connect switch by use of electroholography. *Applied Optics*, 39(5): 746–58.

Ramaswami, R., and K. N. Sivarajan. 1995. Routing and wavelength assignment in all-optical networks. *IEEE/ACM Transactions on Networking*, 3(5): 489–500.

————. 2001. *Optical networks: A practical perspective*. 2d ed. San Francisco: Morgan Kaufmann Publishers.

Riza, N. A., and S. Yuan. 1998. Low optical interchannel crosstalk, fast switching speed, polarization independent 2 × 2 fiber optic switch using ferroelectric liquid crystals. *IEEE Electronics Letters*, 34(13): 1341–42.

Rosberg, Z., H. L. Vu, M. Zukerman, and J. White. 2003. Performance analyses of optical burst-switching networks. *IEEE Journal on Selected Areas in Communications*, 21(7): 1187–97.

Sakata, T., H. Togo, M. Makihara, F. Shimokawa, and K. Kaneko. 2001. Improvement of switching time in a thermocapillarity optical switch. *Journal of Lightwave Technology*, 19(7): 1023–27.

Tapalian, H. C., J.-P. Laine, and P. A. Lane. 2002. Thermooptical switches using coated microsphere resonators. *IEEE Photonics Technology Letters*, 14(8): 1118–20.

Turner, J. S. 1999. *Terabit burst switching*. Journal of High Speed Networks, January, pp. 3–16.

Vu, H. L., A. Zalesky, E. W. M. Wong, Z. Rosberg, S. M. H. Bilgrami, M. Zukerman, and R. S. Tucker. 2005. Scalable performance evaluation of a hybrid optical switch. *Journal of Lightwave Technology*, 23(10): 2961–73.

Optical Cross Connects

Wen-De Zhong, *Nanyang Technological University, Singapore*

INTRODUCTION

Optical cross connects (OXCs) are the fundamental building blocks in a seamless, intelligent, and high-capacity optical transport network. An OXC is an optical switching system that can incorporate several compelling features, including wavelength conversion (making use of all available wavelengths to improve wavelength utilization), improvement of signal quality through reamplifying, reshaping, and retiming of the optical signal (known as *3R regeneration*), and implementation of network protection and restoration to provide the desired optical circuit (lightpath) availability in accordance with the service-level agreement signed with customers. OXCs are essential for provisioning lightpaths in a large optical mesh network automatically without having to perform manual patch panel connections (Iannone and Sabella 1996). This capability is of particular importance in dealing with a large number of wavelengths and nodes in any future large optical transport network. It is also important when the lightpaths in the network need to be reconfigured rapidly to match dynamically changing traffic demands and traffic patterns. The OXCs also play important roles in network management functions, such as performance monitoring and alarm handling. OXCs can detect failures in the network and rapidly reroute lightpaths around the failure.

To establish a lightpath between a pair of source and destination nodes, it is generally required that the same wavelength be assigned to all of the fiber links along the path. This requirement is known as the *wavelength continuity constraint*. Optical networks with such a constraint are generally referred to as *wavelength path* (WP) networks (Sato, Okamoto, and Hadama 1994). A simple example of such a network is shown in Figure 1a; five OXC nodes are interconnected by seven bidirectional fiber links. Assume that each bidirectional fiber link has two fibers transmitting in opposite directions and each fiber has two wavelengths available. As shown in Figure 1a, there are three bidirectional lightpaths in progress in the network, each of which is assigned with a single wavelength. For instance, the first lightpath between nodes 1 and 3 uses wavelength λ_1, the second lightpath between nodes 2 and 4 uses λ_2, and the third lightpath between nodes 1 and 4 uses λ_1. Wavelength λ_1 is used in two lightpaths

simultaneously, while the second lightpath uses λ_2. Now if a new lightpath is requested to be set up between nodes 3 and 5, this lightpath cannot be fulfilled because of wavelength continuity constraint, even though along the path, the links (3, 4) and (4, 5) each have a free wavelength, λ_1 and λ_2, respectively. The wavelength continuity constraint distinguishes a WP network from a circuit-switched network where call blocking occurs only if there is no capacity on any of the links along the path assigned to the call. Therefore, effective routing and wavelength assignment algorithms are essential to ensure the network resources are efficiently utilized in WP networks (Ramaswami and Sivarajan 1995).

Wavelength continuity constraint can be eliminated if a wavelength can be converted to another wavelength at any OXC node in the network. Optical networks that are capable of wavelength conversion are generally referred to as *virtual wavelength path* (VWP) networks (Sato, Okamoto, and Hadama 1994), where a lightpath may have different wavelengths over different links along the route. Under the same situation as that in Figure 1a, Figure 1b shows that a new lightpath request can then be set up between nodes 3 and 5, using wavelength λ_2 on link (4, 5) and wavelength λ_1 on link (3, 4). Studies

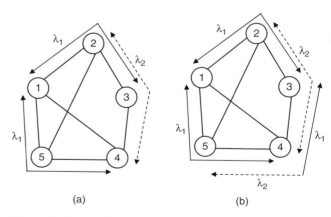

(a)	(b)

Figure 1: A simple example showing lightpaths between nodes for (a) a WP network and (b) a VWP network

in Sato, Okamoto, and Hadama (1994) have shown that a VWP network can improve network blocking performance with relaxed network control and management at the expense of increasing implementation costs because of the requirement of wavelength converters.

This chapter describes and examines various configurations and architectures of OXCs that are reported in the literature. The rest of the chapter is organized as follows. The next section discusses two generic OXC architectures, of which one is for WP networks and the other for VWP networks. The section following after describes and discusses several typical wavelength-selective OXCs. "Wavelength Interchangeable OXCs" describes and investigates OXCs that use either space switching or wavelength switching. The last section before the conclusion presents and discusses OXCs that are capable of multicasting.

GENERIC OXC ARCHITECTURES

Depending on their wavelength conversion capability, OXCs are generally classified as being either *wavelength-selective OXCs* (WS-OXCs) or *wavelength-interchangeable OXCs* (WI-OXCs). A WS-OXC can switch a wavelength channel from any input fiber to any output fiber, but it cannot change its wavelength. Hence, WS-OXCs are used in WP networks. A WI-OXC not only can switch a wavelength channel from any input fiber to any output fiber but also can change an input wavelength to a different output wavelength. WI-OXCs are essential for VWP networks. In practice, WI-OXCs may only have limited wavelength conversion capability. In a limited wavelength convertible OXC, only a subset of the input wavelength channels have a chance to use the wavelength converters (e.g., on a first come, first serve basis), and hence only a subset of the input channels can be converted to different output wavelengths (Chai et al. 2002). In this chapter, we only consider WI-OXCs with full wavelength conversion capability. In both WS-OXC and WI-OXC, wavelength routing (cross connection) is achieved by wavelength-selective elements (such as wavelength multiplexers and demultiplexers and optical

filters) or optical space switches. For example, a fixed wavelength routing OXC will probably use *wavelength-division multiplexers* (WDMs) in a back-to-back configuration to allow the interchange of wavelengths between the input and output fibers in a predetermined pattern. A more advanced and intelligent OXC is usually made with optical space switches or other tunable components so that wavelength channels can be reconfigured arbitrarily. Using such reconfigurable wavelength routing OXCs, each wavelength on any input fiber can be routed to any output fiber provided that the output fiber is not using that wavelength. The capability of reconfiguring wavelength channels is a critical feature in optical networks because the traffic demand and its pattern are unlikely to be static but will change dynamically.

Figure 2a and 2b show the generic architectures for WS-OXCs and WI-OXCs, respectively. Both architectures are based on wavelength multiplexers and space switch matrices. Unless otherwise specified, throughout this chapter we assume that the number of input-output fibers connected to an OXC is N and the number of wavelengths carried in each fiber is M. Hence the total switching capacity is proportional to NMB, where B is the bit rate per wavelength channel. The basic operation for both the WS-OXC and WI-OXC is that they select wavelengths and rearrange them in the spatial domain. Throughout this chapter, an OXC with N inputs and N outputs is generally denoted as an $N \times N$ OXC. Similarly, an optical device with i inputs and j outputs is denoted as an $i \times j$ device.

As shown in Figure 2a and 2b, the incoming WDM signals entering at each input port (fiber) are first demultiplexed using wavelength *demultiplexers* (DMUXs) and then fed into the space switch where individual incoming wavelength channels are routed toward different output fibers. Wavelength channels that are routed to a particular output fiber are combined by a wavelength *multiplexer* (MUX) or an optical coupler. The difference between WS-OXCs and WI-OXCs is the wavelength conversion function that is incorporated within WI-OXCs. In Figure 2b,

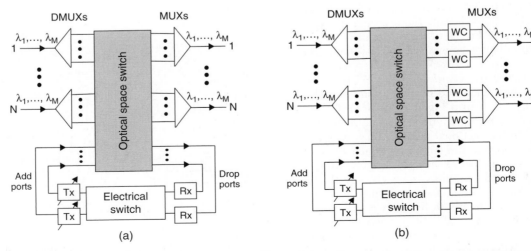

Figure 2: Generic OXC architecture—(a) wavelength-selective OXC and (b) wavelength-interchangeable OXC

the *wavelength converters* (WCs) are placed at the output side of the switch matrix. It is also possible to locate the WCs at the input side of the space-switch matrix. The former case can use fixed wavelength converters, whereas the latter case requires tunable WCs, which are more expensive and complicated than fixed WCs. As illustrated in Figure 2, apart from wavelength channels being cross connected from a particular input fiber to a particular output fiber, some wavelength channels may be terminated (dropped) at the OXC node and new channels may be added to the network from the local node. The dropped wavelengths are converted into electrical signals and then fed into an electrical (packet) switch or router that not only can provide low-speed electronic traffic grooming (aggregation) but also perform packet switching or routing. Traffic grooming is important in high-capacity optical networks, through which many low-speed traffic flows (streams) are packed (multiplexed) into a high-capacity lightpath so as to efficiently utilize optical wavelengths and optimize network throughput. A detailed study on OXCs incorporating traffic grooming can be found in Zhu, Zang, and Muhkerjee (2003). As illustrated in Figure 2, the channels that are added from the electrical switch to the optical switch may have tunable wavelengths.

An OXC is usually referred to as an *optical add-drop multiplexer* (OADM) if the number of input-output fibers is one (Giles 1999). An OADM can be made to be fixed or reconfigurable. A fixed OADM can drop and then add one or more fixed wavelength channels, whereas a reconfigurable OADM can arbitrarily drop any one or more wavelength channels among the incoming wavelength channels and then add the same number of wavelength channels as the dropped ones (Tran et al. 2001). This chapter focuses on OXCs with multiple input and output fibers. For simplicity of description, we will omit add-drop ports and the electronic switch in the description of the various OXCs in the rest of this chapter.

From the point of view of blocking performance, OXCs may be classified as nonblocking and blocking (Clos 1953). A *blocking OXC* may not be able to connect an idle (free) input wavelength channel λ_i on any input fiber to any output fiber, even if λ_i is not being used on that output fiber. *Nonblocking OXCs* are further divided into strictly nonblocking and rearrangeably nonblocking OXCs (Clos 1953). If a WS-OXC is *strictly nonblocking*, then any idle input wavelength channel λ_i on any input fiber can always be connected to any output fiber without disturbing any existing connections, provided that λ_i is not being used on that output fiber. If it is *rearrangeably nonblocking*, then any idle input wavelength channel λ_i on any input fiber can be connected to any output fiber by rerouting some of the existing connections, provided that λ_i is not being used on that output fiber. A strictly nonblocking WI-OXC is capable of connecting any idle input wavelength channel on any input fiber to any output fiber without disturbing any existing connections, provided that that output fiber has at least one free (unused) wavelength. A rearrangeably nonblocking WI-OXC is capable of connecting any idle input wavelength channel on any input fiber to any output fiber by rerouting some of the existing connections, provided that that output fiber has at least one free (unused) wavelength. The blocking performance of the two generic OXCs

in Figure 2a and 2b depend on the blocking properties of the optical space switch matrices used.

Optical space switches are the basic components for OXCs. Various types of optical space switches based on a variety of technologies have been developed. These include electro-optic switches that use lithium niobate (LiNbO$_3$) material in the form of a Mach-Zehnder interferometer, thermo-optic switches that make use of thermo-optic effects to achieve switching, acousto-optic switches, *semiconductor optical amplifier* (SOA) switches, bubble-based optical waveguide switches, and *microelectromechanical system* (MEMS) switches. Large switch matrices can be constructed by smaller switch modules using multistage interconnection networks such as a Clos network (Clos 1953), a Benes network (Benes 1962), or a Spanke network (Spanke 1987).

Apart from space switches, wavelength converters are essential in the implementation of WI-OXCs. There are mainly two different ways to build wavelength converters: an opto-electronic approach and an all-optical approach. An *opto-electronic WC* first converts the input optical signal into an electrical signal, and the electrical signal is then modulated onto another optical light that may be at a different wavelength. Opto-electronic WCs can incorporate 3R regeneration function (reamplifying, reshaping, and retiming) to improve the quality of signals. *All-optical WCs* may use a variety of techniques such as cross-gain modulation, cross-phase modulation, and four-wave mixing in nonlinear optical devices such as SOAs. Details on the operating principles and implementation issues of various wavelength converters can be found in Durhuus et al. (1996) and Yoo (1996).

WAVELENGTH-SELECTIVE OXCs

This section describes and discusses several WS-OXCs that are of different configurations and use different technologies.

WS-OXCs Using Space Switching

Figure 3a and 3b illustrates two different configurations of WS-OXCs in which four input-output fibers each carry four wavelengths—that is, $N = M = 4$. Both configurations use optical space switches to perform switching. In configuration 1, WDM signals entering at each of the input ports are first demultiplexed by wavelength demultiplexers, and channels of the same wavelength are then fed to a specific space switch where they are routed to different output ports; that is, each space switch routes channels of the same wavelength. In contrast, channels of the same wavelength are fed to different space switches in configuration 2—that is, each space switch routes channels of different wavelengths. In general, configuration 1 uses $N \times N$ space switches, whereas configuration 2 employs $M \times N$ space switches where M may not equal to N. In Figure 3, both M and N are equal to 4. Compared to configuration 1, configuration 2 has a better cross-talk performance as reported in Zhou et al. (1996). This is because each space switch in configuration 2 routes channels of different wavelengths and the dominant cross talk arising in the space switches is out-of-band

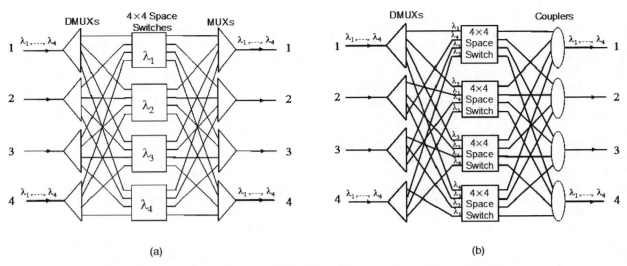

Figure 3: Wavelength selective OXCs—(a) configuration 1 and (b) configuration 2

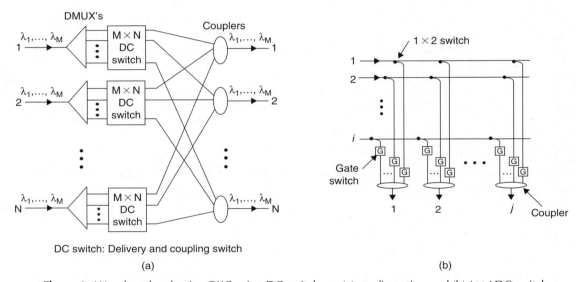

DC switch: Delivery and coupling switch

(a)

(b)

Figure 4: Wavelength-selective OXC using DC switches—(a) configuration and (b) $i \times j$ DC switch

cross talk, whereas the main cross talk in configuration 1 is inband cross talk. The inband cross talk is more detrimental to the main signal than the out-of-band cross talk, because the out-of-band cross talk can always be removed by optical filters. As a result, the cross-talk requirement for the space switches in configuration 1 is more stringent. However, configuration 2 suffers higher power loss because it has to use optical couplers to combine the signals that are switched to the same output fiber, whereas configuration 1 can use optical multiplexers (whose power loss is much smaller than optical couplers, particularly when the number of signals to be combined is large) to combine channels that are directed toward the same output fiber. It may be noted that if the space switches are nonblocking, then both of the above WS-OXCs are also nonblocking.

Figure 4a shows a different WS-OXC using optical *delivery-and-coupling* (DC) switches reported in Okamoto, Watanabe, and Sato (1996). With this WS-OXC, the incoming WDM signal entering at each input fiber is demultiplexed into M wavelength channels, which are then fed to a DC switch. A DC switch is a specific space switch that allows more than one of the incoming optical signals to be connected with any one of the outputs so long as those incoming signals are of different wavelengths. With reference to Figure 4a, it may be seen that the signals that are fed to the same DC switch are of different wavelengths. Following the DC switches, optical couplers are used to combine signals coming from different DC switches that are being directed to the same output fiber. A general $i \times j$ DC switch is reproduced in Figure 4b. This consists of an array of 1×2 switches and a set of couplers, one at each output. A gate

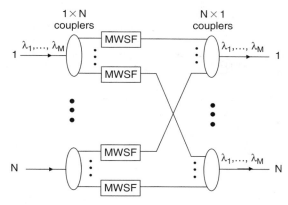

Figure 5: Broadcast-and-select–based OXC using MWSFs

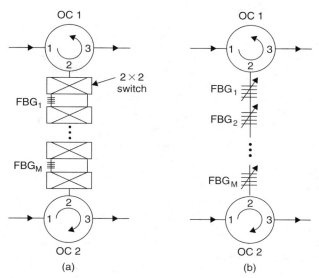

Figure 6: WS-OXC using (a) fixed FBGs and space switches and (b) tunable FBGs

switch is inserted at each input of the couplers, which would significantly suppress the cross talk but at the expense of higher implementation costs. The gate switches may not be necessary if the 1×2 switches induce a cross-talk level less than –30 dB. Each of the i incoming signals can be switched to any one of the j outputs through the array of 1×2 switches. A 1×2 switch can be fabricated in the form of a Mach-Zehnder interferometer with a thermo-phase shifter. A coupler is used to combine the signals coming from the i different inputs. As reported in Watanabe et al. (1996), the DC switch with a large number of inputs and outputs can be fabricated on a silicon board using planer silica waveguide technologies.

Broadcast-and-Select–Based WS-OXCs

Figure 5 illustrates a broadcast-and-select–based WS-OXC (Okamoto, Watanabe, and Sato 1996). It consists of a set of *multiwavelength-selective filters* (MWSFs) and optical couplers. For such an $N \times N$ WS-OXC, one requires $2N$ $1 \times N$ couplers (N of which are used as splitters, and the rest as combiners) and N^2 MWSFs. An MWSF is a specific optical filter that can pass or block any combination of M incoming wavelength channels on each input fiber. Different types of MWSFs have been reported. These include the integrated *acousto-optic tunable filters* (AOTFs) (Simith et al. 1991) and arrayed-waveguide-grating–based filters (Doerr 1998). With this OXC, an input channel can appear at multiple output fibers if it is selected by multiple MWSFs. Hence, this WS-OXC not only can provide a point-to-point connection but also offer point-to-multipoint connections, which is known as *multicasting*. Multicasting is critically important for supporting various multimedia services such as videoconferencing, multiplayer online gaming, and distance learning. More OXC architectures that are capable of multicasting will be discussed later in this chapter.

WS-OXCs Using Fiber Bragg Gratings and Circulators

Apart from the architectures discussed above, WS-OXCs based on optical *fiber Bragg grating* (FBG) are highly attractive and promising, particularly in applications such as interconnecting WDM rings. In such applications, the number of ports required is small. As such, it is cost-effective to use FBGs to build OXCs that are of small size. Figure 6a shows a FBG-based 2×2 WS-OXC in which a series of FBGs with fixed Bragg wavelengths and 2×2 optical space switches are used, with each FBG inserted between two 2×2 space switches (Liaw, Ho, and Chi 1998). Each 2×2 space switch has one of the "cross" and "bar" states at one time. Switching two 2×2 space switches, one before and one after the FBG, to the "cross" state, a channel whose wavelength matches with the center wavelength (also called the *Bragg wavelength*) of the FBG will be reflected back by the FBG, then exit from port 3 of *optical circulator* (OC) 1. Meanwhile, other channels can pass through the FBG chain and appear at port 3 of OC 2. When two or more 2×2 space switches are properly cascaded, multiple-wavelength switching can be realized. Each group of an FBG and a 2×2 optical space switch can be replaced by a tunable FBG, as shown in Figure 6b. Large FBG-based WS-OXCs can be configured using the Benes structure as reported in Wu et al. (2000). Using tunable FBGs and OCs, we can also build bidirectional WS-OXCs that are highly useful for interconnecting bidirectional WDM rings, as reported in Yuan, Zhong, and Hu (2004).

WAVELENGTH-INTERCHANGEABLE OXCs

Wavelength conversion is necessary for VWP optical networks. In this section, we describe and examine several different WI-OXC architectures. Studies have shown that, under many circumstances, WI-OXCs can enhance the efficiency of transmission resources (Sato, Okamoto, and Hadama 1994). This is because the use of WI-OXCs eliminates the requirement for the wavelength continuity constraint in the establishment of lightpaths, so they can considerably reduce the lightpath blocking probability (refer to Figure 1 for an example). More importantly, WI-OXCs allow optical lightpath topologies to be configured and reconfigured more rapidly than WS-OXCs, hence they facilitate optical network management. This is because WI-OXCs allow a lightpath traveling a number of nodes to have a different wavelength over each fiber link along the route and hence simplify establishment of new optical lightpaths and restoration of optical lightpath failures. In other words, using WI-OXCs, wavelengths allocated to optical lightpaths only have local importance, resulting in significant simplification of wavelength assignment in large optical networks; conversely, with the use of WS-OXCs, wavelength assignment has to be done globally, resulting in increased complexity of network management.

In general, there are two approaches to realizing WI-OXCs. The first approach is to employ space switching in conjunction with wavelength conversion, which is generally referred to as the *space-switching* approach. In this case, connecting a wavelength channel from a particular input fiber to a desired output fiber is carried out by optical space switches; wavelength conversion is performed either before or after the space switching, depending on the system architecture. The second approach is to use wavelength routing in conjunction with wavelength conversion (Zhong, Lacey, and Tucker 1996), which is referred to as the *wavelength routing* approach. As we will see subsequently, although some of the WS-OXC architectures described in the previous section may be modified to become WI-OXCs by simply incorporating WCs, others cannot be modified in this fashion.

WI-OXCs Based on Space Switching

Figure 7 illustrates a WI-OXC using the space-switching approach. It is modified from the WS-OXC in Figure 4a. As shown in the figure, after it is demultiplexed, an incoming wavelength channel is converted to a desired output wavelength channel by a *fixed-input, tunable-output wavelength converter* (FTWC). An FTWC can convert an optical signal with a fixed wavelength to any other output wavelength. Following wavelength conversion, individual wavelength channels are then switched by the

DC switches toward their desired output ports. It may be noted that here wavelength conversion is performed before space switching (i.e., before a wavelength channel is routed to a specific output fiber). It is not possible to reverse the order of the wavelength conversion and the space switching, because this WI-OXC uses DC switches, and each output of a DC switch may have more than one wavelength channel. Because a DC switch is strictly nonblocking, this WI-OXC is also strictly nonblocking in both the space and wavelength domains.

Figure 8 shows another WI-OXC structure based on space switching (Hill et al. 1993). In this WI-OXC, each incoming WDM signal is first split into N equal parts and fed to a *tunable input and tunable output wavelength converter* (TTWC). After being selected and wavelength converted by TTWCs, wavelength channels are then individually switched by space switches toward their desired output ports. Figure 9 shows the schematic of a TTWC. The TTWC in the figure uses cross-gain modulation in SOA to perform wavelength conversion, but in general other wavelength conversion techniques can also be used. Details on different wavelength techniques can be found in Durhuus et al. (1996) and Yoo (1996). Because the input signal is a WDM signal, a tunable filter is necessary to select a specific wavelength channel out of M possible input wavelength channels. The selected input wavelength is then converted to a particular output wavelength by tuning the tunable laser. The selected input signal and the continuous light at wavelength λ_{out} generated from the tunable laser are injected into an SOA in opposite directions.

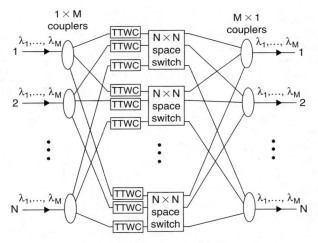

TTWC: Tunable-input tunable-output wavelength converter

Figure 8: WI-OXC using space switches and TTWCs

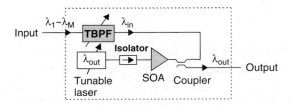

Figure 9: TTWC based on cross-gain modulation in SOA

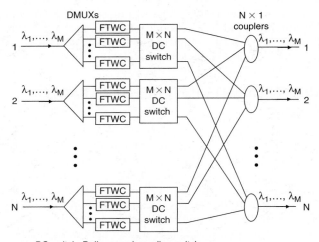

DC switch: Delivery and coupling switch
FTWC: Fixed-input tunable-output wavelength converter

Figure 7: WI-OXC using DC switches and FTWCs

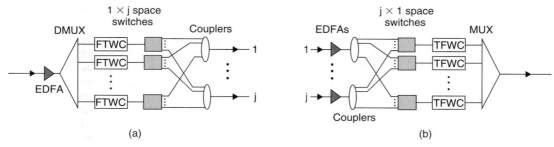

Figure 10: Wavelength interchange device with (a) single input and multiple output and (b) multiple input and single output

This facilitates the separation of the desired output wavelength from the input wavelength. Note that if the incoming signal is of single wavelength, the tunable filter in Figure 9 is not necessary. Such a wavelength converter without a tunable filter at the input is an FTWC. If the tunable laser is replaced with a fixed laser, then the WC in Figure 8 becomes a *tunable-input fixed-output WC* (TFWC). A WC with fixed output wavelength is simpler than a WC with tunable output wavelength because a tunable laser is more complicated and expensive than a fixed wavelength laser. In both of the WI-OXCs in Figures 7 and 8, the WCs are placed before space switching and of tunable output wavelengths. Recently, a new type of WI-OXCs based on space switching is reported in Panda et al. (2004) in which the WCs are located after space switching and are of fixed output wavelengths.

WI-OXCs Based on Wavelength Routing

We next describe a class of WI-OXCs using the wavelength routing approach reported in Zhong, Lacey, Tucker (1996) and Zhong, Lacey, Tucker (1997). These WI-OXCs employ *wavelength interchange devices* (WIDs) and *arrayed waveguide grating multiplexers* (AWGMs) to perform wavelength cross connection. A WID is generally denoted as $i \times j$ WID(u,v,w). This device has i input fibers that between them carry a total of w WDM data channels on u possible wavelengths on each input fiber, and j output fibers that between them carry the same number w of WDM data channels on v possible output wavelengths on each output fiber, where $w \leq \min[iu, jv]$. The basic WIDs that are of particular interest are 1×1 WID(u,v,w), $1 \times j$ WID(u,v,w), and $i \times 1$ WID(u,v,w) because they can be built in a relatively simple way and used as building blocks for various WI-OXCs (refer to Zhong, Lacey, and Tucker 1996, and Zhong et al. 1997 for more details).

Figure 10a shows the schematic configuration of a $1 \times j$ WID(u,v,w) (Zhong et al. 1997). The input WDM signal is amplified by an erbium-doped fiber amplifier (EDFA). After being demultiplexed, each individual wavelength signal is fed to an FTWC where it can be converted to any wavelength out of v possible output wavelengths. The individual signals from the FTWCs are then switched by the optical space switches toward one of j output fibers.

Figure 10b shows the schematic configuration of a $j \times 1$ WID(u, v, w). Each input WDM signal is amplified and then split into v equal parts. Each $j \times 1$ space switch

selects one of the input WDM signals. The selected WDM signal is fed to a TFWC where a specific wavelength out of u possible input wavelengths is selected by a tunable filter and then converted to a preassigned output wavelength. Because the individual wavelengths emerging from the TFWCs are fixed, they can be combined by a multiplexer. The $1 \times j$ WID and the $j \times 1$ WID both become 1×1 WID when all of the space switches and unused input and output fibers and corresponding components are removed.

Figure 11 shows an $N \times N$ WI-OXC using WIDs and AWGMs (Zhong et al. 1996). Each column of WIDs is denoted as a stage. Two adjacent stages are interconnected by an $N \times N$ AWGM that performs wavelength routing. An important property of an $N \times N$ AWGM is that it has a *free spectral range* (FSR) or a frequency period (Dragone 1991; Takahashi et al. 1990). By making use of this property, multiple wavelength connections, each separated by an FSR, can be simultaneously set up through the AWGM between any two WIDs in two adjacent stages.

Figure 12 illustrates an equivalent circuit of a 4×4 AWGM in which a connection between a DMUX and an MUX represents a set of frequencies, each separated by an FSR. Let $f_0, f_1, \ldots, f_{N-1}$ be the N consecutive operating frequencies within an FSR of an $N \times N$ AWGM. The set of frequencies $f_{p,q}$ that connect the ith input to the jth output of an $N \times N$ AWGM can be expressed in terms of f_q and FSR as $f_{p,q} = p \times \text{FSR} + f_q$ where q is determined by $q = (i + j)$ modulo N, and p is an integer indicating the number of FSR periods. The operating frequencies $f_0, f_1, \ldots, f_{N-1}$ can be made to be either equally spaced or unequally spaced for AWGMs. If a wavelength-division channel or connection is looked on as a space-division channel or connection, then each 1×1 WID(u,v,w) is equivalent to a $u \times v$ nonblocking space switch that switches w data channels. Because each 1×1 WID(u,v,w) is equivalent to

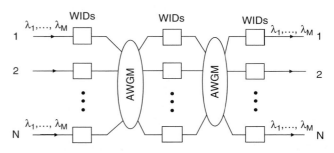

Figure 11: WI-OXC using 1×1 WIDs and AWGMs

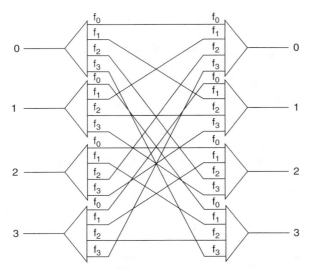

Figure 12: Equivalent circuit of a 4 × 4 AWGM

a $u \times v$ nonblocking space switch and an AWGM can provide multiple wavelength connections (each separated by an FSR) between any two WIDs in adjacent stages, the WI-OXC in Figure 11 can be translated into an equivalent three-stage space-division switching network, which is similar to the Clos network (Clos 1953). It has been shown in Zhong et al. (1996) that the WI-OXC in Figure 11 can be either (1) a strictly nonblocking network if at least two wavelength connections (each separated by an FSR of the AWGMs) are provided between any two WIDs in adjacent stages or (2) a rearrangeably nonblocking network if at least one wavelength connection is provided between any two WIDs in adjacent stages.

Figure 13 illustrates another WI-OXC using WIDs and AWGMs. Unlike the structure in Figure 11, which uses three stages of 1 × 1 WIDs, the WI-OXC in Figure 13 consists of two stages of WIDs, resulting in reduction in the implementation cost. The first stage uses 1 × j WIDs, and the second stage uses $j \times 1$ WIDs. The WIDs in the first stage and the WIDs in the second stage are interconnected by j $N \times N$ AWGMs. In addition to wavelength switching, this WI-OXC also uses space switching to route a wavelength channel from any input fiber to any output fiber. The space switching is carried out within the 1 × j WIDs

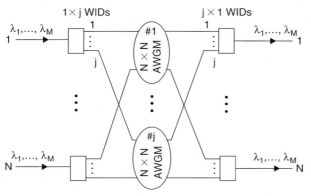

Figure 13: WI-OXC using 1 × j WIDs, j × 1 WIDs, and AWGMs

and the $j \times 1$ WIDs. This WI-OXC is generally a blocking network, but the blocking probability can be made smaller than 10^{-3} for $j \geq 5$ with a relatively high traffic load of 75 percent (Zhong et al. 1997). Several other WI-OXCs using WIDs and AWGMs can be found in Zhong et al. (1996) and Zhong et al. (1997).

MULTICASTING-CAPABLE OXCs

The increasing popularity of multicast services such as videoconferencing, distance learning, and multiplayer online gaming is anticipated to become a major contributor to the growth in Internet traffic demand. These services and applications are quite demanding in their required bandwidth and service quality (i.e., the assurance of bandwidth availability during the life of a particular service session). Their operation inherently requires the simultaneous transmission of information from one source to multiple destinations. Multicasting would be efficient in these applications because it would eliminate the necessity for the source to send an individual copy of the information to each destination. Even though this may be implemented in electrical Internet protocol routers at the Internet layer alone, that would not be an efficient approach in a future Internet over optical network because it would not use the additional flexibility provided by the optical network. In view of this, there has been strong interest in implementing multicasting in the optical layer using multicast-capable OXCs. This section presents several multicasting-capable OXCs.

Multicasting-Capable WS-OXCs

Figure 14a illustrates a multicasting-capable WS-OXC using *splitting-and-delivery* (SD) switches as reported in Hu and Zeng (1998). This multicasting-capable WS-OXC is modified from the WS-OXC in Figure 4a. In fact, the WS-OXC in Figure 4a becomes the multicasting-capable WS-OXC in Figure 14a if the inputs and outputs are swapped. As shown in Figure 14b, an SD switch is the reverse version of a DC switch (refer to Figure 4b).

More specifically, a DC switch becomes an SD switch if the inputs and the outputs of the DC switch are swapped—that is, the inputs of the DC switch are used as the outputs of the SD switch, and vice versa. In an $i \times j$ SD switch, any input signal is split equally into j branches via a 1 × j optical coupler, and each branch is then selected by a 1 × 2 switch. Therefore, the SD switch is able to connect any input signal to any combination of the outputs or all the outputs and hence is strictly nonblocking. It can be shown that the WS-OXC in Figure 14a not only can switch any input wavelength channel to any combination of the N output fibers but also can connect multiple or all wavelength channels entering at the same input fiber to any single output fiber and hence is strictly nonblocking.

Figure 15 shows another multicasting-capable WS-OXC that was reported in Hu and Zeng (1998). This has a configuration similar to that of the WS-OXC in Figure 3a in which the space switches are replaced by SD switches. It consists of a set of N demultiplexers and multiplexers, each associated with an input-output

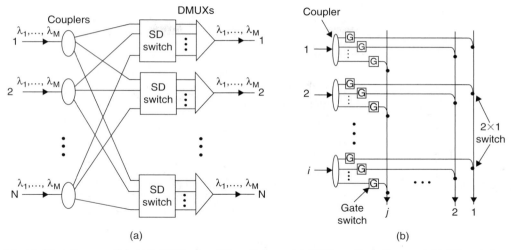

Figure 14: Multicasting-capable WS-OXC using SD switches—(a) OXC configuration and (b) SD switch structure

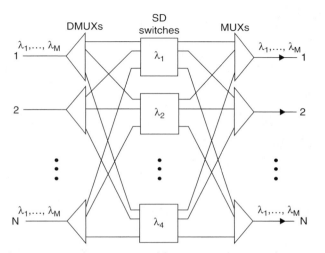

Figure 15: Multicasting-capable WS-OXC reported in Hu and Zeng (1998)

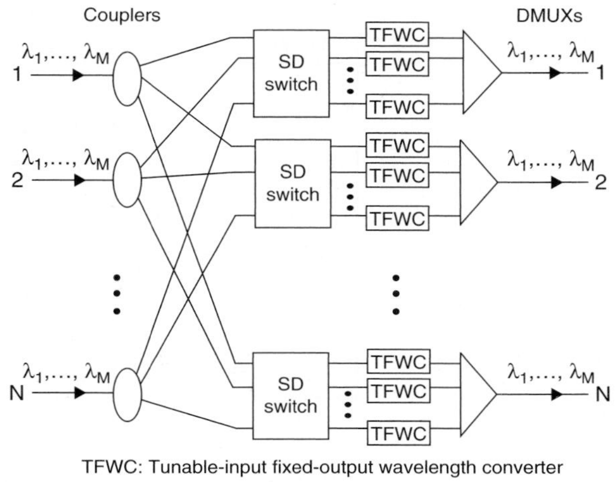

Figure 16: Multicasting-capable WI-OXC using SD switches and TFWCs

fiber, and a set of M $N \times N$ SD switches, each of which handles a single wavelength. After being demultiplexed, all incoming signals with the same wavelength are fed to the same SD switch whereby any signal can be switched to one or more than one output fiber. Signals that are switched to the same output fiber are multiplexed by a multiplexer.

Multicasting-Capable WI-OXCs

By incorporating wavelength conversion, the multicasting-capable WS-OXC in Figure 14a can be modified to be a multicasting-capable WI-OXC as shown in Figure 16 (Hu and Zeng 1998). Here TFWCs are inserted at the outputs of the SD switches. Each incoming WDM signal entering a SD switch can be arbitrarily switched to any combination of M outputs within the SD switch. In each TFWC, a tunable filter is used to select a specific wavelength channel that is subsequently converted to a predetermined output wavelength. Note that the TFWCs cannot be placed at the input side of the SD switches because an optical input channel may

have to be switched to multiple outputs, each of which may be converted to a different wavelength.

CONCLUSION

Optical cross connects play an imperatively important role in future high-capacity and multifunctional optical transport networks. They can be built with different technologies in various configurations. This chapter discussed various OXC architectures and their implementation details. Depending on wavelength conversion capability, OXCs can be classified as wavelength-selective OXCs and wavelength-interchangeable OXCs. Wavelength-selective OXCs can be implemented with optical space-switching technologies, optical multiplexers, or filters. Wavelength-interchangeable OXCs require wavelength converters in addition to optical space switches and multiplexers and filters. Multicasting can also be realized in the optical domain, which may significantly reduce the cost for large-capacity multicast networks. Several multicasting-capable OXCs were described and discussed.

Table 1: List of Acronyms

AOTF	Acousto-optic tunable filter
AWGM	Arrayed waveguide grating multiplexer
DC	Delivery-and-coupling
EDFA	Erbium-doped fiber amplifier
FBG	Fiber Bragg grating
FSR	Free spectrum range
FTWC	Fixed-input tunable-output wavelength converter
MEMS	Micro-electromechanical system
OADM	Optical add-drop multiplexer
OC	Optical circulator
OXC	Optical cross connect
SD	Splitting-and-delivery
SOA	Semiconductor optical amplifier
TFWC	Tunable-input, fixed-output wavelength converter
TTWC	Tunable-input, tunable-output wavelength converter
VWP	Virtual wavelength path
WC	Wavelength converter
WDM	Wavelength-division multiplexing
WID	Wavelength interchange device
WI-OXC	Wavelength-interchangeable optical cross connect
WP	Wavelength path
WS-OXC	Wavelength-selective optical cross connect

GLOSSARY

Blocking Network: A switching network in which a free (idle) input may not be able to be connected to a free output.

Delivery-and-Coupling Switch: A specific optical space switch in which multiple input signals can be connected to the same output as long as these input signals have different wavelengths.

Lightpath: An optical wavelength connection from a source node to a destination node. A lightpath is assigned with a unique wavelength over each intermediate link along the route if the wavelength is not convertible in the network. A lightpath may be assigned with a different wavelength over different links along the route if intermediate nodes are capable of wavelength conversion.

Lightpath Topology: A graph that consists of network nodes with an edge between two nodes if there is a lightpath between them. The lightpath topology refers to the topology seen by the higher network layers using the optical layer.

Multicasting-Capable Optical Cross Connect: An optical cross connect in which an input optical channel can be copied from one input fiber to multiple output fibers.

Optical Space Switching: A switching technique in which an optical wavelength channel is routed from any input port to any output port by optical space switches.

Optical Wavelength Switching: A switching technique in which an optical channel is routed from any input port to any output port by means of wavelength conversion.

Rearrangeably Nonblocking Network: A switching network in which a free input can be connected to a free output by rearranging some of the existing connections.

Split-and-Delivery Switch: A specific optical space switch in which an optical signal can be connected to more than one or all of the outputs of the switch.

Strictly Nonblocking Network: A switching network in which a free input can always be connected to a free output without disturbing any existing connections.

Virtual Wavelength Path (VWP) Network: An optical network capable of wavelength conversion. In such a network, a lightpath from a source node to a destination node may be assigned with a different wavelength over different links along the route. Such a lightpath is usually referred to as a *virtual wavelength path* (or *virtual lightpath*) and hence the network as a *virtual wavelength path* (VWP) *network*.

Wavelength Converter: An optical device that changes the wavelength of an input signal to a different wavelength.

Wavelength Interchangeable Optical Cross Connect (WI-OXC): An optical cross connect in which an input optical channel can be connected from any input fiber to any output fiber, and the wavelength of the input channel can be changed to a different wavelength.

Wavelength Path (WP) Network: An optical network in which wavelength conversion is not possible. In such a network, a lightpath from a source node to a destination node has to be assigned with a unique wavelength over all of the links along the route. Such a lightpath is referred to as *wavelength path,* and hence the network is a *wavelength path* (WP) network.

Wavelength-Selective Optical Cross Connect (WS-OXC): An optical cross connect in which an input optical channel can be connected from any input fiber to any output fiber, but the wavelength of the input channel cannot be changed.

CROSS REFERENCES

See *Optical Fiber Communications; Optical Switching Techniques in WDM Optical Networks; Wavelength Division Multiplexing (WDM).*

REFERENCES

Benes, V. E. 1962. On rearrangeable three-stage switching networks. *Bell System Technical Journal*, 41: 1481–92.

Chai, T. Y., T. H. Cheng, S. K. Bose, C. Lu, and G. Shen. 2002. Crosstalk analysis for limited-wavelength-interchanging cross connects. *IEEE Photonics Technology Letters*, 14: 696–8.

Clos, C. 1953. A study of nonblocking switching networks. *Bell System Technical Journal*, 32: 407–25.

Doerr, C. R. 1998. Proposed WDM cross connect using a planar arrangement of waveguide grating routers and phase shifters. *IEEE Photonics Technology Letters*, 10: 528–30.

Dragone, C. 1991. An $N \times N$ optical multiplexer using a planer arrangement of two star couplers. *IEEE Photonics Technology Letters*, 3: 896–8.

Durhuus, T., B. Mikkelsen, C. Joergensen, S. L. Danielsen, and K. E. Stubkjaer. 1996. All optical wavelength conversion by semiconductor optical amplifiers. *IEEE/OSA Journal of Lightwave Technology*, 14: 942–54.

Giles, C. R. 1999. Wavelength add/drop multiplexer for lightwave communication networks. *Bell Laboratories Technical Journal*, 4, 207–29.

Hill, G. R., P. J. Chidgey, F. Kaufhold, T. Lynch, and O. Sahlen. 1993. A transport network layer based on optical network elements. *IEEE/OSA Journal of Lightwave Technology*, 11: 667–79.

Hu, W. S., and Q. J. Zeng. 1998. Multicasting optical cross connects employing splitter-and-delivery switch. *IEEE Photonics Technology Letters*, 10: 970–2.

Iannone, E., and R. Sabella. 1996. Optical path technologies: A comparison among different cross-connect architectures. *IEEE/OSA Journal of Lightwave Technology*, 14: 2184–96.

International Engineering Consortium. Undated. Optical add/drop switches. Online at: www.iec.org/online/tutorials/add_drop/index.html.

Introduction to all optical switching technologies. Undated. Online at: www.2cool4u.ch/wdm_dwdm/intro_allopticalswitching/intro_allopticalswitching.htm.

Liaw, S. K., K. P. Ho, and S. Chi. 1998. Multichannel add/drop and cross-connect using fibre Bragg gratings and optical switches. *Electronics Letters*, 34: 1601–3.

Okamoto, S., A. Watanabe, and K. Sato. 1996. Optical path cross-connect node architectures for photonic transport network. *IEEE/OSA Journal of Lightwave Technology*, 14: 1410–22.

Panda, M. K., T. Venkatech, V. Sridhar, and Y. N. Singh. 2004. Architecture for a class of scalable optical cross-connects. In *Proceedings of the First International Conference on Broadband Networks*, October, San Jose, CA, USA. pp. 233–42.

Ramaswami, R., and K. N. Sivarajan. 1995. Routing and wavelength assignment in all-optical networks. *IEEE/ACM Transactions on Networking*, 3: 489–500.

Sato, K., S. Okamoto, and H. Hadama. 1994. Network performance and integrity with optical path layer technologies. *IEEE Journal of Selected Areas in Communications*, 12: 159–71.

Simith, D. A., J. J. Johnson, J. E. Baran, and K. W. Cheung. 1990. Integrated acoustically tunable optical filters for WDM networks. *IEEE Journal on Selected Areas in Communications*, 8: 1151–9.

Spanke, R. A. 1987. Architectures for guided-wave optical space switching systems. *IEEE Communications Magazine*, 25: 42–8.

Takahashi, H., S. Suzuki, K. Kato, and I. Nishi. 1990. Arrayed-waveguide grating for wavelength division multi/demultiplexer with nanometer resolution. *Electronics Letters*, 26: 87–8.

Tran, A. V., W. D. Zhong, R. Lauder, and R. S. Tucker. 2001. Optical add-drop multiplexers with low crosstalk. *IEEE Photonics Technology Letters*, 13: 582–4.

Watanabe, A., O. Okamoto, M. Koga, K. Sato, and M. Okuno. 1996. 8×16 delivery and coupling switch board for 320 Gbit/s throughput optical path cross-connect system. *Electronics Letters*, 33: 67–8.

Wu, X. N., Y. F. Shen, C. Lu, T. H. Cheng, and M. K. Rao. 2000. Fiber Bragg crating-based rearrangeable nonblocking optical cross connects using multiport optical circulators. *IEEE Photonics Technology Letters*, 12: 696–8.

Yoo, S. J. B. 1996. Wavelength conversion technologies for WDM network applications. *IEEE/OSA Journal of Lightwave Technology*, 14: 955–66.

Yuan, H., W. D. Zhong, and W. Hu. 2004. FBG-based bidirectional optical crossconnects for bidirectional

WDM ring networks. *IEEE/OSA Journal of Lightwave Technology*, 22: 2710–21.

Zhong, W. D., J. P. R. Lacey, and R. S. Tucker. 1996. New wavelength interchangeable cross-connects with reduced complexity. *IEEE/OSA Journal of Lightwave Technology*, 15: 2029–37.

Zhong, W. D., J. P. R. Lacey, and R. S. Tucker. 1996. Multiwavelength cross-connects for optical transport networks. *IEEE/OSA Journal of Lightwave Technology*, 14: 1613–20.

Zhou, J., R. Caddedu, E. Casaccia, C. Cavazzoni, and M. J. O'Mahony. 1996. Crosstalk in multiwavelength optical cross-connect networks. *IEEE/OSA Journal of Lightwave Technology*, *14*, 1423–35.

Zhu, K., H. Zang, and B. Mukherjee. 2003. A comprehensive study on next-generation optical grooming switches. *IEEE Journal of Selected Areas in Communications*, 21: 1173–85.

Optical Memories

Paul W. Nutter, *The University of Manchester, U.K.*

INTRODUCTION

In today's information society, the demand for high digital data storage capabilities, at increased data rates, has fueled the development of new storage technologies. The dominant data storage technology is magnetic storage—that is, *hard disc drives* (HDD) that offer data storage capacities far in excess of any other storage technology now commercially available. However, although magnetic HDDs offer vast storage capabilities (as much as 1 Terabyte in a single drive), they are limited by the fact that they are fixed, unlike optical memories, which offer relatively large storage capacities (as much as 50 GB on a single 12-cm disc) and the ability to record and erase data using a universal, removable, and reliable disc-based storage medium. The now ubiquitous *compact disc* (CD) and *digital versatile disc* (DVD) have revolutionized the way we archive our data, listen to music and watch movies, and produce our own multimedia content. The next generation of optical memories, such as the *high-definition DVD* (HD-DVD) and the Blu-ray disc, promise superior data storage capabilities with the increased data rates necessary for the recording and viewing of high-definition video content.

This chapter discusses the technology of optical memories and presents an overview of the readout and recording mechanisms in the most popular consumer read-only, write-once, and rewritable disc formats. In addition, the evolution of optical disc memories, from the humble CD to the next generation of ultrahigh-density formats, will be discussed. Finally, new storage technologies being developed for use in future optical memories will be presented, such as near-field recording, magnetic super-resolution techniques for advanced magneto-optical storage, and holographic memories.

OPTICAL DISC STORAGE

Figure 1 illustrates the key components of an optical disc memory, which includes the disc, containing the storage layer where the digital data is stored, and the optical head that is used to retrieve the stored digital data from the disc as well as record the digital data to the disc in recordable formats. The digital data are stored along a spiral track across the storage layer of the disc that originates from the disc center; in the case of the CD, the track is more than 5 km in length. The data are encoded in the form of pits or recorded marks along the track, which are modulated in length according to the data being recorded. The data are recorded to the disc and recovered using a diffraction-limited focused spot, or optical stylus, which scans along the data track as the disc spins beneath the optical head. The optical stylus is produced by focusing the monochromatic laser light produced by a laser diode through the disc substrate onto the surface of the storage layer beneath, as illustrated in the inset of Figure 1. Focusing through the disc substrate is performed to limit the effect that any surface contaminants or dust has on the quality of the optical stylus on the underlying storage layer (Bouwhuis et al. 1985; Marchant 1990; Pohlmann 1989). The design of the objective lens takes into account the spherical aberrations introduced by focusing the laser beam through the disc substrate such that an optimally focused spot is observed at the storage layer.

The storage mechanism depends on the disc format and whether the disc is recordable or not. In the case of read-only formats, such as the CD-ROM, the digital data are embossed into the disc substrate during manufacture as a sequence of phase pits along the data track. In recordable formats, such as the *compact disc–recordable* (CD-R), a focused laser beam, or write beam, which is of a higher intensity compared to that used for readout, is used to record the digital data to the storage layer. A recorded mark is formed by the write beam heating the storage layer to change some physical property of the recording medium, such as its reflectance in phase-change storage media or out-of-plane magnetization in *magneto-optic* (MO) media.

Readout of the digital data from the disc is performed using a low-power focused laser beam, or *read beam*, that

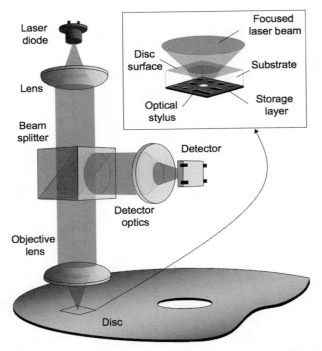

Figure 1: The optical head is used for reading and writing data in optical disc memories. The laser illumination produced by the laser diode is focused by the objective lens to a diffraction limited spot, or optical stylus, on the surface of the storage layer in the disc. The light reflected from the disc is directed to the detection arm of the optical head where it is converted to an electrical form by a detector. Additional detector optics (not illustrated) are used to provide a focus error signal, as well as other optical detection techniques. The inset illustrates the focusing of the laser beam through the disc substrate onto the storage layer beneath

in recordable formats has insufficient power to affect the physical properties of the disc. As the disc spins, the optical stylus scans along the data track and the phase, intensity, or polarization state of the reflected light, depending on the storage mechanism employed, is modulated according to the digital data stored along the data track. The reflected light is then directed to the detection arm of the optical head by a beam splitter and is converted to an electrical form by a detector to produce a high-frequency analog replay waveform. The replay waveform is then processed to recover the digital data—that is, the digital 0's and 1's stored on the disc.

In most consumer optical disc formats, such as the CD and the DVD, a 12-cm diameter disc is typically used. Exceptions are the MiniDisc, which uses a 64-mm disc, and professional optical storage formats, which often use large diameter discs to boost the attainable storage capacity for data archiving.

The Optical Stylus

The data storage capacity of the disc is determined by the size of the features along the storage layer that represent the stored digital data—that is, the pits or marks, along with the track separation, or track pitch. Increased data

storage capacity can be achieved by reducing the size of the recorded features or reducing the track pitch or both. However, ultimately the storage capacity is limited by the size of the optical stylus used for the recording and readout of data. If the pits or recorded marks are too small in comparison with the diameter of the optical stylus, then they will not be "seen" or resolved by the scanning optical stylus and will not contribute to the replay waveform. If the track pitch is too small, then the optical stylus will sense data from tracks adjacent to the main data track, which will introduce cross talk that will degrade the replay waveform, making the recovery of data more prone to error.

The practical size and shape of the optical stylus depends on several factors, including the intensity profile of the laser illumination incident on the objective lens and the presence of any aberrations, such as defocus, in the optical system. The theoretical minimum spot diameter, d_s, expressed in terms of the *full width at half maximum* (FWHM) of the total light intensity, is given by

$$d_s \approx \frac{\lambda}{2.\text{NA}}$$

where λ is the wavelength of the laser illumination and NA is the *numerical aperture* of the objective lens (Bouwhuis et al. 1985). Optical disc memories (CD, DVD, HD-DVD, etc.) have evolved to offer increased storage density by employing an optical stylus of reduced diameter, primarily by a reduction of the wavelength of the incident illumination and an increase in the NA of the objective lens.

Problems such as defocus, in which the disc surface does not lie at the focal point of the objective lens, will affect the quality of the focused spot at the surface of the disc storage layer and act to increase its size, resulting in a loss of resolution and an inability to resolve the pits or recorded marks. An additional problem is the need to hold the optical stylus on the center of the data track as the disc spins because any movement of the optical stylus off-track will result in a loss of signal from the main data track and an increase in the amount of cross talk introduced by the neighboring tracks. The effects of defocus and tracking error require careful consideration; to address these problems, optical disc memories incorporate systems to maintain focus and tracking during the recording and readout of data.

Focusing

The minimum spot size is only maintained over a limited range about the focal point of the objective lens called the *depth of focus*, Δz, which is given by (Bouwhuis et al. 1985)

$$\Delta z \approx \pm \frac{\lambda}{2.\text{NA}^2}.$$

To enable the reliable recording and recovery of data, the storage layer has to be held within the depth of focus of the objective lens as the disc spins beneath, otherwise the storage layer will become out of focus. However, optical discs are not perfectly flat; as a result, the position of the storage layer can vary by as much as ±100 μm as the disc rotates (Mansuripur and Sincerbox 1997) and the disc is invariably out of focus. Vertical

Figure 2: An optical disc player contains a spindle (A), which holds and spins the disc; and an optical head assembly (B), which contains the objective lens (C). The objective lens is mounted in an actuator assembly (D) that allows the positioning of the objective lens vertically for focusing and horizontally for tracking

movement of the disc is particularly prevalent near the outer edge of the disc, which is why the data track starts from the center of the disc. As optical memories have evolved, the amount of defocus that can be tolerated has been reduced as a consequence of the reduction in the wavelength of laser illumination and the increase in the NA of the objective lens. As an example, the depth of focus for the CD is $\approx \pm 1.9$ µm, whereas it is $\approx \pm 0.9$ µm for the DVD. To combat the effect of defocus, an automatic focusing system is required in which the vertical position of the objective lens is adjusted to shift the position of the focused spot about the optical axis to correct for any defocus present. Active positioning of the objective lens is achieved by mounting it in an actuator assembly (see Figure 2) that allows positioning in both the axial (vertical) and radial (horizontal) directions for focusing and tracking, respectively. By applying servo-controlled feedback signals to the actuators, the position of the objective lens in both directions can be precisely controlled (Marchant 1990).

In the case of focusing, the amount and sense of defocus can be measured optically by monitoring the light reflected back from the disc using several optical techniques, including the pupil obscuration method (Bouwhuis et al. 1985) and the commonly used astigmatic method (Braat, Dirkson, and Janssen 2003). The derived focus error signal is fed to the actuator assembly, and any measured defocus is corrected for by moving the objective lens in the appropriate axial direction.

The Pupil Obscuration Method

The pupil obscuration method is based on the principle of the Foucault knife edge (Marchant 1990) whereby the light reflected back from the disc is focused past an obscuration onto a split detector as illustrated in Figure 3 (Bouwhuis et al. 1985; Mansuripur 1995). The obscuration is positioned so that half of the area of the converging light beam is masked so that as the beam moves in and out of focus, the light distribution across the split detector varies.

When the storage layer in the disc is in focus, then the beam is incident on the center of the split detector and the two halves are equally illuminated. However, as the storage layer moves out of focus, the light reflected back from the disc is no longer collimated and is either

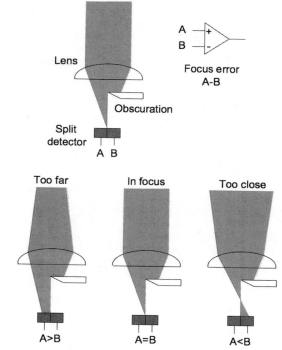

Figure 3: In the pupil obscuration focusing method, the light reflected from the disc is focused onto a split detector. Half of the beam is obscured so that when the disc moves in or out of focus, the light distribution across the split detector varies. The focus error signal is calculated by taking the difference between the signals generated by the two detectors, which is zero when in focus

converging or diverging, depending on the direction of defocus; this is translated into a horizontal shift in the position of the focused light spot on the split detector. The focus error signal is derived by measuring the difference between the signals generated by the two halves of the detector; the magnitude and sign of this signal give the amount and direction of defocus, respectively. An alternative technique, which eases the tolerances on the detector position, involves the replacement of the obscuration and split detector with a pair of prisms and a row of four detectors (see Figure 4), which is also more efficient because of the use of all of the light reflected from the disc (Marchant 1990).

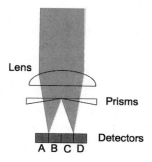

Figure 4: A modified pupil obscuration method involves replacing the obscuration with a pair of prisms and an additional two detectors. The resulting focusing method eases the tolerances on the detector position and is more efficient.

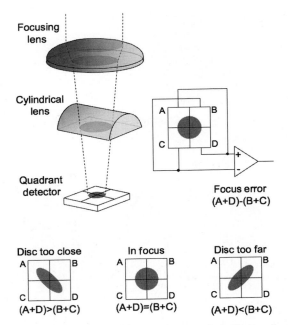

Figure 5: In the astigmatic focusing method, the light reflected from the disc is focused through a cylindrical lens onto a quadrant detector. When in focus, each quadrant receives equal light and the focus error signal is zero. However, as the disc moves out of focus, an astigmatic beam is observed on the quadrant detector and the error signal is given by the sum $(A+D) - (C+D)$ from the outputs from the four detectors

The Astigmatic Method

In the astigmatic method, the light reflected back from the disc is focused through a cylindrical lens onto a four-quadrant detector as illustrated in Figure 5 (Bouwhuis et al. 1985; Bricot et al. 1976).

When the storage layer on the disc is in focus, a circular spot is observed on the detector and each quadrant is equally illuminated. However, as the storage layer moves out of focus, an astigmatic beam is observed on the detector and diagonal pairs of quadrants—that is, A and D, or B and C, receive more light, depending on the direction of defocus. The focus error signal is given by the signal combination $(A + D) - (B + C)$ generated from the output signals from the four quadrants of the detector; the replay waveform is generated by summing the four signals: $(A + B + C + D)$. The sign and magnitude of the focus error signal give the direction and amount of defocus, respectively.

Tracking

In addition to the problem of maintaining focus, the optical stylus must be positioned over the center of the data track, to submicron precision, as the disc spins. Coarse tracking of the optical stylus is achieved by moving the complete optical head assembly across the radius of the disc using a linear actuator. Fine tracking is achieved using servo control of the radial position of the objective lens. Several optical techniques may be used to derive a tracking error signal, and these have been used successfully in commercial optical disc memories. In the same way as focusing techniques, these methods monitor the light reflected back from the disc.

The Three-Spot Method

In the *three-spot* (or *twin-spot*) *method*, two additional focused spots are generated on the surface of the storage medium using a diffraction grating placed after the laser diode. The two satellite spots are projected before and after the main focused spot and are displaced by a quarter of the track pitch off the track center as illustrated in Figure 6 (Bouwhuis and Burgstede 1973). The reflected light resulting from each satellite spot is directed to its own detector, A and B, from which the output signal is low-pass filtered to produce a DC-content signal. The tracking error signal is derived by calculating the difference between these two signals, which is zero when the main spot is on-track and nonzero when it moves off-track. The sign and magnitude of the derived tracking error signal gives the direction and amount of tracking error, respectively. The three-spot method is especially popular in read-only formats (Mansuripur and Sincerbox 1997), although it does suffer from a number of disadvantages: in particular, the need for a precisely aligned diffraction grating, and a loss of optical power resulting from the generation of the satellite beams, which may be a problem for recording.

The Radial Wobble Method

In the *radial wobble method* the optical stylus is forced to oscillate about the track center as the disc spins as illustrated in Figure 7 (Marchant 1990). The resulting tracking error signal is derived from any intensity and phase variations in the light reflected back from the disc. The radial wobble method suffers from several disadvantages such as the introduction of increased cross talk (Braat, Dirkson, and Janssen 2003), the need for the presence of data along the track to enable tracking, and the reduction in the replay waveform resulting from the spot moving off-track (Marchant 1990). A similar technique, which can alleviate some of these problems, involves the use of a wobbled groove on the disc.

The Radial Push-Pull Method

The *radial push-pull method* is well suited for use in storage formats employing a prefabricated phase structure such as read-only disc formats (Mansuripur and Sincerbox 1997). The pit phase structure on the disc acts like a diffraction grating, such that any movement of the main spot off-track introduces a change in the phase difference between the light reflected from the pits and the land (the flat disc surface surrounding the pit), which results in the displacement of the spot across the detector. If the detector is replaced with a split detector, as illustrated in Figure 8, then the tracking error signal can be measured as a difference in the signals from the two halves of the detector as the focused spot moves off-track; the replay waveform is derived by summing the two signals. Again, the sign and magnitude of the tracking error signal give the direction and amount of tracking error, respectively.

One problem with the push-pull method is the need for phase pits on the disc; this makes tracking difficult in the case of recordable formats, such as CD-R, because of

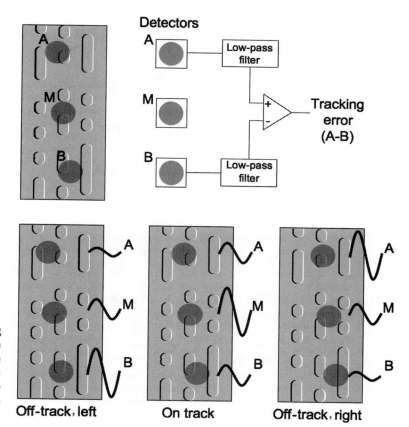

Figure 6: In the three-spot tracking method, tracking is performed using two satellite spots projected in front of and behind the main spot, which are both displaced by a quarter of a track pitch off-track. Each additional spot has its own detector (A and B). The difference between the low-pass signals from the two detectors gives the tracking error signal

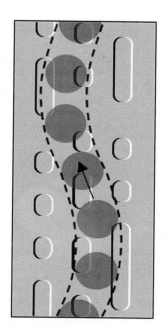

Figure 7: In the radial wobble tracking method, the focused spot is made to oscillate about the track center as it scans along the track. The tracking error signal is calculated from light intensity and phase variations on the main detector

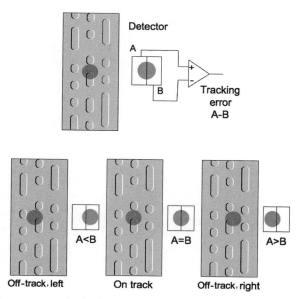

Figure 8: In the radial push-pull tracking method, the main detector is replaced with a split detector. As the scanning spot moves off-track, the phase difference between the pit and land displaces the beam across the split detector. The tracking error signal is found by calculating the difference between the signals from the two halves of the detector

the lack of pits. To remedy this, a prefabricated continuous groove is embossed into the disc substrate during manufacture to form a track for recording and a phase structure for tracking (Mansuripur and Sincerbox 1997). The push-pull method is sensitive to the pit and track depth, and these quantities should be chosen carefully such that they are far enough away from $\lambda/4$ because, in this case, the push-pull signal is zero (Bouwhuis et al. 1985).

Differential Time Detection

An alternative tracking technique commonly used in DVD systems is *differential phase detection* or *differential time detection* (Braat 1998; Braat and Bouwhuis 1978; ECMA International 2001). Here phase changes in the reflected beam introduced as the optical stylus moves off-track give rise to differences in the signals from diagonal pairs of quadrants in a four-quadrant detector; the tracking error signal is then derived from these signal differences.

Data Encoding and the Recovery of Data

The recording and readout process in optical disc memories is inherently imperfect because of errors introduced during the recording process, as well as noise and signal degradations introduced during the readout process arising from the presence of optical aberrations, cross talk, and *intersymbol interference* (ISI). ISI occurs because of the limited frequency response of the optical head, which is illustrated by the *modulation transfer function* given in Figure 9 (Braat, Dirkson, and Janssen 2003).

The frequency response of the optical head is measured in terms of the frequency of the spatial features along the data track, which is translated into a temporal frequency (as seen at the output of the detector) by multiplying it by the disc velocity, v. The so-called spatial frequency response of the optical channel results in a decrease in the amplitude of the replay waveform for high spatial frequency features in the storage layer. The maximum spatial frequency that can be resolved by the optical head is $2NA/\lambda$, which limits the minimum size of the features that can be resolved by the optical stylus (Bouwhuis et al. 1985).

As a result of the limited frequency response of the optical channel, as well as the presence of any signal degradations introduced during readout, the recovery of digital data from the high-frequency analog replay waveform

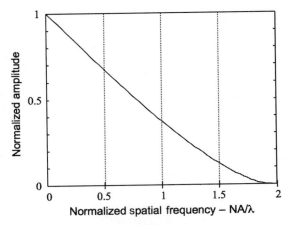

Figure 9: The modulation transfer function illustrates the variation in the amplitude of the high-frequency analog replay waveform as the spatial frequency of the features on the disc storage layer change. The characteristic cutoff frequency, which defines the maximum resolution of the optical head, is given by $2NA/\lambda$. The spatial frequency is translated to a temporal frequency via multiplication by the disc velocity, v

is a complex process. To combat these effects, the digital data are encoded with an error-correction code and a modulation code before recording in order to permit the lossless recovery of stored data. Figure 10 illustrates a block diagram of the read-write channel in a typical optical recording system.

Data Encoding

In storage systems, encoding of the user data involves the addition of both an *error-correcting code* (ECC) and a modulation code to the user digital data. The ECC adds extra redundant data to the original user data to ensure that even under the influence of any signal degradations (random or burst) the user data can still be recovered on readout. The error-correction scheme used in the CD is the cross-interleaved Reed-Solomon code (Bouwhuis et al. 1985; ECMA International 2001), whereas the DVD uses the more powerful Reed-Solomon product code (Schouhamer Immink 2004) because of the greater storage density and the increased susceptibility to aberrations in high NA systems.

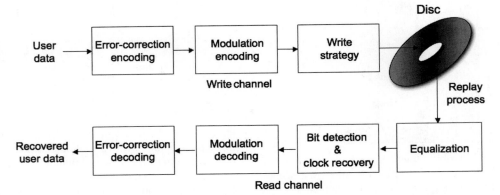

Figure 10: Block diagram of the read-write channel in a typical optical recording system

The choice of modulation, or channel, encoding scheme can be complex, and the scheme must be chosen so that the encoded data closely match the modulation transfer characteristics (Figure 9) of the optical channel and, to some degree, minimize the effects of signal perturbations resulting from the presence of optical aberrations (Schouhamer Immink 2004). The chosen modulation scheme must maximize the data storage density of the medium while maintaining the reliable recovery of data during readout (Bouwhuis et al. 1985). In the case of the CD system, the *eight-to-fourteen modulation* (EFM) scheme adopted is a *run length–limited* (RLL) scheme that serves to restrict the minimum and maximum run-length sequences of like symbols—that is, streams of 0's and 1's in the encoded data. The restriction in the minimum run length controls the highest signal frequency—and hence ISI—in the replay waveform by limiting the minimum length of the pits or recorded marks in the storage layer. The restriction on the maximum run length limits the maximum length of the pits or recorded marks to ensure that sufficient data transitions are available to enable recovery of the data clock (Schouhamer Immink 2004). The encoding process involves the translation of m binary symbols into n binary symbols ($n > m$) using a look-up table. In the case of the EFM scheme, 8-bit blocks of data are converted to 14 bits such that the minimum and maximum pit or recorded mark lengths correspond to run lengths of 3 and 11 like symbols, respectively. The DVD uses the EFMPlus modulation code, which has the same run-length characteristics as EFM but offers an increased code rate (Schouhamer Immink 2004).

After encoding, the data are written to the disc using an appropriate writing strategy such that the encoded data sequence is translated into an appropriate sequence of pits or recorded marks along the data track as illustrated in Figure 11.

The Read Channel

The purpose of the read channel is to take the high-frequency analog replay waveform from the optical head and recover the stored digital data. The read channel can be considered to be the reverse of the write channel, with additional stages to compensate for the frequency limitations of the optical channel and to alleviate ISI (using equalization), as well as sample the analog replay waveform, recover the stored user data (bit detection), and recover the data timing information (clock recovery).

Filtering of the analog replay waveform boosts the high-frequency signal content to compensate for the frequency constraints of the optical channel, as well as counteract any ISI in the replay waveform. The analog waveform is then converted to a digital form using an analog-to-digital converter from which the digital data and data clock are recovered. Two approaches can be used to recover the encoded user data: threshold detection and maximum likelihood detection. *Threshold detection* is the most commonly used approach, which involves comparing the data sampled at the data clock frequency (provided by the recovered clock signal) with a threshold level and making a decision as to whether the sample value corresponds to a stored 0 or 1. The use of *maximum likelihood techniques,* common in magnetic hard drives (Wang and Taratorin 1999), is more complex but more effective in combating the effects of ISI (Mansuripur and Sincerbox 1997). Once the encoded data have been recovered, the modulation code is removed and the error-correction decoder corrects for any introduced errors so that the original stored user data are retrieved.

THE READOUT AND RECORDING PROCESSES IN OPTICAL MEMORIES

The readout and recording mechanisms in optical memories vary, depending on the storage format. The most common formats such as the CD and the DVD use the standard optical head to detect intensity variations in the light reflected back from the disc during readout. The recording process depends on whether the format is read-only, write-once, or rewritable. In formats such as the MiniDisc and some professional storage systems, the recording and readout processes differ considerably because of the use of magneto-optical recording media.

Read-Only Storage

In read-only optical memories such as the CD-ROM and the DVD-ROM, the data are embossed into the polycarbonate disc during manufacture as a series of phase pits along the data track, where the pit lengths are varied according to the data being stored. The high-frequency analog replay waveform is produced as a result of the reflected beam having its amplitude and phase modified by the pit structures as the optical stylus scans along the data track during readout as illustrated in Figure 12. When the optical stylus is incident on the land between pits, the storage layer reflects the majority of the light. However, when scanning over a pit, the light reflected from the bottom of the pit is half a wavelength out of phase compared with that reflected from the land, which results in a reduction in the intensity of the reflected light and hence a reduction in the signal from the detector (Pohlmann 1989).

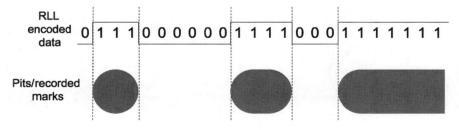

Figure 11: Encoding of the user data restricts the minimum and maximum run-length number of like symbols in the user data. Pits or recorded marks on the disc are formed according to the run length of 1's in the encoded data sequence

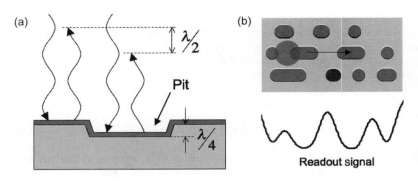

Figure 12: The readout process in read-only formats. In (a), the depth of the pits is a quarter of a wavelength such that light reflected form the pit bottom is half a wavelength out of phase with the light reflected from the land. As a result, in (b) the signal from the detector reduces as the optical stylus scans across a pit

Write-Once Recording

Several recording techniques may be used to implement a *write-once, read many* (or WORM) optical memory such as ablative recording, dye recording, and phase-change recording. In each technique, the recording process changes some physical property of the storage layer in the presence of a write beam as illustrated in Figure 13. Data readout is performed using the conventional optical head, where the detector measures changes in the intensity of the light reflected from the disc.

Ablative Recording

In *ablative recording,* the storage layer is composed of a thin metal film that has a low melting point. When the write beam is applied, the metal film vaporizes to form holes in the storage layer (Marchant 1990). The resulting holes have a much lower reflectivity compared to the unrecorded metal film and, as a result, the amplitude of the replay waveform from the detector reduces as the optical stylus scans over a hole.

Dye Recording

In *dye recording,* the storage layer is composed of a light-absorbing organic film that distorts to form a pitlike structure when exposed to the write beam. The resulting pits in the dye storage layer behave in the same manner as the pits in the read-only formats such that, as the optical stylus scans across a pit during readout, a reduced signal is observed at the output of the detector (Marchant 1990). Dye recording films are used extensively in the recordable CD (CD-R) and recordable DVD (DVD−R/+R) formats.

Phase-Change Recording

In *phase-change recording,* the storage layer is composed of a material that exhibits two structural phases: crystalline and amorphous. Heating an amorphous film using the write beam results in the formation of a crystalline mark that exhibits a slightly increased reflectivity compared to the amorphous state. As a result, the amplitude of the signal at the output of the detector increases as the optical stylus scans across a recorded crystalline

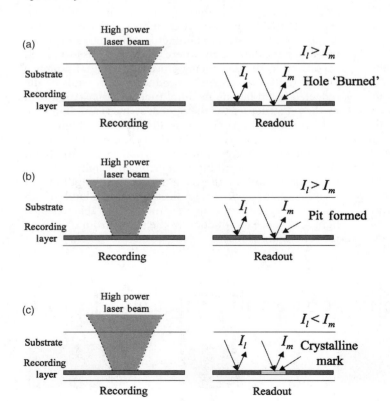

Figure 13: Write-once recording techniques. (a) In ablative recording, the write beam burns a hole in the thin metal storage layer. The light reflected from the hole is of a lower intensity compared with the light reflected from the unrecorded film. (b) In dye recording, the write beam melts the recording layer to form a pitlike structure. The light reflected from the pit is of a lower intensity compared with the light reflected from the unrecorded film. (c) In phase-change recording, the write beam forms a recorded crystalline mark in the amorphous film. The light reflected from the mark is of a higher intensity compared with the light reflected from the unrecorded film

mark (Marchant 1990). The use of phase-change media is viewed as the cleanest of all recording techniques because it does not involve any material removal. However, its use as a write-once storage medium has been restricted because the polarity of the replay waveform differs from that of the other formats, which leads to compatibility issues. Phase-change media have been used extensively in rewritable formats because of the ability to write, read, and erase data.

Rewritable Recording

In rewritable systems, data can be recorded, read, and erased many times. Examples include the CD-RW, the DVD–RW/+RW formats, and the MiniDisc. The two most common rewritable recording techniques use either phase-change media (the CD-RW and the DVD–RW/+RW) or magneto-optical media (the MiniDisc). These two recording techniques are incompatible and require different recording and readout approaches.

Phase-Change Recording

Phase-change recording films have found favor in several rewritable optical disc formats such as CD-RW, DVD–RW/+RW, and the next generation of formats. Here the storage layer is composed of Ag-In-Sb-Te or Ge-Sb-Te type alloys in a complex quadrilayer stack structure (see Figure 14) that is carefully designed to control the thermodynamic recording process (Philips Electronics 1997; Kageyama et al. 1996; Yamada et al. 1991; Mansuripur and Sincerbox 1997).

In its original deposited form, the phase-change storage layer is in an amorphous state (as in the WORM case), which during the manufacturing process is annealed to change the phase of the unrecorded disc to its crystalline state. The state of the unrecorded crystalline storage layer can be changed to an amorphous state by locally heating it above its melting temperature ($\approx$500°C) using a

high-power laser beam and then allowing it to cool, or quench, quickly. If the storage layer is in its amorphous state, then it can be changed back to its (erased) crystalline state by heating it to a temperature below the melting temperature but above the crystallization temperature, $\approx$200°C, using a laser beam of reduced power compared to that used when writing (Philips Electronics 1997; Mansuipur and Sincerbox 1997).

To prevent the formation of asymmetric recorded marks during recording, the write beam is pulsed at a high frequency during the recording of a mark (see Figure 15). Direct overwrite of any existing recorded data in the storage layer—that is, changing any amorphous recorded marks back to the crystalline, or erased, state—is achieved by setting the laser power to the erase power, P_e, between recorded marks. Ge-Sb-Te alloys can tolerate a greater number of overwrite cycles (100,000) compared to Ag-In-Sb-Te alloys (1000), which is why such alloys have found favor in rewritable formats such as CD-RW and DVD–RW/+RW.

Because the amorphous state exhibits a reduced optical reflectivity compared to the crystalline state, the recorded data can be easily recovered by monitoring changes in the intensity of the reflected light using the standard optical head as the optical stylus scans along the recorded data track.

Phase-change media are now being used in professional data-archiving products, such as *ultra density optical* (UDO), because of the long lifetimes (50+ years) they offer (Plasmon 2006).

Magneto-Optical Recording

Magneto-optical (MO) data storage materials have been used in professional storage applications for many years, whereas the application in consumer products has been limited because of the dominance of the CD and DVD formats. However, one commercial success has been the recordable MiniDisc developed by Sony. With a storage

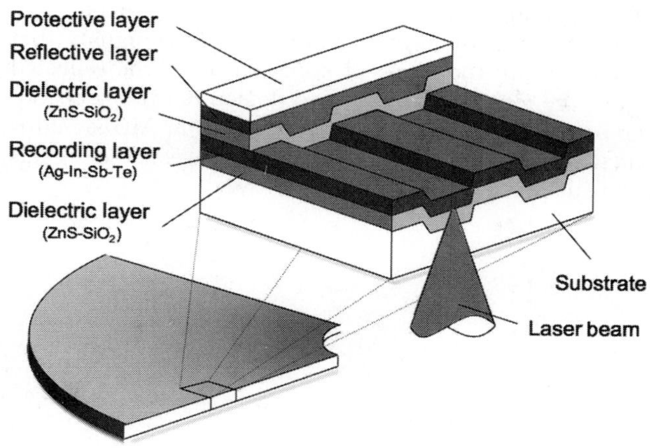

Figure 14: The CD-RW uses a grooved substrate to aid in tracking. The phase-change recording layer (Ag-In-Sb-Te) is sandwiched between two dielectric layers and coated with a metallic reflective layer to form a quadrilayer stack. The design of the stack is optimized to control the writing process.

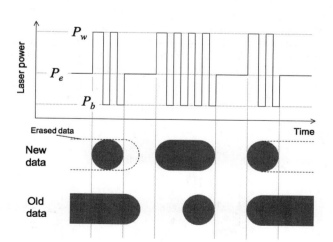

Figure 15: In phase-change recording, a recorded mark is formed in the storage layer by pulsing the write beam at a high frequency. Direct overwriting of prerecorded data is achieved by applying an erase power beam between recorded marks

density of 177 Mb, the MiniDisc allows 74 minutes of compressed audio (using adaptive transform acoustic coding) to be stored to a 64-mm diameter disc (Yoshida 1994).

The recording layer in an MO disc is invariably made from a thin film of an amorphous rare earth and transition metal magnetic alloy, such as Tb-Fe-Co, which exhibits a perpendicular anisotropy—that is, it is magnetized perpendicular to the plane of the disc (Mansuripur 1995; McDaniel and Victora 1997). At room temperature, an MO material exhibits a high coercivity; as a result, it is difficult to change its magnetization state using an externally applied magnetic field. However, the coercivity of the magnetic film can be reduced through heating it using a focused laser beam. If the MO material is heated to its Curie temperature (≈300°C), its magnetization reduces to zero, so its magnetization can be influenced by the presence of an external magnetic field (Mansuripur and Sincerbox 1997; Marchant 1990).

In MO recording, data are recorded to the MO storage layer in the form of recorded domains that are magnetized in the opposite direction to the unrecorded film. These domains are recorded by locally heating the MO storage layer to a temperature just below the film's Curie temperature using a write beam. The application of a small external magnetic field (≈100Oe), generated by an electromagnet placed in close proximity, results in the formation of a magnetic domain when the write beam is removed (see Figure 16). Erasure is achieved by applying an external field aligned in the same direction to the magnetization direction of the bulk MO storage layer.

In MO recording, data can be written in one of two ways: either by application of light-intensity modulation or magnetic field modulation. In *light-intensity modulation recording*, the externally applied magnetic field is held constant with the direction of magnetization aligned in the opposite direction to that of the unrecorded storage layer. The magnetic domains are then written by modulating the write beam according to the data being recorded. Here the size of the recorded domains, and hence storage density, is limited by the size of the optical stylus. In *magnetic field modulation recording*, the write beam is held constant and the externally applied magnetic field is modulated according to the data being recorded. In this case, crescent-shaped recorded domains are written to the MO storage layer, which can be smaller in size (in the data track direction) compared to the optical stylus used to write them, resulting in an increase

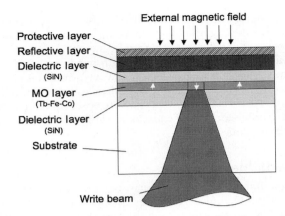

Figure 16: In MO recording, a magnetic domain is written by applying a write beam, which heats the MO layer to a temperature just below the magnetic film's Curie temperature. Application of an external field is then sufficient to allow local magnetization reversal to occur, thereby forming a recorded domain in the storage layer

in the attainable data storage density. In addition, direct overwriting of previously recorded data can be easily achieved using magnetic field modulation, whereas in light-intensity modulation recording the data track has to be completely erased before a new data track can be recorded.

Readout in MO systems is performed using the polar Kerr effect, whereby the plane of polarization of a linearly polarized incident read beam is rotated on reflection from the magnetic storage layer. The sense of rotation depends on the orientation of the magnetization of the MO storage layer as illustrated in Figure 17.

To detect the small rotation of the plane of polarization of the reflected light, the detection optics of the optical head are modified to include polarizing optics to change the rotation in the plane of polarization into a change in light intensity at the two detectors (see Figure 18). The optics are configured in such a way that in the absence of any polar Kerr signal—that is, there is no rotation in the plane of polarization—the detectors are illuminated equally.

However, in the presence of a polar Kerr signal—that is, rotation in the plane of polarization of the reflected light—the signals from the two detectors differ depending on the sense of rotation, and a bipolar MO signal is calculated by taking the difference between the signals (Mansuripur 1995).

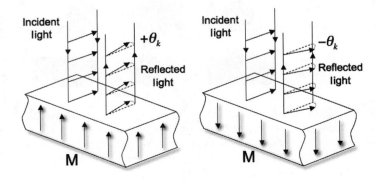

Figure 17: The polar Kerr effect is used to distinguish between the recorded domains in the MO storage layer. On reflection from the perpendicularly magnetized MO layer, the plane of polarization of the incident beam is rotated by a small angle, θ_k. The direction of rotation depends on the direction of the magnetization in the magnetic layer

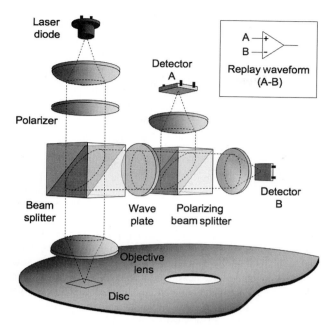

Figure 18: In MO readout, a modified optical head is used to detect the polar Kerr rotation in the plane of polarization of the beam reflected from the disc. A polarizer ensures that the read beam is initially linearly polarized. The detection arm is modified to include a polarizing beam splitter and two detectors (plus additional optical components). Any rotation in the plane of polarization of the beam reflected from the disc results in an imbalance between the signals from the two detectors, A and B. The MO replay waveform is generated by calculating the difference between the signals from the two detectors—that is, A − B.

THE EVOLUTION OF OPTICAL DISC MEMORIES: FROM THE CD TO THE NEXT GENERATION

The first consumer optical disc format was the video disc introduced by Philips in 1978. It used a double-sided 30-cm disc to store as many as 120 minutes of prerecorded video. The video disc was an analog system in which the analog video signal was encoded to the read-only disc during manufacture as a series of phase pits along the data track. The analog replay waveform was then recovered optically using the conventional optical head discussed previously. Ultimately, the video disc failed commercially for several reasons, but mainly because of its inability to record video, unlike the hugely successful, and competing, videocassette recorder. In parallel with the development of the video disc, researchers at Philips started the development of an equivalent system for storing audio. The first optical audio disc system used an analog system similar to that of the video disc. Because of the analog nature of the recording, however, sound fidelity was poor and imperfections introduced during manufacture resulted in audible clicks during replay (Bouwhuis et al. 1985). As a result, a digital system was developed, the compact disc, which utilized error-correction techniques to correct for any such errors (Philips Electronics 2006; Bouwhuis et al. 1985).

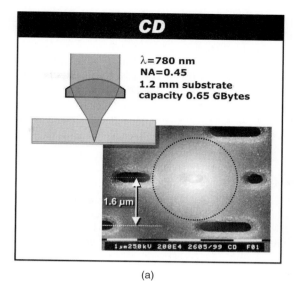

(a)

(b)

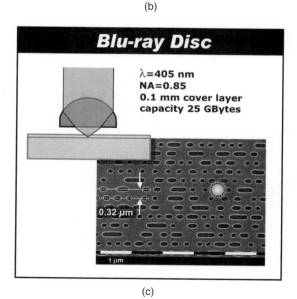

(c)

Figure 19: Electron microscope images (of equal magnification) of the pit structures in the CD, DVD, and Blu-ray disc formats with accompanying laser spots. Courtesy of Philips

Optical disc storage systems have evolved considerably from those early days, with each generation offering increased data storage capacity through technological advances. Figure 19 illustrates the CD-ROM, DVD-ROM, and Blu-ray disc media and clearly demonstrates how the storage density has increased, and the size of the focused spot has been reduced, with each subsequent generation. Table 1 lists the technical differences among the CD, DVD, HD-DVD, and Blu-ray disc formats.

The Compact Disc

The compact disc, developed through a partnership between Philips and Sony, was released to the consumer market in 1982. In its early days, the CD was aimed primarily at the distribution of high-quality, two-channel stereo (16-bit, 44.1-kHz sampling rate) digital audio content (CD digital audio, CD-DA) with the now familiar 1.2-mm thick, 12-cm diameter disc originally chosen to accommodate a 74-minute recording of Beethoven's ninth symphony (Braat, Dirkson, and Janssen 2003).

At the time of its introduction, the CD was revolutionary because it offered a huge increase in storage capacity over what was available at that time (even compared to magnetic storage devices), in addition to offering a removable storage medium that was cheap and simple to mass replicate because of the development of low-cost injection-molding fabrication techniques. The production of CD media begins with a glass master, onto which the recorded data pattern is transferred to a photosensitive resist layer using photolithographic techniques; this is then coated with a silver metal layer. Next, the master is coated with a thick layer of nickel to form a metal stamper; when removed from the master, the stamper has formed a negative replica of the final disc. The stamper is then used in an injection-molding process to form the final disc copy by pressing it against hot plastic (Williams 1996). After the polycarbonate disc substrate has been pressed using the stamper to form the disc, the data side of the disc is coated with a metallic layer to improve the reflectance properties of the disc. Finally, a protective lacquer layer is applied to form the label side of the disc. Figure 20 illustrates the CD disc structure.

Table 1: A Comparison of the Key Optical Disc Parameters for CD, DVD, HD DVD and Blu-ray Disc Formats

	CD	DVD	HD-DVD	Blu-ray Disc
Wavelength (nm)	780 (infrared)	650 (red)	405 (blue)	405 (blue)
Numerical aperture	0.45	0.6	0.65	0.85
Spot size (nm)*	867	542	312	238
Disc diameter (mm)	120			
Disc thickness (mm)	1.2			
Cover layer thickness (mm) (readout side)	1.2	0.6	0.6	0.1
User data capacity (Gb)	0.65–0.7	4.7/8.4/17[a]	15/30[ab], 15[ac], 30/32[ad]	23.3/25/27[e] 46.6/50/54[f]
Minimum bit length (nm)	833	400	204	160/149/138[g]
Track pitch (nm)	1600	740	400	320
Modulation code	(2,10)RLL**		(1,10)RLL**	(1,7)RLL**
Data rate (Mbps) (nominal)	1.44	10	36.5	36
Disc velocity (m/s)	1.2	3.5	5	5
Video compression	MPEG-1 (VCD) MPEG-2 (SVCD)	MPEG-2	MPEG-2 MPEG-4 AVC VC-1	
Video resolution (playing time)	352 × 240/288 VCD 480 × 480/576 SVCD	720 × 480/576(133 mins typical)	1920 × 1080 HDTV(2 hours requires 22 Gb)	

*Theoretical minimum spot size defined by the equation given (FWHM); **RLL = run length limited
[a]In the order single layer/dual layer/dual layer, double-sided; [b]read-only; [c]recordable; [d]rewritable; [e]single layer (variable capacity); [f]dual layer (variable capacity); [g]depends on capacity
Source: Blu-ray 2004; HD DVD Technology 2006; ECMA International 1996 2001; Williams 1996

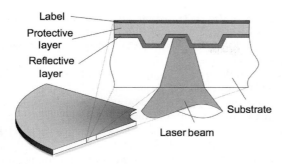

Figure 20: In the CD, the pit structure is embossed into the polycarbonate substrate during manufacture. The substrate is then coated with a metallic layer to improve the disc reflectivity, followed by a protective lacquer layer onto which the label is printed

The introduction of the *compact disc read-only memory* (CD-ROM) revolutionized the way that software was distributed and led to the development of new consumer devices such as game consoles. Because of the success of the personal computer, there soon became need for a recordable CD format for data-archiving purposes. As a result, the write-once CD recordable (CD-R) and CD rewritable (CD-RW) formats were introduced, both of which are backward-compatible with the CD-ROM format and offer the same storage capacity. In addition, they both use the same optical head for the recording and readout of data, but the mechanism by which information is stored on the disc is completely different. In the CD-R format, dye recording is used. Here the recording film is deposited onto a prefabricated groove structure embossed into the polycarbonate disc during manufacture, which forms a track for recording and also aids in tracking. The recording layer is then coated with a reflective metallic layer and a final protective lacquer layer, in much the same way as the CD. The CD-RW disc structure is similar to that of the CD-R, but utilizes a more complex rewritable phase-change recording layer.

The FWHM spot size in the CD system is approximately 0.8 μm, which permits a track pitch of 1.6 μm and a minimum pit length of 0.833 μm (corresponding to a minimum run length of three bits) (ECMA International 1996). A pit depth of λ/4 maximizes the amplitude of the high-frequency replay waveform, although this also minimizes the push-pull tracking signal; hence, a pit depth of approximately λ/6 (≈140 nm) was chosen.

The data transfer rate at which the stored data is read from the CD depends on the speed at which the disc is spun. In older CD-ROM drives, the disc was spun at a *constant linear velocity* so that data were extracted from the disc at a constant rate. To enable this, the speed of the motor was varied, depending on the location of the data on the disc; as a result, the disc was required to spin faster when accessing data nearer the disc center. However, modern drives spin the disc at a *constant angular velocity* (CAV), so the data transfer rate depends on the location of the data on the disc; in this case, the data rate is slower near the center of the disc. The use of a CAV system has allowed the disc velocity to be increased, thus enabling much higher data transfer rates compared to the nominal

(1×) data rate of 150 Kb/s. The maximum data transfer rate in commercial CD-ROM drives is 52× (7.8 Mb/s), although this rate cannot be sustained when transferring data from the whole disc. Increased transfer rates would require spinning the disc faster, which is limited by the strength of the polycarbonate disc and stresses induced when rotating at high speed.

The Digital Versatile Disc

Although the CD was developed for the distribution of digital audio and data, a format called the *video CD* (VCD) was developed for storing digital video. However, the video quality from the VCD was poor because of the MPEG-1 compression standard used. Improved video quality could be achieved using the MPEG-2 compression standard (the *super video compact disc*, or SVCD), but the storage limitations resulted in a limited recording time. Hence, the *digital versatile disc* was developed, driven primarily by the movie industry to offer a means of storing high-quality video and audio content for movie distribution.

At first glance, the CD and DVD appear to be similar, and the fundamental optical principles used for readout and recording remain largely unchanged. However, the DVD offers more than seven times the storage capacity of the CD: 4.7 Gb per disc. This has been achieved by reducing the track width to 0.74 μm, and reducing the minimum pit length to 0.4 μm (corresponding to a run length of two bits). To resolve the reduced feature sizes on the disc, the size of the focused spot in the DVD is much smaller than in the CD; this was achieved by using a shorter-wavelength red laser (650 nm compared to 780 nm in the CD) and a higher NA objective lens (0.6 compared to 0.45 in the CD). One particular problem with increased NA imaging is the reduced tolerance to aberrations, in particular, the depth of focus, which is reduced from ≈±1.9 μm in the case of the CD to ≈±0.9 μm in the DVD. In addition, the act of focusing through the disc substrate leads to the introduction of unwanted coma into the focused spot in the presence of any disc tilt (Braat and Bouwhuis 1978), the amount of distortion being proportional to NA^{-3}. Hence, in the DVD standard the substrate thickness was reduced to 0.6 mm to alleviate these effects but still adequately protect the storage layer (Mansuripur and Sincerbox 1997; Braat, Dirkson, and Janssen 2003). To maintain the standard 1.2-mm thick disc, a DVD disc consists of a substrate containing a single storage layer bonded to a 0.6-mm thick dummy substrate.

The key technical advancement in the DVD standard was the introduction of dual-layer storage in which data can be stored on two closely spaced (≈50nm) storage layers. The data on the bottom layer are read by refocusing the laser through the semitransparent top data layer. In addition to dual-layer recording, the DVD standard offers increased storage capacity by allowing data to be stored to both sides of the disc. In the case of the ROM format, several disc configurations were developed that offered various storage capacities (see Figure 21), ranging from 4.7 Gb on the single layer disc (DVD-5) to 17 Gb over four storage layers using the double-sided dual-layer disc (DVD-17) (ECMA International 2001).

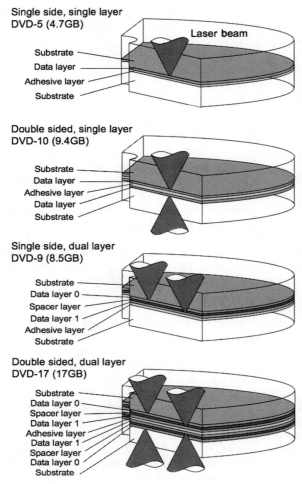

Figure 21: Four types of DVD-ROM discs have varying storage capacity. DVD-5 has a single storage layer and offers 4.7 Gb of storage. DVD-10 has a single storage layer on both sides of the disc and offers 9.4 Gb of storage. DVD-9 has two storage layers on one side of the disc and offers 8.5 Gb of storage capacity. DVD-17 has two storage layers on both sides of the disc and offers 17 Gb of capacity

One problem with the development of the DVD was how to ensure backward compatibility with the CD standard because of the different wavelengths, pit widths, and so on used. Solutions to this included the development of two lens objective assemblies in which the correct objective lens can be switched into the optical path depending on the type of disc being read, and the development of dual focus lens assemblies that, by using a hologram lens, permit the reading of both CD and DVD discs using the same objective lens and optical path.

The development of the DVD standard mirrored that of the CD with the introduction of a read-only format (DVD-ROM) in which information is premanufactured onto the disc like the CD-ROM and on through to the development of recordable and rewritable formats. The development of write-once and rewritable DVD formats resulted in the introduction of three competing DVD recording formats: the DVD-R/DVD-RW and DVD-RAM formats developed by the DVD Forum (2004), the original

developers of the DVD format; and the DVD+R/DVD+RW formats, developed by the breakaway DVD+RW Alliance (2006). The DVD-R/RW and DVD+R/RW formats offer the same storage capacity as the single-layer DVD-ROM disc, are compatible with the majority of DVD players, and offer dual-layer recording capabilities (DVD+RW was the first). However, the two formats are incompatible. The DVD-RAM format offers improved recording features such as random read-write access, much like an HDD, which was made possible through the use of data sectors addressed using embossed land and pit areas on the disc. However, the main disadvantage of the DVD-RAM format, which led to its limited commercial success, was its incompatibility with existing DVD players.

The recording and readout processes in the DVD formats are similar to that of the equivalent read-only, write-once, and rewritable CD-formats: Either a dye recording film is used in the write-once formats, or a phase-change recording medium is used in the rewritable formats. To enable the efficient recording of data at high data transfer rates, media manufacturers encode their discs with recording information that recorders access before recording.

HD-DVD and Blu-ray Disc: The Format War

The next generation of optical disc memories promise storage densities far in excess of the CD and DVD formats and have been developed to satisfy the data storage capabilities and data transfer rates required for the recording and playback of high-definition video (two hours of 1920×1080 pixel resolution video requires 22 Gb). The two competing standards—HD-DVD led by Toshiba and the Blu-ray disc led by Sony—are being promoted by leading industry groups and major Hollywood studios and are sure to ignite a format war similar to that of the competing videocassette formats, Betamax and VHS, in the 1980s. Both standards offer ROM, write-once, and rewritable formats using single- or dual-layer discs (although HD-DVD does not currently support a write-once, dual-layer format) and are aimed at eventually replacing DVD in many applications such as movie distribution, software distribution, and data archiving (Blu-ray 2004; HD DVD Technology 2006).

In both standards, increased storage capacity is achieved through the use of a blue laser (405 nm). However, the main difference between the two standards is that the Blu-ray disc offers a much higher storage capacity (as much as 54 Gb) compared to the HD-DVD system (32 Gb). The increase in storage capacity of the Blu-ray disc has been achieved by adopting an objective lens with a higher NA of 0.85 compared to 0.65 in the HD-DVD standard (Blu-ray 2005; HD DVD Technology 2006). The HD-DVD system is an extension of the DVD format and uses a similar 1.2-mm thick substrate formed by bonding two 0.6-mm thick substrates (DVD Forum 2004). However, the Blu-ray disc uses a 1.1-mm thick disc containing a 0.1-mm protective layer through which the blue laser is focused onto the underlying storage layer.

Because the HD-DVD technology is similar to that of the DVD, little investment is required to modify the disc production line to produce HD-DVD media. However, in the case of the Blu-ray disc, the technology is sufficiently different to require the development of new production lines, which will delay the introduction of Blu-ray consumer products. In addition, the Blu-ray disc system is more susceptible to both scratches and dust on the disc surface because of the reduced thickness of the protective layer as well as from the aberrations introduced as a result of imaging using a higher NA objective lens. Consequently, it was initially believed that Blu-ray media would be enclosed in a cartridge to protect the disc. However, disc manufacturers are developing hard coatings that should provide sufficient disc surface protection (TDK 2006).

THE FUTURE OF OPTICAL MEMORIES

Optical memories have evolved to offer increased data storage densities, primarily by reducing the size of the optical stylus in successive generations. However, any further reduction in the size of the focused spot beyond that of the Blu-ray disc may be difficult for several reasons. Currently, no short-wavelength—that is, *ultraviolet* (UV)—semiconductor lasers are available, and the materials currently used to make discs absorb UV light, thus resulting in low light transmission at these wavelengths. In addition, the tolerances for defocus and depth of focus limit the increase in the NA of the objective lens, which is also limited to a maximum value of 1 in air. Increased storage densities may be achieved through the use of multilayer storage, but this will only offer a short-term solution to extend the capability of today's formats. Consequently, future generations of optical storage products will require the development of new optical imaging techniques and novel data storage mechanisms that will permit recorded features much smaller than those achievable using conventional approaches. There is currently considerable research in both the storage industry and academia on new optical data storage approaches; these include optical imaging systems based on near-field optics such as the solid immersion lens, advanced magnetic recording techniques such as the *magnetically amplifying magneto-optic system* (MAMMOS), and volumetric storage mechanisms using holography.

Near-Field Optical Storage

The minimum size of the focused spot in conventional storage systems is restricted by the diffraction limit in air (although the focused spot is observed in the substrate, the beam diameter is the same as would be observed in air). However, in near-field optics the diffraction limit in air can be circumvented through the use of nano-sized apertures or the more attractive *solid immersion lens* (SIL) (Mansfield and Kino 1990). The SIL is a hemisphere made from a material of high refractive index ($n > 1$) placed such that its flat surface is coincident with the focal point of the objective lens (see Figure 22). Because the speed of light is reduced on propagation through a material of higher refractive index, the wavelength of the light focused inside the SIL is reduced by a factor of $1/n$. Consequently, the effective NA, NA_{eff}, of the optical system is increased to nNA, where NA is the numerical

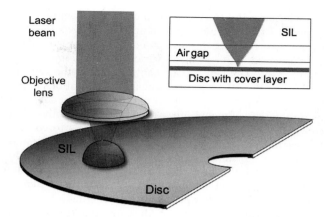

Figure 22: In near-field recording using a solid immersion lens, the SIL is placed close to the focal point of the lens but is separated from the spinning disc by an air gap. The size of the optical stylus is reduced by a factor $1/n$ over that attainable in air. The inset illustrates that, in a practical recording system, the design of the SIL can take account for the presence of any cover layer on the disc, which must have the same refractive index as the SIL material, and that an air gap invariably exists between the flat bottom surface of the SIL and the disc surface

aperture of the focusing objective lens. Hence, the size of the focused spot is reduced by a factor of $1/n$ over that attainable in air. Further improvements in the resolution of an SIL-based imaging system may be achieved through the use of a the stigmatic SIL, or supersphere, which permits a further reduction in the size of the focused spot by a factor of $1/n^2$ over that attainable in air (Terris et al. 1994).

The use of the SIL in optical memories offers several technical difficulties, most notably the inevitable presence of an air gap between the bottom flat surface of the SIL and the surface of the disc because the disc must move independently of the optical head. The air gap reduces the transmission efficiency of the optical system and introduces aberrations that lead to an overall loss in resolution (Mansfield et al. 1993). In a system where $NA_{eff} < 1$, the effect of the air gap is to introduce spherical aberrations. Providing that the air gap is held constant, these aberrations can be alleviated through the careful design of the objective lens. In systems where $NA_{eff} > 1$, rays incident at the SIL–air gap boundary at an angle greater than the critical angle, $\theta_c = \sin(1/n)$, will be totally internally reflected, and the evanescent fields associated with these rays exponentially decay as they propagate across the air gap. As a result, the air gap has to be kept as small as possible—ideally, <100 nm—to maintain the benefits of near-field imaging and maintain a focused spot much smaller than that achievable in air (Hayashi and Kino 1995); this is particularly true in the application of the stigmatic SIL. The design of the SIL can take into account the thickness of any cover layer on the disc, in which case the laser beam is focused onto the surface of the storage layer in the disc as illustrated in the inset of Figure 22 (Hayashi and Kino 1995).

To maintain the benefits of near-field imaging, it is important that the air gap remains constant as the disc spins. As a result, near-field gap servomechanisms have been devised that, using a variety of techniques, can monitor the depth of the air gap and adjust the vertical position of the SIL to compensate for any variations in the air gap's depth. Measurement of the air gap can be achieved using a variety of techniques—for example optically—that can then be used to provide feedback signals to control the vertical position of the SIL above the disc surface and maintain a constant air gap. Philips has devised a technique in which the air gap can be held constant at 25 nm.

Near-field–based storage systems using both phase-change and magneto-optical storage media have been investigated by major optical disc manufacturers, such as Philips, as a possible next-generation optical memory after HD-DVD and Blu-ray disc (Hewett 2005). Storage densities in excess of 4× using Blu-ray may be achievable (Milster 2000). An alternative near-field configuration that has been developed by Callimetrics and involves the fabrication of nano-size SIL-like structures within the disc itself, thus achieving near-field storage capabilities in a DVD-type platform (Guerra et al. 2001). However, the discs may be difficult and expensive to mass replicate.

Other techniques achieve near-field imaging capabilities by employing complex media structures such as the *super-resolution near-field structure* (Super-RENS) approach (Tominaga, Nakano, and Atoda 1998). The Super-RENS system uses a phase-change Ge-Sb-Te storage layer with an additional nonlinear Sb layer. The complex readout mechanism in Super-RENS is not well understood, but the nonlinear layer acts to produce a near-field region when illuminated using a conventional optical head, allowing the imaging of subdiffraction-limited recorded marks of diameter <60 nm in the underlying storage layer.

Advanced Magneto-Optical Recording Techniques

In phase-change recording, the size of the recorded domain is limited by the size of the optical stylus used to record data to the disc. However, in MO recording this is not the case, and marks much smaller than the size of the focused spot can be recorded using magnetic field modulation. However, the size of these features may be beyond the resolving capabilities of the optical head and, as a result, optical techniques such as near-field imaging, or the use of complex media structures, must be adopted to resolve the recorded marks and recover the recorded data.

Magnetic Super Resolution

The *magnetic super resolution* (MSR) technique, as illustrated in Figure 23, offers one way to increase the MO storage capacity and permit the imaging of subdiffraction limit-sized recorded domains using a conventional optical head (Takahashi et al. 1994).

The MSR disc contains two magnetic layers: a perpendicularly magnetized recording layer, to which the data is recorded, and a readout layer, from which the data is recovered. At room temperature the magnetization of the readout layer is in-plane so it exhibits no polar Kerr signal; as a result it masks the underlying recording layer where the high-density domains are stored. Upon application of a focused laser beam, any domain present in the recording layer beneath the focused spot, which would not normally be resolved by the focused laser beam, is copied to the readout layer to contribute to the replay waveform; any surrounding recorded domains are masked by the in-plane magnetization of the rest of the readout layer. As the focused spot scans along the track the domain disappears and the next recorded mark along the data track appears. A commercial MO recording system using MSR is already available, the GIGAMO format developed by Fujitsu and Sony, which offers up to 2.3GB storage on a 3.5-inch disc.

Domain Wall Displacement Detection

Domain wall displacement detection (DWDD) operates in a three-layer magneto-optical recording medium consisting of a bottom recording layer, an intermediate switching layer, and an upper displacement layer (see Figure 24). At room temperature, the domains stored in the recording layer are copied to the displacement layer because of the strong exchange coupling between layers. However, when a focused laser beam is applied, the switching layer is heated above its Curie temperature (which is less than that of the recording and displacement layers), and the exchange coupling between layers disappears. As a result, the small domains in the displacement layer expand temporarily so that they can be resolved by the focused spot (Jenkins et al. 2003). DWDD is used in the latest version of the MiniDisc system, Hi-MD, developed by Sony, which permits a storage density of 1 Gb in the standard MiniDisc form factor.

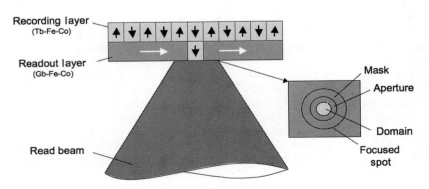

Figure 23: In the MSR technique, the in-plane magnetization of the readout layer masks the underlying perpendicularly magnetized recording layer. On application of a focused laser beam, the readout layer heats up and the recorded domain present in the recording layer beneath the focused spot is copied to the readout layer and contributes to the replay waveform

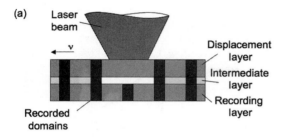

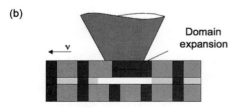

Figure 24: In domain wall displacement detection, the recorded marks, which are too small to be resolved by the focused spot during readout, are copied to the displacement layer. On application of the focused spot, the copied marks expand beneath it and contribute to the replay waveform

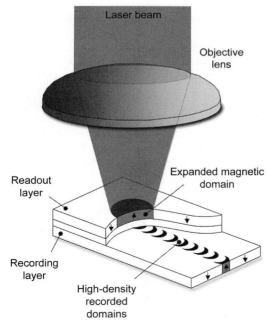

Figure 25: In MAMMOS, the subdiffraction limit-sized recorded domains in the recording layer are copied into the readout layer and expanded when the read beam is applied. The expanded domain diminishes when the laser beam moves away from the recorded domain

The Magnetically Amplifying Magneto-Optic System

MAMMOS is an alternative MSR approach that uses the two-layer storage medium illustrated in Figure 25. The MAMMOS disc structure contains a Tb-Fe-Co recording layer on which high-density magnetic domains are recorded (and which are too small to be resolved by

the optical head) and a Gb-Fe-Co readout layer, from which the recorded data are recovered. Recording is performed using the conventional magnetic field modulation approach. However, during readout, the high-density domain is copied from the recording layer to the readout layer where it magnetically expands to cover the area of the focused spot by a thermal-magnetic process. As a result, the amplitude of the replay waveform is amplified (Awano and Ohta 1998). As soon as the optical stylus moves past the recorded mark, the copied domain immediately shrinks and disappears. This growing and shrinking process continues as the focused spot scans along the recorded track, resulting in a replay waveform exhibiting good signal-to-noise ratio characteristics. Storage densities of more than 150 Gb on a standard 12-cm disc may be possible using this approach; these can be further increased through the application of near-field SIL imaging and the utilization of a blue laser.

Hybrid Recording

Hybrid recording, or *heat-assisted magnetic recording* (HAMR), offers one way of extending the data storage capabilities of magnetic storage systems beyond the coveted milestone of 1 Tbit/in². Although a storage device incorporating hybrid recording is not an optical memory, it does rely on the thermo-magnetic recording process used in MO systems. To achieve a high data storage capacity in magnetic storage systems, recorded domains need to be as small as possible ($\approx$25 nm in diameter for a storage density of 1 Tbit/in²). However, any reduction in the size of the recorded domain leads to thermal instability, so random thermal fluctuations can change the magnetization state of the recording medium. To combat this, recording materials of high coercivity (10KOe) must be used; these are difficult to switch using the magnetic fields produced by conventional magnetic record heads. To overcome the problem of recording to high-coercivity media, a focused laser beam can be used to heat the magnetic recording medium, thus lowering the film's coercivity and allowing the data to be recorded using a conventional recording head. One problem with the practical implementation of HAMR is the design of a suitable light delivery path, and several techniques such as the use of an SIL and nano-apertures are being explored (Challener et al. 2003).

Holographic Memory

The development of holographic storage has been ongoing since long before the introduction of the first optical memory. However, the development of a commercial system has been hampered by the need for complex components such as spatial light modulators and large detector arrays, as well as by the lack of suitable recording media. This type of system has the potential to offer huge storage density improvements and significantly higher data-transfer rates compared to that permitted using conventional optical disc memories. These improvements are made possible because data are recorded to the storage medium in the form of pages of data containing more then a million bits and are correspondingly recovered in a parallel fashion (Inphase Technologies 2006).

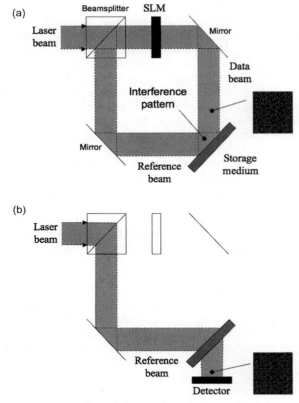

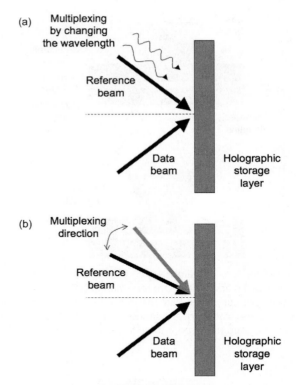

Figure 26: The recording and replay process in holographic storage. (a) Recording is performed using two laser beams derived from the same source. The digital data are encoded onto the data beam as a page of light and dark pixels using a spatial light modulator. The data beam and reference beam interfere in the recording medium, and the resulting interference pattern is recorded. (b) Readout is performed by illuminating the holographic storage medium with a reference beam to regenerate the recorded data. The recovered data are then projected onto a camera, from which each pixel of data is recovered

Figure 27: Multiplexing techniques for addressing pages of data in holographic storage. (a) In wavelength multiplexing, each page of digital data is recorded using a specific wavelength of illumination. The individual pages are recovered by illuminating the storage medium with a reference beam of identical wavelength to that employed in the recording process. (b) In angle multiplexing, each page of data is recorded with the reference beam at a prescribed angle of incidence to the holographic recording medium. The individual pages are then recovered by illuminating the storage medium with the reference beam at the angle used to originally record the desired page

Figure 26 illustrates the recording and readout of data using holography.

In holographic recording, the digital data are encoded onto a data beam as a page of light and dark pixels using a device called a *spatial light modulator*. The data beam interferes with a reference beam in the volume of the storage medium to form an interference pattern. Because the storage medium is light-sensitive, much like photographic film, the light-intensity pattern produced by the interference of the two light beams is recorded. If the recorded area in the medium is illuminated with a reference beam of identical characteristics to that used in the recording process, then the original data beam can be reconstructed and detected electronically using a detector, such as a charge-coupled device (CCD) camera, which is able to detect the individual pixels in the recovered beam (Coufal, Psaltis, and Sincerbox 2000; Ashley et al. 2000). Multiple pages of data can be written to the same position in the medium using some form of addressing technique, such as wavelength or angle multiplexing, as illustrated in Figure 27. Increased storage densities can

also be achieved by focusing the beams onto the recording medium.

In *wavelength multiplexing*, a page of data is recorded to the holographic medium using a reference beam of a particular wavelength; additional pages of data can be recorded to the same volume of the storage medium through the use of a different wavelength. Each page of recorded data can then be recovered by illuminating the storage medium with a laser beam of identical characteristics to that used in the original recording process (i.e., a beam of the same wavelength).

In *angle multiplexing*, a page of data is recorded to the holographic medium with the reference beam aligned to a specific angle; additional pages can be recorded to the same volume of the storage medium by changing the angle of incidence of the reference beam. Each page of data can then be recovered by illuminating the storage medium with a reference beam applied at the same angle used for recording (Coufal, Psaltis, and Sincerbox 2000). Although practically difficult to implement, angle multiplexing has been adopted in commercial holographic storage systems currently under development (InPhase Technologies 2006).

Major obstacles in the commercialization of holographic storage systems have been the availability of both suitable system components and, more importantly, the availability of suitable storage media. However, most of these problems have been solved, and polymer-based write-once media have been developed. Two companies are currently developing commercial holographic memory technologies: InPhase Technologies and Optware. InPhase Technologies (2006) has recently demonstrated the highest data storage capacity of any commercial storage technology; with a capacity of 515 Gbits/in^2, which is far in excess of that achievable in today's magnetic hard disk drives. Inphase hopes to introduce a commercial system on the market soon with an initial storage capacity of 300 Gb on a single disc with a data-transfer rate of 20 Mb/s, with capacities rising to 800 Gb and 1.6 Tb in future generations. However, holographic technologies currently only offer a write-once format aimed primarily at data-archiving applications, and, in addition, the high cost of such systems will initially preclude their use in consumer applications.

CONCLUSION

Over the last twenty-five years, optical memories have evolved to offer increased storage densities and the ability to record and erase digital data in a removable, reliable disc format. From the 650-Mb storage capacity of the CD to the 17-Gb storage capacity of the DVD, the advances in storage capacity have been achieved through the adoption of short-wavelength laser sources and high-NA objective lenses, thus resulting in smaller focused spot sizes for the recording and readout of digital data. The next generation of competing optical disc standards, HD-DVD and Blu-ray disc, promise sufficient storage capabilities to enable the storage of movie-length, high-definition video on a single 12-cm diameter disc. It is difficult to predict which one of these standards will triumph, but it is clear that the consumer will ultimately benefit from the huge data storage capacities offered. Future storage technologies promise even greater storage capabilities, far in excess of the CD and DVD standards, through the adoption of new imaging techniques and the development of innovative storage media.

GLOSSARY

Analog-to-Digital Converter (ADC): An electronic device that converts a continuous analog signal into a sequence of discrete binary digital values, typically at regular time intervals. The value of the digital code at the point of sampling is proportional to the amplitude of the analog signal.

Constant Angular Velocity (CAV): If the disk spins at a constant angular velocity, then it spins at a constant angular rotation per unit time; consequently, the linear speed of the disk with respect to the radial position of the optical head varies along with the rate that the data is read from the disk.

Constant Linear Velocity (CLV): If the disk spins at a constant linear velocity, then the linear speed of the disk with respect to the radial position of the optical head is constant. Consequently, to read data from the disc at a constant data rate, the speed of the disc has to vary (the rotational rate increases as one moves toward the center of the disc).

Eight-to-Fourteen Modulation (EFM): Eight-to-fourteen modulation is a DC-free run-length limited (RLL) coding scheme where each 8-bit block of data is converted into a 14-bit codeword using a lookup table; the encoded data are then recorded to the optical disk. The coding of data using this approach ensures that a regular alternating pattern of digital 0's and 1's are recorded in order to prevent a continuous stream of like symbols being recorded.

Error-Correcting Code (ECC): An error-correcting code is used to enable the recovery of stored data even if they are corrupted during recovery. ECC is added to the recorded data sequence as extra redundant data, the form of which depends on the error-correcting scheme employed.

Full Width at Half Maximum (FWHM): The full width at half maximum is a measure of the width of a function or distribution at half its maximum value. In optics, the FWHM is often used as a measure of the width of the focused spot profile and is the distance between the points where the (typically Gaussian) profile is one-half the amplitude of the maximum (or peak) intensity.

Intersymbol Interference (ISI): Intersymbol interference is a form of signal distortion arising because of the temporal spreading and consequent overlap of replay pulses during replay. ISI results in the inability to distinguish between different recorded states, making recovery of stored data difficult.

Modulation Transfer Function: The modulation transfer function is a measure of the variation in the magnitude of a signal as a function of the spatial frequency distribution of features on the disk.

Numerical Aperture (NA): Numerical aperture is a dimensionless quantity that indicates the resolving power of a lens. The size of the smallest object that can be resolved is proportional to the inverse of the lens NA.

Signal-to-Noise Ratio: The signal-to-noise ratio is a measure of the signal quality with respect to the background noise corrupting it. SNR is defined as the ratio of the signal power to the noise power, and it is often expressed in logarithmic decibel units (dB).

Spatial Light Modulator: A spatial light modulator is an optical device that can be used to spatially modulate the intensity of a light beam.

CROSS REFERENCES

See *Free-Space Optics; Optical Fiber Communications*.

REFERENCES

Ashley, J., M.-P. Bernal, G. W. Burr, H. Coufal, H. Guenther, J. A. Hoffnagle, C. M. Jefferson, B. Marcus, R. M. Macfarlane, R. M. Shelby, and G. T. Sincerbox. 2000.

Holographic data storage. *IBM Journal of Research and Development*, 44: 341–68.

Awano, H., and N. Ohta. 1998. Magnetooptical recording technology toward 100 Gb/in2. *IEEE Journal of Selected Topics in Quantum Electronics*, 4: 815–20.

Blu-ray. 2004. White paper Blu-ray disc format 1.A (retrieved from www.blu-raydisc.com/).

———. 2005. White paper Blu-ray disc format 1.C (retrieved from www.blu-raydisc.com/).

Bouwhuis, G., and P. Burgstede. 1973. The optical scanning system of the Philips "VLP" record player. *Philips Technical Review*, 7, 186–9.

Bouwhuis, G., J. Braat, A. Huijser, J. Pasman, G. Van Rosmalen, and K. Schouhamer Immink. 1985. *Principles of optical disc systems*. Bristol, United Kingdom: Adam Hilger.

Braat, J. J. M. 1998. Differential time detection for radial tracking of optical disks. *Applied Optics*, 37, 6973–82.

Braat, J. J. M., and G. Bouwhuis. 1978. Position sensing in video disk readout. *Applied Optics*, 17: 2013–21.

Braat, J., P. Dirkson, and A. J. E. M. Janssen. 2003. *Diffractive read-out of optical discs*. In Optical imaging and microscopy: Techniques and advanced systems, edited by P. Török and F.-J. Kao. Berlin; London: Springer.

Bricot, C., J. C. Lehureau, C. Puech, and F. Le Carvennec. 1976. Optical readout of videodisc. *IEEE Transactions on Consumer Electronics*, 22: 304–8.

Challener, W. A., T. W. McDaniel, C. D. Mihalcea, K. R. Mountfield, K. Pelhos, and I. K. Sendur. 2003. Light delivery techniques for heat-assisted magnetic recording. *Japanese Journal of Applied Physics*, 42: 981–8.

Coufal, H. J., D. Psaltis, and G. T. Sincerbox, eds. 2000. Holographic data storage. New York: Springer-Verlag.

DVD Forum. 2004. Online at www.dvdforum.org/forum.shtml.

DVD+RW Alliance. 2006. Retrieved from www.dvdrw.com/.

ECMA International. 1996. Standard ECMA-130: Data Interchange on read-only 120 mm optical data disks (CDROM) (retrieved from www.ecma-international.org/publications/standards/Ecma-130.htm).

———. 2001. 120mm DVD—Read-only disk (retrieved from www.ecmainternational.org/publication/standards/Ecma-267.htm).

Guerra, L., D. Vezenov, L. Thulin, W. Haimberger, P. Sullivan, K. Nelson, E. N. Glytsis, and T. M. Gaylord. 2002. Embedded nano-optic media for near-field high density optical data storage: Modeling, fabrication and performance. *Proceedings of SPIE*, 4342: 285–93.

Hayashi, S., and G. S. Kino. 1995. Solid immersion lens for optical storage. *Proceedings of SPIE*, 2412: 80–7.

HD DVD Technology. 2006. Online at http://www.hddvdprg.com/.

Hewett, J. 2005. Near-field optics show data storage promise. *Opto and Laser Europe*, 131: 30–1.

Inphase Technologies. 2006. Online at www.inphase-technologies.com/.

Jenkins, D., W. Clegg, J. Windmill, S. Edmund, P. Davey, D. Newman, C. D. Wright, M. Loze, M. Armand, R. Atkinson, B. Hendren, and P. Nutter. 2003. Advanced optical and magnetooptical recording techniques: A review. *Microsystem Technologies*, 10: 66–75.

Kageyama, Y., H. Iwasaki, M. Harigaya, and Y. Ide. 1996. Compact disc erasable (CD-E) with Ag-In-Sb-Te phase-change recording material. *Japanese Journal of Applied Physics*, 35: 500–1.

Mansfield, S. M., and G. S. Kino. 1990. Solid immersion microscope. *Applied Physics Letters*, 57: 2615–6.

Mansfield, S. M., W. R. Studenmund, G. S. Kino, and K. Osato. 1993. High-numerical-aperture lens system for optical storage. *Optics Letters*, 18, 305–7.

Mansuripur, M. 1995. The physical principles of magneto-optical recording. Cambridge, United Kingdom: Cambridge University Press.

———, and G. Sincerbox. 1997. Principles and techniques of optical data storage. *Proceedings of the IEEE*, 85: 1780–96.

Marchant, A. B. 1990. *Optical recording:* A technical overview. New York: Addison-Wesley.

McDaniel, T. W., and R. H. Victora, eds. 1997. *Handbook of magneto-optical data recording: Materials, subsystems, techniques.* New Jersey: Noyes Publications.

Milster, T. D. 2000. Near-field optics: A new tool for data storage. *Proceedings of the IEEE*, 88: 1480–90.

Philips Electronics. 1997. *CD-ReWritable: How it works.* Eindhoven, Netherlands: Author.

———. 2006. Research dossier: Optical recording (retrieved from www.research.philips.com/newscenter/dossier/optrec/index.html).

Plasmon 2006. Online at www.plasmon.com/udo/.

Pohlmann, K. C. 1989. *The compact disc: A handbook of theory and use.* Oxford, United Kingdom: Oxford University Press.

Schouhamer Immink, K. A. 2004. *Codes for mass data storage systems.* Eindhoven, Netherlands: Shannon Foundation.

Takahashi, A., J. Nakajima, Y. Murakami, K. Ohta, and T. Ishikawa. 1994. Improvement of readout resolution with an in-plane magnetization film for a magneto-optical disk. *IEEE Transaction on Magnetics*, 30: 232–6.

TDK. 2006. Making Blu-ray discs a reality (retrieved from www.tdk.com/professional/marketing/brd1.html).

Terris, B. D., H. J. Mamin, D. Rugar, W. R. Studenmund, and G. S. Kino. 1994. Near-field optical data storage using a solid immersion lens. *Applied Physics Letters*, 65: 388–390.

Tominaga, J., T. Nakano, and N. Atoda. 1998. An approach for recording and readout beyond the diffraction limit. *Applied Physics Letters*, 73: 2078–80.

Wang, S. X., and A. M. Taratorin. 1999. *Magnetic information storage technology.* San Diego: Academic Press.

Williams, E. W. 1996. *The CD-ROM and optical disc recording systems.* New York: Oxford University Press.

Yamada, N., E. Ohno, K. Nishiuchi, N. Akahira, and M. Takao. 1991. Rapid-phase transitions of Ge Te-Sb_2Te_3 pseudobinary amorphous thin films for an optical disk memory. *Journal of Applied Physics*, 69, 2849–2856.

Yoshida, T. 1994. The rewritable minidisc system. *Proceedings of the IEEE*, 82: 1492–1500.

Characterization of Optical Fibers

Liang Chen, John Cameron, and Xiaoyi Bao, *University of Ottawa, Canada*

INTRODUCTION

Work on the characterization of optical fiber began as soon as the first fibers were developed. The National Bureau of Standards (NBS) took the lead in 1976 when telephone companies around the world were just beginning to test optical communications systems in the field. Most of the fiber then available was multimode fiber, in which several hundred optical modes propagate in a core that is typically 50–100 μm in diameter. The typical operating wavelength was approximately 850 nm. Data rates were relatively low, often a few Mb/s. Many of the early problems in optical fiber characterization related directly to multimode propagation in the fiber. Differences in attenuation among the modes led to variations in measured attenuation, depending on how the light was launched into the fiber. Methods of measuring physical parameters such as attenuation, refractive index profile, and fiber geometry such as core and cladding diameters were published in a series of NBS *Technical Notes,* that were later collected in two volumes titled *Optical Fiber Characterization* (Danielson et al. 1982; Chamberlain et al. 1983).

Today, almost all of the communication field fibers operate as single mode. Operating wavelengths now cover 1300 nm to 1600 nm. Compared to multimode fiber, single-mode fiber offers both reduced attenuation and substantially higher bandwidth. Thus, today's long-distance and metropolitan networks consist solely of single-mode fiber. Nevertheless, multimode fiber has found an important niche in high-speed, local area data networks with concepts such as "fiber to the desk" and "Gigabit Ethernet." The larger core fiber offers inexpensive connections, high launching efficiency with large area sources, and the use of inexpensive plastic optics. Therefore, the contribution of NBS's *Optical Fiber Characterization* remains technically relevant to current high-speed local area networks.

Fiber manufacturers commonly perform the following characterizations for their fibers: refractive index profile, fiber geometry such as core and cladding diameters, cladding noncircularity and core cladding nonconcentricity error, mode field diameter at 1310 nm and 1550 nm, effective area at 1310 nm and 1550 nm, and cutoff wavelength. These fabrication parameters are critically important in theoretical prediction of the performance of the resulting fiber.

Therefore, it is important to independently perform these tests when deciding on potential fibers for a new fiber communication network. Their postcharacterization for an existing fiber network becomes somewhat less an issue because one needs to focus on the characterization of the whole network. There are many physical aspects of the network that are not known accurately and that are nearly impossible to prevent from varying because of the dynamic environmental fluctuations, especially aerial field fibers. In this chapter, we will discuss how to characterize the parameters that are important for existing fiber networks.

ATTENUATION

The power of a signal propagating in an optical fiber decreases exponentially with distance, with material absorption and Rayleigh scattering making the dominant contributions to the loss (Agrawal 2001; Saleh and Teich 1991). The attenuation coefficient of a fiber is usually specified in units of dB/km according to the relation $\alpha = (-10/L)\log[P(L)/P(0)]$, where P(0) is the power at the input of the fiber and P(L) is the power at distance L. An example of the attenuation spectrum of an optical fiber is shown in Figure 1.

Rayleigh scattering is caused by variations in the refractive index that occur over distances shorter than the light wavelength, with the refractive index variations resulting from density fluctuations frozen into the fiber material during manufacture (Iannone et al. 1998; Agrawal 1997). The loss resulting from Rayleigh scattering is proportional to $1/\lambda^4$, where λ is the wavelength. For a typical silica fiber, the Rayleigh scattering loss is approximately 0.14 dB/km in the 1550-nm wavelength region (Bickham and Cain 2002b).

Material absorption can be classified as *intrinsic absorption* caused by pure silica or *extrinsic absorption* caused by the presence of impurities (Agrawal 1997). In the attenuation spectrum of Figure 1, the relatively steep increase in attenuation at wavelengths above 1600 nm results from the absorption caused by vibrational resonances of the silica molecules. For the remaining wavelength range of 1200 nm to 1600 nm, the contribution of intrinsic absorption is relatively small. The main

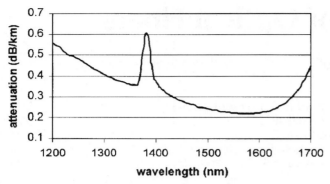

Figure 1: Attenuation spectrum of a silica-germania optical fiber. Reproduced from Bickham and Cain 2002a

source of extrinsic absorption is the presence of OH ions. Overtones of the OH vibrations produce a peak in the attenuation spectrum at 1380 nm, which is clearly visible in Figure 1 (Bickham and Cain 2002b).

In addition to Rayleigh scattering and material absorption, attenuation in an optical fiber can also be caused by two types of bending (Keiser 2003): (1) macroscopic bends with radii that are large compared with the fiber diameter and (2) random microscopic bends of the fiber axis. A long fiber span is normally composed of a number of shorter fiber segments, and the loss of such a span will also include contributions from splices and from the connectors at the ends of the span.

In optical system design, it is important to know the optical power levels at the input of optical amplifiers, at the input of fiber spans, and at the photoreceiver. Therefore, the loss of each fiber span in an optical link must be known. The loss of an installed fiber span is typically characterized through an insertion-loss measurement or through optical time-domain reflectometry. For a more complete characterization, both measurements are taken (Feuerstein 2005) because insertion-loss measurements tend to give the more accurate loss values whereas optical time-domain reflectometry gives valuable information on the spatial distribution of loss along the span.

Figure 2 shows the setup for an insertion-loss measurement of a fiber span using a laser source and optical power meter. The measurement process consists of two steps: (1) a calibration measurement and (2) a measurement through the span. The proper calibration setup depends on the end points defining the loss of the span (Talbot and Michel, undated). As an example, consider the case where the span loss is defined between points A and B in Figure 2b—that is, between the input of the patch panel at the transmit site and the output of the patch panel at the receive site. The span loss then includes the loss of the fiber cable and the losses of the patch panel connectors. In this case, the calibration measurement of step 1 is taken with the laser source connected directly to the power meter with a patch cord as shown in Figure 2a. In step 2, the connections are as shown in Figure 2b, with the laser source connected to the patch panel at the transmit site (using the same patch cord from step 1) and the power meter connected to the patch panel at the receive site (using a second patch cord). Patch cord 1 in Figure 2 should remain connected to the laser source throughout measurement steps 1 and 2 in order to maintain a constant coupling of optical power from the laser to the patch cord. After measurement steps 1 and 2 are completed, the fiber span loss (in dB) is calculated by subtracting the power measured in step 2 from that measured in step 1 (where both powers are expressed in units of dBm).

It can be useful to take loss measurements at multiple wavelengths because the fiber attenuation is wavelength-dependent. For example, measurements of loss can be taken at 1550 nm and 1625 nm to characterize both C and L bands (Feuerstein 2005). The loss can also be characterized as a function of wavelength by using a tunable laser source or by using a broadband source in combination with an optical spectrum analyzer.

A portion of the light propagating in an optical fiber is returned back toward the source because of Rayleigh scattering and Fresnel reflections. An *optical time-domain reflectometer* (OTDR) characterizes loss and reflection as a function of distance along a fiber span by launching a short pulse and analyzing the returning power as

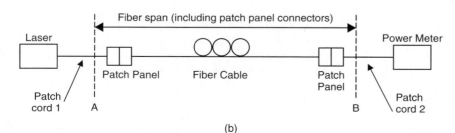

Figure 2: Insertion loss measurement. (a) Setup for the calibration measurement and (b) setup for the measurement through the span

a function of time. In addition to the total span loss, an OTDR can measure the loss and reflectance of the splices, connectors, and fiber segments making up the span.

The features of a typical OTDR trace are shown in Figure 3 (Beller 1998; Keiser 2000). The vertical axis corresponds to the back-reflected power level in dB, calculated as 5log(*power*) rather than 10log(*power*) because of the round-trip nature of the pulse propagation. The horizontal axis corresponds to the distance along the fiber relative to the position of the OTDR. This distance is calculated as $d = tv_g/2$, where d is the distance, v_g is the group velocity (the velocity at which the pulse propagates in the fiber), and t is the time elapsed between the launch of the pulse from the OTDR and the measurement of the back-scattered power. The factor of 2 in the calculation is, again, because of the round-trip nature of the measurement.

The straight-line segments of the OTDR trace are the result of Rayleigh scattering in the fiber. The slope of a straight-line segment is equal to the attenuation coefficient of that fiber segment in units of dB/km.

The spikes in the OTDR trace are the result of discrete reflections. There are three reflections in Figure 3: They occur at the input of the span (because of the connection of the OTDR and fiber), at a connector pair within the span, and at a nonterminated fiber end at the output of the span. The reflections at the input and output of the span may conceal useful information at these locations— for example, the loss and reflectance of patch panel connectors. If desired, this information can be obtained by connecting launch and tail reels of fiber at the input and output of the span. The reels of fiber should be longer than the OTDR dead zone (Feuerstein 2005), where *dead zone* refers to the distance over which information is lost because of saturation of the OTDR receiver as the result of a reflection (Beller 1998).

Abrupt changes in the backscattered power level are caused by discrete sources of loss such as splices and fiber bends. An OTDR measurement of a splice or connector loss will be affected by a difference in the backscattering characteristics of the two fibers spliced or connected. This uncertainty can be overcome through bidirectional OTDR measurements in which measurements are taken from both ends of a span and averaged (Corning Incorporated 2001).

The spatial resolution l in an OTDR measurement is given by $l = v_g\tau/2$, where τ is the width of the OTDR pulse

and it is assumed that the OTDR receiver bandwidth is large enough that the pulse is not significantly broadened on detection (Gold 1985). There is an inherent trade-off that must be made between spatial resolution and dynamic range, another important OTDR parameter that is related to the maximum loss that can be measured as well as the time required (with averaging of the backscattered signal) for the measurement of a given loss (Beller 1998). The dynamic range can be increased through an increase in pulsewidth (which increases the energy of the backscattered signal) and a decrease in the receiver bandwidth (which leads to a reduction in noise power). In contrast, higher spatial resolution calls for a decrease in pulsewidth and a corresponding increase in the receiver bandwidth.

In summary, the loss of a fiber span can be obtained through insertion-loss or OTDR measurements. If possible, both measurements should be taken to give a more complete characterization of the span. Insertion-loss measurements tend to give more accurate values of the end-to-end span loss, whereas the OTDR gives a distributed measure of loss that can identify and locate sources of unexpectedly high loss such as bad splices, macrobends, and even catastrophic failures such as fiber breaks.

Further details on the operational fundamentals and applications of OTDRs can be found in Beller (1998) and Keiser (2000), whereas a detailed discussion of insertion-loss measurements can be found in Hentschel and Derickson (1998).

DISTRIBUTED STRESS AND TEMPERATURE MONITORING OF OPTICAL CABLES

Polarization mode dispersion (PMD) is a limiting factor for high-speed optical communication systems at 10 Gb/s or higher, and PMD is sensitive to cable strains through the environmental conditions, especially wind and large temperature gradients. It is critically important to measure the cable strains, especially for aerial or submarine fibers.

Because communication fibers are in the range of tens to hundreds of kilometers, such a measurement can be achieved with distributed fiber sensors, particularly the Brillouin optical time domain amplification system; this kind of system has the advantages of a long sensing range and the capability of providing the strain at every spatial resolution over the entire sensing fiber, rather than at discrete points, by using the fiber itself as the sensing medium. Spatial information along the length of the fiber can be obtained through optical time domain reflectometry by measuring propagation times for light traveling in the fiber. This allows for continuous distributions of the cable strain in distributed fashion, which can be obtained by the distributed Brillouin scattering or Rayleigh scattering. The most commonly used measurement technique is the Brillouin scattering-based distributed sensing because it provides long sensing length. The longest reported distributed sensor length using spontaneous Brillouin scattering is 57 km with a spatial resolution of 20 m (Maughan, Kee, and Newson 2001), whereas

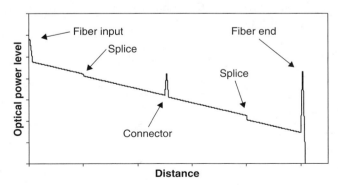

Figure 3: Features of a typical OTDR trace

for a Rayleigh scattering–based distributed sensor, the reported sensor length is in the range of tens of meters (Gifford et al. 2005). The short sensing length in Rayleigh scattering–based distributed sensors is a result of the bandwidth of the broadband source because coherent phase detection is often used as the demodulation process resulting from the weak dependence of the temperature on the Rayleigh scattering comparing to Brillouin scattering (Li, Zhang, and Yoshino 2003). This has limited applications in cable strain monitoring, which requires tens to hundreds of kilometers of fiber to be monitored.

The distributed Brillouin sensor uses Brillouin scattering, which arises from the interaction of light with acoustic phonons propagating in the fiber core. Scattering is in the backward direction with the scattered light experiencing a frequency shift proportional to the velocity of the acoustic phonons. The sensing capability of this scattering phenomenon arises from the dependence of the acoustic velocity, and hence the Brillouin frequency shift, on both strain and temperature.

The concept of using Brillouin scattering for fiber-optic sensing was first proposed in 1989 (Horiguchi and Tateda 1989), and it was termed *Brillouin optical time-domain analysis* (BOTDA). This approach involved launching a short pump pulse into one end of the test fiber and a *continuous wave* (CW) probe beam into the other end. The frequency difference between the two lasers could be set to a particular value corresponding to the Brillouin frequency of the optical fibers, and the CW probe would experience gain at locations along the fiber. The gain as a function of position along the fiber could thus be determined by the time dependence of the detected CW light. By measuring the time-dependent CW signal over a wide range of frequency differences between the pump and probe, the Brillouin frequency for each fiber location could be determined. This allowed for the strain or temperature distribution along the entire fiber length to be established.

The first strain distribution measurement was reported on submarine cables (Tateda et al. 1990) and the use of distributed fiber sensors based on Brillouin scattering. The reported strain distribution was obtained over a 1.3-km cable (Horiguchi, Kurashima and Tateda 1989; Horiguchi and Tateda 1989). Later, another strain test on the bent slot-type optical cables was reported (Horiguchi et al. 1992).

Temperature measurement using Brillouin scattering was proposed in 1989 (Culverhouse et al. 1989) utilizing the linear relationship between Brillouin shift and temperature in a single-mode fiber and measured by a Fabry-Perot interferometer. Then a distributed temperature measurement on a 1.2-km *single-mode fiber* (SMF) with a 3°C temperature resolution and a 100-m spatial resolution was demonstrated with a BOTDA system (Kurashima, Horiguchi, and Tateda 1990) as shown in Figure 4.

The next development in BOTDA was the use of Brillouin loss rather than Brillouin gain (Bao, Webb, and Jackson 1993) to increase the sensing length. Instead of the frequency of the pump being greater than the frequency of the probe, the opposite was implemented. The CW probe therefore experienced loss, rather than gain, at locations along the fiber at which the frequency difference between the lasers matched the Brillouin frequency of the fiber. As the pump pulse is not depleted in this case, longer sensing lengths of 50 kilometers for 10-m spatial resolution was reported using the Brillouin loss mechanism (Bao et al. 1995).

Another development using Brillouin scattering is a single-ended BOTDA system (Fellay et al. 1997). An amplitude modulator generates frequency-shifted sidebands that can serve as a probe. By eliminating the second laser, the cost of the system is reduced. However, the added costs of the frequency modulator, drivers, and *erbium-doped fiber amplifiers* (EDFAs) result in minimal cost savings. This system has been used for temperature monitoring in the field. Fiber was embedded in the Luzzone Dam in the Swiss Alps to monitor the temperature of the concrete during curing (Thévenaz et al. 1998).

Thus, Brillouin scattering–based systems were well suited for long-range sensing, such as communication cable strain or temperature monitoring. On the other hand, strain monitoring for civil engineering and aerospace structures required much shorter spatial resolutions than were achievable, as well as shorter sensing length than communication fibers. Recent research efforts have been directed toward reducing the spatial resolution to the point where it is practical for structural monitoring applications. The first 10-cm spatial resolution was demonstrated in 1999 using BOTDA technique (Bao et al. 1999). This is remarkable: It had been believed that 1-m spatial resolution would be the best that could ever be achieved because of the finite lifetime of the acoustic phonons (Hotate and Hasegawa 1998; Horiguchi et al. 1995). The most recent developments on this technique have been focused on structural health monitoring of various civil structures, which is outside the domain of fiber communications (Ohno et al. 2001).

One problem with the implementation of Brillouin scattering–based sensing systems in the field is the sensitivity of the Brillouin frequency shift to both strain and temperature. This leads to ambiguity in the

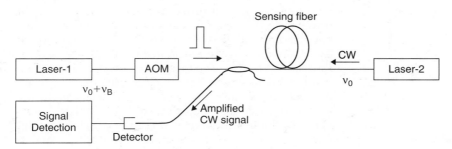

Figure 4: Gain-based BOTDA configuration

measurement because we do not know whether the frequency shift was caused by the strain or temperature changing. In a laboratory environment, the temperature is essentially constant, and its effects can generally be neglected when measuring strain. In many field situations, this is not the case.

An early solution to this problem proposed the use of two fibers placed adjacent to one another, with one fiber isolated from any strain effects (Bao, Webb, and Jackson 1994). The isolated fiber would be used to monitor the temperature, while the other fiber would measure the effect of both strain and temperature. Recent innovative approaches to measuring strain and temperature simultaneously have been developed. By combining the Landau-Placzek ratio with the frequency shift, the temperature and strain were determined simultaneously (in the spontaneous Brillouin scattering regime) at a spatial resolution of 40 m (Parker et al. 1998). Most recently, an improved system of a temperature resolution of 4°C, a strain resolution of 290 micro-strains, and a spatial resolution of 10 m were reportedly achieved for a sensing length of 15 km using the same principle (Huai, Lees, and Newson 2000). Centimeter resolution has been achieved with simultaneous temperature and strain sensing using Brillouin loss-based distributed sensor with polarization-maintained fibers (Bao, Yu, and Chen 2004) and photonic crystal fibers (Zou et al. 2004).

In summary, the Brillouin scattering–based distributed sensors provide long-distance sensors with meter to submeter spatial resolution. With both BOTDA and the Brillouin optical time-domain reflectometer, the measurement range is only limited by the fiber loss. This is especially important for long-haul fiber characterization for strains that would induce PMD as the system limitation for > 10-Gb/s communication systems.

CHROMATIC DISPERSION

The group velocity associated with the fundamental mode in an SMF varies with wavelength, leading to pulse broadening and intersymbol interference in fiber-optic communications (Agrawal 1997). This phenomenon is known as *chromatic dispersion,* and it is the result of two physical mechanisms: material dispersion and waveguide dispersion (Saleh and Teich 1991; Yariv 1997). *Material dispersion* results from the wavelength dependence of the refractive indices of the fiber core and cladding regions. *Waveguide dispersion* is caused by the wavelength dependence of the optical power distribution in the core and cladding; because the phase velocities in the core and cladding are different, the group velocity of the mode varies with wavelength.

The chromatic dispersion of a fiber is characterized by the dispersion parameter D (Agrawal 1997):

$$D = \frac{d}{d\lambda}\left(\frac{1}{v_g}\right) = \frac{1}{L}\frac{d\tau_g}{d\lambda}$$

where λ is the wavelength, v_g is the group velocity, L is the length of the fiber, and τ_g is the group delay (i.e., the time that it takes for a signal to propagate through the fiber).

D is normally specified in units of ps/nm/km. Wavelength components of a signal spaced by $\Delta\lambda$ propagating through a fiber of length L will have a difference in group delay of $DL\Delta\lambda$. Chromatic dispersion thus leads to a broadening of the pulses used in optical communications because the different wavelength components of a pulse have different arrival times at the receiver.

In addition to causing pulse broadening, chromatic dispersion also has a major impact on the nonlinear interactions between channels in *wavelength-division-multiplexed* (WDM) systems (Chraplyvy 1990). The dispersion of an optical link, including contributions from fiber, components, and (potentially) dispersion-compensating fiber, must be kept within the specified limits of a given system to meet the target bit error rate. Measurements of dispersion are carried out by manufacturers of optical fiber and components, optical system vendors, and service providers.

In this section, we provide an overview of three techniques that are commonly used to measure chromatic dispersion: the modulation phase-shift, interferometric, and time-of-flight techniques. The three techniques have the following procedure in common: (1) The relative group delay of different wavelength components (i.e., the variation of the group delay with wavelength) is measured for the *fiber under test* (FUT); (2) these results are then normally smoothed by fitting appropriate equations to the measured data (Cohen 1985); and (3) the dispersion parameter is calculated as a function of wavelength according to

$$D\left(\lambda\right) = \frac{1}{L}\frac{d\tau_r(\lambda)}{d\lambda} \tag{1}$$

where $\tau_r(\lambda)$ is the relative group delay as a function of wavelength. Several fitting equations have been used in step 2, including five- and three-term Sellmeier functions and polynomials of various orders (Cohen 1985). The best choice of fitting equation depends on the type of fiber (for example, dispersion-shifted versus nondispersion-shifted) that is being measured (Hernday 1998). The three chromatic dispersion measurement techniques use different methods to determine the relative group delay as a function of wavelength in step 1.

The *modulation phase-shift method* (Hernday 1998) is used to measure the dispersion of both short and long lengths of optical fiber as well as optical components. Figure 5a shows the measurement setup. The output of a narrowband tunable laser is modulated with a sinusoidal signal before being transmitted through the FUT. At the output of the FUT, the phase of the detected optical signal is measured relative to the phase of a reference signal (as shown in Figure 5a, the electrical modulation source can also provide the reference signal). The measurement is repeated at multiple optical wavelengths, and the difference in the group delays of adjacent wavelengths is given by (Hernday 1998)

$$\Delta\tau(\lambda_{avg}) = -\frac{\phi(\lambda_{avg} + \Delta\lambda) - \phi(\lambda_{avg} - \Delta\lambda)}{360 f_m}$$

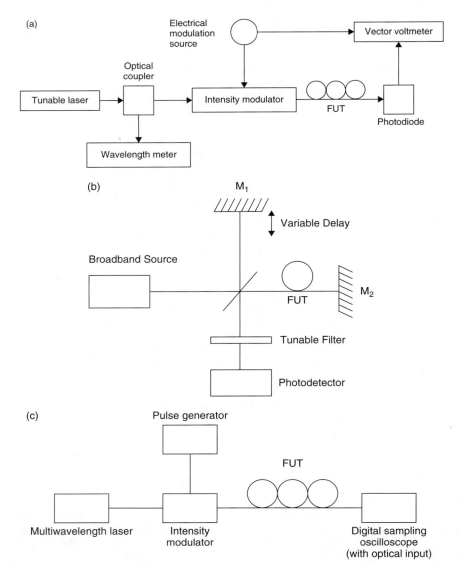

Figure 5: Setup for chromatic dispersion measurement with (a) the modulation phase-shift method (Hernday 1998), (b) the interferometric method, and (c) the time-of-flight method (Maran et al., 2004)

where $\phi(\lambda)$ is the relative phase (in degrees) measured for wavelength λ, f_m is the frequency of the sinusoidal modulation, and λ_{avg} is the average value of the adjacent wavelengths, which are spaced by $2\Delta\lambda$. The relative group delay as a function of wavelength is generated from the values of $\Delta\tau$, the data are smoothed through the appropriate curve fitting, and the dispersion parameter is then calculated through Equation (1).

The *interferometric method* is used to measure the dispersion of short lengths of optical fiber (on the order of 1 m) (Tateda, Shibata, and Seikai 1981; Thévenaz, Pellaux, and Von der Weid 1988) as well as optical components (Knox et al. 1988). The limitation to short lengths of fiber is a consequence of the stability requirements of the interferometer (Thévenaz, Pellaux, and Von der Weid 1988).

The technique has been implemented with both Michelson and Mach-Zehnder interferometers. An implementation with a Michelson interferometer is shown in Figure 5b. The light from a broadband source is split into two beams, with one beam propagating through the FUT and the other through a variable delay line. The variable

delay line has been implemented as an air gap with a movable mirror (Tateda, Shibata, and Seikai 1981; Knox et al. 1988) and as a stretched fiber in an all-fiber interferometer (Thévenaz, Pellaux, and Von der Weid 1988). The beams are reflected off the mirrors M_1 and M_2, recombined, filtered with a tunable optical filter, and detected with the photodetector.

Interference fringes can only be detected when the group delay difference between the signals in the two arms of the interferometer is less than the coherence time of the filtered light. For each setting of the tunable filter, the delay line is swept and the delay corresponding to the center of the fringe pattern is determined. By repeating the measurement at different wavelengths, the relative group delay as a function of wavelength can be determined. The relative group delay data can then be smoothed by curve fitting and the dispersion parameter calculated according to Equation (1).

Thévenaz, Pellaux, and Von der Weid (1988) reported chromatic dispersion measurements with the interferometric method on fibers 1 to 2 meters in length with a resolution of group delay and chromatic dispersion better than 5 fs and 0.1 ps/nm/km, respectively.

In the *time-of-flight method* (Cohen 1985; Maran et al. 2004) of chromatic dispersion measurement, a number of different wavelengths are modulated with narrow pulses and injected into the FUT. The time delay between the pulses in different wavelengths is measured at the output of the FUT using a fast photodetector and a sampling oscilloscope. These relative group delay data are then smoothed by curve fitting and differentiated according to Equation (1) to obtain the dispersion parameter.

The measurement method employed by Maran et al. (2004), shown in Figure 5c, uses an erbium-doped fiber laser with approximately twenty equally spaced laser lines, and all of the wavelengths are transmitted through the FUT simultaneously. This results in a fast measurement of chromatic dispersion that is well suited to long installed fibers.

There is a limit to the lowest value of dispersion that can be accurately measured with the time-of-flight method because the separation of the pulses must be large enough to accurately determine their relative delay. The limit depends on the spacing of the wavelength components and the width of the modulation pulses. For example, with a wavelength spacing of 2 to 3 nm and a pulse width (full width at half maximum) of 83 ps, Maran et al. (2004) found that a minimum length of approximately 10 km of nondispersion-shifted fiber was required to accurately measure dispersion in the C-band.

Inaccuracy in the measurement of dispersion can result from changes in fiber temperature during the measurement. The effects of temperature drift on measurements with the modulation phase-shift method can be reduced by alternating the phase measurements between the test wavelengths and a fixed reference wavelength (Hernday 1998). Changes observed in the phase of the reference wavelength are used to correct the phase measurements of the test wavelengths.

Temperature drift can also impact measurements made with the interferometric method. However, this method is typically used to measure short lengths of fiber for which the temperature would normally be relatively stable. If required, steps can be taken to stabilize the temperature during the measurement. For example, the FUT can be placed in a temperature-controlled chamber.

With the time-of-flight technique, it is possible to obtain a measurement relatively quickly when the pulses in the different wavelengths are transmitted in the FUT simultaneously (Maran et al. 2004). This makes the technique well-suited to the measurement of long installed fibers because the time required for measurement is typically less than the time scale of the temperature drift.

POLARIZATION MODE DISPERSION AND POLARIZATION-DEPENDENT LOSS

Despite the best fabrication effort, the perfect cylindrical symmetry desired for single-mode operation is an ideal almost impossible to achieve technically. Therefore, the core of the SMF is more likely to be in the shape of an ellipse having two orthogonal axes. The "effective" index of refraction of a waveguide, which determines the speed of light, depends on the glass material itself as well as the shape of the waveguide relative to the traveling wave. Therefore, light polarized along one axis travels at a different speed than does the light polarized along the orthogonal axis. As a result, when a light pulse is passing through the optical fiber, some of the light may be polarized in one axis and some may be polarized along the orthogonal axis. To first order this speed difference will cause temporal spreading of the pulse at the output. The propagation time difference between the two axes is termed *differential group delay* (DGD). PMD is a key impairment factor in a single-channel system operating at greater than 10 Gb/s. Another closely related polarization effect is called *polarization-dependent loss* (PDL), which describes the phenomenon of the polarization dependence of the attenuation. For a given fiber network span and at a given wavelength with angular frequency ω, the PDL (defined in dB units) is $\alpha = 10 \log\left(\dfrac{T_{\max}}{T_{\min}}\right)$ where $T_{\max}$ and $T_{\min}$ are the maximum and minimum transmission coefficients. Although PDL could exist in normal SMFs because of imperfect fabrication processes like those resulting in PMD, its dominant contributions in a network come from discrete optical components such as optical modulators, filters, switches, and such active components as EDFAs that can exhibit *polarization-dependent gain*. Further complication arises from the fact that different sections of the fiber network have different DGDs and PDLs, both in terms of their magnitudes and their principal polarization axes, and they vary as a function of time because of dynamic environmental effects such as wind-induced vibration, temperature gradient–induced stress, and microbending at supporting points of aerial fibers. Therefore, the PMD and PDL of a fiber network are a temperature-dependent, stochastic, random process that acts on each WDM channel differently at different times. Thus, their characterization has to be statistical in nature, usually requiring long-term measurement (Waddy, Chen, and Bao 2005).

PMD and PDL interact with each other (Gisin 2004), making the characterization of their statistical properties somewhat involved. For example, the PMD statistics of a network is Maxwellian if PDL can be neglected and if the network can be approximated as a continuous highly mode coupled system (Nelson and Jopson 2004; Gordon 2004). On the other hand, if the network involves some lumped PMD elements, the overall PMD statistics becomes non-Maxwellian (Antonelli and Mecozzi 2004). Furthermore, if the PDL of a network cannot be neglected, then its PMD statistics again becomes non-Maxwellian (Chen, Cameron, and Bao 1999). Interaction of PMD and PDL would naturally cause the PDL of a system to become frequency-dependent (Chen et al. 2003, "Polarization"). Its statistical properties are, however, independent of PMD values in the highly mode coupled continuous limit (Galtarossa and Palmieri 2003).

For a network in which environmental condition changes slowly (e.g., the buried fiber network), one could use many standard PMD and PDL monitoring methods (Williams 2004) to characterize the PMD and

PDL parameters over a given wavelength window. The most notable method is called *Jones matrix eigenanalysis* (Heffner 1992, 1993). However, for a dynamic field fiber network such as aerial fiber cables, the reliable measurement method requires inherently quick speed so that data acquisition time is much less than typical time scales for dynamic environmental fluctuations (Waddy et al. 2001; Waddy, Chen, and Bao 2002). We therefore recommend using the Poincaré sphere method to monitor the complex PMD vector (Chen et al. 2004) for a fiber network because of its minimum scan steps. In this method, one requires a coherent tunable laser source, a polarization controller, and a polarization analyzer (Figure 6). When a coherent tunable laser source is launched into the fiber network having both PMD and PDL, and assuming that all the wavelengths have the same input state of polarization, then its normalized output Stokes vector $\vec{S}(\omega)$ variation as a function of the angular frequency of the light is determined by the complex PMD vector $\vec{W}(\omega) = \vec{\Omega} + i\vec{\wedge}$ (Gisin 2004; Li and Yariv 2000):

$$\frac{d\vec{S}}{d\omega} = \vec{\Omega} \times \vec{S} - (\vec{\wedge} \times \vec{S}) \times \vec{S}$$

By doing three independent laser scans (i.e., for three input state of polarizations) in the measurement wavelength window and measuring their respective normalized output Stokes vector $\vec{S}(\omega)$, one can find the spectrally resolved complex PMD vector $\vec{W}(\omega)$ (Chen et al. 2004). This information can either be used as a feedback signal to drive a PMD compensator or give some detailed fiber status report when one evaluates the autocorrelation of the complex PMD vector (Chen et al. 2003, "Effect"). Once the complex PMD vector is obtained, one can find the corresponding DGD—

$$\tau = \sqrt{\frac{1}{2}\left[\Omega^2 - \wedge^2 + \sqrt{(\Omega^2 - \wedge^2)^2 + 4(\vec{\Omega}.\vec{\wedge})^2}\right]}$$—and the differential attenuation slope (DAS): $\eta = \vec{\Omega}.\vec{\wedge}/\tau$.

The overall PDL of a fiber network can also be monitored using the respective Poincaré sphere method (Chen, Zhang, and Bao 2006) for the PDL vector $\vec{\Gamma}(\omega)$:

$$\frac{d\vec{\Gamma}}{d\omega} = \vec{\wedge} + \vec{\Omega} \times \vec{\Gamma} - \left(\vec{\Gamma}.\vec{\wedge}\right)\vec{\Gamma}$$

By measuring only one such PDL vector $\vec{\Gamma}(\omega_0)$ at a given frequency ω_0 and knowing the corresponding PMD vector, one could integrate the above equation to get the PDL vector at any other wavelength. The relationship between the PDL value in dB and the magnitude of the PDL vector is $PDL_{dB} = 10\log\frac{1+\Gamma}{1-\Gamma}$. Lastly, it is noted that one can increase the measurement speed by replacing the tunable laser with a wideband light source to measure all of the Stokes parameters in "parallel," which will ultimately

be the quickest monitoring set to give the spectrally resolved PMD and PDL information. When the input light source used in the test set cannot guarantee 100 percent polarization, then a modified equation for the Stokes vector $\vec{S}(\omega)$ should be used to find the complex PMD vector $\vec{W}(\omega)$ (Dong et al. 2005).

We mentioned techniques to measure the overall PMD and PDL parameters of a fiber-optic network; it is, however, also possible to use polarization-sensitive reflectometric techniques to measure the distributed PMD values (Galtarossa and Palmieri 2004) even though the circular birefringence component is lost in the round-trip measurement. Therefore, a complete theory of distributed PMD and PDL characterization for a fiber-optic network needs yet to be developed.

NONLINEAR REFRACTIVE INDEX

The nonlinear effects *self-phase modulation* (SPM), *cross-phase modulation* (XPM), and *four-wave mixing* (FWM) have a significant effect on the performance of long-haul optical communication systems. All three effects result from the intensity dependence of the refractive index. This intensity dependence can be seen by writing the refractive index in the form (Agrawal 1997)

$$n = n_0 + n_2 P / A_{eff}$$

where n_0 is the linear part of the refractive index, n_2 is the nonlinear refractive index, P is the optical power, and A_{eff} is the effective core area of the fiber. Measured values of n_2 for different types of silica fiber have been found to range between approximately 2×10^{-20} and 4×10^{-20} m²/W (Agrawal 2001).

In this section, we present a brief description of SPM, XPM, and FWM in fiber-optic systems and introduce measurement techniques for n_2 that are based on these effects. In practice, the measurements obtain the value of n_2/A_{eff}. If required, n_2 can be determined by acquiring the value of A_{eff} in a separate measurement (Namihira 2004).

In SPM, an optical signal experiences a phase shift because of its own intensity, which is given by (Batagelj et al. 2005):

$$\phi_{SPM} = \frac{2\pi}{\lambda}\frac{n_2}{A_{eff}}L_{eff}\,Pm_1 \qquad (2)$$

where λ is the wavelength and m_1 is a parameter that depends on the polarization properties of the signal and the fiber. The effective fiber length is given by $L_{eff} = [1-\exp(-\alpha L)]/\alpha$, where L is the fiber length and α is the fiber attenuation coefficient (in units of km⁻¹). For a pulse propagating in an optical fiber, the nonlinear phase shift resulting from SPM leads to *frequency chirping* in which the instantaneous frequency varies across the pulse (Bayvel and Killey 2002). The frequency chirp,

Figure 6: Setup for PMD measurement—polarization controller (PC) and polarization analyzer (PA)

in combination with chromatic dispersion, leads to pulse distortion, which can result in an increased bit error rate in optical communications. The impact of SPM strongly depends on the sign and magnitude of the chromatic dispersion.

Each measurement technique considered in this section exhibits a dependence on the polarization properties of the signal and the fiber under test. For consistency, we define n_2 throughout this section such that m_1 in Equation (2) takes the value 1 when the signal maintains a linear state of polarization as it propagates through the fiber (e.g., in a polarization-maintaining fiber). In a long (on the order of 1 km or more) telecommunications fiber, the signal polarization state varies randomly with propagation because of PMD; in that case, m_1 in Equation (2) takes the value 8/9 (Kato et al. 1995).

In a measurement method for n_2/A_{eff} based on SPM (Agrawal 2001; Batagelj et al. 2005), the outputs of two CW DFB lasers are combined and launched into the FUT, as shown in Figure 7a. SPM-induced phase modulation generates peaks in the optical spectrum at multiples of the beat frequency between the two lasers. The nonlinear phase shift resulting from SPM is a function of the ratio of these peaks in the optical spectrum. The value of n_2/A_{eff} can be determined using Equation (2) and the measured value of ϕ_{SPM}, with knowledge of the other parameters in the equation.

In XPM, an optical signal experiences a phase shift because of the intensity of a co-propagating signal that is given by (Kato et al. 1995)

$$\phi_{XPM} = \frac{2\pi}{\lambda} \frac{n_2}{A_{eff}} L_{eff} 2m_2 P_2 \qquad (3)$$

where P_2 is the power of the co-propagating signal and m_2 is a polarization-dependent parameter. XPM leads to distortion of a given channel in a WDM system as the phase modulation imparted by the co-propagating channels are converted to intensity fluctuations by chromatic dispersion (Bayvel and Killey 2002).

Figure 7b shows a measurement technique for n_2/A_{eff} based on XPM (Kato et al. 1995). A high-power depolarized pump signal co-propagates in the FUT with a low-power CW probe. With a depolarized pump signal, the polarization factor m_2 has a value of 2/3. Intensity modulation of the pump leads to phase modulation of the probe through XPM. The value of n_2/A_{eff} is obtained by varying the pump power and measuring the frequency components induced in the probe spectrum by the XPM-induced phase modulation.

When three waves with frequencies ω_i, ω_j, and ω_k co-propagate in an optical fiber, a new wave is generated through FWM at frequency $\omega_{ijk} = \omega_i + \omega_j - \omega_k$ (Agrawal 1997). The power of the generated FWM product is given by (Batagelj et al. 2005)

$$P_{ijk} = \left(\frac{D}{3}\right)^2 \left(\frac{2\pi n_2 m_3 L_{eff}}{\lambda A_{eff}}\right)^2 P_i P_j P_k e^{-\alpha L} \eta \qquad (4)$$

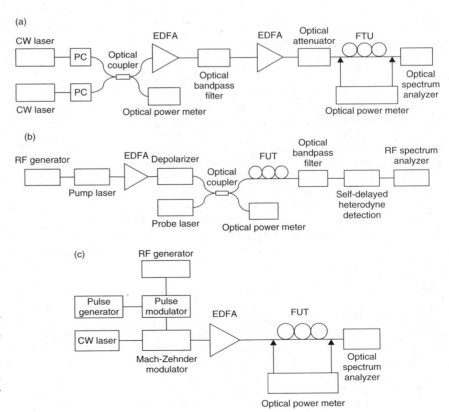

Figure 7: Setup for the measurement of n_2/A_{eff} with methods based on (a) self-phase modulation, (b) cross-phase modulation, and (c) four-wave mixing (Batagelj et al. 2005); polarization controller (PC), erbium-doped fiber amplifier (EDFA), fiber under test (FUT)

where P_i, P_j, and P_k are the input powers of co-polarized waves at frequencies ω_i, ω_j, and ω_k, respectively; η is the FWM efficiency; m_3 is a polarization-dependent parameter that takes the value 8/9 in a long telecommunications fiber (Namihira et al. 2002); and D is the degeneracy factor, which takes the value 3 when $\omega_i = \omega_j$ and the value 6 when $\omega_i \neq \omega_j$. The FWM efficiency η (Song et al. 1999) is a function of the fiber length; the fiber loss coefficient; the frequency values $\omega_{i,j,k}$; the chromatic dispersion; and, because of intensity-dependent phase matching, n_2/A_{eff} and the input powers $P_{i,j,k}$. The FWM efficiency decreases with increasing group velocity mismatch between the interacting signals, so that an increase in the frequency spacing of the signals or an increase in the chromatic dispersion results in a reduced FWM efficiency (Chraplyvy 1990).

FWM leads to interferometric cross talk in WDM systems whenever a FWM product falls at the same frequency as one of the WDM channels. For a system with N channels, the number of products is equal to $1/2[N^3 - N^2]$ (Tkach et al. 1995). FWM can be a major detriment when WDM channels are located in a region of low chromatic dispersion because of the enhancement of the FWM efficiency. For example, C-band channels, with wavelengths close to the zero-dispersion wavelength, may be severely limited by FWM when transmitted through dispersion-shifted fiber.

Measurement of n_2/A_{eff} based on FWM has been implemented using a single laser source (Batagelj, Vidmar, and Tomazic 2005). The measurement setup is shown in Figure 7c. The laser is externally modulated so that two co-polarized sidebands are produced in the optical signal, with their frequency spacing determined by the modulation frequency. The two sidebands interact in the fiber to produce FWM products, and an optical spectrum analyzer is used to measure the power in the optical sidebands and the FWM products at the output of the fiber. The value of n_2/A_{eff} can be obtained with the use of Equation (4) and knowledge of the other relevant parameters.

Note that measured values of the nonlinear refractive index will depend on the pulsewidths or modulation frequencies used in the measurements. In addition to a contribution from the third-order electronic susceptibility, n_2 also includes contributions from the Raman susceptibility and electrostriction; the relative contributions of the latter two mechanisms depend on the pulsewidth or modulation frequency used in the measurement (Agrawal 2001; Buckland and Boyd 1997).

Descriptions of additional techniques for characterization of the nonlinear refractive index can be found in Agrawal (2001) and Batagelj et al. (2005).

CONCLUSION

The performance of existing fiber networks are affected by various dynamic physical parameters. Many of these physical parameters can be quite different from those characterized by fiber manufacturers because of cabling and installation processes as well as dynamic environmental fluctuations. PMD, PDL, stress, and nonlinear effects are critically important to characterize the optical fiber network for high-speed communication systems ($\geq$ 10 Gb/s). In this chapter, we have reviewed different

methods to characterize optical fibers for their linear and nonlinear properties, and methods that are rapid in data acquisition have been emphasized for dynamic field fiber networks. A fiber network should be completely characterized before upgrading to higher bit-rate ($\geq$ 10 Gb/s) communication systems.

GLOSSARY

Attenuation: In an optical fiber, refers to the decrease in the power of a signal as it propagates through the fiber. Material absorption and Rayleigh scattering make the dominant contributions to the attenuation.

Chromatic Dispersion: The group velocity associated with a given mode in an optical fiber varies with frequency, leading to pulse broadening and intersymbol interference in fiber-optic communications.

Nonlinear Refractive Index: The refractive index n of a silica fiber is intensity-dependent, and it can be written in the form $n = n_0 + n_2 \, P/A_{eff}$. The coefficient n_2 is known as the nonlinear refractive index.

Polarization-Dependent Loss (PDL): A measure of the peak-to-peak difference in transmission of an optical component or system with respect to all possible states of polarization. It is the ratio of the maximum and the minimum transmission of an optical device with respect to all polarization states.

Polarization Mode Dispersion (PMD): The type of dispersion that occurs in single-mode fiber because of a lack of perfect symmetry in the fiber and from external pressures on the cable. Light travels over a single-mode fiber in two polarization states. Over long distances, PMD causes each one to arrive at the receiving end at a different time.

Stimulated Brillouin Scattering: An interaction between the optical signal and the acoustic waves in the fiber that causes the optical power to be scattered backward towards the transmitter. It is a narrowband process that individually affects each channel in a DWDM system. It is noticeable in systems that have channel powers in excess of 5 dBm to 6 dBm. In most cases, stimulated Brillouin scattering can be suppressed by modulating the laser transmitter to broaden the linewidth.

CROSS REFERENCES

See *Digital Communications Basics*; *Optical Fiber Communications*.

REFERENCES

Agrawal, G. P. 1997. *Fiber-optic communication systems*. 2nd ed. New York: John Wiley & Sons.

———. 2001. *Nonlinear fiber optics*. 3rd ed. San Diego: Academic Press.

Antonelli, C., and A. Mecozzi. 2004. Non-Maxwellian probability density function of fibers with lumped polarization mode dispersion elements. *Optics Letters*, 29: 1057–9.

Bao, X., A. Brown, M. DeMerchant, and J. Smith. 1999. Characterization of the Brillouin-loss spectrum of single-mode fibers by use of very short (<10-ns) pulses. *Optics Letters*, 24, 510–2.

Bao, X., J. Dhliwayo, N. Heron, D. J. Webb, and D. A. Jackson. 1995. Experimental and theoretical studies on a distributed temperature sensor based on Brillouin scattering. *Journal of Lightwave Technology*, 13: 1340–8.

Bao, X., D. J. Webb, and D. A. Jackson. 1993. 32-km distributed temperature sensor based on Brillouin loss in an optical fiber. *Optics Letters*, 18: 1561–3.

———. 1994. Combined distributed temperature and strain sensor based on Brillouin loss in an optical fiber. *Optics Letters*, 19, 141–2.

Bao, X., Q. Yu, and L. Chen. 2004. Simultaneous strain and temperature measurements with PM fibers and their error analysis using distributed Brillouin loss system. *Optics Letters*, 29, 1341–4.

Batagelj, B., P. Ritosa, M. Vidmar, and S. Tomazic. 2005. Noninterferometric measurement schemes for determination of single mode optical fiber nonlinear coefficient: a comparative study. In *Proceedings of the International Conference on Advanced Optoelectronics and Lasers* (CAOL 2005), 2: 200–7.

Batagelj, B., M. Vidmar, and S. Tomazic. 2005. Fibre non-linear coefficient measurement based on four-wave mixing method with two-tone optical source. In *Proceedings of the IEEE/LEOS Workshop on Fibres and Optical Passive Components*, pp. 152–7.

Bayvel, P., and R. Killey. 2002. Nonlinear optical effects in WDM transmission. In *Optical fiber telecommunications IV*, edited by I. P. Kaminow and T. Li, 611–41. San Diego: Academic Press.

Beller, J. 1998. OTDRs and backscatter measurements. In *Fiber optic test and measurement*, edited by D. Derickson, 434–74. Upper Saddle River, NJ: Prentice-Hall.

Bickham, S. R., and M. B. Cain. 2002a. Submarine fiber. Chap 12 in *Undersea fiber communication systems*, edited by J. Chesnoy, 442. New York: Elsevier.

———. 2002b. Submarine fiber. In *Undersea fiber communication systems*, edited by J. Chesnoy, 435–52. Amsterdam: Academic Press.

Buckland, E. L., and R. W. Boyd. 1997. Measurement of the frequency response of the electrostrictive nonlinearity in optical fibers. *Optics Letters*, 22: 676–8.

Chamberlain, G. E., G. W. Day, D. L. Franzen, R. L. Gallawa, E. M. Kim, and M. Young. 1983. *Optical fiber characterization*. National Bureau of Standards Special Publication 637, Vol. 2. Boulder, CO: NBS.

Chen, L., J. Cameron, and X. Y. Bao. 1999. Statistics of polarization mode dispersion in presence of the polarization dependent loss in single mode fibers. *Optics Communications*, 169: 69–73.

Chen, L., O. Chen, S. Hadjifaradji, and X. Y. Bao. 2004. Polarization mode dispersion measurement in a system with polarization dependent loss or gain. *IEEE Photonics Technology Letters*, 16, 206–9.

Chen, L., S. Hadjifaradji, D. S. Waddy, and X. Y. Bao. 2003. Polarization dependent loss autocorrelation in the presence of combined polarization-mode dispersion and polarization dependent losses in optical fibers. *SPIE*, 5260: 377–81.

———. 2003. Effect of local PMD and PDL direction correlation on the principal state of polarization vector autocorrelation. *Optics Express*, 11: 3141–6.

Chen, L., Z. Y. Zhang, and X. Y. Bao. 2006. Polarization dependent loss vector measurement in a system with polarization mode dispersion. *Journal of Optical Fiber Technology*, 12: 251–4.

Chraplyvy, A. R. 1990. Limitations on lightwave communications imposed by optical-fiber nonlinearities. *Journal of Lightwave Technology*, 8: 1548–57.

Cohen, L. G. 1985. Comparison of single-mode fiber dispersion measurement techniques. *Journal of Lightwave Technology*, 5: 958–66.

Corning Incorporated. 2001. OTDR gainers: What are they? Application Note AN3060 (retrieved from www.corning.com/docs/opticalfiber/an3060_07–01.pdf). Corning, NY: Author.

Culverhouse, D., F. Farahi, C. N. Pannell, and D. A. Jackson. 1989. Potential of stimulated Brillouin scattering as sensing mechanism for distributed temperature sensors. *Electronics Letters*, 25: 913–5.

Danielson, B. L., G. W. Day, D. L. Franzen, E. M. Kim, and M. Young. 1982. *Optical fiber characterization*. National Bureau of Standards Special Publication 637, Vol. 1. Boulder, CO: NBS.

Dong, H., P. Shum, M. Yan, G. X. Ning, Y. D. Gong, and C. Q. Wu. 2005. Generalized frequency dependence of output Stokes parameters in an optical fiber system with PMD and PDL/PDG. *Optics Express*, 13: 8875–81.

Fellay, A., L. Thévenaz, M. Facchini, M. Niklès, and P. Robert. 1997. Distributed sensing using stimulated Brillouin scattering: towards ultimate resolution. *OSA Technical Digest Series*, 16: 324–7.

Feuerstein, R. J. 2005. Field measurements of deployed fiber. In *Proceedings of the Optical Fiber Communication Conference and the National Fiber Optic Engineers Conference* (OFC/NFOEC 2005), March 6–11, Anaheim, CA, USA. NThC4.

Galtarossa, A., and L. Palmieri. 2003. The exact statistics of polarization-dependent loss in fiber-optic links. *IEEE Photonics Technology Letters*, 15: 57–9.

———. 2004. Spatially resolved PMD measurements. *Journal of Lightwave Technology*, 22: 1103–15.

Gifford, K., B. Soller, M. Wolfe, and M. Froggat. 2005. Distributed fiber-optic temperature sensing using Rayleigh backscatter. In *Proceedings of the Thirty-First European Conference on Optical Communication*, We4.P.005, pp. 511–2.

Gisin, N. 2004. PMD & PDL. In *Polarization mode dispersion*, edited by A. Galtarossa and C. R. Menyuk, 113–25. New York: Springer.

Gold, M. P. 1985. Design of a long-range single-mode OTDR. *Journal of Lightwave Technology*, 3: 39–46.

Gordon, P. J. 2004. Statistical properties of polarization mode dispersion. In *Polarization mode dispersion*, edited by A. Galtarossa and C. R. Menyuk, 52–9. New York: Springer.

Heffner, B. L. 1992. Deterministic, analytically complete measurement of polarization-dependent transmission through optical devices. *IEEE Photonics Technology Letters*, 4: 451–4.

———. 1993. Accurate, automated measurement of different group delay dispersion and principal state variation using Jones matrix eigenanalysis. *IEEE Photonics Technology Letters*, 5: 814–7.

Hentschel, C., and D. Derickson. 1998. Insertion loss measurements. In *Fiber optic test and measurement*, edited by D. Derickson, 339–82. Upper Saddle River, NJ: Prentice Hall.

Hernday, P. 1998. Dispersion measurements. In *Fiber optic test and measurement*, edited by D. Derickson, 475–518. Upper Saddle River, NJ: Prentice-Hall.

Horiguchi, T., T. Kurashima, and M. Tateda. 1989. Tensile strain dependence of Brillouin frequency shift in silica optical fibers. *IEEE Photonics Technology Letters*, 1: 107–8.

Horiguchi, T., T. Kurashima, M. Tateda, K. Ishihara, and Y. Wakui. 1992. Brillouin characterization of optical fiber strain in bent slot-type optical-fiber cable. *Journal of Lightwave Technology*, 10: 1196–1201.

Horiguchi, T., K. Shimizu, T. Kurashima, M. Tateda, and Y. Koyamada. 1995. Development of a distributed sensing technique using Brillouin scattering. *Journal of Lightwave Technology*, 13: 1296–1302.

Horiguchi, T., and M. Tateda. 1989. Optical-fiber-attenuation investigation using stimulated Brillouin scattering between a pulse and a continuous wave. *Optics Letters*, 14: 408–10.

Hotate, K., and T. Hasegawa. 1998. Measurement of Brillouin gain spectrum distribution along an optical fiber with a high spatial resolution using a Novel correlation-based technique: Demonstration of 45 cm spatial resolution. *OSA Technical Digest Series*, 16: 337–40.

Huai, H. K., G. P. Lees, and T. P. Newson. 2000. All-fiber system for simultaneous interrogation of distributed strain and temperature sensing by spontaneous Brillouin scattering. *Optics Letters*, 25: 695–7.

Iannone, E., F. Matera, A. Mecozzi, and M. Settembre. 1998. *Nonlinear optical communication networks*. New York: John Wiley & Sons.

Kato, T., Y. Suetsugu, M. Takagi, E. Sasaoka, and M. Nishimura. 1995. Measurement of the nonlinear refractive index in optical fiber by the cross-phase-modulation method with depolarized pump light. *Optics Letters*, 20: 988–90.

Keiser, G. 2000. *Optical fiber communications*. 3rd ed. Boston: McGraw-Hill.

———. 2003. *Optical communications essentials*. New York: McGraw-Hill.

Knox, W. H., N. M. Pearson, K. D. Li, and C. A. Hirlimann. 1988. Interferometric measurements of femtosecond group delay in optical components. *Optics Letters*, 13: 574–6.

Kurashima, T., T. Horiguchi, and M. Tateda. 1990. Distributed-temperature sensing using stimulated Brillouin scattering in optical silica fibers. *Optics Letters*, 15: 1038–40.

Li, Y., and A. Yariv. 2000. Solution to the dynamic equation of polarization-mode dispersion and polarization-dependent loss. *Journal of Optical Society of America B*, 17: 1821–7.

Li, Y., F. Zhang, and T. Yoshino. 2003. Wide temperature-range Brillouin and Rayleigh optical-time-domain reflectometry in a dispersion-shifted fibre. *Applied Optics*, 42: 3772–5.

Maran, J. N., R. Slavík, S. LaRochelle, and M. Karásek. 2004. Chromatic dispersion measurement using a multiwavelength frequency-shifted feedback fiber laser. *IEEE Transactions on Instrumentation and Measurement*, 53: 67–71.

Maughan, S. M., H. H. Kee, and T. P. Newson. 2001. 57-km single-ended spontaneous Brillouin-based distributed fiber temperature sensor using microwave coherent detection. *Optics Letters*, 26: 331–3.

Namihira, Y. 2004. ITU-T round robin measurement for nonlinear coefficient (n_2/A_{eff}) of various single mode optical fibers. In *Proceedings of the Symposium on Optical Fiber Measurements* (SOFM 2004), Sept. 28–30, Boulder, CO, USA, pp. 33–6.

———, et al. 2002. A comparison of six techniques for nonlinear coefficient measurements of various single mode optical fibers. In *Proceedings of the Symposium on Optical Fiber Measurements* (SOFM 2002), Sept. 24–26, Boulder, CO, USA, pp. 15–18.

Nelson, L. E., and R. M. Jopson. 2004. Introduction to polarization mode dispersion in optical systems. In *Polarization mode dispersion*, edited by A. Galtarossa and C. R. Menyuk, 1–33. New York: Springer.

Ohno, H., H. Naruse, M. Kihara, and A. Shimada. 2001. Industrial applications of the BOTDR optical fiber strain sensor. *Optical Fiber Technology*, 7: 45–64.

Parker, T. R., M. Farhadiroushan, R. Feced, and V. A. Habderek. 1998. Simultaneous distributed measurement of strain and temperature from noise-initiated Brillouin scattering in optical fibers. *IEEE Journal of Quantum Electronics*, 34: 645–59.

Saleh, B. E. A., and M. C. Teich. 1991. *Fundamentals of photonics*. New York: John Wiley & Sons.

Song, S., C. T. Allen, K. R. Demarest, and R. Hui. 1999. Intensity-dependent phase-matching effects on four-wave mixing in optical fibers. *Journal of Lightwave Technology*, 17: 2285–90.

Talbot, P., and M. Michel. Undated. Accurate loss testing made easy. EXFO Product Note 006 (retrieved from http://documents.exfo.com/appnotes/pnote006-ang.pdf). Quebec: EXFO.

Tateda, M., T. Horiguchi, T. Kurashima, and K. Ishihara. 1990. First measurement of strain distribution along field-installed optical fibers using Brillouin spectroscopy. *Journal of Lightwave Technology*, 8: 1269–73.

Tateda, M., N. Shibata, and S. Seikai. 1981. Interferometric method for chromatic dispersion measurement in a single-mode optical fiber. *IEEE Journal of Quantum Electronics*, 17: 404–7.

Thévenaz, L., M. Niklès, A. Fellay, M. Facchini, and P. Robert. 1998. Truly distributed strain and temperature sensing using embedded optical fibers. In *Proceedings of SPIE*, 3330, 301–14.

Thévenaz, L., J. P. Pellaux, and J. P. Von der Weid. 1988. All-fiber interferometer for chromatic dispersion measurements. *Journal of Lightwave Technology*, 6, 1–7.

Tkach, R. W., A. R. Chraplyvy, F. Forghieri, A. H. Gnauck, and R. M. Derosier. 1995. Four-photon mixing and high-speed WDM systems. *Journal of Lightwave Technology*, 13: 841–9.

Waddy, D. S., L. Chen, and X. Y. Bao. 2002. Theoretical and experimental study of the dynamics of polarization-mode dispersion. *IEEE Photonics Technology Letters*, 14: 468–70.

———. 2005. Polarization effects in aerial fibers. *Optical Fiber Technology*, 11: 1–19.

Waddy, D. S., P. Lu, L. Chen, and X. Y. Bao. 2001. Fast state of polarization changes in aerial fiber under different climatic conditions. *IEEE Photonics Technology Letters*, 13: 1035–7.

Williams, P. 2004. PMD measurement techniques and how to avoid the pitfalls. In *Polarization mode dispersion*, edited by A. Galtarossa and C. R. Menyuk, 133–54. New York: Springer.

Yariv, A. 1997. *Optical electronics in modern communications*. 5th ed. New York: Oxford University Press.

Zou, L., X. Bao, S. Afshar, and L. Chen. 2004. Dependence of the Brillouin frequency shift on strain and temperature in a photonic crystal fibre. *Optics Letters*, 29: 1485–7.

Optical Couplers and Splitters

Kais Dridi, Mustapha Razzak, and Habib Hamam, *Université de Moncton, Canada*

INTRODUCTION

Why optics? Optical fields show several interesting physical properties that permit any technology that uses light to reach high performance (Born and Wolf 1999). The use of light in advanced technologies allows the production of high-performance components and systems. Some advantages of optical technologies arise in telecommunications applications as well as in nonintrusive sensing methods (Agrawal 2002; Razzak and Hamam 2006). Indeed, by using light, we can benefit from interesting optical properties to attain high immunity and safety. Doubtlessly, optical fiber–based systems are the most commonly used technology to benefit from several advantages of light for information transmission (Taga 1996; Othonos and Kali 1999). This explains why optical fiber and optical components constitute a large part of existing telecommunications components. It is worth mentioning the advantage of using fiber-based components that can easily enable the coupling of light between fiber elements thanks to their small size (a few micrometers) (Hamam 2006). Although optical fields are more desirable for data transmission than electronics signals, the coupling carried out in the optical domain is much more complicated.

Why Optical Coupling?

Optical coupling is a crucial function for many applications, especially for optical communications, where the need for more than simple point-to-point connections is fundamental (Dowd et al. 1996). Multiport connections in optical systems are essential for sharing and monitoring systems. Thus, we need optical components that are able to redistribute optical signals (combining or splitting) throughout the system. An example of the use of such components is in broadcast-and-select networks, where we need to share information between several destinations using a star coupler (Laude 2002; Ruan and Du 2001). So each destination has to filter (i.e., accept or refuse) any received signal. This makes the design and implementation of the system easier. On the other hand, in monitoring and surveillance applications, we sometimes need to regroup several data ports into the same terminal or split the signal into two signals, one of which is of relatively low energy. The latter signal can then be analyzed without disturbing the system signal, thus enabling system characterization under real conditions. Furthermore, this allows the sharing of expensive equipment by means of centralized monitoring (Yilmaz 2006).

An optical coupler is a device able to implement all the functions mentioned above.

What Is an Optical Coupler?

An *optical coupler* (OC) is a device able to connect three or more ends by redistributing the optical power over its ports in a desired ratio. The redistribution may result from combining incoming signals to the output port (the case of an optical combiner) or from splitting the optical power over two or more output ports (the case of an optical splitter). Hence, *optical coupler* is a general term that designates both optical combiners and optical splitters. The manner with which the power is redistributed is not specified here and may differ from one device to another (see the next section). In the electronics field, the term *optical coupler* (or *opto-coupler*) refers to a device that is used to transfer an electrical signal from a circuit to another by using light (GlobalSpec, undated, "About optocouplers"). This opto-coupler also isolates the two circuits from electrical perturbations. The component is also known as an *opto-isolator* or a *photo-coupler*, but it will not be considered here.

How to Fabricate an Optical Coupler

Optical-fiber-based communications systems are among optical technology fields that need optical couplers. To meet the technological constraints regarding fiber dimensions and the nature of the optical signal, couplers based on optical waveguides present an interesting solution that enables cost-efficiency and high performance (Owyang 1981).

The optical waveguide fabrication process—photolithography (Klein 1988), thin-film deposition (Seshan 2002), and ion deposition (Mentzer 1990)—enables the manufacturing of complex circuits that integrate several components into the same substrate. These highly integrated components are commonly known as *optical integrated circuits* (OICs) (Hunsperger 1991; Kyo-Seon and Sotiris 1988). An OIC can contain lasers, guides, filters, detectors, and so on and can be fabricated by means of a hybrid or a monolithic approach. In monolithic integration, the same substrate can be used by choosing an appropriate material to include all components: sources, filters, detectors, and so on. In hybrid integration, on the other hand, several different materials are used, and discrete components are bonded together to form the circuit. The choice of manufacturing technology depends on several parameters such as physical performance and production cost. Recent progresses in optical polymers may make the development of polymer waveguides much less expensive. Spin coating is one technology that can be used for this purpose, although the difference in the thermal expansion coefficients of the polymer and the silica wafer makes thermal stress the main issue in addition to high propagation losses. OC can also be obtained using bulk optics or classical components (lenses, beam splitters, mirrors, gratings, etc.).

Optical Couplers and Switches

Optical couplers and switches can be distinguished as follows. In couplers, connections are fixed, conserving optical path and optical power. In switches, path reconfiguration is possible (Xiaohua 2003). Again, when only power attenuation is considered, we deal with variable optical attenuators (Lagali et al. 2001).

How to Model an Optical Coupler

To explain how the main categories of waveguide-type couplers work, we first introduce the theory underlying waveguides. Coupled-mode theory allows a description of the evolution of the amplitude of each waveguide (Kawano and Kitoh 2001; McCall 2000). This theory is based on coupled-mode theory for microwaves, which was developed in the 1950s (Pierce 1954; Barnes 1964). An overview of the theories used to describe optical couplers is given in the next section.

OVERVIEW OF THEORIES RELATED TO OPTICAL COUPLERS

Because a comprehensive description of the theories related to optical couplers goes beyond the scope of this handbook, we present only a general overview to introduce the theories. For more in-depth study, consult the references at the end of the chapter.

Optical Waveguide Theory

Optical waveguide devices are mostly coplanar structures. Because they can be fabricated with high precision, optical devices can also attain a high degree of integration. This permits the integration of several functions on an extremely small chip (Mentzer 1990).

The fundamental theory that describes couplers as optical waveguides is *electromagnetic theory*. This theory involves mathematical equations that predict the variation of both the electric and the magnetic fields during propagation in the medium. Those mathematical equations are known as *Maxwell's equations* (Pollock and Lipson 2003).

By combining these equations and taking into account the physical properties of the optical waveguide, we obtain what are commonly referred to as the *vector wave equations* for the electric and magnetic fields (Pollock and Lipson 2003). They determine each of the three field components with respect to the coordinate system employed (Cartesian coordinates are frequently used) and time. If we limit our attention to one coordinate—the x component of the field, for example—we obtain a *scalar wave equation* that is commonly referred to as the *Helmholtz equation* (Kawano and Kitoh 2001). Either analytical or numerical methods can be used to solve the Helmholtz equation for a given medium and geometry (Weisstein 1999).

Optical Waveguides

The optical waveguide is the fundamental element that allows the transfer of light energy between several passive or active optical components. To explain the way this transfer occurs, we introduce the concept of guided modes. This concept presents one aspect of the complexity

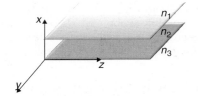

Figure 1: Three-layer planar waveguide structure

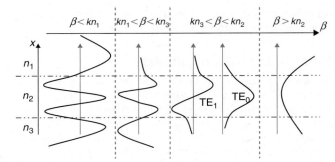

Figure 2: Modes in the planar waveguide

of the problem. It is worth analytically studying simple structures such as planar waveguides because the latter represent the basis of more sophisticated structures (Kawano and Kitoh 2001; McCall 2000; Pierce 1954; Barnes 1964; Pollock and Lipson 2003; Weisstein 1999; Taylor and Yariv 1974).

Planar Waveguides

A planar waveguide as sketched in Figure 1 is a region bounded by parallel infinitely extended planes ($+\infty$ and $-\infty$ for both the y- and z-directions). The planes are separated from each other by a finite distance x_0 in x-direction. We then obtain a three-layer planar waveguide structure. The medium between the two planes has a refractive index of n_2 (core layer). The semi-infinite regions are composed of materials with refractive indexes n_1 and n_3, respectively (the cladding layers). In general, the core refractive index is slightly larger than those of both cladding layers, which are generally identical.

As with any guiding structure, we look for a solution to the wave equation. To determine simple solutions, many assumptions should be made to reduce the problem complexity such as using only *transverse electric* (TE) plane waves (Pollock and Lipson 2003). Again, we will not go into detail here, but the references at the end of the chapter can be consulted for more information.

Waveguide Modes and Guiding Conditions

Solving the wave equation for a given medium and waveguide can sometimes be done by employing rigorous mathematical methods or, more generally, by numerical methods (Kawano and Kitoh 2001; McCall 2000; Pierce 1954; Barnes 1964; Pollock and Lipson 2003; Weisstein 1999; Taylor and Yariv 1974; Belanger 1993). If a solution exists—called a *mode*—it can be interpreted as a form of optical field that can propagate through the medium with guidance. An optical mode in a waveguide is defined as an allowed traveling optical wave that is characterized by relevant spatial optical energy distribution across the waveguide (Kasap 2001).

The modal solutions of the scalar wave equation for the slab waveguide have a wavelike solution in the core and an exponentially decreasing solution into the cladding on either side. The boundary conditions at each of the two interfaces (three layers) also have to be satisfied, leading to a continuous distribution of the field (Pollock and Lipson 2003).

Depending on the value of the modal propagation constant β, several cases are distinguished (Figure 2). The constant β is a complex parameter associated with the transmitted waveguide that describes the behavior of

the wave along the waveguide. It is composed of two parts that describe the signal attenuation and the phase. Consider a waveguide excited by a constant frequency source with the three refractive indexes satisfying $n_2 > n_3 > n_1$. This is the case of many components in which we have a thin layer (layer 2) deposited on a substrate (layer 3) placed in the air (layer 1).

For $kn_3 < \beta < kn_2$ (k is the free-space wave number), we get a field distribution in which we have a sinusoidal distribution in the core and an exponential profile in each cladding. Thus, we have confined guided modes. We notice that β can take only one or more discrete values that depend on the thickness of the waveguide core (region 2). Those modes are referred to as the *zeroth*, *first . . . transverse electric modes* and are denoted as TE_0; $TE_1 . . .$ (or TM_0, $TM_1 . . .$).

In the case of $kn_3 > \beta > kn_1$ (when β can have any continuous value in this range), the confinement can be only on the side of layer 1 where the mode field has an exponential form. In the others layers, it has a sinusoidal form. This mode is carried by the waveguide but is not confined within it because a part of the light escapes as radiation into layer 3. However, it may be considered as a useful effect for coupling light to layer 3.

When $\beta < kn_1$, the field oscillates (sinusoidally) in all regions, leading to an unguided mode.

For $\beta > kn_2$ we find an exponential profile in all three regions. This mode cannot be excited physically and does not propagate and is sometimes referred to as an *evanescent* mode.

There is a lower limit to frequencies that will excite a particular mode. Below this limit, a specific mode is no longer guided—with the exception of the fundamental or first mode, which has the largest value of propagation constant and will always propagate. This kind of guiding condition is referred to as the *cutoff* condition, and it depends on the waveguide's optogeometric characteristics (Pollock and Lipson 2003).

A planar waveguide is a classical structure that is relatively easily analyzed by waveguide theory (Pollock and Lipson 2003). In this structure, the power confinement occurs only in one dimension. In several applications, a two-dimensional confinement (such as channel waveguides or optical fibers) is desired. However, these structures are generally more complex and require heavy mathematical analysis. Simplifying assumptions are generally unavoidable to reduce the complexity of the problem (Nishihara, Haruna, and Suhara 1989). Because optical

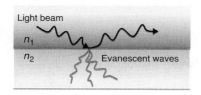

Figure 3: Evanescent wave generation

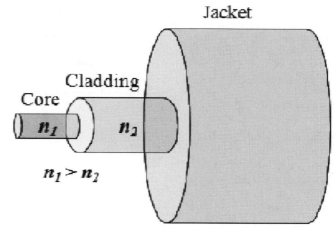

Figure 4: Optical fiber structure

fibers are increasingly being adopted in both sensing and telecommunication applications, we devote the next subsection to this specific waveguide. Moreover, a special subsection is reserved for fiber-optic couplers. However, as stated above, we limit ourselves to an introduction to the theoretical analysis of modes.

Evanescent Wave and Evanescent Wave Coupling

An evanescent wave can be considered as a light guided in the inner part of an optical fiber's cladding. It is a wave that shows an exponential decay with distance. In the optical domain, this wave can be found when sinusoidal waves are totally and internally reflected between two different index waveguides as shown in Figure 3.

In an optical guide coupler, the evanescent wave offers a way to couple power or transport energy from one side arm to the other so that an optical wave will be excited within the second waveguide, which is why it is called *evanescent* wave coupling. Thus, a propagating wave mode can arise.

Optical Fibers

An optical fiber is an optical waveguide that possesses cylindrical symmetry (Belanger 1993; Kasap 2001; Nishihara, Haruna, and Suhara 1989; Buck 1995). In the case of a step profile fiber, the core, with radius (a) and constant refractive index n_1, is surrounded by the cladding, which has a constant refractive index n_2 that is slightly smaller than that of the core (Figure 4). In the standard single-mode fiber used in telecommunications, the core radius is approximately 8 μm, and the diameter of the cladding is approximately 125 μm. For the multimode fiber, the dimensions of both core and cladding are 50/125 and 62.5/125, respectively. Together, core and cladding are protected by a plastic jacket to suppress fiber bending and breakage.

Regarding the symmetry of the fiber, it is convenient to use cylindrical coordinates to solve the wave equations (Belanger 1993). Because the refractive index of the cladding is slightly smaller than that of the core ($n_1 - n_2 = \Delta n \approx 10^{-3}$), we can use the weak guidance approximation to reduce the vector wave equation to a scalar wave equation. We can also assume that the radial and angular field variables are separable. By solving the scalar wave equation in the core and cladding and then matching these solutions through the boundary conditions, we obtain the dispersion equation that allows us to determine the modal fields and propagation constants. Because the mathematical details go beyond the scope of this chapter, see Marcuse (1971) and Snyder and Love (1983).

Mode Conversion and Optical Coupling

Each mode propagates along the z-direction (without loss of generality, the z-axis of the waveguide or fiber denotes the propagation direction) independently of all other propagating modes. Together they constitute an orthogonal basis of modes, so we can decompose each excitation beam in terms of this basis and express it as a sum of these modes. When a beam that is composed of a superposition of modes comes across irregularities in either the geometry or the index profile of the waveguide, light may be coupled into other modes; a power transfer occurs from the initial to the new modes (Nishihara, Haruna, and Suhara 1989).

The theory of the modes coupling (or simply the coupling theory) in the optical wave guide was developed by several researchers including Marcuse (1971), Snyder (1972), and Taylor and Yariv (1974). This theory uses the principle of field decomposition based on the elementary fields. In mathematical terms, it is based on a complete set of solutions of the Helmholtz equations, and each element of this set is a guided mode. To this decomposition, a continuum of modes can be added to describe losses resulting from radiation. These modes are often referred to as *radiation* modes.

Coupled-Wave Theory

Coupled-wave theory, also called *coupled-mode theory* (CMT) (Lifante 2003), provides a mathematical description of the interaction between two or more waves (modes) and the exchange of optical power between them as they propagate (Kawano and Kitoh 2001; McCall 2000). To illustrate this phenomenon in the optical domain, we will take as an example a *fiber Bragg grating* (Kogelnik and Shank 1972; Kashyap 1999).

Principle

The CMT is often used to analyze passives couplers and, more generally, passive structures (Bilbao 2004; Haus

1984). This theory is derived from the variational principle for the propagation constant of the waveguide wave solutions. Simple solutions consist of a linear superposition of the individual modes of the waveguide or fiber. Then the coupled-mode equations are derived.

Now we briefly present the coupling principle for time-dependent oscillators. In a separate subsection, we introduce the principle of coupling in space.

Coupling Modes in Time

Consider two weakly coupled lossless oscillators with different time-frequency dependencies (ω_1 and ω_2) and amplitudes (a_1 and a_2). Under the weakly coupling condition, the formalism describing the coupling of those oscillations is given in Haus and Huang (1991).

The two angular frequencies are assumed to be real. It is interesting to consider the case of two oscillators excited with equal angular frequencies. If the first oscillator is excited ($a_1 = 1$) at $t = 0$ and the second one is unexcited ($a_2 = 0$), then the initial conditions are matched by a superposition of equal amplitude symmetric and antisymmetric solutions. The phases of the two solutions evolve at different rates; after a certain time known as the *beat period* (Haus and Huang 1991), the entire exciting signal is transferred back to the first oscillator. Hence, the excitation oscillates back and forth between the two oscillators. When the frequencies of the two uncoupled oscillators are unequal, and initially only one oscillator is excited, then full transfer cannot occur (Haus and Huang 1991).

Coupling Modes in Space

Let us now consider the coupling of two propagating waves in space with propagation constants β_1 and β_2. In other words, the two waves have the common time-frequency dependence $e^{j\omega t}$ and longitudinal spatial dependencies $e^{-j\beta_1}$ and $e^{-j\beta_2}$, respectively. The coupling can result from either a uniform perturbation or a periodic structure such as a grating (Haus and Huang 1991). In a uniform structure, the interaction between the waves occurs when the propagation constants β_1 and β_2 are of the same sign (i.e., both are either positive or negative) and approximately equal. For periodic structures, coupling among space harmonics (Bloch waves or Brillouin components—see Kittel 1996) becomes possible. A Bloch wave is equivalent to a plane wave modulated by a periodic function (Bloch envelope) (Kittel 1996).

CMT is inherently directional. Two cases exist— codirectional and contradirectional coupling—as depicted in Figures 5 and 6. Similar to the case of time coupling, the total power propagating is conserved.

Power transmitted to each output side of the coupler depends on the coupling length l as shown in both Figures 5 and 6. For example, when we would like to couple some percentage of power from one fiber side coupler to the other side, then the length of the coupler should be a particular coupling length or its odd multiple. This coupling length depends on the wavelength of the propagated light. To have different splitting ratio, we should vary this length.

The power coupled out of each leg of the output side of the coupler is a function of length of the coupler and a periodic function (Lohmeyer et al. 1999).

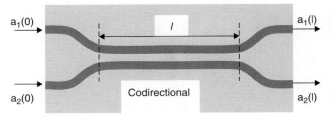

Figure 5: Codirectional coupler

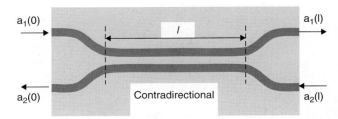

Figure 6: Contradirectional coupler

WAVEGUIDE STRUCTURES AND TECHNOLOGIES

There are several different types of waveguides, depending primarily on the method that is used to fabricate the waveguide.

Buried Waveguide Types

As indicated by its name, a *buried waveguide* has the core buried in the substrate or cladding as shown in Figure 7. Buried waveguides may be formed by, for example, ion-diffusion (Jackel, Ramaswamy, and Lyman 1981; Armenise and De Sario 1982) or ion-exchange (Izawa and Nakagome 1972) techniques. Ion-diffusion techniques use the penetration of titanium (Ti) into lithium niobate crystal or glass to modify their optical properties (Burns et al. 1979; Jiang et al. 1992).

The ion-exchange process uses molten salt or silver film techniques. The substrate is immersed in a bath containing molten salt where the ion exchange occurs. A multistage ion-exchange process is necessary to form

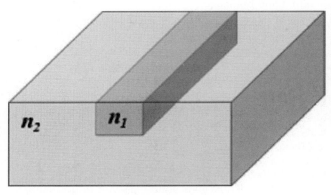

Figure 7: Buried-type optical waveguide

a buried waveguide. An applied electric field is used to better control operations. Others techniques can be used such as light or electron beam irradiation or plasma-enhanced chemical vapor deposition.

Ridge or Relief Waveguide Types

Ridge waveguides (see Figure 8) are formed by removing undesired material from the substrate using a patterning process. The most commonly used technique is

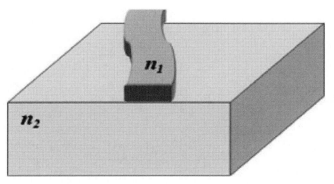

Figure 8: Ridge-type optical waveguide

photolithography (Takato et al. 1988; Herzig 1997). The main photolithography steps are described in Figure 9. A resist that is sensitive to ultraviolet light is spread over a thin film that is spread over the substrate, usually by spin coating. By using a binary amplitude mask, areas of resistance are exposed through the transparent regions of the mask. Photochemical changes occur in these regions of the resist. The exposed areas become more soluble and are removed by using appropriate chemical solutions. The unexposed areas of resist maintain their initial insolubility.

Strip-Loaded Waveguides

One technique of confining a waveguide in two dimensions (x and y) without totally surrounding the waveguide by material with a lower refractive index is to place a dielectric strip on top of the substrate (Figure 10). The added strip should have a refractive index that is lower than that of the dielectric substrate. Thus, the effective index of the set of the strip and the region beneath is lower than the rest of the substrate, which ensures the guidance function of the waveguide (Gray 1986).

Another technique consists of cladding a dielectric medium with a charged metal. The refractive index close

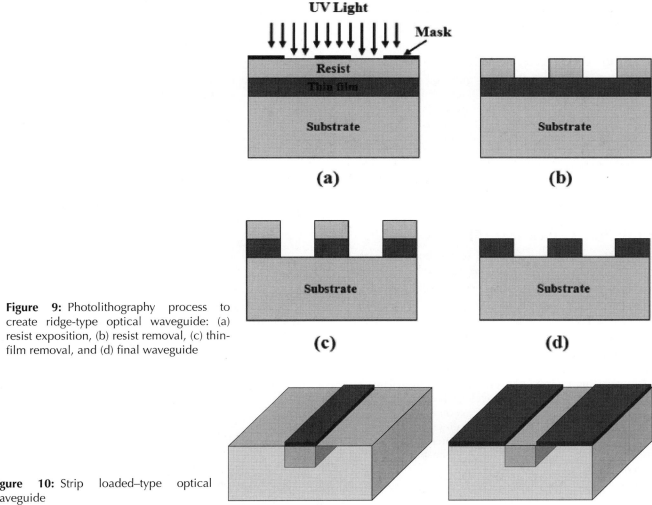

Figure 9: Photolithography process to create ridge-type optical waveguide: (a) resist exposition, (b) resist removal, (c) thin-film removal, and (d) final waveguide

Figure 10: Strip loaded–type optical waveguide

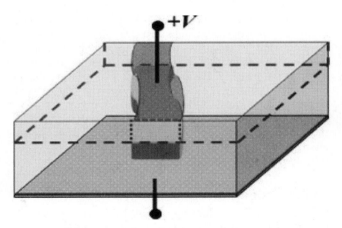

Figure 11: Induced-type optical waveguide

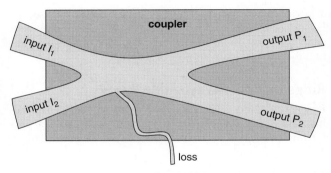

Figure 12: A WDM coupler of type 2 × 2 (the two wavelengths enter through inputs 1 and 2)

to the strip becomes slightly smaller, thus forming the channel waveguide. Metal strip–based waveguides are useful for applications such as electro-optic modulators. Metal strips can also be used as electrodes and to form waveguide functions. One such application is the generation of 50-GHz to 60-GHz *continuous wave, millimeter wave* by applying optical technology for optical-to-radio systems and ubiquitous communications (Park 2006).

Induced Waveguides

By using a material with a high electro-optic coefficient, such as the case of crystals—for example, lithium niobate ($LiNbO_3$) or $NiTiO_3$—an induced waveguide can be formed after applying an electric field generated by planar electrodes placed over the crystal (Yariv 1976; Streetman 1980). The electric field (see Figure 11) induces a small change in the refractive index of the material because of the electro-optics effect (Pockel's effect) and then forms an induced waveguide that is buried.

COUPLING PARAMETERS

In designing optical couplers, it is necessary to quantify parameter values that determine the performance of the device as well as to satisfy the specifications required by the user (i.e., the application).

Center Wavelength and Bandpass

The performance of the coupler depends on the source wavelength. Couplers are usually specified over either one wavelength window or multiple windows. The *center wavelength* is the nominal wavelength of coupler operation. In other words, it is the average wavelength between the wavelengths at the extremes of the coupler's bandwidth. The operation of the coupler normally occurs at this wavelength at the center of the bandwidth. The *bandpass* is the range of values of frequency for which the transmitted signals can pass through the coupler. This said, in many cases, couplers will perform adequately

over a range outside their bandpass, but adherence to specifications would not normally be guaranteed in this region.

Coupling Ratio

The *coupling ratio* or *splitting ratio* is defined as the ratio of the optical power from one output port of the coupler to the sum of the total power from all outputs (see Figure 12). In other words, this ratio defines the optical power distribution of the input signals among the output ports. It is measured at the specified center wavelength and is generally expressed as a percentage. It can be expressed as follows:

$$\text{coupling ratio (\%)} = \frac{\text{optical power from one output port}}{\text{total power from all output ports}} \times 100\% \qquad (1)$$

For a 1×2 *wavelength-division multiplexing* (WDM) coupler (Figure 12) with output powers P_1 and P_2, the two coupling ratios are

$$\text{coupling ratio 1 (\%)} = \frac{P_1}{P_1 + P_2} \times 100\% \qquad (2)$$

and

$$\text{coupling ratio 2 (\%)} = \frac{P_2}{P_1 + P_2} \times 100\% \qquad (3)$$

Excess Loss

The *excess loss* is defined as the ratio of the total optical power from the output ports to the total input power; it is normally expressed in dB as

$$\text{excess loss (dB)} = -10 \log \left(\frac{\text{total optical power from all output ports}}{\text{total input power}} \right) \qquad (4)$$

Insertion Loss

The *insertion loss* is defined as the ratio of the optical power launched at the input port of the coupler to the optical power from any single output port. In other words, it is the fraction of power transferred from input port to one of the output ports and is generally expressed in dB. It includes the coupler splitting loss and excess loss and is the most commonly used parameter in system design. The insertion loss can be expressed by the following formula:

$$\text{insertion loss (dB)}$$
$$= -10\log\left(\frac{\text{optical power of one of the output ports}}{\text{total input power}}\right) \quad (5)$$

Typical Insertion Loss

The *typical insertion loss* is the expected value of the insertion loss measured at the specified center wavelength. Generally, the average insertion loss between input port and one output port at the center wavelength is calculated.

Maximum and Minimum Insertion Losses

Two other parameters are frequently used—namely, the *maximum* and *minimum insertion losses*. These are the upper and lower limits of the insertion loss of the coupler, respectively. These limits are measured with respect to the entire wavelength range specified in the bandpass. In other words, the maximum insertion loss, for example, is the insertion loss between the input port and one output port across the entire bandwidth.

Directivity

The *directivity* expresses the fraction of power transferred from one input port to another input port. It is equal to the insertion loss between these two input ports. Directivity is also referred to as *near-end isolation* or the *near-end cross talk*. It is generally expressed in dBs (positive) and is measured with all output ports optically terminated. The minimum directivity is the lower limit that applies over the entire wavelength range specified in the bandpass.

Return Loss

The *return loss* is the fraction of the optical power launched into an input port to the optical power returning to the same input port. Like directivity, return loss is expressed as positive dB and measured with all output ports optically terminated. Like directivity, the minimum return loss is the lower limit that applies over the entire wavelength range specified in the bandpass.

Reflectance

The *reflectance* is the negative of the return loss. In many instances, reflectance and return loss are used synonymously.

Wavelength Isolation

The *wavelength isolation* expresses the fraction of power in wavelength channel that is blocked from input port to output port. It is equal to the insertion loss at the specific wavelength blocked from input port to output port. It is generally expressed in dBs. In wavelength multiplexing and demultiplexing, wavelength isolation is a measure of how well different wavelengths are separated at the output of a wavelength-division demultiplexer. This isolation is also referred to as *far-end cross talk*.

Minimum Wavelength Isolation

The *minimum wavelength isolation* is the lower limit of the wavelength isolation measured over the entire wavelength range of the specified bandpass.

Uniformity

The *uniformity* for a coupler is defined as the maximum variation of insertion loss between one input port and any two output ports, or between any two input ports and one output port, over the entire bandwidth. In concrete terms, it measures the difference between the highest and lowest insertion losses among all of the coupler output ports. It is generally expressed in dBs. Uniformity is not available for nonuniform couplers and applies only to couplers with a nominally equal coupling ratio.

Flatness

The *flatness* for a coupler is defined as the maximum variation (the peak to peak) of insertion loss between the input port and one output port across the entire bandwidth.

Polarization-Dependent Loss

The *polarization-dependent loss* is the maximum variation of insertion loss between input port and output port over the entire polarization state.

OPTICAL COUPLER FEATURES AND CHARACTERISTICS

The OC is a key component in many applications. Several types of OCs are used in telecommunications and in other fields. We mainly distinguish *optical taps* used for monitoring and *directional couplers* used for power sharing, such as in telecommunications. In the latter case, the equal power at each output port is generally required. In practice, a typical situation occurs when only one optical source is used to deliver one optical signal for many systems or optical paths. However, optical taps used for monitoring systems divert only a small part of the signal from the main optical path to be monitored. Most of the signal's power propagates along the system regardless of whether or not part of the signal is extracted. Other examples of OC uses are given at the end of the chapter.

The power redistribution is not the only factor to distinguish OCs from one another. Distinctions can be made with respect to coupler parameters and the modulation parameter of the optical field (magnitude, phase, polarization, and frequency). This variety of use of OCs gave birth to several types of couplers using different technologies such as bulk optics (discrete-type), fused fibers (fiber-type), and waveguide-type.

It is worth mentioning that optical couplers are completely different from opto-couplers, although the names are similar. *Opto-couplers* facilitate the transfer of an electrical signal between two circuits while electrically isolating the circuits from each other. An opto-coupler is generally composed of an infrared LED-emitting section at the input and a silicon photodetector at the output. Often, other circuitry is included as part of the device. The input for opto-couplers can be AC or DC. The output can be a photocell, a photodiode, a phototransistor, or a photo-darlington (GlobalSpec, undated, "About fiber optic couplers"; Marstone 1999). However, as mentioned previously, this opto-electronic device is outside the scope of this chapter.

Splitting or Coupling

Optical splitters and couplers are indeed linked together. An optical splitter is nothing other than a directional coupler and will be regarded as such in this chapter. The optical splitter can be defined as a transmission coupling device for separately sampling (through a known coupling loss) either the forward (incident) or the backward (reflected) wave in a transmission line. Note that a directional coupler may be used to sample either a forward or a backward wave in a transmission line. Although a unidirectional coupler has available terminals or connections for sampling only one direction of transmission, a bidirectional coupler has available terminals for sampling both directions.

Fiber-Optic Coupler Features

Fiber-optic couplers are optical devices that enable the connection of three or more fiber ends by dividing one input between two or more outputs, or by combining two or more inputs into one output. Both single-mode and multimode fibers may be coupled by means of fiber-optic couplers. Types of couplers include single-window, dual-window, and wideband. Single-window couplers are designed for a single wavelength with a narrow wavelength window. Dual-wavelength couplers are designed for two wavelengths with a wide wavelength window for each. Wideband couplers are designed for a single wavelength with a wider wavelength window. Typical wavelengths for fiber-optic couplers are 633 nm, 830 nm, 1060 nm, 1300 nm, and 1550 nm (Gelikonov, Gelikonov, and Sabanov 2000).

Important coupler performance specifications to consider for fiber optic couplers include: number of input ports, number of output ports, insertion loss, splitting ratio, and polarization-dependent losses. Various coupler types are available (see "Coupler Types" below). Couplers may be typically of star or tee (T) types. Star couplers have M inputs and N outputs ($M \times N$). T couplers have 1 input and N outputs ($1 \times N$).

Insertion loss is the attenuation caused by the insertion of an optical component. The *splitting ratio* is the distribution of power among the output fibers of a coupler, also referred to as *coupling ratio*. The *polarization-dependent losses* are defined as the attenuation caused by polarization.

Common features for fiber-optic couplers include pigtails, rack mounting, polarization maintenance, and bidirectionality. A *pigtail* is a short length of fiber attached to a fiber-optic component such as a laser or coupler. A *rack mountable* coupler can be rack mounted for convenience and efficiency. In a *polarization-maintaining* coupler, the polarization of the incoming signal is preserved between input and output ports. A bidirectional coupler has bidirectional transmission on a single fiber. An important environmental parameter to consider is the operating temperature (Othonos and Kali 1999).

Optical Coupler Characteristics

Because numerous technologies exist to manufacture optical couplers, many couplers have been developed. There is no optimal coupler for all applications. To choose an OC for a specific application, many specifications must be considered in addition to those discussed above in "Coupling Parameters."

Number of Ports

The capacity of an optical coupler is defined as the number M of inputs and the number N of outputs and is generally noted as $M \times N$. For example, a T coupler has one input ($M=1$) and two outputs. This is also the case of Y-branch coupler. However, a star coupler has N inputs and N outputs ($N \times N$). Typically N and M range from 1 to 64 (see the next section).

Bandwidth

The width of the 3-dB zone is centered at the operating wavelength. Depending on the application, the bandwidth should be narrow or large to filter out undesired wavelengths or to behave in a similar way for a large range of wavelengths. A coupler designed for a wavelength band centered at one wavelength is referred to as a *single-window coupler*. Similarly, a dual-window coupler is a device designed for two distinct bands.

Thermal Stability

Losses occur when the temperature changes. Usually, the thermal stability value is obtained by observing the attenuation variation of intensity of the OC over an operating range of temperature.

COUPLER TYPES
Coupler Configurations

Often, the function of the coupler varies according to the number of input and output ports. In the literature, we can discern basic types of couplers that lead to many other types.

Passive and Active Optical Couplers

The OC can be passive or active. The *passive* OC redistributes the optical signal naturally without the need of any other external power (for example, from electro-optic conversion). However, the *active* OC needs an external source of energy to operate properly (Kashima 1995). This should be not confused with an optical switch whereby the coupling ratio changes with the electric field (Xiaohua 2003; Lagali et al. 2001; Kawano and Kitoh 2001; McCall 2000).

Directional Couplers

Unidirectional couplers use only one direction to couple light. However, a *bidirectional* coupler is a coupling device that enables coupling to occur for both the forward and backward wave but in different manners (Yariv 1973). An example of a unidirectional coupler is the planar waveguide optical coupler in which the coupling arises at a characteristic propagation length, which is referred to as the *coupling length*. All of the power coming from the first waveguide is transferred to the second one. Thus, at one-half coupling length, the power is equally divided on the outputs. The control of coupling length and coupling ratio is crucial to devices based on directional couplers. The coupling length is determined by the separation between waveguides as well as by refractive index profiles and frequency; in practice, it is difficult to achieve accurately. Optical couplers based on optical fibers are examples of bidirectional couplers. Many bulk optics-based couplers are also of this type.

Basic Types of Couplers

X Couplers

Principle. An X coupler, named because of its shape, is made by crossing two waveguide cores in the shape of an X (Asous and Shaari 1998) (see Figure 13). At the overlapping region, it is possible that power transfer occurs from the first guide to the other. It is at the same time a splitter and a combiner. It is also commonly called a *2 × 2 coupler*. An X coupler combines the optical signals into one signal and then splits it into the two outputs. An example of an X coupler is the tapered fiber. X couplers are geometrically simple given that they do not require a specific coupling length of the two waveguides. A small cross angle is generally used to avoid radiation mode coupling.

X couplers can be considered as directional couplers. In this case of configuration, directivity measured between the power transmitted to port 2 and the input power in port 1, is given by

$$Directivity\left(dB\right) = -10\log\left(\frac{P2}{P1}\right)$$

By measuring the reflected back power through port 4, directivity is expressed by

$$Directivity\left(dB\right) = -10\log\left(\frac{P4}{P1}\right)$$

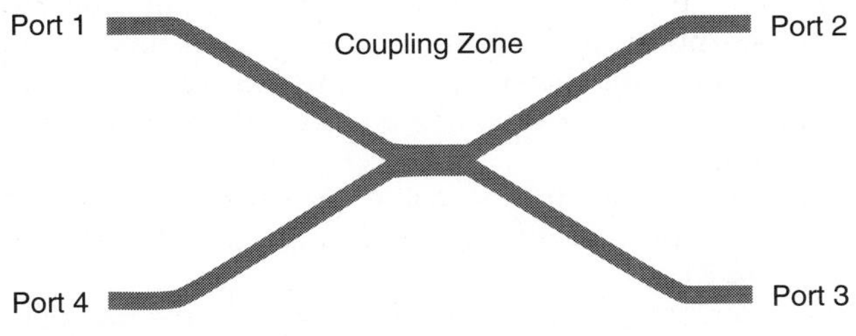

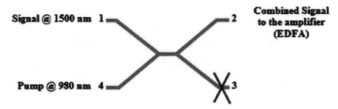

Figure 14: Combiner of different wavelength

This directivity is approximately 40 dB to 45 dB for a typical fused-fiber coupler (Hecht 2002). For this reason, in practice, the 2 × 2 coupler device is often transformed into a 1 × 2 coupler by cutting one fiber end. A particular case of this 2 × 2 coupler is the 3-dB coupler. In fact, one-half of the power entering a particular port at one side of the coupler exits from each of the two output ports.

Applications. This type of coupler is used as a power feed for an erbium-doped fiber amplifier. It intentionally combines or multiplexes two different wavelengths into a single port (see Figure 14). For example, the low-intensity incoming optical signal at 1500 nm can be combined with the high-intensity pump light at 980 nm.

In this configuration, we may choose a coupling length such that 100 percent of the optical signal at port 1 and 100 percent of the pump light at port 4 leave at the same port (2 or 3) (port 2 in Figure 14). This process ensures minimal loss of signal power (Dutton 1998). Such couplers allow the injection of laser pump power into the active medium (erbium-doped fiber) to initiate amplification (Figure 15).

As a second possible application, an optical X coupler can be found in *Passive optical networks* (PONs). In fact, PONs are a challenging technology for local access networks that is competitive with other wired and unwired solutions currently used in digital subscriber lines and broadband wireless delivery. The choice of using only passive components makes PON deployment cheaper than using other optically based networks such as SONET and SDH. Indeed, in PON, no signal conversion is necessary; the signal remains in the optical domain and permits maximum bandwidth access to the end users. PON is well suited for broadcasting-like services (point-to-multipoint architecture) and is a good infrastructure to provide "triple-play" voice, data, and video services. Optical couplers (combiners and splitters) are among the components that are crucial to implement this technology. They allow communication between *optical network units* (ONUs) at remote nodes and the *optical line terminal* (OLT) located at the central office. The use of the word *passive* comes from the fact that this segment of the network (between OLT and ONUs) requires no power supply.

Optical splitters, as depicted in Figure 16, are the essential element that makes a passive distribution of signal from the OLT to as many as sixty-four ONUs. In fact, splitting the signal means splitting the optical power, so this factor must be carefully considered when designing the network, especially the power budget. In a coarse WDM context—a technology that multiplexes multiple optical carrier signals into a single optical fiber by using

Figure 13: X coupler

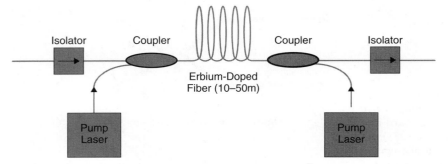

Figure 15: Laser pump injection to an erbium doped fiber amplifier

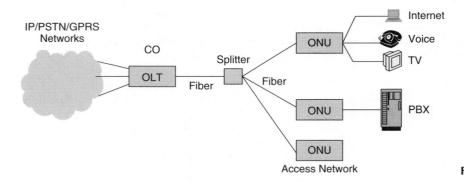

Figure 16: Basic PON in tree architecture

different wavelength to carry different signals—a WDM PON provides a much higher bandwidth compared with that of a standard PON architecture. Moreover, optical add-drop multiplexing brings significant network flexibility by allowing the access of services for a group of subscribers without perturbing the rest of the signal that is designated to other groups.

Another type of network—a loop network—can be implemented by employing several directional couplers. The use of a 2 × 2 coupler enables stations to communicate with each other by sending and receiving information over two different loops (see Figure 17).

Figure 18 shows a four-port configuration that includes a network of 3-dB splitters that divides an input mix of signals into as many outputs as necessary.

Fabry-Perot filters separate each individual signal from the others (Figure 18). These filters can be replaced by fiber Bragg gratings (see Figure 19) and circulators

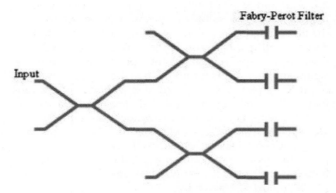

Figure 18: Splitter array with Fabry-Perot filters

(Dutton 1998). This offers more accuracy in selecting signals but at increased cost.

In interferometer applications, optical fiber Michelson interferometers can be set up by using a coupler. Generally, this type of coupler is a 50:50 fiber coupler (Wu 2006). With the Michelson interferometer (Figure 20), physical parameters can be measured by using the difference in phase between the light reflected in the output arms by both the sample and the mirror. For example, this device can be used as a key element for measuring ultrasonic Lamb waves (Pierce, Culshaw, and Philip 1996).

A simple configuration using optical couplers is the fiber-based Mach-Zehnder interferometer as illustrated in Figure 21.

The optical field is split into two parts at the first coupler. Then the two separate parts of the beam traverse

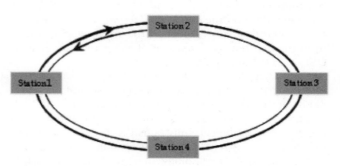

Figure 17: Example of loop network with directional coupler

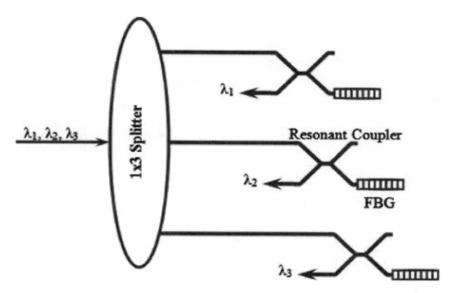

Figure 19: Demultiplexer using in-fiber Bragg gratings with 3-dB couplers

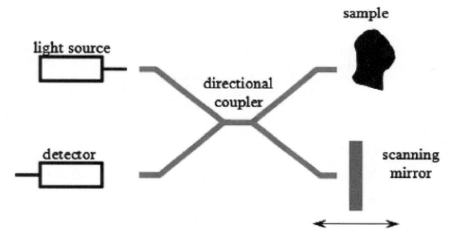

Figure 20: Michelson interferometer

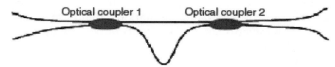

Figure 21: Fiber-based Mach-Zehnder interferometer using two optical couplers

two optical paths of different lengths, leading to a relative phase shift. When recombined together by the second coupler, this phase shift causes fringes that appear in the interference pattern. This device can also be made by using waveguide technology instead of optical fibers.

More sophisticated components using similar configurations include, for example, Mach-Zehnder modulators in which the phase shift is controlled by an external electric signal (Figure 22). In the case of optical sensors, the modulation may be produced by the measurand. The Mach-Zehnder interferometer configuration is not the

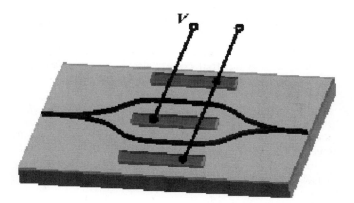

Figure 22: Waveguide-type Mach-Zehnder electro-optical modulator

only physical effect that can be exploited. There are other types of interferometers such as the Fabry-Pérot interferometer, Sagnac interferometer, and so on.

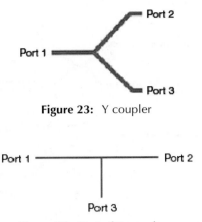

Figure 23: Y coupler

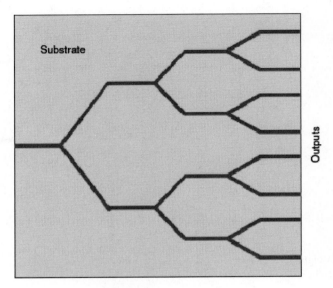

Figure 24: Typical T coupler

Figure 25: 1×8 coupler

Y and T Couplers

Principle. Because of their geometry (Tsuji et al. 2006), Y-shaped couplers (or Y junctions) can be referred to as Y couplers (Figure 23) (Kuznetsov 1985). They are frequently built in planar waveguide technology because of the difficulty of fabrication in fiber technology (Pierce, Culshaw, and Philip 1996). Preferably, these waveguides are created within a glass substrate (Bordes, undated).

Generally, Y couplers split the input power equally into the two outputs ports. Sometimes, this type of coupler is referred to as a *symmetric 50/50 coupler*. However, we can vary this value to another ratio with respect to the given application by introducing a slight asymmetry between the two output arms—for example, 10/90 or other values. Moreover, because of reciprocity, light entering at port 2 will lose 50 percent of its power (i.e., 3-dB insertion loss).

Port 1 can be denoted as the stem port, while ports 2 and 3 are the arm ports branching at a small angle from the one input. This type of coupler is rarely used as a separate planar device because of the costly connection with fiber that can lead to significant loss in power if not properly matched (Dutton 1998).

When only a small fraction of input power is tapped off, the coupler is commonly called a *T coupler* (Figure 24) or an *optical tap*. The T coupler originally had application as an electrical tap that could relay a signal picked up from a passing cable.

Applications. By cascading (*N*–1) Y junctions, we can obtain a 1 × *N* coupler called a *multiport coupler*. The example shown in Figure 25 presents a coupler network of seven Y couplers and eight outputs.

In network communication use, we can create a bus network by connecting several directional couplers or

T couplers in our case. This arrangement permits the connection of a series of stations to a single backbone cable (Figure 26).

For this type of topology, connecting stations can lead to single–direction, bidirectional, or duplex transmission configurations. Note that the transmission loss increases as the number of stations increases.

Optical switching is a function that allows reconfiguring a node in an optical network. Depending on the desired destination, the optical signal has to pass through the switch to be diverted to another destination. The example shown in Figure 27 is a simple 1 × *N* coupler equipped with optical gates at the output ports. The signal can be detected at these ports whether the optical gates are activated or not.

Tree Couplers

Principle. Unfortunately, the elementary coupler normally includes only a limited number of ports (generally, two) because of fabrication limitations. Hence, to obtain a larger number of inputs or outputs or both, many couplers can be cascaded. Tree couplers, or 1 × *N* couplers, have only one input and several output ports (see Figure 28). The single input contains the optical field that is split between the output ports equally or in a desired ratio.

We note that the power of the output beams decreases rapidly with the number of outputs. The maximum number of ports is limited by the technology being used and also by limitations in optical pulse power detection. In a waveguide-type coupler, the limitation in terms of technology arises partly from the maximal angle of the

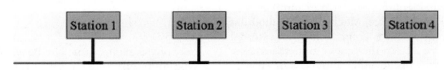

Figure 26: Example of bus network with T couplers

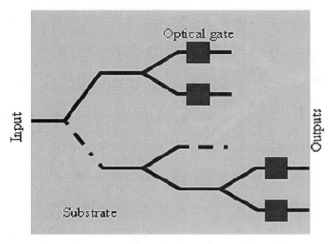

Figure 27: Optical coupler–based optical switch

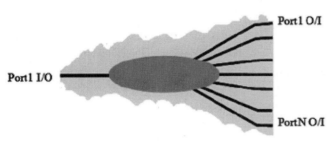

Figure 28: Tree coupler (1:*N*)

Y-branch couplers without incurring significant radiation loss. To increase the number of output ports, we can imagine several Y couplers connected together, the use of Damman gratings (Dammann 1971), or holograms in a bulk optics coupler configuration (Herzig 2004).

In general, tree couplers are directional couplers. Indeed, the optical carrier is split through the outer ports. The signal power decreases rapidly with the number of ports. The permissible number of ports is a function of the receiver sensitivity. If they are used in the opposite direction, they can recombine several inputs into one output—but at the expense of an unacceptably high loss of 3 dB per junction.

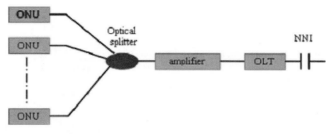

Figure 29: PON access network

Applications. In a laser transmitter module, tree couplers can be integrated. For example, the transmitter (TTCex) provides ten optical outputs. Each output is, in turn, split into thirty-two other outputs by the use of a 1:32 tree coupler. Hence, we can broadcast to 320 destinations (Taylor 2002).

Optical splitters also play an important role in the PON access network (see Figure 29). Because of those devices, subscribers can access a variety of services and applications at an extremely high speed rate. For an even higher split number, a PON repeater could be integrated with an optical amplifier (Gagnon, undated).

Star Couplers

Principle. This multiport coupler can be considered as an X coupler with more than two inputs and outputs that keeps the same functionality of the X coupler (Okuno et al. 1989). The star couplers are made around a central mixing element, allowing multiple inputs and outputs not necessary equal in number. This configuration allows two basic types of coupler (see Figure 30).

The first coupler is directional; signals enter the input ports and are distributed through the output ports and vice versa (Figure 30a). The second coupler is nondirectional and is known as a *reflective star*. It takes the input signals and distributes them equally among all fibers (inputs and outputs together) as with the star coupler shown in Figure 30b.

The advantage of this configuration is that each input delivers power to all outputs. This is a crucial feature that is needed for broadcast-and-select networks. We can also get a similar configuration in a reflective mode. One technique for the fabrication of star couplers uses the fused-taper technique (Yodo, Hasemi, and Shimizu 1993).

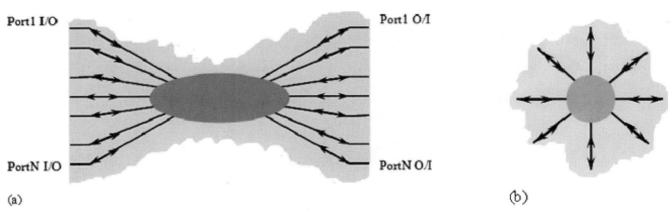

Figure 30: Two types of star couplers—(a) directional and (b) nondirectional

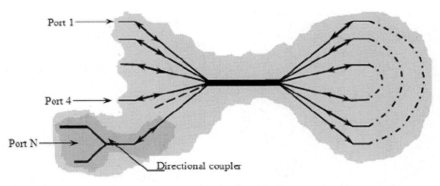

Port 1

Port 4

Port N

Directional coupler

Figure 31: Example of reflective star coupler

Figure 32: Fused-fiber star coupler (Kuznetsov 1985)

Several different types of star couplers can be built. For example, the reflective star coupler can be built by connecting together ports on one side as shown in Figure 31. In this configuration, we use a directional coupler on the opposite side to separate the transmitted and the received signals (Bordes, undated).

To create a fused-fiber star coupler (Figure 32), a number of fibers are twisted together before being heated and elongated under tension (Kuznetsov 1985).

To interconnect multiple 3-dB couplers, we use a concatenation (see Figure 33). This is easy to construct, but

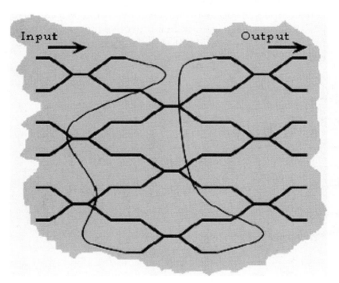

Input

Output

Figure 33: Six-way star

it can result in a considerable loss of optical power because of the arrangement, which often needs extremely tight radii. Moreover, as the number of required ports increases, the cost becomes exponentially greater (Dutton 1998).

Applications. Star couplers can be employed as the central element in a star network (Figure 34). This type of coupler divides all outputs, allowing every station to hear every other station, unless the network adopts a protocol that prevents two stations from communicating simultaneously. But the biggest disadvantage is that this configuration has a large insertion loss, especially when the number of ports (i.e., stations) increases (Force, Inc., undated).

In an OCDMA network, nodes share the optical bandwidth by using optical codes. In this system, each channel corresponds to an OCDMA code. Thus, each station encodes its signal and broadcasts it to all other stations via the star coupler (Figure 35). By using an appropriate code to decode the mixed optical signal, end nodes can detect and recover a particular message (Xue, Ding, and Yoo 2005).

In an all-optical bandpass filter, light emitted from the tunable laser diodes at different wavelength (Figure 36) is fed to the phase modulator through the coupler star (Zeng and Yao 2004).

Wavelength-Selective Coupler
Principle. Wavelength couplers (or WDM couplers or WDM multiplexers) are devices that redistribute optical power with respect to their wavelength (Figure 37). Each wavelength or band is redirected to a particular output.

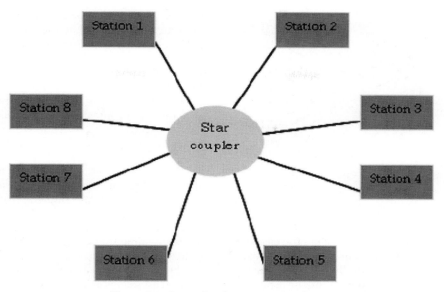

Figure 34: Example of 4 × 4 star topology

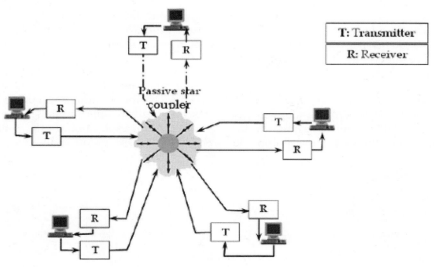

Figure 35: OCDMA network using a star coupler

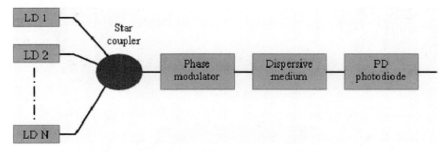

Figure 36: All-optical microwave bandpass filter

Diffractive gratings or prisms have the ability to spatially separate optical spectra. This natural function is the basis of many WDM couplers that exist in the market. Other technologies exist such as arrayed waveguide WDM couplers (Takahashi et al. 1990).

Applications. Because of the high density in dense WDM networks in terms of the use of the 1550-nm erbium-doped fiber amplifier band, the best solution for transporting control information in the 1310-nm band simultaneously is the use of a wavelength-selective coupler. This device

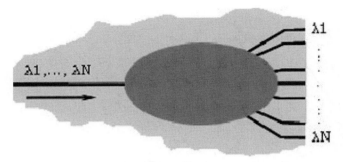

Figure 37: Wavelength-selective coupler

allows coupling 1310-nm signals with other signals in the 1550-nm band (Dutton 1998).

A sparse WDM system integrates wavelength-selective couplers to multiplex (mix) and demultiplex (separate) optical signals. In general, the combiners and separators use 3-dB splitters or Y junctions to mix or separate signals (see Figure 38). This configuration is used for a small number of channels. When the number increases, the combined signal can be amplified (Dutton 1998).

Multimode Interference Couplers

Principle. In *multimode interference* (MMI) couplers, the central multimode waveguide couples the single-mode input waveguides to single-mode output waveguides (see Figure 39).

This coupler is based on the well-known *self-imaging* or *Talbot effect* (Xia et al. 2004). When the input guide is connected to the relatively thick central region, the input beam excites many optical modes in the multimode

region. Note that each mode propagates with a slightly different velocity so that the input is self-imaged at a given Talbot distance. For shorter distances, the phenomenon generates a number of identical images in the cross-section. The number of outputs depends on the length of the coupling region.

The MMI coupler is one of the most extensively used devices in integrated optics because of its special characteristics: large operation bandwidth, fabrication tolerance, and polarization independence (Soldano et al. 1993).

Applications. An optomechanical pressure sensor is composed of two MMI couplers, two arms, and a membrane (see Figure 40). The arms (1 and 2) are placed in the center and at the edge of the membrane, respectively. We can assume that the input MMI coupler behaves like a 3-dB coupler because the input light is split into two equal power lights (Soldano and Pennings 1995).

Two cases can be distinguished. If the membrane does not sustain a pressure, then the light split by the input MMI coupler will recombine with the same phase at the output of the MMI coupler. However, when a pressure is applied to the membrane, a phase shift is observed between the two arms. Two mechanisms are involved: the path length modulation and the photo-elastic effect (Hah, Yoon, and Hong 2000).

In sensor applications, MMI couplers are the most used. For example in a chemical sensor, as depicted in Figure 41, the multimode section of this coupler can be covered with an appropriate sensing material, depending on the given application. In the multimode section, individual modes propagate at different speeds. This difference

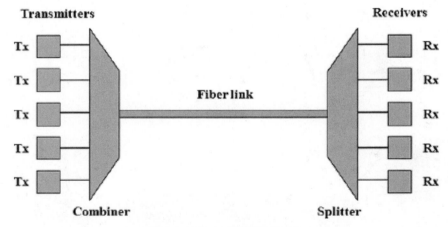

Figure 38: Example of WDM link

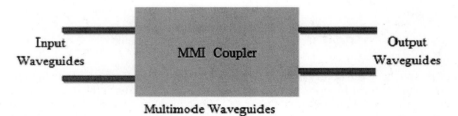

Figure 39: 2×2 MMI coupler

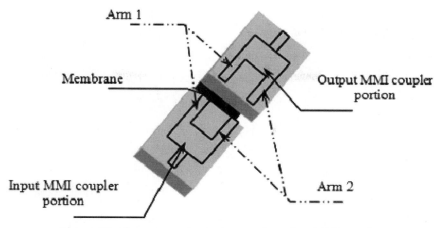

Figure 40: The optomechanical sensor based on MMI coupler

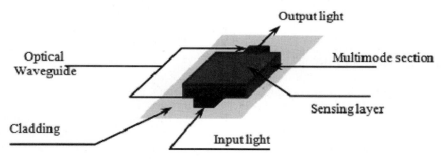

Figure 41: Schematic for a chemical sensor

results from the MMI parameters, including the refractive index of the covering layer (sensing layer in Figure 41) of the multimode section (Kribich et al. 2005). Hence, this difference between mode speeds leads to a phase shift. Therefore, constructive and destructive interferences take place and affect the electromagnetic field intensity profile. As a consequence, the image position shifts, which depends, in turn, on the sensing layer index so that the input intensity profile can be computed (Kribich et al. 2005).

Polarization Couplers

Principle. Controlling the state of light polarization is of interest for several fields including fiber communication and sensing. Although the polarization dependence may be advantageous in a specific application (for example, sensing), it is not relevant in communication systems where intensity is the measurand (Ho 2005). Hence, optical components that can manipulate polarization have application, especially in polarization splitters, polarizers, and circulators.

The polarization splitter is based on two-mode interference in a directional coupler structure. These two modes—the *symmetric* and *asymmetric* modes—are guided for both vertical and horizontal polarizations. These modes are excited by an incoming wave with equal power and propagate with different velocities. At the end of the structure, the power splitting ratio can be determined by measuring the relative accumulated phase of these two modes. This type of splitter is used to separate or to recombine the polarization components TE and

TM (Figure 42) (Herrmann 1998). However, one can find polarization-maintaining couplers based on, for example, Hi-Bi fibers.

Applications. In a dual-frequency stabilization system, the emitting lasers (see Figure 43) excite the two different

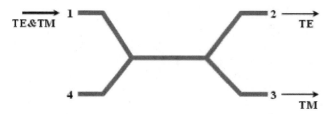

Figure 42: Passive directional coupler as polarization splitter

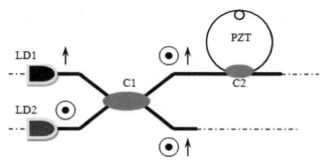

Figure 43: Optical coupling component of the stabilization system

input ports of the first polarization-maintaining coupler (C1). At the output of C1, light propagates along one fiber to reach the second 2 × 2 coupler (C2). The second output fiber of C2 guides lights to photodiodes and to a high-speed photodetector (Batal et al. 1998).

COUPLER TECHNOLOGIES

There are many ways to fabricate couplers. The choice of which technology to use depends on the required performance. In this section, we will address the most commonly used technologies for making OCs.

Macro- and Micro-Optics

Macro-optics, also known as *bulk optics*, include conventional lenses and mirrors that are more commonly used in laboratories. *Micro-optics* are based on planar and lithographic fabrication techniques. Under this aspect, micro-optics employs a micro-technology manufacturing method (Sinzinger and Jahns 2003) to produce extremely small optical components and structures at the micro and nanometer scales. This quality fits well with the fiber components and the fibers themselves. However, both macro- and micro-optics still obey the same classical optical principles.

Figure 44 illustrates an optical coupler made up of bulk optics. An input optical fiber (input 1) delivers an optical field that is collimated by a first lens after passing through a beam splitter. One part of the beam goes to the output fiber 1, and another is directed to the output fiber 2 after traveling through a convergent lens. The beam splitter may be a power or polarization splitter. In addition, a half mirror or other bulk optic device (diffractive grating, thin-film filters, etc.) may be used to split the optical field (Hecht 2002).

Fused-Fiber Couplers

Fused tapered optical couplers can be made by bringing the two cores of two optical fiber closer together through heating and stretching of the two (Figure 45). First, the fibers are stripped of their claddings, and the cladding

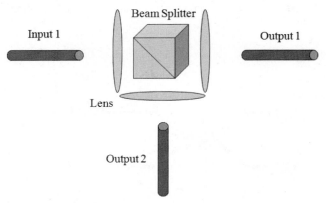

Figure 44: Optical coupler using bulk optics: lenses and beam splitter

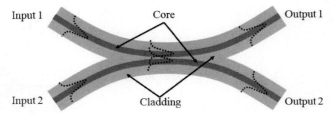

Figure 45: Optical coupler based on fused fibers

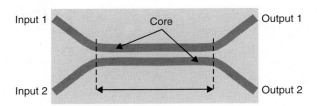

Figure 46: Optical coupler based on planar waveguide

diameters are reduced by immersion in hydrofluoric acid. This close proximity permits power exchange between the evanescent waves traveling within the cladding of the first fiber and then coupled into the core of the second fiber (Yariv 1973; Daxhelet, Lacroix, and Gonthier 1995; Green 1993).

Planar Waveguide Couplers

The structure and the operational principle of the planar waveguide–based optical couplers (Figure 46) are similar to that of fused, tapered fibers except that a planar waveguide is used instead of optical fibers. Waveguide parameters (index of refraction of the core and the surrounding media, the coupling length, etc.) are predetermined to obtain the desired coupling ratio and to match the peak of power to the desired wavelength (Hecht 2002).

CONCLUSION

Optical couplers are basic components with a broad range of practical applications in optical communications generally and sensing systems in particular. The need for such components arises from the large number of applications that require them. In this chapter, we briefly described the basic theories related to these optical devices. By listing some of the parameters, types, technologies, functionalities, and applications of these devices, we have tried to give a design and technology overview of optical couplers and their possible applications in computer network. For further details, the reader should consult the references provided in this chapter. Certainly, such components will have gravitational interest in the near future of networking, especially with the migration toward all-optical networks. Progress in designing, implementing, and using optical couplers is directly linked to advances in telecommunication and sensing systems as well as to fabrication technologies.

GLOSSARY

Circulator: Passive three-port devices that couple light from ports 1 to 2 and ports 2 to 3 and have high isolation in other directions.

Computer Network: Two or more connected computers that share a telecommunication medium for the purpose of communicating and sharing resources.

Continuous Wave: Usually refers to the constant optical output from an optical source when it is biased (i.e., turned on) but not modulated with a signal.

Coupler: An optical device that combines or splits power from optical fibers.

Coupling Ratio: The ratio of optical power from one output port to the total output power expressed as a percentage.

Demultiplexer: A module that separates two or more signals previously combined by compatible multiplexing equipment.

Erbium-Doped Fiber Amplifier: Optical fibers doped with the rare earth element erbium, which can amplify light in the 1550-nm region when pumped by an external light source.

Fabry-Perot (FP): Generally refers to any device, such as a type of laser diode, that uses mirrors in an internal cavity to produce multiple reflections.

Fiber Bragg Grating (FBG): A technique for building optical filtering functions directly into a piece of optical fiber based on interferometric techniques. Usually this is accomplished by making the fiber photosensitive and exposing the fiber to deep ultraviolet light through a grating. This forms regions of higher and lower refractive indexes in the fiber core.

Mode Coupling: The exchange of power among propagating modes in a given waveguide structure. For optical fiber, the nonuniformities in the index of refraction, impurities, and geometric perturbation favor the appearance of mode-coupling phenomena.

Optics: The science that deals with the physical properties of light. It highlights both light propagation and light behavior under different structures.

Passive Optical Network (PON): A point-to-multipoint network architecture in which passive optical splitters are used to enable a single optical fiber to serve multiple buildings.

Pigtail: A short optical fiber permanently attached to a source, detector, or other fiber-optic device at one end and an optical connector at the other.

Star Network: A network in which all terminals are connected through a single point, such as a star coupler or concentrator.

Waveguide Coupler: A coupler in which light gets transferred between planar waveguides.

Wavelength-Division Multiplexing (WDM): Sending several signals through one fiber with different wavelengths of light.

CROSS REFERENCES

See *Optical Fiber Communications; Optical Switching Techniques in WDM Optical Networks; Wavelength Division Multiplexing (WDM)*.

REFERENCES

Agrawal, G. P. 2002. *Fiber-optic communication systems*. 3rd ed. New York: John Wiley & Sons.

Armenise, M. N., and M. De Sario. 1982. Optical rectangular waveguide in titanium-diffused lithium niobate having its optical axis in the transverse plane. In *Journal of the Optical Society of America*, 72(11): 1514ff.

Asous, J. Y., and S. Shaari. 1998. New design of variable X-coupler optical waveguide passive device. In *Proceedings of the Twentieth International Conference on Software Engineering* (ICSE'98), April 19–25, Kyoto, Japan. pp. 204–6.

Barnes, C. W. 1964. Conservative coupling between modes of propagation: A tabular summary. *Proceedings of the IEEE*, 52(1): 64–73.

Batal, A., P. Di Bin, F. Reynaud, and J. Marcou. 1998. Dual laser frequency stabilization with a birefringent fiber ring interferometer for microwave generation. *Microwave Optical Technology Letters*, 19(5): 315–8.

Belanger, P. 1993. *Optical fiber theory: A supplement to applied electromagnetism*. Singapore: World Scientific.

Bilbao, S. 2004. *Wave and scattering methods for numerical simulation*. New York: John Wiley & Sons.

Bordes, N. Undated. What is an optical coupler? (retrieved from http://oldsite.vislab.usyd.edu.au/photonics/devices/networks/coupler0.html).

Born, M., and E. Wolf. 1999. *Principles of optics*. 7th ed. Cambridge, United Kingdom: Cambridge University Press.

Buck, J. A. 1995. *Fundamentals of optical fibers*. New York: John Wiley & Sons.

Burns, W., P. H. Klein, E. J. West, and L. E. Plew. 1979. Ti diffusion in Ti/LiNbO₃ planar and channel optical waveguides. *Journal of Applied Physics*, 50(10): 6175–82.

Chung, P. S. 1986. Integrated electro-optic modulators and switches. *JEEE Australia*, 6(4): 308–20.

Dammann, H. 1971. High-efficiency in-line multiple imaging by means of multiple phase holograms. *Optics Communications*, 3(5): 312–5.

Daxhelet, X., S. Lacroix, and F. Gonthier. 1995. High isolation tapered fiber filters. In *Proceedings of the Twenty-First European Conference on Optical Communication (ECOC'95)*, September, Brussels. Vol. 2: 801–4.

Dowd, P., J. Perreault, J. Chu, D. C. Hoffmeister, R. Minnich, D. Burns, Y.-J. Chen, M. Dagenais, and D. Stone. 1996. Lightning: Network and systems architecture. *Journal of Lightwave Technology*, 14(6): 1371–87.

Dutton, H. J. R. 1998. *Understanding optical communications*. Englewood Cliffs, NJ: Prentice-Hall.

Force, Inc. Undated. Couplers and splitters (retrieved from www.fiber-optics.info/articles/couple-split.htm).

Gagnon, N. Undated. Fiber to the test: PON installation challenges (retrieved from www.exfo.com/en/support/WaveReview/2004-June/WRarticle1.asp).

Gelikonov, V. M., G. V. Gelikonov, and D. V. Sabanov. 2000. Optical-fiber multiplexer for wavelengths of 1.3 and 0.64 μm. *Journal of Optical Technology*, 67(2): 157–60.

GlobalSpec. Undated. About fiber optic couplers (retrieved from http://fiber-optics.globalspec.com/LearnMore/Optics_Optical_Components/Fiber_Optics/Fiber_Optic_Couplers).

———. Undated. About optocouplers (retrieved from http://optoelectronics.globalspec.com/LearnMore/Optics_Optical_Components/Optoelectronics/Optocouplers).

Gray, T. 1986. Thin film deposition technology for hybrid circuits. *Hybrid Circuit Technology*, September.

Green, E. Jr. 1993. *Fiber optics network*. Englewood Cliffs, NJ: Prentice-Hall.

Hah, D., E. Yoon, and S. Hong. 2000. An optomechanical pressure sensor using multimode interference couplers with polymer waveguides on a thin p+ −Si membrane. *Sensors and Actuators* A: Physical, 79(3): 204–10.

Hamam, H. 2006. *Optical fiber components: Design and applications*. Kerala, India: Research Signpost.

Haus, H. A. 1984. *Waves and fields in optoelectronics*. Englewood Cliffs, NJ: Prentice-Hall.

———, and W.-P. Huang. 1991. Coupled-mode theory. *Proceedings of the IEEE*, 79(10): 1505–18.

Hecht, J. 2002. *Understanding fiber optics*. 4th ed. Upper Saddle River, NJ: Prentice-Hall.

Herrmann, H. 1998. Integrated polarization splitters (retrieved from http://fb6www.uni-paderborn.de/ag/ag-sol/research/acousto/splitt.htm).

Herzig, H. P. 1997. *Micro-optics: Elements, systems and applications*. London: Taylor and Francis.

———. 2004. Holography: HOEs, DOEs, and micro-optics. In *Handbook of laser technology and applications*, edited by C. Webb and J. Jones, 2627–42. Bristol, United Kingdom: Institute of Physics Publishing.

Ho, K. P. 2005. *Phase-modulated optical communication systems*. New York: Springer-Verlag.

Hunsperger, R. G. 1991. *Integrated optics: Theory and technology*. 3rd ed. New York: Springer-Verlag.

Izawa, T., and H. Nakagome. 1972. Optical waveguide formed by electrically induced migration of ions in glass plates. *Applied Physics Letters*, 21(12): 584–6.

Jackel, J. L, V. Ramaswamy, and S. P. Lyman. 1981. Elimination of out-diffused surface guiding in titanium-diffused LiNbO₃. *Applied Physics Letters*, 38(7): 509–11.

Jiang, P., F. Zhou, P. J. R. Laybourn, and R. M. De La Rue. 1992. Buried optical waveguide polarizer by titanium in diffusion and proton-exchange in LiNbO₃. *IEEE Photonics Technology Letters*, 4(8): 881–3.

Kasap, S. O. 2001. *Optoelectronics and photonics*. Upper Saddle River, NJ: Prentice Hall.

Kashima, N. 1995. *Passive optical components for optical fiber transmission*. Boston: Artech House Publishers.

Kashyap, R. 1999. *Fiber Bragg gratings*. San Diego: Academic Press.

Kawano, K., and T. Kitoh. 2001. *Introduction to optical waveguide analysis: Solving Maxwell's equation and the Schrödinger equation*. New York: Wiley Interscience.

Kittel, C. 1996. *Introduction to solid state physics*. New York: John Wiley & Sons.

Klein, M. F. 1988. A structured methodology for IC photolithography synthesis in semiconductor manufacturing. *IEEE Transactions on Semiconductor Manufacturing*, 1(1): 28–35.

Kogelnik, H., and C. V. Shank. 1972. Coupled-wave theory of distributed feedback lasers. *Journal of Applied Physics*, 43: 2327–35.

Kribich, K. R., R. Copperwhite, H. Barry, B. Kolodziejczyk, J.-M. Sabattié, K. O'Dwyer, and B. D. MacCraith. 2005.

Novel chemical sensor/biosensor platform based on optical multimode interference (MMI) couplers. *Sensors and Actuators B: Chemical*, 107(1): 188–92.

Kuznetsov, M. 1985. Radiation loss in dielectric waveguide Y-branch structures. *Journal of Lightwave Technology*, 3(3): 674–7.

Kyo-Seon, K., and E. P. Sotiris. 1988. Manufacture of optical waveguide performs by modified chemical vapor deposition. *AlChe Journal*, 34(6): 912–21.

Lagali, N. S., J. F. P. Van Nune, D. Pant, and L. Eldada. 2001. Ultra low power and high dynamic range variable optical attenuator array. In *Proceedings of the Twenty-Seventh European Conference on Optical Communication* (ECOC '01), Sept. 30–Oct. 4, Amsterdam, 3: 430–1.

Laude, J. P. 2002. *DWDM fundamentals: Components and applications*. Boston: Artech House Publishers.

Lifante, G. 2003. *Integrated photonics*. New York: John Wiley & Sons.

Lohmeyer, M., N. Bahlmann, O. Zhuromskyy, and P. Hertel. 1999. Wave-matching simulations of integrated optical coupler structures. In *Proceedings of the Society of Photo-Optical Instrumentation Engineers* (SPIE) *Conference*, April, Bellingham, WA, USA. Vol. 3620: 68–78.

Marcuse, D. 1971. The coupling of degenerate modes in two parallel dielectric waveguides. *Bell Systems Technical Journal*, 50(6): 1791–1816.

Marstone, M. R. 1999. *Optoelectronics circuit manual*. 2nd ed. London: Newnes Technical Books.

McCall, M. 2000. On the application of coupled mode theory for modeling fiber Bragg gratings. *Journal of Lightwave Technology*, 18(2): 236–42.

Mentzer, M. A. 1990. *Principles of optical circuit engineering*. New York: Taylor & Francis.

Nishihara, H., M. Haruna, and T. Suhara. 1989. *Optical integrated circuits*. New York: McGraw-Hill.

Okuno, M., A. Takagi, M. Yasu, and N. Takato. 1989. 2 × 8 single-mode guided-wave star coupler (in Japanese). In *IEICE National Convention Record* (Japan). pp. 290-4.

Othonos, A., and K. Kali. 1999. *Fiber Bragg grating: Fundamentals and applications in telecommunications and sensing*. Boston: Artech House Publishers.

Owyang, G. H. 1981. *Foundations of optical waveguide*. New York: Elsevier.

Park, K. H. 2006. Detection through a dielectric cover on an optical waveguide and the generation of 50- to 60-GHz continuous wave millimeter wave using optical technology for future optical-to-radio systems and ubiquitous communications. *Optical Engineering*, 45(2): 25006–9.

Pierce, J. R. 1954. Coupling of modes of propagation. *Journal of Applied Physics*, 25(2): 179–83.

Pierce, S. G., B. Culshaw, and W. R. Philip. 1996. Synchronized triggering for ultrasonic rated transient detection using optical fibre electric interferometers and application to the measurement of broadband Lamb perspex wave dispersion characteristics. *Measurement Science and Technology*, 7(11): 1665–7.

Pollock, C. R., and M. Lipson. 2003. *Integrated photonics*. New York: Springer-Verlag.

Razzak, M., and H. Hamam. 2006. Optical fiber sensors: An overview. Chap. 7 in *Optical fiber components: Design and applications*, edited by H. Hamam. Kerala, India: Research Signpost.

Ruan, L., and D.-Z. Du. 2001. *Optical networks: Recent advances*. New York: Springer-Verlag.

Seshan, K. 2002. *Handbook of thin film deposition techniques: Principles, methods, equipment and applications*. Ridge Park, NJ: Noyes.

Sinzinger, S., and J. Jahns. 2003. *Microoptics*. 2nd ed. Weinheim, Germany: Wiley-VCH.

Snyder, A. W. 1972. Coupled-mode theory for optical fibers. *Journal of the Optical Society*, 62(11): 1267–77.

Snyder, A. W., and J. D. Love. 1983. *Optical waveguide theory*. London: Chapman and Hall.

Soldano, L. B., M. Bachmann, P. A. Besse, M. K. Smit, and H. Melchior. 1993. Large optical bandwidth of InGaAsP/InP multi-mode interference 3dB couplers. In *Proceedings of the Third European Conference on Integrated Optics* (ECIO'93), April, Neuchatel, Switzerland. pp. 14.10–11.

Soldano, L. B., and E. C. M. Pennings. 1995. Optical multimode interference devices based on self-imaging, principles and applications. *Journal of Lightwave Technology*, 13(4): 615–27.

Streetman, B. G. 1980. *Solid state electronics devices*. 2nd ed. Englewood Cliffs, NJ: Prentice-Hall.

Taga, H. 1996. Long distance transmission experiments using the WDM technology. *Journal of Lightwave Technology*, 14(6): 1287–98.

Takahashi, H., S. Suzuki, K. Kato, and I. Nishi. 1990. Arrayed waveguide grating for wavelength division multi/demultiplexer with nanometre resolution. *Electronics Letters*, 26(2): 87–8.

Takato, N., K. Jinguji, M. Yasu, H. Toba, and M. Kawachi. 1988. Silica-based single mode waveguide on silicon and their application to guided-wave optical interferometers. *Journal of Lightwave Technology*, 6(6): 1003–10.

Taylor, B. G. 2002. *TTC laser transmitter (TTCex, TTCtx, TTCmx) user manual* (RD12 working document) (retrieved from http://ttc.web.cern.ch/TTC/TTCtxManual.pdf).

Taylor, H. F., and A. Yariv. 1974. Guided wave optics. *Proceedings of the IEEE*, 62(8): 1044–60.

Tsuji, Y., K. Hirayama, T. Nomura, K. Sato, and S. Nishiwaki. 2006. Design of an optical circuit devices based on topology optimization. *IEEE Photonics Technology Letters*, 18(7): 850–2.

Weisstein, E. W. 1999. Helmholtz differential equation (retrieved from http://mathworld.wolfram.com/HelmholtzDifferentialEquation.html).

Wu, E. 2006. Measuring chromatic dispersion of single-mode optical fibres using white light interferometry (retrieved from www.phy.auckland.ac.nz/thesis/Elijah_WU_MSc.pdf).

Xia, L., L. Xi-Hua, J. Xiao-Qing, and W. Ming-Hua. 2004. Fabrication of an 8×8 multimode interference optical coupler on BK7 glass substrate by ion-exchange. *Chinese Physics Letters*, 21(8): 1556–7.

Xiaohua, M. 2003. Optical switching technology comparison: Optical MEMS versus other technologies. *IEEE Communications Magazine*, 41(11): S16–23.

Xue, F., Z. Ding, and S. J. B. Yoo. 2005. Performance evaluation of optical CDMA networks with random media access schemes. In *Proceedings of the Optical Fiber Communication Conference*. Paper OThG5.

Yariv, A. 1973. Coupled-mode theory for guided-wave optics. *IEEE Journal of Quantum Electronics*, 9(9): 919–33.

———. 1976. *Introduction to optical electronics*. 2nd ed. New York: Holt, Rinehart and Winston.

Yilmaz, G. 2006. A distributed optical fiber sensor for temperature detection in power cables. *Sensors and Actuators A: Physical*, 125(10): 148–55.

Yodo, S., A. Hasemi, and M. Shimizu. 1993. Single mode 1×8 fused coupler. In *Proceedings of the Conference on Optical/Hybrid Access Networks*, Sept. 7–9, Montreal. pp. 4.05/01–6.

Zeng, F., and J. Yao. 2004. All-optical bandpass microwave filter based on an electro-optic phase modulator. *Optics Express*, 12(16): 3814–9.

Fiber-Optic Filters and Multiplexers

Hamid Hemmati, *Jet Propulsion Laboratory, California Institute of Technology*

INTRODUCTION

The function of an optical filter is to select one wavelength and reject all other wavelengths. Fixed wavelength and tunable optical filters are now playing a crucial role in multichannel optical networks. The recent rapid progress in optical networks has necessitated the availability of more channels at a reduced cost. These trends are underscoring the need to develop filters with large port counts and narrower passbands. Applications of filters in optical networks include *multiplexing* (MUX) and *demultiplexing* (DMUX) of laser wavelengths, noise rejection, and gain equalization after an optical amplifier. Filters are finding an ever-increasing role in *coarse wavelength-division multiplexers* (CWDMs) with channel spacing on the order of 20 nm, and in *dense WDM* (DWDM) networks with channel spacing less than 0.2 nm.

A group of optical filters operate based on absorption, reflection, or diffraction of bands of light, whereas many filters and multiplexers are based on the phenomenon of constructive and destructive interference between monochromatic coherent optical waves. Gratings are an exception and utilize the diffraction property of light. Hybrid filters, in which a number of different filters (for example, gratings and dielectric or absorption filters) are used in conjunction to provide superior performance characteristics over a single filter. Numerous techniques have been developed to achieve high-contrast optical filtering. A given filter's design is driven by its performance requirements and specifications and by physical and environmental requirements and specifications. Some filters operate solely based on changes in the optical properties of an optical material and involve no moving parts. Often, the nonlinear optical material's properties are utilized to achieve the desired characteristics. Examples of such filters include absorption, electro-optic, fixed Fabry-Perot, and Bragg gratings.

The second class of filters involves a moving mechanism such as a *micro-electromechanical system* (MEMS). Examples are movable gratings and Fabry-Perot cavities.

Based on their filtering mechanisms, optical filters can be put into three main categories: thin-film filters, interleaver filters, and grating filters.

1. Thin-film filters include multiple cavity transmission, Fabry-Perot, photonic band-gap, and ring resonator filters. Thin-film interference filters rely on the thickness of each alternating high and low index layer to determine which wavelengths of the incident light are either reflected or transmitted.

2. Interleaver filters include lattice filters (e.g., Mach-Zehnder interferometric and birefringent filters), waveguide-arrayed filters (e.g., waveguide grating router and planar waveguide circuit–based filters), and Michelson interferometer-based (e.g., interference) filters. Therefore, a variety of phenomena is utilized to construct the interleaver filters.

3. Grating filters include bulk gratings, fiber Bragg gratings, and acousto-optic tunable filters. These filters work based on the dispersion power of ruled reflection gratings to separate or combine different wavelengths.

Other filter types include absorption, electro-optic, fused-fiber, gain-flattening, and dispersion-compensation filters. The properties of each filter are summarized below.

The general requirements for the filter response and noise rejection for wavelength-division multiplexing MUX and DMUX applications include:

- low insertion (output-to-input) loss,
- narrow and uniform transmission passband,

- high degree of isolation of out-of-band signals (low magnitude of cross talk),
- polarization independence (all polarizations are accepted without loss),
- high steepness of the filter edges,
- tunability over a wide spectral range with high tuning resolution and speed,
- low dispersive properties and group delay ripple,
- high stability (i.e., environmentally insensitive) and reliability,
- linear phase response and constant time delay (if applicable) for optimum bandwidth utilization, and
- low cost, compactness, light weight, and low power consumption (if active).

Table 1 summarizes the current typical amplitude response characteristics of several commonly used filters. These characteristics are changing rapidly with ongoing developmental research.

Table 1 indicates the availability of a variety of high maturity tunable filters with the capability to accommodate more than one hundred channels, introducing minimal to moderate insertion loss. As expected, the electro-optically tuned filters provide the fastest tenability, whereas mechanically or thermally tuned filters are the slowest in tuning rate.

The undesired dispersive properties of optical filters that affect a WDM system's performance are driven by a filter's dispersive properties. A filter's phase response characteristics consist of the first derivative of the spectral phase response determining the total time delay through the filter, as well as higher-order derivatives of the spectral phase response driving the total time delay through the filter. Lenz et al. (1998, "Dispersive properties," "Optimal dispersion") offer techniques to minimize the dispersion effects. The phase response of filters that demonstrate phase can be derived from their amplitude response through a linear (Hilbert) transformation.

Filters developed based on arrayed-waveguide gratings or fiber Bragg gratings may demonstrate significant group delay ripple. The technique of grating apodization may be necessary to avoid this problem. On the other hand, short path-length Mach-Zehnder interferometer filters demonstrate little delay ripple (Othonos and Kalli 1999). Variations in the group delay spectrum of fiber-optic devices are especially problematic at data-rate regimes exceeding 10 Gb/s.

Figure 1 illustrates the amplitude response and the phase response of an ideal rectangular filter that demonstrates phase responsivity (Lenz et al. 1998, "Dispersive properties"). The phase response is shown to become nonlinear and to diverge at the edges of passband.

Wavelength Add-Drop Multiplexers and Demultiplexers

Optical multiplexers combine, in fiber and free space, individual wavelengths before launch into the fiber. Demultiplexers undo the job of the multiplexer. Multiplexers and demultiplexers utilize a variety of technologies, including interleavers, frequency slicers, thin-film filters, periodic filters, Fabry-Perot cavity filters, acousto-optical tunable filters, Mach-Zehnder interferometers, fiber Bragg gratings, and arrayed-waveguide gratings. This chapter briefly describes most of these technologies. The cascading of multiplexers, demultiplexers, and switches will form static (no switch involved) or dynamic multiple *wavelength cross connects* (WXCs). The static WXCs are functionally limited, whereas dynamic WXCs have a wider range of applications.

A few measurable parameters are commonly utilized to specify a filter. The *passband* is defined as the range of wavelengths that a filter selects. It is characterized by a gain curve representing its boundaries and the spectral distribution of the wavelengths. *Channel spacing* is the minimum frequency spacing between channels to avoid cross talk. Typically, a cross-talk level 30 dB below signal level is desired. The *maximum number of equally*

Table 1: Summary of Certain Characteristics of Filters Commonly Used in Fiber-Optic Networks*

Filter Technology	Maturity	Channel Spacing (GHz)	Cross Talk (dB)	Insertion Loss (dB)	Tuning Range (nm)	Tuning Time (sec)
Dielectric thin film	High	30–200	−15	<1–3	N/A	N/A
Fabry-Perot (FP)	High	50–100	<−10	~1	500	1E2–1E-3
Electrooptic FP	High	50–100		1–3	50	1E-8
FP semiconductor	Low	50–100	−15	1	10	2E-5
Liquid crystal FP	Medium			3	50	1E-5–1E-6
Mach-Zehnder	High	50	−30	1	35	1E-2
Acousto-optic	Medium	100	−20	3 to 5	>700	1E-5
Fiber Bragg grating	High	50	−40	0.1	10	1E-5
Arrayed waveguide grating	High	12–200	−35	3–6	40	1E-2

*Some data are typical while others are state of the art (2007).

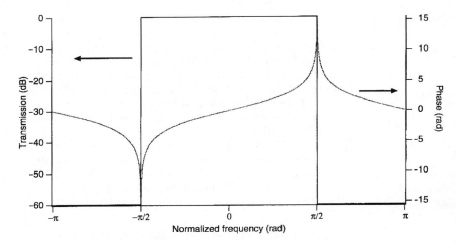

Figure 1: Amplitude response (solid line) and phase response (dotted line) of the ideal rectangular filter, assuming that the filter demonstrates phase responsivity (after Lenz et al. 1998, "Dispersive properties," with permission)

spaced channels is defined as the ratio of the total tuning range for the filter to its channel spacing. The *spectral width* (channel width) represents the spectral content of a channel and is a measure of the deviation from an ideal purely single wavelength channel and is normally described by the 3-dB point. The transfer functions of manufactured optical filters are generally asymmetric accompanied by passband ripple. To a coarse approximation, Butterworth and Bessel functions may be used to describe the filter shape. Some of the most common fiber-optic networking filters applied to signal filtering and multiplexing and demultiplexing are briefly described below.

THIN-FILM FILTERS
Multiple-Cavity Transmission Filters

Multiple-cavity transmission filters constitute a mature technology that is competing well with some of the more advanced filter technologies. The structure of the thin-film multilayer interference filter is based on that of the interferometric effect. Typically, a thin-film filter is composed of one or more cavities and mirrors that together result in a narrow-bandpass filter that is useful to applications such as WDM. *Dielectric thin-film filters* (DTFs) are formed by layers of quarter-wave thick dielectric stacks with alternating high and low indexes of refraction. Silicon dioxide (SiO_2) and titanium dioxide (TiO_2) are among the high-index dielectrics used in the fabrication of these devices. The resulting cavities interfere with the incident light waves, selectively transmitting or reflecting specific wavelengths. This relatively low-cost approach is highly suitable for the development of CWDM and DWDM passband filters (Lin, Kao, and Chi 2003). The narrower the required wavelength spacing (for WDM), the tighter the tolerance on the thickness of a given stack and the larger the number of deposited layers. For example, a 100-GHz bandwidth filter may require as many as 200 layers. High-end coatings require an even distribution of the coating material across the substrate with thickness controlled to the atomic level. Thermally stable DTFs with a flattop passband and extremely sharp skirts for high adjacent channel isolation are now developed routinely. Their use

precludes the need for tight control of laser wavelengths over a system's lifetime. High insertion loss, on the order of a few dBs, for the narrowest passband filters is a drawback for some applications. In general, low insertion loss and passband ripple filters have been developed for WDMs with forty or more channels.

Fabry-Perot Filters

Fabry-Perot (FP) *filters* were derived from the classical FP interferometers, also known as *FP etalons*. An etalon's cavity may consist of two plane parallel mirrors or two spherical mirrors. Other cavity (interferometer) examples include a resonator formed by highly reflective mirrors on the opposing sides of a precisely fabricated transparent refractive material, and, more elegantly, by the polished end surfaces of two fibers aligned relative to each other and separated by air gap <200 μm thick to emulate an air-spaced etalon (Atherton et al. 1981).

In the FP filters, interference of light waves along the optical path of the cavities provides the basis for selecting a particular wavelength. The cavity is electromechanically induced to tune in or out of resonance with the incident light rays. The FP interferometric filter consists of a single input port and a single output port. It is typically used to select one wavelength channel from a series of channels. As described below, several distinguishing characteristics describe an FP filter.

The finesse of an FP interferometer is a measure of the width of the transfer function and thus its wavelength-filtering resolution to determine the maximum number of discernible channels. The *finesse* (F) of an FP cavity is defined by the ratio F = FSR/FWHM, where the *free spectral range* (FSR) is the distance between the transmission peaks and the *full width at half maximum* (FWHM) is defined to be the 3-dB bandwidth of a channel. In effect, the FSR is the period at which the shape of the passband (the transfer function) repeats itself after a certain frequency. Thus, the filter transmits a frequency that is a distance of $n \times$ FSR from the preferred frequency (n = an integer). The finesse of a given cavity is driven by the quality of its mirrors (polishing of substrate, reflectance of and the degree of contamination of coatings), and the angle of incidence of the input beam. The finesse is related to the mirror *Reflectance* (R) by $F = \pi R^{1/2}/(1-R)$. For high-quality FPs, the finesse varies in the range of 100 to more than 1,000,000. The filter bandwidth decreases and the FSR increases as the number of passes through a filter or multiple-filter stage increases. The finesse and FSR together limit the number of channels that can be enclosed within the FSR. The higher the finesse, the more channels can fit within the FSR.

To select different wavelengths, the interferometer may be tuned by adjusting the cavity length or by varying the cavity's index of refraction. This may be accomplished with the aid of a mechanical actuator or an electromechanical transducer—for example, a piezoelectric actuator. Mechanical tuning suffers from low reliability, whereas piezo tuners may suffer from thermal distortions and hysteresis. Alternatively, when the FP cavity's medium is made of liquid crystals or other electro-optical materials, the refractive index can be modulated by an electric current to select individual wavelengths (Hirabayashi 2005). Low power consumption, high tuning bandwidth, fast tuning times (1 µs), and low cost are among the attractive features of these devices (Li, Chiang, and Gambling 2000).

Photonic Band-Gap Filters

Photonic band-gap (PBG) filters are made of photonic band-gap structures that are a subset of photonics structures. Variable narrowband or wideband filtering of incident light can be achieved by constructing a filter consisting of alternating high- and low-index semiconductor, dielectric, metal, or a combination of these layers, typically one-quarter of a wave thick, deposited on a substrate (Scalora, Bloemer, and Baglio 2002). An actuator (e.g., MEMS) varying the air gap between two PBG stacks provides the dynamics for fast filtering and switching (Trimm et al. 2005). These filters have the potential to offer small cost cost-effective filtering and switching for fiber-optic networks.

INTERLEAVER FILTERS

An *interleaver filter* is a periodic optical element for combing or separating a comb of DWDM signals. An interleaver filter inexpensively and effectively doubles the number of channels in a WDM system by separating the WDM signals into two groups of odd and even channels. These filters have a rectangular spectral response that is useful in relaxing the specifications for other fiber-optic devices such as arrayed-waveguide grating. Unlike the single-channel add-drop filters that synthesize a narrowband filter on top of a wide rejection band, the periodic property of the interleaver filter reduces the number of Fourier components required for a flat passband and high-isolation rejection band (Cao et al. 2004). Interleaver filters may be classified based on their structure as *finite impulse response* or *infinite impulse response* (Oguma et al. 2004). Interleaver filters may also be classified under three broad categories: (1) *lattice filters*, which include birefringent filters and Mach-Zehnder filters; (2) *waveguide filters*, which include arrayed-waveguide routers and planar light-wave circuits; and (3) *Michelson interferometer–based filters*, which include interference filters.

Parameters of importance in the design of a interleaver filter are:

1. passband characteristics that include low insertion loss, a wide and nearly flat-top shape with sharp roll-off on the band edges, and minimal chromatic aberration;
2. stopband characteristics that provide high extinction across the passband of the alternate port where, typically, stopband width is traded for the maximum extinction;
3. polarization-dependent characteristics whereby the filter designer's goal is to minimize dependence on the degree of frequency shift between the different polarization states, the polarization-dependent differential insertion loss, and the differential group delay between the two paths (also known as *polarization-mode dispersion*); and
4. reduction of chip size, improved stability, fabrication tolerance, and mass producibility.

Lattice Filters

Lattice filters are constructed based on a cascade of differential delay elements. The delay in each element is an integral multiple of a unit delay. In a large-scale lattice filter, phase adjustment could be cumbersome because of the existence of many delay lines. Between the delay elements, power is exchanged across the different paths. As described below, the category of lattice filters includes Mach-Zehnder interferometric and birefringent filters.

Mach-Zehnder Interferometric Filters

In a *Mach-Zehnder interferometer* (MZI) filter, typically an integrated optic or a fiber-optic device, the input monochromatic beam is channeled into two waveguides that converge into a combiner at its output (Figure 2). A phase difference is induced between the two arms of the interferometer by an adjustable delay element located in one of the two arms. In this manner, 180-degree out-of-phase wavelengths are filtered. Narrowband filtering is accomplished by cascading a number of these devices together. A filter based on a chain of MZIs isolates one of $N = 2^n - 1$ optical channels, where n is the number of interferometers in the chain (Kuznetsov 1994).

MZ interferometers can be tuned the same manner as Fabry-Perot filters and belong to the class of electro-optic filters that may be tuned by varying the voltage on one their arms. The ensuing change in their indexes of refraction affects the phase relationship between the two arms, resulting in different wavelengths at the output of the interferometer. Mechanical compression of one of the waveguides—for example, via a piezoelectric transducer—is another means of tuning an MZI filter. Tuning speed is on the order of several milliseconds, or orders of magnitude less than that for FP-type interferometers.

Birefringent Filters

Birefringent filters rely on the birefringence property of optically anisotropic crystals (e.g., lithium niobate,

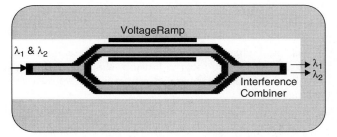

Figure 2: Principles of a Mach-Zehnder interferometric filter

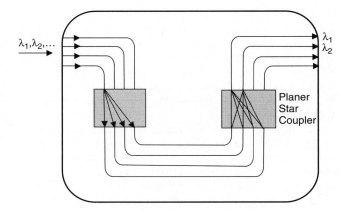

Figure 3: The structure of an arrayed-waveguide grating

LiNbO3), wherein a relative delay between ordinary and extraordinary rays aligned along the fast and slow axes of the material can be produced. As a result, light rays with a single polarization state can be made to interfere with themselves. The line-narrowing property of the birefringence filter (linear retarder) stems from reflection losses at undesired wavelengths. When placed at the Brewster's angle, the selected wavelength (e.g., p-polarized) will experience no reflection loss, whereas the remaining wavelengths with orthogonal (s-polarized) will experience reflection losses. Typically, a stack of (two to four) such filters is required to generate the extremely narrow filter profile. The birefringent filter may be tuned by rotating its crystal plates (Hirabayashi and Kuokawa 1992).

Waveguide Filters

As the name implies, *waveguide photonic fibers* are based in waveguiding effects in a varieties of architectures such as arrayed gratings, planar light-wave circuits, and photonic crystals.

Arrayed-Waveguide Gratings

Arrayed-waveguide gratings (AWGs) are planar devices that utilize the principles of interferometry and are a generalization of the Mach-Zehnder interferometers. Their architecture consists of multiple waveguides with different lengths, all converging at a single point (McGreer 2002). Interference between signals from different waveguides occurs at the crossover point. In an AWG, multiple copies of the same signal, shifted in phase by differing amounts, are added together. Because of its multiple input and output, a single AWG can do the job of multiple Bragg gratings. An AWG may be tuned via thermo-optic tuning. Relatively high insertion loss is the main drawback of these filters. AWGs are typically polarization-dependent, although polarization-independent versions have been demonstrated. Athermal AWGs are now commercially available and do not require extra thermal control. The AWG MUX-DMUX is now a key component of photonic networks. Figure 3 illustrates the structure of an arrayed-waveguide grating.

Planar Light-Wave Circuit Filter

A *planar light-wave circuit* (PLC) filter is formed by a fiber-matched, silica-based waveguide on silicon (Himeno, Kato, and Miya 1998; Yamada et al. 1995). PLC devices can be mass produced to meet the demand for more channels at a reduced cost. Wavelength $N \times N$

MUX-DMUX and programmable filters for high-bandwidth transmission systems have been constructed with PLC devices. Features of PLCs include high channel number, low insertion loss, high reliability, wide wavelength range, wide operating temperature range, excellent design flexibility, compact size, stability, and mass reproducibility. Multiwavelength wideband WDM filter arrays are constructed based on PLC-MZI architecture (Seo et al. 2002).

Michelson Interferometer–Based Filters

Michelson interferometer-based interference filters are multilayer thin-film devices consisting of several layers deposited on a substrate to form one or several cavities arranged in series. Akin to Fabry-Perot interferometers, the filtering of light is based on the destructive interference phenomenon. Width of the gap space (a thick film of dielectric material) between the two reflective surfaces determines which wavelengths are in phase and pass through the coated surfaces and which transmissions are filtered out through destructive interfere. This gap is designed to have a thickness of one-half wave at the desired peak transmission wavelength. The reflecting layers consist of multilayers of thin films, each approximately a quarter-wave thick. The number of layers in the thin-film stack may be adjusted to tailor the width of the bandpass. Interference filters may be designed as a bandpass or as an edge filter. Multicavity filter designs provide sharp cutoffs for spectral passband. Figure 4 illustrates the transmission spectrum and group delay of a thin-film filter with three and five cavities.

GRATING FILTERS

Grating filters are made from passive optical elements that are capable of separating individual wavelengths in their diffraction pattern. Wavelength and angle of incident on the grating determines the reflected light's angle. Compact wavelength demultiplexers have been constructed using a gradient index rod lens and a reflection grating replicated on a glass wedge. Grating-based demultiplexers are well suited for separating a large number of densely spaced wavelength channels.

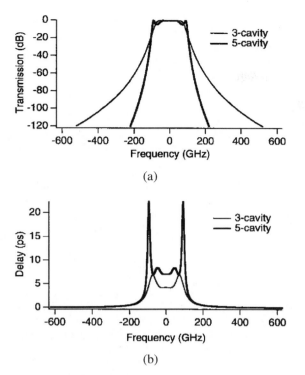

(a)

(b)

Figure 4: (a) Transmission spectrum and (b) group delay of a thin-film filter with three cavities (thin line) and five cavities (thick line). Squarer transmission results with increased number of cavities at the cost of ripple in the passband and higher dispersion near the passband edges (after Lenz et al. 1998, "Dispersive properties," with permission)

Two types of all-fiber filters—fiber Bragg gratings and long-period gratings—are now commercially available. Both are based on gratings written in the core of a single-mode fiber. Both free-space and fiber-based gratings are explained below.

Bulk Gratings

Free-space bulk diffraction gratings utilize the dispersive power of ruled reflection gratings and are used in MUX and DMUX, *reconfigurable optical add-drop multiplexers* (ROADMs), and *wavelength-selective switches* (WSSs). Ruled gratings provide higher dispersion and efficiency than other grating types. Gratings are typically blazed such that the reflected power is maximized for the first order of diffraction. The inherent property of a diffracted peak corresponding to a different angle for different wavelengths is utilized in multiplexing and demultiplexing of light beams with different wavelengths. Figure 5 schematically illustrates the concept of multichannel multiplexing with a bulk grating.

Fiber Bragg Grating

The *fiber Bragg grating* (FBG) is formed by photo-etching a periodical variation of the index of refraction onto the core of the optical fiber or by etching a phase mask into the fiber in the form of a diffractive optical element

(Hill and Meltz 1997). The FBG filter relies on Bragg reflection, wherein the grating's period (distance between the grating lines) is comparable to the incident light's wavelength. The Bragg condition is satisfied when the Bragg spacing (i.e., the grating period) is an integer multiple of the half wavelength. The Bragg grating selectively reflects a specific wavelength back into the fiber's core while transmitting other wavelengths. Figure 6 schematically illustrates a Bragg grating etched into the fiber's core. Figure 7 shows the reflection spectrum and the corresponding group delay of an apodized FBG.

Low insertion loss is a key advantage of these filters because the grating (the filtering mechanism) is an integral part of the fiber itself. Typical performance characteristics include reflectance losses on the order of 1 percent and a wavelength selectivity bandwidth of 0.1 nm. Thermal isolation of the device is required to avoid index-of-refraction fluctuations. FBGs are fairly insensitive to the polarization state of the input signal. FBGs have found applications as filters in add-drop modules and in chromatic-dispersion compensation modules (Kashyap 1999). The channel-selection properties of FBGs are typically excellent. An FBG added to the output of a circulator results in an effective bandpass filter.

Long-Period Fiber Gratings

The *long-period fiber grating* (LPFG) utilizes gratings with a period much longer than the incoming wavelength. On reflection from the grating, the incident light dissipates

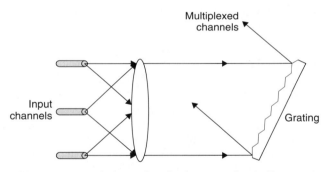

Figure 5: Optical channel multiplexing with a bulk grating

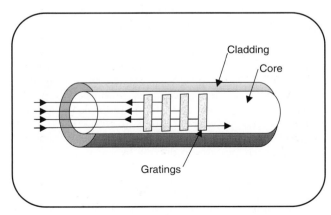

Figure 6: A Bragg grating etched into the fiber's core

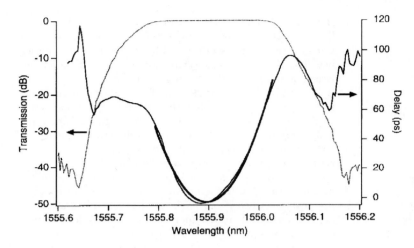

Figure 7: Reflection spectrum (dotted line) and the corresponding group delay (thin solid line) of an apodized fiber Bragg grating (after Lenz et al. 1998, "Dispersive properties," with permission)

into the fiber's lossy cladding modes (contrasted with the FBG, where it is reflected back to the fiber core). Fabrication of these devices is similar to the FBGs. These devices are useful in multichannel optical amplifiers and spectral gain profile flattening. Mechanical and thermal tuning both elongate the fiber, thereby tuning the Bragg grating by controlling the grating's period.

It is possible to make the bandpass curves broader and flatter by utilizing step-index, multimode, large core diameter fibers, where the core diameter of the output fiber is significantly larger than that of the input fiber (Aoyama and Minowa 1979). Also, cascading of multiple gratings, each with a different center wavelength, leads to intricate transmission spectra.

Acousto-Optic Tunable Filters

Acousto-optic tunable filters (AOTFs) are based on the well-developed acousto-optic effect in which a Bragg grating is set up in a waveguide (a crystal) through acoustic waves that are created by an external transducer (e.g., a piezoelectric crystal). The periodicity with which the generated change in the medium's index of refraction (e.g., for $LiNbO_3$ or tellurium dioxide, TeO_2) is equal to the wavelength of the acoustic wave (Chang 1981). The wavelength-filtering effect of these devices results from transmission of those wavelengths that satisfy the Bragg condition. The filter's passband is inversely proportional to the acousto-optic interaction length. Both polarization-dependent and polarization-independent devices have been developed. AOTFs also have applications in wavelength-selective space switches. The undesired cross talk that accompanied some AOTFs has been successfully suppressed by utilizing an optical fiber–based AOTF and multiple nonguiding cladding modes in the fiber (Kim et al. 1997). These filters are particularly suited to active gain flattening because arbitrary filter shapes are producible by simultaneously applying several RF signals to the AOTF.

An AOTF's unique capability to select several wavelengths simultaneously is particularly suitable to the development of a two-input, two-output wavelength cross connects. This is accomplished by simultaneously launching multiple acoustic waves, thereby satisfying the Bragg condition for multiple optical wavelengths. As a tunable filter or wavelength cross connect, current AOTFs benefit from fast tuning time and wide tuning range but suffer from a high level of cross talk and relatively high filter bandwidth (100 GHz). Cascading two such devices can result in nearly 20 dB in suppression of the side lobes.

OTHER FILTERS
Absorption Filters

Absorption filters are commonly manufactured from a selected impurity in a crystal, dyed glass, pigmented gelatin resins, or silicon and germanium deposited as a thin film. Both atomic and molecular absorption bands have been utilized along with induced absorption via the Kerr or the Faraday effect to achieve wavelength selection. The impurities or chemical densities are also varied to adjust the absorption frequency. Absorption filters follow the Kramers-Kronig relations. The transmittance of an absorbing filter is an exponential function of thickness and the absorption coefficient at a given wavelength.

These filters can demonstrate narrowband pass characteristics and are used for frequency stabilization of transmitters (Latrasse et al. 1994). Sharp rejection spectra or interference filters may be fabricated when absorption filters are combined with other filters (Musikant 1985). Because the absorption peak depends on the property of the material forming it, wavelength tuning or absorption edge sharpening is more difficult relative to other filters.

Electro-Optic Filters

The *electro-optic tunable filters* (EOTFs) are constructed from crystals that demonstrate a strong electro-optic effect. An electric field applied to the crystals via electrodes causes a change in the index of refraction. This effect can be used as an interferometric filter to vary the optical path lengths (Green 1993). EOTFs are distinguished by their exceptionally fast tunability feature, which is on the order of nanoseconds (Pinnow et al. 1979). One configuration utilizes a thin (~150 micron thick) platelet of lithium tantalate (LiTaO3) or LiNbO3 crystals within which a spatially periodic electric field is imposed (Pinnow et al. 1979). Light may travel longitudinally or transversely to the birefringent plates formed around the platelet. Transparent or finger electrodes are applied to the electro-optic crystal. The structure of a *Fabry-Perot semiconductor filter* (FPSF) is akin to Fabry-Perot diode lasers. Electrical tuning via injection current of the comblike spectral response of the FPSF allows wavelength selection (i.e., filtering). Wide (~10 nm) wavelength tuning has been achieved. Stepwise wavelength tuning over a range of 9.0 nm with a buildup time as short as a few microseconds has been demonstrated. Flexibility in producing variable filter bandpass, simultaneous operation at multiple wavelengths and side-lobe suppression are among the attractive features of electro-optic filters.

Gain-Flattening Filters

Gain-flattening filters (GFFs) are used primarily with fiber amplifiers. A GFF is typically designed to have a spectral response that closely matches the inverse gain profile of the amplifier (Wysocki, 1997). Etalons, thin-film filters, long-period gratings, chirped fiber Bragg gratings, or a combination of these filters have been utilized to develop this type of filter. In chirped fiber gratings, the Bragg wavelength varies with position. The GFF may be located at the output of amplifiers or between two stages of amplifications. Both passive and dynamic GFFs have been developed. Dynamic channel equalizers can equalize or block individual channels across the C or L bands. In a feedback loop, it can compensate for fluctuations of transmission amplitudes on individual channels or completely block or attenuate a channel. Advanced gain-flattening filters deviate only 0.02 dB from the target shape.

Dispersion-Compensation Filters

At data rates of 10 Gb/s and higher, chromatic dispersion in the fiber becomes a significant factor, causing signal deterioration. An optical *dispersion-compensation filter* must be compact, flexible, cost-effective, and able to simultaneously and over all channels alleviate the channel-to-channel variation of the dispersion and the dispersion slope of the transmission link being utilized. Implementation options include specially designed dispersion-compensating fibers with a large negative dispersion and dispersion slope, chirped fiber Bragg gratings, lattice Mach-Zehnder filters, Michelson interferometer-based (optical all-pass) filters, and specially modulated transmitters (Painchaud et al. 2006; Koch and Brenna 2003).

Fused-Fiber Filters

Single mode fibers may be fused together through application of high temperatures at the fiber joint. *Fused fibers* minimize the packaging requirements and are used in filtering as couplers for multiplexing, ring fiber resonators, and attenuators. For example, a variable loss and coupling add-drop filter–based fused-fiber grating has been developed with controlled transmission properties (Choi, Lee, and Yariv 2002). One configuration of a fused-fiber filter utilizes a long-period grating written into the waist of the coupler (Lauzon 1998). The filter may be tuned to specific wavelengths by adjusting the period of the grating. Such a filter could have approximately 1 nm of wavelength selectivity and is particularly suited to MUX and DMUX in DWDM networks.

Hybrid Filters

By combining two or more filters, we can take advantage of the individual properties of each filter, effectively producing superior characteristics. For example, Lumeau, Glebov, and Smirnov (2006) combined a Fabry-Perot etalon and a volume Bragg grating sequentially to achieve a filter with the narrow spectral band of the etalon and the broad rejection bandwidth of the grating. The spectral sensitivities of the etalon and the Bragg grating were 220 and 320 pm, respectively. The selectivity of the hybrid filter was 220 pm, with separation between channels of 800 pm and a throughput of 95 percent. With a higher-quality etalon, wavelength selectivity down to 10 pm is anticipated.

MULTIPLEXERS

Wavelength-division multiplexing is a powerful technique used to increase the capacity of an imbedded fiber. In this technique, each optical signal is assigned a specific wavelength. Multiple wavelengths are multiplexed and transmitted and amplified as a group through a single fiber. Other features of WDM systems include signal format independence by which data are transmitted irrespective of the data format, wavelength routing whereby wavelength becomes another dimension like time and space, and wavelength switching in which optical layers may be reconfigured efficiently. A fiber-optic multiplexer is an instrument that can optically couple one input channel to tens of different output channels.

Optical filters make up the core of most MUX and DMUX components. For dynamic WDMs with circuit switching at moderate to high speeds that require dynamic filtering functions, tunable optical filters are essential. Static and tunable filters efficiently and selectively add or drop specific wavelength channels from a multiple-wavelength fiber-optic network. Dispersive optical elements such as prisms and diffraction gratings, reflective optics such as interference filters, along with fiber directional couplers and integrated waveguides are utilized in forming MUX and DMUX devices (Senior and Cusworth 1989). Most multiplexers can be used in reverse as demultiplexers, therefore discussion of one type pertains to other applications as well. Table 2 summarizes the generalized characteristics of passive device types for multiplexing and demultiplexing.

A variety of architectures have been developed for wavelength multiplexing and demultiplexing in response to the ever-increasing growth of number of wavelength channels in a WDM system. Table 3 compares the merits of some of the more popular multiplexing and demultiplexing architectures.

Table 2: Typical Devices Characteristics for Multiplexing and Demultiplexing (Generalized)

Device	Insertion Loss (dB)	Channel Bandwidth (nm)	Channel Separation (nm)	Mechanism
Filter	1	4	10	Interference, absorption
Grating	>3	10	40	Dispersive
Prism	>3	20	30	Dispersive
Directional coupler (fiber)	0.2	40	100	Power transfer between adjacent fibers
Waveguide	1.5	100	10	Integrated, no discrete optics

Table 3: Merits of Some Common Multiplexing and Demultiplexing Concepts

Architecture	Approach	Features	Drawbacks
Serial (example: thin film)	Demultiplexes one wavelength at a time	Scalable to a limited number of channels	Moderate loss and uniformity; requires narrow filters
Common stage (example: AWG)	Demultiplexes all wavelengths in a single stage	Low loss and high uniformity	Limited number of channels (<50); requires narrow filters
Multistage (example: lattice)	Divides wavelengths into bands; demultiplexes each band separately	Large number of channels	Requires a guard space between bands
Interleaving (example: AWG)	Interleaves multistage demultiplexers	Modular; wider filters for latter stages	Complex implementation

Table 4: Distinguishing Characteristics of Different Filter Types

Requirement	Suitable Filter
10's of MHz bandpass	Fabry-Perot
A few GHz bandpass	Fiber Bragg grating
<10 channels	Electro-optic or semiconductor
<100 channels	Fabry-Perot or acousto-optic
1 msec tuning time	Mechanically tuned (circuit-switched transmission)
1 μsec tuning time	Acousto-optic (packet switching)
1 nsec tuning time	Electro-optic and semiconductor (packet switching)
500-nm tuning range	Mechanically tuned
250-nm tuning range	Acousto-optically tuned
15-nm tuning range	Electro-optic
<1-dB loss	Semiconductor
Excellent channel selection	Fiber Bragg grating
Good channel selection	Dielectric and arrayed-waveguide grating
Poor channel selection	Fabry-Perot, Mach-Zehnder, acousto-optical

CONCLUSION

In summary, optical filtering that performs channel selection is a major dynamic network functionality in the WDM environment. A wide variety of filters that are capable of selectively isolating single wavelengths from wavelength-multiplexed optical systems have been developed. Each has its own advantages and disadvantages. Many of the filters described here are commercially available. At this time, no filter provides all of the best features simultaneously. Selection of a filter is highly driven by the specifics of an application. For high-speed, highly dynamic networks, electro-optic and acousto-optic tunable filters provide the capability for nsec to μsec tuning speeds.

Table 4 summarizes suitable filters categorized by applications of wavelength and channel selection, tuning speed, tuning range, and multiplexing and demultiplexing requirements.

GLOSSARY

Acousto-Optical Tunable Filter (AOTF): A filter that can be tuned by altering the refractive index by the applied acoustic waves.

Arrayed Waveguide Grating (AWG): A device for multiplexing or demultiplexing multiple wavelengths into a common path (typically, fiber optics).

Demultiplexing (DMUX): Separation of wavelengths arriving on a common path.

Dense Wavelength-Division Multiplexing (DWDM): Multiplexing of a variety of wavelengths that are spaced no more than a few GHz apart.

Dielectric Thin-Film (DTF) Filter: A filter made by depositing alternating layers of quarter-wave film.

Electro-Optical Tunable Filter (EOTF): An optical filter based on polarization conversion.

Fabry Perot Interferometer (FPI): An optical resonator consisting of plane-parallel reflecting ends.

Fiber Bragg Grating (FBG): A grating formed onto a fiber to reflect different wavelengths depending on the grating's period.

Free Spectral Range (FSR): In an FP interferometer, it represents the distance (in frequency space) between adjacent transmission peaks.

Full Width at Half Maximum (FWHM): A value for the extent of a function measured at half of the maximum amplitude.

Gain-Flattening Filter (GFF): A filter used (for example, in an amplifier) to equalize the amplification gain for different wavelengths.

Long-Period Fiber Grating (LPFG): A fiber-optic structure with properties that vary periodically along the length of the fiber.

Mach-Zehnder Interferometer (MZI): An interferometer based on the Twyman-Green interferometer.

Multiple Cavity Transmission (MCT): Thin-film filters are a type of multiple cavity transmission.

Multiplexing (MUX): The combination of several signals onto a common path.

Planar Light-Wave Circuit (PLC): Formed by a fiber-matched, silica-based waveguide on silicon.

Wavelength Cross Connect (WXC): Primarily a device switch connection of input ports to output ports.

Wavelength-Division Multiplexing (WDM): A system that allows the transmission of multiple signals with varying wavelengths over a common path.

CROSS REFERENCES

See *Optical Fiber Communications; Optical Transmitters, Receivers, and Noise; Synchronous Optical Code Division Multiplexing Systems*.

REFERENCES

Aoyama, K., and J. Minowa. 1979. Low-loss optical demultiplexer for WDM systems in the 0.8 μm wavelength range. *Applied Optics*, 18: 2834–6.

Atherton, P. D., N. K. Reay, J. Ring, and T. R. Hicks. 1981. Tunable Fabry-Perot filters. *Optical Engineering*, 20: 806–14.

Cao, S., J. Chen, J. N. Damask, C. R. Doerr, L. Guiziou, G. Harvey, Y. Hibino, H. Li, S. Suzuuki, K.-Y. Wu, and P. Xie. 2004. Interleaver technology: Comparisons and applications requirements. *Journal of Lightwave Technology*, 22: 281–9.

Chang, I. C. 1981. Acousto-optic tunable filters. *Optical Engineering*, 20: 740–2.

Choi J. M., R. K. Lee, and A. Yariv. 2002. Ring fiber resonator based on fused-fiber grating add-drop filters: Application to resonator coupling. *Optics Letters*, 27: 1598–1600.

Green, P. E. 1993. *Fiber optic networks*. Englewood Cliffs, NJ: Prentice Hall.

Hill, K. O., and G. Meltz. 1997. Fiber Bragg grating technology fundamentals and overview. *Journal of Lightwave Technology*, 15: 1263–76.

Himeno, A., K. Kato, and T. Miya. 1998. Silica-based planar lightwave circuits. *IEEE Journal of Selected Topics in Quantum Electronics*, 4: 913–24.

Hirabayashi, K. 2005. PLZT electrooptic ceramic photonic devices for surface-normal operation in trenches cut across arrays of optical fiber. *Journal of Lightwave Technology*, 23: 1393–1402.

———, and T. Kuokawa. 1992. A tunable polarization-independent liquid crystal Fabry-Perot interferometric filters. *IEEE Photonics Technology Letters*, 4: 430–6.

Kashyap, R. 1999. *Fiber Bragg gratings*. New York: Elsevier.

Kim, H. S., S. H. Yun, I. K. Hwang, and B. Y. Kim. 1997. All fiber acousto-optic tunable notch filter with electronically controllable spectral profile. *Optics Letters*, 22: 1476–8.

Koch, B., and J. Brenna III. 2003. Dispersion compensation in an optical communications system with an electroabsorption modulated and a fiber grating. *Photonics Technology Letters*, 15: 1633.

Kuznetsov, M. 1994. Cascaded coupler Mach-Zehnder channel dropping filters for wavelength-division-multiplexed optical systems. *Journal of Lightwave Technology*, 12: 226–30.

Latrasse, C., M. Breton, M. Tetu, N. Cyre, R. Roberge, and B. Villeneuve. 1994. C2HD and C2H2 absorption lines near 1530 nm for semiconductor-laser frequency locking. *Optics Letters*, 19: 1885–7.

Lauzon, J. 1998. Grating assisted fiber filter. U. S. Patent 5,764,831.

Lenz, G., B. J. Eggleton, C. R. Giles, C. K. Madsen, and R. E. Slusher. 1998. Dispersive properties of optical filters for WDM systems. *IEEE Journal of Quantum Electronics*, 34: 1390–1402.

Lenz, G., B. J. Eggleton, C. K. Madsen, C. R. Giles, and G. Nykolak. 1998. Optimal dispersion of optical filters for WDM systems. *Photonics Technology Letters*, 10: 567–9.

Li, S., K. S. Chiang, and W. A. Gambling. 2000. Fast accurate wavelength switching of an erbium-doped fiber laser with a Fabry-Perot semiconductor filter and fiber Bragg gratings. *Applied Physics Letters*, 77(26): 4268–70.

Lin, W.-P., M.-S. Kao, and S. Chi. 2003. A DWDM/SCM self-healing architecture for broad-band subscriber networks. *Journal of Lightwave Technology*, 21: 319–28.

Lumeau, L., L. B. Glebov, and V. Smirnov. 2006. Tunable narrowband filter based on a combination of Fabry-Perot etalon and volume Bragg grating. *Optics Letters*, 31: 2417–9.

McGreer, K. A. 2002. Arrayed waveguide gratings for wavelength routing. *IEEE Communications*, 36: 62–8.

Musikant, S. 1985. *Optical materials: An introduction to selection and application*. New York: Marcel Dekker.

Oguma, M., T. Kitoh, Y. Inoue, T. Mizuno, T. Shibata, M. Kohtoku, and Y. Hibino. 2004. Compact and low-loss interleaver filter employing lattice-form structure and silica-based waveguide. *Journal of Lightwave Technology*, 22: 895–902.

Othonos, A., and K. Kalli. 1999. Fiber Bragg gratings: Fundamentals and applications in telecommunications and sensing. Boston: Artech House.

Painchaud Y., M. Poulin, M. Morin, and M. Guy. 2006. Fiber Bragg grating based dispersion compensator slope matched for LEAF fiber. In *Proceedings of the Optical Fiber Communications Conference*, March 5–10, Anaheim, California.

Pinnow, D. A., R. L. Abrams, D. M. Henderson, T. K. Plant, R. R. Stephens, and C. M. Walker. et al. 1979. An electro-optic tunable filter. *Applied Physics Letters*, 34(6): 391–3.

Scalora, M., M. J. Bloemer, and Baglio S. 2002. Apparatus and method for controlling optics propagation based on a transparent metal stack. U. S. Patent 6,339,493.

Senior, J. M., and S. D. Cusworth. 1989. Devices for wavelength multiplexing and demultiplexing. *IEE Proceedings*, 136: 183–202.

Seo, K., M. Iwaya, M. Shiino, K. Tanaka, and Y. Hadishima. 2002. High-power stable Mach-Zehnder-interferometer-type 15-wavelength multiplexer for 1480nm band pumping. In *Proceedings of the European Conference on Optical Communications* (ECOC), Sept. 8–12, Paris. pp. 1–21.

Trimm, R. H., et al. 2005. Dynamic MEMS-based photonic bandgap filter. *IEEE Sensors Journal*, 5: 1451–61.

Wysocki, P. F., J. Judkins, R. Espindola, M. Andrejco, A. Vengsarkar, and K. Walker. 1997. Erbium-doped fiber amplifier flattened beyond 40 nm using long-period grating. In *Proceedings of Optical Fiber Communication Conference* (OFC97), February. pp. D2ff.

Yamada, Y., S. Suzuki, K. Moriwaki, Y. Hibino, Y. Tohmori, Y. Akutsu, Y. Nakasuga, T. Hashimoto, H. Terui, M. Yanagisawa, Y. Inoue, Y. Akahori, and R. Nagase. 1995. Application of planar lightwave circuit platform to hybrid integrated optical WDM transmitter/receiver module. *Electronics Letters*, 31: 1366–7.

Optical Solitons

Natalia M. Litchinitser, *University of Michigan*

INTRODUCTION

A fascinating phenomenon that is now referred to as a *soliton* was discovered for the first time in 1834 by John Scott Russell, who was conducting experiments in the Union Canal near Edinburgh to determine the most efficient design for canal boats. He noticed "a large solitary elevation, a rounded, smooth and well-defined heap of water, which continued its course along the channel apparently without change of form or diminution of speed" (Russell 1844). He named this phenomenon "the wave of translation." Later, these waves were called "solitary waves" or "solitons."

The name *soliton* was put forward by Zabusky and Kruskal (1965), who performed a detailed numerical study of the interaction of solitary wave solutions of the Korteweg-de Vries equation. It was shown that nonlinear waves can interact elastically and retain their shape after collision. It is noteworthy that the distinction between a "soliton" and a "solitary wave" is often disregarded in optics literature (Ablowitz, Biondini, and Ostrovsky 2000). The term *soliton* is used in optics to describe a localized pulse that travels without a change in shape. However in a strict mathematical sense, solitons only exist for integrable problems—that is, problems that are solvable by inverse scattering theory (IST)—whereas the solitary waves exist for a much broader class of nonlinear wave equations. According to Ablowitz and Clarkson (1991), "a soliton is a solitary wave which asymptotically preserves its shape and velocity upon nonlinear interaction with other solitary waves, or more generally, with another (arbitrary) localized disturbance."

Initially, solitons were primarily the subject of fundamental research in various fields, including optics, mathematics, quantum mechanics, particle physics, and molecular biology. Currently, optical solitons are emerging as promising candidates for building future all-optical networks. The development of all-optical signal processing and computing devices becomes increasingly important as data rates and the capacity of optical communication systems continue to increase. Remarkably, from 1980 to 2000, the capacity of fiber-optics transmission systems increased by a factor of more than 30,000 (Agrawal 2005).

The field of optical solitons is broad and continuously growing. Several excellent books and book chapters are currently available that address the properties and applications of different kinds of solitons, including Akhmediev and Ankiewicz (1997), Trillo and Torruellas (2001), Buryak et al. (2002), Kivshar and Agrawal (2003), and Desyatnikov, Torner, and Kivshar (2005). In this chapter, we focus on those classes of optical solitons that have been demonstrated to have a potential for optical networking applications. In the next section, the theoretical and experimental results demonstrating important properties of the main classes of solitons—including temporal, spatial, spatio-temporal, incoherent, discrete, and Bragg solitons—are summarized. Applications of solitons for optical networking applications are discussed in "Applications of Solitons." Finally, in the summary, we outline future perspectives for the applications of optical solitons.

Optical Soliton Properties

Light propagation in a nonlinear medium is described by the *nonlinear Schrödinger equation* (NLS) (Ablowitz and Clarkson 1991). The particular form and dimensionality of the NLS depends on the geometry and material properties of the nonlinear medium. In this section, we review the mathematical background and main properties of several types of optical solitons.

Temporal Solitons in Telecommunication Systems

Theoretical Background

Temporal solitons in single-mode optical fibers were predicted by Hasegawa and Tappert (1973). Their propagation is described by the NLS equation in the form

$$i\frac{\partial u}{\partial z} - \frac{s}{2}\frac{\partial^2 u}{\partial \tau^2} \pm |u|^2 u = 0 \qquad (1)$$

where the amplitude $u = \dfrac{A}{\sqrt{P_0}}$ is a normalized slowly varying pulse envelope, $z = Z/L_D$ is a normalized longitudinal coordinate, $\tau = (t - \beta_1 Z)/T_0$ is a time coordinate, β_1 is inversely proportional to the group velocity, and $P_0 = (\gamma L_D)^{-1}$ is the soliton peak power, implying the balance between the dispersion and the nonlinearity. The dispersion length $L_D = T_0^2/|\beta_2|$ describes the characteristic length at which dispersion becomes significant. The parameter $\gamma = \dfrac{n_2 \omega_0}{c A_{eff}}$ is the nonlinear coefficient, n_2 is the nonlinear refractive index, ω_0 is the carrier frequency, c is the speed of light in a vacuum, and A_{eff} is the effective mode area. The parameter $s = \mathrm{sgn}(\beta_2) = \pm 1$ is the sign of the *group velocity dispersion* (GVD) parameter β_2, which can be positive or negative depending on the wavelength. The first two terms in Equation (1) describe linear wave propagation, while the third term is responsible for the nonlinear interaction owing to the intensity-dependent refractive index change. The nonlinear term can be positive (as in optical fibers) or negative (as in semiconductors).

In the absence of the nonlinear term, Equation (1) can be solved using a Fourier transform method. The basic idea of this method is illustrated schematically in Figure 1a for the case of temporal wave-packet propagation. The initial data are transformed from the time domain to the spectral domain using a Fourier transform, propagated in time, and then transformed back to the time domain using an inverse Fourier transform. On the other hand, in the nonlinear case, wave propagation is described by the partial differential Equation (1) and cannot be solved by the Fourier transform method because the system is no longer linear. It was first demonstrated by Zakharov and Shabat that Equation (1) can be solved analytically using the IST (Zakharov and Shabat 1973). The schematic for the inverse scattering method is shown in Figure 1b. Interestingly, one of the papers on inverse scattering method by Ablowitz et al. (1974) was entitled

"The Inverse Scattering Transform: Fourier Analysis for Nonlinear Problems." Although the IST is analogous in many ways to the Fourier transform method for the linear problem, the last step in solving the inverse problem is highly nontrivial. Detailed treatments of the IST are available in the original papers by Zakharov and Shabat (1972, 1973) and in many textbooks (see, for example, Ablowitz and Segur 1981; Akhmanov, Vysloukh, and Chirkin 1992).

In the most general form, the bright soliton solution of Equation (1), which is often called a *fundamental soliton*, can be written as (Agrawal 2001)

$$u(z,\tau) = u_s \sec h[u_s(\tau + \omega_s z - \tau_s)] \\ \exp\left[i(u_s^2 - \omega_s^2) z/2 - i\omega_s \tau + i\phi_s\right], \quad (2)$$

where u_s, ω_s, τ_s, and ϕ_s represent the amplitude, frequency, position, and phase of the soliton, respectively. Equation (2) can be simplified, resulting in

$$u(z,\tau) = u_s \sec h(u_s \tau) \exp(i u_s^2 z/2) \quad (3)$$

Equation (3) shows that the soliton width is inversely proportional to the soliton amplitude. This relationship is one of the most important properties of these solitons.

In addition to the bright soliton solution, Equation (1) has a so-called dark soliton solution as shown in Figure 2. The fundamental dark soliton, with zero intensity at its center, is often referred to as a *black* soliton. In addition to the fundamental dark soliton, there is a continuous range of lower-contrast dark solitons, referred to as *gray* solitons.

As shown in Figure 2, a major difference between bright and dark solitons is their symmetry. Fundamental bright solitons are even pulses, with a constant phase across the entire pulse, whereas black solitons are odd pulses, with a π-phase jump at the center (where the intensity is zero). Gray solitons have a similar but smaller phase shift at their center. Like bright solitons, dark solitons are highly robust under perturbation of their width and the shape of the intensity dip (Tomlinson et al. 1989). However, unlike bright solitons (Satsuma and Yajima 1974; Zakharov et al. 1984; Kivshar 1989), dark solitons may be created

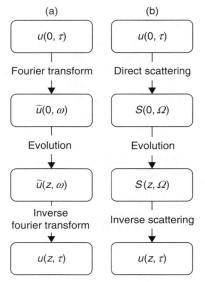

Figure 1: Schematic of (a) Fourier transform method and (b) inverse scattering method

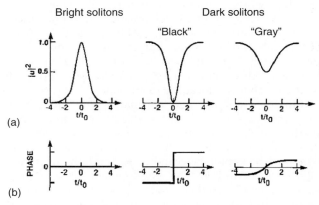

Figure 2: (a) Intensity and (b) phase as functions of normalized time for bright and dark solitons. Adapted from Tomlinson et al. (1989)

without a threshold value in the input pulse power (Gredeskul and Kivshar 1989a, 1989b).

Three major factors affect the signal transmission in long-haul telecommunication systems: dispersion, nonlinearity, and loss. In nonsoliton-based systems, all three factors are generally detrimental for system performance. Optical soliton-based transmission systems have attracted significant attention because solitons use two of these factors—fiber nonlinearity and dispersion— to their advantage. Nevertheless, fiber loss remains a problem because, as the energy and the peak power of the soliton decrease, the nonlinear effects weaken and the pulse broadens resulting from GVD.

To describe the bright temporal soliton propagation in realistic optical fibers with loss, Equation (1) can be modified to include fiber loss:

$$i\frac{\partial u}{\partial z} - \frac{s}{2}\frac{\partial^2 u}{\partial t^2} + |u|^2 u = -i\frac{\alpha}{2}u, \qquad (4)$$

Fiber loss α is usually compensated using either lumped or distributed amplification schemes. Historically, distributed amplification based on *stimulated Raman scattering* (SRS) was proposed first by Hasegawa (1983, 1984). In distributed amplification, losses are compensated locally at every point along the fiber link, making the fiber effectively loss-free. The main advantage of Raman amplification is that it can operate at any wavelength. However, because it is a nonlinear process, it requires especially high pump powers. The invention of *erbium-doped fiber amplifiers* (EDFAs) enabled an alternative, relatively low pump power solution known as *lumped amplification* (Mear et al. 1987). Typically, amplifier length is a few meters and therefore soliton energy increases almost "instantaneously." This rapid change in soliton energy is accompanied by a change in the soliton width and can destroy a soliton. For this reason, the amplifier spacing should be kept much smaller than the characteristic length scale over which the soliton is significantly affected by energy losses (the dispersion length or the soliton period). Because the dispersion length and the soliton period are proportional to the pulse width squared, the above requirement is increasingly difficult to satisfy as the soliton width decreases in order to increase the bit rate. Although lumped amplification has the advantage of the lower pump power requirements, the distributed amplification offers a viable solution at higher bit rates requiring short solitons (soliton width less than 10 ps). Currently, the distributed amplification schemes rely on either SRS or "active" erbium-doped fibers.

Another important factor that can limit the total soliton transmission distance is *timing jitter*, which causes deviations in the soliton position from its original bit position. Several physical mechanisms result in timing jitter, including Gordon-Haus jitter, acoustic jitter, polarization mode dispersion, and soliton interactions (Agrawal 1997). In addition, in *wavelength-division multiplexed* (WDM) systems, additional factors—including soliton collisions and collision-induced jitter—should be accounted for. A comprehensive discussion of WDM technique can be found in Agrawal (2005). Briefly, in a WDM system, several soliton trains are superimposed on each other in the time domain but are launched at different carrier frequencies. WDM has a great potential for using the large spectral bandwidth available in the optical fiber.

Among all of the above-mentioned types of jitter, Gordon-Haus jitter (Gordon and Haus 1986; Elgin 1993) is often considered as a major factor limiting the performance of the transmission system. The origin of Gordon-Haus jitter can be understood as follows. Stimulated emission in EDFAs is always accompanied by a certain amount of spontaneous emission, which adds noise to the signal. In the case of solitons, the added noise produces fluctuations in the pulses' positions and leads to transmission errors at high bit rates or large enough distances. It was predicted by Mecozzi et al. (1992) and Kodama and Hasegawa (1992) that the maximum noise-limited propagation distance of optical solitons can be increased with the addition of optical filters to the transmission system. Such filters remove some of the noise added by the amplifiers. As discussed in the next subsection, a further improvement in transmission distance can be achieved by varying the central frequencies of the filters linearly with distance along the fiber (Mollenauer, Gordon, and Evangelides 1992).

In addition to the loss management described above, modern WDM systems significantly benefit from dispersion management. The concept of dispersion management was first described by Lin, Kogelnik, and Cohen (1980). In one approach, adiabatic dispersion management is utilized. In this approach, the dispersion is changed in proportion to the soliton power in order to reduce dispersive wave radiation and collision-induced frequency shift in WDM systems (Forysiak, Knox, and Doran 1994; Hasegawa, Kumar, and Kodama 1996). An alternative approach uses a nonadiabatic map to cancel out the accumulated dispersion in a transoceanic soliton transmission by periodically inserting dispersion-compensating fibers (Suzuki et al. 1995). In this case, the Gordon-Haus effect, which is proportional to the accumulated dispersion, is successfully reduced. However, when the dispersion is reduced, the corresponding soliton peak power reduces as well, leading to deterioration of the signal-to-noise ratio. This problem was addressed by alternating anomalous dispersion fiber and normal dispersion fiber in a periodic fashion (Smith et al. 1996). The solitons realized in this approach do not actually preserve their shape at every position in the fiber link. However, the parameters repeat from period to period. These solitons are called *dispersion-managed solitons*. Figure 3 shows an example of the evolution of a dispersion-managed soliton over one map period. The design of dispersion-managed soliton systems requires a careful choice of input parameters of the pulse, including the pulse width, energy, and chirp, to ensure that the soliton recovers its input state after each period. The advantages of the dispersion-managed solitons over the standard solitons include a decrease of timing jitter, reduced interaction among neighboring pulses in single-channel systems and of the four-wave mixing as well as significant reduction of the jitter caused by WDM soliton collisions (Mu et al. 1998; Golovchenko, Pilipetskii, and Menyuk 1997).

Several important factors that affect the performance of dispersion-managed soliton-based communication

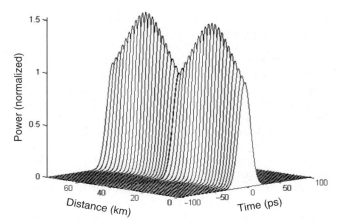

Figure 3: Numerical simulations of the evolution of the dispersion-managed soliton through one map period of 80 km. The parameters of the system used in numerical simulations are input pulse width 21 ps (full width at half maximum), normal dispersion section length 40 km, GVD $\beta_2 = 4ps^2/km$, anomalous dispersion section length approximately 40 km, and $\beta_2 = -4ps^2/km$

systems have been addressed in the literature, including the dispersion map configuration, the interaction between the signal and the noise, and nonlinear interaction between signals (Gabitov and Turitsyn 1996; Kodama, Kumar, and Maruta 1997; Shapiro and Turitsyn 1997; Yang and Kath 1997; Ablowitz and Biondini 1998; Kumar et al. 1998; Yu et al. 1999; Hirooka, Nakada, and Hasegawa 2000; Lushnikov 2001; Poutrina and Agrawal 2002; Poutrina and Agrawal 2003; Del Duce, Killey, and Bayvel 2004). From a practical viewpoint, one of the most important advantages of using dispersion-managed soliton systems is that they can utilize already installed fibers with a zero dispersion wavelength of 1.3 μm combined with existing dispersion-compensation techniques such as dispersion-compensating fibers or fiber Bragg gratings. A long-term debate ranging from whether solitons have advantages over other signal modulation formats to whether solitons are not practical at all for long-haul telecommunication applications still has not completely settled down. Still, a large number of important theoretical results, laboratory experiments, and system demonstrations suggest that solitons have significant potential to find their niche in communication technologies (Menyuk et al. 2002).

Experimental Progress

The earliest example of temporal solitons is related to the discovery of the *self-induced transparency* in 1967 (McCall and Hahn 1967). Temporal solitons and their interactions in optical fibers were experimentally observed for the first time in 1980 (Mollenauer, Stolen, and Gordon 1980) and then in 1987 (Mitschke and Mollenauer 1987). Extensive research in the field of temporal solitons has led to the development of soliton-based telecommunication systems (Hasegawa and Kodama 1995; Iannone et al. 1998). The first commercial fiber-optic telecommunications link using solitons, launched in Australia in 2003, was approximately 3000 km long (McEntee 2003).

As discussed above, the maximum transmission distance of soliton-based systems is limited by several factors,

including the losses, the Gordon-Haus timing jitter, and soliton collisions. In early experiments, Raman amplification was used for loss compensation (Mollenauer, Stolen, and Islam 1985). Using this technique, a soliton transmission of more than 4000 km in a fiber loop with periodic loss compensation was demonstrated in an experiment in 1998 (Mollenauer and Smith 1988). Two main drawbacks associated with Raman amplification are gain variations resulting from polarization fluctuations and relatively high pump power requirements. The emergence of the EDFAs provided a practical solution to these challenges. The first long-distance experiment utilizing an EDFA was reported by Mollenauer et al. (1991). In this experiment, error-free soliton transmission at 2.5 Gbit/s over more than 14,000 km was demonstrated. In the same experiment, a new technique of a fixed-frequency guiding filter was implemented for the first time. As a result, a significant increase in maximum transmission distance owing to the use of the guiding filter technique was demonstrated. For comparison, an error-free distance limited to 11,000 km in a system with no guiding filters was increased to 14,000 km by adding the filter, as shown in Figure 4. However, a soliton transmission utilizing fixed-frequency guiding filters requires additional gain to compensate for the filter attenuation. This extra gain leads to the exponential growth of spontaneous emission and dispersive waves at the soliton center frequency that may destroy solitons.

To avoid this problem, sliding-frequency guiding filters were proposed (Mollenauer, Gordon, and Evangelides 1992; Mollenauer et al. 1993) and resulted in the transmission of a 5 Gbit/s signal over 15,000 km. In addition, in the same work, the bit rate was doubled using the WDM technique. Further improvement in the maximum transmission distance was reported by Morton et al. (1995), and an error-free transmission at 10 Gbit/s was achieved over a distance of 27,000 km. A combination of sliding-frequency filters, a WDM technique, and dispersion-tapered fiber spans allowed for soliton transmission in six and seven WDM channels of 10 Gbit/s each, with measured bit error rates $<10^{-9}$ over distances of 11.4 and 9.4 Mm, respectively (Mollenauer, Mamyshev, and Neubelt 1996). A detailed comparative study of dense WDM systems with and without frequency-sliding guiding filters was reported by Evangelides et al. (1996). In these experiments, the adjacent channel spacing was only

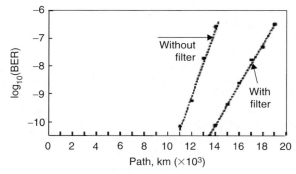

Figure 4: Measured bit-error rate as a function of total path with and without fixed-frequency guiding frequency filter in the loop (Mollenauer et al. 1991)

25 GHz, and error-free transmission of 2.5 Gbit/s at 10 Mm for eight channels without the use of filters was demonstrated. The addition of the filters allowed the number of 2.5 Gbit/s channels to be increased to twelve.

Finally, several experimental studies confirmed the advantages of dispersion-managed solitons for fiber transmission systems (Carter et al. 1997; Morita et al. 1998, 1999; Mollenauer et al. 2000; Mu et al. 2000). The use of dispersion management resulted in demonstration of single-channel soliton transmission at 40 Gbit/s over 8600 km (Morita et al. 1998) and then over 10, 200 km (Morita et al. 1999) without any active transmission control in the transmission link. Massive WDM error-free twenty-seven channel transmission at 10 Gbit/s per channel using dispersion-managed solitons was demonstrated over distances greater than 9000km (Mollenauer et al. 2000) without the use of forward-error correction. A thorough comparison of the experiments and the theory describing the detailed dynamics of the dispersion-managed soliton trains propagating in a recirculating fiber-loop was demonstrated by Mu et al. (2000). An excellent agreement between the experiments and the simulations for the temporal and spectral pulse shapes was demonstrated. Figure 5 shows the comparison of the experimentally measured *full width at half maximum* (FWHM) pulse durations and eye diagrams to those from the simulation results.

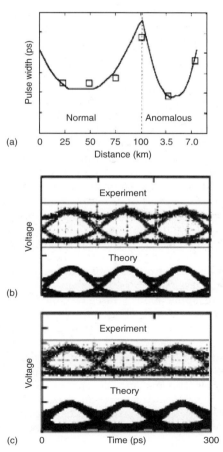

Figure 5: Comparison of the experimentally measured FWHM pulse widths and eye diagrams with those from the simulation results (Mu et al. 1998)

Although theoretical studies predicted that dark solitons may have inherent advantages for long-haul transmission, their implementation was significantly delayed because of relatively difficult generation and detection of dark solitons in comparison with bright solitons. Advantageous properties of dark solitons that have been predicted are reduced Gordon-Haus timing jitter and a longer collision length in comparison to bright solitons (Hamaide, Emplit, and Haelterman 1991; Kivshar et al. 1994). In the initial experiments, a long optical pulse was used as a background for the dark soliton, which appeared as a dip in the center of that pulse (Emplit et al. 1987; Krökel et al. 1988; Weiner et al. 1988). Later, other techniques were implemented, including (1) a spectral filtering approach (Krökel et al. 1988), (2) a continuous train of dark solitons generation using an electro-optic modulator (Zhao and Bourkoff 1990), (3) a quasi-continuous dark soliton train generation by colliding two pulses (Rothenberg 1991; Rothenberg and Heinrich 1992), and (4) beating two continuous wave signals in a dispersion-decreasing fiber (Richardson et al. 1994). The transmission of a pseudo-random 10 Gbit/s data train of dark solitons through 1200 km normal dispersion fiber was demonstrated in a 1995 experiment (Nakazawa and Sizuki 1995). The interactions of dark solitons were observed experimentally in 1996 (Foursa and Emplit 1996) and were shown to be repulsive. Further progress is expected with the development of improved sources for the generation of dark solitons.

Spatial Optical Solitons

Theoretical Background

Spatial optical solitons are self-trapped optical beams that propagate without changing their spatial shape because of the competing effects of diffraction and self-focusing in a nonlinear medium (Chiao, Garmire, and Townes 1964; Kelley 1965; Chiao et al. 1966; Haus 1966; Luther-Davies and Stegeman 2001). In the linear regime, the optical beam experiences a diffraction-induced broadening of its spatial profile. In a nonlinear material with a positive nonlinear index of refraction, light essentially changes the index of refraction of the medium in which it propagates, leading to self-focusing. This self-focusing competes with diffractive effects; at sufficient intensities, it can lead to the formation of a bright soliton owing to the exact balance of diffraction and self-focusing.

Spatial soliton propagation in a bulk medium is described by the generalized NLS:

$$i\frac{\partial u}{\partial z} + \frac{1}{2}\left(\frac{\partial^2 u}{\partial x^2} + \frac{\partial^2 u}{\partial y^2}\right) \pm f\left(\left|u\right|^2\right)u = 0 \qquad (5)$$

where $x=X/w_0$ and $y=Y/w_0$ are the dimensionless transverse coordinates, $z=Z/L_{dif}$ is the dimensionless longitudinal coordinate, the parameter w_0 is the soliton width, $L_{dif} = \beta_0 w_0^2$ is the diffraction length, $\beta_0 = 2\pi n_0/\lambda$ is the propagation constant, n_0 is the linear refractive index, and λ is the optical wavelength in a vacuum. The nonlinear term is written in a generalized form. In contrast to temporal soliton propagation in optical fibers, where the GVD is balanced by a weak Kerr nonlinearity, spatial

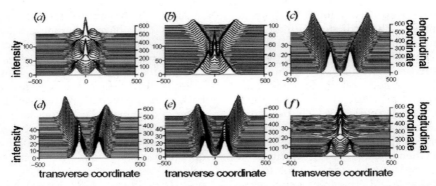

Figure 6: The interactions between two solitons for the following cases: (a) parallel input trajectories, in-phase Kerr solitons; (b) converging input trajectories, in-phase Kerr solitons; (c) parallel input trajectories, out-of-phase Kerr solitons; (d) parallel input trajectories, $\pi/2$ relative phase between Kerr solitons; (e) parallel input trajectories, $3\pi/2$ relative phase between Kerr solitons; and (f) fusion of two solitons input on parallel trajectories in saturating nonlinear media for "small" input separations (Stegeman and Segev 1999)

solitons rely on much larger nonlinearities that counteract the diffraction-induced beam spreading. Such nonlinearities often saturate at high intensities and generally may be not of a Kerr type (Akhmediev and Ankiewicz 1997; Akhmediev 1998; Biswas 2003; Konar and Biswas 2004). Depending on the particular form of the nonlinear (third) term in Equation (5), the solitary wave solutions can possess very different properties, such as the fusion of two solitons in a saturating nonlinear medium.

Stability is one of the most important properties of solitons or solitary waves because only stable or weakly unstable beams can be observed experimentally (Vakhitov and Kolokolov 1973; Kolokolov 1974; Kuznetsov, Rubenchik, and Zakharov 1986; Soto-Crespo et al. 1991; Soto-Crespo, Wright, and Akhmediev 1992; Atai, Chen, and Soto-Crespo 1994; Skryabin and Firth 1998). Self-trapped beams may be unstable in bulk media and may undergo catastrophic self-focusing. However, they are stable when diffraction is limited to one spatial dimension, such as in planar optical waveguides. In such a waveguide, the optical beam forms a one-dimensional spatial soliton in one transverse direction and is confined by the waveguide in another transverse direction. In this case, one of the second-order x or y derivatives in Equation (5) is absent. In the case of Kerr nonlinearity, the spatial soliton is described by the NLS that, from a mathematical standpoint, is identical to Equation (1) for $s = -1$. This observation is known as a *spatio-temporal analogy* (Akhmanov, Vysloukh, and Chirkin 1992), meaning that the propagation coordinate z is treated as the evolution variable and the spatial beam profile along the transverse direction in waveguides is similar to the temporal pulse profile in optical fibers.

Soliton interactions are the most fascinating features of solitons. Different examples of spatial soliton interactions, including in-phase and out-of-phase Kerr soliton collisions and the solitons in a saturating nonlinear medium, are shown in Figure 6. Two examples of more exotic three-dimensional soliton interactions, such as soliton spiraling and soliton fission, are shown in Figure 7 (Buryak and Steblina 1999).

Scalar solitons (or solitons that have only one field component) of an integrable system discussed so far,

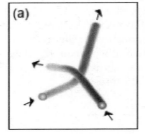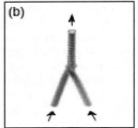

Figure 7: (a) Soliton spiraling and (b) soliton fission (Buryak and Steblina 1999)

such as those in Kerr nonlinear media, remain unaltered during collisions with other solitons, except for a phase shift or a lateral displacement in the case of spatial solitons. This phase shift depends only on the soliton power and velocity, which are conserved quantities. This result can be understood by considering a soliton as a guided mode of its own induced waveguide or induced potential (Snyder et al. 1991). For a Kerr soliton, the induced potential is reflectionless, so scalar Kerr solitons colliding at a nonzero angle cannot exchange energy. Therefore, when two scalar soliton collisions occur sequentially, the outcome of the first collision does not affect the second collision. This is an important property of solitons, demonstrating their robustness, which is important for communication systems applications (Hasegawa and Tappert 1973). However, energy transfer between solitons is essential in applications such as optical computing.

Several approaches to enabling such energy-transferring collisions have been discussed in the literature. In one approach, collisions of solitons in nonintegrable systems, such as spatial solitons in saturable nonlinearities (Stegeman and Segev 1999), can be employed. However, it is problematical to define a "state" in such systems because the number of solitons is not always conserved. Therefore, it would be useful to find a way to transfer information between solitons in an integrable system. Vector solitons consisting of more than one field component in the integrable Manakov system

(Manakov 1974) are good candidates for this application. These solitons can be described by a system of two coupled NLS equations:

$$i\frac{\partial u}{\partial z} + \frac{1}{2}\frac{\partial^2 u}{\partial x^2} + \left(|u|^2 + |v|^2\right)u = 0$$

$$i\frac{\partial v}{\partial z} + \frac{1}{2}\frac{\partial^2 v}{\partial x^2} + \left(|u|^2 + |v|^2\right)v = 0$$

(6)

Both temporal and spatial Manakov solitons have also been described and demonstrated experimentally (Kang, Stegeman, and Aitchison 1996; Chen et al. 1996; Yang 2002). The field components that compose the vector solitons exchange energy upon collision, and at the same time they retain all other conserved quantities of integrable systems. This energy-exchange effect has been proposed as a mechanism for performing computation through interaction of vector solitons (Radhakrishnan, Lakshmanan, and Hietarinta 1997; Jakubowski, Steiglitz, and Squier 1998).

Experimental Progress

The first demonstration of spatial solitons in an atomic vapor was reported by Bjorkholm and Ashkin (1974). Some ten years later, bright spatial solitons were observed in multimode CS_2 waveguides and single-mode glass waveguides (Barthelemy, Maneuf, and Froehly 1985). However, rapid progress in the field of spatial solitons occurred only since the 1990s, stimulated by the availability of appropriate nonlinear materials. One-dimensional bright solitons were subsequently demonstrated in glass (Snyder and Sheppard 1993), semiconductors (Khitrova et al. 1993), and polymers (Torruellas, Lawrence, and Stegeman 1996).

One of the most important issues for the practical realization of solitons is the optical power requirements. Photorefractive materials provide an ideal environment for the propagation of spatial solitons. In a photorefractive medium, the focusing effect, which is necessary for the soliton formation, is produced by an internal nonlocal space-charge DC field as opposed to the local

intensity-dependent Kerr effect. The degree of self-focusing can be controlled by an applied DC voltage across the photorefractive crystal. Because of an especially strong nonlinearity in photorefractive materials, a self-trapping of an optical beam was observed at microwatt power levels (Duree et al. 1993). Figure 8 shows an example of spatial soliton formation in a strontium barium niobate photorefractive crystal (Shih et al. 1995).

As will be discussed in "Applications of Solitons" below, soliton interactions form a basis for various applications of solitons for information transfer, ultrafast switching and processing, optical computing, and logic operations. The first experimental demonstration of spatial soliton interactions was performed by Aitchison et al. (1991). The experimental observations of the trapping of two spatial solitons of the same wavelength but with slightly different propagation directions and the nonlinear interaction between two fundamental spatial solitons with a $\pi/2$ phase difference in carbon disulfide were demonstrated by Shalaby et al. (Shalaby and Barthelemy 1991; Shalaby et al. 1992). It was shown that by adjustment of the phase shift between the two overlapped solitons, it was possible to switch the major part of the input energy to one soliton or the other.

Manakov solitons were first demonstrated in aluminum gallium arsenide (AlGaAs) waveguides in 1996 (Kang et al. 1996). For electric field vectors polarized parallel to the AlGaAs 110 and 001 crystalline axes, it turns out that the self- and cross-phase modulation terms are approximately equal, thus satisfying the requirement for Manakov solitons.

Spatio-Temporal Solitons
Theoretical Background
Spatio-temporal solitons, which are sometimes called *light bullets* (Silberberg 1990), have attracted a lot of attention in the past several years (Malomed et al. 2005; Mihalache et al. 2005). They represent objects that are localized in all of the transverse dimensions of space, as well as in time. Spatio-temporal solitons result from the simultaneous balance of diffraction and dispersion by self-focusing and

Figure 8: Photograph of (top) a 10-μm-wide spatial soliton propagating in a strontium barium niobate photorefractive crystal and (bottom) the same beam diffracting naturally in the linear regime (Shih et al. 1995)

Figure 9: Schematic of the spatiotemporal soliton formation resulting from the simultaneous balance of diffraction and dispersion by nonlinear self-focusing (Malomed et al. 2005)

nonlinear phase modulation, respectively. The schematic of the spatio-temporal soliton formation is shown in Figure 9. Although it is natural to assume that the conditions necessary for the formation of low-dimensional spatial or temporal solitons can be readily extended to the spatio-temporal case, that was not found to be true.

Spatio-temporal solitons are described by the NLS, taking into account the dispersive and diffractive effects:

$$i\frac{\partial u}{\partial z} + \frac{1}{2}\left(\frac{\partial^2 u}{\partial x^2} + \frac{\partial^2 u}{\partial y^2}\right) - \frac{s}{2}\frac{\partial^2 u}{\partial \tau^2} \pm f\left(|u|^2\right)u = 0 \qquad (7)$$

The stability analysis of spatial and spatio-temporal solitons in the case of Kerr nonlinearity shows that only in a one-dimensional case is the shape-preserving solution stable. In two- and three-dimensional cases, the phenomenon of collapse was theoretically predicted (Silberberg 1990). The spatio-temporal collapse is an instability process in which small fluctuations in soliton parameters grow with propagation length. As a result, when the pulse energy exceeds some critical value, the size of the beam decreases both spatially and temporally and the intensity becomes infinitely large at a finite distance. Although the collapse was predicted for a somewhat idealized system in which the effects such as saturation of the Kerr nonlinearity or nonlinear absorption were neglected, in reality these effects could prevent the collapse. Indeed, as it has been first discussed in the original paper by Silberberg (1990), saturation of Kerr nonlinearity can halt the collapse and lead to formation of the aforementioned light bullets (Edmundson and Enns 1993; Enns and Edmundson 1993; Akhmediev and Soto-Crespo 1993; Hayata and Koshiba 1993; Chen and Atai 1995; Edmundson and Enns 1995).

Experimental Progress

The following conditions should be satisfied simultaneously in order to generate a stable, localized spatio-temporal soliton in a homogeneous medium: (1) self-focusing nonlinearity, (2) anomalous group velocity dispersion, and (3) one or more collapse-preventing mechanisms. Eisenberg et al. (2001) demonstrated stable spatio-temporal focusing in a planar waveguide configuration under conditions of the self-focusing Kerr nonlinearity and anomalous group velocity. However, the spatio-temporal soliton as such was not observed. The same mechanisms that prevented collapse, multiphoton ionization, and Raman scattering in this case, eventually

reduced the intensity and caused the pulse to broaden in space and time. Although it should be mentioned that besides the dissipative collapse-preventing processes, there are several mechanisms that conserve energy, such as nonparaxiality and higher-order dispersion, that may lead to new forms of soliton-like propagation (Fibich, Ilan, and Papanicolaou 2002). Soliton-like propagation and beam self-channeling have been observed under conditions of normal group velocity dispersion (Koprinkov et al. 2000; Gaeta and Wise 2001), although the pulses were not temporal solitons.

Although in cubic nonlinear media the formation of stable solitons may be precluded because of the lack of collapse-preventing mechanisms, stable spatio-temporal solitons have been predicted in quadratic nonlinear media with a saturable self-focusing nonlinearity (Karamzin and Sukhorukov 1976; Kanashov and Rubenchik 1981; Liu, Qian, and Wise 1999; Liu, Beckwitt, and Wise 2000). An important step toward the formation of spatio-temporal solitons in quadratic media has been the demonstration of solitons in one transverse spatial dimension and time (Liu, Qian, and Wise 1999; Liu, Beckwitt, and Wise 2000). These pulses were the first experimentally observed optical spatio-temporal solitons, as well as the first temporal solitons directly observed in quadratic media (lithium iodate and barium metaborate) over several characteristic lengths. In these experiments, the effective third-order nonlinearity was produced by the cascade $\chi^{(2)}{:}\chi^{(2)}$ process. The angular dispersion was used to create large and negative group velocity dispersion. The input beam (pulse) size was 50 μm (100 fs). For comparison, if the propagation were linear, the beam (pulse) would have broadened to 300 μm (500 fs) because of diffraction (group velocity dispersion).

Spatio-temporal solitons have an enormous potential for a variety of applications. For instance, a spatio-temporal soliton-based ultrafast logic gate with switching speeds of several Terahertz has been predicted (McLeod, Wagner, and Blair 1995). Various alternative approaches for the realization of spatio-temporal solitons are currently under investigation, including the generation of so-called X-waves, which are stationary and slowly decaying Bessel function–like spatio-temporal beams (Jedrkiewicz et al. 2003; Conti et al. 2003; Di Trapani et al. 2003), and spatio-temporal soliton formation in Bragg gratings formed in a quadratic nonlinear crystal (He and Drummond 1997). Recently, fundamentally new features of spatio-temporal soliton formation were investigated numerically in metamaterials having a negative linear index of refraction (Zharova et al. 2005).

Discrete Optical Solitons
Theoretical Background

Discrete optical solitons are collective excitations of coupled, periodic, nonlinear lattices (Stegeman and Segev 1999; Christodoulides 2003; Buljan et al. 2004; Kartashov, Vysloukh, and Torner 2004; Kartashov et al. 2004; Kartashov, Torner, and Vysloukh 2004; Neshev et al. 2004; Yang et al. 2004a, 2004b; Xu, Kartashov, and Torner 2005; Kevrekidis, Susanto, and Chen 2006; Pezer and Buljan 2006). They are self-localized wave packets, the energy of which resides primarily in distinct waveguide array sites. They are generated through a balance of discrete diffraction and material nonlinearity. Arrays made from materials with intensity-dependent Kerr, quadratic, or photorefractive nonlinearities have been shown to support such discrete localized states (Eisenberg et al. 1998; Pertsch et al. 2002; Fleischer et al. 2003).

Discrete optical solitons possess many properties that are similar to conventional solitons. However, they do not have the translation and rotation invariance typical of their conventional counterparts. As a result, arrays of waveguides support both stable and unstable soliton solutions. The stable states correspond to solitons that are centered on a waveguide and propagate along the waveguide direction. The solitons that are symmetrically centered between two neighboring waveguides are unstable (Morandotti et al. 2003).

Several theoretical approaches have been proposed to study linear and nonlinear propagation in the waveguide arrays. If the waveguides forming the array are sufficiently separated, then a coupled-mode theory or a tight-binding approximation is typically used to study the propagation effects of the soliton within the array (Ashcroft and Mermin 1976). The main assumption of this approach is that the only nearest-neighbor interaction resulting from the evanescently coupled guided modes is taken into account. For ideal, infinite-size, lossless arrays employing the Kerr nonlinearity, the normalized mode amplitude u_n satisfies the discrete nonlinear Schrödinger equation (Christodoulides and Joseph 1988):

$$i\frac{du_n}{dz} + \beta u_n + \kappa\left(u_{n+1} + u_{n-1}\right) + \left|u_n\right|^2 u_n = 0 \qquad (8)$$

where β is the linear propagation constant and κ is the coupling coefficient. No second-order derivatives are included because all dispersive and diffractive effects in each waveguide are usually neglected. It has been shown numerically that at high enough powers, introducing a field distribution to the array such as (Christodoulides and Joseph 1988; Darmanyan et al. 1998)

$$u_n(z) = u_0 sec\, h\left(x_n\right)\exp\left(i\beta z + 2i\kappa z\right) \qquad (9)$$

where $x_n = x_n/x_0$ is the normalized transverse coordinate corresponding to the location of the nth waveguide, $x_n = nd$, and X_0 is the characteristic width, results in a localized propagating distribution. Note that even though no diffraction occurs in each individual waveguide, an input beam spreads over the whole array because of the coupling among the waveguides. This phenomenon is called a *discrete diffraction*.

More recently, array waveguides were also analyzed using Floquet-Bloch theory (Russell 1986). Band theory provides a more formal description not only of the individual waveguides' propagation modes but also of the modes that propagate between waveguides. In this approach, linear optical modes are described using Floquet-Bloch theory, with the corresponding diffraction relation $[k_z = k_z(k_x, k_y)]$ characterized by bands of allowed propagation constants separated by forbidden gaps.

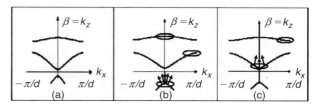

Figure 10: Linear band structure and diffraction properties of a one-dimensional waveguide array (a) consisting of bands of allowed propagation constants separated by forbidden gaps; (b) modes in convex regions experience normal diffraction; (c) modes in concave regions experience anomalous diffraction (Fleischer et al. 2005)

A typical band structure in k-space for a linear one-dimensional waveguide array is shown in Figure 10a (Fleischer et al. 2005). Each mode of the system is an extended Bloch wave with its own propagation constant and direction. During linear propagation, each mode evolves independently of the others. Any wave packet exciting the array can be decomposed in these Bloch modes; because the modes remain the same but attain different relative phases during propagation, the wave packet may have a significantly different profile at the output of the array. Figures 10b and 10c illustrate how the band geometry influences the dynamics of the wave packet. In regions of convex band curvature, the central mode propagates faster than its neighbors, and the beam experiences normal diffraction analogous to that in homogeneous media. By contrast, a group of modes in concave regions of band curvature will diffract anomalously. It is noteworthy that there is an inflection point in each band, implying that wave packets propagating in this direction experience no (lowest-order) diffraction.

When the waveguide array is also nonlinear, propagation dynamics can be further modified. If the beam is narrow, the light modifies the refractive index locally, thus inducing a defect in the periodic structure of the lattice. Such a defect has localized modes, the propagation constant of which now lies outside of the linear transmission band—that is, in a gap. When these nonlinear modes induce the defect and populate it self-consistently, the wave packet becomes self-localized, and its diffractive broadening is eliminated, forming a discrete soliton (Fleischer et al. 2005).

Finally, although discrete solitons were mostly studied through propagation of coherent light beams in nonlinear photonic lattices, the existence of lattice solitons made of incoherent white light originating from an ordinary incandescent light bulb have recently been predicted (Pezer and Buljan 2006).

Experimental Progress

Discrete solitons were first observed experimentally in the AlGaAs nonlinear waveguide array of forty-one waveguides (Eisenberg et al. 1998). Light was coupled to the central waveguide. At low power, the propagating field was spread as it coupled to more waveguides. When sufficient power was injected, the field was localized close to the input waveguides as shown in Figure 11. Figure 12 shows a comparison of experimental measurements

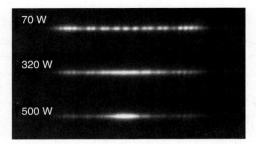

Figure 11: Intensity images at the output of a Kerr AlGaAs array with a waveguide spacing of D = 8μm and operated at 1.53 μm observed at various power levels. At low powers (70 W), the beam discretely diffracts, whereas a discrete soliton forms at 500 W (Eisenberg et al. 1998)

(solid line) with the results of numerical simulations (vertical straight lines) obtained by integrating the discrete NLS equation. It is noteworthy that if an input beam with a phase tilt is launched into several waveguides, the discrete soliton propagates across the waveguides. Also, even without the initial phase tilt, a discrete soliton can be shifted significantly by a small change in the position of the input beam (Morandotti et al. 1999). Several phenomena unique to discrete solitons were demonstrated experimentally. These include power-dependent steering (Eisenberg et al. 1998; Morandotti et al. 1999) and diffraction management (Eisenberg et al. 2000).

The possibility of manipulating discrete soliton motion using engineered structural defects in waveguide arrays was predicted theoretically and demonstrated

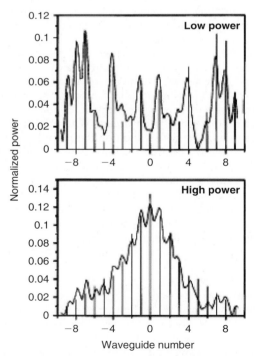

Figure 12: The comparison of experimental and theoretical results. Experimental results are represented by a solid curve and numerical results are shown as vertical lines (Eisenberg et al. 1998)

experimentally in arrays of AlGaAs waveguides (Morandotti et al. 2003). It was shown that the dynamics of a discrete soliton are similar to those of a classical particle in the presence of a potential introduced by the defect. An attractive defect, corresponding to a locally higher effective index, is equivalent to an interaction of the soliton with a potential well. In this case, the soliton will be totally transmitted through the defect at high transverse velocities (or input angle) or reflected from it while it excites a linear guided mode at the defect site at low velocities. At intermediate velocities, the soliton may be trapped by the defect, which induces an attractive potential for the soliton. A repulsive defect, corresponding to a local decrease in the effective index, is equivalent to the interaction of the soliton with a potential barrier. At small transverse velocities, the soliton may be totally reflected from the defect site, whereas at high velocities it is totally transmitted. At intermediate velocities, the soliton exhibits an inelastic collision with the defect and is partially transmitted and partially reflected. Trapping of the soliton to the defect site occurs only at a specific velocity. However, it is highly unstable because of the repulsive nature of the potential barrier.

Experimental observation of two-dimensional discrete or *lattice* solitons was first reported by Fleischer et al. (2003). A two-dimensional photonic lattice was created in real time using an optical induction technique, which is based on the interference of two or more plane waves in a photosensitive material. Then a probe beam was launched into the periodic waveguide array, where it experienced discrete diffraction and, at a sufficiently high nonlinearity, formed a lattice soliton.

Recently, the first observation of discrete optical surface solitons at the interface between a nonlinear self-focusing AlGaAs waveguide lattice and a continuous medium was reported by Suntsov et al. (2006). This approach is attractive because the power response is determined by two easily controllable fabrication parameters: the difference between the propagation constants of the channels and the continuous region, and the coupling strength between adjacent waveguides.

Incoherent Spatial Solitons

Theoretical Background

In most cases, an optical pulse or a wave packet forming a soliton is assumed to be coherent. However, solitons can also be launched using incoherent beams such as incandescent light bulbs (Mitchell et al. 1996; Mitchell and Segev 1997). An *incoherent spatial soliton* is a wave packet self-trapped to form a localized nondiffracting beam in a nonlinear medium with noninstantaneous nonlinearity. The three main requirements for an incoherent soliton to form are: (1) a noninstantaneous nonlinearity, which has a response time much longer than the duration of the phase fluctuations across the beam; (2) the multimode beam should be able to induce a multimode waveguide; and (3) self-consistency (i.e., the multimode beam must be able to guide itself in its own induced waveguide).

Several different approaches have been used to investigate incoherent solitons theoretically. The *coherent-density approach*, in which a partially coherent beam is represented as a superposition of mutually incoherent components, was developed by Christodoulides and co-workers (Christodoulides, Coskun, and Joseph 1997; Christodoulides et al. 1997). In another approach, optical beams in nonlinear media are described in terms of a self-induced multimode waveguide. Stationary soliton propagation is governed by a proper combination of various mutually incoherent linear modes of the self-induced waveguide. This approach has provided both symmetric and asymmetric solutions (Christodoulides et al. 1998; Akhmediev, Królikowski, and Snyder 1998; Carvalho et al. 1999; Litchinitser et al. 1999). An example of a four-mode asymmetric solution is shown in Figure 13.

Until recently, most of the theoretical studies of incoherent solitons use the so-called mean-field approximation (Christodoulides et al. 1997; Mitchell et al. 1997; Shkhunov and Anderson 1998). The mean-field approximation can be justified when the response time of a nonlinear medium is much longer than the correlation time associated with phase fluctuations across the wave front. Within the framework of the mean-field approximation, the nonlinear refractive index of the medium is assumed to depend only on the average intensity of an optical beam. However the mean-field theory does not take into account intensity fluctuations of the source and their effects on generating such solitons. More recently, a general theory of partially coherent optical solitons in slow-responding nonlinear media that takes into account these intensity fluctuations was formulated (Ponomarenko, Litchinitser, and Agrawal 2004). When the source is laser-like with negligible intensity fluctuations, the new theory reduces to the previously reported mean-field theory of partially coherent solitons. However when such fluctuations are significant, the new theory shows that the properties of partially coherent solitons in saturable nonlinear media can be qualitatively different from those predicted by the mean-field theory. Experimental studies verifying the predictions of these two models, however, are not yet available.

Finally, a novel class of incoherent random-phase spatial solitons in fast instantaneous nonlocal nonlinear media has been recently predicted by Cohen et al. (2006). The key mechanism responsible for self-trapping of such incoherent wave packets is played by the nonlocal rather than the traditional noninstantaneous nature of the nonlinearity.

Experimental Progress

Temporally incoherent solitons were discussed by Hasegawa (1975, 1977, 1980) for both waves in bulk dispersive media and nonlinear pulses in multimode fibers. In optical fibers, the wave packet can propagate as a single stationary pulse when the intermodal dispersion is balanced by the cubic nonlinearity. However, intermodal dispersion typically exceeds intramodal dispersion and, as a result, the generation of incoherent solitons in optical fibers requires unrealistically high pulse energies.

The majority of the experimental studies of incoherent solitons were performed in photorefractive materials (Duree et al. 1993; Shih et al. 1995; Iturbe-Castillo et al. 1994; Mamaev et al. 1996; Zozulya et al. 1996). The first demonstration of the self-trapping of a partially spatially incoherent beam was demonstrated by Mitchell et al. (1996) in a biased photorefractive material. A partially incoherent beam was produced by sending an argon laser beam through a rotating diffuser. The self-trapping effect has also been observed using a white light beam that is both spatially and temporally incoherent (Mitchell et al. 1997).

Dark incoherent soliton formation was also demonstrated using a diffuser followed by a mirror with a λ/4 step in the beam center that produced a dark intensity dip on a broad, partially coherent background (Chen et al. 1998).

Most of the studies have focused on the fundamental aspects of incoherent solitons, but these solitons have significant potential for various applications. In particular, the ability of trapping light beams from incoherent sources such as light-emitting diodes suggests possible applications such as optical interconnects and steering light from such sources.

Bragg or Gap Solitons
Theoretical Background

Bragg solitons (also called *gap solitons*) can form in a nonlinear medium with a periodically varying linear refractive index (such as Bragg gratings). Bragg soliton

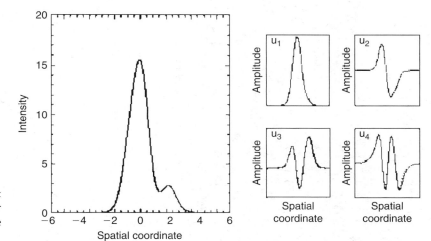

Figure 13: Intensity profile of an asymmetric partially coherent soliton composed of four modes. The inset shows the amplitudes of the constituent modes (Litchinitser et al. 1997)

formation relies on strong GVD of the periodic structure and on a cubic nonlinearity. It is noteworthy that the GVD in fiber Bragg gratings can be as many as six orders of magnitude larger than that in a uniform fiber (Litchinitser, Eggleton, and Patterson 1997). Dispersion is normal on the lower branch of the dispersion relation (ω versus k) and anomalous on the upper branch (Winful 1985; De Sterke and Sipe 1994). A fiber Bragg grating couples forward- and backward-propagating modes and opens up a photonic band gap. While frequencies inside the gap are reflected, those outside the band gap propagate. At low intensities, a transform-limited pulse tuned to a frequency close to the upper edge of the band gap broadens because of the anomalous dispersion introduced by the grating. However in the nonlinear regime, at high intensities *self-phase modulation* (SPM) generates new frequency components that are red-shifted near the leading edge and blue-shifted near the trailing edge. As the upper branch of the dispersion relation exhibits anomalous dispersion, the trailing edge of the pulse travels faster than the leading edge of the pulse. If the incident pulse width is larger than the width of the fundamental soliton, then the pulse undergoes compression initially. In this process, the pulse shape adjusts itself until the SPM and the dispersion compensate each other to maintain a pulse shape, leading to the formation of a Bragg grating soliton.

Bragg solitons were discovered theoretically in the 1980s (Voloshchenko et al. 1981; Winful 1985; Chen 1987a, 1987b; Christodoulides and Joseph 1989; Aceves and Wabnitz 1989) and demonstrated experimentally by Eggleton et al. (1996). Their propagation is described by the *nonlinear coupled mode equations* (NLCMEs). The total optical field inside the grating can be written as the sum of two counterpropagating waves (De Sterke and Sipe 1994):

$$u(z,t) = [u_+(z,t)\exp(ik_B z) + u_-(z,t) \\ \exp(-ik_B z)]\exp(-i\omega_B t) \quad (10)$$

where the slowly varying amplitudes of forward-propagating wave u_+ and backward-propagating wave u_- satisfy the following set of two NLCMEs (De Sterke and Sipe 1994):

$$i\frac{\partial u_+}{\partial z} + i\frac{n}{c}\frac{\partial u_+}{\partial t} + \kappa u_- + \Gamma_s |u_+|^2 u_+ + 2\Gamma_\times |u_-|^2 u_+ = 0,$$

$$-i\frac{\partial u_-}{\partial z} + i\frac{n}{c}\frac{\partial u_-}{\partial t} + \kappa u_+ + \Gamma_s |u_-|^2 u_- + 2\Gamma_\times |u_+|^2 u_- = 0. \quad (11)$$

Here ω_B is Bragg frequency, k_B is the corresponding wave number, n is the average refractive index, c is the speed of light in a vacuum, $\kappa = \pi\Delta n/\lambda_B$ is the coupling coefficient associated with the grating, Δn is linear refractive index modulation depth, λ_B is the Bragg wavelength, and Γ_s and $\Gamma_\times$ are self- and cross-phase modulation parameters, respectively. These equations are nonintegrable, and therefore Bragg solitons are actually shape-preserving solitary waves. Their interactions are similar in many aspects to those of NSL solitons. In fact, in some

limits, the NLCMEs can be reduced to the NLS equation form (De Sterke 1998). A solution of these equations, corresponding to a two-parameter family of Bragg solitons, was found by Aceves and Wabnitz (1989).

Experimental Progress

Experimental demonstration of Bragg solitons in a fiber Bragg grating was first performed by Eggleton et al. (1996). Figure 14a shows measured intensity profiles at the output of fiber Bragg grating for two cases: (1) the optical pulse has its central frequency far from the edge of the band gap (solid line) and (2) the optical pulse has its central frequency close to the band gap (dashed line). In the first case, the grating is transmitting at 100 percent and the dispersion is negligible. As a result, there is no noticeable reshaping in the transmitted pulses. In the second case, the transmission of the grating is still relatively high but the dispersion is extremely strong, resulting in a significant pulse compression. Detailed numerical studies of the evolution of the envelopes of the electric fields along the length of the Bragg grating confirmed predicted soliton-like pulse propagation with

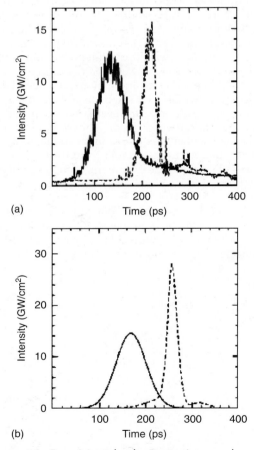

Figure 14: Experimental demonstration and numerical simulations of Bragg solitons. The solid line (broad pulse) corresponds to the launch conditions far from a Bragg resonance when the pulse propagates the fiber without interacting with the grating; the dashed line (narrow pulse) is a Bragg soliton (Eggleton et al. 1996)

an approximately constant shape (Eggleton et al. 1996). Corresponding simulation results are shown in Figure 14b.

High-quality fiber Bragg grating is a mature, relatively inexpensive technology, and its properties—including bandwidth, dispersion, and loss—can be designed and controlled. The peak intensities required for observation of Bragg solitons in silica fiber gratings, however, are typically on the order of 10 GW/cm², which is too high for a majority of practical applications. In addition, from a practical standpoint, soliton formation within the grating band gap is much more challenging to achieve because of the grating's high reflectivity. However, it was recently proposed that stimulated Raman scattering may provide a viable solution: A pump pulse launched far from the stop band can excite a Raman gap soliton that is trapped within the grating (Winful and Perlin 2000). The required peak power can also be reduced by at least two orders of magnitude using highly nonlinear glasses such as chalcogenides (Asobe 1997). Low-power Bragg solitons may have applications in all-optical switching (Taverner et al. 1998) and slow light generation (Mok et al. 2006; Mok, de Sterke, and Eggleton 2006).

APPLICATIONS OF SOLITONS: TOWARD ALL-OPTICAL COMPUTER NETWORKS

As the information transmission speed increases beyond 100 Gbit/s, optical components are likely to replace their electronic counterparts. The ultimate goal of high-speed photonics is a realization of all-optical technology. This section discusses several applications of the unique properties of optical solitons for the realization of all-optical logic elements, interconnects, and soliton-based computing.

Logic Functions

Recent progress in high bit-rate optical communications stimulated the rapid development of all-optical devices for performing routing, switching, multiplexing and demultiplexing, and coding operations without conversion to the electronic domain. Examples of such devices are the nonlinear optical loop mirror (Doran and Wood 1988), the temporal soliton trapping and dragging gates (Islam 1989, 1990; Soccolich et al. 1992), the asymmetric loop mirror (Eiselt 1992; Sokoloff et al. 1993), and the nonlinear directional coupler (Jensen 1982). However, many of these devices do not possess the important properties of a logic gate, such as signal restoration with gain, and as a result require additional amplification stages to use the output of one gate to drive the input to another.

Restoration of the logic level is necessary because of the degradation of the signal level by attenuation or cumulative noise. For an optical gate, logic-level restoration includes power, beam shape and position, pulse duration and timing, wavelength, polarization, and sometimes phase (Blair and Wagner 2000). Large-signal gain implies that the output of the gate is larger than the input necessary to switch the gate. Without large-signal gain, fan-out, in which the output of one gate directly provides the inputs to subsequent gates, is not possible when gates have identical switching thresholds (assuming all gates).

A class of optical logic devices that is based on temporal (Islam 1990) or spatial (Blair, Wagner, and McLeod 1994) optical solitons and satisfies many of the requirements of a logic gate has been proposed. The use of solitons is essential to these optical logic gates because solitons are not affected by dispersion (or diffraction) but use it to their advantage on propagation over distances much longer than the characteristic linear lengths. In one implementation, the trapping-dragging gates use temporal solitons of the same wavelength and orthogonal polarization (Islam 1989). It was shown that orthogonally polarized solitons can trap one another through cross-phase modulation (Islam 1989; Menyuk 1987, 1988). Using soliton trapping in birefringent optical fibers, an ultrafast, all-optical inverter, exclusive-OR, and AND logic gates have been demonstrated (Islam 1989).

These gates are directly cascadable if a wave plate is used to rotate the output pump polarization to the correct state for an input signal or if the definitions of the pump and signal polarization are alternated, and the gate's operation relies on a resolvable spectral shift of the pump soliton. An unshifted pump passes through a spectral bandpass filter, but a pump that is shifted in the presence of the signal does not. This operation results in amplitude keyed logic, which is compatible with common high-speed optical detectors. These trapping gates typically require sufficiently large fiber birefringence to produce the necessary difference in group velocity between the pulse propagating down the slow axis and the pulse propagating down the fast axis. This difference in group velocities is compensated by optical trapping and results in a spectrally resolved frequency shift. Another requirement is that the pump and signal pulses must also be of nearly the same amplitude so the spectral shift will not be weighted toward one of them. As a result, this gate cannot provide significant large-signal gain. Similar trapping gates based on the optical pulses of different central frequencies have been proposed by Friberg (1991) and Kodama and Hasegawa (1991). Because of the chromatic dispersion of the optical fiber, two pulses of different wavelengths propagate with different group velocities. Therefore, these gates are cascadable only through the use of nonlinear frequency shifters or by alternation of the definitions of pump and signal color at every gate. In addition, an ultrafast, all-optical, three-terminal NOR gate with a gain based on temporal rather than frequency phase shift was demonstrated by Islam (1990).

The temporal soliton dragging logic gate utilizes a dispersive fiber delay line to allow a weak signal soliton to drag a strong pump in time (Islam 1992). Even a small spectral shift of the pump can result in a large time delay. Because the pump is a temporal soliton that does not broaden with propagation distance, a resolvable temporal shift can be achieved by choosing an appropriate length of the delay line. Although operation of the majority of non-soliton-based fiber-switching gates is limited by birefringent walk-off (Morioka, Saruwatari, and Takada 1987), the temporal soliton trapping-dragging gate actually uses birefringent walk-off to induce the switching operation.

The first spatial trapping gate demonstrated experimentally was based on spatial solitons of the same polarization (Shalaby and Barthelemy 1991) (i.e., phase-dependent but propagating at different angles that were not necessarily resolvable). The solitons were attracted to each other because of cross-focusing, which is the spatial analogy to cross-phase modulation, and under certain conditions formed a trapped pair. The direct spatial analogy to the temporal trapping and dragging gates (Islam 1989, 1990) is the interaction between spatial solitons in the orthogonal eigen-polarization states of a uniaxial crystal (Wagner and McLeod 1993).

A three-terminal angular deflection gate (Blair, Wagner, and McLeod 1996; Blair and Wagner 1999, 2000) is illustrated in Figure 15 based on the spatial-soliton dragging and collision interactions. The basic principle of operation of such devices is as follows. An undeflected pump soliton passes through an aperture at the output of the gate to form the high-output state. A tilted signal wave nonlinearly induces an angle change (a phase shift) in a strong pump soliton that results in deflection outside of a spatial aperture and a low output. Because the undeflected pump is passed on to subsequent gates where it acts as a signal input, it is important that it propagates as a spatial soliton. This stable propagation allows for restoration of the logic level through complete signal regeneration and the ability to realize nontrivial logic functions via multistage circuits. Therefore the pump acts as the power supply in traditional transistor logic, and the signal acts as the gate voltage. The angular-deflection geometry is independent of the physical mechanism underlying soliton formation, and the use of a spatial interaction has the advantages of being compatible with a variety of nonlinear materials, having an additional spatial degree of freedom, and having substantially reduced latency. Optical gates based on the spatial-soliton dragging and collision interactions are shown in Figure 15.

One of the most important design parameters for an angular-deflection gate is the optical energy needed to obtain the phase shift or the energy for each gate operation. A practical optical logic gate should require less than 1pJ of energy per logic decision (Blair and Wagner 2000) so

that high bit-rate operation can occur with low average power. Operating energies can be reduced by many orders of magnitude when more highly nonlinear materials are used. Two of the most promising nonlinear materials for practical realization of low energy logic gates are non-resonant AlGaAs at half of the band gap (Villeneuve et al. 1995) and resonant semiconductor gain media (Manning et al. 1997). Gain media are attractive because inverted resonance is used to obtain extremely large effective nonlinearity with amplification, although the material response time is increased. Measurements have shown that the response time can be of the order of picoseconds (Hall et al. 1994; Manning and Sherlock 1995), which may be short enough for implementation in 100-Gbit/s systems.

Other proposed approaches use the incoherent interactions of spatial solitons in a multilayered structure consisting of layers of different Kerr media, as well as spatio-temporal soliton-based gates with switching speeds of several Terahertz (McLeod, Wagner, and Blair 1995). The angular steering of spatial solitons' light in nematic liquid crystals was demonstrated and investigated for all-optical switching and logic gates applications (Assanto, Peccianti, and Conti 2003; Peccianti et al. 2004). Figure 16 shows the images of the spatial solitons at different bias voltages and the steering angle as a function of biases. Recently, all-optical AND, NOR, XNOR logic gates based on the interaction between spatial solitons and orthogonally propagating beams in azobenzene liquid crystals were demonstrated (Serak et al. 2006). Spatial solitons were excited at microwatt power levels at 632.8 nm, while gating and switching were achieved using milliwatt beams at 409 nm. Deviation and switching of a spatial soliton and the signal it confines at lens-like defects induced by control optical beams via a trans-cis transformation in liquid crystals was demonstrated. For the AND operation, two defects (A and B) play the role of control bits.

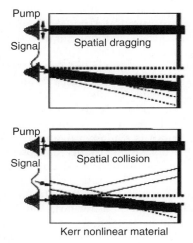

Figure 15: A three-terminal angular-deflection gates based on the spatial-soliton dragging and collision interactions (Blair and Wagner 2000)

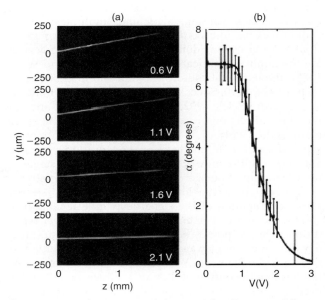

Figure 16: (a) The images of the spatial solitons at different bias voltages and (b) the steering angle as a function of biases (Peccianti et al. 2004)

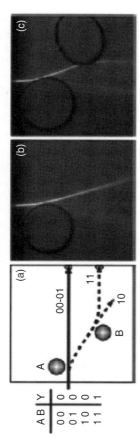

Figure 17: Schematic of the soliton-based AND operation and the experimental realizations that correspond to (A, B, Y) = (100) and (A, B, Y) = (111), respectively (Serak et al. 2006)

The displaced soliton position at the output signifies the logic result. When the soliton is present, the response is 1 (or true), otherwise it is 0 (or false). The corresponding soliton-based scheme is displayed in Figure 17a, with circles representing the isotropic defects induced by external beams onto the liquid crystals. Figure 17b and 17c shows the experimental realizations that correspond to (A, B, Y) = (100) and (A, B, Y) = (111), respectively. The proposed system has a significant potential for realization of complex operations for all-optical computing.

Blocking, Routing, and Time Gating with Discrete Solitons

One of the most important functions of a photonic network is navigating the information from a particular point A to point B. Currently, many of these routing operations also involve opto-electronic conversion. However, opto-electronic conversion will eventually be a limiting factor for the further increase of the speed of information transfer.

The concept of a discrete-soliton optical network was introduced by Christodoulides (Christodoulides and Eugenieva 2001a; Christodoulides and Eugenieva 2001b) and provides a novel platform for all-optical, fast data-processing applications. In such networks, optical beams propagate in a two-dimensional array that behaves as an optical wire. Figure 18 illustrates how discrete

solitons can be routed or blocked at network junctions using vector interactions. Figure 18a shows a Y – 120° intersection involving three array branches. A discrete soliton of the blocking type is positioned at site B at the entrance of the lower branch. A signal soliton travels from left to right, and the two solitons are mutually incoherent. The signal is being routed to the upper branch in an elastic fashion. During this interaction, the blocker always remains in its fixed position. The refractive index around the interaction region is mostly dominated by the high-intensity blocker. The strongly confined discrete soliton blocks the lower pathway and all-optically routes the signal soliton to the upper branch. Without the blocker at the junction, the signal would disintegrate.

Another basic network element is an X junction as shown in Figure 18b. Rerouting at this junction can be accomplished by using two blockers at positions B_1 and B_2, thus terminating two of the three output pathways. These blockers are coherent with each other and are in anti-phase for stability purposes. This process requires both blockers to be present; otherwise, the signal will disintegrate at the junction. Thus, essentially, the X junction functions as an AND logic gate.

In addition, time-gating functions based on discrete soliton propagation have been proposed. Figure 18c shows a T junction with a blocker B placed at the intersection. A signal S, incoherent with respect to the blocker, travels toward the junction on the vertical branch. At the same time, another signal soliton G, coherent with the blocker, moves toward the junction from left to right. The system is designed such that the G signal reaches the junction before the S. Because of the coherent interaction between the blocker and G, the blocker then moves discretely (Bang and Miller 1996) by one slot leftward just in time to open the gate for the signal soliton.

Recently, reconfigurable two-dimensional soliton networks optically induced by arrays of nondiffracting mutually incoherent Bessel beams in Kerr-type nonlinear

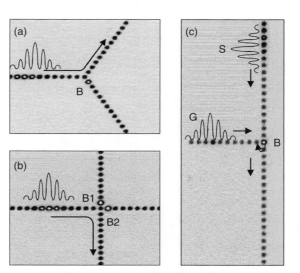

Figure 18: (a) signal router, (b) X junction, and (c) time gating (adapted from Christodoulides and Eugenieva 2001a and Christodoulides and Eugenieva 2001b)

media have been proposed by Xu, Kartashov, and Torner (2005). The dynamics of solitons propagating in such optically induced networks can be used for all-optical manipulation of light similar to that demonstrated in Christodoulides (2001) and Christodoulides and Eugenieva (2001) with additional advantages of the reconfigurability provided by the optical-induction mechanism.

The future success of discrete soliton-based logic schemes relies on the availability of fast-responding highly nonlinear materials. Even though waveguide arrays have thus far been realized in materials that are not ideal in terms their nonlinear properties, research into new materials has the potential to overcome these problems.

Optical Interconnects

Conventionally, when an optical signal reaches a network interconnect, it is converted to an electrical signal, redirected through electrical routers, and then regenerated into an optical signal. Such optical-to-electrical-to-optical conversion often creates significant data traffic jamming. An all-optical interconnect could potentially eliminate this bottleneck by increasing the data-transfer speed, simplifying the network management, and enhancing the interconnection capacity. Both temporal and spatial soliton-based interconnects have been proposed.

Spatial-Soliton Approach

In parallel to rapid progress in the development of temporal soliton-based fiber interconnects, spatial solitons were shown to be promising candidates for the design of dense, reconfigurable, self-induced optical-waveguide interconnects. On one hand, a soliton can effectively induce its own waveguide and guide another beam of a different wavelength or polarization through the effect of induced cross-phase modulation. Such waveguides have several advantages over conventional "fixed" waveguides. They are readily self-reconfigurable, forming a basis for the realization of virtual circuitry. On the other hand, soliton-induced waveguides or waveguide-based circuits can be written in photosensitive materials in which one light-written structure can be erased and replaced by another. The advantage

of using solitons for building optical interconnects is their nondiffracting nature and hence high-packing density for all-optical interconnects. Friedrich et al. (1998) experimentally demonstrated spatial soliton deflection in AlGaAs slab waveguides by an electronically induced prism. It was also shown that a weak signal beam can be guided and steered by a soliton, thus demonstrating the feasibility of a dynamically reconfigurable optical interconnect.

Temporal Soliton-Based Approach

In this approach, a so-called fiber-optic ribbon approach, N parallel bits are sent through corresponding N parallel fibers in a ribbon format, as shown in Figure 19a. This scheme is often called the *space-division-multiplexing* (SDM) scheme. The main drawback of the SDM scheme is that it is extremely difficult to maintain the time alignment of the parallel pulses. This is mainly because, in practice, it is not easy to fabricate identical uniform fibers. An alternative approach based on *bit-parallel-wavelength* (BPW) single-fiber optical links was proposed (Bergman, Mendez, and Lome 1996; Bergman, Morookian, and Yeh 1998; Ostrovskaya et al. 2002). In a BPW scheme, all N bits are wavelength multiplexed and transmitted by the time-aligned solitons through one single-mode optical fiber, as shown in Figure 19b. For bit-parallel optical fiber transmission, the most important issue is maintaining the alignment of pulses corresponding to parallel bits of the same word. The pulse alignment is controlled by employing the pulse-shepherding effect (Yeh and Bergman 1996), which originates from the interaction of co-propagating pulses through the nonlinear *cross-phase modulation* (XPM) effect. In bit-parallel transmission, a strong shepherding pulse traps and constrains a sequence of co-propagating weak pulses to their time slot. It is noteworthy that the XPM effect strongly degrades the pulses in the conventional WDM transmission systems, as discussed previously, and thus should be avoided by all possible means. Ostrovskaya et al. (2002) have shown that because of the XPM interaction of pulses transmitted through the same fiber, they can be treated as fundamental modes of different colors trapped and guided

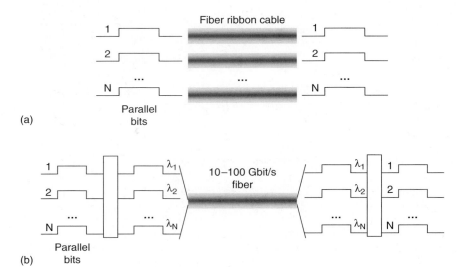

Figure 19: Schematics of the parallel bits transmission through (a) a fiber ribbon link and (b) a bit-parallel single fiber link (Ostrovskaya et al. 2002)

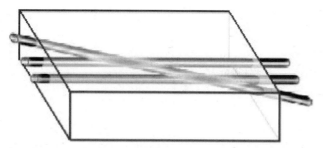

Figure 20: A schematic of a soliton computing device based on the interactions of spatial solitons in a nonlinear medium (Rand, Steiglitz, and Prucnal 2005)

by an effective waveguide induced by the strong shepherd pulse. As a result, the shepherding pulse and all other (weaker) pulses form a new entity: a multicomponent soliton pulse. The BPW soliton propagates in the fiber, preserving the time alignment of its constituents, and therefore enables multichannel bit-parallel transmission.

Optical Computing

A schematic for a soliton computing device is shown in Figure 20 (Rand, Steiglitz, and Prucnal 2005). Input solitons enter on the left and exit on the right. The computation occurs through collisions, and the configuration of input beams determines the operation performed. Unlike typical existing computer architectures in which the data travel between logical elements that are fixed spatially through fabrication on a silicon wafer, the "dynamic" computer architecture in Figure 20 operates without any fixed gates or wires. This scheme is referred to as *nonlithographic* because there is no architecture imprinted on the medium.

To use soliton interactions for all-optical computations, the appropriate soliton parameters responsible for carrying and transferring the information need to be defined. Recall that, for scalar solitons, the only appropriate parameters that are affected by collisions are the carrier phase and position. Unfortunately, the changes in these parameters do not affect the results of subsequent collisions and therefore cannot be used for transferring the information (Jakubowski, Steiglitz, and Squier 2002). On the other hand, Manakov solitons (Manakov 1974) possess extremely rich collisional properties (Radhakrishnan, Lakshmanan, and Hietarinta 1997) and are capable of transferring information via changes in a complex-valued polarization state (Jakubowski, Steiglitz, and Squier 1998). Energy-exchanging interactions between vector solitons were demonstrated experimentally. It was shown that in a sequence of two collisions the outcome of the first collision directly affects the outcome of the second.

Manakov solitons were proposed and realized in various materials, including photorefractive crystals (Chen et al. 1996; Christodoulides et al. 1996; Shih and Segev 1996; Anastassiou et al. 1999, 2001), semiconductor waveguides (Kang, Stegeman, and Aitchison 1996), quadratic media (Steblina et al. 2000), and optical fibers (Menyuk 1989).

CONCLUSION

We have reviewed the basic properties, experimental realizations, and potential applications of several classes of solitons, including: temporal solitons in uniform optical fibers and fiber Bragg gratings; spatial solitons, including coherent and incoherent ones; spatio-temporal solitons; and discrete solitons in waveguide arrays. Although several potential applications of solitons for time gating and various logic functions, optical interconnects, and optical computing have been already demonstrated in laboratory experiments, several practical issues need to be solved before their full potential can be utilized in real-world applications. Further rapid progress is expected in developing new materials with superior properties for the optimization of soliton-based applications.

Finally, although not described in details in this review, yet other kinds of self-trapped beams, optical vortices, and vortex solitons have been recently proposed as promising candidates for such applications as optical storage, distribution, and processing (Desyatnikov, Torner, and Kivshar 2005). Optical vortices have been suggested for designing novel interconnects (Scheuer and Orenstein 1999), free-space communication links (Gibson et al. 2004; Bouchal 2004), and self-induced waveguides (Truscott et al. 1999; Law, Zhang, and Swartzlander 2000; Carlsson et al. 2000; Salguerro et al. 2004).

In summary, optical solitons are an exciting physical phenomenon that offers significant potential for information transfer and optical computing that is likely to be realized in the coming years.

GLOSSARY

Dispersion: The phenomenon that takes place when different components of the signal travel at different velocities in the medium.

Dispersion Management: A technique to cope with the dispersion introduced by the optical fiber.

Erbium-Doped Fiber Amplifier (EDFA): An optical fiber doped with the rare earth element erbium, which can amplify light at 1530 nm to 1610 nm when pumped by an external light source.

Fiber Bragg Grating: A small section of fiber that has been modified to create periodic changes in the index of refraction. Depending on the period (spacing between the index changes), a certain wavelength of light (the Bragg resonance wavelength) is reflected back while all other wavelengths pass through.

Interconnect: An electrical or optical link (or cable) connecting two devices.

Jitter: The deviation in optical pulse parameters, including amplitude, phase timing, and width.

Light Bullet: An optical wave packet confined in three spatial dimensions owing to the combination of self-focusing, diffraction, and dispersion.

Logic Gate: A digital circuit that results in an output whose state (0 or 1) depends on the specific combination of the states of input signals.

Network: A system of cables or other connections that links many terminals or devices, all of which can communicate with each other through the system.

Nonlinear optics: A branch of optics that studies the interaction of intense light with matter. Nonlinear optical phenomena occur when the response of a system to an applied optical field is a nonlinear function of the strength of the optical field.

Optical Computing: The technology that uses optical instead of electronic signals to perform computations.

Optical Demultiplexer: A device that separates two or more optical wavelengths from a single input or fiber into multiple fibers or detectors.

Optical Fiber: A glass or plastic cylindrical waveguide that guides light along its axis.

Optical Multiplexer: A device that combines two or more optical wavelengths into a single output or fiber.

Optical Switch: An optical device that routes an incoming wavelength to a variety of physical output ports.

Raman Amplifier: A fiber that transfers energy from a strong pump beam to amplify a weaker signal at a longer wavelength using stimulated Raman scattering.

Soliton: A solitary wave that asymptotically preserves its shape and velocity upon nonlinear interaction with other solitary waves or, more generally, with another (arbitrary) localized disturbance.

Spatio-Temporal Collapse: An instability process in which small fluctuations in soliton parameters grow with propagation length.

Wavelength-Division Multiplexing (WDM): A fiber-optic transmission technique that increases the capacity of a single fiber by sending independent bit streams at multiple wavelengths.

CROSS REFERENCES

See *Frequency and Phase Modulation; Optical Fiber Communications; Optical Switching Techniques in WDM Optical Networks; Optical Transmitters, Receivers, and Noise.*

REFERENCES

Ablowitz, M. J., and G. Biondini. 1998. Multiscale pulse dynamics in communication systems with strong dispersion management. *Optics Letters*, 23: 1668–70.

Ablowitz, M. J., and L. A. Ostrovsky. 2000. Optical solitons: Perspectives and applications. *Chaos: An Interdisciplinary Journal of Nonlinear Science*, 10: 471–4.

Ablowitz, M. J., and P. A. Clarkson. 1991. *Solitons, nonlinear evolution equations, and inverse scattering*. London Mathematical Society Lecture Note Series, Vol. 149. Cambridge, UK: Cambridge University Press.

Ablowitz, M. J., D. J. Kaup, A. C Newell, and H. Segur. 1974. The inverse scattering transform: Fourier analysis for nonlinear problems. *Studies in Applied Mathematics*, 53: 249–315.

Ablowitz, M. J., and H. Segur. 1981. *Solitons and the inverse scattering transform*. Philadelphia: SIAM.

Aceves, A. B., and S. Wabnitz. 1989. Self-induced transparency solitons in nonlinear refractive periodic media. *Physics Letters*, 141: 37–42.

Agrawal, G. P. 1997. *Fiber-optic communication systems*. New York: John Wiley & Sons.

———. 2001. *Nonlinear fiber optics*. 3rd ed. San Diego: Academic Press.

———. 2005. *Lightwave technology: Telecommunication systems*. New York: John Wiley & Sons.

Aitchison, J. S., A. M. Weiner, Y. Silberberg, D. E. Leaird, M. K. Oliver, J. L. Jackel, and P. W. E. Smith 1991. Experimental observation of spatial soliton interactions. *Optics Letters*, 16: 15–7.

Akhmanov, S. A., V. A. Vysloukh, and A. S. Chirkin. 1992. *Optics of femtosecond laser pulses*. New York: AIP.

Akhmediev, N. N. 1998. Spatial solitons in Kerr and Kerr-like media. *Optical and Quantum Electronics*, 30, 535–69.

Akhmediev, N. N., and A. Ankiewicz. 1997. *Solitons: Nonlinear pulses and beams*. London: Chapman and Hall.

Akhmediev, N. N., W. Królikowski, and A. W. Snyder, 1998. Partially coherent solitons of variable shape. *Physical Review Letters*, 81: 4632–5.

Akhmediev, N. N., and J. M. Soto-Crespo. 1993. Generation of a train of three-dimensional optical solitons in a self-focusing medium. *Physical Review A*, 47: 1358–64.

Anastassiou, C., J. W. Fleischer, T. Carmon, M. Segev, and K. Steiglitz. 2001. Information transfer via cascaded collisions of vector solitons. *Optics Letters*, 26: 1498–1500.

Anastassiou, C., M. Segev, K. Steiglitz, J. A. Giordmaine, M. Mitchell, M.-F. Shih, S. Lan, and J. Martin. 1999. Energy-exchange interactions between colliding vector solitons. *Physical Review Letters*, 83: 2332–5.

Ashcroft, N., and N. Mermin. 1976. *Solid state physics*. Philadelphia: Saunders.

Asobe, M. 1997. Nonlinear optical properties of chalcogenide glass fibers and their application to all-optical switching. *Optical Fiber Technology*, 3: 142–8.

Assanto, G., M. Peccianti, and C. Conti. 2003. Nematicons: Optical spatial solitons in nematic liquid crystals. *Optics and Photonics News*, 14: 44–8.

Atai, J., Y. Chen, and J. M. Soto-Crespo. 1994. Stability of three-dimensional self-trapped beams with a dark spot surrounded by bright rings of varying intensity. *Physical Review*, 49: R3170–3.

Bang, O., and P. D. Miller. 1996. Exploiting discreteness for switching in waveguide arrays. *Optics Letters*, 21: 1105–7.

Barthelemy, A., S. Maneuf, and C. Froehly. 1985. Soliton propagation and self-trapping of laser beams by Kerr optical non-linearity. *Optics Communications*, 55: 201–6.

Bergman, L. A., A. J. Mendez, and L. S. Lome. 1996. Bit-parallel wavelength links for high-performance computer networks. *SPIE Critical Review*, 62: 210–6.

Bergman, L., J. Morookian, and C. Yeh. 1998. An all-optical long-distance multi-Gbytes/s bit-parallel WDM single-fiber link. *Journal of Lightwave Technology*, 16: 1577–82.

Biswas, A. 2003. Quasi-stationary non-Kerr law optical solitons. *Optical and Fiber Technology*, 9: 224–59.

Bjorkholm, J. E., and A. A. Ashkin. 1974. Self-focusing and self-trapping of light in sodium vapor. *Physical Review Letters*, 32: 129–32.

Blair, S., and K. Wagner. 1999. Spatial soliton angular deflection logic gates. *Applied Optics*, 38: 6749–72.

———. 2000. Cascadable spatial soliton logic gates. *Applied Optics*, 39: 6006–18.

———, and R. McLeod. 1994. Asymmetric spatial soliton dragging. *Optics Letters*, 19: 1943–5.

———. 1996. Material figures of merit for spatial soliton interactions in the presence of absorption. *Journal of the Optical Society of America B*, 13: 2141–53.

Buljan, H., et al. 2004. Random-phase solitons in nonlinear periodic lattices. *Physical Review Letters*, 92: 223901–4.

Buryak, A. V., P. Di Trapani, D. Skryabin, and S. Trillo. 2002. Optical solitons due to quadratic nonlinearities: From basic physics to futuristic applications. *Physics Reports*, 370: 63–235.

Buryak, A. V., and V. V. Steblina. 1999. Quadratic solitons: New possibility for all-optical switching. *Australian Journal of Physics*, 52: 697–714.

Carlsson, A. H., J. N. Malmberg, D. Anderson, M. Lisak, E. A. Ostrovskaya, T. J. Alexander, and Y. S. Kivshar. 2000. Linear and nonlinear waveguides induced by optical vortex solitons. *Optics Letters*, 25: 660–2.

Carter, G. M., J. M. Jacob, C. R. Menyuk, E. A. Golovchenko, and A. N. Pilipetskii. 1997. Timing-jitter reduction for a dispersion-managed soliton system: Experimental evidence. *Optics Letters*, 22: 513–5.

Carvalho, M. I., T. H. Coskun, D. N. Christodoulides, M. Mitchell, and M. Segev. 1999. Coherence properties of multimode incoherent spatial solitons in noninstantaneous Kerr media. *Physical Review E*, 59: 1193–9.

Chen, W., and D. L. Mills. 1987a. Gap solitons and the nonlinear optical response of superlattices. *Physical Review Letters*, 58: 160–3.

———. 1987b. Optical response of nonlinear multilayer structures: Bilayers and superlattices. *Physical Review B*, 36: 6269–78.

Chen, Y., and J. Atai. 1995. Dark optical bullets in light self-trapping. *Optics Letters*, 20: 133–6.

Chen, Z., M. Mitchell, M. Segev, T. H. Coskun, and D. N. Christodoulides. 1998. Self-trapping of dark incoherent light beams. *Science*, 280: 889–92.

Chen, Z., M. Segev, T. H. Coskun, and D. N. Christodoulides. 1996. Observation of incoherently coupled photorefractive spatial soliton pairs. *Optics Letters*, 21: 1436–8.

Chiao, R. Y., E. Garmire, and C. H. Townes. 1964. Self-trapping of optical beams. *Physical Review Letters*, 13: 479–82.

Chiao, R., M. Johnson, S. Krinsky, H. Smith, C. Townes, and E. Garmire. 1966. A new class of trapped light filaments. *IEEE Journal of Quantum Electronics*, 2: 467–9.

Christodoulides, D. N., and E. D. Eugenieva. 2001a. Blocking and routing discrete solitons in two-dimensional networks of nonlinear waveguide arrays. *Physical Review Letters*, 87, 233901-4.

Christodoulides, D. N., and E. D. Eugenieva. 2001b. Blocking and routing discrete solitons in two-dimensional networks of nonlinear waveguide arrays. AIP Document No. EPAPS: E-PRLTAO-87-018147 (www.aip.org/pubservs/epaps.html).

Christodoulides, D. N., F. Lederer, and Y. Siberberg 2003. Discretizing light behaviour in linear and nonlinear waveguide lattices. *Nature*, 424: 817–23.

Christodoulides, D. N., T. H. Coskun, and R. I. Joseph. 1997. Incoherent spatialsolitons in saturable nonlinear media. *Optics Letters*, 22: 1080–2.

Christodoulides, D. N., T. H. Coskun, M. Mitchell, and M. Segev. 1997. Theory of incoherent self-focusing in biased photorefractive media. *Physical Review Letters*, 78: 646–9.

———. 1998. Multimode incoherent spatial solitons in logarithmically saturable nonlinear media. *Physical Review Letters*, 80: 2310–3.

Christodoulides, D. N., and R. I. Joseph. 1988. Discrete self-focusing in nonlinear arrays of coupled waveguides. *Optics Letters*, 13: 794–6.

———. 1989. Slow Bragg solitons in nonlinear periodic structures. *Physical Review Letters*, 62: 1746–9.

Christodoulides, D. N., S. R. Singh, M. I. Carvalho, and M. Segev. 1996. Incoherently coupled soliton pairs in biased photorefractive crystals. *Applied Physics Letters*, 68: 1763–5.

Cohen, O., H. Buljan, T. Schwartz, J. W. Fleischer, and M. Segev. 2006. Incoherent solitons in instantaneous nonlocal nonlinear media. *Physical Review E*, 73: 015601–4.

Conti, C., S. Trillo, P. Di Trapani, G. Valiulis, A. Piskarskas, O. Jedrkiewicz, and J. Trull. 2003. Nonlinear electromagnetic X waves. *Physical Review Letters*, 90: 170406–9.

Darmanyan, S., A. Kobyakov, E. Schmidt, and F. Lederer. 1998. Strongly localized vectorial modes in nonlinear waveguide arrays. *Physical Review E*, 57: 3520–30.

Del Duce, A., R. I. Killey, and P. Bayvel. 2004. Comparison of nonlinear pulse interactions in 160-Gb/s quasi-linear and dispersion managed soliton systems. *Journal of Lightwave Technology*, 22: 1263–71.

De Sterke, C. M. 1998. Theory of modulational instability in fiber Bragg gratings. *Journal of the Optical Society of America B*, 15: 2660–7.

———, and J. E. Sipe. 1994. Gap solitons. Chap. 3 in *Progress in Optics XXXIII*, edited by E. Wolf. Amsterdam: Elsevier.

Desyatnikov, A. S., L. Torner, and Y. S. Kivshar. 2005. Optical vortices and vortex solitons. Chap. 5 in *Progress in Optics*, edited by E. Wolf, 291ff. Amsterdam: Elsevier.

Di Trapani, P., G. Valiulis, A. Piskarskas, O. Jedrkiewicz, J. Trull, C. Conti, and S. Trillo. 2003. Spontaneously generated X-shaped light bullets. *Physical Review Letters*, 91: 093904–8.

Doran, N. J., and D. Wood. 1988. Nonlinear-optical loop mirror. *Optics Letters*, 13: 56–8.

Duree, G., J. L. Shultz, G. J. Salamo, M. Segev, A. Yariv, B. Crosignani, P. Di Porto, E. J. Sharp, and R. R. Neurgaonkar. 1993. Observation of self-trapping of an optical beam due to the photorefractive effect. *Physical Review Letters*, 71: 533–6.

Edmundson, D. E., and R. H. Enns. 1993. Fully three-dimensional collisions of bistable light bullets. *Optics Letters*, 18: 1609–11.

———. 1995. Particlelike nature of colliding three-dimensional optical solitons. *Physical Review A*, 51: 2491–8.

Eggleton, B. J., R. E. Slusher, C. M. de Sterke, P. A. Krug, and J. E. Sipe. 1996. Bragg grating solitons. *Physical Review Letters*, 76: 1627–30.

Eiselt, M. 1992. Optical loop mirror with semiconductor laser amplifier. *Electronics Letters*, 28: 1505–7.

Eisenberg, H. S., R. Morandotti, Y. Silberberg, S. Bar-Ad, D. Ross, and J. S. Aitchison. 2001. Kerr spatiotemporal self-focusing in a planar glass waveguide. *Physical Review Letters*, 87: 043902–6.

Eisenberg, H. S., Y. Silberberg, R. Morandotti, and J. S. Aitchison. 2000. Diffraction management. *Physical Review Letters*, 85: 1863–6.

Eisenberg, H. S., Y. Silberberg, R. Morandotti, A. R. Boyd, and J. S. Aitchison. 1998. Discrete spatial optical solitons in waveguide arrays. *Physical Review Letters*, 81: 3383–6.

Elgin, J. N. 1993, Stochastic perturbations of optical solitons. *Physics Letters A*, 181: 54–60.

Emplit, P., J. P. Hamaide, F. Reynaud, C. Froehly, and A. Barthelemy. 1987. Picosecond steps and dark pulses through nonlinear single-mode fibers. *Optics Communications*, 62: 374–9.

Enns, R. H., and D. E. Edmundson. 1993. Guide to fabricating bistable-soliton-supporting media. *Physics Review A*, 47: 4524–7.

Evangelides, S. G. Jr., B. M. Nyman, G. T. Harvey, L. F. Mollenauer, P. V. Mamyshev, M. L. Saylors, S. K. Korotky, U. Koren, T. A. Strasser, J. J. Veselka, J. D. Evankow, A. Lucero, J. Nagel, J. Sulhoff, J. Zyskind, P. C. Corbett, M. A. Mills, and G. A. Ferguson. 1996. Soliton WDM transmission with and without guiding filters. *IEEE* Photonics Technology *Letters*, 8: 1409–11.

Fibich, G., B. Ilan and G. Papanicolaou, 2002. Self focusing with fourth-order dispersion. *SIAM Journal of Applied Mathematics*, 62: 1437–62.

Fleischer, J. W., G. Bartal, O. Cohen, T. Schwartz, O. Manela, B. Freedman, M. Segev, H. Buljan, and N. Efremidis. 2005. Spatial photonics in nonlinear waveguide arrays. *Optics Express*, 13: 1780–96.

Fleischer, J. W., M. Segev, N. K. Efremidis, and D. N. Christodoulides. 2003. Observation of two-dimensional discrete solitons in optically induced nonlinear photonic lattices. *Nature*, 422: 147–50.

Forysiak, W., F. M. Knox, and N. J. Doran. 1994. Average soliton propagation in periodically amplified systems with stepwise dispersion-profiled fiber. *Optics Letters*, 19: 174–6.

Foursa, D., and P. Emplit. 1996. Investigation of black-gray soliton interaction. *Physics Review Letters*, 77: 4011–4.

Friberg, S. R. 1991. Soliton fusion and steering by the stimultaneous launch of two different-color solitons. *Optics Letters*, 16: 1484–6.

Friedrich, L., G. I. Stegeman, P. Millar, C. J. Hamilton, and J. S. Aitchison. 1998. Dynamic, electronically controlled angle steering of spatial solitons in AlGaAs slab waveguides. *Optics Letters*, 23: 1438–40.

Gabitov, I. R., and S. K. Turitsyn. 1996. Averaged pulse dynamics in a cascaded transmission system with passive dispersion compensation. *Optics Letters*, 21: 327–9.

Gaeta, A. L., and F. Wise. 2001. Comment on "Self-compression of high-intensity femtosecond optical pulses and spatiotemporal soliton generation." *Physics Review Letters*, 87(2): 29401–2.

Gibson, G., J. Courtial, M. J. Padgett, M. Vasnetsov, V. Pas'ko, S. M. Barnett, and S. Franke-Arnold. 2004. Free-space information transfer using light beams carrying orbital angular momentum. *Optics Express*, 12: 5448–56.

Golovchenko, E. A., A. N. Pilipetskii, and C. R. Menyuk. 1997. Collision-induced timing jitter reduction by periodic dispersionmanagement in soliton WDM transmission. *Electronics Letters*, 33: 735–7.

Gordon, J. P., and H. A. Haus. 1986. Random walk of coherently amplified solitons in optical fiber transmission. *Optics Letters*, 11: 665–7.

Gredeskul, S. A., and Y. S. Kivshar. 1989a. Generation of dark solitons in optical fibers. *Physical Review Letters*, 62: 977ff.

———. 1989b. Dark-soliton generation in optical fibers. *Optics Letters*, 14: 1281–3.

Hall, K. L., G. Lenz, A. M. Darwish, and E. P. Ippen. 1994. Subpicosecond gain and index nonlinearities in InGaAsP diode lasers. *Optics Communications*, 111: 589–612.

Hamaide, J.-P., P. Emplit, and M. Haelterman. 1991. Dark-soliton jitter in amplified optical transmission systems. *Optics Letters*, 16: 1578–80.

Hasegawa, A. 1975. Dynamics of an ensemble of plane waves in nonlinear dispersive media. *Physics of Fluids*, 18: 77–9.

———. 1977. Envelope soliton of random phase waves. *Physics of Fluids*, 20: 2155–6.

———. 1980. Self-confinement of multimode optical pulse in a glass fiber. *Optics Letters*, 5: 416–7.

———. 1983. Amplification and reshaping of optical solitons in a glass fiber—IV: Use of stimulated Raman process. *Optics Letters*, 8: 650–2.

———. 1984. Numerical study of optical soliton transmission amplified periodically by the stimulated Raman process. *Applied Optics*, 23: 3302–9.

Hasegawa, A., and Y. Kodama. 1995. *Solitons in optical communications*. Oxford, UK: Oxford University Press.

Hasegawa, A., S. Kumar, and Y. Kodama. 1996. Reduction of collision-induced time jitters in dispersion-managed soliton transmission systems. *Optics Letters*, 21: 39–41.

Hasegawa, A., and F. D. Tappert. 1973. Transmission of stationary nonlinear optical pulses in dispersive dielectric fibers. I. Anomalous dispersion. *Applied Physics Letters*, 23: 142–4.

Haus, H. A. 1966. Higher-order trapped light beam solutions. *Applied Physics Letters*, 8: 128–9.

Hayata, K., and M. Koshiba. 1993. Bright-dark solitary-wave solutions of a multidimensional nonlinear Schrödinger equation. *Physics Review E*, 48: 2312–5.

He, H., and P. Drummond. 1997. Ideal soliton environment using parametric band gaps. *Physical Review Letters*, 78: 4311–5.

Hirooka, T., T. Nakada, and A. Hasegawa, 2000. Feasibility of densely dispersion managed soliton transmission at160 Gb/s. *IEEE Photonics Letters*, 12: 633–5.

Iannone, I., F. Matera, A. Mecozzi, and M. Settembre. 1998. *Nonlinear optical communication networks*. New York: John Wiley & Sons.

Islam, M. N. 1989. Ultrafast all-optical logic gates based on soliton trapping in fibers. *Optics Letters*, 14, 1257–9.

———. 1990. All-optical cascadable NOR gate with gain. *Optics Letters*, 15: 417–9.

———. 1992. *Ultrafast fiber switching devices and systems*. Cambridge, UK: Cambridge University Press.

Iturbe-Castillo, M. D., P. A. Marquez Aguilar, J. J. Sanchez-Mondragon, S. Stepanov, and V. Vysloukh. 1994. Spatial solitons in photorefractive Bi12TiO20 with drift mechanism of nonlinearity. *Applied Physics Letters*, 64: 408–10.

Jakubowski, M. H., K. Steiglitz, and R. Squier. 1998. State transformations of colliding optical solitons and possible application to computation in bulk media. *Physics Review E*, 58: 6752–8.

———. 2002. Computing with solitons: A review and prospectus. In *Collision-based computing*, edited by A. Adamatzky, 277–298. New York: Springer-Verlag.

Jedrkiewicz, O., J. Trull, G. Valiulis, A. Piskarskas, C. Conti, S. Trillo, and P. Di Trapani. 2003. Nonlinear X waves in second-harmonic generation: Experimental results. *Physical Review E*, 68: 026610–22.

Jensen, S. M. 1982. Nonlinear coherent coupler. *IEEE Journal of Quantum Electronics*, 18: 1580–3.

Kanashov, A. A., and A. M. Rubenchik. 1981. On diffraction and dispersion effect on three wave interaction *Physica D*, 4: 122–34.

Kang, J. U., G. I. Stegeman, and J. S. Aitchison. 1996. One-dimensional spatial soliton dragging, trapping, and all-optical switching in AlGaAs waveguides. *Optics Letters*, 21: 189–91.

———, and N. Akhmediev. 1996. Observation of Manakov Spatial Solitons in AlGaAs Planar Waveguides. *Physical Review Letters*, 76: 3699–3702.

Karamzin, Y. N., and A. P. Sukhorukov. 1976. Mutual focusing of high-power light beams in media with quadratic nonlinearity. *Soviet Journal of Experimental and Theoretical Physics*, 41: 414–20.

Kartashov, Y., L. Torner, and V. A. Vysloukh. 2004. Parametric amplification of soliton steering in optical lattices. *Optics Letters*, 29: 1102–1104.

Kartashov, Y., V. Vysloukh, and L. Torner. 2004. Soliton trains in photonic lattices *Optics Express*, 12: 2831–7.

Kartashov, Y., A. S. Zelenina, L. Torner, and V. A. Vysloukh. 2004. Spatial soliton switching in quasi-continuous optical arrays. *Optics Letters*, 29: 766ff.

Kelley, P. L. 1965. Self-focusing of optical beams. *Physical Review Letters*, 15: 1005–8.

Kevrekidis, P. G., H. Susanto, and Z. Chen. 2006. High-order-mode soliton structures in two-dimensional lattices with defocusing nonlinearity. *Physical Review E*, 74: 066606–15.

Khitrova, G., H. M. Gibbs, Y. Kawamura, H. Iwamura, T. Ikegami, J. E. Sipe, and L. Ming. 1993. Spatial solitons in a self-focusing semiconductor gain medium. *Physical Review Letters*, 70: 920–3.

Kivshar, Y. S. 1989. Comment: On the soliton generation in optical fibres. *Journal of Physics A*, 22: 337–40.

———, and G. P. Agrawal. 2003. *Optical solitons: From fibers to photonic crystals*. San Diego: Academic Press.

Kivshar, Y. S., M. Haelterman, P. Emplit, and J.-P. Hamaide. 1994. Gordon-Haus effect on dark solitons. *Optics Letters*, 19: 19–21.

Kodama, Y., and A. Hasegawa. 1991. Effects of initial overlap on the propagation of optical solitons at different wavelengths. *Optics Letters*, 16: 208–10.

———. 1992. Generation of asymptotically stable optical solitons and suppression of the Gordon-Haus effect. *Optics Letters*, 17: 31–3.

Kodama, Y., S. Kumar, and A. Maruta. 1997. Chirped nonlinear pulsepropagation in a dispersion-compensated system. *Optics Letters*, 22: 1689–91.

Kolokolov, A. A. 1974. Stability of stationary solutions of nonlinear wave equations. *Radiophysics and Quantum Electronics*, 17: 1016–20.

Konar, S., and A. Biswas. 2004. Chirped optical pulse propagation in saturating nonlinear media. *Optical and Quantum Electronics*, 36: 905–18.

Koprinkov, I. G., A. Suda, P. Wang, and K. Midorikawa. 2000. Self-compression of high-intensity femtosecond optical pulses and spatiotemporal soliton generation. *Physical Review Letters*, 84: 3847–50.

Krökel, D., N. J. Halas, G. Giuliani, and D. Grischkowsky 1988. Dark-pulse propagation in optical fibers. *Physical Review Letters*, 60: 29–32.

Kumar, S., M. Wald, F. Lederer, and A. Hasegawa. 1998. Soliton interactionin strongly dispersion-managed optical fibers. *Optics Letters*, 23: 1019–21.

Kuznetsov, E. A., A. M. Rubenchik, and V. E. Zakharov. 1986. Soliton stability in plasmas and hydrodynamics. *Physics Reports*, 142: 103–65.

Law, C. T., X. Zhang, and G. A. Swartzlander. 2000. Waveguiding properties of optical vortex solitons. *Optics Letters*, 25: 55–7.

Lin, C., H. Kogelnik, and L. G. Cohen. 1980. Optical-pulse equalization of low-dispersion transmission in single-mode fibers in the 1.3–1.7-Mu m spectral region. *Optics Letters*, 5: 476–8.

Litchinitser, N. M., B. J. Eggleton, and D. B. Patterson. 1997 Fiber Bragg gratings for dispersion compensation in transmission: Theoretical model and design criteria for nearly ideal pulse recompression. *Journal of Lightwave Photonics*, 15: 1303–13.

Litchinitser, N. M., W. Królikowski, N. N. Akhmediev, and G. P. Agrawal. 1999. Asymmetric partially coherent solitons in saturable nonlinear media. *Physical Review E*, 60: 2377–80.

Liu, X., K. Beckwitt, and F. Wise. 2000. Two-dimensional optical spatiotemporal solitons in quadratic media. *Physical Review E*, 62: 1328–40.

Liu, X., L. J. Qian, and F. W. Wise. 1999 Generation of optical spatiotemporal solitons. *Physical Review Letters*, 82: 4631–4.

Lushnikov, P. M. 2001. Dispersion-managed soliton in a strong dispersion map limit. *Optics Letters*, 26: 1535–7.

Luther-Davies, B., and G. I. Stegeman. 2001. Materials for spatial solitons. In *Spatial solitons*, edited by S. Trillo and W. Torruellas, 19–35. Berlin: Springer-Verlag.

Malomed, B. A., D. Mihalache, F. Wise, and L. Torner. 2005. Spatiotemporal optical solitons. *Journal of Optics B*, 7: R53–72.

Mamaev, A. V., M. Saffman, D. Z. Anderson, and A. A. Zozulya. 1996. Propagation of light beams in anisotropic nonlinear media: From symmetry breaking to spatial turbulence. *Physics Review A*, 54: 870–9.

Manakov, S. V. 1974. On the theory of two-dimensional stationary self-focusing of electromagnetic waves. *Soviet Journal of Experimental and Theoretical Physics*, 38: 248–53.

Manning, R. J., and G. Sherlock. 1995. Recovery of a Π phase shift in ~12.5 ps in a semiconductor laser amplifier. *Electronics Letters*, 31: 307–8.

Manning, R. J., A. D. Ellis, A. J. Poustie, and K. J. Blow. 1997. Semiconductor laser amplifiers for ultrafast all-optical signal processing. *Journal of the Optical Society of America B*, 14: 3204–16.

Matsumoto, M. 1998. Analysis of interaction between stretched pulses propagating indispersion-managed fibers. *IEEE Photonics Letters*, 10: 373–5.

McCall, S. L., and E. L. Hahn. 1967. Self-induced transparency by pulsed coherent light. *Physical Review Letters*, 18: 908–11.

McEntee, J. 2003. Solitons go the distance for Marconi. *Fibre Systems Europe*, pp. 19–23.

McLeod, R., K. Wagner, and S. Blair. 1995. (3+1)-dimensional optical soliton dragging logic. *Physics Review A*, 52: 3254–78.

Mear, R. J., L. Reekie, M. Jauncey, and D. N. Payne. 1987. Low-noise erbium-doped fiber amplifier operating at 1.54μm. *Electronics Letters*, 23: 1026ff.

Mecozzi, A., J. D. Moores, H. A. Haus, and Y. Lai. 1992. Soliton transmission control. *Optics Letters*, 16: 1841–3.

Menyuk, C. R. 1987 Stability of solitons in birefringent optical fibers. I: Equal propagation amplitudes. *Optics Letters*, 12: 614–6.

———. 1988. Stability of solitons in birefringent optical fibers. II. Arbitrary amplitudes. *Journal of the Optical Society of America B*, 5: 392–402.

———. 1989. Pulse propagation in an elliptically birefringent Kerr medium. *IEEE Journal of Quantum Electronics*, 25: 2674–82.

Menyuk, C. R., G. M. Carter, W. L. Kath, and R.-M. Mu. 2002. Dispersion-managed solitons and chirped return to zero: What is the difference? In *Optical fiber telecommunications IVB: Systems and impairments*, edited by I. Kaminov and T. Li, 305–28. San Diego: Academic Press.

Mihalache, D., D. Mazilu, F. Lederer, B. A. Malomed, Y. V. Kartashov, L.-C. Crasovan, and L. Torner. 2005. Stable spatiotemporal solitons in Bessel optical lattices. *Physical Review Letters*, 95: 023902–6.

Mitchell, M., Z. Chen, M.-F. Shih, and M. Segev. 1996. Self-trapping of partially spatially incoherent light. *Physics Review Letters*, 77: 490–3.

Mitchell, M., and M. Segev. 1997. Self-trapping of incoherent white light. *Nature*, 387: 880–883.

Mitchell, M., T. H. Coskun, and D. N. Christodoulides. 1997. Theory of self-trapped spatially incoherent light beams. *Physical Review Letters*, 79: 4990–3.

Mitschke, F. M., and L. F. Mollenauer. 1987 Ultrashort pulses from the soliton laser. *Optics Letters*, 12: 407–9.

Mok, J. T., C. M. de Sterke, and B. J. Eggleton. 2006. Delay-tunable gap-soliton-based slow-light system. *Optics Express*, 14: 11987–96.

Mok, J. T., C. M. de Sterke, I. C. M. Littler, and B. J. Eggleton. 2006. Dispersionless slow light using gap solitons. *Nature Physics*, 2: 775–80.

Mollenauer, L. F., J. P. Gordon, and S. G. Evangelides. 1992. The sliding-frequency guiding filter: An improved form of soliton jitter control. *Optics Letters*, 17: 1575–7.

Mollenauer, L. F., E. Lichtman, M. J. Neubelt, and G. T. Harvey. 1993. Demonstration, using sliding-frequency guiding filters, of error-free soliton transmission over more than 20 mm at 10Gbit/s, single channel, and over more than 13 mm at 20 Gbits/s in a two-channel WDM. *Electronics Letters*, 29: 910–1.

Mollenauer, L. F., P. V. Mamyshev, J. Gripp, M. J. Neubelt, N. Mamysheva, L. Grüner-Nielsen, and T. Veng. 2000. Demonstration of massive wavelength-division multiplexing over transoceanic distances by use of dispersion-managed solitons. *Optics Letters*, 25: 704–6.

Mollenauer, L. F., P. V. Mamyshev, and M. J. Neubelt. 1996. Demonstration of soliton WDM transmission at 6 and 7 × 10 Gbit/s, error free over transoceanic distances. *Electronics Letters*, 32: 471–3.

Mollenauer, L. F., M. J. Neubelt, M. Haner, E. Lichtman S. G. Evangelides, B. M. Nyman. 1991. Demonstration of error-free soliton transmission at 2.5 Gbit/s over more than 14000 km. *Electronics Letters*, 27: 2055–6.

Mollenauer, L. F., and K. Smith. 1988. Demonstration of soliton transmission over more than 4000 km in fiber with loss periodically compensated by Raman gain. *Optics Letters*, 13: 675–7.

Mollenauer, L. F., R. H. Stolen, and J. P. Gordon. 1980. Experimental observation of picosecond pulse narrowing and solitons in optical fibers. *Physical Review Letters*, 45: 1095–8.

Mollenauer, L. F., R. H. Stolen, and M. N. Islam. 1985. Experimental demonstration of soliton propagation in long fibers: Loss compensated by Raman gain. *Optics Letters*, 10: 229–31.

Morandotti, R., H. S. Eisenberg, D. Mandelik, Y. Silberberg, D. Modotto, M. Sorel, C. R. Stanley, and J. S. Aitchison. 2003. Interactions of discrete solitons with structural defects. *Optics Letters*, 28: 834–6.

Morandotti, R., U. Peschel, J. S. Aitchison, H. S. Eisenberg, and Y. Silberberg. 1999. Dynamics of discrete solitons in optical waveguide arrays. *Physical Review Letters*, 83: 2726-9.

Morioka, T., M Saruwatari, and A. Takada. 1987. Ultrafast optical multi/demultiplexer utilising optical Kerb effect in polarisation-maintaining single-mode fibres. *Electronics Letters*, 23: 453–4.

Morita, I., et al. 1998. 40 Gbit/s single-channel soliton transmission over 8600 km using periodic dispersion compensation. *Electronics Letters*, 34: 1863–5.

Morita, I., M. Suzuki, N. Edagawa, K. Tanaka, and S. Yamamoto. 1999. Long-haul soliton WDM transmission with periodic dispersion compensation and dispersion slope compensation. *Journal of Lightwave Technology*, 17: 80–5.

Morton, P. A., V. Mizrahi, G. T. Harvey, L. F. Mollenauer, T. Tanbun-Ek, R. A. Logan, H. M. Presby, T. Erdogan, A. M. Sergent, and K. W. Wecht. 1995. Packaged hybrid soliton pulse source results 70 terabit.km/secsoliton transmission. *IEEE Photonics Technology Letters*, 7: 111–3.

Mu, R.-M., V. S. Grigoryan, C. R. Menyuk, and G. M. Carter. 2000. Comparison of theory and experiment for dispersion-managed solitons in a recirculating fiber loop. *IEEE Journal of Selected Topics in Quantum Electronics*, 6: 248–57.

Mu, R.-M., V. S. Grigoryan, C. R. Menyuk, E. A. Golovchenko, and A. N. Pilipetskii. 1998. Timing-jitter reduction in a dispersion-managed soliton system. *Optics Letters*, 23: 930–2.

Nakazawa, M., and K. Sizuki. 1995. 10 Gbit/s pseudor-andom dark soliton data transmission over 1200 km. *Electronics Letters*, 31: 1076–7.

Neshev, D., Y. S. Kivshar, H. Martin, and Z. Chen. 2004. Soliton stripes in two-dimensional nonlinear photonic lattices. *Optics Letters*, 29: 486–8.

Ostrovskaya, E. A., Y. S. Kivshar, D. Mihalache, and L. C. Crasovan. 2002. Multichannel soliton transmission and pulse shepherding in bit-parallel-wavelength optical fiber links. *IEEE Journal of Selected Topics in Quantum Electronics*, 8: 591–6.

Peccianti, M., C. Conti, G. Assanto, A. De Luca, and C. Umeton. 2004. Routing of anisotropic spatial solitons and modulational instability in liquid crystals. *Nature*, 432: 733–7.

Pertsch, T., U. Peschel, F. Lederer, J. Meier, R. Schiek, R. Iwanow, G. Stegeman, Y. H. Min, and W. Sohler. 2002. Discrete solitons in quadratic nonlinear waveguide arrays. In *OSA Trends in Optics and Photonics (TOPS)*. Vol. 80, *Nonlinear Guided Waves and Their Applications*. OSA Technical Digest, paper NLTuA1.

Pezer, R., and H. Buljan. 2006. Incoherent white-light solitons in nonlinear periodic lattices. *Physical Review E*, 73: 056608–17.

Ponomarenko, S. A., N. M. Litchinitser, and G. P. Agrawal. 2004 Theory of incoherent optical solitons: Beyond the mean-field approximation. *Physical Review E*, 70: 015603–7.

Poutrina, E., and G. P. Agrawal. 2002. Design rules for dispersion-managed soliton systems. *Optics Communications*, 206: 193–200.

Poutrina, E., and G. P. Agarval. 2003. Impact of dispersion fluctuations on 40-Gb/s dispersion-managed lightwave systems. *Journal of Lightwave Technology*, 21: 990–6.

Radhakrishnan, R., M. Lakshmanan, and J. Hietarinta. 1997. Inelastic collision and switching of coupled bright solitons in optical fibers. *Physical Review E*, 56: 2213–6.

Rand, D., K. Steiglitz, and P. R. Prucnal. 2005. Signal stand-ardization in collision-based soliton computing. *International Journal of Unconventional Computing*, 1: 31–45.

Richardson, D. J., R. P. Chamberlin, L. Dong, and D. N. Payne, 1994. Experimental demonstration of 100 GHz dark soliton generation and propagation using a dispersion decreasing fibre. *Electronics Letters*, 30, 1326–1327.

Rothenberg, J. E. 1991. Dark soliton trains formed by vis-ible pulse collisions in optical fibers. *Optics Communications*, 82: 107–11.

Rothenberg, J. E., and H. K. Heinrich. 1992. Observation of the formation of dark-soliton trains in optical fibers. *Optics Letters*, 17, pp. 261–263.

Russell, J. S. 1844. Report on waves. *Fourteenth Meeting of the British Association for the Advancement of Science*, pp. 311–90.

Russell, P. S. J. 1986. Optics of Floquet-Bloch waves in dielectric gratings. *Applied Physics B*, 39: 231–46.

Salguerro, J. R., A. H. Carlsson, E. Ostrovskaya, and Y. Kivshar. 2004. Second-harmonic generation in vortex-induced waveguides. *Optics Letters*, 29: 593–5.

Satsuma, J., and N. Yajima. 1974. Initial value problems of one-dimensional self-modulation of nonlinear waves in dispersive media. *Progress in Theoretical Physics*, Suppl. 55: 284–306.

Scheuer, J., and M. Orenstein. 1999. Optical vortices crystals: Spontaneous generation in nonlinear semi-conductor microcavities. *Science*, 285: 230–3.

Segev. M., B. Crosignani, A. Yariv, and B. Fischer. 1992. Spatial solitons in photorefractive media. *Physics Review Letters*, 68: 923–6.

Serak, S. V., N. V. Tabiryan, M. Peccianti, and G. Assanto. 2006. Spatial soliton all-optical logic gates. *IEEE Photonics Letters*, 18: 1287–9.

Shalaby, M., and A. Barthelemy. 1991. Experimental spatial soliton trapping and switching. *Optics Letters*, 16: 1472–4.

Shalaby, M., et al. 1992. Experimental observation of spatial soliton interactions with a z/2 relative phase difference. *Optics Letters*, 17: 778–80.

Shapiro, E. G., and S. K. Turitsyn. 1997. Theory of guiding-center breathing soliton propagation in optical communication systems with strong dispersion management *Optics Letters*, 22: 1544–6.

Shih, M. F., and M. Segev. 1996. Incoherent collisions between two-dimensional bright steady-state photore-fractive spatial screening solitons. *Optics Letters*, 21: 1538–40.

———, G. C. Valley, G. Salamo, B. Crosignani, and P. Di Porto. 1995. Observation of two-dimensional steady-state photorefractive screening solitons. *Electronics Letters*, 31: 826–7.

Shkhunov, V. V., and D. Z. Anderson. 1998. Radiation trans-fer model of self-trapping spatially incoherent radiation by nonlinear media. *Physical Review Letters*, 81: 2683–6.

Silberberg, Y. 1990. Collapse of optical pulses. *Optics Letters*, 15: 1282–4.

Skryabin, D., and W. J. Firth. 1998. Dynamics of self-trapped beams with phase dislocation in saturable Kerr and quadratic nonlinear media. *Physical Review E*, 58: 3916–30.

Smith, N. J., F. M. Knox, N. J. Doran, K. J. Blow, and I. Bennion. 1996. Enhanced power solitons in optical fibres with periodic dispersion management. *Electronics Letters*, 32: 54–5.

Snyder, A. W., D. J. Mitchell, L. Poladian, and F. Ladouceur. 1991. Self-induced optical fibers: spatial solitary waves. *Optics Letters*, 16: 21–3.

Snyder, A. W., and A. P. Sheppard. 1993. Collisions, steering, and guidance with spatial solitons. *Optics Letters*, 18: 482–4.

Soccolich, C. E., M. W. Chbat, M. N. Islam, and P. R. Prucnal. 1992. Cascade of ultrafast soliton-dragging and trapping logic gates. *IEEE Photonics Technology Letters*, 4: 1043–6.

Sokoloff, J. P., P. R. Prucnal, I. Glesk, and M. Kane. 1993. A Terahertz optical asymmetric demultiplexer. *IEEE Photonics Technology Letters*, 5: 787–90.

Soto-Crespo, J. M., D. R. Heatley, E. M. Wright, and N. N. Akhmediev. 1991. Stability of the higher-bound states in a saturable self-focusing medium. *Physical Review A*, 44: 636–44.

Soto-Crespo, J. M., E. M. Wright, and N. N. Akhmediev. 1992 Recurrence and azimuthal-symmetry breaking of a cylindrical Gaussian beam in a saturable self-focusing medium. *Physics Review A*, 45: 3168–75.

Steblina, V. V., A. V. Buryak, R. A. Sammut, D. Zhou, M. Segev, and P. Prucnal. 2000. Stable self-guided propagation of two optical harmonics coupled by a microwave or a terahertz wave. *Journal of the Optical Society of America B*, 17: 2026–31.

Stegeman, G. I., and M. Segev. 1999. Optical spatial solitons and their interactions: Universality and diversity. *Science*, 286: 1518–23.

Suntsov, S., K. G. Makris, D. N. Christodoulides, and G. I. Stegeman. 2006. Observation of discrete surface solitons. *Physical Review Letters*, 96: 063901–5.

Suzuki, M., I. Morita, N. Edagawa, S. Yamamoto, H. Taga, and S. Akiba. 1995. Reduction of Gordon-Haus timing jitter by periodic dispersion compensation in soliton transmission. *Electronics Letters*, 31: 2027–9.

Taverner, D., N. G. R. Broderick, D. J. Richardson, R. I. Laming, and M. Ibsen. 1998. Nonlinear self-switching and multiple gap-soliton formation in a fiber Bragg grating. *Optics Letters*, 23: 328–30.

Tomlinson, W. J., R. J. Hawkins, A. M. Weiner, J. P. Heritage, and R. N. Thurston. 1989. Dark optical solitons with finite-width background pulses. *Journal of the Optical Society of America B*, 6: 329–34.

Torruellas, W., B. Lawrence, and G. I. Stegeman. 1996. Self-focusing and 2D spatial solitons in PTS. *Electronics Letters*, 32: 2092–4.

Trillo, S., and W. Torruellas, Eds. 2001. *Spatial solitons*. Berlin: Springer-Verlag.

Truscott, A. G., M. E. J. Friese, N. R. Heckenberg, and H. Rubinsztein-Dunlop. 1999. Optically written waveguide in an atomic vapor. *Physical Review Letters*, 82: 1438–41.

Vakhitov, N. G., and A. A. Kolokolov. 1973. Stationary solutions of the wave equation in a medium with nonlinearity saturation. *Radiophysics and Quantum Electronics*, 16: 783–9.

Villeneuve, A., J. U. Kang, J. S. Aitchison, and G. I. Stegeman, 1995. Unity ratio of cross- to self-phase modulation in bulk AlGaAs and AlGaAs/GaAs multiple quantum well waveguides at half the band gap. *Applied Physics Letters*, 67: 760–2.

Voloshchenko, Y. I., Y. N. Ryzhov, and V. E. Sotin. 1981. Stationary waves in nonlinear, periodically modulated media with large group retardation. *Soviet Physics Technical Physics*, 26: 541–4.

Wagner, K., and R. McLeod. 1993 Spatial soliton dragging gates and light bullets. In Optical Computing, Vol. 7 of 1993 OSA Technical Digest Series, pp. 305–7. Washington, DC: Optical Society of America.

Weiner, A. M., J. P. Heritage, R. J. Hawkins, R. N. Thurston, E. M. Kirschner, D. E. Leaird, and W. J. Tomlinson. 1988. Experimental observation of the fundamental dark soliton in optical fibers. *Physical Review Letters*, 61: 2445–8.

Winful, H. G. 1985. Pulse compression in optical fiber filters. *Applied Physics Letters*, 46: 527–9.

———, and V. Perlin. 2000. Raman gap solitons. *Physical Review Letters*, 84: 3586–9.

Xu, Z., Y. Kartashov, and L. Torner. 2005. Reconfigurable soliton networks optically induced by arrays of nondiffracting Bessel beams. *Optics Express*, 13: 1774–9.

Yang, J. 2002. Suppression of Manakov soliton interference in optical fibers *Physical Review E*, 65: 036606–16.

Yang, J., I. Makasyuk, A. Bezryadina, and Z. Chen. 2004a. Dipole solitons in optically induced two-dimensional photonic lattices. *Optics Letters*, 29: 1662–4.

———. 2004. Dipole and quadrupole solitons in optically induced two-dimensional photonic lattices: Theory and experiment. *Studies in Applied Mathematics*, 113: 389–412.

Yang, J., I. Makasyuk, P. G. Kevrekidis, H. Martin, B. A. Malomed, D. J. Frantzeskakis, and Z. Chen, 2005. Necklacelike Solitons in Optically Induced Photonic Lattices. Physical Review Letters, 94, 11390 2 (4).

Yang, T.-S., and W. L. Kath. 1997. Analysis of enhanced-power solitons in dispersion-managed optical fibers. *Optics Letters*, 22: 985–7.

Yeh, C., and L. Bergman. 1996. Pulse shepherding in nonlinear fiber optics. *Journal of Applied Physics*, 80: 3174–8.

Yu, T., R.-M. Mu, V. S. Grigoryan, and C. R. Menyuk. 1999. Energy enhancement of dispersion-managed solitons in optical fiber transmission systems with lumped amplifiers. *IEEE Photonics Technology Letters*, 11: 75–7.

Zabusky, N. J., and M. D. Kruskal. 1965. Interaction of "solitons" in a collisionless plasma and the recurrence of initial states. *Physical Review Letters*, 15: 240–3.

Zakharov, V. E., and A. B. Shabat. 1972. Exact theory of two-dimensional self-focusing and one-dimensional self-modulation of waves in nonlinear media. *Soviet Journal of Experimental and Theoretical Physics*, 34: 62–9.

———. 1973. Interaction between solitons in a stable medium. *Soviet Journal of Experimental and Theoretical Physics*, 37: 823–8.

Zakharov, V. E., et al. 1984. *Theory of solitons: The inverse scattering transform*. Trans. by Consultant Bureau. Moscow: Nauka.

Zhao, W., and E. Bourkoff. 1990. Generation of dark solitons under CW background using waveguide eo modulators. *Optics Letters*, 15: 405–7.

Zharova, N. A., N. Zharova, A. Zharov, and Y. Kivshar. 2005. Nonlinear transmission and spatiotemporal solitons in metamaterials with negative refraction. *Optics Express*, 13: 1291–8.

Zozulya, A. A., D. Z. Anderson, A. V. Mamaev, and M. Saffman. 1996. Self-focusing and soliton formation in media with anisotropic nonlocal material response. *Europhysics Letters*, 36: 419–24.

Synchronous Optical Code Division Multiplexing Systems

Hideyuki Sotobayashi, *National Institute of Information and Communications Technology, Japan*

INTRODUCTION

The roots of optical code division multiple access are found in spread spectrum communication, which was developed in the mid-1950s, mainly as a form of transmission that could overcome grid restrictions in radio bandwidth allocation (Dixon 1975, 1994; Scholtz 1977; Viterbi 1995; Verdú 1998). It is based on the idea of spreading a narrow band message over a much wider frequency spectrum by means of digital codes (Viterbi 1995; Verdú 1998; Pickholtz, Schilling, and Milstein 1982). Because of the spreading, the transmitted signal arrives at the receiver as a noise-like signal, so message recovery is impossible unless the original code is known. The authorized receiver correlates the received signal using a local code that is a replica of the transmission code. Despreading and signal recovery in the presence of interference from other users can be accomplished. As a result, spread spectrum communications is particularly useful for military applications: Signals can be transmitted in an extremely noisy environment with the highest levels of security. Furthermore, with the emergence of satellite and mobile communications, spread spectrum became the basis of a new multiple access technique: code division multiple access (Sust 1994).

In photonic transport systems, *optical time division multiplexing* (OTDM) and *wavelength division multiplexing* (WDM) are the two primary techniques for multiplexing data onto a single transmission fiber. *Optical code division multiplexing* (OCDM) is an alternate technique. The first work on OCDM began in the late 1970s in the area of fiber delay lines for signal processing (Marom 1978). Since then, many research groups have actively researched OCDM.

In OCDM systems, each channel is optically encoded with the specified code. Only the intended user—the one with the correct code—can recover the encoded information. A careful assignment of optical codes enables signals from all network nodes to be carried without interference between signals. Therefore, simultaneous multiple access can be achieved without using a complex network protocol. As a result, multiple users can share the same transmission bandwidth.

OCDM is generally classified into coherent and incoherent schemes on the basis of the degree of coherence of the signal source. Carrier phase–shifted optical sequences are used for coherent OCDM (Vannucci 1989); intensity-modulated code sequences are used for incoherent OCDM (Salehi 1989). In the coherent case, a phase-shifted bipolar optical chip pulse sequence represents a binary code. Incoherent OCDM uses a unipolar code in which on-off keying modulation is used. The most significant advantage of the coherent scheme is the higher signal-to-interference-noise ratio, which is directly attributed to the superior orthogonality between the codes, which in turn yields higher processing gains. An optical code set is designed so that each *code division multiplexings* (CDM) code has an autocorrelation peak that is as large as possible so that the codes in the set can be easily distinguished. Most of the work in the 1980s focused on incoherent optical codes, but their use results in limited system performance. With the recent advances in optical device technology, most of the difficulties with optical phase encoding have been overcome, so the focus has shifted to coherent optical codes.

There are two types of encoding schemes: encoding in the frequency domain and in the time domain. Encoding in the frequency domain is analogous to the spread spectrum technique (Karafolas and Uttamchandani 1995). In time-domain encoding, time-resolved chip pulses are generated within a one-bit time frame (Kitayama, Sotobayashi, and Wada 1999). The phase of each chip pulse represents an optical code sequence. Matched filtering in the optical domain is one type of dispreading. The matched-filtering detection technique maximizes the signal-to-noise ratio for Gaussian noise. The impulse response of the matched filter on the decoder side is the complex conjugate of an optical encoder. The output of the decoder is expressed by the convolution of the matched filter. If the optical codes between the encoder and decoder match, then the decoded time-despread signal reconstructs the original short pulse. On the other hand, unmatched codes remain randomly spread over a one-bit time frame of T after the decoding.

In coherent OCDM systems, interference noise is a severe problem. The processing gain is expressed as the ratio of one-bit time duration to the gate-time window. Time gating should be used to achieve the highest processing gain. The time gating opens a time window to extract the autocorrelation peak. This operation is equivalent to narrowband filtering in wireless CDM. Placing the optical time gate before the photodetector has a substantial advantage because the requirement for the detector bandwidth is significantly relaxed to the bit rate.

The characteristics of OCDM systems in comparison with those of wireless CDM systems are summarized in Figure 1. OCDM inherits several features from its wireless counterpart: accommodation of a number of channels on a single carrier frequency, tell-and-go access capability, freedom from network-wide timing synchronization, soft capacity on demand, and security (Sotobayashi, Chujo, and Kitayama 2003). Therefore, the potential applications include point-to-point transmission (Sotobayashi, Chujo, and Kitayama 2001; Sotobayashi, Chujo, and Kitayama 2002, "1.6-b/s/Hz"), multiple access (Sotobayashi and Kitayama 1999, "10 Gb/s OCDM/WDM"; Kitayama and Murata 2001), optical path networking (Kitayama 1998; Sotobayashi, Chujo, and Kitayama 2002, "Transparent"), optical secure communications, and label-switching routing (Sotobayashi and Kitayama 2000; Kitayama, Wada, and Sotobayashi 2000).

As shown in Figure 1, a typical OCDM system in the frequency domain (Salehi, Weiner, and Heritage 1990; Sardesai, Chang, and Weiner 1998) uses parallel modulation in the frequency domain to reshape a short pulse into a low-intensity pseudonoise burst. The optical encoder consists of a suitably configured grating and lens apparatus. The first grating spatially decompresses the spectral component of the incident ultrashort light pulse. A phase mask is located at the focal points of the lens, where the optical spectral components experience maximal separation. The mask phase shifts the different spectral components of the initial short pulse, thereby encoding its spectrum. The encoded spectral components are reassembled by the second lens and the second grating. The shape of the encoded pulse resembles a pseudonoise signal. At the receiver, the original signal is recovered by spectral correlation. The matched optical encoder is a complex conjugate of the encoder that restores the original short pulse. If the encoding and decoding phase masks do not match, then the output pulse remains a low-intensity pseudonoise burst. A 30-MHz, 275-fs pulse was encoded using a 63-chip *binary phase shift keying* (BPSK) code. A proof-of-concept experiment using 10-km transmission demonstrated the viability of this concept.

A group at Nippon Telephone and Telegraph used the same spreading-despreading approach to encode and decode femtosecond pulses (Tsuda et al. 1999, "Photonic," "Spectral"). An *arrayed waveguide grating* (AWG) with phase shifters was used for coherent OCDM. The input pulses were spectrally decomposed into their frequency components in the grating. Each phase was binary shifted by an encoding filter. The frequency resolution was 12.6 GHz. Transmission of more than 40 km at 10 Gbit/s using 810-fs pulses was demonstrated.

A group at Southampton University demonstrated both BPSK and *quaternary phase shift keying* (QPSK) encoding in the time domain using superstructure fiber Bragg gratings (Teh et al. 2001, 2002). Such gratings have a rapidly varying refractive modulation of uniform amplitude and pitch onto which an additional slowly varying amplitude or phase CDM code is imposed along its length. The shape of the impulse response directly follows the shape of this special superstructure. Short pulses reflected from gratings are reshaped into coded pulse sequences. Pattern recognition can be achieved by matched filtering of the coded signal using a decoder grating with a conjugate impulse response. The group demonstrated up to 255-chip QPSK optical coding and 2-WDM, 2-OCDM transmission at 1.25 Gbit/s.

Some recent proof of concept demonstrations are reviewed in Prucnal (2005) and "Optical Code in Optical Communications and Networks" (2007).

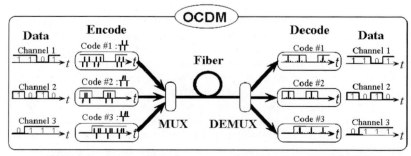

Unique characteristics
- Asynchronous transmission
- Communication security
- Tell-and-go access protocol
- High degree of scalability

Applications of OCDM
Point-to-point transmission
- Multiple access
- Optical path network
- Label switching routing

Figure 1: Optical code division multiplexing

APPLICATION OF SYNCHRONOUS OCDM TO HIGH SPECTRAL EFFICIENCY TRANSPORT SYSTEM

The rapidly increasing demand for more bandwidth by end users is driving the development of flexible network infrastructures with Petabit/s (Pbit/s) capacity. Because of their low transmission loss, optical fibers are ideal for high-capacity signal transmission. However, optical amplifiers have limited gain bandwidths. More than 10-Terabit/s (Tb/s) WDM transmission has been reported by fully utilizing the present amplifier wavelength bands—that is, the S-, C-, and L-band wavelength regions (Fukuchi et al. 2002; Bigo et al. 2002). To achieve Pbit/s capacity, the spectral efficiency must be increased to enable full utilization of the limited wavelength resources. Two approaches to increasing spectrum efficiency are *duo binary encoding* (0.6-bit/s/Hz spectral efficiency) (Ono et al. 1998) and *vestigial sideband filtering* with polarization multiplexing (1.28 bit/s/Hz) (Bigo et al. 2002). The use of OCDM may enable achievement of the ultimate spectral efficiency.

The feasibility of over-Tbit/s BPSK-OCDM/WDM transmission with 0.4-bit/s/Hz spectral efficiency was demonstrated by simultaneous multiwavelength optical encoding of a single *supercontinuum* (SC) source (Sotobayashi, Chujo, and Kitayama 2001). To increase the spectral efficiency, in addition to polarization multiplexing, QPSK optical encoding and decoding was applied at 40 Gbit/s accompanied by ultrafast optical time gating and optical hard thresholding for suppressing interference noise. As a result, 6.4-Tbit/s OCDM/WDM (4 OCDM × 40 WDM × 40 Gbit/s) transmission using only the C-band wavelength region was experimentally demonstrated with 1.6-bit/s/Hz spectral efficiency (Sotobayashi, Chujo, and Kitayama 2002, "1.6-b/s/Hz").

Suppose an optical short pulse, having a much higher frequency spectrum than the data bandwidth, is spread over a one-bit time frame of length T by optical time domain encoding. The sequence of the phases of the N chip pulses in one bit represents an optical code sequence. Matched filtering in the optical domain is the basis of the despreading. The impulse response of the matched filter on the decoder side, $h_d(t)$, along with its Fourier spectrum, $H_d(\omega)$, is the complex conjugate of the optical encoder; it is given by

$$H_d(\omega) = H_e(\omega)^* e^{-j\omega t_0} \tag{1}$$

$$h_d(t) = h_e(t_0 - t) \tag{2}$$

where the impulse response of the optical encoder is $h_e(t)$ and its Fourier spectrum is $H_e(\omega)$. The output of the matched filter is expressed by the convolution of the impulse responses of the encoder and decoder as

$$\begin{aligned} Output &= \int_{-\infty}^{\infty} H_e(\omega) H_d(\omega) e^{j\omega t} df \\ &= \int_{-\infty}^{\infty} |H_e(\omega)|^2 e^{j\omega(t-t_0)} df \\ &= \int_{-\infty}^{\infty} h_e(t') h_e(t' - t + t_0) dt \\ &= \Psi(t - t_0) \end{aligned} \tag{3}$$

where $\Psi(t)$ represents the autocorrelation function of the input optical code, $h_e(t)$. The matched filtering response can be achieved by time reversing the input and output of the optical encoder. When the optical codes between the encoder and decoder match, the decoded time-despread signal reconstructs the original short pulse as an autocorrelation waveform. On the other hand, unmatched codes remain spread over the one-bit time frame of length T after the decoding as a cross-correlation waveform.

Figure 2 shows the operating principle of the QPSK-code OCDM system with optical time gating and optical hard thresholding. Time-spread QPSK pulses are used as optical codes, and optical transversal filters are used as optical encoders and decoders. Each filter consists of tunable taps, 5-ps delay lines, programmable quaternary optical phase shifters, and a combiner. An optical code sequence of three-chip QPSK pulses with a chip interval of

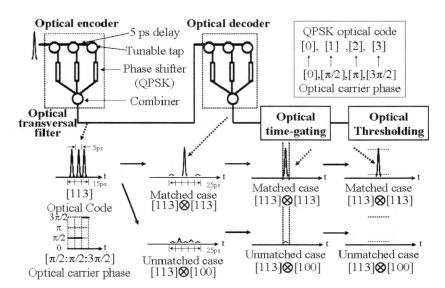

Figure 2: Operating principle of QPSK-code OCDM system with optical time gating and optical hard thresholding

5 ps is generated. The QPSK-encoded signal is despread by the decoder on the receiver side. The QPSK-decoded output shows the correlation waveform with a five-pulse sequence in the time domain. If the receiver's optical code matches the transmitter's optical code, then an autocorrelation waveform, characterized by a sharp central peak, is observed. If they do not match, then a cross-correlation waveform is formed. One bit of the despread signal occupies a 25-ps time frame. Therefore, 40-Gbit/s QPSK optical encoding and decoding is possible. The impulse response of the optical encoding has a frequency periodicity of 200 GHz because of the 5-ps chip interval of the code (Sotobayashi, Chujo, and Kitayama 2001). As a result, simultaneous multiwavelength encoding with 200-GHz WDM channel spacing can be achieved using a single optical encoder when a broadband coherent optical pulse, such as a SC pulse, is used as a chip pulse (Sotobayashi, Chujo, and Kitayama 2001).

In coherent OCDM systems, interference noise is a severe problem. Although optical matched filtering is ideal for beat-noise limited reception, it is only ideal in the absence of intersymbol interference. Introducing optical time gating eliminates interference noise outside the time-gate window. Time gating can realize the exact processing gain in OCDM systems. Looking at Figure 2 again, suppose the time gate opens a time window of $\Delta \tau$ at a repetition rate of $1/T$ to extract only the main lobe of the autocorrelation waveform. The time gate samples only the data-bearing portion of each bit, thereby rejecting the autocorrelation side lobes and the interference codes that fall outside the gate interval. This operation is equivalent to the narrow-bandpass filtering in frequency domain CDM. Placing the optical time gate before the photodetector has a substantial advantage because the requirement for the detector bandwidth is significantly relaxed to the bit rate of $1/T$. If an electrical time gate is placed after the photodetector, then the detector bandwidth needs a chip rate of $1/\Delta \tau$.

When the signal powers of the channels are equal, the signal-to-interference power (SNR) at the receiver is given by

$$SNR = \frac{S}{(K-1)S + \sigma^2} = \frac{1}{(K-1) + \sigma^2/S} \qquad (4)$$

$$\frac{E_b}{N_0} = \frac{ST}{(K-1)S\Delta\tau + \sigma^2\Delta\tau} = \frac{T/\Delta\tau}{(K-1) + \sigma^2} \qquad (5)$$

where K is the number of channels, S is the signal power, and σ^2 is the variance of the additive noise power including the amplified spontaneous emission noise of the optical amplifier, shot noise, and thermal noise. The bit energy-to-interference density ratio, E_b/N_0, (Sotobayashi and Kitayama 1999) after time gating is obtained by multiplying S in the numerator by T and by multiplying the noise by time window $\Delta \tau$.

Compared with the results of Equation 4, the bit energy-to-interference density ratio is enhanced by $T/\Delta\tau$. Therefore, a process gain of $T/\Delta\tau$ can be achieved by introducing optical time gating. For ultrafast operation, a 100-m-long *nonlinear dispersion-shifted fiber* (HNL-DSF)-based *nonlinear optical loop mirror* (NOLM) was used. The control signal consisted of a pulse train with 1.5-ps pulses

at a repetition rate of 10 GHz, so the optical time-gating window ranged from 1.5 to 1.8 ps for all WDM channels.

Even after optical time gating, it is likely that interference noise remains in the time-gate window. As shown in Figure 2, this interference noise is reduced by introducing optical hard thresholding. Optical hard thresholding is achieved by using the nonlinear transmission response of a second NOLM, an optical self-switching device that acts as a pulse shaper by setting an appropriate threshold level. It reflects lower-intensity signals and transmits only the higher intensity signals by limiting its intensity to an appropriate level. Adjusting the power of the input signal suppresses interference noise inside the autocorrelation main lobe after optical time gating of both the 0 and 1 bits. This reduces the power variations in the eye diagrams of the received signal, which improves the *bit-error-rate* (BER) characteristics.

For ultrahigh-speed, wideband operation, the device length, hence the group delay, must be reduced. For this purpose, a 50-m HNL-DSF is used as a hard thresholding NOLM. The group delay for the WDM wavelength range (15,533–1564 nm) is less than 200 fs, resulting in ultrahigh-speed operation as well as wideband operation.

Figure 3 shows the experimental setup used for testing 6.4-Tbit/s OCDM/WDM (4 OCDM × 40 WDM × 40 Gbit/s) transmission (Sotobayashi, Chujo, and Kitayama 2002, "1.6-b/s/Hz"). A 10-GHz, 1.5-ps pulse train transmitted from a *mode-locked laser diode* (MLLD) at 1532 nm was modulated with a 10-Gbit/s data and optically multiplexed to 40 Gbit/s. After being amplified to an average power of 0.48 W, it was launched into a *SC fiber* (SCF) (Sotobayashi and Kitayama 1998). The generated 40-Gbit/s SC signal was linearly polarized and split into eight, and each signal served as the light source for simultaneous multiwavelength optical encoding using a QPSK optical encoder. Two groups of four different optically encoded signals were generated. One group was changed to orthogonally polarized, and both groups of four OCDM signals were multiplexed to orthogonally polarized multiwavelength 2 × 4 OCDM × 40-Gbit/s signals using a polarization beam splitter. Each group had WDM channel spacing of 200 GHz, which corresponds to 1.6-bit/s/Hz spectral efficiency. The transmission line was composed of two spans of a reversed dispersion fiber and single-mode dispersion fiber pair. Each span was 40 km long, so the total length was 80 km. The average zero dispersion wavelength was 1546.59 nm. After the 80-km transmission, signals were split into two, and each beam was demultiplexed using a 20-channel AWG with a channel spacing of 200 GHz. The pass band wavelengths of the two AWGs were separated by 100 GHz (WDM channel 1 = 1532.68 nm; channel 40 = 1563.86 nm). After the demultiplexing, frequency chirping was compensated for and the polarization was demultiplexed. Then the received signals were decoded by an optical decoder. Optical time gating was performed at 10 GHz; it both rejected the interference noise outside the time-gating window and demultiplexed a 40-Gbit/s OTDM signal to a 10 Gbit/s signal.

Optical time gating was performed at 10 GHz using a 100-m HNL-DSF based nonlinear optical loop mirror (Sotobayashi et al. 2002). Optical time gating rejected the interference noise outside the main lobe of the

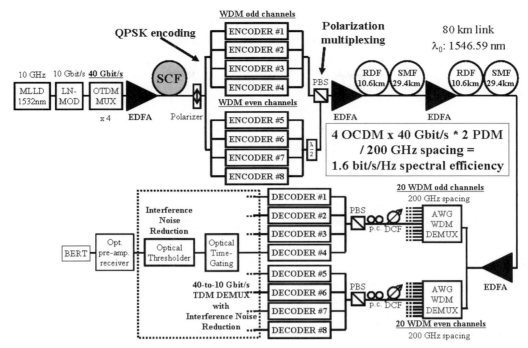

Figure 3: Experimental setup for 6.4-Tbit/s (4 OCDM × 40 WDM × 40 Gbit/s) transmission with 1.6-bit/s/Hz spectral efficiency

autocorrelation waveform. For ultrafast operation, a short HNL-DSF was used. The control pulse used for the time gating was a 1.5-ps pulse from an MLLD at 1562.5 nm for gating of WDM channels 1 to 22 (1533–1549 nm) and at 1542.2 nm for gating of WDM channels 23 to 40 (1550–1564 nm). The walk-off between signal and control pulses was less than 300 fs, resulting in ultrahigh-speed operation. The optical time-gating window ranged from 1.5 to 1.8 ps for all WDM channels. Optical hard thresholding was achieved by using the nonlinear transmission response of the second NOLM. The NOLM acts as a pulse shaper by setting the proper threshold level in the sense that it reflects lower-intensity signals and transmits

a higher-intensity signal by limiting its intensity to an appropriate level. Adjusting the input signal power suppressed the interference noise inside the autocorrelation main lobe after optical time gating, and both the signal 0 and 1 level power variations were greatly reduced. For ultrahigh-speed operation, the device length and group delay must be shortened. Using a short HNL-DSF (50 m) as a hard thresholding NOLM reduced the group delay in all WDM channels (15533–1564 nm) to less than 200 fs, resulting in ultrahigh-speed operation. The BERs were measured using an optical preamplified receiver.

Figure 4 shows the optical spectrum of the SC signal at the output of the SCF, the optical spectra of the

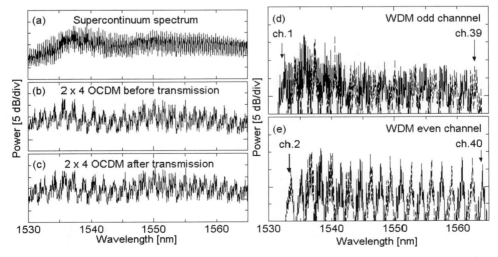

Figure 4: (a) 40-Gbit/s SC spectrum; spectra of 2 × 4 OCDM (b) before and (c) after transmission; spectra of (d) odd and (e) even WDM channels after WDM and polarization DEMUX

WDM ch.1: OC#1   WDM ch.2: OC#5   WDM ch.39: OC#1   WDM ch.40: OC#5

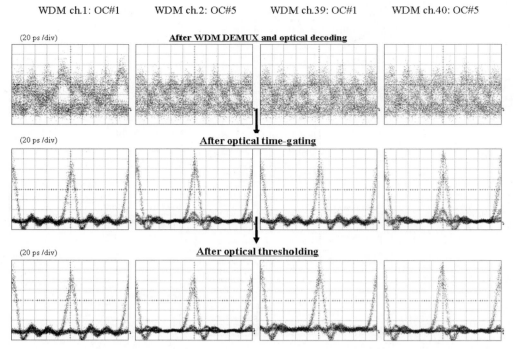

Figure 5: Eye diagrams of optically decoded signals of WDM channels 1, 2, 39, and 40 (a) after optical decoding, (b) after optical time gating, and (c) after optical hard thresholding

multiwavelength 2 × 4 OCDM signals before and after transmission, and the spectra in the odd and even WDM channels after WDM and polarization demultiplexing.

Figure 5a shows the eye diagrams for WDM channels 1, 2, 39, and 40 after optical decoding. The interference noise of the three unmatched codes severely distorted the signal-to-noise ratio. As shown in Figure 5b, the optical time gating of the main lobe of the matched correlation waveforms greatly reduced the interference noise outside the time-gate window. As shown in Figure 5c, the optical hard thresholding greatly reduced the interference noise inside the time-gate window for both the signal 0 and 1 levels, resulting in clear eye openings. The measured BERs of 4-OCDM × 40-WDM data signals were less than 1×10^{-9}.

APPLICATION OF SYNCHRONOUS OCDM TO PHOTONIC ACCESS NODES

In this section, the application of OCDM to photonic access nodes and an experimental demonstration of 10-Gbit/s packet add-drop multiplexing based on optical code correlation will be explained (Kitayama and Murata 2001; Kitayama et al. 2001).

Wavelength add-drop multiplexers enable each wavelength to either add-drop and electronically process packets at the node or optically bypass the node altogether. However, wavelength *add-drop multiplexing* (ADM) has wavelength granularity; moreover, it is limited in that it can only handle traffic on an optical channel and cannot handle traffic on a packet-by-packet basis. This can waste wavelength resources and limit the usage of optical

channels. In contrast, conventional synchronous optical network ADM has a finer granularity for handling traffic and thus can handle traffic on a packet-by-packet basis. It picks up low-speed streams from a high-speed stream and likewise adds low-speed streams to a high-speed stream. However, the speed of the electrical processing eventually becomes a bottleneck because of the limits on overall processing capability. Therefore, there is a growing demand for high-speed multifunctional ADM.

The photonic ADM at each node drops the arriving packets to the node, bypasses the node, or adds packets. It handles traffic on a single wavelength on a packet-by-packet basis. Figure 6a shows the basic architecture of *photonic ADM* (PADM). The fundamental functions are

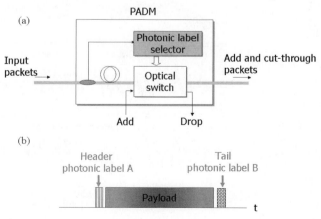

Figure 6: (a) Basic architecture of photonic label-based add-drop multiplexer and (b) optical packet structure

photonic label processing and optical switching. The input and output ports are connected to WDM links of a single wavelength. The photonic label of an arriving packet is processed, and, on the basis of the label, the optical switch is driven by the control signal to direct the packet to the outgoing port either for dropping or bypassing. Figure 6b shows the structure of an optical packet. The label is simply a relatively short fixed-length identifier that bears the information of the destination and source. A flag is attached at the end of the packet to indicate the end. Therefore, two photonic labels—a header label and a tail label—are attached. These two labels enable the handling of variable-length packets. Optical codes (8-chip BPSK) are used for the photonic labels, and optical transversal filters are used as optical encoders and decoders. The decoding is based on matched filtering in the time domain.

As shown in Figure 7, the photonic label selector compares the photonic label of an arriving packet with a local label by optically correlating the optical code of arriving packet with the assigned code of the node. If the incoming label matches the local one, then a control signal is generated that instructs the optical switch to drop the packet. The switch is reset to the bar state by the tail label. If the incoming label does not match the local label, then the switch remains in the bar state, causing the packet to bypass the node. The add multiplexing is performed in the same manner.

Figure 8 shows the experimental setup for testing PADM. Two kinds of optical packets were generated at 10 Gbit/s using two different optical codes. Labels were attached at the head and tail of each packet. After 50-km transmission, the labels were detected using an optical decoder. The generated correlation waveform controlled the optical switch. The measured waveforms of a dropped packet at port 1 and a bypassed packet at port 2 are shown in Figure 9. The dropping and bypassing functions worked well at BERs of less than 10^{-9} on the basis of optical correlation.

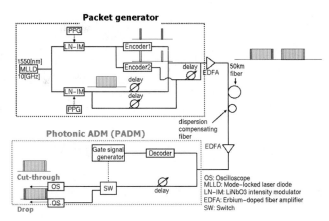

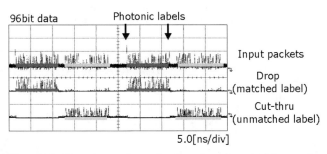

Figure 8: Experimental setup for testing PADM

Figure 9: Experimental results for dropping and bypassing functions of PADM

APPLICATION OF SYNCHRONOUS OCDM TO OPTICAL PATH NETWORKS

OCDM is applicable not only to multiple access networks but also to optical path networks. The *optical code path*, which is defined as the logical path determined by the *optical code* (OC), has been proposed within the concept of OCDM networks (Kitayama 1998; Sotobayashi, Chujo, and Kitayama 2002, "Transparent"). OCDM can be effectively overlaid onto existing WDM path networks. The introduction of OCs provides soft capacity networks and saves network resources. In future hybrid OCDM-WDM networks, flexible OC and wavelength conversions will be key technologies for establishing optical paths. As a node technology, simultaneous optical code and wavelength conversion in the 8.05-Terahertz (THz) bandwidth by supercontinuum generation has been experimentally demonstrated (Sotobayashi, Chujo, and Kitayama 2002, "Transparent"). Furthermore, all-optical 3R regeneration has been has been used to create a transparent network. Finally, an optical code and wavelength-convertible virtual optical code, a virtual optical code path, and virtual wavelength path (VOCP-VWP) network has been experimentally demonstrated that has a total link length of 180 km with four network nodes.

Figure 10 shows the experimental setup used for testing the VOCP-VWP network. For simplicity, data were transported from node A to node C along optical path 1 and

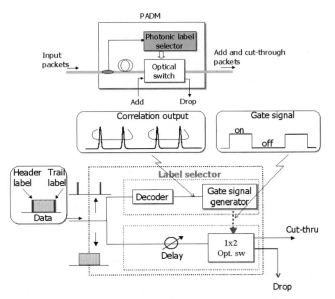

Figure 7: Photonic label-based add-drop multiplexer

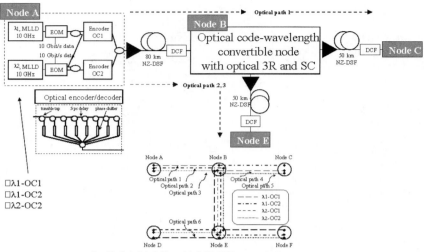

•Opt. Path 1: λ1-OC1 to λ1-OC2 (OC conversion)
•Opt. Path 2: λ1-OC2 to λ2-OC2 (wavelength conversion)
•Opt. Path 3: λ2-OC2 to λ1-OC1 (OC and wavelength conversions)

Figure 10: Experimental setup for testing VOCP-VWP network

OC and wavelength convertible node with optical 3R

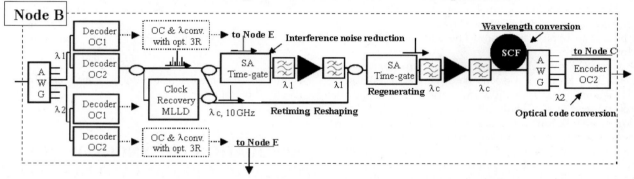

Receiving end

Figure 11: Architectures of (a) node B and (b) nodes C and E

from node A to node E along optical paths 2 and 3. Three types of OC and wavelength conversions were performed at node B: λ1-OC1 to λ1-OC2 (OC conversion), λ1-OC2 to λ2-OC2 (wavelength conversion), and λ2-OC2 to λ1-OC1 (OC and wavelength conversions) for optical paths 1, 2, and 3, respectively. Each network node was linked to several transmission fibers tens of km long.

At node A, λ1-OC1, λ1-OC2, and λ2-OC2 were generated and multiplexed; 10-GHz, 1.5-ps pulse trains from

the mode-locked laser diodes at λ1 and λ2 were 10-Gbit/s modulated. Optical transversal filters were used as 8-chip BPSK optical encoders and decoders. As shown in Figure 11a, at node B, the received signals were decoded, 3R regenerated, wavelength converted by SC generation, and OC converted. First, they were wavelength demultiplexed and decoded by optical decoders. The decoded signals were divided into two. One was fed into the injection-locked MLLD for 10-GHz clock recovery. The clock pulses recovered using the first signals were divided, and half were used as pump pulses for the first semiconductor *saturable absorber* (SA) time gate. After time gating, the decoded signals were, in turn, used as pump pulses for the second SA time gate to gate the clock pulse train. By controlling the optical time gate ON/OFF using decoded signals, the network could transfer the data coding to newly generated, clear optical pulses. Thus, all-optical 3R regeneration was obtained. For wavelength conversion, an SC was produced by pumping using 3R regenerated signals. After spectrum slicing using an AWG at the wavelength to be converted, they were optical encoded with the OC to be converted. Consequently, simultaneous OC and wavelength conversion with optical 3R regeneration was obtained. As shown in Figure 11b, after a subsequent 50-km transmission, OC and wavelength converted signals were detected at node C or E. As was done at node B, after wavelength demultiplexing and decoding, optical time gating was done using the recovered 10-GHz optical clock to reduce interference noise.

The measured eye diagram of the decoded λ1-OC2 signal at node B after 80-km transmission is shown in Figure 12a, and that of the recovered clock–produced optical time-gated signal is shown in Figure 12b. The side lobe and interference noise were greatly reduced in the latter. Figure 12c shows the optical 3R regenerated decoded signal at λc. As obviously shown by comparison

with Figure 12b, the signal-to-noise ratio was higher and the timing jitter was lower.

Figure 13 shows the optical spectrum for a 24-channel WDM spectrum-sliced SC pumped by an optical 3R decoded signal; it ranges from 1524.9 to 1590.0 nm, which corresponds to an 8.05-THz bandwidth. Figure 14 shows the measured BERs back to back, after 80-km transmission, after OC and wavelength conversions with optical 3R regeneration at node B, and at node C or E after subsequent 50-km transmission. Comparison of the BERs for after 80-km transmission with those for after OC and wavelength conversions shows that almost power penalty–free OC and wavelength conversions were achieved by using optical time-gating detection followed by optical 3R regeneration. OC and wavelength-convertible signal transport was also achieved in a VOCP-VWP path network with a total link length of 180 km and four network nodes.

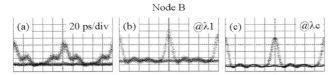

Node B

Figure 12: Eye diagrams (a) of decoded 1-OC2 with interference noise and (b) after optical time-gating to reduce interference noise at λ1 and (c) of decoded signal at λc after optical 3R regeneration

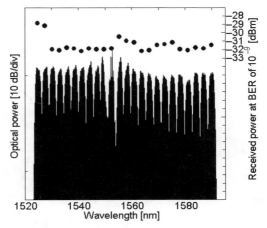

Figure 13: Optical spectrum for 24-channel WDM spectrum-sliced SC pumped by optical 3R decoded signal, and received power at BER of 10^{-9} for each wavelength

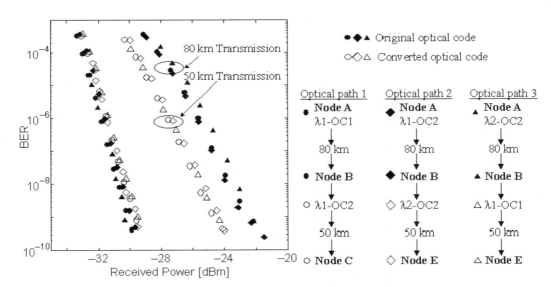

Figure 14: Measured BERs—back-to-back, after 80-km transmission, after optical and wavelength conversion with optical 3R regeneration, and after subsequent 50-km transmission

APPLICATION OF SYNCHRONOUS OCDM TO PHOTONIC ROUTING

A proposed photonic label-switching router (Sotobayashi and Kitayama 2000; Kitayama, Wada, and Sotobayashi 2000) processes labels on the basis of optical code correlation. The use of this scheme is a potential way to overcome the bottlenecks created by electronic routers in Internet protocol over WDM networks. Architectures for a photonic label-switching router, including the photonic label processing, the photonic label swapping, the optical switching, and their optical implementations, are currently being investigated. The results of proof-of-concept experiments for photonic label processing and photonic label swapping should confirm their feasibility.

Figure 15a shows an Internet protocol (IP) over photonic network in which photonic IP routers are used at the nodes instead of electronic routers. Label switching is used to forward the IP packets. A packet is forwarded to its destination via designated intermediate nodes.

The node configuration in an IP over photonic network is shown in Figure 15b. It consists of *photonic label switching routers* (PLSRs) and wavelength multiplexers

and demultiplexers. The PLSRs differ from their electronic counterparts in that the processing of IP packets is mainly performed in the optical domain without optical-to-electrical conversion.

Figure 16 shows the PLSR architecture. Each label is mapped onto a single optical code, and an IP packet is encapsulated in an optical frame. The main building blocks are the photonic label processor, the photonic label swapper, and an optical switch. Exact matching for the table lookup uses optical correlation, which identifies a photonic label only when all of the bits of the label coincide with those of the label entry in the lookup table. The optical payload is gated for routing to the desired port in the switch fabric. The label is swapped at the LSR output in accordance with the entries in the address bank.

Figure 17 shows the principle of the label processing. An input photonic label is optically duplicated by optical amplification and power splitting into as many copies as there are label entries in the table. This enables all of the optical correlations between the copies and the label entries to be performed in parallel. An autocorrelation peak appears in the bit time duration only when the codes match. Unique to the photonic label processing is that no

(a)

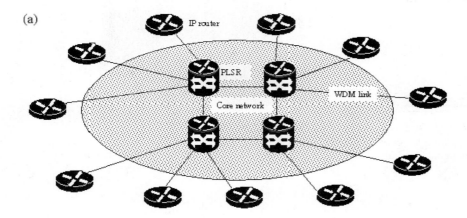

(b)

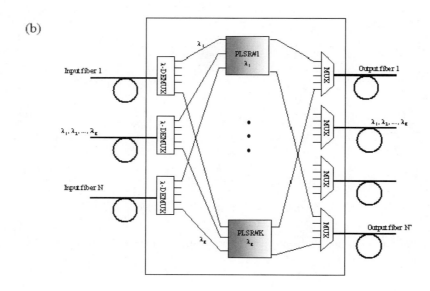

Figure 15: (a) IP over photonic network with PLSRs; (b) node configuration of IP over photonic network

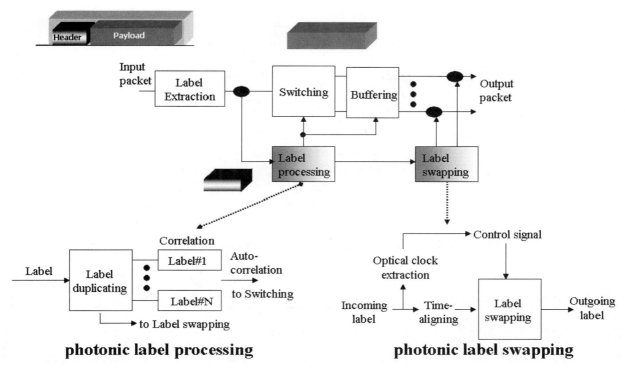

Figure 16: Architecture of PLSR

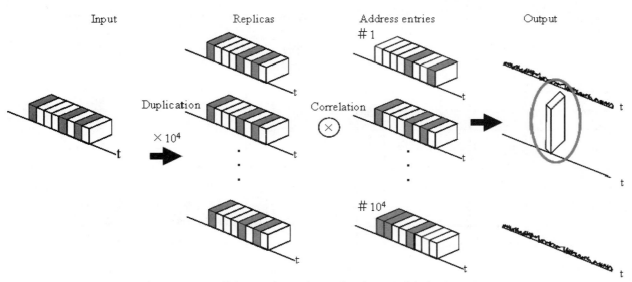

Figure 17: Parallel optical correlation for photonic label processing

optical logic operation is involved—only optical correlation is used. The processing can thus be performed using simple passive optical devices.

Figure 18 shows the experimental setup used for testing the photonic label processing. In the optical transmitter, a photonic label of 8-chip BPSK optical code was generated and a 64-bit-long burst payload data signal was attached. The optical packet was sent to the photonic label processor. The output signal of the autocorrelation peak was detected when the input label matched the label of the correlator. As a result, only the autocorrelation output signal could drive the opening of the optical gate switch

and thereby guide the packet to the target output port. Otherwise, the gate switch remained closed.

Figure 19a shows streak camera traces of a 64-bit-long packet generated with photonic label 1, and Figures 19b and 19c show the auto- and cross-correlation outputs of the packet decoded using label 1 (matched) and label 2 (unmatched). Figures 19d and 19e show the payload data observed at port 1 and port 2 for the two different input packets for which the labels were matched using correlator 1 and correlator 2. These figures clearly show that the address processor alternatively switched the two optical gates as the input optical code switched between labels 1

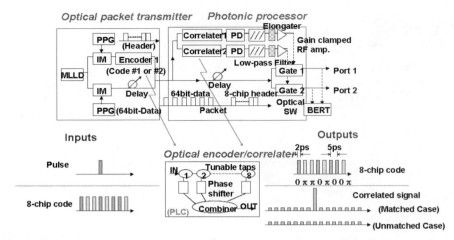

Figure 18: Experimental setup for testing 1×2 photonic label processing

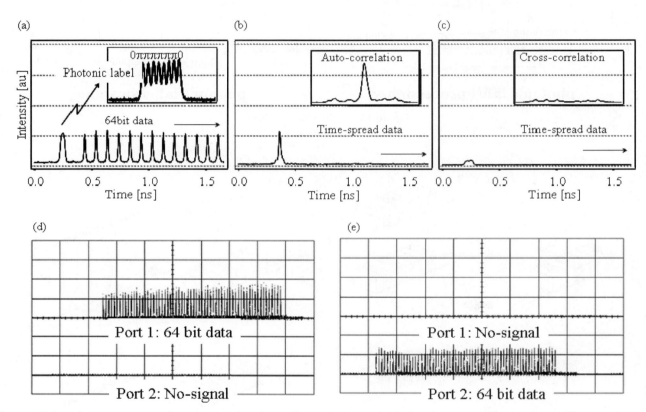

Figure 19: Streak camera traces of (a) generated 64-bit packet with photonic label 1, (b) autocorrelation output of packet decoded with label 1 (matched label), and (c) cross-correlation output decoded with label 2 (unmatched label). Observed payload data at ports 1 and 2 for two input labels: (d) matched with correlator 1 and (e) matched with correlator 2

and 2. This means that the label processor can distinguish eight-chip-long optical codes in packet labels and thereby control the optical switch.

The operation principle of photonic label swapping is shown in Figure 20a. Input photonic labels are swapped to the desired label in the optical domain. Suppose that the label to be swapped propagates along with the control optical pulses in an optical fiber. The use of cross-phase modulation enables the phase to be shifted by π. As a result, label swapping can be obtained by photonic processing.

Figure 20b shows the experimental setup used for testing photonic label swapping. Optical encoders 2 and 3 generated four-chip long BPSK optical code and a control pulse, respectively. Label swapping was performed by cross-phase modulation in a dispersion-shifted fiber. The output swapped label was inspected by correlator 3.

Figure 21a shows the output of correlator 3 without the control pulse. The signal code of [0000] and the setup of the correlator were the same, resulting in an autocorrelation trace. Figures 21b and 21c, respectively, show the

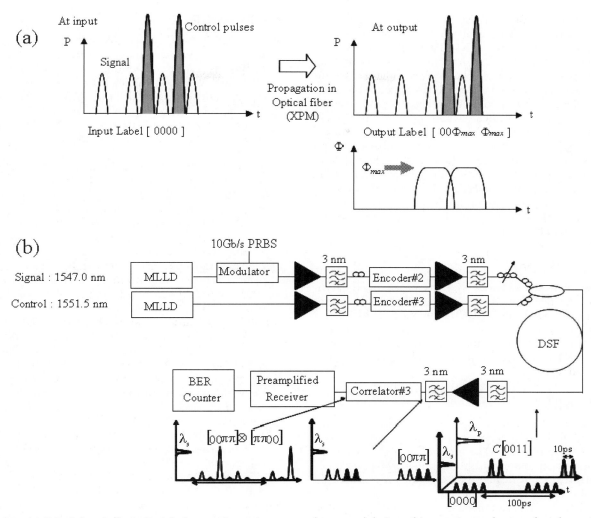

Figure 20: (a) Principle of photonic label swapping using cross-phase modulation; (b) experimental setup for photonic label swapping

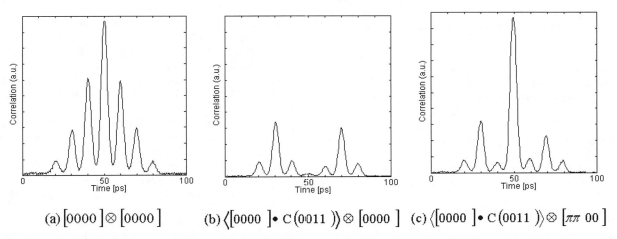

Figure 21: Output of correlator 3: (a) without control pulse, (b) swapped with control pulse (0011), representing cross-correlation decoded with code sequence [0000], and (c) swapped with control pulse (0011), representing cross-correlation decoded with code sequence [0011]

outputs with the control pulse for correlator 3 setups of [0000] and [00$\pi\pi$]. The resultant cross- and autocorrelation waveforms clearly show that label swapping was achieved by optical means. A photonic label-switching router in which the photonic label processing is based on optical code correlation has been investigated. The architectures of PLSRs with photonic label processing, photonic label swapping, and optical switching and their optical implementations have been experimentally demonstrated.

The target performance of a photonic label-switching router is estimated to be multi-Terabit/s. If a 32-chip-long optical code is used for IP routing, then the processing time of the optical correlation is 155 ps. Therefore, the processing speed of the photonic routing is 6.5G packets per second. For a 1000-bit-long packet, the transmission capacity per wavelength is 6.5 Tbit/s.

CONCLUSION

Ultrafast photonic network systems based on the synchronous OCDM have been reviewed. The potential applications of synchronous OCDM include high spectral efficiency transport systems, photonic access nodes, optical path networks, and photonic routers. The synchronous OCDM is thus a promising technique for future photonic networks.

GLOSSARY

Bandwidth: The highest capacity that can be transmitted in information-carrying systems.

Bit error rate (BER): The number of bits that are incorrect as compared with the number transmitted.

Demultiplexer: A device that separates a multiplexed signal into its original channels.

Eye diagram: A simultaneously overlaid display of the rise and fall of a 1 and 0. This generally results in a pattern in the shape of an eye that indicates the bit error rate.

Gigabit per second (Gbit/s): One billion bits per second.

Internet protocol (IP): Standard format for transmitting data on the Internet that uses packet switching.

Optical amplifier: A device that amplifies an optical signal without converting it into an electrical signal.

Point-to-point transmission: Carrying a signal between two points without splitting to other points.

Router: A device that determines the available route to send a packet and instructs the switches accordingly.

Terabit per second (Tbit/s): One trillion bits per second.

Time division multiplexing: Digital multiplexing by taking one pulse at a time from separate signals and combining them into a single stream.

Virtual path: A unidirectional logic connection between two signal destinations.

Wavelength division multiplexing (WDM): Placing multiple simultaneous telecom wavelengths in a single fiber.

CROSS REFERENCES

See *Code Division Multiple Access (CDMA); Frequency Division Multiplexing (FDM); Optical Fiber Communications; Wavelength Division Multiplexing (WDM).*

REFERENCES

Bigo, S., Y. Frignac, G. Charlet, W. Idler, S. Borne, H. Gross, R. Dischler, W. Poehlmann, P. Tran, C. Simonneau, D. Bayart, G. Veith, A. Jourdan, and J. Hamaide. 2002. 10.2Tbit/s (256 × 42.7Gbit/s PDM/WDM) transmission over 100km TeraLight fiber with 1.28bit/s/Hz spectrum efficiency. In *Proceedings of the Optical Fiber Communications Conference 2001* (OFC 2001), March 19–21, Anaheim, CA, USA, postdeadline paper PD25, pp. PD25–1–3.

Dixon, R. C. 1975. Why spread spectrum. *IEEE Communications Society Magazine*, 13(4): 21–5.

———. 1994. *Spread spectrum systems with commercial applications*. New York: Wiley-Interscience.

Fukuchi, K., T. Kasamatsu, M. Morie, R. Ohhira, T. Ito, K. Sekiya, D. Ogasawara, and T. Ono. 2002. 10.92-Tb/s (273 × 40-Gb/s) triple-band/ultra-dense WDM optical repeater transmission experiment. In *Proceedings of the Optical Fiber Communications Conference 2001* (OFC 2001), March 19–21, Anaheim, CA, USA, postdeadline paper PD24, pp. PD24–1–3.

Karafolas, N., and D. Uttamchandani. 1995. Optical CDMA system using bipolar codes and based on narrow passband optical filtering and direct detection. *IEEE Photonics Technology Letters*, 7(9): 1072–4.

Kitayama, K. 1998. Code division multiplexing lightwave networks based upon optical code conversion. *IEEE Journal of Selected Areas in Communications*, 16(9): 1309–19.

Kitayama, K., N. Kataoka, N. Wada, and W. Chujo. 2001. 10 Gbit/s packet-selective photonic label-based ADM experiment. In *Proceedings of the Twenty-Seventh European Conference on Optical Communications*, Sep. 30–Oct. 4, Amsterdam, Th.L.1.6, pp. 548–9.

Kitayama, K., and M. Murata. 2001. Photonic access node using optical code-based label processing and its applications to optical data networking. *IEEE/OSA Journal of Lightwave Technology*, 19(10): 1401–15.

Kitayama, K., H. Sotobayashi, and N. Wada. 1999. Optical code division multiplexing (OCDM) and its application to photonic networks. *IEICE Transactions on Fundamentals of Electronics, Communications and Computer Sciences*, E82-A(12): 2616–26.

Kitayama, K., N. Wada, and H. Sotobayashi. 2000. Architectural considerations for photonic IP router based upon optical code correlation. *IEEE/OSA Journal of Lightwave Technology*, 18(12): 1834–44.

Marom, E. 1978. Optical delay line matched filter. *IEEE Transactions on Circuits and Systems*, 25(6): 360–4.

Ono, T., Y. Yano, K. Fukuchi, T. Ito, H. Yamazaki, M. Yamaguchi, and K. Emura. 1998. Characteristics of optical duobinary signals in terabit/s capacity, high-spectrum efficiency WDM system. *IEEE/OSA Journal of Lightwave Technology*, 16: 788–97.

Optical code in optical communications and networks. 2007. *IEEE Journal of Selected Topics in Quantum Electronics*, special issue.

Pickholtz, R., D. Schilling, and L. Milstein. 1982. Theory of spread spectrum communications: A tutorial. *IEEE Transactions on Communications*, 30(5): 855–84.

Prucnal, P. R. 2005. *Optical code division multiple access: Fundamentals and applications*. New York: CRC Press/ Taylor & Francis.

Salehi, J. A. 1989. Code division multiple access techniques in optical fiber networks: I. Fundamental principles. *IEEE Transactions on Communications*, 37(8): 824–33.

———, A. M. Weiner, and J. P. Heritage. 1990. Coherent ultrashort light pulse code-division multiple access communication systems. *IEEE/OSA Journal of Lightwave Technology*, 8(3): 478–91.

Sardesai, H. P., C. C. Chang, and A. M. Weiner. 1998. A femtosecond code-division multiple-access communication system test bed. *IEEE/OSA Journal of Lightwave Technology*, 16(11): 1953–64.

Scholtz, R. 1977. The spread spectrum concept. *IEEE Transactions on Communications*, 25(8): 748–55.

Sotobayashi, H., W. Chujo, and K. Kitayama. 2001. 1.52 Tbit/s OCDM/WDM (4 OCDM × 19 WDM × 20 Gbit/s) transmission experiment. *IEEE Electronics Letters*, 37(11): 700–1.

———. 2002. 1.6-b/s/Hz 6.4-Tb/s QPSK-OCDM/WDM (4 OCDM × 40 WDM × 40 Gb/s) transmission experiment using optical hard thresholding. *IEE Photonics Technology Letters*, 14(4): 555–7.

———. 2002. Transparent virtual optical code/wavelength path network. *IEEE Journal of Selected Topics in Quantum Electronics*, 8(3): 699–704.

———. 2003. Optical code division multiplexing (OCDM) and its application for peta-bit/s photonic network. *Information Sciences*, 149: 171–82.

Sotobayashi, H., and K. Kitayama. 1998. 325 nm bandwidth supercontinuum generation at 10 Gbit/s using dispersion-flattened and non-decreasing normal dispersion fibre with pulse compression technique. *IEEE Electronics Letters*, 34(13): 1336–7.

———. 1999. 10 Gb/s OCDM/WDM multiple access using spectrum-sliced supercontinuum BPSK pulse code sequences. In *Proceedings of Optical Amplifiers and Their Applications* (OAA '99), June 6–11, PD7, Nara, Japan, pp. Pdp7-1–3.

———. 1999. Transfer response measurements of a programmable bipolar optical transversal filter by using the ASE noise of an EDFA. *IEEE Photonics Technology Letters*, 11(7): 871–3.

———. 2000. Optical code based label swapping for photonic routing. *IEICE Transactions on Communications*, E83-B(10): 2341–7.

Sotobayashi, H., C. Sawaguchi, Y. Koyamada, and W. Chujo. 2002. Ultrafast walk-off free nonlinear optical loop mirror by a simplified configuration for 320 Gbit/s TDM signal demultiplexing. *OSA Optics Letters*, 27(17): 1555–7.

Sust, M. 1994. Code division multiple access for commercial communications. *Review of Radio Science 1992–1994*, pp. 155–179. Ghent, Belgium: International Union of Radio Science.

Teh, P. C., M. Ibsen, J. H. Lee, P. Petropoulos, and D. J. Richardson. 2002. Demonstration of a four-channel WDM/OCDMA system using 255-chip 320-Gchip/s quaternary phase coding gratings. *IEEE Photonics Technology Letters*, 14(2): 227–9.

Teh, P. C., P. Petropoulos, M. Ibsen, and D. J. Richardson. 2001. Phase encoding and decoding of short pulses at 10 Gb/s using superstructured fiber Bragg gratings. *IEEE Photonics Technology Letters*, 13(2): 154–6.

Tsuda, H., H. Takemouchi, T. Ishii, K. Okamamoto, T. Goh, K. Sato, A. Hirono, T. Kutrokawa, and C. Amoto. 1999. Photonic spectral encoder/decoder using an arrayed-waveguide grating for coherent optical code division multiplexing. Optical Fiber Communication Conference, *Technical Digest*, pp. PD32/1—3.

———. 1999. Spectral encoding and decoding of 10 Gbit/s femtosecond pulses using high resolution arrayed-waveguide grating. *IEEE Electronics Letters*, 35(14): 1186–8.

Vannucci, G. 1989. Combining frequency division multiplexing and code division multiplexing for high capacity optical network. *IEEE Network Magazine*, 3(2): 21–30.

Verdú, S. 1998. *Multiuser detection*. New York: Cambridge University Press.

Viterbi, A. J. 1995. *CDMA: Principles of spread spectrum communication*. New York: Addison-Wesley.

Free-Space Optics

John Liu, *Wayne State University*
Mark Schaefer, *OnStar Corporation*

INTRODUCTION

Free-space optics (FSO) is a technology that uses modulated laser beams to communicate without a special transmission medium such as fiber optics. FSO is not without its problems—most notably, its inability to transmit long distances through thick fog. FSO is still in its infancy, with a significant amount of research left to conduct in solutions to its key problems, but it already has become a principle contender in the market for last-mile access.

HISTORY OF FREE-SPACE OPTICS
Heliographs

The recorded history of using light signals for communication goes back to a recounting of Greek history by Xenophon in 405 B.C., who wrote that polished shields were used to make signals from the battlefield. The heliograph was invented in the mid-1800s by Sir Henry Christopher Mance and used extensively by the military; it was one the first devices to provide digital communications over long distances. The telegraph, a wired communication technology, was already in widespread use at that time; however, the heliograph met the need for long distance, portable, wireless communications. Heliographs only operated in direct sunlight because there was no light source powerful enough to be seen at the link distances. Heliograph operators used Morse code, which was already familiar to telegraph operators of the day.

Two primary transmission technologies were used. The original Mance heliograph simply tilted a mirror, which moved the rays of the sunlight away from the receiver to signal letters. A later design improvement added a mechanical shutter to block the light so that the aiming of the mirror was not affected. Heliographs were in wide military use until the mid-1920s when they were superseded by radio communications. The longest recorded heliograph link was 183 miles between Mt. Uncompahgre in Colorado, and Mt. Ellen in Utah. One interesting fact about this link is that the sites were actually obscured by the curvature of the Earth, but in the mornings, an atmospheric effect carried the beam over the horizon allowing the two groups to signal each other (Giddings 1895). Figure 1 shows the use of the heliograph to communicate during the surveying of the U.S.–Canadian boundary in 1910.

Figure 1: Use of heliograph in 1910 (photo courtesy of the National Oceanic and Atmospheric Administration)

Alexander Graham Bell's Photophone

In 1880, Alexander Graham Bell improved on the heliograph by modulating the light signal, similarly to how the telephone modulates a telegraph signal (Korevaar, Kim, and McArthur, undated). Bell used an extremely thin mirror coupled to a microphone to change the intensity of the reflected sunlight. The receiver used selenium, a material whose resistance changes based on the intensity of light received.

The photophone has many of the characteristics of a free-space optics link. Figure 2, from the patent application for Bell's photophone, shows the transmitter side.

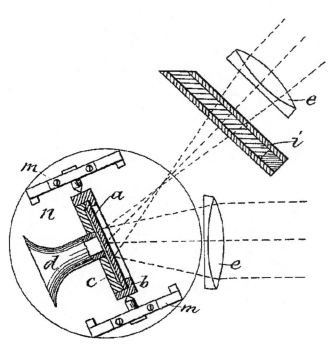

Figure 2: Diagram of Bell's photophone

Sunlight came in through a focusing lens (e), bounced off a thin mirror (a), and was collimated by the output lens (e). The signal was modulated by the audio-induced movement of the thin mirror by the microphone (d). The vibration of the microphone changed the shape of the thin mirror and focused more or less of the incoming sunlight on the target photophone.

Laser

The heliograph and photophone shared one fatal flaw: They required direct sunlight to operate properly. The invention of an electric, high-powered spotlight made communications at nighttime and during cloudy conditions possible. The invention of the laser opened up a new realm of optical communications. Lasers have some features that make them especially useful for long-distance communications. Most digital optical communications today use on-off keying, which turns the transmitter on and off at predetermined intervals to indicate a binary 0 or 1 value. Ordinary electric lights rely on the heat of the filament to provide light, causing a significant ramp-up and ramp-down time, but lasers have nearly instant-on and instant-off capability, providing communication rates in excess of gigabits per second. Another characteristic is *coherence:* All of the light transmitted from a laser is at the same phase. Although this is currently not used to improve FSO communication, significant research has been conducted using coherence as a mechanism for filtering out atmospheric distortion. Lasers also transmit at a single light wavelength. This property allows multiple lasers to be used simultaneously over the same link, a technique called *wavelength division multiplexing* (WDM) (Acampora 2002).

Dispersion in Space

As part of the U.S. manned Apollo missions, corner cube reflectors were installed on the surface of the moon. These reflectors have the property that the light is returned parallel to the incident light. In experiments using these

Figure 3: Laser retroreflector (photo courtesy of NASA)

reflectors, laser light from the Earth was aimed at the reflectors, which then directed the beam back toward the experiment site. The beam from the Earth was shown to disperse to approximately 7 km before reaching the surface of the moon (approximately 385,000 km). The photographs in Figures 3 and 4 show a retroreflector and the McDonald Laser Ranging Station, respectively.

Although the lasers used in this experiment are more powerful and more precise than those typically used for communications, the narrowness of the beam means that much of its energy arrives at the destination, where *radio frequency* (RF) energy spreads more, with less arriving at the destination. Scientists quickly discovered that the dispersion of RF will render the signals too weak to use for deep-space communications, leaving FSO as the principal approach.

A TYPICAL FSO SYSTEM

A simple FSO transceiver is depicted in Figure 5. The transmit laser is located at the bottom of the transceiver. Many FSO systems add forward error correction and link status information to the transmitted beam to reduce errors and provide network status information to the network operator. The incoming beam passes through a lens and is focused onto a *charge-coupled device* (CCD) sensor. The CCD sensor converts the incoming laser signal into electrical impulses that are decoded and transmitted to the rest of the network. Most FSO systems today have made significant improvements to this simple design to optimize the maximum bandwidth and maximum distance while still meeting the constraints of eye safety and reliability.

Figure 4: McDonald Laser Ranging Station (photo courtesy of NASA)

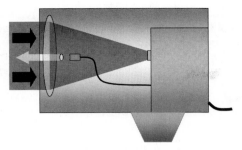

Figure 5: Simple FSO Transceiver

CHALLENGES FOR FREE-SPACE OPTICS
Eye Safety

Although the *infrared* (IR) frequencies used in FSO are invisible to the human eye, FSO laser transmitters can still potentially cause damage to humans if they are of significant power. FSO systems are engineered to provide protection from any eye injury during installation or while the link is active. Because the eye-safety measurement is defined as the power making it outside the FSO transmitter, some tricks can be used to provide more signal energy. For example, multiple eye-safe beams can be used simultaneously, provided they do not overlap in an unsafe manner. Also, a beam that is not safe can be passed through a spreading lens, allowed to expand for a short distance, and then passed through a collimating lens to make the beam parallel. The result is a dispersion of the laser energy over a larger area, which reduces the intensity and thus the possibility of retinal damage.

Weather

Although the attenuation of a laser beam in air under near-ideal conditions is on par with current single-mode fiber technology (on the order of 0.1 dB/km), weather conditions such as haze and fog can quickly reduce visibility, or the maximum range where the laser signaling can be detected. The reliability of FSO systems is primarily dependent on the visibility afforded by weather conditions, especially dense fog, where the laser beam is quickly absorbed (Ketprom et al. 2003; Leitgeb et al. 2002; Ragulsky and Sidorovich 2001). Currently, the only solutions to overcome dense fog are to increase the power of the beam (which is limited by eye safety), and shorten the link distance. Sometimes a series of shorter link segments can be used to create a long link. FSO systems that provide link statistics through a feedback mechanism can raise the power of the beam to overcome weather effects and lower the beam power when visibility improves. The lower beam power allows the system to provide longer service life for the laser transmitter and lower continuous power requirements.

Because link reliability is primarily dependent on weather conditions, FSO vendors rate the reliability of a given FSO link based on the percentage of time the link is available. This is somewhat inconsistent with reliability ratings of other systems, such as fiber. A 99.999 percent reliability of a fiber-based system means that there is a 0.001 percent chance that the link will be down (Kim and Korevaar 2001). The link failure, however, is thought to be dependent on equipment failure. For both FSO and fiber, these measurements do not classify the type of loss. The thought behind 99.999 percent reliability is that the total link downtime in a year averages to approximately 8.5 hours. For fiber, this represents the reliability of the equipment used to establish and maintain the connection but not necessarily the reliability of the medium. For FSO, what is being predicted is primarily the existence of environmental conditions that are conducive to maintaining the link; however, it does not typically account for equipment failure. The reliability prediction for fiber cannot really account for the business risk of catastrophic events such as a fiber cable being cut by construction equipment.

Obstructions and Line of Sight

Although the FSO beam typically disperses to at least 1 meter over typical distances, the beam can still be obstructed by helicopters, large birds, and other objects. Because typical Internet protocol–based communications is resilient to momentary interruptions, brief link loss will not be perceptible to the end user, except for certain time-critical services such as streaming media. One way to overcome obstruction by smaller objects such as dirt or dust on a window is to use multiple transmitting lasers. Larger obstructions are temporary in nature and would be nearly undetectable in most networks, although the affect on streaming media would generally be perceptible. Other line-of-sight problems that cannot be solved by relocating the transmitters are solved by adding multiple hops or by switching to a non–line-of-sight technology.

Scintillation

Scintillation is an optical effect caused by the uneven distribution of heat in the atmosphere. Pockets of hot air have a slightly different index of refraction, which creates small lenses that interrupt the laser beam. Because the pockets are small, the aggregate effect is to reduce the intensity of the incoming beam, which limits the distance the beam can travel (Korevaar, Kim, and McArthur, undated). Scintillation is most significant during the afternoon, when the intensity of the sun is greatest. For humans, scintillation appears as a "shimmering," which is what causes stars to "twinkle." Scintillation can often be overcome by increasing the transmission power. Using multiple transmitters is also effective in overcoming scintillation because the distortion caused by scintillation is highly localized (Willebrand and Ghuman 2001).

Building Movement

Anyone who has been in a skyscraper during a heavy wind will attest to the fact that buildings have significant movement. Movement of the transmitter and receiver is a problem for FSO systems because laser beams are typically extremely narrow and require pinpoint accuracy. Most of the commercial FSO systems available today use some sort of active tracking mechanism to manage the movement of buildings. To overcome higher-frequency artifacts, FSO systems purposefully spread the transmitted beam (Willebrand and Ghuman 2001). Although beam spreading increases resilience to higher-frequency building movement, beam divergence decreases the range of the link and its ability to overcome poor weather conditions.

FREE-SPACE OPTICS DEVICES
Choice of Infrared Laser Wavelength

Two primary laser wavelengths are used for FSO systems: 780–850 nm and 1550 nm. The shorter wavelengths are much easier to produce, and transmitters are approximately 1 percent of the cost of longer-wavelength transmitters. Both wavelengths have similar propagation characteristics through normal weather conditions (Korevaar, Kim, and McArthur, undated). In fact, the only significant reason for choosing the more expensive 1550-nm transmitter is eye safety. The 1550-nm transmitter can have approximately fifty times greater intensity because the majority of the energy in the beam is absorbed by the cornea without being able to focus on the retina (Kim and Korevaar 2001). The increased transmission intensity can be used to increase the availability or link distance.

Active and Passive FSO Devices

Regardless of the physical connection to the existing network, most FSO devices today use internal lasers to actively generate the transmission beam. The manufacturer can then exert more stringent control over the transmission and reception characteristics, which are critical for performance. Having a laser in the FSO device, however, adds latency by introducing, at a minimum, an electrical-to-optical conversion. With optical LAN, an additional conversion is required from optical to electrical. When a manufacturer chooses to generate the transmission beam within the FSO device, extra information can be coded in the transmission path, including forward error correction, beam steering information, and link statistics. The receiving FSO device can use the extra information to improve reliability and other performance characteristics (Li and Uysal 2003).

Passive FSO devices, on the other hand, use only an *erbium-doped fiber amplifier* (EDFA) to amplify the incoming fiber signal in-route, and thus no latency is added. Although this provides complete transparency to the controlling network equipment, the typical wavelengths used in fiber-based optical networking are not specially designed for transmission through the atmosphere, so the link lengths must be reduced to maintain the same reliability characteristics. The FSO system also does not benefit from the beam steering, error correction, and link statistics that are available to active FSO devices.

Active Tracking and Beam Steering

Most commercial systems in use today provide for beam steering to accommodate building movement and some atmospheric problems. The typical solution is to use a large photosensor, which is divided into regions. The intensity of the beam is measured in the different regions, and if the beam is found to be off-center, that information is fed back to the transmitter. The transmitter then adjusts a mirror to point the beam toward the center of the receiver. Different vendors provide different mirror technology, including steerable mirrors and *microelectromechanical systems* (MEMS) mirrors.

Semiconductor Laser Technology

Recent advances in semiconductor lasers are expected to provide benefits for FSO. The most significant of these appears to be *vertical-cavity surface-emitting lasers* (VCSELs). VCSELs are almost exclusively used in high-speed data communications today and are finding more widespread use as sensors. VCSELs offer many advantages over traditional "edge-emitting" semiconductor lasers. VCSELs emit light that is perpendicular to the surface of the wafer. This allows the devices to be tested on-wafer, saving manufacturing cost. VCSELs are brighter and more energy-efficient than edge emitters, allowing more applications. VCSELs output light in a circular Gaussian pattern, with less divergence than edge emitters, which reduces the complexity of coupling optics. VCSELs can also be modulated at much higher speeds than edge emitters, allowing for increased network bandwidth (Guenter et al. 2001; O'Brien et al. 2005).

ALTERNATIVES TO FREE-SPACE OPTICS
Fiber

Although fiber has quickly been established as the medium of choice for service-grade networking, digging fiber trenches in dense cities causes significant problems. Because of resulting traffic congestion and other problems caused by trenching, cities have become more concerned about the disruptions involved in developing fiber-optic networking. Some cities encourage carriers to lay fiber whenever trenches are dug for sewer, water, or even competing fiber lines. Others have outlawed fiber trenching entirely. Some cities and companies have actually run fiber cables through existing sewer lines to avoid the problems associated with trenching. This reaction to fiber trenching is creating a unique opportunity for FSO vendors to build metropolitan mesh networks as an alternative to fiber.

Radio Frequency Links
802.11

Radio frequency links are a significant competitor to FSO. The two primary RF links tend to be 802.11a and b/g. These operate at 5 GHz and 2.4 GHz, respectively, which do not require FCC licenses, and are thus subject to significant interference from other nearby wireless networks. The current 802.11 standards do not allow data rates higher than 54 Mbps, making it suitable only for small company local area network (LAN) traffic over short distances. Some commercial offerings use 802.11 as a slow-speed backup connection for FSO links.

Millimeter-Wave RF Systems

Millimeter-wave (MMW) RF systems carry network traffic at speeds comparable to FSO. However, MMW systems are more affected by weather than 802.11, especially by heavy rain. Because FSO is typically unaffected by heavy rain, MMW-FSO combination systems have made significant inroads because they are capable of sustaining 99.999 percent reliability under most weather conditions.

802.16

The 802.16 standard is designed primarily as a metropolitan area network technology that can supply broadband connectivity to the last mile. The standard is designed to be operated in licensed spectrum near the 2.4-GHz band. An 802.16 cell can support approximately 70 Mbps of shared bandwidth, and new cells can be added as the demand for bandwidth grows. Its operation in licensed spectrum provides protection from interference.

T1 and T3

For lower-bandwidth connections, a T1-T3 link, which is typically routed over copper lines, provides a low-cost, high-reliability link.

ADVANTAGES OF FREE-SPACE OPTICS
Setup Cost

Compared to fiber-optic cable, FSO systems are significantly cheaper to install. The labor involved includes site planning, site preparation (routing cables and power to the transceiver locations), mounting the transceivers, aligning the transceivers, and performing diagnostics (Willebrand and Ghuman 2001).

Security

FSO provides security capabilities on par with fiber optics. The beam dispersion is on the order of 3 meters per kilometer for a typical system. This allows an interceptor to be easily detected. Because the beam often does spread beyond the size of the receiver in building-to-building links, the receivers should be placed against a solid wall to prevent any stray beam from being intercepted.

Freedom from Interference

Because photons do not tend to interfere with each other, FSO systems can be installed in close proximity without risk of interacting with other systems. There is some risk of interference between identical systems mounted in close proximity, but this is easily solved by good site planning.

Because of the scarcity of unlicensed RF bands, low-frequency (2.4 GHz and 5 GHz) point-to-point systems can be greatly affected by interference caused by other devices operating in the same spectrum. Interference is less common with MMW systems because the signal is more directional.

Free Licensing

Because light-based systems are interference-free, the FCC has always allowed free licensing for transmission in the visible, ultraviolet (UV), and IR spectra. This is fortunate because, otherwise, people might not be allowed to wear certain clothes, get UV suntans, or even cook dinners on their stoves.

Because of interference on RF bands, the only enterprise-level option may be to license spectrum for a point-to-point system. This greatly increases the cost of an RF system, although it does guarantee that other nearby systems will not suffer interference.

Line-of-Sight Requirements

One issue in setting up an RF-based point-to-point link is that the signals transmitted between the two towers spread out over the distance of the link. This is caused by the diffraction of the signal in the atmosphere between the transmitting and receiving antennas. The pattern of diffraction is called the *Fresnel zone* and is modeled by an ellipsoid. Any obstructions in the Fresnel zone will affect the transmission, either by attenuating the signal or creating multiple paths. For a 2.4-GHz signal over 1 km, the radius of the Fresnel zone at the midpoint is more than 5 m, whereas at 60 GHz it is only 1 m. Although IR light does have a Fresnel zone, the zone is only 0.1 m.

Bandwidth

Higher bandwidth in an FSO link is usually provided by decreasing the per-symbol time, which reduces the range and reliability of the system. Through some of the technological improvements available today, FSO systems can provide Gigabit speeds. With technologies such as wavelength division multiplexing, which uses multiple light frequencies to transmit more information, FSO can support much higher bandwidth than any other free-space networking technology.

THE GROWTH OF FSO
Mesh Topologies

Mesh topologies allow a long link to be broken into many smaller links. This has allowed network service providers to link multiple clients together by creating multiple-hop optical networks. An additional advantage of mesh networking is that the network can be designed to provide fault tolerance by providing more than one path from a customer site to the service provider (Acampora 2002). For cities where buildings can obstruct each other, a customer with no line of sight to the service provider can be linked through another building with line of sight to both the customer and the network operator. The weather advantages are significant as well. Figure 6 represents an example mesh topology. The node at the top left cannot be reached by a conventional FSO link, so a network has been built, based on existing nodes, to link the farthest node to the fiber end point on the far right. The mesh network depicted also has at least two paths to each node, which provides for failover capability if a link or node fails.

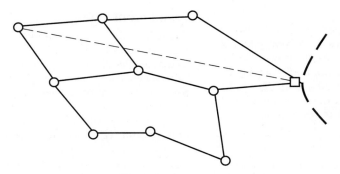

Figure 6: Mesh network topology

Emergency Linking

Although fiber links are extremely reliable, they can be susceptible to excavation problems, seismic activity, and other major failures. Because fiber generally takes months to install, FSO is often used as a disaster-recovery mechanism. Some FSO vendors are even selling so-called disaster kits that include everything needed to set up a temporary link in the case of a severe network outage. For extreme reliability, FSO systems can be installed as a hot standby to another network technology when there is a greater risk of a cable cut or other failure.

Linking in Large Cities

With the rise in mesh networking, FSO has become an enterprise-grade networking system in larger cities where fiber installation is cost-prohibitive (Willebrand and Ghuman 2001). Older buildings were not built with today's networks in mind and lack the bandwidth capability needed for medium to large businesses. FSO becomes an extremely cost-competitive solution with speeds equivalent to fiber, installation time on the order of days, and low system costs compared to fiber. FSO links can even be set up through windows so that roof access is not necessary. Many corporations are using FSO to bridge offices with line of sight without having to lease dedicated bandwidth from a network provider.

The Last Mile

Studies show that 90 percent of businesses with 100 or more employees (Acampora 2002) and 95 percent of buildings (Willebrand and Ghuman 2001) are located within one mile of a fiber backbone. With technologies such as *dense WDM* (DWDM), the backbone supports an almost unlimited bandwidth by today's standards, yet the pipe to most smaller businesses is a T1 or T3 line. FSO provides the unique capability of providing a low-cost optical link to the last mile without the bandwidth limitations of an RF-based system and without the cost of running fiber underground.

THE FUTURE OF COMMERCIAL FSO
WDM and DWDM

Although the propagation characteristics of IR provide a significant advantage in typical weather, multiple wavelengths can be used simultaneously over shorter distances to provide for more bandwidth. This technology in the fiber realm has enabled a single fiber to carry data rates in the Terabits per second range. This can be used to create higher-bandwidth networks over short distances or provide dedicated, wavelength-separated networks.

Passive Optical Networks

The rise of passive optical devices for networking has created the dream of a passive optical network in which backbone traffic could be routed solely by wavelength. This has been made possible by the invention of the EDFA, a device that amplifies laser signals without a loss of its coherent properties. Thus, long-haul networks can be achieved without the latency added by conversion between electronic and optical. Pure optical switches (think of a programmable prism) can reduce the dependence on store-and-forward routing. FSO fits in well with an all-optical solution by providing the capability to expand the network or connect nearby sites without fiber.

Communication to Space

The propagation characteristics of RF preclude its use for deep-space communications. Lasers are being researched extensively because they provide the only viable mechanism for deep-space communications. The two main obstacles for space communications are tracking and atmospheric effects. Eye safety is not as critical because the downlink and uplink stations can be located in restricted areas where human contact and airplane flight paths would not be a concern.

Although the maximum range of a typical eye-safe laser is on the order of 5 km, space agencies have their choice of location (e.g., Antarctica) and can potentially deal with eye safety by restricting the airspace around future satellite and mission ground stations.

The high bandwidth of FSO communications also makes satellite communications via laser a possibility. Recent patents (e.g., 6,912,075) suggest that WDM FSO between satellites could be used to carry a significant amount of data, which would then be communicated to the Earth through RF links.

Quantum Cryptography

A fascinating phenomenon first proposed by Einstein as a proof against quantum mechanics is that two photons can have a relationship that is unaffected by distance. For coupled photons, the relationship is polarization: Two photons can be created simultaneously that will have equal and opposite polarizations. If the polarization of one photon is changed, then the polarization of the other is changed as well. This effect, called *entanglement*, holds until the photon is measured, which destroys the relationship.

This phenomenon is important because, first of all, interception of the photons can be detected easily by comparing the polarizations of the photons at both ends (they should never be equal). In addition, the key, which is distributed over the optical link, means nothing without the information transmitted over a secondary channel. The receiver needs to know both the spin of the photon received and how that photon was changed by the transmitter in order to know the key.

FSO plays an important role because it can be a medium for the secure quantum channel. RF channels do not share the properties of entanglement.

Combined FSO and RF Links

Although FSO cannot meet the enterprise reliability requirements alone, FSO systems can be backed up by RF transmitters to provide continuous coverage in all weather conditions (Kukshya et al. 2002). These combinations generally appear as either a high-data-rate FSO link with a low-cost, low-data-rate RF solution such as 802.11 as a backup during dense fog. Another approach is to use MMW systems of comparable bandwidth that can be load balanced during typical weather conditions and switched over to the surviving system when an outage occurs (Hashmi and Mouftah 2004). A five-year study conducted in Seattle, Washington, tracking hourly visibility and rainfall rates showed that heavy rain, which disrupts MMW systems, and dense fog, which disrupts FSO systems, do not occur simultaneously (Korevaar and Kim 2001). As the bandwidth of FSO solutions increases, even MMW systems, which enjoy Gigabit rates, will become a low-data-rate backup.

RF backup systems guarantee at least some network connectivity in the most adverse weather conditions, although the network performance may not be optimal.

FSO RESEARCH
Multiple Quantum Well Retroreflectors

In discussing dispersion in space, the concept of a retroreflector was covered. Retroreflectors can also be used as a passive, transmit-only node in a FSO network.

The concept is similar to the later modulation scheme used by a heliograph in which a shutter was placed in the line of the beam of light. The difference is that the shutter is placed in front of a passive mirror. The result is a low-power device that can communicate on an FSO network. *Multiple quantum well* (MQW) devices have extremely fast switching times (on the order of 10 GHz), which can enable extremely high-bandwidth communications (O'Brien et al. 2005).

MQW retroreflectors find applications where there is no need for bidirectional communications. A beam of light can be used to query the status of the devices, and modulation schemes could potentially allow multiple devices to communicate simultaneously.

Much of the research in MQW retroreflectors is in the military domain. Because of the small size and low power consumption of these devices, they could be attached to sensors, carried on unmanned aerial vehicles, or even provide status information from soldiers. Low-flying planes or other air vehicles could read the status from the sensors.

Another area of research is wire replacement in space. Copper wiring in space can add significant weight to payloads and is susceptible to vibration during launch and reentry. A communicating node could use a combination of a high-dispersion light source to avoid alignment issues, and a retroreflector to transmit and receive important data.

Reconfigurable FSO Networks

Current commercial implementations of FSO rely on two fixed communications nodes. The mounts are extremely rigid, and the transceivers can only accommodate minimal movement. Although this is acceptable for commercial networking, many potential uses of FSO require communication between nodes at multiple speeds and under multiple conditions. Nodes might be soldiers, helicopters, automobiles, low- and high-flying airplanes, and even satellites.

Indoor FSO Networking

Although the primary market for FSO devices is in outdoor point-to-point networking, FSO research is also finding applications for indoor wire replacement. Although non–line-of-sight systems provide similar performance to 802.11b, higher-performance networking is required to replace the current networking infrastructure. Researchers are proposing a cell-based system so that each transceiver will have a line-of-sight path to one or more base stations. Prototype systems of this type have been demonstrated at bandwidths of 155 Mbps (O'Brien et al. 2005).

CONCLUSION

Free-space optics has developed from a highly intermittent communication technology to one that can provide high-data-rate communications reliably over short distances. FSO provides more significant benefits with increased numbers of customers in close proximity with mesh topologies that can create multiple highly reliable links instead of relying on a single intermittent link.

An FSO's high bandwidth and short setup time give it a unique edge in the network market today. Currently, FSO links are only used where reliability is not as critical or in combination with other technologies because of the possibility of outage.

GLOSSARY

Dense Wavelength Division Multiplexing (DWDM): This technique uses optical properties to transmit multiple simultaneous streams of information on a single optical link. The invention of a few significant devices allows the building of networks based on wavelength. These devices are the *erbium-doped fiber amplifier* (EDFA), which can amplify the entire spectrum of light in a fiber without losing its characteristics; the optical switch; and optical drop-add devices, which can route or add a single wavelength of light into or out of an optical link.

Laser: A device whose name is an acronym for *light amplification by the stimulated emission of radiation.* It produces highly directional and intense light beams by energizing electrons to a specific excitation state. When these electrons return to their rest state, they emit photons at a highly specific wavelength based on the difference in energy between the two states. Different materials emit different wavelengths based on their molecular properties.

Mesh Networking: Networks that are created using multiple links. Mesh networks can also be designed to be more reliable by creating multiple paths to each node on the network. If one link fails, then smart routers in the network can move traffic from the failed link to the remaining link.

Micro-Electromechanical Systems (MEMS): These are microscopic machines created through processing of silicon and other materials at a nanometer level. As an example, MEMS mirrors act like a single bit of RAM but can quickly and accurately switch between two positions. Some projectors use this technology because they support extremely high contrast.

Millimeter Wave (MMW): This refers to radio frequency communications using frequencies in the 60-GHz range. The wavelength of these systems is approximately 1 millimeter. These systems operate within the oxygen absorption band, which means that the maximum link distance is significantly limited. The limiting characteristics of oxygen absorption also increase the security of the MMW links.

Passive Optical Network (PON): A network created by routing of optical signals without requiring conversion to or from electrical impulses. Each wavelength can be routed independently, usually requiring significant setup time and planning, but the advantage is that no latency is added in the optical switches, where electrical switching can add significant latency.

CROSS REFERENCES

See *Optical Fiber Communications; Passive Optical Networks for Broadband Access; Wavelength Division Multiplexing (WDM).*

REFERENCES

Acampora, A. 2002. Last mile by laser. *Scientific American*, June 17, pp. 48–53.

Giddings, H. A. 1895. Army signaling. *Outing*, August, no. 5, pp. 396–9.

Guenter, J. K., J. A. Tatum, A. Clark, R. S. Penner, R. H. Johnson, R. A. Hawthorne, J. R. Biard, and Y. Liu. 2001. Commercialization of Honeywell's VCSEL technology: Further developments, vertical-cavity surface-emitting lasers V. In *Proceedings of the SPIE*, October, Bellingham, WA, USA, vol. 4286, pp. 1–14.

Hashmi, S., and T. Mouftah. 2004. Integrated optical/wireless networking. In *Proceedings of the IEEE Canadian Conference on Electrical and Computer Engineering* (CCECE'2004), May, Niagara Falls, Ontario. pp. 2095–8.

Ketprom, U., Y. Kuga, S. Jaruwatanadilok, and A. Ishamaru. 2003. Numerical studies on time-domain responses of ON/OFF-keyed modulated optical signals through a dense fog. IEEE Topical Conference on Wireless Communication Technology.

Kim, I. I., and E. Korevaar. 2001. Availability of free space optics and hybrid FSO/RF systems. Optical Wireless Communications IV, August, Denver.

Korevaar, E., I. I. Kim, and B. McArthur. Undated. Atmospheric propagation characteristics of highest importance to commercial free space optics. MRV Communications (www.mrv.com), San Diego.

Kukshya, V., T. S. Rappaport, H. Izadpanah, G. Tangonan, R. A. Guerrero, J. K. Mendoza, and B. Lee. 2002. Free-space optics and high-speed RF for next generation networks: Propagation measurements. In *Proceedings of Fall 2002 Vehicular Technology Conference*, Sept. 24–9, Vancouver, Canada. pp. 616–20.

Leitgeb, E., J. Bregenzer, P. Fasser, and M. Gebhart. 2002. Free space optics: Extension to fiber-networks for the "last mile." In *Proceedings of the IEEE/LEOS 2002 Annual Meeting*, Nov. 10–14, Glasgow, Scotland. pp. 459–60.

Li, J., and M. Uysal. 2003. Optical wireless communications: System model, capacity and coding. In *Proceedings of the IEEE Vehicular Technological Conference*, October, Orlando. pp. 168–72.

O'Brien, D. C., G. E. Faulkner, K. Jim, E. B. Zyambo, D. J. Edwards, M. Whitehead, P. Stavrinou, G. Parry, J. Bellon, M. J. Sibley, V. A. Lalithambika, V. M. Joyner, R. J. Samsudin, R. Atkinson, D. M. Holburn, and R. J. Mears. 2005. Integrated transceivers for optical wireless communications. *IEEE Journal on Selected Topics in Quantum Electronics*, 11(1): 173–83.

Ragulsky, V. V., and V. G. Sidorovich. 2001. On the availability of atmospheric optical communication lines. *Optics and Spectroscopy*, 93(1): 161–4.

Willebrand, H. A., and B. S. Ghuman. 2001. Fiber optics without fiber. *IEEE Spectrum*, August, pp. 40–5.

Optical Switching Techniques in WDM Optical Networks

Amor Lazzez and Noureddine Boudriga, *University of the 7th of November at Carthage, Tunisia*
Mohammad S. Obaidat, *Monmouth University*

INTRODUCTION

Optical transmission and switching technologies based on *wavelength division multiplexing* (WDM) have been increasingly deployed over the last decade to satisfy the tremendous demand for bandwidth. WDM transmission technology has been efficiently established, while the development of optical switching technologies has continued to progress rapidly. The result of such efforts has led to the creation of optical networks in which the optical signal undergoes optical-electrical-optical conversion at each intermediate node. Two tendencies have emerged for the design and deployment of WDM networks. The first trend attempts to increase network transparency in order to remove electronic bottlenecks and manage a large set of heterogeneous signals regardless of protocol formats, modulation, and bit rates. The second trend looks for network reconfigurability such that bandwidth can be assigned efficiently to end users in order to accommodate dynamically changing traffic demands. Both trends reflect the vision for future networks in which optical switching technologies play a fundamental role and bandwidth is promptly available to end users.

The migration of switching functions from electronics to optics is a critical issue. It is progressively done through several phases. The first phase is ongoing. It deploys wavelength routing, which offers circuit-switching services at the granularity level of wavelengths. Because of the circuit nature, wavelength-routed networks can be built with commercially available optical switching technologies such as the optomechanical, micro-electromechanical system switches, electro-optic switches, and thermo-optic switches (Papadimitriou, Papazoglou, and Pomportsis 2003; Yano, Yamagishi, and Tsuda 2005); unfortunately, these are still relatively slow. Although wavelength routing represents an important step toward transparent configurable optical networking, optical circuits tend to be inefficient for traffics that have not been multiplexed. In addition, circuit-switching models do not fit well with Internet protocol (IP) packet switching. The second phase undertakes the move toward *optical burst switching* (OBS) (Qiao and Yoo 1999; Baldine et al. 2002) and attempts to minimize the header management at the internal nodes. OBS is generally considered as an attractive technique for supporting improved switching granularity. Because the unit of transmission and switching is a burst, OBS is more efficient than circuit switching when the carried traffic does not utilize full wavelength. In the longer term, *optical packet switching* (OPS) (Yao et al. 2001; Sivalingam and Subramaniam 2005) promises finer switching granularity, providing bandwidth efficiency, flexibility, and data management. The achievement of this third phase, however, faces major difficulties because OPS will necessitate the development of several component and system technologies that are still in their experimental stage (Sivalingam and Subramaniam 2005).

One major issue in optical switching is the provision of differentiated service to support various *quality-of-service* (QoS) requirements. *Multiprotocol label switching* (MPLS) (Rosen, Viswanathan, and Callon 2001) is a recent technology that has been proposed for IP networks to increase node throughput and provide multiclass routing to multiple services. Throughput increase is achieved by packet forwarding at lower layers, whereas QoS differentiation is based on the assignment of a unique label to all of the packets of each flow. To provide more efficiency to MPLS in terms of traffic forwarding and QoS, a technology called *optical label switching* (OLS) has emerged based on the idea of adapting the traditional label-switching technology to WDM networks, which may provide QoS support over WDM networks and resolve some shortcomings. Two approaches are considered: *multiprotocol lambda switching* (MPλS) (Awduche et al. 2002) and photonic label switching. Considering that there are many technologies underlying the data-link and physical layers, the *generalized multiprotocol label switching* (GMPLS) (Mannie 2001; Banerjee et al. 2001) is proposed to extend MPLS to encompass time division, wavelength, and spatial (or fiber) switching. It provides a common control plan that is used to simplify network operation and management by automating end-to-end provisioning of connections and managing network resources.

Signaling is one key issue of interest in the development of optical networks to support switching. It monitors the establishment of several objects and activities such as lightpaths. Specifically, to set up a lightpath, a signaling protocol is required to exchange control information among nodes and reserve resources. Signaling schemes can also be used to manage contention-based optical buffering, wavelength conversion, or deflection methods (Yao et al. 2003). Different signaling protocols have been proposed to implement the aforementioned optical switching techniques. Among theses protocols are the signaling protocols proposed for static and dynamic lightpath establishment over *wavelength routing* (WR) networks (Zang, Jue, and Mukherjee 2000) and the *just-enough-time* (JET) (Yoo and Qiao 1997; Myers and Bayvel 2001) and the just-in-time (JIT) (Wei and McFarland 2000) signaling protocols in OBS networks. Other examples are the signaling protocol that is similar to the *asynchronous transfer mode* (ATM) proposed in Lazzez et al. 2006 for the transmission of packet flows over an optical network in an ATM-like manner, and the MPLS and GMPLS protocols (Rosen, Viswanathan, and Callon 2001; Banerjee et al. 2001; Yao et al. 2003; Ashwood-Smith and Berger 2003; Berger 2003) for the implementation of label-switching technologies over WDM networks.

In this chapter, we discuss the major switching techniques proposed for the development of WDM networks. More precisely, we address the following issues: (1) the description of the architecture of WR networks and related schemes for link and path protection and restoration; (2) the burst switching technology and the issues in designing and implementing OBS networks such as burst assembly, contention resolution, and QoS support; (3) the architecture of an OPS network and the major concerns and difficulties in designing optical packet switching; (4) the label-switching technology and its contribution in terms of traffic forwarding efficiency and QoS support; (5) the MPLS paradigm over WDM optical networks; (6) the most important signaling schemes proposed for WDM; and (7) the advanced issues in network evolution toward an all-optical network.

WAVELENGTH ROUTING NETWORKS
Lightpath Management in WR Network Architecture

In WR networks (Jue and Xiao 2000), an all-optical wavelength path called the *lightpath* can be established between edges of the network. A lightpath is created by dedicating a wavelength channel on every link along the chosen path. After data transfer, the lightpath is released. A WR network is formed by *optical cross-connect* (OXC) devices connected by point-to-point optical fiber links. The OXC devices are capable of differentiating data streams based on their input ports and the wavelengths they use (Elmirghani and Mouftah 2000). The data transmitted in a WR network require no electronic-to-optical conversion, no buffering, and no processing at the intermediate nodes. An OXC device switches optically an incoming wavelength λi on an input fiber to the outgoing wavelength λi of an output fiber. If the OXC is equipped with wavelength converters, then it can also switch λi to different outgoing wavelengths λj of the output fiber. This happens when the wavelength λi of the output fiber is in use. An OXC can also be used as an optical add-drop multiplexer. Thus, it can terminate the optical signal of a number of incoming wavelengths and insert new optical signals on the same output wavelengths.

Lightpath Establishment

Establishing a lightpath is done in a WR network in two steps: path selection and channel assignment. *Path selection* refers to the selection of a path from source to destination based on certain criteria. *Channel assignment* allocates a wavelength channel on every link in the selected path. Path selection can be carried out in several ways. If every source-destination pair has one preselected path, then the selection is referred to as a *fixed-path approach*. If a path is selected depending on the network status from a preselected set of candidate paths, then it is referred to as *dynamic path selection*. With this selection, the set of candidate paths remains the same all of the time and does not change. If the candidate paths are chosen based on the network status, then the path selection process is called *exhaustive routing*.

Traffic Grooming

As shown previously, a lightpath in a WR network occupies an entire wavelength on each hop of the source-destination path. The wavelength can be the same throughout the optical network or differ from one link to another if converters are available at the optical nodes. Nevertheless, many traffic flows do not require the bandwidth of an entire wavelength. In fact, a traffic flow may need only a small portion of a wavelength bandwidth. This results in inefficient network resources utilization because a great part of a lightpath's bandwidth may be unused and unavailable for use by other traffic streams. To solve this problem, the bandwidth of a lightpath is divided into lower subrate units so that it can carry traffic flows transmitted at lower rates. A traffic stream can use one or many subrate units. This allows the unused bandwidth to be available to other traffic streams. Such a technique is referred to as *traffic grooming*, whereby lower-rate traffic streams are multiplexed onto (and demultiplexed from) higher-capacity WDM wavelengths in order to improve wavelength utilization and meet network design goals such as cost minimization (Dutta and Rouskas 2002; Naoya and Kubota 2005; Takahashi 2004; Lazzez et al. 2006).

Quality of Service in WR Networks

A major concern in WR networks is how to provide differentiated services to support various QoS requirements. We present here the general framework proposed in Kaheel et al. (2002) for providing differentiated service in WR networks. This framework extends the previously proposed *differentiated optical services* (DOS) model (Golmie, Ndousse, and Su 2000) and considers other QoS schemes for WR networks. The DOS model considers the unique optical characteristics of lightpaths. A lightpath is identified by a set of optical parameters such as bit error rate, delay, jitter, and behaviors such as protection, monitoring, and security capacities. These parameters and behaviors provide the basis for measuring the quality of optical service available over a given path. The DOS framework is composed of the following six items.

1. Service class: A service class is determined by a set of parameters that characterizes the quality and impairments of the optical signal carried over a lightpath. These parameters are either specified in *quantitative terms* such as delay, average bit error rate, jitter, and bandwidth; or based on *functional abilities* such as protection, security, and monitoring.
2. *Routing and wavelength assignment* (RWA) algorithm: In order to provide QoS support over a WR network, it is obligatory to use an RWA algorithm that manages the QoS characteristics on the wavelength channels. An example for RWA algorithms is presented in Jukan (2001), where the primary idea aims at using adaptive weight functions that characterize the properties of the wavelength channels.
3. Lightpath groups: Lightpaths are classified into groups that reflect the distinctive qualities of the optical transmission. Each lightpath group corresponds to a specific service class.
4. Traffic classifier: Traffic flows are classified at the network ingress into one of the supported service classes. A traffic flow of a given traffic class is transmitted on a lightpath, which is able to provide the required QoS (lightpath groups).
5. Lightpath allocation algorithm: Several algorithms have been proposed in the literature for allocating lightpaths to different service classes.
6. Admission control: An optical resource allocator is used to conduct dynamic provisioning of lightpaths in a WR network. The optical resource allocator keeps track of the resource usage and evaluates the lightpath characteristics and functional capabilities (monitoring, protection, and security). The resource

allocator is also responsible for initiating an end-to-end call setup along the sequence of optical resource allocators representing the different domains traversed by the lightpath.

QoS-Based Lightpath Allocation Algorithms

Lightpath allocation can be static, static with borrowing, or dynamic. In *static* allocation, a fixed subset of lightpaths is assigned to each service class. The number of lightpaths in each group depends on the service class—that is, higher service classes are allocated more lightpaths. When *borrowing* is allowed, different priority classes can borrow lightpaths from each other according to certain criteria. An example of this approach is to permit lower-priority traffic to borrow lightpaths from higher-priority traffic. However, borrowing in the reverse direction is not assigned because lightpaths originally assigned to lower-priority traffic may not satisfy the QoS requirements of higher classes (Kaheel et al. 2002).

Using a *dynamic* lightpaths allocation algorithm, the network begins with no reserved lightpaths. The available set of lightpaths can then be assigned dynamically to any class under the assumption that all lightpaths have similar characteristics and functional capabilities. One approach for dynamic lightpath allocation is to use *proportional differentiation*, which quantitatively adjusts the service differentiation of a particular QoS parameter to be proportional to differentiation factors that a network service provider sets beforehand. More precisely, if P_i is the QoS metric of interest and S_i is the differentiation factor for class i, then the proportional differentiation model shows that $P_i/P_j = S_i/S_j$ for all pairs (i, j). For example, assume that P_i is the packet-loss probability for class I. If $S_1/S_2 = 2$, then the number of lightpaths assigned to Class 1 must be twice the number assigned to Class 2.

OPTICAL BURST-SWITCHING NETWORKS

Optical burst switching has been proposed as a new switching paradigm for optical networks and has emerged as a candidate for the optical transport layer of the next-generation Internet. OBS combines the advantages of optical circuit switching and optical packet switching while overcoming the weaknesses of the circuit switching and the complexity of OPS. OBS is a fast circuit-switching technique that provides a granularity between wavelengths and packets but mandates neither the use of optical header processing nor optical buffering. Two key characteristics differentiate the OBS technology: (1) a hybrid approach in which control information is signaled out of band and processed electronically while data stay in the optical domain all of the time, and (2) the one-pass reservation whereby the transmission of a burst is not delayed until an acknowledgment of successful end-to-end path setup is received but is instead initiated as soon as the burst has been pulled together (COST 266, undated).

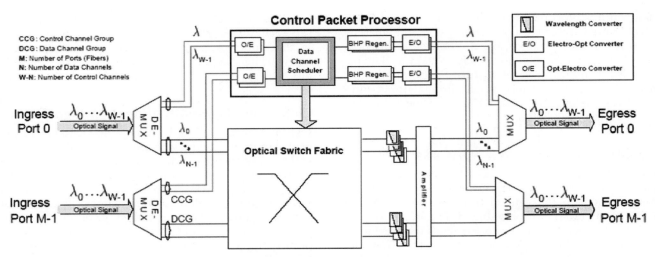

Figure 1: Architecture of an OBS core node

OBS Network Architecture

In an OBS network, data bursts that consist of multiple packets are switched through the network all-optically. Each burst is preceded by a control message—the *burst header packet* (BHP)—to configure the switches along the burst's path. The burst follows the header without waiting for an acknowledgment that resources have been reserved and switches have been configured along the path. An OBS network is composed of edge and core nodes interconnected via WDM fiber links. An optical burst switch transfers a data burst coming on an input port to its destination via an output port. The fiber links carry multiple wavelengths; each wavelength can be seen as a channel. Control traffic may be transmitted in-band over the same channel as data traffic or on a separate control channel. The source edge node (or ingress node) assembles the electronic input packets into an optical data burst, which is sent over the OBS core. The assembled bursts are transmitted all-optically over OBS core routers, without any storage at intermediate nodes to the destination edge node (or egress node). Upon receiving the burst, the egress node disassembles the bursts into packets and forwards the packets to the destination client terminals. In Vokkarane (2004), a basic architecture has been proposed for core and edge nodes in an OBS network.

Core Node Architecture

As depicted in Figure 1, an OBS core node is mainly composed of an *optical switch fabric* (OSF) and a *control packet processor* (CPP) (Vokkarane 2004). The CPP creates and maintains a forwarding table and is responsible for configuring the OSF. When the CPP receives a control packet (the burst header packet), it identifies the intended destination and consults the router signaling processor to find the appropriate output port. If the output port is available when the data burst arrives, then the CPP configures the OSF to let the data burst pass through. If the port is not available, then the OSF is configured depending on the contention-resolution mechanism implemented in the network. Typically, the SCU is responsible for BHP

interpretation, scheduling, contention detection and resolution, forwarding table lookup, wavelength conversion control, BHP rewriting, and OSF control. In the case of a data burst entering the OSF before its control packet, the burst is simply dropped (Vokkarane 2004).

Edge Node Architecture

Edge nodes carry out electrical-optical-electrical conversion and burst assembly and disassembly. Figure 2 depicts the architecture of an OBS edge node, which includes a *routing module* (RM) (Vokkarane 2004), and a *burst assembler* (BA) for each output wavelength channel. The RM selects the appropriate output channel for each packet and sends each packet to the corresponding BA module. The BA assembles bursts from the received packets. Each BA module is composed of a classifier, a separate packet queue for each traffic class, and a scheduler. The scheduler creates a burst based on the adopted burst assembly technique and sends the burst to the output port. At the egress node, a burst disassembly module disassembles the bursts into packets.

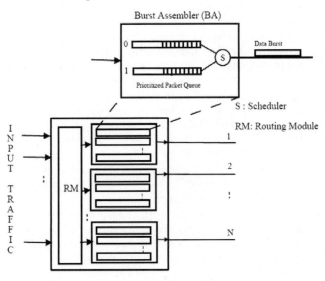

Figure 2: Architecture of an OBS edge node

Burst Assembly

Burst assembly is the procedure of aggregating and assembling input packets from various sources into bursts at the ingress edge nodes of the OBS network. The trigger condition for a burst creation is a key factor in an OBS network because it permits the control of the burst arrival into the OBS core. Different types of burst assembly techniques are developed in the OBS literature. The most frequent burst assembly techniques are timer-based and threshold-based (Vokkarane 2004; Yu, Chen, and Qiao 2002). In timer-based approaches, a timer starts at the beginning of each new assembly cycle. After a fixed time τ, all the packets that arrived during period τ are assembled into a burst. A *timer-based* scheme is used to provide uniform separation between successive bursts from the same ingress node. In *threshold-based* approaches, a limit is placed on the number of packets in each burst. A burst is generated when a new packet arrives, making the total number of current buffered packets exceed the threshold. A threshold-based scheme will generate fixed-length bursts at nonperiodic time intervals.

The time-out value for timer-based approaches must be set properly. If the value is too large, then the packet delay at the edge might be intolerable. If it is extremely small, then too many small bursts will be created, resulting in a higher control overhead. Although timer-based techniques may lead to undesirable burst lengths, threshold-based assembly schemes do not grant any guarantee on the assembly delay that packets will experience. To address the deficiency connected to each type of the aforementioned assembly algorithms, mixed assembly algorithms were proposed in Yu, Chen, and Qiao (2002) in which a burst is sent out when either the timer expires or the burst length exceeds the fixed threshold. A more significant case occurs when packets arriving to an ingress node are of different classes. The choice of a single burst assembly mechanism for all classes of traffic may be inappropriate. To overcome this, a composite burst assembly mechanism was proposed in Vokkarane (2004) whereby packets of different classes may be assembled into a single burst. It has been confirmed that composite burst assembly techniques can provide different levels of service for packets of different classes within the same burst if suitable contention-resolution mechanisms are implemented within the optical core (Vokkarane 2004).

Contention Resolution

Using one-way reservation protocols, an ingress node sends out bursts without having reservation acknowledgments or benefit from global coordination. Thus, it is possible that bursts contend with one another at the intermediate nodes. Contention occurs if multiple data bursts from different input ports are destined for the same output port at the same time. Contention problems can be addressed using techniques such as optical buffering, wavelength conversion, and deflection routing. A combination of contention-resolution techniques may be used to provide high throughput, low delay, and low packet-loss probability (Lazzez et al. 2006).

Optical Buffering

In electronic packet-switched networks, contention is typically handled using *random access memory* (RAM) buffers; however, because of technological constraints, optical RAM-like buffering is not yet available today. In optical networks, *fiber delay lines* (FDLs) can be utilized to delay packets for a fixed amount of time. Using multiple delay lines implemented in stages or in parallel, an optical buffer that can hold a burst for a variable amount of time can be created. Also, different FDL buffer architectures have been proposed in the literature (Chlamtac et al. 1996; Chia et al. 2001). Optical buffers are either *single-step*, meaning that they have only one block of delay lines, or *multistep*—that is, they have several blocks of delay lines. Optical buffers can be also classified into feed-forward, feedback, and hybrid architectures. According to the position of the FDL buffers in the switch, an optical switch is essentially classified into one of three major configurations: input buffering, output buffering, or shared buffering. In input buffering, for example, a set of buffers is dedicated for each input port (Vokkarane 2004).

Wavelength Conversion

Based on the WDM technology, several wavelengths run on a fiber link that connects two OBS nodes. The wavelengths can be operated to minimize contentions. Let us consider that two bursts are destined to the same output port at the same time. Both bursts can still be transmitted but on two different wavelengths. Wavelength conversion is the process of converting the wavelength of an incoming channel to another wavelength at the outgoing channel, thus minimizing burst contentions. Wavelength conversion can be full, limited, fixed, or spare.

Deflection Routing

Using the deflection routing scheme, a contending burst is routed to an output port other than the intended output port and consequently on a different route toward its destination (Vokkarane 2004). Although deflection routing is often not preferred in traditional packet-switched networks because of possible looping and out-of-sequence packet delivery, it may be significant to implement deflection in all-optical burst-switched networks in which buffer capacity is extremely limited to ensure an acceptable level of traffic loss. To further reduce packet loss resulting from contention, another approach called *burst segmentation* has been also proposed (Vokkarane, Jue, and Sitaraman 2002). It aims to drop only those segments of a burst that overlap other bursts.

QoS in OBS Networks

Quality-of-service support is another important issue in OBS networks. Different schemes have been proposed for offering QoS differentiation in OBS networks and providing loss or delay differentiation.

QoS Models

Three models for QoS can be used: relative, proportional, and absolute (Chen, Hamdi, and Tsang 2001; Zhang et al.

2004). In the *relative* QoS model, the performance of each class is defined relatively in comparison to other classes. For example, a high-priority class is guaranteed to experience lower loss probability than a low-priority class. However, the loss probability of the high-priority class depends on the traffic load of the low-priority class; hence, no upper bound on the loss probability is guaranteed for the high-priority class. In the *proportional* differentiation model, the service differentiation of a particular QoS metric is quantitatively adjusted to be proportional to the factors that a network service provider sets. If p_i is a QoS metric and s_i is the differentiation factor for class i, then using the proportional differentiation model, we should have $p_i/p_j = s_i/s_j$, for all (i, j). The achievement of these models requires that each core node maintains traffic statistics. The *absolute* QoS model provides, for the guaranteed traffic, an upper-bound guarantee for any of the supported QoS metrics. This kind of strict QoS guarantee is essential to support applications with delay and bandwidth constraints such as videoconferencing and voice-over-IP applications. Efficient admission-control and resource-provisioning mechanisms are required for the realization of the absolute QoS model over an OBS network.

Relative QoS Differentiation

Several schemes have been proposed to support the relative QoS model. In Yoo, Qiao, and Dixit (2000), an extra offset–based scheme that provides relative loss differentiation was proposed. Using this scheme, higher-priority class bursts are given a larger offset time than the lower-priority class bursts. By providing a larger offset time, the probability of reserving the resources for the higher priority class bursts is increased, and consequently the loss probability experienced by higher-priority class bursts is reduced. The limitations of the extra offset–based scheme are unfavorable end-to-end delay, irregular loss probability differentiation, and a burst-selecting effect (Chen, Hamdi, and Tsang 2001).

Contention-resolution schemes may be used to provide relative QoS differentiation in an OBS network. In Lazzez et al. (2006), a QoS-based contention resolution has been suggested. The proposed scheme combines optical buffering and wavelength conversion techniques. It is based on a differentiated QoS provision in the sense that the selection of the traffic unit to convert or delay in case of contention is done according to the priority of the contending units. Therefore, lower loss probability and lower blocking delay are made to ensure proper operation for the high-priority traffic class. A relative QoS differentiation can be also provided based on the assembling scheme. For example, by using a timer-based single burst assembly mechanism with a specific timeout for each traffic class, we can provide a relative packet delay differentiation.

Proportional QoS over an OBS Network

Different schemes have been proposed to provide proportional QoS differentiation over an optical burst-switched network. In Chen, Hamdi, and Tsang (2001), an intentional burst-dropping scheme has been made available to provide proportionally differentiated loss probability. This will give longer free time periods on the output link capacity, which induces more opportunity for high-priority bursts to be admitted. A limitation of the scheme is that it can result in unnecessary dropping of low-priority bursts. In Loi and Yang Liao (2002), proportional loss probability differentiation is provided by maintaining the number of wavelengths occupied by each class of burst. Every incoming burst is planned based on a usage profile maintained at every node.

To provide a proportional packet delay differentiation over an OBS network, an appropriate assembling scheme has been proposed in Chen, Hamdi, and Tsang (2001). It expands the waited-time-priority scheduler proposed to provide a proportional packet delay over a packet-switched network (Chen, Hamdi, and Tsang 2001), where a queue is kept for each class of packets. A burst will be assembled and transmitted into the OBS backbone when a token is generated at time t. The priority for each queue is given by $p_i(t) = w_i(t)/s_i$, where $w_i(t)$ is the waiting time of the packet at the head of queue i and s_i is the proportional factor for class i. The queue with the largest $p_i(t)$ will be chosen. Therefore, a proportional packet-delay differentiation is provided.

Absolute QoS over an OBS Network

Relative QoS differentiation schemes cannot provide an upper-bound guarantee for the supported QoS metrics; therefore, absolute QoS differentiation schemes are required. An intuitive approach to provide absolute QoS differentiation is to design a hybrid optical backbone network consisting of wavelength-routed lightpaths to carry the guaranteed traffic and a traditional OBS network for nonguaranteed traffic transmission. This approach leads to inefficient bandwidth utilization over the wavelength-routed part of the network. To guarantee efficient bandwidth use, efficient absolute QoS differentiation schemes, in which all wavelengths in the network are available for statistical multiplexing and dynamic bandwidth allocation, are needed.

In Zhang et al. (2004), an absolute QoS model that provides an upper-bound loss probability for guaranteed traffic has been proposed. Two mechanisms have been proposed for providing loss guarantees at OBS core nodes: early dropping and wavelength grouping. The *early dropping* mechanism probabilistically drops the bursts of lower priority class to guarantee the loss probability of higher-priority class traffic. The *wavelength grouping* mechanism provides wavelengths for the guaranteed traffic and schedules the bursts based on provisioning. The integration of the two mechanisms gives a successful solution for providing absolute loss guarantee while significantly reducing the loss probability experienced by the nonguaranteed traffic. In addition, Phung et al. (2004) present a novel signaling and reservation scheme that has been developed to provide an absolute QoS provision for an optical burst-switched network.

OPTICAL PACKET-SWITCHING NETWORKS

Optical packet switching has emerged as a promising solution for the next-generation all-optical networks.

By enabling packet switching in the optical domain, OPS networks can provide cost-efficient and transparent transport services to higher layers. Nevertheless, commercial deployment of OPS requires a careful investigation of several challenges because they are fundamentally different from traditional networks.

OPS Technology

In an OPS network, packets are processed and forwarded hop by hop until they reach their destination node. An OPS network should be able to process and forward packets in the optical domain, which makes the network truly transparent. On the other hand, as optical processing is still in the experimental stage, electronic processing of the packet header is operated until optical processing becomes mature. Therefore, when a packet arrives to a node, the packet header is extracted and converted to the electronic domain in order to be processed, whereas the packet payload is switched to an input FDL to be buffered during packet header processing. OPS benefits from statistical multiplexing, which guarantees better network resource utilization compared to WR and OBS networks. An OPS network can be either synchronous or asynchronous. In *asynchronous* OPS, packets arrive at a switch at nonsynchronized instants. In *synchronous* OPS, time is slotted, and packets arrive at an optical core switch in synchronized and equally spaced time slots. The impact of contention is often less severe in slotted OPS compared to asynchronous OPS. However, slotted OPS requires synchronization at each switch input, which increases the switch cost and complexity. In both slotted and unslotted OPS networks, the packets may be of variable size (Øverby 2005). In slotted OPS with variable-sized packets, a packet is a multiple of time slots, whereas in slotted OPS with fixed-size packets, a packet is contained in a single time slot. Both fixed-size and variable-sized architectures require packet aggregation at the OPS ingress node. This is also required for asynchronous OPS with fixed-size packets. However, packet aggregation can be avoided in asynchronous OPS with variable-sized packets (Øverby 2005).

Figure 3 depicts the functional architecture of a generic OPS node as it is presented in Rouskas and Xu (2004).

The architecture is composed of a set of multiplexers and demultiplexers, an input interface, a switch fabric unit with FDL buffers and wavelength converters, an output interface, and a switch control unit. Packets arriving on an input fiber are first demultiplexed into individual wavelengths and are then sent to the input interface. Each packet has a payload and an optical header that is used for packet routing in the optical domain. The input interface is typically responsible for extracting the optical packet header and forwarding it to the switch control unit for processing. The SCU processes the header information, determines an appropriate output wavelength channel, and configures the switch fabric unit to route the packet accordingly. In case of output port contention, the switch may need to buffer the packet or transfer it to a new wavelength. When the packet arrives at the output interface, the header and the associated data payload are attached and the packet is forwarded on the outgoing wavelength channel to the next switching node. OPS node architectures can be classified using several dimensions, depending on how the switching functions are implemented (Rouskas and Xu 2004).

Synchronous versus Asynchronous Switch Operation

In a synchronous OPS network, time is slotted, and the switch fabric unit at each individual OPS node can only be reconfigured at the beginning of a time slot. As packets enter a node from different links, they may arrive out of phase with one another. Therefore, it is the responsibility of the input interface (which is depicted in Figure 3) to align packets with the switching time slots. In an unslotted network, switch operations may take place at any point in time, and there is no requirement to align arriving packets at the input of a switching node.

Contention-Resolution Strategies

When two packets from different input port–wavelength pairs must be switched to the same output port–wavelength pair at the same time, contention arises and the switch controller and the switch fabric unit have to employ some strategy to resolve the contention—using, for example, wavelength converters, optical buffers, or deflection routing. Contention-resolution strategies are discussed and compared shortly below.

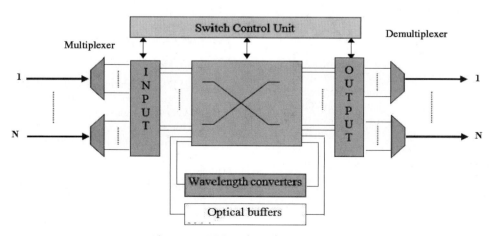

Figure 3: OPS node architecture

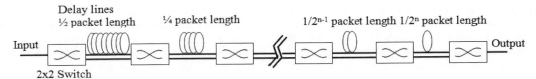

Figure 4: Optical synchronization stage

Packet Delineation and Synchronization

Packet delineation is required for both synchronous and asynchronous networks. The purpose of delineation is to determine the beginning and the end of the arriving packet (Yao 2001). During packet delineation, the incoming bits are locked in phase with the clock in order for the node to read the header information.

In addition to packet delineation, OPS nodes in slotted networks must also synchronize incoming fixed-size packets to the local switching slots. Figure 4 shows a typical synchronization stage that consists of a series of switches and delay lines (Yao 2001). When the header processor recognizes the bit pattern in the header and performs packet delineation, it identifies the packet start time and the control unit can compute the necessary delay and configure the correct path through the switched delay lines. This scheme introduces losses and cross talk, resulting in a significant power loss over long paths. A different strategy takes advantage of the fact that the propagation delay in a highly dispersive fiber depends on the signal wavelength. Each incoming packet is first converted to the appropriate wavelength to achieve the desired delay on such a fiber (Rouskas and Xu 2004).

Contention Resolution

A contention can be resolved using three different approaches: (1) the wavelength-based approach by the use of wavelength converters, (2) the time-based approach by the use of FDL buffers, and (3) the space-based approach by the use of deflection routing. With *wavelength conversion*, one or more tunable wavelength converters are used to convert the input wavelength in the case where two or more packets are intended, at the same time, to the same output fiber and the same output wavelength. *Optical buffering* is implemented by the use of fiber delay lines. The FDLs are made of an optical fiber with fixed length and can store a packet for a time that is proportional to the length of the fiber. When contention occurs, one of the contending packets is sent to the intended output port while the others are deviated to FDLs. Using *deflection routing*, a contended packet is routed to a different fiber to take another way to its destination. Deflected packets often experience a longer delay through the network and risk to arrive out of order to their destination. The most effective combination of contention resolution methods is to use wavelength conversion, FDL buffering, and space deflection together. In Yao et al. (2003), wavelength conversion is proven to be the most effective contention-resolution scheme because neither extra delays nor use of extra network resources are experienced.

QoS in OPS Networks

Generally, QoS techniques in OPS networks aim to provide service differentiation when contention occurs by using wavelengths and FDL assignment algorithms. In Callegati, Corazza, and Raffaelli (2002), two mechanisms have been proposed to provide service differentiation over an OPS network. An overview of these algorithms is given as follows (Kaheel et al. 2002).

Wavelength Allocation

Using *wavelength allocation* (WA), available wavelengths are divided into different groups. Each group is assigned to a different priority level such that higher priority levels get a larger part of the available wavelengths. Wavelength allocation algorithms are similar to those used to provide QoS differentiation over a WR network. Based on the wavelength domain, WA techniques may provide a QoS differentiation over an all-optical OPS network without the need for FDL buffers.

Integrated Wavelength Allocation and Threshold Dropping

In addition to wavelength allocation, integrated *wavelength allocation and threshold dropping* (WATD) uses threshold dropping to ensure a QoS differentiation. If the FDL's buffer occupancy is over a certain limit, lower-priority packets are dropped. By using a different dropping threshold for each priority level, various classes can be supported. Even though it may provide a better differentiation than the bufferless WA, WATD generates a more computational overhead.

The implementation of the aforementioned differentiation techniques over an OPS network can be complex because of the required synchronization between the packet header and packet payload. This process requires the packet payload to be delayed in the FDL buffer until the header is fully processed and the packet is classified. This is done on a packet-by-packet basis, which limits the switching speed. In addition, new techniques will be required to permit an individual access to variable-sized packets stored in fiber delay lines.

OPTICAL LABEL-SWITCHING NETWORKS

IP-over-WDM has been envisioned as the most promising solution for next-generation Internet architectures. IP-over-WDM networking adopts wavelength routing, mainly based on OXCs and a GMPLS control plane (Ashwood-Smith and Berger 2003; Berger 2003). In such an architecture, the minimum granularity of all-optical connections is often a single wavelength, which may lead to an inefficient utilization of resources. OPS technology has emerged as a promising solution for the next-generation IP-over-WDM architecture. OPS would avoid the electronic switching bottleneck and offer a packet-based optical switching solution that matches WDM transmission capabilities. Nevertheless, the achievement of such a task faces significant difficulties because OPS requires the development of component and system technologies that are still not available because of technological constraints. Considering the efficiency of MPLS in terms of signaling, traffic engineering, and QoS requirements, optical label-switching technology, which aims to implement MPLS over WDM networks, seems to be a promising solution. The common label-switching concept implies a natural compatibility of OLS networking with the MPLS architecture and its extensions defined by MPλS and GMPLS.

Forms of MPLS

This subsection discusses the concept of optical label-switching networks in light of interoperability and faultless network upgrades in the context of MPLS, MPλS, and GMPLS.

Multiprotocol Label Switching

MPLS is a switching approach that has been proposed for IP networks with two main objectives: (1) provide a more efficient packet-forwarding mechanism than traditional routing and (2) provide tools for signaling, QoS, and traffic engineering. The principle of MPLS is that every packet is assigned a label, and packets are forwarded along a path where each router makes forwarding decisions based only on the label content. Figure 5 illustrates the principle of the MPLS technology. At each hop, the router substitutes the existing label for a new label, which tells the next hop how to forward the packet. Simple forwarding increases the speed of the forwarding process inside the MPLS network, which may improve the provided QoS in terms of delay and variation of delay (jitter). An IP router that supports MPLS technology is called a *label-switching router* (LSR).

The ingress LSR is the node through which an IP packet enters the MPLS domain. It assigns a label and adds an MPLS header to the packet. If the packet is integrated with a QoS operation, then the ingress LSR will condition the traffic accordingly (e.g., Diffserv). The egress LSR is the router from which the packet leaves

the MPLS domain. It removes the MPLS header that was added by the ingress node and switches the packet to its destination network. Both ingress LSRs and egress LSRs are edge nodes that connect the MPLS network to other networks (e.g., IP networks). The core LSR, also called the *interior LSR*, uses the MPLS header to make forwarding decisions and perform label swapping.

A *label* is a small identifier generated by the ingress LSR and placed in the MPLS header. The implementation of the MPLS technology requires each node to maintain a label-swapping table known as the *label information base* (LIB). By looking up the input port and label in the LIB, the output interface and label are determined. Then the LSR replaces the input label by the output label and forwards the packet. The labels are locally significant only, which means that the label is only useful and pertinent on a single link between adjacent LSRs. The adjacent LSR label tables, however, should form a path through the MPLS network—a virtual connection called a *label-switching path* (LSP). The major advantage of MPLS is its capability to perform traffic engineering. Using MPLS, the LSP is established between two points on a pure packet-switched network. MPLS uses the LSPs in a manner similar to connection-oriented networks (e.g. ATM) while keeping the fundamental efficiency and operation of a packet-switched network. Others benefits of MPLS are in virtual private network applications, multicast, and QoS provision. Although MPLS has added a set of important ATM-like features to IP without accompanying its signaling complexity, MPLS is strictly a data networking protocol that is completely insensible to the abilities of WDM optical networking.

Multiprotocol Lambda Switching

MPλS was proposed to adopt MPLS traffic engineering as the control plane for optical cross-connects. The main idea behind the design of MPλS is to facilitate the provisioning and reconfiguration of lightpaths in OXCs using MPLS traffic-engineering functions. MPλS utilizes the following components of MPLS traffic engineering control plane: resource discovery, state information dissemination,

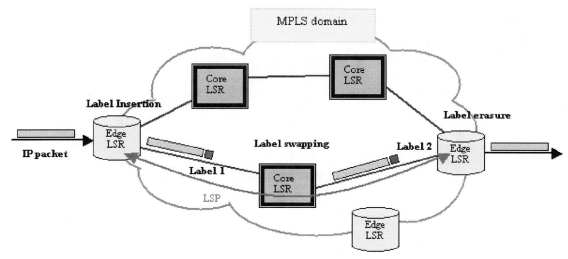

Figure 5: MPLS technology

path selection, and path management (Yoo 2003). MPλS stands for OLS, and the technology concerns routing individual wavelengths—that is, lambdas (λ's). Rather than swap labels on a per-packet basis at each hop, λ's are swapped between the input and output port of OXCs. MPλS may be the key to unify the control plane for all optical elements, and this can help in provisioning services and optical paths while enabling IP network fast reestablishment and traffic engineering. Although MPλS was successful in combining MPLS with WDM, the integration between data networking and optical networking was insufficient. OLS will look for a perfect integration between data and optical networking by means of optical labels (Yoo 2003).

Generalized Multiprotocol Label Switching

GMPLS (Mannie 2001; Banerjee et al. 2001; Yoo 2003) is a multiplatform control plane technology that is designed to control not only packet-switching devices but also devices that perform switching in the time, space, and wavelength domains. Like MPLS, GMPLS ensures the separation between the control and data plane, which may be useful when transparent optical network elements are utilized. Although MPLS is limited to a logical separation between the control and data plane, GMPLS allows the control plane to be physically different from the associated data plane. For example, a packet-switching label path LSP1 may be nested in the subordinate time division multiplexing label-switching path LSP2 (e.g., OC-48), which in turn is enveloped in a lambda-switched label-switching patch denoted by LSP3 (e.g. OC-192). Therefore, the end-to-end LSP can be set up across physically diverse hierarchical LSPs (Yoo 2003). GMPLS allows signaling across the IP, MPLS, and MPλS domains. It basically accommodates any network elements that perform switching in the time, space, and wavelength domains. Interoperability of OLS networks with other networks is achieved via the GMPLS extension known as GMPLS II (Yoo 2003).

Optical Label Switching

The OLS networks utilize a short optical label attached to the data payload, which allows the optical label switching routers (OLSRs) to make decisions about data payloads forwarding. Provided that the optical label is used, the data payload can be of any protocol, format, and length. Therefore, OLS-based circuit switching, burst switching, and packet switching are possible in the optical layer (Yoo 2003). Coming from different networks, the packets are encapsulated, provided with the optical label, and sent through the optical network. To make forwarding decisions, OLSRs only need to look at the optical label. The OLS core network is capable of supporting multiple transport modes with full interoperability between circuit, burst, and packet switching, thus providing a multiservice platform to interface with various client networks.

Figure 6 depicts the structure of an OLS node as it is presented by the National Communications System (2002). When the OLS node receives a packet, both the payload and the header are on the same wavelength; however, the header is on a different subcarrier (1). The optical signal is then split and received by a subcarrier receiver (3) and a fiber delay line (2). The FDL delays the optical signal, whereas the subcarrier receiver forwards the optical label to the optical header processor, which processes the optical label and sets up the switch fabric before the packet arrives from the fiber delay lines (4). Finally, the OLS node receives the packet, deletes the old header information, appends a new optical header, and forwards the packet across the predetermined switched path (5).

OLS provides a means of transmitting the optical header in band and on the same wavelength as the payload; this means that there is no need for the control plane to be separated from the data plane (Yuan and Jue 2004). The data payload is transmitted in the optical domain through an OLS network and therefore requires no electronic processing. However, because of current technological constraints, the optical header must be processed electronically.

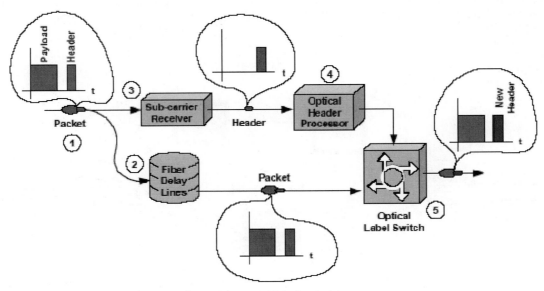

Figure 6: Optical label switching

Contention Resolution in OLS Routers

A contention problem occurs when multiple traffic units contend, at the same time, for the same output fiber and the same output wavelength. In case of contention, the OLSR can use one or a combination among the following three mechanisms: wavelength conversion, FDL buffering, and deflection routing (Yoo 2003). The wavelength dimension available in optical routers provides new capabilities far beyond traditional routers, which use electronic buffering as the main approach for switching conflict resolution.

Wavelength Conversion

Wavelength conversion is done when a contending packet is converted to one of the available wavelengths of the intended output fiber. The alternative wavelength routing may achieve the same propagation delay and number of hops; it avoids the difficulties in sequencing multiple packets. From this point of view, wavelength conversion is attractive compared to FDL buffering and deflection routing.

FDL Buffering

In case of contention, one of the contending packets is sent to the intended output channel while the rest are sent to the appropriate fiber delay lines. A delayed packet will be re-sent later to the same OLSR. The choice of the length of the delay line can be arbitrary; however, there will be a trade-off between the contention-resolution efficiency and the maximum latency. A limited number of delay buffer lines can be included in the optical router, and multiple wavelengths are housed in each optical delay line. The OLSR includes both wavelength conversion and buffering so that packet wavelength can be converted to another wavelength if the buffer is using the original wavelength.

Deflection Routing

In this case, a packet may be deflected to an adjacent OLS node from which it can be forwarded toward its destination. Attention must be taken to prevent a packet from being repeatedly deflected, thus leading to signal degradation and resource wasting. This can be avoided based on *optical time-to-live* (OTTL) control information, which indicates, in a real-time manner, the expected lifetime of the packet. Unlike the traditional time to live (TTL), OTTL does not require rewriting the label.

SIGNALING IN WDM OPTICAL NETWORKS

Signaling protocols are used to set up and remove connections. Different signaling protocols have been proposed for the implementation of the above-presented optical switching techniques. Among theses protocols we can mention lightpath establishment schemes, JET, JIT, and *resource reservation protocol–traffic engineering* (RSVP-TE) in MPLS networks and its extensions for GMPLS.

Signaling in WR Networks

As mentioned in the second section of this chapter, a WR network is an optical circuit-switched network in which the transfer of each data flow is preceded by the establishment of an all-optical lightpath between edges of the network.

Lightpaths

Lightpath establishment in a WR network is done in two steps: path selection and channel assignment. *Path selection* involves selecting a path from source to destination based on certain criteria. *Channel assignment* refers to assigning a wavelength channel on every link of the chosen path. Path selection can be carried out in several ways. If a source-destination pair has one preselected path, then it is referred to as a *fixed-path approach*. If a path is selected depending on the network status from a preselected set of candidate paths, then it is called *dynamic path selection*. With this selection, the set of candidate paths remains the same all of the time and does not change. If the candidate paths are chosen based on the network status, then the path-selection process is referred to as *exhaustive routing*. Channel assignment process ensures the allocation of the appropriate transmission channel on every link of a selected path. This results in (1) a fiber, wavelength, and time slot assignment in the case of a WDM grooming networks, and (2) a fiber and wavelength assignment in a WR WDM network.

When establishing a lightpath over a WR network, the same wavelength is used on every link along the selected path. If the required wavelength is not available at the outgoing fiber of an OXC, then the establishment of the lightpath is blocked. To decrease the probability that a lightpath is blocked, the OXC can be equipped with wavelength converters. Figure 7 shows an example

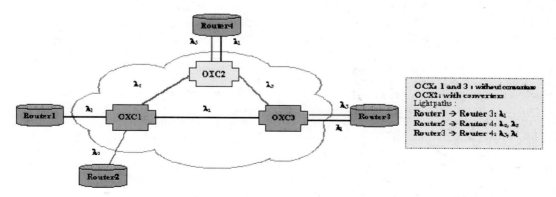

Figure 7: Example of lightpaths

of different lightpaths. The physical topology of a WR network consists of edge nodes, OXCs, and the fibers that connect them. The lightpaths are set up between edge nodes over this physical topology and constitute a logical topology. Each lightpath is assigned a path through the network and a wavelength on that path. Finding routes for the lightpaths through the physical topology and assigning wavelengths to these lightpaths is called the *routing and wavelength assignment problem* (Zang, Jue, and Mukherjee 2000).

Protection and Restoration Schemes

In a wavelength-routed WDM network as well as in other optical networks, the failure of a network element may cause the failure of several optical channels, thereby leading to large data and revenue losses. Therefore, it is imperative to implement appropriate protection and restoration schemes to prevent or reduce data loss. In protection schemes, backup resources are precomputed and reserved for each connection before a failure occurs. In restoration schemes, an alternate path is discovered dynamically for each interrupted connection after a failure occurs. Compared to restoration schemes, protection schemes have faster recovery time and provide guaranteed recovery ability but require more network resources (Yuan and Jue 2004).

Protection Schemes. Protection schemes can be classified as link protection and path protection. In *link protection*, separate backup resources are allocated for each individual link on the working path. In *path protection*, a working path and a disjoint protection path are established for each connection. Path protection usually has lower resource requirements and lower end-to-end propagation delay for the recovered route. Protection schemes can be also divided into dedicated and shared protection schemes. *Dedicated* protection schemes need more network resources, but they are easier to implement. *Shared* protection schemes provide a more efficient resources utilization, but they require more complex signaling (Yuan and Jue 2004).

Dedicated Path Protection. A dedicated link-disjoint backup lightpath is established in advance for each connection that needs to be protected. In 1+1 path protection, the same traffic is transmitted simultaneously on the primary and backup paths. Upon detecting a failure on the primary path, the receiver will switch to continue to receive information from the backup path. This scheme is fast, but there may be a traffic disruption because of the delay difference between the primary and backup paths. In 1:1 path protection scheme, the protected traffic is only transmitted over the primary path; when the primary path fails, the protected traffic is switched to the backup path. Both the sender and the receiver must use signaling to detect the fault and initiate the switchover.

Dedicated Link Protection. Using this dedicated link protection, a backup path and a wavelength are reserved around each link of the primary path during connection setup and are dedicated to that connection. In general, it may not be possible to allocate a dedicated backup path around each link of the primary path.

Shared Path Protection. With the shared path protection scheme, the resources along a backup path may be shared with other backup paths. As a result, backup channels are shared among different failure scenarios that are not expected to occur at the same time; thus, shared path protection provides more efficient resources utilization when compared to dedicated path protection.

Shared Link Protection. Similar to shared path protection, shared link protection reserves backup resources along the backup path and may be shared with other backup paths. Thus, backup channels are shared among different failures scenarios that are not expected to occur simultaneously.

Restoration Schemes

Restoration schemes can be divided into path restoration and link restoration based on the level of network resources involved in the restoration. In link restoration schemes, all of the connections that are concerned with a failed link are rerouted around that link. Source and destination nodes of connections traversing the link are ignorant of the link failure. The end nodes of the link dynamically discover a route around the link for each wavelength that traverses it. They may participate in a distributed procedure to look for new paths for each active wavelength. When a new route is discovered for a wavelength channel, the end nodes of the failed link reconfigure their OXCs to reroute that channel onto the new lightpath. If no new routes are discovered for a wavelength channel, then the connection that utilizes that wavelength is blocked. With path restoration, when a link fails, the source node of each connection that traverses the failed link is informed about the failure. The source node discovers a backup route on an end-to-end basis. When a new route and wavelength channel are discovered for a connection, network elements such as wavelength OXCs are reconfigured appropriately, and the connection switches to the new path. If no new routes are discovered for a failed connection, then that connection is blocked.

Signaling in OBS Networks

Signaling and reservation are important criteria on which OBS can be differentiated from other optical switching technologies. As shown in Figure 8, OBS adopts a signaling approach in which the burst header packet is sent ahead of the associated data burst by an offset time in order to allocate resources and configure optical switches at each node (Vokkarane 2004). In the following subsection, we will look at different design parameters that affect the performance of an OBS signaling technique and also describe the most important signaling protocols proposed for the implementation of an OBS network.

Connection Setup

The connection set up over an OBS network can be either one-way (i.e., tell and go) or two-way (i.e., tell and wait) (Vokkarane 2004). In a one-way connection setup (Figure 9a), the source sends out a control packet requesting the intermediate nodes to allocate the necessary resources for the burst. No control message is sent

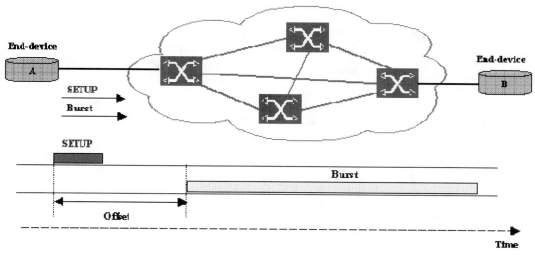

Figure 8: OBS signaling

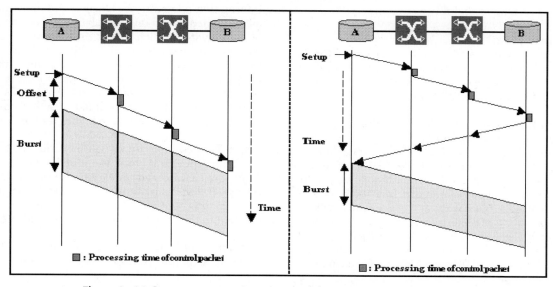

Figure 9: (a) One-way connection setup and (b) two-way connection setup

back to inform the source about the success or failure of the resource reservation. The main objective of the one-way signaling techniques is to reduce the end-to-end data transmission delay. However, this may lead to high data loss because of switching conflict at intermediate nodes. Two-way signaling schemes (Figure 9b) are acknowledgment-based, whereby the data burst is transmitted only after a connection is established successfully. The main objective of the two-way signaling approach is to minimize packet loss; however, it may lead to high data transfer delay because of the round-trip delay during connection establishment.

Resource Reservation and Release

Based on the adopted resources reservation mechanism, OBS signaling techniques can be classified as immediate reservation or delayed reservation (Vokkarane 2004). With the immediate reservation approach, the channel is reserved immediately from the instant that the burst

header packet is processed. In the delayed reservation, the required bandwidth is reserved from the time at which the burst will arrive at the node. In this case, the BHP must carry the offset time between itself and its corresponding data burst. In general, immediate reservation is simple and practical to implement but incurs higher blocking because of inefficient bandwidth allocation. On the other hand, the implementation of delayed reservation is more complex but leads to higher resource utilization and a lower blocking probability (Vokkarane 2004).

A reserved resource can be released in two ways: either implicitly or explicitly (Vokkarane 2004). In an *explicit release* technique, an intermediate node releases the resources allocated to a burst on receipt of an explicit release message. With *implicit release*, the control packet has to carry additional control information such as the burst length. This permits an intermediate node to know when to release its resources. Obviously, an implicit release technique leads to better resource utilization. Based on the reservation and release mechanisms, the

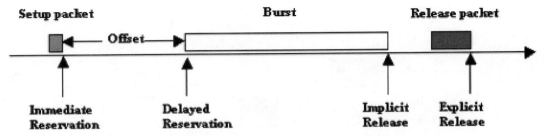

Figure 10: Resource reservation and release schemes

signaling techniques can be classified into four categories (Figure 10): (1) immediate reservation and explicit release, (2) immediate reservation and implicit release, (3) delayed reservation and explicit release, and (4) delayed reservation and implicit release. We can easily observe that techniques that employing delayed reservation and implicit release result in higher bandwidth utilization, and a lower blocking probability.

OBS Signaling Protocols

Different signaling protocols have been proposed for the implementation of the OBS technology. The most important ones are *just enough time, just in time, tell and go* (TAG), and *tell and wait* (TAW).

Just Enough Time. Figure 11a illustrates the work of the just-enough-time signaling protocol (Vokkarane 2004). As shown in the figure, a source node first sends a burst header packet to the destination node. BHP is processed at each intermediate node. If the reservation is successful, then the switch will be configured before the burst's arrival. Meanwhile, the burst waits at the source in the electronic domain. After a predetermined offset time, the burst is sent optically through the established data path. The offset time is calculated based on the number of hops from source to destination and the switching time of a core OBS

node. Offset time is calculated as $OT = h \times \delta + ST$, where h is the number of hops between the source and the destination, δ is the burst header processing time at a given node, and ST is the switch reconfiguration time (Qiao and Yoo 1999). If at any intermediate node the reservation is unsuccessful, then the burst will be dropped.

The implementation of JET requires maintaining information related to the starting and finishing times of all scheduled bursts on each channel of each output port of every switch, which makes the system relatively complex. On the other hand, JET is able to detect situations in which no transmission conflict occurs, although the start time of a new burst may be earlier than the finishing time of an already accepted burst—that is, a burst can be transmitted in between two already reserved bursts. Thus, bursts can be accepted with a higher probability in JET.

Just in Time. Just in time (Baldine et al. 2002) is similar to JET except that it employs immediate reservation and explicit release instead of delayed reservation and implicit release. Based on an immediate reservation approach, the JIT signaling protocol is simpler to implement but less efficient in terms of network resource utilization.

Tell and Wait. Tell and wait (Vokkarane 2004) is a two-way signaling protocol that has been proposed to

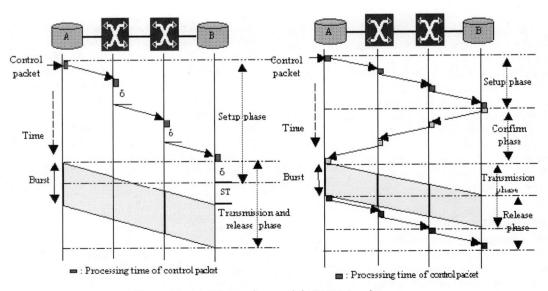

Figure 11: (a) JET signaling and (b) TAW signaling

CLASS_A : destination oriented without TE

00	Destination	Source	Priority	Duration	Exp	QoS	ToS	OTTL

CLASS_B : destination oriented with TE

01	Destination	Source	Priority	Duration	TE	QoS	ToS	OTTL

CLASS_C : label based forwarding

10	Label	Priority	Duration	Exp	QoS	ToS	OTTL

CLASS_D : circuit switching

11	Label	Priority	Set	Exp	QoS	ToS	OTTL

Figure 12: Optical label structure per class

provide a connection setup over an OBS network. In TAW (Figure 11b), BHP is sent along the burst's route to collect channel availability information at every node along the path. At the destination, a channel assignment algorithm is executed, and the reservation period on each link is determined based on the earliest available channel times of all the intermediate nodes. A CONFIRM message is sent in the reverse direction, which reserves the channel for the requested duration at each intermediate node. If the CONFIRM packet reaches the source successfully, then the burst is sent into the core network.

Tell and Go. Another one-way OBS signaling protocol is the tell-and-go approach (Vokkarane 2004). In this method, the data burst must be delayed at each intermediate OBS node to allow time for the burst header to be processed and for the switch to be configured. This requires the use of FDL buffers at each OBS node to delay data bursts, which may increase both the complexity and the cost of a switching node.

Signaling in OLS Networks

The fundamental concept behind OLS is an efficient and transparent packet-forwarding method using an optical label-switching mechanism. New signaling information in the form of an optical signaling label that contains routing and control information such as the source, destination, priority, and the data payload length is associated with each packet. Each optical label-switching router will receive and process this optical label, look up the forwarding table, and take necessary steps to forward the packet. If the packet is to be routed to a wavelength where there is already another packet being routed, OLSR will use one or more of the following three switching conflict-resolution mechanisms: wavelength conversion, FDL buffering, or deflection routing. Different label-based addressing schemes have been proposed for the implementation of OLS technology. Each addressing scheme relies on a specific optical label class. Four optical label

classes have been defined in Yoo (2003): CLASS_A, CLASS_B, CLASS_C, and CLASS_D. Figure 12 shows the structure of these labels.

A CLASS_A label is a simple destination-oriented forwarding label similar to the IP header. It is deterministic and requires no label swapping. *Optical time to live* indicates the expected lifetime of the optical packet. Compared to the conventional TTL, which overestimates the remaining lifetime in long fiber links and underestimates it in low-loss optical routers, the OTTL directly measures the remaining lifetime of the optical packet (Yoo 2003). The entire content of the CLASS_A optical label is deterministic and requires no label swapping. Often there is a need for additional traffic engineering beyond the simple destination-oriented packet forwarding. The CLASS_B label uses the three experimental bits (EXP) for traffic-engineering purposes for a given destination. Therefore, several different label-switching paths can be defined for the same destination. The CLASS_C label abandons the destination-oriented forwarding but relies on label-switching paths set up through the *constraint route label-distribution protocol* CR-LDP or RSVP_TE (Dutta and Rouskas 2002; Kaheel et al. 2002). The CLASS_D optical label is for circuit switching in which OLSR will cease to switch packet by packet or burst by burst; instead, it will be attached to a circuit flow. For packet switching, CLASS_A will be dominantly a popular format even though CLASS_B and CLASS_C may also be used. For burst switching, CLASS_C will be dominantly used, although CLASS_B and CLASS_A can also be used. CLASS_D will be used for circuit switching (Yoo 2003).

Examining Figure 12, we note that for the different proposed optical labels, the priority bits distinguish between the *class of service* (CoS), the QoS defines the quality of service, and the *type of service* (ToS) field defines service type. CoS may be used for a priority-based differentiated packet forwarding, which only provides a relative QoS differentiation and not an absolute QoS guarantee. QoS bits are used to provide a guaranteed assurance of QoS parameters. ToS specifies the type of applications such as real-time applications. For example, IP telephony packets may have low-priority CoS and allow high packet loss QoS but will require real-time ToS.

GMPLS Signaling

The ability to control switched packets, *time division multiplexed* (TDM) network traffic, and optical network components make GMPLS flexible enough to be positioned in the direct migration path from electronic to all-optical network switching. The five main interface types supported by GMPLS are (1) the *packet-switch capable* (PSC) interface, (2) the *layer-2 switch capable* (L2SC) interface, (3) the *time division multiplexing capable* (TDMC) interface, (4) the *lambda switch capable* (LSC) interface, and (5) the *fiber-switch capable* (FSC) interface (National Communications System 2002). The management of these interfaces has required many extensions of the MPLS technology. Obvious modifications to the label have been made, and the necessity for a new method of managing the network links has been identified. Slight modifications have been made to MPLS signaling protocols (e.g., CR-LDP and RSVP-TE) to support the multiple interfaces of GMPLS. Basically, the MPLS protocol has morphed into a more generalized structure to support a larger array of network technologies (National Communications System 2002).

Generalized Label

In MPLS, labels are integrated in the cell and packet structure for in-band control plane signaling. With the different interfaces it is impossible to embed label specific information—in terms of fiber port or wavelength switching—into the traffic packet structure. Therefore, virtual labels have been added to the MPLS label structure. These labels are composed of specific indicators that represent wavelengths, fiber bundles, and fiber ports, and they are distributed to GMPLS nodes via out-of-band GMPLS signaling (National Communications System 2002). GMPLS out-of-band signaling leads to a control channel separation issue. In fact, when we send the control information out of band, the label is separated from the data flow that it is attempting to control. GMPLS provides a means for identifying explicit data channels, which allows the control message to be associated with a particular data flow (National Communications System 2002).

Generalized LSP

The handling of LSPs under GMPLS is different from that of MPLS. MPLS does not provide for bidirectional LSPs. Each directional LSP has to be established in turn. With GMPLS, the LSP can be established bidirectionally. The required traffic engineering for the bidirectional LSP is the same in both directions, and it is established for both directions via only one signaling message. This allows for reductions in latency related setup time.

Another difference between MPLS LSPs and GMPLS LSPs is the ability to handle multiple adjacent links, which may reduce the number of link advertisements that need to be maintained, thus increasing the scalability of GMPLS. Just like MPLS, GMPLS labels only contain information about a single level of hierarchy.

The difference for GMPLS is that this hierarchy can be based on fiber, wavelength, time slot, or packet or cell. For example, if a connection is desired from one PSC interface to another and the traffic traverses physically separate fibers, a unique LSP will have to be established for each level in turn. First, the FSC LSP, then the LSC LSP, then the TDMC LSP, and finally the PSC LSP would have to be established via GMPLS signaling (National Communications System 2002).

Link Management Protocol

The *link management protocol* (LMP) protocol (National Communications System 2002) was developed to address several link specific problems that surfaced when generalizing the MPLS protocol across different interface types.

The following is a list of the proposed responsibilities of LMP as it relates to GMPLS.

- Control channel management: This management is used to establish and maintain control channels between LMP adjacent nodes. The control channel can be used to exchange routing, signaling, and other control messages.
- Link connectivity verification: Such verification is used to confirm the physical connectivity of the data links between the nodes. A pair of nodes exchange tests messages on a periodic basis to verify the physical connectivity of the data links. The verification messaging must be transported through the data channel, not the control channel.
- Fault management: This management provides a fault localization procedure to localize failures. It can localize the path failure by quickly reporting the status of one or more data links. It is designed to work for both unidirectional and bidirectional LSPs.

Network Restoration and Reliability

In addition to the above-presented extensions required for the development of the GMPLS protocol, GMPLS adds techniques for fault detection, fault localization, fault notification, and fault alleviation using either protection or restoration schemes (National Communications System 2002). Fault detection occurs within the equipment nearest to the fault. LMP provides procedures for fault localization within both optical and opto-electronic networks. The protocol sends ChannelFail messages over control channels that are separate from the data plane. Separation of the control and data planes allows support for fault localization independently of the data transmission method, whether it happens to be ATM, synchronous optical network, WDM, or frame relay. GMPLS handles failures using combinations of protection and restoration schemes. GMPLS supports 1+1, 1:1, and 1:N. GMPLS path restoration precomputes alternative restoration paths. To do so, GMPLS accelerates the rerouting of failed LSPs and improves the reliability of the LSP restoration after a failure. GMPLS provides fault notification for restoration with its addition of Notify messages within RSVP-TE (National Communications System 2002).

SWITCHING PERSPECTIVES

The challenges and perspectives of the switching techniques are typically organized around three issues: IP-based switching, network engineering, and QoS provision.

IP-Based Switching

As presented earlier, *IP-over-WDM* (IP-WDM) has been considered the most promising solution for the next-generation Internet backbone. Such IP-WDM architecture will combine IP routers with WDM switching systems to provide a global networking infrastructure for both legacy and emerging IP services. Efforts are being made to reduce the gap between the electrical IP layer and the optical WDM layer. Current IP-WDM networking adopts wavelength routing mainly based on OXCs and the GMPLS control plane. In such an architecture, no wavelength sharing is possible between two distinct all-optical connections, which may lead to inefficient network resource utilization. The realization of subwavelength granularity over a wavelength-routed network requires the use of an optical-electrical-optical conversion at each switch, which leads to a scalability problem of electronic IP routers to match the huge transmission capacity of WDM fibers.

To overcome the problem of inefficient bandwidth utilization, an all-optical WDM switching technology with a finer switching granularity is required for the implementation of the next-generation optical Internet. Recently, optical packet switching, which is capable of packet forwarding at the optical layer, has emerged as a highly promising technology for the optical Internet (Sivalingam and Subramaniam 2005; Papadimitriou, Obaidat, and Pomportsis 2002). This approach would bypass the electronic switching bottleneck and provide an optical switching solution that matches transmission needs. Nevertheless, the accomplishment of such progress faces significant challenges because OPS requires practical, cost-effective, and scalable implementations and necessitates the development of several optical components such as an optical synchronizer for packet delineation, optical memory for packet buffering and traffic engineering, and optical components for all-optical packet header recognition and swapping. To achieve these objectives, different research activities are underway. Photonic memory and optical packet header processing constitute the most important active research areas toward the implementation of the OPS technology.

Network Engineering

Processing packet headers at the optical level is a critical issue. In Naoya and Kubota (2005), an all-optical packet header processing method is proposed. The method assumes that the header has an optical code–based label of the destination node. An optical label processor analyzes the headers optically based on a set of optical correlators working as a label bank, which stores optical codes corresponding to the destination addresses in the routing table. Label recognition is based on parallel optical correlation in the time or frequency domain (or both) between an input optical label (code) and the labels in the label bank. Each correlator decodes the input label of each packet header and outputs the signal, which has high or low value in matched and unmatched cases, respectively. A high-value signal opens a gate switch of a destination port, whereas a low-value signal keeps other switches closed. Three label-processing methods, based on different optical correlators, have been investigated in Naoya and Kubota (2005): (1) those based on planar lightwave circuits with binary phase shift keying code labels, (2) those based on multisection fiber Bragg gratings with multiwavelength labels, and (3) a holographic multiple correlator with on-off keying labels.

In addition to the above-presented propositions toward all-optical header processing, which is needed for high-speed processing for a broadband photonic network, different research activities are being conducted, including (1) the development of easy-to-use optical buffer memory, (2) the definition of efficient techniques for planning and dimensioning WDM optical networks, and (3) the definition of different mechanisms related to traffic management and QoS support. Because of technological constraints, using FDLs remains the most feasible way to implement optical buffers. Recently, in spite of optical technology's relative immaturity, different propositions have been made toward optical buffer development. In fact, an optical memory has various advantages over FDL buffers such as compactness, random access capability, long-term storage, large capacity, and easy control. A prototype of a "photonic" memory has been proposed in Takahashi (2004).

QoS Provision

QoS support constitutes a crucial issue in the development of all-optical WDM networks to provide QoS support for applications with diverse QoS demands. Therefore, different research activities are being conducted in developing QoS support over all-optical WDM networks. The development of the OLS technology constitutes an attempt to have an IP-over-WDM architecture that is able to provide QoS support for IP applications. In fact, OLS constitutes an adaptation of the MPLS technology for all-optical WDM networks, which may provide QoS support, considering the efficiency of MPLS in terms of traffic forwarding, signaling, and QoS guarantees. Several schemes have been proposed to provide a QoS support in IP-WDM architecture. In Chen, Hamdi, and Tsang (2001) and Zhang et al. (2004), an early dropping mechanism and a wavelength grouping scheme have been proposed to provide an absolute QoS guarantee over an OBS network. In Lazzez et al. (2006), a priority-based contention resolution has been proposed to provide a relative QoS differentiation over an OBS network. The analysis of these QoS mechanisms shows that the majority of them represent nothing but simple adaptations of those proposed for traditional electronic networks (e.g., ATM and IP). Unfortunately, this does not allow a high level of resource usage. Thus, the development of appropriate QoS mechanisms, taking into account the optical nature of WDM, will constitute an active area of research.

In addition to QoS support issues, optical networks face another crucial issue: the guarantee of security as required by different applications. Security concerns are part of the QoS provision. WDM networks are vulnerable to various forms of service denials or eavesdropping attacks. Attacks on WDM networks can be classified into three broad categories (Médard, Chinn, and Saengudomlert 2001; Papadimitriou, Papazoglou, and Pomportsis 2003): (1) quality-of-service degradation in which the attacker overpowers legitimate optical signals with attack signals, (2) traffic analysis and eavesdropping in which the attacker analyzes the traffic and attempts to degrade its quality, and (3) service denial in which the optical signal is disrupted by the attackers. Although most of the traditional security issues pertaining to traditional networks are applicable to optical networks equipped with converters, the nature of the signal makes it hard to apply security mechanisms and cope with network speed. The development of mechanisms to prevent and detect these types of attacks is an active area of research but one still in its infancy.

CONCLUSION

The emergence of multimedia applications is driving the demand for high-speed transmission to support ever-increasing bandwidth requirements. WDM technology has the capacity to transmit data at speeds of as much as a Terabit/s. Thus, an all-optical switching technology that is able to match WDM transmission capabilities is required to efficiently use this huge transmission capacity. In the evolution of optical networking, the most important switching techniques are wavelength routing, optical burst switching, optical packet switching, and optical label switching. In this chapter, we have presented a detailed overview of the optical switching techniques and discussed the main issues in the development of these services. Mainly, we have addressed the routing and wavelength assignment problem, protection and restoration, contention resolution, and QoS support—that is, the major concerns in the development of WDM all-optical networks. In addition, we focused on the signaling issue and presented some of the existing schemes proposed in the literature for the development of the considered optical switching techniques.

As optical technology advances and optical switching vision become closer to reality, different challenges emerge. Challenges and perspectives of optical switching techniques are organized around three major issues: IP-based switching, network engineering, and QoS provision; these are active areas of research in the development of all-optical WDM networks. Even though different schemes have been developed, additional schemes may still be necessary to provide better QoS provision and achieve more efficient resource utilization over a WDM optical network.

GLOSSARY

Generalized Multiprotocol Label Switching (GMPLS): A multiplatform control plane technology to support not only devices that perform packet switching but also devices that perform switching in time, space, and wavelength domains. The capacity of controlling not only switched packets but also TDM network traffic and optical network components makes GMPLS flexible enough to be placed in the direct migration path from electronic to all-optical network switching.

Multiprotocol Label Switching (MPLS): A recent switching technology proposed for IP networks for a more efficient packet forwarding, QoS management, and traffic engineering. The principle of MPLS is that packets are assigned a label, and packets are forwarded along a path where each router makes forwarding decisions based solely on the contents of the label.

Optical Burst Switching (OBS): In optical burst switched networks, bursts of data consisting of multiple packets are switched through the network all-optically. A control message is transmitted ahead of the burst to configure the switches along the burst's route. The burst follows the header without waiting for an acknowledgment that resources have been reserved and switches have been configured along the path.

Optical Label Switching (OLS): An extension of MPLS for OPS networks in which new signaling information is added in the form of optical labels. The optical label contains routing and control information such as the source, destination, priority, and packet length that will propagate through the network along with the data payload. Each optical label-switching router will sense the optical label, look up the forwarding table, and take the necessary steps to forward the packet.

Optical Packet Switching (OPS): A packet-switching scheme that is capable of dynamically allocating network resources with decisions made at the packet level. In an OPS network, individual photonic switches are combined to form a network. In packet-switched networks, bit-level synchronization and fast clock recovery are required for packet header recognition and packet delineation.

Optical Switching: The capacity of traffic units switching in the optical domain—that is, without the need of an optical-electrical-optical conversion at switching nodes. Different optical switching techniques have been proposed for WDM optical network. The most important are wavelength routing or optical circuit switching, optical burst switching, optical packet switching, and optical label switching.

Wavelength Division Multiplexing (WDM): A fiber-optic transmission technique that multiplexes different wavelength signals onto a single fiber. Each fiber has a set of parallel optical channels, each using different light wavelengths. It employs light wavelengths to transmit parallel-by-bit or serial-by-character data. WDM is an essential function for optical networks that allows the transmission of data (IP, ATM, SONET-SDH, etc.), over the optical layer.

Wavelength Routing (WR): The first optical switching technique proposed for WDM optical networks. It follows the main concepts of traditional circuit-switched networks. It is used in network backbones. To set up a communication channel, a route between the source-destination pair is chosen with appropriate wavelengths allocated on the links along the route.

CROSS REFERENCES

See *Optical Fiber Communications; Packet Switching; Wavelength Division Multiplexing (WDM)*.

REFERENCES

Ashwood-Smith, P., and L. Berger. 2003. Generalized multi-protocol label switching (GMPLS) signaling constraint-based routed label distribution protocol (CR-LDP) extensions. IETF RFC 3472, January.

Awduche, D., Y. Rekhter, J. Drake, and R. Coltun. 2002. Multi-protocol lambda switching: Combining MPLS traffic engineering control with optical crossconnects. IETF Internet draft, April, http://www3.tools.ietf.org/html/draft-awduche-mpls-te-optical-01.

Baldine, I., G. N. Rouskas, H. G. Perros, and D. Stevenson. 2002. JumpStart: A just-in-time signaling architecture for WDM burst-switched networks. *IEEE Communications*, 40(2): 82–9.

Banerjee, A., J. Drake, J. P. Lang, B. Turner, K. Kompella, and Y. Rekhter. 2001. Generalized multiprotocol label switching: An overview of routing and management enhancements. *IEEE Communications Magazine*, January, pp. 2–8.

Berger, L., ed. 2003. Generalized multi-protocol label switching (GMPLS) signaling, resource reservation protocol-traffic engineering (RSVP-TE) extensions. IETF RFC 3473, January.

Callegati, F., G. Corazza, and C. Raffaelli. 2002. Exploitation of DWDM for optical packet switching with quality of service guarantees. *IEEE Journal on Selected Areas in Communication*, 20(1): 190–201.

Chen, Y., M. Hamdi, and D. H. K. Tsang. 2001. Proportional QoS over OBS network. In *Proceedings of the IEEE Global Communications Conference* (Globecom 2001), San Antonio, TX. Vol. 3: 1510–4.

Chia, M. C., D. K. Hunter, I. Andonovic, P. Ball, S. P. Ferguson, K. M. Guild, and M. J. O'Mahony. 2001. Packet loss and delay performance of feedback and feedforward arrayed-waveguide gratings-based optical packet switches with WDM inputs-outputs. *IEEE/OSA Journal of Lightwave Technology*, 19(9): 1241–54.

Chlamtac, I., A. Fumagalli, L. G. Kazovsky, P. Melman, W. H. Nelson, P. Poggiolini, M. Cerisola, A. N. M. M. Choudhury, T. K. Fong, R. T. Hofmeister, A. C.-L. Mekkittikul, D. J. M. A. Sabido, and E. W. M. C.-J. Suh Wong IX. 1996. CORD: Contention resolution by delay lines. *IEEE Journal on Selected Areas in Communications*, 14(5): pp 1014–29.

COST 266. Undated. Advanced infrastructure for photonic networks. Workgroup 2. Optical Packet and Burst Switching Report (retrieved from http://citeseer.ist.psu.edu/657107.html).

Dutta, R., and G. Rouskas. 2002. Traffic grooming in WDM networks: Past and future. *IEEE Network*, 16(6): 46–56.

Elmirghani, J. M. H., and H.T. Mouftah. 2000. Technologies and architectures for scalable dynamic dense WDM networks. *IEEE Communication Magazine*, 38(2): 58–66.

Golmie, N., T. Ndousse, and D. Su. 2000. A differentiated optical services model for WDM networks. *IEEE Communication Magazine*, 14: 68–73.

Jue, J. P., and G. Xiao. 2000. An adaptive routing algorithm for wavelength routed optical networks with a distributed control scheme. In *Proceedings of the Ninth International Conference on Computer Communications and Networks*, October, Las Vegas, NV, USA. pp. 192–7.

Jukan, A. 2001. *QoS-based wavelength routing in multiservice WDM networks*. New York: Springer.

Kaheel, A., T. Khattab, A. Mohamed, and H. Alnuweiri. 2002. Quality-of-service mechanisms in IP-over-WDM networks. *IEEE Communications Magazine*, 40 : 38–43.

Lazzez, A., Y. Khlifi, N. Boudriga, and M. S. Obaidat. 2006. A novel node architecture for optical networks: Modeling, analysis, and performance evaluation. *Elsevier Computer Communications Journal*, August, 30(5): 999–1014.

Loi, C.-H., and D. Yang Liao. 2002. Service differentiation in optical burst switched networks. In *Proceedings of the IEEE Global Communications Conference* (Globecom 2002), Nov. 17–21, Taipei, Taiwan. Vol. 3: 2313–7.

Mannie, E., ed. 2001. Generalized multi-protocol label switching (GMPLS) architecture. IETF Internet draft-many-gmpls-architecture-00.txt, Feb. (retrieved from http://tools.ietf.org/id/draft-many-gmpls-architecture-00.txt).

Médard, M., S. R. Chinn, and P. Saengudomlert. 2001. Node wrappers for QoS monitoring in transparent optical nodes. *Journal of High Speed Networks*, 10(4): 247–68.

Myers, A., and P. Bayvel. 2001. Performance of the just-enough-time (JET) scheme for optical burst switching. In *Proceedings of the London Communications Symposium* (LCS 2001), Sept. 11–12.

National Communications System. 2002. *Advancements in photonic network architecture migration: The evolution and deployment of multiprotocol label switching (MPLS), generalized multiprotocol label switching (GMPLS), and advanced optical switching*. Technical Information Bulletin 02–4 (NCS TIB 02–4), May (retrieved from www.ncs.gov/library/tech_bulletins/2002/tib_02–4.pdf).

Naoya, W., and F. Kubota. 2005. Ultra-fast optical processing technology and its application to photonic network. *Journal of the National Institute of Information and Communications Technology*, 51(1–2): 151–61.

Øverby, H. 2005. Quality of service differentiation, teletraffic analysis and network layer packet redundancy in optical packet switched networks (doctoral thesis, Norwegian University of Science and Technology, May).

Papadimitriou, G. I., M. S. Obaidat, and A. S. Pomportsis. 2002. Advances in optical networking. *International Journal of Communication Systems*, 15(2–3): 101–14.

Papadimitriou, G. I., C. Papazoglou, and A. S. Pomportsis. 2003. Optical switching: Switch fabrics, techniques, and architectures. *Journal of Lightwave Technology*, 21(2): 384–406.

Papadimitriou, G. I., P. A. Tsimoulas, M. S. Obaidat, and A. S. Pomportsis. 2003. *Multiwavelength optical LANs*. New York: John Wiley & Sons.

Phung, M. H., C. Chua, G. Mohan, M. Motani, and T. C. Wong. 2004. Absolute QoS signaling and reservation in OBS networks. In *Proceedings of the IEEE Communications Conference* (Globecom 2004), Nov. 29–Dec. 3, Dallas, TX, USA. Vol. 3: 2009–13.

Qiao, C., and M. Yoo. 1999. Optical burst switching (OBS): A new paradigm for an optical Internet. *Journal of High Speed Networks*, 8(1): 69–84.

Rosen, E., A. Viswanathan, and R. Callon. 2001. Multi-protocol label switching architecture. RFC 3031, January.

Rouskas, G. N., and L. Xu. 2004. Optical packet switching. Chap. 1 in *Optical WDM networks: Past lessons and path ahead*, edited by K. Sivalingam and S. Subramaniam. Boston: Kluwer.

Sivalingam, K. M., and S. Subramaniam. 2005. *Emerging optical network technologies: Architectures, protocols and performance*. New York: Springer.

Takahashi, R. 2004. Recent progress in optical packet processing technologies for optical packet-switched networks. *NTT Technical Review*, 2(7): 12–56.

Vokkarane, V. M. 2004. Design and analysis of architectures and protocols for optical burst-switched networks (doctoral dissertation, University of Texas at Dallas, August).

———, J. P. Jue, and S. Sitaraman. 2002. Burst segmentation: An approach for reducing packet loss in optical burst switched networks. In *Proceedings of the IEEE International Conference on Communications* (ICC), April, Vol. 5: 2673–2677.

Wei, J. Y., and R. I. McFarland Jr. 2000. Just-in-time signaling for WDM optical burst switching networks. *IEEE Journal of Lightwave Technology*, 18(12): 2019–31.

Yano, M., F. Yamagishi, and T. Tsuda. 2005. Optical MEMS for photonic switching-compact and stable optical crossconnect switches for simple, fast, and flexible wavelength applications in recent photonic networks. *IEEE Journal of Selected Topics in Quantum Electronics*, 11(2): 383–94.

Yao, S. 2001. Design and analysis of optical packet-switched networks (doctoral dissertation, University of California, Davis).

Yao, S., S. J. Ben Yoo, B. Mukherjee, and S. Dixit. 2001. All-optical packet switching for metropolitan area networks: Opportunities and challenges. *IEEE Communications Magazine*, 39(3): 142–8.

Yao, S., B. Mukherjee, S. J. Ben Yoo, and S. Dixit. 2003. A unified study of contention-resolution schemes in optical packet-switched networks. *IEEE Journal of Lightwave Technology*, 21(3): 672–84.

Yoo, M., and C. Qiao. 1997. Just-enough-time (JET): A high speed protocol for bursty traffic in optical networks. In *Proceedings of the IEEE/LEOS Conference on Technologies for a Global Information Infrastructure*, Aug. 11–15, Montreal. pp. 26–7.

Yoo, M., C. Qiao, and S. Dixit. 2000. QoS performance of optical burst switching in IP-Over-WDM networks. *IEEE Journal of Selected Areas of Communications*, 18: 2062–71.

Yoo, S. J. B. 2003. Optical-label switching, MPLS, MPλS, and GMPLS. *Optical Networks Magazine*, May/June, pp. 17–31.

Yu, X., Y. Chen, and C. Qiao. 2002. Study of traffic statistics of assembled burst traffic in optical burst switched networks. In *Proceedings of Opticomm*, July 29–Aug. 2, Boston. Vol. 4874: 149–59.

Yuan, S., and J. P. Jue. 2004. Dynamic lightpath protection in WDM mesh networks under wavelength continuity constraint. In *Proceedings of the IEEE Communications Conference* (Globecom 2004), Nov. 29–Dec. 3, Dallas, TX, USA. Vol. 3: 2019–23.

Zang, H., J. P. Jue, and B. Mukherjee. 2000. A review of routing and wavelength assignment approaches for wavelength-routed optical WDM networks. *SPIE Optical Networks Magazine*, 1(1): 47–60.

Zhang, Q., V. M. Vokkarane, J. P. Jue, and B. Chen. 2004. Absolute QoS differentiation in optical burst-switched networks. *IEEE Journal on Selected Areas in Communications*, 22(9): 1781–95.

SONET and SDH Networks

M. Farooque Mesiya, *Rensselaer Polytechnic Institute*

INTRODUCTION

The *synchronous optical network* (SONET) is a standard for optical transport defined by the American National Standards Institute (ANSI). The standard was initiated by Bellcore (now Telcordia) on behalf of the regional Bell operating companies to provide a common framework for optical telecommunications. A similar standard defined by the European Telecommunications Standards Institute for Europe—the *synchronous digital hierarchy* (SDH)—is now used everywhere outside of North America and Japan.

SONET and SDH is a physical-layer standard that was originally conceived to provide high-capacity links in a circuit-switched network environment. Both SONET and SDH are based on a structure that has a basic frame and speed. Multiple lower-level SONET and SDH signals can be *time division multiplexed* (TDM) to form higher-level signals. SONET defines rates, formats, and optical parameter specifications for optical interfaces ranging from 51.84 Mb/s (OC-1) to 39.8 Gb/s (OC-768) capacities. Other reasons for the worldwide deployment of SONET and SDH transport infrastructures include:

1. highly survivable and reliable networking because of standardized protection switching architectures;
2. powerful *operations, administration, maintenance, and provisioning* (OAM&P) capabilities that allow service providers to efficiently monitor the network performance and operations remotely; and
3. multivendor interworking and interoperability because of mature standards.

It has been widely established that data traffic has overtaken voice traffic in terms of *wide area network* (WAN) bandwidth utilization. Obviously, most of this traffic growth is driven by the growth of the Internet. Demand for high-speed corporate services across wide areas is rapidly growing as companies become increasingly geographically diverse, e-commerce data exchange proliferates, and direct access to offsite data storage is required. Thus, there is growing need to transport *Internet protocol* (IP), Ethernet, and *storage area networking* (SAN) traffic over SONET infrastructures to provide metro and wide-area connectivity. Because the SONET data rate hierarchy was optimized to transport payloads of voice traffic, it requires new mechanisms to carry packet data efficiently. New protocols have been developed to transport all types of packets, including Ethernet frames, using SONET pipes. These mechanisms include *packet over SONET* (POS), virtual concatenation, and emerging protocols such as the *generic framing procedure* (GFP).

The organization of the chapter is as follows. We first examine the SONET system and its layered architecture. SONET's multiplexing hierarchy is covered next along with a discussion of the *synchronous transport signal 1* (STS-1) frame structure and mapping of non-SONET payloads. Then we examine use of pointers to synchronize SONET payload in a SONET frame. The concept of virtual tributaries to map legacy digital hierarchy data signals (DS-1 to DS-3) into a SONET STS-1 frame is covered next. This is followed by a description of SONET overhead, which allows simpler multiplexing and greatly expanded OAM&P capabilities. Next we consider mapping of high-speed nonmultiplexed data payloads into concatenated SONET frames. A description of popular SONET network elements and configurations follows next. The concepts of protection switching and self-healing SONET rings are discussed in following sections. We then describe data transport over SONET and SDH using PPP/HDLC and ATM/AAL5 framing. This is followed by a discussion of GFP and virtual concatenation mechanisms for flexible provisioning of Ethernet, SNA, and other data services that use SONET transport.

SONET SYSTEM ARCHITECTURE

As defined by the American National Standards Institute (ANSI) (1995, "T1.105-2001"), SONET is a hierarchy of links that are terminated by *network elements* (NEs) that incorporate different layers of functionality. In SONET terminology, a *section* is a single fiber span between adjacent SONET network elements or regenerators. A *line* is a span between adjacent multiplexers and usually encompasses multiple sections. A *path* is a span between SONET terminals at the end of network and usually encompasses multiple lines. Figure 1 illustrates the transport hierarchy as defined in SONET standard.

SONET functionality is divided into four layers—optical, section, line, and path—as shown in Figure 2. All of these layers need not be implemented by every SONET network element.

Although SONET has a layered architecture, it is important to note that it mainly deals with the physical layer of the OSI reference model. A layer 3 in SONET has no relationship with the layer 3 (network layer) of the OSI protocol stack. As in layered architectures, each SONET layer requires the services of the layers below it to perform its functions properly. A description of SONET layers follows.

The *optical layer* provides transport of bits across an optical fiber and converts STS-*N* electrical frames into optical carrier (OC) signals.

The *section layer* performs framing, scrambling, and other functions associated with the preparation for physical transport across a single section.

The *line layer* multiplexes multiple path layer payloads into SONET STS-*N* frames. Its main functions are to provide synchronization, line error and status monitoring, and protection switching.

The *path layer* maps non-SONET payloads—DS-1, DS-3, fiber distributed data interface (FDDI), ATM cells, and so on—into SONET signals. It also provides end-to-end error and status monitoring and path protection.

In SONET terminology, a *regenerator* (also called a *repeater*) is called the *section-terminating equipment* (STE). It implements the optical and section layer functions. The SONET equipment that implements three lower-layer functions of the SONET architecture is called the *line-terminating equipment* (LTE). It is either a line multiplexer

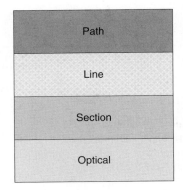

Figure 2: SONET functional layers

(e.g., STS-1 to STS-*N*), an *add-drop multiplexer* (ADM), or a *digital cross-connect system* (DCCS). The equipment that implements all four layers of the SONET architecture is called the *path-terminating equipment* (PTE). The PTE is a SONET terminal or *terminal multiplexer* (TM). For example, an STS-1 SONET terminal assembles twenty-eight DS-1 signals and inserts path overhead to form a 51.84 Mb/s STS-1 signal.

Figure 3 illustrates the functional layers implemented in section-, line-, and path-terminating equipments. Often, PTE and LTE are implemented in one piece of equipment. Note that all SONET equipment types implement the optical and section layer functions. Line layer functions are found in the multiplexers and end terminal equipment. The path layer function occurs only at the end terminal equipment.

SONET MULTIPLEXING HIERARCHY

The SONET standard uses a 51.84 Mbps electrical signal, known as the *synchronous transport signal-1* (STS-1), as a basic building block to extend the digital transmission hierarchy into the multi-Gigabit/second range (ANSI 1995, "T1.105-2001"). Higher-rate SONET signals are produced by interleaving bytes from the lower-level STS signals. For example, an STS-*N* signal is formed by byte-interleaving *N* STS-1 signals. Each STS-*N* electrical signal has a corresponding *optical carrier level-N* (OC-*N*) signal. The optical OC-*N* signal is formed by scrambling the electrical STS-*N* signal using the standardized polynomial and then modulating an optical source. The

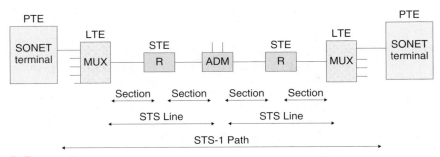

R–Regenerator
MUX–Line Multiplexer
ADM–Add-Drop Multiplexer

Figure 1: Section, line, and path in SONET

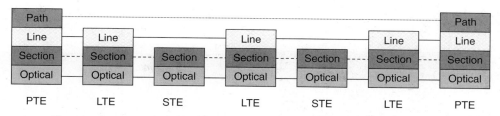

Figure 3: Functional layers in section-, line-, and path-terminating equipment

Table 1: SONET and SDH Hierarchy

SONET Electrical Signal (STS-N)	Optical Signal (OC-N)	Bit Rate (Mbps)	SDH Electrical Signal (STM-N)
STS-1	OC-1	51.84	N/A
STS-3	OC-3	155.52	STM 1
STS-12	OC-12	622.08	STM-4
STS-48	OC-48	2488.32	STM-16
STS-192	OC-192	9953.28	STM-64
STS-768	OC-768	39813.12	STM-256

frame format used by SDH is the *synchronous transport module* (STM), with STM-1 being the base level signal at 155.52 Mb/s [International Telecommunication Union–Telecommunication Standardization Sector (ITU-T) 2003]. The STM-1 signal is converted to an OC-3 optical signal for transmission. Both SONET and SDH have a hierarchy of signaling speeds Table 1 shows the SONET and SDH digital hierarchy. Notice that the rate of an STS or STM-N signal is simply *N* times the rate of an STS or STM-1 signal.

STS-1 Frame

SONET uses a frame structure that has the same 8-kHz repetition rate as traditional telephone TDM systems. Figure 4 illustrates the structure of the SONET STS-1

frame. SONET uses a frame length of 125 μsec or a frame rate of 8000 frames per second. Each STS-1 frame can be viewed as a nine-row by ninety-column structure, a total of 810 bytes. The STS-1 line rate = 8 bits/byte × 9 rows × 90 columns × 8000 frames/sec = 51.84 Mb/s. The order of transmission of bytes is row by row from top to bottom, left to right (the most significant bit first).

The STS-1 frame is divided into two main areas: *transport overhead* and the *synchronous payload envelope* (SPE). The first three columns constitute the transport overhead: a total of twenty-seven bytes. The first three rows (nine bytes) of the transport overhead are used for the *section* overhead. The remaining six rows (eighteen bytes) of the transport overhead are used for the *line* overhead. The SPE may start anywhere within the remaining

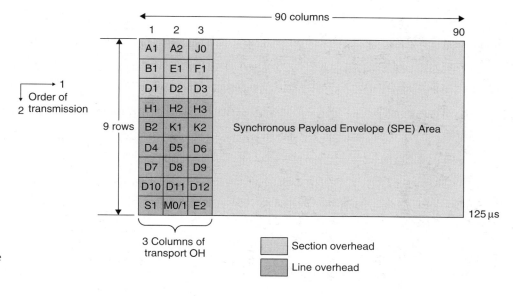

Figure 4: SONET STS-1 frame format

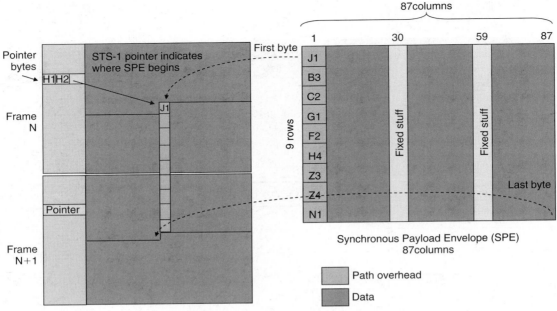

Figure 5: Floating of SPE in two consecutive frames

eighty-seven columns of the STS-1 frame. Unless the SPE happens to start at the fourth column of the first row (rare), it occupies a portion of two consecutive frames as displayed in Figure 5. SPE column 1 (nine bytes) contains the *path overhead* (POH). Two columns in SPE (columns 30 and 59) are not used for payload but are designated as the *fixed stuff* columns. The 756 bytes in the remaining eighty-four columns are designated as the STS-1 *payload* capacity. The bit rate of the STS-1 payload is 8 bits/byte × 9 rows × 84 columns × 8000 frames/sec = 48.384 Mb/s.

Mapping of Non-SONET Payloads

SONET was designed to be highly flexible in the types of services that it can carry in its payload. Any type of service, ranging from voice to high-speed data and video, can be mapped into the payload of an appropriate STS-1

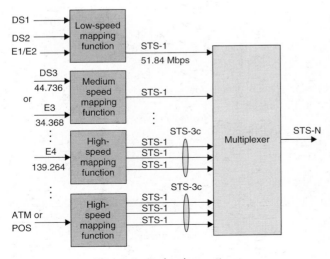

Figure 6: Payload mappings

or higher level signal (ANSI 1995, "T1.105.02-2001"). A slow-speed mapping function allows DS1, DS2, and *European Conference of Postal and Telecommunications Administrations* (CEPT-1) signals to be combined into an STS-1 signal. A DS3 signal can be mapped into an STS-1 signal, and a CEPT-4 signal can be mapped into an STS-3 signal. Mappings have also been defined for streams of packet information into SONET. For example, ATM streams can be mapped into an STS-3c signal. Packet-over-SONET allows IP packet traffic to be mapped into STS-3c or higher level signals. Figure 6 shows how a SONET multiplexer handles a wide range of payloads.

POINTERS

SONET uses *pointers* to compensate for clock variations in the network. Because of slight differences in the clocks at different nodes, the frames originating from them will not be aligned perfectly. To multiplex these signals, it is necessary to decouple the SPE from the STS-1 frame. The pointers allow payload to *float* within the SPE area to accommodate the phase and clock rate differences.

The first two bytes (H1 and H2) of the line overhead in the STS-1 frame are used as a pointer. The pointer bytes perform two functions: (1) locate the first byte of the STS-1 SPE (where the SPE begins) and (2) indicate the need for frequency justification. The sixteen bits of the STS-1 pointer are classified into three fields as shown in Figure 7. A description of the fields follows.

New data flag (NDF): four bits. NDF = 0110 ⇒ normal operation, NDF = 1001 ⇒ ignore previous content of pointer bytes.

Spare field: two bits.

Pointer (offset) value field: ten bits. Indicates the offset in bytes from the H3 byte location to the first byte of the STS-1 SPE. A value of 0 means that the SPE starts in row 4,

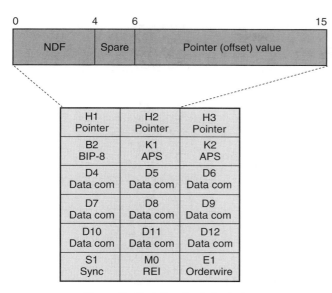

Figure 7: Details of pointer bytes

column 4. The pointer bits are alternately labeled as **IDIDIDIDID**, where I = increment bit, D = decrement bit. The I and D bit designations have additional meaning for positive and negative justification.

Positive Stuffing

When input payload stream is slower than output, a stuff byte is required from time to time so that payload catches up with the frame stream. The additional byte is stuffed in location right after the H3 byte as shown in Figure 8a. This is known as *positive stuffing*. At the receiver, the byte after H3 is ignored. This operation is indicated to the receiver by inverting the I bits of the pointer value. The pointer is incremented by 1 in the next frame (to indicate that the SPE now starts one byte later), and the subsequent pointers contain the new value.

Negative Stuffing

If the input payload stream is faster than the frame rate, an extra SPE byte is transmitted from time to time for the frame to catch up. The extra byte, which is written in the H3 byte location as shown in Figure 8b, is known as *negative stuffing*. This operation is indicated to the receiver by inverting the D bits of the pointer value. Whenever the extra byte is inserted, the pointer is decremented by 1 in the next frame (to indicate that the SPE now starts one byte earlier), and the subsequent pointers contain the new value.

Table 2 illustrates how the pointer field bits are manipulated in a specific example to indicate to the receiver the forthcoming stuffing operation.

STS-*N* FRAME

The STS-*N* frame is an array of *N* × 810 bytes. The STS-*N* frame is produced by interleaving bytes of the *N* synchronized STS-1 signals, in effect producing a frame that has nine rows, 3 × *N* transport overhead columns, and 87 × *N* SPE columns. Before *N* STS-1 signals can be interleaved, each incoming STS-1 signal first needs to be synchronized to the local STS-1 clock of the multiplexer. This is accomplished by terminating the section and line overhead of each incoming STS-1 signal and then mapping its SPE into a new STS-1 frame that is synchronized to the local clock as shown in Figure 9. The pointer in the new STS-1 frame is adjusted as necessary, and the mapping is done on the fly. This procedure ensures that all of the incoming STS-1 frames are mapped into STS-1 frames that are synchronized with respect to each other.

Figure 10 illustrates the structure of an STS-3 frame. Note that the transport overhead of the constituent STS-1 signals are byte-interleaved in the first nine columns of the new STS-3 frame. The composite SPE, formed by byte-interleaving individual SPEs, floats in consecutive STS-3 frames as discussed earlier. To multiplex *k* STS-*N* signals into an STS-*kN* signal, the incoming signals are first de-interleaved into STS-1 signals, and then the above procedure is applied to all *kN* STS-1 signals.

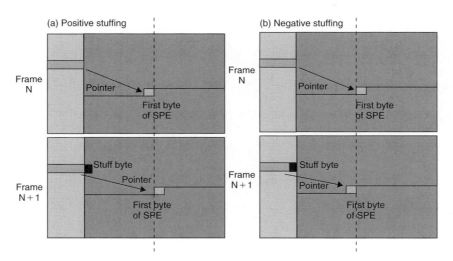

Figure 8: SPE byte stuffing

Table 2: Positive and Negative Stuffing Examples

State	NDF Bits	I D I D I D I D I D	Pointer Value	Frame Number
Initial	0110	0 0 0 1 0 1 1 0 0 1	67	$N-1$
Positive stuff required	0110	1 0 1 1 1 1 0 0 1 1	undefined	N
New pointer value	1001	0 0 0 1 0 1 1 0 1 0	68	$N+1$
	1001	0 0 0 1 0 1 1 0 1 0	68	$N+2$
	1001	0 0 0 1 0 1 1 0 1 0	68	$N+3$
Normal	0110	0 0 0 1 0 1 1 0 1 0	68	$M-1$
Negative stuff required	0110	0 1 0 0 0 0 1 1 1 1	Undefined	M
New pointer value	1001	0 0 0 1 0 1 1 0 0 1	67	$M+1$
	1001	0 0 0 1 0 1 1 0 0 1	67	$M+2$
	1001	0 0 0 1 0 1 1 0 0 1	67	$M+3$

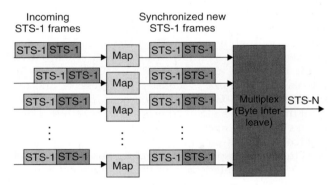

Figure 9: Synchronous multiplexing in SONET

VIRTUAL TRIBUTARIES

SONET is designed to carry broadband payloads. Legacy digital hierarchy data rates (DS-1 to DS-3) are lower than STS-1. To make SONET backward-compatible with the legacy digital hierarchy, SONET defines synchronous formats at sub-STS-1 levels called *virtual tributaries* (VTs). Instead of using all eighty-four payload columns of an STS-1 frame for data from one source, the SPE is divided into VTs that are capable of transporting signals at lower data rates.

Four types of VTs have been defined to accommodate existing digital signals as shown in Table 3. A STS-1 SPE

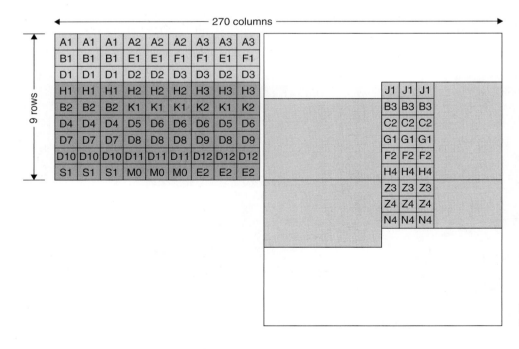

Figure 10: SONET STS-3 frame structure

Table 3: Virtual Tributaries in SONET

VT Type	Payload	Bit Rate (Mb/s)	Size of VT
VT1.5	DS-1	1.728	9 rows, 3 columns
VT2	CEPT-1	2.304	9 rows, 4 columns
VT3	DS-1C	3.456	9 rows, 6 columns
VT6	DS-2	6.912	9 rows, 12 columns

designed to carry VT traffic is divided into seven *virtual tributary groups* (VTGs). Each VTG occupies twelve columns of the STS-1 SPE. A VTG can contain only one size of VTs; however, a different VT size is allowed for each VTG. A VTG may contain four VT1.5s, three VT2s, two VT3s, or one VT6. When two or more VTGs are inserted into an STS-1 frame, they are interleaved column by column. The columns of individual VTs within a VTG are interleaved as well. Because multiplexing is synchronous, an individual VT containing a DS-1 can be extracted without demultiplexing the entire STS-1 signal. This improved accessibility considerably simplifies switching and grooming at the VT or STS level.

Figure 11 illustrates how virtual tributaries are synchronously multiplexed into an STS-1 SPE. Here the STS-1 signal is used to transport seven DS-2 signals using VT6 tributaries.

SONET OVERHEAD

SONET provides substantial overhead information, allowing simpler multiplexing and greatly expanded operations, administration, maintenance, and provisioning capabilities. The path overhead is inserted at the transmit end SONET terminal and terminated at the receive end terminal to carry out necessary path layer functions. The line overhead information is created by adjacent LTEs to communicate with each other to implement line layer functions. The STEs add and terminate section overhead. It is used between adjacent NEs such as regenerators to implement section layer functions such as framing and error detection, among others.

Section Overhead

The section overhead displayed in Figure 12 occupies the first three rows of the transport overhead, which is originated, accessed, and processed by the STE. This overhead supports the following functions: framing, performance monitoring (STS-*N* signal), local orderwire, and data

A1 =0xF6	A2 =0x28	J0/Z0 STS-ID
B1 BIP-8	E1 Orderwire	F1 User
D1 Data com	D2 Data com	D3 Data com

Figure 12: Section overhead bytes in STS-1

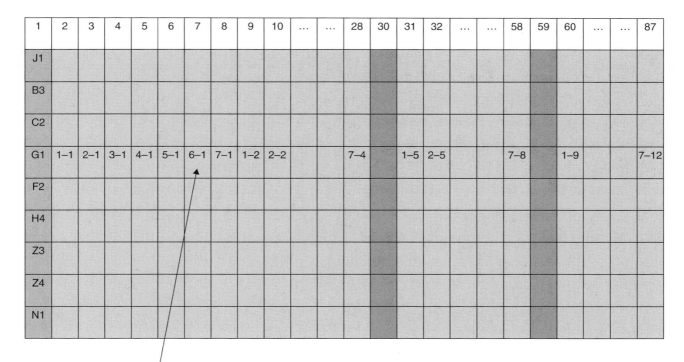

First number is group, second number is column

Figure 11: Mapping of seven VT6 tributaries in STS-1 SPE

communication channels to carry information for OAM&P. A description of section overhead bytes follows.

Framing (A1 and A2): Two bytes, A1 and A2, in each STS-1 indicate the beginning of an STS-1 frame. The A1, A2 bytes pattern is F628 hex. When four consecutive errored framing patterns have been received, an *out-of-frame* condition is declared. When two consecutive error-free framing patterns have been received, an *in-frame* condition is declared. A1 and A2 are not scrambled.

Section BIP-8 (B1): One byte, B1, from the first STS-1 of an STS-*N* is used for section error monitoring. The B1 bytes of the other STS-1s of the STS-*N* frame are not defined. B1 byte is calculated using *bit interleaved parity* (BIP) code. For error checking, bit 1 of the BIP-8 byte is calculated to give even parity over all bit 1's in the previous block. Bit 2 is calculated to give even parity for all bit 2's, bit 3 for bit 3's, and so on through bit 8, which is calculated to give even parity for all bit 8's in the previous block. At the next STE, the parity byte is used to check for bit errors.

Section Trace (J0) or *Section Growth* (Z0): This byte is used to trace the origin of an STS-1 frame. It is not standardized.

Orderwire (E1): One byte, E1, is allocated from the first STS-1 of an STS-*N* frame as a local orderwire channel for voice communication between STEs (e.g., regenerators). One byte of a SONET frame is 8 bits/125 µsec or 64 kb/s, which is the same rate as a PCM voice channel. The E1 bytes of the rest of the STS-*N* frame are not defined.

Section user channel (F1): This byte is located in the first STS-1 of the STS-*N* and is set aside for the network operator. The corresponding byte locations of the second through *n*th STS-1 are not defined.

Section data communication channel (D1, D2, D3): Three bytes—D1, D2, and D3—are allocated from the first STS-1 of an STS-*N* frame. This 192 kb/s message channel can be used for OAM&P and other communication functions between two STEs. The *data communication channel* (DCC) is often called the *embedded operations channel* (EOC) in SONET.

Line Overhead

Line overhead consists of eighteen bytes (in the last six rows of the transport overhead as shown in Figure 13) that are originated, accessed, and terminated by the LTE.

H1 Pointer	H2 Pointer	H3 Pointer
B2 BIP-8	K1 APS	K2 APS
D4 Data com	D5 Data com	D6 Data com
D7 Data com	D8 Data com	D9 Data com
D10 Data com	D11 Data com	D12 Data com
S1 Sync	M0 REI	E1 Orderwire

Figure 13: Line overhead bytes in STS-1

This overhead supports the following functions: locating the SPE in the frame, performance monitoring, automatic protection switching, multiplexing or concatenating signals, and line maintenance. A description of line overhead bytes follows.

Pointer (H1, H2): Two bytes, H1 and H2, in all STS-1 frames within an STS-*N* signal are allocated to a pointer that indicates the offset in bytes between the pointer and the first byte of the STS-1 SPE. The pointer is used to align the STS-1 SPE in an STS-*N* signal as well as to perform frequency justification.

Pointer action byte (H3): One byte, H3, in each of the STS-1 signals of an STS-*N* frame is used for frequency justification purposes. It carries an extra SPE byte in the event of negative justification. Otherwise, its value is not defined.

Line BIP-8 (B2): One byte, B2, in each of the STS-1 signal of an STS-*N* frame is used for line-error monitoring. It is also calculated using BIP code with even parity over all bytes in the previous STS-1 frame before scrambling, and it is placed in the B2 byte location before scrambling.

Automatic protection switching (APS) *channel* (K1, K2): These bytes are located in the first STS-1 of the STS-*N* and are used on the protection line for automatic protection switching signaling between LTEs. These bytes are defined only for the first STS-1 of an STS-*N* signal.

Line data communication channel (D4–D12): Nine bytes, D4–D12, are allocated for line data communication. This 576 kbps message-based DCC can be used for OAM&P and other communication functions between two LTEs. The D4–D12 bytes of the rest of the STS-*N* frame are not defined.

Path Overhead

The POH consists of nine bytes in rows 1 to 9 of the first column of the STS-1 SPE as illustrated in Figure 14. POH provides for communication between the point of creation of an STS SPE and its point of termination. This overhead

JI Trace
B3 BIP-8
C2 Sig label
G1 Path stat
F2 User
H4 Indicator
Z3 Growth
Z4 Growth
Z5 Tandem

Figure 14: Definition of path overhead bytes in STS-1

supports functions such as the following: performance monitoring of the STS SPE, signal label (the content of the STS SPE, including status of mapped payloads), path status, and path trace. A description of path overhead bytes follows.

STS path trace (J1): This byte is used to repetitively transmit a sixty-four-byte, fixed-length string so that a receiving PTE can verify its continued connection to the intended STS transmitting PTE.

Path BIP-8 (B3): This byte is used for path error monitoring. The B3 byte is calculated before scrambling over all bytes of the previous STS SPE using BIP code with even parity.

STS path signal label (C2): This byte is used to indicate the type of payload being transported in the STS SPE, including the status of the mapped payloads. The following is a partial list of C2 byte assignments:

- 0×00, unequipped
- 0×01, equipped, nonspecific payload
- 0×02, VT-structured STS-1 SPE
- 0×04, asynchronous DS-3 mapping
- 0×13, ATM cell mapping
- 0×15, asynchronous FDDI mapping
- 0×16, POS mapping

Path status (G1): This byte conveys information about the path-termination status or performance back to the PTE that originated the STS.

Path user channel (F2): This byte is for network operator communications between STS path-terminating NEs.

CONTIGUOUS CONCATENATION

Superrate services, such as the transport of a router or ATM switch output or uncompressed high-quality or high-definition video signals, require multiples of STS-1 rate. To enable this high-bandwidth transport, multiple contiguous SPEs are transported (and switched) across the SONET or SDH network as a *single concatenated SONET* (STS-*Nc*) frame, where *c* indicates concatenated. Because concatenated signals STS-*Nc* are not channelized, the access to individual STS-1 signals is neither required nor provided Table 4. outlines supported contiguous concatenation for

Table 4: Contiguous Concatenation Containers for SONET and SDH

SONET	SDH	Payload Capacity (Mb/s)
STS-1	VC-3	48.38
STS-3c	VC-4	149.76
STS-12c	VC-4-4c	599.04
STS-48c	VC-4-16c	2396.16
STS-192c	VC-4-64c	9584.64

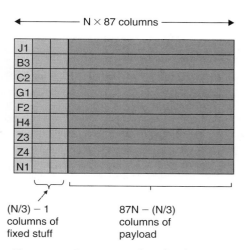

Figure 15: Concatenated payload STS-*Nc*

both SONET and SDH. For the SONET standard, these are denoted as STS*Nc*, and for SDH as VC-4-*Nc*. Most SONET interfaces on routers are concatenated.

An STS-*Nc* contains a single synchronous payload envelope as well as a single column of path overhead, which always appears in the first STS-1 as shown in Figure 15. The number of fixed-stuff columns is given by $N/3 - 1$. Thus, an STC-3c contains $3/3 - 1 = 0$, or no fixed-stuff columns, whereas an STC-12c contains $12/3 - 1 = 3$ fixed-stuff columns. STS-*Nc* payload $= N \times 780$ bytes. Thus, the number of bytes in the payload of the STS-3c frame is more than that of STS-3 by 18 bytes. One can think of an STS-3c as three STS-1 frames pasted together to create a single, larger frame. SONET equipment treats these interfaces as a single entity.

Figure 16 illustrates which overhead bytes are used with an STS-3c concatenated SONET frame. The unused bytes cannot be used for payload and are simply ignored. For example, the B1 byte in the section overhead and the K1 and K2 APS bytes in the line overhead are undefined and ignored except in the first STS-1 of the STS-3c. The SONET standard specifies use of the H1 and H2 bytes in the line overhead section to indicate whether or not the frames are channelized. The first set of pointers (H1, H2) performs exactly the same functions as STS-1 payload pointer does. For example, if (H1, H2) = 0110 00 0000000001, then the pointer offset is 1. All other pointer bytes (H1*, H2*) should set bits 7 to 16 to 1, and set the new data flag bits to 1001. In other words, (H1*, H2*) use values of 10010011 and 11111111 for these bytes. Channelized interfaces use the H1 and H2 bytes to form a ten-bit pointer that indicates the byte location where a new frame begins. The pointer supports values between 0 and 782. An STS-1 includes eighty-seven columns of SPE. An STS-3c includes $3 \times 87 = 261$ columns. However, the H1 or H2 pointer field is ten bits. Receiving SONET interfaces resolve this problem by tripling the value in the pointer field of the first STS stream when the value falls within the range of 0 and 782. Thus, it sees a pointer value of 1 as 3, and a pointer value of 782 as 2346. For (H1, H2) = 0110 00 0000000001, the J1 byte will reside in column 13.

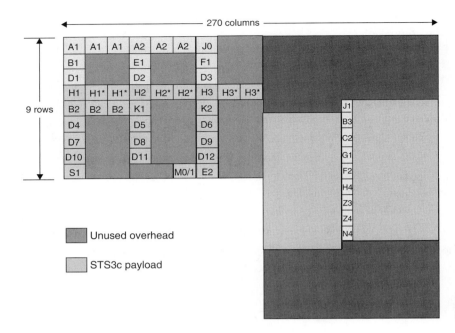

Figure 16: Definition of overhead bytes in STS-3*c*

SONET NETWORKS

SONET transport networks primarily deploy following three broad classes of network elements: terminal multiplexers, add-drop multiplexers, and digital cross-connect systems.

The *terminal multiplexer* is an end-point device in the SONET network. TMs are used to provide access to the SONET network for various types of traffic using legacy interfaces such as DS-1 and DS-3 or in data-oriented forms such as FDDI via an appropriate bridge or router. TM multiplexes these signals into STS payloads for transport over an OC-*N* fiber link. The demultiplexer portion of a TM terminates an OC-*N* fiber link on the network side and provides access to individual signals. The TM is a point-to-point device and is commonly deployed in a point-to-point SONET link.

The add-drop multiplexer is the most widely deployed SONET NE. An ADM is a fully synchronous, byte-oriented multiplexer capable of adding and dropping legacy DS-*n* or SONET OC-*M* ($M \leq N$) signals onto one of two SONET OC-*N* signals. Note that SONET ADMs have two sets of OC (line) interfaces instead of one as in the TM. At an add-drop site, only those signals that need to be dropped or inserted are accessed. The remaining traffic continues through the network. An ADM enables *drop and repeat* (also known as *drop and continue*), a key capability in CATV application. With drop and repeat, a signal terminates at one node, is duplicated (repeated), and is then sent to the next and subsequent nodes.

The DCCS has a switching fabric capable of cross-connecting STS-*M* and STS-*N* line-side ports. Normally, *N* is greater than the *M*, but it can be the same. If $N > M$, an incoming STS-*N* is first demultiplexed into a number (*N*/*M* at most) of STSMs, which are switched through the STS-*M* fabric and reassembled into STS-*N* if they are continuing on, or are dropped in the office as STS-*M*s through the ports shown at the bottom. There could be many (thousands) of STS-*N* and STS-*M* ports on a single DCCS.

All three types of NEs shown in Figure 17. have been widely deployed in the network and continue to be deployed in significant volumes. In intercity networks, a typical ADM being installed today would likely have STS-48 or STS-192 line-side ports and a mix of STS-3 and STS-12 drop-side ports.

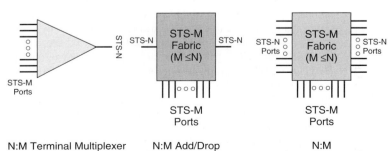

N:M Terminal Multiplexer   N:M Add/Drop Multiplexer(ADM)   N:M Digital Cross-Connect System (DCCS)

Figure 17: Widely deployed SONET network elements

SONET Network Configurations

A *point-to-point* link, as shown in Figure 18, consists of two SONET multiplexers linked by a fiber pair with or without a regenerator in the path. This implementation represents the simplest SONET configuration.

A *point-to-multipoint* (*linear* add-drop) link consists of ADMs interconnected in a linear fashion to facilitate adding and dropping tributary channels at intermediate points in the network. At each ADM, only the signals that are destined for that site are accessed and dropped, and transit signals are passed through. Signals generated locally and destined for other sites are inserted at the ADM. Figure 19 displays a SONET linear add-drop system.

SONET *rings* are formed by interconnecting a number of ADMs (as many as sixteen) to form a closed loop network. A ring provides redundant bandwidth to protect services against failures; if a fiber cable is cut, the SONET nodes have the intelligence to send the services affected via an alternate path through the ring without interruption. Figure 20 illustrates a SONET ring topology.

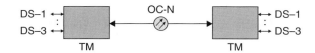

Figure 18: Point-to-point SONET link

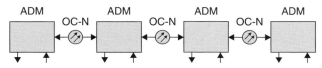

Figure 19: Point-to-multipoint SONET link

PROTECTION SWITCHING

The SONET standard defines automatic protection switching schemes that provide linear protection against failures at the line layer. Recall that in SONET terminology, a line connects two multiplexers with a single OC-*N* optical signal. Therefore, protection at the line level applies to a multiplexed signal while it traverses the line between two multiplexers. Figure 21 shows two such SONET multiplexers connected in a 1+1 ("one plus one") configuration using two SONET lines: a *working* line and a *protection* line.

At the upstream node, the signal is *bridged* electrically into working and protection lines that carry the same payload across the two lines. At the downstream node, the two received signals are monitored for failures. The monitoring looks for loss of signal, loss of framing, bit-error-rate levels, as well as alarm signals in the overhead. A selector in the downstream node picks the better signal based on the information provided by the two monitors and does not need to coordinate with the upstream node. Recovery from failures can be done quickly because the monitoring and selection functions are typically implemented in hardware. However, the 1+1 APS scheme is inefficient because it uses twice the bandwidth required by an unprotected signal.

Figure 22 shows a 1:1 ("one for one") APS arrangement. In this approach, the signal is only transmitted in the working line during normal operation. The optical signal that is received in the working line is monitored for degradation, and a request to switch to the protection line is sent on a reverse signaling channel when a failure is detected. On receipt of the request, the upstream node switches the signal to the protection line. The 1:1 APS scheme takes more time to recover from failure than the 1+1 APS scheme because of the need to signal for

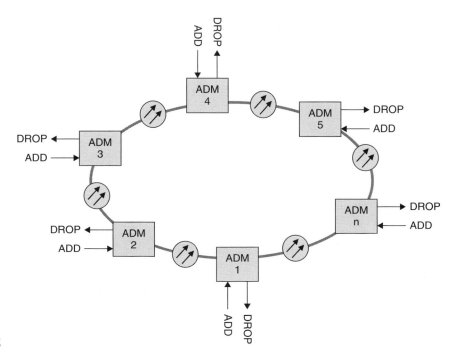

Figure 20: SONET ring

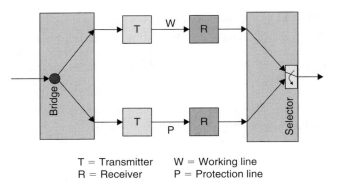

T = Transmitter   W = Working line
R = Receiver   P = Protection line

Figure 21: 1+1 linear APS scheme

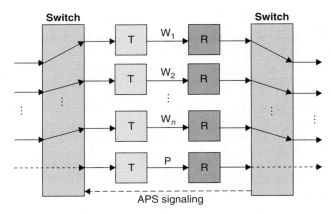

Figure 23: 1: *n* linear APS scheme

a switchover. However, the 1:1 scheme can be more efficient in bandwidth usage because the protection line can be used to carry extra traffic when there are no failures. The extra traffic is preempted when the protection line is needed to protect working traffic. The K1 and K2 bytes in the line overhead of a SONET frame are used to exchange requests and acknowledgments for protection switch actions.

Figure 23 shows that the 1:1 APS scheme can be generalized to a l:*n* APS scheme where one protection line protects *n* working lines. The scheme assumes that the working lines are unlikely to fail at the same time. This assumption is reasonable if the lines use diverse transmission routes. In both 1:1 and l:*n* APS schemes, the working signal is switched back to its original line once the fault has been repaired.

The SONET linear APS specifications require that fault recovery be completed within 50 milliseconds after the fault has been detected in all of the above schemes.

SELF-HEALING SONET RINGS

The main advantage of ring topology is protection: The ring offers two different ways of passing traffic from ingress to egress. The two main standardized ring protection architectures are the two- and four-fiber SONET *bidirectional line switched rings* (BLSRs) and *unidirectional path switched rings* (UPSRs) (ANSI 1995, "T1.105.01-2000"; Wu 1995). In SDH terminology (ITU- T 1998), BLSRs are

called *multiplex section shared protection rings* (MSPRings) and UPSRs are referred to as *subnetwork connection protection* (deployed in) *physical rings* (SNCPRings).

Unidirectional Path Switched Ring

The unidirectional path switched ring provides protection at the path level. Figure 24 shows a two-fiber ring in which data travel in one direction in one ring and in the opposite direction in the other ring. By convention, working traffic flows clockwise and protection traffic

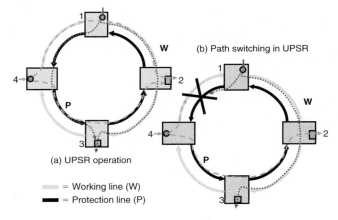

(a) UPSR operation

= Working line (W)
= Protection line (P)

Figure 24: Protection switching in UPSR

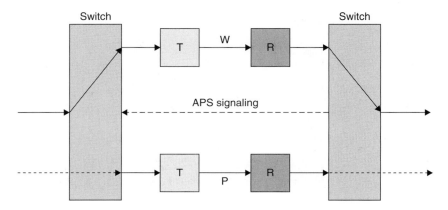

Figure 22: 1:1 linear APS scheme

flows counterclockwise. At each ADM—say, node 1 in Figure 24a—the path signal to another node—say, 3—is bridged into both the working fiber and the protection fiber. Thus, information can flow between any pair of nodes in the ring along two paths, providing 1 + 1 protection at the path level. For example, Figure 24a shows a path signal inserted at node 4 that travels around the ring in both directions and exits at node 2. In UPSR, each exit node monitors the two received path signals and selects the better one. For example, suppose that a fiber is cut between two nodes—say, nodes 4 and 1 in Figure 24b. Node 1 can no longer receive the working signal in the clockwise direction, so it inserts a path alarm indication in the overhead of every affected path signal. A selector at the receiver then selects the path that arrives in the protection fiber as shown in Figure 24b. In this example, we see that the selector in node 2 switches to the counterclockwise signal to receive the path signal from node 4.

UPSR rings can provide fast path protection, but they are inefficient in terms of bandwidth usage because two paths are used to carry every signal. If a path uses an STS-N signal, then the path will use STS-N in every hop in both rings. The UPSR is most often deployed for hubbed transport scenarios. The lower speed UPSR rings in the access portion of a network collect traffic from various remote sites and carry to a large central hub where a DCS directs the traffic to other parts of the network.

Bidirectional Line Switched Ring

SONET rings can also be configured to provide protection at the line level. In a four-fiber bidirectional line switched ring, adjacent ADMs in the ring are connected by a working fiber pair and a protection fiber pair. Suppose that failure disrupts the working pair between nodes 2 and 3 as shown in Figure 25. The BLSR operation recovers from this failure by switching both working channels to the protection channels between nodes 2 and 3. In effect, line APS protection is used in identical fashion to linear ADM networks. This protection scheme is called *span switching*.

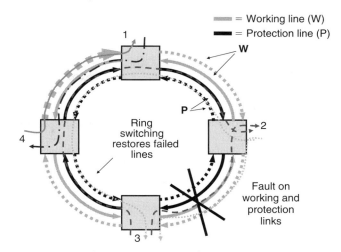

Figure 26: Ring switching in BLSR

Now suppose that the working pair and the protection pair between adjacent nodes fail together as shown in Figure 26. In this case, BLSR uses the protection pair in the directions away from the failure to restore the two working lines that spanned the failure. The nodes on either side of the failure bridge their working line onto the protection line that flows in the direction away from the failure. In effect, the working lines that traversed the failed path are now routed to their adjacent node the long way around the ring as shown in Figure 26. This protection scheme is called *ring switching*. SONET requires that fault recovery using either path or ring switching be completed within 50 milliseconds after the fault has been detected.

In the four-fiber BLSR, each fiber span supports full ring bandwidth. Thus, the total network bandwidth can be calculated using the following formula:

Four-fiber BLSR bandwidth = ring speed × number of spans − total STS pass-through node traffic

Thus, in a perfect BLSR network, where all traffic originates and terminates on adjacent nodes, the total ring bandwidth equals N × ring speed, where N = number of spans. If the BLSR in Figures 25 and 26 is operating at OC-48, then the maximum ring bandwidth is OC-192. This bandwidth capability is in stark contrast to a UPSR based OC-48 network, where the total ring capacity is equal to the ring speed (OC-48). The reason for this lies in the fact that for each circuit created, the UPSR restoration mechanism creates two copies of the circuit, routing one copy on each of the counter rotating fibers. These two copies consume bandwidth on each fiber span around the entire ring. BLSR, therefore, offers more bandwidth around the ring and flexibility to manage it efficiently compared with UPSR. Further, the protection fibers in BLSR can be used to carry extra traffic when there are no faults in the ring. On the other hand, BLSR requires fairly complex signaling to implement span or ring switching. The capability of BLSRs to manage bandwidth flexibly and recover from fault within 50 msec are key reasons for

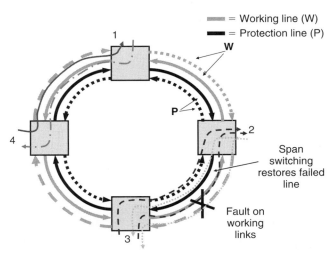

Figure 25: Span switching in BLSR

their wide scale deployment in interexchange carrier and incumbent local exchange carrier backbone networks.

DATA TRANSPORT OVER SONET OR SDH

SONET and SDH standards were developed primarily for the transport of constant bit rate applications. This is evident in many characteristics of these technologies. As an example, bandwidth is provisioned via a rigid hierarchy of bit rates (STS-1, STS-3, STS-12, STS-48, etc.). However, with the explosion of IP and other packet-switched data traffic, solutions for the transport of data over SONET and SDH systems were developed. Because SONET and SDH are connection-oriented layer 1 protocols and IP is a layer 3 protocol, the transport of IP over SONET and SDH requires a layer 2 protocol. The following framing protocols are used to encapsulate IP packets: packet over SONET, frame relay, and asynchronous transfer mode.

Packet over SONET

IP datagrams are encapsulated into *point-to-point protocol* (PPP) data frames (Malis and Simpson 1999). The PPP formats data frames using a byte-oriented version of the HDLC protocol. The PPP data frames are then mapped byte-synchronously into contiguously concatenated SONET frames (e.g., STS-12*c*, STS-48*c*). HDLC provides flag-based delineation of the IP datagrams across the synchronous transport link. Byte stuffing is used to enable transparent operation. Each HDLC frame begins and ends with the flag byte 0 × 7E as shown in Figure 27. At the transmit side, the data bytes in each datagram are monitored for the flag sequence and an escape sequence (0 × 7D). If the flag sequence occurs anywhere within the information field of the HDLC frame, it is changed to the sequence 0 × 7D 0 × 5C. Likewise, the occurrences of the escape sequence, 0×7D, are converted to 0×7D 0 × 5D. As a result, the signal to be transported grows by

one byte for each byte requiring transparency processing. At the receive end of transmission, the stuffed patterns are removed and replaced with the original fields. The byte-stuffed transparency processing becomes difficult to implement in 10 Gb/s and 40 Gb/s SONET equipment.

IP or ATM over SONET

This approach utilizes ATM as the data-link layer with its excellent traffic management capabilities as a significant bonus for multimedia applications. The IP over ATM mapping can be described as a three-step process. First, each IP datagram is encapsulated into an *ATM adaptation layer type* 5 (AAL5) frame using multiprotocol logic link control and *subnetwork attachment point* (SNAP) encapsulation (Grossman and Heinanen 1999). Second, the resulting AAL5 common part convergence sublayer *protocol data unit* (PDU) is segmented into forty-eight-byte payloads for ATM cells as illustrated in Figure 28. Lastly, the ATM cells are mapped into a contiguously concatenated SONET or SDH (e.g., STS-48*c* or VC-4-16*c*) frame. This protocol stack introduces a certain bandwidth overhead. It has been repeatedly reported that the classical IP over ATM mapping results in an overhead ("cell tax") of 18–25 percent, in addition to the approximately fixed 4 percent overhead needed for SONET.

Example: Mapping of ATM Cells in STS3c Frame

ATM cells are mapped into SONET STS-3*c* SPE "directly" (without any additional overhead) as shown in Figure 29. The only requirement is that the STS-3*c* byte boundaries are preserved in such a mapping (i.e., bytes of the ATM cell coincide with those of the STS-3*c* SPE). Because the STS-3*c* payload capacity (260 × 9 = 2340 bytes) is not an integer multiple of the ATM cell length (53 bytes), a cell is allowed to cross the SPE boundary. For instance, if an ATM cell starts right after the POH J1 byte (that defines the beginning of the SPE), the SPE will contain forty-four full ATM cells and eight bytes of the forty-fifth

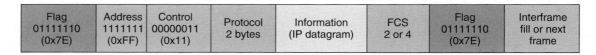

Figure 27: Frame format for PPP/HDLC frame

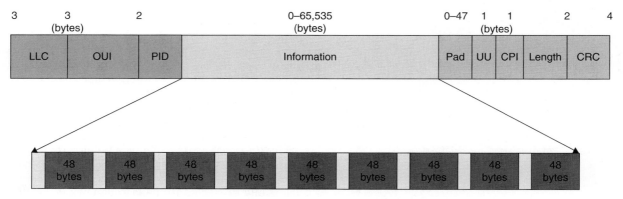

Figure 28: Frame format for ATM/AAL5 frame

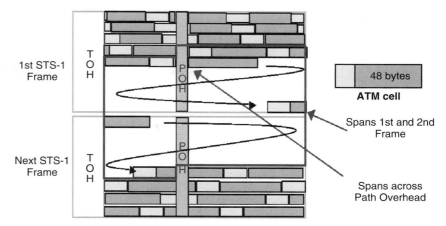

Figure 29: Mapping of ATM cells in STS-3*c* frame

ATM cell. The "tail" forty-five bytes of the forty-fifth cell will begin directly following the POH J1 byte of the next SPE. Thus, ATM cells always span the SPEs. That is of no concern to SONET or SDH, because the cell delineation is an ATM layer function. Cells are mapped row-wise into the frame. Cells could contain data or be empty. The SONET delivers bytes in the SPE to an ATM switch, which has to make sense out of the bytes. The STS-3*c* payload rate is $9 \times 260 \times 8/125\text{msec} = 149.76$ Mb/s, which provides maximum ATM payload capacity of 149.76 Mb/s $\times$ (48/53) = 135.63 Mb/s $\Rightarrow$ 87.21 percent efficiency.

The tremendous acceptance of Ethernet and *Gigabit Ethernet* (GbE), *enterprise system connect* (ESCON), *fiber connection* (FICON), *fiber channel* (FC), and *storage area networking* (SAN) applications has created pressure on carriers for efficient transport of these services in metropolitan area and wide area network environments. Unfortunately, the line and data rates of GbE, Fiber Channel, ESCON, and FICON are not well matched to standard SONET or SDH contiguously concatenated payload rates. For example, the 1.0-Gb/s data rate of GbE does not fit into STS-12*c* or VC-4-4*c* at 622 Mb/s and wastes bandwidth if mapped singly into a 2.5-Gb/s STS-48*c* or VC-4-16*c*. This has led to a new set of enhancements that will make the transport network better suited to carrying data signals, driving its evolution toward increased efficiency and flexibility in supporting new data over transport services. These include the generic framing procedure, virtual concatenation, and the *link capacity adjustment scheme* (LCAS). Virtual concatenation, GFP, and LCAS enable generalized mappings of variable-length multiprotocol packets into SONET or SDH, and they also allow for flexible and elastic data transport over SONET or SDH networks (Scholten et al. 2002; Hernandez-Valencia, Scholten, and Zhu 2002; Bonenfant and Rodriguez-Moral 2002).

GENERIC FRAMING PROCEDURE

Generic framing procedure is a recently standardized (ITU-T 2005) framing procedure that provides a standard means of mapping, in a highly efficient way, a wide variety of data signals into SONET or SDH frames. GFP provides a generic mechanism to adapt traffic from higher-layer client signals over SONET or SDH. Client signals may be

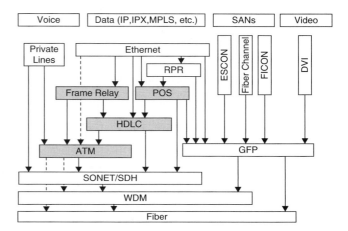

Figure 30: Protocol stacks for mapping data services over GFP

variable-length packets (e.g., IP or PPP or Ethernet MAC) or block code–oriented constant-bit-rate streams such as ESCON, FICON, or FC. GFP has extremely low overhead requirements and robust frame-delineation qualities, making it a more efficient and flexible data-services mapping scheme. Figure 30 illustrates choice of transport options for end-user applications such as voice, data, storage, and video traffic over the public network infrastructure. Note that IP data services that have previously been mapped to SONET and SDH through ATM and HDLC can now be mapped efficiently through Ethernet and GFP. In addition, nontraditional data services such as fiber channel, ESCON, and FICON can also be encapsulated using GFP, thereby eliminating the need for proprietary mapping solutions into SONET and SDH frames.

Two types of GFP frames have been defined by the ITU standard: *frame-mapped GFP* (GFP-F) and *transparent mapped GFP* (GFP-T). The decision on which mode to use depends on the underlying service to be transported.

Frame-mapped GFP is a mapping mechanism in which a single client protocol data unit (e.g., an IP packet or Ethernet frame) is received and mapped in its entirety into a single GFP frame. In this adaptation mode, the client or GFP adaptation function may operate at the data-link layer (or higher layer) of the client signal. Client PDU visibility is required. GFP-F mappings are currently defined for Ethernet MAC payloads (10/100/1000M/GbE) and IP or PPP payloads.

Transparent-mapped GFP frames are slightly different. GFP-T mapping provides a block code–oriented adaptation mode in which the client or GFP adaptation function operates on the coded character stream rather than on the incoming client PDUs. Transparent GFP provides a way for a number of client data characters to be mapped into efficient block codes for transport within a GFP frame. With this type of mapping, block-coded client characters are decoded and then mapped into the payload area of a fixed-length GFP frame and may be transmitted immediately without waiting for the reception of an entire client data frame (as in the case of GFP-F). Transparent mapping is intended to facilitate the transport of 8B or 10B block-coded client signals for services that require especially low transmission latency, making GFP-T ideally suited for FC, ESCON, and FICON transport service.

A GFP frame consists of three main components: the core header, the payload header, and the payload area. Figure 31 illustrates the format of a GFP frame. The GFP *core header* carries information about the size of the GFP frame itself and allows GFP frame delineation independent of the content of the higher-layer PDUs. The GFP core header is four bytes long and consists of two fields:

- The *payload length indicator* (PLI) field is a two-byte field indicating the size in bytes of the GFP payload area. It indicates the beginning of the next GFP frame in the incoming bit stream as an offset from the last byte in the current GFP core header. PLI values in the range 0–3 are reserved for GFP internal usage and are referred to as GFP *control* frames. All other frames are referred to as GFP *client* frames.

- The *core header error control* (cHEC) field is a two-byte field containing a *cyclic redundancy check* (CRC-16) sequence that protects the integrity of the core header. The cHEC sequence is computed over the core header bytes using standard CRC-16. The CRC-16 enables both single-bit error correction and multibit error detection.

The GFP *payload area* covers all remaining bytes of the GFP frame following the GFP core header. It consists of a payload header and a payload information field. The variable-length payload information field may include from 0 to 65,531 bytes. The payload information field may optionally be followed by a payload *frame check sequence* (FCS).

- The *payload header* is a variable-length area 4–64 bytes long. It carries information about the payload type (Ethernet, fiber channel, etc.) and consists of two mandatory fields: the type field and an accompanying *type header error correction* (tHEC) field.

- The *payload type* field is a mandatory two-byte field of the payload header that indicates the content and format of the GFP payload information. As shown in Figure 31, the type field consists of a *payload type identifier* (PTI), a *payload FCS indicator* (PFI), a *extension header identifier* (EXI) and a *user payload identifier* (UPI).

- The tHEC field is a two-byte field that contains ISO CRC-16 sequence to protect the integrity of the type field. The tHEC sequence is computed over the type field bytes, enabling both single-bit error correction and multibit error detection.

- The *payload frame check sequence* (pFCS) is an optional four-byte-long frame check sequence. It contains a CRC-32 check sequence that protects the contents of the GFP payload information field.

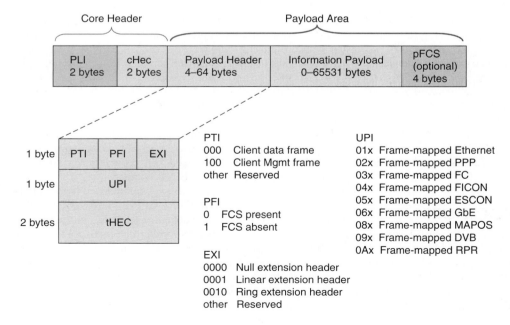

Figure 31: GFP frame format

VIRTUAL CONCATENATION

Earlier we discussed contiguous concatenation to accommodate high-speed data applications that use protocols such as ATM, POS, and others that require high-bandwidth mappings over SONET and SDH. Although contiguous concatenation has been successfully introduced and deployed for years, it presents major deficiencies. Contiguous concatenation keeps the SONET payload concatenated through the whole SONET and SDH transport. Therefore, all NEs along the path must support contiguous concatenation. In addition, data and line rates of GbE, fiber channel, ESCON, and FICON are not well matched to standard SONET or SDH contiguously concatenated payload rates, so using GFP with current contiguous concatenation schemes results in suboptimal use of the bandwidth. As an example, the 1.0 Gb/s data rate of GbE does not fit into STS-12c or VC-4-4c at 622 Mb/s and results in approximately 60 percent of wasted bandwidth if mapped into a 2.5-Gb/s STS-48c or VC-4-16c.

To address these limitations, virtual concatenation, defined in ITU standard G.707 (ITU-T 2003), was developed to allow any number of SONET or SDH channels to be bonded to create a customized *virtual concatenation group* (VCG) that can be any multiple of some basic SONET or SDH rate. In high-order virtual concatenation, this basic rate would be an STS-1, VC-3, STS-3c, or VC-4. Thus, virtual concatenation is an inverse multiplexing procedure where a VCG can be created in multiples of 50 or 150 Mb/s, and multiple LAN or SAN data signals can be transported over single OC-48, STM-16, OC-192, or STM-64 lines with much better bandwidth utilization. Control packets, which contain the necessary information for reassembling the original data stream at its destination PTE, are inserted in some of the currently unused SONET or SDH overhead bytes (H4 byte for high order, and Z7 (SONET) and K4 (SDH) for low order). Furthermore, each virtually concatenated group of signals is transported as individual SPEs across the SONET or SDH network without requiring any upgrades. The receiving end PTE is responsible for reassembling the original byte stream. In this manner, virtually concatenated channels may be deployed on the existing SONET or SDH network with a simple end-point node upgrade.

As presented in Table 5, VCAT provides a much more efficient use of the transport bandwidth for data user interfaces. With VCAT, an OC-48 link can carry two full GbE signals with 95 percent of the link used through seven virtual STS-3cs or VC-4s each instead of just one GbE signal with 42 percent of the link used through an STS-48c or VC-4-16c.

In summary, virtual concatenation enables SONET or SDH transport pipes to be filled more efficiently with data services by grouping individual SONET or SDH containers into a virtual high-bandwidth "link" matched to the required service bandwidth.

Link Capacity Adjustment Scheme

The link capacity adjustment scheme as defined by the ITU (ITU-T 2004; Bonenfant and Rodriguez-Moral 2002) is a complementary technology to virtual concatenation. LCAS is a method to dynamically increase or decrease the bandwidth of VCGs. This brings *bandwidth-on-demand* capability for data clients such as Ethernet when mapped into VCGs. Signaling messages are exchanged within the SONET or SDH overhead (H4 or Z7/K4 bytes) in order to change the number of tributaries being used by a VCG. The number of tributaries can be increased or decreased in response to an identified change in service bandwidth requirement or in response to a fault condition of an existing VCG member. LCAS works by ensuring synchronization between the sender (PTE) and receiver (PTE) during the increase or decrease of the size of a virtually concatenated circuit in such a way that it does not interfere with the underlying data service. In addition to providing a resiliency mechanism for VCAT, LCAS gives service providers the flexibility to tailor service bandwidth for customers on demand.

In summary, VCAT and LCAS combined can be extremely useful when provisioning data packet transport services over an existing SONET network. In this case, VCAT is used to provision point-to-point connections over the SONET network, and LCAS provides resiliency to VCAT connections and allows for fine tuning of the network transport resources.

CONCLUSION

SONET and SDH systems have stood the test of time and have been the preferred optical transport technology for more than two decades now. The reasons for the wide popularity of networks based on SONET or SDH standards include multivendor interworking, self-healing

Table 5: Bandwidth Efficiency Using Virtual Concatenation

Service	Bit Rate (Mb/s)	Efficiency	
		Without VCAT	**With VCAT**
Ethernet	10	STS-1 (20%), VC-2 (20%)	VT1.5-7v (93%), VC-12-5v (97%)
Fast Ethernet	100	STS-3c (47%), VC-4 (67%)	STS-1-2v (99%), VC-3-2v (99%)
Gb Ethernet	1000	STS-48c (42%), VC-4-16c (42%)	STS-3c-7v (95%), VC-4-7v (95%)
Fiber channel	1062.5	STS-48c (43%), VC-4-16c (43%)	STS-3c-6v (98%), VC-4-7v (98%)

architectures, enhanced OAM&P capabilities, and ease of signal grooming and multiplexing. Until recently, however, SONET networks have been primarily used to transport multiplexed voice signals and private-line frame relay and ATM services. The growth of these high revenue–generating services over the years has resulted in large-scale deployments of metropolitan and long-haul SONET and SDH networks worldwide. Today, however, data transport is driving the demand for increased bandwidth in WANs. Although several ATM and HDLC-based data mappings over SONET and SDH are widely deployed, each has its own limitations. GFP provides—for the first time—a standard means of mapping, in an extremely efficient way, a wide variety of data signals into SONET and SDH frames, enabling compliant equipment from different manufacturers to transport both traditional and nontraditional data signals over a SONET or SDH infrastructure. Coupled with complementary developments in the standardization of virtual concatenation and automatic link capacity adjustment schemes, GFP holds the promise of rendering existing SONET and SDH transport networks capable of increasingly efficient data transport, leveraging existing infrastructures to offer new services.

GLOSSARY

Add-Drop Multiplexer (ADM):   A time division multiplexer capable of extracting and inserting lower-rate signals from a higher-rate multiplexed signal without completely demultiplexing the signal.

Automatic Protection Switching (APS):   The ability of a network element to detect a failed working line and switch the traffic to a spare (protection) line.

Concatenated STS-*Nc*:   An STS-*Nc* signal in which synchronous payload envelopes from the N STS-1s have been combined to carry the high-capacity payload. It is transported as a single entity unlike an STS-N signal.

Concatenated Virtual Tributary: A virtual tributary (VT × Nc) that is composed of N × VTs combined. Its payload is transported as a single entity rather than separate signals.

Contiguous Concatenation: The process of joining multiple consecutive SONET STS-1 signals to create a single, larger capacity concatenated SONET frame.

Digital Cross-Connect System (DCCS):   Network equipment that allows lower-level TDM bit streams to be rearranged and interconnected among higher-level TDM signals. DCCS can be used for "grooming" telecommunications traffic, switching traffic from one circuit to another in the event of a network failure, and supporting automated provisioning, among other applications.

Enterprise System Connection (ESCON):   An optical serial interface between IBM mainframe computers and peripheral devices such as storage and tape drives. ESCON is capable of half-duplex communication at a rate of 17 Mbytes/second over distances of as much as 43 kilometers.

Fiber Channel (FC):   Technology designed for especially high-performance, low-latency data transfer among various types of devices as defined by a family of ANSI standards. Data rates of 100, 200, 400, and 1200 Mbytes/sec are defined for fiber-optic links for distances as much as 50 kilometers.

Fiber Connection (FICON):   An input-output technology developed by IBM to connect mainframes to storage devices at higher speeds and greater distances than the earlier ESCON. FICON supports full duplex data rates of 100, 200, and 400 Mbytes/second and distances of as much as 100 kilometers.

Fixed Stuff: A bit or byte that has a reserved function. Fixed stuff locations, sometimes called *reserved* locations, do not carry overhead or payload.

Generic Framing Procedure (GFP):   Allows mapping of variable-length, higher-layer client signals over a transport network such as SDH and SONET. The client signals can be protocol data unit (PDU)–oriented (such as IP, PPP, and Ethernet frame) or can block code–oriented (such as fiber channel).

Gigabit Ethernet (GbE):   Describes various technologies for transmitting Ethernet packets at a rate of 1 Gigabit per second as defined by the IEEE 802.3-2005 standard.

Grooming: Consolidating or segregating traffic for efficiency.

Line: One or more SONET sections, including network elements at each end, that are capable of accessing, generating, and processing line overhead.

Line Overhead: Eighteen bytes of overhead accessed, generated, and processed by line-terminating equipment. This overhead supports functions such as locating the SPE in the frame, multiplexing or concatenating signals, performance monitoring, automatic protection switching, and line maintenance.

Line-Terminating Equipment (LTE):   Network elements such as add-drop multiplexers or digital cross-connect systems that can access, generate, and process line overhead.

Link Capacity Adjustment Scheme (LCAS):   A method to dynamically increase or decrease the bandwidth of virtual concatenated containers. The LCAS protocol is specified in ITU-T G.7042.

Network Element (NE):   Equipment that is part of a SONET transmission path and serves one or more of the section, line, and path-terminating functions.

Optical Carrier Level 1 (OC-1):   The optical equivalent of an STS-1 signal.

Optical Carrier Level *N* (OC-*N*):   The optical equivalent of an STS-*N* signal.

Overhead: Extra bytes (or bits) in a digital stream used to carry information besides user data. Transport overhead in a STS-1 frame is an example of overhead information.

Path: A logical connection between a point where an STS or VT is multiplexed to the point where it is demultiplexed.

Path Overhead (POH):   Overhead accessed, generated, and processed by path-terminating equipment. Path overhead consists of nine bytes in the first column of the STS-1 SPE. POH provides for communication between the point of creation of an STS SPE and its point of disassembly.

Path-Terminating Equipment (PTE):   Network element that terminates the SONET STS path layer.

PTE interprets and modifies or creates the STS path overhead.

Payload: The portion of the SONET signal available to carry user information such as DS1 and DS3.

Pointer: Portion of the line overhead (2 bytes) that locates the beginning of an SPE.

Section: The span between two SONET network elements capable of accessing, generating, and processing only SONET section overhead.

Section Overhead: Nine bytes of overhead accessed, generated, and processed by section-terminating equipment. This overhead supports functions such as framing the signal and performance monitoring.

Section-Terminating Equipment (STE): Equipment that terminates the SONET section layer. STE interprets and modifies or creates the section overhead.

Synchronous: A network in which transmission system payloads are synchronized to a master (network) clock and traced to a reference clock.

Synchronous Digital Hierarchy (SDH): The ITU-T defined world standard of transmission with a base transmission rate of 155.52 Mb/s (STM-1); it is equivalent to SONET's STS-3.

Synchronous Optical Network (SONET): An ANSI standard for optical transport that defines optical carrier levels and their electrically equivalent synchronous transport signals.

Synchronous Payload Envelope (SPE): The major portion of the SONET frame format used to transport user payload and STS path overhead. The STS SPE may begin anywhere in the frame's SPE.

Synchronous Transfer Module (STM): An element of the SDH transmission hierarchy. STM-1 is SDH's base-level transmission rate equal to 155.52 Mb/s. Higher rates of STM-4, STM-16, STM-64, and STM-256 are also defined.

Synchronous Transport Signal Level 1 (STS-1): The basic SONET building block signal transmitted at 51.84 Mb/s data rate.

Synchronous Transport Signal Level N (STS-N): The signal obtained by multiplexing N STS-1 signals together.

Virtual Concatenation (VCAT): An inverse multiplexing technique used to split SONET or SDH bandwidth into logical groups that may be transported or routed independently.

Virtual Tributary (VT): A signal designed for transport and switching of sub-STS-1 payloads.

Virtual Tributary Group (VTG): A nine row by twelve column structure (108 bytes) that carries one or more VTs of the same size. Seven VT groups can be fitted into one STS-1 payload.

CROSS REFERENCES

See *DSL (Digital Subscriber Line); Frame Relay; Passive Optical Networks for Broadband Access.*

REFERENCES

American National Standards Institute (ANSI). 1995. Synchronous optical network (SONET): Basic description including multiplex structure, rates and formats. T1.105-2001 (retrieved from http://webstore.ansi.org/ansidocstore/product.asp?sku=T1%2E105%2D2001).

———.1995. Synchronous optical network (SONET): Automatic protection. T1.105.01-2000 (R2005) (retrieved from http://webstore.ansi.org/ansidocstore/product.asp?sku=T1%2E105%2E01%2D2000+%28 R2005%29).

———. 1995. Synchronous optical network (SONET): Payload mappings. T1.105.02-2001 (retrieved from http://webstore.ansi.org/ansidocstore/product.asp?sku=T1%2E105%2E02%2D2001).

Bonenfant, P., and A. Rodriguez-Moral. 2002. Generic framing procedure (GFP): The catalyst for efficient data over transport. *IEEE Communications Magazine,* May, pp. 72–9.

Grossman, D., and J. Heinanen. 1999. Multiprotocol encapsulation over ATM adaptation layer 5. IETF RFC 2684, May.

Hernandez-Valencia, E., M. Scholten, and Z. Zhu. 2002. The generic framing procedure (GFP): An overview. *IEEE Communications Magazine,* May, pp. 63–71.

International Telecommunication Union Telecommunication Standardization Sector (ITU-T). 1998. Types and characteristics of SDH network protection architectures. Rec. G.841, October.

———. 2003. Network node interface for the synchronous digital hierarchy (SDH). Rec. G.707, December.

———. 2004. Link capacity adjustment scheme (LCAS) for virtually concatenated signals. Rec. G.7042/Y.1305, February 2004.

———. 2005. Generic framing procedure (GFP). Rec. G.7041/Y.1303, August.

Malis, A., and W. Simpson. 1999. PPP over SONET/SDH. IETF RFC 2615, June.

Scholten, M., Z. Zhu, E. Hernandez-Valencia, and J. Hawkins. 2002. Data transport applications using GFP. *IEEE Communications Magazine,* May, pp. 96–103.

Wu, T. 1995. Emerging technologies for fiber network survivability. *IEEE Communications Magazine,* February, pp. 58–9, 62–74.

Passive Optical Networks for Broadband Access

Nirwan Ansari and Yuanqiu Luo, *New Jersey Institute of Technology*

INTRODUCTION

The access network is part of a carrier network that connects subscribers to a service provider's *central office* (CO) over the public ground (Wikipedia, undated). With the recent development of optical fiber technologies, a dramatic increase in bandwidth has been facilitated in the backbone network through the penetration of *wavelength-division multiplexing* (WDM) technology, which provides tens of Gigabits per second (Gbps) per wavelength. At the same time, *local area networks* (LANs) have been scaled up from 10 Mbps to 100 Mbps and are being upgraded to Gigabit Ethernet speeds. However, the access network in between only runs at sub-Megabit or even kilobit bandwidth speeds. The tremendous growth of Internet traffic has accentuated the growing gap between the capacities of the backbone and local networks, and the serious bottleneck of the much lower capacities of these in-between access networks. Such a mismatch is the so-called last mile problem from the service provider's point of view—or the first mile problem from the end users' perspective—and it calls for the upgrading of the current access network with a low-cost and high-speed solution to provide broadband access services.

The most widely deployed broadband access solutions are the *digital subscriber line* (DSL) and the cable modem. For truly high-speed broadband access, significant worldwide efforts of fiber-optic access—in particular, the deployment of *fiber to the home* (FTTH)—are led by telecommunications giants such as AT&T, Verizon, and NTT. Among diverse approaches, the *passive optical network* (PON) is especially attractive. Compared to DSL and cable modem, a PON lowers the cost of network deployment and maintenance with the provisioning of much higher bandwidth. The PON standards of current interest include *broadband PON* (B-PON) [International Telecommunication Union, Telecommunications (ITU-T) 1998], *Ethernet PON* (EPON) [Institute of Electrical and Electronics Engineers (IEEE) 2004], and *Gigabit-capable PON* (G-PON) (ITU-T 2003a). The next-generation fiber-optic access network is likely to take advantages of WDM

technologies to achieve the ultimate bandwidth, and WDM-PON is considered a promising solution.

This chapter presents an overview of the wired access technologies, including DSL, cable modem, and diverse PONs. The rest of this section covers the introduction of DSL, cable modem, and major features of fiber-optic access. The second section presents various PONs in detail, including the network architecture, enabling technologies, and *media access control* (MAC). The chapter conclusion provides a summary of the ongoing developments in the area of PONs. Readers who are interested in wireless broadband access technologies can refer to the chapter "Wireless Broadband Access" for more details.

ACCESS TECHNOLOGIES
The Digital Subscriber Line

Telecommunications typically use twisted-pair copper wires to provide voice services to their customers. The demand for more bandwidth has resulted in the deployment of DSL equipment to provide simultaneous voice and higher-speed data services. DSL modems contain an internal signal splitter that carries voice signals on low frequencies (from 0 to 4kHz) and data signals on the unused higher frequencies (Mervana and Le 2001), allowing simultaneous access to the wire by the telephone and the computer.

As shown in Figure 1, DSL services are *point-to-point* (P2P) dedicated public network access between a service provider's CO and the customer's site (Ooghe et al. 2003). The term *xDSL* covers several similar yet competing forms of DSL including *asymmetric DSL* (ADSL), symmetric DSL, high-data-rate DSL, rate-adaptive DSL, and very-high-speed DSL (Starr et al. 2002). DSL is distance-sensitive, and the supported data rate varies with transmission length. Essentially, customers with longer telephone line runs from their houses to the CO experience lower performance rates compared to neighbors who might live closer to the CO (Ouyang et al. 2003). A typical ADSL system provides 8 Mbps downstream

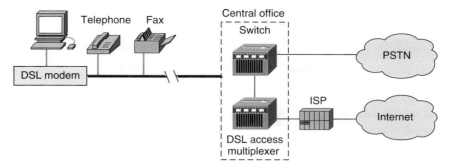

Figure 1: DSL network

bandwidth with a wire length of 9000 feet or 1.5 Mbps downstream bandwidth with 18,000 feet. DSL draws significant attention from service providers because it delivers data services to dispersed locations with relatively small changes to the existing telecommunications infrastructure.

The major problems with sending a high-frequency signal such as that used in DSL over an unshielded pair of copper wires include signal fading and cross talk. As the length of wires increases, the signal at the customer side may become too weak to be correctly detected. If the power is increased at the CO, then the signals tend to transfer to wires in the same bundle, resulting in cross talk and severely impaired performance.

Cable Modem

Cable companies offer Internet access through the traditional *cable TV* (CATV) network. The Internet access requires two types of equipment: a cable modem at the customer's end and a *cable modem termination system* (CMTS) at the cable provider's end (Fellows and Jones 2001). The CMTS located at the cable operator's network hub is a data switching system specifically designed to route data from many cable modem users over a multiplexed network interface. It controls access to cable modems on the network. Traffic is routed from the CMTS

to the backbone of a cable *Internet service provider* (commonly called an ISP), which in turn connects to the Internet (International Engineering Consortium, undated).

Figure 2 illustrates the elements and services in the cable modem network. Data traveling upstream from individual users to the CMTS are filtered by upstream demodulators for further processing by the CMTS. For data traveling downstream from CMTS to the users, a cable headend combines the data channels with the video, audio, and local programs and transmits them throughout the cable distribution network. At the user location, a one-to-two splitter separates the coaxial cable line serving the cable modem from the line that serves the TV sets.

Different from DSL, cable modem service uses a shared cable line to provide service to an entire neighborhood (Dutta-Roy 2001). Essentially, all cable customers in the region belong to the same LAN. Cable modem speeds vary widely. Although cable modem technology can theoretically support rates as high as 30 Mbps, most providers offer service with between 1 Mbps and 6 Mbps bandwidth for downstream (from CMTS to individual users) and bandwidth between 128 Kbps and 768 Kbps (Azzam 1997) for upstream (from individual users to CMTS).

Besides the signal fading and cross-talk problems, cable modem has its own technical difficulties. One is that the original CATV infrastructure is designed to

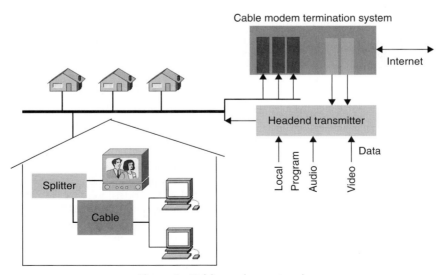

Figure 2: Cable modem network

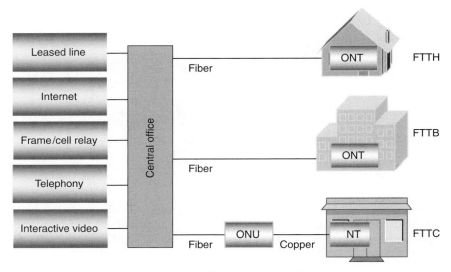

Figure 3: Fiber-optic network

broadcast TV signals in just one direction: from the CATV provider to home end users. The Internet, however, is a two-way system in which data also need to flow from the subscriber to the service provider. To enable the two-way transmission, the upstream channel capacity has to be significantly increased by encroaching on the service provider's content bandwidth. Moreover, cable modem technology is based on shared bandwidth, and many factors may influence the delivered services. The speed of shared bandwidth fluctuates, depending on the number of subscribers in the network, and it is difficult to gauge an exact download speed. In rural areas with fewer subscribers, cable modem is bound to provide faster download speeds than in a metropolitan area. In DSL, the connection between the subscriber and the CO is dedicated, and the customers tend to have a more constant transmission speed.

Fiber-Optic Access

With the expansion of services offered over the Internet, neither DSL nor cable modem can remain successful as bandwidth demands grow significantly beyond their supported levels. Besides, DSL has severe problems with respect to distance and noise limitations, and cable modem is not optimized to carry data traffic because of its inherent asymmetry in capacities for upstream and downstream data transmission (Green 2004). It is desired to upgrade the current access network with a low-cost and high-speed solution for broadband access services.

Recent developments in optical fiber technologies, especially the maturity of integration and new packaging technologies, have enabled fiber-optic access network as a promising solution for the provisioning of high bit rate at a reasonable cost. Fiber-optic technology offers a mechanism that enables sufficient network bandwidth for the delivery of new services and applications. The supported access network architecture includes FTTH, *fiber to the building* (FTTB), and *fiber to the curb* (FTTC) (Keiser 2006). In the FTTH and FTTB architectures, an optical fiber is extended into the subscriber's home or building;

in the FTTC architecture, the optical fiber reaches a small cabinet located near the subscribers from where the signal is converted to feed the subscribers over copper telephone wires or coaxial cables (see Figure 3).

The connection between the CO to the subscriber could be P2P or *point-to-multipoint* (P2MP). In the P2P connection, each subscriber is connected to a CO through a dedicated fiber. Network upgrading for higher capacity is straightforward and the power budget is sufficient for an extremely long link reach. To provide the P2P connection, each subscriber requires a separate fiber port in the CO, and the transceiver count must be twice the number of subscribers. The overall cost of running and managing active components at both ends of a fiber is prohibitive for broadband access. Without the benefits of large-scale cost sharing as in the backbone network, the access network must strive to minimize cost. Therefore, the P2MP connection is a better option because it provides sharing among multiple subscribers. This enables cost sharing of a transceiver and a large portion of the fiber infrastructure, reducing system costs significantly. On the other hand, MAC protocols are required to allocate the shared network resources among the associated subscribers.

PASSIVE OPTICAL NETWORKS

With the goal of eliminating the bottleneck of broadband access, passive optical networks are drawing much attention from both research communities and service providers. As illustrated in Figure 4, a typical PON consists of one *optical line terminal* (OLT), which is located at the provider CO, and n associated *optical network units* (ONUs) or optical network terminals (ONTs) that deliver data to end users. In the FTTC architecture, an ONU terminates the circuit at the subscriber's end, whereas an ONT terminates the circuit in the FTTH and FTTB architecture. A single fiber extends from the OLT to a 1:n passive optical splitter, fanning out n single fiber drops to connect to the associated ONUs and ONTs (Luo and Ansari 2005a).

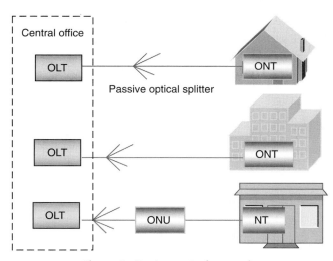

Figure 4: Passive optical network

PON networking is a full duplex technology that uses inexpensive optical splitters to divide a single fiber coming from the backbone network into separate drops feeding individual subscribers in the access network. The passive elements of a PON include fiber-optical cables and a passive optical splitter. The splitter is a simple device with no electronics. It allows the downstream traffic from the OLT and the upstream traffic to the OLT to be split from and combined onto the shared portion of the fiber. The less expensive and longer-lived passive components are located in the optical distribution network, replacing the active electronic components such as regenerators, repeaters, and amplifiers in DSL or cable modem. The employment of passive optical splitters reduces the feeder fiber counts in PONs. The OLT, ONUs, and ONTs are the active elements, being located at the end points of a PON. The OLT supports management functionalities at the CO and is capable of managing tens of downstream links in a PON. ONUs and ONTs are known as the *customer premise equipment* and must support only their own link to the CO. As a result, the ONU and ONT devices are less expensive whereas the OLT devices tend to be more capable and more expensive. By eliminating the intermediate powering, PONs are easier to maintain and provide lower overall system cost to the service providers.

The basic communications architecture in a PON is a P2MP network in which the OLT serves as the control point for the entire PON and the ONU or ONT serves as the subscriber points or controlled points. Optical signals transmitted across a PON are either split into multiple fibers in the downstream from the OLT to ONUs or ONTs, or combined onto a single fiber in the upstream from ONUs or ONTs to the OLT by the optical splitter. Compared to the P2P network, a PON has the advantage of minimizing the number of optical transceivers and reducing the CO wiring and space requirements. The aforementioned PON architecture is beneficial under the following scenarios (Corning Cable Systems 2005). First, no active devices are desired in the outside plant, and deploying large electronics platform is restricted. Second, the service coverage is typically in the distance of 10 km to approximately 20 km. Third, the expensive

fiber installation and maintenance cost prevents dedicated P2P connection.

The available medium access technologies are *wavelength-division multiple access* (WDMA), *code-division multiple access* (CDMA), and *time-division multiple access* (TDMA) (Kramer and Mukherjee 2001). In WDMA, each ONU or ONT transmits its data to the OLT using a specific wavelength laser. The OLT must have a transmitter array to support multiple ONUs or ONTs, thus increasing the cost of the access network. CDMA encodes data with a special code associated with each channel, and the interchannel interference increases as the number of ONUs or ONTs increases. Reducing such interference calls for complicated signal-processing chips and would add more cost to maintain a CDMA-based access network. Furthermore, to provide CDMA among the data from different ONUs or ONTs, the network components must be able to handle a signal rate that is much higher than the data rate, thereby raising the network price tremendously. By dividing the upstream channel into time slots, TDMA allows ONUs and ONTs to transmit their data in different exclusive time slots (as exemplified in Figure 5b). Only one transmitter is needed at the OLT to multiplex the upstream data no matter how many ONUs or ONTs are connected. A new ONU or ONT can be easily added by the control protocol. To support TDMA, synchronization is required between the OLT and the ONUs or ONTs. Without the benefits of large-scale cost sharing, access networks must strive to minimize cost. Service providers desire to fulfill the medium access with as low a cost as possible while achieving as fine a granularity as possible and building the access networks as scalable as possible. Toward this end, TDMA and *time-division multiplexing* (TDM) were chosen by the PON standard bodies (IEEE 2004; ITU-T 1998, 2001, 2003a, 2003b, 2004a, 2004b) for upstream and downstream data transmission, respectively.

Employing TDMA in the upstream transmission requires a tight synchronization mechanism between the OLT and the associated ONUs or ONTs (Van Caenegem 2004). Consequently, the ranging procedure during activation and registration is necessary to automatically adjust time offsets of individual ONUs or ONTs. Ranging ensures that the bursts coming from different ONUs or ONTs are lined up in the right time slots and correctly received by the OLT. Employing TDM in the downstream transmission brings on the concern of data security. Each ONU or ONT receives the same copy of downstream data, and a proper data-encryption mechanism is required to prevent eavesdropping.

The process of transporting data downstream to the end users in a PON is different from that of transporting data upstream to the OLT. Different wavelengths are employed for the two directions to avoid collisions and interactions between the downstream and upstream traffic flows. As illustrated in Figure 5a, in the downstream transmission, data are broadcasted from the OLT to each ONU or ONT using the entire bandwidth of the downstream channel, and all of the downstream data are carried in one wavelength (e.g., 1490 nm). ONUs and ONTs selectively receive frames destined to themselves by matching the addresses in the received data. The "broadcast and select" architecture allows downstream multimedia services

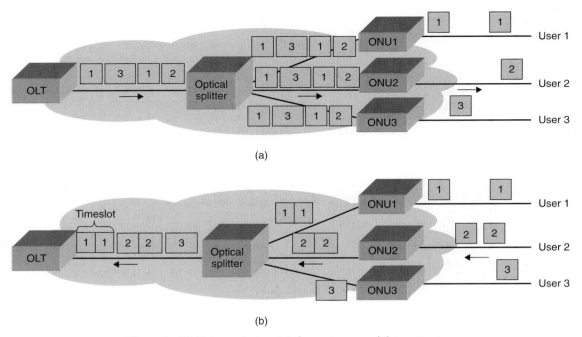

Figure 5: PON transmission: (a) downstream and (b) upstream

such as video broadcasting. In the upstream direction, as illustrated in Figure 5b, multiple ONUs or ONTs share the common upstream channel, and another wavelength (e.g., 1310 nm) is employed for the upstream traffic. Only a single ONU or ONT may transmit during a time slot in order to avoid data collisions. Because of the directional nature of the passive optical splitter, each ONU or ONT transmits directly to the OLT but not to other ONUs or ONTs. An ONU or ONT buffers the data from the end users until its time slot arrives. The buffered data would be "bursted" out to the OLT in the exclusively assigned time slot at the full channel speed. The result is that the basic P2MP architecture of a PON can support P2P communications between the OLT and an ONU or ONT.

PON technologies are evolving according to the development of optical devices and high-speed networking. Several different PON standards—including B-PON, EPON, and G-PON—have been approved to facilitate broadband access. The most significant difference between each "flavor" of PON is the supported line rates and the type of bearer packets. The rest of this section will elaborate on their characteristics.

Broadband PONs

Asynchronous transfer mode (ATM) PON, or APON, was introduced in the 1990s by the Full Service Access Network (FSAN) group. The International Telecommunications Union (ITU) ratified ITU-T G.983 recommendation (ITU-T 1998) with extensions such as ONU and ONT management and control interface specification, survivability, and *dynamic bandwidth assignment* (DBA). In addition, the name APON was soon changed to *broadband PON* (B-PON) to more appropriately reflect its functionality. B-PON adopts ATM cells as the transmission data unit and inherits the features of the ATM technology

such as multiservice capability and support of different quality-of-service (QoS) classes.

In the downstream transmission from the OLT to ONUs or ONTs, each frame is composed of fifty-six ATM cells for the basic line rate of 155 Mbps, or two hundred and twenty-four ATM cells for 622 Mbps. *Physical layer operation, administration, and maintenance* (PLOAM) cells are inserted into the downstream frame, containing grants for upstream transmission as well as *operation, administration, and maintenance* (OAM) and *OAM and provisioning* (OAM&P) messages ("APON" 2002). Upstream transmission from ONUs or ONTs to the OLT is in the form of ATM cell bursts. Each ATM cell is appended with a three-byte physical overhead, allowing burst transmission and reception. The basic upstream line rate of 155 Mbps is constructed by the data frame of fifty-three cells. The typical link rates over B-PON are asymmetrical 622 Mbps/155 Mbps and symmetrical 155 Mbps or 622 Mbps. A new amendment with a 1.25-Gbps downstream line rate was added in 2003. Figure 6 shows the B-PON frame format of the symmetric 155-Mbps line rate.

B-PON is the leading PON technology in North America, making up 81 percent of its PON revenue in year 2004. Verizon planned to pass 3 million premises by the end of 2005, and AT&T is deploying PONs at the rate of 300,000 homes a year ("PON and FTTx, update" 2005).

Ethernet PONs

A B-PON suffers from the complexity of the ATM transport layer, and it faces the problems posed by the provisioning (i.e., it requires ATM-based CO equipment), complexity (in timing requirements and protocol complexity), and subsequent cost of components. EPON was proposed by the IEEE 802.3ah Ethernet in the First Mile (EFM) Task Force (IEEE, 802.3ah Task Force 2004) to

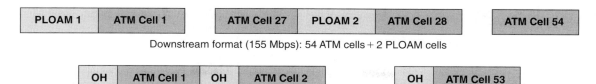

Downstream format (155 Mbps): 54 ATM cells + 2 PLOAM cells

Upstream format (155 Mbps): 53 cells (53-byte ATM cell + 3-byte Overhead)

Figure 6: B-PON frame format

tackle the aforementioned issues, and it has been ratified as the IEEE 802.3ah standard (2004). It adopts Ethernet frames as the transmission data unit and simplifies timing and lowers costs by using symmetrical 1.25-Gbps data streams using standard Ethernet optical components.

EPON relies on the *multipoint control protocol* (MPCP) (Luo and Ansari 2005a) to control the P2MP connection between each OLT and its associated ONUs or ONTs. MPCP is a frame-based protocol, defined as a function within the MAC control sublayer. It uses messages, state machines, and timers to control the access to a P2MP topology, and it introduces five new 64-byte MAC control messages to provide the transmission of Ethernet frames over EPON (Luo and Ansari 2005b). REGISTER_REQUEST, REGISTER, and REGISTER_ACK messages are utilized in the auto_discovery process to register a new ONU or ONT. GATE and REPORT messages are used for upstream bandwidth negotiation. As shown in Figure 7, the GATE message is sent downstream by the OLT, informing a particular ONU or ONT of its dedicated transmission time slot, whereas the REPORT message is sent by an ONU or ONT to the OLT, containing the transmission request. By allocating the upstream transmission from ONUs or ONTs into exclusively dedicated time slots, an EPON avoids data collision and is able to support higher speed than the original Ethernet in which carrier sense multiple access with collision detection is applied.

As compared to B-PON, EPON is tailor-made to carry the rapidly growing Internet protocol (IP) traffic. Transporting IP traffic over B-PON is quite inefficient. B-PON has to segment the variable-length IP packets into many fixed-length and much shorter ATM cells. This excessive segmentation causes a considerable delay in the communication process. Furthermore, the so-called ATM cell tax—that is, the 5-byte cell header—causes an onerous overhead in the transmission of IP packets over B-PON. By contrast, EPON encapsulates the IP packets in the Ethernet frames, with the length ranging from 64 bytes to 1518 bytes, thus reducing the time-consuming segmentation process relative to B-PON. In addition, Ethernet is a widely used LAN

protocol all over the network world. If Ethernet were used in the access network, then it would be unnecessary to convert between protocols as required in B-PON.

The REPORT and GATE mechanism is provided for bandwidth negotiation without specifying any particular bandwidth allocation algorithm (Luo and Ansari 2005c). Therefore, as compared to B-PON, EPON MAC does not support QoS directly, and the proper upstream DBA architecture over EPON is of high interest to both industry and academia (Ma, Zhu, and Cheng 2003). The typical proposals are *fixed bandwidth allocation* (FBA) (Kramer, Mukherjee, and Pesavento 2002), *limited bandwidth allocation* (LBA) (Kramer, Mukherjee, and Pesavento 2002), *excessive bandwidth reallocation* (EBR) (Assi et al. 2003), and *limited sharing with traffic prediction* (LSTP) (Luo and Ansari 2005d).

FBA grants each ONU or ONT a fixed time-slot length in every service cycle. A *service cycle* is defined as the time that each ONU or ONT transmits its data once to the OLT. Without the overhead of the queue status report and the transmission grant, FBA is simple to implement. On the other hand, an ONU or ONT will occupy the upstream channel for its assigned time slot even if there is no frame to transmit, thus resulting in the increased delay for all of the Ethernet frames buffered in other ONUs or ONTs. Many frames could be backlogged in the buffers while the upstream channel is lightly loaded or even idle, hence leading to underutilization of the upstream channel.

LBA tracks the traffic load by adopting the REPORT and GATE mechanism to facilitate the bandwidth negotiation. Each ONU or ONT reports the local queue status by piggybacking a REPORT message at the end of its time slot. The granted time-slot length by the OLT varies according to the dynamic traffic, and the time-slot length is upper-bounded by the maximum bandwidth parameter in the service level agreement.

Extended from LBA, EBR exploits the leftover bandwidth from the lightly loaded ONUs or ONTs by redistributing it among the heavily loaded ONUs. Therefore, each

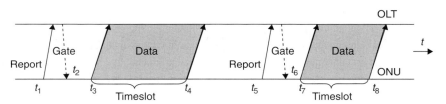

Figure 7: An example of bandwidth negotiation over EPON

heavily loaded ONU or ONT may obtain an additional bandwidth to facilitate its upward data delivery.

During the time of bandwidth negotiation, each ONU or ONT experiences a waiting time, which ranges from sending the bandwidth requirement to sending the buffered data. More data will be enqueued at the buffer during the waiting time. LSTP reduces data delay and loss by taking consideration of the data arrived during the waiting time. In LSTP, online traffic prediction is conducted based on network traffic self-similarity, and ONUs or ONTs prereserve a portion of the upstream bandwidth to transmit these data, thus resulting in latency reduction and improved bandwidth utilization.

EPON is firmly entrenched in Asia. NTT had reached 1.7 million EPON customers by fall 2004 and expects to reach 30 million subscribers by 2010. In 2004, Asia/Pacific accounted for 93 percent of the world PON subscribers, and most of them are supported by EPON ("PON and FTTx update," 2005).

Gigabit-Capable PONs

G-PON is the continuation and evolution of B-PON. It supports Ethernet, ATM, and TDM traffic over the P2MP PON network topology. The ITU-T G.984 recommendation (ITU-T 2003a) family specifies a physical media dependent layer (ITU-T 2003b), a transmission convergence layer (ITU-T 2004a), and the ONU and ONT control interface over G-PON (ITU-T 2004b). The G.984 series differs from the previous G.983 series primarily in that higher line bit rates are described. G-PON offers the line rate of as much as 2.5 Gbps upstream and 2.5 Gbps downstream. The B-PON and G-PON systems are not interoperable. As a consequence of this difference, the G.984 series deals with many technical issues and features in a manner different from the G.983 series, including frame format, ranging method, OAM functionalities, data security, and physical layer requirements and specifications.

G-PON surpasses B-PON capabilities because of its more efficient packet transport protocol and the support for forward error correction. The *G-PON encapsulation method* (GEM) is defined in G-PON to transport packet based services. GEM maps all traffic across the G-PON network using a variant of generic framing procedure (ITU-T 2001). It facilitates the transmission of Ethernet,

ATM, and TDM data units by traffic flow identification and packet and fragment delineation through the GEM header (Van Caenegem 2004). The GEM header contains important information such as payload length, port ID, payload type, and error detection. The encapsulation of ATM cells is an evolution of the existing B-PON standard. GEM fragments the packets, reassembles them at the receiver, and forwards them to the higher layer, thus supporting a native transport of triple play with voice, video, and data services. With B-PON, all services must be mapped over an ATM layer. With EPON, all services must be mapped over Ethernet. The employment of GEM does not require an added encapsulation layer, resulting in a dramatic increase of bandwidth utilization: Both of the downstream and upstream line rates are as high as 2.5 Gbps—a significant increase over B-PON and EPON.

As shown in Figure 8, G-PON defines a framing format of 125 μs for the downstream services, with the header of each frame containing the OAM information. The fixed frame delivers 8 kHz of clock information, facilitating synchronization between the OLT and ONUs or ONTs. In the upstream, ONUs and ONTs burst out their data. The burst payload consists of a variable number of GEM packets carrying Ethernet and TDM traffic. An ATM partition may be contained in a burst to carry multiple ATM cells (Angelopoulos et al. 2004).

G-PON inherits the OAM mechanism from B-PON by taking over the PLOAM message and major features of the ONU and ONT management and control interface. The ITU-T G.984.4 recommendation (ITU-T 2004b) specifies the information exchange between the OLT and ONUs or ONTs, including connection establishment and release across the ONU or ONT and a configuration request, as well as automatic system event notification. These salient characteristics enable G-PON with QoS support to provide diverse broadband services.

Compared to EPON, G-PON provides higher line rate with more flexibilities (1.25 Gbps or 2.5 Gbps in the downstream, and 155 Mbps, 622 Mbps, 1.25 Gbps, or 2.5 Gbps in the upstream), facilitating standard compatibility and the capability of tuning to various deployments. Because asymmetry is the distinct feature of access network traffic, the line rate flexibility in G-PON enables the service provider to configure the rates according to the real needs. In addition, G-PON improves data security by embedding

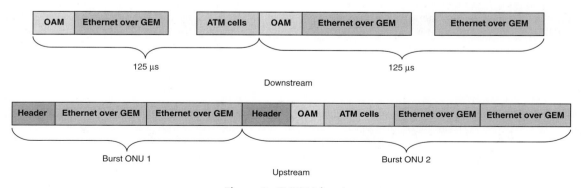

Figure 8: G-PON framing

Table 1: B-PON, EPON, and G-PON

	B-PON	**EPON**	**G-PON**
Driven by	ITU-T/FSAN	IEEE EFM	ITU-T/FSAN
Standards	G. 983	802.3ah	G. 984
Max line rate (downstream)	1.25 Gbps	1.25 Gbps	2.5 Gbps
Max line rate (upstream)	622 Mbps	1.25 Gbps	2.5 Gbps
Typical split ratios	1:32	1:16	1:128
Payload	ATM	Ethernet	ATM, TDM, Ethernet
Distance	≤20 km	≤20 km	≤20 km

data encryption using the advanced encryption standard in the downstream broadcast channel (Nortel 2004). The current concern about G-PON is the cost of supporting equipment. The requirement to support 2.5 Gbps in the upstream direction significantly increases the cost of both the transmitter in ONUs or ONTs and the receiver in the OLT (Ossieur et al. 2005). G-PON is likely to be deployed on a larger scale in Northern America, because its larger capacity in the downstream can support in-band video services. Various features of B-PONs, EPONs, and G-PONs are compared in Table 1.

Wavelength-Division Multiplexed PONs

The aforementioned PONs are all TDM-PONs that employ TDM or TDMA for data transmission with the maximum line rate of 2.5 Gbps. Each subscriber can only access the OLT within a limited time interval. The limited bandwidth as a result of this time sharing is not expected to satisfy future bandwidth consuming applications such as high definition TV. As more broadband applications appear, demands from PON subscribers will soon outgrow the TDM-PON capacity. To enable cost sharing among multiple ONUs or ONTs, the corresponding MAC protocols are rather complicated and may hinder the

TDM-PON upgrade. Moreover, the security of the communication link is not guaranteed because each subscriber on the TDM-PON receives all of the data sent to others in the network. This results in a major concern for potential business subscribers. WDM-PON is being studied as the next-generation wired broadband access solution to tackle these issues.

As illustrated in Figure 9, WDM-PON allocates different wavelengths to each ONU or ONT, providing a separate P2P connection between each ONU or ONT and the OLT. The transmission data rate is expected to be much higher than that of TDM-PON. The cost of the wavelength router is shared among all ONUs and ONTs, and the network management is much simpler than TDM-PON. In addition, the P2P connection guarantees downstream data privacy, and only the destined subscribers can receive the data. Independent of the transmission data format and line rate, the P2P connection in WDM-PON is able to further exploit the larger capacity of optical fibers. By delivering all services over a single network platform, this common network architecture will satisfy all future needs for both residential and business subscribers.

Because cost is the main obstacle in the implementation of WDM-PON, tremendous effort is being dedicated to provide scalability (Amitabha et al. 2005), thus reducing

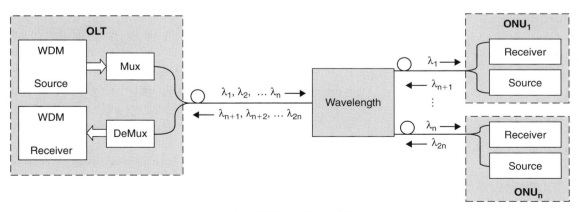

Figure 9: A WDM-PON architecture

the cost to support the ever-growing number of subscribers. Besides, research effort on the WDM-PON frame format, coarse WDM, wavelength sources, wavelength routers, network architecture, and suitable protocols works as the impetus to the development of WDM-PON.

CONCLUSION

Driven by both ITU and IEEE, PON is gaining more and more support from the service providers as the solution for broadband access. As compared to DSL and the cable modem, the PON lowers the cost of network deployment and maintenance by eliminating the active electronic components and replacing them with less expensive passive optical splitters. In addition, PON covers longer distances from the service provider CO to customer sites and provides line rates as high as 2.5 Gbps. The cost benefits and capacity improvement of a PON verify the assumption that it will be a dominant architecture for broadband service provisioning. This chapter has illustrated broadband access technologies, especially PON technology for fiber-optic access and the line rates and transmission data units that characterize different "flavors" of TDM-PON. The three existing TDM-PON standards—B-PON, EPON, and G-PON—have been overviewed with emphasis on frame format, bandwidth negotiation, and GEM protocol layer, respectively. They offer packet-based transport at Gigabit per second speeds and will dominate the broadband market in the near future. Nevertheless, WDM-PON has attracted much attention recently because of its high capacity, secure P2P connection, and independency of line rate and frame format. WDM-PON holds promise as the next-generation PON technology of broadband access.

GLOSSARY

Broadband Passive Optical Network (B-PON): A PON standard ratified by ITU-T G.983 recommendations. It uses ATM cells as transmission data units.
Cable Modem: An access technology designed to modulate a data signal over cable television (CATV) infrastructure.
Digital Subscriber Line (DSL): A family of technologies that provide digital data transmission over the wires used in the local telephone network.
Ethernet Passive Optical Network (EPON): A PON standard ratified by the IEEE 802.3ah standard. It uses Ethernet frames as transmission data units.
Generic Framing Procedure: A mapping method defined by ITU-T Recommendation G.7041. It allows mapping of variable-length, higher-layer client signals over a transport network such as SDH or SONET.
Gigabit-Capable Passive Optical Network (G-PON): A PON standard ratified by ITU-T G.984 recommendations. It uses the *G-PON encapsulation method* (GEM) to transmit Ethernet, ATM, and TDM data units.
G-PON Encapsulation Method (GEM): A mapping method adopted in a Gigabit-capable passive optical network (G-PON). It allows a G-PON to natively carry both Ethernet and TDM traffic.
Optical Line Terminal (OLT): The central controller of PONs. It is located at the central office (CO),

supervising all signal activity and arbitrating the data transmission.
Optical Network Terminal (ONT): The active device that delivers broadband access services to the subscribers. It is located in homes or in buildings.
Optical Network Unit (ONU): The active device that delivers broadband access services to subscribers. It is located near to the subscribers (e.g., "in the curb").
Passive Optical Network (PON): A fiber-to-the-premises configuration in which passive optical splitters are used to enable a single optical fiber to serve multiple premises. A PON consists of an optical line terminal (OLT) at the service provider's central office and a number of associated optical network units (ONUs) or optical network terminals (ONTs) near or at end users.
Wavelength-Division Multiplexing (WDM): A technology that multiplexes multiple optical carrier signals onto a single optical fiber by using different wavelengths.
Wavelength-Division Multiplexed Passive Optical Network (WDM-PON): A PON technology using WDM to reach multiple subscribers.

CROSS REFERENCES

See *Cable Modems; DSL (Digital Subscriber Line); Ethernet LANs; Wavelength Division Multiplexing (WDM).*

REFERENCES
Amitabha, B., Y. Park, F. Clarke, H. Song, S. Yang, G. Kramer, K. Kim, and B. Mukherjee. 2005. Wavelength-division-multiplexed passive optical network (WDM-PON) technologies for broadband access: A review. *Journal of Optical Networking*, 4: 737–58.
Angelopoulos, J. D., H.-C. Leligou, T. Argyriou, S. Zontos, E. Ringoot, and T. Van Caenegem. 2004. Efficient transport of packets with QoS in an FSAN-aligned GPON. *IEEE Communications Magazine*, 42: 92–8.
APON: ATM based PONs. 2002 (retrieved from www.ponforum.org/technology/apon.asp).
Assi, C., Y. Ye, D. Sudhir, and M. A. Ali. 2003. Dynamic bandwidth allocation for quality-of-service over Ethernet PONs. *IEEE Journal on Selected Areas in Communications*, 21: 1467–7.
Azzam, A. A. 1997. *High-speed cable modems*. New York: McGraw-Hill.
Corning Cable Systems. 2005. Access solutions design guide. Appendix: Migration to an all-optical network (retrieved from www.corningcablesystems.com/web/pubnet/ftppub.nsf/download/migration.pdf/).
Dutta-Roy, A. 2001. An overview of cable modem technology and market perspectives. *IEEE Communications Magazine*, 39: 81–8.
Fellows, D., and D. Jones. 2001. DOCSISTM cable modem technology. *IEEE Communications Magazine*, 39: 202–9.
Green, P. E. 2004. Fiber to the home: The next big broadband thing. *IEEE Communications Magazine*, 42: 100–6.
Institute of Electrical and Electronics Engineers (IEEE). 2004. IEEE Standard 802.3ah-2004 (retrieved from

http://standards.ieee.org/reading/ieee/interp/802.3ah-2004.html).

———, 802.3ah Task Force. 2004. Ethernet in the first mile (retrieved from www.ieee802.org/3/ah/index.html).

International Engineering Consortium. Undated. Cable modems (retrieved from www.iec.org/online/tutorials/cable_mod/).

International Telecommunication Union, Telecommunications (ITU-T). 1998. Recommendation G.983.1 Broadband optical access systems based on passive optical networks (PON).

———. 2001. Recommendation G.7041. Generic Framing Procedure.

———. 2003a. Recommendation G.984.1. Gigabit-capable passive optical networks (GPON): General characteristics.

———. 2003b. Recommendation G.984.2. Gigabit-capable passive optical networks (GPON): Physical media dependent (PMD) layer specification.

———. 2004a. Recommendation G.984.3. Gigabit-capable passive optical networks (G-PON): Transmission convergence layer specification.

———. 2004b. Recommendation G.984.4. Gigabit-capable passive optical networks (G-PON): ONT management and control interface specification.

Keiser, G. 2006. *FTTX concepts and applications*. New York: Wiley-IEEE Press (Wiley Series in Telecommunications and Signal Processing).

Kramer, G., and B. Mukherjee. 2001. Ethernet PON: Design and analysis of an optical access network. *Photonic Network Communications*, 3: 307–19.

———, and Pesavento, G. 2002. IPACT: A dynamic protocol for an Ethernet PON (EPON). *IEEE Communications Magazine*, 40: 74–80.

Luo, Y., and N. Ansari. 2005a. Bandwidth allocation for multiservice access on EPONs. *IEEE (Optical) Communications Magazine*, 43: S16–21.

———. 2005b. Bandwidth management and delay control over EPONs. In *IEEE Workshop on High Performance Switching and Routing*, May, Hong Kong, China. pp. 457–61.

———. 2005c. Dynamic upstream bandwidth allocation over Ethernet PONs. In IEEE International Conference on Communications, May, Seoul, Korea. Vol. 3: 1853–7.

———. 2005d. Limited sharing with traffic prediction for dynamic bandwidth allocation and QoS provisioning over EPONs. *Journal of Optical Networking*, 4: 561–72.

Ma, M., Y. Zhu, and T. H. Cheng. 2003. A bandwidth guaranteed polling MAC protocol for Ethernet passive optical networks. In *IEEE International Conference on Computer Communications* (INFOCOM), March, San Francisco. pp. 22–31.

Mervana, S., and C. Le. 2001. *Design and implementation of DSL-based access solutions*. Indianapolis: Cisco Press.

Nortel. 2004. Pondering passive optical networking deployment (retrieved from www.nortel.com/solutions/brdbndaccss/collateral/nn109280-092304.pdf).

Ooghe, S., J. De Clercq, I. Van de Voorde, Y. T'Joens, and J. De Jaegher. 2003. Impact of the evolution of the metropolitan network on the DSL access architecture. *IEEE Communications Magazine*, 41: 140–5.

Ossieur, P., D. Verhulst, Y. Martens, W. Chen, J. Bauwelinck, X. Z. Qiu, and J. Vandewege. 2005. A 1.25-gb/s burst-mode receiver for GPON applications. *IEEE Journal of Solid-State Circuits*, 40: 1180–9.

Ouyang, F., P. Duvaut, O. Moreno, and L. Pierrugues. 2003. The first step of long-reach ADSL: Smart DSL technology, READSL. *IEEE Communications Magazine*, 41: 124–31.

PON and FTTx update. 2005. Retrieved from www.lightreading.com.

Starr, T., M. Sorbara, J. M. Cioffi, and P. J. Silverman. 2002. *DSL advances*. Upper Saddle River, NJ: Prentice Hall.

Van Caenegem, T. 2004. B-PON, G-PON and E-PON: A guided tour. FTTH 2004 Conference and Expo, October, Orlando, FL, USA (retrieved from www.ftthcouncil.org/documents/215896.pdf).

Wikipedia. Undated. Access network (retrieved from http://en.wikipedia.org/wiki/Access_network).

Reviewers List

Abaza, Mahmoud, Athabasca University, Canada

Abbas, Kaja, University of California, Irvine

Abdel Hamid, Ayman Adel, Arab Academy for Science, Technology, and Maritime Transport, Egypt

Abdeljabbar, Wael, Mission College

Abdel-Wahab, Hussein, Old Dominion University

Abdu, Hasina, The University of Michigan, Dearborn

Ablowitz, Mark J., University of Colorado, Boulder

Abolmaesumi, Purang, Queen's University, Canada

Adams, Chris, University of Colorado, Boulder

Agathoklis, Pan, University of Victoria, Canada

Agrawal, Gopal, Texas A&M University, Texarkana

Akkaya, Kemal, Southern Illinois University

Akl, Robert, University of North Texas

Albright, Richard, Goldey-Beacom College

Ali, Sanwar, Indiana University of Pennsylvania

Aliyazicioglu, Zekeriya, California State Polytechnic University, Pomona

Al-Jaroodi, Jameela, University of Bahrain, Kingdom of Bahrain

Allan, Robert J., Daresbury Laboratory, UK

Allen, James M., University of North Dakota

AlRegib, Ghassan, Georgia Institute of Technology

Al-Shaer, Ehab, DePaul University

Altay, Gökmen, Bahcesehir University, Turkey

Altintas, Ayhan, Bilkent University, Turkey

Amin, Mohammad, National University

Amjad Umar, Fordham University

Anderson, Anne H., Sun Microsystems, Inc.

André, Paulo Sérgio de Brito, Universidade de Aveiro, Portugal

Andreozzi, Sergio, Istituto Nazionale di Fisica Nucleare (INFN), Italy

Ankiewicz, Adrian, Australian National University, Australia

Antonio, Patricia San, University of Maryland, Baltimore County

Anwar, Zahid, Intel Corporation

Ardakani, Masoud, University of Alberta, Canada

Argles, David, University of Southampton, UK

Argüello, Francisco, University of Santiago de Compostela, Spain

Arifler, Dogu, Eastern Mediterranean University, North Cyprus

Astani, Marzie, Winona State University

Atai, Javid, University of Sydney, Australia

Atti, Venkatraman, Arizona State University

Avoine, Gildas, Massachusetts Institute of Technology

Awan, Asad, Purdue University

Azad, Abul K. M., Northern Illinois University

Baaren-Hopper, Joanna van, University of Connecticut

Babula, Eduard, Universidad Carlos III de Madrid, Spain

Babulak, Eduard, University of Pardubice, Czech Republic

Badia, Leonardo, Università degli Studi di Padova, Italy

Baehr, Craig, Texas Tech University

Baeza-Yates, Ricardo, Yahoo! Research, Spain

Baggag, Abdelkader, McGill University, Canada

Bakos, Jason D., University of South Carolina

Baldwin, Rusty O., Air Force Institute of Technology

Barnes, Frank, University of Colorado, Boulder

Barnes, Stuart J., University of East Anglia, UK

Barnhart, Billy S., Webster University and AT&T

Bartolacci, Michael R., Penn State University, Berks

Basu, Kalyan, University of Texas, Arlington

Baudoin, Geneviève, ESIEE, France

Baumgartner, Robert, Vienna University of Technology, Austria

Beavers, Gordon, University of Arkansas

Bedell, Paul, Independent Consultant

Bellardo, John M., California Polytechnic State University

Bellavista, Paolo, DEIS—Università degli Studi di Bologna, Italy

Ben Slimane, Slimane, The Royal Institute of Technlogy (KTH), Sweden

Benhaddou, Driss, University of Houston

Benkabou, Fatima Zohr, Université de Moncton, Canada

Bennette, Daniel, University of Maryland University College Europe

Benvenuto, Nevio, University of Padova, Italy

Berg, George, University at Albany, SUNY

Berkes, Jem E., University of Waterloo, Canada

Berlemann, Lars, Swisscom Innovations, Switzerland

Berman, David J., DBM Technology Consulting

Bernstein, Larry, Stevens Institute of Technology

Bertoss, Alan A., University of Bologna, Italy

Biagioni, Edoardo S., University of Hawaii, Mānoa

Bianc, Andrea, Politecnico di Torino, Italy

Binsted, Kim, University of Hawaii, Manoa

Birant, Derya, Dokuz Eylul University, Turkey

Birru, Dagnachew (Dan), Philips Research North America

Biswas, Abhijit, Jet Propulsion Laboratory, California Institute of Technology

Biswas, Anjan, Delaware State University

Bjerke, Bjorn A., Qualcomm, Inc.

Bocchino Jr., Robert L., University of Illinois

Bocquet, Wladimir, France Telecom R&D, Japan

Bode, Arndt, Technische Universität München, Germany

Bodnar, Bohdan L., Motorola, Inc.

Bohn, Jürgen, Wernher von Braun Center for Advanced Research, Brazil

Bollen, Johan, Los Alamos National Laboratory

Bolyard, John W., University of West Florida

Bonnel, Wanda, University of Kansas

Boppana, Rajendra V., University of Texas, San Antonio

Border, Charles, Rochester Institute of Technology

Boroson, Don M., MIT Lincoln Laboratory

Bose, Sanjay K., Nanyang Technological University, Singapore

Bostian, Charles W., Virginia Tech

Bouras, Christos, University of Patras, Greece

Brännström, Robert, Luleå University of Technology, Sweden

Braun, Mark J., Gustavus Adolphus College

Braun, Torsten, University of Bern, Switzerland

Brewster, Gregory, DePaul University

Briscoe, Bob, BT, UK

Broughton, S. Allen, Rose-Hulman Institute of Technology

Brown, Andrew, University of Southampton, UK

Brown, Eric Paul, Canyon College

Brown, Stuart M., New York University

Bryan, David A., College of William and Mary and SIPeerior Technologies, Inc.

Buchholz, Dale, DePaul University

Bucy, Erik P., Indiana University

Buhari, M. I. Seyed Mohamed, University Brunei Darussalam, Brunei

Burn, David R., Southern Illinois University, Carbondale

Burpee III, Howard A., Southern Maine Community College

Butler, Donald, University of Texas, Arlington

Byrd, Gregory T., North Carolina State University

Cabri, Danijela, University of California, Berkeley

Cai, Qingbo, Case Western Reserve University

Cai, Yu, Michigan Technological University

Caini, Carlo, Università di Bologna, Italy

Calabresi, Leonello, Univerity of Maryland, University College

Ćalić, Janko, University of Bristol, UK

Callahan, Dale, University of Alabama, Birmingham

Camarillo, Gonzalo, Ericsson

Can Vuran, Mehmet, Georgia Institute of Technology

Candan, K. Selcuk, Arizona State University

Cannistra, Robert M., Marist College

Cantrell, Cyrus D., The University of Texas, Dallas

Cao, Lei, The University of Mississippi

Cao, Xiaojun, Rochester Institute of Technology

Cardei, Ionut, Florida Atlantic University

Cardell-Oliver, Rachel, The University of Western Australia, Australia

Careglio, Davide, Universitat Politècnica de Catalunya, Spain

Carlson, David E., University of Florida

Carroll, Bill D., The University of Texas, Arlington

Castane, Laurent, Onera, France

Castillo, Carlos, Yahoo! Research, Spain

Cernocky, Jan "Honza," Brno University of Technology, Czech Republic

Chaffin, Dorothea S., Park University

Chambers, Robert, Lightspeed Systems

Champion, Jean-Luc, UN/CEFACT Forum, Belgium

Chan, Sammy, City University of Hong Kong, Hong Kong

Chan, Tom S., Southern New Hampshire University

Chandra, Vigs, Eastern Kentucky University

Chandrashekhara, K., University of Missouri, Rolla

Chaudet, Claude, GET/ENST, France

Che, Hao, University of Texas, Arlington

Chen, Chien-Chung, National Taiwan University, Taiwan

Chen, Jim Q., University of Maryland, University College

Chen, Ju-Ya, National Sun Yat-Sen University, Taiwan

Chen, Li-Wei, Vanu Inc.

Chen, Runhua, The University of Texas, Austin

Chen, Whai-En, National Chiao Tung University, Taiwan

Chen, Yu-Che, Northern Illinois University

Cheng, Tee Hiang, Nanyang Technological University, Singapore

Chepkevich, Richard A., "Sam," Hawaii Pacific University

Chess, David M., IBM Watson Research Center

Chiani, Marco, DEIS, University of Bologna, Italy

Chiao, J. C., The University of Texas, Arlington

Cho, Pak S., CeLight, Inc.

Choi, Byung K., Michigan Technological University

Choi, Young B., James Madison University

Choksy, Carol E. B., Indiana University, Bloomington

Christensen, Ken, University of South Florida

Chuah, Chen-Nee, University of California, Davis

Chuah, Teong-Chee, Multimedia University, Malaysia

Chudoba, Katherine M., Florida State University

Chung, Chia-Jung, California State University, Sacramento

Chung, Sam, University of Washington, Tacoma

Clarke, Roger, Xamax Consultancy Pty Ltd, Australia, and University of Hong Kong

Cohen, Daniel, George Mason University

Cohen, David J., University of Maryland, University College

Collings, Neil, University of Cambridge, UK

Collins, J. Stephanie, Southern New Hampshire University

Colonna, Danilo, ENEA C. R. Frascati, Italy

Comellas, Jaume, Universitat Politècnica de Catalunya, Spain

Connel, Mark, State University of New York, Cortland

Conti, Claudio, Research Center Enrico Fermi, Italy

Coopman, Ted M., University of Washington

Corazza, Giovanni E., University of Bologna, Italy

Cordeiro, Carlos, Philips Research North America

Craenen, B. G. W., Napier University, UK

Craig, Richard, San Jose State University

Crawford, George W., Penn State McKeesport

Crnkovic, Jakov, University at Albany (SUNY)

Cronin, Eric, University of Pennsylvania

Crowcroft, Jon, University of Cambridge, UK

Cui, Dongzhe, Bell Labs—Lucent Technologies

Cui, Yi, Vanderbilt University

Dai, Huaiyu, North Carolina State University

Dai, Yuan-Shun, Indiana University Purdue University Indianapolis

Daniels, Robert C., The University of Texas, Austin

Danielson, David R., Stanford University

Daoud, Moh, Las Positas College

Daskalopulu, Aspassia, University of Thessaly, Greece

David, John J., Wake Forest University

De Leenheer, Marc, Ghent University, Germany

Debbah, Merouane, Eurecom Institute, France

Debrunne, Christian H., Colorado School of Mines

DeJoie, Anthony, Telcordia Technologies

Dellacca, David, Indiana University-Purdue University Indianapolis (IUPUI)

Desai, Uday B., Indian Institute of Technology, India

Deters, Ralph, University of Saskatchewan, Canada

Develi, Ibrahim, Engineering Erciyes University, Turkey

Dhadwal, Harbans S., State University of New York, Stony Brook

Di Cecca, Angelo, Alcatel Alenia Space

Diaz, Michel, LAAS-CNRS, France

Dick, Steven J., Southern Illinois University, Carbondale

Dietrich, Sven, CERT

Ding, Hao, Norwegian University of Science and Technology, Norway

Ding, Qin, Pennsylvania State University, Harrisburg

Ding, Wei, The University of Houston, Clear Lake

Dor, Jean-Baptiste, France Telecom, France

Doran, K. Brewer, Salem State College

Dorsz, Jeff, Saddleback College

Downing, Rob, IP Infusion

Drábek, Vladimír, Brno University of Technology, Czech Republic

Dringus, Laurie P., Nova Southeastern University

Drummond, Lúcia Maria de A., Universidade Federal Fluminense, Brazil

Durbano, James P., EM Photonics, Inc.

Dyo, Vladimir, University College London, UK

Edd, Wesley M., Verizon Federal Network Systems / NASA Glenn Research Center

Eddie Rabinovitch, ECI Technology

Edirisinghe, Ruwini Kodikara, Monash University, Australia

Edwards, Paul N., University of Michigan, Ann Arbor

Efstathiou, Elias C., Athens University of Economics and Business, Greece

Egbert, Brian G., Sprint Nextel

Egedigwe, Eges, Eastfield College of Dallas County Community College System

Ehrensberger, Juergen, HEIG-VD, Switzerland

Ehrich, Thomas A., Golden Gate University

Ekbia, Hamid R., Indiana University

El Fatmi, Sihem Guemara, High School of Communications, Tunisia

Elin, Larry, Syracuse University

Elliot, Stephen John, Purdue University

Elmusrati, Mohammed Salem, University of Vaasa, Finland

Enck, William, The Pennsylvania State University

Erbacher, Robert F., Utah State University

Erenshteyn, Roman, Goldey-Beacom College

Erol, Ali, University of Nevada, Reno

Esmahi, Larbi, Athabasca University, Canada

Evans, Gary, Southern Methodist University

Ewert, Craig, University of Maryland University College (UMUC)

Faber, Brenton, Clarkson University

Falconer, David, Carleton University, Canada

Fallah, M. Hosein, Stevens Institute of Technology

Fan, Guangbin, Intel Research, China

Farahat, Nader, Polytechnic University of Puerto Rico

Farhang-Boroujeny, Behrouz, University of Utah

Farley, Toni, Arizona State University

Farren, Margaret, Dublin City University, Ireland

Faruque, Abdullah, Southern Polytechnic State University

Fazel, Khaled, Ericsson GmbH, Germany

Feiler, Michael, Merritt College

Feng, Jack, Bradley University

Fernandes, Stenio F. L., Federal Center for Education in Technology (CEFET), Brazil

Fernback, Jan, Temple University

Ferner, Clayton, University of North Carolina, Wilmington

Ficek, Zbigniew, The University of Queensland, Australia

Figg, William C., Dakota State University

Fitkov-Norris, Elena, Kingston University, UK

Fitzek, Frank H. P., Aalborg University, Denmark

Fitzgibbons, Patrick W., SUNY Institute of Technology

Fitzpatrick, John, University College Dublin, Ireland

Fleisc, Brett D., University of California, Riverside

Fleischmann, Kenneth R., Florida State University, and Drexel University

Fonseka, John P., University of Texas, Dallas

Ford, Davis, Zeno Consulting, Inc.

Ford, Steve, Northeastern State University

Foschini, Luca, DEIS—Università degli Studi di Bologna, Italy

Fowler, Thomas B., Mitretek Systems

Fox, Geoffrey, Indiana University

Fox, Louis, University of Washington

Frank, Michael P., FAMU-FSU College of Engineering

Frantti, Tapio, Technical Research Centre, Finland

Freed, Shirley Ann, Andrews University

Freelan, Joseph Curtis, University of Notre Dame

Fricke, Justus Ch., University of Kiel, Germany

Friesen, Norm, Simon Fraser University, Canada

Fritts, Jason E., Saint Louis University

Frolik, Jeff, University of Vermont

Fu, Xiang, Georgia Southwestern State University

Fukami, Cynthia V., University of Denver

Fuller, Dorothy P., Black Hills State University

Gallagher, Helen, Computer Clarity, Glenview, Illinois

Gao, Jie, State University of New York, Stony Brook

Gao, Liang, Huazhong University of Science and Technology, China

Garcia-Armada, Ana, University Carlos III de Madrid, Spain

Gauch, John M., The University of Kansas

Gavrilenko, Vladimir, Norfolk State University

Gebali, Fayez, University of Victoria, Canada

Gentzsch, Wolfgang, University of North Carolina, Chapel Hill

Ghafouri-Shiraz, H., University of Birmingham, UK

Giambene, Giovanni, University of Siena, Italy

Giangarra, Paul P., IBM

Glick, Madeleine, Intel Research Cambridge, UK

Glushko, Robert J., University of California, Berkeley

Goffe, William L., State University of New York, Oswego

Gong, Yili, Chinese Academy of Sciences, China

Gonzalez Benitez, Ruben A., Universidad Veracruzana, Mexico

Goodarzy, Hormoz, Cambridge College

Goodsell, David S., The Scripps Research Institute

Gordon, Jr., Horace C., University of South Florida

Govindavajhala, Sudhakar, Princeton University

Grandy, Holger, University of Augsburg, Germany

Graupner, Sven, Hewlett-Packard Laboratories, Palo Alto

Gray, Charles G., Oklahoma State University

Greaves, David, University of Cambridge, UK

Grimaud, Gilles, INRIA/CNRS/ University, France

Groth, Dennis P., Indiana University

Guan, Yong Liang, Nanyang Technological University, Singapore

Guenach, Mamoun, Department of Telecommunication and Information Processing

Gunther, Jake, Utah State University

Guo, Jinhua, University of Michigan, Dearborn

Guo, Li-Qiang, University of Limerick, Ireland

Guo, Yile, Nokia

Gurses, Eren, The Norwegian University of Science and Technology, Norway

Gurusamy, Mohan, National University of Singapore, Singapore

Haddadi, Hamed, University College London, UK

Hadidi, Rassule, University of Illinois, Springfield

Hadjicostis, Christoforos, University of Illinois, Urbana-Champaign

Haenggi, Martin, University of Notre Dame

Haghverdi, Esfandiar, Indiana University, Bloomington

Hague, Rob, Independent Consultant, UK

Hammell II, Robert J., Towson University

Hammer, Florian, Telecommunications Research Center Vienna (ftw.), Austria

Han, Youngnam, Information and Communications University, Korea

Hanchey, Cindy Meyer, Oklahoma Baptist University

Hansse, Øyvind, University of Tromsø, Norway

Haque, Saira N., Syracuse University

Härmä, Aki, Philips Research Laboratories

Harper, Christopher, Temple University

Harris, Jr., Frederick C., University of Nevada, Reno

Hartel, Pieter, University of Twente, The Netherlands

Hasan, Aamir, University of Texas, Austin

Hasan, Mohammad Masud, University of Texas, Dallas

Hasina Abdu, The University of Michigan, Dearborn

Havill, Jessen T., Denison University

Hawkin, Joseph, University of Alaska, Fairbanks

Hayden, Patrick, McGill University, Canada

Hayee, M. Imran, University of Minnesota, Duluth

He, Dan, University of Surrey, UK

Heckenberg, Norman, The University of Queensland, Australia

Heidari, Sam, Ikanos Communications, Inc.

Heijenk, Geert, Uniiversity of Twente, The Netherlands

Heim, Gregory R., Boston College

Heintzelman, Matthew Z., Saint John's University

Helfers, Eric C., University of Maryland, University College, and Johns Hopkins University

Helm, Pamela C., Radford University

Henkel, Werner, International University Bremen (IUB), Germany

Henry, Joel, University of Montana, Missoula

Hershey, John E., GE, Research

Hesselbach-Serra, Xavier, Universitat Politècnica de Catalunya, Spain

Hettak, Khelifa, Industry Canada, Canada

Higgs, Bryan J., Rivier College

Hiwasaki, Yusuke, NTT Corp., Japan

Hizlan, Murad, Cleveland State University

Ho, Chen-Shie, National Taiwan University, Taiwan

Hoag, John C., Ohio University

Hoffmeyer, Jim, Western Telecom Consultants, Inc.

Hogrefe, Dieter, Georg-August-Universitaet Goettingen, Germany

Hole, Kjell Jørgen, University of Bergen, Norway

Holzer, Richard, University of Passau, Germany

Hong, Edwin, University of Washington, Tacoma

Horan, Stephen, New Mexico State University

Horikis, Theodoros P., University of Colorado, Boulder

Hostetler, Michael, Park University

Howenstine, Erick, Northeastern Illinois University

Hu, Yuh-Jong, National Chengchi University, Taiwan

Huang, Chin-Tser, University of South Carolina

Huang, Freeman Yufei, Queen's University, Canada

Hudson, James M., Georgia Institute of Technology

Huemer, Mario, University of Erlangen-Nuremberg, Germany

Hunsinger, Jeremy, Virginia Polytechnic Institute and State University

Hurley, Stephen, Cardiff University, UK

Hussmann, Heinrich, University of Munich, Germany

Huston, Geoff, Asia Pacific Network Information Center (APNIC)

Ibrahim, Hassan, University of Maryland

Iftode, Liviu, Rutgers University

Ilk, H. Gokhan, Ankara University, Turkey

Ingram, Mary Ann, Georgia Institute of Technology

Ionescu, Dan, University of Ottawa, Canada

Iraqi, Youssef, Dhofar University, Oman

Ishaq, A. Faiz M., The University of Lahore, Pakistan

Iskander, Cyril-Daniel, The MathWorks Inc.

Islam, M. Saif, University of California, Davis

Iversen, Jakob Holden, University of Wisconsin, Oshkosh

Jablonski, Dan, John Hopkins University

Jackson, Henry L. "Jack," Austin Community College

Jacobs, Raymond A., Ashland University

Jajszczyk, Andrzej, AGH University of Science and Technology, Poland

Jank, Wolfgang, University of Maryland

Jayakar, Krishna, The Pennsylvania State University

Jenkins, David, University of Plymouth, UK

Jenq, Yih-Chyun, Portland State University

Ji, Ping, City University of New York

Jia, Weijia, City University of Hong Kong, Hong Kong

Jiang, Tao, University of Michigan, Dearborn

Jiang, Yuming, Norwegian University of Science and Technology, Norway

Jin, Hai, Huazhong University of Science and Technology, China

Joadat, Reza, Richmond University, UK

Johnson, J. T., Institute for Analytic Journalism

Johnson, Michael P., Carnegie Mellon Universitiy

Jones III, Creed, Seattle Pacific University

Jones, James G., University of North Texas

Jordan, Kurt, Calumet College of St. Joseph

Jun, Jaeyeon, Mazu Networks

Kabara, Joseph, University of Pittsburgh

Kan, Min-Yen, National University of Singapore, Singapore

Kandus, Gorazd, Jozef Stefan Institute, Slovenia

Kang, Jaewon, Rutgers University

Kang, Joonhyuk, Information & Communications University, Korea

Kapfhammer, Gregory M., Allegheny College

Karandikar, Abhay, Indian Institute of Technology, India

Karapetyan, Aram, Yerevan State University, Armenia

Karp, Tanja, Texas Tech University

Karush, Gerald, Southern New Hampshire University

Kato, Nei, Tohoku University, Japan

Katos, Vasilios, University of Portsmouth, UK

Katzy, Bernhard R., University Bw Munich (D) and Leiden University (NL), Germany

Kawanish, Tetsuya, National Institute of Information and Communications Technology, Japan

Kayssi, Ayman, American University of Beirut, Lebanon

Keenan, Susan M., University of Northern Colorado

Keliher, Liam, Mount Allison University, Canada

Kent, M. Allen, Montana State University

Kerrigan, John E., University of Medicine and Dentistry of New Jersey

Kesden, Gregory, Carnegie Mellon University

Keselman, Yakov, Microsoft Corporation

Kesidis, George, Pennsylvania State University

Keys, Anthony C., University of Wisconsin, Eau Claire

Khatri, Farzana I., MIT Lincoln Laboratory

Kholodovych, Vladyslav, University of Medicine & Dentistry of New Jersey

Khosla, Raj, Colorado State University

Khunboa, Chatchai, Khon Kaen University, Thailand

Kim, Jinoh, University of Minnesota

Kim, JongWon, Gwangju Institute of Science & Technology, Korea

Kim, Su Myeon, Samsung Advanced Institute of Technology

Kimmel, Howard, New Jersey Institute of Technology

Kivshar, Yuri, Australian National University, Australia

Kleist, Virginia Franke, West Virginia University

Knolle, Jonathan W., California State University, Chico

Kobtsev, Sergey, Novosibirsk State University, Russia

Kocyigit, Altan, Middle East Technical University, Turkey

Kodi, Avinash, University of Arizona

Kolias, Christos, University of Southern California

Kolumban, Geza, Budapest University of Technology and Economics, Hungary

Kong, Albert, The University of the West Indies, Trinidad & Tobago

Koppler, Alois, Kukla Electronics, Austria

Kornhauser, Alain L., Princeton University

Korpeoglu, Ibrahim, Bilkent University, Turkey

Koucheryavy, Yevgeni, Tampere University of Technology, Finland

Kretschmer, Tobias, London School of Economics, UK

Kriehn, Gregory R., California State University, Fresno

Krishnamurthy, Prashant, University of Pittsburgh

Krishnan, Iyengar N., Johns Hopkins University

Kritzinger, Pieter S., University of Cape Town, South Africa

Krotov, Vlad, University of Houston

Kruger, Anton, The University of Iowa

Kruger, Lennard G., Library of Congress

Kuhn, Marc, Institut für Kommunikationstechnik, Switzerland

Kumar, Aarti, Motorola Inc.

Kumar, Chiranjeev, Indian School of Mines University (ISM), India

Kumar, Santosh, University of Memphis

Kumar, Saurabh, University of Southern California

Kummerfeld, Sarah, Stanford University

Kumwilaisak, Wuttipong, King Mongkut's University of Technology, Thailand

Kurkovsky, Stan, Central Connecticut State University

Kurkowski, Stuart, Colorado School of Mines

Kursh, Steven R., Northeastern University

Kut, Alp, Dokuz Eylul University, Turkey

Kwok, Yu-Kwong Ricky, The University of Hong Kong, Hong Kong

Kwon, James Minseok, Rochester Institute of Technology

Kyperountas, Spyros, Motorola Labs

Kyprianou, Andreas, University of Cyprus, Cyprus

Lacity, Mary C., University of Missouri

Lagerstrom, Eric J. "Rick," Golden Gate University

Lamblin, Claude, France Telecom R&D, France

Land, Martin, Hadassah College, Israel

Landfeldt, Bjorn, University of Sydney, Australia

Langar, Rami, University of Waterloo, Canada

Langendoen, Koen, Delft University of Technology, The Netherlands

Larson, Robert E., University of Washington

Lassous, Isabelle Guerin, INRIA ARES/CITI, France

Law, K. L. Eddie, Ryerson University, Canada

Lawrence, Ramon, University of British Columbia Okanagan, Canada

Leangsuksun, Chokchai, Louisiana Tech University

LeBlanc, Cathie, Plymouth State University

Lee, Gyungho, University of Illinois, Chicago

Lee, Jung Woo, Stanford University

Lehman, Ann C., University of Illinois, Urbana-Champaign

Lehr, William, Massachusetts Institute of Technology

Leitgeb, Erich, Graz University of Technology, Austria

Leonardo Badia, IMT Lucca, taly

Li, Chih-Peng, National Sun Yat-Sen University, Taiwan

Li, Frank Y., University of Oslo, Norway

Li, Honglin, North Dakota State University

Li, Jun, University of Oregon

Li, Tongtong, Michigan State University

Li, Zexian, Nokia

Liang, Chuck C., Hofstra University

Liang, Jie, Simon Fraser University, Canada

Liebenau, Jonathan, London School of Economics, UK

Light, Jennifer S., Northwestern University

LiKamWa, Patrick, University of Central Florida

Lin, Bin, Northwestern University

Lin, Xiaojun, Purdue University

Lineman, Jeffrey P., Northwest Nazarene University

Liszka, Kathy J., The University of Akron

Liu, Boan, Tsinghua University, China

Liu, Chang, Northern Illinois University

Liu, Fenghai, Mintera Corporation

Liu, Huaping, Oregon State University

Liu, Xiang, Bell Labs, Lucent Technologies

Liu, Xiangqian, University of Louisville

Llewellyn, Mark, University of Central Florida

Lo, Shou-Chih, National Dong Hwa University, Taiwan

Lodwig, Sunita, University of South Florida

Löh, Hermann, CeTIM, Germany

Lorenz, Pascal, University of Haute Alsace, France

Losada, David E., University of Santiago de Compostela, Spain

Love, John, Australian National University, Australia

Lozano-Nieto, Albert, The Pennsylvania State University

Lu, Guo-Wei, The Chinese University of Hong Kong, Hong Kong

Lu, Yuanqiu, New Jersey Institute of Technology

Lugmayr, Artur R., Tampere University of Technology

Luo, Jun, Ecole Polytechnique Fédérale de Lausanne (EPFL), Switzerland

Ma, Maode, Nanyang Technological University, Singapore

Mabry, Edward A., University of Wisconsin, Milwaukee

Mache, Jens Mache, Lewis & Clark College, Oregon

Magistretti, Eugenio, DEIS—Università degli Studi di Bologna, Italy

Maguire, Paul, Dublin City University (DCU), Ireland

Mahanti, Anirban, University of Calgary, Canada

Mai, Bin, Northwestern State University, Louisiana

Mailaender, Laurence, Lucent Technologies, Bell Labs

Majumdar, Abhik, University of California, Berkeley

Makani, Joyline, Dalhousie University, Canada

Malkevitch, Joseph, York College (CUNY)

Mambretti, Joe, Northwestern University

Mandujano, Salvador, Intel Corporation

Mann, Catherine L., Brandeis University and Peterson Institute for International Economics

Mano, Chad D., University of Notre Dame

Mao, Shiwen, Auburn University

Mapp, Glenford, Middlesex University, UK

Markman, Kris M., Bridgewater State College

Marks, Gregory A., University of Michigan and Merit Network

Marsic, Ivan, Rutgers University

Marsteller, Matthew R., Carnegie Mellon University

Martel, Normand M., Medical Technology Research Corp.

Martin, Jim, Clemson University

Martin, Richard K., The Air Force Institute of Technology (AFIT)

Martins, Luis L., Georgia Institute of Technology

Mashburn, Ronald, West Texas A & M University

Mason, Sharon P., Rochester Institute of Technology

Mateti, Prabhaker, Wright State University

McConn, Charlotte Eudy, Penn State University

McFadden, Anna C., The University of Alabama

McFarland, Daniel J., Rowan University

McKeever, Susan, Dublin Institute of Technology, Ireland

Mehlenbacher, Brad, North Carilina State

Menif, Mourad, Ecole Supérieure des Communications (SupCom), Tunisia

Menth, Michael, University of Wuerzburg, Germany

Mertins, Alfred, University of Oldenburg, Germany

Metesh, Ed, Montana Tech

Miers, Judson, University of Kansas

Mihaila, George Andrei, IBM Research

Milenkovic, Aleksandar, The University of Alabama, Huntsville

Millard, Bruce R., Arizona State University

Miller, Holmes E., Muhlenberg College

Miller, Joseph B., University of Kentucky

Milosevic, Milos, Schlumberger Technology Corporation

Minoli, Daniel, Stevens Institute of Technology

Mirchandani, Vinod, The University of Sydney, Australia

Miscetti, Stefano, Laboratori Nazionali di Frascati dell' INFN, Italy

Mishra, Piyush, Michigan Technological University

Misra, Christopher, University of Massachusetts, Amherst

Mitchell, John, University College London, UK

Mitchell, Joseph N., Southwest Research Institute, San Antonio

Moerman, Ingrid, Ghent University, Belgium

Mohanty, Saraju P., University of North Texas

Moision, Bruce, Jet Propulsion Laboratory (JPL), California Institute of Technology

Mokhtar, Simohamed Lotfy, Ecole Militaire Polytechnique, Algeria

Monberg, John, University of Kansas

Montante, Robert, Bloomsburg University of Pennsylvania

Montpetit, Marie-Jose, Motorola Connected Home Solutions

Morgan, Brian M., Marshall University

Moser, Allen W., Everett Community College

Mostafa, Javed, Indiana University, Bloomington

Motlagh, Bahman S., University of Central Florida

Mucchi, Lorenzo, University of Florence, Italy

Mueller, Milton L., Syracuse University

Murata, Masayuki, Osaka University, Japan

Murphy, John, University College Dublin, Ireland

Murphy, Richard, Southwest Research Institute, San Antonio, Texas

Murray, Alan, Ohio State University

Naimi, Linda L., Purdue University

Nair, Suku, Southern Methodist Unversity

Natarajan, Preethi, University of Delaware

Nelson, David Allen, University of Central Oklahoma

Nesbary, Dale, Oakland University

Neufeld, Derrick J., The University of Western Ontario, Canada

Neuman, Clifford, University of Southern California

Ngom, Alioune, University of Windsor, Canada

Ni, Jun, University of Iowa

Niar, Smail, University of Valenciennes, France

Nickerson, Matthew, Southern Utah University

Nithiyanandam, N., Sri Venkateswara College of Engineering, India

Noble, Bradley L., Southern Illinois University, Edwardsville

Nohlberg, Marcus, University of Skövde, Sweden

Noll, John, Santa Clara University

Nolle, Daniel E., United States Treasury Department

Noonan, Liam, Tipperary Institute, Ireland

Nuaymi, Loutfi, ENST Bretagne, France

Okazaki, Shintaro, Autonomous University of Madrid, Spain

Olan, Michael J., Richard Stockton College

Oldham, Joseph D., Centre College

Ole Bernsen, Niels, University of Southern Denmark, Denmark

Oliver Jr., Walter E., Howard University

Olsen, Torodd, Telenor Research and Innovation

Ong, Hong, Oak Ridge National Laboratory (ORNL)

Ortiz, Therezita K., St Petersburg College

Östling, Per-Erik, Aalborg University, Denmark

Ostrowski, John W., California State University, Long Beach

Ozmen, Andy, University of Cambridge, UK

Pagli, Linda, Dipartimento di Informatica, Pisa, Italy

Pak Shing, Cho, CeLight, Inc.

Palazzo, Sergio, Università di Catania, Italy

Paliwal, Kuldip K., Griffith University, Australia

Panetta, Karen, Tufts University

Pang, Qixiang, The University of British Columbia, Canada

Pangburn, Michael S., University of Oregon

Pantos, George, National Technical University of Athens, Greece

Paolo, Bellavista, DEIS—Università degli Studi di Bologna, Italy

Paprzycki, Marcin, Polish Academy of Science, Poland

Paragas, Fernando, University of the Philippines, Philippines

Parks, Lance Michael, Cosumnes River College

Parlos, Alexander G., Texas A&M University

Parssian, Amir, Instituto de Empresa

Passarella, Andrea, University of Cambridge, UK

Patel, Nilesh, University of Michigan, Dearborn

Patel, Ram Bahadur, M. M. Engineering College, India

Patrick, Eric, Northwestern University

Pelish, Matthew D., University at Albany, SUNY

Pérez, Jorge, Kennesaw State University

Perkis, Andrew, The Norwegian University of Science and Technology, Norway

Perlot, Nicolas, German Aerospace Center (DLR), Germany

Peroni, Isidoro, Università degli Studi di Roma, Italy

Perrig, Adrian, Carnegie Mellon University

Phanse, Kaustubh S., Luleå University of Technology, Sweden

Phifer, Lisa, Core Competence Inc.

Phillips, W. Greg, Royal Military College of Canada, Canada

Piotrowski, Victor, University of Wisconsin, Superior

Place, Jerry P., University of Missouri, Kansas City

Podell, Harold J., Johns Hopkins University

Polajnar, Andrej, University of Maribor, Slovenia

Poland, Ron A., Clinton Community College

Polycarpou, Andreas H., University of Denver

Ponterio, Robert, SUNY College, Cortland

Pontes, Marlene, WiNGS Telecom, Brazil

Poole, Melissa J., University of Missouri, Columbia

Porter, J. David, Oregon State University

Porter, Jr., Lon A., Wabash College

Potkonjak, Miodrag, University of California, Los Angeles

Poutrina, Ekaterina, University of Rochester

Pratter, Frederick E., Eastern Oregon University

Preece, Alun, University of Aberdeen, UK

Preston, Jon A., Clayton State University

Pritsky, N. Todd, Hill Associates, Inc., and Champlain College

Prunier, James (Tom), Southwestern College

Pucella, Riccardo, Northeastern University

Puliafito, Antonio, Università di Messina, Italy

Qad, Ala, University of Nebraska, Lincoln

Ra, Ikyeun, University of Colorado, Denver and Health Sciences Center

Raatikainen, Pertti, VTT Telecommunications, Finland

Rachidi, Tajje-eddine, Al Akhawayn Univertsity, Morocco

Radu, Mihaela E., Rose-Hulman Institute of Technology

Raghuwanshi, Pravin M., DeVry University

Raja, M. Yasin Akhtar, University of North Carolina, Charlotte

Rajput, Saeed, Think-Sync, Inc.

Rakocevic, Veselin, City University, UK

Rao, Soma Venugopal, Indian Institute of Technology, India

Rapeli, Juha, University of Oulu, Finland

Rasmussen, Jeremy, Sypris Electronics, LLC

Raynal, Michel, Irisa Université de Rennes 1, France

Razaghi, Peyman, University of Toronto, Canada

Razavi, Mohsen, Massachusetts Institute of Technology

Razmov, Valentin, University of Washington

Recor, Jeff, CTG, Inc.

Redi, Jason K., BBN Technologies

Reed, Lisa J., University of Portland

Refai, Hakki H., The University of Oklahoma, Tulsa

Rehrl, Karl, Salzburg Research, Austria

Reichinger, Kurt, Vienna University of Technology, Austria

Reichl, Peter, Telecommunications Research Center Vienna (ftw.), Austria

Reiher, Peter, University of California, Los Angles

Reinschmidt, Kenneth F., Texas A&M University

Reiter, Joshua J., Johns Hopkins University

Ren, Jian, Michigan State University

Requicha, Aristides A. G., University of Southern California

Riabov, Vladimir V., Rivier College

Richard A. Stanley, Worcester Polytechnic Institute

Robila, Stefan A., Montclair State University

Rogers, David V., Communications Research Centre, Canada

Rollins, Sami, Mount Holyoke College

Romero, Alfonso E., University of Granada, Spain

Rose, Chris, Erudio College

Roset, Cesare, University of Rome "Tor Vergata," Italy

Rosu, Marcel C., IBM T. J. Watson Research Center

Rovati, Luigi, University of Modena and Reggio Emilia, Italy

Rupf, John A., Southern Polytechnic State University

Ryan, Kevin, Stevens Institute of Technology

Ryoo, Jungwoo, Pennsylvania State University, Altoona

Sabelli, Nora H., SRI International

Sachdev, D. K., SpaceTel Consultancy LLC and George Mason University

Saengudomlert, Poompat, Asian Institute of Technology, Thailand

Safaai Jazi, Ahmad, Vigina Tech

Salane, Douglas E., John Jay College of Criminal Justice

Saliba, Anthony, Charles Sturt University, Australia

Saligheh Rad, Hamidreza, Harvard University

Sampei, Seiichi, Osaka University, Japan

Sandy, Mary F., DePaul University

Sankar, Ravi, University of South Florida

Sarac, Kamil, University of Texas, Dallas

Satterlee, Brian, Liberty University

Savoie, Michael J., The University of Texas, Dallas

Schaumont, Patrick, Virginia Tech

Scheets, George, Oklahoma State University

Schlager, Mark, SRI International

Schmidt, Dieter S., University of Cincinnati

Schmitz, Corby, Loyola University Chicago

Schneider, Gerardo, University of Oslo, Norway

Schoute, Frits C., Delft University of Technology, The Netherlands

Schreiner, Wolfgang, Johannes Kepler University, Austria

Schubin, Mark, Technological Consultant

Schultz, E. Eugene, High Tower Software

Schwaig, Kathy S., Kennesaw State University

Schwarz, Thomas, S. J., Santa Clara University

Schwebel, Joseph P., University of St. Thomas

Scornavacc, Eusebio, Victoria University of Wellington, New Zealand

Seltzer, Wendy, Berkman Center for Internet & Society, Harvard Law

Selviah, David R., University College London, UK

Semrau, Penelope, California State University, Los Angeles

Servetti, Antonio, Politecnico di Torino, Italy

Sessions, Chad, Essex Corporation

Sethi, Adarshpal, University of Delaware

Shah, Dinesh S., Portland State University

Shah, Rahul, Intel Corporation

Shalunov, Stanislav, Internet2

Shamsi, Mehrdad, University of Toronto, Canada

Shand, Brian, University of Cambridge, UK

Shank, Patti, Learning Peaks LLC

Shao, Zili, The Hong Kong Polytechnic University, Hong Kong

Sharma, Vimal, Cardiff University, UK

Shay, William, University of Wisconsin, Green Bay

Shedletsky, Leonard J., University of Southern Maine

Shen, Dou, Hong Kong University of Science and Technology, Hong Kong

Shepard, Scott, University of Central Florida

Sherman, Richard C., Miami University

Shi, Qicai, Motorola Labs

Shimeall, Timothy J., Carnegie Mellon University

Shin, Dongwan, New Mexico Tech

Shokrani, Arash, Carlton University, Canada

Shrestha, Deepesh Man, Ajou University, South Korea

Shumba, Rose, Indiana University of Pennsylvania

Siekkinen, Matti, University of Oslo, Norvay

Simco, Greg, Nova Southeastern University

Simmons, Ken, Augusta Technical College

Simpson, Jr., Charles Robert (Robby), Georgia Institute of Technology

Singh, Manpreet, Cornell University and Google

Singh, Nirvikar, University of California, Santa Cruz

Singh, Vijay P., University of Kentucky

Sisalem, Dorgham, Tekelec Inc.

Sivrikaya, Fikret, Rensselaer Polytechnic Institute

Skoglund, Mikael, Royal Institute of Technology, Sweden

Slay, Jill, University of South Australia, Australia

Slimani, Yahya, Sciences of Tunis, Tunisia

Sloan, Joseph H., Webster University

Smith, Alan, BT Group

Smit, Anthony H., Purdue University

Smith II, Raife F., Southern University

Smith, Garry, University of Edinburgh, UK

Smith, Lloyd M., University of Wisconsin, Madison

Smith, Richard E., University of St. Thomas

Snow, Charles, George Mason University

Somasundaram, Siva, Stevens Institute of Technology

Song, Hongjun, University of Memphis

Song, Xiaoyu, Portland State University

Sopitkamol, Monchai, Kasetsart University, Thailand

Spegel, Marjan, J. Stefan Institute, Slovenia

Speidel, Joachim, University of Stuttgart, Germany

Spon, Kenneth, Federal Reserve Bank of Kansas City

Srinivasan, Bhaskar, Robert Bosch Corporation

Stachursk, Dale, University of Maryland, University College

Stackpole, Bill R., Rochester Institute of Technology

Stahl, Bernd Carsten, De Montfort University, UK

Stamp, Mark, San Jose State University

Stan, Sorin G., Philips Consumer Electronics, The Netherlands

Stastny, Richard, OeFEG Telekom, Austria

Stavrou, Angelos, Columbia University

Stavrou, Stavros, University of Surrey, UK

Steckler, Brian D., Naval Postgraduate School

Stefanov, Andrej, Polytechnic University

Stefanovic, Darko, University of New Mexico

Stern, Harold P. E., University of Alabama

Stevens, J. Richard, Southern Methodist University

Stiber, Michael, University of Washington, Bothell

Stiemerling, Oliver, ecambria systems GmbH, Germany

Stolfo, Salvatore J., Columbia University

Stork, Milan, University of West Bohemia, Czech Republic

Stout, Glenn Allan, Colorado Technical University

Striegel, Aaron, University of Notre Dame

Stylianos Drakatos, Florida International University

Sud, Seema, George Mason University

Suh, Changsu, Hanback Electronic, Republic of Korea

Sullivan, Richard J., Federal Reserve Bank of Kansas City

Sun, Chen, ATR Wave Engineering Laboratories, Japan

Sun, Hongxia, University of Calgary, Canada

Sun, Zhili, University of Surrey, UK

Sunda, S. Shyam, Penn State University

Sung, Dan Keun, Korea Advanced Institute of Science and Technology, Korea

Sur, Sayantan, The Ohio State University

Swedin, Eric G., Weber State University

Tabak, Leon, Cornell College

Tang, Zaiyong, Louisiana Tech University

Tangsangiumvisai, Nisachon, Chulalongkorn University, Thailand

Tarhuni, Naser G., Helsinki University of Technology, Finland

Tayahi, Moncef Benjamin, University of Nevada, Reno

Taylor, Nolan J., Indiana University, Indianapolis

Teitelbaum, Ben, Internet2 and BitTorrent

Tel, Gerard, University of Utrecht, The Netherlands

Temelkuran, Burak, Omniguide, Inc.

Terrell, Thomas F., University of South Florida

Tewari, Hitesh, Trinity College, Ireland

Teyeb, Oumer M., Aalborg University, Denmark

Thiruvathukal, George K., Loyola University, Chicago

Thomas, George, University of Louisiana, Lafayette

Thomas, Joseph R., University of Maryland

Thompson, Charles, Univeristy of Massachusetts, Lowell

Thompson, Dale R., University of Arkansas

Thompson, Steve C., University of California, San Diego

Thorne, Steven L., The Pennsylvania State University

Tirkel, Andrew, Monash University, Australia

Todd, Byron, Tallahassee Community College

Tomasin, Stefano, University of Padova, Italy

Tomažič, Sačo, University of Ljubljana, Slovenia

Tomlin, Chas, University of Southampton, UK

Toniatti, Tiziana, Siemens Networks

Toppin, Ian N., Clayton State University

Toumpis, Stavros, University of Cyprus, Cyprus

Trabelsi, Chokri, Lucent Technologies

Tran, Duc A., University of Dayton

Traynor, Patrick, Penn State University

Trigon, Niki, University of London, UK

Trostmann, Manfred F., University of Maryland, University College, Europe

Troxel, Ian, University of Florida

Tucker, Catherine, Massachusetts Institute of Technology

Turner, Stephen W., The University of Michigan, Flint

Tweedy, Edward, Rockingham Community College

Tyrer, Harry W., University of Missouri, Columbia

Ugur, Ahmet, Central Michigan University

Ugweje, Okechukwu, The University of Akron

Ulusoy, Özgür, Bilkent University, Turkey

Umar, Amjad, University of Pennsylvania

Uyar, Ahmet, At Mersin University, Mersin, Turkey

Valcourt, Scott A., University of New Hampshire

Van Camp, Julie C., California State University, Long Beach

Van den Boom, Henrie, Eindhoven University of Technology, The Netherlands

Van Engelen, Robert, Florida State University

Van Hook, Pamela, DeVry University

VanDeGrift, Tammy, University of Portland

Vanderster, Daniel C., University of Victoria, Canada

Vanelli-Coralli, Alessandro, University of Bologna, Italy

Varela, Martin, VTT Electronics, Finland

Vartiainen, Matti, Helsinki University of Technology, Finland

Vasconcelos, Wamberto Weber, University of Aberdeen, UK

Vaughan, Norman Vaughan, The University of Calgary, Canada

Venables, Phil, Independent Consultant

Verdurmen, E. J. M., Eindhoven University of Technology, The Netherlands

Verticale, Giacomo, Politecnico di Milano, Italy

Vidács, Attila, Budapest University of Technology and Economics, Hungary

Viehland, Dennis, Massey University, New Zealand

Villanti, Marco, DEIS—University of Bologna, Italy

Vishnevsky, Vladimir M., Russian Academy of Sciences, Russia

Viswanathan, Harish, Bell Labs, Alcatel-Lucent

Vivekanandan, Vijayanth, The University of British Columbia, Canada

Vogel, Christine, University of Texas, Austin

Vyavahare, Prakash, SGSITS, India

Wahl, Mark, University of Texas, Austin

Walden, Eric, Texas Tech University

Wall, Kevin W., Qwest Information Technologies, Inc.

Wallace, Layne, University of North Florida

Wan, Tat-Chee, Universiti Sains Malaysia, Malaysia

Wang, David C., Verizon Communications

Wang, Haomin, Dakota State University

Wang, Lan, University of Memphis

Wang, Minhua, State University of New York, Canton

Wang, Qian, Dublin Institute of Technology, Ireland

Wang, Suosheng, Indiana University

Wang, Yongge, University of North Carolina, Charlotte

Wang, Yu, University of North Carolina, Charlotte

Wang, Zhicheng, Clark Atlanta University

Warfield, Andrew, University of Cambridge, UK

Weatherspoon, Hakim, University of California, Berkeley

Webb, William, Ofcom, UK

Weinig, Shelly, Colombia University

Wellens, Matthias, RWTH Aachen University, Germany

Werstein, Paul, University of Otago, New Zealand

Whitaker, Roger, Cardiff University, UK

White, Curt M., DePaul University

White, Gregory B., The University of Texas, San Antonio

White, Stephanie, Long Island University

Wietfeld, Christian, University of Dortmund, Germany

Wijesekera, Duminda, George Mason University

Wilkerson, Trena Lashley, Baylor University

Wilkinson, Anthony Barry, University of North Carolina, Charlotte

Wilkinson, Timothy D., University of Cambridge, UK

Williams, Kevin, University of Cambridge, UK

Williamson, Carey, University of Calgary, Canada

Wilson, C. Diane, Central Missouri State University

Wing, William R., Oak Ridge National Labs

Witschnig, Harald, Philips Semiconductors, Austria

Wolff, Richard S., Montana State University

Wong, Yue-Ling, Wake Forest University

Wood, David, MITRE Corporation

Woolley, Sandra I., University of Birmingham, UK

Wu, Jingxian, Sonoma State University

Wu, Ke-Li, The Chinese University of Hong Kong, Hong Kong

Wu, Kui, University of Victoria, Canada

Wu, Ningning, University of Arkansas, Little Rock

Wu, Zhiqiang (John), Wright State University

Wulich, Dov, Ben-Gurion University, Israel

Wykle, Helen H., University of North Carolina, Asheville

Xiao, Yang, The University of Memphis

Xie, Shizhong, Tsinghua University, China

Xu, Kaixin, Scalable Network Technologies, Inc.

Xu, Xizhen, New Jersey Institute of Technology

Xue, Fei, University of California, Davis

Yagami, Raymond, University of Maryland

Yam, Scott S-H., Queen's University, Canada

Yamagiwa, Shinichi, INESC-ID/IST, Portugal

Yang, Cheer-Sun, West Chester University

Yang, Laurence T., St. Francis Xavier University, Canada

Yang, Lie-Liang, University of Southampton, UK

Yang, Shanchieh Jay, Rochester Institute of Technology

Yang, Xiuge, Ansoft Corporation

Yang, Y. R., Yale University

Yao, JingTao, University of Regina, Canada

Yao, Wenbing, Brunel University, UK

Yaprak, Ece, Wayne State University

Yedavalli, Kiran, University of Southern California

Yee, Wai Gen, Illinois Institute of Technology

Yi, Kwan, University of Kentucky

Yi, Yunjung, Honeywell Inc.

Yildiz, Melda N., William Paterson University

Yin, Lijun, State University of New York, Binghamton

Yin, Si, New Jersey Institute of Technology

Yoneki, Eiko, University of Cambridge, UK

Yoon, Jaewan, Old Dominion University

Youssef, Mahmoud, Rutgers University

Yu, Ming, State University of New York

Yu, William Emmanuel S., Ateneo de Manila University, Philippines

Yu, Chansu, Cleveland State University

Yuksel, Murat, Rensselaer Polytechnic Institute

Zaharov, Viktor, Polytechnic University of Puerto Rico

Zakhidov, Erkin, Uzbekistan Academy of Sciences, Uzbekistan

Zaki, Mohammed J., Rensselaer Polytechnic Institute

Zaman, Muhammad H., The University of Texas, Austin

Zawacki-Richter, Olaf, HfB—Business School of Finance & Management, Germany

Zehm, Brenda, Axia College of Western International University

Zekavat, Seyed Alireza (Reza), Michigan Technological University

Zeng, Qing-An, University of Cincinnati

Zerfos, Petros, Deutsche Telekom Laboratories, Germany

Zghal, Mourad, Sup'Com, Tunisie

Zhang, Chi, Florida International University

Zhang, Jinye, University of Victoria, Canada

Zhang, Liqiang, Indiana University, South Bend

Zhang, Zhao, Iowa State University

Zhao, Jiying, University of Ottawa, Canada

Zhao, Julie Yuhua, Miami University

Zho, Bo, University of Surrey, UK

Zhou, Luying, Institute for Infocomm Research, Singapore

Zhou, Zhaoxian, University of Southern Mississippi

Zhu Liu, AT&T Labs, Research

Zhu, Yifeng, University of Maine

Zimermann, Alfred E., Hawai'i Pacific University

Zou, Hanli, Broadcom Corporation

Zubairi, Junaid Ahmed, State University of New York, Fredonia

Zuo, Yongrong, Qualcomm Incorporated

Zuuring, Hans, University of Montana

Zvonar, Zoran, Analog Devices

Index